D0768548

Handbook of

North American Indians

1 Introduction
2 Indians in Contemporary Society
3 Environment, Origins, and Population
4 History of Indian-White Relations
5 Arctic
6 Subarctic, 1981
7 Northwest Coast
8 California, 1978
9 Southwest, 1979
VOLUME 10 **Southwest, 1983**
11 Great Basin
12 Plateau
13 Plains
14 Southeast
15 Northeast, 1978
16 Technology and Visual Arts
17 Languages
18 Biographical Dictionary
19 Biographical Dictionary
20 Index

Handbook of North American Indians

WILLIAM C. STURTEVANT

General Editor

VOLUME 10

Southwest

ALFONSO ORTIZ
Volume Editor

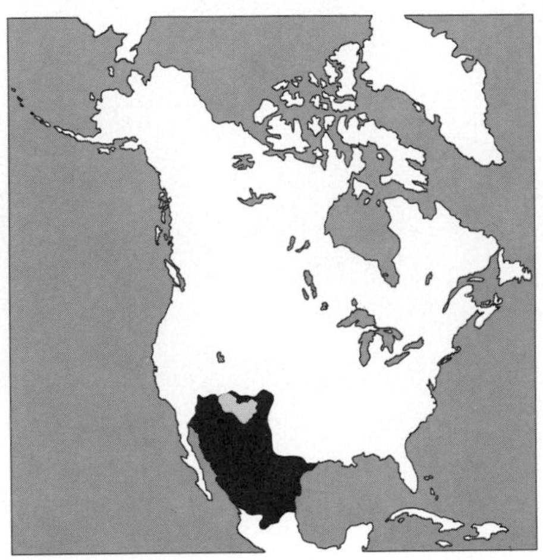

SMITHSONIAN INSTITUTION

WASHINGTON

1983

For sale by the Superintendent of Documents,
U.S. Government Printing Office, Washington, D.C. 20402.

Library of Congress Cataloging in Publication Data

Handbook of North American Indians.

Bibliography: pp. 780–839
Includes index.
CONTENTS:

v. 10 Southwest.

1. Indians of North America. 2. Eskimos.
I. Sturtevant, William C.

E77.H25 970'.004'97 77–17162

Southwest Volumes Planning Committee

Alfonso Ortiz, Volume Editor

William C. Sturtevant, General Editor

Edward P. Dozier

Fred Eggan

Kenneth L. Hale

Albert H. Schroeder

Douglas W. Schwartz

Gary Witherspoon

Richard B. Woodbury

Contents

This map is a diagrammatic guide to the coverage of this volume and volume 9. The prehistory of the whole region is treated in volume 9; for the historic and recent periods the groups indicated in tone are described in this volume while the others (the Pueblo peoples) are described in volume 9. This is not an authoritative depiction of tribal ranges, for several reasons. Sharp boundaries have been drawn and no territory is unassigned. Tribal units are sometimes arbitrarily defined, subdivisions are not mapped, no joint or disputed occupations are shown, and different kinds of land use are not distinguished. Since the map depicts the situation at the earliest periods for which evidence is available, the ranges mapped for different tribes often refer to quite different periods, and there may have been intervening movements, extinctions, and changes in range. Not shown are groups that came into separate political existence later than the map period for their areas. In general, the Pueblo areas are simplifications of the locations known for the 16th century, while the adjoining areas of Athapaskan groups are approximately as in the 18th century as are the boundaries along the Colorado River. The extreme southwestern region shows the 17th-century distribution. Boundaries in the large area south and southeast of the Chiricahua and Mescalero are especially arbitrary, due to the lack of evidence for the 17th and 18th centuries. For more specific information see the maps and text in the accompanying chapters in this volume and volume 9.

Key to Tribal Territories
115°
110°
105°
100°
95°
35°
30°
25°
Hopi
Navajo
R. Grande
Keresans
Jemez
Tewa
N. Tiwa
Jicarilla
Apache
Tano
Pecos
Zuni
Acoma
Laguna
S. Tiwa
Tompiro
Piro
Walapai
Havasupai
Mohave
Yavapai
Western Apache
Halchidhoma
Quechan
Maricopa
Cocopa
Chiricahua
Apache
Mescalero Apache
Papago and Upper Pima
Jocome and Jano
Suma
Jumano
Opata
Eudeve
Seri
Jova
Eudeve
Lower Pima
Yaqui
Guarijío
Tarahumara
Concho
Toboso
Tubar
Mayo
Guasave
Acaxee
Xixime
Tahue
Tepehuan
Zacatec
Poorly Known Groups of the Gulf Coastal Plain and Interior
Karankawa
Pame
Gulf of California
Pacific Ocean
Tropic of Cancer
Gulf of Mexico
0
100
200
Miles
Kilometers
0
100
200

Technical Alphabet

Consonants

		bilabial	*labiodental*	*dental*	*alveolar*	*alveopalatal*	*velar*	*back velar*	*glottal*
stop	vl	*p*		*t*	*t*		*k*	*q*	*ʔ*
	vd	*b*		*d*	*d*		*g*	*ġ*	
affricate	vl			*θ̂*	*c*	*č*			
	vd			*δ̂*	*ʒ*	*ǯ*			
fricative	vl	*ϕ*	*f*	*θ*	*s*	*š*	*x*	*x̣*	*h*
	vd	*β*	*v*	*δ*	*z*	*ž*	*γ*	*γ̇*	
nasal	vl	*M*		*N*			*Ŋ*		
	vd	*m*		*n*			*ŋ*	*ŋ̇*	
lateral	vl				*ł*				
	vd				*l*				
semivowel	vl	*W*				*Y*			
	vd	*w*				*y*			

vl = voiceless; vd = voiced

Other symbols include: *λ* (voiced lateral affricate), *ƛ* (voiceless lateral affricate), *ʕ* (voiced pharyngeal fricative), *ḥ* (voiceless pharyngeal fricative), *r* (medial flap, trill, or retroflex approximant). Where in contrast, *r* is a flap and *R* is a continuant.

Vowels

	front	*central*	*back*
high	*i (ü)*	*ɨ*	*u (ɨ)*
	ɪ		*ʊ*
mid	*e (ö)*	*ə*	*o*
	ɛ		*ɔ*
		ʌ	
low	*æ*	*a*	*a*

Unparenthesized vowels are unrounded if front or central, and rounded if back; *ü* and *ö* are rounded; *ɨ* is unrounded. The special symbols for lax vowels (*ɪ, ʊ, ɛ, ɔ*) are generally used only where it is necessary to differentiate between tense and lax high or mid vowels. *ɨ* and *a* are used for both central and back vowels, as the two values seldom contrast in a given language.

Modifications indicated for consonants are: glottalization (*ť, ƙ*, etc.), retroflexion (*ṭ, ç, ʒ̣*), palatalization (*tʸ, kʸ, nʸ, lʸ*), labialization (*kʷ*), aspiration (*tʰ*), length (*t·*). For vowels: length (*a·*), three-mora length (*a:*), nasalization (*ą*), voicelessness (*A*). The commonest prosodic markings are, for stress: *á* (primary) and *à* (secondary), and for pitch: *á* (high), *à* (low), *â* (falling), and *ǎ* (rising); however, the details of prosodic systems and the uses of accents differ widely from language to language.

Words in Indian languages cited in italics in this volume are of two types. Those in Nahuatl (the language of the Aztecs) are in the regularized orthography of Siméon (1963). Italicized words in other Indian languages are written in phonemic transcription. That is, the letters and symbols are used in specific values defined for them by the structure of the sound system of the particular language. However, as far as possible, these phonemic transcriptions use letters and symbols in generally consistent values, as specified by the standard technical alphabet of the *Handbook*. Deviations from these standard values as well as specific details of the phonology of each language (or references to where they may be found) are given in an orthographic footnote in each tribal chapter or an early chapter in each tribal section. Italicized Navajo, Mescalero, Western Apache, and Pima-Papago words are in practical orthographies; these are phonemic but the Apachean orthographies use digraphs and trigraphs for some single phonemes. Special conventions for transcription and italics are used in "Apachean Languages" and "Uto-Aztecan Languages."

No italicized Indian word is broken at a line end except when a hyphen would be present anyway as part of the word. Words in italicized phonemic transcription are never capitalized, except that the practical orthographies follow the English rules of capitalization. Pronunciations or phonetic values given in the standard technical alphabet without regard to phonemic analysis are put in roman in square brackets rather than in italics. The glosses, or conventionalized translations, of Indian words are enclosed in single quotation marks.

Indian words recorded by nonspecialists or before the phonemic systems of their languages had been analyzed are often not written accurately enough to allow respelling in phonemic transcription. Where phonemic retranscription has been possible the citation of source has been modified by the label "phonemicized" or "from." A few words that could not be phonemicized have been "normalized"—rewritten by mechanical substitution of the symbols of the standard technical alphabet. Others have been rationalized by eliminating redundant or potentially misleading diacritics and substituting nontechnical symbols. Words that do not use the standard technical alphabet occasionally contain some letters used according to the values of other technical alphabets or traditional orthographies. The most common of these are c for the *Handbook*'s *š*; b and v for *β*; ts and tz for *c*; tsh, tj, and tc for *č*; dj for *ǯ*; pʻ and ph for *pʰ* (and similarly with some other consonants); hl for *ł*; j for *ž, ǯ*, or *y*; ʼ for *ʔ*; ʻ for *h* (or nondistinctive aspiration); oñ or oⁿ for *ǫ* (and with other vowels, for nasalization); ar for *a* and er for *ə*; u for *ɨ*; and x or j for *š, x*, or *h*, and z for *c* (in early Spanish sources). Other common variants in Spanish are discussed on p. xv. All nonphonemic transcriptions give only incomplete, and sometimes imprecise, approximations of the correct pronunciation.

Nontechnical Equivalents

Correct pronunciation, as with any foreign language, requires extensive training and practice, but simplified (incorrect) pronunciations may be obtained by ignoring the diacritics and reading the vowels as in Italian or Spanish and the consonants as in English. For a closer approximation to the pronunciation or to rewrite into a nontechnical transcription the substitutions indicated in the following table may be made.

technical	*nontechnical*
æ	ae
β	bh
c	ts
č	ch
δ	dh
δ̂	ddh
ε	e
γ	gh
ł	lh
λ	dl
ƛ	tlh
M	mh
N	nh
ŋ	ng
Ŋ	ngh
ɔ	o
θ	th
θ̂	tth
ɸ	ph
š	sh
W	wh
x	kh
Y	yh
ž	zh
ʒ	dz
ǯ	j
ʔ	'
k̓, p̓, t̓, etc.	k', p', t', etc.
a·,e·, k·, s·, etc.	aa, ee, kk, ss, etc.
ą, ę, etc.	an, en, etc.
kʸ, tʸ, etc.	ky, ty, etc.
kʷ	kw

English Pronunciations

The English pronunciations of the names of tribes and a few other words are indicated parenthetically in a dictionary-style orthography in which most letters have their usual English pronunciation. Special symbols are listed below, with sample words to be pronounced as in nonregional United States English. Approximate phonetic values are given in parentheses in the standard technical alphabet.

ŋ: thing (*ŋ*)
θ: thin (*θ*)
ð: this (*δ*)
zh: vision (*ž*)
ă: bat (*æ*)
ä: father (*a*)
ā: bait (*ey*)
e: bet (*ε*)
ē: beat (*iy*)
ə: about, gallop (*ə*)
ĭ: bit (*ɪ*)
ī: bite (*ay*)
ô: bought (*ɔ*)
ō: boat (*ow*)
o͝o: book (*ʊ*)
o͞o: boot (*uw*)
u: but (*ʌ*)

'(primary stress), ˌ(secondary stress): elevator ('eləˌvātər) (*ɛ́ləvèytər*)

Conventions for Illustrations

Map Symbols

●	Indian settlement
○	Abandoned settlement
■	Non-Indian town
□	Abandoned non-Indian town
	Mountain range, peak
— - - — - - —	National boundary
— - - - — - -	State boundary
- - - - - - - - - - - -	County boundary
(line)	River or stream
(broken line)	Intermittent or dry stream
Sonora	Settlement, site, reservation
Gila R.	Geographical feature

Toned areas on tribal maps represent estimated territory.

Credits and Captions

Credit lines give the original source of the illustrations or the collections where the artifacts shown are located. The numbers that follow are the catalog or inventory numbers of that repository. When the photographer mentioned in the caption is the source of the print reproduced, no credit line appears. "After" means that the *Handbook* illustrators have redrawn, rearranged, or abstracted the illustration from the one in the cited source. All maps and drawings not otherwise credited are by the *Handbook* illustrators. Measurements in captions are to the nearest millimeter if available; "about" indicates an estimate or a measurement converted from inches to centimeters. The following abbreviations are used in credit lines:

Amer.	American	Hist.	History
Anthr.	Anthropology, Anthropological	Histl.	Historical
		Ind.	Indian
Arch.	Archives	Inst.	Institute
Arch(a)eol.	Arch(a)eology, Arch(a)eological	Instn.	Institution
		Lib.	Library
Assoc.	Association	Mus.	Museum
Co.	County	NAA	National Anthropological Archives
Coll.	Collection(s)		
Dept.	Department	Nat.	Natural
Div.	Division	Natl.	National
Ethnol.	Ethnology, Ethnological	opp.	opposite
fol.	folio	pl(s).	plate(s)
Ft.	Fort	Soc.	Society
		U.	University

Metric Equivalents

10 mm = 1 cm	10 cm = 3.937 in.	1 km = .62 mi.	1 in. = 2.54 cm	25 ft. = 7.62 m
100 cm = 1 m	1 m = 39.37 in.	5 km = 3.1 mi.	1 ft. = 30.48 cm	1 mi. = 1.60 km
1,000 m = 1 km	10 m = 32.81 ft.	10 km = 6.2 mi.	1 yd. = 91.44 cm	5 mi. = 8.02 km

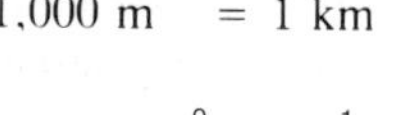

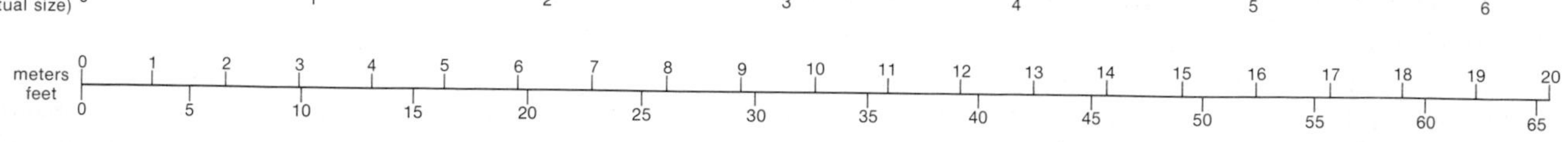

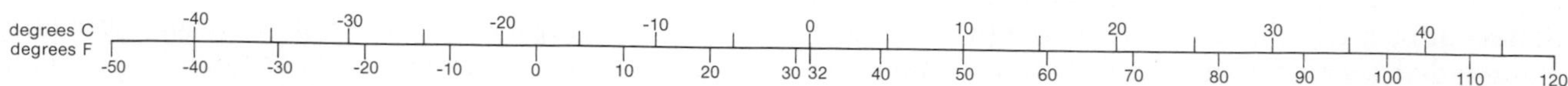

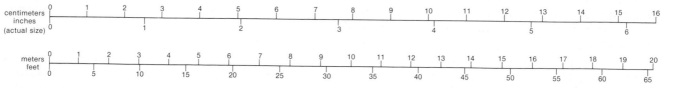

Preface

This is the fifth volume to be published of a 20-volume set planned to give an encyclopedic summary of what is known about the prehistory, history, and cultures of the aboriginal peoples of North America who lived north of the urban civilization of central Mexico. Volumes 5–8 and 11–15 treat the other major culture areas of this region (see p. i).

The Southwest is the only culture area requiring two volumes. This is because of the great amount of anthropological knowledge of the many peoples of this region, due in part to the fact that distinctive traditional cultures have survived here to a greater extent than elswhere on the continent. The present volume covers the cultures, histories, and languages of the non-Pueblo peoples of the Southwest, the groups sometimes referred to as Circum-Pueblo and those on the northern fringe of Mesoamerica (see p. ix). In volume 9 are comparable treatments of the Pueblo peoples, and also several discussions that deal with the whole Southwest, including the areas otherwise covered in this volume: the history of Southwestern anthropological research, the prehistory of the entire region, and the volume editor's introduction to both volumes. Conversely, the final five chapters in this volume are surveys that cover Pueblo as well as non-Pueblo cultures. Each of the two volumes is independently indexed; the introductory pages, including the prefaces, are also specific for each.

The editors recognize that there is an unfortunate difference in thoroughness of coverage of most of the societies in present Mexico, as compared to those now north of the international border. Much less research has been conducted on most northern Mexican societies; Mexican and Mexicanist anthropologists and historians have focused on the more populous and complex regions south of the area covered by this volume, while most United States and North American specialists have also ignored northern Mexico. Thus many Indian societies in this region are essentially unknown. Much less historical and archeological research has been done, and the ethnography is also less well covered than it is to the north. The ethnographic research that has been conducted (and is summarized in this volume) has usually had somewhat different emphases. In the United States, most attention has been devoted to aspects of culture that seemed particularly "Indian," while the relation of the societies to their non-Indian neighbors has usually not been well studied. In Mexico this distinction has been less important, so that we sometimes have more well-rounded knowledge of those societies at the period of research, but often have less knowledge about their cultural and social antecedents. Our lack of knowledge of many north Mexican Indian societies is also due to the distinct economic, social, and political history of the region. This was to have been discussed in a chapter titled "The Modern Capitalist World System and North Mexican Native Societies" that Ángel Palerm had agreed to provide. His death on June 10, 1980, deprived us of an important contribution that no one else was qualified to write. An indication of its themes can be found in an article he published (Palerm 1979).

Some topics relevant to the Southwest area are excluded from volumes 9 and 10 because they are more appropriately discussed on a continent-wide basis. Readers should refer to volume 1, Introduction, for general descriptions of anthropological and historical methods and sources and for summaries for the whole continent of certain topics regarding social and political organization, religion, and the performing arts. Volume 2 contains detailed accounts of the different kinds of Indian and Eskimo communities in the twentieth century, especially during its third quarter, and describes their relations with one another and with the surrounding non-Indian societies and nations. Volume 3 gives the environmental and biological backgrounds within which Native American societies developed, summarizes the early and late human biology or physical anthropology of Indians and Eskimos, and surveys the earliest prehistoric cultures. (Therefore the Paleo-Indian or Early Man period in the Southwest receives major treatment in volume 3 rather than in volume 9.) Volume 4 contains details on the history of Indian-White relations. Volume 16 is a continent-wide survey of technology and the visual arts—of material cultures broadly defined. Volume 17 surveys the native languages of North America, their characteristics and historical relationships. Volumes 18 and 19 are a biographical dictionary; included in the listing are many Southwest Indians. Volume 20 contains an index to the whole, which will serve to locate materials on Southwest Indians in other volumes as well as in this one; it also includes a list of errata found in all preceding volumes.

Preliminary discussions on the feasibility of the *Handbook* and alternatives for producing it began in 1965 in what was then the Smithsonian's Office of Anthropology. A history of the early development of the *Handbook* and a listing of the entire editorial staff will be found in volume 1. Detailed planning for the Southwest volumes was undertaken at a meeting of the General Editor and the Volume Editor with a specially selected Planning Committee (listed on page v) held in Santa Fe, New Mexico, January 7–9, 1971. At that time a tentative table of contents was drawn up, and qualified specialists on each topic were listed as potential authors. The chapter headings in the final volumes reproduce almost exactly the list decided upon at that meeting, and about two-thirds of the authors were those first invited. Inevitably, some replacements had to be made as people were unable to accept invitations or later found that they could not meet their commitment to write.

At the time they were invited, contributors were sent brief indications of the topics to be covered, prepared by the Volume Editor (with assistance, for the prehistory chapters, by Richard B. Woodbury and Douglas W. Schwartz; for the Yuman chapters by Kenneth M. Stewart; for the Navajo chapters by Gary Witherspoon; and for the Pima and Papago chapters by Donald M. Bahr). They were also sent a Guide for Contributors prepared by the General Editor describing the general aims and methods of the *Handbook* and the editorial conventions. One convention has been to avoid the present tense, where possible, in historical and cultural descriptions. Thus a statement in the past tense, with a recent date or approximate date, may also hold true for the time of writing. As they were received, the manuscripts were reviewed by the General Editor, the Volume Editor, and usually one or more referees (frequently including a member of the Planning Committee). Suggestions for changes and additions often resulted. During final preparation of the volume, many manuscripts received much earlier were significantly revised and updated, usually by the original authors. The published versions frequently reflect more editorial intervention than is customary for academic writings, since the encyclopedic aims and format of this publication made it necessary to attempt to eliminate duplication, avoid gaps in coverage, prevent contradictions, impose some standardization of organization and terminology, and keep within strict constraints on length.

This volume was planned and initially prepared at the same time as volume 9. However, when intensive work was begun in 1976 to complete volume 9 for publication, editorial work on volume 10 was postponed. In January 1981 intensive work on volume 10 began, with the revision and supplementing of manuscripts then in hand, and focused work on the illustrations and on final editing.

The first manuscript submitted for this volume was received on March 9, 1972, and the last on December 29, 1981; the first final acceptance of an author's manuscript was on February 2, 1973, and the last on January 21, 1982. Edited manuscripts were sent from the Washington office to authors for their approval between May 15, 1981, and March 17, 1982. These dates for all chapters are given in the list of Contributors. Late dates may reflect late invitations as well as late submissions.

Linguistic Editing

All cited words in Indian languages were referred to consultants with expert knowledge of the respective languages and, as far as possible, rewritten by them in the appropriate technical orthography. The consultants and the spelling systems are identified in an orthographic footnote to each tribal chapter or set of chapters; these footnotes were drafted by the Linguistic Editor, Ives Goddard.

Statements about the genetic relationships of Indian languages have also been checked with linguist consultants to ensure conformity with recent findings and terminology in comparative linguistics and to avoid conflicting statements within the *Handbook*. In general, only the less remote genetic relationships are mentioned in the individual tribal chapters. More remote relationships are treated in the chapters on Yuman, Uto-Aztecan, and Apachean languages in this volume, on "Historical Linguistics and Archeology" in volume 9, and in volume 17.

The Linguistic Editor served as coordinator and editor of these efforts by linguist consultants. A special debt is owed to these consultants, many of whom took time from their own research to check words with native speakers, for all provided advice and assistance without compensation. The Linguistic Editor is especially grateful to Robert W. Young, Kenneth L. Hale, Philip J. Greenfeld, Lynn Gordon, and Marie-Louise Liebe-Harkort.

In the case of words that could not be respelled in a technical orthography, an attempt has been made to rationalize the transcriptions used in earlier anthropological writings in order to eliminate phonetic symbols that are obsolete and diacritics that might convey a false impression of phonetic accuracy.

Synonymies

Toward the end of each tribal chapter (or, sometimes, in an early chapter of a set covering a single tribe or several closely related tribal groupings) is a section called Synonymy. This describes the various names that have been applied to the groups and subgroups treated in that chapter (or set of chapters), giving the principal variant spellings used in English and in Spanish, and often the names applied to the groups in neighboring Indian languages.

Not all spelling variants of names in the earlier Spanish sources have been included: alternations among u, v, and b; between j and x (and occasionally h and g); and between hu and gu (representing [w]), occur more often than indicated. Also ç (for [s]) in manuscript sources has sometimes been miscopied as c (normally used for [k]). Older Spanish spellings also often omit or write the accent in violation of modern rules for accentuation, and they often omit the dierisis over u, writing ambiguously gu for [g] and [gw] (word-medial [(γ)W]) and qu for [k] and [kw].

Most of the synonymies have been expanded or reworked by the Linguistic Editor, who has added names and analyses from the literature, from other manuscripts submitted for the *Handbook* (from which they have then been deleted), and as provided by linguist consultants. In this work the Linguistic Editor had the valuable assistance, in 1980–1981, of Willem J. de Reuse. When a synonymy is wholly or substantially the work of the Linguistic Editor or his assistant, a footnote specifying authorship is given.

These sections should assist in the identification of groups mentioned in the earlier historical and anthropological literature. They should also be examined for evidence on changes in the identifications and affiliations of groups, as seen by their own members as well as by neighbors and by outside observers.

Radiocarbon Dates

Authors were instructed to convert radiocarbon dates into dates in the Christian calendar. Such conversions normally have been made from the dates as originally published, without taking account of changes that may be required by developing research on revisions of the half-life of carbon 14, long-term changes in the amount of carbon 14 in the atmosphere, and other factors that may require modifications of absolute dates based on radiocarbon determinations.

Binomials

The scientific names of plant and animal genera and species, printed in italics, have been checked by the General Editor to ensure that they reflect modern usage by biological taxonomists. Scientific plant names have been brought into agreement with those accepted by Kearney et al. (1960), while zoological nomenclature has been revised in consultation with Smithsonian staff in the appropriate departments.

Bibliography

All references cited by contributors have been unified in a single list at the end of the volume. Citations within the text, by author, date, and often page, identify the works in this unified list. Wherever possible the *Handbook* Bibliographer, Lorraine H. Jacoby, has resolved conflicts between citations of different editions, corrected inaccuracies and omissions, and checked direct quotations against the originals. The bibliographic information has been verified by examination of the original work or from standard reliable library catalogs (especially the National Union Catalog and the published catalog of the Harvard Peabody Museum Library). The unified bibliography lists all and only the sources cited in the text of the volume, except personal communications. In the text, "personal communications" to an author are distinguished from personal "communications to editors." The sections headed Sources at the ends of most chapters provide general guidance to the most important sources of information on the topics covered.

Illustrations

Authors were requested to submit suggestions for illustrations: photographs, maps, drawings, and lists and locations of objects that might be illustrated. To varying degrees they compiled with this request. Yet considerations of space, balance, reproducibility, and availability required modifications in what was submitted. In addition much original material was provided by editorial staff members, from research they conducted in museums and other repositories, in the published literature, and from correspondence. Locating suitable photographs and earlier drawings and paintings was the responsibility of the Illustrations Researchers, while the Artifact Researcher found artifacts suitable for illustrating. These duties were divided as follows:

Jo Ann Moore, Scientific Illustrator—prepared all uncredited drawings except 17 drawn by Brigid Sullivan; supervised layout and design of all illustrations;

Gayle Barsamian, Artifact Researcher—all chapters 1979–1982;

Joanna Cohan Scherer, Illustrations Researcher—all chapters except as specified below;

Laura J. Greenberg, Illustrations Researcher—all chapters 1976–1980 and Navajo illustrations 1980–1982;

Anne F. Morgan, Assistant Illustrations Researcher—Apache illustrations 1981–1982.

All maps were drawn by the *Handbook* Cartographer, Judith Crawley Wojcik, who redrew some submitted by authors and compiled many new ones using information from the chapter manuscripts and from other sources. The base maps for all are authoritative standard ones, especially U.S. Geological Survey sheets and

Universal Jet Navigation Charts (from the National Oceanic and Atmospheric Administration). When possible, the hydrography has been reconstructed for the date of each map.

Captions for illustrations were usually composed by Scherer, Greenberg, Barsamian, or Moore, and for maps by Wojcik. However, all illustrations, including maps and drawings, and all captions have been approved by the General Editor, the Volume Editor, and the authors of the chapters in which they appear, and authors, referees, and editors frequently have participated actively in the selection process and in the improvement of captions.

We are indebted to individuals on the staffs of many museums for much time and effort spent in their collections locating photographs and artifacts and providing documentation on them. Many individuals, including professional photographers, have generously provided photographs free or at cost. Donnelly Cartographic Services (especially Sidney P. Marland, III, general manager) devoted meticulous care to converting the map artwork into final film.

Acknowledgments

Especially valuable suggestions for improving and editing chapters were provided by several scholars. Donald M. Bahr was particularly helpful in this respect for the Pima and Papago chapters. Bernard L. Fontana provided advice on the Papago and Pima illustrations. William L. Merrill assisted with the chapters on northwest Mexico and guided the selection and captioning of Tarahumara illustrations. Keith H. Basso supervised illustrations research for all the Apache chapters, composing nearly all the captions for photographs. Morris E. Opler also assisted with Apache illustrations, and Veronica Tiller with those of the Jicarilla Apache. Gary Witherspoon served as a consultant for the Navajo chapters through 1976; after then, David F. Aberle gave significant assistance on these chapters, while Joe Ben Wheat checked the final captions regarding Navajo artifacts. Stephen C. Jett provided important assistance on Navajo house types. Throughout, Ives Goddard was of particular assistance on matters of historical accuracy as well as on decisions made by the General Editor regarding organization, consistency, and other editorial procedures. The help of many other individuals is acknowledged in footnotes, in credit lines, and as communications to editors.

During the first few years of this project, the *Handbook* editorial staff in Washington worked on materials for all volumes of the series. Since intensive preparation of this volume began in 1981, especially important contributions were provided by: the Editorial Assistant, Nikki L. Lanza; the Production Manager and Manuscript Editor, Diane Della-Loggia; the Bibliographer, Lorraine H. Jacoby; the Scientific Illustrator, Jo Ann Moore; the Assistant Illustrator, Molly Kelly Ryan; the Cartographer, Judith Crawley Wojcik; the Illustrations Researchers, Joanna Cohan Scherer and Laura J. Greenberg; the Artifact Researcher, Gayle Barsamian; the Assistant Illustrations Researchers, Anne F. Morgan and Sheila Hoban; the Management Services Assistant, Melvina Jackson; and the Secretary, Valerie Ann Smith.

The Department of Anthropology, National Museum of Natural History, Smithsonian Institution, released the General Editor and the Linguistic Editor from part of their curatorial and research time.

Preparation and publication of this volume have been supported by federal appropriations made to the Smithsonian Institution, in part through its Bicentennial Programs.

The volume editor, Alfonso Ortiz, acknowledges the research and secretarial assistance of Nancy Soulé Arnon during the critical first year of 1971–1972, when the initial great flood of correspondence with authors for both volume 9 and 10 had to be attended to. Rebecca Ann Foulk provided a similar level of assistance during 1972–1973, when the largest number of manuscripts were edited and accepted. His greatest debt, however, is to Margaret Davisson Ortiz, for serving as editorial aid for volume 10.

Four months of direct support from a Travel and Study Grant from the Ford Foundation in 1971–1972 enabled the Volume Editor to devote much of his time to the *Handbook* during that period. Reduced teaching loads at Princeton University during 1972–1973 and at the University of New Mexico during 1974–1975 further expedited editorial work.

March 26, 1982

William C. Sturtevant
Alfonso Ortiz

Yumans: Introduction

KENNETH M. STEWART

Kroeber (1943:21) classified the Yuman languages into four groups:

(1) Delta—Cocopa, Kahwan, and Halyikwamai, the three southernmost languages along the lower Colorado River. In the nineteenth century the Kahwan and Halyikwamai lost their tribal identity, merging into the Maricopa tribe.

(2) River—Quechan (or Yuma) and Mohave, residents along the lower Colorado River where it forms the boundary between California and Arizona, plus the Yumans living along the Middle Gila River in Arizona, the Maricopa proper, Halchidhoma, and Kavelchadom. The tribes of the Gila River, now merged into the Maricopa, were former residents along the lower Colorado.

(3) Upland (northwest or upland Arizona; called Arizona by Kroeber)—Walapai, Havasupai, and Yavapai.

(4) California (Mexican and American California north of 31° north latitude)—Diegueño, Kamia, Paipai (or Akwa'ala), and Kiliwa.

Kroeber's linguistic classification has been considerably revised by research done in the 1960s and 1970s ("Yuman Languages," this vol.), but the units he set up correspond well to the major cultural subgroups of the Yumans and will be used in the cultural overview of the Yumans given in this chapter.

The territory of the Yumans was nearly all desert or semidesert, but annual overflows along the Colorado and to a lesser extent the Gila made possible riverine agricultural oases with relatively dense populations. In the deserts away from the rivers the food quest was more arduous, and in most places little or no agriculture was possible for peoples of simple technology.

The Desert tradition of archeology was undoubtedly ancestral to the Yuman cultures. In particular, the Mexican Yumans and the Upland Arizona Yumans remained closer to the ancient cultural substratum than did the Yumans of the River and Delta groups. In this respect, the cultures of the Mexican and Upland Arizona Yumans resembled those of the Paiutes of the Great Basin in low intensity and lack of specialization, although they were influenced to varying degrees by adjacent tribes. Thus, the Diegueño were culturally much like their Shoshonean-speaking Mission Indian neighbors in southern California, and they also manifested cultural influences from the more distant River Yumans.

The Delta and River Yumans

Although it remains to be ascertained how long Yumans have lived along the Colorado and from whence they came, archeologists concur in the conclusion that probable ancestors of the River Yumans have resided in the area for at least 1,000 years (Rogers 1945; Colton 1945; Schroeder 1952b). The rather scanty cultural materials that have been recovered in the few archeological surveys and excavations along the lower Colorado suggest a mode of life in prehistoric times essentially similar to that of the historic Yumans.

The cultures of the River and Delta Yumans were so similar to each other that they may be considered together. The River and Delta Yumans constituted a series of agricultural tribes along the lower Colorado and Gila rivers. Persistent warfare between the tribes had precipitated numerous population shifts and amalgamations, until by the middle of the nineteenth century the Yuman tribes on the Colorado had been reduced to three: Mohave, Quechan, and Cocopa. The ancestral homeland of the northernmost tribe, the Mohave, was in the Mohave Valley, and the Mohave also claimed the northern part of the Colorado Valley, locale of the present Colorado River Reservation, by virtue of earlier residence. From it they ousted the Halchidhoma tribe between 1827 and 1829 (Dobyns, Ezell, and Ezell 1963). To the south and centering around the confluence of the Gila and Colorado rivers, the Quechan occupied a rather extensive territory that reached north to the vicinity of the present community of Blythe, California, where they were intermingled with the Mohave. South of the Quechan, in the delta country at the head of the Gulf of California, were the Cocopa, a tribe to which the Quechan and Mohave were hostile.

By the early nineteenth century the Maricopa were living along the middle Gila, in south-central Arizona, although at an undetermined time before 1700 they are thought to have been resident on the lower Colorado (Spier 1933:11ff.). By 1840 they had been joined by remnants of the Halyikwamai, Kahwan, Halchidhoma, and Kavelchadom, weary of being battered about by the Quechan-Mohave alliance. The weakened tribes had shifted their locations periodically and were reported in varying places by different explorers. For instance, according to the chroniclers of the Juan de Oñate expedition of 1604, the Halchidhoma were the first tribe on the Colorado below the mouth of the Gila (Hammond and Rey 1953), while Father Eusebio Kino, a century later, reported them north of the Gila. Francisco Garcés, in 1776, found the Halchidhoma occupying a 40-mile stretch in the northern part of the Colorado Valley (Coues 1900, 1:125), which they abandoned to the Mohave half a century later. They had shifted northward to escape their enemies, the Quechan, but this only brought them closer to the at least equally formidable Mohave.

Oñate found the Halyikwamai on the east bank of the Colorado near the Cocopa, and Garcés reported them north of the Cocopa and south of the Kahwan. To the north of the Kahwan were the Kamia and Quechan. The Kahwan were living with the Halchidhoma at the time when remnants of the Halchidhoma departed from the Colorado Valley. The Kavelchadom were situated on the lower Gila in the early nineteenth century; they were said to be a Halchidhoma group who had earlier left the Colorado because of dissension (Spier 1933:9). The Kavelchadom joined the Maricopa at about the same time as the other remnant tribes (Spier 1933:3).

All the River Yumans practiced floodwater agriculture, growing corn, beans, and cucurbits in the rich silt deposited in the bottomlands as the spring floods receded. Their diet also included mesquite beans and other wild plant foods, plus fish and small game such as rabbits.

The River Yumans did not live in compact villages; rather, their settlements were of the rancheria type, each house being separated from its nearest neighbor by 100 yards or more. The Colorado River tribes lived in low, rectangular, earth-covered houses, but the Maricopa of the Gila had adopted the round houses of their Piman neighbors. Technology was of little interest to the River Yumans, and remained at a low level of development.

Informality characterized the political and social organization of the River Yumans; however, they manifested a characteristic rare in the Southwest: a veritable tribal unity. With this sense of nationality went a minimum of organization for social control. Tribal chiefs have been reported for the Mohave, Quechan, and Maricopa, but they had slight authority. In each settlement were men of prominence who were recognized as leaders, but who again had little or no power of coercion. The tribes were loosely divided into bands and local groups.

Marriage was simple and without ceremony, and while most marriages were monogamous, divorce was so easy and frequent that there was an approach to serial monogamy. Residence after marriage was flexible, but with a patrilocal bias. The nuclear family was the basic unit of economic and social cooperation, although an extended family constituted the core of a settlement. There was a system of patrilineal, exogamous clans, which were almost functionless, except that all the women of the clan were known by the clan name rather than by personal names.

The religions of the River Yumans centered around a most unusual conception of prenatal dreaming, in which the unborn soul of the dreamer was projected back in time to the scene of creation, where power was conferred by the deities. Not all people had "great dreams," but power for success as a warrior, a chief, a shaman, or a singer had to be dreamed rather than learned. Ceremonialism, which was little developed, was replaced by the singing of lengthy cycles of songs, which were supposed to have been dreamed.

Warfare was another emphasis in River Yuman culture, and those who had dreamed power were the leaders. The principal weapons were clubs of hard wood; the weak bows and untipped arrows of the River Yumans were relatively ineffective.

Little attention was paid to the earlier stages of the life cycle, and observances in connection with them were without ritual. The greatest emphasis was placed upon death; the cremations of the River Yumans involved relatively elaborate procedures and prescriptions.

The Upland Yumans

A large area in northwest and north-central Arizona was sparsely populated by bands of Yuman-speaking Indians conventionally subgrouped under the names Walapai, Havasupai, and Yavapai. Although it has been customary to distinguish between the Walapai and Havasupai tribes, which are politically separate groups, they were ethnically one people, speaking the same language and participating in the same basic culture. Their enemies, the Yavapai of the mountains and deserts of central and west-central Arizona, have been classed with the Walapai and Havasupai as Upland Yumans.

The Havasupai farmed along a creek in a side branch of the Grand Canyon. They spent the winter months hunting and gathering over the Coconino Plateau, to the south of their inaccessible canyon. The Walapai ranged over a large and very arid territory to the south and west of the Havasupai, hunting all available game animals and collecting a variety of wild plant foods. The Yavapai similarly relied mainly on hunting and gathering, roaming over a vast area of 20,000 square miles of mountain and desert to the south and east of the Walapai. Three subtribes of the Yavapai have been distinguished—Yavepe (Northeastern), Tolkapaya (Western), and Kewevkapaya (Southeastern), each of which was further subdivided into bands.

The Upland Yumans resembled the Paiutes of the Great Basin in specific cultural details as well as in the general simplicity of their cultures, and they inhabited a similar environment. Subsistence patterns and technology of the Upland Yumans were reminiscent of the Great Basin, as were social organization and religion. Unlike the agricultural River Yumans, the Upland Yumans remained essentially hunters and gatherers, although the Havasupai were able to farm in a well-watered canyon, and some Walapais and Yavapais did a little farming in a few favorable localities. Cultural differences among the Upland Yumans were the result both of differential contacts with other tribes and of ecological adjustments to varying environments.

The Upland Yumans lived in dome-shaped shelters thatched with grass, they dressed in buckskin, and they wove basketry as their principal craft. Upland Yuman chiefs were men of prominence rather than authority, who were respected for their oratorical abilities and prowess in war. Ceremonialism was meager, and concepts of the supernatural were not carefully worked out. Shamanism was prominent, the shaman being primarily a medical practitioner.

California Yumans

On a cultural basis the California Yumans can be divided into the Diegueño and the Mexican Yumans. The Diegueño are treated in "Tipai-Ipai" (vol. 8). The Mexican Yumans, who are culturally similar but do not form a linguistic subgroup, fall outside the territory covered by the *Handbook*. The communities that retain some Indian identity have been described by Owen (1969), and further information on earlier periods is in Massey (1966) and Spicer (1969).

History of Ethnographic Research

Before the turn of the twentieth century the Yumans were little known. Yuman territory was remote and seldom visited during Spanish and Mexican times, and the few accounts by Spanish explorers contain a paucity of ethnographic information. The best account is that of Garcés, who in 1776 journeyed from the Quechan to the Mohave, then overland eastward to the Walapai and Havasupai (K.M. Stewart 1966a). The fur trappers who traveled through Yuman territory in the 1820s and 1830s, including Jedediah Smith, James O. Pattie, and George C. Yount, wrote documents that contain only minimal information about the Yumans (K.M. Stewart 1966). The accounts of the railroad and steamboat explorers of the 1850s (among them Amiel Whipple and Joseph C. Ives) were somewhat more informative (K.M. Stewart 1969). For the late nineteenth century there are the brief descriptions of the Mohave by Bourke (1889), of the Havasupai by Cushing (1882), and of the Yavapai by Corbusier (1886). But no fieldwork that meets modern anthropological standards was done among the Yumans prior to 1900, and with the outstanding exception of A.L. Kroeber's Mohave studies, the Yumans were neglected by anthropologists until the 1920s and 1930s.

Kroeber did his pioneering work among the Mohave between 1900 and 1911, and published his preliminary report in 1902. His fuller account of the Mohave (Kroeber 1925) was the forerunner of a series of ethnographic studies of Yuman tribes, sponsored or inspired by the University of California, although in part conducted by anthropologists affiliated with other institutions. The result was a series of basic monographs and papers on the Yumans, including those by Spier on the southern Diegueño (1923), Havasupai (1928), and Maricopa (1933); those by Gifford on the Kamia (1931), Cocopa (1933), Kewevkapaya Yavapai (1932), and Yavepe and Tolkapaya Yavapai (1936); by Gifford and Lowie (1928) on the Akwa'ala; by Forde (1931) on the Quechan; and by Meigs (1939) on the Kiliwa. During the 1930s also George Devereux made the first of his many field trips to the Mohave, which continued at intervals to 1950. Philip Drucker obtained culture trait lists from Yuman tribes in 1934 and 1938 as part of the University of California program of the culture element distribution survey of western North America. Castetter and Bell (1951) began their field studies of Yuman agriculture in 1937.

During the 1940s studies of the Cocopa by W.H. Kelly (1942, 1949, 1949a) appeared, and Abraham Halpern (1946–1947) published articles on the Quechan language. Kenneth M. Stewart, William J. Wallace, and George Fathauer did fieldwork among the Mohave, as did Elman Service among the Havasupai. In the 1950s additional work among the Yumans was stimulated by the Indian Claims Commission cases. Among the anthropologists who did research on the Yumans and testified as expert witnesses were A.L. Kroeber and Kenneth M. Stewart on the Mohave; Robert C. Euler, Henry Dobyns, and Robert A. Manners on the Walapai; and Paul Ezell and Alfonso Ortiz on the Maricopa. The 1960s brought a new wave of studies, more specialized in nature than the earlier general ethnographies. These included the works of Bee (1963) on Quechan social organization, Martin (1966) on Havasupai economics, Sherer (1965) on Mohave clans, and Fontana (1963) on the history of the Colorado River Reservation. Kenneth M. Stewart returned to the Mohave for further ethnographic studies in the 1970s.

Yuman Languages

MARTHA B. KENDALL

The Yuman ('yo͞omən) languages are relatively closely related compared to those in other North American language families. They were spoken in the 1980s in the same general areas where they were first encountered by the Spaniards in the sixteenth century, in western Arizona and southern California, in the valley of the lower Colorado River, and in northern Baja California. There were no complete or systematic descriptions of these languages until the mid-1940s, although partial word lists and short texts occasionally accompanied more ethnographically or historically oriented discussions of Yuman-speaking groups (for example, Gatschet 1887–1892; Harrington 1908). A summary of the early literature that included linguistic materials is in Wares (1968).

The first comprehensive study based on modern linguistic principles was Halpern's (1946–1947) description of Quechan (Yuma), based on fieldwork conducted in 1935 and 1938. Scholarly interest in these languages picked up in the 1950s and increased in the 1960s and 1970s, resulting in descriptions of all the extant languages and of many individual dialects (Crawford 1966; Gorbet 1976; Gordon 1980; Hardy 1979; L. Hinton 1977; Joël 1966; Kendall 1976; Langdon 1970; Mixco 1972; Munro 1976; Redden 1966). In addition to individual studies, reports on this work have appeared in Langdon and Silver (1976:87–174), Klar, Langdon, and Silver (1980), and in the proceedings of a series of Yuman language and Hokan language workshops (Redden 1976, 1977, 1978, 1979, 1980).

Classification

As a result of these descriptions and discussions, a classification and subgrouping has been worked out that is generally accepted by Yuman language specialists (see table 1). This classification distinguishes four branches for the Yuman family: Pai, River, Delta-California, and Kiliwa. The Pai subgroup consists of Upland Yuman (comprising the peoples known as Yavapai, Walapai, and Havasupai) and Paipai. The River subgroup includes Mohave, Quechan, and Maricopa, along with the extinct dialects Halchidhoma and Kavelchadom. The Delta-California branch consists of two languages: a dialectally diverse language that linguists call Diegueño, spoken by the peoples known as Tipai, Ipai, and Kamia; and Cocopa, together with the extinct dialects Halyikwamai and Kahwan, which were closely related to Cocopa linguistically but were amalgamated into Maricopa in the nineteenth century. Kiliwa is a single language. Because it is so divergent from the other three branches of the Yuman family, Kiliwa could possibly be classified as coordinate with them, which would result in classification dividing Yuman into two subgroups, Kiliwa and Core Yuman, with Core Yuman subdivided into the first three branches of table 1.

An earlier classification of the Yuman languages, influential for many years, was that of Kroeber (1943), who recognized four Yuman subgroups: Arizona (the equivalent of Upland Yuman), River, Delta (embracing Cocopa and its extinct congeners), and California (composed of Tipai, Ipai, Kamia, Kiliwa, and Paipai, the last identified as Akwa'ala). At the time he proposed this classification, Kroeber noted that the materials available for the California branch were sketchy, and he expressed some reservations about the integrity of this subgroup. When data did become available on Paipai and Kiliwa, these languages were separated out and

Table 1. The Yuman Languages

Branch	*Location*
Pai branch	
Paipai	Baja California
Upland Yuman or Northern Pai (Havasupai, Yavapai, Walapai)	Arizona
River branch	Colorado River
Mohave	
Quechan	
Maricopa (and Halchidhoma, Kavelchadom)	
Delta-California branch	
Diegueño (Tipai, Ipai, Kamia)	San Diego and Imperial counties and Baja California
Cocopa (and Halyikwamai, Kahwan)	Lower Colorado River
Kiliwa branch	Baja California
Kiliwa	

NOTE: Names in parentheses are groups speaking dialects of a single language.

SOURCES: Langdon 1976b; Langdon and Munro 1980:122.

set up as distinct branches, making a total of six (Joël 1964). Further work led to the subgrouping of Paipai with Upland Yuman (W. Winter 1967) and of the former Delta branch with the Diegueño dialects, which was all that remained of Kroeber's California branch (Langdon 1976b). The classification of the extinct varieties of Yuman follows Kroeber (1943), who based his conclusions on the opinions of elderly Indians interviewed in the 1930s and a Kahwan vocabulary obtained in the same period. Kroeber is essentially confirmed on these points by the classification Francisco Garcés made in 1776 on the basis of firsthand contacts (reported in Coues 1900, 2:443).

The nearest linguistic relative of Yuman is Cochimi, a small family containing an uncertain number of poorly documented extinct languages formerly spoken in Baja California south of the Kiliwa (Troike 1976; Mixco 1976). More distant relationships have been postulated with languages in the Hokan stock, although the precise extent and inclusiveness of this grouping was not established by the early 1980s (Langdon 1977).

The languages of the Yuman family are spoken in parts of three culture areas conventionally and somewhat arbitrarily distinguished by anthropologists: California, the Southwest, and Baja California. The fact that the Yuman-speaking populations are divided up in this way is an indication of the arbitrariness of any attempt to draw sharp lines among Indian groups on the basis of cultural criteria; Yuman languages, and to some extent Yuman cultures, form a recognizable continuum across their geographical spread. The Yuman tribes of California are considered in volume 8 ("Tipai-Ipai") and those of Baja California are described by Owen (1969).

Survey of Languages

Upland

Upland Yuman (Northern Pai, Arizona Yuman) is a single language, although it is spoken by peoples usually classified under three different ethnic labels: Havasupai, Walapai, and Yavapai. These labels do not actually correspond to the dialectal subunits of the language, since there is more diversity among the Yavapai dialects than there is between those of the Walapai and Havasupai, which are nearly identical (Kendall 1975). Nevertheless, the standard tripartite division is used here as the basis of this discussion of Upland Yuman, both because it corresponds to the usual political classification and because it is in conformity with the strong sense of linguistic distinctiveness felt especially by the Walapai and Havasupai.

• WALAPAI In 1980 there were between 900 and 1,100 Walapais, most of whom spoke or understood the language. Walapai was formerly spoken in six regional dialects (with centers near the present towns of Peach Springs, Kingman, Hackberry-Valentine, Big Sandy, Chloride, and Seligman), but dialect leveling took place after 1873, when the United States government settled all the Walapai subunits together. By 1959 Walapai was developing age-graded dialects with the younger speakers tending to favor Walapai structures that parallel English and tending to use more English words than older speakers. By 1963 the last monolingual speakers of the dialect had died, which left a population composed entirely of Walapai-English bilinguals (Redden 1966, 1). The Walapai have developed a vigorous literacy program in their native idiom since 1977, publishing and distributing materials of local interest such as newsletters, pamphlets, and collections of texts. In addition, the Walapai were compiling a comprehensive bilingual Walapai-English dictionary in late 1981, and Walapai scholars were contributing papers on their dialect to scholarly conferences (Powskey, Watahomigie, and Yamamoto 1980; Watahomigie, Powskey, and Yamamoto 1979).

• HAVASUPAI Havasupai has about 500 speakers, the total Havasupai population being able to speak and understand the tribal idiom. According to L. Hinton (1980) the dialect is stratified generationally, with younger speakers making obligatory phonological adjustments in the production of person-marking prefixes that older speakers make only optionally. In addition, Havasupai speakers generally have a marked tendency to voice bilabial and velar stops in contexts where speakers of Yavapai and other Yuman languages produce voiceless sounds, and Havasupais have apparently replaced the old Yuman tapped or trilled *r* with a modern Havasupai voiced stop [d].

Havasupai is both thriving and changing. The Havasupai people can for the most part read and write their dialect and are developing textual materials to be used in their schools. How the stabilizing forces of literacy will interact with the Havasupais' tendencies to innovate linguistically is unknown, but in any case, the future of this dialect looks remarkably promising.

• YAVAPAI The term Yavapai does not refer to a single political or linguistic entity, but to a collection of locally organized groups speaking mutually intelligible but nevertheless differentiable subdialects. Gifford (1932, 1936) grouped this set of Yavapai bands into three main divisions, identified as Yavepe (Northeastern Yavapai), Tolkapaya (Western Yavapai) and Kewevkapaya (Southeastern Yavapai). The Northeastern Yavapai division is represented linguistically in speech varieties called Yavepe (spoken by people in the Verde Valley and Beaver Creek regions, along with those located in the Jerome tablelands) and Wipukpaya (spoken by people who come from the Oak Creek Canyon area). These two subdialects were barely distinguishable in the 1980s. What distinguished Yavepe from Wipukpaya in earlier times were apparently vocabulary differences on the order of *bag* versus *sack* or *soda* versus *pop* in American English, but there may have been pronunciation discriminations as well. The information that would permit a lucid discussion of speech variation in Yavepe is no longer available and is unrecoverable from Gifford's materials. Furthermore, it is difficult to assess exactly how many subdialects this division included, for it is possible that more local varieties existed than Gifford or his consultants recognized, a statement that could also be made for the Tolkapaya and Kewevkapaya. Fortunately, systematic comparison of Yavepe and Tolkapaya became possible in the late 1970s, providing some needed insights into the internal diversity of what is generally called Yavapai (Chung 1976; Hardy 1979; Hardy and Gordon 1979; Kendall 1975, 1976).

In precontact times, the total population incorporated into the three classic divisions was about 1,500. In the early 1980s, after a century of intermarriage with Apaches and other Indians, there were few full-blooded Yavapais under 45 years of age. This has had linguistic consequences. The language was spoken by 100 to 150 individuals in one form or another, but only the generation born before 1925 used it to tell stories or recite speeches, and even then these speakers were distributed over at least five geographically separated speech communities, which further limited their opportunities for daily conversation. Children did not learn Yavapai unless they lived with grandparents, which meant that if they learned the language at all, they could not speak it with their age-mates. This situation is remarkably different from that described for the Havasupai and Walapai peoples, but it reflects a very different set of historical circumstances. The total Yavapai population in 1875 was a little over 1,000; in 1905 it was half that (Spicer 1962). The decline in Yavapai numbers, a consequence of their incarceration at San Carlos, Arizona, practically required that they marry out of their tribe, there being so few eligible partners available within it at any given time. When the Yavapais married out, they tended to marry Apaches, with whom they do not share a language but with whom they were traditionally associated. They did not tend to marry Walapais or Havasupais, with whom they do share a language, because they considered the Walapais their enemies and considered the Havasupais the allies of their foe. Intermarriages between Yavapais and Apaches did result in a number of Yavapai-Apache bilinguals (Mierau 1963), but more usually it contributed to the acquisition of a lingua franca, English or occasionally Spanish, which was in any case being forced on the children of both groups through compulsory education. In the late 1960s there were approximately 25 Apache-Yavapai bilinguals in the Clarkdale, Cottonwood, and Camp Verde areas, with an undetermined number at Middle Verde, Fort McDowell, Prescott, and San Carlos. Of the Clarkdale group surveyed, most reported an imperfect command of their second Indian language, and most reported that they had considerably fewer opportunities to use it than to use English (Kendall 1968). These factors are contributing to the slow but steady replacement of Yavapai by English.

Speakers of Verde Valley Yavapai, if asked to characterize the difference between Yavepe and Walapai, typically provide sets of words that they use differently from Walapai speakers. The number of words on the list would of course depend on the depth and richness of contact the Yavapai had had with Walapais, but in any case, it would represent what strikes native Yavapai speakers as the most salient feature distinguishing their speech from varieties found farther north. Most Verde Valley Yavapais, for example, know that the word they use for 'horse' (*ʔhat*) is the same word that Walapais and Havasupais use for 'dog', and most also know that the Yavapai word meaning 'dog' (*kθar*) is like the Walapai word for 'coyote' (*kθat*). Table 2 presents examples that native speakers are likely to cite as discriminating Yavapai from Havasupai and Walapai.

The Havasupai and Walapai word for 'dog' is the older form, since it, or a cognate form (*ʔxat*) appears in Mohave, Maricopa, Diegueño, and Cocopa. This seems to mean that the Yavapais replaced their old word for 'dog' with the word formerly meaning 'coyote', and used the 'dog' word for the animal that the Spaniards introduced into the New World: the horse. The Walapais and Havasupais on the other hand adopted the Spanish word for 'horse' in a modified form. From this information the argument might be made for a

Table 2. Comparison of a Yavapai dialect with Walapai and Havasupai

	Yavepe	*Walapai/ Havasupai*
dog	*kθar*	*ʔhat*
horse	*ʔhat*	*vʔolo* (from Spanish *caballo*)
coyote	*kθar ʔkʷara* (*ʔkʷar* 'desert')	*kθat*
cat	*nʸmi*	*muso* (ultimately from Spanish *mizo*, perhaps via Hopi)
bobcat	*ymita*	*nʸmi*
mountain lion	*ʔhat ʔkʷila*	*nʸmita*
wolf		*ʔhatʔkʷila*
deer	*qʷaqa*	*qʷaqa*
cow	*qʷaqta*	*waksi* (ultimately from Spanish *vaca*)

SOURCE: Kendall 1980.

separation of Yavapai from Walapai and Havasupai predating the arrival of the Spaniards, and a different history of interaction with Spanish speakers postdating the contact. There is of course other evidence that this was the case and table 2 provides additional hints. For example, it looks as if the Yavapais applied the old Yuman word for 'bobcat', *nʸmi*, to house cats and used the old 'mountain lion' in its stead for 'bobcat'. The Walapais and Havasupais on the other hand borrowed another foreign word to refer to domesticated cats and retained the old Yuman 'bobcat' and 'mountain lion' terms in their original meanings. It also looks as if the Yavapais made up a term for 'cow' based on their indigenous word for 'deer' (*qwaqta* = *qwaqa* 'deer', *ta* 'big, mature'), but the Havasupai and Walapai borrowed the Spanish term *vaca,* most likely through an Indian intermediary like Zuni *wa·kaši*.

While Yavepe speakers are more likely to cite vocabulary differences than grammatical distinctions between the way they talk and the way their neighbors to the north do, it is the grammatical differences that strike non-Yumans as most obvious. The northern dialects, Walapai and Havasupai, indicate tense or aspect in their sentences with a combination of auxiliary verbs and aspect markers; the southern dialects, Yavepe, Wipukpaya, and Tolkapaya, use compound tense-markers (Chung 1976) to accomplish similar grammatical functions. Thus in Yavepe and Wipukpaya a verb describing an on-going action or an enduring state normally ends in the compound tense-marker suffix *-kəm,* for example: *smá·kəm* 'he is sleeping' (*smá·* 'sleep') and *himá·kəm* 'he is dancing' (*himá·* 'dance'). In Walapai and Havasupai, on-going action is indicated with an active auxiliary verb following the main verb, and enduring states are indicated with a stative auxiliary following the main verb, for example: *smá·g yù* 'he is sleeping' and *himá·g wì* 'he is dancing'. *yu* is the stative auxiliary, *wi* is the active auxiliary, and *g* indicates same subject. Tolkapaya's compound tense-markers seem to incorporate the active-stative distinction that Walapai and Havasupai's auxiliaries manifest, and at the same time, to freeze them into verbal suffixes rather than employ them as auxiliaries: *smá·kyum* 'he is sleeping' and *himá·kwim* 'he is dancing'. The evidence for the "frozenness" of Tolkapaya and Yavepe tense-markers shows up in first- and second-person forms of verbs, which must be inflected for subject. Compare Yavepe *ˀsmá·kəm* 'I am sleeping' and *məsmá·kəm* 'you are sleeping' with Tolkapaya *məsmá·kyum* 'you are sleeping'. These forms show that only the verb takes a person-marking prefix. In Havasupai and Walapai either the verb or the auxiliary may be marked by a first-person prefix *ˀ-*, and both the verb and the auxiliary will accept second person indicating *m-*. The age of the speaker is important in this regard since younger Havasupai speakers show a tendency not to pronounce the first-person morpheme in initial position on verbs (see L. Hinton 1980 for details).

Havasupai and Walapai have *ˀsma·(g)ˀyu* 'I am sleeping' and *məsma·ŋŋu* 'you are sleeping'. The second-person form, *məsma·ŋŋu,* could be represented abstractly as *m-sma·-g m-yu,* where the two *m*s indicate the subject of the verb-auxiliary couplet, *sma·* is the main verb, *yu* is the auxiliary, and *g* (which appears in Yavapai as *k*) is a referencing morpheme indicating that the verb and auxiliary have identical subjects. The sequence *-g m-* undergoes an assimilation process, resulting in the velarization of the nasal segment. The first-person paradigm is a little more complicated, since older speakers seem to alternate between pronouncing the sequence *ˀsma·gyu, ˀsma·ˀyu,* and, more rarely, *ˀsma·gˀyu*; and younger speakers leave off the initial glottal stop. At any rate, Yavapai speakers do not introduce the subject pronoun morphemes between the reference morpheme *-k(-g)* and the auxiliary. The Yavapai verb endings *-kəm, -kyum,* and *-kwim* are synchronically monomorphemic, although they are obviously reduced forms of the verb-auxiliary sequences that Havasupai and Walapai retain. Evidence from Tolkapaya shows this most clearly (Chung 1976; Hardy 1979).

This kind of speech variation, no matter how great or small it appears to nonspeakers of Upland Yuman, does not impede communication when native speakers from one dialect area talk to people from another (Biggs 1957; W. Winter 1957) or when people of one generation talk to people of another. People do notice and comment on the difference between the way they talk and the way others do, but clearly the similarities they notice outweigh the distinctions. What these speech patterns represent is partially shared social histories, combined with and working against tendencies to innovate or conserve. The Upland Yuman dialects overlap considerably, but there are still enough distinctions among them to make them compelling ethnic or social indexes.

Paipai

Paipai (formerly identified by the Mohave term Akwa'ala, as in Kroeber 1943; Gifford and Lowie 1928) is spoken in several small speech communities in northern Baja California, near San Miguel, Santa Catarina, and San Isidoro. There are probably fewer than 100 speakers of Paipai, the majority of them over 50 years of age.

The relationship of Paipai to Upland Yuman has been the subject of a lively debate since Kroeber (1943) noticed a strong resemblance between this language and Walapai, with which he had had some firsthand experience, but he could not believe that resemblance was anything other than accidental. He hypothesized that the northern Arizona dialects and Paipai were similar because they were all examples of a conservative or

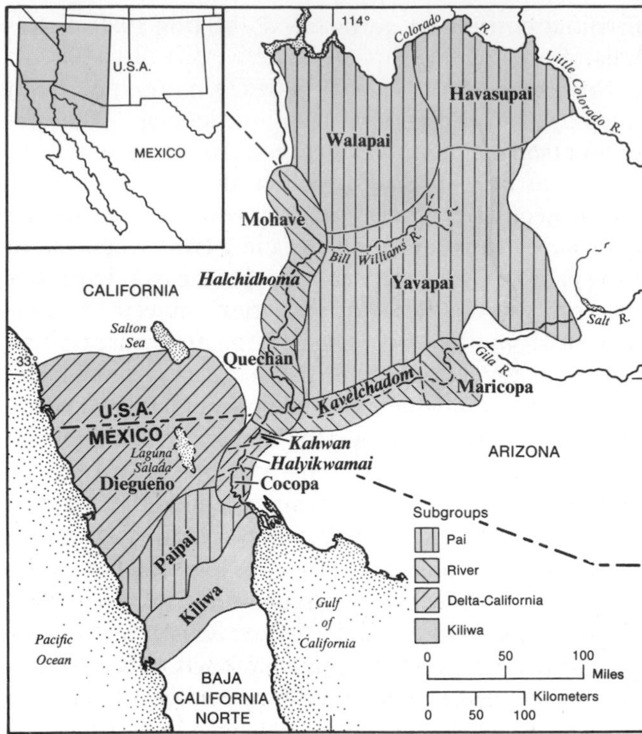

Fig. 1. Approximate distribution of Yuman languages at time of European contact. Extinct languages are in italics.

"generalized Yuman" structure, while the intervening languages were unlike them due to linguistic specializations. Kroeber (1943:25) found "nothing to indicate a tribal migration from desert to desert across the Colorado; at least not as compared with the likelihood of speech specialization along the river."

Joël (1964) amplified the "generalized Yuman" hypothesis in her discussion of the internal relationships of the Yuman family. She suggested that the development of agriculture and subsequent establishment of trade networks with non-Yuman tribes had served as the impetus to linguistic specialization among the River Yumans.

> A prime requisite for rapid change is the stimulation of ideas from varied sources. The Yumans on the river received frequent visits from people of surrounding tribes, including some non-Yumans (e.g., Hopi, Pima). In this way, presumably, influences reached them from a wide area. Such a situation would be favorable for a fairly rapid rate of cultural change and probably not only facilitated the developments mentioned above but also stimulated further changes. The linguistic specialization of these tribes, thus, can be regarded as a part of their relatively rapid over-all cultural specialization (Joël 1964:104).

This statement of course ignores certain well-established facts concerning contact between the Northern Yuman peoples and non-Yuman groups. The Havasupai practiced agriculture, and this practice allowed them to trade with the Hopi and Navajo. The Yavapai and the Apache were closely allied; the Walapai were in contact with the Paiutes to their north. There is no reason to suppose that such economic and military leagues did not leave their impress on the Upland Yuman speakers. However, following the "River specialization" hypothesis, Joël established Paipai as a branch of Yuman coordinate with Upland but not in the same subgroup.

W. Winter (1967) argued for the revision of Joël's proposed classification, presenting evidence that Paipai ought to be included as a separate language within what had formerly been called the Arizona division. In essence, Winter rejected the "generalized Yuman" hypothesis that both Kroeber and Joël espoused, maintaining that the similarities everyone observed between Paipai and Upland Yuman indicated a common history. As evidence, he presented cognate sets linking Paipai to Yavapai, rather than to Walapai, and alluded to a Yavepe Yavapai tale concerning tribal fission in recent historic times. This tale is about a man and a woman who were forbidden to marry because they were cousins. Angry and frustrated, they marshalled such kinsmen and friends as they could and decamped from Arizona, heading west. If this tale refers to the origin of the Paipai, it receives a small boost from the fact that the word *paya* in Yavepe Yavapai refers to the children of one's mother's brother or the children of one's father's sister, that is, to cross-cousins. This would mean that the word Paipai comes from *paya* 'cross-cousin' and *ʔpay* 'people', so that the Paipai would call themselves 'people who are cross-cousins' or 'cousin people'. That this group split off from the Yavapai in early historic times might account for the fact that there is no archeological evidence of Paipai migration. The problem with this hypothesis is that there is a genuine gap in intelligibility between Paipai and Upland Yuman. Yavapai speakers can understand many Paipai words or even whole Paipai phrases, but they cannot converse freely, nor can they understand casual Paipai conversation. This demonstrates that substantial linguistic change has taken place since the split between Upland Yuman and its sister language in Baja California, which suggests greater time-depth for the divergence than the migration hypothesis would allow.

Mohave

When Chafe (1962) estimated the number of speakers of North American Indian languages, he listed the figure of around 1,000 for Mohave, providing the additional information that these speakers were of all different ages. However, Munro (1976) estimated that probably only a few hundred people used the language conversationally, the majority of these being people advanced in years. Still, members of the Mohave community have developed a practical orthography, have produced a dictionary, and have been writing the language since the early 1970s.

Mohave is one of the best attested of the Yuman languages. There exists a comprehensive grammatical description (Munro 1976), native language texts with English analyses (J. Crawford 1976; Munro 1976a), and an impressive series of topical studies, covering diverse subjects such as baby talk and diminutive forms (Munro 1977); personal nouns (Munro 1980); number systems (Langdon and Munro 1980); modal constructions (Munro 1976); and various grammatical processes (J. Crawford 1976a). References to the bulk of papers and monographs on Mohave can be located in Redden (1976, 1977, 1978, 1979, 1980) and Klar, Langdon, and Silver (1980).

Quechan

Quechan was the first Yuman language to receive a systematic description and is the first to be restudied after a significant period of time had passed (Langdon 1977; Norwood 1976; Slater 1976; Sundheim 1976). Studies conducted 40 years after the pioneer fieldwork by Halpern reveal that the language had changed remarkably, but in "very Yuman ways." That Quechan has followed courses recognizable as occurring or having occurred in other Yuman languages means that modern developments cannot be attributed solely to the influence of bilingualism or to interference from English. It also means that Quechan is spoken differently by different generations, and that therefore its dialects are generational rather than regional, precisely the situation one finds with Havasupai. Quechan in the 1970s displayed phonological innovations not present in the Quechan of the 1930s; for example, an old alternation between [t^s] and [č] as pronunciations of the phoneme *c* has been resolved in favor of the consistent use of [t^s], a phenomenon that might have something to do with Quechan speakers' feelings that [t^s] is an unambiguously Quechan sound, while [č] occurs in both their own language and that of the Mohaves (Langdon 1977:44). In other words, [t^s] may be interpretable as an index of Quechan ethnicity.

In addition to the phonological innovations Quechan speakers have made between the 1930s and the 1970s, they have also done some morphosyntactic reshaping of their language. Specifically, they have developed a new demonstrative, restructured the case system, and reanalyzed several suffixes as prefixes for following syntactic units (the last process is also reported for Paipai, and observed sporadically in Yavapai).

The precise number of Quechan speakers in the 1980s had not been determined, but it was probably less than 700. The language was still spoken by young people as well as by the elderly. A practical orthography was developed for Quechan in 1975 by Christine Emerson and Cynthia Wilson, speakers of the language, in collaboration with linguists at the University of California at San Diego (Langdon 1977:43, 51).

Maricopa

The last of the Yuman languages to receive modern systematic treatment, Maricopa in 1981 was spoken in two geographically separate speech communities in Laveen and Lehigh, Arizona. The members of these communities recognized linguistic differences distinguishing them but held these differences to be inconsequential. More significant socially are the generational dialects that have been emerging since the first quarter of the twentieth century. Most Maricopa speakers over 40 understand and use the language, while in the generation of people 20 to 40 the extent of fluency varies radically. Older speakers expressed distress that young adults replaced Maricopa words with English borrowings and were concerned that the language was not being taught systematically to children in the group. The social situation in which Maricopa finds itself is quite reminiscent of the situation with Yavapai; Maricopas are frequently forced to seek marriage partners outside the tribe since their communities are so small, and this often means that the language of the home will not be the Maricopa partner's native idiom. In 1980 the number of Maricopa speakers was estimated to be less than 300 and declining. The Maricopa had an incipient literacy program. As of 1980 a single orthography had not been officially selected from among the five proposed by non-Maricopa linguists and anthropologists, although the Maricopa tribal council did publish one of them in the tribal newsletter.

The exact relationship of Maricopa to Quechan is not entirely clear. Scholars have proposed that the two speech forms are mutually intelligible, although such speculation seems to have resulted from comparing word lists rather than stretches of articulated speech. Syntactic analysis makes dubious the claim that Maricopa and Quechan are dialects, as do reports from native speakers. Certainly much lexicon and morphology is common to Maricopa and Quechan, although the shared elements do not always have corresponding functions or meanings in both. Furthermore, native speakers of Maricopa do not always agree on the degree to which Quechan speech is intelligible, and vice versa. The two kinds of speech are so closely related structurally that decisions about their status as languages or dialects must rest on social criteria, and these criteria are differently perceived in different segments of Maricopa and Quechan societies.

Diegueño

Diegueño is the name applied by linguists to a collection of dialects spoken in San Diego and Imperial counties in California and in northern Baja California. Three main dialect groupings of this language exist: northern Diegueño, spoken by people who call themselves *ʔi·pay*, is found at Mesa Grande, Santa Ysabel, San Pasqual, and Barona, California; southern Diegueño, spoken by people who designate themselves *kumeya·y* (Kamia), is found at Baron Long, Campo, Iñaja, and Imperial, California; and Tiipay, spoken by the *ti·pay*, is found at La Huerta, San Jose de la Zorra, Neji, and Haʔa, in Baja California, and at Jamul, California. The dialects form a linguistic continuum without sharp breaks, which means that at least some of these local speech varieties could be classified in more than one fashion (Langdon 1970, 1976).

The Diegueño dialects north of Mexico were spoken mostly by people over 60 years of age in 1980. The Mexican dialects were still spoken by people of all ages, but in every case Diegueño speech communities are small, at least relative to Yuman speech communities in Arizona. Several Diegueño-speaking groups have instituted language classes, notably those of Mesa Grande, Baron Long, Barona, and Jamul (Gorbet 1976); and the Mesa Grande community produced a dictionary (Couro and Hutcheson 1973), a pedagogical grammar (Couro and Langdon 1975), and various items for local distribution.

Cocopa

Cocopa is spoken on both sides of the Mexican-American border where the Colorado River empties into the Gulf of California. In 1980 there were approximately 300 speakers on each side of the border, and the number appeared to be increasing in spite of the fact that young children learned the language less and less frequently. Most Cocopas over 25 were fluent in their native language, with less fluency found among those below this age. The Cocopa had not established a literacy program nor a practical orthography as of 1979, although there were at that time non-Cocopa missionaries living among them, trying to teach them to read religious materials and to write.

The speech form called Kahwan, which merged with Maricopa in the nineteenth century, was apparently so closely related to Cocopa as to be considered one of its dialects, and indeed Cocopa specialists who have examined the Kahwan word list Kroeber used to classify this dialect assert that Kahwan and Cocopa are nearly identical structurally (James M. Crawford, personal communication 1981). Although there were in 1980 people who identified themselves as Kahwan living in Maricopa speech communities, they apparently spoke Maricopa or Cocopa, or, more expectedly, Maricopa with a number of Cocopa words interlarded.

Cocopa is most closely related to Diegueño within the Yuman family, although its geographical location and social history ally it to Kiliwa and Paipai on the one hand, and to the River languages on the other. In some ways Cocopa is unique: it is the only Yuman language to lack ʔ- as a first-person subject marker, and its sound correspondences show some idiosyncracies not shared with Diegueño.

Kiliwa

Kiliwa is spoken in Baja California, in the same areas where Paipai is found, with a major population concentration near Santa Catarina. There is a great deal of social exchange between the speakers of these two languages, with attendant, but asymmetrical bilingualism: most Kiliwas speak Paipai, while Paipais in general do not command Kiliwa. In spite of the fact that Paipai and Kiliwa are in separate branches of the language family, they appear to share a syntactic trait not attested elsewhere in Yuman. Kiliwa distinguishes between oblique and nonoblique relativizing morphemes: the latter [k^{w}-] is cognate with the relativizer [k-] or [k^{w}-] in other Yuman languages; the former [-uʔ] is apparently a Kiliwa innovation. Paipai also has a suffix [-uʔ], which functions syntactically like the corresponding Kiliwa form. The fact that this innovation is shared across language boundaries suggests that Kiliwa was formerly spoken more extensively in Paipai communities than was the case in the 1980s and that the asymmetrical bilingualism is therefore a relatively recent development (Mixco 1976). If Kiliwa and Paipai bilingualism did give rise to this shared innovation, it ought to have given rise to other shared features as well, but as of the mid-1970s no additional evidence of shared syntax or morphology (other than that expected for two languages in the same language family) had been discovered.

Criteria for Grouping

Table 3 gives the consonants and stressed vowels reconstructible for Proto-Yuman and summarizes their reflexes in the modern Yuman languages.

Inspection of the table immediately reveals two distinct types of vowel systems: the River and Pai branches of the family show 10 phonemic vowels; the Delta-California and Kiliwa branches show six. Within the Pai branch, the mid-vowels *e, e·, o,* and *o·* appear relatively less frequently than the contrasting high and low-back vowels, and diphthongs are rare. In the River languages diphthongs are not at all uncommon, nor are mid-vowels. Thus even within the two branches of the family that show a 10-vowel system, there are discriminations to be made in the type of system manifested. Langdon (1976a) suggests that the Pai languages became differentiated from the others by developing rules of diph-

Table 3. Sound Correspondences within the Yuman Family

Proto-Yuman		Pai		River			Delta-California		
		Paipai	Upland Yuman	Mohave	Maricopa	Quechan	Cocopa	Diegueño	Kiliwa
**p*[a]	non–root-initial	*v*	*v*	*v*	*v*	*v*	*p*	*p*	*p*
	elsewhere	*p*	*p*	*p*	*p*	*p*	*p*	*p*	*p*
**t*	root-final	*t*	*t*	*t*	*t*	*ṭ*	*ṭ*	*ṭ*	*t*
	elsewhere	*t*	*t*	*t*	*t*	*t*	*č*	*t*	*t*
**č*		*č*	*č*	*č*	*c*	*c*	*s*	*č*	*č/t*[b]
*k^y		*ky*	*ky*	k^y	k^y	k^y	*k*	*k*	—
**k*		*k*	*k*	*k*	*k*	*k*	*k*	*k*	*k*
*k^w		k^w	k^w	k^w	k^w	k^w	k^w	k^w	k^w
**q*		*q*	*q*	*q*	*q*	*q*	*q*	*q*	*q*
**ʔ*		*ʔ*	*ʔ*	*ʔ*	*ʔ*	*ʔ*	*ʔ*	*ʔ*	*ʔ*
**s*		*s*	*θ*	*θ*	*s*	*s*	*ṣ*	*s*	*s*
**ṣ*		*š* [ṣ]	*s*	*s*	*š* [ṣ]	*š* [ṣ]	*š* [š]	*ṣ/x*[c]	*s*
**x*		*x*	*h*	*h*	*x*	*x*	*x*	*x*	*h/x*
*x^w		x^w	h^w	h^w	x^w	x^w	x^w	x^w	h^w
**m*		*m*	*m*	*m*	*m*	*m*	*m*	*m*	*m*
**n*		*n*	*n*	*n*	*n*	*n*	n^y	*n*	*n*
*n^y		n^y	n^y	n^y	n^y	n^y	n^y	n^y	n^y
**l*		*l*	*l*	*l*	*l*	*l*	*l/ɬ*	*l/ɬ*	*l*
*l^y		*l*	*l*	l^y	l^y	l^y	$ɬ^y$	$ɬ^y$	*l*
**r*		*r*	*r*	*r*	*r*	*r*	*r*	*ṛ*	*r*
**y*	root-initial	*y*	*y*	*δ*	*δ*	*δ*	*y*	*y*	*y*
	elsewhere	*y*	*y*	*y*	*y*	*y*	*y*	*y*	*y*
**w*[a]	root-initial	*w*	*w*	*v*	*v*	*v*	*w*	*w*	*w*
	elsewhere	*w*	*w*	*w*	*w*	*w*	*w*	*w*	*w*
**i*[d]		*i/e*	*i/e*	*i/e*	*i/e*	*i/e*	*i*	*i*	*i*
**i·*		*i·*	*i·*	*i·*	*i·*	*i·*	*i·*	*i·*	*i·*
**u*		*u/o*	*u/o*	*u/o*	*u/o*	*u/o*	*u*	*u*	*u*
**u·*		*u·*	*u·*	*u·*	*u·*	*u·*	*u·*	*u·*	*u·*
**a*		*a/e*	*a/e*	*a/e*	*a/e*	*a/e*	*a*	*a*	*a*
**a·*		*a·*	*a·*	*a·*	*a·*	*a·*	*a·*	*a·*	*a·*

SOURCE: Langdon and Munro 1980:126.

[a] The question of the reflexes of **p* and **w* is treated in detail in Munro (1972) and Langdon (1975b).

[b] The reflex of **č* is *t* in Kiliwa after stress.

[c] The reflex of **ṣ* is *x* in Mesa Grande Diegueño under conditions not yet fully understood.

[d] The most comprehensive treatment of Proto-Yuman vowels is in Langdon (1976), but a number of problems remain. In addition to the correspondences above, diphthongs often have single-vowel reflexes. For example, in Pai **ay* > *e* and **a·y* > *ay*, and final **a·y* > *a·* in Cocopa.

thong reduction but are otherwise conservative in their vocalic systems, just as they are conservative in their consonantal systems. Both the River and Pai languages followed a course common to all the Yuman daughter languages of lowering high vowels and raising low vowels in particular conditioning contexts, but only these two divisions went on to establish the resulting mid-vowels as phonemic. The Delta-California and Kiliwa branches have phonetic but not phonemic mid-vowels.

It is clear from examining the consonantal portions of table 3 that no two languages have exactly the same phonemes, although the similarities and differences cluster within the family as a whole. The River languages, for example, all manifest the voiced interdental spirant *δ* where the other languages show *y*, and the voiced bilabial fricative *v* ([β]) where all other branches have a labial semivowel *w*. The Delta-California languages have a voiceless lateral *ɬ* distinguishing them from languages in the other divisions and have *k* as modern reflexes of both **k* and *k^y. Delta-California languages also have an alveolar stop *ṭ* that shows up only in this branch and in Quechan. Additionally Diegueño and Cocopa have retained Proto-Yuman **p* (non–root-initially) where River and Pai branches have developed *v* ([β]), sharing this conservatism only with Kiliwa. The Pai languages show the identical split of **p* into *p* and *v* that the River languages do but conserve **y* and **w* where the River languages have innovated. Within the Pai branch, Paipai retains Proto-Yuman **x*, *x^w, and **s* where Upland Yuman shows the reflexes *h*, h^w, and *θ*. It is also the case that the Paipai retention of **ṣ* is not shared with the Upland dialects, which resemble Mohave more in showing *s*. Kiliwa stands alone in lacking a modern reflex of **k*, but it shares with Upland and Mohave the correspondences of *h* and h^w to **x* and $*x^w$. Cocopa has at least two idiosyncratic features: *č* from **t* and *s* from **č*.

Overlapping and cross-cutting these phonological criteria for subgrouping are others based on lexical (Wares 1968; N. Webb 1977) and morphosyntactic correspondences (Hinton and Langdon 1976; Langdon and Munro 1980) as well as on information concerning interlingual intelligibility (Biggs 1957; W. Winter 1957). Comparing lexical items across languages, N. Webb (1977) confirmed the existence of a Delta-California branch composed of the Diegueño dialects and Cocopa but argued that Cocopa must properly be viewed as a link to the River languages since it shares many words in common with them. In the same vein, she was able to show that Mohave stands out among the River idioms in using many forms found in the Upland dialects. On the other hand, the lexical evidence Webb used showed strong resemblances between Paipai and Kiliwa, and between Paipai and Upland, which led her to group Kiliwa with what other scholars have established as a separate (Pai) branch. There is no question that the geographical proximity and social interrelatedness of Paipai and Kiliwa have led to mutual lexical borrowing, which means that there is good reason to consider the merging of Kiliwa with Pai to be premature.

While Kiliwa shares some vocabulary with Paipai, it nevertheless displays several completely idiosyncratic morphological and syntactic features in various semantic domains. For example, in its numerical system Kiliwa exhibits a stative prefix *m-* in place of the more usual Yuman stative prefix ˀ- in certain verbs, along with unique forms of the words for 'four' and 'ten', and a divergent form of the word meaning 'nine'. Furthermore, Kiliwa is the only Yuman language to display any tendencies toward developing a decimal system (Langdon and Munro 1980).

Examining Yuman numerical systems produces interesting results from the point of view of classification. In general the words for 'one', 'two', 'three', and 'five' are reconstructible in relatively straightforward ways ('four' is problematic but this may be attributed to its special ritual and cosmological significances as much as anything else). Numbers from 'five' to 'ten' are too diverse to reconstruct, although they may be categorized synchronically according to two patterns—one additive, the other multiplicative. In the additive systems, the numbers 'six' through 'eight' are derived by adding the lower reconstructible integers to the base five, so that 'six' is represented as 'five plus one', 'seven' is represented as 'five plus two', and 'eight' as 'five plus three'. Upland, Mohave, and Kiliwa have additive systems, at least the last two do with respect to attributive numbers. Kiliwa's actual forms for 'nine' and 'ten' do not correspond systematically to those found in Upland, although the logic underlying the two systems is equivalent: 'nine' is expressed as 'minus one (from ten)' and 'ten' is either a new morpheme or a new construction. The Mohave number 'ten' is not additive, but multiplicative, expressed in terms of its factors (2 times 5). This means that Mohave once again stands out from the other River languages in showing affinities with Upland. The River and Delta-California languages generally have multiplicative systems where nonprime numbers are factored (that is, 'six' equals 'three twos'; 'eight' equals 'four twos'; 'nine' equals 'three threes'; and 'ten' equals 'five twos') and the prime number 'seven' is treated separately. In Quechan, Maricopa, Diegueño, and Cocopa the numbers 'six', 'seven', 'eight', and 'nine' correspond transparently to factors while the word for 'ten' is frequently based on constructions meaning 'hand' or 'two hands'. Paipai shows a mixed system, having both additive and multiplicative features, along with an apparent borrowing from Spanish in its word for 'ten' (Langdon and Munro 1980).

What all these types of correspondences add up to is a tightly knit group of languages sorting themselves into fairly clear subgroups, with particular languages showing mixed features no doubt arising out of social contact. Cocopa, spoken in an area where River Yuman comes into contact with California and Baja California Yuman, shows many mixed features, as does Mohave, apparently the linguistic bridge between Pai and River branches. Paipai's affinities are most clearly with Upland Yuman, but it has not been unaffected by its contact with Kiliwa and Diegueño.

It could hardly be otherwise in the course of human social exchanges. Even if the only things ever exchanged are words, the very process of communicating across a language barrier affects the way speech can be produced and comprehended. Social history and language history are not after all separable.

Havasupai

DOUGLAS W. SCHWARTZ

The Havasupai (ˌhăvə'so͞opī), a Yuman-speaking group,* are closely related to the Walapai and Yavapai, their neighbors in northwestern Arizona. In the past the Havasupai tribe lived in bands composed of a few related but autonomous families. During the nineteenth and twentieth centuries, these bands became consolidated both territorially and politically as pressure from White settlers and government reduced their territorial size and increased the need for a single group voice. Since 1939, tribal unity has been formalized under a constitution and by-laws that provide for a partly elected tribal council.

Territory and Environment

The Havasupai occupied a territory approximately 90 miles wide by 75 miles long (Spier 1928:91) on the Coconino Plateau, a range including the drainage area of Cataract Creek Canyon through which flows a tributary of the Colorado River. The territory extended from the south bank of the Colorado River within Grand Canyon south to Bill Williams Mountain and the San Francisco Peaks, and from the Aubrey Cliffs east at least to the edge of the Coconino Plateau above the Little Colorado River (fig. 1). Only during winter was the whole of this range occupied, since summer was spent on the well-watered farmlands of Cataract Creek Canyon.

Since the nineteenth century the Havasupai have faced increasing competition for land from the Walapai on the west, the Navajo on the east, and particularly from Anglo-American cattlemen. This encroachment not only reduced Havasupai territory but also destroyed wild plant and game resources upon which the tribe was partially dependent. Consequently, by mid-twentieth century, the Havasupai were restricted to a 500-acre reservation in Cataract Creek Canyon within Grand Canyon. Because agriculture alone was unable to support the entire population, a growing proportion of the tribe began living and working off the reservation, especially in connection with the tourist trade at Grand Canyon.

From about 1971 to 1974 Havasupais were involved in a fight to regain land that was formerly theirs. In 1974 Congress passed a bill (signed into law in 1975) establishing a 160,000-acre reservation, and allocating 95,000 acres of Grand Canyon National Park for their permanent use (Hirst 1976).

Both the Coconino Plateau and Cataract Creek Canyon are semiarid environments, although a large permanent spring is found at the lower elevation, resulting in a lush creek-side environment. In the canyon, this spring gives birth to Cataract Creek, which contains ample flow for irrigation. During the violent summer thunderstorms common to the region, runoff from the

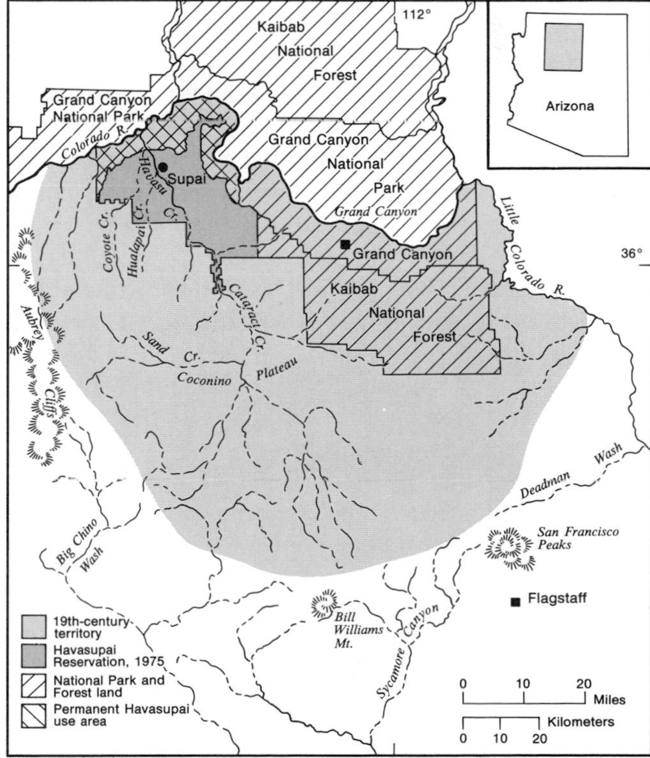

Fig. 1. Tribal territory in the 19th century.

*The phonemes of Havasupai are: (voiceless unaspirated stops and affricate) *p*, *t* (dental), *č*, *k*, k^w, k^y, *q*, ʔ; (fricatives) *v* ([β]), *θ*, *s*, *š*, *h*, h^w; (lateral) *l*; (alveolar flap) *r*; (nasals) *m*, *n*, n^y, *ŋ*; (semivowels) *w*, *y*; (short vowels) *i*, *e*, *a*, *o*, *u*, *ə*; (long vowels) *i·*, *e·*, *a·*, *o·*, *u·*; (stress) v́. In the speech of younger speakers sequences of *h* followed by a stop or affricate are replaced by aspirates, giving rise to an additional phonemic series: p^h, t^h (dental), $ṭ^h$ (alveolar), $č^h$, k^h, k^{wh}, q^h.

Information on Havasupai phonology and the phonemicizations of Havasupai words were provided by Leanne Hinton (communications to editors 1974, 1981). A discussion of the development of a practical orthography for Havasupai is in Crook, Hinton, and Stenson (1977).

plateau often sends disastrous floods through Cataract Canyon, destroying homes and fields alike.

Temperatures are relatively mild, ranging on the plateau from a winter average of 30° F to about 70° F in midsummer. Within the canyon, temperatures vary from a winter average of 44° F to a summer average of about 70° F with summer highs well above 100° F. The growing season in the canyon extends from April through September.

Vegetation is that of the Sonoran life-zone, characterized on the plateau by juniper, piñon pine, and in some areas by ponderosa pine. At lower elevations, trees are scarce, and desert plants such as sagebrush, grasses, yucca, and prickly pear become dominant. Near the canyon floor grow a number of edible plants, including agave, prickly pear, mesquite, Mormon tea, and grasses from which seeds could be harvested. Dense thickets of willows line the banks of Cataract Creek, while cottonwoods and introduced fruit trees are also common.

Prior to settlement by Whites, the Coconino Plateau supported an abundant fauna. Antelope, deer, and mountain sheep were plentiful, along with smaller game such as rabbits and squirrels. This environment offered the Havasupai a large variety of potential resources within a relatively small territory and made possible a wide range of economic activities.

External Relations

The Havasupai are most closely related culturally and linguistically to the Walapai. Each tribe occupied a territory from which it took a distinctive name. The Havasupai and Walapai were distinguished by name as early as 1776, and were perhaps distinct much earlier (Schwartz 1959; Dobyns and Euler 1970 believe it was not until 1882). The two groups may have become more politically and economically differentiated only after intensive White contact in the nineteenth and twentieth centuries (Martin 1966:11–14). Not only did Whites distinguish the two groups conceptually, but also differing historical events served to segregate the Havasupai from the Walapai. This trend culminated in the establishment of separate reservations for the two tribes and their separate administration.

Throughout historic times, the Havasupai have maintained consistently friendly relations with the Walapai. The two groups have been known to combine in offensive action against common enemies, to conduct extensive trade, and often to intermarry.

Both the Havasupai and the Walapai carried on hostile relations with the Yavapai, by whom they were frequently raided during the harvest season. Western Apache groups also joined in some of these raids. Due to their small population, Havasupai response was usually limited to defense and occasional brief retaliatory attacks; offensive action was seldom undertaken. About 1865 the Havasupai and Yavapai agreed to end hostilities, and they have conducted peaceful trade relations since then.

Similarly, earliest contacts with the Navajo in the mid-nineteenth century were antagonistic, but relations of trade and friendship developed subsequently. The same was probably true of Havasupai relations with the Paiute. The Hopi, on the other hand, have for many years been friends, allies, and trading partners with the Havasupai.

Prehistory

The Havasupai are probably the direct descendants of a prehistoric group known to archeologists as the Cohonina (Schwartz 1956; for another view on Havasupai prehistory, see Euler 1958). This culture first appeared in the plateau region south of the Grand Canyon around A.D. 600. Population, quite small at first, tripled by A.D. 800 and doubled again within the next century, probably resulting from a successful adaptation to an agricultural economy (Schwartz 1956a). By about A.D. 1050, population pressure for available land had increased to such proportions that new farmland in the canyon floors began to be cultivated on a permanent basis. Thus originated, in all likelihood, the characteristic Havasupai economic pattern based on summer irrigation agriculture in the canyon and winter hunting-gathering on the plateau.

Between 1050 and 1200, the Havasupai completely abandoned the Coconino Plateau for Cataract Creek Canyon in what appears to have been a defensive move. The cliffs lining the canyon contain dwellings dating to the second half of this period that have the appearance of being protective; however, other explanations, such as space pressure, must also be considered for the withdrawal. After 1300 the defensive pressure was removed, allowing the Havasupai to return to the Coconino Plateau. However, increased aridity on the Coconino Plateau, which occurred as a result of climatic change affecting the entire northern Southwest, prevented extensive farming. Therefore, the Havasupai at this time began a double economic life, farming Cataract Creek Canyon in the summer and supplementing their stored agricultural food resources by hunting and gathering on the plateau in winter. Year-round occupation of the Coconino Plateau was never re-established (Schwartz 1959).

History

Early Spanish explorers mention wandering tribes seen in the general area later certainly occupied by the Havasupai (Dobyns and Euler 1960). These observers include: Cardenas in 1540, Marcos Farfan in 1578, and Fray Esteban de Perea in 1598 (Schroeder 1953:45,46). According to Schroeder, the first reference by name to the existence of the Havasupai is in 1665 when Governor Peñalosa testified to subduing the Coninas (Havasupai) and the Cruzados (Yavapai) (Schroeder 1953:46). After 1700, references to the Coninas appear more frequently. In 1776 Father Francisco Garcés was guided to Cataract Creek Canyon by a group of Walapais. Spanish influence upon the Havasupai was negligible except for European items such as horses, cloth, and fruit trees, which were obtained indirectly through the Hopi.

Beginning about 1776, the Havasupai had sporadic contacts with European trappers and explorers (Schwartz 1956:82), including the expeditions led by Lorenzo Sitgreaves (1853) and Amiel Whipple (Whipple, Ewbank and Turner 1855) in 1853 and by Joseph C. Ives (1861) in 1857–1858. Acculturation was minimal during these decades and took place chiefly with respect to material items. During the late nineteenth century, White cattle ranchers began to encroach increasingly upon Havasupai land, and mining prospectors began to be interested in the copper deposits in Cataract Canyon itself. Therefore, a reservation was established within the canyon in 1880, after which the rate of acculturation rapidly accelerated. In 1895 a Bureau of Indian Affairs subagency and day school were set up on the reservation, and families were urged to remain there year-round while their children attended class. This restriction was aggravated by loss of territory and natural resources to cattlemen, until by the 1940s the annual migration to the plateau for hunting and gathering ceased to be part of the Havasupai way of life.

After the 1940s, acculturation increased as growing numbers of Havasupais came into individual contact with Whites in the course of wage employment and as federal government involvement in tribal affairs grew in intensity.

Traditional Culture

Subsistence

The economic system of the Havasupai involved a seasonal dichotomy between summer agriculture in the canyon and winter hunting-gathering on the plateau. In early spring, families began moving into Cataract Canyon to repair their summer homes and ready their fields for planting in mid-April. Corn, beans, and squash were raised in abundance with the aid of the hoe, the digging stick, and a simple network of irrigation ditches. A variety of other crops, including peaches, sunflowers, apricots, and figs, were added to the Havasupais' diet in historic times. Horse-raising has also become an important activity since the late nineteenth century.

Planting began in mid-April with corn harvesting starting in June and continuing until early fall, by which time all crops and many kinds of wild plant foods had been picked and processed for storage. Drying was the usual method employed in preserving food for winter use.

By the middle of October, families began moving back to their semipermanent camps scattered over the plateau, to spend the winter hunting deer, antelope, and rabbit, and gathering piñon nuts, mescal, and other wild plant foods. Camps were moved when necessary to follow newly available resources. When spring again brought planting time, the cycle began with migration back to summer homes and farmland on the canyon floor.

Trade was another important economic activity, although most trading expeditions were equally opportunities for visiting and diversion. The Havasupai participated in a trade network extending from the Hopi in the east, through the Navajo and Walapai, to the Mohave in the west. Buckskins, foodstuffs, and basketry were the main items of Havasupai commerce, for which they received cotton goods, horses, pottery, jewelry, and buffalo hides.

Division of labor by sex was not strict, with the exception of certain handicrafts. All members of the family helped with agricultural tasks and housebuilding, although men usually held the greatest responsibility for these chores and for hunting. While both sexes probably took part in tanning hides, the subsequent manufacture of clothing was done by males alone (fig. 2). Items made solely by women included sleeping mats, cradleboards, baskets, and pottery; however, most of their time was taken up by cooking (fig. 3) and child care. Women gathered wild plants growing near their camps, but large-scale gathering expeditions involved the entire family. There was no strong craft specialization within the groups, but merely the recognition of certain individuals as being particularly skilled in making various items.

Social and Political Organization

The sole component group in Havasupai society was the family, either nuclear or extended, which functioned as both an independent economic unit and a local residential group. Family composition was not rigidly fixed but changed frequently as nuclear families merged or separated. Most common was the patrilocal extended family, composed of a man, his wife, their unmarried children, and their married sons and families. However, patrilocal residence (that is, with the husband's family) was normally preceded by a period of temporary matrilocality (residence with the wife's parents) immediately after marriage.

The Havasupai possessed no other social divisions

left. Calif. Histl. Soc., Los Angeles: Title Insurance Coll., 3396. right. Amer. Mus. of Nat. Hist., New York: 50.2/1266.

Fig. 2. Leather work. left, Preparing buckskin, a man seated on a Navajo blanket stretches a hide to make it more pliable. Photograph by Charles C. Pierce or George Wharton James, 1890s. right, Woman's leather dress made in 2 parts. Front piece has loop to go over neck and ties at the waist. The breast flap is sometimes decorated, and the loops around it that are from the tanning pegs are ornamental. Extending from breast to ankles, it is put on after the back skirt, which hangs from the waist. Both are fringed at the sides and bottom and worn over a short under-apron. A leather belt is tied around the dress with a Hopi sash added (Spier 1928:183–188). A similar garment stained red was worn by a girl as a puberty dress even when cloth had replaced leather for everyday clothing (Smithson 1959:65). Length of dress front 129.0 cm, collected by Leslie Spier in 1918.

such as clans, moieties, or ceremonial sodalities. Neither was there any system of social classes or ranking; instead, prestige was acquired simply by individual merit, based on skill, industriousness, or other admired characteristics.

Kinship was traced bilaterally, but kin terms were rarely used either in reference or address. Indeed, genealogical knowledge does not seem to have been of very great interest or importance to the Havasupai. Marriage with any blood relative was at least theoretically forbidden, but since kinship ties were usually forgotten after several generations' distance, third and fourth cousins often felt free to marry one another.

Certain individuals were recognized as tribal chiefs (fig. 4), but their leadership took the form of advice and persuasion, not of any true authority or power. While chiefship tended to be inherited patrilineally, a potential successor would be bypassed if he failed to meet certain standards of personal merit, including bravery in war, wisdom, dignity, and good temper. One man was considered to be the head chief, the others being of lesser prestige, but few differences in function accompanied this distinction. The ranking of chiefs was based simply on individual achievement and did not correspond to any formal status positions.

Actual councils were rarely held. Instead, most issues were dealt with informally by the men as they relaxed around the sweatlodge.

For another view on the social and political organization of the Havasupai, see Dobyns and Euler (1970).

Structures

The Havasupai constructed two main types of houses. (fig. 5). Winter homes, located in dense piñon or juniper thickets for warmth, were domed or conical structures of thatch or dirt over a log-and-pole frame. Summer dwellings were of the same type or of a rectangular design with dirt-covered roof and thatched walls. In addition, various kinds of shade structures were utilized in summer camps, such as an open post frame with a thatched roof. During hot canyon days, nearly all activities took place outdoors or under shades, the houses actually being used only for sleeping.

Another important structure was the sweathouse, a low, dome-shaped building roughly two meters in di-

Harold M. Smithson, Salt Lake City, Utah.

Fig. 3. Food preparation. left, Nettie Nora making tortillas, summer 1958. Tortillas are made from wheat flour, salt, water, and baking powder. They are baked on a wire rack over an open fire that has been reduced to coals. Tortillas are a mainstay of the meal and are often used instead of a spoon to carry soft food to the mouth (Smithson 1959:150). right, Mariam and Edith Putesoy drying peaches in the open air, 1950–1951. Photographs by Carma Lee Smithson.

ameter set over a shallow pit (fig. 6). In the 1950s, all sweatlodges were earth-covered, but formerly the pole frame was often covered with blankets. Heated rocks were carried into the lodge and sprinkled with water, producing steam at temperatures up to 150° F. While it held certain therapeutic functions, the lodge also served as a sort of clubhouse where men weekly gathered to visit, gossip, or discuss matters of importance.

Clothing and Adornment

Traditionally clothing was manufactured mainly from skins, although some loom products were acquired in trade. A man wore a shirt, breechclout, leggings, moccasins, and headband; a woman's clothing consisted of a short under-apron, a long buckskin dress, moccasins, and a rabbitskin blanket. Children went naked until the age of six or seven, but girls began to wear full dress somewhat earlier than boys. Ornamentation was not elaborate, consisting mainly of necklaces, earrings, and some face painting.

Technology

Basket weaving was the most important craft, for baskets were used in a great number of contexts (fig. 8). Burden baskets, pitch-smeared water bottles, parching trays, and stone-boiling containers were all found in the basketmaker's repertoire. Plain, utilitarian pottery was also made at one time but by 1900 had been completely replaced by metal containers. Women used stone grinding slabs or mortars for preparing cornmeal and grinding seeds, while men hunted with both bows and arrows and traps.

Property

Farmland was considered private property as long as it was in use. Failure to cultivate a plot for a few years resulted in property rights reverting to the community, and another household could then lay claim to the land. Title usually belonged to men, and all sons shared in the inheritance.

Life Cycle

The life cycle of the Havasupai was marked by little ritual and few rites of passage. A woman was aided in childbirth by her mother or other close relative and rested for four days after delivery on a bed of sand over heated rocks. The infant's face and body were often painted with red ocher, and its head and limbs were symbolically molded by the attendant to insure that the child would be well-formed. At about two weeks old, the baby was tightly bound on a cradleboard where it would spend much of its first year of life (fig. 9). As the child learned to walk, it made a gradual transition from cradleboard to play group, frequently being placed in the care of an older sibling. Names, usually assumed between the ages of three and seven, were simply nicknames referring to an amusing incident or a peculiar trait.

top, Mus. of N. Mex., School of Amer. Research Coll.: 16341; bottom, Calif. Histl. Soc., Los Angeles: Title Insurance Coll., 4691.

Fig. 4. Havasupai chiefs. top, Captain Jack with some of his followers. The men directly behind him wear face paint and one holds a fringed decorated quiver. The women wear Navajo blankets. Photograph by Ben Wittick, about 1883. bottom, Chief Navajo, a leader during the Ghost Dance period, who died about 1900 (Dobyns and Euler 1967:25; Spier 1928:240), wearing buckskin moccasins and seated on a Navajo blanket. Photograph by George Wharton James, 1898.

Infants and children received a great deal of affection and attention from all members of the household but were never made to feel that they occupied a special or privileged position. Young children were allowed to play freely but, as they grew older, were expected to assist more and more with the daily chores. Through verbal instruction and by example, children were taught to perform the tasks that would be required of them as adults and were continually admonished to work hard and not be lazy. Discipline was mild, punishment being infrequent and administered verbally, although it was said to have been much more severe in the past. Grandparents often played an important role in child rearing and developed close, affectionate relations with their grandchildren.

Puberty ritual was observed only for girls, at the onset of the menses. The girl was given a special buckskin dress stained red with powdered ocher, which she wore for four days and nights. Most of this time was spent on a bed of sand spread over heated rocks, but each day at sunrise the girl ran toward the east, and at sunset toward the west, to insure that she would always perform her work quickly and untiringly. Several taboos were observed during the puberty ceremony and all subsequent menstrual periods; meat eating, for example, was forbidden. Although the puberty ritual marked a change in a girl's status from child to near-adult, it was not followed by any great shift in her daily activities or her eligibility to marry.

Marriage was not accompanied by ceremony but was simply recognized when two people began to cohabit openly. Parental approval was essential, for the young couple would need economic support from one or both families. When a boy had chosen a particular girl, he might ask his father to arrange the marriage for him. If the girl's family approved, they usually received a gift such as a horse or a blanket, and the boy then moved into his new wife's home. Another form of marriage took place when a boy crept into a girl's home at night, and, if she accepted him, remained there until morning. If she did not like the boy, she would drive him away, though her parents might encourage him to try again if they liked the young man.

Polygyny was not forbidden, but few men had more than one wife. Divorce, comparatively rare, took place at the desire of either party, adultery being the most common cause.

Havasupai mortuary customs were relatively simple prior to the late nineteenth century. The body was cremated, and most of the deceased's personal property, including his house, one or two horses, and all or part of his crops, was destroyed. Open mourning was brief, and there was no formal funeral ceremony.

Religion and Ceremonies

Spier (1928:289) observed that religion and ceremonialism were not elaborately developed and occupied only a minor place in Havasupai life. Religious beliefs were expressed, as among other Yuman tribes, chiefly in the importance attached to shamanism, curing by means of spirits, and dreams.

Each person was believed to possess a soul associated with his heart. The soul left the body during dreams and at death, when it journeyed to the land of the dead in the sky. The place was conceived as a huge dome that came down to meet the flat earth at its edges. After death, souls could reappear as ghosts, which if seen could cause illness and death. For this reason, the Havasupais professed great fear of going about at night, lest they happen upon a ghost.

The Havasupai had few specific deities. Spier (1928:276) identified *Pakiyóka* 'he who draws people after', who draws souls into the sky, and *Pakiyóva* 'he who makes people live again', who is probably a version of the Christian god and who causes people to live after death. Two other characters, a boy and his grandmother, figured prominently in Havasupai mythology. The boy lived in the east, but traveled to the west each year to visit his grandmother, bringing with him rain, wind, and seeds to scatter upon the earth.

The major ceremony of the Havasupai was the round dance held each year at harvest time. Although the dance was to help bring rain and prosperity, its purpose was equally social and religious. Navajos, Hopis, and Walapais were invited, and the two- or three-day festival saw much visiting, feasting, and bartering. During interludes in the dancing, chiefs would harangue the crowd on proper behavior or other matters of importance.

Until about 1900, masked dances borrowed from the Hopi were held for the purpose of bringing rain. It may be that these dances ceased as a result of confinement in Cataract Canyon, where rain was unnecessary and usually did more damage than good.

Shamanism and Curing

Four types of shamans were known to the Havasuapai, the most important being the general curing shaman. Others were the weather and the hunt shamans, and those who specialized in treating wounds, fractures, or snake bites. Each curing shaman possessed a spirit that had come to him in a dream, whom he could send out to discover things such as the cause of a patient's illness. Although a man could inherit his spirit from a former shaman, dreaming was still essential to the process of becoming a practitioner. It was in dreams that the shaman learned the songs he would need for the curing ceremony.

Illness was believed to have supernatural causes such as sorcery, ghosts, spirits, and harmful dreams. Shamans themselves were sometimes thought to have caused one's sickness. In treating a patient, the shaman sang over him in an all-night ceremony, sending his spirit into the patient to seek out the cause of illness. Upon diagnosis, the shaman either sucked out any harmful objects that had been sent into the patient's body or, if appropriate, exhorted the malevolent spirit to leave the patient alone.

Sociocultural Situation in the 1960s

In 1964, Havasupai population stood at approximately 350. This figure represents the upper limit of a population size range that has remained remarkably stable for two centuries (table 1). The low of 177 followed a disastrous measles epidemic, and the high of 350 undoubtedly reflects the impact of modern medical care. Alvarado (1970) has pointed out a number of cultural practices that act to control Havasupai population, among them the spermicidal effect of the sweatbath.

Havasupai government in the 1960s consisted of a seven-member tribal council, of which three members were chiefs serving for life and four were councilmen elected for two-year terms. The council had responsibility for managing tribal affairs, making contracts, hiring personnel, and enacting ordinances. Because the council was seen by the general populace as little more than an instrument of the Bureau of Indian Affairs, its actions were frequently met with opposition. Since 1957, the Havasupai have also possessed a tribal court operating under a law and order code modeled after White concepts of law. Because Havasupai culture does not share these concepts, the court has been largely ineffectual. Despite these institutions imposed by the federal government, the extended family remained the fundamental unit in Havasupai social organization.

The Havasupai in the 1960s possessed a cash economy based mainly on the tourist trade, welfare, and wage employment. About 1940, the cooperative Havasupai Development Enterprise was founded with the aid of a federal grant, for the threefold purpose of developing a tourist industry on the reservation, establishing a tribal

Table 1. Population

Date	*Population*	*Source*
1776	34 families	Garcés (Coues 1900)
1858	200	Ives 1861
1881	235	Cushing 1882
1896	253	Coues 1900
1902	233	Spier 1928
1919	177	Spier 1928
1964	350	Martin 1968

top left, U. of Ariz., Ariz. State Mus., Tucson:30201; center left, Smithsonian, NAA: 76-6293; center right, Calif. Histl. Soc., Los Angeles: Title Insurance Coll. 4689; bottom, Mus. of N. Mex., School of Amer. Research Coll., 16109.

Fig. 5. Dwellings. top left, Contemporary houses and fields in Cataract Canyon, in a view toward the north from East Rim Gorge; photograph by Helga Teiwes, Nov. 1970. top right, Brenda Jones at home; photograph by Lyntha Scott Eiler, 1973. center left, Woman seated in front of a typical domed, thatched house; a heavy wooden door is visible, with a burden basket at left; photograph by Edward S. Curtis, copyright July 1903. center right, Flat-roofed rectangular summer house with thatch and bark covering in Cataract Canyon; fur bags hang from the left pole of the house and women are making baskets in front; photograph possibly by Charles C. Pierce or George Wharton James, 1890s. bottom, Double lean-to in Supai Canyon; a burden basket is behind the women wearing Navajo blankets; photograph by Ben Wittick, about 1883.

grocery store, and improving farmlands and farming techniques. The Farming Enterprise was bankrupt and inactive by the 1960s. After reaching a peak in the 1930s under government pressure and subsidy, agricultural production declined until a mere 8.2 acres were under cultivation in 1963 (Martin 1966:42). However, land itself remained of great economic importance, for it was used as pasture for the horses needed to pack tourists in and out of the canyon. Indeed, increased emphasis on individual, as opposed to community, property rights began to develop after about 1950, along with a tendency for one son to be singled out as heir.

top, Milwaukee Public Mus., Wis.: 44513.

Fig. 6. Dome-shaped sweathouses. top, Earlier type made of pole frame covered with Navajo blankets; photograph by Sumner W. Matteson, Cataract Canyon, 1899–1905. bottom, Man and his son placing heated stones into an earth-covered sweatlodge of recent type; photograph by Terry Eiler, 1973.

Chief among the sources of cash income was the tourist business, which accounted for $34,000, or roughly half the tribal income, in 1963–1964 (Martin 1966:39). Of this sum, $17,000 went to individual packers who rented horses to carry tourists and supplies into the canyon. The Tourist Enterprise owned two lodges and a campground that brought income to the tribe as a whole. Several salaried positions were also created by the Tourist Enterprise, including a tourist manager and the personnel employed at the lodges.

After about 1940, the availability of wage employment for Havasupais steadily increased. The federal government and tribal enterprises provided a few jobs on the reservation itself, and developments in tourism at Grand Canyon Village opened up new employment opportunities off the reservation. Those who held permanent positions at Grand Canyon Village on the South Rim in the 1970s comprised a small settlement near that city, and each tourist season saw an influx of temporary

Smithsonian, Dept. of Anthr.: top, 210,070; bottom, 210,071.

Fig. 7. Grooming. top, Hairbrush of mescal fiber with piece of leather folded over one end and bound on with leather thong. As the fibers break the end is evened by burning, thus the blackened tips here. The brush is used primarily by women (Spier 1928:193–194). bottom, Bone scratcher with incised and blackened designs, human and bird figures on convex side and geometric pattern on flat side; hole at the top holds a leather thong used to tie it to a garment. Length of top 12.5 cm, bottom same scale; both collected by J.H. Bratley in 1901.

Smithsonian, Dept. of Anthr.: a, 213,258; Denver Mus. of Nat. Hist.: b, 5647; c, 5632; d, Mus. of Northern Ariz., Flagstaff: 1070/E677; e, U. of Ariz., Ariz. State Mus., Tucson: E-9384.

Fig. 8. Basketry. Twined utility ware was common and ancient; coiled baskets were rare until after 1890, when they were increasingly produced for trade to Hopis and Navajos and sale to Whites. a, Typical close-coiled container sewn counterclockwise on a 3-rod triangular foundation with design in black. b, Humans and animals, such as the deer here, were represented in addition to geometric motifs. c, Lidded jar with aniline dyed pattern, produced around 1900, a period of innovation in basket design and shape. An hourglass-shaped basket was also made during this period. d, Tray by Edith Putesoy with black wind design, characteristic of the high quality ware made during the 1930s, when utilitarian baskets were rarely made and more care was taken with coiled basketry made for sale. e, Twined bowl made by Katie Hamidreek. After World War II basket production and quality declined, but in the 1970s a revitalization began of both coiled and twined baskets. (See McKee, McKee, and Herold 1975; Herold 1979.) a, Diameter 35.5 cm, rest to same scale, collected by Walter Hough in 1902. b-c, Collected by J.H. Bratley 1900–1901. d, Collected by Barbara and Edwin McKee in 1934. e, Collected by Helga Teiwes in 1970.

employees for kitchen and laundry work, maid service, and the like. Young men could also find occasional jobs as ranch hands. However, due to its usual short-term nature, off-reservation employment accounted for only about one-fifth of tribal income in 1963–1964. Welfare provided one-third.

Havasupai material culture in the 1960s had been largely replaced by that of the Whites. Houses were built of purchased materials, and manufactured clothing was bought in nearby towns or through mail-order catalogs. Native craft items had been supplanted by factory-made tools and implements, although a few baskets were still made for sale to tourists.

The life cycle of the Havasupai was in the 1960s devoid of what little ritual it had previously entailed. The puberty ceremony was infrequently held, and marriage had become a gradual developmental process unmarked by ritual at any stage. New opportunities for economic independence made parental approval of marriage no longer crucial. In addition, young people had greater freedom to develop close personal relationships while attending federal boarding schools and accordingly took the initiative in arranging their own marriages. Temporary matrilocal residence after marriage ceased to be the statistical norm, residence being determined instead by pragmatic interests.

Mission activity has been carried out among the Havasupai since 1927, but response to White religion was consistently apathetic. By the mid-1950s a moderate church membership was achieved by the United Indian Missions, but the church never became important in community organization. At the same time, indigenous religion seemed also to lose its hold. Medical care by White doctors replaced curing by shamans; the last resident shaman died about 1963. The only ceremonies still being held in the 1960s were the annual dance at harvest time, informal dances during the summer, and funerals. The funerals consisted of a ceremony borrowed from the Paiute and Mohave via the Walapai. Cremation and the practice of destroying the deceased's property had ceased, though some uncertainty exists as to exactly when these customs disappeared.

Amer. Mus. of Nat. Hist., New York: 316864.

Fig. 9. Fannie with her son Lorenzo in a willow cradleboard with wicker hood. Cradleboards are made by women, usually the child's grandmother (Spier 1928:302–303). Photograph by Joseph K. Dixon, John D. Scott, or W.B. Cline on Wanamaker Expedition, 1913.

Mus. of N. Mex., Santa Fe: 37711.

Fig. 10. Footraces, usually for stakes, were run to and from a point 50–125 meters distant. This diversion was superseded by horse races, run on a similar course (Spier 1928:337). Photograph by William H. Simpson, 1901.

top, Calif. Histl. Soc., Los Angeles: Title Insurance Coll., 4690; bottom, Harold M. Smithson, Salt Lake City, Utah.

Fig. 11. The game of stick dice. Each of 2 teams has a small stick marker, which is moved around the stone circle starting at the gap. Moves are counted, stone by stone, according to scores made by 3 dice (flat wooden billets marked in red on one side) that are bounced off the flat central rock. The first team to complete the circle wins (Spier 1928:341–342). top, Photograph by George Wharton James, copyright 1898; bottom, photograph by Carma Lee Smithson, 1950–1951.

Synonymy†

The Havasupai call themselves *havasúwə ˀəpá* (pl. *havasuwə ˀəpačə)* 'person (people) of the blue or green water'; *ha-* represents *ˀəha* 'water' and *vasúwə* is a color term referring to any of the parts of the spectrum called 'blue', 'blue-green', or 'green' in English (Leanne Hinton, communication to editors 1974). Similar names are found in other Yuman languages: Walapai Ha-ba-soo-py-a 'green water people' (Corbusier 1923–1925:2); Yavapai Ha-ba-soo-pī´-ya 'people of the green or blue water' (Corbusier 1921:3), ăhă´ háβasú 'apā́ 'blue water people' (Freire-Marreco 1910–1912); Mohave *havasu·pay* 'blue or green person' (Pamela L. Munro, communication to editors 1981); Quechan *xavašú·k apáy* 'blue people' (Abraham M. Halpern, communication to editors 1981). It is noteworthy that the Mohave and Quechan names make no overt reference to 'water' (since in these languages the syllable *ha-* or *xa-* is part of the color term), and that the English name Havasupai must come from a language in which 'person' is *-pai* (*-pay*) or *-paya*, rather than from Havasupai itself (which has *ˀəpa*). The name was first recorded by Francisco Garcés in 1776 in the Spanish spelling Jabesúa; he also used the compound name Yabipais Jabesua and Yabipai Jabesua (Coues 1900, 2:335, 340, 414, 444). Col-

†This synonymy was written by Ives Goddard, incorporating some references supplied by Douglas W. Schwartz.

loquial English has also an abbreviated form spelled Supai or Suppai (also Supies), the second of these being for a time the official government designation (Hodge 1907–1910, 1:538–539; Coues 1900, 2:346). Havasupai was perhaps used first by Cushing (1882) in the spelling Ha-va-su-paí.

An earlier name for the Havasupai in Spanish documents is written Coninas, 1665 (Diego de Peñalosa in Hackett 1923–1937, 3:264, as interpreted by Schroeder 1953:46), or Cogninas, 1672 (Bloom and Mitchell 1938:116), and Cosninas, 1775, or Cosninos, 1779 (Vélez de Escalante in Coues 1900, 2:472; Twitchell 1914, 2:269). This name, applied vaguely to Indians west of the Hopi, is derived from a name variants of which appear in a number of Indian languages but the origin of which has not been determined: Third Mesa Hopi *kô·nina* (pl. *-mɨ*) (Voegelin and Voegelin 1957:49); First Mesa Hopi Kóhonino or Kóhonini (Stephen 1936, 2:1232); Zuni *kohni·kʷe* (Dennis Tedlock, communication to editors 1977), also recorded as kuhnikwe (Kroeber 1916:275) and kochninakwe (Ten Kate 1885:300); Navajo *Góóhníinii* (Young and Morgan 1980:370); Hopi-Tewa *kuˀni* (Paul V. Kroskrity, communication to editors 1977) and koxníní (Mooney 1895, normalized); Isleta *kų́niníde* (pl. *kųnínin*) (C.T. Harrington 1920:47). In Navajo and Hopi this name may be used for the Walapai as well as for the Havasupai; Harrington (1913a) reported an Oraibi Hopi distinction between kó‘nīnă ‘Walapai’ and sətákó‘nīnă ‘Havasupai’, the latter differentiated by the addition of the word for red ocher (*sɨ̂·ta*), a substance obtained from the Havasupai (Stephen 1936, 2:1195). Many renderings of this name appear in nineteenth-century American and European sources referring to the Havasupai or other Upland Yumans, including Casnino, Coçoninos, Cohoninos, Cojnino, Cojonina, Cosninas, 1853 (S. Eastman in Schoolcraft 1851–1857, 4:24), Cosninos, 1854 (A.W. Whipple in Foreman 1941:204, 206), Koninos, and others listed by Hodge (1907–1910, 1:538–539).

The Havasupai are sometimes referred to as Yampais, 1858 (Ives 1861:108), or Yampas (Bell 1869:243), but variants of this name are more frequently applied to the Yavapai (see the synonymies in "Walapai" and "Yavapai," this vol.).

Other names recorded for the Havasupai are Pima su´-palᵗt (Russell 1902–1903) and Western Apache Dĕzhī´piklakŭlh ‘women dress in bark’ (Curtis 1907–1930, 1:134) and t‘ádùtł‘ìjǹ ‘blue water people’ (Goodwin 1942:92).

Sources

Among the Spanish chronicles of the seventeenth and eighteenth centuries, only that of Father Francisco Garcés (Coues 1900) contains an eyewitness account of the Havasupai. Several American explorers mentioned the Havasupai during the 1800s, among them Ives (1861), but it was not until Cushing (1882) that any detailed ethnographic information was available. A popular account of both the Havasupai and the Walapai was written by Iliff (1954), based on her experiences as a reservation schoolteacher in the early 1900s.

The classic work on the Havasupai is Spier (1928), which furnished the bulk of the information on traditional culture for this chapter. Also of major importance is Smithson's (1959) monograph on the Havasupai woman, which updates many of Spier's topics. Smithson and Euler (1964) provide information on religion and myth.

Martin (1966, 1968) studied social and economic organization. Alvarado (1970) has discussed the cultural factors in Havasupai population stability.

Information on Havasupai prehistory can be found in Schwartz (1955, 1956, 1959) and Euler (1958).

Walapai

THOMAS R. MCGUIRE

The Walapai (ˈwälə,pī), a Yuman-speaking group* with close cultural affinities to the Havasupai and Yavapai, occupied an extensive territory in northwestern Arizona (fig. 1). Rugged canyons of the Colorado River marked the northern boundary. To the west the often hostile Mohaves restricted Walapai movement past the Black Mountains. Hostile Yavapais bordered Walapai territory along the Bill Williams and Santa Maria rivers to the south. The eastern boundary was less clearly defined, running northward across the Coconino Plateau to Cataract Creek Canyon, inhabited by the Havasupai.

This expanse of more than five million acres was never heavily populated. In 1882, following a period of warfare and exposure to epidemic diseases, 667 Walapais were counted in a U.S. Army census (U.S. Congress. Senate 1936:142). Martin (1973:1462) estimates that one-third of the aboriginal Walapai may have been lost by then. But the fluid nature of Walapai hunting and gathering bands, as well as the difficulty early explorers encountered in distinguishing Walapais from neighboring groups, work against an adequate reconstruction of demographic patterns. By 1900, Walapais numbered only 584 (U.S. Congress. Senate 1936:192), but their population has risen, under conditions of settled reservation life, to approximately 1,000 in the 1970s (Dobyns, Stoffle, and Jones 1975:164).

Environment

Preceding belligerent contact with Anglo settlers and soldiers in the mid-nineteenth century, the Walapais ranged over a territory that was relatively abundant in plant and animal resources and diverse in physiographic features. Several perennial streams drain this predominantly arid range. Along the southern frontier of traditional Walapai territory, the Bill Williams system is fed by year-long flow from the Big Sandy and, less consistently, from Burro Creek. To the north, the Peach Springs–Diamond Creek network and the Meriwhitica empty into the gorges of the Colorado River. A number of usually dry arroyos carry flood waters into the basins during violent summer cloudbursts, but most of this water is quickly absorbed into the soil or lost through evaporation. These cloudbursts, occurring almost daily in July and August, and mild rainstorms during the winter months, contribute some water to tanks in the clay soil and to perennial springs along the base of mountain ranges.

Summers are hot and winters mild over most of the Walapai territory, though temperatures vary markedly with altitude. Truxton Canyon in the mesquite-covered valley at 3,800 feet is representative of much of traditional Walapai territory. Mean July temperature is 80.4° F, dropping to a mean of 41.3° F for January. Mean yearly precipitation for the period 1931 to 1972 was 10.56 inches (Sellers and Hill 1974:520).

Chaparral and desert-grassland vegetation characterize most of the valley and basins of the region. Cacti of various species—prickly pear, saguaro, barrel, agave—and trees such as mesquite, creosote bush, and paloverde served the Walapai as important food resources and raw materials for manufactured goods. At higher elevations and along stream sources, juniper, oak, walnut, and piñon abound in association with varieties of cane used as arrowshafts. Thick stands of mesquite are found in lower riparian environments (Lowe 1964).

Faunal resources played an equally important role in Walapai subsistence. Rabbits, rodents, deer, and antelope inhabited the grasslands of the basins. Higher ranges provided a favorable environment for mountain sheep and varieties of birds. With these relatively abundant and diverse faunal and floral resources, Walapais were able to procure adequate food despite the prevailing aridity of their territory (Kroeber 1935:27–37).

Origins: Mythology

The origin and diversification of the Yuman tribes of northwestern Arizona have been recorded in myth. There are three main figures in the Walapai origin myth, Coyote ($k^h a\theta ar$) and the twins *matvila,* the older brother,

*The phonemes of Walapai are: (voiceless unaspirated stops and affricate) *p*, *t* (dental), *č*, k^y, *k*, k^w, *q*, q^w, ʔ; (aspirated stops and affricate) p^h, t^h (dental), $\underset{.}{t}^h$ (alveolar), $\check{c}^h$, k^h, k^{wh}; (voiced spirants) *v* ([v] - [β]), *δ*; (voiceless spirants) *f*, *θ*, *s*, *h*, h^w; (lateral) *l*; (nasals) *m*, *n*, n^y, *ŋ*; (flap) *r*; (semivowels) *w*, *y*; (short vowels) *i*, *e*, *æ*, *a*, *o*, *u*, *ə*; (long vowels) *i·*, *e·*, *æ·*, *a·*, *o·*, *u·*; (stress) v́.

Information on Walapai phonology has been furnished by Akira Yamamoto and Lucille J. Watahomigie (communications to editors 1981), who also provided the phonemic transcriptions of Walapai words.

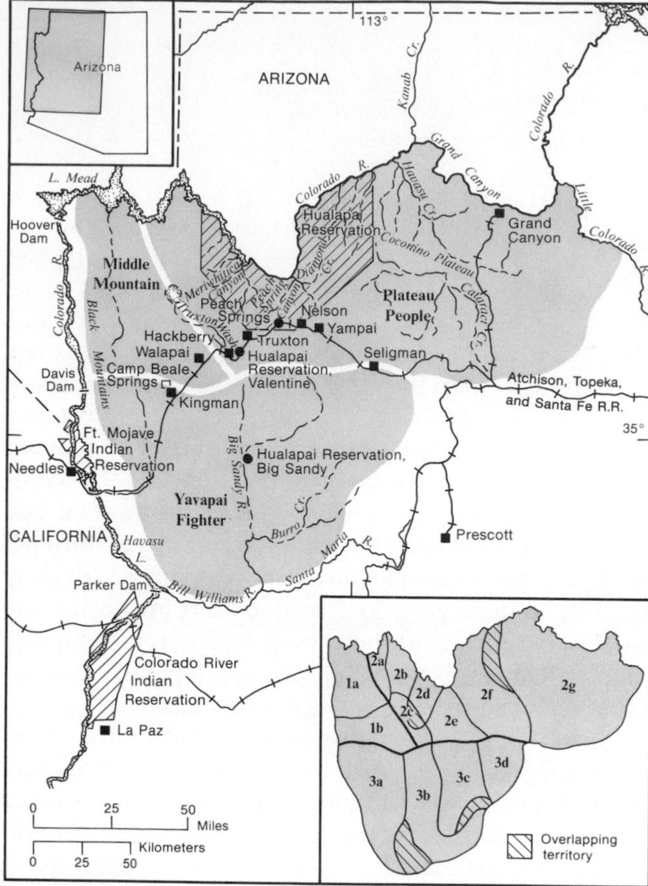

Fig. 1. Tribal territory in the 19th century. Inset shows subtribes. 1, Middle Mountain: 1a, Red Rock (Wi gahwa đa Ba:'); 1b, Cerbat Mountain (Ha' emđe: Ba:'). 2, Plateau People: 2a, Clay Springs (Haduva Ba:'); 2b, Grass Springs (Đanyka Ba:'); 2c, Hackberry (Qwaq We' Ba:'); 2d, Milkweed Springs (He:l Ba:'); 2e, Peach Springs ('I qađ Ba:'); 2f, Pine Springs (Hak saha Ba:'); 2g, Cataract Canyon (Hav'su:wa Ba:'). 3, Yavapai Fighter: 3a, Hualapai Mountain (Mađ hwa:la Ba:'); 3b, Big Sandy River (Haksigaela Ba:'); 3c, Mahone Mountain (Ha gi a:ja Ba:'); 3d, Juniper Mountain (Hwalgijapa Ba:'). Subtribe names are from Dobyns and Euler (1970) respelled in the Walapai practical orthography by Lucille Watahomigie (communication to editors 1982).

and *turčupa* (or *čurpa·*), the younger brother (Akira Yamamoto and Lucille J. Watahomigie, communications to editors 1981). Different recorded versions do not completely agree on the roles and names of the three, *turčupa* being called Tu´djupa by Kroeber (1935:12, 203) and Kathat Kanave 'Told the Coyote' by Ewing (1961); other sources agree that *kʰaθar kana·ve* '(What) Coyote told, Coyote's teachings' is not the name of a character but a general designation of the contents of the origin myth and the primeval period it describes (Kroeber 1935:203; Lucille J. Watahomigie, communication to editors 1981).

In the version of the origin myth recorded by Ewing (1961), Kathat Kanave was directed by the Great Spirit to a place on the west bank of the Colorado River, where a great bed of canes grew. In company with Coyote, Kathat Kanave was instructed to cut large bundles of cane, laying the tops toward the east. During the night, the Great Spirit would create human beings out of these canes. Kathat Kanave relayed instructions to Coyote to remain quiet in the night, and many people would come to life. Coyote could not restrain his glee, becoming boisterous. This disobedience infuriated Kathat Kanave and the Great Spirit. Consequently, only a few people were created, instead of the great multitude.

Kathat Kanave rounded up these new people, instructed them in many things, and led them east to the sacred canyon *matwita* (Meriwhitica canyon), in the territory of the historic Walapai. Here he taught them to farm by irrigation, to hunt, to collect wild foods on the high mesas, and to make weapons. After several generations of harmless play, boys of different families divided into sides and began to throw mud at each other in mimic warfare. Some were injured. Their parents, instead of halting the game, encouraged the children to retaliate with bows and arrows. Bellicose Yavapai parents were the main instigators, soon taking over the fight from their children. After widening the breach in the once-friendly relations with the rest of Kathat Kanave's people, the Yavapai were expelled to the southeast, always to remain at war with their former friends.

For a time, the remaining families lived in peace and prospered. But they grew so numerous that Kathat Kanave had to order them to search for new homes. Mohaves moved west to the valley of the Colorado River. Paiutes went across the river to the north. Navajos, Hopis, and Havasupais wandered east.

Origins: Prehistory

In search of more precise clues to Walapai origins, archeologists have studied the region. A lack of consensus, as well as a lack of data, is reflected in the use of different designations for overlapping prehistoric traditions: Yuman (Gladwin and Gladwin 1930), Patayan (Colton 1939; Euler 1958), and Hakatayan (Schroeder 1957, 1960).

Euler (1958) and Dobyns (1974) marshall evidence to tie the historic Walapai to the Cerbat branch of the prehistoric Upland Patayan tradition. Tizon brownware, an oxidized, paddle-and-anvil plainware, is the key to this probable linkage. Found in Cerbat sites as early as A.D. 655, up to 1300 (Linford 1979:38), it is also present in four historic Walapai sites excavated by Euler. Further, there is one surviving ethnographic speciman of Tizon ware, the famous "Wilder pot." Lillie Wilder, a Walapai from Peach Springs, obtained it from her parents-in-law around 1900, who told her it was made by a Walapai (Dobyns 1974:147–148). By inference from these lines of evidence, then, the prehistoric Cerbat tradition was directly ancestral to the

Walapai (for a skeptical view of this evidence, see Linford 1979; see Schwartz 1956 for alternative reconstructions of Walapai and Havasupai antecedents).

History

In the sixteenth and seventeenth centuries, Spanish explorers and missionaries made excursions into the areas inhabited by the Colorado River Yumans, the Havasupai, and the Hopi (see Schroeder 1952 for a summary of these contacts). But not until the 1776 expedition of the Franciscan missionary Francisco Garcés was direct Spanish contact made with Walapais. Hoping to expand the mission frontier, Garcés traveled through the region around present-day Kingman and Peach Springs. He was welcomed and fed by Indians he identified as Jaguallapais (Coues 1900,1:316).

Garcés's explorations terminated when he was killed by Yumans along the Colorado River in 1781. The Walapai apparently remained isolated from Anglo or Spanish incursions for the next 70 years. In the 1850s, the United States Army began to sponsor explorations through northern Arizona, seeking railroad routes to the west coast. Capt. Lorenzo Sitgreaves led a party into Walapai territory in 1851, where he established peaceful contacts with some bands but suffered attacks from other Walapais. The Sitgreaves expedition was followed by two others in 1853–1854. A party of well-armed New Mexican explorers under François Aubry traded shots with Walapais in the vicinity of Truxton Canyon, while Lt. Amiel W. Whipple's railroad surveyors met with little hostility from the few Walapais they encountered (Dobyns and Euler 1960:51).

Lt. Edward F. Beale's road-building expedition through northern Arizona in 1857–1858 presaged hostile contact between Walapais and Anglo settlers. Wagon trains began to move along the road cutting Walapai territory, bound for California via the Needles landing on the Colorado River. Mohaves, in 1858, were the first to retaliate against the incursion, killing 18 settlers from Iowa and forcing their wagons back to Albuquerque. Walapais continued the harassment from inaccessible retreats overlooking the trail.

A crushing military defeat of the Mohaves, and the establishment of an army garrison at Fort Mohave in 1859 initiated a short period of enforced peace between settlers and Yuman groups. Large numbers of prospectors rushed to northwestern Arizona with the discovery of gold near Prescott in 1863. Friction soon developed between settlers and Walapais. In 1866, Anglos killed a respected Walapai leader, Wauba Yuma, bringing immediate retaliation. Assembling a fighting force of perhaps 250 men, Walapais engaged U.S. troops in several large-scale battles during the following year. However, the better-armed and better-mounted Anglo soldiers under Lt. Col. William R. Price waged a successful campaign, burning Walapai rancherias, destroying crops and food caches. By 1869, the most recalcitrant leaders, Cherum and Leve Leve, had surrendered, and the Walapai War ended (Dobyns and Euler 1960, 1970).

The defeated Walapai were interned at Camp Beale Springs in 1871 but removed three years later by the army to La Paz, on the Colorado River Indian Reservation. Conditions on the reservation were unacceptable to the Walapais: diseases killed many; miserly government rations left others hungry; and the labors of hay cutting and ditch digging in the sweltering lowlands were arduous (Dobyns and Euler 1960:55). In 1875, the Walapai fled this riverine internment to return to their accustomed territory (U.S. Congress. Senate 1936).

During the brief absence of the Walapai, Anglo ranchers and miners had effectively colonized the habitable areas, taken over the springs, and started to herd cattle over large tracts of grassland. Unable to return to their traditional subsistence activities, Walapais looked for jobs in the mines. A 900,000-acre reservation, representing only a fraction of their original land, was established in 1883. Anglos desired the reservation more than Walapais, for it kept the Indians off the land already appropriated by ranchers (U.S. Congress. Senate 1936:139).

The stress of living under Anglo domination did not diminish with the demarcation of reservation boundaries. Heavy grazing of cattle had quickly altered the vegetation, virtually exterminating several of the food plants upon which Walapais relied. Direct physical threats by ranchers and miners were also common. Moreover, epidemic diseases—smallpox, whooping cough, gonorrhea, and syphilis—had drastic effects on Walapai population. Many died, while birth rates declined markedly due to the effects of venereal diseases (Dobyns and Euler 1967:38–39).

Under these conditions, Walapais readily accepted the millenarian Ghost Dance, introduced to them by Southern Paiutes in 1889. Ideologically, the Ghost Dance had two goals: the removal of Anglos from traditional Walapai territory, allowing a return to previous subsistence patterns; and the resurrection of dead ancestors. For several years, Walapais avidly attended Ghost Dances in their territory, causing a brief period of fear among Anglos. It soon became clear that Ghost Dance adherents would resort only to magical means to attain their ends, not force. Consequently, military power was not used to curtail the movement.

By 1891 the cult began to lose intensity because of repeated failures to revive the dead and expel the Anglos. Walapais held their final Ghost Dance in 1895 (Dobyns and Euler 1967).

Few Walapais remained on their unproductive reservation, which Oliver Gates, superintendent in 1905, characterized as "730,880 [sic] acres of the most valueless land on earth for agricultural purposes. It is unsurveyed and unallotted. Scarcely a dozen families live on the reservation" (U.S. Congress. Senate 1936:201). Many others sought jobs in towns on the railroad, or with miners and ranchers. They sent their children to schools in Kingman and Hackberry, Arizona, to be instructed in Christian customs and Anglo social patterns (figs. 3–4).

Reservation Life

Two developments of the 1930s laid the groundwork for life on the Walapai reservation. With the Depression, many Walapais left the insecure job market in urban centers, returning to the reservation to find employment with the Civilian Conservation Corps building roads and making other improvements. When this program was terminated, most chose to remain on the reservation and to resume tending small herds of cattle. By 1960 half the 702 Walapais on tribal rolls (Coult 1961:12) lived permanently in the reservation town of Peach Springs, Arizona. Many of the remaining members continued to reside in railroad towns between Kingman and Seligman.

Also in the 1930s, the Indian Reorganization Act established the political structure of the tribe: a nine-member tribal council, with each elected member serving a three-year term. A tenth seat on the council was created for the hereditary chief of the tribe, but Walapais disagree over who should fill this position (Dobyns and Euler 1970:56). Consequently, this seat has remained vacant for a number of years (Coult 1961).

Calif. Histl. Soc., Los Angeles: Title Insurance Coll., 3189, 3202.

Fig. 2. Leaders during the Walapai War of 1866–1869. left, Susquatama or Walapai Charley, who later became a scout for the U.S. Army and then led the assimilationist element of the tribe (Dobyns and Euler 1976:36, opp. p. 42); photograph by George Wharton James, 1895–1901. right, Quasula, son of the great leader Wauba Yuma and father of Phillip Quasula, who in 1938 was elected as the first tribal council president; photograph probably by George Wharton James, 1895–1901.

Calif. Histl. Soc., Los Angeles: Title Insurance Coll., 3162.

Fig. 3. Woman with facial paint and children posed with F.S. Calfee, missionary-schoolteacher sent by the Massachusetts Indian Association to Hackberry, Ariz., in 1894 to open an Indian school. A disassembled cradle is at right. Photograph probably by George Wharton James, about 1895.

The tribal council is responsible for making laws, administering tribal property, and supervising all tribal economic affairs; however, ordinances passed by the council must be approved by the Bureau of Indian Affairs and the secretary of the interior. Coult (1961:149) sees this stipulation as effectively limiting the role of the tribal council to one of making recommendations to the Department of the Interior. A more important limitation on the council's ability to govern lies in the lack of adequate information available to it. The council has few channels for gathering information other than the BIA and owners of enterprises petitioning for use of Walapai land. Often these sources of information are biased, forcing the council to make hasty decisions or to allocate funds (Dajevskis 1974:30).

In the 1960s, chronic unemployment compounded the difficulties faced by the tribal council. A state government survey (Arizona. State Employment Service 1970) found only 92 permanently employed Walapais out of a total available work force (those over 16 years old) of 394. In addition, 120 were temporarily employed, but 46 percent of this labor force had no jobs at all.

In the 1970s there were signs of change. Tribal enterprises received the impetus of $2,950,000, awarded as a result of the Indian Claims Commission decision in 1968, representing a compromise over the valuation of 4,459,500 acres of Walapai land appropriated by the United States in 1883 (Manners 1974). A doll factory was funded in 1973, creating steady income for two dozen Walapais (fig. 5) (Dobyns and Euler 1976:97). The trading post and grocery store was infused with the capital necessary to function as a welfare agency, extending credit to unemployed families and cattle owners short of cash in the months prior to stock auctions. Additionally, the Walapai tribal cattle herd was culled and shaped into a high-quality breeding herd of 1,000 head. From this herd, Walapai cattlemen obtain stock on deferred payment plans with low interest rates and, for nominal fees, can secure the use of bulls. In 1981 some 4,000 head of cattle were run on the reservation ranges, providing supplemental income to many Walapai families.

The tribal council has taken a serious interest in the natural and recreational resources on the reservation. Where Diamond Creek empties into the Colorado River, enterprising Walapais began charging fees to haul out the rafts of river-runners. Of more fundamental economic impact was the attention being devoted to Walapai timber. A forestry project was instituted in 1978, under which five million board-feet of lumber were harvested by two dozen tribal employees, and plans were laid for sustained-yield operations on 50,000 acres of reservation land (Anonymous 1979b).

The continued development of tribal enterprises may overturn the established pattern of off-reservation wage work, though more than half the enrolled members of the tribe have been forced to reside in the Anglo towns along the railroad (Dobyns, Stoffle, and Jones 1975:164). Moreover, sustained economic viability on the reservation may correct the discouraging picture drawn by the anthropologist Coult (1961). In the late 1950s, social life on the reservation was marked by hostility in interpersonal relations. Coult attributed this situation in part to the absence of economic cooperation within and between families. In part, also, he noted the lack of well-developed mechanisms for social control, stemming from a failure to maintain feelings of tribal identity.

Dobyns and Euler (1967:54) point to an alternative interpretation for this pattern of overt aggression. It is a recurrent response among Walapais to strains emanating from life in an Anglo-dominated society. The pattern began when Walapais returned from captivity on the Colorado River Reservation in 1882 to find their original territory taken over by White ranchers and miners. Walapais soon learned that any overt hostility against Anglos resulted in quick and effective physical punishment. Aside from the brief respite that the Ghost Dance movement provided, the only emotional alternative to these stresses has been in-group aggression.

With careful investment of tribal funds, with the growing self-confidence of tribal officials in making hard decisions, with renewed interest in Walapai arts, crafts, and history, the stresses generated by unemployment and poverty will be lessened.

Calif. Histl. Soc., Los Angeles: Title Insurance Coll., 3188.

Fig. 4. Classroom of the Bureau of Indian Affairs day school in Kingman, Ariz., which opened in Oct. 1896 with an enrollment of about 35 Walapai students. Susquatama stands in the back at right; the White man, next to him, may be Agent Henry P. Ewing (Dobyns and Euler 1976:opp. p. 72). The students, girls to the left and the boys to the right, wear school uniforms and have had their hair closely cropped. The blackboards list assignments for first, second, and third grades, and the walls above have depictions of the continents. Photograph by George Wharton James, soon after 1896.

Culture

Sociopolitical Organization

Prior to the destructive Walapai War and settlement on reservations, Walapais were organized into a tribe with three divisions. Each of these divisions or "subtribes" encompassed several bands, which in turn were composed of camps and families (fig. 6) (Dobyns and Euler 1970; see Manners 1957, and Kroeber 1935, for alternative views of Walapai social and political organization).

The smallest unit—the nuclear family of parents and children—was seldom isolated from other units of similar composition. For most of the year, several families cooperated economically and resided together in camps. Numbering about 25 persons, each camp recognized a headman, who offered advice, made the decisions necessary to coordinate subsistence activities, and admonished children. Headship was often inherited from fathers, provided the sons demonstrated the essential leadership qualities of wisdom and bravery.

Neighboring camps, exploiting the same set of resources within a restricted geographical area, united politically into a band. There were 13 of these bands, each named for an important geographical feature within their customary range. During temporary periods of abundant resources, all camps of a band resided together under the leadership of a chief, drawn from the ranks of the local camp headmen. No rules prohibited marriage within the band. Often, however, marriage partners were sought outside the band, for lack of eligible, nonkin individuals within the band (Dobyns and Euler 1970:10–35).

Bands with adjacent territorial ranges grouped politically into three subtribes: the Middle Mountain People in the northwest extreme of the Walapai region, the Yavapai Fighters to the south, and the Plateau People to the east. The Plateau People may have included the Havasupai as one of its bands until the 1880s, when the United States government established separate reservations for the Walapai and Havasupai. (See "Havasupai," this vol., for an alternative interpretation that traces the Havasupai as a separate entity back to prehistoric times.)

Subtribal boundaries were not clearly demarcated, either spatially or socially. Bands from one subtribe were welcome in the territory of another subtribe during periods of abundant food resources. Moreover, marriage occurred across subtribal distinctions, although such marriages were less common than ones within the subtribe.

The Walapai tribe was the most inclusive political entity, characterized by a common dialect and cultural homogeneity. Most important in the definition of the tribe was the Walapais' own conception of themselves. They designated themselves, collectively, as *ʔpaʔ* (or *paʔ*) 'people', though Dobyns and Euler (1970:3) claim that the gloss 'people' fails to convey the emotional force of this word, an ethnocentric conception of themselves as chosen people.

The organizing potential of this flexible sociopolitical structure is lost in a simple description of its component parts. Cherum, the subtribal chief in Middle Mountain territory at the time of the Walapai War, understood this potential, and the sketchy details of his political career are therefore illuminating. Initially, Cherum had little hereditary claim to band chieftainship: his father had not been chief, but reportedly Cherum's father's father had held such a position (Dobyns and Euler 1970:46). As an acknowledged war leader of the Middle Mountain subtribe, though, Cherum prepared diligently for the impending confrontation with the United States Army and Anglo prospectors. He armed himself and his relatives well, through a clever trade network: woven goods from the Pueblos were taken to the Mohave and exchanged for horses, which Cherum then traded to the Southern Paiute in return for firearms they had secured from the Utah Mormons. During the height of the Walapai War, Cherum reportedly marshalled close to 70 arms and a fighting force of 250 Walapais (Dobyns and Euler 1970:39). But his influence did not stem simply from military prowess. Cherum also married well. Coming from the smallest of the Walapai subtribes, he necessarily extended his marriage ties outside the Middle Mountain People, and in the process garnered political influence through the tribe. Within his own subtribe he soon obtained the position

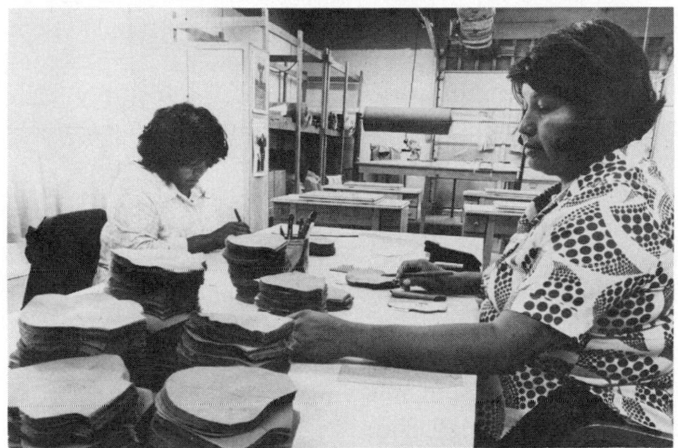

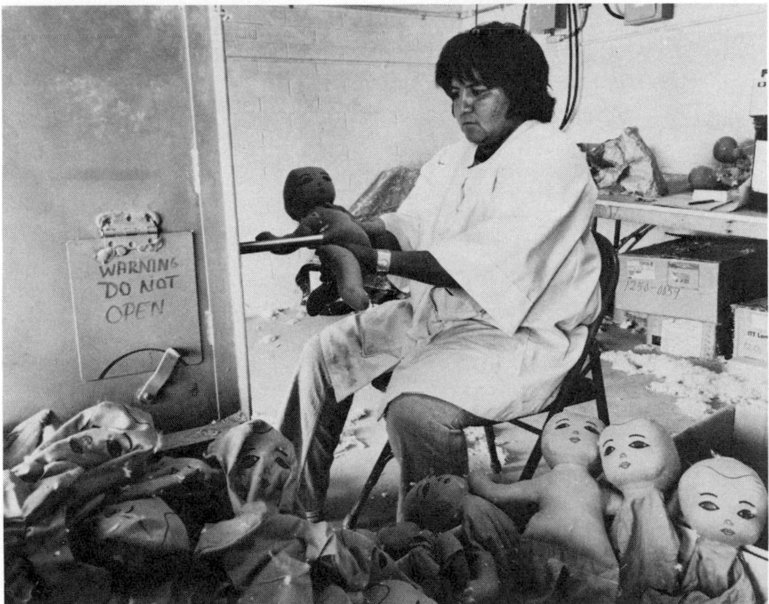

Fig. 5. The Walapai doll factory at Peach Springs, Ariz., opened by the tribal council in Nov. 1973 and closed in 1980. top, One of about 24 employees painting the facial features; bottom left, stuffing the dolls; bottom right, Winifred Paya holding the finished product. Photographs by Jerry Jacka, Oct. 1977.

of chief under not uncommon demographic circumstances. He married the daughter of the hereditary subtribal chief. When this chief was killed during the Walapai War, leaving no male heirs, Cherum simply assumed his father-in-law's status. Subsequently, Cherum won recognition as the head chief of all the Walapai, a position fabricated by the United States Army in its misunderstanding of the nominal equality of the three subtribal chiefs of traditional Walapai social organization (Dobyns and Euler 1970:46).

Subsistence

In an arid but physiographically diverse environment, Walapais based their economy primarily on hunting and gathering seasonally available wild resources. Moving frequently within the vaguely defined band and subtribal territories, groups visited specific locations where resources were known to be abundant. This annual round—a fairly regular pattern of movement—focused on several key plant foods (Kroeber 1935:48–76).

In the spring, activity centered on the gathering and processing of wild mescal or agave (*Agave* spp.) in canyons and foothills. Mescal stalks were baked for several days in an earth oven. When cooked, the nonfibrous inner core was eaten immediately, while the outer layers were crushed into a pulp, dried in the sun, and then stored. In the form of slabs, mescal could then be boiled and eaten or mixed with water to produce a beverage (Kroeber 1935:52–53).

Following the mescal harvest, families or larger camps moved down to the valley and basin floors to gather *sleʔ* (stick-leaf, *Mentzelia albicaulis*), a wild plant producing seeds that are rich in carbohydrates and protein (C.G. Smith 1973).

By midsummer, fruits of several cactus species ripened, and Walapai camps shifted back into the canyons and foothills. Seeds and fruits of saguaro, tuna and prickly pear (*Opuntia* spp.), barrel cactus, and yucca (*Yucca baccata*) were all procured, either to be processed into beverages or stored for future use.

Late summer and early fall were devoted to nut gathering. Piñon cones (*Pinus edulis*) were obtained in mountain groves, baked and dried, then processed into a paste or soup. The berries of juniper (*Juniperus osteosperma*) and sumac (*Rhus trilobata*) were gathered at the same time, to be crushed and soaked in water to make a drink.

Winter encampments were larger and more sedentary. Although few vegetal resources were available during this season, subsistence was adequately based on hunting and the consumption of stored foods.

Women bore primary responsibility for the gathering activities, while men and boys hunted, employing a variety of techniques. For small game such as rabbits and rodents, vital to the Walapai diet, the favorite technique was a drive under the direction of a temporary leader. Mule deer, bighorn sheep, and pronghorn antelope were hunted, either by a drive involving several men, or by individual stalking (Kroeber 1935:70–76).

In its scale and flexibility, Walapai social organization was well suited to this economy of gathering and hunting. Martin (1973) argues convincingly that the Walapai camps, averaging about 25 individuals of all ages, were of optimum size to hunt and gather efficiently. Four cooperating, mature hunters—the number expected in a social group of 25—would be sufficient to drive and ambush deer and bighorn sheep and surround rabbits but would put less pressure on local resources than larger concentrations of related individuals. The wives of these hunters, in turn, would constitute an efficient gathering force, large enough to overcome the temporary withdrawal from gathering activities of pregnant and nursing women (Martin 1973:1452). Continued survival of such camps was predicated upon mutable residence rules. Upon marriage, a man was expected to live for a time in the camp of his wife's family, then return with his spouse to his own family's camp. Kroeber's ethnographic work discovered, predictably, that such expectations were quickly ignored: young couples went where they were most needed in the quest for food (Kroeber 1935:142–143).

Unresolved controversy surrounds the extent to which the historic Walapai relied on agriculture. Until the Indian Claims Commission research conducted by Henry Dobyns and Robert Euler in the 1950s, Kroeber's report on the brief Laboratory of Anthropology field study offered the accepted position: cultivation was at best intermittent. Indeed, Gordon MacGregor of Kroeber's party was almost scornful of the Walapai efforts to farm six or seven acres in Meriwhitica Canyon: "It is clear that even the pitiful attempt at farming consistently made at Matewitide impressed the imagination of the whole tribe far beyond warrant of the actual economic results" (Kroeber 1935:58). Dobyns and Euler suggest

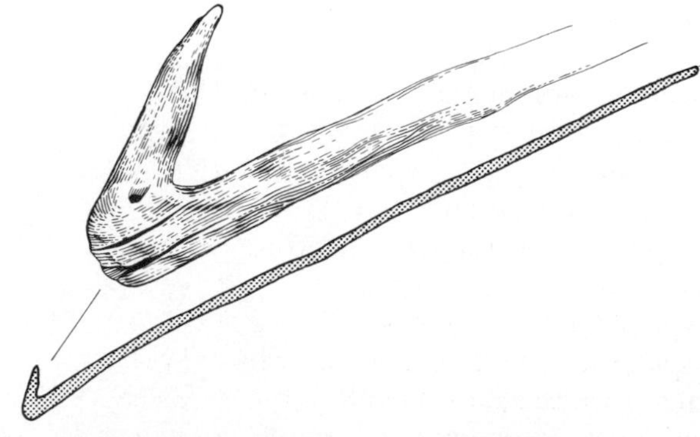

Mus. of N. Mex., Santa Fe: School of Amer. Research Coll., 10857/12.

Fig. 6. Wooden stick, barbed at one end, used to pull chuckwallas (the only lizard eaten) from rock crevices. Woodrats, another food source, were also drawn from their holes with a hooked stick. Length about 94.0 cm, collected by A.L. Kroeber in 1929.

that Kroeber and his associates saw only the residue of Walapai agriculture, long after traditional residences and economic patterns were disrupted by the Walapai War and the ensuing Anglo-American occupation, opening up more profitable wage labor opportunities. On the basis of oral testimonies, Dobyns and Euler (1976:10–12) reconstruct a pattern of extensive and quite sophisticated Walapai farming in the nineteenth century. Along the Big Sandy and Bill Williams rivers and their tributaries, in the deep canyons of Cataract Creek and Diamond Creek, flowing into the Colorado River, Walapais built diversion dams to irrigate gardens of squash, maize, beans, watermelons, and wheat. Numerous springs in the cliff faces were channeled to flood adjacent fields as well. And natural, unchanneled runoff from mountain springs was put to use for crops, in a fashion very similar to that of Hopi agriculture at the mesa bases.

Mus. of N. Mex., Santa Fe: School of Amer. Research Coll., 16256.

Fig. 7. Camp at Grand Canyon with at least 3 brush shelters (see Kroeber 1935:pl. 1 for another view). Several large conical seed-gathering baskets are at left. The woman shading her eyes seems to wear dark paint over much of her face and may also have close-cropped hair (perhaps in mourning); in front of her is a slab metate with a large, rough mano on top. Photograph by Ben Wittick, 1880s.

Trade

Despite this impressive range of crops and cultivation techniques, the Walapai actively traded with neighboring Indians for agricultural products. When at peace with the Mohave, Walapai bartered meat for supplies of corn, pumpkins, and beans grown along the Colorado River floodplain. Likewise, cultivated foods were obtained from the closely related Havasupai of Cataract Creek, in return for deer and mountain sheep skins (Kroeber 1935:64–66). But these trade linkages extended well beyond adjacent groups. Walapai introduced their own specialized products—dried mescal, red hematite, and prized basketry—into an exchange system connecting Pacific Coast Indians to the Pueblos of New Mexico (Kristine L. Jones, personal communication 1980). Cherum, the great subtribal chief, effectively used these extensive networks to arm himself for the conquest of the United States Army.

Structures

Shelters consisting of little more than branches and leaves laid against a low tree limb offered protection from the summer sun (fig. 7). Kroeber's ethnographic field party observed Walapai living in semipermanent winter homes, roughly 14 feet long, with an eight-foot domed roof and thatched with arrowwood or covered with juniper bark. Archeological evidence fails to support the antiquity of such construction; post-holes have not been found. Circular rock outlines—the material remains of rough brush wickiups—have been uncovered, as well as habitation debris in caves and rockshelters (Linford 1979:38). During the period of settled reservation life, the Walapai also built eight-sided hogans and tar-paper shacks (Kristine L. Jones, personal communication 1980) and sweathouses, large enough to accommodate two to four people, covered with a thick mat of branches and bark. Rarely were these sweathouses covered by earth, although the Walapai were aware of this mode of construction among the Hopi and Navajo (Kroeber 1935:77–79).

Technology

Basketry (fig. 8), highly valued in the trade network, provided one of the major outlets for artistic expression among Walapai women. Prior to the rising tourist demand for Indian crafts, most Walapai baskets were made by twining techniques into functional containers: large burden or firewood baskets, conical seed-gathering baskets, flat trays used for winnowing and parching seeds, and water bottles coated with red paint and piñon pitch (Kroeber 1935:79–86).

Walapai pottery manufacture did not survive the influx of metal utensils during the reservation period (Dobyns 1974:163). A member of Kroeber's Laboratory of Anthropology party observed in the 1930s that "the art has fallen into disuse and it seems impossible to find a creditable Walapai potter" (Kroeber 1935:86). Ceramic decoration on the specimens that Kroeber's party commissioned consisted simply of red paint applied in geometric shapes or straight lines.

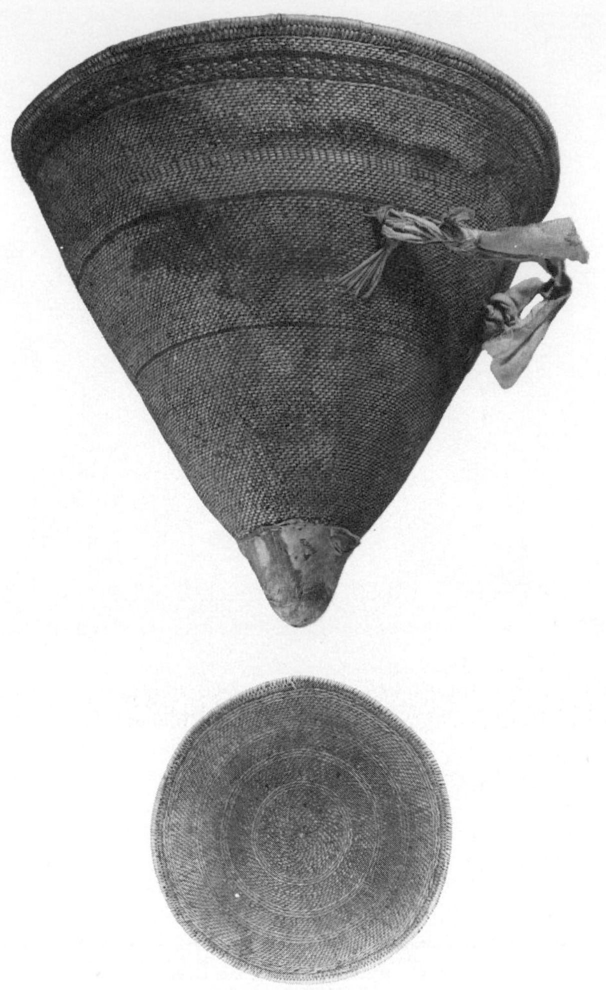

top, Field Mus., Chicago: 63091; bottom, Mus. of N. Mex., Santa Fe: School of Amer. Research Coll., 10925/12.

Fig. 8. Basketry. Traditional forms included: top, conical basket for gathering and carrying seeds, made of twined willow shoot with tip reinforced with leather, with rawhide loops on side with cotton cloth carrying strap attached; bottom, diagonally twined tray used to winnow and parch seeds. Other common types were seed beaters and pitched water bottles. Such forms are no longer produced but bowl-shaped baskets of twined sumac twig with colored decorative bands are made for the tourist market (Robinson 1954:119–122). left, Diameter 74.0 cm, collected by Stephen Simms at Truxton Canyon in 1901; right, same scale; collected by A.L. Kroeber in 1929.

Clothing and Adornment

Buckskin and juniper bark were the primary materials for men's and women's clothing. Traditional women's dress consisted of a double apron belted at the waist, and buckskin tied around the calf for travel through brush. A short-sleeved hide shirt, breechclout, and moccasins completed the Walapai male costume (Kroeber 1935:99–111).

Face painting and shell neck pendants were important modes of personal decoration. Obtained in trade from Mohaves and Quechans, shell decorations served as charms or amulets guarding the wearer against disease

Mus. für Völkerkunde, Berlin: IV B 12911.

Fig. 9. Group from Diamond Creek. The men wear either sleeveless or longsleeved shirts, and moccasins with upturned toes. The woman wears low moccasins with plain toes; her garment may be of Hopi or Navajo woven cloth. Watercolor by Heinrich Balduin Möllhausen, on Joseph C. Ives Colorado River Expedition, March-April 1858.

(Ewing 1960). Paint for temporary facial decorations was procured from red hematite from the mine in Middle Mountain band territory. A moderate amount of facial or limb tattooing was also customary, with simple designs picked into the skin by cactus needles (fig. 11) (Kroeber 1935:110).

Life Cycle

Few formal ceremonies and rather flexible standards of behavior characterized the traditional Walapai life cycle. The most stringent rules surrounded pregnancy and birth, where both the expectant mother and her husband were required to observe taboos. Women were admonished not to laugh at strange animals or funny jokes and to avoid salty or fatty foods. In addition, some foods were avoided for fear of having twins. Several of Kroeber's informants reported that twins were unwanted, weak, and likely to cause the mother's death during birth (Kroeber 1935:129). In a population as small as that of the Walapais, twins were probably not very common.

A pregnant woman was assisted at delivery by her husband and three women. Shortly after birth, the baby was placed in a cradleboard (fig. 12), and the mother returned to her household tasks. Babies were kept in cradleboards for about a year, nursing until they teethed (Kroeber 1935:129–135).

Childhood and adolescence were periods of casual education. Boys at an early age were taught to hunt rabbits and other small game. Later they accompanied their fathers on hunting trips in pursuit of larger animals (Kroeber 1935:136–138).

Girls passed through a simple puberty ceremony following their first menses. While they were lying on a blanket-covered bed of hot stones, initiates were bathed and shampooed with yucca-root by their mothers. For a short time thereafter, girls were required to wear a yucca leaf belt and refrain from bathing. The value of hard work was inculcated into the adolescents at this time, backed up by threats of afflictions such as loss of hair or teeth (Kroeber 1935:138–140).

Marriage was not marked by any formal ceremony, coming about instead through repeated presentations of gifts by the male suitor to the girl's father. If the father regarded the young man as an acceptable spouse for his daughter, he would continue to take the gifts and eventually urge his daughter to receive the man (Kroeber 1935:140).

Divorce, according to several informants, was frequent and easy, commonly caused by incompatibility, jealousy, and adultery (Kroeber 1935:145–146). By the 1960s this pattern had reversed. Coult (1961) found very few cases of divorce among Walapais living on the reservation, despite a relatively high level of tension between spouses.

Burial practices, like divorce rates, have undergone changes. Traditionally, Walapai dead were cremated along with their material possessions. The souls of the good people departed for the ancestral land of Tudjupa, in the west, to the accompaniment of ceremonial crying by the living relatives and friends (Kroeber 1935:148). In the late nineteenth century, the practice of cremation was altered by order of United States soldiers, pressing for Christian burials, and by the demands of the Ghost Dance movement. Walapais found burial in rock slides and cairns more conducive to an ideology calling for the return to life of deceased ancestors and relatives (Dobyns and Euler 1967:35). Mourning ceremonies for the dead, the most elaborate ritual occasions for the Colorado River Yumans, have persisted in attenuated form among the Walapais.

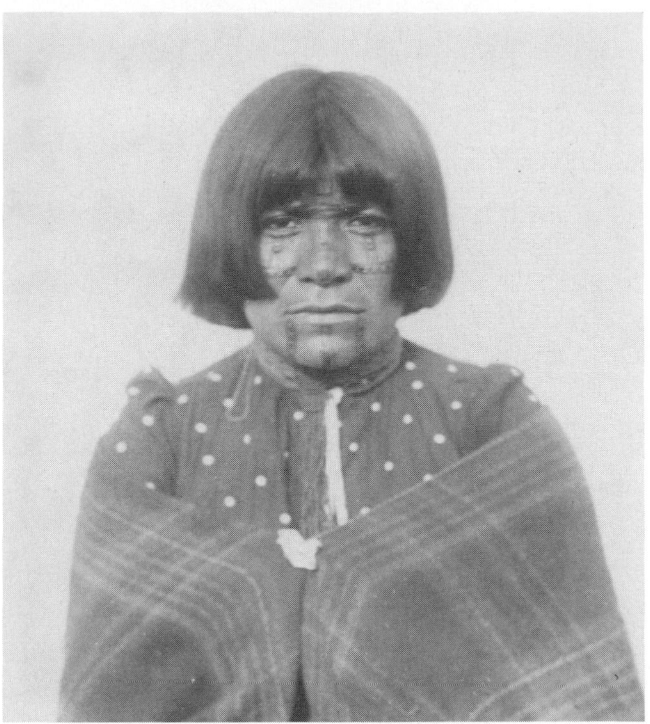

Smithsonian, NAA: 81-5347.

Fig. 11. Woman with facial decoration, evidently a tattooed line in center of chin (and perhaps on forehead), with the rest painted. The tattooing was made with a cactus needle pricking over a design drawn in ground charcoal; more charcoal was applied after the blood was washed off (Kroeber 1935:104–105). Photograph by Aleš Hrdlička, Truxton Canyon, 1900.

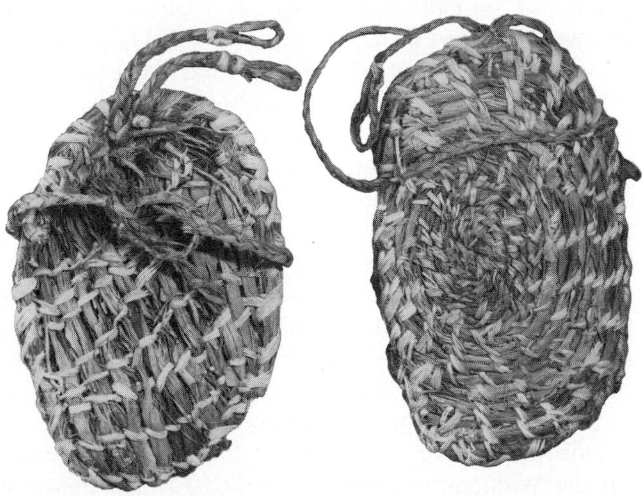

Mus. of N. Mex., Santa Fe: School of Amer. Research Coll., 10905/12.

Fig. 10. Yucca-fiber sandals with coiled sole (right) and twined upper (left) were stuffed with chokilala fiber. They were tied onto the foot with the attached braided strings and were worn by poor hunters who lacked the leather to make other footwear (Kroeber 1935:100–107). Length about 29.2 cm, collected by A.L. Kroeber in 1929.

Religion and Shamanism

Apart from mourning ceremonies, little knowledge of traditional religious practices and of the formerly complex cosmology seems to have survived among Walapais, perhaps due to the tribe's acceptance of religious movements from outsiders during the nineteenth century. Dobyns and Euler (1967:2) suggest that by borrowing the Southern Paiute Ghost Dance, rather than developing a nativistic movement within the structure of traditional Walapai religion, they opened the way for subsequent religious diversification. And indeed, Walapais have been subjected to repeated missionary activity during the twentieth century; however, Baptists, Mormons, and the revivalistic Four Square Gospel mission have met with little success. Coult (1961:145) attributes this failure to the Walapais' empirical attitude toward life.

Shamanism was an important facet of traditional Walapai culture and continued to be so when Kroeber's

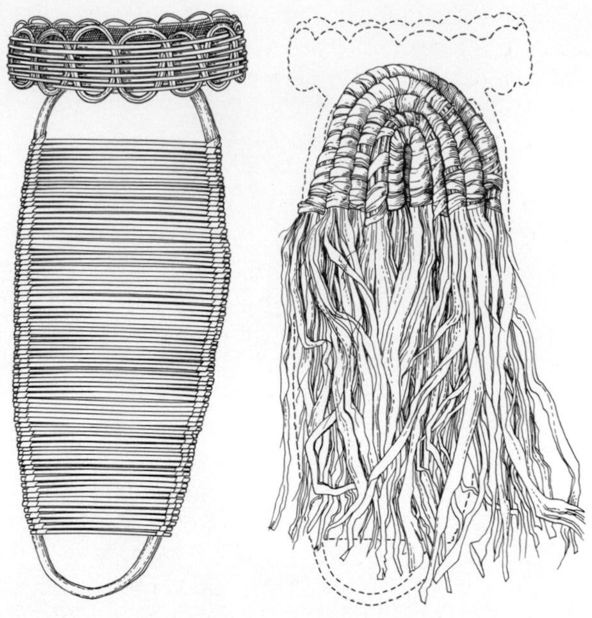

Mus. of N. Mex., Santa Fe: School of Amer. Research Coll. 10833/12; after Kroeber 1935:pl. 6.

Fig. 12. Cradleboards consist of a frame made of a stick bent into an oval or U-shape with from 30 to 90 close-set thin sticks across it and tied on with leather thongs or fiber and a wickerwork hood, which is tied to the head of the frame. A fiber cradle pad of shredded bark bundles wrapped near their centers and bound together in a U-shape is placed on top of the frame as bedding; the child's head lies on the bound end. Length about 60.0 cm, collected by A.L. Kroeber in 1929.

party visited the Walapai in 1929. The spirit of a deceased relative alerted the prospective shaman to his calling through a series of dreams. A candidate might then bolster his power by allying himself with the resident spirits of geographical features in Walapai territory. Thus prepared, the shaman began to operate in the realm of curative medicine. Treatment of diseases and snakebites consisted of singing over the patient and sucking the wound. Shamans would then produce a small object—stone, a piece of bone, or string—believed to be the residing place of malignant spirits. If the patient recovered, the shaman was paid in buckskins or cash. If the patient died, the shaman was liable to be killed by relatives of the deceased (Kroeber 1935:185–194).

Synonymy†

The name Walapai is first attested in English in reports of the Colorado Exploring Expedition of 1857–1858, appearing in the invariant form Hualpais as singular, plural, and attributive (Ives 1861:94, 97). It was apparently learned from the Mohave guides on the expedition (Dobyns and Euler 1970:70) and reflects Mohave *huwa·lʸapay,* literally 'pine person', a reference to the mountain territory of the Walapai (Pamela Munro, communication to editors 1981). Other spellings of this name in the nineteenth century include Hualapais, Huallapais, Hualipais, Hualopais, Huallopi, and others listed by Hodge (1907–1910, 2:899–900). The spelling Walapais first appears in secondary sources, apparently introduced by authors who incorrectly took the Hu- to be the Spanish equivalent of English W- (Bell 1869:243). Hualapai is the official spelling used by the tribe and the Bureau of Indian Affairs, but Walapai has become more common in the anthropological literature.

The Mohave name was recorded by Francisco Garcés in Spanish orthography as Jaguallapai(s), 1776 (Coues 1900, 1:231, 308–312), which would be phonetically [xawalʸapay]. An equivalent name is used in several other Yuman languages: Havasupai *hʷa·lpáy* (Leanne Hinton, communication to editors 1981); Quechan *xawálʸ apáy* (Abraham M. Halpern, communication to editors 1981); Maricopa *xwalʸpay* (Lynn Gordon, communication to editors 1981); Cocopa wālyapai (Kroeber 1943:38). In Walapai itself the corresponding term *hwa·la ˀpay* 'ponderosa pine people' (Lucille J. Watahomigie, communication to editors 1981) was originally confined to a single band living west of the Hualapai Mountains (Kroeber 1935:39, 43; Dobyns and Euler 1970:70). The Walapai self-designation is *ˀpaˀ* 'people'.

Other names recorded for the Walapai include Havasupai Θulgámpayȧ and guehegaíȧ (Spier 1946:17); Yavapai mă-tä-vē-kē pä-yä 'people on the north' and Hoo-wäl-yä-pīä (Corbusier 1921:3); and Southern Paiute ɔa·rɨp·aiatsiŋWɨ (Sapir 1930–1931:593), a loanword.

Names used for both the Walapai and Havasupai (and in some cases the Yavapai or other Yumans) include variants of Yampais (S. Eastman, 1853, in Schoolcraft 1851–1857, 4:24), among them "the Yum-pis" and "the Jum-py, or Ya-pa-pi tribe," described as living in the mountains east of the Colorado River nearly opposite the Chemehuevi (Heintzelman 1857:38, 44), and of Coconino or Cosnino, such as Navajo *Góóhníinii* (Young and Morgan 1980:370) and Third Mesa Hopi *kô·nina* (Voegelin and Voegelin 1957:49). Additional variants of these general or ambiguous names are in the synonymy in "Havasupai" (this vol.).

Dobyns and Euler (1970) use the term Pai Indians for the Walapai including, according to their analysis, the Havasupai.

Sources

Several early explorers—Spaniards and, later, Anglos—mention encounters with Indians living in or near

†This synonymy was written by Thomas R. McGuire and Ives Goddard.

traditional Walapai territory, but the terminological confusion surrounding tribal designations makes many of these accounts suspect. Manners (1974) provides an excellent summary of the reports. However, his ethnohistorical reconstruction of Walapai land use (ibid., also Manners 1957) should be compared carefully with the various works of Dobyns and Euler, anthropologists who served as expert witnesses for the Walapai Tribe before the Indian Claims Commission; Manners served in the same capacity for the defendants, the United States government.

The standard reference for Walapai social life and material culture is by Kroeber (1935). This work is the outcome of eight weeks of fieldwork in Kingman, Arizona, by Kroeber and a party of four graduate students, under the auspices of the Laboratory of Anthropology, Santa Fe. Additional ethnographic information comes from two manuscripts by Henry P. Ewing (1960, 1961), an agent to the Walapai and Havasupai between 1895 and 1903.

Coult (1961) gathered much useful information on economic and social aspects of Walapai reservation life; during six months of fieldwork at Peach Springs in 1959, Coult administered Murray Thematic Apperception Tests in an attempt to understand Walapai personality.

Linguistic analyses of the Walapai and related Yuman speakers have been published by Spier (1946), W. Winter (1957), and Wares (1968). W. Winter (1963), who collected stories and songs in Walapai and English from an elderly Walapai informant, provides a short analysis of the influences of the Yuman language on English.

Walapai Papers, published as a public document by the U.S. Congress. Senate (1936), is a valuable compendium of historical reports, Army and Department of Indian Affairs correspondences, and documents covering primarily the nineteenth century.

Discussions of the prehistory of the Walapai area can be found in Colton (1939), Dobyns (1974), and Euler (1958). Two theses, Heuett (1974) and Matson (1971), add significantly to the earlier archeological work. Linford (1979) summarizes the argument over the antiquity of Walapai occupation in the region.

Yavapai

SIGRID KHERA AND PATRICIA S. MARIELLA

Language and Territory

Before Anglo-American encroachment into their territory in the 1860s the Yavapai (ˈyävəˌpī) lived in the area that today constitutes central and west-central Arizona. They considered themselves one people who had originated in the Sedona Red Rock country, spoke the same language, followed the same way of life, married among each other, and could call upon each other in warfare against other groups.

Yavapai may be considered a dialect of an Upland Yuman language of which Walapai and Havasupai constitute the two other major dialects* (W. Winter 1957; Biggs 1957). The Yavapai recognize this linguistic similarity but consider themselves a separate people who at one time had split from the others (Gifford 1936:247; Williams and Khera 1975:94).

The northern boundary of Yavapai territory ranged from the San Francisco Peaks to the area of present-day Williams and Ash Fork, to north of the Santa Maria and Bill Williams rivers (fig. 1). When Yavapais occasionally frequented areas as far north as Seligman and Kingman, conflict with the Walapai usually resulted. The westernmost expansion of the Yavapai included the mountains and at times even the lowlands along the Colorado River as far south as Yuma. The mountains north of the Gila River constituted the southwestern border of their territory. From the lower Verde Valley, the territory of the Yavapai reached through the Superstition Mountains to the Pinal Mountains and through the Tonto Basin north to the Mogollon Rim (Schroeder 1974:122; Khera 1977:1; Gifford 1936:249).

Modern Yavapais recognize four regional subtribes with minor dialectal differences: Tolkapaya (*tòlkpáya*), Kewevkapaya (*kwèvkpáya*), Wipukpaya (*ˀwipukpáya*), and Yavepe (*yavpé*). Gifford (1932:177, 1936:249), who wrote the major ethnographies on the Yavapai, speaks of only three subtribes, since he lumps together the Wipukpaya and Yavepe as the Northeastern Yavapai; he calls the Tolkapaya the Western Yavapai and the Kewevkapaya the Southeastern Yavapai.

The Tolkapaya (Western Yavapai) ranged from the Colorado River to the western slopes of the Kirkland Valley. The Kewevkapaya (Southeastern Yavapai) lived in the Bradshaw Mountains, the Verde Valley, as far north as Fossil Creek, the Tonto Basin, and the Superstition and Pinal mountains. The Wipukpaya (Northeastern Yavapai) lived in the middle Verde Valley, the Bradshaw Mountains, and the Sedona Red Rock country as far north as the San Francisco Peaks. The Yavepe (Central Yavapai) occupied the area around present-day Prescott and Jerome Mountain.

In general, Yavapais born around or before the 1920s distinguish individuals of their own or older generations as belonging to a particular subtribe. Most younger people emphasize a person's membership in one of the four Yavapai reservation communities: Fort McDowell, Prescott, Middle Verde, and Clarkdale.

Since the Fort McDowell Reservation was established in 1903 it has been designated a "Mohave-Apache Reservation" by the federal government. Only the reservation in Prescott, officially established in 1935, was designated a "Yavapai Reservation." This has resulted in the erroneous assumption by the public and even some government officials that the Prescott and Fort McDowell Reservations are inhabited by people of two different tribes—one being Yavapai and the other a branch of the Apache or a mixture of Mohave and Apache—whereas both are Yavapai.

Environment

The prereservation Yavapai population occupied an area of approximately 10 million acres in central and western Arizona. This vast range includes Sonoran desert, mountain, and transition zone environments of which the transition itself is a highly varied topographic and climatic region. While specific local bands did not generally range over this entire area, most bands had access to all three environmental zones. This extensive and

*The phonemes of Yavapai are: (stops and affricate) *p, t, č,* k^{y}, *k,* k^{w}, *q,* q^{w}, ˀ; (voiced spirant) *v* ([β]); (voiceless spirants) *θ, s, š, h,* h^{w}; (lateral) *l*; (nasals) *m, n,* n^{y}; (tap) *r*; (semivowels) *w, y*; (short vowels) *i, e, a, o, u, ə* (ə not phonemic in some analyses); (long vowels) *i·, e·, a·, o·, u·*; (stress) v́ (primary), v̀ (secondary). At least for some speakers a series of aspirated stops must also be recognized: p^{h}, t^{h}, k^{h}, k^{wh}; these and some further details are discussed by Shaterian (1976).

Information on Yavapai phonology was obtained from Kendall and Shaterian (1975) and Martha B. Kendall (communication to editors 1981), who also provided the phonemic transcriptions of Yavapai words.

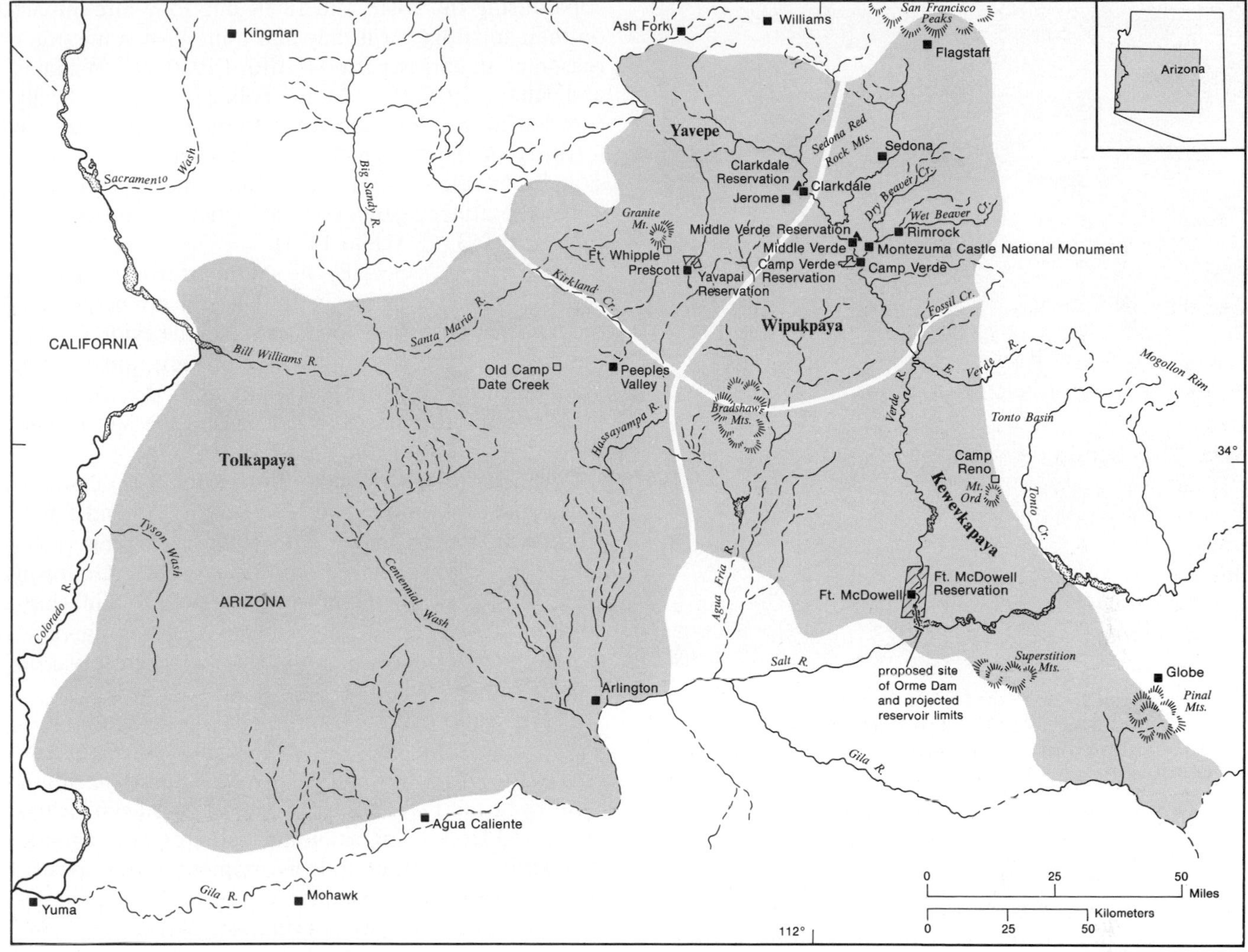

Fig. 1. Tribal territory in the mid-19th century, with subtribes.

comparatively rich land base provided the mobile hunter and gatherers with a steady and varied food supply of plants and animals. The Yavapai range also included the Colorado, Verde (fig. 2), and Salt rivers, which were free-flowing all year, as well as springs, numerous streams, and seasonal tanks of water in the western desert region.

Vegetation ranged from pines in the mountains to juniper-oak woodlands below. Chaparral, shrub, and grasses continued in the lower elevations merging into Sonoran cactus as well as paloverde and riparian mesquite trees. Deer, pronghorn antelope, and mountain sheep were hunted in the mountains, and small birds and rodents were found in all zones.

Prehistory

The Verde River valley and central western desert of Arizona, which encompass the historical range of the Yavapai, are among the Southwestern areas least studied archeologically. Most work there is of a general and exploratory nature (Fish and Fish 1977:6).

Yavapai origin myths do not mention the displacement of previous inhabitants of the area. Schroeder (1975) cites this as supportive data for his suggestion that the Hakataya tradition that developed in the Verde Valley was the most likely ancestor of the Yavapai. According to Schroeder's analysis, Hakataya was the basic "folk culture" of the region, which had considerable influence from Hohokam and Sinagua populations. The Hakataya reemerged as the dominant population after the decline of the more sedentary peoples.

A variation of Schroeder's hypothesis suggests that the Yavapais are the descendants of the Prescott and southern Sinagua peoples, with the change from a more sedentary and agricultural way of life being due to a variety of disruptive climatic and social factors (Pilles 1979:14). A third hypothesis proposed by Rogers (1945:190) and further developed by Euler and Dobyns

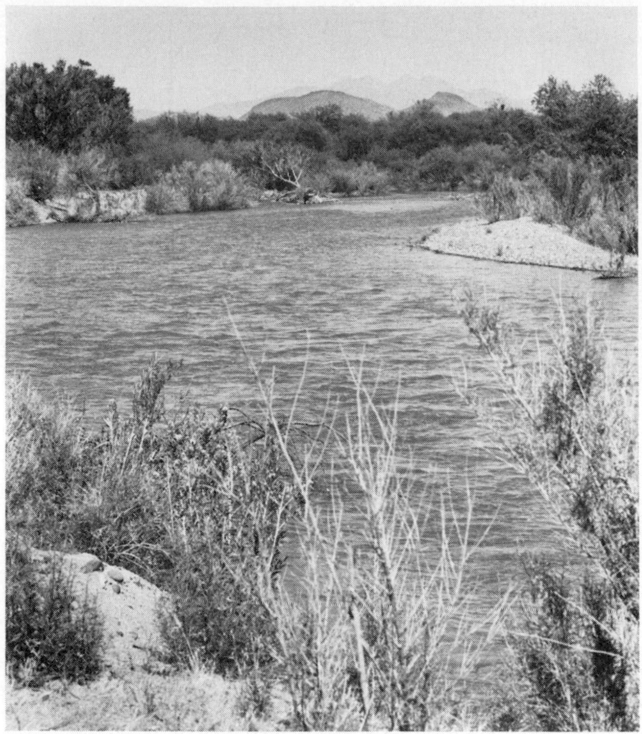

Fig. 2. The Verde River on the Fort McDowell reservation bordered by lush vegetation. The Four Peaks, the sacred mountain of the Yavapai, are visible in the distance. Photograph by Melissa Jones, 1976.

(in Pilles 1979:15) suggests a Yuman migration from the west into Arizona after A.D. 1100, displacing contemporaneous Arizona populations. Reports by the Spanish indicate that the ancestors of the modern Yavapai were the major inhabitants of the middle Verde Valley by the 1600s (Schroeder 1952a).

External Relations

During the nineteenth century the Yavapai had hostile relations with their northwestern neighbors, the Walapai and Havasupai, and their southern neighbors the Papago, Pima, and Maricopa. Hostilities with these people to the south had also been typical during the eighteenth century. Oral history relates that specific conflicts of individuals and local bands generated these hostilities with the northwestern and southern neighbors.

Yavapais sometimes visited Navajos and Hopis to exchange mescal and buckskin for woven blankets and silver jewelry. Stories of the hosts ambushing Yavapais attest that these occasional relations were often less than friendly.

Relations with the Mohave and Quechan on the Colorado River were relatively peaceful. Several Cocopa families trace their ancestry to Tolkapayas. It is not clear, though, if these Tolkapayas had joined the Cocopa during the 1850s and 1860s due to White impact on their territory, or if they had joined for some other reason at an earlier period (Gifford 1936:297; Williams and Khera 1975:218). Many Tolkapayas periodically traveled to the Colorado River to plant crops near the territory of the Quechan. The Quechan in turn occasionally traveled into the mountain ranges of the Tolkapaya to utilize resources from higher elevations (Gifford 1936:263; C. White 1974).

The Yavapai, especially the southeastern population, had their closest relations with their eastern neighbors, the Apache. Historical documents include evidence that the Apache were moving into the eastern range of the Yavapai after 1700; however, not until the 1850s are there specific references to Apaches in the Verde Valley.

Corbusier (1969:16) and Gifford (1932:197) mention occasional hostilities between Kewevkapaya and Tonto Apache in the eastern Verde Valley, sometimes resulting in "wife-stealing" from the Apaches. Goodwin (1942:88–92) describes more cooperative relationships between Kewevkapaya and Western Apaches, agreeing that some intermarriage took place in prereservation times.

There were definite similarities in the culture of Yavapais and Apaches, a fact that must have contributed to the misunderstanding of Whites about the ethnic identity of the two peoples. Some of these similarities originated from living as hunter-gatherers and agriculturalists in a similar natural environment. Other specific culture traits held in common are basically Pueblo-derived (Schroeder 1975:61). In contrast, Gifford (1932:249) suggests that Yavapais borrowed these traits from the Apache. It is also probable that the Apache, as latecomers to the Southwest, derived them from the Yavapai.

History

Until the early 1860s when gold was discovered in central Arizona, and Anglo-Americans began to settle in the area, Yavapais had little contact with Whites.

Between 1583 and 1605 the Spaniards Antonio de Espejo, Marcos Farfan, and Juan de Oñate traveled through the southern portions of Yavapai territory, and during the eighteenth and nineteenth centuries Yavapais occasionally visited Spanish missions to the south. Anglo-Americans made several expeditions into the Yavapais' home areas during the early nineteenth century.

Unlike the Apache, Yavapais did not undertake raiding expeditions into Mexico, and with a very few exceptions they did not have guns. This lack of effective weapons must have been a major reason why the Yavapai tried to avoid clashes with miners and other Anglo invaders of their homelands in the early 1860s. Despite occasional "peace treaties" initiated by individual Whites, attacks by Anglos upon Yavapais, whom they called "Apache," were the rule (Schroeder 1974:12). Under continuous attack and severe pressure on their resources, including their game and agricultural land, Yavapais began fighting back during the mid-1860s (Schroeder 1974:18). However, as written documents and oral history attest, Yavapais were also ready to accept a peace if it would have allowed them a place where they could have lived in security and that could have provided them reasonable sustenance.

Under these expectations, about 2,000 Yavapais, most likely Tolkapayas, agreed to settle on the Colorado River Reservation in 1865 (Farish 1915–1918, 3:322). This place, which they had to share with several other tribes, was not large enough to raise sufficient crops. To have enough food, they had to return to the mountains for hunting and gathering for at least part of the year (Feudge 1866).

The willingness of the Kewevkapaya to settle on a reservation had no permanent results, though attempts were made to settle them next to the military post of Camp McDowell in the lower Verde Valley. After a short trial period these Yavapais left; not only would they have had to depend on insufficient food rations, but also they found that their personal safety was constantly endangered by the White soldiers and Pima Indians who were employed as U.S. military scouts. A reservation near Camp Reno in the Tonto Basin near Mount Ord was promised to them and they found it acceptable, but it was never established (Smart 1868; Feudge 1866; Devin 1868; D.Curtis 1871).

On November 9, 1871, an executive order approved the establishment of the Rio Verde Reservation located in the middle Verde Valley. On December 21, Gen. George Crook ordered that all "roving Apache" were to be on this reservation by February 15, 1872, or be treated as hostile (Schroeder 1974:93).

In the course of forcing all Yavapais onto the reservation, the army wiped out a large band of Kewevkapaya in the Salt River Canyon on December 27, 1872. These people were killed by soldiers who shot into a cave in which they had taken refuge. Of all the massacres during the 1860s and 1870s (for example, at Bloody Basin, Skull Valley, and Date Creek) the one at "Skeleton Cave" is remembered as the most horrendous in Yavapai history (Williams and Khera 1975:1).

By 1873 most Yavapais had been brought onto the Rio Verde Reservation near Camp Verde. Despite a serious epidemic and other adverse conditions typical of forced settlement of a conquered people, these Yavapai, mainly by means of their own aboriginal tools, managed to excavate an irrigation ditch and produce several successful harvests (Corbusier 1969:17).

A group of Tucson contractors who supplied Indian reservations was alarmed by the growing self-sufficiency of the Rio Verde Reservation population. These contractors pressed for a government order to transfer these Indians onto the Apache Reservation at San Carlos (Corbusier 1969:260). General Crook, who had protested this move (Crook 1946:184), told the Yavapai that they would be allowed to return to their homelands and receive their own reservation after they had learned the "White people's ways" and shown their loyalty as army scouts. Relocation to San Carlos took the form of a forced march in 1875 over approximately 180 miles of extremely rough terrain with insufficient supplies in midwinter. According to Corbusier (1969) 115 of the Rio Verde Indians died during this march.

Sitgreaves 1853:pl. 17.

Fig. 3. *Yampai Indians*. Lithograph after unknown original sketch by Richard H. Kern, cartographer and artist for the Sitgreaves Expedition down the Zuni and Colorado rivers, Oct. 1851.

Some Yavapais escaped during the trip to San Carlos while others managed to remain behind. These individuals remained within their familiar home ranges making a meager living by farming and working for White settlers (Thrapp 1964:156; Crawford 1894).

At San Carlos, the Yavapais were settled in an area separate from the Apaches. Relations with the Apache were basically peaceful, and intermarriage took place occasionally. Agriculture was an important part of subsistence; but due to extreme difficulties in developing a permanent irrigation system, hunting and gathering was necessary to provide supplementary food.

In the 1880s and 1890s the Indian agents at San Carlos allowed many Yavapais to return to their homelands (ARCIA 1898:130). Their land at San Carlos, including the so-called Mineral Strip, was then free for leasing to White interests (U.S. Commissioner of Indian Affairs 1881, 1900). Several hundred Yavapais did remain at San Carlos; many intermarried with Apaches, and their descendants are integrated into the reservation community (Spicer 1962:274; Anonymous 1894).

Most Yavapais returned to their home areas and tried to make a living by working on farms, ranches, mines, smelters, road construction, and wherever else there was an opportunity for earning wages. In addition, gathering of wild plants and, when possible, hunting and agriculture were practiced for food supplementation.

A number of Yavapais, mainly Wipukpayas, were able to rent patches of agricultural land from White farmers in the middle Verde Valley for some time (Anonymous 1900a). Some Tolkapayas tried homesteading north of the Gila River around Mohawk, Agua Caliente, Palomas, and Arlington (James 1903; R.G. Vivian 1965; Williams and Khera 1975). The Tolkapayas were the only subtribal population that never had a reservation established for them. The Kewevkapayas, who soon were joined by members of the other subtribes, tried to settle at the abandoned military post at Fort McDowell.

Fort McDowell

The history of the Fort McDowell Reservation from its establishment into the 1980s is marked by a continuing struggle of the community members to maintain rights over their resources, in particular land and water.

After it had been abandoned as a military post, Anglo and Mexican squatters, some of them land speculators, occupied all the arable land.

With the assistance of a sympathetic Anglo appointed as government mediator, and despite threats from the local Indian agent, Yavapai delegations went to Washington twice to ask for exclusive use of the land. The leader of these undertakings, by majority vote, was Chief Yuma Frank (fig. 4). The money for sending the delegations was raised by the Yavapais at McDowell (N. Curtis 1919; Khera 1977:10).

Eventually, the non-Indian settlers were bought out by the federal government and the entire reservation was turned over to the Yavapais living at McDowell in 1904. Within the first year problems developed with the irrigation system; the periodic floods of the Verde River, which runs through the middle of the reservation and is the source of irrigation water, washed out the brush diversion dams and canals. The McDowell farmers labored constantly in attempts to maintain the irrigation system because without irrigation the land at McDowell cannot be farmed (Mariella 1977).

In 1906 the Indian Irrigation Service of the Bureau of Indian Affairs recommended that no more funds be spent on the irrigation system of McDowell. Instead, it was proposed to relocate the McDowell farmers onto the neighboring Salt River Pima Maricopa Reservation; this land was under the Bureau of Reclamation's Salt River Project canal. According to the Indian Irrigation Service, such a move would have been less expensive for the government than developing a permanent irrigation dam at McDowell. This recommendation assumed that the McDowell water rights could be legally transferred to the Salt River Reservation and that the McDowell farmers would agree to removal.

Smithsonian, NAA: 2806-a.

Fig. 4. Yuma Frank (Kapalwa or Tearing), a Tolkapaya married to a Kewevkapaya, chosen chief of the Fort McDowell reservation about 1900 and a leader of delegations to Washington to negotiate the Indians' exclusive rights to the land at Fort McDowell (Khera 1977:9–12). Photograph by DeLancey Gill, Washington, 1911.

The federal government never settled the legal problem involving the transfer of water rights, and the Fort McDowell community members did not agree that it was in their best interests to move to land without a water right. Beginning in 1910, the Fort McDowell Yavapais fought for land with water rights. This struggle was led by Dr. Carlos Montezuma until his death in 1923. Dr. Montezuma was a full-blood Yavapai who had been captured as a child, reared in Anglo society, and become a physician; he was able to contact his relatives at McDowell and spent a great deal of his time and resources aiding the tribal members in their continual battle to avoid relocation and to develop irrigation at McDowell (U.S. Congress. House of Representatives. Indian Affairs Committee 1911).

In 1907, the federal government entered into *Hurley* v. *Abbott,* a law suit initiated by members of the Salt River Valley Water Users Association. This suit was supposed to result in allocation of Salt River valley water. Fort McDowell was allotted only a temporary supply based on estimates of water used during a period when the ditches and brush dams were washed out. The allocation was temporary because of the planned removal of the Fort McDowell community to the Salt River Reservation (Kent Decree, Arizona Territorial Court 1910:No. 4564). The small amount of water allocated to Yavapais by the court decree (390 miner's inches) then limited the amount of land that could be irrigated.

The legal and administrative decisions concerning Fort McDowell were closely tied to political and economic growth of the Salt River Valley Water Users Association, a part of the Salt River Project. The United States government had spent over nine million dollars for the Salt River Project for non-Indian farmers. There was no further federal or local interest in spending money for irrigation projects for a small population of Indians.

The McDowell farmers continued to resist removal, but as irrigation labor costs continued to rise for smaller returns, many community members turned to more profitable ways to make a living. Many Yavapais traveled to work in the mines of the Middle Verde valley and near Globe, or on ranches, or to pick cotton in the nearby non-Indian farms. Wage labor was becoming the most important source of income.

Many at McDowell also turned to cattle raising to make a partial living from the reservation land. As cattle raising developed, most farmers grew feed as supplement to open range grazing. However, the water supply continued to be unreliable as water was controlled by the Salt River Project in reservoirs upstream (Mariella 1977).

The city of Phoenix water plant built on the reservation in the middle 1940s provided local employment. The city has been diverting water for domestic use from the Verde River at McDowell through a pipeline since 1920 (Schaffer 1978).

A major issue facing the Fort McDowell community in increasing intensity since 1948 has been the proposed Orme Dam and reservoir, which was planned to provide flood control and to create a storage basin for the Colorado River water that the Central Arizona Project will bring into the Salt River valley. Construction of this dam would result in almost 65 percent of the reservation (15,960 of 24,967 acres) being flooded (U.S. Bureau of Reclamation 1976:123). These acres consist of all the fertile river bottomlands used for farming, cattle grazing, wood cutting, housing, and recreation. The remaining acres are the higher desert areas unsuited for most economic pursuits.

The planned Orme Dam has been the hindering factor in economic developments at McDowell: federal aid for improvements in housing, health, and agriculture was withheld because of the proposed dam. It is not clear to what extent, if at all, the tribe was informed of the dam project during the 1940s and 1950s; however, the Fort McDowell community that would be most affected by the dam was consistently left out, while almost every non-Indian interest group was consulted (Anonymous 1964).

In an informal referendum at McDowell in 1966, the majority of voters did not approve of the dam (Coffeen 1972:363). Nevertheless, on September 30, 1968, Congress passed the Colorado River Basin Project Construction Act (Public Law 90–537), which included Orme Dam or a suitable alternative. It was more than four years later that the Bureau of Reclamation met with the whole community in Fort McDowell for the first time, telling them about the proposed flooding of the reservation and relocation of the community. Attending government officials received a strong negative response.

On September 25, 1976, the Fort McDowell community, including over 50 members who live off the reservation, held an offical referendum on the dam. The results of this vote were 144 against the dam, 57 people for the dam (Butler 1977:19).

In 1981 the Department of the Interior Bureau of Reclamation and the Army Corps of Engineers was evaluating the regional water needs for central Arizona and still considering building Orme Dam. The Fort McDowell community's opposition to the dam remained adamant.

Camp Verde, Middle Verde, and Clarkdale

Many of the Yavapai returnees from San Carlos settled near the abandoned military post at Fort Verde, and in 1907 the BIA established an Indian day school there. In 1910, 40 acres with water rights were set aside for these returnees. As only 18 of these acres were suitable for farming, most Yavapais living there continued working for wages.

In 1912 there were so many Yavapais working in the copper mines and at the smelter at Clarkdale, 18 miles northwest of Camp Verde, that the BIA opened a day school there. After World War I the power of the mine unions was broken, and the number of Yavapai miners increased (Spicer 1962:257).

In 1914 and 1916 an additional 448 acres with water rights were set up for the Yavapai eight miles west of Camp Verde at Middle Verde. This place was more suitable for farming, and many people from Camp Verde moved to Middle Verde (Morris 1971).

The slowdown and finally closure of the mines in central Arizona during the 1930s and 1940s greatly affected the Yavapai workers. Consequently, more people returned to the reservations, and farming and cattle raising activities were expanded; however, off-reservation employment still provided most of the earned income into the 1980s.

A tribal project designed to provide greater local employment opportunities for reservation members is a tourist center complex associated with the Montezuma Castle National Monument, a prehistoric cliff-dwelling site.

In 1969, 60 acres near the former mining community of Clarkdale were established as reservation land for the Yavapais who had been living there while working for the mines. A Department of Housing and Urban Development program helped to provide new homes (fig. 5).

Camp Verde, Middle Verde, and Clarkdale all combine to elect one council under an Indian Reorganization Act constitution.

Prescott

Some Yavapais who escaped earlier or returned from San Carlos in the late 1890s settled in the area around the town of Prescott near the abandoned Fort Whipple. This area lies within traditional Yavepe territory.

These Yavapai families, like those in the middle Verde Valley and at Fort McDowell, made a living by a combination of traditional hunting and gathering skills and wage labor in the local areas. Mining was one source of wage labor. Working as domestic servants for non-Indian families in Prescott was also a source of cash income for many Yavapai women. The day-to-day association of these Yavapai women with non-Indians was also a source of information about the non-Indian way of life (Patricia McGee, personal communication 1981).

Religion was another sphere of interaction between the Yavapai and non-Indians in Prescott. In 1922 a one-room Indian Mission was established at the entrance of the Yavapai community. One of the leaders of this Yavapai Presbyterian church was Viola Jimulla, whose husband, Sam Jimulla, was the political leader of the Prescott Yavapai community in the early 1900s (Barnett 1968:10).

In 1933 and 1934 a housing project was undertaken in the Prescott Yavapai community. Due in part to the difficulties the Yavapai had experienced in securing federal funds for such development projects, a major effort was begun by the Yavapai and their allies in the non-Indian community to obtain reservation status. On June 7, 1935, 75 acres from the former Fort Whipple military reserve were transferred from the Veterans Administration to the Interior Department for a reservation. On May 18, 1956, 1,320 acres were added to the reservation from the Fort Whipple lands. This enlarged reservation borders the city of Prescott on three sides.

The formal establishment of the reservation had many political implications. One of the national Indian issues in 1935 when the reservation was established was the Indian Reorganization Act, which detailed procedures for forming federally recognized tribal councils. The Prescott Yavapai had several concerns when deciding whether to organize under the Indian Reorganization Act. Most Indians living on reservations in Arizona could not vote in county or general elections until 1948. The legal decision that officially ended this discrimination was the result of a suit filed by two Yavapais, Frank Harrison and Harry Austin, who lived on the Fort McDowell Reservation (*Harrison* v. *Laveen* 67 ARIZ. 337, 196 P2d 456). Once the Prescott Yavapai had achieved reservation status for their lands, there was a question whether community members would be allowed to vote in off-reservation elections. Furthermore, the community had a working, traditional form of leadership; a chief or chieftess was supported by a group of councilors made up of family heads. This traditional organization was codified and submitted by the Yavapai community in Prescott to the federal government. Following Indian Reorganization Act policy the government officials responded that the traditional government was not "democratic" and was therefore unacceptable. These pronouncements from distant Washington and the implications for the loss of independence led to the rejection of the Indian Reorganization Act within the Yavapai-Prescott community. After Sam Jimulla's death in 1940, his widow, Viola, became the

Fig. 5. Modern housing on the Clarkdale Reservation, inhabited by both Yavapai and Apache. The Sedona Red Rock Mountains are in the distance. Photograph by Jerry Jacka, April 1978.

Sharlot Hall Mus., Prescott, Ariz.: IN-Y-2108PA.
Fig. 6. Viola Jimulla (b. 1878, d. 1966), an important leader in the Yavapai Indian Presbyterian Church and head of the tribe after 1940 (Barnett 1968). Photograph by Charles Troncy, 1951.

community's chieftess (fig. 6). Traditional community leadership continues to pass down through this family: in August 1967 the Yavapai-Prescott community appointed Viola's daughter, Grace Mitchell, as chieftess; following her death, her sister, Lucy Miller, was appointed chieftess in July 1976.

After rejection of the Indian Reorganization Act, an administrative government centering around a board of directors was organized under Articles of Association adopted December 5, 1962. This board consists of a president, vice-president, secretary-treasurer, and two board members. Each officer and member is elected at large every two years.

As in the case of Middle Verde, many tribal members have been forced to live off the Prescott Reservation to be near work. However, following the enlargement of the reservation, the construction of new housing, and increasing job opportunities, many tribal members have returned. The tribe has plans underway for development of an industrial park to benefit from the expansion of the city of Prescott. In 1980 tribal enrollment consisted of 108 members, 68 of whom were residents on the reservation (table 1).

Off the Reservations

Some Yavapais hold and live on small parcels of land outside the official reservations. These lands are near the Camp Verde Salt Mine, Rimrock, Peeples Valley, and Arlington. Many Yavapais have relatives living in all the reservation communities. Social and cultural ties are maintained by visits between individuals and groups on the reservations as well as with those Yavapais living off the reservations, including those in urban areas (Khera 1974–1980; Mariella 1975–1980).

Population

Nineteenth-century population estimates were made at a time when the Yavapai were stunned by warfare, disease, and displacement by White settlers. The estimate of 1,500 in the 1860s (table 1) is derived from the population on the Rio Verde Reservation, which had just experienced intensive fighting with the U.S. army.

The population figures imply a very low density, about one person per 13 square miles. Even within an area containing microenvironments with poor resources, this density seems quite low (Fish and Fish 1977:24).

Forced onto small, unsanitary reservations after a decade of tremendous stress and malnutrition, Yavapais then encountered epidemic diseases that took a great toll of lives. The army physician at Rio Verde noted that so many Indians died of a combination of diseases (dysentery, malaria, and "epizootic") that there were not enough people to collect the wood needed to cremate the dead, as was traditional Yavapai practice (Corbusier 1969:16).

Table 1. Population

Date	*Population*	*Location*	*Source*
1860s	1,500		Gifford 1936:252
	2,000		Schroeder 1974:261
1874	1,500		Corbusier 1969:32
1906	195	Fort McDowell	ARCIA 1906:481
	300	Upper Verde Valley	
	100	Beaver Creek	
1978	355	Fort McDowell Reservation	Schaffer 1978
	68	Prescott	BIA Annual Report 1978
	460	Camp Verde, Middle Verde, Clarkdale Reservations	BIA Annual Report 1978

In the 1900s many Yavapais died of tuberculosis, particularly the Tolkapayas, once the most numerous subtribe. The 1918 world influenza epidemic also killed many Yavapais (Montezuma 1901–1922). Not until the 1960s did the historic Yavapai population begin to experience growth; the population had been stationary or decreasing since the 1860s.

Culture

Subsistence

In general, the Yavapai subsistence cycle followed the ripening of different plant foods; local bands would camp in areas where food was available during each part of the year. Though the Yavapai were primarily hunters and gatherers, they also practiced agriculture, as did most Southwestern native peoples.

The specifics of the prereservation Yavapai subsistence cycle varied according to the features of different locales, but in general the Yavapai had their greatest food supply in the fall. This was when the nuts (sweet acorn, piñon, and walnuts), seeds (sunflower, goldeneye, wild grasses), and berries (manzanita, juniper, cedar, mulberry, hackberry, lemon berries) of the higher elevations were ripening as well as the fruit of the banana yucca. The summer agricultural crop would be harvested, and the wild summer fruits, seeds, and berries were gathered and stored.

As usual for hunters and gatherers, women were responsible for most of the gathering and processing of wild plant food. Men often stood guard as women gathered in areas that were vulnerable to attack (Gifford 1932:180; Burns 1977:36). Many of the seeds and nuts were ground on grinding stones of the trough or concave type that were either found or less often made and occasionally individualized by some marking. Bedrock mortars were also utilized particularly in caves. The processed foods were stored in earthen pots and baskets sealed with plant gum. These containers were then kept in caches or in the back of caves in the warmer elevations for use in winter when fresh plant foods were scarce. Some tubers (wild garlic, wild potatoes) were dug and gathered year-round but most often in winter (table 2).

Cooking techniques included boiling in pots over a fire or stone-boiling, in which heated stones were dropped into a cooking vessel. Foods were also roasted and parched with hot coals in baskets.

In the spring, leafy greens (chenopod, amaranth) were collected and boiled. In mid-summer the desert fruits and seeds, mainly cacti, mesquite, and paloverde, became ripe. Saguaro fruits were picked with a stick consisting of two long saguaro ribs tied together with a wooden hook at the end. The fruits were eaten raw as they were picked or mixed with water for juice. The seeds were washed, dried, and ground for immediate consumption or for storage.

Some foods were available year-round. The agave ripened in higher elevations throughout the year and Gifford's informants suggest that it provided a staple food (mescal) that could be relied on in times of need. The base was dug out and the sharp ends of the leaves cut off. The hearts were cooked in large roasting pits for several days. As with most other foods, mescal was both eaten after being cooked as well as dried and stored for future use; it was usually eaten in combination with other foods providing a more nutritionally complete diet. As much as three to four months might be spent in one area preparing mescal, and large stands of agave were points where local bands came together (Gifford 1936:260).

Men and older boys did essentially all the bow and arrow hunting of large game and small birds (particularly quail), as well as hunting of smaller animals with a throwing stick. Deer were driven into blinds by several men hunting together, or stalked at close range by individual hunters camouflaged with deer-head masks. Almost every part of a deer was utilized for food, clothing, or tools. Baited traps and snares were used to catch coyotes, wildcats, and foxes. Men as well as women and children might participate in animal drives, for example, for rabbits and antelope. Men and women of all ages occasionally collected lizards, locusts, grasshoppers, and caterpillars for food (Gifford 1936:264).

In the Anglo historic period, agriculture contributed considerably fewer calories to the diet than hunted and gathered foods. Prehistoric sites suggest that more intensive agriculture was practiced by the populations that are possible ancestors of the Yavapais. The early Spanish records also mention rancherias that were most likely Yavapai that had prominent gardens (Schroeder 1974). Ethnographic sources also stress that warfare seriously disrupted the agricultural aspects of the subsistence cycle. Intertribal warfare, especially with the Pima and Maricopa, made any sedentary tasks a considerable liability. This situation was exacerbated by the United States army campaigns in the 1860s and 1870s, which included destroying caches and agricultural crops and raiding. This forced continuous movement of local bands, devastating the balanced cycle that was the basis for the Yavapais' subsistence.

Table 2. Seasonal Gathering of Wild Plant Foods

Spring
- chenopod
- amaranth
- thistle (*Cirsium neomexicanum*)
- wild spinach

Summer and autumn
- cactus fruit (*Peniocereus greggii, Opuntia* spp.)
- wild grapes (*Vitis arizonica*)
- squawberry, lemonberry (*Rhus trilobata*)
- manzanita (*Arctostaphylos pungens*)
- mesquite (*Prosopis juliflora*)
- palo verde (*Cercidium floridum*)
- juniper (*Juniperus deppeana*)
- cedar (*Juniperus osteostoma*)
- mulberry (*Morus microphylla*)
- hackberry (*Celtis reticulata*)
- acorn (*Quercus emoryi*)
- goldeneye (*Cordylanthus*)
- sunflower (*Helianthus*)
- wild grasses (many varieties)
- banana yucca (*Yucca baccata*)
- piñon (*Pinus edulis*)
- walnuts (*Juglans major*)

Winter
- wild garlic or onion
- wild potatoes

Yavapais planted corn, beans, and squash as well as tobacco in washes, streams, and near springs. Corn was planted most often and in the greatest quantities. The amount of crops planted probably varied from band to band and over time. Members of local bands would plant gardens and then leave to gather and to hunt, returning intermittently and finally for harvest. Some green corn was roasted and boiled as it ripened. The rest was picked when mature and processed into meal (Mariella 1977).

Some modern Yavapais tell of relatives digging small irrigation ditches with digging sticks, commenting that this was a practice that was said to antedate White influence. On occasion crops might be watered by hand with ollas (Williams and Khera 1975).

Further evidence of the importance of agriculture is found in the early military reservation records. At Camp

Date Creek the officers consistently quoted Yavapai headmen asking for land to plant (Brinkerhoff 1964). While a tendency to exaggerate the sedentary desires of potential "wards" might be imagined, this desire is backed up with data concerning agriculture on the early reservations. Once forced onto the Rio Verde Reservation, Yavapais took up farming with a vigor that startled their military overseers, particularly as they used only their aboriginal tools, such as digging sticks, to produce corn, beans, and squash as well as crops introduced by the military, such as wheat, barley, and potatoes (Corbusier 1969:17). Forced onto a small reservation and denied access to their vast hunting and gathering ranges, they had to produce crops or they would have starved.

The intensive irrigation agriculture required by the small amount of land available on the early reservations led to increased ditch digging. Brush dams were built as needed, and ditch digging, maintenance, and water allocation were supervised by a ditch rider or boss (Mariella 1977).

Social Organization

General statements concerning Yavapai bands correspond with data from other Southwestern rancheria populations. Several extended families with members that were related consanguineally and affinally would camp together during times of the year when resources could be gathered, grown, and hunted efficiently by a local band. On occasion, smaller family groups would move to new harvest areas on their own. Conversely, larger numbers of families would gather in areas where food resources were plentiful; up to 10 families might camp and travel together (Gifford 1936:254, 297). Up to 100 households of Kewevkapaya gathered once a year in winter during the 1850s and 1860s in an easily defended area (Gifford 1932:181). The composition of local bands was flexible in that individuals and families who might have disagreements could leave and join other bands in which they had relatives (Gifford 1932:189).

No one was supposed to marry relatives; relatives were reckoned bilaterally and kin terms reflected this bilaterality. First cousins were never allowed to marry. Individuals who violated this prohibition were either killed or banished from the area. Oral tradition states that some banished couples settled along the lower Colorado River and in Baja California and that their descendants are found among the Cocopa and Paipai (Williams and Khera 1975). Gifford (1936:297) mentions a tendency to subtribal endogamy; although individuals did marry into other subtribes, the tendency to endogamy is supported by the dialectal and other differences (albeit minor) that existed between the subtribes.

If a man were a successful hunter who could provide adequately for more than one wife, the wife's family might encourage the husband to take a sister in marriage; however, polygyny was rare. When a husband died, his brother or other close male relative would often marry the widow. Similarly, if a wife died the widower was often encouraged to accept a sister in marriage. Personal factors would influence these tendencies.

Divorce might result from marital infidelities, failure to perform the expected duties, or from incompatibility. Gifford's (1932, 1936) informants stated that divorce was not common before the reservation period.

Men had to be adequate hunters before a girl's family would take notice and encourage a marriage. Yavepes and Tolkapayas said that a man often did not marry before the age of 25 (Gifford 1936:296). Girls were considered marriageable after they had reached puberty. Marriage was secured by the exchange of gifts between the families of the couple. A man continued to provide hunted animal products for his in-laws throughout his marriage.

Gifford suggested that there was a matrilocal tendency, though postmarital residence seemed to begin first with the bride's group after which there was a stay with the groom's local group. (The bride and groom's local group could be the same.) Then a couple apparently decided where they wanted to live (Williams and Khera 1975:217). Interband quarrels or disagreements led to dispersing of population according to one of Gifford's (1932:189) informants.

• CLANS? Gifford (1932) details the existence of nontotemic but exogamous matrilineal clans among the Kewevkapaya, considering the clans as evidence of contact with the Western Apache. Given the similarity of many demographic and ecological factors of the Western Apache and Yavapai it would seem inappropriate to analyze matriclans as borrowed without understanding why clan organization would have been incorporated into Yavapai social organization.

What was the nature of these clans? The same Yavapai informant that spoke with Gifford used the English word family rather than clan in his own manuscript (Burns 1977). Mike Burns, a Kewevkapaya, stated that people from certain families identified with specific local areas could not marry each other. They must belong to different families and their children could not marry any of their father's relatives. The manuscript also mentions the existence of a mother-in-law taboo.

Gifford (1932) uses the word *tyúče* for 'clan', which he says has the literal meaning of 'relative'. This word means simply 'relatives' to modern Kewevkapayas at Fort McDowell. Also Gifford pointed out that no relatives should marry. In a small bandlike society, this prohibition would encompass local clan members. Marrying relatives was also prohibited by the Tolkapaya, Wipukpaya, and Yavepe and fits with the general, bilateral organization demonstrated in other social organizational features among the Yavapai.

Yavapais at Fort McDowell in the 1980s did not recognize clans. A Kewevkapaya informant who was familiar with the "clan" names listed by Gifford stated that these words (place-names followed by the suffix *-pa* meaning 'people') meant "people who had been born and grew up in that area." It would seem that Gifford may have given a fairly rigid label to something that was more bilateral and flexible. It is possible, also, that intermarriage with Western Apache had encouraged the extended unilineal recognition of family ties by some Yavapai. However, Gifford (1932:190) cites two cases of "patrilineal descent" when Yavapai men had married Apache women. Goodwin (1942) noted that children of marriages between Northern Tonto Apache and Yavapai were members of their mother's tribe. Clearly there was some intermarriage during the early historical period and even more regular interactions when the two populations were put together on the Rio Verde and San Carlos reservations.

Political Organization

Local groups of different subtribes used to join for war expeditions, each group under its own war chief. A runner brought the message about a planned expedition to other local groups who would then decide whether or not to join. War chiefs were men who had distinguished themselves by outstanding fortitude and skill in battle.

Each local group also had an older man, often a former war chief, as civic leader. He advised people where and when to hunt and gather food and was often a persuasive orator who regularly gave a public lecture in the morning about "right behavior." Advisory chiefs continued to encourage people with these morning speeches throughout the 1930s (and in some cases even longer) in places such as mining camps where numerous Yavapai families lived together (Williams and Khera 1975:214).

Life Cycle

There was no birth feast for a newborn child, but two to three weeks later relatives assembled to congratulate the parents. The name for the baby was usually chosen by the mother, who did not name a baby after anyone else, dead or alive (Gifford 1936:299). People who lived in the vicinity of Montezuma Well sometimes used its water for bathing the newborn (Harrison and Williams 1977:40).

At menarche a girl had to get up in the morning before everybody else for four days, bring in water and firewood, and do other tasks connected with her future role as a woman. She was also placed on a bed of cedar branches over a shallow pit lined with warm coals. This was to keep her body warm during these critical four days. An older woman, renowned for her excellent work and good character, massaged the girl's body for proper growth (Williams and Khera 1975). A few families observed this ritual into the 1980s.

When a boy's voice changed, he had to get up before everyone else for four mornings. He had to watch the gray rocks of the fireplace intently in order to make his eyes sharp for seeing the dull-colored game animals. To make him a good hunter, he had to run distances and to receive little food during the four-day period. Boys and girls were told to use a scratching stick and a drinking tube made of cane during the four days of their puberty rites (Gifford 1932:198, 1936:301; Williams and Khera 1975).

Into the early 1900s the dead were disposed of by cremation (James 1903). Tolkapayas usually burned their dead in a shallow pit while members of the other subtribes usually cremated the body in the house where the person had died. The deceased's property was destroyed and the place abandoned (Gifford 1932:232, 1936:302). A year or so after the cremation people gathered for a memorial ritual in which goods were burned on behalf of the deceased (Williams and Khera 1975).

Since the early 1900s the dead have been buried. Burying and sometimes burning of at least part of the deceased's property and last gifts from relatives and friends have remained customary for many modern Yavapais.

Technology

Sturdy and lightweight basketry was the most important kind of container in prereservation times. Burden baskets for large loads were made as well as tightly coiled baskets for carrying, storing, winnowing, and roasting. Water ollas were made by coating tightly woven baskets with pitch. Women were the primary basketmakers, and baskets were involved in tasks that women performed.

Coiled baskets (fig. 7) were also a trade specialty of the Yavapai. Ethnographic information indicates that baskets were traded with neighboring populations such as the Navajo. When metal pots and pans came into greater use during the early reservation period, the basket trade took on a new economic importance. Baskets, then as now sold through Anglo traders for the tourist market, became a major source of cash.

BIA reports at San Carlos and McDowell as well as other historical sources (James 1903) indicate that Yavapai basketry was of the highest quality. It continued in the 1980s to be a highly skilled craft that was practiced by women in all the Yavapai reservation com-

left, U. of Calif., Lowie Mus., Berkeley: 2-14180, 2-14182, 2-10320.

Fig. 7. Coiled basketry. left, Trays stitched with devils-claw and cottonwood around coils of 3 unsplit willow twigs. The star design is a common motif although women create unique patterns by the way they individually arrange such symbols. The baskets resemble and are often confused with those of the San Carlos Apache (Robinson 1954:97). Diameter of top left 29.8 cm, rest to same scale; all collected by E.W. Gifford, 1932. right, Bessie Mike stitching a coiled basket. Photograph by Melissa Jones, Fort McDowell reservation, 1975.

munities. The women generally collect their own materials.

Gifford (1936) implied that the Yavapai had learned basketry from the Apache when he organized his list of traits supposedly shared by the two populations. However, all the Upland Yumans have similar design elements. The contention that the Yavapai learned from the Apache is specifically contradicted by stylistic and informant data (Robinson 1954). As basketmaking is an idiosyncratic craft and most basketmakers can repeat designs that they are exposed to in the reservation context it may be more fruitful to discuss individual styles as well as cultural traditions.

Unlike basketry, pottery did not flourish in the early historic period and fell largely into disuse. Descriptions of Yavapai pottery are recorded by Corbusier (1886) and by Yavapais who remembered the techniques. There was some technical variation in shaping between the various Yavapai populations (Gifford 1932, 1936). Kewevkapayas sometimes added pigments to create a red-colored pottery (Pilles 1979:8), and sometimes pots were decorated with yucca brushes (Williams and Khera 1975).

Structures

In the winter during the prereservation era, many Yavapai families and bands camped in caves or rockshelters that were readily heated by fires. Sometimes partial windbreaks of stone and mud plaster were constructed at the opening. In areas where caves were not available, pole-domed huts, thatched with strong grass fibers, were built (fig. 8). The base of these brush huts was often covered with dirt, and the domed tops could be protected from water with skins, replaced in historical times by canvas sheets. Larger, mud-covered houses (approximately 12 feet square) were also built though they required more time and labor than a hut. These mud homes were strong enough to support the weight of a man who delivered the morning speech on behavior (Gifford 1932:203; Williams and Khera 1975:173, 213).

Shades or ramadas were also utilized during the hot summer months. These were rectangular coverings consisting of four strong posts of wood pushed into the ground with a few cross-beams covered with cottonwood branches. The open sides allowed for maximum ventilation while providing shade from the intense heat.

Smithsonian, NAA: top, 76-5680; bottom, 56,888.

Fig. 8. Yavapai house types. top, Domed brush houses; baskets are evident, including carrying baskets and pitched water containers, and a trade blanket, probably Navajo, is on the roof at extreme left. The women, wearing multiple-strand bead necklaces, cook in metal pots. The boy carries a small bow and arrow. Photograph by A.F. Randall, before March 1888. bottom, Woman stitching a basket in front of a brush and pole shelter. Photograph by George Wharton James, Palomas, Ariz., before 1903.

Tools and Weapons

While most hunting tools also doubled as weapons there were some specializations. Hunting tools consisted of bows and arrows as well as clubs, throwing sticks, and snares or traps. Bows were made from desert mulberry and sized according to the hunter's height and the size of the prey. Arrows were crafted from light materials such as cane. Arrowheads or points were usually pressure-flaked chert or obsidian, often side-notched in Upland Yuman and Great Basin style (Pilles 1979:13). The point was attached to a wooden foreshaft that was then fitted into the shaft. If the arrow was for small game, the tip might simply be sharpened and used without a stone point. At the end of the shaft, three feathers (usually hawk or eagle) were added for balance.

Some small animals were hunted with snares made of sticks and string set up in bushes and branches as well as with baited traps made of logs and stones. Animals were also clubbed or stunned with throwing sticks.

Bows and arrows as well as clubs were also used as weapons, and a round shield often protected warriors who fought at close range. The shield was made of untanned hide that retained the hair for added thickness and protection; the hide was stretched over a wooden frame. A club was carried by many Yavapais, including women, for killing small animals and for protection against attack. For offense it was used by the strongest and most agile fighters. The club was made of heavy wood (usually ironwood), about two feet long, with a round hitting end and a handle shaft; the round end was covered by hide. One advantage of the club over the bow and arrow was that it was essentially noiseless and did not reveal the attacker's location (McCarty 1977:57).

The lance was basically an oversized arrow with a large point attached at the tip. The other end had a carrying handle of buckskin. The lance was rarely thrown; rather it was pushed into the prey or victim. Loss of the lance would leave the attacker defenseless (McCarty 1977:56).

Clothing and Adornment

There was some regional variation in clothing, hair styling, and adornment, but the early White chroniclers depict a generally similar Yavapai style. Men and women wore bangs down to their eyebrows. Women's hair was worn loose and to the shoulders while men's hair was often long and tied back. Men and women often painted their bodies for protection from the sun and for adornment; red clay was generally used (Corbusier 1969). Facial tattooing with a cactus needle and charcoal was practiced to some extent by women.

In hot weather men wore a hide breechclout besides moccasins. In winter a blanket or skin poncho was added as well as leggings. Sometimes blankets were woven from willow bark.

Women generally wore two buckskins draped over a belt and a buckskin top, poncho style, or of two pieces sewed together. High or low moccasins or leggings were worn according to weather and activity (fig. 9). Men and women wore ornaments of beads as necklaces, bracelets, as well as ear and nose rings (Corbusier 1969; Gifford 1932, 1936).

A good hunter provided his wife with buckskin moccassins, while a less successful hunter had to rely on yucca plant fibers to make sandals.

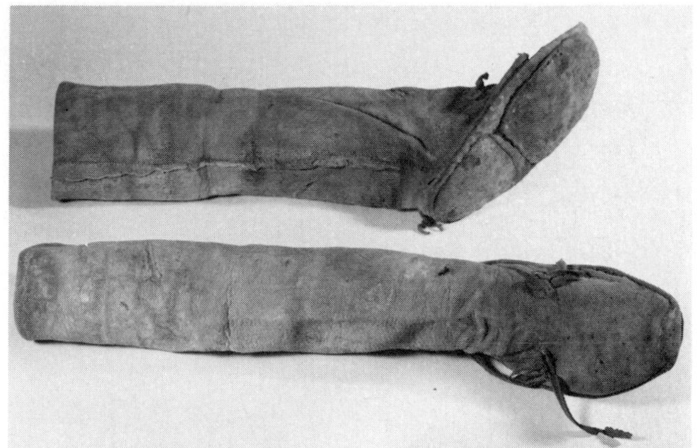

U. of Calif., Lowie Mus., Berkeley: 2-14172

Fig. 9. Woman's leather boots with cowhide soles, tied around the ankles with leather ties. The knee-high upper was worn folded down when traveling (Gifford 1936:275). Length about 41.0 cm, collected by E.W. Gifford in 1932.

Cosmology, Mythology, and Religion

The Yavapai conceive of the world as having been destroyed by catastrophes three times, a fourth destruction to be expected in the future. The places where specific events occurred during these four ages are located in the middle Verde Valley and in the Sedona Red Rock area. All these places are deeply revered by the Yavapai.

From the underground world, all beings—human and animal—ascended to this world on the first maize plant. The hole through which they entered this world then filled with water; it is Montezuma Well, to the Yavapai one of the most sacred places. Its water is considered to carry a special blessing (Gifford 1932:243; Harrison and Williams 1977:40).

After the second world was destroyed by fire, a flood came as the third catastrophe. One woman survived in a hollow log and landed in the Sedona Red Rock Mountains where she lived in a cave in Boynton Canyon. The Red Bluff where the cave is situated is the most sacred site to the Yavapai. First Woman was impregnated when she opened her body to Sun and Cloud, and she gave birth to a daughter. This daughter also became impregnated by Sun and Cloud, and gave birth to a son, *skàrə kˀa·mčə* 'the one who wanders in the cloud edges' (Lofty Wanderer). As the boy's mother was killed by monster eagles, he was brought up by his grandmother, *qmwírmə pukkwí·ya* 'old woman who has a (magical) stone' (Old Lady White Stone or Old Woman of the Verde Valley Foothills) (Kendall 1980). Later he cleared the world of all the monsters. He searched for and found his fathers, Sun and Cloud, receiving special powers from them. Returning with lightning, he made his aged grandmother young again.

Before he left this world, he called all beings together in a cave in the Red Rock Mountains. He taught each their right ways and then sent the different groups of humans to different places throughout the world. The Yavapai alone stayed at the Center of the World where everything had begun (Gifford 1932:243; Harrison and Williams 1977:42; Williams and Khera 1975:94).

"Praying for each other," particularly to encourage good health, is a crucial feature of Yavapai religion. Relatives and friends pray for and often over a person when asked to do so or when they feel such help is needed.

There are certain individuals, medicine people, who have great spiritual power and a great deal of knowledge about the forces that can influence people's lives; their prayer is considered the most effective. To become a medicine person a certain innate quality is necessary. Also, people who do not possess special qualities necessary to become a medicine person can sleep in the Red Rock Mountain caves to receive power. People also go there, especially to the Cave of First Woman in Boynton Canyon, for prayer at any time. Real estate developments, blocking the entrances to some of the canyons with sacred places, have become a serious problem for the Yavapais' exercise of their religion.

For most praying and for all rituals the participants indicate their position in the middle of the world by either a cross, a square, or diamond. If drawn on the ground, the person stands in the middle of this symbol, the arms of the cross and the corners of the square or diamond representing the four directions.

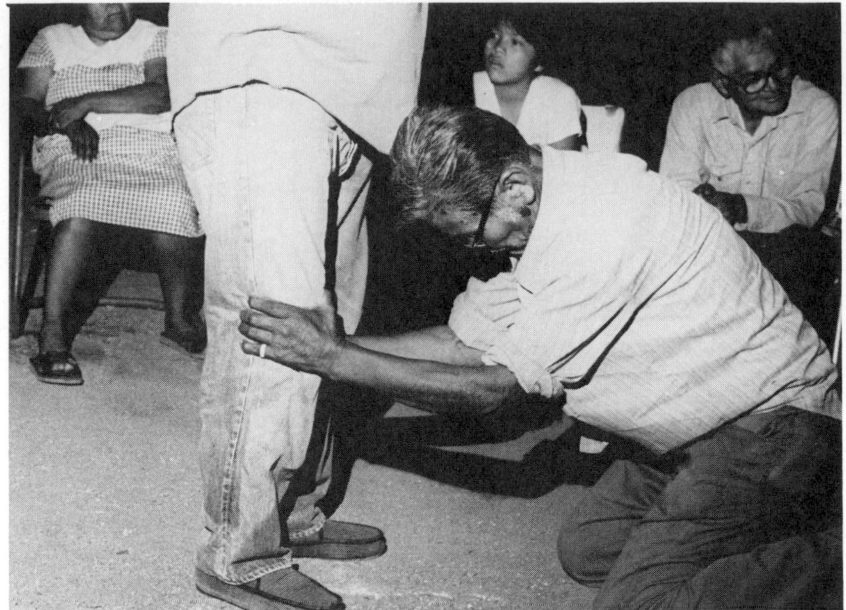

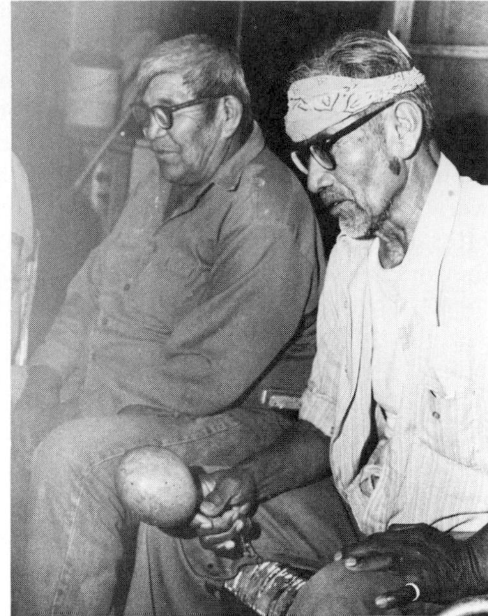

Fig. 10. A Yavapai healing ceremony in progress at Fort McDowell Reservation. left, Jim White, a Cocopa curer who had been a student of the Yavapai curer Mike Nelson, performing in the ceremony. right, John Williams, a Yavapai elder, on the left and Jim White on the right, in another part of the ceremony. Photographs by Melissa Jones, summer 1976.

Each direction is associated with a particular color. The life-giving new daylight rising in the east is symbolized by the yellow cattail pollen; this pollen is used in all prayers and rituals.

Cattail pollen, the medicinal plant blackroot, and turquoise and white beads were given to the people for their well-being by Lofty Wanderer. Turquoise and white beads protect against sickness and bad luck. Small parts of blackroot are blown onto the sore body part of a patient by the medicine man during the healing ritual.

Lofty Wanderer also gave to the people four musical instruments: the rattle and pot drum are used by the medicine man mainly when healing; the bull-roarer and flute are used mostly when calling for rain. Singing and dancing, which are part of every ritual, are considered a special form of prayer.

The bald eagle, several pairs of which are still nesting at Fort McDowell, and golden eagles are considered messengers of the spirit world who possess special knowledge. Their feathers, in particular the down, are essential for most rituals and are carried by individuals to gain special knowledge.

The dome-shaped sweat lodge was used by men only, for frequent purification. Since the late 1950s it has been rarely used, though efforts to renew its use were underway in 1980 in Fort McDowell.

Of the forces appealed to for help in ritual and individual prayer, the most important are those of Old Lady White Stone, who had planted all the healing herbs, and those of her grandson Lofty Wanderer who had put the present world in order, who could bring the dead back to life, and who taught people the right song for everything.

Help comes also from the *qaqáqə* 'little people' who live in certain mountains (among others in the Sedona Red Rock Mountains, Granite Mountain near Prescott, Four Peaks, Superstition Mountains, and McDowell Mountains). The *qaqáqə* are about three feet tall, have round heads with only eyes and a mouth but no nose; they wear skirts of fresh cedar twigs (Gifford 1932:234, 1936:313; Harrison and Williams 1977:44; Williams and Khera 1975:108).

Many Yavapais say the *qaqáqə* are "the same as the kachinas of the Hopi." They sometimes appear as a small whirlwind, and occasionally one can hear them hollering in the mountains (Harrison and Williams 1977:45).

The *qaqáqə* are represented in the Crown Dance ritual. Yavapais say they gave this ritual up when they were held at San Carlos and the Apache began to copy certain features of it (Williams and Khera 1975:110).

Individuals also call on various forces of nature and on their own personal power for help (Gifford 1932:236, 1936:308; Harrison and Williams 1977:46).

A Presbyterian mission was started at Fort McDowell in 1905. From the 1950s on, missions were established also by Southern Baptists, Mormons, Pentecostals, and Seventh Day Adventists. The Adventists ceased being active at Fort McDowell in the late 1950s. In Prescott, Viola Jimulla was instrumental in organizing a Presbyterian church in the early 1920s (Barnett 1968).

The Yavapais' rituals have continued alongside the Christian church activities. During the early 1920s the Holy Ground Church, which was started by the White Mountain Apache Silas John Edwards, was also accepted by many at Fort McDowell (Goodwin and Kaut

1954:385). It contains most of the basic elements of Yavapai ritual and emphasizes the sacredness of the land on which the people live and by which they are sustained. With some interruptions, the Holy Ground Church has remained of importance at Fort McDowell into the 1980s (Williams and Khera 1975:145).

Synonymy†

Some twentieth-century Yavapais use the name *yavpáy* as a general self-designation, but in older usage this was merely the plural of *yavpé,* the name for a member of the largest Yavapai subdivision (Martha B. Kendall, communication to editors 1981). The Yavapai were not politically united and had no name for themselves as a separate group, but other Yuman languages do call them all by a name similar to Yavapai: Quechan *ya·vapáy* (Abraham M. Halpern, communication to editors 1981); Mohave *yavapay* (Pamela Munro, communication to editors 1981); Maricopa *yavʔi·pay* (Kroeber 1943:38; Lynn Gordon, communication to editors 1981); Walapai *nʸavpeʔ* 'people living in the direction of the sunrise' (Lucille J. Watahomigie, communication to editors 1981); Havasupai *nʸavpéʔe* (Leanne Hinton, communication to editors 1981). It seems likely, therefore, that the name Yavapai was borrowed into Spanish and English from one of these other languages. Francisco Garcés, who was the first to use this name, as Yabipai, 1774, reported that it was employed by the Mohave, and he compounded it with other names to refer to a number of other Indian groups (Bolton 1930, 2:381, 383; Coues 1900, 2:444, 446). The Spanish spelling yavipais also appears. The Maricopa name is applied to both the Yavapai and the Western Apache (Spier 1946:17–18).

An extensive historical survey of names applied to the Yavapai in the historical sources has been compiled by Schroeder (1974:49–75, 267–276). The more common and definite of those used by the Spaniards include: Cruzados (1598) and Cruciferos (1716); Tacabuy (1605), probably intended for Taçabuy, and Tas(s)abuess (1775); Nijor (1699), Nijoras, Nijores, Niforas, Nifores, Nixoras, Nichoras, Nixotas, and Nijotes; and Tejuas (1776), Tehuas, and Teguas. American writers in the second half of the nineteenth century usually referred to the groups of Yavapais separately until the name Yavapai came into general use.

Since at least 1686 the Yavapai have often been referred to in Spanish and in English as Apaches (Schroeder 1974:268). This usage appears to be an extension of the term used for the Athapaskan-speaking Apacheans since 1598 and not based on the coincidentally similar Yavapai word *ʔpačə* 'people', which some modern Yavapai give as the source. The name Cohonina (and variants) has been applied to the Yavapai as well as the Havasupai and Walapai (see the synonymies in "Havasupai" and "Walapai," this vol.); this appears as the Western Apache name *gó·hń* 'Yavapai' (Goodwin 1942:575). Yampai has also been applied to all the Upland Yumans.

The Western Apache call the Yavapai *dilzhę́'é* (Curtis 1907–1930, 1:134, phonemicized); one source gives also a longer variant Har-dil-zhay 'red soil with red ants' (J.B. White 1873–1875), but this and other translations offered for this name may be only folk etymologies. This name is also said to refer to 'San Carlos and Bylas people' (Perry 1972:64) and to the Southern Tonto component of the Western Apache, though it is "strongly resented," at least by some (Goodwin 1942:259). The Navajo call the Yavapai *Dilzhí'í* (Young and Morgan 1980:320), *Dilzhé'é* (Haile 1950–1951, 1:89), or *Dilzhę́hé* (Hoijer 1974:276), the last actually attested as referring to "a group of Apaches in the White Mountain country."

Subgroups

The Yavepe (*yavpé*), also called the Northeastern Yavapai (Gifford 1932, 1936), were referred to by Corbusier (1886:276) as "the Apache-Mojaves, Yavapais, or Kohenins," these being the names in use by speakers of English (and Spanish?), Yuman, and Athapaskan, respectively. J.B. White (1873–1875) gives We´-le-id-ger-par´ as the Tonto (Kewevkapaya) name for the "Apache Mohave." The Yavapai form *yavpé* lacks any clear meaning and has been given several conflicting explanations; the apparent cognates in other Upland Yuman languages mean 'eastern people'. The Maricopa name is *yavʔi·payxan* (Lynn Gordon, communication to editors 1981).

The Tolkapaya (*tòlkpáya*) or Western Yavapai were known as the Apache-Yumas in the second half of the nineteenth century. Their Apache name was given as natchous 'lizards' (Corbusier 1886:276). *tòlkpáya* does not have a transparent meaning in modern Yavapai but has been explained as 'western people' (Martha B. Kendall, communication to editors 1981) and 'central people' (Corbusier 1923–1925). The Maricopa call them *yavʔi·pay kve* (Lynn Gordon, communication to editors 1981).

The Kewevkapaya (*kwèvkpáya*) or Southeastern Yavapai were known as Apache-Tontos, Tonto Apaches, or Tontos. This group intermarried extensively with Apaches and the name Tonto has also been applied to the Apaches that were in contact with them or descended from the mixed Yavapai and Apache bands of the nineteenth century (Corbusier 1886:277; J.B. White 1873–1875a). *kwèvkpáya* means 'southern people' (Martha B. Kendall, communication to editors 1981); a writing of the name as Co-wá-ver. Co-pi´-yar (J.B. White 1873–1875) led to the appearance of the parts

†This synonymy was written by Ives Goddard.

before and after the internal period as two separate names in some secondary sources (Gatschet 1877–1892:370; Hodge 1907–1910, 2:836).

Sources

In general, there are comparatively few works that deal with the Yavapai. The only ethnographic works on the Yavapai are those of Gifford (1932, 1936), based on several months of fieldwork in the early 1930s. There is a manuscript by Mike Burns, Gifford's only Kewevkapaya informant, which is published in part, in Khera (1977); copies are located in the Sharlot Hall Museum library, Prescott, Arizona, as well as in the Hayden Collection of the Arizona State University library, Tempe.

There are several discussions of the Yavapai in the 1860s and 1870s by army personnel, the most informative being those of Corbusier (1886, 1969), who was the physician on the Rio Verde Reservation, and Bourke's (1891) discussion of General Crook's campaigns.

Schroeder's (1952a, 1974) works for the U.S. Indian Claims Commission case definitively detail historical and ethnographic material concerning the aboriginal territory of the Yavapai and the records of their early interactions with non-Indians.

A partial collection of Dr. Carlos Montezuma's correspondence concerning Fort McDowell is held in the Hayden Collection of the Arizona State University library; a preliminary analysis of these documents has been made by Chamberlain (1975). A collection of all Dr. Montezuma's papers will be forthcoming through a research project edited by John Larner.

There is a brief discussion of Fort McDowell in the 1950s by Heider (1956). C.P. Morris's (1971, 1972) articles provide brief social and economic histories of the Middle Verde and Camp Verde reservations, while a summary history of the Jimulla family of Prescott is found in Barnett (1968). Coffeen (1972) discusses the impacts of the proposed Orme Dam on the Fort McDowell community. Khera (1977), a book designed for the Fort McDowell community as well as the public, contains articles on Yavapai history, farming, and tools, and on Orme Dam as well as excerpts from manuscripts. Williams and Khera's (1975) ethnohistory is the result of a long-term collaboration between a noted Yavapai oral historian and an anthropologist.

Mohave

KENNETH M. STEWART

Northernmost and largest of the Yuman-speaking* tribes of the lower Colorado River in aboriginal times, the Mohave (mō'hävē) comprise two divisions—former residents of the Fort Mojave Reservation in Arizona who have lived since the 1930s across the river in the town of Needles, California, and the Mohaves of the Colorado River Reservation, 60 miles downstream (fig. 1). These are approximately the same localities that the Mohave were occupying when the Spaniards first encountered them in the seventeenth and eighteenth centuries. The Mohave then constituted a true tribe, with a loose division into bands that did not weaken the tribal unity for purposes of attack or defense, possessing a national consciousness despite a minimal political organization.

The core and most heavily populated part of the Mohave territory in precontact times was the Mohave Valley, where no other tribe has ever been reported. The Mohave, if Schroeder is correct in identifying them with the prehistoric group he calls the Amacava, may have come out of the Mohave Desert to the west to settle along the river in the Mohave Valley as early as A.D. 1150 (Schroeder 1952b:29). Mohave settlements in the valley extended from about 15 miles north of the present Davis Dam down to the peaks known as The Needles, just south of Topock, Arizona. The Mohave apparently considered, too, that they owned the country along the Colorado south to the Bill Williams River, although in the nineteenth century they allowed the Chemehuevi, migratory desert Indians, to infiltrate and farm along the river in what is now known as the Chemehuevi Valley.

Mohaves were also living in the Colorado River Valley, near the present Colorado River Reservation, when they were first seen by Spaniards of the Juan de Oñate expedition in 1604 (K.M. Stewart 1969a). That valley was later in part occupied by a hostile tribe, the Halchidhoma, who after protracted warfare were finally expelled from the valley between 1827 and 1829. Some Mohaves then moved into the northern part of the valley to establish possession once again. In 1859 a larger group of Mohaves was induced to move south from the Mohave Valley by Chief Irrateba (*ˀiraté·və*), and others joined them when the Colorado River Reservation was established in 1865. A conservative faction, under a rival chief, *hamosé·-kʷaˀahot* ('good star'), refused to leave their ancestral homeland in the Mohave Valley, and ever since that time the Mohaves have remained split into two groups, one in the Mohave Valley and the other on the Colorado River Reservation (K.M. Stewart 1969). Despite the differences between the two Mohave communities, there is considerable visiting between them and some intermarriage.

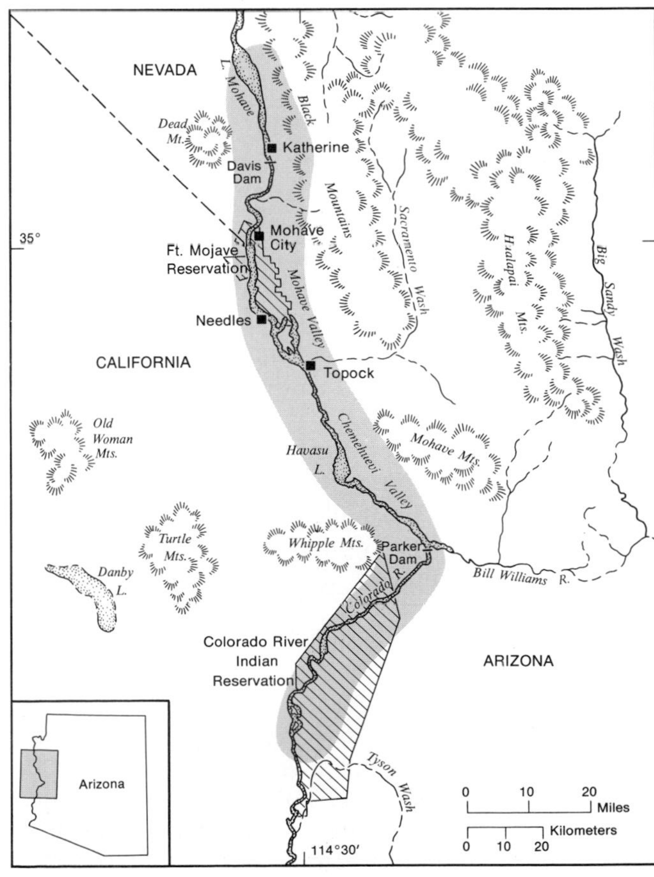

Fig. 1. Tribal territory in the mid-19th century (reservations and hydrography are modern).

*The phonemes of Mohave are: (voiceless unaspirated stops and affricate) *p*, *t* (dental), *ṭ* (back alveolar), *č*, *kʸ*, *k*, *kʷ*, *q*, *qʷ*, *ˀ*; (voiced spirants) *v* ([β]), *δ*; (voiceless spirants) *θ*, *s*, *š*, *h*, *hʷ*; (laterals) *l*, *lʸ*; (nasals) *m*, *n*, *ṇ*, *nʸ*, *ŋ*; (trill) *r*; (semivowels) *w*, *y*; (short vowels) *i*, *e*, *a*, *o*, *u*, *ə*; (long vowels) *i·*, *e·*, *a·*, *o·*, *u·*; (stress) v́ (primary), v̀ (secondary). Word-final /ə/ is optionally dropped.

Information on Mohave phonology was provided by Pamela Munro (communications to editors 1974, 1976), who furnished the transcriptions of the Mohave words cited in italics in the *Handbook*.

External Relations

The Mohave were culturally very much like their Quechan friends and allies and were also similar in culture to the antagonistic Halchidhoma, Maricopa, and Cocopa. The Pima (and to a lesser degree, the Papago) were allies of the Maricopa and thus were considered to be enemies by the Mohave. The Yavapai, on the other hand, were friendly to both the Quechan and Mohave, whom they sometimes joined in expeditions against the Maricopa. Relations between the Mohave and the Walapai were mixed; at times they were friendly enough to permit trade, while fighting between them occurred at other periods.

The Cahuilla, Tipai-Ipai, and other Mission Indians of southern California were regarded by the Mohave as good people. In the deserts to the north and west of Mohave territory were the Southern Paiute, close relatives of the Chemehuevi. Poor and nomadic, the Chemehuevi were allowed to come on the river to farm in the early nineteenth century. But war broke out between Mohave and Chemehuevi between 1865 and 1867, and the Chemehuevi were temporarily driven back into the desert. They were allowed to return when peace was made, and they were later incorporated into the Colorado River Reservation community (K.M. Stewart 1968a).

Environment

The Mohave country is a region of mild winters, oppressively hot summers, and extremely low annual precipitation. Back from the bottomlands along the river, vegetation is prevailingly xerophytic. Were it not for the beneficence of the great Colorado River, the land would doubtless have been only thinly populated by hunters and gatherers. But annual flooding made possible relatively dense populations in the lush oases of the river valleys.

The Colorado River, originating high in the Rocky Mountains, is fed by numerous tributaries in a drainage area of a quarter of a million square miles. Emerging from the chasm of the Grand Canyon, it rounds a bend at the present boundary of Arizona and Nevada and turns southward, flowing alternately through constricted canyons and floodplains en route to the Gulf of California.

Once an untamed torrent, the silt-laden Colorado was prone to overflow its banks in the spring of the year, swollen with the melting snows of the Rockies. Ordinarily the floods were not destructive, spreading gently over the bottomlands for distances of as much as a mile or two from the river. In late June the waters began to recede, leaving behind a deposit of rich silt on the floodplains. In these alluvial sediments the Mohave planted their crops, which ripened rapidly in the intense summer heat.

In the bottoms are dense thickets of cane and arrowweed, and groves of cottonwood and willows. The terrain away from the river rises gradually to a sandy mesa, where there are stands of mesquite trees, which do not tolerate marshy conditions. Where the root systems can no longer reach the subsurface moisture, abrupt changes in flora occur. Beyond the arid mesa, where the vegetation consists mainly of cacti and creosote bushes, rise jagged and utterly barren mountains.

Few larger game animals were found at the lower elevations, although deer occasionally strayed into the thickets near the river. More common were rabbits and various rodents. In the river were fish such as humpbacks and mullets, which have been supplanted by introduced species.

History

The Spaniards of the sixteenth and seventeenth centuries, far to the south in Mexico, knew of the Mohaves mainly by hearsay. Too remote from the Spanish centers of ecclesiastical and temporal influence to be very directly affected by the activities of the Spaniards, the Mohave were visited only at protracted intervals.

The first Spaniard known to have contacted Mohaves was Oñate, who in 1604 met them near the junction of the Colorado and Bill Williams rivers and farther south. Father Francisco Garcés was in 1776 the first Spaniard to reach the Mohave Valley. He estimated the Mohave population to be 3,000 (table 1).

No missions or Spanish settlements were ever established in Mohave territory; the Mohave maintained their independence throughout Hispanic times. The rather sparse accounts of the Mohave left by the Spanish explorers reveal a picture of Mohave life similar in its essentials to that later reported by ethnographers. There were few changes in Mohave culture during the Hispanic period. The Mohave obtained wheat at second hand from the Quechan, and they acquired a few horses, some of them obtained in raids upon the Spanish mission communities in California.

After Mexican independence from Spain in 1821, the Mohave for a while continued their traditional way of life without hindrance. But during the 1820s a new breed of aliens, the Anglo-American trappers and fur traders, began to travel through Mohave country. Among them were the parties of Jedediah Smith and James O. Pattie in 1826 and 1827. At this period the Mohave were unpredictable in their reception of strangers, and blood was spilled on several occasions (K.M. Stewart 1966). Some of the parties of Anglo-Americans passing through their territory in subsequent years also had trouble with the Mohave; for example, the Lorenzo Sitgreaves ex-

Table 1. Population

Date	*Estimate*	*Source*
1770	3,000	Kroeber 1925:883
1776	3,000	Garcés (Coues 1900, 2:450)
1872	4,000 (828 on the Colorado River Reservation, 700 at Fort Mojave)	ARCIA 1872:58, 323
1910	1,050	Kroeber 1925:883
1965	1,500	Wallace (Spencer and Jennings 1965:273)

pedition, seeking a route for a transcontinental railroad, was attacked in 1851.

Other railroad explorers, including Amiel W. Whipple in 1854, and steamboat captains seeking to determine the navigability of the Colorado, among them Joseph C. Ives in 1858, penetrated Mohave territory at a time when the long period of intertribal warfare among the River Yumans was coming to an end. In 1857 the Quechan-Mohave allies suffered a disastrous defeat at the hands of a combination of Pima and Maricopa warriors.

Still smarting from their defeat, and apprehensive about the increasingly frequent intrusions of Whites into Mohave country, the Mohave warriors in 1858 attacked a wagon train bound for California. As a consequence, a United States military post, later to be named Fort Mohave, was established in the Mohave Valley. However, the Mohave were still defiant, and in 1859 a battle was fought in which the Mohave warriors were mowed down by the rifle fire of the soldiers. This defeat ended the resistance of the Mohaves and paved the way for their subsequent acculturation (K.M. Stewart 1969).

During the period between about 1870 and 1890 the Mohaves, plagued with disease and living in abject poverty, went through a demoralizing interlude. Around the turn of the century things began to improve for them somewhat, although many problems persisted. Recent years have brought increasing prosperity to the Mohave of the Colorado River Reservation in particular, with the development of irrigated farmlands and income from leases of reservation land to Whites.

Mus. für Völkerkunde, Berlin: IV B12910.

Fig. 2. Mohave appearance in the 1850s. The woman holds an infant on one hip and a basket on her head and wears a double skirt of bark fiber. The designs on her arms and cheeks were painted, while her chin may have been tattooed. The men wear long breechclouts and hair rolls, are painted on legs, chests, and arms, and wear feather head ornaments. Watercolor by Heinrich Balduin Möllhausen on Joseph C. Ives Expedition, 1857–1858.

Culture, 1860–1890

Settlement Pattern

The Mohave had no true villages but lived in sprawling settlements or rural neighborhoods that were scattered throughout the valleys near arable land. The houses were usually situated on low rises above the floodplain. The houses of a particular settlement might be spread out over a distance of a mile or two, with perhaps four or five miles separating them from the next settlement. The settlement constituted a local group, the nucleus of which was an extended family, either patrilocal or bilocal, although because of much shifting around of population, and also because of marital instability, unrelated families might be resident in a settlement (K.M. Stewart 1970–1971).

Structures

During much of the year the Mohaves slept under flat-topped, open-sided ramadas (shades), resorting to their more substantial sand-covered houses only in cold weather. The winter houses (fig. 5) were low and rectangular in floor plan. Four large cottonwood posts supported a sloping roof of poles, which was covered with a thatch of arrowweed. The sides and ends of the house, consisting of vertical poles, were also sloping. A layer of sand and earth or river mud several inches in thickness was piled over the exterior of the house (Kroeber 1925:731–735). Native-style houses have not been built since the beginning of the twentieth century.

Subsistence

The Mohave were basically dependent upon farming in the bottomlands along the river, supplementing their diet by gathering wild plants, by fishing in the river, and by doing some hunting. The principal crop was maize, mainly flour corn of the white variety. Tepary

left, Bancroft Lib., U. of Calif., Berkeley; right, Boston Public Lib., Print Dept.

Fig. 3. Clothing of the 1860s. left, Woman at Ft. Mojave. Her torso and probably her arms and legs bear vertical painted stripes, and she wears a bark skirt overlaid by a decorative cloth. Photograph by R. D'Heureuse, 1863. right, Group at Ft. Mojave. The man standing beside Maj. William Redwood Price (8th Cavalry) wears a rabbitskin robe over one shoulder, while the Indian man at right wears a military coat and hat. The women wear bead necklaces and skirts made of twisted cloth and yarn strips tied with waist bands. Photograph by Alexander Gardner, while on the Kansas Pacific Railroad, early 1868.

beans of several varieties were second in importance, and pumpkins and melons were also raised.

Mohave agricultural methods were relatively simple. The men did most of the work in clearing the land, and in planting and cultivating the crop, often assisted by the women, who did much of the harvesting. The Mohave farmer used a planting stick with a wedge-shaped point, punching holes in the moist soil, four to six inches deep and a pace apart, making no attempt to align the holes in regular rows. A woman usually followed a planter, dropping a half-dozen seeds in each hole, then replacing the soil and pressing it down by hand.

No crop rotation was practiced, and artificial fertilization was superfluous, since the fertility of the fields was maintained by the deposition of silt in the annual overflows. The growing plants received little attention other than that required to clear away weeds with sword-shaped wooden hoes.

Harvesting of the main crop started in late September and continued into October. The corn was husked in the fields by the women, and that portion of the crop that was not roasted and eaten while still green was thoroughly dried in the sun on the roofs of ramadas. After that it was stored away in huge basketry granaries, woven of arrowweed branches with the leaves still on them, and so coarse in their weave that they have been compared to giant birds' nests.

A man might appropriate any piece of land not already in use, clearing the land by breaking down the shrubby growth and burning it. Once under cultivation, the land was regarded as private property. The shape of the fields varied in accordance with the topography, but the fields were rarely more than an acre or two in size. Boundaries were marked with ridges of dirt, or with arrowweed markers set up along the edges of the field. Disputes over boundaries sometimes occurred, when flooding changed the configuration of the land or obliterated the dividing ridges. A rough pushing match or stick fight between the disputants, each backed by supporters, might then be the way to settle the matter. Each party would attempt to drive the other back across the contested territory, thus definitely establishing claim to the land.

Famines were rare, and in normal years the Mohaves

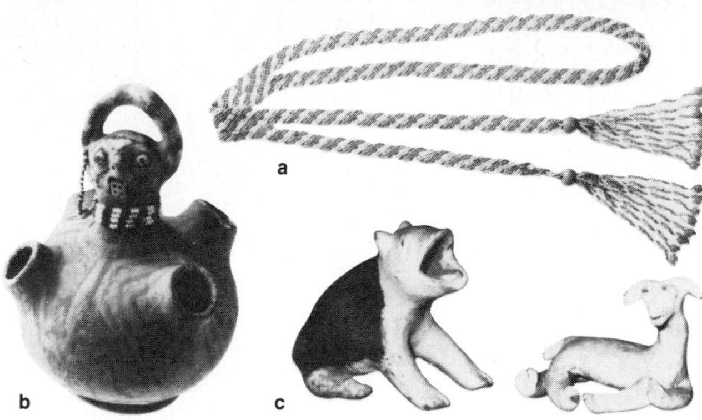

top, Southwest Mus., Los Angeles: 1376; Smithsonian, Dept. of Anthr.: a, 348,977; b, 278,080; c, U. of Colo. Mus., Boulder: 963.

Fig. 4. Tourist trade. top, Women selling bead necklaces to tourists. Photograph by Warren Dickerson at Needles, Calif., about 1890s. Crafts sold at the Needles, Calif., train station—a scheduled meal stop—included: a, necklace of braided strands of light blue and white seed beads accented with larger light blue beads; b, painted pottery vessel with 4 spouts and handle in shape of a human head with blue and white seed bead earring and necklace added (figurines similar to those of the Quechan were also made); c, whimsical animal figures that may also have been made as toys (Kroeber and Harner 1955:2). Length of a, 94 cm, collected before 1930. Height of b, 15 cm, rest to same scale, b and c collected by J.P. Harrington in 1911.

had enough to eat. But in years of drought the river might fail to rise sufficiently to flood the fields, and then the harvest was lean. At such times the Mohaves were obliged to rely more heavily for their food supply on hunting, gathering, and fishing. These activities were also carried on at other times but became of crucial importance in times of poor harvest (K.M. Stewart 1966b; Kroeber 1925:735–737; Castetter and Bell 1951).

The women collected a variety of wild seeds in the bottomlands after the recession of the floods. They also went out in small parties to collect cactus fruits and other desert plants on the adjacent mesas. The most important wild food plants were the beanlike pods of the mesquite and screwbean (tornillo) (K.M. Stewart 1965; Castetter and Bell 1951).

Fish were the principal source of flesh food in the Mohave diet, although the fish native to the Colorado were rather soft and unpalatable. They were taken in dip nets, with seines or drag nets, in traps or weirs, or with large, canoe-shaped basketry scoops with long handles, both in the river and in muddy sloughs and ponds (fig. 6). The fish were eaten fresh, after broiling on hot coals or boiling with corn in a kind of stew that the Mohaves particularly relished (K.M. Stewart 1957; Wallace 1955).

Hunting was of relatively little significance to Mohave subsistence, since game was scarce along the river, and the Mohave only occasionally went farther afield to hunt. The Mohave had only a feeble development of hunting techniques and devices, making no use of pitfalls or deerhead disguises. The deer hunter either waited in ambush or stalked the animal with a bow and arrow. Deer hunters sometimes made special excursions to the mountains east of the river. The hunter traded the game to other Mohaves for fish and farm products, since it was believed to be bad luck for a hunter to eat his own kill. Rabbits were caught in snares or nets, or shot with bows and arrows, or bowled over with curved throwing sticks, sometimes in communal rabbit drives (K.M. Stewart 1947b).

Technology

Artifacts, for the most part unadorned, were fashioned to meet only minimum requirements of utility. Little value was placed upon anything technological, but the Mohave indifference to craftsmanship may be in part attributable to the fact that all the property of an individual was destroyed at his death, and there was thus no inheritance of personal possessions. Mohave basketry was carelessly woven, and pottery (fig. 7) was no better than mediocre. Few artifacts were made of stone or bone, and the craft of woodworking remained rudimentary (Kroeber 1925:737–740).

Clothing and Adornment

Since the weather was hot or warm for the greater part of the year, a minimum of clothing was necessary. Children went naked, and the garments of both men and women were scanty. Men wore breechclouts, woven of strands from the inner bark of willow. Women were clad in knee-length skirts of willow bark.

Both sexes took pride in the glossy appearance of their long hair, which for cleansing purposes was frequently plastered with a mixture of mud and boiled mesquite bark. The hair of the women hung in a loose mass over their shoulders, while men's hair was rolled into some 20 to 30 ropelike strands that hung down the back (Kroeber 1925:729).

top left, Mus. für Völkerkunde, Berlin; top right and bottom, Mus. of N. Mex., Santa Fe.

Fig. 5. Habitations. top left, Low-roofed winter house made of wattle-and-daub with earth-covered roof and open ramada. At left foreground is a basketry granary with 2 pottery vessels. A hoop-and-pole game is in progress. Watercolor by Heinrich Balduin Möllhausen, on Whipple Expedition, 1854. top right, A low-roofed house inundated by the annual spring flooding of the Colorado River. A basketry granary stands on the platform on left. bottom, Semisubterranean house under construction. The large posts are made from cottonwood trees and the covering is of arrowweed under a layer of sand. Thatch and sand remain to be added on the side walls (cf. Kroeber 1925:731–734). Corn is drying on the house roof as well as on the storage platform to right. The men wear long breechclouts and the traditional hair rolls. In front are pottery vessels of at least 5 shape types including a large shallow parcher for corn and wheat (cf. Kroeber and Harner 1955). top right and bottom, Photographs by Ben Wittick, 1890s.

Transport

Despite the importance of the river to the subsistence of the Mohave, they had no true boats. They were good swimmers, and often swam across the river, a swimmer sometimes ferrying goods or small children by pushing them ahead of him in a large pottery vessel. A man might straddle a single log to float downstream, and occasionally log rafts were made when an entire family wanted to travel downriver. On foot, the men could cover great distances across the desert in a single day, sometimes as much as 100 miles, in a steady, jogging trot. Women carried burdens in a rough, netted structure that was supported by a framework of sticks and was attached to a tumpline passed over the woman's forehead (Kroeber 1925:738–739).

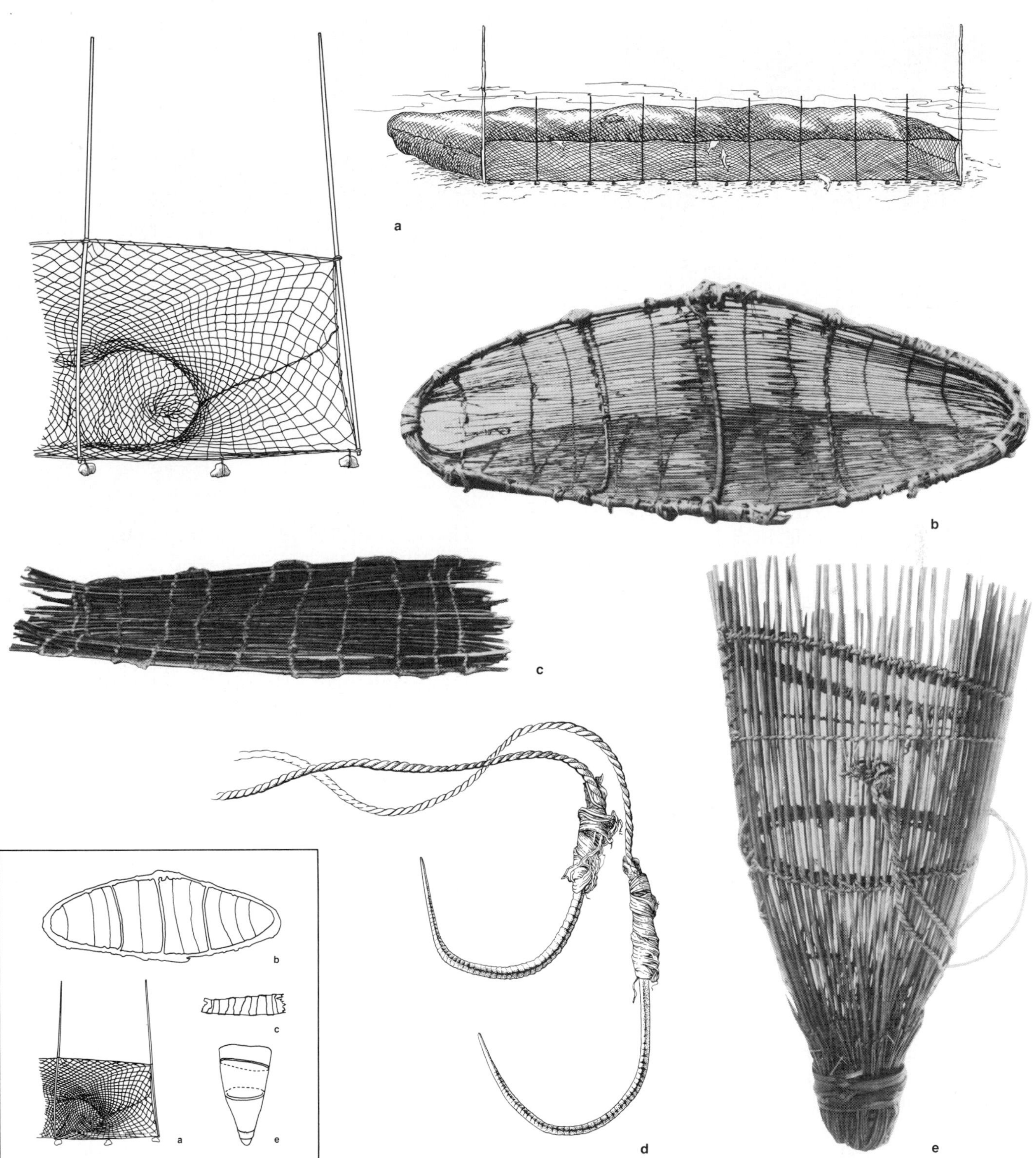

Smithsonian, Dept. of Anthr.: a, 277,907, d, 24,181; e, 278,007; b, San Diego Mus. of Man, Calif.: 16,838; c, U. of Colo. Mus., Boulder: 981.

Fig. 6. Fishing equipment. Fish were caught in the Colorado River and in the lagoons and sloughs left by its spring flooding. One of the most common techniques used a seine or drag net (a) with poles attached to each end and sticks spaced vertically across the net with stones serving as weights. The net was worked by 2 men at opposite ends who dragged it through the water. A large basketry scoop (b) of willow lashed with bast would have a long handle attached across the center and was used by one man, although not on the river. Fish were also caught in sieves (c), dip nets, and weirs, and were shot with bow and arrow (Wallace 1955; K.M. Stewart 1957). Angling was not so common, but fishhooks (d) were made from cactus spines that had been moistened, heated, and bent. They were attached with fiber line to willow poles. A conical basket of willow twigs (e), carried on the back, was used to hold fish. d, collected by Edward Palmer in 1871; c, collected by J.P. Harrington and Junius Henderson in 1911; a,b,e collected by J.P. Harrington, b in 1914, rest in 1911. a, length of stick 120 cm; b, length about 183 cm; c, length 66 cm; d, length 5 cm; e, length 68 cm. Key at lower left indicates relative sizes (except for fishhooks).

Smithsonian, Dept. of Anthr.: 278,042, 10,320.

Fig. 7. Painted pottery. left, Bowl, *kʷáθki· valʸtáy* 'big bowl', painted with red geometric pattern on interior, with fiber wound around the rim for strengthening. Water was added to pounded mesquite beans in the bowl and, after stirring, the slightly sweet beverage was drunk. right, Water bottle with red on buff design. left, Diameter 30 cm (other to same scale), collected by J.P. Harrington in 1911; right collected by Edward Palmer in 1871.

Calif. Histl. Soc., Los Angeles: Title Insurance Coll., 1908.

Fig. 8. Nopie wearing strands of rolled hair wound around his head. He also has a bone nose ornament through his nasal septum. A ramada is behind him. Photograph possibly by Charles C. Pierce or George Wharton James, 1890s.

Political Organization

The Mohave, regardless of place of residence, thought of themselves as one people, living in a true nation with a well-defined territory. Despite a loose division into bands and local groups, the tribal cohesion was such that the Mohave were able to present a united front in warfare against all enemies. At least three bands within the Mohave tribe have been identified: *mathálʸa·ðom*, the northern division; *ható·pa*, the central division; and *kavé·lʸa·ðom*, the southern division. Each band was subdivided into settlements or local groups. To the Mohave, the locality of residence was unimportant in contrast to membership in the tribe, and people moved freely from one locality to another within the tribal territory.

The Mohave had a head chief for the tribe, although it is uncertain how long the status had existed prior to extensive contact with Whites. The chieftainship may have developed out of the status of local group leader. Although the head chief was supposed to have dreamed his power, which is in full accord with Mohave ideology, the office also became hereditary in the male line, which is un-Mohave-like. It is clear, in any case, that despite the tribal cohesiveness, the governmental machinery of the Mohave was minimal, with relatively slight institutionalization. No one individual or group of persons was in a position of significant authority over other Mohaves. There was no organized tribal council, although the chief might at times ask the prominent men from each settlement to meet with him for informal discussion of matters of importance. The chief had little authority but was expected to look after tribal welfare. He exerted a moral rather than a commanding influence over the people. The chief's importance increased for a brief period around 1859, when Mohave independence was coming to an end, but factionalism subsequently developed, with rival claimants to the chieftainship.

There were subchiefs in the several bands of the Mohave: one in the north, one in the south, and five in the more populous central division, according to informants. In the various settlements also were an indefinite number of local group leaders who, like the chiefs, were believed to have attained their positions by dreaming. They were expected to be skillful speakers, who addressed the people from the rooftops in the morning. People deferred to their wishes because they respected them, not because they had any real authority.

top right and bottom left, Mus. of N. Mex., Santa Fe: School of Amer. Research Coll., 15959, 15956; bottom right, Smithsonian, NAA: 2801-b-6; top left, Douglas Co. Mus., Roseburg, Oreg.

Fig. 9. Adornment. Both men and women customarily had tattooed chins and frequently wore elaborate facial painting in a large variety of designs (see Taylor and Wallace 1947; Kroeber 1925:730, 732–733 for other patterns). top left, Olive Oatman, a White woman who was tattooed by the Mohave while she was a captive among them 1852–1856 (K.M. Stewart 1969:220); photograph by Powelson of Rochester, N.Y., about 1858. top right, Unidentified woman from Needles, Calif.; photograph by Ben Wittick, about 1883. bottom left, Hanje; photograph by Ben Wittick, about 1883. bottom right, Unidentified woman; photograph by Ben Wittick, 1880s. Two of the women wear jew's harps suspended from their multi-strand bead necklaces.

The main religious leaders were the *kohótə* ('the one who is good'), of whom there were several in different parts of Mohave territory. They performed religious functions that were believed to strengthen the integration of the tribe, and they were also festival chiefs, giving feasts and arranging victory celebrations. They, too, were speakers, addressing the people at funerals and on other occasions. They may at one time have been the principal tribal leaders, but their importance declined considerably during the early contact period, as that of the chief increased (Kroeber 1925:725, 745–747; K.M. Stewart 1970–1971; Fathauer 1954).

Warfare

Mohave warfare was carried on primarily by the *kʷənəmí·* ('brave, willing'), those men who had experienced "great dreams" conferring power in battle, although in a major expedition men who had not had the proper war dreams might also participate. In Mohave belief, warfare was instituted by the culture hero, *mastamhó*, who decreed that in each generation some men would have dreams giving power in war. Thus the *kʷənəmí·* were eager to validate their dreams, so to speak, by demonstrating prowess in battle. A few *kʷənəmí·*, those with stronger dreams, were recognized as war leaders.

A raid might be undertaken by 10 or 12 *kʷənəmí·* whenever they wished to go out and fight, but more preparation preceded a major campaign. Scouts or spies, who had dreamed specific powers, first reconnoitered the route to be traversed, locating water holes and enemy habitations. Attack on an outlying enemy settlement was at dawn, by surprise, but if the Mohave continued farther into the enemy Maricopa territory they might encounter a battle array of Maricopa and Pima warriors. Challengers from the opposing sides would then meet in single combat before a general melee started. The Quechan usually joined the Mohave for campaigns, and sometimes they invited the Mohave to come downriver to join them in an attack on the Cocopa.

The Mohave had a divided armament in which some warriors bore long bows with untipped arrows of sharpened arrowweed, while others carried hardwood clubs, which did most of the damage in hand-to-hand fighting. Most effective was a mallet-headed club (fig. 10) shaped like an old-fashioned potato masher, which was wielded by the *kʷənəmí·*.

On each major expedition a special scalper, who had dreamed his power to scalp, treated warriors who had fallen ill because of contact with the evil power of the enemy. The return of the warriors was celebrated with a victory dance around enemy scalps mounted on poles. Prisoners were almost exclusively girls or young women, who were given to the old men as an insult to the enemy

top, U. of Ariz., Ariz. State Mus., Tucson: E-4971; bottom, Yale U., Peabody Mus.: 19127.

Fig. 10. War equipment. top, Warrior's traveling kit consisting of bow with twine string and arrows with sharpened tips, painted ends with 3 feathers. Attached to bow are items a man would need: cloth cap, hide sandals, wooden club painted black except for red ends, gourd water bottle with wood stopper hung in twine netting, hair ornament of flicker feathers. Missing is a small bag of mesquite beans for food. Made by Romeo Burton. bottom, War standard, made of pointed stick with feathers attached. Quills are bound with red yarn to either end of a short string, which is then tied to the staff by a continuous cord. This example was probably made for use at a mourning ceremony since those used in battle were usually heavier (Spier 1955:12). Each war party had a standard bearer who carried no other weapon and was obliged not to flee (K.M. Stewart 1947:265–266). top, Length of bow 120.0 cm, bottom to same scale, collected in 1962; bottom collected by Leslie Spier in 1932.

(K.M. Stewart 1947; Fathauer 1954; Kroeber 1925: 751–753).

Social Organization

Marriage among the Mohave was casual, arranged without formality by the couple themselves, subject to the observance of clan exogamy and the avoidance of marriage between close relatives. Wedding ceremonies were lacking; the couple simply began living together. Most marriages were monogamous, although polygynous unions occurred occasionally. There was no mandatory rule about place of residence after marriage. Where the newlyweds lived seems in practice to have been a matter of preference or convenience. The Mohave had neither in-law avoidances nor prescribed behaviors toward affinal relatives. Marital instability was common, divorce entailing merely a separation at the will of either party (Kroeber 1925:745; K.M. Stewart 1970–1971).

Status differences between families were insignificant. The nuclear family was the essential unit in daily social and economic life, although the members of an extended family sometimes cooperated in tasks such as farming (K.M. Stewart 1970–1971).

While lacking both phratries and moieties, the Mohave had a rather unusual system of patrilineal, exogamous clans. Whatever functions the clans may have had in the precontact period have been lost, other than the sometimes-ignored exogamic prescriptions. There were no clan leaders, and the clans played no significant part in either religious or secular life.

The Mohave word for a clan is *símulʸ* (also 'clan name'; cf. *imulʸ* 'personal name'). The names of the clans, 22 in number, were believed to have been given by the deity *mataví·lʸə* in the mythical period. All the women of a particular clan were called by the clan name rather than by a personal name, while the men were silent carriers of the name, being known by nicknames. The clan names were of totemic import, pertaining to plants, animals, or natural phenomena, although the words were archaic rather than those in current usage. There were no taboos on killing or eating the totems, nor were the totems venerated. Not all members of a clan lived in the same locality (Kroeber 1925:741–744; Spier 1953; K.M. Stewart 1970–1971).

Religion

Mohave religion featured an unusual conception of dreaming, which was in fact a pivotal concept in their culture as a whole, permeating almost every phase of Mohave thought and endeavor. All special talents and skills, and all noteworthy success in life, whether in warfare, lovemaking, gambling, or as a shaman, were believed to be dependent upon proper dreaming.

Dreams were constantly discussed and meditated upon by the Mohave. This intense preoccupation with dreams was accompanied by an indifference to learning. The Mohave were aware, of course, that skills could be improved by practice and that songs and myths could be assimilated by listening to them. But the acquisition of knowledge in such ways seemed of little value to the Mohave, since information and skills were regarded as ineffectual unless a person had the requisite power-bestowing dreams.

Although the Mohave were interested in dreams of all kinds, they made a clear distinction between ordinary dreams and the "great dreams" that brought power. All dreams were believed to have a meaning, so the ordinary dreams were regarded as "omen dreams," which when properly interpreted might foretell coming events.

The "great dreams," called *sumáč ˀahót* or *su·máč ˀahót* 'good dream', came to relatively few people, but the chosen ones who had them were the leaders in Mohave society—chiefs, braves, shamans, singers, and funeral orators. The dream was thought to occur first while the unborn child was still in the mother's womb. In Mohave belief the prenatal dream was forgotten by the dreamer but was dreamed over again later in life, usually during adolescence. The youth, conditioned throughout his life by the cultural emphasis upon dream power, longed for and anticipated having a "great dream." Having heard others tell their dreams, again and again, in the stereotyped mythological pattern, the boy might have, or believe that he had, similar dreams. The test of the authenticity of his dreams depended upon whether he was able to validate them in successful undertakings.

Public ceremonies were almost totally lacking among the Mohave, and even dancing occurred only incidentally as an adjunct to the singing of certain song cycles. The Mohave had no masks, almost no ceremonial regalia and paraphernalia, and practically no symbolism or fetishism. There were no rituals intended to bring rain or promote the growth of crops.

Instead, the Mohave emphasized the recitation of dream experiences and the singing of song cycles. The song cycles, numbering about 30 in all, were supposed to have been dreamed by the singer. Each cycle consisted of from 50 to 200 songs, and the singing of a complete cycle required an entire night or more. The singer alternately sang and recited mythological episodes, for some cycles accompanying his singing by shaking a gourd rattle or beating rhythmically with a stick on an overturned basket (Kroeber 1925:754–755; Wallace 1947; K.M. Stewart 1970–1971; Devereux 1956, 1957).

Mythology

Mohave myths were extremely long and detailed, and the narrations were replete with details of name and place and trivial events. In general, they described the journeys of mythical personages and told of their eventual transformation into animals or landmarks.

In the Mohave cosmogony, Sky and Earth were male and female respectively. From them was born the deity *mataví·lʸə* who built a sacred house, the Great Dark House, where Mohave dreamers would later receive power. He offended his daughter, Frog Woman, who bewitched him, causing his death. *mataví·lʸə* was cremated, and the Great Dark House was burned, setting the precedent for future Mohave funerals.

A younger deity and culture hero, *mastamhó,* then assumed leadership and proceeded to put the land into shape, making the Colorado River and heaping up the sacred mountain, *ˀavì·kʷaˀamé,* where he conferred upon the unborn souls the powers of which they would later dream. *mastamhó* taught the people to speak, to get food, to cook in pottery; he also instituted the clan system and separated the various tribes. His work completed, *mastamhó* transformed himself into a fish eagle and flew away. Since *mataví·lʸə* and *mastamhó* no longer existed as divinities, the Mohave neither worshiped them nor invoked them in prayer. Other supernaturals were not numerous and did not figure prominently in Mohave myths (Kroeber 1925:770–775, 1948, 1972).

Shamanism and Sorcery

Shamans, who were believed to have received their power from *mastamhó* at the time of creation, had perhaps the most elaborate "great dreams" of any Mohaves. The Mohave shaman (*kʷáθ ˀidé·*) was typically a specialist, who had dreamed the power to cure only one or several kinds of illness, such as sickness attributed to contact with aliens, to "bad dreaming," to loss of one's soul, to witchcraft, to sickness caused by ghosts, to arrow wounds, or to the bites of rattlesnakes and other poisonous animals. The shaman's power to cure depended upon which portion of the creation myth he had dreamed, and upon which powers *mastamhó* had conferred upon him. When curing, the shaman would brush the patient with his hands, blow a spray of saliva over him, and sing the songs learned in his "great dream." See "Southwestern Ceremonialism," figure 2, this volume, for a shaman's pipe.

A shaman could cause disease as well as cure it. Mohaves were apprehensive that a doctor might become a witch as he grew older, being most apt to bewitch his own relatives, or those of whom he was fond, or to whom he was attracted, in order to segregate them in a special place as his "followers." There, he was believed to be able to visit them in dreams. A shaman was thought to be powerless to bewitch anyone who was "mean," or whom he hated or disliked. The Mohave distinguished between "fast witching," in which the witch shot power into a person, killing him almost instantly, generally at a public gathering such as a funeral, and "slow witching," in which the witch came to the victim in dreams and caused him to gradually waste away and die. Successful treatment of a bewitched person was possible if not too long delayed.

The shaman lived a precarious life, since if he were suspected of witchcraft, or if he lost too many patients, he might be killed. Usually, the braves were the witch-killers. Shamans are said to have met their fate with an accepting stoicism, sometimes even deliberately provoking people and inviting them to kill them. The reason for the shaman's indifference to death was that a special fate was believed to await him in the afterworld, but only if he died in a violent manner. If the death were too long delayed, his retinue of "followers" might be kidnapped by another witch, or if he died a natural death the souls of the bewitched were automatically released to pass on to *salʸaˀáytə,* the land of the dead (K.M. Stewart 1970, 1973, 1974a; Kroeber 1925:775–779).

Life Cycle

Mohave observances in connection with pregnancy and birth were of a simple and nonritualistic nature. But the period of pregnancy was significant to future life, since it was believed to be then that the "great dreams" first occurred, with the soul of the dreamer being impelled backward in time to the "first times." Also, the fetus was believed to have a conscious existence of its own, and it could cause difficulty for the mother if it were unhappy or angry.

The enculturation of the young Mohave was informal and gradual, and the parents were indulgent and permissive throughout the childhood of their offspring. Disciplinary methods were mild, and were mostly of an admonitory nature.

Children spent much of their time in play activities, many of which were in imitation of adult occupations. Education of the child was casual, and little pressure was put upon the children to acquire skills rapidly. Specific instruction was minimal, since in Mohave belief myths and songs were dreamed, and special abilities could be acquired only in dreams.

Puberty rites had only a feeble development among the Mohave. The very minor observances at the time of a girl's first menstruation were considered a private, family affair, and they were not occasions for singing, dancing, or public performances. For four days the girl was secluded in a corner of the house, remaining quiescent and eating only sparingly, while avoiding meat and salt. Each night she lay in a warmed pit. Her dreams at this time were considered significant as omens of the future (Wallace 1947a, 1948; Devereux 1950).

• DEATH PRACTICES In a society with few ceremonial occasions and a minimum of ritualism, the most important observances were concerned with death, specifically with the funeral (fig. 11) and the subsequent commemorative mourning ceremony.

When a death was believed to be imminent, friends and relatives would assemble and begin to sing and wail. As soon as possible after death had occurred, the deceased was cremated upon a funeral pyre along with his or her possessions. Funeral orators made speeches extolling the virtues of the departed, and song cycles were sung. The mourners wailed, the tempo increasing when the fire was lighted, and some then cast their own belongings into the flames. It was believed that, by burning, these things would be transmitted to the land of the dead along with the soul. The house and granary of the deceased were burned. There was a stringent taboo on mentioning the name of a dead person, and one of the greatest insults was to mention, one by one, the names of a person's dead relatives (K.M. Stewart 1974; Kroeber 1925:749–751).

The Mohave did not believe in eternal life after death. The ghost was believed to spend four days after the

top left, Calif. Histl. Soc., Los Angeles: Title Insurance Coll.: 1403; bottom left, after Densmore 1932; right, Mus. of the Amer. Ind., Heye Foundation, New York: 24580.
Fig. 11. Cremation. top left, Cremation of a Mohave leader. Wailing, funeral speeches, and songs preceded and accompanied the cremation, at which were also burned the combustible possessions of the dead and mortuary gifts from others (K.M. Stewart 1974). Photograph by Charles C. Pierce & Co., copyright 1902. bottom left, Construction of the funeral pyre, formerly of cottonwood and willow logs, but recently largely mesquite. right, Burial of the ashes in a pit beneath the pyre. Photograph by Edward H. Davis at Parker, Ariz., in 1921.

cremation revisiting the scenes of the events of its life, after which it went to *salʸaʔáytə,* the land of the dead, which was believed to be located in sand hills downriver from the Mohave Valley, near the peaks known as The Needles. Deceased relatives greeted the soul there, in a pleasant place where souls were believed to live on much as before death, but with no sickness, pain, or troubles, and always with plenty of watermelons and other good things to eat. Regardless of a person's behavior while alive, the soul went to *salʸaʔáytə,* with only a few exceptions, such as the victims of witchcraft, and those who died without having been tattooed, who were believed to pass down a rat hole at death. The soul did not live forever; eventually it died again and was cremated by other ghosts. After passing through a series of metamorphoses, the ghost ceased to exist altogether, ending up as charcoal on the desert (K.M. Stewart 1977).

A commemorative mourning ceremony was held subsequent to the funeral in honor of the death of prominent warriors or chiefs. The ceremony, which lasted for a day and a night, featured a ritual enactment of warfare. For hours 10 men, in war regalia, ran back and forth carrying ceremonial replicas of weapons. A funeral orator told of the death of the god, *mataví·lʸə* who had provided the first cremation. At dawn a large shade, which had been specially constructed to house the spectators, was set afire. The weapons were thrown into the flames, and the runners rushed to the river and jumped in, for purification purposes (K.M. Stewart 1947a; Kroeber 1925:750–751).

Sociocultural Situation in 1970

By 1970 little of the traditional Mohave culture remained, and the Mohave had been largely acculturated to the Euro-American way of life. Although pride in identity as Mohaves persisted among the people, many were apprehensive that the identity would be lost in the near future, as intermarriage with other ethnic groups became more common, and as Whites moved into Mohave territory in increasing numbers.

Even the Mohave language was lapsing among the younger people, although their elders still conversed in it frequently. Most of the Mohaves had attended school and were able to read and write in English.

The old mode of subsistence was gone; fishing, hunting, and gathering were no longer of importance. Some farming was still done, but with canal irrigation and the use of modern implements and techniques. Most of the food was purchased in grocery stores.

The old material culture had disappeared almost entirely. Craftwork was of negligible importance. The Mohaves were living in wooden cottages or modern houses of cement-block construction. The White styles of clothing alone were worn.

There had been no successor to the last chief, who died in 1947. Both reservation communities were governed by elected tribal councils with chairmen, under the provisions of the Indian Reorganization Act of 1934.

The clan system was being rapidly forgotten, and many people disregarded exogamy or did not even know their clan affiliations.

Belief in the Mohave religion persisted among some of the older people, although many Mohaves had been converted to Christianity, affiliating mainly with the Presbyterian, Nazarene, or Assembly of God churches. Some had resisted conversion, and some older Mohaves maintained that they believed in both the Mohave religion and the Christian religion and tried to equate them.

One elderly shaman still occasionally treated people on the Colorado River Reservation, although most people went for treatment to the government hospital. Some of the older people speculated about whether certain youngsters might have had the proper dreams for curing power, but had not yet "shown themselves." Older people, at least, continued to believe in witchcraft, and certain individuals were commonly suspected of being witches.

Marriage and divorce were conducted by legal methods, often through the tribal council, but marital instability was still rather common. Many Mohaves had been married more than once.

Native games were seldom played any longer. Few singers of the ancient song cycles were still living, and only a few older people remembered fragments of myths and folktales. It was doubtful that anyone any longer experienced a "great dream," although the Mohaves were still very much interested in dreams as omens. But the manifest content of the dreams had come to reflect contemporary conditions rather than the traditional Mohave culture.

Most Mohaves were still cremated on funeral pyres, to the accompanient of wailing. Some of the property of the deceased was still being burned, but houses were

top, Colo. River Tribal Lib.-Mus., Parker, Ariz.: BBB-14-823; center, Smithsonian, Dept. of Anthr.: 210,954.

Fig. 12. Beaded collars and belts. top, Cha-cha Cox (d. 1941), Irrateba's granddaughter, wearing an elaborate netted bead collar of the type that became popular in the late 19th century. center, Beaded collar. Netted openwork body of blue and white seed beads in fret pattern with drawstring neckline and fringe of strands of seed beads ending with large white glass beads. Depth 23.0 cm, collected before 1901. bottom, Flora Sands beading a belt at the home for the elderly on the Colorado River Indian Reservation. Photographed by Jerry Jacka, Nov. 1977.

no longer put to the torch. The commemorative mourning ceremony was no longer held.

Approximately 1,000 Mohaves were living on the Colorado River Reservation, and some 500 former residents of the Fort Mojave Reservation were living on the outskirts of Needles, California. A higher standard of living had been attained by many Mohaves during the 1960s, when it became possible to lease reservation lands to development corporations and large-scale farming operations. By 1970 most of the Mohave income was in wages and land-lease money, with a lesser income from farming (K.M. Stewart 1970–1971).

Synonymy†

The Mohave have generally been referred to by variants of their name for themselves, *hàmakhá·v*. Many Mohave speakers identify the syllable *ha-* with the word *ʔahá·* (or *há·*) 'water', but linguists have not recorded the apparent form *ʔahàmakhá·v* given as the "true Indian name" by Sherer (1967:2, 28–29, phonemicized), though explained as pronounced "so that it sounds as though it begins with an *H*." Some speakers give no literal meaning to this name, others translate it as 'people who live along the water' or relate it to an old word for the traditional grass skirt. The shortened form *makhá·v* is also in use (Pamela Munro, communication to editors 1974).

The translation of the name Mohave as 'three mountains' (Gatschet 1877–1892, 1:378; Hodge 1907–1910, 1:919) is a guess based on knowledge of the Mohave words *hamók* 'three' and *ʔaví·* 'mountain', but these words do not appear in *hàmakhá·v* and would in any case have to be used in the order *ʔaví· hamók* to give the meaning 'three mountains' (Sherer 1967:4; Pamela Munro, communication to editors 1974).

The earliest known recording of *hàmakhá·v* is as Amacava, 1605 (Escobar in Bolton 1919:28), later Spanish spellings being Amacaua, Amacaba, Amacabos (Sherer 1967:5–6, 29), and the Jamajab of Garcés, 1776 (Coues 1900, 2:443), and Jamajá of Font, 1776 (Bolton 1930, 4:484). The first recordings by English speakers refer to incidents in the late 1820s: Ammuchabas and Amuchabas, 1826 (Jedediah Smith), Mohawa (J.O. Pattie), Mahauvies, Mohauvies, and Mohavies (G.C. Yount as recorded by O. Clark), and Mohave (Christopher Carson as recorded by D.C. Peters; all in Sherer 1967:8–13, 30–32). Later forms are Mohahve (obtained by J.C. Frémont in 1843, probably from Carson), and in the 1850s Mojave, a Spanish or pseudo-Spanish spelling first used by Whipple (1941), 1853–1854, and found interchangeably with Mohave since (Sherer 1967:11–18). Other forms are given by Hodge (1907–1910, 1:921) and Sherer (1967). The spelling Mojave has been officially adopted by the Fort Mojave and Colorado River tribal councils; Mohave is used by the Bureau of Indian Affairs.

Related or borrowed forms of the name Mohave in other Indian languages include the following: Havasupai *wamk*^{h}*áv* (Leanne Hinton, communication to editors 1981); Walapai wa-mo-ka-ba (Corbusier 1923–1925) or wamaka´v^{a} or wamuka´va (Kroeber 1935:39); Yavapai makhava (Gifford 1932:182, 1936:253); Quechan *xamakxáv* (Abraham M. Halpern, communication to editors 1981); Maricopa xamākxa´va (Kroeber 1943:38) and *makxav* (Lynn Gordon, communication to editors 1981); Cocopa xam^{a}kxā´p (Kroeber 1943:38); Hopi 'amák'ăvă (Harrington 1925–1926). Other names are Pima-Papago *nakṣaḍ* or the English loanword *mahá·wi·* (Saxton and Saxton 1969:156), and the historical Spanish Soyopas, 1774 (Bolton 1930, 2:365).

†This synonymy was written by Ives Goddard, incorporating some references supplied by Kenneth M. Stewart.

Sources

The early Spanish chronicles contain rather meager descriptions of the Mohave. The best account of the Mohave in Hispanic times is that of Garcés (Coues 1900). The writings of the Anglo-American fur trappers in the early nineteenth century contain scant ethnographic information, since the trappers were little given to the observation of cultural details, and their encounters with the Mohave were often hostile (K.M. Stewart 1966).

For the mid-nineteenth century there are accounts of railroad explorers and steamboat captains, as well as Stratton's (1857) sensationalistic and in part inaccurate book on the captivity of the Oatman girls among the Mohave. And, from the Annual Reports to the Commissioner of Indian Affairs between 1865 and 1892 it is possible to glean a fragmented conception of the culture and conditions of the Mohave during the early reservation period. The nearest approach to an anthropological account of the Mohave during the nineteenth century was Bourke's (1889) article, based on a brief visit in 1886.

The basic and definitive ethnographic work among the Mohave was done by A.L. Kroeber between 1900 and 1911. His chapters on the Mohave (Kroeber 1925) remain the standard and most complete source on this tribe.

No phase of Mohave culture has been neglected by anthropologists, who have generally written articles on particular aspects of Mohave culture rather than comprehensive books or monographs. The few books on the Mohave include Devereux's (1961) work on ethnopsychiatry. Mohave subsistence is explained by Castetter and Bell (1951). The information in print on Mohave culture is actually rather copious, but it is widely scattered in many journals, some of which are relatively obscure and available only in large libraries with extensive holdings. The most important articles on the Mohave have been written by Kroeber (1925, 1948, 1972), Devereux (1937, 1950, 1951, 1951a, 1956, 1957), Sherer (1965, 1966, 1967), Fathauer (1951, 1951a, 1954), Wallace (1947, 1947a, 1948, 1953, 1955), K.M. Stewart (1946, 1947, 1947a, 1947b, 1957, 1965, 1966, 1966a, 1966b, 1968, 1969, 1969a, 1969b, 1970, 1970–1971, 1974, 1974a, 1977), and Spier (1953, 1955).

The best museum collections of Mohave artifacts are at the University of California Lowie Museum, Berkeley, and the National Museum of Natural History, Smithsonian Institution, Washington.

Maricopa

HENRY O. HARWELL AND MARSHA C.S. KELLY

The term Maricopa (ˌmărĭˈkōpu) applies to Yuman-speaking groups traditionally occupying locales along or near the Gila River and its tributaries in what is now southern Arizona. Culturally the people given the name Maricopa share much in common with both the Quechan and Mohave, underscoring common origins and sustained diachronic contact. Prominent shared traits included patrilateral or bilateral descent, emphasis on personal dreams, cremation, and floodwater agriculture. Maricopa material culture was essentially similar to that of the Quechan and Mohave.

Language

The Maricopa language is closely related to Quechan and Mohave, these three languages being generally classified as members of the River branch of the Yuman language family (see Joël 1964). The relationship with Quechan is particularly close in terms of mutual intelligibility, as many mature speakers of Maricopa will readily acknowledge. Maricopa also bears similarities to the Upland and the Delta-California languages of the Yuman family.*

Environment

Thrusting 3,000 feet from the Gila River's shimmering plain, the Estrella Range of the Sierra Madre Occidental forges a bold western skyline for some 372,000 acres shared by the Pima and Maricopa people of the Gila River Indian Community (fig. 1). Along the Estrellas' southern march, Montezuma's Head overlooks Maricopa Wells and a promontory known as Pima Butte. The mountains in this land are emblazoned in Maricopa thought. The northwestern flanks of the Sierra Estrella are dominated by a peak called 'berdache mountain' in Maricopa, recalling epithets hurled by opposing bands of Yuman warriors taunting each other to skirmish. On the Salt River Range to the east Coyote wiped his paw after eating the heart of Chipas (*čpa·s*), the culture hero, plucked from the funeral pyre at the Colorado River. The core of Maricopa land, at least since the early nineteenth century, was here in the Gila Valley circumscribed by these three landmarks and a fourth, called 'water divider', an outlier of the Sierra Estrella just west of the Gila-Salt confluence (Spier 1933:252–254).

Reverence for the majesty and mystery of these peaks remained strong in Maricopa during the 1970s: younger men, finding special routes into the higher and less accessible reaches of the Estrellas, returned to report fresh springs, mountain sheep, and treasure stashed by outlaws. Miners, they say, still keep the unwary at a distance with rifle fire. Lower, on the flanks and alluvial outwash, wild pigs may be sighted. Deer, rabbits, and quail populate lower ravines and washes near the riverbed.

Before its flow was impounded upstream and beavers eliminated along its channels, the Gila supported lush stands of cottonwood, cattails, and other riparian plant life that, in turn, fed waterfowl, turtles, fish, and crustaceans. Away from water courses, the Sonoran life-zone ecology favors xerophytes such as cactus, along with other tough, woody, and thorny survivors like mesquite, creosote, paloverde, and ironwood in the uplands. Dramatic thunderstorms, often driving rain mixed with blowing dust and sand, relieve summer temperatures that may approach 120° F. Winters are mild, allowing a growing season exceeding 260 days between killing frosts.

Territory

In this rugged country of rock and withering heat tempered here and there with soft green splashes and brown, the Maricopa people occupy two settlement areas amid the detrital plain cut by the Salt and Gila rivers. To the east, a community near the banks of the Salt River on the Salt River Reservation is often referred to as Lehi, after an area of Mormon farms north of Mesa. This locale is bounded visually to the north and east by the McDowell Range and, in the distance, the Super-

*The phonemes of Maricopa are: (stops and affricate) *p*, *t* (dental), *ṭ* (alveopalatal or retroflex), *č*, *k*ʸ, *k*, *k*ʷ, *q*, *q*ʷ, ʔ; (voiceless fricatives) *s*, *ṣ* (retroflex), *x*, *x*ʷ; (voiced fricatives) *v*, *δ*; (nasals) *m*, *n*, *n*ʸ; (laterals) *l*, *l*ʸ; (trill, or tap) *r*; (semivowels) *w*, *y*; (short vowels) *i*, *e*, *a*, *o*, *u*; (long vowels) *i·*, *e·*, *a·*, *o·*, *u·*. Primary stress falls on the last vowel of the root, regardless of what prefixes or suffixes occur.

Information on Maricopa phonology given here is from Gordon (1981:6–9) and the transcriptions of Maricopa words were furnished by Lynn Gordon (communication to editors 1981). Here *t* and *ṭ* are not distinguished.

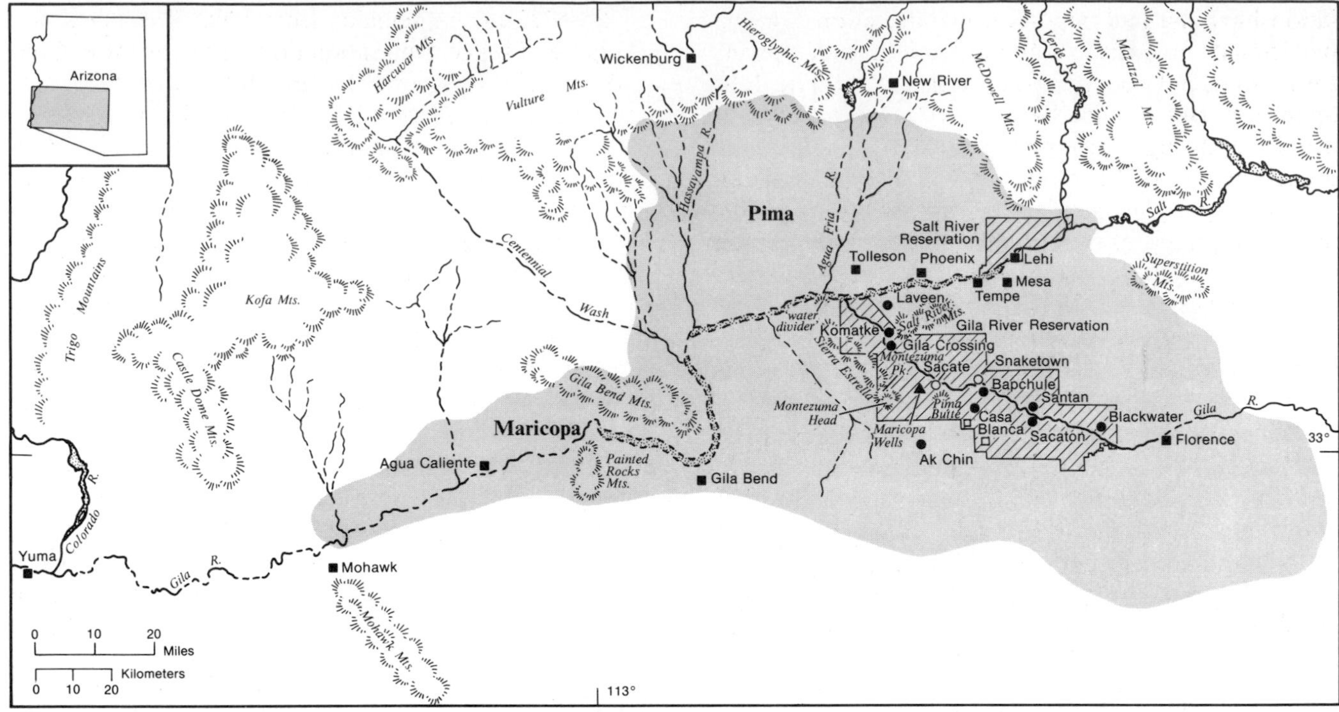

Fig. 1. Pima and Maricopa territory in the 18th century, and modern reservations.

stition Mountains. At the confluence of the Salt and Gila, southwest across the Phoenix Valley, a larger community in the shadow of the Sierra Estrella is usually referred to as Laveen after a small farm and trade center several miles east. Together the 1980 population of these settlements numbered about 700, not counting those who may live for periods in nearby urban centers, particularly Phoenix and Los Angeles, or elsewhere that careers may lead.

The Lehi people usually prefer the designation Halchidhoma (see M.C. Kelly 1972), referring to those in the Laveen community as *pi·pa·kveṣ* 'Western Maricopa'. Laveen residents simply call themselves *pi·pa·ṣ* 'people'. Although they constitute politically separate districts on their respective reservations, both communities share land and resources with their Pima neighbors, a reciprocity underscored through many years of intermarriage, political alliance, and mutual cooperation in work and warfare. Ties are maintained through frequent family visits and ceremonial activities.

These two reservation districts are but a pale reflection of the geographic range once known to Maricopa people and their ancestors. Prior to Arizona statehood in 1912, certain local groups stayed for a time at different locales along the Salt River, in areas as widely dispersed as Mesa, Tempe, and the southwestern edge of Phoenix, a distance of about 30 miles. Sites along Hassayampa River yielded the clays prized for pottery and black pigments, which were also collected from Vulture Mountain farther west. Seasonally, families relocated to the uplands north of Wickenburg to gather cactus fruit and hunt mountain sheep.

A sphere of joint military activity with Pima allies was remembered in the 1970s by Maricopa elders, based on the distance a scouting party could cover on foot in a day, not having to rest horses the following day before returning home (Harwell 1971–1978). From the Superstition Mountains on the east, the perimeter extended north to *k*^{w}*tn*^{y} ^{ʔ}*al*^{y} *x*^{ʔ}*ar* 'black racer's tail', a peak near New River, and to the west, well beyond the Hassayampa. Actually, this broad sweep of terrain merely defined an area equally available to Apache and Yavapai, who frequently penetrated it. The Mohawk Mountains marked the westernmost point of earlier territorial claims, known also to Papago groups as well as Quechan and Cocopa.

External Relations

Beyond this horizon, trail networks linked the middle and lower Gila overland to Halchidhoma and Mohave country on the Colorado. The connections were very old—perhaps predating Yuman people—and brought trade goods from the Gulf and Pacific coasts (Farmer 1935; Colton 1945). On the week-long journey to the delta country, for instance, Maricopas obtained the Paipai's ^{ʔ}*u·v ṣax* 'rotten tobacco' through the Cocopa.

Gila Yuman contacts throughout the trans-Colorado region are also reflected in a pattern of intergroup relationships that had important manifestations for local participants in terms of war and raiding, trade, alliance formation, and spouse acquisition. By the late 1700s Spanish horses provided an important object of trade, acquired through bartering captives gained in intergroup raids (Dobyns et al. 1957). This Yuman traffic may well have preconditioned the access that Cocomaricopas later exercised in carrying mail between Mexico City and California during the time of Mexican independence (Ezell 1968).

For Gila Yuman participants in this regional system, warfare defined a set of nominal allies—prominently Pima, Cocopa, and Halchidhoma—as well as foes—Quechan, Mohave, Yavapai, and Apache. Weapons and tactics used in war mirrored Quechan and Mohave customs, formally arranged pitched battles being fought with clubs. Engagements with Yavapai and Apache, on the other hand, relied upon quick strikes with bow and arrow (Spier 1933:162). Some writers (for example, Spier 1936:5) have taken these relationships of amicability and hostility to underscore the "national" character of the tribal groups involved. This perception was manifest in Hernando de Alarcón's report for the Gulf of California in 1540 that "they had warre and that very great, and upon exceeding small occasions" (Hakluyt 1969, 9:262).

Other discussants have since focused on material factors such as drought and food shortages in triggering raids and battles (C. White 1974; Stone 1981). This analysis may correlate low water stages on the Colorado and Gila with the periodicity of from four to six years in Maricopa initiatives, felt by them to be pre-emptive or defensive in nature (Spier 1933:160–163). Whatever the sources of these complex relationships, the American presence effectively terminated their military expression after the last major confrontation with the Quechan in the winter of 1857–1858 near Maricopa Wells.

Prehistory

The weight of scientifically accepted evidence indicates that the present Maricopa people are closely related to other Yuman groups living along the Colorado River, based on numerous cultural and linguistic similarities (Rogers 1945; Law 1961). Indeed, stories related by many Maricopas in Laveen tell of traditional life remembered first on the Colorado River describing their foods, their Yuman relatives, and the Chemehuevi, nearby Shoshonean speakers, in an otherwise uniform Yuman-speaking area. These tales include mention of difficult times on the river and a joint decision by their leaders to leave this region, resulting in a dispersion of people in several directions including California, the lower Gila River, and Sonora in Mexico (Sunn and Harwell 1976).

Post-Hohokam remains from Gila River sites near Gila Bend suggest migration there from the lower Colorado, possibly triggered by drought and other climatic conditions during the 1200s. The association of various ceramic styles in Hakataya sites west of Gila Bend led Schroeder (1961) to propose dual or even multiple occupancy of that area by culturally distinguishable groups. The groups involved have been identified as the historically known Opa and Cocomaricopa, but while these peoples may well be reflected in these archeological finds, conclusive material links to present Yuman groups remain elusive (see Breternitz 1957; R.G. Vivian 1965). It is also noteworthy that the current-day Maricopas do not accept these historical terms as applying to themselves and deny that these groups were Maricopa. Although it is not currently accepted as archeological evidence, some Maricopa also trace their ancestry to the Hohokam culture through the continued practice of cremation. Their Pima neighbors do likewise, based on farming practices and material items.

History

Maricopa history can best be approached by looking inside the Maricopa communities of today. These communities—really, several neighborhoods of ethnically diverse groups speaking a similar language—have melded into one with distinctions depending on "where you came from." Overall the Maricopa are one people for the purposes of identification by the various White-oriented governmental and provincial functions. Who the Maricopa are and how they came to be there are compelling issues, absolutely crucial to the Maricopa sense of peoplehood, their feeling for history and their destiny. For those old enough to know, the answers to these questions arise naturally from oral narratives recalling places known and events driving their ancestors onward. Within the community, each story charts one's lineage or family line.

As literature, these narratives generally are metaphorical and cyclical, classifying all events within a fourfold visionary framework spanning episodes of unity, strife, crisis, and resolution. Some accounts, though by no means all, agree that their people originated on the Colorado south of the Mohave; one joint account tells of a meeting of chiefs to decide to move the people, met with a ritual four days and four nights of dancing and feasting and then leave-taking (Harwell 1971–1978). Later, they found new homes along the Gila, in the Gila Valley, and finally in Laveen or Lehi.

The history of this amalgam of Yuman subgroups, drawn from the Halchidhoma, Kavelchadom, the Kahwan, and the Halyikwamai, starts before the earliest of White explorers and missionaries. What is known of this time can be reconstructed through migration accounts and also in part through fragmentary glimpses provided by early European contact in the region. Tracing the peoples represented in these terms suggests overall patterns of historical movement, generally from the Colorado onto the Gila starting perhaps in the late thirteenth or the fourteenth centuries (see Schroeder 1961; Spicer 1962:262–263). Micro-movements within these general patterns are, of course, much less easy to resolve.

Yuman communities have been known historically or reliably reported along the lower Gila River since the Jesuit explorations of Eusebio Kino and his associates, beginning in 1694 (Bolton 1919a, 1:127–129; Ezell 1963: 2). Settlements at their westernmost extent are noted just east of the Mohawk Mountains and were typically reported west to the vicinity of Agua Caliente. From Gila Bend upstream in this period, occupation is documented into the Gila-Salt confluence. Many recorded native names associated with these settlements seem to be of Piman origin, pointing to mixed settlements occupied by ancestors of today's Maricopa and Pima (Spier 1933:25–41; Winter 1973:69).

Although matching external group labels with those early contacts along the Gila is problematic it has been usefully resolved by Ezell (1963:19–26). Maricopa corresponds in a specific sense to Opa, living from earliest record in settlements upstream from the Painted Rocks Mountains. Since there are family lines without traditions of migration from the Colorado River area, this specific sense of Maricopa retains some utility. The designation 'Cocomaricopa' first referred to groups living along the Gila downstream from Gila Bend and Painted Rocks; these are the people called Kavelchadom by Spier (1933:25–41). The term Kavelchadom is also used to designate Yumans ancestral to the Gila groups living along the Colorado River south of Parker and the Mohave. Their migration traditions suggest that groups filtered out from the Colorado, leaving goods and seeds in pots for a new start cached in a cave inside a hill near present Poston (Harwell 1979:164–166).

At the beginnning of the nineteenth century the term Halchidhoma or its variants designated Yumans along the Colorado River south of the Mohave. After about 1825 some segments of these people relocated via the Mohawk Mountain district on the Gila to Magdalena, in Sonora. By 1840 Halchidhomas came to the Gila Valley near Sacate where, by this time, many other Yumans from the Gila Bend districts had also located (Spier 1933:12–16; Swanton 1952:350; Kroeber 1974: 69–76). Juan de Oñate's party in 1604–1605 had recorded a group, by name Halchedoma or Alebdoma, on the east Colorado bank south of the Gila confluence (Bolton 1916:276; Hammond and Rey 1953, 2:1021; Ezell 1963:9). This group name and position in the delta correspond with that of the Alchedomas reported to Kino in 1699 (Bolton 1919a, 1:195), south of Yumas (Quechan) and Cutganes (Kahwan). Jalchedunes were encountered 75 years later farther north on the river by Garcés (in Coues 1900, 2:443, 450), and one indication of ethnic continuity between the Halchidhoma populations is provided in those Kahwan families taking up residence near or with the Halchidhoma north of the Quechan (Kroeber 1925:801). In 1980, Halchidhoma were most closely associated with the Lehi community on the Salt River Reservation, but many individuals living at Laveen were of Halchidhoma ancestry also. Typically, those who refer to any connection with the Colorado area in their family ancestry are summarily dubbed Halchidhoma.

Descendant Kahwan families within the Maricopa community present a strong continuing tradition. Between 1820 and 1840 members of this group, with Halchidhoma families, had relocated into the Gila Valley area around Sacate–Maricopa Wells. As late as 1850 Kahwan in the Gila Crossing area were reputed to have an independent headman. Affiliated through intermarriage with the Kahwan are Halyikwamai, whose connections with them seem to stem from a much earlier period of joint residence in the delta area near the Quechan (Spier 1933:16–17; Swanton 1952:350–351, 353–354; Kroeber 1974:69–70, 75).

When Americans finally crossed the desert in force during the mid-nineteenth century, Pima and Yumans had already consolidated on the plain above Gila Cross-

The Huntington Lib., San Marino, Calif.

Fig. 2. Idealized view of a Maricopa village near the Gila River, looking south. The mountain range is almost certainly the Estrellas with Montezuma Peak to right. The Gila River, not shown, is to the left. The small clustering of houses seems accurate, but the domes were somewhat flatter and they were covered with river mud, especially around the base. The doors were generally oriented east and north to help block the afternoon winds. There is a ramada on the right and a large enclosure for animals in the background. The man is carrying a feathered lance, bow, and quiver. Two of the women carry Pima baskets, which were frequently obtained in trade. The women's skirts were probably thick fringes of willowbark strands (Spier 1933:95); the man's skirt is the artist's invention to cover his almost bare body, for he probably wore only a breechclout. Drawing by William Hayes Hilton, Oct. 1859.

ing. External pressure had a hand in bringing them there, through interaction among Spaniards, Apaches, and the Colorado groups. Here their mutual security was enhanced with the Sierra Estrella to their back, deflecting Apaches bound for Sonora to the Jornada, open country west of Maricopa Wells. Toward the Salt confluence (thick with mesquite), and beyond the river's great bend around the Estrellas and flanking ranges, Yavapais and Quechans might also be encountered.

By this time Gila Pima and Yumans showed many results of Euro-American contact, particularly in terms of material acquisitions. Besides cattle, horses, and mules (which Maricopa may not have then bred), wheat and possibly barley had become familiar items (Ezell 1961:33–35). Some Yumans spoke Spanish well, from travel and courier service in Mexico and California, even acting as interpreters for the Pima as need arose (Emory 1848:82; Bartlett 1854, 2:213; Ezell 1968:31–32). Hispanic contact is still reflected by a number of Spanish loanwords in the Maricopa lexicon.

Travelers among them noted few outward features to distinguish Pima settlements from those of Yumans in the 15–20 mile strip taken up near the Gila's southern channel (Bartlett 1854, 2:232–233). Yuman tracts ran for about five miles in the western portion short of Gila Crossing, their houses clustered amid fields and ditches. United States agents put their population under 500 during this time (table 1), but such counts may have focused on village sites and missed traveling Maricopa altogether.

As White Americans in increasing numbers secured their own presence in the Gila Valley, native populations experienced losses that may have exceeded those ever known through indigenous warfare. Epidemics of cholera struck in 1844–1845 followed by a three-year siege of malaria in 1866–1869, appearing in the autumn and winter. The malaria apparently exacted a heavy toll on children (Ruggles 1870). There were incidents of measles in 1871–1872 and 1898–1899, tuberculosis in 1882–1883, and smallpox in 1896 (Russell 1908:42–64; M.A. Cook 1976:188–189).

The spread of these diseases, unknown and unmanageable through customary techniques, triggered additional effects in local groups, as curers became increasingly suspect of causing disease through witchcraft or not trying honestly to save the patient (see Spier 1933:285; cf. Kroeber 1925:778–779 and K.M. Stewart 1973:320). Among the Pima, four medicine men were killed at Gila Crossing at 1844–1845 in conjunction with the cholera outbreak (Russell 1908:42–43). One attempt on the life of a man reputed to know cures for arrow wounds occurred among the Maricopa in about 1870 and remained an ideological component of community folklore in the 1970s.

American involvement in Pima and Maricopa affairs entered a new phase in 1859 when Congress created the Gila River Reservation. Following the American Civil War an influx of Whites increasingly drew water from the Gila for their own irrigation purposes near the new towns of Adamsville, settled about 1866, and Florence, founded in 1869 (Hackenberg and Fontana 1974). Coupled with natural low-water cycles, this diversion meant little water for Maricopa and Pima farmers downstream.

In the face of these pressures on their very existence some native people in the Gila Valley moved to areas where conditions were simply better. A number of Pima and Yuman families went northwest to settle along the Salt River east of Phoenix. Other families, mainly Yuman in heritage, relocated south of Phoenix along the Salt, while still others leveled and cleared arable tracts in the gently rolling, hummocky lands of the Gila-Salt confluence. The exact timing of these events is hazy; by 1879 the executive order setting aside Salt River tracts farther east added the northwestern sector to the Gila Reservation.

Table 1. Population

Date	*Population*	*Location*	*Source*
1680	2,000	Gila River	Swanton 1952:354
1742	6,000 Maricopa + Pima combined	Gila River	Venegas 1759
1775	3,000	Gila River	Garcés (in Coues 1900)
1859	472	Yuman settlements, with Pima, in Gila Valley upstream from Gila Crossing	St. John 1859
1870	382	same as above	Grossman 1873
1905	350	Gila River Reservation	Swanton 1952:356
1910	386	Gila River Reservation	Swanton 1952:356
1915–1922	297[a]	Gila River Reservation	Anonymous 1913–1922
1930	310	Gila River Reservation	Swanton 1952:356
1965	107	Lehi	Munsell 1967
1977	607	Gila River Reservation, District 7	Lewis 1977

[a] Includes approximately 35 persons receiving late allotments in Laveen.

left, Smithsonian, NAA: 45,856-A; right, Sharlot Hall Mus., Prescott, Ariz.: IN-M-604P.

Fig. 3. Maricopa hairstyles. left, "The interpreter of the Pimos, by birth a Coco Maricopas," shows male hairstyle of short bangs and rolls or braids down the back (Spier 1933:98). He wears a nasal ornament, which was usually "either a small fragment of sheep leg bone, ground to disk-shape and bored, or of blue shell" (Spier 1933:103). Lithograph from Emory (1848:opp. p. 82) after unknown original painted from life by John Mix Stanley, Nov. 1846. right, Maricopa woman. Photograph by Albert S. Reynolds, 1890s.

According to oral tradition, families filtered into the confluence area over a period of about 20 years. They came in small, related groups formed around two or three families, a habitual mode for fishing parties and gathering mesquite. Most of the last arrivals in the 1890s came because they were pushed in this direction by White farmers expanding their holdings outward from Phoenix. A few others may have come during this time or earlier from downriver near Gila Bend, where Papago groups had recently located (Harwell 1979:198–203).

Settling where land was ample to clear and irrigate, these families coalesced into several adjacent clusters or neighborhoods that retained distinct traces of their lineal and ethnic heritage rooted in Gila Valley locales. Halchidhoma lineages formed a primary core in one neighborhood, while lineage cores elsewhere reflected varied Yuman constituents of the Gila Valley settlements, including those who traced their line primarily to Sacate and Maricopa Wells. The sense of lineal continuity and collective identity, so vital in the Laveen community in the 1980s, derives from the neighborhoods of this nascent community.

Closer American involvement with Maricopa life began after about 1890 when a government stockman was in residence at the Laveen colony (Lumholtz 1912). A day school (fig. 4) was established around the turn of the century, as was the first Christian church, a Presbyterian one, built with community help near the stockman's hacienda between the spring of 1899 and the fall of 1900. Community members were first selected as elders from this Laveen congregation in 1902. At the Lehi Maricopa community a Presbyterian chapel was built in 1901 and its congregation organized in 1904 (Hamilton 1948:44–49).

These developments reflected federal government policy, but it was perhaps even more the local and regional response that rippled throughout the Maricopa community. In fact, Gila Valley Yumans had been conceptually integrating the Anglo-American incursion for a generation or more, a process reverberating particularly throughout traditional leadership specialties.

River Yumans enjoyed independence of action; Spaniards and Mexicans, in their dealings, gave out gold-tipped staffs and the title *capitán,* allowing local leadership to continue. United States agents, however, insisted on dealing with one individual acting for all the people. Since U.S. hegemony began, components of the Maricopa have been divided over which person should be designated as their "leader."

The Americans also recruited Maricopas for scouting parties in their Indian wars and later employed some

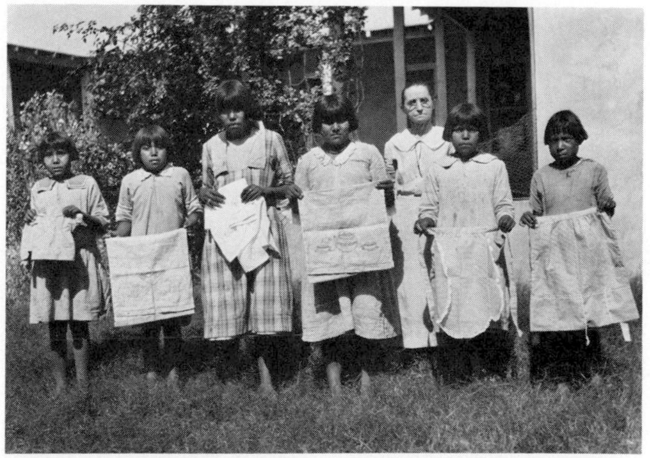

U. of Ariz., Ariz. State Mus., Tucson: top, 6520 x 10; bottom: 6520 x 1.

Fig. 4. Maricopa Day School in the Laveen community. top, Girls with their sewing. Ameila Linderman looks on. bottom, Student farmers. Photographs by Daniel B. Linderman, teacher at the school, 1924–1929.

of these men, for instance *č?or kʷes* ('Yellow Hawk'), to uphold their laws in the community itself and make sure that children got to school (Harwell 1971–1978). Ministers recruited Pimas and Maricopas to roles in their churches—elders, deacons, and translators.

These initiatives cut two ways, transparently aiming to create a new class of specialists to supplant the old. The whole area of leadership, in short, went through a period of upheaval that climaxed when traditional spokesmen among the Gila Pima and Maricopa—remembered in the 1970s as "Montezumas"—were jailed for holding out against White assignment of allotment tracts in community land after 1915 (see Spicer 1962:530–531; Hertzberg 1971:44–45).

Culture

The "Cocomaricopa villages" of Anglo reports were, in all likelihood, several neighborhoods, each formed locally around the houses of a few related families. A few cluster locales were probably associated with family groups or bands coming from particular geographic areas. The sites of these clusters constantly shifted, since an owner's house and belongings were burned after cremation and other residents relocated. Local groups also segmented with some frequency, so there was a state of flux throughout the Yuman zone. Internally, neighborhood "families" (as Maricopas in 1980 referred to them) comprised patrilineages grouped in a set of clans (*ṣimulʸ*) sharing certain symbolic aspects. Though nominal descent was traced through male ancestors, female links were often critical in establishing relationships. A woman's personal name typically derived from some quality of hers associated with an aspect of her clan; her husband's people could address her directly through the clan name.

Technically, clan exogamy meant that two persons from lineages in the same clan should not marry, but there were departures from this in practice. People married between clans but also, and perhaps predominantly, between local groups. Marriage and divorce were fluid arrangements, family genealogies typically reflecting serial marriage for both men and women. These practices interrelated people throughout the "Cocomaricopa" region during the nineteenth century.

During all but the coldest weather, Maricopas used brush-covered rectangular shades for shelter and work space. These ramadas generally adjoined houses, which like those of the Pima resembled a flattened dome supported by a rectangular frame laid across four stout mesquite or cottonwood uprights; encircling willow ribs bent overhead to meet the roof frame beneath an arrowweed thatch, packed with earth as were the banked walls (Bartlett 1854, 2:233–235; Spier 1933:82–87). Hence the Western Apache called the Papago, Pima, and Maricopa all 'sand-house people' (Goodwin 1942:86–87).

Maricopas built a number of other structures using similar materials and methods, including oval gabled structures excavated knee deep for keeping melons and pumpkins. Woven basket granaries, too, were half-buried on brush or raised to keep a household's grain stores dry and safe from rodents (Bartlett 1854, 2:234–236; Spier 1933:89–91).

Pottery (figs. 5–8) was made by women by using the paddle and anvil finishing method (Spier 1933:104–110). Vessels were in a wide variety of shapes with smaller forms being decorated with red or white clay slips or black paint made from woody portions of mesquite trees. Weaving was done by both men and women and included small blankets, cradle ties and bands (fig. 9), mens' headbands and belts, and girls' skirts worn during puberty rituals. Cotton was the only material used on both the belt and horizontal looms. Basketry, woven burden baskets made by coiling methods, and other items from native fibers were used, but many such ar-

U. of Ariz., Ariz. State Mus., Tucson: top left, 21188; top right, 21212; bottom left, 21207; bottom center, 21214; bottom right, 21216.

Fig. 5. Ida Redbird and her pottery. top left, Pulverizing and grinding dried local clay with a stone pestle. The clay is then screened and mixed with water and kneaded to the proper consistency. Shaping begins using the bottom of an old pot as a mold or anvil (top right) while the clay is beaten with a wooden paddle to the desired thickness. The sides of the pot are then built up with clay rolls. The pot is sun-dried briefly and shaped and polished with a smooth pebble. Next the pot is sun-dried thoroughly, turning it to prevent cracking. If the pot is a cooking or water vessel, it is now ready for firing. If the pot is to be decorated the bowl is covered with a red slip made from ground hematite, repolished (bottom left), and thoroughly sun-dried before firing. The pots are placed in a tin protector (bottom center) and fired with mesquite wood (bottom right). Any designs desired are then added, and after the paint has dried the vessel is fired again (Sayles 1948). Photographs by Edward B. Sayles, near Laveen, Ariz., 1940s.

ticles were traded from Pima makers. Slab grinding stones or metates and the handstone were made from granite or sandstone or taken from prehistoric ruins. Wooden mortars made by hollowing the end of a cottonwood or mesquite log and stone pestles were used to pulverize mesquite beans. Hides were rarely used but did provide tough material for sandles, shield covers, thongs, and quivers.

At puberty young women were secluded in circular, unexcavated huts of a type serving also as a woman's shelter during birth and as a warrior's purification site (Spier 1933:91). Small sweathouses, located near dwellings, had the same use of intense heat inside as larger meeting houses. Built at an elder's urging in the middle of their settlements, the meeting houses served as a focal point among men for community discussion and nonbinding decisions (Spier 1933:92, 158–159).

Daily life combined aspects of hunting and gathering with semi-intensive agriculture. Training of children centered around informal learning of adult family tasks, and endurance of pain was a trait valued in both girls and boys; to prepare them for war, boys were tested by killing bees while sitting near a hive. A public dance in a young woman's honor followed her first menstrual seclusion, and her face was then tattooed: the tattooing continued among some families well into the 1970s.

From the early 1800s on, Yumans in the Gila Valley integrated brush dams with ditch and lateral systems to grow a variety of crops including maize, wheat, beans, squash, and cotton. The climate permitted two growing seasons, harvests coming in May and June and in late October and November. This technology effectively displaced floodwater methods practiced earlier in the Gila Bend districts: it probably derived from residence near the Pima, who were then turning to agriculture for a greater share of their food (Winter 1973:70–75).

Much food, however, still came from resources provided by the land. Though within easy reach of home, Maricopa were frequently away to gather seeds maturing in late fall or early winter, and berries that ripened in May and June. From early July through August groups of women collected seed-bearing pods from mesquite trees, while men hunted or fished nearby, standing ready to protect the women. Several varieties of mesquite beans provided the primary share of caloric and protein requirements, supplemented by rabbits and other game and fish. Stripped from their pods and laid out atop roofs to dry, mesquite beans were then ground to flour for baked cakes (Spier 1933:48–53). For fishing parties or treks overland, the meal was mixed with water (often with parched, ground wheat) making pinole, a delicious and fortifying drink.

In work and war, ties internal to Maricopa localities and outward to Pima settlements provided a loose but apparently effective coordination for joint action. Within Yuman neighborhoods, a headman or *pi·pa·-vtay* ('big man') called men out to work at daybreak, announcing also public news from his rooftop; typically, ditch work was involved between adjoining tracts, since men cleared their own land individually.

Some men were assumed to be "subchief," "chief,"

a b c d

a, Smithsonian, Dept. of Anthr.: 9378; U. of Wash., Wash. State Mus., Seattle: b, 2-11880; d, 2-11935; c, Mus. of the Amer. Ind., Heye Foundation, New York: 24/3731; top right, U. of Ariz., Ariz. State Mus., Tucson: 21109.

Fig. 6. Painted pottery. a, Early utilitarian bowl, unusual in having black geometric designs painted on a red ground; however, it does lack the highly polished surfaces and thin walls common to later pottery made for the tourist market. A variety of sizes and shapes, including b, small bowl, and d, effigy pot, are made for sale. c, Long-necked vase, made by Ida Redbird, is one well-known form. Designs are primarily geometric in recent times, often inspired by prehistoric Hohokam patterns. A revival effort around 1936 encouraged improvement of declining quality and sought wider markets. Redbird was president of a short-lived pottery cooperative at that time. Pottery making never developed into a thriving family business; women continued to work alone at their craft. For a discussion of the development and changes in pottery shape and design see Fernald (1973). a, Diameter 32 cm, rest to same scale. a, collected by Edward Palmer in 1870; b, collected by Leslie Spier in 1929; c, collected in 1970; d, collected in 1924. top right, Design in mesquite sap being added to pot with a pointed stick applicator by Redbird; photograph by Edward B. Sayles, near Laveen, Ariz., 1940s.

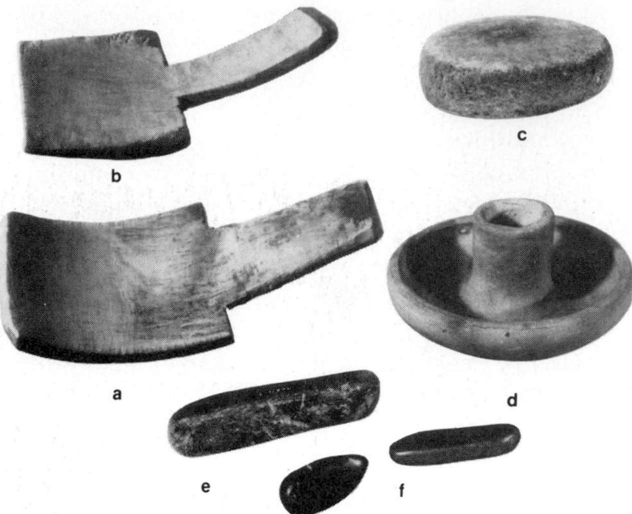

Yale U., Peabody Mus.: a, 19088; b, 19086; c, Smithsonian, Dept. of Anthr.: 317,606; U. of Wash., Wash State Mus., Seattle: d, 2-11909; e, 2-11905; f, 2-11907-8.

Fig. 7. Paddle-and-anvil technique pottery manufacture. a, Wooden paddle made from a barrel stave used initially to flatten the clay, forming a base and sides over a mold. b, Smaller triangular-shaped wooden paddle used to pat the surface, thinning the walls and erasing marks made by the larger paddle. Small bowls may be formed entirely over the mold, but larger vessels are removed and then turned over; coils are added to the rim to enlarge the pot. Anvils of a stone (c) or pottery (d), held inside the vessel with the potter's left hand while the outside is simultaneously shaped with the paddle (Fernald 1973:14–18). When completed the pot is smoothed with a stone (e), dipped in the water. After the slip has been applied further rubbing is done with polishing stones (f), resulting in the characteristic high gloss surface. a, Length 21.6 cm, rest to same scale. a and b collected by Leslie Spier in 1932; c, collected by Francis Densmore in 1922; d–f collected by Spier in 1929.

or "*capitán*" by Euro-Americans; for instance, Jose Juan and Francisco Dukey (Bartlett 1854, 2:213; St. John 1859). They probably acted as spokesmen, mediating between communities: in the 1930s a settlement near Maricopa Wells, *ṣa·k vʔaw* 'standing bone', was remembered as the primary chief's residence a century earlier, incorrectly rendered in Spanish as Huesa Parada. A few leaders such as Frogbeater and Dog's Paw, typically those connected with prominent lineages, were remembered in the 1970s for their military prowess.

Traditionally, leadership in Maricopa terms went beyond nominal chiefs (who exerted little authority) to recognized specialists who controlled several domains of knowledge and skill. In truth, the viability of living patterns emergent in the Gila Valley arose in no small measure through the callings of these traditional practitioners—curers, calendar-stick keepers, singers, and potters—who met needs shared by all; collectively they provided direction and coherence, a sense of place in the universe.

Through their calendar sticks and stories, certain elders told who the ancestors were, where they traveled, settled, fought, and died. As among the Pima and Papago, calendar sticks served the Maricopa as mnemonic devices to record year dates of significant events through special notches cut by the keeper of the stick; this feature allowed senior persons in the community to know their own birthdates precisely. Later, the staff itself could be purchased commercially (Spier 1933:138–142).

The nature of disease, curing, and personal prophecy was understood by the k^{w}*siδe*, a term encompassing different kinds of doctors and medicine men. Other

Fig. 8. Barbara Johnson making pottery by the paddle-and-anvil method. left, Rolling a piece of clay until it reaches a uniform diameter. right, The roll is placed on the rim and beaten with a curved paddle against a stone anvil until it merges smoothly into the pot body. Rolls are added until the desired neck shape is achieved (Spier 1933:107). Photographs by Jerry Jacka, Oct. 1977.

Mus. of Northern Ariz., Flagstaff: MS-118-5-28 and 29.

Fig. 9. Mary Juan demonstrating the making of a cradle band using commercial cotton yarn. The loom "consisted of four stakes driven into the ground, to which two warp bars were tied, parallel to each other and horizontal. The warp was laid directly over these bars" (Spier 1933:115). Designs, usually simple, indicated the sex of the infant. The specimen shown here was collected by Spier unfinished (Spier 1933:119). Photographs by Leslie Spier, 1929–1932.

ceremonial specialists built funeral pyres, led dances, and sang at public events including funerals.

Access to specialists as often as not was a function of kin relationships and kindred links extended throughout the neighborhoods of local communities. Patterns seem to have emerged from the recent past with more newly established neighborhoods having some kinds of specialists available but not showing all traditional skills in any one group. Hence, their calling brought them in contact with persons beyond the local group, providing another level of integration in Maricopa society. In difficult cases of sickness, for instance, close relatives might call out several *k*ʷ*siδe* from their respective neighborhoods, invoking appropriate kin relations between curer and patient.

Those who told history (whether through stories or calendar sticks) also compared their knowledge amongst themselves, a practice probably taking them beyond their local settlement. Singers, for their part, honored families through funeral performances, giving the songs "liked" by the deceased and calling upon the generations of ancestors already gone to the other world that lay to the west. Elaborate song cycles were associated with the *l*ʸ*ʔoṣ* 'buzzard', *xavčas* 'corn', and several other clans.

Because the deceased might have relatives in far places, a singer's repertoire included songs from throughout the Yuman network. Generally, most people could recognize which was a Mohave or Quechan song, if only through association with a clan known to be strong there. This suggests extensive learning and wide contacts extending beyond the Gila Valley; in Yuman theory, the songs all came originally through dreams although not necessarily to the singer of the moment.

The dream experience permeated the entire field of professional involvement, profound in guiding all Maricopas to special ability. Though apprenticeship and application might be a practical aspect in achievement, this in itself was no guarantee of recognition: "Everyone who is prosperous or successful must have dreamed of something. It is not because he is a good worker that he is prosperous, but because he dreamed" (Last Star, cited by Spier 1933:236).

Power to cure, bewitch, foretell the future, and sing ritual songs all came by dreaming, which could be induced. Even conception must be dreamt; bad dreams with blood as an aspect, on the other hand, figured as a common cause of illness. Spirit familiars in dreams were most often birds; the mockingbird (*k*ʷ*ṣila*) gave skill in oratory and battle. Other animals, insects, mountains, or stars were also the spiritual powers imparting knowledge or skills. One potter, for instance, saw designs on the walls of a room beneath the Colorado, and these became her seal; a man is remembered for his dreams or vision of *čmδu·l*ʸ 'black ants' that covered the ground and bespoke White influence.

Prestige in all roles was associated with social maturity and experience. Shamans, for instance, became highly valued after a period of associating with one or more mature guides to learn cures for diseases and specific wounds, providing they had their dream experience. In alerting other groups to the need for joint

left, Ariz. State U., Ariz. Histl. Foundation, Tempe: Barry Goldwater Coll.; right, Smithsonian, NAA: 52,544.

Fig. 10. Juan Chivaria (Xantapacheria, Kingfisher's Beak), a war leader and shaman (k^{w}*siδe*). left, Seated in center wearing striped tie and surrounded by men who served in the all-Maricopa volunteer unit in the Civil War, photographed about 1865; right, portrait wearing a turban, photographed about 1869.

action, word was sent via an older spokesman, a man of recognized oratorical skills. Since oratory involved formal linguistic devices not found in everyday speech, the role required inborn talent, skill, and practice. Spier's informant Kutox (remembered as a work boss) lamented that for an old man being too old was no good. This principle applied widely throughout Maricopa society as older people lost personal vitality and were not listened to seriously.

Sociocultural Situation in 1980

Reservation roads, ditches, and allotment boundaries mark off potential sites for homes, disrupting older neighborhoods. Federally subsidized frame and cement block houses have displaced homes of the old style. A few Pima-style "sandwich houses" packed with adobe between slats and upright timbers are to be seen, along with stucco homes built around 1900. Surplus structures brought from nearby federal facilities and the Japanese internment camps of World War II provide additional house styles, along with increasing numbers of mobile homes.

Most Maricopas no longer farm, gather, or hunt, being drawn instead to wage work offered off-reservation or to getting by on a combination of lease money, retirement, and social security payments. Children attend schools outside the community, usually in one of three state-run elementary institutions in the nearby towns of Tolleson, Laveen, and Lehi. Some children attend a well-respected Roman Catholic school at Saint Johns near Gila Crossing. Few Maricopas attend the Bureau of Indian Affairs Indian School in Phoenix, although in the past many children were sent there or to Esquella in Tucson or to California after completing their training in the local day school.

In 1980 none of these schools had active language maintenance or culture programs in place, although a community college near the Lehi community had optional courses of this nature. Sporadic attempts have been made to utilize Maricopa-based teaching materials in Sunday school and community-run educational programs. A few Maricopas had progressed beyond high school to college, the training often being ministry-related. Many elders had good technical grounding in several trades.

These signs of heavy acculturation were matched with numerous indicators of cultural continuity. While most food was purchased, many women prepared fry bread for bake sales and special observances. Several Christian churches were connected to preallotment neighborhoods through their congregational affiliations. Cultural continuity was certainly manifest in the importance of dream-invoked experience. Elders continued to have certain prerogatives until their vitality waned. Many aspects of lineage organization were to be found, perhaps most strikingly in the concept of history as a social property, to be shared cautiously with outsiders. Clans were not openly discussed.

Contacts continued in force throughout the Gila-Colorado River drainage, in the forms of annual camp meetings, choir practices for Christians, and funerals. Visits to relatives were frequent. Personal achievement, once proved through physical endurance, seemed transformed in part to getting experience in the outside world. Intergroup competition had a clear analogue in the athletic events regularly scheduled among Maricopa, Pima, and Apache teams.

Politically, the Maricopa communities were chartered as separate districts in the Gila River Reservation and Salt River Reservation governments. Their representatives, respectively, one and two, were distinctly in the minority, yet voting stances of District 7 (Laveen) and District 6 (Gila Crossing) were often aligned. At Laveen, a council of elders essentially directed the administrative component of the tribal government that was located there. Although the required representative forms were present, the Maricopa Colony still maintained as its own decision-making process community meetings attended by mature members; this body had as an advisory group the Maricopa Resident Board, which acted for the community when larger meetings were unfeasible.

In the areas of economic development and health severe problems exist. Irrigation water is of insufficient quantity since the allocation was based on the amount of land cleared in the early twentieth century. The water is too alkaline for domestic gardens, being suited only to cash crops such as alfalfa and cotton (Resident Board Meeting Minutes 1981). The lack of domestic water hookups is a significant factor in a plethora of bureaucratic obstacles to acquiring additional housing.

Health-related problems were especially acute for the elderly. Medical services tend to shuffle them between distant points where they must endure limited service or long waits for doctoring and advice that is often inapplicable to their living situation. Lower limb amputations were common, owing to diabetes-related circulatory problems.

Robberies and assaults on the elderly, even in their own homes, seem to be without previous parallel but were reminiscent of assaults on shamans during the nineteenth century once their powers were suspected of misuse or ineffectiveness. The current phenomena are often directed toward elders who have no kin to protect them or who are living in an isolated reservation area. This is a matter of some concern to community leadership and is thought to be an internal problem that some reservation conditions have stimulated.

U. of Ariz., Ariz. State Mus., Tucson: 31724.

Fig. 11. Key punch operators in a business in which the Gila River Indian community tribal government has controlling interest. Photograph by Helga Teiwes, 1972.

Synonymy†

The name Maricopa first appears in the reports of the Kearney expedition of 1846 (Ezell 1963:20); it is an English abbreviation of the name Cocomaricopa, first used by Father Eusebio Kino in the 1690s (Bolton 1916:444; Ezell 1963) and the standard Spanish designation subsequently. Although this name appears to be of Yuman origin it has not been recorded in any Yuman linguistic materials and hence has no determinable etymology. Guesses and folk-etymologies based on the shortened form Maricopa clearly have little value (Harrington 1908; Spier 1933:6). The earliest record in English may be the Cocomarecopper of Pattie (1833); Hodge (1907–1910, 1:807) lists other variants, mostly miscopyings and the like. Garcés, 1776 (Coues 1900, 1:113–114, 123), equated the Cocomaricopas with the Opas, also on the Gila River: "the Opa nation, or Cocomaricopa, which is the same;" "this Opa or Cocomaricopa nation, which is all one." After Garcés the name Opa appears to be no longer used (Ezell 1963:12), but earlier sources locate them as a distinct group upstream (east) of the Cocomaricopa (Spier 1933:36–37).

The Maricopa call themselves *pi·pa·ṣ* 'the people'.

The names for the Maricopa in Mohave (*hačpa ʔanʸa*) and Quechan (*xatpá· ʔanʸá·*) appear to mean 'Eastern Pima', though this is not geographically accurate (Pamela Munro and Abraham M. Halpern, communications to editors 1981); apparently the same expression appears in Cocopa xačupa´nya´ (Kroeber 1943:38). The Pima-Papago name is *ʔÓʔobab* (Saxton and Saxton 1969:78). The attested Apache, Navajo, and Yavapai names are general terms covering the Pima-Papago as well as the Maricopa, and sometimes other River Yumans: Western Apache *sáíkįhné* 'sand-house people' (J.B. White 1873–1875a; Philip J. Greenfeld, communication to editors 1981); Navajo Bĕ Ĕsá Ntsái 'those with large jars' (Curtis 1907–1930, 1:138); Yavapai Widge´-e-te-ca-par´ (J.B. White 1873–1875) and táxpa (Gatschet 1877–1892, 3:98). A Yavapai name Atchihwá for the Maricopa alone is given by Gatschet (1877–1892:123).

†This synonymy was written by Ives Goddard, incorporating some references from Marsha C.S. Kelly and Henry O. Harwell.

Incorporated Groups

Halchidhoma. This name first appears, as Halchedoma, in accounts of Juan de Oñate's expedition of 1604 (Zárate Salmerón in Bolton 1916:276); Garcés appears to be mistaken in his statement that the name Alchedum was used in accounts by associates of Francisco Vásquez de Coronado in 1540 (Coues 1900, 2:488). Garcés himself used Jalchedun, pl. Jalchedunes (Coues 1900, 2:443, 450), other Spanish spellings being Halchedunes and Galchedunes (Bolton 1930, 5:332, 375) and Chidumas (Escalante in Garcés in Coues 1900, 2:474). Miscopied forms are Hud-Coadan, 1764 (Nentvig 1980:17, 72), Alebdoma (Hammond and Rey 1953, 2:1021), and others in Hodge (1907–1910, 1:36) under the heading Alchedoma (cf. Kino in Coues 1900, 2:544). The spelling Halchidhoma is Kroeber's rendering of the Mohave name (Hodge 1907–1910, 1:36).

The names recorded for the Halchidhoma in Yuman languages are: Quechan *xa·lʸcaδu·m,* perhaps 'those who turned or faced far off in a different direction' (Abraham M. Halpern, communication to editors 1981); Maricopa *xalʸčδu·m* (Lynn Gordon, communication to editors 1981), Cocopa xalsiyúm (Kroeber 1943:38).

Halyikwamai. The name Halyikwamai first appears uncorrupted, as Jalliquamai and Jalliquamay, in Garcés's report of his 1775–1776 journey (Coues 1900, 2:434, 443); earlier miscopied or garbled forms of this include Agalec-qua-maya, 1605, and spellings like Talliguamays with initial Tl- or T- for J- (Hammond and Rey 1953, 2:1021; Hodge 1907–1910, 2:340). Garcés gives Jalliquamay as synonymous with Quiquima (Coues 1900, 1:176), a name used in the earlier Spanish sources (Hodge in Coues 1900, 1:176–178, with variants). In the earliest account mentioning the Quiquima, that of Hernando de Alarcón in 1540, the name appears as Quicama, Chicama (an Italianization), Quicoma, and Quicana (Hammond and Rey 1940:140, 141, 142, 150). Hodge (1907–1910, 2:340) discusses this group under the name Quigyumas, evidently an imperfectly transmitted form of the name, perhaps contaminated by the name Yuma (Quechan).

The recorded names for the Halyikwamai in Yuman languages are: Quechan *xalʸí· kʷaʔamáy* 'upper *xalʸí·*' (Abraham M. Halpern, communication to editors 1981); Maricopa xelyi´kuma´i (Kroeber 1943:38); Cocopa łi'kwa'ama´i (Kroeber 1943:38) or *xàlʸkʷmáy* (James M. Crawford, communication to editors 1981). The element *xalʸí·* in the Quechan name is reminiscent of that of the Haglli (phonetically [axlʸi]?) reported to be neighbors of the Tlalliquamallas (i.e., Halliquamai), though upstream from them, in 1604 (Zárate Salmerón in Bolton 1916:276).

Kahwan. The Kahwan are first mentioned in Alarcón's 1540 account as the Coana, Coama, Coano, and apparently Cumana (Hammond and Rey 1940:140, 141, 150, 153–154). Garcés used the form Cajuenche, 1776 (Coues 1900, 2:443; Hodge 1907–1910, 1:187), and Cajuenes also appears (Bolton 1930, 5:375). The Coahuanas visited by Juan de Oñate in 1604–1605 were mistakenly identified with the Quechan by Hodge (1907–1910, 2:1010), though correctly equated with the Kahwan in the general synonymy (Hodge 1907–1910, 2:1045). Other names given by Hodge in the Quechan synonymy that actually refer to the Kahwan are: Cetguanes; Cuatganes; Cueganas; Cutcanas (Nentvig 1863:25, 1894:132), which appears in a later edition as Cuhanas and Cuhuanas (Nentvig 1980:17–18, 72); Cuteanas and Cutganas (Kino in Coues 1900, 2:551), clearly Kahwan from the context; Cutganes and Cutguanes, both from citations of Kino in secondary sources; and the garbled Octguanes (Hodge 1907–1910, 2:1010–1011).

Spier (1933) used the spelling Kohuana, and Kroeber (1943) used Kahwan.

The names recorded for the Kahwan in Yuman languages are: Quechan *kʷaxʷá·n* (Abraham M. Halpern, communication to editors 1981); Cocopa *kxʷa·n* (James M. Crawford, communication to editors 1981); Maricopa *kʷxʷa·n* (Lynn Gordon, communication to editors 1981), given as kaxwā´n, sg. kahwe´n, by Kroeber (1943:38–39).

Kavelchadom. The Kavelchadom are not known historically under this name. Discussions of whether they may be included under the names Opa, Cocomaricopa, or both, are in Spier (1933:25–41) and Ezell (1963). Spier (1933:9) introduced the spelling Kaveltcadom, describing them as "a hitherto unrecorded people . . . living west of the Maricopa" whose name meant 'west or downriver dwellers'; in this spelling the -tc- represents an obsolete phonetic notation of the sound [č] (normal English ch). This name is cognate with Quechan *kavé·lʸ caδóm* 'those who turned or faced into the south (literally, downstream)', the name of one of the three sections of the Quechan. Kroeber (1943:38) used the spelling Kavelchadhom and gives the Kahwan name as inyéhčiyum. Maricopa has *kvelʸčδu·m* (Lynn Gordon, communication to editors 1981).

Sources

Spier's (1933) work concentrated on reconstructing culture among the Maricopa prior to the American period. Castetter and Bell (1951) dealt more exclusively with agriculture and subsistence, their fieldwork following Spier's by about a decade in the Laveen community. Spier (1936) and Drucker (1941) summarized culture element traits. Drucker's findings remain extremely useful in comprehending culture area development, especially in detailing linkages between adjoining areas.

Glaringly absent are thorough-going descriptions of the Maricopa as they were at the time of research. This gap can be partially remedied by recourse to Spier's fieldnotes (at the Museum of Northern Arizona, Flagstaff) in comparison with Forde's (1931) Quechan ethnography. The extensive works published by Dobyns et al. (for example, 1957, 1963) and by Ezell (1963) deal with critical historical issues. Field research prepared for the Indian Claims Commission case (Fontana 1958; Hackenberg and Fontana 1974) provides extensive and valuable documentation for earlier periods. Additional historical surveys have been conducted in connection with the transmission line for a nuclear generating station at Palo Verde (Woods 1980). M. C. Kelly's (1972) research at the Lehi community focused scholarly attention on historical issues with contemporary implications. Similarly, community formation in the late preallotment period has been examined by Harwell (1979).

Field research in culture and language since the early 1960s provides good data, typically for restricted domains (for example, Frisch and Schutz 1967). Alpher's (1970) fieldnotes were circulated privately among an intent group of Yumanists awaiting fresh data for Maricopa. Gordon's (1981) thesis marks the first comprehensive treatment of Maricopa syntax. Fernald (1973) and Chenowith (1976) provide good detail on developments in Maricopa pottery, as do the collections of the Heard Museum in Phoenix.

The situation probably relates, in part, to the skill that Maricopas have in regulating outside knowledge of their culture. Field research by single investigators with a small number of informants remains a continuing problem. Maricopa social organization, for instance, remains incompletely understood, especially with regard to other communities in the Yuman network. Critical in this regard would be detailed biographical information. The social use of language and culture-linked semantics remain fertile areas for future research among the Maricopa.

Quechan

ROBERT L. BEE

Language and Territory

The Quechan (kwə'chän), also popularly known as Yuma, are linguistic members of the Yuman subfamily of the Hokan family.*

The Quechans' reservation lies near the confluence of the Gila and Colorado rivers (fig. 1), their aboriginal territory now divided between the states of California and Arizona. Unlike the tribes of the Plains and the East in this country, these people have not been moved out of their home territory by the whims of federal Indian policy or the pressure of White settlers. Older Quechan can still, if they wish, glance to the north at the looming thumb of Picacho Peak as they recall legends about spiritual encounters around its summit. Yet it is not known when the ancestors of these people first settled near the river junction. No group of that name was mentioned by the first European into the area, Hernando de Alarcón, who passed through on his way to a meeting with Francisco Vásquez de Coronado's expedition in 1540. The earliest specific reference to the Quechan appeared in Spanish documents of the late seventeenth century. By then they were settled in the confluence area, as well as to the north and south along the Colorado and east along the Gila.

The Quechan themselves tell of a southward migration of their ancestors from a sacred mountain, *ˀaví·kʷamé·* (Newberry Mountain, located north of the modern community of Needles, California). They had been created there, along with the Cocopa, Maricopa, eastern Tipai, and Mohave, by Kwikumat (or Kukumat; *kʷakʷamá·ṭ*), who later died from sorcery worked by Frog Woman, his own daughter (Forde 1931:214). Anthropological evidence points—tentatively—to an accretion of small, probably patrilineal, bands into larger "tribal" groups between the thirteenth and eighteenth centuries, a trend fostered in part perhaps by group proximity during horticultural activities on the river bottomland, by linguistic affinity, and by the effects of warfare (see Forbes 1965:36 ff.; Steward 1955:159–161).

Culture

This account of traditional Quechan culture is based on conditions existing between 1780 and 1860. During this period the Quechan were sporadically subjected to Spanish, Mexican, and Anglo influences of varying intensity; undoubtedly this modified some of the earlier, precontact patterns of behavior.

Subsistence

The people were primarily growers and gatherers rather than hunters (Forde 1931:107, 118). The forbidding desert terrain immediately beyond the rivers' floodplains yielded little game for a relatively high labor output, so the productivity of growing or gathering plant foods was much greater. Forde (1931:115–116) was unable to estimate the ratio of gathered to cultivated plants in the Quechan diet but concluded on the basis of Spanish reports that horticulture was "no mere accessory" to gathering. Castetter and Bell (1951:238) estimated that the proportion of cultivated foods in the aboriginal diet of Colorado River Indians ranged between a low of about 30 percent for the Quechans' southern neighbors, the Cocopa, to a high of about 50 percent among the Mohave, their friends to the north. But no estimates were made for the Quechan themselves. There were occasional crop failures when the Colorado-Gila overflow was not so extensive as usual, and there was some danger of late flooding, which would destroy the sown fields (Forbes 1965:189; Castetter and Bell 1951:8). But all in all, in early postcontact times the flooding of the river and the richness of silt left after the waters receded made food growing a relatively low-risk enterprise with high potential yield.

The Quechan were able to seed some of their fields several times during the year. A little maize and some

*The phonemes of Quechan are: (voiceless unaspirated stops and affricate) *p, t, tʸ, ṭ* (retroflex), *c* ([c] ~ [č]), *kʸ, k, kʷ, q, qʷ, ˀ*; (voiced spirants) *v* ([β]), *δ*; (voiceless spirants) *s, š, x, xʷ*; (voiced laterals) *l, lʸ*; (voiceless laterals) *ł, łʸ*; (nasals) *m, n, nʸ, ṇ*; (trill) *r*; (semivowels) *w, y*; (short vowels) *a, e, i, o, u, ə*; (long vowels) *a·, e·, i·, o·, u·*; (accent) v́ (high falling tone, except before another accent, where it is high tone; usually accompanied by stress). Initial glottal stop contrasts with initial vowels, which are pronounced with preceding aspiration.

Information on Quechan phonology was obtained from Halpern (1946–1947, 1:25–33, 2:150; Abraham M. Halpern, communication to editors 1981), based on studies of the language in the late 1930s. Innovations in the phonology of the language as spoken in the 1970s are described by Langdon (1977).

melons were planted in February and were not dependent on the natural irrigation provided by the river (Forde 1931:109). Clearing the brush from the main fields began immediately prior to the spring flooding, and the year's major planting took place when cracks appeared in the surface of the postflood silt deposits, usually in July. The people first planted teparies, maize, and watermelons, then black-eyed beans, pumpkins, and muskmelons (Castetter and Bell 1951:149). In the fall the Quechan sowed winter wheat to be harvested just prior to the spring floods.†

In addition, the people planted the seeds of wild grasses on less fertile portions of land. The harvested seeds were ground into meal and baked or dried into cakes.

Care of the planted fields was not a particularly demanding or time-consuming chore. Wheat was not weeded. Teparies were weeded once during the growing season; maize, pumpkins, and black-eyed beans were weeded twice. Members of an extended family might cooperate for the weeding chores. Men were usually responsible for the heavier phases of the work, like clearing away the brush from the fields, digging the planting holes, weeding, and gathering the harvest. Women sowed the seeds and stored the harvested foodstuffs. This division of labor was by no means a strict one, however; and women could help in any of the agricultural chores they wished to (Bee 1969).

The chief sources of wild food were mesquite and screw-bean pods (Castetter and Bell 1951:179), with the former being the more popular and more resistant to drought. The people crushed mesquite pods in a mortar to remove the sweetish-tasting pulp, the only part of the pod that was eaten. The pulp could be dried, then ground into flour and mixed with water to form cakes that would last indefinitely. The crushed pods could also be steeped in water to make a nourishing drink that, with fermentation, could be mildly intoxicating (Castetter and Bell 1951:185–186). Mesquite and screw bean were always important portions of the diet and were probably the main source of nourishment when there were crop failures or during the lean times between harvests. The mesquite trees were not considered private property unless they grew close to a family's shelter; however, there was a tendency for families to return to the same grove each year to harvest the ripe pods. Castetter and Bell (1951:187–188) provide an extensive list of other wild plant foods utilized by the Quechan and their riverine neighbors.

†Watermelons, black-eyed beans, muskmelons, and wheat were postcontact introductions. Forde (1931:110) mentions that in Alarcón's 16th-century account of peoples of the lower Colorado, wheat and beans were not among the crops then being grown. Heintzelman's (1857) detailed report does not mention wheat as a cultigen. Thus, to the extent these reports are accurate, wheat was popular for no more than 200 years and may have been introduced by Father Eusebio Kino, in 1702 (Forbes 1965:124).

Settlement Pattern

The Quechan recognized themselves as a single tribal group but were geographically separated into a series of settlements or rancherias (see Spicer 1961:12–14) scattered north and south of the confluence along the Colorado and east along the Gila. Forde (1931:map 2) places the northernmost Quechan rancheria on the Colorado some 20 miles north of the confluence, although Quechan living in 1966 noted that some of their tribesmen (called collectively "the Blythe group") moved into the confluence area during the last half of the nineteenth century from a rancheria in the Palo Verde valley some 60 miles to the north. The southernmost extent of settlement was probably the rancheria *xuksílʸ* during the ethnographic baseline period. Quechan rancherias were encountered by the Spaniards as far as about 26 miles east of the confluence, along the Gila. Settlement west of the riverine floodplain was limited by extensive sand dunes. The exact number of rancherias existing during the baseline period is not known. Forde (1931:map 2) lists the locations of four "village sites"; Bee's informants named six locations that they believed were in existence in the late nineteenth century (fig. 1).

Geographical arrangement of components of the rancherias shifted during the year, which adds to present difficulties in pinpointing past locations. Extended family groups in each rancheria dispersed to locations

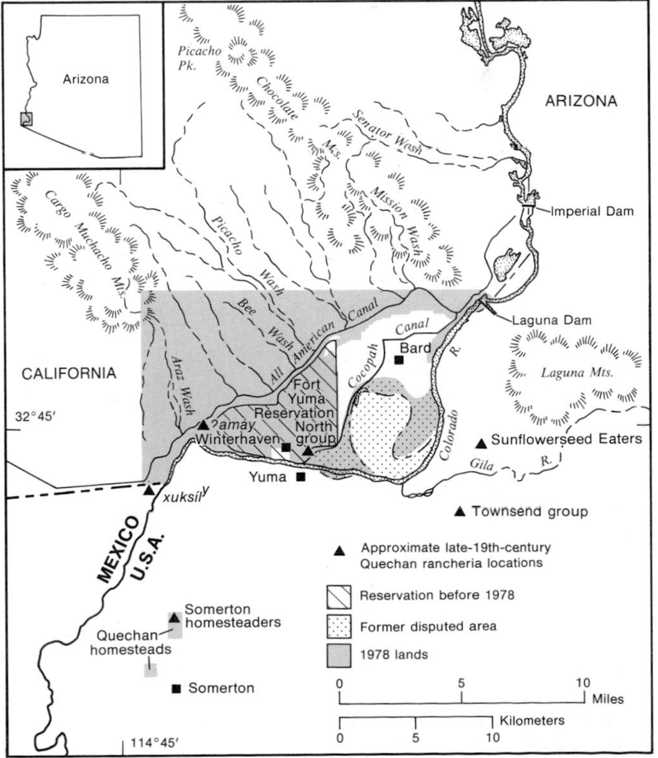

Fig. 1. Central area of Quechan settlement in the late 19th century and reservation in 1978.

close to their bottomlands during spring and summer farming seasons. The families drew together again on high ground, away from the river, during the winter and spring flood periods (Bee 1963:209). Also, the high ground locations of the rancherias themselves apparently shifted up and down both banks of the rivers at irregular intervals: Spanish journals reported an absence of Quechan on the Gila in 1774–1775 (Forbes 1965:127; Forde 1931:100). Patrick Miguel (1950:4), a gifted Quechan who was one of Forde's informants, wrote of groups moving north and south along the Colorado during the nineteenth century in response to food shortages and conflicts with Mexican and Anglo military units. One such movement was witnessed by Heintzelman (1857:36).

Several hundred people lived in each rancheria. The largest, *xuksíl*^{y}, had a population estimated at over 800 by Spanish observers in 1774 (Forde 1931:101). Those living in the same rancheria considered themselves to be related, and, while the "tribal" orientation was strong (Forde 1931:140), they probably felt that their own rancheria group was somehow superior to the others (Bee 1963:209). The rancherias were agamous—that is, a man was free to seek a mate from either his own or a different rancheria—however, in practice there may have been a slightly higher frequency of marriages between persons belonging to the same rancheria (Bee 1963:209–210).

These major groupings were in turn composed of extended family households, whose membership was probably augmented by individual adults (usually related to the family) having no place else to live. Ideally, residence after marriage was with the man's family, but in fact the newly married couple often moved in with the woman's family; thus the residence pattern is best described as bilocal. The extended family household was the basic cooperative unit of subsistence. It was not

Calif. Histl. Soc., Los Angeles: Title Insurance Coll.: top, 3517, bottom, 3522.

Fig. 2. Quechan houses. top, Dome-shaped arrowweed house to right and ramada to left. bottom, Earth-covered house, usually occupied by the most important leader of a rancheria. Photographs possibly by Charles C. Pierce, about 1900.

uncommon for several extended families to pool their labor for the more demanding agricultural tasks of clearing land, weeding, or harvesting (Bee 1969; cf. Castetter and Bell 1951:140). The families lived under ramadas or in dome-shaped arrowweed shelters near their fields during the farming season, then moved into arrowweed shelters or camped under ramadas on high ground (Forde 1931:120). In each rancheria were one or two large shelters covered on three sides with earth; the front was walled with posts and horizontal slats, between which arrowweed was stuffed. These shelters were typically occupied by the rancheria leaders' families but could accommodate a small crowd in extremely cold weather (Forde 1931:122). The rancheria leaders dispensed hospitality from these earth-covered shelters, and climbed up on their rooftops to address the assembled community.

The geographical dispersion of the households within rancheria groups was thus closely correlated with the condition of the rivers and the technology of riverine agriculture. The threat of enemy attack may also have been a factor, particularly in the eighteenth and nineteenth centuries. If the Quechan patterns of warfare in all aspects closely paralleled those reported for their close allies, the Mohave, then Fathauer's (1954:98) observation that the Mohave assembled for large war parties "after the harvest" may be most relevant (see also K.M. Stewart 1947). It was at this time that the rancheria families were less dispersed and thus perhaps less vulnerable to surprise counterattack by the enemy. Forde's (1931:162) informants mentioned attacks on villages rather than isolated extended families in major war expeditions.

The bilocal extended family household seemed an optimal unit of agricultural exploitation; it provided a cooperating work force large enough to lessen the amount of heavy individual labor, yet small enough to reduce conflict over personal versus group economic interests. The bilocal pattern indicated that the family was as flexible as possible in incorporating new members for the labor force.

Property

Given the apparent functional importance of the extended family, it is difficult to account for the report that the farm plots themselves were individually owned by males. Individual ownership is even less understandable in view of the fact that these lands were not inherited by kinsmen upon the death of the owner but were instead abandoned, perhaps in later seasons to be used by nonkinsmen (Forde 1931:114–115). The family of the deceased usually sought replacement plots from among the bottomlands not then being utilized by others. Castetter and Bell's Mohave and Quechan informants recalled that extended family holdings were demarcated by reference to terrain features in the reservation period, and that "usually there were no individual boundaries within this larger area" (1951:144). This was probably typical in the prereservation period as well. In view of these conditions, it seems safest to assume, with Castetter and Bell (1951:144), that "land ownership was little formalized." This conclusion, coupled with the pattern of abandoning plots at the death of a family member, implies that during the prereservation period land was not a particularly scarce resource among the Quechan, even though occasional interfamily brawls erupted over the precise locations of family plots (Forde 1931:114–115).

In fact, the inheritance of any sort of material property was probably never a source of conflict in prereservation times. This is because all possessions of the deceased (including the family home) were destroyed or given away by kinsmen in an attempt to erase the painful reminders of the person's existence. Often this left the surviving kinsmen in destitution, and they were provided for by friends and rancheria leaders until they could recoup their losses.

Perhaps in part because of the noninheritance pattern, the people did not show much interest in the accumulation of material goods beyond the immediate needs of the family group or the surplus maintained by local leaders to provide for impoverished families within their rancheria. Family groups often donated a portion of their harvest to the leaders for eventual redistribution. There were no marked gradations in wealth, a condition fostered by the mourning practices as well as the social pressure in favor of sharing of one's abundance with others who were less fortunate (Bee 1966; see also Forde 1931:137).

Technology

Forde (1931) and Trippel (1889) describe the material culture in some detail. In general the Quechan were not preoccupied with technological or decorative elaboration beyond the demands of minimal utility, although Trippel (1889:575–576) was favorably impressed with the painted geometric designs on late nineteenth-century pottery (fig. 3). Their arrows, propelled from simple, unbacked bows, had relatively weak penetrating power, made weaker when used (as they frequently were) without points. Sharpened staffs served as digging sticks, or, when cut in longer lengths, as weapons.

Clothing and Adornment

Neither males nor females wore much clothing: two-piece aprons (front and rear) made of the inner bark of willow were the standard female dress; males frequently wore nothing. In cooler weather members of

Smithsonian, Dept. of Anthr.: left, 5509; right, 76,179.

Fig. 3. Painted pottery. left, Water jar with red horizontal stripes on buff ground. right, Red bowl with black geometric designs on exterior and interior rim and cord wrapped around neck. Used for squash or mush. Diameter of right 27.5 cm, both collected by Edward Palmer, left in 1867, right in 1885.

both sexes carried firebrands for warmth (Forbes 1965:49) or wrapped themselves in rabbitskin robes or blankets obtained in trade with the Hopi.

Males were particularly proud of their long hair and alternately rolled it in long rolls (fig. 5) treated with mesquite sap or plastered it with reddish mud. Both sexes liked to paint their faces with yellow, red, white, black, or green pigment (Trippel 1889:565). Males daubed light pigment over their entire body (fig. 6) for warfare. Men often had their nasal septum perforated, as well as their ear tissue, for the attachment of bits of decorative shell or beads. The warm climate and lack of precipitation made substantial housing unnecessary for most of the year. The relatively few earth-covered lodges were apparently adequate for winter quarters. Clearly in this milieu of fairly low food-production anxiety, the emphasis was on other than the material aspects of the Quechans' way of life.

Social and Political Organization

• KIN GROUPS The Quechan recognized a series of patrilineal clan groupings whose past importance and functions are not entirely clear. The clan name was borne only by females; and each had linked with it one or more "namesakes" (as Forde's informants described them) or totemic associations (for example, corn, frog, red mud, red ant, moon, coyote, rattlesnake). The clans were once exogamous units and may have been informally ranked in importance: both Forde (1931:142) and Bee (1961) were told that *xavcá·c kʷacá·n* was the leading clan. There is a suggestion that some of the clans functioned as units in the mourning ceremonies (Bee 1963:217; cf. Forde 1931:145). Clan membership did not necessarily correspond to rancheria affiliation,

Smithsonian, Dept. of Anthr.: a, 152,697; b, 325,194; c, 325,193; d, 325,182; e, U. of Ariz., Ariz. State Mus., Tucson: 23055 x 6.

Fig. 4. Clay figurines, which may once have had a ceremonial function but in the 19th century were already being sold to tourists (Trippel 1889:576). They are usually dressed in traditional style although some recent examples show modern clothing. Wigs of either human or horse hair are glued into a depression at the top of the head (see drawing) and held in place by string wound around the head. Seed beads are added around the neck and through pierced ears. Painted designs represent body painting and tattooing. a, Male in red flannel breechclout secured with blue thread has extensive body patterns painted in red on white. Blue and white beads are threaded through ear holes and blue beads serve as the typical necklace. Legs are always straight and stiff but b and c show some of the variations in arm position. (Both probably have lost bead necklaces because of neck breakage). The female has fiber back skirt and red and blue yarn front with red cloth overskirt. The male wears red cloth breechclout and light blue and gold earrings ending with red yarn tassels. Both have black tattooing lines on chin, minimal red body paint, typical incised mouth and large eyes outlined in black. d, Baby in cradleboard complete with fiber blankets and black and white plaited band binding it to cradle. Female figures are made in more positions than males, including holding pots or children (Kaemlein 1954–1955). e, Child carried in distinctive manner on the skirt bustle. a, collected by Edward Palmer in 1890–1891; b–d collected by Frances Densmore in 1922; e, collected by Herbert Brown 1895–1913. Length of a 23 cm, rest to same scale.

although some coincidence was reported in the Sunflowerseed Eaters rancheria near the Gila in the late nineteenth century (Bee 1967:218). This is to be expected given the fact that the rancherias were agamous, residence was ideally patrilocal, and clan affiliation was patrilineal.

Some clan names are either alien or make reference to alien groups, and others may have originated in groups like the Mohave, Maricopa, or Tipai-Ipai (Forde 1931:142–143). Forde (1931:146) reported that there was nothing to indicate the clans developed out of a series of localized lineages. Yet evidence cited at the beginning of this chapter could be used to support the assertion that the Quechan clans were once small, relatively autonomous local groups that became merged into the tribal group at the expense of their formal

top, Calif. Histl. Soc., Los Angeles: Title Insurance Coll., 3471; bottom, Smithsonian, NAA: 2793-a.

Fig. 5. Quechan hair styles. top, Billy Escallante with traditional rolled hairstyle. Photograph possibly by Charles C. Pierce, 1890s. bottom, José Pocati wearing a nose ring and turban. Photograph by Alexander Gardner, in Washington, Oct. 1872.

Smithsonian, NAA: 56,961.

Fig. 6. Young boy with elaborate body paint, multi-strand bead necklaces, and a breechclout over a yarn or bark twine girdle, covered with a trade kerchief. Photograph by E.A. Bonine, 1870s.

Mus. of N. Mex., Santa Fe: School of Amer. Research Coll.

Fig. 7. Pau-vi, Polly, with chin and cheek decoration, probably painted, and painted stripes on her hair. Photograph by Ben Wittick, about 1880s.

functional importance. In the 1960s, clans were still regarded as exogamous units; but, particularly among the younger Quechans, one's own clan affiliation was not always known, and past clan functions were largely forgotten.

• THE TRIBE The Quechan tribal structure became apparent in large-scale war expeditions against the neighboring tribes, when the relevant structural principles were sex, skill in the use of a particular type of weapon, and "Quechan" (rather than rancheria or clan) affiliation (see Gearing 1962 for the "structural pose" concept). There were also annual tribal harvest celebrations in which members of all rancherias would gather for feasting and visiting, each family contributing food or labor. And almost every year there were large tribal mourning ceremonies in which the ceremonial roles were assigned on the basis of sex and kin-group affiliation (Forde 1931:221 ff.; Bee 1963:217). What structural units comprised "the tribe" at any given time was thus in part a question of what sort of activities "the tribe" was engaged in.

Smithsonian, Dept. of Anthr.: 325,202.

Fig. 8. Ornament of red, white, and black braided horsehair hung as a charm on a child's neck to stop excessive drooling and insure strength and rapid growth. Length 27 cm, collected by Frances Densmore in 1922.

• LEADERSHIP Spanish and Anglo sources consistently reported the existence of two tribal leadership statuses, one (*kʷaxóṭ*) for civil affairs, the other (*kʷanamí·*) for war. Forde's account (1931:133 ff.) accepts this dichotomy, but how accurately it reflects the traditional Quechan situation—as distinct from one imposed by foreigners accustomed to executive hierarchies—is not clear. Abraham M. Halpern (personal communication 1981) feels that the *kʷaxóṭ* was most likely the kind, generous embodiment of spiritual power described by Forde (1931:135), but that his role in handling civil affairs was not particularly influential. Likewise, the *kʷanamí·* is consistently described by Quechans themselves as an extremely brave and skillful warrior, but it is not clear that he was preeminent in tactical or strategic decision-making.

Each rancheria had one or more headmen (sg. *paʔi·pá· taʔaxán* 'real person' or 'genuine man'), who probably not only handled the bulk of the leadership responsibilities in each rancheria but also met in council to resolve issues of tribal concern (Forde 1931:139). Leadership statuses tended to remain in "eminent" families, but only so long as other, more important criteria were met by candidates (Forde 1931:136). The authority of the local headmen was extremely circumscribed by public support, and they held their statuses only so long as they were able to demonstrate their competence to do so. Important matters at either the rancheria or tribal level were always decided by consensus, sometimes after long debates dominated by the better and more forceful speakers.

The primary criterion of leadership was competence, and competence in turn stemmed from personal power bestowed by special types of dreams. The candidate for a leadership status quite literally dreamed his way into office. A group of elderly men listened to a candidate's accounts of his dreams, then decided on his qualification for office. The power of a leader's dreams had to be continually manifested in his success in handling practical matters, however; the "right" dreams alone were not enough to secure his status (Forde 1931:137).

The proper sorts of dreams were also prerequisites to other achieved statuses in Quechan society: for singers, speakers, and curers. Other individuals reckoned the success or failure of proposed undertakings on the basis of dreams.

Warfare

Much of the Quechans' attention and energy centered upon warfare. Accounts of battles and reenactment of battle tactics permeated their myths and rituals, and war was considered an essential source of the tribe's life stuff, spiritual power. In some aspects it seemed atypical of the almost nonchalant organization and execution of other community activities (Forde 1931:161–162). For example, in some of the larger war expeditions, the lines of battle were arranged roughly according to the various warrior functions: the first group behind the leader were the spearmen and clubmen; behind them, the archers; horsemen armed with spears comprised a third group (when horses were available); and there was a rear element of hefty Quechan women bearing stout staffs to finish off the enemy wounded (Bee 1961, 1967:16; Forde 1931:167).

The Quechan distinguished between two sorts of warfare: the war party ("going to the enemy") and the small raiding party ("waking the enemy"). The raid was conceived as a surprise attack, not necessarily to kill but to stir up mischief and maybe to steal some horses or captives. Usually these raids were launched from individual rancherias by a group of younger men who grew restless for action. The larger parties were tribal affairs, launched ostensibly for revenge against losses suffered at the hands of the enemy. At times these encounters were rather like brutal team sport: prearranged appointments for combat, agreement of types of weapons to be used, one side delaying the attack until the other side drew up in battle formation, exchange of a series of insults with opponents before closing with them, and other acts (Forde 1931:162 ff.).

Warfare was probably incessant but usually not very costly in lives among the combatants. Often one side would break off the conflict if it looked as though too many of its men were being lost; however, there were occasions when the battle continued until one side had been all but obliterated. The last such clash is said to have occurred in 1857, and the Quechan were the losers (Forde 1931:163–164).

The Cocopa and Maricopa (who sometimes were allied with the Pima) were the major enemies. Quechan allied themselves frequently with the Mohave in striking out against the tribes to the east of the Colorado, and they were good friends with some of the Sand Papago groups (Castetter and Bell 1951:58–59).

It is possible that warfare among the riverine peoples increased in both scale and intensity during the eighteenth and early nineteenth centuries (Forbes 1965:134). The factors seem to have been economic: to gain captives for trade to Spaniards or other tribes for horses or other goods. If so, then Forde's statement (1931:161) that there was no economic motivation in Quechan warfare must be qualified. During this period the Mohave and Quechan pushed the Halchidhoma out of the broad river valley near Blythe, California, and availed themselves of the fertile bottomlands in the area (Forde 1931:103). The Quechan later abandoned this area and moved southward to lands closer to the confluence. Elsewhere, along the Gila to the east and the Colorado to the south, the Quechan showed no particular desire to seize and occupy the land of their enemies. Again, the inference is that population pressure on available farming land was not particularly severe.

Smithsonian, Dept. of Anthr.: 325,203.

Fig. 9. War club for close combat, of solid hardwood with head painted black. The leather thong, threaded through 2 holes in the handle, was looped around the wrist and the sharply pointed tip was jabbed in the opponent's stomach. When the victim doubled over the club was brought up and the broad end was smashed into his face (Forde 1931:170). Length 37.5 cm, collected by Frances Densmore in 1922.

Mourning

Commemoration of the dead was another concern of the Quechan, ranking along with patterned dreaming and warfare in the emphasis it received in their traditional lifeways. The tribal mourning ceremony, *karʔúk,* was performed usually after an important leader had died, or when there had been an accumulation of deaths of other persons whose families wished to dedicate a ceremony to their memory.

Like the rituals of many societies, the *karʔúk* was a microcosm of the Quechan way of life in its totality. An important element of the ritual was a sham battle, including all the tactical steps of a real foray against the enemy. It was at the same time a reenactment of the original *karʔúk* staged after the death of the creator, Kwikumat. Corn, one of the staples of the Quechan diet, was sprinkled liberally at intervals to serve as a purifying element. Tasks were assigned according to the ideal sexual division of labor and perhaps on the basis of clan affiliation. Older men, some of whom had dreamed of their ritual role (Forde 1931:204), assumed important leadership functions.

It was also in effect a second funeral for the deceased, complete with copious wailing, destruction of property and ritual paraphernalia at the climax of the rite, and the cremation of elaborately dressed images as representatives of the dead (the making of images may have diffused in about 1890 from the Tipai-Ipai—Forde 1931:221). The *kar?úk,* like the war party, required organization and coordination relatively more elaborate than that of the usual extempore pattern described by Forde, although it was certainly more flexible than ceremonial arrangements among groups like the Pueblos.

History

The Quechans' territory at the confluence of two major rivers was of major strategic importance to the Spaniards, Mexicans, and Anglos in the eighteenth and nineteenth centuries. It afforded the most logical crossing for soldiers and settlers moving between California and points to the south and east. Most of the Spanish efforts among the Quechan were thus aimed at ensuring their friendliness, and to this end a leader (Salvador Palma) and three other Quechans were wined and dined in Mexico City in 1776–1777 (Forbes 1965:177). Spanish Franciscan priests were perhaps the most familiar contact agents at that time and were fairly well accepted by the Indians even though the priests persistently condemned the aboriginal patterns of polygyny and shamanism (Font 1951:201–208).

Near the close of the eighteenth century, the Spanish decided that the most effective way to consolidate their interests in the crossing was to establish two settlements near it, occupied by farm families, four priests, and a small detachment of soldiers. What had theretofore been a generally amicable, if intermittent, relationship between two cultures became increasingly hostile as the settlers turned to Quechan fields for food and forage for their cattle and Spanish discipline by the lash made the Quechan recalcitrant hosts (Forbes 1965:175–220). The Indians finally destroyed both settlements in 1781, killed the priests and some others, and abruptly ended Spanish control of the crossing. Spanish and, later, Mexican military and civilian expeditions passed through the area, but it was not until the mid-nineteenth century that alien influence was permanently reestablished among the Quechan. After one unsuccessful try, the United States Army in 1852 built a small garrison, Fort Yuma, on a bluff near the confluence. The fort served to ward off Indian attacks against Anglos streaming into California.

The commanders of the garrison were generally content to let the Quechan live their lives, so long as they remained peaceful. The first commandant, Maj. Samuel P. Heintzelman, deposed one Quechan leader for attacking the Cocopa (Heintzelman 1857:46) and later appointed a man, Pasqual (fig. 10), who enjoyed the status of "tribal chief" for the next three decades.

The fort's presence assured the growth of steamship and railroad travel through the area, and with it the emergence of a small town on the opposite side of the Colorado from the garrison. Quechan men found work as laborers on the steamships or in town, and Quechan women worked as domestic help in the increasing number of Anglo homes. By 1884, when the government established a reservation for the Quechan on the west side of the Colorado, the Anglo town of Yuma had become a flourishing transportation center, and Anglo settlers were becoming increasingly envious of the Quechans' farm plots on the fertile bottomlands. In 1893 the Quechan were persuaded to sign an agreement that would limit their holdings to five acres for each person living at that time (a local application of the Dawes

Smithsonian, NAA: 53,564.

Fig. 10. Pasqual, a principal leader (perhaps the last *k*ʷ*axoṭ*) from 1854 until his death in 1887, with nasal pendant and wearing a military coat over his breechclout; his walking cane leans in front. At his sides are possibly L.J.F. Jaeger and his wife, who were proprietors of a store and ferry boat at Yuma, Ariz. The 2 men in the background are not identified. Photographed in 1870s.

Natl. Geographic Soc., Washington.

Fig. 11. The "Yuma Indian Band," with Quechan and non-Indian members in pan-Indian uniforms. Its successor, the Quechan Indian Band, in 1981 included Quechan, Mohave, and other Indians. Photograph supplied by the Yuma, Ariz., Chamber of Commerce in Nov. 1927.

Severalty Act of 1887). The remainder of the land was to be sold at public auction. The Quechan have vigorously challenged the legality of this document for years, charging that it was made under duress and that the government never fulfilled its terms. The agreement nevertheless served as partial justification for financial charges levied against the tribe for irrigation systems, water usage, and other goods and services (Bee 1969). After prolonged negotiations between the tribe and Department of the Interior solicitors, 25,000 acres of the original 1884 reservation were restored to the tribe in December 1978 on the grounds that the agreement's conditions in fact had not been fully met by the government.

The reservation was finally allotted in 1912, with each person receiving 10 acres instead of the five originally dictated by the 1893 agreement. In the interval, a dam had been built on the Colorado upstream from the reservation, reducing the annual floods and yearly deposits of silt. The Quechan children were being educated in a government school created from the old Fort Yuma buildings (the facilities were transferred to Department of the Interior in 1884). By the time of the allotment, most of the people had abandoned their outlying rancherias and had moved into the area of the reservation. Only one small group of Quechan "homesteaders" remained to the south (fig. 1), outside the reservation boundaries (Bee 1981:48–84).

By the 1920s and 1930s, farming was no longer a lucrative vocation for most Quechans. They had by then become wage earners in nearby Yuma, serving as laborers or domestic help; or, they lived on the money received from leasing their allotments to farmers. A government agricultural development program of the late 1920s did not appreciably alter this economic pattern, and during the depression of the 1930s the Quechan suffered along with communities of unskilled wage-laborers elsewhere. Between 1884 and 1965 the Quechans' land holdings shrank from the 45,000 acres of the original reservation to slightly over 8,000 acres, much of it unproductive (Bee 1981:48–84).

The proper sort of dreams were an irrelevant criterion for the government's selection of community leaders very early in the twentieth century (although some Quechan may still have considered it important for leaders they themselves recognized as legitimate). It may also have lingered as a requirement for certain singers, speakers, and curers. Government "papers" of certification became a crucial prerequisite for "official" tribal leaders, and the government was at best inconsistent in granting such validation. It was perhaps inevitable that political factions would form around would-be Quechan leaders and their kinsmen-followers in the resulting power vacuum. Factional squabbling scuttled the attempts to form tribal representative bodies, even when both the Quechan and the government wanted such organizations. Between the early 1890s and 1936, there was no Quechan who enjoyed unequivocal leadership status (Bee 1981:48–84).

Under the provisions of the Indian Reorganization Act of 1934, the Quechan narrowly ratified a tribal constitution and elected a seven-man tribal council in 1936. The act also provided for the ratification of a tribal business charter, but the Quechan have never voted to become a chartered business corporation. The tribe's police force and court were abolished in 1953, when Public Law 83-280 transferred local law enforcement responsibility to the state of California (Bee 1981:88–119).

In the 1940s and 1950s, the tribal council's primary concerns were the economic development of the tribe

Natl. Arch., Washington: 75-N-Colr.-4.

Fig. 12. A man using a disk harrow in a field on the Ft. Yuma Reservation, Calif. His hair is in the traditional rolled style. Photographed in 1940.

and a favorable solution to various reservation boundary disputes. In 1940 the council drew up an agricultural development plan to bolster family farming on allotted land, but the federal government did not respond. The reservation remained in the economic doldrums. In the boundary disputes, the council's attention focused on a large portion of rich bottomland lying on the west bank of the Colorado near the confluence with the Gila. This tract was exposed in 1920 by a sudden eastward shift of the river channel. The reservation's eastern boundary was described in relation to the river channel, without further description of the location of the channel itself. The Quechan reasoned that if the river moved, so did the eastern boundary, and the bottomland should belong to the tribe. The government waffled on the issue, and in the meantime non-Indian families moved in and established substantial farming operations. This made an amicable solution of the issue all the more difficult (Bee 1981:88–119).

In 1960, frustrated by the delay of government officials in resolving the dispute, the tribal council unilaterally reconstituted its tribal court and police force and blockaded access roads into the disputed territory. Tribal members manned the blockades and demanded toll payments from non-Indian drivers wishing to enter the area. Tempers flared, the Quechan voluntarily disarmed themselves to prevent violence, and after five days the blockade was lifted. The land was not restored to the tribe by this action, but by 1970 the tribe had taken a long-term government lease on the tract and the non-Indian farmers were moving out. In 1973 the Quechan again blockaded a portion of land (this time to the west of the reservation) whose ownership was being contested between the tribe and Imperial County, California. That issue was resolved by the 25,000-acre restoration in 1978.

By 1966 the Quechan found themselves in the midst of a series of federal anti-poverty and community development programs. Some of their plywood prefabricated homes, obtained from the government after World War II, were being replaced with new cinderblock houses built by the Quechan themselves. The reservation received a new water system, a community action program including public health and preschool education facilities, a credit union, and several different vocational rehabilitation projects. The vocational projects were especially popular with the people, who were feeling an acute need for employment (the average yearly family income in 1965 was estimated at less than $2,000 for 150 of the reservation's 180 families) (Bee 1970:156). There were problems in the administration of some of the development programs (Bee 1969a, 1970), but in 1969 the programs' material impact on the reservation itself was most evident. The effect on the life-styles of the people was less apparent.

By 1974 the tribe had launched two on-reservation farming operations that offered the potential for significant and permanent income for many of its members. One was a hydroponic tomato and cucumber farm; the other, a farm that included 600 acres of the leased bottomlands plus several hundred additional acres leased by the tribe from individual Quechan allottees. Under tribal management, both enterprises flourished at first. Then an unfortunate combination of crop disease, a hurricane, competition from lower-priced produce imported from Mexico, and management problems forced the tribe to relinquish its management role and lease both operations to non-Indians in 1980.

In 1980, the reservation's 1,000 or more inhabitants lived along its major hard-surfaced roads, where communication with others and access to the stores in the nearby towns of Yuma, Arizona, or Winterhaven, California, was made easier. Their homes were scattered at 10-acre intervals in a pattern not markedly different form that of Anglo families living near the reservation. Many of the Quechan family households were still extended, a condition forced in part by the need to pool family income from a variety of sources.

Quechan children attend the nearby San Pasqual Consolidated School, where they are not in the ethnic majority. A considerable number of Indian high-school graduates have taken advantage of the government program for vocational training as medical assistants or automobile mechanics. According to one Bureau of Indian Affairs official, the Quechan do relatively well in vocational programs requiring them to move into urban areas such as Los Angeles or Oakland. They are still close enough to the reservation to return for brief visits, and experiences such as shopping in nearby Yuma serve them well in a more intensely urban environment (Bee 1967:79).

The tribe still gathers on the national holiday of Memorial Day to pay homage to its dead, and occasionally truncated versions of the *karʔúk* are sponsored by bereaved families when they accumulate the considerable amount of money required. On both occasions, and at

U. of Ariz., Ariz. State Mus., Tucson: 41867.

Fig. 13. The Quechan Community Center, looking north-northeast, Ft. Yuma Indian Reservation, Calif. Photograph by Helga Teiwes, July 1975.

funerals, there are still the songs and speeches in Quechan, still the wailing, still the destruction of clothing and other personal items, still the military themes. In fact, this mourning pattern has remained the most massively resistant to alien intervention, even though the destruction of property has bothered federal administrators for nearly a century. Land is too scarce to abandon now after a death, and no family would think of destroying a serviceable house. But in the commemoration of the dead the public expressions of Quechanness are never more visible.

Population

Forbes (1965:343) concludes that there were perhaps 4,000 Quechans at the time of their first contact with Spaniards. The population diminished to about 3,000 due to European diseases and increased warfare, "and it remained fairly stable at that figure until it declined to 2,700–2,800 in 1852. Thereafter, the decline was even more rapid, reaching 2,000 in 1872, 1,100–1,200 in the 1880's, and a low in 1910 (at least as far as the reservation was concerned)," of 834 (Forbes 1965:343).

There are some puzzling ambiguities about the reported totals, even allowing for inaccurate estimates by brief visitors to the area. Father Francisco Garcés in 1774 estimated 3,500 Quechans, yet one year later, Juan Bautista de Anza reported only 2,400, with no mention of major catastrophe in the intervening period. This difficulty continues into the 1960s. The tribal roll of April 1, 1963, listed a total membership of 1,544, while government figures cited by Forbes (1965:343) gave a total of 2,125 in 1950. It is possible that the government figures refer to all Indians under the jurisdiction of the Fort Yuma Subagency, which includes some Cocopa.

Synonymy‡

The name Quechan is from the Quechan name for themselves, *kʷacá·n,* literally meaning 'those who descended'. This is interpreted as a reference to the account of the creation of the Quechan and their neighbors on the sacred mountain *ʔaví· kʷamé·*. In one version, the name is a shortening of *xá·m kʷacá·n* 'those who descended by a different way' (Corbusier 1925–1926; Forde 1931:88; Kroeber 1943:39); in another version the full phrase is *xám kʷacá·n* 'those who descended by way of the water' (Abraham M. Halpern, communication to editors 1981).

Related or borrowed names for the Quechan in other Yuman languages are: Mohave *kʷičá·n* (Pamela Munro, communication to editors 1981); Walapai kachan (Corbusier 1923–1925); Maricopa *kʷča·n* (Lynn Gordon, communication to editors 1981); Kahwan kwasá·nt and Cocopa kwasanʸ (Kroeber 1943:38).

The Spanish name for the Quechan was Yuma, perhaps first recorded by Eusebio Kino in 1699 (Coues 1900, 2:544); this name shows virtually no variation, spellings like Huma (Kino in Bolton 1916:445) being merely misprints or the like. Spanish Yuma appears to be a borrowing of Pima-Papago *yu·mĭ* 'Quechan' (Saxton and Saxton 1969:51); Cahuilla *yú·mu,* glossed 'Yuman', shows the same word in another Uto-Aztecan language (Seiler and Hioki 1979:255).

The earliest English accounts sometimes use the Spanish Yuma (Ives 1861:42) and sometimes adaptations of *kʷacá·n*: Cutchanas (Möllhausen 1858, 2:245), Cuchaus (misprint for Cuchans), Cuchian, Cuichan, Cushans (Hodge 1907–1910, 2:1010). Heintzelman (1857:35–36, 51) refers to the "Cu-cha-no, or as they are usually called, the Yuma Indians," or simply Cuchano, and distinguishes them from the "Yum, or New River Indians," apparently members of the Kamia group of Tipai.

Spellings of Yumas in English include Umahs, and Umeas; another form is Yahmáyo, Yumayas, Yurmarjars (Hodge 1907–1910, 2:1011). Yuma has been the name commonly used by anthropologists and linguists, but Quechan has been officially adopted by the Quechan tribal council and has since become prevalent in scholarly studies. The spelling Kwtsaan, based on the practical orthography representation of the pronunciation of *kʷacá·n* used in the 1970s, appears in some linguistic studies as the English name of the language (Norwood 1976; Langdon 1977).

Some sources give the Spanish name Garroteros, "or Club Indians," or versions of this (Hodge 1907–1910, 2:1010; Möllhausen 1858, 2:246).

For spellings of the name of the Kahwan in historical sources that were erroneously taken by Hodge (1907–1910, 2:1010) to refer to the Quechan, see the synonymy for Kahwan in "Maricopa" (this vol.).

Sources

Early Spanish explorers and missionaries left brief and scattered accounts of the Quechan lifeways, perhaps the most extensive of which is Pedro Font's (1951). Much of this early material has been collected and arranged into a readable volume by Forbes (1965).

Heintzelman (1857) included a brief ethnographic account in his report to the secretary of war regarding the problems of establishing Fort Yuma; but Trippel's (1889) articles about the Quechan comprise the earliest comprehensive ethnographic treatment, portraying the culture as it existed at the end of the nineteenth century. Forde (1931) produced the best single source on traditional Quechan life; since it was aimed at ethno-

‡This synonymy was written by Ives Goddard, incorporating references supplied by Robert L. Bee.

graphic reconstruction, his work contains practically no information on the twentieth-century reservation community. Bee (1963, 1967, 1969a, 1970, 1981) focused on kinship structure and sociocultural change, particularly the changing tribal political process and the impact of federal "development" programs during the twentieth century.

In a more specialized vein, Halpern (1942, 1946–1947) visited the Quechan in the early 1940s to collect linguistic data and kinship terminology. He returned in the 1970s to collect folklore and oral history materials. Castetter and Bell (1951) included a detailed discussion of Quechan horticultural techniques and products in their extensive survey of Yuman agriculture.

Cocopa

ANITA ALVAREZ DE WILLIAMS

The Cocopa ('kōkə,pä) are speakers of a language of the Yuman family* who live on the lower Colorado River and its delta, in the southwestern United States and northwestern Mexico (fig. 1). Prior to the construction of dams and irrigation systems in the twentieth century, their habitat was unique, with the Colorado River providing ample moisture, particularly in summer floods (fig. 2), so as to convert the delta into a land rich in flora and fauna.

External Relations

Although the lower Colorado is the acknowledged homeland of the Cocopa, they are known to have had contacts as far west as the Pacific coast, northwest as far as the Pomo of northern California, north to the Chemehuevi and Walapai, northeast to the Navajo (all of Arizona), and southeast to the Seri of Sonora, Mexico. Their more usual association was with other Yuman peoples, particularly the Maricopa of Arizona and the Paipai and Tipai of southern and Baja California. However, they maintain friendly contacts with some non-Yuman groups, such as the Luiseño and Papago (A. Williams 1974:27). Historical evidence from the eighteenth century indicates that the Cocopa were part of an alliance system that included the Maricopa and Gila Pima people, as well as the eastern Papago, the Halchidhoma, Walapai-Havasupai, Cahuilla, Paipai, Tipai, and Kiliwa. They opposed another league that centered in the Quechan. Some groups, such as the Halyikwamais and the Imperial Valley Kamia, alternated between friendship and enmity with the Cocopa. Early warfare between these groups seems to have been for the purpose of maintaining tribal prestige, mystical values, individual honors, and supernatural power (W.H. Kelly 1977:129–131). On several occasions opposing war leagues banded together to fight a common enemy such as the Spaniards at Santa Catarina Mission (Forbes 1965:80, 276, 292).

Origins

The origins of the Cocopa people are allegorically stated in their mythology, transmitted through oratory and in song cycles. Their creation myths, like those of other Yumans, include a belief in the existence of twin gods who began under the waters, eventually emerging to create the firmament, the earth, and its creatures, things,

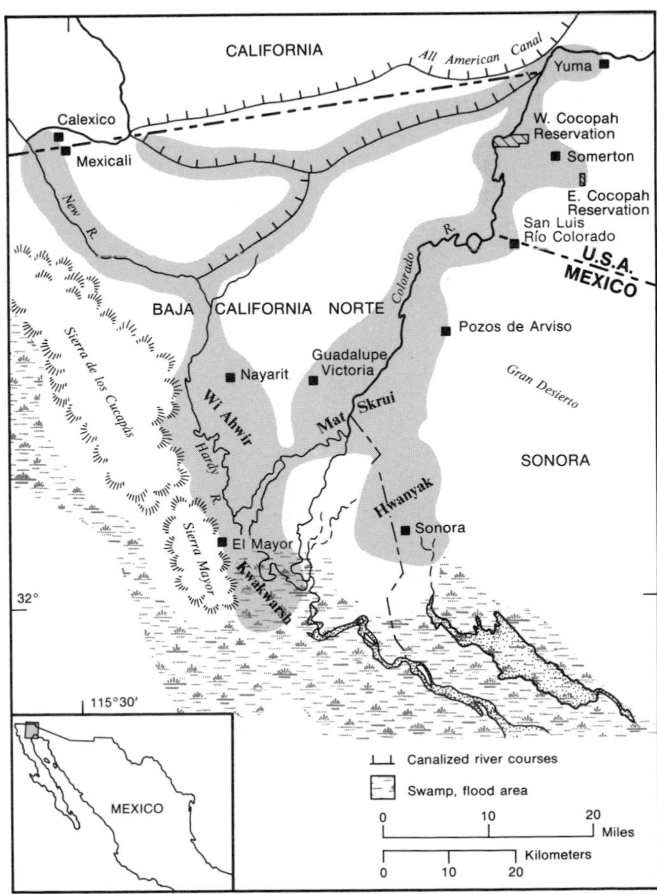

Fig. 1. Tribal territory and band locations in the late 19th century.

*The phonemes of Cocopa are: (stops and affricate) *p*, *t* (dental), *ṭ* (postalveolar), *č*, *k*, *kʷ*, *q*, *qʷ*, *ʔ*; (fricatives) *s*, *ṣ*, *š*, *x*, *xʷ*; (voiceless laterals) *ł*, *łʸ*; (voiced laterals) *l*, *lʸ*; (nasals) *m*, *n*, *nʸ*; (semivowels) *w*, *y*; (dental flap) *r*; (short vowels) *i*, *a*, *u*; (long vowels) *a·*, *i·*, *u·*; (stress) v́ (primary), v̀ (secondary), unmarked (unstressed). Spanish loanwords have also *v*, *δ* and *d* (perhaps one phoneme), *f*, *ŋ*, and in the speech of some *e* and *o*.

Information on Cocopa phonology was obtained from Crawford (1978:18) and James M. Crawford (communication to editors 1981), who also provided the phonemic transcriptions of the Cocopa words cited in italics. In the 1960s no speaker of Cocopa could be found who had heard of the band whose name was recorded in 1943 as Kwakwarsh 'yellow people' (W.H. Kelly 1977:79); the phonemicization *kʷaqʷáṣ*, which would mean 'those who are yellow', is a conjecture based on this.

and customs. Cocopa beliefs concerning death prevented any direct mention of the deceased, so that much of the past is veiled in a mythology richly populated with villains and heroes in the forms of animals, birds, and insects displaying very human traits (W.H. Kelly 1977:115; Uriarte Castañeda 1974:165).

Archeological studies indicate that the ancestors of the Cocopa and other Yuman speakers migrated from the north, perhaps the Great Basin, to the lower valleys of the Gila and the Colorado rivers sometime between 1000 B.C. and the time of Christ. During a pluvial period around A.D. 900 a large lake formed in the Imperial-Mexicali Valley, a lake referred to in the twentieth century as Blake Sea or Lake Cahuilla. Many Yuman speakers were attracted to settle on its shores; however, the Cocopa remained on the river. The desiccation of that lake between A.D. 1400 and 1500 nevertheless affected the Cocopa drastically when the Quechan and the Mohave returned to the river, displacing the Cocopa and forcing them downriver to the southern delta into an area that had been submerged during the earlier pluvial period (A. Williams 1975a:3–6).

Fig. 2. Flooding of the Baja California Cocopa school (in distance at right) and houses by Colorado River overflow into the Hardy River, a rare occurrence since the construction of the Hoover and Morelos dams. Photograph by Anita Alvarez de Williams, spring, 1980.

History

The Colorado River was a natural route for traffic, so the ancestors of the Cocopa may have been among the first native Americans in the Southwest to encounter Europeans. Interesting fragments of dated information about Cocopa culture have been recorded throughout historical times.

The Spanish explorer Hernando de Alarcón made the earliest recorded contact with the people living at the mouth of the Colorado River in 1540. He wrote of tall, well-built people, who carried wooden maces and bows and arrows and adorned themselves with face and body painting. The men wore loincloths, and the women hung bundles of painted and glued feathers from their waists in front and in back. These people offered gifts of shells, beads, well-tanned leathers, and food, including corn and corn cakes, to Alarcón and his men. By certain rituals they demonstrated reverence for the sun. The men hung shell ornaments from their pierced ears and noses, and they wrapped a wide band of cordage around the upper arm, from which they suspended deer-bone blades to clean off perspiration as well as bamboo tubes for a purpose not recorded. Small bags served as wristbands when handling the bow. These bags were filled with seeds that were used in beverage preparation. Alarcón wrote of seeing 1,000 men at one point, 5,000–6,000 farther on, and of groups of hundreds, indicating a heavy native population in the delta at that time (Ramusio 1554–1603, 3; A. Williams 1975:19–29).

Also in 1540, Melchior Diaz visited the river people. He wrote a description of their semisubterranean houses covered with straw. They were long structures, with entrances at both ends large enough to enable a person to enter without stooping, that could shelter 100 people at a time (Hammond and Rey 1940). In his 1604–1605 diary Francisco de Escobar reported that there were nine Cocopa living complexes (called *rancherías* by the Spaniards), of which he and his party actually observed only two, containing between them about 1,500 people (Bolton 1919; A. Williams 1975:33).

Father Eusebio Kino encountered Indians believed to have been Cocopa during his visit to the Colorado delta in 1702. They told him that some small pots in their possession had been obtained from the Pacific coast. The river people lived in small rancherias growing corn, beans, and pumpkins, setting aside areas for drying pumpkin (A. Williams 1975:35). In 1923 strips of this vegetable were still being hung from horizontal poles in a Cocopa rancheria (A. Williams 1975a:facing p. 100).

Another priest, Father Francisco Garcés, visited the people between 1771 and 1776. He attempted to missionize the delta Indians and failed. Garcés visited many rancherias of the Cocopa, groups of 200–300 people, most of them on the west side of the river. To the list of foods mentioned by earlier travelers he added watermelon. In the writings of Garcés there is a record of intertribal hostility among the Jalliquamay or Quiquima (Halyikwamai), the Quemaya (Kamia), and the Cajuenche (Kahwan) and Yuma (Quechan) (Coues 1900; W.H. Kelly 1977:6–7).

The Cocopa probably heard the English language for the first time during an extended visit to the delta by Lt. R.W.H. Hardy in 1826. He wrote of the similarity between the houses of the Seri of Tiburon Island and those of the Cocopa, mentioned women dressed in willow-bark skirts, saw the use of native tobacco, and described native mesquite bread. The Cocopa traded melons, pumpkins, corn, fish, and cotton with Hardy. He was impressed by the quality of their fine large ollas and well-made fishing nets. Merely by chance, he became the first person to write down a bit of Cocopa music. Hardy stated that once 5,000–6,000 Indians assembled near his boat (Hardy 1829; A. Williams 1975:45–68; W.H. Kelly 1977:8).

When James Ohio Pattie visited the Cocopa in 1827 they invited him to participate in ceremonial smoking, after which they all feasted on fatted dog. The Cocopa regaled him with oratory. When they saw that he had some "Umea" (Yuma, that is Quechan) scalps, they demonstrated their animosity toward those people by what seems to have been a version of the Cocopa scalp dance (W.H. Kelly 1977:136). Pattie wrote that the Paipai (mountain people of Baja California) had a winter camp on the river just below the Cocopa (Pattie 1833; A. Williams 1975:69–81).

George R. Derby and Maj. Samuel P. Heintzelman investigated the Cocopa below Fort Yuma in the 1850s. The most notable thing about their observations concerning weapons, food, and agriculture of the Cocopa is that they were relatively unchanged from those mentioned by Alarcón 300 years earlier (Derby 1852; Heintzelman 1857:50; A. Williams 1975:83–90). Derby specified that they lived near the tidal bore from the gulf, and that an area of unoccupied neutral ground separated them from the "Cu-cha-nos" (Quechans). This period saw the beginnings of more intensive contact and communication between the Cocopa and the non-Indian people who no longer came to the lower Colorado river valley as travelers, but as settlers.

The Gadsden Purchase in 1853 established an international boundary through what was the Cocopa territory (A. Williams 1974:36). Influenced by pioneer settlement, the American and Mexican Cocopa began becoming bilingual in their own and the dominant language, and in some cases trilingual (speaking English, Spanish, and Cocopa). When visiting between the two nations, particularly upon ceremonial occasions, Cocopas speak their native language (Ricardo Sandoval, personal communication 1975).

The first written mention of Cocopa living near Yuma, Arizona, was made by Jacobo Blanco in 1873, who found them occupying land between Fort Yuma and the mouth of the river. The Cocopa are said to have occupied both the east and the west sides of the river. Articles in the *Arizona Sentinel,* published in Yuma, mention the Cocopa there from 1878 through 1900, and the *Calexico Chronicle* mentions them in Calexico, California, in 1908 (Blanco 1873:998; Chittenden 1901:198; Densmore 1932:7–8; North 1910:314).

In the last half of the nineteenth century the Cocopa became very active in the river trade, supplying steamboats on the Colorado with wood for fuel. Until the turn of the century when the river trade died out, the Cocopa were well known for their skill as river pilots and navigators. They, better than any non-Indian, knew the intricate and changeable waterways of the delta (A. Williams 1975:93, 111–113).

Smithsonian, NAA: 2819.

Fig. 3. Yuman men, probably Cocopa, on board Commander (later Admiral) George Dewey's hydrological survey ship *Narragansett*. Cocopa cloth breechclouts in this period were longer in back than in front (Kelly 1977:55). Photograph by Henry von Bayer, at the mouth of the Colorado River, 1874.

In 1900 the ethnologist W J McGee briefly visited the Cocopa. He wrote that they were divided into seven groups, each one identified by the name of its leader. However, he mentions only five "Captains" by their first name, and adds the name of Capt. Pablo Colorado, saying that he is "head chief of all Indians on lower Colo." One of these captains is reported by McGee to have spoken "Apache" and another Diegueño. The Cocopa leader Frank Tehana guided the expedition, and photographer DeLancey Gill photographed him and many other Cocopas of that period (fig. 5).

Four politically autonomous bands or groups of Cocopa lived in dispersed rancherias in the delta in the early 1900s: the Wi Ahwir (*wi· ˀaxʷí·r*) in Baja California, Mexico, from El Mayor to 15–20 miles north of there; the Kwakwarsh (*kʷaqʷáṣ?*) south of El Mayor to the freshwater limit; and the Mat Skrui (*maṭ škru·wí·*) and Hwanyak (*xʷanʸá·k*) south of San Luís, Sonora. Early in the twentieth century most Wi Ahwir Cocopa moved into the area of Mexicali and along the railroad on the Baja California border, but some of them moved to Pozos de Arvizu, south of San Luís, and a few others to land near Somerton, Arizona. Most of the Hwanyak also settled in the vicinity of Somerton, excepting those who went to live with the Mat Skrui people near San Luís. The development of irrigation systems in the northern part of the delta and in the Imperial and Yuma valleys, with consequent opportunity for employment as day laborers, was probably the major factor in determining these moves, and from that period on individuals and families moved back and forth frequently between these areas. However, a large por-

Sherman Lib. and Gardens, Corona Del Mar, Calif.

Fig. 4. Indian laborers on a Colorado River steamboat between 1902 and 1904. left, Cocopa boatmen with hair rolled on top of their heads and covered with cloth, a characteristic early 20th-century hairstyle (Kelly 1977:58). top right, Indian crew loading wood onto the river boat at Pescadero Landing, Colorado River. bottom right, Steamboat *Cochan* (Capt. Mellon, Master) at Pescadero Landing, such as employed Cocopas as pilots and crew. Indian men stand on the bow near stacked wood. Photographer not recorded.

tion of the Hwanyak Cocopa established themselves permanently near Somerton by 1910 (W.H. Kelly 1977:13).

In 1917 government decrees gave the American Cocopa legal title to three small areas of land as a reservation under the jurisdiction of the Yuma agency (W.H. Kelly 1977:13). This was the last that the Cocopa were to hear from the national government for a long time. Culturally and linguistically isolated, ordinary school systems hardly touched them, and generally they responded to the rapidly expanding non-Indian community by withdrawing from it (A. Williams 1974:81).

Then, in 1961, the Cocopa in Arizona began to organize. In the next few years, with help from private sources and with government assistance, they worked to improve their housing. Electricity was introduced. They built their first Cocopa tribal building. In 1968, with some advice from the Navajo, they revised their tribal constitution. Ceremonial buildings were built on East and West Reservations, and in the 1970s the Cocopa began to focus their attention on education. They began with an Operation Headstart program, followed by an individualized Indian instruction program (Elementary and Secondary Education Act, Public Law 93-380, Title III), and in 1976 they were provided with special tutoring at the high school level in a learning center on East Reservation. Another problem is handled through a center that directs rehabilitation for alcoholics.

In the 1970s the Cocopa were also reviving their traditional crafts, such as beadwork (fig. 6), and developing their ability in the fine arts. Young Cocopas were learning songs and legends from their elders in appreciation of their ancient culture. At the same time, through the various educational programs they were becoming better adapted to living and working alongside their non-Indian neighbors. The tribal council directed projects for economic development benefiting the Arizona Cocopa people. Their octagonal tribal building was completed in 1976 (Peter Soto, personal communication 1976).

The tribal council consists of five members and a chairman with jurisdiction over Cocopa West Reservation, Cocopa East Reservation, and Cocopa Lots Five and Six. The entire area consists of approximately 1,800 acres.

In 1981 one group of the Mexican Cocopa still lived in the area of the Hardy River in Baja California. In 1976 they benefited from a presidential decree that confirmed their communal rights to 143,000 hectares of land, most of it desert, including the Cucapá Mountains. In 1981 they were awaiting another decree that

Smithsonian, NAA: 2821.

Fig. 5. left to right: Clam, a Cocopa shaman; woman married to a Cocopa said to have been a captive Apache, dressed in full-length dress, cloth cloak, netted beadwork collar and multi-strand bead necklaces, with a jew's harp suspended from her neck; and Frank Tehana, a guide for WJ McGee's 1900 expedition, who became headman in 1927 (A. Williams 1974:42). Photograph by DeLancey Gill, at a village near mouth of the Colorado River, Sonora, 1900.

Fig. 6. Ricardo Sandoval Portillo making a netted beadwork collar. Photograph by Anita Alvarez de Williams, Hardy River Cocopa community, Baja California, 1975.

would expand their holdings to include irrigable farmland near the Hardy River. They worked on nearby ranches and at Hardy River tourist camps; whenever possible, they farmed on a small scale and raised poultry or animals for meat. They fished regularly and hunted small game. The Mexican Cocopa are excellent beadworkers, often producing wide bead necklaces for their own adornment and for sale to outsiders. Under Mexico's program for rural development, the Cocopa were eligible for participation in several economic programs.

A smaller number of Mexican Cocopa lived in Sonora in 1981. Most of these people were located near Pozos de Arvizu south of San Luís. They had the reputation of being the most conservative of the surviving Cocopa in the observance of their traditional customs. Otherwise they lived much as other rural northern Mexican folk. Education is available to all Mexican Cocopa children, but as was true of the American Cocopa earlier in the century, there are certain cultural differences to be resolved before many of them can take full advantage of existing educational possibilities.

In 1981 the Cocopa continued to maintain their identity as an ethnic group, although many elements of their material culture have disappeared. One dramatic change in the lives of the Cocopa people in the twentieth century is that after hundreds, perhaps thousands, of years of being river people, most of them no longer live on the river. Several dams and diversions have reduced the Colorado River to almost nothing in the lower delta. The meager section of river that flows past one small piece of American Cocopa land has been put to use by the U.S. government for agricultural drainage. The Mexican government uses the Hardy River for the same purpose and also for drainage from nearby geothermal steam wells. The lives of the Cocopa people once depended upon the river, but the river's functions have been severely altered by non-Indians. By the end of the twentieth century the Cocopa may no longer be river people at all.

Population

Since there are neither United States nor Mexican government censuses for the Cocopa before the twentieth century, and since they themselves kept no records, previous population estimates must be taken for what they were: what the travelers saw, or thought they saw, or what they wanted someone to believe they saw. Alarcón must have included more than just Cocopa, while some later estimates probably included only a portion of the Cocopa population. The general picture presented during historical times is of a dense initial population of the delta—5,000 is the number most often mentioned. Escobar estimated 5,000–6,000 in 1604–1605 (Bolton 1919), Garcés estimated 3,000 in 1776 (Coues 1900), and the population seems to have diminished gradually until the mid-nineteenth century when, coincident with a growing non-Indian population, the native population began to diminish more rapidly. Heintzelman (1857:50) supposed that formerly there were as many as 5,000 Cocopa warriors, whereas by 1853 he thought there were no more than 300 warriors. In 1873 a total estimated Cocopa population of 2,300 to 3,000 included also some Quechans (Blanco 1873:998). A smallpox epidemic in 1900 in Yuma affected the Quechan people; although it is not recorded among the Cocopa, probably it was partially responsible for the drop in their numbers at that time (Crowe and Brinckerhoff 1976:16). Lumholtz (1912; A. Williams 1975:129–135) reported a 1900 census that numbered the Cocopa at 1,200. The explorer Chittenden estimated "at least 450" about a year later (Chittenden 1901; A. Williams 1975:103–109).

In 1974 the enrolled membership of the American Cocopa was 504 (A. Williams 1974:97); in 1980, it was 571 (Paul Soto, personal communication 1981). A 1976 census counted 145 Cocopas in Baja California, while at this period some 60 Cocopas were reported living in Sonora.

Culture

The Cocopa once used wild tobacco for ceremonial smoking. They kept dogs as pets, as well as doves, young eagles, hawks, and other wild birds; this was still true in the 1970s, with the exception of the eagles and hawks (Drucker 1941:131; Onesimo Gonzalez, personal communication 1975).

Subsistence

The Cocopa possessed no formal calendar but spoke in terms of the coming of warm and cool seasons, the floods and their recessions, and of planting and harvesting (W.H. Kelly 1977:23).

During the first months of the year food was scarce. By then, the Cocopa had eaten most of their harvest, and it was a season when wild food sources, including fish, game, and vegetable foods were reduced. During this period the Cocopa traveled to the high desert in search of bisnaga cactus and agave. In the spring the people went by raft downriver to the islands near the gulf to harvest wild rice. By midsummer there were more fish in the river. As the seasonal floodwaters receded the Cocopa followed, making planting holes with long digging sticks, and hand planting several varieties of corn, squash, and beans. When harvested in the fall (some squash in midsummer), these crops along with certain wild foods were stored in baskets on high racks, safe from late flash floods and from hungry animals. Moisture sufficient to mature farm crops was secured from saturated soil and high water tables resulting from annual summer floods. In addition, in some areas dikes and dams were used to control and distribute river flood water. For some crops the Cocopa carried water for irrigation, and for others they constructed small earthen dikes to retain water for later distribution. Remnants of these agricultural systems were still to be seen and photographed early in the twentieth century (W.H. Kelly 1977:27–28). One special technique used in planting a certain grass seed consisted of broadcasting the seed by spraying it from the mouth (Drucker 1941:94–95; W.H. Kelly 1977:38).

Prior to 1900 mesquite was probably the most important wild plant food known to the Cocopa. It still was widely used throughout the first half of the twentieth century. Since then it has been used mostly for animal food, particularly for goats, or at times for small numbers of horses or cattle (Güera Maclis, personal communication 1975). Preparation of mesquite for human consumption meant grinding the dry pods in a mortar, eliminating the seeds, and then either forming the mesquite meal into cakes or using it to make a drink. Screw beans, a relative of mesquite, were placed in a pit to ripen and ground in a mortar. The Cocopa gathered and ate cattail reed pollen and tule roots as well as certain grass seeds. These they threshed with a stick seedbeater in a tray (Drucker 1941:96; W.H. Kelly 1977:32–39).

Bathing, fasting, and continence preceded the Cocopa hunt for deer and wild boar, which were once plentiful in the delta. Hunters stalked game individually with bow and arrow or banded together in communal rabbit drives employing fire and trapping the rabbits or other small animals in snares or nets. Wood rats, raccoons, and beavers were also caught and eaten, as well as various insects (Drucker 1941:98–99; W.H. Kelly 1977:24). Wild geese and duck once abounded in the delta, and in the 1970s the Mexican Cocopa still trapped and hunted dove, quail, and duck (Anonymous 1900; Onesimo Gonzalez, personal communication 1975).

Fish no longer form an important part of the diet of the American Cocopa because of dwindling access to the river, but the Baja California Cocopa still count heavily on fish as a food source. They trap fish in large nets or catch them in small nets. More ancient fishing methods included the use of basketry traps and scoops, and spearing, or even shooting the fish with bow and arrow. But in 1981 these methods were rarely practiced. Extra meat and fish were dried and stored for later use (Adelaida Saiz, personal communication 1975).

right, Smithsonian, NAA: 2844-A; Smithsonian, Dept. of Anthr.: a, 209,788; b, 209,766; c, 209,741; d, 209,809.

Fig. 7. Food preparation and household goods. right, Woman grinding corn. She wears a basketry hat and a cloth skirt, which replaced the willow-bark skirt. To her right is a gourd jug with a corn cob stopper, probably used for water (Gifford 1933:270). Photograph by DeLancey Gill, at a village near mouth of Colorado River, 1900. a, Twined basket with strip of black cotton cloth sewn around the rim, worn by women as a hat (especially when grinding corn) (Kelly 1977:56) and also used as a scoop for seeds and flour. Corn and other seeds were roasted on pottery pans, ground into flour, and made into cakes or used in a mush. b, Mush stirrer made of 5 sticks twined together with string. c, Gourd container in fiber netting used as a water canteen. Gourds were also used to hold seeds and were made into dishes. d, Reddish buff-colored pottery ladle with handle shaped to resemble an animal head. Diameter of a, 19.5 cm, rest to same scale. All collected by WJ McGee in 1900.

By tradition Cocopa women are the family cooks. Food preparation (fig. 7) was originally done over wood fires in pottery vessels on pot-rests of stone or clay. Earth ovens sometimes served to cook meat or vegetables. Seeds were toasted in pottery trays. Since the Mexican Cocopa did not have electricity or gas in 1981 they did most of their cooking on a simple home-built wood stove, or on one using tanked gas, but pottery and gourd utensils have been replaced by metal pots and pans, and plastic or china tableware (Drucker 1941:107–109; W.H. Kelly 1977:48).

Structures

The original dwellings of the Cocopa were of several types. Their winter house was a rectangular structure with excavated floor. It was supported by a four-post frame with connecting beams, or by two posts supporting a longitudinal beam. Short side posts supported the hip roof. The walls, sometimes inclined and sometimes vertical, were made of sticks covered with arrowweed and earth. On the floor was a hearth (Drucker 1941:104; W.H. Kelly 1977:46).

Another type of dwelling was the round or oval domed-to-conical postless hut supported by its own wall of inward bent poles. This brush-covered frame served as a summer home along with or in place of a simple ramada (Drucker 1941:104–105; W.H. Kelly 1977:46).

The Cocopa sometimes constructed a circular to semicircular unroofed windbreak of brush, used as a temporary dwelling or in connection with a house for a cooking area (W.H. Kelly 1977:46). This particular form of shelter may be more ancient than the others: it was observed in use in 1767 (A. Williams 1975:34).

The twentieth-century dwellings of the American Cocopa are built of wood or cement blocks, reflecting government programs for community development and generally improved living conditions. The Mexican Cocopa continue to live in adaptations of the Mexican wattle-and-daub jacal. The oval or round dwellings were no longer seen in the 1970s. When unusual flooding of the Colorado River drove many of these people from their homes in 1980, the Mexican government provided modular plywood houses with asbestos roofs for them on higher ground.

Technology

Household equipment once included a large wooden mortar, smaller mortars of twined arrowweed, a fire

top left, Natl. Arch., Washington: 22 WB-8300; top right and bottom right, Mus. of the Amer. Ind., Heye Foundation, New York: 24504, 24513.

Fig. 8. Structures. top left, House on Hardy River, with walls of vertical reeds or brush fastened down on outside by horizontal poles; flat roof, evidently of brush and earth, supporting storage baskets; shade entrance at left; photograph by E.A. Goldman, April 1905. top right, Semisubterranean earth-covered winter house on Cocopa Reservation, Ariz.; behind it is a flat-roofed, rectangular thatched dwelling with ramada to right; photograph by Edward H. Davis, 1923. bottom left, House of Adelaida Saiz Dominguez on the Hardy River; photograph by Anita Alvarez de Williams, fall 1980. bottom right, House at Alamo, Sonora; wattle-and-daub structure is at the left and ramadas at right; pumpkin strips are drying over the ramada rail; photograph by Edward H. Davis, 1923.

drill, and variously shaped stone metates and manos. Stone and clamshell knives, and wooden and bone awls served as tools. The Cocopa made nets from vegetable fibers for use in trapping, fishing, carrying, and storage. Pottery vessels were many and varied for storage and cooking, and the people used canteens made of gourds or of clay for travel (Drucker 1941:122–123; Gifford 1933:270; W.H. Kelly 1977:48).

Pottery manufacture was introduced to the Cocopa around A.D. 700, and the Cocopa became very skilled in this art, which they practiced through the first half of the twentieth century. They virtually abandoned the art for awhile, but in 1976 some of them began to make pottery again, through interest in ancient ways and as an attractive item for sale to tourists.

The traditional method for pottery making includes gathering, grinding, and winnowing the clay, then adding a temper of ground sherds. The concave bottom of the vessel is formed by working the clay over an old pot, or the knee, and then rolls of clay are added by pinching them into place in order to build up the sides of the vessel. The potter uses a wooden paddle and a mushroom-shaped pottery anvil or a smooth stone for shaping the vessel. Firing is done in an open area or in a shallow pit using mesquite chips, arrowwood, and dung for fuel (Drucker 1941:107; Gifford 1933:318–320; W.H. Kelly 1977:48–51).

The basketry of the Cocopa seems to have been confined to large, loosely woven storage baskets (fig. 9) and a few crude small bird's-nest weave baskets (Gifford 1933:270; W.H. Kelly 1977:51–52).

The Cocopa made U-shaped willow-wood cradleboards padded with shredded willow bark. The child was bound into place, with head shaded by a hood, which was sometimes decorated with paint and hung with feathers to indicate a boy child or with shell beads to indicate a girl. The mother carried this cradleboard horizontally on the head, or on her hip, or hung it by cords from a house pole (Drucker 1941:110–111; Güera Maclis, personal communication 1975; W.H. Kelly 1977:53–54).

The weapons of the Cocopa included hardwood daggers, spears, wooden war clubs, lances, and bows and arrows. Bows were five feet or more in length, consisting of a simple curve with abruptly curved tips, bound with sinew at the stress points. The belly of the bow

The Huntington Lib., San Marino, Calif.
Fig. 9. Cooking in a summer house at the lower delta of the Colorado River. On top of house are large food storage baskets, with woven circular walls sometimes over 4 feet in diameter, for which the house roof served as bottom (Kelly 1977:48, 51). Photograph by Frederick I. Monsen, 1891–1902.

was painted, and the three-ply bowstring was made of sinew or plant fiber. Arrows were made of untipped arrowweed or of cane with hardwood point, and before 1900, with foreshaft and stone arrowpoint. These were at times gall-tipped for poison. The Cocopa used quivers of skin or fiber and bow guards (Drucker 1941:118–119).

Clothing and Adornment

One textile reported for the Cocopa was the rabbitskin blanket or robe, which was made of strips of fur twined onto vegetable fiber cords and held together by wefts of plant fiber. Another was the shredded bark skirt made of the inner bark of the willow or cottonwood tree (fig. 10). The Cocopa still wore and occasionally made these skirts in the last quarter of the nineteenth century. In 1981 they were occasionally made for sale to collectors and museums.

They also tanned animal skins, using a stone scraper to dehair the skins, which had been soaked in a lye solution for two or more days. A certain white earth found near the Hardy River was employed to soften hides (Drucker 1941:44; Adelaida Saiz, personal communication 1975). The people used tanned skins for storage bags and for breechclouts (Drucker 1941:114–115). Untreated skins were used with the hair side up for sandals (Güera Maclis, personal communication 1975; W.H. Kelly 1977:55–57).

The traditional men's hairdress of the Cocopa consisted of thin twisted ropes or braids of hair worn as long as possible. They sometimes wore forehead bangs (fig. 11) and plucked their facial hair. A light coating of mud was sometimes employed as added adornment and to keep the hair in place (Drucker 1941:115–116; Gifford 1933:279). Around 1900 they began tucking their hair up under a bandanna wrapped around the head. At least one San Luís Cocopa did this in 1981. Women wore their hair long and straight with forehead bangs. Mourning rites called for the cutting off of hair. Both men and women used mesquite-sap dye and mudpacks as a vermin remover and for general beautification. Feather adornments were used in men's ceremonial headdresses (fig. 12) (W.H. Kelly 1977:58).

Cocopa men and women practiced ornamental and ceremonial face and body painting well into the first half of the twentieth century (Gifford 1933:277). In 1981 the Cocopa were almost indistinguishable in dress from their neighbors in both Mexico and the United States.

Transport

For river travel, the Cocopa used the tule balsa, dugouts of cottonwood, or rafts of logs or brush guided by paddles or poles. For transporting small items or ferrying children they used large baskets or ollas, pushing them as they swam along beside them (Drucker 1941:124). In the 1970s many Cocopa on both sides of the border had automobiles, but foot travel and horseback riding were still used by some Mexican Cocopa to cover long distances, sometimes involving journeys of several days.

Warfare

Dreams and fasting formed an important part of Cocopa preparations for war in times past. Warriors practiced continence before battle, and both men and women participated in dances of incitement in which they used scalps taken in former battles. A shaman accompanied the war parties for purposes of healing his own men and intimidating the enemy, and to perform divination. In formal battle warriors, led by a war leader, were divided into bowmen, clubmen, and lancebearers variously adorned with feather headdresses and red and black body paint, which was believed to improve fighting ability. To taunt the enemy they carried old scalps into battle along with ceremonial feathered staffs. Sometimes the Cocopa staged pitched battles, but night raids were more common. Some took scalps from the bravest enemy slain, taking into account the length and elegance of their hair, believing these to be a source of power. Young women and children were taken captive for purposes of marriage and adoption. Returning warriors, especially the enemy-slayers and scalp-takers, had to observe certain purification rituals. Victory celebrations consisted of speeches and dancing and a display of the scalps taken. The scalps, having undergone special treatment, were retained in sealed ollas in a small specially made structure that was cared for by the war leader. Defensive tactics of the Cocopa consisted simply in posting sentinels to warn of possible raids (Drucker 1941:134; W.H. Kelly 1977:53).

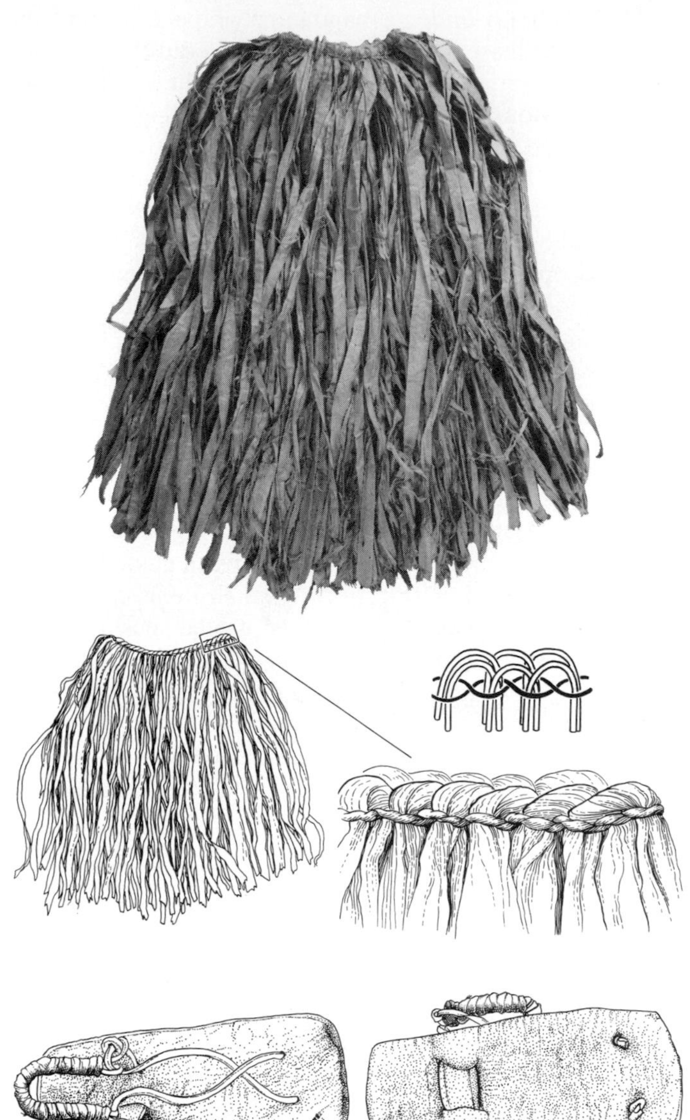

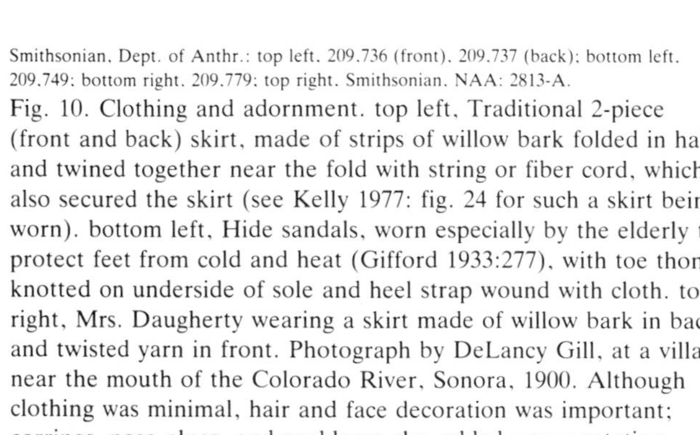

Smithsonian, Dept. of Anthr.: top left, 209.736 (front), 209.737 (back); bottom left, 209.749; bottom right, 209.779; top right, Smithsonian, NAA: 2813-A.

Fig. 10. Clothing and adornment. top left, Traditional 2-piece (front and back) skirt, made of strips of willow bark folded in half and twined together near the fold with string or fiber cord, which also secured the skirt (see Kelly 1977: fig. 24 for such a skirt being worn). bottom left, Hide sandals, worn especially by the elderly to protect feet from cold and heat (Gifford 1933:277), with toe thongs knotted on underside of sole and heel strap wound with cloth. top right, Mrs. Daugherty wearing a skirt made of willow bark in back and twisted yarn in front. Photograph by DeLancy Gill, at a village near the mouth of the Colorado River, Sonora, 1900. Although clothing was minimal, hair and face decoration was important; earrings, nose plugs, and necklaces also added ornamentation. bottom right, Shell pendant (design cut in clam shell) with blue and white seed beads hung from a cloth-wrapped string. Ends have shells, beads, and a cartridge case attached. Such necklaces were worn by both men and women. Length of skirt front 74.5 cm, length of sandals 27.0 cm, length of pendant 56.0 cm. All collected by WJ McGee in 1900.

Mus. of the Amer. Ind., Heye Foundation, New York: 24507.

Fig. 11. Man identified as Took. His hair is loose in a traditional style and in it is a feather ornament. He wears a string of beads across his chest and arm wrappings (perhaps of fiber) with bead-decorated leather pendants. He holds a painted shinny stick (Gifford 1933:281, pl. 39) used in a team ball game (A. Williams 1974:56). Photograph by Edward H. Davis, Sonora, 1923.

Smithsonian, Dept. of Anthr.: 9,390.

Fig. 12. Headdress made of feathers of the great currassow (*Crax rubra*). The end of each feather is wrapped with string and all are tied together forming a radiating crown worn at the back of a man's head. Eagle and hawk feathers were worn only by certain shamans and twins (Gifford 1933:279). Diameter 30.5 cm; collected by Edward Palmer in 1869.

Music and Games

The musical instruments of the Cocopa once included the scraped and drummed basket, the gourd rattle, cane flutes and whistles, and the bull-roarer (Drucker 1941:124–125; Densmore 1932:147–153; W.H. Kelly 1977:58). In 1981 the gourd rattle was the sole accompaniment in traditional singing.

Their games included shinny, kickball races, hoop and pole, ring-and-pin, stick dice, and a gambling hand game called *peón* in Spanish. In 1981 *peón* was a favored though not common game. Cat's cradle, in which each figure symbolized an object or situation, was well known to the Cocopa. Men engaged in games of competitive archery (A. Williams 1974:50–62).

Social Organization

Leadership was and is determined by ability and experience among the Cocopa. Figures of importance were also believed to derive their powers from dreams. Dreaming of a particular mythical creature involved in certain situations enabled a man to undertake healing work, serve as a leader or an orator, do well in war, or perform some other task capably. In the nineteenth century war leaders figured importantly, but in the twentieth century the ability to speak well and to serve as a consultant and advisor to the people bears most weight in the selection of the *capitán* of the Mexican Cocopa or the tribal chairman of the American Cocopa. Funeral orators, singers, and, until the 1950s, healing shamans were traditional figures of importance in Cocopa society (W.H. Kelly 1977:73, 80–82; Robert Barley, personal communication 1975).

The clans or lineages (*šyamuł*ʸ) of the Cocopa have been described as patrilineal, exogamous, nonlocalized, and nonautonomous. Each clan is identified with a certain animal, plant, or natural phenomenon that may be considered its totem. All the women of a clan shared a common personal name. The people believed that the totem and clan names were provided by the creator at the beginning of time. Out of 50 clans with their totems, 10 are noted to have been derived from Paipai, Tipai, and Kamia clans (W.H. Kelly 1977:109). Most of the Cocopa in the second half of the twentieth century used anglicized or hispanicized last names, such as Wilson or Gonzalez, but traces of the ancient clan systems survive in some instances. For example, the *xčʔam* clan (totem: crow, wildcat) is spoken of by contemporary Mexican Cocopa as the Paipai-related *hatʔam* clan and is represented by members of the widespread Tambo family (W.H. Kelly 1977:110; Ricardo Sandoval, personal communication 1975). Exogamous marriage is no longer important to most of the Cocopa.

Life Cycle

A simple gift offering marked the marriage ceremony of the Cocopa and even this was not often observed. Divorce was informal, and consisted of a simple parting of the ways (W.H. Kelly 1977:61, 65, 140).

The birth of a Cocopa child involved certain food restrictions for the mother before and cleansing rites after to assure the well-being of all concerned. A clamshell knife was used to cut the umbilical cord. Perhaps because of the twin gods in the creation myths of the people, twins were specially privileged in Cocopa culture (W.H. Kelly 1977:68–69).

Young men were initiated into manhood by having their nasal septums pierced, a ceremony that was accompanied by diet restrictions and footraces to a specified secluded point in the Sierra Cucapá where the initiates painted symbols on the rocks (Onesimo Gonzalez, personal communication 1975; W.H. Kelly 1977:98).

Puberty rites for girls consisted of eight days of special behavior for their first four menstrual periods. They engaged in ritual bathing, quiet, and diet restrictions, and were required to use a scratching stick. On the evening of the first four days the girl lay face down in a fire-warmed, branch-lined trench, and a small female relative walked on her back, after which she was given a new two-piece willow-bark dress to wear. During the last four days her hair was dressed with arrowweed-root mud, and her body was dusted with red pigment. After her sixth or seventh menstruation a woman friend tattooed her chin with mesquite thorns and charcoal. This ritual tattooing and the perforation of the nasal septum in boys was prerequisite to comfort and happiness in the afterworld (Gifford 1933:291; W.H. Kelly 1977:93, 99).

By far the most elaborate social and ritual events of the Cocopa have been and still are those associated with their traditions concerning death and the dead (Uriarte Castañeda 1974:58–74; W.H. Kelly 1977:86–89). Wailing by relatives announces a death and accompanies the final dressing of the corpse. The body is dressed in the best clothes, and in the last quarter of the twentieth century some Cocopa still observed the tradition of painting the face with designs in the old style, and of painting the hair with red. The deceased goes fully adorned, which may include watches and jewelry. Cremation is the custom of the people and is still practiced formally by the American Cocopa. The Mexican Cocopa have been required by law to bury their dead, but cremations occurred in Sonora at least as late as 1962.

Originally, the house of the dead and all his belongings were burned with the intention of erasing every memory or sign of that person's existence. Even footprints were eradicated. The idea was that everything belonging to the deceased might accompany him into the next world so that he or she might not remain or return and bother the living for the lack of anything. To insure against this happening, commemorative ceremonies, the Kerauk (*kraʔúk*) and sometimes the Chekap (*či·ká·p*), are held. The Chekap is similar to the Kerauk, but older and less elaborate. These ceremonies are described in Cocopa myths and song cycles and are believed to have existed since the time of creation, at which time their procedure is said to have been prescribed.

The traditional belief of the Cocopa is that the soul leaves the body at the time of cremation and goes to live for an indefinite period of time in a spirit land of plenty and festivity in the area of the salt flats near the mouth of the Colorado River. Twins are believed to go to a different place and to be continuously reincarnated, thus being assured of living forever, an idea that may have had its origins in the belief in the twin creators, Sipa and Komat (*sipá* and *kma·ṭ*, shortened forms of *sipàkmá·ṭ* and *kùkmá·ṭ*).

A funeral orator leads the people in the ceremonial procedure, comforting the family and describing in detail the life of the dead person, to the accompaniment of highly ritualized wailing and interspersed with singing of verses from the appropriate song cycle. The funeral procession leads to the pyre and relatives bid farewell. Nearby some men and women dance in line, arm in arm, moving back and forth to the accompaniment of rattle and song. The funeral orator then addresses the dead, encouraging him to break all earthly ties and to abandon completely the material world. The relatives again dance, this time four times around the funeral pyre, and then return to a ramada while the fire is lit. Wailing intensifies, and as the fire burns, offerings of clothes, jewelry, money, and other items are thrown on the fire.

When the body is nearly consumed, women relatives sitting with their backs to the fire cut off their hair as a sign of mourning. This is followed by inhaling of smoke and ritual bathing to remove all memory of the dead and their possible dangerous influence. Traditionally for some days after this certain food restrictions are observed: no meat, fats, or salt. Formerly the house and all belongings of the dead were burned (as they occasionally were in 1981), but more recently belongings, including pets and cattle, were usually sold or given away, and the money was given to those attending the funeral. Cars, formerly burned, are now usually sold or traded in. The Mexican Cocopa abandon the house of a dead person.

Traditionally a year or later after the funeral the Kerauk ceremony is held in memory of one or more dead. A leader is appointed who takes charge of notifying people and preparation of a ceremonial structure, and delivers the ceremonial speeches made during its construction. The American Cocopa have a permanent structure for this purpose (fig. 13). They make an image and dress it to represent the most important person to be commemorated, and others are represented by children dressed and painted to resemble the deceased. These children are called by the names of the deceased during this ceremony only, and they are required to imitate the behavior of each person they represent. After ritual dancing and bathing for purification, food and money are distributed to the persons attending the ceremony. The ceremonial image is then burned, and ritual wailing intensifies. Originally the entire ceremonial structure was also burned.

The memorial and funeral ceremonies are considered highly dangerous, and all who attend are believed to risk illness or even death from malevolent souls that might linger in the area. A death occurring near the time of either of these ceremonies can be attributed to these dangers. However, such occasions also serve as get-togethers, and those not directly involved in mourning play traditional games, eat, and visit (W.H. Kelly 1977:86–89; Ralph Michelsen, personal communication 1974).

Fig. 13. The Cry House at West Reservation where funeral and memorial services are held. The building was constructed in 1968 with the aid of the Bureau of Indian Affairs and the Office of Economic Opportunity, allowing the Cocopa to maintain their mourning ceremony. Another Cry House was built and dedicated at East Reservation in 1973 (A. Williams 1974:86–91). Photograph by Anita Alvarez de Williams, 1974.

Synonymy†

The name Cocopa is a borrowing of the name used for this group in their own and other Yuman languages. It first appears, as Cocapa, in the 1605 account of Francisco de Escobar (Bolton 1919:33), the source of its use also by Zárate Salmerón, 1626 (Bolton 1916:276). A later rendering in Spanish sources is Cucapá, 1775 (Garcés in Coues 1900, 1:175), which is the form used in Mexico in the twentieth century. Additional spellings in nineteenth-century English-language sources include Cacopas, 1863; Cacupas, 1853; Cochopas, 1857; Co-co-pah, 1852; Co-co-pas, 1853; Cucapachas and Cupachas, 1853; Cucassus (misprint for Cucapas), 1878; Cucopa, 1839; Cu-cu-pahs, 1854; Kokopa, 1877 (Hodge 1907–1910, 1:319–320). The spelling Cocopah, first used by Chittenden (1901), was officially chosen by the Cocopas enrolled near Somerton, Arizona, in 1974.

†This synonymy was written by Ives Goddard, incorporating some references from Anita Alvarez de Williams.

The Cocopa name for themselves, as obtained in the 1960s, was *kʷapá* (James M. Crawford, communication to editors 1981); this was recorded in 1930 as kokwapá (Kroeber 1943:38). Forms in other Yuman languages are: Mohave *kokʷaʔapa* (Pamela L. Munro, communication to editors 1981); Quechan *kʷakʷʔa·pá*, usually shortened to *kʷaʔa·pá* or *kʷa·pá* (Abraham M. Halpern, communication to editors 1981); Maricopa *kʷpa* (Spier 1933:11; Lynn Gordon, communication to editors 1981); Kahwan kwikapat (Kroeber 1943:38); Yavapai ē-kwē-ka-pi´-ya (Corbusier 1921:3). This name has no clear etymology; the derivation from a supposed root kuk 'proud, strut' (Kroeber 1943:39) is considered very doubtful by Yuman specialists (Abraham M. Halpern, communication to editors 1981). Papago has the loanword *koapa* or *kuapa*, pl. *kukapa* (Saxton and Saxton 1969:61, 156).

Sources

Gifford's (1933) general account of Cocopa ethnography was based on winter visits between 1916 and 1930. At about the same time the geographer Kniffen (1931) provided an interesting view of the delta and its people. Densmore (1932) published important specialized information concerning Cocopa music, while Castetter and Bell (1951) described Cocopa agriculture and other subsistence techniques along with those of other Yuman peoples. Drucker (1941) is another useful reference, especially for comparisons of Cocopa material culture with that of their neighbors. The most important ethnographic work is that of W.H. Kelly (1977) from information provided by the Cocopa between 1940 and 1952. An unpublished study of the Cocopa language is by Crawford (1966). A. Williams has written about Cocopa culture and history in English (1974) and Spanish (1975a) and has published a collection of relevant extracts from historical sources (1975). C.B. Kroeber (1980) discusses Cocopa warfare in the 1850s.

Photographs by DeLancey Gill taken in 1900 are in the National Anthropological Archives, Smithsonian Institution. Another handsome set of photographs of the Cocopa taken by an unidentified photographer from this period is in the archives of the Sherman Foundation, Corona Del Mar, California. The Museum of the American Indian, Heye Foundation, New York, is another valuable source of pictures of the Cocopa.

Uto-Aztecan Languages

WICK R. MILLER

In terms of number of speakers, number of languages, and area covered, Uto-Aztecan is one of the largest families of languages in the New World. It has also received more than its share of attention from linguistic scholars. The languages are spoken in three geographic areas, a fact that delayed the recognition of Uto-Aztecan as a linguistic unit. The southernmost are in central Mexico and Central America, and the northernmost in the western United States, primarily in the Great Basin and southern California (the Shoshonean languages) (fig. 1).

The Uto-Aztecan languages were first encountered and recorded by Europeans in a south-to-north direction. The variety of Aztec (or Nahuatl) that Hernando Cortez heard in the sixteenth century in Mexico is now known as Classical Aztec. It was spoken natively in the Valley of Mexico, and as a second language throughout the Aztec empire and beyond (Dakin 1981). Numerous manuscripts exist from this early period, as well as some very good grammatical descriptions (see Anderson, Berdan, and Lockhart 1976; Newman 1967:179–181).

The Sonoran languages first received attention in the seventeenth and eighteenth centuries from Jesuit missionaries: for Cora, Ortega (1732); for Cahita, see Velasco (1890); for Tarahumara, Guadalajara (1683); for Ópata, Lombardo (1702) and Barbastro (1792); for Eudeve, B.T. Smith (1861); for Northern Tepehuan, Rinaldini (1743); for Lower Pima or Névome, see Pennington (1979–1980, 1). Bright (1967) provides a fuller discussion of this material. Knowledge from this early period is spotty, because not all Sonoran languages received attention, and some languages became extinct before they were recorded.

The northernmost languages were almost totally unknown until the nineteenth century. Tubatulabal, at the turn of the century, was the last extant Uto-Aztecan language to be identified (Lamb 1964). Most of the good, useful material for these languages dates from the twentieth century, especially the second half. A very full bibliography on Uto-Aztecan languages is given by Langacker (1976, 1977).

Determination of Genetic Relationships

The term Uto-Aztecan was first used by Brinton (1891). But work on genetic relationship had begun earlier, with the work of Johann Carl Eduard Buschmann, a German scholar working in the middle of the nineteenth century. Similarities among the languages of northwest Mexico seem to have been recognized by the early Jesuit missionaries, but Buschmann (1859), who provided the term Sonoran for those languages, was the first to present evidence and to present a genetic hypothesis. The more northerly languages, which were given the name Shoshonean by Bancroft in 1875 (1874–1876, 3), were just becoming known. Buschmann presented evidence for genetically relating these two language groups. Similarities with Aztec were noted, but curiously Buschmann ascribed this to borrowing by the Aztecs.

In spite of the large amount of evidence available by the turn of the century, the validity of Uto-Aztecan was questioned by some because of the influence of Powell (1891),whose highly respected classification of American Indian languages kept apart Shoshonean and Sonoran (the latter called Piman), and Aztec. (Aztec was not classified since it was in Mexico.) It was not until after Sapir (1913–1914) published his detailed comparison of Southern Paiute and Nahuatl that the genetic relationship of Uto-Aztecan was generally accepted. Lamb (1964) provides a fuller discussion of the history of Uto-Aztecan studies.

Some subgroups of Uto-Aztecan languages are so closely related that their genetic unity is obvious on inspection. This is the case with Numic, the most northerly Shoshonean languages. When words in Numic are similar, they are almost identical, as is clear from table 1, which gives lexical data from four Numic languages. Such a relationship is obvious even with fragmentary and poorly recorded material, and the similarities are obvious to the speakers of the languages, as well. The more distant relationships within Uto-Aztecan as a whole are not this easy to see at first glance. Their common descent has left all Uto-Aztecan languages with certain similarities in lexicon (word stock), phonology (sound system), and grammar, but recognizing them often cannot be done by inspection but involves analysis to discover recurring patterns.

Lexicon

A casual inspection shows similarities in the basic vocabulary of even widely separated Uto-Aztecan languages (table 2). The basic vocabulary includes the everyday words that are learned early in life such as those for body parts, natural phenomena, basic conditions, basic qualities, basic activities, and the like; in general, these words are less apt to be borrowed and more resistant to change than others. For example, the word for 'ear' is similar in all seven languages illustrated; for 'stone', it is similar in all but Hopi. These sets of similar words are cognates, that is, each set descends from a single word in the ancestral language. In some of the languages certain of the basic vocabulary items appear dissimilar, but once sound correspondences are identified, some of these will turn out to be cognate also. In other cases as a consequence of changes in meaning, cognates must be found by looking further afield. For example, the word for 'dog' seems to be similar in only Tubatulabal and Hopi; however, there is a cognate in Shoshoni, *punku,* that means 'horse, pet', and one in Tarahumara, *bukú*, that means 'cattle, pet'. The word in the ancestral language probably meant 'pet', which was then extended to the most typical 'pet' or domesticated animal.

Even after identifying those cognates that involve meaning changes and sound changes, many basic vocabulary items seem unrelatable across the Uto-Aztecan languages, but this is hardly surprising for a family whose member languages are not closely related. More importantly, the large number of similarities that can be identified make a genetic hypothesis unavoidable, since they are too numerous to be due to chance, and the borrowing of so many basic vocabulary items in such a large number of geographically separated languages never occurs.

Sound Correspondences

The procedure of identifying sound correspondences can be illustrated in the closely related Numic lan-

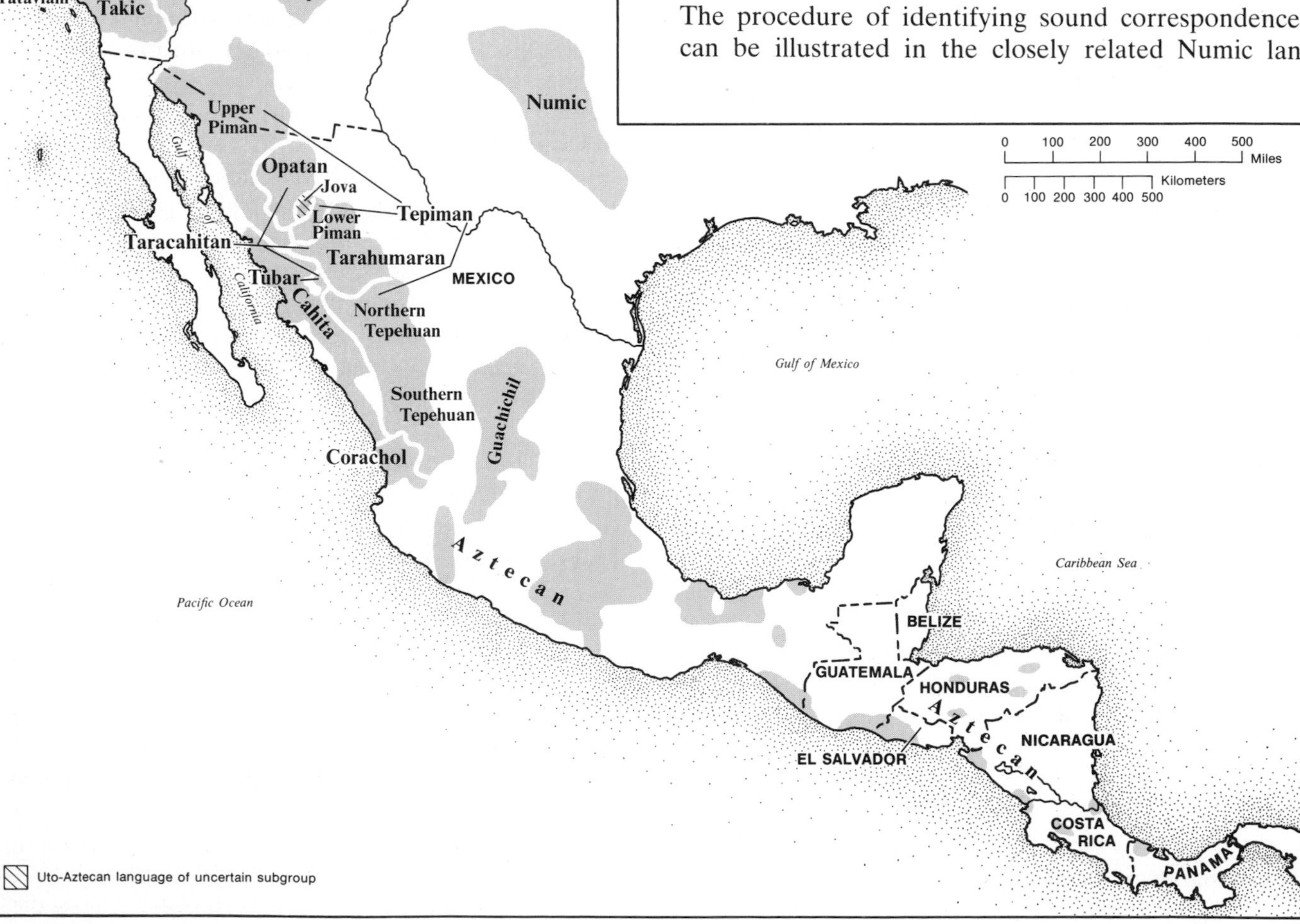

Fig. 1. Approximate distribution of Uto-Aztecan languages and language groups at the times of first European contact. Not mapped are groups for which no linguistic data survive. For a detailed classification see table 8.

Table 1. **Lexical Similarities in Four Numic Languages**

gloss	*Mono*	*Shoshoni*	*S. Paiute*	*Kawaiisu*	*Proto-Numic*
nose	*mupi*	*mupi*	*mupi*	*muvi·-*	**mupi*
older brother	*papi*	*papi*	*papi*	*pavi-*	**papi*
pine nut	*tɨpa*	*tɨpa*	*tɨpa*	*tɨva-pɨ*	**tɨpa*
sleep	(*ɨwi*)	*ɨppɨi*	*appɨi*	*ɨpi·*	**ɨppɨwi*
belly	(*qohi*)	*sappɨh*	*sappɨ*	*sapɨ-vɨ*	**sappɨ*
cedar	*waʔappɨ*	*wa·ppi*	*waʔappɨ*	(*waʔada-*)	**waʔappɨ*
cloud	*to·ppɨ*	*to·ppɨh*	(*pakina*)	(*kɨna-vɨ*)	**to·ppɨ*
stone	*tɨppi*	*tɨmpi*	*tɨmpi*	*tɨbi-čɨ*	**tɨmpi*
mouth	*tɨppe*	*tɨmpe*	*tɨmpa*	*tɨbi-vɨ*	**tɨmpe*
foot	(*kɨ·kɨ*)	*nampe*	*nampa*	*nabi-vɨ*	**nampe*

NOTE: Items that are not cognate with those in the other languages are placed in parentheses.

guages, where it is easy to distinguish between cognate and noncognate material. As illustrated in table 1, where Mono has word-initial *p,* as in 'older brother', the cognates in the other Numic languages have the same. In this case the corresponding sounds are identical in all the languages, and Proto-Numic can be reconstructed as also having initial **p-*. But in word-medial position, as a result of sound changes in some of the languages, the corresponding sounds are not identical. Nevertheless, because sound change in language is regular, these sound correspondences are regular and make it possible to reconstruct the word-medial sounds as well (table 3). Because of the close relationship of the Numic languages, the Proto-Numic sound system can be reconstructed in great detail, along with a great deal of the vocabulary.

The same principles that apply to the Numic subgroup apply to Uto-Aztecan as a whole. Since the relationship is more distant, cognates are not always so obvious, the sound system cannot be reconstructed in so great detail, and the reconstructible vocabulary is smaller, but the principles are the same. Because of the regularity of sound change, cognates can sometimes be verified even when they appear quite dissimilar. For example, the Aztec element *i·š-* in the word for 'eye' is cognate with the words in all the other Uto-Aztecan languages, even though there is little resemblance. In Aztec initial PUA (Proto–Uto-Aztecan) **p-* is lost (see also 'water,' 'road', and 'heavy'), **u* becomes *i*(·) (see 'die'), **s* becomes *š* before **i* (see 'urinate'), and under certain conditions vowels in noninitial syllables are lost.

The vocabulary items in table 2 are listed again in table 4, but with noncognate items omitted and with the order rearranged so as to illustrate the vowel correspondences in the initial syllable, which are then listed in table 5. Table 6 gives the initial consonant correspondences, only some of which are illustrated in the cognates of table 4. Because some consonant changes are restricted to certain phonetic environments, multiple correspondences result. For example, **w* becomes Hopi *l* before **a* and **o* but remains *w* before other vowels; **t* becomes Aztec *tl* before **a* but remains *t* before other vowels. (Also, there are sound changes reflected by the cognates of table 4 that are not explainable in terms of present knowledge.)

Sapir (1913–1914) was the first to identify the major sound changes in the Uto-Aztecan languages, and to reconstruct much of the PUA sound system. Whorf (1935) elaborated and expanded on Sapir's work. Voegelin, Voegelin, and Hale (1962) and Miller (1967) summarized and added to this work and also provided a large body of Uto-Aztecan cognates.

The PUA vowels and consonants of initial syllables can be reconstructed in considerable detail, but there are still many problems for noninitial syllables, in part because of changes brought about by morphological and grammatical processes, including in particular suffixation. More work with the intermediate proto-languages of Numic and other subgroups will help in the solution of these problems. But because of the distance involved for the whole of Uto-Aztecan, it is unrealistic to think that there will not always be a sizable unexplained residue.

Grammar

Uto-Aztecan languages share a number of grammatical similarities. While most are the legacy of their common ancestry, some are more useful than others in demonstrating that ancestry. Three will be considered here: the relative order of direct object and verb, the form of direct objects in dependent clauses, and the absolutive noun suffix.

Most Uto-Aztecan languages place the verb after the direct object. Compare Shoshoni *setɨn nittɨn tahan pi·a pekkanu* (word for word: 'that:one' 'must' 'our' 'mother' 'killed') 'She must have killed our mother'; and Cupeño *nišmálimi kuʔut mipəmʔə́wluninwən pə́či qay pəmčíxpi* ('girls' 'they:say' 'they-initiate' 'with' 'not' 'die') 'They used to initiate girls, in order that they would not die.' In some languages (like Shoshoni), the verb is almost always placed after the object, whereas in others its

Table 2. Basic Vocabulary Items in Seven Uto-Aztecan Languages

gloss	*Shoshoni*	*Tubatulabal*	*Luiseño*	*Hopi*	*Tarahumara*	*Cora*	*Aztec*
nose	*mupi*	*mupi-t*	*mú·vi-l*	*yáqa*	*aká*	*cúʔuri*	*yaka-tl*
ear	*nenki*	*naŋha-l*	*náq-la*	*náq-vɨ*	*naká*	*našái*	*naká·-s-tli*
eye	*puih*	*punʒi-l*	*púš-la*	*pó·si*	*busí*	*hɨʔɨ*	*i·š-telolo-tl*
tooth	*tama*	*taman-t*	*tamá-t*	*táma*	*ramé*	*tamé*	*tlan-tli*
breast	*pici*	*pi·-l*	*pí-t*	*pí·-hɨ*	*kasó*	*ciʔi-mé*	*čičiwal-li*
heart	*pihyɨ*	*su·na-l*	*ṣún-la*	*ɨnáŋʷɨ*	*sulú*	*sáihnʸuʔuka-ri*	*yo·l-o·-tl*
bone	*cuhni*	*o-n*	*kulá·wu-t*	*ő·qa*	*oʔčí*	*karí*	*omi-tl*
urinate	*si·*	*šiʔ-ɨt*	*ší·ʔa-*	*sisíwkɨ*	*isí*	*séʔe*	*a·-šiša*
excrement	*kʷita-ppɨh*	*ša·-l*	*ṣá·ʔi-š*	*kʷíta*	*witá*	*čʷitá*	*kʷitla-tl*
tail	*kʷesi*	*wiši·*	*-píqʷsiv*	*sɨ́ri*	*wasí*	*kʷasí*	*kʷitla-pil-li*
dog	*sati·*	*puku-biš-t*	*awá·-l*	*pó·ko*	*kočí*	*čɨʔɨ*	*či·či·*
moon	*mɨa*	*mɨ·ya-bis-t*	*móy-la*	*mɨ́·yawɨ*	*mečá*	*máškɨraʔi*	*me·c-tli*
water	*pa·*	*pa·-l*	*pá·-la*	*pá·-hɨ*	*baʔwí*	*háh*	*a·-tl*
stone	*tɨm-pi*	*tɨn-t*	*tó·-ta*	*ówa*	*ré·*	*tʸetʸé*	*te-tl*
salt	*ona-pi*	*o·na-l*	*éŋ-la*	*őŋa*	*koná*	*unáh*	*ista-tl*
road	*poʔe*	*poh-t*	*pé-t*	*pő-hɨ*	*bowé*	*huyé*	*oʔ-tli*
one	*sɨmmɨ*	*či·č*	*supú-l*	*sɨ́·ka*	*bilé*	*séi*	*se·*
two	*waha-*	*wo·*	*wéh*	*lő·yö-m*	*okwá*	*wáʔapwa*	*o·-me*
dry	*pasa*	*wa·g-ɨt*	*a-wáx-ve*	*lá·qu*	*wakí*	*wáči*	*i·š-wa·k-ki*
heavy	*pɨttɨ*	*pɨliʔ*	*wíma-*	*pɨ́tɨ*	*beté*	*tʸí-hetʸe*	*eti-k*
stand	*wɨnɨ-*	*ɨ·win-*	*wí·ta-*	*wɨ́nɨ*	*wilí*	*áh-če-si*	*iʔka·-c*
give	*uttu*	*maha*	*óvi-*	*máqa*	*yá*	*-ša*	*maka*
die	*tiai*	*mu·g-ɨt*	*píʔ-muk*	*mó·k*	*mukú*	*mɨʔɨ*	*miki*

position is more variable, as for example in Guarijío: *noʔ-kiʔá pié mahuána patári* ('me-give' 'one' 'bottle' 'mescal') 'Give me a mescal bottle.' and *pié espáda noʔ-kiʔá* ('one' 'shovel' 'me-give') 'Give me a shovel.' But Aztec more often places the verb before the object: *auh i·wa·n niman iʔkʷa·k kitlatike in teo·kalli* ('and' 'also' 'then' 'when' 'they-burned' 'the temple') 'And it was also when they burned the temple.' Aztec is no less Uto-Aztecan than Shoshoni or Guarijío, but grammar, like other aspects of language, can change, and Aztec in this case has innovated.

Because most Uto-Aztecan languages place the verb after the object, and because of other considerations (Langacker 1977:24), it can be established that this was also a feature of PUA grammar. However, this feature cannot be used to prove the genetic relationship, because there are only two possible orders.

Proto–Uto-Aztecan placed the subject of most dependent clauses in the object form rather than the subject form. Most of the daughter languages still do this, for example: Shoshoni *nɨwi tiʔopikka-ku, nɨwi cayɨcippɨhkantɨn* ('person' 'sick-when', 'person' 'raises: up') 'When a person gets sick, He cures them.' 'Person' is *nɨwɨ* in subject form, *nɨwi* in object form. Tubatulabal has *piškič tu·mupi-n anaŋat čičwanaʔaš a·bu·-i unaŋa·l-aŋ* ('then' 'child-her' 'crying' 'always' 'mother-her' 'goes:to:pound-when') 'Then her child is crying all the time when her mother goes pounding.' 'Her mother' is *a·bu·-n* in subject form, *a·bu·-i* in object form. Guarijío has *woʔí tukéruma tamó mociká-ci iʔwá* ('Coyote' 'asked' 'we' 'lived-where' 'here') 'Coyote asked where we lived.' 'We' in subject form is *remé*; 'us', object, is *tamó*. The use of the object form for the subject of dependent clauses is a more specific grammatical feature than the placement of verb and object and thus more useful for determining genetic relationship. But there are some Uto-Aztecan languages that have lost this feature and some non–Uto-Aztecan languages that have similar features (cf. English 'Coyote asked *us* to come.').

PUA had a suffix called the absolutive suffix that was added to nouns. A reflex of the suffix is found in almost every Uto-Aztecan language (see table 7). In most languages it plays an important role in the grammar, but in some it is found in only vestigial form. In most of

Table 3. Some Numic Correspondences in Medial Position

Mono	*Shoshoni*	*S. Paiute*	*Kawaiisu*	*Proto-Numic*	*glosses of examples on table 1*
-p-	*-p-*	*-p-*	*-v-*	**-p-*	nose, older brother, pine nut
-pp-	*-pp-*	*-pp-*	*-p-*	**-pp-*	sleep, belly, cedar, cloud
-pp-	*-mp-*	*-mp-*	*-b-*	**-mp-*	stone, mouth, foot

Table 4. Some Uto-Aztecan Cognate Sets

gloss	*Shoshoni*	*Tubatulabal*	*Luiseño*	*Hopi*	*Tarahumara*	*Cora*	*Aztec*
water	*pa·*	*pa·-*	*pá·-*	*pá·-*	*baʔwí*	*háh*	*a·-*
tooth	*tama*	*taman-*	*tamá-*	*táma*	*ramé*	*tamé*	*tlan-*
dry		*wa·g-*	*-wáx-*	*lá·qu*	*wakí*	*wáči*	*-wa·k-*
nose (1)				*yáqa*	*aká*		*yaka-*
ear	*nenki*	*naŋha-*	*náq-*	*náq-*	*naká*	*našái*	*naká·-*
tail	*kʷeši*	*wiši·*[a]	*-qʷsi-*		*wasí*	*kʷasí*	
stone	*tɨm-*	*tɨn-*	*tó·-*		*ré·*	*tʸetʸé*	*te-*
heavy	*pɨttɨ*	*pɨlɨʔ*		*pítɨ*	*beté*	*-hetʸe*	*eti-*
moon	*mɨa*	*mɨ·ya-*	*móy-*	*mɨ́·ya-*	*mečá*		*me·c-*
road	*poʔe*	*poh-*	*pé-*	*pő-*	*bowé*	*huyé*	*oʔ-*
bone		*o-*		*ő·qa*	*oʔčí*		*omi-*
two		*wo·*	*wéh*	*lő·yö-*	*okwá*		*o·-*
salt	*ona-*	*o·na-*	*éŋ-*	*őŋa*	*koná*[b]	*unáh*	
breast	*pici*	*pi·-*	*pí-*	*pí·-*			
urinate	*si·*	*šiʔ-*	*ší·ʔa-*	*sisí-*	*isí*		*-šiša*
excrement	*kʷita-*			*kʷíta*	*witá*	*čʷitá*	*kʷitla-*
eye	*puih*	*punʒi-*	*púš-*	*pó·si*	*busí*	*hɨ́ʔɨ*	*i·š-*
nose (2)	*mupi*	*mupi-*	*mú·vi-*				
heart		*su·na-*	*ṣún-*		*sulú*		
die		*mu·g-*	*-muk*	*mó·k*	*mukú*	*mɨʔɨ*	*miki*

[a] Probably cognate but first vowel does not match regular correspondences.
[b] Probably cognate but initial *k-* is of obscure origin.

the languages, the suffix has little or no meaning but is added when the noun is used alone. For example Aztec *pil-li* 'son' has the absolutive (in the shape *-li*), but the same stem has no suffix when used with the prefix *no-*: *no-pil* 'my son'. *a·-tl* 'water' has absolutive *-tli,* which is absent when the stem is compounded with a following root: *a·-kal-li* 'canoe' (literally 'water-house-*li*'). In some languages, for example Hopi, the absolutive suffix is involved in the formation of the object form of the noun. In Tarahumara, the suffix is used to distinguish an item from all others and is often best translated into English by 'the'. In some languages, for example Papago and Shoshoni, it is found in vestigial form only, in Papago to connect a noun with certain postpositions and in Shoshoni as an object suffix with only a handful of nouns.

Of the three grammatical features, the absolutive is the most useful for establishing genetic relationship. It has changed its grammatical meaning and function in a number of languages, but always in ways that can be understood by common historical processes. It plays an important role in the grammar of most of the languages, but in almost all other Uto-Aztecan languages it is found in at least vestigial form in some nook or cranny. The forms can be phonetically related to one another (from PUA *-*ta,* perhaps also *-*la*). And most importantly it is very particular, a kind of grammatical feature that is seldom found in other languages.

Work on PUA grammar postdates that on reconstruction of the sound system (Crapo 1970; Steele 1973, 1975; Langacker 1976, 1977, 1977a; Heath 1977–1978). More attention has been paid to syntax, but morphology (the formation of complex forms through prefixation, suffixation, and compounding) has not been entirely ignored. Morphological changes are difficult to study in the absence of a thorough understanding of the phonology, since morphological development can be extensively affected by phonological changes. Morphology is the area of historical research that should be the most fruitful in the 1980s, since it has received the least attention and will aid in understanding and reconstructing both the sound system and the syntax of PUA.

History of Classification

A family-tree classification, which divides a language family into branches and subbranches, if taken as a model of prehistory would imply an ancestral speech community that split into two or more communities, with little or no contact between them. In actual fact, sharp divisions seldom occur. The separations may be more or less gradual, leading first to a chain of interrelated dialects before developing into distinct languages. In this case languages that developed out of dialects that occupied in-between positions still reflect their original intermediate position (see fig. 2). Uto-Aztecan presents a classic case of this situation, so that any classification into distinct subgroups will distort the nature of the interrelationships to a greater or lesser extent. Certain aspects have always been difficult and subject to disagreement among informed scholars.

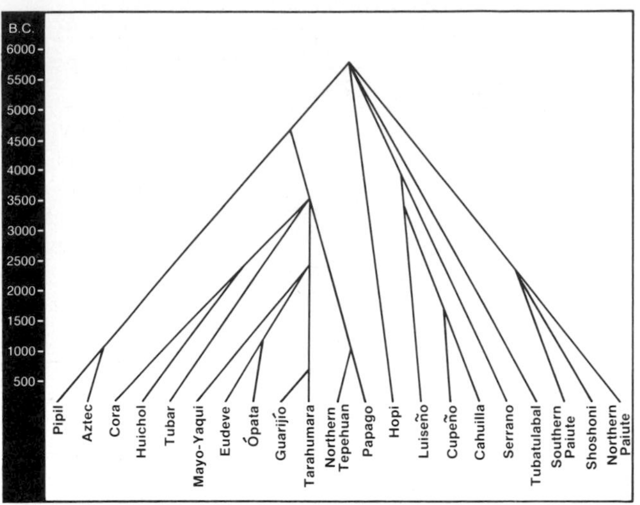

Fig. 2. Family-tree diagram of relationships in the Uto-Aztecan family showing estimated dates of separation.

The earliest classifications, which began appearing in the nineteenth century, are now of historical interest only, since they were based on fragmentary data (see Lamb 1964). The first adequate classification, made by Kroeber (1907), concerned only the northern, or Shoshonean languages. Based almost entirely on lexical evidence, Kroeber divided Shoshonean into four branches—Plateau, Kern River, Southern Californian, and Pueblo. His terms have been replaced by modern ones—Numic, Tubatulabal, Takic, and Hopi—but the divisions have stood the test of later scholarship.

A number of conflicting classifications of the Sonoran languages have been proposed (Kroeber 1934; Mason 1936, 1940; Whorf 1936a; Lamb 1964). The conflicts are small and stem from the scantiness of the data for certain extinct languages and, until after 1950, for some crucial languages.

Most controversy in classification pertains to the largest divisions within the family. Early work in the twentieth century implicitly or explicitly recognized three large divisions, Aztecan, Sonoran, and Shoshonean. Kroeber (1934:6) departed from this scheme when he suggested that Sonoran languages did not form a unit but instead consisted of several independent branches within Uto-Aztecan. In a review of Kroeber, Whorf (1935b) suggested that the same was true of the Shoshonean languages. This view, sometimes with slight variations, has been endorsed by Mason (1940), Lamb (1964), and Miller (1964). The earlier tripartite approach has been followed by Voegelin, Voegelin, and Hale (1962:1), Hale (1958), Langacker (1977:1), Heath (1977–1978:27), and Steele (1979), sometimes with variations in which Sonoran is placed in a larger grouping with either Aztecan or Shoshonean. Most discussions are notable for the skimpiness of evidence brought to bear. The one exception is Hale (1959), and in this case Lamb (1964:122) and Miller (1964:147) suggest that Hale's data could better be used to support their position.

Miller's (1980) classification, using primarily lexical evidence and secondarily phonological evidence, has the advantage of being based on fuller and more accurate data than preceding classifications (table 8). It is a hybrid of the two approaches, with Sonoran, but not Shoshonean, recognized as a unit. There are five main branches, with the first four being the same ones that constituted Kroeber's Shoshonean. Sonoran is grouped with Aztecan to form a larger group, Southern Uto-Aztecan. As with all classifications, intermediate and chain relationships go unrecognized, but they are evident in the data. Particular mention must be made of the Numic and Aztecan groups, the two most dissimilar sets of language in Uto-Aztecan, which must have represented opposite ends of the old Uto-Aztecan dialect chain.

Numic Languages

The Numic languages, consisting of three closely related groups, occupy the greatest area of any branch of Uto-Aztecan, covering all of the Great Basin, as well as parts of the Plateau and Plains areas to the north and east.

Western Numic consists of Mono and Paviotso. Mono is spoken in California, on both sides of the Sierra Nevada mountains, by the Monache and the Owens Valley Paiute. There are a few hundred speakers, almost all middle aged or older. The Northfork dialect of Mono has been described by Lamb (1958b). Paviotso, also known as Northern Paiute, is found in adjoining areas of California, Nevada, and Oregon, and includes, linguistically, the Bannock of southern Idaho. The language was still widely used by 1,000–2,000 speakers in 1981, but few children were learning it. The language has been extensively studied, but little has been published on it (Liljeblad 1950, 1939–1981; Nichols 1971, 1973).

Panamint, Shoshoni, and Comanche comprise Central Numic. Panamint, spoken by probably fewer than 50 older people, in and near Death Valley in California and Nevada, has been studied in the field by Dayley (1971) and Miller (1968). Locally, and sometimes in the ethnographic literature, the Panamint are known as Shoshoni. The Koso are, properly speaking, the southwesternmost Panamint, but this name is sometimes used for all of the Panamint. Shoshoni is spoken by a few thousand speakers over a wide area from southwest Nevada to southwestern Wyoming. Though the language was widely used in 1981, few children were learning it. The language is described in Miller (1972) and in the sketch in volume 17. Comanche, once widely spoken in the southern Plains, was used in 1981 only

Table 5. Uto-Aztecan Correspondences of Vowels in Initial Syllables

Shoshoni	*Tubatulabal*	*Luiseño*	*Hopi*	*Tarahumara*	*Cora*	*Aztecan*	*PUA*	*glosses of examples on table 4*
a,e	*a*	*a*	*a*	*a*	*a*	*a*	**a*	water, tooth, dry, nose (1), ear, tail
ɨ	*ɨ*	*o*	*ɨ*	*e*	*e*	*e*	**ɨ*	stone, heavy, moon
o	*o*	*e*	*ö*	*o*	*u*	*o*	**o*	road, bone, two, salt
i	*i*	*i*	*i*	*i*	*i*	*i*	**i*	breast, urinate, excrement
u	*u*	*u*	*o*	*u*	*ɨ*	*i*	**u*	eye, nose (2), heart, die

by a handful of older speakers in two communities near Lawton, Oklahoma. Canonge (1958) did extensive field work with the language and has published a set of texts and vocabulary. Using primarily the notes of Canonge, Wistrand-Robinson (1980) has prepared a dictionary to which Armagost (1980) has appended a grammatical sketch.

Southern Numic consists of Kawaiisu and Ute. Kawaiisu, in 1981 spoken by about 20 old people in Tehachapi and Bakersfield, California, has been studied by Klein (1959), Booth (1979), and Munro (1976b), and by Zigmond who has prepared a dictionary (1975). The Ute language is spoken in the southern portions of Nevada, Utah, and Colorado by the Chemehuevi, Southern Paiute, and Ute tribal groups. One of the best grammars, and the first thorough description of a Uto-Aztecan language, was Sapir's (1930–1931) treatment of Southern Paiute. Also available is a dictionary of the Ute dialect (Givón 1979) and a grammar and vocabulary of Chemehuevi (Press 1975), a dialect that is perhaps divergent enough to be considered a separate language. There were a few thousand speakers of the various dialects of Ute in 1981, and the language was widely used, though few children were learning it.

Comparative work in Numic has been done by I. Davis (1966), Nichols (1973), Iannucci (1972), and Miller (1980b). Freeze and Iannucci (1979) provide a detailed discussion of the Numic internal classification and arrive at conclusions different from those of Kroeber (1907:97–98) and Miller (1980).

Tubatulabal

The Tubatulabal branch is made up of a single language of the same name. Aboriginally it was spoken by 500 to 1,000 people in the Kern River valley near Bakersfield. In 1972 only six older people spoke the language (vol. 8:439). The language has been treated by Voegelin (1935, 1935a, 1958) and Munro (Mace and Munro 1981).

Tubatulabal has a number of features that place it in an intermediate position between Numic and Takic (Kroeber 1907:99; Miller 1980).

Takic Languages

The Takic languages were spoken in southern California. Like Numic, there were three internal divisions, but their linguistic relationships to each other were much more distant. The Serran and Gabrielino languages are extinct, and the Cupan languages were spoken by only a small number of older people in 1981.

Table 6. Uto-Aztecan Initial Consonant Correspondences

Shoshoni	*Tubatulabal*	*Luiseño*	*Hopi*	*Tarahumara*	*Cora*	*Aztecan*	*PUA*
p-	*p-*	*p-*	*p-*	*b-*	*h-*	∅	**p-*
t-	*t-*	*t-*	*t-*	*r-*	*t-,tʸ-*	*t-,tl-*	**t-*
c-	*c-*	*c-*	*c-*	*č-*	*c-*	*c-,č-*	**c-*
k-	*k-,h-*	*k-,q-*	*k-,q-*	*k-*	*k-,č-*	*k-*	**k-*
kʷ-	*w-*	*kʷ-,qʷ-*	*kʷ-*	*w-*	*kʷ-,čʷ-*	*kʷ-*	**kʷ-*
s-	*s-,š-*	*s-,ṣ-,š-*	*s-*	*s-*	*s-*	*s-,š-*	**s-*
m-	*m-*	*m-*	*m-*	*m-*	*mw-*	*m-*	**m-*
n-	*n-*	*n-*	*n-*	*n-*	*n-*	*n-*	**n-*
w-	*w-*	*w-*	*w-,l-*	*w-*	*w-*	*w-*	**w-*
y-	*y-*	*y-*	*y-*	∅	*y-*	*y-*	**y-*
h-	∅	*h-*	*h-*	∅	∅	∅	**h-*

(∅ indicates no initial consonant)

The closely related Serran languages, Serrano and Kitanemuk, the northernmost Takic languages, were formerly spoken by about 3,000 people (vol. 8:88). Kitanemuk is known from notes made by Harrington (1917), and Serrano from work by K.C. Hill (1967) and Crook (1974–1976).

Gabrielino (or Gabrielino-Fernandino) was probably a single language with diverse dialects. It may have formed an independent Takic group, or it may have been aligned with Serran (Miller 1980). It was spoken in the area of present-day Los Angeles, was recorded by Kroeber (1907) and Harrington (1914–1930), and died out in the early twentieth century (vol. 8:541).

The Cupan languages, Cupeño, Cahuilla, and Luiseño, were the southernmost Takic languages. Cupeño, the smallest of the three in area and numbers (about 1,000), has been recorded by Hill (J.H. Hill 1966; Hill and Nolasquez 1973). The other two languages had about 5,000 speakers each. Luiseño is available from a number of sources (Kroeber and Grace 1960; Bright 1968; Hyde 1971). Seiler and his students provided several reports on Cahuilla (Seiler 1970, 1977; Seiler and Hioki 1979). Cupan is well provided with historical studies. Bright and Hill (1967) have reconstructed the phonological system, along with much of the vocabulary, and Jacobs (1975) has studied Cupan historical grammar.

Hopi

Hopi, like Tubatulabal, is a branch made up of a single language. It is spoken with slight dialect variation in several Pueblos in northeast Arizona. The population in 1970 was 4,857 (vol. 9:221). Whorf (1935a, 1946) has described the language, and Voegelin and Voegelin (1957) have published lexical material.

Southern Uto-Aztecan Languages

Sonoran Languages

The Sonoran languages are found in the coastal plains and mountains of northwest Mexico from Nayarit to Sonora, and across the international border into southern Arizona. Some Sonoran languages are extinct; others are still widely spoken, but because of pressures from European colonization over the past four centuries it is difficult or impossible to reconstruct aboriginal locations and numbers. There are six groups: Tepiman, Tarahumaran, Opatan, Cahitan, Tubar, and Corachol. Three of the groups, Tarahumaran, Opatan, and Cahitan, share a number of similarities and perhaps can be grouped under the heading Taracahitan. But since the similarities are not striking, when contrasted with other Sonoran languages, and since the three were in geographic proximity, it may be an apparent subgrouping resulting from contact and from their central position within Sonoran.

The northernmost Sonoran group, Tepiman, consists of four closely related languages—Upper Piman, Lower Piman, Northern Tepehuan, and Southern Tepehuan. The group is also known as Piman, but this has resulted in some terminological confusion, since Piman is also used for the two northernmost languages, as well as for some dialects of the northernmost language, and was the term Powell (1891:98–99) used for Sonoran. Aboriginally, Tepiman was spoken in a long band stretching from southern Arizona to Durango, but with a gap between the two Piman and two Tepehuan languages, which was filled by intervening Tarahumaran and Cahitan speakers. Upper Piman was spoken in 1981 in two areas, by the Pima-Papago of southern Arizona and contiguous northern Sonora, and by the Névome in Ónavas, in south-central Sonora. Pima-Papago was widely used by 5,000 or more adults and children. Saxton and Saxton (1969) provide a dictionary and grammatical sketch. Névome, a markedly different dialect from Pima-Papago of Arizona, had two speakers in 1971 (Hale, quoted in Bascom 1965:161). Because it is geographically closer to Lower Piman, Névome has sometimes been mistakenly placed with it, but it is clear that linguistically Névome belongs with Pima-Pagago (Bascom 1965:5). Lower Piman (or Mountain Piman) was spoken in 1981 in several places in the mountains of southern Sonora and contiguous Chihuahua by 1,000 or more people (Pennington 1979–1980, 1:47–53; Bascom 1965:5). Northern Tepehuan was spoken by about 3,500 people in the mountains of southwestern Chihuahua (Bascom 1965:6). There is an early Jesuit vocabulary (Rinaldini 1743). Bascom (1965) has conducted extensive research. Southern Tepehuan, which also includes the extinct Tepecano dialect (Mason 1917), was spoken by approximately 8,000 people in Durango and Jalisco (Bascom 1965:5). Elizabeth and Thomas L. Willett have done extensive fieldwork with the language (see Willett 1978). Bascom (1965) has reconstructed Proto-Tepiman phonology and vocabulary.

Tarahumaran consists of two closely related lan-

Table 7. Absolutive Suffix in Several Uto-Aztecan Languages

Shoshoni *-tta: naipi-tta* 'girl' (obj. form)
Tubatulabal *-l, -t: pa·-l* 'water', *ma·-l* 'hand', *pom-t* 'egg'
Luiseño *-la, -ta, -ča, -l, -t, -š: pá·-la* 'water', *pá·ni-l* 'egg', *má-t* 'hand'
Cahuilla *-(a)l, -(i)l*ʸ, *-(a)t, -iš: pá-l* 'water', *héma-l* 'hand', *púč-il*ʸ 'eye'
Hopi *-ta: pá·sa-ta* 'field' (obj. form)
Papago *-t, -č: kúkui č ʔɨḍ* 'in the trees' (lit. 'trees-*č*-in')
Tarahumara *-la: moʔó-la* 'head', *saʔpá-la* 'meat'
Aztec *-tl, -tli, -li: a·-tl* 'water', *oʔ-tli* 'road', *pil-li* 'son'

guages, Tarahumara and Guarijío. With about 50,000 speakers in 1981, Tarahumara is the second largest language, after Aztec, with many speakers being monolingual. The Tarahumaras live in the mountain and canyon country of southwestern Chihuahua, and there is considerable dialect diversity. The eastern dialect is one of the best documented Uto-Aztecan languages, because of the extensive work in the twentieth century by Jesuit missionaries (Brambila 1953, 1980; Lionnet 1968, 1972). Burgess (1977, 1978, 1979, 1981) has studied the very different western dialect. The Guarijío, numbering about 2,000 in 1981, live to the west of the Tarahumara in the canyon and foothill country in and near the Río Mayo of Chihuahua and Sonora. The language consists of two markedly different dialects, an upland dialect (Miller 1977, 1978), and a lowland dialect (Stoltzfus 1979, 1979a).

Opatan consisted of the extinct Eudeve (also called Heve and Dohema), and Ópata, which survived into the twentieth century, but is thought to have become extinct by the 1960s (Escalante H. 1964). These languages were located in the mountains of Sonora, generally east of the Upper Piman. The Ópata were the politically and numerically dominant people of the area. The early Jesuit missionaries left much linguistic material (Lombardo 1702; Barbastro 1792; Pennington 1981; B.T. Smith 1861).

There are about 33,000 Cahitan speakers (Lastra 1975:183). Cahitan consists of two dialects, Mayo and Yaqui, which are spoken on the coastal plain of Sonora and Sinaloa. Yaqui is also spoken in several communities in Arizona, the result of migrations that took place at the beginning of the twentieth century. The language is well described (Velasco 1890; J.B. Johnson 1962; Collard and Collard 1962; Lindenfeld 1973; Lionnet 1977).

Tubar was the language of a small group sandwiched between the Tarahumara, Northern Tepehuan, and Mayo. Material gathered during the Lumholtz expedition of 1893 has been published by Lionnet (1978). The language is thought to be extinct.

Cora and Huichol, which make up the Corachol subbranch, were in 1981 spoken by about 20,000 to 25,000 people in Nayarit and Jalisco. While they belong to the Sonoran branch, they share some similarities with the Aztecan languages, indicating that they probably were the ones closest to the Aztecan languages in the old Sonoran dialect chain. Cora has been studied by Preuss (1932), McMahon and Aiton de McMahon (1959), and Casad (1981). Huichol has been studied by Grimes (1964) and McIntosh (1949).

Aztecan Languages

Aztecan consists of three languages, Aztec (also called Nahuatl or Mexicano), Pipil, and Pochutec. The three are very closely related, but Aztec and Pipil are more closely related to each other than to Pochutec.

Aztec had in the 1980s about half a million speakers throughout a wide area of central and southern Mexico and displayed considerable dialect variation. In some places it was being replaced by Spanish, but in others it maintained a vigorous existence. There is a continuous tradition of study from the time of the conquest to the present (Lastra 1975:172–177).

Pipil is a dying language, spoken in the 1970s or formerly in several isolated enclaves in Central America. The dialect Nicarao, in Nicaragua, is grouped by some with Pipil (for example, Campbell and Langacker 1978:87) and by others with Nahuatl (for example, Lastra 1975:173). Pochutec, spoken in Oaxaca, is extinct but was documented by Boas (1917), who did fieldwork with some of the last speakers.

Aztecan phonology, along with a great deal of the vocabulary, has been reconstructed by Campbell and Langacker (1978), and Dakin (1979) has reconstructed some important aspects of the morphology. Lastra (in

Table 8. Classification of Uto-Aztecan Languages

Numic
- Western Numic: Mono, Paviotso or Northern Paiute (Bannock)
- Central Numic: Panamint, Shoshoni, Comanche
- Southern Numic: Kawaiisu, Ute (Chemehuevi, Southern Pauite, Ute)

Tubatulabal

Takic
- Serrano-Gabrielino
  - Serran: Serrano, Kitanemuk
  - Gabrielino (Gabrielino, Fernandeño)
- Cupan
  - Cupeño, Cahuilla
  - Luiseño

Hopi

Southern Uto-Aztecan
- Sonoran
  - Tepiman: Upper Piman (Papago, Pima, Névome), Lower Piman, Northern Tepehuan, Southern Tepehuan (Southern Tepehuan, Tepecano)
  - Taracahitan
    - Tarahumaran: Tarahumara (Eastern Tarahumara, Western Tarahumara, Southern Tarahumara), Guarijío (Upland Guarijío, Lowland Guarijío)
    - Opatan: Ópata, Eudeve
    - Cahita (Mayo, Yaqui)
  - Tubar
  - Corachol: Cora, Huichol
- Aztecan
  - General Aztec: Pipil, Aztec (Classical Aztec, Tetelcingo, Zacapoaxtla, and others)
  - Pochutec

SOURCE: Miller 1980.
NOTE: Names in parentheses are dialects of the preceding language.

preparation) has completed a massive dialect survey of contemporary Nahuatl.

Extinct Languages

Some languages in southern California and northern Mexico became extinct before little or anything of them was recorded and thus are difficult to place.

Those in California were Tataviam (Bright 1975; vol. 8:535–537), San Nicolas (Kroeber 1907:153), Giamina (Lamb 1964:110; Kroeber 1907:126–128, 1909a:263–265), and Vanyume (Kroeber 1907:139–140; Bright 1975; vol. 8:570, *570*). Most likely these were Takic languages, though both Kroeber and Lamb suggest that Giamina might have been a language constituting a separate branch within Uto-Aztecan, like Tubatulabal and Hopi. Vanyume was clearly Takic, and perhaps simply a dialect of Serrano.

The extinct groups in northern (mostly northwestern) Mexico are discussed very carefully by Sauer (1934) and reviewed again by Miller (1981). In spite of the fact that there are no data for some of the languages, it has often been assumed that these languages were Uto-Aztecan, simply because almost all the neighboring languages are. For two coastal tribes with a maritime economy, Guasave and Naarinuquia (or Themurete), this is especially problematic; the Seri are the only other maritime people in the area, and they speak a language that is assumed to be most closely related to the Yuman languages. The Seri were in 1981 the only Indian people in northwest Mexico to speak a non–Uto-Aztecan language.

There are enough data for Jova to indicate clearly that it is Sonoran, probably Taracahitan. Since the Jova lived next to the Ópata and Eudeve, it has usually been assumed that Jova fits in this group, but the data are too scanty to confirm this.

Based mostly on comments of the early missionaries, it is probable that Chínipa, Guasapar, and Témori were Tarahumaran, probably dialects of Guarijío, and that Conicari, Tepahue, Macoyahui, Baciroa, Comanito, Mocorito, Acaxee, and Tahue were Cahitan. These languages were spoken principally in what is now Sonora and Sinaloa. Huite, Zoe, Nio, Ocoroni, and Xixime were, for the most part, spoken in the foothills of Sinaloa. Being surrounded by speakers of Sonoran languages, it is likely that these, too, were Sonoran languages, but only for Ocoroni is there some supporting evidence.

Farther south, in the Corachol area, were languages aligned with this branch: Totorame with Cora, and Tecual and Guachichil with Huichol. In 1940 a vocabulary was recorded from some traveling musicians who claimed to speak Zacatec, a language of Zacatecas that was supposed to be extinct (H.R. Harvey 1972:300). The vocabulary was so similar to Huichol that Miller (1981) speculated that it was in fact Huichol rather than Zacatec.

In the plains to the east of the main body of extant Sonoran languages, there were a number of languages that have been seen by some to be Uto-Aztecan, more specifically Sonoran: Lagunero, Toboso, Concho, Jumano, and Suma (Pennington 1969:11–12; Kroeber 1934:13, 15; Sauer 1934:65; Miller 1981). Pennington suggests that Lagunero is affiliated with Zacatec, and that Toboso goes with Concho, but there are no linguistic data available for either language. The three words of Concho that were recorded in 1581 look like they may be those of a Uto-Aztecan language. It has been established that the Jumano and Suma spoke the same language. Three words have been recorded for this language, also, but in this case there is not even enough evidence for it to suggest a Uto-Aztecan affiliation.

More Distant Relationships

A number of suggestions have been made for more distant relationships. The only one for which convincing evidence has been published is with Kiowa-Tanoan (Whorf and Trager 1937), which, with Uto-Aztecan, comprises the Aztec-Tanoan family. Table 9 presents some of the evidence. The relationship is so distant that little reconstruction of the proto-language is possible.

Whorf (1935) suggested that Aztec-Tanoan is more distantly related to Penutian, Mayan, and Totonac but presented no evidence. Swadesh has suggested even more inclusive groupings, but again without published evidence. Greenberg (1980, 1981) has claimed evidence for a Uto-Aztecan, Kiowa-Tanoan, and Otomanguean relationship, as well as for more distant relationships.

Time and Place

By gauging the difference between two related languages, it is possible to estimate the time-depth for the proto-language. One method is based simply on intuition. Linguists have some notion how much difference to expect for a given period of time because of experience with languages, such as European languages, that have a long written history. A nonintuitive quantitative technique, called glottochronology (Swadesh 1955; Hymes 1960), developed to measure degree of vocabulary differences, has been applied to Uto-Aztecan languages (Swadesh 1963; Hale 1958, 1959; Lamb 1958; Goss 1965; Bascom 1965:4; Campbell and Langacker 1978:87).There are critics who question the accuracy of glottochronology; nevertheless, if used in conjunction with the older intuitive method, it is useful for obtaining rough dates that one can feel quite comfortable with (see fig. 2).

Table 9. Some Uto-Aztecan and Kiowa-Tanoan Cognates

	Uto-Aztecan languages			*Kiowa-Tanoan languages*	
Glosses	*Shoshoni*	*Tarahumara*	*Aztec*	*Taos*	*Kiowa*
'older brother/sister'	*papi, paci*	*baˀčí*	*a·č-tli*	*pòpò-na*	*pabí*
'three'	*pahi*	*beikiá*	*e·i*	*póyno*	*pʰą́ˀo*
'water'	*pa·*	*baˀwí*	*a·-tl*	*ṗòˀo-ne*	*ṗɔ-*
'road'	*poˀe*	*bowé*	*oˀ-tli*	*ṗìē-*	
'hair, fur, skin'	*poˀa*	*boá*		*pʰó-na*	*pʰɔ-*

SOURCES: Trager and Trager 1959; Whorf and Trager 1937.

A problem with both dating techniques is that greater similarity can result from contact, in which both languages influence the direction of change. This is especially the case in families like Uto-Aztecan in which the slow dissolution of dialects into languages is the rule, and clean cleavages between branches are rare. But this can be turned to advantage, by reconstructing old contacts and dialect chains. Thus the glottochronological figures show Tubatulabal to be intermediate between Numic and Takic, a position that cannot be represented in a family-tree classification.

When information on dating, diversity, and similarity due to contact is coupled with information on location, much historical information can be gained. The Numic languages display little internal diversity, yet they cover a huge area. Clearly, movement has taken place in relatively recent times. Lamb (1958) has shown that the Numic homeland is in the southwestern part of the Great Basin, since that is the area in which the three Numic subbranches exhibit the greatest degree of internal diversity. He suggests that the divisions into Northern, Central, and Southern Numic took place 2,000 or more years ago, and then about 1,000 years ago each of the three branches started moving into the Basin. His conclusions have been substantiated by other linguistic data: the distribution of place-names, and the distribution of reconstructed terms for flora and fauna (Fowler 1972).

The Takic languages present a contrasting picture. There is much greater internal diversity, yet they cover a much smaller area than the Numic languages. Thus they have been in or near their present location for a much longer time.

Since Tubatulabal and Hopi comprise branches each made up of a single language, internal diversity can be no help in establishing time and location of residence. Since lexical as well as other evidence (Miller 1980) shows Tubatulabal to be intermediate between Numic and Takic, it is likely that the language has been in southern California for some time, at or near its present location. Lexical evidence does not show Hopi to have close affiliations with any other Uto-Aztecan branch, but phonetically it shares some features with some of the Takic languages. Based on this, and some nonlinguistic evidence, Miller (1966:93–94) has suggested the Hopi may have come from a more western location.

The division between the two branches of Southern Uto-Aztecan, Sonoran and Aztecan, is profound, going back almost to the time of Proto–Uto-Aztecan. The Aztecan branch consists of few languages, very closely related, with a shallow time-depth. By contrast, the many Sonoran languages are well diversified, with a considerable time-depth, almost as deep as Takic. Thus, it is clear that the Sonoran languages have been in northwest Mexico for a long time. Miller (1981) has suggested that the Sonoran homeland might be in the foothill area between the Río Mayo and Río Sinaloa, because of a hint of greater diversity in that area.

The distribution of the Tepiman languages is anomalous. The four languages occupy a long band from north to south, but with a gap in the middle that was occupied by a number of other Sonoran languages. A glance at the spatial arrangement would make it appear that perhaps the band was once continuous and was cut in two by the intrusion of others. But because the Tepiman languages are so closely related, and because the languages in the gap are diverse, it is much more likely that the Tepimans have moved within the last millennium into their present location. Fowler (1980) and Miller (1981) have suggested that the movement was from south to north, but the evidence is not conclusive.

Lexical Evidence

The comparative method, which allows the reconstruction of proto-words, offers the cultural prehistorian a powerful tool. If a word and its gloss can be reconstructed, then that item must have also been present in the proto-language. Thus, the existence of the word for 'grinding stone', reconstructed as **mata*, attests to the use of this object in Proto–Uto-Aztecan times, by people who were hunters and gatherers and depended particularly on wild seeds for food. Information can sometimes be gleaned by showing that a change of meaning has taken place. Thus the word that means 'bow' or 'firearm' in most of the languages can be reconstructed with the probable gloss of 'spear thrower' or 'atlatl'. The comparative method also allows the isolation of loanwords. Thus, most of the Sonoran languages have a similar word for 'beans', but since the regular changes are not reflected in some of the languages, it is clear that at least some of the languages have borrowed from others (Miller 1966:100–101). More recent borrowings can also be illuminating. Thus many Sonoran languages have a word very similar to Guarijío *pirikó* 'wheat' as a borrowing from Spanish *trigo*. Since the phonetic changes involved are unusual, it is unlikely that each language borrowed directly from Spanish, but rather than one borrowed from Spanish, and the word was then passed from one Sonoran language to another. There are a few words for introduced food items that reflect this history.

The first lexical study in Uto-Aztecan was done by Romney (1957). Unfortunately, Uto-Aztecan studies were not then well developed, so that many of his conclusions were wrong (Miller 1966:94–101). Later work, and the most careful in Uto-Aztecan, has been done by Fowler, with Numic and nearby Uto-Aztecan languages (1972) and Sonoran (1980).

Sources

Examples given without citation in the tables and elsewhere in this chapter are from the following sources: Andrews 1975; Brambila 1953, 1980; Bright 1968; Hill and Nolasquez 1973; Kroeber and Grace 1960; Lamb 1958a; Langacker 1977; Lionnet 1972; Mace and Munro 1981; Miller 1966, 1967, 1972, 1977, 1980, 1980a; Molina 1977; Sapir 1930–1931; Seiler 1977; Seiler and Hioki 1979; Sullivan 1976; Swadesh and Sancho 1966; Voegelin 1935, 1935a, 1958; Voegelin and Voegelin 1957; Whorf 1935a; Zigmond 1975.

The Hopi forms are principally Third Mesa dialect. Aztec is given in a phonemic transcription based on a synthesis of available sources. Most Cora words are from Eugene Casad (personal communication 1980).

Pima and Papago: Introduction

BERNARD L. FONTANA

The Pima ('pēmu) and Papago ('päpə,gō) Indians speak a Piman language of the Uto-Aztecan language family. No one knows how long they have lived scattered throughout what are today the western two-thirds of southern Arizona and northern Sonora, Mexico. The Spaniards called them Pimas Altos, meaning Upper Pima Indians, to distinguish them from their linguistic brethren, the Pima Bajo (Lower Pima), who lived far to the south in lower Sonora.

During the late seventeenth, eighteenth, and early nineteenth centuries Spaniards further recognized different groups of Upper Pimans, variously labeling these as Pima, Papago, Sobaipuri, Soba, Gileños, and Piatos, the last presumably an abbreviation for Pimas Altos. Although the labels were not always applied consistently and they changed through time, in general Pimas were river-dwelling people; Sobaipuris lived at Bac on the Santa Cruz River and along the San Pedro River; Papagos were farmers who lived away from the rivers; Piatos were apostate Pimas who lived in the Altar Valley; Gileños were Pimas of the Gila River; and Sobas lived in the west and southwestern portions of the northern Sonoran Desert.

Although these terms indicate that Spaniards were aware of cultural and geographical differences among Upper Piman Indians, they also betray Spanish ignorance of definitions employed by the Indians themselves. All Upper Pimans call themselves *ˀóˀodham*, meaning 'we, the people'.* In modern times the Gila River Pimas have called themselves *ˀákĭmel ˀóˀodham* ('river people') as distinct from the *tóhono ˀóˀodham* ('desert people'), their Papago neighbors to the south. Beyond these distinctions, Upper Pimans further recognize dialect differences in their common language. Thus, among the Papago Indians of today the dialects are the *Hú·huˀula, ˀA·ngam, Gígimai, Húhuwoṣ, Koló·di, Ge ˀÁji, Kóhadk* (Quajote), *Tótoguañ,* and *Híac ˀeḍ ˀÓˀodham* 'Sand Papago' (Saxton and Saxton 1969:183–185). The Gila River Pimas may formerly have spoken more than a single dialect of Piman, and certainly there were additional dialects in use among Pimas living on other rivers, the names of which have been lost to history.

The living descendants of the Upper Piman Indians are known as the Pima and Papago Indians. The Pimas live on the Gila River, Salt River, and Ak Chin reservations in southern Arizona and off-reservation in adjacent Casa Grande, Chandler, Coolidge, and the greater Phoenix metropolitan area. The Papagos, perhaps as many as 16,000 of them, live on the Papago (Sells), San Xavier, Ak Chin, and Gila Bend reservations as well as off-reservation at Ajo, Marana, Gila Bend, Florence, and in the greater Tucson and Phoenix metropolitan areas, and Los Angeles and San Jose, California. There continue to be small and isolated settlements of Papagos living in Sonora, Mexico, as well, none of them more than 100 miles south of the international boundary. Most of the fewer than 200 Mexican Papagos lived in Caborca, Sonora, in 1980, where they were employed as laborers. Many of them maintained an interest in a ranch, however small, which they would visit on occasion. Their ownership of lands in Sonora, except for the Papago ejido of Poso Verde, was in a precarious status in 1980, although Mexico's Instituto Nacional Indigenista was making efforts to secure Papagos in their title to their few remaining lands (Fabila 1957; Fontana 1981a:68–84; Nolasco Armas 1964).

Environmental Adaptation

To view Upper Piman life as it may have existed in its various modes before European culture began to exert

*Pima-Papago words written in italics in the *Handbook* are in a version of the practical alphabet developed by Hale and Alvarez (1972). The following phonemes are recognized: (fortis stops and affricate, with voiceless approach; preaspirated postvocalically) *p, t, c* ([č]), *k*; (lenis, with voiced approach) *b, d, ḍ, j* ([ǯ]), *g*; (voiceless fricatives) *s, ṣ*; (nasals) *m, n, ñ* ([nʸ]); (retroflex lateral, with flap release) *l*; (semivowels) *w, y*; (laryngeals) *h, ˀ*; (short vowels) *i, e* ([ɨ]), *a, o, u*; (long vowels) *i·, e·* ([ɨ·]), *a·, o·, u·*; (extrashort vowels) *ĭ, ĕ* ([ɨ̆]), *ă, ŏ, ŭ*; (stress) v́. In the Pima dialect *w* is phonetically [β] ([ɸ] when devoiced). Differences among Papago dialects are generally very slight (Hale 1965:304; Saxton and Saxton 1969:107–108).

Several different orthographies are in use to write Pima-Papago. The long vowels, here written with a raised dot (*i·*), are also written with a colon—i: (Hale and Alvarez 1972); vowel plus h—ih (Saxton and Saxton 1969); and vowel doubling—ii (Mathiot 1973). Other differences are as follows: Saxton and Saxton (1969) write D for *ḍ*, sh for *ṣ*, ch for *c*, n or ni for *ñ*, and apostrophe (') for *ˀ* (omitted word-initially). Saxton and Saxton (1973) is the same but uses th for *d* and d for *ḍ*. Mathiot (1973) writes d̹ for *ḍ*, x for *ṣ*, and v for *w*.

Information on the transcription of Papago words has been furnished by Kenneth L. Hale (communications to editors 1972, 1973, 1975, 1981).

its steady influence in the late seventeenth century, it becomes necessary to rely on the written observations of admittedly partial European missionaries, soldiers, and government officials as well as on twentieth-century efforts of anthropologists and others to elucidate Piman Indian culture. Archeology has thus far been of very little help in the effort to reconstruct "aboriginal" Piman life.

To extrapolate from knowledge gleaned from Pimans living in the twentieth century to describe their seventeenth-century ancestors, even when adding this information to early non-Indian evaluations and statements of fact, is a precarious exercise. However, when these sources are combined with a further knowledge of the environment in which Upper Pimans carried out their lives, it becomes reasonably possible to sketch in what were at least the outlines of native Piman culture. It appears that in Pimeria Alta—the land of the Upper Piman Indians—there were three major modes of human adaptation.

To understand these modes of adaptation it is important to know that nearly the whole of Pimeria Alta lies within portions of the Sonoran Desert. The Sonoran Desert covers about 100,000 square miles of southwestern Arizona, southeastern California, western Sonora, and northeastern Baja California (Dunbier 1968: map facing title page). Some students would add the whole of central Baja California and another 20,000 square miles to this figure (Shreve and Wiggins 1964, 1:12).

The Sonoran Desert has seven vegetational subdivisions, two of which, the Lower Colorado Valley and Arizona Upland, come close to demarcating the aboriginal domain of the Upper Piman Indians (see Shreve and Wiggins 1964: map 1). These late seventeenth-century boundaries seem to have been the Gila River on the north, the San Pedro and San Miguel rivers on the east, the Río Magdalena and Río de la Concepción on the south, the Gulf of California on the southwest, and the Colorado River to the west (fig. 1). In the 1690s there was a single Pima village on the headwaters of the Río Sonora, east of the Río San Miguel, but the Spaniards saw to its early removal (Spicer 1962:118–119).

The Sobaipuris of the San Pedro Valley were beyond the eastern limits of the Sonoran Desert as were the Pimas of the Upper Santa Cruz River and its tributaries and nearby mountains. But the numbers of Pimans living in these locales were always a small proportion of the total, and it was from these areas that they were first dislodged by Apache Indians in the eighteenth century. Moreover, these nondesert lands were probably the last ones to be occupied by Pimans during the prehistoric or protohistoric periods, and in a very real sense Pimans were beyond their range in desert-grassland and evergreen-woodland country.

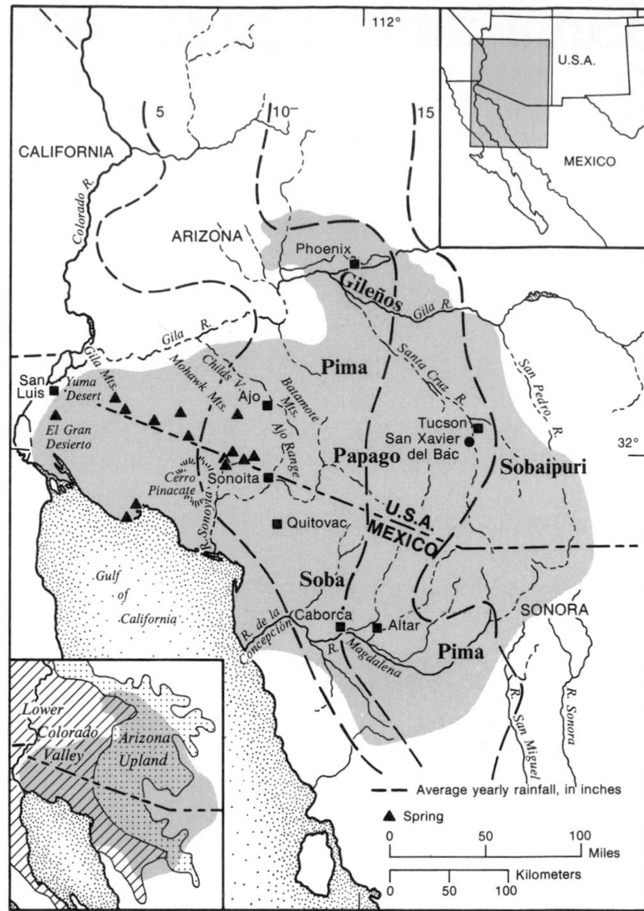

Fig. 1. Upper Piman territory in the late 17th century with locations of groups recognized by the Spaniards. Inset shows northern regions of the Sonoran Desert. Rainfall and Sonoran Desert subdivisions after Shreve and Wiggins (1964, 1: maps 1 and 3).

The Pimeria Alta portions of the Sonoran Desert are divided into three major subdivisions in terms of the availability of water. There are the extremely dry western section, with from 0 to 5 inches of annual rainfall; a central section with from 5 to 10 inches of rainfall each year; and riverine perimeters, at least some of which on the east and south are the beneficiaries of from 10 to 15 inches of rain per year. In short, moving from the west toward the east and then out toward the northern, eastern, and southern perimeters, increasing amounts of water are available. It is therefore not surprising to find corresponding environmental adaptations among the Upper Piman Indians who lived here.

No Villagers

Lying south of Interstate Highway 8 beteen Gila Bend and Yuma, Arizona, are some of the driest and, in many ways, most forbidding lands in the United States. San Luis, south of Yuma and at the northwestern tip of Sonora, got 0.003 inches of rainfall in 1956, and between

1963 and 1967 its mean yearly average was a dry 0.9 of an inch (Hastings 1964; Hastings and Humphrey 1969:68). Yuma averages a scant 3.48 inches of annual rainfall, while various weather stations in the desert east of Yuma and south of the Gila River give yearly rainfall readings such as 4.28 inches, 5.06 inches, 4.13 inches, and 6.88 inches (Turnage and Mallery 1941:4–5). The Pinacate Plateau in Sonora is dampened by an annual 5.61 inches of rain, while at Quitovac and Sonoita, both also in northwestern Sonora, it is a somewhat wetter 11.26 inches and 7.70 inches, respectively (Hastings and Humphrey 1969:29, 33).

These yearly averages conceal the important fact that what little rain there is comes in two seasons, July-August and December-January. The summer downpours derive from convective storms that are highly localized and that originate in the Gulf of Mexico. The winter storms, cyclonic in nature, generally cover the whole sky. These move in from the Pacific Ocean and the Gulf of California. This western area of Pimeria Alta gets slightly more than half its rain during the winter, the remainder usually falling during the summer. The trend is for the percentage of summer to winter rainfall to increase as one moves from west to east and from south to north in the Sonoran Desert (Hastings and Turner 1965:11–12).

The western Pimeria Alta is its driest portion, so is it the hottest. Highs in Yuma have gone to 120° F and in Ajo to 115° F. Although the region is generally frost-free, the thermometer has been known to dip as low as 17° F in Ajo and 22° F in Yuma. The highs usually occur in July; the lows in January (Hastings and Turner 1965:16; H.L. Simmons 1965:10).

Two of the major ingredients upon which human beings depend to remain alive, water and food, are in short supply in the western Pimeria. Without the use of modern technology to drill for and to pump underground water or to import water artificially for long distances, farming is virtually an impossibility. It was certainly so for the Upper Pimans whose homeland this once was. These Indians, then, were of environmental necessity food collectors rather than food producers, and they were forced to travel by foot over great expanses of desert in search of the water, wild plants, and native animals that might sustain them. They led what was essentially a camping, nomadic existence, marked by

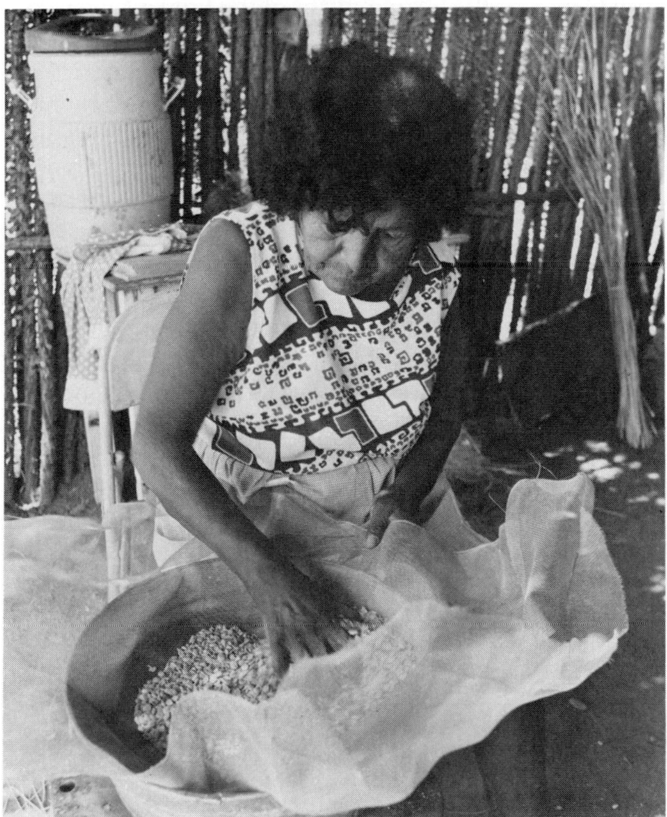

U. of Ariz., Ariz. State Mus., Tucson: left, 42545; right, 42565.

Fig. 2. Mesquite beans, formerly an important staple, were dried thoroughly, then crushed in bedrock mortars (left) and winnowed or sifted (right) to separate the crushed meal from uncrushed seeds. The ground meal has a sweetish taste and is said to be very nourishing (Russell 1908:75). Photographs of Juanita Ahil of Ali Chukson (Little Tucson), Papago Reservation, Ariz., by Helga Teiwes, Sept. 1975.

U. of Ariz., Ariz. State Mus., Tucson: left, 35201; center, 35205; right, 35216.

Fig. 3. Cholla buds, formerly an important food staple. The buds, which ripened in May, were picked using tongs (left, made of saguaro rib). They were then cooked in a pit layered with saltbrush and hot stones. The top was covered with earth and the mound left overnight. The next day the cactus buds were removed from the pit, spread out, dried, and rubbed with a stick to remove the thorns. The buds were then boiled, salted, and eaten with pinole (Russell 1908:71). center, Juanita Ahil pouring the buds into a wire mesh box to remove the spines from the buds. right, Marinating the dried buds in a vinegar mixture. Photographs by Helga Teiwes at Ali Chukson (Little Tucson), Papago Reservation, Ariz., May 1973.

seasonal intervals when they bartered salt, seashells, and ceremonies in return for pottery and the agricultural products of Yuman Indians of the Lower Colorado River.

The quantities and seasons of rainfall in western Pimeria as well as the variations within limited geographic areas of the larger region are related to the water supply and vegetation, as well as ultimately to the fauna, through the physiography of the Sonoran Desert. This is because the amount of effective precipitation (that which is available to plants in the soil without percolating on through) depends in part on the nature of the soil, the gradient of slopes, and on the amount of runoff contrasted with the amount of penetration.

All of Pimeria Alta lies within the Desert Region of the Basin and Range Province (Wilson 1962:fig. 13). Mountain ranges alternate with valleys, both oriented generally from southeast to northwest and both generally gaining in altitude as one moves away from the Colorado River and heads toward Tucson and the Santa Cruz Valley. The western sector of Pimeria Alta in Arizona has eight of these southeast-northwest "rows" of mountains and five intervening "plains" or "valleys." The 500-foot high Yuma Desert on the east runs into the Gila–Tinajas Altas mountains and their 3,150-foot maximum elevation; and the eastern line of western Pimeria is marked by the Childs Valley–Valley of the Ajo–Sonoyta Valley (1,500 feet) and the Batamote-Redondo-Ajo mountains (4,770 feet).

Northwestern Sonora is essentially a low-lying mesa marked by the Great Sand Dunes (*El Gran Desierto*), a few small and scattered mountain clusters, and by the dominating Cerro Pinacate, which looms to 4,235 feet above sea level (see J. Powell 1964, 1966; Ives 1964).

The gradients of the upper mountain slopes in western Pimeria are quite steep, and their bajadas (the outwash slopes between the upper slopes and the valleys or floodplains) are short. Soils are formed chiefly by the disintegrating action of 60°–70° F rain hitting basaltic rocks that have been heated to 150°–160° F by the sun's unrelenting rays. The net effect of these factors is the production of very little effective precipitation. Coarse and sandy soils are almost devoid of humus, and the total amount of rainfall is generally insufficient to allow runoff to carry all the way to the sea. The result is that a series of landlocked basins become deposits of soluble salts—a further detriment to the growth of plants.

Nearly all of western Pimeria Alta lies within the Lower Colorado Valley vegetational subdivision. Some 85 percent of this area is comprised of valleys and bajadas, and 90–95 percent of the plant cover consists of *Larrea tridentata* (creosote bush) and *Franseria dumosa* (white bursage, burro weed). Although the leaves of creosote bush can be boiled to make a tea, and although this plant hosts an insect that produces a lacquer suitable for mending earthenware pottery, it fails to qualify as a food source for man. Bursage is similarly inedible.

However, a few microenvironments—especially the banks of drainageways (arroyos or washes) on the bajadas and plains as well as parts of the bajadas themselves—support a vegetation more characteristic of other parts of the Pimeria Alta. These plants, many of which have edible parts in season, include mesquite (*Prosopis juliflora*), blue paloverde (*Cercidium floridum*), foothill

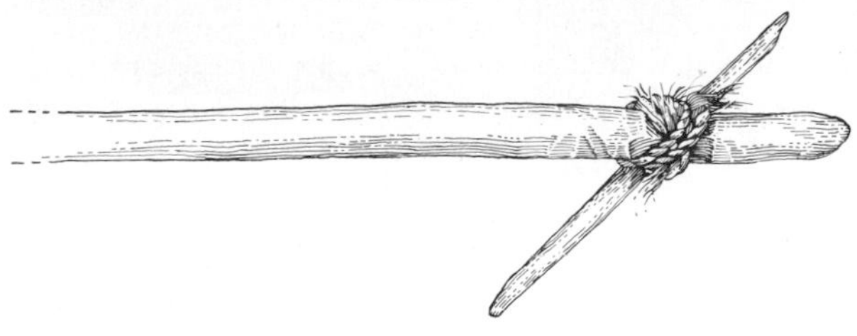

top, U. of Ariz., Ariz. State Mus., Tucson: 19207; bottom, Smithsonian, Dept. of Anthr.: 218,038.

Fig. 4. Saguaro harvest. From June to mid-July the ripe red fruit gathered from the top of the 20–40 foot cactus is knocked to the ground with a pole. bottom, Pima pole with hook made of a piece of wood attached with maguey fiber to the cactus rib handle. Length of hook 16.5 cm, collected by Frank Russell at Sacaton, Ariz., 1902. top, The Noceo family harvesting saguaro fruit several miles southwest of Sil Nakya, Papago Reservation, Ariz.; photograph by Helga Teiwes, July 1968.

paloverde (*C. microphyllum*), ironwood (*Olneya tesota*), and cat's-claw (*Acacia greggii*). In addition to these trees there are several perennial cacti and shrubs, most notably chollas (*Opuntia* spp.), prickly pears (*Opuntia* spp.), saguaro (*Carnegiea gigantea*) (figs. 4–5), organpipe (*Lemaireocereus thurberi*), desert agave (*Agave deserti*) and sotol (*Dasylirion wheeleri*). Finally, there are innumerable perennial plants, especially in herbaceous species, which provide seasonal food sources for fauna, including man (see Shreve and Wiggins 1964, 1:136–142).

Animal life, by no means abundant, includes desert bighorn sheep (*Ovis canadensis*), the gray fox (*Urocyon cinereoargenteus*), the kit fox (*Vulpes macrotis*), bats (*Chiroptera*), pack rats (*Neotoma* spp.), javelina (*Tayassu tajacu*), mule deer (*Odocoileus hemionus*), white-tailed deer (*O. virginianus*), and Sonoran pronghorn antelope (*Antilocapra americana sonoriensis*). There are also the coyote (*Canis latrans*), hares, bobcat (*Felix rufus*), spotted skunk (*Spilogale putorius*), badger (*Taxidea taxus*), various rodents including the kangaroo rat (*Dipodomys* spp.), desert cottontail (*Sylvilagus audubonii*), and the ringtail (*Bassariscus astutus yumanensis*). Dozens of additional species of small mammals are listed by Cockrum (1960).

In addition to innumerable genera and species of snakes and lizards, there is bird life, including the golden eagle, ducks and geese, hawks, and the white-necked raven (*Corvus cryptoleucus*), to say nothing of the many smaller birds (see Phillips, Marshall, and Monson 1964).

Simmons (1967:133) has aptly observed "that the apparently rugged landscape of this arid area is by nature more delicately balanced between stability and deterioration than that of most such areas. The desert plants and animals are more highly specialized and easily destroyed."

Recalling that the southwestern perimeter of western Pimeria Alta is the head of the Gulf of California, it needs finally to be pointed out that in addition to desert flora and fauna, Pimans living here also had available to them—when they could be gotten—a comparatively abundant supply of fish, shellfish, sea turtle, ocean-going mammals, and shore and sea birds. However, there is no evidence that Pimans ever took to sea in rafts or boats of any kind, and the impression one gains is that they were merely occasional visitors to the sea, never littoral peoples like the neighboring Seris to the south.

The final point to be made in this discussion of environmental adaptation of the Piman No Villagers is that the great desideratum is water. Permanent sources of water in western Pimeria are rare. Discounting the boundary-marking lower Gila and Colorado rivers, of which only the Colorado is permanently flowing, the only other river is the Sonoyta. It is intermittent, flowing after rains, and interrupted, flowing only over short portions of its course all year long (in the vicinity of Sonoita, Sonora). The few western Pimans who lived here, the so-called Areneños, apparently engaged in small-scale farming and had fixed settlements.

The other sources of water include about a dozen fracture and fault springs, most importantly those at Quitovac and Quitobaquito and at the head of the Gulf of California; ephemeral streams, those which run only after a rainfall; lakes, ponds, and charcos, which depend on immediate rainfall; and rock tanks, watering places "consisting of a cavity or depression in rock which fills periodically with rain or flood water. Most Mexicans and many Americans use the Spanish word 'tinaja,' meaning a bowl or jar, in speaking of a rock tank" (Bryan 1925:123). About two dozen of these tinajas are scattered throughout western Pimeria Alta, and near all of them are the scattered potsherds, stone flakes, and other archeological evidences of man's former campsites, all giving testimony to the man's dependence

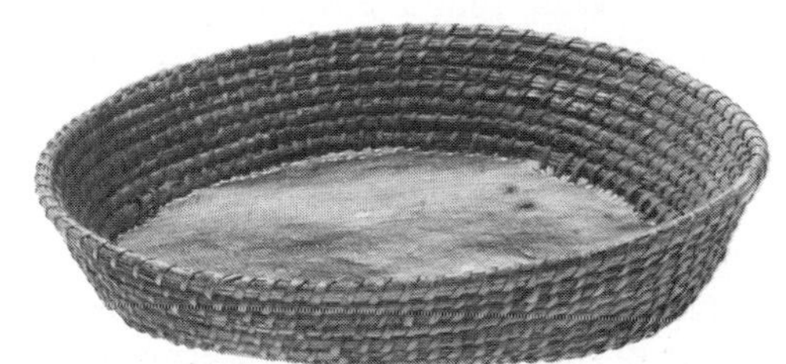

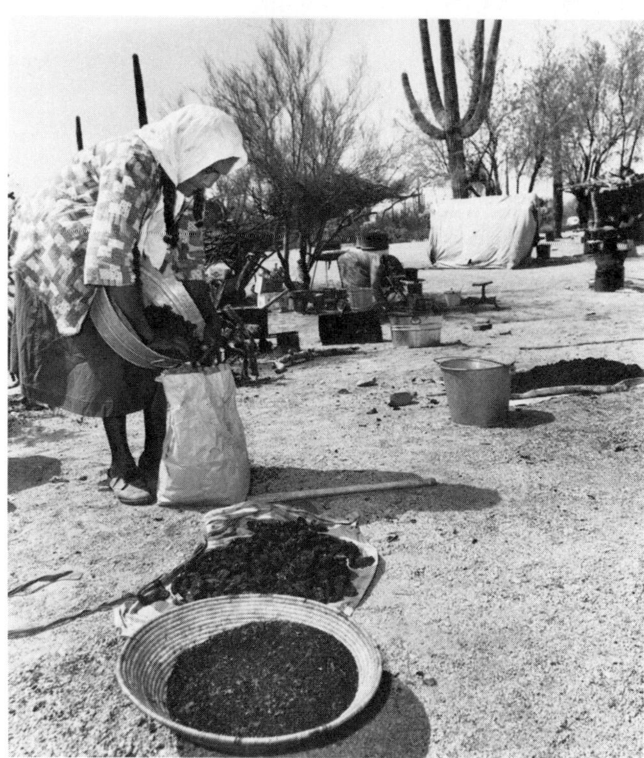

top, Natl. Geographic Soc. (Western Ways), Washington; center left, Smithsonian, Dept. of Anthr.: 218,036; U. of Ariz., Ariz. State Mus., Tucson: bottom left, 19231; bottom right, 27587.

Fig. 5. Saguaro fruit preparation. Fruit of the saguaro is eaten raw, dried, or made into syrup and jam. The syrup is prepared by boiling the crushed fruit and straining the liquid through a sieve of twilled basketry (top), burlap (bottom left), or wire mesh. The sieve, center left, is a Pima coiled basket with wire netting attached. Diameter 26 cm, collected by Frank Russell at Sacaton, Ariz., 1902. The syrup is stored in pottery vessels covered with broken pottery, cloth, or tin and sealed with mud; some of it is later fermented into ceremonial wine. bottom right, Some seeds are separated from the pulp, dried and ground into meal. Dried fruit is put into a sack by Laura Williams, Papago, for later use. Photograph by Helga Teiwes, west of Saguaro National Monument, Ariz., 1970. top, The Hillman and Ventura families, Papagos, from Santa Rosa. Photograph by Charles W. Herbert, before Jan. 1952. bottom left, Noceo family camp. Photograph by Helga Teiwes near Sil Nakya, Papago Reservation, Ariz., 1968.

on these sources of water. Prehistoric trails as well as modern jeep tracks run from water source to water source.

It is not surprising, given the environmental circumstances, that the Pimans whom the Spaniards encountered in the late seventeenth century "were poor and hungry, living on roots, locusts and shell fish." They were "poor people who lived by eating roots of wild sweet potatoes, honey, mesquite beans and other fruits. They traveled about naked; only the women had their bodies covered with hare furs" (Manje 1954:14, 17, 30).

These Sand Papagos, as they have been called in the twentieth century, were truly nomadic No Villagers. "Home" was most of the Lower Colorado Valley. People lived in an undetermined number of bands probably comprised of extended families, and band size probably never exceeded 80 or 90 people. Even this would have been exceptionally large. Seafood, reptiles, insects, and small mammals were the principal ingredients of their diet; their tools were few (they made no pottery of their own); and they relied heavily on native flora to remain alive. Their shelters, judging from all the archeological and documentary evidence available, were nothing more than small rings of stone laid out as temporary windbreaks, so-called sleeping circles (see Fontana 1964 for a summary of the archeology and Fontana 1968–1974, 2; Hayden 1967; Lumholtz 1912; R.K. Thomas 1953; and Childs 1954 for additional data concerning western Pimans).

The nomads of western Pimeria Alta no longer exist as cultural entities. They appear to have died from epidemic diseases and from murder at the hands of Mexicans and Anglo-Americans in the last half of the nineteenth century. Others simply wandered off to lose themselves in mining camps and non-Indian settlements in southern Arizona and northern Sonora during the same period. One Piman hermit, Juan Caravajales, continued to live in the Pinacate Mountains until his death early in the twentieth century, but with his passing the Piman No Villagers disappeared into history (Bell, Anderson, and Stewart 1980; Hayden 1967:341–342).

Two Villagers

Thanks to the efforts of Underhill (1936, 1938, 1939, 1946), more is known by non-Indians about the Two Villagers than about any other Pimans. These are the people known as the Papagos, and it was among them that Underhill did most of her fieldwork during the 1930s.

Papagos live in the central portion of Pimeria Alta—away from permanent streams but in a region whose biseasonal rainfall pattern brings consistently more water (5–10 inches) annually than that in the arid west. Lying almost wholly within the Arizona Upland vegetation zone of the Sonoran Desert, central Pimeria Alta—known as the Papagueria—is characterized by higher mountain ranges and intermontane valleys, with less than half the area being made up of a low-gradient bajadas and plains; mountain slopes are less steep than in the west and valleys are less flat and more sloping; and the soil, especially at the mouths of mountain drainageways, is rich alluvium capable of supporting abundant plant life. Although all the streams are interrupted, intermittent, and ephemeral, central Pimeria lacks landlocked basins and dry lake beds.

Foothill paloverde, chollas, and prickly pears tend to dominate in central Pimeria in place of creosote bush and bursage, and there are more and larger saguaros, mesquites, acacias, and ironwoods as well as succulents like the barrel cactus (*Ferocactus wislizeni*) growing in comparative profusion. The higher reaches of mountain ranges in central Pimeria also include juniper, oak, Mexican piñon (*Pinus cembroides*), Mormon tea (*Ephedra trifurca*), and bear grass (*Nolina microcarpa*).

Water sources include springs in almost every range of mountains as well as semipermanent charcos in the flats. The inventory of fauna, like that of flora, is much the same as in western Pimeria, except that here the population sizes are much greater. Deer, which are comparatively scarce in the western desert, for example, tend to be in abundant supply in central Pimeria.

The Pimans who lived in this section of the Sonoran Desert were Two Village people in that they had winter dwellings in the mountain foothills next to the permanent springs of water as well as summer dwellings in the intermontane plains where they farmed at the mouths of washes after the summer rains had watered their fields. The people followed seasonal migration patterns, moving back and forth between their winter or "spring" or "well" villages and their summer or "field" villages in the valleys.

Before the summer rains began men climbed the mountainsides to erect temporary rock dams in the upper drainageways. The purpose of this was to channel the runoff from rainfall so it would eventually end up in one major arroyo where it entered the valley plain. With the onset of summer rains there would be flash floods down the arroyos and the men would water the fields at their mouths by erecting brush spreader dams across them. This akchin agriculture (*ʔákĭ cíñ* 'arroyo mouth') was characteristic of Papago farming. It had been described in considerable detail by Castetter and Bell (1942).

The social consequences of this kind of Piman environmental adaptation are described in "Pima and Papago Social Organization," this volume. Two Village families harvested from zero to 45 percent of their food supply in a given year, depending on the amount of rainfall and the location of particular fields, and harvested goods accounted for about 17 percent of their annual average consumption. The latter figure takes

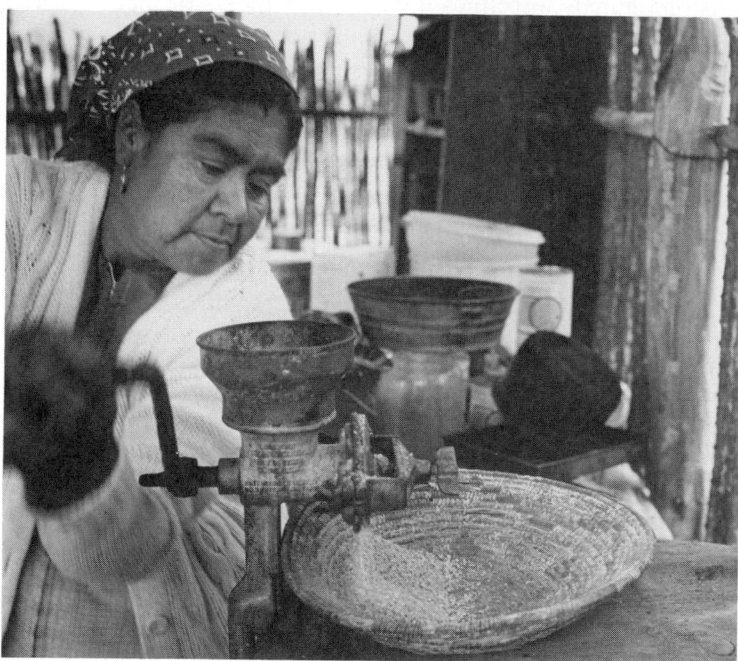

top left, Calif. Histl. Soc., Los Angeles: Title Insurance Coll.: 771; U. of Ariz., Ariz. State Mus., Tucson: top right, 42180, bottom left, 55433, bottom right, 55432.

Fig. 6. Food preparation. top left, Pima woman winnowing mesquite beans; photograph probably by Charles C. Pierce, about 1900. top right, Clara Stone, Pima, winnowing wheat. The large wooden mortar and stone pestle were used to crush large amounts of mesquite beans (Russell 1908:75). Photograph by Helga Teiwes, Stotonik, Gila River Reservation, Ariz., 1974. bottom left, Anita Victor, Papago, grinding wheat with traditional stone mano and metate and, bottom right, in commercial grinder, her usual method. Photographs by Helga Teiwes, Menager's Dam village (Ali Chuk), Ariz., 1981.

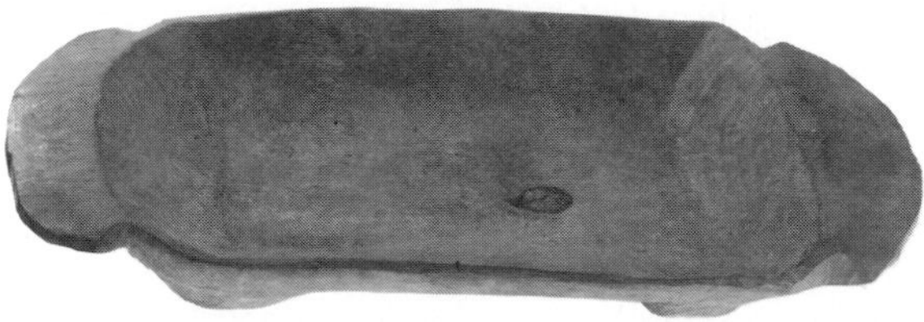

Smithsonian, Dept. of Anthr.: left 218,022; right 174,437.

Fig. 7. Wheat preparation. left, Papago pottery pan in which the grain is usually parched with coals before being ground. The ashes are blown away and several jerks move the coals to the side of the pan where they can be scraped off when parching is completed. right, Pima wooden bowl used to mix dough for the unleavened bread that is made from the ground wheat. Diameter of left at handles 44 cm; collected by WJ McGee at San Xavier, Ariz., 1894–1895. right, same scale, collected by Frank Russell at Sacaton, Ariz., 1902.

into account Papago traditions involving gift-giving, barter, and wagering.

The most noteworthy addition of material culture to the Piman inventory of goods found among Papagos but not among the No Villagers is the brush house. This form of house requires no water in its construction, a fact that gives Piman settlement pattern the flavor of "camping" rather than that of a fully sedentary people. This is true even among the riverine Pimans.

One Villagers

The most permanently fixed of the Upper Piman Indians were those who lived on the riverine perimeters of Pimeria Alta. The best known of their modern descendants are the Pima Indians of the Gila River (Russell 1908). The living descendants of the Sobaipuri and Pima Indians of the San Pedro and Santa Cruz rivers and of rivers in northern Sonora have become amalgamated with Indians known today as Papagos on both sides of the international boundary.

The villages of riverine Pimans were the largest. Wild plants and animals were in greatest abundance along the streams, and the alluvial floodplains of the rivers were the best suited to agriculture in the Arizona Upland vegetation zone. The Sobaipuri Indians at Bac on the Santa Cruz River were involved in canal irrigation when the Spaniards arrived in the 1690s, and although the matter of canal irrigation among other riverine Pimans at this early date is equivocal, it is certain that soon after the arrival of Spaniards—and especially with the introduction of wheat, a winter crop—canal or ditch irrigation became extremely important in the subsistence of these natives.

Although the rainfall along the riverine perimeters of Pimeria Alta is not uniformly higher than in central Pimeria, what is important is that the streams, if interrupted, are at least perennial over parts of their courses. And at that, riverine Piman settlements such as Magdalena and Tucson in the twentieth century got average annual rainfalls of 16.59 inches and 11.29 inches each year (see Bryan 1925: 34–40; Hastings and Humphrey 1969:8, 19).

In addition to the relatively greater abundance of flora and fauna along the rivers, and in addition to the fact that floodplain and irrigation farming are more reliable and were a source for most Piman foods, the rivers also supplied freshwater fishes (see Lowe 1964:133–151 for a list).

While it is true that riverine Pimans often maintained fields one or two miles away from their regular settlements, it was nonetheless along rivers that Piman life assumed its most anchored form. From No Villagers to One Villagers, the Sonoran Desert provided habitats that demanded different adaptations on the part of the Upper Piman Indians who lived in its northern sector.

Smithsonian, NAA: top, 2767-A; center, 4548; bottom, U. of Ariz., Ariz. State Mus., Tucson: 55452.

Fig. 8. Preparing wheat tortillas. top, Johanna Victoriana, Papago, cooking outside her house of ocotillo stalks with adobe and volcanic breccia fill; photograph by William Dinwiddie near Pitiquito, Sonora, 1894. center, Papago woman cooking inside a cornstalk shelter while a girl scrapes corn kernels into a basket; photograph by H.T. Cory, 1916. bottom, Clara Aguilla, Papago, cooking at Anita Victor's house on St. Joseph's day. The cooking area is surrounded by a cactus wall of ocotillo stalks and saguaro ribs. Photograph by Helga Teiwes, Menager's Dam village (Ali Chuk), Ariz., 1981.

Synonymy†

Pima

The name Pima has been used in Spanish at least since the late seventeenth century, the earliest use listed by Hodge (1907–1910, 2:252) being by Father Eusebio Kino in 1692. Variants in Spanish, probably all errors or misprints, include Paymas, Pimes, Pimicas, and Pirnas. Nineteenth-century English sources have Pema, Pemos, Pijmos, Pimos, and Pimoles. A longer variant of the name is found in early Spanish sources as Pima Aytos or Pimahitos, 1565 (Obregón in Hammond and Rey 1928:164, 194), also wrongly written Primahaitu, 1536 (cited by B.T. Smith in Shea 1861:7). The Pima appear to have been named by the Spanish after their word for 'nothing', which was pimahaitu in the eighteenth century (B.T. Smith in Shea 1861:7); compare *pím* 'no' in the twentieth-century dialect of Ónavas (Obregón in Hammond and Rey 1928:164, 194; Kenneth L. Hale, communication to editors 1973). This would have handily distinguished them from the Yaqui-Mayo speakers, whom the Spaniards called Cahita after their phrase *kaita* (from *kaa hita*) 'nothing' (Kenneth L. Hale, communication to editors 1973).

In the earliest Spanish usage the name Pima covered all the Pimans, that is the Pima Bajo and the Pima Alto, the latter including the Papago. The ancestors of the modern Pima of Arizona were sometimes distinguished as Pimas Gileños (or Ileños) 'Pima of the Gila River' or simply Gileños (Nentvig 1980:72).

The Pima and Papago refer to themselves as *ˀóˀodham* 'tribesman, person, human' (Saxton and Saxton 1969:36). The Pima are specified as *ˀákĭmel ˀóˀodham* 'river people', and the loanword *pí·ma* is also used (Saxton and Saxton 1969:84, 156).

Names for the Pima in other Indian languages include: Navajo *Naakétł'áhí* 'foot-sole foreigners' or *Kétł'áhí* 'foot-sole ones' (presumably an allusion to the wearing of sandals; Young and Morgan 1980); Jemez hapǫ ya wų̀ ts'aaš (Harrington 1909); Yavapai ^{idja}hwága '^{a}hắna 'the enemy par excellence; Pima, Maricopa' (Freire-Marreco 1910–1912); Maricopa *txpa·* (Lynn Gordon, communication to editors 1981); Mohave *hačpa* (Pamela Munro, communication to editors 1981), earlier recorded as hat-pá (Mowry in Gibbs 1856); Quechan *xatpá·* (Abraham M. Halpern, communication to editors 1981), earlier recorded hat-spa (Corbusier 1925–1926:2) and also applied to the Papago (G.H. Thomas 1868); Cocopa hats-pás (McGee 1900:184); Western Apache *sáíkį̨hné* 'sand-house people' (Philip J. Greenfeld, communication to editors 1981), also including the Papago (Gatschet 1883:98). Some languages use a loanword from Spanish: Zuni *pima·k^{w}e* (Dennis Tedlock, communication to editors 1977); Hopi pímọ (Harrington 1913b:15).

Papago

The name Papago became established in Spanish in the eighteenth century, at least as early as 1748 (Villa-Señor, in Hodge 1907–1910, 2:201). It is written accented in some sources: pápagos, 1762 (Nentvig in Bandelier 1890–1892, 1:73), Pápagos, 1774 (Bolton 1930, perhaps normalized), 1775 (Coues 1900, 1:64); but not in others (Nentvig 1980). The earliest recording of the name appears to be Papabotas, 1699 (Manje 1954: 102, 236, wrongly ascribed to Kino by Hodge 1907–1910, 2:201; Fontana 1981a:35). Variants of this include: Papabi-Ootam, 1794 (Pfefferkorn), and Papapootam, 1762 (Nentvig, in Bandelier 1890–1892, 1:73), miscopied as Papap-Otam and Papa-Otam by Bandelier (1890–1892, 1:72), and as Papapootans (Nentvig 1980:71). This longer name was shortened in Spanish to Papabos and Papavos, 1742 (Mota-Padilla, in Hodge 1907–1910, 2:201), which with the shift of the third consonant from [β] to [γ] gave Pápago. A variant Papalotes, 1746, and many miscopyings and misprints of the forms listed here are in Hodge (1907–1910, 2:201).

Manje (Fernández del Castillo 1926:309) glossed the name Papabotas in Spanish as 'pimas frijoleros' or 'bean Pimas'; this translation is confirmed by the agreement between Pfefferkorn's more precise spelling Papabi-Ootam and the Pima scholar José Lewis Brennan's päpä´fi 'â'âtäm 'Papago person, Papago people', explained as a reference to a species of bean called päf that tastes different from ordinary beans (in Hewitt 1897). The first element of the name *bá·bawĭ-ˀóˀodham* 'bean Piman(s); Papago(s)' is in fact *bá·bawĭ* 'tepary beans' (sg. *báwĭ*) (Philip J. Greenfeld and Kenneth L. Hale, communications to editors 1981).

The English name Papago is taken from the Spanish spelling. Early forms written impressionistically on the basis of pronunciation include: Papaga, 1839; Pa-Pagoe, 1869; Papawar, 1833 (Pattie); Papigo, 1856 (all in Hodge 1907–1910, 2:201).

The Papago call themselves *Tóhono ˀÓˀodham* 'desert Pimans' to distinguish themselves from the Pima, Lower Pima, and Sand Papagos (Saxton and Saxton 1969:156).

Names for the Papago in other Indian languages (where indicated, referring also to the Pima) include: Navajo *Kégiizhí* 'foot gap ones' (an allusion to the wearing of sandals with the thong between the toes; Young and Morgan 1980); Yavapai d^{a}hapá (Freire-Marreco 1910–1912); Havasupai *pa· n^{y}a·ˀa* 'Pima-Papago' (Leanne Hinton, communication to editors 1981); Maricopa *txpa·may* (Lynn Gordon, communication to editors 1981); Mohave *hačpa ˀamay* 'above the Pima' (Pamela Munro,

†This synonymy was written by Ives Goddard.

communication to editors 1981); Cocopa ha-pas-má (McGee 1900); Seri papani (Pinart 1879) or *ʔapáai* (Moser and Moser 1976:294); Yaqui *papawim*, pl. (Lindenfeld 1973:123).

Sources

This sources section refers to all chapters on the Pima and Papago. It is limited to major published sources concerning the ethnography and history of these groups, to museum collections, and to sources of photographs.

The standard ethnography of the Pima Indians, based on fieldwork carried out in 1901–1902, continues to be that of Russell (1908). A re-edition of this book by the University of Arizona Press contains an introduction, citation sources, and an up-to-date Pima bibliography by Bernard L. Fontana (Russell 1975). Pima history, from the Spanish colonial period to the 1920s, besides being touched upon in Russell (1908), is found in Ezell (1961), C. Hayden (1965), and Hackenberg and Fontana (1974). Pima oral traditions are published in Shaw (1968, 1974), Webb (1959), and Lloyd (1911).

Pima Indian basketry has been described in Breazeale (1923) and Kissell (1916), the latter having been reprinted in 1972 by the Rio Grande Press. Pima ethnobotany is found in Curtin (1949); Pima political organization and business management was described by the Bureau of Ethnic Research (1971).

The remainder of published sources concerning the Pima appear almost exclusively as sections of books or in serial publications. Most of these are cited in Russell (1975:443–460).

Thanks largely to the efforts of Ruth Underhill, published books concerning the ethnography of the Papago Indians are much more extensive than for that of the Pima. Underhill has described Papago social organization as it existed in the nineteenth century (1939); Papago religion (1938a, 1946; Underhill et al. 1979); and general Papago ethnography (1940, 1951). She has published an account of Papago oral history (1938), and her autobiography of a Papago woman in both its original (1936) and more recent (1979) versions is a classic of its kind.

The earliest book-length description of the Papago Indians is that written by the naturalist Carl Lumholtz (1912). It is a volume in the category of "description and travel." In 1917–1918 all the Papagos' aboriginal domain within the United States was explored and described in great geographical detail by the geologist Kirk Bryan (1925), and in 1920 the ethnomusicologist Frances Densmore carried out fieldwork that culminated in her pioneering study of Papago music (1929). Her modern heir-apparent in the study of Papago music is Richard Haefer (1977).

Both Pima and Papago Indian agriculture and Papago ethnobiology have been examined by Castetter and Bell (1942) and Castetter and Underhill (1935). The effects of modern technology, especially drilling for underground water, as this has affected Papagos is considered by Bowden (1977).

In 1942–1943 a team of anthropologists worked among Papagos under the auspices of the Indian Education Research Project of the University of Chicago and the U.S. Bureau of Indian Affairs. Their efforts resulted in an ethnography emphasizing Papago youth and the enculturation process (Joseph, Spicer, and Chesky 1949). Later overviews of Papago culture and history have been provided by Dobyns (1972) and Fontana (1981a). An excellent discussion of twentieth-century Papago political and economic history, especially good for 1932–1948, was written by the second chairman of the Papago tribal council (Blaine 1981).

Papago oral traditions have appeared in three single-volume works (Bahr 1975; Saxton and Saxton 1973; Wright 1929); Papago dictionaries have been compiled by Mathiot (1973) and Saxton and Saxton (1969), and Mathiot (1968) used Papago exclusively in her examination of the cognitive study of language. The Papago grammars of W. Kurath (1945) and Mason (1950) have been superseded on most points by the treatments by Saxton and Saxton (1969:114–151), Hale (1959a, 1965), and Alvarez and Hale (1970).

Papago—and by extension, Pima—beliefs concerning the etiology and cure of sickness are described in voluminous detail by Bahr et al. (1974). The Papago *wí·gida* ceremony at Quitobac, Sonora, is the subject of a monograph by E.H. Davis (1920), and a bibliography relating to the subject of the *wí·gida* is in Jones (1971).

The history of the Papago Indians is summarized in Dobyns (1972), Fontana (1974, 1976, 1981a), and Hackenberg (1974a); a study of the impact of Spain on northern Pimans is found in Bringas de Manzaneda y Encinas (1977); and the story of Papagos in Sonora is told in Fontana (1981a) and Nolasco Armas (1965). Dobyns (1951) and Waddell (1969) concern themselves with off-reservation Papagos in southern Arizona.

Papago basketry is the subject of publications by DeWald (1979) and Kissell (1916); Papago pottery has been described by Fontana et al. (1962).

Finally, there are numerous volumes relating to the prehistory and protohistory of Pima and Papago country, but perhaps the most useful because of their extensive bibliographies on the subject are those by Haury (1976) and Masse (1980).

Important holdings of Pima and Papago Indian material culture are to be found in the general collections of the University of Arizona, Arizona State Museum, Tucson; the Southwest Museum (especially basketry), Los Angeles; and the Heard Museum, Phoenix, Arizona. The American Museum of Natural History, New York, is the repository for the Papago materials collected by Carl Lumholtz; the Field Museum of Natural History, Chicago, has the S.C. Simms Pima materials; the National Museum of Natural History, Washington, houses Papago and Pima collections by Edward Palmer, Frank Russell, and WJ McGee, among others; and the Museum of the American Indian, Heye Foundation, New York, has the Papago collections of Edward Davis. Papago, and to a lesser extent, Pima, basketry is found in natural history and anthropology museums throughout the world. Papago and Pima materials in European museums are listed in Kaemlein (1967), with perhaps one of the most important of these being the specimens collected by S. Jacobsen between 1882 and 1884 and now being cared for in the Museum für Völkerkunde, Berlin-Dahlem, Germany.

Photographic and archival materials concerning the northern Pimans are in the Arizona State Museum; the Southwest Museum; the American Museum of Natural History; the Museum of the American Indian, Heye Foundation; the California Historical Society, Los Angeles; Denver Museum of Natural History, Colorado; and the National Museum of Natural History, National Anthropological Archives. The last houses the superb photographs of Pimas taken in 1901–1902 by Frank Russell and the William Dinwiddie photographs of Papagos taken during the WJ McGee expedition of 1894.

History of the Papago

BERNARD L. FONTANA

The history of the Papago Indians of necessity begins with the documentary period of Hispanic history in the region. This is because the historical nature of Piman oral traditions is too poorly understood by non-Indians to make their interpretation as non-Indian history possible and because archeologists have thus far been unable to make a convincing case concerning the prehistoric beginnings of Piman culture in the Pimeria Alta. In spite of the archeological efforts of Di Peso (1953, 1956), Ezell (1963a), Hayden (1970) and others, there remain various theories but little conclusive evidence concerning Piman prehistory (vol. 9:176).

Spanish Period, 1687–1821

It is known that when Father Eusebio Kino and his fellow Jesuits penetrated the Pimeria Alta beginning in 1687, the Pimans were already there. They were probably there as well in the 1539–1540 period when Fray Marcos de Niza and Francisco Vásquez de Coronado were in the region enroute to New Mexico and the Pueblo Indians, but even this is not a certainty.

The Jesuit thrust spearheaded by Father Kino brought about the establishment of missions among the riverine Pimans and brought the Two Villagers and No Villagers into their first extensive contacts with Europeans. Father Kino introduced among the Upper Piman Indians many European foodstuffs, especially wheat, and including what were to become the all-important domestic animals: cattle and horses.

Although some students have regarded these Jesuit-period (1687–1767) contacts with Upper Pimans as sporadic and unthreatening to the Indians, there were major Piman revolts against the Spaniards in 1695 and in 1751, and throughout the entire period of Spanish and Mexican domination (1687–1856) Whites could never be certain of the constancy of their Piman neighbors. This was especially the case among riverine Pimans, where most Spanish missionization and settlement took place.

Summarizing from the works of Bolton (1960), Bringas de Manzaneda y Encinas (1977), Kessell (1970, 1976), and Kino (1948, 1971), it becomes possible to offer an overview of what happened to Piman Indians during the Spanish and Mexican periods (see also Fontana 1974, 1976:245, 1981a:32–62).

When Kino arrived in Pimeria Alta, various groups of Apache Indians were pressing hard on its eastern limits. Hostilities broke out between Spaniards and Apaches in the 1680s, and the Spaniards were only too happy to enlist Piman Indians as allies, especially the Sobaipuris and Pimas of riverine Sonora, to serve as a buffer between themselves and Apache enemies. This Sobaipuri-Spaniard versus Apache warfare by the end of the 1760s had resulted in the evacuation of Sobaipuris from eastern Pimeria and in the Apache takeover of lands formerly in Piman control. It had also resulted in the establishment of Spanish presidios in this sector of Pimeria Alta. The site of one of them, Terrenate, was changed four times in a fruitless effort to stay the Apache incursion from the northeast.

After Father Kino died in 1711, the work begun by him continued under his fellow Jesuits. By the time the Society of Jesus was expelled from New Spain by edict of the King of Spain in 1767, more than two dozen missions and mission-visiting stations (*visitas*) had been constructed by Jesuits at Piman riverine settlements. Efforts to christianize Pimans had taken place in a triangle-shaped area between the missions at Dolores, Sonoita, and San Xavier del Bac. The river valleys had further witnessed the founding of missions at Cocospera, Magdalena, Remedios, Guevavi, Tumacacori, Caborca, Pitiquito, Oquitoa, Saric, San Ignacio, and Tubutama, to name some of the more important ones (fig. 1).

Jesuit missions and missionaries were not the only early eighteenth-century bearers of European culture among Upper Pimans. A silver strike in 1736 near the present Arizona-Sonora border brought a rush of Spanish fortune seekers into Pimeria. Moreover, although there had been Spanish soldiers in the Pimeria since the 1680s, the 1751 revolt of Piman Indians headed by Luis Oacpicagigua of Saric occasioned the construction of two more Pimeria presidios in 1752, one at Tubac in Arizona and another at Altar in Sonora.

Presidial troops had to be fed, and inevitably, the presence of presidios attracted Spanish civilian farmers and ranchers. The Apache threat continued, and in 1775 the Tubac presidial garrison was ordered to move to Tucson, another Piman village on the Santa Cruz River and a mission *visita* of San Xavier del Bac.

The expelled Jesuits were replaced in 1768 by Fran-

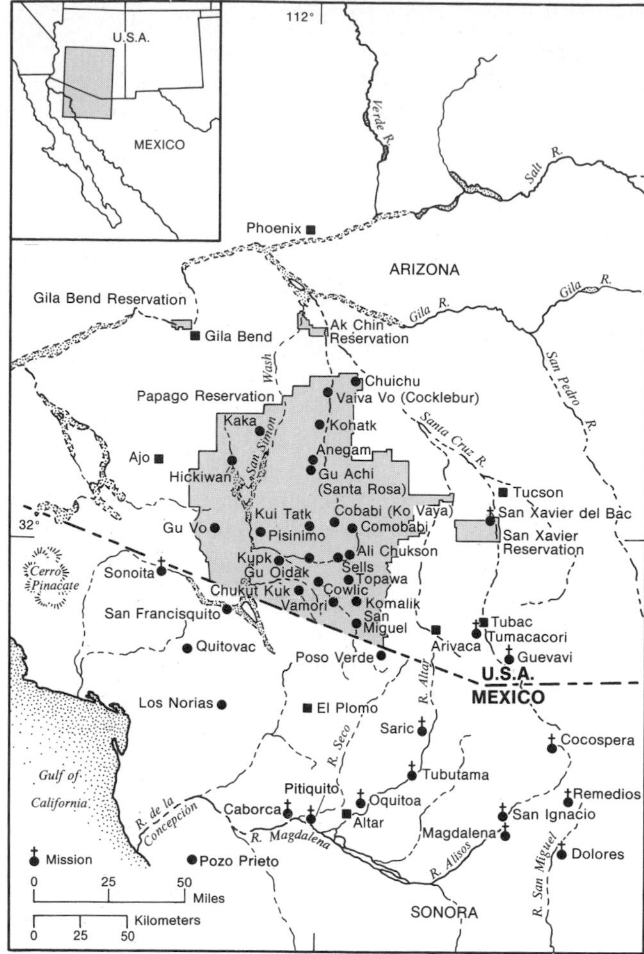

Fig. 1. Central area of Papago settlement.

ciscan friars from the College of Santa Cruz de Querétaro in Mexico, and the christianization program started by Kino continued under new missionaries in many of the same mission stations. Franciscans erected new structures on Jesuit sites.

In spite of various difficulties that faced the Franciscans—both from within in the form of internal power struggles and seemingly endless reorganizations of programs, and from without in the form of Apache raids and the danger of Piman apostacy—the friars managed to enlarge mission herds and fields during the closing decades of the eighteenth century and into the first four decades of the nineteenth. The friars were also able to recruit Two Villager Pimans to become One Villagers in the mission settlements on the rivers. Epidemics continually ran along river courses during the Spanish period, and combined with the population loss occasioned by Apaches' attacks, it became necessary for the Franciscans to entice Papagos to the mission communities through offers of land to work and the promise of a more abundant life.

In 1786 the Spaniards inaugurated a peace policy on their Apache frontier, and several Apache bands were induced to forgo their raiding and warfare habits in exchange for farmlands next to Spanish settlements and for rations and obsolete Spanish firearms to enable them to hunt. It was thus that an Apache "peace establishment" was created on the outskirts of Tucson, and Pimans and their long-time enemies were brought into a state of peaceful coexistence at least in this one location. In the meantime, many Pimans had been recruited into the Spanish army on the frontier and many others had begun to become integrated into segments of Spanish society via baptism and godparentage in both mission and presidial settlements.

The Spanish empire had left its impact on the Upper Pimans. Their economy had been greatly affected by the introduction of European crops, most notably wheat, and of European domestic animals, especially cattle and horses. Mining and cattle ranching had also involved an untold number of Upper Pimans directly in the cash and barter economy of New Spain. Piman soldiers were paid in cash—a medium wholly foreign to native economy—and their service in the Spanish army doubtless had its effects on Piman ideas of warfare and military organization.

Native Piman religion was affected to the extent that the forms of a new religion, Roman Catholicism, were melded into an aboriginal system of beliefs. Besides native curing songs, people could now sing hymns in Spanish and recite prayers in Latin. Baptism by 1856 was something that could be performed twice: once by a native medicine man and again by a Roman Catholic priest. Indeed, it may be that the "native" name-giving ceremony of Pimans was a Catholic-inspired one.

It may also be that the Spaniards had affected the

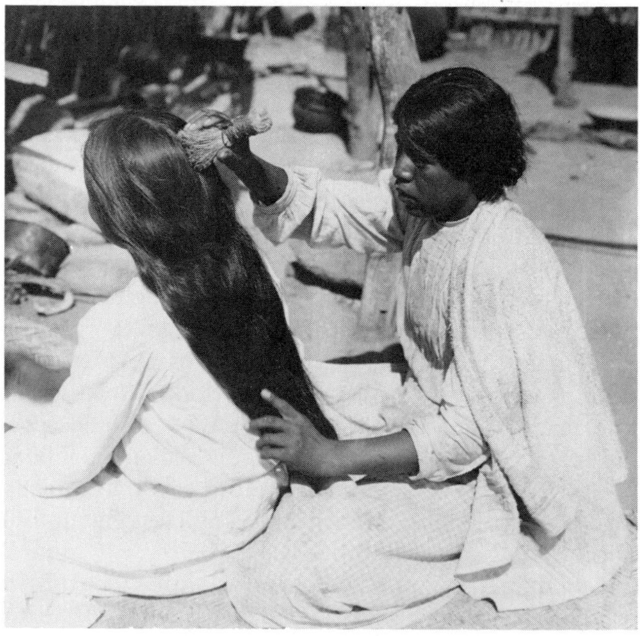

Smithsonian, NAA: 4539.

Fig. 2. Grooming hair, using a brush possibly made of sacaton grass roots (Russell 1908:118). Photograph possibly by H.T. Cory, 1916.

U. of Ariz., Ariz. State Mus., Tucson: left, 9131; right, 56495.
Fig. 3. The *wí·gida* 'Prayerstick Festival' ("Kachinas and Masking," fig. 5, this vol.). left, Papago clown (*náwijhu*) carrying bow and arrows in the wrong hands since such clowns do everything backwards. Photograph by Joseph Menager, probably at Achi (Santa Rosa), Ariz., 1920s. right, Joseph Flores from Menager's Dam village, Ariz., serving as a cornmeal sprinkler, standing inside a brush enclosure. He wears a handwoven belt over a commercial blanket, an eagle feather band across his chest, and a headband with feather and other decorations. He also holds a small shell container for the cornmeal. Photograph by Richard Nonis at Quitovac, Sonora, July 1963.

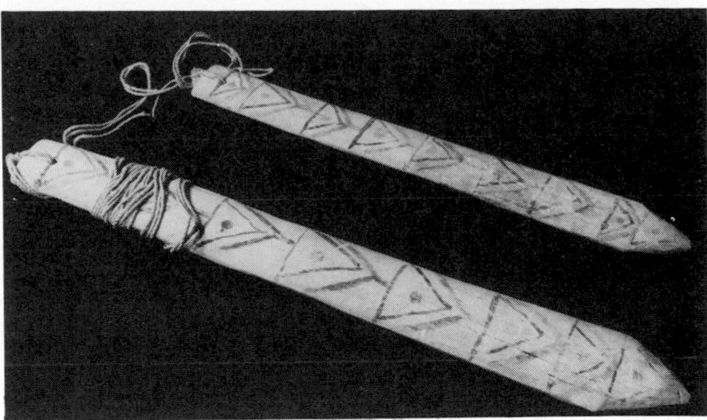

Amer. Mus. of Nat. Hist., New York: 50.1/4586.
Fig. 4. Bull-roarer made of 2 pieces of wood, painted white with red, blue, and yellow geometric designs, connected with cord. The shorter piece serves as a handle while the longer blade is swung through the air. These buzzing instruments were used by men and boys in the Papago *wí·gida* to give the signals for assembling and for other events (see Densmore 1929:141). Length of longer blade 51 cm, collected by Carl Lumholtz, Santa Rosa, Ariz., 1911.

native political organization as well, especially in the mission villages. Here there were Spanish-appointed Piman governors and other village officials bearing Spanish titles for their roles. How many Piman governors appointed in this way were already recognized headmen is impossible to say, but it seems probable that at least a few notions of government alien to Piman ways crept into the political organization of Upper Pimans during this period.

Finally, it needs to be emphasized that all Upper Pimans were not affected by White domination of their country to the same degree or in precisely the same way. Spanish settlement never penetrated the heartland of the Two Villagers, for example, and the No Villagers seem to have responded to European contact either by dying off or by becoming rapidly assimilated in Spanish mining camps. Even the Gila River Pimas never had a resident missionary among them in Hispanic times. The influence of New Spain in Upper Pimeria instead made itself felt most immediately along the eastern and southern river systems of the region. These were the best lands for farmers and cattlemen; they were the highways through the desert.

Mexican Period, 1821–1848

In 1821 Mexico won the war with Spain to become an independent nation, and the Franciscans living and working among the riverine Pimans found themselves in a difficult situation. Members of their order, and especially the religious of the College of Santa Cruz de Querétaro, were regarded by Mexicans as being conservative supporters of Spain. It was only because of the remoteness of the Pimeria Alta frontier from the heartland of Mexico and because of the unstable situation vis-à-vis Apaches that the Franciscans avoided secularization of the missions and managed to continue to work among at least some Pimans until the 1840s. Finally, with their priestly numbers reduced beyond the breaking point, the Franciscans relinquished their hold on the churches of the Pimeria, and what religious care the Upper Pimans received at the hands of Christians was from secular clergy.

The early years of Mexican independence from Spain were also marked by an increase of Mexican migration to the north. Farmers, ranchers, and miners moved in growing numbers into Papago country in the vicinity of Caborca, taking up Papago lands and water holes with utter disregard for Papago rights. Matters finally came to such a pass that Papagos engaged Mexicans in armed conflict starting in May 1840, continuing in what amounted to a state of war until June 1843. Hostilities ended with the capitulation of the Papagos (Fontana 1981a:57, 60).

In 1853, when the Gadsden Purchase left half of Pimeria Alta in Arizona and half in Sonora, there were more than 40 villages in Sonora that were either wholly Papago or of which Papagos formed a significant part. These extended from the new international boundary to a few miles south of Hermosillo, and they included No Villagers in the Pinacate Mountains as well as One Villagers in the Altar Valley.

For many years after 1854 Papagos continued to live and to behave as if the boundary did not exist. They passed freely back and forth over this artificial border, and in time they discovered that one could flee over the line in either direction as a means of escaping Mexican or Anglo-American justice, as the case may be. It was not uncommon for Mexicans and Papagos to steal horses in Sonora, sell them to Papagos living in Arizona, and to have the Papagos dispose of them to the Gila River Pimas. The sanctity of national boundaries, heeded more by Mexicans and Anglos whose borders these were than by Indians whose borders they were not, made such horse-stealing and related operations easier than they would otherwise have been.

Until the 1890s most Sonoran Papagos managed to continue living on and using lands that had always been theirs, either by adjusting their ways of life to Mexican economy or by losing themselves in the general rural

U. of Ariz., Ariz. State Mus., Tucson: top left, 984; bottom left, 44652; bottom right, 38504.

Fig. 5. The *célkona* ceremony, which included speeches, gift-giving, a dance (involving hopping or skipping, Papago *célko*), races, games with betting, and feasting. In the dance participants carried ceremonial objects (dream symbols) usually depicting something natural such as a bird, mountain, cloud, or rainbow. Although formerly set within a framework of intervillage rivalries, this ceremony, usually held in autumn, was partly a harvest celebration or winter rain dance. In 1980 the dance served as entertainment or as a contest at powwows, rodeos, or Indian celebration days (Haefer 1980:239–273). top left, Participants with white dots painted on legs and arms, carrying bird figures. The man at left wears a belt decorated with feathers. Photograph by Charles Morgan Wood, San Xavier, Ariz., 1920s. top right, Participants with white-painted faces parading with bird, mountain, and cloud symbols. Photograph by James Griffith, San Xavier, 1968. bottom left, Rain dance, during Feast of the Sacred Heart at Covered Wells, Papago Reservation, Ariz. Participants carry symbols of mountains, birds, clouds, and rainbows. Photograph by Helga Teiwes, 1977. bottom right, Cardboard figures of birds are carried during Tucson Rodeo Week. Photograph by Helga Teiwes, 1974.

U. of Ariz., Ariz. State Mus., Tucson: left, 867; right, 44254.

Fig. 6. Shrines where visitors leave offerings such as tobacco. left, "Children's grave," near Santa Rosa, Ariz., made of piles of stones open to all 4 directions. "The stones, says tradition, cover a hole through which once the ocean water threatened to issue in a flood. It was stopped by the sacrifice of four children, a boy and a girl from each moiety. They were thrown into the hole, but remain alive underground; they are the patron supernaturals of the locality" (Underhill 1946:23). Photograph by E.W. Haury, May 1941. right, Rock painted with stylized U.S. flag at a new shrine north of Gu Vo, Ariz. Photograph by Helga Teiwes, March 1977.

Sonoran population. A great deal of intermarriage took place between Papagos and Mexican peasants, such that the identity of many Papagos quietly disappeared.

By the late 1890s Papagos found themselves in a last attempt to protect their meager Sonoran holdings, confronted as they were by an ever-burgeoning number of Mexican cattlemen, ranchers, miners, and farmers. In 1898 small-scale warfare exploded in northernmost Sonora at a mining town called El Ploma (see Dolan 1972). Mexicans and Papagos got into a serious quarrel over some stolen cattle. The argument resulted in a Papago raid on El Plomo, in the death of some of the Indian attackers, and, ultimately, in a general exodus of Mexican Papagos to the United States. Papagos' willingness to leave Sonora was further abetted by their ability to find more and better wage work in Arizona than they could south of the line.

Those Pimans who remained in Sonora throughout the nineteenth century had been under more continuous influence of Roman Catholic priests than their cousins on the Arizona side. It was probably early in the eighteenth century that there developed in Magdalena, Sonora, an annual religious celebration that became extremely important in the lives of Papagos. This is the Feast of Saint Francis (*fiesta de San Francisco*), held on October 4, the feast day of Saint Francis of Assisi, patron of the Franciscan order. The image of Saint Francis of Xavier, the great Jesuit saint, was used in the celebration, and thus the Pimans managed to fuse together the patron of both Jesuits and Franciscans to create a generalized Saint Francis. The fiesta continues to attract Indians, as well as Mexicans, from throughout Sonora and southern Arizona (Fontana 1981).

It was also among Pimans living in Sonora that there developed a kind of Catholic religious practice without benefit of clergy. The practice spread to the Two Villagers into Arizona and there came to be what has been called Sonoran Catholicism. It represented Papagos' efforts to carry out Christian rituals—complete with homemade chapels and an attendant ceremonial and feasting area adjacent to the chapels—that they had been taught, only now the teachers were no longer present.

Following the El Plomo incident, in 1908 Mexican soldiers dispossessed Papagos of their farmlands at Caborca and Pitiquito. In 1927 a similar fate befell some of the Papagos living at Sonoita.

It was 1928 before the Mexican government finally took measures to secure at least a few Papagos in the rights to some of their remaining lands. On April 12, 1928, President Elias Calles signed a proclamation creating the ejido—a community land grant entitling its occupants to its exclusive use—of the Congrecación de Pozo Verde. This gave the Papago Indians at Pozo Verde community rights to 2,832 hectares (about 7,675 acres).

Papagos continued in the 1980s to be a part of Mexico's population, although minuscule in numbers. Fabila (1957) estimated that in 1957 there were 745 of them living in 11 settlements, both villages and ranches, in three Sonoran *municipios* (Caborca, Saric, and Altar). Fabila said they lived largely at a subsistence level, lacking credit and unable to acquire capital to drill wells or build small dams. This meant their cattle ranches and tiny farms were not competitive with commercial Mexican farms and ranches.

The anthropologist Nolasco Armas (1964) counted some 450 Sonoran Papagos; the census taken in 1979 by the Instituto Nacional Indigenista, Mexico, enumerated about 195. The anthropologist who conducted that census discovered that most "Sonoran" Papagos were living in Arizona communities adjacent to, but not on, the Papago Indian Reservation. Interviews among them indicated these people were rearing their families in the United States and few expressed any intention of returning to ancestral homes in Sonora (Fontana 1981a:75–76).

In the 1980s most Mexican Papagos lived in Caborca, the largest city in northwestern Sonora. They worked as laborers in town or on nearby large commercial farms or ranches, occasionally paying visits to their country homes. The Mexican government identified six major Papago "communities" in 1979: Las Norias, El Bajio, San Francisquito, Pozo Prieto, Quitovac, and Pozo Verde. "Major" can be taken to mean that at least one or two people might be expected to be in residence at any given moment (Fontana 1981a:78).

In spite of the more than 100-year presence of the international boundary, Sonoran Papagos remain in at least loose contact with their Arizona relatives. Many Papagos deeply resent the tighter controls on crossing that were instituted along the border in the late 1960s and in the 1970s, but it is a situation that they have been forced to accept.

Ariz. Dept. of Lib., Arch. and Public Records, Phoenix.

Fig. 7. Group of warriors, perhaps including (in the doorway) Chief Con Quien, war leader of the *Tótoguañ* Papagos. The men are dressed in Spanish-Mexican military style and hold either rifles or bow and arrows. An unidentified White man stands in foreground to left of the doorway. Photograph by William Bell, Dec. 1867, at the fortified hacienda of Cerro Colorado (the Heintzelman Mine) at the foot of the Atascosa Range, Pima Co., Ariz. (Bell 1869, 2:94–132).

American Period, 1848–

The American period of Papago history is discussed by Fontana (1974, 1976), Manuel, Ramon, and Fontana (1978), and Dobyns (1972).

The first face-to-face contacts between English- and French-speaking peoples and Upper Pimans were probably those between Anglo and French fur trappers and Gila River Pimas in the early nineteenth century. The war between the United States and Mexico in 1846 brought American troops through Piman country enroute to California, and the California gold rush of 1849 brought a flood of Americans (and, it seems, of virtually everyone else) down the Gila and Santa Cruz rivers as well as across the Camino del Diablo through the domain of the No Villagers.

Hardly had the United States Senate ratified the provisions of the Gadsden Purchase in 1854 when Anglo-American miners and mining promoters moved into Upper Piman country in the Santa Cruz Valley area, near Arivaca, and to the west at Ajo. It was not until June 1857 that the United States extended its federal Indian policy to the Papagos (and Pimas) in the form of Col. John Walker of Rogersville, Tennessee. It was then that Walker arrived in Tucson to become the Papagos' first Indian agent. In 1861 he left Arizona to take part in the Civil War, and it was more than a year before the Indians got another agent. In the meantime, in 1859 the Catholic Church at Santa Fe, New Mexico, sent a French priest to pay a visit to the Papagos at San Xavier del Bac, paving the way toward a reopening of Papago and Catholic church ties.

Papago agents and Catholic clergy came and went until at last in 1874 the Papagos got their first Indian reservation. This was the 71,000+-acre San Xavier Reservation created by executive order on July 1, 1874.

Smithsonian, Dept. of Anthr.: 107,529.

Fig. 8. Shield. The front is a fabric resembling burlap, painted black with white spokes around a black center, sewn to a twilled basketry base. The wooden handle on the back is attached with leather thongs. In design but not material this example resembles the rawhide shield used in battle by a club bearer who carried it while leaping from side to side to avoid arrows. The motion of the shield when rotated was supposed to have power over the enemy. Diameter 49 cm, collected by E.W. Nelson in Ariz. in 1884.

And the Roman Catholics established themselves permanently in Tucson, sending secular clergy to San Xavier Mission (fig. 9) to say weekly Masses and in 1873 sending nuns of the Order of Saint Joseph of Carondelet to become teachers for Papago children living at San Xavier.

For a brief period during the 1880s Presbyterians rather than Catholics were school teachers for Papagos at San Xavier, and in the late 1880s the Presbyterians opened an Indian boarding school in Tucson largely to accommodate Piman students. The Sisters of Saint Joseph took over the teaching duties at San Xavier again in 1889, and in 1932 they were replaced there by the Franciscan Sisters of Manitowac, Wisconsin, who continued to run the parochial elementary school at San Xavier in 1981.

In 1891 the federal government opened the Phoenix Indian School, the largest Indian boarding school in the territory. That same year the government inaugurated the "outing system" for Pimas, Papagos, Apaches, and other students at the Phoenix school, an arrangement whereby pupils were given jobs in non-Indian homes as a regular part of the teaching program. For the next several years innumerable Papago girls were trained in the outing program, most of them getting jobs as domestics and coming into prolonged and close contact with non-Indians for the first time in their lives.

Federally operated Indian boarding schools were opened elsewhere in the United States, and Papago children were sent to many of them. In 1900, 54 Papagos were enrolled in the industrial training school at Grand Junction, Colorado. In 1901, 22 pupils were sent to the school at Chilocco, Oklahoma, and in 1903, 53 Papago children were sent to the government boarding school in Santa Fe, New Mexico.

During the early part of the 1900s, more and more Papagos moved to Tucson, by then the largest city in Arizona, to settle permanently. In 1905 the federal government bought two acres of land in the "Native American Addition" in the city on which to build a day school to accommodate the growing number of Papago children living there. Classes began in 1907 with two teachers and 38 pupils. The venture was not long-lived. In 1921 Congress authorized the secretary of the interior to sell the two-acre tract.

In May 1911 the first attempt in history was made to form a Papago-wide political organization: the Papago Indian Good Government League. Backed by the Indian Rights Association of Philadelphia, the Good Government League was organized to enable Papagos to speak with some semblance of unity on matters that concerned the whole group. It was partially through the efforts of this organization that President William H. Taft set aside two tiny tracts of land for day schools at Indian Oasis (later called Sells) and San Miguel in 1911. Three years later Congress appropriated the money to build day schools at Indian Oasis, San Miguel, Cocklebur, and Gila Bend. An executive order reservation of 10,337 acres had been created for Papagos at Gila Bend in 1882.

By 1916 three of these four schools were completed and two more were under construction at Kohatk and Vamori.

bottom, Amer. Mus. of Nat. Hist., New York: 316542; top, U. of Ariz., Ariz. State Mus., Tucson: 34125.

Fig. 9. San Xavier Mission, Ariz. bottom, Papago houses and schoolteachers' convent near the mission. Photograph by John D. Scott or W.B. Cline on Wanamaker expedition, 1908–1913. top, Procession at the Feast of the Assumption of the Virgin Mary. Photograph by Helga Teiwes, Aug. 1972.

U. of Ariz., Ariz. State Mus., Tucson: left, 56496; right, 56499.

Fig. 10. San José Mission at Pisinimo Village, Papago Reservation. left, Facade of the church, redecorated by Frank Mariano, Papago, with black and white designs reminiscent of Papago pottery designs. Crosses are affixed to the top of saguaro cacti. Photograph by Bernard L. Fontana, Dec. 1965. right, Father Camillus Cavagnaro, O.F.M., at the altar. The fresco of the Last Supper was painted by the Apache artist David Sine. The altar cloth and the border of the priest's long alb are decorated with Papago designs. Photograph by Fritz Kaeser, 1966.

In the meantime, the Roman Catholic church had not remained idle in the matter of day schools for Papagos. Indeed, it was a Franciscan friar, Bonaventure Oblasser, who laid the foundations for the school system still in operation in the 1980s on the Papago Reservation.

When Father Bonaventure began living regularly among Papagos in 1912, most Indian children in Arizona who attended school were being forcibly removed from their homes and taken away to government boarding schools. Such compulsory attendance at boarding schools had not appreciably affected the Two Villagers in 1912, so this Franciscan set out to establish day schools in the villages. Father Bonaventure felt strongly that schools should come first; churches could follow. The result was that in 1912 the first day school in the Papagueria opened at Little Tucson. It was followed that same year by another at Topawa and in 1914 by schools at San Miguel, Chuichu, and Gila Bend. Two more opened in Cowlic and Cababi in 1915, and another parochial day school held classes for the first time in Anegam in 1916.

By January 14, 1916, when the Papago Indian Reservation proper was created by executive order, Catholics, Presbyterians, and the federal government had joined, even if they had not cooperated enthusiastically, in bringing to the Papago a new kind of education. And although probably fewer than 1,000 children had been to school at all by 1917, a system had been set in operation that would become as much a part of Papago culture as it was already that of Whites.

As important and lasting as the impact of schools on the Papagos may have been, just as important has been the impact of cattle. The modern Papago Reservation is characterized by two different kinds of cattle operations. Taken together, they represent the most significant aspect of modern reservation economy in terms of an industry whose control lies in Papagos' hands rather than in those of outsiders.

One kind of Papago cattle operation is that most familiar to non-Indians. It consists of a select and small number of Papago families who control very large herds of cattle, herds that sometimes are more than 1,000 head. These cattle are raised commercially in the sense that they are raised for cash and economic profit. The Papago cattlemen who are involved in this cattle business emulate the model of Anglo cattlemen throughout Arizona (fig. 12).

The other kind of Papago cattle operation is not a "business" in the economic profit-motive sense at all. It is instead a small family subsistence enterprise in which a Papago individual or family may have from one to 10 or 20 head of cattle, livestock being viewed in the manner of a four-footed savings account. But this account, which is drawn on only in times of need, is walk-

Smithsonian, NAA: 81-8922.

Fig. 11. Farm equipment including rake, shovels, ax, and horse collars, issued at the Papago Reservation (now the San Xavier Res.), Ariz. According to the photographer the Farmer-in-charge (J.W. Berger) required that these Papagos be photographed. Photograph by W.B. DeRue, Oct. 1898.

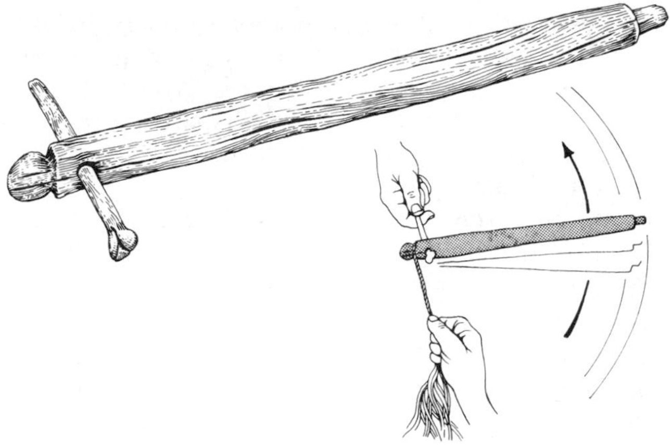

U. of Ariz., Ariz. State Mus., Tucson: E-8968.

Fig. 13. Rope twister, an artifact probably ultimately of European origin, carved from 2 pieces of wood. The handle (smaller piece) fits through a hole in the larger (spindle), which has a knob at one end where fiber is attached. One person holds the loose fiber, feeding it out, and another holds and turns the implement, thus twisting the fiber, which is sometimes twisted this way a second time. Horsehair and maguey are made into cord by this process. Length 49.6 cm, collected in Ariz., 1969.

ing on the range instead of reclining in a bank. In 1960 it was estimated that some 400 Papago families owned from one to nine head of cattle; 48 families had 10–499 head; five families had between 500 and 999 head; and two families owned more than 1,000 cattle (Metzler 1960:6). The Jesuits' introduction of these horned creatures had left a Papago legacy of cattle barons and of an unusual form of savings. Indeed, the modern Papago institutions surrounding livestock raising are extremely complex (see Fontana 1976a; Manuel, Ramon, and Fontana 1978).

By the 1930s Papago Indians had become irreversibly tied to non-Indian cash economy for their livelihood, although gift-giving, wagering, and bartering had not altogether stopped. But as early as the 1880s and 1890s Papagos began in growing numbers to sell their labor to mines and ranches and their wood, farm produce, and crafts (such as earthenware pottery and baskets) to non-Indians in communities throughout southern Arizona. After 1917 the production of long staple cotton became one of southern Arizona's most important industries, and for almost four decades Papagos provided the backbone of the cotton farm labor force in off-reservation cotton fields between the Gila River and the Sonoran border. The mechanization of cotton farming that took place in the 1960s brought an end to the dominance of cotton economy over the lives of many Papagos, although a large number continued to be employed on non-Indian farms in 1981.

Fig. 12. Weighing cattle at Papago livestock center west of Sells, Ariz. Photograph by Jerry Jacka, March 1978.

Land on the Papago and Gila Bend reservations has always been tribally owned; but in 1890 land at San Xavier was allotted under the terms of the Dawes Severalty Act of 1887. Most of the acreage at San Xavier continued in 1981 to be held in trust allotments, a situation carrying with it all the problems of fractionalized heirship interests characteristic of allotted reservations everywhere (see Fontana 1975).

The headquarters for the Papago Indian Agency of the Bureau of Indian Affairs was moved from the San Xavier Reservation to Sells on the Papago Reservation in 1919. Since that time the Bureau of Indian Affairs has continued to exercise a daily and direct influence on the lives of the Papago. The Depression of the 1930s witnessed a small economic boom on the Papago Reservation in the form of a variety of federally sponsored programs, and many Papagos who had moved away from the reservation were attracted to return to work

U. of Ariz., Ariz. State Mus., Tucson: a, E-5449; b, E-4718; c, E-4884; d, E-4715; e, E-9192; g, E-4645. f, Mus. of New Mex., Santa Fe: 25498/12.

Fig. 14. Modern basketry. Baskets have been made for sale to trading posts and travelers since the late 1880s, but in 1938 markets were expanded with the development of the Papago Arts and Crafts Board by the Office of Indian Affairs in the Department of the Interior. The Board bought and sold baskets and encouraged basket making. These examples are non-traditional in size, shape, materials, or technique: a, Miniature with traditional design; b, miniature of horsehair; c, miniature with cover; d, miniature with straight sides; e, basket with cover, cattail stem foundation sewn with yucca in a split-stitch pattern; f, scene depicting sgauaro cactus harvest; a miniature basket is attached to the base beside the woman; g, dog-shaped basket, the head serving as a lid; human and other animal forms are also made. a, Diameter 8.0 cm, others same scale. a, Collected in 1963; b and d, in 1941–1951; c, in 1962; e, in 1970; f, in 1959; g, in 1961.

on a variety of road improvement, range improvement, and water development projects. All were under the direction of the BIA.

1980s

In 1981 about half of the approximately 16,000 Papago Indians lived on their three reservations: San Xavier (71,095 acres), Gila Bend (10,337 acres), and the Papago Reservation (2,774,370 acres) at Sells. Some live on Ak Chin, which is administered by the Gila River Indian Community.

The Papago Tribe was organized in 1937 under terms of the Indian Reorganization Act of 1934, and it is divided into 11 political districts: one each for San Xavier and Gila Bend and nine (Schuk Toak, Baboquivari, Gu Achi, Sells, Chukut Kuk, Pisinimo, Gu Vo, Hickiwan, and Sif Oidak) on the Papago Reservation. Each district has its own council in addition to which it elects two councilmen to represent it on the Papago Tribal Council. In addition to the 22 councilmen there are elected at large by the whole tribe, a chairman, vice-chairman, secretary, and treasurer.

One of the problems that arose when this form of government was introduced to Papagos was that Papagos did not understand the concept of "representative government" in the same way in which that term is generally understood by non-Indians, including BIA administrators. Papagos were generally taught from the time of childhood onward that every human being was "his own man," so to speak, and that he could think for only himself and not for others. Each Papago was responsible for his own thoughts and actions and could not presume to know what lies in the hearts and minds of others. In this sense, then, the notion of "representing" someone else in tribal or community affairs was wholly foreign to Papagos.

The result was that until a particularly bitter dispute arose over the tenure of a tribal attorney in the 1970s, Papago tribal councilmen (both men and women) tended to run tribal council meetings as if they were old-fashioned village or community meetings. They were swayed by the opinions of others present at the council meeting rather than by abstract considerations of "representing" the "constituents" back home. Thus it was that for years in vote after vote of the council there were no dissenting ballots. In 1973, with the dispute over retention of the tribe's attorney, this pattern began to change.

The loci of power on the Papago Indian Reservation are found in the Papago Indian Tribe and its extensive bureaucracy, which originated with Office of Economic Opportunity programs in 1965 and has been abetted by increased business and leasing activities of the Tribe; the Papago Agency of the BIA; the U.S. Public Health Service, which has been responsible for the non-Indian health care of Papagos since 1955; the Indian Oasis Public School District (Pima County School District #40), in operation since 1963 and with an all-Indian school board; various church organizations, Protestant and Catholic, most notably Franciscan missionaries. It is estimated that about 90 percent of all Papagos are at least nominally Roman Catholic; many of them are devoutly so.

By 1981 the Papago Tribe in the form of the tribal body politic had become the single most powerful institution on the reservation. A large measure of former village and district autonomy had been usurped by the central tribal government because of the complete control by that government over massive sums of federal money intended for Papagos. Sells, as the administrative headquarters for the reservation, had become the

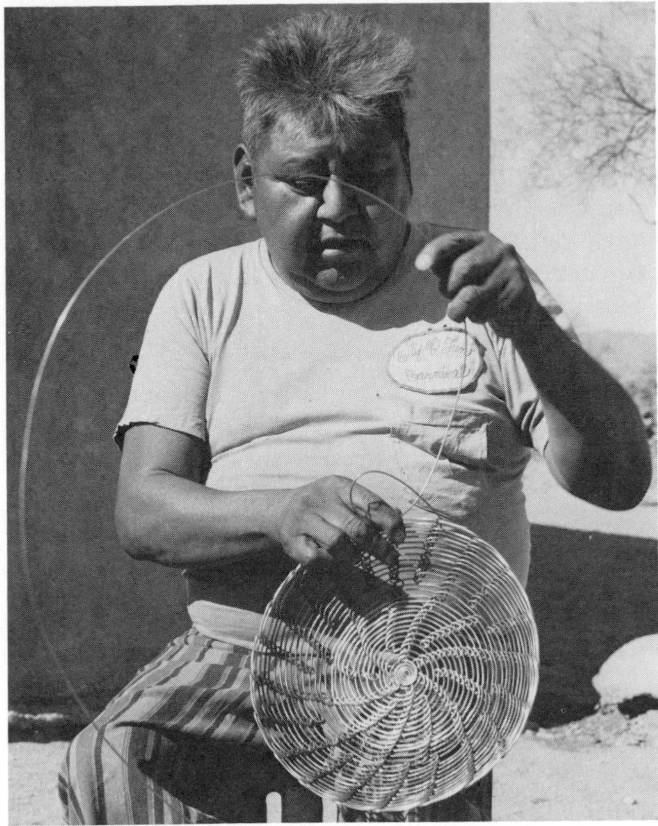

U. of Ariz., Ariz. State Mus., Tucson: left, 44475; right, 44210.

Fig. 15. Contemporary crafts. left, Eugene Lopez of Sells, making a basket of wire used both in the home and for sale. right, Antone Lewis of Coldfields, making a horsehair hatband. Photographs by Helga Teiwes, March 1977.

real seat of authority and influence. Programs in education, housing, welfare, alcohol and drug addiction, and youth employment, to name but a few, received federal grants, all to be channeled through the Papago Tribe.

Thus the Tribe and the other institutions impinge to a very large degree on the lives of the reservation's residents, most of whom live in population centers at Sells, Santa Rosa, Chuichu, and San Xavier, the remainder living in more than 40 settlements scattered from one end of the reservation to another. Children who cannot walk to school are carried in buses over paved roads; by 1981 most villages had been supplied with electricity through the Papago Tribal Utility Authority; houses are built by contractors out of non-native materials; hundreds of people are employed in tribal programs or by the BIA, the schools, and the Public Health Service.

An additional modern source of income funneled through the Tribe is that which accrues from the leasing of copper mining properties. Half of this income goes to the district council of the district in which the lease is located; the other half goes to the Tribe. At San Xavier most of the leased land is allotted, individual allottees getting most of the money rather than the district or the Tribe. The principal mining operations, involving millions of dollars in leases and royalties, have taken place in the Sif Oidak and San Xavier districts.

The Papagos at San Xavier began in the early 1970s to operate a cooperative farm, and there have been well-organized cattlemen's associations on the main reservation to improve income from that source. The Tribe

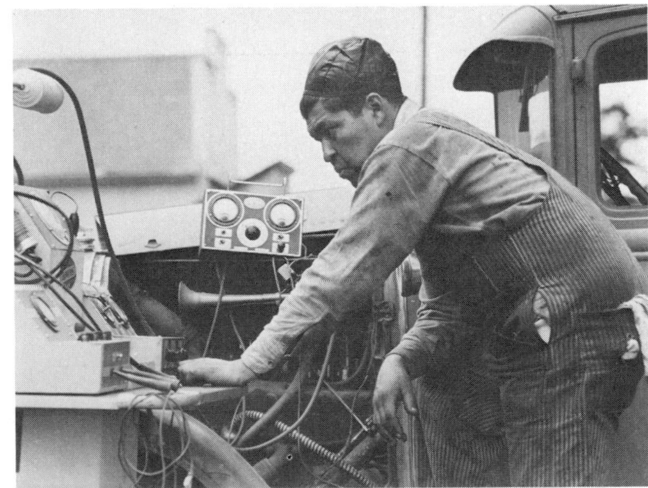

Smithsonian, NAA: 81-11583.

Fig. 16. Albert Noriego, a 21-year-old Papago from Sells, Ariz. in Civilian Conservation Corps training at the San Carlos (Apache) Agency, Ariz. Photograph by Harry Stevens, before Feb. 1941.

also leases the land for Kitt Peak National Observatory to the National Science Foundation and the Association of Universities for Research in Astronomy. And in 1976 the Tribe was awarded $26,000,000 by the federal government as a settlement for land and mineral claims. As of 1981 none of that money had been spent, partly because the Tribe had not completed compilation of a tribal roll that would identify potential beneficiaries.

Taking the most recent developments in Papago economy into account, it looks as if Papagos find themselves appended to a much larger economic, political, and technological system over which they exercise no direct control. Cash economy was not of their own making. Neither were federal programs nor even their present form of government. However, in time, through the increasing influence of education in the lives of Papago young people they will come to possess at least that same degree of autonomy in their own affairs as enjoyed by citizens of any other political jurisdiction in the United States.

History of the Pima

PAUL H. EZELL

In the beginning, the Spaniards generally referred to the people of the Santa Cruz and San Pedro valleys as Sobaipuris (Bolton 1948, 1:119, 122; Carrasco 1698) or Pimas Sobaipuris (Fernández del Castillo 1926:75). The Spaniards occasionally set down Indians' own names for themselves, but no instance has been found where a Spaniard recorded *ʔákĭmel ʔóʔodham* 'River People' or *tóhono ʔóʔodham* 'Country People' as expressing concepts of fundamental difference between two ways of life (Ezell 1961). Manje (Fernández del Castillo 1926:259) wrote in 1699 that the Jesuit priests and he had "found, seen, and tamed the greater number of the Pima nation, Soba and Sobaipuris, which, although in different regions and factions, is one and the same [as is] the language they speak with little difference between this and that verb and noun . . . Papabotas [Papagos] who live to the northwest [of Dolores, Sonora] of the same tongue, and the Yumas and Cocomaricopas of a totally distinct [tongue]." Thus Manje introduced into the record the two terms, albeit the one was later changed to Papagos, by which these two populations of Upper Pimas have come to be commonly called.

The terms Pima and Papago have come to connote ethnic differences beyond what the people themselves perceive; they have not forgotten what Manje observed, that they were both parts of a larger "Pima nation." The clearest exposition of the artificiality of too rigid a distinction between Pima and Papago has been provided by Dobyns (1974a:317–327) in his analysis of one former settlement. Kohatk would now be classed as Pima during the winter, but as Papago during the summer, according to where the people were living and farming when categorized.

The disappearance of the Sobaipuris of the San Pedro as an ethnic group was a side effect of missionization as increasing wealth was produced in Pimeria Alta: the region between San Ignacio on the south, the Gila and Salt valleys on the north, and San Pedro Valley on the east, and the Colorado Valley on the west (fig. 1). Establishment of the missions was followed by an increase in Apache economic raiding for produce, domestic animals, cloth, tools, and weapons, especially from the people of the San Pedro and Gila-Salt valleys whose homelands were closest to those of the Apaches. One result of this raiding was that the San Pedro Valley peoples began to take refuge with their congeners in the Santa Cruz and Gila valleys. By 1762 Nentvig (1951:79) reported that the San Pedro Valley had been abandoned, but this abandonment may not have been as voluntary as Lafora (1939:123) claimed. Elias reported to the Spanish governor of Sonora on March 22, 1762, on his having "settled" the Sobaipuris at Tucson (Dobyns 1976:19–22). Evidently not all who moved to the Santa Cruz were content there, for Anza (1770) wrote that some of the refugees had left Tucson for the Gila Valley, and after that time the Sobaipuris were no longer named as an ethnic enclave. The occupants of the Gila Valley were already being singled out as a separate group, as Nentvig (1951:15) referred to "the Pimas, called Gilenos . . . of the river Gila" or the Gila River Pimas.

As overland travel increased, especially following the discovery of gold in California, the presence just downriver from the Pimas of Yuman-speaking groups originally from the Colorado was partly the source of growing friction between the Pimas and the Quechan. This friction contributed to Quechan fears that too great political advantage and power were accruing to the combined Pimas and Maricopas because of their traffic with, first, the Spaniards, then the Mexicans, and finally the Americans (Dobyns et al. 1957:46–71). These fears led to increasing raids and counter raids between Pimas and Quechans, culminating in the elimination of many of the Maricopas and the greater portion of the Quechan warriors on the plains of the Middle Gila in 1857 (Ezell and Ezell 1970). This left the Pimas as the dominant native group along the southern continental route between the San Pedro and Colorado rivers.

Prehistory

In attempting to reconstruct Pima culture as it was upon the first direct contact between them and the Spaniards in 1694 (Bolton 1919a, 1:127–129) one is faced with the question of whether any genetic or cultural connection could be established between the Pimas and earlier peoples in the Gila and Salt valleys. Since the work of Bandelier (1890–1892, 2:463–464), the consensus among Southwesternists has been that such a connection must have existed (Gladwin et al. 1937:28; Haury 1945:212, 1976:38, 357; Schroeder 1954:599; Ezell 1963; Ham-

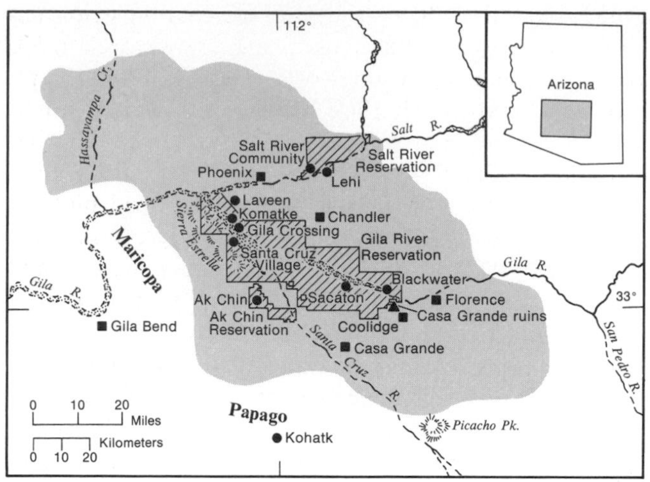

Fig. 1. Pima territory in about 1700 with modern settlements and reservations.

mack 1969:27; D.E. Weaver 1977:27, 90, 97). Yet the evidence to support an assertion that such a continuum existed was not forthcoming, so the idea of a "gap," a kind of Dark Ages between the end of the Hohokam Classic period at about A.D. 1450 (Haury 1976:357) and the beginning of the written record, continued to be entertained. As Haury (1976:357) observed: "to assert that there was no connection between the Piman people and the Hohokam requires the removal of the latter from the area by about A.D. 1450 and the introduction of the Pimas with an impressively similar lifeway almost immediately." The principal alternative to the "gap hypothesis" has been proposed by Di Peso, who found at San Cayetano de Tumacagori, in the Santa Cruz Valley, evidence that he argued supported the alternative that Hohokam elements survived in the indigenous culture until the arrival of the Spaniards (1956:562–566). Dobyns (1981:49) has reservations about the accuracy of the archeological dating of late sites in the Gila-Sonoran area and concludes that there was no Hohokam-Pima gap.

The principal obstacle to acceptance of a continuum, thereby necessitating the hypothesis of a Dark Ages, has been the perceived attenuation of Piman cultural inventory at the time of contact when compared with that of the Classic period Hohokam. M.E. McAllister (1980) had more success in reconstructing Hohokam social organization from archeological data than have had the archeologists in closing the gap. Environmental deterioration brought about by irrigation has often been adduced as a possible explanation for the technico-economic collapse of the Hohokam (Haury 1976:355). No equally plausible explanation has been advanced to account for a secondary obstacle, the shift from cremation as the preferred funerary practice among the Hohokam to interment as the customary rite among the Pimas.

There had been conjecture, but only conjecture, as to the possibility of introduced epidemic disease having had a bearing on culture changes in the area during the years preceding the arrival of the Spaniards (Ezell 1961:16, 1963:65). Although Aschmann (1959) had discussed the effects of epidemic diseases on the aboriginal population of Baja California, the idea was not extended to the mainland. Dobyns (1963) documented the spread of smallpox from the Valley of Mexico through Central America to the Andean area by 1526, only six years after its appearance among the Aztecs (Sahagún 1978:64). Others (Dobyns 1966, 1981; Crosby 1972, 1976; McNeill 1976) have demonstrated growing understanding of the economic and social consequences of epidemic diseases suddenly introduced into what Crosby (1976) has aptly characterized as "virgin soil."

In light of the foregoing, it seems time for a reassessment of the situation in Pimeria Alta during the period 1520–1694. Since the airline distance between Mexico City and Lima, Peru, is 2,639 miles (Dobyns 1981:50), one can approximate the rate of spread of the diseases at more than 400 miles per year. One of the characteristics of populations experiencing plagues is spread of the disease by fugitives from the locale of the outbreak (Crosby 1976:297), and it is unlikely that Aztec plague carriers moved only southeast. The airline distance between Mexico City and the Middle Gila Valley in Arizona is approximately 1,600 miles, over terrain no more difficult of transit than that between Mexico City and Peru. Therefore, it can be argued that disease did not wait upon Spanish explorers but preceded them by being spread by fugitives from infected communities and that one or more epidemics had struck Pimeria by 1524.

Proceeding upon that assumption, it is argued that the Spaniards met in 1694 a society reeling under the onslaughts of repeated epidemics over a period of approximately 170 years. As Hohokam numbers were reduced by successive plagues, each followed by only partial recovery, there would have had to occur a retrenchment in all aspects of life from the Hohokam culture as reflected in the great ruins. It is doubtless oversimplification, but applying Dobyns's (1966:414) " 'standard' depopulation ratio of 20 to 1" to the first population figures given for the Pimas, one arrives at an estimate of from 44,600 to 61,000 population for 1520, for example. Whatever the figures, any such population decline would have had a catastrophic effect. Some appreciation of the scope and nature of that retrenchment, undocumented though it may be, can be gained by examining the cases of other systems that have been similarly affected (Crosby 1976; McNeill 1976:199–234).

Pima Culture in 1700

When the written record for the Pimas begins, they occupied at least seven rancherias separated from each other by distances of from seven to nearly 40 miles. One of these, Santa Catarina, was on the Santa Cruz River west of Picacho Peak (Bolton 1919a, 1:206; Fernández del Castillo 1926:255; Martín Bernal 1858:806; Carrasco 1698); five were on the south side of the Gila between Casa Grande Ruins and a few miles above Gila Bend (Bolton 1919a, 1:128; Fernández del Castillo 1926:253–254; Carrasco 1698); and one was on the north bank of the Gila above the junction of the Salt River (Fernández del Castillo 1926:270). Population figures given as of about 1700 range from 2,230 to 3,050 (Bolton 1919a, 1:206; Fernández del Castillo 1926:253–254; Martín Bernal 1858:805, 806; Carrasco 1698). As with the rancheria count, this estimation may well have been low in view of the sporadic and inconsistent tallying and the evidence of Pimas resident in Opa ("Maricopa") settlements (Bolton 1919a, 1:186; Kino 1698; Carrasco 1698; Fernandez del Castillo 1926:301). As with the other Pimans, individual domiciles were separated from one another by hundreds of yards, each house being set in the midst of fields (Sedelmayr 1939; Pfefferkorn 1949:174; Barbastro 1793; Howard 1907:141).

Theirs was a digging-stick economy, like that of the rest of the Pimans, relying on irrigation with the waters of the Gila, the Salt, and the Santa Cruz (Anza 1776; Bolton 1930, 2:304). Diversion dams of logs and brush were built in the Gila River (Garcés 1770; Bolton 1930, 2:44), and an extensive system of canals and feeder ditches distributed the water to fields (Sedelmayr 1744). In addition to their own produce, the Pimas traded with the Papagos to the south of them for commodities scarce in their homeland such as hides (Barbastro 1793), mescal, and *chiltipiquines* (Russell 1908:78), a small wild pepper much used for seasoning in the Southwest.

Gathering of wild plant foods was an important source of supplementary or emergency food (Martín Bernal 1858:804, 805; Bolton 1930, 3:44). Hunting (Bolton 1930, 3:14) was of less importance, with deer being the largest game taken (Hayes 1849–1850; Whittemore 1893:69), although mountain sheep may have been important in pre-Hispanic times (Fernández del Castillo 1926:254), but rabbits were the animals most frequently sought (Whittemore 1893:69; Russell 1908:39). Fishing, usually with nets (Bolton 1919a, 1:195; Bartlett 1854, 2:240, 241; Grossman 1873:416), provided additional animal protein but evidently was not regularly practiced at all settlements. Exploitation of those resources, as well as war-making and religious requirements (wood for bows and hawk and eagle chicks for ritual paraphernalia and observances), led the Pimas to range beyond the river valleys on the bajadas, the slopes leading up from the valleys to the mountains, even in the face of possible danger from raiders (S.M. Hall 1907:415, 416; Russell 1908:42, 43, 44, 45; Kilcrease 1939:298).

Surpluses of food were stored in very large jars and coiled basket granaries inside the houses (Bolton 1930, 2:389; Goulding 1849); squashes were cut in strips and dried on the tops of the houses, later to be stored inside in the supporting framework (Russell 1908:91, pl. XXXVa; Southworth 1949). In addition to foodstuffs, the Pimas grew native cotton (Fernández del Castillo 1926:256; Sedelmayr 1939; Fewkes 1912:148–156; Gladwin et al. 1937:162) and cultivated plots of devil's claw for ornamentation of their baskets (Alamán 1825; Russell 1908:133). For illustrations of pottery and basketry see "Pima and Papago Social Organization," this volume.

Pima pottery, although technically fairly well made, was not especially artistically notable (Bolton 1930, 3:215), but Pima coiled basketry aroused admiration both for its technical excellence and for its artistic qualities (Pfefferkorn 1949:56–57; Goulding 1849). Among the Pima (and Piman) basketry constructions was the *gího* (Pfefferkorn 1949:194; Bartlett 1854, 2:236; Grossman 1873:408), a carrying frame made by fastening a net of yucca fiber cords to a framework of four poles. Also admired were the woven cotton blankets (fig. 2), which antedated by a century or more the Navajo blankets as a prized article of commerce (Goulding 1849; Barbastro 1793; Whipple, Eubank, and Turner 1855:32).

Pima settlements were largely self-sufficient economically and politically. Each settlement had a civil leader (Martín Bernal 1858:804, 805) and one or more shamans (Fernández del Castillo 1926:315; Nentvig 1951:59; Sedelmayr 1856:852). Each shaman was credited with only one specialty, different shamans being consulted for curing, control over weather, or promotion of success in war (Fernandez del Castillo 1926:315; Pfefferkorn 1949:221, 227; Nentvig 1951:58–59). It is unlikely that they had a paramount chief this early, but there is some evidence that one settlement, Shodakshon (Fernández del Castillo 1926:254; Bolton 1919a, 1:173; Sedelmayr 1939), owing to its size and central location, exerted a certain amount of influence over the others through its leader. Dobyns (1974a:317–327) has adduced evidence to show that, even prior to the first visit of the Spaniards to the Gila, the Shodakshon leader had initiated contact between the Spaniards and the northernmost Pimans by leading a party beyond the mission frontier into Sonora, where he was baptised Juan de Palacios.

The basic unit of social structure was the patrilineal extended family, composed of a couple (or a surviving member), married sons, and unmarried daughters (Fernández del Castillo 1926:315, 316; Whittemore 1893:58, 67, 76; Russell 1908:182–184; Ezell 1951–1954). Social organization above the family level included clans organized into moieties (Russell 1908:197; Herzog 1936:520–521), but their function had become obscured or forgotten or was perhaps concealed from the investigators when inquiries about them finally came to be made. Since clan affiliation descended in the male line,

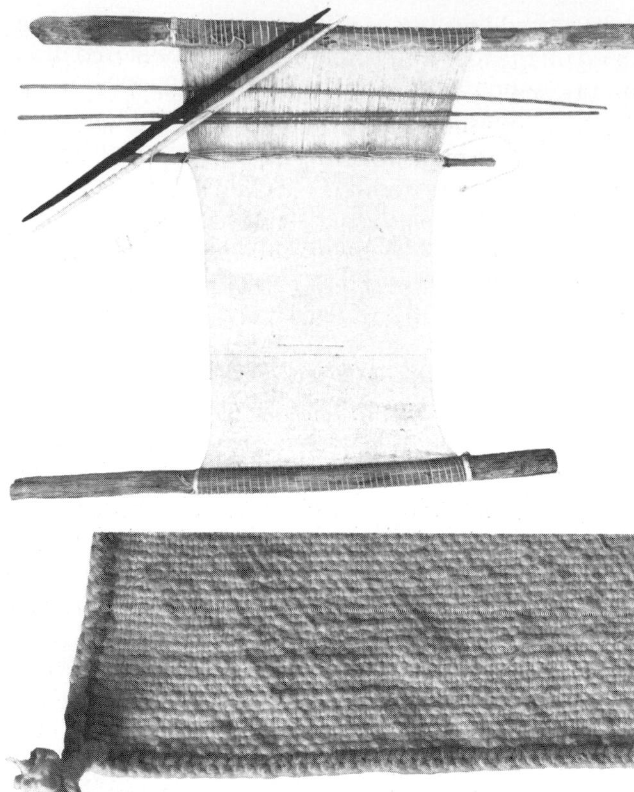

Smithsonian, Dept. of Anthr.: top, 76,008, bottom, 27,828.

Fig. 2. Loom and cotton blanket. The loom was stretched horizontally and tied to 4 stakes in the ground; sand was spread underneath to protect the fabric. The warp and weft are handspun undyed cotton producing the typically plain material that was used for wearing and sleeping blankets. The work in process here has several red weft threads; occasionally selvage threads were ocher-colored; otherwise no decoration was added. bottom, Detail of a blanket. top, Width of fabric 58 cm, collected by Edward Palmer in 1885; bottom, width of detail 15 cm, collected by G. Stout, Ariz., 1877.

children of non-Pima fathers did not acquire it; hence it at least served a kind of legitimating function (Parsons 1928:455; Ezell 1951–1954). A form of ritual kinship similar to the compadrazgo also united the individual with a group wider than the family (Nentvig 1951:63–64), but there was no evidence of age-grading or rites of passage except possibly a puberty ceremony for girls. Marriage was unattended by any ceremony, the couple simply taking up residence together; and divorce and remarriage were equally informal (Fernandez del Castillo 1926:315–316). Ideally, parents were supposed to arrange marriages for their children (Pfefferkorn 1949:187; Ezell 1951–1954), but in practice considerable liberty of choice was allowed. Consanguinity was reckoned over five generations, thus providing a set of incest rules (Fernandez del Castillo 1926:315; Ezell 1951–1954).

The principal supernatural being recognized by the Pimas was *ʔÍʔitoi* (Fernández del Castillo 1926:315), accorded the role of culture hero. Coyote was the trickster he so commonly was among American Indians, and in addition Pima mythology described a man-devouring monster (Fernández del Castillo 1926:261) called *hóʔok* (Russell 1908:222–223, 225). The Pimas had an extensive body of legend (Russell 1908:206–242; Lloyd 1911; Hayden 1935; Shaw 1968) that includes a period of social unrest in their past (Fernández del Castillo 1926:253). Reed (1954) and Schroeder (1954) have seen this as having been true of the Southwest generally during the approximately 400 years preceding Spanish entry, and it may be that the disruptions attributed to the impacts of epidemics have become merged in the larger picture. The large ruins, such as the Casa Grande (Fernández del Castillo 1926:311–312; Sedelmayr 1939), caves (Steen and Jones 1935:288–292; Haury 1945:202–203; Ezell 1951–1954), and the burial places of notable shamans (Russell 1908:255, pl. XLIc; R.F. Van Valkenburgh 1946a:20; Hayden 1935), were regarded as sacred places where offerings were deposited.

Reconstruction of Gila Pima supernaturalism (Ezell 1961:86–98) has not been so successful as that of technology or economics, for lack of data. Considering their similarities in other elements of culture, it would be permissible to extrapolate from the Papagos, who have been better documented in this respect. One difference might be the lustration ceremony for a man who had killed an Apache (Grossman 1873:416–417), since it required bathing in a stream.

In summation, at the beginning of their recorded history the Pimas lived in a loosely organized society, with an economy that was stable when compared with the hunters and gatherers around them and that was capable of providing them with surpluses. They were on amicable terms with the Papagos to the south (Carrasco 1698; Fernández del Castillo 1926:313) but, because they were allied with the Yuman peoples (Bolton 1919a, 1:128) now called Maricopas (Ezell 1963a) who lived in close proximity on the Gila and Salt rivers, Pimas were at odds with other Yumans, notably the Quechan of the Colorado (Bolton 1919a, 1:247; Fernández del Castillo 1926:267) and the Yavapais (Bolton 1919a, 1:202, 235). Pima surpluses were already attracting the attention of the Apaches to the east (Bolton 1919a, 1:198, 237, 247; Fernandez del Castillo 1926:248, 254, 255), adding another pressure to Pima life, but there had not yet developed the tensions among Pima communities that were to come later.

Hispanic Period, 1694–1853

The nature of Hispanic-Pima contacts through the period 1694–1854 (Ezell 1957) is better understood if set against the background of Sonoran frontier life (Dobyns 1976; Kessell 1976). Close relations with and communication among the Pimas Gileños, Pimas Altos, and Papagos meant that news about events in the south was constantly transmitted beyond the "Rim of Christendom" to the Gila-Salt valleys. Any discontent in the south with the Spanish colonization program was quickly transmitted north, as was the likelihood of rebellion. Because they lived so far beyond the Hispanic frontier, which never extended north of Tucson, the Gila Pimas generally escaped involvement in those events, although they did not always escape suspicion in the minds of the Spanish, and later Mexican, authorities: in 1752 the Jesuit Philip Segesser felt that the Gila River Pimas should be "curbed" (Dobyns 1976:12), and Middendorf (Gardiner 1957) accused Gabanimo (his rendition of the Piman name *Háwañ Mó?ŏ* 'Crows Head') of leading the attack on San Xavier del Bac in 1756; but Middendorf's account of the punitive expedition he accompanied following the raid makes it clear that *Háwañ Mó?ŏ* was an Opa/Cocomaricopa, groups ancestral to the modern Maricopas (Ezell 1963a). In the main, however, the Gila Pimas managed to stand aside from the turbulence in the south. The growth of Apache, Yavapai, and Quechan raiding so occupied the Pimas' resources that diverting any part of those resources to adventures in the south would have been unwise (Comaduran 1843).

While some Gila Pimas joined in the revolt of 1843, enough of them led by their "General," that is, governor, Culo Azul abstained to support the Hispanic assumption of their loyalty (Alamán 1825; Comaduran 1843a; Figueroa 1825). Thus, they benefited from the Hispanic concern that the productive (as contrasted with the foraging) indigenes be secure in the possession of their lands as a means of bringing them into the Spanish, or later Mexican, commonwealth. Gálvez's (1769) instruction on this point was reiterated by Corbalan (1778) and A. García (1798) and continued after Mexican independence down to the Gadsden Purchase in 1853 (Elias 1826; Ezell 1955). This policy went as far as the legal requirement that titles to land be issued and clarifies Mowry's (1858:298) assertion that the Pimas had a Spanish or Mexican title to their lands.

Archivum Romanum Societatis Jesu, Rome.

Fig. 3. The earliest known depiction of Pimas, drawn by Eusebio Kino in 1696–1697 on his manuscript map of Pimeria and neighboring areas. The warriors are shown shooting the Jesuit missionary Francisco Xavier Saeta in 1695; Kino was then among the Pimas, where he had been since 1687. For the full map and transcriptions and identifications of the many place-names, see Burrus 1965:7, 43–46, pl. 9.

The geopolitical advantages enjoyed by the Gila Pimas in their relations with the colonizing authorities thus structured their transculturation experience. They acquired a "most favored nation" status that worked to their advantage until 1868. Despite recommendations (Sedelmayr 1744; Escovar 1745; Bonillas 1774; Crespo 1774) and approval (Maria of Portugal 1759; Arriaga 1775), no presidio was ever established nearer to the Gila Pimas than Tucson; in fact, no Spanish or Mexican community of any kind was ever founded on the Gila, although J.F. Velasco (1850:161) urged it as the only means of retaining the territory. Instead of that kind of sustained interaction, contact and culture change occurred in three other ways that permitted them to escape imposition of cultural changes incompatible with their own value system. First, Gila Pima visits to Hispanic communities, which began even before the Spaniards reached the Gila, increased in frequency and duration as Pima production and commerce increased. Gila Pimas therefore could borrow not only from the Europeans but also from acculturated Sonoran Pimas. The Spanish and Mexican expeditions along the Gila served as a second vehicle for culture change; as the expeditions diminished in importance, a third means developed approximately concurrently. This was immigration to the Pima settlements by acculturated Upper Pimas from Sonora.

The Gila River Pimas demonstrated their pragmatism by the items they selected from the Spaniards and the Mexicans (Ezell 1961:137–146). The item accepted from the Spaniards that most changed Pima life was wheat, for the chain reaction set up by its introduction ultimately affected virtually every aspect of their culture. As it could be planted in the fall and harvested in the spring, it complemented rather than conflicted with the indigenous staple, maize, and thus doubled their production. Furthermore, as wheat was more esteemed by the Euro-Americans than maize, the colonization of Sonora provided a growing market for it, which in turn led to a market for other Pima products such as blankets, basketry, and captives (Escudero 1849:142–143). Separate storage structures for produce surpluses had not been mentioned by any previous reporters, but as

top, U.S. Military Academy, The West Point Mus. Coll., N.Y.: bottom, The John Carter Brown Lib., Brown U., Providence, R.I.

Fig. 4. Early drawings of Pima villages on the Gila River. top, A village in 1848. "The women dressed in a skirt of cotton cloth or strips of the inner bark of the cottonwood, they wore padding on the hips and behind under their skirts, in fact regular bustles. The men went almost naked, although a few had on shirts obtained from Graham's command; they had an odd fashion of filling their hair full of mud from the Gila, and then twisting it up into a helmet-like form and letting it dry" (S.E. Chamberlain 1956:286). Gouache by Samuel Chamberlain. bottom, A village in 1852. Watercolor by Seth Eastman in 1853 from lost original sketch probably by John Russell Bartlett, 1852.

Griffin noted in 1846 that "we saw many of their store-houses full of pumpkins, mellons, corn &c--" (Walcott 1943:43) it appears that storage facilities too were a consequence of the expanding market. The Pimas were thereby introduced to the idea of commerce instead of gift exchange, to the concept of a medium of exchange, and to the marketplace, a potent vehicle for culture change (H.G. Barnett 1953:46).

As the market grew, more land was brought under cultivation, and the growing involvement with irrigation agriculture provided one stimulus leading to increasing cooperation among the Pimas. Cooperation in turn led to more institutionalization and formalization of the structure of Pima society and to the emergence of a number of new occupational specialties. The division of labor became more sharply defined as men took over more of the work of farming while women concentrated on manufacturing articles for commerce.

The introduction of wheat also resulted in changes in the relations between the Pimas and their Apache and Yavapai neighbors. Campaigning against Upper Pima and Seri rebels in 1769, the Spaniards withdrew all but token garrisons from the frontier. When the Apaches discovered how weakened the presidios had become, their raids shortly were extended as far as Durango (Bohorquez 1792), and the wealthy Pima towns came in for a share of the attention. The Pima response was to increase the sentinal duty they already had (Dobyns 1974a:319) and to introduce, if they did not have it, arms drill for all adult males (Goulding 1849; Bartlett 1854, 2:249; Russell 1908:39)—in short, universal military service—and to shift from vengeance raids to planned punitive campaigns modeled on those of the Spaniards (Urrea 1773; Alamán 1825; Russell 1908:38, 55). Although the Pimas continued to place a high value on peace, prowess in battle came to carry respect and admiration; a growing orientation toward war can be discerned. Further impetus to this trend was provided through a growing trade in children captured by the Pimas and sold to settlers in Sonora, where they became known as Nixoras (Dobyns et al. 1960).

The combination of intensified farming and raiding brought about (through a settlement contraction at the east and west ends) a denser settlement pattern, with its consequent requirements for even more coordination and formalizing of society. If the office of paramount chief had not become formally recognized before as governor, it became so with Culo Azul and, furthermore, became hereditary. By the end of the Hispanic period, the Pimas qualified for the designation of "nation" accorded them by the Spaniards, the Mexicans, and later the Anglo-Americans (Emory 1848:111). At the same time, the total area exploited by the Pimas expanded when more land was brought under cultivation, and as the technological and ritual demands of war increased, so did the demand for resources obtainable only by venturing into the bajadas and mountains.

Other changes emerged during this period, producing an assemblage of traits that characterized Gila Pima culture for a generation, especially in the realms of subsistence and technology. The sources available for 1846 (Bigler 1962; H.G. Boyle 1931; Cooke 1848; Emory 1848; A.R. Johnston 1848; Tyler 1881) list 17 elements characteristic of Gila Pima life that were introduced during Hispanic times. Only the letters of recommendation called "passports" by the Pimas (Couts 1961:134) were not related to subsistence. Of the other 16, only peas (H.G. Boyle 1931) and wheat were listed among the introduced crops. Cattle, horses, mules, donkeys (Bigler 1962:37), sheep (Cooke 1964:163; Tyler 1881:235), chickens, and ducks were the livestock noted. Axes, harrows, hoes, shovels, plows, and fences were the farm equipment mentioned; the recorders made a point that only the axes were of metal, all the other tools being of wood. The hoe was presumably the aboriginal weeding blade, since that form, with a metal blade, was later described and sketched by Goulding (1849). Plows such as that described and sketched by Goulding (1849) were implicit in Emory's (1951:134) statement that the few cattle were "used in tillage" although he did not mention plows until his letter to Gallatin (Emory 1848:130); plows probably were few for lack of draft animals.

Changes in Pima world view had also taken place but were much less marked and far-reaching in their impacts. For example, the articles of clothing that were accepted were limited to male attire and were regarded as prestige items, implying that the transculturative interchanges had been between men only (Emory 1951:133). The idea of validation of authority through appointment by a Hispanic official (Emory 1951:137) had been accepted as an element of leadership. Pima vocabulary had been enlarged by the adoption of the Spanish words for borrowed items; examples are *káwiyu* from *caballo* 'horse', *íspul* from *espuela* 'spur' (Whipple, Ewbank, and Turner 1855), and *kósin* from *cocina* 'kitchen' (Ezell 1951–1954). Baptism was accepted as an additional curing rite rather than a symbol of religious conversion, as were crucifixes and saints' medals (Dumke 1945:153; Guardián de San Bernardo 1849). Otherwise Pima religion remained largely unaffected by Christianity (Hayes 1849–1850).

By the beginning of the American period, the Gila Pimas had become an economic force in Sonora. Escudero (1849:142–143) reported an annual "fair" on the Gila to which "multitudes" came from as far south as the San Ignacio Valley, and Bartlett (1854, 2:259) wrote of three Mexican traders from Tucson in one of the Pima settlements in 1852. Virtually every source described the Pimas as the only effective military force restraining the Apaches. As a consequence of those two developments the Pimas had become a power bloc among the aboriginal peoples of the Southwest. At the same time, they had become disillusioned with the Hispanics

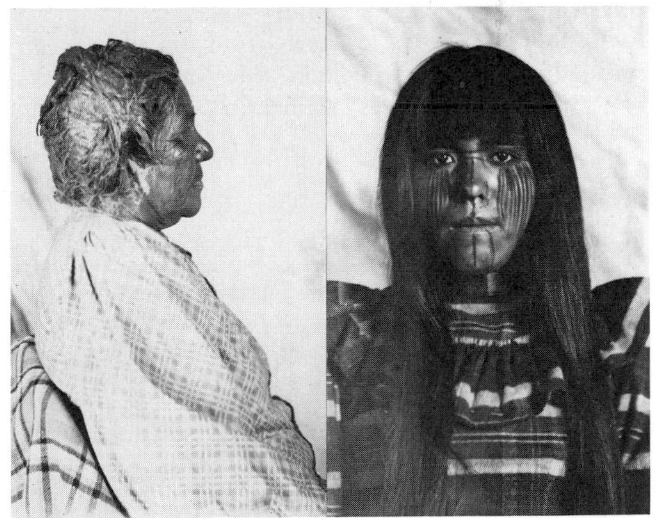

Smithsonian, NAA: left, 2635-d; right, 2629.

Fig. 5. Women's hair dressing and face painting. left, Chulis with hair dressed with plaster made of black river mud mixed with mesquite gum, which was allowed to remain on the hair overnight. The mixture was said to kill vermin and clean the hair. The gum was also thought to darken the hair and prevent graying. Such grooming frequently occurred about once a week (Russell 1908:159). right, Lieta with face painted in obsolete style, a reconstruction for the photographer (Russell 1908:161). Photographs by Frank Russell, 1902.

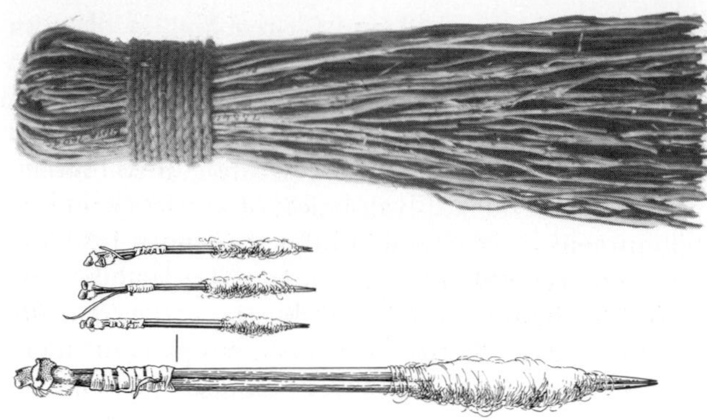

Smithsonian, Dept. of Anthr.: top, 76,044; bottom, 217,935.

Fig. 6. Grooming. top, Hairbrush of sacaton grass folded over and wrapped with fiber cord, used primarily by women. Maguey fiber was also made into brushes. bottom, Tattooing kit. Both men and women formerly had face tattoos. The line was made using cactus spines tied together with cotton; charcoal was rubbed in during the 2 operations that were necessary and for 4 days afterward (Russell 1908:161–162). Length of top 15.5 cm; collected by Edward Palmer, 1885; bottom, same scale, collected by Frank Russell, 1902.

in Sonora. Promises of missions in Pima territory, with all the anticipated benefits, were never fulfilled, but the Spaniards had attempted an abortive establishment of a mission for the Pimas' enemies, the Quechan (Palou 1926:201). When the conflict erupted between America and Mexico, the Pimas again chose neutrality (Emory 1848:601) rather than support the Mexicans.

American Period, 1853–

For the first decade and a half of the American period, the Pimas and their allies, the Maricopas, continued to enjoy a "favored nation" status for the same reasons as heretofore. The stresses that were to lead to the Civil War attracted most of the federal government's attention and resources and slowed immigration into the area until after that conflict.

Lacking adequate troops to deal effectively with the marauding Indians, the government had to have the help of the productive Indians against the raiders. One of the first combined operations involving Americans and the Indians of the Gila was recorded by Juan Thomas, a Pima of Blackwater, Arizona, in 1856–1857 (the Pima year beginning with the saguaro fruit harvest in June—Russell 1908:35): "The Pimas and Maricopas joined the white soldiers in a campaign against the Apaches under White Hat" (Russell 1908:46). Chapman characterized them as having "acted in the capacity, and with even more efficiency than a frontier military" (Knight 1858).

Without settlers, the government had to depend on the farming Indians for provisions, which became increasingly important in a very short time. On May 9, 1857, the secretary of the interior issued instructions on the construction of a wagon road to link El Paso, Texas, with Fort Yuma, Arizona, including this comment: "It is suggested that Fort Yuma being an unsuitable place for recruiting your party and animals, you had better fall back on the Pimas Villages, having made arrangements for such supplies as you may need to be in readiness for you at that place" (J. Thompson 1857). Since "recruit" meant "rest and recuperate" in that context, not "enroll" as it does today, the Pimas were to be notified of an increased market for their produce. In August-September of that same year the semimonthly San Antonio, Texas–San Diego, California, stage line began operation (Browne 1869). Both projects required food and shelter for men and animals and replacement

Smithsonian, NAA: 57,275.

Fig. 7. Mounted scouts from the campaign of 1886. About 31 Pimas and 8 soldiers pursued Geronimo and his Apache followers into Mexico. The Apaches were captured by soldiers before the scouts overtook them (Russell 1908:60). Photograph possibly by A. Frank Randall, 1886.

animals. By 1859 a mill and a number of trading posts had been established, counting on the Pimas as both producers and consumers (Browne 1869).

Concurrently, the foundations for the Pima-Maricopa distrust and suspicion of government personnel were being laid even before the Gadsden Purchase brought the Indians under American control. Whether soldier, goldseeker, or member of a boundary commission crew, the Americans all shared a quality that, more than language, distinguished them from the Spaniards and Mexicans: they possessed more goods that could become available to the Pimas. Unlike the civilians, however, the government people operated under constraints other than expediency when it came to the disposal of their goods. However well or poorly perceived or understood by the Indians, federal regulations influenced their attitudes toward government personnel from the beginning of their contacts.

When Pima Gov. Juan Antonio Llunas (Emory 1848:82) asked him for guns, Major Graham "told him that he would represent their wants to our great chief in Cal.a and if he could spare them, they should have them" (Couts 1961:67). When asked for spades that the troops were carrying, Graham explained his denial by pointing out the depletion of their equipment resulting from their Mexican campaign, then compounded the situation by saying "*but that* if we *had come from the U.S.* we would of course have many presents for them . . ." (Couts 1961:68). In January 1858 Lt. Chapman had been in command of the escort that accompanied the newly appointed Indian Agent John Walker to the Pima settlements where Walker "assured them that the government was prepared to furnish them with plows, spades, shovels, axes, and every article necessary for their comfort" (Knight 1858). On a subsequent stop some months later, the chief offered three dollars each for spades and axes, exhibiting a "handful of gold"; when Chapman explained that he could not sell government property the offer was doubled. Chapman repeated his explanation and the chief was reported to have responded: "I believe your people are a nation of liars, and *you are a liar individually*; you came with your agent and you heard what he said—you sanctioned it. . . . I trust you no more." G. Bailey (1858:204) attributed those remarks to the Maricopa chief, but in view of some of the comments from Antonio Azul (fig. 9) reported by Mowry (1860:354) they could equally well have come from him.

Other actions by government personnel contributed to the Pimas' and Maricopas' negative reaction. When Sylvester Mowry, a special commissioner to the Indian Bureau reporting on the inhabitants of the Gadsden Purchase, was finally able to distribute tools and other goods, Antonio Azul expressed the Indians' resentment that their enemies, the Apaches, had already been given them while the Pimas and Maricopas had been neglected (Mowry 1860:354). The Pimas' resentment was

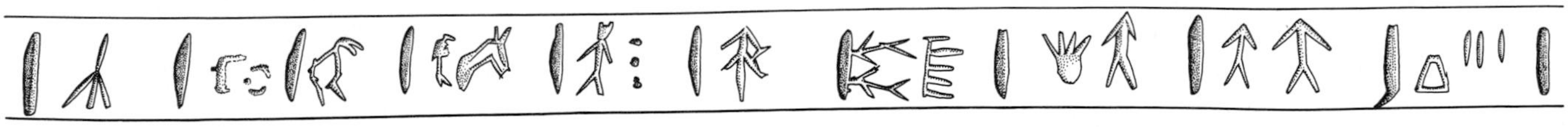

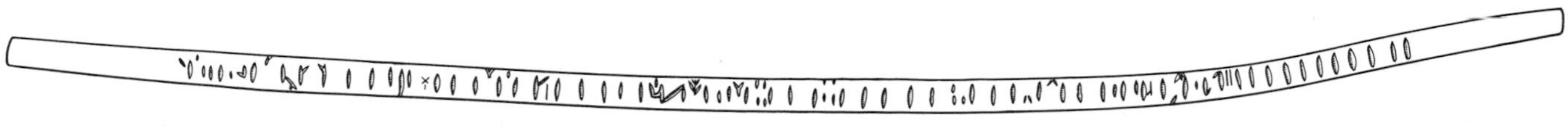

top, Mus. of Amer. Ind., Heye Foundation, New York: 24596; Smithsonian, Dept. of Anthr.: center, 218,135 (detail); bottom, 218,130.

Fig. 8. Calendar sticks. top, Joseph Head, left, reading a calendar stick to Henry Soalikee. These sticks were mnemonic devices with each notch representing a year, "the owner being expected to remember the events of that year" (Spier 1933:138). They were so personal that they were usually destroyed at the death of the individual. Photograph by Edward H. Davis, Gila Crossing, Ariz., 1921. Calendar sticks, carved with notches to set off years (reckoned from July—the saguaro harvest) and dots and other nonstandardized symbols to represent events during the year. Red and blue coloring is added to some of the markings. center, Small portion of stick from Blackwater, which was recarved from memory by the man who had lost the original but who had continued the history on paper, perhaps resulting in these more pictorial signs (Russell 1908:135). bottom, Stick from Casa Blanca, slightly flattened on the one side covered with symbols. Length of Casa Blanca stick 93.0 cm, total length of Blackwater stick 139.5; both collected by Frank Russell in 1902.

heightened by their knowledge that the Apaches had little or no use for the implements of labor. At the 1859 meeting Mowry (1860:354) told the Indians "that they were children," and Superintendent of Indian Affairs Charles D. Poston acted in ways that could have done little to allay their suspicions (Altschuler 1977:23–42).

Nevertheless, in spite of (or, perhaps, owing to) government neglect, the Pimas enjoyed an expanding economy during those first 15 years of American rule. Even though traders paid as little as possible for Pima produce (Rusling 1874:370), the Indians were at least able to buy for themselves some of the things they needed to increase the acreage under cultivation, hence increasing production, until the end of the Civil War freed thousands of land-hungry settlers to bring about what every agent had warned against: the depletion of the Pimas' Gila River water.

From the beginning, the Pimas had made known their anxiety about their water in the Gila River, and that anxiety was communicated to the commissioner of Indian affairs by the agents. The initial reservation surveyed in November 1859 (Mowry 1860:358–359) included only the cultivated land that Mowry and Andrew B. Gray, surveyor, saw at the time, and the Pimas were told that if they could prove their claim to land upstream from their fields the survey would be adjusted. Too little was done too late (McGinnies, Goldman, and Paylore 1971:52–53; Schroeder 1973:245–257). As early as 1863 Poston (1864:506) warned that "If, . . . the land above them should be occupied by Americans, and their supply of water reduced, it might produce discontent." Four years later marked the end for Pima economic stability and the way of life they had known for centuries. In 1867 the ex-Confederate J.W. Swilling began construction of a canal intended to reclaim 4,000 acres of land, using the water from the Salt River; completed in 1868, all the lands it served were occupied by settlers during the following two years and the city of Phoenix was born (Farish 1915–1918, 2:252–253). By July 1, 1870, settlers had located above the Pima reservation, opened large canals, and were wasting water instead of returning it to the Gila (R. Jones 1870:219–220). Clashes were occurring, and the only reason the settlers had not yet tried to eject the Indians was fear of the nearly 1,000 warriors the Pimas and Maricopas could field. At a council held on May 11, 1872, Antonio Azul told Agent John H. Stout that about 300 men had gone over to Salt River to farm because of lack of water in the Gila (Stout 1872:167; Howard 1872:153). On June 14, 1879, that new settlement was recognized by the establishment of the Salt River Indian Reservation (Barnes 1960:192).

Ironically, at the same time the Pimas started into their own depression, they also received the chance to try to cross the last threshold between themselves and other American farmers. On January 1, 1871, the missionary Charles H. Cook "received an appointment as government teacher" (Whittemore 1893:31), and some Pimas began their exposure to elements of education (and Christianity). As a side effect, the process of changing their society in other ways began, as agents and teachers came to supplant chiefs and parents as wisdom and authority figures. An enduring and pervasive consequence of the missionary couple's work was the elimination of large areas of Pima supernatural concept, and Pima religious culture took on a strong flavor of Presbyterian Christianity. This change was so deep and far-reaching that, when the Roman Catholic Church established its first missions, around 1900, resentment was aroused by the effort to convert people from one form of Christianity to another thus adding one more source of tension in Pima culture (Ezell 1951–1954).

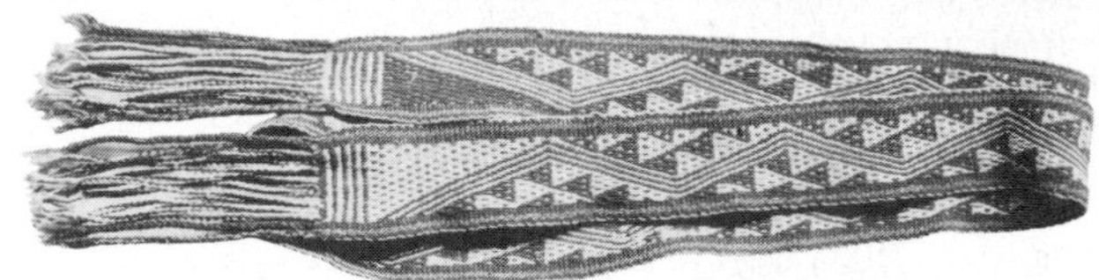

top, Smithsonian, NAA: 2611-b; bottom, Smithsonian, Dept. of Anthr.: 178,911.
Fig. 9. Headbands. top, Antonio Azul, wearing a woven cotton headband over hair that very likely was long and twisted in rolls (Russell 1908:152–153, 159). The headband was worn to increase the bulk of the hair. Horsetail hair was sometimes braided and added into the hairstyle for this purpose. His earlocks are braided. Photograph by Alexander Gardner, Washington, Oct. 1872. bottom, Double-weave headband in blue, red, yellow, and white cotton with braided fringe at ends. Such bands were woven on a horizontal loom. Length 200 cm, collected by John Russell Bartlett, 1850–1853.

The Pimas refer to the 40 years following the disastrous withdrawal of their water by 1871 as the "years

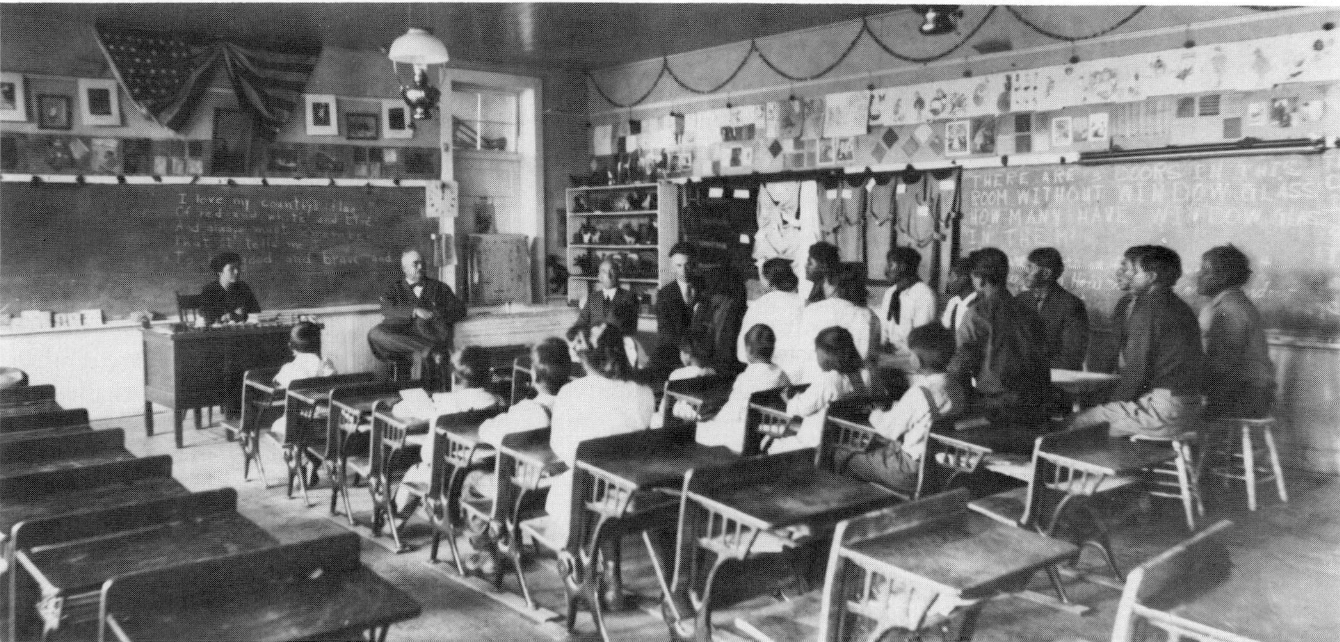

top left, Calif. Histl. Soc., Los Angeles: Title Insurance Coll., 3561; top right, U. of Ariz., Ariz. State Mus., Tucson: 32851; bottom, Natl. Geographic Soc., Washington.

Fig. 10. Schools. top left, School and Presbyterian mission at Gila Crossing, Ariz. Photograph probably by Charles C. Pierce, about 1900. top right, School bus on the Gila River Indian Reservation, St. Johns, Ariz., in front of a building formerly used for all classes, then later as an art center. Both the bus and building are decorated with basketry designs. Photograph by Helga Teiwes, 1972. bottom, Inside a school on Pima Indian Reservation, Ariz. Photograph by McCulloch Brothers, before March 1928.

of famine," and Ortiz chose 1910 as an end date because the Pimas themselves most often used it, but he also commented that any terminal date would be "arbitrary at best" (Schroeder 1973:245, 252). At any rate, the Pimas were plunged from the status of independent farmers competing successfully with White farmers to that of wage laborers (fig. 11) and even welfare recipients (Ludlam 1880:4). Russell (1908:32–34, 54, 56–66) synopsized the water deprivation and chronicled the consequences: alcoholism, increased killing as Indians quarreled more, and increased intercommunity strife.

Wittfogel (1957:27) perceived cooperation as the key organizational device in hydraulic societies. One of the most serious changes after 1871 was the erosion of the web of cooperation that had knit the Pima communities into an irrigation, if not a hydraulic, society, as individual groups sought solutions apart from the society as a whole, such as the founding of Blackwater (Grossman 1871:14). Both that move and the founding of the Salt River community were only of short-term benefit to portions of the society, and both settlements soon found themselves once more short of water as were the rest of the Pimas. Deprivation of irrigation water turned the Pimas into a "peasant" society for three generations; as such they were subjected to the attributes G.M. Foster (1962:44–47) has described for such societies—impotence in the face of the outside world and absolute limitation of resources. As such, they could be said to share in the "culture of poverty," one component of which has been described as isolation from the main stream of change, magnified by reservation status (Cowles

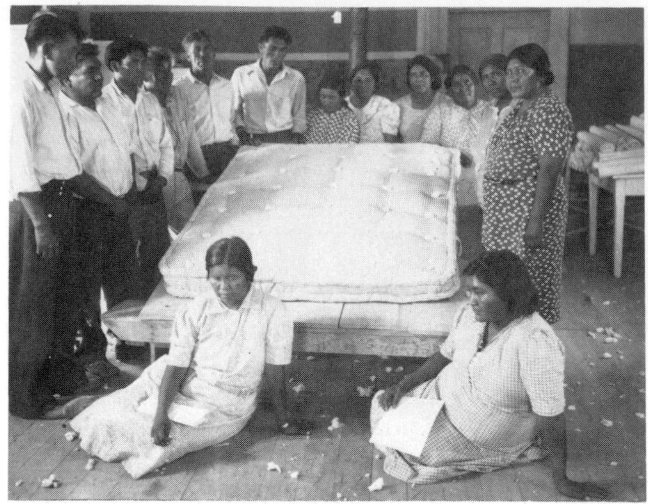

left, Mus. of the Amer. Ind., Heye Foundation, New York: 32998; right, U. of Ariz., Ariz. State Mus., Tucson: 32886.

Fig. 11. Wage labor, a factor in 20th-century life. left, Mattress factory on Pima Reservation, Ariz. Photograph by Odd Halseth, 1920–1925. right, Pima-owned canvas factory in the Gila River Indian Community, Ariz. Gladys White is at the machine in the foreground. Photograph by Helga Teiwes, 1972.

1969:11). Thus, from the deprivation of water stemmed another kind of deprivation—that of the learning situation in childhood, which promotes learning in later life (Crow, Murray, and Smythe 1966:117). And as that deprivation was continued over generations it came to constitute the kind of self-perpetuating mechanism described by Frost and Hawkes (1966:7–8). When Southworth (1949) wrote that "the Pimas had grown as rusty as their tools," he anticipated some insights by a generation.

Other changes in American culture afforded the Pimas opportunities to demonstrate their survival potential. One of those changes was the invention of the battery-powered radio. Although Pimas had been acquiring English in interaction with Whites and, since 1871, in schools, most communication was in Pima (Russell 1908:17). From daily exposure to English on the radio Pimas born after World War I experienced a reinforcement of their grasp of English not available to their parents.

World War II took young men, accustomed to English, away from the reservation and exposed them to places, people, and experiences that brought some out of the insulating shell of apathy that so many of their elders had developed to endure the vicissitudes of their times. Some of those veterans returned with a more sophisticated knowledge of the world and with a determination to take a more aggressive approach to the stultification that had kept Pima life narrow and provincial for so long.

Postwar developments provided impetus to the changes stemming from the battery-powered radio and military service. The Indian Reorganization Act of 1934 had provided a situation favorable for the agent to become more paternalistic, and the council merely to approve his decisions. The old-style agent retired, and the new agent brought to his job the conviction that the Indians must make their own decisions. A young Pima veteran was elected council chairman (governor), from which post he helped persuade his fellows toward a new, more positive approach. The Pimas retained their own legal counsel who, together with some of the Bureau of Indian Affairs personnel, joined the Pimas in challenging the White world by maneuvers such as renegotiating leases of Indian properties, drilling wells, and in other ways raising that part of the tribal income not under the control of the BIA. A young Pima educated at the College of Agriculture of the University of Arizona was appointed manager of the tribal community farm and within a short time it was showing a profit. A woman, for the first time in Pima history, was elected to the tribal council.

Since then, a freeway has been built through the reservation and a restaurant built near it, where young Pimas meet tourists, as they had not since 1848, and listen to popular music. Television aerials over an increasing number of Pima homes show that modern Pimas are continuing the process of intellectual expansion begun with the battery-powered radio. A community arts and crafts center offering Indian creations from many tribes collects tourists (and their dollars) and brings more people of different cultures in contact with each other. The Indian Claims Commission has accepted essentially the Pima-Maricopa territorial claim (Hackenberg and Fontana 1974:319–354) as stated by them in 1857. When the claim is settled the Pimas will once more have in their hands the primary tool of the modern world, their own capital. Just as their ancestors raised their gross national income as they acquired spades and plows and draft animals, the Pimas now can build their own schools and hospitals and hire their own teachers and doctors and learn from their own mistakes.

Pima and Papago Ecological Adaptations

ROBERT A. HACKENBERG

The adaptation of the Pima and Papago Indians to their southern Arizona environment has been a study in contrasts (Russell 1908; Joseph, Spicer, and Chesky 1949; Castetter and Bell 1942; Hackenberg 1962, 1974, 1974a). For several millennia (Haury 1945, 1950; cf. Ezell 1963a; Sayles 1962) they have continuously occupied a precarious environment characterized by radical oscillations between periods of abundance and scarcity. Their persistence must be attributed to a survival strategy providing maximum security against the threats implicit in their unpredictable surroundings.

Environment: Variety and Constraint

The wider limits of Pima and Papago territory from prehistoric times to the nineteenth century encompassed a vast tract extending from the Gulf of California across the Salt River in central Arizona, which falls within the Sonoran Desert. The nature and extent of this desert is described in "Pima and Papago: Introduction," this volume. During the historical period the Pima and Papago were confined mostly to the central zone of the Sonoran Desert, bounded by the valleys of the Gila, Santa Cruz, and Sonoyta rivers and on the west by a line drawn through the modern towns of Ajo and Gila Bend. This central zone, known as the Arizona Upland (Shreve 1951), has been called "the most diverse of the provinces of the Sonoran Desert" (Hastings and Turner 1965:185) in terms of elevation, rainfall, and vegetation.

The Papagueria, a region extending westward from the Baboquivari Mountains near Tucson, is the traditional homeland of the Papago Indians. It consists of three life-zones, each with average annual rainfall and elevation descending in stepwise fashion. The valley floor near the Baboquivari range (fig. 1), which rises to 8,000 feet, is high and well-watered, supporting perennial grasses and providing grazing for large antelope herds during aboriginal times. The central zone combines rich desert vegetation with wide shallow slopes suitable for collecting runoff water, which was used for floodwater farming activities. The western portion, consisting of valleys below 1,800 feet, represents the hottest, driest, and most impoverished vegetation zone.

Two patterns of Papago adaptation were recorded during the nineteenth century. The Sand Papago (No Villagers), a small seminomadic band, made a scant living from the fish and wild plant resources of the western zone. They failed to survive the nineteenth century.* The larger and more permanent Papagos (Two Villagers) were located in the central zone, where the wild plant food yield of the bajada slopes was heaviest, and in the grassy eastern valleys where superior conditions for both cultivation and hunting prevailed.

U. of Ariz., Ariz. State Mus., Tucson: 34866.
Fig. 1. The eastern section of Sells, Papago Reservation, Ariz., with Baboquivari Peak to the right. Photograph by Helga Teiwes, 1972.

Since earliest times, the Pimas (One Villagers) were located on the Gila River above its junction with the

*The Sand Papago or Areneños intermittently occupied the forbidding Sierra Pinacate region of Sonora, west of the Ajo Mountains and south of the present international boundary (Childs 1954). This band, which probably never exceeded 150 members, had a deviant subsistence pattern consisting of fish, shellfish, and a few highly specialized plants of the region of which the most important was sandroot (*Ammobroma sonorae*). They ranged from the Gulf of California to the Tinajas Altas in Arizona and inhabited the driest part of the Sonoran Desert. Like all Piman peoples, their subsistence pattern was diversified, including mountain sheep and other game. They also planted at least one field at Suvuk in the Sierra Pinacate (Lumholtz 1912:329–331, 394–397; Castetter and Bell 1942:63). The Gila River Pima did not locate permanent settlements on the Salt River until the 1870s, but fishing parties visiting the area camped there frequently.

Salt River, extending to the vicinity of Casa Grande National Monument. Elevation is low there (1,280 feet) and temperatures are hot. Large villages, and at times the entire tribe, were concentrated in the vicinity of modern Casa Blanca, where a peculiar terrace system formed a floodplain four miles in width (Hoover 1929:46–48). The fertility of this terrace was continually restored by periodic flooding, which also provided natural irrigation for a richly productive agriculture.

Under "average" climatic conditions, the central Papagueria and middle Gila Valley provided abundantly for their Papago and Pima occupants, who were never more than 25,000 in number, and may have numbered far less in prehistoric times. However, societies must survive under the wide range of actual environmental conditions encountered year to year from which the average is constructed. In determining the prospects for continuous occupancy in such an environment it is more important to know the extremes than the average.

The unpredictability of the yield of plant and animal foods from year to year throughout this region verges on environmental treachery. The wide range of subsistence activities and settlement pattern alternatives utilized by all Pimans were essential adaptive mechanisms required to cope with this range of variation. For where the environment was potentially rich in variety, the climatic uncertainties imposed constraints.

Some patterns of climatic variation are historical, unfolding over centuries in cycles of aridity and excessive precipitation; and some patterns are contemporary year-to-year or month-to-month variations within the long term trends. Thornthwaite, Sharpe, and Dosch (1942:125–157) note that "areas normally semiarid may be arid one year and subhumid the next. Differences between the precipitation for corresponding months in different years is even more striking." Through dendrochronology it is possible to reconstruct climatic events of the past 2,000 years (Schulman 1938). The weather cycles provide insights into problems of Pima-Papago environmental adaptation. The quarter-century of drought at the end of the thirteenth century forced the abandonment of the area (Jett 1964) and was the driest interval in 2,000 years. But rainfall during the following century exceeded that of any interval in the chronology!

For the next several centuries, rainfall was near the average for the two millennia until 1570, only to end the sixteenth century with another severe 30-year drought. The wet seventeenth century was followed by the below-normal eighteenth; following this, a trend toward dry conditions brought a minimum near 1880. A series of destructive storms and floods ushered in the twentieth century, following which there occurred since 1920, "a quarter century of the most severe drought since the late 1200's" (Schulman 1956:67). The tree-ring record confirms an erratic pattern of excesses and deficiencies, rather than "average conditions," defining the pattern of precipitation since the thirteenth century.

The radical shifts in rainfall over the centuries have changed the balance of geological processes from alluviation (soil-building) to degradation (erosion and soil removal) several times. Bryan (1941) notes three cycles of alluviation and degradation in the geological history of the Southwest, observing that rapid degradation has been taking place in response to aridity throughout the region since the 1870s.

The major environmental damage occurs through loss of vegetation whose root structures formerly held the banks of streams and rivers firmly in place. Removal of these plants causes the rapid runoff following heavy rains to widen the channels with breathtaking speed. The runoff velocity is itself accelerated by denuding of vegetation on the watershed resulting from aridity and erosion. Widened channels are cut deeper by subsequent rapid runoff, and the result is an arroyo, a deep trench cut to a depth of 50 feet or more into the terrain (Cooke and Reeves 1976). These trenches, in turn, lower the groundwater level by draining soil moisture from the adjoining terrain. Leopold (1951) argued that a change in rainfall intensity since 1850 may have also contributed to arroyo-cutting.

Since the mid-nineteenth century, the combination of aridity, arroyo-cutting and declining groundwater level has had catastrophic consequences. Living streams with narrow channels, ideal for irrigation with primitive tools, became intermittent flood channels with crumbling and widening banks—impossible to control. The Gila River channel increased from 100 feet to over a mile in width (Hackenberg 1974). The Santa Cruz River, used for irrigation by the San Xavier Papago, met the same fate (Castetter and Bell 1942). Xerophytic shrubs replaced grass throughout the Gila River watershed and Santa Cruz Valley (Humphrey 1958; Buffington and Herbel 1965; A.L. Brown 1950). River beds and banks were rapidly choked with forests of phreatophytes, mostly mesquite and salt-cedar, replacing earlier stands of cottonwood and desert willow (Gatewood 1950).

Within this twentieth-century pattern of aridity and environmental degradation, there are great short-range fluctuations. The Carnegie Desert Laboratory, near Tucson, which maintained records from 1905 to 1933, reported that rainfall in the highest year was 23.3 inches, and in the lowest year 5.8 inches! "The greatest single daily fall was 5.01 inches which was 86% of the lowest annual total" (Shreve 1934:132). During the same period there were 94 intervals of 30 days or more without rain, comprising 55 percent of the elapsed time for the years reported.

Since earliest times, Papagos have relied upon a form of agriculture called akchin farming, rains falling on foothill slopes, funneled into alluvial fans where fields were saturated and then planted. However, the erratic rainfall patterns (Shreve 1951) would have made these fields an uncertain proposition if they were the exclusive source of village subsistence.

Traditional Pima farming relied on the floodwaters of the Gila to spread over the broad lower terrace at Casa Blanca, which contained their largest expanse of fields to perform the same field-preparing function. These floods were produced by runoff from the watershed upstream. The mean annual flow of the Gila at Kelvin, Arizona, was 444,000 acre-feet a year from 1900 to 1950; however, annual runoff during that period ranged from zero to 4.5 million acre-feet (Dunbier 1968:84).

While the Pima and Papago utilized different sources of water for farming, neither source appears to have been very reliable in an environment where radical reversals were more frequent than "average conditions." Over time, the grasslands advanced and retreated, arroyos were excavated and filled again, and drought alternated with deluge.

Adaptive Mechanisms

The key mechanism that explains Piman survival over time in their unpredictable environment has been diversification. At different periods of history all Pimans made use of the major subsistence patterns—hunting and gathering, grazing domestic animals, and agriculture. While they have been united by a common language and features of social organization and religion, they can be differentiated in terms of their selective intensification of subsistence alternatives.

The Papago, who called themselves the Desert People, relied upon wild crops and animal products for 75 percent of their annual food intake in the prehistoric period (Castetter and Bell 1942:57), including, according to Mark (1961:46)

> seeds, buds, fruits and joints of various cacti; seeds of the mesquite, ironwood, palo verde, amaranth, saltbush, lambsquarter, mustard, horsebean and squash; acorns and other wild nuts; screwbean, the greens of lambsquarter, saltbush, canaigre, amaranth and pigweed; boxthorn and other berries; roots and bulbs of the sandroot (wild potato), covenas and others; and the yucca fruit.
>
> . . . deer, antelope, mountain sheep and goats, peccary, muskrats, bears, rabbits, quail, dove, mockingbird, wild ducks, geese, bittern, heron, snipe, wild turkey, rats, terrapin, lizards, grasshoppers, moth larvae, locusts, iguanas, snakes, toads, and beaver.

In addition, 25 percent of the prehistoric Papago diet came from the traditional maize, bean, and squash agriculture of the region.

The Pima, who called themselves the River People, relied primarily upon agriculture for 60 percent of their subsistence before the coming of the Spaniards (Castetter and Bell 1942:57). The wild foods in their diet were less diversified, although Russell (1908:69–78) lists 50 edible plants that were used in addition to cultivated foods.

Two mechanisms of food exchange between Pimas and Papagos occurred before the coming of the Europeans. Fruit diversity between their environments facilitated exchange of wild foods by the Papago for the cultivated crops of the Pimas. Second, in dry years when the Papagos had little to trade, they "hired out" as migratory farm labor, earning a share of the crop in exchange from their Pima neighbors to the north, and from analogous One Villager populations in river valleys to the east and south of the Papagueria.

The rhythm of food production displayed marked seasonal variation. Wild foods were only abundant during the spring and summer, when they were consumed at that time by both tribes. Since the Pima could employ flood water from the melting snows of the New Mexico portion of the Gila watershed for planting, they started their summer crops much earlier than the Papago who were forced to wait for the July rains before they could plant. They were often able to obtain two corn crops during the summer (harvested in July and October) while the Papago harvested only once in the autumn. Winter planting might have taken advantage of soil moisture and avoided the summer floods, but the aboriginal people had no frost-resistant crops, and killing frosts were apt to occur between mid-October and mid-April. Acquisition of winter wheat from the Spaniards at the end of the seventeenth century provided a suitable crop for this interval.

The basic security system of both tribes consisted of shifting from one resource to another with the passage of the seasons. The harvest of grain and vegetables was saved for the winter months when the desert was devoid of plant growth. But, even within the constraints imposed by the unpredictable environment, several options in resource management were available.

The maximization strategy is associated with modern societies throughout the world. It consists of deploying all resources to optimize productions during each crop year. The surplus produced is carried forward to the following year as insurance against possible crop failure. Effectiveness depends on holding damage to the resource base to a minimum. Soil depletion, overgrazing, and a rising ground water table (from excessive irrigation) are all danger. Maximization also assumes that recognition of private ownership of property will protect a farmer's stored surplus against the claims of relatives and neighbors.

The second possible strategy is the "minimax option" (minimum gains with maximum security). It assumes that holding resource exploitation to the minimum needs of the population each year, and rotation of resources so that all are drawn upon evenly, will guarantee the continued productivity of the environment. Under this option, environmental damage is unlikely and there is no need for a concept of personal property to preserve surpluses.

From prehistoric times to the present, the Papago have adhered to a form of the minimax strategy described as "restricted interdependence" (Hackenberg 1972). The Pima adhered to the same minimax strategy prehistorically and during early European contact but shifted to maximization during the nineteenth century. The contrast between the two strategies during the late historical period provides the framework of a natural experiment, providing the opportunity to evaluate the consequences of each strategy for its adherents.

Subsistence Strategies Before Contact

Papago

As first revealed by early historical and archeological accounts, the Papago tribe was pursuing a risk-spreading strategy aimed at providing security rather than surpluses. The spatial configuration of Papago subsistence changed along a west-to-east gradient as moisture conditions improved and the environment became more suitable for the cultivation of crops. The size and permanence of settlements also scaled along this gradient. The smallest groups are said to have been found among the Sand Papago, whose movement was almost continuous. The central Papago occupied large súmmer field villages during the season when food was more plentiful, breaking into family groups for the winter season in the mountains. The river settlements of the Santa Cruz Valley were continuously occupied.

This narrative does not exhaust the spatial and temporal alternatives contributing to the Papago adaptive pattern. Another dimension was a willingness to leave a region entirely in difficult years, as was remarked upon by Anza (Bolton 1930, 2:17–19) in 1774: "Because of their nearness to our settlements, both of Spaniards and Indians, the Pápagos frequently live in them, especially in the winter, in which season they almost completely desert their own country." This mobility pattern can be generalized from native traditions and historical notes (Hackenberg 1972:115–116). Each of the four sides of the Papagueria contained a refuge area "belonging" to someone else to whom nearby Papagos could retreat in times of extreme need. Each refuge area was under the control of a strong, warlike people and was associated with irrigated agriculture. The areas included the Altar Valley to the south, occupied by the Ópata; the Santa Cruz Valley to the east, controlled by the Sobaipuri; the Casa Grande Valley on the north, held by the Pima; the Gila Bend region to the northwest where the Maricopa resided; and the floodplain of the Sonoita River to the southwest (unoccupied until it became a Mexican rancheria).

Each refuge area was visited by Papagos of a particular regional band who maintained friendly relations with the hosts. The Papago visitors either planted temporary fields near those of their hosts or exchanged labor with them for a share of their crop. In effect this practice greatly amplified the range of water resources available to the Papago. The headwaters of the three river systems primarily employed (Santa Cruz, Gila, and Altar) were remote from the Papagueria. Given the great variation in the micro-environments of the Southwest, it was highly unlikely that all these locations would suffer from adverse weather conditions at the same time.

A second spatial dimension of survival was in a distributive mechanism that made it possible for Papago villages to "place a claim" upon the goods possessed by each other. Gambling was a principal instrument in this. A village in need would challenge a more affluent neighbor to compete against its champion runners, kickball players, or race horses. The challenging village would bet its real property (such as horses and blankets) upon the outcome of the contest. If they won, they received food supplies equal to the value of the wager; if they lost, they could be wiped out. However, Papago etiquette required that challengers should not be sent away empty handed, and if a village had nothing with which to gamble, as a last resort they could employ a "begging dance" (Castetter and Bell 1942:46). This was a song and dance cycle lasting for several nights; the spectator village was expected to reward the performers with gifts of food.

The mix of resources upon which Papagos relied depended on the weather. The Spaniards of the Anza expedition, 1774–1775, seemed to regard the Papago as a nation of beggars because their arrival coincided with the driest part of the declining rainfall cycle lasting throughout the eighteenth century. At that time, Papago access to their neighbors' resources was heavily exploited. Other variations occurred when circumstances were unusually favorable. During the fourteenth century, when precipitation was the heaviest in centuries, the archeological record shows that substantial irrigation canals were in use in the central Papagueria (Castetter and Bell 1942:162). About 1914, in the midst of another favorable rainfall interval, the Papago excavated irrigation canals in several parts of the area that became their major reservation. These incidents confirm that the Papago commanded a wide range of economic alternatives and chose from among them to match the vagaries of the environment.

It was widely reported by early chroniclers that the Papago were without government, and Underhill (1939) and Drucker (1941) agree that village chiefs of the type found among them in the twentieth century were a Spanish innovation. But, since they were able to mobilize and direct large reserves of manpower for canal excavation when desired, Papago social organization was not necessarily as dispersed and fragmented as the records of their survival under arid conditions suggest.† Perhaps the Spanish diarists were committing the ethnographer's error of assuming that whatever institutional activity is observed during his visit constitutes "the culture," then and forever.

Pima

Before the arrival of the Spaniards provided a technological basis for transforming their agriculture, the Pima practiced a risk-spreading strategy similar to that of their desert-dwelling neighbors. Like the Papago, the Pima at the beginning of the eighteenth century were dispersed in small, scattered settlements. These extended for 53 miles (21 leagues) from the vicinity of Casa Grande monument to the confluence of the Gila and Salt rivers, according to Manje (Kino 1948, 1:196) and contained no more than 2,000 inhabitants in 5 to 10 locations. The villages were placed on both banks of the Gila and quite near the water's edge (Russell 1908:30).

The Pima did not need irrigation by means of canals or ditches to pursue the maize-bean-squash agriculture typical of the region, and there is no mention in the early Spanish accounts that they practiced it. During the seventeenth century, which saw the Spanish *entrada*, rainfall tended to be above normal; Cooley (1962), on the basis of geological processes, asserts that the seventeenth century was typified by slow-moving rivers, formation of swamps, and runoff spread over floodplains. The regime of the river was compatible with the existence of islands in the Gila River, a feature described in early historical records. These would have been suitable for planting without irrigation since the water table would have been near the surface (Nentvig 1980; C. Hayden 1965).

A prehistoric canal excavated by the Hohokam was cut across a shallow bend of the Gila River in the vicinity of Blackwater, forming the largest of the islands above Casa Blanca district. Below it was a similar region, known as *má·s ʔákĭmel*. Southworth (1919:138) reported that these islands were cultivated without plowing or irrigation.

Mekolas John, a Pima whose observations were recorded by Castetter and Bell in their 1939 field notes, said that "in the old days" Pimas did not irrigate with ditches but were able to divert river water by throwing a log across the channel. He insisted that "the Pima always knew how to irrigate with ditches" but employed less strenuous methods when topography and rainfall permitted.

The islands of the Gila were especially suitable for farming without ditches because they were situated below rock reefs, which crossed the channel of the Gila and brought the underground flow of water to the surface. These formations, first described by Meskimons in 1904 (Southworth 1919), appear at three locations below the Casa Grande monument. Two provide sources of seepage water in the vicinity of the Little Gila island, and the third delivers water to the *má·s ʔákĭmel* district. The methods described by Mekolas John were well-suited to the requirements of these locations. Spier (1933:58–59) described similar practices in use by the Maricopa in the vicinity of Gila Bend.

Village dispersal and lack of irrigation were consistent with a Pima strategy of minimal intervention with the environment. Intervention was also limited by technological impoverishment. The Pima farmer had only two implements—a digging stick for planting and a flat board with sharpened edges used both for hoeing and for harvesting (Castetter and Bell 1942:135).

A final component of the risk-spreading strategy employed by both tribes was the selection of drought-resistant seed varieties. The most important aboriginal subsistence crop was maize, which, when cultivated without modern tools, yielded 10 to 12 bushels an acre (Castetter and Bell 1942:37). The crop produced a small harvest, and observers agreed that ears were almost miniature in size. The peculiar characteristic of this native variety was its early maturity. Informants alleged that it produced ears within two months after planting, thus making the best possible use of the uncertain water supply. Next in importance was the tepary bean, preferred once more because of its capacity to survive drought conditions (Nabhan 1979, 1979a). Both these plants, it was claimed, would mature with one irrigation before planting. Because of their rapid maturity it was sometimes possible to obtain two crops in the course of one summer season.

The restrictions on crop production imposed by strategy, technology, and seed varieties determined that the Pima could not rely exclusively on farming. Water failure withered crops in one of five years (Russell 1908:66). Father Eusebio Kino, the first European visitor to the Pima villages in 1697, remarked that the Pima had no cornmeal because of a recent flood, and they offered him mesquite instead (Russell 1908:38). The mesquite bean provided the Pima with emergency rations from thickets near their villages. Many Spanish visitors came away convinced that it was their primary food source. Saguaro fruit, the other important gathered food, was obtained in nearby mountains.

There was no visible socioeconomic differentiation among either Pima or Papago villagers, as was consistent with an absence of wealth. According to Velarde,

†The adaptability of both the Pima and Apache to gang labor during the historic period confounds most stereotypes concerning resistance of "hunting and gathering bands" to more compact forms of social organization. In 1905, Papagos volunteered to work on the reconstruction program in California following the Salton Sea disaster.

who visited the Gila River in 1716, they had no government "other than the one who incites them to fight . . . or who gives the signal for the time to hunt" (Di Peso 1953:25–26). Both the simplicity of social structure and the adherence to the minimax strategy among Pima and Papago at this time are consistent with Steward's (1955) description of the primitive band rather than the agricultural village.

Subsistence Strategies After Contact

Papago

Because of diminishing rainfall during the century following the Spanish *entrada*, the Papago were relatively easy to collect at the mission stations of the Altar and Santa Cruz valleys. In addition to expanded opportunities for irrigation and farm labor, the Spaniards provided a variety of new domestic plants and farm animals to both Pima and Papago. Father Kino distributed "wheat, chick peas, bastard chick peas, lentils, cow peas, cabbages, lettuce, onions, leeks, garlic, anise, pepper, mustard, mint, melons, watermelons and cane, also grapevines, roses and lilies, plum, pomegranate and fig" (Kino 1948, 2:265). He also established livestock ranches "with cattle, oxen, horses, mules, burros, goats, sheep and chickens" (Wetzler 1949:50).

Castetter and Bell (1942:114) describe wheat as the most important of the Spanish contributions to Piman agriculture because "it came as an off-season crop, ripening in May when the fall harvest of maize, teparies and pumpkins was exhausted, and before the giant cactus harvest." Winter wheat was of less importance to the Papago than to the Pima in Kino's time because their valleys were deficient in winter rainfall. Livestock were accepted by the Papago but, since they were unfamiliar with herding practices, cattle were turned loose on the open range and hunted when meat was desired.

top, Smithsonian, NAA: 2763-C; bottom, Smithsonian, Dept. of Anthr.: 217,973.
Fig. 2. Wooden yokes, modeled on Spanish types. top, Papago yoke tied with rawhide to the horns of the cattle. Photograph by William Dinwiddie, Fresnal, Ariz., 1894. bottom, Pima yoke; the tongue or harnessing pole of the wooden plow (also based on Spanish types) would be attached at the center. Length 146.0 cm, collected by Frank Russell at Sacaton, Ariz., 1902.

U. of Ariz., Ariz. State Mus., Tucson: 864.
Fig. 3. A stone mill at Cowlic, Papago Reservation, Ariz., probably for grinding wheat (and perhaps maize), the tongue being rotated by a horse, mule, or ox. Photograph by E.W. Haury, 1939 or 1940.

New crops, coupled with the eighteenth-century tendency toward aridity in the central Papagueria, might have motivated the Papago to occupy available river valley sites and become irrigators. They were deterred by the accelerating tempo of Apache raiding, which forced the warlike Sobaipuri to abandon their homes in the Santa Cruz Valley in 1762. At the time of the Spanish contact, the Sobaipuri Indians, close relatives of the Gila Pima, occupied villages of substantial size on the San Pedro and Santa Cruz rivers (Di Peso 1953). Spaniards recruited the Sobaipuri as allies against the Apache. After a series of severe defeats they were eliminated from their homeland. By 1768, the Papago had replaced the Sobaipuri in their former locations at Tubac, Tumacacori, and Calabasas in the Santa Cruz Valley. Within the next century, the Papago replaced the Sobaipuri at San Xavier, which received some protection from the Spanish presidio at Tucson; they abandoned the locations to the south. The Apache were drawn primarily by the livestock herds at the Spanish missions.

Though Papagos occupied a few sites on the Santa Cruz River until the Mexican revolution, the nineteenth-century withdrawal of Spanish outposts from Arizona and Sonora forced them to retreat to defense villages deep in their desert homeland. These fortified positions were placed adjacent to flood-irrigated fields in low, open country so that crops could be defended.

The central Papagueria is drained by three main systems of arroyos along which all 10 defense villages were located (Hoover 1935). San Simon wash in the western zone contained Kaka (*gágga, gágka*), Hickiwan (*híkĭwañ*), and Gu Vo (*ge wóˀŏ*); Vamori wash in the south central zone included Kupk (*kú·pĭk*), Kui Tatk (*kúi tátk*), Komalik (*komálk*), and Chukut Kuk (*cúkuḍ kúhŭk*); Santa Rosa wash in the north was the site of Gu Achi (*ge ˀáji*), Anegam (*ˀá·ngam*), and Kohatk (*kóhadk*). With the exception of Komalik in the present district of Baboquivari, the entire eastern half of the Papagueria was abandoned for most of the nineteenth century. Despite these precautions, a terrible defeat was sustained at Kui Tatk near the center of the Papago defense perimeter in 1852.

This retreat to defense positions would have been disastrous in the arid eighteenth century because the territory given up by the Papago contained the best-watered parts of their homeland. But Schumm and Hadley (1957:162) describe the period from 1826 to 1870 as an interval of maximum tree growth correlated with the lush vegetation described in travelers' accounts. Because the central Papagueria containing the defense villages receives an even division of summer and winter rainfall, an increase in precipitation would have made it possible for them to raise winter wheat and to remain at these settlements for the greater part of the year.

Eyewitness accounts indicate that wheat was still being grown "when winter rainfall is unusually great" in the southern districts in 1893; however, rain during all three months, December-February, was necessary for the crop to mature (Whited 1894:140–142). In the 1930s Underhill's informants from Santa Rosa could remember when wheat was produced regularly at this centrally located defense village.

In 1854 the Gadsden Purchase was ratified and political jurisdiction over Pima and Papago villages passed to the United States. Following the Civil War, government action was taken against the Apache menace, and the raiders were finally subdued in the early 1870s. Schumm and Hadley (1957:162) remark that 1870 also initiated a recurrence of pervasive drought conditions. The Papago defense villages were disbanded and the tribal settlement pattern assumed its modern configuration.

Components of the formerly concentrated settlements dispersed as sets of "mother-and-daughter" villages, which Underhill (1939:58) attributes to the cessation of Apache raids: "usually the main villages are found in the middle of the north to south valleys, with their daughter villages stretching along the valley in both directions and their wells perched in the mountain walls on either side." Village dispersal and the reoccupation of the southeastern territory expanded the areas that could be used for summer crops; however, diminishing rainfall must have severely limited wheat production. Whited (1894:140–142) reported that they could count on a wheat crop only once in six years! At the same time, political separation from Mexico and the declining fortunes of their Pima neighbors restricted recourse to traditional refuge areas.

The problem was met by the development of a subsistence alternative that became the keystone of modern Papago village economy: the livestock industry. Because of its partial abandonment during the Apache wars, a heavy grass cover was established in the southeastern Papagueria where cattle were first introduced after the Civil War. The ancestral stock of the Papago herds were apparently stolen from Mexican ranches near the border. A letter from the prefect of Altar (Redondo 1957) complains of the theft of 500 cattle and 300 horses during a four-month period by the Papago of Tecolote village.

Cattle were family property in the beginning. Underhill (1930) and G. Harrington (1930) agree that each village herded cattle together and kept them in a common corral. The village official presiding over cattle operations modeled his behavior on that of the former hunting chief. Herding, like hunting, employed the manpower of the entire village, but the activities associated with livestock tending were annual rather than seasonal in nature. Entry into the cattle business probably strengthened the political organization of the villages because of the communal labor requirement and the need to make a number of joint economic decisions. Village chiefs and councils of family heads were certainly functioning at this time.

Modernization of Papago society accelerated with the penetration of mine operators into their territory in the 1870s. Camps were established near rich copper deposits at Ajo and the gold and silver of the Baboquivari, Comobabi, and Quijotoa Mountains. Wells were dug at each location, and the Indians were quick to appreciate their usefulness for livestock. Permanent Papago villages such as Fresnal, Cababi, and Vainom Kug were formed near the mines and inhabited year around.

The government established reservations for the Papago at San Xavier in 1874, Gila Bend in 1882, Ak Chin in 1912, and Sells in 1916. The last of these, the Papago Indian Reservation, contained 2,774,370 acres in 1981 ("History of the Papago," fig. 1, this vol.). The reservations were expected to facilitate permanent settlement and agricultural development. These initiatives were largely nullified by the cycle of erosion, arroyo-cutting, and extreme drought that began in the 1870s and has persisted throughout the Southwest through the 1980s with only occasional relief. The Mexican Boundary Survey (1898) observed that the Papago ranges were badly overstocked, and by 1900 the grass cover of the Baboquivari Valley was becoming thin and contracting rapidly. Mesquite invasion was visible everywhere (Humphrey 1958).

top, Smithsonian, NAA: 2785-e; U. of Ariz., Ariz. State Mus., Tucson: bottom left, 25681; bottom right, 43374.

Fig. 4. The manufacture and use of adobe. top, Adobe house of the chief of Fresnal. A ramada is to the right with household items on its roof. The woman in foreground is cooking corn; a burden basket leans against the house wall. Photograph by William Dinwiddie, 1894. bottom left, Mr. Esalio with adobe bricks for house he is making in background. Photograph by Helga Teiwes, Cobabi (Ko Vaya), Papago Reservation, Ariz., 1970. bottom right, The Antone ramada made of mesquite posts overlain with saguaro ribs. Behind them is the adobe house surrounded by a fence of ocotillo stalks. left to right: Ascension Antone, his grandson Mike, Margaret Acosta (a niece), and Laura Antone. Photograph by Helga Teiwes, Poso Verde, Sonora, 1976.

At the threshold of the twentieth century, Papago settlements were dispersed and their subsistence pattern was diversified across a range of aboriginal and introduced alternatives. The Mexican Boundary Survey (1898:20–26) gives unusually complete detail concerning the variety of subsistence resources employed in the 1890s. The annual cycle included the saguaro harvest, three to four months of farming at the field locations, autumn trips to the mountains to gather acorns, seasonal collection of mesquite beans and grass seeds, occasional planting of winter wheat, and continuing stockraising activities. It was in keeping with the security orientation of the culture that its treatment of the introduced plants and animals was additive rather than substitutive.

Pima

The gift of winter wheat, combined with climatic change and the increasing tempo of warfare with the Apaches, led to a complete reorganization of Pima community life during the eighteenth century. Wheat could be planted on the Gila when the November rains brought the river to life after the dry month of October. Because of its heavier yield of grain it more than doubled the capacity of a unit of irrigated land to support human life.

The opportunity to support a denser population with more dependence on agriculture was utilized for several reasons. During the Spanish period, population increased to about 3,000, adverse climatic conditions required a heavier manpower investment in irrigation,

Smithsonian, Dept. of Anthr.: 217,999.

Fig. 5. Pima wooden shovel, the type used in the construction of irrigation ditches to remove the earth loosened with a digging stick. Before Spanish contact baskets probably served the same function (Castetter and Bell 1942:137). Length 85 cm, collected by Frank Russell at Sacaton, Ariz., 1902.

and the increasing tempo of Apache warfare limited distances that could be traveled safely for hunting and gathering. The most dramatic Pima action consisted of a contraction in their range of settlements.

Between Manje's (1954) account of 1699 and Bartlett's (1854) 1852 visit, the distance separating Pima villages had been reduced from 52.5 miles (21 leagues) to 15 miles (C. Hayden 1965). All villages were withdrawn from the north bank of the Gila, and residences were removed from the south bank to higher and more distant ground for strategic reasons. Villages containing the bulk of the population were placed together, forming an inner circle in Casa Blanca district, surrounded by fences, ditches, and irrigated fields that made them difficult to approach undetected. Bartlett (1854, 2:249) observed that the purpose was to form a defense perimeter and that all villages were literally within shouting distance of one another.

The Spanish accounts that document the changing settlement pattern also report new developments in social organization as required by the higher population density. In 1746 the cultivation of wheat and the use of irrigation were simultaneously observed in the village of Shodakshon by Sedelmayr. In 1761 a tribal chief was functioning in the same village with jurisdiction over all communities. By 1775 all villages were employing irrigation ditches and growing wheat, a tribal council was in operation, communal labor was being employed, and Papago migrants were participating in the wheat harvest said Anza. In 1775 the Pima were said to be constructing a dam to raise the river to the level of their ditch intakes according to Font. All references are from C. Hayden (1965).

Increased grain production not only fed the larger Pima population but also provided substantial surpluses for trade with Papago and Mexican villages. The rich content of this barter exchange is described by Russell (1908:93–94), who notes that edible delicacies and luxury items were brought in by the Papagos to exchange for substantial amounts of Pima farm produce and basketry materials. Prosperity was facilitated by the construction of an elaborate network of intersecting canals (fig. 6) described by Southworth (1919), which efficiently irrigated the entire Casa Blanca plain from the

top, Calif. Histl. Soc., Los Angeles: Title Insurance Coll., 3609; center, Smithsonian, NAA: 57,273; bottom, U. of Ariz., Ariz. State Mus., Tucson: 36036.

Fig. 6. Conservation and utilization of water. top, Pimas building a dam to turn the water into the irrigation canals. The bank at left across the channel is lined with thick brush or possibly mesquite poles; tree trunks (cut on right) were also used by placing them in the river with stones and brush piled against them to serve as a dam. Main canals were communally owned and were built and maintained by all the men in a district (Castetter and Bell 1942:158–160). The man with the top hat is Vaugh-kum, a medicine man. Photograph probably by Charles C. Pierce, about 1900. center, Man from Sacaton, probably Pima, maintaining an irrigation canal on the Gila River Reservation, Ariz. Photograph by Walter J. Lubken, about 1904–1911. bottom, Harrison Azul, Pima, siphoning water into cotton fields of the San Xavier Tribal Farms Co-op. Photograph by Helga Teiwes, 1973.

Little Gila. However, previous linkage of moisture conditions to production implies that these achievements would not have taken place unless precipitation was exceptionally favorable. The years from 1826 to 1870 were a period of heavy rainfall (Schumm and Hadley 1957:162).

The north bank of the Gila came under American jurisdiction in 1848, and the south bank in 1854. Between these two dates, Bancroft (1889) estimates that 60,000 American gold-seekers passed through the Pima villages en route to the California gold fields. They camped at a site near Maricopa Wells, west of the Indian settlements, and traded for provisions. Prices went steadily upward over time, and the medium of exchange shifted from barter to gold and silver (Bartlett 1854, 2:259).

Production was increased under American political control. The Overland Mail Company established a route through their villages in 1858 and contracted for the entire Pima wheat crop to ship to the California settlements. In 1859, the Pima and Maricopa villages were enclosed within a 100-square-mile reservation, and they were granted $10,000 worth of farm implements by Congress. The gift included thousands of axes, shovels, picks, hoes, and harrows. With these steel implements they extended their ditches and enlarged their fields by 3,000 acres! Wheat production was doubled in 1859, reaching 225,000 pounds, and it climbed steadily to 3,000,000 pounds by 1870 (St. John 1859; Fontana 1976b:51).

While part of this increase can be attributed to expanded markets during the Civil War, and to favorable weather conditions, a basic change in the adaptive strategy of the tribe was a more fundamental factor. With the arrival of the Americans, surplus crops could be exchanged for cash and consumer goods. The notion of private property and even wealth as a personal distinction replaced earlier distributive sanctions. Motivated individuals persuaded fellow villagers to compete with American settlers for farmlands above the reservation. New Indian irrigation ditches were opened at Blackwater in 1862, Old Santan in 1865, Cholla Mountain in 1865, and Cayau in 1869 to challenge the pioneer communities located by non-Indians at Adamsville in 1864 and Florence in 1867 (Southworth 1919).

Manpower for this expansion was provided by population increase. In 1858, 518 Maricopas and 4,117 Pimas were counted within the newly established reservation. A more decisive factor in releasing manpower was the termination of Apache raiding. Pima calendar sticks (Russell 1908:38–66) disclose that there were only two recorded attacks on Pima villages after 1864; the cessation of attacks coincides with the construction of Fort McDowell and Fort Grant to protect both the Pima villages and the new American settlements in 1865.

Demobilization of the Pima military establishment, which had created elaborate systems of sentries, patrols, and pursuit groups (Hackenberg 1955), released manpower for farming at the same time that the need to maintain a compact defense perimeter was removed. Given the opportunity to acquire wealth presented by the new markets, sudden expansion of the range of settlement and the acreage cultivated were the results. Drucker (1941:194) observed that the complex political organization and irrigation management achieved by the Pima after 1775 were the result of constraints imposed on them by the Apaches.

With the end of hostilities there was no further need for strict tribal discipline, and the fabric of Pima society began to unravel. The changing social order was symbolized by the transformation of the chieftainship. In 1846 and 1852, Emory and Bartlett found Antonio Azul, the principal chief, to be a poor man working his own fields but immensely respected by his people. In 1866, Agent Lord reported that he was "without selfishness or desire to hoard money" and was impoverished by providing support to the indigent members of the tribe (ARCIA 1866:113). Little more than a decade later, Agent Ludlam in 1879 described him as "a man of consideration and wealth having a large accumulation of cattle . . . who is a sensible business man," although he was "without authority to act" in tribal matters, for "if he should cause an arrest and punishment his own life would be in danger" (ARCIA 1879:6). The chieftainship had been a position of power and no wealth; it became a position of wealth and no power.

Despite the shift from cooperation to competition (exemplified in the efforts by individual villages to secure more advantageous locations for irrigation by moving upstream in the 1862–1869 period), the transition from spartan militarism to acquisitive mercantilism might have been achieved except for a devastating climatic reversal. Beginning in 1870, the driest conditions in 600 years returned to the Gila watershed. Destructive floods, deepening of the river channel, and disappearance of entire canal systems were announced by the disastrous flood of 1868, which wiped out three villages. By 1870, Agent Grossman reported that less than 3,000 acres (20% of the area farmed in 1859) were cultivated by the Pima (ARCIA 1870:338).

No longer restrained by the Apache and threatened with famine, the Pima sought to resume their former security-oriented pattern of dispersed dependence on a variety of food resources. Two more ditches were opened east of the reservation in 1872 (Sacaton Flats and Cottonwood), and three were excavated in the west between 1873 and 1877 (Hoover, John Thomas, and Simon Webb). Despite efforts to restrain them by the agents, the Pima had by this time expanded their range of settlements to the dimensions of 1699.

There were immediate difficulties. The population was now twice the size previously supported in dispersed settlements. The mesquite trees above and below Casa Blanca district had been consumed as fuel by the two steam flour mills operated during the boom years. Agent Stout (1878:3–4) reported that the Casa Blanca flood plain, which provided the bumper crops of the previous decade, was abandoned and "a dry, barren waste. . . . The crop of mesquit beans . . . has been an entire failure."

Those occupants of the lower villages who had not reoccupied the *má·s ʔákĭmel* district to the west during 1873–1877 moved to the Salt River and occupied land above Phoenix at this time. After failing to dislodge them, the government established the Salt River Reservation in 1879. Seven additions were made to the Gila River Reservation between 1876 and 1915, bringing it to 372,000 acres and including the territory of the expanded range of settlements. But, while the government sought to solve the problem with additional land, the basic issue was water. There were partial or total crop failures in eight years between 1870 and 1880, and it was the winter wheat crop around which the new cash economy was oriented that usually failed.

Under the strain of these converging evils the social order continued to disintegrate. In 1879–1880, intervillage warfare broke out between Santan and Blackwater over the allocation of seepage water. Between 1878 and 1898, Russell (1908) reports 24 murders "during drinking bouts." There were 18 additional witch-killings between 1860 and 1887 according to the calendar sticks collected by Russell and Southworth, indicating the level of anxiety within a society under severe stress (Kluckhohn 1944).

The final reverses of the nineteenth century followed a brief change in weather. Rainfall was abundant between 1881 and 1884, promoting a temporary land boom near Florence. The Florence Canal Company constructed a diversion dam intended to appropriate the entire flow of the Gila for the non-Indian settlements in 1887; by the time it was completed the long drought returned and the company failed. In the same brief interval, abundant grass cover appeared on the Gila watershed and the first cattle ranch was established at Solomonville in 1884. Population growth and cattle operations accelerated the environmental damage caused by the deteriorating climate, which continued to impose extreme aridity through 1904.

Beginning in 1895, an appropriation of $30,000 per year was provided to the Pima Agency to buy wheat for the indigent Indians. The 225,000 pounds provided was equal to the surplus sold by Pima farmers in 1859, the year the reservation was established. Yet hardship was unequally distributed. A number of individual families had acquired cattle wealth (5 to 25 head) by this time, and the several villages with access to the underground flow of seepage water (Santan and Gila Crossing) were obtaining and selling annual crops of wheat (Southworth 1919).

Despite the hardships following 1870, the Pima continued to pursue the goals of production and personal property. The difference between the tribes at this time is exemplified by cattle operations, which were pursued by villages among the Papago but by individual families among the Pima. Pimas with property were not required to share with those less fortunate, who were sent to the BIA Agency for "rations." Inequality was sanctioned by the Protestant ethic. Following the baptism of Antonio Azul into a Presbyterian church in 1893, 1,800 other tribal members joined in the same decade (Hamilton 1948).

Subsistence Strategies in the Twentieth Century

At the turn of the century, the Papago adhered to the minimax strategy of diversification of resources and distribution of gains to all villagers. This resulted in the preservation of village organization despite adverse weather conditions and intrusion of non-Indian miners and ranchers. The Pima, seeking to maximize production and modernize their institutions, found these changes undermined by a hostile environment. Their traditional economic and political institutions had passed into "memory culture," where they remain in the 1980s.

Since 1900, both tribes have received substantial government assistance intended primarily to develop the cattle industry among the Papago and to rehabilitate agriculture among the Pima. The comprehensive program of the Bureau of Indian Affairs also encompassed health and education and added two new dimensions to the adaptive processes of both tribes: massive technological intervention and explosive population growth.

In conformity with the national philosophy guiding Indian adjustment, the mechanisms for tribal improvement were to be the allotment program (Dawes Severalty Act of 1887) and the formation of business enterprises to be operated under reconstituted tribal governments (Indian Reorganization Act of 1934). But development planning reckoned without the intervention of climatic conditions in the ever-changing Southwest. Beginning in 1905, 15 years of the "wettest conditions in many centuries" were followed by four decades of "most severe drought since the late 1200's" (Schulman 1956:66–67). Many adaptive problems created for both Pimas and Papagos by these processes remain unsolved in the 1980s.

Papago

The San Xavier Reservation was the only valuable resource of the tribe that came under the allotment program, largely without damage to the land or its occupants. The BIA provided wells (fig. 7) and pumps after 1912 to compensate for damage to the channel of the Santa Cruz River caused by severe erosion during the 1890s, and the land under cultivation was said to be four times that which was farmed in 1880 (Castetter and Bell 1942:165).

Development on the large Papago Indian Reservation in the early decades consisted of the location of permanent artesian wells, for both livestock and domestic use, at 11 villages between 1914 and 1916. These were also years (1905–1920) of excessive rainfall, and farming and stockraising prospered without interference. Tucson residents recall the arrival of wagon caravans of Papago wheat at local flour mills.

The consequences resembled those among the Pima in the 1860s. As wealth accumulated, village livestock operations became individualized. Family herds were separated from those of the community, and individual ranches were formed (D.J. Jones 1962). In 1914, 5,662 Papagos on the reservation were reported to be cultivating 9,177 acres; cattle holdings were estimated at 15,000 head (Castetter and Bell 1942:53). However, a 1934 livestock census noted that 44.6 percent of the cattle were located in the two southeastern districts of Baboquivari and Chukut Kuk where both rainfall and permanent grass were heaviest. While most were divided into 12–15 large herds, one-sixth were owned by a single family (G. Harrington 1930).

The resulting social differentiation produced inevitable rivalries over grazing and water rights. These were intensified by drought conditions during the 1930s, since cattle accumulations of the 1920s had left the range overstocked. To promote effective management, the tribe (over the opposition of the larger ranchers) decided to partition the reservation into nine fenced grazing districts. Each district corresponded to a group of related villages descended from one of the old defense centers of the nineteenth century.

The first Papago tribal council, established under the Indian Reorganization Act, convened in 1937. Because of the prior formation of the grazing districts, from which council members were elected, the tribal government had considerable decentralization and local autonomy. Centralized BIA technical assistance meanwhile remodeled the reservation landscape. Wells, storage tanks, masonry dams, flood irrigation projects, and registered breeding stock were all introduced (Hackenberg 1972:171; Fontana 1976a).

But the terrain became dessicated at a more rapid rate than could be countered by these efforts. In 1955,

left, Natl. Geographic Soc., Washington; right, U. of Ariz., Ariz. State Mus., Tucson: 43428.

Fig. 7. Wells. Permanent villages developed around wells, built by the federal governments of the U.S. and Mexico. Formerly, "permanent springs were widely scattered, and the women spent more time fetching water than gathering food" (Castetter and Bell 1942:42). left, Papago woman at San Xavier Reservation filling her jar with water. A head ring used to support the pot is on the ground. Photograph by Putnam and Valentine, before Aug. 1915. right, A pump-driven walk-in well at the Papago village of Poso Verde, Sonora. Photograph by Helga Teiwes, 1976.

only 14,000 head of cattle were being supported on the Papago Indian Reservation, and only 40 percent of the range was within reach of permanent water. Flood farming had shrunk to 2,500 acres, most of which was in the old Two Village heartland (Baboquivari District). The 1964 Papago development program aimed at renovating reservation agriculture estimated that $28,000,000 would be required for all phases of the work. But by then, reservation agriculture was irrelevant.

The tribal population reached 10,587 persons in 1960, although only 4,779 (45%) were reservation residents. There were 4,028 Papagos in Arizona cities and towns; 1,225 had left the state and others were in Mexico or residing on non-Papago reservations (Hackenberg 1967). The tribe had overgrown its resource base despite all efforts at development. The major factors in Papago ecological adaptation have been the rapid growth of wage work opportunities on non-Indian farms and access to welfare support.

As cotton farming became the mainstay of Arizona's irrigated agriculture during the 1930s, seasonal farm labor became the basis of Papago household economy for both reservation and nonreservation families (Joseph, Spicer, and Chesky 1949; Padfield and Martin 1965). By 1960, the occupational commitment of two-thirds of economically active reservation residents was to employment in non-Indian communities (Hackenberg 1968).

An unseen complication obstructing Papago economic development was explosive population growth. The Papago birth rate of 38.8 and death rate of 8.8 between 1950 and 1960 yielded a net increase of 3 percent a year—sufficient to double the population every 23 years! The push of overpopulation and the pull of off-reservation wage work combined to insure that, for any Papago born on the reservation after 1930, the probability of permanent residence in a non-Indian community was high (Hackenberg and Wilson 1972:180).

Pima

Tribal fortunes for the Pimas reached bottom during the first decade of the twentieth century. Cultivated acreage, which averaged close to 9,000 acres per year between 1880–1889, shrank to an average of 6,700 for 1890–1894, and further to 3,600 for 1895–1899. An investigating committee discovered in 1904 that there had been no crops for six years and most cattle herds had been sold for subsistence. In 1895, 462 cords of mesquite wood were cut and sold for firewood by Indians whose crops had failed; by 1905, nearly 12,000 cords a year were being cut and sold in Phoenix.

The contemporary economic adjustment of the tribe reflects a progressively more inclusive and expensive effort by the federal government to solve the irrigation problem. In 1905, a half-million dollars were spent on a pump irrigation scheme to develop 10,000 acres in Santan district. Since this plan involved the sale of tribal lands for reimbursement of government expenses, it was strongly opposed by Indian defense organizations

top, Calif. Histl. Soc., Los Angeles: Title Insurance Coll.: 3616; center, U. of Ariz., Ariz. State Mus., Tucson; bottom, Mus. of the Amer. Ind., Heye Foundation, New York: 26582.

Fig. 8. The traditional Pima round, flat-roofed house (*ki·*). top, Framework, showing the central supporting beams possibly of mesquite, screwbean, or cottonwood and outer framework probably of willow. Photograph by Charles C. Pierce, about 1900. center, Framework covered with material such as arrowweed, wheat straw, or cattail reeds, over which was a layer of earth (Russell 1908:154). Photograph by Daniel Boone Linderman, 1912. bottom, Thatch dwelling, which has no smoke hole and in which doorways were closed using old blankets. Clothing and possessions such as a metal bucket and wash tub and pottery are at hand. Photograph by Frank C. Churchill, near Gila Crossing, Ariz., 1904.

Calif. Histl. Soc., Los Angeles: Title Insurance Coll., top left, 3640; top right, 3566; bottom left, Ariz. Histl. Soc. Lib., Tucson: 5585; bottom right, Mus. of New Mex., Santa Fe: 56644.

Fig. 9. Rectangular structures, which served as both storage rooms and temporary summer (field) dwellings. top left, A Pima *ki·* is in the background with the summer house in front at left and the ramada at right. A saddle hangs from the ramada rafters as does an empty baby hammock. top right, Pima storage shed with large granary baskets. top left and right, Photographs probably by Charles C. Pierce, about 1900. bottom left, Pima farm house on the north bank of Gila River near Casa Grande, Ariz. The walls are of saguaro and mud covered with arrowweed secured by saguaro ribs. The chimney (far right) was of adobe. To the left is the detached ramada with pottery ollas on the ground. Photograph by F.D. Nichols, 1938. bottom right, Papago house at Badger's Well (Cobabi or Ko Vaya), Ariz. A baby hammock is suspended in the ramada at left. Photographed in 1916.

and canceled. Efforts began, instead, to restore the surface flow of the Gila to the Pima reservation. The Florence–Casa Grande Project Act of 1924 authorized the construction of a storage reservoir. The San Carlos Project Act of 1924 authorized the construction of storage facilities to impound the entire flow of the Gila and to provide for the irrigation of 50,000 acres of Indian and 50,000 acres of non-Indian land. It was expected to provide a permanent solution to the problem of Pima livelihood.

Meanwhile, between 1914 and 1921, each member of the tribe received a 10-acre allotment, and precipitation conditions had improved to the point where water was abundant. Cultivated acreage increased to an average of 16,000 for 1910–1914 and continued upward to the record-breaking average of 32,000 for 1915–1919. It was during this favorable interval that non-Indian farmers introduced cotton cultivation in the Casa Grande Valley, south of the Gila. By 1924, 18,000 acres of cotton were being produced there with water supplied primarily from 140 deep wells. Such wells were encouraged when the climate turned arid after 1920, and when the high price of cotton compensated for pump installation.

Unable to meet the competition of off-reservation pump irrigation, Indian production dropped to between 5,000 and 12,000 acres during the years in which the San Carlos Project was under construction (1925–1930). However, the modernizing impact of the project on Indian agriculture was, literally, a metamorphosis. Lands were leveled, cleared, surveyed, titled, adjusted for gradient, and provided with ditches and headgates. An auxiliary pumping plant was installed, and district farmers' associations were organized to promulgate agricultural extension work. These developments were viv-

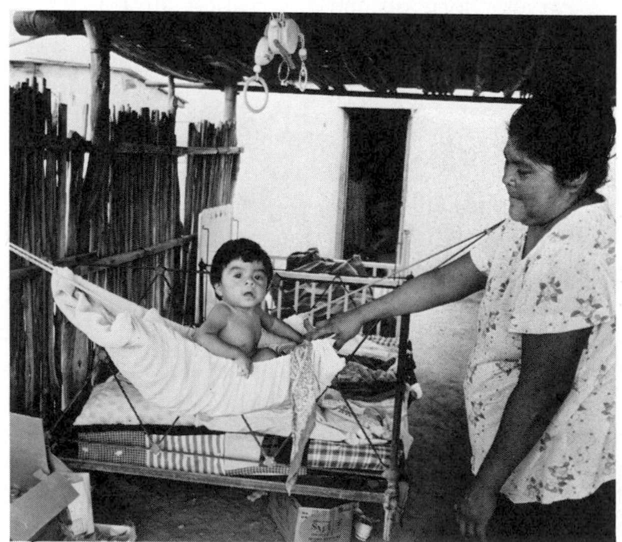

U. of Ariz., Ariz. State Mus., Tucson: 45457.

Fig. 10. Dimitri Antone in a hammock cradle made of blanket and ropes, with mother Juanita Antone. Photograph by Helga Teiwes, Fresnal, Papago Reservation, Ariz., 1977.

U. of Ariz., Ariz. State Mus., Tucson: top, 42190; bottom, 31743.
Fig. 11. Contemporary Pima houses on the Gila River Reservation, Ariz. top, Melons stored under a ramada, with a brush roof. The house, located near Interstate highway 10, is called a "sandwich house," and is made by packing mud (adobe) between a temporary frame made of both inner and outer planks. bottom, Older adobe house and shed next to modern house with siding, at Bapchule, Ariz. Photographs by Helga Teiwes: top, 1974; bottom, 1972.

idly described by the agency superintendent who conducted them (Kneale 1950).

By 1940, Indian farm acreage had risen to 30,265, or two-thirds of the land intended for the Pima under the San Carlos Project. In 1936 the tribe accepted self-government under the Indian Reorganization Act, and the Gila River Reservation was divided into districts from which council members were elected. But instead of economic and political revival under these joint stimuli, further reversals rapidly took place.

Surveys conducted by agricultural economists in 1935 and 1940 disclosed that average family income declined from $708 to $484 during this interval. Since irrigation water was not available to Pimas in quantity until 1934 because of the complicated land operations required to prepare their fields, this was the same interval during which the project had come into full operation. The loss of Indian income took place in the face of a $25 million investment in development.

Several determinants worked to cancel the benefits of the San Carlos Project. Between 1925 and 1934, the Pima had grown accustomed to wage work provided by the construction phase of the project. The payroll was suddenly withdrawn in 1934 and they were reluctant to return to subsistence farming. Instead, they sought wage work among off-reservation cotton growers, whose acreage increased from 15,000 in 1934 to 32,000 in 1937. By 1942 non-Indian irrigated farms in Pinal County included 130,000 acres.

A second factor was the complexity of a bureaucratically administered system of water management. Watermasters and ditch riders, all government employees, were interposed between the Indian farmer and the source of water. Indians were required to grow alfalfa and barley instead of their traditional crops of wheat and cotton to promote soil-building in areas that were never intended for farming. The upper terrace of the Gila, brought under cultivation for the first time by the San Carlos Project, required this treatment, which ran counter to Indian custom.

Agent Kneale (1950) justified his paternalism with the need to get land into production; Indians were unable to manage irrigated farms averaging 50 acres without equipment or credit. The Agency owned machinery and hired drivers to perform the operations required. Later, these operations were contracted for by Indians directly with mill owners who deducted the cost of the operations and transportation from the sale price of feed grains, giving the Indian a check for the balance. Under the San Carlos Project, the Pima were farm owners, but they were no longer operators.

Indian frustration at the outcome of the development program was signified by the tribal council's 1937 decision to refuse to pay for the operation and maintenance of the San Carlos Project. The BIA assumed control of a 12,000-acre tract of unallotted project land that it managed as an Agency farm to pay these charges for the Indians. If this amount is deducted from the average of 30,000 acres irrigated during 1935–1939, the magnitude of Indian farm operations was no greater than in the 1860s.

A third significant factor was the dismal record of the San Carlos Project. The reservoir was never filled to more than two-thirds of its rated capacity (1,285,000 acre-feet) and that level was reached only once in 1942. Reservoir capacity was estimated on the basis of runoff at 460,000 acre-feet per year (recorded between 1899–1928), but for the years following the completion of the project (1929–1967), the average annual runoff was only 215,000 acre-feet.

The remedy was for all irrigation farmers in the region to use more ground water, tapped by deep wells. In this competition the Indian, who was growing pasture crops for cattle feed, was at a disadvantage. Non-Indian farmers have met increasing costs by shifting to specialty crops such as lettuce and safflower, which commanded a higher profit margin than cotton.

A final factor in the demise of Pima farming was heirship, the nemesis of the allotment program, and its companion problem of land fragmentation. By 1952, 86 percent of the original allotments covering 98,000 acres were in heirship status. In the same year, median family income from agriculture was estimated at $750, while those relying upon migratory farm work were earning $1,500. More than 40 percent of the 952 families on the Gila River Reservation were receiving welfare support, the average payment being $490 per family (W.H. Kelly 1953).

In 1952 the Agency farm of 12,000 acres was transferred to the tribe. Subsequently it has operated as a tribal enterprise with part of its area planted to cotton and part leased to non-Indian operators. Revenues have been substantial, but most of the profits have been used to defray the costs of tribal government or to subsidize services provided by the tribe to individual farmers. The most visible benefit from the farm has been in wages to be paid to Indian employees.

A survey conducted in 1961 enumerated 11,246 living descendants from the ancestral populations of the Gila and Salt River reservations. Of these, 60 percent were Pima reservation residents (6,797), while 3,097 were living in Arizona cities and towns, 1,044 were outside Arizona, and the remainder could be found on reservations belonging to other tribes. Only 97 persons gave their primary occupation as farm owner-operator, although 891 said they were engaged in farm work for wages. In 1961, the Pima birth rate of 39.3 produced a net annual increase in population greater than 3 percent.

Increasing numbers of Indians must be provided with a higher standard of living from a diminished resource base. Having failed to meet this goal from tribal economic development, the federal government established a relocation program in the early 1950s to assist city-bound migrants to obtain industrial employment. Much Pima-Papago "surplus" population settled in California cities.

The 1960s

The "Indian problem" has ceased to be a federal responsibility assigned to a single agency, the Bureau of Indian Affairs within the Department of the Interior. In 1954 health care was assigned to the U.S. Public Health Service; several years later, assistance to indigents was assumed by state welfare departments. In the 1960s public school districts incorporated reservation communities, extension work was moved to the Department of Agriculture, law enforcement was shared with state and county agencies, and development initiatives were assumed by a plethora of new agencies under the impetus of social and economic programs. While Indians benefited substantially from Model Cities, Head Start, VISTA, and Job Corps operations, they were treated, essentially, "like everyone else" under a piecemeal administrative network of semiautonomous agencies.

In the 1980s the federal government no longer treated Indian economic development as a special obligation. The terms of the Indian Reorganization Act no longer define government policy, and there is no further effort to provide services through channels that will preserve Indian self-determination and the integrity of tribal society and its distinct resource base. The political integration of Indian tribes into non-Indian jurisdictions has its economic counterpart. Indian resources have been incorporated into regional growth patterns, directed by the non-Indian economy.

For the Pima-Papago, as for other peoples in the Southwest, the instrument employed has been the long-term development lease. Through it, representatives of external businesses enter working relationships with members of tribal governments. An important role in this new approach has been played by tribal attorneys. The outcome has been a series of agreements covering the establishment of corporate farms, mineral exploration and development operations, industrial plants and parks, tourism, and recreational facilities within reservation boundaries under non-Indian management. The tribes receive lease revenue and guarantees concerning the employment of tribal members.

For the Pima, the San Carlos Project lands have served as a powerful magnet to attract non-Indian investment, but the location of an interstate highway connecting the reservation with nearby Phoenix was even more important. The Papago lease development efforts were accelerated by the award of reservation mineral rights to the tribe in 1964. Financial receipts from mineral leases were the most important factor in Papago tribal government income in the 1980s. In this alliance for progress, the tribal government and the non-Indian enterprise seeking access to reservation resources have become partner corporations.

The role of the individual tribal member in this big business atmosphere remains ill-defined. The range and intensity of services provided to Indian homes and villages has ramified and expanded year by year. Houses, electricity, domestic water supply, and comprehensive health care together with surplus commodities and many other benefits are provided. The range, quality, and access to educational facilities are vastly superior. An expansion of employment has resulted from the growth of the bureaucracies that administer the programs, but these programs have succeeded at the cost of breaking down boundary mechanisms that maintained Indian social and cultural autonomy through three centuries of contact with Europeans and Americans. Indians migrate in ever-increasing numbers while the reverse trend brings in non-Indian corporations to exploit reservation resources through development leases. These trends can only promote assimilation.

Conclusion

The record of environmental challenge and response is incomplete. Portions of both tribes still occupy their traditional homelands. Each resource base remains intact and development efforts continue. There is no proper end to this account, but only another beginning. It would be premature to conclude that the adaptive capacity of either tribe has been destroyed, but even less accurate to assert that native cultures have persisted. It is more correct to observe that both systems, Pima and Papago, are evolving.

The Papago continue to meet their subsistence requirements as they have in centuries past: by drawing upon surrounding territory to supplement their own resource base in quest of maximum security. Local farm and grazing areas have not been forced to provide the purchase price of pickup trucks and television sets, which are the universal status symbols. Consumer goods are tangible results of extended periods of off-reservation wage work. Papagos still regard their cattle as savings, not spending money (G. Harrington 1930). The reservation remains a buffer against non-Indian institutions.

Papago resources have been preserved through decentralization of authority. Each district council acts to preserve the undivided interest of its ancestral families in community resources against both enterprising residents and outsiders. Within the past decade, several business ventures proposed to the tribal council have been vetoed by the districts within which they sought to locate, vindicating the premise of district autonomy.

Papago social organization must remain simple since decision making is decentralized. Since districts as "parts" impede efforts of the tribal council to represent the "whole," there can be no reservation-wide development schemes, a situation designated restricted interdependence (Hackenberg 1972). Thus, resource utilization fails to advance but exploitative damage is retarded—an effective survival strategy in a region of few resources.

The Pima, from earliest times, have sought to remodel their environment in order to yield maximum productivity. Despite climatic reversals they never went far in search of subsistence until forced to migrate by population growth; even then, most have gone no farther than Phoenix. They have preferred to manipulate an uncertain water supply to the best of their ability to increase the productivity of their land base.

This strategy required them to create a tribal-wide irrigation system and related complex social organization that has (Hackenberg 1962:193) been compared to Wittfogel's (1957) hydraulic society model. The basis of this development was the wheat economy of the 1860s, and its loss before 1900 caused the collapse of Pima society and disappearance of traditional institutions (Spicer 1962:408–409).

The restoration of the tribe to irrigated agriculture through a centrally managed water system took place under the San Carlos Project. A similar system, on a vastly simplified scale, previously existed in the 1860s. That system required central institutions for its management and maintenance, but there were discrete villages with independent subchiefs to mitigate the central decisions in terms of local needs. The San Carlos Project management was less subject to modification by local interests.

Contemporary contrasts with Papago tribal organization reflect these differences. The Pima tribal council is more clearly empowered to make binding decisions on behalf of the tribe. In 1966 it enacted a comprehensive development program (Weaver 1973–1976, 2) to advance the transformation of the land base begun under the San Carlos Project. Its commitment to central planning and total resource management appears complete. Growth of tribal government activities since 1960 has been documented by Hackenberg (1961) and Weaver (1971).

The ecological niche defended by Pima farmer-warriors since the nineteenth century is no longer recognizable. The ancient fields and ditches themselves have been erased (Hackenberg 1974). The San Carlos Project offers a "high technology" solution to the uncertainties of the environment, but mastery over this desert country and river has not yet been achieved.

While each strategy has produced a distinct structural outcome, both tribes remain poor, overpopulated, and with ineffectively utilized resources. Task-oriented social structures and indigenous means for social control are conspicuously lacking. Only the illusion of progress has been created by expanded federal assistance across a broad spectrum of projects.

Considering the changes over three centuries, the forces of climate and population growth appear to dwarf the efforts of human societies, Indian and non-Indian alike, to repeal their consequences by whatever strategy or level of intervention. One conclusion is indisputable: both tribes were independent agriculturists throughout their previous histories, and neither remained so in the 1980s.

Pima and Papago Social Organization

DONALD M. BAHR

In discussing the contemporary Pimas, Lester Lewis distinguishes between the "lying-on-top" institutions that came through Anglo-American contact and the deeper "lasting" ones that stem from the aboriginal past and constitute for him the true basis of propriety ("Contemporary Pima," this vol.). Concentrating on testimony from the mid-nineteenth century, this chapter portrays Piman social organization as it was before the top layer was added.

While European contact certainly had an impact on the Upper Pimans by 1850, the contacts had been sporadic and unthreatening. This chapter actually is an interpretation of the mid-nineteenth century, not a direct reading from the documents, for it makes inferences back to this period from recent observations and it covers well-documented, as well as poorly documented, nineteenth-century groups. It tries to bring the scattered record of Upper Piman societies under a single focus.

Three modes of Piman adaptation have been defined in "Pima and Papago: Introduction," this volume. They are: a sedentary One Village adaptation (Pima) found where there was permanent running water, a "back and forth" or Two Village mode (Papago) where people moved between summer field villages and winter mountain wells, and a completely migratory No Village adaptation (Sand Papago) in the driest regions.

Structures

It appears that Pimans settled into farming villages whenever possible and that water (for drinking and crops) was critical to the degree in which they settled. The more lasting the water supply, the more lasting would be a people's attachment to the village and the more substantial would be the very structures that made it up. It is significant that water was not used for housebuilding during the nineteenth century.

Whereas the prehistoric Hohokam used mud as a building material, this apparently was not done by any nineteenth-century Pimans. The sole dwelling type was a round building with brush walls and a dry earth roof. This was the architecture of the Two Village adaptation, which was understandable because by their testimony, water was at a premium. Making houses of mud was felt to be impossible until the United States government drilled wells in the early 1900s. To paraphrase a contemporary Papago: "We admire the Hohokam because they were rich in water. For ourselves before the wells were dug, we had to save water for drinking. The ponds of the summer villages supplied drinking water for the longest period possible and even without making mud with it, it ran out before the fall harvest so the women had to carry water from the mountains in jars. Nobody wanted to move to the mountain villages before his crops were harvested" (Baptisto Lopez, personal communication 1971).

Also understandable on environmental grounds was the absence of any house-building at all among the No Village people. Constantly on the move, their architecture literally was a matter of camp-making rather than village-building. The No Villagers were limited to brush enclosures that lacked roofs. Other Pimans built roofed although mudless houses. Supporting the roof were mesquite or ironwood posts as well as rafters of mesquite or saguaro cactus wood. These durable items were passed through generations.

The principle of environmental limitation does not serve for the domestic architecture of the Pima. Although the Hohokam used mud for their houses, the Pima did not. In architecture and in other respects, the One Village people appear more like the other, migratory, Pimans than like deeply rooted town dwellers.

The private buildings belonged to family and household groups. The council house was the center for local group or village integration. The ceremonial grounds, while tied to the settled territory of a local group, were sites for ceremonies that integrated the regional bands. Whether permanent or evanescent, Piman settlements were built on a similar plan, essentially camplike. The area of human settlement was always interspersed with unclaimed patches of nature. The settled or "claimed" area contained structures of two broad categories, private and public. Structures of the first type—family houses, brush shelters, cooking enclosures—were grouped in household compounds. The single public structure was the site of nightly council meetings for the men.

Among the Pima and Papago, the meeting area included a round dwelling-type house in which nobody lived. East of it was an open-roofed sunshade and under the shade or a few feet farther to the east was a fireplace

U. of Ariz., Ariz. State Mus., Tucson: top left, 25586; bottom left, 25588; top right, 42523; bottom right, 42532.

Fig. 1. The Papago wine ceremony or *náwait*, a ritual to bring rain. The liquid made from saguaro cactus fruit is sometimes stored and fermented in the roundhouse (Underhill 1938a:23–25) or in a house where sacred objects are kept. top left and bottom left, Santa Rosa roundhouse at Anegan. The wine jar is stored in the depression in floor. right, *dâhiwua k ʔí·ʔe* (sit and drink) ceremony at Ali Chukson, Ariz., which is preceded by 2 nights of dancing (Waddell 1973:217–228). top right, Cup bearers bring out the wine. bottom right, The wine maker gives a welcoming speech. After the speech the 8 cup bearers, 2 from each of the 4 cardinal points, sing the songs of the directions and distribute the wine. The ceremony lasts for several hours with the chief rain shaman singing repetitive cycles of the rain song and ends only when all the wine is consumed. The wine maker holds a rod with a feather at top, probably a divining rod. Photographs by Helga Teiwes, left, 1970; right, 1975.

for the nightly meetings. The meetings were not held inside the house.

Among the No Villagers the meeting area was simply a fireplace; this is all that was really necessary. The inside of the public house was used primarily for one ritual, a summer wine feast (fig. 1).

The meeting place had to be within shouting distance of the farthest family's house, for announcements were made from it in that manner. Normally, it was near the compound of the local group headman, for he was in charge of its upkeep and, more important, his office was symbolized in the right to build the fire for each meeting.

Among the One and Two Village Pimans the public building was called the 'smoking house' (*jé·ñgidakuḍ kí·*), for 'smoking' was an idiom for 'to have a meeting'. Alternately, it was called *wáʔaki*, a word commonly translated as 'rain house'. In the twentieth century it is also called by a third term, *ʔó·las kí·* 'round house', since in contemporary villages this is the only building still constructed on the old round mudless plan.

Settlement Pattern

Where there was agriculture, the household compounds sometimes were surrounded by fields, a practice that encouraged settlements to spread or sprawl. There were counterbalancing forces promoting concentration: the need for defense, desire to be near communal waterholes, desire to build on ridges of high ground to avoid flooding. Whether concentrated or dispersed, the clusters of private buildings never touched each other, a principle evident in contemporary Piman architecture by the practice of surrounding compounds with barbed-wire fences. There is normally an unclaimed space, perhaps only three feet wide, between the fences.

Conceptually midway between the "built up" areas of the settlement and the unclaimed desert was another type of land use, the cleared spaces for ceremonies. One such space was immediately to the east of the council house—in effect, the settlement's plaza. When not in use, it was indistinguishable from the desert except that it was carefully stripped of all wild vegetation. Scattered about the settlement but usually on the periphery in the sense of being far from the council house were open spaces set aside for rituals. These peripheral ceremonial grounds were held rigidly distinct from the "everyday" areas of the settlement. People were not to set foot on them except during rituals. The firewood, cooking utensils, and brush enclosures left over after rituals were considered dangerous and were not tampered with by passersby. In a word, these were sacred grounds.

The sacred grounds were used for rites called collectively the "ceremonial cycle": a corn harvest and deer-hunting ritual called *má?amaga*; an early winter harvest and "prayerstick" ritual called *wí·gida*; and three different "purification" rites—for eagle killing, warfare, and salt expeditions to the Gulf of California.

Two other rituals took place on the central plaza: a summer cactus wine feast and a "naming ceremony" by which local groups honored and entertained each other. Finally, there were rituals at private houses centered on particular individuals: a puberty dance for girls, a purification ceremony following the birth of a child, ritual cures for sickness, and, by the 1900s, folk Roman Catholic rites primarily concerning death: wakes, dinners on the anniversary of a death, and all souls' observances. Underhill, Bahr, Lopez, Pancho, and Lopez (1979) concentrate on the "public" and "native" portions of the religious system. Waddell (1973) studied the Papago wine feast.

There was considerable overlap in the content of the various ceremonies and considerable variation from group to group in the content of any one type of ceremony. A theme through all of them is that the power needed to sustain human society is gotten by men on journeys away from home. The songs, oratory, and drama that accompanied each ceremony focused on how individual men could get things—scalps, rain, luck, feathers, seeds—on which the general welfare depended.

Last of all, and normally at some distance from the settlement, were graves. In some cases burials were concentrated in cemeteries; in other cases, individuals were buried in isolation. In either case, mountainous locations were preferred; intentionally or not, a water-course normally separates any present-day village or part of a village from its cemetery.

Overall, the Piman settlement plan is more suggestive of a camping people than a sedentary one. Lacking was the kind of dense and compact village plan in which one knows decisively whether he is "in" or "out" of the village, and in which every square foot within the village either belongs to somebody or is maintained for public use. The Piman plan, like a camp, leaves untended desert between everything. There was always room for an additional family to construct its buildings. Moreover, the center of the public life, the meeting place, was remarkably simple: a fireplace or a fireplace plus a brush house.

Family and Household

Each family or unmarried adult had a house (or brush enclosure) in which to sleep and to store personal property. These separate dwellings were grouped into household compounds, the household normally headed by an old man. In addition to the separate dwellings, household compounds contained structures that everybody used in common: a roofless cooking enclosure; a roofed, open-walled sunshade, lacking among the No Villagers; food storage houses, lacking among the No Villagers, probably scarce among the Two Villagers and perhaps scarce even among the One Villagers before the farming boom of the mid-nineteenth century; a brush hut for the seclusion of menstruating women (fig. 2), presumably lacking among the No Villagers; a corral and a privy since the 1900s at least.

In the twentieth century, there is an additional important feature, an outside place for washing clothes.

As families grew, they tended to equip themselves as independent households by constructing their own set of "common" buildings. A man would want his own corral; his wife or wives would want their own place to cook. This process of cutting loose through building your own things could be started while the family kept its sleeping house at the original location. The result,

Denver Mus. of Nat. Hist., Col.: UN82-001.

Fig. 2. Papago brush menstruation hut. Photograph by Ruth Underhill, 1931–1933.

left, U. of Ariz., Ariz. State Mus., Tucson: 35734; a, Amer. Mus. of Nat. Hist., New York: 50.1/4754; Smithsonian, Dept. of Anthr.: b, 76113; c, 76122; d, 174,452.

Fig. 3. Pottery. left, Laura Kermen roughing edge of pot before placing another coil on it. The pot is cushioned in a cloth ring, and the wooden paddle used to thin the sides of the pot is to her left in foreground. Photograph by Helga Teiwes, Topawa, Ariz., 1972. right, Pottery constructed with the paddle and anvil technique: A feather or the tip of a stem of devils-claw (*Proboscidea parviflora*) is used as a paint brush. Both vessel shape and decoration vary: a, Interior of Papago bowl of highly polished redware with black pattern, characteristic of pottery made for sale to non-Indians. b, Pima jar with black (mesquite bark) design painted on a white ground, probably used for storing dry materials. c, Pima vessel with a red (hematite) pattern on white ground; undecorated pots of this shape were probably used for water storage and decorated ones for wine (Fontana et al. 1962:47). d, Papago twilled yucca fiber headring with characteristic folded over construction (Kissell 1916:159–164) used to carry large pots. b, Height 17.0 cm; rest same scale. a, Collected by Carl Lumholtz in 1911, b and c collected by Edward Palmer in 1885, d collected by WJ McGee in 1894–1895.

at least in modern villages, would be household compounds that are intricately divided into several private, duplicating domains: fenced compounds crisscrossed internally by still more fences, visible and invisible. The final step for separating a household would be the construction of an entirely new compound centered around a new sleeping house.

Postmarital Residence and Inheritance

Underhill obtained an extremely valuable record in the 1930s of aged Papagos' recollections on household composition during the period 1859–1890. She reconstructed the membership, kin relations, work arrangements, and gift-giving customs for the households of eight different local groups (Underhill 1939:211–234).

The eight local groups are: Kuitatk (*kúi tátk* 'mesquite root'), Sikorhimat (*síkol hímadk* 'whirlpool village'), Wahw Kihk (*wáw kéˑkk* 'standing rock'), San Pedro (*wíwpul* 'wild tobacco'), Tciaur (*jíawul dáhăk* 'barrel cactus sitting'), Anegam (*ʔáˑngam* 'desert willow place'), Imikah (*ʔíˑmĭga* 'relatives'), and Tecolote (*kolóˑdi; cúkuḍ kúhŭk* 'owl hooting'). These data show the importance of bilateral ties in residence and inheritance.

Table 1, derived from her information, concerns both residence and inheritance, for it tabulates the ways in which men gained the right to use agricultural fields. The table includes all the men in her census who worked old fields, that is, fields that they did not personally clear and construct. It lumps together old men, such as heads of households, and younger men, such as married or unmarried sons co-resident in the households; thus, it is not a table of ownership for many of the young

Natl. Geographic Soc.

Fig. 4. Papago women from San Xavier carrying pottery vessels filled with water. They use woven headrings to cushion the round-bottomed jar. Photograph by Putnam and Valentine, before Aug. 1915.

Table 1. Inheritance of Rights to Fields

Village	*Inherited through father*	*Inherited through mother's father*	*Granted by wife's father*
Kuitatk	5	7	1
Sikorhimat	15	9	4
Wahw Kihk	7	—	4
San Pedro	7	2	2
Tciaur	13	—	—
Anegam	5	—	1
Imikah	4	—	—
Tecolote	15	3	2
Total	67	21	14

SOURCE: Underhill 1939:app. 1.

men counted in it would not have been considered owners of the fields they helped to cultivate.

It should be emphasized that the relation between men and fields was constantly in flux as new fields were constructed, for land was not scarce. Households split up into their component families and cleared new land, and young men moved from place to place in search of opportunities or in answer to calls for help. In short, there was a pool of men exercising varying degrees of ownership over a smaller number of fields. (The land situation may have been more restricted for the Pimas.)

Table 2 shows how 15 additional men from the same eight villages came to construct new fields of their own. Unlike the men counted in table 1, each of these was the sole or senior owner of a field (if such a man had co-resident sons, the sons were counted as individuals whose right to the field had been obtained through the father). The relationship of interest is between the new field's owner and the headman of the local group, for the construction of new fields had to be approved by the community at large, and the headman was crucial to this process. In two-thirds of the cases, this relation

Table 2. Attainment of Rights to Construct New Fields

Village	*Owner related to headman through father*	*Owner related to headman through mother*	*Owner related to headman through wife*
Kuitatk	—	—	—
Sikorhimat	—	—	—
Wahw Kihk	—	1	2
San Pedro	5	—	—
Tciaur	—	—	2
Anegam	3	—	—
Imikah	—	—	—
Tecolote	2	—	—
Total	10	1	4

SOURCE: Underhill 1939:app. 1.

Table 3. Married Women Residing in Local Groups

		Women reared in local group	
Village	*Women from outside local group*	*Husband from outside local group*	*Husband from within local group*
Kuitatk	8	1	1
Sikorhimat	7	6	8
Wawh Kihk	9	7	—
Tciaur	3	—	—
Anegam	3	1	—
Imikah	2	—	—
Tecolote	3	3	—
Total	35	18	9

SOURCE: Underhill 1939: app. 1.

was through the owner's father; the rest were through women.

Table 3 concerns the married women residing in seven of the eight local groups (data on San Pedro were lacking). The table shows the extent of patrilocal versus matrilocal residence and it indicates the high frequency of marriage between persons whose original homes were in different local groups.

Although comparative data are lacking from the Pima and the No Village peoples, the following generalizations seem in order. Residence after marriage was predominantly in the household of the husband's father. Men tended to stay in close association with their paternal lands and relatives. If they separated themselves, which as many as one-third of them did, they were as likely to establish a new residence through maternal relatives as through affinal relatives.

The flexibility that shows in these figures on field inheritance and postmarital residence is only part of a general emphasis in Piman social organization on maintaining multiple and far-flung contacts. The decision to change one's place of residence would be made only once or twice in a lifetime, while underneath that was a constant movement of people for shorter periods between the households of relatives and friends in different local groups.

Local Groups

Local groups were typically named after geographic features or legendary events, for example: Black Water, Standing Rock, Mouth of the Wash, Saddle Hanging, Devil Sitting, and Witches Songs. Many of these names are mentioned in the eighteenth-century documents; thus it was not a question of local groups forming and dissolving every few decades.

One clear case is known of a group retaining its name long after it had moved from the place referred to in the name. This is the Papago village of Anegam. The

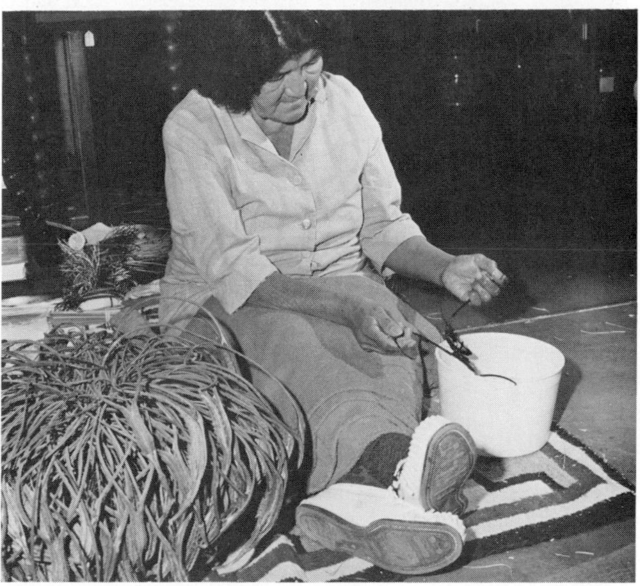

U. of Ariz., Ariz. State Mus., Tucson: top, 35425; center, 35415; bottom, 35450.

Fig. 5. Juanita Ahil, Papago, collecting and preparing material used in making baskets. top, Cutting green yucca. center, Warren Ahil aids in cutting beargrass. bottom, Dried devils claw (*Proboscidea parviflora*), foreground, purchased from San Xavier village. The black pod is soaked and split, and when used with the white willow gives a striking design. Photographs by Helga Teiwes. top and center, Photographed in Oracle, Ariz., Dec. 1972; bottom, photographed at Desert Arts Craft Shop, Tucson, Jan. 1973.

name, meaning 'place of the willows', is said to derive from the group's sixteenth- or seventeenth-century location along Queen Creek ('willow wash') north of the present Pima Reservation. Sometime before 1698, when Father Eusebio Kino visited them, the Anegam people settled in Papago territory approximately 70 miles to the south of Queen Creek. This explains why their present village is called Anegam, even though nearby there are no willow trees.

Besides the retention of a name, local groups commonly kept a plaited basket containing relics from legendary times. The baskets were carefully preserved and brought out from safekeeping for the major ceremonies. They were not kept in the council house but were secreted in the desert, a practice in keeping with the camplike nature of Piman settlement, for the care of this bundle did not require a permanent building or fixed place of residence. Underhill mentions the sacred baskets of several Papago villages; information is lacking on their use among the No Village and Pima people.

Public Offices

The indispensable pair of positions for any group's public life was a headman and a medicine man or shaman. Of the two, only the headman was absolutely necessary because, while shamans were essential for ceremonies, they could be called in from outside the group. The headman was indispensable because the public life focused on him and he ideally lit the fire each night in the central fireplace.

The relation between headman and shaman was as follows: the headman was at the center of public life, while the shaman avoided it. Shamans participated in public as shamans only when asked by the headman, and they were asked only after prior discussion around the council fire. Of course, in the capacity of ordinary citizens, they could attend meetings, but some twentieth-century shamans at least are said to prefer to stay at home.

Among the Pimans, as with most tribes, the shaman's career was different from the public leader's. The shaman's ideal, which was socially valued, was to avoid crowds and political involvement, while the headman thrived on it. As one shaman put it: "Whenever people are gathered for something fun, the shaman won't be in the middle of them; he should stay outside watching"

coarse coiling
fine coiling

(Juan Gregorio, personal communication 1970). It need only be added that politics was viewed by the successful headman as fun, a fact that frequently has been missed by observers of Piman society. Thus, ideally at least, the headman was never a shaman. So far as is known, this was true in fact, at least for the most famous headmen and shamans.

The road to authority at the nightly council meetings was gift giving. The headman ruled public life only in the sense of being in control of the agenda of the meetings and in being able to speak first and last on any issue. He could not compel agreement, and, in fact, strong argument over an issue—whether to go to war, when to work on communal irrigation ditches, when to hold a ceremony, whether sorcery was being practiced—was studiously avoided. After the headman stated his opinion, the rest in attendance ventured theirs in full awareness that open disagreement meant a split.

Thus, a headman had to sense the group's feelings and avoid pushing too hard or fast. His security was a backlog of respect earned through industry and generosity. This was the "great man" aspect of headmanship referred to in certain titles for the office. It was essential to becoming headman, for there was no strict rule of succession. It was also the requirement for keeping the position, and the problems involved with it helped to keep groups in flux and to keep authority soft-spoken.

If there were rivalry for leadership, the headman's industry and generosity could be interpreted as aggressive or self-aggrandizing. To judge from contemporary villages, rivalry of this kind is considered normal. Furthermore, the industrious man faced a built-in dilemma in that a large local group would contain people unrelated to him while some of his relatives were not in the local group. His most likely rivals were nonrelatives. Should he give to them (who would resent it anyway), his outside relatives could complain. If he favored the relatives, his control over potential local rivals was diminished.

Shamans, being defined as outside the normal governmental process, were always suspected of antisocial activities. "The shaman was the only individualist in Papago society. He received genuine pay for his services, while others, even those with power visions, worked only for their food. He was not afraid of being rich, nor did he resent the epithet of 'stingy,' which would blight another man. But he paid for his eminence with the constant risk of his life" (Underhill 1946:263).

In contrast to the outward tests of gift giving, which separated a headman from his rivals, the process of becoming a shaman was through totally private contacts with spirits. The shaman and headman were at opposite positions with respect to involvement in the mundane affairs of the group, the shaman staying out of them at the risk of execution for sorcery, the headman drawn to them at the risk of being blamed by rivalrous fellow villagers or disappointed kinsmen elsewhere.

Each vocation had its positive side. Shamans were the primary heroic type celebrated in the ceremonial cycle, as may be seen in the songs and oratory; the headmen, as men of action, had Piman government in their hands.

• OFFICES DERIVED FROM HEADMAN Associated with the progression from the least to the most sedentary adaptations was an increase in the number of local group offices. This increase can be understood as a splitting off or differentiation from the two primary positions of headman and shaman. The process did not involve a change in the basic group structure, for on the headman's side, the additional offices and activities associated with them still were channeled through the nightly meetings. On the shaman's side, the increase did not affect the public life. It was a proliferation in the private area of curing.

The following titles have been used by one or another Papago group for the office of headman: Wise Speaker, Fire Maker, Keeper of the Smoke, Keeper of Meeting, Keeper of the Plaited Basket, The One Above, The One Ahead, and The One Made Big (Underhill 1939:72).They are descriptive of four different aspects of the office, two of which could readily be divided among members of the band.

In the capacity of ritual orator, the title Wise Speaker refers to the long poetic orations given at each ritual of the ceremonial cycle. This duty commonly was divided

Smithsonian, Dept. of Anthr.: top left, 217,879; top center, 76,041; top right, 107,527; center left, Calif. Histl. Soc., Los Angeles, Title Insurance Coll., 3648; center right, U. of Ariz., Ariz. State Mus., Tucson: 51274; bottom left, Ariz. Histl. Soc. Lib., Tucson: 26024; bottom right, after Kissell 1916: 207–208.

Fig. 6. Coiled basketry. top, Close-coiled basketry bowls, which are multi-purpose household items. Such baskets are started with a plaited rather than a coiled center (bottom right). An awl is used in the coiling, and patterns are created with a black element. top left, Typical whorl design and profile of a Pima basket. Papago baskets tend to be broader and flatter in profile (Kissell 1916:197). Other shapes began to be made only with the tourist trade (see "History of the Papago," fig. 14, this vol.). Other traditional patterns are: top center, the simple fret, and top right, stepped zigzags. The designs apparently have no symbolic meaning. top left, diameter 52 cm (rest to same scale) collected by Frank Russell, Sacaton, Ariz., 1901. top center, Pima, collected by Edward Palmer in 1885, and top right, Papago, collected by E.W. Nelson in Ariz., 1884. center left, Etta Morgan, Pima, making a basket. Photograph probably by Charles C. Pierce about 1900. center right, Aloisa Juan, Papago from Bigfields. Photograph by Helga Teiwes, 1979. bottom left, A Pima woman weaving a large granary basket of coarse coiling (Kissell 1916:179–190). Such baskets were so large they had to be made from within. Photograph by Putnam and Valentine, probably at Sacaton or Snaketown on Gila River, Ariz., about 1900.

among a corps of ceremonial officiants. As the group ceremonial life became more complex, an ever larger number of orations and hereditary orators appeared. The effect of this process is seen in the different genres of ritual oratory, for while given on different occasions—for example, salt ceremonies as opposed to war ceremonies—the rules for composition were constant and many episodes were interchangeable. It was a process of enlarging the oratorical repertoire and multiplying the number of individuals entitled to perform that particular priestly function, or, in other words, of spreading opportunities for official involvement in the public life. The orations were normally passed from father to son, so a village with 10 different orations could well have 10 different lines of ceremonial officiants.

The second responsibility was as organizer and main speaker at council meetings (Fire Maker, Keeper of the Smoke, Keeper of the Meeting). This aspect would not be divided.

The role of keeper of the group's sacred bundle (Keeper of the Plaited Basket) was a duty that would not be divided, for along with building the fire, it was a symbol and prerogative of the office.

The fourth aspect of headman, social status in the sense of great man (The One Above, The One Ahead, The One Made Big) is reflected in titles that refer to the political process of headmanship and specifically to the manner in which one obtained and held the office. This aspect of the office was readily divisible in that greatness could not be monopolized.

Among the Papago, Underhill found that old headmen were given younger assistants to serve as their 'Legs', 'Eyes', and 'Voice', in other words, to act as substitutes for the old man's failing senses. This is a clear case of parceling out aspects of the office without changing its basic character; no young man was appointed to be the 'Head', 'Memory', or 'Heart'.

The headman's wife organized group-wide gathering expeditions for the women.

Other special offices among the Papago were: War Leader, Hunt Leader, Game Leader, and Song Leader. These positions were priestly as much as practical, for the activities, especially war and hunting, were ritualized. Thus, although Underhill (1939:75–78) does not mention them in this context, the list could be extended to include all experts involved in the ceremonial cycle.

Finally, there was the secular position of ditch boss. The men worked cooperatively under a leader to maintain communal waterholes and irrigation ditches. For example, the nineteenth-century Papago at *Káij Mék* (now Santa Rosa) had a communal system with about three miles of ditches about eight feet wide and six feet deep.

• OFFICES DERIVED FROM SHAMAN The ceremonial cycle was run by the headman and his priestly adjuncts. The shaman's role in these ceremonies was always the same. Using a few simple tools plus spirit helpers and his intrinsic power, he foretold the future (where the enemy would be found, when it would rain, etc.), and he worked magic to reduce the strength of whatever the group was interested in (enemies, game, athletic teams from other villages, etc.). The tools were a divining instrument made from eagle wing feathers, a shining crystal, tobacco, and a rattle ("Pima and Papago Medicine and Philosophy," fig. 3, this vol.). The spirit helpers were summoned with songs, and the intrinsic powers were derived from the shaman's breath and heart (the two were intimately connected in Piman theory).

In the field of curing, shamanism engendered a class of nonshaman ritual curers who duplicated the shaman's tools and techniques. They sang songs, blew smoke, and fanned with feathers, but they lacked powers of their own. The efficacy of their shamanlike actions was said to derive from the sicknesses they cured, or more precisely, from various 'ways' that both caused and cured sickness (see "Pima and Papago Medicine and Philosophy," this vol.).

Ritual curers came into action only after a shaman's diagnosis. While the curers' techniques looked on the surface almost identical with the shamans' diagnostic techniques, the two types of event were conceptually distinct. This permitted elaboration in the field of curing. In the simplest case, the shaman could change caps, so to speak, after the diagnosis and commence with the appropriate cure. At the very least, this would involve a battery of special songs dedicated to the 'way' causing the sickness. Under elaboration, as among the Papago and Pima, the cure could include a chorus of singers and refinements, such as dancing, sand painting, and oratory.

All this was outside the public sphere in that patients chose the shaman and arranged for curers without bringing the matter before the headman's meetings.

Regional Band

Encompassing the local group was a larger entity corresponding linguistically to a dialect of the Piman language. Eight of these groups are recognized for the Papago (Saxton and Saxton 1969). The corresponding divisions for the other peoples are uncertain.

Socially the regional bands were nearly insignificant. Folklore existed on the quirks and brutal qualities of each band, but this did not prevent interband marriage and a thorough crisscrossing of the regional boundaries. The only reported serious interband hostility was between the No Village peoples and any other Pimans who entered their territory.

Groups within the same regional band normally attended one another's ceremonies; in fact, certain ceremonies such as the prayerstick festival and the summer cactus wine feasts required the attendance of several different local groups. They were performed on a directional scheme with the representatives of different local groups holding the appropriate cardinal positions. It was in this sense that the group's ceremonial ground was the basis for regional integration.

Bilateral Kindred

The kindred consisting of an individual's blood relatives was not a group in the sense that family, household, local group, and regional band were. The people in an individual's kindred extended far and wide, and they would practically never have occasion to think of themselves as a special body by virtue of their blood relation with the individual. Except for full siblings, each person's kindred contained different people and, conversely, each person had different positions in the family trees of hundreds of other individuals. For Pimans in historic times, marriages, baptisms, and funerals provide endless discoveries of how people are distantly related to each other.

A force that kept one's kindred large was the prohibition against marrying close relatives, second cousins according to Underhill (1939). As table 3 shows, marriages were predominantly but not exclusively between people of different local groups. This stands to reason when local groups were small, but it was also considered advantageous for a household to establish ties by marriage with other local groups. It is worth noting in this respect that the Piman expressions commonly used in reference to the "distance" of relationships—'near relative' versus 'far relative' (*mía hájuñ* versus *mé·k hájuñ*)—have both a spatial and a genealogical aspect. The ideal 'near relative' is a second cousin or closer who belongs to the same local group; the ideal 'far relative' is outside the local group and genealogically more remote than second cousin. The remaining two "mixed" possibilities might be called 'near' or 'far' depending on one's feeling toward the individuals involved, or, for example, whether one is regularly exchanging gifts or visits with them.

Clan and Moiety

All Pimans used a set of five patrilineal clan names that were grouped in turn into a pair of patrilineal moieties, three clans in the Buzzard moiety and two in the Coyote moiety. Clan and moiety membership did not figure into the choice of spouses. Moiety was the basis for some teasing and was recognized in certain ceremonies. In some bands, the Coyote moiety outnumbers the Buzzard, and this is explained in myth as the result of an ancient conquest. Clan membership determined the kin term used in addressing one's father.

Subsistence

Agricultural Efficiency

It is estimated that agriculture accounted for from 4 to 30 percent of the Papago people's food supply, and for from 25 to nearly 100 percent of the Pimas' food (Castetter and Bell 1942:56). With these figures, Castetter and Bell wished to indicate variations among households in the percentage of agricultural food consumed. They arrived at the figures through estimates of average yield and variations in field size per household.

Their conclusions may be modified in light of the fact that a household's consumption was not a direct reflection of the amount of food grown in its field. Between harvest and consumption was a series of food exchanges that Castetter and Bell did not reckon with. The effect was to equalize differences in harvest within and even between local groups.

To represent consumption, the range of variation should be collapsed to something nearer an average figure, say 17 percent for the Papago and 60 percent for the Pima. On the other hand, to represent variations in amount harvested per household, the range should expand beyond that given by Castetter and Bell for the Papago. Owing to the risks of rains, frost, and insect pests, a Papago's field could yield anything from zero to perhaps one and one-half times the figure given (Castetter and Bell 1942 calculated on an average yield of 12 bushels per acre). Yields among the Pimas were more stable because the rivers provided a dependable water supply, and this in turn permitted planting early enough to avoid the frost. Total failures would have been rare.

There is evidence that Pima production was limited by the demand for crops rather than by lack of resources or technology. Shortly after the Anglo-Americans appeared in the Gila Valley, Pima agriculture entered a brief golden age, 1850–1875. The golden age was short-lived because the new settlers speedily pre-empted the Pimas' water supply by draining the Gila River upstream.

The Papago did not increase their production with the opening of this market because their land and water situation was not suitable for it. Some of them responded by moving permanently into Pima territory (for example, the case histories of Whirling Water House B and Anegam House D in Underhill 1939:215, 228). More migrated seasonally to Pima country to work as harvest hands.

Thus, on the eve of Anglo-American contact, the Papago agricultural adaptation was working near the environmental limit, while the Pima adaptation was working at less than full capacity. The same set of social organizational factors may lie behind both situations, effectively spreading the yields in the context of Papago agriculture while holding Pima agriculture to a level that

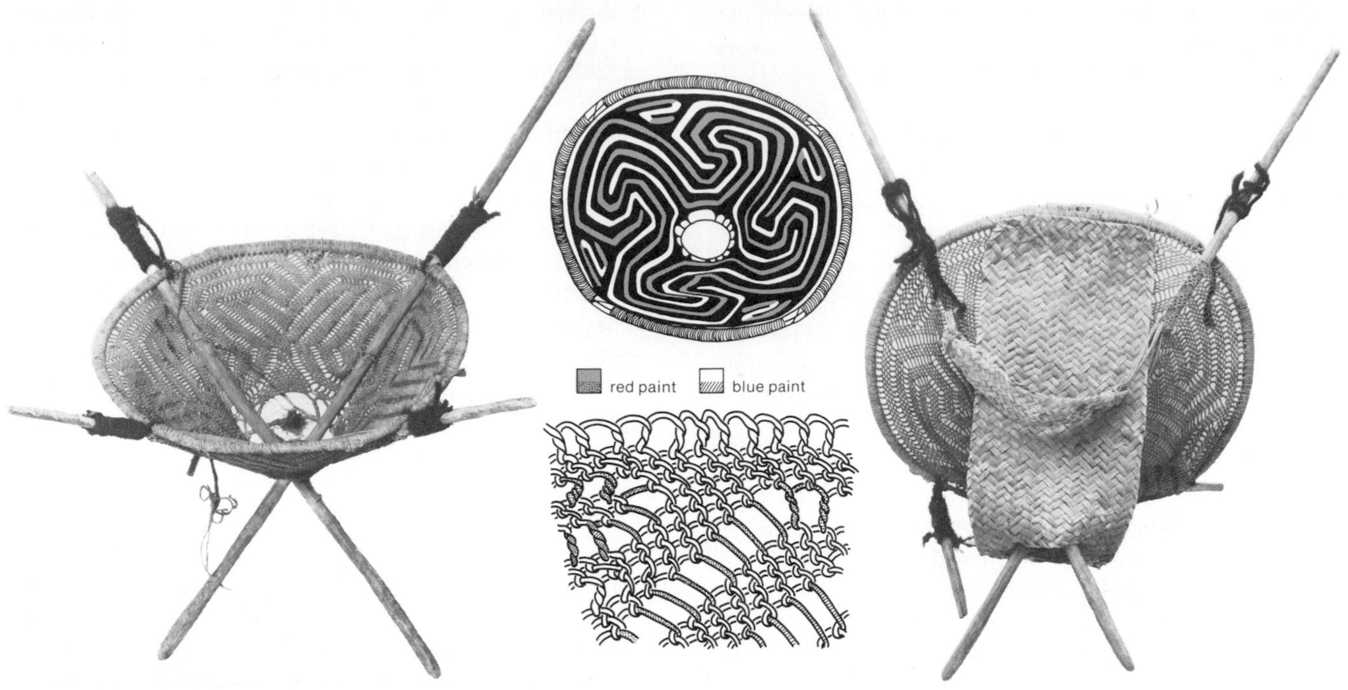
red paint
blue paint

was modest relative to their performance during their farming boom.

Papago agriculture is risky because most of the yearly rainfall of about 10 inches is confined to localized thundershowers during July and August. Instead of sinking into the ground, the water from these showers runs off in "washes" so that, roughly speaking, the washes leading to the fields of five contiguous villages may tap the runoff from 500 square miles of hinterland. Fields and "field villages" were built at the 'mouth' (*cíñ*) of these washes where the collected water spread out, normally with the aid of irrigation channels maintained by the community. A typical highly localized thundershower would water the drainage of only a few washes, resulting in irrigation for some of a village's fields while other fields would remain dry.

A good soaking was needed before a field could be planted and three or four mild soakings were needed to guarantee a crop. Too much water would kill the young plants. The rainy season begins in July, but a given field may not receive its first soaking until August. Castetter and Bell (1942:150) found that the latest safe date for planting or replanting corn was August 17. For tepary beans, the date was August 20–25. Crops planted later would be killed by frost. With the summer rains and the sprouting plants came the additional hazard of pests, particularly grasshoppers and, especially since the 1920s, cattle.

Thus, farming required thundershowers but crops could be ruined by them. A man had about a month to decide when, how much, and what to plant. On balance, the remarkable thing about Piman agriculture was that it was done wherever remotely possible. Only the No Village people, with an annual rainfall sometimes as low as 1 millimeter and a maximum yearly average of 6.88 inches, did not attempt it.

The key to how this system limited the demand for agricultural production among the One Village Pimas is given in Underhill's (1939:90) remark that Piman economics were basically those of abundance. It is apparent that among the Papagos this outlook was expressed in harvest sharing and food giving. Agriculture had the aspect of a hobby or a passionate avocation; however, it was the Papagos' means par excellence for achieving concentrations of people. The field villages were larger in size than the winter mountain retreats, and the public ceremonial life was also concentrated in them. The ceremonies theselves, even when manifestly about war, had abundant crops as their stated goal.

The same system of compulsory generosity with harvests and precisely the same ceremonial cycle prevailed among the Pima. In effect they produced no more than they could conveniently give away or otherwise dispose of according to the customs of economics and government.

Movement

Much of the quality of Piman life can be subsumed under the theme of "movement." Most obvious was the seasonal movement of households or entire local groups in all but the One Village adaptation. Furthermore, characteristic of daily life under each adaptation was considerable movement as each adult member of a household went about his work, for literally hundreds of different tasks for women as well as men were done in the desert, that is, in the unclaimed "wild" spaces that surrounded and interpenetrated the settlements. This discussion presents the features of social life under a "minimax" cultural ecology, as described in "Pima and Papago Ecological Adaptations," this volume.

Perhaps the most characteristic woman's artifact was the burden basket (fig. 7), a triangular webbed frame carried on the back in which firewood, water jars, and wild food were carried from gathering places to the home. According to myth, the baskets walked by themselves up to a certain point in the Piman migration from the underworld and they became the women's burden because Coyote, a more experienced inhabitant of the earth's surface, laughed on seeing them in motion.

Smithsonian, Dept. of Anthr.: top left, 360,860; top right, 174,523. center left, Smithsonian, NAA: 2749-c; center right, Calif. Histl. Soc., Los Angeles: Title Insurance Coll. 3604; Ariz. Histl. Soc. Lib., Tucson: bottom left, 4778; bottom right, 24808.

Fig. 7. Burden baskets or *gíhos*. All loads were formerly carried by women using either headrings or these carrying baskets. The distinctive baskets are made of maguey or agave cord worked in simple (and some twisted) looping to create a lacelike pattern. To begin a small fiber loop is made and a few inches are completed when the loop is slipped over the big toe and work continues outward forming a conical shape. Looping is done with fingers, sharpened stick, thorn needle, umbrella rib, or other handy tool. The designs created by the netting varied; the layout styles are circling, 4-part, and overall (Tanner 1965:71). The finished piece is bound with cord to a circular stick, which forms the rim. This body is then dampened and stretched to fit a framework of 4 saguaro rib poles and tied with human hair or horsehair cord, making a light, strong basket. Also attached are a twilled back mat (which might have shredded bark or cloth stuffed between it and the body to protect the back) and headband. As a finishing touch the pattern is highlighted or varied with blue and red paint (Kissell 1916:225–244). top left, Diameter 59 cm (both to same scale), Pima, collected before 1931. top right, Papago, collected by WJ McGee in 1894 or 1895. center left, Papago woman painting a design on the basket. The red was obtained from a native clay and the blue from the juice of prickly pear cactus fruit or later from laundry bluing (Tanner 1965:62). Photograph by William Dinwiddie, San Xavier Reservation, Ariz., 1894. center right, Si-rup, Pima, lifting a load of fire wood using a special helping stick; the loads could weigh nearly 100 pounds (Russell 1908:100). Photograph probably by Charles C. Pierce, about 1900. bottom left, Papago women resting with their *gíhos* around them. Photographer and date not recorded. bottom right, Papago woman carrying a load of pots, including ollas and bean boiling pots, in a southern Arizona town. Photographed about 1900.

Symbolic of man's daily travels was the wooden kickball, which men habitually kept in motion while traveling between distant places "to keep in practice," it was said, "for races." Running was preferred to walking as a form of locomotion, and the ball was used to keep up the pace over treks that commonly covered 20 or 30 miles.

A third aspect of the theme of movement was the movement of goods, particularly food, through gifts. Piman economics were dominated by this ideology, which receives its most striking expression in cases from relatively small Papago local groups of the 1860s. "One family gave two large wooden spoonfuls to every household at every meal; another cooked, for each meal, a four gallon pot and distributed it all, sometimes leaving nothing for the home household which subsisted on gifts" (Underhill 1939:100).

The ideal even in the largest local groups was: each household grows, gathers, stores, cooks, in short owns, its food. At mealtime, this owned food becomes the dinner of every other household of the local group. In strictest application, the ideal of gift giving prevented one from eating his own food. In physical terms, this meant that the settlement would be crisscrossed every evening with food deliveries.

Cooperation

The mealtime ideology was only the climax of a thorough-going emphasis on cooperation among households; thus, the emphasis on movement by men and women during the day. This work commonly was organized by special officers within the local group; but even when it was the project of a single household, other households were implicitly involved.

In gathering wild plant resources, especially the fruit of saguaro cactus ("Pima and Papago: Introduction," fig. 4, this vol.), the plants themselves were considered free; but each household had its customary gathering grounds. Expeditions into another household's grounds normally were cleared with that household ahead of time. Each person was an assiduous student of his neighbor's footprints, and in the twentieth century, of wagon tracks and tire marks. Although the desert's wild resources were not actually defended by particular individuals or households, the paths toward them were routinely studied to see who was following or departing from his customary route.

There was a basis for this informal territoriality in the geographic scale and yearly variation in wild resources. The size of each household's territory was so large and so vaguely defined at the edges that in a good year the household could not possibly exploit every tree, cactus, or rabbit within it; and in a bad year, it would not bother. People tended to gravitate toward the best pickings, sometimes letting others use their grounds and sometimes using the grounds of others. Underhill (1939:98) quotes a Papago as saying: "But I would not say anything [about others picking cactus in his grove]. The cactus is for all. We did not make it and the people who pick it are bringing rain."

The situation with farming, at least among the Papago, was an intensification of the same principle. In addition to its own fields, each household held options on the fields of friends and relatives. If its own field paid off handsomely, much of the harvest went to others; if the field failed, its storage bins were filled from others' harvests.

> Harvest was in a class by itself for, at this time, the workers were often paid in produce. To invite relatives to help at harvest was a favor to them and families invited distant ones . . . in different years. . . . [One] group took turns in inviting the wife's relatives and the husband's. As pay, they asked them to help themselves but the amount they took would be regulated by what they thought they could repay. One informant mentioned two sacks of wheat out of ten or "a pile" of unhusked corn or beans about three feet in diameter (Underhill 1939:104).

The same principle of accumulating options on others' crops applied to the earlier stages of cultivation: weeding and planting. By helping different households in widely scattered locations, and by being helped by them at each stage of the farming process, each household's fields became a well-cushioned bet against the risks of Papago agriculture.

Types of Exchange

Two major types of exchange carried the burden of Piman economic life, the gift and the wager. Much rarer was the sale. Of the two institutionalized types, the gift was more important in the sense that the production and distribution of food were channeled almost exclusively through it. The goods that moved through wagering, while considerable by Western standards of gambling, were for the most part surplus items and symbols of wealth.

Gifts, wagers, and sales are separated into three distinct types of exchange. In the case of a gift, the initiator has possession of the only item or good that will be passed in the exchange. He simply gives this item to the respondent, often no doubt with the expectation of receiving something in return. But the return, whether another material gift or a favor of some kind, is not immediately forthcoming; and when it comes, its amount and nature are left to the discretion of the respondent. Another defining feature of the gift is that the respondent should not refuse to accept the thing the initiator offers. Gifts may be vehicles for sharp and highly self-interested economic relationships. These relationships are typically studied from the point of view of the initiator who asserts his power, earns prestige, or obligates his respondents through strategic gift giving.

left, U. of Ariz., Ariz. State Mus., Tucson: 991; right, Smithsonian, Dept. of Anthr.: bottom, 76,016 and top, 76,014.

Fig. 8. Footraces. left, Papago runner with white clay decoration that helped his team identify him (Underhill 1939:148), urged on by onlookers. Photograph by Charles Morgan Wood at San Xavier, Ariz., 1920s. right, Pima balls used in men's races, usually covered with creosote gum; bottom, wooden core; top, stone core showing through deteriorated covering. They are kicked with the bare foot while running. Diameter of bottom right, 7 cm (other same scale); collected by Edward Palmer in Ariz., 1885.

The sale is also to be studied from the initiator's point of view. In this case, he offers an item to the respondent, or perhaps to the public at large, for which he will receive an immediate payment. Sales differ from gifts also in that the respondent may refuse to purchase the item if, for example, his close inspection reveals that it does not fill his needs; and the initiator may also, without prejudice, refuse to conclude the bargain by rejecting what the respondent offers in payment. As mechanisms for exchange sales are more "above board" than gifts primarily because they make allowance for open bargaining while gifts mask or prevent bargaining, covering the exchange with an etiquette of generosity.

Wagers, like sales, permit a careful, on-the-spot matching of items between the initiator and the respondent, for example by setting the wagered objects side by side in full public view. They differ from sales in that the outcome of the exchange depends on an event such as a dice game or a footrace (fig. 8). One party wins everything. Wagers resemble sales in another respect,

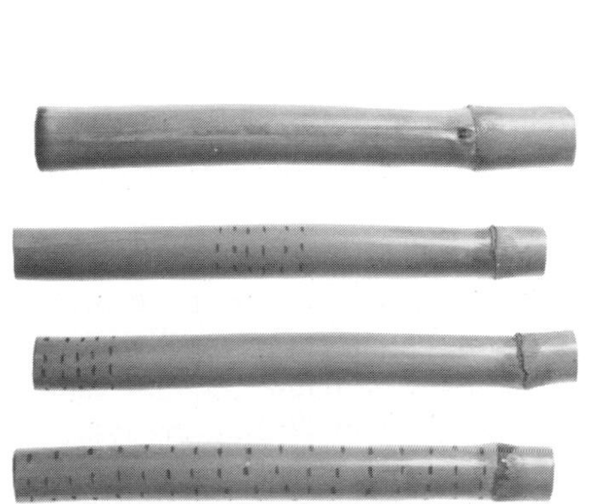

left, Smithsonian, Dept. of Anthr.: 218,043; right, Smithsonian, NAA: 2772-B.

Fig. 9. The game of *wópdai* 'slender things laid down'. left, Pima cane tubes used in game, with natural joint closing one end and a pattern on the outside made by cutting notches into the tube and darkening them with soot. Length 22 cm, collected by Frank Russell at Sacaton, Ariz., 1902. right, One team hides a bean or other small object in one tube and all 4 are filled with sand. The opposing team must then guess which tube holds the bean (Underhill 1939:139–144). left to right, Matias Encinas (emptying sand from a tube), Jose Lewis, Hugh Norris, and an unidentified Papago man. Photograph by William Dinwiddie, San Xavier, Ariz., 1894.

U. of Ariz., Ariz. State Mus., Tucson: top, 981; bottom, 52206.

Fig. 10. Papago women's *tóka* (double ball) game, played with a bent stick made of cat's-claw and a double ball usually of 2 small sticks tied together by a short cord. The aim of the game is to throw the ball past the opponent's goal (Underhill 1939:149). top, At San Xavier mission; photograph by Charles Morgan Wood, 1920s. bottom, At Santa Rosa Indian Day; photograph by Helga Teiwes, Sept. 1979.

namely, that they are concluded on the spot, while gifts, by contrast, lend themselves to prolonged relationships of gift and return.

Among the Pimans the gift was the staple form of exchange, no doubt because it fostered prolonged friendly relationships that were excluded by definition from the wager. Gifts were routinized to the point of establishing measures by which quantities could be judged in anticipation of a return gift ("Inter-Indian Exchange in the Southwest," fig. 11, this vol.). "The usual container was a basket bowl with a black pattern involving many lines parallel to the rim. A person receiving such a basket would note to what line the corn or beans reached and then fill it to the same point for the return gift. To fill it even higher was an act of virtue but to fill it short of the line was to commit social suicide" (Underhill 1939:101).

The term trade should be avoided in describing Piman exchanges because this term stands midway between the definitions of gift and sale. The "trades" described in the Piman ethnographies are derivatives of the more basic Piman institution of gift giving. Despite the existence of measures for equivalence, the Piman method of "trading" actually was a form of gift and countergift rather than an on-the-spot, openly bargained, and freely refused sale. Thus, in the example quoted above, the respondent could not refuse the proffered basket of goods without offending the giver and it was the respondent's prerogative to return it with an act of virtue or to commit social suicide. The initiator of this "trade," unlike the initiator of a sale, could only wait and see what course of action the other would follow.

The basic gift form was elaborated also to permit initiators to receive speedy return gifts of items that they could not otherwise obtain. For example, if a deer were being butchered at another household, one could send a small "trigger gift" of beans with the tacit understanding that a return gift of deer meat was desired. This act would be judged against the background of past gift exchanges between the two households. In any case, what was forbidden by etiquette was for the hunter's household to advertise that a deer had been killed and to receive bids from the neighbors for portions of the meat.

Similarly the services of shamans were recompensed in the form of gifts, no price having been set formally ahead of time. But there were subterfuges; for example, a family who wanted a shaman's presence sent a messenger who placed some cornmeal in his hand or some manure, if they planned to pay him with a horse or a cow (Underhill 1946:272). On his part, the shaman could introduce hints about the desired form of payment into the songs he sang while making a diagnosis: "Don't give me beads, I am not young and handsome. Give me a horse! a horse!" (Underhill 1946:277).

Pima and Papago Medicine and Philosophy

DONALD M. BAHR

Shamans or medicine men (fig. 1) have traditionally dominated Piman intellectual life both as the principal heroic type celebrated in popular song and poetry and as the main source for critical reflection on social issues. In addition, they have developed a specialized area of contemporary Piman thought, a theory of sickness, which has emerged as a central issue in the Piman scene.

In the late nineteenth century when American civilization first reached the Pimans in force, shamans were singled out for abuse by Whites and Indians alike. They were considered "an annoyance and a hindrance" by missionaries and to "have done more to destroy the efforts of Indian agents to improve the condition of the Indian, both in school-work and in moral elevation, than all the other undermining and checking influences combined. . . . The Indians crave excitement and amusement. Since the hunt and chase are things of the past, a substitute of some kind is required" (Cook 1893:63–64).

Among Indians, shamans were held responsible for disease. For example, there was a plague in 1860–1861 at Gila Crossing. "Three medicine-men who were suspected of causing the disease by their magic were killed, 'and nobody was sick any more'" (Russell 1908:48). In the 69 years covered by one Piman calendar stick published by Russell there were seven instances of shamans being killed after epidemic sicknesses. For other examples, see "History of the Pima," figure 8 (this vol.).

In the 1970s the prevailing attitude toward shamans is, when will they be gone? They have no place in the official schemes for Indian development—Christian, medical, legal, or commercial—but they are treated with respect as the last devotees of an almost vanished vocation.

The nineteenth-century Piman social organization is said to have had shamans and village headmen at opposite positions with respect to the running of public affairs. Headmen were at the center of the public life while the shamans stayed on the fringe except when called upon to do some particular piece of work. The headmen were responsible for mobilizing people and for keeping the traditional ceremonial cycle intact; the shamans' role was to perform magic during the public ceremonies, for example, to cast spells over the enemy or to divine the location of rain clouds.

While the shaman played a minor role in organizing the ceremonial life, his experience, as celebrated in song, drama, and oratory, dominated the content of every ceremony. The ritual oratory, for example, was a poetic form based on the idea of shamanic journeys from the earth to the sky or underworld and back to earth again. These speeches, which figured into almost every kind of public ceremony, were passed through generations of orators who were not normally shamans. The same holds for the ceremonial songs and drama: they celebrated shamanism, but they were performed by laymen.

As the period of Anglo-American influence wore on and the ceremonial cycle faltered and collapsed, shamans have taken abuse, but it was the headmen and the holders of various hereditary offices, such as orators and masked dancers ("Kachinas and Masking," fig. 5, this vol.), who quit or died without replacement. In

Calif. Histl. Soc., Los Angeles: Title Insurance Coll., 3639.

Fig. 1. Vaugh-kum, a Pima medicine man wearing a top hat, a status symbol. He probably holds a shovel, since he was helping to build a dam when this photograph was taken. Photograph by Charles C. Pierce, about 1900.

1976 the old ceremonies were mostly gone, headmanship of the old kind was greatly challenged by new institutions of government, and yet shamanism was strong. The main field left open to shamans is curing, or more precisely, the definition and diagnosis of sickness; curing is left to others.

For the shamans this is a reduction in scope from the old times. Where formerly they used their magic in war, sports, hunting, and making rain—in almost every venture that the headmen organized—they work now in private practice, so to speak, on sickness, the one legitimate aspect of shamanism that was not a public affair.

The fact that this work is private makes it difficult to know how many shamans there are, how many patients they treat, and indeed what to count as a shamanistic treatment of sickness. There is no official coming out for shamans and no objective way to identify them when they are not at work. People tend to keep the news of their sickness from circulating. Furthermore, a certain prestige attaches to the possibility that one might be a shaman, that one has the skill but rarely uses it.

One village had in 1972 about 400 residents and three well-known shamans plus several "possible" ones. "Well-known" meant known throughout the village and outside it as well. "Possible" meant reputed by some villagers to have the power to treat sickness. A well-known shaman might see two or three patients in a busy day. Especially since cars and trucks became common, people did not necessarily visit the shaman who lived nearest to them.

What is a Shaman?

This chapter concerns the theory of a Papago shaman named Juan Gregorio who was well known in the sense of receiving patients from throughout the Piman area, Pimas as well as Papagos, and Papagos from Mexico as well as from the United States (Bahr et al. 1974). According to Gregorio, the critical distinction among shamans, called *má·kai* in Piman, is the ability to perform a night-long diagnostic session called *dóajida*. In the *dóajida* one must bring spirit helpers into play by singing to them. It is the most powerful form of diagnosis.

Short of the *dóajida* and suitable for simpler diagnostic problems is a technique called *kúlañmada*, which does not require spirits and which is done in the daytime, identifying sicknesses by "illuminating" them with tobacco smoke blown over the patient's body. This technique may be attempted by anyone with tobacco and, more important, with the intuition that his breath, when accompanied by smoke, will illuminate sickness. Apparently many people are willing to experiment with it, even children.

left, U. of Ariz., Ariz. State Mus., Tucson: 34249; right, Mus. of the Amer. Ind., Heye Foundation, New York: 3805.

Fig. 2. Pima medicine men. left, The *dóajida* ceremony, to diagnose sickness, in progress (Bahr et al. 1974:113). The medicine man is singing while holding a rattle in one hand and a feather in another. The coffee can in front of the woman is used as a place to dispose of the strengths (Bahr et al. 1974:131–138) sucked from the patient. Painting by Louis Valdez, a Papago, 1961. right, A blind medicine man holding a gourd rattle and a feather wand. Photograph by Edward H. Davis, Salt River Reservation, Ariz., 1920.

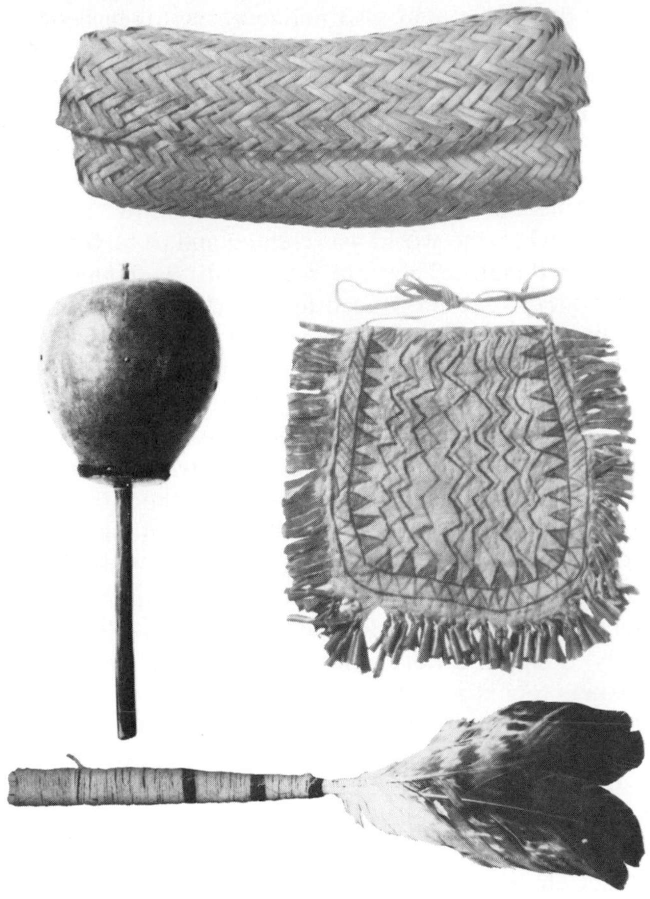

Smithsonian, Dept. of Anthr.: top, 174,531; center left, 27,839; center right, 107,520; bottom, Amer. Mus. of Natural Hist., New York: 50.1/4624.

Fig. 3. Shaman's equipment. top, Papago oblong twilled basket with lid used to hold feathers and other paraphernalia. center left, Papago gourd rattle, the only instrument used with songs to bring rain and treat the sick (Densmore 1929:3). Here the gourd has metal tacks and small perforations in the shape of various animals; the handle is wooden. center right, Pima leather pouch used to hold tobacco, the smoke of which is used to augment the shaman's breath when blowing over a patient's body (Bahr et al. 1974:189). bottom, Papago divining plume of eagle feathers set into a wooden handle bound with cloth and twine. top, Length 36 cm, rest to same scale; top, collected by WJ McGee in 1894–1895; center left, collected by E.W. Nelson in 1884; center right, collected in 1877; bottom, collected by Carl Lumholtz at Santa Rosa, Ariz., in 1911.

The longer and more strenuous *dóajida* is more serious because it requires proof of the shaman's ties with spirits. Each song is understood to have been given to him by a spirit, and so as he works through his repertoire of songs he calls out his lifetime collection of spirits.

The relation between these two kinds of diagnosis can be summed up as "*dóajida* is the *kúlañmada* and more," for like *kúlañmada, dóajida* includes the act of blowing smoke over the patient's body. This is done after the singing of every song and also between the singing of groups of *dóajida* songs. If the shaman has many songs, he will do the equivalent of many *kúlañmada*s during the night. It is the combination of blowing on the body and singing to the spirits and the fact that the combination is repeated several times that makes the *dóajida* more effective.

There is evidence that this definition of a real shaman is a standard one. It fits perfectly with the succession of daytime and nighttime techniques described by Russell (1908). In this case history, two shamans worked over a patient unsuccessfully during the day using smoke. A third and more powerful shaman succeeded in making the diagnosis at night after singing (Russell 1908:260–261).

Staying Sickness

With the theory of sickness, Pimans have worked out an intellectual response to the coming of Anglo-American culture. It is a rationale for the continuation of shamanism. The problem it seeks to solve is: What is the relation between Anglo-American medicine, in the broad sense of kinds of sickness and kinds of cure, and Piman medicine? The answer involves a basic distinction between 'wandering' (*ˀóimeḍam*) and 'staying' (*ká·cim*) sickness, the former belonging to Anglo-American medicine and the latter to Piman shamanism.

The critical distinction between the names 'wandering' and 'staying' has a triple application. It refers to infectiousness, so that the wandering sicknesses are infectious and the staying ones are not; it refers to origins, so the wandering sicknesses originate with foreigners (Anglo-Americans, Mexicans, Asians) while the staying sicknesses were created locally along with the Pimans; finally the terms contrast on the idea of permanency. Wandering sicknesses, such as measles, flu, and chicken pox, are observed to be here today and gone tomorrow, not only as epidemics move on, but also as new germs or viruses evolve, spread around the world, and finally disappear with the development of new medicines.

The various strains of Asian flu are illustrative of the three aspects of wandering sickness. This flu is notoriously infectious, and it is understood by Pimans to have come to America from Asia. They also understand that each year's invasion of flu is slightly different from the epidemics of previous years, which is why a different immunization is required against each new type. An older example of wandering sickness, still infamous because of its virulence in the nineteenth century, is smallpox.

The staying sicknesses by contrast are likened to the ocean. They always have existed and they always will. They never leave the Pimans to afflict other races, they never even pass by contagion from one Piman to another, and while they may be cured when they afflict patients, they will never be cured in the sense of being wiped out or removed from the face of the earth.

As Gregorio expressed it:

What is the meaning of staying sickness?
Look, something is called that way
of the diversity of our sicknesses,
and it never wanders,
Look, I will explain something clearly,
which is that the ocean lies over there,
and it never wanders.
It just stays there through the years
for as long as it lies, that one.

If these are the meanings conveyed by the names, what are the causal mechanisms for each kind of sickness? For each kind, the Piman theory is interested in the relation between symptoms within the patient's body and dangerous substances outside the body. In the case of wandering sicknesses, the dangerous substance is germs, particles too small to be seen by the naked eye and in fact below the threshhold of all the human senses. It is understood that germs enter the human body to cause the symptoms of wandering sickness such as the sores of chicken pox or the running nose and fever of flu. In other words, germs make themselves felt by entering the body. Otherwise people would have no evidence of their existence. With this much understood, it is easy to see why Pimans were terrified of wandering sicknesses. They personified them. "Smallpox was regarded as an evil spirit of which they did not dare to show fear. They said, 'I like Smallpox,' thinking that he would be thus placated. At one time they attempted inoculation from persons that had light attacks, but the experiment resulted in many deaths" (Russell 1908:267). When personified, the wandering sicknesses seem exquisitely bad. Their sole purpose is to inflict people and to this end they blow around the world seeking any victim whatsoever.

The present shamanic theory leaves the cure of these scourges to Western medicine. The technique of inoculation is still known, but it is held in reserve. It is considered to be an Anglo-American technique that Indians would only use in an emergency, and then only in preference to telling lies to the sickness.

The causal scheme for staying sicknesses involves a different, more complex, and typically American Indian set of terms: the 'strength' and 'way' of 'dangerous objects'. Outside the body are the various kinds of dangerous objects. A total of 38 have been mentioned (Russell 1908; Underhill 1936, 1938a, 1946; Bahr et al. 1974): badger, bear, bee, butterfly, buzzard, cat, caterpillar, cow, coyote, deer, devil, dog, eagle, enemy, frog, Gila monster, "ground squirrel of the mesas," hawk, horned toad, housefly, *húidam* (a serpent), datura (jimsonweed), lightning, lizard (*cúsugal*), lizard (*jénaṣaḍ*), mouse, ocean, owl, peyote, quail, rabbit, rattlesnake, roadrunner, saint, turtle, *wí·gida* (a ceremony), wind, whore.

Unlike germs, these outside objects are perceptible to all the senses and also unlike germs, they do not enter directly into the body to produce symptoms. The casual chain linking them with a patient's symptoms is as follows. Each kind of dangerous object has a 'way' (*hímdag*), which in practical terms means a number of things that humans must do when they meet up with a dangerous object. The ways are said to have been instituted when the world was created and to be binding only on Pimans. They are referred to as 'commandments' (*cíhañig*) and traced to the god 'Elder Brother Shaman' (*sí·s má·kai*). One can get a staying sickness only by transgressing on a way; he cannot get it by contagion from another sick person and he cannot get it merely by meeting up with a dangerous object. In these respects, dangerous objects differ from germs.

Sometime after his transgression, the 'strength' (*géwkadag*) of the dangerous object will enter his body to produce the symptoms of the sickness. Strength is said to be a liquidlike substance that shamans can suck out and that, if left unattended, will permeate the entire body. Strength is not identical with the symptoms of a sickness for, in its initial phase, each kind of strength produces distinct symptoms—wrinkled and itchy skin for coyote sickness, diarrhea for ocean sickness, swollen limbs for bear sickness—while the strength exists in the body as a liquid.

Strength is not imparted directly from the dangerous object. It is "the strength of the kind or species of dangerous object," but it is not localized in any individual dangerous object. In other words, it is not the same kind of thing as rattlesnake venom.

The theory does not identify a physical point of origin for strength. Gregorio said strength comes because a 'way' has been violated, as if a 'way' were a god watching over the treatment received by every individual dangerous object, but he did not refer to 'way' as a god, that is, as a spiritual person who looks over the world and dispatches strength to punish wrongdoers. He was indefinite as to just what kind of thing 'way' is, whether a spirit or an impersonal moral force.

The causal scheme for wandering sickness is simpler than that for staying sickness: it involves fewer terms and fewer steps. What is gained by imposing the extra steps of 'way' and 'strength' between the 'dangerous objects' and the symptoms? First, the distinction between 'way' and 'dangerous object' prevents the objects from being the direct cause of the sickness. (Dangerous objects don't enter the body like germs.) Another consequence is that the physical prowess of a thing has nothing to do with its selection as a dangerous object. Certain dangerous objects such as rattlesnake and bear are killers or maimers in their own right, but most of them, such as mice, horned toads, and rabbits, are not. The insertion of the 'way' causal chain has permitted the selection of dangerous objects for reasons other than their physical power over humans. As close observers of nature, the Pimans have a large empirical lore on noxious bugs, snakes, and germs, but this lore is largely outside the system of staying sickness.

The rationales behind the last two distinctions, between 'way' and 'strength' and between 'strength' and symptoms, will be understood with reference to the shaman's techniques for diagnosis.

Diagnosis

The test of a true shaman is the ability to make a difficult diagnosis called *dóajida* during the night. Diagnoses are difficult when they involve strengths from several kinds of dangerous objects. The body is viewed as an archive for these strengths. People pick them up unknowlingly through misadventures that start in childhood, in fact before they are born, and continue until they die. Certain 'ways' are particularly likely to be violated by children, others by the parents of unborn children—in which case the sickness comes to the baby—and others by the adults. Thus, the typical adult patient who, by definition, is sick without knowing the reason why presents the shaman a body full of strengths, tokens of a lifetime of encounters with dangerous objects. The strengths to be diagnosed are spoken of as the 'consequences' (*cúʔijig*) of his past actions. In sorting through them, the shaman makes the patient dig into his past.

Latency, Depth, and Permeation

The theory holds that strengths enter the body imperceptibly. Once present, a strength may either begin to make itself felt immediately by causing a distinctive set of symptoms, for example, the itchy skin and wrinkles of coyote sickness, or it may remain latent and unfelt. If it remains latent it is likely to be supplemented by other strengths. Thus a distinction is made in diagnosis between 'deep' and 'shallow' strengths, the deepest being the oldest. Finally, it is said that any strength, once active, tends to 'permeate' (*cé·moʔo*) the body, "like cancer." As it permeates, it mixes with other strengths and moves toward the patient's heart. Permeated strengths produce highly generalized symptoms: the patient aches all over, is feverish, and is barely conscious. Death occurs when permeated strengths reach the patient's heart.

The general picture, then, is of strengths that may begin by producing distinct symptoms but that can remain latent and be buried by others. When they finally become active, they have lost their distinctiveness. The difficult diagnosis centers on the patient with several nearly permeated strengths in him. The shaman will separate them one by one and move them back from the heart to their points of entry, clarifying them. His attention is on the patient's body, which he molds, blows on, and massages. Once a strength is separated from the mass, he sucks it out. This process lasts all night.

The *dóajida* goes in stages. Individual songs are sung and punctuated by the blowing of smoke over the patient. At the end of groups of songs (normally four), the shaman massages and sucks strengths from the patient's body. The only role attributed to spirits in this theory of the Piman *dóajida* is that spirits help in identifying the deep and permeated strengths. It is said that the shaman's blowing and massaging will not be sufficient. As he sings, spirits presumably give him the extra help he needs to reach a diagnosis.

Ritual Cures

Sucking the strength is not sufficient to get rid of it. It is said that some will remain, diagnosed but unremoved. The final cure will be in the hands of nonshamans who are expert in performing rituals for the 'ways' of the dangerous objects in question. These rituals typically include blowing smoke and singing songs descriptive of the 'way'. In this sense, 'way' designates distinctive quirks of the dangerous object. For example, a 'coyote way' song:

> Little grey Coyote!
> Indeed, a dirty girdle
> You make for yourself of snakes (Underhill 1946:289)

and a 'frog way':

> Narrow mountain upon
> A big green frog was hopping
> On the summit a mist
> Was lying (Underhill 1946:290).

Representative collections of curing songs have been published (Russell 1908; Densmore 1929; Underhill 1946). Of special interest is the presence of certain songs in more than one collection, for this indicates that the content of cures is the same throughout the Piman area. Bahr and Haefer (1978) and Bahr, Giff, and Havier (1979) provide the most detailed analyses of how selected curing song sets function as music and as literature and how they convey a curative "message" to the patient.

The cures for certain ways include dancing as well as singing. Others (rabbit and deer) include eating the flesh of the dangerous object. Others (wind, owl, and horned toad) involve sandpaintings (fig. 4). In short, the cure for each 'way' is a distinct cult.

Cures are said to work like prayers through the intervention of a spirit associated with each 'way'. Upon hearing its way celebrated, the spirit will lift the remaining strength from the patient's body. Patients are said to experience a great relief on hearing the songs. People who have been feverish and unable to rest for weeks may fall into a deep sleep after the curers have gone home.

Content of the Ways

The shaman completes his part of a diagnosis by identifying one or more kinds of strength. Then the patient searches his past for an application. Through this creative act, the patient contributes to the vitality of the system, for the sharp imagery of his remembered past action will point the way for future patients.

The following are examples of sharp imagery:

> A man's child was diagnosed for rabbit sickness. The father remembered that during the summer before the child was born, the family traveled by wagon to a village where there was to be a dance. The man saw a rabbit and got off the wagon to shoot it. The rest of the family had to lie on the floor of the wagon covered by a canvas because nobody is permitted to look at a rabbit while it dies. Even the hunter is supposed to look the other way after shooting it. It was too hot there and the wife got out and saw the rabbit. That's why their next son got rabbit sickness.
>
> Bear sickness: you are not supposed to bother anything that belongs to a bear. A lady found out that she had this kind of sickness even though she had never seen a bear. Then she remembered that as a little girl she was walking alone in a sandy wash in the mountains and came upon a large track. She didn't know what animal had made it and decided to step in it. Now she found out it must have been a bear.

U. of Ariz., Ariz. State Mus., Tucson: 56500.

Fig. 4. Benito Segundo, Papago, singing in front of a sandpainting he made. The painting, a type used to cure "wind sickness" or arthritis symptoms such as pains in legs or back (Bahr et al. 1974:298), is surrounded by sticks, fringed with split and peeled bark. He accompanies himself on a makeshift drum. Photograph by Gwyneth Xavier, in an arroyo just east of Tucson, Ariz., 1940.

It is difficult to summarize the dangers represented in the various 'ways' because each 'way' is open to a large range of transgressions. It is not a question of a few well-defined taboos, but of broad principles extending across many 'ways', which have the potential for thousands of mentally reconstructed sharp images. Some of the most commonly mentioned principles are listed and illustrated here, but there are many more. These examples came from cases mentioned by Gregorio.

Harming the body or the 'property' (*cúʔidag*) of any dangerous object is a violation of its way. The concept of 'property' is of particular interest, for it covers houses, burrows, or nests as well as the paw tracks quoted in the example above. It also includes an animal's food, for example:

> Mice eat leftovers from our tables at night. This means they claim the leftovers for their property. If you eat something a mouse has chewed on, even without realizing it, you will get sick.

Finally, the concept of 'property' may bind together things that otherwise would not seem connected. 'Devil way' covers fancy clothes, especially cowboy clothes, because the devil is thought to dress like a Mexican cowboy. In line with cowboys, if you are kicked by a horse or if you mistreat a cow, you get devil sickness. The ceremony called *wí·gida* is a dangerous object. Everything in it—the food, the firewood, the effigies, the dishes—is the 'property' of the ceremony and, if mishandled, will bring *wí·gida* sickness.

To return to the theme of bodily injury: several 'ways' focus on how, owing to the habits or appearance of the dangerous object, it is difficult even for the most careful person to avoid inflicting injury:

> Horned toads are almost the color of the ground and they move slowly. Hence they are difficult to see. If you step on one you get sick.
>
> Rattlesnakes make their houses beneath the ground or under the brush where you can't see them. If you crush the house or burn it accidentally while burning brush in a field, that's against the 'way'.
>
> Butterflies and frogs must not be harmed, but in the summer they are all over the road. It's hard to miss them while you drive.

Practically every 'way' presents a special problem to parents. They literally have their children to look out for in questions of dangerous objects, for when a parent violates most 'ways' the sickness may bypass the parent and strike the child. This was the case in the rabbit-killing example above, only there the line of cause was actually more complicated: the father shot the rabbit, the mother looked at it, and the unborn child was sickened.

Further examples of the dangers special to the parental generation are: pregnant women should not watch cows being butchered at fiestas. If you cut firewood from a tree that has been struck by lightning, your children will get lightning sickness; their faces will be pock-marked. If a hawk pecks a chicken egg, you should not eat it unless you are old. Young people would bring hawk sickness onto their children. One should kill his first Apache before he is married. If you get married first, your children are likely to be sickened. Menstruating and pregnant women must stay away from the ceremonies following war in any case. Any person who is sick will be made worse by the approach of a menstruating or pregnant woman.

As the example of bear sickness shows, childhood is a dangerous time. The idea is that children will attempt things where adults would know better, for example:

'Turtle way' requires that turtles, great travelers, not be impeded in their journeys. When one meets a turtle, the proper thing to say is, "Well turtle, you seem to be going somewhere. Now where would you be going?" and let him proceed. Children are inclined to impede them by putting rocks on their back or by putting obstacles in their path. If they kill them in this manner, they will get turtle sickness.

Jimsonweed has white, bell-shaped flowers that children play with because they resemble doll dresses. This results in jimsonweed sickness.

When whirlwinds come by, children like to run inside them. The stones carried by the winds will strike their backs and this causes wind sickness.

The cigarettes used in various ritual cures must be thrown far away from the village because otherwise children will find them. They will pretend to smoke them and get the sickness.

The old are exempted from the dangers specific to other ages, but they are not altogether free:

'Owl way' means ghosts. If you think too much about a person who has died, this will make you sick.

'Devil way' covers the horsehair baskets made by old women, the best basket weavers. These are very fine and worth a lot of money, but the makers can get devil sickness.

"Ceremonial Lapse" Sickness

The adaptability of late twentieth-century shamanism is nowhere more clearly evident than with respect to what Underhill (1946) called the "ceremonial lapse" sicknesses. These do not come from encounters with dangerous objects in their natural environments, but rather from misbehavior toward objects used in the old ceremonial cycle. There are six such sicknesses: deer, eagle, enemy, ocean, saint, and *wí·gida*. They are associated with the following ceremonies: a corn harvesting and deer hunting ritual (*máʔamaga*), eagle purification, warrior purification, salt purification, saint purification, and the "prayerstick" ritual (*wí·gida*).

The six rituals have the status of dangerous objects and the paraphernalia used in them are conceived as the 'property' (*cúʔidag*) of the dangerous object. Quite likely these sicknesses were incorporated into the theory by extension of the idea of dangerous object from species to event. This has permitted a wide range of new things to be classed as hazards from which sickness may come: artifacts such as cooking pots and clothing used in ceremonies, and man-made icons or effigies such as the cloth models of the sun used for the *wí·gida*. Even mythical heroes and Apaches are brought into the field of staying sickness. Each of these sicknesses is cured by performing an abbreviated form of the normally public ceremony at the patient's house.

Of the six dangerous public ceremonies, only the one concerned with saints is still widely carried out. 'Saint way' covers primarily the saints' images obtained on religious pilgrimages to the fiesta of San Francisco at Magdalena, Sonora, Mexico. These images have to be baptized and 'purified' before they can be kept safely in Piman villages. Failure to do so results in saint sickness. Getting the saints' images on pilgrimages is analogous with the old and now extinct quests for scalps, eagle feathers, and salt. In each case a journey was undertaken to obtain a powerful object and a ritual purification was required before the acquisition and the acquirer could be admitted into the village. Thus the one vigorous expression of the old ceremonial cycle remaining is this Christian "quest" into Mexico.

As for the other dangerous ceremonies, by 1976 only the old people have been exposed to them and when the last witness of, for example, a warrior purification, has died, that sickness should be extinct. However, the shamans' diagnoses have kept the memory of these ceremonies alive and relevant for as long as 50 years after the ceremony itself has ended.

Conclusion

Piman shamans are generally old people. It seems that one does not build up a large clientele until after middle age. Thus the shamans of the 1970s are people who grew up when the ceremonial cycle was still in force.

As individuals they are sympathetic to the old Indian religion; however, they are not tied to it, and in becoming shamans they are supposed to have forgone the priestly and political careers associated with the public life. Accordingly in the 1970s they may equally serve the Christian priests in diagnosing saint's sickness or the headmen of years past in diagnosing ocean, eagle, deer, or *wí·gida* sickness. Their main task is to keep their diagnoses meaningful and up to date, or in other words to define sickness for their people.

In an atmosphere of pride in being Indian, the shamanic theory could last simply because it gives people opportunity to tie themselves with an Indian tradition. The 'staying sicknesses' could be mere patriotic gestures; however, it appears that for many Pimans they are more than that, since the acceptance of a diagnosis makes the patient think through his life in terms of the dangerous objects and their ways. It draws him in.

Other Studies On Piman Thought

This synopsis of one medicine man's theory is the most detailed study of that aspect of Piman culture. The question arises, how representative is his theory? Gregorio's ideas are in accord with what Russell (1908) wrote about the Pimas and Underhill (1946) wrote on the Papagos, especially on distinctions between *kúlañmada* and *dóajida*, diagnosis and cure, and staying and wandering sickness. Where the earlier works contain those distinctions in implicit form, this theory elaborates them. Conversation with many Pimas and Papagos in addition to the study with Gregorio and the observation of two other men's *dóajida*s and a dozen-odd ritual cures are convincing that Gregorio's theory represents a broadly shared Piman cultural reality. Of course equally detailed studies of other shamans' theories are much to be desired.

The articles by Hale and Alvarez (1972) and Alvarez and Hale (1970) on linguistics provide important data from a native viewpoint. In each instance Pimans have spoken at length, analytically and in their language, on an aspect of their culture. Also valuable are the autobiography of a Papago woman (Underhill 1936) and the autobiographical reminiscences of a Pima man (Webb 1959). Finally there are numerous works on song, oratory, and prose myth texts, the best being Underhill (1938a), Lloyd (1911), Giff (1980) on Pima swallow songs, and a study of the Papago ceremonial year with emphasis on its oratory (Underhill et al. 1979).

Papago Semantics

MADELEINE MATHIOT

This presentation gives an overview of some of the most striking semantic characteristics of Papago grammatical categories, based on Mathiot (1973, 1:29–134). Grammatical categories are understood here in the traditional sense proposed by Boas (1911:24–43) and Hockett (1958:230–239) among others. They are those forms of a language that manifest meanings such as person, gender, tense, and aspect. Traditionally, grammatical categories have been regarded as being manifested in two types of forms, simple forms and compound forms such as the English simple and compound tenses. Simple forms are those consisting of a major word each, such as a verb form by itself (e.g., English "eats", "ate"). Compound forms are those consisting of a major word accompanied by an auxiliary (e.g., English "has eaten", "is eating").

This traditional conception applies to Papago with the following further specifications.

Papago can be called a "highly inflected" language, as most Papago words are characterized by a fairly elaborate inflectional paradigm added to the theme (root portion) of the word. The theme, in turn, consists of a stem (inner root portion) with or without derivational affixes, which are prefixes or, in the overwhelming majority of cases, suffixes. Table 1 shows examples of Papago themes; hyphens indicate morpheme boundaries. The inflectional paradigm consists of the process of reduplication affecting the theme and the affixes. These affixes are of two types: categorial affixes and incorporated forms. Categorial affixes are those that manifest grammatical categories. An example is the durative marker, *-da-*, *-d*, a member of the category of extensionality. Incorporated forms are those that in other contexts function either as words or as stems. An example of the first case is the incorporated locational *-ˀámjeḍ* 'from', as in *kí·him-t-ˀámjeḍ* 'from town', which can also function as a postposition. An example of the second case is the incorporated stem *d-* (third-person indefinite human) as in '*D-ó·p uḍ?*' 'Who are you (sg.)?', which can also function as a stem in the personal pronouns *hé-ḍa-ˀi* (sg.) and *hé-ḍa-m* (pl.) 'whoever'.

Two main types of Papago words can be distinguished: inflected words, which have an inflectional paradigm, and uninflected words.

Inflected words can be further differentiated into auxiliaries and major words: auxiliaries are occurrence-dependent and they belong to classes of restricted membership. All other inflected words are major words.

Seven classes of major words can be distinguished by their respective inflections: nouns, verbs, modifiers (adjectives and adverbs), cardinal numerals, postpositions, personal pronouns (including demonstrative pronouns), and locative pronouns.

Five classes of auxiliaries can be distinguished by their respective inflections: the subject-complex words; the two sets of demonstrative auxiliaries—*ˀí·daˀa* (sg.), *ˀídam* (pl.) 'this, these' and *hégaˀi* (sg.), *hégam* (pl.) 'that, those'; the locative auxiliaries; the three indefinite quantifiers (*ha* 'a little', *héma* 'a', and *háˀi* 'a few'); the two indefinite manner qualifiers (*ha-b* 'in a certain familiar way', *ha-s* 'in a certain unfamiliar way'). Tables 2 and 3 give a detailed account of the subject-complex words and of the locative auxiliaries, respectively. The symbol Ø indicates a zero allomorph. All major words can occur as simple forms. The auxiliaries, on the other hand, combine with major words to make compound forms.

For the purposes of this survey only two types of uninflected words will be distinguished on the basis of their respective syntactic functioning—conjunctions and particles. Conjunctions enter into the internal structure

Table 1. Examples of Papago Themes

kéhi-wa	'to trample object'
kéhi-ñ-wa	'to push down hard on object with the foot'
kéhi-ñ-u-n	'to push down on object applying slow and regular pressure with one's feet'
kéhi-w-i-n	'to grind, crumble object by stepping on it'
kéi-hi-n	'to kick object once'
kéi-hi-ṣ	'to give object reiterated kicks'
kéi-c-k-wa	'to give a violent kick to object'
kéi-k-o-n	'to miss a step'
kéi-t-pa-g	'to push object down with the foot by repeated light pushes or short poundings'
kéi-ṣ-p	'to step on object'
kéi-ṣ-p-iˀok	'to take one's foot off object'
kéi-ṣ-u-n	'to crush object by stepping on it on purpose'
kéi-ṣ-u-ḍ	'to crush object by stepping on it by chance'
kéki-wa	'to stand up (sg. subj.)'
ké·-ṣ	'to choose object'
ké·-k	'to be standing (sg. subj.)'

Table 2. Internal Structure of the Subject-Complex Words

Prefixes			*Suffixes*			
2	*1*	*Stem*	*1*	*2*	*3*	*4*
b-	*ñe·-*	Subject	*-ḍ*	*-s*	*-p*	*-s*
d-	*wa-*	personals			*-kĭ*	
ṣ-	*na-,n-,naʔa-*	discussed				
	-a·-,-o·-	below		*-t*	*-ṣ*	
	ku-,k-					
	ma-,m-					

NOTE: The functions of these morphemes are as follows. Incorporated stems: *b-* (indefinite locative), *d-* (indefinite human), *ṣ-* (indefinite manner). Markers of grammatical categories labeled in parentheses: (statement mode) *ñe·-* promptive, *wa-* assertive, *na-* (etc.) interrogative; (connectivity) *k(u)-* disconnective, *m(a)-* connective; (aspectual distance) *-ḍ* remote; (aspectual boundedness) *-t* bounded; (incognizance) *-s* incognizant; (attestation) *-kĭ* evidential, *-p* potential, *-ṣ* quotative.

of clauses, whereas particles enter into that of phrases. Conjunctions, therefore, are not simple forms, but neither are they a part of the construction of compound forms. Particles combine with major words (with or without auxiliaries) to make compound forms.

Table 4 shows Papago word types and subtypes together with some examples of Papago conjunctions and particles.

The traditional conception of simple forms and compound forms can now be specified for Papago as follows: a simple form consists of a single major word. A compound form consists of a major word with one or more auxiliaries, or with one or more particles, or with both. The following analyzed sentences illustrate compound forms.

In examples (1)–(3) the compound form is coextensive with the entire sentence. (1) *Na-p-t o píastam?* 'Are you (sg.) on your way to the feast?' The verb *píastam* forms a compound form with the auxiliary *na-p-t* (a subject-complex word containing the morphemes for interrogative, second person sg., and bounded, respectively) and the particle *o* (nonfactual). (2) *Na-p-t ʔam o píastam?* 'Do you (sg.) intend to go to the feast?' The compound form has the same constituents as in (1) with in addition the auxiliary *ʔam* (locative indicating infradistal non-lateral position). (3) *B g ʔi dá·ʔi.* 'Jump down this way (toward me).' The verb makes a compound form with the auxiliaries *b* (infradistal facing position) and *g* (imperative) and the particle *ʔi* (punctual).

In examples (4)–(5) there is more than one compound form in each sentence. (4) *Na-t ʔab-hú ʔi mel g Húsi?* 'Did Jose drive up this way?' This contains a verbal compound form followed by a nominal compound form. The verbal compound form has the verb *mel* with the auxiliaries *na-t* (subject-complex word: interrogative, bounded) and *ʔab-hú* (infradistal facing position; unfocused). The nominal compound form consists of the noun *Húsi* and the noun marker *g*. (5) *Ku-p-t-p heg o ñéid-k, ʔan ʔi ʔóida-him-k o cé·, ʔa-t-p héms.* 'You (sg.) may see that, and having followed it you may find him, perhaps.' This sentence contains three verbal compound forms and three additional words: the personal pronoun *heg* (demonstrative, distal), the auxiliary *ʔa-t-p* (subject-complex word: neutral, third person, bounded, potential), and the particle *héms*. The first compound form, which is discontinuous (with a pronoun that is not part of it in its midst), has the verb *ñéid-k* 'see (correlative mode)' with the auxiliary *ku-p-t-p* (subject-complex word: disconnective, second singular, bounded, potential) and the nonfactual particle *o*. The second has the verb *ʔóida-him-k* 'follow (interruptive aspect, correlative mode)' with the auxiliary *ʔan* (infradistal lateral position) and the punctual particle *ʔi*. The third has the verb *cé·* 'find' and the nonfactual particle *o*.

An exhaustive investigation of the grammatical categories manifested in the simple and compound forms of Papago should therefore include a consideration of the inflectional paradigms of the major words, the auxiliaries, and the particles. In this chapter, only the inflectional paradigms of the major words and the auxiliaries will be considered. The particles—with the exception of the nonfactual *wo*—have been left out, their meaning not being known at this stage in sufficient depth to allow the inference of what grammatical categories are manifested in them (Hale 1969 analyzes one other particle).

Table 3. Locative Auxiliaries

		Position		
		Facing	*Not facing*	
Spatial Distance	*Visibility*		*Lateral*	*Not lateral*
Proximal *ʔia, ʔi*			*ʔi-n*	*ʔi-m*
Infradistal		*ʔab*	*ʔan*	*ʔam*
Distal	*g-ḍ*	*ga-∅*	*ga-nai*	*ga-mai*
Ultradistal	*gá-·-š*	*gá·-j*	*gá·-n*	*gá·-m*

NOTE: Markers of grammatical categories (labeled in parentheses): (spatial distance) *ʔia, ʔi* proximal, no marker: infradistal, *ga-* distal, *ga·-* ultradistal; (visibility) *-ḍ, -ṣ* out of sight, no marker: in sight; (position)*ʔab, -∅, -j* facing, *ʔan, -n, -nai* lateral, *ʔam, -m, -mai* neutral.

Table 4. Papago Word Types and Subtypes

Inflected		*Uninflected*	
Major Word Classes	*Auxiliaries*	*Conjunctions*	
Nouns	Subject-complex words	*hékid*	'when'
Verbs	Demonstrative auxiliaries	*heg hékaj*	'in order that'
Modifiers	Locative auxiliaries		
Numerals (cardinal)	Indefinite quantifiers		
Postpositions	Indefinite manner qualifiers		
Personal pronouns (including demonstratives)		*Particles*	
Locative pronouns		nonfactual	*wo*
		punctual	*ʔi*
		"ineffectual"	*cum*
		copula	*wuḍ*
		noun marker	*g*

The most striking semantic characteristics of the grammatical categories manifested in the simple and compound forms are: the extreme elaboration of the concept of multiplicity; the handling of time; and the elaboration of the concept of knowledge status, that is, the nature of the knowledge that is being transmitted (whether it is based on evidence or hearsay, whether it is factual or nonfactual, whether it involves familiarity or lack of familiarity with the referent, etc.).

In thc Papago manifestations of the concept of multiplicity three semantic variables are at play: the number of entities, the number of occurrences, and the number of loci (where by locus is meant the culturally defined whereabouts of entities and occurrences). These semantic variables may operate separately or jointly. They operate separately in grammatical categories entailing multiplicity of entity, multiplicity of occurrence, and multiplicity of locus. They operate jointly in grammatical categories entailing localized multiplicity. It would be possible to reduce the number of grammatical categories by ascertaining their predictability in terms of certain conditions; however, these conditions are quite complex.

When the number of entities is indicated the semantic opposition is between one and sèveral (singular versus plural). This opposition is manifested in four grammatical categories: subject number, object number, extended number, and referential number.

Subject number and object number are part of the inflection of verbs, and tables 5 and 6 give examples of the various ways in which these two grammatical categories are manifested.

Table 5. Subject Number

	Singular Subject	*Plural Subject*	
The plural subject is manifested by reduplication of the first syllable of the stem.	*hím*	*híhim*	'to walk, go on foot'
	bágat	*bábgat*	'to get angry'
	ʔe-báhigid	*ʔe-bá·bhaigid*	'to wag one's tail'
	cúdwa	*cú·cudwa*	'to land on both feet'
	wóʔo	*wó·pĭ* (animate)	'to be lying'
	céṣad	*cé·ci(ṣa)d*	'to rise'
	bíjim	*bí·bi(ji)m*	'to go around slowly'
	ʔíbhup (semelfactive) *ʔíbhupaṣ* (reiterative)	*ʔíʔibhup* (semelfactive) *ʔíʔibhupaṣ* (rciterative)	'to pant'
The plural subject is manifested by suppletion, i.e., substitution of a wholly different stem or theme.	*méḍ*	*vó·poʔo*	'to run, drive'
	céʔuimeḍ	*céʔuiop*	'to go and pick obj. one by one'
	jíwa	*dáda, dáiw*	'to arrive (unitive)'
	jíjjiwa	*dáiwup*	'to arrive (nonunitive)'
	mú·ki-	*kóʔi-*	'to die'
	múmku	*kóko*	'to be sick'
	ké·k	*gégok* (animate) *cú·c* (inanimate)	'to be standing'
	béhimeḍ (sg. obj.) *ʔúʔameḍ* (pl. obj.)	*béhiop* (sg. obj.) *ʔúʔiop* (pl. obj.)	'to go and get object'

Table 6. Object Number

	Singular Object	Plural Object	
The plural object is manifested by reduplication of the first syllable of the stem.	*bágacud*	*bábgacud*	'to make object get angry'
	táḍan, táḍañ	*tá·taḍan, ta·taḍañ*	'to spread object open'
	dá·ṣ (unitive) *dádṣa* (nonunitive)	*dádṣp* (unitive) *dádṣṣap* (nonunitive)	'to put object in a sitting position'
	cú·ṣ	*cú·cṣ*	'to extinguish object (such as a fire)'
	húḍ(u)ñid	*húhuḍsid*	'to take object down'
	wáwan	*wáwpan*	'to stretch object open'
	wáid	*wápaid*	'to ask object to come'
	swía	*swípia*	'to ruin object'
The plural object is manifested by suppletion.	*béhĕ*	*ˀúˀu*	'to get object'
	béhimeḍ (sg. subj.) *béhiop* (pl. subj.)	*ˀúˀameḍ* (sg. subj.) *ˀúˀiop* (pl. subj.)	'to go and get object'

Extended number is also part of the inflection of verbs. This category indicates the number of entities to which a given action or condition extends without these entities being directly involved as either subjects or objects of the action or condition. Thus, in the verb *kí·cud* 'to build a house for somebody' extended number indicates how many houses are being built, not how many people are doing the building or how many the building is being done for. There are two extended numbers: the single and the multiple (table 7).

Referential number is part of the inflection of the modifiers (adjectives and adverbs) and of the indefinite quantifiers. This category makes reference to the number of entities indicated by one of the number categories that may be manifested in the noun or the verb that a given modifier or quantifier modifies. There are two referential numbers: singular-referent and plural-referent, referring, respectively, to the single or plural entities indicated by the modified noun or verb. Table 8 shows how referential number is manifested in the modifiers. Examples of this category in the indefinite quantifiers are the following (cf. table 14): *héma ñ-ˀáliga* 'one of my children, a child of mine'; *háˀi ñ-ˀáˀalga* 'several of my children, several children of mine'.

When the number of occurrences is indicated the semantic opposition is between one occurrence and several occurrences. This opposition is manifested in two grammatical categories, nonlocalized aspectual number and successionality.

Nonlocalized aspectual number is part of the inflection of verbs. It indicates the number of times an action is performed without regard to its locus. There are two nonlocalized aspectual numbers: the semelfactive and the reiterative. The semelfactive indicates a single action; the reiterative indicates several identical actions repeated in rapid succession (table 9).

Successionality is part of the inflection of verbs. This category indictes whether or not several actors perform

Table 7. Extended Number

Single	Multiple	
kí·t	*kí·kĭt*	'to build one/several house(s)'
gógsga	*gógogsga*	'to have one/several dog(s)'
cíwa	*cíciwa*	'to settle somewhere (one/several familie(s)'
jégaḍ	*jé·jegaḍ*	'to pierce one/several hole(s) through object'
ˀe-cíndad	*ˀe-cícindad*	'to kiss each other (one/several pair(s))'
cékṣan (nondistributive) *céckṣan* (distributive)	*cékṣṣas* (nondistributive) *céckṣṣas* (distributive)	'to draw one/several unbroken line(s)'

Table 8. Referential Number in the Modifiers

Singular referent	Plural referent	
s-mói k	*s-mómoik*	'soft'
s-doa	*s-dóda*	'healthy'
ˀáj	*ˀáˀaj*	'narrow'
s-ṣéliñ	*s-ṣé·ṣeliñ*	'straight'
s-tóhă	*s-tó·ta*	'white'
s-ké·g	*s-kéheg*	'nice, beautiful'
s-wí·nk	*s-wípink*	'hard'
s-dápk	*s-dádpk*	'smooth'
s-káwk	*s-káwpk*	'strong'
kówk	*kówpk*	'thick'
géwk	*géwpk*	'strong'
cém	*céˀecem*	'small'
ṣáwaḍk	*ṣáˀaṣwaḍ*	'thick'
gákoḍk	*gáˀagkoḍk*	'crooked'
sípolk	*síˀispolk*	'piled'
gíwulk	*gíˀigwulk*	'tapered'

the same action one after the other. There are two successional aspects: the successive and the nonsuccessive (table 10).

Whenever multiplicity of locus is indicated the semantic opposition is between one locus and several. This opposition is manifested in three grammatical categories: postpositional number, numeral number, and locative number.

Postpositional number is part of the inflection of the postpositions. This category indicates the number of loci in which the action or condition associated with the postposition occurs. There are two postpositional numbers: the postpositional singular and the postpositional distributive. The postpositional singular indicates a single locus; the postpositional distributive, several loci (table 11).

Numeral number is the only inflectional category of the cardinal numerals. This category indicates the application (single or distributive) of a given cardinal numeral (e.g. 'two' versus 'two by two, in groups of two'). There are two numeral numbers: the singular numeral and the distributive numeral. For example, corresponding to the singular numerals *hémako* 'one', *gó·k* 'two', *wáik* 'three', and *húmukt* 'nine' there are the distributive numerals *héhemako* 'one here and there', *góˀogok* 'two by two, in groups of two', *wáˀawaik* 'three by three', and *húhumukt* 'nine by nine'. An example is: (6) *B ˀo hi a ˀal héhemako dá·dad.* 'There is one (cottonball) on (the plant) here and there.'

Locative number is part of the inflection of locative pronouns. It indicates the number of loci to which reference is made in connection with the particular location specified by the locative pronoun itself (e.g., 'there, in one place' versus 'there, in several places'). There are two locative numbers: the singular locative and the distributive locative. The inflection of the locative pronouns for locative number is as follows: (singular locative) *ˀábaˀi* 'up there (in one place)' and *ˀámaˀi* 'down there (in one place)'; (distributive locative) *ˀáˀabai* 'up there (in several places)' and *ˀáˀamai* 'down there (in several places)'.

Table 9. Nonlocalized Aspectual Number

Semelfactive ('once')	*Reiterative* ('several times')	
ṣámk-	*ṣámk-e*	'to make a rustling noise'
bísck	*bísc-e-k*	'to sneeze'
bébedk	*bébed-e-k*	'to thunder'
ṣónck-	*ṣónc-e-k*	'to cut object by striking it'
ˀíapa	*ˀíapa-ṣa*	'to come back from gathering saguaro fruits'
jéwa	*jéwa-ṣ*	'to rot'
wáke	*wáke-ṣ*	'to milk a cow'
dágĭto	*dágĭto-ṣ*	'to let go of object'
ˀíbhup	*ˀíbhupa-ṣ*	'to pant (sg. subj.)'
cékṣaḍ	*céṣaḍa-ṣ*	'to draw a broken line on object'
cúˀakaḍ	*cúˀakaḍa-ṣ*	'to puncture, stab object'
kópo-ñ	*kóp-ke*	'to explode'
hói-ñ	*hói-ke*	'to move, undulate'
wú·ṣa-ñ	*wúš-ke*	'to come out'
ˀúli-n	*ˀúli-ṣ*	'to hand out object'
cépoi-n	*cépoi-ṣ*	'to peck at object'
kápa-ñ	*kápa-ṣ*	'to make a slapping noise'

Whenever localized multiplicity is indicated there are two semantic oppositions: on the one hand that between one entity or occurrence and several, and on the other hand that between one locus and several. This dual opposition is manifested in three grammatical categories: nominal number, localized aspectual number, and personal number.

Nominal number (table 12) is part of the inflection of nouns. This category indicates both the number of entities and the number of loci in which these entities are located. Nominal numbers form contrastive sets of two or three depending on the substantive status, mass, aggregate, and individual type of the noun (Mathiot 1967:208–209). With individual type 1 nouns nominal numbers form a contrastive set of three: the nominal singular, the nominal plural, and the nominal distributive. With aggregate nouns nominal numbers form a contrastive set of two: the nominal nondistributive and the nominal distributive. With mass nouns and individual type 2 nouns nominal numbers also form a contrastive set of two: the nominal singular and the nominal nonsingular. The nominal singular indicates a single entity at a single locus; the nominal plural indicates several entities at a single locus. The nominal nondistributive indicates a single locus without specifying the number of entities. Both the nominal nonsingular and the nominal distributive indicate several entities at several loci, without specifying the number of entities per locus. The relation between locus and entity in Papago is as follows: Entities referred to by mass or individual type 2 nouns are viewed as being coterminous with their respective loci. The locus of entities referred to by aggregate nouns is viewed as being the groups to which these entities belong, for example, a herd. The locus of entities referred to by individual type 1 nouns, which typically refer to domesticated animals and tools, is viewed as being their owners or makers.

Localized aspectual number is part of the inflection of verbs. This category indicates the number of times an action is performed or a condition occurs as well as the number of loci in which these performances or occurrences take place. Localized aspectual numbers form contrastive sets of two or three depending on the status yet to be ascertained systematically of the verb. With some verbs the localized aspectual numbers form a contrastive set of two: either the nondistributive and the distributive or the unitive and the nonunitive. With other verbs the localized aspectual numbers form a contras-

Table 10. Successionality

Successional 'one after the other'	*Nonsuccessional*	
jé·ñi-d, jé·ñi-ʔad (unitive)	*jé·ñ,* (unitive)	'to smoke object'
jéjjenʔi-ad, jéjjena-d (nonunitive)	*jéjjen* (nonunitive)	
béhi-ʔad (sg. obj., singular)	*béhi-* (sg. obj.)	'to get object'
bé·bhei-ad (sg. obj., multiple)		
ʔúʔi-ad (pl. obj., singular)	*ʔúʔi-* (pl. obj.)	
ʔúʔui-ad (pl. obj., multiple)		
ʔíʔi-ad	*ʔíʔi-*	'to drink object'
ṣóṣaʔañi-ʔad	*ṣóṣañ-*	'to cry (pl. subj.)'

tive set of three: the unitive, the repetitive, and the distributive. The unitive indicates a single action or condition at a single locus. The repetitive indicates several identical actions at a single locus. The nondistributive indicates a single locus, without specifying the number of actions or conditions. Both the nonunitive and the distributive indicate several identical actions or conditions at several loci (table 13).

Personal number is obligatorily associated with the category of person in: the personal pronouns; the demonstrative pronouns and auxiliaries; the subject personals, which constitute the stems of the subject-complex words; the object personals, which are part of the inflection of nouns, verbs, and postpositions; and the verb forms in the imperative. The category of personal number indicates either the number of entities referred to by the category of person or the number of loci in which the referents of the category of person are found.

In accordance with these two possibilities, personal numbers form two contrastive sets of two each. The contrastive set that enumerates loci is found only in the demonstratives (pronouns and auxiliaries), and the set that enumerates entities is found in all the other forms. The two personal numbers of the first contrastive set are the personal nondistributive and the personal distributive. The paradigm of the demonstrative pronouns and auxiliaries is: (nondistributive) *ʔí·da-ʔa, ʔíd-Ø*, proximal, and *héga-ʔi, hég-Ø*, distal; (distributive) *ʔíd(a)-m*, proximal, and *hég(a)-m*, distal. In these forms the nondistributive marker is *-ʔa, -ʔi, -Ø*, and the distributive marker is *-m*.

The personal nondistributive indicates a single locus, with one or several entities in it (for example, *hégaʔi há·ṣañ* 'that saguaro cactus' and *hégaʔi háhaṣañ* 'those saguaro cacti in a single cluster'). The personal distributive indicates several loci, with one or more entities per locus (*hégam háhaṣañ* 'those saguaro cacti, either several individual saguaros or several clusters of saguaros, here and there').

The two personal numbers of the other contrastive set, which is found in all forms except the demonstratives, are the personal singular and the personal nonsingular (or plural). The personal singular indicates a single entity, at a single locus. The personal nonsingular indicates several entities, at one or more loci. The paradigm of the personal pronouns is given in table 14. Except in the human familiar forms the singular marker is *-ʔi* and the plural marker *-m*; personal number is not a category in the nonhuman pronouns.

The subject personals are inflected for a contrast of number only in the first and second persons. When occurring without other elements in the subject-complex word the subject personals are: (first singular) *ʔañ*, (first plural) *ʔac*, (second singular) *ʔap*, (second plural) *ʔam*, (third person, nonindefinite nonhuman) *ʔo*, (third person indefinite human) *ʔam*. In the first and second person forms personal number and person are indicated jointly, with no segmentation into separate markers; personal number is not distinguished in the third person. When these elements are in second position in the subject-complex word (table 2) they are found in reduced form: first singular *-ñ, -n* (in *ma-ñ, ma-n-t, ku-ñ, ku-n-t*), first plural *-c, -t* (in *ma-c, ma-t-t, ku-c, ku-t-t*), second singular *-p* (in *ma-p, ma-p-t, ku-p, ku-p-t*), second plural *-m* (in *ma-m, ma-m-t, ku-m, ku-m-t*), third person nonindefinite nonhuman *-o, -Ø* (in *m-o, ma-Ø-t, k-o, ku-Ø-t*), third-person indefinite human *-m* (in the same combinations as the second plural subject personal, with which it is homonymous).

Table 11. Postpositional Number

Postpositional singular	*Postpositional distributive*	
bá·ṣo	*bábṣo*	'against'
míabidc	*mímiabidc*	'near, next to'
gáhi	*gá·ghai*	'across'
ʔéḍa	*ʔéʔeḍa*	'inside'
ʔóidk, ʔóidc	*ʔóʔoidk, ʔóʔoidc*	'behind, after'
ʔámjeḍ	*ʔáʔamjeḍ*	'from'
wéco	*wépco, wéʔeweco*	'under, below'
báʔij	*báʔabaʔij, bábaij*	'in front of'
dá·m	*dáʔadam*	'above'
tá·gio	*táʔatagio*	'in the direction of'
wé·gaj	*wéʔegaj, wéʔewegaj*	'behind'
wé·m	*wéʔewem*	'with'
wúi	*wúʔuwui*	'toward, to'

Table 12. Nominal Number

Individual 1 Nouns			
Singular	*Plural*	*Distributive*	
ṣóiga	*ṣóṣoiga*	*ṣóṣṣoiga*	'horse, pet'
wísilo	*wípsilo*	*wíppsilo*	'calf'
ká·wul	*kákawul*	*kákkawul*	'sheep'
káwiyu	*kákawiyu*	*kákkawiyu*	'horse'
dáikuḍ	*dáḍaikuḍ*	*dáḍḍaikuḍ*	'chair'
ˀíagta	*ˀíˀagta*	*ˀíˀˀagta*	'offering'

Individual 2 Nouns		
Singular	*Nonsingular*	
bán	*bá·ban*	'coyote'
gógs	*gógogs*	'dog'
máihogĭ	*mámaihog(ĭ)*	'centipede'
bí·	*víbi*	'food on a plate'
cíñ	*cí·ciñ, cé·ciñ*	'mouth'
móˀŏ	*mó·mĭ*	'head'
wúhĭ	*wú·pui*	'eye'
dóˀag	*dó·daˀag*	'mountain'

Mass Nouns		
Singular	*Nonsingular*	
wá·ga	*wá·paga*	'dough'
póṣol	*pópṣoˀol*	'corn gruel'
tóki	*tótki*	'cotton'
náwait	*náwppait*	'saguaro cactus wine'
mátai	*mámtai*	'ashes'
ˀóˀohia	*ˀóˀˀohia*	'sand'
ṣúdagĭ	*ṣúṣudagĭ*	'water'

Aggregate Nouns		
Nondistributive	*Distributive*	
háiwañ	*háhaiwañ*	'cattle, cow'
táḍai	*tátaḍai*	'road runner'
cúcul	*cúccul*	'chicken'
tótoñ	*tóttoñ*	'ant'
sígal	*sísigal*	'cigarette'
ˀáhid	*ˀáˀahid*	'year'
ñíˀokĭ	*ñíˀñeokĭ*	'words'

The paradigms of the object personals are given in table 15. In these number is indicated suppletively in the first person: *ñ-* singular, *t-* plural. Third person singular is indicated by *-j* in nouns, ∅- in verbs, and *g-* or ∅- in postpositions; third plural is *ha-* in all three paradigms. The second singular is *m-*; the second plural *ˀem-* is analyzed as containing this *m-* plus a nonsingular marker *ˀe-*.

In the imperative the singular is indicated by *-ñ* and the nonsingular by *-wo, -io, -o*. These markers are suffixed to the verb when nothing precedes it: (singular) *hími-ñ* 'go; walk!'; *béhi-ñ* 'get it!'; *síswa-ñ* 'spit!'; (plural) *híhimi-ñ-o, híhimi-o, híhim-o*; *béhi-wo, béhi-o*; *síswa-io*. When the verb is preceded by other material the imperative particle *g* is used, followed by the plural marker but no singular marker: (singular) . . . *g hím* 'go; walk!'; . . . *g bé·ˀi* 'get it!'; . . . *g síswa* 'spit!'; (plural) . . . *g-o híhim*; . . . *g-o bé·ˀi*; . . . *g-o síswa*.

Table 13. Localized Aspectual Number

Class 1 Verbs			
Unitive	*Repetitive*	*Distributive*	
bái, báhă	*bábbhe*	*bá·bhe*	'to ripen'
nái	*ná·nda*	*ná·nad*	'to make a fire'
hab céˀi-	*hab céce*	*hab cécce*	'to say something (primofactive)'
ˀíˀi-	*ˀí·ˀe*	*ˀí·ˀe*	'to drink (obj.)'
béhĕ	*bébbhe*	*bé·bhe*	'to get (sg. obj.)'
ˀúˀu	*ˀúˀˀu*	*ˀú·ˀu*	'to get (pl. obj.)'
béhidameḍ	*béhidammeḍ*	*bé·bheidop, bé·bheidameḍ*	'to go and get object for somebody'

Class 2 Verbs		
Unitive	*Nonunitive*	
héhem	*héhhem*	'to laugh'
wáhawa	*wáhawup*	'to take off object'
hím (sg. subj.) *híhim* (pl. subj.)	*híhhim*	'to walk'
hab júñ	*hab új̃ju*	'to do something (primofactive)'
jíwa (sg. subj.) *dada, dáiw* (pl. subj.)	*jíjiwha* (sg. subj.) *dáiwup* (pl. subj.)	'to arrive'
wó·ñ, wo·pon-	*wóppon*	'to pluck object'
ˀéi, ˀéṣ	*ˀéˀeṣa*	'to plant from seeds'
wá·g-	*wápga*	'to irrigate object'
céṣad (sg. subj.) *cé·ci(ṣa)d* (pl. subj.)	*cécṣaj*	'to rise'
kámṣ	*kámṣṣa*	'to put object in one's mouth'

Class 3 Verbs		
Nondistributive	*Distributive*	
cíkpan	*cíckpan*	'to work'
wóˀŏ (sg. subj.) *wó·pĭ* (pl. subj.)	*wóˀowop*	'to lie (animates)'
ká·c (sg. subj.) *wé·c* (pl. subj.)	*wéˀewec*	'to lie (inanimates)'
cékṣan (singular) *cékṣṣaṣ* (multiple)	*cécks̩an* (singular) *céckṣṣaṣ* (multiple)	'to draw one/several broken line(s) on object'

Table 14. Personal Number in Personal Pronouns other than Demonstratives

	Personal singular	Personal nonsingular
1st person	*ʔá·ñi-ʔi*	*ʔá·ci-m*
2d person	*ʔá·pi-ʔi*	*ʔá·pi-m*
3d person indefinite		
Nonhuman		
Unfamiliar	*há-s-cu*	
Familiar	*há-ʔi-cu*	
Human		
Unfamiliar	*hé-ḍa-ʔi*	*hé-ḍ(a)-m*
Familiar	*héma*	*háʔi*

-*ʔi* = personal singular marker
-*m* = personal nonsingular marker
NOTE: Personal number does not apply to the 3d-person nonhuman pronouns.

The first thing to observed about the way in which time is handled in Papago grammatical categories is the absence of a tense system. A tense system is a deictic system involving time, that is, a system in which there are one or more points of reference in terms of which temporal coordinates are established.

The only Papago grammatical category that comes close to this definition is aspectual distance. This category is part of the inflection of the subject complex words (see table 2). In the compound verb forms containing a subject complex word and a verb, aspectual distance indicates the degree of distance of the particular event or condition referred to by the verb. There are two members of the category of aspectual distance: the remote and the nonremote. The remote indicates that the statement in question is an account of a particular event or condition that is remote from the speaker's point of reference. The remote marker (-*ḍ*) is used very infrequently, only in myths and Juan Dolores's (1909–1951) autobiography. The category of aspectual distance is either limited to formal language or being lost. Examples of the occurrence of the remote marker (-*ḍ*) in Papago utterances are: (7) *Ku-t-ḍ ʔam híhhim.* 'We used to go there repeatedly.' (8) *Ku-ḍ-s héms hí uḍ hégam si wépeg ʔemáṣcamokam.* '(At the time) I thought wrongly that they were the first ones to go to school.'

The determination of whether or not aspectual distance is a tense system in Papago should be based on whether or not the notion of distance entails temporal relations to the exclusion of spatial ones. This does not seem to be the case, since the notion of distance is found in another grammatical category, spatial distance. Spatial distance enters into the constitution of the stems of the demonstratives, both pronouns and auxiliaries (*ʔí·daʔa* 'this (one)', *ʔídam* 'these', *hégaʔi* 'that (one)', *hégam* 'those'. It is also part of the inflection of the locatives, both pronouns and auxiliaries (see table 3). Spatial distance indicates how far away either the entity or location referred to is from the speaker's point of reference. Spatial distance is manifested in contrastive sets of either two degrees or four degrees of distance depending on whether it occurs with the demonstratives or the locatives. In the demonstratives the two degrees of distance are: proximal and distal. In the locatives the degrees of distance are: proximal, infradistal, distal, and extradistal. The proximal indicates that the referent is close to the speaker's point of reference; the infradistal indicates that it is neither close nor far; the distal that it is far; the extradistal that it is very far.

The above indicates that the manifestations of the two grammatical categories of aspectual distance and spatial distance are variations of the same underlying notion and that tense variations are due to associations with verbs and nouns. Moreover, since the notion of distance in Papago entails both temporal and spatial relations, it has to be interpreted as pertaining to a broader notion that covers both types of relations. Tópology might be such a notion.

The assertion that Papago has a tense system could also be made mistakenly in connection with another inflectional category, aspectual boundedness, and a particle, the nonfactual *wo*, which are often translated into English by the marking of tense on verb forms.

Aspectual boundedness (table 16) is part of the inflection of the subject-complex words (see table 2). In

Table 15. Personal Number in the Object Personals

		Personal singular		Personal nonsingular	
Nouns	1st person	*ñ-kí·*	'my house'	*t-kí·*	'our house'
	2d person	*m-kí·*	'your house'	*ʔe-m-kí·*	'your house'
	3d person	*kí·-j*	'his/her/its house'	*ha-kí·*	'their house'
Verbs	1st person	*ñ-má·*	'gave me'	*t-má·*	'gave us'
	2d person	*m-má·*	'gave you'	*ʔe-m-má·*	'gave you'
	3d person	*∅-má·*	'gave him/her/it'	*ha-má·*	'gave them'
Postpositions	1st person	*ñ-wé·m*	'with me'	*t-wé·m*	'with us'
	2d person	*m-wé·m*	'with you'	*ʔe-m-wé·m*	'with you'
	3d person	*g-wé·m, ∅-wé·m*	'with him/her/it'	*ha-wé·m*	'with them'

the compound verb forms containing a subject-complex word and a verb, aspectual boundedness indicates whether or not the event or condition referred to by the verb is viewed as being bounded, as having a beginning and an end. There are two members of the category of aspectual boundedness, bounded and nonbounded. The bounded indicates that the event or condition referred to by the verb is viewed as having a beginning and an end, whether or not it has duration. The nonbounded indicates that the event or condition referred to by the verb is viewed as not having a beginning or an end (Alvarez 1969:2 corroborates this interpretation).

The bounded is indicated by the bounded marker *-t* in the subject-complex word, with the short variant of the verb theme except in the durative; the nonbounded lacks the *-t* and has the long variant of the verb theme. In the bounded, the durative (marked by *-d* after the long theme) is found only with the nonfactual particle *wo* (here in the form *o*); the nondurative occurs with and without *wo* (*o*).

The nonfactual particle *wo* indicates that the statement in which it occurs "has reality only in the heart of the speaker; it is an idea or thought" (Alvarez 1969:11, 79).

The present analysis rules out the category of aspectual boundedness and the nonfactual particle as candidates for a tense system in Papago. It also shows that the nonfactual particle does not involve time in any way but rather the concept of knowledge status. Aspectual boundedness, on the other hand, does involve time since the contrast between having boundaries and not having boundaries with respect to the events or conditions referred to by the verb has to do with their having a beginning and an end in time.

The notion of events having or not having temporal boundaries is implicit in another Papago grammatical category, namely ranking. Ranking is part of the inflection of verbs. This category indicates whether or not the action takes place for the first time, or by extension as a unique occurrence. There are two ranking aspects: the primofactive and the habituative. The primofactive indicates that the action is taking place for the first time, or as a unique occurrence; the habituative indicates that the action is a habitual one, or one among a series. The category of ranking seems to be limited to a very small number of verbs. The verbs to which it applies, however, occur extremely frequently. Examples are: (primofactive) *hab céˀi-* 'to say something, to talk in a certain way', *hab júñ-* 'to do something, to act in a certain way', *húgi-* 'to eat object'; (habituative) *hab káij* 'to say something, etc.', *hab wúa* 'to do something, etc.', *kúˀa* 'to eat object'. The forms illustrated for the primofactive of 'say' and 'do' are in the unitive localized aspectual number; the corresponding habituative verbs do not indicate the oppositions of this grammatical category, shown for the primofactive verbs in table 16.

The major difference between aspectual boundedness and ranking is whether the linguistic context or the cultural context serves as the frame of reference in terms of which temporal boundaries can be said to be present or absent.

In the case of aspectual boundedness the frame of reference is provided by the immediate linguistic context. Thus one event (e.g., getting somewhere) may or may not mark the boundaries of another event (e.g., singing). It does in the bounded: 'he started/finished singing when I got there'. It does not in the nonbounded: 'he was singing when I got there'. In the case of ranking the frame of reference is provided by the cultural context. The latter may be a gathering within which somebody 'speaks for the first time' (the primofactive) as opposed to 'having a conversation with somebody else' (the habituative). The cultural context may also be the culture as a whole, as when certain food or customs were introduced, that is 'were eaten for the first time' (primofactive) as opposed to 'eaten as a staple food' (habituative).

The notion of boundedness in Papago does not necessarily involve temporal boundaries. In the case of

Table 16. Aspectual Boundedness

Bounded	without *-wo* (nondurative)	*Húan ˀat cíkp.*	'John worked.'
		Húan ˀat ñío.	'John spoke.'
		Húan ˀat héhe.	'John laughed.'
	with *-wo* (durative and nondurative)	*Húan ˀat o cíkp.*	'John will work.'
		Húan ˀat o cíkpana-d.	'John will be working.'
		Húan ˀat o ñío.	'John will speak.'
		Húan ˀat o ñíoka-d.	'John will be speaking.'
		Húan ˀat o héhe.	'John will laugh.'
		Húan ˀat o héhema-d.	'John will be laughing.'
Nonbounded		*Húan ˀo cíkpan.*	'John is/was working, works.'
		Húan ˀo ñíok.	'John is/was speaking, speaks.'
		Húan ˀo héhem.	'John is/was laughing, laughs.'

SOURCE: Alvarez 1969:1.

another grammatical category, entity boundedness, the reference is to spatial rather than temporal boundaries. Entity boundedness is manifested in the indefinite quantifiers that are auxiliaries in compound nominal forms such as 'a little water' in contrast to 'a few beans'. This category indicates a contrast between having boundaries and not having boundaries for the entities referred to by the nouns or nominal expressions entering into compound nominal forms. It has to do with these entities having a beginning and an end in space.

The manifestations of the two grammatical categories of aspectual boundedness and entity boundedness seem to be variations of the same underlying notion, boundedness. These variations are due to associations with verbs or nouns. Hence the common denominator again is topological.

An additional way in which time is expressed in the Papago inflectional system is through the two aspectual categories of extensionality and resumptivity.

Extensionality is part of the inflection of verbs. This category indicates the duration of the action or condition referred to by the verb. There are two extensional aspects: the durative and the immediative. The durative indicates an action or condition that has extension. The immediative indicates that the action immediately precedes another action, which can be either stated or implied. Examples of the durative (marked by *-da-, -d*) are: (9) *Wágt-da-ñ!* 'Be digging it!' (10) *M g abṣ ˀi híma-d!* 'Just keep on walking!' (11) *M g abṣ ˀi híma-d-c o ˀip hékid gḍhú jíwa!* 'Keep on walking until you get there!' (12) *Ññé·nḍa-d-k!* 'Wait for me (implied: so I can go with you)!' (13) *ˀAn ˀapt o híma-d!* 'You will keep on walking!' Examples of the immediative (marked by *-kaˀi*) are: (14) . . . *jíwa-kaˀi* '. . . immediately upon arriving' (15) . . . *ˀam ˀi tóˀa-him-kaˀi-k gmhú hí·* '. . . right after he had been putting them there he left'.

Resumptivity is part of the inflection of verbs. This category indicates whether or not a given action or condition can be resumed after an interruption. There are two resumptive aspects: the interruptive and the completive. The interruptive indicates that the action or condition can be resumed after an interruption, or that the action occurs in interrupted portions. The completive indicates that the action is definitely terminated. Examples of the interruptive (marked by *-him, -hi-*) are: (16) *Cíkpana-him ˀo.* 'He has been working, he was working (i.e., he is not working now but he may be working again).' (17) *Nt o mél-hi-d.* 'I'll be running in spurts (running for a while and then walking and then running again).' Examples of the completive (marked by *-okaˀi, -ok*) are: (18) *Pt o ˀíˀ-okaˀi napt wóho ˀi abṣ o jíwa!* 'Have a drink (and finish it) although you did not come for that reason!' (polite formula). (19) *Kupt hégi o ñéid-ok wo ˀi ˀói!* 'After you have seen it, follow it!' (20) *Nt o kú·p-ok g tíanna k o mˀói.* 'I'll close the store and then I'll go with you (I'll go with you after I have closed the store).' (21) *M g ˀip ˀegégusid-ok!* 'Go ahead and finish eating first (implied: before you do something else)!' (22) *B ˀapt o kú·p-okaˀi!* 'Make sure that you have closed it (implied: before you do something else)!'

A final way in which time is expressed in the Papago inflectional system is through the locative auxiliaries (see table 3). In the absence of an analysis in depth of the nonlocative meanings of the locative auxiliaries the following tentative observations can be offered: There is no equation of locative auxiliaries to the notions of present, past, and future. Rather, aspectual meanings involving duration, immediacy, and indefiniteness are conveyed through some of them. These meanings are illustrated in Papago utterances obtained in texts in examples (23)–(36). The locative auxiliary *ˀi* apparently indicates immediacy: (23) *ˀI ˀat hú o ˀágckwa g tó·lo!* 'The bull is going to horn him momentarily!' The auxiliary *ˀan* seems to indicate continuous action: (24) *ˀan méḍ* 'to flow (for a river), to drive'. (25) *ˀan dáˀa-* 'to fly (for a bird)'. (26) *ˀan hím* 'He is going, walking.' (27) *ˀan abṣ hímhim* 'He is just wandering around.' (28) *Mantp ˀanhu hébi o ˀi béi g cíkpan k ˀan o cíkpank hékaj o gégus g ñhúˀul.* 'Whenever I get a job I'll work (on and on) in order to feed my grandmother.' The auxiliary *ˀam* perhaps marks indefinite time: (29) *Napt ˀam o píastam?* 'Do you intend to go to the feast (sometime)?' (30) *No ˀam a shú·k?* 'Is it (ever) warm?' (31) *ˀAm ˀi géˀege hégaˀi baˀag-má·maḍ.* 'They became big, those baby eagles.' (32) *Tatṣ mo ˀom cú·c* . . . 'The coming days (i.e. the days that stand somewhere) . . .'. (33) *Nt a ˀá·ñi héjel ˀam o ˀi vú·ṣank ˀam o ˀemˀá·gĭ matt hékid o ˀi háˀas tjé·ñgĭ.* 'I'll go out alone (sometime), and then (later) I'll tell you people when we should close our meeting.' (34) *ˀAm ˀi ˀehohónt.* 'They got married (recently).' (35) . . . *mañ ˀamhú hab ˀá·g.* '. . . which I have already talked about.' (36) . . . *ˀam áha ˀi ˀáˀamic g ˀú·pio mat hás másma wabṣ spéhegim o béi g cú·kug* '. . . later on Skunk figured out an easy way of getting the meat'.

The semantic characteristics of Papago may reveal something of Papago world view.

Regarding the way in which the concept of multiplicity is manifested the following observations can be made. First, multiplicity in Papago involves an unusual number of ways of conceiving of the opposition between one and more than one since three semantic variables are at play, namely, entities, occurrences, and loci, which can function either independently of one another or in conjunction with one another. Second, the notion of locus is defined in spatial terms. It is given priority over the notions of entity and of occurrence when it functions jointly with either one or the other (Mathiot 1967:210). The importance given to the notion of locus is reflected in the proposal that the cognitive content of the category of nominal number is manifested in an opposition between closeness and dispersion (Mathiot 1967:234–235). Third, no distinction is made between entities and occurrences in the way they relate to the notion of locus: both entities and occurrences may or may not function jointly with locus.

These observations raise the following questions regarding Papago world view: Why is there so much emphasis on single versus multiple? Why is so much importance given to space? And finally, to what extent are entities and occurrences viewed as having similar attributes and consequently as being basically similar rather than different?

The tentative answers to these questions rest on obvious ethnographic information for the first two and more subtle linguistic and ethnolinguistic corroborative evidence for the third.

The Papago tribe is and apparently has always been constituted by several thousand members grouped in small villages that are widely scattered over an immense and arid territory. It is tempting therefore to suggest that the emphasis given to the notion of single versus multiple and to space is in keeping with the ecology. It remains to be investigated whether or not languages whose speakers live in a similar ecology (relatively few people scattered over a wide and difficult territory) give as much importance as Papago does to the two notions of multiplicity and space. Note that what is to be inquired into is the relative part played by these notions in the language as a whole. The particular ways in which these notions are manifested in a given language (for example, in the lexicon rather than in the grammar, as interrelated or independent of one another) raise additional questions not directly pertinent to the relation of language to ecology.

The possibility of entities and occurrences being regarded as basically similar is very intriguing to the western mind in view of the Aristotelian tradition of opposing these notions. The Papago grammatical categories manifesting the notions of distance and boundedness provide corroborative evidence for the possibility of entities and occurrences being regarded as similar by the Papagos. Both entities and occurrences can be characterized in terms of distance and boundedness since it was argued that both distance and boundedness are topological notions rather than temporal or spatial ones on the basis that they apply equally to entities and to occurrences. Kenneth L. Hale (personal communication 1974) suggested "it is still possible" that some events are regarded by Papagos as having will (*cégĭtoidag*), although this idea comes not from Papago grammar but from Papago philosophy. In the analysis in depth of Papago nominal number, having will was shown to be the distinguishing attribute of animate entities (Mathiot 1967:223–224). Once again, then, entities and occurrences are characterized in terms of the same attribute, that of having or not having will.

These observations raise two interrelated and unanswered questions. Do the Papagos distinguish between entities and occurrences in their taxonomy of the world? What is the meaning of "nounhood" and "verbhood" in Papago? In other words, to what phenomena or qualities of phenomena do the word class statuses of noun and verb correspond?

Regarding the handling of time in Papago grammatical categories two general obervations can be made. First, although no tense system exists in the grammar the native lexicon has a system for specific time designations that covers what a Westerner would call the present, the past, and the future (*ˀíd ˀi táṣkaj* 'today', *hému* 'now'; *táko* 'yesterday'; *háˀakid* 'last year', *gḍhú héma ˀi tóñiabĭk* 'two summers ago', *hékĭhú* 'a long time ago'; *síˀalim* 'tomorrow', *gḍ héma síˀalim* 'the day after tomorrow'). Second, in the analysis of the grammatical categories manifesting distance and boundedness, rather than dealing with time and space as separate notions it was found necessary to postulate a broader notion that would combine them. Topology was suggested as such a notion without further inquiring into the relationship between time and space.

These observations raise one basic question regarding Papago world view: What is the relationship between time and space in Papago? In other words, how do time and space fit into the Papago taxonomy of the world? Two alternative answers suggest themselves: Time and space are on a par with one another as variants of a single broad notion, namely, topology; or time is subordinate to space in the sense that it is conceived of in spatialized terms; consequently the single broad notion needed is space and not topology; or the second alternative is the one that impressionistically seems to be most likely. It is interesting to note that it goes against the assertion, attributed to Benjamin Lee Whorf, that time is never treated like space in American Indian languages.

The effort to inquire into what some of the striking semantic characteristics of Papago grammatical categories reveal of Papago world view has raised three broad problem areas: the relationship between language and ecology, the Papago taxonomy of the world, and the relationship between word-class status and a given taxonomy of the world. It is clear that in order to deal with these problem areas one cannot remain within the confines of grammatical categories but should take into consideration every aspect of language—the grammar as a whole as well as the lexicon.

Contemporary Pima

SALLY GIFF PABLO

The history and culture change of the Pima are described in other chapters in this volume. This chapter considers the present and future: how the Pima may shape themselves. Two different examples of present-day Pima thought on government in the broadest sense—the public good—are presented. Tape recorded in 1973, these narratives were unrehearsed but eloquent as the words of old men can be. Literally hundreds of other speeches by numerous individuals would have served the purpose equally well, but these two speeches were selected because they depict, so differently, the present and the desired future.

The first perspective is expressed by Gov. Alexander Lewis, Sr. (fig. 1), who has faced many issues involving both individual tribal members who lived in a modernistic world and the future of the tribe as a whole. The second viewpoint is presented by Lester Lewis, an elderly spokesman for an organized segment of the population who viewed contemporary Pima life as a loss of old Pima ways and as an unwise use of land, water, and self-government. (These men are not related.) Each man was confident that he was expressing a view shared by other members of the tribe. Governor Lewis emphasized education, industrialization, land leasing, and the continuation of a way of life the Pima obtained through daily interaction with a dominant outside culture over a period of years. On this view the great change was from the old Pima ways into a new order that arrived with American civilization. The future means the completion of this process primarily by obtaining more education for the next generation.

U. of Ariz., Ariz. State Mus., Tucson: 25851.
Fig. 1. Inauguration of Gila River Indian community officers. Gov. Alexander Lewis, Sr., sworn in by Judge William Roy Rhodes. Photograph by Helga Teiwes, Jan. 1973.

The other speaker, Lester Lewis, does not completely accept the new civilization, which he terms a 'lying-on-top (kind of) saying' (*dá·m wóʔokam háʔicu ʔá·ga*), an expression referring primarily to regulation of the tribe through the Indian Reorganization Act of 1934. Under this legislation the tribe was to exercise powers of self-government and to establish a tribal council as its central governing body. But for Lester Lewis the true base of Pima life was and should be an aspect of the old ways, which he refers to as 'lasting well-being' (*ká·cim ʔápʔedag*). For him the desired future is basically a defense of the land on which the Pima may continue to farm on a family basis or, at most, with families cooperating with relatives and neighbors within local communities. Industrialization, and especially industrialization under central control, are not for him.

The two speeches were selected from many speeches, given in the Pima language, at public meetings. Governor Lewis gave his speech in his chambers in the tribal administration building in June 1973 for the purpose of the *Handbook*. The intent of the interviewer was to obtain a view of Pima life as perceived by the person in the highest position in the tribal government. Governor Lewis found it natural to stress the various developmental programs that his administration had been involved in, while Lester Lewis, speaking in a village at a conservative Farmers Association meeting, put an expected stress on the traditional activities and values of farming.

The Gila River Indian Community is located in south-central Arizona about 35 miles south of Phoenix and 69 miles north of Tucson ("History of the Pima," fig. 1, this vol.). The reservation is comprised of 372,000 acres of land. The Gila River sustained a native agricultural economy until the usurpation of water by upstream farmers. Governor Lewis addresses this problem and states that this is the reason why the tribe must look to other economic sources. Beginning in 1914 a program of allotting two 10-acre parcels to members of the tribe went into effect, ending in 1921. Each person received a 10-acre "primary" parcel with water provided, and a 10-acre "secondary" parcel in the desert with no water. At least in some cases very young allottees received their entire 20 acres in unirrigated desert land. This program required the registration of the original 20-acre plots and the division of the plots by probate according to Arizona State law among the heirs of an original allottee. It resulted in fragmentation of the original parcels into uneconomic units and in heirship problems. These problems continued when water was partially restored in 1925–1930 when the federal government constructed the San Carlos Irrigation Project for the Pima (they were not its only beneficiaries; half of the water went to non-Indians surrounding the reservation). The result was that many Pimas found it more feasible to lease their irrigated land than to farm it on a family basis as in the past. The leases are administered through a central office operated by the Bureau of Indian Affairs.

The Gila River Indian Community is governed by a 17-member tribal council with a governor and lieutenant governor who are elected every three years. A tribal constitution, which was adopted in 1960, dictates the procedures for the election of these officers. Council members are elected from seven political districts, based on population, and serve staggered terms.

The tribal council meets twice a month, as do the five standing committees (Economic Development, Natural Resources, Government and Management, Health and Social, and Education). Membership on the standing committees consists of four council members and one member from the community-at-large. There is also an executive committee.

The Gila River Farmers Association was organized in the 1930s to form a cohesive group who could deal effectively with the federal government on water issues facing the tribe. In 1981 the membership of the Association consisted mainly of the original members, who are now elderly men and few in number. Other members include elderly women plus a few young people who adhere to the basic philosophy of the Association, which is self-reliance, and nongovernment intrusion, and subsistence farming from the land. The occasion of Lester Lewis's speech was a regular semimonthly meeting of the Farmers Association, which was held at his residence in Wet Camp in July 1973. Present at the meeting were two young tribal council members who were sympathetic to the cause of the group and who assumed their representative roles by maintaining communication with the Association and by supporting their views at the tribal council level.

Acceptance of the two young council members by the group was indicated by many speeches and instructions directed to them. Although Lester Lewis's speech was directed to the entire Association membership present at the meeting, his speech also includes instructions and encouragement for the two council members. As a former member of the tribal council and an elderly tribesman, Lester Lewis was free to bring up the dark side of government, touching on matters such as self-gain and misuse of authority.

Speech by Alexander Lewis, Sr.

I will tell you something about the present Pima way of life here on the Gila River Indian Reservation.

Pima Farmers

Through the generations we have been told that the people living on this earth worked the soil and raised food crops for sustenance. It was at that time that large amounts of water flowed in the rivers and from this they received life and continued their existence and received their well-being. From this they remembered their creator who created the earth for them that they may dwell and work on the land. As years went by leadership was by appointment of someone who was respected and well thought of. The descendants of his house would take over the leadership when the appointed one passed on, and from this there would be the new leadership. Then through the years it happened that the Whites made something for the Indian people that they should use to govern themselves, which is called the Indian Reorganization Act. It happened that from this the people (*ʔÓʔodham*) made their laws for self-government. They go by these laws, which are for the benefit of all the *ʔÓʔodham*, but from these changes many [disadvantageous] things emerged.

Loss of Water

In the past our people worked the land. But then it happened that the water was gone and no longer could anything grow again on their land because gone was the water, and we [must] see things differently now. From this poverty approached the *ʔÓʔodham*.

The *ʔÓʔdham* have always had a deep concern toward one another and were content with their way of life. In the past there was no need to change this way of life. Today we see that this is not satisfactory. As children are born and grow, each generation will want some kind of change.

As a result of the self-government that I spoke about the *ʔÓʔodham* wanted more education than what the government had been providing for them. In the past the *ʔÓʔodham* were able to live satisfactorily on the crops they harvested from their land. Today this is not possible, for no longer can we work the land as in the past. For this reason the *ʔÓʔodham* recognized the need for education; the need to learn new skills; the need for employment opportunities in well-paid jobs. All this will change our way of life, how we live, and how we will live in the future.

Land Use

Self-government has allowed the *ʔÓʔodham* to administer reservation lands. Lands are now being leased in exchange for monetary gains in contrast to working the land for their livelihood.

The tribe designated certain tribal lands for industrial parks to bring industry to the reservation and to create employment where people will be employed in well-paid jobs from which they can become self-sufficient. Through this self-sufficiency they may acquire more education and teach their children the value of higher education. In the past there were no jobs for the people where they could earn money to send their children to schools where money is needed, such as public schools and universities. Now that jobs are available through the industrial parks, families can earn sufficient income to improve their standard of living and to provide advanced education for their children. The young Pimas are encouraged to pursue higher education and to return to the reservation to use their skills [technical and professional] in working for the good of the tribe and for their own well-being.

Health

Through the many studies that have been done on the *ʔÓʔodham* it has been learned that our death rates are greater than that of White people. Our health is generally poor and we live shorter lives. The poor living conditions of the Pima may bring about the high death rates and short life span. We do not have adequate housing, nor do we have running water in our homes as White people have in their homes.

Education

Many of our people do not have the education and training necessary for certain high-paying jobs and for that reason cannot get jobs. There stands this school [Gila River Career Center] where one can learn [a trade] in whatever he chooses to work. But it happens that people do not seem to understand very well the reason why they are learning something. Do they understand where this will lead them? Will it be to their benefit or not to their benefit to enter training? Many times it happens that they do not complete their educational plans. Something happens and they fall short and do not finish that which they went to learn.

As we look at the people's way of life it appears that the people must understand that what they do will be to their benefit, for the benefit of those for whom they work, and by this their way of life on this earth will be good.

Speech by Lester Lewis

I will speak of this self-government that we talk about, which began in the 1930s. It states that we are the government, I, you, all *ʔÓʔodham* living on this earth. I have a right; you have a right; we have the right in all things. Because you elected your councilman, your governor, your lieutenant governor, they only serve you.

What has happened today? Many who are bucking us [the Farmers Association] say that the association is no longer needed. They say that the association was useful only at the time when we fought for our irrigation water. They say that it is over and it is meaningless and we speak uselessly. Many have said that we are just old people who gather to eat together and call these gathering meetings. Why is it that this one person who is elected to a position speaks to me in this manner, then he asks me, "What do you know? Did you go where the old men gathered?" I answer, "They are old people.

U. of Ariz., Ariz. State Mus., Tucson: 35841.

Fig. 2. Basket dancers during the Mul-Chu-Tha (*mélcuda* 'running'), an annual fair in Sacaton that raises money for youth activities. The women wear skirts decorated with traditional basketry designs and carry feather wands. Photograph by Helga Teiwes, Sacaton, Ariz., Feb. 1973.

It is nothing to you. Only to me is it meaningful. For what reason should I tell you what they discuss? If I were to tell you, you would not understand."

It is true they first met at Blackwater and named themselves "Farmers Association." They sat and planned for the purpose of getting our water back. Already the water was shut off and they sent word to Washington and the water was turned back on.

And it is that you speak of Harvey Adams, that he is not a resident. This man's relatives lived here before they moved to Salt River [Reservation]. They live there and have all rights just as we have here. These rights were passed on to us and called a 'lying-on-top saying'. It is not good that 'lying-on-top saying'. It is this that we speak that is the truth.

All this is the truth that you who were elected to the tribal council must not be afraid of. There lay our records from way back that the Pima are gentle people. They just sit and listen and observe what they are doing to us. It is not right. Well, you are turning around now and finally saying what you think. You are challenging and you are taking part. You are speaking the truth. You are standing on the truth now, do not fear it. From this I am not just talking. The truth is spoken for what is yours, what is your well-being, true sayings, lasting sayings. Look, it is this. The ancient people said that lasting sayings (*ká·cim ʔá·ga*) is the truth and it is *ʔÓʔodham* well-being (*ʔápʔedag*) and it is the *ʔÓʔodham* way of life.

And there came to me someone and said, "How can we say 'peace' in the Pima language? What is it called?" I said, "The ancient ones would say *ká·cim ʔápʔedag* 'lasting well being', it is a lasting saying (*ká·cim ʔá·ga*) and it is peace."

Land Use

There is a question about the land. Many from the outside have asked to lease Indian land. What will happen to the people? Where will they build their homes? Where will they live? When I was on the tribal council there were requests to lease land. I opposed these requests because we are a growing tribe and we are crowding up this ground that is our property. The land is ours and we own a portion of that water and will use it to plant crops. The ones who want to lease our lands are saying that the *ʔÓʔodhum* are lazy and are not farming. They say that we don't know how to farm. It is not so. Back in 1930 there were government workers in every district; so-called farmers who sat and waited for the *ʔÓʔodham* farmers to ripen their crops of wheat, beans, and whatever other crops were planted. Only then would the government worker pay the farmers a visit to ask what kind of crops, and how much, was harvested. The information was recorded and reports sent to the government in Washington. They would tell them that they taught the Indians how to farm. Never did they walk among the people, but they got a good name and got promoted in their work. This is how it is. But they say that the Pima cannot make it on farming. Do not believe this. They are making money on Indian land. What are we, the owners of the land, to do? There will be people who will want to bribe you to get Indian lands. Do not believe them. This will get you nowhere. This is the way it has been for many years. You've got to talk and you've got to know what to say. . . .

Conclusion

Why are the recorded Pima words of these two elders presented here rather than an academic discussion of the contemporary scene? To state it very simply, this is the Pima way. Our tribe has what is by White American standards an extreme interest in holding forth on the public good. This is all done orally at many village meetings where old people express their views and instruct the younger generation of Pimas on traditional Pima life. It would therefore be unusual for a relatively young Pima to write an article based on personal conclusions. My purpose is to convey what is normal for the Pima rather than to innovate.

The translations are based on actual talks, which are now stored on tape and in bilingual transcript. I have deleted certain portions of the original, condensed some portions by changing the word order in sentences, and felt free to use my own interpretation and sentence structure of the Pima language into English.

In conclusion I submit the following information taken from the latest reports on the status of the Gila River Indian Community. (Another independently governed community of Pimas lives on the Salt River Reservation east of Scottsdale, Arizona. Historically they are offshoots of the Gila River Pimas. Both reservation communities include Maricopa Indians as well as Pimas. The Maricopa speak a language unrelated to Pima-Papago but are longstanding friends and allies of the Pima.)

A 1977 reservation housing and population census (Gila River Indian Community 1977) showed an on-reservation population of 6,744. An additional 2,000 may be dispersed throughout the United States. Of the 6,744, 11 percent were under 4 years; 26 percent were 4–14 years; 22 percent were 15–24 years; 23 percent were 25–44 years; 12 percent were 45–59 years; 6 percent were 65 years and older.

Total housing units occupied were 1,456, 60 percent of them considered to be substandard. Substandard homes lacked one or more of: electricity, indoor plumbing or water, and certain structural or construction features.

Elementary school education on the reservation is provided by two Bureau of Indian Affairs schools; two

Roman Catholic schools; one public school; and one community school for kindergarten and first grade. Some children attend the off-reservation elementary schools in nearby towns. High school students attend public schools in Chandler, Casa Grande, Coolidge, Tempe, Tolleson, Phoenix, and BIA boarding schools in Phoenix, Arizona; Riverside, California; and Brigham City, Utah. The majority of college students attend junior colleges and universities in Arizona. Others are in universities throughout the United States. The number of students receiving financial aid from the BIA and the tribe in 1981 totaled 117. Other students were on scholarships and private funds. It can be estimated that at least 200 tribal members were enrolled in institutions of higher education.

The three main categories of employment on the reservation are agriculture, industry, and government. In 1977 the median family income was $5,417 with per capita income at $1,217. Table 1, from a January 1981 report of the tribal Office of Economic Development, shows sources of employment on the reservation. The 1981 unemployment rates fluctuate between 30 and 35 percent, a decrease from the early 1970s when unemployment rates were 45–50 percent.

Public transportation is nonexistent on the reservation. This interferes with securing and retaining employment. Automobile ownership is a necessity, and those without automobiles depend on others for transportation, often involving monetary exchange for the service. The five grocery stores on the reservation are sometimes the only means of obtaining groceries for those without transportation. Most people purchase groceries in the nearby towns of Chandler, Coolidge, Case Grande, and Phoenix at prices much lower than the reservation-based stores. Of the five grocery stores, one is owned and managed by a tribal member.

In general there is mutual respect among federal, state, and tribal governments. Tribal administration of certain federal and state funds provides services to the people without jeopardizing the sovereignty of the Gila River Indian Community.

Table 1. Employment on Gila River Reservation, 1981

Source of Employment	*Indian Employees*	*Total Employees*
Gila River tribe	508	536
Bureau of Indian Affairs	115	136
Public school system	62	135
Federal Indian Health Service	59	80
Career Center (county)	7	42
Industrial parks (3)	208	597
Commercial	33	62
Tourism (Arts and Crafts Center)	25	26
Agriculture (tribal farms)	103	146
Other	40	119

SOURCE: Gila River Indian Community 1981.

Lower Pima

TIMOTHY DUNNIGAN

Identity

Most Mexican Pimas claim a special social and legal status apart from non-Indians, whom they call *blancos* (Spanish for 'Whites'), *dúdkam* or *ǯúǯkam* (the Pima word for 'Mexicans'), or, in Spanish, *yoris* (borrowed from the Yaqui to mean 'non-Indians'). This terminology is used by the Pimas when forced to argue the primacy of indigenous rights over competitive claims from outside the community. The Pimas are an enclaved and threatened minority living for the most part in small satellite settlements around the larger Mestizo-controlled towns. Even where they are physically integrated with the non-Indian population, social boundaries continue to separate the two groups.

As subsistence farmers, the Pimas appear to differ little from the poor Mestizos in material culture. This is particularly true of the more assimilated lowland groups where a common sense of Indian heritage may serve only to promote family alliances in political matters. The more conservative highland Pimas display a greater number of culture differences from the local non-Indian population, although these are not elaborated to the same extent as among their eastern neighbors the Tarahumara or the Yaqui Indians to the west.

Much remains to be learned about Pima cultural antecedents. Field research has tended to focus on isolated traits that appear to be uniquely Pima or at least Indian. This kind of salvage ethnography has not produced a great deal of information. The rapid culture change that the Pimas have undergone in historic times has made reconstructions extremely difficult. The most significant facts to be studied relate to the dynamics of interethnic relationships and the processes of social group maintenance that have allowed the Pimas to survive.

Language

The only areas where linguistic research on Lower Pima has been conducted in modern times are Onavas and Maycoba. Faubert (1975) reported that only one elderly person had an extensive knowledge of Pima at Onavas. The dialect of Onavas is quite similar, at least in its morphophonemic aspects, to that of the Upper Pima–Papago (Hale 1965) but is markedly different in both phonology and syntax from the Pima dialects spoken in the mountains around Maycoba. The two principal divisions of the Lower Pima, the highland *ʔóob* and the lowland *ʔóʔodam*, have but slight knowledge of each other, although they do recognize their linguistic affinities.*

There appear to be at least two subdialects of highland or Yécora Pima. The Pimas residing at Yécora and Maycoba characterize the speech of those living in the vicinity of Yepachi as an intelligible version of Pima, that is, *ʔóob nóʔŏk*, but one that is articulated differently and contains some special vocabulary not widely known outside the area. Almost all the older Maycoba Pimas and a majority of those under 25 years of age speak their native language as well as the local dialect of Spanish. A few women claim to understand only Pima. Informants report that the same patterns of language fluency exist among the Yepacheños.

The following outline summarizes the present-day geographic, cultural, and linguistic divisions of the Lower Pimas:

Highland Pima (Yécoras or *ʔóob*)
- Yécora, Maycoba, and satellite ranchos (*máykiṣ ʔóob*)
- Yepachi, Tutuaca, and satellite ranchos (*yúpiṣ ʔóob*)

Lowland Pima (*ʔóʔodam*)
- Onavas (Névome)
- Ures, Horcasitas, and satellite ranchos (Ures)

Territory

The Lower Pimas of northwestern Mexico once occupied a large portion of east-central Sonora and adjacent areas in extreme western Chihuahua. According to Sauer (1934:38), the Lower Pimas were divided into three populations. The Yécoras inhabited the high valleys of the Sierra Madre Occidental between Yécora and Tutuaca. The Névomes, who lived on both sides of the

*The lowland Lower Pima speak a dialect of Pima-Papago that can be written in the orthography described in the orthographic footnote in "Pima and Papago: Introduction" (this vol.).

The language of the highland Lower Pima has the following phonemes: (voiceless stops and affricate) *p*, *t* (dental), *č* (lamino-alveolar), *k*, *ʔ*; (voiced stops and affricate) *b*, *d*, *ǯ*, *g*; (voiceless fricatives) *s* (apico-alveolar slit), *ṣ* (apico-domal), *h*; (voiced fricative) *v* (labio-dental); (nasals) *m*, *n*, *nʸ*; (liquids) *l*, *lʸ*, *r* (flap); (semivowels) *w*, *y*; (vowels) *i*, *a*, *o*, *u*, *ɨ* (high back unrounded); (stress) v́. Long vowels are indicated by gemination; extra-short vowels, marked v̌, are voiceless word-finally after a voiceless consonant.

middle Yaqui River in the *tierra caliente*, ranged from Onavas south to Nuri, and west as far as San José de Pimas on the Mátape River. The Ures, another lowland group, were located near the confluence of the Sonora and San Miguel rivers, the most concentrated settlements being at Ures and San Miguel de Horcasitas (fig. 1).

Seventeenth-century missionary records, the earliest pertaining to the Pima area, frequently fail to give adequate cultural or linguistic identification of the aboriginal populations. According to Pérez de Ribas (1944a:160) and Bannon (1955:33), the natives of Nuri spoke a language different from the Névome Pimas of Onavas, possibly one related to Yaqui. Bannon (1955:131) also indicates that the Movas inhabitants were partially Ópata speakers.

Adding to the confusion created by these rather tentative identifications based on an incomplete knowledge of the local languages are the purely geographic divisions mentioned by Pérez de Ribas (1944a:147) in which certain Pima settlements east of the Yaqui River were referred to as belonging to the Névomes Altos, while those west of the Yaqui River were said to be of the Névomes Bajos. Sauer (1934:38) maintains that this distinction merely points to the fact that the eastern settlements were situated in the foothills of the Sierra, whereas those to the west were located in low, wide basins. However, it should be noted that the towns of Onavas, Movas, and Nuri are also within relatively low river valleys in the *tierra caliente*. A more extensive division of the mission field that has been preserved in the ethnographic literature separates the Upper Pima–Papago of northern Sonora and southern Arizona from the Lower Pima to the south.

Population

The status of the Névomes and Ures is not fully known. Hinton (1959:26) reported that there were probably between 200 and 250 Pimas in the Ures area and that additional Pima descendants lived around San Miguel de Horcasitas. Hinton gives a population figure of 125 for the Onavas Pimas, "62 of whom are assertedly unmixed." Pennington (1979–1980) counted 34 pure Pimas at Onavas. Other settlements listed by Pennington as having one or several Pima families are Pueblo de Alamos, Tónichi, El Cajón, and San Miguel de Horcasitas. Some families from Onavas have settled near Ciudad Obregón and Hermosillo. Although Pennington recorded a total of only 62 pure lowland or Névome Pimas (average family size 3.0), he believed that the actual number was probably somewhat larger.

Population estimates for the highland Pimas located farther east along the Sonora-Chihuahua border vary between 3,000 (Faubert 1975) and 1,500 (Dunnigan 1970:28). The greatest number of Pima homesteads or

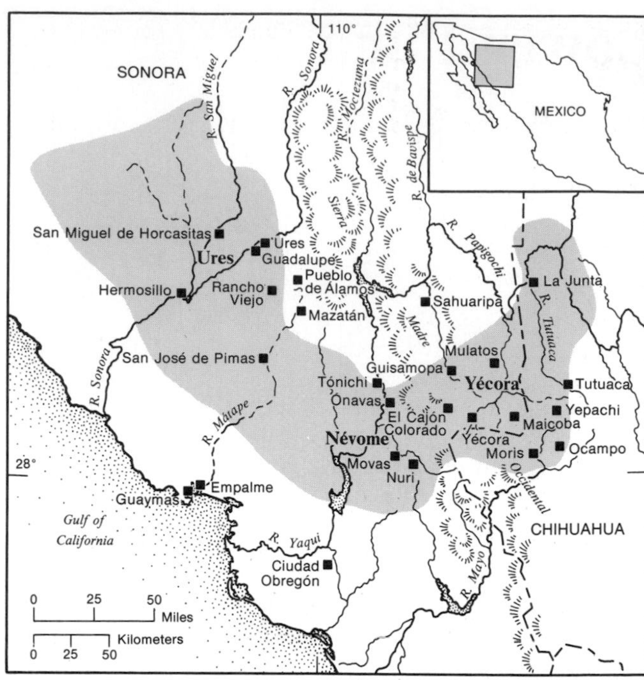

Fig. 1. Tribal territory in the 17th century, with named subdivisions after Sauer (1934:38).

ranchos is found in the vicinity of Maycoba and Yepachic. From these areas, Pimas have moved to Yécora, Mulatos, La Juta, and other predominantly non-Indian settlements. Lumholtz (1902, 1:128) visited Yepachi in 1891 and encountered about 20 Indian families. After reconnoitering the area, he concluded that "there are probably not more than 60 Pima families within the State of Chihuahua, unless there are more than I think near Dolores." Official census figures on the indigenous populations of Chihuahua for 1940 (Passin 1944:147; Plancarte 1954:101) placed the total number of Pimas residing in the vicinity of Moris, Ocampo, and Guerrero at 86 individuals. By 1945 their number had increased to 105 (Plancarte 1954:102). It is doubtful whether very many identifiable Pimas were locatable in 1976 in these places. The Maycoba Pimas in 1968 were unanimous in the opinion that all but a few families had been absorbed into the Mestizo population. Based on statements given by tribal representatives at Yepachi, Pennington (1979–1980) estimated that some 690 individuals and 150 families within the *comunidad* can be considered Pima in terms of immediate ancestry. A May 1971 census taken by officials at La Junta (Pennington 1979–1980) listed 115 Pimas out of a total of 323 inhabitants. Six Pima families were said by Faubert (1975:map 4) to be living at Tutuaca to the west of Yepachi.

Saxton (1956) conducted a brief survey of the Sonoran Pimas, counting 140 at Yécora. At the time, a large sawmill was operating in the area, and many Indians had congregated there in order to find work. Four years later, after the sawmill had shut down, Escalante

(1960) found only 30 resident Pimas at Yécora. As of January 1968 approximately 54 Pimas maintained some kind of residence at Yécora (Dunnigan 1970:27), but 22 of these were temporarily located at the sawmill of La Tijera. Later in the year, when work cutbacks began at the mill, the Pima families left to look for employment elsewhere. They returned to Yécora, applied for work at other sawmills, or journeyed to the Ciudad Obregón area to labor as agricultural field hands. Four Pima families numbering 16 individuals had, prior to this time, established residence in the lowlands.

While Saxton (1956) counted only 175 Maycoba Pimas, Escalante (1960) gives a figure of 279. A 1962 census cited by Pennington (1979–1980) showed 313 Pimas to be living in the vicinity of Maycoba. Pennington's own 1970 survey of the area resulted in a still higher estimate of 408 Pimas residing within the Maycoba Ejido, which encompasses a number of ranchos. Only 15 Pimas lived in the village proper along with 70 Whites.

The inconsistency of these figures reflects the difficulties involved in thoroughly studying a population that is grouped into many small and widely separated clusters, each consisting typically of a few closely related nuclear families. The frequency with which the Pimas are forced to shift residence in search of work also impedes accurate census taking. Therefore, it is only an estimate that the lowland Pimas probably numbered in excess of 100 persons, whereas all the highland groups combined totaled between 1,500 and 2,000 in 1975.

Environment

The general elevation of the upland country in which the Pimas live is about 1,600 meters, with the main settlements situated at elevations between 1,500 and 1,800 meters. The region is crossed north to south by a series of mountain ridges, which occasionally reach heights above 2,000 meters. A few broad and relatively level valleys occur in the area, but this is the exception. Along the many tributaries of the Tutuaca and Mulatos rivers, the two major drainages, extensive stream dissection has veined the area with deep, narrow valleys. On the flanks of streams in the valley bottoms occur stretches of rich alluvium. Pimas have traditionally located their small, single-family ranchos near these alluvial deposits but are gradually being pushed off some of the more desirable lands by White ranchers. Elsewhere, settlement tends to be quite sparse since the soil, being rocky and quite thin, is less suitable for agriculture.

The mean temperature for the months of June through August at Yécora (elevation 1,652 meters) is 18.8°C. The months of December through February average 6.7°C. Annual rainfall averages 1,071 mm, but there are wide fluctuations in total precipitation from year to year. The heavy summer rains begin in late June or early July and taper off in September. October and November have clear days occasionally interrupted by showers. In December begin the winter *equipatas*, which are steady, light rains sometimes lasting several days. A few inches of snow usually fall in the higher valleys, such as at Yécora and Maycoba. The mountain peaks are covered by a foot or more snow during most of December and January. A long dry season commences in late February, with April or May having the least rainfall of the year. By the time the June rains begin, the Sierra is usually parched and the Pimas are using their last reserves of food.

The vegetation types of this region are listed by Félix Valdés (1966–1967:19–20). In large part, Pennington's (1963:33–36) description of the western upland of Tarahumara also applies to the highland Pima territory. At the higher elevations are found large, valuable stands of pine trees, some of which are still under control of the Pimas. Grasses thrive on the open mesas and on the hillsides where scrub oak is the primary tree form.

Because of the marked variations in elevation, drainage, soil quality, and precipitation, the region produces many kinds of plants that are of considerable utility to the Pimas. Most of these are valued chiefly for their medicinal properties (see Dunnigan 1970:81–83). Mason and Brugge (1958:285) mention the use of herbs by native shamans but do not give detailed information on the subject. A wild plant particularly important to the Pimas is bear grass or *mohŏ* (chiefly *Nolina microcarpa*), which the women use to weave their baskets and sleeping mats. Hats are sometimes made of beargrass, but the more common material is palm fiber (figs. 2–4), which does not grow in the Sierra so must be brought in from the desert foothills to the west and north. Pimas will make occasional trips to places like Guisamopa in order to obtain palm fiber and to sell some of their handicrafts and medicinal plants to the White Mexicans. Most income is derived from agriculture and wage work. Yet the gathering of food plants, hunting, and fish trapping with narcotic plants can become very important during short periods when drought has greatly depressed the Sierra economy and created serious food shortage.

History

Jesuit priests first contacted the Lower Pimas in 1591 when they visited a group of Pimas who had left Nuri and moved south to Spanish Bamoa on the Sinaloa River. After almost three decades of friendly visits by Pima deputations from the north, the Jesuits began establishing missions along the middle Yaqui and Mátape rivers. Except for minor disturbances at a few mission centers in the 1630s, there was no serious resistance to Spanish rule until some of the lowland Pimas revolted

Mus. of the Amer. Ind., Heye Foundation, New York: 24717.
Fig. 2. Guadalupe Tanori making a palm fiber hat. Photograph by Edward H. Davis, Onavas, Sonora, 1924.

along with Yaquis and Mayos in 1740. At several times in the late 1700s Pimas are also reported to have assisted other Indians in their fight against the Spaniards (Spicer 1962:89). There is little mention of the lowland Pimas in later historical records, which probably reflects their rapid acculturation.

Spicer (1962:89) has summarized the limited population data on the Lower Pimas that exist for the mission period:

> In 1678 there were reported to be a little more than four thousand Lower Pimas living in the vicinity of the nine missions which had been established in their country as far east as Maicoba, the largest settlement being Onavas where there were reported to be 875 Indians. About a hundred years later, in 1769, the Lower Pimas were reported to number about three thousand. There were then eight missions in operation serving fifteen pueblos. Within the same area, where there were many small mines, there were reported to be 792 Spaniards, or *gente de razón*.

The Jesuits initiated their mission work among the highland Pimas in the middle of the seventeenth century. By the late 1670s a system of head missions and dependent *visitas* was established in the area. The only threat to Spanish authority occurred in 1697 and 1698 when some of the highland Pimas rebelled on the side of neighboring Tarahumara. Otherwise, relations between priest and Indian continued unbroken for almost 100 years. During this time, the missionaries tried to

Fig. 3. Semisubterranean structure of logs, stone, and earth (*húukī*), near Maycoba and Yepachi, Sonora, formerly used to store grasses needed for weaving baskets and mats. It was also a place where one could weave protected from the elements. This type of structure may also formerly have been used as a menstrual hut (Campbell W. Pennington, personal communication 1981). Photograph by Campbell W. Pennington, 1968.

gather the Pimas into centrally located villages. This program of reduction was only partially successful, since many Pimas preferred rancho life and could not be persuaded to take up residence at the mission center. The lack of extensive arable lands at places like Maycoba further impeded reduction. The resettlement that did occur was to some extent offset by a high death rate attributable to diseases transmitted from the Europeans, including miners who developed several rich strikes in the area and increased the traffic between the Sierra and Spanish settlements in the lowlands.

Apache raiding forced the withdrawal of almost all Europeans from the Sierra late in the eighteenth cen-

Mus. of New Mex., Santa Fe: left, 23684/12; right, 23679/12.
Fig. 4. Baskets of beargrass (*Nolina*). Made in a variety of shapes and sizes, all are basically round containers made with a structurally square weave (twilled). Palm fiber imported from the lowlands is used for finer work. In dry weather women weave in the *húukī* to keep fiber, which has been placed there a day before and sprinkled with water, moist and pliable. At other times they work outside (Brugge 1956). Baskets and particularly hats are sometimes sold to Mexicans. left, Height about 20.3 cm, right same scale; collected by David Brugge at Yécora, Sonora, 1957.

tury (Brugge 1961:8), and missionary activity practically ceased. It is difficult to say how many non-Indian settlers were present before the outbreak of Apache hostilities, but they could be found in the Sahuaripa valley and at Yécora in small numbers. Subsequent to the reopening of the Sierra in the second half of the nineteenth century, the influx of ranchers and farmers outnumbered miners and missionaries. The natives were quickly displaced from the broad valleys most suitable for cattle raising, such as Yécora and Sahuaripa. The invasion of Whites farther east remained sufficiently limited prior to the Mexican Revolution of 1910 so that open conflict was avoided. When strong territorial pressures were exerted by non-Indians, there was still enough reserve land so that internal migration could alleviate the problem for the Pimas.

The Revolution temporarily interrupted the trend toward greater contacts between Whites and Pimas. Oral testimony of the Pimas (Dunnigan 1970:237) states that White settlement increased markedly in the 1930s and caused a critical land shortage, which impelled many Indians to seek work at newly opened mines and sawmills. Even families that could subsist by traditional means started sending some of their members to labor for Whites as a way of obtaining added income and acquiring store goods. By the late 1940s a majority of the Pima men had worked for wages.

In the 1930s indigenous civil and religious institutions at places like Maycoba were intact, and the Pimas governed their own affairs while tolerating the White presence. White Mexicans have since emerged as the stronger political force.

Culture

The residents of Onavas divide themselves into four racial types (Pennington 1979–1980); the labels are Spanish. The Pima *inditos* have pure Indian ancestry, whereas the Whites (*blancos*) claim to be entirely non-Indian. Mestizos result from Pima-White marriages, and *mezclados* belong to families that are in part White, mestizo, and Pima. Membership in the Onavas Ejido includes most of the Pimas, but non-Indians are also represented. Several Pimas reported in 1966 (Dunnigan 1966) that they resented non-Indians settling in the area, an attitude reflecting the usual antagonisms that exist in villages where the *ejidatarios* periodically dispute with private ranchers and farmers over land. The Pimas who hold office in the Ejido are extremely influential in the village. The only evidence found by Hinton (1959:27) of a surviving Pima culture at Onavas is a much reduced ceremonial calendar carried on by the Indians in their ancient mission church. Pimas supervise the celebrations of Catholic feast days, and all segments of the population participate to some degree.

The division between Pima and White is more sharply drawn in Sierran communities. The two groups remain apart socially and to some extent physically. At large settlements such as Yécora, the few resident Pimas live on the town periphery and associate with non-Indians primarily as the clients of higher-status *patrones*. At places like Maycoba and Yepachi, the Whites control the center of town, while the more numerous Indians are scattered over the surrounding countryside. Despite the friendships that exist between some Pimas and Whites, interethnic relations tend to be antagonistic as well as symbiotic. The boundaries of Indian land have not been precisely established by law. In this uncertain situation, Pima peasants and White ranchers are extremely defensive about their rights. The violence that formerly characterized interethnic conflicts has subsided, but the hostilities remain. Both sides derive some economic benefit from mutual cooperation and continue to tolerate each other as long as the tense balance is not upset by a major confrontation.

Because the highland Pimas represent a substantial cultural enclave, they have been better studied than the less numerous and highly acculturated Pimas of the lowland. The following description of Lower Pima culture, unless otherwise indicated, pertains to the mountain communities of eastern Sonora.

Subsistence

The small farms (fig. 5) or ranchos of the Pimas seldom encompass more than a few hectares each, most of which is rocky hillside or hilltop terrain unsuitable for plow agriculture. About two-fifths of rancho land consists of small, arable tracts in the valley bottoms. This means that a Pima peasant will have, on the average, one acre that he can work intensively and four acres that he can utilize for grazing or hoe cultivation.

The two basic crops of the Pimas are beans and maize. The maize is grown almost exclusively in the better fields, while beans can be successfully raised in fairly rocky soils. By rotating these two crops in the rich bottomlands, a Pima can cultivate his small parcel of land year after year. The types of maize most commonly grown are a long- and a short-eared variety of the chapalote race, and a small-eared sweet corn (Mason and Brugge 1958:286). To these have been added several hybrids introduced into the Sierra from the Sonoran lowlands by migrant workers returning home and then traded among the Pima families. Several varieties of squash are sowed with the maize or planted in hillside *majueches*, which are small plots cultivated with a hoe. Other major crops include wheat and, sometimes, potatoes. In the small, fenced gardens located near Pima dwellings are grown, in addition to a large variety of flowers, crops such as tomatoes, green beans, chiles, onions, garlic, and any other vegetables for which seeds can be obtained locally or in the lowland. The number

Fig. 5. Farming. left, Oxen pulling a plow with a homemade wooden tip. Many farmers own plows, but few own oxen. right, A man weeding his cornfield using a hoe. His hat is native made. Photographs by Campbell W. Pennington, left in 1970, right in 1968.

of fruit trees growing on a rancho is seldom very large. Pear and peach trees are sometimes cultivated, and there has been some experimentation with apple trees.

Additional income is derived from chickens and turkeys. A few Pimas still maintain small herds of cattle. All rancho families desire a pair of oxen for plowing, but rarely can they afford them. About 10 percent of the families have one or more pigs, while goats and sheep are no longer of any economic importance. Faubert (1975:9–10) reports that Pima women in the Yepachi area still weave wool blankets for their own families on looms similar to those of the Tarahumara. The wool is supplied from herds located farther west, some of which are owned by Pimas. Small profits are made on the rent or sale of riding and pack animals, usually burros. Only rarely are Pimas able to acquire a mule or horse.

San Diego Mus. of Man, Calif.: 1979-57-3.

Fig. 6. Corn husking peg made of wooden stick pointed at one end and blunt at the other with grooves holding a leather handle. It is used to remove partially dry ears from stalks (Pennington 1979–1980, 1:59). When not in use it is often carried stuck in a man's hat (Mason and Brugge 1958:290). Length 15.2 cm, made by Sergio Estrella in Onavas, Sonora, 1979.

Structures

Most Pima dwellings are constructed by nailing pine boards or shingles over a one-room, pole framework. The addition of an enclosed porch to some houses provides a cooking area in bad weather. More substantial structures with walls of adobe or unshaped stone are owned by a few Pimas in and near the town of Maycoba. The simplest habitations are brush-roofed ramadas with low half-walls of piled stones. These are usually just temporary structures used in the warmer seasons when working away from home. Rockshelters are also sometimes occupied by Pimas (fig. 8). Two examples occur at Los Pilares. Vertical planks enclose a portion of one shelter, thereby creating a one-room dwelling entered by a hinged door. At another, a small sleeping area is partly walled by horizontal planking and loosely piled rocks. The rest of the shelter is used for storage and cooking.

Fig. 7. Corral in Sierras, recently moved from the dark area on right, which will then be planted utilizing the natural fertilizer generated by the stock. Photograph by Campbell W. Pennington, 1970.

Fig. 8. Dwellings. top, Rockshelter house of José Lau Ban in Los Pilares, Sonora. bottom, Family seated outside a house in Maycoba, Sonora. The house is made of a wall of unshaped stones, shinglelike strips of wood for the roof, held down with logs. The man lying down wears sandals with soles of old tire tread. Photographs by Timothy Dunnigan, top in Sept. 1967, bottom in April 1970.

Close by some Pima dwellings are found semisubterranean, one-room structures (*húukĭ*) used for basket and hat weaving (fig. 3). Few were used in the 1970s, although the Pima women still manufactured woven articles (see Mason and Brugge 1958; Brugge 1961).

Social Organization

The residence unit that works the rancho land is typically the nuclear family. To this basic group are sometimes added other relatives. A widowed parent, a son-in-law, uncle, brother, or brother-in-law may become part of the rancho unit on a permanent or long-time basis. There are also a number of other arrangements that can occur, and all have a similar organization. At the core of the group are the landholding members. This includes, at a minimum, a woman who performs the domestic chores of cooking, housekeeping, and washing and at least one adult male who does the heavy labor of farming. These two persons may be an unmarried brother and sister, a widowed parent and unmarried child, or some other relative pair. One or more unmarried kin may attach themselves to the core group, and children are sometimes added through informal adoption. The total membership is never very large, since the rancho could not support them.

Some members of the residence group are often absent from the rancho for long periods of time while they pursue one of the adjunct occupations open to Pimas. In a large family, several sons might sign on at a sawmill during the slack periods in the agricultural cycle. The wages earned make up for whatever crop shortages occur and help finance the next planting. So long as there are jobs available, the sawmill workers spend relatively little time on the rancho; however, they are important members of the agricultural unit and consider the rancho to be their permanent residence.

Because of the patterns of Pima inheritance and the practice of lending land to close affines and compadres, the residents of associated ranchos share many bonds of kinship. A community such as Maycoba is made up of a number of these detached neighborhoods, each of which exerts a special political influence within the ejido.

• KINSHIP Kinship usage varies among different segments of Pima society. Generally, persons under 40 years of age and those living in White communities tend to use terminology considerably modified in the direction of the White Mexican model (Dunnigan 1970:64–67). This modification has occurred in two ways. First,

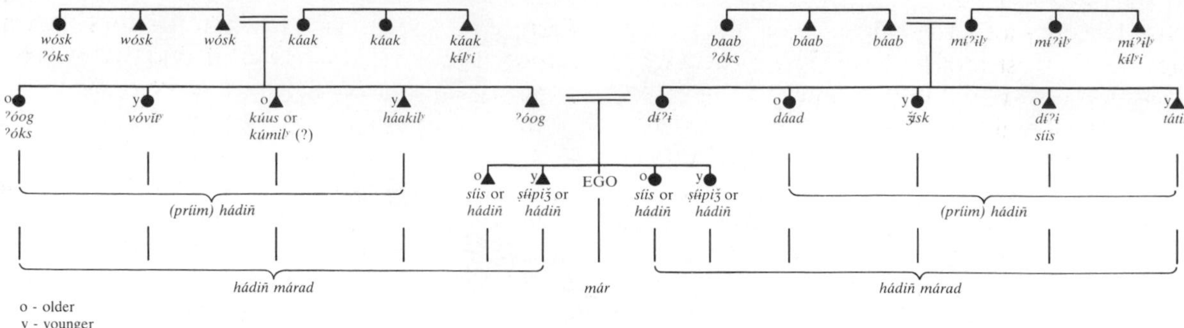

Fig. 9. Kinship terminology of the highland Pima for male or female ego.

there has been a reduction in the number of kin categories normally recognized in speech; second, modified Spanish words have been extensively substituted for Pima terms. Regarding the reduction in native categories, the bifurcate collateral classification for parents' siblings utilized by some of the older people (fig. 9) has been collapsed into a lineal system through the equating of different terms. These changes reflect the bilateral character of Pima kinship relations. Within the broad range of his bilateral descent group, a Pima selects members of certain families with whom to establish social and economic alliances. Preference may be given either father's or mother's consanguineal kin depending on circumstances external to the fact of kinship itself.

A majority of Pimas regard subsistence agriculture as their primary occupation, and for them a determining factor in family alliances is the distribution of rights in land and livestock. The father apportions land and, in some cases, part of his livestock herds among his sons and daughters when they marry. Final division of property occurs when both parents die. The children receive equal shares, but land remains integral within the sibship, and there is no alienation to persons outside the family.

With the gradual loss of lands, adjustments in Pima inheritance procedures had to be made. If land and cattle are scarce in relation to the number of sons, daughters frequently come away with very little at marriage. They go to the ranchos of their husbands, and not until later, when final division of the parents' property is made, can they expect some share in the movable goods. The rights of daughters to land exist in principle but can be exercised only if their husbands enter into planting partnerships with the brothers holding the land. If a father has only daughters or has surplus land, one or more of his sons-in-law may help work his fields, which the daughters later inherit. When landholdings are small, one adult son stays with the father while the other male offspring of working age seek employment at sawmills, ranches, or in Mexican towns. At the death of the parents, the sons and daughters must negotiate with one another for what remains to be inherited. Siblings who have permanently settled elsewhere and are working for wages or earning a living from the property of their fathers-in-law seldom share in the inheritance. Ideally, they retain rights in the land, but these rights have no force in fact unless legitimized by continued occupancy and use of the fields. It is up to those still in actual possession of inheritable property to decide its distribution.

Due to the small size of the Indian population, the pattern of establishing affinal ties between Pima families has become highly involuted. The noncorporate bilateral kindred of the Pimas typically consists of families that have repeatedly married into one another to the point where many persons share both an affinal and a descent connection. The implicit strategy in such alliances appears to center on keeping land wealth within a small group and preventing its dispersion into plots of unworkable size. The question of land represents for the Maycoba Pimas a particularly important justification for communal endogamy. Their legal possession of the territories of Maycoba depends upon the Pimas continuing as the descendants of the original members of the ejido as it was mapped and allotted in 1905.

Bonds of descent and affinity are complemented by a form of fictive kinship established through the ritual of baptism. Every Pima child is sponsored in baptism by two or more adults. At a minimum, the initiate (*vák már*) has one godfather (*vák ʔóog*) and one godmother (*vák dáad*). Baptismal sponsors are usually selected from close blood relatives and affines of the parents, but a certain number will be drawn from a wider circle of relatives and friends. Store owners, ranchers, mill bosses, and other influential Whites are sometimes asked to be one of several godparents for a Pima child. These interethnic compacts are rarely sought by the Pimas despite the possibility of receiving preferred treatment from the White coparents. The choice of a Pima *kompáalʸ* and *komáalʸ* (Spanish *compadre* and *comadre*) provides a more reliable basis for long-term social and economic reciprocity.

The ritual of baptism has particular significance for the Maycobeños. Every year on the feast day of San

Francisco (October 4) parents bring their unbaptized children to Maycoba, sometimes from great distances, so that they can be christened by the priest and formally registered as a member of the town. In this way, the Maycoba baptismal register has come to be a sort of tribal roll, a list of those who still have rights in the ejido.

• THE TOWN The social structure of a Pima town, including its relationship to the outlying satellite ranchos, has been partially described for Maycoba (Mason and Brugge 1958; Nolasco Armas 1969; Dunnigan 1970) and Yepachi (Faubert 1975). The White families tend to reside near the center of town in large adobe houses with white plastered facades. The smaller and less stable in-town Indian population is scattered toward the periphery in poorer housing of wood or piled stone construction. The majority of Pimas live on the ranchos a few minutes' to several hours' walk distant from the town. The rancho dwellers come to town in order to look for work, buy supplies, confer with the Pima *gobernador* (governor), and attend the major fiestas.

Religion

The principal religious symbols of Indian solidarity are the village mission church and its statues or *ṣaṣánt* (Spanish *santos*). The ancient church at Yepachi has been well maintained and continues to be at least partially under the control of the Pimas, who share use rights with other Roman Catholics. At Maycoba, the old mission church stands just off the plaza to the rear of a newer church built by the Whites in the 1950s. Now a roofless structure of melting adobe walls, the Indian mission has a large main chamber with a smaller room on one side. The main chamber is a meeting place for Pimas when they wish to hold an open forum on pueblo or ejido affairs. It is also the site of various rituals associated with Easter. The smaller room housed the *ṣaṣánt* of San Francisco and San José until it fell into disrepair. Whites have since removed the statue to their church over the objections of the Pimas.

There are only two community-wide fiestas when large numbers of Pimas travel to Maycoba. These are the feast day of San Francisco and Easter. The Virgin of Guadalupe's feast day (December 12) and the Day of the Cross (May 3) are of lesser importance. The June 24 feast day of San Juan, which marks the beginning of the summer rains, is celebrated at the different ranchos by ritual bathing in the morning followed by an afternoon of visiting and drinking tiswin or *hún váki*, a type of weakly fermented corn beer. Although the fiesta of San Francisco has become a secularized affair run by Whites, there are a number of sacred devotions, which, in addition to the baptisms, confirmations, marriages, and special masses said by visiting priests, include the display of San Francisco by the Pimas in processions around the town plaza.

The most elaborate Pima rituals take place during Easter Week (figs. 10–11) when a semimilitary organization of *fariseos* 'Pharisees' is installed by the Pima governor to run the community from Wednesday to noon on Saturday. Each year the young men either volunteer for service or are forced to join as the result of capture. Older, less vigorous men enter the ranks on Holy Saturday for the concluding ceremonies. The *fariseos* keep a strenuous vigil protecting some of the tribe's holy relics, which have been placed in two specially constructed litters for daily processions. In one litter is placed an ancient crucifix. The other contains a square stone referred to as the *cuadro* of the Virgin Mary.

Under the direction of a *káapiš* 'captain', *káv* 'sergeant', and *ˀúušigam* 'baton bearer', the *fariseos* make regular patrols of the town and nearby ranchos to insure the general order and to enforce prohibitions on bathing and unnecessary work. These tasks were formerly shared by the Pima *judíos*, but the group has been taken over and secularized by teenage Whites. Faubert (1975:17) mentions that both organizations remain under the control of the Pimas in the Yepachi area. The Pimas of Yepachi have also continued the role of the pascola dancer, which has not been practiced in Maycoba for several decades.

The Easter traditions of the Pimas and local Whites articulate at a number of points, but the rules of interaction change as political power shifts (Dunnigan 1981). The Pimas can no longer control the activities of the Whites or even demand their cooperation as they have done in the past. Easter is a time when each side tests its prerogatives over the other. The basic conflict is most dramatically expressed on Holy Saturday when the two groups, the *fariseos* representing the Pimas and the young male adults from the most prominent White families, contest each other in wrestling matches held in the mission church.

The Yepachi Pimas hold a number of sacred dances called in Spanish *yumaris* during the year. Most often they are held before a large wooden cross in a clearing not far from the church. Participation in these dances, which lasts three days and two nights, is region wide and often involves performances by *pascoleros*. In describing the Yepachi *yumari*, Faubert (1975:16) remarks on their similarity to the *yumaris* of the Tarahumara and Guarijío.

Political Organization

The Maycoba Pimas elect a governor for a term of four to six years. He has the responbility of overseeing the affairs of the town or pueblo, including those ranchos lying within a radius of roughly two or three miles. Areas beyond these limits are said to be under the jurisdiction of six Pima ejidal officers, but such officers have been relatively powerless in a situation where the

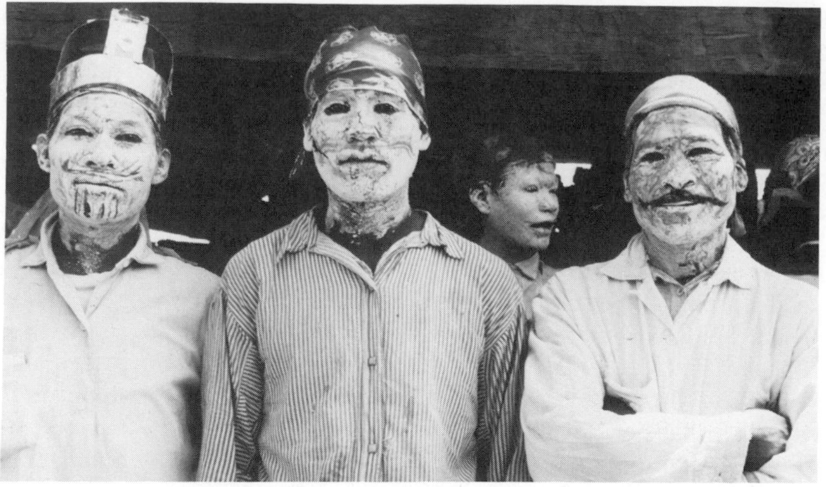

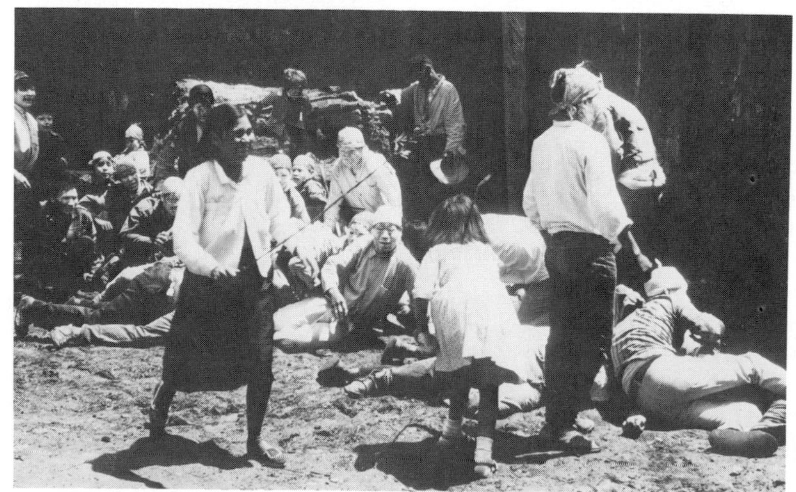

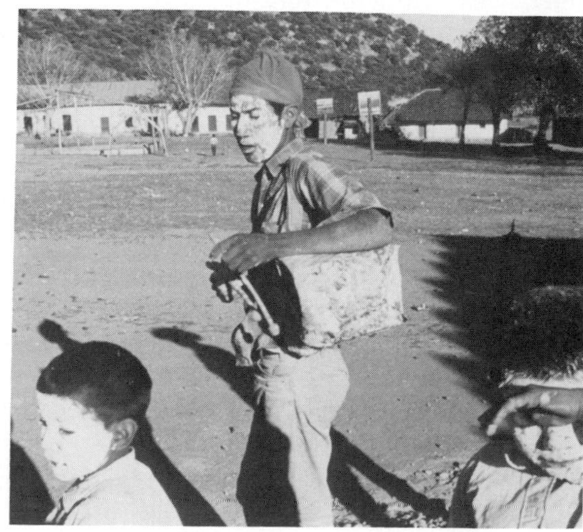

Fig. 10. *Fariseos* during Easter week in Maycoba, Sonora, 1970. top left, Face painting with a feather. Over the white clay, designs are painted with pigments made from ground charcoal, red earth, green willow and mulberry leaves, yellow clay, and a bluish residue from peach leaves. top right, Completed facial decorations. Common painted designs include black beards, large curling mustaches, and gogglelike outlines around the eyes. Alternating colors of parallel lines sometimes are drawn on the chin, cheeks, and upper lip. center, *Fariseos* playfully tossing pieces of pottery. bottom left, A woman and child switch the fallen men. bottom right, Drummer keeping the younger *fariseos* in line. Photographs by Timothy Dunnigan.

limits of authority are confused and the Whites are contesting Indian ejido rights.

The governor or his assistant is sometimes called upon to arbitrate disputes between Pimas. In cases of assault, he tries to see that compensation is paid the victim and that the aggressor is restrained from further violence. The governor formerly had the authority to fine and jail law violators. This must now be left to the local *comisario*. Official census records on the Indian population are kept by the governor, who is likely to be one of the very few literate Pimas.

The power of the governor comes as much from his position as a crucial link to the non-Indian community as it does from being an elected official who handles the internal affairs of the Pimas. He drafts Indian petitions to the Mexican authorities and is expected to plead their case, especially when the issue of indigenous land rights is called into question. When the local Whites need the services of organized Pima work groups for public projects such as road improvement, the hiring and handling of the payroll is done through the governor. State and federal agencies use the same point of contact with the Pimas. On the other hand, competitive pressures from non-Indians have caused dissension among the Maycoba Pimas and encouraged the formation of factions, which tends to undermine the influence of the governor among his own people.

Pimas in White Mexican Society

Outside the environs of Maycoba, Yepachi, and La Junta, the largest concentration of highland Pimas is at the ranching town of Yécora, which had about 1,500 White residents and just 16 Pima families with a total of 54 members in 1968. Twenty-two of these Pimas spent most of the year working at distant sawmills, returning to their houses on the outskirts of Yécora only during the important fiestas, when laid off work, or when ill and requiring the service of the local doctor. The others depended on the occasional wage jobs found locally. Seven families maintained some kind of a garden each year, and three families cultivated from one-half to a full acre of maize, beans, and squash at the ranchos of Los Pilares near the western edge of Maycoba Ejido.

The Pima residents of Yécora, who share close ties through descent and marriage, have not fully integrated into the town's sociopolitical structure. Except for a few persons from Mulatos of Yepachi, they are all former

Fig. 11. Constructing the scarecrow Judas figure during the Easter ceremony. Photograph by Timothy Dunnigan, Maycoba, Sonora, 1970.

inhabitants of the Maycoba area, and it is as citizens of the Maycoba ranchos that they regard themselves. The issues affecting the ejido continue to concern them, but as their stay in Yécora lengthens there tends to be less direct participation on their part in Maycoba politics. However, most of the Pimas continue to have their children baptized and registered in Maycoba.

Pimas who have established regular client-*patrón* relationships with Whites in Yécora are more likely to be classed with the non-Indian poor, that is, as part of the *clase humilde*. The other Pimas are regarded by the Whites as transients or squatters for whom the pueblo may perform an occasional act of charity without feeling any further obligation toward them.

The Sawmill

The 50 to 60 Pima workers at sawmills around Yécora can be divided into three groups of approximately equal size on the basis of subsistence and residence patterns. One group comes directly from the ranchos of Maycoba. Sawmill work is for them merely an adjunct occupation that carries them over the difficult period after their food crops have been exhausted. The preparation and sowing of their fields usually keeps them away from the mill during the late spring and early summer months. In October and November, they are back on the rancho in order to harvest the crops. July and August are slack periods at the sawmills if the rains are too heavy, so that the rancho Pimas are more likely to seek employment at a sawmill during the winter and early spring. This group also regularly attends the fiestas of Maycoba, even when they stand to lose valuable pay by being absent from their mill jobs.

A second group of Pimas consists of those who maintain residence in Yécora but work at the sawmills of the Sierra as long as possible. Unlike the rancho Pimas, they cannot readily fall back on subsistence farming when the lumbering camps close down. Unless they enter into a temporary partnership with a relative who has land to cultivate and needs capital, they must rely on local ranchers to employ them or travel outside the area in order to obtain work. Because jobs are scarce, some of the younger adult males make the 165-mile trip to the lowland around Ciudad Obregón to hire out as agricultural laborers.

A third group of sawmill workers is geographically mobile laborers, some with families, who move from job to job and have no permanent residence. They migrate between the lowlands and the Sierra, working for a while out of migrant labor camps and small agricultural settlements until the heat and humidity of the Obregón irrigation district coupled with an improved job situation in the Sierra cause them to return temporarily to a mountain sawmill.

The Sonoran Lowlands

Employment on the large farms in the Yaqui valley is for some Pimas a regular source of seasonal income. Every year during slack work periods in the Sierra, about 20 or so rancho and Yécora Pimas leave their families behind and walk or hitch rides on lumber trucks to the Obregón area to work as field hands. If sawmills are not hiring, the more mobile Pimas move their families to the lowlands. The average stay of the mobile group tends to be much longer than that of the Pimas who maintain residences in the Sierra, in some cases lasting as long as six years.

Because a Pima family may remain for a considerable period in the lowlands and still not become permanent residents there, it is difficult to identify those who have made a lasting adjustment outside of Pima society. Of 45 persons living in the Ciudad Obregón area in 1967–1968, 35 had lived three or more consecutive years in the lowlands. Among these were three Pima men and two Pima women who had non-Indian spouses, a type of union that is much more rare in the Sierra. Hinton (1959:29) has stated that some 20 Pima families formerly lived year-round in Ciudad Obregón.

Pimas residing in the lowlands, like those of the Sierra, show a preference for sibling associations. Families located at the same settlements are frequently headed by brothers. Alliances are also formed between brothers-in-law and first cousins, who often choose one another as compadres. Continuous contacts have been maintained between the Obregón and Sierra groups. The Sierra Pimas visit their relatives when searching for work in the lowlands. Conversely, the Obregón Pimas try to get back to the Sierra every few years on important holidays, and a few send money to help support parents who have remained behind in the mountains.

The primary occupation of the Pima men is unskilled agricultural labor. The women supplement the family's income by taking in washing and performing other domestic chores for pay. Temporary employment can also be found for men at construction sites where there is a need for hod carriers and mixers of cement. Seldom is a Pima able to obtain steady work. Almost everyone complains of the competition for jobs, but they agree that their economic situation is much better than it had been in the Sierra. A number of children over six years of age are attending school, an opportunity that few Pimas had in the highlands outside of Yepachi. In other mountain communities the schools have either failed or the Pima parents have withdrawn their children from what they perceive to be a hostile environment. The lowland Pima families hope that their students will acquire the skills necessary for a well-paying occupation.

Assimilation

Since the early 1950s, more of the younger Pima men from Maycoba have been making tentative work contacts far from home. After a period of moving between rancho and place of employment, a small percentage of these seasonal wage workers transfer residence to a White town like Yécora. This is a major occupational adjustment, since those permanently quitting the rancho become day laborers who have no more than a secondary reliance on agriculture. Work is easier to obtain at the White settlements, and, if jobs are scarce locally, a Pima has ready access to other centers of employment. He can then proceed in one of two directions. By severing relations with other Pimas and acquiring a White Mexican style of living, he may attain non-Indian status. But this is a difficult achievement requiring considerable time for one's Indian origins to be forgotten. The more practical alternative is for a Pima to take up residence in or near a lowland urban center where he can merge immediately into the lower classes, which already include many migrants from the rural hinterland. Before a Pima's adaptation to the *tierra caliente* is complete, he often returns to the Sierra when opportunities for work are good, but in depressed times the move is always back to the city or lowland farm community.

Despite the strong pressures that encourage out-migration, the highland Pimas have refused to leave their homeland in great numbers. Attachment to the land and the hope that Indian rights will be protected encourage a strong sense of solidarity among the Pimas. Oral traditions supporting Indian claims are well circulated, and there are frequent rumors about an impending expulsion of the Whites from the Maycoba Ejido, which is supposedly to be carried out by the Mexican federal government. Their expectations of outside help may not be entirely realistic, but the Pimas are being more assertive regarding the control of land and timber. In view of this growing militancy, Lower Pima culture seems much more likely to survive in the Sierra than in the lowlands.

Anthropologists need to be more aware of the perdurable nature of Pima society. Because of the great amount of cultural replacement, Pima practices and institutions are often characterized as representing conventional Mexican types. However, research should reveal social differentiation between Indian and non-Indian and the processes of cultural maintenance that reinforce these distinctions.

Synonymy

The lowland Pimas of Onavas identify themselves as *ˀóˀodham* and refer to the highland Pimas as *táramil ˀóˀodham*, meaning the 'Tarahumara-like people'. The highland Pimas of Maycoba call all members of their tribe *ˀóob*, including those of the *tierra caliente*, and call the lowland Pimas *ˀóˀodam*. The term *ˀó·b* also exists in Arizona Papago but with the entirely different meaning of 'Apache' or 'enemy'. Whether the two words are cognate is not known.

The distinction between Lower Pima or Pima Bajo and Upper Pima was established during the mission period when a north-south division was drawn to separate the *pimería alta* from the *pimería baja* for administrative purposes. Unfortunately, the term Pima Bajo is taken by the Pimas themselves as denigrating, connoting 'low' or 'base'.

The most frequently cited folk etymology for the origin of the word Pima is that it is a corruption of the *ˀóˀodham* expression *pi ˀanʸmáat*, literally 'I don't know'. Supposedly, this was the native's answer to the first interrogations in Spanish. For a different but related explanation see the synonymy in "Pima and Papago: Introduction" (this vol.).

Sources

Researchers from the Instituto Nacional de Antropología e Historia centers in Mexico City and Hermosillo, Sonora, have made the most extensive collections of Lower Pima material culture. The Hermosillo collection includes items found only among the Chihuahua groups, such as violins, flutes, and wool blankets, which show a strong Tarahumara influence.

A comprehensive review and analysis of Lower Pima history is provided by Spicer (1962). For the early mission period, a great deal of information has been published on the lowland groups (Acosta 1949; Alegre 1956–1960; Almada 1952; Bannon 1955; Calvo Berber 1958; Eckhart 1960; Ocaranza 1937–1939, 2, 1942; Pérez de Ribas 1944a). A detailed history of the Névome Pimas, including the ejido period in Onavas, is provided by Pennington (1979–1980). The more isolated highland Pimas were missionized relatively late and have received much less attention from historians. The gaps in Lower Pima history could be reduced by additional research on documents pertaining to the mission period, but critical work remains to be done in the area of native oral traditions.

The genetic relationships between the highland dialects of lower Pima and other languages in the Tepehuan-Piman subfamily have not been precisely determined. Except for a brief phonological study of the Maycoba dialect by Escalante (1962), collected materials (Dunnigan 1966) have not been fully analyzed. In view of the large proportion of highland Pimas who speak their native language, this is a very promising area of descriptive and comparative research. Lowland Pima appears to be nearly extinct, but extensive recordings of the Onavas dialect were made by Cornell (1971). Valuable data on the grammar (B.T. Smith 1862) and vocabulary (Pennington 1979–1980) of an eighteenth-century dialect of Névome Pima are available.

An ethnographic baseline has been described for the Lower Pima and adjacent indigenous groups in northern Mexico by Beals (1932a). Articles on Lower Pima culture pertaining to recent times are those of Mason and Brugge (1958), Nolasco Armas (1969), and Hinton's (1959, 1969) areal surveys, which include comparative data on other so-called remnant tribes. The best source on lowland Pima material culture is Pennington (1979–1980). Highland Pima subsistence, social organization, and rituals are discussed by Dunnigan (1970, 1981, 1981a) and Pennington (1979–1980). Other useful ethnographic sources are Escalante (1960) and Faubert (1975).

Seri

THOMAS BOWEN

The Seri ('serē) numbered in 1980 about 475 individuals living along the arid central coast of Sonora, Mexico, between Bahía Kino and Puerto Libertad (fig. 1). They are the remnant of a substantially larger but scattered population that occupied a much greater stretch of coast as well as Islas Tiburón and San Esteban in the Gulf of California. At the time of Spanish contact they shared boundaries with the Yaqui on the south and with the Pima and Papago on the east and north. Directly across the Gulf, about 25 miles west of Isla San Esteban, were the various Cochimi groups who occupied the central peninsula of Baja California.

Language

The Seri language at one time consisted of at least three mutually intelligible dialects. Only one was still spoken by the late nineteenth century although fragments of two other dialects are still accessible (Moser 1963:17).*

Since Jesuit times, Seri (or Serian) has been considered a difficult and distinctive language, and there has been considerable disagreement on its classification. Much comparative work has focused on whether Seri and Yuman are genetically related, with often conflicting conclusions (Powell 1891:136–137; Hewitt 1898:300; Kroeber 1915, 1931:31; Swadesh 1967:100; J.G. Crawford 1976b; "Historical Linguistics and Archeology," vol. 9). A relationship with Chontal (Tequistlatec) has also been proposed and debated (Kroeber 1915; Bright 1956; Turner 1967, 1976), and subgroupings have been suggested that would affiliate Serian with certain California languages, notably Salinan and Chumash (Sapir 1925:525; Langdon 1974:86). Although Serian is generally assigned to the Hokan stock, it is often classified as an isolate (Voegelin and Voegelin 1966a).

*The phonemes of Seri are: (voiceless stops) *p*, *t* (dental), *k*, *kʷ*, ʔ; (voiceless fricatives) *f* ([ɸ]), *s*, *š*, *x*, *x̣* (back velar with uvular trill), *x̣ʷ*; (nasals) *m*, *n*, *ŋ*; (voiced resonants) *l*, *r* (flap), *y*; (voiceless resonants) *W*, *ɬ*; (vowels) *i*, *e* (low front), *a*, *o*; (stress) v́. Vowels may occur nasalized (v̨) and in sequences of two or three (in certain combinations). Initial glottal stop contrasts with its absence. Information on Seri phonology and transcriptions was obtained from Moser and Moser (1965, 1976).

Environment

Seri country is rugged, hot, and dry (Felger 1966). On the mainland the Sierra Seri separates the sloping coastal bajada from the desolate sandy plain of the interior. These mountains extend much of the length of the territory occupied by the Seri since about 1920, and they served as a fairly effective barrier against the encroachment of the Euro-Americans virtually until the mid-twentieth century. In contrast, the unprotected plain of the Río Sonora and the vast Llanuras de San Juan Bautista to the south, once Seri territory, have been completely taken over by Mexican agricultural projects watered by pump irrigation.

Isla Tiburón, the largest of the two formerly inhabited islands, is dominated by two ranges separated by a broad valley. Isla San Esteban consists of a narrow central valley surrounded by mountains.

Rainfall is meager, less than 10 inches annually, and its biological utility is low. Much of it comes in a few torrential summer downpours, causing extensive sheet and gully erosion. Summer temperatures regularly exceed 100° F and the evaporation rate is excessive. The flora includes succulents such as pitahaya, saguaro, and cardon. Of the terrestrial fauna, the most important to the Seri are deer and rabbits.

Although some Seri groups appear to have relied primarily on terrestrial food resources (Moser 1963:22–24), the sea sharply differentiates Seri habitat and culture from most North American desert environments and peoples. An important traditional staple has been eelgrass (*Zostera marina*), a seed-bearing marine plant (Felger and Moser 1973). The archeological record indicates a long reliance on shellfish, fish, and sea turtle, which continues in the 1980s. However, traditional Seri fishing technology was not always capable of yielding large or regular catches, and shellfish, while readily available, are unsatisfactory as a staple. Food has sometimes been in precarious supply, and the Seri have frequently known hunger despite the resources of the sea.

Potable water is scarce and sources are dispersed in the form of natural tanks, springs, seasonal accumulations in playas, and localities where subsurface ground water can be trapped by shallow excavation. Although older Seris recall nearly 100 such sources on the mainland and islands, the vast majority are ephemeral, and

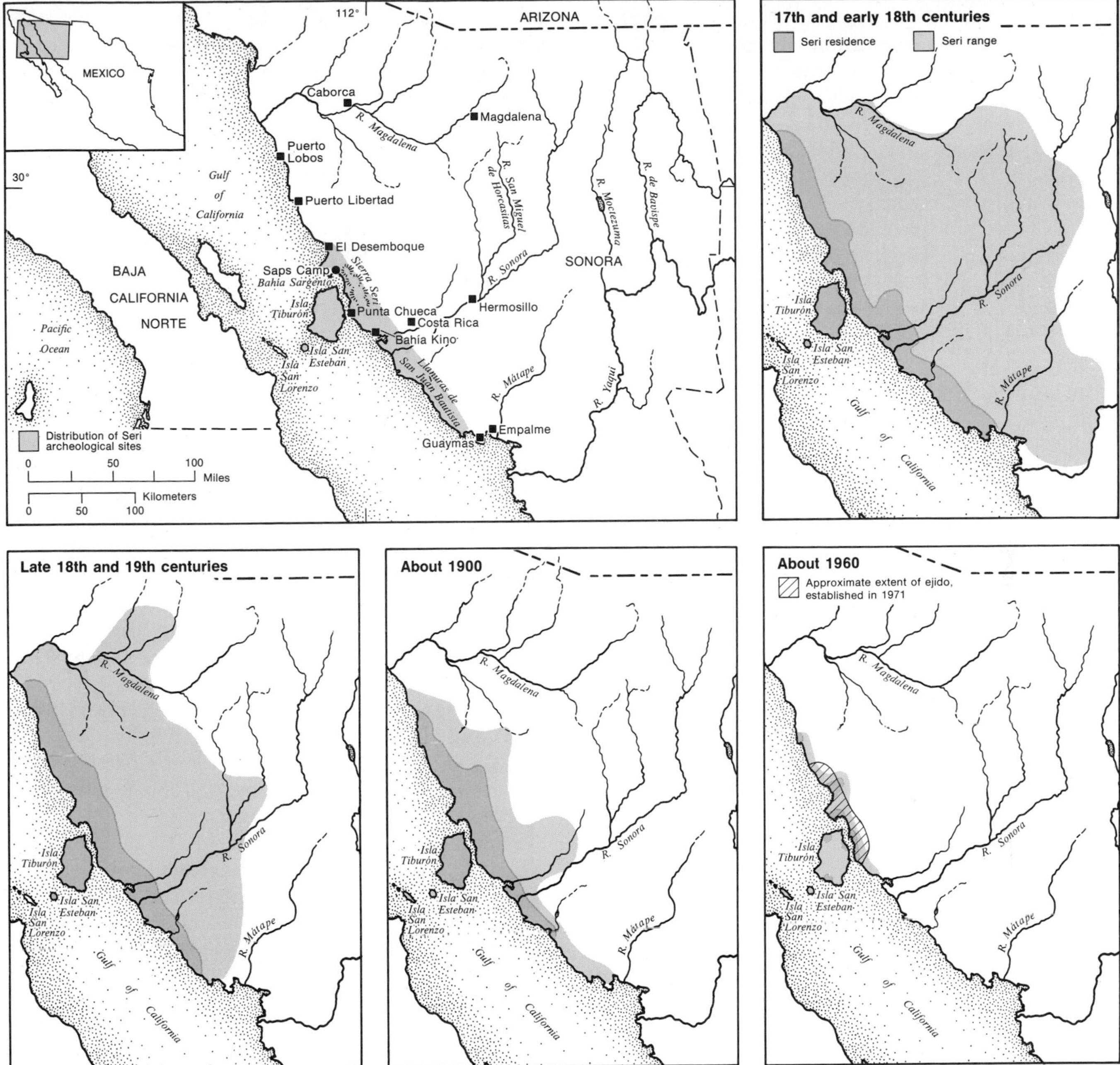

Fig. 1. Fluctuations in tribal territory (after Bahre 1967) from the time of first European contact until 1971.

lack of water has occasionally led to crisis situations (Quinn and Quinn 1965:157–158, 178; Felger and Moser 1970:164–165). Encroachment on Seri territory by Whites was considerably delayed by water scarcity, both real and perceived. In 1894 the Mexican ranchers queried by McGee (1898:30) knew of only six water sources (three of which were ephemeral) in the Seri region.

Bands and Territory

The twentieth-century Seri are an amalgamated remnant of several distinct bands. These units were politically independent, occupied separate territories, and were sometimes hostile toward one another. Band differences in culture and dialect, as well as territory, were sufficient for some Europeans to recognize separate "nations."

There has been disagreement regarding the validity and location of the Serian-speaking groups distinguished by the Europeans. Three groups seem to have been consistently identified and located. These were, from south to north, the Guaymas, Seris (or Tiburones), and Tepocas (Bahre 1967:50–51, 1980). Inconsistent identification and positioning of other groups in the early records reflects infrequency of Spanish visits to the coast, limited knowledge of coastal geography, and ineffective communication of such information among the early Europeans. It is also likely that territories have shifted, especially during the Mexican period when hostilities and resultant population decline destroyed the structural and functional integrity of these groups.

Seri oral history recognizes six bands speaking three mutually intelligible dialects (Moser 1963). Only two of these, Bands I and III in Moser's (1963) terminology, correlate well with Spanish designations (Tepocas and Seris-Tiburones, respectively). The Band V people, situated between them, are said to have come from the south and may represent a relict of the Guaymas or Upanguaymas. The coastal strip between Guaymas and Bahía Kino, attributed to Band II, includes territory that must have once belonged to the Guaymas band. Band II corresponds with Kroeber's (1931) Tastioteños but was probably not distinguished from the Seris-Tiburones by the early Europeans. Band IV, unrecognized by the Europeans, occupied the interior of Isla Tiburón. Band VI, also unnamed, was based on Isla San Esteban and periodically occupied the southern coast of Tiburón Island (see Moser 1963:fig. 2).

The changes through time in residence and range of the Serian speakers have been discussed by Bahre (1967). Figure 1 summarizes these changes and shows the geographic extent of the Seri Ejido established in 1971.

Prehistory

Information pertaining to the prehistory of the Seri coast is meager and derives solely from limited surface reconnaissance and artifact collections (Bowen 1976a). Early occupation is suggested by a few isolated surface occurrences of Clovis points (Robles Ortiz and Manzo Taylor 1972). Several nonceramic sites are known but most are surface deposits and not clearly preceramic in age. By far the majority of sites postdate the appearance of a thin and superbly made pottery, Tiburón Plain. In addition to pottery, these sites exhibit a standard basic assemblage consisting of unworked mollusk shells, unmodified or battered rocks, limited lithic debitage, and simple manos and metates. The close resemblance between these sites and recently abandoned Seri camps, plus factors of ceramic continuity (Bowen and Moser 1968) and correspondence between site distribution and historic Seri territory all indicate that the Seri have occupied the central coast since the beginning of ceramic times, which a single radiocarbon assay places no later than A.D. 220 ± 130.

To the Spaniards as well as to later observers, the Seri have been conspicuous as the only major group of nonsedentary food collectors in Sonora. In subsistence base, in the simplicity of their material culture, and in certain specific cultural features, they resemble peninsular Baja California groups. Coupled with their geographic location, these factors have led to speculation, as yet unverified, that the Seri originally came from Baja California (Kroeber 1931:5–6, 52–55; Rogers 1945:194; Bowen 1976a).

Historic documents and Seri oral tradition attest to contact with every neighboring group (Yaqui, Pima, Papago, and Cochimi), and many features of contemporary Seri culture may have derived from these sources. Studies of specific aspects of Seri culture indicate extensive borrowing, in some cases with little subsequent modification, of, for example, songs, dances, and musical instruments from the Yaqui and basketry techniques and designs from the Papago (Bowen and Moser 1970a:190; Moser 1973; Bowen 1973). In many cases borrowing in comparatively recent times may have served to replace elements of indigenous culture lost during three centuries of recurrent hostilities (Kroeber 1931:3).

History

Comparatively few specifics of Seri culture were recorded until the close of the nineteenth century. The Spanish documents deal largely with military encounters and resistance to mission life (see McGee 1898; Griffen 1961; Spicer 1962; Bahre 1967; Tweed 1973, 1975; Sheridan 1979). The major recorded events of contact are summarized in table 1. Table 2 gives population estimates.

In evaluating the development of Seri-European relations, it is important to recognize that early contact, particularly, was with the minority of Seri who traveled inland to prey upon the missions and European settlements. It was these Seris who were responsible for the early reputation of thievery, slovenliness, and laziness as well as for the eventual eruption of open warfare.

Although the Seri came to be regarded, with considerable justification, as a fierce people, there is no indication that they were initially or fundamentally hostile to outsiders. With the single exception of the killing of Fray Juan Crisóstomo Gil de Bernabé the Seri living on the coast and the islands received nonagressive visitors hospitably from earliest contact to the late nineteenth century.

The inland movement of certain groups and their reorientation to stealing and raiding was largely an opportunistic adjustment to a new subsistence resource. Although adventurous motives may have entered in and encouraged the persistence of Seri raiding in the face of retaliatory measures, the level of violence and destruction was low prior to 1750. Most killings seem to have occurred during Spanish reprisals rather than the Seri raids, and the Spaniards seem to have regarded them more as a nuisance than a serious threat.

Table 1. Summary of History

Date	Event
1536	Álvar Núñez Cabeza de Vaca described Seri
1539	Francisco de Ulloa discovered I. Tiburón; Marcos de Niza party encountered Seris
1541	Skirmish, possibly with Seris
1620s	Some Guaymas baptized by Jesuits, given towns on R. Yaqui
by 1660s	Seris raided Pima missions
1662	First known battle between Seris and Spaniards
1678	Nuestra Señora de Bethlem (Belem) founded for Guaymas band
1679	Seris requested Father Juan Fernández; Nuestra Señora del Pópulo founded
1683	Fernández transferred, mission Seris reverted to nomadism
1685	Father Eusebio Kino visited Seri on coast
1688	Father Adam Gilg re-established Pópulo mission
1691	Gilg founded St. Thaddeus and St. Eustatius missions; the latter destroyed
1699	Padre Melchior Bartiromo founded Santa Magdalena de Tepocas mission; Domingo Jironza led reprisal for Seri stealing
1700	Juan Bautista de Escalante led reprisal, first invasion of I. Tiburón
1709	Padre Juan Maria Salvatierra visited Seris on coast
1721	Padre Juan de Ugarte visited Seris on coast
1742	Pitic presidio and San Pedro de la Conquista de los Seris mission founded (near modern Hermosillo)
1749	Pitic presidio moved, Gov. Diego Ortiz Parilla deported Seri women
1750	Parilla war of extermination
1751–1770s	Seris raided from Cerro Prieto, Spanish campaigns against Cerro Prieto
1767	Jesuits expelled from Mexico, replaced by Franciscans
ca. 1770	Villa de Seris founded (near modern Hermosillo)
1772	Carrizal mission founded on Seri coast under Fray Juan Crisóstomo Gil de Bernabé
1773	Gil de Bernabé killed by Seris, mission abandoned
1776	Seris raided Santa Magdalena mission
ca. 1780–1790	Relative peace prevailed
1790s	Seri raids and Spanish reprisals resumed
1826	Hardy (1829) visited Seris on coast
1844	Victor Araiza campaign killed Seris on coast, Francisco Andrade–Tomás Espence campaign captured coastal and island Seris
1844	Pascual Encinas established Rancho San Francisco de Costa Rica
1854	Seris kidnapped Lola Casanova
ca. 1855–1865	Encinas War, half of Seris killed

Table 1. Cont'd.

Date	Event
1894	2 White men killed on I. Tiburón
1896	Prospectors killed; George Porter and John Johnson killed on I. Tiburón
1904	Rafael Izábal led last formal campaign against the Seri
ca. 1900–1920	Most Seris on I. Tiburón
1920s	Seris shifted to Bahía Kino; Roberto Thomson became liaison to Seri
late 1920s	Kino Bay Club exposed Seri to Americans
1930s	Seri took up shark fishing
1938	Fishing cooperative founded, Seris shifted to El Desemboque
1952	School built by American and Mexican Friends Service Committee
1952	Mexican evangelical church established
1958	National Indian Institute revived fishing cooperative
1959, 1960	Sonoran medical team assessed Seri health
1960	Agricultural projects attempted, were unsuccessful
1961	Ironwood carving began
1960s	United States tourists arrived in numbers
1965	I. Tiburón declared game refuge, Seri forbidden to hunt
1970–1972	Fishing decline, ironwood carving major source of income, Seris buy used automobiles
1971	Seri land established as ejido; school established at Punta Chueca

The pivotal episodes in Seri-European relations took place around 1750 when the presidio at Pitic (now Hermosillo) was moved and the resident Seris deprived of their lands. Their protests were met with prompt arrests of the men and deportation of the women. This triggered a fierce attack on the Spaniards, countered by the first of a series of campaigns to exterminate the Seris. These failed, but they established a policy toward the Seri revived periodically until the twentieth century. Distinctions among Seri bands were largely ignored by the European forces, and Seris who had never taken part in raiding found themselves under attack. The present Seri believe that the remote Isla San Esteban band, which had rarely even visited the mainland, was virtually exterminated in this manner (Moser 1963:25–26). After 1750 the embittered Seri raided with increased violence and destruction, and their reputation as merciless killers became firmly established.

Until 1904 a perpetual cycle of Seri raids followed by retaliatory campaigns reduced the Seri in numbers and gradually pushed them into the refuge of Isla Tiburón and the adjacent coast. Seri-European relations prob-

Table 2. **Population Estimates**

Date	*Population*	*Source*
1692	3,000	Di Peso and Matson 1965:48
1780	2,000	McGee 1898:135
1824	1,000 plus	McGee 1898:135
1826	1,000–1,500[a]	McGee 1898:135
1826	3,000–4,000	McGee 1898:135
1841	1,500	McGee 1898:135
1844	550	McGee 1898:135
1846	less than 500	McGee 1898:135
about 1855	500–600	McGee 1898:135
about 1865	250–300	McGee 1898:135
1894	250–350	McGee 1898:134
1922	200	Quinn and Quinn 1965:164
1930	175	Kroeber 1931:30
1941	160	Hayden 1942:41
1952	215	Moser, personal communication 1972–1980
1955	242	Griffen 1959:6
1963	280	Moser 1963:14
1967	320	Moser, personal communication 1972–1980
1970	363	Moser, personal communication 1972–1980
1973	400	Moser 1973
1975	415	Moser, personal communication 1980
1980	475	Moser, personal communication 1980

NOTE: Estimates are substantially accurate after 1855.
[a] I. Tiburón only.

ably reached an all-time low during the "Encinas War" of the 1850s when half the Seri population was hunted down and killed by Pascual Encinas's cowboys (McGee 1898:113). Occasional killings on both sides continued into the 1920s, and bitter memories among the older adults persisted through the 1960s.

Little is known of the Seri between 1900 and 1920. While some evidently continued to prey intermittently on ranch livestock, most retreated to Isla Tiburón and resumed a life of food collecting. The development of the Mexican fishing industry at Bahía Kino during the late 1920s attracted some Seris and gradually reoriented their life toward the sea. Although their initial relationship with the Mexican fishermen was strained by mutual mistrust and occasional violence, they slowly adopted Mexican fishing techniques and equipment. The short-lived Kino Bay Club introduced the Seri to North American sportsmen around 1930. The beginnings of Seri commercial fishing, stimulated in the 1930s by a market for shark fins and later for shark livers, led to the establishment of a fishing cooperative in 1938.

By the early 1940s the commercial market for fish transformed El Desemboque de los Seris from a seasonal camp into a permanently occupied center of Seri activity. Beginning in the late 1940s a succession of anthropologists, linguists, evangelists, school teachers, traders, and service groups set up temporary or permanent residence. By 1953 El Desemboque was a multilingual community of Seris, Mexicans, and United States citizens.

During the 1960s improved roads and the appearance of recreational vehicles brought large numbers of North American tourists into Seri county, encouraging a minor revival of traditional crafts and adding measurably to cash income. However a radical shift in the economy came about through the sale of carved ironwood figurines, an entirely new craft that began in 1961 (fig. 2). The sale of these items was so successful that by 1970 carving had largely replaced all other subsistence activities.

Cash income from the sale of these figurines also stimulated considerable material interests among the Seri. The more conspicuous items introduced since 1970 are double beds, chairs, dinette sets, propane stoves (some with ovens), 12-string guitars, tape recorders, binoculars, cameras, bicycles, and motor bikes. By 1972 at least 18 Seris owned used automobiles and trucks.

The Seri have used cash for many years in transactions with outsiders, but it was rarely used among themselves before 1970. As a result of the rapid conversion to cash, favors are less frequently carried out, the traditional begging system has become less effective as a means of obtaining food, and the system of gift exchange among relatives has been increasingly ignored. Many vehicle owners have begun to charge other Seris high fees for rides between camps, and some are using their vehicles to import food and soda pop for sale. By 1972 marriage had become difficult to contract without including a used automobile, if the young man's family owned one, as part of the bride price.

Partly in response to the burgeoning tourist trade, Punta Chueca became the second permanently settled Seri community by 1972. Its population, and that of El Desemboque, fluctuates greatly as the Seri move freely between the two villages. Services in both communities include an ice house, where Mexican fish-buyers load the Seri catch. El Desemboque also has a school, clinic, and Protestant church. However, activities in both villages focus on the resident Mexican traders' stores.

Among themselves the Seri speak their own language exclusively. Most speak a little Spanish; some speak it with ease. A number of Seris can read and write limited Spanish. Intermarriage with Mexicans is only beginning; apart from occasional mixing with other Indians in the distant past marriage has been almost completely endogamous. Medical facilities of the clinic are regularly sought and have virtually replaced traditional curing techniques. About 30 adults have accepted the be-

U. of Ariz., Ariz. State Mus., Tucson: center left, E-7912; center right, E-9696.

Fig. 2. Ironwood figurines, a nontraditional craft sold to outsiders. The first carvings were done in the early 1960s by José Astorga. Market demand for the pieces created family enterprises with most adult men and women and even children contributing to production. Figures are roughly shaped with a machete or butcher knife, and then worked with a rasp or a file as shown by Rosita Méndez (top); photograph by Diane Littler, probably at Punta Chueca, 1981. Sandpaper is used to smooth the surface, which is finally rubbed with motor oil or shoe polish to achieve a lustrous finish. Subjects include animals and fish native to the area such as the quail (center left) and porpoise (center right) as well as those made in response to tourist requests or copied from other sources. center left, Length 19.7 cm (other to same scale), made by José Astorga, El Desemboque, Sonora, 1968; center right, collected in Punta Chueca, Sonora, 1971. bottom, Tourist's car in El Desemboque surrounded by Seri women hoping to sell their carvings. Photograph by David Burckhalter, 1972.

liefs of the evangelical church, and nearly all the Seri have been affected by its teachings.

Social life continues to operate according to traditional patterns with comparatively little influence from Mexican culture. In the two permanent communities, Seris and Mexicans interact comfortably in affairs of mutual concern; otherwise they remain socially and culturally separate.

The Seri have never had any formal political structure, and they have not developed any kind of tribal organization. As a result they have lacked effective means of ensuring rights to the territory they consider to be theirs. They have retained their present territory only because it has long been unchallenged; however, since the 1950s the Seri coast has been viewed by the government in terms of its tourist potential. Tourist facilities developed rapidly at Bahía Kino and the development of other parts of the coast has been under discussion. Seri hunting on Isla Tiburón was banned in 1965 when the island was declared a wildlife preserve. By 1980 access to the interior of Tiburón (and most other Gulf islands) was restricted, and neither Seri nor other unauthorized visitors were permitted beyond the immediate beach zone. In practical terms Seri territory in 1980 consisted primarily of a strip of coast set aside as an ejido by the federal government in 1971 (fig. 1).

The rate of culture change since the 1950s has been very rapid and continues to accelerate, but change has been confined primarily to the economic and technological spheres. Although much esoteric knowledge is not being perpetuated, social institutions have been only superficially modified. Ethnic identification remains strong and the Seri show little interest in becoming participants in Mexican national life. Many Seri youths have visited Hermosillo briefly, but few have traveled farther and almost all have experienced difficulty functioning in Mexican culture. Thus neither the population nor the culture is being absorbed into the Mexican milieu.

Culture in 1692

In a letter to a superior written in 1692, Father Adam Gilg produced the earliest substantial description of Seri (Tepoca) culture (fig. 3). Because it is unique, its contents are abstracted in table 3, based on Matson's translation (Di Peso and Matson 1965).

Even though Gilg confined most of his remarks to overt aspects of Seri culture, the accuracy of his description is difficult to evaluate because few of the features mentioned were described again for more than 200 years. Some statements, such as those pertaining to kinship terminology, are unquestionably correct. Curiously, he makes no mention of arrow poison, a topic that uniformly fascinated other early writers. In some cases the discrepancies between Gilg's remarks and twentieth-century descriptions are due to demonstrable culture change. For example, the practice of piercing the nasal septum and inserting stones is corroborated by other eighteenth-century observers and by Hardy (1829) in 1826 but had disappeared by the time of McGee's visit in 1894. However, Gilg's erroneous statements concerning the language and his claim that the Seri lacked any kind of religion suggest that his understanding of Seri culture was rather shallow.

Archivum Romanum Societatis Jesu, Rome: Bohemiae 108.

Fig. 3. Seris on the march. Drawn by Father Adam Gilg as detail on a map accompanying a letter he wrote from Seri country in Feb. 1692 (Di Peso and Matson 1965:39, 49). According to Gilg's description, the men's breechclouts are simple fox pelts while the woman's skirt is made of animal skins (perhaps the precursor of the pelican-skin skirt of the 19th century). The child's tunic contrasts with Gilg's statement that children were naked. Gilg mentions that much jewelry was worn, such as the necklaces and nose ornaments depicted here; the nose ornaments persisted into the 19th century. The man at left is probably wearing an elaborate hair arrangement rather than a hat. The other man and the child appear to have feathers inserted in headbands. Both men carry knives tucked in armbands on their left arms (later knives were carried in the belt). According to Gilg, mats such as the woman carries on her back were woven of palm or reeds. The basket is supported by a headring, in the method women still use to carry burdens. The carrying yoke with loads suspended from each end in nets (left) is the traditional method men use for transport. Although bows and arrows were used as late as the 20th century, it is unlikely that bows were ever recurved like these.

Table 3. Seri Culture in 1692, after Gilg

Language: Bands speak mutually unintelligible dialects. Language contains few words and no abstract concepts, many words correspond to German, lack of negation morpheme. (All these statements are erroneous. Gilg was later accused of being unable to learn the language.)

Population: No more than 3,000 Seris. Infant mortality high; longevity great unless killed or died (presumably from disease) after exposure to the missions.

Band distinctions: Different "tribes" of Seris. Tepocas cited specifically.

Subsistence: Gathering, seasonal nomadism, fishing, raiding, and thievery, no mention of hunting. Foods included vegetation, fruits, herbs, and seeds, cactus fruit; rats, marmots, grasshoppers, worms, carrion, lice, fish. Tiswin prepared.

Weapons: Bow and arrow, quiver. Stone points formerly used. Knife carried in braided skin armlet worn on left arm.

Structures: None, open campsites.

Watercraft: Three-bundle cane balsa, heavy stone used as anchor.

Technology: Large pottery vessels, baskets (carried on headring), woven mats. Skins tanned with brains and tallow. Material inventory meager and lack of interest in accumulating goods.

Clothing: Married men wear fox skin over genitals and buttocks. Animal-skin skirt for women. Tubular kilt of rabbit furs sewed with thongs worn in cold weather. Deerskin sandals. Some European clothing worn. Complete nakedness was common, particularly boys to 16 years and old men.

Adornment: Necklace of seeds, fruits, beads, polished round shell pendant; girdle of various materials; feathers; black dots tattooed about the eyes and mouth; body, especially breast, buttocks, and cheeks, painted blue or red. Ears and nasal septum pierced soon after birth. Shells or colored ribbons placed in earlobes; shell (for children) and blue stone or skewer (for adults) placed in nasal septum. Hair hangs loose, is twisted about the temples, or tied up over head with thong.

Marriage and sex: Polygyny and premarital sexual activity absent. (Gilg was probably deluded on both counts.)

Avoidance taboos: father- and son-in-law do not approach or talk with each other.

Kinship: Extraordinary number of kinship terms. Older and younger brothers distinguish each other terminologically. Term for father depends on sex of offspring.

Religion: No religion and no magic (although one visionary experience that included dancing is described).

Table 3. (Cont'd)

Death: Body placed in trees and surrounded by thorny branches (see M.B. Moser 1970). Wailing for a day, women sing certain death songs at dawn and at night. Parents shave heads, paint faces black, and strip off clothing upon death of child. If death is by ambush, mourning continues until death is avenged by relatives.
Medicine: Unspecified effective herbal(?) cures for illness and venomous bites; singe and burn the skin for scorpion bite, illness, and chills. The sick are well cared for.
Gambling: A frequent pastime. Game played with small wooden pieces; European clothing serves as stakes.
Myth: Giants live across the sea, wade across the gulf.
Warfare: Generally nocturnal ambush or raid.
External relations: Plundering of Pima missions, constant warfare with Cocomacaketz (Pima).
Personality characteristics: Wild, vain, stupid, dirty, lazy, fickle, unstable, deceitful, cheerful, good-humored, generous, possessing good memories. Lacking in malice, greed, drunkenness, lewdness, or blasphemy.

SOURCE: Adam Gilg (DiPeso and Matson 1965).

Culture in the 1950s–1970s

This summary, based primarily on studies conducted between about 1955 and 1980, reflects the Seri of this period, unless otherwise indicated.

Subsistence

The Seri have never practiced agriculture. Traditional subsistence was based on hunting, fishing, shellfish gathering, and collecting wild plant foods; these activities survived in some degree to 1980. While Seri bands still functioned independently, the emphasis on these techniques differed considerably from one band to another (Moser 1963:22–24). Raiding and stealing livestock was added as a subsistence activity by some groups in the early seventeenth century; by the late 1800s all the surviving Seris probably depended on this source of food to some extent. Livestock stealing was largely replaced by subsistence fishing by the 1920s. As commercial fishing developed during the 1930s some food items began to be purchased with cash. By 1960 commercial fishing had become the basis of the Seri economy. Hunting had declined sharply and subsistence fishing had become supplementary to foods purchased with cash. However, a shift in the income base occurred during the late 1960s as the market for carved ironwood figurines expanded and Mexican and foreign fishing fleets seriously depleted Gulf resources (Ryerson 1976). By 1970 nearly all foods were bought with income derived from figurines; and fishing, both commercial and subsistence, and gathering had become relegated to a minor role.

Changes in subsistence activities since the turn of the century have been accompanied by major changes in diet. This is reflected in the difference between McGee's (1898:214) and Kroeber's (1931:20) estimates of the proportion of sea products, plant foods, and game consumed (although neither of these estimates may have been accurate). In the 1950s Malkin (1962:17, 54) ranked fish as the most important animal food followed by sea turtles, mollusks, and mammals (primarily rabbits, deer, bighorn, and peccary). Among the animals no longer commonly eaten are sea mammals and pelicans.

Several European domesticated animals are eaten including cattle, horses, burros, and goats. Chickens are kept but only their eggs are eaten (Griffen 1959:13).

Although the Seri have frequently been branded as cannibals, especially in the more sensational writings, there is no convincing evidence that human flesh was eaten either for sustenance or ritual.

Some 75 species of plants serve as traditional food sources (Felger 1976). One of the most important is mesquite, harvested in July. The pods and seeds were ground into flour. Eelgrass seeds, harvested in April, are toasted or ground and made into atole with the addition of turtle oil. Pitahaya, cardon, and saguaro fruits are harvested in summer and eaten; formerly the juice was fermented. Other plant foods include tree cholla fruit and agave hearts, the latter taken in January and February and roasted in pits (Felger and Moser 1970:160, 1971, 1973, 1974a).

Foods purchased from local traders that have become staples include corn flour, bread, rice, beans, potatoes, tomatoes, oranges, melons, canned meat, coffee, sugar, cookies, candy, and carbonated beverages. The most important item is wheat flour, which is made into pan-fried bread (Griffen 1959:13).

Most foods are boiled but meat and fish are often roasted. Cooking usually takes place outside on small fires. It is generally done by women, but it may be done by either sex and at any time.

Hunting is exclusively a male activity carried out on an individual basis by tracking and stalking. In the past, stuffed deer and rabbit heads were used as decoys. Larger game is hunted with rifles. Wooden clubs were formerly used for small game and for animals that can be taken by surprise, such as sea mammals.

Rifles began to be used around 1900 and had essentially replaced the bow and arrow by the 1930s, although W.N. Smith (1970:6) reports that a deer was killed with a bow and arrow as late as 1950 by a man who had run out of bullets. Bows were about five feet long, and arrows had removable foreshafts. Stone points and fire-hardened foreshafts survived until the late nineteenth century when glass and metal arrow points came into use. Arrow poison seems to have been last used in the

1860s (McGee 1898:112). According to Seris in the 1970s, it was made from the sap of *yerba de flecha* (*Sapium biloculare*), not putrefied liver injected with rattlesnake venom as commonly stated.

Fishing, also a male activity, is carried out mainly from boats. The traditional fishing implement is a spear with a two-pronged hardwood head, now made of metal. Hook and line fishing, without poles, was introduced to the Seri during the 1920s and has become the standard technique. Nets for catching sea bass were introduced in the 1940s.

Most maritime activity centers around sea turtles (fig. 4) when seasonally abundant, although in some localities they may be taken all year (Felger, Clifton, and Regal 1976). The weapon is a harpoon with a detachable barbed metal head sunk in a wooden plug (Ascher 1962).

The indigenous watercraft from which the Seri fished was the cane balsa, powered by a double-bladed paddle (fig. 5). A few were still in use during the early 1920s but were completely replaced shortly thereafter by small flat-bottomed boats often made from driftwood. Later boats, modeled after the dory used by the Mexican fishermen, were constructed of planks and painted in bright colors. Single-bladed paddles were used and boats were outfitted with masts, a blanket sometimes serving as the sail. By about 1950 small outboard motors were being rented to the Seri. By 1970 several Seris owned motors, and by the late 1970s the wood dory had been replaced by molded fiberglass boats.

Women gather most plant foods, but men sometimes help. A knife or wooden digging stick is used to cut or uproot plants. Mesquite pods are crushed in a bedrock or earth mortar with a hardwood pestle (Felger and Moser 1971:55–56). Most seeds are ground with a metate and mano consisting of unshaped cobbles found on the beaches or scavenged from archeological sites.

Structures and Settlement Pattern

The traditional style of house, built by women, was in use in 1894 and has persisted through the 1970s, although used only at temporary camps. It takes the form of a Quonset hut about nine feet long, with an open end or an opening in one side. Its framework is formed by successive parallel arches of bent ocotillo branches, connected by lengthwise branches and fastened with supple twigs, string, wire, or any other suitable material. The framework was formerly covered with brush,

Fig. 4. Turtle feasts. left, Leatherback turtle being painted by Aurora Comito at Saps camp, south of Estero Sargento, opposite I. Tiburón. These huge turtles are rarely caught; between 1953 and 1970 only 4 are known. A catch is followed by a ceremony during which the turtle is painted (here in blue and white) before it is eaten. The turtle's head is covered with branches of *Bursera microphylla*, a sacred bush of the Seri (Mary Beck Moser, communication to editors 1981). Photograph by Mary Beck Moser, March 24, 1981. right, Cooking a green turtle. Photograph by Richard Felger, probably at Punta Chueca, near Bahía Kino, about 1972.

Mus. of the Amer. Ind., Heye Foundation, New York: top, 24086; bottom, 23784.
Fig. 5. Water transportation. top, One-man balsa of carrizo cane on Bahía Kino, supposedly the last one made by the Seri. The man holds a long harpoon used in turtle hunting, which occasionally doubled as a paddle. The typical double-bladed paddle rests on the balsa. bottom, Plank boat at I. Tiburón, with painted paddle. Made by hand and modeled after the Mexican dory, this type of boat replaced the balsa in the 1920s. Photographs by Edward H. Davis, 1922 and 1924.

seaweed, and turtle shells; more recently cardboard, canvas, and plastic have also been used (fig. 7).

Each dwelling generally shelters a single nuclear family, although a recently married son and his wife may attach their house onto that of his parents. Otherwise, location with respect to other people is a matter of individual preference. At camps on the coast, houses are usually placed just below the crest of a dune.

Traditional camp locations are known to all the Seri. When occupied, the population of a camp may be as great as 15 families. When abandoned, houses are left standing and new ones built when the camp is next occupied.

In the two permanent communities of El Desemboque and Punta Chueca, the traditional settlement pattern persists but the traditional house has been completely replaced by more substantial structures with vertical walls and flat roofs. Some are built in the style of the rural Mexican jacal with a mud-plastered ocotillo

Mus. of the Amer. Ind., Heye Foundation, New York: 24032.
Fig. 6. Alberto Molina and Guadalupe Astorga, obtaining liquid from a barrel cactus. Photograph by Edward H. Davis, at Johnson Mt., Sonora, 1929.

frame; others utilize a wood frame covered with tarpaper. The heavier work involved in their construction is undertaken by men; women perform the lighter tasks. Many families in both communities moved into cinderblock houses constructed by the Mexican government during the late 1970s.

The traditional house form has always been considered a temporary shelter. It contains little or no furniture and nearly all activities are conducted outside the house; however, houses in the two villages are more permanent. Some are very well furnished and there has been a concomitant shift to bringing certain activities, such as cooking, indoors.

Technology

Pottery was made by women and continued to be used until the middle 1930s when metal containers and cooking vessels completely replaced it. Since then it has been produced only for tourist consumption.

Contemporary pottery is weak and friable due to its high content of rabbit dung temper and low firing temperatures. Vessels are made by coiling on a small molded base. Bivalve shells were used for thinning; now objects such as spoons may be used. Decoration in red, white, blue-gray, or bright blue consists of simple, mostly linear designs, and is applied with the finger. Olla forms predominate (Bowen and Moser 1968).

Baskets are made by women. They were formerly a woman's most important single utensil. By 1960 some were still made for use but most were produced for sale. Some contemporary baskets are of excellent technical quality.

Except for a single plaited form, Seri baskets are close-coiled on a bundle foundation (fig. 8). *Torote* (*Jatropha cuneata*) is used for foundation and stitching splints. Present forms are primarily shallow bowls and ollas. Utilitarian baskets are undecorated or incorporate a single colored coil. Others, particularly those

Smithsonian, NAA: top 4281-B, center left 81-11581; center right, U. of Ariz., Ariz. State Mus., Tucson: 25021.

Fig. 7. Habitations. top, Camp at Pascual Encinas's Ranch, San Francisco de Costa Rica, Sonora. Photograph by William Dinwiddie, Nov. 1894. center left, Camp with departing hunters. Photograph by J.F. Reynolds Scott, 1925. center right, Lolita Astorga preparing fry bread in front of a permanent Mexican-style jacal house made of ocotillo stems caulked with mud. Some household goods are stored on the earth-covered roof. The man is Chico Sesma. Photograph by James W. Manson, Feb. 1963. bottom left, El Desemboque with Seri houses in the foreground. The whitewashed structures include Mexican traders' stores and the schoolhouse (far left). Wooden fishing motorboats are beached. The boats are pointed at both ends with a mount for the outboard motor added on the stern. Photograph by Thomas Bowen, April 1967. bottom right, Saps camp south of Estero Sargento, opposite I. Tiburón. Frame of uncompleted traditional Quonset-shaped house at left has been covered with corrugated tar paper. Beef or deer meat is hanging on an ocotillo-stem drying rack. The woman standing in the center may be Angelina Torres. Photograph by Mary Beck Moser, 1981.

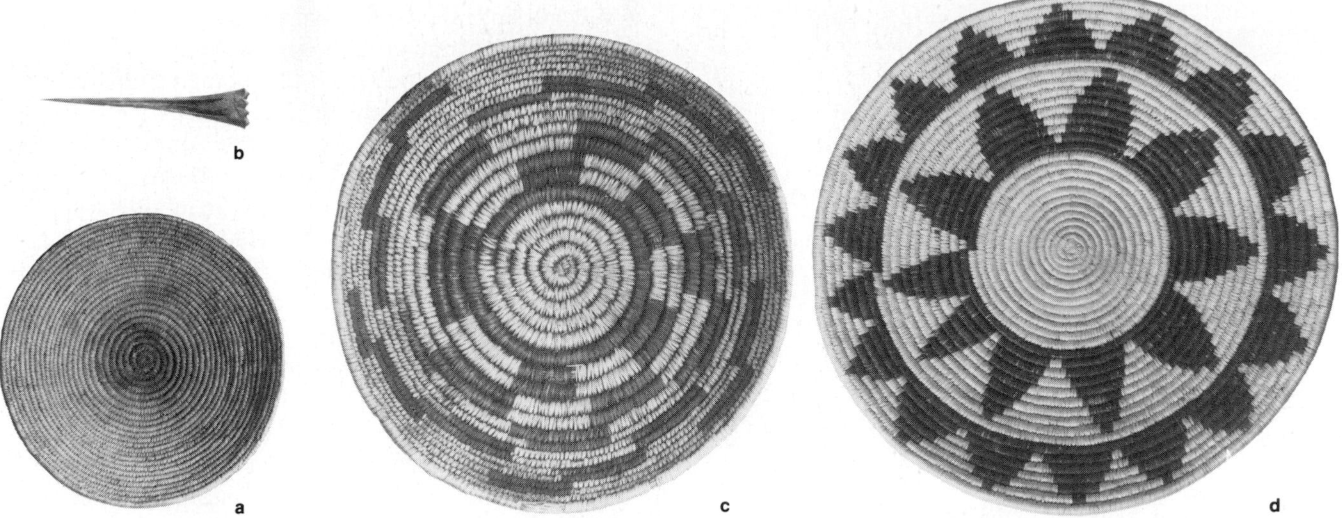

Smithsonian, Dept. of Anthr.: a, 174,528; b, 222,653; c, 381,025; d, 409,811.

Fig. 8. Coiled basketry. a, Shallow tray, once regarded by the Seri as a woman's most important household utensil. Although the basic construction technique, including the use of b, a deer bone awl, to perforate the coils has largely been preserved, baskets are now made exclusively for sale, having been replaced for Seri use by metal and plastic containers. It is not certain whether any baskets were decorated before 1900, although characteristic reddish-brown designs appeared shortly thereafter and had become common by the 1920s (c). Nearly all late 20th-century baskets are decorated (d), and the commercial market has encouraged many novel designs and basket forms. Diameter of a, 23.5 cm, rest to same scale; a and b collected by WJ McGee in 1894–1895; c collected by Charles Sheldon in 1921–1922; d collected in 1967.

made for sale, are decorated with designs in red-brown and a more recent black. Considerable Papago influence on basketry is visible (Moser 1973; Bowen 1973).

Ironwood carving has become the major craft activity (Ryerson 1976; Hills 1977). The carvings are mostly stylized animal figures, and most of the animals known to the Seri have been represented. The process begins by roughing out the figure with a machete or small hatchet, this usually being men's work. Further shaping with a hack saw, filing the figure to final form, sanding, and hand polishing may also be done by the men although many women take over after rough shaping. An entire family may contribute to various stages of production (B. Johnston 1968).

Careful attention is paid to coordinating the natural grain of the wood with the lines of the figure. From both aesthetic and technical standpoints some of the best pieces are exquisite.

Transport

Women traditionally placed burdens in a basket that was carried on the head with the aid of a headring (fig. 9). This mode of transport continues but metal washbasins are now the characteristic containers. Men carry a wooden yoke over one shoulder with loads suspended from each end in nets. Formerly, balsas or boats were important means of transporting loads. The acquisition of automobiles since 1970 has largely eliminated the need for long-distance carrying.

Clothing and Adornment

The clothes worn by most Seri men are no different from those of rural Mexicans. Many Seris own shoes although sandals and bare feet are common in camp. Every male owns a straw cowboy hat, and sunglasses are popular. Hair is generally cut as among the Mexican population although some men continue to wear their hair long, either loose or in a single or double braid. Those who retain long hair also wear a bright cloth kilt over their conventional trousers, a survival of the pelican-skin kilt that disappeared shortly after 1900 (fig. 10).

Many women continue to wear distinctive clothing, which they sew by hand, although commercial clothing is increasingly worn. Skirts are full and ankle length. Handmade blouses are long sleeved, typically a bright color with piping of contrasting color. Women wear sandals in the desert but many go barefoot in camp. Hair is parted in the middle and worn long, either loose or in braids. Standard headgear is a cotton shawl. Shell necklaces (fig. 11) are occasionally worn by older women.

Face painting among men had nearly disappeared by the early 1950s. By the late 1960s it had become rare among Seri women though occasional painting continues. Design is typically a single line across the cheeks and nose with pendant designs. Colors are blue, red, white, yellow, and black. Men's and women's designs differed and some designs may have been characteristic of specific families (Xavier 1946). Typically, unmarried

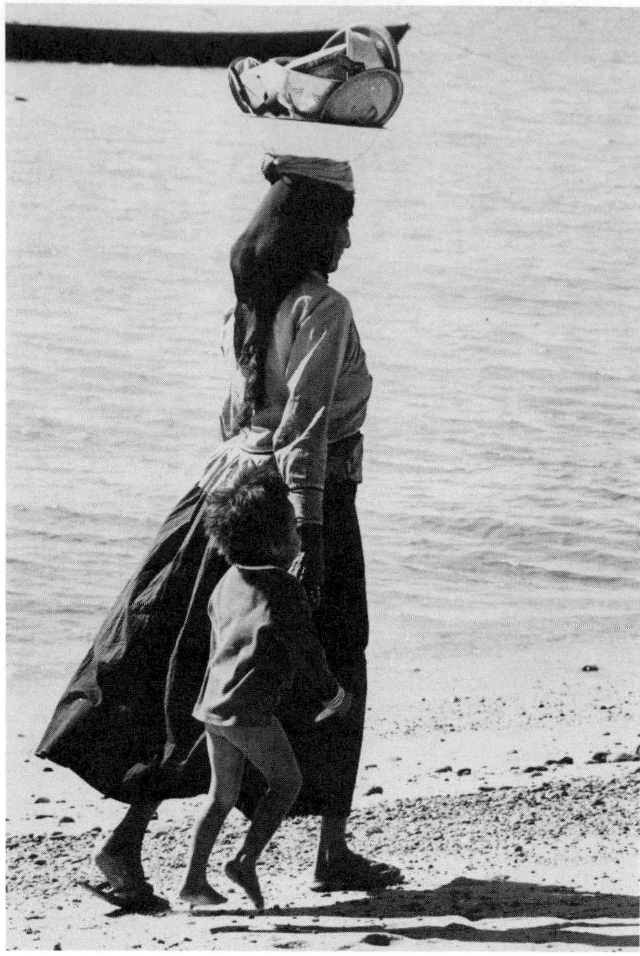

Fig. 9. Transportation of household goods using a head-ring support. Lupe Comito in traditional hand-sewn skirt and blouse carrying an enameled basin filled with kitchen utensils. Photograph by David L. Burckhalter, El Desemboque, 1971.

women painted their faces with more care and intricacy than married women (fig. 12).

A few women have a tattooed line descending from the lower lip, which formerly served to identify captured Seris (Moser and White 1968:145). Many women use lipstick and several have experimented with tinted hair.

Life Cycle

Children are regarded as economic assets and are therefore desired. Twins are welcomed. Girls are generally preferred for the bride price they will later bring.

Conception is believed to occur when the baby's spirit enters the woman's body. This may be induced or prevented by drinking certain herbal preparations.

Throughout pregnancy the expectant mother and father continue normal activity. No food taboos are presently observed. However, women should avoid contact with certain objects to insure normal delivery and the health of the child. Women often conceive while a child is still nursing; this has been a major cause of malnutrition and death among young children.

Delivery usually occurs in the woman's house and is attended by a paid midwife. Herbal teas are drunk to speed delivery. The husband either continues routine activity or stays close to the house. Shortly after birth, a charcoal cross may be painted on the infant's forehead to prevent harm. Later he is placed on a cradleboard.

There are several postdelivery restrictions and observances for both parents. A ritual fire must be maintained. The mother is not permitted to eat animal flesh for eight days, the father for four days. Four days after the birth the parents must wash their hair in salt water. Formerly, neither parent engaged in work for four days although this restriction has been relaxed.

The child receives a Spanish name soon after birth and a Seri name after about a year. Often derived from a characteristic of the child, the Seri name is used in address until puberty; thereafter, only in reference. Individuals may receive a variety of nicknames throughout their lifetimes. Spanish names may be conferred by a Seri or a non-Seri. Among a few families nominal *compadrazgo* relationships are recognized, but these do not seem to involve obligations of any kind.

Partial adoption may occur if a couple has lost a child. A child may be donated to the couple, who feed and clothe him, but the child returns to his parents' house at night. The child eventually reverts to his parents but maintains certain life-long rights and obligations with his foster family. An adult who has lost most of his relatives may request adoption into another family. He lives apart but functionally becomes their youngest child (M.B. Moser 1970a; Griffen 1959:22–23).

A ceremony is given immediately upon a girl's reaching physical maturity. The puberty fiesta, lasting four days, is the only major ceremonial event remaining in Seri culture.

The sponsor of the ceremony is one of several individuals who stand in a special relationship with the girl known as *ʔamák*. The girl's mother decides which *ʔamák* must actually fulfill this obligation, usually choosing a female, and one whom she likes or who she believes has the means to provide the best fiesta. This *ʔamák* in turn designates one of her *ʔamákx* as an assistant. The girl is taken to the house of her *ʔamák* where she remains in seclusion for four days. Her face is painted but she must not look at herself. She must abstain from meat for eight days.

The accompanying fiesta is public. The central feature is dancing on a foot drum, which provides syncopated accompaniment to a paid singer with a tin-can rattle. Young girls engage in a betting game during this time, and food is provided by the family of the *ʔamák*. Dancing continues throughout the fourth night. Before dawn the girl is taken to the sea where she washes her hair. The fiesta ends when the rising sun first strikes

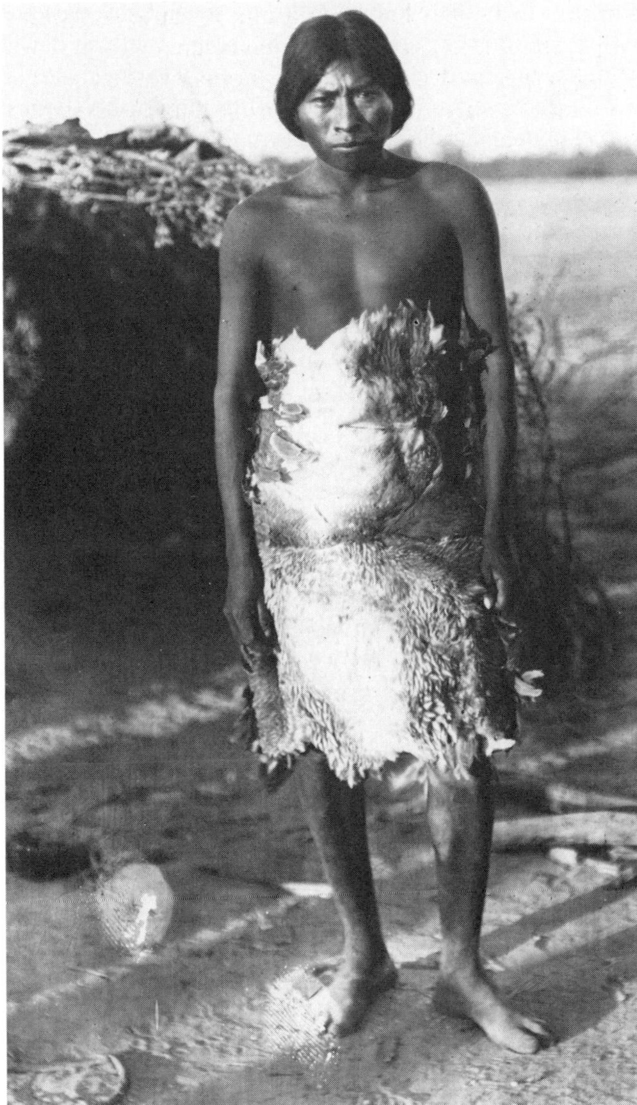

left, Smithsonian, NAA: 4262.

Fig. 10. Men's apparel. left, Juan Chávez wearing pelican-skin kilt fastened with a belt of mesquite fiber. Photograph by William Dinwiddie, Rancho San Francisco de Costa Rica, Sonora, Nov. 1894. right, Miguel Barnet (b. 1915) wearing traditional long hair and a cloth kilt over cotton trousers. Photograph by Thomas Bowen, at El Desemboque, 1967.

the dancer, whereupon the *ʔamák* throws a basket of gifts to the spectators (Griffen 1959:23–25; Hinton 1955).

A similar ceremony was formerly performed for pubescent boys.

Polygyny was occasionally practiced, but all present marriages are monogamous. Marriage is contracted outside one's kin group and excludes all cousins, who are equated terminologically with siblings. Marriages are typically arranged by the parents with little influence from the prospective couple. Sometimes a boy can initiate proceedings by giving a present to a girl of his choice, whereupon his family takes over negotiations, if it approves. Elopement may have been common in the past. After the proposal is tentatively accepted by the girl's parents the boy's family and relatives must raise a substantial bride price to secure final approval. Upon final payment, the bride moves in with the husband. There is no ceremony of any kind.

Bride service obligations continue after marriage. Initial residence is flexible but frequently patrilocal; after a short time the couple may reside anywhere.

Divorce is not common. The bride price is not returned, and the woman is responsible for the children unless other arrangements are made.

When death occurs, one of the male *ʔamákx* of the deceased is charged with the responsibility for burying the body and performing the other necessary activities. This *ʔamák* must paint black lines on the back of his hands and fingers to protect himself against dangers associated with burial. Unless he has buried four people previously, he abstains from eating meat for the next four days.

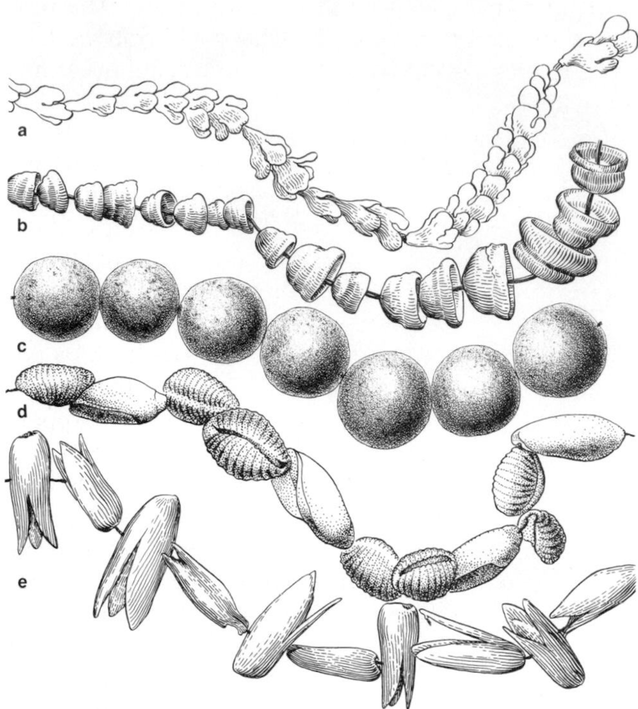

a, Smithsonian, Dept. of Anthr.: 174,499; U. of Ariz., Ariz. State Mus., Tucson: b, E-8594, c, E-6034, d, E-6056, e, E-6093.

Fig. 11. Necklaces. Traditionally an important item of adornment, they were made of a variety of materials, including dried flowers (a). Although worn since at least the 17th century, necklaces in the 1980s were produced almost exclusively for the tourist market. Examples are: b, octopus suction cups; c, unfired blue beads; d, shell; e, ocotillo buds. a, collected by WJ McGee in 1894–1895; b, collected before 1969; c, collected in 1963–1964; d, collected in 1963; e, collected in 1964. All shown actual size.

There is no ceremony at the burial and anyone may attend. The body is wrapped in a blanket; if a coffin is not used the body is positioned on its side with the knees flexed and forearms laid across the abdomen. The head must be to the west so that the spirit, which makes a flip upon leaving the body, will be properly oriented for its journey to the afterworld in the western sky. The grave is covered with stones or brush to thwart predatory animals.

Stillborns and aborted fetuses are placed in cardon branches. Rare instances of disposal of adults in this manner are remembered, but if this was ever a common practice for adults it has long since been replaced by inhumation (M.B. Moser 1970).

After the burial the *ʔamák* builds a new house for himself and his family. The possessions of the deceased's family and those of the *ʔamák* are exchanged, and the family of the dead person takes up residence in the old dwelling of the *ʔamák*. In the past, the deceased's house was burned.

Anyone may mourn a death. Men sob quietly for a few days at most. For women, there are two separate expressions of mourning, a wailing and a low moan during which the woman talks as though to the deceased. Women mourn away from camp, chiefly at dawn or dusk, and may continue as long as a year.

The deceased is not referred to by any of his names or nicknames, but he can be designated by kinship terms. He is ostensibly forgotten quickly. The surviving spouse may remarry but widowers seem less desirable as spouses than young widows. Neither the levirate nor sororate is practiced (Griffen 1959:25–30).

Social Organization

The nuclear family forms the core of contemporary Seri social life and is the basic production and consumption unit. Nearly all subsistence needs can be met by the family, and the few manufactured items (unless intended for the tourist market) stay within the household. Ownership of tangible property is largely vested in the household, with the exception of personal items and those associated with specific sex roles, such as fishing gear. Exchange between nuclear families occurs primarily as a result of the bride price and often assumes major proportions. The bride's family may also receive some contribution of labor from the bride's husband, but the new couple and the bride's family attend to the majority of their needs as independent nuclear families.

Kinship terminology is bifurcate collateral (Yuman). One of the distinguishing features of the system is the unusual number of terminological distinctions. Griffen (1959:40–42) lists 57 terms of address plus another 17 forms that connote affection but that cannot be used unless the speaker is intoxicated.

As Gilg stated (table 3), a son and daughter call their father by different terms; however, a single term for mother is used regardless of the sex of the child. These, like many Seri terms, have reciprocals; a man distinguishes his son and daughter but a woman uses a single term for both (although a word indicating gender may be added).

Sibling terminology extends to cousins. Siblings are distinguished by sex, and those of the same sex are further distinguished by age. In addressing an individual classed as an older sister, male and female speakers use separate terms. In the ascending generation father's older and younger brothers are distinguished as are mother's older and younger brothers and sisters. Father's sisters are addressed by a single term regardless of relative age or sex of the speaker (Kroeber 1931:9–11; Griffen 1959:36–42).

Several sets of avoidance relations are observed, such as between parents-in-law and their children-in-law, between a woman and her husband's oldest brother, and between a man and all his wife's sisters but the youngest. As Kroeber (1931:8) noted, strict avoidance would be difficult to maintain in a very small society, and for this reason Griffen (1959:38) refers to these as "non-speaking relations." In instances of unavoidable contact a man may exchange a few necessary words with his wife's brothers, and avoidance restrictions are lifted when the persons affected are intoxicated or have reached old age. Under current conditions of rapid population increase, avoidance relations may be easier to adhere to than in the past. However, since the trend toward leniency is firmly established it may well continue.

Joking relations exist between a woman and her husband's younger brothers but between only her youngest sister and her husband. It is expressed by mildly obscene language and actions.

Teknonymy, based on the child's Seri nickname, is a common form of address; otherwise Spanish names are gaining favor over kinship terms. Griffen (1959:39–40) attributes this to the increasing importance of relationships other than those based on kinship as Seri life changes.

Since the late nineteenth century there have been no functioning social units larger than the nuclear family (apart from the entire Seri tribe itself). Two important groupings existed in the past, although their characteristics are not well known. Both Seri tradition and European documents agree that the Seri were formerly dispersed into some half-dozen territorially defined, politically independent, and to some extent culturally and dialectally distinct units. These, the maximum units of traditional social structure, were often designated "tribes" or "nations" by the early writers and have been referred to as bands (Griffen 1959:47; Moser 1963; Owen 1965). According to Seri oral history (Moser 1963) three of the bands were subdivided into smaller units called *iʔišitim*, and it is this unit that was central in Seri life. The *iʔišitim* was apparently a well-integrated grouping based on principles of patrilineal descent, patrilocal residence, and exogamy. Each such unit was named and associated with a specific territory. Although Moser (1963:21) has referred to them as clans (following Murdock 1949) they may have resembled the rancherias of the peninsular Indians of Baja California (see also Bahre 1980). Seris maintain that the collapse of band and *iʔišitim* structure occurred in the late nineteenth century, after which descent became bilateral, residence retained only vestiges of patrilocality, the exogamous prescription necessarily dissolved, and the present Seri tribe, composed simply of all Seris, emerged as a de facto social entity. Although the tribe is viewed by contemporary Seri as a valid social grouping, it functions principally as a unit of ethnic identification.

Seri culture maintains few formal status positions. While the *iʔišitim* were functioning some authority may have been vested in older males. At present husbands serve as informal heads of their households. A war leader existed in the past but his authority was confined to military matters. Certain individual shamans have had some political power, but it is unlikely that power was ever institutionalized in the status itself. The role played by twentieth-century "chiefs" is restricted to dealings with outsiders and does not carry over into internal affairs.

In addition to kinship the *ʔamák* system, consisting of a set of reciprocal obligations between specific individuals for puberty fiesta and burial sponsorship, constitutes a separate system of social relationships. Since the structure of the system has not been fully analyzed, the following remarks are tentative. *ʔamák* relationships normally exist between siblings of several, often unrelated families. The system perpetuates itself by the offspring of two individuals who stand in the *ʔamák* relationship becoming *ʔamákx* to each other. Apparently, this has not created any broader bonds between families; ties exist only between those individuals who stand in the *ʔamák* relationship.

In theory, one's *ʔamákx* seem to be determined bilaterally and by generation: ego's *ʔamákx* are the descendants of the *ʔamákx* of any direct ancestor of ego who are also on ego's generation level. In practice, a Seri recognizes as his *ʔamákx* only the grandchildren of the *ʔamákx* of his four grandparents, and certain of these are unlikely to be pressed into service. The person chosen to sponsor a puberty fiesta is usually a woman and almost always a descendant of the girl's mother's mother's *ʔamák*. Burial is always performed by a male and almost always by the son of the dead person's father's *ʔamák*. Thus the sex of the *ʔamák* largely determines whether the obligation to the reciprocal is for burial or fiesta sponsorship. In rare cases a male might be burdened with both fiesta and burial responsibilities for a female reciprocal.

The *ʔamák* system appeared in the 1970s to be breaking down in operation if not in principle. This is particularly noticeable with respect to burial obligations, as considerable effort is sometimes expended in persuading outsiders to bury the dead (Griffen 1959:44–46).

Religion

Traditional religion is poorly known. Kroeber (1931:4) and Gilg (DiPeso and Matson 1965) before him believed the Seri to be "remarkably religionless." Undoubtedly both observers missed the many inconspicuous ritual observances that pervaded most activities, and Gilg may have misinterpreted the public ceremonies as amusement because of their outwardly secular appearance.

Seri religion was oriented around belief in a large number of malevolent spirits who were placated by individual and public ritual. Shamans, who served principally as medical practitioners, received their power by direct contact with the spirits by means of a vision quest.

As a functioning system, Seri religion is dead. Tra-

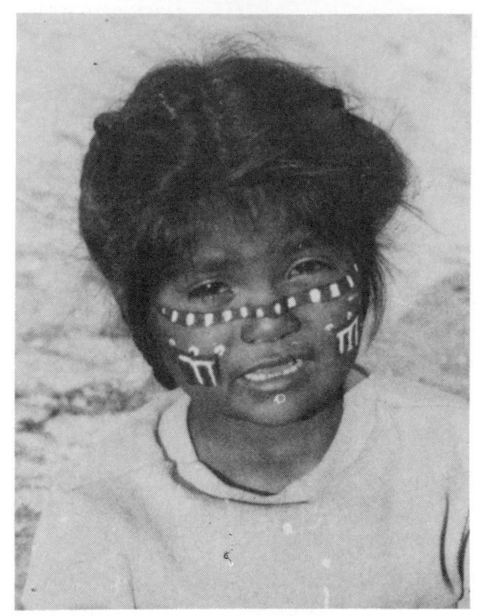

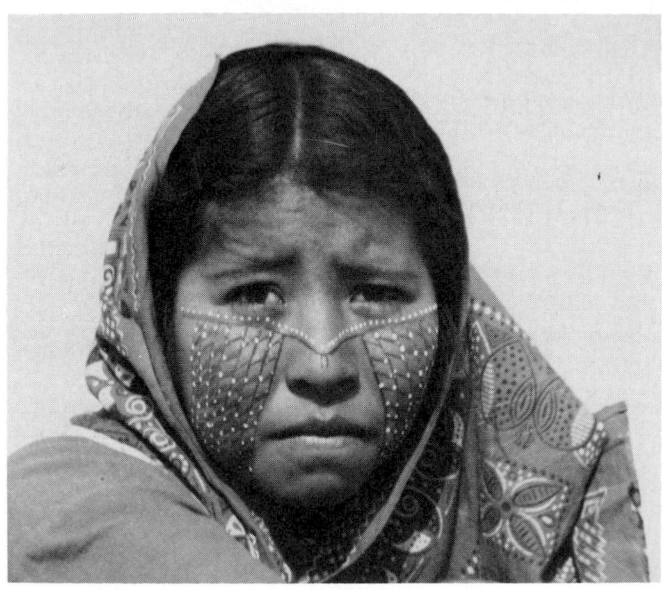

top center, Mus. of the Amer. Ind., Heye Foundation, New York: 23875; top right, Smithsonian, NAA: 4265-A-1; center left, U. of Ariz., Ariz. State Mus., Tucson: 24967; center right: Mus. of the Amer. Ind., Heye Foundation, New York: 24044; bottom left, U. of Ariz., Ariz. State Mus., Tucson: 25096; bottom center, Natl. Geographic Soc., Washington; bottom right, San Diego Mus. of Man, Calif.: 1963-23-67, 1963-23-71, 1963-23-68 ab.

Fig. 12. Face painting. The paints were obtained from mineral pigments sometimes gathered from sources as distant as I. San Esteban. Various designs were used, and women sometimes painted and removed 3 different designs in a day (Quinn and Quinn 1965:160). top left, María de la Luz Díaz at a leatherback turtle feast. Photograph by Mary Beck Moser at Saps camp, south of Estero Sargento, opposite I. Tiburón, 1981. top center, Girl from I. Tiburón, Sonora. Photograph by Edward H. Davis, 1929. top right, Candelaria wearing a decoration in blue, red, and white. Photograph by William Dinwiddie at Pascual Encinas's Ranch, San Francisco de Costa Rica, Sonora, 1894. center left, Graciela Cesma (b. 1941). Photograph by James Manson, I. Tiburón or Bahía Kino, Sonora, 1957. center right, Miguel Barnet at Bahía Kino, Sonora, having his face painted by Lola Astorga. Photograph by Edward H. Davis, 1934. bottom left, Sara with winged style of face paint. Photograph by James Manson, I. Tiburón or Bahía Kino, Sonora, 1960. bottom center, Applying face paint using a mirror. Before mirrors were available, people painting their own faces used a bowl of water in the shade reflecting the face in sunlight (McGee 1898:166). Photograph by Walter M. Edwards, north of Bahía Kino, Sonora, 1971. bottom right, Face painting kit includes a palette of flat circular granite. Dried blue paint is visible; on the reverse side is a blue X. Dry paints, often kept in a shell as here, are ground with a hard stone on the palette and then mixed with water. Diameter of palette about 11.0 cm, rest to same scale. All collected by Ralph C. Michelsen in El Desemboque, Sonora, 1964.

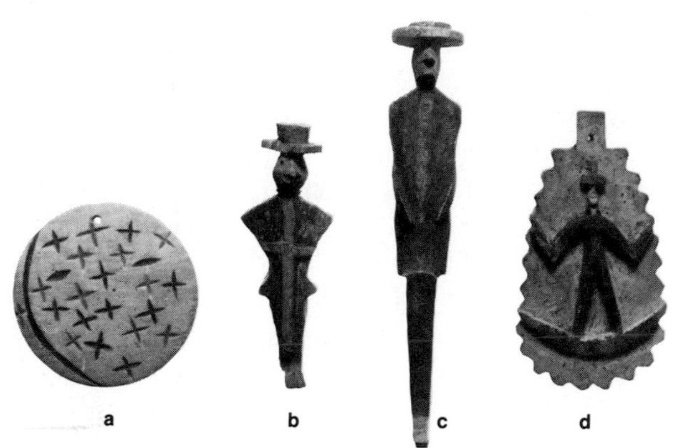

U. of Ariz., Ariz. State Mus., Tucson: a, E-5223, b, E-952, c, E-945, d, E-819.

Fig. 13. Religious items. a, Wooden amulet, with red and blue designs on both sides. The others, wooden santos, painted blue and red, are made and used by shamans who also rent them to their clients to prevent illness. a, Diameter 5.9 cm (rest to same scale), collected by William Griffen in El Desemboque, Sonora, 1955. Rest collected by Gwyneth Harrington, b and c in El Desemboque, Sonora, in 1941, d in Bahía Kino area in 1940.

ditional beliefs have been discarded by all but a few of the older people. Christian beliefs and concepts are only poorly understood by the majority of Seris, but the teachings of the evangelical church have become an effective replacement for some 30 converts. Similarly, European medicine and healing by prayer among the Christianized Seris have completely replaced the curing function of shamans. The last vision quest occurred about 1930.

A great many individual ritual acts are still observed, but since the underlying belief system has disintegrated, they are performed largely out of tradition. Four public ceremonies are still performed but only the girls' puberty fiesta occurs regularly. The festive atmosphere surrounding the four surviving ceremonies, and others no longer performed, was based on the theory that festive behavior helps pacify potentially dangerous spirits. While the form of the ceremonies has survived, they are now viewed principally as celebrations of important events.

Music

Music is most often sung and played for enjoyment, even though most songs bear a religious connotation or originated as shamans' songs. Besides enjoyment, songs have traditionally been sung for purposes such as curing, luck in gambling or hunting, influencing a marriage arrangement, placing a curse, and fulfilling ritual requirements after killing an enemy. Both sexes sing but women may not sing in public unless intoxicated.

Musical instruments include a one-string box-shaped fiddle, musical bow, mouth bow, flutes and whistles, rasping stick, a variety of rattles, and foot drum (fig. 14). Most are used to accompany singing or dancing but some are also solo instruments. Several instruments were formerly played by women as well as men.

Traditional Seri music is not a folk idiom. It appears to be uninfluenced by Spanish or Mexican forms, but the Seri attribute some of their songs to the Yaqui. Many instruments played by the Seri have wide distributions but some, such as the cocoon rattle, are clearly of Yaqui origin. The only instrument derived from a European form is the one-string fiddle, but the idea of the fiddle probably reached the Seri through the Yaqui. Characteristically, the instrument was simplified by the Seri.

Because of the radio and increasing mobility, Mexican popular music is more commonly heard than is traditional music. Many of the younger Seris own guitars or other European instruments and are adept musicians. Traditional music is not being taught to the younger generation (Bowen and Moser 1970a).

Synonymy†

The name Seri comes into English from Spanish, in which it has been in use since the seventeenth century. The first use is in the form Heris, 1645 (Pérez de Ribas

†This synonymy was written by Thomas Bowen, with additions by Ives Goddard.

1944:149). Father Adam Gilg, who used Seris as a cover term for several related peoples (including specifically the Tepocas), stated that the name was Spanish (DiPeso and Matson 1965:41). However, no Spanish etymology has been established, Gatschet's (1877–1892, 4:3) derivation from *sera* 'large basket' being unsupportable; Gilg's form Sera, 1692 (DiPeso and Matson 1965:46) is apparently only a Latin inflectional form. McGee (1898:9, 129) wrote that their name was from an Ópata word that "may be translated 'spry'," giving Se-ere as the "etymologic form." The Pima-Papago name is *ṣé·l* ([ṣɨ·ḷ] (Saxton and Saxton 1969:90, 156). Perhaps the name was of Uto-Aztecan origin, and Gilg's statement refers only to the fact that it is not the Seri self-designation.

top, U. of Ariz., Ariz. State Mus., Tucson: 25169.

Fig. 14. Musical instruments. top, Miguel Barnet playing a one-string fiddle, a Seri instrument type ultimately derived from the European 4-string violin. Photograph by James Manson at El Desemboque, Sonora, about 1960. bottom, Luis Guicho supporting himself with poles while playing a foot drum—dancing on a board over a pit—accompanied by a seated singer with tin can rattle. Photograph by Edward Moser at a girl's puberty fiesta at El Desemboque, 1970.

The Seri call themselves *koŋkáak* '(the) people'; the singular is *k^wį́kke* 'person' (Moser and Moser 1976:294). These forms were recorded by Alphonse Pinart in 1879 as komkak, sg. kmike (McGee 1898:129).

Despite disagreement on the existence of certain bands, the names have been rendered uniformly during the twentieth century: Seri(s), Tepocas, Tiburones, Salineros, Tastioteños, Guaymas, and Upanguaymas. McGee presents a detailed list of historical spelling variants (1898:128–130), of which the most divergent are listed here. Seri: Heris, 1645 (Pérez de Ribas); Ceris, 1745 (Villa-Señor); Ceres (Hardy, 1826); Sadi (*San Francisco Chronicle*, 1896); Soris (Deniker, 1900). Tepocas: Topoquis (Kino's map, 1701); Tepeco (Disturnell's map, 1847). Guaymas: Uayemas (*Carta Anua*, 1628, in Griffen 1961:14); Gueimas (Villa-Señor, 1748); Baymas (Ortega, 1754); Guaymi (Bancroft, 1882). Upanguaymas: Jupangueimas (Villa-Señor, 1748); Opan Guaimas (Nentvig, 1763); Houpin Guaymas (Hardy, 1829); Jumpanguaymas (Velasco, 1860).

Sources

Mention of the Seri in the historic records is sometimes extensive but generally with little specific information about the culture (Polzer 1976). Many sources merely repeat statements, sometimes erroneous, of earlier observers. The significant exceptions are Gilg's 1692 description (Di Peso and Matson 1965) and Hardy's (1829) firsthand observations. The best historical summaries are by McGee (1898), Griffen (1961), Spicer (1962), Bahre (1967), Tweed (1973, 1975), Kessell (1975), and Sheridan (1979). A comprehensive bibliography has been prepared by Moser (1976).

Several general accounts of the Seri are available. McGee's monograph (1898) is the result of the first ethnological investigations ("History of Ethnological Research," fig. 4, vol. 9). Unfortunately McGee's data are not clearly separated from his inferences, which are based on a rather fertile imagination and theoretical dogma no longer tenable (see Fontana 1971). Despite many errors, it is still an important work; the historical summary is valuable and the photographs are unique.

Valuable and largely accurate notes based on several visits to the Seri during the 1920s by Davis and Sheldon have been published (Quinn and Quinn 1965; Sheldon 1979); both works contain important photographs. Kroeber's (1931) short monograph is sketchy but an important and generally accurate study. Of special interest are his comparative data. One of the most widely known (and sensational) descriptions of the Seri is by Coolidge and Coolidge (1939); unfortunately, it is also one of the more inaccurate accounts. Hayden's (1942) article is based on careful observations and contains several photographs and drawings. A series of photographs from about 1950 has been published by W.N.

Smith (1974). Hinton's (1969) summary incorporates several good photographs. W.N. Smith's (1970) introduction to a collection of Ted De Grazia paintings of the Seri is both well-rounded and informative. B. Johnston's (1970) and Burckhalter's (1976) books are basically photographic essays with minimal texts. The best general work in Spanish is Nolasco Armas's (1967) monograph, incorporating original field data and copious photographs.

The basic source on contemporary Seri culture is Griffen's concise monograph (1959), the result of fieldwork. It is the first published treatment of several major areas of Seri culture, many of which have not been dealt with since. It remains the most important single study.

The archeology of the Seri coast has been evaluated briefly by Hayden (1956) and Bowen (1976), and more extensively by Bowen (1976a). Holzkamper (1956), Owen (1956), Dockstader (1961), and Moser and White (1968) have described artifact collections; and Fay (1955) has described a surface survey. R.J. Hills (1973) has discussed settlement in relation to the ecology of the area.

Physical characteristics of the Seri are dealt with by Kroeber (1931) and Cano Avila (1960).

Phonology of the Seri language is described by Moser and Moser (1965), and aspects of morphology are covered by Moser (1961), M.B. Moser (1978), and Moser and Moser (1976). A Seri-Spanish dictionary has been compiled by Moser and Moser (1961). The history of comparative work with Seri is summarized by Langdon (1974) and J.G. Crawford (1976b).

Malkin's (1962) ethnozoological study is detailed but hastily prepared. Seri knowledge of sea turtle ecology is covered by Felger, Clifton, and Regal (1976). A comprehensive ethnobotanical monograph by R. Felger and M. Moser is in progress; partial results have appeared in several short papers (Felger and Moser 1970, 1971, 1973, 1974, 1974a).

A number of topical articles on Seri culture, some detailed, have appeared. These discuss band structure (Moser 1963; Bahre 1980), the puberty fiesta (Hinton 1955), recent influences on the culture (W.N. Smith 1951; J.A. Woodward 1966; see also Bahre 1967), life cycle (M.B. Moser 1970a), instrumental music (Bowen and Moser 1970a), elevated burial (Lindig 1964; M.B. Moser 1970), the Lola Casanova legend (Lowell 1970), face painting (Xavier 1946; M.B. Moser 1964; Peirce 1964), headgear (Bowen and Moser 1970), pottery (Bowen and Moser 1968), basketry (B. Johnson 1959; W.N. Smith 1959; Moser 1973; Bowen 1973), and ironwood carving (B. Johnston 1968; Ryerson 1976; Hills 1977).

Since about 1900 a great many articles about the Seri have appeared in the popular press. With few exceptions, they tend toward sensationalism and the perpetuation of misinformation.

Major collections of material culture have been obtained by the Smithsonian Institution; Museum of the American Indian, Heye Foundation, New York; Arizona State Museum, Tucson; Museo Nacional de Antropología, Mexico City. Archeological specimens from the Seri coast are housed in the Centro Regional del Noroeste (Instituto Nacional de Antropología e Historia) in Hermosillo and the Arizona State Museum. Collections of Seri photographs can be found in the Smithsonian Institution; Museum of the American Indian, Heye Foundation; Arizona State Museum; and Museo Nacional de Antropología. A film of the Seri by William N. Smith has been deposited with the Arizona State Museum. A tape of Seri music is on file in the Archives of Traditional Music, Indiana University.

Yaqui

EDWARD H. SPICER

Language

The Yaqui (ˈyäkē) speak a dialect of Cahita (ˈkäēˌtu, käˈētu), a language or language grouping that once contained 18 or more closely related dialects spoken by culturally similar natives of the region now included in southern Sonora and the state of Sinaloa on the west coast of Mexico. All but two of these—Yaqui and Mayo—ceased to be spoken perhaps as early as the end of the 1700s. The two surviving dialects are mutually intelligible.* The Yaqui and Mayo speech communities have since 1700 absorbed thousands of individuals who spoke others of the Cahita dialects, and in the process differences among these dialects were leveled, as is apparent in the two that survive.

Cahita is a member of the Uto-Aztecan language family, most closely related to Tarahumara and Guarijío, and the extinct Ópata and others. These languages have sometimes been grouped together as a distinct branch of Uto-Aztecan called Taracahitan or Taracahitic (Mason 1940:81; Lamb 1964:110; Steele 1979:451, 509; "Uto-Aztecan Languages," this vol.).

Territory

Throughout their known history Yaquis have been very conscious of territorial boundaries. When they first encountered Europeans in 1533—a party of Spaniards under Diego de Guzmán—a Yaqui leader and spokesman drew a line in the dirt on the south bank of the Río Yaqui and announced that if any Spanish soldier stepped across there would be a battle. The Spaniards defied the Yaquis and were forced to turn back when the Yaquis inflicted heavy losses on them. This was the first of several successful defenses of Yaqui territory against Spaniards.

Beginning apparently in the early 1800s a mythology concerning a sacred tribal territory took form under the increasing pressures from Spaniards and later Mexicans attempting to invade and take possession of Yaqui land. The territory to which Yaquis laid claim consisted of some 6,000 square miles and included the locations of what became two of the largest cities in Sonora, Guaymas and Ciudad Obregón (fig. 1). In Yaqui belief the boundaries of this territory were made sacred by the

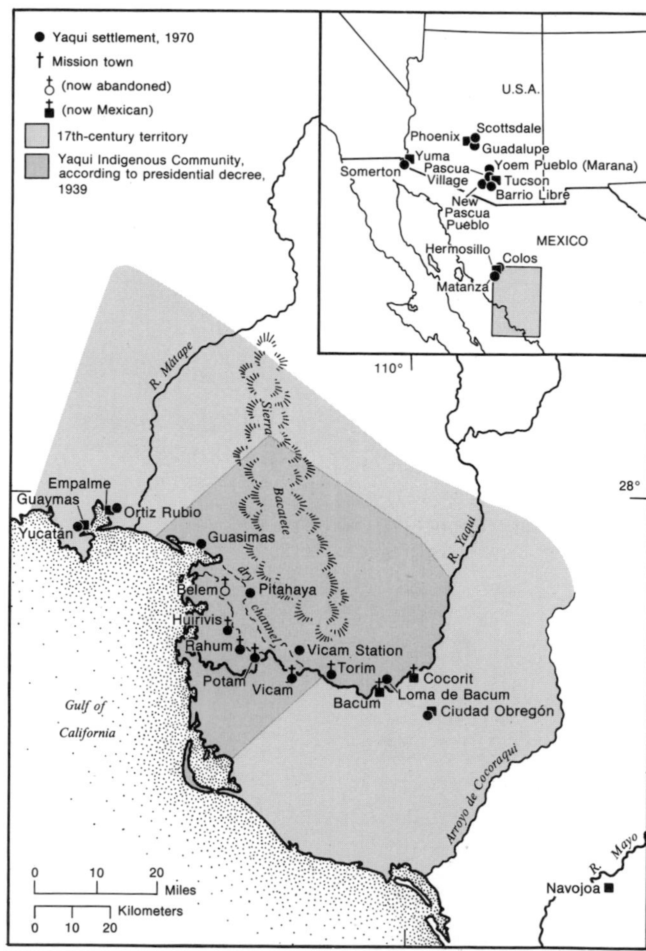

Fig. 1. Territory in the 17th century and modern Yaqui population centers.

*The phonemes of Yaqui are: (voiceless stops and affricate) *p, t, č, k, ʔ*; (voiced stops) *b* ([b] ~ [β] ~ [v]), *bw, d, g*; (voiceless fricatives) *f, s, h*; (nasals) *m, n,* n^y; (lateral) *l*; (flap) *r*; (semivowels) *w, y*; (vowels) *i, e, a, o, u*. Of these, *d, f,* and n^y are found only in words borrowed from Spanish. Long consonants and vowels are interpreted as clusters of identical segments. Every word (except possibly some monosyllables) has one primary stress, most often on the second mora, or sometimes two, but this is not written as it is considered to be predictable.

Information on Yaqui phonology is from Lindenfeld (1973:3–5); the analysis of J.B. Johnson (1962) differs in writing stress and in treating the unit *bw* as a sequence *bu*. The transcriptions of Yaqui words cited in this chapter in italics were provided by Jacqueline Lindenfeld (communication to editors 1974); phonemic transcriptions were not available for the nonitalicized place-names.

Table 1. Population Estimates, 1617–1981

Year	Total	United States	Sonora Outside River Area	Río Yaqui Area	Source
Precontact	35,000			35,000	Sauer 1935:17
1617	30,000			30,000	Pérez de Ribas 1645, 2:64
1760	62,000		40,000	22,000–23,000	Tamarón y Romeral 1937:244–246
1822	11,501		6,000	5,501	J.F. Velasco 1850:54
1829	40,000–60,000[a]				Hardy 1829:438
1849	54,000–57,000			54,000–57,000	Escudero 1849:100
1875	14,000–20,000[b]			14,000–20,000	Troncoso 1905:24
1889	10,000		10,000		McKenzie 1889:299–300
1900	14,000		8,000	6,000	Troncoso 1905:6, 342
1901	20,000		20,000		Balbás 1927:114
1904	14,051[c]				Hrdlička 1908:6
1932	7,000–9,000			7,000–9,000	Beals 1945:1
1937	16,000–20,000	several thousand		8,400–9,600	Beals 1945:1
1938	10,000			9,531+	Fabila 1940:13
1947	16,000	2,800	3,000	10,200	Spicer 1947:11, corrected
1958	21,391		8,000	13,391	Fabila 1958:19
1974				20,000	Gouy 1976:214–215
1981		5,400			Valenzuela 1981:3

[a] Includes Mayos.
[b] Higher figure based on 3,000 fighting men; lower figure on effects of constant war and smallpox.
[c] Official Mexican statistics.

singing of angels who traversed it in mythological times, *batnaataka*.

Traditional Yaqui territory embraced one of the most fertile regions of northwestern Mexico. Steadily during the nineteenth century Mexicans attempted to settle it and bring it into the hacienda land system with Yaquis as agricultural laborers. Yaquis fought to keep Mexicans out, with periodic success between the 1820s and the 1890s. In 1887, with President Porfirio Díaz supplying federal troops, the Mexicans were able to establish military occupation of the whole Yaqui territory. The Yaqui population within the tribal lands was reduced from about 20,000 to less than 3,000 as a result of ruthless warfare, deportation of thousands to Oaxaca and Yucatán, and the emigration of more thousands to other parts of Sonora and to the United States (table 1).

After the fall of Díaz in 1910 Yaquis began a return to their tribal territory, resettling the sacred sites of their towns wherever possible. In 1939 President Lázaro Cárdenas decreed exclusive Yaqui ownership in an area about one-third of the traditional lands, giving this the legal status of an "Indigenous Community" (Fabila 1940:306–310). At the same time an extensive federally supported program of agricultural development was initiated, which included the Yaqui area.

Settlement Pattern

Yaqui settlement patterns have undergone three major changes. Prior to the arrival of the Jesuit missionaries in 1617, Yaquis lived in 80 rancherias irregularly distributed along the lower 60 miles of the Río Yaqui. These were settlements of rarely more than 250 people consisting of clusters of dome-shaped, cane mat–covered houses. The locations were at the edges of the river bottomlands and probably shifted frequently as the recurring floods temporarily altered the course of the river.

The missionaries instituted a successful program of concentrating the scattered Yaqui population. Within a dozen years after their arrival the Jesuits had persuaded Yaquis to settle close to eight churches built at intervals of six to eight miles from near the mouth of the river to 50 miles upstream. The adobe-walled churches became the focus of town plazas around which buildings to house the newly instituted civil, military, and ceremonial organizations were grouped. Yaquis did not accept the grid plan of town layout urged by the Spaniards. They built their houses, adopting the new-style rectangular wattle-and-daub structures, irregularly spaced in the vicinity of the churches. Every household group, always including enramadas as well as walled rooms,

Smithsonian, NAA: 81-7675.

Fig. 2. José María Leyva, known to the Yaquis as Cajeme (b. 1837), an important leader of the Sonoran Yaqui until his execution by the Mexicans in 1887. Leyva's military successes were well accepted, but his attempts to become a civil "chief" over all the Yaqui towns failed. Photographed in 1887.

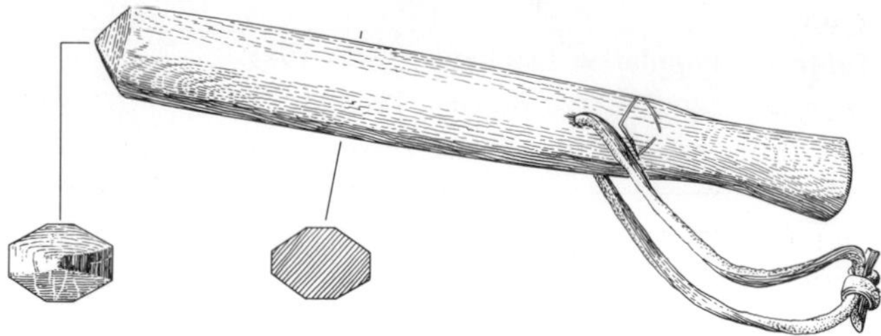

Smithsonian, Dept. of Anthr.: 129,849.

Fig. 3. Ironwood warclub, octagonal in cross-section, with pointed end. A design of double Vs is incised on both sides of the rounded grip below the hole through which a buckskin carrying thong is tied. Length 40.5 cm, collected by Edward Palmer in Sonora, 1887.

was surrounded by a cane fence; there was little clearing of the natural growth outside the fenced household compounds.

Three major features characterized this new settlement pattern. First, settlements were on the average 10 times larger than before, from 2,000 to 4,000 persons. Second, enlarged population was focused around a prominent group of public buildings the center of which was the church. Third, sharper contrast of a rural-urban sort became apparent in the Yaqui country, that is, concentrated population centers contrasting with former scattered house clusters blending into the natural growth. This form of the Yaqui town retained great stability for more than 250 years, from the 1620s until the 1880s.

A second major change took place at the end of the nineteenth century. With military occupation by the Mexicans in 1887, the Spanish-Mexican grid plan of settlement was introduced into the larger Yaqui towns. The result was a dual settlement pattern; a portion of the town where Mexican troops and some assimilated Yaquis lived was characterized by contiguous Mexican-style houses along streets, but surrounding the central grid on all sides were the irregularly scattered fenced compounds of the Yaquis. During the twentieth century the dual pattern became established in the major Yaqui towns. However, there were also pure forms of both the Mexican grid pattern (e.g., Vicam Station) and the Yaqui mission town (e.g., Vicam Pueblo).

The third type of settlement pattern developed during the forced migration of Yaquis into Sonora and Arizona cities. In Empalme, Guaymas, Hermosillo, Tucson, and near Phoenix, Yaquis adapted to the urban situation by forming church-centered communities. Wherever they settled they eventually built small open-front churches adapted to their distinctive ceremonial needs. Where practical, Yaqui families settled near the churches, but this was by no means always possible. The church with its small concentration of Yaqui households in the vicinity became the focus of community life of Yaquis who lived widely scattered in and around the cities. The pattern of the church-centered urban community, often called a barrio by Yaquis, became stabilized during the 1930s in Arizona and somewhat earlier in Sonora.

Wherever Yaquis settled they maintained some degree of devotion to the towns originally established under Jesuit guidance on the Río Yaqui. They became sacred in Yaqui thought as the *wohnaiki pweplum* (The Eight Towns); characteristically, as in so much of post-Spanish Yaqui culture, the word *pweplum*, from Spanish *pueblo*, as well as the institution of the town structure were borrowed from the Spaniards but very extensively modified to fit Yaqui needs. The names of the Eight Towns, believed by Yaquis to have been founded by prophets on sacred ground, became standarized in the following forms (in Spanish spellings and as traditionally listed by Yaquis from east to west): Cocorit 'chile peppers', Bacum 'where the water comes out', Torim 'wood rats', Vicam 'arrow points,' Potam 'ground moles', Rahum (?), Huirivis 'a bird', and Belem from Yaqui *beene* 'a flat sloping place' (see "Southern Periphery: West," fig. 2, this vol.).

During the 1970s there were 21 Yaqui communities. Of these 18 maintained their own churches and thus were self-sufficient centers of Yaqui traditional life. These consisted of nine towns along the Yaqui River, five barrios in Sonoran cities, and four communities in Arizona. Yoem Pueblo in Marana was a satellite of Pascua, Scottsdale was a satellite of Guadalupe, and the Yuma settlement set up a church only on special occasions.

Culture

Yaqui culture as first reported by Spaniards in the 1500s was a product of adaptation to the Lower Sonoran natural region, a "desert" habitat. Yaquis were sedentary, but they were frequently forced to change location because of floods. Their dome-shaped, often mat-covered houses were placed close to the river. Yaquis were cultivators but also relied heavily on the abundant wild foods—mesquite beans, cactus fruits (such as pitahaya, or "organpipe") in great variety, succulent roots, grass seeds (and of amaranth, which was also cultivated); wild game including deer, rabbits, and (of considerable importance) a large gray tree-dwelling rodent; and many kinds of shellfish and large saltwater fish, such as sea bass, on the gulf coast.

Technology

A notable technological adaptation consisted in the utilization of cane, which grew in heavy brakes along the river, for a great variety of important functions. The indigenous origin of the cane has been questioned (Holden et al. 1936:117), but there is no doubt that it was in use in the early 1600s in many aspects of Yaqui life: heavy twilled mats of split cane stalks as roof and wall materials, and as sleeping mats (fig. 4); household compound fences; household implements and furnishings such as cutting instruments, spoons, birdcages, swinging shelves; ceremonial headdresses, dance wands, and canes of office; and numerous other uses.

Craft arts, including weaving of blankets in both cotton and wool, were well developed until the disturbed

bottom left, Mus. of the Amer. Ind., Heye Foundation, New York: 24454.

Fig. 4. Dwellings. top, Adobe house belonging to the head *malehto* or ritual leader of Pascua Village, Ariz. Unused adobe bricks are curing at right. The Santa Catalina Mountains are in the background. Photograph by David J. Jones, Jr., 1936. bottom left, Brush-sheltered kitchen area with young children, chickens, and cooking equipment—including a stone mano and metate on elevated forked log platform. The infant crawls on a twilled carrizo mat, and a second mat (of different weave) hangs to the left. Carrizo cane mats, made by men as well as women, are used in house construction and for sleeping while lighter ones of palmetto are used for seats or for sleeping cushions. Photograph by Edward H. Davis, Potam, Sonora, 1924. bottom right, Two structures constituting a single household, with breezeway between, in Potam, Sonora. The walls are of woven cane covered with mud (left) and upright canes, one covered with twilled carrizo cane mats (right). Corn and pumpkins are stored on the roof, which is of earth over mats or small branches resting on the beams. Photograph by Tad Nichols, 1942.

times of the nineteenth century when they died out. This was true also of pottery making. The only craft art survivals into the twentieth century were carving of wooden masks ("Kachinas and Masking," fig. 13, this vol.), making of undecorated brownware bowls for the death anniversary services, and weaving of heavy split cane mats for commercial sale.

Subsistence

Yaquis used the reliable annual floods of the Río Yaqui and also the summer rains, respectively, for irrigated and nonirrigated agriculture. Irrigation was carried on with simple ditches dug into the floodplain from the edge of the river. This system was only slightly improved by the Jesuits. The crops were corn, beans, squash, amaranth, and cotton at the time the Spaniards arrived. Jesuits added wheat, pomegranates, peaches, figs, and a few other crops. Applying more regular work schedules and intensive techniques, the Jesuits made the Yaqui valley one of the most productive areas in the whole province of Sonora-Sinaloa, which led to its becoming one of the most desired areas for Spanish and Mexican settlement. The Jesuits also introduced cattle, sheep, goats, and horses; and the Yaqui country became a major livestock-producing region during the eighteenth century. An agricultural surplus was produced for a century or more before Mexican encroachments, after 1821, led to bitter warfare and steadily declining production during the nineteenth century.

Mexican military occupation of the Yaqui country began in 1887. Mexicans initiated larger irrigation canals, and in 1890 the first steps were taken toward what became one of the largest irrigation developments in North America utilizing the waters of the Río Yaqui. During the 1940s the Alvaro Obregón Dam was built upstream from the Yaqui towns, and by 1956 water no longer ran in the Río Yaqui bed. Yaquis paid water rent and were subject to the management plans of several different Mexican governmental agencies. Under the new direction almost all subsistence crops were eliminated; Yaqui lands were devoted to the cash crops of wheat, cotton, and vegetable oils such as ajonjoli. A cattle-raising cooperative was instituted utilizing the whole Bacatete Mountain area as a single unit, and at Guasimas on the coast a fishing cooperative was set up. The profits from these enterprises, according to the plans, went to Yaquis, but management was in the hands of the government agencies. Thus there was total transformation of Yaqui economy after 1956 when the new irrigation system was opened.

Kinship and Ritual Kinship

All aspects of pre-Spanish social organization have been obscured by the processes of acculturation. There is no evidence of unilineal descent groups. Kinship affiliation was reckoned bilaterally. No rules regarding postmarital residence have been discovered, although the wedding ceremony suggests former immediate residence in the groom's parents' household. Rancheria exogamy is asserted by some investigators (Beals 1943:52), but no form of exogamy has been recorded since the foundation of the Eight Towns. The term *wawaim* 'kinfolk' was widely used as a kind of community affiliation term and as an aid in drawing boundaries between Yaquis and non-Yaquis.

top, Mus. of the Amer. Ind., Heye Foundation, New York: 24444; bottom, U. of Ariz., Ariz. State Mus., Tucson: 43,617.

Fig. 5. Cooking. top, Kitchen in Potam, Sonora. A stone metate and mano rest on a box behind the woman bending over the cooking fire. Photograph by Edward H. Davis, 1924. bottom, Maria Murrietta placing a tortilla on a grill over a fire in a wash tub. Her house of plywood is in Old Pascua, Ariz. Photograph by Helga Teiwes, June 1976.

Those who called themselves Yaquis in the 1960s must be regarded, contrary to all popular and some scholarly literature, as greatly mixed genetically with neighboring Indian and Mexican mestizo populations.

There is accumulating evidence that Yaqui population was on the increase from first Spanish contacts until at least the mid-nineteenth century, in contrast with neighboring Ópatas, Mayos, and Lower Pimas. The Yaqui country was less infiltrated by Spaniards and served as a refuge area for those inclined to militant resistance to Spanish and Mexican encroachment. This together with the breakup of families as a result of deportation during the 20 years preceding 1910 have probably influenced Yaqui household composition. It is notable that Yaquis have not maintained any standard kin composition in the household. A household may consist of any number of nuclear families related in any of a variety of ways; moreover, the families may be related only through ritual kinship.

Since at least the early 1600s, ritual kinship has been of importance in Yaqui life. The Jesuits reported ceremonies of ritual sponsorship (Pérez de Ribas 1645:40–41; Beals 1943:66–68), probably customs similar to those among Western Pueblos in connection with ceremonial fathers and mothers. The Jesuits introduced the European godparent system at the time of very first contact, requiring ceremonial sponsors for Christian baptism. The two systems fused, becoming elaborated into a complex system of coparenthood (Spicer 1940:91–116). An individual Yaqui might have as many as a dozen, or even more, pairs of godparents, each of whom was obligated in important ways to one another as well as to the godchild and the godchild's parents.

At what point in Yaqui cultural history this system attained its great complexity is not known. It seems probable that what had already become a fairly complex and important institution in Yaqui life, as the result of the fusion of European and native sponsoring institutions, assumed new functions during the period of Yaqui dispersal at the end of the nineteenth century. In the face of deportation and forced migration, Yaquis found themselves frequently with no kin anywhere near, or at best only one or two persons known to be related. Under these circumstances as Yaquis reorganized, they could have fallen back on the established institution of fictive, or ritual, kinship. New households and new cooperative groups were founded on the basis of the coparent (*kompai*) relationship. Probably at this time, from 1887 until the 1920s, the important and many-faceted system of ritual kinship assumed its unusual level of complexity.

Ceremonial Organization

In 1617, along with the European godparent system, the Jesuits introduced another European institution that became of great importance after it too had undergone much modification by Yaquis. This was the cofradia, an organization (sometimes called a brotherhood) of laymen dedicated to the service of a Christian saint or other supernatural. The cofradia was fused by Yaquis with ceremonial sodalities of the Western Pueblo type (Spicer 1954:78–93), and these became the major vehicles of Yaqui religious tradition after the expulsion of the Jesuits in 1767. Three sodalities for men were the most notable: the Horsemen (*kabayum*) dedicated to the Child Jesus, the Judases (*hurasim*, Spanish *fariseos*), dedicated to Christ crucified, and the Matachines dedicated to the Virgin Mary. The first two played the central role in dramatizing the last days of Jesus, during Lent and Holy Week in the Christian ceremonial calendar. The Judas sodality developed a distinctive version of the Passion, not duplicated outside of northwestern Mexico. The major actors, a segment of the sodality called *čapayekam*, wore helmet masks similar to Pueblo kachina masks. They behaved as ceremonial clowns (Parsons and Beals 1934) and also took the roles of evil beings in the religious drama. The Horsemen assisted and managed the Judases.

During the nineteenth century this pair of sodalities became the focus of Yaqui solidarity and distinctiveness. During Holy Week each year they took control of the church and the civil and military organization of the town. In this joint role they were called the *kohtumbre yaʔura* 'custom chieftainship'. During their period of ascendancy they were responsible for law and order and administered the Spanish-introduced punishments of whipping and incarceration in stocks. They enforced sexual and other taboos during Lent and carried out all burials. The *čapayekam*, or devil-clowns, behaved with complete license, mocking every sacred institution. The period of dominance of the *kohtumbre* extended from sometime in January or February (marked by Ash Wednesday in the Christian calendar) to May (the Day of the Finding of the Holy Cross). This winter-spring season was a time of sadness, penitence, and in the final crisis during Holy Week symbolic disruption of all normal life (fig. 6).

In contrast the summer-autumn ceremonial season was characterized by gay and colorful dances and a general atmosphere of relaxed enjoyment of the benefits conferred by the Virgin who was identified with the Mother Church, trees, and flowers. The most prominent sodality was the men's dance group known as the Matachines (fig. 7), whose appearances were sharply restricted during the other ceremonial season. The Matachine sodality was under the overall direction of a church governor (*teopo kobanao*), as were two women's sodalities (*kopariam* 'singers' and *kiyohteim* 'altar-tenders'). The church governor in turn was under the command of a policy-making group for the church consisting of the head *kiyohtei,* the head *sacristán*, and the leader of the church ritual—the head *malehto* (Spanish *maestro*). This church organization, dominant during most of the year, was in part suspended and subordinated to the *kohtumbre* in their season.

bottom center, Smithsonian, NAA: 81-7674; bottom right, Ariz. Histl. Soc. Lib., Tucson: 47219.

Fig. 6. *waehma*, the major Yaqui religious ceremonies. These ritual dramas are performed during Lent under the direction of the *kohtumbre*, the sodalities of Horsemen and Judases (Spicer 1980:70–88). The Judases include participants known as the Soldiers of Rome (headed by those playing Pontius Pilate) and the *čapayekam* (clowns wearing helmet-masks, belts of deer-hoof rattles, and cocoon leg rattles, and carrying painted wooden daggers and swords). top left, The church at Potam during Palm Sunday. At the foot of the cross are Yaqui pottery bowls, in which black cords are burned at church-household ceremonies held on the anniversaries of deaths. At left background *čapayekam* and Soldiers of Rome are marching. Photograph by Rosamond B. Spicer, 1942. top center, Ritual paraphernalia around a houseyard cross in Potam during a resting interval in a Lenten household ceremony. Included are the cross-tipped red flag of the Judas society, lances of 3 Pontius Pilates, and *čapayeka* masks and swords. Photograph by Rosamond B. Spicer, 1942. top right, *čapayeka* at Pascua Village, beating his dagger on his sword to interfere with a church service. The mask caricatures an "American Indian." Photograph by David J. Jones, Jr., 1937. bottom left, Beginning his ceremonial clowning, this *čapayeka* at Pascua sneaks into town. Photograph by David J. Jones, Jr., 1937. bottom center, Soldiers of Rome preparing a straw-stuffed figure of Judas dressed as a *čapayeka*. Photograph by Walter B. Hough, Tucson, Ariz., probably 1932. bottom right, Burning the Judas figure and the masks and swords of the *čapayekam* and the Soldiers of Rome, the finale of the *waehma* ceremonies. Photographed about 1930s.

Entirely outside the church or custom chieftainship, in no way linked organizationally but in constant cooperation with those groups, was another set of ceremonial performers. These were the pascolas and Deer Dancers and their respective musicians (figs. 8–9). They worked under their own administrative officer (*moroyaʔut*) and maintained headquarters, when preparing for ceremonies, at private houses or at a public building in the town plaza. The pascolas (*pahkoʔolam*) were ceremonial hosts required for most ceremonies; they were linked through important rituals with the sacred ceremonies but carried out their dances and other activities in an enramada built separately alongside the sacred, or altar, enramada. Along with the pascolas the Deer Dancer (*maso*) performed his naturalistic dance and joined in pantomime and dramatic action with them. Typically, the pascola-Deer activities were carried out from sunset until sometime after sunrise. The songs, dances, and pantomimes followed a fixed time schedule during the night.

Military Organization

A military organization followed the basic pattern of the cofradia-influenced ceremonial sodalities. Its members made vows (*mandas*) to the Virgin of Guadalupe and served for life. The officers bore military titles and constituted a hierarchy of command following the introduced Spanish pattern. Like the men's dance sodalities they marched always in two parallel files, with a flagbearer at the head of each carrying their insignia of a bluish-gray flag. They had duties designed to maintain the security of the governors and of the whole town. Important ritual duties consisted of a bow-and-rosary ceremony weekly in the church, heading a procession each Sunday symbolic of Yaqui identification with their tribal territory, daily salutes with drum and flag to the sun, and the "Coyote" dance on special occasions such as military victory. By the 1950s the Military Society had died out in the Arizona settlements but remained as an important part of the ceremonial organization in Sonora.

Political Organization

Except during times of military conflict, there was no overall tribal organization. A captain of the Military Society of one of the towns was elected as field commander by common consent of all the military societies in time of war. He had no command powers outside of military affairs, and his authority over all the towns ended with the need for military action. Contrary to the persistent belief of Mexicans, a Yaqui military leader made no decisions regarding peace treaties.

The maximum political unit was the town, each of the Eight Towns duplicating in its organization that of every other town. The town government, like the ceremonial and military organizations, was a fusion of European and aboriginal features of local government. The town was composed of *yaʔuram* (best translated as 'authorities'), who always worked in conjunction with the people of the town as a whole. Elders, who had served frequently in other town offices, were recognized as spokesmen for the people. Collectively these elders were sometimes called *prinsipalim*; individually the most respected and active elders were called *yoʔotui*. Any man or woman could speak in the town council meetings, but one or two of the *yoʔotui* had the obligation to speak in every meeting.

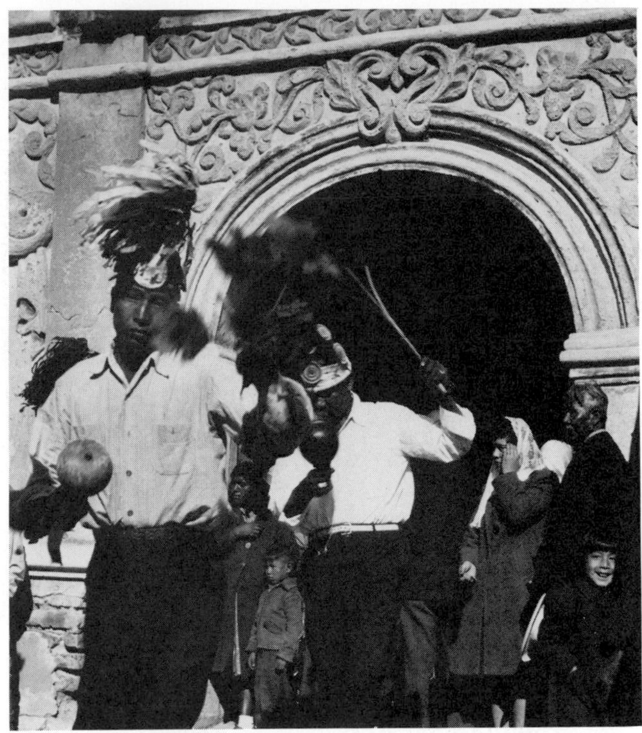

U. of Ariz., Ariz. State Mus., Tucson: 21788.

Fig. 7. Yaqui Matachine dancers, at the Papago fiesta of St. Francis Xavier in front of San Xavier Mission near Tucson. Matachines are members of a sodality directed by the church governor that dominates the ceremonial season from May to January. Their headdresses are of colored paper and cloth over cane frames, with colored disks or mirrors and paper or cloth streamers. Each carries a red-painted rattle and a trident wand with dyed feathers at the end, and they dance to violin and guitar music (Spicer 1980:87, 100–102). Photograph by E.B. Sayles, Dec. 1945.

The town authorities (*yaʔuram*) consisted of five hierarchically organized groups: the church (*teopo*), the governors (*kobanoam* or *kobanahuak*), the military (*yoemsontaom*), the *kohtumbre*, and the *pahkome* ('fiesta makers'). There were five governors with five assistants elected annually, each of whom carried a cane of office; the first governor supported by the others acted as chairman of meetings. The five governors were administrators and transmitters of decisions to the people and

top right, U. of Ariz., Ariz. State Mus., Tucson: 43,109; bottom left, Ariz. Histl. Soc. Lib., Tucson: 22609. bottom right, U. of Ariz., Ariz. State Mus., Tucson: 43,092.

Fig. 8. Pascolas. These solo performers are essentially secular, dancing and clowning to amuse the crowd at ceremonies such as children's funerals, saint's day fiestas, weddings, and Holy Week ceremonies. They wear masks, kilts, heavy belts with metal bells suspended from them, and cocoon rattles on their lower legs. They are always accompanied by musicians playing either a drum and whistle, or harps and violins. The Deer Dancer appears only with pascolas, wearing a stuffed deerhead, shaking red gourd rattles, and accompanied by his own musicians who play on rasping sticks and a half-gourd floating in a container of water (Spicer 1940:176–182, 1980:102–110). top left, Arriving at a fiesta in Potam, Sonora, pascolas led by their manager visit the houseyard cross (to right) and then enter the dance ramada blessing the house. Photograph by Rosamond B. Spicer, March 1942. top right, Dancer retying a cocoon ankle-rattle. The red yarn tassels on the cords for the rattle and for the topknot in his hair are called 'flowers' and symbolize divine grace. Photograph by George Iacono at Pascua Village, Ariz., July 1955. bottom left, In the dance ramada at Pascua Village, pascolas touch their canes to the harp, permitting the music to flow into the dancers so they can perform (Spicer 1980:108). Photographed July 1955. bottom right, Pascolas alternate between two types of dance, one (as here) with their masks pushed aside and sistrum rattle stuck in their belts while violinists and harpists play, and the other with masks over their faces, shaking the sistrum, to the accompaniment of a drum and whistle. Photograph by George Iacono at Pascua Village, July 1955. opposite page, top left, Pascolas, Deer Dancer, and musicians performing on Palm Sunday in Pascua Village. Photograph by David J. Jones, Jr., 1937. opposite page, bottom left, Deer Dancer on Palm Sunday, Potam, Sonora. Photograph by Rosamond B. Spicer, 1942.

Smithsonian, Dept. of Anthr.: a, 129,851; b, 178,076; c, 152,695; d, 9394; e, U. of Ariz., Ariz. State Mus., Tucson: E-1391 and E-529.

Fig. 9. Pascola equipment. top, Masks depicting men (another type represents a sheep or goat), carved wood painted black with white and red designs. White horsehair eyebrows, cheek tufts, and beard represent the old man aspect of the pascola. a, Mask with sharply pointed nose, teeth inset around mouth, and crosses on both forehead and chin; b, Mask with cross only on the forehead with large patches of white around the eyes. Pascola masks made for sale to outsiders since about 1930 often lack the forehead cross (Griffith 1972:192). bottom, Musical instruments: c, Cane whistle of 2 sections fitted together with whistle at the end of one and stops at the opposite end of the other (2 holes in front and one in back). Sinew is wound around the body to prevent splitting (Beals 1943:31); more recent examples are bound with thread. d, Wooden sistrum rattle with carved handle and metal disks attached with nails. The dancer shakes this in his right hand and also beats it against his left palm. e, Double-headed drum; a wider wooden frame separates the 2 heads of rawhide stretched and laced over thinner wooden hoops. The drum is beaten with one plain stick, and the performer simultaneously plays the whistle. a, 21.0 cm long, excluding beard, rest to same scale. a–d, Collected by Edward Palmer in Sonora; a in 1887, b in 1897, c in 1891 and d in 1870; e, collected by Edward Spicer in Ariz., drum in 1942, beater in 1940.

spokesmen for the town with all outsiders. The Military Society administered all sanctions ordered by the governors and always accompanied the governors as their protectors in the carrying out of any official business. The church and the *kohtumbre* played important roles in the annual selection of governors as well as fulfilling what Yaquis regarded as the most important of functions, namely, the maintenance of the sacred "Yaqui Law." The *pahkome* (Spanish *fiesteros*), carried out all burials outside the *kohtumbre* ceremonial season and played vital roles in the weekly ceremonies affirming the sacred relationship to the land. In addition, they were responsible for what, next to the Lent-Easter ceremonies, were the most important events in the ceremonial calendar, namely, the annual honoring of the patron saints of the towns.

The separate hierarchically organized groups thus had their own clearly marked jurisdictions, but in matters of general welfare they functioned together and none was dominant. General meetings of all the authorities were called whenever necessary to make decisions affecting the whole town or to decide disputes or try criminal cases. The management of the land, an important function, was generally carried out without general meetings by the civil governors. In a town meeting all persons could speak, providing they observed the traditional rules of order. A decision was reached only when no one spoke against a defined course of action. If there was dissent, decision was postponed or never reached.

Under Mexican influence efforts were repeatedly made to create an overall tribal structure, residents of Vicam where military headquarters was established by Mexicans being most prominent in the efforts. Such an organization, not officially sanctioned by the town governments, has been in existence since the 1930s.

Tribal Integration

Although every town was politically autonomous, a process of wider integration operated constantly. The ceremonial sodalities linked all the towns in a network of ritual interaction. The ceremonial organizations were duplicates of one another, which enabled householders in one town to invite sodalities of various towns to perform ceremonial functions on their behalf. During the winter season the Horsemen and the Judases were constantly in demand not only in their own towns but also in all the others, and this was also true of the Matachines during the summer season. The performance of a group from another town lent distinction to the ceremony. Thus the Yaqui country was constantly criss-crossed throughout the year by members of the various sodalities traveling from town to town, and various kinds of interaction were stimulated among the towns. Essentially what was involved was the exchange of ceremonial labor (cf. L.S. Crumrine 1969). A climax in the Matachine ceremonial exchanges came in early July with the fiesta of the Virgin of the Road in the town of Bacum. On this occasion the Matachine sodalities from all towns gathered at Bacum and danced severally and collectively in the Bacum town patron celebration. Often more than 200 Matachine dancers danced in the climactic ceremonies; this was the closest to a general tribal ceremony.

Religion

Yaqui religious belief and practice are not well described in early Spanish accounts. A few odds and ends seem clear (Beals 1943:59, 64–65), such as individual supernatural power through visions of animals and the making of ground paintings. From descriptions made by travelers and ethnographers since the mid-nineteenth century emerge five major focuses of Yaqui religion: honoring of and concern for ancestors, fulfillment of obligations for help in curing, maintaining and distributing the benevolent power of Our Mother (*itom ae*), honoring the patron supernaturals of the Eight Towns, and affirming the sacred relationships between Yaquis and their tribal territory. The relative emphasis on these dominant orientations has probably shifted in response to contact relations with Spaniards, Mexicans, and Anglo-Americans. The elaborate ceremonialism of the patron saints of the towns cannot have developed before the 1620s when the Jesuits consolidated the scattered small rancherias into the Eight Towns. The curing focus with strong emphasis on various manifestations of Christ may well be pre-Spanish but embodying a new synthesis of aboriginal supernaturals with the Christian. The Virgin Mary was identified with a supernatural called Our Mother whose associations with trees and flowers and the earth were reworked into superficially Christian forms. The honoring of the dead was an important accompaniment of nearly every other ceremonial activity, but in itself simpler and less focused than the other cults; its pervasiveness suggests but does not prove that it is the oldest emphasis in Yaqui ceremonialism. The land ceremonials seem the most recent, being neither elaborate nor pervasive in the system. Perhaps this cult became increasingly important as Mexican land pressures intensified during the nineteenth century.

Essential elements in the ceremonialism of the ancestors were monthly rituals at the graves surrounding the church of a town, all-night funeral services at the household of the dead person, a commemorative ceremony one year after death when formal mourning for relatives ended, and the annual visits of spirits of the dead to the town during October followed by a formal farewell feast when the spirits left on November 1-2 (All Souls–All Saints in the Catholic calendar). All these were household-centered ceremonies, including the funeral, which, although involving all organized groups of the town if the person were participant in many organizations, took place at the household with relatives as sponsors. Each kin group (not precisely defined with reference to kin roles included) maintained a Book of the Dead containing the names of all ancestors of the group and the offices they held in the town organization. Ideally the books were taken to every ceremony and placed on the altar where it was believed the spirits were able to enjoy the ceremonies through contact with the benevolent supernaturals. The concept of hell was rejected by Yaquis, but the dwelling place of the ancestral spirits was at least in part identified with heaven.

The interest in curing was expressed in every activity of the ceremonial sodalities, including the Military Society, for recruitment of all participants was a result of illness and their continued activity was the means of warding off the original illness as well as maintaining the goodwill of Jesus and Mary in the constant effort to keep their power working for the people of the town. Jesus was understood to have been a great curer. The most elaborate ceremony of the year, which enlisted the effort of everyone, was the *waehma* (from Spanish *Cuaresma* 'Lent'). This included Holy Week, the ceremonial climax of the year, when the drama of Christ's last days was enacted with the Horseman and Judas sodalities taking the leading roles. The central theme, in Yaqui conception overriding the Passion itself, was the accumulation of evil in the town (represented in the increase in numbers of the *čapayekam* during the 40 days) and the ultimate destruction of that evil on Holy Saturday. Central in the drama was the symbolism of flowers, by means of which the evil of the masked *čapayekam* was ritually destroyed during a ceremonial battle in front of the church.

Of equal importance was the ceremony of the supernatural patrons of the towns. These were carried out during four days that included the name day of the saint and hence occurred at different times in different towns. Most took place from late May to early July. The *pahkome* were the managers and the ones responsible for assembling the large amounts of food necessary, for these were great feasting ceremonies. The *pahkome* were divided into two groups—the Moors and the Christians; and the fiestas were organized into two distinct, but duplicate and articulating, parts, associated with the colors red (Moors) and blue (Christians). The two fiestas were competing in every respect: in lavishness of supplies, in quality of the pascola and Deer Dancers and their music, and in superiority in a game involving the ritual stealing of the pascola musicians' drums and a mass pushing contest at night in the town plaza. The ritual opposition culminated in a ceremonial battle over a symbolic structure representing a castle in which the Blues, or Christians, triumphed—obviously based on the missionary-introduced War of the Moors and Christians.

The land orientation in Yaqui ceremonialism was expressed primarily in a weekly procession led by the Military Society around the cemetery in which four crosses were permanently planted representing the Four Gospels and the four corners of the Yaqui tribal territory. This was called *konti*, or the Surrounding. The mythology of the tribal territory was well known. It included a flood myth recounting how great supernatural figures and some animals were saved from the flood on the most prominent peaks of the Bacatete Mountains, these peaks having both biblical and Yaqui names. A second myth told how the tribal territory was defined; angels and prophets in mythical time moved from a notched peak called *takalaim* (San Carlos Bay on current maps) to a place called *mogonea* (now sunken near the mouth of Cocoraqui Arroyo) singing and making sacred a boundary line. This boundary was regarded as forever inviolable. A third important myth in this complex described the founding of the Eight Towns at eight sacred places.

The Arts

Yaqui arts as known in detail consist of dance, music, religious drama, and oral literature. There is no record of important pictorial or geometrical decorative art in weaving, basketry, pottery, or other forms. Ground paintings were made with a number of colors, but there is no sure record of what was represented. A single exception to the absence of decorative art was the painted geometric designs in red, green, black, and white on the heads of the lances used by members of the Judas sodality representing Pontius Pilate, the titular head of that organization.

Dance and drama were the great Yaqui arts, which survived the war-disturbed century from the 1820s through the 1920s. Yaqui dance was ritual dance. Social dances for men and women were entirely absent. An occasional woman, at the end of the usual night of ceremony, danced the pascola dance, and there are accounts of one or two women having become professional pascolas, but this was exceptional. Only men participated in the ceremonial dancing. In the Matachine dances boys dressed as women represented the female figure of Malinche.

There were three types of ritual dance: animal representation, pascola solo, and sacred group. None of these was strictly for entertainment, although the first two developed such characteristics as they were danced at the request of non-Yaqui audiences during the twentieth century.

Only one animal dance survived into the twentieth century of the several that existed as late as the 1870s. This was the Deer Dance—an intense, classically restrained, partly naturalistic interpretation of deer movements by a solo dancer. It was performed to songs dealing with natural phenomena, especially flowers, and a land "beneath the dawn." The singers accompanied themselves with gourd-resonated wooden rasps and a gourd water drum.

The pascola solo dance was an integral part of the many-faceted activities of the pascola in his role as ceremonial host for most sacred ceremonies. The dance was a combination of rapid shuffle and toe-and-heel drags, one pattern when the dancer wore a mask and the other when the mask was pushed to the side of the head, which alternated throughout a night of dancing. Pascola musicians played Mexican harps, violins, and a drum-and-whistle combination; and the pascola himself beat rhythms with a wood-and-metal rattle to his masked dance. The pascola also maintained an almost constant patter of comment on current events, dialogues with members of the crowd, absurd narratives in which he was often the foolish protagonist, and pantomime dramas with the Deer Dancer. A pascola drew on an extensive oral literature, employing symbolic terms known to the crowd, and himself contributed to that traditional literature during a lifetime of pascola dancing.

The sacred Matachine dances consisted of group performances in front of or inside the church with groups of as many as 50 dancing at a time. Steps bore resemblance to those of other North American Indian dances but also to European country dances of the sixteenth century and earlier. The ground patterns of the group dances closely resembled quadrille, Kerry Dance, and other European figures. The music was always string, violin, and guitar in the twentieth century, but the Matachine organization also made use of a double-headed drum for announcement and processions.

Knowledge

The most systematic interest in codified knowledge, other than the ritual knowledge necessary for the elaborate ceremonials, was in history. Yaqui elders maintained schools for young men in which myths, such as the land myths, were taught. The sacred oral mythical texts were supplemented with selections translated into Yaqui from historical accounts written by Spaniards or Mexicans in Spanish.

Synonymy

The first Jesuit missionary to the Yaquis, Andrés Pérez de Ribas, established the tribal term by which Yaquis have been known to non-Yaquis ever since. Pérez de Ribas (1645:284 passim) repeatedly used the word hiaqui in this first historical and ethnographic description. The term was connected with the name used by the Spaniards for the river on which the people lived, the Yaquimi (perhaps a plural form), but no sure meaning for it is known. It is still used in Yaqui as *hiaki* (Lindenfeld 1973:12–13). Despite Pérez's clear distinction between Hiaquis and peoples farther south on the Río el Fuerte, the Cinaloas, a confusion later crept into the literature. Hervas (1800–1805, 1:322) in his catalogue of American languages and nations identified the Hiaquis and the Cinaloas (Sinaloas) as the same tribe.

Also in the early 1600s, a Jesuit who wrote the first grammar of Yaqui used the term Cahita. Velasco's (1890) grammar dealt with three dialects—Hiaqui, Mayo, and Tehueco—that he said constituted a single language, Cahita. In 1678 Zapata (1853–1857, 3:393) wrote an account of Jesuit missions in which he used a variant of the term, caita, with a similar, but broader meaning. A number of Mexican scholars during the mid-nineteenth century adopted Cahita in the same sense, as a generic term for the three dialects and some others similar to them (Cancio 1853–1857, 2:246; Pimentel 1874–1875, 1:485; Orozco y Berra 1864:35). They also used the spelling Yaqui for the original Hiaqui. The most influential use of Cahita was that of Velasco's *Arte de la Lengua Cahita*. The usual form of this name in Spanish is *Cahita* (Santamaría 1974:180), but some sources use *Cáhita* (Velasco 1890).

Kroeber pointed out (Thomas and Swanton 1911:12) that Cahita was inappropriate because Yaqui *kaita* means 'nothing' or 'I don't know' and its use was probably due to a misunderstanding, but Brinton (1891:125), Sauer (1934:23 and 1935:15), and Beals (1943) all used the term in approximately Velasco's sense. Beals (1945) further used Cahita not only as a linguistic but also as a cultural designation. Most maps of language distribution in the twentieth century employed Cahita in the same way (Sauer 1934; Mason 1940; F. Johnson 1940; Spicer 1980). On the other hand, Thomas and Swanton (1911:11), following Kroeber's suggestion, designated the Yaqui, Mayo, Tehueco, and neighboring languages by the phrase the Yaqui Group. The standard name for both language and people by 1980 in both Mexican and United States government usage was Yaqui.

Meanwhile the Yaquis' own name for themselves came very slowly into use. In Velasco's grammar of the early 1600s a variant form of the Yaqui word *yoeme* (pl. *yoemem*) appeared. The Mayo form, *yoreme*, was listed in a Yaqui vocabulary in Hernandez (1902:214). Beals (1945:217) recorded Mayo *yoreme* as applying to both Mayos and Yaquis. Giddings (1959:100) used the Yaqui form in one tale. Spicer (1980:5, passim), used *yoeme* in several publications, but nevertheless employed Yaqui as the primary designation. The first publication to use Yoeme in the title as the tribal name in English uses Yaqui in the text (Kaczkurkin 1977:59).

The Pima-Papago name for the Yaqui is *hiakim*, plural *hihakim* (Saxton and Saxton 1969:101).

Sources

For the Jesuit phase of Yaqui cultural history, 1617–1767, the most important sources are Pérez de Ribas's (1645) firsthand account of the beginnings of the missionary-directed change program; Navarro García's (1966) painstaking chronological summary of materials from the Seville archives, especially the civil records; and Tamarón y Romeral's (1937) 1765 work, one section of which describes the Yaqui towns and their environment.

For the period of Yaqui resistance to absorption into the hacienda system, 1768–1910, two works provide much insight into Yaqui-White relations: Hardy's (1829) description of events in southern Sonora during the rebellion of the Yaqui leader Juan de la Bandera and Hernández's (1902) viewpoint of a Mexican doctor during the climax of the nineteenth-century conflict.

While there are many books and articles dealing with particular phases of Yaqui history subsequent to 1910, probably the best connected narrative placing Yaqui life in the context of Sonoran economic and social development is by Dabdoub (1964). Spicer (1980, more briefly in 1961) is a study of the whole panorama of Yaqui cultural history from 1533 to 1980.

Ethnographic knowledge of the Yaquis rests on only a few studies. Pioneering work treating Yaqui culture as part of the larger whole of "Cahitan" culture was published by Beals on aboriginal culture (1943), which is an extremely useful summary of materials from all the Spanish sources, and on contemporary culture (1945), which describes the results of Beals's 1930–1932 fieldwork. Intensive community studies on Pascua in Arizona (Spicer 1940) and Potam in Sonora (Spicer 1954) provide an ethnographic baseline regarding functioning Yaqui culture in its two major varieties as of 1930–1950. Interesting supplementary notes are to be found in Holden et al. (1936), Fabila (1940), and Moisés, Kelley, and Holden (1971). Spicer's (1980) cultural history puts in a single synthesis most of the historical and ethnographic facts.

The undocumented material in this chapter is chiefly from field notes of E.H. Spicer and R.B. Spicer (1936–1937, 1942, 1947, 1970) and from the publications of E.H. Spicer (1940, 1954, 1980).

Mayo

N. ROSS CRUMRINE

Language, Territory, and Environment

The Mayo (ˈmäyō) speak a dialect of the Cahita language, which includes also Yaqui and the extinct Tehueco, Cinaloa, and Zuaque (Mason 1940).* Cahita is classified as a member of the Taracahitan branch of the Uto-Aztecan family.

Mayo natural, social, and cultural boundaries are not completely clear due both to gaps in the information available and to shifts that have been taking place since at least the time of Spanish contact. In the 1970s Mayo-speaking peoples were concentrated along the lower Río Mayo valley in southern Sonora and along the lower Río el Fuerte valley in northern Sinaloa. Although the concentration increases as one moves down the river valleys toward the Gulf of California, Mayo peoples are found up the Mayo valley at least as far as the Alamos-Macusari area and up the Fuerte valley at least as far as the Tehueco and El Fuerte area, a distance of about 60 miles from the mouth of the rivers (fig. 1). Although in 1965–1974 some of the lands between and beyond the river valleys had been opened to irrigation agriculture, these areas were sparsely populated desert regions covered with thorn forest of numerous varieties of large and small cactus and mesquite trees. Contested by the Yaquis, concentrated in the Río Yaqui valley to the north, the northern Mayo boundary runs along the Arroyo de Cocoraqui parallel to and some 20 miles north of the Mayo valley. The Cocoraqui splits the desert region between the Yaqui and the Mayo valleys into two approximately equal areas. The Fuerte valley lies almost 100 miles south of the Mayo with the Arroyo de Masiaca breaking up this long stretch of coastal desert. Groups of Mayos also live in the Ocoroni and Sinaloa river valleys, the two river valleys farther south of the Fuerte valley (Beals 1945:1). Although inhabited in the 1970s by Mayos and Mestizos, at the time of Spanish contact this northern Sinaloa area was occupied by a set of separate dialect groups: Zuaque, Oquera, Cinaloa, Ocoroni, Baciroa, Nio, Guasave, and Mocorito (Beals 1932a:map 1).

In the 1970s the common Mayo language and dialect, migration and movement of individuals, and ceremonial labor and exchange tie together: Río Mayo Mayos with one another, Ríos Mayo and Fuerte Mayos with each other, and occasional Río Mayo Mayos with Mayos from farther south than the Fuerte valley. In addition, although split by the dialect divergence, some persons born in the Yaqui valley and still recognized as originally Yaqui now live in the Mayo valley and participate in Mayo ceremonialism, in some cases assuming rather important ceremonial roles. In summary, Mayo social and cultural boundaries are marked chiefly in terms of language and dialect spoken and social and ceremonial labor and exchange.

Mayo territory and natural environment are intertwined in a dramatic opposition between the fertile luxuriant Mayo and Fuerte valleys with their high population concentration and the thorn forest desert areas useful for their fruits, woods, and animal products. These desert areas divide the two river valleys and separate Mayos from Yaquis on the north and Mayos from the

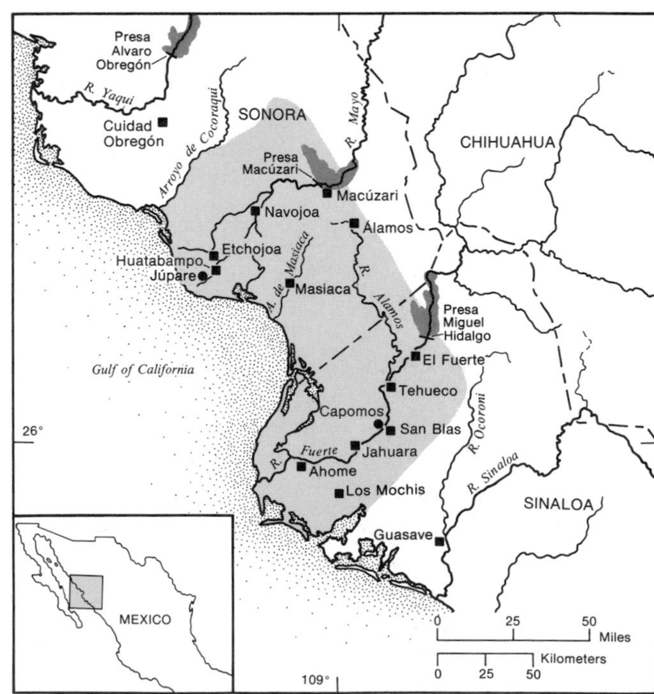

Fig. 1. Tribal territory, 1900 to 1980s. This probably corresponds to the precontact area.

*Mayo has the same native phonemic inventory as Yaqui and may be written with the same letters (see the orthographic footnote in "Yaqui," this vol.). The editors have transcribed the Mayo words in this chapter on the basis of the transcriptions in Collard and Collard (1962) and information on Yaqui.

extinct divergent dialect groups on the south. Originating in the mountainous region of the rugged Sierra Madre Occidental the Mayo and Fuerte rivers drain westward on to the narrow coastal plain of the Gulf of California. This hot lowland coastal Mayo area, called the Sonoran Desert, consists of a subtropical section south of the Río Mayo and a hot dry section with highly distinctive desert vegetation north of the Mayo. The major heavy rains in July and August and slow winter rains in December and January produce 40 to 80 centimeters of rainfall a year. This means that early lower river Mayos had to rely upon river flooding to water their crops of corn, beans, and squash while modern Mayos irrigated their fields of cotton, wheat, and safflower. Yet the wild areas coupled with the river and the gulf still provided a varied diet such as deer, small game, fish, shellfish, fruits of numerous cacti, beans of the mesquite, agave plants, and many other seed- and fruit-producing plants.

From the gulf up the modern Mayo valley there existed three ecological zones besides the area of intense vegetation along the river itself. The river zone consisted of huge cottonwood, oak, and mesquite trees and cane. First, the beach and dune coastline produced abundant supplies of fish, shellfish, and salt. Second, the coastal plain proper, with numerous cacti and thick growth of scrub desert plants, provided building materials, medicines, and natural fruits and seeds. Third, in the upper river valley, the foothills zone consisted of thorn forest with a great range of vegetation such as mesquite trees, cacti, agaves, and larger hardwood trees. This zone produced hardwoods for tool handles, construction, and cooking fire fuel and was rich in a range of animal, fish, and bird life. Rainfall and temperature also varied with the three zones with higher temperatures and more rainfall in the upper valley.

External Relations

Very little is known about Mayo precontact external relations. The relative lack of dialectal variation among the local Uto-Aztecan languages indicates population movement and migrating shifting tribal groups in the 1400s and 1500s (Spicer 1969:782, 1980). The almost immediate willingness of Mayos to ally themselves with the Spaniards and to attack the Yaquis to the north as well as earlier explorer and prospector reports of Yaqui attacks against Mayos suggest a prehispanic pattern of interriverine warfare. The arrival of the Spaniards in the early 1600s stabilized the tribal groups around missions up and down the Río Mayo valley, mines in the Alamos area, and haciendas that slowly spread down the Mayo valley from the Alamos area. During the 1700s and 1800s Mayos both accepted Spanish and later Mestizo intrusions, accompanied by continued loss of lands and political powers, yet also revolted against "foreign" usurpations, sometimes even burning villages and killing their inhabitants. In the 1880s the Mayos as an independent "nation" were finally pacified, and since that time they have been under the political control of the states of Sonora and Sinaloa and of the national government of Mexico. Politically the Mayo valley is divided into four *municipios* (municipalities), each of which is governed by an elected president and a council. The municipality is divided into subareas (*comisarías*) headed by a town or village and governed by a sheriff, appointed by the municipal president and his council. Within each *comisaría* are satellite villages or hamlets usually called rancherias, which are governed by a deputy sheriff. The deputy sheriff is appointed by the municipal president but is immediately responsible to the *comisaría* sheriff. Although governed by this political organization, Mayos complained that it was not a Mayo political system, that the officials were Mestizos and not Mayos, and that Mayos had almost no voice in their selection since modern Mexican politics were controlled by a single party, the party of the Mexican Revolution of 1910, which Mayos wish to back in loyal support of the principles of the Revolution.

Component Local Groups

In precontact times, Mayos lived in loose clusters of houses (rancherias) generally consisting of under 300 related persons although occasional ones may have reached 1,000 persons. After contact, the new churches constructed by the Jesuit missionaries provided a focus for mission communities that consolidated some of the Mayos into seven towns of 2,000 to 3,000 persons. In spite of Jesuit and later influences, many twentieth-century Mayo families still constructed their homes in small rancheria communities. Modern Mayos live: in several hundred scattered rancherias, in more than 40 small pueblos of one to several hundred people, in urban districts of the four larger Mexican towns and small cities of the area, and in ejido communities (communal land-holding units established by federal authority under the 1910 Revolution). With the exception of some rancherias, modern Mayos resided interspersed with non-Mayos although some communities had larger percentages of Mayos than did others. Almost all communities include at least 10 to 20 percent Mestizos and a large number consisted of more than half Mestizos. More specifically Erasmus (1967:7) notes that of 18 rancherias in the Navojoa *comisaría* of Camoa only three were all Mayo and five all Mestizo, while 10 were mixed, with 1,200 persons in all, of which 60 percent were Mayo. Nevertheless, in many Mayo households and churches the Mayo language was still preferred, and Mayos maintained at least the ideal if not the reality of a separate *yoréme* (Mayo) way of life (Crumrine 1981, 1981a). The Mayo structure of the component local groups was best seen in the context of Mayo ritual and ceremonial exchange. These social contexts revealed Mayos integrated at four separate levels: household and rancheria, local ceremonial center or village, municipal ceremonial center or town, and intermunicipal ceremonial exchange and feasting (Crumrine 1977).

Culture

This culture sketch is based upon Crumrine's (1961–1972) field research. The data refer specifically to one village in the Huatabampo *municipio* in the lower Mayo valley, although they are generally applicable to the whole river valley. It is essential to realize that the way of life being outlined belongs to an enclaved group and involves the fusion of aboriginal beliefs, rituals, and symbols with sixteenth- and seventeenth-century Roman Catholic beliefs and with modern Mexican traditions (Crumrine 1977). This description emphasizes the indigenous and uniquely Mayo aspects of this fused sociocultural tradition, but the Mexican national economy, political organization, and symbolism also play a crucial role in Mayo everyday life.

Subsistence

Mayo modern subsistence revolved around farming and wage labor. Relying upon river flooding, preconquest Mayos raised two crops of corn, beans, and squash a year, depended upon fish from both the river and the gulf, and collected cactus fruit and beans from local trees. Wild foods constituted perhaps up to 40 percent of the diet (Spicer 1961:12, 1980). Jesuit introduction of sheep, goats, cattle, wheat, and irrigation agriculture increased the efficiency of the Mayo economy but did not basically modify it. But the investment involved in modern irrigation and farm technology has fundamentally changed Mayo subsistence. In 1972 Mayos still utilized the thorn forest for firewood and building materials and with long sticks knocked down pitahaya cactus fruit in July. Several villages directly on the coast housed Mayos who specialized in fishing from small boats, while some Mayo farmers also fished but from the shore by blocking an estuary and at low tide picking up the stranded fish from the mud and salting them (Crumrine and Crumrine 1967). The fishing families ate some of the fish but in the main they sold them to other Mayos or in the market. Although Mayos used to shoot wild hog and deer with a bow and arrow or take them with a snare, by 1972 few if any lower valley Mayos did any hunting for what deer or hog still remained. Thus wild foods constituted an extremely small percentage of the modern Mayo diet.

Many rural families held ejido plots of 10 to 12 acres while more Mayos, about three-fourths of the total rural families, had some landholdings. In the towns and villages larger numbers of families, sometimes as many as half the village, held no lands at all (Erasmus 1967:71). These families as well as most of the landholding group had to rely upon wage labor either as a supplement or a major means of subsistence. Although many families had garden areas where they grew the traditional and preferred subsistence crops (corn, beans, squash, and melons), the cash crops (cotton, wheat, barley for commercial beer production, safflower, and alfalfa) were raised by Mayos in most fields. In the early 1960s cotton was extremely popular, but by the late 1960s and early 1970s it often had been replaced by wheat or safflower. Since cotton requires a larger wage labor pool, this shift affected many a Mayo's hope for employment. Mayos, in order to obtain seed and pay land and irrigation water taxes, had to obtain capital in the form of loans either from the Banco Ejidal, a store owner, or a private financier. The lending agency, in order to receive its repayment, often stipulated a cash crop. Many Mayo households also kept chickens while others cared for pigs, turkeys, cows, and horses. Away from the irrigated areas, herding of cattle and more often sheep and goats became more popular. For some special occasion an animal was slaughtered so the family had fresh meat with some left over for gifts to relatives or compadres.

Prepared foods, tools, most clothing, and manufactured items were purchased in the market or in local stores. All families had to buy sugar, coffee, lard, and occasional fruit while some even purchased wheat flour and cornmeal. Many modern women ground cornmeal in a crank type meat grinder while some still used the mano and metate for the grinding of wild seeds and coffee beans, which Mayos purchased green and toasted, adding sugar to produce a black crystalline mass of toasted beans and melted sugar. Mayos ate a full range of stews supplemented by flour and corn tortillas followed by coffee with a generous amount of sugar.

Material Culture

Most of the slightly wealthier families owned one or several bicycles and a radio, and a few had a sewing machine. Walking or riding on bicycles, two-wheeled horse-drawn carts, buses, or large trucks provided the major modes of individual and produce transport. Large mats and rather small baskets were still woven from cane (fig. 2), collected along the edges of the river. The mats were utilized for sleeping and constructing walls. Mayos slept either simply on a mat thrown on the ground, on a folding cot, or on a mat placed on a bed constructed of a wooden frame with tightly stretched rawhide thongs between. Several small wooden chairs, benches, a wooden table, and one or several suitcases or wooden trunks for pictures, valuables, and documents made up the household furnishings. At the wooden table, Mayos ate from enamel or glass bowls with enamel spoons. Some native blankets and sashes (fig. 3) were still woven

Mus. of the Amer. Ind., Heye Found., New York: top left, 24752; top right, 24770; bottom, 24805.

Fig. 2. Weaving. top left, Ruperto Zazuera of Masiaca, Sonora, probably making a horsehair band. top right, Woman weaving a blanket. bottom, Woman from Navivaxia, Sonora, making twilled cane sleeping or sitting mat. Photographs by Edward H. Davis, Sonora, in 1924 except bottom, 1922.

and larger pots (figs. 4–5) were still manufactured, although most Mayos utilized store-bought blankets and clothing and cooked and carried water in metal pots or large square oil and lard tins. A major exception was the large water cooling pot that rested at the front of most Mayo houses in a three-branched fork of a tree trunk at about chest height.

Most men and boys wore shoes or sandals; blue, gray, or tan wash trousers; a colored or white shirt; and a Western straw hat. Most women and girls wore shoes or sandals, a blouse, a rebozo, and a medium-length skirt, although by 1972 short skirts were worn by some younger women. An occasional woman wore slacks, some of those of the younger women being very bright and of the latest United States styles. Young girls wore a dress and were always covered with rag diapers. While in 1961 some young boys wore only a small shirt, by 1972 most little boys were also covered with rag diapers.

Settlement

Mayo architecture and settlement patterns reveal the history of the area, cultural fusion, and social duality. In 1972 there were four major settlement types, each

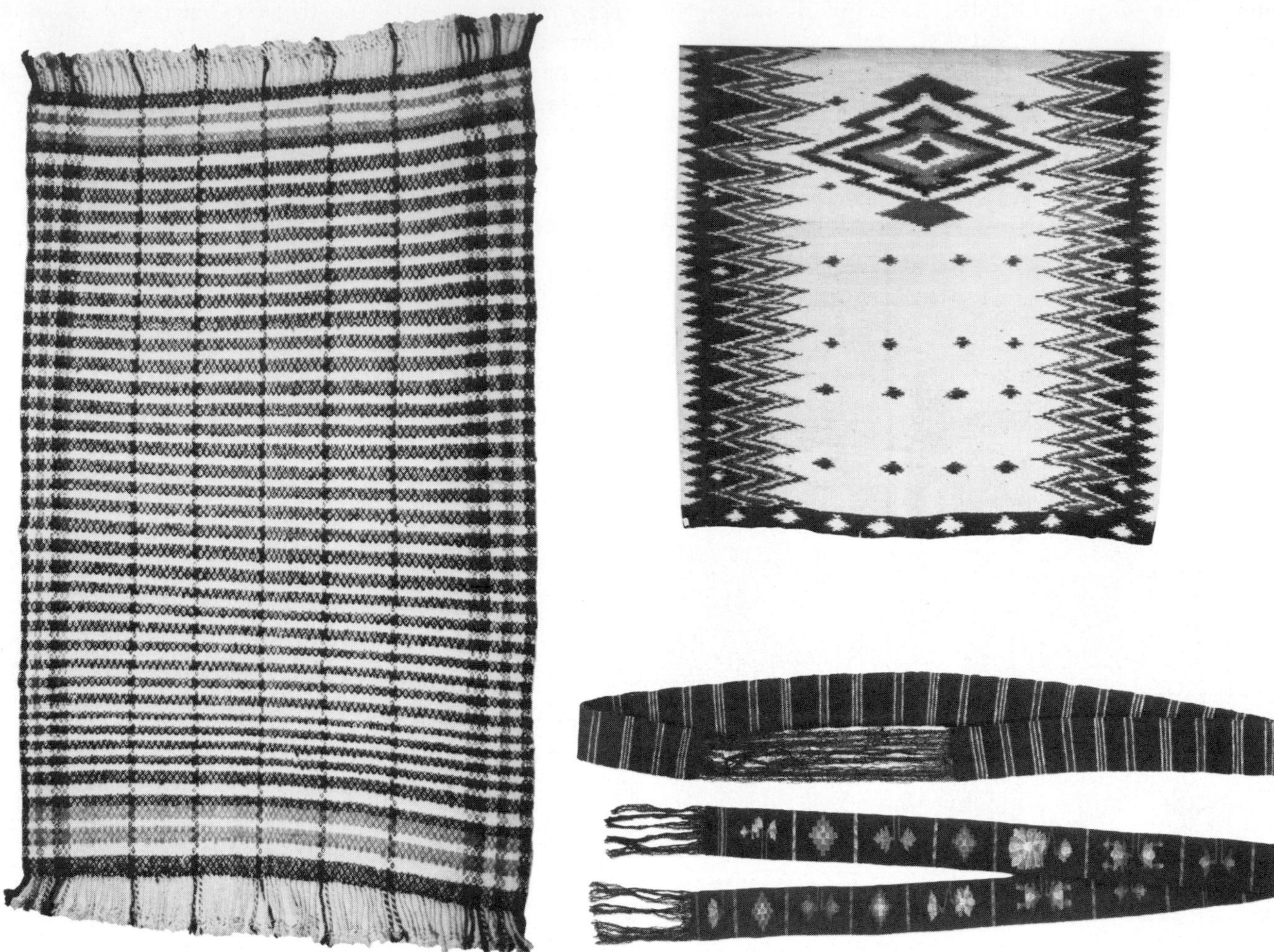

left, San Diego Mus. of Man, Calif.: 1980-6-24; U. of Calif., Lowie Mus., Berkeley: top right, 3-3424; center right, 3-3340; bottom right, 3-3328.

Fig. 3. Textiles. Blankets of handspun wool woven by women on the horizontal loom are of 2 types, those made for native use or for sale. left, Blanket (Spanish *cobija*), made for native use, is white, tan, and dark brown natural colored wool in the fish-eye pattern. Other examples are striped (or plaid when a colored warp is used). top right, Serape (portion shown), made for sale to Mexicans and tourists. Also in natural colors, serapes are often finer and more tightly woven. They are distinguished by having border designs at the ends and sometimes at the sides, often with a diamond shape in the center. They are probably based, directly or indirectly, on the Saltillo serapes (B.T. Burns 1979:54). center right and bottom right, Woolen sashes, black ground with brightly colored patterns also woven on horizontal looms. left, 189 by 130 cm, made by Rosario Gastelum, Las Bocas, Huatabampo, Sonora, in the 1970s; rest same scale, collected by Ralph Beals in the Navojoa district, Sonora, 1930–1931.

reflecting cultural traits from specific historical periods and carrying different social implications: the rancheria type or scattered rural household clusters, a precontact pattern; the modified Spanish village ceremonial center, basically a Spanish mission type of pattern; the modern northwest Mexican urban market center type; and the ejido community type. With houses scattered in small clusters at the edges of the fields and in the bush, the rancheria pattern meant distance from neighbors, relative privacy, and less frequent contact with strangers. An example of the village ceremonial center type was characterized by dual focuses, the Mayo part of town consisting of an unordered scattering of Mayo homes around the church-cemetery area and the Mestizo section with homes, the rural school, the stores, and the public governmental buildings radiating out from the central plaza in a square grid pattern. The Huatabampo municipal seat exemplified the growth of urban Mexican market centers in the river valley. In this town, originally a Mayo ceremonial center, Mayos had been crowded into Mayo sections at the outermost edges of the town and replaced by the wealthy houses of the large landowners, several schools, a new social security building, a police station, a large number of stores, saloons, and a central plaza consisting of a municipal palace, banks, a mestizo church, a bandstand, a centralized enclosed market, and a central park. The fourth type of settlement, found in recently established ejido villages, was based entirely upon a grid pattern and included a central cluster of public buildings. In these communities Mayo and Mestizo household compounds appeared to be interspersed with little ethnic zoning, although Mayo relatives tended to own groups of houses near to one another. Mayo churches or cemeteries did not exist in these communities so their Mayo families were members of a Mayo village congregation or of another local Mayo ceremonial center. The crowded ugly fishing communities that combined grid and random settlement patterns were of necessity only found on the barren sand hills of the coast. Their component houses were constructed of tin scraps or planks gathered on the beach due to the lack of adobe and organic building materials in this area (Crumrine 1977).

Structures

Generally Mayo houses were constructed of several heavy mesquite posts supporting heavy beams upon which lay lighter cross-members and a flat earthen roof. The walls were formed of either adobe brick or woven branches plastered with mud (fig. 6). A household generally consisted of an enclosed sleeping room for each nuclear family and a single open cooking ramada shared by the women of the household. The women cooked over an

Mus. of the Amer. Ind., Heye Foundation, New York: left, 24753, right, 24767.

Fig. 4. Pottery. left, Petra Buitemaya and a young girl of Masiaca, Sonora, carrying jars using circular head rings. right, Large cooking vessels. Photographs by Edward H. Davis, Sonora, 1924.

left, U. of Ariz., Ariz. State Mus., Tucson: E-10092; U. of Calif., Lowie Mus., Berkeley: center, 3-3290, right, 3-3361.

Fig. 5. Pottery. Usually made by only a few women in a community and sold to others (Beals 1945:41), this earthenware is usually made in undecorated utilitarian forms. left, Small brown bowl with handles and rim painted red. center, Bowl in more ornamental shape. right, Miniature bull with bowl on its back to hold burning embers, used for at least 2 of the 4 yearly feasts dedicated to San Juan (Fontana, Faubert, and Burns 1977:30). left, Diameter 25.2 cm (rest same scale); collected by James Griffith in Capomos, Sinaloa, in 1968. center and right, Collected by Ralph Beals in the Navojoa district, Sonora, in 1930–1931.

Mus. of the Amer. Ind., Heye Foundation, New York: top, 24763; bottom, 24794.
Fig. 6. Structures. top, Thatch house with adjoining ramada in Masiaca, Sonora. Man at left is twisting fibers; behind him is a large cooking vessel. bottom, Cactus fence around a house (at left) with a brush ramada for the animals inside the enclosure. Photographs by Edward H. Davis, Sonora, 1924 (top) and 1922 (bottom).

open fire surrounded on three sides with a short adobe mud or brick wall that supported the round metal cooking griddle, above the fire. The women of the rancherias usually carried water from a nearby well or canal and relied upon kerosene torches for light, while Mayos of many villages and of the urban areas often had a running-water tap located near their homes and electric power used only for one or two light bulbs. On the west wall of the sleeping room, Mayos had a shelf or table that served as an altar, supporting the pictures of the saints that have some special meaning to the family. Across the house patio, generally to the east of the house, Mayos placed a three- to four-foot-high wooden cross. In the past households members used to join in morning prayers by the house cross and in evening prayers in front of the household altar.

Social Organization

Wealth took two major forms for modern Mayos: lands and productivity; and health, respect, and Holy Flowers. With lands and good crops one could feed and aid his family and relatives as well as support Mayo ceremonials. The hoarding of food, material goods, or money was distinctly evil and could injure not only the individual but also his relatives or anyone who touched the tainted money. On the other hand, freely giving of the productivity of one's fields, especially in the support of Mayo ceremonialism and of the saints, produced health, respect, social prestige, and heavenly rewards after death (Holy Flowers).

The division of labor was based chiefly upon age and sex. Young through mature adults carried out the major production roles with individuals and households acting as the major production units and households the major consumption units. Girls and boys began to learn their respective adult roles quite early. But by 1972 schooling had become more important and children assumed adult production roles later in life. Older people became repositories of knowledge and highly respected as such. A household that had escaped serious sickness and contained a large percentage of young adults tended to be well fed, accumulated wealth, and increased its ceremonial participation. Since single-household productivity ebbs and wanes through time, no highly stratified social system based upon wealth had developed. Nevertheless, Mayos did recognize that some households were better off than others and that there were good and bad families although wealth was not necessarily as crucial a variable as was the behavior of family members. For adults, the sexual division of labor was crucial in precontact times, when men farmed and hunted and women assisted in the farming and collected wild foods. This division remained important in 1972 as men farmed and participated in the major commercial transactions and women maintained the households and made small purchases in the market and at the stores. The following production specializations, although only part-time, still were practiced in 1972: wool blanket and cane mat weaving, fireworks making, fishing, certain ceremonial dance and musical specializations, native curing, and certain ceremonial roles. In summary, modern Mayo household production was consumed or expended in two separate and quite different economic systems—the national Mexican market economy and Mayo ceremonialism, a redistributional fiesta economy.

Mayo social organization focused upon the family, household, ceremonial kindred, and the ceremonial center consisting of the ritual sodalities and the church officers. In the precontact period descent was traced bilaterally, kinship terminology patterned as bifurcate collateral with an emphasis on relative age of siblings, rancheria exogamy was practiced, and supra-rancheria political organization existed only during periods of warfare while in peacetime the rancheria was governed by an informal council of elders in conjunction with the adult male members (see Spicer 1969, 1980). In the 1960s confusion existed among Mayos regarding the traditional kinship system; although Mayo terms were remembered, many families utilized a modified Mexican kinship system, lineal and Eskimo, with Mayo terms applied to parents, siblings, and children and Spanish terms for aunts, uncles, cousins, and in-laws (Crumrine 1977). Although nuclear family households existed, often a modern Mayo household included several old people or one or more siblings with their own families. In fact, for Mayos, households without old people were indeed poor and weak in supernatural power. At times of birth, marriage, and ceremonial labor, Mayo parents selected godparents for the newborn, the marrying couple, or the initiate. Through sponsorship the new godparents became coparents with the actual parents of the individual being sponsored. The group of coparents, *kompan^{y}ía*, became a cooperative unit and offered aid especially when an individual sponsored a large ceremonial. An occasional household also included members who were ceremonial rather than real kin.

The Jesuit missionaries emphasized ceremonial kinship and godparenthood, certain ceremonial sodalities, and village government that had parallels to the older rancheria political organization. Both political systems valued equality and individuality of adults but consisted of hierarchical ceremonial sodalities. The heads of these sodalities met in open town councils at which each household had some representation. Even though modern Mayos have lost much of their political control and the secular village governors have become part of the church organization, this type of village government still existed in a modified form in some Mayo villages in 1972.

In addition to being the locus of production and consumption, the household also played a major part in the individual's life cycle and the rites of passage. The rituals associated with these events provided unifying social situations for the members of the household. Although by 1972 most women went to the hospital, formerly childbirth involved a midwife who used herbs and massage to aid in the birth, a female member of the household for general aid, and a male "holder" who sat behind the pregnant woman and squeezed around her waist with each contraction. Babies were held and played with a great deal by all members of the family and were nursed until another child was born. When children began to walk they were cared for more by their older siblings and ceased to be the center of attention, which appeared to be a difficult adjustment for the children as they turned fussy and demanding. As children approached six years of age they entered school, took part in the Easter ceremonial, and several years later passed through a kind of initiation ritual when both boys and girls danced in the Matachine (the church dance sodality) and made a pilgrimage to the neighboring municipality to attend the saint's day ceremony for the Holy Spirit. Some girls in their mid- or late teens joined a female church sodality and the boys often became *fariseos* (Mayo *parisero*) (the male Lenten sodality), during Lent for a period of three years (see Crumrine 1968, 1969).

Mus. of the Amer. Ind., Heye Foundation, New York: 24766.

Fig. 7. Baking bread in a beehive oven. Photograph by Edward H. Davis, Masiaca, Sonora, 1924.

Although in the past it was a quite elaborate household ritual, in 1972 the wedding was either simple or not held as the couple eloped or simply began living together. Evidence indicates (see Robertson 1964:188) the elopement pattern had some historical depth and was employed to avoid church costs associated with a wedding. As individuals matured, some became leaders in church-Pueblo sodalities and most acted at one time or another as *pahkóme*, ceremonial sponsors.

Curing

When a Mayo became ill, Mayo traditions provided several alternatives, depending upon the type of illness. Foods were classified in terms of intrinsic qualities such as hot or cold, and for certain kinds of illness or body states one had to eat only hot foods while for other states one had to eat cold foods. While Mayos visited medical doctors and purchased medicines in the local drug stores, they also employed native Mayo curers who, with the aid of the power of God, could cure witch-caused diseases. Also a Mayo could make a promise (Spanish *manda*) to God or an especially powerful saint and if one were cured he or she had to pay the supernatural by making a ceremony or cycle of ceremonies in the saint's honor. Sometimes none of these attempts was successful and death resulted. After death, the *kompan^{y}ía* formed, consisting of the deceased's real and ceremonial kin, and a wake took place in the home. The following day, the deceased was taken to the church where the lay minister (Spanish *maestro*) read parts of the Mass for the dead and then to the cemetery for burial. Several remembrance rituals took place in the household, especially on the eight-day and one-year anniversary of the death when more elaborate foods were provided for the *maestro* and other persons attending. All the dead were remembered the first days of each November when Mayo families decorated the

Fig. 8. *čapayékam* (or *čapakobam*), masked participants in the Easter ceremonies, and members of the *fariseo* (Mayo *parisero*) sodality. The large mask covers the entire head and may represent an animal (bottom left), man, or a woman (top left). They are always hairy and frequently have long sharp noses and large pointed ears. The men who act the *fariseos* are usually in their late teens; at one time or another most men in the village take on this role (Crumrine 1977:89). top left and right, Photographs by David Burckhalter, Júpare, Sonora, 1980. bottom left and right, Photographs by James Boudreau, Júpare, 1971.

graves and remained in the cemetery to pray, light candles, and attend the graves into the night.

Religion

Many Mayo precontact beliefs, rituals, and ceremonial sodalities were combined with traditions taught by the Jesuits. Modified yet still practicing as the modern native curer and "living" saint (see Crumrine 1975, 1977; Crumrine and Macklin 1974), the precontact shaman diagnosed diseases, controlled weather, foresaw future events, and cured diseases by sucking or constructing a painting of colored sand. Precontact ceremonial sodalities often utilized masks and fermented corn or cactus fruit drinks and included a hierarchy of officers and a formal initiation with a ritual sponsor. Enriching the native Mayo belief system, Jesuits introduced new supernaturals such as the Virgin of Guadalupe, Jesus, a number of saints, the Christian flood myth, and Roman Catholic brotherhoods and sisterhoods. The unique Mayo fusion or combination of indigenous beliefs and organizations with those introduced by the Jesuits and the linking of this sacred system to the village government has resulted in the highly integrated modern Mayo folk culture (Crumrine 1981, 1982). The modern church-pueblo organization consisted of five church governors and five helpers generally elected for two terms of three years each, the *maestros*, the Matachine dance sodality, the *fariseo* sodality, and the *pahkóme*, who promised to serve the saint by producing the saint's day ceremony, praying, and providing the fireworks, food, and entertainment in the form of pascola (*pahkóʔora*) and deer dancers. The *fariseos* are shown in figure 8 and "Kachinas and Masking," fig. 9, this volume. The ceremonial cycle generally followed the outline of the life of Christ. From Christmas through the elaborate Easter

U. of Calif., Lowie Mus., Berkeley: 3-3430.

Fig. 9. Harp, of cottonwood and ironwood, derived from an early Spanish form. It is usually played by men during the pascola dance (Beals 1945:42). Height about 137.0 cm, collected by Ralph Beals in the Navojoa district, Sonora, 1930–1931.

ceremonial, Mayos reenacted the life, death, and resurrection of Christ (Crumrine 1974, 1977a, 1981, 1982). The ceremonies of the Exaltation of the Holy Cross took place on May 3, San Isidro on May 19, the Holy Spirit and Holy Trinity in late May or early June, and the nativity of San Juan on June 24. The dead ancestors returned to the villages in October and November, and the church governors were confirmed in office in the first week of January.

The realms of nature as well as Mayo church and ritual organization were structured in terms of a Holy Family model: *ítom áčai*, God, 'our Father'; *ítom áčai ússi* 'our Father's Son', Jesus; and *ítom aíye* 'Our Mother', the Virgin Mary (see Crumrine 1977). The sun was identified as *ítom áčai*, the moon as *ítom aíye*, and the stars as *íli ússim* 'little children'; as the animals of the forest and the fish of the sea were the little children of their supernatural parents and protectors. *ítom áčai*, the power of the sun, protected man against serpents that lived under the earth and wished to surface and eat man up. Also cycles of myths were associated with the different ceremonials of the yearly round (Crumrine 1981, 1982). Some of these myths integrated recent historical events, such as a church burning (see Crumrine 1977), into Mayo ceremonialism while individual prophets combined elements of myths and rituals into new messianic cults (see Crumrine 1975, 1977; Erasmus 1967:102–107). Thus although modern Mayos had essentially lost control of the secular political structure of the river valley, in the 1960s and early 1970s they were revitalizing and elaborating Mayo secular and sacred church organization and traditional myths and rituals.

Prehistory

Specific identifications with prehistoric cultures proved to be minimal because no extensive archeological reports have been published on the Mayo or Fuerte valleys. However, excavation has been completed by Pailes (1972) in the Alamos foothills area. Reconnaissance and excavations were made at Guasave in the Río Sinaloa valley south of the Fuerte in the 1930s (Ekholm 1939). Meighan's (1971:757) revised sequence lists only a Huatabampo phase from around A.D. 900 to around A.D. 1200–1250 for the Mayo valley and the Huatabampo phase from around A.D. 900 to A.D. 1050–1100 and the Guasave phase from A.D. 1050–1100 to A.D. 1400 for the Sinaloa valley. Early conquest documents indicate a heavy population and a remarkable cultural complexity on the Sinaloa coastal plain. An extremely destructive conquest appears to have depopulated the area. In this area just south of the Mayo, the native peoples were prosperous farmers who supported chiefs and wore cotton garments decorated in blue and white as well as ornaments of shell, pearls, copper bells, gold, and silver.

History

The earliest records of sporadic Mayo-Yaqui contact with the Spaniards describe a Spanish slave raid in 1533 and a Spanish prospecting expedition in 1564. Capt. Diego Martínez de Hurdaide conquered the Indians south of the Mayos by early 1600, and immediately Jesuit missionaries were at work among them. In 1609 Hurdaide made a treaty with the Mayos and he and his Mayo supporters were defeated by a huge force of some 7,000 Yaquis. After this heavy battle the Yaquis proposed peace, and both Mayos and Yaquis requested missionaries who were sent in 1614 to the Mayos and in 1617 to the Yaquis. Several Jesuits were able to produce broad changes in Mayo belief and technological systems through their successful missionization techniques—learning and teaching in the Mayo language, working through native Mayo leaders, living with the Mayos, and relying upon the army as little as possible. The mission villages created by the Jesuits became economic as well as religious centers. With the exception of the epidemics that killed around half the Mayo population in the first half-century (table 1), the Mayo river

Table 1. Population Estimates

Date	*Population*	*Remarks*	*Source*
early 1600s	25,000		Pérez de Ribas 1944a
late 1600s	13,000		
1760	6,500	in 7 villages when many were away working in mines and on haciendas	Acosta 1949:100–101
1950	31,053	2,509 monolingual in Mayo	Marino Flores 1967:22; 1950 census
1958	30,000–34,000	in Sonora	Erasmus 1967:6
1960	13,317	R. Mayo valley	1960 census
1963	15,000	R. Mayo valley	Nolasco Armas 1969:48
1970	27,848	Mayo speakers	1970 census

valley was relatively quiet until 1684 when one of the richest silver mines of northwest Mexico was discovered at Alamos just above the river valley. As increasing numbers of Mayos were taken to work in the mines and as Spanish settlers moved down the river valley, resentment grew until 1740, a date that marks a general Indian revolt. After the situation quieted down, the Jesuits returned to the river valley only to be expelled from the New World in 1767. After three years of unsuccessful Franciscan missionization, the secular clergy were assigned to the area in 1771. Thus Mayos became pawns in the classic conflict between missionaries seeking souls and the founding of mission towns on the one hand and secular authorities pursuing cheap lands and labor for the mines and haciendas on the other.

Spanish authority weakened, and in the 1820s Mexico became a free and independent nation. Lacking power, the new Occident State government (Sonora and Sinaloa combined) failed to integrate the Mayos through their projected program of land distribution, taxation, and localization of political power in non-Indian villages. Continued Mestizo land encroachment in part triggered a number of highly destructive revolts that ultimately resulted in Mayo pacification during the 1880s. A number of Mayo prophets, among them "Santa" Teresa (Crumrine 1974, 1977), appeared in the years preceding 1890, and in September of that year many Mayo prophets were deported to the mines in Baja California. From at least the 1880s up to 1910, the period of Porfirio Díaz, many Mayos were virtually enslaved on the haciendas in the Río Mayo valley. After a visit by the future revolutionary Francisco Madero, many Mayos joined Alvaro Obregón, later president of Mexico, and left with him in 1912 to fight in the Revolution. Returning in 1915, many found their families and homes destroyed and their lands gone even though the law establishing the ejidos and small properties was enacted in this same year. In 1926 President Plutarco Elías Calles, attempting to enforce Mexico's antichurch legislation, ordered local Mestizos to burn the churches and santos in the Mayo valley. Although similar church burnings took place all over Mexico, Mayos believed that the local powers took this occasion as a revenge by burning Mayo churches and not destroying those of the rich and powerful Mestizos. In the late 1920s and the early 1930s lands were actually redistributed in the river valley, and a number of ejidos were set up. One Mayo village reconstructed a church in 1938. Since that time Mayos have been reviving and adjusting their "traditional" way of life. This brief historical sketch points out the importance of the following processes of culture change: initial contact and missionization, slowly eroding sociopolitical autonomy and land loss, prophetic movements, revolution, reconstruction and revival of a way of life (Crumrine 1977).

1960s and Early 1970s

Since Mayos are an enclaved group, this section consists of an outline of the social structure of contact between Mayos and Mestizos. The following social situations exist in which there was a potential for cultural integration and adaptation between the dominant Mestizo culture and society and that of the Mayos. However, in actuality, when Mayos and Mestizos interacted, the basis of the relationship proved to be either between two individual persons, irrespective of their ethnic identity, or between an individual, the Mayo, and a Mestizo who is representing (playing a role rooted in) a Mestizo social unit. It was almost never between a Mayo, representing a Mayo social status, and a Mestizo individual or a Mestizo representing a Mestizo social status. Mayos resided as neighbors with Mestizos; but the place of residence, the degree of neighboring, the settlement of house plot inheritance, and land disputes tended to have become individual and nuclear family matters, rather than those of a Mayo societal corporate unit like a lineage, clan, or sodality. Intermarriage and close friendship ties with Mestizos also depended upon individual rather than ethnic identity. In principle Mayos disliked intermarriage, but due to war and migration, marriage was quite brittle, intensifying the number of spouses per individual and increasing chances for intermarriage. From data on 170 marriages collected in five Mayo and Fuerte river villages, Erasmus (1967:8) found one-eighth were mixed marriages. Also Mayos ideally preferred Mayo compadres to Mestizo ones. As individuals, Mayos accepted and respected certain Mestizo in-laws, neighbors, and compadres. In terms of employer–employee relationships, Mestizos acted as employers and utilized Mayos and Mestizos as low-paid unskilled farm wage labor without regard to their ethnic identity. Lower-class social dances produced by either Mayo or lower-class Mestizo families brought together members of both groups. Yet Mayo social dances also involved a *velación*, or religious ceremony dedicated to a saint, while most Mestizo dances were expressly secular (Crumrine and Crumrine 1977).

A few Mestizos did make promises that had to be consummated in Mayo churches. But the majority of Mestizos who attended Mayo ceremonials were either curious or selling clothing, trinkets, food and drink, or side-show rides. This commercial exploitation of Mayo ritual was explicitly regarded by Mayos as a violation of sacred ground, as one should give freely and not sell in the churchyard area. On the other hand, all Mayos participated as individual Mexicans in Mestizo societal units. Mayos held a high value for schooling and knowledge and encouraged their children to get a good education. Yet the poor quality of the rural schools, sheer economic hardships, and the use of the Mayo language at home and Spanish in school meant that until the mid-twentieth century few Mayos experienced more than six months or at the most several years in school.

The ejido may be either the infrequent collective or the parceled type. Erasmus (1967:16) found that in 22 of 35 Mayo area ejidos, "90 percent or more of the members spoke Cahita as well as Spanish and in three, 90 percent of the members spoke only Spanish. In the remaining ten, the monolingual Spanish speakers were slightly in the majority." Even though in the majority, Mayo members often complained that they had very little control of ejido politics. Military service, Mayos believed, was one means of getting ahead yet remaining a Mayo. Nevertheless, army life provided a new experience that was Mestizo and not Mayo in structure, aim, and quality.

In summarizing this diversity of data, Crumrine and Crumrine (1969:55) abstracted the dominant type of integration, "individual integration in which either individuals are integrated with individuals (regardless of their Mayo or mestizo identity) or individual Mayos are integrated with mestizo societal units" and treated as if they were peasant Mexican farmers. Thus Mayo societal units were essentially not recognized by Mexican social and political structures. And interaction took place in terms of non-Mayo aims, goals, and values. Within this kind of social structure of contact, Mayos were utilizing several responses. Some Mayo individuals assimilated, becoming Mestizos—in local Spanish *yoris rebueltos* 'turned Mestizo', a term used by the Mayo with a great deal of hostility toward the defectors. But in assimilating a Mayo had very few real alternatives and had to reject his traditional culture and enter Mestizo society at the bottom level, that of peasant farmer with little hope of upward mobility. Thus, other Mayos preferred to seek prestige within their traditional culture and society, which they had converted into a symbol and a value in itself. They were actively adapting and revitalizing as much of their "traditional" way of life as was possible in the modern Mayo valley (Crumrine 1981, 1981a).

Synonymy

Acosta (1949:37) suggests that the term Mayo signifies 'boundary' and was applied to the people living along the Mayo or Mayambo River because they were "locked in" their boundaries or did not wish to communicate with outsiders. For the name Cahita, see the synonymy in "Yaqui" (this vol.).

Sources

Beals (1932a, 1943) discusses the aboriginal Mayo culture in detail and provides an excellent comparative ethnology of pre-1750 northern Mexico. The major English summary and source on Mayo history is the amazingly detailed and accurate presentation of Southwest history and culture change, 1533–1960, by Spicer (1962). See also the Spanish sources (Acosta 1949; Navarro García 1967; M. Gill 1957; Pérez de Ribas 1944a; Troncoso 1905). The three major contemporary field studies are: Beals's (1945) pioneering descriptive ethnography of the upper Mayo valley, Navojoa area; Erasmus's (1961, 1967) in-depth study of socioeconomic conditions and Mayo-Mestizo relations in southern Sonora and northern Sinaloa; and Crumrine's (1964, 1968, 1969, 1970, 1974, 1975, 1976, 1977, 1977a, 1978, 1979, 1981, 1981a, 1982) examination of lower Mayo River valley Mayos' ethnic identity, ceremonialism, and processes of cultural integration and change.

Tarahumara

CAMPBELL W. PENNINGTON

The Tarahumara (ˌtärəhōōˈmäru), who speak a Uto-Aztecan language,* live within the southwest of the Mexican state of Chihuahua, occupying approximately 35,000 square kilometers, about one-half the territory they dominated at first European contact (figs. 1a–b). They have proved resistant to culture change; in spite of almost four centuries of influence from missionaries, farmers, cattlemen, and miners their basic pattern of settlement, population, and economy has remained essentially unaltered.

Prehistory

Exactly when the Tarahumara occupied western Chihuahua is not known. Archeological investigations have been made only in the upper reaches of the Río Urique near Norogachi, in the canyon country near Batopilas, and at Waterfall Cave in southern Chihuahua (Zingg 1940; Ascher and Clune 1960; Clune 1960; Cutler 1960). Zingg demonstrated a marginal affiliation of his material with the Basketmaker culture of the American Southwest; therefore, the Tarahumara presumably have been in western Chihuahua for at least 2,000 years. The Waterfall Cave material has been dated between A.D. 100 and 1600. Where the Tarahumara came from is not known. Tradition indicates that they came from the Apache country to the north and east (Lumholtz 1894:296). Some substance is given to this tradition by a comment made by Verlarde in the eighteenth century (Manje 1954:223); this priest noted that Apaches living northwest of the Gila River were called Tarasoma by the Gila Pima. Tarasoma may be linked with the name Tarahumara.

History

Jesuits appeared in southeastern aboriginal Tarahumara country in 1610 (Pérez de Ribas 1944a, 3:159–160) and at the time of their expulsion from Mexico in 1767 maintained 29 missions and at least 55 *visitas* within the Indian country (Lizasoain 1763; Tamarón y Romeral 1937:120, 131–134, 140–149, 169–174). Franciscans replaced Jesuits, but there was a rapid decline in missionary activities, and between 1825 and the return of Jesuits in 1900 the church exerted little influence upon the Tarahumara (Pennington 1963:16–17). Efforts of Spanish military forces in putting down rebellions in the seventeenth and eighteenth centuries as well as activities of Spanish farmers and cattlemen in the eastern plains, foothill country, and in the northern portion of uplands occupied by the Indians during the same period caused surviving aborigines who did not merge into the Mestizo world to retreat into southwestern Chihuahua. These alien pressures further resulted in a movement of some Tarahumaras westward (fig. 1), into territory once dominated by the Jova, Lower Pima, Guarijío, Chínipa, Guazápar, Témori, and Tubar (Pennington 1963:6–11, 23). Spanish miners maintained sporadic mining operations in the Tarahumara country during the seventeenth and eighteenth centuries (Pennington 1963:21), but the influence of such activities was minimal. Of all outside influences, those of the Jesuits have been the most lasting, since from introductions by these missionaries the Tarahumara selected culture traits most appropriate for life in their rugged habitat.

Three major influences affect the Tarahumara—those of the Jesuits, the Mexican federal government, and the ever-increasing Mestizo population around margins of the Indian country. Jesuit missions (fig. 1) emphasize religious and educational instruction and provide medical attention at Sisoguichi, Norogachi, and Creel. The federal government, operating essentially from a station established at Guachochi in 1952 (Lister and Lister 1966:307), concentrates upon bringing the Tarahumara into the mainstream of Mexican cultural life, most attention being given to programs geared to improve the Indian economic position within the Mestizo world of western Chihuahua. Within prehistoric and historic times the Tarahumara seem not to have been influenced by, nor have they influenced, the Tepehuan, whose habitat is within the most southern Chihuahua *municipio* in the sierras (Pennington 1969:235–373). Further, there is

*The phonemes of Tarahumara are: (voiceless stops and affricate) *p, t, č* ([č, c]), *k, ʔ*; (voiced stops) *b, g*; (voiceless fricatives) *s* ([s, š]), *h*; (nasals) *m, n*; (liquids) *r* (flap), *l* ([l, l̩]); (semi-vowels) *w, y*; (vowels) *i, e, a, o, u*; (stress) v́.

The sources for the phonemic spelling of the Tarahumara words cited in italics in this chapter are Hilton (1959) and Lionnet (1972); the editors are responsible for the interpretation of these sources. In the absence of a comprehensive study of Tarahumara dialectology the details of some forms remain uncertain.

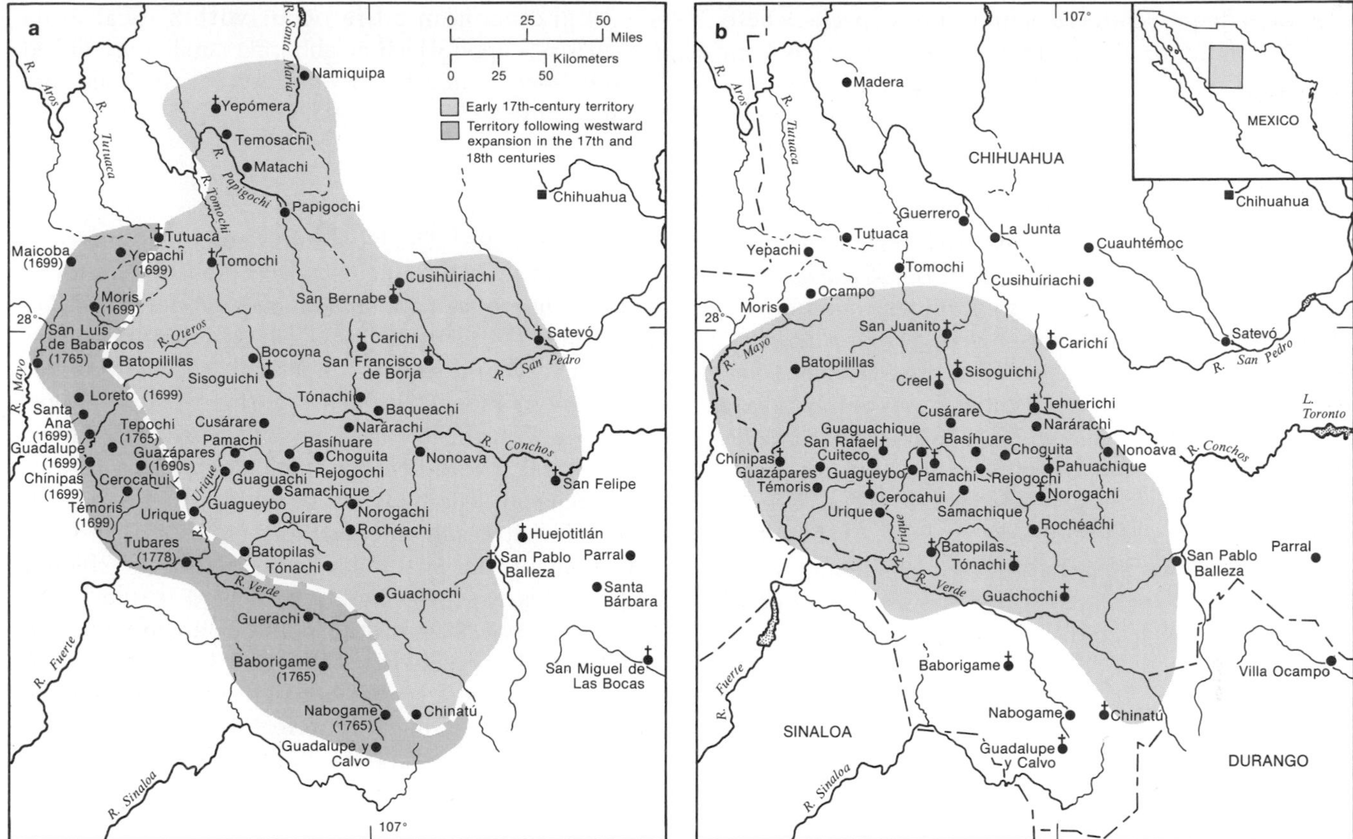

Fig. 1. a, 17th- and 18th-century Tarahumara territory with Jesuit missions in 1700. Dates following village names refer to earliest reference to Tarahumara settlement west and south of the early 17th-century boundary. b, Territory and missions in 1980.

little recorded evidence of influence of the Tarahumara upon or by other surviving aboriginal people of the sierras, such as the Guarijío, who have long occupied the upper Río Mayo country, and Lower Pima who live near Yepachi, Chihuahua (see Bye, Burgess, and Mares Trías 1975).

Population

The most useful twentieth-century census of the Tarahumara was taken in 1945 (Plancarte 1954:101–102); this census listed a total of 44,141 Indians, a figure consistent with data obtained in a Jesuit survey made in 1920 (Ocampo 1950:100), in which more than 46,000 Tarahumaras were reported. Available data for the colonial and modern periods suggest that the Indian population has remained rather static (Pennington 1963:24). Whatever the total number of aborigines, their way of life has come under steady pressure by Mestizos in southwestern Chihuahua. There were approximately 100,000 non-Indians in the 23 *municipios* that contained Tarahumaras in 1920, 107,000 in 1930, 126,000 in 1940, 152,000 in 1950, and 190,000 in 1960 (Plancarte 1954:103–105; México. Dirección General de Estadística 1963:23–24).

Environment

At contact the Tarahumara were clustered along streamways of great canyons, upland meadows and valleys, foothill country, plains, and basin and range country of central and western Chihuahua. Uplands and canyon country occupied by twentieth-century Tarahumara include some of the most rugged terrain in North America. Precipitation in southwestern Chihuahua averages about 35.7 centimeters annually (Pennington 1963:26–30), and erosion by westward-flowing streams has greatly dissected the uplands, carving canyons several thousands of feet in depth. Most of the annual precipitation occurs during the summer, and the early part of the rainy season is marked by much hail. Except for higher portions of the upland plateau, where elevations average about 2,000 meters, the climate is mild, with an average annual temperature of 15.2° C. July is the hottest month, with a mean reading of 22.4° C. An average temperature of 7.4° C characterizes December, the coldest month. Snow may fall in the uplands during December, January, and February but rarely remains upon the ground for more than two weeks except on protected slopes (Pennington 1963:28).

Species of pine dominate the upland vegetation complex, there being scattered stands of oak species where edaphic conditions are suitable, or where pine has been removed. Conspicuous smaller forms include species of *Cercocarpus, Arctostaphylos, Arbutus*, and juniper. Grass is not abundant except along streamways and in meadows that have developed since introduction of the metal ax. Upper portions of the canyons are distinguished by species of pine and oak that give way to a middle slope association dominated by species of oak, *Acacia, Achras, Platanus, Agave*, and *Dasylirion*, which in turn are replaced at lower elevations by species of *Baccharis, Mimosa, Guazuma*, and *Lysiloma*, there being some examples of tall cacti. Conspicuous forms of the canyon bottoms include species of *Ficus*, Rubiaceae, and *Pithecellobium*. The most useful soils within the Tarahumara country are those located in the central portions of narrow or broad flat-bottomed valleys, or those that appear as narrow stretches of alluvium flanking the streams. Elsewhere, the soils are thin and stony (Pennington 1963:31–32, 34).

Culture

Political Organization

Seventeenth-century Jesuits introduced the concept of a hierarchy of native officials that persists in the late twentieth century on the pueblo level. The principal officer is a governor, who with his assistants oversees secular and religious affairs, particularly the organization of fiestas, adjudication of disputes between and within families, meting out punishment, and the promotion of and arrangement for marriages. The governor (elected by popular vote) and his assistants (chosen by popular vote or appointed by the governor), who are known in Spanish by terms such as *mayor, capitán, teniente, fiscal*, and *soldado*, carry a special staff when executing their responsibilities. There is no significant connection between officials of the pueblos and the official machinery of municipal, local, and national government (Fried 1969:860–862), and except in instances of murder state authorities rarely give attention to Indian disputes.

Within Tarahumara society, which lacks effective tribal leadership or councils, the pueblo is the basic territorial unit, the boundary of each pueblo enclosing an area of about 15 miles in radius. Indians frequently converge upon the religio-administrative center of each pueblo for gossip, settlement of disputes, religious fiestas, arrangement of affairs common to the pueblo, and footraces. Affairs in each pueblo are controlled and directed by native officials. Contacts among pueblos are maintained by attendance at fiestas, seasonal mobility, attendance at *tesgüinadas* (drinking parties), and trading relationships. The most significant contacts that affect social and economic life occur within local units (rancherias), upon which neighboring families are linked by religio-economic fiestas and mutual work-aid and lending patterns (Fried 1969:860).

Subsistence

• AGRICULTURE The basic subsistence items are corn, beans, and squash, remains of which have been found in pre-Columbian Tarahumara sites (Cutler 1960:277–278; Zingg 1940:19, 37, 49–50, 54–56). Minor cropping of the Old World wheat is practiced at locales marked by strong missionary influence during the colonial period, as at Guagueybo and Pamachi, or where the Mexican federal government has implemented its tillage, as at Guachochi. The Old World sorghum and barley are known but little cultivated. Jesuits and Franciscans promoted sugarcane in suitable areas during the colonial period; this cane was rarely cultivated in the 1970s. Species of sweet and white potatoes are occasionally cultivated. It is likely that aboriginal Tarahumaras cultivated one or more species of amaranth, since the Franciscan record for Guaguachi refers to a plant that must have been an amaranth (Relación de Guaguachic 1777). Cultivation of the bottle gourd used in manufacturing utensils and rattles is common, as is tillage of the introduced Job's tears as a source of seeds utilized as beads. The bottle gourd was probably cultivated in aboriginal times (Zingg 1940:37, 49, 54–56; Cutler 1960:278). The introduced watermelon is occasionally cultivated in western canyons.

Introduction of metal ax, plow, and cattle permitted the Tarahumara to move away from a dibble tillage restricted to plots developed on alluvial deposits adjacent to streams. The Indians prepare fields along streamway floodplains, on slopes of upland meadows, on well-drained meadow flats, in terraced arroyos, and on canyon slopes that may or may not be terraced (Pennington 1963:47). It is not known whether aboriginal Tarahumaras girdled trees, but undoubtedly some land was cleared by fires set to destroy animals (Steffel 1809–1811, 1:323). Field plots are cleared individually or with aid of neighbors who expect reciprocity at some future time. Fertilizer from corrals or cave shelters may be placed upon fields, or corrals may be moved from place to place in the fields to facilitate spreading of manure (Pennington 1963:50–51). The wooden plow used in preparing plots has changed little since its introduction in the seventeenth century.

Men, women, and children participate in planting and harvesting activities. Corn is usually sowed in April and May and harvested in October and November (fig. 2). Cucurbits are planted after the corn is hilled. Beans are seeded in June or July and harvested in August and September. Wheat is sowed before the spring rains and harvested in late summer (Pennington 1963:53–54). A

bottom right, U. of Ariz., Ariz. State Mus., Tucson: 55932.

Fig. 2. The cultivation of maize. In March or April the ground is prepared for planting by plowing with a wooden plow. "The oxen are yoked to a special yoke regulated to space the furrows at a distance so that the growing corn can be cultivated later by oxen and plows" (bottom left) (Bennett and Zingg 1935:29). When the furrows are ready, the planting begins using planting-sticks (top left). Much of the planting is done cooperatively, typically accompanied by drinking maize beer. top right, Maize curing ceremony, usually performed every year and sometimes several times during the growing season (Bennett and Zingg 1935:281). A Tarahumara doctor is delivering a speech to maize plants to encourage their proper growth. The other men carry containers of medicines that they sprinkle on the plants to protect them from pests and aid their growth. bottom right, Maize is hand picked, shucked and put in a basket made of wood hoops, sticks, and probably twisted rope (Fontana, Faubert, and Burns 1977:76, fig. 53) at Rancho Rijisuchi near Panalachi, Chihuahua. Photograph by Bernard L. Fontana, Nov. 1978. Other photographs by William L. Merrill at Rejogochi, Chihuahua, top left, April 1978, top right and bottom left, June and July 1981.

wooden dibble or an iron rod is used in making holes in which corn, beans, and cucurbits are seeded.

Some Tarahumaras use a metal hoe for weeding, whereas others utilize a crudely fashioned wooden hoe that is probably derived from a sharp pointed stick used in the eighteenth century for weeding (Relación de Guazápares 1777). The wooden plow is used for cultivation of corn. During the growing season livestock are carefully tended during the day and maintained in corrals at night. Log fences are constructed. Birds and wild animals that damage crops are destroyed whenever possible, or the fields are guarded by crop watchers. Little can be done about damage to crops by insects and cornworms.

Men, women, and children gather crops, which are stored in stone, plank, or log cribs constructed so that animals cannot enter (Pennington 1963:59). The Tarahumara once utilized storage cribs constructed on faces of cliffs that overhang streamways (Zingg 1940:44).

• HORTICULTURE Crops that require careful attention are cultivated in garden plots that are protected against predators in the same fashion as fields. Important greens are the New World peppergrass (*Lepidium virginicum*) and two Old World mustards (*Brassica juncea, B. campestris*). Condiments include the Old World coriander (*Coriandrum sativum*) and the New World chili pepper (*Capsicum annuum*). The true tobacco (*Nicotiana tabacum*) is supplemented by wild tobaccos (*N. trigonophylla, N. glauca*). Old World fruits—peach, apricot, apple, and pear—are occasionally grown, as are native fruits, such as the sapote (*Achras zapota*), cherry (*Prunus serotina*), plums (*Spondias mombin*), and mulberry (*Morus microphylla*). Canyon Tarahumaras occasionally propagate the Old World citrus fruits and the native avocado (*Persea americana*). Some Tarahumaras sell fruits to Mestizos (Pennington 1963:65–74).

• FOOD AND BEVERAGES Maize is the principal foodstuff, and the important corn dishes are roasting ears, pinole, *esquiate*, atole, tortillas (fig. 3), and tamales. The staple dish throughout the year is pinole, which is prepared by grinding parched and burst corn grains into a meal that is mixed with water or milk. Fresh squash is pit baked, baked in ashes, or boiled. Toasted squash seeds are an esteemed food. Green beans are boiled. Dried beans are commonly toasted in an olla that contains sand; then they are ground and mixed with water that is boiled until the mixture thickens (Pennington 1963:75–83).

Tiswin (*batári* or *sugí*) is the ubiquitous beverage prepared by the Tarahumara, either from juice expressed from *elote* cornstalks or from sprouted corn. The juice is boiled and material from certain local plants serves as a catalyst (for detailed information on exactly what plants serve as catalysts see Pennington 1963:151). A day or so of fermentation is required. A fermented drink may be prepared from juice expressed from baked hearts of *Agave* and *Dasylirion* species. Fruits obtained from tall cacti that grow in the canyons to the west and from several species of small cacti that appear almost everywhere except in the essentially pine-clad uplands serve in the preparation of fermented drinks, as do fruits of several species of Ericaceae (Pennington 1963:149–151). The antiquity of fermented drinks prepared from maguey or mescal roots is demonstrated by an account of San Pablo Balleza dated 1662 (Figueroa 1853–1857, 3:219).

• HUNTING AND FISHING Foods derived from hunting and fishing give variety to the basic Indian diet throughout the year, and such foods are exceedingly important, particularly when crops are poor or when corn that might have been saved for food or planting is utilized in making tiswin. Animals and birds that prey upon livestock or crops are hunted, and certain wild game serve as a source of skins and grease used in preparation of medicinal potions.

Wild turkeys, cranes, ducks, wild pigeons, quail, swallows, and magpie are mentioned by the Tarahumara as sources of food. Animals that serve as foodstuff include the cottontail, hare, three species of squirrels, three species of rodents (fig. 4), otter, badger, peccary, white-tailed deer, and mule deer. Among important predators are squirrels, gophers, pumas, jaguars, bobcats, coyotes, gray foxes, wolves, peccaries, and bears. Cottontail, hare, jaguar, otter, gray fox, coyote, bear, and deer provide skins utilized in the preparation of sleeping or sitting mats. Medicinal preparations are made from grease obtained from skunk, otter, ring-tailed cat, raccoon, coati, badger, opossum, coyote, and bear (Pennington 1963: 89–102).

Techniques used in bringing down fowl and game are ancient and new. Bow and arrow were rarely used in the 1970s, but their use certainly dates back to the seventeenth century (Neumann 1682), and probably earlier since remains of a reed paint container that historically has been associated with paint used for decorating arrows was found in a prehistoric Tarahumara site (Zingg 1940:16, 42, 58–59). Large and small bows are fashioned from wood obtained from at least nine species of trees (Pennington 1969:278–279). Tips of bows are notched, and bow strings are prepared from istle and deer sinew. Arrows are commonly made without heads or foreshafts; however, an Old World cane is sometimes used in making foreshafted arrows (Pennington 1969:281). Arrowheads are fashioned from wood, obsidian, and flint and hafted with gut, sinew, or istle fiber. Two or three halved feathers are anchored to the arrows with sinew. Arrow poison is apparently no longer used, but it was prepared from a plant during the eighteenth century (Neumann 1682). A wristguard is worn, and a quiver is fashioned from skin of the gray fox. Few Tarahumara possess rifles. Dogs are used in hunting.

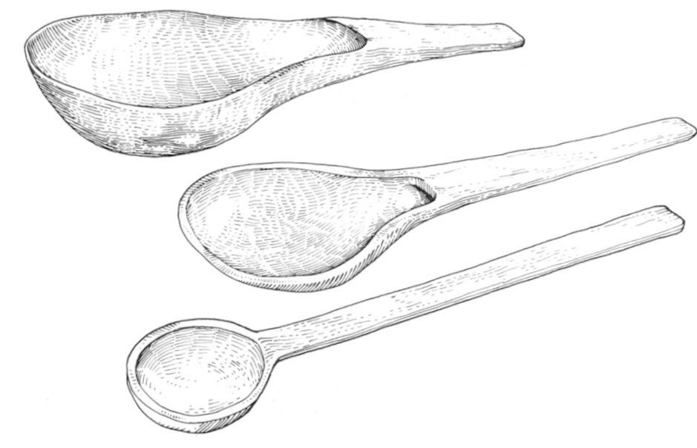

top right, Amer. Mus. of Nat. Hist., New York: top to bottom, 65/984, 65/854, 65/853; bottom left, U. of Ariz., Ariz. State Mus., Tucson: R3/5.

Fig. 3. Making tortillas. To remove the kernel covering, the maize is first boiled in water mixed with lime or oak ashes and then washed several times. The end product is called *napíware*, in Spanish *nixtamal*. top left, Washing boiled maize kernels in an open-weave basket using a gourd dipper. The washing removes the ash or lime. Photograph by Luis Verplancken, vicinity of Basíhuare, Chihuahua, about 1975. The *napíware* is then mashed or ground twice (bottom left) using stone mano and metate. The man is eating tortillas and beans from the bowl in front of his feet. Photograph by Franz J. Bogdany, Río Batopilas, Chihuahua, 1979. After being ground the dough is shaped and cooked on a flat metal griddle (bottom right). A pottery griddle is next to the wall. The women wear full skirts in several layers, loose blouses, handwoven belts, and scarfs. The women here prepare tortillas on the porch of a former mule station (for the mines in Batopilas) for the fiesta of Corpus Christi. Two clay pots full of maize beer stand against the wall in the corner. Photograph by William L. Merrill, Basíhuare, Chihuahua, June 1981. top right, Wooden spoons used in food preparation. Bennett and Zingg (1935:72) point out that these spoons are almost identical to Pima and Papago ones, suggesting extensive cultural exchange between the groups following the arrival of missionaries in the area. Length of top, 32.0 cm, rest to same scale, all collected by Carl Lumholtz in 1893.

Deer are driven over cliffs; and turkeys, rabbits, and deer are run down. Individual hunters stalk deer along well-known trails. Stake and snare traps are constructed for deer. The figure-four release trap is commonly used for capturing small animals and birds. Log traps are used in bringing down coyotes. A lance is used for killing peccaries cornered in caves or in brush. Meat is boiled or roasted.

Fish are sought everywhere in the Tarahumara country, and they are caught with hook and line, within funnel-shaped traps of vegetable materials, behind converging stone walls closed by weirs, and with seines. In addition, any one of at least 29 species of plants may be crushed and tossed into slowly moving or quiet water as a pisicide agent (see Pennington 1963:104–110 for an extended discussion of specific plants used in fish stupefaction).

• GATHERING Species of pine, juniper, oak, walnut, and *Carya* provide nuts for the Tarahumara. Important sources of fruits in season include species of *Ulmus,*

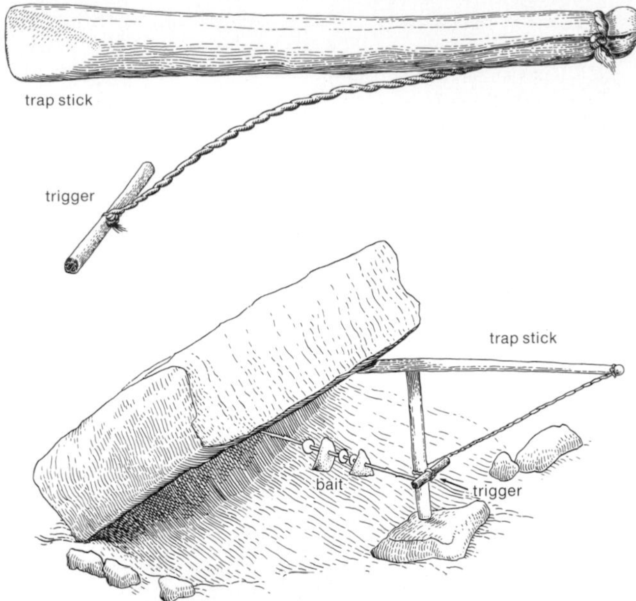

Amer. Mus. of Nat. Hist., New York: 65/1043.
Fig. 4. Trap used for catching mice and other small rodents. Made of wood, a twisted fiber cord, and a twig, the trap is set, using more sticks, in a figure-4 with a rock leaning against it as a deadfall. Bait is skewered through the trip stick (shown) or put on the ground under the rock. The rodents are roasted and eaten. Length 16.0 cm, collected by Carl Lumholtz at Guachochi, Chihuahua, in 1892.

Celtis, Ficus, Phoradendron, Rivina, Fragaria, Potentilla, Rubus, Prunus, Pithecellobium, Casimiroa, Citrus, Thryallis, Karwinskia, Vitis, Pachycereus, Lemaireocereus, Cephalocereus, Opuntia, Ferocactus, Mammillaria, Eugenia, Psidium, Arbutus, Achras, Ipomoea, Physalis, and *Randia*. Among significant sources of seeds are the common horsetail, catkins of willows, amaranth, legumes, and the kapok tree.

Edible greens are sought from various species of *Quercus, Salix, Celtis, Morus, Urtica, Chenopodium, Amaranthus, Arenaria, Lepidium, Oxalis, Tragia, Viola, Begonia, Oenothera, Arracacia, Eryngium, Fraxinus, Asclepias, Ipomoea, Lippia, Mentha, Solanum, Mimulus, Proboscidea, Plantago, Hieracium, Cosmos, Bidens, Sonchus*, and certain examples of plants that have been introduced from Europe, those belonging to the genera *Erodium, Portulaca*, and *Brassica*. Greens, which are commonly boiled, drained, and lightly salted, provide a welcome respite from the predominant corn diet.

Roots from palma (*Sabal uresana*), sotol (*Dasylirion durangense, D. wheeleri*), agave (*Agave patonii, A. schottii, A. chihuahuana, A. hartmani*), *Eriogonum atrorubens, Oxalis decaphylla*, kapok (*Ceiba acuminata*), *Prionosciadium serratum*, and jicama (*Exogonium bracteatum*) are prepared as food. Particularly important are the hearts of the agaves, which are pit baked. For a detailed résumé of specific species of plant life that serve as a source of collected foods among the Tarahumara see Pennington (1963:294–311).

Miscellaneous collected foods include the following: mushrooms, a grub from a cocoon found upon species of *Arbutus*, flies, cornworm, locusts, grasshoppers, honey from nests of escaped bees, frogs, tadpoles, lizards, and rattlesnake meat. The insects are commonly toasted upon coals, and the amphibian and reptile foods are spitted for roasting or are boiled.

• ANIMAL HUSBANDRY Cattle reached the Tarahumara in the late seventeenth century (Pennington 1963:138–139), and oxen became quickly established in the agricultural complex. Oxen are owned by a few Indians who share the beasts with others in return for labor, corn, beans, tiswin, or a sheep or goat. Cows are used for sacrificial purposes in religious or funeral ceremonies. There is little milking except for use in making cheese, an important trade item. Sheep and goats supply raw material used for the manufacture of blankets and sashes. Horses, which once were fairly common among the Tarahumara (Neumann 1682), are rarely maintained, and the important pack animal is the burro. Pigs are commonly kept and are prized as a source of food and fat used in cooking and preparation of medicinal potions. Dogs occupy a significant place in Tarahumara life, not only as pets but also as assistants in caring for flocks (fig. 5) and in hunting small game. Cats are maintained by some Tarahumara families.

Medicine

A great variety and number of plants from more than 50 plant families and many unidentified plants are sought for use in preparation of potions taken for fever, head-

Smithsonian, NAA: 55,132.
Fig. 5. A girl and dog herding goats near Quírare, Chihuahua. Goats are the most numerous domestic animals and are valued for their meat, skin, and manure (which is used to fertilize fields). Tanned goat skin is used for sitting mats, pack saddle blankets, and sleeping mats (Bennett and Zingg 1935:21–22, 79). Photograph by Anne T. Blaker, 1964.

ache, backache, lung congestion, infections caused by wounds or bruises, toothache, and "fright." For a detailed comment on specific species utilized in preparing medicines see Pennington (1963:177–194). Extensive utilization of the plant world in preparing medicinal potions is documented for the eighteenth century (Pennington 1963:194), but whether such references reflect earlier customs of the Indians or missionary influence is unknown.

Technology

• LEATHER GOODS Sandals (fig. 6), ropes, quirts, a carrying basket, rattling belts, slings, tumplines, saddle blankets, sleeping or sitting mats, and bags of different sizes and shapes are manufactured from processed skins of goat, oxen, cow, mule deer, and white-tailed deer. Prehistoric Tarahumara sites indicate that rabbit fur was once used in making blankets (Zingg 1940:20), and as recently as the eighteenth century deerskin was utilized in making clothing (Relación de Tutuaca 1777; Relación de Cusihuiriachic 1777; Relación de Guaguachic 1777). Leather sandals are doubtless a postcontact innovation since the earliest historical reference to hide sandals is that in an eighteenth-century account (Steffel 1809–1811, 1:341).

• FIBER GOODS Prehistoric Tarahumaras utilized fibers of the agave in the manufacture of aprons and blankets (Zingg 1940:31), and such use persisted until well into the eighteenth century (Steffel 1809–1811, 1:311–312, 344 and Relación de Cerocahui 1777). Istle was used in the 1970s in the manufacture of nets for carrying baskets, nets used in straining tiswin, and headbands, but its most important use was as a source of cordage for tying bundles of wood and other objects

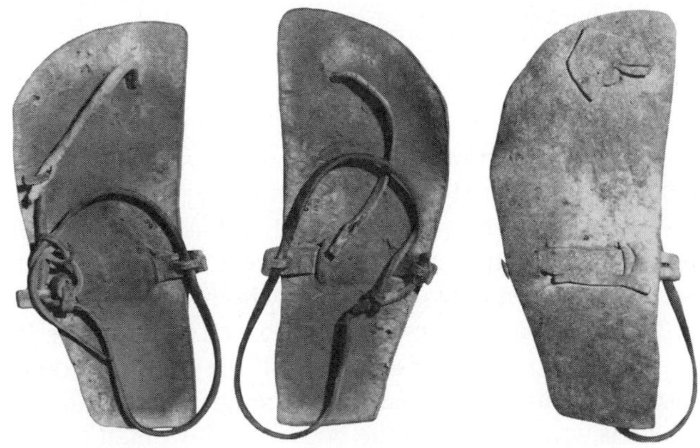

Amer. Mus. of Nat. Hist., New York: 65/1192.

Fig. 6. Leather sandals. The sole is cut slightly larger than the foot and leather ties are attached at 3 points. The toe strap on this pair is kept on by a widening of the thong at the end rather than a knot. The heel ties are attached to a cross-strap, which is put into slits in the sole. Sandals are worn by both men and women. Length 24.5 cm; collected by Carl Lumholtz in 1898.

bottom, U. of Ariz., Ariz. State Mus., Tucson: 77-33-348.

Fig. 7. Pottery. top, Potter, with sleeping child on her back, preparing to fire pottery. Pottery is sun-dried and then fired until the dried manure, cedar, juniper, pine, or oak stacked around articles burns down (Pennington 1963:217). The metal barrel on the fire contains a mixture of water and ground maize, which is cooked and later fermented into beer. Photograph by Cecilia Troop Merrill, at Rejogochi, Chihuahua, Feb. 1979. bottom, Pottery water jar with white sunlike designs painted on red ground. Eating bowls and various storage pots may also be decorated but tiswin pots usually are plain; pottery is not painted in all areas (Fontana 1979a). Height 29.0 cm, collected by Edmond Faubert in Tónachi, Chihuahua, 1977.

upon burros. Yucca (*Yucca decipiens, Dasylirion durangense, D. simplex, D. wheeleri*), nolina (*Nolina durangensis, N. matapensis*), and a palm (*Sabal uresana*) are used in the manufacture of simple twilled baskets (Pennington 1963:199–200). Such baskets are analogues of containers found in prehistoric Tarahumara sites (Zingg 1940:15–16, 25–26, 37). Coiled basketry practiced by prehistoric Tarahumara (ibid.:15–16) has not been documented for the historical period. Sleeping or sitting mats are fashioned from leaves of various species of *Liliaceae, Sabal uresana, Phragmites communis*, and young shoots of the Old World *Arundo donax* (Pennington 1963:200). Prehistoric Tarahumaras manufactured such articles from fibers of species of nolina, agave, and yucca (Zingg 1940:28–29). Single-

left, Amer. Mus. of Nat. Hist., New York: 43965; right, Smithsonian, NAA: 55,646.

Fig. 8. Men's clothing. left, Juan Ignacio and his son wearing breechclouts secured with native woven sashes and sandals made of leather. The son wears a multi-strand bead necklace, and the father wears a short native-woven wool shirt with small slits at side. Photograph by Carl Lumholtz, 1890–1898. right, Men (wearing 2-piece breechclouts) carrying sticks for a game called *hubáre*, which is often played while traveling. One player tosses a goal stick ahead and each competitor throws two or three playing sticks at it; the closest stick in each throw wins. The clothes of the man on the left show Western influence, including rubber-tire sandals, kerchief for headband, and several Euro-American shirts. The man on right wears more Tarahumara-style clothing including a long folded cloth headband and native-made shirt. Both carry slings of cloth, which often contain food for the trip. The man on left has a length of cloth called *činí* folded up in his sling; this is used for carrying things and as an outer wrap. Photograph by Raymond D. Parker, south of Creel, southwestern Chihuahua, 1964.

or double-twilled hats are fashioned from leaves of *Dasylirion wheeleri, Sabal uresana, Nolina matapensis*, and *N. durangensis*. Western canyon Indians utilize *Sabal uresana* and any available species of *Liliaceae* in preparing thatch. *Yucca decipiens* is used in the fashioning of crude sandals (Pennington 1963:201, 202).

• HOUSEHOLD ARTICLES Hard-shelled fruits of the bottle gourd serve in preparing small containers or dippers, as they did in prehistoric times (Zingg 1940:38). Crude ollas, griddles, and bowls are made by the women who use a coiling technique (fig. 7). The age of pottery among the Tarahumara is not known, but the presence of mano and metate in the Waterfall Cave site suggests that pottery was made in prehistoric times (Ascher and Clune 1960:272). Contemporary metates are fashioned without legs, from a hard flat rock that is chipped to form a depression for the grinding stone. An abrading stone, a pestlelike hammer or pounding stone, and stone knives play a minor role in modern Tarahumara culture. These artifacts are analogues of prehistoric stone objects (Zingg 1940:31, 62). An elongated wooden bowl is fashioned from large knots upon roots of species of *Arbutus*, the easily worked wood of the Mexican elm, lower portions of species of *Ficus*, knots upon the trunks of a species of *Platanus*, and the soft wood of species of *Populus*. Sleeping boards are made from easily worked pine (Pennington 1963:220). A small broom used for removing ground corn from the metate to the pinole container is made from tall spikes of a species of *Muhlenbergia*.

Clothing and Adornment

During warmer months most adult males wear sandals, headband or hair ribbon, sash, and a breechclout (figs. 8–9). Other males wear a shirt or blouse, and a small poncholike garment may be worn over this article. Hats are not commonly worn. Indians who live near Mestizo settlements have adopted the Mexican *calzones* or inexpensive cotton trousers and shirts. During colder months the male costume is supplemented by a blanket, which is wrapped about the body. Adult women usually wear a headband or hair ribbon, a loosely made shirt or blouse, a sash, and very wide skirts. Few women possess footgear. Women may wear an extra shirt, blouse, or skirt in cold weather or drape a small blanket over their shoulders. Clothing worn by children differs little from that typical of adults except that children rarely wear sandals. Cotton cloth utilized by the women in making garments is obtained from itinerant Mestizo traders or from stores at Mestizo settlements.

Blankets and sashes are woven by the women upon horizontal looms located in a sunny and protected area outside the Indian dwellings. Antiquity of a loom among the Tarahumara is demonstrated by beautifully made pita blankets found in prehistoric sites (Zingg 1940:56). Girdles and blankets are decorated with woolen threads dyed with dyestuff obtained from traders or prepared from plants available in the Indian country (Pennington 1963:209–212).

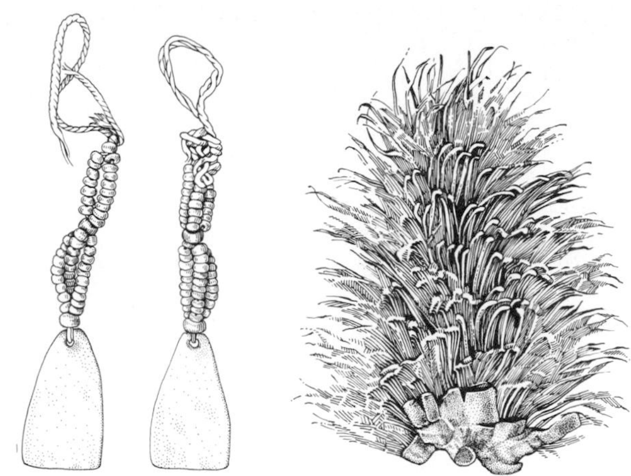

Amer. Mus. of Nat. Hist., New York: left, 65/1240; right 65/977.

Fig. 10. Personal adornment. left, Earrings made of strands of glass beads ending in a shell pendant. In the 1980s brightly colored plastic replaced shell, with strings of multi-colored seed beads replacing dark-colored glass beads, but the style is the same. right, Pine cone with outer covering removed, used as comb. Length of left 8.0 cm, of right, 15.0 cm; both collected by Carl Lumholtz, right in 1893, left in 1898.

As a substitute for commercial soap, the Tarahumara utilize saponaceous qualities of local plants. Crushed roots of species of yucca, agave, *Cucurbita, Sicyos*, or *Dyssodia* are soaked and smeared upon blankets or clothing, which are soaked for several hours (Pennington 1963:212). The Tarahumara once used a red soil as a detergent (Relación de Tónachic 1777).

The Tarahumara no longer tattoo, but during the seventeenth century men were distinguished by marks that had been burned into their faces (Ratkay 1683). In the eighteenth century thorns were used to prick dotted wavy lines upon foreheads and lips of small girls. A round "wheel" was pricked upon both cheeks, and charcoal dust was rubbed into the pricks to produce a permanent design (Steffel 1809–1811, 1:330–331).

Pine-cone combs are prepared from fruits of at least four species of pine. The bristly covering of fruit from one of the tall cacti common to western canyons serves as a hairbrush. Seeds of species of Job's tears, *Arbutus*, and *Erythrina flabelliformis* serve in fashioning necklaces. Wooden crosses worn by men or women are made from the easily worked wood of the hop tree (Pennington 1963:213–214).

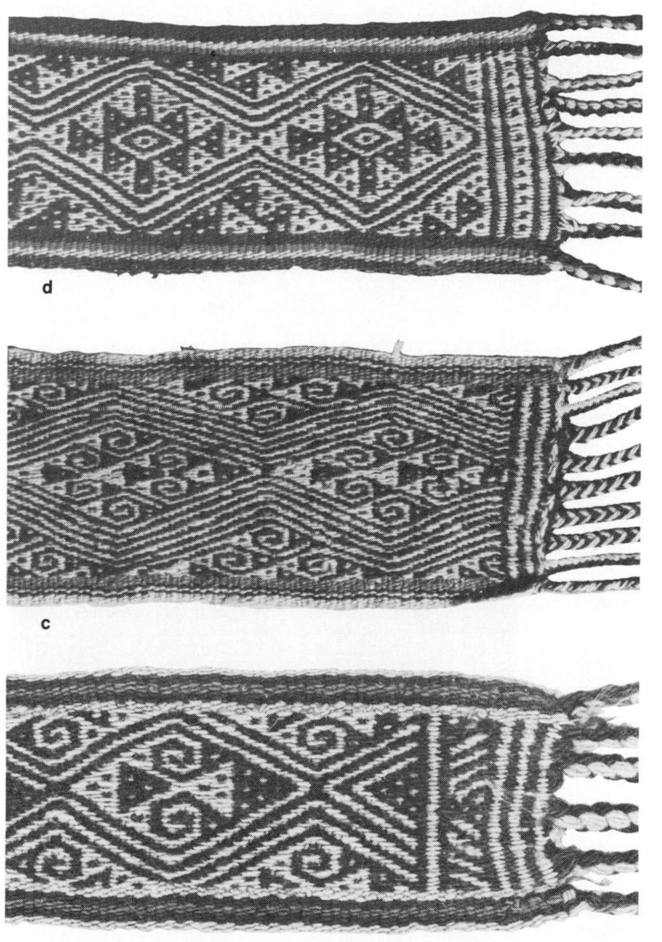

Milwaukee Public Mus, Wis.: a, 39538/10312; Amer. Mus. of Nat. Hist., New York: b, 65/1085; c, 65/1086; Smithsonian, Dept. of Anthr.: d, 126,666.

Fig. 9. Sashes. Woven on a narrower version of the horizontal blanket loom more skill is required to create the patterns in these warp-faced belts. The wool is more finely spun than in blankets, and pick-up sticks are used to make the pattern. These typical examples have stripes—including one or 2 of bright color—along the selvedges to frame the central design panel, which is worked in natural white and dark brown; the ends are braided. Sashes are worn around the waist by men and women. Several simpler style sashes are also woven (Fontana, Faubert, and Burns 1977:63). a, Total length 274.0 cm, collected by Wendell C. Bennett and Robert M. Zingg in 1931. b–d, detail only. b, c collected by Carl Lumholtz in 1892, 1893. d, collected by Edward Palmer in 1885.

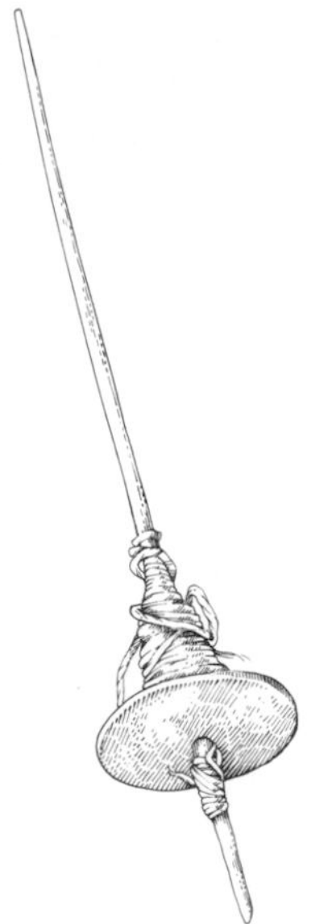

top left, Amer. Mus. of Nat. Hist., New York: 65/1229; Milwaukee Public Mus., Wis.: bottom center, 39326/10312, bottom right, 39280/10312; center, Field Mus., Chicago: 48508.

Fig. 11. Spinning and weaving. Wool is washed in a stream, dried, carded by hand, pulled into loose stands, and rolled into large balls for storage. top right, Photograph by John G. Kennedy at Inápuchi, 1960. When ready to spin it, a woman first twists the loose strands together The wool is then spun using (top left) a wooden spindle and whorl. Length 71.0 cm, collected by Carl Lumholtz in Guajochi, Chihuahua, in 1898. Yarn for the warp usually is spun tighter than that for the weft. Weaving is done on the horizontal loom (bottom left). Photograph by Jacob Fried, at Guachochi Pueblo, Chihuahua, 1951. Blankets have a predominantly brown or white background of natural-colored wool with decorative bands colored with either natural or commercial dyes. center, Brown background (slightly more than half shown); bottom, portions of 2 blankets. Men use the blankets in cold weather wrapped around the body, and both men and women use them for sleeping. center, Width about 125.5 cm, collected by Lumholtz in 1893; bottom collected by Wendell C. Bennett and Robert M. Zingg in 1930.

Structures

In prehistoric times the Tarahumara lived in caves, and some caves were so large that several families dwelled therein (Pérez de Ribas 1944a, 3:159). Caves are still occupied by the Tarahumara but are less elaborate than they once were (Zingg 1940:46–48). Rectangular stone houses with wooden plank doors enclosed by a wooden jamb are constructed in the open by communal activity. Roofs for such structures consist of pine troughs, sometimes covered with stone and earth. A portion of the hardpacked floor serves as a hearth. Chimneys are rare. A more common house type consists of a rectangular-shaped log frame roofed with troughs and enclosed by boards leaned upright against the frame, there being no door. Entry or egress is made by removing a few boards. A small gable-on-the-ground structure, with stones piled to form triangular end walls connected by a ridge pole, against which boards or saplings are leaned, is typical of eastern Tarahumara country. Crudely built notched log cabins roofed with pine troughs are found near Mestizo settlements. The Tarahumara no longer construct small conical brush huts as they did in the seventeenth century (Ratkay 1683).

Games and Music

The reticence of the Tarahumara is broken only during games (fig. 12) and festivals, which are marked by music and much drinking of tiswin. Two classes of games are played, those of chance and dexterity. In the former, articles similar to dice are thrown or struck at random, and sticks or pebbles are used to enumerate the sum of the counts. This game is on the order of the Spanish board game *quince*. Games of dexterity include the kickball game, a crude lacrosse or shinny, archery, throwing of sticks, and quoits, all of which are played exclusively by males, and two games played by women—a hoop race and a game in which team members strive to reach a goal with two chunks of wood that are tied together by a leather thong or fiber cord. Anciently, the Tarahumara played a rubber ball game similar to that played by peoples of the south. For a description of games played within historical times see Pennington (1963, 1970). An important prelude to almost all games played at festivals is betting, and most Indian possessions are subject to wager.

Musical instruments include a leather-covered drum, a reed flute, an instrument that vaguely resembles a

Amer. Mus. of Nat. Hist., New York: bottom left, 65/1034; top right, 65/1005; bottom right, Smithsonian, Dept. of Anthr.: 422,482.

Fig. 12. Games. top left, Girls in a race, using a curved stick to toss hoops. The woman and 2 boys are encouraging them. Photograph by William L. Merrill, Rejogochi, Chihuahua, Aug. 1981. bottom left, Pole and hoops made of fiber with yarn twisted around them. Diameter of hoop 13.5 cm, collected by Carl Lumholtz in 1892. Men race with a wooden ball that they kick ahead of them with their feet. During long races men or women may wear rattling belts tied around their waists and hanging at the rear to keep themselves awake and in a pleasant frame of mind. Betting accompanies all races and includes wagers of cloth, knives, clothes, yarn, sheep, goats, or cattle (Pennington 1963:169). top right, Leather belt with deer dewclaws and cane strung on thong and tied on; bottom right, similar belt with small tins and cartridge cases added in place of lost dewclaws. top right, Length 92.0 cm, collected by Carl Lumholtz in 1892; bottom right, same scale, collected by William L. Merrill in 1981 in Rejogochi, Chihuahua.

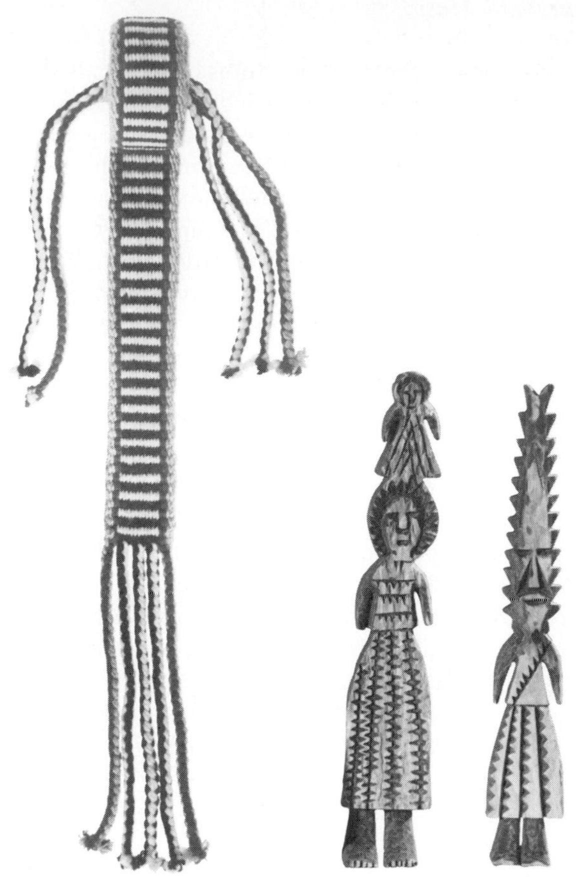

Smithsonian, Dept. of Anthr.: left, 422,519; U. of Ariz., Ariz. State Mus., Tucson: center, 78-37-13, right, 78-37-15.

Fig. 13. Tourist crafts. left, Belt woven with commercial yarn for sale in tourist shops. Contemporary Tarahumaras also make such belts for their own use. center and right, Ponderosa pine bark carvings, made only since the 1960s; they are changing from simple flat forms to fully sculpted and clothed figures (Fontana 1979b:25). Cloth dolls, wooden toys, baskets, and painted pottery also are made for sale. left, Width 6.0 cm, total length (not shown) 192.0 cm, collected by William L. Merrill in Chihuahua, Chihuahua, 1981. center and right, to same scale, both collected by Barney T. Burns in Creel, Chihuahua, 1978.

musical bow, handled rattles fashioned from thin pieces of easily worked wood or dried bottle gourds, a rattling belt prepared from a cocoon, and crude violins; all these noise-making instruments are manufactured by the Indians. Relative antiquity of at least two of these articles, the musical bow and gourd rattle, is demonstrated by material from archeological sites (Zingg 1940:63–64).

Synonymy†

The name Tarahumara was from the beginning the only one used for the Tarahumara Mission and the converted Indians living on the territory assigned to it (Pennington 1963:2). The earliest use was by the Jesuit Juan Fonte, who applied it to a group of slightly over 3,000 Indians encountered between 1607 and 1611 in the extreme southern portion of the later mission territory; as the missionaries extended the mission territory north and west in the course of the seventeenth century the name Tarahumara was spread with it to eventually cover all Indians of the western Sierra Madre between 28° and 33° north latitude (Pérez de Ribas 1944a, 3:159–161; Deimel 1980:31, 1980a:43–44). It is not known if Tarahumara was a self-designation used by the group first encountered or a name used in a language spoken farther to the south.

The Tarahumaras call themselves *rarámuri*, a name first attested in 1826 in Miguel Tellechea's Tarahumara grammar (Deimel 1980:31, 1980a:43). This name has no agreed-upon etymology, and Tarahumaras consider it merely a name (Deimel 1980:36, 1980a:52; William L. Merrill, communication to editors 1981). Derivations from *rará* 'foot' or *raramúri* 'struck by lightning' have not been shown to be consistent with established patterns of Tarahumara word-formation. A survey of suggested explanations is in Deimel (1980:31–36, 1980a:43–53).

†This synonymy was written by Ives Goddard.

Sources

The first major ethnography of the Tarahumara was that of Lumholtz (1902) who traveled extensively in western Chihuahua during the 1890s. The earlier account by the newspaperman Schwatka (1893) has been largely ignored by students of the Tarahumara. Basauri (1929) visited the Tarahumara in 1925–1926. His brief but important monograph and the very detailed study of Bennett and Zingg (1935), who lived among the Tarahumara during 1930 and 1931, demonstrate little Tarahumara acculturation during the period 1890–1930. Valuable ethnographic data are available in the neglected account by Gómez González (1948), who traveled among the Tarahumara in 1941. Plancarte's (1954) résumé of Tarahumara culture is significant because it is based upon more than six years of residence in southern Chihuahua. Pennington completed fieldwork among the Tarahumara during the mid-1950s; his (1963) study further demonstrates persistence of the Tarahumara way of life and includes numerous comments pertaining to Tarahumara material culture found in archival materials in the United States and Mexico. Fried (1969) presented a fine summary of Tarahumara culture, deriving much of his data from fieldwork done in 1950–1951. Kennedy (1970a, 1978) provides the only detailed description of a gentile Tarahumara community, based on his investigation of 1959–1960. Bye traveled widely in Tarahumara country between 1971 and 1975, gathering data for his extensive study of Tarahumara ethnobotany (1976). Merrill's (1981) report, based on data collected between 1977 and 1979, is the only in-depth study of Tarahumara world view. Kennedy and López (1981) compare Holy Week ceremonies in three Tarahumara pueblos, documenting substantial regional variation. Fontana's (1979) and Deimel's (1980, 1980a) overviews of Tarahumara history and culture are intended for a general audience.

Short papers published after 1940 focus upon various aspects of Tarahumara life. Zingg (1942) discussed values in Tarahumara culture. Passin (1943) reported on kinship and social organization, while Fried (1953, 1969) gave attention to social control and interpersonal relations. The important role of tiswin in Tarahumara culture was considered by Kennedy (1963) and Merrill (1978). Theoretical implications of Tarahumara joking relationships were discussed by Kennedy (1966, 1970a). Bye (1979a, 1981) documented the importance of several different kinds of greens in Tarahumara diet, examining in detail the ecological relationships between these plants and the Tarahumaras. Snyder et al. (1969) presented a study of dentition among Tarahumaras and Mestizos in western Chihuahua. Fontana, Faubert, and Burns (1977) provided an overview of the material culture of the Tarahumara and other northern Mexican Indian groups. Pennington (1969, 1970) compared in detail Tarahumara and Tepehuan material culture and discussed the origin of the kickball race played by Tarahumara males. Kennedy (1969) examined the significance of this game in twentieth-century Tarahumara culture, and Balke and Snow (1965) studied the physiological characteristics of the runners. López Batista et al. (1981) describe in Tarahumara and Spanish the various sports and games the Tarahumara play.

The most valuable printed sources dealing in a general way with Jesuit activities among the Tarahumara are those of Pérez de Ribas (1944a), Neumann (1725, 1969), Tamerón y Romeral (1937), Alegre (1956–1960), Decorme (1941), Dunne (1944, 1948), and Ocampo (1950, 1966). For the Franciscan period there are general accounts by Arlegui (1851) and Alcocer (1958). Data pertaining to material culture are found in eighteenth-century Franciscan *relaciones*, particularly those of Baqueachic, Batopilillas, Cerocahui, Chínipas, Cusihuiriachic, Guaguachic, Guazápares, Nabogame, San Miguel de Las Bocas, Tomóchic, Tónachic, and Tutuaca, all from 1777, and the Relación de Santa Eulalia de Chihuahua, from 1778. Some of these *relaciones* have been published (Paso y Troncoso 1950), but errors in copying the originals and editorial omissions lessen their value. A descriptive account of missions also reveals material culture details (Anonymous 1853–1857, 4:92–131). Civil, military, and ecclesiastical documents referring to the Tarahumara during the colonial period are found in Hackett (1923–1937, 2), Sheridan and Naylor (1979), and in Documentos para la Historia de Méjico (1853–1857).

Much unused archival material pertaining to the Tarahumara is available in the United States, Mexico, and Europe, not only for a more complete study of Tarahumara culture at contact but also for an examination of the relations between the Tarahumaras and missionaries, cattlemen, miners, and farmers during the colonial and modern periods. Important materials are found in the Bancroft Library, University of California at Berkeley (especially the Bolton Transcripts); the Latin American Collection, particularly the Stephens Collection, University of Texas, Austin; the Archivo del Parral, Hidalgo del Parral, Chihuahua; the Archivo General de la Nación, Mexico City; and the Archivum Romanum Societatis Iesu, Rome.

Significant material pertaining to the Tarahumara language is found in Steffel (1809–1811), Thord-Gray (1955), Hilton (1959), and especially Brambila (1980). Data for Tarahumara grammar range in importance from the preliminary study by Tellechea (1826) to the scholarly grammars by Brambila (1953) and Lionnet (1972). Burgess (1970) provides detailed information on the phonology of the western dialect of Tarahumara.

Scant archeological data are available for western Chihuahua. Zingg (1940) presented tentative conclusions concerning pre-Columbian culture history of the Tarahumara, basing his statements upon work done by Bennett and Zingg near Norogachi and Batopilas in 1930–1931. Material from the Waterfall Cave site in southern Chihuahua is discussed in Ascher and Clune (1960), Clune (1960), and Cutler (1960).

Tarahumara Social Organization, Political Organization, and Religion

WILLIAM L. MERRILL

The Tarahumara reside in dispersed settlements scattered across a mountainous terrain approximately 35,000 square kilometers in area. There is considerable regional variation among the Tarahumara in language, world view, ritual, settlement patterns, subsistence strategies, dress, and many other domains of their culture. Some of these variations represent different adaptive responses to divergent environmental zones, which in the Tarahumara homeland range from upland pine-oak forests to subtropical canyon bottoms. Others reflect the differential impact that non-Tarahumaras—principally Whites and Mestizos but other Native American groups as well—have had on the Tarahumara of different regions. The distances between settlements and physical barriers to travel such as deep canyons and seasonally impassable streams have hampered interaction among the members of widely separated communities, contributing to the emergence and persistence of these variations.

Despite these variations, there appear to be many things that most if not all Tarahumaras share, but ethnographic coverage of the Tarahumaras is uneven. Since the majority of anthropological treatments deal with the Tarahumaras of the central, upland region, and the writer's experience with the Tarahumaras has been confined largely to the pueblo of Basíhuare, also located in the upland area, the generalizations given here may not apply to the Tarahumaras as a whole. Although most of the references cited date from well before 1981, all the information presented here was current in 1981, unless otherwise noted.

Social Organization

The Household

The Tarahumara reckon descent bilaterally, considering a person to be equally related to the kin of both parents. Because they address and refer to all their cousins with the same terms that they employ for their siblings, their kinship terminology is classified as Neo-Hawaiian (Murdock 1949; Bennett and Zingg 1935:220–223; Passin 1943; Kennedy 1970:176–187).

The basic unit of Tarahumara social organization is the nuclear family, composed of a husband and wife and their unmarried children. As a rule Tarahumara men marry for the first time in their late teens or early twenties, and women, slightly younger (for discussions of Tarahumara marriage practices, see Bennett and Zingg 1935:224–232 and Passin 1943:482–488). Sometimes a couple will decide on their own to live together as husband and wife; more frequently, parents or Tarahumara officials known as *mayóli** (from the Spanish *mayor* 'major') act as intermediaries or instigators in arranging marriages. The principal duties of the *mayóli* are finding spouses for unmarried people, performing the Tarahumaras' brief marriage ritual, and attempting to resolve marital difficulties. The Roman Catholic Church, which began proselytizing among the Tarahumaras in the early 1600s, does not recognize the marriages performed by the *mayóli*, but only in those areas most heavily influenced by Catholic missionaries do Tarahumaras seek out priests to marry them.

In arranged marriages, the prospective husbands and wives usually know each other, although occasionally they are total strangers. People are not forced to marry against their will, but there is considerable social pressure for every adult to have a spouse. The Tarahumaras view single adults as potential threats to the marriages of others and consider marriage the proper context for procreation as well as the most logical arrangement for living, since the skills that men and women learn as children are complementary (Merrill 1981:55–57).

Most Tarahumara marriages are monogamous, but polygyny and, according to Fried (1969:859), polyandry do occur. The quality the Tarahumaras most desire when looking for a spouse is industriousness, although physical attractiveness and wealth also can be considerations. The relative ages of potential spouses seldom is of significance; most couples are of about the same age, but cases in which one spouse, husband or wife, is 10 or more years older than the other are not uncommon.

Some Tarahumaras marry but once during their lives while many others have a succession of spouses, because

*The Tarahumara words in this chapter were recorded by William L. Merrill. They are transcribed in the orthography described in "Tarahumara," this vol.

former mates die or the unions are incompatible. Couples dissolve their marriages simply by no longer living together, but divorce is not rampant among the Tarahumaras. Most unstable are the unions of young people. Since the Tarahumaras discourage interaction between unrelated men and women, many first marriages represent little more than opportunities to become better acquainted with someone of the opposite sex who is not a relative. Once children are born, the majority of couples remain together until one dies.

The members of Tarahumara nuclear families usually live together year-round, often joining other kin for all or part of the year to form extended family households. A couple's economic circumstances as well as the tenor of their relations with their immediate kin usually determine whether they live alone or with other members of their families. Many young couples reside with the parents of one or both spouses until they have the resources to set themselves up as independent households, and elderly people frequently move in with their children or other relatives when they can no longer support themselves. Even when it is economically feasible for the members of a nuclear family to establish a separate household, they sometimes will live with the relatives of one spouse because they enjoy their company (Kennedy 1978:176–179).

The members of most Tarahumara households share their food and eat together, although in many extended family households each nuclear family stores its maize supplies separately. They also cooperate in farming and performing domestic chores and generally enjoy free access to one another's possessions, except clothing. However, as Bennett and Zingg (1935:188) emphasize, a distinction must be made in the Tarahumara case between joint use and joint ownership. Almost every item of property in the household, regardless if used communally or individually, is owned by a specific member of the household, including the house in which they reside and the fields they plant. The property a person leaves behind at death passes not to the household as a group but to individual heirs, usually to the deceased's children rather than spouse, with sons and daughters ideally sharing equally in the inheritance (Bennett and Zingg 1935:189–192).

The majority of Tarahumaras live in small hamlets, known in Spanish as *ranchos*, composed of from one to 20 or so homesteads scattered along the drainages of the streams that dissect their mountainous homeland. They usually build their houses on or adjacent to their fields, often preferring an elevated spot from which they can watch their crops and the activities of their neighbors.

Many Tarahumara households shift residence during the year to farm the often widely scattered plots of land that their members own, to establish themselves in more comfortable habitations during the colder months of the year, or both. That the members of a single household should own fields in several dispersed locations derives from the operation of certain principles of Tarahumara inheritance and mate selection. The Tarahumara prefer to marry people to whom they are completely unrelated, although marriages between distant relatives are accepted and occur with some frequency. Since people who reside near one another tend to be close relatives, prospective spouses typically live and inherit land in different places. Some households own sufficient land in one locality to meet their needs, often because one spouse purchases or trades for land adjacent to that inherited by the other. In such cases, they usually remain there throughout the growing season, leaving their plots in other places fallow or lending them to other people to plant. However, many households must cultivate most or all of their members' fields to sustain themselves and must shift their residence to do so. When such households are extended families, the members sometimes split up for short periods, usually along nuclear family lines, to farm different plots (Passin 1943:367; Kennedy 1978:80–81).

Movement to special winter residences takes place primarily among those Tarahumaras who live adjacent to the deep canyons of southwestern Tarahumara country. Here many families descend from the uplands to winter with their flocks of sheep and goats in the warmer canyons (Plancarte 1954:19–20; Kennedy 1978:65–67). The direction of this winter movement is reversed in the transitional zone between the uplands and the canyons where the most suitable winter quarters—usually rockshelters—are found on the mountainsides above the valley floors. Not all households in this area shift to these winter residences, but those who do say they prefer them to their valley homes because they are better shielded from the wind, closer to firewood sources, and exposed earlier to the warming rays of the morning sun (Fried 1969:853; Merrill 1981:52–53).

Another form of seasonal mobility is practiced by the residents of the more eastern and southern Tarahumara communities. Primarily after the maize harvest, but at other times of the year as well, some members of these communities travel to predominantly White and Mestizo centers in the states of Chihuahua, Durango, and Sinaloa, usually returning to their homes before planting time in the spring. While there they sell or trade items such as medicinal plants, textiles, and baskets, purchase goods not available in their home communities, work as laborers, and quite frequently ask the residents of these places to share their food, money, and clothing with them (Plancarte 1954:20; Françoise Brouzés, personal communication 1981). As of 1981, no study had been undertaken of this seasonal migration, but the number of Tarahumaras involved apparently varies from year to year, depending in part upon the success of the maize harvest.

top, Amer. Mus. of Nat. Hist., New York: 44388; bottom left, U. of Ariz., Ariz. State Mus., Tucson: R1/24A.

Fig. 1. Tarahumara dwellings of various types. top, Thatch-roofed A-frame structure in the uplands, described as a "winter house." To the right are 2 stone and mud storehouses, which held corn, beans, clothing, and other valuables. In the 1980s, thatch roofs were restricted to the canyon country. Photograph by Carl Lumholtz, 1890–1898. center left, Rockshelter at Wisarórare, near Panalachi, being used during the early summer. Rockshelters are typically used as temporary dwellings in the winter. Photograph by Luis Verplancken, 1960. center right, Wood plank house at Sitéachi, near Cusárare, Chihuahua. Photograph by Luis Verplancken, 1971. bottom left, Rectangular stone structure, possibly a house, with earth roof held in place by large stones and one plank. Photograph by Franz J. Bogdany, Río Batopilas, Chihuahua, 1979. bottom right, Extended family compound consisting of 2 separate log houses, an area enclosed by a stone wall between them for cooking, eating, and sleeping in good weather, and one storehouse (obscured from view) against which hand-hewn planks are leaning to form a space protected from the elements for working and storage. The log house with a roof of overlapping hand-hewn, grooved planks, or troughs, was the most common Tarahumara house type in the 1980s. Photograph by William L. Merrill, Rejogochi, Chihuahua, June 1981.

Interhousehold Relations

Tarahumara individuals spend much of their time alone or with their families, performing household tasks or relaxing. In those areas where the distances separating households are not too great, neighbors also frequently visit in one another's homes, usually in the early morning or late afternoon, or join to herd their flocks of sheep and goats, to compete at games, or to collect wild foods. However, the principal contexts within which the adult members of different households interact are drinking parties, in which both men and women participate with equal enthusiasm (for descriptions of these parties see Kennedy 1978:97–110 and Merrill 1981:64–78).

Each drinking get-together is sponsored by one or occasionally a few households, who supply their guests with home-brewed alcoholic beverages, usually tiswin, a maize beer known in Tarahumara as *batári* or *sugí* and in Spanish as *tesgüino* (fig. 2) (Pennington 1963:149–157). The quantity of alcohol a household prepares for a party can vary from as little as 10 gallons to 100 gallons or more, depending upon the amount of maize they feel they can expend for the purpose and their motivation for holding the party. Ideally they ferment enough for everyone they invite to become intoxicated.

Some households lack the resources to sponsor even one drinking party a year, but many others hold several to which they invite their poorer neighbors. Tarahumara households organize drinking parties for various reasons, but rarely is the desire to drink with their fellows the sole motivation. The expressed purpose usually is to obtain the assistance of others in completing some project such as planting maize or staging a ritual, with the alcoholic drinks prepared for the occasion serving to compensate the guests for their help (Plancarte 1954:52–53; Kennedy 1963).

These parties occur regularly throughout the year and are the foci around which Tarahumara social life above the household level revolves. They represent the Tarahumaras' principal form of recreation as well as constituting one of the major contexts within which community affairs are discussed, marriages arranged, and interpersonal conflicts expressed. Individuals typically begin attending drinking parties as full participants soon after they reach puberty, signaling thereby that they have reached adulthood and a marriageable age; the Tarahumaras perform no rituals to commemorate this transition. The importance of these parties to the Tarahumaras is reflected in Kennedy's (1963:635) estimate that the average individual participates in between 40 and 60 drinking parties annually, spending at least 100 days a year preparing alcoholic beverages, attending drinking parties, and recovering afterward.

Attendance at drinking parties usually is by invitation only. Most households include among their guests the members of adjacent households as well as friends and kinsmen from other *ranchos*. However, neighboring households rarely invite exactly the same groups of individuals to drink with them. Rather, their guest lists tend to overlap, engendering what Kennedy (1963:625–626) has labeled "the tesguino network." This network consists of the connections among households that derive from the participation of their members in one another's drinking parties. A household is linked not only to the various households with which it exchanges drinking invitations but also indirectly to those to which these households extend invitations but it does not. The result, as Kennedy (1963:625) writes, is "a general net-like system of household-centered, overlapping interaction systems, stretching across the region."

Political Organization

At the time of European contact, the basic units of Tarahumara political organization appear to have been *ranchos*, each composed of several contiguous households, the affairs of which were directed to a limited degree by a headman and a body of elders. The members of different *ranchos* sometimes congregated for judicial, governmental, and ceremonial purposes and joined forces in times of conflict under the direction of war captains (Fried 1977; Bennett and Zingg 1935:372). Although vestiges of this political system can be found among twentieth-century Tarahumaras, it was largely supplanted by the more complex and centralized pueblo organization imposed in the colonial period by Spanish officials and Catholic missionaries (Bancroft 1886–1889, 1:346, 689; Spicer 1962:371–395).

A Tarahumara pueblo is not a compact settlement but a group of *ranchos* whose residents congregate at the same church, the site of which serves as the administrative and religious center of the pueblo. All Tarahumara pueblos include among their residents at least some individuals of European or mixed European-Indian heritage, who as a group are known in local Spanish as *blancos* 'Whites', *mestizos* 'Mestizos', *gente de razon* 'people of reason', or *chabochis*, the last from Tarahumara *čabóči* 'non-Indian' (designated *chabochis* in this chapter). However, only Tarahumaras participate in the pueblo political organizations.

The pueblo political officials (fig. 3), whose numbers and titles vary from pueblo to pueblo, invariably are males chosen and approved by the other male members of the pueblo. If they fail to perform their duties to their constituents' satisfaction, they can be removed from office. The responsibilities of these officials are outlined in "Tarahumara," this volume, and discussed in detail by Bennett and Zingg (1935:201–209) and Plancarte (1954:37–41).

Some Tarahumaras are only marginally involved in

top left, Amer. Mus. of Nat. Hist., New York: 65/865; U. of Ariz., Ariz. State Mus., Tucson: bottom left, R 2/36; bottom right, 77-33-276.

Fig. 2. Maize beer preparation, which requires about 7 days. The maize kernels must first be soaked in water and sprouted, then ground (top center), mixed with water, and simmered for 12–15 hours (top right). The resulting tannish liquid is cooled and poured through a basket strainer (center left). Then it is poured into a small-mouthed jar (center), often together with one or more plants designed to render the brew strong. Fermentation usually takes 18–24 hours (see Pennington 1963:149–153 for details). center right, Tarahumara doctor passing flaming pine splints around the jars of maize beer to eradicate any evil or otherwise dangerous substance possibly associated with the beer. Photographs by William L. Merrill: center right, Upache, near Rejogochi, Chihuahua, Jan. 1979, others, Rejogochi, June 1981. bottom left, A drinking party at a dwelling near the Río Batopilas, Chihuahua. Photograph by Franz J. Bogdany, 1979. top left, Twilled basketry strainer, height including handle, 23.0 cm; collected by Carl Lumholtz near Panalachi, Chihuahua, 1894. bottom right, Plainware ceramic jar used for fermentation; height 70.0 cm; collected by Edmond Faubert in Choguita, Chihuahua, 1977.

the political organization and activities of the pueblos with which they are affiliated. This is particularly true of the members of the few Tarahumara communities who traditionally have refused the Catholic sacrament of baptism and consequently are known in Spanish as *gentiles* 'heathens' (Tarahumara *hentile*) or *cimarrones* 'wild people' (Tarahumara *simaróne*) (Kennedy 1970, 1978). These *gentiles* tend to have their own sets of officials, fewer in number and less formal than those of the pueblo political organizations, who perform their duties primarily in the context of drinking parties rather than in the pueblo centers (Kennedy 1963:621, 626–627, 1978:181–209).

Although individuals from different pueblos interact with some frequency and marriages across pueblo boundaries are common, there has never existed among the Tarahumaras an effective interpueblo political organization. During the first half of the twentieth century, a few Tarahumara leaders in different parts of the Sierra Tarahumara extended their influence over several adjacent pueblos but never over the region as a whole (Passin 1943:366; Aguirre Beltrán 1953:85; León Pacheco 1974:8–9). In 1981, the closest approximation to an interpueblo organization was the Consejo Supremo Tarahumara, established in 1939 primarily through the efforts of several Tarahumara school teachers supported by government representatives. These individuals envisioned the principal role of the Consejo to be one of working to improve the lot of the Tarahumaras and to hasten their integration into the national economy and culture, goals that largely coincided with those of the Mexican government (Aguirre Beltrán 1953:86–93). Through its lobbying efforts, the Consejo has attempted to resolve a variety of problems confronting the Tarahumaras and other residents of the region, concentrating particularly in the areas of education, land tenure, and the exploitation of local forest resources (León Pacheco 1974). However, it has never wielded any real political power and as late as 1981 many Tarahumaras were unaware of its existence.

Fig. 3. Tarahumara officials of Samachique Pueblo resolving a disagreement among the people seated on the ground before them. One official, presumably the *siríame* 'governor', holds a special staff, symbolic of his office. Community officials are asked to adjudicate a variety of cases, ranging from disputes over inheritances to charges of theft and assault. Photograph by Jacob Fried, 1951.

The influence of non-Indians, or *chabochis*, in the political affairs of the Tarahumara area, although present to some degree since the seventeenth century, increased dramatically in the twentieth. Between 1920 and 1960 the *chabochi* population in the area almost doubled, from 100,000 to 190,000, about four times that of the Tarahumaras. The cessation of major mining activity in the Sierra Tarahumara during the early twentieth century forced many *chabochis* to adopt agriculture as their means for survival. This circumstance, combined with the construction of a railway and a network of roads through the region and the emergence of new economic opportunities associated primarily with lumber, led to an expansion of *chabochis* into many localities formerly occupied only by Tarahumaras. In some areas, the Tarahumaras accepted their arrival with equanimity, but in others, particularly where *chabochis* displaced Tarahumaras from the better agricultural lands, the two groups came in conflict, a situation that in many cases had not been resolved by 1981 (Plancarte 1954; Bennett and Zingg 1935:181; Champion 1955).

Although some Tarahumaras and *chabochis* reside quite near one another, they usually live in separate settlements, and relations between the two groups tend to be superficial. Each maintains a negative stereotype of the other: the *chabochis* view the Tarahumaras as uncivilized, superstitious, dirty, of inferior intelligence, and childlike, while the Tarahumaras consider the *chabochis* to be immoral, unscrupulous, shameless, and offensively forward in their interactions with others. Tarahumaras sometimes ask *chabochis* to serve as godparents for their children in church baptisms, but *chabochis* seldom request the same of Tarahumaras, and rarely if ever do the elaborate relations of compadrazgo found among *chabochis* emerge between *chabochis* and Tarahumaras. As a rule, few close friendships develop between Tarahumaras and *chabochis*, and intermarriage is discouraged by both groups (Bennett and Zingg 1935:181–182; Passin 1943:367, 483).

Most contacts between Tarahumaras and *chabochis* are economic. Tarahumara girls and women sometimes serve as maids in *chabochis* households, particularly in the larger towns in and near the Sierra. Tarahumara men work for *chabochis* as laborers in farming, lumbering, and road construction, and both men and women purchase goods in *chabochi*-owned stores. The *chabochis*, in addition to hiring Tarahumaras and selling things to them, buy farm animals, crops, and items the Tarahumaras manufacture such as baskets, blankets, and pottery, either for their own use or to resell for a profit.

Tarahumaras and *chabochis*, primarily men, also interact in two distinct political organizations, the first of which is the ejido organization. Ejidos are communal economic units that hold ultimate title to all land that falls within their boundaries and usually operate commercial ventures like sawmills, the profits of which are distributed among their members. The first ejidos in the Sierra Tarahumara were established in the 1920s and 1930s as part of the national program of agrarian reform; by 1981 the vast majority of Tarahumaras and a sizable proportion of their non-Indian neighbors were members of ejidos (Anonymous 1950:166–167). Tarahumaras outnumber *chabochis* in many ejidos, but because ejido business requires literacy and some familiarity with the workings of the state and national economy, *chabochis* often control the official positions and affairs (Plancarte 1954:63).

The Tarahumaras and local *chabochis* also fall under the jurisdiction of the state of Chihuahua and ultimately the federal government of Mexico. Chihuahua is divided into a number of *municipios*, comparable to counties in the United States. These *municipios* in turn are divided into 'sections' (*secciones*), each of which encompasses several police districts (*comisarías*) (Plancarte 1954:37).

Tarahumara participation in this political organization is quite limited, restricted primarily to reporting births, deaths, and the sale of cattle to the section president and paying a minimal tax each year. Disputes between Tarahumaras and *chabochis* also are handled by officials of this political organization, and Tarahumaras who commit serious crimes like murder or grand larceny usually are turned over by the Tarahumara pueblo officials to the *municipio* officials to be jailed. Tarahumaras sometimes serve as commissioners of police districts and section presidents but higher-level positions almost invariably are filled by *chabochis* (Kennedy 1978:30–31; Plancarte 1954:89).

World View and Religion

Twentieth-century Tarahumara world view and religion blend indigenous beliefs and practices with ones introduced since the seventeenth century by representatives of European and European-derived cultures. Catholic missionaries in particular have had a substantial impact on these domains of Tarahumara culture. Members of the Jesuit order were active among the Tarahumaras from the early seventeenth century until their expulsion from the New World in 1767. Franciscans continued the Jesuits' work through the first few decades of the nineteenth century, but political upheavals and financial problems led to the decline and eventual abandonment of the Tarahumara mission system until the Jesuits reestablished it in 1900. Presumably beginning with their first exposure to them, the Tarahumaras have interpreted Catholic rituals and theological notions in terms of ideas they inherited from the precontact era. However, the Church's general neglect of the Tarahumaras for most of the nineteenth century allowed them particular freedom to do so. The resulting synthesis has in turn undergone modification as the Tarahumaras have accommodated their thinking and behavior to the changes that have occurred in their world, a dynamic process that still continues (Dunne 1948; Almada 1955; Spicer 1962; Ocampo 1966; Sheridan and Naylor 1979).

Cosmography

The Tarahumara universe consists of a hierarchy of seven levels, with the underside of each level constituting the sky of the one below. All these levels are more or less identical in appearance, being flat, surrounded by water, and inhabited by people, plants, and animals. God, identified by many Tarahumaras as the sun, resides on the highest plane, the Devil inhabits the lowest, and the earth is in the middle; the remaining four levels do not figure prominently in Tarahumara cosmography (Merrill 1981:90–130; Bennett and Zingg 1935:322).

The Tarahumaras attribute the origin of the universe to God and his elder brother, the Devil. God created the earth and the levels above it, the Devil those below, after which they formed human beings, plants, and animals to populate the various levels of the universe (Bennett and Zingg 1935:321; Merrill 1977–1981).

The present-day earth is but the most recent in a series of worlds; most people say it is the fourth. The Tarahumaras state they are uncertain about the nature of the previous worlds and the circumstances of their demise, although tradition holds that the third world was destroyed by flood. They presume that the present earth also will come to an end when it is old, to be replaced by a new one in a never-ending succession of worlds (Lumholtz 1902, 1:296; Merrill 1977–1981).

The Tarahumaras maintain a number of accounts that describe the events that transpired in the distant past, when the fourth world was new (Lumholtz 1902, 1:296–310; Burgess McGuire 1970; Irigoyen Rascón 1974:106–118; Mares Trías 1975; López Batista 1980). This was a miraculous time, during which major geological features such as mountains and canyons were formed, giants and other monsters roamed the earth, and human beings were capable of transforming themselves into animals, an ability they no longer possess except after death.

The original residents of the fourth world, placed on earth by God, were like Tarahumaras physically but possessed none of the plants and animals upon which the Tarahumara of today rely for their sustenance. As a consequence, they ate one another. Angered by their behavior, God as the sun descended very close to the ground and burned them up. He then sent new people down from heaven to populate the earth, provisioning them with all manner of plants and animals, both domestic and wild. At the same time, he dictated in great detail the manner in which they were to conduct their lives. These people became the ancestors of the contemporary Tarahumaras and the instructions God gave them, passed down from one generation to the next, form the basis of present-day Tarahumara culture (Lumholtz 1902, 1:192–193; Bennett and Zingg 1935:322; Merrill 1977–1981).

The Tarahumaras divide the contemporary human inhabitants of the universe into two major categories: *rarámuri* and *čabóči* (Passin 1943:366). *rarámuri* is the Tarahumaras' name for themselves, but they employ the term in a more general sense to include all Native Americans. *čabóči* in turn designates all other people, although when the Tarahumaras wish to distinguish local non-Indians from other kinds of *čabóči*, they label the former as *čabóči* and the latter with terms adopted from Spanish, such as *brínki* (Spanish *gringo*) 'American', *alemáni* 'German', or *číno* 'Chinese'.

The Tarahumaras rely primarily on physical characteristics to decide whether a person is a *rarámuri* or *čabóči*; in fact, *čabóči* literally means 'whiskered one(s)' (Brambila 1980:100–101). Cultural factors come to the fore when they are confronted with people of mixed Indian and non-Indian ancestry. Although they sometimes characterize such individuals as *nasóame* 'mixed', the Tarahumaras will classify them as either *rarámuri* or *čabóči* depending on whether they identify with and practice a *rarámuri* or *čabóči* way of life.

The dichotomy between *rarámuri* and *čabóči* is linked to that between God and the Devil, for God is said to be the father of the *rarámuri* and the Devil the father of the *čabóči*. These two deities protect and provide for the needs of their respective children. However, while God seldom intentionally harms *čabóči*, the Devil constantly endeavors to make the Tarahumaras miserable by sending pests to destroy their crops, illnesses to make them sick, and a variety of malevolent beings to steal their souls. He also encourages the Tarahumaras to argue, fight, commit adultery, steal, and bewitch one another. Individuals who behave in such a fashion are said to have accepted as true the Devil's way of thinking; those who do not are considered to be following God's thinking and consequently are highly thought of by others.

The names the Tarahumaras apply to God include most prominently *onorúame* 'one who is father', *táta riósi* 'father god', and *mi paní bitéame* 'one who lives above'. God resides in the highest heaven with his wife, whom the Tarahumaras call 'mother' (*yéra* or *číči*); she is identified with both the moon and the Virgin Mary (Lumholtz 1902, 1:295; Bennett and Zingg 1935:320–321). Joining them are a number of other people who assist God and his wife by providing food for them and delivering their messages to the inhabitants of the other levels of the universe.

The souls of most Tarahumaras enter the ranks of these helpers at death. Excluded are individuals who commit offenses such as murder or theft and consequently are sent by God to be burned up in a large fire the Devil maintains on his level of the universe (Bennett and Zingg 1935:323; Merrill 1981:288–298). Also, Tarahumaras who engage in sexual intercourse with *čabóči* exchange places with their sexual partners in the afterlife, the Tarahumaras descending to reside with the Devil, the *čabóči* ascending to live with God (Merrill 1981:110–111, 116).

The Devil, known in Tarahumara as *riáblo* (from the Spanish *diablo*) and *riré bitéame* 'one who lives below', makes his home on the bottommost level of the universe. Like God, the Devil is married but the Tarahumaras make little mention of his wife beyond the fact that she is the mother of the *čabóči* and cooperates with the Devil in caring for them (Lumholtz 1902, 1:296). The Devil never punishes *čabóči*; however, some Tarahumaras propose that God destroys the souls of *čabóči* who have been particularly mean during their lives in a fire he keeps for this purpose. The Tarahumaras do not consider the Devil's plane to be an unpleasant place; it is identical in most respects to all the other levels of the universe and represents the *čabóči* equivalent of heaven.

God and the Devil, located at opposite extremes of

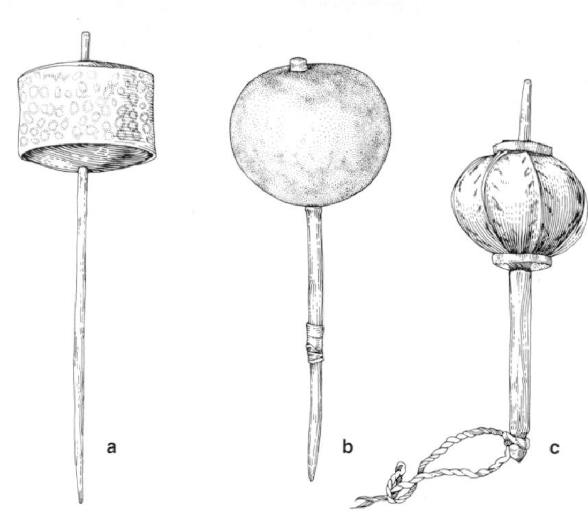
a
b
c

the universe, constitute the poles around which are clustered the basic oppositions that demarcate Tarahumara moral space. The Tarahumaras associate God—their provider and protector—with happiness, beauty, health, life, and goodness, and the Devil—their enemy—with sadness, ugliness, sickness, death, and evil. However, the attitudes these deities assume toward the Tarahumaras are not constant but vary according to the actions the Tarahumaras undertake with respect to them. The Tarahumaras' relationship with God is based on balanced reciprocity; to insure God's continued beneficence, they must reciprocate his attentions by dancing, offering him food, and generally behaving in conformance with his teachings (Lumholtz 1902, 1:330–331). If they fail to do so, God will not protect them from the Devil, will withhold the rain upon which their crops depend, or cause people to fall ill and die. Similarly, the Tarahumaras can neutralize the Devil's maleficence by giving him food, which they frequently do during fiestas. Although the Devil will never help them, he will be grateful for their gift and will refrain from harming them, at least temporarily (Merrill 1981:122–127).

Ritual Activities

The Tarahumaras undertake the vast majority of their rituals (fig. 4) primarily to perpetuate or restore the well-being of particular individuals or the community as a whole. They stage some of their rituals at specific times year after year—for example, the elaborate ceremonies held in conjunction with certain Catholic holy days—while performing others, such as curing rituals and death fiestas, when the circumstances that call for them arise (Bennett and Zingg 1935; Lumholtz 1902, 1:330–355). Despite differences in periodicity, all these rituals include many of the same elements. (The rituals of *gentil* Tarahumaras vary in several respects from those of baptized Tarahumaras. For a discussion of these differences, see Kennedy 1978:127–156.)

• HOLY DAY OBSERVANCES The principal Catholic holy days celebrated by the Tarahumaras are those of the Virgin of Guadalupe (December 12), Christmas Eve (December 24), Epiphany (January 6), and Holy Week. The Immaculate Conception (December 8), Candlemas (February 2), Palm Sunday, Corpus Christi, and certain saints' days also are observed in some areas (Bennett and Zingg 1935:297; Plancarte 1954:52; Merrill 1977–1981).

The Tarahumaras stage their holy day ceremonies primarily in and around their churches and, except for those of Holy Week, all these ceremonies involve basically the same activities (Bennett and Zingg 1935:296–318). Most are organized by one or more sponsors (*pistéro*, from Spanish *fiestero*), assisted by their relatives and other community members. Usually designated a year in advance, these sponsors tend to assume the responsibility voluntarily but seldom for two years in succession because the expenditures are so great. Each must provide meat, usually a head of cattle, as well as maize for food and beer in sufficient quantities for all present to partake, often 100 people or more. In Basíhuare pueblo, local *chabochis* occasionally have served as *pistéro*, but the overwhelming majority of sponsors have been Tarahumaras (Merrill 1977–1981).

Most of these fiestas begin on the eve of the holy day in question and conclude 18–24 hours later. They are vibrant, colorful affairs, highlighted by the Matachine Dance, performed by brightly costumed male dancers known in Tarahumara as *awíame* 'dancer(s)' and *matachíne*. Introduced by Catholic missionaries presumably in the colonial era, the Matachine Dance is executed to the accompaniment of violins and sometimes guitars, with the dancers shaking rattles in time with the music (Basauri 1929:70–73; Kurath 1967). The matachines dance at intervals throughout the fiesta, usually both inside the church and around several wooden crosses (typically three) erected on a dance patio near where the women prepare the food.

top, Amer. Mus. of Nat. Hist., New York: 44412; center right, Amer. Mus. of Nat. Hist., New York: a, 65/1015, b, 65/1012; c, Smithsonian, Dept. of Anthr.: 420,825.

Fig. 4. Tarahumara fiestas, staged at homes and churches throughout the year. In both settings, the focus of ritual activities is the dance patio and altar, the altar composed of one or more wooden crosses and a plank, sheet, or blanket upon which food offerings are placed. top, Conclusion of a performance of *tutugúri* (called *rutubúri* by Lumholtz 1902, 1:349) at a fiesta in Narárachi, Chihuahua. Three chanters stand with rattles on the edge of a dance patio in front of an altar; women stand to the chanters' right, men to their left. A violinist is seated to the right; a matachine dancer is partly visible standing beside him. Photograph by Carl Lumholtz, 1890–1898. center left, Food offerings at a fiesta in front of the church in Basíhuare, Chihuahua. Matachine dancers perform in the background. The canes of office carried by the local Tarahumara officials lean against the raised plank bearing the offerings. Photograph by Luis Verplancken, 1971. center right, Rattles, which both chanters and matachine dancers shake in their performances. In some areas, chanters use only gourd rattles and matachine dancers only those made of wood strips; in others, both types are used interchangeably. a, The head is a thin wooden strip, painted with red circles, overlapped and glued with wooden top and bottom pierced by the stick handle. b, Plain gourd rattle with white string wound around the center of the stick handle. c, Petal-shaped strips of wood with designs made with blue crayons are bent and held in place by glue and 2 wooden disks. A yarn loop is wound around the wooden handle. Length of c 26 cm (rest to same scale), collected by Donald Cordry around 1970; a–b collected by Carl Lumholtz in 1892. bottom, A matachine dancer and chanter perform simultaneously at a fiesta to cure maize, goats, and sheep. The man standing with folded arms is a *čapío* (Spanish *chapeón*), who directs the matachine dance. Food offerings rest on the planks in front of the crosses. The metal containers beside the crosses hold medicines to cure the maize and animals. Photograph by William L. Merrill, Rejogochi, Chihuahua, June 1981.

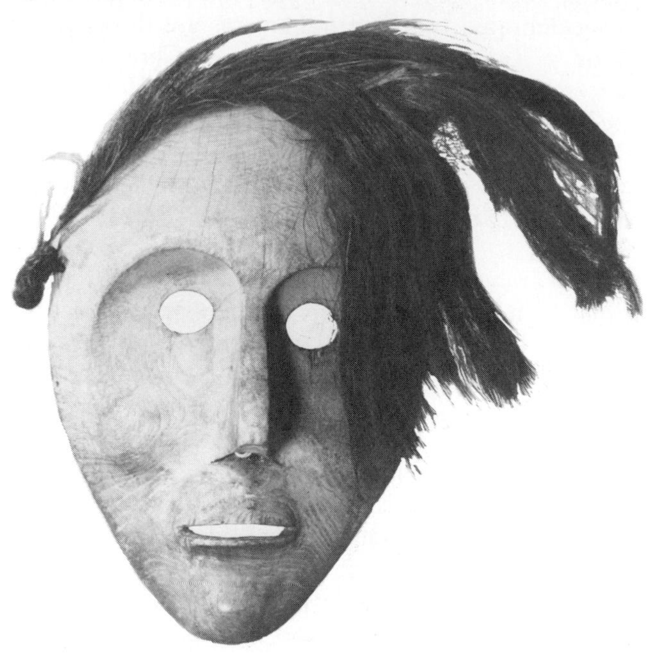

Amer. Mus. of Nat. Hist., New York: 65/1031.

Fig. 5. Mask of unpainted wood with strips of horsehair glued to the top. Such masks sometimes are worn during performances of the Matachine Dance by *čapíos* who oversee the Matachine dancers and insure that they receive food and drink. Height 29.0 cm, collected by Carl Lumholtz in El Cumbre de la Barranca de Cobre, Chihuahua, 1892.

bottom, Smithsonian, Dept. of Anthr.: 93,570.

Fig. 6. Violins and bows of native manufacture, originally patterned after instruments from Renaissance Europe. top, Violinists performing at a fiesta. The pottery jar at their feet holds maize beer. Photograph by Jacob Fried, 1951. bottom, Bow carved of a single piece of wood, bearing a horsehair string. The violin has one metal string and 3 of gut. A piece of rosin for preparing the bow string is attached to the back of the violin neck. Length 60.0 cm, collected by Edward Palmer, Chihuahua, in 1885.

This dance patio also is the stage upon which one or more chanters (*wikaráame* or *sawéame*) enact an indigenous rite known as *tutugúri*, or *yúmari*.† Frequently performed simultaneously with the Matachine Dance, the *tutugúri* is solemn by comparison. The chanter shakes a rattle in his right hand while singing over and over a limited number of musical phrases, which in most areas have no intelligible words. He moves back and forth across the patio in front of and, at times, around the wooden crosses, often accompanied by several men and women who follow his movements but do not join him in song. Resting every half hour or so, the chanter continues until the food being prepared for the occasion is ready.

While these activities are in progress, most of the women present are engaged in cooking meat, making tortillas and tamales, and parching maize kernels that they grind into two dishes known as *kobísi* (Spanish *pinole*) and *ki?orí* (Spanish *esquiate*). They usually complete their work around dawn, at which time containers of the food are placed in front of the crosses. Several men then offer portions to God at the cardinal directions in a counterclockwise circuit around the crosses while the matachines and chanter perform. At the conclusion of the offering, which marks the climax of the fiesta, women supervise the distribution of the food and people eat a bit, saving the rest to take home.

The remainder of the fiesta is devoted to drinking alcoholic beverages, almost invariably maize kernel beer, the consumption of which constitutes a necessary component of most Tarahumara rituals. Having commenced imbibing earlier in the fiesta, the participants finish the beer that is left and either return to their houses or, as

†In many localities, *tutugúri* (or *tutubúri*) and *yúmari* label somewhat different dances, but authors disagree about which term applies to which dance (Bennett and Zingg 1935:271–275; Plancarte 1954:50, 59; Kennedy 1978:141–143). In addition, the Tarahumaras in some areas do not employ the term *yúmari* at all, designating both dances as *tutugúri* (Merrill 1977–1981).

frequently occurs, continue their drinking and revelry in private homes, sometimes for another day or so.

The principal reason for which the Tarahumaras organize these holy day fiestas is to please God so that he will continue to care and provide for them. Everyone in attendance and especially the chanter and matachines is said to be *wikálawi tánia*, a phrase that literally means 'asking forgiveness' (Brambila 1980) but which most Tarahumaras translate as 'asking God for long and healthy lives, many children, abundant crops, and productive herds' (Lumholtz 1902, 1:332; Merrill 1981:289). These requests are never spoken but conveyed through the participants' actions, which also are designed to make God look upon them with favor. The performances of the chanter and matachines, for example, are felt to give God pleasure because they are beautiful, and the food offerings to fulfill at least partially their obligations to him for having given them plants and animals upon which to subsist.

The Tarahumaras' Holy Week observances (fig. 7), the most elaborate religious ceremonies they perform, share few elements with other holy day celebrations and, as Kennedy and López (1981) document, vary substantially from one pueblo to another. The major performers are the members of two opposing sodalities, known in different regions by variants of the Spanish terms *fariseos* 'Pharisees' and *soldados* 'soldiers', *fariseos* and *moros* 'Moors', or *Judas* and *fariseos* (Kennedy and López 1981). The individuals in these sodalities are distinguished from one another in various ways: in Basíhuare pueblo, for example, the Pharisees smear their bodies with white pigment, carry painted wooden swords, wear hats crowned with turkey feathers, and are led by a flagbearer who waves a white banner; the soldiers are unpainted, bear wooden staffs tipped with bayonets, and their banner is red (Merrill 1977–1981).

The leaders of these sodalities often are appointed

left, U. of Ariz., Ariz. State Mus., Tucson: 55935, center, Smithsonian, Dept. of Anthr.: 422,485; right, Amer. Mus. of Nat. Hist., New York: 65/1020; bottom, U. of Calif., Mus. of Cultural Hist., Los Angeles: X66-2416, X66-2324.

Fig. 7. Easter Week ceremony. left, Pharisees parade a Judas figure erected on a pole. Photograph by Bernard L. Fontana, at a village in the eastern highlands of the Sierra Madre Oriental, Chihuahua, 1978. center, Goatskin double-headed drum painted in red ocher with different designs on each side, with a snare strung with 2 blue beads. The drumstick is pine with a knob on the end covered with cloth secured with goat sinew. right, Whistle to accompany drums during the Easter ceremonies. It is made of cane with a bill cut at one end and a convex piece of reed tied to it to form a mouthpiece. bottom, Wooden swords painted with mostly geometric designs carried by Pharisees (see Kennedy and López 1981). center, Diameter 51.5 cm (rest to same scale), collected by William L. Merrill, Rejogochi, Chihuahua, 1981; right, collected by Carl Lumholtz, 1892; bottom, collected by Raúl López, 1966.

prior to Holy Week by the pueblo officials and approved by the other Tarahumara men of the pueblo. During Holy Week, the majority of men and boys in attendance affiliate with one or the other sodality. In some areas, a person's affiliation is determined by where he lives with respect to the church while in others each person decides on his own which group to join (Kennedy and López 1981). In most pueblos, these sodalities are active only during Holy Week and a short period before.

The principal events of Holy Week take place on Maundy Thursday and Good Friday (Kennedy and López 1981; Bennett and Zingg 1935:312–317). The two sodalities devote most of these days to completing processions around the church, in which women, the community officials, and unaffiliated males also participate; standing guard in front of the altar and church; and performing a special dance seen only in this and a few preceding weeks. Both the processions and the dancing are accompanied by drums and reed flutes, which are played exclusively during the Easter season. Also during this time, one of the sodalities appears with a human figure, usually constructed of long grasses tied over a wooden frame and dressed in Western clothing. This image, identified as Judas, is paraded about for a time and later hidden by its creators.

In most Tarahumara pueblos, the Holy Week activities conclude on Holy Saturday. In many areas, dancers known in Spanish as *pascoleros* perform, and wrestling matches are staged between the members of the two sodalities (Kennedy and López 1981; Murray 1981). The climax comes when the members of one sodality destroy the Judas figure made by the other, assuming they can find it. Then everyone leaves the church area for nearby *ranchos* to consume the beer prepared by the leaders of the two sodalities, the principal community officials, or others. In certain areas, some drinking takes place earlier in the week, but usually in moderation; however, occasionally the events of Holy Saturday are abbreviated or eliminated altogether because the people begin drinking in earnest during the evening of Good Friday.

Little has been published on the Tarahumaras' interpretations of the Holy Week ceremonies (Kennedy and López 1981:54–61). The residents of the Basíhuare pueblo regard Holy Week as an especially portentous period, for each year at this time God and his wife are believed to be in a weakened state and thus vulnerable to the Devil's attacks. If the Devil should overcome them, he would destroy the world. Consequently, most of the activities in which they engage between Maundy Thursday and Holy Saturday are intended to protect and strengthen God and his wife until they can recover and defend themselves personally (Merrill 1977–1981).

• OTHER FIESTAS During the course of a year, the Tarahumaras usually sponsor a number of fiestas in addition to their major holy day celebrations (Bennett and Zingg 1935:268–290). These fiestas include many of the same ritual activities as the holy day ceremonies but differ from them in several respects. People hold them at their homes rather than in the vicinity of the church, and attendance is by invitation, not open to all. Goats or sheep often are slaughtered in place of cattle and, while chanters almost invariably perform, matachines frequently do not. Furthermore, in most instances the sponsorship of these fiestas is not a formal obligation, as is the case for holy day fiestas, nor is the scheduling of them necessarily determined by the Catholic ritual calendar, being instead at the discretion of the households who organize them.

Tarahumara households stage these fiestas for a variety of reasons (Plancarte 1954:49). An individual may be instructed to do so in his dreams by God (Lumholtz 1902, 1:333–334) or a family may feel they are in special need of God's care because several of their members have recently died. Sometimes the motivation is less individualistic, as in the case of the fiestas held to offer the first fruits of the agricultural season to God, which often are sponsored cooperatively by several neighboring households (Bennett and Zingg 1935:282–283). The Tarahumaras also organize some fiestas because they provide the contexts within which certain special purpose rituals must be performed, such as curing the community's crops and domestic animals or offering food and other items to the dead. Regardless of why any particular fiesta is given, the general purpose of all of them, like those on holy days, is to engender or maintain a positive relationship with God.

• CURING RITUALS The Tarahumaras attribute sickness to a wide range of causes (García Manzanedo 1963; Merrill 1981:231–275). Consuming bitter foods, for example, can lead to the accumulation inside the body of a yellowish, mucuslike substance called *awagásine*, which causes lethargy and loss of appetite. An invisible white thread known as *rumugá*, which grows from the crown of the head, can induce illness by wrapping around the body and can further threaten an individual by attracting lightning and hail. Other ailments such as headcolds, measles, and scarlet fever are sent by the Devil. These maladies, known as *nawirí*, have human form but are like fog or wind and infiltrate the bodies of their victims. The proper functioning of the body also can be impeded by the intrusion of foreign objects such as wire, bottles, knives, stones, and chilis, placed there by sorcerers.

Ailments such as these, in which the affliction is concentrated in the body, tend to be minor when compared to those involving a person's souls. All individuals possess many souls, distributed throughout their bodies, which endow them with vitality, sentience, and the ability to think. Should any harm befall their souls, they will be adversely affected and potentially will die (Merrill 1981).

The universe is populated by a number of beings who threaten the Tarahumaras' souls, most of whom are allied with the Devil. The water people (*bawičí piréame*) capture the souls of individuals who are startled at or near water, holding them for ransom (Bennett and Zingg 1935:259–260). More dangerous are sorcerers who attempt to injure or kill the souls of their fellows, usually those who have angered them but sometimes others as well. Rather than undertaking the attack themselves, sorcerers (both men and women) sometimes will dispatch their *oromá*—fierce, long-beaked birds identified with shooting stars—which rip their victims' hearts to shreds, drink their blood, and carry their souls back to their homes to devour (Lumholtz 1902, 1:315–326; Bennett and Zingg 1935:266; Passin 1942). On occasion, even God will remove the souls of people who have displeased him, causing them to die.

The Tarahumaras confront the numerous threats to their health with a variety of curing rituals, some of which are designed to prevent illnesses and others to alleviate them. Preventative curing is undertaken not only for people but also for domesticated plants and animals, principally maize, goats, sheep, and cattle (Bennett and Zingg 1935:276–282; Kennedy 1978: 140–149). In these rituals, Tarahumara doctors (*owirúame*), who can be men or women, perform things such as cutting or burning the threadlike *rumugá* from their patients' heads, administering one or more medicines to them, and blowing their breath, or soul, over their bodies and, when the patients are human, into their mouths. A baby is cured in this fashion on several separate occasions (four if a girl, three if a boy), with the doctor naming the child and assuming responsibility for its future health; these rituals represent the Tarahumara equivalent of the Christian baptism. These curings are intended to strengthen the subjects' souls so they can repel the attacks of malevolent beings and to protect them from harm in general. When children, plants, and animals are involved, another goal of the curing is to encourage their proper growth (Merrill 1981:241–242).

If preventative measures fail and a person falls ill, the Tarahumaras resort to alleviative curing. When people are only mildly sick and fairly confident of the cause of their ailments, they may attempt to cure themselves, usually by taking remedies prepared from local plants or commercially manufactured medicines (Bye 1976; Pennington 1963:177–194). However, if their illnesses are serious or persistent or if they are unsure of the proper diagnoses, they will request the assistance of Tarahumara doctors.

Most Tarahumara communities include several individuals who are doctors, predominantly men but women as well, some of whom usually are considered more competent than others. People can become doctors only if God endows them with the ability to cure, but they learn the specifics of the trade from other doctors, often relatives (Lumholtz 1902, 1:322; Bennett and Zingg 1935:255–256). To practice effectively, they must be familiar with basic curing techniques and have strong, resilient souls so that they can defend the souls of their neighbors from the attacks of evil beings in the night and search for these souls if they are captured or otherwise lost. Many doctors maintain in addition one or more specialities, such as breaking up the mushrooms (*amaséware*) that sometimes grow in people's stomachs, extracting worms and other objects from their patients' bodies, or performing the elaborate rituals associated with peyote (fig. 8) and a similarly esteemed and feared plant known as *bakánawi* (Lumholtz 1902, 1:356–379; Bennett and Zingg 1935:291–295; Bye 1979; Merrill 1977–1981).

The activities in which doctors engage to cure their patients vary according to the ailments they are diagnosed as having (Bennett and Zingg 1935:258–264; García Manzanedo 1963). They may search for their souls in their dreams, massage their bodies, prescribe medicines, or subject them to sweatbaths, among other things. Regardless of the specific treatment, doctors usually perform a general curing ritual for their patients designed to strengthen them and their souls so they can recover and resist future illnesses. Quite often on the same occasion, members of the patient's family are cured in a similar fashion to protect them from illness. Such curings typically take place during drinking parties and household fiestas, with the doctors receiving alcoholic beverages, food, and sometimes money as compensation for their services.

If a cure is ineffective, the patient frequently will conclude that the original doctor was incompetent or the diagnosis incorrect and call upon a different doctor. Since the same set of symptoms often can have different underlying causes, a variety of diagnoses may be offered and a series of treatments applied until the patient is healed or dies. Also, in the 1970s and 1980s, many Tarahumaras were turning with increasing frequency to physicians at mission and government health facilities when their own curing efforts failed (Merrill 1977–1981).

• DEATH RITUALS Death originated in the distant past at the instigation of the horned lizard (*wikókere*). Being short, fat, and a slow walker, the horned lizard feared that, because no one ever died, the Tarahumaras eventually would multiply to such numbers that he would be trampled. Consequently, he petitioned God to begin periodically calling the souls of some of them to heaven, and people have died ever since (Bennett and Zingg 1935:127; Merrill 1977–1981).

At death a person's body begins gradually decomposing into clay while the souls commence an independent existence, unless they are destroyed because of misdeeds committed during life. The souls of the dead continue to inhabit the same universe as the living

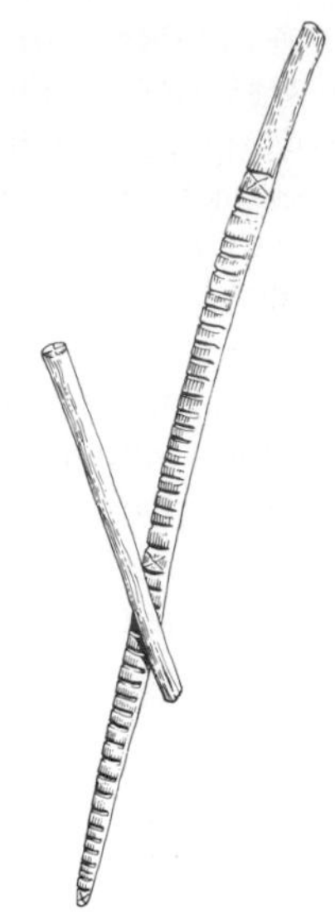

Amer. Mus. of Nat. Hist., New York: left, 43481; right, 65/1218.

Fig. 8. The peyote ceremony. left, Peyote specialist, seated third from right, accompanies his song with rasping sticks. The other participants dance and assist him. The dancer wearing the dark blanket holds straps of leather with deer-hoof rattles on the end. According to Lumholtz (1902, 1:359), the Tarahumara attributed to peyote the power to give health and long life and to purify the body and soul. Photograph by Carl Lumholtz, Guajochi, Chihuahua, 1890–1898. right, Rasp consisting of a notched wooden stick that is rested on an overturned gourd or pottery vessel (serving as a resonator) and a smooth round stick that is run up and down the notched piece. Length of longest 75 cm, collected by Carl Lumholtz at Guajochi, Chihuahua, in 1898.

but their perceptions of it are reversed. For them, night is day and day is night, they plant when the living harvest and harvest when the living plant, and they believe themselves to be alive and the living dead (Bennett and Zingg 1935:251).

The Tarahumaras are much more concerned with their existence here on earth than with the afterlife. They envision heaven to be no more or less a paradise than any of the other levels of the universe and assume that most Tarahumaras will join God there after they die, not as a reward for lives well spent but simply because they are his children. People who commit acts during their lives that preclude their entry into heaven can do nothing to alter their fate. However, any punishment they warrant—such as the destruction of their souls in the case of serious crimes—will be quickly administered and of short duration. The Christian notions of repentance, salvation, and eternal damnation and suffering do not figure in the Tarahumara scheme of things.

When a person dies, the activities in which the surviving relatives engage are basically the same regardless if the deceased is male or female except that, as in all other domains of Tarahumara culture, things associated with males are done or organized in series of threes and those associated with females in series of fours. These activities are designed to prevent the deceased from harming the living and to provide for him until he can establish himself in the afterlife (Bennett and Zingg 1935:236–251; Basauri 1929:44–47; Lumholtz 1902, 1:380–390).

In the interim between death and burial, food, clothing, and other items are placed near the body, which is covered with a blanket, and a fire kindled in the house where it lies. The adults in the household inscribe crosses on the foreheads of the children with ashes and often send them to another home to sleep, for children are especially vulnerable to the dead, who endeavor to take the souls of their relatives with them.

The corpse is buried as soon as possible, usually the day following death. The adult males of the household, sometimes assisted by other men in the neighborhood, carry the body wrapped in a blanket to a cemetery or, in some areas, a rockshelter where they place it in the grave together with articles of clothing and bits of food (Bennett and Zingg 1935:237; Kennedy 1978:150). Then one of the group delivers a speech, reminding the deceased that he is now dead and should leave the living alone, informing him that his family will provide for his needs in the coming weeks and months, and encouraging him to have strength for his impending journey. The grave is then closed and the members of the burial party protect themselves against sickness potentially arising from their contact with the dead by bathing in cedar or juniper smoke and taking certain medicines (Bennett and Zingg 1935:238).

A dead person's relatives begin to fulfill their major obligations three days after death, or four if the departed is female. They prepare food and assemble the possessions left behind, often adding money and other goods they want the souls of the deceased to have. These souls arrive at the former home to retrieve the offerings, frequently in the company of previously departed relatives, who share in the food and aid in transporting the other items to the deceased's new abode in heaven.

Following this initial prestation, the dead person's immediate family sponsors at least three (four if female) additional fiestas, although they may give things at other times, typically during drinking parties (Bennett and Zingg 1935:249). More distant relatives also may make offerings on these or other occasions if they desire and, in certain areas, the dead person's joking relatives—principally siblings-in-law and grandparents or grandchildren—rather than spouse, parents, or children assume the responsibility for staging these fiestas (Kennedy 1978:152).

In some Tarahumara communities, one of these fiestas, usually the last, is more elaborate than the others, but all contain basically the same elements and differ little from other Tarahumara fiestas except for the activities directed specifically to the dead (Bennett and Zingg 1935:239–248). Often one or more individuals who can communicate with the dead supervise these special activities, which include things such as offering the dead food, beer, clothing, and tools, delivering speeches admonishing them to refrain from harming the living, scattering ashes around the homestead to discourage them from returning, and administering medicines to the living and applying ashes in the form of crosses to their foreheads to protect them from the dead.

These death fiestas are times for dancing, joking, feasting, and getting drunk, not for mourning. Occasionally people may begin to cry or show signs of melancholy, but their companions quickly encourage them to cheer up and have strength. The Tarahumaras strive to avoid becoming overly sad when a loved one dies because they are afraid their souls will abandon their bodies to join the deceased. At the same time, they want these fiestas to be happy affairs because they are intended not only to provision the dead but to entertain them so that they will leave in good spirits and be content in the afterlife (Plancarte 1954:57; Merrill 1981: 276–305).

Northern Tepehuan

CAMPBELL W. PENNINGTON

Language and Territory

The Northern Tepehuan, who speak a Uto-Aztecan language (Bascom 1965:2),* are scattered throughout southern Chihuahua south of the Río Verde (fig. 1), occupying about 10,500 square kilometers within the *municipios* of Guadalupe y Calvo and Morelos. They share this territory with approximately 33,000 Mestizos (Pennington 1969:5). How long these indigenes have occupied this territory is not determined. However, archival materials suggest that they were in the same area when first contacted by Spaniards and that their lands extended northward beyond the Río Verde, into the valleys of the San Pablo de Balleza and the Río Valle de Allende. These Tepehuan are undoubtedly a northern remnant of an aboriginal people who once occupied a vast territory that extended from what is now Nayarit and Jalisco to southern Chihuahua (Pennington 1969:6–22).

The Northern Tepehuan have apparently not influenced, nor have they been influenced by, the more numerous Tarahumara who are found immediately to the north, either in prehistoric or historic times (Pennington 1969:235–373).

Environment

The Northern Tepehuan live within a much-dissected portion of the Sierra Madre, and their lands may be roughly classified as either canyon country or rolling upland, there being within these subdivisions a great variety of individual physiographic features and concomitant types of vegetation. The average elevation is about 7,800 feet, with much deviation from this average in some areas. Native folk refer (in Spanish) to the uplands as *tierra templada* and the canyon lands as *tierra caliente*. Two distinct annual periods of precipitation may be identified, the rainy season from March until late August, and a somewhat drier period during the remainder of the year. Tepehuans and Mestizos state that only portions of their land ever experience really serious drought—especially upon the great mesas that form the heartland of the upland Tepehuan country.

Species of *Pinus, Cupressus*, and *Pseudotsuga* dominate the larger stands of vegetation at higher levels of southern Chihuahua. These stands are marked by an understory of vegetation dominated by species of *Arctostaphylos, Arbutus, Garrya, Salix, Populus*, and *Ceanothus* in favorable ecological situations. Downslope from the uplands, where there is less moisture and poor soil, the vegetation is dominated by genera such as *Ceiba, Bursera, Willardia, Caesalpina, Lysiloma*, and *Acacia*, there being an understory of shrubs belonging to the generas *Mimosa, Erythrina, Eysenhardtia, Calliandra*, and *Hydrangea*. The great variety of vegetation associated with the canyons is demonstrated by the appearance of examples of *Sebastiana, Sapium, Alnus, Piscidia, Jatropha, Fouquieria, Haematoxylon, Pithecellobium, Pachycereus, Prosopis, Ficus, Randia, and Acacia*. Other than amidst pines of the uplands there are many examples of species of *Opuntia, Echinocereus, Dasylirion, Nolina*, and *Yucca*, and everywhere species of *Bromus* compete with harsh bunch grasses (*Muhlenbergia*).

History

The role of Franciscan and Jesuit missionaries during the colonial period was important, since it was via these orders that significant introductions of European plants and animals were made. Contributions of the Jesuits were the more lasting, since Franciscans directly influenced the Tepehuan only for a short time in the seventeenth century, in their most northerly location in the Valle de Allende (Pennington 1969:19). Jesuit missions were established at Nabogame and Baborigame shortly after 1700. These missions were maintained until expulsion of the Jesuits in 1767, at which date the missions were assigned to the Franciscans, who retained nominal control until secularization in the nineteenth century.

*The native words appearing in this chapter in italics are Spanish, with the exception of *kukúduli, úgai, yoríki*, and *ódami*, which are Northern Tepehuan.

The phonemes of Northern Tepehuan are: (voiceless stops) *p, t* (dental), *t^y* (alveopalatal), *k*; (voiced stops) *b, d, d^y, g*; (affricate) *č*; (spirants) *v* ([β]), *s* (alveolar), *š* (alveopalatal), *h* ([x]); (nasals) *m, n, n^y*; (lateral) *l*; (flap) *r* (with spirantized and trilled allophones); (semivowels) *w, y*; (high vowels) *i, ɨ* (central, unrounded), *u*; (low vowels) *e, a, o*; (tones) high (v́) and low (unmarked). Vowel length is interpreted as vowel gemination.

Information on Northern Tepehuan phonology and the transcription of words was furnished by Burt Bascom (communication to editors 1981).

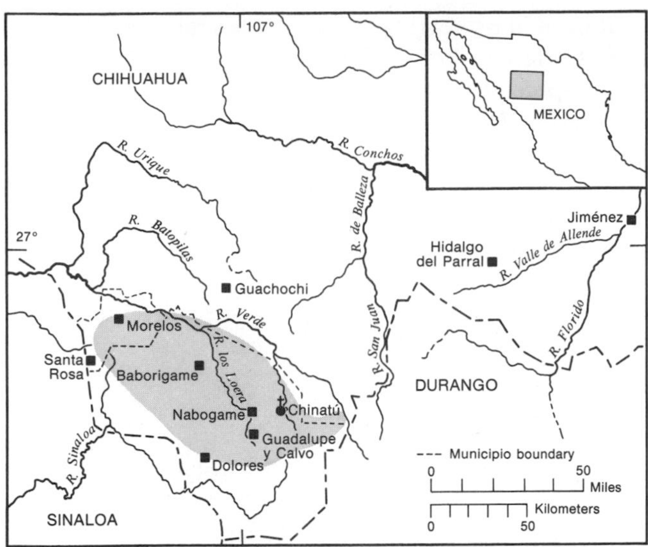

Fig. 1. Territory in the 20th century.

Jesuits returned to the sierras shortly after 1900; however, their influence upon the Northern Tepehuan in the twentieth century is apparently minimal, there being few Tepehuan who make use of religious and educational instruction available at Chinatú in southern Chihuahua.

Two major influences affect the Northern Tepehuan in the 1980s, the federal government and the increasing Mestizo population in southern Chihuahua. A government station established at Guachochi in 1952 (Lister and Lister 1966:307) provides services that contribute to bringing the indigenes into the mainstream of Mexican cultural and economic activities. The ratio of indigene to Mestizo was about four to one in the 1960s (Pennington 1969:373). It is likely that the proportion of Mestizos will become greater during the late twentieth century, because of increased ranching, mining, and lumbering activities in southern Chihuahua. This development was made possible by construction of a gravel road from Parral to Guadalupe y Calvo and thence northward into the heartland of the Tepehuan country. The result will surely be a rapid merger of Tepehuan within the Mestizo complex, accompanied by disappearance of ancient customs pertaining to material culture, and perhaps even the language, which was spoken by most Tepehuan adults in 1981.

Contemporary Northern Tepehuans live in relative isolation, being scattered in rancheria settlements that are located upon the great mesas or along streamways that lead down to the deep canyons. Location of rancherias is determined by availability of good soil and potable water. Rarely are there more than four or five related families occupying a rancheria. There are five large clusters of rancherias, each of which is tributary to one of the following pueblos: Baborigame, Cinco Llagas, Santa Rosa, Nabogame, and Dolores. These settlements are essentially Mestizo in population.

At each of these pueblos there is an elaborate hierarchy of officials made up of Tepehuans. Activities of these officials represent a blend of aboriginal and colonial customs. Generally, except in cases where rape and murder are involved, Indian officials handle disputes among themselves.

Population

The number of Northern Tepehuans cannot be determined, there being no agreement as to definitions of Indian and Mestizo, not only among Indians and mestizos in southern Chihuahua but also among government census takers. Published figures range from between 3,000 and 4,000 (Service 1969:822) to 8,000 (Pennington 1969:25); the higher figure is based upon an extensive survey made in the heartland of Northern Tepehuan country (Llano Grande) where aboriginal connections are denied even where they patently exist (Pennington 1969:24–25).

Culture

Religion

Contemporary Northern Tepehuan are nominally Roman Catholic, and their religious concepts represent elements of Catholicism introduced by Franciscans and Jesuits that were later modified by contacts with Mestizos (Service 1969:827). A creator is recognized, there being helpers who apparently represent ancient figures among the aborigines. *kukúduli* is the master of the deer and determines whether or not such an animal is brought down (Pennington 1969:131). Another god is *úgai*, a spirit that manifests itself as a light in the sky at the death of someone. There is a spirit that creates wind (Service 1969:827). Contemporary rituals are essentially Christian in origin, there being an emphasis upon making the sign of the cross and the use of phrases such as *nombre de Dios*. Like Mestizos in southern Chihuahua, the Tepehuans follow essentially standard Catholic dramas during the Christmas season, Holy Week, and the October Fiesta of San Francisco (Service 1969:828). Drinking of tiswin (*tesgüino*), dancing, and food offerings placed before a cross are characteristic of fiestas held at the scattered rancherias; these ceremonies are held to insure good crops, to honor the dead, and to promote health of men and animals.

Subsistence

• AGRICULTURE More than 95 percent of the Tepehuan families practice some type of agriculture, and the basic crops are corn, beans, and squash. Relative antiquity of these crops among the Chihuahua Tepehuan is demonstrated by analogues of contemporary items found in the Río Zape site in northern Durango, a site that is clearly within Northern Tepehuan aboriginal territory, which has been dated at about A.D. 600 (Pennington 1969:53–55, 58). Contemporary races and varieties of maize bespeak ancient and widespread Mexican corns. Northern Tepehuans have apparently long experimented with teosinte (*Zea mexicana*) in their cornfields. Most beans are repsentatives of *Phaseolus vulgaris*; there is also a variety of the scarlet runner bean (*P. coccineus*). The European cowpea is an important staple. Four species of edible cucurbits are widely cultivated, as is the bottle gourd, that indispensable source of materials used in the manufacture of dippers, storage containers, and rattles. Under favorable ecological conditions the Old World watermelon and wheat are grown. *Amaranthus hypochondriacus* is cultivated by some of the Northern Tepehuan (Pennington 1969:52, 237–242).

Field plots utilized by the Tepehuan are small and generally located either upon edges of the mesas that dominate so much of Chihuahua south of the Río Verde or along arroyos that trend downward from those mesas to the canyons. Few Indians utilize canyon floodplains, due to the lack of good soil there. The relative infertility of southern Chihuahua upland soils requires preparation of new field plots every few years; these plots are cleared with a metal ax and tilled with a wooden plow drawn by oxen. That stone axes may have anciently served in clearing plots is suggested by the occasional appearance of such articles in fields.

The sharp contrast between upland and canyon environments is emphasized by the fact that only one season for cropping exists in the uplands, whereas two growing periods (one extending from November until May or June, the other from July to November) are typical of the canyons (Pennington 1969:65–66). A wooden dibble serves in making holes in plowed ground for seeding of corn, beans, or squash. Although some Tepehuan seed beans and corn together, most aborigines plant their bean plots apart from maize, in plots located upslope from the corn fields. Edible cucurbits are seeded in fields near habitations. The ubiquitous bottle gourd is seeded in corrals, upon trash heaps, in fields, or upon ant hills (Pennington 1969:67). Field or garden products are generally stored in cribs, which may be integral parts of log houses or else constructed apart from the habitations. Tepehuans who live immediately south of the Río Verde, in very hot country, sometimes construct round or square storage huts of stone and mud mortar, topped by a conical frame covered with brush (Pennington 1969:76).

Rail fences are occasionally constructed in the uplands for protection of crops against damage by cattle. Rail and stone fences are built in the canyons. Although most weeding is done by hand there is some use of metal and wooden hoes. Crop watchers and scarecrows are utilized in protecting young plants against predatory birds. Little can be done to prevent crop damage by grasshoppers, locusts, and the corn worm, which are omnipresent (Pennington 1969:69–71). The antiquity of the hoe among the Tepehuan is not determined; however, the eighteenth-century Tepehuan vocabulary composed by Rinaldini at Nabogame includes a term that refers to an implement used for tilling corn (Pennington 1969:38, 71).

• HORTICULTURE Crops that require more attention and protection than field crops are cultivated in small plots located near habitations. Such plants may be protected by enclosures of wood or stone. Most garden plants are Old World in origin, the following being the most commonly cultivated: three species of sorghum utilized as a source of seeds for preparing pinole or for fresh sprouts used in preparing tiswin, sugarcane that provides sprouts used in preparing tiswin, two species of *Allium* (onions), a wild mustard (*Brassica campestris*), cabbage, garden pea, chickpea, a vetchling (*Lathyrus vernus*), a horsebean (*Vicia faba*), coriander, white potatoes (*Solanum tuberosum*), tomatoes (*Lycopersicon esculentum*), domesticated chile (*Capsicum annuum*), tobacco (*Nicotiana tabacum*), watermelon, and lettuce. Two species of native *Opuntia* cactus are occasionally cultivated in garden plots. The meager supply of *Nicotiana tabacum* is supplemented in canyons by leaves from the wild *N. trigonophylla* and *N. glauca*. That tobacco smoking is relatively ancient among the Northern Tepehuan is demonstrated by the appearance of a native term for *chupador de tabaco* ('tobacco sucker') in the eighteenth-century vocabulary (Pennington 1969:89–92). Tobacco is smoked in corn shucks. The utilization of a pipe is denied.

Fruit trees maintained near habitations in the uplands include the introduced fig, pomegranate, peach, and apple trees. Old World fruit trees are represented in the canyons by orange and lemon trees (Pennington 1969:93–96).

• FOOD AND BEVERAGES Corn dishes constitute the principal foodstuff among the Tepehuan, the important dishes being variants of gruels (pinole, *esquiate*, atole, *yoríki*, and *pozole*), tortillas, tamales, and *esquite* (parched corn). Fresh corn is boiled or roasted in season. Upland Tepehuan prepare pinole, *esquiate*, and tamales from wheat. Squash foods are prepared from fresh or dried material. Relatively simple modes are utilized in preparing pea and bean dishes; these legumes are not soaked before being boiled. Introduced condiments (*Brassica campestris, Coriandrum sativum*), fruits and leaves of wild and domesticated chile, leaves of two varieties of *Chenopodium, Chimaphila umbellata, Oxalis albicans*, seeds of coriander, and leaves of an introduced species of *Raphanus* serve to make bean and pea foods more palatable. Potatoes are baked in ashes. An important quelite dish is prepared from processed leaves of the *Amaranthus hypochondriacus* (Pennington 1969:99–105).

The important beverage among the Northern Tepehuan is tiswin, and the juice that serves as the base of this fermented drink is commonly obtained from maize sprouts. A fermented beverage is also prepared from juice expelled from cooked hearts of at least four species of *Agave*. Juice from these hearts, or from crushed maize sprouts, is boiled before being put aside for fermentation. Certain additives utilized in preparing tiswin accelerate a chemical change during fermentation: seeds and plumes of species of *Bromus*; bark of a species of oak; a small herb (*Chimaphila umbellata* or *C. maculata*); and roots of several unidentified plants. Relative antiquity of fermented beverages among the Northern Tepehuan is demonstrated in seventeenth-century documentary materials for southern Chihuahua (Pennington 1969:105–111).

• HUNTING AND FISHING Hunting and fishing are important not only as supplements to the diet of corn, beans, and squash but also because of their significance as sport. A cottontail, several species of squirrel, an armadillo, a small black mole, a large gopher, several species of rats, skunks, puma, jaguar, jaguarundi, ocelot, nutria, ring-tailed cat, raccoon, coati, gray fox, coyote, wolf, peccary, and deer are hunted, either as sources of skin or food, or because the creatures are known to prey upon stock and crops. Techniques utilized in bringing down these creatures are both old and new, including a figure-four release trap, bow and arrow (fig. 2), lance, stake trap, snare, dog, and rifle (Pennington 1969:119–132).

Fish do not serve as a significant element in the Tepehuan diet but do provide variety. Fishing techniques include the use of hook and line, stupefying agents derived from plant life, and dynamite. Important stupefying agents are obtained from the following: species of *Agave, Juglans major, Argemone ochroleuca* subsp. *ochroleuca*, four species of *Prunus, Tephrosia nicaraguensis, T. thurberi, Lupinus* sp., *Brongniartia* sp., *Hura crepitans, Lasianthaea podecephala*, and at least five unidentified species (Pennington 1969:132–135).

• COLLECTING Fruits in season provide an important supplement to the diet. Piñon nuts, walnut, and certain species of acorns are sought as foodstuff (Pennington 1969:135–138). Collected greens are sought chiefly during the rainy season and are particularly important in the uplands where potherbs appear in moist areas in pine-clad country, in plowed fields, along borders of fields, along arroyos, and in the gardens. These quelites include both native and introduced plants. Among important examples of plants used before contact are species of *Rumex, Eriogonum, Chenopodium, Amaranthus, Phytolacca, Descurainia, Rorippa, Oxalis, Oenothera, Tauschia, Osmorhiza, Fraxinus, Phacelia, Mimulus*, and *Cirsium*. Species of *Rumex, Portulaca,*

Fig. 2. A family living near Llano Grande, on the Mesa de Milpillas in southern Chihuahua. The man holds a bow and arrows. The boy to the far left wears leather sandals, and the woman and young girl wear bandanas. Photograph by Campbell W. Pennington, summer 1960.

Nasturtium, Brassica, Coriandrum, and *Solanum* are important examples of edible greens introduced from the Old World (Pennington 1969:138–140).

Roots are not really important as a foodstuff among the Northern Tepehuan. However, some utilization is made of species of *Dasylirion, Yucca, Agave, Ceiba, Exogonium, Solanum*, and *Valeriana* (Pennington 1969:140–142).

Like other aborigines of northwestern Mexico, the Chihuahua Tepehuan seek certain insects and reptiles as a source of foodstuff. A crude honey is obtained from hives of a bumble bee (*Bombus formosus*), a wasp *Polybia diguetana*), wild native bees, and from at least one species of the escaped European bee (*Apis mellifera*). A grub removed from a cocoon found upon species of *Arbutus* is an esteemed addition to the corn dish *yoríki*. Rattlesnake meat is occasionally eaten (Pennington 1969:142–144).

• ANIMAL HUSBANDRY European stock surely reached the Northern Tepehuan when Franciscan and Jesuit missionaries appeared in what is now northern Durango and southern Chihuahua in the seventeenth century. However, it appears that Tepehuan south of the Río Verde did not commonly use oxen as draft animals until during the nineteenth century. Even so, there is a scarcity of oxen in the 1980s, and the difficulties encountered because of primitive methods at plowing time are compounded because of a reluctance to use mules, burros, or horses as draft animals. Those Indians who possess oxen rent them to their neighbors. Sheep and goats are numerous and are valued because their wool serves in the manufacture of sashes and blankets and because they serve as foodstuff during celebrations. Ownership of horses, burros, and mules brings prestige to Tepehuans. Horses serve for human transport, mules and burros as pack animals. Most Tepehuans maintain dogs, whereas few keep cats. Upland Tepehuans raise poultry more than do canyon folk (Pennington 1969: 152–154).

Medicine

Respiratory infections (influenza, pneumonia, and the common cold), two types of measles, a modified form of smallpox, snake bites, constipation, and aches and pains of one sort or another are frequently mentioned by the Tepehuan. They obtain relief from discomforts caused by such ailments through use of poultices, infusions, and teas prepared from roots, leaves, stems, or seeds of at least 56 plant families. Many unidentified specimens are also used (see Pennington 1969:177–190 for a full discussion of plant life used in the preparation of medicines).

Technology

Skins of certain wild animals, cows, oxen, and goats serve in the manufacture of sandals, sleeping and sitting mats, carrying baskets, saddle bags, small bags used for carrying seed or pinole, wrist guards, and quivers. A tanning agent used in processing these skins may be obtained from the bark of any one of eight species of oak, from *Acacia pennatula*, and a species of *Wimmeria*. The antiquity of processing hide is not determined, but anciently skins must have been used in the manufacture of a quiver, in view of a seventeenth-century reference to arms used by the Northern Tepehuan. Arrows were mentioned, and they must have been carried in a quiver, which probably was an analogue of the modern quiver fashioned from the skin of a gray fox (Pennington 1969:193–194).

The indispensable baskets (square or round, of the single- or double-twilled variety) and mats are fashioned from fibers obtained from *Yucca decipiens, Nolina matapensis, N. durangensis, Dasylirion simplex*, and *D. wheeleri*. Maguey plants are important as a source of istle utilized in the manufacture of cordage. *Dasylirion simplex, Nolina matapensis*, and *N. durangensis* provide fibers used in the manufacture of simple twilled hats. Crude sandals may be fashioned from large leaves of *Yucca decipiens*. That basketry is relatively ancient among the Northern Tepehuan is attested to by the remains of plaited material in the Río Zape site of northern Durango. There is a seventeenth-century reference to the use of mats among the Northern Tepehuan. Antiquity of istle as a source of cordage is demonstrated by fragments of agave leaves in the Río Zape site (Pennington 1969:195–200).

Canteens, dippers, and bowls are manufactured from fruits of at least six cultivated varieties of the bottle gourd. The indispensable pottery is manufactured from

U. of Pa., U. Mus., Philadelphia: 50090.

Fig. 3. The interior of a house with woman grinding corn into a wooden bowl using stone mano and metate. Several ceramic ollas are on the raised shelf and the cooking platform is to the left. The platform, usually in an end room of the dwelling, is built of mud mortar, measuring 4 by 5 feet on top and about 2.5 feet high (Pennington 1969:223–225). Photograph by J. Alden Mason, Baborigame, Chihuahua, 1951.

clay obtained from arroyos. A coiling technique is employed in making ollas, which range in size from very small containers used in storing seeds to large containers used for fermenting tiswin. Cooking pots are commonly supported by several stones or sticks of wood. Some Tepehuan habitations include a cooking platform fashioned from stone and mud mortar (fig. 3). Small pieces of bone are used in cleaning the comal. Broken pottery is mended with glue prepared from roots of *Nolina matapensis*. Legless stone metates are utilized for grinding corn. A stone of the proper dimension is obtained from a creek bed for use as a mano. Wood from *Arbutus arizonica, A. xalapensis, A. glandulosa, Salix* sp., and a species of *Thevetia* serves in the fashioning of wooden household articles such as headrests, benches, bowls, and stools. That pottery is an ancient item among the Northern Tepehuan is clear, in view of the recovery of sherds from the Río Zape site in northern Durango. Crude metates and manos were also found in that site (Pennington 1969:211–221).

Clothing and Adornment

Tepehuan men commonly wear ready-made cotton shirts and jeans, sandals of leather or rubber, a headband of cotton cloth, a woolen or cotton sash (fig. 4), and frequently a bandana about the neck. Breechclouts fash-

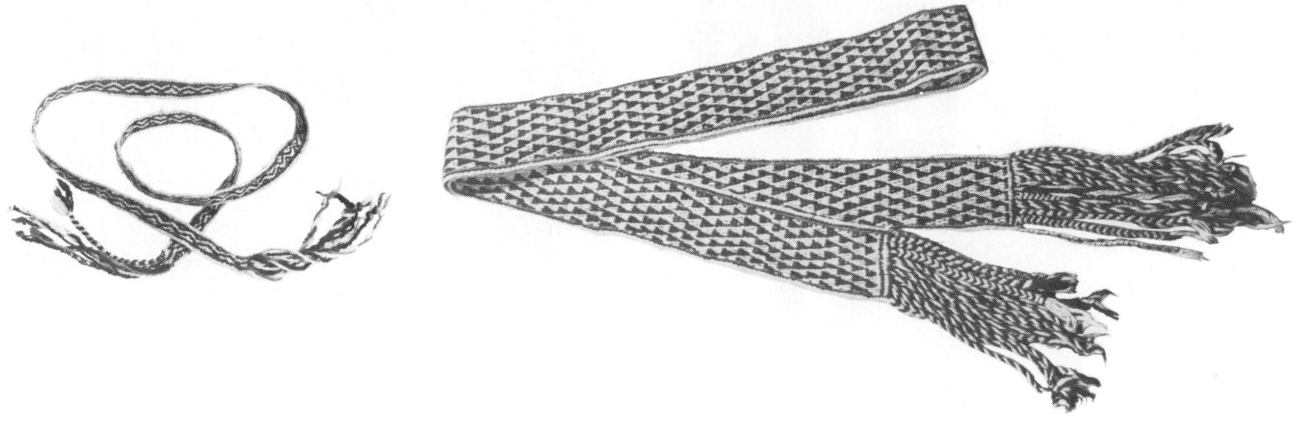

left, Field Mus., Chicago; right, Amer. Mus. of Nat. Hist., New York: 65/1089.

Fig. 4. Textiles. left, Wool headband. right, Wool belt with warp patterned geometric designs in dark brown and off-white with some red in border. Fringes are twisted and braided. Length of right 248 cm, including fringe, left same scale. Both collected by Carl Lumholtz at Baborigame, Chihuahua, in 1893.

ioned from cotton cloth are sometimes worn in remote areas. The shirts are commonly made by the women. Male children usually dress as adult males, although in remote areas small boys wear a cotton breechclout or go nude except in winter. Woolen blankets (fig. 5) fashioned by the women are worn by men in extremely cold weather, being wrapped about the body. These blankets, which may be decorated with a few black, brown, or yellow stripes of varying width, are woven upon a horizontal loom. Adult women commonly wear a bandana about the head, a cotton blouse, and a short cotton skirt. Occasionally, women wear a woolen or cotton sash or belt. Very old women wear a one-piece dress with several narrow ruffles at the bottom of the skirt. Blankets are rarely worn by women during cold weather. Rather, they wear an additional skirt or blouse. Sandals are infrequently worn by women, who prefer the cheap shoes that may be obtained from traders or from stores maintained by Mestizos in southern Chihuahua. Girls dress as do their mothers (Pennington 1969:200–202).

Saponaceous characteristics of plants serve in preparing substances utilized in washing blankets, clothes, and hair (fig. 6). Hair is generally worn by men in the form of a page boy, and in the form of braids by women and girls. Necklaces fashioned from red seeds of *Erythrina glabelliformis*, grass seeds, and shells traded in from the west are worn by the women. These articles are strung upon pita fiber cordage (Pennington 1969:206–208).

The antiquity of the loom and of the use of pita and cotton fibers among the Northern Tepehuan is clearly established. The Jesuit report of 1596 referred to cotton clothing worn by Tepehuan of northern Durango, and the seventeenth-century account by Pérez de Ribas explicitly mentions cotton and pita fiber. These fibers were woven into mantas and aprons or skirts on a loom (Pennington 1969:205).

Structures

Upland Tepehuan dwellings are constructed of timber, whereas canyon dwellings are built with stone held together by mud mortar. Rush and grass huts covered

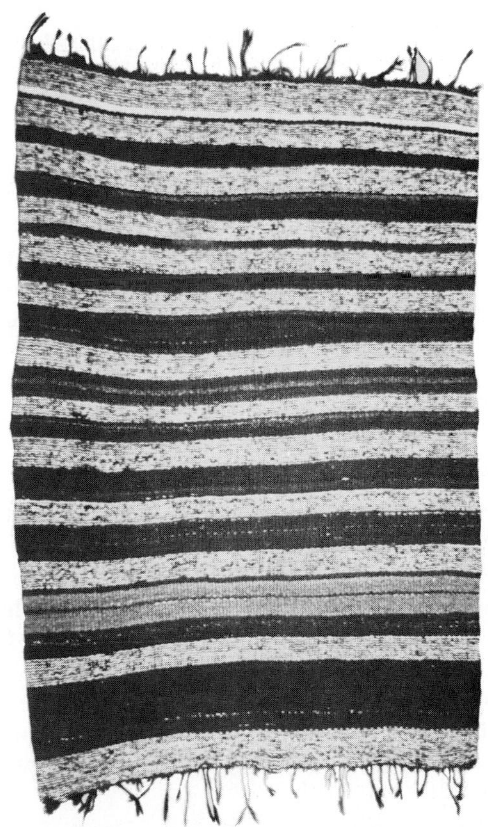

San Diego Mus. of Man, Calif.: 1980-6-21.

Fig. 5. Blanket of handspun, undyed wool, with white, dark brown, and mixed stripes. Women weave these heavy blankets on the horizontal loom. Made about 1971, 122 by 175 cm, collected by Edmond Faubert near Baborigame, Chihuahua.

Fig. 6. A lye hopper, an inverted pyramidal lattice frame of *torote* stalks lined with grass and supported by 4 posts. It contains ashes from oak logs, through which water and occasionally urine is poured and collected in a pottery bowl beneath the hopper. This liquid is boiled for a short time and then pig stomach and fat are added. The mixture is boiled for several hours, strained, and put aside to harden into soap. Photograph by Campbell W. Pennington, summer 1965.

Fig. 7. Dwellings. top, Permanent house, which includes storage crib on left, on the margin of Mesa de Milpillas in southern Chihuahua. The gable roof is covered with shingles held down with stones; in case of fire it is therefore relatively easy to remove the burning portion of the roof. Garden plots are often integrated into the dwelling complex, as here. bottom, Summer house near Llano Grande on the Mesa de Milpillas. This type of temporary dwelling, with storage room an integral part of the structure, is used when the Tepehuan guard their distant fields against stock depredations. Photographs by Campbell W. Pennington, summer 1960.

with thatch were rare in the canyons in the 1960s, but they were common there in the early twentieth century. The log structures may range in size and complexity from simple dwellings about 12 feet square, characterized by open-ended gable roofs of logs covered with shingles anchored by stones (fig. 7), to large multiroomed structures with high gabled rooms. The upland Tepehuan sometimes construct a single-room dwelling that is essentially a frame of carefully smoothed and notched logs upon which shakes are placed. Wooden structures are invariably fitted with door jambs, and doors are often characterized by intricate wooden locks (Pennington 1969:221–225).

Twentieth-century Tepehuan dwellings of Chihuahua may be considered as sophisticated analogues of structures built by Tepehuan in northern Durango in the seventeenth century. Such structures were described as being built of wood and saplings, stone and mud, branches and straw (Pennington 1969:221).

Games and Music

The most important game among the Northern Tepehuan in the 1960s was a kickball race (fig. 8), which involves the kicking of a wooden ball about a prescribed course that may be straight or circuitous in design. There are commonly two teams, each team utilizing a distinctively marked ball. Eighteenth-century Tepehuan played a rubber-ball game upon a court. Tepehuan women use a wooden hoop in a game that is played upon a straight or circuitous course; a straight stick is used to toss the hoop along the course. Women also play a stick game that involves the tossing of two sticks that have been anchored together with thongs of istle fiber or leather. This object is tossed with a long stick. Men and women play an exceedingly rough game that involves the driving of a wooden ball back and forth along a court established in an open area, there being goal lines established at either end of the playing field. A spoonlike device serves in tossing the ball back and forth. *Quince* (fig. 9) is played by either men or women. In another game of chance the knuckle bone of a deer is tossed into the air. Points are awarded according to the position of the bone after it falls to the ground. Two

U. of Pa., U. Mus., Philadelphia: left, 50097; right, 50099.

Fig. 8. A kickball game at Baborigame, Chihuahua. There are two teams in kickball, with 1–20 individuals on a team. The number of participants depends upon the importance of the occasion. Important races are also accompanied by violin music and drums (Pennington 1969:168–171). left, Musicians with violins and drum. right, Runners participating in the game. Photographs by J. Alden Mason, 1951.

stone disks are utilized by men in playing quoits (Pennington 1969:168–175).

Reed flutes, a rasping stick, drums, violins, and rattles fashioned from gourds serve in making music that is an integral part of celebrations held by the Northern Tepehuan (Pennington 1969:165–168).

Relative antiquity of a crude form of shinny, *quince*, an arrow game, a running game played by women, and a rubber-ball game is attested to by data found in an eighteenth-century vocabulary (Pennington 1969: 171,173–174). The kickball game so important in the 1960s was probably not known to aboriginal Tepehuan, in view of the fact that there are no known references to the game for Indians living east of the Sierra Madre Occidental before the eighteenth century.

Synonymy†

The name Tepehuan is from Spanish Tepehuán (pl. Tepehuanes); Tepehuano (pl. Tepehuanos) is also used (Santamaría 1974:1033). Like the name of the entirely distinct Tepehua Indians of Veracruz, Tepehuan is apparently ultimately from Nahuatl *tepetl* 'mountain'; the simplest explanation would be that it is a Spanish adaptation of Nahuatl *tepehua* 'hill or mountain owner' (for the formation see Andrews 1975:215–217, 471). Various opinions on the etymology have been summarized by Pennington (1969:3); these include a suggestion by Pimentel of a derivation from Nahuatl *tepeuani* 'conqueror', which seems to be based solely on the partial similarity of these words.

Contemporary Tepehuans have no knowledge of the origin of the Spanish name and designate themselves *ódami* 'Indian people'; this was recorded in the eighteenth century as odame 'people, nation' (Rinaldini 1743).

†This synonymy was written by Campbell W. Pennington and Ives Goddard.

Sources

Few Mexican students have given attention to the Chihuahua Tepehuan. Cerda Silva (1943), Gámiz (1948), and Basauri (1940) have written about the Tepehuan, but most attention was given to the southern remnants of this group. The existence of several thousand Tepehuan in Chihuahua was hardly recognized.

Lumholtz (1902) visited Chihuahua during the 1890s,

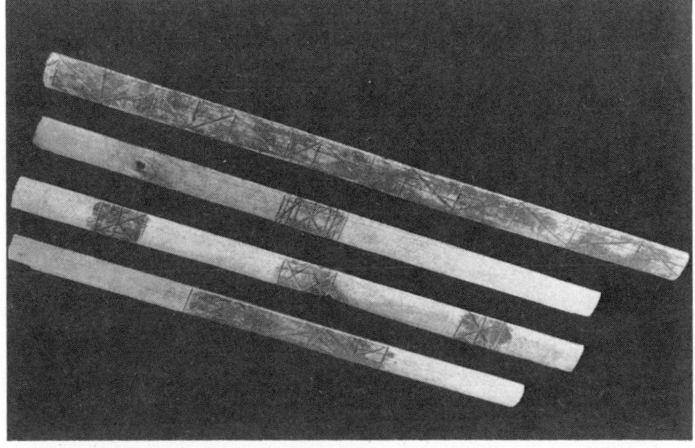

Amer. Mus. of Nat. Hist., New York: 65/1039.

Fig. 9. Cane dice, with flat sides marked with incised lines and red stains, rounded sides plain, used to determine the moves of a stone marker around holes made in a square court in a game called *quince* in local Spanish (see Pennington 1969:172–173). Length of longest, 34.0 cm; collected by Carl Lumholtz in 1892.

and his account of aborigines in the northern portion of the Sierra Madre Occidental includes a few important comments on Tepehuan material culture.

The first comprehensive ethnographic study of Northern Tepehuan was made by Pennington (1969). This contribution and short articles by Mason (1948, 1952) and Service (1969) constitute the only substantive studies of these people made in the field. Detailed data pertaining to agriculture, horticulture, food preparation, hunting, gathering, fishing, animal husbandry, ceremonies, games, medicinal plants, leather goods, fiber products, textiles, personal adornment, dwellings, and an extended comment on the question of possible influence of Tarahumara upon the Tepehuan are found in Pennington (1969).

Needed are extensive archeological investigations in southern Chihuahua. Tentative data pertaining to some aspects of ancient Tepehuan culture are available in the reports on material found in the Waterfall Cave site of southern Chihuahua (Ascher and Clune 1960; Clune 1960; Cutler 1960). Comments by Brooks et al. (1962) on material found in the Río Zape site of northern Durango are particularly important since the data are clearly related to material culture of the contemporary Chihuahua Tepehuan. In-depth sociological studies should be made before the surviving Northern Tepehuan are further merged into the Mestizo complex.

Bascom's (1965) study constitutes the sole important modern research on the Tepehuan language. Rinaldini's (1743) grammar and vocabulary are important, not only because of the details concerning grammar but also because of the wealth of ethnographic data in the vocabulary; this work was composed at Nabogame where Rinaldini served as missionary for more than 20 years (Pennington 1969:38–39).

General information pertaining to activities of Jesuits among the Northern Tepehuan is found in Anonymous (1596), Pérez de Ribas (1944), Zapata (1678), Lizasoain (1763), Tamarón y Romeral (1937), Alegre (1956–1960), Burrus (1963), Decorme (1941), Dunne (1944, 1948), and Bandelier and Bandelier (1923–1937, 2). Some data pertaining to Franciscan activities among the Tepehuan are found in Hackett (1923–1937, 2), Anonymous (1777–1825, 1778), and Villagra (1777).

Southern Periphery: West

THOMAS B. HINTON

Territory

One of the oldest controversies in American anthropology involves the southern limits of the American Southwest and the connections of this area with lands to the south in Mexico. This question, which has never been completely resolved, continues to influence and perhaps distort ideas of the true relationships among the native peoples on this part of the continent. Traditionally, for both archeology and ethnology, the Southwest has included Arizona, New Mexico, and portions of adjoining states, along with an indefinite part of northern Mexico, extending sometimes into the third tier of Mexican states. This area, termed the Greater Southwest, has been the area where Indian, Hispano-Mexican, and Anglo-American cultures have met and mixed to the point that all have been greatly modified.

The delineations of the northern regions of the Southwest, with their Puebloan, Athapaskan, and Upland Yuman configurations, are clear-cut and generally accepted. Cultural affinities of these peoples with groups to the south become obscure and confused. Should the southern tribes be included in a single cultural cotradition with the Pueblo Southwest? It would be far more in line with ethnographic fact to recognize a cultural dividing line just north of the Gila River in southern Arizona as the separation between the northern, or plateau, portion of the Southwest and the lands and peoples of southern Arizona and northwest Mexico. Geographically, this line roughly coincides in central Arizona with the northern boundaries of the Sonoran Desert ecological zone. Included in the area would be the Arizona Pimans and all the native Indian groups of northwestern Mexico except those of Baja California and the extinct coastal populations of southern Sinaloa and Nayarit. The peoples of the region stretching from the Gila River in Arizona to the Río Grande de Santiago in Jalisco emerge, when their basic patterns are examined, as a unit composed of closely related cultures distinct from those to the north and south. Other writers have recognized the distinctiveness of northwest Mexican culture. Beals (1932a) points out that the area should be studied in its own right and not solely as a corridor between the Pueblo Southwest and Meso-America. Most scholars dealing with these groups have generally treated northwest Mexico as an area sharing many features but not at all identical with the upper Southwest (Beals 1932a; Sauer 1934; Underhill 1948; J.B. Johnson 1950; Ellis 1968; Spicer 1962).

Much of the original unity within the northwest Mexican area has been obscured by centuries of Hispanic acculturation, but it becomes readily apparent when underlying features are compared. Over this entire region, all the known historical languages and all existing speech, except that of the Seri and the intrusive Apache, are varieties of Uto-Aztecan. All the Uto-Aztecan groups lived in communities composed of groups of associated rancherias (clusters of scattered dwellings), and all cultivated maize as their staple. Aboriginal social organization centered about a bilateral family and a loose community organization, while kinship terminologies, primarily bifurcate collateral with Hawaiian cousin terms, appear to have been cast in a common mold (Spicer 1964; Shimkin 1941). The matrilineal clans of the Western Pueblos and the closely settled pueblo towns common to all the Pueblos are completely absent. Substantial religious similarities appear throughout the whole area (Spicer 1964). Material culture was simple and utilitarian; lacking was the sophisticated technology and the elaborate art forms of those Mexican cultures that bordered northwest Mexico on the south. The parallels that exist both to the north and south of this area have been pointed out in abundance (Beals 1932a; Underhill 1948), but they do not obscure the evidence for far closer ties among the groups within this region itself.

The aboriginal cultures of the Mexican Northwest appear to have been very simplified versions of the basic Meso-American agricultural complex, and the closest affiliations of this area are to the south. Indeed, the only native peoples in all the Mexican Northwest whose relationships are primarily with North America are the Seri and the Yuman groups of Baja California. While the area probably represents an earlier and less complex Uto-Aztecan base the picture is complicated by the presence of sophisticated Meso-American cultures in the south, which influenced the southern group extensively. Complex Meso-American cultures were present on the coast areas west of the Sierra Madre as far north as north-central Sinaloa, and some of them spoke languages similar to those of the rancheria tribes of the Sierra—Totorame (Cora) and Tecual (Huichol) (Sauer 1934). This strong Meso-American influence is apparent in the southern Sierra Madre area among the Cora, Huichol, Tepecano, Southern Tepehuan, and the extinct Acaxee and Xixime of the Sinaloa-Durango boundary. While these southernmost groups remained rancheria dwellers with a simple technology and social organization, Central Mexican features significantly colored their lifeways. Beals (1932a) found that at contact in the southern Sierra 70 percent of known culture traits were shared with southern Mexico. The long contact with and the marginal participation of these groups in Meso-America is established by archeology as well. Slash-and-burn agriculture, rancherias affiliated with a ceremonial center, temples (if simple ones), idols, sacrifice and cannibalism, and shared ceremonial and mythological concepts point to this area as one of a Meso-American rather than North American influence. This can be stated without negating the existence of a northwest Mexican cultural unit or ignoring some ceremonial similarities of this area with the Pueblo area of the American Southwest. The Pueblo Southwest was itself subject to some of the same Meso-American influences but represents a different cultural adjustment and distinct recombination of these elements.

The northern peoples—Pima-Papago, Northern Tepehuan, Yaqui-Mayo, Ópata, Tarahumara, and Guarijío—were more removed from close central Mexican influence, and their cultures at the time of the conquest show little of late Meso-American origin.

The native peoples of this area who have survived into the mid-twentieth century are of three Uto-Aztecan subgroups: Piman, comprising the American or Gila Pima, the Papago, the Lower Pima (Pima Bajo), and the Northern and Southern Tepehuan of the Sierra Madre Occidental; Taracahitan, comprising the Cahitan Yaqui and Mayo and the Tarahumara and Guarijío; and Cora and Huichol, jointly referred to as Coric (Lamb 1964) or Corachol (Steele 1979:451). Recognized descendants of the Taracahitan Ópatas still existed in Sonora in the 1970s but were almost culturally extinct. Likewise the Tepecano, the once numerous southernmost branch of the Tepehuan, were nearly extinct culturally, but their descendants were recognized in the village of Azqueltán, Jalisco. The non–Uto-Aztecan Seri and now absent Apache complete this list. All other native tribes of mainland western Mexico north of Jalisco have long since disappeared. Among these are the coastal populations of Nayarit and southern Sinaloa and the Acaxee-Xixime of the Sinaloa-Durango border, a warlike group that may have been related to the Cahita. Each of the remaining peoples has absorbed remnants of related groups or is itself a contraction or consolidation of previous tribal units.

The continuity of the original northwest Mexico area has long been broken. The southern groups, the Cora-Huichol and Southern Tepehuan, whose lifeways in the late twentieth century belong to the modern Indian cultures of Middle America with their community *cargo* systems and elaborate religious *costumbre* are separated by hundreds of miles from the northern peoples. The northern rancheria tribes extend into the United States with the Pima-Papago, and all have been involved to some extent with North American groups, if only as subjects of Apache raids. Most have shared in the common history of the Southwest United States–Northwest Mexico borderlands, and they have traditionally been within the area of interest of students of the North American Indian. On this basis a contemporary boundary can be drawn between those groups within the orbit of North America and those within the ethnographic sphere of Middle America. This boundary, running east-west across northern Sinaloa and Durango, divides the northwest Mexican rancheria area into two subareas. Passing just to the south of the Cahita, and separating the Northern from the Southern Tepehuan, it reflects the increased Middle American influence to be found in both the aboriginal and the contemporary cultures farther south.

While there are many intriguing problems involving parallels between the Cora-Huichol peoples and the Pima-Papago and even the American Pueblo peoples, much of the evidence is sparse and ambiguous. Nonetheless, additional investigation, especially in the realm of religious practice, could yield rich results in understanding the cultural history of North America. This chapter deals with the present peoples native to what is generally considered the borderlands of the American Southwest—Pima-Papago, Northern Tepehuan, Yaqui-Mayo, Guarijío, the descendants of the Ópata, and Apache and Seri (fig. 1). The common term "Sonoran" is used to refer to the Uto-Aztecan peoples of Sonora, northern Sinaloa, and southern Arizona. Since the Tarahumara are discussed in other chapters, they will be referred to here only minimally. Likewise, the Yuman groups on the northwest frontier of the area, who have different cultural affiliations, are not included.

This discussion does not attempt to supply ethnographic material available in the tribal summaries. Indeed in the last part of the twentieth century, factors such as the historical presence of the international border, demographic changes, and economic development in the American Southwest–Mexican Northwest have far overshadowed ethnographic survivals of earlier times or continuing interactions between native groups as prime factors in the Indian life of this region.

Environment

The Sonoran Desert, Sierra Madre, and adjoining regions offer a wide variety of habitat; mountain, plateau, grassland, desert mountain, lowland desert, seacoast, and subtropical steppe are all present. However, the sedentary groups, with very few exceptions, located their

Fig. 1. Ópata and Jova territory and surrounding groups in the western Southern Periphery. For groups outside the area shown, see the Key to Tribal Territories (p. *ix*) and maps in individual chapters.

rancherias on narrow strips of land along the permanent streams where the availability of water and alluvial soils made agriculture possible. Every watercourse from the Gila River to the Río Sinaloa was utilized, and there the Indians were able to cultivate enough maize, beans, and squash (with the postconquest addition of wheat, garbanzos, and livestock) to produce fairly stable and comfortable societies. Crops were produced using diversion ditches, hand irrigation, and flood farming. While it is doubtful that the shortage of water was ever a serious problem in the days before the introduction of livestock and the construction of upriver dams, good riverbottom land was limited in some areas, such as northern and eastern Sonora. The mountain ranges and deserts that lie between the rivers were used for hunting and gathering and in later times for grazing. Only the Seri and the desert Papago, who occupied lands with few streams, were not closely tied to the rivers. However, even the most remote Papago groups were at least partially dependent on river agriculture in that they visited the river peoples to trade and to work for a part of the harvest.

The tribes of this area were not so constricted in their ecological adjustments as were the American Pueblo peoples, especially as compared with the dry-farming Western Pueblos. With superior water resources, the major groups—Yaqui, Mayo, Ópata, and Tarahumara—had populations as large or greater than that of all the Pueblos combined (J.B. Johnson 1950).

Riverine concentrations of the Indian populations greatly facilitated their conquest and missionization. In many places, the arrival of European settlers to these attractive valleys led to mixing, submersion, and eventual disappearance of the native population. Many of these same river systems are the sites of twentieth-century industrialization in the Southwest and northern Mexico. The damming of rivers, irrigation of their valleys, and the pumping of the groundwater reserves of the floodplains for additional water have resulted in a heavy growth of population and have altered the environment of the surviving Indians, so that the ramifications of this situation are apparent in every group.

The main mass of the Sierra Madre Occidental, which bounds the area to the east, is essentially an elevated plateau that breaks away on the Pacific slope in a major escarpment. The plateau and some of its outlying ranges support growths of oak and pine, but fingers of low-country vegetation extend far into the mountains along the precipitous barrancas (gorges) of the major rivers and their tributaries. It seems probable that all the historic groups that inhabited the western slopes of the Sierra Madre were basically barranca dwellers, since these narrow valleys are the only possible sites for cultivation in most areas. Rugged as these mountains are, they have never been a barrier to Indians who passed back and forth freely on foot. In the early eighteenth century, the Sierra Madre and its detached western ranges became the headquarters for bands of Apache, who followed the mountains as far south as the upper Río Mayo fanning out in their raiding expeditions. With the arrival of the Apaches, most of the sedentary Indians, Jovas and Ópatas, living in the barrancas migrated westward to the comparative safety of the mission villages in the larger valleys, such as that of the Sahuaripa. In the 1970s the population of the Sierra bounding Sonora was basically non-Indian, except for Lower Pima of the Yepachi and Maycoba areas of the Sonora-Chihuahua border, but to the south of there, the Guarijío at the headwaters of the Río Mayo and the Tarahumara and Northern Tepehuan still lived as mountain peoples.

Coasts of the Gulf of California, north of Guaymas, including the remote and almost uninhabited region left to the Seris, remained a frontier area until the mid-twentieth century. Since the 1950s there has been a rush of development radiating from the Hermosillo and Caborca areas as pump irrigation has brought mechanized agriculture and a large non-Indian population. The subsequent spread of roads, tourism, and land speculation has completely transformed the economic and cultural situation on Sonora's coastal desert.

Native Peoples

There is only an obscure picture of the premission cultures on the southwestern peripheries of the Southwest. While there is a sizable amount of documentation on the Spanish settlement of the area, there is little real ethnographic detail from contact times (fig. 2). To add to this difficulty, the archeology of the area to the south of the American-Mexican border has yet to be extensively investigated, so there is little knowledge of either the preconquest culture or any possible sequence in this region. Another complicating factor is the possible influences from the Indians of central Mexico in early colonial times that may have greatly altered the native patterns in the region. There is reason to suspect, for instance, that pinole, maize parched and ground to a powder, was the staple food there rather than the tortillas that are universal in the twentieth century (Pfefferkorn 1949). Such problems may never be solved.

While the aboriginal cultural pattern of the area south of the Papago may never be known with any detailed accuracy, one fact is immediately apparent in nearly every group within the boundaries. This is the overwhelming hispanicization that has significantly remade the cultural complexions and even influenced the physical types of these peoples. To investigate the surviving Indians of Sonora and northern Sinaloa in the 1970s was to deal with ethnic enclaves whose cultural patterns are more those of Mexican subcultures than those original to the area. These observations are less applicable to the northern, or American, portion of the area where contact was later and where mission control and later Mexican contact were much less intense. In all this vast region, only the Seris of Mexico and the Gila Pimas and Papagos of Arizona retained lifeways (until the twentieth century) that were predominantly non-European. Even these three more isolated groups were profoundly influenced by Spanish ideas and material culture. This is to say that the traditional culture of the Sonoran tribes, which developed in mission times and is only now fading, was an amalgamation of Indian and European under the direction of European agents of change, much as was that in central Mexico, with the difference that the simpler Sonoran cultures and much smaller entities involved produced a Spanish-Indian amalgamation on the northern frontiers of Mexico that was not identical with those farther south.

Changed as they are, the major tribal-linguistic entities of this area at contact still exist in the 1980s, with the exception of the detribalized Ópatas and the associated Jovas. Even the descendants of these two Indian peoples retain some degree of ethnic distinctness, although their native languages and social organizations are extinct. The tendency has been for the numerous divisions of each language group to become consolidated and become a single unit with a single name (Spicer 1962). Thus, the remnants of the Seri, Tepocas, Salineros, Guaymas, and related groups are now all Seri. The result is that instead of the several scores of tribes, subtribes, dialects, and other divisions named by the Spanish writers for this part of Mexico, there remain only five (or six, counting Ópata). While this undoubtedly represents the incorporation of remnant populations, it also suggests that many of the earlier divisions were based on only slight differences of dialect or on local geographic designation.

Pima

Speakers of Piman languages are generally divided into the Pima-Papago of the Arizona-Sonora area and the Tepehuan of the Sierra Madre of southern Chihuahua, southern Durango, and Nayarit. The Pima-Papago groups are again divided into the Upper Pima of Arizona and northwestern Sonora and the Lower Pima of central and southeastern Sonora, each with subdivisions (Sauer 1934). These divisions seem to be based as much on geography as dialect and can hardly be defended ethnologically.

Like other Sonoran Indians the Lower Pima were concentrated into mission settlements, and there was much mixing with Ópatas and others in the colonial missions. As with the other groups, the Pimas scattered to work in mines and on ranches. The result was much detribalization, so that in the late twentieth century it was much more difficult to find acknowledged Pima descendants, even in their former villages, than it is, for example, to encounter known descendants of the Ópatas. The few remaining enclaves of Lower Pimas appear to be nearing extinction.

The Upper Pima, who once spread from the Huachuca Mountains in southeastern Arizona to the shores of the Gulf of California and from the Gila River to the Seri coast, are now reduced to the American Pima and the Papago. Former Pima areas, the valleys of the upper Sonora, upper San Miguel, Magdalena, upper Altar in Mexico and the Santa Cruz, except at Tucson, and San Pedro in the United States, have become completely non-Indian. These peoples were driven out by the Apaches, reduced by epidemics, displaced by settlers, or assimilated. Some joined the Papagos or Gila Pimas (see "History of the Papago," this vol.). The Soba Pimas of the lower Altar River, who were estimated at 4,000 in 1700 (Sauer 1935), have survived as Caborca Papagos, of whom in 1975 there were fewer than 100.

The Pimas were never so close to the Spaniards as

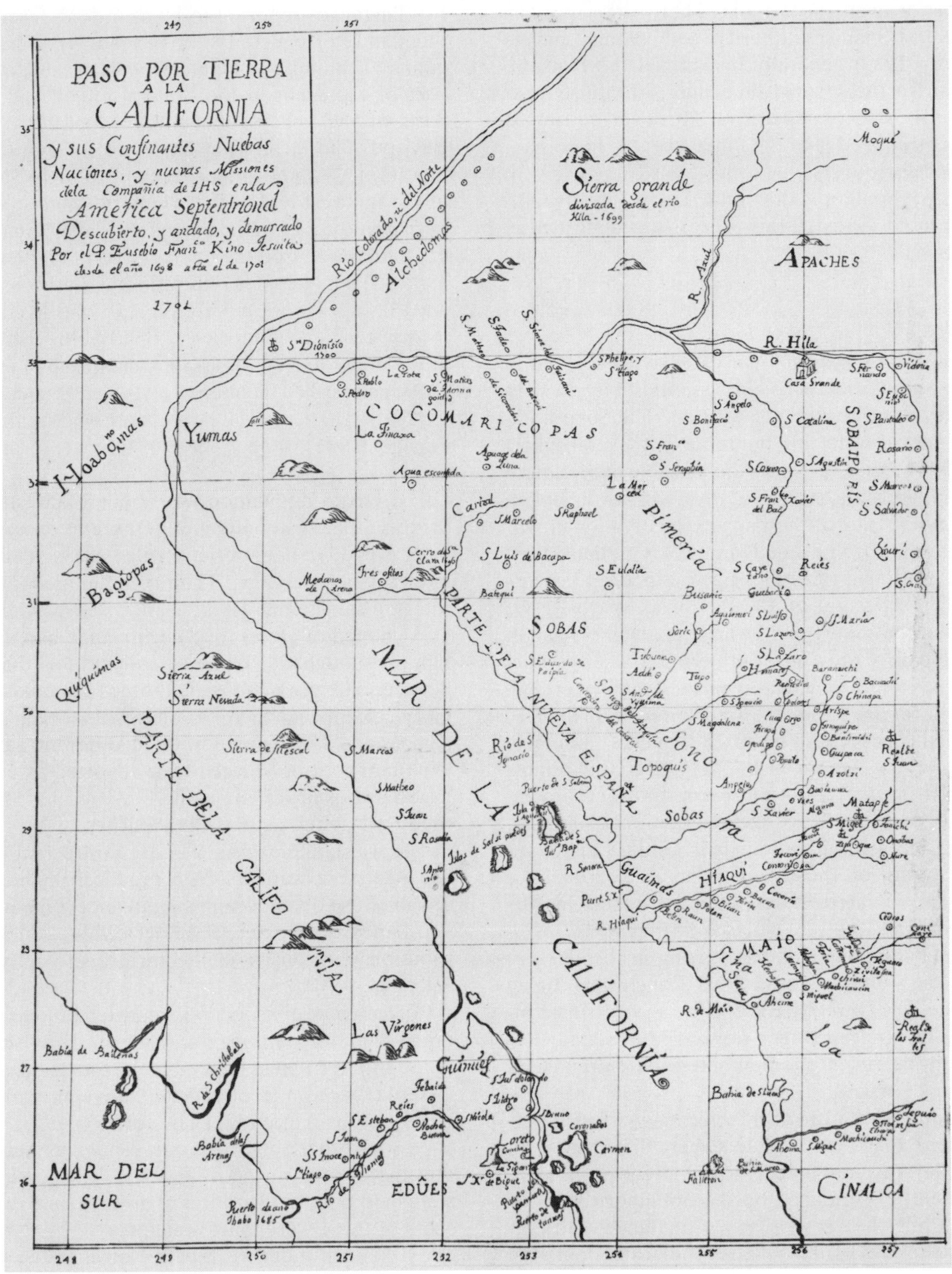

Archives des Jésuites de la Province de France, Chantilly.

Fig. 2. The best surviving copy of several lost manuscript maps of northwestern New Spain prepared in 1701 by the Jesuit Eusebio Francisco Kino (1645–1711), who had served in the region since 1683 as missionary, explorer, and cartographer. The following tribes are clearly marked: Moqui (Hopi), Apaches, Alchedomas (Halchidhoma), Yumas (Quechan), Hoabonomas (perhaps Cocopa), Bagiopas (perhaps Cocopa), Cocomaricopas (Maricopa), Sobaiporis (Sobaipuri Pima), Sobas (Soba Pima), Topoquis (Tepoca Seri), Guaimas (Guaymas Seri), Hiaqui (Yaqui), Maio (Mayo), and 3 in Baja California. Many missions and Indian towns are located. The 8 sacred towns of the Yaqui are mapped, but with their names displaced (in copying?); they are, in modern spellings: Belem (here Belen, dot north of the river), Huirivis (name omitted; dot labeled Raun), Rahum (dot labeled Potan), Potam (dot labeled Bican), Vicam (dot labeled Torin), Torim (dot labeled Bacun), Bacum (dot labeled Cocorin), Cocorit (dot unlabeled). For discussion, and reproduction of a modern copy of this original, see Burrus 1965:46–50, pl. XI. Photograph from slightly retouched Xerox copy of the original manuscript, 44 by 33 cm.

the Ópatas or even the Yaquis. There were sporadic revolts against Spanish authority, and colonial sources (Pfefferkorn 1949) generally disparaged the Pimas in comparison to the Opatas—meaning, of course, that the former were less cooperative. However, resistance was never prolonged, and the Pimas seem to have readily become Mexicanized and to have easily merged with the Mestizo population that grew up in this area. In lowland Sonora, at least, this process was almost complete by the 1980s.

Papago

Since the Arizona Papagos are extensively covered in the tribal summaries, this discussion is largely concerned with those residing in Mexico. The Sonora Papagos are not a distinct unit but represent several dialect groups. All the dialects, with the possible exception of that of the Caborca area, are identical with those spoken on the southern part of the Papago Reservation in Arizona. There has been a steady migration to the United States, where Papago families have joined settlements of their own subgroup on the Arizona Papago Reservation. This continuing northward movement began in the middle part of the nineteenth century when conflict arose with Sonoran ranchers over land and water. Minor clashes (in 1840 and the El Plomo War in 1898) expedited the process. The migration was extremely easy because the American Papago differed in almost no respect from the Sonoran group, and for many individuals even in the 1970s the international boundary is an artificial line separating their families and communities. Many of those remaining in Sonora have worked in the United States, attended school in Arizona, and speak English (Nolasco Armas 1964).

McGee (1898) found Papagos living in the 1890s at points as far south as Costa Rica Ranch near Bahía Kino in the Seri country. Except for an occasional individual, they are no longer present in this area. Relations with the Seri are remembered, but normal contact no longer occurs.

A combination of historical factors has served to perpetuate the Papago as a viable society. Their location vis-à-vis the Apaches preserved them from the front line of assault experienced by the Sobaipuri Pimas of Arizona, while the very presence of the Apaches inhibited the spread of the Spanish-Mexican population into their northern area. The desert environment was attractive only to a few cattlemen and miners. Finally, the international border and the large Arizona Papago Reservation have served as refuge for those pushed out of other territories.

Ópata

The Ópata (ˈōpäˌtä) of central and eastern Sonora spoke two languages reported to be as little different as Castilian and Portuguese (Nentvig 1980:54).* One was Teguima (Tehuima), or Ópata proper, of the northeastern part of the area, in the Sonora Valley and northern parts of the valleys of the Río Moctezuma and Río Bavispe. The second was Eudeve (Eudebe, Heve, Hehue, Egue, Aibine), the speech of the Río San Miguel in the far west and of the southern Ópatas, who lived from Mátape east to the Sahuaripa Valley. Spanish writers sometimes used the names of communities as tribal names. Thus, peoples referred to as Batucos, Sonoras, and Bavispes were merely Ópatas who lived in those towns or valleys. The Jova (ˈhōˌvä) of the Sierra Madre are usually referred to as a third subgroup of the Ópata. The Ópatas called themselves joyl-ra-ua (Bandelier 1890–1892, 1:57). The word Ópata corresponds to their Pima-Papago name *ʔó·badi*, but its ultimate origin is unknown.

The Ópata population was about 20,000 at contact. Sauer's (1935) estimate of 60,000 seems excessive. The Ópatas lived in narrow but fertile valleys, well watered by permanent streams. Their communities (at first, associated rancherias; later, mission towns) were guided by a council of elders, and each village had a war captain. Although the types of cooperation that existed between villages in aboriginal times are unknown, it is fairly certain that there was never an Ópata tribal organization. The communities of different valleys and even neighboring villages were reported as having engaged in hostilities (Bandelier 1890–1892, 1). In later times, all united against the Apaches.

The war complex was well developed. All able-bodied men were warriors. War practices included attack at dawn, use of a bow and a light lance, taking of scalps and hands as trophies, a victory celebration, total distribution of spoils, and the torture of captives (J.B. Johnson 1950).

Ceremonial sponsorship is reported among the Ópatas as a major pattern, occurring in many social contexts. In later times, the compadrazgo, associated with Catholic baptism, replaced the native custom and was itself greatly elaborated (J.B. Johnson 1950).

As with other Sonoran groups, shamans were present and there were no native priests. Village ceremonies were held for rain, war, rites of passage, and recreation. Most of these were quickly suppressed by the missionaries. Several modified Ópata dances lasted until late into the nineteenth century. The *daguimaca* (a gift exchange between peoples of different villages), the mariachi (called an obscene dance by mission priests), and the *taguaro* (involving the ceremonial shooting of a fig-

*No accurate analysis of the sound system of Ópata is available and the language is now extinct. The words *daguimaca* and *taguaro* appearing in the description of Ópata culture are Spanish spellings of unidentified Indian words; the former is given as Daui-Namaca by Bandelier (1890–1892, 1:68).

ure placed on a pole) are the best known of these. The *taguaro* was still held during Easter Week in the San Miguel valley in the 1970s.

The Ópata towns were established between 1628 and 1650 by missionaries, who organized the local rancherias into small Spanish-type communities, as they had done earlier among the Mayo, Yaqui, and Pima. These settlements were organized after the Spanish town plan, with civil and religious officials under the direction of the priests. Forms of this organization lasted until 1858, when the Indian communities were abolished by the reform laws of the Mexican Republic. The old Ópata villages of mission days number about 40, and many still existed in 1970. Most of the descendants of the Ópata still live in these communities, where certain families are considered as Indian, but are culturally hardly distinguishable from non-Indians. The mission towns of Cucurpe, Tuape, and Opodepe were on the Río San Miguel. On the Río Sonora, Ópata towns were Chinipas, Arispe, Sinoquipe, Banamichi, Huepac, Aconchi, Babiacora, and Masocahui. On the Moctezuma branch of the Río Yaqui were Nacozari, Cumpas, Oposura (now Moctezuma), Batuc and Tepupa (both relocated because of the El Novillo Reservoir), Mátape, Soyopa, Rebeico, and Tónichi. The Ópata mission towns on the Río Bavispe were Huasabas, Oputo, Bavispe, Bacerac, Huachinera, with Bacadehuachi and Nácori Chico in the foothills of the Sierra Madre. In the Sahuaripa Valley were Sahuaripa, Santo Tomas (Jova), Pónida (Jova), and Arivechi. Other former Ópata mission towns—Bacanora, Mazatán, Nácori, and Pueblo de Alamos—were all located east of Hermosillo on minor streams. All these Sonoran towns contained a predominantly Mestizo population in the 1970s.

Some early writers have reported "towns" for the aboriginal Ópatas (Sauer 1934), but most speak of large rancherias. Rancherias would be more consistent with what is known of the area, and it is probable that the "towns" were a number of large rancheria settlements in one area; however, this has not been resolved.

From the beginning, the Ópatas impressed all comers by being eager converts to Christianity and enthusiastic followers of Spanish patterns. The Spaniards considered them of all the Sonoran Indians as model converts, industrious workers, and loyal and brave soldiers. The Ópatas fully reciprocated this esteem, and the two groups merged. The Indians, always known as formidable fighters, were quickly recruited as allies against the Apaches, who by the end of the seventeenth century had become a threat to both groups. The Ópatas likewise turned to the Spaniards for protection. Many villages had an Indian militia under a native war captain that was called on to pursue and fight the Apache raiders who became Sonora's major problem in the eighteenth and nineteenth centuries. Mutual dependence for safety led to deep involvement of the Ópatas in the Spanish establishment and accelerated the progress of acculturation.

However, in the nineteenth century, in the early years of the Republic, some Ópata towns were involved in military action against constituted authority. The first involvement occurred in 1820–1825, led by the Dorame brothers, who were war captains at Bacerac. Alleging mistreatment, they led the Ópata militias of several towns in two short-lived revolts, ending in a major battle with Mexican troops at Tónichi (Villa 1951). Ópata troops under Dolores Gutiérrez joined the Yaqui Juan Banderas in the 1830s to fight against the Sonoran government, believing that the Ópata would become a part of an Indian government in Sonora. Again, in the 1860s the Ópata general, Refugio Tánori, with his army supported the French-backed royalists and was defeated at Mátape by Mexican troops (also largely Ópata). Tánori was executed. After this time, Ópata troops no longer fought as units (Villa 1951).

The nineteenth century saw the demise of the Ópata culture and the assimilation of the group. The language gave way to Spanish sometime after 1850. Bandelier (1890–1892, 1) related how, at the time of his visit in 1887, there were hardly 30 Ópata-speaking individuals on the upper Río Yaqui. Hrdlička (1904) in 1902 encountered Ópata speakers only near Tuape in the San Miguel valley, where, surprisingly, he found a small community of Ópatas still using the language. By 1955 Owen (1959) could find no trace of this group and was able to discover only a few words remembered by the people in the Tuape area. Probably the last speakers of Ópata died in the 1940s. Throughout Sonora, their descendants relate how their grandparents were ashamed to speak the language lest they be considered ignorant, backward Indians.

In 1955 Hinton (1959) found a few villages in Sonora with a recognizable Ópata population, but these people had few cultural features to distinguish them from their non-Indian neighbors. Tepupa was the largest of these. Before inundation by El Novillo Reservoir, its people were resettled in Hermosillo and near Ures. Other towns have a number of Ópata families, usually the poorest people, who tend to live in jacales (wattle-and-daub structures) on the outskirts of towns or on ranches. These families differ from the poor Mestizos with whom they tend to identify. These families are generally called *inditos*, the diminutive of the Spanish word for 'Indian', by their neighbors, but they dislike the term. There is a tendency for such families to intermarry with other *inditos* from the local village or other communities (Owen 1959; Hinton 1959). It is impossible to give any realistic estimates of Ópata population, since assimilation has gone so far. Hinton estimated about 4,000 *inditos* in 1955 and about 500 nearly pure Ópatas. Both groups are diminishing, the first by continued assimilation and the others by the passing of the older generation.

Fig. 3. Leaders of the Ópata *fariseo* society repairing the church prior to the Easter week celebrations. Photograph by Roger C. Owen in north-central Sonora, 1956.

Fig. 4. Ópata *fariseo* society members going from house to house during Easter week soliciting food and drink. Man on the mule holds the Judas figures; in front of him is a masked *fariseo*. Some members carry branches used as switches, and one man is playing a guitar. Photograph by Roger C. Owen in north-central Sonora, 1956.

Modern Ópata descendants retain few memories of their former Indian culture. The social organization is totally contemporary Mexican, and earlier forms are not even known by the people. In a few villages, elderly people keep the village documents from past times. The retention of Indian identity seems tied in with knowledge of traditional folk Catholic forms, especially the Easter ceremony (figs. 3–5; "Kachinas and Masking," fig. 11, this vol.). The elderly *inditos* are generally considered the knowledgeable ones on these aspects of life and are deferred to and take major responsibility in these matters. However, the Easter ceremony is actively discouraged by some of the clergy, leading to its demise in many places.

Jova

The Jova (Joba, Hoba, Hova, Ova) at Spanish contact were located in the extremely rugged portion of the Sierra Madre Occidental on the Aros (Papiogochi) branch of the upper Río Yaqui. This area lies between the Ópata proper and the northernmost Tarahumara, and there is a strong suggestion that the Jova may have been an intermediate people. One eighteenth-century source (Nentvig 1980:54) reports that they originally spoke an entirely separate language that was replaced by Ópata in the eighteenth century; however, all other references speak of Jova as a dialect of Ópata, and there is little else to support the idea of a distinct language. They were described as rude mountain dwellers, whose barranca gardens were supplemented by hunting and gathering and who had a reputation for being brave and hardy warriors against the Apache.

Jova missions in the Sierra were located at Setachi, Nátora, and Teópari. The first two were abandoned because of the Apache; and the Indians moved to Santo Tomás, Pónida, Rebeico, and elsewhere to join the Ópata. In 1955 a few dozen admitted descendants of the Jova could be found in the Valley of Sahuaripa, especially at Pónida. They are identical to the Ópata and, like the Ópata, strongly mestizoized (Hinton 1959).

Yaqui and Mayo

The Yaqui and Mayo occupied all the rivers and their tributaries from the borders of Culiacán north to Río Yaqui and from the Sierra de Tarahumara to the coast of the Gulf of California. Where there were many Cahitan-speaking groups aboriginally, there were in the twentieth-century only the Yaqui and the Mayo, with the Mayo now encompassing the descendants of many earlier tribes. These foothill and lowland peoples shared a common culture and still exhibited in the 1970s similar

Mus. of the Amer. Ind., Heye Foundation, New York: top left, 20/5213; top right, 20/5184; bottom, U. of Ariz., Ariz. State Mus., Tucson: E-2346.

Fig. 5. Ópata *fariseo* equipment. top, Masks, carved from balsa wood and painted, represent traditional characters (Johnson 1950:41)—humans, animals, and monsters. Men wear them during Easter week festivities and then give them away to young boys or keep them to use again. bottom, Wooden ratchet, used to call people to church Wednesday through Saturday of Easter week, the period when bells are not used. During the year it is stored in the church with the drum and other items of the *fariseo* society. top right, Length 23.0 cm, rest same scale; top collected by Jean B. Johnson at Tónichi, Sonora, 1940; bottom, collected at Tuape, Sonora, 1947.

cultural traits. They have become the best known of the modern Sonoran Indians as a result of the extensive ethnographic literature on them.

The Yaquis and Mayos, whose numbers are twice those of all the other Indian groups of the Sonoran Desert region, share with the Ópatas and Pimas much of the traditional Sonoran Indian culture that developed under mission influences.

Guarijío

The Guarijío (Varojío, Warihio, Huaraijía, Hio, Hia) are located in the canyons and mountains of the upper Río Mayo and the Chínipas branch of the Río El Fuerte. Their rancherias are dispersed from Macoyahui and San Bernardo in Sonora as far as the regions of La Trompa, Arechuybo, Loreto, and San Augustín in Chihuahua. Total population of the group was estimated at about 1,600 in 1936 (Gentry 1963).Those in the lower country in Sonora were much acculturated in the 1970s and appeared to be losing their identity; upriver they remained very distinct.

The Guarijío are one of the least known of north Mexican tribes. They had been thought extinct until rediscovered by Sauer in 1931. Gentry (1963), a botanist, worked in the area in the 1930s and produced a short ethnography of the group, the only real body of information on the tribe. Some writers have been inclined to classify the Guarijío as a subgroup of the Tarahumara (Sauer 1934; Passin 1944), while others (Gentry 1963; Kroeber 1934) have regarded them as separate.† Historically the Guarijío have been removed from the main body of the Tarahumara, being associated more with the extinct Chínipas, Témoris, and Guazapares, who were probably their close relatives.

The Guarijío were proselytized in the seventeenth century, being gathered into missions at Guadelupe, Loreto, and Santa Ana, where they came to share many of the features of Spanish colonial Indian culture while retaining their language and the basic patterns of their aboriginal lifeways. The Guarijío never became cooperative Christians. They engaged in revolts and returned to the Sierra when force was removed (Pérez de Ribas 1645).

The Guarijío lead much the same solitary lives as do the Tarahumara. Poor subsistence cultivators, gatherers of wild plants, and sometime ranch workers, they manage to survive on few resources. Guarijío households and rancherias are linked by *tuwúri* gatherings—fiestas held several times a year following the agricultural cycle (and cognate with the *tutubúri* ceremonies of the Tarahumara). The *tuwúri* fiestas are combined social and religious gatherings and are presided over by a *turélo* 'singer' (or seleme). There are four overlapping territories in the Guarijío country based on the attendance at *tuwúri* fiestas by the various rancherias (Gentry 1963). Such informal areas of interaction and contact may have been the basis of the pre-Columbian community in this part of the Sierra Madre Occidental.

Guarijío material culture is similar to that of their neighbors (Mayo, Tarahumara, Lower Pima) with the manufacture of coil and scrape pottery; the twilling of baskets, mats, and hats; and the weaving of a few woolen blankets (fig. 6) and sashes. Dress in the 1970s was much like that of the rural Mestizos although Gentry (1963) reported the use of loincloths and long hair by the men into the 1930s.

Extinct Groups of the Foothills and Barrancas

The Spaniards found the western parts of the Sierra and the barrancas of Durango and Sinaloa west of the Tepehuan occupied by two closely related tribes, the Acaxee and the Xixime. These peoples lived in scattered rancherias and engaged in endemic warfare with frequent cannibalism. Their languages are unknown, but they may have spoken a variety of Cahita (Spicer 1962). They appear to have been influenced by the fully Meso-

†The phonemes of the Guarijío language are: (voiceless stops and affricate) *p, t, č, k*; (voiced continuants) *β, r, γ*; (voiceless fricative) *s*; (nasals) *m, n*; (liquid) *l*; (semivowels) *w, y*; (glottals) *h, ʔ*; (vowels) *i, e, a, o, u*; (stress) v́. Information on Guarijío phonology and transcriptions of Guarijío words were provided by Wick R. Miller (communication to editors 1981).

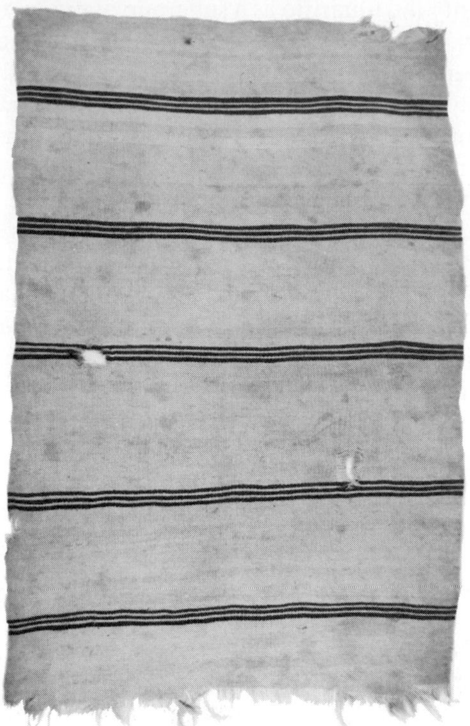

U. of Ariz., Ariz. State Mus., Tucson: 75-7-2.
Fig. 6. Guarijío blanket of handspun, undyed white and brown wool in plain tapestry weave, made in 1930s by Guadalupe Buitema of Babicora, Sonora. Size 127.0 cm by 185.4 cm. Collected by Edmond Faubert in 1975.

American cultures of the coast to the west (Beals 1933). These peoples did not survive the conquest. In the twentieth century the area is apparently totally Mestizo.

North of the Acaxee on the Mayo and Fuerte rivers were several small tribes whose affiliations are likewise obscure. Some of these were most certainly Cahita and their descendents are numbered among the Mayo. These were the Tepahue, Macoyahui, Baciroa, Conicari, and Tehueco. East of here in the uplands several Tarahumaran groups—Guazapar, Témori, Chínipas, and Tubar—occupied the areas around the present towns of these same names. The Chínipas were reported by the early missionaries to have been more populous and better agriculturists than the others. They were relocated in lowland Sinaloa in 1632 after a combined attack of the Guarijío, Témori, and Guazapar destroyed their missions and drove the Spaniards from the area for several years. The Témori and Guazapar likewise disappeared in early mission times, their remnants becoming mestizoized or absorbed by the Guarijío and Tarahumara. The Tubar, another small tribe with a Tarahumaran language, survived until the 1890s when Lumholtz (1902) encountered the last few speakers of the language, near Morelos, Chihuahua. The Huite and Zoe, two other small groups bordering the Tubar to the west and south, have left only their names; their lifeways and languages are unknown.

The coastal estuaries and swamps of northern Sinaloa were the territory of the Guasave, who are reported as living by fishing and gathering (Pérez de Ribas 1645). The Guasave language, which had four dialects, was apparently a variety of Cahita, like the other languages of northern Sinaloa. The Guasave disappeared into the colonial missions; their descendents probably are represented among the Mayo.

Seri and Apache

The Seris have been surrounded by the Uto-Aztecan agriculturists of Sonora for many centuries. As a group that probably had its origins in Baja California, its whole cultural profile is alien to the mainland of northwestern Mexico, and Seri history and acculturation have been unique. While a definitive study of the Seris has yet to appear, the group is becoming fairly well known through numerous minor works. In 1975 this viable society consisted of 415 people.

The entrance of Apache raiding parties into northern Sonora occurred no later than 1680 (Goodwin 1942). The Jocome and Jano referred to in still earlier accounts were absorbed or replaced by the Apache, if indeed they were not Athapaskan themselves. Both the Western Apaches and the Chiricahuas ranged over Sonora, and their raids were experienced by all sedentary groups of northern Mexico, with the possible exception of the Mayo. The effects of long periods of warfare and ever-present fear in this area are difficult to overestimate.

The Apaches changed the ethnic map of southwestern United States and northern Mexico, having an impact second only to the coming of the Europeans. The northward expansion of Spanish-Mexican civilization was checked by the enmity of the Apaches. The agricultural groups of this area, particularly the Pima and Ópata, bore the brunt of their incursions. The eastern Pimas of the San Pedro–Huachuca area and the Santa Cruz River valley in Arizona and the exposed areas in northern Sonora retreated westward as their societies disintegrated under Apache pressure. The Gila Pimas concentrated themselves into larger settlements, as did the Papagos in the desert. The Ópatas in their rich valleys came under early attack by the northern raiders and existed for 200 years under constant alert. The Jovas abandoned their Sierra Madre homes in the eighteenth century and joined the Ópatas. Ópatas, Pimas, Spaniards, and Mexicans united to hold the Apaches in check, greatly increasing their interdependence.

Apache raids were a problem through much of this area until the final surrender of the Chiricahuas in 1886, and they are by no means forgotten, being the subject of endless tales in nearly every village and ranch in Sonora.

In these centuries of hostile contact, considerable Mexican and Sonoran Indian influence crept into Apache culture, something that is often ignored by those attributing Apache borrowings largely to the Pueblo groups. Not only were hundreds of Mexican, Ópata, and Pima children carried away to be raised as Apaches, but also at times during these centuries Apaches as individuals and small groups made their way to the Mexican settlements and attached themselves at the encouragement of the Spanish and Mexican military, who gave them rations and used them as scouts to pursue enemy Apaches. Such Apache groups were, at times, to be found at Tucson and Tubac in Arizona, at Fronteras and Santa Cruz in Sonora, and near Janos in Chihuahua. These *Apaches mansos* 'tame Apaches' apparently returned to the mountains at will. Because of their wide distribution, they were probably not a separate band but stragglers or outlaws from the Chiricahua and Western Apache peoples. Some *Apaches mansos* were assimilated by both the Mexican and Papago populations.

Mexican contact was responsible for certain elements in Apache religion, folktales, and much of Apache dress, including the long skirts of the late nineteenth century and modern times. The tiswin, or tulapai (corn beer) used extensively by the Apache is identical with a beverage produced in northern Mexico. Many Apaches once spoke Spanish and knew Sonora as well as they did their own country (Goodwin 1942). Some Apache war practices, such as apprenticeship of warriors, recall the Ópata.

With the removal of the Apaches to reservations in the United States, their contacts with Mexico ceased. A handful of Chiricahua Apaches (20 to 30) remained in the Sierra Madre in the upper Bavispe area of Sonora until the 1930s. These last holdouts remained hostile to the Mexicans and were gradually exterminated. An Apache known as Juan or Big Foot, purported to be their leader, was killed with several of his followers in the early 1930s by a posse of ranchers from the surrounding area, and at this time two small children were taken captive. No Apaches have been reported in the Sierra Madre for many years.

Traditional Culture

Similar lifeways developed among the Yaquis, Mayos, Lower Pimas, and Ópatas as the result of their Spanish acculturation. In this complex, the outlying Papagos were marginal participants and like the Gila Pimas borrowed many Spanish material items (horses, cattle, wheat, and the Spanish plow), while remaining largely independent. The Apaches and Seris at the northern and western margins preyed upon the hispanicized groups, but these two peoples never became a permanent part of the Spanish system. The Ópatas, Pimas, Yaquis, Mayos, and Guarijíos—christianized, hispanicized, and tied economically and politically to Spanish-Mexican institutions—ultimately became peasantlike Mexican Indians, while the Papagos, Gila Pimas, Seris, and Apaches remained independent tribal peoples.

The hispanicized culture that replaced the aboriginal in the generations after the conquest has survived in modified form among most Sonoran Indians. In colonial days, the mission communities were given land grants and allowed to select village officials. This traditional organization was swept away in most areas by the political events of the nineteenth century. Only the Yaquis retain a modified version in their home villages (Spicer 1962). Elsewhere, Indian political forms are nonexistent. With the breakdown of the mission towns as strictly Indian villages, the Indians have tended to live on the outskirts of rural towns and on ranches. In the 1970s many resided in the growing cities of coastal Sonora. The Yaqui-Mayos often settle together to form "Yaqui" settlements, as at Hermosillo, Guaymas, Ciudad Obregón, Phoenix, and Tucson.

Most Sonoran Indians have been bilingual for generations, although some monolinguals remain among the Yaqui-Mayos. Kinship forms vary, all being more or less Mexicanized, except, of course, for the Seri, who are not included in this discussion.

Subsistence agriculture, supplemented by outside wage labor, has been the economic base for centuries. To work for pay is an old pattern there, probably going back to pre-Spanish days when poverty-stricken groups from the desert, such as the Papago and possibly even the Seri, paid annual visits to the cultivated valleys to assist and to share in the harvest. This pattern continued until 1910 in northern Sonora. Since mission times, Indians have labored in the mines, on ranches, on the railroads, and as house servants and have served in the army. Colonial days saw Sonoran Indians in the great mines of Parral, Chihuahua, and Nacozari, Sonora, and elsewhere. Many Yaquis, Ópatas, and later Papagos specialized in mining. Many hundreds of Sonoran Indians took part in the California gold rush. Since 1880, Sonoran Indians, especially the Yaquis, have worked all over the western United States and Mexico. Outside work has thrown many Indians into the general population, both in Mexico and the United States, and has been a strong factor in their acculturation. Wage work is of continuing importance everywhere there as rural independence fades and the urban areas develop.

Material culture is consistent with that of northern Mexico's rural poor. A traditional dwelling for Indians is the wattle-and-daub jacal (hut) with the brush ramada (fig. 7), with a shift toward the Mexican adobe as Indian status is forgotten or income improves (Hrdlička 1904; Hinton 1959). Dress and diet differ little from that of poorer non-Indians. Only a few traces of native forms remain, such as the sandals worn by some Pimas, Yaquis, and Mayos. Some Ópatas still wear teguas, crude moccasins, long used in eastern Sonora. A few wild foods, especially cactus fruits, are gathered as a delicacy or, in the case of mesquite and camachile pods, as a food supplement in hard times. The weaving of palm (fig. 8) into hats and *guares* (a type of basket), once universal, is fast disappearing. Pottery, still made by Mayos, Ópatas (fig. 9), and Pimas by the coil-and-scrape method and by Papago women by paddle-and-anvil, is likewise declining rapidly.

Religious patterns are varieties of folk Catholicism, which have developed since mission days. Aboriginal elements were incorporated to some degree, but it is often difficult to recognize them. The aboriginal ceremonial life in this area centered about the agricultural cycle, rites of passage, and war ceremonies (J. B. Johnson 1950; Spicer 1962). These were forcibly displaced by a new complex of Spanish-derived ceremonies, which may have contained native elements. This complex gave rise to the traditional Indian dances of northwestern Mexico. The Holy Week observances, the masked clowns, and the European Matachine Dances are common forms. Also present is the ritual battle of the Moors and Christians. The well-known pascola and Deer Dance, which have come to be considered characteristic of the Yaqui, were once common in all these groups.

Sociocultural Situation in the 1970s

New forces are affecting the life of the southern Arizona–Sonoran Indians in ways not previously experi-

top, Smithsonian, NAA 81-5346.

Fig. 7. Structures. top, Ópata brush dwelling in Tuape, Sonora. The walls of the house and enclosure at right are ocotillo stalks. A fenced-in area is on right, and on the roof of the ramada adjacent to the house is a cross, replaced once a year. Photograph by Aleš Hrdlička, probably 1898. bottom left, Upland Guarijío stone house with thatched roof in La Barranca, Chihuahua. The girl is filling a large pottery jar with water carried in a metal bucket. Squash are drying over the pole above her head. bottom right, Corn storage structure of the Upland Guarijío in Chiltepín, Chihuahua. bottom left and right, Photographs by Wick Miller, 1976–1977.

Mus. of the Amer. Ind., Heye Foundation, New York: left, 20/5217; center, 20/5220; right, 20/5219.

Fig. 8. Ópata palm fiber basketry, woven by women in semisubterranean structures like those used elsewhere in northern Mexico ("Lower Pima," figs. 3–4, this vol.). left, Unfinished twilled hat; center, coiled openwork basket; right, twilled basket. right, Height about 14.6 cm, rest to same scale. All collected by Jean B. Johnson at Tónichi, Sonora, 1940.

enced, leading to a new acculturation and inevitably in some cases to a final loss of their identity. The great shift toward corporate agriculture and industrialization in both Sonora and Arizona has upset the equilibrium of all groups as nothing has since initial mission contact. In the 1950s began the end of centuries of geographic isolation and greatly increased pressures toward integration of the Indian tribes into the national culture. To the south, the once remote Yaqui-Mayo valleys are served by paved roads and watered by the great dams on the Yaqui, Mayo, and Fuerte rivers, and each year more of the monte (brush jungle) is being brought under cultivation. These processes are leading to a breakdown in the semi-independent economic adjustments common to subsistence farmers. Wage work and cash-crop farming are rapidly taking their place. In 1955 the Yaquis were still basically subsistence farmers. in 1975 they were largely cash-crop producers, relying on credit and direction from the Banco Ejidal (National Agrarian Bank). Erasmus (1961) has similar comments for the Mayos. The thin remnants of the Mexican Pimas and Papagos are likewise becoming more involved in outside employment. Subsistence farming in the old Ópata and Pima areas of eastern Sonora still exists, but yearly more of the inhabitants of these areas go to the coasts to work and to live.

About 1960 the remote and independent Seris began to lose their isolation and sociocultural autonomy with the development of highways and increasing outside contact. Fishing and gathering have quickly given way to the production of tourist items, especially the ironwood carvings, which have made the Seris dependent on North American trade; presumably they now will stand or fall with the American economy. The Seris between 1968 and 1975 wholeheartedly adopted modern items, such as automobiles bought on credit, tape recorders, motorbikes, and similar items. And it appears that sociocultural life is following the trend toward extensive change.

Loss of isolation, both cultural and economic, will mean loss of identity for some of the groups. In Mexico in 1975, only the Yaqui and Seri were still viable Indian societies, but even they are facing the greatest threats to their continued existence since the conquest. The nature of modern acculturation forces is so all-encompassing that the whole situation constitutes a phase with wholly new dimensions, compared to the simpler pressures of earlier times.

The American tribes—Gila Pima and Papago—are firmly oriented toward American culture rather than

left, San Diego Mus. of Man, Calif.: 1980-6-6; right, U. of Ariz., Ariz. State Mus., Tucson: E-2950.

Fig. 9. Pottery. left, Guarijío redware water jar with white painted floral designs. right, Ópata redware vessel with scrape marks on body and incised decoration below rim. left, Height 32 cm, collected by Edmond Faubert at Jicamorachi, Chihuahua, about 1978; right, same scale, collected by Thomas B. Hinton at San Pedro de la Cueva, Sonora, in 1955.

toward their former Mexican connections. Their interaction network is no longer limited to the Southwest, and they have developed wide associations with other Indian groups in the United States. Each generation, ties with their Sonoran counterparts become more obscure and relationships more vague. In 1975 only a few of the Papagos had contact with the Sonoran Indians. The Gila Pimas had no modern contact with the Mexican Pimas. Apache interactions with Mexico have ceased except for an occasional tourist trip to a border town.

In summary, the Sonoran groups after centuries of gradual acculturation toward Mexican ways were in the 1970s undergoing a rapid acceleration toward complete incorporation into Mexican society.

The Arizona peoples, the Pima-Papago, who once constituted a single culture unit with the northwest Mexicans, are likewise undergoing far-reaching changes, but they are likely to exist indefinitely as an American ethnic group.

Sources

There is extensive colonial documentation for northwest Mexico and adjacent parts of the United States. Such archival sources were used extensively by Beals (1932a), Sauer (1932, 1934, 1935), and Kroeber (1934) in delineating the peoples and languages of northwestern Mexico at the time of the conquest. The published works of the seventeenth-century priest Pérez de Ribas (1645) are the best available early source for much of western Mexico for the area as far north as central Sonora. For the eighteenth century, the *Rudo Ensayo* (Nentvig 1980) and the description of Sonora by the Jesuit, Pfefferkorn (1949) give information on the natives a century after missionization.

Bandelier (1890–1892, 1), Lumholtz (1902, 1912), McGee (1898), and Hrdlička (1904) furnish ethnographic and social data on the tribes of southern Arizona and Sonora. While their reports are essentially observations from survey trips, they furnish significant information on the Pima, Papago, Ópata, Yaqui, Mayo, and Seri of the time. The historian Bancroft (1886–1889) brings together many sources on the area. While some of his data are inaccurate, his work as a whole is a valuable source.

The above-mentioned works of Beals, Sauer, and Kroeber deal with northwest Mexico as a whole and relate it to the southwest United States; they are basic to an overall view of the aboriginal scene and are notable for their accuracy. Hinton (1959) surveyed the surviving Indians of Sonora, locating descendants of the Ópatas, Pimas, and Jovas. Spicer (1962) produced what is unquestionably the most comprehensive work; he integrates the Indian groups of northern Mexico and the southwestern United States and analyzes the course of change in each tribe. Spicer (1969) likewise summarized the Mexican Northwest. Modern anthropological literature on the individual groups of the area is spotty, with some tribes, such as the Yaqui and Papago, being well documented, with others, such as the Lower Pima and Ópata, having scanty coverage.

Southern Periphery: East

WILLIAM B. GRIFFEN

Several groups of people inhabited the area of north-central and northeast Mexico north of the Meso-American border, an area that Kirchhoff (1944) has called Arid-America. It runs approximately from the state of San Luis Potosí on the south to about the latitude of El Paso on the north and it therefore includes the Mexican state of Chihuahua and extends eastward into the old Spanish province of Texas and to the gulf coast (fig. 1).

In broadest overview, the area consisted of several large "tribal" groupings. From south to north these were the Chichimeca-Pame-Jonaz, Guamar, Zacatec, Cuachichil, Lagunero, Toboso, Cacaxte, Coahuiltecan, Concho, Suma-Jumano, and Jano-Jocome.*

Languages

The linguistic affiliation of these large tribal groupings is not well known. The only surviving language in 1975 was Pame in the state of San Luis Potosí (with a very small group of Chichimeca in northeastern Guanajuato), related to Otomí and a member of the larger linguistic family of Otomanguean of Meso-America (Manrique Castañeda 1967:332–333; Driver and Driver 1963; Voegelin and Voegelin 1965:16–17, 1966:71). Historically, the Pame extended into southwestern Tamaulipas and are related linguistically to the Jonaz (Eguilaz 1966; Saldívar 1943:14–16; Swadesh 1959).

To the north, in the area of Tamaulipas, Nuevo León, Coahuila, and Texas, the classification of languages is in considerable doubt and will remain so until solid linguistic data are discovered. Swadesh (1959) considered the region of Tamaulipas, from the Huasteco speakers in the south on the Meso-American border to slightly below the Rio Grande, to have been Uto-Aztecan speaking; others have doubted his evidence and simply use the older catch-all label Tamaulipeco for this area. To the north, extending through the Spanish Province of Texas as treated here, were a great number of languages and dialects once generally lumped together as Coahuiltecan (Swanton 1915) but since the 1960s regarded as largely unrelatable (I. Goddard 1979:375–379). To the west, along the eastern Sierra Madre and extending into the higher plateau country on the west of the mountains were several languages that have remained unclassified and are in even greater doubt and dispute. These include Borrado, Janambre-Pisón, Negrito, and Bocalo, as well as Guamar and Cuachichil, which border the Mesoamerican Tarascans on the south. Cuachichil extends as far northward as the Laguna district (the general area of modern Torreón). While these languages may have been Uto-Aztecan, it is probably safest to leave them unclassified (Del Hoyo 1960; Sauer 1934; Swadesh 1959).

Westward of the Cuachichil were the Zacatec, perhaps a Uto-Aztecan group. To the north of the Zacatec and Cuachichil is the Laguna district. Historically, Zacatec, Cuachichil, and Tepehuan (Uto-Aztecan), and Irritila were reported spoken in and around this district. Indeed, early Spanish observers said that a number of

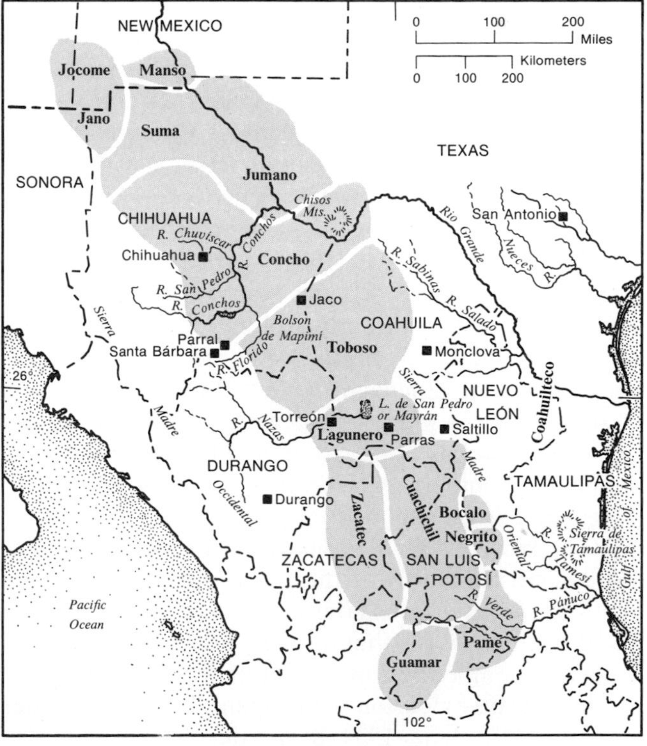

Fig. 1. Territory of eastern Southern Periphery tribes.

*The English names of the historic Indian groups in Mexico are taken directly from Spanish and are to be pronounced according to the regular Spanish rules.

languages were spoken here, although perhaps these were only dialects of one language. Several hundred different names for groups are mentioned for the general area, but no doubt a great many belonged either to the Irritila people or to those later called Cabeza, who had associations with lower Rio Grande groups. Whether or not any other major language divisions were represented in this area may be determined by further research. The same lack of solid data obtains regarding the corridor to the north of the Laguna district, which includes Toboso and Cacaxte. However, slightly farther north, across the Rio Grande east of the Chisos Mountains, a Uto-Aztecan word for salt (ona) was recorded in 1674. In any event, the entire question of linguistic classification and boundaries with the Coahuiltecan speakers of northern Tamaulipas, south Texas, Nuevo León, and Coahuila remains practically unanswerable (Del Hoyo 1960; Eguilaz 1965, 1966; Griffen 1969:133ff.; Sauer 1934; Swadesh 1959; Voegelin and Voegelin 1965:142, 1966:85).

To the northwest of the Toboso, along the Conchos and Rio Grande rivers, the evidence that the Conchos and Chisos (an eastern extension of the Conchos who have lent their name to the Chisos Mountains in Big Bend National Park, Texas) spoke a Uto-Aztecan language is considerably better. The two were reported to speak the same language on several occasions and Kroeber (1934:13–14) published three words from them that he claimed indicated a linguistic affinity to Cahitan (the word for salt, noted above, is also Cahitan in type) (Griffen 1979:133–134; Sauer 1934; Swadesh 1959).

Finally, the Suma and Jumano, who overlapped into northern Chihuahua and for an unknown distance into southwest Texas, have been considered by Sauer and Kroeber as most probably Uto-Aztecan on the basis of four words recorded with meanings (particularly the word for 'water') and a number of personal names without meaning. However, this evidence is very scanty and does not permit placing these peoples definitively in any specific language family (Kroeber 1934:15; Sauer 1934:65). A group called the Manso found around El Paso at the time of the early explorations is of unknown linguistic affiliation. The Jano and the Jocome (said to speak the same language) were to the north and west of the Suma and Manso, respectively. They have often been identified as Athapaskan and consequently forerunners of southern Apache groups in this area. However, there is no linguistic evidence for this, and in the 1750s they were still identified as distinct from Apaches in the parish records of the Janos presidio. It is true that their territory was later taken over by Athapaskan speakers, but so was that of many other groups as contacts and competition increased under the pressure of the northward extension of the Spanish colonial frontier (Griffen 1979; Sauer 1934; Schroeder 1974b:36; see also Forbes 1959a, for a different view).

Territories

Geographically the area of north-central Mexico and southern Texas can be divided into two broad provinces, the lowlands on the east and the higher plateau country on the west. The eastern gulflands are hot and humid. Demarcating this region on the west is the low-lying Sierra Madre Oriental or eastern Sierra Madre chain. West of this series of low mountains is the slightly cooler and much drier central Mexican Basin, which runs to the eastern skirt of the Sierra Madre Occidental. From approximately 2,000 feet altitude in the north, the land tilts upward, as one moves south and southeastward toward San Luis Potosí. The region covered here, then, aside from the section of Texas from San Antonio south, includes some seven modern Mexican states and comprises a total area of approximately 680,000 square kilometers.

The Indian peoples who inhabited this great area were basically nomadic or wandering hunters and gatherers. As such they existed as very small social groups, most accurately referred to as bands. Many of these bands were closely related to one another in several ways: specifically, they were often tied together from area to area by kinship and marriage, and they were related also by a common culture and because they generally spoke dialects that were mutually intelligible variants of the same language. The Indians of north Mexico and south Texas from a broader linguistic and, to some extent, cultural perspective can conveniently be classified into tribes and these "tribes" then given general names such as Concho, Toboso, or Cuachichil.

In the southern portion of the area, there were several tribal groups considered to have been essentially nomadic who bordered the sedentary peoples of Meso-America. These were, first, the Cuachichil, who inhabited a vast section of the central area considered here. They inhabited the eastern part of the present-day state of Zacatecas, extended into San Luis Potosí, and north to approximately the towns of Saltillo and Parras. On the west were the Zacatec, whose territory extended to Tepehuan country and the eastern slope of the western Sierra Madre. The northward extent of these Zacatec reached to about the town of Parras and the Laguna district. To the immediate south of the Cuachichil were the Guamar, culturally virtually unknown. On the east of the Guamar and bordering on the east of the central Cuachichil were the Chichimeca-Jonaz and Pame who, while not properly part of Meso-America, together with some of the Tamaulipec to the east of them manifested some Meso-American influences. The Pame are the only group in all north-central Mexico who survived in the 1970s, although in very small numbers. Immediately east, in northern Veracruz and southern Tamaulipas, over to the gulf coast, is the most northern extension of Meso-American peoples, the Huastec.

North of the Pame and the Huastec were a great number of bands, many of which have been referred to collectively as Coahuiltecan on the basis of their assumed linguistic relationship. These included peoples occupying several Spanish colonial provinces. In Nuevo Santander (roughly the present Tamaulipas and south Texas to the Nueces River), lived the Janambre, the Pamorano, the Comecrudo, and the Pachal. The Borrado, Cabeza, and Contotor people lived in Nuevo León or in the border area between Nuevo León and Coahuila. Farther northwest in the Rio Grande country of northern Coahuila dwelled the Terocodame and the Hueyhueyquetzal. In the Texas province the Payaya, Aranama, Tamique, and Orejón were prominent. These peoples comprised a large number of quite small and widely dispersed bands, apparently speaking a number of distinct languages. Another tribal group, the Karankawa, was located along the coastal prairie or littoral. Karankawa territory ran from the west side of Galveston Bay southwestward to Corpus Christi Bay and included all the offshore islands (Eguilaz 1965, 1966; W.W. Newcomb 1961:59; "Coahuiltecans and Their Neighbors" and "Karankawa," this vol.).

In the district of the Laguna de San Pedro at the time of the Jesuit mission system there were several groups of people whose cultures may have been slightly different from those of the surrounding desert groups. If so, this variation stemmed mainly from the different environmental opportunities afforded by the drainage of the lower Río Nazas, including the Laguna de Mayrán itself, also called Mayrán. It is not certain that more than one language family was represented in the Laguna district although distinct languages were reported here historically, together with the slightly different cultural emphases (Griffen 1969:6ff., 136; Martínez del Río 1954; Pérez de Ribas 1944a:251–253, 256).

North of the Laguna country along the eastern fringe of Tepehuan country must be included a few bands of Tepehuan Indians proper (for example, Los Negritos, not to be confused with the Negrito group east of the Cuachichil) (Griffen 1969:163) who were apparently essentially an eastern nomadic, hunting-gathering extension of the more sedentary mountain-dwelling Tepehuan. North of the Laguna country and east of the Tepehuan were the Toboso who inhabited the general area of the Bolsón de Mapimí, geographically a region of internal drainage. North and west of the Toboso, north of Tepehuan country of the Santa Bárbara district, and east of the sedentary mountain-dwelling Tarahumara, were the Concho Indians. While there is little information on the Concho people, a great many of their settlements seem to have been concentrated along the river systems of the Florido, Conchos, San Pedro, and Chuvíscar. There were desert-dwelling extensions of the Concho—the Chiso in the Big Bend country to the east, and the Chinarra in north-central Chihuahua. Many of the river-dwelling Concho may have been more sedentary than is often implied in the sources. The culture of these early Concho most likely will never be known, since the Spaniards seem to have moved first up the river courses appropriating native lands and disrupting the social system while putting the natives themselves to work on these lands. Consequently, little was ever recorded regarding the first Indians subjugated (Griffen 1979; Sauer 1934).

In the lower Conchos River valley, north of Concho territory, on the Rio Grande at La Junta, was a group of people who were definitely sedentary and who lived in pueblo-like towns. These peoples were given several different names during the colonial period, but most probably belonged to a sedentary branch of the Jumano, some of whom at one time or another were reported farther north on the Plains hunting buffalo. These town-dwelling Jumano in and around the mouth of the Río Conchos were probably related to the much less sedentary Suma, who lived westward upriver in northern Chihuahua (Griffen 1979; J.C. Kelley 1952–1953, 1955; W.W. Newcomb 1961:225ff.; Sauer 1934).

Finally, in the northwest corner of the present state of Chihuahua and overlapping into southwest New Mexico, southeast Arizona, and adjacent Sonora were the nomadic Jano and Jocome, who disappeared with most of the Suma early in the eighteenth century. Their territorial extent is vague, but they may have routinely ranged as far north as the Gila River. By the time much is heard of them, processes leading to their extinction seem to have been fairly advanced; they ceased to be referred to as a tribal entity soon after 1700, although a few were living at the Janos presidio in 1750 (Griffen 1979; Sauer 1934).

Culture

Subsistence

The peoples of north-central and northeast Mexico were basically hunters and gatherers. Horticulture was reportedly practiced in a few areas, but, with the possible exception of a few places in the west and southwest of this area, it was subsidiary and supplementary to collecting activities at the time of contact.

Hunting was, without a doubt, important for all groups. For the most part, any animal that could be taken was utilized for food; specifically rabbits, deer, antelope, peccary, turtles, and other smaller animals are often mentioned, as well as birds of various types. For those people living closer to the Rio Grande, especially on the north side of the river, the hunting of bison was important aboriginally during certain seasons (Beals 1932a:103; Eguilaz 1965:83; Griffen 1969:112–114; W.W. Newcomb 1961:39–41; P.W. Powell 1952:41).

During the colonial period, ecological changes caused shifts in the numbers and distribution of the wild fauna, and the native groups, or what was left of them, adjusted to these shifts. One major new element in the hunting complex of the north Mexican Indians was the introduction of European types of domestic livestock, principally horses, donkeys, and their sterile offspring, mules. For those peoples who learned to rely on raiding Spanish holdings goats, sheep, and pigs were considerably less important. In any event, contact with European domestic animals occurred in two different ways. On the one hand, many of these animals, particularly horses and donkeys, became wild and substituted ecologically, in part, for deer, antelope, and other native American fauna. These were hunted for food like any wild animal, although Indians learned how to capture wild mustangs so they could then use them for riding. On the other hand, these animals were often stolen from Spanish settlements for food and raw materials, such as hides and sinew. As a consequence, the native hunting patterns were adjusted to the new circumstances brought about by the arrival of the Europeans (Griffen 1969:112–114; Del Hoyo 1972:311ff.; P.W. Powell 1945).

All known edible vegetable products were utilized. These included tunas, or cactus apples, mesquite beans, lechuguilla, and maguey and its derivatives honey water (aguamiel) and mescal. Seeds, fruits, and roots of all kinds were eaten. Pecans were used near the Nueces River and may have been used more widely in the south Texas–Coahuila area. Herbs were mentioned specifically by one writer. Alcoholic beverages seem to have been made from a number of plants. The use of the hallucinogen, peyote, was a general characteristic of the area. A major technique of processing these vegetable products was by grinding, either on a stone grinding slab (metate), a stone mortar, or, at least in Nuevo León, a wooden mortar. The resulting powder or flour was then used to make gruel, cakes, or bread patties. The cooking or roasting of bread as well as of agave or mescal leaves was often done in pits. Meat was also barbecued in pits or roasted on sticks (Beals 1932a:105, 163–164, 168, 216; Eguilaz 1965:82–85; Griffen 1969:110–111; W.W. Newcomb 1961:40–43; P.W. Powell 1952:40–41).

Fishing and shellfish collecting were carried on where the opportunity existed along rivers and other bodies of water. These included the Rio Grande; the Río Conchos, and the Río Florido in Chihuahua; the Río Sabinas and its tributaries in Coahuila and Nuevo León; the coast and various rivers in Tamaulipas, such as the Pánuco, Verde, and Tamesí in the south; and the Río Nazas and its lower drainage area, including the Laguna de San Pedro or Mayrán. The people in this general Laguna and Parras area were said to rely quite heavily at some times of the year on both fish and waterfowl that could be caught in the San Pedro basin. Other lakes and lagoons of the region, such as Encinillas, Jaco, Los Gigantes, Los Frailes, and Patos, no doubt also were sources of subsistence items (Beals 1932a:116; Eguilaz 1965:83; Griffen 1969:109–111, 1979:119; W.W. Newcomb 1961:40).

The harvesting of these wild foods was extremely important and virtually determined the movements of bands. In the summer, during the rainy season, there was an abundance of foodstuffs. Winter was known as a period of starvation because rainfall subsided and natural foods disappeared. This seasonal fluctuation in available food also was correlated with the amount of interband and intergroup warfare that occurred at the end of the rainy season (Griffen 1969:109ff., 119ff.; W.W. Newcomb 1961:39–40).

While these people are generally considered nonagricultural, a number of references indicate that digging-stick horticulture of corn, beans, and squash was practiced in some areas. These included the Zacatec region, the Parras-Laguna district, along the Conchos and Rio Grande rivers, and the Sierra de Tamaulipas. Colonial references are on occasion somewhat contradictory or unclear, and agriculture of a simple type may have been more extensive than indicated. Even Tobosos were reported to plant squash, for example (Beals 1932a:98ff.; Eguilaz 1965:87; Griffen 1969:111–112; P.W. Powell 1952:40).

Technology

The major weapon for the chase, as well as war, was the bow and arrow. Bows were made of local woods, mesquite often being mentioned, with a bowstring of either sinew or plant fibers. Arrows were made in several different styles, although in general they were of lechuguilla flower stalk or cane, probably often had hardwood foreshafts, were fletched with turkey or other feathers, and were armed with fire-hardened tips or with points of flint. The bow and arrow were also used for fishing when this was appropriate (Beals 1932a:104, 115–116, 167, 194–195; Eguilaz 1965:84; Griffen 1969:109ff.; W.W. Newcomb 1961:43–44; P.W. Powell 1952:47–49).

Various kinds of traps, snares, and pitfalls, sometimes with sharpened stakes at the bottom, were also used, although references are very scarce in the literature. Decoys, such as the heads of deer, were used for stalking. For hunting waterfowl, a technique reported from Tamaulipas and the Laguna district was that of placing a calabash, with holes cut in it for the eyes, on the head and then with only the gourd above water approaching and catching the swimming birds by the legs. The use of fences for game drives and surrounds as well as running down of deer until they became exhausted were other widespread techniques. Communal hunting was practiced employing surrounds and brush and grass fires (Beals 1932a:104, 166; Eguilaz 1965:83–84, 87; Griffen 1969:109ff.; W.W. Newcomb 1961:40).

Other items of material culture included sticks used for all kinds of purposes, from digging up tubers and rodents to throwing at small game. Knives, scrapers, and hammers were made of chert. Gourds were utilized for keeping flour and water and as cups for drinking water. The leaves of the prickly pear cactus were also hollowed out and used for containers. Baskets were made and employed for the same purpose by most if not all the peoples in the area. Mats (petates) were made from local desert palm. Fiber-net bags and carrying crates or frames (*cacastes* and *guacales*) were used, most notably at the Laguna of Mayrán but also in other areas. Rafts, such as were reported at Mayrán, were constructed of bundles of cypress or sedge tied together. Basket seines or weirs made out of willow branches or similar materials were used to catch fish in both rivers and lakes as apparently were nets, and fish poisoning is reported for Tamaulipas. These kinds of historically reported basketry, netting, matting, and weaving work are also illustrated in reports on the archeological sites in the area, particularly caves. During the colonial period deer skins and mule hides, as well as buffalo hides, were utilized by the natives. The thin skins of rabbits were cut into strips and woven into blankets. Carrying was done on the back with a tumpline to the forehead. One reference in the middle of the eighteenth century stated that Chiso Indians carried water in horse intestines, apparently slung over the backs of their beasts when they moved from camp to camp (Beals 1932a:167, 186; Eguilaz 1965:87; Griffen 1969:106–109; W.W. Newcomb 1961:43–44).

Clothing and Adornment

Native-style dress before the advent of Spanish clothing is poorly reported (there are Spanish claims that the Indians went about nude). In general, dress consisted of breechclouts or loincloths, belts, leather or fiber sandals, cloaks made of skin (rabbit or other), and considerable face and body painting, tattooing, and scarification. On some occasions headdresses made of feathers were reported, and necklaces and bracelets of bones and shells of snail or other animals were also utilized. Nose and ear piercing with associated pendants was reported from Tamaulipas and Nuevo León. Several types of hairstyles are reported, from tonsure to simply hanging long and loose (Beals 1932a:172–176; Eguilaz 1965:85–86, 93; Griffen 1969:104, 106; W.W. Newcomb 1961:39; P.W. Powell 1952:39–40).

Structures

Dwellings were classified by the Spaniards as huts although their construction and design is not well described. However, these huts invariably consisted of some kind of framework covered with different materials. In some cases, such as the Toboso of the Bolsón de Mapimí country, these were covered with skins. At other times, in the same general area, these huts were reported to be covered with grass. The shape of Toboso dwellings seems to have been semicircular and arched or, as one writer put it, in the form of caves. For the south Texas–Coahuila area huts or shelters seem to have been portable, and reed mats as well as hides were placed over the framework. Seemingly, these reed mats and hides were then carried from camp to camp as the settlement was moved about. The wattle-and-mud house type at La Junta on the Rio Grande and in the Tamaulipas range was radically different from the rest of the houses of the area (Beals 1932a:176–177, 192; Eguilaz 1965:86–88; Griffen 1969:106–107, 1979:120ff.; W.W. Newcomb 1961:43, 241–243).

Material Culture After Contact

A number of material culture items evince direct and indirect contact with outsiders, not only with Europeans but also with Meso-Americans through culture elements brought in by Europeans. The number of these items is too great to specify in detail particularly because the practice of raiding for various goods—foodstuffs and many manufactured products—became institutionalized among the native groups during the colonial period. The many items of European origin that found their way into native camps included flint and steel for fire-making, pictures or paintings, boxes and chests, iron knives of diffent types, and other metal objects, including weapons such as swords and harquebuses. Other things discovered at Indian camps were blankets, Spanish horse trappings, and many religious items—stoles, crosses, bells, rosaries, and candles. In all, it appears that articles of Spanish clothing and adornment, including skirts, jackets, shirts, hats, beads, earrings, belts, and ribbons, became some of the most important items that Indians acquired in their raiding activities (Griffen 1969:107–109).

Weapons used by Indians during the colonial period show considerable contact with the Spaniards. Occasionally, a harquebus or other firearm was encountered in the hands of the Indians, but certain limitations restricted the wide utilization of such weapons before the advent of bullets mounted in shells with their own charge of powder. Powder and ball also had to be captured and the powder cared for in specific ways so it did not become too dry or too wet. Such problems simply prohibited the extensive use of European firearms by the natives. Indeed, Indian arrows were quite efficient for many purposes; although they did not have the same range as the firearms, they could be discharged more rapidly. Other items of battle (aside from the ubiquitous employment of naturally occurring missiles such as rocks and stones) were swords and lances, some of which may have been of strictly native design or manufacture. However, the reported use of pikes, fashioned by hafting Spanish swords on long poles, was a product of contact. Also, spears, clubs, and slings were reported from some places. Shields or *chimales*, unstated whether of north Mexican or of outside origin, were utilized as were Spanish leather military jackets (*cueras*) (Beals 1932a:194–197; Eguilaz 1965:84; Griffen 1969:107–109; P.W. Powell 1952:47–49).

Social Organization

Except for a few places such as at La Junta where fairly large permanent villages existed, Indian society in the north Mexican area in general was characterized by a group of 20 to 50 people living in a rather mobile camp, here designated a band, but often called a nation by the Spaniards. Except for occasional alliances among bands, the band served as the social group for the average person; it formed the limits of most of his dealings with other people. The band was also the largest group within which binding decisions were made for the allocation of resources, control of people and their movements, and the like. Consequently, the band may be said to have functioned as the largest autonomous political unit. Of course, alliances among bands occasionally occurred for specific purposes such as war and raiding. At the same time, early reports indicate that band territory was fairly well delineated. Such territory was sacred to the band members, and outsiders and trespassers were attacked if they did not have the proper introduction. Indeed, such trespassing was often an excuse for war (Eguilaz 1965:97; Griffen 1969:114ff.).

Moreover, some bands, at least from colonial accounts, were associated (by name) with one another more than they were with other bands. While some of this may be because of faulty identification of bands, some of the clustering certainly is because of factors such as geographical proximity and the exploitation of concentrated natural resources, including water, with the result that kinship ties were closer and other obligations more binding. Consequently, these groupings would have been naturally occurring resource-use communities. Also, under the influences of the Spanish colonial system, some band names became more and more generic, that is, of wider and wider application. A name like Cabeza was clearly used to designate the members of several more specific bands. Both these factors—the natural environment and pressures from colonial frontier society—probably contributed to the clustering of certain groups of bands, an organizational phenomenon that occurred over and above the basic characteristics of bands (Griffen 1969:14ff., 174–175; Ruecking 1954a, 1955a).

Leadership roles were held by people designated as chiefs or captains. For some groups at least there seems to have been a patrilineal aspect to the selection of men for these positions. Clearly, however, general ability and bravery as exhibited in warfare, and possibly elsewhere, were also part of the criteria for recruitment, as probably were wisdom and generosity. From the pattern in the greater Southwestern area one might expect both war and peace chiefs, but evidence for this does not often come out clearly in the documents of the colonial period. This is quite possibly because the descriptions of these groups often occurred at time of conflict and hence the only chiefs encountered were war or raiding leaders. In some cases, at least, the possession of supernatural power was an attribute of leadership also, and for Tamaulipas physical combat with the existing chief by a pretender was at least part of the process of leadership succession (Eguilaz 1965:92; Griffen 1969:118–119; W.W. Newcomb 1961:44–45, 71).

The makeup of the band seems to have been that of a large extended family. Much of the available evidence indicates that residence was patrilocal, in which case the result would have been that such bands were essentially groups of patrilineally related kinsmen. But apparently not all groups were patrilocal; there is some evidence that the Tobosos were matrilocal and matrilineal, for example. Some of the peoples in the Parras-Laguna area also practiced matrilocality or matriliny. Earlier in the sixteenth century Gonzalo de las Casas reported that some Chichimeca, that is, Cuachichil, to the south of the Parras-Laguna region, also were characterized by matrilocal residence. While more information is needed on the postmarital residence rule in specific cases, people could and did shift residence depending on where they had kinsmen. Probably some of this movement was done in attempts to adjust to colonial contact conditions. On occasion a man moved in with his wife's relatives, and presumably before marriage he could move and live with his mother's kinsmen (Griffen 1969:114–119; Las Casas 1936; W.W. Newcomb 1961:44–46; P.W. Powell 1952:43).

Marriage in the north Mexican area apparently was arranged by parents and kinsmen of the couple. This is not surprising since a marriage would unite people of exogamous bands and, hence, was important to all the bands' members, that is, the kinsmen of the contracting parties. Premarital chastity does not appear to have had much importance and, indeed, according to some reports, there seems to have been considerable premarital sexual freedom. There was no ceremony for marriage, although there was gift giving and one report states that there was a ceremonial feast at the time the proposal was accepted. It appears very likely that both the levirate and the sororate were practiced to some extent. Berdaches are reported from the area of the Texas-Coahuila country (Beals 1932a:205; Eguilaz 1965:90;

Griffen 1969:117–118; W.W. Newcomb 1961:50, 72–75).

Marriages, particularly if there were no children, were rather brittle and may have fluctuated to some extent in accordance with the relations between bands. Generally, marriage was monogamous, but leaders, including shamans, do appear occasionally to have had more than one wife. Indeed, some evidence from the Bolsón country indicates that sororal polygyny was practiced. Gifts to the bride's parents and even suitor service also were noted in the accounts of some areas (Beals 1932a:204; Eguilaz 1965:94–95; Griffen 1969:117–118; W.W. Newcomb 1961:50, 72–74; P.W. Powell 1952:43).

Evidence on childbirth and pregnancy is slight. In some areas there was no sexual intercourse after a pregnancy was known, or for two years following the birth of a child. Intercourse was also prohibited during the menstrual period. Pregnant women were relieved of carrying heavy loads, and certain ceremonial restrictions were placed on their husbands. Birth was away from camp. A woman, squatting, would be attended and assisted by one or more female friends. When the child arrived, both mother and child were bathed as soon as possible. After the birth, the placenta was treated ceremonially. The couvade is reported for the Laguna and Tamaulipas areas. This is a practice whereby the father would retire to bed or to rest for a certain period of time, usually four days, although one account states a week. Twins were not accepted as normal and one was buried. If a baby was born deformed, it was also done away with by burial. When Cabeza de Vaca was in the general area of Texas and Coahuila, he observed female infanticide, and other reports note that children were sometimes killed because of dreams and other omens (Beals 1932a:205; Eguilaz 1965:89; Griffen 1969:127–130; W.W. Newcomb 1961:48–49).

There is little information on childrearing and general education. Boys began to practice with small or miniature bows and arrows at an early age, both for the chase and for war. Boys were also taken on hunts and raids to serve as lookouts and to perform simple chores, including keeping camp and making arrows. Apparently, the practice often was to confer on a child two types of names, a secret, personal name and one or more public nicknames for some particular or outstanding characteristic. While such information is very scanty for these peoples, such naming practices are not uncommon in other areas of the Greater Southwest.

Adoption between bands was common and probably followed the lines of the kinship systems. However, during warfare children were often captured, and those who were not done away with were kept and raised until they were recaptured or negotiated for by their own kinsmen, or else they grew up to be a member of the captor's band (Eguilaz 1965:90; Griffen 1969:120–122; W.W. Newcomb 1961:49, 72).

Division of labor was essentially by sex as there were few other roles involving any degree of specialization. One of the most prominent, aside from the leadership role, was that of shaman or medicine man. The roles of hunter or warrior were really aspects of the general adult male role. Those men who could not accept the adult male role simply took the female role, becoming berdaches. From direct evidence the prestige-ranking system is apparent only for males, and this was based principally on bravery in war and raiding activity. How women were ranked can only be guessed; from general ethnographic knowledge their prestige would stem from how well, as individuals, they performed the female role as well as some status that would accrue to them from the males with whom they were associated (Griffen 1969:109ff., 127; W.W. Newcomb 1961:50, 73–74).

Ceremonial and Religious Life

Ceremonies involving dancing, chanting, and feasting (sometimes called mitotes) are reported for a number of different occasions. These included puberty and curing rites, celebrations of harvest and thanksgiving, and of war, peace, and alliance making. In general, these ceremonies were most frequent during the summer, toward the end of the rainy season when food resources were most plentiful.

Puberty ceremonies (as part of the life cycle as well as part of the ceremonial cycle), led by shamans, were reported for the areas of Coahuila, Texas, and the Laguna de Mayrán, although the practice was no doubt of wider distribution. In the Texas-Coahuila area these ceremonies involved tattooing and certain necessary feats for the neophytes. Tattooing and scarification were carried out by rubbing charcoal, resin, and other matter into cuts in the skin in order to cause a raising of the ruptured area. In the region of Parras, dances were reportedly held for several days, sometimes for as many as eight. They were mainly held at night, although some ceremonial activity was also carried out in the daytime. These dances involved considerable amounts of feasting, including the taking of peyote. A number of references note inebriation with peyote during ceremonies concerned with curing (for example, when plagues attacked) and warfare. In ceremonies associated with war, some testimonies noted that the flesh of captives was often eaten or their ground bones consumed with peyote. On an occasion or two the meetings of bands to cement alliances were accompanied by the sacrifice of human beings, whose bodies were eaten with peyote (Beals 1932a:216; Eguilaz 1965:95–97; Griffen 1969:122–124; W.W. Newcomb 1961:49–50, 53–55).

Little or nothing is known directly of the mythology of the north-central Mexican groups. Something of religious beliefs can be deduced from the general social context in which ceremonial behavior took place. Curing by shamans is noted for several specific peoples and was, no doubt, universal. Many kinds of ritual behavior were cited—keeping of hawks' claws and other fetishes, the use of snakes and fire, and the like. Curing was accomplished by sucking wounds and sores, blowing on the afflicted body parts, apparently some actual cauterizing of wounds, and the magical extraction of sticks, stones, vermin, and other foreign objects from the patient's body. Visions were a part of shamanistic activity and power, and medicine men were paid for their efforts. The importance of curing activity is underscored by the experience of Alvar Núñez Cabeza de Vaca, who traveled through the area in the early part of the sixteenth century. He and his companions were forced to become healer-shamans and this, in effect, was their passport for safe conduct from one group to another. In the Parras-Laguna district, group dances, often apparently led by shamans, were employed as an attempt to turn the tide of plagues (Eguilaz 1965:98–99; Griffen 1969:127–130; W.W. Newcomb 1961:51–53). The Jesuits in the early years of their contact in the Parras-Laguna district reported a number of incidents in which natives had been visited by the supernatural. Such visitations came in the form of animals (deer, snakes), human beings, or fire. One colonial writer, Pérez de Ribas, gives evidence that the belief in a guardian spirit was held by groups in the Laguna district. The sun was reported to be an important supernatural among the Pame (Beals 1932a:212–213; Eguilaz 1965:98; Griffen 1969:29–30; Pérez de Ribas 1944a:284).

In general, disposal of the dead was by burial, although cremation is also reported for groups in Nuevo León (perhaps especially for shamans). Other widespread practices were burying personal property with the deceased and the cutting of hair and the destruction of property of survivors. Mourning behavior, especially as carried out by the women, was reported as quite extreme. The mourners set up tremendous wails, beat upon themselves and fell on the ground; in some places the hair was torn out at the crown of the head and a person slashed himself with a flint knife. The length of mourning is unknown, although it was reported on the northeast periphery that it endured as much as a year. Varying periods of confinement were required of the survivors. Endocannibalism, the eating of deceased kinsmen, was practiced in Nuevo León (Beals 1932a:205–207; Eguilaz 1965:99–100; Griffen 1969:130–132; W.W. Newcomb 1961:51, 74).

Warfare and War Ceremonialism

War loomed large in the reports by Europeans during the colonial period. While war was practiced prehistorically, it took a different focus with the Spanish conquest of the area. The new emphasis stemmed in part from the increased need to defend one's territory and in part from the availability of new goods, especially food, animals, and clothing but also other material items that could be obtained rather easily by raiding. At the same time, warfare was connected with the ceremonial cycle of the native groups (Griffen 1969:119–122, 143ff.; W.W. Newcomb 1961:47; P.W. Powell 1952:44ff.).

For precontact or early postcontact times, wars were reported to have been endemic, although they took place especially in the dry season, when fighting occurred over water and other resources. Essentially, such fighting involved small parties of men who conducted a surprise attack. Raids were usually carried out at night, and pitched battles were rare. When necessary, a group took refuge on the higher mountain peaks and prominences and then made their escape during the night. Only occasionally were larger interband alliances and large war parties organized. Certain measures were taken against surprise attacks. Huts were hidden in clumps of vegetation or placed in out-of-the-way places and occasionally they were protected by trenches or other defensive works (Eguilaz 1965:94; Griffen 1969:119–122; W.W. Newcomb 1961:47; P.W. Powell 1952:44ff.).

Preparations for the warpath consisted of ritual dancing, feasting, and body painting. Taunting and goading remarks to the warriors, especially by the older women, reminded them of past grievances band members had with their neighbors. Such revenge seems to have been the immediate and major reason motivating fights.

After battles, it was customary to have a ceremony of purification. These postbattle rituals included dancing with heads, scalps, and other items of booty taken from the enemy and, if captives were taken, often the torture and eating of these captives. Returning warriors were met before they entered camp. Booty from the enemy was treated ceremonially to purify it and to expunge the supernaturally dangerous forces it contained as a result of contact with the enemy. Scalps and some other items were placed on poles before the ceremony started (Eguilaz 1965:93; Griffen 1969:119–122, 124–126; W.W. Newcomb 1961:47–48; P.W. Powell 1952:50–54).

As the colonial period advanced, much of the ceremonialism associated with warfare may have been discontinued, particularly during periods of regular pursuit by Spanish punitive forces. However, captured Spaniards who escaped often reported some ceremonial behavior. At the same time, it appears that warfare organization as well as interband alliances became somewhat more complex or intricate under the new conditions brought about by contact with European society. The small raiding party continued, as it was quite efficient for running off sizable herds of horses and mules. (These were the animals mainly sought by raiding Indians, since other animals such as cattle, sheep, and goats were too slow as well as too erratic to herd when there was a possibility of being followed by Spanish forces.) As Indians of north-central and northeastern Mexico accepted the horse and their mobility became greater, several bands from wider areas often joined for raids and attacks on Spanish holdings. On some occasions the organization of these native war parties included both infantry and cavalry; rarely, fifers, drummers, and Spanish-style standard bearers were reported, although the last in some form probably existed in the native times. While a few groups of Cuachichil, Toboso, Coahuileño (people specifically from the area of Coahuila), and others at one time or another were well known for their raiding activities and they often united into fairly large attacking forces, it cannot be said that these were wars of conquest. Fighting was motivated by economic and religious factors, but the natives had no administrative structure through which to manage, control, and hold conquered land. Despite slight shifts in size of battles and probably in the frequency of warfare on the north Mexican frontier, such organized fighting remained, as in precontact times, most aptly described as raids on neighbors (Griffen 1969:19–22; P.W. Powell 1952:42–54).

History

Sixteenth Century

The peoples of north-central Mexico and Texas were first contacted during the sixteenth century. However, for most of the natives of the area it was only toward the end of that century and into the next that the major impact of the arrival of Europeans was felt.

The first Spaniards were those of the party of Alvar Núñez Cabeza de Vaca who, with three other men, spent some eight years, from 1528 to 1536, wandering through the area after having been shipwrecked on the south Texas coast. They traveled as medicine men and traders visiting coastal as well as Coahuiltecan and Jumano peoples. They eventually crossed the Rio Grande and arrived back in Spanish-controlled country on the west Mexican coast (Hodge 1907).

Subsequently several expeditions spearheaded the introduction of Spanish civilization into the area. While Spaniards had pushed northward from the valley of Mexico, within three or four years of the fall of Tenochtitlan in 1521, the first major event in the European movement northward was the discovery of silver in 1546 at Zacatecas. This brought with it a great rush of people from farther south, and for the next 30 years or so the principal task on the northern frontier was the political and economic consolidation of the region between Zacatecas and Mexico City (Alessio Robles 1938:60; Jiménez Moreno 1958:99–100; P.W. Powell 1952:3–15).

For the two decades or so after the founding of Zacatecas, considerable energy was devoted to exploration into the northern regions, mostly for precious metals and slaves, and mission settlements for the natives were established. Explorations were carried out by adventurers such as Francisco de Ibarra, who by 1563 had founded the city of Durango and a new province, Nueva Vizcaya. Exploration and settlement continued to the northwest, where the mines and town of Santa Bárbara were established in 1565, along with a number of other places of lesser importance that were founded about this time. In 1570 the town of Valle de San Bartolomé, near Santa Bárbara, was begun, and this district, which after 1630 included Parral, became one of the focal points of Spanish-Indian contact (Bancroft 1886–1889, 1:99–103; Dunne 1948:10–11; Jiménez Moreno 1958:99–100; López-Velarde López 1964:49–52; Mecham 1927:101ff.; Saravia 1956, 3:263; West 1949:10–12).

On the eastern side of this area, the town of Nombre de Dios was founded in 1555 as a mission among the Zacatec Indians. In 1565, the Franciscan Pedro de Espinareda made the first expedition into Coahuila, and a year later Francisco Cano discovered the Río Las Palmas and a lake he called the Laguna de Nuevo Mexico, apparently the Laguna de Patos. Mazapil was founded in 1569, one year after minerals were discovered there (Alessio Robles 1938:63–67, 140; Jiménez Moreno 1958:99; López-Velarde López 1964:50–58).

Northward from Mazapil, the Saltillo-Monterrey district was first penetrated in 1577, and the New Kingdom of León, which included parts of San Luis Potosí, Tamaulipas, and Texas, was given formal royal sanction in 1579. The town founded was short-lived, but Monterrey itself was resettled around 1582–1583 as the Villa de San Luis. Spanish activity in this area continued into the 1590s, when the Jesuits moved in and opened their missions at Parras and San Pedro de la Laguna on the Río Nazas, founding a mission system that lasted until 1646 when it was secularized.

Finally, in the western portion of the area, beginning in 1581 and 1582 with the parties of Augustín Rodríguez and Antonio de Espejo, several groups explored northward across the Rio Grande into New Mexico, out of the Santa Bárbara district (Alegre 1956–1960, 2:41–42, 57; Alessio Robles 1938:38, 89–93, 102–108, 140–142; Dunne 1944:20ff., 1948:13ff.; López-Velarde López 1964:88–90).

Seventeenth and Eighteenth Centuries

The seventeenth century saw considerable expansion in northern New Spain, much in the realm of missionization. Aside from the Jesuit work, first in Tepehuan country and later in mid-century in the Tarahumara, as well as up the Mexican west coast, the Franciscan Order developed and maintained several administrative units (provinces and custodias) from which they operated. The custodia of Río Verde on the southern periphery saw active mission construction and expansion during the 1600s and early 1700s. Approximately 19 missions were constructed on the Río Verde proper and in the adjacent parts of the present states of San Luis Potosí and Tamaulipas (Dunne 1944, 1948; López-Velarde López 1964:105–121; Spicer 1962:25ff., 46ff., 86ff.).

One of the most active provinces of the Franciscans was that of Zacatecas, originally named after the Zacatec Indians, whom the men of this order first began to missionize. From the city of Zacatecas, Franciscan missions were pushed out in three directions: to the south and southwest into Sierra Madre country; to the north, where the custodia of Parral was eventually established; and to the northeast, where the custodia of Nuevo León was founded.

In the northerly direction, following along the lower elevations of the western Sierra Madre, a chain of missions was established in the lower river valleys of the present state of Chihuahua, first among Concho Indians (with some overlap into Tarahumara country). Soon it had pushed into Suma and Jano-Jocome country in the region of the Casas Grandes valley. The first Franciscan establishment had actually begun about 1570 when Spaniards first went into Tepehuan territory in the Santa Bárbara district. Then, Fray Alonso de la Oliva started work among Concho Indians in the 1590s, establishing the first mission for these people in 1604, with reportedly 4,000 neophytes. More missions were soon founded for Concho Indians at San Pedro de Conchos with a number of satellite conversions, and at Babonoyaba and Namiquipa. Missions at Santa Ana del Torreón, San Antonio de Casas Grandes, and Carretas were for Suma and neighboring groups. After the Pueblo Revolt of 1680 in New Mexico missions were founded at El Paso for Suma and other Indians. Finally, in the early 1700s mines were opened up in what later became the Chihuahua district, and considerable economic development and population influx followed (Griffen 1979:10–11, 158–261; Jiménez Moreno 1958:146–147; López-Velarde López 1964:48–84, 97–98, 104; Torquemada 1943–1944, 3:345).

In the Coahuila and Nuevo León areas, expansion continued in the late 1500s following the foundings of Saltillo and Monterrey and associated settlements. In Nuevo León proper, towns were founded during the 1600s, and many later received Franciscan missions. This missionary push continued into the eighteenth century (López-Velarde López 1964:88–97).

In the late seventeenth century priests from the Franciscan province of Jalisco also began missionization north of Saltillo in the province of Coahuila. Some missionary work had been carried out before 1644. However, in the years following 1673 there was a renewed attempt at missionization of these northern regions toward the Rio Grande. It was not an easy matter to keep Spanish settlements going; a number of missions and Spanish towns failed (Alessio Robles 1938:354–357; López-Velarde López 1964:127–134).

In the vicissitudes suffered by the Coahuila missions some were abandoned and refounded several times. A few missions of this area were founded in the eighteenth century, the best known probably being San Francisco Vizarrón, which was founded in 1737. In addition, around the years 1748 and 1750 some 15 missions were established in the lowland coastal area in the present-day state of Tamaulipas (Alessio Robles 1938:529ff.; López-Velarde López 1964:134–141, 156–159).

In the late 1680s, Spaniards gave some attention to the Texas coastal areas, notably the Bay of Espíritu Santo, in response to French incursions into the region; however, these missions were abandoned by 1694. In the late 1710s several short-lived missions were again installed in the area. Beginning in 1718 the San Antonio district was settled, with some five missions founded by 1731. It was this district, which became the Spanish province of Texas, that served as an area of contact for the native populations of the region (Alessio Robles 1938:424–436, 443–470).

By the middle of the eighteenth century, approximately 200 years after silver had been discovered at Zacatecas, north Mexico and south Texas had been explored by Europeans and a number of places settled. By this time, many native Indian groups had been decimated by the impact of the conquest. In the last half of the century many of the remaining natives were at missions or were living and working at Spanish holdings such as haciendas. A smaller number apparently had joined incoming Apache bands and raiding local settlements, an alternative to conquest that had developed during the contact period (Griffen 1969, 1979).

Spanish Policy and the Frontier

Much of the missionary activity, as well as other types of contact, developed in part from the policy that had been forged in the sixteenth century out of the frontier conditions of early contact between Europeans and Indians, especially after the founding of Zacatecas and the silver rush into that area. The first phase of the policy was to put down Indian hostilities by military means alone. This resulted in such an increase in military activities that the practice was eventually seen to be self-defeating. From about the year 1590 it became the practice of the colonial government to attempt to purchase peace from the Indians with gifts and handouts, while control by military force was diminished. The development of this alternative gave tremendous impetus to missionization, marked especially at the time by the entrance of the Jesuits into the mission field. Their activity was concentrated mostly in the western Sierra Madre and near the west coast, but it also included the region of the Laguna de San Pedro and Parras. The Franciscans, already in the field since the conquest, also stepped up their activities on the frontier.

At the same time, there was a reduction of the presidio or military fort system. By the seventeenth century northern Mexico had a very few permanent military defense posts. It was not felt that these were needed since military and, increasingly, religious personnel, were employed as go-betweens in peace negotiations and settlements. The missionaries made direct efforts at educating and civilizing the Indians. All during the seventeenth century what formal military activity existed was carried out on a local basis and was sponsored by town merchants and other community organizations. Local citizenry, landowners as well as others, held military titles and were frequently pressed into duty in times of emergency. At the same time many Indians from various Indian communities under the control of Spaniards were called to service as auxiliary troops. Around the year 1670, there were about three presidios in the entire north Mexican area, including one on the coast and another at Cerro Gordo, south of the Bolsón de Mapimí country. The total number of soldiers was less than 100 (Hackett 1923–1937, 2:21–25; Haring 1947:124–225; P.W. Powell 1952:189–203, 205, 222–233).

Another change took place after the major revolts in the 1680s. While they continued to try to induce Indians to peace by nonviolent means, often more honored in the letter than in practice, the Europeans clearly increased their reliance on military control of the frontier. Two years after the Pueblo Revolt of 1680 the presidio of El Paso del Norte was established, and after the 1684 revolt in northern Nueva Vizcaya, the presidios of El Pasaje, El Gallo, San Francisco de Conchos, and Janos were set up. From the last decade of the 1600s into the eighteenth century, a rather elaborate presidio system was established, across the northern frontier both westward into Sonora from the Chihuahua area and eastward into Coahuila and Nuevo León (although in 1674 a presidio had been founded at San Francisco de Coahuila in the vicinity of Monclova). In 1703 another presidio was constructed in the east, San Juan Bautista del Río Grande, which was a major power center for the early eighteenth century in this area, as San Francisco de Conchos was in the west. Concurrently, an additional alternative to meeting the frontier threat was developed, that of deporting the most recalcitrant of the raiding Indians from the northern provinces. The final presidio system in the late 1700s, during the Bernardo de Gálvez reforms, belongs to the Apache period and is not properly a part of this chapter (Alessio Robles 1938:237, 274, 376–377; Griffen 1969:4–5, 63ff.; Hackett 1923–1937, 2:24–26, 384).

Cultural Change During the Colonial Period

• THE STRUCTURE OF CONTACT The results of Indian-European contact in north Mexico and south Texas can best be understood by examining the conditions under which the two groups met. While these contact conditions varied over space and time, the general structure was that of a number of small, politically autonomous, and mobile societies meeting the more heterogeneous and more politically and economically powerful European society. The latter, with its formal political-administrative system, eventually became dominant and directed much of the contact processes in accordance with its own goals, while the Indian groups had to react and to adjust to this dominance. The long-range goals of Spanish society were to civilize (christianize) the Indians and to incorporate them into Spanish society. More immediate goals were often to utilize the labor of the natives in some form (Spicer 1961:517–544).

Institutional contexts in which contact occurred can be reduced to four—mine, ranch, mission, and military. Much of the expansion into the northern regions of New Spain was motivated by the attraction of new wealth, mostly in the form of precious metals. Considerable exploration and early settlement (by no means always recorded) was by miners searching for minerals. The establishment of mines was responsible for the development of communities where not only mining but associated activities could be carried out.

A major supportive activity to these settlements was farming and ranching. Some of the livestock were important not only for food but also for power and transportation. At the same time, cattle ranches became prime targets for Indian raiding activities. Often, mines would fail but farming-ranching activities were continued as support to the remainder of the settlements (Del Hoyo 1972, 1:330ff.; Griffen 1969, 1979).

A necessity for these settlements was labor. Exactly how the rather heavy demands for this commodity were met is poorly documented for the northern areas of New Spain, although the sources and the control of the labor can be outlined. Spanish legal theory regarding the protection of Indians aside, it is quite evident that colonists on the frontier felt they had a right to native labor. Indians found on a piece of land were pressed into service. When these people were found to be insufficient for labor needs, because of high mortality or increased economic activity, workers were sought from farther away. Often this took the form of outright raiding, sometimes under a legal fiction that the band of Indians attacked had been granted to the colonist by the Spanish governor. Such raids resulted in individuals and communities being settled on haciendas and at mines. There were also repartimiento-like forced labor drafts where natives continued to live in their own communities, and voluntary migrant labor also occurred. For the most of the area there seems to have been no tribute collecting from the local natives, such as was common elsewhere in the Spanish colonies.

Despite the legal irregularities in the above arrangements, in theory the European owner had certain legal obligations regarding payments to Indians and the provision for minimum conditions of living. Consequently, it was often easier, as West (1949) reports for the Parral mining district, to develop a "free" type of labor, employing Indians as wage laborers, a system that quickly turned into debt peonage. Under this system, because of a lack of a contract with the Crown, Spanish employers no longer had even a modicum of obligation to provide education, civilization, or good treatment for Indians.

Finally, the importation of Indians from distant areas was a regular practice. Often nomadic Indians were captured, given a criminal sentence that legalized their enslavement, and then sent to the mines at Parral or Zacatecas. Natives from the Mexican west coast and from New Mexico were regularly taken to mining areas of northern New Spain (Eguilaz 1965:103–107; Griffen 1979:147–153; Del Hoyo 1972, 1:315–317; Hackett 1923–1937, 2:249; Porras Muñoz 1966:277–278, 512–517; L.B. Simpson 1950; West 1949:47–53, 72–74).

Political incorporation of Indian groups involved bringing people who were used to political decisions being made in an informal context of family, band, or camp into the more formal situations of town, mission, or non–kinship-based work units. Often, of course, in the new contexts political decisions were made entirely by the Europeans, although at the missions it was attempted to have the Indians participate in a community organization of Spanish type. The Spaniards conferred on Indians, frequently as part of mission community organization, titles of *gobernador* (governor), *teniente de gobernador* (lieutenant governor), *capitán* (captain), *sargento* (sergeant), *alférez* (ensign), *alcalde* (mayor), *alguacil* (constable), *fiscal* (public prosecutor), *topil* (constable), *sacristán* (sexton), and *cantor* (singer). Also regional units for the administration of Indians, such as *corregimientos*, which were managed directly by Spaniards, were set up. Concho and Jumano Indians in the Río Conchos basin, because of the rather heavy reliance upon agricultural workers from this area, were placed under an Indian regional governor to facilitate the recruitment of laborers as well as of auxiliary troops (Griffen 1979:138–147).

The Spanish policy of *reducción*, or the congregating of dispersed native groups into nucleated settlements as carried out at the missions, included educational and other community development activities. With the new forms of social organization in community administration, the godparent system and other cultural practices, especially in the areas of agriculture and religion (such as customs of marriage and baptism), were introduced. Consequently the mission was less directly exploitative than were mines, ranches, and military units, while its educational activities often directly attacked the realms of nonmaterial culture, such as the replacement of native ideology, with which the other institutions were not immediately concerned (Griffen 1979:274–278; Spicer 1968:172).

Most of the area of concern here was worked by Franciscans, and consequently there was a certain uniformity in the cultural practices of the missionaries. The exception was the Jesuits at San Pedro de la Laguna and Santa María de las Parras, a single mission district. In contrast to the Jesuits, Franciscans used the Indian languages less (including the Nahuatl tongue), and they transferred their men more often (usually every three years), which meant that they could not establish lasting ties with their flocks. Franciscan establishments were often located close to Spanish civil settlements and therefore they felt the demands for Indian labor and troops directly. In addition, different Indian groups were frequently made to settle at the same mission, and a number of missions (for example, San Francisco de Conchos, Santa Cruz de Tapacolmes) were multi-ethnic for much of their history (Griffen 1979:158ff., 171–177).

During the first century or so of colonial contact Indians were regularly drafted into service for military campaigns, often accounting for the major part of the military force, as fighters as well as scouts and couriers. Frequently, virtually all the able-bodied males of a band would be pressed into service. Later, Indian auxiliary troops were used less and then in more specialized ways, as scouts and special fighting forces of quite acculturated individuals. By the eighteenth century, the presidio system consisted of regular soldiers who were Mestizos, Spaniards, and other hispanicized individuals (Griffen 1979:153–157).

• REACTIONS TO CONQUEST Responses of the native populations to conquest occurred in several ways. On the biological level there was a reduction of the population, largely as a result of the introduction of diseases for which the Indians had little immunity, but overwork on Spanish holdings, famines, war, executions, and deportations also played a part.

On the cultural level, the common response of politically autonomous groups was an increase in hostility toward the Europeans, leading to a virtually perpetual state of war. For those peoples who became subordinate to the Spanish empire, there is no good accounting of how many groups ever settled down permanently and became assimilated. Many bands took up raiding activities for considerable periods of time. Then, later, when their numbers had been decimated by the processes mentioned above, their few remaining descendants were found at missions, haciendas, or other places. A few others joined neighboring groups or invading newcomers such as the Apache.

Because of this similarity in response, warfare on the north-central Mexican frontier became regular. While the distinction is sometimes difficult to maintain, this endemic war-raiding-retaliation should not be confused with revolts or rebellions. The rebellions occurred under slightly different conditions, when peoples were settled and quiet for considerable periods of time and then as grievances accumulated several different groups rose at the same time, maintaining active and concerted hostilities with the Spaniards until some agreement for peace was reached, and the hostilities again abated for a number of years.

At least in the western portion of the area, particularly in the Concho-Jumano river valley region, revolts rather than endemic warfare seem to characterize the reaction to conquest. Precise reasons for this difference in response still need to be adequately documented, but they include the original native type of society, particularly the level of sociopolitical sophistication, in addition to the type, intensity, and stage of Spanish contact. While little is known of the nature of Concho society, certainly the Jumano in the La Junta region were much more sedentary and socially complex than were the hinterland desert dwellers.

After some initial hostilities of raiding and retaliation, the Concho-Jumano groups remained quiet until 1644 when a short-lived but rather intense rebellion occurred. These peoples, although joined by the endemic raiders, were rather quickly brought to peace and did not again take up arms until 1684, four years following the Pueblo Revolt in New Mexico. This is the last time the Concho-Jumano acted as any kind of unit. Only the Jumano at La Junta were able to retain their unity during most of the first half of the 1700s. Afterward the descendants of these groups were found living at various Spanish holdings with increasing assimilation to hispanic society. This is after their numbers had been quite reduced; however, it now seems that a greater percentage of these people were eventually absorbed into north-central Mexican society than in areas farther east. It was also about at the turn of the eighteenth century that the Tarahumara to the west ceased to be overtly hostile to the Spaniards. Much of the Tarahumara country as it existed then became a zone of refuge, while Concho-Jumano country became a zone of hispanicization (Aguirre Beltrán 1967; Griffen 1979).

The pattern of warfare in the north-central desert region was somewhat different. By around 1600, the Cuachichil and their neighbors had diminished their hostilities, partly in response to changing Spanish policy. However, in the mountains to the west, the Tepehuan carried out a bloody rebellion beginning in 1617, in which a few neighboring peoples, notably the Concho in the Santa Bárbara district, participated.

War-raiding-retaliation continued with the desert hinterland groups, although slowly the focus of the zone of hostilities (*tierra de guerra*) shifted northward. After the 1644 revolt, the Spanish governor of Nueva Vizcaya moved his residence to the Parral district. Hostilities continued especially from the Parral district to the east, and from Parras and Saltillo north, for the next few decades. About the year 1690 a major raiding group, the Cabeza, composed of people from a number of specific bands in the general area and up to the Rio Grande, capitulated and settled at the town of Parras.

This left a niche into which various groups of Toboso and other Coahuila peoples moved. Within the next two or three decades some of these groups were settled in towns or deported. Most notably, some Coahuileño were settled at Santos Cinco Señores in the 1710s, and most of the Toboso and many Coahuileño were deported out of the northern provinces in the 1720s. This again left a niche, soon occupied by Apache from across the Rio Grande and refugees and remnants of local native groups. Within a very few years after the 1750s, practically the only remaining hostile groups in the general region were Apaches, while Spanish governmental and military power again shifted northward to Chihuahua city and areas near the present United States–Mexican border (Griffen 1979:42–44).

In the twentieth century all the original Indian groups of the area are culturally extinct. For a time in the later colonial period and into the Mexican national period there existed two different kinds of people called Indians or *indios*. One consisted of people occupying marginal places in the Spanish social system and generally the lowest stratum. They were partly or largely hispanicized and basically Spanish speaking, forming part of the less skilled labor force. People of low socioeconomic status were still on occasion referred to as *indios* in the 1970s.

The other kind of Indian was those groups not incorporated into Spanish society who continued to dwell in the hinterland in direct continuity with the earlier native way of life. These often became the specialized, wide-ranging, and hard-hitting raiders of Spanish colonial settlements who, mounted on horseback, adopted a number of items of Spanish material culture (such as knives, clothing) into their ways of life. A number of different peoples, such as the Cuachichil, Toboso, and Coahuileños, evolved into this type of society before they became extinct. The best remembered are the Apache, the last of a long line of colonial raiding specialists, who entered the area in the late seventeenth and the eighteenth centuries (Griffen 1969:103, 142, 1979:274ff.; P.W. Powell 1952).

Synonymy

Aranama: Aranames (Eguilaz 1966), Xaranames, Jaranames (I. Goddard 1979:373).

Bobol: occasionally Babol, Vovol, etc.

Cabeza: Cabesa, Cabessa, Caveza, Cavessa, Cavesa; 'head' in Spanish.

Cacaxte: Cacaste, Cacaxtle; 'carrying frame' in Mexican Spanish.

Carrizo: Carriso; 'reed' in Spanish. This name was

applied to several distinct groups that lived in a riverine environment (I. Goddard 1979:369–370).

Coahuileño: A general term used for people from Coahuila (later adopted as the name for the modern Mexican state), a native term said to mean 'lowlands' with variants used from 1605 into the early half of the 1700s: Cuaguila, Quahuila, Cauila, Cuaguilla (Griffen 1969:159; Jiménez Moreno 1958:106).

Contotor: Contotol, Contotoli.

Cuachichil: Guachichil.

Hueyhueyquetzal: This name has a great many variants, the one used here being a Spanish rendering of a Nahuatl reduplicated form meaning 'great big green feather'. Many of the variations that occur apparently depend upon how familiar writer or scribe was with Nahuatl: Heyquetzal, Gueiquesal, Guesal, Quequesal, Quesal, Quechal, Guicasal, Guical, Guijacal, Gusiquesal, Guesol, Kesale (Griffen 1969:160, 165; W.W. Newcomb 1961:39).

Jocome: rarely Jacome.

Jumano: Jumana, Xumana, Humano, Zumana, Chouman (a French rendition), apparently also Zuma, Suma, and Yuma; the Suma were the western branch, the Jumano the eastern (Sauer 1934:68).

Katuhano: Catajuno, Catujan, Catujano, Catuxano, Catuxanes.

Suma: Zuma, Yuma (Jumano).

Toboso: Tobosso, Tovoso, Tovosso, Toboço.

Terocodame: Terococodames, Teodocodamos, Terkodams.

See also the synonymy in "Coahuiltecans and Their Neighbors," this volume.

Sources

There are a good many works on the northern, central, and eastern portions of New Spain in the colonial period. Major secondary sources that summarize relevant facts of the political, social, and cultural history of the area include Alessio Robles (1938), Bancroft (1886–1889), Bolton (1930a, 1970), Forbes (1960), Saravia (1956, 3), and Santa Maria (1929–1930). Almada (1968) gives much specific history on various sites. Decorme (1941) covers the Jesuit period, and Del Hoyo's (1972) history is excellent. López-Velarde López (1964) covers the Franciscan expansion into the area. Porras Muñoz (1966) gives valuable information on the structure of Spanish society in the western part of the area. P.W. Powell (1952) covers Spanish contact with Indians in the northern region and the development of policy in the sixteenth century. Four writers from the colonial period itself give an invaluable perspective—Alegre (1956–1960), Arlegui (1851), Mota y Escobar (1940), and Pérez de Ribas (1944a).

Works that deal more specificallly with the ethnography and tribal distributions will give a good introduction to the area. Ethnographic summaries past and present as well as explorations in the area during the colonial period are included: Beals (1932a), Bolton (1911, 1930a), Casañas (1927), Driver and Driver (1963), Eguilaz (1965, 1966), Del Hoyo (1972), Leon (1909), Griffen (1969, 1979), Hackett (1923–1937), Pichardo (1931–1946), Gallegos Lamero (1927), Hodge (1907, 1911), Jiménez Moreno (1958), Kroeber (1934), Lafora (1939), Las Casas (1936), Manrique Castañeda (1969), Martínez del Río (1954), Miranda (1871), Morfí (1958), W.W. Newcomb (1961), Orozco y Berra (1864), Portillo (1886), Ruecking (1955a), Saldívar (1943, 1945), Sauer (1934), Soustelle (1937), Tamarón y Romeral (1937), and Tello (1858–1866, 2, 1891).

There are a number of documentary collections that cover the area. While some have been utilized more than others, probably none has been exhausted regarding the ethnography and culture history of the region. Generally, the amount of direct information on social and cultural practices, languages, contact among groups and processes of change in any one source is slight, and a number of sources must be consulted to obtain any kind of comprehensive picture. Consequently, much remains to be done, especially for the earlier years of the period and in the utilization of local archives, church parish archives, and private collections. Major collections are the Archivo General de la Nación, Mexico City; the Biblioteca Nacional, Mexico City; University of California at Berkeley, Bancroft Library; the Documents Division and the Latin American Collection at the University of Texas, Austin; the collection of Padre Pablo Pastells at Saint Louis University, Missouri; the collection of Fray Marcelino de Civezza (Franciscan documents on the late colonial period), University of Arizona, Tucson; copies of documents held at the Centro de Documentación, Castillo de Chapultepec (Mexico City), and the published collection of *Documentos para la Historia de México*. Specifically, for the western portion of the old province of Nueva Vizcaya local documents from the following places have been consulted quite exhaustively: Archive of the Jesuit Church, Parras de la Fuente, Coahuila; in Chihuahua, parish archives at Aldama, Aquiles Serdán, Bachíniva, Buenaventura, Camargo, Casa Grandes Viejo, Chihuahua City (Cathedral), General Trías, Julimes, Namiquipa, Ojinaga, Parral (Cathedral), Rosales, and Valle de Allende. The most significant municipal archives are those of Janos (records of the old Janos presidio) now deposited specifically in the local church and at the Latin American Collection, University of Texas, Austin, with some copies at the University of Texas, El Paso, and the archives at Parral, a veritable mine of the records of the capital of the Province of Nueva Vizcaya now on microfilm (over 300 reels) and available at a number of major libraries.

Coahuiltecans and Their Neighbors

T.N. CAMPBELL

The lowland portion of northeastern Mexico and adjacent southern Texas was originally occupied by hundreds of small, apparently autonomous, distinctively named local groups or bands of Indians, most of whom seem to have lived by hunting and gathering. During the Spanish colonial period these groups were extensively displaced from their traditional foraging territories by Europeans from the south and by Apaches from the north.

In their documents the Spanish immigrants did not describe Indians in much detail, and they had little interest in developing a formal classification of the numerous ethnic units. For these hunting and gathering peoples there was no obvious basis for classification. Major cultural contrasts were not noted, and a tribal form of organization was not evident. Few Europeans were able to recognize significant similarities and differences in the native languages and dialects spoken. Each Indian group was commonly referred to as a *nación*; and when Spaniards referred to Indians collectively, it was usually done in practical but superficial ways. The Indians were most often grouped on the basis of association with major terrain features or with Spanish jurisdictional units; however, in Nuevo León certain Indian populations were linked on the basis of shared cultural peculiarities, such as styles of hairdress and body decoration. All this has made it difficult for modern scholars to achieve a sorting of these hunting and gathering groups that reflects valid differences in language and culture.

The first attempt at classification, which was based on language, came after most of the Indian groups had become extinct. In the mid-nineteenth century Mexican linguists (Orozco y Berra 1864:61–69; Pimentel 1862–1865, 2:409–413) designated some of the Indian groups as Coahuilteco because it was believed that they had spoken various dialects of a language known to have been spoken in Coahuila and Texas. (Coahuilteco is a Spanish adjective formed from the name Coahuila.) This language is mainly documented by published manuals prepared by two friars for use in administering church ritual in one native language at certain missions of southern Texas and northeastern Coahuila (García 1760; Vergara 1965). Unfortunately, neither these manuals nor other documents specify the names of all Indian groups who originally spoke Coahuilteco. Remnants of other linguistic groups also entered the same missions, and some of these had learned to speak Coahuilteco because it had become the dominant language spoken by Indians at those missions.

This inability to identify all the named Indian groups who originally spoke Coahuilteco has been a perennial stumbling-block in efforts to distinguish them from their neighbors. After a few additional language samples became known for the region, linguists concluded that these represented languages related to Coahuilteco and grouped them in a Coahuiltecan family (Powell 1891; Sapir 1920; Swanton 1940). This encouraged ethnohistorians and anthropologists to believe that the region was occupied by numerous small Indian groups who spoke related languages and shared the same basic culture. A "Coahuiltecan culture" was constructed by assembling bits of both specific and generalized information recorded by Spaniards at various times for widely scattered and very limited portions of the region (Ruecking 1953, 1954, 1954a, 1955, 1955a; see also W.W. Newcomb 1961). Later, this belief in a widespread linguistic and cultural uniformity was seriously questioned. In Nuevo León evidence of at least one language not relatable to Coahuilteco has come to light (Gursky 1964), and linguists are beginning to doubt that any of the other language samples recorded for the region are good enough for demonstrating relationships with Coahuilteco (I. Goddard 1979). Thus, interpretive opinion about the region as a whole is now in a state of confusion, but it is becoming evident that the Coahuiltecan concept has been extended beyond the bounds of credibility.

Regional Definition

The identifiable Coahuiltecans and many of their numerous neighbors were associated with an extensive coastal plain environment of northeastern Mexico and Texas (fig. 1). This plain includes the northern part of what in Mexico is called the Gulf Coastal Lowlands and the southern part of what in the United States is called the Gulf Coastal Plain (R.C. West 1964). Except on the northeast, this region has clear-cut boundaries: the shore line of the Gulf of Mexico on the east, the northwest-trending mountain chain of Mexico on the west, and the eroded southern margin of the Edwards Plateau of Texas on the north. East and southeast of San Antonio, Texas, the boundary is somewhat arbitrary. The southeastward course of the Guadalupe River to the Gulf of Mexico is chosen here because it marks certain changes in plant and animal life, as well as in Indian languages and culture. Thus the region, as here defined, includes southern Texas, northeastern Coahuila, and the greater parts of both Nuevo León and Tamaulipas.

Most of this region is characterized by flat to gently rolling terrain, particularly in Texas, but in Nuevo León and Tamaulipas several isolated mountain masses occur east of the Sierra Madre Oriental. The region is dominated by one drainage system, that of the Rio Grande, which flows across its middle portion and has a delta on the coast. Important but smaller drainages are found both north and south of the Rio Grande. The coast line from the Guadalupe River of Texas southward to central Tamaulipas is notable for its chain of elongated, offshore barrier islands, behind which are shallow bays and lagoons. The region's climate is best described as megathermal and generally semiarid. Rainfall declines with greater distance from the coast, but no part of the region can be classified as true desert.

In this region horticulture among Indians was confined to certain groups of southern Tamaulipas; elsewhere hunting and gathering subsistence techniques prevailed. The region roughly coincides with the Tamaulipan Biotic Province of biologists (Blair 1950; R.C. West 1964), which has a wide range of soil types that fosters localized abundance of wild plants yielding edible foodstuffs, such as mesquite bean pods, maguey root crowns, prickly pear fruit, pecans, acorns, and various kinds of roots and tubers. The introduction of European livestock altered vegetation patterns, and extensive grassland areas were invaded by thorny brush vegetation.

The deer was the most widespread and readily available large game animal. Bison were confined mainly to southern Texas, with one notable southward extension across the Rio Grande into northeastern Coahuila. Smaller game animals widely available included the peccary and armadillo, rabbits, rats and mice, various birds, and numerous species of snakes, lizards, frogs, toads, and land snails. Fish were found in all perennial streams, and both fish and shellfish were available in saline waters along the Gulf coast.

Prior to European colonization this region was known only from observations recorded in documents pertaining to the travels of Álvar Núñez Cabeza de Vaca in 1534–1535. The Mexican portion of the region was colonized over a period of approximately 150 years, beginning about 1590. The colonists came by land from southern Mexico, principally by an inland route west of the Sierra Madre Oriental, crossing the mountains by easy passes west and northwest of Monterrey, Nuevo León. Effective colonization of northern Tamaulipas and southern Texas came relatively late, mainly in the eighteenth century.

This is one of the most poorly known regions of Indian North America. The reasons why it is so poorly known have never been clearly stated. Since all its native Indian groups are extinct, what can be learned about each group must come from miscellaneous observations sparingly recorded in various kinds of documents written before its extinction. Early drawings and paintings by Europeans, artifact collections in museums, and limited archeological excavations have yet to yield much information that can be linked with specific Indian groups of the historic period. In the archives of Europe and America the innumerable unpublished documents that pertain to this region have not been thoroughly searched, and the information collected has not been meticulously evaluated and analyzed for the purpose of making, for each identifiable Indian group, reliable statements about its earliest known territorial range, the language originally spoken, and the nature of its culture before displacement. Little effort has been made to study group names and their orthographic variants in order to reduce confusion about the actual number of ethnic units present in the region. Minimal attention has been paid to definition of the major factors involved in Indian group displacement, population decline, and extinction or absorption. After initial dis-

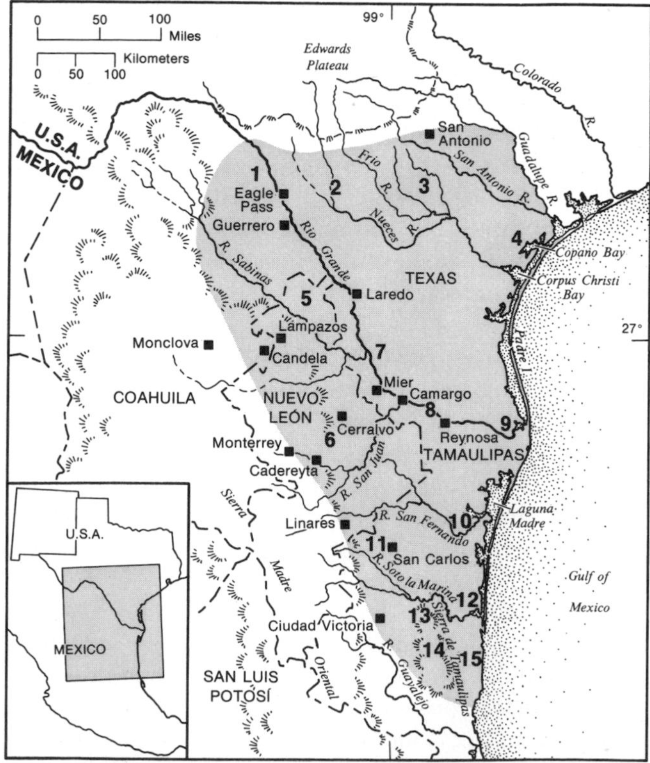

Fig. 1. Territory of the Coahuiltecans and their neighbors. Numbers refer to areas described at the end of the chapter and in the synonymy.

placement, the movements of very few Indian groups have been painstakingly traced through dated documents. Many groups were last recorded as remnant populations associated with Spanish missions, but little use has been made of information recorded in mission registers and censuses. Assessments of group territorial range and population size, both before and after displacement, have been superficial, and there have been few attempts to ascertain the extent of changes in language and culture during the historic period. With such limitations, it is evident that most statements about Indians of this region must be general in nature and largely tentative.

In early attempts to define culture areas or provinces in North America this region was found to be difficult to categorize. Initially parts of the region were assigned to other, better-known cultural provinces. O.T. Mason (1896) divided the Texas portion between a Gulf Coast and a Plains area. Wissler (1917) assigned parts of the region to three culture areas: Southeastern, Southwestern, and Nahua. Kroeber (1939) recognized more unity when he designated a Northwest Gulf Coast area, but this extended eastward almost to the Mississippi River. W.W. Newcomb (1956) defined a smaller Western Gulf area that terminated at Galveston Bay in southeastern Texas. These later conceptualizations recognized occupation of an extensive coastal plain by Indian peoples who subsisted without benefit of horticulture and who exhibited a relatively low level of cultural complexity. It appears that more cultural unity can be demonstrated for Newcomb's Western Gulf province if its northeastern boundary is moved westward to the lower Guadalupe River of Texas. Even with this modification, Newcomb's Western Gulf is still not a sharply defined cultural province.

Displacement

One continuing theme throughout the Spanish colonial period was displacement of hunting and gathering groups, which resulted in fragmentation and population decline. This displacement phenomenon was complex, and there has been no intensive study of it in this region comparable to that of Griffen (1969) for central northern Mexico. The indigenous Indian groups were displaced by two invading populations—Spaniards from southern Mexico and Apaches from the Plains area of northwestern Texas.

The best-documented displacements resulted from the slow, uneven northward advance of the Spanish settlement frontier. Displaced Indian groups tended to move northward away from a Spanish settlement, but sometimes there were movements to the east or west. As the frontier moved northward, some groups that had been previously displaced were displaced again. In some areas it is evident that European-introduced diseases, such as smallpox and measles, had moved ahead of the Spanish frontier and had reduced the size of many groups before they were initially displaced (Figueroa Torres 1963).

When Spanish settlers arrived in a new area they often occupied the favored Indian encampment localities. They brought livestock that competed with wild grazing and browsing animals. Game animals were thinned or driven away by Spanish hunters with firearms. The Indians turned to livestock as a substitute for game animals, and loss of livestock brought punitive action by Spaniards. European goods that had come to be desired by Indians were taken by theft, by raids on isolated ranches, and sometimes by attacks on Spanish supply trains. Frustration and accumulated resentments led to poorly organized Indian rebellions that were invariably followed by Spanish retaliation. Eventually most of the Indians left the immediate area, although some chose to remain and coexist with Spaniards (Alessio Robles 1938; Espinosa 1964; León, Bautista Chapa, and Sánchez de Zamora 1961).

Displacement by Apaches occurred only in the northern part of this region, where the northward-advancing Spanish frontier converged with the leading edge of the southeastward expansion of Apaches from the southern Plains. In the first half of the seventeenth century these Apaches acquired horses from Spanish colonists of New Mexico and soon dominated their southern Plains environment. In 1683–1684 Juan Domínguez de Mendoza traveled from El Paso eastward into the western part of the Edwards Plateau of Texas, and his itinerary clearly indicates Apache dominance by that date (Mendoza, in Bolton 1916; J.W. Williams 1962). This southeastward expansion seems to have been intensified by the Pueblo Indian Revolt of 1680, during which all Spanish colonists were driven from New Mexico and the Apaches lost their prime source of good horses. Their attention was apparently drawn to the Spanish settlements of Coahuila, where horses were to be had. In his itinerary Domínguez de Mendoza recorded the names of numerous Indian groups east of the lower Pecos River who had been or were being displaced by Apaches in 1683–1684. Variants of many of these group names were found in later documents that pertain to northeastern Coahuila and the adjoining part of Texas, for example, Abau (found later as Hiabu), Acani (Ocana), Humez (Hume), Papan (Papanac), Pucha (Patzau), Puguahian or Paguachian (Pacuache), and Tojuma (Toamar).

By the middle eighteenth century the Apaches themselves were displaced from the highlands of central Texas by Comanches and moved down onto the coastal plain of southern Texas, where they were commonly referred to as Lipan Apaches. These Apaches in turn displaced the last Indian groups native to southern Texas, most of whom ended up at Spanish missions in San Antonio (fig. 2) (Campbell and Campbell 1981). By 1790 Spaniards were little concerned with the remnants of aboriginal hunting and gathering groups and faced the problem of containing various Apache groups in a large area that extended from the Gulf coast of southern Texas westward across northern Coahuila and Chihuahua.

In one area the combined effects of Spanish and Apache displacements led to unusual ethnic complexity: northeastern Coahuila and the adjacent part of Texas. Here the Indian groups native to the area were joined by groups displaced from the south by Spaniards, from the north by Apaches, and from the west as a result of the Spanish-Indian wars of the middle seventeenth century in western Coahuila and Chihuahua (Griffen 1969). Some groups, in order to escape from both Spaniards and Apaches, combined and migrated northeastward into open areas east of the central Texas highlands. Among those who are best documented by records of travel across that part of Texas are Ervipiame, Pamaya, Sijame, Ticmamar (Tumamar), and Xarame (Bolton 1970; Campbell 1975, 1979). Failure to chart the recorded movements of displaced peoples in this especially complex area has been the source of much confusion in ethnic group identification and classification.

Spanish Missions

In this region Spanish missions were especially numerous. Although rationalized by Europeans in a variety of ways, the Christian missions of northeastern New Spain represented an institution that provided places of refuge for remnants of displaced and declining Indian populations. Each mission was established on the forefront of the advancing Spanish frontier. New missions were built as the irregular line of settlements moved forward, and older missions were left behind to decline in importance. Each mission was agriculturally based and could not be maintained very long unless it continued to receive recruits to replace its normally declining Indian population, which constituted the mission's labor force.

The missions were unevenly distributed. Some were more or less isolated; others were clustered, two to five in number, in relatively small areas, as in northeastern Coahuila and southern Texas, where the number of displaced Indian groups was large because of combined Spanish and Apache pressures. Clustered missions always had a nearby protective military garrison (presidio). Some missions had a very short life span, lasting only a few years, but others lasted as long as a century. A few were moved one or more times because of inadequate subsistence resources or because of desertion by their Indians. Eventually all missions were either abandoned or transformed into parish churches.

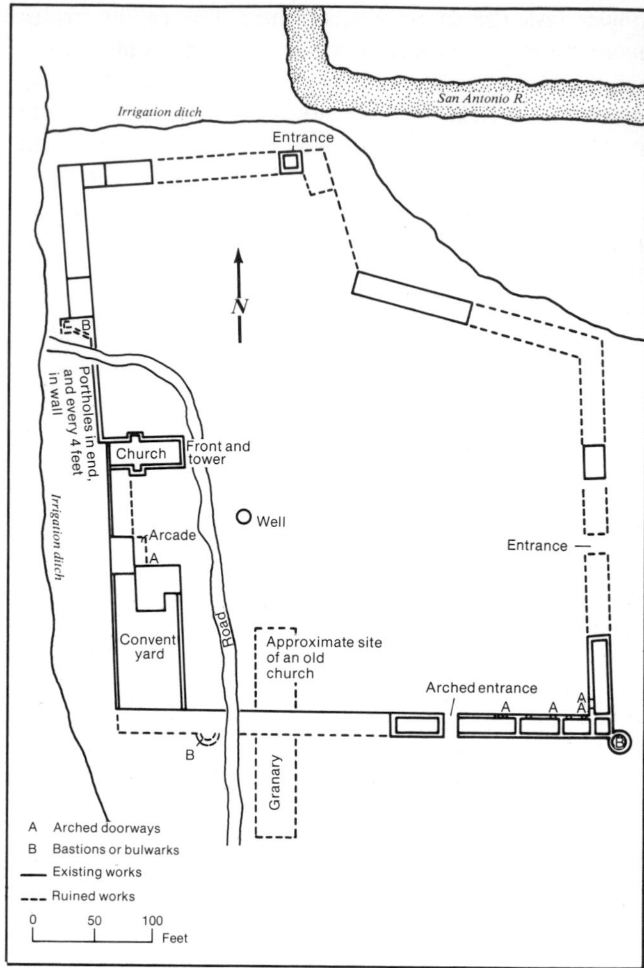

after Corner 1890.

Fig. 2. Plan of Mission San Francisco de la Espada at San Antonio, Tex. The Indian quarters built of stone and mortar formed the walls of the mission compound. The mission was one of the centers of Indian activity during the 18th century until after partial secularization in 1794, when it was abandoned by the Indians and the fields neglected (Berlandier 1969:8). In 1762, 207 Indians lived in the mission; by 1794 there were about 40 (Habig 1968:270).

The evidence is limited, but it appears that the total number of separate Indian groups represented at particular missions throughout their existence was highly variable, ranging from less than 20 groups to as many as 100 (Hodge 1907–1910, various mission entries; Campbell 1979). Many Indian groups were represented at a mission by less than 10 individuals, sometimes by one individual only. Missions in existence the longest usually had more groups represented, particularly in the north. At no time does any mission Indian village seem to have been notably large, usually consisting of no more than a few hundred Indians.

Each mission had a different mix of Indian groups. Remnants of many groups came from a relatively large area surrounding a particular mission, but some remnants came from distant areas, reflecting complex movement patterns of groups displaced at different times over a large part of northern Mexico and Texas (Campbell 1979). Sometimes all surviving Indians of a single group seem to have entered one particular mission, but individuals and families of a single ethnic group might enter as many as five or six different missions. The available evidence suggests that remnants of some Indian groups never entered a Spanish mission.

Extinction and Absorption

Most groups lost their identities as free-moving units during the seventeenth and eighteenth centuries, their distinctive names, one by one, disappearing from written records. Their decline was the result of prolonged attrition: deaths in periodic epidemics, deaths in warfare (early rebellions against Spanish control, disputes with other local groups, and attacks by intrusive Apaches), migration of remnants to other regions, punitive dispersion by Spaniards to work at distant plantations and mines, high infant mortality, and general demoralization (Alessio Robles 1938; Bolton 1970; Campbell 1975; Del Hoyo 1972; León, Bautista Chapa, and Sánchez de Zamora 1961; Saldívar 1945). Small remnants of some groups lost their identities by merging with larger remnants of other groups. By 1800 the names of very few ethnic units were noted in documents, and by 1900 the names of all Indian groups native to the region had disappeared (Swanton 1940).

The last bastions of ethnic identity were Spanish missions and small, unstable refugee communities near a few Spanish or Mexican towns. The communities were tolerated because the Indians caused little trouble and the communities were convenient reservoirs of unskilled labor. In both missions and refugee communities the original ethnic names ceased to be important because of intermarriages. By the close of the eighteenth century most missions had been terminated and Indian families were given small parcels of mission land. Eventually all surviving Indians passed into the lower economic levels of Mexican society. In 1981 descendants of some aboriginal groups still lived in various communities of Mexico and Texas, but few attempts have been made to discover individuals who can demonstrate this descent.

Ethnic Group Identification

For this region and various areas immediately adjacent to it scholars have encountered over 1,000 ethnic group names in documents that cover a period of approximately 350 years. This remarkably large number of names poses questions that have seldom been asked. Does each recorded name signify a separate and distinct ethnic unit, or were some units known by two or more names at the same time or at different times? Do these names signify groups that were native to the region, or do some names refer to groups displaced from adjoining regions? How many of the names refer to groups that were in existence at particular selected dates?

Critical studies of ethnic group names have barely begun, but those that have been made show that the total number of recorded names exceeds the number of actual ethnic units, possibly by as much as 25 percent. Group names are recorded very unevenly. Some names are known from a single document, which may or may not indicate a geographic location. Other names may appear in 10 or 12 documents, and still others may appear in hundreds of documents, making it possible to demonstrate ethnic continuity over a long span of time. Sometimes documents clearly indicate that two or more names refer to the same ethnic unit. It has been shown that a substantial number of names refer to Indian groups that were displaced from adjoining areas (Campbell 1979). Some groups evidently became extinct very early or later became known by different names.

One knotty problem in ethnic identification arises when modern scholars misinterpret orthographic variants of the same group name. Phonetically complex names of native origin have been rendered by Spanish writers in an astonishing number of ways, sometimes 50 or more. Some name variants are so badly distorted that scholars have concluded that they signify additional ethnic units. One special study of name variants in southern Texas indicates that 18 renditions of one name had been mistakenly interpreted as referring to six separate ethnic units instead of one (Campbell 1977). Similar studies may further reduce the total number of Indian groups believed to have lived in this region.

The best information on the meanings of native group names comes from Nuevo León documents, in which Spanish translations of native names are often given (Del Hoyo 1960). Over 60 percent of these names refer to localized topographic and vegetational features. Other names refer to specific plants and animals and to body decoration. Group names of Spanish origin are not numerous, less than 10 percent of all recorded names, and usually refer to physical characteristics, cultural traits, and environmental details. Although documentary evidence is hard to find, there is enough to suggest that some Spanish names duplicate native group names already recorded.

Modern attempts to standardize the spelling of Indian group names for this region have either been limited in scope (Hodge 1907–1910) or impractical (Ruecking 1954a). The pronunciation of ethnic group names of native origin cannot be indicated with authority because all Indian groups are extinct and samples of very few languages spoken were ever recorded (I. Goddard 1979).

Spanish writers rarely placed accent marks on Indian names to indicate stress. In the twentieth century it has become customary to follow Spanish phonetics and place stress on the next to last syllable when the native name ends in a vowel or in *n* or *s*, and on the last syllable when the name ends in other consonants.

Identifying Coahuiltecan Groups

There is no question about the reality of a language known as Coahuilteco, but it is not at present possible to identify all the Indian groups who spoke dialects of this language. Since cultural description is so limited, it is not possible to identify groups as Coahuiltecans by using strictly cultural criteria.

Although far from satisfactory, the best information on Coahuilteco-speaking groups comes from statements made by two missionaries, Damián Mazanet and Bartholomé García. In 1690 and again in 1691 Mazanet traveled northeastward from a mission near Candela in eastern Coahuila to the vicinity of present San Antonio, Texas, and recorded the names of 39 Indian groups encountered (Gómez Canedo 1968). In his account of the 1691 journey Mazanet stated that a single language was spoken throughout the area traversed. This language was apparently Coahuilteco, since some of the recorded and translated place-names are identifiable as Coahuilteco words (I. Goddard 1979). Coahuilteco was probably the dominant language of the area, but some groups may have spoken Coahuilteco only as a second language. By 1690 the area traversed by Mazanet must have received some groups displaced by Apaches, and for two groups named by Mazanet, Jumano and Hape, there is acceptable evidence of such displacement (Campbell 1979). It is doubtful that the native language of all groups displaced southward by Apaches was Coahuilteco.

García (1760), in a manual for the administration of church ritual in the Coahuilteco language, listed the names of 18 Indian groups at missions in southern Texas (San Antonio) and northeastern Coahuila (Guerrero) who spoke dialects of Coahuilteco (fig. 3). It is evident from other documents that some of the groups named did not originally speak dialects of Coahuilteco, and García himself noted that in four groups only the young people could speak Coahuilteco. It is not surprising to find on García's list no more than three names that also apear on Mazanet's lists of 1690–1691. Many groups had lost their ethnic identities during the intervening years. The García list is especially informative because it identifies as Coahuilteco speakers a number of poorly known groups who lived nearer to the Gulf coast of southern Texas than the groups seen farther inland by Mazanet.

Table 1 contains the names of all groups who probably spoke dialects of Coahuilteco before being displaced, or at least before their remnants entered Spanish missions. Most names are derived from the lists of Mazanet and García; names of other groups are given when various kinds of circumstantial evidence in documents suggest that they may have spoken Coahuilteco. Some groups long believed to have been Coahuilteco speakers are excluded from table 1 because of evidence that shows that another language was spoken (Campbell and Campbell 1981; I. Goddard 1979).

This list of probable Coahuiltecans, which is based on none too reliable information about the language spoken by any specific group, indicates that all the Indians who can reasonably be designated as Coahuiltecans were confined to southern Texas and extreme northeastern Coahuila, with perhaps some extension into northern Nuevo León, as was indicated by the nineteenth-century Mexican linguists who created the term Coahuilteco. Because of inadequate information on various other languages spoken in the surrounding areas, it is not now possible to compile similar lists of Indian groups who spoke those languages. The belief, under question, that all the Indians of Newcomb's Western Gulf province spoke languages related to Coahuilteco, is the prime reason why so many Indian groups have been brought into the Coahuiltecan orbit. For some time it has been customary to assume that any Indian group of the coastal lowlands that did not speak a Karankawa or a Tonkawa language must have spoken Coahuilteco (for example, see W.W. Newcomb 1961; Ruecking 1953, 1954; Swanton 1940). Since the Tonkawans and Karankawans were largely confined to areas farther north and northeast, only one classificatory pigeonhole was available, and hence most of the Indians of southern Texas and northeastern Mexico came to be loosely thought of as Coahuiltecans. Additional studies are needed in order to demonstrate whether this interpretation is essentially correct or whether it is an oversimplification.

Territory and Population

Inadequate documentation and displacement over such a long period make it difficult to determine the original territorial ranges of most of the hunting and gathering groups of this region. Few attempts have been made to plot the locations of specific groups as indicated by a sequence of dated documents or to identify the earliest location recorded for each group. For any particular Indian group the earlier European observers rarely recorded the locations of two or more encampments, and when they did it was usually for warm seasons when Europeans did their traveling on horseback. Winter encampments were rarely recorded. This problem is further complicated by the fact that encampments were often shared by two or more separately named Indian groups, which in many cases seems to indicate associ-

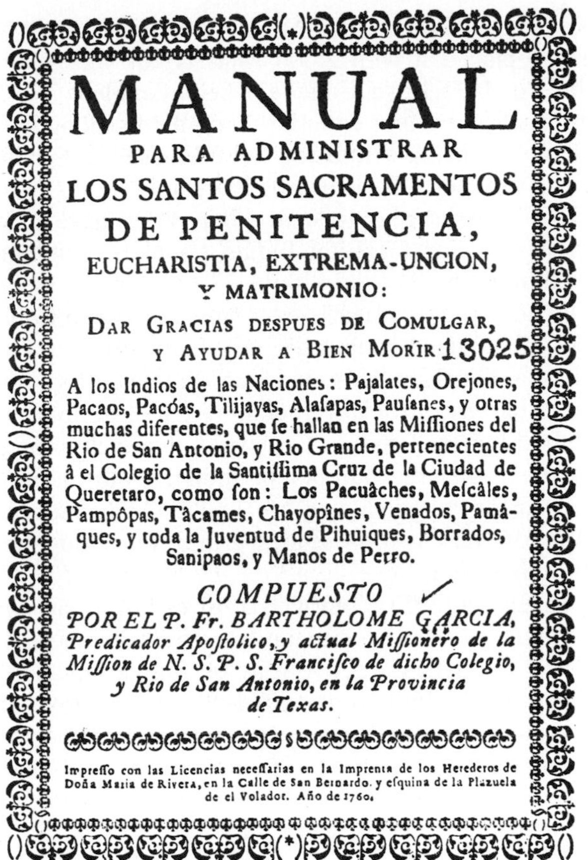

MANUAL
PARA ADMINISTRAR
LOS SANTOS SACRAMENTOS
DE PENITENCIA,
EUCHARISTIA, EXTREMA-UNCION,
Y MATRIMONIO:
DAR GRACIAS DESPUES DE COMULGAR,
Y AYUDAR A BIEN MORIR 13025

A los Indios de las Naciones: Pajalates, Orejones, Pacaos, Pacóas, Tilijayas, Alasapas, Pausanes, y otras muchas diferentes, que se hallan en las Missiones del Rio de San Antonio, y Rio Grande, pertenecientes à el Colegio de la Santissima Cruz de la Ciudad de Queretaro, como son: Los Pacuâches, Mescâles, Pampôpas, Tâcames, Chayopînes, Venados, Pamâques, y toda la Juventud de Pihuiques, Borrados, Sanipaos, y Manos de Perro.

COMPUESTO
POR EL P. Fr. BARTHOLOME GARCIA,
Predicador Apostolico, y actual Missionero de la Mission de N. S. P. S. Francisco de dicho Colegio, y Rio de San Antonio, en la Provincia de Texas.

Impresso con las Licencias necessarias en la Imprenta de los Herederos de Doña Maria de Rivera, en la Calle de San Bernardo, y esquina de la Plazuela de el Volador. Año de 1760.

78 DEL SACRAMENTO

Es tu Padrastro? Japujuâi po ê?	Es tu Entenado? Japámmám po é? Es tu Entenada? Japalúm po é?

Hermano con Hermana.

Es tu Hermano mayor? Jacuânitáp po ê (*vel* jat'atál po ê?) Es tu Hermano menor? Jamácutzân po ê?	Es tu Hermana menor? Jayat'án po é? Es tu Hermana mayor? Jatâl poé? (*v.* jaquitál poê?)

Pero preguntando al Hermano mayor por el menor, ó al contrario, dicen assi.

Es tu Hermano mayor? Jajat'ál po é? Es tu Primo hermano? Jamamôu po ê?	Es tu Hermano menor? Jamatzân po é? Es tu Prima hermana? Jamámochám po é?

Y preguntando à la Hermana mayor por la menor, ò à el contrario, dicen assi.

Es tu Hermana mayor? Jatzâal po ê?	Es tu Hermana menor? Jatzûtzan po ê? (*vel* jamatzûtzan po é?)

Tios con Sobrinos, Yerno con Suegros, y al contrario.

Es tu Tio paterno mayor? Jacôu po é?	Es tu Sobrino? Jap'ái po é? Es tu Sobrina? Jap'ái po ê? Es

García 1760: title, 78.

Fig. 3. Title page (left) from a 1760 manual for administering the church sacraments to missionized Coahuilteco-speaking Indians, and some of the questions (right) by which the priest could determine the kinship relations, if any, of couples desiring to be married. Each Spanish question is followed by a Coahuilteco equivalent, but the arrangement, basically according to Coahuilteco kinship categories, reveals a remarkable understanding of the structure of the Indian system and its differences from the Spanish system. Reciprocal terms are given side by side in parallel columns. The faint pencil marks on this copy were made by John R. Swanton while compiling his lexicon (Swanton 1940:10–54).

Table 1. Probable Coahuilteco Speakers

Aguapalam[a]	Pachaque[a]	Pulacuam[a]
Aguastaya	Pacoa[a]	Quem[a]
Anxau[a]	Pacpul[a]	Sacuache
Apaysi[a]	Pacuache[a]	Samampac[a]
Arcahomo	Pajalat[a]	Sampanal[a]
Ataxal[a]	Pamaya[a]	Sanaque[a]
Cachopostal	Pampopa[a]	Saracuam[a]
Cauya[a]	Papanac[a]	Semonan[a]
Chayopin[a]	Pastaloca[a]	Siaguan[a]
Geyer[a]	Pastia	Siquipil
Juanca[a]	Patacal	Sonayan[a]
Manico[a]	Pataguo[a]	Sulujam
Mescal[a]	Patumaco	Tacame[a]
Mesquite	Patzau[a]	Tilijae[a]
Ocana[a]	Pausane[a]	Tilpacopal
Paac[a]	Payaya[a]	Tepacuache
Paachiqui[a]	Payuguan[a]	Yorica[a]
Pacao[a]	Pitahay[a]	
Pachal[a]	Pitalac	

[a] Named by García (1760) or Mazanet (Gómez Canedo 1968).

ations of displaced groups. Detailed descriptions of individual encampments have yet to be found in documents.

It appears naive to assume that each of the Indian groups of this region once had an exclusive foraging territory and that, after prolonged research, it will eventually be possible to compile a map showing the mosaic of territorial ranges. Some of Cabeza de Vaca's south Texas groups, who were observed prior to European colonization, apparently had exclusive territories during the winter, but in summer they shared a distant area with other groups because it was rich in foodstuffs (Campbell and Campbell 1981). The Mariames, for example, ranged over two areas separated by a distance of at least 80 miles. If drawn on a map, the Mariame territorial range might be described as bilobate in form, the two lobes being connected by a narrow corridor of leisurely travel on foot. Cartographers will find it frustrating to show such oddly shaped, overlapping territories on a map.

The summer range of the Payaya Indians of southern

Texas has been determined on the basis of 10 encampments observed between 1690 and 1709 by summer-traveling Spaniards (Campbell 1975). Its maximum dimension was approximately 30 miles. Just where the Payaya lived in winter remains unknown. Limited data for two other groups of southern Texas, Pampopa and Pastia, indicate annual movement over a territory having a length of at least 85 miles (Campbell and Campbell 1981). These ranges suggest that in southern Texas the annual food quest of many groups covered an area of considerable size. Comparable information for Indian groups of northeastern Mexico has not yet been found.

For this region few reliable statements can be made about its total Indian population or the sizes of its basic population units. It is not now possible to determine with any precision the number of valid ethnic groups for the region as a whole, nor is it possible to determine just which groups were in existence at any selected date. For remarkably few single ethnic units were population figures recorded at any time. Although recorded population figures appear to be fairly abundant, many of these refer to aggregations of displaced group remnants sharing the native encampment locality or living in a mission Indian village. Most population figures refer to the northern part of the region, which became a refuge area for groups displaced by both Spaniards and Apaches. For impressions of group size prior to European colonization one must resort to scanty information given in the Núñez Cabeza de Vaca (1542) documents.

Perhaps the most valuable information lies in the largest figures recorded for specific groups at any time, since these suggest an upper limit for groups of hunting and gathering peoples in a generally semiarid region. Apparently the largest figure on record for a single group is 512, reported by a missionary in 1674 for Gueiquesal in northeastern Coahuila (Steck 1932), but this figure may have included remnants of other groups not recognized by the observer. The Pacuache of the middle Nueces River drainage of southern Texas were estimated by another missionary to number about 350 in 1727 (Campbell 1979). Many documents for the period 1747–1772 suggest that the Comecrudo of northeastern Tamaulipas may have had a population of at least 400. Thus very few groups of the region at any time seem to have had a population of more than 400. Limited figures for other groups suggest that most units had populations ranging from 100 to 300. Scattered bits of quantified data given by Cabeza de Vaca for the Mariames in 1533–1534 indicate a population of about 200 (Campell and Campbell 1981).

Estimating the total population of the entire region at any particular time is hazardous, and the few estimates that cover the region, or parts of it, have not been based on detailed ethnohistoric research. Mooney (1928) estimated that in 1690 the "Coahuiltecan tribes" of southern Texas had a total population of 15,000. Kroeber (1939) regarded Mooney's estimate as too large and replaced it with 2,000. This is not very realistic, since in 1675 Bosque made a head count of 2,247 individuals in various Indian encampments along his line of travel during a journey from Monclova, Coahuila, northward into the Edwards Plateau of Texas (Bolton 1916). For the year 1690 Kroeber (1939) gave a figure of 100,000 for the total Indian population of nonagricultural "northeastern Mexico," in which he included true desertlands at least as far west as the Río Conchos of Chihuahua. Kroeber did not seem surprised by the fact that this figure indicated a population destiny greater than that given for any Indian agricultural area in the United States. Kroeber was evidently much impressed by the very large number of Indian group names recorded for "northeastern Mexico" and was inclined to think of them as representing groups that flourished at the same time.

Ruecking (1953) compiled a list of 614 group names for northeastern Mexico and southern Texas and referred to them collectively as Coahuiltecans. He believed that he had found sufficient evidence to indicate that those names represented groups having an average population of 140, and by multiplication he obtained a total population of approximately 86,000. Ruecking's estimate was not linked with any specific year or short period and, like Kroeber, he assumed that all these groups were in existence at the same time. It seems reasonable to conclude that not enough is presently known about this region for anyone to do much more than make an arbitrary statement about its total Indian population at any particular time.

Culture

For this entire region there are very few reliable descriptions of Indian groups that were written fairly early and that are sufficiently coherent and detailed to give informative impressions of what life was like among some of the hunting and gathering groups before their displacement. Two such descriptions, although dissimilar in scope and separated by a century of time, are especially valuable because they constitute important primary evidence. Preoccupation with problems of linguistic and cultural classification has obscured this value.

The first of these is Cabeza de Vaca's description of the Mariames of southern Texas, among whom he lived for about 18 months in 1533–1534; the second is Alonso de León's (in Léon, Bautista Chapa, and Sánchez de Zamora 1961) generalized description of various unspecified Indian groups he knew as a soldier in Nuevo León before the year 1649, groups who ranged over or near the area that extends from Monterrey and Cadereyta northeastward to Cerralvo. These two descriptions fortunately cover some of the same categories of culture, particularly material culture, and indicate notable differences in the cultures of groups separated by a distance of at least 150 miles. The description of León records significant differences between the cultures of various Indian groups associated with a restricted area. The two descriptions, when considered together, suggest that those who have attributed so much cultural uniformity to the Western Gulf province have overemphasized the generic similarities in its hunting and gathering cultures and have paid little attention to the recorded evidence that indicates cultural differences.

Mariames

The Mariames (not to be confused with the later Aranamas) appear to have been one of 11 Indian groups who occupied an inland area between the lower sections of the Guadalupe and Nueces rivers of southern Texas (Núñez Cabeza de Vaca 1542; Oviedo y Valdés 1851–1855, 3). These groups shared an apparently unique subsistence pattern that involved seasonal migration westward and southwestward to harvest prickly pear fruit in an area west of Corpus Christi Bay (Campell and Campbell 1981). Cabeza de Vaca provides much more descriptive detail for the Mariames than for the other groups, and to this day the Mariames remain the best described single Indian group of northeastern Mexico and southern Texas.

The Mariames spent about nine months of each year (fall, winter, spring) ranging along the valley of the Guadalupe River just above its junction with the San Antonio River. Summer was spent in an area some 80 miles to the southwest, where prickly pear cactus thickets yielded fruit in great profusion.

The population of about 200 individuals normally lived in a single settlement that was moved when the food resources of a locality were depleted. The number of houses probably did not exceed 40. Each house was round in floor plan and had a framework of four flexible poles, both ends of each pole being set in the ground. This domed framework was covered with mats, and both poles and mats were transported when a settlement was moved.

Unlike later times, bison were apparently not common in Mariame territory during the time of Cabeza de Vaca. Bison hunting is not mentioned, but limited use of bison hides is indicated. Deer were hunted in several ways. A hunter might run a deer long enough for the animal to become exhausted. In the Guadalupe River area special two-day hunting trips for deer were made two or three times a year. Such trips involved leaving the wooded valley and going out into the adjacent grasslands. Wood and water were carried for these overnight trips. Dry grass was set on fire to control movements of the game. A third method was more complex and was used only when the Mariames were traveling to the prickly pear collecting grounds and passed along the western shoreline of Copano Bay. When an offshore breeze was blowing, hunters spread out and drove deer into the bay, keeping them there until they drowned and were beached by onshore winds.

Rats and mice were hunted, but rabbits are never mentioned. Snakes were eaten and their bones were saved, pulverized, and eaten. Land snails were collected and eaten when the Mariames were in the prickly pear thickets. Insects of various unspecified kinds were also eaten, some in egg or larval form. Other faunal foods, especially in the Guadalupe River area, included frogs, lizards, salamanders, and spiders. Earth, wood, and deer droppings were sometimes eaten when food was scarce.

Fish were obtained by unspecified methods from the Guadalupe River. Apparently fish were eaten in quantity only during the April-May flood season, when they were taken from shallow pools after floodwaters had subsided. Fish bones were also pulverized and eaten.

Two plant foods can be identified as seasonal staples—pecans and the fruit of prickly pear cactus. In autumn pecans formed the dominant foodstuff when Mariames were living along the Guadalupe River. When the pecan crop was abundant, other Indian groups came to the river for nuts. Mashed nut meats were sometimes eaten mixed with small seeds. The chief attraction of the prickly pear area to the southwest was the presence of fruit in quantity during most of the summer. When water was locally unavailable there, the Mariames expressed fruit juice in a hole in the earth and drank it as a water substitute.

Roots of several unspecified plants were the principal source of food in winter. Plants with edible roots were said to be thinly distributed, hard to find, and difficult to dig. Women searched areas around an encampment for distances of five to eight miles, beginning the search at daybreak. Roots were baked for two days in some sort of oven, and women spent considerable time at night preparing ovens and baking roots. Some roots were bitter and caused the abdomen to swell.

Mariame clothing and ornaments are not described, and little is said about handicrafts. A net, said to have been about 5.5 feet square, may have been used to carry bulky foodstuffs. Much matting must have been made, since it was used to cover house frames. Pottery is never mentioned, and the only container referred to is either a woven bag or a flexible basket. The only offensive weapon mentioned is the bow and arrow. The Mariames had small undescribed shields covered with bison hide.

Several factors seem to have prevented overpopulation among the Mariames: female infanticide was practiced; occasionally male children were killed because of unfavorable dream omens; and men refrained from sexual intercourse with their wives from the first indication of pregnancy until the child was about two years old.

Women continued breast feeding of children until they were about 12 years of age, and there seems to have been a taboo against male contact with any menstruating woman. Since female infanticide was the rule, it is evident that Mariame males obtained wives from surrounding ethnic groups. The "bride price" was said to have been a good bow and two arrows or, in lieu of these, a net. No Mariame male seems to have had two or more wives. Divorce was permitted but no grounds were specified other than "dissatisfaction." Female infanticide and ethnic group exogamy indicate a patrilineal descent system.

Cabeza de Vaca briefly described a dispute between two adult males over a woman. A fight ensued in which only fists and sticks were used. After the fight each man dismantled his house and left the encampment. Very little is said about Mariame warfare.

Among the Mariames some behavior was motivated by dreams, which were a source of omens. The documents cite 12 cases in which male children were killed or buried alive because of unfavorable dream omens. No descriptive detail is given about ceremonies, although it is clearly stated that some behavior involved group feasting and dancing. This activity went on despite winter food shortages and reached a peak during the summer season in the prickly pear area.

Indians of Nuevo León

In an early history of Nuevo León that was first published in 1649 appears a description of the Indians of the area by León (León, Bautista Chapa, and Sánchez de Zamora 1961; English translation in Davenport 1924). In the same volume Juan Bautista Chapa listed the names of 231 Indian groups, many of whom must be covered by León's description. It is clear that some of the groups described by León were those collectively known to Spaniards by names such as Borrados, Pintos, Rayados, and Pelones, and that some of them spoke dialects of a language designated as Quinigua (Del Hoyo 1960; Gursky 1964).

All the groups known to Alonso de León subsisted by hunting, fishing, and gathering. Foodstuffs were usually consumed shortly after they were obtained. Sizes of foraging territories are not indicated, but part of a territory might be shared with another group by common consent if food was abundant.

Settlements, which were moved frequently, varied in size but most were relatively small. It is not stated how many different encampments were simultaneously occupied by the same ethnic group, although it is said that one or more families might withdraw from an encampment at any time and seek foodstuffs separately. One particular settlement is described as consisting of 15 houses, which were arranged in a semicircle with one offset house at each end. When necessary, water was transported by women, each woman placing 12 to 14 water-filled prickly-pear pad pouches in a netted carrying frame, which was placed on the back and controlled by a tumpline. Ceramic containers were not used. In summer prickly pear fruit juice was sometimes drunk as a water substitute.

Houses, presumably circular in floor plan, were covered by cane or grass and had very low entrances. In the center of each house floor was a small hearth area, its fire said to have been used mainly for illumination. Fire was produced by a wooden hand drill. Occupants slept on the house floor, using grass and deerskins for bedding. House materials were not transported when a settlement was moved. The number of individuals associated with each house was eight to 10 or more. The settlement mentioned as consisting of 15 houses would thus have had a population of about 150.

All animals available in the environment were hunted except toads and lizards. Animals actually mentioned include deer, rabbits, rats, birds, and snakes. Deer was the most important game animal; and when a deer was killed, a trail from the kill site to the encampment was marked by the hunter, and women were sent to bring the carcass home. The man who killed a deer received only its hide; the rest of the animal was butchered and portions distributed throughout the encampment. Two weapons are specified, the bow and arrow and a curved wooden club. The club seems to have been a multipurpose device, serving variously as an aid in walking, as a club, and as a handy tool for probing and prying. At night each man kept his club in easy reach while he slept.

Fishing, participated in by both sexes, was done in several ways: shooting the fish with bow and arrow at night by torchlight; use of nets; and underwater capture by hand from holes or pockets along steep or overhanging stream banks.

Maguey root crowns and the roots and tubers of various unspecified plants were the principal winter foods. In summer the most important foods were prickly pear fruits and mesquite bean pods. Small fruits from other plants were eaten as they ripened. Maguey crowns were baked for two days in some kind of oven. The fibers in this food were not swallowed but expectorated in small masses or quids. When there was a food shortage, quids were sometimes salvaged, pulverized, and eaten.

Both flowers and fruits of the prickly pear cactus were eaten. Green fruit was roasted, and ripe fruit was eaten immediately or sun-dried on mats. The bean pods of mesquite trees, said to have been abundant in the area, were eaten both when green and when matured to a dry state. The dry pods were pulverized in a wooden mortar, and the flour, either sifted or still containing the hard-cased seeds, was temporarily stored in woven bags or in prickly pear pad pouches. The pod flour was eaten either cooked or uncooked. Salt was added to various foods, and the ash of at least one plant was used as a salt substitute.

It is clear that in Nuevo León there were striking group differences in clothing, hairdress, and face and body decoration. Men wore little clothing. No garment covered the pubic zone, and sandals were worn only when traversing thorny terrain. In some groups men wore rabbitskin robes. Women covered the pubic area with grass or cordage, and over this some women at times wore a slit skirt composed of two deerskins, one skin in front, the other behind. To the rear deerskin was attached an extension of deerskin long enough to drag on the ground, and to its hem small, sound-producing objects were attached: beads, snail shells, animal teeth, seeds, and small hard fruits. On special occasions some women also wore robes of unspecified animal skins, or in some groups a rabbitskin robe.

Sex differences in hairdress are not clearly indicated. In general, hair was worn long and allowed to hang free down to the waist, deerskin thongs sometimes holding the hair ends together at waist level. In some groups (apparently the Pelones) hair was plucked out in bands of varying width between the forehead and the top of the head. Ornaments consisting of feathers, sticks, and bones were inserted in perforations in ears, noses, and breasts.

Ethnic identity seems to have been indicated by painted or tattooed patterns on the face and body. On the face were various combinations of undescribed lines; and among those who had hair plucked from the front part of the head, lines extended upward from the root of the nose. Body patterns included broad lines, straight or wavy, that ran the full length of the torso (probably giving rise to the Spanish designations Borrados, Rayados, and Pintos).

Although the descriptions of Cabeza de Vaca and Alonso de León are not strictly comparable, they nevertheless give clear impressions of the amount of cultural diversity that must have existed among the hunting and gathering peoples of the region. Especially notable in these two descriptions are differences in foodstuffs and subsistence techniques, houses, containers, transportation devices, weapons, clothing, and body decoration.

Location of Indian Groups

Most of the Indian groups recorded for this large region can be associated with 15 areas. These areas do not correspond to concentrations of Indian populations but to places where locational information was most often collected, as along routes of early travel or near Spanish frontier settlements and missions. The 15 areas are numbered on the regional map (fig. 1) and in the Synonymy.

Area 1

Area 1 includes the nonmountainous part of northeastern Coahuila west of the railroad that connects Eagle Pass, Texas, with Monclova, Coahuila, and extends northward across the Rio Grande to the southern edge of the Edwards Plateau in Texas. At least 49 groups linked with this area in the late seventeenth century cannot now be identified as having been displaced from other regions. A small sample of one language, Solano, has been attributed to the Terocodame and associated groups (I. Goddard 1979). As the Solano sample was long believed to represent a Coahuilteco-related language, many of the 49 groups listed have at one time or another been considered as Coahuiltecans.

Area 2

The core of Area 2 extends from the vicinity of Guerrero, Coahuila, northeastward toward San Antonio, Texas, as far as the Frio River. It was frequently traversed by Spanish travelers during the late seventeenth century (Gómez Canedo 1968), and the names of 33 Indian groups are recorded in the travel records, most of them encountered near the Rio Grande, Nueces, and Frio rivers. Some of these groups at times ranged as far south of the Rio Grande as the Río Sabinas of northeastern Coahuila. Many of the groups Mazanet reported as speaking Coahuilteco appear on the list for Area 2 (see table 1).

Area 3

At least 19 Indian groups can be associated with Area 3, which extends about 100 miles southward from San Antonio, Texas. These groups ranged over lands lying between the upper half of the San Antonio River and the two great bends of the Nueces River. Some of the names appear in table 1 as probable Coahuilteco speakers, but for the remainder there are no recorded indications of the language spoken.

Area 4

Area 4 lies between the lower sections of the Guadalupe and Nueces rivers of southern Texas. Because of a gap of some 150 years in the records, the Indians of this area known to Cabeza de Vaca are listed separately from groups recorded in the eighteenth century. Of Cabeza de Vaca's groups, only the Mariames can be clearly identified in the eighteenth century documents, where they appear as the Muruam (Campbell and Campbell 1981:21–22). The later groups include some identified as probable Coahuilteco speakers (table 1), but the remaining groups apparently spoke other languages.

Area 5

Area 5, which includes extreme northern Nuevo León and closely adjacent parts of northeastern Coahuila, is given separate status because documents connected with a late seventeenth-century mission at present Lampazos, Nuevo León, refer to a number of groups who spoke the same language (Espinosa in Maas 1915). This language may have been Coahuilteco, but the evidence is not conclusive. Most of the names do not appear on the lists of Indian groups recorded by Chapa for Area 6.

Area 6

Area 6 refers to the central part of northern Nuevo León and is based on the lists of Indian groups recorded by Chapa (León, Bautista Chapa, and Sánchez de Zamora 1961), who is unique in that he attempted to compile complete lists of Indian groups known in specified areas. Some of his group names are so similar that they may represent duplications, but this is not certain. Those of his groups that are recognizable as refugees from other regions do not appear in the synonymy for Area 6. In the synonymy, names without letter symbols are derived from other sources, such as documents cited by various historians of Nuevo León (Cavazos Garza 1964, 1966, 1966a; González 1885, 1887; Del Hoyo 1960, 1963). Asterisks indicate groups who may have spoken dialects of the Quinigua language identified by Gursky (1964) and Del Hoyo (1960). Alonso de León's generalized description of Nuevo León Indians undoubtedly covers many groups named for Area 6.

Area 7

For the valley of the Rio Grande between Mier and Laredo a few refugee groups were recorded in the middle eighteenth century. Most of the names are Spanish and apparently refer to amalgamated remnants of many groups whose original native names cannot now be ascertained. The name Carrizos (fig. 4) was often applied by Spaniards to any Indians who lived in houses covered with reeds or grass.

Area 8

Area 8 refers to a section of the lower Rio Grande valley. The names, mainly of Spanish origin, refer to Indian groups represented at the missions of Reynosa and Camargo (about 1750) that cannot be linked with other areas until later. The names probably include some groups native to the area as well as groups displaced from nearby parts of Tamaulipas and Nuevo León.

The Thomas Gilcrease Inst. of Amer. Hist. and Art, Tulsa, Okla.

Fig. 4. *Carrizos.* The man wears a breechclout and has a bow slung across his chest with arrows in a quiver on his back. He holds a gun. The woman wears a long dress of trade cloth. Watercolor by Lino Sánchez y Tapia, 1834–1838.

Area 9

At least 34 Indian groups are rather clearly associated with the Rio Grande delta and its environs. This delta, which consists of some 3,000 square miles, has its western apex near Reynosa, Tamaulipas, and widens toward the Gulf of Mexico to include some 75 airline miles of shoreline that is about equally divided between Tamaulipas and Texas. The middle eighteenth-century documents refer to abundance of wood, water, game, and fish, and they also note the well-nourished appearance of the Indians. One Spaniard guessed that some 2,500 Indian families lived in the delta area. Of the 34 groups, 21 are said to have ranged mainly south of the Rio Grande channel (Saldívar 1943). Some delta groups are said to have spoken the same language, which may have been Cotoname, a sample of which has been recorded (Swanton 1940; I. Goddard 1979).

Area 10

For the decade 1750–1760 at least seven Indian groups can be associated with the lower Río San Fernando and the nearby shores of the Laguna Madre of northern Tamaulipas. One group, the Pintos, may have been displaced from some area to the west. The Comecrudo, who seem to have been more numerous than the others, are of special interest because samples of their language were recorded in the nineteenth century, after their displacement to the north (Swanton 1940; I. Goddard 1979).

Area 11

Area 11 includes the mountains that surround the town of San Carlos, Tamaulipas, which is east-southeast of Linares, Nuevo León. It seems evident that, when first known about 1750, the Indian groups recorded for the area had already been displaced, and it is not possible to determine which groups were native to the area. Since most of the names are of Spanish origin, some of the groups may have been recorded elsewhere under native names. The Bocas Prietas seem to have been the dominant group numerically.

Area 12

Between 1747 and 1750 five groups were recorded for the area around the mouth of the Soto la Marina of the middle Tamaulipas coast. Descriptive details are not recorded, and it is not known if the groups were native to the area. Saldívar (1943) suggests that they were closely related linguistically and culturally but cites no evidence.

Area 13

For the northern part of the Sierra de Tamaulipas, east of Ciudad Victoria, 24 Indian groups were recorded during the middle eighteenth century. Although displaced, most of them being recorded only at Spanish missions, many of the groups were probably native to the general area. Of these 24 groups, five are identified as growing crops (corn, beans, squash). Saldívar (1943), without explanation, gives some names on the list as synonyms for others, but documentary confirmation of this has not been found.

Area 14

Ten groups can be associated with the southern part of the Sierra de Tamaulipas, and four of these are briefly described in the middle eighteenth century as practicing horticulture and manufacturing pottery. In his attempt to define a hunting and gathering "Coahuiltecan culture," Ruecking (1953, 1954, 1955, 1955a) drew heavily from Santa María's (1929–1930) generalized description for Indians of southern Tamaulipas without noting that some of Santa María's informants were identified as Maratín, Mariguan, and Simariguan, all recorded as horticultural groups in Area 14. A short text recorded in the Maratín language has been analyzed by Swanton (1940).

Area 15

Along the coast of southern Tamaulipas, southward from the mouth of the Soto la Marina, 11 Indian groups were recorded in the 1750s. About half of these practiced horticulture, and some are said to have made pottery and lived in houses with mud walls and thatched roofs. Some of these groups may have been displaced from the Sierra de Tamaulipas immediately to the west.

Synonymy

The following lists of group names are in alphabetical order, separated by geographical area, with the numbers corresponding to those in figure 1. In parentheses are some synonymous names as well as badly distorted variants. Some group names are omitted here because of inadequate knowledge of their location.

Area 1

Aquitadotdacam, Babane, Bibiamar (Baniamama), Bacora (Bacoram, Bacaranan, Bascoram), Bagname (Baguame, Pagaiame), Bibit (Vivit), Bobol (Babol, Babor, Baburi, Boboram, Pabor, Vovol), Cacaxte (Cacaste, Cataxtle), Coaxa, Cubsuvi, Dacacmuri, Doaquioydacam (Oydican), Ervipiame (Barbipian, Berttipame, Chivipane, Gueripiamo, Hueripane, Hierbipiam, Yeripiame), Escaba, Espopulam (Isipopolam), Gicocoge (Xicocoje, Xicocossi), Guariqueche, Guerjuadan (Guergaida, Guerjuatida), Gueiquesal (Coetzal, Guericochal, Guisole, Huequetzal, Huisocal, Quesal), Guiguigoa, Heniocane (Ceniocane, Gioricane), Huhuygam, Hume (Lume, Xomi, Yumi), Jicaragrande, Macapao, Manos Coloradas, Manos Prietas, Matuimi, Maubedan, Obayo (Opaia), Piedras Chiquitas (Piedras Chicas), Pinanaca, Piniquu, Saesse (Ciaesier, Haeser, Siaexe, Siansi, Siausi, Xaeser), Seromet, Sijame (Cijame, Hihame, Injame, Jijame, Scipxamc, Sixacama, Tziame, Xixame), Teneinamar (Teneymama), Terocodame (Hieroquodame, Perocodame, Teodoran, Toxocodame), Tet, Tiltiqui, Toamar (Toarma, Tojuma), Tobocore, Tocamomon, Tumamar (Feimamar, Jaimamar, Ticmamar, Tuimama), Xiancocodam, Xupulame (Sinpulame), Yerguiba, Yorica (Corica, Goxica, Hiorna, Lorica, Torica, Yoxica), Ysbupue.

Area 2

Agualohe, Aguapalam, Apaysi (Apayi), Ataxal (Atacal), Geyer (Geie, Heye, Jae), Juanca (Huacacasa, Jaucar, Juamaca, Juampa, Juncata, Puncataguo, Tuamca), Manico (Minicau, Mirrica, Muncu), Mescal (see also Area 6) (Mescata), Momon, Ocana (Acani, Cane, Ocam), Odoesmade, Paac (Pajaca, Paxac), Paachiqui, Pachal (Pacgal, Pachan, Pachat, Paschal, Pasteal, Patehal), Pacoa (Pacoatal, Pacuq), Pacpul, Pacuache (Nacuache, Pacahuche, Pacuachiam, Pacuasin, Pagnache, Puguahiam, Taguache), Pamaya, Papanac (Panac, Papani, Paponal, Popan), Pastaloca (Pachaloco, Pastulac,

Pataloco), Pataguo (Patagu, Pataguaque, Patao, Patou), Patzau (Paceo, Pacha, Pachaug, Pacho, Pasxa, Patzar, Psaupsau, Pucha), Payuguan (Paiabun, Paiapan, Payahan, Payavan, Payoan), Piedras Blancos, Pitahay (Pitanay, Piutaay, Putai), Quem, Sacuache, Samampac, Sampanal, Siaguan (Chaguan, Chanaguan, Choguan, Mahuame, Ohaguame, Siaban, Xhiahuan, Ziaban), Sonayan (Samioj, Sanaian, Sanyau), Tepacuache, Xarame (Charame, Charrom, Harame, Jalam, Jurame, Schiarame, Xalan).

Area 3

Aguastaya, Anxau (Anna, Asau), Arcahomo (Acoma), Assar, Cachopostal (Cachopostate, Cachsaputal), Cauya (Cabia), Chayopin, Mesquite (see also Area 13), Pacao, Pampopa (Campoa, Panpoc, Pumpoa), Pastia, Payaya, Pitalac (Alobja, Patalca), Pulacuam (Pulacman), Sanipao, Saracuam, Semonan, Siupam, Sulujam (Chaadulam, Chulajam, Juliam, Zolahan).

Area 4

• CABEZA DE VACA'S GROUPS, 1534–1535 Acubadaos, Anegados, Atayos, Avavares, Camoles (coastal), Coayos, Comos, Cutalchuches, Fig People (coastal), Guaycones (coastal), Maliacones, Mariames, Quitoles (coastal), Susolas, Yguazes.

• 18TH-CENTURY GROUPS Manos de Perro; Muruame; Orejón; Pajalat; Pamaque, with the subdivisions Camasuqua, Sarapjon, Taguaguan, Tinapihuaya, Viayan; Pasnacan; Patumaco; Pausane (Paisano, Pauxane, Paysan); Piguique (Pihuiques); Siquipil; Tacame (Tâcames); Tilpacopal.

Area 5

Alasapa (see also Area 6), Canua (Cana, Cano, Canon), Catujan (see also Area 6), Cenizo (Censoc, Saczo, Seniczo, Sinicu, Sinixzo), Exmalquio, Jacao (Cacaje, Gacafe, Xacaje), Milijae, Pasalve (Pajalve), Pastancoya (see also Area 6), Pita (Pittal), Pomulum (Molia, Mulian, Pamulian, Panulam), Tacaguista, Tilijae (Alijae, Filixaye, Tilijayas, Tiloja, Titijay, Tolujaa), Xantigui.

Area 6

Letters following group names below indicate on which of Chapa's four lists the name was found: Ca, Cadereyta area; Ce, Cerralvo area; M, Monterrey area; NL, Nuevo León in general. Names without these symbols are derived from other sources. Asterisks indicate groups who may be linked with the Quinigua language.

*Abasusiniguara NL, Acancuara NL, Acatoyan M, Admitial Ca, Aguacero, Aguacoata, Aguana NL, Aguaque M, Aguarnauguara NL, Aguata M (Ahuata, Agata), Aguatinejo, Aguica M, *Aguiniguara Ca and NL, *Aguiquegua, Aguirtiguera NL, Aigual (Aguial, Aygual), Ajuipiaijaigo NL, Alaoqui M, Alasapa Ce (see also Area 5), Aleguapiame M, *Amacuaguaramara NL, Amacuyero Ce, Amanasu M, Amancoa Ca, Amapoala Ce, Amaraquisp M, Amatam M, Ameguara NL (cf. Amiguara), *Amiguara Ca (cf. Ameguara), Amito Ce, *Amituaga Ce (Amitagua), *Amiyaya, Amoama Ce (cf. Amoguama), Amoguama Ce and M (cf. Amoama), Anasgua NL, *Añiraniguara Ca, Anquimamiomo NL, Aocola NL, Apamona, Apitala M, Aquijampo NL (Aguijampo), *Arichimamoica, *Ariscapana (cf. Iscapana), Aristeti NL, Asequimoa NL, Axipaya, Ayagua (Ajijagua), *Ayancuara, *Ayenguara NL, *Ayeraguara, Ayerapaguana NL, *Ayundiguiguira NL, Baquiziziguara Ca, Batajagua M, *Bazaniguara NL (Bayaguaniguara), Boiguera NL (cf. Boquiguera) (Boijero), *Boquiguera NL (cf. Boiguera), Boquiniguera NL, Cabicujapa M, Cabyamaraguam, Cacamara, Cacamegua Ca, NL (Cocamegua, Cacamacao, Cayacacamegua?, Guacacamegua?), Cacapam, Caculpaluniame Ce (Cacuilipalina), *Caguaumama, Caguayoguam Ce (Cayaguam), Cagubiguama M, Caguchuarca M (cf. Caguchuasca), Caguchuasca Ce (cf. Caguchuarca), *Caguiamiguara Ca (cf. Cuaguijamiguara), Caguilipan Ce (Coquiapan), Caguiniguara NL (cf. Caguisniguara), Caguiraniguara Ca and NL, *Caguisniguara Ca (cf. Caguiniguara), Caguisniguara Ca (cf. Caguiniguara), Cajanibi Ca, Cajapanama NL (Canapanama), Cajaquepa Ce, Cajubama M, Calancheño, Calipocate Ce, Canabecuma M, Camacaluira M, Camacuro Ce, Camahan (Camasán), Camaiguara Ca (cf. Camaniguara), Camalucano Ce, Camaniguara NL (cf. Camaiguara), Camatonaja Ca, Camayopalo Ca, Cami-isubaba M, *Camiopajamara, Camisnimat NL, *Camuchinibara Ce, Canacabala Ce, *Canaguiague Ca, Canaine Ce (cf. Canayna), Canaitoca NL, Canamarigui Ca, Canamau M, Canameo Ce, Cananarito NL, Canapanama (cf. Guanapujamo), Canapeo Ce (Canapú), Canaranaguio NL, *Canayna Ca (cf. Canaine), Canbroiniguera NL, Capache, Capae Ce, Capagui Ce, Capatuu M, Capujaquin Ce, *Caramapana NL, *Caramaperiguan NL, *Caramunigua NL, Caraña Ce, Casaga, Cataara Ce, Catareaguemara NL, Catomavo NL (see also Area 9) (Catomao), Catujano Ce and M (see also Area 5), Caurame (Carbame, Caruama, Coaruama, Guarama, Queroama), Cauripan (Cauaripan), Cauyguama, Cayaguaguin Ce (Cayaguaga), Cayague Ce (Guayagua), Cayanaguanaja NL, Cayanapuro Ce, Cayupine NL, Cazulpaniale M, Coalimoje Ce, Coapuliguan, Cocoaipara Ca (cf. Cocojupara), Cocojupara NL (cf. Cocoaipara), Come Pescado, Comité Ce, Comocaura Ca, Congue Ce, Conicoricho Ce, Copuchiniguara NL, Cotipiniguara Ca, *Cotoayagua, Coyoquipiguara (Sanamiguara), Coyote Ce, Cuaguijamiguara Ca (cf.

Caguiamiguara), Cuaquinacaniguara NL, Cuatache M (Ayuguama, Coatae, Cojate, Cuatahe, Suatae), *Guatiguara Ca, Cuchinochi (Cuchinochil), Cuepane Ce, Cuiminipaco NL (Quiminipao), Escabel Ce, Estecuenopo NL (cf. Estiajenepo) (Estequenepo), Estegueno M, Estguama M, Estiajenepo NL (cf. Estecuenopo), Guacachina M, Guadepa, Guagui Ce, Guajolote Ce (see also Area 11), Gualegua Ce (Aquelegua), Guamepeje Ce (cf. Guampexte), Guamoayagua M, Guampexte Ce (cf. Guamepeje), Guanapujamo Ce (cf. Canapanama), Guampe Ce, *Guarastiguara Ca and NL, Guelamoye Ce, *Gueyacapo NL (Cuyacapo), Guicopasico NL, Guinaima Ce (Quinaimo), Guinala M, Hualahuis Ca (Gualahuis), Icabia, Icaura (Icuara, Incaura), Icuano (Iguana), Iguaracata (Guaracata), Iliguigue Ce (Elixguegue, Lisguegue), Imiacolomo NL, Imimule Ce, Imipecte Ce, Incuero (Inquero), *Ipajuiguara Ca (Opaguiguara, Upahuiguara), Iscapana NL (cf. Ariscapana), Jacoquin, Janapas Ce, Jaquiripamona NL, *Jiminiguara NL, Jimiopa Ce (cf. Jiniapa) (Ximiapa), Jiniapa Ca (cf. Jimiopa), *Jiniguara Ca (Jinipiguara), Joqualan M (Juaquialan), Lespoama Ce, Locaguiniguara NL, Lomotugua NL, *Maapiguara NL, Macacuy M, Macapaqui M, *Macatiguin NL (Macatiguire), Macatu NL, Maciguara Ce, Macomala Ce (Niacomala), Macoraena Ca, Macuarera NL (Macorajora?), Majanale Ca, Malicococa NL, Mal Nombre (see also Area 7), Manunejo Ca, Mapaniguara NL, Mapili NL, *Maquispamacopini NL (Maguipamacopini), Matahuinala, Matascuco Ce, Matatiquiri NL (Matetiguara), Matolagua, Mayaguiguara, Mayajuanguara Ca, Mayeguara, Michiaba M, Mimiola, *Minacaguapo NL, Miscal M (see also Area 2) (Mezcal), Mohiguara, Moquiaguin Ce (Miquiaguin), Munapume NL, Nam, Nepajan M, Noreo Ce, Oguecolomo, Pachizerco NL, Paciguima Ca, Pajamara NL, Palaguin Ce, Pantiguara Ca and NL (Paritiguara), *Pantipora NL (Patipora), Parajota Ca, *Passaguaniguara, Pastanquia M (see also Area 5), Patoo NL, Paxalto (Pafalto), Peguampaxte Ce (Teguampaxte), Pericaguera (Pelicaguaro, Perico?), Pijiniguara Ca, Piograpapaguarca NL, Pionicuagura NL, Pitisfiafuil, Plutuo NL, Pomaliqui M, Popocatoque M, Pusuama (Posnama), *Pueripatama NL (Puanipuatama), Quejanaquia Ca, Queremeteco, Quetapon Ce, Quiatolte M, Quibobima M, Quibonoa, Quien, Quiguantiguara NL, Quiguasguama Ce (Quiauaane?), Quimicoa, Quinegaayo Ce, Quinemeguete Ce, *Quiniapin, Quinigual Ca, Quiniguio NL (Quiniquijo), Quinimicheco NL, Quiriquitiniguera NL, Quitaguriaguilo NL, *Saguimaniguara NL (Aguimaniguara, Xaguimaniguara), Sainipame NL, *Saratiguara NL, Sayulime Ce, Siamomo M, Soloagua Ca, Sologuegue Ce, Sucuyama (Cucuyama), Tacopate NL, Tacuanama Ce, Táncacoama Ce, Tapayotoque, Tascuache Ca, Tatoama Ce and M, Tatocuene Ce, Teminaguico NL, Tiaquesco NL, Tochoquin M, Tociniguara Ca, Upaseppta Ca, Yaquinigua Ca, Yechimicual Ce, Zalaia (Zalai), Zimitagui.

Area 7

Cacalotes, Carrizos (applied to several distinct groups; see also Area 10), Garza (see also Atanaguaypacam in Area 9), Malnombre (see also Area 6), Tepemaca, Tortugas.

Area 8

Comosellamos, Cueros Crudos, Cueros Quemados, Guape, Huaraque, Malaguita, Narizes, Nazas, Pajaritos, Tampacua (Campacua, Tanpacuaze), Tareguano, Tejones, Venados.

Area 9

Alcalerpaguet (Calexpaquet), Apennapem, Aretpeguem, Atanaguaypacam ('sea people' in Comecrudo; the same as the Garza found later in Area 7) (I. Goddard 1979:369–370), Auyapaguim, Auyapem, Clancluiguyguen (Tlanchuguin), Concuyapem, Coospacam, Cotoname (Catanamepaque, Cootajam, Cotomavo—see also Area 6), Goajopocayo (Giajepocotiyo), Guiguipacam (Iguiguipacam), Gummesacapem (Comesacapem), Inyopacan, Lugplapiagulam (Hueplapiaguilam), Manyateno, Masacuajulam (Assaca?, Ymasaquajulam), Mayapem (Mallopeme, Mauliapeño), Parampamatuju, Perpacug (Pezpacuz), Perpepug (Perpapug; 'white-head' in a language similar to Comecrudo) (I. Goddard 1979:369), Peupuetam (Peumepuem), Samacoalapem (Sumagualapem), Saulapaguem (Alapaguem, Salaphueme, Talapaguem), Saulapaguet, Segujulapem, Segutmapacam, Sepinpacam ('salt people' in Comecrudo) (Goddard 1979:369), Sicujulampaguet (Sicajayapaguet), Tenicapem (Paniquiapem, Tanaquiapem), Tugumlepem (Tunlepem), Umalayapem, Unpuncliegut (Hunzpuzlugut), Uscapem (Usapam).

Area 10

Comecrudo (later, on the Rio Grande, called Mulato and Carrizo) (I. Goddard 1979:369), Maquiapem, Pamoran, Pintos, Quedejeño (Querejeño, Tedexeño), Quiniacapem (Canaguiapem, Guianapaqueno), Quinicuan.

Area 11

Antiguos; Bocas Prietas, with subgroups Clanapan (Tlanapanam), Comeperros, Dienteños, and Santiagueños; Cadima; Chapulines; Comepescados; Cometunas (Comenopales); Guajolotes (see also Area 6);

Malincheños; Odamich (Damiche); Palmitos; Politos (Ypolitos); Zacatil.

Area 12

Chapoteños, Morales, Palmeños, Sinacanai, Villegas.

Area 13

Ancashiguay (horticulture), Anichapanama, Aracate, Barrosos, Camaleones, Caribay (horticulture) (Aribay), Comecamotes (horticulture), Conejeros, Conipigua, Inapanam (Manimapacan, Napanam), Inocoplo, Matucapam, Mesquites (see also Area 3), Molina, Monan, Mulatos, Ojos de la Tierra, Pasita (horticulture), Picacheños, Sarnosas (Sainoscos), Sincoalne, Tagualillo (horticulture) (Tagualito), Tumapacam.

Area 14

Aracuay, Characuay (Taracuay), Maratín (horticulture) (Maratino, Martín), Mariguan (horticulture), Moraleños, Palalgueque, Simariguan (horticulture) (Casimariguan, Chinarihuan), Trueños, Vejaranos, Yamacán (horticulture).

Area 15

Anacan (horticulture), Aretin (horticulture), Caramariguan (horticulture), Caramiguay (horticulture), Cataican (Caicana), Maporcan, Mapulcan (horticulture?), Panguay (horticulture) (Tanguay), Pachima, Yecan (Yacana), Zapoteros.

Sources

Most of the basic information on the Indians of this region is contained in documents of the major archives of Spain and Mexico, especially Archivo General de Indias, Seville, and Archivo General de la Nación, Mexico City. For northeastern Mexico and Texas the best guide to these documents is that of Bolton (1913).

The first attempt to compile a list of Indian group names for Mexico was that of Orozco y Berra (1864), who collected names from numerous uncited documents and arranged them according to their associations with the various Mexican states. Hodge (1907–1910) listed and presented limited information on many Indian groups of Texas and northeastern Coahuila. Most of this information was provided by Bolton (1915a, 1916), who sometimes failed to recognize distorted group name variants and identified more Indian groups than actually existed. Bolton presented such information as he had found on group locations, linguistic affiliation, and association with Spanish missions, but he seldom included any cultural detail. Despite these limitations, Bolton's entries in Hodge are still very useful.

Although somewhat uneven in quality, a number of formal histories have been published that contain unusual amounts of information on Indian populations and their interaction with Europeans. These vary in scope but mainly cover Spanish colonial provinces or the modern states of Coahuila, Nuevo León, Tamaulipas, and Texas. Some are organized collections of documents in various archives (Alessio Robles 1938; Bolton 1915a; Castañeda 1936–1958; Espinosa 1964; Figueroa Torres 1963; Gómez Canedo 1968; Habig 1968; Del Hoyo 1972; León, Bautista Chapa, and Sánchez de Zamora 1961; Maas 1915; Morfí 1935; Oberste 1942; Portillo 1886; Prieto 1873; Saldívar 1943, 1945; Santa María 1929–1930; Weddle 1968, 1973). The best interpretation of the route of Cabeza de Vaca across this region is that of Krieger (1955, 1961).

The overwhelming number of Indian groups recorded for this region has discouraged attempts to prepare maps showing their locations at various times. Saldívar (1943) has published an informative map that identifies localities where various Indian groups of Tamaulipas were reported in the eighteenth century. Jiménez Moreno (1944) extended Saldívar's map to cover northeastern Mexico, but the number of Indian groups shown for Coahuila and Nuevo León is small because of inadequate locational information. Ruecking's (1955) map covering the entire region follows Saldívar and Jiménez Moreno, but the number of groups shown by Ruecking for southern Texas is quite small. General maps showing the distribution of North American Indians, such as that of Driver and Massey (1957), are not very informative for northeastern Mexico and southern Texas because only a few group names appear out of hundreds that might have been included. The various linguistic maps covering this region are not very informative.

Karankawa

W.W. NEWCOMB, JR.

Environment and Territory

The flat, low-lying Texas coast is fringed with a series of barrier islands and sand bars, separated from the mainland by shallow lagoons and bays. These and the Gulf of Mexico waters are rich in mussels, oysters, turtles, marine mammals, and many kinds of fish. Birds of many kinds are plentiful. Paralleling the coast from the San Antonio River to the Sabine and extending inland 50 to 75 miles are coastal prairies. Toward the south rainfall decreases and thorny brush, cactus, and other xerophytic plants become more common; northeastward rainfall increases and the vegetation becomes more luxuriant. Meandering across the coastal prairies are a number of streams, generally flowing in a southeasterly direction and emptying into shallow bays. Their valleys support a denser growth of trees and other vegetation than the adjacent prairies. Deer were the most important and common big-game animal of the coastal prairies, but bison were present seasonally, sometimes in substantial numbers in early historic times. Collared peccaries, bears, and many smaller mammals also frequented the region.

The human inhabitants of this varied coastal environment, from Galveston Bay on the northeast to Corpus Christi Bay on the south, have been collectively termed Karankawa (kəˈräŋkəˌwu) after one of its groups (fig. 1). The term is convenient and well established, but it obscures the facts that at the beginning of historic time these coastal people were not a political or possibly even a homogeneous cultural entity, and that some of them are so poorly known that only their names, or some of them, survive. Sporadically, over a span of more than three centuries, an assortment of Spanish, French, and American castaways, explorers, missionaries, soldiers, and others came in contact with these coastal natives, during which time their culture—or cultures—underwent dramatic changes and their numbers dwindled to ultimate extinction. Fortunately, one of the first shipwreck victims to be cast up on the Texas coast, Álvar Núñez Cabeza de Vaca, lived with the natives in the vicinity of Galveston Island, came to know them intimately, and left the most complete account of these coastal people. His observations are the primary source for the following cultural summary, supplemented by scattered data from later centuries.

History

In the fall of 1528 in a desperate attempt to flee what is now the panhandle of Florida, the members of the Spanish expedition of Pánfilo Narváez built five crude barges and launched them in the Gulf of Mexico. All of the barges were apparently cast up on the Texas coast. Two were blown ashore perhaps on Galveston Island, but more probably on the peninsula (apparently then an island) just to the southwest. Cabeza de Vaca and the other survivors of one of the barges were met and cared for by friendly natives, and after an unsuccessful attempt to relaunch their vessel, the naked and chilled survivors were taken to the natives' camp where quarters had been prepared for them. Soon afterward these shipwreck victims made contact with the crew of the other barge that had been beached four or five miles away; they too had been accorded a friendly reception.

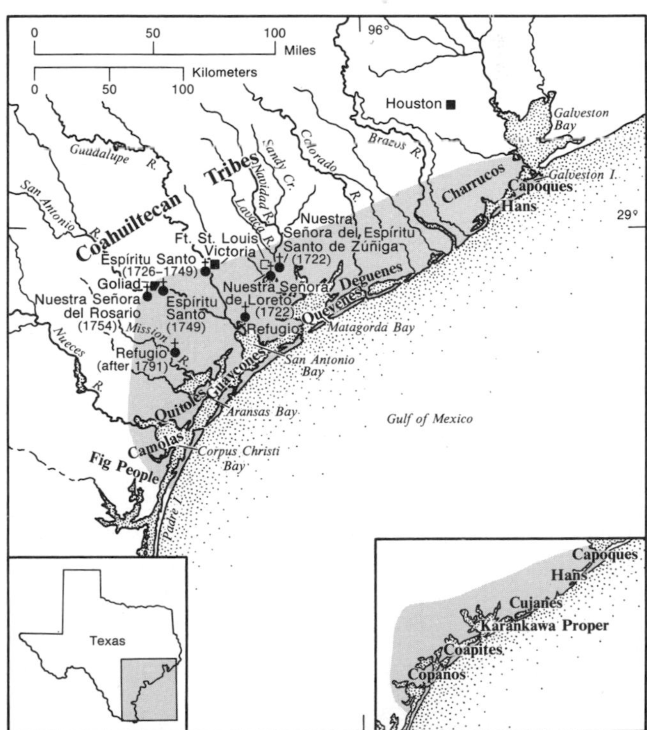

Fig. 1. 16th-century territory with band locations recorded by Núñez Cabeza de Vaca (1904). Inset shows current band designations.

Cabeza de Vaca said that the island was inhabited by two groups, the Capoques (or Coaques or Cocos), who spoke a different language from the second group, the Hans. He neglected to specify which group he was with, but implied that other than linguistically the two were friendly and culturally identical (Núñez Cabeza de Vaca 1904:54ff.). It has been argued that the Hans were Akokisas, an Atakapa tribe, on the grounds that the name resembles Atakapa aŋ 'house' (Hodge 1907:54; Swanton 1946:85). But even Galveston Island is outside the territory later occupied by Akokisas (the westernmost Atakapa tribe), and it seems unlikely that two linguistically disparate groups should have coexisted amicably on such a small island. The name Han is also similar to that of a Karankawa band located farther down the coast and known in later years as the Kouans (table 1).

About 90 Spaniards had been shipwrecked on the island, and they soon overtaxed the local resources as well as the hospitality of the natives. By spring most of the Spaniards had succumbed to famine or sickness, and a stomach disorder they introduced had reduced the native population by half. Twelve surviving Spaniards were able to move on, but a seriously ill Cabeza de Vaca and another castaway remained behind. Though forced to labor strenuously for the Indians, Cabeza de Vaca slowly recovered and managed to leave them after about a year, joining a group on the mainland known as the Charrucos (or Chorrucas). These people treated him relatively well as he became a trader for them, bartering seashells and other coastal products for hides, red ocher, flint, and other things that inland enemy tribes possessed. As a trader he said he was able to explore inland as far as he wanted and along the coast for 120–150 miles, but he failed to record anything about the terrain or its natives. He spent nearly six years in this fashion, finally escaping to join three other survivors of the expedition. In addition to the Capoques, Hans, and mainland Charrucos, Cabeza de Vaca listed six other coastal groups. Proceeding down the coast they were the Deguenes (or Deaguanes), Quevenes (or Guevenes), both of whom he first may have encountered while employed as a trader, and the Guaycones, Quitoles, Camolas (or Camoles), and "those of the figs" (table 1) (Núñez Cabeza de Vaca 1904:123–124; Krieger 1955, 1961; Campbell and Campbell 1981:11–13). He did not have any contact with the last four of these groups. But he learned that the Camolas had killed the survivors of one of the Spanish barges blown ashore in their territory, and in 1534 he saw some of their clothing and weapons that had been traded to an inland group. Cabeza de Vaca also was told by natives that two Spanish survivors had been seen among the Fig People (Campbell and Campbell 1981:12–13).

The Karankawas were not visited again by Europeans for more than a century and a half. Then, in 1685, the expedition of the Frenchman, René-Robert Cavelier de La Salle, landed at Matagorda Bay and established Fort Saint Louis on Garcitas Creek in the heart of Karankawa country. La Salle undertook two expeditions

Table 1. Chronological Synonymy of Karankawan Tribes

Location	*Cabeza de Vaca, 16th century* (Núñez Cabeza de Vaca 1904)	*LaSalle, 17th century* (Cox 1905)	*Spanish Mission, 18th century* (DeSolís 1931)	*Current Designation*
Galveston Island and vicinity	Capoques Hans Charrucos (mainland)	 Quaras (Kouraras)	Capoques (Coaque, Cocos)	Capoques
Mouth of Colorado and vicinity	Deguenes (Deaguanes)	Kouans (Quouan) Korenkake (Koïenkahe)	Cujanes (Coxanes, Cujanos, Quxanes, etc.)	Cujanes
Matagorda Bay and peninsula, San Antonio Bay	Quevenes (Guevenes)	Bahamos (Bracamos) Quinets Quoaquis	Karankawa (Carancaguases, Talancagues, etc.)	Karankawa proper
Aransas Bay, Matagorda and St. Joseph islands[a]	Guaycones		Coapites (Guapites)	Coapites
Between Corpus Christi and Copano bays[a]	Quitoles		Copanos (Coopanes, Cobanes)	Copanos
Vicinity of Corpus Christi Bay[a]	Camolas			
South of Corpus Christi Bay	Fig People			

[a] Locations are from Campbell and Campbell 1981.

from Fort Saint Louis to search for the mouth of the Mississippi where he had intended to establish his colony, and on the second he was murdered by some of his men. The struggling colony at Fort Saint Louis had already suffered heavy losses from disease and Karankawa attacks, and word of the French settlement had also reached Spanish ears. An expedition was dispatched in 1689 to destroy it, but by the time the Spaniards found the fort Karankawas had already overrun it, killing all but five of its residents. In 1690 Alonso de Léon returned to burn the fort (West 1905; Bolton 1915).

Fort Saint Louis had been established in the territory of a people the French called Bahamos or Bracamos. Initially the Bahamos were friendly, but relations soon deteriorated. The Quinets also lived in the vicinity of the French settlement and they too became enemies of the French. A third nearby people, the Quoaquis, were distinguished from the wandering Bahamos and Quinets by a member of La Salle's colony, Father Anastasius Douay, who claimed that they raised "Indian corn and have horses cheap"(Shea 1852:207; Cox 1905, 1:237). However, the statement about corn appears to be inaccurate or misleading.

Apart from these three peoples the French had little contact with other Karankawas. La Salle's two expeditions soon carried him away from the coast, though some of the peoples who were said by Henri Joutel, a trusted subordinate of La Salle's, to live between the fort and the Maligne River (the Colorado or Brazos) have traditionally been considered Karankawas. Thus, Gatschet (1891:23–25) equates the Korenkake (variously Koïenkahé) with the Karankawas, and the Kouans (or Quoans) with the Cujanes (Cox 1905, 2:114; Margry 1876–1886, 3:288). These, as well as a number of other tribes or villages mentioned in these lists, may or may not have been Karankawas. But if Korenkake and Clamcoches are renderings of the same name (see Synonymy), they were the first uses of the term now written Karankawa, which became the generic name for these coastal groups. In later years the Karankawas (Karankawa proper) continued to inhabit the region of Matagorda Bay and Peninsula.

In 1722 the mission of Nuestra Señora del Espíritu Santo de Zúñiga, usually called La Bahía, was founded by the Marqués San Miguel de Aguayo expedition on Garcitas Creek opposite the ruins of La Salle's Fort Saint Louis. A presidio, Nuestra Señora de Loreto, was established on the old ruins to protect the mission and to prevent any new attempts by the French to settle there. But the mission was not a success. The Karankawas for whom it was founded—the Capoques, Cujanes, and Karankawa proper—could not be persuaded to enter the mission, and in 1726 the presidio and mission were moved to the Guadalupe River, southeast of present Victoria, in the territory of the Aranama Indians, an unrelated tribe. In 1749 the mission and presidio were again moved, this time to the San Antonio River, modern Goliad growing up at the site of the presidio. For many years the Karankawas caused trouble at the mission, raiding the herds and making a nuisance of themselves in other ways (Buckley 1911–1912; Bolton 1970:296ff.).

In 1754 the mission of Nuestra Señora del Rosario was established for the Cujanes, Coapites (Guapites), Karankawa proper, and Copanos about four miles west of present Goliad. The name Cujanes was sometimes employed as the generic term for these four groups during this period (Bolton 1970:306). For a time the mission prospered, an extensive cattle ranch was developed, and many of these coastal Indians were at least sporadically attracted to it. Another mission, Nuestra Señora del Refugio, was built in 1791 near the mouth of Mission River for the Karankawas, and it persisted until 1828. But despite their efforts the Spaniards were never able to establish entirely amicable relations with the Karankawas, and few of them embraced mission life. By the end of the Spanish reign the effects of introduced diseases and the other by-products of European invasion had reduced the Karankawas to a numerically weak remnant (Castañeda 1936–1958; Bolton 1906; Oberste 1942).

In 1817 Jean Laffite, the buccaneer, established the village of Campeche on the eastern end of Galveston Island. At first Laffite and his men got along well with the few Karankawas remaining on the island, no doubt because they were hospitable and generous with presents. The wrestling matches and archery contests the Indians staged were a popular spectator sport in the village, and the Indians were of great help in repairing damages to the village after a hurricane in 1818. There were even two marriages between Whites and Indians. But eventually petty thievery forced Laffite to bar the Indians from the settlement, and soon afterward a party of Laffite's men while deer hunting discovered the camp of the Karankawas on a ridge known as the Three Trees. The men abducted a woman, or perhaps a woman for each man, and in retaliation the Karankawas ambushed the next buccaneer hunting party. Laffite responded by sending a force of 200 men equipped with two artillery pieces to attack the Karankawas. The buccaneers quickly drove the Karankawas from their camp at Three Trees, and the Indians resorted to guerrilla tactics for several days before abandoning the island. Unfortunately, fact and fiction are so tangled that even the year in which this episode took place is in doubt (Gracy 1964).

The breakdown in amicable relations between Laffite and the Karankawas presaged the conditions that characterized the usual relationships between Anglo-American settlers and Karankawas. Some of Stephen F. Austin's first colonists arrived by schooner in 1821, but the vessel was wrecked and most of the survivors killed by

Karankawas, though oddly, the Indians escorted some of the settlers to their destination. Continuing conflicts led Austin to undertake a campaign against the Karankawas in 1825, and he soundly defeated them. The Indians appealed to the priests and civil authorities at Goliad, and a peace treaty was signed. But Karankawas continued to harass the colonists, and the Mexican government finally dispatched a body of troops to assist the Whites. In a ruthless campaign troops and colonists pursued the Karankawas to Matagorda Bay. About half the Capoques and Karankawa proper were killed; the remainder sued for peace, and in 1827 another treaty was signed with them.

During the Texas revolution, 1835–1836, the Karankawas seem to have switched sides several times, and while fighting alongside the Texans lost about 20 warriors and a chief. In 1843 a band apparently gained permission from the Mexican government to settle west of the Nueces River. Others may have moved south of the Rio Grande, and apparently a band lived at least seasonally on Padre Island. A Mexican ranging company almost annihilated a band living some 50 miles southwest of Corpus Christi in 1844. In 1858 some Karankawas fled back across the Rio Grande from Mexico and were exterminated by a party of ranchers. If other Karankawas survived in Mexico or the United States, all trace of them has since disappeared (Huson 1953:38–43; Hodge 1907–1910, 1:657; Gatschet 1891:47–50).

The Thomas Gilcrease Inst. of Amer. Hist. and Art, Tulsa, Okla.

Fig. 2. *Carancahueses*. The man wears a breechclout; his garters, anklets, and feathered circlet are probably of plant fibers. He carries a bow and quiver, as well as a powder horn and shot pouch. The woman wears buckskin garments including a fringed V-shaped top of the early southern Plains type (Berlandier 1969:162). The fish on the ground presumably indicated a principal food. Watercolor by Lino Sánchez y Tapia, 1834–1838.

Language, Relationships, and Prehistory

The relationships of the Karankawas to other peoples are not clear-cut. They have been associated linguistically and culturally with neighboring peoples of northeastern Mexico and south Texas (Swanton 1952:320; W.W. Newcomb 1956), but this linguistic relationship has been called into serious question (I. Goddard 1979). In the 1720s a French sea captain, Jean Béranger, obtained a Karankawa vocabulary along with an Atakapa one (Villiers du Terrage and Rivet 1919). Gatschet (1891) published two Karankawa vocabularies, one secured from a Tonkawa who knew a little of the Karankawa language, the other from a White woman who as a girl had lived near the Karankawas and acquired some knowledge of it. These are not sufficiently precise or extensive enough to determine their linguistic affiliations.* Landar (1968), using these materials plus a vocabulary obtained by Raphael Chowell about 1829 (I. Goddard 1979:367), asserts that they spoke a Carib language. This linguistic interpretation has not received support, and Landar's hypothetical migration of Carib-Karankawas to the Texas coast in the sixteenth century is controverted by all that is known about their prehistoric past and their culture. There is every indication that they were longtime residents of the Texas coast, and the historic Karankawas lacked seafaring equipment and were not a maritime people.

The Karankawa adaptation to the gulf littoral may obscure an ancient and basic affiliation with their inland neighbors, but it is also possible that the similarities to them in various aspects of material culture, social organization, and ceremonial life are not very deep-seated. That the Karankawas had a separate and independent heritage is suggested by their distinct physical type. They were an exceptionally tall, long-headed, robust people, physically distinct from most neighboring inland tribes. Such skeletal evidence as exists confirms their distinctive physical nature (Woodbury and Woodbury 1935; Woodbury 1937; Clauser 1947). The Karankawas have been linked archeologically to the Rockport focus, a complex of the central Texas coast, which probably began about A.D. 1000 and persisted into historic times, since metal coins, arrowpoints chipped from bottle glass, and other European materials have been found in some sites (Campbell 1956, 1960:168; Fitzpatrick, Fitzpatrick, and Campbell 1964). The Rockport focus was preceded, at least in the region of Aransas and San Antonio bays, by an Archaic complex known as the Aransas focus. The relationships between the two complexes have not yet been fully determined, but it seems

*Because of the inadequacy of the surviving documentation of the Karankawa language (I. Goddard 1979) no determination of the phonemic system is possible, and words and names can only be cited in the orthography of the sources.

likely that the Rockport focus was a continuation of the older complex, also adapted to a hunting, gathering, and fishing existence, and differing from it principally by the addition of pottery. In short, it appears that the Karankawas were ancient occupants of the central Texas coast.

Culture

Clothing and Adornment

Karankawa men normally wore little or no clothing; women, a short skirt of skin or Spanish moss. In cold weather skins were thrown about the body. Cabeza de Vaca noted that the lower lip and one or both nipples of the men had been perforated for cane or reed ornaments. Both sexes painted their bodies, in part at least to indicate marital status, and men painted their bodies in distinctive ways when going to war. Tattooing was also practiced.

Subsistence

Subsistence was extremely varied; from lagoons and the gulf they took oysters, clams, scallops, other mollusks, turtles, a wide variety of fish, porpoises, tubers of the water chinquapin or yellow lotus (*Nelumbo lutea*), and perhaps other marine plants. Alligators were sought in creeks and estuaries. Deer were hunted as were bison when they appeared near the coast. Bear, peccary, and smaller mammals were also taken when the opportunity arose. Birds and their eggs were seasonally important to subsistence, and berries, nuts, seeds, and other plant foods, such as tubers of the bamboo briar (*Smilax* sp.) were gathered (Bollaert 1956:349).

To take advantage of these varied food sources Karankawa bands led a roving life, seldom spending more than a few weeks at any one campsite, but returning year after year to favored localities. Campsites were often on shell middens—refuse heaps built up by years of intermittent occupation. When possible they were located near sources of fresh water and firewood, and they were always accessible to lagoons and bays. The Capoques and/or Hans, with whom Cabeza de Vaca was so familiar, camped on the offshore islands, catching fish in cane weirs and eating the root of an underwater plant in the fall. By mid-winter or soon after, these plants had begun to grow, making the root inedible, and they were forced to move. They subsisted until spring exclusively upon oysters, found along the shore of the mainland; then for a month they ate blackberries. The summer months were again spent on the coastal islands. Other bands probably followed a similar seasonal round, their movements being determined chiefly by the availability of foods and secondarily by climatic considerations.

Transport

The Karankawas' nomadic, riparian existence was made possible by the use of dugout canoes. Fashioned from tree trunks without removing the bark, one side was trimmed flat, its ends blunted, and then it was hollowed out, probably with the aid of fire and much scraping. A solid section forming a triangular deck was left at either end. The dugouts were large enough to hold a man, his wife, children, and household goods. Propelled by poles, such craft were fit for voyages across the shallow, placid waters of lagoons and bays, but they were not sufficiently seaworthy for use in stormy weather or in the open gulf. The Karankawas were excellent swimmers.

Structures

The movable dwellings of the Karankawas were constructed of a dozen or so slender willow poles approximately 18 feet long and pointed at one or both ends. The sharpened ends were forced into the ground in a circle, the upper ends interlaced and tied with thongs to form an oval framework over which skins and woven rush mats were thrown. Often only the windward side was covered, so it could as well be called a windbreak as a hut. The size of huts varied, but normally they were 10 or 12 feet in diameter and accommodated seven or eight people. They could be rapidly dismantled by the women, who had a special knack for twisting the poles together to stow in the dugouts. Fires for cooking and for heat were built in the center of the huts, the smoke easily finding its way out. Skins were used to sit on and to wrap up in when sleeping.

Technology

Karankawas manufactured distinctive pottery vessels, frequently coated inside and decorated outside with asphaltum, a substance that washes up on the gulf beaches. They made wide-mouthed jars, globular ollas, bowls, and perhaps bottles called Rockport Black-on-gray (Campbell 1958:435–437; Fitzpatrick, Fitzpatrick, and Campbell 1964). Meat, fish, and other foods were cooked in these vessels, their rounded bottoms being sunk in ashes and live coals. Oysters were thrown into the fire or live coals and were raked out and eaten when they began to open. Nuts and seeds were crushed with milling stones. They appear to have made basketry as a number of lumps of asphaltum that have impressions of twined basketry (Campbell 1952:74) have been found in Karankawa archeological sites (Rockport focus).

The Karankawas were superb bowmen, using a bow as long as they were tall, with correspondingly long arrows. Bows were of cedar and bowstrings were fashioned from a number of fine deer sinews twisted together. Arrows were of cane with wooden foreshafts, feathered with three feathers. The bowstring was drawn to the left cheek in shooting, and a guard was worn on the left wrist. The Karankawas also used lances, clubs (fig. 3), and tomahawks. The bow and arrow was the chief weapon used in fishing, though cane weirs were also employed. In 1829 Berlandier (1969:148) saw Karankawas attract fish "by flailing the water around their pirogues" then shooting the fish that came to the surface with bows and arrows. The Karankawas had barkless dogs, and it has been claimed that the name, Karankawa, means 'dog-lovers' (Gatschet 1891:44).

Political Organization

Little is known about the size, nature, and interrelationships of the eight groups (or nine if the Charrucos are included) Cabeza de Vaca encountered or heard about while he was on or near the Texas coast. The Capoques and Hans were evidently friendly neighbors, and they apparently held no animosity for the nearby mainland Charrucos. Cabeza de Vaca implied that the Capoques and Hans greeted an acquaintance from the other group (or perhaps an acquaintance of their own group) by weeping for half an hour. The visitor was then given all that his host possessed and the two might then part without saying a word (Núñez Cabeza de Vaca 1904:72). The Charrucos "entreated" Cabeza de Vaca to become a trader because of their chronic warfare with other, presumably inland people (Núñez Cabeza de Vaca 1904:74). But the more southerly Camolas and Fig People appear to have had friendly contacts with inland natives, who visited and traded with them (Campbell and Campbell 1981:12–13). It is also evident from Cabeza de Vaca's remarks about his journey down the coast that the coastal groups were in close communication with one another, and for example, had detailed knowledge about where the other scattered Spaniards were and what disposition had been made of them.

In later years there were five tribes or subdivisions—the Capoques, Cujanes, Coapites, Karankawa proper, and Copanos—each of which appears to have been originally composed of at least several and probably more divisions. In their declining years, and probably during the winter season of scarcity, Karankawas foraged throughout their territories in small bands. But there are indications that in earlier days much larger groups were common and perhaps characteristic. In a matter of hours after Cabeza de Vaca and his companions were marooned, for example, 100 "archers" confronted them (Núñez Cabeza de Vaca 1904:55). Similarly, the camp visited by La Salle when he first contacted the Karankawas "consisted of about fifty cottages" (Cox 1905, 2:45). With seven or eight persons per dwelling, this camp would have numbered between 350 and 500 persons, which also would be a likely size for the camp or band from which Cabeza de Vaca's "archers" were drawn. That considerable numbers of Karankawas sometimes congregated in one place also may be indicated by La Salle's brother, who noted while in the Kouraras village three days' journey from Fort Saint Louis that he saw there a party of 700 to 800 warriors triumphantly returning with 150 prisoners (Cox 1905, 1:289). The identification of the village as Karankawa is, however, uncertain.

Sparse data, then, suggest that in the sixteenth and seventeenth centuries Karankawa bands numbered somewhere around 400 persons. They appear to have been in rather close communication with one another. During the eighteenth century their numbers dwindled, and by the following century they had been reduced to small remnants scattered along the Texas coast.

In the sixteenth century Cabeza de Vaca asserted that there was "no ruler among them" (Núñez Cabeza de Vaca 1904:71), but according to Gatschet (1891:63) the Karankawas had two kinds of tribal chiefs: those who were responsible for the civil government and war chiefs probably appointed by the civil chiefs. Succession to civil chieftainship was hereditary "in the rule line." The Spanish priest De Solís (1931:41) in the eighteenth century described an ordeal of bloody scarification, iso-

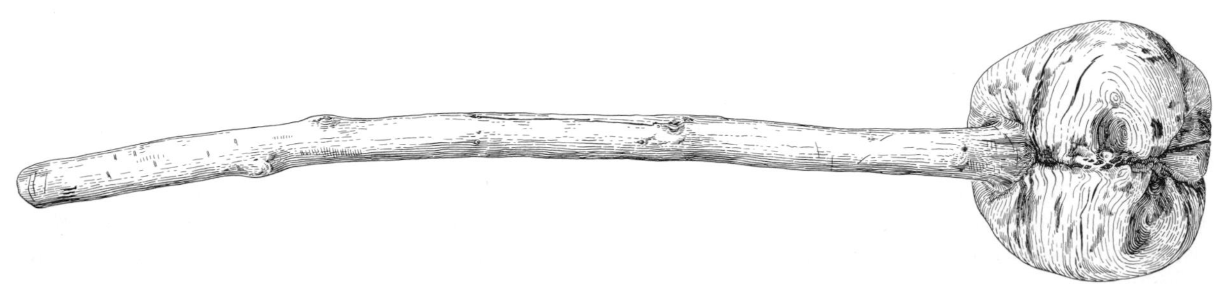

Smithsonian, Dept. of Anthr.: 5,458.

Fig. 3. War club of ironwood used in close combat. The head of this example is a natural burl and the handle a branch projecting from it. Length 46.0 cm, collected in 1838 or before (see Berlandier 1969:176).

lation, and fasting for those who aspired to the office of chief. It is likely that this office was a response to changed conditions brought about by the European presence.

Mooney (1928:13) estimated that in 1690 the Karankawa population was 2,800. Swanton (1952:321), for unstated reasons, believed this estimate was "decidedly too high, but there are practically no data upon which to make a satisfactory determination." It is apparent, even from the limited data drawn on here, that these estimates are too low for 1690, and too low for the preceding century. Assuming that there were eight or nine bands in the contact period, each composed of about 400 persons, the total Karankawa population would have been 3,200 to 3,600. This probably represents a minimal estimate of population in the sixteenth century, considering that they were strung out along the Texas coast for 200 miles and that the existence of some bands may not have been recorded.

Life Cycle

The Karankawas were known to Cabeza de Vaca as being extremely fond of their children. The explorer was amazed to learn that children were nursed until they were 12 years old, by which time they were able to fend for themselves. He was told that it was because of the frequent necessity to go several days without food that children had to be allowed to suckle for so long a time; otherwise they would starve or at best be weak. Mothers carried their children "wrapped in the loop of the skin worn by her" (Gatschet 1891:122). Children were given two names, one a nickname that was used in public and among outsiders, the other a secret name, probably having magical significance.

Puberty rites are unknown, though it appears that tattooing may have taken place to mark this transition. The women did much of the gathering and were charged with most of the onerous chores of the camp—erecting and dismantling the huts, cooking, collecting firewood, and other similar tasks. Men bore the brunt of the hunting and fishing, and they were the warriors. Men and boys competed in shooting arrows at targets, in throwing knives and other weapons, and they played some kind of ball game. They also enjoyed wrestling matches, a custom that set them apart in the eyes of nearby tribes. In this flat, mostly treeless coastal land, smoke signals provided a good means of communication, and scattered groups could quickly join one another for social events, defense, or other purposes.

Marriage was arranged by a man with a girl's parents and included gifts for her parents. Apparently a couple simply settled down in their own hut after the marriage arrangements had been concluded. A form of bride service was practiced in which a man gave all the fruits of the chase to his bride, who took them to her father's hut. Neither bride nor groom dared touch a morsel of this food, but the bride's parents in turn gave her food to take to her husband. At the conclusion of such service the recently married pair normally joined the family or band of the husband. A man was forbidden from entering his parents-in-law's or brother-in-law's dwellings, and similarly they could not enter his. They never spoke to one another, and if they happened to come face to face, both parties turned aside and averted their eyes.

Divorce was rare if a couple had children, common if they had none. Karankawas were normally monogamous, but shamans were allowed multiple wives, and Cabeza de Vaca remarked that their two or three wives lived together harmoniously. De Solís (1931:42), ever contemptuous of Karankawa customs and habits, claimed that they exchanged or bartered their wives, and that "they lend them to their friends in order that they may use them, they sell them for a horse, or gunpowder, balls, beads of glass and other things which they esteem." Homosexual men (berdaches) were also found among the Karankawas.

Death was attended by much ceremony and ritual. This was particularly true for boys and young men who were mourned for an entire year. Before dawn, at noon, and at sunset of each day the parents and kin wept for the departed boy. When the year had passed the mourners cleansed themselves of the paint they had continually worn, and the period of mourning was at an end. Cabeza de Vaca also mentioned that when a son or brother died the members of his household did not attempt to supply themselves with food for three months. Relatives and neighbors attempted to do so, but when epidemics swept through their camps, as they did shortly after the Spaniards were cast up on their shores, it resulted in extreme hardship and starvation. The aged were not mourned for it was felt that they were a burden to others, got little pleasure from life, and were better off dead. Ordinary persons were buried in shallow graves on or near campsites; few tools or ornaments were interred with them. Shamans were not buried but were cremated during a ceremonial dance. One year later the shaman's ashes were mixed with water and drunk by his relatives who also scarified their bodies on this occasion.

Religion

The Karankawas are said to have believed in the existence of two divinities (De Solís 1931:41), but little else is known about their theological beliefs. They held several kinds of religious ceremonies or festivals for different purposes and involving different activities. One, quite obviously considered to be of great religious importance, was a dancing and drinking bout celebrated after successful fishing and hunting ventures. A fire was made inside an enlarged hut, and on this fire large quantities of a yellow, frothy tea were prepared from the leaves of the yaupon shrub (*Ilex vomitoria*). If a woman chanced to pass by while the liquid was cooking and the pot happened to be uncovered, the contents were considered to be contaminated and had to be thrown away. Drinking the contaminated beverage was thought to cause a man to fall sick and die.

Privileged with multiple wives and accorded special treatment at death, Karankawa shamans played an important role in society, but otherwise little is known about them. In Cabeza de Vaca's time they treated the sick by blowing, cutting, and sucking on affected parts of the body. They also successfully cauterized wounds and sores with fire.

The Karankawas have traditionally been described as ferocious cannibals, usually in the sense that they were supposed to have consumed human flesh simply as a result of their ghoulish appetites. There appears to be little to substantiate this reputation. Cabeza de Vaca, for example, reported that the Capoques and/or Hans were disgusted and horrified when they learned that some of the Spanish castaways had consumed their companions who had died. Father De Solís, who was not an eyewitness, alleged that Karankawas ate half-roasted bits and pieces of still living captives in front of their victims, and that after the captives' lingering death they consumed the rest of their bodies. This kind of cannibalism, if De Solís's description is accurate, was quite plainly performed for purposes of revenge and out of religious belief. As such it was widely shared with neighboring peoples, including the Atakapans, Caddoans, and Tonkawa to say nothing of many other American Indians. It was quite clearly an inappropriate criterion for anthropologists to use to consign the Karankawas to a quasi-human "cultural sink" (Swanton 1924; Kroeber 1939:74; see W.W. Newcomb 1956). The Karankawas' reputation has afforded journalistic sensationalists a field day to malign a rather inoffensive, poorly known, much put upon, extinct, coastal people.

Synonymy†

The name Karankawa first appears in the seventeenth century. It was used in Spanish, French, and English in a variety of spellings, though many of those listed by Hodge (1907–1910, 1:658) are clearly miscopyings or misprints.

The accounts of La Salle's contact with the Karankawa and its aftermath have the name as Koïenkahé and Korenkake—different transcriptions of Henri Joutel (Margry 1876–1886, 3:288; French 1846–1875, 1:137), perhaps originally written Korenkahé, and as Clamcöets (Joutel 1713:74), Clamcoches (Villiers du Terrage and Rivet 1929:307), Quelamoueches (De l'Isle in Winsor 1884–1886, 2:294), Quélancouchis (Iberville in Margry 1876–1886, 4:316), and others listed by Villiers du Terrage and Rivet (1919:415). Spanish documents use Carancaguazes, Carancahuases, Carancahuazes, and similar forms. Berlandier (1969:102, 147) used Tarancahuases, Tarancahueses, and Carancahueses. English spellings include Carancouas (Sibley 1806:72, 1832:722), miscopied as Charankouas beside Carankoways (Schoolcraft 1851–1857, 3:544, 5:571), Coronkawa, Karankaways, and Karankoo-as (Hodge 1907–1910, 1:658).

The Tonkawa called the Karankawa kéles 'wrestlers' (Gatschet 1884) and included them under the general name for the Texas coast Indians *yakokxon-kapay* 'no moccasins' (Gatschet 1884, phonemicized after Hoijer 1949:29, 40). Their name in Lipan was nda kun-dadéhe 'people walking in the water' (Gatschet 1884a).

†This synonymy was written by Ives Goddard.

Sources

Cabeza de Vaca's account of the Capoques and Hans, though fragmentary and written after he returned to Spain, is the fullest account of the Karankawas in existence. His narrative was first printed in 1542 and it has been reprinted many times. The Bandelier (1904) translation has been used here. Others in English include Smith (1851, second edition edited by Shea, 1871). Hodge (1907) reprinted the Smith (1871) translation. Cabeza de Vaca and two other survivors, Andrés Dorantes and Alonso del Castillo, also made a written report in 1537. Oviedo y Valdés (1851–1855) condensed this report, and it supplements Cabeza de Vaca's narrative. Translations of Oviedo may be found in Davenport (1924), Covey (1961), and Hedrick and Riley (1974). There has long been disagreement among scholars about the route the Spaniards followed from Galveston Island to Culiacán (see for example Sauer 1971). The route proposed by Krieger (1955, 1961), as modified by Campbell and Campbell (1981) is most in accord with the geographic, ethnographic, and environmental facts and is relied on here, particularly as regards the location and affinity of the coastal tribes.

A number of participants in La Salle's expedition left accounts of their experiences in Texas; unfortunately, they have little to say about Karankawa culture. Cox (1905) and Margry (1876–1886, 3) have been used here; also see French (1846–1875, 1).

The principal source of information about Karankawas during the Spanish mission era of the eighteenth century is De Solís (1931); however, the value of his description of Karankawa life may be questioned because of his violent bias against the tribe. Morfí (1932), writing somewhat later, depended heavily on the De

Solís report. A considerable amount of scattered information, drawn from the mission documents, may be found in Castañeda (1936–1958, 4, 5) and Bolton (1970).

Nineteenth-century sources are fragmentary and most are of doubtful reliability. Some useful material may be found in Bollaert (1956), Berlandier (1969), and Kuykendall (1903). Gatschet (1891) was the first anthropologist to describe the history and culture of the Karankawas. While dated, his study remains a valuable source of information. Schaedel (1949) has summarized Karankawa culture as has W.W. Newcomb (1961). See also Mayhall (1939).

Spanish mission documents likely contain additional data about the Karankawas, but no exhaustive search has been made of them. While these untapped sources and as yet undiscovered documents may provide fruitful new information about the Karankawas, it is unlikely that the yield ever will be ample. Nevertheless, these coastal people represent a challenge to the curious scholar dedicated to cultural reconstruction. For if he is willing to use every scrap of documentary, archeological, environmental, linguistic, and other evidence he can find, then make appropriate and judicious ethnological inferences, a much more rounded and complete comprehension of these Texas coastal natives should be attainable.

The Apachean Culture Pattern and Its Origins

MORRIS E. OPLER

Territory and Language

There are seven recognized Southern Athapaskan– or Apachean-speaking tribes: Chiricahua, Jicarilla, Kiowa-Apache, Lipan, Mescalero, Navajo, and Western Apache. The traditional territories associated with the Apacheans included a good deal of eastern Arizona, much of New Mexico, adjoining sections of Mexico, southeastern Colorado, western Oklahoma, the Oklahoma and Texas Panhandles, and western, central, and southern Texas. How much more extensive their territories are conceived to have been in the past depends upon one's view of claims that the Querechos, Vaqueros, Teyas, Janos, Jocomes, Mansos, Sumas, Cholomes, Jumanos, Cíbolos, Pelones, Padoucas, and various other groups named in early Spanish and French records were Apacheans and that the creators of the Fremont, Promontory, and Dismal River archeological cultures were likewise Apacheans (Forbes 1959a; Wedel 1961a; cf. Schroeder 1974b:50–56; "Southern Periphery: East," this vol.; synonymy below). The acceptance of such assertions would spread the aboriginal Apachean domain into Kansas, Nebraska, Utah, Wyoming, and farther south in Mexico.

Hoijer (1971), mainly on lexicostatistical grounds, asserts that Navajo, Western Apache, Chiricahua, Mescalero, Jicarilla, and Lipan are closely related dialects of a single language (southwestern Apachean) and that Kiowa-Apache is a second Apachean language. Because distinctive features separate Jicarilla and Lipan from other southwestern Apachean dialects, Hoijer (1971:5) thinks that the ancestors of the Navajo, Western Apache, Chiricahua, and Mescalero were the first to move southward, "followed by but still in contact with the Jicarilla and Lipan." Since he accepts Mooney's (1898) dictum that the Kiowa-Apache were associated with the Kiowa from a very early period in the north and never had ties with the southwestern Apacheans, he suggests that the basic linguistic differentiation between southwestern Apachean and Kiowa-Apache occurred "before any considerable movement southward took place." However, Bittle (1971:2, 19–22, 25) has shown that the Kiowa-Apache tie with the Kiowa has always been tenuous, and it is becoming increasingly evident that Mooney never conducted any serious fieldwork among the Kiowa-Apache but depended on what Kiowa informants told him about them. Moreover, Mooney's reconstruction of early Kiowa history has been challenged (Lowie 1953; E.W. Voegelin 1933).

Lexicostatistical data show that Kiowa-Apache did indeed differentiate from Jicarilla and Lipan earlier than these latter two dialects separated from each other. Yet the gap in time is not so great as may be supposed; the divergence time of Jicarilla and Lipan is a little over 200 years (Hoijer 1956a; Hymes 1957). The Kiowa-Apache divergence from Lipan and Jicarilla, as indicated in the lexicostatistical work of Bittle (1961), occurred about 200 years earlier (429 and 401 years, respectively). The time difference may even be considerably narrower than available evidence can reveal. The federal government policy of consolidating southwestern Apacheans on a few reservations, begun in the 1870s, forced these six tribes into common speech communities and may, as Hoijer (1956a:226) has pointed out, "account in part for the generally low times of divergence." Kiowa-Apache and southwestern Apachean cultural correspondences are so numerous that it is difficult to believe that the separation took place too long ago or very far from the area in which the major differentiation of the Apacheans proceeded.

For Apachean prehistory see also "Historical Linguistics and Archeology" and "Southern Athapaskan Archeology," volume 9, and "Comparative Social Organization," and "Apachean Languages," this volume.

Culture: Uniformities and Variations

Mythology

Apachean mythology is marked by an account of two culture heroes, one associated with the sun or fire and the other with water, who vanquish a number of monsters that threaten man's survival. Another important myth common to all Apacheans describes a hidden-ball game played "in the beginning" between evil animals and the beneficent animals and birds to determine whether there should be perpetual darkness. Coyote is a participant whose loyalties fluctuate with the fortunes of the game, and characteristics of many birds and animals are explained by reference to events of the contest. All Apacheans likewise possessed remarkably similar trickster cycles in which Coyote was the protagonist (D. French 1942). Most of Coyote's behavior is reprehensible, but he occasionally performs a service, as when he secures fire from those who are hoarding it.

Myths and tales that are shared by only some of the Apacheans indicate alignments that dispute claims of their cultural distance and separate origin. For instance, the same account of the beginning of agriculture, involving a man who travels down a waterway in a hollow log and is aided by his pet turkey, appears among the Navajo, Western Apache, Jicarilla, and Lipan and is absent in the other three groups. The same four tribes have an account of emergence from an underworld. These and many other common concepts argue against early separation of the Navajo and Western Apache from the Jicarilla and Lipan (Goodwin 1939; Matthews 1897; McAllister 1949; Opler 1938a, 1940, 1942).

Social Organization

Apachean social organization was everywhere characterized by an extended family with matrilocal residence. Each nuclear family had a separate dwelling, but several of them ordinarily formed a cluster of homes occupied by persons related by blood and marriage who constituted the basic cooperative work unit. The women were lifetime members of this social group; the men, who entered it through marriage, were obligated to contribute to its support and defense. A respected elder of the group acted as its spokesman, and the unit was usually associated with his name.

A number of extended families who lived in the same general area and together exploited its resources comprised the local group. The local group was capable of supporting economic, ceremonial, and martial enterprises for which the extended family was too small. Since it brought unrelated families into a larger encampment or rancheria, marriages often occurred between members of the local group, though there was no rule of local group endogamy. Leadership and authority, weakly developed at best among Apacheans, reached its strongest expression in the local group; the most dynamic family headman was acknowledged as leader or "chief." Though an active and eloquent leader might exercise a good deal of influence, his main assets were the continued success of his policies and his ability to persuade. He enjoyed no coercive power, and any who lost faith in his direction were free to go elsewhere. The office was not hereditary, and often a leader who lost effectiveness through age or infirmity was succeeded by a nonrelative.

In most Apache tribes local groups that were in loose contact and could call upon one another for ambitious undertakings and emergencies constituted named bands. True bands have not been reported for the Navajo; possibly the need to remain close to pasturages, as the Navajo turned to sheepherding, interfered with the maintenance of extensive band territories. During the last half of the nineteenth century the Kiowa-Apache were apparently too few in number to require a division into bands (Bittle 1971:25; McAllister 1955:165–166), but there are hints in the literature of band organization among them at an earlier period (Thwaites 1904–1907, 16:105, 117). Mescalero bands have been discussed by Castetter and Opler (1936:6–8), Opler (1969:13), and Basehart (1971:35–48), though the last does not clearly distinguish between the band and local group. In any case, band organization among the Mescalero was weakly developed, and this is true also of the Lipan (Opler 1974). Among the other tribes band consciousness was relatively strong; it was particularly significant among the Chiricahua (Opler 1941:1–4, 463) and the Western Apache (Basso 1970:5, 1971:14; Goodwin 1942:5–62).

Because the population was thinly scattered over large territories and political control was concentrated at the local-group level, tribal cohesion was minimal among Apacheans. It amounted mainly to a recognition that one owed a modicum of hospitality to those of the same speech, dress, and customs.

There were also some social units that developed in response to local conditions or the influence of neighboring peoples. Kluckhohn and Leighton (1946:62–63) described what they call "the outfit" for the Navajo, a body of kindred more numerous than the extended family but less comprehensive than a community or local group. Though bilateral kinship reckoning was the rule for the others, the Navajo and Western Apache, possibly inspired by Western Pueblo examples, developed strong matrilineal clans and linked clans or phratries. Among the Western Apache were found five subtribal groups that were something more than bands and something less than tribes; they were themselves divided into bands (Goodwin 1942:12–50). The Jicarilla bands are best described as moieties, for the two sides engaged in rivalry and were jointly responsible for certain ceremonial functions (Opler 1946:116–134). The influence of the northeastern Pueblos may be suspected in this Jicarilla development, for one of the prime functions of the bands was to pit their youths against one another in a relay race that greatly resembles a similar event that takes place annually at Taos, San Juan, and Isleta (Opler 1944, 1946:1–2, 116–134).

• BLOOD KIN In Apachean kinship usages there was emphasis upon the role of the grandparents, particularly on the maternal side, in instruction and disciplining. This became very formalized in the Jicarilla system but was present in principle everywhere. Siblings of the same sex were expected to be boon companions; great restraint in speech and behavior was observed between siblings of opposite sex. Cousins were either regarded as siblings (parallel cousins) or were addressed by separate terms (cross-cousins). A teasing-rivalry relationship between cross-cousins of the same sex prevailed in which the mate of the cross-cousin was often a foil. In the case of cross-cousins of the opposite sex, restraint was extreme and sometimes culminated in total avoidance. Among the tribes showing most Plains orientation (Kiowa-Apache, Jicarilla, Lipan) the supervisory function of the adult male in regard to his sister was marked. The mother's brother was everywhere a key figure in the fortunes of his nephew and niece. Among the Jicarilla, for instance, the maternal uncle engaged in rough play and rivalry, particularly with his nephew, designed to spur on his young relative to adult standards (Opler 1936b).

• MARRIAGE AND AFFINES In preliminaries to marriage among Apacheans the initiative was taken by the relatives of the boy. Presents were always given by the relatives of the boy to the kin of the girl; occasionally gifts of smaller magnitude were made by the girl's family in return. The corporate concern for the marriageable child was evident; kin who had taken an interest in the child were consulted about the marriage choice, and the presents received were divided among them. Though the arrangements were made by their elders, the feelings of the young principals were usually respected. Once an understanding between families was reached, the marriage took place with a minimum of formality: in six of the seven tribes the procedure consisted simply of building a new dwelling for the couple near the home of the bride's parents. Only the Navajo performed a marriage ceremony in addition: the bride and groom washed each other's hands, ate of a basket of corn mush, and listened to Blessingway songs at dawn (Leighton and Kluckhohn 1947:81–82).

The Apachean preference for matrilocal residence was only one strand in a web of conventions that bound a husband securely to his wife's extended family. An Apachean male was trained to feel that he should provide for his wife's parents and obey their instructions. He was obligated to be restrained in speech and action while in the company of his wife's close kin. According to tribe and the affinal relatives involved, these conventions of restraint ran the gamut from simple, self-imposed circumspection through "polite form" (indirect speech) to "avoidance" practices in which the principals were barred from coming into each other's presence. The Chiricahua had the most extensive system of affinal avoidances and polite forms. The Lipan practiced no total avoidances of affinities, though they showed them other tokens of respect. Avoidance and all other Apachean forms of respect relations implied economic, military, and moral assistance and continued even after the death of the mate who had been the link between the affinal relatives.

In all tribes but the Lipan, polygyny was practiced, though it was not particularly encouraged. Because of the difficulty of providing for more than one family, only a few wealthy and prominent men could afford it. Since the burden of satisfying the demands of duplicate sets of affinals could be a crushing one, sororal polygyny was favored.

Despite the seriousness of the marriage tie, a divorce was not difficult to obtain. A cruel or lazy husband might find himself driven from his wife's parents' encampment. Incompatibility and unfaithfulness were grounds for divorce. If it was the woman who misbehaved, her relatives could not complain if her husband departed. When the aggrieved man was a good provider, a woman might be disciplined by her own kin in an effort to retain him. Among the Jicarilla and the Kiowa-Apache a brother might curb an erring woman whose conduct jeopardized family economy, stability, and honor.

It was much more difficult for a man to secure his freedom when he became a widower; the degree of his obligation to a family rather than to the deceased individual then became apparent. He was expected to continue to help provide for his dead wife's relatives, to mourn for as long as a year, and to enter into a sororate marriage with an eligible sister or cousin of his deceased spouse. The levirate, too, was practiced by the Apacheans. In case of the husband's death, his wife, after an appropriate mourning period, could be asked to accept his unmarried brother or cousin as her mate. These usages were the Apachean manner of healing family scars left by death and of providing for surviving mates and children. The marriage of a widow or widower to an outsider without permission inevitably precipitated a feud between families. When a family had no eligible mate to offer the survivor, it ordinarily freed him and allowed him to make his own future marital arrangements.

Subsistence

The Apacheans were essentially hunters and gatherers, though sheep-raising and agriculture became very important for the Navajo in historic times. The Western Apache, Jicarilla, and Lipan also cultivated crops, but less intensively; the Chiricahua and Mescalero farmed very little (two of the three Chiricahua bands disclaim any cultivation), and the Kiowa-Apache not at all. Some think that the Apacheans were already agriculturists when they entered the Southwest and southern Plains. However, the uneven distribution and differential intensity of agriculture among the Apacheans, as well as the Southwestern cast of the associated ritual traits (such as prayersticks, cornmeal, rain ceremonies) that were part of the farming complex, especially among the Navajo and the Western Apache, raise questions about this.

Division of Labor

A sexual division of labor prevailed among the Apacheans, but its lines were not rigidly drawn. Gathering was usually women's work, but the men joined in the collection and roasting of the crowns of the agave (mescal) ("Western Apache," fig. 2, this vol.). Hunting was men's business (figs. 1–2), but the Lipan women participated in rabbit surrounds and antelope hunts. Women were expected to tan hides, but men might assist in the preparation of large and heavy skins. In general the care of children was in the hands of women, but the grandfather, the maternal uncle, and the father were often active in this task. The women sewed leather and made clothes, but the men were capable of repairing clothing when on hunting or raiding trips. Moreover, men sometimes participated in the manufacture of artifacts of hide designed for their own use, such as the quiver. Gathering fuel and cooking fell to the lot of women during ordinary camp life, but men were trained to take care of their own needs in these respects when they were alone. Except for the Navajo, house construction (the wickiup in the highlands and the tepee on the plains) was the women's task; the Navajo men took main responsibility for the building of the hogan, though the women helped in the plastering and some of the lighter work (Kluckhohn, Hill, and Kluckhohn 1971:146, 427).

In general, men and women made, owned, and repaired the artifacts required in their work: women made baskets and household utensils; and men fashioned weapons (fig. 3), rope, and most of the gear for the horse. Ceremonial activities were not monopolized by the men; in those in which herbalism was important, female practitioners predominated. Female shamans were common and competed on even terms with their male counterparts among the Chiricahua and Mescalero; Navajo diviners were often women. Even in more traditional and less shamanistic ceremonies, such as the girls' puberty rite, female ceremonialists played an essential part. Though most singers of the Navajo chants were males, women, too, have served in this role (Rei-

top, Sharlot Hall Mus., Prescott, Ariz.: In-A 174p; bottom, Smithsonian, Dept. of Anthr.: 21,525.

Fig. 1. Hunting. top, Western Apache hunter in posture and costume for stalking deer. He holds bow and arrows and is wearing a mask made from the head of a mule deer or blacktail deer. Photograph by D.F. Mitchell, probably early 1870s. bottom, Antelope head mask worn when hunting antelope, an animal even more difficult to approach than deer. A twig is bent into a circle and lashed with leather to the base of the mask, which rests on the hunter's shoulders. The features of the skinned-out head would be stuffed with grass; the horns are missing here. Length 26.5 cm, collected in Ariz. before 1876.

Smithsonian, NAA:2491-a.

Fig. 2. Young Apache hunters. One wears knitted socks, probably army-issue. Photograph by A. Frank Randall, 1888.

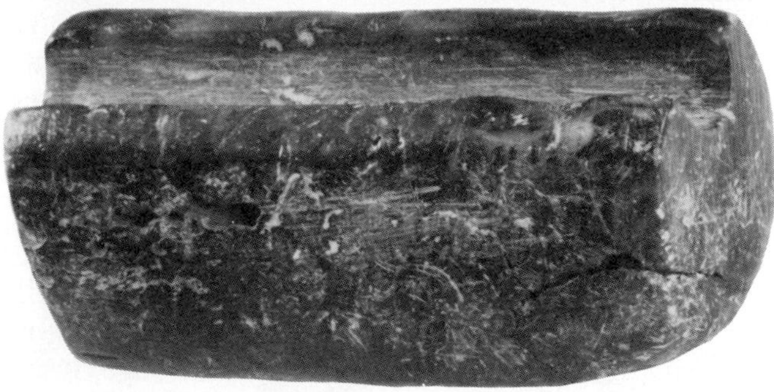

top, Amer. Mus. of Nat. Hist., New York: 14329; bottom, Smithsonian, Dept. of Anthr.: 5527.

Fig. 3. Arrow making. top, Casa Maria, Jicarilla Apache, smoothing arrow shaft with grooved stone. Photograph by Pliny E. Goddard, 1909–1910. bottom, Rectangular stone with lengthwise groove used to smooth arrow shafts. Length 7.5 cm, collected by Edward Palmer in Ariz., 1868.

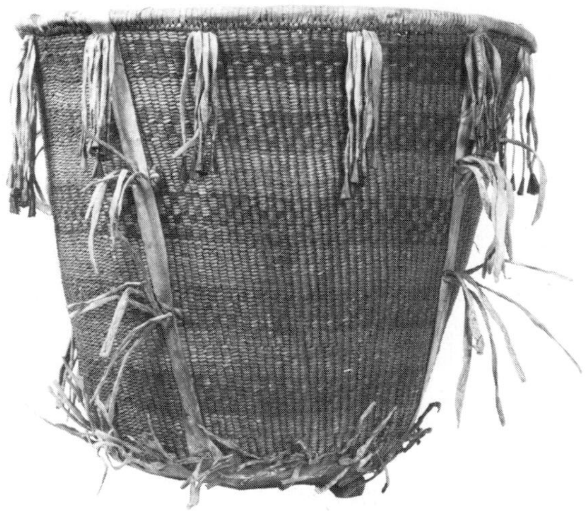

top, Smithsonian, NAA:76–6288; bottom, Smithsonian, Dept. of Anthr.: 21,487.

Fig. 4. Transportation. top, White Mountain Apache woman on horseback; burden basket and pitch-covered, woven water carrier are attached to the saddle. Photograph by Edward S. Curtis, copyright 1906. bottom, Twined burden basket with bands of red and blue on natural ground, decorated with leather fringe and cone-shaped tin pendants. A piece of rawhide on the bottom strengthens the basket. Such baskets were also carried on a woman's back, supported by a carrying strap. Height 38.5 cm, collected in Ariz., before 1876.

chard 1950, 1:xliv). McAllister (1955:130) reports that Kiowa-Apache women "might even possess 'worship bundles,' and one woman had the important 'buffalo medicine' curing power." Brant (1951:45, 1969:5), too, found evidence that Kiowa-Apache women were recipients of supernatural power.

Religion

Apachean religion was everywhere a combination of shamanism and priestcraft. For example, most Chiricahua and Mescalero rites were acquired through an individual vision experience; yet, with the permission of the power source, they could be taught to others. Furthermore, the girls' puberty ceremony of these tribes was learned by rote from active practitioners by those interested in perpetuating it (Opler 1941: 84–87, 210–211).

Standardized, nonshamanistic rituals, which included the girls' puberty rite (figs. 5–6), the chants of the

Navajo, the "long-life ceremonies" of the Jicarilla, and the sacred-bundle ceremonies of the Kiowa-Apache, were more numerous in some tribes than in others. Yet everywhere they assumed considerable importance. Among the Jicarilla they were considered to be more efficacious than the shamanistic rites (which required less preparation and expense and were mainly used in emergencies), and among the Western Apache shamanism consisted principally in learning embellishments for established rites through personal experiences with supernatural power (Goodwin 1938:28–30; Opler 1936b:214–215).

Underlying all ceremonies, whether shamanistic or priestly, was the conception of supernatural power that pervaded the universe and could be utilized for human purposes by ritual procedures known to priests or learned in personal revelation by shamans. Most Apachean deities were personifications of natural forces. Witchcraft fears loomed large among the Apacheans, for power was susceptible to use for malicious purposes as well as for good. Prolonged sickness was often attributed to witchcraft, and Apachean ritual, in which curative rites predominated, was repeatedly interpreted as a contest between witchcraft and power used for beneficial ends. Sorcery was usually accomplished by the "shooting" of foreign substances, often bits of bone and hair of the dead, into the victim. The location and extraction of the "arrow" of the witch by sucking or other means was consequently a prominent feature of Apachean curing rites.

In Apachean religious ideology sickness and misfortune could also be caused by the anger of a deity or by failure to treat respectfully some personified natural force, such as Lightning. In addition, there were animals and birds—among them the owl, snake, bear, and coyote—that were intrinsically dangerous and that sickened people by sight, odor, or touch. Even to cross the trail of one of these creatures, to be frightened by it, or to rest where it had lain could have dire results, as a diagnostic ceremony might reveal. Witches were often suspected of instigating encounters with such contaminating beings. The owl and the coyote were favorite forms in which the spirits of dead sorcerers and restless ghosts of relatives appeared to unfortunate Apacheans. A common threat that ran through Apachean ideas about witchcraft was that sorcerers were prone to the equally heinous crime of incest; consequently anyone charged with incest was automatically treated as a witch and was in danger of being tortured, forced to confess, and executed (Basso 1969; Kluckhohn 1944; Opler 1941:242–257).

The generous use by the Apacheans of masked impersonators of the supernaturals, including clowns, strongly suggests Pueblo influence and considerable Apachean time-depth in the Southwest. The only Apachean group for which this trait has not been explicitly reported is the Kiowa-Apache, though it may have been present even among them (Battey 1968:127–129). The frequent employment of sandpaintings in Apachean ritual, especially among the Navajo, Western Apache, and Jicarilla, also suggests diffusion from Pueblo sources. In some instances the Pueblo stimulus for Apachean ritual features is obvious; the Jicarilla ceremonial relay race is a case in point (Opler 1944). The special internal relations of Apacheans in respect to ritual are of interest for clues to history, too. Some Navajo and Jicarilla ceremonies are so strikingly similar, in general conception and details, that it is difficult to accept theories of separate routes of dispersion and long separation for these two peoples (Opler 1943).

Raid and Warfare

The Apacheans made a sharp distinction, terminologically and behaviorally, between raid and warfare. A raid was undertaken to acquire enemy horses and booty. The object was to avoid encounters with the enemy. The ritual associated with the raid was directed toward enhancing successful concealment and thwarting pursuit. Those who led a raid were persons who felt that the possessions of the encampment, particularly horses, were in short supply. Of course, raiders, if discovered, had to be prepared to fight, but even then the emphasis was on successful escape with as much booty and as few casualties as possible rather than upon confrontation.

In contrast, a war party had as its purpose the avenging of Apachean casualties previously suffered. If the enemy were routed and his camps abandoned, booty was taken, but this was subordinated to revenge. It was the relatives of slain Apacheans who agitated for a war party and took a prominent part in it. The dance that preceded the expedition was usually a demonstration of what heroics warriors meant to perform. If the effort was successful, the dance and celebration that followed pantomimed the military accomplishments.

It was Apachean practice to prepare boys for the rigors of raid and war by a strenuous training process that involved running, wrestling, mock fights, and other tests of agility, strength, and stamina. A youth's first expeditions were usually raiding parties, and as a novice he was treated in a special manner, had certain restrictions on his conduct, and was the recipient of much instruction. Usually he was considered to be in a sacred status, and there was reluctance to expose him to danger. In most of the tribes, perhaps all (clear evidence on this point is lacking for the Lipan and Kiowa-Apache), the youth was taught a special raid and warfare vocabulary that he was obliged to use in place of ordinary terms for common objects during his first ventures (Basso 1971:264–267; Opler 1938a:244, 1936b:210, 1938b:14, 38, 42, 1946:141, 145–146; Opler and Hoijer 1940; Reichard 1950, 1:269, 270, 273, 374, 2:453, 454).

U. of Ariz., Ariz. State Mus., Tucson: this page—top left, 54901, bottom left, 54927, top right, 54943, bottom right, 54973; opposite page—top left, 54954, bottom left, 54991~~, top right~~, 54960, bottom right, 54999.

Fig. 5. Girls' puberty ceremony (Sunrise Dance). A major ritual among the Western Apache, this ceremony symbolically invests young women with physical and psychological attributes needed to fulfill adult responsibilities. The girl is dressed to represent White Painted Woman (Changing Woman, White Shell Woman), a prominent figure in Apache mythology whom the girl "becomes" for a 4-day period. As proceedings begin, the girl, holding a decorated cane she will keep for use in old age, stands with a young companion before a pile of rugs and a tanned buckskin (this page, top left). The girl's "sponsor," a woman of exemplary character and reputation who belongs to a different matrilineal clan, replaces the companion and ties a piece of abalone shell in the girl's hair—another symbol of her identification with White Painted Woman (bottom left). The sponsor, dancing in place to a chant sung by a medicine man (hand cupped over mouth), watches as the girl assumes the kneeling posture in which White Painted Woman was made pregnant in mythological times by Sun, another important Western Apache deity (top right). Other participants in the ceremony, many of whom are female relatives of the girl and her sponsor, link arms and dance together (opposite page, top left). While she lies face-down, the girl's shoulders, back, and legs are massaged by her sponsor, an action that assures the girl of physical strength as an adult (top right). She is then instructed to run in each of the four directions, an act that is intended to provide her with quickness and endurance (this page, bottom right). Later, shortly before the ceremony ends, the girl and her sponsor are blessed with holy pollen by the girl's parents (opposite page, bottom left), and by all other participants who care to repeat the blessings. The ceremony concludes with the distribution of fruit and candy to all in attendance (bottom right). Photographs by Helga Teiwes at Bylas, Ariz., March 28, 1981. Caption by Keith H. Basso.

In general, Apachean attitudes toward warfare contrasted with those of the Plains Indians. Little enthusiasm was shown for standing ground in a deteriorating fight. The Apachean strategy was to scatter when the situation seemed hopeless and to reassemble at a prearranged place. Except for the Kiowa-Apache there were no warrior societies: even here there were only two such societies, fewer than the number possessed by the surrounding Plains tribes. Moreover, Kiowa-Apache men were not eager to join the society that extolled brash war deeds (Brant 1951:51; McAllister 1955:150, 153). Counting coup on a fallen enemy was considered meritorious only by the Kiowa-Apache and the Lipan; all other Apacheans felt that to kill an enemy was the bravest possible act. The Apacheans had little interest in the acquisition of scalps or body parts of the enemy as trophies or embellishments for clothes, shields, or dwellings. Most groups claimed that what scalping they practiced was in retaliation for similar indignities constantly visited upon them. Apparently the Apachean fear of contamination from the dead was instrumental in shaping this attitude. For example, no Jicarilla who was not ritually prepared could take a scalp; he had to find some tribesman who could do so with impunity. If the Jicarillas had lost more men than had the enemy, any scalps taken had to be abandoned. For the homeward journey scalps were placed in the custody of persons who were ritually protected from attendant dangers, and the scalps were kept at a distance from the camping site. When the home encampment was reached, the scalps were given to elderly ceremonialists, who cared for them far from the settled area (Opler 1936b:211–213).

Eschatology

In a study of Navajo eschatology, Wyman, Hill, and Osanai (1942:42), noting "the parallels with the various Apache groups," declared, "they are numerous enough almost to warrant speaking of a Southern Athapascan eschatological pattern assemblage with minor Navajo, Chiricahua Apache, etc., variants." This view is supported by further data (Goodwin 1942:518–521; Opler 1941:14–15, 229–237, 301–305, 472–478, 1945, 1946c, 1960; Opler and Bittle 1961).

At the time of each individual's death, according to

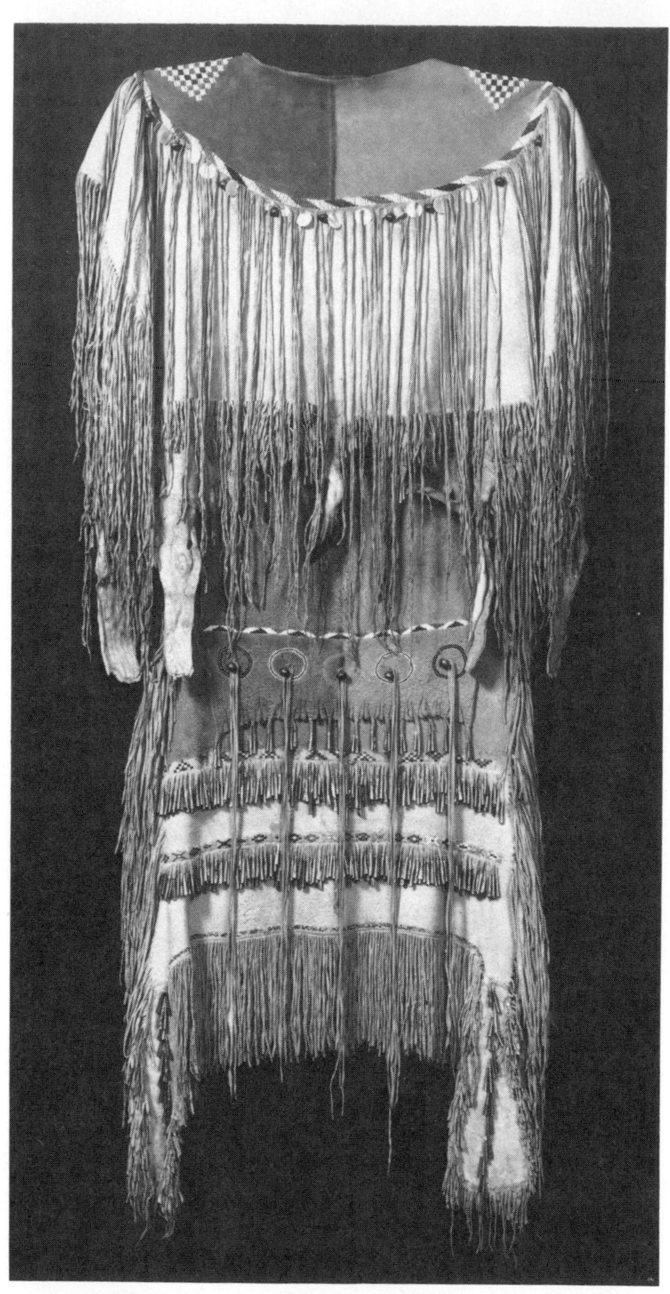

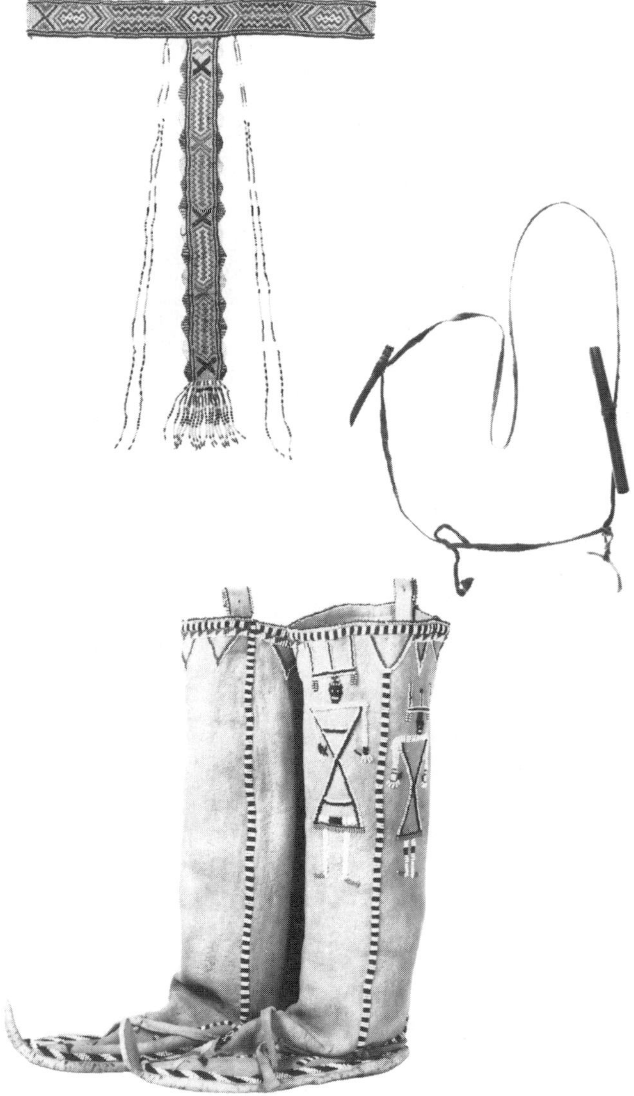

left, Denver Art Mus., Col.: 1953.358; bottom right, Smithsonian, Dept. of Anthr.: 270,013; U. of Ariz., Ariz. State Mus., Tucson: center right, 21,869, top right, 21,497.

Fig. 6. Girls' puberty ceremony clothing and accessories. Although not from the same costume, these pieces, in varied form, would be present together. left, Mescalero Apache 2-piece buckskin dress decorated with coloring, fringe, beadwork, cone-shaped tin pendants, bells, and shells. bottom right, Moccasins with yellow-colored buckskin uppers, rawhide soles, beaded trim, and figures representing masked dancers. The disc toe often appears on Chiricahua and Western Apache footwear. These buckskin garments, made of the finest materials, are now made only for ceremonial occasions. center right, White Mountain Apache scratcher, hollow tube, and part of a shell bracelet tied on a yellow cord. The girl had to use the stick rather than her nails to scratch herself and to use the tube to drink. When not in use these items were tied to her dress. top right, T-shaped necklace of black, yellow, red, blue, green, and white beads, probably inspired by doctrines of the Silas John cult. left, Width at shoulders 152.3 cm, rest to same scale. Collected: left, on Mescalero Reservation in 1953; bottom right, before 1910 probably at Ft. Sill, Okla.; center right, on White Mountain Reservation, 1936; top right, in Rice, Ariz., 1936.

Smithsonian, Dept. of Anthr.: 21,520.

Fig. 7. Shaman's garment, a rectangular piece of buckskin, with hole cut for the head, edges notched, sides left open. The symbols painted in blue, red, and yellow on the front and back, together with the feathers and bead decoration, are associated with the owner's power source. Length about 45.0 cm, collected in Ariz., before 1876.

Apachean belief, a ghost was released that was capable of doing great injury to the living unless it promptly traveled to the afterworld and remained there. A dead kinsman appeared to the dying and led him on a four-day journey to the north to an underworld. The newly deceased often resisted leaving the surroundings familiar to him and severing bonds of kinship and association. How peaceably he departed depended on whether funerary practices had been properly performed. Even after entering the underworld a ghost might return to the land of the living to avenge some past injury. The visit of a ghost never failed to threaten, sicken, or destroy. Therefore, the protective measures considered appropriate at the time of death were immediately invoked and scrupulously followed.

As soon as a death occurred, close relatives went into mourning. Men wept, women wailed, and both sexes cut the ends of the hair and donned old clothing. One or two elderly relatives (death was particularly contaminating to the young) washed the body, combed the hair, and dressed the deceased in his finest clothes. Burial took place during the daytime and as soon as possible. The deceased was placed on his favorite horse with as many of his personal possessions as could be carried and taken far from the habitations of the people, into hilly or mountainous country, if possible. Because of the risk of contamination, the burial party was small. It proceeded silently, and tribesmen it encountered turned away. A crevice in the rocks that could be covered with earth, brush, and stones was sought as a grave. Some personal possessions were buried with the corpse; the rest were broken and left at the burial site. The horse was killed at the graveside, for the dead person needed his mount as well as his belongings in the afterworld. The burial party returned by a different route, and its members refrained from looking back toward the grave or discussing its location with others. Upon their return they discarded the clothes they had worn and thoroughly washed themselves. They and the other mourners burned sage, juniper, or some pungent plant considered to be "ghost medicine" and bathed themselves in the smoke. Ashes, too, were liberally used on their persons and around the camp to discourage any lingering or returning ghost.

While the burial was in progress, other relatives carried out requirements at home. Personal possessions of the dead that had not been taken to the grave were broken or burned. Even possessions of others that the dead person had lately used or handled a great deal were destroyed. Nothing that would constantly remind the living of their dead relative was retained, for to think of the dead was to attract the ghost. As a precaution, the name of the deceased was not uttered; if it was absolutely necessary to refer to him, a circumlocution was used. Since ghosts strove to return to their former homes, the encampment in which a death occurred was moved, even though sometimes the shift was to a nearby location and was more symbolic than substantial. The mourning relatives remained isolated for a time, shunning social events.

Ghosts almost always chose the night to strike. They often appeared in human guise in dreams or as black, amorphous objects. They made whistling noises to frighten their victims; therefore whistling at night was discouraged. The owl and the coyote were favorite vehicles through which ghosts approached their victims. Consequently the hooting of an owl or the presence of a coyote around the camps instilled terror. Fainting spells, persistent bad dreams, palpitation of the heart, hysteria, seizures, insanity, and paralysis affecting the face or upper body were usually diagnosed as ghost sickness and required curative ceremonies such as the owl ceremony of the Mescalero and Chiricahua or the Enemyway rite of the Navajo.

The acute fear of the dead and of ghosts was related to two main conceptions. The first was that the denizens of the underworld were "lonely" and sought new recruits. Therefore a ghost experience was the harbinger of one's own death or that of a close relative. The

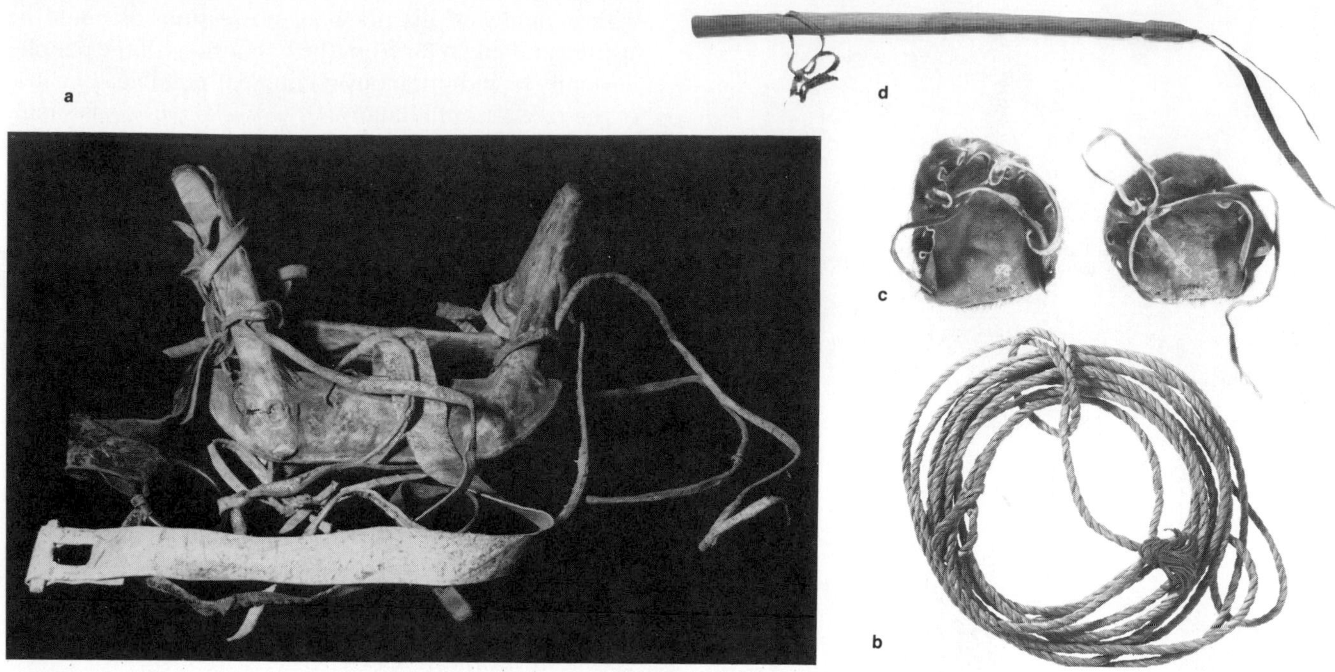

a, Amer. Mus. of Nat. Hist., New York: 50/8229; b, Smithsonian, Dept. of Anthr.: 17,354; U. of Ariz., Ariz. State Mus., Tucson: c, 21,406; d, 21,374.

Fig. 8. Equipment for the horse. a, Mescalero Apache saddle made of rawhide stretched over a wooden frame and based on Mexican examples. Packsaddles were made of 2 rolls of rawhide stuffed with grass, one on each side of the horse and tied together with leather thong. b, Rope made from 2 pieces of rawhide twisted together, used for bridles; c, White Mountain Apache horseshoes of rawhide with thong for lashing to horse's feet, often used to protect the feet of an animal going lame; d, White Mountain Apache quirt, with wooden handle, rawhide whip, and thong carrying strap. a, Length 38.0 cm, rest to same scale, collected by Pliny E. Goddard on the Mescalero Reservation, 1909; b collected on Wheeler Expedition in 1875; c and d collected by Grenville Goodwin in Bylas, Ariz., 1936.

second was that some ghosts returned out of malice because of friction in the past or a sin of commission or omission. There was an ideological link between fear of the ghost and of the witch: both were capable of persecuting those who had aroused their ire. Inevitably, then, ghosts were often described by Apacheans as the shades of those who had been witches, even though they might have successfully concealed this during their stay on earth. Consequently, if an individual with a fiery temper or an unsavory reputation died while one was at odds with him, it was cause for worry. Also, if an Apachean felt that a person who died had had reason to resent his behavior, he might be apprehensive. Since most Apachean interactions and obligations involved relatives by blood or marriage, it was inevitable that the majority of attacks of ghost sickness were attributed to the activitities of dead kinsmen (Opler 1936a).

The anxieties and extraordinary precautions concerning death, burial, and the visits of ghosts were greatly relaxed when it was an infant or a very old person who died. An infant could not have developed animosities, it was thought, and an aged person who had lived out his life fully was considered beyond rancor. It was the person who died with his promise and hopes unfulfilled who was to be feared.

The details of the death complex that have been enumerated thus far are pan-Apachean. Special features and emphasis shared by only some of the tribes are also of interest for determining whether consistent alignments within the Apachean fold existed. The Jicarilla and the Kiowa-Apache believed that in the course of life, because of frustrations, disappointments, and interpersonal conflicts, evil tendencies accumulated in the individual, became associated with the corpse at death, and furnished motive power to the ghost. They contrasted the ghost with a breathlike spirit that also persisted after death but that there was no need to fear. The Navajo, Western Apache, and Kiowa-Apache did not remove a corpse through the doorway of a dwelling, but through a hole broken in a side wall. Among the Navajo, the Kiowa-Apache, and the Lipan the reluctance of relatives to handle a corpse was so great that outsiders (in the case of the Navajo, captive slaves) were sought to bury the body. The Navajo sometimes practiced hogan burial; the Kiowa-Apache occasionally used the tepee in the same manner. Among the Lipan, the Kiowa-Apache, and the Western Apache mourners were comforted by nonrelatives from surrounding camps. The Navajo and Kiowa-Apache both believed that the ghost could return in the form of a whirlwind; consequently the Kiowa-Apache shielded the face of a baby from the sight of a whirlwind. Because the deceased's name was not supposed to be mentioned, the Western Apache and the Kiowa-Apache hesitated to name an infant until they were sure it would survive. The Lipan, Jicarilla, Western Apache, and Navajo pictured a separation of

top, Mus. of N. Mex., Santa Fe: 56,138; bottom, Smithsonian, Dept. of Anthr.: left, 11,319; center, 21,532; right, 5517.

Fig. 9. Warriors. top, Mescalero Apache delegation led by 2 prominent chiefs, at the tercentenary celebration of Santa Fe in July 1883. Their tepees are in the background. Photograph by Ben Wittick. bottom, Weapons and accessories, made by each man; design and decoration were highly individual. left, White Mountain Apache rawhide shield, the front painted blue and black with a strip of red wool to which feathers are attached with a rawhide cord. Some hair remains on the back, and there are twisted rawhide handles. center, Buckskin hat topped with cut feathers and bordered with a strip of red wool, blue-painted rawhide in a saw-toothed design, and white buttons. The cloth chin-strap is also decorated with white buttons. Such hats were ordinarily worn only by shamans who carried out protective ceremonies before a war expedition. right, War club with horsehair tail. Between the head, which is rawhide stretched over a stone, and the handle, which has a wooden core, the rawhide is slashed and twisted to give flexibility and to prevent the handle from breaking on impact. A rawhide carrying strap is tied through the handle and designs are scratched on the head and handle. bottom left, Diameter 46.5 cm, rest same scale. Collected: left, by W.F.M. Arny in Ariz., 1872; center, in Ariz., before 1876; right, by Edward Palmer in Ariz., 1868.

the afterworld into two sections—a pleasant land for the good, and a cheerless, barren section for those who had been witches. In the view of the Lipan and Navajo the underworld to which the dead journeyed was the place from which the people originally emerged. Yet the Jicarilla and the Western Apache, who also had a myth of emergence, did not associate the land of the dead with the place of emergence. Not only were the Lipan, Mescalero, and Chiricahua without fear of an aged person who was at the point of death, but they sought a blessing from the dying elder so that their own lives might be prolonged. The Navajo, Jicarilla, Lipan, and Chiricahua were concerned about sickness from the ghosts of slain foes; the others expressed no such fear. According to the Chiricahua, Kiowa-Apache, Lipan, Mescalero, and Western Apache, the favorite vehicle utilized by the ghost for its return was the owl; for the Jicarilla it was the coyote, and for the Navajo it was either.

From this review of Apachean eschatology two conclusions emerge: that the beliefs and practices of all seven tribes are remarkably alike in respect to this subject area and that the correspondences in variations that do exist appear to be random. The alignments do not reveal sharp geographical cleavages of a kind that would suggest markedly different histories or prolonged separation; an Apachean tribe of the east is as likely to share some special features of eschatology with an Apachean tribe of the west as it is with any other. The inner unity can be gauged in another manner: even when a seemingly unique occurrence is found for a particular Apachean tribe, it is likely to be an extension or intensification of a basic Apachean concept. Thus, because of the vulnerability of children to the attacks of ghosts, the Kiowa-Apache placed a protective stick across the cradleboard at the chest when an infant had to be left unattended and erased footprints made in soft earth by a child who was learning to walk. Similarly, a Tantalus motif was introduced into the Jicarilla conception of the fate of witches after death, and the Navajo peopled the unpleasant portion of the underworld with suicides as well as with witches.

Influences from Non-Apacheans

The major departures of particular tribes from the basic Apachean culture pattern can largely be accounted for by geographical position and contact with non-Apachean peoples. Only the Navajo and the Western Apache have developed matrilineal clans; these are the tribes that had most interaction with the matrilineal Western Pueblos. The Jicarilla, who enjoyed close relations with Taos, Picuris, and San Juan over a long period, developed a moiety system that was doubtless inspired by northern Rio Grande Pueblo models. The Apacheans—the Navajo, Western Apache, and Jicarilla—who interacted most with the Pueblos were the ones who gave the greatest attention to agriculture. There is little doubt that Navajo loom weaving owes its elaboration, if not its origin, to Pueblo examples. In the realm of religion, the masked dancer cult—again most complex among the Navajo, Jicarilla, and Western Apache—is attributable to Pueblo influence. The Jicarilla ceremonial relay is a synthesis of a comparable event in three Rio Grande Pueblos. Yet it should be kept in mind that even where outside influence was pronounced, there was no slavish imitation. The basic ideas and the content were reworked to harmonize with Apachean conceptions and purposes. Moreover, influence did not flow solely from the outside to the Apacheans. Parsons (1939, 2:1039–1064) refers to a large number of Pueblo concepts and traits that may be of Apachean derivation.

There is frequent mention in the literature of "Plains Apache," but this is an ambiguous term that, if used at all, should be employed with caution. When appeal is made to it, the tribal unit or the part of it to which reference is made should be identified, and it should be specified whether geographical or tribal criteria, or both, are involved. This would be clarifying, since one section of an Apachean tribe was sometimes more Plains-like in certain respects than another. Thus, the eastern moiety of the Jicarilla used the tepee as a dwelling more consistently than did their tribesmen to the west, and the eastern band of the Chiricahua was more prone to employ the tepee and Plains-like garb than the other two Chiricahua bands.

Whether any of the Jicarilla can properly be termed "Plains Apache" is a question; although they hunted buffaloes on the Plains, they lacked many other traits characteristic of Plains life, such as warrior and women's societies, the camp circle, the Sun Dance, medicine bundles of tribal significance, heraldic tepees, shield groups, and graded war deeds. Nor have they participated in movements that swept the Plains in later times, such as the Ghost Dance and Peyote religion. Their important rituals, such as the adolescence ceremony, the masked dancer cult, and the ceremonial relay race, most certainly did not stem from the Plains. Their fear of the ghosts of enemies and the restrictions with which they surrounded the taking of enemy scalps were anything but Plains-like. Industries for which they have been long noted, such as the manufacture of baskets and pottery, also separate them from "typical" Plains representatives.

The Lipan showed more Plains orientation than did the Jicarilla. They depended on hide receptacles rather than on baskets and pots, made more use of the tepee, were less concerned about contamination from the dead enemy, and deemed it a virtue to be the first to strike a fallen foe. Yet they, too, lacked the Sun Dance, the camp circle, warrior and women's societies, heraldic tepees, shield groups, tribal medicine bundles, and other prime characteristics of Plains culture. Moreover, non-Plains elements such as an emergence legend, agriculture, masked supernatural impersonators, and an elaborate girls' puberty rite were present in their culture.

The Kiowa-Apache have the best claim, in view of their location and total culture, to be considered "Plains Apache." They depended on the buffalo, made much use of the horse travois, at times practiced scaffold burial, gashed the body and sometimes cut off a finger joint in mourning, counted coup, occasionally passed down heraldic tepees in inheritance, formed shield groups, and treasured tribal medicine bundles. They also possessed dancing societies for men, women, and children and in other ways exhibited a Plains bond that must be conceded some time-depth. Yet even here caution in interpretation must be exercised. The Kiowa-Apache societies were not so numerous or functionally important as those of their Plains neighbors, and their shield groups were weakly developed (McAllister 1955:166–168). Although they are credited with a Sun Dance and camp circle, it is more accurate to say that at the time of the Kiowa Sun Dance they were permitted to be present and were assigned a place in the Kiowa camp circle. On this occasion the Kiowa were in full control; there is no evidence that the Kiowa-Apache role was anything more than a subordinate one or that a Kiowa-Apache ever acted as a pledger of the Sun Dance (McAllister 1955:100). In spite of all the talk about "Plains Apache," general Apachean culture was probably more greatly enriched by Southwestern than by Plains contacts and currents of influence. The basic culture is neither Pueblo nor Plains but uniquely Apachean.

Migration and Dispersion

Ethnological material can give some conception of the central tendencies and variations in contemporary Apachean cultures and clues to the direction from which the ancestral peoples came and to the approximate length of time their spatial and cultural journeys must have taken. Yet such tentative conclusions need to be tested, amplified, and refined by evidence from linguistics, archeology, and history. Apachean specialists agree that the Apacheans came from the north, from the great hive of Athapaskan speakers in the Mackenzie Basin of Canada (Sapir 1936). There is less consensus regarding the amount of time involved in the southern movement, the route or routes followed by the early migrants, and whether more than one migration was involved.

Serious linguistic research was begun among the Apacheans in 1883 when Gatschet (1883, 1884a, 1884d) gathered vocabulary, phrase, and text material from Western Apache, Lipan, and Kiowa-Apache informants. Russell (1898) contributed a Jicarilla vocabulary. Goddard collected San Carlos texts (1919), Mescalero and Lipan texts (1906, 1909), Jicarilla texts (1911), and White Mountain texts (1920a). A dictionary of Navajo was based on material gathered mainly by Father Berard Haile (Franciscan Fathers 1910). Thus, during the last two decades of the nineteenth century and the first decade of the twentieth enough linguistic data accumulated to establish that the lexical variations and the sound shifts that differentiate the contemporary Apachean dialects and languages were already present. It seems reasonable, then, to take the year 1900 as a base line from which the temporal divergences revealed by lexicostatistics can be projected backward in time.

The greatest divergence time among the Apacheans, 601 years, exists between the Western Apache and the Kiowa-Apache (Bittle 1961). This indicates that until A.D. 1300 the Apacheans were a single group or a number of very closely related groups. Mooney (1898:247–248), Harrington (1940:520), and Gunnerson and Gunnerson (1971:19) have suggested a relatively recent tie between the Apacheans and the Sarcee, the most southern of the northern Athapaskan tribes. However, lexicostatistics show the smallest divergence time between the Sarcee and any Apachean tribe to be 928 years (Bittle 1961; Hoijer 1956a:228–229). Moreover, Brant (1953:197–199) has called attention to the concomitant cultural distance between the Sarcee and the Kiowa-Apache, the Apachean group most often mentioned in connection with Sarcee-Apachean ties. Thus the Apacheans enjoyed an independent existence for over 300 years before they began to differentiate among themselves linguistically and, presumably, spatially and culturally.

To demonstrate that the Apacheans were internally united though differentiated from others in the year 1300 still does not explain where they lived at this time horizon, what line or lines of migration they took from the Mackenzie Basin to their historic territories, or how, when, and where tribal separation proceeded. Because the Apacheans were basically mobile hunters and gatherers, especially during prehistoric and protohistoric times, archeological evidence concerning them is meager. Almost all firm Apachean archeological data pertain to the Navajo, who built sturdier homes than their linguistic congeners. Archeological investigations have located forked-stick hogans with a tripod base (an early house form that the Navajo continued to erect well into the historic period) in northwestern New Mexico that, on the basis of dendrochronology, have been assigned to the late fifteenth and early sixteenth centuries (Dittert, Hester, and Eddy 1961:247; Hall 1944a:7, 1944:100; Hester 1962:63, 80, 82; Riley 1954:51, 52, 58; R.G. Vivian 1960:155–157; Vogt 1961:280; Young 1968). It is unrealistic to suppose that the oldest hogans that were built have resisted the ravages of time or even that the very oldest have been discovered. Since most Apacheans are known to have lived in dwellings less substantial than the Navajo hogan, there is no certainty that this was the earliest Apachean house type of the area; on comparative grounds it is possible to argue that the forked-stick hogan was a specialization developed after the Navajo had lived for some time in their traditional homeland.

Moreover, it is unnecessary to assume that the ancestors of the modern Navajo were the very first Apacheans to enter the San Juan River basin. Lexicostatistical computations have shown that the greatest divergence between Apacheans is not between the Kiowa-Apache and the Navajo, but between the Kiowa-Apache and the Western Apache. This suggests that the Western Apache, whose territories lay south and west of the Navajo, may well have preceded the Navajo into the

San Juan basin and later moved west and south to their historic territories, just as the Navajo subsequently did. This is the sequence suggested by Goodwin (1942:71–72) and Forbes (1966:336). Before the lexicostatistical data were available, D.A. Gunnerson (1956:346, 363) estimated that the Apacheans first reached the Southwest about 1525. It seems more reasonable to assume that the entry was made by 1400. By some this may even be considered too conservative. Forbes (1960:xiv–xxiii) is sharply critical of theories of a very recent southern migration of the Apacheans and holds that they were probably present in the Southwest by the thirteenth or fourteenth century.

Two contrasting hypotheses concerning the route by which the Apacheans reached the Southwest have been presented. An intermontane route through Utah or Colorado and the Great Basin has had a number of adherents. Steward (1937a:86, 87, 1940:472–474) favored the intermontane explanation and suggested that the Promontory people who once occupied the caves of the Salt Lake Basin were southward-bound Apacheans. Huscher and Huscher (1942, 1943) are even more vigorous proponents of an intermontane route or, at the very least, of a movement west of the Continental Divide. On the basis of excavations and surveys carried out in western Colorado they concluded that the builders of circular stone structures who oriented the doors of their homes to the east, practiced a hunting economy, and made pointed-bottomed pottery were Apacheans whose ultimate destination was the Southwest. Huscher and Huscher have argued that the Apacheans were essentially mountain dwellers who usually sought the safety of the highlands at a time of danger even though they sometimes ventured into the plains. They point out the similarity between the intermontane approaches to the Southwest and the territory occupied by the Northern Athapaskans. The same observation, incidentally, has been made by Goodwin (1942:71). After a comprehensive review of Navajo archeology, Riley (1954:58), too, leaned toward a western path of migration, and the historian Worcester (1947:13) came to the same conclusion. In emphasizing the Great Basin character of Navajo material and economic culture, Hill (1938:190) and Farmer (1942:78–79) have also implied their acceptance of the western route concept.

A much different view of Apachean dispersion is held by a second group of investigators. They believed that the Querechos, Teyas, and Vaqueros, whom the Spanish explorers of the sixteenth century encountered on the southern Plains, were all Apacheans. They are also convinced that the creators of the Dismal River aspect of the Plains, 1675–1725, whose cultural remains have been excavated in Nebraska, eastern Colorado, and western Kansas, were Apacheans as well and that therefore the Apacheans must be considered to have inhabited the central Plains for a long period. Accordingly, they envisage an Apachean migration southward through the northwestern and central Plains close to the eastern edge of the mountains. The presence of the Apacheans in New Mexico, Arizona, and northern Mexico is considered by them to have resulted from a fairly late movement westward from the Plains into the Southwest on the part of some of the Apacheans. Gunnerson (1956:72, 1960:252) even interprets the Promontory culture of Utah to be "an early protohistoric thrust by a buffalo-hunting Athabascan group into the Great Basin from the Plains." Aikens (1966:iii, 87, 1967:198, 199, 204–205) reverses the direction and sequence of events and,

left, U. of Ariz., Ariz. State Mus., Tucson: 18237; right, Smithsonian, NAA: 75–8318.

Fig. 10. Western Apache scouts. left, Dressed in uniforms issued by U.S. Army, probably at San Carlos, Ariz. Man on left wears tweezers on a bead necklace. Caps worn by scouts on right, which were believed to impart quickness and agility in combat, are adorned with turkey and quail feathers. right, Probably members of a Tonto band, stationed at Ft. Wingate, N. Mex. Cap of scout second from left shows distinctive style but serves functions similar to those of caps in photograph at left. left, Photographer unknown, probably 1883–1886; right, photograph by Charles Barthelmess, 1881–1886.

on the grounds that Promontory and Fremont, which he considers to be variants of the same culture, precede Dismal River in time, concludes that Fremont-Promontory Apacheans moved eastward from the Great Basin to the Plains to initiate the Dismal River aspect. Despite such differences concerning details, these researchers, mainly archeologists who have concentrated on problems of the Plains, emphasize a Plains background for the Apacheans (Champe 1949; D.A. Gunnerson 1956, 1974; Gunnerson 1960, 1968, 1969; Gunnerson and Gunnerson 1971; Hester 1962; Wedel 1940, 1947, 1947a, 1950, 1953, 1953a, 1953b, 1961, 1961a, 1964).

In view of the fact that only one contemporary Apachean tribe, the Kiowa-Apache, shows any thoroughgoing Plains orientation, the thesis of long-continued Plains residence and influence requires careful examination. The term Querecho was at first used of any wandering people the Spaniards encountered on the southern or central Plains, much as Chichimeca was at one time employed as a generic label for the unsettled peoples of northern Mexico. It was only later, with the addition of qualifiers or descriptive adjectives (Mountain Querechos, Apache Vaqueros) that the designations began to take on anything approaching tribal significance. The description of the Querechos met east of Pecos by the Francisco Vásquez de Coronado expedition in 1541 is so general that most of the features mentioned (tepee, buffalo hunting, jerked meat, pemmican, use of the dog and the dog travois for transporting goods, sign language) would fit any plainsmen of the times. Whenever the traits described are more specific, they do not seem to be particularly Apachean. For instance, the Querechos are said to have drunk fresh animal blood as a regular staple of diet; identified Apacheans drank fresh blood only in special circumstances as a health measure (Opler 1969:105–106).

There is even less correspondence between some of the most important traits of the Dismal River aspect of the Plains and the practices and artifacts of Apacheans as they are known from the historical or ethnographic record. Gunnerson (1960:160, 246, 1968: 175) has repeatedly called pottery the "most diagnostic" artifact of the Dismal River aspect and has constantly referred to its uniformity throughout the Dismal River range. Dismal River pottery was abundant, the paste was gritty, it was tempered with fine sand or mica, it was lump modeled (or, at least, an anvil and paddle were used at some stage in shaping it), and simple stamping was the common surface treatment. In contrast, among most Apachean tribes no pottery or little pottery was manufactured (Hill 1937:7). Only the Jicarilla made any considerable amount, and there is no evidence that the Kiowa-Apache, the most "Plains-like" of the Apacheans, ever made any. What pottery Apacheans made was highly variable in size, shape, and tempering material. The Navajo shaped pointed-bottom pots; the Jicarilla did not. Most Apachean pottery was constructed by the coiled technique, but the Lipan claim to have modeled pots from the mass, and the Jicarilla, who coiled their larger vessels, molded small ones from the lump. There is no hint of the use of anvil and paddle or of simple stamping in Apachean pottery (Opler 1971).

Comparison of house forms is just as unsatisfactory. The Dismal River home had a five-post foundation and a diameter of about 25 feet (7.62 meters). It is obvious that a structure of this size was meant to house more than one nuclear family. On the other hand, each Apa-

Smithsonian, NAA: 74–11687.

Fig. 11. Issue day at Camp San Carlos, Ariz. Rations consisted mainly of flour, lard, and coffee. Occasionally, meat and cloth were also distributed. Photograph by Camillus S. Fly, probably early 1880s.

chean small family occupied a separate dwelling about one-third the size of the Dismal River home: the need for privacy was dictated in part by the complicated system of restraint relations prevalent among Apacheans. Furthermore, it was not feasible for them to build very large and substantial houses in view of their mobility and their death practices, which forced the abandonment of the dwelling and, indeed, of the whole campsite at a time of bereavement. With this in mind, it is difficult to accept the suggestion that even more massive structures, such as seven-room pueblitos in Scott County, western Kansas, and in northeastern New Mexico near Ocate were the handiwork of Dismal River Apacheans (Gunnerson 1960:250, 1969:25–30).

No remains of the horse have been found in Dismal River sites. Yet the Apacheans are known to have acquired horses shortly after the beginning of the seventeenth century, were using horses for food as well as for mounts by 1630, and were riding armored horses into battle by 1689 (Forbes 1959; Worcester 1941:5–6, 1944). Moreover, the bones of horses have been found in Navajo sites of approximate Dismal River date (Farmer 1942:67, 69, 74; R.G. Vivian 1960:153, 179, 220). There are a good many other reasons for doubting, on comparative cultural grounds, that Dismal River sites are Apachean. For example, Apacheans have an acute fear of the coyote, but the Dismal River people used beads of coyote bone. The flesh of the dog was a staple of Dismal River diet, but the Apacheans, with the exception of the Kiowa-Apache, who may have eaten dog meat during times of scarcity, abhorred the very idea of such food. Other non-Apachean traits found at Dismal River sites include a flageolet of bone and a bone eyed needle.

Smithsonian, Dept. of Anthr.: 10,730.

Fig. 12. Rawhide playing cards, based on Spanish printed decks used for the game of *monte*. There are 40 cards in a deck divided into 4 suits of swords, coins, clubs, and cups, with 7 numbered cards and 3 figure cards—page, king, and mounted knight. Cards are cut with rounded corners to about the size of printed decks, and figures are painted on one side in blue, red, and black (Wayland 1962, 1972). Wagering on games was a favorite Apache pastime. Length of most 8.5 cm, collected in Ariz., by George Gibbs in 1871.

Since the Apacheans arrived in the Southwest in protohistoric times, the historical documentation concerning their whereabouts in the area is largely a function of the pace and direction of Spanish penetration. As soon as the Spaniards entered an area of the Southwest, they usually found evidence that Apacheans were nearby. In 1540 the expedition of Coronado moved north across southeastern Arizona and at a pass called Chichilticale met hunters and gatherers who lived in rancherias. These Indians undoubtedly were Apaches (Forbes 1960:8–9; Goodwin 1942:67) and most likely were Chiricahuas. So, too, were the "Mountain Querechos" about whom Antonio de Espejo and his followers learned in 1583 while exploring for mineral wealth near Acoma (Bolton 1916:182–183). Soon after the colonization of New Mexico in 1598, Juan de Oñate's first capital, San Gabriel, at the confluence of the Chama River and the Rio Grande, was repeatedly attacked by the Navajo. This was largely responsible for moving the capital to Santa Fe in 1610 (Worcester 1951:103–104). By 1638 Father Juan de Prada was complaining of Apaches who surrounded the Pueblos (Hackett 1923–1937, 3:106). Even before this Alonso de Benavides had preached to the Chiricahua Apache on the west side of the Rio Grande and the Mescalero Apache on the east side (Benavides 1945:80–85). No sooner was San Antonio founded in Texas in 1718 than the Lipan began to raid its horse herd (W.E. Dunn 1911:201, 204–205). Thus it is clear from historical sources as well as from the other criteria introduced that once the Apacheans reached the Southwest, their linguistic and political differentiation proceeded rather rapidly and that by the beginning of the eighteenth century they were distinct tribes, each occupying what it had come to consider to be its traditional territory.

Summary and Conclusions

While much ethnological, linguistic, archeological, and ethnohistorical research on the Apacheans is in progress, the available evidence can be summarized for what it provides concerning present knowledge. The glottochronological data (Bittle 1961; Hoijer 1956a; Hymes 1957) indicate that Apachean linguistic differentiation began in approximately A.D. 1300. It probably started with some divergence between Western Apache and

Ariz. Histl. Soc. Lib., Tucson: Hannah Coll.

Fig. 13. Western Apache couple on a visit to Globe, Ariz., to purchase supplies. Photograph by Forman G. Hannah, about 1905–1918.

Kiowa-Apache shortly before the Apacheans entered the Southwest around A.D. 1400. On the grounds that some of the Apacheans, particularly the Western Apache and the Chiricahua, show so few Plains and so many Great Basin characteristics, it is probable that the route was intermontane. The fact that Kiowa-Apache culture has an underlying Apachean base but a Plains orientation suggests that this tribe separated from its linguistic kinsmen before Puebloan and Southwest influence upon the Apacheans became very pronounced (Bittle 1971:2; Brant 1949, 1951:77–117, 129–134, 1953, 1969:1–2). Still, the Kiowa-Apache must have lived for a century at the northeastern fringe of the early Apachean range in the Southwest, for the Kiowa-Apache language did not diverge from Jicarilla and Lipan until about A.D. 1500. At this time or shortly afterward the Kiowa-Apache must have committed themselves to the Plains and moved both north and south at subsequent periods as they entered into temporary alliances with the Kiowa and other tribes of the southern Plains. At the very time the Kiowa-Apache were moving eastward it is very likely that the ancestral Western Apache, soon to be followed by the Navajo, were drifting westward and southward. The Navajo movement west and south has been clearly verified by archeological research. By 1600 the Jicarilla and the Lipan were presumably no longer in contact with the Western Apache and the Navajo. Within the next century the Lipan and Jicarilla had differentiated from each other linguistically and culturally. The Jicarilla remained at the northeastern edge of Apachean territory in the Southwest and cautiously advanced toward the Plains, ultimately establishing themselves in northern New Mexico and southern Colorado in lands roughly bounded by the Arkansas River on the north, Chama on the west, Estancia on the south, and the Canadian River on the east (Opler 1936b:202, 1946:1, 1971a:309–315). The Lipan migrated east and south into more decidedly Plains terrain and occupied central and south Texas, perhaps as early as the second half of the seventeenth century (Secoy 1953:22; Worcester 1944:227). The ancestral Chiricahua and Mescalero, in all likelihood not yet tribally distinct, moved south through the Rio Grande valley during the sixteenth and early seventeenth centuries. As they diverged, the Chiricahua established their range west of the river, in southwestern New Mexico, southeastern Arizona, and the adjoining section of Mexico. The Mescalero roamed the land to the east, to the Pecos River and beyond, and found their way into northwestern Texas as well. Because of their central position the Chiricahua-Mescalero group was able to maintain contact with most other Apacheans (with the exception of the early breakaway segment, the Kiowa-Apache) for a relatively long time and probably were the last Apacheans to realize separate tribal identities.

Synonymy*

The English word Apache is from Spanish *Apache*, which was first used by Juan de Oñate, on September 9, 1598, at San Juan Pueblo (Hammond and Rey 1953, 1:345). The most widely accepted source for this word is Zuni *ˀa·paču* 'Navajos', the plural of *paču* 'Navajo'; in Oñate's time no distinction was drawn between Apaches and Navajos (Hodge 1907–1910, 1:63; Dennis Tedlock, communication to editors 1977). Harrington (1940:513), and other authors before him, derive the word Apache from the Yavapai word 'axwáača 'Apaches', perhaps through confusion with *ˀpačə* ([ˀəpá·čə]) 'people'. Similar words are found in other Yuman languages. These hypotheses are weakened by the fact that at the time he used this name Oñate had not yet encountered either the Zunis or any of the Yuman peoples (Schroeder 1974a:232, 239). A third, rather improbable etymology derives Apache from *apache*, a rare spelling variant of the Spanish *mapache* 'raccoon' (Santamaría 1974:69). Evidence supporting this possibility is given in D.A. Gunnerson (1974:58–59). Early Spanish spelling variants and misprints include Apades, Apiches (from Oñate 1598) (Hodge 1907–1910, 1:67), and aphaches (Tamarón y Romeral 1937:350). A Spanish masculine *Apacho* and a feminine *Apacha* sometimes occur (Harrington 1940). Santamaría (1974:69) gives a feminine *Apachesa*. The first occurrences in a text orginally written in English are found in the accounts of Zebulon Montgomery Pike's expeditions: Appache, 1805–1807 (Coues 1895, 2:633). Other early English spelling variants are Appeche (Schermerhorn 1814:29) and Apa-

*This synonymy was written by Willem J. de Reuse.

chies, 1846 (Schroeder 1974a:400); other variants are listed in Hodge (1907–1910, 1:67).

Oñate himself used the word as a cultural term, and although the first use of the term included Athapaskans, it also included other tribes that were linguistically unrelated to the Athapaskan Apache but confused with them or assumed to be sufficiently similar to them to justify the same name (Harrington 1940:513). Later, Bancroft (1874–1876, 1:476) stated that the Apache may sometimes include Comanches and Mohaves. When attributive terms were added to the word Apache to distinguish among the various groups, the identity of these non-Athapaskan Apaches becomes clearer. After 1605 and till the 1850s the Yavapai, and perhaps the Havasupai, were often called Apaches, Apaches Cruzados or Apaches Coninas (Schroeder 1974b:23, 28). Around 1860, the terms Garroteros Apaches, Hualapai Apaches, Tonto Apaches, Apache-Mohave, and Apache-Yuma appear, all of which refer to divisions of the Yavapai (Schroeder 1974b:401, 414, 415, 438). Schroeder (1974b:438–441) shows that up until 1863 the name Tonto or Tonto Apache was applied to Yumans only. The term Apache also originally included the Navajo (see the synonymy in "Navajo Prehistory and History to 1850," this vol.). Among all Apache tribes, the term used to designate themselves is the word for 'person, people'; see the synonymies in "Chiricahua Apache," "Mescalero Apache," "Jicarilla Apache," and "Western Apache" (this vol.) for the various phonemic spellings of this word.

The following paragraphs give the general word for Apache in non-Athapaskan American Indian languages.

The Taos word is *xiwana* (Amy Zaharlick, communication to editors 1981), also spelled xiwanæ (pl. xiwaną) (Harrington 1918:274), q́iwænæ (pl. q́iwæną) (Harrington 1918a); its etymology is unknown, but it is related to Picuris *xəwiane* (Amy Zaharlick, communication to editors 1981), or *yew'enę*. Picuris has also the following nickname for Apache: *h'ǫʔemǫ́ x'əʔene* 'cedar seed' (George L. Trager in Parsons 1939:214).

The Rio Grande Tewa word is *sáve*, of obscure etymology (Harrington 1916:573). It is used for every kind of Apachean.

The Sandia word is Apa´tche tai´nin 'gente de Apaches' (Gatschet 1899:38), and the Isleta word is *apáchide* (pl. *apáchin*); one Isleta informant stated that this is a loanword from Zuni (William Leap, communication to editors 1977). Terms given by nineteenth-century authors are p'o´nin 'an Apache man' (Gatschet 1879–1885:4) and Tāt-li-em-a-nūn 'Apaches and Navajos' (Gibbs 1868).

The Keresan terms are Cochiti Kirauash (Bandelier 1890–1892, 2:116–117), Santo Domingo tcháska or cháhshm (Gatschet 1890:32), Santa Ana *čʰišé·*, Zia ˈChi´-she (Stevenson 1894:15), Laguna Chïshyë´ (Hodge 1907–1910, 1:67), and Acoma *čʰíšé* (Miller 1965:210). The four last forms are clearly the same word and may be derived from the Navajo word for the Chiricahua, *chíshí*. Acoma also has a loanword, *apâ·čʰi*, from Spanish or from English (Miller 1965:210).

The Jemez name for Apachean is *k̓ʸǽlǽ*, plural *k̓ʸǽlǽcoš* (Joe S. Sando, communication to editors 1978). The Pecos term is Tágukerésh (Hodge 1907–1910, 1:67), which may be identical with the Jemez name for the Jicarilla.

Zuni does not seem to have a truly general word for Apache; most often *wilacʔu·kwe* (Newman 1958:51) is given with the meaning 'Apache', but this seems to refer specifically to the White Mountain Apache; the word specifically referring to the San Carlos Apache can apparently also be used as a general word (Harrington 1913); see the synonymy in "Western Apache" (this vol.). The Third Mesa Hopi term is *yótseʔe* (pl. *yótseʔemɨ*) (Voegelin and Voegelin 1957:49); Gatschet (1899) has Utchi and glosses it 'cactus people'.

Hopi-Tewa has the expected general Tewa term *sá·be*, and *yuc'e·ʔe*, apparently a Hopi loanword (Paul V. Kroskrity, communication to editors 1977). Mooney (1892–1898) gives yuq-yé 'grass beds'.

The Havasupai term is *hʷá·ʔa*, pl. *hʷa·če* (Leanne Hinton, communication to editors 1981), and perhaps İgihúa-a (Gatschet 1877–1892, 3:98). Yavapai has 'axwá, plural 'axwáatca (Harrington 1940:513); the loanword from Spanish can occur before this term: a´patche-áhua 'an Apache' (Gatschet 1883a:6). The same word in Mojave, a-hŭ-á-cha (Lt. Mowry) is glossed 'Mescalero Apache' but perhaps used as the general term as well; other terms are *kuhwa·lʸt* (cf. *hwa·lʸ* 'pine, wood') and *ʔahʷé* 'enemy' (Pamela Munro, communications to editors 1974, 1981). Quechan has *ʔapáč*, apparently a loanword, which covers all the Apacheans (Abraham Halpern, communication to editors 1981). The Pima and Papago general term is *ʔó·b* (Mathiot 1973:466) or *ʔó·bĭ* (Philip Greenfeld, communication to editors 1981), which also has the broader meaning of 'enemy' (Saxton and Saxton 1969:34, 67). Maricopa uses *yavʔi·pay* for the Apache and, with various modifiers, for the Yavapai; there is also *yavʔi·pay xʷet* (Lynn Gordon, communication to editors 1981).

The Indians of northern Mexico generally have a term that is borrowed from the Spanish word for Apache (Harrington 1940): Tubar has the plural A-pa-tci´m (Hewitt 1893), and Seri has *ʔáppaats* (Moser and Moser 1976:295).

Navajo makes sharp distinctions among the White Mountain, Chiricahua, Mescalero, and Jicarilla Apache groups but does not seem to have a general term for 'Apache'. Only Harrington (1940) gives *Shgalí Dine'é* as a general term used for Athapaskans, distinct from the Navajo *Mashgalí* 'Mescalero Apaches' and used to distinguish the Athapaskans from the Plains and Pueblo tribes.

Some Numic terms are Ute (from Spanish Fork Canyon, Utah) A-vwa´-tsu (Powell 1873–1874:54); Southern Ute *ʔaváa-cI* 'Apache person' (Givón 1979:98), which both might be loanwords; and Panamint ai-a´-ta (Henshaw 1883:184).

The Comanche generic term for 'Apache' is also the specific name for Kiowa-Apache; Gatschet (1884e:112) has Tá-ashi, tashihiⁿ, and Mooney (1898:245) has Tashĭn.

Other terms from the Plains are Tonkawa Apátche (Gatschet 1884e:4), and Pawnee *katahka* 'Apache; alien tribe; to be inside out'; 'Apache woman' is *ckatahka*. This last word should not be confused with *cka·-ta·ka* 'white face' as was done in Gunnerson and Gunnerson (1971:15) (Douglas R. Parks, communication to editors 1972). Caddo has *ʔíšikwitaʔ* (Wallace L. Chafe, communication to editors 1973), a borrowing of the Comanche term for 'Mescalero Apache'. As in the case of Comanche, the Kiowa generic term for Apache is also the specific term for Kiowa-Apache: *tʰɔ̀gûy* (Laurel Watkins, communication to editors 1979). It is glossed as 'lazy, indolent' (Gatschet 1884e:184), or 'poor outside' (Harrington 1939–1945). Another name that also seems to apply both specifically to the Kiowa-Apaches and to Apaches generically is k̀ʸaapææ-towp 'the ones that whet a knife' (Harrington 1939–1945), also given as Kawăpa´tu 'whetting knife' (Gatschet 1884e) and K'á-pätop 'knife-whetters, or whetstone people' (Mooney 1898:245). The last reference notes that this name became obsolete about 1892 in consequence of the death of a Kiowa chief named K'á-pä´te.

Mooney (1896a:1081) gives for Kiowa-Apache Arapaho Tha'kahinĕ´na 'knife-whetting men' and Cheyenne Mûtsiănătä´niuw´ 'whetstone people', but it is safe to assume that like the Kiowa word with the same meaning these words also mean 'Apachean' in general, because for one thing the 'knife whetting' sign of the sign-language is used for 'Apache', 'Lipan', and 'Navajo'. The English-Cheyenne student dictionary (Northern Cheyenne Language and Culture Center 1976) gives 'Apache' as *motsė-héone-tane*, pl. *motsė-héone-taneoʔo*, with the literal translation 'occupied-camp person'. This is a better transcription than Mooney's, but his gloss is presumably the correct one.

Lakhota (Teton Dakota) has a term *čʰį́čakįze* 'squeak by striking against wood' that is said to refer to the Arapahos (Boas and Deloria 1941:8) and to the Apache (Buechel 1970:103).

Obsolete Group Names

The following names are discussed here because they are no longer in use and cannot be made to correspond neatly with the modern division of the Apache into four tribes. These are obsolete names for groups or tribes that are assumed, with various degrees of certainty, to have been Apachean, or at least to have included some Apacheans. They are discussed in rough chronological order. The older Plains Apaches are included here, because at least part of the modern southwestern Apaches are descended from them. Those Plains Apache names that are clearly identifiable with the modern Lipan Apaches or Kiowa-Apaches only are treated in volume 13.

Chichimeca. Chichimeca is a Nahuatl term of uncertain meaning that was used by the Spaniards in the Spanish forms Chichimecas or Chichimecos as a generic label for the unsettled peoples of northern Mexico and the southwest. An example of Chichimecos that certainly includes Apaches is found in Diego Pérez de Luxán's account of the Espejo expedition (Hammond and Rey 1966:189).

Querecho. Querechos was first used for a nomadic people encountered by the Francisco Vásquez de Coronado expedition (Hammond and Rey 1940:261–262), but the description of the Querechos is so general that most of the features mentioned would fit any Plains Indians of the time (Opler 1969:105–106). Later, in 1583, Querecho is also used for Apache groups living in the mountains west of the Rio Grande near Acoma (Bolton 1916:183).

The Oñate documents in some places appear to distinguish between the Querechos or Vaqueros and the Apaches (Schroeder 1974a:238; cf. D.A. Gunnerson 1974:8); by the 1630s the term Apache had spread and completely replaced Querecho (Schroeder 1974a:32).

Querecho is probably derived from the Pecos equivalent of Jemez *k̀ʸǽlǽcoš* (pl.) 'Navajo, Apache' (Harrington 1916:573, phonemicized). Variant spellings of Querecho are: Quereches, Guereches (Harrington 1916:573), and Corechos (Hammond and Rey 1929:97).

Teya. Teyas was the name of another nomadic people first encountered on the plains by the Coronado expedition (Hammond and Rey 1940:258, 261–262); apparently it does not appear in later sources. Schroeder (1974a:99–101) presented evidence showing that the Teyas must have been a Caddoan group, whereas D.A. Gunnerson (1974:18) argued for the identification of the Teyas as Apacheans. Harrington's (1916:573) conjecture of a connection with a Jemez (and presumably also Pecos) word meaning 'east Navajo, east Athapaskan' involves phonetic difficulties.

Vaquero. Vaqueros was probably first used as a synonym of Querecho by Obregón (Hammond and Rey 1928:303) in 1584 in his secondhand accounts of the Francisco Sánchez Chamuscado–Agustín Rodríguez and Espejo expeditions (D.A. Gunnerson 1974:37). Vaquero, 'cowboy' in modern Spanish (Santamaría 1974:1106), came to be applied to the nomadic plains tribes because of their dependency on the buffalo, which were called *vacas* 'cows' by the early Spanish explorers. According to D.A. Gunnerson (1974:80), the Vaqueros probably included both non-Apachean groups and the

Apachean groups later called Cuartelejos and Palomas. Schroeder (1974a:479) states that the bulk of the Vaqueros became the Lipan, some of whom probably joined the Mescaleros. In the seventeenth century the term Vaquero gradually gave way to Vaquero Apache or Apache. Oñate was the first one to recognize the identity of the Apaches and the Vaqueros and adopted the term Apaches for them in 1601 (Schroeder 1974a:239); Zárate Salmerón (1899–1900:45, 180) still used Vaqueros and Apaches Vaqueros; Benavides (1630:70) only has Apaches Vaqueros. A notable spelling variant is Baqueros (Scholes 1944:339).

Manso. Mansos was a term employed for Apaches who were friendly to the Spaniards and Mexicans and used especially for a small group of Apache continually friendly with Mexicans and Papagos who lived in an area south of Tucson (Goodwin 1942:572). Manso also was used, first by Oñate in 1598, to refer to a group around El Paso. They were called *mansos* 'tame, peaceful ones' by the Spaniards because it was one of the first words these Indians used to greet them (Hammond and Rey 1953, 1:315). The first descriptions of the Mansos never give any evidence that they were Apacheans, and the denomination Apaches Mansos may well be due to the fact that they became close allies of the Apaches (Schroeder 1974a:217–221; D.A. Gunnerson 1974:102). Zárate Salmerón (1899–1900:183) and Benavides (1630:9) give Gorretas 'caps', as an equivalent of Mansos, because their haircut gave the impression that they were wearing caps (Benavides 1954:10).

Apaches de Quinía. The earliest mention of this group was made by Zárate Salmerón, about 1629, who referred to "the lands of the great Captain Quinia" (1899–1900:47). Benavides (1630:53) mentioned the "Rancherías del Capitan Quinîa" and later stated that the Apaches of Quinía were governed by an Indian called Quinía (1945:89). Their identity is obscure, but they might have been a division of the Navajos (Schroeder 1974a:247); the Apaches of Quinía were never referred to after Benavides's time.

Apaches del Perrillo. Benavides (1630:14) probably was the first to use this name in print. Spanish *perrillo* 'little dog' was the name of a spring in the Jornada del Muerto that was discovered by a small dog during the Oñate expedition in 1598 (Hodge in Benavides 1945:307). There seems to be a general agreement on the fact that the Apaches del Perrillo may have been partly composed of bands later identified as Mescalero Apache (Schroeder 1974a:480–481).

Sierra Blanca. In the course of history, this name, meaning in Spanish 'white mountain' or 'white mountain range', has been applied to three different Apachean groups: the Sierra Blanca Apaches that were the lineal descendants of the Apaches del Perrillo (Schroeder 1974a:483), who were first reported in the Sierra Blanca mountains of New Mexico in 1653 (Scholes 1940:281) and may have become known as Faraones after the Pueblo rebellion of 1680–1692 (Schroeder 1974a:488, 506); the Sierra Blanca who lived north of the Raton River in southeastern Colorado at the beginning of the eighteenth century and were identical with the Carlanas (Gunnerson and Gunnerson 1971:11; Schroeder 1974a:498); and the Sierra Blanca Apaches who are the White Mountain Apaches of the nineteenth and twentieth centuries.

Eighteenth-Century Groups. In the late eighteenth century two lists of Apache bands with both their Spanish and Apache names were compiled. Hugo de O'Conor, writing in the 1770s, listed the Chiricagui (in Apache Segilande), Gileños (Setocendé), Mimbrereños (Chiquendé), Mezcaleros (Zetosendé), Faraones (Selcaisanendé), Rancheria of Pasqual (Culcahende), Rancheria of El Ligero (Chahugindé), Rancheria of Alonso (Yncagende), Rancheria of Capitán Vigotes (Sigilande), and Natagé (Zetocendé). The rancherias presumably included the Apaches elsewhere called Llaneros and Lipan; in another place the Lipan are mentioned by name as being accustomed to join the Mezcaleros. O'Conor specifies the Apaches west of the Rio Grande as "the Apaches of the west that inhabit the mountains of Chiricagui, Gila, and Los Mimbres," obviously the first three groups on his list, but he seems to have been unfamiliar with the northern Apachean groups, notably the Navajo (Brugge 1961a:60–62). The second list was that compiled by Antonio Cordero in 1796 (Matson and Schroeder 1957:336): Tontos (Vinni ettinen-ne), Chiricaguis (Segatajen-ne), Gileños (Tjuiccujen-ne), Mimbreños (Iccujen-ne), Faraones (Yntajen-ne), Mescaleros (Sejen-ne), Llaneros (Cuelcajen-ne), Lipanes (Lipajen-ne), and Navajós (Yutajen-ne).

Apaches de Gila. This term was probably first mentioned by Benavides (1630:53) with the spelling Apaches de Xila. The name Gila most often refers to the Gila river, but sometimes it refers to the Sierra de Gila or Gila Mountains. The largest part of the Gila Apaches were probably the forerunners of the Mogollon Apaches; some southern Gila Apaches of New Mexico may have evolved after the 1690s into the group called Chiricahua (Schroeder 1974b:17, 48–49). The name was extremely vague: in the eighteenth century, the Apaches of southeastern Arizona and western New Mexico were called Apaches or Apaches de Gila, rather than by different names; at that time, only the Navajos and other Apachean groups east of the Rio Grande were distinguished by specific names. Only after 1772 did the Spaniards begin to make distinctions among the various groups located west of the Rio Grande (Schroeder 1974b:21, 73–75). When specific groups were named, the Spaniards sometimes used the term Apaches de Gila for the Western Apaches encountered along the Gila river, east of the San Carlos drainage, in the Gila mountains (Schroeder 1974b:529), although these were usually called

Coyoteros. The Spaniards almost never confused the Gila Apaches with the Western Apaches as a whole, and the Central Chiricahua Apaches were always kept distinct from them (Schroeder 1974b:121, 135). In the early American period, the term Gila Apache was usually replaced by Mogollon or Coppermine Apache, but it was sometimes retained and sometimes applied to the Mimbres (Schroeder 1974b:192). In the middle of the nineteenth century, there was again considerable confusion as to which groups were Gila Apaches. The name is often used as a cover term for the Coyoteros, Mogollones, Tontos, and Mimbreños; but sometimes it contains the Pinaleños, Chiricahuas, and the (Yavapai) Garroteros as well (Schroeder 1974b:185–189). The following remarks can be made on the synonyms and variant spellings of the term. Before the late 1700s the Spanish name is Apaches de Gila or Apaches de la Sierra de Gila (Schroeder 1974b:18, 21). In the late 1700s the terms Apaches Gileños and Gileños appear (Schroeder 1974b:18, 247); Francisco Garcés uses Yabipais Gileños in 1775–1776 (Coues 1900, 2:452). Orozco y Berra (1864:59) uses both Xileños and Gileños. The Spaniards also used the term Gileños to refer to the Pimas Gileños, who were the Pimas living on the Gila River (ten Kate 1885:24); other spellings are Pimas Cileños and Xileños (Coues 1900, 1:27, 85; synonymy in "Pima and Papago: Introduction," this vol.). Synonyms and garbled spellings occurring in English texts are: Gilenas (Bender 1974a:10), Gilans, Apaches of the Gila (Coues 1895, 2:748), Gilanians, Gila Apache (Goodwin 1942:571), and Gilleños (Worcester 1949:240).

Two Apache names for the Gila Apaches are found in Spanish reports: O'Conor, 1771–1776, has Setocendé but uses spelling variants of the same name for the Mescaleros, Zetosendé, and for the Natagés, Zetocendé (Brugge 1961a:55–60). Cordero, 1796, has Tjuiccujen-ne (Orozco y Berra 1864:369; Matson and Schroeder 1957:336).

Salineros. This is a Spanish word referring to several groups connected in some way with salt or with salines. In one case, they may have been a group of Gila Apaches who lived in the Gallo-Mangas mountain area south of the Zuni salt lakes (Schroeder 1974a:281–282). The first occurrence of the name (Benavides 1630:77) apparently refers to a different group living near the Manzano Salines, in Torrance County, New Mexico (Benavides 1954:57). Another group of Salineros, perhaps identical with the preceding one, were Natagés living on the Rio Salado (the Pecos) in 1745 (Schroeder 1974a:519).

Cuartelejo. El Cuartelejo was a place-name applied to a Plains Apache group of western Kansas, for the first time at about 1650: 'people of El Cuartelejo, on the frontier of Quivira' (Hackett 1923–1937, 3:263–264). Spanish *cuartel* means 'quarters, barracks', and *cuartelejo* is its depreciative (Harrington 1940:511). In the 1600s *cuartelejo* was used to refer to an area containing semisedentary, hut-dwelling Apacheans (Tyler and Taylor 1958:306). By 1719 the Apaches of El Cuartelejo began to merge with other Plains Apache tribes (Gunnerson and Gunnerson 1971:12). The last contemporary reference to El Cuartelejo in Apache territory is from 1727 (Gunnerson and Gunnerson 1971:12). Spelling variants of the term used as a tribal name include Apaches de Quartelejo, 1696 (Forbes 1960:268); apaches de quartelejos, Barriero's map of about 1728 (D.A. Gunnerson 1974:171); Quartelêxos, 1736, and cuartelejos, 1742 (Harrington 1939–1945).

Palomas. The Palomas are a Plains Apache tribe that lived northeast of El Cuartelejo; the northernmost of the Palomas may have been the Kiowa-Apaches (Gunnerson and Gunnerson 1971:13). In 1719 the Palomas had been driven out of their territory by the Pawnees and went to live with the Cuartelejos as refugees (Gunnerson and Gunnerson 1971:12) and lost their identity as a group separate from Plains Apache tribes about 1754 (Gunnerson and Gunnerson 1971:13). *Paloma* means 'dove' in Spanish, but the origin of Paloma as a tribal name is unknown (Gunnerson and Gunnerson 1971:12). A synonym is apaches Palomas, on Barriero's map of about 1728 (D.A. Gunnerson 1974:171). Calchufines (Thomas 1935:130), or Escalchufines (Thomas 1935:257), of unknown etymology, is generally considered to be a rarer equivalent of Palomas.

Carlanas. This is the name of a Plains Apache division also known as Sierra Blanca that lived in the Raton Mesa area of southeastern Colorado. By 1726 they had apparently gone to live with the Cuartelejos and Palomas and absorbed them. In and after 1730 the Carlanas, Palomas, and Cuartelejos began to live with the Jicarillas, perhaps sometimes even being identified as Jicarillas (Gunnerson and Gunnerson 1971:11, 12, 13). Later names for part of the Carlanas are Lipiyanes or Llaneros (D.A. Gunnerson 1974:xiv, 277); after 1750, only Jicarilla was used as a term for Apaches north of Pecos Pueblo (Schroeder 1974a:379). Gunnerson and Gunnerson (1971:13) suggest that the Carlanas, Palomas, and Cuartelejos had become the Plains (Llanero) band of the modern Jicarilla, whereas Schroeder (1974a:379) thinks that the Jicarilla division called Dáchizh-ó-zhín by Mooney (1897b) may be the former Carlanas. However, there is evidence that the term was still used under the form Carlanes in 1812, apparently as a synonym for the much more widespread Jicarilla (Carroll and Haggard 1942:128, 246). The etymology of the name Carlana is unknown. This group was apparently so called after the name of one of their chiefs (Thomas 1935:114–116). A synonym is apaches Carlanes, on Barriero's map of about 1728 (D.A. Gunnerson 1974:171).

Apaches de Siete Ríos. This was a group living in an area called Los Siete Ríos 'seven rivers', between the Guadalupe Mountains and the Pecos River (Schroeder

1974a:482). The name is mentioned for the first time in 1659 (Scholes 1937:396). The Apaches de Siete Ríos were also called Faraones up to 1726, when these two names were replaced by Natagés (Schroeder 1974a:506). A synonym is Apaches de los Siete Rios, 1710; the name was still found on European maps long after the name had disappeared on documents. Examples are Sept. Rivieres, 1755, 1789; 7 Rivieren, 1785, Sette Fiumi, 1798 (Schroeder 1974a:486).

Faraones. This group was probably first mentioned in 1675 as "Apaches called Paraonez" (Forbes 1960:171). The name is derived from Spanish *Faraón* 'Pharaoh', because these Indians were according to Torquemada, 1723, "the barbarians who did not know God or respect God, like the other Pharaoh" (Schroeder 1974b:491). The Faraones have not been firmly identified with a modern Apache tribe, but it seems likely that they merged with the Mescaleros (Gunnerson and Gunnerson 1971:10, 21). Cordero, 1796, states that the Jicarillas are a branch of the Faraones, which is doubtful, as he is the only one to say so (Orozco y Berra 1864:369). According to Reeve (1958:207), the name was used about 1692 for Apaches living south of Zuni, on the west side of the Rio Grande, and also for Apaches living on the east side of the Rio Grande, so it did not have a specific meaning for a particular geographical group at that date. In the course of time, the name became restricted to the eastern group and other names came into use for the bands west of the Rio Grande. By 1720 and up to 1726, it was applied to all the Apaches between the Pecos River and the Rio Grande, and from the Santa Fe region south to the Conchos River in Mexico (Thomas 1935:166; Schroeder 1974a:506). From 1726 on, the name Natagé replaced Faraón in the southern part of the area. The name Faraón disappeared from contemporary use and was replaced by Mescalero in 1814 but continued to be noted on maps up to 1858 (Schroeder 1974a:506). Variant spellings include Pharaones, 1736 (Harrington 1939–1945), taraones, 1742 (Harrington 1939–1945), apaches faraones, 1765 (Tamarón y Romeral 1937:354), Taracones, 1799 (Schroeder 1974a:541), Apaches Faraone (Coues 1895, 2:632). Orozco y Berra (1864:59) gives a list of supposedly Faraón subdivisions, most of which are actually other Apachean tribes, non-Apachean Southwestern tribes, and non-Apachean Plains tribes; some of them are rare unidentifiable names. One of these, cuampes, was already considered a division of the Faraones in 1748 (Schroeder 1974a:386).

Apaches de Chilmo. These Apaches lived west of the Rio Grande, north of the Mansos and south of Acoma and were probably forerunners of the Warm Spring Apaches (Schroeder 1974b). They were considered separate from the Gila Apaches (Schroeder 1974a:291). The name is apparently derived from their chief's name El Chilmo; it seems to appear in 1667 and to disappear by about 1705 (Schroeder 1974b:21–23; Reeve 1958:223). The synonym Chilmos was used in 1702 (Schroeder 1974a:320).

Apaches del Acho. This name was first used under the form Apaches of the Achos nation by Gov. Antonio de Otermín in the 1680s (Hackett 1942:98). Their identity has never been established, but they should not be confused with the Acha of the 1540s mentioned by Pedro de Castañeda (Schroeder 1974a:271). When first mentioned, they lived in an area near or east of the Sangre de Cristo Mountains (Schroeder 1974a:319). Reeve (1957:51) considers them Jicarillas, whereas Schroeder (1974a:320–322, 363, 495) shows that they would have been a western faction of the Lipan Apaches. The name Achos appears for the last time in contemporary documents in 1706 (Ulibarrí in Thomas 1940:5). In a later document (1746–1748) the spelling Hachos is used (Gunnerson and Gunnerson 1971:17).

Cancy. Cancy is a French name that was used for several Plains Apache tribes. It is usually applied to the Kiowa-Apache and the Lipan, but it may also have been used for the Faraones (Gunnerson and Gunnerson 1971:19) or for the Conejeros (Schroeder 1974a:113). This name is a French rendering of Caddo *k̓ánʔciʔ* 'Kiowa-Apache', literally 'little duck' (Wallace L. Chafe, communication to editors 1973); Mooney (1898:245) gives Kántsi as a Caddo collective name for the Apache tribes but claims it means 'liars'. The term seems to have been first used, as Cantcy, by Joutel in 1687 (Margry 1876–1886, 3:409). Spelling variants are canecy, from Beaurain and La Harpe, 1719 (Margry 1876–1886, 6:289–290), Canze, from Casañas, 1691 (Schroeder 1974a:173), canchy or Connessi from Bienville, 1700 (Gunnerson and Gunnerson 1971:19 where other variants are given), Cannecy (Schroeder 1974a:114). Maybe the Cancers of Valverde, 1719, are also Cancy (Schroeder 1974a:360).

Apaches Colorados. This name was apparently first used by Diego de Vargas in 1694 (Forbes 1960:254). It might refer to the Vaqueros living on the Canadian River, which was known to the Spaniards as Río Colorado (Schroeder 1974a:280). It should not be confused with an identical name that possibly referred to some Gila Apaches located somewhere southwest of Acoma (Schroeder 1974a:281).

Apaches del Mechón. This term was used by Diego de Vargas in 1694 (Forbes 1960:254). As *mechón* means 'large lock of hair' in Spanish, the name almost certainly refers to a peculiar kind of hairstyle. Schroeder (1974a:286, 1974b:80) speculates that they may have been a group of Gila Apaches or perhaps Navajos.

Apaches Conejeros. Also spelled Conexeros, this is another name given by Diego de Vargas in 1695 (Forbes 1960:262) and means 'rabbit eaters' or 'rabbit hunters'. Schroeder has assumed they were the Cancy (1974a:113), a Jicarilla division (1974a:380), or a Lipan division (1974a:495).

Chilpaines. Although at least part of this Plains Apache group may be the ancestors of the Lipans, it has been tentatively identified with many other groups or parts of groups. Schroeder states that Chilpaines (Chipaynes) is a synonym for Trementinas and for Lemitas (Limitas) and that these three names refer to one and the same division of the Lipan Apaches who lived on the Canadian River around 1700 (Schroeder 1974a:343, 344). The Chilpaines then joined the Jicarillas and lived with them as an identifiable group up to the late 1750s, when the name disappeared (Schroeder 1974a:379, 436). Schroeder (1974a:380) also states that some Chilpaines could have joined the Mescaleros in the 1740s and the late 1760s. Evidence for this may be the fact that the Chilpaines were called Sejines in their own language (Schroeder 1974a:343–344), which matches the Mescalero self-denomination Sejen-ne given by Cordero, 1796 (Orozco y Berra 1864:369). However, this term has also been considered a synonym for Faraón in 1715 (Thomas 1935:80, 98) and a name for a subordinate group of the Carlanas in 1745 (Schroeder 1974a:378).

The etymology of the name Chilpaines is unknown, and whether it is nothing but a variant of the term Lipan is still an open question. The first occurrence seems to date from Diego de Vargas, 1695 (D.A. Gunnerson 1974:120) and is Apaches de los Chipaynes. Other spelling variants are: Chipaynes, Cipaynes, 1715 (Thomas 1935:80); Cipayno (Thomas 1935:98); Chilpanines, 1754 (Thomas 1940:135); and Chilpaines (Orozco y Berra 1864:59).

Apaches de Trementina. This term was first recorded in 1702 (J.M. Espinosa 1942:337). Schroeder (1974a:336) believes that they were Chilpaines or Lipans and shows that they were separate from the Faraones (1974a:496). The origin of the name is unknown, but *trementina* is Spanish for 'turpentine', which is evidence that this name has nothing to do with an unidentified branch of Apaches of Arizona called Tremblers, first noted in 1848, "who acquired their name for their emotions at meeting the whites" (Hodge 1907–1910, 2:814). Goodwin (1942:572) states that this term was applied once to the San Carlos or the White Mountain Apaches. Synonyms for the Apaches de Trementina were Trementinas, 1715 (Thomas 1935:82), 1748 (Villaseñor y Sánchez 1748, 2:412) and a misspelling Nementinas, 1706 (Thomas 1935:60–75).

Lemitas. The first occurrence of this name dates from 1706 (Thomas 1935:60–75). What Schroeder states about the identity of the Lemitas is identical to what he states about the Trementinas. The etymology of the name is uncertain. Variant spellings are Apaches Lemitas, Barriero's map of about 1728 (D.A. Gunnerson 1974:171), and Limitas, 1715 (Thomas 1935:80).

Penxayes. Penxayes was used in 1706 to refer to a Plains Apache tribe that might have been part of the Carlanas (Thomas 1935:60–75) or one that was closely associated with them (Schroeder 1974a:495).

Flechas de Palo. Flechas de Palo, Spanish for 'wooden arrows' was used in 1706 as the name for another Plains Apache division that might have been part of the Carlanas or associated with them. As the term is not mentioned in 1719, Schroeder (1974a:363–364) has speculated that this division had been absorbed by the Carlanas or perhaps by the Cuartelejos by that time.

Pelones. Pelones 'hairless ones' in Spanish, was a Plains Apache group name that also first appears in 1706 (Schroeder 1974a:343). They were said in 1745 to have lived on the Red River and to be identical with the Ypandis (the Lipans) (W.E. Dunn 1911:266–268). D.A. Gunnerson (1974:255) thinks that they were perhaps Carlanas. The Pelones from the Lower Rio Grande referred to in Hodge (1907–1910, 2:223) are probably an unrelated group.

Nifora. Niforas was a cover term used by the Papagos, Pimas, and Maricopas for any captive taken from enemy tribes and sold to the Mexicans of Sonora (Goodwin 1942:572). It has also been considered a Pima Gileño name for the Yabipais (Coues 1900, 2:446). The term is apparently first used in 1716 (Schroeder 1974b:340). Spelling variants include Nichoras (Pfefferkorn 1949:29); Nijoras, 1811; Nijotes, and Nixoras (Goodwin 1942:572). See the synonymy in "Yavapai" (this vol.).

Padouca. Padouca was a cover term used by the French to designate several Plains tribes. The French were aware of the fact that at least some of the Padoucas were Apaches. In eighteenth-century French usage, Padouca seems to have finally replaced all other terms for Apacheans (Gunnerson and Gunnerson 1971:20). The Apachean Padoucas encountered by the French on the Plains were probably Cuartelejo Apaches (D.A. Gunnerson 1974:121). The etymology of the name is unknown, but it is said to be of Siouan origin. One of the earliest occurrences of it seems to be on the Vermale map of 1717: "Païs des Appaches ou Padoucas orientaux" (Gunnerson and Gunnerson 1971:20). Later in the eighteenth century Padouca is applied to the Comanche, who replaced the Plains Apaches in many areas.

Yabipai. Yabipais, which is the same word as Yavapai, was used by Francisco Garcés as a term of Mohave origin synonymous with the Spanish word Apache as used at that time and with the same broad reference (Coues 1900, 2:446, 457). The term is used in the same way in Orozco y Berra's classification: *familia Apache ó yavipai* (1864:40).

Llanero. Llaneros, Spanish for 'plains dwellers', was probably never the name for an entity but rather the name of several groups that congregated seasonally in the High Plains for the buffalo hunt (Schroeder

1974a:539). Before the name Llaneros came into use these Indians were simply called Apaches de los Llanos 'Apaches of the plains', 1702 (J.M. Espinosa 1942:337). The number and names of tribes covered by this term has changed in the course of history. In 1777 Bernardo de Miera y Pacheco stated that Carlanas, Natagés, and Lipans were included (Bolton 1950:249). For Cordero, 1796, the Llaneros included the Natagés, the Lipiyanes, and the Llaneros proper (Orozco y Berra 1864:381–382; Matson and Schroeder 1957:355). D.A. Gunnerson remarks that the Natagés were allies of the Llaneros rather than part of them, but that it is possible that the Llaneros absorbed the Natagés (1974:277); she also suggests that the Llaneros were part of the Carlanas and were also called Lipiyanes (1974:xiv, 253, 277). The term Llaneros is in the 1980s applied to a Jicarilla division, and there has also been a Mescalero division with the same name. The Apache name of the Llaneros given by Cordero, 1796, is Cuelcajen-ne (Orozco y Berra 1864:369), which corresponds exactly to the self-denominations of these Jicarilla and Mescalero divisions.

Lipiyán. Lipiyanes, of unknown etymology, is probably an Athapaskan word. The identity of this group was discussed in the preceding section; historical documents disagree as to whether it is just a synonym for Llaneros or a synonym for Natagés. The singular was Lipiyán, 1787, and a spelling Lipillanes, 1798, also occurs (D.A. Gunnerson 1974:266, 282).

Natagé. Natagés came to be used around 1726 to replace progressively the denominations Siete Ríos Apache, Sierra Blanca Apache, and Faraón of southeastern New Mexico (Schroeder 1974a:211, 506). By 1745, the Natagés were said to consist of two groups, the Mescaleros, in the El Paso and Organ Mountain region, and the Salineros, in the Rio Salado area; but these probably referred to the same group encountered in different locations (W.E. Dunn 1911:266–267). In 1749 and up to the late 1700s, the names Natagés and Mescaleros were used interchangeably; then Mescalero gradually replaced Natagé (Schroeder 1974a:512, 514, 525). Its last mention in contemporary documents dates from 1791, but it was still mentioned on maps in 1820 (Schroeder 1974a:513). The name, probably Apache in origin, may be related to Nataina 'mescal people', a division of the Mescaleros (Mooney in Hodge 1907–1910, 2:34), or it may be borrowed from the Lipan name for the Mescaleros, nátahĕ´ (Hodge 1907–1910, 1:846). Spelling variants and synonyms are Natagees, 1726, perhaps the first occurrence (Hackett 1931–1941, 3:236); Apaches del Natagè, Barriero's map of about 1728 (D.A. Gunnerson 1974:171); a misspelling of this is Apaches del Natafé (G.P. Villagrá 1900:94); Natagêes, 1736 (Harrington 1939–1945); Yabipais Natagé (Coues 1900, 2:452); Natageses; Natajes (D.A. Gunnerson 1974:232, 253).

Chafalotes. Chafalotes refers to a little documented group of southern New Mexico, first mentioned in 1775 (Thomas 1932:156). They were presumably called after Chief Chafalote, who was said to be a Gila Apache.

Calvo. Calvos, also spelled Calbos, is derived from one of the chiefs of this group, Captain Calvo, 'the bald one' in Spanish, also known as Brazo de Hierro 'iron arm' and Picaxande. The Calvos are mentioned in 1791, and Schroeder (1974a:537–539) feels that the facts suggest that they were Mescaleros who ranged east into the Staked Plains to join with the Lipans during the buffalo hunting season. Several other obscure Apache groups of little historical interest can be found in Hodge (1907–1910). Examples are the Alacranes and the Colina (Hodge 1907–1910, 1:34–35, 322).

Apachean Languages

ROBERT W. YOUNG

The Apachean languages, consisting of Navajo, Western Apache, Chiricahua, Mescalero, Jicarilla, Lipan, and Kiowa-Apache, comprise the southernmost geographic division of the Athapaskan language family (fig. 1). The two related divisions are the Pacific Coastal, containing eight languages spoken or formerly spoken in California and Oregon, and the Northern, embracing 23 languages distributed over a wide area in western Canada and interior Alaska. The languages of the Apachean group constitute a dialect complex derived from a common ancestral prototype.

Prehistory

Although anthropologists and linguists had hypothesized a northern origin for the Apacheans since at least William W. Turner in 1852 (Krauss 1980), it remained for Sapir (1936) to present the first formal evidence in support of the hypothesis.

Available evidence, derived primarily from comparative linguistic studies, points to a comparatively recent period as the probable time at which Proto-Apachean separated from the Northern language complex, and glottochronology has estimated the date of "separation" as about A.D. 950–1000 (Hoijer 1956a). (Glottochronological dates of "separation" are theoretical constructs with a complex relation to actual prehistoric interruptions of communication; they are used by some comparative linguists to give rough estimates of linguistic prehistory.) Some time later the ancestral Apacheans began the southward movement along the eastern flank of the Rocky Mountains that culminated in their appearance in the American Southwest only a few centuries ago.

Archeological evidence is scant, except for the ancestral Navajo segment during the period following their arrival in the Navajo Reservoir–Gobernador–Largo Canyon region of southern Colorado and northern New Mexico, a general location known in Navajo tradition as *Dinétah* 'Navajoland' (literally 'among-the-people'). Tree-ring specimens from Navajo sites in Gobernador Canyon date from the period 1491–1514 (Hall 1944), supporting the belief that at least one Apachean group had arrived in the Southwest as long ago as A.D. 1500 (Dittert, Hester, and Eddy 1961; Hester 1962; Hester and Shiner 1963; Schroeder 1974b; Ellis 1974). Later studies have argued for a slightly later date ("Comparative Social Organization," this vol.; see also "Historical Linguistics and Archeology" and "Southern Athapaskan Archeology," vol. 9).

Wedel (1959) suggests the possibility that archeological sites relating to the Dismal River aspect in western Nebraska, western Kansas, eastern Colorado, and southeastern Wyoming may be associated with Plains Athapaskans, possibly Apacheans, although the earliest tree-ring dates so far discovered do not precede A.D. 1650.

The ancestral Apacheans drifted piecemeal into the Southwest and gradually spread to occupy a broad expanse of territory surrounding the Pueblos, including much of southeastern Colorado; northern, eastern, and southwestern New Mexico; western Texas; northern Mexico; and central and southeastern Arizona.

Spanish chronicles mention a few nomads in New Mexico west of the Rio Grande as early as 1583, but the number of such non-Pueblo people is not represented as substantial until the 1620s. The designation Apache first appears in Spanish documents of 1598. It appears, from Spanish accounts, that a western group, called collectively the Gila Apaches, spread south and west from the Manzano-Datil Mountains of New Mexico, with a subsequent movement northwestward into southeastern Arizona sometime between the late 1500s and the 1680s (Schroeder 1974b). All the Apacheans living west of the Rio Grande were indiscriminately termed Gila Apaches until the close of the seventeenth century, after which time distinctive band names came into use, for example, Chiricahua, Mogollon, Pinal, Mimbres, Arivaipa (Schroeder 1974b).

Schroeder (1974b:15) and Wedel (1947) cite archeological evidence pointing to cultural changes that were taking place on the Plains in the mid-sixteenth century, at a period contemporaneous, coincidentally, with the advent of the first Europeans in the region. Francisco Vásquez de Coronado reports encounters with nomadic hunters during his trek into the Plains in 1541, to whom his chroniclers applied the names Querechos and Teyas. The name Querechos was borrowed by the Spaniards from the Pecos name later used for the Apacheans, and it almost certainly referred at least in part to Apacheans in the sixteenth century (see the synonymy in "The Apachean Culture Pattern and its Origins," this vol.).

Chronology

Application to Athapaskan of the lexicostatistical method of estimating the time of first separation of genetically related languages shows dates of "separation" for the several Apachean languages from Sarcee, their nearest geographical relative in the Northern Athapaskan division, at about A.D. 1000 (Hoijer 1956a).

The high proportion of lexical cognates within the Apachean languages, and the relatively narrow limits of phonological and morphological diversity that characterize them in their relationship to one another, indicate that the Proto-Apacheans were a homogeneous ethnic group, sharing a relatively uniform common language at the time of their separation from the Northern complex. This basic homogeneity was shared by at least a part of the ancestral Apacheans at the time of their arrival in the Southwest. The close kinship among the Apachean languages is reflected in the relative dates of their "separation" from one another, ranging up to 419 years for that between the San Carlos dialect of Western Apache and Lipan, the westernmost and easternmost of the languages compared (Hoijer 1956a).

The periods of time separating the Apachean languages from one another are brief, and Benavides's comments of 1630 are perhaps pertinent when in his section on the "huge Apache nation" he notes that "although, being one nation, it is all one language, since it is so extensive it does not fail to vary somewhat in some bands (*rancherías*), but not such that it cannot be very well understood" (1916:131–132). This observation implies that the Apachean languages were still quite similar to one another in the early seventeenth century, at least those that came to Benavides's attention.

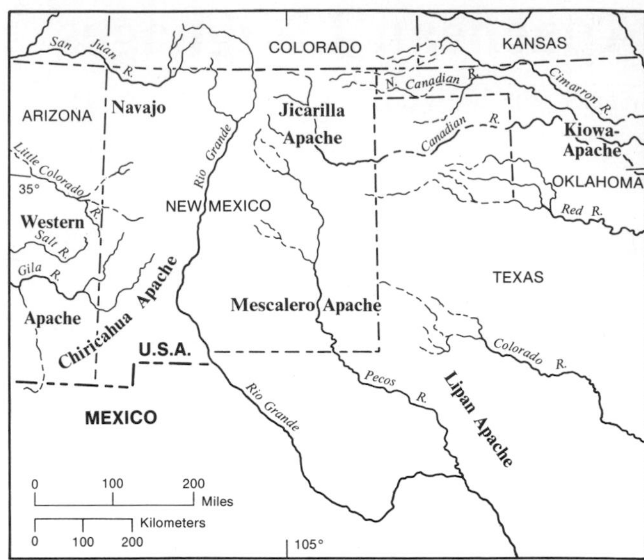

Fig. 1. Approximate locations of Apachean groups in the 18th century.

Historical Phonology

In the 1920s Edward Sapir introduced the science of comparative linguistics to the study of the Athapaskan languages (Krauss 1980), an approach that he first applied to include one of the Apachean languages in Sapir (1931). This study was concerned with the comparative development of three reconstructed Proto-Athapaskan consonant series, in stem-initial position, in four languages representing three widely separated geographic areas within the Athapaskan language family: Hupa (Pacific Coastal), Navajo (Apachean), and Sarcee and Chipewyan (Northern).

The results of this important study, summarized in table 1 with reference to Navajo, showed that the Proto-Athapaskan phonemes in Sapir's series I and II were retained intact by Navajo, while four of those in series III had merged with the corresponding phonemes of series I. This merger, involving the shift of Proto-Athapaskan *g̯-/*k̯-/*k̯̓- to Navajo *ʒ-/c-/ċ-* (orthographic dz-/ts-/ts'-), respectively, was highly significant, for it set Navajo apart from the Pacific and Northern languages, where the developmental history of the same Proto-Athapaskan phonemes was shown to have followed a different course. This discovery suggested that Navajo, along with the other Apachean languages, might conceivably constitute a separate and distinct dialect complex.

Although Sapir did not pursue the matter further in print, one of his students, Harry Hoijer, using data placed at his disposal by Sapir, set about the task of determining the linguistic position of the Southern Athapaskan (Apachean) languages both with respect to one another and to the related languages spoken on the Pacific Coast and in the North. The broadened data base included not only additional languages but also the full inventory of reconstructed Proto-Athapaskan consonants. And for Apachean the analysis included the languages within the southwestern complex. The most significant of Hoijer's (1938) findings included:

1. The merger of Proto-Athapaskan *g̯-/*k̯-/*k̯̓- to *ʒ-/c-/ċ-*, as demonstrated for Navajo by Sapir's (1931) analysis, was shared by all the Apachean languages. (This conclusion had to be revised in the 1960s when new information showed that Kiowa-Apache had a different treatment of this series of phonemes.)

2. Proto-Athapaskan *x̯- became *s-* in all the Apachean languages with the exception of Kiowa-Apache, where it appeared as *š-*.

3. Stem-initial Proto-Athapaskan *k- was retained in all the Apachean languages, except that in Kiowa-Apache *k- appeared as *č-* before the vowels *e* and *i*, remaining as *k-* only before *a* and *o*.

4. Stem-initial Proto-Athapaskan *t- was retained in Navajo, Western Apache, Chiricahua, and Mescalero

Table 1. Merger of Phonemes in Navajo

Series I			*Series II*			*Series III*		
Proto-Athapaskan		*Navajo*	*Proto-Athapaskan*		*Navajo*	*Proto-Athapaskan*		*Navajo*
**s-*	>	*s-*	**š-*	>	*š-*	**x̭-*	>	*s-*
**z-*	>	*z-*	**ž-*	>	*ž-*	**y-*	>	*y-* and *γ-*[a]
**ʒ-*	>	*ʒ-*	**ǯ-*	>	*ǯ-*	**ĝ -*	>	*ʒ-*
**c-*	>	*c-*	**č-*	>	*č-*	**k̭-*	>	*c-*
**c̓-*	>	*c̓-*	**č̓-*	>	*č̓-*	**k̭̓-*	>	*c̓-*

[a] Proto-Athapaskan **y-* becomes Navajo *γ-* before front vowels, but this is written *y* in the Navajo orthography.
SOURCES: Sapir 1931; Hoijer 1963.

but became *k-* in Jicarilla and Lipan; in Kiowa-Apache also **t-* fell together with **k-*, taking the form *k-* before the vowels *a* and *o*, but *č-* before *e* and *i*.

5. Stem-initial Proto-Athapaskan **n-* was retained as *n-* only in Navajo, having become ^{n}d- in Western Apache, Chiricahua, Mescalero, Jicarilla, and Lipan, and *d-* in Kiowa-Apache.

6. In all the Apachean languages, again with the exception of Kiowa-Apache, stem-initial Proto-Athapaskan **y-* retained the shape *y-* before the vowels *a* and *o* and appeared as *γ-* before *e* and *i*. In Kiowa-Apache **y-* appeared as *ž-* in all phonological environments. (This conclusion may also require slight modification in the light of Greenfeld's (1978) evidence that /y/ and /γ/ remain distinct before front vowels in Western Apache.)

Hoijer's (1938) study was also extended to include the differential development of certain Proto-Athapaskan consonants, depending upon their position in the word: that is, whether stem-initial, stem-final, or prefix-initial. It was apparent that positional developments did not follow a uniform pattern throughout the Apachean languages. Proto-Athapaskan **-d*, as a stem-final consonant, for example, was retained as *-d* by Navajo and Western Apache, but it had undergone phonetic change in Jicarilla, where it appeared as -ˀ, and in the other Apachean languages, where *-d* had dropped entirely. Likewise, Proto-Athapaskan **n-* as the initial consonant of a paradigmatic prefix remained as *n-* only in Navajo. In Jicarilla and Lipan this **n-* appeared as ^{n}d-, and in the remaining Apachean languages it became *d-*.

It was obvious that Kiowa-Apache was an exception to the general rule in virtually every instance, but in 1938 the available evidence seemed to support a hypothesis that the divergence of this one language was a regional development within a historically homogeneous language complex.

Table 2 summarizes Hoijer's (1938) major findings but includes subsequent revisions (Hoijer 1963) with reference to the development of Proto-Athapaskan **ĝ -*/**k̭-*/**k̭̓-* in Kiowa Apache, where merger produced *ǯ-*/*č-*/*č̓-* rather than *ʒ-*/*c-*/*c̓-*, as in the other six Apachean languages.

Analysis of the data available in 1938 led to the conclusions that (1) the Apachean languages are divergent descendants from a common ancestral prototype, constituting, as a group, a basically homogeneous dialect complex distinct from the Pacific and Northern complexes; (2) based on the differential treatment of Proto-Athapaskan **t-* and **k-* the Apachean languages fall

Table 2. Some Apachean Sound Correspondences

Proto-Athapaskan		*Navajo*	*Western Apache*	*Chiricahua-Mescalero*	*Jicarilla*	*Lipan*	*Kiowa-Apache*
**t-*	>	*t-*	*t-*	*t-*	*k-*	*k-*	*k-* and *č-*[a]
**k-*	>	*k-*	*k-*	*k-*	*k-*	*k-*	*k-* and *č-*[a]
**n-*	>	*n-*	*n-*	^{n}d-	^{n}d-	^{n}d-	*d-*
**x̭-*	>	*s-*	*s-*	*s-*	*s-*	*s-*	*š-*
**y-*							
before *a* and *o*	>	*y-*	*y-*	*y-*	*y-*	*y-*	*ž-*
before *e* and *i*	>	*γ-*(y-,gh-)	*γ-*[b]	*γ-*	*γ-*	*γ-*	*ž-*
**ĝ -*	>	*ʒ-*(dz)	*ʒ-*	*ʒ-*	*ʒ-*	*ʒ-*	*ǯ-*
**k̭-*	>	*c-*(ts-)	*c-*	*c-*	*c-*	*c-*	*č-*
**k̭̓-*	>	*c̓-*(ts'-)	*c̓-*	*c̓-*	*c̓-*	*c̓-*	*č̓-*

[a] Kiowa-Apache *k-* before *a* and *o*, *č-* before *e* and *i*.
[b] Western Apache retains *y-* according to Greenfeld's (1978) data.
SOURCES: Hoijer 1938, 1963.

into two separate groups: a Western and an Eastern division; and (3) Navajo and Kiowa-Apache diverged, at an early period, from the Western and Eastern divisions respectively, within which they were classified.

These conclusions were summarized in a schematic classification—essentially a family-tree type representation—in which the Apachean languages comprised a limb (from the Athapaskan trunk) that forked into an Eastern and a Western extension, but with Navajo and Kiowa-Apache diverging from their sister languages as later outgrowths.

Subsequently, Hoijer (1960) prepared a comparative study of the Athapaskan languages of the Pacific Coast and a comprehensive analysis of phonological change and development in 38 Athapaskan languages of Alaska, western Canada, the Pacific Coast, and the American Southwest (Hoijer 1963). An objective of this analysis was extension to the entire Athapaskan family of the family-tree classification format developed in 1938 for the Apachean languages.

Hoijer's (1963) article treated the Apachean languages summarily except to note that Kiowa-Apache was an exception to the previous position (Hoijer 1938) that all the Apachean languages had followed the same developmental course in the merger of Proto-Athapaskan **ĝ -/*k̯-/*k̯̓-* as that shown by Sapir (1931) for Navajo. Kiowa-Apache had merged this series with the Proto-Athapaskan **č*-series (Sapir's series II) to produce *ǯ-/č-/č̓-*, in contrast with the remaining Apachean languages, which had merged the **k̯*-series with the **c*-series (series I) to produce *ʒ-/c-/c̓-*.

A Second Proto-System for Athapaskan

Continuing comparative studies (Krauss 1964, 1964a, 1979), coupled with an ever-increasing fund of knowledge of the Northern Athapaskan languages, revealed the fact that there were major differences between the development of three series of the reconstructed Proto-Athapaskan consonants in certain Northern languages (Ingalik, Lower Tanana, Kutchin, Han, and Tsetsaut) and their development in the Athapaskan languages of northwestern Canada, the Pacific Coast, and the American Southwest. The Northern languages mentioned retained as distinct a Proto-Athapaskan series **ǯʷ/čʷ/č̓ʷ*, which in the other Athapaskan languages had merged with the Proto-Athapaskan series **ǯ/č/č̓*.

The wide distribution of this merger led Hoijer (1971) to propose a second, later, proto-system, to be called Proto–Canadian-Pacific-Apachean (PCPA), a system for which he hypothesized a northern development long before the Proto-Apacheans and the ancestral Pacific Coastal Athapaskan peoples began their migration from the North. Krauss, in contrast, ascribes the additional series to Proto-Athapaskan and does not reconstruct a second, intermediate, common language ("Northern Athapaskan Languages," vol. 6).

The new information pointed to the compelling need for revision of the 1938 classification of the Apachean languages, especially with reference to their portrayal as two separate groups, an Eastern and a Western, based upon the differential development of Proto-Athapaskan **t*- in Jicarilla, Lipan, and Kiowa-Apache (the Eastern division) and Navajo, Western Apache, Chiricahua, and Mescalero (the Western group), respectively. Hoijer (1971) was also greatly influenced in his revision by some newly developed unpublished lexicostatistical information. This reflected the range of shared lexical cognates at 90–97 percent within a six-language group including Navajo, Western Apache, Chiricahua, Mescalero, Jicarilla, and Lipan, in sharp contrast with a 74–76 percent range between these same languages and Kiowa-Apache. The six languages appeared to comprise a single closely related dialect complex, derived from a single ancestral prototype, while Kiowa-Apache appeared to be a second and distinct Apachean language, equidistant from each of the other six.

The differential treatment of the **ĝ -/*k̯-/*k̯̓-* series and of **n*- between the six languages and Kiowa-Apache, along with the lexicostatistical evidence cited above, were interpreted as suggesting that the Athapaskan peoples did not, as previously believed, migrate into the Southwest as a homogeneous linguistic entity. It appeared that the falling together of **t*- with the reflexes of **k*-, taken in 1938 as a major criterion for classification of the Apachean languages in two groups, had occurred also in the North. Furthermore, the need to reconstruct Proto-Apachean with all three of Sapir's (1931) consonant series distinct meant that Proto-Apachean matched the pattern of many Northern languages and was not unique in its treatment of this part of Proto-Athapaskan phonology. The linguistic data now suggested to Hoijer that the migration was led by an ancestral Navajo–Western Apache–Mescalero–Chiricahua group, followed closely by the Jicarilla-Lipan, and much later by the Kiowa-Apache.

Addressing the question of which language or language group is most closely related to Apachean, Hoijer cites lexicostatistical evidence pointing to a greater degree of proximity to the Northern Athapaskan languages than to those of the Pacific Coast. This is in agreement with the suggestion of Krauss (1979:874) that Apachean may have certain "affinities" with Sarcee.

Morphology and Structure: A Common Pattern

The Apachean languages, including Kiowa-Apache, diverge from one another to varying degrees in details of phonology, morphology, and structure, but basically they share a common pattern—a close bond of kinship within the Apachean dialect complex and one that is somewhat more remote between Apachean and its closest relatives in the North.

The Apachean languages share the same word classes: nouns, postpositions, verbs, and particles (the particles including pronouns, numerals, conjunctions, adverbs, and other uninflected elements). The constituents of the several word classes are similarly formed and, for nouns, postpositions, and verbs, similarly inflected.

As in all Athapaskan languages, noun inflection is limited to the possessive, where it involves prefixation of a set of possessive pronouns to the noun base. Similarly, a set of object pronoun prefixes, identical in shape with those prefixed to the nouns, are added to the postpositional base to mark the object of the postposition (a word class corresponding semantically to the prepositions of English). Compare, for example, Navajo *čah* 'hat': *šičah* 'my hat', *ničah* 'your hat', *bičah* 'his, her, their hat(s)'; and the postposition *-k'i* 'on': *šik'i* 'on me', *nik'i* 'on you', *bik'i* 'on him, her, it, them'.*

Also as in all Athapaskan languages, the Apachean verb is a complex construction composed of a stem, representing the verbal concept in abstract form, preceded by varying numbers and types of prefixes that serve to mark subject, object, number, and other grammatical features (the paradigmatic prefixes), or that function adverbially to modify the stem and derive lexical meaning (the derivational prefixes).

Whether nominal, postpositional, or verbal, the stem nearly always has the shape CV (consonant + vowel) or CVC (consonant + vowel + consonant), and the prefixes have the form CV or simply C. These features are illustrated by the noun stem *tsé* (CV), 'stone' in Navajo, Jicarilla, Chiricahua, and Mescalero, *łid* (CVC), 'smoke' in Navajo and San Carlos, *li'* (CVC), 'smoke' in Jicarilla, and *łi* (CV), 'smoke' in Chiricahua and Mescalero, and by the postpositional stems *-ċą́ą́'* (CVC) and *-ċą́* (CV), in Navajo and Chiricahua respectively, both meaning 'away from'; also note the verb stems *-dá* (CV), 'one subject sits' in all the Apachean languages except San Carlos (where it has the shape *-dáá*), and *-béėž*/*-béėš* (CVC), 'boil' in Navajo and Kiowa-Apache respectively.

The components of the verb—the stem and prefixes—must be arranged in a fixed relative order, usually described in terms of numbered positional slots counting backwards from the stem, which is always the final element in the verb construction proper. Thus, the Navajo verb *hadahidookah* 'they will climb up one after another' is composed of the adverbial (derivational) prefix *ha-* 'up' + the paradigmatic prefixes *da-*, distributive plural marker; + *hi-*, a seriative marker; + *di-*, inceptive; + *yi-*, progressive mode marker (*di-* + *yi-* contract to produce *doo-* in the third person of the future paradigm); + *-kah*, the verb stem, meaning 'plural subjects go'.

The study of comparative Athapaskan morphology is not yet far enough advanced for it to be possible to give a comprehensive survey of the distinct morphological innovations of Apachean, but the treatment of some important morphological categories can be mentioned. For example, the original negative paradigm has been lost, but the first-person plural subject prefix *-i·d- is retained (compare "Northern Athapaskan Languages," fig. 2, vol. 6).

The Apachean languages share not only many features of phonology and morphology with one another and with the Athapaskan languages generally but also many cognate stems and prefix morphemes. These may vary in shape from language to language, corresponding to differential phonological developments, including rules of juncture that govern the contraction or reduction of prefixes as they come together in the word. The progressive mode marker has the base form *yi-* in Navajo, *γi-* in Kiowa-Apache, and *ho-* in Chiricahua, for example, and when combined with the inceptive prefix *di-* to form the paradigm of the future, a characteristic series of contractions occurs in which the progressive prefix loses its base form, except in Kiowa-Apache. Thus, Navajo *di-* + *yi-* + *-š-* (the first-person singular subject pronoun prefix) become *deeš-*, Chiricahua *di-* + *ho-* + *-š-* appear as *dooš-*, and Kiowa-Apache *di-* + *γi-* + *-š-* remain uncontracted as *diγiš-*.

Phonological differences that distinguish even the most closely related members of the Apachean dialect complex, superficial though they may be, in conjunction with other divergent features, place limitations on the extent to which the several languages are mutually intelligible. Mescalero and Chiricahua are so close that mutual intelligibility is virtually unimpaired, while between Mescalero and Navajo or Jicarilla it is limited. However, speakers of one of the Apachean languages seem readily to learn to speak and understand another, at least in some cases.

Table 3 provides a representative list of cognates in all the Apachean languages and includes Sarcee as a representative of the Northern Athapaskan complex, for comparative purposes.

Apachean Speech Communities

Navajo

The Navajo constitute the largest Indian tribe in the United States, with a reported population of 166,519

*In this chapter all phonemes and words in the Apachean languages are transcribed phonemically in a scientific orthography consistent with that used elsewhere in the *Handbook* for Athapaskan languages (see "Northern Athapaskan Languages," vol. 6). In some cases the equivalents in the Navajo practical orthography are added in roman in parentheses.

Table 3. Selected Cognates in the Apachean Languages and Sarcee

	Navajo	*Western Apache*	*Chiricahua*	*Mescalero*	*Jicarilla*	*Lipan*	*Kiowa-Apache*	*Sarcee*
'I'	*ší*	*ší·*	*ší*	*ší*	*ší*	*ší*	*ši-*[a]	*síni*
'you (sg.)'	*ni*	*″di*	*″dí*	*″dí*	*ni*	*″dí*	*di-*[a]	*níni*
'we'	*nihí*	*nohʷí·*	*nahí*	*nahí*	*nahí*	*nahí*	*daxí-*[a]	*ná·ni*
'two'	*na·ki*	*na·ki*	*na·ki*	*na·ki*	*na·ki*	*na·ki*	*″da·čiˀ*	*akî·ˀ*
'long'	*-ne·z*	*-″de·z*	*-″de·z*	*-″de·z*	*-″de·s*	*-″di·s*	*-de·s*	*-nà·z*
'woman'	*ˀasʒání*	*ˀisʒánhń*	*ˀisʒáń*	*ˀisʒáń*	*ˀisʒání*	*ˀisʒání*		*ċiká*
'man'	*diné*	*n″dé·*	*n″dé*	*n″dé*[b]	*di″dé*	*di″dí*	*dį·dé*[b]	*diná*
'fish'	*łó·ˀ*	*łóg*	*łóíˀ*	*łų́·ye*	*łóge·*	*łǫ́ˀ*		*ƛúƙá*
'louse'	*ya·ˀ*	*ya·ˀ*	*ya·*	*ya·ˀ*	*ya·ˀ*	*ya·*	*ža·h*	*yàˀ*
'leaf'	*-ł̓ą·ˀ*	*-ł̓ą·ˀ*	*-ł̓ą·*	*-ł̓ą·ˀ*	*-ł̓ą·ˀ*	*-ł̓ą·ˀ*	*-ł̓ą·*	*ił̓ɑ́·sí*
'blood'	*dił*	*dił*	*dił*	*dił*	*dił*	*dił*	*dił*	*díλa*
'bone'	*ċin*	*-ċin*	*ċįˀ*	*-ċine*	*-ċin*	*-ċįh*	*-ċį·*	*-ćín*
'feather'	*-ł̓aˀ*	*-ł̓aˀ*	*-ł̓aˀ*	*-ł̓aˀ*	*-ł̓aˀ*	*-ł̓aˀ*	*-ł̓áˀ*	*-ł̓àh*
'head'	*-ci·ˀ*	*-ci·*	*-ci·*	*-ciˀ*	*-ci·*	*-ci·ˀ*	*-ci·*	*-cìˀ*
'eye'	*-ná·ˀ*	*-″dá·*	*-″dâ·*	*-″dâ·ˀ*	*″dá·*	*-″dâ·*	*-dá·ˀ*	*-néγa*
'nose'	*-íčį́·h*	*-čį́h*	*-íčį́*	*-(í)čį́*	*-čį́š*	*-íčį́š*	*-į́·čį·š*	*-cì*
'tooth'	*-γo·ˀ*	*-γo·ˀ*	*-γo·*	*-γu·ˀ*	*-γo·*	*-γo·ˀ*	*-γo·*	*-γò·ˀ*
'tongue'	*-co·ˀ; -za·d*[c]	*-za·d*	*-za·de*	*-zu·de*	*-za·di*	*-za·di*	*-za·*[c]	*-còˀ; -zaˀ*[c]
'star'	*sǫˀ*	*ċi·łsǫ·sé*	*sǫ·s*	*sų·s*	*sǫ·s*	*sǫ·s*	*sǫ·*	*sòh*
'water'	*tó*	*tó·*	*tó*	*tú*	*kó*	*kó*	*kó·*	*tú*
'stone'	*cé*	*cé·*	*cé*	*cé*	*cé*	*cí*	*ce·h*	*cá*
'sand'	*sáí, séí*	*sáí*	*sáíˀ*	*sáí, séí*	*sáí*	*sáí*	*sé·*[d]	*cáʒìł*
'earth'	*niˀ*	*niˀ*	*ni·*	*ni·*	*ni·*	*ni·ˀ*	*nǫ·*	*ni*
'cloud'	*ƙos*	*yá·ƙos*	*ƙos*	*ƙus*	*ńłcą́*[e]	*ƙos*	*ƙos*[f]	*ƙos*
'smoke'	*łid*	*łid*	*łiˀ*	*łi*	*łiˀ*	*łih*	*łiˀ*	*ƛi*
'fire'	*koˀ*	*koˀ*	*ko·*	*ku·*	*koˀ*	*ko·ˀ*	*koˀ*	*kòˀ*
'sun'	*ǯóhona·ˀáí*	*ya·ˀáí*	*ǯígona·ˀáí*	*ǯíguna·ˀáí*	*ǯígona·ˀáí*	*ǯį́·ˀna·ˀáí*	*ša·*	*č̓à·ł̓áγá*
'stand'	*-zį́*	*-zį́*	*-zį́*	*-zį́*	*-zį́*	*-zį́*		*-zíˀ*
'lie (sg.)'	*-tį́*	*-tį́*	*-tį́*	*-tį́*	*-kį́*	*-kį́*		*-tí(n-)*
'fly (verb)'	*-ł̓á·h*	*-ł̓áh*	*-ł̓á*	*-ł̓á*	*-ł̓áíh*	*-ł̓áh*		*-ł̓ɑ́h*
'sit (sg.)'	*-dá*	*-dá·*	*-dá*	*-dá*	*-dá*	*-dá*		*-dɑ́*

[a] Pronominal prefixes used in various functions; *daxí-* is also 'you (pl.)'.
[b] 'People'.
[c] 'Language'.
[d] 'Dust'.
[e] Compare Navajo *níłcą́* 'rain'.
[f] 'Sky'.

SOURCES: Hoijer 1938a, 1956a; Bittle 1963; Young 1940; Scott Rushforth, personal communication 1981.

in 1981 (table 4), of which 106,199 were resident on the Navajo Reservation and adjoining area (Navajo Tribal Office, Census Report, personal communication 1981). This number constitutes 89 percent of all Apacheans. The area of Navajo use and occupancy, including tribal, allotted, and leased lands, embraces about 24,000 square miles in northwestern New Mexico, northeastern Arizona, and an adjoining strip in southeastern Utah.

Until the 1940s the Navajo were predominantly a rural people, dependent on stockraising and subsistence farming for a livelihood, and carrying on a traditional culture within which the Navajo language was almost exclusively the medium for communication. It was not until the 1950s that a majority of the Navajo population had an opportunity to attend school (Young 1961).

Although urban settlements were established at key locations over the Navajo country in the late nineteenth and early twentieth centuries, largely around agencies, boarding schools, and medical installations (Fort Defiance, Window Rock, Shiprock, Crownpoint, Tuba City, Chinle, and Leupp) they remained small and attracted few permanent Navajo residents aside from federal government employees until about 1950. The boarding schools reached only a small segment of the tribal population. As a result, the knowledge of English in addition to Navajo was an exception to the rule.

During World War II, and in the period that followed, many changes took place. Expanding federal and tribal programs reflected in rapid growth of the reservation communities and urban growth, coupled with an expanded educational system, led to a shift away from the Navajo language toward English in the population centers. In addition, many Navajo people resided outside the reservation, in areas where employment opportunities were available, and their children attended public schools, where only English was spoken. This pattern was borne out by language use and maintenance studies of six-year-old Navajo children, sponsored by the University of New Mexico in 1969–1970 (Spolsky 1970–1971), which clearly indicated that relative isolation from centers of acculturation was a leading factor in the choice of home language and in the degree of maintenance of Navajo. The isolation factor has been declining at an accelerating rate for a generation or more, and if these studies were updated to 1982 the effects of acculturation on language maintenance during the past decade would be significant.

As a result of the changes that have taken place since 1950, there has been a steady decline in the use of the Navajo language except, perhaps, in the remaining isolated areas of the Navajo country, and excluding tribal members 40 or more years old. Accurate information with regard to language maintenance is not available, but estimates by federal and tribal officials suggest that about 75 percent of the reservation population are able to speak and understand Navajo. If this estimate is realistic, there are about 80,000 Navajo speakers still within the reservation population and, if as many as 40 percent of the off-reservation population can still speak the language it follows that the total number of Navajo speakers, in 1981, was about 100,000.

The Navajo language has been written in a variety of orthographies and for a variety of purposes since the 1880s, when ethnological studies were initiated by Washington Matthews. Later Bible translations, religious tracts, and catechisms were produced by missionary groups, and scientific studies were completed by linguists and ethnologists in the twentieth century. In 1981 there was a very large volume of published material in and about the Navajo language, including grammars, dictionaries, and textbooks designed for instructional purposes (see Young and Morgan 1980 and the surveys in Krauss 1973, 1979).

Universities in Arizona and New Mexico offer courses in spoken Navajo, and bilingual instructional programs are operated by some of the 52 reservation schools. In 1981, 85 percent of the reservation first-graders were Navajo speakers, and there were more than 50 bilingual classrooms, designed both to meet the needs of Navajo children who enter school unable to speak English and to further Navajo language maintenance. However, about four-fifths of the schools on the reservation had no form of Navajo instruction, not even a bilingual teacher's aide (Anita Pfeiffer, communication to editors 1981). Teaching materials are produced by some of the schools themselves, and by the Native American Materials Development Center, established in 1976, under the sponsorship of the Ramah Navajo School Board. The orthography employed for the writing of Navajo is that adopted by the Bureau of Indian Affairs in 1940 (Young 1977).

Table 4. Apachean Languages, 1981

		Speak the Language	
Tribe	*Population*	*Number*	*Percent*
Navajo	166,519	100,000	62%
Jicarilla	2,308	800	35%
Lipan	not counted separately	3	—
Kiowa-Apache	833	20	2%
Western Apache (San Carlos–White Mountain)	15,825	12,000	75%
Mescalero	2,415	1,700	70%
Chiricahua	not counted separately	?	?
	187,900	114,523	62%

SOURCES: BIA agency superintendents, Keith Basso, and Scott Rushforth, personal communications 1981.

Jicarilla

The Jicarilla Apache Tribe, with a membership of 2,308 in 1981 on the tribal roll, live on a 740,323-acre reservation located in Rio Arriba County, in northwestern New Mexico. The entire tribal population is shown as resident on the reservation in the 1981 Labor Force Report compiled by the Bureau of Indian Affairs.

Formerly subsistence farmers and stockmen, Jicarillas have since the end of World War II been moving from rural toward urban areas and a wage economy in and around Dulce, headquarters for the BIA and the tribal government, and site of the public schools serving the tribe.

Urbanization of the population has been accompanied by a decline in the use of the Jicarilla language, spoken in 1981 by an estimated 30–35 percent of the adult members of the tribe, primarily by those aged 35–40 years or older (about 800 persons).

Jicarilla Apache has been documented in scientific articles (Goddard 1911; Hoijer 1945–1949). A practical alphabet has been devised, patterned after the system in use for Navajo, and in 1981 an effort was being made by older tribal members to revive interest in the language. However, few parents speak Jicarilla to their children, and children generally cannot speak it (Liebe-Harkort 1980).

Lipan

Lipan Apache was virtually extinct, in 1981, with a reported population of two or three old women living on the Mescalero Apache Reservation in New Mexico (Scott Rushforth, personal communication 1981).

Kiowa-Apache

Known officially as The Apache Tribe of Oklahoma and as The Plains Apache Tribe of Oklahoma, the Kiowa-Apache had an enrollment of 833 members, in 1981, of whom an estimated 20 adults could still speak the language fluently (BIA, Anadarko Agency, personal communication 1981).

Bittle (1963) estimated the number of Kiowa-Apaches at 400, with about 100 fluent speakers, presumably in 1952–1955 during the period of his fieldwork, and Liebe-Harkort (1980) reports an enrollment of more than 800, including about 10 fluent speakers.

Spoken only by elderly tribesmen, Kiowa-Apache was moribund in 1981.

Western Apache

Western Apache includes the San Carlos, White River, Cibecue, Southern Tonto, and Northern Tonto dialects. It is spoken on the 1,876,256-acre San Carlos Reservation and on the adjoining 1,664,872-acre Fort Apache Reservation. The San Carlos numbered 7,545 in 1981, and Fort Apache groups aggregated 8,280 (BIA, San Carlos and Ft. Apache Agencies, personal communications 1981).

Although Liebe-Harkort (1980) saw a decline in the use of the Apache language in 1976, a resurgence of interest in the language and culture was reported in 1982. At least 75 percent of the total population of 15,825 were able to speak the tribal language, a somewhat larger percentage at Fort Apache than at San Carlos (Keith Basso, personal communication 1982). Children and parents use the language in the home, and children use it to communicate with one another. With about 12,000 speakers, the Western Apache dialect group was the most viable of all the Apachean languages in 1982.

Liebe-Harkort (1980) reports the compilation of a Comprehensive Education Plan by the White Mountain Apaches, in which a major concern of the parents was stated as continuation of the White Mountain language and culture. A practical orthography was devised in 1972, patterned after that in use for Navajo, and a number of publications have been issued by the White Mountain Culture Center, Fort Apache, Arizona, and others, including a small Western Apache dictionary, a list of plant names, and a translation of the New Testament. The language was previously documented by Goddard (1920a) and by Hoijer (1945–1949). The San Carlos dialect was similarly documented by Goddard (1919), and by Hoijer, and a number of children's books have been produced since 1972, with adoption of a practical orthography patterned after the Navajo alphabet (Liebe-Harkort 1980).

The population on the San Carlos Reservation includes an unreported number of Western Chiricahuas, but their dialectal distinctness, if any, has not been studied.

Mescalero

The Mescalero Apaches, with a population of 2,415 in 1981, live on a 460,242-acre reservation in southeastern New Mexico. The population includes the last remnants of the Lipan, as well as an unreported number of Chiricahuas. The Chiricahuas are descendants of those who, in 1913, elected to reside on the Mescalero Reservation rather than remain in Oklahoma where they had been held as prisoners of war since 1894. Although Chiricahua is still spoken in some households, Mescalero Apache is the dominant language, spoken by all.

The majority of the Mescaleros live in or near the tribal and Agency headquarters, at Mescalero, New Mexico, where school facilities, services, and work opportunities are available.

An estimated 70–75 percent of tribal members, in all age groups, continue to speak the tribal language, although about 25 percent of the children under the age of five speak no Apache.

The language has been documented in texts (Hoijer 1938a) and grammatical studies (Hoijer 1945–1949). In addition, a practical orthography has been devised and has been used for the production of several children's books. A dictionary of Mescalero Apache is in preparation.

Chiricahua

The Chiricahua Apaches have no separate reservation. It was the Chiricahuas, under Geronimo and other leaders, who held out against the U.S. Army troops until 1886, at which time they surrendered and were taken as prisoners of war, first to Florida, and subsequently to Alabama and finally Oklahoma. In 1913 they were offered the choice of relocation on the Mescalero Reservation in New Mexico or allotments in the vicinity of Apache, Oklahoma. About two-thirds of the tribe chose to move to New Mexico, and the remainder, known as the Fort Sill Apaches, accepted allotments and remained in Oklahoma. The language is moribund, replaced largely by Mescalero, and it is difficult to estimate how different it may have been from Mescalero at some earlier time.

An unknown number of Chiricahuas are reportedly included in the San Carlos Reservation population.

The Fort Sill Apache population was reported at 272 in 1981 (BIA, Anadarko Agency, personal communication 1981), and the number of speakers of Chiricahua there was estimated at five, all over 50 years of age.

Chiricahua Apache

MORRIS E. OPLER

The Chiricahua (ˌchĭrəˈkäwu) are one of the seven Apachean-speaking tribes of the American Southwest, the southern Plains, and northern Mexico.*

Territory and Tribal Subdivisions

The tribe was based on common territory, language, and culture. The hunting and gathering economy in a rugged area required the population to be thinly spread. Consequently tribal cohesion was minimal, and central political direction nonexistent. There was not even a recognized Apachean name to designate the entire tribe, though there were ways of expressing the community of traits and interests that Chiricahuas shared.

The Chiricahua tribe was divided into three named bands (fig. 1). One of these, because of its geographical position, may be called the Eastern Chiricahua. The Chiricahua name for it is 'red paint people' (*číhéne*; Hoijer *čí·héne·ˀ*). To the Eastern Chiricahua belonged almost all the Chiricahua territory west of the Rio Grande in New Mexico. Their lands joined those of the Mescalero Apache at the Rio Grande and included the sites of contemporary landmarks such as Quemado, Spur Lake, Luna, Reserve, Glenwood, Cuchillo, Hot Springs, and the Datil, Mimbres, Pino Altos, Florida, and Tres Hermanas ranges. Thus this band was the most northern and eastern of the Chiricahua. The terms Mimbreños Apaches, Coppermine Apaches, Warm Spring Apaches, and Mogollon Apaches have been used of various sections of this band.

West and south of the 'red paint people' stretched the territory of a second band, which for convenience may be termed the Central Chiricahua. The Apache word for this band (*č̓ók̓ánéń*; Hoijer *č̓o·k̓anén*) does not yield to analysis. Present-day Duncan, Willcox, Benson, and Elgin in Arizona mark the western boundary of the Central Chiricahua, and their mountain strongholds included rugged ranges such as the Dos Cabezas, Chiricahua, Dragoon, Mule, and Huachuca mountains. A small part of the band territory lay south of the present international line, in Mexico. It was one of its local groups that was first called the Chiricahua. This band, or part of it, has been referred to as the Cochise Apaches, since Cochise was one of its prominent members.

The territory of the third band, the Southern Chiricahua, was mainly in Mexico, though its members ranged through a small section of southwestern New Mexico, as well. In their own tongue they called themselves 'enemy people' (*ⁿdé'iⁿda·í*; Hoijer *nédna·ˀí*) with the implication that they were fearsome to all foes (Opler 1941:1–2). This band, or part of it, has sometimes been called Pinery Apaches or Bronco Apaches.

History

Spanish and Mexican Periods

It is generally agreed that the Chiricahua came to their southwestern territory from a region considerably to the north, but there are differences of opinion concerning the route they took and the approximate date of migration. Because the first Spanish party of exploration to pass through southeastern Arizona, that of Fray Marcos de Niza in 1539, and the second one, the Francisco Vásquez de Coronado expedition of 1540–1542, made no specific mention of encounters with Apaches in the Chiricahua region, some believe that these Indians must have entered the area after the middle of the sixteenth century, presumably from the east. However, Goodwin (1942:66–67) points out that Apaches with mountain retreats who feared attack were not easily detected by those who passed through their country. Moreover, it is by no means certain that the Coronado expedition failed to learn about the proximity of Apaches. After reaching a pass in southeastern Arizona that they called Chichilticale, Coronado's men traveled through the country of a nomadic people who dwelled in rancherias and lived by hunting and gathering. Both Forbes

*The phonemes of Chiricahua are: (voiceless unaspirated stops and affricates) *b*, *d*, *ƛ*, *ʒ*, *ǯ*, *g*, *ˀ*; (voiceless aspirated stops and affricates) *t*, *ƛ̄*, *c*, *č*, *k*; (glottalized stops and affricates) *t̓*, *ƛ̓*, *c̓*, *č̓*, *k̓*; (voiceless continuants) *ł*, *s*, *š*, *x*, *h*; (voiced continuants) *l*, *z*, *ž*, *γ*; (nasals) *m*, *n*; (nasals with stop release) *ᵐb*, *ⁿd*; (semivowel) *y*; (short oral vowels) *i*, *e*, *a*, *o* ([ɔ-u]); (long oral vowels) *i·*, *e·*, *a·*, *o·* ([o·-u·]); (short nasal vowels) *į*, *ę*, *ą*, *ǫ*; (long nasal vowels) *į·*, *ę·*, *ą·*, *ǫ·*; (tones) unmarked (low), v́ (high), v̂ (falling), v̌ (rising). The syllabic nasal is indicated by a tone mark: *ń* or *ǹ*.

Information on Chiricahua phonology is from Hoijer (1946). The Chiricahua words cited are in the transcription of Hoijer (1938a:59, 74), except that low tone is not marked on vowels and the band names are given as recorded by Opler (1941:1–2) and Hoijer (1939).

(1960:8–9, 1966:345–346) and Goodwin (1942:67) believe that these people were Apaches, and Goodwin suggests that "they were a part of the Chiricahua."

In 1583 Antonio de Espejo and his followers wished to explore the mountains near Acoma in west-central New Mexico for mineral wealth, but they abandoned the plan because of the occupation of the nearby highlands by a numerous and warlike people whom the Pueblo dwellers called Querechos. These Querechos traded with the inhabitants of Acoma, exchanging salt, meat, and tanned skins for cloth and other Pueblo possessions (Bolton 1916:182–183). In all likelihood these "mountain Querechos" were a part of the Eastern Chiricahua band.

Father Alonso de Benavides arrived in New Mexico in 1626 to preach and to direct the missionary work of the priests. His discussions of the Indians of the region and their locations are important sources for the period. Benavides (1945:82, 84–85) distinguished the Xila (Gila) Apache, who lived west of the Rio Grande, from the Perrillo (Mescalero) Apache, who lived east of it.

In 1686, in response to an inquiry by the Spanish king and the Council of the Indies, Fray Alonso de Posada, who had served as a missionary and church official in New Mexico from 1650 to 1665, wrote a report dealing with New Spain's northern frontier during these years. In it he undertook to locate the various branches of "the Apacha nation" and included among them a group that constantly invaded Sonora from a mountainous region about 50 leagues (approximately 125 miles) to the north. It is probable that he was referring to the Chiricahua, though he may also have had some Western Apache in mind (Tyler and Taylor 1958:301).

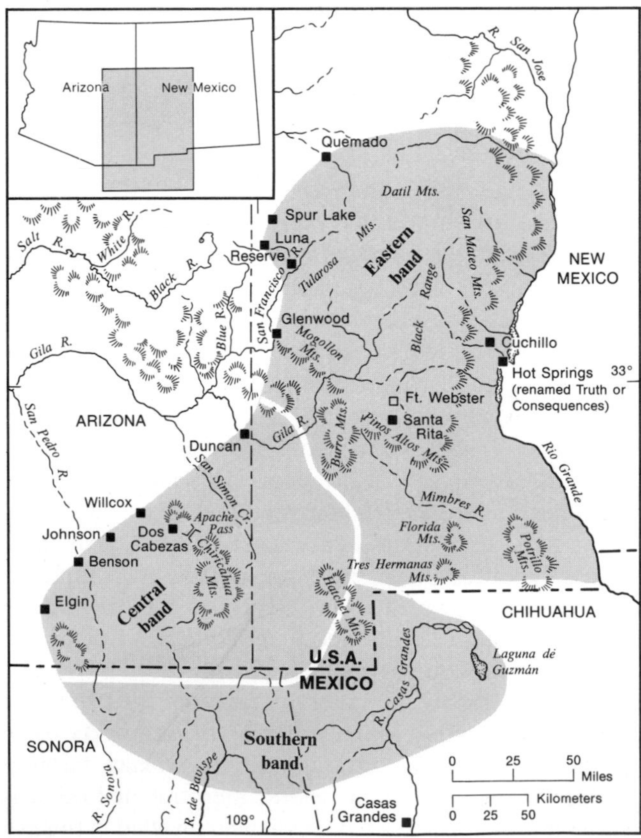

Fig. 1. Mid-19th-century territory.

In the spring of 1687 Father Eusebio Kino, a Jesuit priest, was sent to the Spanish frontier to missionize the Upper Pimas. Father Kino was an indefatigable traveler and explorer and came to know the area better than any European of his day. The Gila River, wrote Kino, "issues from the confines of New Mexico through the Apachería," a region that lay between the lands of the Pima and "the province of Moqui [Hopi] and Zuñi" (Bolton 1916:444). The Apache, Jocome, and Jano, who were allied and were enemies of the Spaniards in Sonora, lived "in the sierras of Chiguicagui [Chiricahua Mountains]" (Bolton 1916:446, 447, 451). Spicer (1962:231–235) believes that the Jocome and Jano were Apachean speakers and suggests that they are to be identified with branches of the Chiricahua. Forbes (1960:140, 141, 183, 245, 248, 275, 277) marshals evidence to make the same points and, like Spicer, indicates that the Spaniards were applying the term Apache to the Jocome and Jano by 1698. On the other hand Schroeder (1974a, 1974b) presents arguments that the Jocome and Jano were not Apaches, and that no Apaches lived south of the Gila River before the 1680s ("Southern Periphery: East," this vol.).

In his report on the country and its people, Capt. Juan Manje, who often accompanied the padre, corroborated Father Kino's account of Apache groupings and territory. He, too, linked the Apache, Jocome, and Jano in activities and location and wrote of encounters with Apaches in the Florida and Chiricahua mountains (Manje 1954:63, 67, 69, 70, 79, 83, 84, 96–98). Other letters and reports of Spanish officers and administrators written in the late seventeenth century (Hackett 1923–1937, 2:371–375, 377–381, 387–409) indicate that Apaches, presumably Chiricahuas, were strongly entrenched in this same area. Sauer (1934:54, 72, 73, 75, 77, 81), too, leans to the opinion that the Jano and Jocome were Apache groups, that they are to be recognized as branches of the Chiricahua, and that they were established in historic Chiricahua territory before the end of the seventeenth century.

Spanish documents of the eighteenth century reveal that in spite of numerous military forays, little progress was made in dislodging the Chiricahua from their territories. The missionary who followed Father Kino wrote in 1746 of the strong position of the Apaches south and west of Acoma along the Gila, in the area of the Datil Mountains, and in other regions that have become associated with the Chiricahua (Ives 1939:104, 106, 113, 114). Pfefferkorn (1949:35, 36, 43, 61, 144–151), whose missionary labors were interrupted by the expulsion of the Jesuits from the Spanish colonies in 1767, penned an account of the province of Sonora of the early 1760s that indicated that Sonora was being attacked from both the east and the north by Apaches. He also presented an example of the treachery and enslavement that turned the Apache into such bitter foes of the Spaniards, and he offered what was rare for the period—a fairly accurate description of aspects of Apache culture.

In 1765 Carlos III of Spain commissioned the Marqués de Rubí to inspect all presidios in the viceroyalty of New Spain and to draw up a plan for improving defenses. The Marqués's journey took place in 1766–1768 and has been described at length by his cartographer, Nicolás de Lafora. Lafora pointed out how useful the presidio of Janos was in controlling Apaches who lived along the banks of the Gila, San Francisco, and Mimbres rivers. He called one section of the Chiricahua the Chafalotes after the name of one of their leaders. "This group," he said, "maintains a sort of capital in Los Mimbres mountains." Other sections of these Gileños were said to hunt and to gather mescal through the Hatchet, Florida, Burro, and Potrillo mountains of southwestern New Mexico, the Chiricahua Mountains of southeastern Arizona, the Sierra Caballeros in northwestern Chihuahua, El Tabaco (a range northwest of Lago de Guzmán, Mexico), and El Capulín west of Casas Grandes valley, Mexico (Lafora 1958:78, 79, 81, 106, 127).

Some additional information on the distribution of the Chiricahua in the middle of the eighteenth century is provided by accounts of the missionary efforts of Fray Juan Miguel Menchero in New Mexico. After preaching to the Navajo, he "went to another nation of heathen Apaches at a place called La Cebolleta" (a little north of Laguna). He also sought to induce Apaches at Encinal (17 miles west of Laguna) to become Christians, and he prematurely submitted glowing reports of his progress. These Apaches must have been Eastern Chiricahua (Hackett 1923–1937, 3:420–422, 433–438).

A good deal of light is shed on the location of the Chiricahua and the Spanish efforts to contain them during the second half of the eighteenth century by the reports and letters of Juan Bautista de Anza, governor of New Mexico from 1777 to 1787, and of his military commanders. Anza's aggressive plans for bringing the Chiricahua to terms led to military strikes in the Chiricahua, Mogollon, Mimbres, Socorro, Florida, Hatchet, and Burro mountains, and at Ojo Caliente—all sanctuaries of Chiricahua local groups (Thomas 1932:1, 4, 5, 7, 11, 12, 156, 192, 209, 218, 221, 320). The concentration of Spanish military effort upon the New Mexico sector of Chiricahua territory, especially during the period 1775–1789, has been graphically diagrammed (Beck and Haase 1969:map 18). As these and other sources (Thomas 1959:19–32) indicate, the Chiricahua yielded little ground during this period.

In the early years of the nineteenth century the decline of Spain as a European power and the intervention of Napoleon in Spanish politics encouraged an independence movement in New Spain. Revolt flared in 1810, Spanish authority was reestablished in 1815, the independence of Mexico from Spain was proclaimed in 1821, a short-lived monarchy came into existence in 1822, and a federal republic emerged in 1824. During this period of instability campaigns against hostile Indians lapsed. Instead, there were conciliatory gestures that led to treaties of peace and to permission for mining operations in Chiricahua territory. However, the independence of action of the Mexican states and of the Chiricahua bands and local groups resulted in irritating incidents, and the truce was a brittle one (Thomas 1959:33–34).

American Period

Soon it was the United States with whom the Chiricahua had to reckon. The expansionist policies of Presidents John Tyler and James K. Polk precipitated war with Mexico. In 1845, just before leaving office, Tyler effected the annexation of Texas, the former province of Mexico. In 1846 a dispute over the western boundary of Texas led to a clash between American and Mexican forces, and Polk called for war with Mexico. By the Treaty of Guadalupe Hidalgo of 1848, which ended the war, the United States acquired a vast additional domain, which included much of present-day Arizona and New Mexico. The Gadsden Purchase of 1853 added land south of the Gila River. Most of Chiricahua territory was within the United States at mid-century, and the United States was responsible for any incursions of Chiricahuas into Mexico.

The attitude of the Americans toward the Apacheans was defined early in their rule. When Gen. Stephen Watts Kearny entered New Mexico, in his first proclamation to the conquered inhabitants he reminded them of their sufferings at the hands of the Navajo and Apache and promised protection. The Americans were eager to exploit the mineral wealth of the region, to link the newly acquired lands with the west coast by safe military and commercial roads, to provide lands for veterans of the Mexican War who chose to remain in the West after being mustered out, and to encourage new settlements where agriculture, stock-raising, and trade might flourish. These aims were incompatible with the unrestricted presence of nomadic Indians jealous of their extensive hunting and gathering territories. The situation was made still more acute by the discovery of gold in the lower Sacramento Valley of California in 1848. In the gold rush that followed, thousands of men, most of them impatient with any Indian presence and claim to rights, moved through Chiricahua country on their way to seek their fortunes. Clashes between the immigrants and Indians were frequent, and it became the settled policy of the army to "overawe" the Indians and to punish them for any defense of their hunting grounds or for any retaliation because of mistreatment. To guard settlements and routes, in present New Mexico alone nine forts were built between 1846 and 1855 (Gregg 1968). By 1860 four more military posts were established to control the Indians of the area. Present-day Arizona was being blanketed with forts by 1862 (Brandes 1960; U.S. National Park Service 1963).

In 1852 Americans wanted to reopen the Santa Rita copper mines in Eastern Chiricahua country, and Fort Webster was established nearby to protect them. Then gold was discovered at Pinos Altos, not far from Santa Rita, and there was an influx of prospectors to that site. Their immediate contribution to Indian-American relations was to flog and thoroughly alienate Mangas Coloradas, the most prominent leader of his time of the Eastern Chiricahua band. As mining and agricultural communities multiplied, the Apache presence in their traditional territories was less and less welcome. Restrictions on their movements and depletion of game were increasing the need of the Indians, and charges of Indian "depredations" became more frequent; from 1852 on, the Chiricahua, who had been conciliatory toward the Americans, became more aggressive (Bartlett 1854, 1:308–340).

Government response fluctuated wildly. In 1855 an appropriation was voted by Congress for the purpose of concentrating the Eastern Chiricahua, providing them with necessities, and encouraging them to farm. This venture was to be guided by Michael Steck, one of the few sympathetic resident agents the Chiricahua were to know. Most of the Chiricahua over whom Steck exercised control were from the Mimbres Mountain region, but in due course he hoped to persuade their bandsmen of the Mogollon Mountain area to join them. His hopes were thwarted when, to his dismay, Col. B.L. Bonneville launched a vigorous military campaign against the Mogollon group that scattered them and killed many of them. Later Steck met with Central Chiricahuas near Apache Pass and was promised that they would not attack immigrants along the overland route. Despite provocations, they kept their word until Cochise, a leader of the Central Chiricahua, and four other prominent men were arrested through deception by a hot-headed young officer and charged with acts in which they had had no part. Cochise cut his way though a tent and escaped, but his companions were executed, and Cochise vented his anger on any who dared use Apache Pass.

Meanwhile Steck found what he considered to be the ideal locality for a Chiricahua reservation 15 miles south of the Mogollon Mountains on a tributary of the Gila River. In 1860 he was authorized to settle as many of the Eastern Chiricahua there as possible, and he voiced the hope that the reservation would be made permanent and that the Central Chiricahua would soon be willing to settle there also. This time it was the Civil War and the invasion of New Mexico Territory by Confederate forces from Texas that intervened (Ogle 1970:31–45; ARCIA 1851–1861).

Early in 1862 the government ordered a regiment of California volunteers, commanded by Gen. James H. Carleton, to the Rio Grande to secure New Mexico. The goal was reached and the mission accomplished, but not before Carleton's soldiers had fought Cochise's Central Chiricahua at Apache Pass and lost nine men (ARCIA 1862:238–239). Carleton's thinking reflected the gold fever that prevailed in the far West of his day. He referred to his soldiers as a regiment of "practical miners"; many of his forays were thinly veiled explorations to find rumored mineral wealth. He wrote more than once that he considered his main mission to "brush" the Apache aside so that mineral exploration and exploitation might proceed unhampered. He developed the idea of concentrating all the Navajo and Apache on a 40-square-mile reservation on the Pecos River near Fort Sumner (Bosque Redondo), which was deficient in water and fuel as well as space for the purpose. Carleton had his best success with the Mescalero Apache and Navajo, many of whom he managed to concentrate at the Bosque. His course brought him into sharp conflict with Steck, who had become the superintendent of Indian affairs for the New Mexico Territory. Steck recognized the limitations of Bosque Redondo very early and was still certain that he could settle the Chiricahua peaceably on a suitable reservation in their own territory (ARCIA 1863).

One of the more dubious achievements of Carleton's forces was to lure the Eastern Chiricahua chief, Mangas Coloradas, into custody under a flag of truce and a promise of treaty talks on January 17, 1863, and to torture and shoot him the next day (Conner 1956:34–42). This was the prelude to a series of attacks on the Eastern and Central Chiricahua. By May 1865 Carleton thought that the Eastern Chiricahua were sufficiently weakened to agree to move to the Bosque. He sent Capt. N.H. Davis to deliver his ultimatum. Davis was told by Victorio and other chiefs with whom he met that they wanted to see the Bosque before they agreed to take their people there. A delegation of leaders was chosen to make the inspection, but they did not appear at the appointed place and time. Davis, enraged, returned and made his report, ending it with the words, "Death to the Apache, and peace and prosperity to this land" (U.S. Congress. Senate 1867).

By late 1866 Carleton's harsh policies had been discredited, and he was transferred from the area to another command. Their Indian agent again tried to calm and concentrate the Chiricahua. By 1869 a large number of Eastern Chiricahuas were camping around Cañada

Alamosa, near Fort McRae, waiting to hear what reserve the government would set aside for them. Loco, one of their spokesmen, said that they wanted it to be established in the same general area in which they were then camping. However, during the years since Agent Steck had tried to settle the Chiricahua in the Rio Grande valley west of the river, settlers had moved in, many of them squatters on government land. They were in an ugly mood at the prospect of being displaced by the Indians. By the time Vincent Colyer, the special commissioner appointed by President Ulysses S. Grant to set up reserves for the western Indians, arrived, the Chiricahua had fled to the hills in fear of attack. Colyer decided that there would be constant friction with the settlers in the Cañada Alamosa region and that it would be too expensive to pay for the improvements the settlers claimed to have made. As an alternative he chose another site farther west in the Tularosa Valley and surrounding highlands near the Arizona border (Colyer 1872; ARCIA 1869:95–104, 1871:2, 3, 46–49, 93, 94, 369). In an order of November 20, 1871, Lt. Gen. Philip H. Sheridan directed Indians at Cañada Alamosa and all roving bands of Apaches of New Mexico Territory to report to the new Tularosa Reservation. He stated that a military post would be established there as soon as possible and that Apaches who failed to comply with the order in due time would be subject to attack as hostiles. In spite of the threats, there was an exodus of Chiricahuas, and army officers supervising the removal could find only 450 of the more than 1,600 who had gathered to await the verdict. Cochise, who had camped close to Cañada Alamosa with his Central Chiricahua followers while the issue was being decided, left for his old country (ARCIA 1872:176).

In 1872 a determined attempt was made to settle the Central Chiricahua on a reservation. Gen. O.O. Howard was sent to confer with Cochise and other leaders and make the decision. With the help of Thomas Jeffords, one of the few White men the Chiricahua trusted, he reached Cochise's encampment and held the meeting. Southern Chiricahua representatives, as well as Central Chiricahua, were present at this conference, which resulted in the establishment of a Chiricahua Reservation in the southeast corner of Arizona Territory abutting the international line (Howard 1907:184–225; Sladen 1880). Jeffords was named special Indian agent, and the Indians promised to remain within the reservation limits (ARCIA 1872:148–178). The new reservation seemed promising at first: Cochise took his pledge to maintain peace very seriously, and Jeffords exercised remarkable control over the Indians. But the troubles of other reserves plagued the Chiricahua Reservation. Fugitive Eastern Chiricahuas from the unpopular Tularosa Valley Reservation arrived in numbers and depleted the rations. Coyoteros (White Mountain Apaches) who had been forced to move to San Carlos came because of feuds with San Carlos Apaches. Because of the proximity of the reservation to the border, any thefts in northern Mexico were charged to the Indians of the Chiricahua Reservation. In mid-June 1874, just when Jeffords needed his support most, Cochise died. Earlier in 1874 the failure of the Tularosa Valley reserve was admitted, the Cañada Alamosa (Hot Springs) Reservation was reestablished, and Cochise was asked to take his followers there. The old chief, already ill, had replied that "the Government had not enough troops to move them, as they would rather die here than move there" (ARCIA 1874:288).

Nevertheless, it had already been decided to abolish the Chiricahua Reservation, and a pretext soon presented itself. A man named Rogers, who lived at a mail station in the vicinity of the reservation, sold whiskey to some of the Indians and was killed for his pains when they returned for more and were refused. Shortly afterward John Clum arrived with armed men to announce that the Chiricahua Reservation was being abolished and that he was instructed to escort its inhabitants to San Carlos. Of the more than 1,000 Chiricahuas who had lived on the reservation, Clum was able to find only 42 men and 280 women and children by the time he started his homeward journey on June 12, 1876 (ARCIA 1873:291–293, 1874:287–288, 1875:209, 1876:3–4, 10–11).

Now the Hot Springs Reservation attracted many displaced and disaffected Chiricahuas, and so in the next year it suffered a like fate. On April 20, 1877, John Clum arrived with an armed force to compel the Apaches living at Hot Springs to march to San Carlos. Prominent Southern Chiricahuas, such as Juh, Nolgee, and Geronimo, who had fled from the Chiricahua Reservation to Hot Springs rather than obey the order to report at San Carlos, were arrested and taken to San Carlos in irons. There they were subjected to confinement and hard labor for some time (ARCIA 1877:20, 34–35).

San Carlos soon seethed with resentment and rebellion. The San Carlos Apache considered their unhappy guests to be intruders. The uprooted Apaches detested the hot, humid lands to which they were confined. The military officers and the civilian administrators quarreled incessantly over lines of authority. Indian leaders who had been unchallenged in their own local groups found themselves in conflict with representatives of other units. The army officers had their favorite informers, Indians were encouraged to spy on their fellows, punishments were harsh and arbitrary, and the place rocked with rumor and fear. The Indians were swindled out of the meager supplies appropriated for them; the agent, a pious fraud, was heavily implicated, and even the commissioner of Indian affairs was found to be manipulating Apache reservation assets in his own interest and was dismissed in disgrace (B. Davis 1963; Ogle 1970:179–215).

It was not long before Chiricahuas began to desert San Carlos. In early September 1877 about 300 bolted. Thirteen were killed and 30 women were returned by pursuers, but the rest escaped. Eleven days later 187 were discovered at Fort Wingate and surrendered. They were taken as captives to Hot Springs, where there was still a military post. Other wandering Apaches who were gathered up were sent to join them. A year later when it was announced that they would be returned to San Carlos, about 80 escaped to the hills. In December 1878, 63 of them appeared at Mescalero in destitute condition and begged to be allowed to stay (ARCIA 1879:xxxviii–xl).

In February 1879 Victorio and 22 followers who had been in Mexico approached the military post at Hot Springs and expressed willingness to surrender under certain conditions. He was pressed to agree to go to Mescalero. He resisted this, and he and his party escaped to the nearby San Mateo Mountains. Later, he appeared at Mescalero and talked with the agent. He expressed fear that the real intent was to seize him and send him to San Carlos. The agent reassured him, and he and his followers came in and were enrolled with a sizable body of fugitive Chiricahuas already there. His stay was to be a brief one. In July 1879 three indictments were returned in Grant County against Victorio, and he learned of this. A few days later a hunting party that included a judge and a prosecuting attorney of Grant County passed through the reservation. Their presence was interpreted by the jittery Indians as preliminary to the arrest of Victorio and perhaps of all the Chiricahuas. The alarmed Indians fled the reservation and were pursued by the military. A bloody war erupted that resulted in the death of Victorio and most of his followers on October 15, 1880, in a battle with Mexican soldiers in Mexico, where they had been driven by American forces. The irony of the costly Victorio campaign was that it had virtually been decided to restore the Hot Springs Reservation for the use of the Chiricahua, when the outbreak occurred and the recommendation was suspended (Ogle 1970:210; ARCIA 1879:xl, 113–114, 1880:xlv).

In 1881 fighting broke out between American soldiers and the Western Apache when an attempt was made to arrest a shaman whose ritual was thought to have anti-White overtones. The Chiricahua were alarmed by the display of force evoked, and a large number of them took advantage of the preoccupation with the Western Apache to flee southward. In April 1882 a force of 60 Chiricahua warriors slipped quietly back on the reservation. Their purpose was not to stay but to induce the rest of the Chiricahuas to join them outside the reservation. In this they succeeded, and the enlarged group reached Mexico, with American forces in hot pursuit. In their anxiety to outdistance the Americans, the Chiricahuas fell into a Mexican ambush, and they suffered frightful casualties, especially of women and children.

In the spring of 1883 Gen. George Crook was ordered by Gen. Sheridan to recapture the elusive Chiricahuas, who now had their main camp in the rugged Sierra Madre range of Mexico. An agreement between the two governments, signed on July 29, 1882, permitted American troops to cross the border in pursuit of Indians, and plans for a joint effort were made by the military leaders of the two sides (Crook 1946:246). Crook's force consisted of about 50 White soldiers and 200 Indian scouts drawn from Apache and other tribes. The heavy reliance on Indians was a tactic that caused Sheridan uneasiness. Crook's command administered no decisive defeat to the Chiricahuas, but it did penetrate Chiricahua fastnesses, demonstrated to the hostiles that they were nowhere safe, and forced their leaders into parley. The upshot of the meetings was a promise by the Chiricahuas to return to the reservation if no punishment were exacted for their flight. The main body of 335 returnees arrived at San Carlos on June 23, 1883, but three other smaller groups did not arrive until the fall of the year and the spring of 1884 (Bourke 1891). As an aftermath of the outbreak an agreement was worked out between the Departments of War and the Interior whereby full control of the Chiricahua was placed in Crook's hands and police control of the reservation was entirely vested in the military (Bourke 1886; Thrapp 1972).

The army interpreted its police powers very broadly: almost every phase of life, even agriculture, was judged to have a peace-keeping component. The agent chafed at this erosion of his authority, and the Indians were pawns in the tug-of-war. In the efforts of both sides to assert authority there was a great deal of resented intrusion into the family life and customs of the Chiri-

Mus. of N. Mex., Santa Fe: 11649.

Fig. 2. An Anglo-American boy, Santiago (Jimmy) McKinn, in front of a group of Chiricahua Apache children at the camp of the Central Chiricahua Long Sinew of the Back. Captured in 1885 on a raid along the Mimbres River, N. Mex., McKinn was later freed. Contrary to popular belief, Apache raiders took few adult captives and tortured fewer still. Photograph by Camillus S. Fly, 1886.

Smithsonian, NAA:82–963.

Fig. 3. Apache men, women, and children at Ft. Bowie, Ariz., 1886. These people are Chiricahuas captured after months of eluding mounted U.S. troops. Moccasins of man squatting are worn through, and the women's clothes are soiled and their hair is uncombed. Constantly on the move, small bands of Chiricahuas were forced to survive for long periods of time on very little food, and it was impending starvation—as well as military pressure—that brought about their eventual defeat. Photograph by A. Frank Randall.

Mus. of N. Mex., Santa Fe: 2108.

Fig. 4. Alfred Chatto, an Apache leader. He is wearing a silver peace medal bearing the likeness of Pres. Chester A. Arthur. This was presented to him in July 1886, when he accompanied a delegation of Chiricahua to Washington to discuss a separate reservation for their people in Ariz. Taken by an unknown photographer on the Mescalero Reservation in N. Mex., 1927.

cahua. In this atmosphere rivalries and animosities flourished among the Indians themselves; Chiricahuas suspected tribesmen, often with good reason, of bearing tales to White officers or conniving in some manner to discredit them (Bourke 1891:457–476; Crook 1971:10,14; B. Davis 1963). In mid-May 1885 two prominent Chiricahuas, Geronimo and Mangus, heard the rumor that they were to be arrested. Actually, plans had been made for Geronimo's arrest (Ogle 1970:232). On May 17, 42 Chiricahua men, many of them close relatives and relatives-in-law of the two men and subject to their orders, headed for Mexico with their wives and children. The majority of the Chiricahua refused to join the exodus and, indeed, by scouting activities and by acting as intermediaries, played a major role in achieving the final surrender of the fugitives.

The flight of these Chiricahuas resulted in two major campaigns against them, the first led by Gen. George Crook and the second by his successor, Gen. Nelson A. Miles (Crook 1971; C.B. Gatewood 1929; Miles 1896:450–532). The Chiricahuas also had to contend with the Mexican forces arrayed against them. In neither campaign was a decisive military defeat administered to the Apaches. They surrendered to Crook because they had run low on supplies and ammunition in a contest in which the foe was constantly replenished in men and provisions. What is more, it was only because Crook made liberal use of Apache scouts that he was able to find and penetrate their sanctuaries. When, on March 27, 1886, they agreed to surrender, it was on terms that the Chiricahuas proposed and Crook accepted. These terms became an embarrassment to Crook, for they were repudiated by President Grover Cleveland, who, considerably after the event, demanded unconditional surrender (B. Davis 1963; Geronimo 1887; U.S. Congress. Senate 1890).

The erstwhile fugitives retained their arms as they moved toward the border. Satisfied that the officer in charge would safely shepherd the hostiles to the reservation, Crook left for Fort Bowie. Soon after his arrival a courier brought the news that Naiche and Geronimo, their apprehensions fired by liquor that an unscrupulous trader had sold them, had again disappeared, taking with them their close relatives and a sprinkling of followers. The others continued their journey north. President Cleveland and General Sheridan were furious with Crook. Sheridan hinted that the Apache scouts must have been in collusion. This Crook stoutly denied, and on April 1 he asked to be relieved of his command. His resignation was accepted, and General Miles was immediately named to succeed him.

Then the full wrath of the government was leveled against the Chiricahuas. Those fugitives who had shown good faith and had marched in were hastily gathered up, and all 77 were entrained for confinement in Fort

Marion, Florida, arriving there on April 13, 1886. Meanwhile Miles was making elaborate plans to find and subjugate the small fugitive band of 17 men, encumbered with 19 women and children. Against this handful Miles pitted an army of 5,000 soldiers and had the cooperation of the Mexican army besides. In spite of his boast that he improved on Crook's methods, Miles had to depend on Apache scouts to a great extent. Twenty percent of the force that most effectively harried Geronimo and Naiche were Apache scouts. Again there were no decisive military victories over the hostiles. Surrender came only after two Chiricahua Apache scouts were sent ahead alone to seek the hostiles and to invite them to a parley with the American command, and these two were able safely to enter the fugitives' mountain fortress only because they had relatives there (B. Davis 1963; Opler 1938).

At this time there was a public clamor to remove all Apaches, particularly the Chiricahua, from Arizona Territory. Partly because of this, and partly because it was thought good strategy to isolate the hostiles and to give them an inducement to surrender, the decision was made to move all the Chiricahuas at San Carlos to Fort Marion. These were Indians who had not fled the reservation, and many of the men had served or were serving terms as United States Army scouts. Thus it was that when the Chiricahua hostiles emerged to discuss surrender conditions, they learned that their comrades in arms had been sent to Florida five months before and that the rest of their people were even then being moved out of the state. The dejected fugitives surrendered to Miles on September 3, 1886, and in five days they, too, were on their way to Florida (figs. 5–6). Even at the end of this episode the Chiricahuas had reason to feel deceived. The men had been promised by Miles that they would be housed at Fort Marion with their wives and children. Instead, Naiche, Geronimo, and 15 other men were incarcerated in Fort Pickens, Florida, on the other side of the state (fig. 7) (Opler 1938; Geronimo 1887; Welsh 1887).

Before the main contingent of Chiricahua was sent to Fort Marion, the adjutant general asked the officer in charge how many additional persons the place could accommodate. He was told that a maximum of 75 more could be absorbed. Instead, the fort received almost 400 additional members of the tribe. It was not long before the crowded conditions, the related insanitation, the transfer of a mountain people to hot, humid lowlands, the privations of the recent past, the enforced idleness, and the fears and uncertainties concerning the future began to take their toll. Before the end of 1889, 119 of the total of 498 Chiricahuas who had been sent to Florida had died, a casualty rate for the short period of over 20 percent.

Daughters of the Republic of Tex. at the Alamo, San Antonio:Misc. 94.

Fig. 5. Chiricahua Apaches being held at San Antonio, Tex. After surrendering to Gen. Nelson Miles they were placed on a train for Florida, but owing to confusion over the surrender terms they were ordered to wait in San Antonio while their fate was debated. Photographer unknown, Sept. or Oct. 1886.

Soon after the arrival of the Chiricahua at Fort Marion, protests concerning their treatment and location, voiced by the Indian Rights Association and by Gen. Crook, who was outraged at the tribulations of his former Chiricahua Indian scouts, began to be heard. In response, those at Fort Marion were moved to Mount Vernon Barracks near Mobile, Alabama, in April 1887, and those confined at Fort Pickens were allowed to join them in May 1888. Alabama proved little healthier than Florida for the Chiricahua. Consequently, in 1894 the tribe was transferred to a reservation at Fort Sill, Oklahoma (fig. 9). Here they arranged themselves into "villages" much like the old local groups, each with its leader, and took up cattle-raising and farming in earnest (U.S. Congress. Senate 1890).

In 1913 full freedom was restored to the Chiricahua, and they were given the choice of accepting lands in severalty in the vicinity of the towns of Fletcher and Apache, just north of Fort Sill, or of going to south-central New Mexico to share a reservation with the Mescalero Apache. The opportunity of returning to the mountainous country of the Southwest had great appeal for the majority of the Chiricahua. Of the 271 individuals to which the tribe was reduced, 187 elected to go to Mescalero and 84 chose to remain in what had become Oklahoma. The Oklahoma contingent is popularly known as the Fort Sill Apache (ARCIA 1913:69, 1914:58, 1915:29).

At Mescalero, Whitetail, a section of the reservation remote from the agency and from Mescalero Apache settlements, was assigned to the Chiricahua, and initially an attempt was made to provide separate health, educational, and other services there for them. However, the better work opportunities, trader's supplies, medical services, and other facilities closer to the agency beckoned, and intermarriage with Mescaleros and Lipans induced mobility.

In the 1970s the outlying communities, including the more remote Mescalero settlements as well, were virtually abandoned. Because of the proximity of the schools, the hospital, the traders' stores, the post office, the administrative center, and access to roads leading to the surrounding towns in New Mexico, most of the nearly 2,000 Apache residents of the reservation lived in one large community in the vicinity of the agency center. The descendants of the three Apache tribes—the Chiricahua, the Mescalero, and the Lipan—who have been housed on the reservation have amalgamated politically and economically and, after some initial resistance, have intermarried freely. Of the 1,190 persons listed on the Mescalero Reservation agency rolls in 1956, 502 were said to be Chiricahuas. How Chiricahua affiliation was determined was not specified. Certainly by this time many of these "Chiricahuas" must have been the product of mixed marriages, for in 1959 only 7 percent of the approximately 1,300 Indians at Mescalero were full Chiricahuas and 78 percent were of mixed ancestry (Boyer 1962:32, 33; Kunstadter 1961:148). Intertribal synthesis is characteristic of most aspects of modern reservation life at Mescalero. The majority of the members of the business committee are of mixed ancestry; the native language spoken is an amalgam of the ancestral Apachean dialects, with Mescalero perhaps dominating.

The Oklahoma branch of the Chiricahua, the Fort Sill Apache, has succeeded little better in maintaining its tribal identity. When the Chiricahua were first brought to Fort Sill and settled in "villages," extended families

left, Ariz. Histl. Soc. Lib., Tucson: 17,345; right, Smithsonian, Dept. of Anthr.: 270,093.

Fig. 6. Geronimo in captivity. left, Geronimo at San Antonio, Tex. He seems to be wearing army boots and socks. Photographer unknown, Sept. or Oct. 1886. right, Quiver and bow said to have been made by Geronimo. While a prisoner he made many items for sale to army officers and others, charging a higher price for the pieces he autographed (Debo 1976:353, 383). Length of bow 106.0 cm, collected by Allyn K. Capron before 1909.

Ariz. Histl. Soc. Lib., Tucson: 30425.
Fig. 7. Chiricahua chiefs Geronimo, Naiche, and Mangus at Ft. Pickens, Fla., where the leaders of the 1885–1886 outbreak were imprisoned for several months. Photographer unknown, 1887.

remained together and a good deal of work was carried on cooperatively (Opler 1931–1934; Pollard 1965:136–142). Pressure for conformity to tribal standards could be exerted upon families and individuals. In 1913, at the time of separation, it was the more traditional of the Chiricahua who departed for Mescalero and the more acculturated who remained behind. Those who stayed were settled on separate, scattered allotments on the outskirts of Apache and Fletcher, Oklahoma, purchased for them from the heirs of deceased Kiowa, Comanche, and Kiowa-Apache Indians. The Fort Sill Apache have never organized formally under government auspices, though they have an informal business committee that meets to consider matters of common interest. The Apache Reformed Church of Apache, Oklahoma, is the site of these meetings and of what socializing goes on within the group. Common agricultural interests used to hold the group together to some extent, but when large-scale agriculture came to Oklahoma in the 1940s and 1950s, the Chiricahua found that they could not afford the new machines or efficiently use them on plots of the size they owned (80 to 160 acres), and they largely withdrew from farming. As a result, dispersion has become still more pronounced, for breadwinners must seek work where they can find it. Intermarriage has further eroded tribal cohesion. In 1962 there were approximately 115 persons who were considered to be Fort Sill Apache. Even then over 30 percent of the adults were married to members of other tribes or to Caucasians (Pollard 1965:167). There is no reason to believe that this trend toward dispersion of the Fort Sill Apache and their absorption into the general population of the region will be reversed.

Population

It is possible that the full tribal strength was over 500 in 1886, for a large part of the Southern Chiricahua range lay in Mexico and it is known that remnants of this band survived in Mexico for some time. Chiricahua population statistics are very unreliable because the whole

Smithsonian, NAA: top, 52542; bottom, 52543.
Fig. 8. Chiricahua Apache children at Carlisle Indian School, Pa. top, Upon arrival from Ft. Marion, Fla., Nov. 4, 1886. front row, left to right: Clement Seanilzay, Beatrice Kiahtel, Janette Pahgostatum, Margaret Y. Nadasthilah, Frederick Eskelsejah; back row, left to right: Humphrey Escharzay, Samson Noran, Hugh Chee, Basil Ekarden, Bishop Eahtennah, and Ernest Hogee. bottom, 4 months later, seated left to right: Hogee, Escharzay, Kiahtel, Pahgostatum, Eatennah, Ekarden; standing left to right: Noran, Nadasthilah, Eskelsejah, Seanilzay, and Chee. Photographs by J.N. Choate.

Smithsonian, NAA; Ms. 2847.
Fig. 9. Housing built in 1896–1897 by the army at Fort Sill, Okla., for the Chiricahua local group led by Naiche. Photographer and date unknown.

tribe, until it had been decimated by wars, disease, and privation, was never enumerated. For a long time the existence of the Southern Chiricahua was not known to the American authorities, and the name Chiricahua was often used of the Central Chiricahua alone. In 1866, 1867, and 1868 the Bureau of Indian Affairs reported the population of the Eastern Chiricahua (Mimbreños and Mogollones groups combined) as 1,500 (ARCIA 1866:147, 1868:160). In 1873 and 1874 Agent Jeffords was able to congregate approximately 1,000 Central and Southern Chiricahuas on the Chiricahua Reservation (ARCIA 1874:291). Thus there is good reason to think that during the period 1866–1874 the full strength of the tribe was in excess of 2,500 persons. Since by this time the Chiricahua had already lost heavily in encounters with settlers and the American military forces, the tribal population very likely was 3,000 or more in 1850. That it was ever very much more is doubtful.

Culture at 1850

Political Organization

The Chiricahua band, like the tribe, lacked a chief and any vestige of organized political authority. Its boundaries were well known, and its members felt a strong attachment to their range. In aboriginal times the Chiricahua seldom sought mates outside the band. Band territories were ample enough so that most individuals carried on their ordinary tasks within band boundaries.

The bands were in turn divided into local groups, units of 10 to 30 extended families who inhabited and exploited a given section of band territory. The local group was always named after some prominent natural landmark of its range, though it could also be referred to by the name of its leader or "chief." The local group usually had a headquarters, a site favored for natural advantages such as ease of defense and access to water, firewood, and grazing land for the horses. Here a nucleus of the local group membership could usually be found, and though there were constant departures of groups and individuals on various errands, the 'settlement' (*go·ta, ko·ta*) could be expected to persist for some time. Yet these encampments were not permanent: penetration by an enemy, epidemics, a large number of deaths associated with the locality, failure of the water supply, overgrazing, a sharp reduction in the animal or plant resources of the immediate vicinity, the fouling of the locality through long occupation by too many people, or still other reasons might result in a move (Opler 1937:179–182).

It was in the context of the local group that as much central authority as the Chiricahua would tolerate was to be found. Each local group had a 'chief' or 'leader' (*nańtá, na·tá*) who had gained prominence because of esteemed personal traits such as sagacity, bravery, generosity, and eloquence. Frequently his stature was enhanced by ceremonial knowledge. Despite the fact that they are often represented in the literature as band or even tribal spokesmen, the historical figures Mangas Coloradas, Cochise, Victorio, Naiche, Chihuahua, Juh, Nane, and Loco were local group chiefs. Though the chief was undoubtedly the most influential individual of the local group, he exercised very little arbitrary or coercive power over his followers. He seldom decided any course of action without conferring with the other family heads. One of the important functions of the local group leader was to prevent or mitigate internal disharmony.

The office of chief was not hereditary. It had to be earned and to be validated constantly by appropriate activities and behavior. Consequently debility and age were factors in the retirement of a chief. A chief's children were expected to have had the benefit of excellent guidance and training, and therefore there was a tendency for a chief's son to succeed to his father's post. Yet this was by no means inevitable: the sons of the famed leaders Victorio and Naiche, for instance, were never considered of chieftainship caliber (Opler 1937:233–235).

The local group had very significant functions in regard to Chiricahua social and economic institutions. Though there was no strict rule of local group endogamy, the majority of marriages were contracted within the local group. Marriage entailed so many obligations and was so fateful for support of the extended family that it was considered essential for a family to be well acquainted in advance with the partner chosen for their child and with his kin. Moreover, it was an advantage to find a marriage partner who was thoroughly conversant with the resources of the local group territory. Families related by marriage were expected to interact with and support each other.

As a result of confidence in the local group chief, familiarity with local group territory, and the network of ties of blood relationship and affinity found within it, the local group was a strong and relatively stable social and spatial unit. Most economic pursuits were carried on within its boundaries, ordinarily war and raiding parties were drawn from men of a single local group, and the sponsors and visitors at ceremonial and social events were usually members of the same local group. Even when representatives of more than one local group joined in some undertaking, the members of each unit remained under the direction of their own leader. Viewed in this light, the band can be considered a loose confederation of local groups, and the tribe emerges as an equally loose union of the three bands.

There were apparently three to five local groups in each band. No person or family was committed to live in the same local group for his entire life. Marriage to a woman of another local group required a change of residence and affiliation for a man. Also, interfamily feuds, fears of witchcraft, economic reverses, or loss of confidence in the leader might induce a family to move from its local group territory. If this happened, the relocation usually would take the family to another local group of the same band.

Social Organization

Another important Chiricahua social unit is the extended domestic family. It was called by the same term used to designate the local group or large encampment (*go·ta*). Literally, the stem of this word conveys the concept of being among or with others. When it is used of the extended family, it is always coupled with the name of the family head, as in 'Naiche's family' (*na·'iči gogo·ta*). Since matrilocal residence was the rule, the extended family ideally was composed of a man and his wife, their unmarried sons and daughters, their married daughters, and the husbands and children of these women. At marriage sons moved to their wives' encampments, although this might not take them too far from their blood kin if the alliance was within the same local group. Yet, however near they remained, their principal obligations were henceforth to their wives' extended families.

The members of the extended family lived in close proximity to one another. Their dwellings formed a separate cluster, though each elementary family occupied its own home. The individual dwellings were necessary because of the avoidances and special usages that obtained between affinal relatives. When combined with the name of the family head, the term for home or dwelling (*go·γą, ko·γą*) had the force of 'household' or 'elementary family'.

Since the male component of the extended family fluctuated as marriages were contracted, the women were the anchors of this social unit. Mothers and daughters formed a work team that endured for the lifetime of its members. Because the tie between an extended family and a local group was usually permanent, the women matured and remained in a familiar natural setting and learned to exploit its resources efficiently. Their considerable contribution, economically and socially, had an important bearing on the high status of women in Chiricahua culture.

Most of the necessary economic tasks were planned and executed by the members of the extended family. The women departed together to gather wild food harvests and cooperated to process the foodstuffs upon their return. They cooked at a central place, usually the home of the oldest woman, and each married woman carried her share of the prepared food to her home for her husband and children. These women also assisted each other in tanning and sewing hides. Skins and game were shared with needy members of the extended family. Hunters who left in pairs or small groups were likely to be from the same extended family, and they shared the game with their companions: a successful hunter invariably offered anyone who accompanied him the hide and a portion of the meat. Though a war party for revenge drew from the local group, warriors of the extended family that had suffered the loss that precipitated the expedition were expected to play a major role in the conflict. In most matters the Chiricahua was sensitive about his individual rights. Yet the extended family was so central a social unit that he was taught to subordinate his personal wishes to its welfare (Opler 1937:182–184).

Subsistence

Chiricahua food economy was heavily dependent upon hunting and the gathering of wild plant foods. Obtaining game was the man's responsibility: it was considered inappropriate for a woman to be along on the hunt in any capacity. Even the presence of a woven basket, that symbol of female industry, was thought to be detrimental to success in the hunt. Deer was the principal game animal and, though efforts to obtain it intensified in the fall when the meat and hides were considered to be at their best, it was sought at any time of the year according to need. Men left for the deer hunt singly or in small groups; if they started out in groups, they scattered when the hunting ground was reached. A successful hunter was expected to share his kill with a tribesman who came upon him while he was butchering, and it was customary, even after a hunter brought in meat, to show generosity to neighbors and to the needy.

U. of Okla., Mus. of Art, Norman: 1569.

Fig. 10. Apache family on horseback. Horses occupied a prominent place in Chiricahua culture, serving as a primary means of transportation and, when times were hard, as a source of food. Owning many horses was a sign of general good fortune and prowess in raiding. The Apaches were superb horsemen, described by Gen. George C. Crook as the "finest light cavalry the world has seen." Tempera painting by Chiricahua artist Allan Houser, 1938.

The antelope was another very important game animal. Since it was usually found in fairly open country, it was considered more difficult to stalk than the deer, and additional techniques were employed to obtain it. An antelope-head mask was often used to get close enough to shoot ("The Apachean Culture Pattern and Its Origins," fig. 1, this vol.). When antelopes were plentiful in a locality, a surround in which mounted men participated was arranged. Relays of horsemen sometimes ran antelopes to exhaustion. The wapiti or elk was not present in the southern part of the Chiricahua range but was hunted wherever found. Other acceptable meat sources were wood rats, squirrels, cottontail rabbits, and opossums. Surplus horses and mules were eaten also. Wild cattle augmented the meat supply, and on raids, especially into Mexico, domestic cattle as well as horses and mules were captured.

There were a number of animals found within their tribal range that the Chiricahua would not eat. It was believed that the bear was an evil animal and that to smell it, to come in contact with its tracks or droppings, to touch its carcass, or even to look at it could cause sickness. The indiscriminate food habits of the peccary and turkey, especially their willingness to eat snakes and insects, were reasons for their rejection. Fish were excluded from the diet because their "slickness" reminded the Chiricahua of the dreaded snake (Opler 1941:316–332).

The Chiricahua diet depended as much upon the wild plant harvests as upon game, and much of the time and energy of the women went into gathering and processing this kind of food. In this work the women of an extended family acted as the producing unit. Because the plants that were sought grew at different elevations and matured at different seasons, Chiricahua families had to move frequently within the local group territory during the growing seasons. The search for plant food began in the early spring, when the new stalks of the yucca started to sprout, and lasted until late fall, when the nuts of trees were ready. Perhaps the most important staple was the agave or century plant. Its tender shoot was roasted, and its crown was dug up, trimmed, and baked in an underground oven. An effort was made to gather a great many crowns and to steam them together, and in this strenuous undertaking the men assisted in transporting the heavy crowns to a central point, digging the pit, gathering the rocks that lined the oven, and guarding the temporary camp. The baked agave or "mescal" was sun-dried and stored, and it supplied a sweet and nutritious food for many months.

Other important plant foods besides mescal were yucca (its stalk, blossoms, and fruit were used), mesquite beans, the fruit of the screw bean, agarita berries, sumac berries, juniper berries, the rootstocks of the tule, locust blossoms, onions, potatoes, many varieties of greens, sunflower seeds, the seeds of many grasses, acorns, pine nuts, piñon nuts, walnuts, prickly pear and other cactus fruits, raspberries, strawberries, chokecherries, mulberries, and grapes. The inner bark of pine was scraped to provide a sweetener, and the women were alert for the hives of honey bees in the stalks of the agave, sotol, and yucca and for ground hives. Foraging for vegetal foods was only a part of women's gathering activities; other plants were sought for medicinal purposes and for the making of artifacts such as baskets (Castetter and Opler 1936; Opler 1941:354–365).

The Chiricahua practiced a little agriculture, but not enough to affect the food economy significantly. Almost all the agriculture attempted was carried on by the Eastern Chiricahua, who had suitable lands just west of the Rio Grande in the Hot Springs area and who had considerable contact with early Mexican settlers of the region. Corn and melons were the initial crops raised. Pumpkins, squash, beans, chilis, onions, and potatoes were gradually added to the list. Ditch irrigation was employed, and both men and women shared the work. Only a minority of the families ever farmed, and the practice was probably of historic origin. By the time the Eastern Chiricahua became seriously interested in cultivation they were already so often threatened, assaulted, and uprooted that it was almost futile for them to attempt to farm (Opler 1941:372–374).

Division of Labor

Besides gathering, processing, and storing the plant foods in parfleches or cave caches, women busied themselves with many other tasks. They erected and maintained the home, usually a wickiup, a simple dome-shaped structure of poles and thatch, though occasionally, especially among the Eastern Chiricahua, a tepee was constructed. Drying and storing meat, carrying water, collecting fuel, cooking, and caring for the children fell to their lot also. In addition, women tanned, dyed, and sewed buckskins for clothes and bags, made the saddlebags, wove baskets of various sizes and shapes, applied the piñon pitch to the woven water jar, ground seeds and other foods on the metate, and fashioned spoons and dippers from gourd and wood. Not all Chiricahua groups used the parfleche, but where it was found, it was the women who manufactured and decorated it. A few Chiricahua women made unpainted pottery, sometimes incised along the rim. Men and women cooperated in the making of the quiver and bow cover. The women prepared the skins, the men cut out the pieces to be used, and the women did the sewing. The making of tiswin, a weak corn beer, was the women's prerogative (Opler 1941:375–386).

Men were occupied with hunting, raiding activities, and warfare much of the time. Each man made his own weapons (bow, arrows, shield, wristguard, lance, stone knife, war club, and sling) and kept them in repair. A man decorated his shield and other personal possessions (fig. 11). He braided rope of horsetail hair or rawhide, and he was responsible for the equipment for the horse—the saddle, stirrups, bridle, bit, and quirt. When a bullboat was needed in crossing a stream, it was the men who made it. Musical instruments, such as the flute or the "Apache fiddle," a simple stringed instrument, were also prepared by men (Opler 1941:386–396).

Life Cycle

Soon after birth a child's earlobes were pierced by his mother or maternal grandmother so that he would hear appropriate things and obey. Young children were considered vulnerable to evil influences, and so protective amulets were placed on their persons or cradleboards. Four days after birth or soon thereafter, a ceremony was held and the infant was laid in the cradleboard. When the child was ready to walk, clothes were made for him, and he donned them in a ceremony called "putting on moccasins." He was led through a pollen trail to the east in his new moccasins—a symbolic prayer for a long and successful journey through life. During the following spring a haircutting rite took place. All but a few tufts of hair were shorn; these were left to encourage the growth of new hair and, by extension, to insure the healthy growth of the child in all respects (Opler 1941:5–45).

Child training was eminently practical; a child was encouraged to perform useful tasks appropriate to his sex as quickly as he could manage them. Storytelling sessions acquainted children with the traditions and made them aware of the expectations of their elders. Children often witnessed ceremonies and soon became familiar with the belief system. Well before puberty children of both sexes went through a process of physical hardening and training. Emphasis was placed on arising early, running often, and engaging in strenuous tasks (Opler 1941:65–76).

When a girl reached puberty, an important ritual was arranged for her in which all her close relatives were sponsors, sharing the expenses and the labor. Special clothes were made and special food was prepared for her. Early in the morning of the first day of the four-day rite, a female ceremonialist who had been engaged for the purpose fed and clothed her ritually. This older woman was to advise and guide her for the remainder of the rite. Then the girl was led to a large structure by a male ceremonialist hired to sing songs to safeguard her health and longevity while she performed stylized dances. The girl was called by the name of the culture heroine during this rite, and she was subject to certain restraints. Many well-wishers were invited to the event and were entertained and fed by the girl's relatives. Masked dancers, impersonators of important protective mountain-dwelling deities, appeared in the early evening (fig. 12); social dancing by the visitors followed.

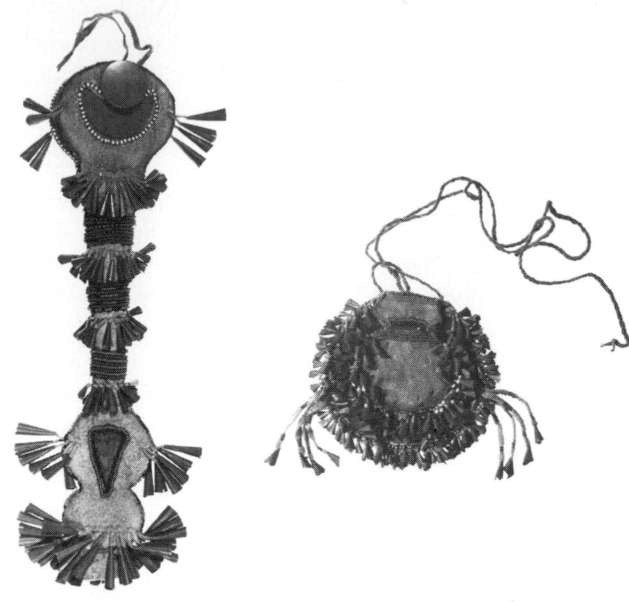

U. of Ariz., Ariz. State Mus., Tucson: left, E-5072; right E-5077.
Fig. 11. Containers attached to a warrior's belt. left, Buckskin pouch, with painted lines, beadwork, and cone-shaped tin pendants, which was probably used to carry tobacco; right, buckskin awl case decorated with beads, cone-shaped tin pendants, and red flannel. Both may have belonged to Juh. Length of left 10.2 cm, right to same scale; both collected by George W. Kingsbury in 1881.

For the boy the counterpart of the girl's puberty rite was his first four raiding expeditions. On these occasions the youth was addressed by the name of the culture hero, was subject to some of the same restrictions that had been placed upon the girl at the time of her puberty rite, and had to learn a special vocabulary to use during these ventures. At the successful conclusion of this period of trial, he, too, had earned adult status (Opler 1941:77–139; Opler and Hoijer 1940).

Marriages were arranged by family elders, though the young people involved were usually consulted to make sure they had no strong objection. The initiative was taken by the family of the boy, who often used the services of a go-between, and substantial presents were offered by the boy's relatives to the family of the girl. When a girl's family was approached, all close relatives who had supported her in some way were consulted; the presents, if accepted, were divided among them. After a marriage was agreed upon, there was little delay and no ceremony. Since matrilocal residence was the rule, a wickiup was built for the new bride near that of her mother and married sisters, and the groom joined her there as soon as the household was physically established.

Though his wife remained in familiar surroundings, the marriage state was a sharp transition for the husband. He was called upon to practice avoidance with his mother-in-law and his father-in-law and with his wife's grandmothers if they were still living. Though the parents-in-law could not come into the son-in-law's presence, they sent messages through their daughter concerning tasks that they wished him to perform. Still other members of his wife's family could call upon him for avoidance, and with some he used a "polite" form of speech. All these special forms implied respect, consideration, and economic help. Even the death of his wife or divorce did not automatically terminate them: the permission of his former wife's family was essential before a man was free to go his own way. Polygyny, though it was not particularly encouraged, was permitted to those who could afford it; almost always it was sororal polygyny. The sororate and levirate were both favored, and this assured children of a concerned stepparent when death struck one of a married pair. The constant interaction between siblings or cousins of the same sex contrasted with the marked restraint that existed between siblings or cousins of the opposite sex (Opler 1937:200–224, 1941:154–185).

The elderly were greatly respected in Chiricahua society: since there was an acute health anxiety and dangers to well being were many, to live to old age was considered a triumph over inimical forces. There was a constant effort made in ritual to improve a young person's chances for longevity by associating him with the symbols of old age. The ghosts of the dead could be very malignant and draw the living to them prematurely; but it was the unrequited ghosts of those who had died in the prime of life that were feared, and not of those who had lived fully and long and were past envy and contention.

At death a body was buried with dispatch in some rocky crevice at a distance from the encampment. The

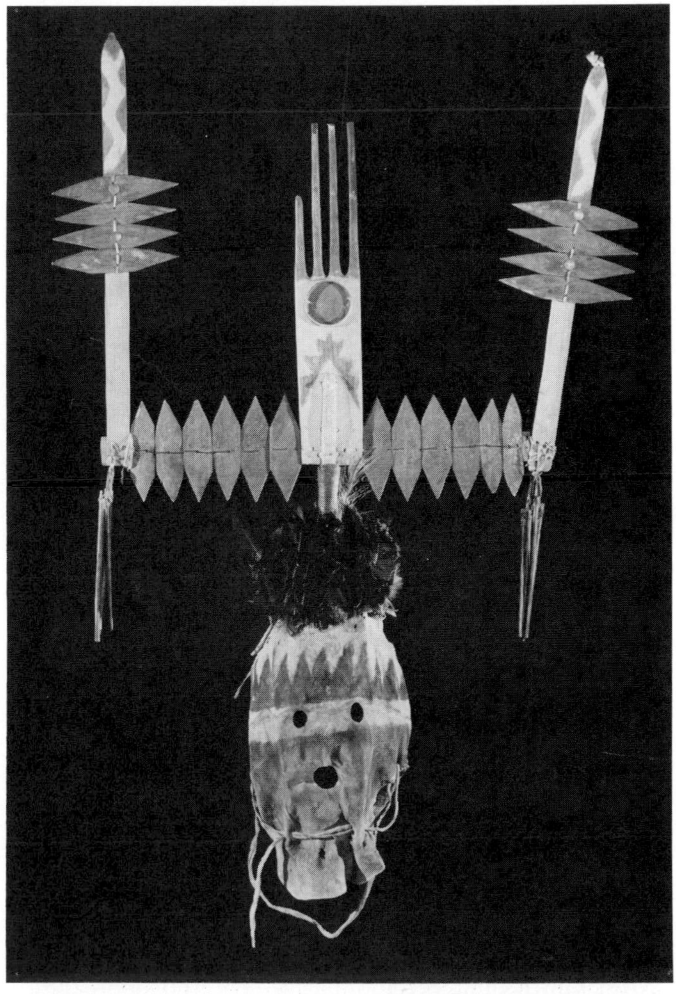

right, Denver Art Mus., Col.: 1947.260.

Fig. 12. Crown dancers. left, Three men dressed and painted to represent Mountain Spirits by David Fatty, a shaman (kneeling with drum), and his helpers, Matthew Fatty (left) and John Tonitu (center). This photograph was taken in the hills before they descended to take part in a puberty ceremony. Photograph by Morris E. Opler, July 1935. right, Mask used by crown dancer. Hood is painted buckskin (later examples are of cloth) topped with turkey feathers. Painted wooden uprights or horns are tied together with thong (see Opler 1941:110). Length 99.7 cm, collected by Morris Opler about 1935.

fewest possible relatives disposed of the corpse, and young people, who were "tender" and more susceptible to contamination, were kept from the scene. The wickiup in which death had taken place was destroyed; the personal possessions of the dead were either buried with him or burned. The close kin of the deceased wailed and cut the ends of their hair. So that they would not dream of the dead person or court persecution by his ghost, they bathed themselves in the smoke of burning sage and made liberal use of ashes, black obsidian blades, and other prophylactics. For a long time after his demise a dead person was not discussed, and his name was not mentioned. An angry ghost assumed the form of an owl, so the hoot of an owl at a time of bereavement was especially terrifying.

Ultimately the dead person had to begin his journey to the land of the dead. A deceased relative came to lead him: hence the strong belief that dreams or thoughts of the dead were harbingers of one's own early demise. The dead person was conducted by his ghostly escort to the edge of a break in the earth. At that point there was a cone of loose sand that crumbled when it was stepped on and carried the dead person below. Efforts to ascend it were futile. The underworld was a paradise filled with encampments of dead people who had been restored to health and vigor and who carried on the activities they had liked best during life. The new arrival was guided to the homes of the relatives who had died before him and joined his ancestors in this ideal replica of the culture he had known above (Opler 1936a, 1941:472–478).

Religion

The Chiricahua had a vague belief in a personified first cause, Life Giver, sometimes pictured as a sky god. Though prayers were occasionally addressed to him, he was not otherwise involved in the ceremonial round. Of more immediate importance were the divine culture heroine, White-Painted Woman, and her son, Child of the Water. The principal sacred myth described the birth of the culture hero, his triumphs over the personified evils that beset the Chiricahua in their earliest period, and the legacy of custom that he and his mother left to the tribe. Another group of deities were the mountain spirits, who lived in the highlands bounding Chiricahua territory and prevented epidemic disease and enemies from assailing their worshippers (Opler 1942:2–21, 74–79, 1946b).

Most Chiricahua ceremonialism centered upon the individual acquisition and manipulation of supernatural power. It was believed that the universe was pervaded by diffuse supernatural power that was eager to be of service to the pious but that could approach an individual (either a man or a woman) and teach him what he must do only through the medium of familiar beings and objects. Thus animals, plants, and celestial bodies became channels through which supernatural power appeared to individuals in vision experiences and conveyed to them the details of useful rites.

A typical ceremony lasted from one to four days and nights. It began with a formal request made to a shaman and the presentation to him of four ritual objects required by the "power" to insure its participation, for it was the power that achieved the cure or objective—the shaman was merely the intermediary. In the course of a ceremony there were likely to be ritual smoking; prayer; singing; the marking of the central figure with pollen, white clay, red or yellow ocher, charcoal, or specular iron ore; brushing with feathers; sucking at an afflicted spot with a tube; and the administration of herbal decoctions or special foods. There was much reference to the cardinal directions and associated colors and a marked tendency to group songs, prayers, and ritual acts in sets of four. The shaman was well paid at the conclusion of the rite with practical rewards such as horses, buckskins, and meat. Often food or behavior restrictions were imposed upon the patient to prevent a relapse. Ceremonies were most often conducted for curing purposes, but rites were also practiced to locate and confound the enemy, to find lost persons and objects, to diagnose rather than to cure an illness, and to improve luck in hunting, games of chance, and the pursuit of the other sex. A shaman might have multiple powers and ceremonies, each from a different source.

Chiricahua ceremonialism was complicated by witchcraft beliefs. Supernatural power, once it entered the human realm, was easily angered. The possible presence of power with evil intent and the known existence of malicious men who might be tempted to manipulate power for evil raised the specter of witchcraft, or ceremonies designed to harm rather than to aid. Accused witches were sometimes seized, tortured, forced to confess, and executed if they could not restore those named as their victims. Incest and witchcraft were associated and, indeed, almost equated: they were considered to be the two most heinous crimes, and a person suspected of incest was almost automatically labeled a witch (Opler 1935, 1941:224–315, 1946a, 1947).

Synonymy†

The Chiricahua Apaches are named after the Chiricahua Mountains in their former territory in southeastern Arizona. They are first mentioned in 1784 in Spanish sources that use the spelling Chiricagui (Thomas 1932:246, 249). The name of these mountains is of Ópata

†This synonymy was written by Ives Goddard.

Mus. of the Amer. Ind., Heye Foundation, New York: 16/1342.

Fig. 13. Ceremonial cord of 4 strands, each probably originally colored, with beads, feathers, and a wooden cross attached. The cross was to prevent the owner from getting lost (Bourke 1892:553). Length about 63.5 cm, collected by John G. Bourke before 1891.

origin (Nentvig 1980:21, 125). Variants of the Spanish name are Apaches de Chiricahui (Harrington 1940:519) and Chiricahues (Schroeder 1974b:127). Nineteenth-century English sources sometimes have spellings with *l* for *r*: Chilicague, 1861; Chilecagez, 1861 (Schroeder 1974b:188, 244). The spelling Chiricagua has also been used in English. The name was extended to include the Eastern Chiricahua only in the reservation period.

The Navajo name for the Chiricahua is *Chíshí* (Young and Morgan 1980:272); formerly this was used for the southern Apaches generally and included the Mescalero (Gatschet 1883b:78; Harrington 1936–1941; synonymy in "The Apachean Culture Pattern and Its Origins," this vol.). A similar Jicarilla name číšín (Harrington 1936, normalized) or chĭsh-hĭnd (Mooney 1892a), glossed 'red paint people', refers to the Chiricahua and, according to some sources, also to the Western Apache and other groups (Curtis 1907–1930, 1:135). Other specific names for the Chiricahua are borrowings: Mescalero *Chidikaagu* (Scott Rushforth, communication to editors 1981); Tewa tsirakawa (*sáve*) (Harrington 1916:573). The Apache who were familiar with the Chiricahua in premodern times appear to have named the bands separately; a table correlating some of these names is in Schroeder (1974b:264). Yavapai names, the scope of which is not clear, are kŭ-chḗ-sä (Corbusier 1921a:3) or kidjī´sa (Freire-Marreco 1910–1912) and Par-lar´-we 'play cards' (J.B. White 1873–1875); the first of these is matched by English Cochise (ˌkō'chēs) Apaches and was the source of the nickname of the Chiricahua leader Cochise. The Kiowa name *tò·k̀ɔ̀nsènhâ·gɔ̀* (Mooney 1892a, 4:25; Laurel Watkins, communication to editors 1979) has the same meaning 'turned-up moccasins' as the Tonkawa name given for the Mescalero (synonymy in "Mescalero Apache," this vol.). In Western Apache, the Chiricahua are sometimes included in a general name that refers to several Apache groups: *Ha'i'ą́há* 'Mescalero' (Perry 1972:48), 'Mescaleros and Chiricahuas' (Gatschet 1883:96), 'Mescalero, Jicarilla, and Chiricahua' (Philip Greenfeld, communication to editors 1981); several sources give the literal meaning of this name as 'eastern people'.

The Chiricahua refer to themselves as *ⁿdé* 'man, person, Apache' or by the borrowing *čidiká·go* (Hoijer 1938a:45, 104).

Bands

A number of subdivisions of the Indians now recognized as Chiricahua Apaches are separately named in the historical literature. In Opler's opinion (communication to editors 1975) names like "Pinery Apaches, Warm Springs (Hot Springs, Ojo Caliente) Apaches, Bronco Apaches, Coppermine Apaches, Mogollon Apaches, and Mimbres Apaches . . . properly designate no more than local groups or bands of the Chiricahua" even though they have been used by some "as though they referred to autonomous Apache tribes surrounding the Chiricahua." At the same time "from the point of view of the Chiricahua Apache the band was more important than the tribe. This is reflected in nomenclature. There is no true native tribal name for the Chiricahua, but . . . the [three] bands are named" (Opler 1937:179). These named bands, and their constituent sections, are listed above.

A different view is presented by Schroeder (1974b:9–326), who concluded that the Chiricahua of Opler had been in pre-reservation times five distinct bands with separate home territories: Mogollon, Copper Mine, Mimbres, Warm Spring, and Chiricahua proper. Of these the first four together (Schroeder's "Eastern Group") correspond to Opler's Eastern Chiricahua, and the last subsumes Opler's Central and Southern Chiricahuas. The Chiricahua proper continue the Chiricaguis of Cordero's 1796 account and the Eastern Group continues Cordero's Gileños and Mimbreños; presumably the Mogollon and Copper Mine correspond to the Gileños, and the Warm Spring and Mimbres to the Mimbreños (Matson and Schroeder 1957:336; Schroeder 1974b:189–192).

The lists of Chiricahua bands given in earlier sources can be largely identified and correlated on the basis of Schroeder (1974b:264) and Harrington (1936, 1937, 1939). In 1796 Antonio Cordero (Matson and Schroeder 1957:336) distinguished the Chiricaguis (called by the Apaches Segatajen-ne), Gileños (Tjuiccujen-ne), and Mimbreños (Iccujen-ne). A source from the 1770s gives the names of these three groups as, respectively, Segilande, Setocendé, and Chiquendé (Brugge 1961a:59–60). In 1874 Indian Agent Thomas J. Jeffords enumerated the Apaches on the temporary Chiricahua reservation at Sulphur Springs in three groups: Mimbres, Mogollon, and Coyotero; Cochise's band; and Southern Chiricahuas. Jeffords' three groups correlate with those of Opler, except that the Coyotero were a Western Apache band (Schroeder 1974b:261). Bourke (1890:115) named the bands encountered in 1883 as Chokonni 'juniper' (equivalent to Cochise's band; Central Chiricahua), Tidendaye or Nindáhe 'strangers' (Southern Chiricahua), Nadohotzosn (Coyotero), Chi-é 'red paint people' (Warm Spring), and Iya-áye (perhaps Mogollon, though the name matches that of a Western Apache clan—Goodwin 1942:600). Geronimo (Barrett 1906:12–14) listed as "fast friends" the Be-don-ko-he (his own band), Chi-hen-ne (Victorio's band, Warm Spring Apache), Cho-kon-nen or Chiricahua (in the narrow sense; Cochise's band), and Ned-ni (Opler's Southern Chiricahua). Curtis (1907–1930, 1:133–134) gives the Western Apache names for the Chiricahua "clans" as Aiahá^{n} 'people of the east', Ndĕ Ndái 'Apache half Mexican', Cho Kŭnḗ 'ridge on the mountain-side', and Cha^{n} Ha^{n} 'red people'; he also gives Aiahá^{n} as the Western Apache name for the Chiricahua, and the other three names, which are confirmed by Goodwin (1942:83), appear to correlate with Opler's divisions. Mescalero names for Chiricahua bands are: *Chíížhénde* 'red-ocher people' (Victorio's band); *Ch'úk'ánénde*, *Chishhénde* 'firewood people', and *Tséghát'ahénde* 'rock-pocket people' (bands under Cochise); and *Shá'i'ánde* 'people of the sunset (or West)' (Geronimo's band) (Scott Rushforth, communication to editors 1981). Mescalero *Tséghát'ahénde*, though not recorded in other recent lists, seems to match exactly Segatajen-ne, given by Cordero for the Chiricahua proper.

Sources

Though there are a good many books and papers dealing with the history and ethnology of the American Southwest that contain some material about the Chiricahua Apache, there are relatively few that deal wholly or largely with the culture of this tribe. In fact, the only study that attempts to offer a rounded picture of Chiricahua life before it was substantially altered by White contact is Opler's (1941). Opler (1942) published a volume on Chiricahua mythology and a detailed account of Chiricahua Apache social organization (1937). Because the harvesting of wild plants was so important in Chiricahua subsistence, Castetter and Opler (1936) described the ethnobotany of the Chiricahua and Mescalero Apache.

Because of the Chiricahua practice of living in mountain fastnesses or retreating to them when threatened, little reliable material existed about their divisions and territory until the mid-nineteenth century. Indeed they were seldom differentiated from the Western Apache before this period. Probably the best historical sources that chronicle the increasing awareness about the Chiricahua over time are by Forbes (1960), Lafora (1958), and Thomas (1932, 1959). The last was written for the land claims case being pressed against the U.S. government by the Chiricahua. For the events leading up to the final conflict with the Chiricahua and their temporary removal from the West, compact sources are the *Annual Reports of the Commissioner of Indian Affairs*, particularly for the years 1871–1877, and Welsh's (1887) report on the Apache prisoners in Florida.

Since the Chiricahua were one of the last of the American Indian tribes to be subdued and reduced to reservation life, and since by that time large numbers of settlers had moved onto Western lands and raised a great hue and cry about their perils and the savagery of their Indian antagonists, much public attention was centered upon the conflict at the time. Consequently, the events of the period are abundantly, if not evenhandedly, documented, and a good deal has been written about the military campaigns and the leadership on both sides (Bourke 1891, 1886; Davis 1963; Debo 1976; Thrapp 1972, 1974).

Mescalero Apache

MORRIS E. OPLER

Territory and Environment

The Mescalero (ˌmĕskəˈlārō) are an Apachean-speaking tribe* of the American Southwest, the southern Plains, and northern Mexico. The historical record shows that from the seventeenth century, when the Mescalero were first distinguished as a separate tribe, until the beginning of the reservation period in the third quarter of the nineteenth century the Mescalero continuously occupied essentially the same territories (fig. 1). Their western boundary was the Rio Grande, and though their settlements were located west of the Pecos River, buffalo and antelope hunts, expeditions for salt and horses, and forays against enemies frequently took them farther east. Their living sites and main activities lay south of 34° north latitude, but they have been known to travel farther north for short periods on economic errands. On the south their domain extended into northwestern Texas and the northern parts of the Mexican states of Chihuahua and Coahuila to the arid Bolsón de Mapimí.

Thus, the lands of the Mescalero were extensive, but they were not conducive to a large and concentrated population. The area associated with them is characterized by a series of mountain ranges with peaks that soar to 12,000 feet, separated by valleys and flats. The highlands are formidable barriers to travel, and the descent to the flats is often precipitous. Contrasts in climate, vegetation, and fauna match the sharp differences in elevation. Winters are severe in the mountains, and the short growing season there discouraged cultivation. The flats are hot and dry, especially in summer, and never supported a sizable population until large-scale irrigation was introduced. These topographical and climatic factors greatly influenced the economy and po-

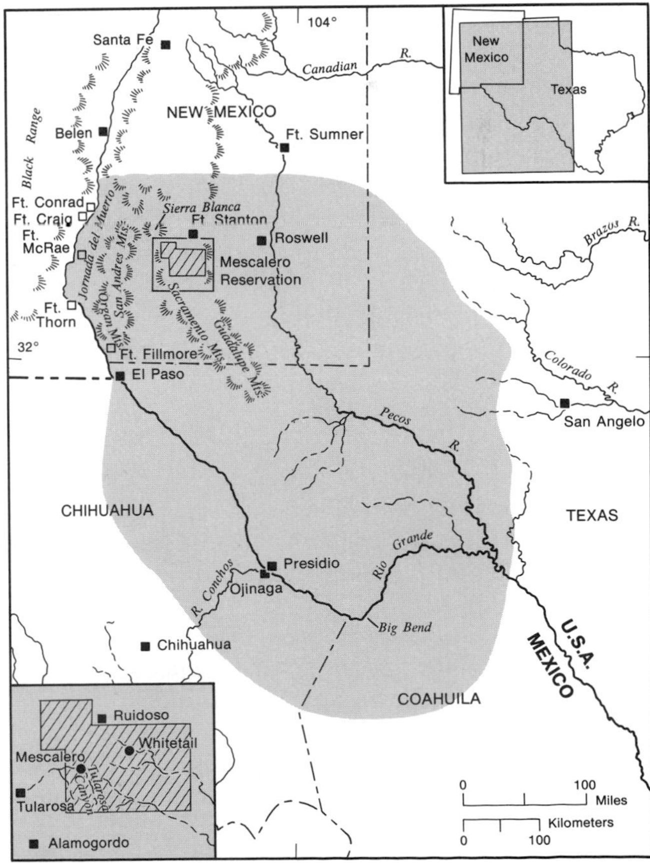

Fig. 1. Tribal territory in about 1830.

*Mescalero Apache words appearing in italics in the *Handbook* are written in the standard practical orthography used by the Mescalero Apache tribe's dictionary project, which uses essentially the same conventions as the Navajo orthography ("Navajo Prehistory and History to 1850," this vol.). The graphemic units are the following: (lenis unaspirated stops and affricates) *b, d, dl, dz, j, g,* '; (voiceless aspirated stops and affricates) *t, tł, ts, ch, k*; (glottalized stops and affricates) *t', tł', ts', ch', k'*; (voiceless continuants) *ł, s, sh, x, h*; (voiced continuants) *l, z, zh, gh*; (nasals) *m, n*; (nasals with stop release) *mb, nd*; (semivowels) *w, y*; (short oral vowels) *i, e, a, u*; (long oral vowels) *ii, ee, aa, uu*; (short nasalized vowels) *į, ę, ą, ų*; (long nasalized vowels) *įį, ęę, ąą, ųų*; (tones) unmarked (low), v́ and v́v́ (high), v́v (falling), vv́ (rising). In contrast to Navajo, the Mescalero orthography uses *x* consistently for /x/ and uses *gh* for /γ/ in all positions in prefixes and stems (pronounced [γʸ] before *i* and [γʷ] before *u*); *w* and *y* are used only in loanwords. Syllabic *n* is written *n* (low tone) or *ń* (high tone); in the pronunciation [ᵈn] it may be written *dn*.

Written in the *Handbook* technical alphabet (between slashes) the phonemes of Mescalero corresponding to these graphemic units and given in the same order are: /b/, /d/, /λ/, /ʒ/, /ǯ/, /g/, /ˀ/; /t/, /ƛ/, /c/, /č/, /k/; /t̓/, /ƛ̓/, /c̓/, /č̓/, /k̓/; /ł/, /s/, /š/, /x/, /h/; /l/, /z/, /ž/, /γ/; /m/, /n/; /ᵐb/, /ⁿd/; /w/, /y/; /i/, /e/, /a/, /u/; /i·/, /e·/, /a·/, /u·/; /į/, /ę/, /ą/, /ų/; /į·/, /ę·/, /ą·/, /ų·/; /v/, /v́/, /v̂/, /v̌/.

Information on the phonemic transcription of Mescalero words has been furnished by Scott Rushforth and Evelyn Breuninger (communications to editors 1981, 1982). A description of Mescalero phonology and some of the Mescalero forms cited are in Hoijer (1938a). The word 'icá applied to a widower was unknown in 1982 and could not be phonemicized.

litical structure of the Mescalero, who remained until the late historic period a numerically small tribe of hunters and gatherers scattered in small groups throughout their territory.

History

Spanish and Mexican Periods

It is very likely that the Mescalero were already in the territories with which they have been historically associated by the time Spanish exploration of the Southwest began. Certainly the Indians whom Father Alonso de Benavides found east of the Rio Grande in the early part of the seventeenth century in the region of New Mexico that came to be known as the Jornada del Muerto and whom he called Apaches de Perrillo after a local landmark were Mescalero (Hodge 1895:234). Benavides (1916:41) also bears witness to the cruelties and slave trafficking to which the Apache, including the Mescalero, were subjected and that fanned the hostilities that persisted for over two centuries. In 1653 Capt. Juan Domínguez de Mendoza led a force on a punitive mission against Apache of the Sierra Blanca (Scholes and Mera 1940:281), which can be identified as White Mountain, still one of the landmarks of Mescalero country as it has been throughout the recorded history of the Southwest. During the Pueblo Revolt of 1680 the Mescalero harried the defeated Spaniards as they marched south to reach safety. In 1682 Gov. Antonio de Otermín, bent on retaliation, invaded the Organ Mountains, a Mescalero stronghold. He saw evidences of Mescalero occupation, but the Indians were able to elude his force (Hackett 1942, 1:ccv). In 1684 Mendoza, still pursuing the Mescalero, led his troops down the Rio Grande from El Paso to La Junta at the junction with the Rio Conchos, then north to the Pecos near Horsehead Crossing, and from there to the Concho River near the present-day Texas city of San Angelo. At several points in his journey he learned of the presence of Mescaleros in the vicinity, and he was attacked by the Mescalero when he stopped to camp on the Concho (Bolton 1916:331, 335, 337–338). In 1692, during the reconquest of the Pueblos, Gov. Diego de Vargas also had difficulties with the Mescalero, who raided as far south as El Paso for horses and cattle (J.M. Espinosa 1940:200).

There was little improvement in Spanish-Mescalero relations during the first part of the eighteenth century. Spain did not recognize any Indian title to land and encouraged the exploration and colonization of conquered lands. Therefore, tribes who sought to defend their homelands against intrusion were harshly treated. Dealing in slaves, though illegal under Spanish law, was countenanced. It was difficult for the town-dwelling Pueblo Indians to resist the superior Spanish arms or to prevent the destruction or confiscation of their crops when they challenged the intruders. But the more mobile Apacheans could strike, flee, and usually elude pursuit. By this time not only were the Mescalero and other tribes east of the Rio Grande constantly attacking the Spanish settlements and animal herds, but also the raiding activities of the Apacheans west of the Rio Grande were increasing in frequency and ferocity. By mid-century the strain on Spanish military, financial, and administrative resources was evident, and the northern border was imperiled.

To cope with the growing danger, a comprehensive review of the possibilities for the defense of the northern frontier was authorized, one intended to provide a plan for a more effective distribution of presidios and forces. The Marqués de Rubí was delegated to make the study, and he began his inquiry in 1766. One of his tasks, of course, was to identify the tribes to be controlled, and his work and that of his cartographer, Nicolás de Lafora, yield a good deal of information about the location and movements of the Mescalero during the third quarter of the eighteenth century. The area that Rubí associates with the Mescalero is essentially that which has been previously described as their homeland. Lafora (1958) even charts the routes the Mescalero took when they traveled to and from their home bases within the territory. Hugo de O'Conor, who was allotted the task of implementing Rubí's recommendations for military action against the Mescalero and other disaffected tribes, spent four years trying to carry out his assignment. He had only limited success in subduing the Mescalero, but he did verify Rubí's account of the extent of Mescalero lands. His encounters with the Apache also made it evident that the terms Natagé, Faraones, and Mescalero were equivalent names for the same people or for branches of them (Thomas 1932:6, 10–11, 64). Since O'Conor's strenuous efforts failed to subdue the Mescalero or reduce their attacks, in 1776 the Spanish authorities created a commandancy-general of New Spain and named Teodoro de Croix as commander-general.

Croix attempted a number of strategies in dealing with the Mescalero. He launched several military campaigns against them. During his term of command, which lasted until 1783, his forces fought them in Coahuila, in what is today Chihuahua, in what is now the Big Bend of Texas, and in various places along the Pecos and Rio Grande rivers in modern New Mexico. Spanish expeditions penetrated the Sacramento Mountains, the Guadalupe Mountains, the Organ Mountains, and the Sierra Blanca range in attempts to dislodge Mescalero encampments. Because they favored mountain retreats and were less frequently found in an exposed position on the plains, Croix considered the Mescalero a more formidable foe for his soldiers than the Lipan.

Another device through which Croix sought to weaken the Mescalero was to set the Lipan and Mescalero against each other by granting favors to one tribe when it withheld assistance from the other or when it aided the Spanish forces. Still another approach of Croix was to induce sections of the tribe to settle on lands that would be reserved for them and where they could remain unmolested. One such settlement was established at the junction of the Conchos and Rio Grande rivers, but before long the Spaniards were charging that it was being used as a base for raiding, and hostilities began anew (Thomas 1941:37, 61, 89–90, 93, 125–127).

During the last years of the Spanish empire, policy toward the Mescalero alternated between military action and attempts to settle them in specified areas (Nelson 1936, 1940; Thomas 1932:5–9). Toward the end of the period of Spanish rule, when resources and energies were required for internal problems, the emphasis was on conciliation. In 1793 a large number of Mescalero agreed to stay at a tract along the Rio Grande near the present-day town of Belen, New Mexico. Even earlier another attempt had been made to locate a group of Mescalero near the mouth of the Conchos River. In 1810 the Spanish authorities entered into a treaty with the Mescalero whereby they were granted rations and the right to occupy a sizable area in Chihuahua and lands in New Mexico stretching from the vicinity of El Paso northward to the Sacramento Mountains. This treaty seems to have been effective and agreeable to both sides, for it was reaffirmed in 1832, 11 years after control had passed from Spanish to Mexican hands. Despite lapses into hostilities, usually originating in charges that Mescalero raiding parties had struck some settlement, attempts to pacify the Mescalero continued. Mexican officials engaged in treaty negotiations with Mescalero leaders as late as 1842, for they were eager to reduce their internal problems. The separation of Texas and the growing friction with the United States presented them with troubles enough (Thomas 1932:5–9). However, the Mescalero, who had little understanding of the political changes that were taking place but who had a deep sense of grievance over the indignities they had suffered at Spanish hands, transferred their animosity against Spain to Mexico, and the peace with Mexico was always brittle. When the Texans revolted, the Mescalero aided the insurgents. Later, when warfare erupted between the United States and Mexico, they favored the Americans. Unfortunately both Texas and the United States promptly squandered this good will and precipitated prolonged conflict with the Mescalero that probably could have been averted.

American Period

When titles to the lands of Texas and New Mexico were acquired from Mexico, it was assumed that the Spanish-Mexican precepts, which recognized no Indian claim to the land, also governed. Thus the Indians were considered squatters, obliged to move at the convenience of the Whites. Obviously the stage was set for misunderstanding and resistance. At first, when the American population was small and when large areas were without any White settlers and were even considered relatively worthless, it was thought that there was room enough for all without conflict. However, the determination of the American military leaders to link the West Coast with the East by good military roads, the discovery of mineral wealth in newly acquired western lands, and the tendency of discharged soldiers to remain in the West after the Mexican War swelled the population much faster than anyone had anticipated. Moreover, the conditions under which Texas entered the Union in 1845 gravely affected the Indians, including the Mescalero, who lived there. When Texas became a state, it retained all its lands and agreed to pay all its debts. These were substantial because of the costs of the revolt against Mexican rule. The federal government, since it retained no lands for itself in Texas, could not make the provision for the Indians that it did in other states and its territories. Whatever would be done for Indians in that direction would have to come from Texas. The Texans, for their part, were in no mood to consign lands to Indians. The land was the one resource from which they could raise capital to pay their debts and with which they could attract colonists and encourage development. In regard to the Indians, they felt that it was the responsibility of the federal government either to remove them to federal lands in Indian Territory to the north or to exterminate them. The Indians, who were continually dispossessed as the frontier moved northward and westward, were driven to acts of desperation. Forts and military units to man them moved westward with the population, and the federal forces, who considered themselves obliged to protect American citizens wherever they were menaced, found themselves increasingly involved in the struggle between the advancing tide of White settlers and the Indians. Finally, in 1855, two tiny reserves were set aside in the north of the state for some of the Texas Indians, and there was some talk of a separate reservation for the Lipan and Mescalero. However, in 1859, before any plan of this kind was implemented, vigilantes raided the existing reserves, and the resident Indians were hastily evacuated to Indian Territory. Major Robert S. Neighbors, United States superintendent of Indian affairs for Texas, who had supervised the exodus and who had sought to protect the Indians and their property, was assassinated from ambush as he was preparing to return to his home in Texas. His murderer was tracked down and shot by a posse the following year (Neighbours 1958, 1960). After the elimination of the Texas reservations, the Mescalero were considered fair game wherever they appeared in Texas.

In New Mexico also political and military events greatly affected the Mescalero. In 1845, when Congress voted to annex Texas, the move was bitterly resented by Mexico, and it sharpened boundary disputes between the United States and Mexico. War broke out between the two countries in 1846, and in 1848 a defeated Mexico ceded most of present-day New Mexico and Arizona to the victor. The rest, the southern part of these states, was acquired by the United States in the Gadsden Purchase of 1853. As a result of these developments, a very large percentage of the Mescalero came, at least technically, under United States control. The opening of new lands, the discovery of gold in California and Colorado, and the expansionist spirit that was stimulated by the war brought a heavy influx of people to the region. The land that the Mescalero considered their own was increasingly occupied by these strangers, and the game and foodstuffs on which they depended were steadily depleted. When they retaliated, military forces were dispatched to punish them. Strategically placed army installations played an important part in keeping the Indians in check. Between 1851 and 1855 six forts—Fort Conrad, Fort Craig, Fort Fillmore, Fort McRae, Fort Stanton, and Fort Thorn—were established in or near Mescalero centers in New Mexico, and from them campaigns were constantly launched (Gregg 1968; Frazer 1965). From 1856 on, there was frequent mention of settling all Mescalero on a reservation. This concept ignored the devotion of the Mescalero to their homeland and the fact that any single site chosen was sure to be the traditional home of only a small fraction of the Indians who would be forced to live there. Usually the locations considered were not climatically suited to the economic activities of the Indians since they were selected to accommodate the American conquerors. If mineral wealth was found on any reserve or if White settlers coveted some part of it, the boundaries were revised or the Indians were moved elsewhere. For instance, the borders of the present Mescalero reservation were altered more than once in response to the demands of miners.

At the beginning of the Civil War the Confederate and Union forces were preoccupied with their struggle over the territory, and the Mescalero were temporarily free of many restraints. As soon as he achieved military control, Gen. James H. Carleton resolved to remedy this. He planned a three-pronged campaign and ordered that none of the Mescalero men caught in the trap be spared unless they presented themselves at Fort Sumner or their leaders promptly came to Santa Fe and surrendered. One elderly Mescalero leader was slain as he traveled north to comply with these conditions.

Carleton was determined to concentrate the Mescalero at Bosque Redondo, a 40-square-mile area on the Pecos River at Fort Sumner. Some of the Mescalero escaped to the plains or made their way to west Texas or Mexico, but eventually most of those remaining in New Mexico were cornered and were confined at the Bosque under the eye of the military. Michael Steck, superintendent of Indian affairs for New Mexico, had told General Carleton that the Bosque would support only a limited number of Indians, that the drinking water was alkaline, and that fuel was in short supply. Nevertheless, Carleton decided that a large number of Navajo prisoners he had taken should also be sent to this reservation. Ultimately he concentrated over 9,000 Navajos and 500 Mescaleros in the limited space. By 1864 conditions at Bosque Redondo had deteriorated badly. Hail, frost, and crop failure led to hunger and discontent. There was armed conflict between the Navajo and the outnumbered Mescalero. In 1865 the crops failed again, this time because of cutworms. In November of that year all but nine of the Mescaleros slipped away from the Bosque and made their way to their former territories. General Carleton and his policies came under increasing attack, and he was relieved of his command in September 1866. By 1868 it was acknowleged that the Bosque was unsuitable for a reservation, and the Navajo, too, were allowed to return to their former homes (Bailey 1970; Thompson 1976; see "Navajo History, 1850–1923," this vol.).

In 1869 the army assumed control of the Indians of New Mexico. A.G. Hennissee, who was stationed at Fort Stanton, was ordered to take charge of the Mescalero, but the members of the tribe, fearing a repetition of the Bosque Redondo experience, sedulously avoided the fort and the lieutenant. In 1870, before Hennissee could overcome the suspicions of the Indians and make meaningful contact with them, the "peace policy" of President Ulysses S. Grant went into effect, military control was abolished, and a church-related agent was appointed to the Mescalero post.

One of the features of the new policy was the establishment of a Board of Indian Commissioners, composed of a group of eminent men who were to serve without compensation and advise the secretary of the interior concerning Indian matters. One of their members, Vincent Colyer, visited the Southwest and included recommendations for the pacification and settlement of the Mescalero in his report (Reeve 1938). Gradually the Mescalero became less distrustful and gathered in greater numbers near Fort Stanton to receive rations. In 1871 the agent, A.J. Curtis, was able to reach an agreement with one of the prominent leaders whereby the Mescalero were to be allowed to retain all their stock and would receive protection, a school for their children, and land for cultivation in return for remaining at peace in the vicinity of Fort Stanton. In 1872 attempts were inaugurated to define the specific boundaries of a reservation for the Mescalero, and in 1873 a reservation consisting mostly of the eastern slopes of the White and Sacramento mountains was created by executive order. The Indians complained that the area reserved for them was too small, and it should have been obvious that the elevation would make farming precarious. A good deal of suffering occurred, too, because the boundaries were such that the Indians had to remain in the high mountains in severe winter weather, a period during which they were used to camping at lower elevations. Yet a pass system was instituted, the boundary lines were enforced, and any member of the tribe found outside the limits of the reservation was treated as a "hostile" (Kappler 1904, 1:870–871; Reeve 1938:268).

The establishment of the reservation had other unpleasant consequences as well. The concentration of the Indian population and the influx of Whites in surrounding localities led to outbreaks of disease against which the Mescalero had little immunity. In 1877 there was a serious smallpox epidemic, the first of several such disasters. In a grim turn of affairs the confined Mescalero, who had been called thieves and plunderers for nearly three centuries, lost stock and possessions to bands of White outlaws and hostile settlers. In 1878 the Lincoln County War, a bloody contest between two rival groups of cattlemen, was waged in the vicinity of the reservation. The officials of the agency became involved in the struggle. The agent, a partisan of one of the factions, was relieved of his position, and the agency clerk was killed. Two hundred lives were lost during the hostilities, and the Indians were kept in a state of turmoil for some time (Opler and Opler 1950:27).

Still more difficulties lay in store for the Mescalero. The Desert Land Act of 1877 opened up additional western lands to settlement, and as both the White population and land hunger increased, sentiment grew for the concentration of the Indians on fewer and smaller reservations. The Chiricahua Apache, who lived just west of the Mescalero, were ordered to leave their homes and take up residence at San Carlos in Western Apache country. Some of the members of the Warm Spring band refused to comply and, led by Victorio, fled instead. The Mescalero were accused of giving him temporary sanctuary and of augmenting his forces as he continued south. To prevent them from giving any further aid to Victorio, the army moved quickly to disarm and imprison the Mescalero. In early April 1880 they were ordered to Fort Stanton, were persuaded by deliberate falsehoods to surrender their arms and mounts, and then were surrounded by 1,000 soldiers and forced into a corral where the manure lay several inches thick. Fourteen Mescaleros who resisted were killed. Others who had not responded to the orders to appear at Fort Stanton were hunted down and attacked. Their horses and possessions were appropriated by Indian scouts from other tribes who accompanied the troops, and they were imprisoned in the filthy corral until spreading sickness forced their release. Even then, though their rations were meager, they were not permitted to travel far enough from the fort to hunt and gather successfully. These miserable conditions continued without relaxation until Victorio was killed in battle in Mexico. The agent, S.A. Russell, was almost as indignant as the Apache over this episode, for he, as well as the Indians, had been deceived about the purpose of the order to assemble at Fort Stanton and had assured his charges that no harm would befall them if they obeyed orders (Thrapp 1974:268–274).

Although the Mescalero considered the reservation assigned to them too small for their needs, they were soon called upon to share it with the members of another tribe. The curtailment of Indian lands and the concentration of Indian populations had been an underlying feature of Indian-White relations since the time of first contact. Even the well-intentioned assumed this as inevitable. In his report on the Indians of the Southwest, Vincent Colyer, for instance, called for the housing of the Jicarilla Apache of the northern part of the state with the Mescalero and had discussed the possibility with Jicarilla leaders. Twelve years later, in 1883, the suggestion was implemented, and the Jicarilla were ordered to report to the Mescalero reservation. One of the reasons the Mescalero accepted the arrival of the Jicarilla without too much protest was that they had no clear title to the land set aside for them by executive order. Though they repeatedly pleaded for such action, it was not until 1922 that Congress confirmed the Indian title to the Mescalero reservation. Until then the Mescalero were constantly fearful of further constriction or removal, and through the years they several times had good reason for their anxiety.

If the Mescalero were not too happy with the turn of events, neither were the Jicarilla, who were discontented from the beginning of their stay on the Mescalero reservation. The members of the two tribes did not get along particularly well; there were enough linguistic and cultural differences to breed distrust. A Jicarilla exodus began in 1886, and by 1887 all the Jicarilla had left Mescalero and had made their way north to their former territory.

During the decade beginning with 1870 vast changes were taking place in American technology, economy, and outlook that would challenge aspects of former Mescalero life. In 1874 barbed wire became available, and the movements of men and animals were thereafter increasingly controlled. The completion of the Union Pacific Railroad divided the buffalo and brought hordes of buffalo hunters to the area. The southern herd was exterminated by 1875; the northern herd met a like fate by 1880. As a result of the changed conditions, the conviction grew among Americans concerned for the future of the Apache and among the Indians themselves that their survival depended on better educational and health facilities and on the acceptance of the principal features of American culture.

The implementation of these new ideas began modestly. In 1877 a day school was started at Mescalero for a limited number of children. In 1881 the Albuquerque

Indian School was founded for Pueblo and Mescalero children old enough to live away from home. The next year Mescalero parents were persuaded to allow three children to enroll. A boarding school was also established on the reservation in 1884. This became a hated institution to many Mescalero, for a number of agents, on the assumption that the only way to "civilize" the young was to keep them separated from their elders, did not allow them to visit their relatives and even denied them summer vacations. In 1883, the year of the Tertio-millennial celebration of New Mexico, a large contingent of Mescalero went to Santa Fe as representatives of the tribe. There they met with members of other tribes, state officials, and persons from all sections of the White community. They brought with them examples of Mescalero handiwork and in general made a good impression. It was one of the first times so many Mescaleros had traveled far from their own territory to engage with foreigners in peaceful pursuits.

Christianity was introduced to the Mescalero reservation in 1884, when a priest from Lincoln County baptized 173 members of the tribe into the Roman Catholic faith. Most of the Mescalero remained Catholic, at least nominally, in 1981. In 1885 a Court of Indian Offenses was set up, with Indians conducting the hearings and meting out sentences for minor violations. The next year attempts to improve health and curb epidemic disease were inaugurated with the vaccination of all the children against smallpox. Many a battle was to be lost on the health front before the tribe could prosper, however. For instance, contacts with outsiders, greater crowding, and poor nutrition brought a devastating tuberculosis scourge, one so serious that it threatened for a time to destroy the tribe. Certainly vast changes in housing, dress, economy, population size, education, and much else have occurred since then, but one can say that by 1885 the Mescalero had abandoned any thought of successful resistance against settler intrusion into their traditional territories and were reconciled to reservation life (Opler and Opler 1950:30–36). The Mescalero had entered the modern period, and its general pattern, though not its details, was evident. Yet regardless of all external changes, an inner core of cultural precept and belief survived, and despite all the buffetings to which it has been exposed over the years, it is still an active element of Mescalero behavior.

In 1981 the Mescalero reservation was occupied by members of three Apachean tribes—Mescalero, Lipan, and Chiricahua—who have intermarried and have become increasingly amalgamated. In 1903, 37 Lipans who had been driven into Mexico from Texas were brought to Mescalero to live. In 1913 the 271 surviving Chiricahua who had been settled in the vicinity of Fort Sill, Oklahoma, since 1894 were freed of their prisoner-of-war status, imposed after the Geronimo campaign and their removal from the West, and were given the option of taking allotments of land in Oklahoma or moving to the Mescalero reservation. One hundred and eighty-seven of them chose to go to Mescalero.

• SOCIAL AND ECONOMIC DEVELOPMENTS SINCE 1885 Though the Mescalero were pacified by the mid-1880s, their small numbers, their lack of U.S. citizenship and the franchise, their inability to obtain title to their reservation, and the misunderstandings bred by the contrasts between their culture and that of their White conquerors left their future very uncertain (Dobyns 1977; Kunstadter 1961:147–149). After a number of boundary adjustments to accommodate special interests, the reservation assumed approximately its present dimensions in 1883 (McCord 1946:22–23). In 1909 President Theodore Roosevelt issued Executive Order No. 862, which added the reservation to an adjoining national forest. Only a grace period in the Roosevelt edict and the rescinding of the order by President William Howard Taft (Executive Order No. 1481) prevented the Mescalero from being rendered homeless. Then, beginning in 1912, Sen. Albert B. Fall of New Mexico, who had acquired land adjacent to the Mescalero reservation, sponsored legislation that would have dispossessed the Indians and turned their homeland into a national park. It was not until 1922 that the Indian title to the land was confirmed and the threat of eviction and removal was dispelled (Dobyns 1973:80; Sonnichsen 1958:206–207).

Obviously the constant alarms and the uncertainties about the future did little to encourage economic and social stability. Moreover, the policy of consolidating Indian groups on fewer reserves was still in force, and it was some time before the tribal elements that came to constitute the resident population of the reservation were determined.

When the Mescalero were first settled on their reservation, they sought to maintain their traditional sociopolitical organization as well as they could in the curtailed space. Local group centers and house clusters grew up in different areas of the reservation, all at some distance from the agency headquarters and separated from one another. The local group leaders acted as spokesmen for their followers, and, as far as possible in the changed surroundings, former customs continued. During the period when the Jicarilla Apache were stationed at Mescalero, each of their two bands lived at different localities. They were separated from the other settlements, too, and therefore had very little contact with the Mescalero. When the Lipan first came in 1903, they also lived apart from others in one section of the reservation. Even in 1913, when the Chiricahua arrived, the Apache pattern of spatial separation prevailed, and they were concentrated in isolation at Whitetail, in the north-central part of the reservation. At first the only inducement that brought representatives of all the Indians to the agency periodically was the distribution of rations (Opler 1975:13–15).

The agency headquarters, initially at Fort Stanton,

were soon moved to a convenient spot along Tularosa Canyon, on the wagon road that ran through the reservation from northeast to southwest, which became U.S. Highway 70. It is still the only major road through the reservation and links Ruidoso and Roswell on the north and east with Alamogordo and Tularosa on the southwest. As government services multiplied the agency facilities were located along this road for the convenience of employees and to insure access to supplies. Even though the government concentrated its own personnel in one area, it favored the dispersion of the Indians over the reservation. This contradiction led to a duplication of services and a burgeoning of expenses. It became necessary to have schools, stores, health officers, and extension workers in each major local group settlement. The strain on the agency resources became intolerable, and the benefits to the Indians were meager. For its size and number of Indians, the Mescalero reservation became one of the most expensive in the country to maintain.

For a long time the Indians were satisfied to remain in the outlying settlements. They distrusted the agency officials, feared the agency hospital where deaths had occurred, and were sure their children would be mistreated and alienated at the agency school. Gradually some of these fears were overcome, jobs became available at the new facilities, and the trader's store offered a variety of products and a central meeting place. In response, a population drift toward the agency center began. The interaction among members of different groups led to intermarriage, and tribal and local group boundaries became increasingly blurred. When modern political life began in 1915, it was a matter of the recognized leaders of the several local groups meeting informally with the agency superintendent. They had little influence on decisions and no real power: they were called into council mainly to learn of courses of action already determined in Washington or at the agency headquarters and to relay information to their followers in the settlements. In 1982, when practically everyone lives in the town of Mescalero that has grown up around the agency buildings, the members of the Mescalero tribal business committee, the ruling body, are elected at large and constantly make important decisions. Though pride of heritage is treasured by some individuals, tribal distinctions have been sacrificed to the amalgamation process and to economic realities. All three tribes represented had different grievances to lay before the court of the Indian Claims Commission that was established by the government in 1946. To prevent gross inequities and friction if awards varied greatly, it was agreed that all would share equally in any compensation. The primacy of community over tribal interests reached its culmination in late 1964 when the tribal constitution, first formulated under the Indian Reorganization Act in 1936, was revised to make explicit the new relationships that had grown up. In this document all residents of the

U. of Ariz. Lib., Tucson: Special Coll.

Fig. 2. Baseball team, Cloudcroft, N. Mex. Photographer unknown, about 1908–1916.

reservation were defined as members of the "Mescalero Apache Tribe" regardless of historical tribal or subtribal ties. The feeling of all the Apache groups for bilateral descent was recognized, for it was declared that the children of one Mescalero parent would be accepted as members of the tribe and shareholders in it. Throughout this process of amalgamation the traditional Mescalero Apache have contributed much more than their name. They greatly outnumbered the Lipan and had gone far in absorbing them by the time the Chiricahua appeared. They had more than twice the numerical strength of the Chiricahua who chose to move to the reservation, and so they have been a potent force in the modifications—political, economic, and linguistic—that have taken place since. In regard to language changes, for instance, though all the languages of the three tribes resident on the reservation were mutually intelligible, there were phonetic, idiomatic, and grammatical differences. The Apache that is heard in the 1980s is somewhat closer to older Mescalero than to the others. Among the young, this generalized form of speech is slowly giving way to English.

The concentration of population near the Tularosa Canyon agency center has continued. Older houses that were worth saving were moved to the locality, and new housing has been built to accommodate the influx. In the vicinity are to be found the health facilities and, nearby, housing for elderly people who need medical supervision. Here is also situated a community building in which there are amenities such as an indoor swimming pool, bowling alleys, and meeting rooms and offices for the tribal business committee. At the northern edge is a flat area reserved for religious events, such as the girl's puberty rite, held in early July. Adjoining this is an outdoor stadium for the associated rodeo and other features of entertainment offered to the public during this four-day period when religious exercises are not in progress. At Bent, south of the agency center but just off the reservation, is a public elementary school attended by children of the reservation, Bent, and Tularosa (Dobyns 1973:85–86, 88; Opler 1975:5, 15–21; A.M. Smith 1966:71).

Vast changes have occurred in the social and economic status of the Mescalero since the reservation period began. At that time they were lowly wards of the government, dependent on rations, with no title to land, and with few possessions of any kind. Most of the cattle on the range belonged to White ranchers of the vicinity, who brazenly used the reservation for pasture without offering compensation. Many of the early agents were venal and colluded with suppliers to cheat the Indians of the meager rations allotted to them. Actual starvation was common, and malnutrition undermined Mescalero health for decades. Frequently agency officials were tyrants, imposing their warped ideas upon a hapless population about whose culture they had little understanding. Even so, at times the field agents knew more about the Indians than the Washington officials whose decrees they were called upon to enforce. It was not until Indian title to the reservation land was confirmed and all Indians were ruled to be citizens of the United States that the Mescalero were safe from caprice and sheer indifference. Another important milestone was reached in 1948, when, in a court decision, all Indians in New Mexico were granted the franchise (Anonymous 1948; Jefferis 1915; Kunstadter 1961:82–126; Meritt 1915, 1920; F.C. Morgan 1922:2; Stecker 1920; Stottler 1897).

Initially, agriculture was considered to be the means of making the Mescalero more self-sufficient, but rainfall on the reservation was sparse, barely 20 inches a year, and it was found that only a limited amount of small grains for fodder could be produced. The growing of vegetables on irrigated land for home consumption and the El Paso market seemed a likely prospect, but after dividing the waters of the Tularosa River with the Tularosa townspeople as the courts had decreed, it was found that there was enough left for the irrigation of only 300 acres. In stock-raising, sheep and goats were first emphasized. However, it was too expensive to issue large flocks to every family, and the token allotments that were made did not warrant the work and the expense of maintaining a sheep camp. Moreover, the high, broken, brushy country and the severe winters were not ideal for sheep-raising. Before long most of the sheep had been eaten or were in the hands of a few families who were more experienced than the others or who took a special interest in this kind of work.

Next it was decided that the abundant grazing lands were better suited to the raising of cattle. A tribal herd of registered Herefords was established, and, as it grew, the arrangements with surrounding cattlemen, who had finally been forced to pay a grazing fee, were canceled. A Cattle Growers' Association was organized to buy, sell, and run cattle and to care for the range. In order to provide some income for themselves, individuals were encouraged to purchase cattle on a reimbursable plan. These cattle and their issue received the owner's brand and were grazed and cared for in the tribal herd. For this service the owners paid the Cattle Growers' Association 25 percent of what their brand brought at cattle sales. Cattle owners were invited to contribute work on the range in lieu of payment, but this avenue was not open to women, the aged, and the inexperienced. There were years when drought damaged the range and made it necessary to reduce the size of the herd. Yet these were the very times when the costs of supplementary fodder and procuring water were high. Consequently there were periods, as in 1956, when the books showed a loss rather than a profit. Thus, while it generally produced a yield, it became clear that the cattle industry would not be the ample and dependable source of revenue that some had predicted.

For several years the fine stands of timber on the reservation were the mainstay of tribal income; but the market and price for timber fluctuated with the general economy, so that intermittently the gain here, too, was small. Moreover, timber cannot be cut at a lively pace indefinitely; there comes a time when the forest must be left to renew itself and alternative resources must be sought. Moreover, the earnings from timber were small comfort to the Mescalero, who were looking for per capita payments for themselves, since most of the income was used to defray the costs of running the reservation, including the salaries of White personnel and the maintenance of roads that were of more use to non-Indians at this time than they were to the Apache.

One of the assets the Mescalero tribe has sought to capitalize upon is the natural beauty of their reservation setting and its potential for recreational activities and tourism. Some of the ventures in this direction have been financed with funds awarded to them in claims court cases. Perhaps the most ambitious enterprise of this kind is a luxury resort hotel, the Inn of the Mountain Gods, with its magnificent view of the Sierra Blanca, an artificial lake, a golf course, and other attractions (fig. 3). The Mescalero have also invested in a popular ski-run area with five lifts and various other amenities, a motel-restaurant-gift shop complex, and a fish hatchery from which to restock the streams that flow through the reservation. These activities require substantial expenditures, both initially and in maintenance, yet they are extremely sensitive to the state of the economy.

The Mescalero tribe in 1982 owned and managed a general store once the property of a licensed trader, and this provided lower prices and some employment. However, this tribal venture cannot be expected to show large profits because it does not have the purchasing power or expert direction of the Tularosa chain stores and there is a reluctance to deny credit to relatives, friends, and neighbors. Its main function, perhaps, is to act as a training ground for Apaches interested in learning the rudiments of business management. Attempts have been made to develop an industrial park, and one or two enterprises, attracted by the prospects of cheap labor, have located there. However, the costs of transporting raw materials to and the finished product out of this rugged scenic paradise are higher than they would be in some other areas. Furthermore, Mescalero work habits, which traditionally favor alternate spurts of effort and relaxation, have not entirely accommodated themselves to the steady pace that industrial work demands. This is a factor that has been felt throughout the modern reservation economy. Because Mescalero is far from any large center, the people have tended to look inward for opportunity and security. Yet the types of enterprises best suited to the reservation—stock-raising, lumbering, and tourism—employ relatively few people. Unemployment and underemployment have been chronic, often involving 70 percent and more of the work force, and are reflected in the large amount of gambling and drinking that take place.

In 1948, in an attempt to cope with unemployment, the Bureau of Indian Affairs launched a program of relocating young Indians in jobs in urban centers. However, the close family ties and the long years of living in a segregated society did not prepare the Mescalero for the loneliness that developed in a city environment, and before long most of them returned. As a result, more attention focused on employing Apache in the enterprises close at hand sponsored by the tribe. In addition, greater effort was made to train young people for the positions that are available around the reservation. The economy must be varied and dynamic and the work force must be Apache and efficient if the Mescalero are to reach the standard of living their leaders have in view for them.

In this process higher levels of performance and greater educational opportunity are expected to play a large role. After enduring decades of the regimented reservation day school and the equally objectionable boarding schools on and off the reservation, Mescalero children began to be admitted to the public schools. By 1953 all Mescalero children were in the public schools that serve the Mescalero area (fig. 4). They tend to be shy and withdrawn in classroom situations, and their mere presence in integrated schools does not automatically mean that they are interacting freely with their non-Apache classmates. Yet slowly confidence is building up and barriers are falling. An increasing percentage of young people finish high school, and a greater number have been entering college. The interest of the tribe in such stirrings is demonstrated by the material help it is offering to finance college education; it has invested $600,000 of the claims money it received in a fund whose earnings are used to defray the college expenses of Mescalero students. It is a good omen that the Mescalero look to their young people and to the quality of their training in their efforts to build a better future (Crittenden and Maddison 1958; Dobyns 1973:81–101; Ferran 1964; R.K. Hall 1961; McCord 1946; McGraw 1975; Scott 1959; A.M. Smith 1966:71–80; Sonnichsen 1958:247–270; U.S. Congress. Senate. Committee on Indian Affairs 1931; U.S. Department of Commerce. Economic Development Administration 1971:267–268).

Traditional Counseling Program, Mescalero Apache Tribe, Mescalero, N. Mex.
Fig. 3. Inn of the Mountain Gods, a tribally owned resort. Photograph by Molly McGill, Feb. 1982.

Population

Estimates of Mescalero population at the middle of the nineteenth century vary from 750 to 6,000. Most of the figures are suspect, since much of Mescalero territory was imperfectly known at that time, the composition of the tribe was not well understood, and the numbers given sometimes reflected fears of the settlers and an appeal for military assistance rather than reliable fact.

Traditional Counseling Program, Mescalero Apache Tribe, Mescalero, N. Mex.
Fig. 4. Headstart children performing the Mountain Gods dance at the White Mountain Middle School, Ruidoso, N. Mex. Photograph by Molly McGill, Nov. 1981.

It is probable that there were about 2,500 to 3,000 Mescaleros about 1850. The wars of extermination waged against them by the Spaniards, Mexicans, Texans, and Americans, together with the malnutrition and epidemic diseases that followed in their wake, steadily reduced the tribe in numbers until the mid-twentieth century. At the low point, in 1888, there were only 431 Mescalero Apaches left. For several years thereafter the figure hovered around 450 and then slowly began to rise. Although intermarriage with Lipan, Chiricahua, and other tribal and ethnic groups makes a count of those who are predominantly Mescalero in lineage difficult, it is likely that in 1981 there were at least 1,000 individuals who could make this claim.

Culture about 1850†

Political Organization

• THE TRIBE Mescalero tribal cohesion depended upon unity in language, belief, and cultural practices rather than on concentrated leadership. There was no chief or leader who spoke for the entire tribe, and the units of the tribe were only loosely affiliated. Yet there is no difficulty in identifying the distinctive features of Mescalero culture.

It is impossible to tell whether the Mescalero ever had a well-defined band or moiety system. Their neighbors to the west, the Chiricahua Apache, were divided into named bands, and minor cultural specializations followed along band lines. In contrast, Mescalero culture was uniform throughout. Their fellow Apacheans to the north, the Jicarilla, had a moiety organization, with special functions allotted to each half of the tribe.

The subtribal divisions of the Mescalero are much less clearly defined. A terminological distinction was made between those who lived east of the mountains, 'the people of the plains' (*Gułgahénde*), and those who lived in the mountains, 'earth crevice people' (*Ni'i'ahénde*). Yet the difference between the two groups appears to be more geographical and semantic than functional. Though the terms carry the implication of an east-west division, no definite boundaries are specified. Leadership, the movement of people, and settlement patterns were little affected by the division.

• THE LOCAL GROUP AND ITS LEADERSHIP It may be that the importance of the buffalo hunt in Mescalero economy militated against the formation of any strong bands or moieties with well-defined and jealously guarded boundaries. The buffalo were available only in the lowlands to the east. Those who lived much of the year in the western section of the tribal territory and in the mountains could reach the buffalo grounds and share in this major tribal economic resource only by traveling without impediment through the eastern sections of the tribal territory. The Chiricahua could establish band territories within each of which the total round of subsistence practices could take place; the Mescalero required a more fluid arrangement.

The absence of strong, central tribal or band authority did not mean that the Mescalero were without leaders or a sense of community. At places considered fairly safe from enemy attack and easily defended, reasonably close to water, fuel, and forage for horses, and strategically positioned for purposes of the food quest, people tended to gather under trusted leadership. Such as assemblage of people associated with a specific area and leader can be termed a local group. Many of the residents of the local group would undoubtedly be kinsmen of the "chief" or leader, related to him by blood or marriage. Others would be friends and acquaintances of the leader or of residents, attracted by the qualities of the leader or the attributes of the local group territories. A local group might include as many as 30 families, but most were composed of considerably fewer such units. Though each local group was marked by a headquarters or settlement (*kuuta*), this was mainly a place from which to lay plans to exploit the surrounding area. Sometimes a local group was identified by reference to its leader. At other times the name of the place where the homes of its members were clustered was used in speaking of it. Seldom was the total population in residence at one time; small parties were constantly leaving the local group center on economic errands or returning to process what they had acquired. There were periods, as in the spring when the agave crowns were to be harvested and baked or in fall when buffalo fur and meat were at their best, when there was a general exodus and only a few old people and young children were left at the center.

The term for chief or leader of a local group (*nant'á*) and an analysis of his role and of the manner in which he was selected and replaced tell a good deal about Mescalero sociopolitical organization. The leader was invariably a man, though the society was matrilocal. This suggests that he was a person who had served his wife's kin well and had earned their good will and support. The office was not hereditary, though there was a feeling that the son of a leader, because he had an excellent model before him and the possibility of superior training, might be worth considering when his father was to be replaced. The office, once acquired, was not necessarily a lifetime position. The post constantly had to be validated by performance; when ill health, advancing age, or anything else interfered with a leader's effectiveness, he was quietly and often gradually replaced. Someone whose word carried more weight came to the fore, and before long it was this individual's

†This cultural summary is based primarily on field notes (Opler 1931–1935). For other overviews of aspects of Mescalero culture, see Castetter and Opler (1936:3–34) and Opler (1969:9–36).

Smithsonian, NAA: 2575-e-2.

Fig. 5. San Juan, a prominent leader. He wears a quiver and bowcase made from mountain lion skin, the material prized for this purpose. Photograph by R.W. Russell, 1880s.

advice that was shaping local group activities. Sometimes, of course, a leader retained his faculties, his drive, and his sagacity to the end of his life.

Once a plan of action had been decided upon in a local group, it was important that the leader guide its members toward the goal. Still, in determining that goal, he had been more of a sounding board than an originator of policy. He had great control over his own kinsmen, but unrelated members of the local group might drift away to other alliances if they felt that he had become too arbitrary or was an avid proponent of a questionable cause. A successful leader was sensitive to the views of other family heads and sought consensus rather than the acceptance of his own personal views. The word for 'leader' (*nant'á*) has a number of component shades of meaning, such as 'he who commands', 'he who leads', 'he who directs', 'he who advises'. Of these, the advisory role contributed most to his continued success. The head of a Mescalero local group who not only offered his advice but also tried to enforce it against determined opposition would soon see his following melt away.

The local group leader had to do more than sound out sentiment, give it voice, and offer advice. He had to be brave in battle and generous with the spoils of war and raid, especially to the needy. He was expected to be eloquent, for he was usually called upon to speak on public occasions. It did him no harm to possess a ceremony or two, for those who lacked the protection of supernatural power were considered vulnerable to attacks that could impair their health or judgment. Above all, he had to prevent or counter disruptive quarrels between local group members. The Mescalero sense of family solidarity and honor was strong, and consequently there were frequent tests of his skills as an arbiter of disputes and of his powers of persuasion.

Social Organization

• THE EXTENDED FAMILY Though the leader of a local group was the most respected and influential family head of the settlement and ordinarily had the backing of a family strong in numbers and prestige, the welfare and survival of the group depended on the presence and cooperation of other families much like that of the leader in structure. This resilient social unit, ready to join others in common endeavors but capable of accomplishing a good deal by itself when necessary, was the extended domestic family. Ideally it was composed of a married couple, their unmarried children, their married daughters, the husbands of these women, and the issue of these marriages. As this indicates, matrilocal residence was practiced: young men left their natal home to reside at the encampment of their parents-in-law; young women remained at the encampment of their parents and were joined by their husbands. All members of an extended domestic family did not live in one dwelling. Each elementary family of parents and children occupied a separate home. When a girl married, a new dwelling, positioned close to her parents' home, was erected for the new pair. Consequently, if an older married couple had a number of daughters, their encampment would consist of a cluster of dwellings in which they, their unmarried sons, their daughters, their sons-in-law, and their grandchildren (daughters' children) resided.

The social and economic lives of the Mescalero were in basic harmony with this family form. Girls were trained to work closely with their mothers and sisters and were taught that they would share the labors and fortunes of these relatives throughout their lives. Boys were urged to develop their bodies and their skills so that when they married and were called upon to provide for their families and contribute to the defense and support of their relatives-in-law, they would not be found wanting. At marriage a man might become attached to a local group other than the one in which he had been reared and might have to learn much about the resources of unfamiliar territory. Often, however, he married within the local group of his birth and was able to continue his activities in an area well known to him and to visit his relatives and receive support and counsel from them. In such an endogamous marriage the man's transition was less severe, but the obligation to obey, honor, and work for his parents-in-law persisted in any case.

These marriage and work arrangements offered considerable security to the Mescalero woman. After marriage her labors continued in familiar surroundings and in the company of those with whom she was used to cooperating in domestic chores. She was protected from abuse, for her husband owed deference and obedience to her parents, and any harshness on his part toward her could be reported to them.

The extended domestic family allowed the sharing of many duties. The men could hunt together and could carry out a good many other economic activities without the necessity of recruiting manpower from outside the family circle. The women could go out together on food-gathering forays of modest scope without calling upon others. They could also join in such work as the supervision of children, the making or repairing of articles of clothing, and the cooking of food for the households. In fact, it was common practice for the women to cook the food at the home of their parents or at some central place and then for each of the married women to carry an appropriate portion of the meal to her own home for her immediate family.

Even though it was the Mescalero man who was forced to make the major adaptations at marriage, it should not be thought that his lot was always unduly difficult. If he was a good provider and a considerate husband and father, his parents-in-law thought highly of him and would even reprimand their daughter if they felt that she was neglecting or alienating him. As time went on, the married man's identification with the local group became more pronounced; if he sired daughters, he would one day become the head of his own extended family and would have sons-in-law to do his bidding. Eventually, if he gained a reputation for courage and wisdom, he might become the leader of the local group into which he had married.

It should be remembered that while much of the routine work could be accomplished by members of the extended family, there were situations and endeavors in which the presence of a still larger group of people was most valuable and, indeed, crucial. The concentration of a sizable number of people discouraged enemy attacks or made their repulse more likely. The buffalo hunt and the gathering, baking, and transportation of the agave required many hands. To have the fairly self-sufficient extended families functioning in the larger local group setting provided for both ongoing tasks and less frequent emergencies.

• INTRAFAMILY RELATIONS Marriage arrangements were initiated by the parents of an eligible young man, often at the suggestion of the boy himself if he had a strong preference for a girl he had met or seen. Before taking any action, the parents ordinarily discussed the suitability of the alliance with other relatives, whose approval was usually accompanied by a contribution to the gifts that would be presented to the family of the girl. The father, or an eloquent go-between whom he selected to act as spokesman, then approached the girl's parents, spoke of the family's interest in their daughter as a wife for their son, detailed the manly virtues of the young man, and described the presents that would be given if the marriage were approved. The girl's parents were likely to say that they had great respect for the boy and his family but would have to consult relatives who had given them so much help in rearing and training their daughter. If the relatives raised no objections, the young man's family was notified, the promised gifts were delivered, the mother of the girl and some of her relatives built a separate dwelling near the parental home, and without any fanfare or ceremony the young man joined his wife in the new home. The presents, a token of the economic help the newly married man would henceforth render his wife's kinsmen, were distributed to those who had shared in the support and protection of the girl over the years.

Since residence after marriage was matrilocal, the work habits and associations of the girl continued much as before. However, her husband's companions in hunting and military ventures would now be his father-in-law, his unmarried brothers-in-law, and the husbands of his wife's sisters. He was expected to treat his wife's kin with great deference and respect. He was obliged to avoid coming face-to-face with his mother-in-law and his wife's maternal and paternal grandmothers. There were also other relatives of his wife who might request avoidance from the newly married man if they so chose. Such requests were great compliments, signifying approval of the marriage and affection for the kinswoman through whom the relationship had been established. Avoidance carried with it the obligation to defend the good name of the other party to the relationship and to extend economic aid and defense when necessary. The obligations were lifelong and could be abrogated only under unusual circumstances. Though the young married man did not avoid his father-in-law, he was required to address him in "polite form," a special type of speech that implied respect and mutual aid. There were other relatives of his wife who might request polite form to indicate their satisfaction with the marriage and their desire to establish formal bonds of regard and support with their new relative-in-law. The married man had serious and enduring ties to his wife's extended family, and there are good reasons why such usages developed: the girl's extended family lost their own young men at marriage and had to depend for survival on the loyalty and sense of duty of those who entered their ranks as in-laws. In keeping with this, though the Mescalero permitted polygyny, normally only sororal polygyny was encouraged: if a married couple had many children and the woman was overburdened with work, her husband might ease the situation for her by taking one of her sisters or female cousins (terminological sisters) as his second wife.

The extended family had safeguards even against the eroding force of death. When a woman died, her husband was said to become 'one who belongs to' ('icá) her relatives. If he had been a poor husband and provider, they might tell him that he was free to go. If, on the other hand, he had been an asset, they could invoke the sororate. After a decent interval of mourning, they would suggest that he marry a sister or cousin of his dead wife, and he could not very well refuse. Should he be resistant to their request, he would remain in the "belonging" category, and no family would allow one of their girls to marry a man in this state, for the issue of such an unsanctioned union would, it was believed, sicken and die. The tendency to close ranks in the face of death and preserve the full strength of the family went even further: the sororate was balanced by a levirate in Mescalero marriage practices. If a married man died, the widow was said to "belong to" her deceased husband's family. In case the family that had suffered the bereavement was a prominent one or they wished to make sure that the children of their dead relative would be well cared for, they could request that one of his brothers or his cousin marry the widow. Of course, if the marriage had been unsatisfactory, they would refrain from exercising their rights in the matter and tell the woman that she was free to marry outside of their family. Even though a marriage was disrupted by death, the avoidance and polite-form understandings to which it had given rise persisted during the life of the principals.

The maternal grandparents played a special role in the training and instruction of the young. They usually cared for the children when younger adults were away, and they took responsibility for imparting the first practical skills to their grandchildren. They were the traditional storytellers of the society and not only entertained the children with secular tales but also introduced them to Mescalero religious concepts and symbols through their recitals of the sacred myths of the tribe.

Siblings and cousins of the same sex enjoyed a very relaxed and cooperative relationship. The boys played and worked together, and even after being scattered in marriage they strove to remain in contact. An even more sustained bond existed among the girls, who had a lifelong obligation to work in harmony. The informality of these interactions contrasted sharply with the behavior of siblings or cousins of opposite sex toward one another. Such relatives took care not to be alone together, avoided physical contact, could not listen to anything salacious in the presence of the other, and in their encounters were formal, dignified, and sparing in speech. Any conspicuous departure from these standards started gossip and could inspire charges of incest and witchcraft, concepts associated in Mescalero thought.

Am. Mus. of Nat. Hist., New York: 50/8280.
Fig. 6. Doll made of cloth and dressed in typical woman's buckskin costume. Length 28.0 cm, collected by Pliny E. Goddard in 1909.

Subsistence

Mescalero economy rested on the hunting of wild game and the harvesting of wild plant products, though a little agriculture, inspired by the example of cultivators of the region, was also practiced by at least a few of the families. Of the game animals found at the higher elevations, deer were the most abundant, but elk and bighorn were sought, too. On the plains the buffalo was the principal source of meat, though the antelope and cottontail rabbit were hunted as well. Opossums and wood rats were taken when possible, and after their introduction by the Spaniards, horses, mules, and wild steers became important as food sources. Birds, such as turkey, quail, and dove, though hunted and eaten by some, were disdained by many others on the grounds that they ate insects, worms, and "nasty things." Fish, whose smooth, scaly surface reminded the Mescalero of the dreaded snake, were eaten by only a few. Completely avoided were the coyote, bear, snake, and owl, which were considered polluting and capable of sickening any who came in contact with them. The flesh of some animals—among them the squirrel, prairie dog, ringtail, and peccary—was acceptable to some but rejected by others. Several animals, such as the mink, beaver, muskrat, and weasel, were hunted, not for their meat, but for their skins and body parts, which were valuable for ceremonial use.

A large number of men joined together for the buffalo hunt, and men, women, and children cooperated in the rabbit surround, but most hunting was carried out by men singly, in pairs, or in small groups. Occasionally head masks were used to get near enough to shoot deer and antelope, or head nooses were placed along deer trails to snare the animals. Relays of mounted men might run antelopes to exhaustion. However, these were not common practices.

The uncertainties of the hunt and the Mescalero emphasis on generosity are reflected in the conventions of the chase. If a hunter who had tried in vain to make a badly needed kill came upon a more fortunate tribesman, he was entitled to as much as one-half of the meat and the hide. In any case, the hunter was likely to be approached by some infirm or needy person as he returned through the camps from a successful hunt, and he would rarely turn the suppliant away empty-handed.

The women occasionally aided in obtaining wood rats and prairie dogs and joined in rabbit surrounds. They accompanied the men to the buffalo grounds to help in the butchering of the meat, the preservation of the skins, and the transportation of what had been obtained on the hunt to the local group settlements. They took no further part in hunting, especially of large game, for they were exceedingly busy with the gathering of the wild plant harvests.

Agave (mescal) was especially plentiful in Mescalero territory, and there was great dependence on this food staple. In late spring, when the reddish flower stalks began to grow, the women traveled to an area where the plants were abundant to pry up the crowns that lay at the base of the new stalk growths and bake them in underground ovens. Men accompanied the women to help them dig the large roasting pit, to assist in carrying the heavy crowns to the oven, to stand guard while the work continued, and to help in the transportation of the baked material to the home encampments. Mescal was eaten fresh, was sun-dried and stored in parfleches for later use, or was placed in sealed caves for emergencies or times of scarcity. There was little edible plant material within the Mescalero range that the women overlooked. Sotol, though its crowns were smaller than those of mescal, was prepared in the same manner. The stalks of bear grass and amole were roasted, peeled, and eaten. The fruits and even the flowers of datil were utilized. The tunas of the prickly pear cactus, once the spines were brushed from them, were roasted, split, and eaten, and the fruits of many other cacti were gathered and relished. Mesquite pods, the pods of vetch and the wild pea, the pods and flowers of the locust, the screwbean, the fruits of the white evening primrose, the tubers of the sedge, rootstocks of the cattail, wild potatoes, juniper berries, and agarita berries were a significant part of the diet. Lamb's-quarters, shepherd's purse, purslane, and wood sorrel were sources of greens. The nuts of the piñon pine, western white pine, and western yellow pine, as well as acorns and walnuts, were gathered and were often mixed with other foods in cooking. A flat, baked bread was made from the seeds of pigweed, tumbleweed, and grasses such as dropseed. Sunflower seeds were harvested whenever possible. Strawberries, mulberries, raspberries, gooseberries, currants, grapes, hawthorne fruits, chokecherries, elderberries, and hackberries were part of the Mescalero diet. Mint, wild onion, sage, wild celery, pennyroyal, horsemint, and hops provided condiments. The inner bark and sap of the box elder and the inner bark of the pine and aspen yielded sweeteners.

Many of the plants that the women knew so well and could easily locate had multiple uses. The cattail, for instance, which has been mentioned as a source of food, also supplied pollen, indispensable for ceremonies, and foreshafts for arrows.

Division of Labor

Though men and women shared some of the tasks necessary to the garnering of the food supply and the maintenance of the family, there was a division of labor according to sex that guided most activities. Besides her responsibility for gathering the wild food harvests, the woman preserved and stored surplus foodstuffs; fleshed (fig. 7), tanned, and sewed skins for clothes and other purposes; made and painted parfleches; built the wickiup or erected the tepee; gathered firewood; kept a fresh supply of water at hand; prepared meals; cared for the children; wove baskets and pitch-covered water jars; fashioned the cradleboard (figs. 8–9); and brewed the weak corn beer (*túłibaí*) that the Mescalero considered so important to health and social occasions alike.

His hunting duties took a good deal of the time of the man. In addition he was entrusted with the safety of the camp, an obligation that required long hours of vigil when enemies were in the vicinity. He cared for the horse herd, sought to protect it from raiders, and went in pursuit when any were stolen. If the horse supply dwindled, it was his responsibility to catch and break wild horses to replenish the supply or to acquire more horses on a dangerous raiding expedition to enemy country. When his group suffered serious losses at enemy hands, he was expected to join a war party to exact revenge. If the casualties included any of his kin, he might even initiate such a war party. The man made and decorated his own weapons, the gear for his horses ("The Apachean Culture Pattern and Its Origins," fig. 8, this vol.), and his ceremonial paraphernalia. In any spare time he repaired his weapons, made additional

Mus. of N. Mex., Santa Fe: 36052.
Fig. 7. Woman fleshing deer hide, with a tool probably made from the rib of a deer or elk. Photograph by H.F. Robinson, 1908.

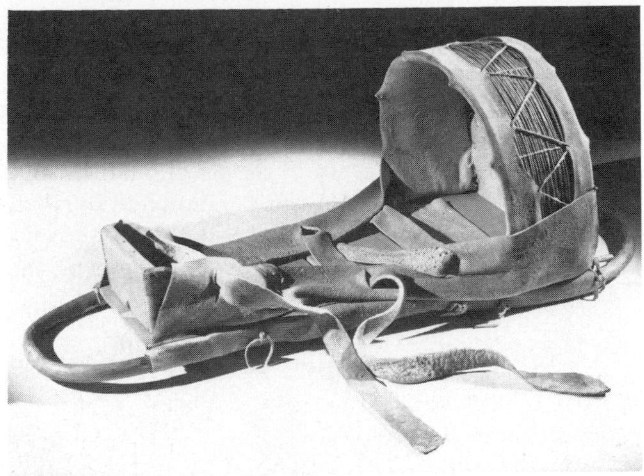

U. of Ariz., Ariz. State Mus., Tucson: E-3301.
Fig. 8. Cradleboard with ovoid frame of shaped branch with wood back slats and foot piece. The hood is of twigs, lined inside and out with tanned leather, which is also attached to the frame sides. Layers of crushed cedar bark or cloth cushioned the child who was wrapped in a blanket and strapped in with the buckskin ties. Length 86.0 cm, collected in 1957.

arrows, braided strands of rawhide into rope, or twisted buffalo hair or horsehair into rope with a distaff-type device.

Technology

Since the Mescalero were essentially nonagricultural and very mobile, their inventory of possessions was small, and their artifacts had to be portable. In the mountains the home was a dome-shaped structure or wickiup consisting of a framework of sturdy but pliable branches covered with grass thatching or hides; on the plains it was a skin tepee (figs. 10–11). In a household would be found pitch-covered woven water jars (for camp use, since on the march the Mescalero carried water containers made from the stomachs or intestines of animals), coiled tray baskets (fig. 12), large burden baskets of twined technique, dippers and spoons of split gourds, ladles of split mountain sheep horn, crude stone manos and metates, rock pounders, stone axes hafted to wooden handles, the distaff twisting tool for winding animal hair into rope, fire drills, drills of the lower leg bone of the deer, saddles, bridles, stirrups, cinches, whips, and saddlebags. For grooming there would be combs of mountain mahogany and brushes of folded and pounded mescal or sotol leaves. Hunting and warfare would be represented by shields with painted buckskin covers, bows and arrows, quivers, bow covers, wrist guards, spears, rawhide slings, flint knives, and war clubs of several types. The camps would contain musical instruments, too, such as hoof rattles, gourd rattles for use in the Peyote rite, drums, musical bows, flageolets, and one-stringed fiddles made of the flowering stalk of sotol. Though there probably would not be examples of them in a camp, when it was necessary to ford streams the Mescalero constructed a crude bull-boat of skins stretched over a circular wooden framework, or they built a raftlike structure.

Belief and Ceremony

The Mescalero had no large pantheon of gods and goddesses, but they did revere two powerful supernaturals: their culture hero, Child of the Water, and his mother, White-Painted Woman, whose exploits are recounted in their most important ritual narrative. According to this myth, in the early days of man's existence, his survival was threatened by a merciless giant and several other "monsters." To remedy this, a divine maiden came among the people, allowed water from overhanging rocks to drip upon her head, and miraculously conceived. She bore a son, Child of the Water, and protected him from the suspicious giant by various strategems. When the child was only four years old, he began to challenge the monsters and, in a series of daring feats, destroyed them all. The behavior of the culture hero and his mother during this stressful period and a great many objects and substances they used in vanquishing the monsters became incorporated into Mescalero ritual practice.

After the destruction of the monsters the people prospered and multiplied. The helpful supernaturals left the scene. Some of the inhabitants began to move away from the area. As they did, their language and their customs changed. One group remained in the original homeland and preserved the ancient language, usages, and memory of the contributions of the supernaturals. These were the Mescalero. Though the culture hero and his mother set the pattern of ceremonial concept and behavior and were frequently mentioned in ritual songs and prayers, once they departed they were no longer actively involved in the ongoing ceremonies. At the girl's puberty rite the maiden impersonated White-Painted Woman, but the divine woman was thought of as a model, rather than as a presence (Opler 1946d).

A number of life-cycle rites, designed to safeguard the individual from birth to maturity, were observed by the Mescalero. The first of these was the cradle ceremony, in which the infant was placed, with ritual gestures and prayers, in a carrier especially prepared for him. When a child took his first steps, another ceremony

left, The Reformed Church in Amer. Arch., New Brunswick, N.J.; right, U. of Ariz., Ariz. State Mus., Tucson:1012.

Fig. 9. Cradleboards. left, Woman on horseback with cradleboard and child. Photographer unknown, 1920s or 1930s. right, Woman carrying cradleboard. Lightweight and easily handled, cradleboards provided protection for infants and a safe means of transporting them. The bell hanging from the hood of the cradleboard is to entertain the baby. Photograph by Charles Morgan Wood, possibly in 1925.

Mus. of N. Mex., Santa Fe: left, 14524, right, 21553.

Fig. 10. Dwellings. left, Camp at Tularosa Canyon, N. Mex. Photograph by J.R. Riddle, 1885. right, Tepees in winter. The frame of a brush wickiup is visible at center. In prereservation times wickiups were used in high, rugged country, and tepees were used on the plains. Photograph by Kenneth Chapman, about 1915.

Natl. Geographic Soc., Washington: 100536-A.

Fig. 11. Woman seated in front of brush wickiup. Tepee is behind wickiup. Drying meat hangs from pole extending from top of wickiup. Photograph by Richard H. Stewart, 1936.

Smithsonian, Dept. of Anthr.: top, 204,653; bottom, 204,646.

Fig. 12. Baskets with distinctive wide flexible coil in natural white, yellow, and brown. Large simple patterns such as these star motifs are common. top, Diameter 44.5 cm, bottom to same scale; both collected by Walter Hough in 1900.

occurred: he was dressed in new moccasins and was led to the east through four footprints outlined in pollen. At a slightly older age, in springtime, when new growth was apparent in nature, the child's hair was cut for the first time while prayers were recited for his good health and long life. To encourage luxuriant growth thereafter, little tufts of hair were left at various places on his head. At the time when the boy was being trained for raid and war there were special observances of a protective nature. On the first four expeditions of this kind that he joined he could drink water only through a short length of hollow reed and had to refrain from scratching his person with his fingernails, using a small stick instead. He was supposed to remain grave in demeanor, to be respectful and obedient to the older men he was accompanying, to talk little, and to refer to a number of common objects by a vocabulary of circumlocutions that he had been taught.

The observances for the girl at puberty were much more formal and detailed. Since this event was a costly and intricate affair, the extended family began preparations well in advance. A woman who had the proper ceremonial knowledge was hired to supervise the making of the new clothes that the girl was to wear ("The Apachean Culture Pattern and Its Origins," fig. 6, this vol.), to dress her ritually, and to instruct her in the proper behavior for the occasion. A male ceremonialist, who was to lead her to the large structure (fig. 13) prepared for the more public aspects of the rite and who had mastered the large body of songs to which she would dance, was also engaged. It was customary for masked dancers, men who impersonated Mountain Spirits capable of protecting the Mescalero from hostile forces and epidemic disease, to appear at the girl's puberty rite and perform around a fire at night. A ceremonialist who had the right to costume these impersonators and to sing the ritual songs to which they would dance therefore had to be persuaded to cooperate as well.

The rite continued for four days and nights and ended on the fifth morning. Very early on the first morning the ceremonial tepee was erected, with the door facing the east. Meanwhile the girl was being clothed and blessed by her female mentor in a different place. When she was ready, she was led to the "Big Tepee" by the singer, who guided her with an eagle feather and sang as he went. In front of the Big Tepee other exercises took place, climaxed by four ritual runs to the east, which the girl made around a tray basket filled with objects to be employed in the rite.

In the evening the girl was again led to the tepee, and the ritual singing and dancing took place. The dance step performed was a difficult one, quite different from those in any social dance. The songs figuratively carried the girl through a long, fecund, and prosperous life. All the Mescalero symbols of health and happiness were invoked in the verses. The singing and dancing inside

Smithsonian, NAA: 44767-G.

Fig. 13. Camp prepared for a girls' puberty ceremony at Mescalero, N. Mex., July 1956. The brush-covered tepee seen at left, sometimes referred to as the Big Tepee, served as the focal point for the public aspects of the ritual. Photographer unknown.

the tepee went on late into the first night. Meanwhile there was social dancing in front of the ceremonial structure. After three types of social dancing had taken place in a given order, the masked dancers appeared and carried on their vigorous and colorful performance.

There was no morning ceremony on the second, third, and fourth days. The time was given over to visiting, feasting, playing games, and other social activities. The events of the second and third nights were little different from those of the first. However, on the fourth night the singing and dancing continued until dawn. At sunrise the singer painted a sun symbol on the palm of his hand with colored materials, and, as the sun's rays entered the tepee, he rubbed the design over the girl's head. The girl was then led to the east of the tepee, where a buckskin, decorated with footprints, had been laid. The tray basket had been placed well to the east of the tepee, filled with all the materials used in the rite. The girl walked toward the east through the footprints and began four ritual runs around the tray basket. Each time she completed a circuit the basket was moved closer to the tepee, which was in the process of being dismantled. By the time the girl was ready for the last run, only a skeleton of four poles remained. As she returned from her last run, they were pushed to the east, and the ceremony ended.

The song cycle of the girl's puberty rite was so long and the details so intricate that the singer had to learn it from someone who had been carrying it on before him and who was willing to instruct him. While he might be strongly motivated to perform the ceremony and might believe sincerely in its efficacy, he was perpetuating a tradition that he had acquired through study and practice, and not by ecstasy or inspiration. Thus he was a priest rather than a shaman.

Most Mescalero ceremonies were of a different type. They were obtained not from another person, but directly in a supernatural experience (Opler 1935). The Mescalero believed that their world was flooded with undifferentiated supernatural power (*dighį*), which was more than willing to help man if it was properly approached. Power had to reach man through some "channel." In the usual pattern of acquiring a shamanistic ceremony, power approached a Mescalero in a vision experience in the guise of an animal or natural force, offered him help in overcoming his difficulties, and, if encouraged, led him to a holy home, perhaps a cave, where a ceremony was shown him and its uses explained. Ceremonies obtained in this manner might serve various purposes, but, perhaps because sickness and debility were so catastrophic to hunters and gatherers, a high percentage of them were curative rites.

The Mescalero shamanistic system was extremely flexible. Ceremonies could be obtained by both men and women. A shaman might use his rite only in the service of his own family, or he might let it be known that he would be willing to help others, too. Because of excellent and prolonged rapport with power, the shaman might begin to feel that his ceremony had become more effective than it was originally. On the other hand, failures might diminish his faith in his rite, and he might cease to use it. Sometimes individuals who were very religious believed that they had received power grants from more than one source and were said to be "loaded up" with power. The inventory of shamans and ceremonies was always in flux.

The manipulation of supernatural power was not without risk. Power might be evil (*'éntį́*) rather than beneficent and might not reveal this to the recipient until he was well within its meshes. Persons who had posed as kindly shamans might turn out to be witches, bent on the destruction of those against whom they had some secret grievance or dislike. They might cause deaths and serious sicknesses until they were exposed in dramatic exhibitions by genuine shamans. The Mescalero world of shamanism and ceremony teemed with challenge and excitement, charge and countercharge.

• DEATH AND AFTERLIFE The Mescalero reaction to death was to repress the consciousness and memory of the sad event as completely as possible (Opler 1946c). There were no elaborate funerary rites. The young, who were easily contaminated, were kept away from the death scene. The corpse was washed and prepared by as few persons as were needed for the task, and the deceased was buried, with some of his possessions, as quickly as could be managed in a rocky crevice remote from the camps (fig. 14). The home in which the dead person had lived was destroyed, the rest of his possessions were burned or broken, the other elementary families of his extended family moved their homes, if only a short distance, to make sure that the encampment did not appear just as it had been when their relative was

Mus. of N. Mex., Santa Fe: 36076.
Fig. 14. Pieces of a cradleboard, together with other property associated with a deceased baby, were placed in a tree and allowed to disintegrate. The body was buried. The Mescalero believed that retention of possessions of the dead would stimulate acute grief and invite the return of ghosts. Photograph by H.F. Robinson, 1906.

alive. After his death the name of the deceased could not be used, particularly before his relatives. The bereaved created a smudge by burning sage or other pungent plants that were obnoxious to ghosts. Close kin cut their hair as a sign of mourning and shunned social activities for some time to show respect for the departed. Everything possible was done to encourage the ghost to enter the afterworld without delay. What was desired was a clear line of demarcation between the dead and the living: a ghost that lingered near the place of death or the dwellings of the living could sicken others and draw them to the "death side."

The land to which the dead went was pictured as an underground paradise. It was a land of clear streams, tall grass, and pleasant groves where the animals and plants that were the favorite food sources of the Mescalero abounded. It was a world without disease or sorcery, where the inhabitants could pursue forever the activities and pleasures that had given them most enjoyment during life.

Cultural Orientation

A number of streams of influence can be discerned in Mescalero culture. Some of the elements that suggest Pueblo inspiration are the presence of masked dancers who impersonate the supernaturals, the beginning of an agricultural complex, the use of the mano and metate, the appearance of pollen, turquoise, and abalone in ceremonies, the liberal employment of color-directional symbolism, and the utilization of the throwing stick. For that matter, Mescalero witchcraft lore may have received some impetus from the Pueblos.

It is obvious, too, that the proximity to the plains, the lure of the buffalo hunt, and the contact with Plains tribes have also left their impact, especially in regard to material traits. Clothing and hairdress show Plains influence. The Mescalero man wore a bucksin shirt, breechclout, leggings, and hard-soled, low-cut moccasins. His hair was braided and wrapped. The Mescalero woman, too, often wore leggings and braided her hair, though she did not wrap it. Mescaleros also plucked their eyebrows. When on the plains the Mescalero lived in a Plains-type tepee and employed a horse travois for dragging along the tepee poles and carrying the tepee cover. Parfleches were made, and geometric designs were painted on some of them. For a short time the Peyote cult, so common among the Plains Indians, was present among the Mescalero, but it was much altered in character in the Mescalero context and was early abandoned. The Mescalero war complex shows some Plains-like features. Upon their return from battle, for instance, the Mescalero warriors described their exploits and called upon others to bear witness to their veracity and bravery.

It is questionable whether Mescalero-Plains resemblances go much beyond surface manifestations. The travois was used, but it was crudely made and was not often employed to carry people or any amount of baggage. Some scalping was practiced, but its victims were ordinarily Mexicans, and it was considered a retaliation for the bounties that Mexican officials had placed on Apache scalps. Because of death fears these trophies were not retained as they were by Plains Indians. Moreover, characteristic features of Plains culture, such as graded war deeds, the Sun Dance, the camp circle, and men's and women's societies, did not exist, even in embryo, in Mescalero culture. In spite of other contacts that undeniably have left their imprint, it is within the general Apachean pattern that satisfying explanations of Mescalero thought and action are to be found.

Synonymy‡

The name Mescalero was borrowed into English from Spanish. Early uses in English sources are Apaches Mescaleros and Apaches Mescalorez, 1811 (Pike in Coues 1895, 2:632), Mezcaleros (J. Gregg 1844, 1:290), Muscallaros (Pattie 1833:117), and others listed by Hodge (1907–1910, 1:846).

In Spanish Mescaleros (also spelled Mezcaleros) means 'people of the mescal', a reference to the Mescaleros' use of this plant (*Agave* spp.), also called century plant, as a staple food; the name does not refer to mescal beans (*Sophora secundiflora*) or peyote. According to W.E. Dunn (1911:266–267) the first mention of the

‡This synonymy was written by Ives Goddard.

Mescalero by this name was in 1745, when Mescaleros and Salineros were given as the two names that the Spaniards in different areas gave to the Natagés, who ranged between El Paso and the Pecos River.

The first distinct Spanish reference to Indians that are likely to have been Mescaleros was the mention of the Apaches de Perrillo of the 1620s by Benavides (1945:84, 307). Other groups referred to in the later Mescalero territory and presumably in whole or in part Mescalero antecedents are the Sierra Blanca Apaches (of the White Mountain area of New Mexico), Apaches de los Siete Ríos, and Faraones (synonymy in "The Apachean Culture Pattern and Its Origins," this vol.). In 1726 the name Natagé (also Natagee) appears (Hackett 1931–1941, 3:236), and it is subsequently used as a synonym of Mescalero; sometimes the Mescalero are given as a subgroup of the Natagé or both are given together as if distinct but associated. Eventually the name Mescalero replaces Natagé, in the south, and Faraón, in the north (Schroeder 1974a:511–526).

In Hugo de O'Conor's list of Apache groups from the 1770s (Brugge 1961a:60–62) the Mezcaleros, Faraones, and Natagé are given separately, but the Apache names for the Mezcaleros and Natagé seem to be identical (Zetosendé and Zetocendé) and that of the Faraones is Selcaisanendé, which appears to be based on Mescalero *Dziłgais'ání*, the name of White Mountain (Hoijer 1938a:188, 213). Antonio Cordero's list of 1796 (Matson and Schroeder 1957:336) includes the Faraones (Yntajen-ne) and Mescaleros (Sejen-ne). A 1787 list of Apache groups (D.A. Gunnerson 1974:266) includes the Mescalero, Sendé (cf. Cordero's Sejen-ne), and Nitajende (cf. the *Ni't'ahénde* division of the Mescalero).

The names of the territorial divisions in the nineteenth century have been discussed by Basehart (1974:130–139). These are generally transparently geographical in reference, as for example the Agua Nueva Apaches (Agua Nuevo Apaches, Agua Nuevas), named after a town in Chihuahua, and the Apaches of the Organ Mountains.

The name Natagé is borrowed from an Apachean language and is based on the word for mescal (e.g., Chiricahua *ˀina·da*, Hoijer 1938a:47); perhaps the source is Lipan *ˀina·dahį́·* 'the Mescalero' (Hoijer 1975:7, 12, 13), nátahĕ´, ndátahĕ´, ĭnátahĭn 'mescal people' (Mooney 1897b). A corresponding Mescalero expression was recorded by Mooney (1897b) as the name of a division; nata-ĭ´ni or nata-hinde 'mescal people', but others have obtained this as a general self-designation (Bennett 1889–1894; Opler 1931–1935; Basehart 1974:157, 164). The fact that the earlier Spanish sources do not give this as the Apache name of the Mescalero (or even of the Natagé) suggests that its use in reservation-period Mescalero may not be old as a general term. Jicarilla also has nátahĭ´n (Mooney 1897b).

The Mescalero self-designation is *ndé* 'Indians, men' (Hoijer 1938a:189), also given as ǹ-^{n}dé 'person' (Hoijer 1938:77), or the borrowing *Mashgaléne* (Hoijer 1938a:188) or *Mashgalénde* (Scott Rushforth, communication to editors 1981).

Navajo uses a borrowed form *Mashgalí* and a partially assimilated *Naashgalí*, as if with *naa-* 'enemy' (Young and Morgan 1980:595), another recording being *Naashgálí* (Harrington 1940:520; Hoijer 1967:81). Chiricahua has *mašgaléń* (Hoijer 1938a:36, 37), and Western Apache has *Mashgalé*, beside *Ha'i'ą́há* 'easterners', a name also applied to the Chiricahuas (Perry 1972:48; Curtis 1907–1930, 1:134). A borrowed or unassimilated form of Mescalero is also attested in Sandia (Gatschet 1899:38), Zuni (Harrington 1913), and Kiowa-Apache (Harrington 1944).

The Comanche name for the Mescalero is *ˀesikwitaˀ* 'gray feces' (Casagrande 1954:231) or 'brown feces', a condition believed caused by the eating of mescal (Mooney in Gatschet 1884c:112). This name was borrowed as Kiowa *ésèkwìtà·-gɔ̀* (Laurel Watkins, communication to editors 1979).

Other names recorded for the Mescalero are Jemez *nį̨́ˀkʷa ḱʸǽlæ* 'southern Navajo' (Joe S. Sando, communication to editors 1978); Isleta tixitíwahû p'onín (Gatschet 1880:24); and Tonkawa *yakokxon-ˀecewin* 'turned-up moccasins' (Hoijer 1949:8, 40). The meaning of the Tonkawa name matches that of the Kiowa name for the Chiricahua (see the synonymy in "Chiricahua Apache," this vol.). Harrington (1916:574–575, partly phonemicized) gives three Tewa names for the Mescalero: p̓o-*yán sáve* 'water-willow Apachean' (gloss uncertain), tsise *sáve*, and *fa· sáve* 'yucca Apachean'. For the second of these see the synonymy in "The Apachean Culture Pattern and Its Origins" (this vol.); the last appears also as Tesuque Tewa pa-ha-sa-be´ (ten Kate 1884:8), showing [pʰa·] for *fa·* [ɸa·].

In Arizona the name Mescalero has been applied to southern Western Apaches (synonymy in "Western Apache," this vol.). Names glossed 'Mescalero' in early vocabularies of the languages of the Colorado River and southern Arizona may well refer to Western Apaches.

Sources

References to the Mescalero in books and articles of a general nature or mainly devoted to the study of other tribes of the Southwest are plentiful, but there are very few books and monographs that deal exclusively with the Mescalero or discuss their history and culture at great length. One of the exceptions is Sonnichsen's, (1958), which emphasizes Apache history from the early Spanish period to the present but also includes material on the culture. Dobyns (1973) gives a similar, though briefer, account. Opler (1969) contributes a Mescalero life history, copiously annotated to show the interplay between the individual and the culture. The first section is a general overview of Mescalero history and culture, intended to orient the reader and set the stage for the narrative that follows. Hoijer's (1938a) collection of texts was written with the linguist in view, but it contains ethnological as well as linguistic notes and offers a good introduction to Mescalero mythology. Two well-known historians have provided scholarly studies of the Mescalero. Thomas's (1974) monograph is an overview of the tribal history from 1653 to 1874. Bender (1974) covers the 1846–1880 period and is much more detailed. A monograph by Castetter, a botanist, and Opler, an anthropologist (1936), offers an introduction to the cultures as well as detailed ethnobotanical data.

Jicarilla Apache

VERONICA E. TILLER

The Jicarilla (ˌhĭkəˈrēyu) Apache are one of the six groups of Southern Athapaskans who migrated into the southwest between about A.D. 1300 and 1500. The route of the migration and the length of time involved continues to be in dispute among Apachean scholars. D.A. Gunnerson (1974:5) places the arrival of the Southern Athapaskans in the southwest at about 1525. Some scholars believe that the Jicarilla were part of the migrants who chose the route that led south into the north-central plains along the eastern edge of the Rocky Mountains. These Apaches settled into the region of western Nebraska, eastern Colorado, and western Kansas; they were the creators of the Dismal River aspect, 1675–1725 (D.A. Gunnerson 1956, 1974; Gunnerson 1960:252; Wedel 1961). This interpretation is based on archeological research and early Spanish records.

During the migration the bands separated, which led to a divergence among their languages. The Jicarilla language* is a dialect of Apachean (Southern Athapaskan), but along with Lipan it has distinct features that separate it from the others. This suggested to Hoijer (1956a:232) that these two groups migrated south at a later date than the Navajo, Western Apache, Chiricahua, and Mescalero and that the Jicarilla separated from the Lipan about 1300. (See "Apachean Languages," this vol.).

Environment

The native lands of the Jicarilla Apache (fig. 1) consist of the high plains country rising westward into plateaus and mesas with intermontane basins. The Southern Rockies, which extend from southern Colorado into north-central New Mexico, make up the western part. The elevation ranges from 3,800 feet in the Canadian River valley in the southeast to about 14,000 feet in the Rockies. The climate is moderate and pleasant. The precipitation ranges from 8 to 30 inches a year, most of it during the summer months, with winter rain and snow occurring chiefly in the mountains. The growing season varies from about 40 to 200 days. The vegetation consists mainly of short grasses and scrub pine. Approximately 67 percent of the area is grasslands; 16 percent produces coniferous forests, primarily of pine, spruce, and fir; 12 percent is woodland made up of piñon and juniper; and the remaining 5 percent is covered with desert shrub such as sagebrush and greasewood. The major rivers and streams include the Rio Grande, the Canadian, Vermejo, Purgatoire, Arkansas, Conchas, and Pecos rivers, and Ute Creek (*Jicarilla Apache Tribe* v. *United States* 24 Ind. Cl. Comm. 123).

Cultural Position and Tribal Divisions

The Apachean-speaking bands settled in separate locations after their migration from the north. They preserved much of their Athapaskan culture, but their ways of life were modified. These Athapaskans were influenced by the buffalo they encountered, the introduction of the horse, and their contact with other Indian groups such as the Pueblos. Over the years these influences blended into a combination of Plains traits and sedentary traits, which became typical of the Jicarilla and other tribes in this region. The Spaniards were the first to observe in them a way of life with two orientations, one of a semisettled agricultural people who lived in rancherias, and another of migrants who followed the buffalo out on the plains but returned to New Mexico to trade with and winter near the Pueblos of Taos, Pecos, and Picuris (Curtis 1907–1930, 1:54; Goddard 1911).

The cultural position of the Jicarilla has been defined as having elements of three cultural groups.

> The material culture and the war-path and raiding complexes show a decided orientation toward the Plains, [while] contact with the Pueblo peoples of the upper Rio Grande has left its impress in the development of a Jicarilla corn complex and in the ritual life. But despite the interesting differentiation towards Plains and Pueblo characteristics, Jicarilla culture is in fundamental agreement with a round of beliefs and traits which the Southern Athabaskan-speaking tribes share with one another. Jicarilla culture can best be comprehended as a growth and modification of this basic Southern Athabaskan pattern in terms of Plains and Pueblo influence (Opler 1936b:202).

In the late 1800s ethnologists who worked among the

*No separate study of Jicarilla Apache phonology is available to the editors, but apparently the language may be written with the same symbols as those used for Chiricahua Apache (see the orthographic footnote in "Chiricahua Apache," this vol.). The Jicarilla words cited in italics in this chapter are transcribed following Opler (1936b:202–204).

Jicarilla discovered two bands that had two orientations and were referred to in Spanish as Olleros (Potters) and Llaneros (Plainsmen) (fig. 1).

The Llaneros were composed of the Carlana, Cuartelejos, and Paloma bands, which occupied the region east of the Rio Grande through southeastern Colorado and southwest Nebraska. These bands migrated south into Texas during the mid-1700s and returned to northern New Mexico by the 1800s at which time they merged with the Jicarilla. Gradually the term Llanero was dropped in favor of Jicarilla (D.A. Gunnerson 1974:221–228).

Gunnerson claims that the Llaneros who are associated with the Lipans, Lipiyanes, and Natagees in the historical literature are the eastern band of the modern Jicarilla; but Moorhead (1968:202) and Kenner (1969:60) do not recognize them as Jicarilla.

There are no cultural or linguistic differences between the two bands, membership being simply a matter of residence. In 1880 and 1887 when they were located on reservations they lived in separate areas, and during the late 1800s they were also politically aligned against each other over the location of their reservation (Tiller 1976:86). By the mid-1900s the Llaneros were referred to as conservatives and the Olleros, as progressives (Basehart and Sasaki 1964:286).

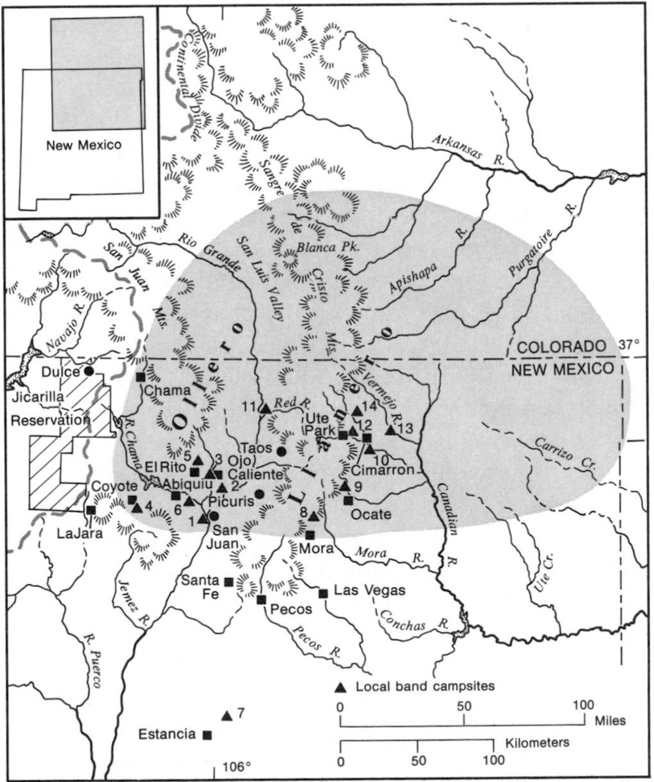

Fig. 1. Tribal territory with locations of bands and camping grounds of local groups, about 1850 (after Opler 1946, 1971a, Morris E. Opler, communication to editors 1982). Numbers refer to descriptions in the text.

Culture

Subsistence

The physical environment made it possible for the Jicarilla to carry on various economic activities, including agriculture; however, their mainstay was hunting and gathering. The large animals that they hunted were primarily the buffalo in the eastern plains, mountain sheep in the Southern Rockies, antelope in the eastern flatlands of New Mexico, and deer and elk throughout the mountains and foothills (Opler 1936b). Smaller animals such as the beaver, rabbit, squirrel, chipmunk, porcupine, and prairie dog were also hunted. Horses and burros were also used for food but only in emergencies as in a time of famine; they were not part of the regular diet.

These animals provided the material goods used by the Jicarilla. The large animals provided hides for tepee covers; sinew for thread; rawhide for ropes and straps; tanned skins for clothing, moccasins (fig. 2), and a host of household items. Some birds and animals, such as eagles, mountain lions, wildcats, and land turtles, were taken for their feathers, furs, or other body parts that were useful for clothing or ceremonial purposes (Opler 1936b:207).

In addition to hunting, the Jicarilla gathered wild berries and fruit of all varieties, acorns, piñon nuts, and seed-bearing grasses. A good portion of the herbs, tubers, and leaves that were gathered were used for medicinal purposes.

• AGRICULTURE Agriculture has been practiced by the Jicarilla since the late 1600s when their ancestors were described by the Spaniards as living in flat-roofed houses or rancherias, with their fields of maize, melons, squash, and beans in near proximity. Irrigation was used to supplement the scanty rainfall.

The development of agriculture was uneven because of the danger of raids by the Plains Indians who destroyed the crops. By the time of American occupation, the agricultural complex had fully developed. The Jicarilla were raising irrigated crops along the streams in the Cimarron and Abiquiu regions. There was a slowdown in these agricultural pursuits by 1848 due to constant encroachment by the Whites. With this decline the Jicarilla were forced to rely on rations issued by the United States government, and they also resorted to raiding the settlements. In 1887 when they were permanently settled on a reservation they continued to plant crops but the climate and soil were not conducive to farming so it was done on a very limited scale.

The origin of agriculture is attributed to the efforts of a man in Jicarilla mythology and for this reason it was the men who prepared the fields, worked the irrigation ditches, and helped with the harvest. The women did the seeding, hoeing, weeding, and harvesting. The

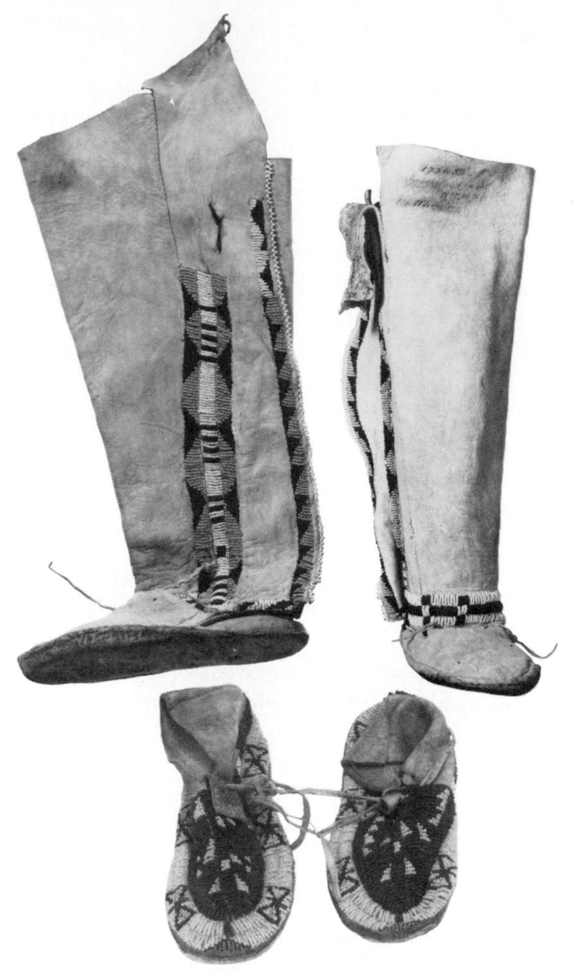

top, Smithsonian, Dept. of Anthr.: 17,345; bottom, U. of Pa., U. Mus., Philadelphia: NA 2170.

Fig. 2. Moccasins. top, Woman's moccasins with leggings attached and rawhide soles. Beadwork is white, blues, and green on the outer side of the leggings and around the ankle. bottom, Men's moccasins, Plains type, with rawhide soles and beadwork on the top and around the heel. top, Height 43 cm, collected at Tierra Amarilla, N. Mex., by the Wheeler Expedition in 1875. bottom, to same scale, collected at Dulce, N. Mex., in 1911.

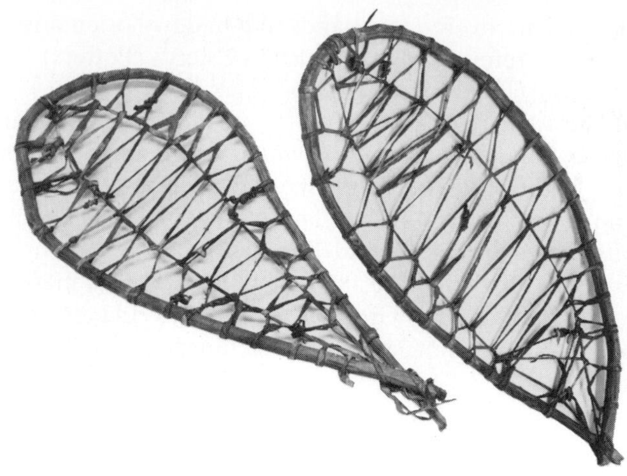

U. of Ariz., Ariz. State Mus., Tucson: E-17.

Fig. 3. Snowshoes, oval-shaped wooden rim tied together at heel end with cowhide lacing. They were formerly used in deep snow. Length 80.0 cm, collected by Grenville Goodwin in 1938.

whole process was a family effort, since the children also helped where they were able (Opler 1972:1141).

• HUNTING The hunting of large game animals was the duty of the men. Training for this role began in childhood, when the use of a bow and arrow was first demonstrated by the grandfather. A young boy was taught the use of proper whistles to attract birds and animals, the various trapping methods, and to recognize the animals and learn their habits. Horsemanship also was taught at a very early age. When the boy was proficient as a marksman, he was taken on his first big hunt in the company of experienced hunters. This was usually around the age of 12. During the first hunt, if the boy made a kill, this was the occasion to initiate him into the fraternity of hunters. He began learning all the elaborate and complex rules and rituals necessary to become a respected and lucky hunter. It was believed that each animal had its own habits and mystique, and it was imperative that they be respected. Even the wives and families had to observe strict rules of behavior while their men were out hunting.

Raiding and Warfare

An important corollary to hunting activities was raiding. It developed into an art after the horse was introduced into Jicarilla culture. The horse made it easier to hunt the buffalo, but sometimes horses could not be acquired except by stealing them from others, mainly the Plains Indians. Raids occurred whenever there was a need for horses. Gradually the raid, like the hunt, developed into a body of beliefs and rituals. It was attended by rigorous training that began at an early age. The proper rituals had to be performed before the raiders set out for the plains, and while on the plains the men had to observe strict rules of behavior.

Raiding naturally led to retaliation. When a Jicarilla was killed by the enemy, this called for revenge and war parties were organized. Again rituals were performed before the journey began. When the enemy was found combat ensued. The object was to inflict more casualites upon the enemy than he was able to do in return. Unlike the Plains Indians who counted coup, the Jicarilla preferred to kill their enemies. Individual Jicarillas did not take scalps but deferred this priviledge to the leader of the party, who had performed the prior necessary ceremonies with a tribal shaman before leaving on the warpath. This was directly related to the fear of death common to all Southern Athapaskans.

The raiding-war complex draws its influence from the Plains Indians with the exception of the scalping practices. As a matter of practicality, the Jicarilla adopted the material culture of the Plains Indians—the tepee,

U. of Ariz., Ariz. State Mus., Tucson: E-18.

Fig. 4. Parfleche, a rawhide container used to carry food or other goods, an adoption from Plains material culture. Painted in blue, yellow, red, black, and green on the 2 front flaps and the inner surface, the characteristic small triangles outlining the main design units were called "fringe" (Morrow 1975:86). Width 43 cm, collected by Grenville Goodwin in 1938.

travois, and parfleche (fig. 4), for example. However, they remained basically Athapaskan because they were never quite at home on the plains (Opler 1936b:205–211).

Social Organization

Like that of all other Southern Athapaskans, the Jicarilla social organization was characterized by the extended family with matrilocal residence. The family was the basic social unit, consisting of parents, unmarried children, married daughters, their husbands and children. The next larger unit was the local group made up of a cluster of families. These groups moved around together, shared common territory, and were led by elderly men and women, who were chosen for their sagacity, experience, powers of persuasion, and other leadership qualities. Members were free to come and go as they pleased. There was no formal political organization among the Jicarilla, but there was a hierarchy of leading religious leaders, warriors, and politicians, who dealt with other tribes and the Spaniards and Americans. In the period of American occupation, there were several chiefs for the Llaneros and several of the Olleros, and their chieftainships were usually handed down to their sons or close relatives (Tiller 1976).

The local bands had favorite camping grounds near some familiar landmark, a mountain or river. This pattern of residence was evident ever since the first contacts with the Spaniards, who associated different Apache bands with different landmark areas and so named the bands. This continued through 1850 when there were 14 local groups throughout northern New Mexico (see fig. 1). Six belonged to the Olleros and eight to the Llaneros. The Olleros were located: (1) west of San Juan Pueblo, (2) south of Ojo Caliente, (3) northwest of Ojo Caliente, (4) at Coyote, (5) along the canyons

Denver Mus. of Nat. Hist., Dept. of Anthr., Col.: left, 80–010; top right, 720/2; bottom right, U. of Ariz., Ariz. State Mus., Tucson: E-20.

Fig. 5. Domestic equipment. left, Adobe fireplace built inside house around a framework of bricks. It served as the focal point for cooking, eating, and other domestic activity. Photograph by Hendrina Hospers, 1945. right, Pottery of micaceous clay made by women (Opler 1971). top right, Bean pot, height 19.6 cm, collected in 1960; bottom right, pitcher, same scale, collected by Grenville Goodwin in 1938.

at El Rito, and (6) on the Chama River a little east of Abiquiu. The Llaneros lived (7) near Estancia, on the west side of Pedernal Mountain, (8) north of Mora, (9) north of Ocate, (10) near Cimarron, (11) on the Red River, (12) at Ute Park, (13) at the south end of the Vermejo River before it joins the Canadian River, and (14) along the Ponil River (Opler 1971a:317). These places must have been permanent camping spots, as Hibben (1934) identified more than 80 sites for the Jicarilla Apache in their claims before the Indian Claims Commission in 1958. Hibben based this work on his research in 1933 and 1934, when he was accompanied by Juan De Dios, an aged member of the tribe, who pointed out these sites used by his people after the American Civil War.

The key to the Jicarilla social system is kinship (see Opler 1936b:216–220). There are two determinants for one's social relationship, the one to which one is born and the other into which one marries. In the first ascending generation the father's brother is classified with the father, while the mother's sister is addressed as mother; hence all paternal uncles are surrogate fathers, and all maternal aunts are surrogate mothers. All parallel cousins are grouped with one's brothers and sisters, so that only cross-cousins are considered true cousins. Children of siblings and cousins of the opposite sex are called nephew and niece. There are two terms for grandparents, one for grandmother and one for grandfather, and there is no distinction between maternal or paternal grandparents. There is one term for grandchild, regardless of sex.

Marriages among the Jicarillas were generally monogamous; only in exceptional cases were they ever polygynous. A young girl was considered eligible for marriage after she reached puberty, but a young man was eligible if he could prove he was capable of providing for a family. The marriage was consummated when the man asked the parents for the hand of the bride, a dowry was offered, and gifts exchanged. A "long-life" ceremony could be held if the couple so wished, but otherwise the residence of the young man with his in-laws was enough to announce the marriage. Divorces occurred for many reasons, but they were not very frequent until the late 1940s and 1950s. If a spouse were to die the other partner could remarry within a year after the proper mourning period was observed and the proper cleansing rituals were performed.

Mythology

The Jicarilla describe their creation as the emergence of *hą·šč̓ín*, the supernatural spirit who was born of the union of Black Sky and Earth Mother who existed alone in the beginning. The parent supernatural beings lived in darkness in the inner womb of the earth; they dwelt within the body of their mother, the Earth. In the darkness of this underworld *hą·šč̓ín* was their leader. He created the animals, birds, Ancestral Man and Ancestral Woman. The first people were descendants of these two.

In this inner world, the sun and moon were created by the supernaturals and provided light for the underworld. Soon after, a conflict arose when the shamans

Denver Mus. of Nat. Hist., Dept. of Anthr., Col.: left, 73–093; right, 73–007.

Fig. 6. Women preparing food. left, Grinding corn with mano and metate, Dulce, N. Mex.; photograph by Hendrina Hospers, 1930–1940. right, Preparing tiswin, a mild alcoholic beverage made from sprouted corn that is ground, placed in water, and boiled down to the proper strength and consistency; photograph by Gertrude VanRoekel, 1940.

Denver Mus. of Nat. Hist., Dept. of Anthr., Col.: top, 80–024; bottom, 719/4.

Fig. 7. Women's clothing. top, Woman wearing one-piece dress with a wide leather belt. Items such as an awl case or small pouch were carried attached to the belt. Her hairstyle shows Pueblo influence. Photograph by Hendrina Hospers, 1920–1930. bottom, Dress of flowered cotton with slit in yoke for the head and loose sleeves. Length about 122.0 cm, collected around 1940.

began to claim that they had made the heavenly bodies and that they could control them. This disturbed *hą·šč̇ín* so much that he allowed the sun and moon to escape to the upper world.

The emergence of the people from the underworld to the upper world was the attempt to recover their sources of light. Twelve shamans who became known as *c̓a·na·tíh* were given powers comparable to those of *hą·šč̇ín*.

In the transition period, all powers were used to aid the ascent from the underworld. All the powers helped create the mountains, but they were not high enough to let the people reach the sun and moon. *hą·šč̇ín* constructed four ladders of sunbeams and the journey upward continued. Two old people were forced to remain behind in the underworld, when the worn-out ladder could no longer be used. They warned the people that all would eventually return to this underworld at death.

At the place of emergence, the supernaturals gave instructions and ceremonies to the people. The animals could no longer talk, and they were deprived of all their human attributes, but they were allowed to retain some of the powers they had used to facilitate the emergence. For this reason they were held in reverence by the Jicarilla, and special ceremonies were necessary before hunting them for food. If any rules were violated, the animals still possessed the power to punish the offenders.

The Earth acquired female attributes and for this reason the Jicarilla believed that people emerged from the underworld as man is born of woman today.

After the people arrived on earth they searched for suitable places to live. While the adults were thus occupied, the children during their play invented new languages and began numerous new dialects. Those who retained the original language remained together, and together they reached a region in the heart of the earth, which became the true home of the Jicarilla. These people considered themselves to be the sole descendants of the people of the emergence. During this time a strong tie was developing between the people and their lands.

On earth everything became a personification of *hą·šč̇ín*; all natural objects and living things became representations of his powers. The rocks and mountains were equated with bones of the human body, a structure necessary to life. The flowing rivers and streams are the lifeblood of all existence just as plant life is necessary to sustain life.

After they emerged from the underworld, the people discovered that the earth was inhabited by monsters, but these were slain by culture heroes who eliminated all obstacles that made the earth uninhabitable. The main character was the coyote trickster who was responsible for acquiring all cultural and behavioral traits of man through theft and cunning rather than physical aggression. All social institutions can be traced to this trickster. The emergence story and the related mythology became the basis for the ceremonial and ritual life among the Jicarilla (see Russell 1898a; Mooney 1898a; Goddard 1911). "The keynote of the Jicarilla world conception is a tremendous enthusiasm for life; a conception of a personified universe with which man may identify himself" (Opler 1936b:203–205).

Religion and Ceremonies

The rites may be classified into two general categories: the personal or shamanistic and the traditional or long-life ceremony (Opler 1936b:214). The power for the personal ceremony is derived from an animal, a celestial body, or some natural phenomenon, which selects its candidates from the newborn children of the tribe. In later years the power appears to the individual, and overtures for acceptance are made. The person may or may not accept the invitation to become a shaman. If the person acquiesces, he or she is put through an initiation to test his courage and if he proves capable, he undergoes a rigorous training period usually under the guidance of an established shaman. The individual has to learn a wide array of prayers, songs, and rituals, which could involve several years. During this time the recipient of the power has formed a tight bond with his power, which is finite; that is, the person is practically controlled by the power, which demands the observation of a rigid code of behavior. Punishment is administered if the rules are not adhered to. The power obtained can be either for good or evil.

The long-life ceremony has its origin and rationalization in the mythology of the emergence. This does not require a person to have a direct encounter with the supernaturals; rather, it can be taught by elders to promising and willing boys and girls. The most difficult long-life ceremony is the Holiness Rite or Bear Dance, which is a curing rite that has its spiritual sanction in the story of two girls who were stolen by the Bear and Snake during the emergence from the underworld and who were rescued and returned by the White and Black Gods. This rite has to be performed to cure Bear or Snake sickness. Other sicknesses, such as wind and fire sickness, can also be cured.

The ceremony is usually performed three days prior to the appearance of the full moon. It takes place within a large corral-like enclosure made of pine, spruce, or piñon, with an opening to the east. Within this corral there is a tepee where the patients are confined. On the first night, a person impersonating the Bear makes an appearance. If the patients are frightened by this, it confirms that they indeed have one of the various illnesses. The shamans preside over the patients and sing an average of 24 songs each night. On the fourth night the sacred clowns, who are painted with black-brown stripes, and the 12 *č̓a·na·tíh*, who represent the snake, make their appearance. All help to cure the patients with their special prayers and powers. Although Opler (1943) has emphasized the grotesque, obscene language and behavior of these clowns, this is only a minor part of the ritual. The major part of their role is to cure the patients and to pray for guidance and grace from the spirits. The clowns also give out a special bread, and women are allowed to dance single file on the south side of the corral. This ceremony is a major undertaking. Outside the corral, camps are set up to serve food and drinks to all who come; this goes on for four days and nights. During the ceremony, the women and men are allowed to dance to the songs. On the fourth night the tribal members are not permitted to leave the encirclement, even if it rains. In the morning all participants and patients may enter the tepee, receive the blessings, and exit to the east where all ailments are "deposited" on a tree, which had been prepared by the medicine men. Blankets are shaken out and cornmeal and pollen are scattered on the tree after the final prayers are said. They then all run back into the corral without looking back, where the medicine men paint their faces.

Another of the long-life ceremonies is the Jicarilla Relay Race, which takes place each year on September 13–15 (figs. 8–9). It is a combination ceremony–harvest festival. It derives its rationale from the mythological concepts of racing for sun and moon, with benefits for longevity and health to the runners and other participants. It also represents the duality of the food supply for the Jicarilla, who were primarily hunters and gatherers. The ideological background is to insure a balanced and regular food supply, for the Sun and Moon had enlisted the aid of the culture hero, the deities, the plants, and the animals. The race is between the Olleros, who represent the sun and the animals and the Llaneros, who represent the moon and the plants (Opler 1946:118).

The ceremonial track is laid out on an east-west course with circular structures at the end of each track, the doors opening to the east and west (although in the 1950s the doors were changed to open to the north). Preparations are made during the two days prior to the race, which include a preliminary race to determine the head runners, the ground drawing or sacred sandpainting, and the preparation of materials for the decorative painting of the runners. On the third day, the young boys run the relay. If the Olleros win, there will be an abundance of plant foods, and if the Llaneros win, animals will be plentiful during the coming year.

Since this Jicarilla ceremony is similar to several Pueblo races, it has been argued that it was borrowed from the Pueblos. However, Opler (1944:97) argues that "to all that they could learn from the Pueblos . . . the Jicarilla [already] have the social structure to accommodate it (the two bands), and a long-standing respect for Sun and Moon as important supernaturals, but, being primarily hunters and gatherers, they were spurred by a profound interest in a dual food supply, an even-handed interest which the more agricultural Pueblos could not match."

Whereas this ceremony emphasizes the role of the young boys, there is also a ceremony that highlights the girls who have reached puberty. This is the Puberty fiesta or Adolescence rite. Like the Holiness Rite or Bear Dance, this is a four-day affair, but it is held within a tepee presided over by several elderly men. The purpose of this ceremony is to pray that the girl can enjoy a long and fruitful life. She is usually accompanied by a young boy although there have been instances where the girl was accompanied by another girl or had the ceremony performed alone. During the four days the girl listens to the prayers and songs that tell of the origins of the Jicarilla, emphasizing the good and positive traits she should strive to imitate during her life.

Like the Bear Dance, this is a major undertaking for the family and relatives of both the girl and the boy. It is also a time for socializing, politicking, and renewing acquaintances. The Jicarilla Apache tribal council began a program of subsidizing this program in the late 1960s as part of its cultural preservation efforts. The end of the ceremony formerly signified that the girl was eligible for marriage; however, by the 1940s it was understood that this did not necessarily apply.

History

In the mid-sixteenth century when the Spaniards arrived in the Southwest they encountered Apaches in northeastern New Mexico, southeastern Colorado, and the immediate plains region to the east. The Jicarilla were a part of this larger group of Apache recorded in the early chronicles of Spaniards, who often called the bands by the name of the chieftain, their physical location, or their ecological practices. Their identity was also obscured by the tendency of the Spaniards to use only the generic name Apache to refer to all these groups (D.A. Gunnerson 1974:5; Thomas 1958).

If this line of reasoning is accepted then the Querechos whom Francisco Vásquez de Coronado and his men met on the plains between the Canadian and Red rivers in 1541 were ancestors of the Llanero Jicarilla. These Indians followed the buffalo and satisfied all their needs from this animal. Pedro de Castañeda mentioned that they were called Querechos by the people of the terraced houses and that they traded dressed skins with them and wintered near the Pueblos. D.A. Gunnerson (1974) points out that the early Apache traded with the Pueblos of Taos, Picuris, and Pecos and this fact is significant in establishing early Jicarilla identity. However, not all scholars accept this explanation (Harrington 1940:510).

The second Spanish contact with the ancestors of the Jicarilla was in 1595 when Juan de Oñate began settling the province of New Mexico. He dispatched Vicente de Zaldívar in September 1598 to the Canadian River region where he found Indians whom he called Vaqueros. His description of their lifeways was similar to that of Coronado's Querechos. Thomas (1958) and D.A. Gunnerson (1974:62) cite them as being one and the same.

As part of the Spanish policy that required the christianization of the Indians, Oñate assigned Fray Francisco de Zamora to the province of Picuris, which included the Apaches in the north and east. Fray de San Miguel was assigned to the province of Pecos including the Vaqueros of that area. This was the first time that a distinction was made between the mountain Apaches and the Vaqueros to the east. It was also the first mention of Apaches in the region where the Jicarilla emerge into recorded history in 1700 (D.A. Gunnerson 1974:57).

Benavides (1945) shed more light on the Apaches living in the mountains in the Taos and Picuris region in 1630. He reported the religious conversion of a group of Apaches who resided in rancherias about 10 leagues north of Taos under the leadership of a Captain Quinia. D.A. Gunnerson (1974:70–71) claims that philological research has linked the name Quinia specifically with modern Jicarilla. The terms Quinia and Kiñya´-īnde both could mean people who reside in houses: the Mescalero Apaches and Navajo still call the Jicarilla kiñya´-īnde. Later in history these Apaches are again encountered living in much the same fashion as was described by Benavides. (For another view, see the synonymy in "The Apachean Culture Pattern and Its Origins," this vol.).

Early contacts between Spaniards and Apaches apparently were limited, since references to the Jicarilla and other tribes are rather obscure in the records from 1630 to 1690. Relations between the Spaniards and the Pueblos were strained: some Pueblos began to take refuge among the Apaches. Due to their influence, the Apaches began to adopt a semisedentary way of life, including horticulture along with irrigation and pottery making (D.A. Gunnerson 1974:90).

During the Pueblo Revolt of 1680 the Achos were the only Apaches who joined with Taos and Picuris in killing the Spanish residents of that area (D.A. Gunnerson 1974:100). But when Diego de Vargas reconquered New Mexico and journeyed north to Taos in search of Ute Indians who had given aid to the Pueblos in the revolt, he found only Apaches living in the mountains northeast of Taos. These Apaches demonstrated a continuity in their lifeway, showing both orientations—toward the plains existence and settled ways. They are identified as Cuartelejos by D.A. Gunnerson (1974:96).

During the late seventeenth and the eighteenth centuries, two important factors affected the Jicarilla lifeway and territory. One factor was that the Comanches began pushing the Apaches out of the eastern plains as

top left, Peabody Mus., Harvard U.; center, Smithsonian, NAA: Ms. 2847; bottom, Mus. of N. Mex., Santa Fe: 2075; top right, *Jicarilla Chieftain*, Dulce, N. Mex.

Fig. 8. Annual relay race determines the relative abundance of meat or plant foods for the ensuing year. top left, Each side builds a circular structure or "kiva" on the first day of the ceremony. On the day of the relay race, a ground drawing is traced and the runners are decorated inside the structure. As the runners leave for the race, singing and dancing, they walk over the ground drawing, obliterating it, and absorbing its symbols and strength into their bodies. center, Each side has a large wooden drum that is only used for this 3-day ceremony. The old men of the side that wins signal the end of the race by hitting their opponent's drum 4 times. bottom, Each side also has a banner. The Ollero carry a white banner with a round yellow sun symbol in the center. The Llanero banner is traditionally red with a new yellow moon. At the top of each pole are tied 2 eagle feathers and 2 ears of corn. top right, The lead runners for each side are determined by preliminary races held on the second day of the ceremony. In this 1980 race the lead runner for the Ollero was Caron Elote. top left and center, Photographs by Frank Russell, 1898; bottom, photograph by T. Harmon Parkhurst, around 1935; top right, photograph by Glen Edmonds.

left, Smithsonian, NAA: Ms. 2847; right, after Opler 1946:129.

Fig. 9. Runners in the annual relay race. left, Runners painted, decorated with feathers, and with yucca leaves tied around the ankles and wrists; photograph by Frank Russell, 1898. right, Dress and decoration of the lead runners: Llanero at left, Ollero at right.

they migrated south. They were dreaded by the Apaches because they were able to obtain guns from the French to the north, while the Spaniards had a policy that did not allow the selling of arms to the Indians. This gave the Comanches decisive superiority as they made war on the Apaches, who were forced into the mountains and foothills of northeastern New Mexico and other areas.

The second situation was the beginning of French activities along the Mississippi River and their penetration into the plains northeast of new Mexico. This French presence increased Spanish concern over their own control of the northern frontier. As a result of these two events the Jicarilla identity was clearly established. However, the name Jicarilla was first recorded in 1700 when Gov. Pedro Rodríguez Cubero ordered that a condemned criminal's head be stuck upon a pole in Taos to warn the "apaches de la xicarilla" not to harbor Spanish fugitives.

In 1706, when the Picuris asked the Spanish officials in Santa Fe for assistance against the Apaches, Capt. Juan de Ulibarrí was sent to help rescue the Picuris who had been taken captive. Ulibarrí did not find the Picuris but instead he came upon the Jicarilla who were living in rancherias, cultivating the soil, and manifesting friendship for the Spaniards. He met their leader El Cojo or El Coxo ('the lame one') who was still alive in 1719 when he was again identified as Jicarilla (D.A. Gunnerson 1974:176). On this march Ulibarrí traversed the mountain region bearing the name "serro de la Jicarilla." His journey also verified the presence of the French as well as the intensification of hostilities between the Apaches and Comanches.

There is no further mention of the Jicarilla until the Faraones Apaches began rampaging along the eastern frontier of New Mexico in 1714. They were harassing both the Spanish and Pueblo settlements but "wreaked their worst havoc upon their northern neighbors, the Jicarillas, who were gravely weakened by the Ute-Comanche onslaught and thus vulnerable to any foe" (John 1975:235). In this same year the Spaniards included the Jicarilla among the friendly Indians in their campaign against the Faraones. This was also the beginning of the use of Jicarillas as auxiliaries to the Spanish army.

More devastating than the Faraones were the Comanches who had the Carlanas, Cuartelejos, and Jicarilla in full retreat by 1719, when they also began raiding the Spanish settlements. In 1720 Viceroy Marques de Valero advocated the establishment of a presidio at a place called La Jicarilla to protect the frontier from the Comanches and to check the French advance. Unfortunately, this presidio was not built and the depredations of the Comanches continued. The Carlanas threw in their lot with the Jicarillas (John 1975:251). In 1723 the two tribes asked Gov. Juan Domingo de Bustamente for aid against the Comanches and in turn promised to settle down and become Christians (Thomas 1935:29). They even pledged themselves as vassals of the King of Spain (John 1975:255). They hoped this would induce the Spaniards to reconsider the presidio, but it was not to be established. One of the reasons for this lack of action was the abatement of the French threat by 1726. Instead of offering aid against the Comanche, the Spaniards suggested that the Jicarilla settle closer to the Pueblos for protection from their enemies (Thomas 1935:42; D.A. Gunnerson 1974:202).

Between 1730 and 1750, the Comanche-Jicarilla wars raged on although not without long periods of truce. For this reason the Jicarilla did settle closer to the Pueblos. In 1733 a mission was founded for the Jicarilla five leagues north of Taos by Fray José Ortero de Velasco, but the governor cut off their trade in hides and drove them back into the mountains (Thomas 1932:96–97).

The pressure of the Comanches forced the merger of the eastern plains Apaches with the mountain Jicarillas. From 1733 to 1750 the Cuartelejos, Palomas, and Carlanas became obscure in the Spanish records. It is speculated that these Apache groups began to live in the Sangre de Cristo Mountains and then developed closer ties with the Jicarilla (D.A. Gunnerson 1974: 212–214). In 1752 the records again mention the Carlanas in relation to their association with the Jicarilla who were trading at Pecos. At this time it was discovered that they, the Cuartelejos, and the Palomas had been living in the neighborhood of Pecos but made their homes as far south as the Texas Plains to get away from the Comanches (D.A. Gunnerson 1974:228). They were referred to as Lipiyanes and Llaneros by the Spanish. "The Lipiyanes were part of, or the same as, the Llaneros who eventually proved to be the Llaneros Band of the modern Jicarilla" (D.A. Gunnerson 1974:253). Evidently some of the Carlanas joined the Lipans and the rest joined the Llaneros. Eventually they were all called Llaneros. After 1786 they asked for asylum in New Mexico but were refused by the Spanish officials, so they continued to live out in the plains but maintained relations with the Jicarilla. In 1801 they arrived back in New Mexico despite Spanish objections, insisting that they were part of the Jicarilla, and took up residence in eastern New Mexico. They merged with the Jicarilla and were not again called Llaneros until the late 1800s when ethnologists were conducting research among the Jicarilla.

In the 1760s the Spaniards became more concerned about the hostile Comanches and made a greater effort to quiet them. In 1768 Gov. Fermín de Mendinueta campaigned against them along the Arkansas River, using Jicarilla Apaches as guides and auxiliaries. This did not deter the Comanches and hostilities continued sporadically. In August and September 1779 the Comanches faced a combined force of Gov. Juan Bautista de Anza's 600 men including Pueblos, Utes, and Jicarillas and were defeated. This success was followed by other campaigns until the Comanches sued for peace in 1786. The Jicarilla and their relatives were then confined to the regions of northeastern New Mexico and southeastern Colorado, but they continued to hunt farther out in the plains.

In the late seventeenth and the eighteenth centuries, the lands of the Jicarilla between Santa Fe and Taos were gradually settled by the Hispanic people. This provided the rationale for the Spanish government to award land grants to its subjects in this region prior to 1821, when it broke with its Mexican state. Under the new Mexican government more land grants were given to private citizens. Mexico was anxious to develop the far regions of New Mexico and to establish peace with the Indians. Since the peace of 1786 Spanish-Indian relations had progressively deteriorated and it was the hope of the infant state to transfer the responsibility for peacekeeping to private groups and individuals by inviting petitions for land grants from them. Numerous citizens applied, including Americans who had obtained Mexican citizenship for this very purpose. They had entered New Mexico about 1820, when Mexico established free trade with the United States.

Mexico granted thousands of acres of traditional Jicarilla territory to her citizens without either the knowledge or the permission of the Jicarilla. In the Mexican Colonization Law of 1828, the governors were authorized to award land grants but were to allow the Indians continued use and occupation. A full title was not to be given until the Indians of their own free will would choose to leave, but this law was not enforced to the letter (Cutter 1974:261).

In 1841, the largest land grant that affected the Jicarilla was awarded to Carlos Beubien and Guadalupe Miranda—a grant involving about 1.7 million acres of land in northeastern New Mexico. The new owners permitted the Jicarilla undisturbed use and continued occupation of these lands, mainly because they could not realistically expect the Jicarilla to move off the land without either causing a war or breaking the law.

In 1847 this grant was purchased by Lucien B. Maxwell. The Maxwell Land Grant was recognized by the United States Court of Claims in 1860 as required by the 1848 Treaty of Guadalupe Hidalgo (Keleher 1942:29). This was done without the recognition of prior and continuing rights of the Jicarilla Apache.

In 1850 Jicarilla hunting territory had been defined as extending from the Arkansas River, south to Mora, New Mexico, and from the Canadian River on the east to Chama, New Mexico, on the west (Opler 1936b:202). In spite of this, the government recognized the land grants and set the stage for the total dispossession of the Jicarilla in the following three decades.

The 1850 boundaries were enlarged by the Indian Claims Commission in 1969, which defined the aboriginal boundaries of the Jicarilla as "beginning from Trinidad, Colorado, on the north, along the Texas and Oklahoma borders on the east, the Sangre de Cristo on the west and a line beginning at McIntosh, New Mexico, east of Albuquerque and running below Santa Rosa and Tucumcari, New Mexico on the south" (*Jicarilla Apache*

Tribe v. *United States* 1969). This area consisted of 9,218,532.77 acres.

1846 to 1887

After the Jicarilla lands came under the jurisdiction of the United States in 1848, American settlers began moving into the country around Cimarron, Las Vegas, Taos, and Mora, New Mexico. These lands were already occupied in part by the Hispanic people but the influx of more settlers upset the economic system. The Jicarilla could no longer pursue their way of life, while at the same time they did not have any alternative. Therefore, the new government had to solve the dilemma.

When Gen. Stephen Watts Kearny entered New Mexico in 1846, the prevailing attitude of the New Mexicans toward the Indians was colored by a long history of conflict. This attitude influenced the policies of the military. Kearny proclaimed that New Mexico was going to be protected from the Indians, a position that was reinforced by the Treaty of Guadalupe Hidalgo in 1848. While the position of the military was clear, there was no definitive civilian Indian policy for New Mexico, especially with regard to the Jicarilla. As a result, there was dual control over Indian affairs until about 1856.

In 1846 Kearny appointed Charles Bent as temporary civil governor until Congress decided on the status of the territory. In Bent's first official report to Kearny he stated that there were about 100 lodges of 500 Jicarillas throughout New Mexico. He described them as an indolent and cowardly people having no permanent residence and roaming throughout the settlements, living principally by theft (Walter 1933:111–112). This attitude developed into a stereotype for the Jicarilla, and it became the rationale for the ill treatment that they received from the government.

Indian hostilities in which the Jicarilla participated flared up all over the territory in the first few years. Indians began attacking wagon trains and raiding the settlements from the San Luis Valley on the north, along the Santa Fe Trail east, west to the Rio Grande River, and south to the Pecos Valley. In October 1849 a combined group of Jicarilla and Ute warriors attacked a wagon train near the Point of Rocks on the Cimarron cutoff of the Santa Fe Trail, and a month later, they raided an eastbound mail party on the Trail (Abel 1915). It was becoming clear that they were not a cowardly people but a force that had to be reckoned with, and pressure was growing to rid the country of them; but the military remained ineffective against their guerrilla tactics.

This cycle of raiding and military pursuit continued until 1850 when the army began reorganizing its development. Several forts were built in the heart of Jicarilla country—Fort Union near Las Vegas, Cantonment Burgwin at Taos, and Fort Massachusetts at the foot of Blanca Peak in Colorado (Utley 1967:85–87). This reorganization had some positive results.

A portion of the Jicarilla were convinced that they preferred maintaining peaceful relations with the newcomers to their country. In 1851 a treaty was signed with the tribe, which was represented by several chiefs and leading men—Francisco Chacon, Lobo Blanco, Huero Mundo, and Josecito Largo. This was not a treaty of land cession, but one by which the Jicarilla agreed to submission to the United States, confinement within certain territorial limits, cultivation of the soil, the cessation of hostilities, and the delivery of all captives and stolen property. In turn the United States offered annuities and other forms of aid. This treaty was not ratified by Congress; nevertheless, in the period between 1851 and 1853, the tribe attempted to live up to its terms, although small Jicarilla war parties continued their sporadic raiding activities. Gov. James S. Calhoun established cordial relations with the Jicarilla and distributed some rations, but this was the extent of the aid given them.

In 1852, William Carr Lane, Calhoun's successor, began implementing a program of settling the Jicarilla on lands west of the Rio Grande River, without specific instruction or support from Washington (Tiller 1976:60; Utley 1967:143). One band led by Chacon was particularly cooperative, choosing lands near Abiquiu on the Chama River, clearing over 100 acres, and planting corn, wheat, squash, pumpkins, and melons. This program offered a solution to the raiding as well as an alternative to the hunting and gathering economy, which was no longer feasible. Despite its apparent success, the commissioner of Indian affairs ordered Lane to suspend all operations that he considered to be too costly and that exceeded the funds available for the support of the Indians of New Mexico. Thereupon, when the Jicarilla again resorted to raiding, the acting governor on April 10, 1854, declared war on the Jicarilla and their Ute allies, although not all the Jicarilla were outright belligerents.

For a year, the army pursued the Indians throughout the rugged mountains of northern New Mexico and southern Colorado without decisive action. In March 1855 a new campaign was begun to subdue the Indians. By August both the Jicarilla and the Utes, weary of being pursued, opened negotiations with the governor, which resulted in the signing of a treaty of peace at Abiquiu on September 10, 1855 (M.F. Taylor 1969:269–291, 1970; Utley 1967:143–146).

By the terms of the treaty a reservation was to be set aside for them in Rio Arriba County, but the treaty was not ratified, so for the next several decades the Jicarilla lived amongst the communities in Rio Arriba, Taos, San Miguel, and Mora counties. However, the Abiquiu and Taos Indian Agencies were created in 1856 to issue rations in the hope of preventing depredations.

This was the extent of the responsibilities assumed by these agencies. Five years later the Cimarron Agency on the Maxwell Land Grant was established to replace the Taos Agency, which was abolished. The Jicarilla remained in the vicinity of Cimarron and Abiquiu where they raised some crops and hunted and gathered in the mountains and plains. The Cimarron Agency was abolished in 1876 as was the one at Abiquiu in 1879.

After the cessation of hostilities in 1855, there was a clarification of Indian policy for New Mexico. The old policy was continued, but more consistently, of consolidating and settling the Indians on reservations and providing them with technical assistance and gratuities to help them become assimilated peoples. All the New Mexico tribes were located on reservations by 1873, with the exception of the Jicarilla who were the victims of bureaucratic indecision. Between 1855 and 1887, the government entertained numerous plans for locating them. One suggestion was to put them with the Gila Apaches in southern Arizona; another advocated the Bosque Redondo Reservation before it was abandoned; and still another was to consolidate them with the Utes in Colorado. All these were abortive but two others were kept under consideration: the establishment of a northern reservation and consolidation with the Mescalero Apaches in southern New Mexico (Tiller 1976:94–113). Both plans were implemented.

On December 10, 1873, an agreement was entered into between the Jicarillas and the United States. As a result, a Jicarilla Apache Reservation on the headwaters of the San Juan River in northwestern New Mexico was established on March 25, 1874, by executive order. This order was abrogated on July 10, 1876, because the land was desired by the White settlers and because the Jicarilla had not taken possession of it.

In spite of the creation of the 1874 reservation, the Indian Office continued to plan the Jicarilla-Mescalero merger and it even made several unsuccessful attempts to move the Jicarilla south. In the meantime, their leaders asked the government whether they could go to Washington to settle this affair once and for all. To their surprise a delegation of principal men was invited to Washington. On September 21, 1880, another reservation was established in Rio Arriba County near the Navajo River in north-central New Mexico. Again interest groups began pressuring the Department of the Interior to move the Jicarilla to the Mescalero Reservation. Also, a good portion of the Jicarilla found the Rio Arriba area not to their liking, but another faction wanted to remain there. On August 20, 1883, the government succeeded in removing all the Jicarilla to the Mescalero Apache Reservation where they remained until several of their leaders began making plans in 1886 to get back their northern reservation. With the help of Gen. Nelson A. Miles and the governor of New Mexico, the Indian Office was coerced into again considering the 1880 reservation, which on February 10, 1887, was declared permanent (Tiller 1976:116–142). The mining area on the west side was excluded but comparable acreage was added to the eastern side.

During the period from 1870 to 1887 there was a growing trend toward greater tribal consciousness. Although the Ollero and Llanero leaders disagreed on the location of the reservation, they put this issue aside in order to find themselves a permanent home. The 1873 agreement marked the first time that they had acted together; and in 1886 they again decided as a tribe that they would return north. Prior to this time the main emphasis had been on the welfare of the bands rather than the entire tribe.

1887 to 1934

In the same year that the Jicarilla Apache Reservation was created, the Dawes Severalty Act of 1887 was passed. This outlined the specific procedures for the allotment of Indian lands into 160-acre plots. Titles or patents-in-fee to these allotments were to be held in trust by the federal government for 25 years. After that, the competent Indians were to receive title to their lands. The intent of this act was to make the Indians productive citizen-farmers. They were to give up their tribal cultures and become assimilated into the body politic. Thus the government would sever its relationship with the Indians forever.

By the authority of this act the reservation was to be allotted to eligible Jicarillas to form the basis for the intended farming community, but several factors immediately ordained the failure of this plan. The rugged mountainous terrain, the unfavorable climate, the presence of bona fide settlers within the boundaries of the reservation, and the indifference of the government all contributed to thwart implementation of the legislation. As a consequence the Jicarilla were denied a reliable means of support, their poverty worsened, and the stage was set for their near extinction in the first decades of the twentieth century.

Their reservation, located in north-central New Mexico, consisted of about 416,000 acres. It straddles the continental divide where the altitude is between 6,000 and 8,000 feet. The terrain is rugged, with many canyon valleys. Timber in the higher elevations is mainly ponderosa pine, with some fir, aspen, and spruce. The valleys produce grama grass, other wheat grasses, and sagebrush. The growing season is short, rainfall undependable, and the soil is unsuited for farming. There are three small natural lakes in the east, and the northwest section touches on a small stretch of the Navajo River.

On these lands, allotments were made in 1891, but shortly thereafter, it was discovered that the surveys were incomplete and hopelessly confused. This neces-

Bureau of Ind. Affairs, Forestry Service, Dulce, N. Mex.

Fig. 10. Tug of war between Apache and Navajo women at July fourth intertribal gathering. Photograph by W.J. Enbom, 1938–1939.

sitated the cancellation of the entire survey, and land assignments could not be made. The situation was not cleared up until 1909 when the reservation was resurveyed and reallotted (Tiller 1976:149–153).

The allotment process was also hindered by the presence of White settlers, who had homesteaded prior to 1887. Their claims, which were recognized in the executive order, were to the majority of the arable lands and to control of the limited water resources, leaving the barren and unproductive lands to the Jicarilla. The government maintained that it would be unjust to eject any settler who had a legitimate claim. Although government inspectors continued to recommend that the settlers be bought out so that the Jicarilla could have the full use of their reservation, the government chose not to take this advice and thereby undermined its own policies (Nicklason 1972:6–16).

Since the arable lands had been pre-empted, the Jicarilla did not succeed as farmers. Very few crops were raised, drought was a constant threat, and the Jicarillas became more and more dependent on government rations. A suggested alternative was that the timber be sold and livestock purchased with the proceeds. On August 15, 1894, Congress passed an act that made this possible but it specified that the timber on only the unallotted lands be sold. Since the best timber was on the allotted lands, Jicarilla leaders agreed to sell the timber from all lands, put the proceeds into a common fund, and purchase livestock for distribution to all members on an equitable basis. Congress refused to allow this.

Conditions among the Jicarilla went from bad to worse and several bands temporarily left the reservation in search of a better way of life. In 1906 legislation finally permitted the sale of timber from both types of land. The money realized was deposited in a U.S. Treasury account for the Jicarilla, where it remained for several more years.

In anticipation of replacing the faltering farming economy with one based on livestock, an addition to the reservation, known as the southern part, was made in 1907 with minor changes the following year. It consists of a fairly level area with deep arroyos and high mesas. The elevation is between 4,500 and 6,500 feet and the climate is milder than in the northern part. This addition provided the solution to the wintering of livestock in a climate where there would not be high losses due to cold. The northern part became the summer grazing range and the southern section, the winter range. The total area of the reservation was then 742,315 acres.

With the enlargement of the reservation, the sale of timber, and the reorganization of the allotments, only

Bureau of Ind. Affairs, Office of Technical Assistance and Training, Brigham City, Utah: 301-69-165.

Fig. 11. Men at sawmill. From 1907 to the 1920s the timber industry was active on the reservation, and it revived in the late 1950s. Photographer unknown, probably 1930s.

the purchase and distribution of the livestock were necessary for the Jicarilla to become self-sustaining. However, this did not occur. Instead, the funds were tied up in the U.S. Treasury. A tribal herd was purchased and put under the management of the BIA Agency in 1914. Consequently, all hopes for a decent livelihood ended.

The years from 1905 to 1920 were critical ones. The people were still laboring to subsist on their unproductive allotments, employment opportunities were severely limited, and rations had been curtailed. Living conditions continued to deteriorate in the wake of economic deprivation. Diseases of all types ravaged the population, but the most devastating was tuberculosis. Poor and insufficient nutrition contributed to the low resistence to diseases. Between 1905 and 1925, the Jicarilla population decreased, largely due to deaths from tuberculosis (table 1).

By 1920 the government was forced to start a program of economic and health rehabilitation. A sanatorium for the tubercular patients was established. Sheep from the tribal herd were issued to each member of the tribe. These two programs helped put the Jicarilla on the road to recovery, although the health situation was not brought under control until the late 1920s. The economic recovery was instrumental in improving the standard of living. During the 1920s the Jicarilla sheep industry grew and prospered to a point where it was making substantial profits. This trend continued through 1932, when nearly 70 percent of the animals were lost during a severe winter. Within a year Congress extended a loan to restock the reservation, but the recovery was not so spectacular as it had been in the previous decade. However, this industry was the basis of the prosperity that the Jicarilla were to experience during the 1940s (fig. 12) (Tiller 1976:167–170).

Formal education had always been valued by the Jicarilla. Since the days when the Olleros lived in the vicinity of the Abiquiu Agency in the 1860s and 1870s, requests were made for a day school by Jicarilla leaders, but the requests fell on deaf ears. Throughout the removal years (1870–1887) the state of tribal affairs was in such turmoil that schooling was of little concern to both the Jicarilla and the government. From 1883 to 1886, some of the Jicarilla children attended the government schools on the Mescalero Apache Reservation.

Upon return to the 1887 reservation, a few children were sent to the boarding schools at Fort Lewis, Colorado, and the Ramona Indian School, Santa Fe. Throughout the 1890s the majority of the school-aged children were not in school anywhere. In 1899 the Jicarilla BIA Agent reported that there were 251 children of school age who were not attending any school (ARCIA 1899:254).

In 1903 a government boarding school with a capacity of 120 students was built in Dulce. Since all Jicarilla

Table 1. Population

Year	Population
1900	815
1905	795
1910	743
1915	642
1920	588
1925	635
1930	647
1935	640
1940	735
1945	811
1950	920
1955	1,062
1960	1,305
1965	1,548
1970	1,869
1975	2,053
1981	2,308

SOURCE: Jicarilla Apache Tribal Census Rolls.

children from ages 6 to 18 were required to attend school, they were all eligible to use the facilities. In the first few years the grades went only to the fourth grade but by 1918 the fifth and sixth grades had been added. The curriculum consisted of the regular academic courses common to all American schools of the period. English as a spoken language was given more attention since it posed the greatest problem for the students.

In addition to the academic curriculum vocational training was emphasized. A small farm and domestic cottage were established in 1913 to teach agricultural and domestic arts. For half a day the boys helped with the chores on the school farm and the girls helped with the cooking, laundry, and housekeeping as part of their vocational training.

Between 1903 and 1908 the school was filled beyond capacity. Two reservation day schools were established in 1907 and 1908 at Dulce and LaJara, but this did not solve the problems at the boarding school. The lack of adequate living quarters enhanced the spread of tuberculosis, which by 1907 was spreading rapidly among the school children as well as the adult population. The day schools were forced to close down due to high attrition rates caused by tuberculosis and other diseases. In 1917 the superintendent at the Jicarilla Agency reported that 90 percent of the students were afflicted with tuberculosis, and a year later the boarding school was closed. Between 1918 and 1921 the boarding school was converted into the Southern Ute Mountain Sanatorium as part of the health recovery program initiated by the government. Since the sanatorium was for tubercular students, the government entered into an agreement with the Dutch Reformed Church of America, which was located in Dulce, to operate a school for the healthy children. The school opened in 1921.

Natl. Arch., Washington.

Fig. 12. Sheep shearing done by professional traveling shearers who brought their own equipment to the Jicarilla Reservation. These professionals were often Navajos, as here, or Mexicans. Photographer unknown, possibly 1930.

The period from 1918 to 1923 was one of slow recovery. In 1923 the Mission School had only 43 students and the sanatorium started with 28 student-patients. Attendance at the Mission School for the years 1922 to 1930 remained at approximately 45–50 students. At the Mission School, the Jicarilla students were offered the same courses offered by the boarding school, and emphasis was put on vocational training, but here the students were also required to take Bible studies. In 1926 a new program of physical examinations began; this approach proved to be quite successful and by 1930 the sanatorium was filled to its capacity at 80. As the patients regained their strength, they were allowed to receive academic instruction for half a day. When they recovered they were transferred to the Mission School.

During the 1930s the tuberculosis rate among the Jicarilla decreased at a steady rate. In 1938 of 227 children of school age, 156 were considered healthy enough to attend school but 32 of these students were not in school. In this year there were only 39 remaining at the sanatorium. In 1940 the sanatorium was closed and the remaining patients were transferred to other facilities throughout the Southwest.

From 1887 to 1953, the Jicarilla did not make the social progress that had been anticipated nor did they give up their traditional culture. They maintained their close kinship ties and continued to practice their native religion. This can be attributed to their physical isolation, the lack of missionary activities up to 1910, the delay in establishing a school until 1903, and economic hardships. By the 1920s some noticeable social adjustments had taken place. More marriage licenses were obtained through the county offices, more members dressed in American fashion, and traveled off the reservation, there was greater use of the English language, and a large number of people had accepted Christianity.

The economic recovery also revitalized the traditional religious practices. For example, the people could better afford the cost of sponsoring the Puberty Fiestas and Bear Dances, which seemed to have dropped off between 1900 and 1920. Although the number of men who accepted roles as religious leaders had declined considerably, this was not enough to affect the religious zeal of the people.

There was a growing problem with alcoholic beverages and this led to arrests related to its use. After 1887 tribal police helped to maintain law and order, and this small force was sufficient to meet the need. Less than five major crimes were committed by Jicarillas between 1887 and 1935. By that year the social order was a cross between the traditional and the American rural lifeway.

1934 to 1960

The Indian Reorganization Act of 1934 inaugurated a new era for the Jicarilla Apache. Under its provisions the tribe organized its first formal government, adopting a constitution and by-laws on July 3, 1937, documents approved by the secretary of the interior on August 4 (fig. 13). This constitution provided for a tribal government to consist of an elected representative tribal

top, Bureau of Ind. Affairs, Office of Technical Assistance and Training, Brigham City, Utah: 301-68-75; bottom, Howard's Photography, Farmington, N. Mex.

Fig. 13. Jicarilla tribal councils. top, The first elected council: standing, Antonio Veneno, Cevero Caramillo, Dotayo Veneno, Juan Vigil, Agency Superintendent A.E. Stover, De Jesus Compos Serafin, Garfield Velarde, Sr., Anastacio Juilan, Norman Tecube, Jack Ladd Vicenti; sitting, Agapito Baltazar, Ramon Tafoya, Sixto Atole, Albert Velarde, Sr., Grover Vigil, John Mills Baltazar, Sr., Laell Vicenti, Henry "Buster" Vicenti, Lindo Vigil. Photographer unknown, August 4, 1937. bottom, 1980 tribal council: standing, Harrison Elote, Rudolfo Velarde, Calvin Veneno, Wainwright Velarde; sitting, Edwin Sandoval, Raleigh Tafoya, President Leonard Atole, and Cora Gomez. Vice-president Richard Tecube was absent. Photograph by Howard Jones; submitted by Jicarilla Tribal Council, Dulce, N. Mex.

Smithsonian, NAA: 52337.

Fig. 14. Dulce, N. Mex., headquarters for Jicarilla Apache agency. The Emmet Wirt Trading post (far left) was founded in the late 1890s and continued operating until the store was sold to the tribe in 1938. Wirt was the sole post trader. Photographer unknown, about 1918.

council of 18 members from the six reservation districts. A council member must have reached 28 years of age and be resident in the district. The term of office was four years. Members of the tribe who were 21 years or older could cast their votes in their respective districts. Membership was defined as all persons of Indian blood whose names appeared on the 1937 official census roll. The council could elect its own officers. It was to meet twice a year, and 10 members constituted a quorum. Any tribal member could be removed from the council for improper conduct or neglect of duty by a three-fourths vote of the council itself.

A corporate charter was adopted on September 4, 1937, that took the name Jicarilla Apache Tribe. The tribal council was its governing body. The charter's basic purpose was to direct economic growth, protect the tribe's natural resources, and oversee its financial affairs. Under this charter, the tribe borrowed $85,000 from the Revolving Credit Fund made available by the Indian Reorganization Act to purchase the Wirt Trading Post (fig. 14), which was renamed the Jicarilla Apache Cooperative. The loan was repaid within eight years.

The next step was to relinquish all land allotments in favor of tribal ownership, although the people were permitted to maintain their previous land allotments. They were to register their assignments under the regulations set forth in a tribal range code that governed land use. A tribal member was entitled to his land as long as he put it to beneficial use, but once he did not put it to use another member could apply for it.

The livestock industry grew rapidly. In 1940 the income from livestock and its subsidiaries was approximately $120,000, rising to about $320,000 by 1948. The number of families having incomes over $1,000 increased during this decade, which brought about improvement in the standard of living. This prosperity had other beneficial effects. There were more children in school, health conditions improved dramatically, population increased, and the morale of the people shot upward, in sharp contrast to previous years.

Another important change in federal Indian policies that directly affected the Jicarilla occurred in 1946, when the Indian Claims Commission was set up to hear all legitimate claims against the United States. The Jicarilla filed their land claim as part of the *Apache Nation* v. *United States*, Docket No. 22, on February 3, 1948 (becoming the *Jicarilla Apache Tribe of the Jicarilla Apache Reservation* v. *United States of America*, Docket No. 22-A, on January 5, 1958). The Jicarilla claim was for damages based upon the expropriation in 1883 by the United States of 14,026,000 acres of land in northeastern New Mexico, southeastern Colorado, and portions of the Oklahoma panhandle, without compensation to the Jicarilla.

The Commission excluded 4,859,576.23 acres that made up the Spanish and Mexican land grants, for which it disclaimed liability. The final award of 9,218,532.77 acres valued at the fair market price of $9,950,000 was made on December 2, 1970. Of this the government was awarded an offset of $800,000; legal fees were set at 10 percent; and the Jicarilla received the remainder.

During the 1950s the federal government severed its trust relationship with several Indian tribes under its "termination" policies. The Jicarilla were not affected directly. They were considered ineligible because they did not meet the criterion of demonstrating competency in managing their own affairs nor did they have a solid economic base of support. However, the federal objective continued to be eventual termination after the Jicarilla were well on their way to self-sufficiency. Moreover, their tribal income from natural resources had the potential for the development of a reservation economy that could support the tribal population.

The reservation had potential due to its natural resources—gas, oil, and timber. Tribal income rose dramatically during the 1950s from several hundred thousand to just over one million dollars by 1960. The bulk of the income came from gas and oil revenues. This made it possible to diversify the economy, which was predominantly dependent on livestock raising, by developing other small industries that would provide employment opportunities for the tribal members.

There were other trends occurring within Jicarilla society that determined the feasibility of this economic policy and led to its implementation. There was a decline in the sheep industry in the early 1950s and a parallel migration into the town of Dulce, the reservation headquarters, by 1954. In that year 80 percent of the people lived within seven miles of the Agency, 10 percent lived at least 15 miles away, and 2 percent lived off the reservation. At the end of the decade 90 percent lived in the vicinity of Dulce (H.C. Wilson 1964).

The majority of the Jicarilla also did not take advantage of "termination" policies that provided for relocation in the cities and assistance in finding jobs; instead they remained on the reservation.

Upon migration to Dulce the new arrivals were faced with lack of employment, shortage of housing, and inadequate community service facilities. The new income accommodated the movement into town. In 1953 the first per capita payments derived from the natural resources revenue were authorized by the Bureau of Indian Affairs to be distributed to all tribal members. The subsequent annual payments helped to sustain the community although they had decreased in amount by the 1960s and were distributed quarterly.

Since it was clear that the per capita payments were not going to be adequate, and by 1955 the population of Dulce had reached 1,000, the program to diversify the economy was stepped up. Retail enterprises such as a service station, an automobile repair shop, a restaurant, a laundromat, and other service industries were supported; and by the late 1950s a greater portion of the tribal budget was allocated for these purposes. Although some progress was made, the community development programs did not begin in earnest until the following decade. Prior to 1950, the superintendent of the BIA Agency exercised the main control over Jicarilla affairs although he consulted the tribal council on some important matters. Then the increase in tribal income, migration to town, and the new economic policy inaugurated a new era for tribal government. The participation of the tribal council in directing its own affairs increased. The annual income of the tribe grew to over several million dollars by early 1960, causing an increase in tribal business that was reflected in the greater frequency of council meetings and in the number of resolutions passed. As a result, the BIA decided to promote the gradual assumption of tribal council control over its own affairs. It began with the administration of its own operating budget and other procedural business. The substantive control relating to trust responsibilities and control over natural resources remained with the Agency Superintendent (H.C. Wilson 1964; Basehart and Sasaki 1964).

The formal structure of the tribal government likewise underwent changes. The district system had become obsolete in light of changing residential patterns. In 1958 the tribal constitution was amended, reducing the council from 18 to 10 members who were elected at-large by popular vote rather than by districts. The positions of chairman and vice-chairman were also created. The voting age was lowered from 21 to 18 and tribal membership was extended to those Jicarilla children born off the reservation but who had parents listed on the 1937 rolls. All these provisions were incorporated into a completely revised constitution that was accepted by the people on July 11, 1960. The constitution was further amended on Feburary 11, 1963, and again in 1968.

The 1968 version, which superseded all previous constitutions, reorganized the tribal government into three divisions—executive, legislative, and judicial—and defined their powers and terms of office. A tribal law and order code was made a part of the constitution. Basically Jicarilla members have the same rights and privileges as other American citizens in their relationship with their government.

The tribal income benefited not only the economy but also education and social welfare. In 1955 one million dollars was set aside under the Chester E. Faris Scholarship Fund for all tribal members who desired vocational training or a college education. As the number of Jicarilla students who wanted advanced education increased and college costs rose, it became necessary for the tribe to obtain matching funds from the BIA.

In the 1940s school enrollment soared; health was no longer a serious problem, and the Jicarilla produced the first students who completed the eighth grade and went on to Santa Fe or Albuquerque Indian School or other schools for a high school education. By 1950 there were about 10 Jicarillas with high school diplomas.

During the 1951–1952 school year there were 295 Jicarilla students in federal boarding schools, and the majority were at the Dulce boarding school; 16 were attending public schools on and off the reservation. In 1956 a county public school was established in Dulce, and the 331 Jicarilla students attended the new Dulce public school, but they continued to live during the school year at the boarding school. In 1959 the public school combined with two other schools in the nearby area to form the Dulce Independent School District. By the mid-1960s there was an increasing number of Jicarilla students who became day students since their parents lived in and around Dulce. After 1970 all the students were attending school from their own homes.

In 1963 there were 18 high school graduates. From 1956 to 1965 there were 61 scholarships given for vocational training and 51 for college from the Chester E. Faris Scholarship Fund. The attrition rate among these students was rather high; 40 of 61 completed vocational training, and 24 of 51 completed college (Jicarilla Apache Agency report to BIA, Department of Education).

Sociocultural Situation in the 1960s

The groundwork for economic development was laid toward the end of the 1950s with the aid of the income from natural resources, the changing federal Indian policies, and the migration to the Agency town. The traditional subsistence activities became only nostalgic memories. However, the tribal government recognized the potential that lay in developing its tourism and recreational facilities to supplement tribal income and create employment opportunities for the people. In cooperation with the New Mexico State Department of Game and Fish, wildlife resources were developed. Instead of observing an open season, even the Jicarillas had to obtain licenses to hunt and fish on the reservation. In 1969, the total income from fishing and hunting permits was $86,040. The people also derived additional income from providing camping facilities, equipment, and guide services to hunters and other tourists. Hunting and fishing became a sport for most Jicarillas, although a good number still depended on wild game to supplement their food resources.

The traditional gathering activities continued on a very limited basis, mainly confined to the older generation. The majority of jobs available were service-type, the federal government and the tribe being the principal employers. Other jobs were provided by local businesses on the reservation, the livestock industry, construction and maintenance, and occasional fire-fighting.

By the mid-1960s Dulce had become the largest community on the reservation. Here the offices of the tribe, the BIA, and the Public Health Service were located.

The movement into Dulce, with its concomitant economic and social changes gave rise to a number of social ills. There were problems with juvenile delinquency, alcoholism, child neglect, a rise in the suicide rate, unemployment, and withal a lack of social skills necessary to accommodate the rapid economic growth. The underlying reasons seemed to be related to the general poor quality of life on the reservation, in spite of the increase in tribal wealth. With the proliferation of these problems, the tribal council and the Agency began to direct their efforts toward creating more employment and giving particular attention to the education and training of both the youth and the adults.

The social legislation provided by the federal government during the 1960s through the Department of Labor, Department of Health, Education, and Welfare (Public Health Service), Department of Commerce (Economic Development Administration), Department of Housing and Urban Development, and the Office of Economic Opportunity served to stimulate and assist the Jicarilla in developing their economy and in solving their social problems. By 1969, with matching funds, loans, and grants, the tribe had acquired a supermarket and general store, a motel, restaurant and lounge, banking facilities, a beauty and barber shop, a service station, a laundromat, and an electronics plant—the Jicarilla Apache Tribe Industries. This plant has provided employment for about 60 individuals.

The development of the natural resources of the reservation also has continued with a comprehensive program undertaken to improve the commercial forests under the guidance of the BIA. In addition, the improvement of the range, and the conservation of the soil, water resources, and real property have received considerable attention.

Community services have also been expanded. Like other tribes, the Jicarilla have benefited from programs such as Head Start, funds for special services given to the public schools under the Johnson O'Malley Act, adult education, and day care services. Other types of social services were made available with the help of federal agencies: a variety of counseling services, rehabilitation services for the handicapped, employment programs, and alcoholism programs.

Housing, which was deplorable, has received top priority. By 1969 25 units of public housing had been built, and 55 units of mutual help housing were under construction, in addition to those new units built by individuals.

With the shift from a lifestock to a wage economy in the 1950s and 1960s social changes have also occurred. One of the most noticeable changes has been in the traditional kinship system. The relationships in the extended families were weakened by the increased assumption of social welfare services by the tribe and the Agency. Since 1940, the tribe has provided for the care of the aged with proceeds from the old people's herd, a flock of sheep managed by the Agency. This pattern was continued and extended by the addition of tribal and state welfare for the elderly. The former family responsibilities, such as the care of foster children by relatives and the settlement of family disputes, were assumed by the tribe and state welfare agencies. A tribal court system was set up to handle the legal aspects. The traditional responsibility of the kinship group gradually was disregarded. However, kinship ties are still evident, especially in distributing jobs, loans, scholarships, and long assignments.

The traditional band delineations, which for many years existed primarily for the purpose of determining the opponents in the ceremonial Relay Races, were in 1981 no longer strictly adhered to.

The kinship system declined as the sources of family income changed. The immediate family unit remains the basic unit in present-day Jicarilla society with a strong tie to the tribe, rather than the extended family group.

The Jicarilla religion and beliefs have remained an important part of Jicarilla life. Perhaps 70 percent of the Jicarilla continue to practice their native religion, in spite of the drastic decline in the number of tribal members who assume the role of religious leaders. The number of Puberty Fiestas and Bear Dances increased in the late 1960s and the 1970s in contrast to the 1950s, when they were performed somewhat less frequently. The tribal council has offered financial assistance to those ceremonials, and it has declared a two-day tribal holiday on September 14 and 15 for the ceremonial Relay Race.

Smithsonian, Dept. of Anthr.: left, 378,867; top right, 222,678; bottom right, 409,816.

Fig. 15. Coiled basketry. top right, Design elements in red (possibly vegetal dye), barely visible. More common especially since 1920 are bold motifs worked in bright aniline-dye colors such as, left, straight-sided waste basket with red, green, and orange designs, and bottom right, bowl with magenta and purple. top right, Height 18.5, (rest to same scale), collected in 1903; left, collected before 1937; bottom right, collected in 1967.

In addition to encouraging the traditional religion, the council also established a Jicarilla Arts and Crafts Industry in 1964 to preserve the traditional arts of beadwork, buckskin tanning, basket making (fig. 15), and leather work. This industry has provided steady employment for about 20 people. All these crafts are on display at the Jicarilla Museum in Dulce. The public schools have also made efforts to teach Jicarilla culture and language. In the early 1970s about 60 percent of the tribal members could speak in their native tongue.

A large number of Jicarillas are Christians. The sectarian breakdown includes the Dutch Reformed Church, which has the largest number of converts, the Baptist Church, the Church of Latter Day Saints, the Roman Catholic Church, and the Church of Christ, all located in the vicinity of Dulce.

Synonymy†

The name Jicarilla originated in the Spanish expression Apaches de (la) Jicarilla—also Apaches de (la) Xicarilla, Apaches Xicarillas, and simply Gicarillas (D.A. Gunnerson 1974:167--171, 282). It was first used, as "apaches de la xicarilla," in 1700 (Cubero in D.A. Gunnerson 1974:167), and according to José Pichardo, writing in 1805, it came from the name of a hill or peak called Cerro de la Xicarilla, apparently 'little-chocolate-cup(-shaped) peak'. This hill was referred to by this

† This synonymy was written by Ives Goddard. Uncredited forms are from anonymous sources.

name in 1706 by Juan de Ulibarrí, who passed nearby northeast of the Jicarilla villages (D.A. Gunnerson 1974:157–160). Explanations of the name Jicarilla that assume a reference to baskets or pottery lack a clear historical context.

Self-designations recorded for the Jicarilla are: haísndayĭn 'people who came from below' (Curtis 1907–1930, 1:135); and the apparent loanwords apæči, from Spanish or English (E.F. Wilson 1889:2, normalized), and awačI̩, from Ute (Russell 1898:65, normalized). Other sources report the use of dì-ⁿdé 'person' (Mooney 1898a:197; Goddard 1911:137; Hoijer 1938:77).

Names for the Jicarilla in other languages include Navajo *Beehai* (Young and Morgan 1980:160); Jemez *tò·-k̓ælæ* (pl. *-cóš*) 'painted Apachean' (Joe Sando, communication to editors 1978); Taos p̓úaɬ̓ę̨ną̨ (pl. p̓uaɬ̓ę̨nę̨) (Harrington 1918); Kiowa *k̓óp-tʰɔ̀gûy* 'mountain Apache' (Laurel Watkins, communication to editors 1979). Tewa *sáve* 'Apachean' applies especially to the Jicarilla; Har̦rington (1916:574) obtained the specific Tewa names *tún sáve* 'basket Apachean' (which, as he points out, is likely to be a translation from Spanish) and *p̓i sáve* 'red Apachean' (Harrington 1920), given by other sources as the name for the Western Apache. Mescalero uses the loanword *Higaalí* (Scott Rushforth, communication to editors 1981); other names, recorded by Mooney (1897b), are kiñya´-ĭnde (or -ĭni) and tashĭ´nĕ.

The two Jicarilla divisions are the *gułgahén* 'plains people, Llanero' and *sáidindé* 'sand people, Ollero' (Opler 1936b:202–203); adaptations of the Spanish names for these bands have also been recorded in Jicarilla (Goddard 1911:141). Harrington's (1940:511) conclusion that the Spanish name of the Olleros, who were mountain-dwellers, should be Hoyeros 'people of the mountain dells' (a dialect form from *hoya* 'dell') has been supported by D.A. Gunnerson (1974:161).

Sources

There are few general works that cover Jicarilla Apache history from the colonial period to the recent past. The standard source, which relies primarily on Spanish documents but provides an overview of Jicarilla cultural life and history through 1800, is by D.A. Gunnerson (1974). Mails (1974) contains a section on the Jicarilla. Tiller (1982) is a study of the economic, social, and political history of the tribe. Crocchiola (1967) and Van Roekel (1971) are poorly documented; the latter is essentially a memoir of missionary activity on the Jicarilla Reservation.

Several reliable monographs deal tangentially with Jicarilla history during the colonial period: Thomas (1932, 1935), Moorhead (1968), and Forbes (1960).

More studies cover the territorial period from the 1840s to 1900, but they, too, treat Jicarillas as part of the larger Southwestern historical picture. Among them is Bancroft (1889). Still the most valuable source on early Jicarilla relations with the federal government is Abel's (1915) volume of the edited correspondence of James S. Calhoun while he was an Indian agent and superintendent of Indian affairs in New Mexico.

Galloway (1905) and Carson (1964) also document Jicarilla relations with Indian agents. The 1873 agreement between the federal government and the Jicarilla Apaches is recounted by T.A. Dolan (1929).

On the Jicarilla Apaches' role in the War of 1854 and 1855 see especially Utley (1967) and M.F. Taylor (1969, 1970). Military histories and memoirs including chapters or sections on the Jicarilla War are Cooke (1952), Bender (1952), and Miles (1896).

Books on northeastern New Mexico history, particularly with reference to the famed Maxwell Land Grant, deal to some degree with the Jicarilla occupation of that region (Keleher 1942; Pearson 1961). Murphy (1972, 1972a) focuses on the American settlement and the interaction between the White populace and the Jicarilla Apaches. Dale (1949) covers the same period but concentrates more on federal Indian policies and treats the Jicarillas only indirectly.

Studies resulting from the Indian Claims Commission litigation on the Jicarilla land claims offer well-argued and documented information on Jicarilla history and ethnography, although the authors were commissioned specifically to support particular legal positions (Atwater 1974; Bender 1974b; Cutter 1974; B.L. Gordon et al. 1974; J.W. Nelson 1974; Schroeder 1974c).

Materials on the period after 1887 are rare. Hamlin Garland gave an interesting literary account of life on the Jicarilla Reservation (Underhill and Littlefield 1976). Nicklason (1980) is a specialized study of the Jicarilla-federal relationship.

Works on the Jicarilla in the twentieth century are as limited as for previous periods. L.A. Cornell's (1929) thesis provides a cursory and narrow overview. Collier (1962) gives a brief account of government programs under the Indian Reorganization Act of 1934 on the Jicarilla Reservation. The role of Collier and the Indian Reorganization Act in the economic history of the Jicarilla can best be evaluated by consulting Philp (1977).

A comprehensive study of Jicarilla life in the 1950s is by H.C. Wilson (1964). Basehart and Sasaki (1964) treat political organization, and Sasaki and Basehart (1961–1962) discuss economy in the same era. The Stanford Research Institute's (1958) five volumes contain much documented information on the economic and political system of the Jicarilla Apache Tribe. Kerr's (1959) thesis explored reservation education in the 1950s. Ethnographic studies of the Jicarilla Apaches are as scarce as the historical studies; most of them are the works of Opler, whose general works (1936b, 1971a) are most useful. More detailed works by Opler describe the Jicarilla ceremonial relay race (1944), mythology (1938a), the Adolescence rite (1942a), the Holiness rite (1943), and childhood and youth (1946). Other good sources dealing with Jicarilla ethnology are Curtis (1907–1930, 1), Goddard (1911), and Mooney (1898a).

The largest repository of primary documents concerning the Jicarilla Apaches are the federal records centers of the National Archives, mainly within Record Group 75, Records of the Bureau of Indian Affairs, but also within other categories like Record Group 48, the Records of the Secretary of the Interior, Indian Division, Record Group 279, the Records of the Indian Claims Commission, Docket 22-A: The Jicarilla Apache Land Claims Case. These records date from 1848 to 1952.

Some correspondence concerning the Jicarilla Apache War of 1854–1855 is in the William Ritch Papers in the Huntington Library, San Marino, California. At the Newberry Library, Chicago, the Benjamin H. Grierson Papers include a few pieces on the settlement of the Jicarilla Reservation in 1887. The Benjamin Thomas Collection at the Museum of New Mexico Library, Santa Fe, has a small file of correspondence of Thomas, the Indian agent for the Jicarilla Apaches in the 1870s.

Western Apache

KEITH H. BASSO

Of the hundreds of peoples that lived and flourished in native North America, few have been so consistently misrepresented as the Apacheans of Arizona and New Mexico. Glorified by novelists, sensationalized by historians, and distorted beyond credulity by commercial film makers, the popular image of "the Apache"—a brutish, terrifying semihuman bent upon wanton death and destruction—is almost entirely a product of irresponsible caricature and exaggeration. Indeed, there can be little doubt that the Apache has been transformed from a native American into an American legend, the fanciful and fallacious creation of a non-Indian citizenry whose inability to recognize the massive treachery of ethnic and cultural stereotypes has been matched only by its willingness to sustain and inflate them.

Stereotypes invariably come attached to their own inaccurate versions of history, and the Apaches are no exception. It is commonly supposed, for example, that these were a single people undifferentiated by geographical location, language, or culture. This is untrue. There were a number of distinct Apache groups, each one characterized by a unique constellation of cultural features that set it apart from all the others. There is also a widespread belief that the Apache, having met defeat at the hands of the United States Cavalry, were forcibly removed from their homelands and thereafter quietly perished. This, too, is untrue. In 1978 Arizona alone boasted an Apache population of well over 10,000 individuals. Finally, one may encounter the view that modern Apaches, at last aware of the "error" of their "primitive" ways, have abandoned all traces of their former customs and beliefs. False once again. Although it is true that far-reaching changes have taken place since the establishment of reservations in the 1870s, large sectors of Apache culture have been maintained and survive to the present in vigorous form.

Kroeber (1939:35–36) observed: "In terms of precise ethnological knowledge, the Apache are, with the possible exception of the Ojibwa [an Algonquian-speaking people of the Northeast] the least-known surviving North American group among any of like areal extent or historic importance." Even though impressive advances have been made in Apachean ethnology since the time of his writing, it cannot be claimed that the deficiency he noted has been fully rectified. To the contrary, much of Apache history—undocumented and irretrievable—will never be known, and the dynamics of contemporary Apache societies have proved difficult to understand.

Twentieth-century Apaches, observant and astute, are fully aware that aspects of their culture and behavior seem puzzling and perplexing to outsiders. Modern Apaches are firmly convinced that anyone who is not an Apache can never know what it means to *be* an Apache, and they are unquestionably correct. But they are willing to acknowledge the possibility that honest attempts to unravel the threads of their history and comprehend their current way of life can facilitate more effective cooperation with non-Indians. This attitude was expressed in 1961 by Leon Beatty, a Western Apache shaman:

> I don't know why you want to learn these things about Apaches, these things of long ago and how it rests with these same people today. Perhaps you will take these things and give them to the Whitemen. I do not know if you will do this, but if that is what you want to do it is alright. It is alright as long as what you tell them is spoken with respect. . . . You say that the Whitemen can receive such things with respect. I hope what you say is true. It has not been true before. But if it is true it will be good. You can try. Up to now, these people [the Apache] have been afraid to speak out for themselves. But some of them are becoming bold and soon many more will speak out. They will not have to learn what to say. They will know what to say because they have known it all their lives. Perhaps you can help the Whitemen get ready for them. You can try. The time has come.

Language and Territory

The term Western Apache has been used in the anthropological and historical literature in two distinct senses, thus giving rise to confusion about the proper identity of these people. Some writers have used the term to refer inclusively to all Southern Athapaskan tribes, except the Navajo, who lived west of the Rio Grande (Kroeber 1939; Forbes 1960; Spicer 1962; Thrapp 1967; Moorhead 1968; Dobyns 1971). This usage is misleading because it fails to distinguish the Chiricahua from other Apacheans in the region, thereby creating the erroneous impression that despite important cultural differences all the groups were essentially alike. A more restricted definition, and the one adopted here, avoids this difficulty by designating as Western Apache "all those Apache peoples [excluding the Navajo] who have lived within the present boundaries of the state of Arizona during historic times with the exception of the Chiricahua, Warm Springs, and allied Apache, and a small band of Apaches known as the Apache Mansos, who lived in the vicinity of Tucson" (Goodwin 1935:55).

By 1850, and perhaps well before, the totality of people thus identified as Western Apache was divided into five major groups that occupied contiguous territories in east-central Arizona (fig. 1). The White Mountain Apache was the easternmost group, ranging over an extensive area bounded by the Piñaleno Mountains on the south and the White Mountains on the north. To the southwest, in the foothills of the Santa Catalina and Galiuro mountains, and on both sides of the San Pedro and Gila rivers, lived the San Carlos Apaches. The territory of a third division, the Cibecue Apache, extended north from the Salt River to well beyond the Mogollon Rim. The western boundary of Cibecue territory was marked by the Sierra Ancha, which, together with the Mazatzal Mountains and the East Verde River, defined the area occupied by the Southern Tonto Apache. The Northern Tonto inhabited the upper reaches of the Verde River and ranged as far north as the San Francisco Mountains.

Although the Western Apache made lexical distinctions corresponding to Goodwin's (1935) White Mountain, San Carlos, Cibecue, and Tonto categories, they did not partition the Tonto group with different names for northern and southern divisions. This distinction was made by Goodwin (1942:41, 47, 197–200) on the basis of geographical and dialectal criteria but has no other counterpart in Western Apache culture. To the contrary, the Tontos have always regarded themselves as a single entity, undifferentiated internally except for distinctions based on local group and clan affiliations. Goodwin's classification has been retained in the historical sections of this essay simply because it is basic to an understanding of his interpretation of Western Apache social organization prior to 1850.

The Western Apache spoke a language* belonging to the Athapaskan stock. Dialect differences existed among the five Western Apache groups, but these differences were minor and did not interfere with effective verbal communication.

Prehistory and Early History

Owing to the almost complete absence of excavated Western Apache archeological sites and to an equally small number of early Spanish documents concerning these people, the reconstruction of Western Apache prehistory is made extremely difficult. However, this has not prevented anthropologists and historians from speculating on the matter. A review of some of their theories reveals the extent to which responsible scholars disagree and underscores the fact that their interpretations, though provocative and certainly worthwhile, are highly tentative and should be regarded with a commensurate amount of caution. Compare "Southern Athapaskan Archeology" and "Historical Linguistics and Archeology," volume 9; and "The Apachean Culture Pattern and Its Origins," "Apachean Languages," and "Navajo Prehistory and History to 1850," this volume.

It seems probable that by 1525 Athapaskan-speaking peoples who had earlier migrated southward from points in northern Canada were established on the plains of Texas and New Mexico (D.A. Gunnerson 1956; Vogt 1961; Gunnerson 1969; Gunnerson and Gunnerson 1971; Hester 1962). In the centuries that followed, some of these latecomers to the Southwest increased in population and, for reasons that remain obscure, moved to occupy territories west of the Rio Grande. A few of these people pressed on into the heart of what is now Arizona and there, responding to a new set of environmental conditions (including, of course, the presence of other human populations) began to develop the linguistic, social, and cultural characteristics that were eventually to distinguish them as Western Apache. Prior

*Western Apache words appearing in italics in the *Handbook* are written in the standard practical orthography of Perry (1972), which uses essentially the same conventions as the Navajo orthography ("Navajo Prehistory and History to 1850," this vol.). The graphemic units are the following: (lenis unaspirated stops and affricates) *b*, *d*, *dl*, *dz*, *j*, *g*, *'*; (voiceless aspirated stops and affricates) *t*, *tł*, *ts*, *ch*, *k*, *kw*; (glottalized stops and affricates) *t'*, *tł'*, *ts'*, *ch'*, *k'*; (voiceless continuants) *ł*, *s*, *sh*, *h* (- *x* - *hw*); (voiced continuants) *l*, *z*, *zh*, *gh* (- *w* - *y*); (nasals) *m*, *n*; (nasal with stop release) *n̲* - *d̲*; (semivowel) *y*; (short oral vowels) *i*, *e*, *a*, *o*; (long oral vowels) *ii*, *ee*, *aa*, *oo*; (short nasalized vowels) *į*, *ę*, *ą*, *ǫ*; (long nasalized vowels) *įį*, *ęę*, *ąą*, *ǫǫ*; (tones) unmarked (low) v́ and v́v́ (high), v́v (falling). The practical orthography allows for spelling *o* as u "when the sound is definitely as in 'to'" (Perry 1972:107). The underlined letters *d̲* and *n̲*, given as free variants, are pronounced [^{n}d] or [n] in the San Carlos dialect and [d] in the White Mountain dialect (F. Hill 1963:149).

Written in the *Handbook* technical alphabet (between slashes) the phonemes of Western Apache corresponding to these graphemic units and given in the same order are: /b/, /d/, /λ/, /ʒ/, /ǯ/, /g/, /ʔ/; /t/, /ƛ/, /c/, /č/, /k/, /k^{w}/; /t̓/, /ƛ̓/, /c̓/, /č̓/, /k̓/; /ł/, /s/, /š/, /x/ ([x(^{w}) - h(^{w})]); (voiced continuants) /l/, /z/, /ž/, /γ/ ([γ - γ^{w} - γ^{y}]); /m/, /n/; /^{n}d/; /y/; /i/, /e/, /a/, /o/; /i·/, /e·/, /a·/, /o·/; /į/, /ę/, /ą/, /ǫ/; /į·/, /ę·/, /ą·/, /ǫ·/; /v/, /v́/, /v̂/. To this list Greenfeld (1978) adds three rare phonemes: /p/ (voiceless aspirate), /^{m}b/ (varying with /b/), and /^{n}g/.

In the practical orthography the rule for writing /x/ as *x* is the same as Navajo. The phonemes /x/ and /γ/ are labialized when adjacent to an *o*-vowel, and these labialized allophones are written with the distinct graphemes *hw* and *w*, respectively. The phoneme /γ/, if not labialized by a preceding *o*-vowel, is palatalized to [γ^{y}] before a front vowel, and this allophone is written *y*, identically with the distinct phoneme /y/.

Western Apache words are from Perry (1972) or have been phonemicized on the advice of Philip J. Greenfeld (communications to editors 1981) and Marie-Louise Liebe-Harkort (communications to editors 1982). In the cases of disagreement among the sources the editors are responsible for selecting among them.

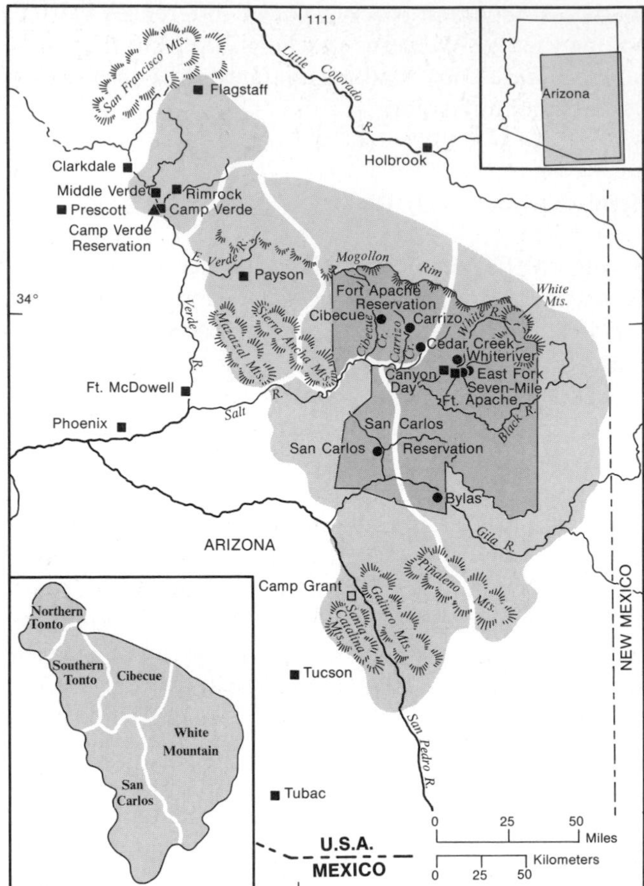

Fig. 1. Tribal territory in 1850 with reservations established in the 1870s.

to the onset of this process of differentiation, which in other regions took other forms and resulted in the emergence of other Apachean societies, anthropologists suppose that Southern Athapaskan culture was uniform and relatively simple. This hypothesis is based upon inferences drawn from comparative studies of historic Apachean cultural systems that have attempted to reconstruct the common base, or "proto-Apachean" system, from which the historic Apache presumably evolved (Opler 1936; Kroeber 1937; Murdock 1949; Bellah 1952; Hoijer 1956; C.B. White 1957; Kaut 1956, 1957; Vogt 1961).

The Proto-Apacheans were seminomadic hunters and gatherers. Adult males armed with the sinew-backed bow pursued bison, antelope, deer, and smaller game, while females collected wild plant foods. Material culture was unelaborate and easily transported. The typical Proto-Apachean dwelling probably consisted of a conical frame of wooden poles covered with hides. The fire drill was used by these people, and it seems fairly certain that they made undecorated pointed-bottom pottery. Clothing and footwear were fashioned from the tanned skins of deer and antelope, and prior to the acquisition of horses the dog served as an important beast of burden (D.A. Gunnerson 1956).

It is believed that the Proto-Apacheans lived in small scattered encampments, which were composed of bilocal or matrilocal extended families that periodically detached themselves from the larger group to follow herds of game and exploit floral resources. Political organization was minimal beyond the limits of the extended family, the activities of each camp being directed by an older man whose main responsibilities were to organize hunting parties, supervise overland treks, and mediate interpersonal disputes.

Descent was probably bilateral (C.B. White 1957), although Murdock (1949) believes that the Southern Athapaskans may have arrived in the Southwest with vestiges of an archaic matrilineal system. C.B. White (1957) has suggested that Proto-Apachean kinship nomenclature was characterized by Hawaiian cousin terminology and bifurcate merging terminology on the first ascending generation, a conclusion with which Kaut (1957) concurs. However, Hymes and Driver (1958) have challenged this point, reaffirming the position taken by Hoijer (1956) and earlier by Opler (1936) and Kroeber (1937) that bifurcate collateral terminology was more likely.

Vogt (1961:289) provided a summary of basic themes in Proto-Apachean religion: "Ceremonial organization was probably focused around a shaman who derived power from visions, or other supernatural manifestations, and performed curing ceremonies. Girls' puberty was emphasized ceremonially as an important rite of passage. Strong beliefs included fear of the dead and ghosts and that disease is caused by contact with lightning and with certain animals, such as the bear."

If the Proto-Apacheans are destined to remain obscure, so too are the circumstances surrounding the proliferation of their descendants and the expansion of these populations into territories west of the Rio Grande. Prior to the occupation of this region by Apacheans, it was inhabited by Puebloan peoples, and for many years prehistorians and ethnologists attributed the disappearance of these sedentary agriculturalists to the devastating effects of a "Southern Athapaskan invasion" (V. Mindeleff 1891; Kidder 1924; Gladwin and Gladwin 1935). This hypothesis has been called into question (cf. Schroeder 1952, 1963; D.A. Gunnerson 1956; Hester 1962; Carlson 1965). Archeological data suggest that by A.D. 1400–1450 the Puebloan villagers (except the Piro) had vacated all areas aside from those in which they continue to reside today. Conversely, there is no really solid evidence that Southern Athapaskans lived west of the Rio Grande until at least a century later (Schroeder 1963). In summary, it appears that the Puebloans abandoned their lands long before they were discovered and taken over by Apacheans.

During the 1500s Plains-dwelling Apaches established trading relationships with several Pueblos on the Rio Grande and by 1625 were firmly settled west of the river itself (Forbes 1960). In 1630 Friar Alonso de Benavides, a Franciscan missionary, reported that a people he called Gila Apaches (*Apaches de Xila*) were living in small rancherias on the pine-covered slopes of mountains in west-central New Mexico. Farther north, Benavides noted, were "Navajo Apaches" who led a more settled way of life and practiced a limited amount of agriculture (Benavides 1954). The earliest record of Athapaskan speakers living west of the Rio Grande was made by Antonio de Espejo who encountered a group of Apacheans (*Querechos*) near the Pueblo of Zuni in 1582 (Hammond and Rey 1966). Although many historians have identified these people as Navajo, it is entirely possible that they were Gila Apaches (Schroeder 1963). In fact, on the basis of Navajo archeology it seems unlikely that the Navajo advanced as far south as Zuni until the mid-1700s (R.G. Vivian 1960; Hester 1962; Carlson 1965; Bannister 1964; Jeffrey S.Dean, personal communication 1972).

It is uncertain when ancestors of the Western Apache first penetrated Arizona. Nor is it understood what the conditions were that enabled these people to establish themselves and secure the territories they held by 1850. The lack of information is a direct reflection of the fact that Europeans rarely ventured north of the Gila River before 1800 (cf. Spicer 1962); ever since Francisco Vásquez de Coronado's epoch-making expedition in 1542 the major thrust of Spanish exploration and colonization had been directed farther east. Consequently, the central and northern portions of Arizona saw relatively few outsiders; and in comparison to Indian peoples in New Mexico and Texas, the Western Apache remained isolated and aloof, their locations and numbers poorly known, the course of their cultural development a mystery.

Nevertheless, the picture is not a total blank. When the northern frontier of the Spanish empire finally reached into southern Arizona, Apacheans were securely installed on both sides of the Gila River (Bolton 1916; Kino 1948; Wyllys 1931; Ives 1939; Spicer 1962). In the late 1600s Father Luis Velarde was informed by Pimans that Apaches had closed to travel a route leading north from Casa Grande (Wyllys 1931), and in 1743 when another priest, Ignacio Keller, attempted to use the same trail he was forced to turn back because Apaches stole his horses (Ives 1939). It is possible, then, that as early as 1600–1625 a phalanx of Benavides's Gila Apaches or Espejo's Querechos (who may or may not have been Navajos) entered Arizona in the vicinity of the Little Colorado River (David Brugge, personal communication 1972). And it can be stated with a measure of confidence that by 1700 these same people, who later came to be known as Western Apache, had successfully laid claim to an extensive territory that stretched south from the Mogollon Rim across the Natanes Plateau to the Gila River. This interpretation coincides with a number of Western Apache clan legends that tell of a southward migration from points north of the Mogollon Rim followed by expansions to the east and west (Goodwin 1939, 1942; Goddard 1920, 1920a). Forbes (1960) has asserted that Indians seen by Espejo in 1583 in the Northern Tonto area were in fact Western Apache; however, most authorities agree with Bandelier (1890–1892, 1) that the people in question were Yavapai (Bolton 1916; Schroeder 1952; Hammond and Rey 1966). Spanish sources from the early 1700s place Yuman speakers in the Tonto Basin–Verde River region at that time (Wyllys 1931), and Schroeder (1955–1956) has argued that Apacheans did not expand into the Tonto area until after 1750. On present evidence, this interpretation seems to be the most reasonable.

Although very little is known about the content of Western Apache culture in the seventeenth and eighteenth centuries, several important elements had been added to it that were absent from the Proto-Apachean system. One of these was agriculture. Having acquired the techniques of farming from the Western Pueblos or Navajo, the Western Apache adapted them to local conditions and thereafter managed to cultivate limited quantities of maize, beans, and squash (Goodwin 1935, 1942; Buskirk 1949). Although agriculture never replaced wild-plant gathering and hunting as the dominant modes of subsistence, it did become sufficiently important to alter the economic cycle of Apache society from year-round nomadism to one involving periods of sedentary residence near farm sites. This shift and its concomitant association of kin-based sodalities with particular localities has led some authorities to suggest that agriculture fostered the development of unilineal descent groups among the Western Apache, a feature of social organization they shared with no other Southern Athapaskan people except the Navajo (Kaut 1957).

Another important addition to the cultural inventory of the Western Apache was the horse (Forbes 1959). Introduced into the Southwest by Coronado, this animal became highly valued as a beast of burden and a source of food. Simultaneously, it served as a means of transportation that enabled the Apache to increase their geographical range greatly and to exploit economic resources far beyond the boundaries of their own territories. By the middle of the eighteenth century, the Western Apache had established an intricate network of trading and raiding relationships that involved at least a dozen other cultural groups and reached all the way from the Hopi villages in northern Arizona to Spanish settlements in central Sonora (table 1). The development and maintenance of such an extensive system would have been totally impossible without the mobility afforded by the horse.

The degree to which contacts between the Western Apache and other Indian societies resulted in cultural borrowing is poorly understood. Some anthropologists

Table 1. Western Apache Raiding and Trading Relationships about 1850

Division	*Maricopa*	*Pima*	*Ópata*	*Papago*	*Havasupai*	*Walapai*	*Yavapai*	*Hopi*	*Chiricahua*	*Zuni*	*Navajo*
White Mountain	R	R	R	R	0	0	T,R	0	T	T	T,R
San Carlos	R	R	R	R	0	0	T,R	0	0	T	0
Cibecue	R	R	R	R	0	0	T,R	T	T	0	T,R
Southern Tonto	R	R	0	0	R	R	T	T	0	0	0
Northern Tonto	R	R	0	0	R	R	T	T	0	0	T,R

NOTE: T = trading, R = raiding, 0 = no contact.

(for example, Gifford 1940; Underhill 1948) have speculated that prominent elements of Western Apache religion were taken over from the Hopi, and others (for example, Kroeber 1937) believe that matrilineal clans, certainly among the most basic components of Western Apache social organization, were borrowed from these same people. Intriguing though such proposals may be, they are extremely difficult to document and therefore virtually impossible to prove. Nonetheless, it seems highly probable that certain spheres of Western Apache culture, most notably religion and material culture, were influenced by ideas and techniques acquired from outside sources (Underhill 1948; Goodwin 1942, 1945).

History: Spaniards and Mexicans

Indian peoples of the Southwest responded to the impact of Spanish colonialism in different ways (cf. Spicer 1962). Among the Western Apache the most conspicuous reaction, though by no means the only one, took the form of vigorous raiding and warfare. It is not known when the Apache first began to attack Spanish settlements on a regular basis, but raiding was probably a well-established practice by the middle of the eighteenth century. Present evidence suggests that the Western Apache did not organize raids for the purpose of increasing their already vast territory; nor was their aim to drive away or destroy the Europeans who had settled along its margins (Goodwin 1942; Spicer 1962; Basso 1971). To the contrary, these populations were viewed as valuable economic resources that could be counted on throughout the year to produce substantial amounts of cereal grain and livestock. It was to the Apaches' distinct advantage that such resources remain viable, and this may help explain why mass killing and the widescale destruction of enemy property never figured prominently in the raiding complex (Basso 1971).

Spanish attempts to control and defeat the Western Apache by military means met with failure (Spicer 1962; Thrapp 1967; Moorhead 1968). Presidios were established at various points on the northern frontier—Arispe, Fronteras, Tubac, and later at Tucson—but this was a porous line of defense that Apache raiding parties, well-mounted and supremely elusive, were able to puncture at will. Between 1765 and 1780 hostilities intensified, and the Spaniards, confronted with a situation they could not control, were forced to admit that their plan to exterminate the Apache was unrealistic and unfeasible. In 1786, following a reorganization of the administrative structure of New Spain, a new Indian policy was conceived and implemented by Viceroy Bernardo de Gálvez.

Gálvez's policy decreed that immediate offensive action be taken against all Indian tribes still at war. Once the "hostiles" had sued for peace, they were to be settled in villages near presidios where they would be supplied with cloth, food, inferior firearms, and alcoholic beverages. These gifts, Gálvez reasoned, would be so highly esteemed that the Indians would soon develop a wish to remain at peace and abandon all thoughts of war. Simultaneously, their weapons would become inoperative, thus weakening their ability to revolt. They would also develop an abiding fondness for liquor. On this last point, Gálvez was clear: "The supplying of drink to the Indians will be a means of gaining their goodwill, discovering their secrets, calming them so they will think less often of conceiving and executing their hostilities, and creating for them a new necessity which will oblige them to recognize their dependence upon us more directly" (in Faulk 1970:45). Cynical and subversive, but distinctly utilitarian nevertheless, the intent of Gálvez's plan was to subdue the Apache by promoting social disorganization and corrupting their will to fight. In this way, it was hoped, the Indians would become docile and dependent, a harmless appendage of the Spanish crown instead of one of its most determined adversaries.

For nearly 25 years the new policy worked with moderate success. Some Western Apache groups did make peace, and a few took up residence in the vicinity of Spanish presidios. By 1825 the incidence of raids had dropped significantly, and a quarter-century later Spanish mines and ranches began to appear in northern Sonora and southern Arizona. In the meantime, an uneasy symbiotic relationship came into being between Spaniards and Apaches, the Apaches acquiring weekly rations and, in the words of a Franciscan missionary living in Tucson, "all of the Spanish vices and none of the Spanish virtues" (in Faulk 1970:46). Indeed, the strategy of pacification through dependency might have been permanently successful if circumstances produced by the Mexican War of Independence had not prevented its continuation (Spicer 1962).

After 1821, the year in which Mexico's independence

was finally achieved, the situation of the northern frontier began to deteriorate. Beset with serious financial problems, the new Mexican government could not continue to subsidize the rationing system, and more and more Apaches, displeased at this turn of events, drifted away from presidios and started to regroup in their homelands to the north. Simultaneously, as a result of the shortage of funds and a depleted supply of troops and equipment, the presidios themselves ceased to function effectively. In 1831 the Western Apache resumed intensive raiding, and Sonora, weakened and confused, was thrown once again into turmoil.

The reaction of the Mexicans was impulsive and unwise. Rejecting outright the possibility of treaties with the Indians, it was decided instead to pursue a policy of extermination similar to the one that had failed six decades earlier. A volunteer army was raised but met with little success. Confident and rejuvenated, the Apache struck deeper into Mexico than ever before. From the mid-1830s until Anglo-Americans assumed control of Arizona in 1853, the population of Sonora declined. The capital city of Arispe, which had 7,000 inhabitants in 1821, was reduced to 1,500 in 1846 (Faulk 1970:53). Tucson and Tubac were besieged on several occasions by large numbers of Apaches, but these attacks were repelled without extensive loss of life. Nevertheless, it was perfectly clear that the Mexican policy had backfired and the "Indian problem" remained unsolved.

In reference to the development of raiding as an important subsistence strategy, Spicer (1962:229) has observed that "contact with Spaniards more completely revolutionized the life of the Apaches than it did any other Southwestern people."

This is certainly correct, but it needs to be emphasized that the impact of raiding was felt most profoundly in the sphere of economics and that other sectors of Apache culture—language, mythology, ritual, and basic forms of social organization—did not undergo significant alteration. In large part, this may be attributed to the fact that throughout the Spanish and Mexican periods the Western Apache remained marginal to the colonial administrative-missionization system (Spicer 1962). Western Apache territory never became the scene of Spanish settlements, and there was never any acceptance by the Indians of Spanish political domination. As a result, the conditions under which contact took place, as well as the purposes it served, could be determined and regulated by the Apache, thus enabling them to select for permanent adoption only those elements of Spanish culture that were congruent with preexisting institutions. Primarily, it appears, these elements consisted of items of material culture: the lance, perhaps the shield, the saddle and stirrup, the bridle, firearms, cloth, and playing cards.

Spanish and Mexican captives, the majority of whom were females taken as young children, undoubtedly altered the genetic composition of Western Apache populations, but there is little evidence to indicate that they played a major role as agents of culture change. To the contrary, most of them were fully enculturated as Apaches, willingly assumed the rights and duties of Apache women, and thereafter had neither the incentive nor the power to alter what they regarded as a coherent and satisfying way of life. Captives were responsible for introducing a few Spanish words into the Western Apache lexicon, several new forms of gambling, and certain modifications in dress and the preparation of food. However, beyond these and other essentially minor contributions, their influence upon Apache culture seems to have been negligible.

Culture about 1850

Practically no reliable ethnographic information was available on the Western Apache until the early 1900s when Pliny E. Goddard (1920, 1920a), one of the founders of American anthropology, collected a number of Apache myths at Fort Apache and San Carlos. The reports and memoirs of military officers were also published (Bourke 1886, 1891, 1892; B. Davis 1963; Cruse 1941; Crook 1946; Bigelow 1958; Betzinez 1959; Reagan 1931), as were the journals and recollections of travelers (Cozzens 1876; Blount 1919), and missionaries (Guenther 1958). In the main, however, the cultural data contained in these accounts were meager and superficial, and it was not until the early 1920s, by which time the Western Apache had been placed on reservations, that ethnographic work was begun in earnest. The most significant research of this period was conducted by Grenville Goodwin, a self-trained ethnographer of impressive talents, who lived among the Western Apache for nearly 10 years. His publications represent the first successful attempt to describe Western Apache culture as an integrated system (Goodwin 1933, 1935, 1938, 1938a, 1939, 1942). Working with a large group of elderly Apache informants, most of whom belonged to the White Mountain, San Carlos, and Cibecue divisions, Goodwin acquired massive amounts of data on the conditions of prereservation life. This material provided the basis for his major work (1942), which is a detailed historical reconstruction of Apache society as it existed in the mid-1800s before the coming of the White Americans.

Subsistence

The territory controlled by the Western Apache covered an area of approximately 90,000 square miles (Getty 1964). Characterized by extreme ecological diversity, it is a region of rugged mountains and deep canyons, of well-watered valleys, deciduous and coniferous forests, and arid desert. Elevations rise from around 2,000 feet to slightly less than 12,000, and mean temperatures fluctuate from below zero in the winter to near 100 degrees during the months of July and August (Lowe 1964). Rainfall is concentrated in the summer and winter, ranging from four inches annually at low elevations to 20–30 inches at higher altitudes. The flora varies correspondingly from essentially desert types, including a large number of cactus species and riparian shrubs to heavy stands of ponderosa pine, Douglas fir, cottonwood, and oak. The fauna is equally varied, and game in the form of deer, bear, elk, and antelope was plentiful.

In spite of numerous similarities in language and culture, significant variation existed among the five Western Apache divisions with respect to population, size of territory, use of the horse, and dependence upon agriculture. The White Mountain Apache were the largest division with an estimated population of 1,400 to 1,500, followed by the San Carlos and Cibecue Apache (900 to 1,000 each), the Southern Tonto (800 to 900), and the Northern Tonto (400 to 500). This ranking corresponded exactly to the relative amount of territory controlled by each division as well as the extent to which its members utilized the horse. Only in regard to intensity of agriculture was the ordering partially disturbed; in this dimension the Cibecue Apache ranked first, the White Mountain Apache second, the San Carlos Apache third, and the Southern and Northern Tonto fourth and fifth respectively (Goodwin 1942:59–65).

Although the Western Apache engaged in farming, their subsistence economy was based upon hunting and gathering. Goodwin (1935) estimates that agricultural products made up only 25 percent of all the food consumed in a year, the remainder being a combination of meat and undomesticated plants. Because the Apache could not rely on a surplus of crops, they were compelled to travel widely in search of food and, as a consequence, did not establish permanent residences in any one place. Indeed, except for the winter months, when plant-gathering activities came to a virtual standstill, they were almost constantly on the move.

In April, the people took leave of winter camps in the Salt, Black, and Gila river valleys and proceeded north to farm sites located on the banks of streams in the mountains. Here they constructed dome-shaped wickiups called *gową*, repaired irrigation ditches, and, after breaking the earth with pointed digging sticks, seeded plots of corn, beans, and pumpkin (Goodwin 1935, 1942; Buskirk 1949). Immediately after sprouts appeared in May, gathering parties set forth to collect mescal tubers, which were pounded into a coarse pulp, shaped into flat rectangular cakes, roasted in pit ovens (fig. 2), and packed for transportation in large, finely woven baskets. Meanwhile, older people, the disabled, and young children remained behind at the farm sites

top, Smithsonian, NAA: 76 4665; center, Amer. Mus. of Nat. Hist., New York: 242717; bottom, U. of Ariz., Ariz. State Mus., Tucson: 18183.

Fig. 2. Preparation of mescal. A staple food in all the Apache groups, mescal was treated with singular respect, and roasting it involved a sequence of prayers and ritual actions. top, Western Apache woman uprooting mescal plant with pointed stick and stone hammer. center, Base portions of the plant, or crowns, after the leaves were shorn off, being roasted in a large underground oven. bottom, Cooked mescal pounded into flat cakes that were spread to dry (as here) and saved for future use. top, Photograph by Edward S. Curtis, 1906. center, Photograph by Pliny E. Goddard, at Calva, Ariz., 1909. bottom, Photograph by Grenville Goodwin, early 1930s, probably on San Carlos Reservation.

to cultivate the crops and protect them from destructive birds and animals.

In late June and early July, the fruit of the saguaro (*Carnegiea gigantea*), prickly pear (*Opuntia* spp.), and cholla (*Opuntia* spp.) cacti reached maturity, and once again gathering expeditions fanned out to exploit floral resources. These expeditions involved from eight to a dozen women all of whom were related by close ties of matrilineal kinship. Normally, such a group consisted of three or four fully adult sisters and their married and unmarried daughters. These women and their families lived together year-round and helped work one another's fields, thus forming an enduring social unit that functioned conspicuously in all economic pursuits except raiding (Goodwin 1942). Mesquite beans (*Prosopis* spp.), the fruit of the Spanish bayonet (*Yucca* spp.), and acorns of Emory's oak (*Quercus emoryi*) were collected in July and August, but toward the end of September, when domesticated crops began to ripen, gathering activities were temporarily suspended. Corn was harvested in October. Most of the yield was roasted and eaten on the spot, but a portion was dried in the sun and carefully stored in ground caches for use as seed the following year. Hunting was best in the late fall, and while women and children amassed large quantities of piñon nuts and juniper berries men journeyed afield in search of deer and antelope. In November, when a good supply of meat had been secured and transformed into smoked jerky, the people abandoned their farm sites and headed for lower altitudes and winter camps.

From December to March, the focus of Western Apache economic life shifted from hunting and gathering to raiding. The exact frequency of raiding is not known, but Goodwin (1942:158) asserts categorically that it reached its peak during the winter months. This, of course, was the time when severe shortages of food were most apt to occur, a fact that underscores the vital contribution made by raiding—chiefly in the form of stolen livestock—to the maintenance and survival of Apache society. Throughout the winter, women, who did not participate in raids, attended to other tasks. Foremost among these were the tanning of hides and

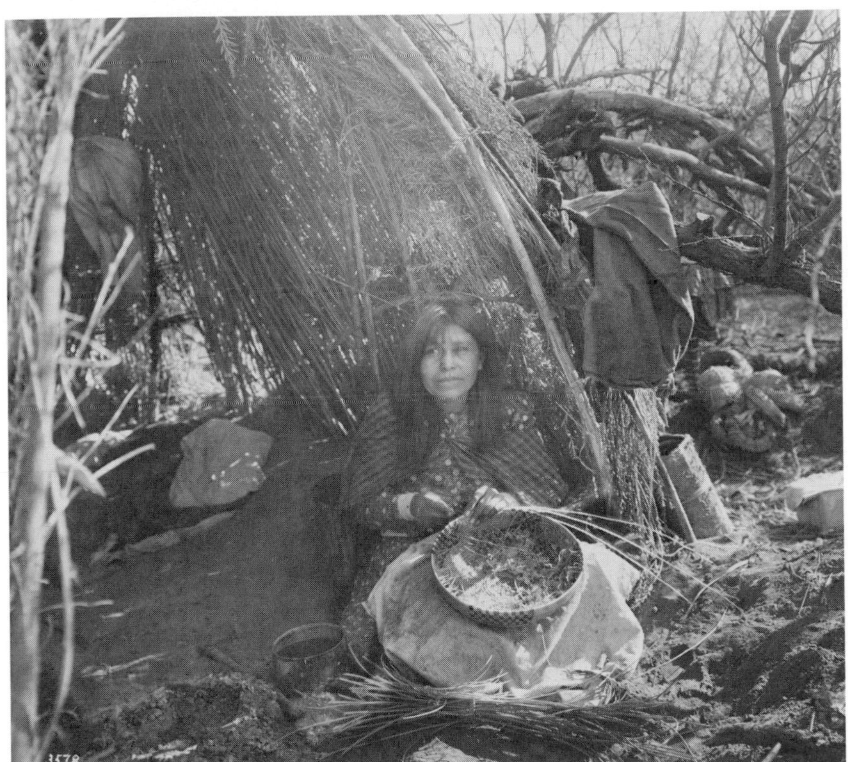

left, Calif. Histl. Soc., Los Angeles: Title Insurance Coll. 3578; Smithsonian, Dept. of Anthr.: top right, 328,067, bottom right, 360,758.

Fig. 3. Coiled basketry. left, Woman weaving basket in front of wickiup. Fibers are first softened in water (held in small pail). Dark-colored designs served primarily decorative purposes but might also identify the clan of the basketmaker. Bundles of unprepared materials lie on ground at right of wickiup. Photograph by C.C. Pierce, probably about 1900. top right, San Carlos Apache shallow tray with overall pattern in black. bottom right, White Mountain Apache olla-shaped basket with typical animal and human figures in black. These baskets were made for sale and were often quite large. top right, Diameter 44.0 cm, other to same scale, collected before 1925; bottom right, collected before 1931.

top right, Smithsonian, Dept. of Anthr.: 392,743; bottom left, Amer. Mus. of Nat. Hist., New York: 242,698; bottom right, U. of Ariz., Ariz. State Mus., Tucson: 21,378.

Fig. 4. Water bottles. top left, White Mountain Apache woman grinding juniper leaves for use in preparation of water basket. top center, She rubs the mashed leaves and ground hematite onto the surface of the twined basket to begin the waterproofing process and add a slight orange color (Tanner 1946). Both photographs by Tad Nichols, July 1941. bottom left, Completion of waterproofing by applying heated piñon pitch tothe inside and outside of the container. Photograph by Pliny E. Goddard, 1914. bottom right, White Mountain Apache brush made of yucca, shredded at one end, used to apply pitch to basket. Length about 20.3 cm, collected by Grenville Goodwin in 1936. top right, White Mountain Apache completed pitch-covered basket. The 2 twig handles could be used to attach a carrying strap that passed across the forehead or shoulders; such baskets were also used to hold beer. Height 31.0 cm, collected before 1954.

the manufacture of buckskin clothing. Older girls helped in these and other activities, while boys, armed with slings and small bows and arrows, added packrats, birds, and an occasional rabbit to the family larder. Even with the spoils of raiding to sustain them, winter was not a season of plenty for the Western Apache, and it was always with great anticipation that they greeted the first signs of spring. Late in March they packed their belongings in anticipation of the day when they could depart once again for their farm sites in the mountains and begin the annual cycle anew.

Social Organization

Although the five Western Apache divisions had varying degrees of contact with one another, each was considered distinct. Open conflict between the groups was rare—indeed, a limited amount of intermarriage took place among them—but it must be emphasized that they were autonomous and never acted as a unified body. Each division was made up of from two to five bands. According to Goodwin (1942), band distinctions were not so pronounced in some divisions as in others, but each possessed its own clearly defined hunting grounds and, except when pressed by lack of food, did not encroach upon those of its neighbors. Using military censuses presented in Goodwin (1942:582–587), it is possible to compute a mean size for Western Apache bands around 1880. This figure comes to 387 individuals, but there was considerable variation. For example, the San Carlos band (one of four in the San Carlos division) had only 53 members, whereas the Eastern White Mountain band of the White Mountain division had 748. Although bands were characterized by an internal unity somewhat greater than that of whole divisions, they did not participate in any form of joint political action. As Goodwin (1935:55) observed: "Bands were units only in the sense of territorial limitations and minor linguistic similarities."

Bands were formed of what were unquestionably the most important segments of Western Apache society, what Goodwin referred to as local groups. These were the basic units around which the social organization, government, and religious activities of the Apache revolved. Local groups varied in size from as few as 35 persons to as many as 200, but each local group had exclusive claims to certain farm sites and hunting localities, and each was headed by a chief who was in charge of collective enterprises such as trading expeditions, irrigation projects, and moving camp. The lack of solidarity characteristic of bands and divisions was replaced at the level of the local group by a high degree of social cohesiveness, primarily because most of the individuals who comprised these units were related by blood or marriage and were bound together by obligations of mutual support. A substantial number of marriages involved persons from the same local group, and, in fact, this seems to have been the preferred arrangement. Kaut (1957:63–64) has offered what is probably a sound explanation of this practice:

> Basically, people who had grown up in the same general area could operate together as a better economic team. Matrilocality required that the woman remain in the area to which she had been educated in terms of farming and gathering activities. Gathering activities, especially, required a very specific knowledge of rough terrain which could only be gained over a period of many years. The man's main economic activities were centered around hunting and raiding, which also required extensive training and integration into a tightly organized group. A man hunted best on his home ground, both because he knew it so well and because he garnered power from the very ground itself—a power which he lost when he entered other hunting grounds. He was trained for war and raiding by his mother's parents, his father, his elder brothers, and his mother's brothers. . . . For these reasons, a local group composed of extended families which drew their members from the same general area could operate more efficiently than one which contained many men who were strangers to its hunting territory and ceremonial organization.

Local groups were composed of from two to six smaller units that Goodwin (1942) described as family clusters. In most cases, a family cluster was no more than a large matrilocal extended family, that is, three to eight nuclear households each of which contained at least one female member who was a sibling or lineal descendant of an older woman in the group. There were exceptions because in spite of a prevailing tendancy for married men to reside in their wives' family cluster, it was not unusual for an elder son—especially an only son—to remain with his parents and sisters and bring his wife to live with them. Persons belonging to the matrilineage that formed the core of a family cluster shared membership in the same clan. This was significant because a family cluster, unlike local groups and bands, was not named after its territorial location but by the clan of its core lineage. Thus Goodwin (1942:128) writes: "The Apache readily identifies a family cluster by its nuclear clan, and will often say, 'The people in that cluster are

U. of Ariz., Ariz. State Mus., Tucson: left, 21,413; right, 21,439; center, Milwaukee Public Mus., Wis.: 3702/1693.

Fig. 5. Saddlebags. left, San Carlos Apache double saddlebag of leather with red flannel behind the leather cutwork, and decorative fringe. center, White Mountain saddlebag with red and black cloth behind leather cutwork and decorated with fringe and cone-shaped tin pendants. Goods were stored through the slit in the center section, which was placed over the horse's back with one bag hanging on each side. As leather became harder to acquire bags of the same design were made of cloth. right, White Mountain Apache canvas double saddlebag with colored calico appliqué and cloth fringe. left, 250.0 cm, rest to same scale; left and right collected by Grenville Goodwin in 1936, center, by Charles L. Owen, 1900–1905.

of such and such a clan,' although actually they may be composed of members of several clans. . . . By mentioning the nuclear clan of the unit he emphasizes a bond holding the unit together. . . ."

Every family cluster was under the leadership of a headman. Although this individual might be a member of the cluster's core lineage, he was more often an outsider, a relative by marriage. At first, a man who married into a family cluster was obliged to work for his wife's parents and found himself at their complete disposal. As he grew older, became the father of children, and developed the qualities necessary for leadership, he was released from these duties and assumed more and more responsibility for the family cluster as a whole. Eventually, the cluster's headman would come to him and say: "I have been looking out for those people for many years. But now I am growing weak. I have done what I can do. Your children are part of these people now, so I think it should be you who watches out for our camps" (Basso 1970:27). On the initiative and advice of their headman, the members of a family cluster undertook farm labors, prepared for certain types of ceremonials, and settled interpersonal disputes. It was also customary for a headman to lecture his followers before sunrise every morning. These speeches were primarily concerned with food-gathering activities and how to conduct them. The following excerpt is a typical example.

> Do not be lazy. Even if there is a deep canyon or a steep place to climb, you must go up it. Thus, it will be easy for you to get deer. If any of you go out hunting this morning, tomorrow, or the following day, look after yourselves while you are alone. When you trail deer you may step on a rock. If the rock slips from under you, you may fall and get hurt. If there is a thick growth of trees ahead of you, don't go in it. There might be a mountain lion in a tree ready to attack you. Always go on the upper side or the lower side of such a clump. If there is thick brush ahead, there may be a bear or some wolves in it. Go above or below it. When you trail a deer and you come upon him, if he should start to run, don't run after him for a deer can run faster than you, and you cannot overtake him. You women who go out to gather acorns and walnuts, don't go alone. Go in a party of three or four. Look after each other. If you get a mescal head ready to cut off, don't stand on the lower side of it; always work on the upper side. If you stand below it while you cut, it will roll on you, and its sharp points will stick into you. If you cut it off and are about to chop away the leaves from the head, don't open your eyes wide. Close them halfway so the juice won't get in them and blind you (Goodwin 1942:166).

Western Apache social organization included a system of matrilineal clans. Whereas bands, local groups, and family clusters were spatially distinct (that is, residence groups), clans were not. Members of the same clan were scattered throughout Western Apache territory, thus creating an extensive and intricate network of relationships that cut across bands and local groups but at the same time served to link them together. The members of a clan considered themselves related through the maternal line, the descendants of a group of women who, according to mythology, established farms at the clan's place of origin. These locations provided the names for clans (for example, 'juniper standing alone people', 'two rows of yellow spruce coming together people') and were held to be sacred. Altogether there were 60 clans.

Marriage between members of the same clan was not allowed, although marriage into the clan of one's father was permissible and, there is some evidence to suggest, even preferred (Goodwin 1942). Persons belonging to the same clan were expected to aid one another in a variety of ways, and if it was deemed necessary the entire clan might be called upon to avenge a wrong done to one of its members. Beyond these personal responsibilities, there was nothing in the way of clan government or law. The clan's main functions were to regulate marriage, extend reciprocal obligations beyond the local group, and facilitate concerted action in projects requiring more manpower than was available within the family cluster.

Most of the 60 Western Apache clans claimed ultimate descent from one of three archaic clans, and on this basis were grouped into phratries (Kaut 1956, 1957). The structure of the phratry is best approached through a consideration of the types of relationships that existed between its constituent clans, these being expressed by the Apache as 'closely related', 'related', or 'distantly related'.

A single clan was 'closely related' to from 2 to 10 others. The members of 'closely related' clans were not permitted to marry and were bound by reciprocal obligations only slightly less demanding than those between persons belonging to the same clan. Closely related clans formed an exogamous segment—called a section by Goodwin—which related to all other clans as a unit. In other words, with regard to one another, as well as to clans outside their section, 'closely related' clans shared identical marriage restrictions.

'Related' clans belonged to separate sections but were nonetheless bound by ties almost as close as those that existed between 'closely related' clans. Marriage was prohibited and mutual obligations were strong; however, with respect to other clans, two sections of 'related' clans rarely observed the same marriage restrictions. For example, if one section (A) was 'related' to another (B), which in turn was related to a third (C), the relationship between A and B did not necessarily imply a corresponding relationship between A and C. As Kaut (1957:41) has observed, "The term 'related' implied a bond of obligation and marriage restriction between two separate groups of 'closely related' clans (*i.e.* sections)." 'Distant relationship' between two clans (or sections) generally meant that each was related to a third clan in common. The members of 'distantly re-

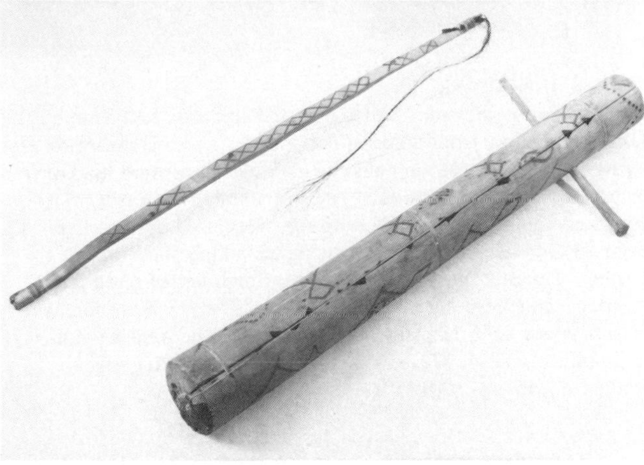

top, Southwest Mus., Los Angeles: 22540; bottom, Field Mus. of Nat. Hist., Chicago: 68,791.

Fig. 6. Fiddles. top, Amos Gustina, White Mountain Apache, with fiddles he made. Fiddles are fashioned from hollowed-out agave stalks and strung with horsehair or deer sinew. The instrument is played by placing the lower end against the chest, stopping the string with fingers on the left hand, and moving the bow with the right. Decorations consist primarily of geometric designs and patterns of small holes, usually triangular, drilled into the body of the fiddle. Photograph by C.P. Baldwin, May 16, 1939. bottom, White Mountain Apache fiddle with painted designs. The bow is also decorated; the horsehair string is broken. Instruments made for Apache use were smaller than those (such as examples by Gustina) made for sale (Ferg 1981). Length about 39.5 cm, collected by Charles L. Owen in 1901.

top, Smithsonian, NAA: 45987-C; bottom, Mus. of N. Mex., Santa Fe: 16138.

Fig. 7. Hoop and pole game, a men's gambling game that women were not allowed to observe. top, Start of a play (a woman is in the distant background). The aim of the 2 contestants is to roll the hoop (marked with notches and colored bands) to a designated area in such a way that it falls over the butt end of the pole, which has also been notched. The relation of notches and bands on hoop and pole yields a point count toward the score needed to win. Copyrighted by Katherine T. Dodge, Jan. 1899. bottom, Determining a count at the end of a play. Although this game required considerable skill and dexterity, it also involved the use of supernatural forces, or 'powers', which players called upon to help them perform more effectively. Thus, hoop and pole was more than mere entertainment; it was a ritual form as well. Photograph by Ben Wittick, around 1890s.

lated' clans could marry and were under weaker obligations of support.

It is important to recall that persons sharing membership in the same phratry lived in local groups dispersed throughout the whole of Western Apache country. By establishing bonds of kinship among these individuals, some of whom lived at great distances from one another, the phratry system bound them together and, in so doing, helped keep in check the divisive tendencies inherent in local group isolation. Concomitantly, the phratry system provided the primary means for recruiting participants in activities whose success depended upon the cooperation of large numbers of people. In this way, "the phratry in its relations with other phratries formed a close approach to tribal organization" (Kaut 1957:41).

Marriage

Rules of clan exogamy, together with restrictions prohibiting marriage with close paternal kin, were the most significant factors determining the eligibility of potential spouses. On very rare occasions, paternal parallel cousins married each other, as did persons belonging to 'related' clans, but these unions were condemned as being openly incestuous and, if not terminated abruptly, were believed to bring insanity or death to the parties involved (Goodwin 1942). The overwhelming majority of marriages involved members of unrelated clans, thereby serving the important function of creating reciprocal obligations between persons belonging to different phratries.

Western Apache women usually entered marriage before the age of 18, men in their early twenties. Although proven ability in economic activities was desirable in a spouse it was not essential, for often youths were inexperienced in hunting and raiding and girls were unskilled in the full range of female tasks. However, laziness, truculence, and physical disabilities that prevented the performance of adult labors were vital hindrances. The practical aspects of marriage were uppermost in the minds of parents, and in many cases it was they who arranged the alliance. Family status was an important consideration and marriage ties with a large, wealthy family were preferred. Such a family was able to make generous gifts prior to marriage and could be counted on for small contributions in the years that followed. Despite the importance attached to economic factors, Apache parents did not insist upon marriages in which their children were reluctant to participate. Love was regarded as an essential component in lasting unions, and its absence was recognized as having destructive effects. However, young people were consciously trained to see that other considerations had comparable importance and for this reason were usually willing to accept the judgment of their parents.

The most common method of proposal was for a

Smithsonian, NAA:81-5353.

Fig. 8. Girls constructing a miniature camp of sticks and grass, consisting of several dome wickiups and 2 square shades or ramadas. Wickiups were used primarily for sleeping, ramadas for most domestic activities. Girls also played at cooking and weaving baskets and with dolls. Boys were encouraged at an early age to play at riding horses and hunting with small bows. Most forms of play were patterned on essential adult activities and so served as a kind of informal training for subsequent responsibilities. Photograph by Aleš Hrdlička, Rice School, San Carlos Reservation, 1900 or 1905.

Max R. Sarvis, Boise, Idaho.

Fig. 9. Apache wickiups, San Carlos Reservation. top, Frame is fashioned mainly from limbs of cottonwood tied together with strips of yucca. Except in cold and rain, wickiups were not covered over completely, as this would prevent ventilation. Easily constructed and taken down, wickiups were used by Apaches primarily for sleeping, all other activities taking place outside. bottom, Camp of individuals related through ties of kinship and marriage, thus forming a "family cluster." Two or more family clusters made up a "local group," which was the basic economic and political unit of Western Apache society. Photographs by Walter J. Lubken, 1904-1911.

member of the young man's family to inform the family of the girl of his wishes, this declaration of intent being followed by a small gift. Unless the proposal was rejected, the youth's kinsmen continued with the marriage arrangements, returning in several weeks with large quantities of food, buckskins, horses, and other prized items. When these goods had been received by the girl's parents, the marriage was considered final and the young man remained behind in the camp of his new wife. Shortly thereafter, the girl's kinsmen reciprocated with gifts of their own, thus initiating a series of exchanges that frequently continued for three or four years. Goodwin (1942:321) reports that "the boy's family was expected to make the largest gifts, and to a certain extent this was considered to be a price paid for the girl . . . As Apache sometimes remark: 'In those days you couldn't get a girl for nothing. You had to give something to her family first, and it could be an expensive undertaking.'"

Divorce was not infrequent, and there was nothing to prevent a husband or wife from marrying again, sometimes almost immediately. Remarriages were accorded far less attention than initial ones and did not entail protracted sequences of gift-giving. Acceptable grounds for divorce included laziness, incompetence in the performance of expected duties, continual bickering, unreasonable jealousy, infidelity, and the failure of a man to observe proper forms of respect with his wife's parents. Most divorces were precipitated by heated quarrels after which the husband gathered up his essential belongings and returned to his natal family cluster.

In prereservation times a few Western Apache men had more than one wife. Goodwin (1942) recorded only 12 polygynous marriages for the period before 1880, and in all of these the men were either local group chiefs or persons of unusual influence. All other marriages were monogamous. Ten of the 12 polygynous unions were with women of the same clan or phratry and three involved marriage to sisters.

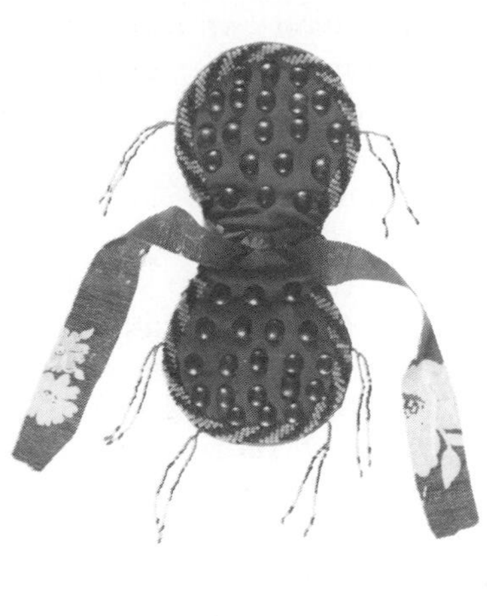

left, Smithsonian, NAA:76–5682; right, U. of Ariz., Ariz. State Mus., Tucson: 21,323.
Fig. 10. Women's hair ornaments. left, White Mountain Apache woman with hair drawn back, folded, and bound with ornament indicating that she is of marriageable age. Photograph by A.F. Randall, probably 1883–1888. right, White Mountain Apache hourglass-shaped leather ornament covered with cloth and decorated with beadwork and brass tacks. The cloth ribbons are used to tie up the wearer's hair with the ends hanging down her back. Length 23.0 cm, collected by Grenville Goodwin in 1936.

Leadership

The most prominent leaders in Western Apache society were the chiefs of local groups. These individuals were selected from the ranks of family cluster headmen on the basis of skill in hunting or raiding and the possession of personal qualities that inspired confidence, allegiance, and respect. Among the Western Apache, as among other Apachean groups, chiefs lacked absolute authority over their followers and did not control by means of coercion. Without recourse to force, manifest or implied, chiefs governed effectively by strength of character, an ability to promote consensus within the group, and the exemplary fashion in which they conducted their own lives. In short, they served as models for others to emulate and, in so doing, personified a set of moral values to which the Apache attached singular importance. These values included:

(1) Industriousness: A chief was not idle. He rose early, ate and drank sparingly, and spent his day actively involved in productive pursuits.

(2) Generosity: A chief was always prepared to share his food and belongings with persons in need of them.

(3) Impartiality: In dealing with other people, and especially when arbitrating disputes, a chief did not rule unfairly in favor of kinsmen or personal friends.

(4) Forbearance: A chief kept control of his temper at all times. He refrained from harsh criticism and did not display anger, displeasure, or indignation toward any member of the local group.

(5) Conscientiousness: A chief did not make decisions hurriedly or by himself. In all matters of importance, he consulted at length with other adult members of the local group and weighed their opinions carefully against his own.

(6) Eloquence: A chief was a "good talker," especially when exhorting his followers to consider a course of action he was convinced would be beneficial to their collective interests.

The dignity of a chief placed him above the performance of menial tasks such as gathering firewood, and the dwellings in his camp tended to be somewhat larger than those of other people. He never traveled alone, and if by some extraordinary circumstances he was killed his followers retaliated with all the force they could muster. It is highly significant, as Goodwin (1942:181) notes, that "no Apache could recall an unsatisfactory chief nor one who had been removed because of incompetence. The people knew their men far too well to make a faulty choice in leaders."

Raiding and Warfare

The Western Apache drew a sharp distinction between raiding (literally 'to search out enemy property') and warfare ('to take death from an enemy'). Raiding expeditions were organized for the primary purpose of stealing livestock. War parties, on the other hand, had as their main objective to avenge the death of a kinsmen who had lost his life in battle. The differences went considerably further than this, and it is useful to consider the distinctive features of each.

Raids were organized in response to a shortage of food. Whenever it became apparent that the meat supply of a local group was running low, some individual, usually an older woman, would publicly draw attention to the fact and urge that plans be made to capture enemy livestock. Within a few days it was expected that the local group's chief would step forth and volunteer his services as leader. Having announced when he intended to leave and against whom the raid would be directed he issued a call for followers. All able-bodied men were eligible to go, providing they had participated successfully in the so-called novice complex, an extended period of instruction during which adolescent boys were introduced to both the practical and ritual aspects of raiding (cf. Basso 1971).

Raiding parties were normally composed of from 5 to 15 men. (Larger numbers were discouraged because the success of a raid depended almost entirely upon being able to travel without being seen). The party proceeded slowly until it moved into enemy territory. Here the pace quickened, special measures at concealment were taken, and a number of taboos went into effect, including the use of a special "warpath language." More than anything else, Western Apache raiders attempted to avoid armed conflict—not out of fear, but because it would reveal their position and numbers, alert the enemy for miles around, and increase the chances of being intercepted on the way home.

Raids normally took place in the early hours of the morning. Two or three men approached the enemy's herd on foot and moved it as silently as possible in the direction of an open trail. Here the livestock was encircled by the remainder of the party and driven off. Speed was imperative on the journey home, and it was not unusual for returning raiders to go without sleep for as many as four or five days. As soon as the party was secure within the borders of its own territory, a messenger was sent ahead to inform those who had stayed behind in the local group that the venture had been a success.

A man who captured livestock was entitled to give it away to whomever he chose, in most cases to close kinsmen; however, he could be prevailed upon by widows and divorcees who, by singing or dancing for the raider, obligated him to present them with at least one animal. This custom had important economic consequences because it helped assure the distribution of livestock throughout the local group and not just to the families of raiders (see Basso 1971).

Whereas raiding parties drew their personnel entirely from the men of a single local group, war expeditions were recruited primarily on the basis of clan and phratry. It was up to a warrior's maternal kinsmen to avenge his death, and this responsibility applied to clan and phratry members as well as to those more immediate relatives who resided in his local group. Although the latter took it upon themselves to sponsor the expedition, the former were always called upon to participate and, apparently, rarely refused.

When the decision was made to prepare for war, the chief of the slain warrior's local group sent messages to other local groups inviting kinsmen of the deceased to convene at an appointed spot. Here, all men who planned to take part in the expedition joined in a ceremonial termed *'ikał sitą́ą́'* (literally, 'stiff hide spread on the ground'). Warriors from each clan were called upon to dance, and speeches were made encouraging them to "think of angriness, fighting, and death" (Basso 1971). This was in sharp contrast to the members of raiding parties, who were instructed to avoid combat unless it was absolutely necessary.

War parties were composed of as many as 200 men under the direction of a single leader. In addition, they contained at least one shaman, or medicine man, whose primary duties were to encourage proper conduct on the journey to enemy territory and, with the aid of a supernatural power, to look into the future and predict the outcome of impending conflict. Prior to battle, if the chances of a victory appeared good, the shaman might also perform a short ceremonial that was believed to afford protection against the enemy and instill the will to fight.

Western Apache warriors preferred to atack the town or settlement where their kinsman had lost his life, and sometimes it was possible to single out the individual who had done the actual killing; however, ordinarily the identity of the slayer was not known and the expedition attacked any encampment they came across in enemy territory. In either case the basic strategy was the same: send out scouts to locate the target, surround it in full force during the night, and then, in early morning ambush, kill as many of the enemy as possible. When the fighting was over, the expedition's leader might suggest that his men keep going and attack elsewhere, but in most instances a single victory was considered sufficient, especially if moving on meant the forfeiture of captured livestock.

Religion and World View

A substantial portion of the Western Apache world view was expressed in a cycle of rich and intricate myths that explained the creation of the universe and the sequence of stages by which it reached its present form. These myths, together with those comprising another cycle dealing with the origin of ceremonials and supernatural powers, were considered sacred by the Apache and could be narrated only under special circumstances to audiences composed exclusively of older men. Two other cycles of myths, which recounted the adventures of Coyote and Big Owl, were free of such restrictions and served as vehicles of instruction and amusement for both children and adults. For a sample of Western Apache myths and tales see Goddard (1920, 1920a) and Goodwin (1939).

Under the watchful supervision of an amorphous and impersonal deity, Life Giver, the earth was shaped by Black Wind, Black Metal, Black Thunder, and Black Water. But the earth was bare and suffered in the cold. Seeing this, Black Thunder gave hair to the earth in the form of grasses and trees. Then Black Water gave blood to the earth in the form of streams and rivers. Black Metal next gave bones to the earth in the form of rocks and mountains. Finally, Black Wind gave breath to the earth in the form of breeze. Now the earth was alive.

The first human beings to inhabit the earth emerged from beneath its surface, but life was difficult for them because of the presence of wicked creatures who devoured them and stole away the women. During this difficult time, a young maiden named Changing Woman became pregnant and gave birth to twin sons. One of them was the son of Sun, the other the son of Black Water. When the first twin, called Slayer of Monsters, reached adolescence he journeyed to the home of his father. At first, Sun refused to acknowledge that the boy was his own offspring and forced him to undergo a number of arduous tests to prove it. With the help of Spider Woman, Fly, Gopher, and other helpful powers, Slayer of Monsters passed all the tests. Now Sun was satisfied and gave the boy proper Apache clothing, a bow and arrows, and horses. Slayer of Monsters returned to earth with these things and taught the people how to use them. Then he and his half-brother killed the evil creatures who had been causing trouble and death. At last the earth was a good place to live.

Of all the figures in Western Apache mythology, none was so fondly regarded as Coyote. Exemplifying all the strengths and weaknesses of man himself, Coyote was both admirable and pathetic, dignified and ridiculous. It was Coyote who first showed the Apache how to make a living, teaching them to plant corn, gather mescal, make baskets, construct roasting pits, and smoke tobacco. But it was also Coyote who tried to steal fire from Sun and burned his tail, who lied to Rabbit and subsequently lost his eyesight, and who boasted of his physical prowess to Badger and got horribly mauled in the competition that followed. Whenever Coyote behaved foolishly there was a moral lesson behind his actions, and Apache parents were quick to point it out to children. "Don't do like Coyote did," they would say. "He did many bad things long ago such as marrying his daughter and stealing. But because he did these things, don't you do them. You see, Coyote tried to marry his own daughter and for this reason some of our own people still think about such things. But you must not do as he did. It is very bad" (Goodwin 1939:ix).

The term *diyį̨h* 'supernatural power' was used by the Western Apache to denote one or all of a set of abstract and invisible forces that were believed to emanate from certain types of animals, plants, minerals, celestial bodies, and meteorological phenomena. These forces were construed as being every bit as tangible and "real" as their visible sources, and although they had access to supraterrestrial regions denied to man they regularly intruded into his midst and became involved in his affairs. According to Apache belief, there was an inexhaustible supply of each type of power in the universe. A small amount could be acquired by man and brought under his control, but the remainder stayed free to act on its own. This portion did not possess moral sanctity and was not inherently benevolent. To the contrary, if a power was antagonized by what it considered disrespectful behavior, or if it was used by someone motivated by "evil thoughts," it was capable of causing illness and misfortune.

Powers could be acquired in one of two ways. In the first of these, called *diyį̨h yaanyáá* 'power comes to him', a power acting on its own accord chose some person to be its "owner." In the second, called *diyį̨h baanyáá* 'he goes to power', the situation was reversed: a would-be owner selected a power. Individuals who were sought out by a power (normally in the form of a dream) were considered especially worthy and well qualified. After all, the reasoning went, they did not have to search for power, it came to them. Conversely, individuals who were not sought out lacked this tacit sign of approval with the result that their claim to power might be questioned. Regardless of how a power was acquired, it was controlled and manipulated with a set of chants and prayers that bore its name and, according to mythology, were given as gifts to the Western Apache shortly after the earth was created. These chants and prayers were said to "belong" to the power and, simultaneously, to be a "part" of it. Indeed, the association between the two was so close that the term *diyį̨h* was used to refer to either one or both.

Powers could be put to a variety of purposes, and every Apache who owned one had to learn through trial and error what his was capable of doing. If a power failed at one type of activity, its owner took note and refrained from using it for that purpose again. Alternatively, if the power succeeded at some task, its owner gained confidence and was encouraged to call for a repeat performance. In this way through protracted experimentation, an Apache was able to discover what his power could accomplish. Individuals who had possessed a power for many years knew exactly what to expect of it, whereas those who had only recently acquired power were less certain (Basso 1970:39). Some of the uses to which supernatural powers were put, aside from the prevention and curing of illness, are discussed in Goodwin (1942) and Basso (1969, 1970).

Besides aiding its owner in the performance of specific tasks, a power acted in the more generalized capacity of providing protection against adversity. Under normal circumstances, this was not a service that an Apache felt compelled to request. He simply assumed that if he behaved toward his power in the appropriate fashion, taking care not to offend it, protection would follow as a matter of course. However, in the event that amicable relations were upset, the power could withdraw its custody, thereby exposing its owner to sickness and danger. The surest way to maintain effective contact with a power was to accord it the same courtesies customarily extended to human beings. For example, the wishes of a power should be carried out without complaint or suppressed ill feeling. When making requests, a power should be addressed politely and spoken to in a low, unhurried key; it should never be "bossed around." Having rendered a service, it should be given tangible payment, either with prayers of thanks, or by singing several of its associated chants. In short, viable and productive interaction with a power, like viable and productive interaction with other people, required conscious effort and constant attention. Failure to observe the appropriate social forms engendered hostility, which in turn could lead to a termination of the relationship.

The Western Apache drew a sharp distinction between persons who possessed a supernatural power and those who did not. Members of the former category were partitioned into two subclasses labeled by the terms *diyin* 'shaman, medicine man' and *'ínłgashn* 'witch, sorcerer'. Shamans admitted to the possession of power and some of them used it publicly in the context of ceremonials. Witches, on the other hand, kept their powers hidden, manipulating them in private to cause sickness, certain forms of insanity, and "accidents" that resulted in death, bodily injury, or the destruction of personal property.

The clandestine activities of witches made them extremely difficult to apprehend and convict, and on those rare occasions when it was absolutely certain that one person had used witchcraft against another the victim's kinsmen were entitled to retaliate with murder (Goodwin 1942). Normally, however, the suspect's guilt was uncertain and he was given a trial (*'ínłgashn baa yá'iti'* 'witch trial', literally 'they are talking about witches'). Directed by local group headmen, trials followed a definite pattern. The suspect was flatly accused of his crime and evidence in support of his accusation was presented. If the suspect could not defend himself or if he refused to confess, he was strung up by the wrists from the limb of a tree so that his toes barely touched the ground. If he continued to deny his guilt, he was left hanging for several hours and a fire might be lit beneath him to hasten his confession. Goodwin (1942:420) reports that witch suspects were sometimes killed whether they confessed or not, but more commonly were released, terrified and weakened, on the condition that they must leave the local group and never attempt to return. Western Apache witchcraft as it operates today is treated in detail in Basso (1969).

The knowledge necessary to perform ceremonials was detailed and extensive and a Western Apache could acquire it only through specialized instruction from an established shaman. This instruction, which focused primarily on the acquisition of chants, required payment (usually in the form of large quantities of food) and frequently lasted several years. During the period of instruction, student and teacher lived together, alone, and at a distance from other people that allowed them to work undisturbed.

The feat of mastering a corpus of ceremonial chants takes on impressive intellectual proportions when it is understood that as many as 80 chants might be involved and that a single chant contained up to 32 separate verses. Moreover, practice had to continue until each chant could be flawlessly performed with each word, each line, and each verse in its proper place and sequence. To complicate matters further, many chants contained archaic words and phrases that differed strikingly from conventional spoken Apache. Thus, in a very real sense, someone learning a ceremonial was also obliged to learn a new language. In addition to mental agility and a tenacious memory, the acquisition of a ceremonial demanded physical strength. Chants were not easy to sing. They were apt to range over more than one octave and frequently involved abrupt and difficult changes in tempo and pitch. Then, too, they were supposed to be sung with as much force as the singer could muster so that the power to whom they belonged would know that its owner, like itself, was strong. In short, the performance of even one chant required considerable effort. When one considers that a full day of practice might involve the singing of over two dozen chants, it is no wonder that neophyte shamans sometimes found themselves close to exhaustion.

Despite the effort and expense involved, the rewards of acquiring a ceremonial far outweighed the costs. Confident in the ritual's ability to benefit himself as well as other people, a shaman felt well equipped to deal with life's uncertainties and hardships. In addition, a ceremonial placed in the shaman's hands a valuable means to achieve status. If his performances were successful more often than not, thereby attesting to both the strength and cooperativeness of his power, he quickly reached a position from which he could demand and receive widespread respect. Equally important, his expertise in ritual matters became a source of personal gratification and pride among members of his local group. The training of a new shaman was welcomed by the Apache as an event from which everyone stood to benefit, for shamans functioned as indispensable links between the realm of men and the realm of supernatural powers. When relations between the inhabitants of these realms were disturbed, bringing harm and misfortune to man, only persons with ceremonials could intervene, repair the damage, and restore the original balance.

It was a fundamental postulate of Western Apache culture that serious forms of physical and mental illness could result from behaving "without respect" toward things that were 'sacred' (*godiyį̨hgo*). More specifically, sickness occurred when an Apache violated one or more of the taboos surrounding objects from which power emanated or in which it had come to reside. For example, one should not boil the stomach of a deer, or eat its tongue, or sever the tail from its hide. Wood from trees struck by lightning should not be used in cooking fires. It was dangerous to fan a fire with one's hat, and to allow the hairs combed from a horse's tail to touch the ground. One should not urinate in streams and rivers or defecate near a cornfield. Taboos of this sort numbered in the hundreds. Many pertained to men and the activities they customarily performed; others were relevant only to women. But all had one thing in common: they served to define "respectful" and, in Apache terms, "safe" behavior toward sources of power.

A power antagonized by the violation of taboos could produce symptoms of illness within a few days or lie dormant for several years. At any time it might activate itself and then, suddenly and without warning, the signs of illness would appear. Two courses of action were open to the person whose health was threatened. He could do nothing, in which case his symptoms might intensify and possibly prove fatal, or he could seek diagnosis and treatment in the form of ceremonials.

The ceremonial system of the Western Apache approached that of the Navajo in complexity, and there is evidence to suggest that the number of distinct rituals was comparable (Goodwin 1945). The majority of these rituals were connected with curing or the bestowal of protection against illness, but several, including very important ceremonials relating to hunting, warfare, and the onset of male and female puberty (see Basso 1966), were held for other purposes (see "Southwestern Ceremonialism," this vol.). Curing ceremonials were divided into two major classes, each of which had one-, two-, four-, and eight-night forms. Those termed *goch'itaał* began at sundown and continued until dawn the following day; ceremonials of this type contrasted with *'idot'áát*, which started at the same time but came to a close shortly before midnight. Differences in duration were paralleled by differences in function. The shorter ceremonials were held chiefly for diagnostic purposes, that is, to determine what power was causing the illness and to prescribe subsequent treatment. The longer rituals were aimed at neutralizing the power, thereby eliminating the illness itself.

Curing ceremonials had a definite structure, an overarching framework into which discrete elements were inserted. These elements—items of ritual paraphernalia, sand paintings, masked dancers, stylized gestures, and chants and prayers—were dictated by fixed associations and the preferences of individual shamans. Although many of the same elements appeared in different ceremonials, a few were restricted to particular types. Thus, while each type contained some elements that were unique, much of the total inventory was common to all. For example, there were always turquoise beads, eagle feathers, drums, cattail pollen (used in blessing the patient), and objects and colors designating the four directions. Invariably, chants from the Deer, Lightning, and Bear corpuses were sung, and prayers were offered to Changing Woman, Sun, and Life Giver. And at all ceremonials the presiding shaman made a preliminary speech exhorting everyone in attendance to behave properly and think "thoughts of goodness" (Basso 1970).

The principal therapeutic effects of Western Apache curing ceremonials were accomplished through the provision of encouragement and reassurance. Long before a ceremonial took place—in fact, prior to diagnosis—the patient was informed by members of his local group that a cure would be forthcoming. On the eve of the ritual, myths describing its origin and potency reiterated the same theme and during the actual proceedings, chants and prayers requested over and over again that sickness be sent away to have "goodness" return in its place. The spectators at ceremonials included nearly all the persons of importance to the patient—his kinsmen, children, and friends. These same people, the patient knew, had focused attention upon him and were genuinely concerned about his condition. They wanted to see him well again. There was also the prestige and authority of the shaman who by his very presence and esoteric knowledge assured the patient that everything possible was being done to bring about his recovery. Finally, it was very likely that the patient had witnessed performances of the ceremonial before and had seen it work for others. This, too, gave him confidence.

The most salient benefits of Western Apache curing ceremonials were psychological. For many centuries skillful physicians have recognized that a desire to get well, together with a belief that one will eventually recover, can be tremendously beneficial. Furthermore, it is a well-established fact that a variety of physical disabilities ultimately stem from psychic disorders. Curing ceremonials produced positive results by strongly reinforcing the patient's own desire to be cured. In so doing, these rituals relieved him of anxiety and fear and instilled a sense of security that enabled him to face the future with revitalized optimism and hope.

History: Anglo-Americans

When the Gadsden Purchase was finally ratified in 1853 all of Arizona came under the control of the United States of America, and shortly thereafter Anglo settlers and prospectors, lured by hopes of taking wealth from the land, began to intrude upon the domain of the Western Apache. At first the Indians were wary but peaceful, thinking that the Anglos, like themselves, would continue to fight the Mexicans. As soon as it became apparent that the Anglos wished to put an end to Apache raiding, and on top of this would stop at nothing to carve out mines, mistrust flared into open hostility. The result was a harsh, tragic, and bitterly immoral war that lasted nearly 40 years and ended with the irreversible defeat of the Western Apache and their consignment to reservations.

Throughout the 1850s Anglo attention was focused on the Chiricahua Apache who had become a major obstacle to the settlement of the newly formed Territory of New Mexico. Treaties were made with several Chiricahua bands and an agreement was reached in which they promised to give safe passage to the Overland Mail. It semed for a while that a durable peace might be achieved. But peace was not to come. In 1861 a young cavalry officer attempted to recover a Mexican captive from the Central Chiricahua band by holding hostage the band's leader, Cochise, and several of his subchiefs. Cochise was able to fashion an escape but his companions were summarily murdered. The Chiricahua leader retaliated by killing an Anglo trader, and war was on. Treaties were forgotten, attacks on the Overland Mail resumed, and the U.S. government declared its intention to destroy the Apache as soon as possible.

Initially, the struggle was confined to western New Mexico and southeastern Arizona, leaving all but a few of the Western Apache bands unmolested and free to continue their raids into Mexico. But in 1863, the year Arizona became a territory, gold was discovered in the heart of Northern Tonto country and troubles began. Soldiers stationed at Fort Whipple near Prescott killed indiscriminately, and private citizens took to organizing "Indian-hunting parties." On one infamous occasion, a group of Apaches was fed poisoned food while participating in what they had been told was a peace conference. Understandably, the Indians responded with massacres of their own, and for a time it appeared that the Anglos would be forced to abandon central Arizona.

In 1864 Camp Goodwin (named after the first governor of Arizona) was established on the Gila River in White Mountain territory. This was an event of major significance, especially for Apaches living farther north. Sandwiched between the Tonto and Chiricahua, the White Mountain and Cibecue Apache were geographically isolated and had remained comparatively undisturbed by Anglo military operations. Led by several powerful chiefs, they were anxious to avoid the fate that had befallen their neighbors to the east and west and so, when U.S. troops arrived at Camp Goodwin and made offers of peace, they accepted. In the years that followed, White Mountain and Cibecue raiding expeditions continued to make forays into Mexico but, with the exception of minor skirmishes, open warfare with the Anglo soldiers was avoided. Simultaneously, an uneasy friendship developed that was to have two important consequences. One was the unresisted founding of Camp Ord (later Fort Apache) on the White River in 1868; the other was the willingness of White Mountain and Cibecue Apaches to serve as scouts for Gen. George Crook in later campaigns against the Tonto and Chiricahua.

By 1870 it was becoming increasingly clear that the Territory of Arizona lacked the military means to exterminate the Apaches. The number of forts continued to grow, but the army was undermanned and, more important, unable to formulate a clear and effective plan for dealing with the problem. Following the Camp Grant Massacre in 1871, during which a mob of enraged citizens from Tucson and a group of Papago Indians slaughtered more than 75 Western Apache women and children, the federal government implemented a new "peace policy" in Arizona. This policy was designed to put an end to the army's fumblings and to curtail the illicit activities of corrupt civilian agents.

The peace policy called for the collection of all Apaches on reservations. The Indians would be settled on their own lands, given protection against Anglos, and encouraged to make a living through agriculture and the raising of livestock. In 1871–1872 four areas were hurriedly designated as Apache reservations. A large tract of land was marked off around Fort Apache, this to be the home of the Cibecue people and the northern bands of the White Mountain division. In central Arizona, Camp Verde became headquarters for the Northern and Southern Tonto as well as some bands of Yavapai. An area around Camp Grant was set aside for the San Carlos Apache and the southern White Mountain bands. And in western New Mexico, near Ojo Caliente, a reservation was set aside for the Chiricahua.

Meanwhile, General Crook assumed formal command of the Department of Arizona. Crook was skeptical of the new peace policy from the outset. Some Apaches had moved onto reservations but a large number, fearful of treachery, stayed away. Everywhere the Indians were restless and fearful. Camp Grant was abandoned when fresh troubles arose, and new headquarters were established at San Carlos on the Gila River. Sporadic raids by the Apache continued, and the suspicion grew that a massive outbreak was imminent. Crook was convinced that forceful action was necessary and when attacks intensified in the Prescott region he embarked upon a campaign to round up all Apaches who were not already settled on reservation lands. In the winter of 1872, he began a series of vigorous operations against the Tonto Apache and within a few months succeeded in dealing them a resounding defeat. Several hundred Tontos lay dead and the remnants of their families were taken captive at Camp Verde. The survivors were warned not to attempt escape and were urged to cooperate with Indian Bureau personnel in the development of agriculture. A degree of tranquillity was restored to central Arizona, and General Crook was hailed a hero.

In 1874 the Department of the Interior embarked upon a "removal program" that had as its main objective the concentration of all Western Apache, Chiricahua, and Yavapai on a single reservation—San Carlos (fig. 11). Centralizing the Indians, it was hoped, would make them easier to control, thus reducing the threat they posed to the Anglo settlement of Arizona. From Washington the removal strategy looked sound, but its implementation had unforeseen consequences—none of them altogether surprising—that probably did more to prolong the Apache wars than bring them to a close.

In February 1875 more than 1,400 Tonto Apaches and Yavapais were brought to San Carlos from Camp Verde. They were followed several months later by a large body of White Mountain and Cibecue people from the region around Fort Apache. In 1875 a group of 325 Chiricahuas came in to San Carlos, although the most hostile factions, under the leadership of recalcitrants such as Juh and Geronimo, remained at large. With the removal in 1877 of the Chiricahua chief Victorio and some 400 of his followers the number of Indians gathered at San Carlos rose to above 5,000.

There were serious problems from the start. Many of the groups living at San Carlos had never before been associated with one another, and their new proximity gave rise to tension and suspicion. In addition, factional disputes arose within single groups, especially the Chiricahua. Some elements, weary of the hardships of war, favored peace and were prepared to settle down. Others found the conditions at San Carlos unbearable and waited for a chance to escape. Among all Apaches there was a feeling that the future was uncertain and that anything could happen at any time.

Victorio bolted from San Carlos six months after he

top, Smithsonian, NAA: 43005-J; bottom, U. of Ariz., Ariz. State Mus., Tucson: 43685.

Fig. 11. San Carlos, Ariz. top, Camp San Carlos. Site was chosen in part because its openness facilitated easy surveillance of Apache by U.S. military personnel. In 1914, following construction of Coolidge Dam, the entire area was flooded. Photograph by Camillus S. Fly, 1879–1901. bottom, New community, also named San Carlos, established nearby on the San Carlos River. Photograph by Helga Teiwes, Sept. 1976.

arrived, taking with him over 300 men, women, and children. He surrendered voluntarily at Ojo Caliente in the fall of 1879, only to break again and launch upon a series of depredations that threw the entire Southwest into panic. In 1881, after a number of Anglo troops were killed at Cibecue while attempting to arrest the leader of a nascent nativistic cult, more Apaches fled from San Carlos and it appeared that the removal program had backfired completely. Two years went by before the nearly 1,000 Indians who had escaped were hunted down and returned to reservations. The most significant blow was struck by Crook himself who, in 1883, led a force composed largely of White Mountain Apaches deep into Sonora's Sierra Madre and there entered into negotiations with Geronimo that ultimately resulted in the surrender of nearly 400 Chiricahuas.

By 1884 peace had been restored and several groups of Apaches, including Geronimo and a small band of dissident Chiricahuas, were taken to Fort Apache. Here, under strick military control, they set about the construction of irrigation dams and the planting of crops. Crook relied heavily on Apache police to preserve order and favored a policy of trial by native juries. Most of the Indians at Fort Apache adjusted to the new conditions as best they could. Internal strife was kept to a minimum and there were no outbreaks.

The calm was shattered in the spring of 1885 when Geronimo, incensed at Crook's refusal to allow the Apache to brew their own intoxicants, broke from Fort Apache with 33 men, 8 boys of fighting age, and 92 women and children. Remarkably, the Indians avoided capture for 16 months but finally, having once again been pursued into Mexico, they agreed to surrender. Not long thereafter, they were taken to a railroad heading at Holbrook, Arizona, loaded into boxcars, and shipped to Fort Marion, Florida. The next few years saw scattered renegade action around Fort Apache and San Carolos, but no more large-scale outbreaks occurred and the Indians on both reservations became less restive. By 1890 the Apache wars were over.

Throughout the conflict the Western Apache suffered less severely than the Chiricahua. Fewer Western Apache were killed, and except for their removal to San Carlos in the middle 1870s they were not forcibly uprooted from their original homelands. Of all the Western Apache divisions, the Tontos were unquestionably the hardest hit, but even they recovered and have managed to survive at Camp Verde, Middle Verde, Rimrock, Clarkdale, and a small community near Payson, Arizona. From the beginning, the Cibecue and White Mountain Apache were the least disturbed and responded to reservation conditions with only a moderate amount of social upheaval. But the awful truth remained that a way of life had been destroyed, and Apaches everywhere knew that it could never be restored. The Anglo conquerors were in complete control.

Reservations and Directed Culture Change

With the fighting finally over, the United States government turned its attention to the modification of Western Apache culture in an attempt to prepare the Indians for eventual assimilation into Anglo society. Three objectives were accorded primary importance. One of these was the economic development of reservations to a point that would provide the Indians with a reliable and sufficient means of support. Another was the opening of schools so that Apache children could be taught the rudiments of "civilization" and at the same time be persuaded to relinquish their native language and customs. The third objective was the establishment of churches and the eventual conversion of all Apaches to belief in Christianity. Nearly a century after these efforts were begun, it can safely be said that none of them has been wholly successful. Although exploitation of reservation resources has increased steadily, many Apaches find themselves the victims of poverty. Practically all Apache children now learn English, but their first and preferred language is still Western Apache. Christian missionaries have made converts, some of them genuinely devout, but native ceremonials are still conducted by shamans, belief in witchcraft persists, and traditional myths are still invoked to explain the origin and constitution of the universe. In short, despite important economic and social changes that have occurred since the founding of reservations, contemporary Western Apaches remain marginal to national American society and retain a cultural system that is distinctly Apachean and entirely their own.

Economic Change

Economic development proceeded slowly at first, especially on the Fort Apache Reservation where the old pursuits of hunting and gathering, together with intensified agricultural activity, sufficed to meet basic subsistence needs and made extensive rationing unnecessary. However, shortly before the turn of the century, when the Indian population was estimated at 1,811, significant numbers of Apaches began to work for wages and augment their traditional foodstuffs with flour, coffee, sugar, and beans. In 1907 over 80 men were employed by the U.S. Cavalry to cut hay for horses stabled at Fort Apache, and by 1910 several dozen others worked as cowboys for Anglo cattle ranchers who leased portions of the reservation for grazing land. Eleven years later, in 1918, the population had risen to 2,456 and the federal government issued 400 cattle to the Apache themselves, starting 80 families in the livestock business by giving five beeves to each family head. This experiment almost failed, but it was not abandoned, and by 1931 there were approximately 20,000 head of cattle on the Fort Apache Reservation (see Getty 1963). Since then cattle raising has become a major industry on both Fort Apache and San Carlos reservations (fig. 12). The economic base of reservation society was further expanded during the early 1920s through the establishment of a lumbering operation, which has since become a major industry, processing over 50,000,000 board feet annually and providing employment for approximately 200 men (fig. 13). And in 1954 the White Mountain Apache Tribe, by this time a legally constituted body governed by an elected tribal council, responded to the outdoor interests of increasing numbers of tourists by creating a Recreation Enterprise to sell hunting and fishing licenses, develop camping areas, and construct summer cabins and homes.

In spite of these and other attempts to make the Fort Apache Reservation self-supporting, a great many of its residents remained without jobs and lived in indigence. In 1969, when the reservation population had reached 6,000, a study of manpower resources showed that the rate of unemployment was 7.3%, roughly twice the national average (Taylor and O'Connor 1969:55). The same study indicated that 49 percent of the Indian families on Fort Apache had an annual income (including public assistance benefits) of less than $1,000 and that the median income of all individuals was close

Fig. 12. Apache cattle round-up, White River. The Fort Apache and San Carlos Reservations are each divided into several cattle districts, which are supervised by a stockman and a small crew of permanent cowboys. Cattle themselves are owned by individuals. Photographs by Robert Sissom, Oct. 19, 1962.

to $500 (Taylor and O'Connor 1969:74). Another study reported that 80 percent of 1,163 Apache dwellings were substandard (Century Geophysical Corporation 1970). The average dwelling consisted of two rooms and the occupancy per room was 2.9 persons. To make matters worse, environmental and sanitation conditions in existing housing were extremely poor. In 1969, 90 percent of the Indian homes on Fort Apache were without butane heat, 74 percent lacked indoor plumbing, and 46 percent had no electricity. Under these devastating conditions, it should come as no surprise that 58 percent of all out-patients at the United States Public Health Service hospital at Whiteriver were children below the age of 15. In 1968, the national mortality rate for babies was 22 deaths per 1,000 live births; the rate for Arizona Indians in the same year was 39 per 1,000. The infant mortality rate for the Fort Apache Reservation was an appalling 78.1 per 1,000 (Century Geophysical Corporation 1970:20).

Long before Whites set foot in Western Apache territory, the Indians produced an intoxicating beverage called tulapai (*túłbáí* 'gray water'). Made from corn, it was quite mild and unless consumed quickly and in large quantities had only the slightest inebriating effects. For the most part, drinking was restricted to social occasions, including ceremonials, when groups of people came together to participate in collective enterprises. In these contexts it served the useful purpose of heightening good will and promoting esprit de corps. Placed on reservations, the Apache continued to make tulapai, but deprived and confused, they frequently drank to excess. No longer a lubricant for social relations, tulapai functioned as an anesthetic against uncertainty and anxiety. Other forms of alcohol became available and the native brew was replaced with beer, wine, and whiskey. Subsequently, alcoholism has developed into a major problem that permeated virtually every aspect of Apache life. Drinking is involved in over 85 percent of major crimes committed on the Fort Apache and San Carlos Reservations, and it is directly or indirectly responsible for a wide range of ancillary illnesses. Attempts to curb alcohol abuse among Apaches have been ineffective, and the problem has grown more acute, especially among women and teenagers (Richard C. Cooley, personal communication 1972). For discussion of various aspects of Western Apache drinking in its ethnographic context see Everett (1970, 1971, 1971a, 1972).

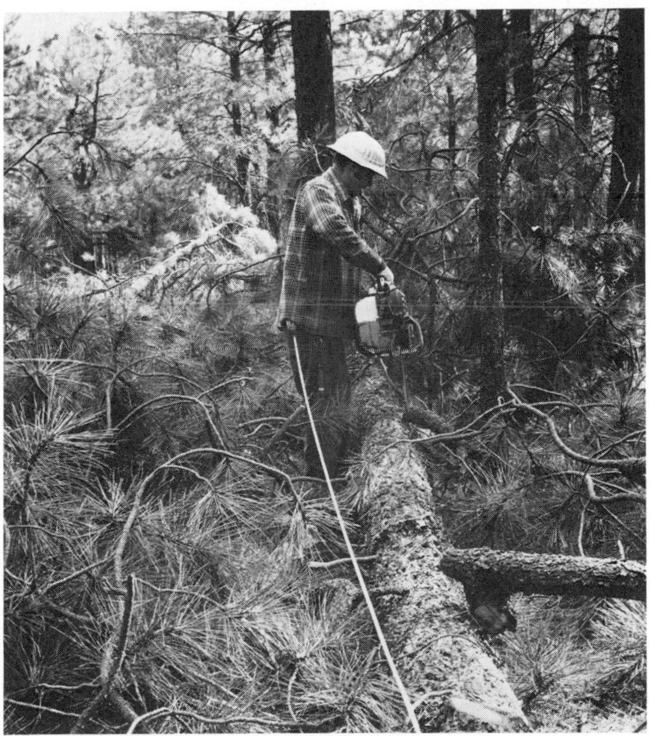

Fig. 13. White Mountain Apache man felling a ponderosa pine near Whiteriver, Ariz. The lumber industry has developed into a major enterprise on the Fort Apache Reservation. In 1981 the industry provided employment for several hundred men and women. Photograph by Jerry Jacka, 1976.

Unfortunately, the situation at Fort Apache is no different from that which prevails on the San Carlos and Camp Verde Reservations, and despite the separate histories of these populations it is clear that their economic problems stem from a similar set of factors. To begin with, there is a shortage of full-time on-reservation jobs that appeal to Apaches. Second, any job—regardless of its location—that threatens to separate an Apache from his family and kinsmen for long periods of time is likely to be rejected. Third, alcoholism and its attendant disabilities prevent some individuals from securing employment or holding down a job for more than a few days. Fourth, a significant number of Apaches, especially women, have come to rely heavily on welfare payments, which, though less remunerative than working for wages, permit them to stay at home with children and friends. A fifth factor highlights the significant role played by persisting traditional values.

> In pre-reservation times, the economic goal was limited to subsistence; to the satisfaction of immediate needs at the highest possible level of fulfillment. Throughout Apache productive activity there seems to be little concept of the production of surplus, or provision for the future through the acquisition and maintenance of exchangeable property. Emphasis was on production for immediate consumption at a high level, not on production for acquisition. The limited resources of the Western Apaches imposed severe restrictions on the accumulation of property, and it is not surprising that property played little part in the economic scheme. The traditions of the culture, in any event, showed comparatively little concern for or interest in the distant future; attention and interest were focused on the needs of the present.
>
> After a half century of exposure to the American capital economy, Apache productive activity remained geared to a subsistence level, as it was in prereservation times. The Apache had apparently never accepted the concept of capital. The underlying motivation for all economic activity was the maintenance of as high a level of immediate consumption as is practicable. Even though capitalization provided the potential means, the production of surplus seemed to be as little contemplated in 1954 as it was a century earlier (Adams and Krutz 1971:127).

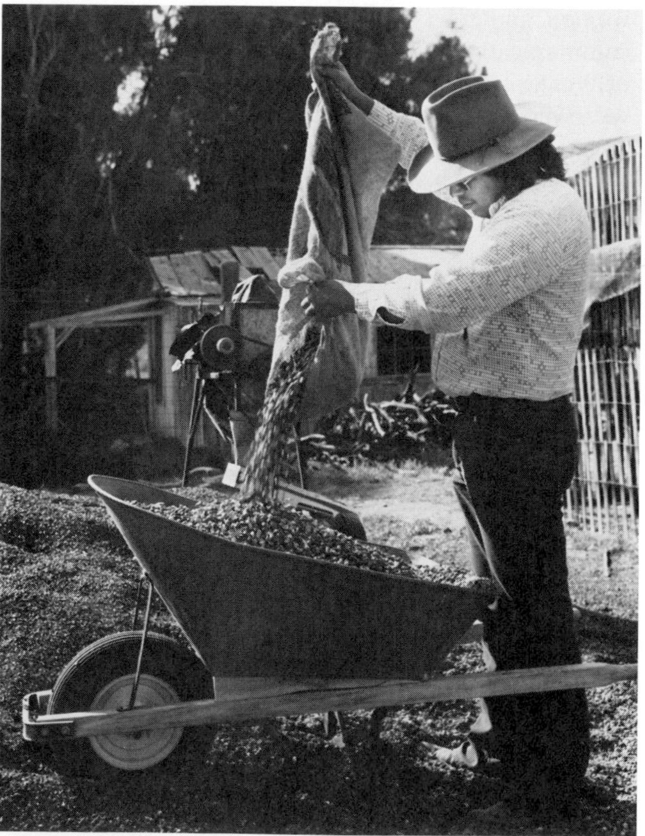

Fig. 14. Pouring nuts outside the jojoba processing plant at San Carlos, Ariz. The jojoba nut industry is managed by a marketing cooperative on the San Carlos Reservation. A high-quality liquid wax is extracted from the small nuts, harvested from an uncommon shrub that flourishes on the reservation. The wax has properties similar to whale oil and is used as a lubricant for watches, as a base for fine cosmetics, and to manufacture candles. Photograph by Jerry Jacka, 1977.

Social Change

The forces that have altered Western Apache economy also produced changes in social organization. Foremost among these was the formation of settlements around trading posts and schools and the concomitant disappearance of bands and local groups. For example, in 1893 there were 13 local groups in the Cibecue area with a combined population of 943 (Goodwin 1942:97). Collectively, these groups comprised three bands: the Canyon Creek band with five constituent local groups, the Carrizo band with four, and the Cibecue band proper, also with four. After the conflict in 1881 a subagency was established in Cibecue Creek, and it was not long before local groups in the surrounding territory began to settle near it. With the opening of a school and the enforcement of regular attendance the old pattern of "wintering below" in the Salt and Gila river valleys came to an end, and people from Canyon Creek and Carrizo set up permanent residences in and around Cibecue. In this way, distinctions between bands and local groups were blurred and then obliterated, and the modern "community" had its genesis (table 2). Simultaneously, residential isolation ceased to be a major factor in the organization of social life, and the clan system assumed greater importance than ever before (Kaut 1957). In Cibecue, as in other Western Apache settlements, clan members whose local groups had formerly been separated by great distances found themselves in daily contact with the result that concerted action as a group became decidedly easier than in prereservation times.

As used by modern Apaches, the term *hát'i'íí* may refer to a single clan or, more specifically, to those of its members who live together in the same settlement. Bilinguals may use the English term "branch" to distinguish this latter sense of *hát'i'íí* from the former,

Table 2. Western Apache Population in Arizona, 1972

Fort Apache Reservation	
Whiteriver – North Fork	1,868
East Fork (Seven-Mile)	1,075
Canyon Day	900
Cedar Creek	278
Carrizo	255
Cibecue	1,015
Remote locations	37
San Carlos Reservation	
San Carlos	2,320
Bylas	1,094
Camp Verde Reservation (including Clarkdale and Middle Verde)	700
Payson	80
Total	9,622

which is sometimes translated as 'line'. Members of the same clan "branch" regularly turn to each other in times of crisis and make a point of exchanging small favors whenever possible. Nowhere, however, is the unity of the clan "branch" so evident as in the long and costly preparations that precede major ceremonials, most notably the girl's puberty rite (Basso 1966, 1970), called in local English a Sunrise Dance. Work is begun fully two months in advance and throughout the preliminaries clan relatives of the pubescent girl contribute heavily with gifts of food and long hours of physical labor. The distinction between an entire clan and its residentially localized "branches" is significant, for although clan membership still serves to establish meaningful relationships between individuals in different settlements, Apaches openly admit that their closest ties and most demanding obligations are with clan kinsmen who live nearby. This points up an important feature of contemporary Western Apache social organization: whereas the solidarity of "branches" is still viable, ties that formerly bound distinct "branches" together have been weakened.

There are also signs of instability in phratry structure. Members of the same clan occasionally marry, and within the past 20 years at least a dozen marriages on the Fort Apache Reservation have taken place between persons whose clans are 'related' or 'closely related'. Although these marriages were widely publicized and roundly denounced, it is evident that the exogamous proscriptions that once applied to all clans within a clan section are beginning to break down. That they have remained in force this long is remarkable considering that evidence of their violation at San Carlos was recorded as early as 1935 when Goodwin (1935:60) wrote that "the clan system remains only partially intact . . . marriage between related clans is sometimes allowed. . . ."

In prereservation times, major subsistence activities were carried out by groups of kinsmen who felt compelled to share the rewards of their labor with one another. This was no longer true in the late twentieth century. The cash and credit system that was imposed upon the Western Apache placed unprecedented value on the willingness of individuals to work for and by themselves, thus producing significant modifications in the composition of work parties and the functions of kinship groups. The most noticeable of these changes has been the emergence of the nuclear household as a primary economic unit and the decline in this capacity of the family cluster.

The members of a nuclear household cooperate very closely, and most of whatever income they receive is kept within the family to purchase essentials such as food and clothing; however, despite its increasing self-sufficiency, the nuclear household has not yet become an autonomous social unit. To the contrary, its welfare is intimately bound up with several other households located nearby, which collectively comprise a family cluster. Although the modern family cluster no longer provides the organizational framework for activities such as food gathering, the loss of the function has in no way damaged its internal cohesiveness. The women whose lineage forms its core and from whose clan its name derives are together almost constantly—washing clothes, grinding corn, collecting firewood, cooking, and helping care for one another's children. It is common for Apaches to liken these women to the trunk of a tree, their children to the tree's branches, and their husbands to its leaves. "The leaves drop off," it is said, "but the trunk and the branches never break."

Education

As part of the program to assimilate the Western Apache into Anglo-American society, several government and mission schools were founded on the Fort Apache and San Carlos Reservations between 1895 and 1922. At these institutions Apache children were taught to speak the English language, to read and write, and to farm, make clothing, and prepare "proper foods." At the same time, the children were subjected to excessively harsh discipline. Classroom regimes involved strict separation of the sexes, the exclusive use of English, and forms of punishment that included whipping, shackling to a ball and chain, and periods of solitary confinement with only bread and water to eat (Spicer 1962). Runaways were common and many Apaches developed a profound hatred for Anglo methods of education.

Educational facilities as well as instructional techniques have been improved, but even so serious problems remain. By any standard Apache students do poorly in school. The scholastic achievement of teenagers falls consistently (and often drastically) below non-Indian norms, absenteeism is chronic, and dropout and withdrawal rates are high. Few Apaches advance beyond high school and only a handful have graduated from college. According to Parmee (1968), who made a study of the school system at San Carlos in 1961, most Apache parents are ignorant of the aims of the education program, and a number oppose it because it conflicts with traditional values. Moreover, there is growing resentment because Apaches have for so long been denied a voice in policy-making decisions.

Equally acute are problems within the school sytem itself. Anglo teachers at the primary levels lack the special training to aid their Apache-speaking pupils, and, as the pupils advance from grade to grade, their difficulty with the English language is compounded. Bewildered and frustrated, teachers complain of feeling "lost" and frequently resort to unimaginative and confusing methods. As a consequence of these and other difficulties, most Apache students who reach high school are not prepared to meet existing requirements. Evaluating the education program as he found it in 1961, Parmee concluded that the "orientation of the entire program was towards the assimilation of Apaches into the Anglo culture, an aim which was diametrically opposed to the desires of most Apaches. . . . Efforts to bring the goals and operation of the program into more extended agreement with the needs and desires of the Apache people were either weak or non-existent" (Parmee 1968:8). Although attempts have been made to solve these problems, Apache children continue to go to school in the face of severe obstacles that the educational system does as much to intensify as to alleviate.

Missionaries and Religious Change

Christian missionaries have been present on the San Carlos and Fort Apache Reservations since about 1900. Following on the heels of the U.S. cavalry, they came on foot and by wagon and built churches of sun-baked adobe. At these outposts, they raised the cross, planted gardens, and began to preach the gospel. The pagan population they sought to convert was anything but receptive. Still recovering from the shock of defeat and the indignities of subjugation, the Western Apache were far more concerned with survival than salvation. Prior to 1920 the missionaries experienced little active resistance, but neither did they make such progress. For the most part, it appears, the Apache simply ignored them.

In response to the deprivation and tensions generated by a new and unsatisfactory style of living, the indigenous ceremonial system flourished vigorously. In 1901 a visitor to Fort Apache reported that "there was a ceremony almost every night. Somewhere drums are always to be heard" (Reagan 1931). The years after 1900 were marked by the emergence of several extremely influential shamans, two of whom founded cults that expressed discontent with existing conditions. One of these movements, headed by a medicine man called Big John, was referred to as *daagodighá* (literally 'spiritual movement starts', interpreted as 'they will be raised upward') and spanned the period from 1903 to 1907. Big John instructed his followers to wear white clothing and silver jewelry in anticipation of a day when they would ascend into the sky and watch the destruction of evil forces on earth. Later, when a better world had come into being, those whom Big John had saved would return to their former homes and spend the rest of their lives in happiness, plenty, and peace. The circumstances surrounding the genesis and disintegration of this movement are very obscure. According to Goodwin and Kaut (1954), its demise did not result from the intervention of Anglo authorities but from a loss of faith among Big John's followers when his predictions failed to come true.

The other cult took form in 1921 under the leadership of Silas John Edwards, an Apache shaman from the community of East Fork on the Fort Apache Reservation (fig. 15), who had begun having dreams in 1904. Silas John, as he was called by his disciples, received a vision from *yúsen* (the Apache deity equated with the Christian God) in which he was instructed to found a religion that stressed allegiance to strict canons of moral behavior and a rejection of many traditional curing

Amer. Mus. of Nat. Hist., New York: 14468; inset, U. of Ariz., Ariz. State Mus., Tucson: 21,453.

Fig. 15. Silas John cult. White Mountain Apache dwelling with crescent cross, the symbol of affiliation with a native religious movement founded by Silas John Edwards, an Apache shaman from the community of East Fork on the Fort Apache Reservation. Inspired by a series of dreams starting in 1904, Edwards proclaimed himself a prophet and traveled widely throughout the Southwest in search of followers. By 1930, Edwards's religion had established itself in communities on both Western Apache and Mescalero reservations. Photograph by Pliny E. Goddard, 1909–1916. inset, Cross and crescent of metal used as an insigne of the movement. They were carried in pouches or worn as necklaces. Length 5.0 cm, collected by Grenville Goodwin in 1936.

practices. In place of the curing practices, Silas John substituted an entirely new set of ceremonial forms that were conducted at special locations called "holy grounds" and sometimes involved the handling of poisonous snakes. At these ceremonials, Silas John warned against the evils of using "secret knowledge" (that is, witchcraft) and urged his followers to abstain from drinking, fighting, and other kinds of disruptive behavior. The Silas John movement was rejected in what were then the two most conservative Apache communities—Cibecue and Carrizo—but received varying degrees of support in all the others. Eventually, it spread to the Mescalero Apache Reservation in New Mexico as well as to several non-Apachean tribes. In 1938 Silas John was falsely accused of the murder of his wife and sentenced to prison. He was released in 1954 and returned to San Carlos where he resumed his place as head of the cult, which by that time had become institutionalized and a regular part of reservation religious life.

Through all these events, the Anglo missionaries stayed on, and when the turbulence of the early reservation years had died down, their numbers increased. Adobe churches were replaced by churches of wood and stone, and interpreters were found to translate the Bible. All the while, the missionaries preached. Extolling the benefits of Christianity, they condemned with equal conviction the "Apache way." Much of their criticism was directed against shamans like Silas John, whom one missionary described as "a dog, an agent of the Devil." It is difficult to ascertain how the Apache reacted to this kind of proselytism, but by 1940 there were definite signs that factors having no connection with the missionary effort were undermining the ceremonial system.

For one thing, ceremonials were becoming more and more costly. The major expense in any ceremonial undertaking was tied up with procuring enough food to provide all who attended with a generous meal. During prereservation times, herds of stolen livestock and the spoils of year-round hunting provided the necessary surplus. But raiding had become a thing of the past, and with the confinement of the Apache to reservations hunting had been limited to government-imposed "seasons." As the traditional economy gave way to a system based on monetary exchange, the Apache were forced to rely more and more on trading posts. Here, of course, purchases had to be made with U.S. currency or other commodities to which Anglos attached equivalent worth. However, money was not plentiful, and few families had personal possessions valuable enough to buy food in the quantity necessary for ceremonial feasts. No doubt the clan system, with its network of reciprocal obligations, worked to defray the cost of ritual undertakings. But it was also at this point in Western Apache history—1930 to 1940—that Goodwin (1942) observed the clan system breaking down.

On the basis of testimony given by Apaches born before 1910, the effects of these changes in the ceremonial system were threefold: fewer ceremonials were given, and there was a sharp decline in rituals requiring more than one night to perform; ceremonials not directly concerned with curing were held less and less frequently; aspiring shamans tended to acquire those types of rituals for which there was a steady demand (that is, curing ceremonials), and other ceremonial forms became destined for extinction.

Although modern Western Apache ritual is decidely cure-oriented, it does not conflict directly with the medical services provided by Anglo hospitals. The Apache recognize that a wide range of physical symptoms responds effectively to Western medicine and, in most cases, show little reluctance in bringing them to the attention of White physicians. But they also believe that in other critical areas, such as the treatment of psychological disorders and the bestowal of protection against illnesses caused by supernatural powers, shamans are unquestionably more skillful (Everett 1971a). For as long as this attitude persists Apache curing ceremonials will remain viable, providing relief and assurance of a kind that is essential to the people's welfare and available from no other source.

Synonymy†

The name Western Apache was coined by anthropologists to designate the Apaches whose twentieth-century reservations are in Arizona and their immediate historical predecessors. Earlier uses of this name in a more general or vaguer sense are cited in the body of this chapter. The language of the Western Apache is also called Western Apache (Perry 1972). In earlier studies it was sometimes called San Carlos Apache, apparently because linguistic data from members of the San Carlos band were used to represent the whole language: San Carlos Group (Hoijer 1938:86), "San Carlos Apache and a number of other mutually intelligible dialects" (Hoijer 1946:11), or simply "San Carlos" (Hoijer 1943:38).

Officially the Western Apache are referred to as the White Mountain Apache and the San Carlos Apache, after the names of their two reservations. These names were originally proper to only two of the five Western Apache band-groups, and the name San Carlos originated as that of a single band of what was later called the San Carlos band-group (Goodwin 1942:3, 35).

There is no native self-designation for the Western Apache as a distinct group. For self-reference the word *n̲dee* ~ *n̲n̲ee* 'man, person, Apache' may be used (Perry 1972:47).

†This synonymy was written by Ives Goddard.

The name given for the Western Apache in other languages is usually the general name for Apache; this is the case, for example, in the neighboring Yuman languages (see synonymy in "The Apachean Culture Pattern and Its Origins," this vol.). A specific name for the Western Apache is Chiricahua *bini·ˀédiné* (Goodwin 1942:6) and Mescalero *Binii'édinendé* (Scott Rushforth, communication to editors 1981), meaning 'people without minds', that is 'crazy people' or 'wild people' (cf. J.B. White 1873–1875a:104; Harrington 1939–1945). This name was recorded by Cordero in 1796 as Vinni ettinen-ne, a major grouping of Apaches called by the Spaniards Tontos 'crazy people' (Matson and Schroeder 1957:336). The name may be an allusion to their different way of talking. The Spanish name Tontos was later restricted to the westernmost bands of the Western Apache. Tewa has *p̓í sáve* 'red Apachean' for the Western Apache.

In some languages separate designations are found for White Mountain and San Carlos. Names for the White Mountain Apache are: Navajo *Dziłghą́'í* 'mountain-top people' (Young and Morgan 1980:360), or with assimilation *Dziłghą́'ą́* (Hoijer 1974:273); Zuni *wilacˀu·kʷe*, sometimes used as a general term (Kroeber 1916:275; Newman 1958:51; Dennis Tedlock, communication to editors 1977). The English name White River Apache is widely used in the Southwest. Zuni also has *čišše·kʷe* 'San Carlos Apache' (Kroeber 1916:275; Dennis Tedlock, communication to editors 1977), to be compared to the general word for Apache in a number of languages.

Groups and Bands

An extended discussion of the names of the Western Apache bands and band-groups is in Goodwin (1942:1–50). Goodwin recognized five band-groups: White Mountain (with Eastern and Western bands); Cibecue (with Carrizo, Cibecue proper, and Canyon Creek bands); San Carlos (with Pinal, Arivaipa, San Carlos proper, and Apache Peaks bands); Southern Tonto (with the Mazatzal band and six unnamed semibands); and Northern Tonto (with Mormon Lake, Fossil Creek, Bald Mountain, and Oak Creek bands). Schroeder (1974b:640) has criticized this classification as based on informants' recollections of early reservation times rather than the prereservation situation of the mid-nineteenth century. He concludes that the Northern and Southern Tonto were original Yavapai bands that intermarried with Apaches; that the San Carlos group subsumed the earlier separate Pinaleño and Arivaipa Apaches; and that the White Mountain group contained the Sierra Blanca ('White Mountain') in the north and the Coyotero in the south. The names Pinaleño (or Pinal) and Coyotero are sometimes used in historical sources in more general senses, implying two major divisions of the Western Apache under these names, but there is no complete consistency in this. Sometimes Coyotero is virtually equivalent to Western Apache (Schroeder 1974b:529, 540–542), and this seems to be how this name was used by Cordero in 1796 when he equated it with Tontos (Matson and Schroeder 1957:351). Some southern Western Apaches were called Mescaleros in the early American period (Schroeder 1974b:420, 584), and this was the Spanish name used at Zuni for Western Apache (Schroeder 1974b:359, 363; Harrington 1934–1939).

Names of Western Apache bands in historical sources and as collected by investigators before Goodwin are in Schroeder (1974b), Bourke (1890), Gatschet (1883), J.B. White (1873–1875a), and Hodge (1907–1910, 1:87, 209, 356, 2:254, 255, 783–784, 861, 945). Goodwin (1942:573–576) identifies most of these.

Sources

Reliable sources of information about Western Apache culture and society are few. A brief but accurate overview of Western Apache history appears in Spicer (1962). Thrapp (1967) gives an excellent account of the military conflict that arose between Apaches and U.S. troops during the second half of the nineteenth century. Other works of immediate relevance include Betzinez (1959), Bigelow (1958), Bourke (1886, 1891), Clum (1936), Crook (1946), Cruse (1941), B. Davis (1963) and Thrapp (1964).

The best works on prereservation Western Apache culture are by Goodwin, especially his work on social organization (1942) and on myths and tales (1939).

Literature dealing with the contemporary Western Apache is limited to the contributions of a handful of investigators. Kaut (1957) has written an important monograph on the structure and evolution of the Western Apache clan system. Basso (1970) has published a short ethnography of a community on the Fort Apache Reservation, together with more technical studies of Western Apache witchcraft (1969) and ritual symbolism (1966). Parmee (1968) presents an illuminating analysis of the formal educational system on the San Carlos Reservation, and Everett (1971, 1971a) considers a number of problems associated with Apache alcoholism. The most thorough and proficient study in the realm of Western Apache linguistics is Greenfeld's (1972) treatment of White Mountain Apache phonology.

Navajo Prehistory and History to 1850

DAVID M. BRUGGE

Prehistory

No consensus exists as to the date of the arrival in the Southwest of the people called by the Spanish colonists of the seventeenth century *Apaches de Nabajó*, opinions varying from dates as early as A.D. 1000 (Kluckhohn and Leighton 1962:33) to 1525 (D.A. Gunnerson 1956). Nor is the route by which they came clearly defined, some students preferring the High Plains (D.A. Gunnerson 1956), some the mountain chain of the Rockies (Huscher and Huscher 1942), and others the Great Basin (Steward 1936:62). Until early archeological remains undeniably attributable to these Athapaskans are identified, a reconstruction of the culture with which they arrived will depend in part on one's views regarding these matters, as well as the related problems of manner of separation between the *Apaches de Nabajó* and the other Apachean tribes.*

It is probable that the Apacheans left the north as one group or as closely related bands, perhaps some 1,000 years ago. The migration was not as a concerted movement with any fixed destination, but a steady expansion into new territory, quite likely stimulated by famine as periodic ecological disasters threatened a growing population. Helm (1965) describes a social and ecological condition among the early northern Athapaskans that might well have led to such a migration. The Rocky Mountains provided an area that was ecologically similar to that left behind in higher latitudes, and the central movement was along the mountain chains, spreading into country on each side as techniques for exploiting new environments were mastered. This led to two more distinct bands with orientations in opposite directions from the center, but still having sufficient contact that exchange of cultural innovations was possible. When they left the north a generalized description of their culture would include economic dependence on hunting, fishing, and gathering; use of the sinew-backed bow, single-piece arrow shafts, side-notched projectile points, harpoons, chute-and-pound game drives; tailored skin clothing with porcupine quill decoration; use of conical dwellings with details varying according to local circumstances but with the forked-pole principle being employed on occasion; twined and flat, coiled baskets, no pottery; use of dogs and snowshoes for transportation; religion based on shamanism

*Navajo (ˈnăvəˌhō) words appearing in italics in the *Handbook* are written in the version of the standard Navajo practical orthography used in Young and Morgan (1980). The graphemic units are the following: (voiceless stops and affricates) *b, d, dl, dz, j, g,* '; (aspirated stops and affricates) *t, tł, ts, ch, k, kw*; (glottalized stops and affricates) *t', tł', ts', ch', k'*; (voiceless continuants) *ł, s, sh, h (~x), hw*; (voiced continuants) *l, z, zh, y (~gh), w*; (nasals) *m, n*; (short oral vowels) *i, e, a, o*; (long oral vowels) *ii, ee, aa, oo*; (short nasal vowels) *į, ę, ą, ǫ*; (long nasal vowels) *įį, ęę, ąą, ǫǫ*; (high tone) v́, v́v́, (falling tone) v́v, (rising tone) vv́, (low tone) not marked.

Written in the *Handbook* technical alphabet (between slashes) the phonemes of Navajo corresponding to these graphemic units and given in the same order are: /b/, /d/, /λ/, /ʒ/, /ǯ/, /g/ and /g^w/, /ʔ/; /t/, /ƛ/, /c/, /č/, /k/, /k^w/; /t̓/, /ƛ̓/, /c̓/, /č̓/, /k̓/, /ł/, /s/, /š/, /h/ and /x/, /h^w/ and /x^w/; /l/, /z/, /ž/, /y/ and /γ/, /γ/ and /$γ^w$/; /m/, /n/; /i/, /e/, /a/, /o/; /i·/, /e·/, /a·/, /o·/; /į/, /ę/, /ą/, /ǫ/; /į·/, /ę·/, /ą·/, /ǫ·/; v́, v̂, v̌, v̀. The glottalized resonants /m̓/, /n̓/, and /y̓/ are treated in the practical orthography as clusters of glottal stop and resonant: *'m, 'n, 'y*. This phonemic transcription follows the usual Athapaskanist practice of using voiced stop and affricate symbols for the corresponding voiceless consonants, and voiceless symbols for the aspirated consonants. In the case of *t* the aspiration is usually heavy, realized as a velar affrication [t^x]. Heavy aspiration of this kind used with other consonants to indicate an augmentative or pejorative sense is written *x*.

The practical orthography does not distinguish between /g/ and /g^w/, /h/ and /x/, /h^w/ and /x^w/, and /y/ and /γ/, all oppositions of restricted occurrence, low contrastive yield, and very similar or overlapping phonetic realizations. /x/ is found only stem-initially and /h/ only elsewhere; /x/ and /h/ are usually written *h*, but /sx/ is written *sx* to distinguish it from /š/, written *sh* (/sh/ does not occur). /γ/ is written *gh* before *a*, *y* before *i* or *e*, and *w* before *o*. /g^w/ occurs only before /o/, but contrasting /go/ and /g^wo/ are both written *go*.

The practical orthography described here differs from that recommended by the Albuquerque Conference on Navajo Orthography (Ohannessian 1969) only in writing word-initial glottal stop ('). Many writers use other slight variations, for example writing tl and tl' for *tł* and *tł'* (Platero 1974), writing ghi for *yi* and ghe for *ye* in stem syllables, or indicating a low-tone syllablic /n/ with a grave accent (ǹ instead of *n*).

Although Navajo has a standard writing system, in the sense that the practical orthography provides a consistent way of transcribing sounds, there is no standard Navajo language. There is considerable variation among speakers from different areas and of different ages and degrees of experience with the language, though without sharply distinct dialects. Different literate speakers may write some words differently, following their own individual uses. In the *Handbook* the usage of Young and Morgan (1980; Robert W. Young communications to editors 1980, 1981) has been followed as far as possible, but chapters by Navajo speakers in some cases have words or forms based on their own speech or experience. Other sources on Navajo phonology and dialectology are Hoijer (1945), Reichard (1945a, 1948a), Sapir and Hoijer (1967), and Kari (1976).

and curing; music accompanied by hoof and possibly hide rattles; a loose band organization, a flexible bilateral kinship system, and the accomplishment of special jobs by temporary task groups, with leadership roles of an informal type for band and family and authority over the task groups lasting only so long as the group functioned.

Most of this cultural inventory was probably intact upon arrival in the Southwest. It is possible that limited knowledge of agriculture and ceramics was acquired during the migration; but without knowledge of the peoples met on the way, the extent of change is difficult to assess. It seems likely that late western remnants of Woodland peoples and survivals of the Fremont culture were encountered or even absorbed by some segments of the bands (Hall 1944; Aikens 1967, 1972:63–64). By 1300 the Apacheans must have been close to the northern periphery of the Anasazi region. It is still uncertain whether they had any influence on the Puebloan abandonment of vast regions about this time (Jett 1964:290–297), but areas such as the San Juan and Chama river basins must have been occupied by them at a relatively early date following the Anasazi withdrawal to precede occupation by Shoshonian- or Yuman-speaking peoples or a reexpansion of Puebloan settlement.

Early History

When the Spaniards arrived in New Mexico the Pueblos were almost entirely surrounded by Apachean peoples, only the Hopis on the extreme west having some non-Athapaskan neighbors. The Spaniards first referred to the Southern Athapaskans as *Querechos* but soon settled on the term *Apache*, giving each tribe a regional or descriptive epithet. Thus, the people living west of the northern Pueblos, north of the Western Keresans and Zuni and east of the Hopi were termed the *Apaches de Nabajó*, their neighbors to the north and northeast the *Apaches de Quinía*, and those west of the southern Pueblos the *Apaches de Gila*, while various other tribes and bands were recognized to the east. Only the *Apaches de Nabajó* practiced agriculture to such a de-

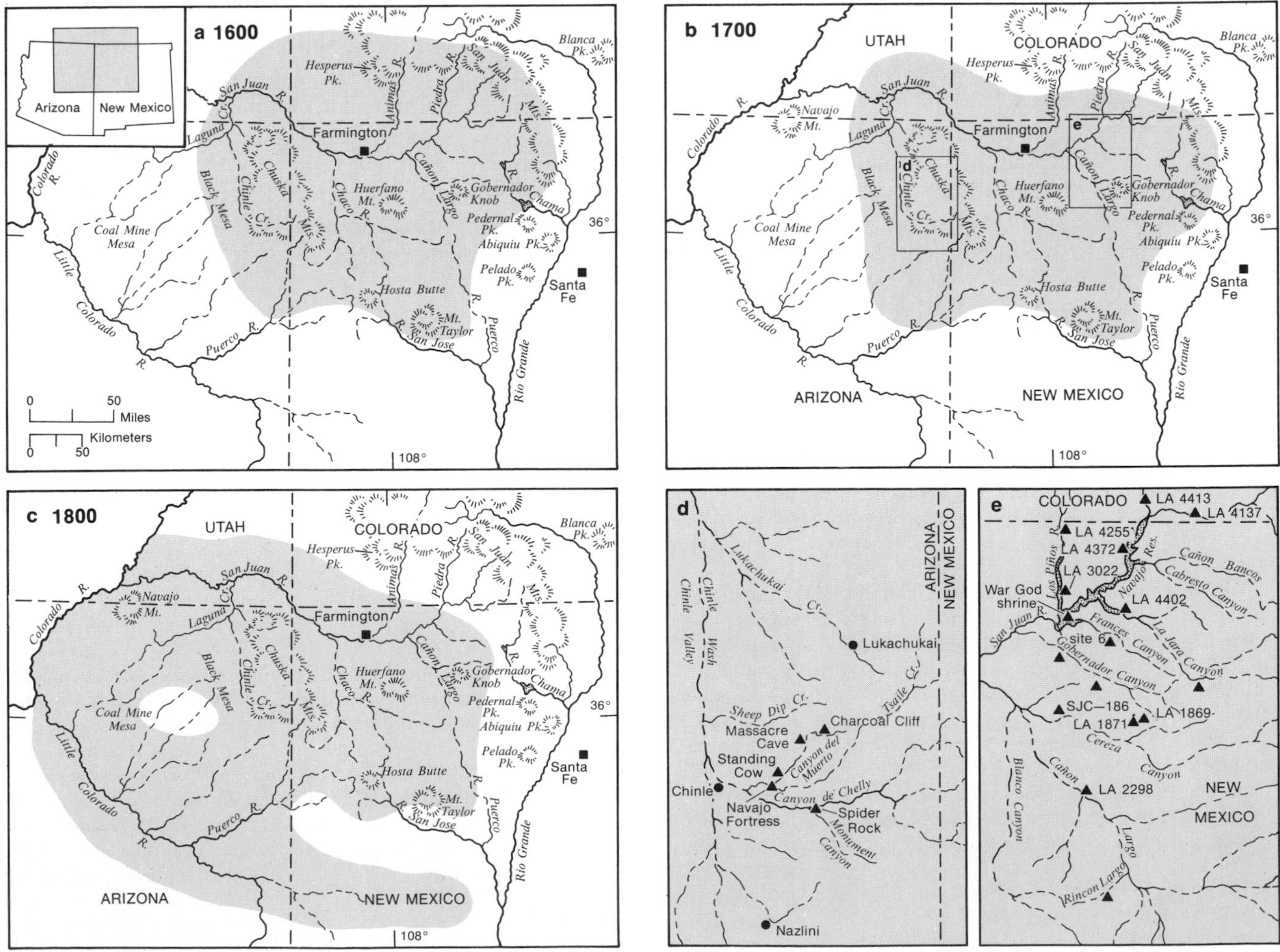

490 Fig. 1. Approximate Navajo settlement areas. a–c, 1600–1800; d, Canyon de Chelly; e, Navajo Reservoir archeological site concentrations.

gree that it was noted by the early Spaniards. This alone has been sufficient to suggest a somewhat different history from that of the other Apacheans prior to initial contact. The fact that the area of occupation was similar to that abandoned by the prehistoric Anasazi suggests that there may have been some similarities in ecological adaptations between the earlier occupants and the later. That this was a highly successful adaptation based on a diversity of resources and a degree of mobility lacking in the later Pueblo periods seems certain, for early accounts indicate a very large population (Benavides 1945, 1954). While the precise figures given are obviously exaggerated, the implication of a large and powerful tribe cannot be ignored. It seems reasonable that the demographic pattern described by Dobyns (1966) for most tribes, involving a drastic decline in total population in the decades following initial contact with Europeans as a result of epidemic disease and warfare, followed by a recovery if the population nadir did not lead to extinction, must be valid for the Navajos as well, particularly since the contemporary documentary evidence would accord with this interpretation. The Navajos differ from other tribes only in that their recovery was under more favorable conditions, resulting in a more spectacular increase.

The best indications of *Apache de Nabajó* culture about the time of initial contact are the accounts of the Antonio de Espejo expedition of 1582–1583 (Pérez de Luxán 1929:86, 111–114) and the Benavides memorials of 1630 (1954) and 1634 (1945), the latter based on observations during the years 1625 to 1629, plus a few scattered observations. These describe a semisedentary people who planted maize and perhaps other crops but moved to areas distant from their fields for hunting; traded meat, hides, and mineral products, primarily salt and alum, to the Puebloans; lived in "underground" homes in rancherias and built special structures for the storage of their harvests; were variously friendly or hostile with the Pueblos under different poorly defined circumstances; had clothing with feathered headgear, arrows tipped with stone points; had many local headmen including war chiefs and one or more caciques or peace chiefs; practiced polygamy; and were quite skillful in war. The only distinctively Puebloan traits added to those brought from the north are agriculture and a more formal political structure. Benavides describes an elaborate ritualized encounter between Tewa emissaries and Navajo hosts that demonstrates a sharing of certain ceremonial concepts, including the use of a feather-tipped arrow as a symbol of peace and the mutual smoking of a cane cigarette. It is probable that all or most of the northern traits listed above were still extant and that ceramics and cloth were not yet produced by the tribe, but acquired in trade in limited quantities.

The earliest recorded contact of tribal members with Spaniards, that of Espejo at the base of Mount Taylor, was friendly at first but soon led to fighting, in part as a result of the Spaniards' desire to retain Navajo captives obtained from the Hopis. A similar course of events may easily be postulated for Navajo-Spanish relations after the colonists arrived in the Tewa country. The first mention of people who were apparently Navajos indicates the assignment of missionaries and, following the destruction of Acoma in 1599, the placing of old captives from that Pueblo with Navajos. It was not long before bitter warfare became the rule and throughout the seventeenth century relations were predominantly hostile. The Navajos have been credited with being a factor in the abandonment of San Gabriel in favor of Santa Fe as the capital of New Mexico (Forbes 1960:113) and were closely allied with the Pueblos in their efforts to throw off Spanish rule (Brugge 1969). The trade in captives was one of the major causes of hostilities during this period (Brugge 1968:135), although the Indians may have attributed introduced diseases to black magic on the part of the Spaniards.

Cultural changes during the period prior to the Reconquest may be traced to two major influences, the arrival of occasional Pueblo fugitives and the impact of European culture. The former doubtless led to increased Puebloan influences, although they cannot be traced in any detail, and the latter to the adoption of a few items of the most obvious utility. The major items identified in the documentary record are horses and metal objects, both tools and trinkets. It is highly probable that the use of horses for transport and the use of metal, including minor reworking of worn tools and scraps by cutting and abrasion, were incorporated in the culture during this period.

The Dinetah

The Navajos participated in the Pueblo Revolt of 1680 and shared in the captives taken (Reeve 1959:16–17; Brugge 1968:43), but it is difficult to separate their part from that of other Apacheans. The Reconquest was another matter, and Navajo aid as a retreat for the many refugees was to have a profound effect on Navajo culture. As the Spaniards defeated one minor alliance after another of the divided Pueblos, the people most closely involved in the movement fled, some to the Plains Apaches and others to Hopi, while many poured into the valley of the San Juan above present-day Farmington, New Mexico. Here they camped with their Navajo allies and plotted the eventual expulsion of their enemy. The superior arms and organization of the Spaniards allowed them to consolidate their rule throughout the New Mexico Pueblos, and the Reconquest was halted only at Hopi by the destruction of Awatovi in 1700. Within a generation the refugees among the Nav-

top left, Natl. Park Service, Washington.

Fig. 2. Rock paintings depicting Spanish horsemen, Canyon del Muerto, Ariz. top left, Detail of painting in brown, black, and white showing mounted Spaniards with lances. Photograph by David de Harport. top right, Charcoal Cliff: Spanish cavalcade. bottom, Standing Cow Ruin: riders (in red and white) wearing long capes and broad-brimmed hats and carrying flintlock guns may depict soldiers of Lt. Antonio Narbona on their 1805 raid against the Navajo (Grant 1978:228). The artist may have been *Dibé Yázhí Nééz* 'Tall Lamb', who lived there at or soon after this date (Grant 1978:220-223, 228, 259; McNitt 1972:opp. p. 244). In addition to such naturalistic figures of men and animals, Navajo rock art dating as early as the 18th century includes ceremonial subjects and astronomical diagrams (see Schaafsma 1980). top right and bottom, Photographs by Stephen Jett.

ajos had lost all hope of freeing their former homes and began to settle in to stay with their hosts.

Archeological sites reported in the Chama drainage may include pre-Reconquest components. Their significance to Navajo prehistory needs to be evaluated (C.F. Schaafsma 1979).

The earliest clearly identifiable and datable Navajo archeological remains are those from the Navajo Reservoir area on the upper San Juan. The pottery there is the most strongly Puebloan of any from Navajo sites, including a high proportion of the indented variety of Dinetah Utility, Jemez Black-on-white, and some polychromes and late glazes. The local Frances Polychrome is the predecessor to Gobernador Polychrome (Carlson 1965:51–57). This complex is usually mixed with later and more distictively Navajo types such as Dinetah Utility, Gobernador Polychrome, and non-glaze trade polychromes (fig. 3). The later complex is found in generally purer form in the somewhat later sites up the canyons tributary to the San Juan. The riverside sites lack elaborate architectural development and may best be interpreted as the camps established by the refugees along with Navajo allies in the early days of the Reconquest. Here the two peoples farmed and the refugees probably remained fairly settled while their Athapaskan hosts ranged more widely on hunting and gathering expeditions. Although the proportions of Athapaskan and Pueblo in this population are unknown, there can be little doubt that the Puebloan element was relatively large. Ceramic styles suggest both Tewa and Jemez immigrants (Carlson 1965:57), while Navajo clan origins mention Keresans and Zuni as well. Jemez tradition supports other evidence of their inclusions (Reiter 1938:38). In addition to the refugees in the Dinetah, as this rather poorly defined region has come to be known, Hopi refugees from the Pueblo of Awatovi fled to join the western Navajos in the upper Chinle drainage. With this influx of refugees the two major ancestral roots of traditional Navajo culture, Athapaskan-Apachean and Anasazi-Puebloan, were joined. The development of Navajo culture as it is known today was far from complete, but the two peoples quickly merged sufficiently to form a single tribal entity with the *Apaches de Nabajó* providing the political unit and linguistic unity while the theology of the Pueblo Revolt gave sanction to the Puebloan participation.

More permanent settlement by the refugee population, by this time probably well mixed with the Athapaskan element, seems to have begun between 1710 and 1715 in the canyons tributary to the San Juan, including Largo Canyon, Gobernador Canyon, Frances Canyon, La Jara Canyon and others on the south and the Los Pinos and Animas rivers on the north. Sites of this period are characterized by pueblitos (fig. 4), small Puebloan-style structures ranging from one room to many, usually built in defensive locations and with associated hogans, towers, and defensive walls (Carlson 1965; Brugge 1972; Eddy 1966). Warfare with the Spaniards continued until about 1716, after which time peace with the Whites developed gradually as both found a new enemy in the Utes (Reeve 1958:229–230). The Pueblo-style strongholds of this period were of little value for defense against well-supplied armies but were well suited to warding off raids by Indian war parties. During the next few decades the pueblito tradition flourished alongside that of the hogan, but the hogan was being built more solidly than previously with more general use of the forked-pole principle (fig. 5; for modern examples see "Navajo Social Organization," this vol.). The Dinetah became the center of a cultural development that has no equal in Apachean history. The Puebloans had brought with them their rich ceremonial lore, and ceremonies of great complexity were performed. The abundant rock art of the Dinetah attests vividly to the interest taken in religion during this period (Schaafsma 1963), as do many of the collections from the pueblito sites (Hester 1962:105–122; Carlson 1965:20–50). It is noteworthy that despite the strong religious interest, the kiva was not introduced by the refugees. The hogan was the kiva's counterpart in the

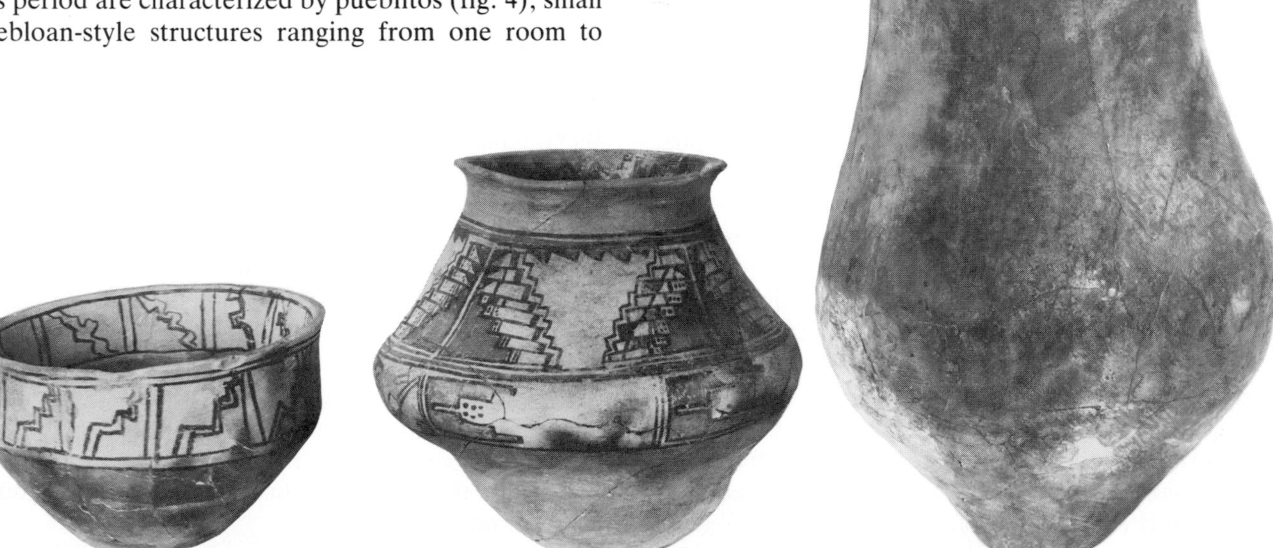

U. of Colo. Mus., Boulder: right, 210; center, 383; left, 401.

Fig. 3. Pottery. right, Dinetah Utility ware vessel of the 18th century, dark gray with surface striations probably caused by scraping with a corncob. For examples of modern Navajo cooking vessels see "Navajo Arts and Crafts," this vol. center and left, Gobernador Polychrome vessels of the early 18th century with typical black and red painted decoration on yellow ground are probably derived from Rio Grande pottery styles, possibly learned by the Navajo from Pueblo refugee women (Carlson 1965:57). center, Height 20.5 cm, left, 11.1 cm. Both collected by Earl Morris from burial knoll northwest of Ruin #4, Gobernador Canyon, Rio Arriba Co., N. Mex., 1915. right, Height 35.0 cm, collected by William Ross from rock niche, Gobernador Canyon, Rio Arriba Co., N. Mex., 1914.

Fig. 4. Pueblito of the early 18th century, near Cañon Largo, N. Mex., with remaining walls about 5 feet high. These Pueblo-style masonry structures were usually rectangular in plan (this one has curved walls) and were often built in defensive positions. This is a small example; others ranged from one room to about 40. Multistoried tower pueblitos were another variant. Hogans and pueblitos are found at the same sites. Pueblito construction ceased about 1753 in the Dinetah. A few pueblitos were built about 1764 in the region from Lobo Mesa west to Klagetoh and Nazlini and Spanish accounts indicate use of defensive stone towers into the 1790s. Photograph by David M. Brugge.

Fig. 5. Remains of a forked-pole hogan dating about 1760 on a fortified mesa near Mariano Lake, N. Mex. This is probably the earliest type of hogan; it is circular in plan, conical in section, and has poles leaned against a tripod foundation of forked poles then covered with bark and earth. For a discussion of geographic and structural differences in the hogan through time see Jett and Spencer (1981). Photograph by David M. Brugge.

old Athapaskan way, and hogans appear in the plazas of those pueblitos sufficiently large that kivas might be expected.

Puebloan cultural influence was very strong. The ceramics of the period are predominantly Puebloan in all except the shape of utility jars. This vessel shape is very similar to that of the prehistoric Largo-Gallina culture of the same general region and was probably copied from jars found in nearby prehistoric ruins, the stimulus for this perhaps being a nativistic orientation in the beliefs of the refugees. Pictographs and petroglyphs show many strongly Puebloan features, such as kachinas, including the Hunchback deity, sun shields with macaw feathers, and heart lines in animal figures, as well as stylistic resemblances to prehistoric kiva murals (Schaasfma 1963). Other Puebloan traits included cane arrow shafts, macaw images, sandals, close-coiled basketry, tubular pipes, tablitas, masks, gourd dippers and canteens, woven cloth, and tools for spinning and weaving (Hester 1962:105–125). A number of items of uncertain origin also appear. European traits introduced by the refugees were fewer in number but of great importance, including cattle, sheep and wool, probably goats and cheesemaking, new crops including peaches and cotton, perhaps improved gear for use with horses, and chimneys. Navajo tradition suggests that the dominant character of Pueblo culture was fully as strong as the trait lists would suggest and even included the European custom of whipping for punishment (Underhill 1956:50). Contemporary documentation shows that the people were particularly noted for their skill in working buckskin, making baskets, and weaving cloth, all of which were important items of trade, while additional traits included dams for stock water, irrigation, and cotton (Hill 1940).

On the basis of the earliest transcription of the Navajo origin tradition, it may be postulated that clans, unification of linguistic usage, and the tribal assembly or *naachid* also began during the Dinetah period (Matthews 1897). Some clans were based on previous Apachean band groups and others on refugee groups from different Pueblos and perhaps in some cases even diverse clans from the same Pueblo, while a few had origin with captives. Multiple "origins" for some clans may be postulated as well, resulting in branches within the clans with slightly differing ancestries. One description of the *naachid* (Van Valkenburgh 1946) is highly suggestive in its ground plan of a large Pueblo with the major action taking place in a central plaza and in an underground structure in the plaza. The loss of fishing may have come about during this period by the introduction of the taboo on use of fish as food found at certain Pueblos.

Exodus

That conflicts arose between the Puebloan and Apachean values of the two ancestral groups of the population is predictable. While the Dinetah remained an area of cultural growth and wealth these could be worked out slowly and with little strain, but when severe pressures on the people came about toward the middle of the eighteenth century in the form of drought and intensified Ute attacks these internal conflicts were aggravated and solutions sought in more drastic ways. Among a people with a strong interest in religion and with some of the nativistic concepts of the Pueblo Revolt still present in their thinking, a religious validation of any solution might be expected. Two solutions were attempted, one being conversion to Roman Catholicism and settling under the protection of the Spaniards, which was shortly found to be too foreign to the ways of those who tried it, and the other being a revitalization movement of native origin, which placed a strong emphasis on the Apachean values but allowed retention of those introduced traits and complexes most compatible with these values. There was a rejection of the more overtly Anasazi elements among the Pueblo introductions, specifically stone houses and highly decorated ceramics, and of those traits that tended to structure society too rigidly, such as use of whipping for social control and some religious practices. The raising of livestock by a people living in a dispersed settlement pattern with sufficient mobility to escape enemies and utilize the diverse resources of the environment offered the solutions needed to both the economic and military problems. Blessingway, the central ceremony in Navajo religion, gave the supernatural sanction that brought about the change, although whether Blessingway originated at this time or merely was raised in status with some reworking is not at all certain (Brugge 1963). The changes were not made without difficulties and were uneven. Destruction of pottery at the time of emigration from the Dinetah has been noted at at least one site (Carlson 1965:21), and some of the emigrants continued to build pueblitos for a very brief time. A transitional period from about 1753 to 1770 is indicated by the archeological data (Brugge 1972) and suggested by some Navajo tradition.

Warfare

The end of this transitional period coincides quite closely with the resumption of warfare with the Spaniards, in 1774, when the Navajos successfully drove encroaching Spanish settlers from the eastern portion of their land (Reeve 1959:39–40, 1960:206–210). The success of the war and the general success of the new way of life apparent by this time seem to have been sufficient to gain its acceptance by all factions. The conflicts between the Puebloan and Apachean traditions had been resolved in such a way that a relatively well-integrated pattern very like what is now known as traditional Navajo culture had emerged.

Agriculture, animal husbandry, hunting, gathering, and manufacturing (primarily the weaving of woolen cloth) formed the economic base (fig. 6). V. Troncoso's (1788) account of Navajo culture shows little difference from that known ethnologically except for the high quality of coiled basketry then produced and some continued use of cotton. The adjustments to the natural environment and to the tactical demands of a period when warfare was rampant were quite good, and territorial expansion was again possible. Lands held in the upper Chama valley had long since been lost to the Ute advance, but movement to the west and south was possible. The alliance that the Spaniards had forged against the southern Apaches had reduced their numbers and driven them to settle in peace at the presidios in Chihuahua and Sonora (Navarro García 1964:457–459). On the east the Navajos held their own with fair success against the pressures of the expanding Spanish population, while on the west they allied themselves with, and in time absorbed, some of the Southern Paiutes. Farther west they moved into country once held by the Havasupais, there being some evidence that there was accompanying warfare between the two peoples (Chacón 1801; Cadelo 1801:203).

U. of N. Mex., Maxwell Mus. of Anthr., Albuquerque: 63.34.69.

Fig. 6. Textile fragments (among the earliest known pieces of Navajo weaving) from Massacre Cave, Ariz., have stripes in 3 shades of brown, on a beige ground, all of undyed wool. Based on Pueblo tradition (Wheat 1981), striped blankets were woven into the 1890s. Size 119 by 134.5 cm, woven before 1805.

A new factor was introduced with Mexican independence. The opening of trade with the Anglo-Americans gave the New Mexicans better supplies of firearms, and for the first time since before the Pueblo Revolt the Navajos became a major target of the suppliers of captives for the slave trade. This was set off by the José Antonio Vizcarra campaign of 1823 and continued until the end of warfare in the 1860s (Brugge 1968:147–149). During the early and middle 1820s there were numerous baptisms of Navajo captives in the churches of New Mexico. The tribe, suffering from the aggressiveness of the New Mexicans as well as from drought, tried to avoid war, but with limited success. By 1833 warfare was rapidly escalating. The Navajos gained a major victory in 1835 when they routed a large Mexican force in Washington Pass, killing its leader among others (Brugge 1968:57–60). In 1837 when New Mexico suffered a local revolt the Navajos found allies among the western Pueblos and aided them in their abortive bid for freedom (Brugge 1969:196–197). As the number of Navajo captives among the New Mexicans grew, attacks were launched from both sides with increasing frequency and the issue of return of their lost people became the major Navajo concern at treaty negotiations (Brugge 1968:61–66). The demands of war were increasingly hard on the economies of both peoples. The New Mexicans were able to solve the problem by taxing the Anglo-American traders who came regularly over the Santa Fe Trail (Brugge 1965:25–26), but for the Navajos there was no source of outside support. The strains resulted in internal divisions within the tribe. As early as 1818 a group favoring peace with the Spaniards had detached themselves from the rest of the tribe to form the nucleus of the so-called Enemy Navajo (*diné 'ana'í*), who later settled at Cañoncito (McNitt 1972:48, 434). The basic issue was whether to have war or peace with the Whites, specifically the New Mexicans. Explanations of the differences of opinion within the tribe vary, some being in terms of rich versus poor (Brugge 1968:66) and others on a regional basis, the Navajos closest to the White settlements being those who most favored peace (Simpson 1964:lxxviii–lxxix). Detailed analysis of the data shows that both versions were at best only partially true (Littell 1967:37–44). It is probable that many factors influenced the attitudes of individual Navajos.

With the arrival of the United States Army in 1846 a new and untested force was introduced into the conflicts. American officers wavered between attempts to treat both sides fairly and outright espousal of the New Mexicans' cause but lacked insight into local conditions. By 1850 three treaties had been signed between the United States and the Navajo Tribe, but the private war between the tribe and the New Mexicans continued in sporadic fashion (Brugge 1968:67–72).

Synonymy†

The English name Navajo is from Spanish *Navajó,* which first came into use in the seventeenth century as the name of the territory then inhabited by the Navajo in northwestern New Mexico. Zárate Salmerón (1899–1900, 4:183, 1966:94), about 1629, referred to the Apaches de Nabajú, and Benavides (1630:59 [i.e. 57]) to the Apaches de Nauajò, which he explained as meaning 'large planted fields' (*sementeras grandes*), a reference to the fact that these Indians were great farmers (*muy grandes labradores*). Spanish *Navajó* seems to be a borrowing of Tewa *navahu·*, a compound of *nava* 'field' and *hu·* 'wide arroyo, valley' used to designate a large arroyo in which there are cultivated fields (Hewett 1906; Harrington 1940:518). It is not known whether the Tewa expression was a specific place-name in the Navajo area or a descriptive term; it is known to be the name of an abandoned pueblo near Puye. In any case, the Spaniards adopted it to designate the Largo Canyon area south of the San Juan River, where the Navajo lived (Reeve 1956:298–303). Provinsia de Nabajo and Provinsia de Navajo are used on Menchero's map of about 1745, and Provincia de Nabajoo appears on Miera y Pacheco's 1776 map ("History of Pueblo-Spanish Relations to 1821," figs. 3, 6, vol. 9). In the nineteenth century *Navajó* became the most common Spanish name for the tribe, the plural being *Navajoses*; *Navajoso* (pl. *Navajosos,* fem. *Navajosa*) is also used (Harrington 1940:517). Variant spellings have b for v and x for j. Early Spanish plurals are Navajós (Coues 1900, 2:458; Orozco y Berra 1864:369) and Navajoes (Bloom 1928:177). Other early Spanish variants are Navejo, Nabejo (Harrington 1940b), Napao and Apaches Nabajai (Coues 1900, 2:351, 369), navajoas, 1765 (Tamarón y Romeral 1937:350), and Abajoses (D.A. Gunnerson 1974:282).

The first occurrences in a text originally written in English are found in the accounts of Zebulon Montgomery Pike's expeditions: Nahjo, Nanahaws, 1805–1807 (Coues 1895:730, 746). From this last form, the misspellings Namakaus (Schermerhorn 1814:29) and nanahas (Orozco y Berra 1864:385) are derived. Other early occurrences are Nabeho, 1821–1822 (J. Fowler 1898:123); Navahoes, 1821–1823 (T. James 1953:136); Nabijos (Anonymous 1824); Nabahoes (Pattie 1833:41); Navajoes, Navajó, 1831–1839 (Josiah Gregg in Thwaites 1904–1907, 20:56, 103); Navahoes, 1835–1837 (Parker 1942:32); Navijos, 1846 (Sage 1956, 2:90); Nebajos, 1848 (J.S. Robinson 1932:29). Ten Kate (1885:160) has Návojos, and Deniker (1907:525) Nodehs.

The modern English spellings are Navaho and Navajo, now generally pluralized as Navahos and Navajos, though in the nineteenth century the plurals Navahoes and Navajoes were frequent. Both the anglicized spelling Navaho and the Spanish spelling Navajo have been considered correct, but there has been some discussion about which one should be preferred. Navajo was the prevailing spelling for centuries in local use and is the only one officially recognized by the Board on Geographic Names of the Department of the Interior (Har-

†This synonymy was written by David M. Brugge, Ives Goddard, and Willem J. de Reuse. Uncredited phonemic transcriptions are from sources that prefer to be anonymous. Some of the 19th-century spellings are from Kluckhohn and Spencer (1940:11–12).

rington 1945a). After the Tewa origin of the name was pointed out by Hewett (1906), the spelling Navaho was officially adopted by the Bureau of American Ethnology (Hodge 1907–1910, 2:41) and the Bureau of Indian Affairs. This was used during the first two thirds of the twentieth century by many authorities but never became popular. Hodge (1949:78) was strongly in favor of the BAE's decision, on the grounds that it is pointless to write a word of Tewa origin with a Spanish spelling; an extended discussion is in Haile (1949). However, the spelling Navajo was officially adopted by the Navajo Nation in 1969 and has been officially adopted by the BIA and the *Handbook*.

When the Navajos were first identified by name by the Spaniards in the seventeenth century they were considered a subdivision of the Apaches and called *Apaches de Navajó* (see above). The term Apache came to be used less as Navajo culture began to diverge more clearly from that of other Southern Athapaskans, but it is still used in some rural Spanish-speaking New Mexico communities to include the Navajos. For the name Apache and its synonyms, see the synonymy in "The Apachean Culture Pattern and Its Origins" (this vol.). Francisco Garcés, who used the Yuman term Yabipai to include both Upland Yumans and Apacheans, called the Navajo Yabipais Nabajay (Coues 1900, 2:457).

In the Navajo language, the usual self-denomination is *Diné* (plural or collective *Dine'é*). This term is sometimes used in a more general sense to include related peoples such as members of a clan or all Apacheans or even all Indians or all peoples of the world, its literal meaning being 'person', 'people', or 'human beings'. It is occasionally used to refer to the gods or other supernatural beings. It is sometimes even used, when appropriately modified, to identify classes of animals. For this reason more specific terms are available for use in some contexts. *T'áá diné* (with the particularizing particle *t'áá*) may fill this function, as may *Naabeehó,* the latter clearly a loanword of recent origin (Young and Morgan 1980:321; Wyman and Bailey 1964:18). An old Navajo man once stated that when some Navajos were robbing a Tewa cornfield, the Tewa Indians shouted [naapeexwóh] (i.e., *naabeehó*) as a warning, and that this is how the Navajos know that the Tewas call them this (Howard Gorman in Harrington 1940a). What appears to be an older pronunciation nāwehó was recorded by the Franciscan Fathers (1912:132), who also give the sobriquet goyő́dĕ, from Spanish *coyote,* as another possible Navajo self-denomination. Apparently derived from the Navajo term *diné* are the following Keresan and Zuni words for 'Navajo': Cochiti Dinne (Bandelier 1890:175), Laguna *téné* (Harrington 1944a, phonemicized), Acoma *tʰené*, Zuni tʸynɛ́ or tʸynǽ (Harrington 1913, normalized).

The oldest Apache term recorded that refers specifically to the Navajos is Yutajen-né, 1796 (Antonio Cordero in Matson and Schroeder 1957:336). It is not clear which Apache group called the Navajos by this term, but it is probably related to the Western Apache word for 'Navajo', *yúdahą́* (Perry et al. 1972). Goodwin (1942:71) has *yúúdahą́* 'people above', said to be used because they lived directly to the north of the Western Apache. Variants of the same word that cannot be explained merely as different spellings are yúttahi (Harrington 1945) and Yú-tah-kah (Eaton 1854).

Among other Apachean words for 'Navajo' is a Jicarilla form variously given as Inltanĕ́ 'corn planters', (Curtis 1907–1930, 1:135), īnLt'anne (Goddard 1911:130), nłt'ă´ni 'farmers, corn raisers' (Franciscan Fathers 1912:132), iⁿl-tŏn-ɐ (Russell 1898:65), and Nl'-dû´nĕ 'katydids' (Mooney 1897a). This is apparently cognate with Navajo *'anilt'ánii* 'ripener (variety of insects associated with ripening such as lacewing flies, tree crickets, ant-lions)' (Young and Morgan 1980:116). The same name has been recorded in Mescalero Apache (Franciscan Fathers 1912:132), but the current Mescalero term for 'Navajo' is *ndaabixúńde,* literally 'White man's prisoner', referring to the Navajos' captivity in Fort Sumner (Scott Rushforth, communication to editors 1981).

Chiricahua Apache has Naväχú (Gatschet 1884b:5), from Spanish, and tl'ests'ōsi bizhă´ha 'small G-strings' (Franciscan Fathers 1912:132), apparently a nickname. Kiowa-Apache has da·bahû· (Harrington 1944), also of Spanish origin.

Various other names for the Navajo are used by Pueblo Indians. Zuni has *paču* (pl. *ˀa·paču* less often *paču·kʷe*) (Dennis Tedlock, communication to editors 1977), which may be the origin of the term Apache. Taos has the borrowing Nawahonæ, pl. Nawahoną (Harrington 1918), also spelled nábahunæ, pl. nábahuną̀ or nabahúnæmą (Harrington 1918a), and milenă 'the heathen, the gentiles' (Harrington in Franciscan Fathers 1912:132). Picuris has k⁽ʰ⁾ulénà, which means 'captive' in Taos (Harrington 1918), or *kˀulone* (Amy Zaharlick, communication to editors 1981). Rio Grande Tewa has *wǽn-sáve* 'Jemez Apachean' (*wǽn* 'Jemez Indian' and *sáve* 'Apachean'), so called because the Navajo live in the country west of Jemez, the nearest Pueblo to their historical location. Harrington (1916:573, 575 normalized) recorded [ŋwæn-saβè]. Hopi-Tewa has the corresponding *sá·be, wónsá·be* (Paul V. Kroskrity, communication to editors 1977). Mooney (1892–1898) glosses *sá·be* (which he spells shä´bi) as 'people to look out for'. Southern Tiwa has Sandia *tˀęłimpede,* pl. *tˀęłimnen* (Elizabeth A. Brandt, communication to editors 1981), and Isleta *tę łémide,* pl. *tę łémnin* (William L. Leap, communication to editors 1977). Gatschet (1879–1885:22) derives this word from te´ 'liep 'without pity, hard-minded'. Gibbs (1868) gives a plural Tāt-li-em-a-nūn glossed 'Apaches and Navajos', an indication that the word earlier had a broader meaning. The Franciscan Fathers (1912:132) give Isleta nabē'łi 'dried skins', apparently a nickname.

Several Keresan terms do not come from Navajo *diné*. Cochiti has Moshome (Bandelier 1890:175), given by Harrington as mo´rzhrumæ 'the gentiles, the heathen' (in Franciscan Fathers 1912:132); this corresponds to Santa Ana *ṁúsumi* 'enemy'. In later notes Harrington (1944b) states that the borrowing navahǫ́ is the only common name. Zia has 'Ché-shap (Stevenson 1889–1890:15). Laguna has Navajó (Harrington 1944a) and sōk'ĕīn´ or sōk'ĕ´ină, for which no etymology is given (Franciscan Fathers 1912:132), but which resembles Laguna *śáuk̓î·ni* 'my friend'. Jemez has *k̓ʸǽlǽ*, pl. *k̓ʸǽlǽcoš* (Joe S. Sando, communication to editors 1978), which is the same word as Pecos Keretsâ (Hodge 1910:339), the source of the name Querecho.

Hopi names for 'Navajo' are Third Mesa *tasávɨ*, pl. *tasávɨmɨ* (Voegelin and Voegelin 1957:49), and Mishongnovi *tásʔavà*, pl. *tásʔavàm* (Whorf 1936:1301). This term is probably a loanword from Tewa (see above), although Ten Kate (1885:259) glosses Tasámewé as 'bastards'. The word is doubtless related to the name transcribed in Spanish in the seventeen and eighteen centuries as Tacabuy (i.e. Taçabuy) or Tassabuess, although there is some evidence that these early names refer to the people now called Western Apaches (Forbes 1960:104–106). Another Hopi name is Third Mesa *qaláyʔtaqa* 'one who has a prominent forehead' (Voegelin and Voegelin 1957:49). An obsolete term for 'Navajo' is yútahani (Stephen 1936, 2:1325), probably a borrowing of the Western Apache term.

Yuman tribes also have various names for the Navajo. Havasupai has *hʷa·múʔu* (Leanne Hinton, communication to editors 1981), also recorded as hua'ámu´'u or hwa'mu (Spier 1946:18), apparently representing *hʷa·ʔmúʔu*. This term was first recorded by Francisco Garcés as Guamua (Coues 1900, 2:404) although he did not explain that it was another name for those he called Yabipais Nabajay and may not have made the connection himself. Yavapai has *mu·ka kyula* 'tall Hopi' and *čihʷahmu·ča* (Martha B. Kendall, communication to editors 1981); earlier forms are Yutila pa´ 'Navajo man' (Gatschet 1883:6), pl. Yat-́e-lat-lar´-we (J.B. White 1873–1875), which may be related to the Western Apache term, and plural χwamṓ (Freire-Marreco 1910–1912), obviously related to the Havasupai term. Mohave has Navahúa (Gibbs 1856), Quechan has *navaxó* (Abraham Halpern, communication to editors 1981), and Cocopa has *navaxú* or *navaxú·* (James Crawford, communication to editors 1981), all from Spanish Navajó. Quechan *ʔapač*, presumably from Spanish too, can also refer to the Navajo (Abraham Halpern, communication to editors 1981).

The Pima and Papago name is *ná·waho* (Saxton and Saxton 1969:156). Pima and Papago *ʔó·b* refers specifically to the Apache (Saxton and Saxton 1969:35, 156; Mathiot 1973, 2:466) but in its original broader meaning of 'enemy' it included the Navajos.

The Great Basin Numic names all seem closely related in form but show some variation in meaning. Southern Paiute has *paγaŋʷi·ciŋʷɨ*, literally 'cane-knife people' (Sapir 1930–1931, 3:605, phonemicized). The Southern Ute name *paγáwĭ·čI* is explained as 'walking knife' and also means 'dragon-fly' (Givón et al. 1979:154), but the meaning given for an early recording, Ute Pá-gu-wēts 'reed knives' (Powell 1874:26), agrees with Southern Paiute. Gosiute Shoshoni has *paka-wi·cci* [paγa wi·č·i] 'arrow knife' (Miller 1972:165), with a word for 'arrow' cognate with Ute and Southern Paiute 'cane, reed'.

Panamint has yu-ī´-ta (Henshaw 1883:184), but the recorder was apparently not certain that this word referred to the Navajos. It may be related to the Western Apache word for 'Navajo'. Comanche has *navó·* (Casagrande 1954:231). Earlier spellings seem to be closer to the Spanish or English: nábaho· nö´ 'the Navajo people' (Gatschet 1884c:113), or Nă´-vȧ-hō (Detrick 1894:184). Other Comanche terms, taken down by Gatschet from a trader's vocabulary, are of very uncertain spelling and unknown etymology: Marho, moodus-sey (Gatschet 1884c:87).

The Kiowa name is *àbàhô·-gɔ̀* (pl.) or *kʰó·-cén-gɔ̀* (pl.); the second word is analyzable into 'body' and 'mud' (Laurel Watkins, communication to editors 1979). Mooney (1898:391) states that Ä´bähóko is the old name, derived from the word 'Navajo', and that the more frequent name is Kotsénto 'muddy bodies', from an alleged custom of painting themselves with clay. Besides the words given by Mooney and Watkins, Harrington (1943) has a form nǽbǽhów-gɔ̀ (pl.) perhaps influenced by the English word Navajo (cf. Harrington 1928:123).

Sources‡

This sources section refers to all the chapters on the Navajo. With a very few exceptions, it is limited to monographs that provide significant historical or ethnographic information, to museum collections, and to sources of photographs.

Iverson (1976) is an introduction to the voluminous literature on the Navajo. Correll, Watson, and Brugge (1969, 1973) is a more extensive bibliography. One may also consult Vogt (1961) for a synthesis of much of the central work completed to that date.

Underhill (1956) is the most comprehensive narrative of Navajo history. Other useful overviews include Van

‡This section is by Peter Iverson, except that the paragraph on manuscripts and the listing of museum collections is by Susan Brown McGreevy, and the paragraph on illustrations is by Laura J. Greenberg.

Valkenburgh (1974) and Young (1968). Iverson (1981) emphasizes the period since World War II. Other studies that focus on critical eras in the Navajo past include McNitt (1972), Thompson (1976), Kelly (1968), and Parman (1976).

In addition, Navajo oral history accounts have been collected in volumes published by the Navajo Community College Press. These include Ruth Roessel (1973), Roessel and Johnson (1974), and B. Johnson (1977, 1977a). Other collections are Sapir and Hoijer (1942) and Young and Morgan (1954),which have selections printed in both Navajo and English.

One of the most prominent American anthropologists, Clyde Kluckhohn, devoted much of his career to study of the Navajo; as an introduction to the people, Kluckhohn and Leighton (1962) remains essential. Kluckhohn and Leighton (1947) on the Navajo individual and a classic study of witchcraft (Kluckhohn 1944) are also important. Kluckhohn's influence may also be measured by the work carried on by dozens of his students in the "Rimrock" (Ramah, New Mexico) area. Another important ethnographer who studied the Navajo was W.W. Hill, who treated warfare (1936), agriculture and hunting (1938), humor (1943), and trading (1948).

Navajo religious ceremonies and religious thought have encouraged many works. Matthews (1887, 1902) was a pioneering observer. Haile (1938, 1943, 1950) contributed the translation of texts of many ceremonies. Reichard published on medicine men (1939), on prayer (1944), and a monumental examination of most aspects of Navajo religion (1950). Spencer (1947, 1957) and Wheelwright (1946, 1949, 1956) dealt with origin and chantway myths. Wyman and Kluckhohn (1938, 1940) analyzed ceremonial practice, and Wyman (1957, 1970a, 1975) edited versions of ceremonies recorded and translated by Haile as well as other ceremonies (1962, 1965). O'Bryan (1956) reviewed origin myths, while Yazzie (1971) edited origin stories published by the Navajos. Luckert (1979) studied Coyoteway.

Reichard (1928, 1939) also provided valuable analyses of Navajo social life. Later interpreters of Navajo society include Aberle (1961a), Shepardson and Hammond (1970), Witherspoon (1975a), and Lamphere (1977). Downs's (1964) study of animal husbandry is also useful. Other aspects of Navajo society are revealed in autobiographical accounts, including Dyk (1967), Dyk and Dyk (1980), Mitchell and Allen (1967), Mitchell (1978), and I. Stewart (1980). Among the students of Navajo philosophy have been Ladd (1957) and McNeley (1981). McAllester (1954) has examined social and aesthetic values as reflected in music. Aberle's (1967) fine work on the growth of Peyotism tells much about social change.

The evolution of Navajo government in the twentieth century has been traced by Shepardson (1963), Williams (1970), and Young (1978). Adams (1963) and McNitt (1962) have recorded the role of the trader in Navajo country. Sasaki (1960) has studied one Navajo community in transition. Aberle (1969) provided a critical review of economic development, and Reno (1981) analyzed the economy. Kammer (1980) has investigated the Navajo-Hopi land dispute.

The definitive study of Navajo grammar and lexicon is by Young and Morgan (1980). A still useful early ethnographic dictionary, topically organized, is by the Franciscan Fathers (1910). Witherspoon (1977) has examined the role of language and art in Navajo life and culture.

Navajo arts and crafts have inspired many works. Kluckhohn, Hill, and Kluckhohn (1971) provide a thorough survey of Navajo traditional material culture (except for weaving, silversmithing, and sandpainting). Important treatments of weaving are by Amsden (1934), Reichard (1936), Mera (1947), King (1976), Kent (1961), Trimble (1981), Rodee (1981), Berlant and Kahlenberg (1977), and Kahlenberg and Berlant (1972). Young and Bryan (1940) discuss native dyes in weaving. Adair (1944) is the basic treatment of silversmithing, on which Mera (1960), King (1976), L. Frank (1978), and Bedinger (1973) are also useful. Tschopik (1940) is the standard work on basketry, and Hill (1937), Tschopik (1941), and Brugge (1963) on pottery. Jett and Spencer (1981) is a thorough treatment of both traditional and recent Navajo architecture. Newcomb (1964) has provided a biography of Hosteen Klah, a singer, weaver, and sandpainter. Tanner (1957), Dunn (1968), and Brody (1971) have devoted significant attention to modern Navajo painters, while Monthan (1978) is a collection of the lithographs of R.C. Gorman, an important contemporary Navajo artist.

Manuscript sources on Navajo history and culture include federal records in the National Archives, Washington; the papers of Clyde Kluckhohn (incorporating materials by his students and coworkers) in the Harvard University Archives, Cambridge; those of Franc Newcomb in the Maxwell Museum of Anthropology, University of New Mexico, Albuquerque; of Berard Haile, Gladys Reichard, and Leland C. Wyman in the Museum of Northern Arizona, Flagstaff; and of Washington Matthews in the Wheelwright Museum of the American Indian, Santa Fe, New Mexico.

Photographic records of the Navajo dating to at least the 1860s are extensive, though not always very well documented. The following listing is representative rather than exhaustive. Notable among the earliest photographs are studio portraits and views of Fort Sumner from the Bosque Redondo period; both are included in the Meem collection in the Museum of New Mexico, Santa Fe, with copies elsewhere (Frink 1968), and Fort Sumner views are included with other materials in the U.S. Signal Corps collection, National Archives, Washington. Many fine studio portraits of prominent Navajos, often identified by name, exist from this and somewhat later periods (Roessel 1980); the National Anthropological Archives at the Smithsonian Institution, Washington, is a particularly good source of these and other early photographs, including a series of portraits of members of the 1871 delegation to Washington. From the 1880s until about 1910, after the railroad came to Navajo country and with the increasing popularity of photography, numerous professional and semiprofessional photographers took excellent photographs of Navajo and other Southwestern subjects. These included Adam C. Vroman (in the collection of the Los Angeles County Museum of Natural History and elsewhere; see Webb and Weinstein 1973), Frederick Monsen, some of whose work (Huntington Library, San Marino, California) has been misattributed to Vroman (Kristina Foss, communication to editors 1982), Santa Fe photographer Ben Wittick (in the collections of the Museum of New Mexico), J.H. Bratley (Denver Museum of Natural History), G. Wharton James (Southwest Museum and Title Insurance collection of the California Historical Society, Los Angeles), and the somewhat romantic photographer of Indians, Edward S. Curtis (1907–1930, 1). A particularly valuable series of photographs documenting Navajo ceremonial and other subjects was taken by Simeon Schwemberger, a Franciscan monk who operated a camera studio in Gallup and Window Rock (Rudisill 1973:52), whose original glass negatives are in collections of the Saint Michael's Mission, Arizona, and the Mullarky Camera Shop, Gallup. In the same era, more specialized anthropological photography began with architectural photographs by Cosmos Mindeleff, photographs documenting specific technologies like tanning by army surgeon R.W. Shufeldt, and photographs by the ethnographer James Mooney (all in the National Anthropological Archives), and by photographers, such as George Pepper (Heye Foundation), accompanying ethnological or archeological expeditions. Other sources of historic photographs are the collections at large museums such as the American Museum of Natural History, New York, and the Field Museum, Chicago, and local archives such as the Arizona Historical Society, Tucson. The 1920s through 1950s are covered by a miscellany of amateur and professional photographers; photographs from this era can be found, among other places, in the collections of the Museum of Northern Arizona, Flagstaff, and the Navajo Tribal Museum, Window Rock. Many of the snapshot photographs, which could serve for research if not for publication, that probably exist from this era have not been systematically assembled. Beginning in the 1930s and continuing through to at least the 1950s, there are several excellent collections by professional photographers, among them those by Charlie Wunder in the Mazzulla collection and those by Laura Gilpin, both in the Amon Carter Museum, Forth Worth, Texas. Milton Snow, photographing for the U.S. Indian Service in these years, provided an extremely valuable record of some of the programs and changes taking place in the John Collier era and later; negatives of his photographs are in the Snow collection in the Window Rock area office of the Bureau of Indian Affairs, with many prints in the Bureau of Indian Affairs collection of the National Archives and in the possession of individuals. The Snow collection and many of the photographs from anthropological documentation projects of the 1950s, which are valuable visual records, were not, in 1980–1981, sufficiently catalogued to be easily accessible. For example, photographs from Roberts's (1951) inventory of Navajo households were in cartons in Roberts's garage, the collection of Ramah materials accumulated by Clyde Kluckhohn and Harry Tschopik, although in the Peabody Museum at Harvard University, were temporarily unavailable, and the extensive photographs of John Collier, Jr. (taken in connection with Tremblay, Collier, and Sasaki 1954) and John Adair, each in the possession of those individuals, were for purely logistic reasons incompletely accessible. Photographs taken in conjunction with the films by the American Indian Films Group in the early 1960s were available directly from the photographer in 1980–1981 (see "Navajo Ceremonial System," this vol.), but the film footage was largely uncatalogued. The period after 1960 is documented by the work of many excellent professional photographers (several of whom are represented in this volume), mostly obtainable directly from them. In a few cases (for example, the Helga Teiwes photographs in the Arizona State Museum, Tucson), such photographs are in museum collections. The central office of the BIA discontinued its photographic library in 1980 (donating the majority of its collection to the National Archives), but many of the BIA area offices and branches continue to assemble and maintain photographic records, as do other government agencies, such as the Public Health Service in the Department of Health and Human Services.

Collections in United States Museums

• TEXTILES (including blankets, dresses, rugs, and sashes). In the West and Southwest: AF; ASM, general collection; CAS, Elkus Collection; DAM, important examples; DMNH, Hubbell, Harvey, Crane, Kohlberg, and Bratley Collections, especially strong in Germantowns; HM, large holdings, Harvey and Read Mullen Collections; LACM, important holdings, William Randolph Hearst Collection; LMA, documented early pieces; MMA, large holdings, Maxwell Collection; MNA; MNMLA; MRM, strong collection; NTM, Amsden Collection; SDMM; SAR, important collection including Chief White Antelope blanket; SWM, extensive holdings; TM, large collection; UCOM, extensive, well-documented holdings; ISUM, Gates Collection; WMAI, strong collection, Klah sandpainting weavings. In the Midwest: CIS; FMNH, documented early pieces; ISM; LMAB; MPM; NG. In the East and Southeast: Many early anthropologists made systematic collections for Eastern institutions; thus these museums are major repositories of early, well-documented objects: AMNH; MAI; NMNH; PMH; PMS. Other textile collections are at BMFA; BM; FSM; HRM; LAM, Barton Collection; RMS, including two early pieces collected by Frank Hamilton Cushing; UMP.

• SILVER (including jewelry, ornaments, bridles, bowguards, pouches, etc.). In the West and Southwest: ASM, turquoise; CAS, Elkus Collection; DMNH; HM, Harvey Collection; LACM, documented early examples; MMA, modern jewelry only; MNA; MNMLA, Witter Bynner Collection; MRM, early examples; SDMM, early examples; TM, strong early collection; UCOM, Bedinger and Wheat Collections; WMAI, good early collection. In the Midwest: FMNH, documented early examples; ISM; MPM; MIA, Donihi Collection; NG. In the East and Southeast: AMNH; HRM; MAI; NMNH; PMH all have early, well-documented collections.

• BASKETRY AND POTTERY AMNH; ASM; DMNH; FMNH; MAI; MMA; MNA; MNMLA; MPM; NMNH; SAR; UCOM; WMAI.

• CEREMONIAL OBJECTS AMNH; FMNH; HM; MAI; MNA; NMNH; NHCC; WMAI.

• SANDPAINTING REPRODUCTIONS DMNH; MNA; MMA, Newcomb; NHCC; NMNH; TM, Huckel Collection; WMAI, Newcomb and Oakes.

• CRADLEBOARDS, DOLLS, TOYS, GAMES DMNH; HM; MAI; NMNH; WMAI.

• TOOLS AND IMPLEMENTS DMNH; FMNH; HM; MAI; MMA; MRM; MNA; MNMLA; NMNH; WMAI.

• WEAPONS DMNH; HM; MAI; MNA; NMNH; WMAI.

• WOOD CARVINGS ASM; DMNH, Tom Yazzie; WMAI, Alfred Walleto.

• KEY TO ABBREVIATIONS AF: Amerind Foundation, Dragoon, Arizona. AMNH: American Museum of Natural History, New York. ASM: Arizona State Museum, University of Arizona, Tucson. BMFA: Boston Museum of Fine Arts. BM: Brooklyn Museum, New York. CAS: California Academy of Science, San Francisco. CIS: Cranbrook Institute of Science, Bloomfield Hills, Michigan. DAM: Denver Art Museum, Colorado. DMNH: Denver Museum of Natural History, Colorado. FMNH: Field Museum of Natural History, Chicago. FSM: Florida State Museum, Gainesville. HM: Heard Museum of Anthropology and Primitive Art, Phoenix, Arizona. HRM: Haffenreffer Museum of Anthropology, Brown University, Bristol, Rhode Island. ISM: Illinois State Museum, Springfield. ISUM: Idaho State University Museum, Pocatello. LACM: Natural History Museum of Los Angeles County. LAM: Lowe Art Museum, Coral Gables, Florida. LMA: Lowie Museum of Anthropology, University of California, Berkeley. LMAB: Logan Museum of Anthropology, Beloit College, Beloit, Wisconsin. MAI: Museum of the American Indian, Heye Foundation, New York. MIA: Minnesota Institute of Arts, Minneapolis. MMA: Maxwell Museum of Anthropology, University of New Mexico, Albuquerque. MNA: Museum of Northern Arizona, Flagstaff. MNMLA: Museum of New Mexico, Laboratory of Anthropology, Santa Fe. MPM: Milwaukee Public Museum, Wisconsin. MRM: Millicent Rogers Museum, Taos, New Mexico. NHCC: Ned Hatathli Cultural Center, Navajo Community College, Tsaile, Arizona. NG: Nelson Gallery, Kansas City, Missouri. NMNH: National Museum of Natural History, Smithsonian Institution, Washington. NTM: Navajo Tribal Museum, Window Rock, Arizona. PMH: Peabody Museum, Harvard University, Cambridge, Massachusetts. PMS: Peabody Museum, Salem, Massachusetts. RMS: Rochester Museum and Science Center, New York. SDMM: San Diego Museum of Man, California. SAR: School of American Research, Indian Arts Fund Collection, Santa Fe, New Mexico. SWM: Southwest Museum, Highland Park, California. TM: Taylor Museum, Colorado Springs Fine Arts Center, Colorado. UCOM: University of Colorado Museum, Boulder. UMP: University Museum, University of Pennsylvania, Philadelphia. WMAI: Wheelwright Museum of the American Indian, Santa Fe, New Mexico.

Navajo Views of Their Origin

SAM D. GILL

Navajos tell stories of the origin of their people and their world, Navajoland (*dinétah*), which often reach grand proportions and comprise a number of distinct story traditions. Navajos are quite conscious of story variations, and storytellers are often familiar with the versions of others and will indicate how their particular story differs from them and perhaps how it is more correct or complete. In any case, the many versions of these stories have in common a description of the origin as a series of primordial events occurring in two phases, a journey ascending through several worlds below the surface of the earth followed by a cosmic ordering process once the earth surface is reached. While there are many variations, the general outline of these stories may be described.

The Emergence

The origin story begins with a description of a journey of emergence upward through a subterranean domain of unaccounted origin. This domain amounts to worlds described as either platters or hemispheres, numbering variously from 2 to 14, stacked one on top of another. These worlds are identified by number and distinguishing color as well as by the events that transpire on them. The sun and moon do not exist in these lower worlds, so time is reckoned by colored clouds or columns that appear in sequence around the four quadrants. The color and position tell the time of day.

In this setting, the emergence process begins in the center of the lowest world and proceeds upward, world after world, with a series of events recounted for each world. A given telling may be but an outline in simplest fashion of the essential events that lead to the emergence onto the present earth surface, or it may use this outline as a frame to support a great many stories elaborately developed.

In the beginning, the underworlds are inhabited by insect (usually ant) or animal peoples. There may also be a number of special figures like First Man, First Woman, and Coyote. Some versions feature major creator figures. While the primordial peoples have some insect or animal traits, they have the power of speech and they live and act according to manners and customs in common with those of the yet-to-be-created Navajo people. These primordial peoples have been placed in their world to live peacefully and happily, but, as the stories recount, they have difficulty in doing so. Quarreling and jealousies disrupt their lives. Incest and adultery erupt into violence and destruction. The powers who live in the peripheral worlds in the four directions repeatedly warn the people that they must revise their ways and live properly and peacefully. But despite repeated efforts to do so, they always fail. In exasperation and disgust, those who control the surrounding oceans unleash their destructive powers upon the world. As the people see the great walls of water converging upon them (or fire, in some accounts) threatening destruction, they take flight seeking entrance into the next world. A helper familiar with the world above shows them the opening through which they may enter. They find that other peoples already occupy the new location. As they establish their homes they pledge anew their desire to live an orderly life.

In each new world, a world with a different hue and with new acquaintances, the pattern is repeated. With good intentions life is begun, but its promise for happiness is dissolved as disruptive acts lead to strife, violence, and eventually to the destruction of the world. Throughout the emergence process there is an unmistakable association of the repeated world destructions and these acts of misconduct. Set in worlds that are somewhat impoverished, yet clearly identifiable as projections of the yet-to-be-created Navajo world, the stories of emergence portray images of disorder, disruption, and broken laws. The stories reveal a Navajo world in chaos and disorder.

One of the most dramatic of stories, which is usually set in one of these lower worlds, is that of the separation of men and women. While this story is told in many versions it always involves some set of misdeeds leading to the men moving across a river and leaving the women behind. The story tells of the difficulties and failed attempts of the sexes to get along without one another. A final reconciliation reunites them with new understanding.

In some versions of the story, aspects of the Navajo world, although usually in prototype form, are created before emergence onto the earth surface. These creations may include the sacred mountains (varying in number from four to seven or more), corn, and even people. Witchcraft is established here, for the underworld is its domain. Hunting and agricultural procedures are sometimes established. The future carriers of the sun and moon may be created. In these versions the event of emergence onto the earth surface is a final culmination to the process of creation. Based on established prototypes, the world on the earth surface is given its form. Life, as well as death, begins in the Navajo world.

Earth-Surface Origins

In some versions the repetition of this failure to successfully exist, world after world, creates an increasing urgency to find that place upon which an orderly world might be founded. While there seems to be little progress toward this goal, there is some. First Man, First Woman, and other figures who will take part in the creation of the Navajo world come into being as does the sacred medicine bundle, the collection of objects and powers from which will come the Navajo world. These appearances serve as the background for the creation of the world as told particularly in Blessingway, a ritual and story tradition that forms the core of a major Navajo view.

In this story tradition, a new era in the creation process begins with the emergence onto the earth surface. The rim of the emergence place stands at the center of the Navajo sacred geography and sacred history. This new world is markedly different from the others. It is covered with water under the control of water birds. Defeated in contests the water birds flee and the waters recede. The winds of the four directions are called upon to dry the earth, and in the undistinguished landscape that is revealed, First Man and First Woman think and talk about how this new world shall be. This demonstrates the important Navajo notion that thought, speech, and planning are essentially creative acts. With their plan in mind, First Man and First Woman demonstrate the powers of the sacred medicine bundle by opening it and transforming the medicine objects into their spiritual counterpart, holy figures in humanlike form. Then they build a ceremonial house (hogan) in which to create the Navajo world. This creation hogan is the paradigm for all Navajo ceremonial and house structures (see "Navajo Social Organization," figs. 9–10). It is a microcosm standing at the center of the world, at the emergence place. Its four main support pillars are personified as spiritual forces and correspond with the cardinal directions. The party of creators enters this primordial structure and First Man places objects

left, Mus. of Northern Ariz., Flagstaff: 2371/C656; right, Amon Carter Mus., Ft. Worth, Tex.: Laura Gilpin Coll.

Fig. 1. Sacred mountain of the east. left, *East Mountain*, one of a set of 4 paintings by Navajo artist Harrison Begay, each representing a sacred mountain associated with a specific color and direction. Begay, who spent most of his early life away from the Navajo reservation, based the paintings on a fairly literal interpretation of part of the origin myth published by Matthews (1897; H. Begay 1967). The painting depicts the male and female inner forms of the mountain in characteristic human form, sprinkling pollen upon the 2 eggs placed on its summit by First Man and First Woman. The mountain, decorated with white shells, corn, and lightning, is fastened to earth (represented by a black band similar to that used in sandpaintings) by a bolt of lightning (Matthews 1897:78–79). Painted in 1959, following a similar set (see Dunn 1968: pl. XX), 3 of which went to a singer as payment for an Enemyway performed for Begay. right, Blanca Peak, Colo., sometimes identified as the sacred mountain of the east (R. Roessel 1971:7), which has also been correlated with Pelado Peak in N.Mex. (Matthews 1897:221; Franciscan Fathers 1910:136); see Reichard 1950, 1:20, 2:452–453; Wyman 1957:35–39 for discussion of geographical identifications of the Navajo sacred mountains. Photograph by Laura Gilpin, Feb. 1953.

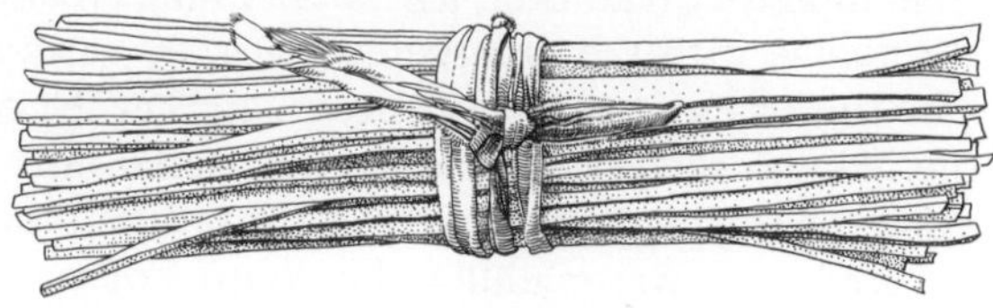

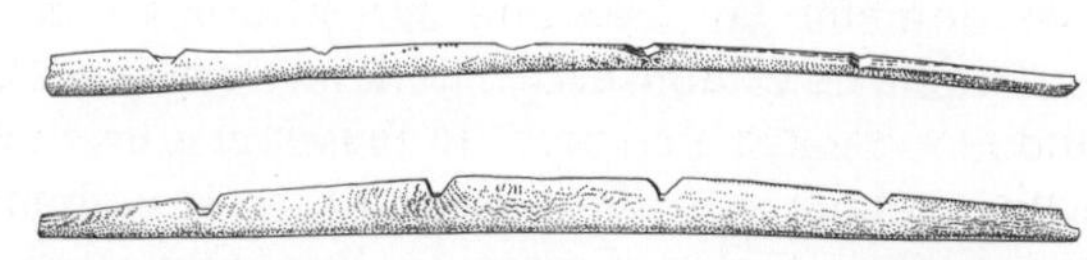

top, Smithsonian, Dept. of Anthr.: 74,741; bottom left, Navajo Community College Press: R. Roessel 1971:14; bottom right, James T. Bialac, Phoenix, Ariz.

Fig. 2. Moccasin game, a Navajo gambling game, first played between the nocturnal and diurnal animals to determine whether daylight or darkness would prevail and now played as a social game. bottom left, Pen and ink drawing of the first moccasin game by Raymond Johnson, published as an illustration for a contemporary Navajo version of the origin myth (see also G. Begay in Wheelwright 1949:61–62; Matthews 1889:4–6; Yazzie 1971:24–27). Nocturnal animals (at right) face diurnal animals (at left); One Walking Giant (*Yé'iitsoh Łá'í Naagháii*), instigator of the game, is at extreme left, and Coyote (center) observes the proceedings, which resulted in the alternation of day and night. Pointer, ball, and yucca counters in background are all used in the game, which is a form of hidden ball game (see Culin 1907:335–382). bottom right, *Moccasin Game*, painting of a contemporary game by the Navajo artist Robert Chee, 1961 (see Kluckhohn, Hill, and Kluckhohn 1971:388–395 for modern variants of the game). top, Yucca leaf counters used in the moccasin game. The side eventually holding all the counters (102) is the winner. The 2 notched counters are given out last and according to Matthews (1889:3) "One of the party receiving them sticks them up in the rafters of the *hogan* (lodge) and says to them 'Go seek your grandchildren' (*i.e.*, bring the other counters back to our side). The possession of the 'grandmothers' [notched counters] is supposed to bring good luck." Average length 23 cm, collected by Washington Matthews at Ft. Wingate, N. Mex., in 1884.

from the medicine bundle upon the floor of the hogan in a manner resembling a painting in sand. He arranges in human shape the objects representing the life forms of all the living things that are to constitute the Navajo world. Then these inner life forms are dressed in representations of the physical forms they will take: plants, animals, and other living forms. So too are created the months of the year, the celestial bodies, and the living landscape.

This ceremony lasts throughout the night. The acts of creation being performed are described in the sequence of songs that are sung. At dawn this world, created in microcosm with objects from the sacred medicine bundle, is transformed into the Navajo world, the world in which Navajo people have since lived. This transformation is achieved by the preparation of smoke to serve as a vehicle to transport the representational forms to their proper places. The recitation of a prayer to the inner forms of the earth is the transforming power giving birth to the earth.

When all is done, the human-shaped forms of dawn and evening twilight are sent on a tour of the newly created earth. They ascend each of the mountains and their inspection reveals that the world is extremely beautiful. Indeed, this state of order, a state in which all living things are in their places and in proper relationship with all living things, constitutes the very definition of the concept of beauty (*hózhǫ́*), which is central to Navajo world view. It stands in contrast with the preemergence condition of disorder, chaos, and ugliness (*hóchxǫ́ǫ́'*).

This is the environment into which the benevolent creator, Changing Woman, is born. Her parents are identified with the most sacred objects, those representing the powers of thought and speech, in the medicine bundle held by First Man. She is reared by First Man and First Woman and upon achieving womanhood, Changing Woman gains possession of the medicine bundle. Her twin sons, Monster Slayer and Born for Water, fathered by the Sun, clear the world of the monsters that had appeared because of adulterous acts of the Sun or others. This done, Changing Woman continues her era of creation by using her powers to create corn. Then performing ritual acts over balls of epidermal waste that she has rubbed from her body and mingled with cornmeal, she creates the first Navajo people. The first four pairs are the progenitors of the four original Navajo clans and from them stem all Navajo people.

The creation of the Navajo world concludes with the departure of the Holy People who were active in the creation to their own spiritual domains. Those who emerged from the lower worlds return there, for their origin gave them association with disorder and therefore with witchcraft, death, and other forms of malevolence. The human-shaped forms of other Holy People depart announcing that they will never again be seen in their primordial forms, but that they will be forever overlooking and directing life in the Navajo world.

Importance of the Origin Stories

While it must be remembered that there are many and widely varying stories of the cosmic creation and the origin of the Navajo people, these accounts are nonetheless central to Navajo world view; indeed, they are primary statements of it. The order and character of the world and of the place of human beings in that world, including their relationships with one another and with all other living things, is defined in these stories.

With the era of cosmic creation concluded, the responsibility for maintaining the created world passes to the Navajo people. Whether it is the ordinary daily activities of planting, herding, and tending children or the more formal ceremonial acts of reparation performed at times of sickness and suffering, or creative acts at times of birth and renewals, the Navajo view their creation known to them through stories as the basic model.

Sources

Twenty-three versions of the Navajo stories of origin dating from as early as 1883 are presented with brief synopses by Spencer (1947), whose primary intent was to discern aspects of contemporary Navajo social life in these stories. Other versions have since been published, notably in Wheelwright (1949), Fishler (1953), O'Bryan (1956), and Wyman (1965, 1970a). Wyman (1965) presents an extensive comparative analysis of the themes and motifs in the major recorded versions published to 1965 including: Matthews (1883a, 1897), Stephen (1930), Curtis (1907–1930, 1), Wheelwright (1949), which is a version recorded by Father Berard Haile in 1908, Goddard (1934), Wheelwright (1942), Sapir and Hoijer (1942), Oakes (1943), Fishler (1953), and O'Bryan (1956), in which comparison with other versions is included. Wyman (1970a) published three versions recorded by Father Berard Haile of the portion of the origin story cycle known as Blessingway, which includes only postemergence events. Wyman (1970a) analyzes the motifs and themes of Blessingway mythology in its several recorded versions. For a general summary and review of the entire body of relevant Navajo oral tradition, see Gill (1979, 1980).

Navajo History, 1850–1923

ROBERT A. ROESSEL, JR.

Navajo history during the period 1850–1923 could well be described as "what might have been." At times during this period there were Americans in positions of action and authority who understood the Navajo and recognized the fact they were more sinned against than sinning. Yet, unfortunately and tragically these men were transferred, resigned, or killed. Consequently, the Navajo were usually dealt with by men who neither understood them nor were sympathetic to their needs and predicament. Historical accounts dealing with the Navajo during this period are full of biased and one-sided reporting, to the effect that the Navajos were untrustworthy.

Later authors have suggested a very different picture of the Navajos. Forbes (1960:281–285) stated that the Spaniards and not the Athapaskans were responsible for the increased warfare after the arrival of the Spaniards. Bailey (1966:73) declared that the documentary record shows that "the Navajos did not make war just to steal and kill; they earned their reputation as warriors fighting to protect their lands, property and families—and a just cause it was."

Events Leading to the Long Walk

The Murder of Narbona

On August 31, 1849, Col. John Washington, accompanied by Indian Agent James Calhoun, met in the Chuska Mountains with a group of Navajos under the leadership of Narbona and José Largo. At the conclusion of the meeting, a Mexican with the American troops declared he saw a horse that had been stolen from him with the Navajo. Washington demanded that the horse be turned over to the Mexican. The Navajos refused and turned to leave. The order to fire on the departing Navajos was given, and Narbona was shot in the back and killed along with six other Navajos. As the Navajos fled on horseback several shots were fired from the artillery. Richard H. Kern, an artist on the Simpson expedition, wrote in his journal that Narbona, the head chief (fig. 1), was shot in four or five places and scalped (McNitt 1972:138–146; Simpson 1964; Hine 1962:77).

This incident created additional mistrust in the minds of the Navajo; how could it have had any other effect? Actually, Narbona was one of the most influential Navajo leaders, who tried to keep a state of peace between his people and the New Mexicans. His death, and the manner in which it occurred, did nothing to allay the fears the Navajos felt toward the intruders. While the Navajo were usually required to return prisoners and allegedly stolen livestock, the New Mexicans were never forced to do so; combining this with incidents of gross criminal action, such as the murder of Narbona, on the part of the Army or others with no corrective action taken, helps explain the hopelessness and disbelief in obtaining justice that the Navajos must have felt in their dealings with the Army, the New Mexicans, and other outsiders.

The Fort Fauntleroy Massacre

A large group of Navajos went to Fort Fauntleroy in September 1861 to receive rations as negotiated by Maj. Edward R.S. Canby in his treaty with the Navajos of February 15, 1861. The treaty stipulations indicated an understanding of the Navajos and of the fact that they had been subjected to devastating slave raids. Canby in a February 27, 1861, letter to Army Department Commander T.T. Fauntleroy deplored the continuing slave raids by the New Mexicans despite the treaty, adding that he himself would "have no hesitation in treating as enemies of the United States any parties of Mexicans or Pueblo Indians who may be found in the country assigned to the Navajos" (Bailey 1964:139).

In keeping with the treaty, Navajos went to Fort Fauntleroy periodically to receive their promised rations. On the ration day of September 22, 1861, 12 Navajo women and children were shamelessly shot by soldiers under the command of Col. Manuel Chaves. Chaves was an "experienced Indian fighter" who had earlier raided the Navajo for slaves.

On this as well as on most ration days, a series of horse races was held (fig. 5), with heavy betting between the soldiers and the Navajos. The featured race pitted a thoroughbred owned by the post's assistant surgeon, Finis Kavanaugh, against one of the best Navajo horses. Both got off to a fast start, but it became evident within a few seconds that the Navajo horse and rider were in serious difficulty as the Navajo horse ran off the track uncontrolled. Upon examination it was apparent that

Academy of Nat. Sciences, Philadelphia: Coll. 146 #44.

Fig. 1. Watercolor portrait of Narbona, by Edward M. Kern from a sketch made by Richard H. Kern on the day of Narbona's death, Aug. 31, 1849. One of a set of watercolors by the Kern brothers, many of which were published as lithographs in the expedition's report (Simpson 1850).

Smithsonian, Dept. of Anthr.: 281,473.

Fig. 2. Man's shoulder blanket of black, white, red (bayeta), dark and light blue wool. Often called chief blankets, although not associated with rank, the earliest were striped only. In the second phase a block design was added to the stripes and in the third phase, shown here, the blocks were replaced by a diamond motif. When worn, the joining of the ends at the front of the body forms a repeat of the diamond on the back. First woven about 1800, the various chief blanket patterns continue to be made. Size 162.5 by 198.0 cm, collected by Washington Matthews, 1880–1882.

the bridle reins had been slashed with a knife so only a slight pull resulted in a broken rein that caused the rider to lose control of his mount. The Navajos thought they had been tricked, but the judges of the race, all soldiers, decided otherwise, and Kavanaugh's horse was declared the winner. The Navajos were dissatisfied and so indicated. In this state of confusion shots were fired.

Chaves declared that the Navajos attempted to rush the fort so he ordered the troops to fire. An investigation showed that a single drunken Indian tried to get into the fort. A shot was fired by the sentry and the Indian fell. The troops then began killing other Navajos, despite the attempts of at least two sergeants to stop the slaughter, and Col. Chaves ordered his howitzers to fire on the Indians.

An effort to court-martial Chaves was unsuccessful. This incident was one of many that "impressed the Navajos as being unjust, inexcusable and unforgiveable" (Keleher 1952:297–300; McNitt 1972:426–442).

Slave Trade

Thousands of Indians were held as slaves in the territory of New Mexico (Keleher 1952:366, 482–483, 497; McNitt 1972:379, 386, 399, 406–409, 441–446; Bailey 1966:73, 114, 116, 177–178, 180–181, 188). On a list of 148 Indian captives held in two Colorado counties in July 1865, 112 were identified as Navajo (McNitt 1972:443–446). The slave traders wanted to keep war going between the Navajos and the government so as to continue their opportunities for raids to capture Navajos.

Even after the Civil War, Navajos were held as slaves by residents of New Mexico. In 1865 Julius Graves was appointed by the Office of Indian Affairs to examine the practice of Indian slavery. He reported it to be widespread, with the superintendent of Indian affairs for New Mexico himself owning six slaves, and suggested that the loss of their children to slavers was a Navajo motive for warfare (Bailey 1966:180–182).

Land and Gold Pressures

As the Mexicans and Anglos expanded into territories claimed by the Navajo, tensions and problems increased.

On February 10, 1854, Maj. Henry L. Kendrick wrote New Mexico Gov. David Meriwether that he was infuriated by the encroachment of large flocks of non-Navajo sheep deep into Navajo grazing lands, the owners of the flocks being utterly indifferent to complaints by Navajos. He pointed out that this could endanger all his and Agent Henry Dodge's efforts to develop peaceful relations with the Navajos (McNitt 1972:247).

The Bonneville Treaty of 1858 materially reduced the size of the land recognized as belonging to the Navajo. Agent Samuel Yost realized the consequences of "depriving the best of the Indians of the grounds they cultivate and graze—whereon they raise corn and wheat enough to support the whole nation . . . thus forcing them either to violate the agreement forced upon them, or . . . to abandon cultivating the soil and stock raising or become pensioners on the government, or plunderers" (Bailey 1964:102).

While the New Mexicans pressed into the eastern portion of Navajo country, others felt that their land held untold riches in gold, silver, and other minerals. Brig. Gen. James H. Carleton frequently spoke of moving the Navajo from their homeland so miners could reap the mineral wealth of their land, and in 1863 he was influenced by gold-mining potentials in reaching decisions on military matters (Keleher 1952:338–339, 340–341).

The Death of Jim and Related Army Actions

When the Navajos had honest, capable, and open-minded agents who were supported by like-minded Army or government officials there was peace and understanding. Unfortunately, this combination was exceedingly rare, the outstanding example being Agent Dodge and Major Kendrick. This partnership was coupled with the understanding, if only for a time, of Governor Meriwether. Dodge lived with the Navajo after he was appointed agent in 1853 and married one of them, but while hunting deer south of Zuni Pueblo in November 1856 he was killed by a party of Mogollon and Coyotero Apaches. With his loss, all hope for mutual understanding and a peaceful settlement to New Mexican and Navajo problems ended. Major Kendrick left Fort Defiance in 1857 for an assignment at West Point. Shortly thereafter Capt. William T.H. Brooks became the commanding officer at Fort Defiance. He was biased, hotheaded, and vehemently anti-Navajo.

On July 12, 1858, a Navajo shot a Negro slave named Jim, who was the personal servant of Captain Brooks. An ultimatum was given to the Navajos to turn the killer over to Army authorities immediately, or else war would be declared on them. A group of Navajos tried unsuccessfully to deceive the Army by bringing a body of an individual they falsely claimed to be the murderer of Jim (McNitt 1972:325–337).

Objections by the majority of the lower-ranking officers at Fort Defiance that the demands placed upon the Navajos were unjust and that the reports of New Mexican losses attributed to Navajos had been falsified or padded were to no avail. On the other hand, Superintendent of New Mexico James L. Collins wrote on September 17, 1858, to the commissioner of Indian affairs that the Navajos "deserve no mercy at our hands, and should be taught to expect none" (Bailey 1964:114). Col. Dixon Miles issued a formal declaration of war on September 8, 1858 (Bailey 1964:90).

Mus. of N. Mex., Santa Fe:38200.

Fig. 3. Studio portrait of Navajo man, with accoutrements of war. He wears a tight-fitting cap, apparently decorated with pearl shell buttons, and possibly made from the crown of a felt hat (Frink 1968:73) in imitation of the more traditional animal skin caps worn by men and associated with war (see Kluckhohn, Hill, and Kluckhohn 1971:272–275). A fur and skin quiver and bow case is slung from his neck, and on his left wrist he wears an undecorated metal or leather bow guard. Photographer unidentified, taken about 1865–1868.

Abraham Rencher, governor of New Mexico, wrote to the secretary of state on October 16, 1858, complaining that Brooks should not have issued his ultimatum without referring the matter to a higher authority, and followed this with a letter on November 2 stating that "the war, in my opinion, was unwisely precipitated upon the Indians and [might] have been avoided by prudence and firmness on the part of the Indian agent. The rendition of the murderer of the Negro boy was improperly made a *sine qua non*"

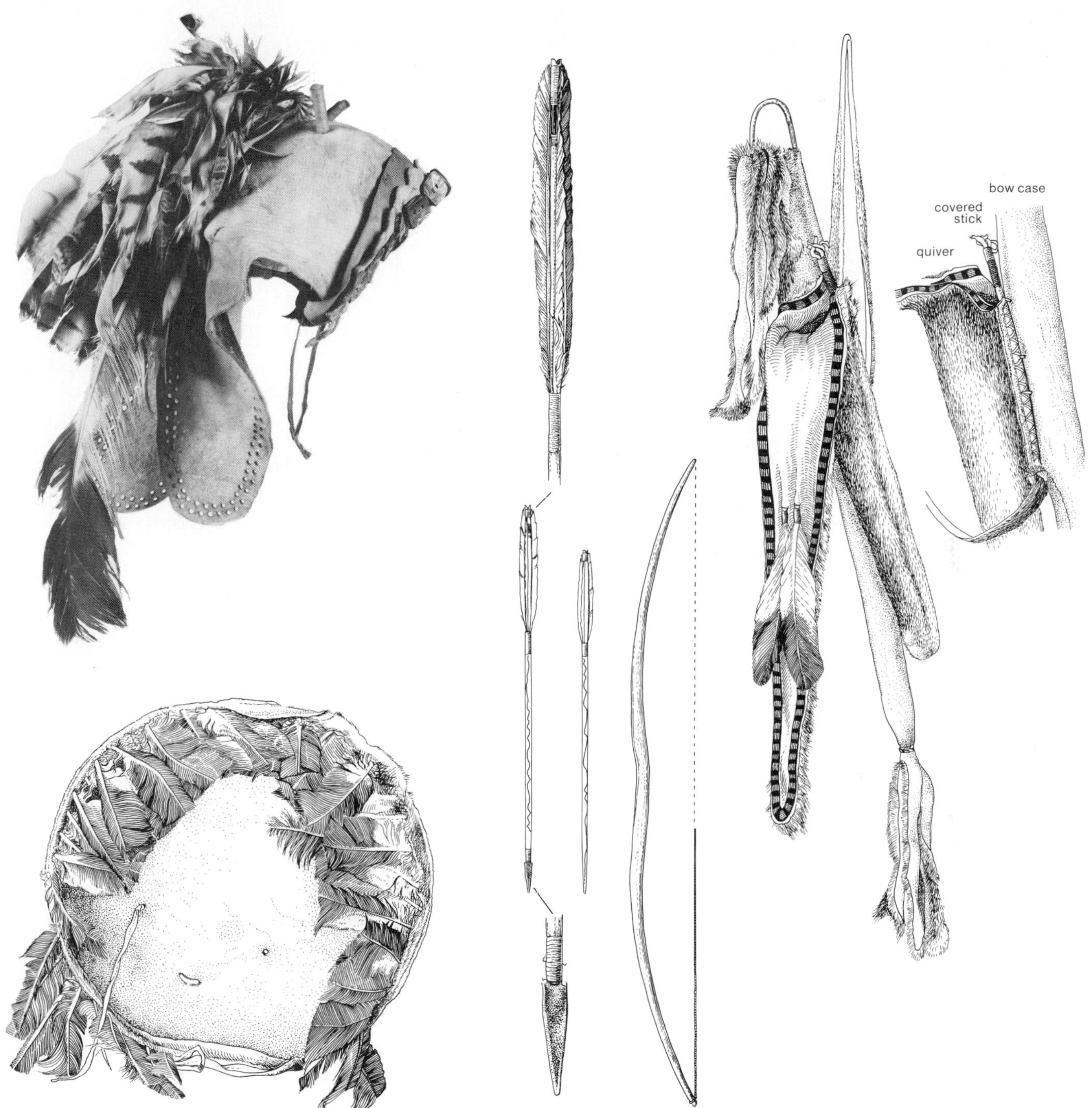

bottom left, Mus. of N. Mex., Santa Fe: 1877/12; Smithsonian, Dept. of Anthr.: right, 166,614, top left, 129,572.

Fig. 4. War equipment of Navajo men traditionally included a shield, bow and arrows, lance, and sometimes a club. bottom left, Painted rawhide shield decorated with a strip of red flannel hung with feathers. right, Combination quiver and bow case of sinew-sewn mountain lion skin; the bow case has the fur side in and is fringed at both ends and has a wooden stiffener inside; the quiver has the fur side out, with a feather-decorated flap lined with red flannel edged with black tape decorated with white seed beads; the 2 containers are lashed together with a decorated cloth-covered stick between them. Although sinew backed bows were often used in warfare, this is a simple wood bow used for hunting game as well. The arrows are fletched with 3 split feathers lashed on with sinew, and have incised zigzags on the shafts (probably representing lightning); one has a hafted metal point, the other a sharpened end. The secondary arrow release was used and a piece of leather served as a wrist guard. Multi-layer leather shirts were sometimes worn as armor and a decorated hat completed the outfit. top left, War hat of tanned leather with 2 flaps with perforated edges in back and a plume of owl feathers attached to the top with 2 pieces of rolled leather in front of it. The front edge is decorated with a strip of green cloth over which is a piece of scalloped leather with abalone shell attached. Whether the hat design signified status or clan is unclear. Shields and war hats were evidently not used after 1870, but bows and arrows were used until about 1890. For descriptions of war equipment and its use see Hill (1936), and Kluckhohn, Hill, and Kluckhohn (1971). top left, Length 29 cm; bottom left, width about 60 cm, rest to same scale; right, collected by James Mooney in 1893, top left by Washington Mathews in 1887.

Smithsonian, NAA:74–7224.

Fig. 5. Navajo horse race, with numerous spectators in attendance, about 1904–1906. Navajo horse-racing, with associated wagering, was fairly common at this time, with horses specifically trained to race (Franciscan Fathers 1910:154). In earlier times, races were more normally run with only two horses at a time, often the best horse from each of 2 groups or communities (Kluckhohn, Hill, and Kluckhohn 1971:387–388). Photograph by Simeon Schwemberger, probably in the vicinity of St. Michael's, Ariz.

(McNitt 1972:359). Capt. John G. Walker in a report written on August 3, 1859, stated:

> I would remark that the Navajoes everywhere evinced the most earnest desire for peace. I am not prepared to say what would be the better line of policy towards them, but there is no doubt that a war made upon them now by us would fall the heaviest upon the least guilty, would transform a nation which has already made considerable progress in civilized arts into a race of beggars, vagabonds and robbers. What consideration such views should have in the settlement of our difficulties with them—difficulties based upon exaggerated demands—which every animal in the Navajo country would scarcely be sufficient to satisfy, it is not for one to suggest, but before severe measures are resolved on and a course of policy initiated that would entail poverty and wretchedness upon the entire tribe, it may be that some little forbearance might be the part of true wisdom (McNitt 1972:368–369).

After meeting with Navajo headmen at Laguna Negra on September 25, 1858, Maj. John Smith Simonson expressed a similar view and pointed out that "the treaty binds the Navajoes to make restitution, but leaves them without redress for injuries inflicted upon them" by New Mexicans and Pueblo Indians, despite clear evidence "that the Navajoes understood that restitution was to be mutual" (McNitt 1972:375). Despite such advice, the military authorities went ahead with their punitive campaign.

Navajos Attack Fort Defiance

Unable to find understanding or justice and goaded into retaliation by increased slave raids by the New Mexicans, the Navajo in the early morning hours of April 30, 1860, attacked Fort Defiance, which had been founded in the heart of the Navajo country in 1851. There have been only a few documented attacks by Indian tribes against established Army forts. Although most were armed with bows and arrows, the Navajos almost succeeded in capturing the fort before they were finally repulsed. On July 9, 1860, the secretary of war ordered that active operations be instituted against the Navajos as soon as possible, using no volunteers, only regular troops (McNitt 1972:384). These orders were a response to the action of Governor Rencher, who had given his approval for the formation of two companies of volunteers, declaring that "these people prefer to carry on Indian wars in their own way" (McNitt 1972:385), that is, presumably, as a means to capture slaves. When Rencher later cooperated with the Army and opposed the volunteers, he was subjected to criticism from both sides (Keleher 1952:105–107; U.S. Congress. Senate 1861, 2:64).

The Long Walk

Planning the Long Walk

In the fall of 1862, Brigadier General Carleton became the new military commander for New Mexico. He arrived as commanding officer of a column of troops from California whose purposes were to subjugate the Indians, protect the territory from a Confederate invasion, and open an overland mail route (Keleher 1952:229). However, after a 10-month trip from the Pacific to the Rio Grande the column arrived too late to be involved with any fights with the Confederates. Carleton's California troops wanted action or a discharge, and he almost immediately began making plans to curb Indian hostilities (Keleher 1952:277–278; Thompson 1976:11).

Gov. Henry Connelly and Brigadier General Carleton agreed to start a war first against the Mescalero Apaches and then against the Navajos (Keleher 1952:279), placing Col. Christopher (Kit) Carson in command of the troops in the field. Carson was not at all enthusiastic about undertaking the campaign as he believed the Indians could be brought to terms without war. Furthermore, he had resigned as Indian agent during the Civil War in order to defend the Territory of New Mexico from the Confederates and not to fight Indians. He was clearly a reluctant campaigner who succeeded through perseverance rather than military ability (Kelly 1970:7–12; Keleher 1952:279).

The war with the 500 or so Mescalero Apaches lasted only five months (Bailey 1964:146). Carleton had made arrangements to move the vanquished Mescalero Apache to a new military post he established on the Pecos River, which he named Fort Sumner (also known as Bosque Redondo). Actually, a board of officers who visited the site prior to the establishment of the Fort recommended to Carleton that another location be selected because of poor water, lack of wood, and threat of floods (Bailey 1964:146–147); nevertheless, Carleton had his mind made up and Fort Sumner was created at the place he had selected in east-central New Mexico as the home for captured Mescalero Apaches and Navajos.

With the subjugation of the Mescalero Apache, Carleton and Carson (fig. 8) were prepared to move against the Navajo. In April 1863 Carleton met with leaders of the peaceful Navajo and told them they would have to move to Fort Sumner (Kelly 1970:20). Then, on June 15, 1863, he issued General Order Number 15, which stated:

> For a long time past the Navajoe Indians have murdered and robbed the people of New Mexico. Last winter when eighteen of their chiefs came to Santa Fe to have a talk, they were warned—and were told to inform their people—that for these murders and robberies the tribe must be punished, unless some binding guarantees should be given that in future these outrages should cease. No such guarantees have yet been given: But on the contrary, additional murders, and additional robberies have been perpetrated upon the persons and property of our unoffending citizens. It is therefore ordered, that Colonel CHRISTOPHER CARSON, with a proper military force proceed without delay . . . and . . . prosecute a vigorous war upon the men of this tribe until it is considered at these Head Quarters that they have been effectually punished for their long continued atrocities. . . . These troops will march from Los Pinos [near Albuquerque] for the Navajoe country on Wednesday, July 1, 1863 (Kelly 1970:21–23).

In a letter dated June 23, 1863, to Lt. Col. J. Francisco Chaves, commanding officer at Fort Wingate, Carleton ordered him to call in the peaceful Navajo leaders again and "tell them they can have until the twentieth day of July of this year to come in—they and all those who belong to what they call the peace party. *That after that day every Navajoe that is seen will be considered as hostile, and treated accordingly*" (Kelly 1970:21).

While issuing these demands to the "peace party" Carleton was making preparations for war on the general population of the Navajo, whom he regarded as hostile. He made no attempt to communicate his ultimatum to all the Navajo, who were scattered throughout a 30,000-square-mile territory, and he ordered Carson and his troops into Navajo country three weeks before the July 20 deadline, on July 1. Carson arrived at Fort Defiance exactly on July 20 and began military operations two days later (Keleher 1952:303; Kelly 1970:26–29).

The Long Walk Itself

Not only did the Navajo have to contend with the United States Army and Kit Carson, but also their land was filled with other Indians (Ute and Pueblo) and New Mexicans determined to pillage and capture slaves, particularly women and children, to be sold as domestics. Companies of irregulars were being organized and equipped with Carleton's blessings. The frontier towns of Cubero, Cebolleta, and Abiquiu served as jumping-off points for the slave-raiders, who were disguised as "volunteer troops" (Bailey 1964:154).

By September 1863 Carleton had developed and begun implementation of his campaign policy. In a letter to Carson dated September 19, 1863, Carleton stated: "Say to them, 'Go to the Bosque Redondo [Fort Sumner], or we will pursue and destroy you. We will not make peace with you on any other terms. You have deceived us too often and robbed and murdered our people too long—to trust you again at large in your own country. This war will be pursued against you if it takes years . . . until you cease to exist or move' " (Kelly 1970:52).

In Carleton's own words Fort Sumner would serve as a "spacious tribal reformatory, away from the haunts and hills and hiding places of their country" (fig. 9). He further said that the Navajos were not to be trusted any more than "the wolves that run through the mountains" (Keleher 1952:310, 311).

While forbidding the use of captured Navajos as slaves, Carleton did authorize payment of a bounty to each soldier for the capture of horses, mules, and sheep (Kelly 1970:31–32). The scorched-earth policy of Carleton, in which the troops destroyed cornfields, peach trees, hogans, water holes, animals, and people, began to pay dividends as the Navajo had nowhere to hide and little or nothing to eat. The statistics for 1863

Calif. Histl. Soc., Los Angeles: Title Insurance Coll.:3236, 3263.

Fig. 6. Navajo riders about 1900. Horses were reported among the Navajo as early as the 1650s (Haines 1966:11; see also Forbes 1959) and quickly became valued. left, Navajo woman, wearing Pendleton blanket, in front of a forked roof, mud-covered hogan. The horse has a silver-mounted bridle and a decorated bit similar to those of native manufacture described as early as 1856 (Kluckhohn, Hill, and Kluckhohn 1971:82). right, Navajo man. Both he and the woman are mounted on horses with Navajo (Spanish-derived) saddles, consisting of wooden saddletrees covered with rawhide and decorated with brass-head tacks. The men's and women's saddles were differentiated by the pommel construction; the woman's saddle had a horn designed to accommodate a cradleboard (Kluckhohn, Hill, and Kluckhohn 1971:84–85). Photographs possibly both by G. Wharton James (left copyrighted by James and Pierce 1901).

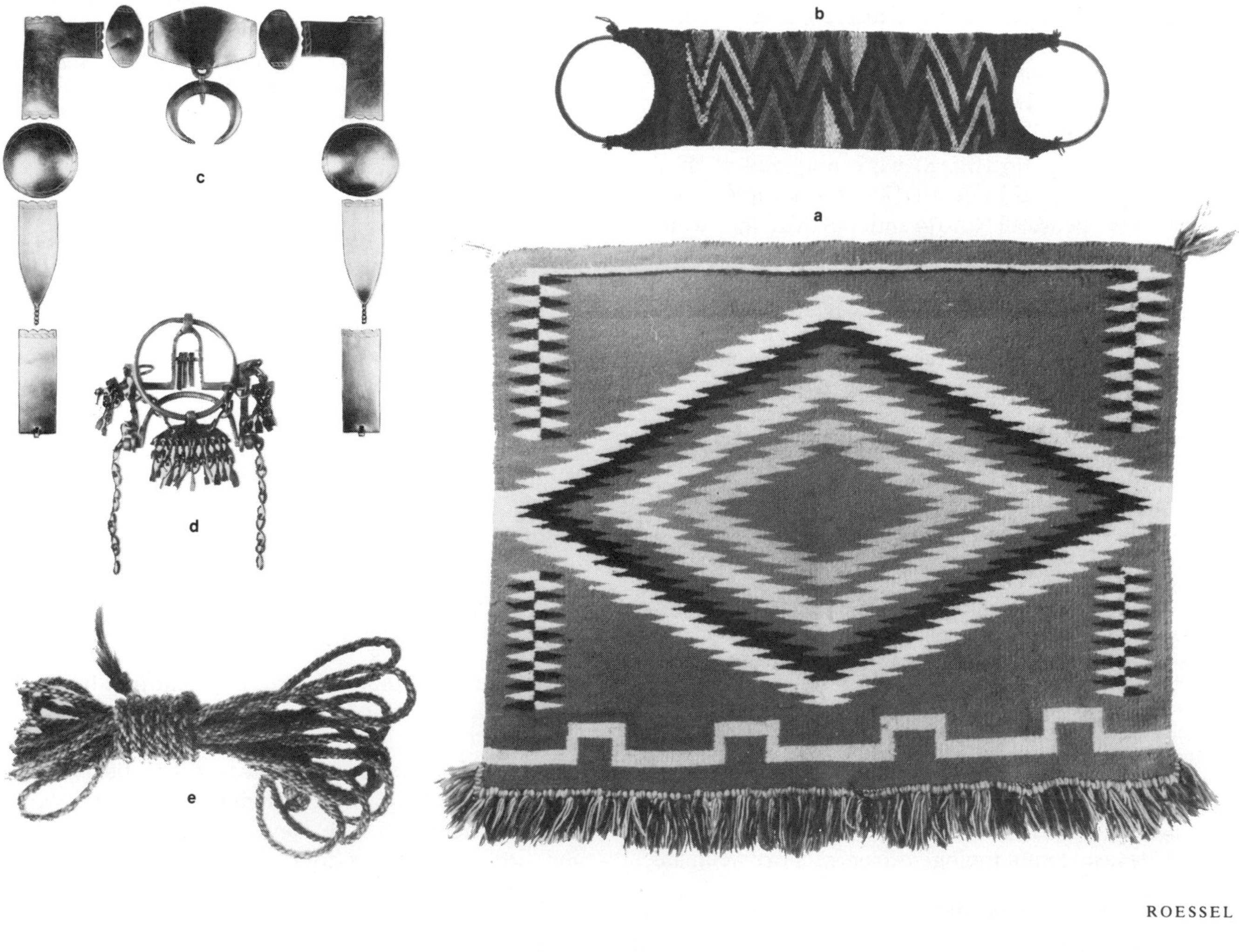

Mus. of N. Mex., Santa Fe.:9826.

Fig. 8. Col. Christopher (Kit) Carson (left), commander of the 1863–1864 campaign against the Navajos and later Military Superintendent of Indians at Ft. Sumner, with Brig. Gen. James H. Carleton, advocate and designer of the Ft. Sumner reservation scheme. The original concept of Navajo removal to a remote reservation, though not the details of the plan, had been inherited from Maj. E.R.S. Canby, whom Carleton replaced as departmental commander of N. Mex. in Sept. 1862 (Thompson 1976:7–9). Detail from a group portrait of Masons, taken at the Masonic Temple in Santa Fe, N. Mex., by Nicholas Brown, Dec. 26, 1866.

showed that the Navajo campaign resulted in 301 Indians killed, 87 wounded, 703 captured. The losses for the Army numbered 14 soldiers killed, 21 wounded, 3 officers killed, and 4 wounded (Keleher 1952:315).

On January 6, 1864, Carson departed with 375 troops for Canyon de Chelly. It was bitter cold and there was heavy snow on the ground. Sixteen days later he returned to Fort Canby (Fort Defiance) with more than 200 prisoners. Carson was generous in his treatment of those who surrendered, and his kindness toward the captives was one reason so many surrendered (Kelly 1970:97). The Navajos at Canyon de Chelly told Carson that their people were starving and that many had already died. Many captives had eaten only berries and piñon nuts for many days preceding their surrender. The captive Navajo women, dressed in rags, feared that their children would be taken from them (Keleher 1952:316).

During the remainder of the winter of 1864, many Navajos surrendered at Fort Canby as well as at Fort Wingate. On February 26, 1864, Capt. Joseph Berney and his troops left Los Pinos with 1,445 Navajos for Fort Sumner (fig. 10) (Kelly 1970:114–116).

In early March 1864 a second convoy of over 2,500 Navajos left Fort Canby for Fort Sumner. Counting those Navajos that died at the Fort before leaving with those that died on the way, 323 Navajos died before reaching Fort Sumner, which was a death figure in excess of 10 percent for the second convoy.

Frequently on the fearful trip to Fort Sumner, New Mexicans would capture Navajo stragglers as well as Navajo livestock. Army reports mention these losses but nothing was ever done to recapture or prevent them (R. Roessel 1973:187–239; Kelly 1970:166, 120, 125, 130). The journey was one of hardship and terror. Navajos remember that "there were a few wagons to haul some personal belongings, but the trip was made on foot [over a distance of 300 miles]. People were shot down on the spot if they complained about being tired or sick, or if they stopped to help someone. If a woman became in labor with a baby, she was killed. There was absolutely no mercy" (R. Roessel 1973:103–104).

Carleton had estimated the total number of Navajos at 5,000; by late February 1864 over 3,000 had surrendered. He felt the war was nearly over and his experiment at Fort Sumner ready to succeed. Unfortunately for the Navajos and for Carleton's plans there were many more Navajos than Carleton had anticipated. A census prepared by Capt. Francis McCabe showed, as of December 31, 1864, a total of 8,354 Navajos at Fort Sumner (Keleher 1952:502), and by March 1865 there were 9,022 Navajos (Bailey 1964:214). From that date until the return of the Navajos in 1868, the number of

Smithsonian, Dept. of Anthr.: a, 129,959; b, 16,498; d, 16,501, e, 401,383; c, Mus. of the Amer. Ind., Heye Foundation, New York: 22/8176.

Fig. 7. Horse equipment. a, Saddle throw of red, yellow, yellow-green, light orange, dark blue, and white wool, used on top of the saddle for comfort and show. A blanket about twice as long (often twilled) was folded in half for use under the saddle. b, Saddle girth or cinch of black, red, white, green, and light orange wool, used to fasten the saddle to the horse. The warp is attached directly to the iron rings and the cinch was woven between them (Matthews 1884:382–383). c, Silver headstalls, probably copied from Spaniards (Adair 1944:41), are attached to the leather bridle by loops on the backs of the silver pieces. This simply engraved example, complete with naja (Navajo *názhahí* 'crescentic pendant'), is by the early smith Atsidi Chon. Later examples are stamped and may have turquoise settings. Silver conchas also appear as bridle decorations. d, Iron bits with a metal fringe to jingle as the horse walks were based on Mexican examples; this one is said to be made from horseshoe nails. e, Ropes were an important part of a rider's equipment. This one is 4 strands of twisted brown and tan horsehair. Ropes are also made of leather or wool. Whips or quirts were made of leather or horsehair. Length of b 59.5 cm, rest to same scale; a, collected by Washington Matthews, 1888; b and d collected by W.F.M. Arny, 1875; c, collected 1880–1885 and e, collected 1898.

Natl. Arch.: U.S. Signal Corps. Coll.: 111-SC-87964, 111-SC 87966, 111-SC-87973.

Fig. 9. Navajos at Ft. Sumner. top, Navajo group being counted by soldiers. Several of the men appear to be carrying bows, and all are wearing blankets (the striped ones of native manufacture, and the dark ones probably government issue). center, Navajos at the Provost Marshall's office, waiting to be issued ration tickets. Rations varied both in frequency and amount, often shrinking drastically despite vast amounts of money spent on supplies. In 1864, for example, the food rations alone cost over three quarters of a million dollars, or more than 26¢ per day per person, while the crops grown by the Indians were estimated to have offset only about one-tenth that amount (Thompson 1976:100–101). bottom, Indian building crew constructing quarters for the troops from adobe bricks. The Navajos lived in makeshift hogans and semi-subterranean dwellings. Photographer unknown, all 1863–1868.

Navajos at Fort Sumner decreased. Navajo prisoners, slowly starving to death, homesick and broken hearted, many desperately ill, deserted Fort Sumner in large numbers: some successfully escaped and returned to their native land.

Not all Navajos went on the Long Walk. Estimates vary with respect to how many Navajos avoided the ordeal by being captured and sold into slavery or by hiding out in inaccessible locations like the Grand Canyon and Navajo Mountain. It would appear that at least

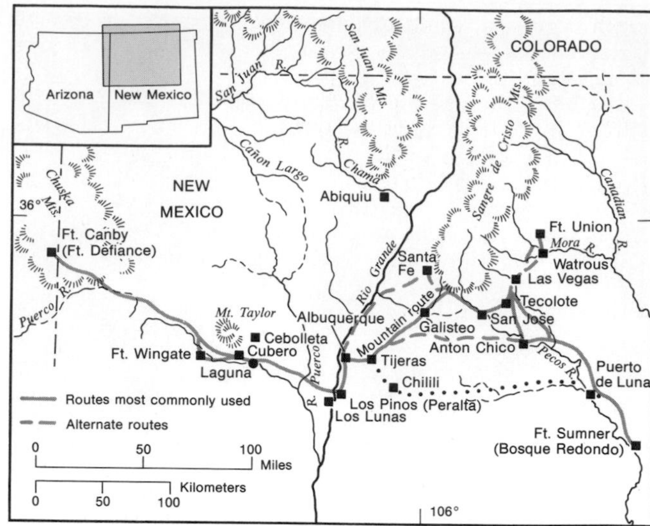

after McNitt 1973:146.

Fig. 10. Routes of the Long Walk of the Navajos, 1863–1867. The mountain route was the one most commonly used by the military escorting the Navajos to Bosque Redondo because supplies were more plentiful and it afforded some protection from the elements. The shorter southern route (dotted line) was preferred by the Navajos and was possibly used by them when escaping from or voluntarily returning to Bosque Redondo (see McNitt 1973).

several thousand Navajos did not go on the Long Walk. According to Navajo traditions, 1,000–2,000 or more escaped being sent to Fort Sumner by moving below Navajo Mountain. Other Navajos went north of the San Juan and Colorado rivers to avoid capture (R. Roessel 1973:41). Some Navajos even eluded the troops by going into the territory of the Chiricahua Apache (Goldtooth in R. Roessel 1973:152).

Problems at Fort Sumner

Carleton's remolding of the Navajo was doomed to failure if for no other reason than that inadequate arrangements had been made to feed and care for the thousands of Navajos who had been brought to Fort Sumner.

Life at Fort Sumner was precarious and difficult. Most accounts of the terrible years there have come from official reports made by men who had certain responsibilities and interest in the situation. However, there are some stories that tell the experience from the Navajos' point of view. One person recounted: "According to my great-grandmother, when the journey to Fort Sumner began the *Diné* [Navajo] had hardly anything to comfort them or to keep warm, like blankets. Women carried their babies on their backs and walked all the way hundreds of miles. They didn't know where they were headed" (Florence Charley in R. Roessel 1973:149).

Howard Gorman (in R. Roessel 1973:32–33) related:

> The Navajos had hardly anything at that time; and they ate rations but couldn't get used to them. Most of them got sick and had stomach trouble. The children also had stom-

ach ache, and some of them died of it. Others died of starvation. . . . Some boys would wander off to where the mules and horses were corraled. There they would poke around in the manure to take undigested corn out of it. Then they would roast the corn in hot ashes to be eaten. . . . They said among themselves, "What did we do wrong? We people here didn't do any harm. We were gathered up for no reason. . . . We harmless people are held here, and we want to go back to our lands right away." Also the water was bad and salty, which gave them dysentery.

Rita Wheeler (in R. Roessel 1973:84) stated that: "The people were given small shovels with which they built their shelters, which were just holes dug in the ground with some tree branches for shade over the top part. . . . Different tribes of enemies would sneak upon the camp to attack the Navajos. Wolves also were one of the worst enemies."

According to Akinabh Burbank (in R. Roessel 1973:132–133) "during confinement at Fort Sumner a lot of people perished from diarrhea because of the change in diet and the poor quality of the food. Also, various diseases had spread. . . . Some cows were slaughtered and the hides used for shade and windbreaks. After the bushes and small trees had been cut and burned, the people had to dig . . . (mesquite roots) for firewood. The women wore woven wool dresses. . . . The men's clothing usually was made of deer hides."

General Carleton and His Critics

The problems of food, water, wood, and raids by other tribes combined to make visible the circumstances of the Navajo at Fort Sumner. General Carleton had declared martial law, which remained in effect from 1861 to 1865 and to a great degree prevented public criticism of his policy. Nevertheless, two men and a newspaper were vocal in their denunciation of Carleton and his programs.

The two most vehement critics were Dr. Michael Steck, superintendent of Indian affairs for New Mexico from 1863 until forced to resign in 1865, and Judge Joseph Knapp, a judge of the New Mexico Territorial Supreme Court assigned to the third judicial district from 1861 until forced to resign in 1864. Both men lost their jobs because of their disagreement with the military commander of New Mexico, General Carleton, over the placement and confinement of the Navajos at Fort Sumner as well as other matters.

Judge Knapp publicly attacked Carleton and his policies. In an 1864 letter addressed to President Abraham Lincoln, Knapp criticized Carleton for imprisoning citizens without conviction or trial, taking away property without just compensation, and setting up courts to try citizens for offenses unknown to the law. Even after removal from his office, Judge Knapp continued to challenge Carleton. In a letter directed to General Carleton published in the *Santa Fe New Mexican,* an anti-Carleton newspaper, in February 1865, Knapp suggested that Carleton never wanted peace with the Navajos. Referring to Carleton's deadline to the Navajos of July 20, 1863, to surrender or be killed, Knapp declared:

> You send them word, but do not say whether it ever reached them. In a word, you specify nothing; you appoint no place of rendezvous; offer no means of conveyance or food for the journey, but require "these pagans" with their women and helpless children to "come in and go down to the Bosque,". . . . and that you cannot "discriminate between the innocent and guilty." Do you, on calm reflection, on sober second thought, now believe that your "plan" was not rather calculated to alienate and sour the minds of those peace Indians, than to make them more friendly? (Keleher 1952:449).

In a second open letter, published in the same newspaper on April 7, 1865, Judge Knapp contended that Carleton had no authority to begin a war against the Indians:

> Soon after the command of the Department of New Mexico came into your possession, you declared war against the Apaches and Navajos. . . . In this, you exceeded your powers and usurped those belonging to others. The constitution has given this authority to Congress. . . . It does not follow . . . that every Brigadier General is vested with it, without regard to any action of Congress. . . . You cannot avoid this position by asserting that individual Indians had committed murders and robberies on the inhabitants, and that your acts, in declaring war against the entire nation or bands of Indians, were necessary for the protection of this Territory. Individuals are liable personally for their own acts, but the nation is not. . . .
>
> The peaceful Navajos, seeing Colonel Carson in their country, and trusting to his word and promises, also surrendered themselves, and you have taken them to the Bosque [Fort Sumner], as prisoners of war. Old men and women too decrepit to walk, little ones equally, yes more helpless, women and children, non combatants, and those not able to take care of themselves much less to fight, are all held as prisoners of war—persons who have voluntarily come in for their protection and food, are treated in the same manner as those taken with arms in their hands, if indeed, you have one such in your possession. Where do you find the rule for such conduct? Certainly not in any code of civilized warfare (Keleher 1952:450–451).

Dr. Steck's opposition was less intense and perhaps was focused differently but was nonetheless powerful. Steck wrote on December 10, 1863, to Commissioner of Indian Affairs William P. Dole explaining his opposition to settling the Navajos at Bosque Redondo: "First, the arable land in the valley is not sufficient for both [Navajo and Mescalero Apache] tribes; and secondary, it would be difficult to manage two powerful tribes upon the same reservation" (Bailey 1964:182).

Steck's lack of respect for Indian culture is shown by his belief that the Navajos and Apaches could only learn such "civilized" traits as respecting "the value of property" if their "wild religious superstitions" could be eradicated (Keleher 1952:412). His opposition to

Mus. of N. Mex., Santa Fe.

Fig. 11. Navajo couple of the 1880s, identified only as Pedro and Anselina. The man wears loose trousers of white muslin with slits up the sides of the legs (a pattern of Spanish-Mexican origin) and a V-necked shirt made of calico in the same pattern as the white muslin shirts worn earlier. The woman's old style native-woven woolen dress (a type modeled after the Pueblo manta) was possibly worn for the occasion of this studio portrait since by this time calico shirts (similar to those worn by men) and calico or denim skirts were commonly worn by women as everyday wear; commercially made clothing and fabrics were distributed by government and sold by traders, while native wool was sold for export (Underhill 1953:195). Both wear commercially manufactured blankets, traditional leggings (probably of tanned, red-dyed buckskin), and moccasins. Photograph by Ben Wittick, Santa Fe, N. Mex.

Bosque Redondo was not entirely for humanitarian reasons. One of his main concerns, expressed in 1864, was the cost to the government of keeping the Navajos at Fort Sumner, which he estimated would be two million dollars in 1865, while he believed they could be fed in their own country at an annual cost of $200,000 until they could again plant and grow their own crops (Keleher 1952:421). Steck pointed out that in 1860 Major Canby had proposed building a military post on the Little Colorado around which the Navajos could plant crops and raise sheep. Steck felt that if Canby's plans had been carried out "the Navajos would this day be at peace, and supporting themselves, instead of being an enormous tax upon the treasury" (Keleher 1952:421).

The opposition to General Carleton and his Fort Sumner experiment grew. New Mexicans, who had earlier welcomed and supported him and his policies, became his foes. The land held by the Navajos at Fort Sumner was coveted by livestock interests. The mere presence of such a large group of Indians east of the Rio Grande created concern and opposition. The increasing disfavor to Carleton's Fort Sumner program on the part of his former supporters, combined with natural disasters and health and starvation problems at Fort Sumner, finally took their toll.

Carleton Removed and Navajos Freed

On September 19, 1866, the secretary of war relieved General Carleton as commander of the Department of New Mexico (Keleher 1952:457). Shortly afterward, in January 1867, the control over the Navajo was shifted from the Army to the Bureau of Indian Affairs.

Directly related to these actions was the growing repudiation of the Fort Sumner experiment. Ever recurring blight, grasshoppers, disease, drought, and other natural catastrophes had prevented the Navajos at Fort Sumner from raising the crops needed to prevent starvation. The crops failed consistently from 1864 to 1867.

Following the removal of Carleton there was another investigation aimed at evaluating Bosque Redondo. Lt. R. McDonald in a report dated November 12, 1867, recommended that the enterprise be abandoned and the Navajos removed elsewhere (Keleher 1952:460–461). The die was cast and it was only a matter of time before the mounting pressures to move the Navajos from Fort Sumner would prevail. A peace commission was established by Congress in 1867. It assailed the present treatment of Indians and sent its members to meet and to treat with different Indian groups.

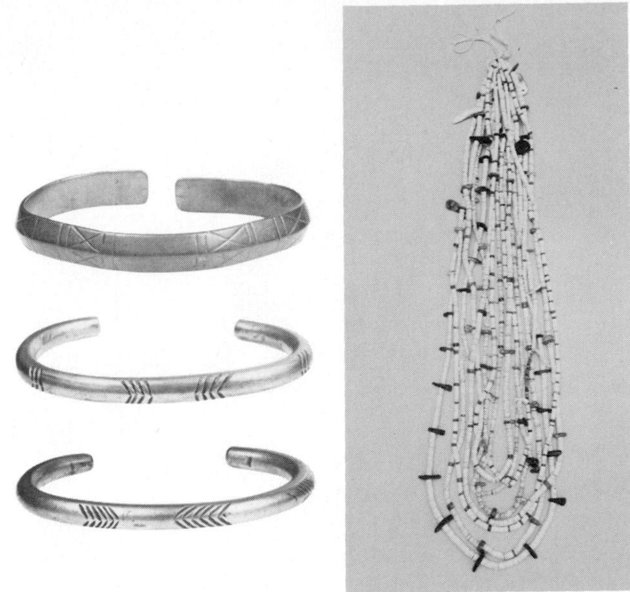

right, Wheelwright Mus., Santa Fe, N. Mex.: 74/118; left, Smithsonian, Dept. of Anthr.: 210,962, 131,366.

Fig. 13. Jewelry. right, Necklace made of shell and turquoise, worn especially at ceremonies and gatherings, and often acquired from the Pueblos. Even after silver necklaces became popular the shell type was still worn, often together with the silver. left, Bracelets, one of the most common and varied items of jewelry. The earliest were probably of brass or copper (top left) with engraved designs. Copper may still be used by the apprentice smith. center and bottom left, Early silver bracelets, C-shaped in cross-section, with engraved chevron designs. For later more elaborate jewelry styles see "Navajo Arts and Crafts," this vol. Width of top left 7.0 cm, collected before 1910; bottom and center left, collected 1890. right, Formerly owned by medicine man Hosteen Klah, acquired after his death in 1937.

On May 28, 1868, Gen. William T. Sherman and Col. Samuel F. Tappan were sent to Fort Sumner as peace commissioners to make a treaty with the Navajos. There was discussion about moving the Navajos to Texas or to Indian territory. The proceedings of the treaty session revealed the desperate desire of the Navajo to return to their native land. Barboncito appeared as the principal spokesman for the Navajo. He declared: "I hope to God you will not ask me to go to any other country except my own. . . . We do not want to go to the right or left, but straight back to our own country"

Smithsonian, Dept. of Anthr.: bottom left, 207,780; top, 210,963; bottom right, Mus. of the Amer. Ind., Heye Foundation, New York: 2622.

Fig. 12. Clothing and accessories. bottom left, Woman's dress of 2 identical wool pieces, black body with red and dark blue borders, which would be sewn together at the sides and shoulders (as shown in drawing). Women also wore shoulder blankets. The dress was belted with a woven sash or later a concha belt. top, Belt with 7 conchas probably made from silver dollars. The outer edge is slightly scalloped with punched holes. The belt leather is strung through the conchas and there is a simple silver buckle. Each concha is backed with leather, saving wear on cloth, and a stamped design is visible on several of the leather backing pieces. Such belts were worn by both sexes. bottom right, Leather pouch, a type used by men, with plain silver buttons on the shoulder strap and a single silver ornament on the flap. Tobacco, firemaking equipment, and other small items were carried in the pouch. bottom left, 127 by 172 cm, collected before 1900; top, length 98 cm, collected before 1901; bottom right, length about 76.2 cm, collected before 1905.

Smithsonian, NAA:2410–C.

Fig. 14. Delegation of Navajo dignitaries, who met with Pres. U.S. Grant in Dec. 1874, to discuss provisions of the treaty of 1868, conflicts with the Mormons and miners who were entering their lands, and a possible land exchange. seated, left to right, Carnero Mucho, Mariano, Juanita Pal ti-to (wife of Manuelito), Manuelito, Manuelito Segundo (son of Manuelito and Juanita), Tiene-su-se; standing, left to right, "Wild Hank" Sharp or Easton (an Anglo acting as interpreter), Ganado Mucho, Barbas Güeras, William F.M. Arny (Indian agent for the Navajos at Ft. Defiance since 1873), "Rocky Mountain Bill" Taylor (Anglo interpreter), Cabra Negra, Cayetanito, Narbona Primero, and Jesus Arviso or Alviso (a Mexican by birth who lived among the Navajo, acting as interpreter). According to McNitt (1962:144–159) and Link (1968:20–21), the visit to Washington was engineered by Arny as part of a scheme to defraud the Navajos of mineral-rich lands. The scheme was foiled, largely through the efforts of Thomas V. Keam (later a trading post owner); Arny resigned following a Navajo petition for his removal. Photograph possibly by studio photographer C.M. Bell, Washington, 1874.

(R. Roessel 1971:32). The treaty was concluded on June 1, 1868, and ratified by Congress July 25, 1868 (fig. 14). On June 18, a column of Navajos 10 miles long left Fort Sumner under escort of four cavalry companies. They reached their destination by the end of July (Bailey 1966:234–235).

Navajos relate stories of certain ceremonies that were held to assist them in being able to return home (R. Roessel 1973:85, 136, 167, 178–179, 212, 215, 222, 227, 238, 244, 261, 265). The ceremony mentioned most frequently was called *Mą'ii Bizéé' naast'ą́* (Put a Bead in Coyote's Mouth) ceremony. People formed a big circle and started closing in. There was a coyote within the circle. Barboncito approached the coyote, a female, who was facing east. "Barboncito caught the animal and put a piece of white shell, tapered at both ends, with a hole in the center, into its mouth. As he let the coyote go free, she turned clockwise and walked . . . toward the west, Barboncito remarked: 'There it is, we will be set free' " (Mose Denejolie in R. Roessel 1973:244). And they were! Many Navajos continue to believe that this ceremony resulted in their release from bondage.

Nothing in heaven or earth could have been more terrifying and traumatic to the Navajo than the experience of the Long Walk. They were a free people who lived in their own country with its sacred mountains and familiar landmarks. They were people who were independent and self-sufficient: a people who had a way of life that was satisfying and meaningful. They were people who related to Navajoland in a spiritual manner since it was given and made safe for them by the Holy People. To be forced to leave their beloved land with its sacred mountains and shrines, and to cross three rivers, all of which their traditions warned them never to do, was to subject the Navajo to unparalleled anguish and heartache. When this anguish and heartache is combined with the unequaled physical suffering experienced at Fort Sumner, a faint glimpse of the impact this tragedy had, and continues to have, for the Navajo may be

Smithsonian, NAA: left, 55766; right, 2390.

Fig. 15. Navajo leaders of the Bosque Redondo period and afterward. left, Barboncito (Spanish for 'little bearded one'), known in Navajo as *Dághaa'í* 'the one with the mustache' (or *Hastiin Bidághaa'í* 'the man with the mustache') and by his war name *Hashké yich'į' Dahilwo'* 'he is anxious to run at warriors' (or *Yich'į' Dahilwo'* 'he is anxious to run at them') (Sapir and Hoijer 1942:360, 366; Underhill 1953:151, 157, 1956:133). Possibly wielding more authority than would have been accorded him by strictly tribal custom because of the status granted to him by Whites (Underhill 1956:133, based on conversations with Navajo leader Henry Chee Dodge), Barboncito played a leading role in the treaty negotations of 1868 (see U.S. Treaties, etc. 1865–1869) and was subsequently appointed head chief of the Navajo by the Indian agent, with Ganado Mucho (*Tótsohnii Hastiin* 'Big Water Clan man') and Manuelito (*Dahána Baadaaní* 'Texan's son-in-law') appointed as subchiefs (Franciscan Fathers 1910:125; Sapir and Hoijer 1942:371). Photograph probably by studio photographers Nicholas Brown and Son, Santa Fe, N.Mex., sometime before Barboncito's death in 1870. right, Manuelito, noted Navajo war chief and ranking chief in the 1874 delegation to Washington. Photograph, probably by C.M. Bell, Washington, 1874.

realized. The experience at Fort Sumner could well have totally destroyed the heart and mind of a less determined people. The Army's efforts to remold the Navajo into Pueblo dwellers, the constant presence of starvation, the continued raids by other Indians, the anguish of sickness and death—all could have resulted in the destruction of Navajo culture. But by using their ceremonies and relying on their fortitude, the Navajo held on until they were allowed to return home.

After the Long Walk

Return from Fort Sumner

The return from Fort Sumner must have been a joyous occasion for many Navajos, even though the trip back was long and hard. A Navajo story of the event related:

> Children and food were put on the wagons. A great multitude journeyed over hill after hill, some on foot, some on horses, others in the wagons. When they reached Fort Wingate many were in a hurry and started taking off, saying, "We're lonely for our beloved country. . . ." At Fort Defiance, besides the other things, the men received hoes and axes and were told to work with them. They were told to go back to your lands but to return within 14 days . . . [when] two sheep were given to each person, from babies born the night before to old people. . . . So *Diné* [Navajo] gathered together and put on a ceremonial chant to sacrifice . . . (precious stones). The ceremony was held for about four days, and that is the reason why our population has increased rapidly up to these days. If it had not been for the ceremony it wouldn't have been like this (Francis Toledo in R. Roessel 1973:147).

The Reservation

The original reservation set up under provisions of article 2 of the treaty of June 1, 1868, contained 3,414,528 acres (fig. 16). Confusion surely existed as to its extent or boundaries: the Navajos felt they were returning to

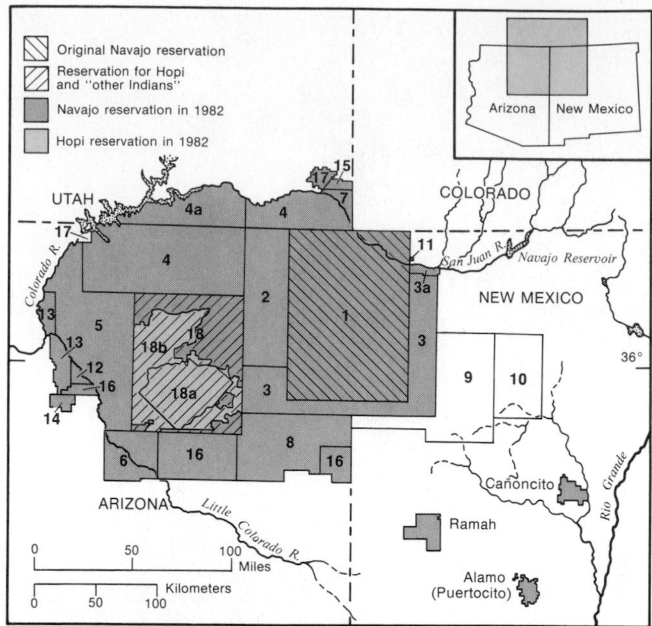

Fig. 16. Navajo lands, 1868–1977. Original treaty reservation with executive order additions and withdrawals: 1, reservation, June 1, 1868; 2, addition Oct. 29, 1878; 3, addition Jan. 6, 1880; 3a, originally part of 3, withdrawn from reservation May 17, 1884, restored to reservation April 24, 1886; 4, additions May 17, 1884; 4a, "Paiute Strip," originally a part of 4, restored to public domain 1892, withdrawn for use of various Indians 1908, restored to public domain 1922, withdrawn again in 1929, permanently transferred to Navajo reservation March 1, 1933; 5, addition Jan. 8, 1900; 6, addition Nov. 14, 1901; 7, addition May 15, 1905; 8, addition Nov. 9, 1907; 9, addition Nov. 9, 1907, restored to public domain Jan. 16, 1911; 10, addition Nov. 9, 1907, restored to public domain Dec. 30, 1908; 11, addition Dec. 1, 1913; 12, addition May 7, 1917, and Jan. 19, 1918. Additions to the Navajo reservation by acts of Congress: 13, act of May 23, 1930; 14, act of Feb. 21, 1931; 15, act of March 1, 1933; 16, act of June 14, 1934; 17, act of Sept. 2, 1958 authorizing exchange of lands at Glen Canyon Dam and Page, Ariz., for lands in Utah (see also Correll and Dehiya 1972). Hopi reservation lands: 18, original executive order reservation created "for the use and occupancy of the Moqui, and such other Indians as the Secretary of the Interior may see fit to settle thereon," Dec. 16, 1882; 18a, Hopi reservation outlined in a decision by the U.S. District Court for the District of Arizona Sept. 28, 1962, with remaining part of 18 designated Hopi-Navajo Joint Use Area; 18b, Hopi reservation outlined along "Mediator's Line" according to an Order of Partition issued by the U.S. District Court for the District of Arizona Feb. 10, 1977. Remaining area within 18 was ordered to become Navajo land. The satellite reservations of Alamo, Cañoncito, and Ramah were created from individual Navajo allotments and purchases and exchanges by the federal government and the Navajo Tribe.

the land they lived on prior to Fort Sumner but in reality the 1868 reservation contained no more than 10 percent of the land they earlier owned and used. Following Fort Sumner, as non-Navajo ranchers and sheepmen began to move with livestock into the area in which Navajos lived but that was not a part of the treaty reservation, trouble and conflict took place. The original reservation was first expanded in 1878 as a result of an executive order that added to the west side a reported 957,817 acres. Executive orders in 1880 added a reported 996,403 acres on the east and south sides, and in 1882 and 1884, 2,373,870 acres to the west and north sides. The next addition was by executive order issued in 1900, which increased the area by 1,575,369 acres. In 1901, another executive order added 425,171 acres to the southwest portion of the reservation, and one in 1905 incorporated 67,000 acres in southeastern Utah. In 1907 and 1908 executive orders increased the size of the reservation by adding 1,208,486 acres. But in 1911 lands in New Mexico were restored to the public domain. Minor revisions were made in 1912, 1913, 1914, 1915, and 1917. In 1917 and 1918 executive orders added 94,000 acres of land in Coconino County, Arizona. In 1930 and 1931 a total of 179,110 acres were added by congressional acts. In 1933 Congress permanently set aside 552,000 acres in Utah as an addition to the Navajo reservation. Another act of Congress in 1934 provided some smaller additions, and minor changes were made in 1948, 1949, and 1958. Court decisions in 1962, 1963, and 1977 reallocated some areas to the Hopi.

In addition to the land listed above as belonging to the Navajo reservation there are three noncontiguous areas of Navajo reservation land. The Cañoncito Navajo reservation in New Mexico consists of 57,863 acres of trust land surveyed in 1910, 1915, and 1954 with the present boundaries established in 1960. The Alamo (or Puertocito) Navajo reservation established in 1964 consists of 62,000 acres, and the Ramah Reservation, established in 1931, contains 91,456 acres (Littell 1967; Correll and Dehiya 1972).

Trading Posts

Trading posts played a major role in the growth and change of the Navajo people, particularly after 1867. In this period, traders lived with and were members of the Navajo community in which their post was located (fig. 17). Obviously, not all traders were loved but all played a most important part in exposing the Navajo to the world around them and to its contents. McNitt (1962) tells of the impact the traders had on Navajo life: in mediating problems, both family and tribal; selling goods; buying rugs and silver and improving markets for Navajo crafts; burying Navajo dead; filling out forms and writing letters.

Round Rock was one of the first trading posts operated within the reservation. It was established in 1885. It stands as a thick walled rock structure with living quarters attached.

Education

The treaty of 1868 stipulated that Navajo children would be compelled to attend school and that for every 30 children between the ages of 6 and 16, a school and a teacher would be provided. In 1869 a school was

top and bottom left, Mus. of N. Mex., Santa Fe; bottom right, Natl. Park Service, Ganado, Ariz.

Fig. 17. Hubbell's Trading Post at Ganado, Ariz., owned by Lorenzo Hubbell, one of the best known and best liked traders (Anonymous 1979). top, Hubbell (seated) examining a late-style Chief's blanket, possibly woven by the Navajo woman with him. The post, one of several owned by Hubbell, was purchased by him in 1878 and named after his friend Ganado Mucho, who lived in the area. Hubbell was instrumental in promoting Navajo rugs by encouraging good quality yarns, and certain patterns. He also encouraged the weaving of blankets so large they could only be used as rugs; the double-faced rug on the fence at extreme right (now in the collection of the Mus. of Northern Ariz.), is 12 feet wide and more than 18 feet long (McNitt 1962:200–212, Amsden 1934:186–204). bottom left, Hubbell's warehouse at Ganado, containing crates of staple foodstuffs and tobacco, goatskins (probably obtained from the Navajo), and harnesses. The large scale was used for weighing wool and possibly woven blankets (which were sometimes sold by the pound). Photographs by Ben Wittick, 1890s. bottom right, View of the rug room at Hubbell's Trading Post (designated a National Historic Site in 1967), hung with framed oil paintings of rug patterns. These copies of actual rugs, principally painted by artist E.A. Burbank in the early 1900s, were used as patterns for Navajo weavers to follow. Photograph by Elizabeth Bauer, 1981.

Los Angeles Co. Mus. of Nat. Hist.: A.5141.42–192.

Fig. 18. Pictorial rug showing trains and buildings. The arrival of the railroad in 1882 changed reservation life in many ways including influencing the style of jewelry and rugs through sale in Fred Harvey Company curio shops, which were run in conjunction with the Santa Fe Railroad. With a commercial market, Navajo weavers changed during 1880 to 1900 from making blankets to producing rugs for the tourist trade (Kent 1981). Although not a common style in this period, pictorials frequently show objects new to Navajo experience (Cerny 1975). Size 185.4 by 132.0 cm.

opened at Fort Defiance under the supervision of the Presbyterian church, with the first teacher Charity Gaston. The school was a failure due to poor attendance and was closed.

At Round Rock in 1893 Agent Dana L. Shipley attempted literally to capture Navajo children and haul them off to Fort Defiance Boarding School. He was rebuffed and almost killed by Black Horse (fig. 19) and his group of Navajos while at Round Rock. This incident reflected the attitude many Navajos had toward education at that time.

In the early 1900s additional boarding schools were built in various parts of the reservation. Here again there was considerable opposition on the part of the Navajo who resented and often resisted sending their children to distant schools, some located off the reservation, where they might not come home even in the summer.

Education was looked upon as a threat and a foe to the Navajo way of life as well as a threat to the Navajo family.

Smithsonian, NAA.

Fig. 19. Black Horse (*Bilį́į́' Łizhinii*), left, a headman of Round Rock area, with *Tayoonih* (Squeezer), a headman of the Ganado region. Photograph by Simeon Schwemberger, 1905 or before.

Culture Change after 1867

The Navajo people were both increasing in population and expanding in territory during the years following the Long Walk. They came back as beaten people and hardly had more than the clothes on their backs. Yet, in spite of all adversity the strength of their culture carried them through this period of rebuilding. Navajo culture was changing very rapidly. Trading posts were established. Blanket weaving for Navajo consumption changed into rug weaving for sale to tourists; silverwork became yet another expression of Navajo harmony and beauty. Children were sent to boarding schools, learning in an alien environment. Railroads were constructed, which created jobs as well as new markets for Navajo arts and crafts. Labor-saving devices entered Navajoland such as wagons, metal plows, roads, automobiles, and trucks. The presence of the federal government expanded on the reservation; health facilities and medical doctors became available for the first time. Missionaries and missions scattered themselves throughout the land. Navajo population increased, as did Navajo livestock holdings.

Perhaps no other period in Navajo history reveals as clearly the capacity for Navajo culture to adjust, to change, and to bend yet never to break, as does the period immediately following the return of the Navajo from the Long Walk.

The First Tribal Council

After their return from Fort Sumner the Navajo were governed by a head chief, who was appointed by the agent and approved by the secretary of the interior. In addition, there were regional leaders (*naat'áanii*), of which there were 30 in 1900. Should a problem arise, the Indian agent would contact the head chief, who in turn would call the *naat'áanii* of that region and summon him to Fort Defiance. "When the *naat'áanii* arrived, the problem of his region would be discussed with the "Head Chief" and any leaders who might be involved. Since the Agent was supported by the military at Fort Wingate, there was little dickering or disobedience. The *naat'áanii* [were] directly responsible to the "Head Chief" who was responsible to the Agent. . . . About once a year all *naat'áanii* were 'called in,' and then only problems of tribal importance were discussed" (Van Valkenburgh 1945:72, with Navajo spelling corrected).

The discovery of oil in 1921 within the boundaries of the Navajo reservation forced a revision in the system of tribal government placed upon the Navajo by the federal government. The Midwest Refinery Company was authorized to negotiate with the Navajos in the discovery area, San Juan Jurisdiction (Northern Navajo), for an oil and gas development lease. A "general council" of the Indian residents in that jurisdiction was called, and a lease was approved on 4,800 acres of land. However legal the "general council" system might have been, it was at best clumsy and limited in terms of its application on a reservation-wide basis. Originally, the thinking of the Department of the Interior was to the effect that the oil and gas resources belonged exclusively to the Indians of that jurisdiction.

As additional leases were sought, the Department's policy changed to the concept that any resources discovered within the Navajo reservation belonged to the Navajo tribe as a whole. The implementation of this new philosophy made the "general council" concept unfeasible and focused the Department of the Interior's attention on the necessity to develop a representative tribal government, which would include membership from all jurisdictions (Kelly 1968:61–65).

On January 27, 1923, Commissioner of Indian Affairs Charles H. Burke issued a document entitled "Regulations Relating to the Navajo Tribe of Indians." These regulations were revised and amended later in 1923. One of the provisions of the regulations provided for a Commissioner of the Navajo Tribe to be appointed by the secretary of the interior. The revised regulations installed a tribal council council composed of 12 delegates (earlier regulations allowed only 6 delegates) and 12 alternates, with each jurisdiction having two delegates. The six jurisdictions were San Juan, Western Navajo, Southern Navajo, Pueblo Bonito, Leupp, and Moqui. The chairman was to be chosen from candidates outside the council membership (earlier regulations had the chairman elected by the Council delegates), while the vice chairman was chosen by vote of the delegates (Young 1961:374–376).

The first session of the newly appointed Council occurred July 7, 1923, at Toadlena, New Mexico. The purpose of the meeting was to obtain approval from the delegates to lease their oil and gas properties. The Council approved a resolution, drawn up by Bureau of Indian Affairs officials, granting the Commissioner of the Navajo Tribe the authority to sign on behalf of the Navajo Indians all oil and gas mining leases granted within the Navajo reservation (Kelly 1968:68–69).

This early tribal council was completely the creation of the Department of the Interior; in fact, one provision of the 1923 regulations required the tribal commissioner to be present at all tribal council meetings. In addition, the secretary of the interior reserved the right to remove any member of the tribal council, for cause, and to require the election or appointment of another to take his place (Young 1961:395).

Navajo Social Organization

GARY WITHERSPOON

Social Categories

The social universe of the Navajo is labeled *dine'é* 'people'. This universe is divided into two categories: *diyin dine'é* 'holy people' and *nihookáá' dine'é* 'earth-surface people'. Earth-surface people are also often referred to as 'the ones with five fingers'. The earth-surface people are again divided into two categories: *diné* 'Navajos' and *'ana'í* 'non-Navajos'. The non-Navajos are further divided into various groups of Indians and non-Indians. The Navajos are further divided into 60 or more matrilineal clans called *dine'é* or *dóone'é* 'a particular kind of Navajo' (for a list see Young and Morgan 1980: *s.v. dóone'é*). The clans are grouped into approximately 15 unnamed phratries.

The matrilineal clans of the Navajo are based on the mother-child bond, and the child becomes a member of his mother's clan. Because the clans are exogamous, the child's father must necessarily be of a different clan than the mother. The child is said to be 'born for' his father's clan, while in essence he is born 'in' or 'of' his mother's clan. As undifferentiated categories, the child considers all those of his mother's clan to be 'mothers' and all those of his father's clan to be 'fathers'.

The father-child relationship, or the 'born for' concept, is used to delineate two more categories of relatives. Those who are born for the same clan (that is, those whose fathers are of the same clan) consider themselves to be 'siblings'. In addition, a male ego considers all those born for his own clan (that is, all those whose fathers are of his own clan) to be his 'children'. A female ego considers this same category to be either 'paternal grandchildren' or 'cross-cousins' (table 1).

Because of rules of clan exogamy, ego's maternal grandfather will be of still a different clan from either that of his or her mother or father. Ego considers all those of his or her maternal grandfather's clan to be 'maternal grandfathers'. Likewise, those of the paternal grandfather's clan are considered to be 'paternal grandfathers'.

Types of Solidarity

Ego considers everyone who fits any one or more of these six categories to be related to him by *k'é*. In fact, he refers to all these categories as *shik'éí* 'my relative(s),

Table 1. ***Shik'éí*** **'my relatives'**

Paternal Grandfather's Clan 5 Considered: Paternal Grandfathers	Maternal Grandfather's Clan 6 Considered: Maternal Grandfathers
Father's Clan 2 Considered: Fathers	Mother's Clan 1 Considered: Mothers
Born for Father's Clan 3 Considered: Siblings	Born for Mother's Clan 4 Considered: Children or cross-cousins

those to whom I am related according to *k'é*'. *K'é** means 'kindness, love, cooperation, thoughtfulness, friendliness, and peacefulness'. *K'é* is the ideal that orders all social relations, but it is especially true for those who are related to one another according to the categories mentioned in table 1.

K'é is one of two main kinds of solidarity that hold the *Diné* 'Navajos' together as a society or tribal group. The other type of solidarity can be characterized as reciprocity. The former might be called kinship solidarity and the latter nonkinship solidarity, for reciprocity is the pattern of social relations among those not related by *k'é*.

In the Enemyway ceremony the participants divide into two main groups. One is organized around the main patient, and the other is organized around the person who is often called the stick-receiver. Solidarity within the two groups takes the form of unsystematic sharing, while solidarity between the two groups takes the form of reciprocity. Those of the patient's group are all related by *k'é*, and they share the cost of the ceremonial performance. The same is true for the stick-receiver's group. But the main patient and the stick-receiver must not be related by *k'é*. The two groups relate to each other on the basis of systematic exchange or reciprocity. Numerous items are exchanged between the two groups during the ceremony, including a major

**K'é* is a noun, also used as a verbal prefix. When the noun-forming enclitic *-í* is added to make *-k'éí*, the resulting stem means 'those to whom one is related according to *k'é*'.

left, Amon Carter Mus., Ft. Worth, Tex.: Mazzulla Coll.; top right, U. of Okla. Lib., Western Hist. Coll., Norman: W.E. Hollon Coll. #147, bottom right, Smithsonian, Dept. of Anthr.: 9536.

Fig. 1. Hairdressing, a frequent household activity, generally performed by women for both sexes (Kluckhohn, Hill, and Kluckhohn 1971:269). The traditional hairstyle (in which the hair is brushed back, folded up, and tied in the middle with any of a variety of hair ties) is essentially the same for men, women, and children. left, Woman combing a man's hair, probably her husband's or possibly an unmarried brother's, with a grass brush. In the background, women (presumably members of the same household) are carding wool and working at a loom. top right, Woman tying the hair of a young woman, probably her daughter, with a skein of yarn, which is sometimes decorated with a bead of turquoise or shell. bottom right, Hair brush of grass stems tied together with a strip of white cloth. left, Photograph by Charlie Wunder, probably 1930s or 1940s. top right, Photograph by Chuck Abbott, Ariz., probably 1930s or 1940s. bottom right, Length 30.0 cm, collected by Edward Palmer, 1869.

gift exchange (Witherspoon 1970:165–188). Thus *k'é* is the form of solidarity characterized by love and unsystematic sharing, while nonkinship solidarity is characterized by reciprocity or systematic exchange.

The primary bond of *k'é* in Navajo culture is found in the mother-child bond, which is the closest and strongest of all relationships in the Navajo social system. Motherhood in Navajo culture is defined in terms of the reproduction and sustenance of life, and it is expressed in affection, care, kindness, and unsystematic sharing.

The primary bond of nonkinship or affinal solidarity in Navajo culture is found in the husband-wife relationship. The husband-wife relationship is a contractual one that involves exchange, one form of which is the bridewealth that the husband's kin group provides for the wife's kin group. This relationship can be very strong, but it is often very fragile, particularly in its early stages.

A main difference between these two relationships is that it is not because she expects the same in return that a mother gives life, sustenance, and care. A mother continues to love even when she may be despised and continues to give when her gifts are not appreciated. On the other hand, when a husband is irresponsible or immoral, a wife usually sends him away. If a wife is barren, a husband usually goes elsewhere. In other words, if either sees the relationship as without merit to himself or herself, it will likely be dissolved. The relationship is supposed to be advantageous to both parties through mutual obligations. Such is not true of the mother-child bond.

Social Organization

The residence group is the fundamental unit of Navajo social organization. It is organized around a head mother, a sheep herd, a customary land-use area, and sometimes agricultural fields, all of which are called mother. The residence group is both a social and an economic unit. It is a cooperative unit organized, structured, and integrated by the symbols of motherhood.

The personnel of the residence group are organized around a head mother. All rights of residence within the group are ultimately derived from the head mother of the unit. Residence rules are based on the primary bonds of kinship (mother-child) and affinity (husband-

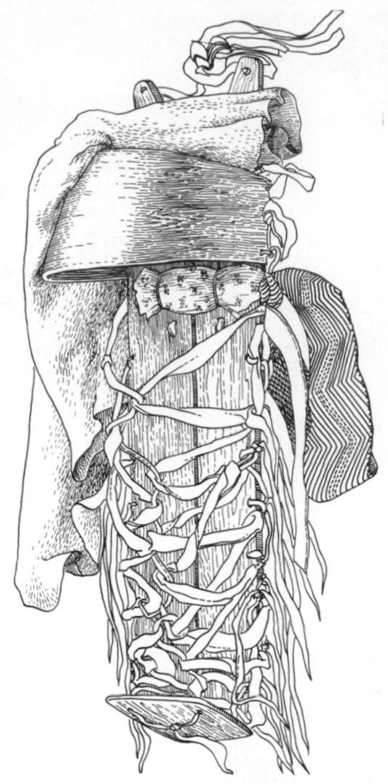

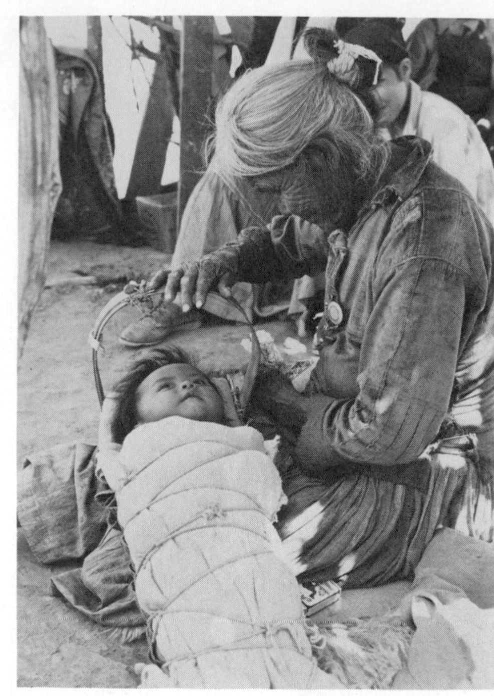

center, Smithsonian, Dept. of Anthr.:127,615; Amon Carter Mus., Ft. Worth, Tex., Laura Gilpin Coll: left, 4255 [1], right, 4256 [1].

Fig. 2. Cradleboards. center, Split-back cradleboard (Kluckhohn, Hill, and Kluckhohn 1971:191–197) consisting of 2 pieces of board lashed together to form the back, a footrest, and a hood or canopy strip from which a piece of leather is draped as an awning. Shredded bark serves as an absorbent material and a piece of fur as padding. The baby is strapped on with the leather ties. Cradleboards are reused; this one served 3 children. In transit they are carried, worn on the back, or placed in front of the rider on a horse. left, Man constructing a cradleboard possibly for his child or grandchild. right, Woman with her grandchild. A small ornament or possibly a charm consisting of pieces of turquoise or shell is attached to the bow-shaped canopy support. Both photographs by Laura Gilpin, 1951 and 1954. center, Length 84.0 cm, collected by R.W. Shufeldt, 1886.

wife). A Navajo may live wherever his mother has the right to live. In addition, a Navajo may live wherever his or her spouse has the right to live. Thus residence rights are acquired from one's mother and one's spouse.

All residence rights are ultimately derived from a head mother. The husband of the head mother resides in the unit on the basis of his marriage; the spouses of the children reside in the unit by virtue of their marriages; the head mother's paternal grandchildren reside in the unit by their right to reside with their mother, by their mother's right to reside with her husband, and by her husband's right to reside with his mother.

There are two important breaks that can occur in this chain of residence rights based on the mother-child and husband-wife bonds. One of these is divorce and the other is death. When divorce occurs residence rights by virtue of marriage are lost. Thus when a couple living with the wife's mother's unit is divorced, the husband must leave while the wife and children remain. When a couple living with the husband's mother's unit is divorced, the husband remains and the wife and children must leave.

If the husband dies when the couple is living at his mother's unit, the wife is expected to remarry within the unit or return to her natal unit. However, sometimes she may remain as long as she does not remarry outside the unit. If the wife dies when a couple is living at her mother's unit, the husband must eventually either remarry into the unit or return to his natal unit. The children will remain in the unit, raised either by their maternal grandmother or one of their deceased mother's sisters.

When a young couple marry (fig. 4), they can live at either spouse's natal unit. There is a preference and an expectation that they will live at the wife's mother's unit, but if circumstances so dictate they may live at the husband's mother's unit. Examples of such circumstances would be that the wife's natal unit was overcrowded or the husband's natal unit was in need of assistance.

The initial choice of residence of the married couple does not cause them to forfeit their rights to live at the unit that they did not choose. Some couples switch their residence back and forth between the wife's and husband's natal units several times before finally settling at one place or the other. This switching back and forth may continue as long as the mothers of both spouses are alive.

In the past when the head mother died (or sometimes after both the head mother and her husband had died), the unit usually divided into several new residence groups with her daughters and daughters-in-law becoming the head mothers of new units. These new residence groups will often consist of what were household or

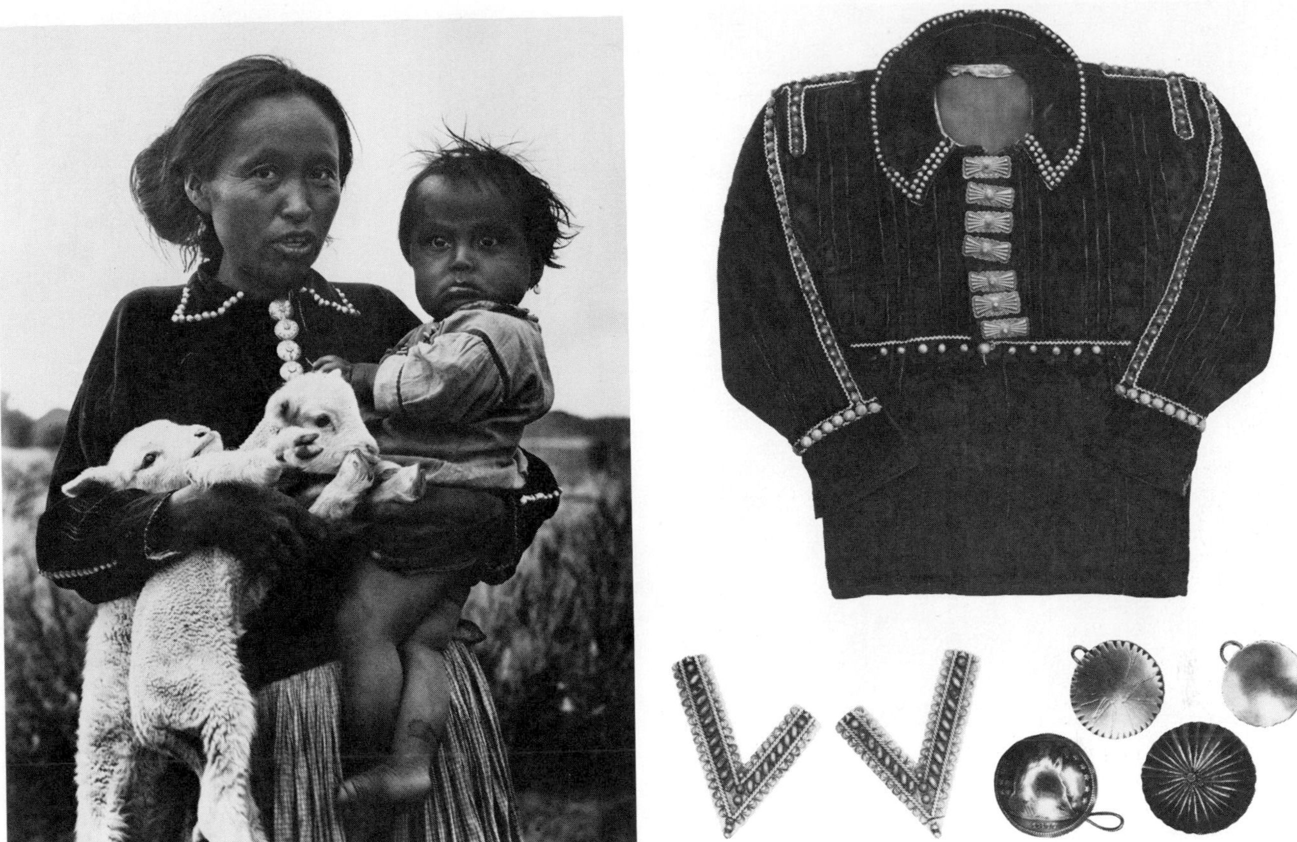

Wheelwright Mus., Santa Fe, N. Mex.: top right, 44/526; bottom left, 47/243; bottom right, Smithsonian, Dept. of Anthr.: a, 74,167, b, 74,166, c, 131,377; left, Amon Carter Mus., Ft. Worth, Tex.: Laura Gilpin Coll. 7995/90.

Fig. 3. Woman's blouse and silver ornaments. left, Woman wearing a velveteen blouse with decorative stitching on the sleeves, large stamped silver buttons, and small fluted buttons used as studs. top right, Velveteen blouses (modeled after the earlier calico style) have been worn since about 1900, with a long full cotton skirt. Design features such as sleeve stitching may differ regionally (Gilpin 1968:72). Silver buttons (bottom right), often made in sets, are common blouse ornaments and are made in a variety of forms ranging from a coin with a loop on the back to cast pieces. In addition to plain and fluted buttons this green blouse also has 7 butterfly buttons, a shape also developed into slides used on concha belts. Men use buttons on moccasins and pouches and formerly on leggings and leather trousers. The collar tabs (bottom left), set with turquoise and stamped, were attached to collar points as decoration, especially during the 1930s. Ornaments were moved from blouse to blouse as occasion demanded. left, Photograph by Laura Gilpin, probably 1930s. Length of blouse, about 63.5 cm, collar tabs about 8.5 cm, largest button, 2.5 cm.

nuclear-family groups within the former residence group. As time passes the children in these new residence groups will get older, marry, have children, and maybe even grandchildren. Thus the constitution of the residence group in terms of numbers of persons, families, and generations will vary according to its developmental stages.

In the late twentieth century normal fissions in the developmental cycle of residence groups are often impractical if not impossible. The scarcity of land and the rapid increase of population are the main causes of this condition. One adaptation to this situation that many Navajos are taking is to reside outside the traditional residence groups and live by means of wage work. Such people often maintain close ties with their natal units without depending on their limited resources for a livelihood.

Most residence groups usually consist of more than one household. Normally every married couple in the residence group has its own household, which they share with their children if they have any. Often mature women with children but without husbands will have their own households. A household can be identified as the group that eats and sleeps together. Household groups tend to merge in the winter and disperse in the summer (figs. 7–8). This is mostly due to the great difficulty of acquiring sufficient firewood to heat numerous separate households.

Economic Organization

Residence groups are also organized around a sheep herd. Members of a distinct residence group put their sheep in a common herd and share in the tasks of caring for the herd. So at the residence group level, social groups correspond to the groupings of sheep into herds.

left, Bureau of Ind. Affairs, Washington; right, Smithsonian, Dept. of Anthr.: 168,804.

Fig. 4. Traditional wedding. left, Ceremony; participants unidentified. As reported by Reichard (1928:139–141), a wedding is held in the evening at the woman's hogan. A small container of water with gourd ladle (center foreground) and a wedding basket containing ceremonial gruel or mush are set out by the bride's father. As part of the ceremony, he draws lines with pollen (in a manner similar to sandpainting) across the gruel basket—first from east to west with white pollen and then south to north with yellow pollen—and circles the basket. After dipping water from the water bottle over each other's hands, the bride and groom eat gruel from the east, south, west, north, and center of the wedding basket, with remaining portions eaten by the guests. Then the presents (which have been brought by the groom's family) are distributed to the bride's family and general feasting begins. Photographer unknown, possibly early 1970s. right, Wedding basket, coiled, with design in red (inner row of triangles) and black (outer row). The opening or "trail" in the pattern is placed toward the east when in use. Such baskets, made to Navajo standards, are now usually obtained from the Ute or Paiute, possibly because of the ritual restrictions placed on their construction by Navajos (Tschopik 1938). The same type of basket when inverted (bottom right) serves as a drum for other ceremonies (Matthews 1894). Diameter 34.0 cm, collected by Washington Matthews, 1894.

When the distance between houses does not clearly indicate which households form distinct residence groups, the matter can be clarified by ascertaining who puts their sheep in which herd.

The sheep herd is an important symbol of social integration within the residence group. The sheep herd is a cooperative enterprise of the individual owners. Nearly everyone in the unit has some sheep and therefore has an interest in the welfare of the herd. Children are given lambs to begin building their flocks as soon as they are able to share in the tasks of caring for the sheep, and this is usually around five years of age. It is in the sheep herd, more than anywhere else, that the divergent interests of the individual members of the units are converged into this very meaningful and cooperative endeavor.

The identity, welfare, and status of the residence group is closely linked to the size and well-being of the sheep herd. Community members judge the character and qualities of those within the residence group on the basis of the size and appearance of their sheep herd. No one will be respected in the community or elected to positions of leadership if his family's herd gives the appearance of improper care and attention.

An individual's identity and social position is also closely linked to his sheep. Most often the person who wields the most power and influence within a residence group is the person who has the most sheep in the herd. Sheep are also an important aspect of the way in which an in-marrying affine is integrated into the residence group of his spouse. The in-marrying affine may bring none or only a few of his sheep to his wife's home at the beginning of their marriage, leaving the majority of his sheep in the herd of his natal group. Later as children come and his marriage becomes more stable, he will bring more or most of his herd to his wife's home. Sometimes it might not be until after 10 or 20 years of marriage that a man will finally have placed all his sheep in his wife's herd (Shepardson and Hammond 1966:90). Having fully tied his identity and loyalty to his new residence group, the in-marrying affine is likely to begin to have more influence over the affairs of the group and may soon become its leader. From this it may be concluded that a person's status within

left, James T. Bialac, Phoenix, Ariz.; right, Smithsonian, Dept. of Anthr.: 9557.

Fig. 5. Gambling games. left, *Navajos at Play*, painting by Navajo artist Raymond Johnson (Ne-chah-He), 1967 or earlier. A group of men and women play cards under the ramada or shade at right. (See Tanner 1973:fig. 7.78 for somewhat different treatment of the same subject by Navajo artist James Wayne Yazzie.) Women play the stick dice game at lower left. Three dice are used in this game, usually played by women only; they are tossed on a flat rock in the center of a circle created by pebbles. Unshaped sticks serve as counters. For description of the game and the lore associated with it see Aberle (1942). right, Dice of cottonwood, convex and unpainted on one side, flat and blackened on the other. Length 20.5 cm, collected by Edward Palmer, 1869.

and loyalty to a particular residence group or groups largely correspond to the location and position of his sheep in a particular herd or herds.

Sheep are also a means of incorporating children into the life and communal economy of the residence group. The children's receipt of lambs as the nucleus of a future herd is an earned right because it comes when they get old enough to share in the tasks of caring for the herd (Shepardson and Hammond 1966:90). Thus children have a direct interest in the welfare of the herd, just like their parents. It is in this corporate enterprise or institution that the child learns the meaning, necessity, and nature of group or communal life. He is initiated into this group at a young age, and it is this experience, more than any other, that forms his social personality. In this light it is not hard to understand why the Navajos bitterly resisted attempts by the United States government in the 1930s to reduce their sheep. Their main complaint was, "Who will raise the children when you take away the sheep?"

Since the early part of the twentieth century, Navajos have shown a gradual tendency to replace some of their sheep with cattle. This shift could result in significant economic and social changes. Sheep provide a minimal

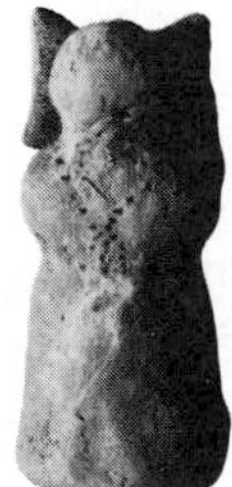

Smithsonian, Dept. of Anthr.: 350,273.

Fig. 6. Figurines of sun-dried clay, made as toys by Navajo children. These, part of a set made by a 4 year old, depict sheep, goat, horse, cat, dog, cradleboard, and humans. Fewkes (1923) points out their resemblances to fetishes found at Southwestern archeological sites. Length of left, 3.5 cm, collected by W.H. Spinks, Chinle, Ariz., 1923.

cash income from the sale of lambs and wool, but they provide many other useful and consumable items within the residence group. Among these are meat for food; wool for clothing, bedding, and weaving; and sinew for bows. Cattle, on the other hand, provide a proportionally greater amount of cash income but a proportionally smaller amount of consumable products. Very few Navajos ever butcher their own cattle, and so cattle are only useful to provide cash income from the sale of calves.

In terms of social organization, cattle require less care and do not need to be herded. Also, cattle require more male labor in their care than sheep do. Therefore, the gradual move toward more cattle and less sheep may mean an expanded move toward a cash economy, the breakdown of the residence group as the fundamental unit of social organization, and the greater importance of men in social and economic organization.

Before 1868 agriculture was an important part of Navajo subsistence. In order to compel the Navajos to surrender, Col. Christopher (Kit) Carson destroyed thousands of acres of agricultural fields and fruit trees. After their return to Navajoland from Fort Sumner Navajos were given some sheep and cattle with which to subsist. Although they continued to do some farming, livestock has been the center of the Navajo economy up to the middle of the twentieth century. With the expansion of irrigated land on the Navajo reservation, agriculture may again become an important part of the Navajo economy.

WITHERSPOON

top left. ©Natl. Geographic Soc., Washington; center left, Ariz. State Mus., Tucson:22616; bottom left, Natl. Park Service, Canyon de Chelly, Natl. Monument, Ariz.; top and bottom right, Amon Carter Mus., Ft. Worth, Tex.: Laura Gilpin Coll.:4245[1], 4246[1].

Fig. 7. Navajo hogans, traditional Navajo dwelling structures of enclosed and covered design, associated with the winter months. Jett and Spencer (1981:29) report a classification of Navajo dwellings based on Navajo linguistic distinctions: the *hooghan*; the *kin* 'house', which is "rectilinear in plan, with vertical walls and of largely or totally foreign—Puebloan or European—derivation"; and the *chaha'oh* 'shade', "relatively insubstantial summer or temporary shelters of various plans and origins which are, more often than not, at least partially wall-less." Mindeleff (1898:487) reported a twofold distinction, also based on Navajo terminology, between: *keehai* 'winter residence' and *keeshį́* 'summer residence'. These terms seem based on function or use rather than structure as such: hogans are associated with winter and shades or shelters with summer use. The identifications provided here generally follow the taxonomic system (based primarily on construction techniques) devised by Jett and Spencer (1981:fig. 3.1); these are reconciled where practicable with other reported Navajo classifications and categories (Young and Morgan 1980:459; Franciscan Fathers 1910:335–340; Mindeleff 1898:514–517). top left, "round hogan" (*yaadah(')askání* 'under the round roof') (Franciscan Fathers 1910:332), contrasting with the distinctive conical shape of the older forked-pole hogan, which has a conical roof. This is probably a leaning-log hogan, which is constructed by leaning logs and boughs against a framework composed of vertical posts and horizontal stringers, with the whole then chinked and covered with mud. A hogan using such a skeleton or framework is called a *hooghan bijáád hólóní* 'hogan with legs' (Young and Morgan 1980:459) in general and a "4-legged house" (Underhill 1953:pl. 161) when 4 vertical posts are used. Photograph by Clifford Adams, near Tuba City, Ariz., 1928. center left, Palisaded hogan, *náneeskáál hooghan*; this type is generally also a *hooghan bijáád hólóní*. The palisaded walls are created from upright logs or timbers, most likely set in a trench. Photograph by Helga Teiwes, north of Shiprock, N. Mex., April 1968. bottom left, Polygonal cribbed log hogan, *hooghan dah diitł'iní* (Young and Morgan 1980:459), a hogan in which parallel logs are vertically stacked. Corbelled log hogan (*hooghan yistł'óní*) (Young and Morgan 1980:459; Jett and Spencer 1981:80), has logs in staggered rather than parallel formation. Photograph by Fred Mang, Jr., vicinity of Spider Rock, Ariz., 1971. top right, Hexagonal stone hogan, *tsé bee hooghan*, one of several varieties of masonry hogan. Photograph by Laura Gilpin, near Red Rock, N. Mex., 1953. bottom right, Interior view of stone hogan shows the domed roof of corbelled construction and central hearth below the smoke hole. The roof would probably be covered with mud and resemble that shown at bottom left. Both general orientation (doorway to east) and functional use of interior space within a hogan are traditionally defined by direction. Photograph by Laura Gilpin, 1953.

Political Organization

In traditional Navajo social or political organization, there was no clearly defined group larger than the residence group. In some areas residence groups that in the previous generation were one unit formed a larger unit sometimes called the "outfit," but the outfit did not have any really important functions. It was used as a means of recruiting assistance for major ceremonies and for settling internal disputes or uniting against external foes.

Until the early part of the twentieth century there were loosely defined local groups organized around a local headman (*naat'áanii*). This local group was usually mobilized only for the purpose of dealing with outsiders. This meant both offensive and defensive warfare and negotiations with other Navajo groups, other Indian tribes, and non-Indians. It was the leaders of such

left, Calif. Histl. Soc., Los Angeles: Title Insurance Coll. 1009; right, Amon Carter Mus., Ft. Worth, Tex.: Laura Gilpin Coll. 4250[1].

Fig. 8. Summer shelters. left, Lean-to shelter or shade (compare with Mindeleff 1898:pl. LXXVI), occupied by a family group (woman at right is grinding corn). Photograph possibly by G. Wharton James, location unidentified (©James and Pierce 1901). right, Windbreak or brush circle shade (compare with Kluckhohn, Hill, and Kluckhohn 1971:fig.109a), exploiting a natural formation of low cedar and juniper trees, with canvas hung over the sleeping area and loom (at right). The shelter is occupied by a group that includes 5 generations of women (Gilpin 1968:69–71). Photograph by Laura Gilpin, Navajo Mt. area (southeastern Utah), 1954. Like the more enclosed hogans, shades and shelters can be constructed using a variety of techniques and materials, including those used for hogans. They traditonally occur either as separate residences, or in combination with winter hogans or houses (either attached or in proximity). Modern housing also exhibits this versatility and variation (Tremblay, Collier, and Sasaki 1954).

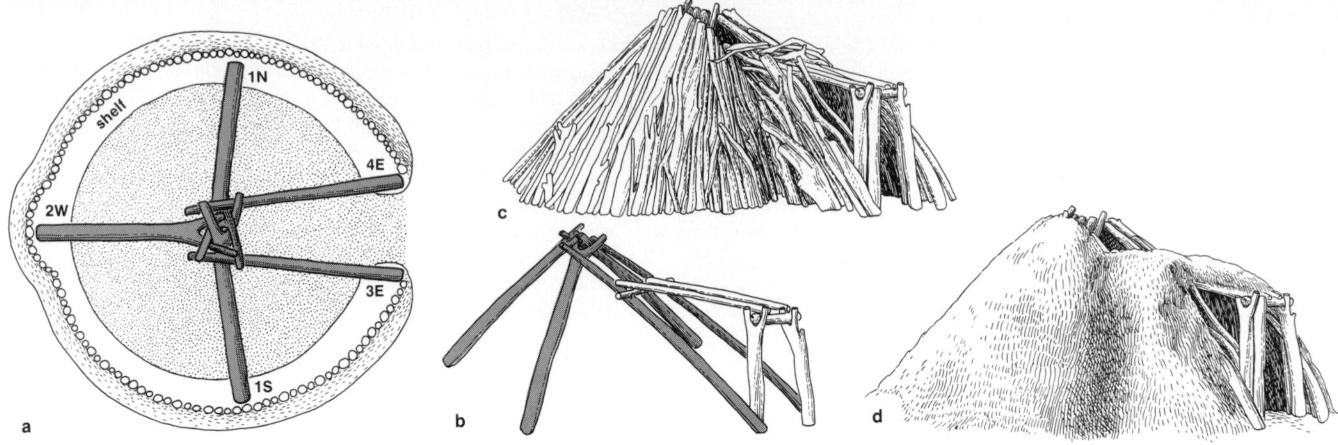

a,b, after diagrams and description Mindeleff 1898:489–493; c–d, after Kluckhohn, Hill, and Kluckhohn 1971:fig. 107c; d, Smithsonian, NAA.

Fig. 9. Traditional conical forked-pole hogan, *'ałch'į' 'adeez'á* ('(the supporting poles) extend toward one another') (Young and Morgan 1980:459; cf. Franciscan Fathers 1910:335; Mindeleff 1898:514), probably the oldest form of Navajo hogan. The framework (*sahdii*) consists of 3 forked interlocking poles (each named for a cardinal direction) with 2 straight poles defining the entrance; the straight poles collectively form the east timber or pole. (See Mindeleff 1898:489–493 and Franciscan Fathers 1910:330–332 for details of construction and Jett and Spencer 1981:22 for Navajo terms.) The skeleton is then filled in with shorter timbers, narrow strips of wood and cedar bark, and finally a thick coating of mud or earth. a, Diagram of the framework, showing 5 named timbers and the order in which they are erected; stipple indicates excavated areas. The periphery of the floor is left unexcavated, forming a storage shelf along the interior walls of the finished hogan. b, Perspective view of this same framework, to which timbers forming the extended doorway have been added. The space between the apex of the hogan and the horizontal timber placed across the east timbers becomes the smoke hole. c, Framework (in tone) to which smaller timbers have been added. d, Final chinking and coating. Conical hogans range in interior diameter from less than 12 to about 30 feet (3.66 to 9.14 m) averaging nearer the low end of the scale (Jett and Spencer 1981:62).

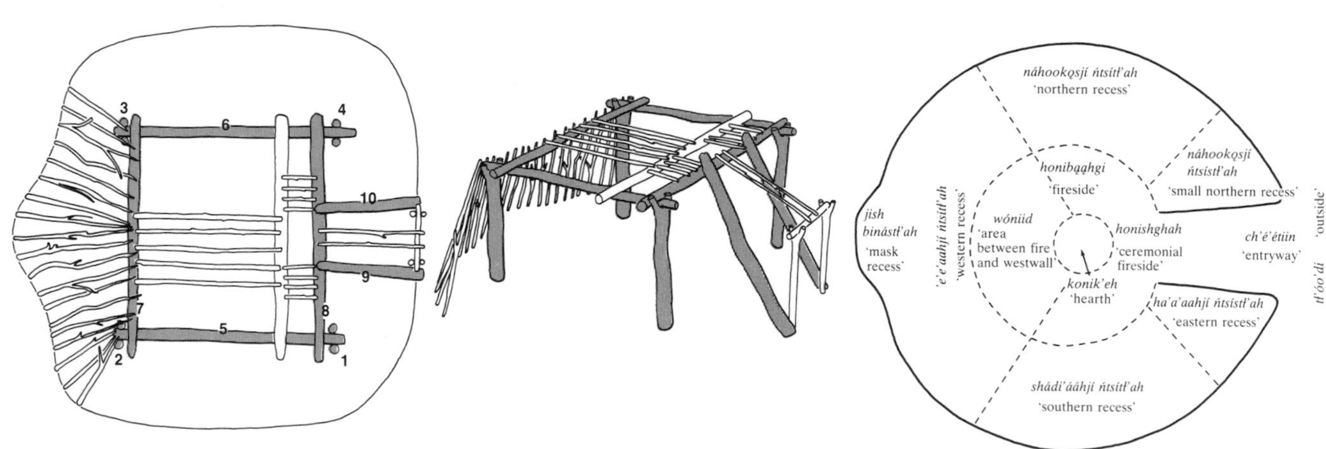

left and center, after Mindeleff 1898:figs. 241–243; right, after Mindeleff 1898:pl.XC; Jett and Spencer 1981: fig. 2.6; Young and Morgan 1980:746.

Fig. 10. left, *Hooghan bijáád hólóní* 'hogan with legs' with leaning log walls. Both this hogan and the conical forked-pole hogan are mentioned in legend and associated with ceremonial use; this type is more often associated with ceremonials such as the Nightway, which require considerable floorspace. left, Diagram of the *sahdii* (framework or skeleton) of the hogan, which consists of 10 timbers (theoretically erected in the order shown): 4 forked upright posts or 'legs' (named according to directional orientation), 4 beams, and 2 poles delineating the doorway. The structure is then completed with smaller timbers (some of which are shown), bark, and packed earth. A flat roof is typical on a 4-legged hogan. For those with more than 4 legs or supports, *hooghan bijáád łani* 'its legs are many', a domed (corbelled) roof is often used (Jett and Spencer 1981:74). center, Perspective drawing. right, Schematic diagram of a hogan, showing named divisions of interior and exterior space. The naming generally corresponds to the directional orientation of the hogan. The names for the eastern recess and the small northern recess relate to the 2 doorway poles, designated north and south timbers, that together form the east pole in the forked-pole hogan. There are further spatial divisions based on sexual and honorific criteria, according to Jett and Spencer (1981:22–23), who provide additional terms and analyses.

groups who negotiated and signed peace treaties, even though they could speak only for their own group.

It is not likely that the Navajo ever had any important central political organization before the development of the Navajo Tribal Council. There have been reports that the Navajo once had 12 peace chiefs and 12 war chiefs who met together annually in a *naachid* ceremony. The last such ceremony probably occurred around the middle of the nineteenth century, but very little is known about it or about the peace and war chiefs.

In the twentieth century local communities have developed around trading centers, schools, and missions. These have become formalized in more than 100 local chapters of the Tribal Council. These chapters have been organized into 18 districts, and the districts make up the tribe as a whole. A tribal council was organized in 1923 for the purpose of signing oil leases, and it has gradually grown in importance and acceptance as the valid central government of the Navajo Nation.

Sources of Flexibility

Published reports on Navajo social organization are often confusing and contradictory. There are several reasons for this. One is that the Navajo have been studied by a variety of people with different backgrounds and theoretical orientations. These people have also studied the Navajo in varying degrees of depth and have come to varying degrees of understanding and misunderstanding of Navajo social life. A second reason for contradictory or confusing reports is that the Navajo social system is flexible to the extent that it provides a number of alternatives according to which a person may make his choice. In addition, Navajos emphasize the freedom of the individual to pursue his own course. Within this flexibility and emphasis upon individual freedom, there is a strong orientation toward pragmatism.

Aberle (1963:7) has argued that flexibility in Navajo social organization is due to rapid change, resource instability, expanding population, and the conflict between acculturation and kinship organization in a tribal society. These factors combined with flexibility, individualism, and pragmatism are the principal ingredients that make a very complicated social system. Much of the confusion about Navajo social organization in published works is the result of the failure of observers to comprehend this social system. For example, there have been published reports on the Navajo emphasizing the communal and cooperative nature of Navajo social life (Witherspoon 1970; Aberle 1967a) and reports that emphasize the individualistic orientation of Navajo social life (Downs 1964; Shepardson and Hammond 1970). Actually both individualism and communalism operate in Navajo social organization, but they are more complementary than contradictory.

According to Navajo cultural concepts each being in the world has the right to live, to eat, and to act for itself. These rights to life and freedom extend to plants and animals, as well as to human beings. Only real and immediate human need justifies the killing of an animal or the cutting down of a tree. On such occasions a prayer should be said to the plant or animal explaining one's need and asking for the pardon and indulgence of the soul of the animal or plant. As Reichard (1950, 1:22, 144) observed: "The Navaho have a sentimental attitude toward plants, which they treat with incredible respect. . . . To pick them without taking them into ritual, to let them wither as cut flowers is quite out of order, even dangerous, there being no aesthetic compensation for the fear such sacrilege may engender."

Navajo attitudes toward the unnecessary taking of animal life are similar. For example, Navajo resentment of the stock reduction program has been attributed "in large part . . . to the government's allowing thousands of sheep to die in holding pens or en route to the railroads. Such behavior, perfectly understandable in white economic terms, was viewed as utter barbarism by the Navajo" (Downs 1964:92–93).

Navajos believe that each person has the right to speak for himself and to act as he pleases. This attitude is manifested in both dyadic and intragroup relations. The mutual rights and duties of kinsmen normally discussed under the concept of jural relations are best described as mutual expectations, rather than obligations. This distinction is a matter of emphasis and degree but is very real and worth noting. Desirable actions on the part of others are hoped for and even expected, but they are not required or demanded. Coercion is always deplored.

In intragroup relations no individual, regardless of position or status, has the right to impose his will or decision on the group. Likewise, the group does not have the right to impose its will on the individual. Unanimity is the only basis of collective action. Although a system of majority rule has been imposed on the Navajos since the 1920s, the extent to which the principle of unanimity continues to pervade almost all social and political deliberations is amazing.

Downs (1964) described this Navajo attitude as a belief in the "inviolability of the individual." The social implications of this belief are very important: "Despite close and absolutely essential familial ties, the Navajo remain highly individualistic people. Their primary social premise might be said to be that no person has the right to speak for or to direct the actions of another" (Downs 1964:69).

In searching for a key to the Navajo social system, Shepardson and Hammond came upon the phrase "It's up to him." They note that "just as this is a Navajo

bottom, Calif. Histl. Soc., Los Angeles: Title Insurance Coll.:4623.

Fig. 11. Sheepherding. top, Early morning view of a sheep corral, with nearby hogan. The hogan is of the hexagonal cribbed-log variety. See Jett and Spencer (1981) for details of corral and fence construction. Photograph by John Collier, Jr., near Wide Ruins, Ariz., 1950. bottom, Sheep herd at a watering hole, about 1900. Herding is accomplished on horseback or on foot. Goats are often included in a sheep herd, sometimes acting as leaders or sentinels (as is probably the case with the single goat included in this herd). Photograph (©C.C. Pierce and Co.) possibly by G. Wharton James.

left, Bureau of Ind. Affairs, Washington; right, Smithsonian, NAA:55440.

Fig. 12. Dipping and shearing of sheep. left, Sheep dipping, the procedure whereby sheep are partially cleaned and rid of ticks and other vermin, requires concerted communal effort. Individual herds enter a holding pen (shown here at far end) one by one to be examined and vaccinated; they are then driven through chutes to the dipping vat, and are finally placed in dripping vats to dry off. (See Downs 1964:43–46 for description and diagram of this operation.) Men, women, and often children work at prodding the sheep with long forked poles as they swim through the dipping vat. Photographer unknown, probably 1950s. right, Men shearing sheep with commercial clippers (one of which rests on fence at left). Shearing is generally accomplished by members of the nuclear rather than the extended family (Downs 1964:46) or by individual owners. Photograph taken 1961 or earlier by unidentified photographer.

informant's regular response to questions about expected behavior, so it is his view of society's patterned relations" (Shepardson and Hammond 1970:241). Although there are patterned expectations in social relations, these expectations are balanced by an emphasis upon individualism and pragmatism.

In the sheep herd operation (fig. 11) individualism is manifested in several ways. First, the sheep are individually owned and one's involvement in the communal herding is voluntary. He may separate his sheep from the others at any time, either for the purpose of selling them or for placing them in a separate or different herd. Second, he is not required to help with the care of the herd, although he is expected to do so whenever possible.

Communalism operates not only in the placing of individually owned sheep into a common herd but also in the sharing of the products of the herd. Food from the herd is shared among everyone in the residence group. Usually an informal rotation is followed in the periodic butchering of sheep. The permission of individual owners is not necessary to butcher their sheep if the meat is to be shared within the residence group. Wool from the herd is not sacked and sold individually. It is sold together and the proceeds are used by the head of the group to buy food and other things for the entire group. The head of the group may also buy individual things for people in the group but there is no clear attempt to distribute the proceeds either equally or proportionately to the size of each individual's number of sheep in the herd.

The sheep herd enterprise also provides an interesting convergence of the ethical concepts of egoism and altruism. In a study of the Navajo moral code, Ladd (1957:303–304), a philosopher, concluded:

> Western moralists have generally assumed that egoism and altruism are incompatible; and therefore, that one of them must be rejected. . . .
>
> According to the Navaho ethical system which I have outlined, it is impossible to be a good egoist without at the same time being a good altruist. Although all the moral prescriptions listed are ultimately based upon an egoistic premise, in content they are altruistic. . . .
>
> The basic factual belief which unites egoistic premises with altruistic conclusions is that the welfare of each individual is dependent upon that of every other individual in the group. What is good for the individual is good for everyone else, and what is good for everybody is good for the individual.

The particular social group in which the concepts of egoism and individualism converge with the concepts of altruism and communalism is the residence group. This convergence occurs most forcefully and profoundly in the operation of the sheep herd. The welfare of one's own sheep is intrinsically related to the welfare of the entire herd. In providing good care for his own sheep, the individual is providing good care for everybody else's sheep and vice versa. The inviolability and inviability of the individual and his sheep are both asserted and demonstrated through putting one's own sheep in the common herd, and the common herd beautifully symbolizes both the individualism and the communalism of the residence group.

The sheep herd provides the major insurance of the group against hunger and starvation. Because food is shared among all members of the group, the increase or decrease of an individual's sheep increases or decreases the food supply for everyone. Thus doing good for oneself is inseparably related to doing good for others. Ladd (1957:224, 253) found this thinking to be basic in Navajo economic theory, which

> assumes that there is a potential abundance of goods, and that through cooperation the amount of goods will be increased for everyone; in other words, they would deny the basic assumption upon which much of our own economic theory depends, namely, the scarcity of goods. . . .
>
> No man is thought to be in competition with his fellow. Rather, it is assumed that a neighbor's success will contribute to one's own welfare.

By putting his sheep in the common herd, the interests of the individual become voluntarily attached to the interests of others in the group. By maintaining individual ownership while at the same time making the sheep herd a communal enterprise, Navajos are able to successfully merge the concepts of individualism and egoism with those of communalism and altruism.

Navajo Ceremonial System

LELAND C. WYMAN

There is no word or phrase in the Navajo language that can be translated as 'religion' in the sense of that term in European languages. However, this word is the most convenient label for Navajo beliefs concerning the dynamics of the universe and their techniques for controlling them when rational means fail, and for their belief in what may be called the "supernatural," although Navajos do not place such matters in a separate category of experience. It is a tribute to what has been called the Navajos' "genius for adaptability" that they have been able to preserve practically intact their traditional cultural inventory of these beliefs and practices in the face of long and vigorous pressure from European culture and the enormous number of acculturative changes in the last few decades. Their religion, or ceremonial system to use a more accurate term, was adhered to by the majority of Navajos in 1972.

When the Peyote religion of the Native American Church first appeared among the Navajo it was opposed by many medicine men (although Peyotists were never antagonistic to traditional Navajo religion), and until the 1960s it seemed to some observers that its influence might cause a decline in the traditional ceremonial system. However, this did not happen. By the 1970s the Native American Church was seen by most Navajo people as simply another chantway, *'azee'jí* or Medicine Way. Members of the NAC were active in traditional ceremonialism, and a good number of traditional Navajo medicine men had also become Roadmen in the Native American Church (Gary Witherspoon, communication to editors 1974).

A survey conducted by Chi'ao (1971:91–94) in 1965 among 284 Navajo students in Bureau of Indian Affairs schools found that although the majority of Navajo young people believed that sickness and misfortune were caused by supernatural agencies and would like to learn more about their ceremonialism, few were inclined to study to become practitioners of it. Much of the reason for this is the long time required for learning and participating in ceremonials; therefore, Chi'ao suggested that one solution to the problem of lagging recruitment of practitioners is to shorten and simplify the ceremonials and to use some learning aids such as taking notes of ceremonial songs or using tape recorders.

Ceremonialism is the system the Navajos have developed to cope with the uncertainties and dangers of their universe. They regard the universe as an orderly, all-inclusive, unitary system of interrelated elements. The tiniest object, being, or power, even minute insects; the most stupendous, the great mountains that bound the Navajo country and the thunder and lightning that crash above them; and man himself—all have their place and significant function in the universal continuum. Being all-inclusive, the universe contains evil as well as good, not as abstract ethical concepts but as complementary components of it—the controlled, harmonious, orderly, and the uncontrolled, unharmonious, disorderly portions of every unit or complex in it. Every human being, no matter how good in life, has an evil component that becomes a dangerous ghost after death, which may harm the living if not controlled. Evil and danger come from disturbance of the normal order, harmony, or balance among the elements of the universe and absence of control, which depends upon knowledge (Reichard 1950, 1:5–7). There are numerous things or powers in the universe that are indifferent or good when under control and in harmony with man but that may be potentially evil when uncontrolled. Some, such as ghosts of the dead or certain animals like snakes, coyote, or bear, or natural phenomena such as lightning or whirlwinds, have greater potentiality for evil than others, but they may be controlled and even made to help in restoring the normal order of things upon the application of sufficient knowledge. Other elements are predominantly good unless related to excessive activity. Improper contact with inherently dangerous powers (even if indirect, unintentional, or unconscious), the breaching of traditional restrictions on human behavior in relation to the supernatural (taboos), or excesses in gambling, sexual activity, or even harmless pursuits such as weaving, may lead to disturbance of the normal harmony or balance among elements in the universe and to the price man pays for it usually manifested as illness. Moreover, such improper behavior on the part of a parent of an unborn child, especially the mother, may affect the child by causing it to suffer sickness later in its life. That is why women are barred from witnessing or participating in certain aspects of ceremonial procedure, such as the making of drypaintings. Such a theory of evil is based on contagion rather than sin. Murder is potentially dangerous not because of the deed itself but because of contact with the dead. Excesses are not considered sins but are thought of as symptoms of disease amenable to ritual cure. The principle of reciprocity governs human relations with the many elements in the universe, including other humans. Thus injury for injury, sickness for misbehavior, and favor for favor to set things right are the circumstances to be expected in this dangerous world.

The Ceremonial System

The knowledge and correct performance of traditional orderly procedures, that is, ritual, are the means for bringing the dangerous under control, exorcising ghosts, restoring harmony in the relations of an individual or a group with the world, and rendering a sick person immune to renewed contamination by the same supernatural factors. Various procedures sometimes called "white magic" are employed in this ritual—compulsion by repetition, the principle of like cures like, identification of participants with supernatural beings. Ceremonials governed by this ritual are permeated with colorful symbolism expressed in the word imagery of songs, prayers, and myths; in the sound of the music accompanying them; in the behavior of participants; in material paraphernalia and drypaintings with their symbols of color, sex, and direction.

The Holy People, supernatural beings attracted to the ceremonial by invocatory prayers and offerings, judge the correctness and completeness of the performance and if satisfied they are compelled by the ethic of reciprocity to come and "set things right"—to cure the patient, to restore universal harmony. Prayers and offerings in Navajo ceremonials are not for the purpose of glorifying or thanking the holy ones but are invocatory and compulsive, to attract and obligate them.

Although the chief aim of Navajo ceremonialism stated philosophically is the restoration of universal harmony once it has been disturbed, the practical-minded Navajo if questioned would say that ceremonials are carried out, first, to restore and maintain health; second, to obtain increase of wealth, the well-being of home, flocks, and fields, the security of himself and his relatives; and perhaps third, to acquire certain ceremonial property, such as the white shell or turquoise bead token to wear as protection from lightning and snakes. Unspoken benefits would be the prestige value of giving costly ceremonials and the opportunity for social gatherings. A Navajo might sum it all up in a single Navajo word, *hózhǫ́*, a term that has no single equivalent in English. This term, often translated as 'it is pleasant, beautiful, or blessed', covers everything that a Navajo thinks is good or favorable to man, as opposed to that which is evil, unfavorable, or doubtful. It expresses for the Navajo what the words beauty, perfection, harmony, goodness, normality, success, well-being, blessedness, order, and ideal do for English speakers. It is the central idea in Navajo religious thinking and their basic value concept (see Reichard 1944:32–33, 1950, 1:318; Wyman 1950:346, 1957:15, 1959:16, 1970a:7–8). Adding the enclitic *-jí* 'in the direction of, side, manner, way' results in the name of a rite designed to bring about the conditions expressed by the word *hózhǫ́ǫ́jí*, which is translated as 'Blessingway'.

The majority of Navajo ceremonials are primarily for curing disease, actual or anticipated; thus every performance is given for an individual patient, with occasionally one or two copatients, relatives or children of the patient, who is called 'the one sung over'. Even in a Blessingway rite that is not specifically concerned with curing but is performed for other purposes there is usually one sung over or a 'patient'. No doubt the Navajo's predisposition to worry over health (it is his "type worry"), exacerbated by the prevalence of actual disease, caused him to combine his religious and medical practices. Thus his ceremonialism differs markedly from that of his neighbors, the Pueblo Indians of Arizona and New Mexico, whose ceremonials thoroughly integrated with their social organization are primarily for bringing rain and fertility with curing only secondary. Moreover, Pueblo ceremonials are conducted by organized priesthoods, religious societies, or other groups, and are carried out in an annual round according to a set religious calendar. Their focus is the common good and the individual is subordinated. The Navajo have no organized priesthoods or religious societies, but their ceremonials are conducted by trained specialists called *hataałii* 'singers' (figs. 1–2), because the singing that accompanies every important act in the ritual is held to be the one essential element of the ceremonial. In fact the name for a performance of one of the largest group of ceremonials, the chantways, is *hatáál* 'sing' or 'singing'. Moreover, Navajo ceremonialism touches their social organization in only a few rather minor ways, and it is not integrated with any sort of calendar, except for a few seasonal restrictions; rather, ceremonials are held whenever they are needed. Thus Navajo practice is more individualistic than that of the Pueblo, although along with the cure of an individual patient there may come blessings that extend to the family, the local community, even to the whole tribe, such as rain in time of drought. According to Reichard (1945:206), "between the Pueblo and Navaho there is no difference of purpose, but only a difference of emphasis," and "they differ in their interpretation of what well-being consists of and how it is to be achieved."

Curing ceremonials often do cure the patient, especially when the ailment being treated is largely of psychosomatic origin. A few of the procedures in Navajo ceremonials may have actual organic effects, but above

Leland C. Wyman, Sonderborg, Denmark.
Fig. 1. Ceremonial singers Hastin Gani (left), of Beautiful Valley, Ariz., and Red Moustache of Kinlichee, Ariz. Both hold rawhide rattles, traditionally used in chantways. Baskets in foreground hold some of their ceremonial equipment, such as the otter fur collar (to be used by either singer or patient in chantways, such as the Shootingway). Hastin Gani, whose specialty was the Beauty Chant (Reichard 1950:xvi), died in 1948 or 1949. Photograph by Gladys A. Reichard (whom Red Moustache had instructed in the Big Star and Endurance Chants) (Reichard 1950), 1930s or 1940s.

Leland C. Wyman, Sonderborg, Denmark.
Fig. 2. Frank Mitchell of Chinle, Ariz., a noted Blessingway singer, with his mountain soil bundle (upright in basket). It consists of 4 small packages each containing earth from one of the sacred mountains, placed around a mirage stone and a perfect white shell, which "resembles Mother Earth" and into which valued substances such as corn pollen have been placed, all wrapped in buckskin from an "unwounded" (ritually suffocated) deer (Mitchell 1978:203–204). Photograph by Charlotte Johnson Frisbie, at Chinle, May 1965.

all the ceremonials constitute a powerful system of suggestive psychotherapy, which relieves psychosomatic ills and enables the patient to bear organic troubles with more fortitude. The prestige and authority of the singer, the mysticism of the performance itself, the rallying of relatives and friends to aid in his cure—all contribute to his feeling of well-being. Moreover, the psychotherapy extends to all the spectators, while the ceremonial reaffirms the basic tenets of their faith and, by providing a fixed point in an existence of bewildering change, gives them comfort, societal security, and something to hold to in an unstable world (Kluckhohn 1942).

Singers learn ceremonials by studying with older experts often for long periods of time. The apprentice ratifies his knowledge by payment to his teacher. A singer specializes in one or two or at most a half-dozen complete chants, because each one is a vast complex requiring accurate knowledge of hundreds of songs, long prayers, plant medicines, material properties, symbolic drypaintings, and ritual acts. Some singers have claimed to know as many as eight ceremonials, but some of these were doubtless brief procedures. Besides his specialties a singer may know how to perform portions of several others. Women seldom become singers, probably because of fear of prenatal contagion, for there is no rule against it and there have been a few highly respected female practitioners.

Sometimes certain individuals, not always or even often singers, are accused or suspected of malevolently misusing certain types of ritual knowledge to harm others, that is, of practicing witchcraft. Troubles thought to have been caused by witches are especially difficult to deal with, sometimes being refractory to ceremonial treatment and requiring special techniques such as the sucking cure (see Haile 1950). Therefore, the witch is hated and feared, and this fear persists even among Navajos who have ceased to believe in the efficacy of the ceremonials (Kluckhohn 1944:33). Chi'ao (1971:91) in his study of Navajo students found that the majority of them feared witches and the older they were the greater their fear.

The Holy People

Each ceremonial has special relations with certain groups of supernatural beings, but of course there is considerable overlapping. The Navajo universe contains innumerable personalized powers, most of them believed to be beings something like humans, or capable of assuming human form at will if they are animals or plants. Mountains, the cardinal points, and other natural phenomena have anthropomorphic inner forms (Wyman 1970a:24–26). This concept applied to man himself is perhaps the closest Navajo parallel to the idea of a soul (Haile 1943a). Even material objects such as arrows may be endowed with power and conceived of as "people." Thus there are Snake, Bear, Porcupine, Deer, Ant, Cactus, and Corn People; Thunders; Winds; mythological creatures such as Big Snake (*Tł'iistsoh*), Endless Snake (*Tł'iish doo ninít'i'í*), Water Monster (*Tééhooltsódii*);* and a host of others. Navajos say that the animals and plants "used to be people." Nearly every element in the universe may be thus personalized, and even the least of these such as tiny Chipmunk and those little insect helpers and mentors of deity and man in the myths, Big Fly (*Dǫ'tsoh*) and Ripener (Corn Beetle) Girl (*'Anílt'ánii 'At'ééd*) (Wyman and Bailey 1964:29–30, 51, 137–144), are as necessary for the harmonious balance of the universe as is the great Sun. They vary, of course, with respect to properties and powers, but each being "has charge of" a given group of things and all are interdependent, complementary parts of the whole. However, there is no evidence that they form a well-ordered hierarchy, although Reichard (1950, 1:4, 5, 52, 75–76) suggested that a Sun cult is outstanding. Factors that complicate an analysis of the Navajo pantheon are the equivalence of beings appearing under different names or as various actors in the myths, the multiplication of deities in time and space, the duplication of functions among different deities, and the immanence of supernatural power. Changing Woman (*'Asdzą́ą́ Nádleehé*), who is intimately concerned with the myth and practice of the Blessingway rite, is certainly the most beloved deity. Her twin children, Monster Slayer (*Naayéé' Neizghání*) and Born for Water (*Tó Bájíshchíní*) (fig. 3), sired by the Sun, slew the monsters that were threatening mankind and thus represent war power. She, the Slayer Twins, and the Sun form a sort of "holy family," prominent in myth and ritual. Immediately after the Emergence of the Holy People from the underworlds a "first family"—First Man (*'Áłtsé Hastiin*), First Woman (*'Áłtsé 'Asdzáán*), First Boy (*'Áłtsé 'Ashkii*), and First Girl (*'Áłtsé 'At'ééd*)—and their companions, Coyote (*'Áłtsé 'Ashké* 'First Scolder'), the exponent of trickery, and *Begochídí* were prominent in early events on the earth while it was being made inhabitable for mankind. Members of a group of Holy People known as the Yeis (*Yé'ii*, sg. and pl.), led by Talking God (*Haashch'ééłti'í*) (fig. 4), are impersonated by masked dancers in the public performances of a few ceremonials such as the Night Chant and the Mountain Chant.

The Navajo name for supernatural beings, the Holy People (*Diyin Dine'é*), does not imply that they are virtuously holy but that they are powerful and therefore dangerous. It is man's responsibility to maintain harmonious relations between himself and the Holy People, or at least to avoid them, lest he become injured or ill from their power. Thus an attack from the Holy People is not necessarily because they are inimical to man but because man himself has been the transgressor, whereas an attack by a ghost or a witch may be unprovoked, although a ghost is usually provoked into returning by an improper burial or disturbance of the grave. The Holy People for the most part are indifferent to man but may be persuaded or coerced into aiding in the restoration of a person who has become ill through contact with them.

Rite, Chant, and Ritual

In discussing the terms the Navajo use for their ceremonials, Haile (1938a:639, 1938:10) revealed a grand dichotomy of the entire ceremonial system. He claimed that they employ the term *hatáál*, rendered 'chant', only for ceremonials in which the singing is accompanied by a rattle (there are a few exceptions to this rule) and, lacking a single Navajo equivalent, suggested that all other ceremonials be called "rites." The Navajo do set two of their major song ceremonial complexes, the Blessingway (*Hózhǫ́ǫ́jí*) and the Enemyway (*'Anaa'jí*) rites, quite apart from the chantways (the suffix '-way' is a translation of the enclitics *-jí* and *-(y)ee* used to form the Navajo names for ceremonials). However, these two should have little or nothing to do with each other. Blessingway is concerned with peace, harmony, and good things exclusively, while Enemyway, a rite designed to exorcise the ghosts of aliens, makes much of war, violence, and ugliness; in fact it belongs in a native category of ceremonials usually translated as Evilway (*Hóchxǫ́'íjí*).

The Blessingway rites, of which there are some five kinds that differ only slightly from each other, are used for a multitude of reasons; in general they are not for curing but "for good hope," for good luck, to avert misfortune, to invoke positive blessings that man needs for a long and happy life and for the protection and increase of his possessions. Thus they are used to protect livestock, aid childbirth, bless a new hogan, consecrate ceremonial paraphernalia, install a tribal officer,

*The Navajo names of supernatural beings and ceremonies cited in this chapter, as well as a few technical terms of ritual, have been added by the editors, chiefly on the basis of Young and Morgan (1980). In the names of the "first family" the element meaning 'first', here given as *'áłtsé*, is also found as *'átsé*, a form common in some earlier sources and preferred by some speakers. There is wide disagreement on the preferred shape of the name *Begochídí*, also given as *Bégóchidí*, *Beego'chídí*, and *Be'gochídí*.

top, William R. Heick Photography, Mill Valley, Calif.; Mus. of the Amer. Ind., Heye Foundation, New York; a, 22/9162; b, 22/9164; c, 22/9167.

Fig. 3. Yeibichai masks. top, Consultation over a mask being repainted for use in a Nightway. The mask is that of one of the Slayer Twins, Born for Water (*Tó Bájíschíní*), which is painted red, except for a triangular white-bordered black section at the middle (into which the eye-holes and mouth have been cut) and a series of white queue symbols (see Matthews 1902:22–24). These symbols, said to represent the scalps of enemies taken in war, also appear on the rattle stick used in the Enemyway and as representations of scalps also refer to the traditional Navajo way of wearing the hair. This 9-day Nightway was filmed and recorded by the Amer. Ind. Films Group; unedited footage and tapes are in the Lowie Mus., Amer. Ind. Films Coll., Berkeley, Calif. Photograph by William R. Heick, Dec. 1963. bottom, Masks worn for ceremonies such as the Night Chant, which required up to 24 masked dancers (Matthews 1902). The buckskin masks are decorated to represent specific gods. a, Male God, *Haashch' ééh Bika'*, has a mouth made from a gourd surrounded by kit fox hair. b, Female God, *Haashch' ééh Ba'áád*, is characterized by the ear flaps with notched edges on either side of the face. Men do dress as females, but especially in public exhibitions women will serve as Female God impersonators. c, The mask of Born for Water's brother, Monster Slayer, *Naayéé' Neizghání*, with olivella shells attached to the eye and mouth openings. For more detailed description of masks and their trimmings when worn see Haile (1947a). Traditionally masks were to be made only of unwounded buckskin but imitations were made for other than ceremonial purposes (Franciscan Fathers 1910:393). c, Length about 38.1 cm, rest to same scale. All collected by Stewart Culin, Cottonwood Pass, Ariz., 1903.

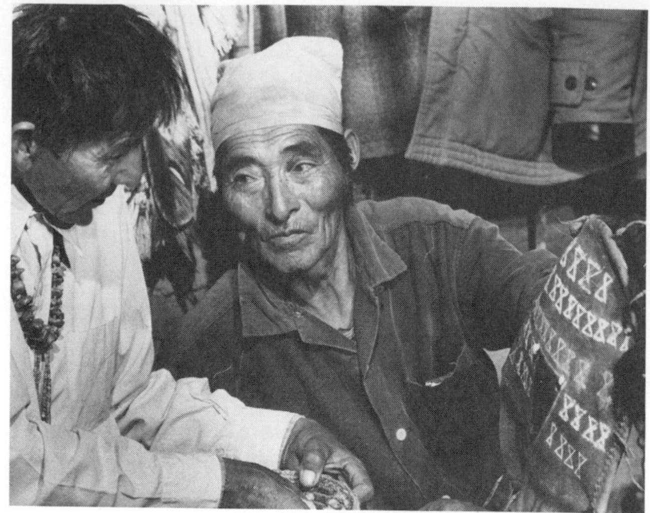

protect a departing or returning soldier, strengthen a neophyte singer, and consecrate a marriage (Wyman 1970a:3–9). The *kinaaldá*, the girl's adolescence rite, is a Blessingway rite (fig. 5) (Frisbie 1967), as is the rain ceremony, the obsolete salt-gathering rites, and probably the obsolescent hunting rites (Gameway, *Dini'ee*). The Navajos regard Blessingway as the backbone of their religion and give it historical precedence over all other ceremonials. Although set apart from the chantways it is said to control all of them. Every chant, and even the Enemyway rite, includes a Blessingway song near the end to correct possible errors and insure the effectiveness of the performance.

Although not for curing, a person who is sung over represents the group to be benefited. The rite is comparatively short and simple lasting only two nights, from sundown of one day to dawn of the second day after that. (Navajos reckon time by nights, that is, from sundown to sundown, instead of by days.) After consecration of the hogan with cornmeal, there are a few prayers and songs and perhaps a long litany while the one sung over holds the mountain soil bundle in front of his chest on the first evening. The next day there is a ritual bath in the forenoon, sometimes drypaintings made of variously colored cornmeal, pulverized flower petals, and pollens strewn on a buckskin or a cloth substitute spread on the ground, with more songs and prayers. The final night is taken up with all-night singing, and the ceremonial closes with the dawn procedures (Wyman 1970a:104–106). The only essential piece of equipment for performing a Blessingway rite is the mountain soil bundle, a buckskin bundle containing little buckskin packages of pinches of soil from the summits of the sacred mountains and certain stone objects. Also one or more pairs of talking prayersticks are in most if not all Blessingway singers' pouches. These are usually made of two cylinders of aragonite (mirage stone) tied

Smithsonian, NAA.

Fig. 4. Talking God (*Haashch'ééłti'í*) at left, with the Gray God (*Haashch'ééłbáhí*), center, and Female God (*Haashch'ééh Ba'áád*). These three yei impersonators are among those known as begging gods or food soliciters, who are sent out to solicit gifts of food, tobacco, or other items, on the sixth or subsequent days of a Night Chant (Matthews 1902:126–127). Talking God's whitened buckskin mask, which includes outlined circular holes for eyes and mouth, a distinctive band of yellow at the base, and a representation of a double-eared stalk of corn in the center, is worn with a fringe of hair, a spruce collar, and a fan-like head ornament of eagle plumes (Matthews 1902:9–10). The impersonator is draped in a buckskin and carries a deerskin pouch filled with pollen. Talking God, the leader of the yeis, appears elsewhere in the Night Chant and in other chantways. Photograph by Simeon Schwemberger, about 1905.

together (Wyman 1970a:16–24, 27). Small sacks of pollen are also present.

No herb medicines are administered in Blessingway rites, but pollen is eaten along with prayer, and the rite makes much of this substance. Usually it is corn pollen shaken from the tassel but the pollen of certain wild plants, such as cattail flag, may be used. Pollen is personified as Corn Pollen Boy (*Tádídíín 'Ashkii*) and his companion, Corn Beetle Girl, symbols of fertility, happiness, and life itself (Wyman and Bailey 1964:29, 131–132, 142–144; Wyman 1970a:30–32). Pollen is applied to everything for consecration and sanctification—patient, hogan, paraphernalia, drypaintings, spectators. Pollen prayer consists of taking a pinch from a sack, putting some in the mouth and on the top of the head, and sprinkling the remainder or a fresh pinch upward while muttering a brief prayer. Ceremonies are often closed with communal pollen prayer in which a sack of pollen is passed to all the spectators, beginning south of the door of the hogan and so on to south, west, and north (sunwise), each one partaking as above.

The Enemyway rite, one of the mostly obsolescent group of ancient war ceremonials (Wyman and Kluckhohn 1938:7, 33), which was used to protect warriors from the ghosts of slain enemies, has been preserved and no doubt elaborated as a cure for sickness thought to be caused by ghosts of non-Navajos. It is now classed with the other Ghostway (Evilway) ceremonials. It differs from other song ceremonials in that it lasts three or five nights, portions of it are conducted in different places, it is not in charge of a single singer but has more than one leader, and it is not restricted to four repetitions (see Haile 1938).

The chantways used for curing or preventing illness

William R. Heick Photography, Mill Valley, Calif.

Fig. 5. Marie Shirley during the fourth night of her second *kinaaldá* at which her grandfather, Frank Mitchell, officiated (see Frisbie 1967:29–66). The silver and turquoise bracelets (4 on the right arm, 3 on the left), turquoise necklaces, ceremonial sash, and concho belt (belonging to Mitchell), were taken from a ceremonial basket during successive days of the *kinaaldá* as part of the ritual dressing. Other ceremonies in the *kinaaldá* include ritual hair combing and tying, molding (which involves symbolically pressing the girl's body into a woman's shape), the running of races, ritual corngrinding, and various blessings (see Frisbie 1967:71–88). Photograph by William R. Heick (in connection with filming by the Amer. Ind. Films Group), at Chinle, Ariz., June 1963.

are by far the largest group of song ceremonials. Formerly there were some 24 chantway systems, but only about eight were well known and frequently performed in the 1970s. At least six are extinct (Hailway, Mothway, Dogway, Ravenway, Awlway, Earthway), and three or four are obsolescent if not extinct (Waterway, Excessway, Coyoteway, Big Godway). Navajos may differentiate chants according to the ritual governing them, male and female branches (a distinction probably depending on the sex of the protagonist of the myth and marked by comparatively slight differences in procedure), and a few other considerations, so that from 40 to 50 names for song ceremonials are used by them.

A chantway is dominated by one of three rituals or patterns of behavior governing procedure: Holyway, Evilway, and Lifeway. Most chantways are performed according to Holyway ritual, theoretically directed by the Holy People, and are concerned with the attraction of good and the restoration of the patient. This in turn is subject to one of two subrituals, Peacefulway characterized by a preponderance of procedures to attract good and summon the Holy People, and Injuryway (Angryway, Fightingway, Weaponway), which has exorcistic emphasis. Any Holyway ceremonial is to be regarded as Peacefulway unless the contrary is stated. Injuryway is employed when the patient has been or is thought to have been subjected to direct attack by the etiological factors involved, struck by lightning, bitten by a snake, mauled by a bear, and so on. Such ceremonials are called red-inside because the red parts of red and blue elements in sandpaintings and on praysticks are placed opposite to their normal outside positions.

Evilway (Ghostway; literally Uglyway, see Haile 1938a:650) ritual is characterized by techniques for exorcising native ghosts and chasing away evil influences, such as big hoop ceremonies (fig. 6); garment or cincture ceremonies (fig. 7); overshooting; blackening the patient; and lightning-herb, ash-blowing, and brushing procedures (Wyman 1965:31–42, 58–62). Evilway chants are used to treat disease traced to contact with Navajo ghosts and to combat the effects of witchcraft. The Enemyway rite for dealing with alien ghost sickness is associated with them. In 1972, Shootingway, Red Antway, Big Starway, and Hand-Tremblingway were known to be performed according to this ritual, and there was an exclusively and probably fundamental Evilway ceremonial called Upward-reachingway (Wyman and Bailey 1943). In fact, Big Starway is usually, if not always, an Evilway chant, and Hand-Trembling Evilway is more common than the Holyway form. Symptoms of ghost sickness or bewitchment may be bad dreams, insomnia, fainting, nervousness, mental disturbances, feelings of suffocation, loss of appetite, loss of weight, or other alarming disturbances. Sinister unknown influences, perhaps never to be known, may be removed by Evilway ritual.

Finally, Shootingway, and formerly Hand-Tremblingway, may be conducted according to Lifeway ritual, which is specific for treating injuries resulting from accidents. Besides, there is a fundamental Lifeway chant called Flintway. Such chants are simpler than the others, lasting only two nights although their duration may not be fixed, a ceremonial being continued as long as needed. The distinctive feature of Lifeway ritual is painting the patient red, the color of flesh and blood, symbolizing return to life and health (Haile 1943; Wyman and Bailey 1945).

It may never be known if all the chantways were once conducted according to all three rituals. In the 1970s Shootingway was the only one that employed all three, the choice depending on the purpose involved. There

Wheelwright Mus., Santa Fe., N. Mex.: 60/1370–1399.

Fig. 6. Big Hoop ceremony, one of the exorcising techniques used in Evilway ritual. The patient, a young boy, is under the white cloth (replacing the buckskin representing Coyote's hide that is normally worn and shed during this ceremony). Painted hoops (in red, blue, yellow, and black) are being held by 4 men as the patient's grandmother (left, obscuring the view of the fourth man) assists the patient through the hoops and into the ceremonial hogan. See Wyman (1965:31, 46–47, 58–59) for description of ceremony, shown here on the fifth morning of a Red Antway Holyway. Photograph by Kenneth Foster, Valley Store, Ariz., June 17, 1963.

Wheelwright Mus., Santa Fe, N. Mex.: 60/1370–1399.

Fig. 7. Patient wrapped in garment of Douglas fir for the garment ceremony of a Nightway. The patient is divested of her evergreen garment by impersonators of the Slayer Twins. As described by Matthews (1902:82–85), the garment ceremony occurred on the evening of the second day of the Nightway, and the patient normally wears a yucca mask (differentiated according to whether the patient is male or female). Photograph by Kenneth E. Foster, Totso Trading Post (Lukachukai, Ariz.), 1963.

is some evidence that certain rituals for some chants are only recently extinct. Actually all Holyway chants contain both invocatory and exorcistic elements. Nearly all Holyway chants have or had two-night and five-night forms, and some, perhaps most of them, had nine-night forms. Several still do, and they are achieved by spacing the components (ceremonies) found in the five-night form over a longer period rather than by adding new procedures. Since two of the three principal ceremonies of the first four days of a nine-night performance, unraveling and the sweat-emetic, have an exorcistic flavor, while only one, the offering ceremony, is invocatory, and since all the main ceremonies of the last five days are invocatory, it may be that the first part was derived from an earlier, mainly exorcistic pattern of ritual behavior and that the second part was attached to it later. Perhaps the elements of the first part were brought along by the early Athapaskans in their southward migrations and the second was derived from the drypainting practices of the Pueblo Indians after the arrival of the Athapaskans in the Southwest. Whether these two parts were first fitted together into a five-night ceremonial that was later expanded into a nine-night form or condensed into a two-night form, or whether they were first attached to each other linearly in a nine-night form that was condensed later is a moot point. Evilway ritual, then, may have come about by the elaboration of the first, predominantly exorcistic portion. There are, of course, still other possible explanations (Wyman and Kluckhohn 1938:10; Kluckhohn and Wyman 1940:106; Wyman and Bailey 1943:45; Wyman 1957:12).

The Holyway Chantways

The Navajo think of certain ceremonials as "going together" or as partner chants, making such associations because of interrelations in the origin myths of the chants, efficacy against the same etiological factors, procedures peculiar to the group, and so on. Although all Navajos in all regions do not group the ceremonials in exactly the same way, there is enough uniformity in the statements of informants to derive therefrom a native classification that is generally valid for most members of the tribe (Wyman and Kluckhohn 1938:5–7; Reichard 1950, 1:322–323; Kluckhohn 1960:69–70). Thus the Holyway chant complexes may be placed in seven subgroups (table 1). Only six of the chantways were performed frequently in 1972—Shootingway, Mountainway, Nightway, Navajo and Chiricahua Windways, and Hand-Tremblingway. Red Antway, Big Starway (Evilway ritual), Beautyway, and Plumeway are known and may be performed as complete chants but much less often than the other six, and Eagleway and Beadway are very uncommon, perhaps obsolescent. Singers sometimes know a few songs but not the entire repertory from the obsolescent or extinct ones.

Excerpts or a single or a few procedures from a chantway lasting only a portion of a day or night may be carried out, often as a test performance, and if the patient seems to be benefited the whole ceremonial may be given for him. Theoretically a chant that has cured a person should be given for him a total of four times, usually in alternate five-night and two-night forms. However, repetition of performances may be strung over a period of many years or may be dispensed with entirely.

Each chant is concerned with particular factors that are thought to cause the disease or diseases for which it is believed to be an efficacious cure. In fact the ceremonial is directed toward appeasing or exorcising such factors rather than toward treating the physical symptoms of the illness itself. There are a multitude of things with which improper contact is believed to cause sickness (fig. 8). Among them are numerous animals with snakes, bear, porcupine, weasel, deer, coyote, eagle, and ants figuring prominently; cactus plants; natural phenomena with lightning (Thunder) and winds predominating; ceremonials themselves or actually the Holy People associated with them who may be present while the performance is in progress; and ghosts of dead people, both Navajo and alien, against which Evilway ritual is employed. Besides, the machinations of witches, incest, and excessive activity of any kind may cause illness. Improper contact may occur while hunting, trapping, killing, eating, mishandling, or being injured by an animal, using things it has been in contact with, such as firewood, stones, and the like; burning cactus for firewood, especially for cooking; being struck by whirlwinds or by lightning, or seeing or eating animals killed by it, or having anything to do with objects affected by it; mistakes or neglect in ceremonial procedure, or transgressions of ceremonial restrictions; improper burial of the dead, using their possessions, or any sort of contact with them or their belongings; or even dreaming of any of these things.

The association of these etiological factors with specific diseases or disease categories is extremely loose. In fact almost any human ailment may be attributed to any one of them, although certain ones are thought to be more likely to cause certain symptoms than others. When an illness has been traced to a certain factor or group of factors the chant most closely associated with them, through its origin myth or its symbolism, is indicated as a cure.

In the Shooting Chant subgroup the recently extinct Hailway and the obsolescent Waterway (Haile 1979) were used for persons injured by water, frost, or snow and hail; for resuscitation from drowning; for frostbite; and for lameness or muscle soreness. The Shootingways, which have more ramifications in regard to rituals, subrituals, phases, branches, and etiological fac-

Leland C. Wyman, Sonderborg, Denmark.

Fig. 8. Red Ant Holyway (Peacefulway subritual), held for a patient who had improper contact with ants. On the eighth and last afternoon of this ceremony, conducted by singer *Deeshchii'nii ni' Nééz Biye'* 'Son of the late Tall Red Streak Clansman', a sandpainting representing Blue Corn People was made, and various procedures, including those shown here, followed (see Wyman 1965:48–49). left, Patient being painted by an assistant who has just applied a yellow Thunder design to his back. Part of the sandpainting, which has been sprinkled with cornmeal, is visible in left foreground. right, Patient, fully painted (principally with designs representing thunder, black clouds, and lightning), seated on one of the Blue Corn People in the sandpainting. Bundle prayersticks (at left) and spruce uprights (behind patient at right) are part of the sandpainting set-up. Photographs by Charlotte Johnson Frisbie, Valley Store, Ariz., June 20, 1963.

tors than any other chantway, were among the most popular and most frequently performed song ceremonials in the 1970s. They have preserved more of the elements of a chantway complex and have more sandpaintings associated with them than any other ceremonial (Newcomb and Reichard 1937; Reichard 1939, 1950; Wyman 1970). They are used to alleviate troubles attributed to the effects of thunder and lightning or to their cognate earthly symbols, snakes and arrows. Chest and lung troubles and gastrointestinal diseases are often ascribed to these factors, but most any ailment may be traced to them if convenient. Red Antway is good for diseases coming from ants, horned toads (fig. 9), and secondarily from lightning and bears. These are primarily genitourinary troubles, but gastrointestinal distress, skin diseases, sore throat, or rheumatism may be treated by the chant. Urinating on an anthill or disturbing one in any way, or inadvertently swallowing an ant in food or drink, or being bitten by one, may be sources of ant infection (Wyman 1965:25–27). Big Starway, although probably once concerned with heavenly bodies, is now done according to Evilway ritual and used to treat any illness thought to be caused by native ghosts or by witches (Wheelwright 1956:106–110). There is presumptive evidence that the Windways and also Flintway, the fundamental Lifeway chant, may belong in the Shooting Chant subgroup instead of comprising separate ones (Wyman 1962:48, 51, 66, 1970:4).

In the Mountain Chant subgroup there are, of course, the Mountainways themselves (Matthews 1887; Haile 1946; Wyman 1975) and the closely related Beautyway (Wyman 1957), and two obsolescent or extinct chantways, Excessway and Mothway (Haile 1978; Luckert 1978). The etiological factors that Mountainway deals with are animals that live in the mountains, first and foremost the bear, porcupines, weasels, squirrels and chipmunks, badgers, skunks, and wild turkeys. Bear disease seems to be firmly associated with two groups of illnesses, arthritis and mental disturbances. Porcupine disease may be manifested as gastrointestinal trouble or kidney and bladder disturbances. Killing squirrels may lead to nasal discomfort or coughing. Itching, pimples, and skin diseases may be traced to killing or eating a turkey; deafness and eye troubles, to the mountain sheep. There are other associations of sickness with animals, but primarily Mountainway may be considered a cure for bear disease. Beautyway, which could be considered to be Mountainway's sister chant, is above all concerned with snakes of every description as etiological factors; in fact it is so firmly associated with snake infection that English-speaking Navajos sometimes call it "the snake chant." Lizards, certain water creatures such as frogs, toads, and possibly weasels might be included among Beautyway's etiological factors. Among the diseases sometimes traced to snake infection are rheumatism, sore throat, stomach trouble, kidney and bladder trouble, and skin diseases or sores, in short almost any human misery. Care must be exercised in diagnosis because snakes are also important etiological

William R. Heick Photography, Mill Valley, Calif.

Fig. 9. Blue horned toad and anthill sandpainting from a Red Ant Holyway. In contrast to the Corn People sandpainting painted for this same chantway, sandpaintings of horned toads and anthills, Ant People, and Horned Toad People are generally confined to the Red Antway (Wyman 1965:233). This rendering (in blue with a trail in blue and red from the toad's mouth to the entrance of the anthill) was made for the sweat-emetic ceremony on the morning of the second day. Beside it is a basket of herbs and a sweat-emetic hoop (through which the patient is to vomit) placed over a basin made of sand. The sweat-emetic ceremony was performed on 4 successive mornings, with a similar painting of a horned toad with bow and arrow and lightning arrows, each day rendered in a different color. Photograph by William R. Heick, at Valley Store, Ariz., June 14, 1963. Filmed and recorded by the Amer. Ind. Films Group.

Table 1. Holyway Chantways Subgroups

Shooting Chant	Wind Chant (*Níłch'ijí*)
Hailway (*Ńlóee*)[a]	Navajo Windway (*Diné Biníłch'ijí*)
Waterway (*Tóee*)[a]	Chiricahua Windway (*Chíshí Biníłch'ijí*)
Shootingway (*Na'at'oyee*)	Hand-Trembling Chant
Red Antway (*Wóláchíí'jí*)	Hand-Tremblingway (*N'dilniihjí*)
Big Starway (*Sǫ'tsohjí*)	Eagle Trapping
Flintway (*Béshee*)(?)	Eagleway (*'Atsáájí*)[a]
Mountain Chant	Beadway (*Yoo'ee*)[a]
Mountainway (*Dziłk'ijí*)	Of uncertain affiliation
Beautyway (*Hoozhónee*)	Awlway (*Tsahaa*)[a]
Excessway (*'Ajiłee*)[a]	Earthway (*Ni'jí*)[a]
Mothway (*'Iich'ąhjí*)[a]	Reared-in-Earthway (*Ni' Honeeyą́ą́jí*)(?)[a]
God-Impersonators (*Yé'ii Hólóní*)	
Nightway (*Tł'éé'jí*)	
Big Godway (*Haashch'éétsohee*)[a]	
Plumeway (*'Ats'osee*)	
Coyoteway (*Mą'iijí*)[a]	
Dogway (*Łééchąą'íjí*)[a]	
Ravenway (*Gáagiijí*)[a]	

[a] Extinct, obsolescent, or extremely rare.

factors for Shootingway and for Navajo Windway. Here is an instance where an appropriate choice among the three chantways might be determined by an experimental trial of excerpted ceremonies. The extinct or decidedly obsolescent Excessway was doubtless closely related to the extinct Mothway, and both may have been associated with Coyoteway (Wyman and Bailey 1964:32–33, 148). These chants were cures for the effects of breaking ceremonial restrictions, all sorts of recklessness including sexual excesses, incest, and sexual irregularities of any kind. Contact with moths or butterflies may cause insanity, a desire to jump into the fire like a moth, or an impulse to commit clan incest. Witches are said to apply a powder containing setae from the wings of a moth or butterfly to the body of a victim to cause insanity. The text of a myth of Excessway recorded by Haile and two English versions have been published (Pepper 1908; Kluckhohn 1944:21–24, 96–108; Haile 1978), but little is known about Mothway. The Gameway version of Excessway was recorded by Luckert (1978).

The God-Impersonators subgroup (those that have impersonators of the supernaturals) is so called because in nine-night performances masked impersonators of the group of Holy People known as the Yeis appear as dancers in the public exhibition of the final night. The subgroup includes the well-known and popular Nightways and the closely related Big Godway (which may be only a branch of Nightway and not an independent ceremonial), Plumeway, the obsolescent Coyoteway, and two extinct chants, Dogway and Ravenway. The Night Chant, along with the Mountain Chant, is one of the Navajo ceremonials best known to non-Navajos, because of the spectacular dances of the final night, the peculiar, stirring singing that accompanies them, public performance of these dances outside of ceremonial practice (as in the Intertribal Indian Ceremonial at Gallup, New Mexico), and the fact that some of the first substantial descriptions of a Navajo ceremonial were devoted to this chant (J. Stevenson 1891; Matthews 1902; Tozzer 1909). The Yeis themselves are etiological factors and the chant is considered to be an efficacious cure for all sorts of head ailments, including eye and ear diseases and mental disturbances, but like all chants it may be used for other illnesses if they are attributed to the proper etiological sources. The myth of Big Godway is the story of the Stricken Twins, crippled and blind, and the chant is used for stiffness, paralysis, and blindness. Because the leader of the Yeis is Talking God, who is also called maternal grandfather or great-uncle of the Yeis (*Yé'ii Bicheii* 'Grandfather-of-the-gods'), the anglicization of this alternate name of his as Yeibichai is loosely applied not only to him but also to all the masked impersonators (Haile 1947a), to their dance, and to the Night Chant itself. Plumeway, also called Downway or the Feather Chant, like Nightway represents the Yeis in its sandpaintings and its dances, although in the 1970s it was rarely performed. Also like Nightway it is used for diseases of the head or other ailments, such as rheumatism, but when these are attributed to infection from game animals, especially deer, such troubles may be called "deer disease." Game and hunting and the origins of agriculture are stressed in the myth, and deer and other game animals and domesticated plants are featured in the sandpaintings. Coyoteway is obsolescent and comparatively little was known about it (Wheelwright 1956:91–111, 150–157) until Luckert (1979) recorded it in 1974 (fig. 10). Apparently it was used for the same group of troubles as Excessway and Mothway—the results of sexual aberrations such as incest—for it seems to have been related to the moth-incest-insanity complex. A more orthodox Navajo pattern emerges, in tune with the hunter tradition, from the Gameway version of Excessway (Luckert 1978). Even less is known about Dogway and Ravenway, for they are certainly extinct. Some informants have held that Ravenway was related to Coyoteway, was used in cases of incest, and involved blackening the patient and ash blowing, which are Evilway procedures (Kluckhohn and Wyman 1940:188; Wyman 1951:44).

The diseases alleged to be benefited by performances of either Navajo or Chiricahua Windway and the causal factors concerned are mostly the same. Among these factors winds of all kinds, but especially whirlwinds, come first. Snakes are usually mentioned next and sometimes their cognate lightning (Thunder). Cactus is the third most frequently invoked factor, and Sun and Moon have been mentioned for Chiricahua Windway. All these are represented in the sandpaintings of the Windways. A long list of ailments may be ascribed to these factors (see Wyman 1962:20–22), but stomach trouble due to snake infection, eye trouble and itching due to cactus infection, and heart and lung diseases are often mentioned. Navajo Windway is subject to more or less elaboration. It has male and female branches, a male branch performed according to Injuryway subritual, which is called Striped Windway and, rarely, nine-night forms, which may include the With-many-sandpaintings phase, in which as many as 12 sandpaintings may be made in a single performance, or the Chant-with-the-house phase, which features a Rainbow's House, a painted wooden reredos like the Sun's House screen of male Shootingway, which is set up at the back of the hogan during the last four days when sandpaintings are made (Wyman 1962:23–26; Kluckhohn and Wyman 1940:111–139). Chiricahua Windway, one of the briefest but also one of the most popular of Navajo chants, seems to be of comparatively recent origin, probably from the period of the captivity at Fort Sumner, 1864–1868, or perhaps a few years earlier (Kluckhohn and Wyman 1940:140–154; Wyman 1962:214ff.). Apparently an Apache ceremonial was transformed

U. of Ariz. Press, Tucson and Mus. of Northern Ariz. Press, Flagstaff.

Fig. 10. Eighth day of a Coyoteway. After the completion of a sandpainting inside the ceremonial hogan and the preparation outside of gear to be worn or carried by the yei impersonators, 3 impersonators with Talking God in the lead approach the ceremonial hogan from which the patient (at left) emerges to be blessed. Talking God, in mask with radiating eagle plumes, is followed by two "Coyote Girls," in this case impersonated by a man and woman, each wearing the blue mask of Female God. The first of these 2, Blue Coyote Carrier, carries the representational stuffed Blue Coyote (*Mą'ii Dootł'izhí*, i.e. 'kit fox') that completes his identity, while the second, Female God, carries a feather-festooned wedding basket containing white and yellow ears of corn. The fourth figure, with cowboy hat, is a prompter. Photograph by Karl Luckert, Black Mesa area, Jan. 1974.

into a typical Navajo chantway by borrowing from the older native Windway. It seems that there is or was a five-night form, but in the 1970s the two-night form prevailed. Chiricahua Windway features usually rather small sandpaintings of the Sun and Moon, and the manufacture, application to the patient, and disposal of a rather complicated cactus prayerstick offering. The myths stress hunting episodes. Its simplicity, brevity, and the concomitant economy in sponsoring a performance undoubtedly account for its widespread practice.

Hand-Tremblingway, which appears to have no partner chants, is said by some Navajo to date from earliest mythological times, but others have said that it too was learned from the Apache like Chiricahua Windway and in fact is related to the latter chant. Its characteristics do indicate that it is a relatively late composition from Chiricahua-Mescalero ceremonials, hand-trembling divination rites, and the Navajo Big Starway (Wyman and Kluckhohn 1938:28; Kluckhohn and Wyman 1940:169–183; Wyman 1962:214–216). The Gila Monster is prominent in the songs and prayers of the chant and along with stars and Big Flies is featured in the sandpaintings. Hand-Tremblingway may be used to treat any illness coming from practicing or overpracticing hand-trembling divination or star-gazing, such as nervousness or mental upsets, paralysis of the arms, impaired vision, or chest disease.

The Eagle Trapping subgroup contains two chants, Eagleway and Beadway. There is some difference of opinion among Navajos as to whether Eagleway and perhaps Beadway also should be grouped with the Gameway hunting rites or with the Holyway chants. Possibly they were once hunting rites that developed into chantways as the hunting rites became obsolescent. The close link between Gameway hunting and Gameway healing in general supports this inference (cf. Luckert 1975, 1978). Both Eagleway and Beadway are specific for eagle infection, which may be manifested as head ailments such as earache, itching, boils and sores, or sore throat. The myth and the sandpaintings of Beadway together present about the best example of the paintings as narrative illustrations of the story (Reichard 1939). Usually sandpaintings are seldom frankly narrative but simply serve as reminders of the cardinal episodes of the myths. However, the sandpaintings of Beadway illustrate quite well the adventures of the hero, Scavenger, with the Pueblo Indians and the Eagle and Hawk People.

Finally, a group of extinct ceremonials of uncertain affiliation contains Awlway, Earthway, and possibly a third called Reared-in-Earthway. These have been extinct for many years, perhaps since the mid-nineteenth century, so only a few disconnected scraps of information about them and a few sandpaintings alleged to have been used in them are known.

Some of the chants have male and female branches (*biką'jí* and *ba'áádjí*). Perhaps most of them did at one time have them, but no evidence remains for the existence of the two branches for the majority of them. The ones known to have or have had male and female branches are Shootingway, Red Antway, Mountainway, Excessway, Beautyway, and Navajo Windway. Male and female branches are not distinguished according to the sex of the person being treated, for either one may be sung over a man or a woman. Haile thought that the distinction depended upon the sex of the protagonist of the myth of the chant. There has been no systematic study of the differences in practice of the two branches. Probably they are comparatively slight, resting mainly in the songs and prayers.

Besides the song ceremonials there are prayer ceremonials, long prayers being said without singing, lasting four nights (Navajo reckoning). Drypaintings of pollen on buckskin may be made. The prayer ceremonials are mainly associated with Blessingway although some are given in connection with Evilway ceremonials. They may be added to chants at the request of the sponsor and can be given by the singer conducting the chant or by a prayer maker who is called in. Prayer ceremonials are the best protection against witchcraft and the best cure for its effects. Some are considered powerful in cases of severe injury.

Ceremonial Procedure

When anthropologists began to study the Navajo ceremonial system many were dismayed by its apparently stupendous complexity. In fact, however, a Navajo chant is a framework into which are fitted more or less discrete units, some of which are fixed and are used over and over again in different chants, sometimes with slight modifications, and others that may be inserted or omitted in accord with the practice of the singer, the wishes of the patient or his family, the nature of the illness, or other circumstances. Within a unit there may also be acts and procedures that are similarly manipulated. Thus the intricacy of Navajo ceremonialism is not quite so overpowering once it is understood. Following Haile Navajo specialists have used the term 'ceremony' for these units, each of which fulfills a specific function, as distinct from 'ceremonial', which refers to a complex of ceremonies that has a name and origin legend and is conducted according to a particular set of rules or ritual. One or a few ceremonies may be used as test excerpts.

Theoretically a ceremonial should be carried out only in the traditional, roughly circular hogan or Navajo house, which has a door opening to the east, the direction whence comes good, and a smoke hole in the center of the roof for the egress of evil. The family hogan is emptied and swept for a chant, but sometimes a large hogan is built to accommodate the large sandpaintings and many spectators in one of the nine-night winter chants, such as Nightway. Blessingway is preoccupied with the hogan and every Blessingway rite must begin with the hogan songs (Wyman 1970a:10–16).

Ceremonial Equipment

'Bundle' and 'pouch' are renderings of the same Navajo word (*jish*) and have been used interchangeably by English-speaking Navajos and by writers. However, 'bundle' more precisely refers to all the concrete objects that a singer uses in carrying out a ceremonial and that he usually keeps in a buckskin bag or even a commercial sugar or flour sack, while 'pouch' signifies a package of equipment specific for a given ceremonial. Since most of the articles must be made during a ceremonial, often only a single item during a given performance, to obtain a complete outfit entails the sponsoring of many ex-

left, Wheelwright Mus., Santa Fe, N. Mex.: 49/153. right, William R. Heick Photography, Mill Valley, Calif.

Fig. 11. Ceremonial equipment. right, Singer Tonnie Zonnie Yazzie of Naschitti (in plaid shirt at center), with layout of ceremonial equipment during a Mountain Chant, just before the messengers or *'ak'áán ndeinilii* 'flour sprinklers' (shown in Link 1968:53) are sent out. Photograph by William R. Heick (in conjunction with filming by the Amer. Ind. Films Group), at Totso Trading Post, Lukachukai, Ariz., Oct. 1963. Baskets, calico and other spreads, and buckskin (at back) would have been provided by patient (seated at right). left, Talking prayersticks, usually included in a ceremonial layout. The male mirage stone (right) and the female haze stone, with several prayer stones and images, are bound together with a leather thong on a bed of multicolored fabrics and feathers. Length about 17.0 cm; collected by Mary Wheelwright in the 1920s.

pensive ceremonials; hence, a bundle is valued highly. Upon the death of a singer his bundle may be buried with him or it may be inherited by his or his sister's children or some other relative who knows how to use it.

A singer's bundle (Wyman 1972) contains many items of nonspecific equipment that may be used in various ceremonials, some perhaps in all ceremonials (Kluckhohn and Wyman 1940:22–48). Among these are gourd, rawhide, or deer or bison hoof rattles; a bull-roarer, a flat stick pointed at one end, with a buckskin thong attached to the other, which is whirled to make a sound like thunder and thus intimidate evil; medicine stoppers, small feathered wands used to protect, stir, taste, sprinkle, and apply medicines; smooth canes or digging sticks, to remove medicines from sacks; talking prayersticks (fig. 11) of wood or stone; tie-ons (chant tokens, head feather bundles), little bundles of fluffy eagle plumes one of which is tied to the patient's forelock on the last day of a chant to facilitate recognition by supernaturals and humans; a brush of eagle quill feathers used for asperging, protecting medicines, and exorcising evil; a fur collar, a badge of recognition for singer or patient (Shootingway requires one of otter or beaver skin), with an attached eagle wing bone whistle to signal, summon, and attract the Holy People; a fire drill handle, tip, and fireboard (hearth); woolen unraveling strings with eagle plume feathers tied to the ends; medicine cups of abalone or turtle shell; prehistoric arrowheads, spearpoints, knives, drills, and the like, which have exorcistic properties and are used to cut ceremonial materials (flints); a stone club, Monster Slayer's weapon; materials for jewel (bits of turquoise, abalone and white shell, and jet), reed ("cigarette"), and cut wooden prayerstick offerings; interesting or oddly shaped stones, concretions, or fossils, and small cylinders or animal figurines made of banded or white aragonite; quartz crystals; and many small sacks of paints, cornmeal, pollens, and herbal medicines.

Equipment for Evilway ritual, besides many of the above items, consists of a pair of miniature bows; shoulder bands (bandoliers) and wristlets of hide or the skin of an unwounded deer (Kluckhohn, Hill, and Kluckhohn 1971:210) with attached flints, animal claws, and eagle talons, worn by impersonators of the Slayer Twins during garment or cincture and overshooting ceremonies, and by the patient in blackening ceremonies; and mountain lion, wildcat, wolf, or bear claws, used to split yucca leaves.

The pouch contains variously shaped wooden objects, painted and decorated with feathers, which may be called bundle prayersticks (as opposed to temporary prayerstick offerings). These are specific for a given ceremonial. For instance, the bundle prayersticks of male Shootingway include four wide boards, paddle-shaped wooden objects painted with designs; four plumed wands (held-to-water-sticks), wooden shafts with turkey tail feathers and little wooden hoops attached to them; and five arrows, earthly imitations of the jewel arrows of the Sun, made of wood or big reeds, fletched with various feathers, and decorated with jewel beads and pendants. The pouch of Navajo Windway contains a number of painted and feathered sticks shaped like snakes.

Certain items of equipment are made during a ceremonial, such as the drumstick of yucca leaves used to beat a basket to accompany singing, or the arrows used in overshooting. Such articles are usually taken apart and disposed of at the end of the ceremonial.

Among the medicines, usually herbal, needed for a chant are the infusion specific (*zaa'nił* 'objects are put into mouths'), a preparation specific for a given chant; the chant lotion (*kétłoh* 'foot lotion'), a cold infusion of fragrant herbs such as mints, for external application; the fumigant, containing herbs, cornmeal, sulphur, and birds' feathers, which is sprinkled on glowing coals and the fumes inhaled, usually as the concluding act of a ceremony; the emetic, made of freshly gathered herbs with some ingredients from the bundle added; and other preparations used for specific purposes (Kluckhohn and Wyman 1940:48–57). A special infusion of twigs from a tree that has been struck by lightning and of herbs

Wheelwright Mus., Santa Fe., N. Mex.:49/185.

Fig. 12. Plumed wands, set up as guardians around sandpaintings and other sacred areas, are constructed in a prescribed manner (Matthews 1893:233–236). These are female wands made of a willow stick with turkey and eagle feathers bound on with cotton string. Length about 35.5 cm. Formerly owned by medicine man Hosteen Klah, acquired after his death in 1937.

gathered around it is used in Evilway ceremonials. A ball of pollen and other dry ingredients made by the singer and given to the patient during a sandpainting ceremony represents the Agate or Turquoise Man who stands within a person for life (inner form) and makes him invincible. For the performance of a chantway of the God-Impersonator type, various painted deerskin masks representing different gods are called for (Haile 1947a).

Equipment provided by the sponsor or patient includes baskets, buckskin or a white cloth substitute, lengths of calico for spreads, and materials for sandpaintings.

Holyway Ceremonies

A typical Holyway chant consists of about 12 ceremonies, quasi-independent complexes of acts set off by pauses of activity. Accompanying these there are certain procedures that occur throughout all chants. Most important is the singing, usually accompanied by a rattle, led by the singer but joined by all (usually men) who know how. Singing accompanies nearly every act and in Navajo thought it is the one indispensable part of any ceremonial; without it there can be no cure, indeed no chantway. A few songs, if nothing else, may do some good. Knowledge of several hundred songs is required for most chants. Prayers are said at intervals and communal pollen prayer occurs at or near the close of ceremonies. The singer's equipment, especially the contents of the pouch, is laid out in a fixed order upon a calico spread at the west in the hogan (layout), or it may be arranged in a basket (Navajo or Paiute) for certain procedures (basket layout). Objects from it, especially the bundle prayersticks, or other articles such as the bull-roarer or unraveler items, are applied to the body of the patient by the singer while he voices a sound symbolic for the chant (sound symbolism), in the ceremonial order, that is, from the feet upward to the top of the head. Anything applied to the patient—medicines, cornmeal, pollen, sand from drypaintings, bath suds—is applied in this order. All movement of people or objects is likewise in a ceremonial order called "sunwise," that is, from left to right or from east to south, to west, to north. Herbal medicines are prepared and administered to the patient. The bull-roarer is whirled outside the hogan at the cardinal points. Fumigation closes most ceremonies. Following each ceremony materials and objects that have served their purpose are disposed of by trusted helpers in stated directions and situations well away from the hogan, often with meal or pollen prayer. During the ceremonial and for four days thereafter the patient must observe numerous restrictions on behavior, sexual continence (which also applies to the singer), prohibition on bathing thus preserving the body paint, and care in all activities lest he harm someone else, for he is powerful like one of the Holy People and therefore dangerous.

A ceremonial is opened at sundown the first evening by consecration of the hogan. The singer rubs cornmeal on four roof beams in the cardinal directions and places twigs of wavyleaf oak (*Quercus undulata*) above them, with prayers and Blessingway songs. Seeing these the Holy People realize that the hogan is being used for a chant.

Following this after sundown, and on each of the three succeeding evenings in a five or nine-night chant, there may be an unraveling ceremony, lasting about an hour. A stated number (4 to 15) of unravelers are made, bundles of herbs and feathers tied together with a wool string by crochet knots so that when the end is pulled it will unravel and come free. These are applied to the patient's body and unraveled in ceremonial order, symbolizing release from evil, danger, and harm (untying).

A short singing ceremony lasting an hour or so follows unraveling, or occurs after sundown on the first four evenings if unraveling is omitted. The songs may be accompanied by basket drumming, beating an inverted Navajo basket covered with a blanket with a special drumstick of yucca leaves made for the occasion.

Just before dawn on each day that a sandpainting is to be made a setting-out ceremony notifies human and supernatural beings alike of the procedures within the hogan. The singer accompanied by the patient brings out the basket layout, and seated before a small mound of earth about six feet east of the hogan door he sticks the bundle prayersticks upright in the mound in a fixed order. Cornmeal is sprinkled liberally over the mound. Singing and a litany accompany this procedure.

Just after dawn on each of the first four mornings a sweat and emetic ceremony drives evil away through internal and external purification. On the first morning a fire is kindled with a fire drill, and coals from it kindle all fires throughout the chant. Four small sandpaintings, often of snakes, may be made at the cardinal points around the central fireplace, and ritually prepared wooden fire pokers are laid beside them. Another small painting is made northwest of the fire on which the patient's basket of emetic is placed (fig. 9). The patient, singer, and others who wish to participate undress, the men retaining a breechclout and the women a skirt. An enormous fire induces copious sweating. A warm decoction of many kinds of plants is prepared in a pail and dispensed in a basket for the patient, in pans for others. Everyone washes with it, from the feet up, and the patient and others who wish drink some and vomit into a basin of sand, which is later disposed of. A procession around the fire may occur, and finally the singer sprinkles everyone with a cool, fragrant herb lotion by means of the eagle-feather brush. Then all go out to cool off.

After breakfast on the first four days an invocatory offering ceremony attracts the Holy People (fig. 13). Offerings are made for them of jewels (bits of turquoise, shell, and jet), of short lengths of painted reeds stuffed with wild tobacco and other materials ("cigarettes"), and of prayersticks (small cut and painted wooden sticks), or of some of these. The patient holds these while repeating a long prayer, sentence by sentence, after the singer (litany). Then a special, reliable helper deposits them at some distance from the hogan in carefully specified places where the Holy People can find them. If they are correct the Holy People, by reciprocity, are obliged to come and render aid.

In the forenoon of the last day (next to last night, Navajo reckoning) a bath ceremony purifies the patient still further (fig. 14). A platform of sand, often covered with herbs, is made and a basket placed upon it. Water and a piece of yucca root placed in it is whipped into a stiff mound of suds. Designs of pollen and powdered herbs are strewed on the suds, which are then applied to the patient in ceremonial order by the singer. Then the patient kneels, washes his hair, and bathes, assisted by helpers, is dried with cornmeal, and is dressed in clean clothes.

Following the bath or the offering ceremonies the sandpainting (*'iikááh*) is begun. This is a symbolic picture, often large and complicated, of the protagonist of the myth that sanctions and explains the ceremonial or the Holy People he encounters in his mythical adventures, accompanied by many subsidiary symbols. It is made on the floor of the hogan by trickling dry pigments from between the thumb and flexed forefinger on a background of tan-colored sand smoothed out with a weaving batten. The pigments are red, yellow, and white sandstone, charcoal pulverized on a grinding stone, and a few mixtures—charcoal and white sand for a bluish color, red and black for brown, and red and white for pink. Any man who knows how may work on them under the direction of the singer who seldom takes part except to lay down some fundamental lines. Women do not take part or even watch for fear of injury from the powers invoked, although a woman past childbearing age may grind the pigments. When the Holy People taught the protagonists of the myths how to reproduce their sacred pictures, which they kept rolled up on clouds, they forbade their reproduction in permanent form lest they be soiled or damaged, so the designs that are rigidly prescribed are transmitted in memory from singer to apprentice. A sandpainting may be a foot or less in diameter or one around 20 feet across made in a special large hogan. The average painting made in a family hogan is about six feet in diameter. Depending on its complexity it may be completed by from four to six men in three to five hours.

When the sandpainting is completed in the late forenoon or early afternoon the ceremony begins. The bundle prayersticks are brought in from the set-out mound and set upright around the painting. Cornmeal is sprinkled on it by singer and patient. Sometime during the singing the patient, stripped to a breechclout if a man and wearing a single skirt if a woman, sits on some figure in the painting (fig. 8). While singing the singer applies his palms moistened with herb medicine to various parts of the painted figures' bodies and then applies the adhering sand to corresponding parts of the patient's body. This identifies the patient with the Holy People represented who have been attracted to the scene to look at their portraits, making him strong and immune to further harm like them. The patient also absorbs their powers from the sands, exchanging evil for good. The singer also applies the bundle prayersticks from the set-up and parts of his own body to the patient in ceremonial order, and since he personifies a Holy Person this reinforces the identification making the patient himself a Holy Person for a time. Thus his acquired power could harm others, hence the necessity for the postceremonial restrictions. Finally the patient leaves the hogan, the singer erases the sandpainting, and the now infectious sand is carried out and deposited north of the hogan where it can do no harm.

William R. Heick Photography, Mill Valley, Calif.

Fig. 13. Preparation of reed prayerstick bundle offerings to the Holy People on one of the first 4 mornings of a Nightway. The singer at left is placing a painted reed (cigarette) or wooden stick on one of the 4 bundles being prepared; patient sits at right. In this as in other ceremonies, orientation, sequencing, and color differentiations are all of significance. Photograph by William R. Heick, at Totso Trading Post (Lukachukai, Ariz.), Dec. 1963, in conjunction with the Amer. Ind. Films Group.

On the last day only the patient's body is painted from head to foot with symbolic designs by means of mineral pigments for still further identification with the holy ones (figure painting), the tie-on (chant token) is tied in his hair, and a personal token (a shell bead for women or turquoise bead for men, which the patient may keep) is also tied to his hair (token tying). This is a mark of recognition for the Holy People and a protection from further danger.

William R. Heick Photography, Mill Valley, Calif.

Fig. 14. Bath ceremony from a Nightway. left, Patient (woman at right) watches as an assistant prepares yucca root suds to be used in the bath. Singer (in white headband) is holding gourd rattle used to accompany singing through much of the ceremony; Talking God mask and garb used by yeibichai impersonators in other ceremonies in this chantway are along the wall. right, Assistant helps the patient with the bath by using gourd ladle to pour water from pitched water container. Photographs by William R. Heick, at Totso Trading Post (Lukachukai, Ariz.), Dec. 1963. Filmed and recorded by the Amer. Ind. Films Group.

No one, not even the Navajos, knows how many different drypainting designs are known and used. Moreover, a Navajo count would be very different from a non-Navajo one, since Navajos regard paintings that appear different as the same if they depict the same supernatural beings, whereas a slight, barely noticeable change can make an important ritual difference for them. All Holyway chants, most or perhaps all Evilway chants, and the Blessingway rites are known or are alleged to have employed drypaintings. The number pertaining to a given ceremonial from which a singer may select one for a two-night or four for a five- or nine-night performance varies from scarcely more than the required four for chants such as Hand-Tremblingway and Eagleway to about 100 for Shootingway, although here the Navajo count might be closer to 50. The singer selects one or four of those he knows, according to his or the patient's wishes, the factors supprosed to have caused the patient's troubles, or some such consideration. Over 500 different designs have been recorded by White artists and a few Navajos. Perhaps around 1,000 distinguishable designs are known, but this is conjecture. A Navajo estimate would be much smaller.

One familiar with the symbolism of the drypaintings and the ceremonial myths can correlate the two, but few are actually narrative. The statement that the sandpaintings are illustrations to a book of Navajo mythology is, therefore, misleading. Most of them show the Holy People in pairs, quartets, or larger multiples to increase their power, standing around on rainbow-bars, their means of transportation, or on black foundation bars representing the earth, as if waiting for something to happen. To a Navajo the pictures are full of motion symbolically indicated. These Holy People may have human forms or they may be anthropomorphized animals, plants, natural phenomena, or even material objects. The pairs are called male and female although actually representing distinctions of power. Animals and plants may also be drawn in more or less naturalistic forms, and there are standard abstractions for natural phenomena, heavenly bodies, and mythological creatures. Place is important to a Navajo; and a locality symbol—the center in radial compositions, the foundation bar in linear ones—is conspicuous. The main theme symbols are arranged according to one of three types of composition (fig. 15): linear, with figures in a row or rows; radial, with important symbols cardinally oriented in a Greek cross and with subsidiary symbols in the quadrants in a Saint Andrew's cross, around a center symbolizing the spring, pool, mountain, or dwelling where the commemorated episode took place; and extended center, with a central motif occupying most of the space. Sequences of color have directional, sexual, or other ritual meanings. Finally the entire picture is surrounded by an encircling guardian, usually the red and blue Rainbow deity or garland, open to the east for the entrance of good and the expulsion of evil. Sometimes a pair of small symbols enhances control of this eastern aperture.

Again, the complication of drypainting designs is more apparent than real for a limited number of symbols are combined in numerous ways to produce artistically if not symbolically different designs. Since the normally invisible powers made visible in the symbols of sand are dangerous if mishandled, the designs for safety's sake are now frozen within the limits of ritual prescription. Much has been written about Navajo drypainting and many paintings have been published (Matthews 1887, 1902; Newcomb and Reichard 1937; Reichard 1939; Kluckhohn and Wyman 1940; Wyman 1952, 1959, 1960, 1962, 1965, 1970, 1970a, 1975; Wheelwright 1946, 1949, 1956; Klah 1942; Foster 1964; Witherspoon 1977; Luckert 1979a; Haile 1979).

On the final night there is an all-night singing culminating in the dawn songs, which are begun when the first faint streak of dawn in the east can be detected. After these the patient may leave the hogan, face the east, and "breathe in the dawn" four times. The ceremonial ends with a final prayer and a Blessingway song to avert ill consequences from any errors in songs, prayers, or procedure during the chant.

Certain optional ceremonies may be added to the ceremonial at extra expense if requested by the patient. The ritual eating of cornmeal mush from a basket commemorates early foodstuff. Ritual consumption of a mixed stew of meat and internal organs of game and domestic animals removes the necessity of later food restrictions or remedies violations of them. The shock rite may be added to most any ceremonial as a test to determine if the treatment being used is the correct one. A special sandpainting may be made for it surrounded by a low bank of earth, or merely a circular ridge of earth, enclosing a space surrounded by spruce tree tops forming a sort of bower in which the patient sits. A man covered with spruce branches, impersonating a bear, springs out from a dark corner as if to terrify the patient. If the patient faints or has a fit after four such appearances it shows that the correct ceremonial has been chosen, and he is then resuscitated by a restoration rite (Wyman and Bailey 1944:332–337; Wyman 1965:45, 56–58).

Any Holyway chant includes one or more phases, that is, emphasis upon a given type of ceremony (Wyman and Kluckhohn 1938:11). Chant-with-sandpaintings (*'Iikááh Bee Hatáál*) would apply to most any performance and With-many-sandpaintings (*'Iikááh łáníjí*) is known for Navajo Windway, and so is Chant-with-the-house (*Kin Bee Hatáál*) in which the wooden screen is used. Chant-with-Sun's-house (*Jóhonaa'éí Bighan Bee Hatáál*) is an elaborate form of Shootingway featuring the Sun's House screen, which represents the Sun's home (Wyman 1970:15–18, 35, pl. 7). Chant-with-cut-sticks (prayersticks) (*K'eet'áán Bee Hatáál*) and Chant-with-jewels (*Ntł'iz Bee Hatáál*) are phases in which there is special emphasis on these two types of invocatory offerings. In the first a very large number of wooden prayersticks may be prepared and deposited (Haile 1947). The phases best known outside the Navajo community are God-Impersonators (Yeibichai) and the Dark Circle of Branches (*'Ił Náshjin*). The first, known for chants of the God-Impersonators subgroup but especially for Nightway, presents its masked dancers on the final night, but when the public exhibition cannot be held the chant is called an Interior Chant or Just Visiting Chant. The Dark Circle of Branches, popularly called the Corral Dance or Fire Dance because this all-night exhibition is carried out in a great circle or corral of evergreen branches and culminates with nearly naked, clay-daubed dancers running about brandishing torches of cedar bark amid showers of sparks, usually occupies the final night of a Mountain Chant, but other ceremonials, especially Shootingway, may have this phase (Matthews 1887; Haile 1946). When Shootingway borrows this phase from Mountainway the performance is called Mountain-Shootingway (Wyman 1970:25–27). In this phase various acts such as dances or magical illusions are performed not only by teams representing the parent chant but also by groups representing various other chantways. The whole is like a sacred vaudeville show. In theory the patient benefits not only from the chant itself but also from every other ceremonial whose specialty has been presented; thus, it is an economical way of obtaining such benefits without sponsoring numerous chants. A chant that includes this phase (and God-Impersonators as well) must last nine nights and any nine-night ceremonial may not be performed before the first killing frost in the fall nor after the first thunderstorm in the spring; that is, it may be given only when rattlesnakes and bears are hibernating and there is no danger from lightning. Only two- or five-night chants may be held in the frostless months. See "Navajo Music," this volume, for illustrations of some of these ceremonies.

Evilway Ceremonies

Evilway ceremonials are made up of the same kinds of ceremonies as described above for Holyway chants except for setting-out and the usual type of offering ceremony. There may be a ghost's offering of a plume stuck in charcoal or blue glass beads and ashes to appease the ghost or attract it so it may be "shot." Some of the ceremonies may be modified for Evilway ritual. Instead of painting designs on the patient's body (figure-painting) he is entirely covered with red grease paint (reddening) or more often with mixed charcoal burned from all the kinds of plants used in the ceremonial (blackening), and besides tying the chant token two crossed shoulder bands and the wristlets are placed on him. Sandpaintings may be made at night, sometimes on buckskin or cloth, and the patient spends the night on a covering placed over some of the sand.

Certain procedures and ceremonies are especially associated with Evilway ritual. Brushing the patient with the eagle-feather brush or a native grass broom dipped in ashes, or having the patient blow ashes toward the smoke hole from a feather or from a flint, are exorcistic acts that brush or blow away evil and sickness (Kluckhohn and Wyman 1940:72–73). The lightning herb infusion may be administered.

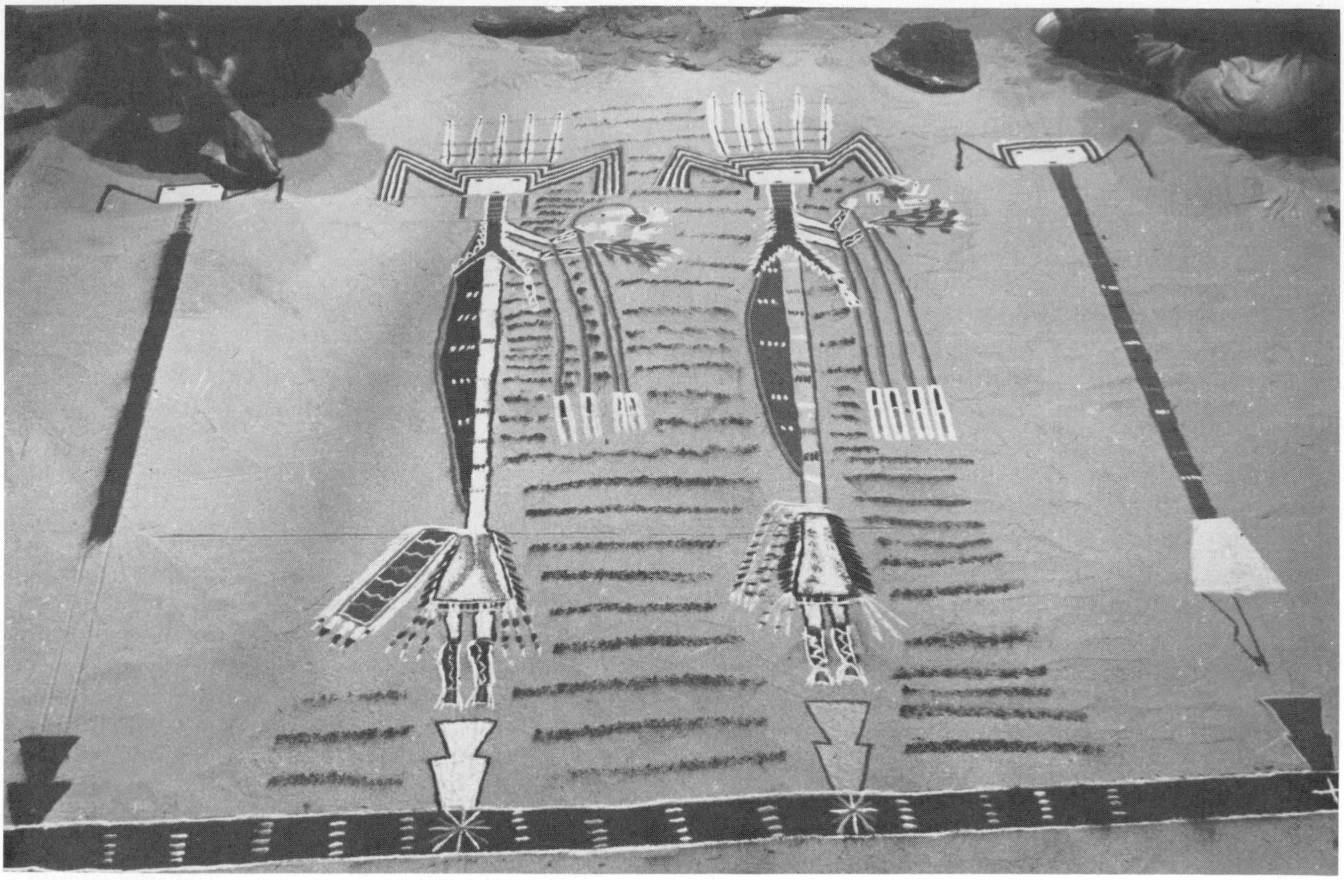

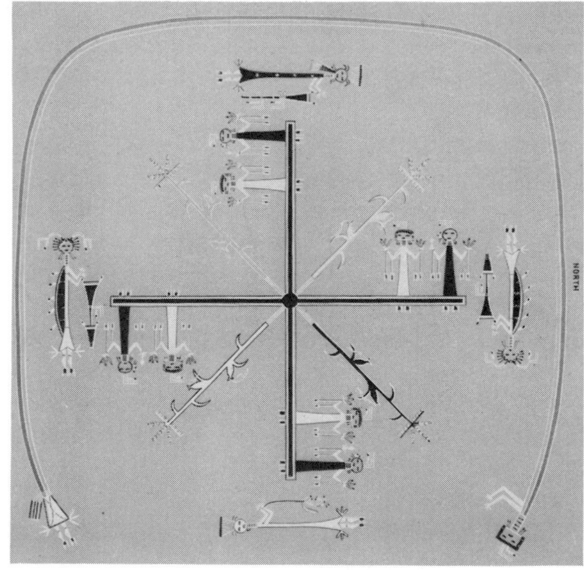

top and bottom left, William R. Heick Photography, Mill Valley, Calif.; bottom right, after Matthews 1902:pl. VI; top opposite page, Mus. of Northern Ariz., Flagstaff.

Fig. 15. Sandpaintings illustrative of 3 compositional types. top, Linear composition. Sandpainting of 4 Holy People or yeis (on black foundation bar representing the earth) being painted for a Nightway. Photograph by William R. Heick, Totso Trading Post (Lukachukai, Ariz.), Dec. 1963. bottom left, Radial composition. Sandpainting (with plumed wand set-up) from same Nightway as above. Photograph by William R. Heick. bottom right, Similar sandpainting (Matthews 1902:121–123, pl. VI), painted on the sixth day of a Nightway. Said to represent the myth of the Whirling Logs (Matthews 1902:121,183–184), the black cross represents the logs crossing one another, with 4 stalks of corn (each of appropriate color) on the shores of the lake. Eight yeis are seated on the logs, one male (black outer figure with characteristic round head) and one female (white inner figure with squared head) on each log, with additional yei figures around the periphery, partially surrounded by an anthropomorphic rainbow. As described by Matthews (1902:121) the painting process takes from 4 to 7 hours. top opposite page, Extended center composition. Sandpainting representing Moon with Rays (used in the Navajo Windway ceremony) being painted by singer John Burnside of Pine Springs, Ariz., at demonstration at the Mus. of Northern Ariz. He is working on the arms of the rainbow. Photograph by Paul V. Long, Aug. 1963.

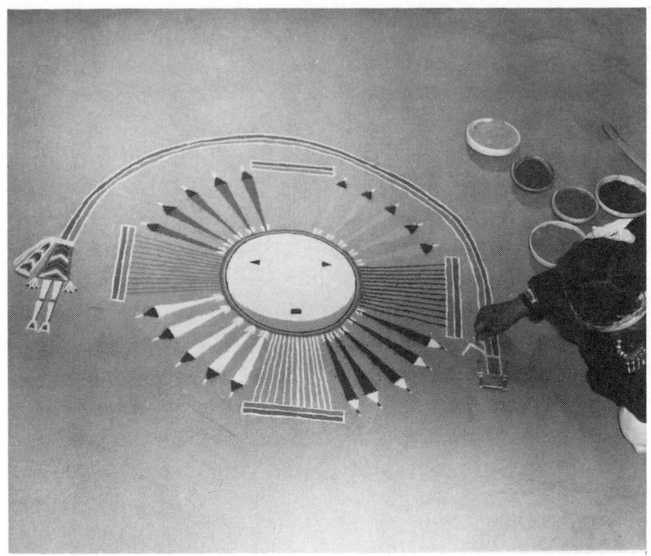

In the big hoop ceremony (hoop transformation rite) the patient enters the hogan for the sweat-emetic ceremony through a series of four or five big hoops made of flexible branches, the last one of wild rose, which have been set up in front of the hogan door, over a drypainted trail, often of mountains and bear tracks, which leads through the hoops into the hogan. He wears a buckskin or cloth over his head and shoulders, which is pulled off gradually by the singer as he passes through the hoops. This symbolizes the restoration to normality of a mythic hero who had been transformed into a snake or a coyote, when the supernatural beast had magically blown or otherwise placed his hide upon the heroic victim, so the act is exorcistic in nature (Wyman and Bailey 1943:27–32; Haile 1950:66–72, 84–88, 192–196, 201–202; Reichard 1950, 1:161, 182, 2, 649–657; Wyman 1965:40, 58–60, 1966). The big hoop ceremony may be followed immediately by the sweat-emetic or by a prayer ceremony, the liberation prayer or prayer on buckskin.

Overshooting usually followed by cincture or garment ceremonies is performed in the evening, ordinarily four times or only once on the final night. Two men smeared with ashes and charcoal and wearing yucca cinctures, shoulder bands, and wristlets impersonate the Slayer Twins, Monster Slayer and Born for Water. Standing on opposite sides of the patient and holding the miniature bows in one hand they pass two chant arrows especially made for the ceremony of pine branchlets, herbs, and feathers over the patient and finally over the hogan outside while voicing the sound symbolism of the Slayer Twins. Eventually the chant arrows are disassembled and disposed of (Wyman and Bailey 1943:19–26; Reichard 1950, 2:657–666). This ceremony is, of course, exorcistic.

In cincture and fir or plant garment ceremonies, narrow strips of yucca leaves slit with mountain lion claws, or long garlands of bundles of Douglas fir or other evergreens, and/or various plants tied to long yucca thongs or otherwise put together, or a tentlike structure of Douglas fir boughs and yucca strips (fir hogan) are tied, wrapped, or otherwise placed around or over the patient (fig. 7). The impersonators of the Slayer Twins cut these to pieces with flints and remove them from the patient. These ceremonies, like unraveling, symbolize release from evil and danger, freeing the patient from the tied-in bonds of disease.

In the Enemyway rite directed against alien ghosts and thus Evilway in ritual, a specially decorated staff known as the rattlestick is carried throughout the ceremonial by a female virgin. The singing is accompanied by a pot drum instead of a rattle. This rite is better known (in English) as the Squaw Dance because of a social feature in the evenings in which girls choose their partners for a kind of dance.

Evilway chants are confined to five nights or fewer and are not subject to the rule of repetition four times if they have benefited a patient.

Ceremonial Organization

The component ceremonies of a ceremonial may vary somewhat depending upon its purpose, the subgroup to which it belongs, and the ritual according to which it is performed. Table 2 shows the characteristic organization of the dozen or so standard ceremonies of most Holyway chants. The time of day given is approximate only and varies with circumstances. Some ceremonies, such as consecration of the hogan, the bath, figure painting, token tying, all-night singing, and the dawn procedures occur only once in any chant. Others are performed four times in five- or nine-night ceremonials. Because the sweat-emetic ceremony must be carried out four times if at all, it cannot be included in a two-night chant. Of course the other ceremonies that are done four times in longer chants can be performed only once in the two-night condensation. A nine-night chant is achieved, not by adding new ceremonies, but by moving the short singing, setting-out, and sandpainting ceremonies ahead to the fifth to eighth days, and of course the bath and final night are on the eighth and ninth.

When a Navajo feels that he requires ceremonial aid because of illness, bad dreams, recollection of violated restrictions, fear of witchcraft, or some other reason, a family conference may decide upon the etiological factors and choose a ceremonial and a singer. Failing this a diagnostician, a specialist in divination, usually not a singer and quite often a woman, is employed (Wyman 1936). The technique used in the 1970s was usually hand trembling. The diagnostician, who lays claim to unusual powers, interprets involuntary motions made by his own hand while he is in a trancelike state. Very occasionally the older techniques of star gazing or listening, interpreting things seen or heard, are used. An intermediary, usually a kinsman of the patient, goes to the home of the chosen singer to make an offer in behalf of the sponsor. Unless there is urgency, the singer usually agrees to come in four days and the intermediary brings the singer's bundle to the patient's home.

The cost of a ceremonial in the 1960s varied from the equivalent of 25 dollars for a two-night performance to several thousand dollars for a nine-night ceremonial when hundreds of spectators must be hospitably fed by the patient and his kinsmen. The singer's money fee, perhaps 10–25 dollars for a five-night chant, must be paid in advance. The singer also keeps all calico spreads, buckskin, and baskets used in the chant.

Mythology

The Navajo ceremonial system, which is transmitted orally from singer to apprentice, is sanctioned and explained in a large body of mythology, likewise transmitted orally from generation to generation. This consists of two major parts, the general origin myth including the story of the Emergence from the underworlds, and the origin legends of the separate ceremonials, which branch off from the origin myth at various points.† The legends usually relate the misadventures of a hero or heroine who through intentional or unintentional misbehavior gets into a series of predicaments requiring supernatural assistance for survival and causing injury or illness calling for ritual restoration. Thus the hero acquires the ceremonial knowledge and power for establishing a chantway and teaches it to his people. In spite of its apparent complexity, Navajo mythology like the ceremonial system has an underlying simplicity, because many of the same mythic motifs are used over and over with specific modifications in the myths of different ceremonials (Spencer 1957; Wyman 1962:29–58). A singer need not know the myths pertaining to his specialty ceremonials, but it is felt that he should and the best singers do. Moreover, ideally, when he relates a myth he should begin with the origin myth and tell it up to where the chant myth branches off from it, but this is not always done.

†According to Karl W. Luckert (communication to editors 1981), the Deerway (a hunting rite) and Deerway *'Ajiłee* (a healing ceremonial involving Deerway mythology) show no evidence of having originally been based on Emergence mythology. In contrast to the Emergence mythos, which by all indications was adopted from the Pueblo Indians, these Deerway traditions appear to be rooted in the Athapaskan hunter stratum (cf. Luckert 1975, 1978, and the editor's introduction in Haile 1981).

Toward New Perspectives‡

Leland Wyman's data for this chapter were gathered by him during approximately four decades prior to his writing in 1972. Since that time several new Navajo ceremonial texts have been published, some bilingually (Wyman 1975; Haile 1978, 1979, 1981, 1981a; Luckert 1975, 1977, 1978, 1979a). The foremost aim of all these publications was to present primary materials. Differences among writers and editors can generally be explained as differences in academic perspectives. Henceforth, the study of Navajo ceremonials should be a multidisciplinary effort, with the various academic disciplines emphasizing field observation while maintaining a critical view regarding the ideological history of their respective methodologies.

The linguistic studies of key ontological and ceremonial concepts by Witherspoon (1974, 1975, 1977) and McNeley (1981) help round out the general picture of Navajo religious thought. The structural analysis of

‡This postscript was written in May 1981 by Karl W. Luckert, who also added to Wyman's text a few references to work published since 1972.

Table 2. Ceremonies of Holyway Chants

	Two-night	*Five-night*	*Nine-night*	*Time of day*
Consecration of hogan	1	1	1	At sundown
Unraveling	1	1 2 3 4	1 2 3 4	Early evening
Short singing	1	1 2 3 4	5 6 7 8	Evening
Setting-out	1	1 2 3 4	5 6 7 8	Before dawn
Sweat and emetic	0	1 2 3 4	1 2 3 4	At dawn
Offering	1	1 2 3 4	1 2 3 4	Early forenoon
Bath	1	4	8	Forenoon
Sandpainting	1	1 2 3 4	5 6 7 8	Afternoon
Figure painting and token tying	1	4	8	During sandpainting
All-night singing	2	5	9	Late evening
Dawn procedures	2	5	9	At dawn

Note: Numerals indicate the days on which the ceremonies occur according to Navajo reckoning.

Navajo prayer by Gill (1974, 1977), together with the wonderfully complete autobiography of a renowned Navajo singer by Mitchell (1978), add to the understanding of ceremonial practice. Additional work on Shootingway has been published by McAllester (1980), and Frisbie's ongoing research on *jish* is reported in three preliminary essays (Frisbie 1977, 1977a, 1978).

The general psychological and psychoanalytic perspective, earlier brought to Navajo studies so forcefully by Kluckhohn and the Leightons, is now represented by the work of Levy (1963), Sandner (1979), and Bergman (1973). The last became involved in teaching psychoanalysis to medicine men and their apprentices at the Rough Rock training program for medicine men. If indeed the declining interest in learning Navajo chantways is caused by economic needs among the student population, as is claimed, the Rough Rock experiment could become a model for similar efforts among other tribes who wish to revitalize waning ceremonial traditions.

The perspective of a historian of religions differs from the psychological approach. He views Navajo ceremonials not as forerunners or prototypes of modern psychoanalysis but as religious responses to reality in their own right—that is, responses in narrational historical time (Luckert 1979b). By the same token, Navajo Holy People (gods) are conceived to be greater-than-human configurations of reality who are actually encountered in the Navajo environment. Not even the most analytically inclined Navajo singer will think of his gods as personified processes. The distinction between nature and supernature being foreign to Navajo tradition, singers also do not think of their gods as "supernaturals." In Navajo ceremonial contexts personal beings, discovered as such and not "personified," tend to outnumber "elements" or less than human "things." Navajo ceremonialists are priestly singers who perform chantways and mediate *for* the people, but they sing and pray *to* their gods. Certainly, like priestly practitioners in all religions, Navajo priests can be tempted into adopting more manipulative or more "efficient" techniques. But such a change in attitude invariably undermines their priestly role. Traditionally, Navajo priestly singers who became too assertive were identified as witches and persecuted accordingly.

Perhaps it is misleading to view Navajo ceremonialism as a single "system." The struggle that many expected to develop between the Native American Church and the traditional Navajo ceremonial "system" failed to occur precisely because there is no such thing as a Navajo ceremonial system. Navajo chantways are systematic, and each ceremonial unit may indeed be called a system. But beyond particular ceremonial systematics, Navajo singers and ethnologists alike (Wyman among them) have been able to produce only variant classifications of chantways. A previously unknown and entirely different classification of Navajo chantways, from the point of view of Upwardmoving Way (*ha'neełnéhee*) singers, appears in a volume by Haile (1981). Moreover Wyman himself may not really have believed in the existence of a singular Navajo ceremonial system. When Navajo chantways were referred to as self-contained mini-religions, each having its own distinct history and soteriology (Luckert 1979a:7), Wyman answered that he was "intrigued by [the] appellation" (personal communication to Luckert 1975).

Peyote Religion Among the Navajo

DAVID F. ABERLE

The spread of the Native American Church to the Navajo country started a struggle that was to pit church members against non-Peyotist Navajos, the Navajo tribal council, the governments of several states, and the Bureau of Indian Affairs and other branches of the federal government, for decades.

The Peyote Religion

The Peyote religion, often called the Peyote cult, is a pan-Indian, semi-Christian, nativistic, redemptive religious movement in the course of whose ritual believers eat the Peyote cactus (*Lophophora williamsii*), a substance containing more than 10 alkaloids, the best known of which is mescaline, some of which have psychotropic effects. It is pan-Indian in the sense that its membership is drawn from many tribes and that its ideology emphasizes the unity of Indians and their distinctness from Whites. Some of its symbolism is Christian, and God, Jesus, Mary, and the Heavenly Angels figure in prayers, but much more symbolism is Indian, and supernaturals of various tribes also appear in prayers; hence it may be called semi-Christian. It is nativistic in its stress on maintaining an Indian religion for Indians and in its ritual details. It is redemptive, rather than transformative, in seeking a major change in the soul of the believer, rather than in the social order. Whether one's criterion is the worship of supernatural beings, the symbolic presentation of ultimate values, or a symbolic effort to close the gaps between things as they are and things as they should be, it is a religion, and since it is one that actively proselytizes in the face of opposition, it is a religious movement. Peyote itself is nonaddictive. It serves as a religious adjunct, making ordinary people capable of extraordinary experiences, whether through visions or through long reflection on their problems and paths.

Membership

There is no accurate count of the number of Navajo Peyotists. A survey by Window Rock Area Office (Navajo reservation) BIA employees in 1951 provided a rough estimate of a membership of 12 to 14 percent of a tribe then numbering perhaps 70,000 people, or 8,400–9,800 adherents (Aberle and Stewart 1957:110; Aberle 1967:110, 352; Aberle 1967:124 is an error). Estimates for later dates are: 22,000 in 1956 (Dustin 1960), 30,000 in 1960 (Dustin 1960), 25,000 to 40,000 in 1962 (Aberle 1967:124), 30,000 in 1965 (U.S. Congress. Senate. Committee on the Judiciary. Subcommittee on Constitutional Rights 1965:165), 35,000 in 1965 (Aberle 1967:124). All estimates except the first two are provided by officials of the Native American Church. All may be overestimates. They suggest an absolute and relative increase over the years. In 1972, of some 130,000 Navajos on and off the reservation, between 40 and 60 percent, adults and children, were adherents of the Peyote religion. There were more Peyotists in the Navajo tribe than in any other single tribe in North America, although on a percentage basis other tribes may stand higher.

Organization

In 1972 Navajo Peyotists were members of the Native American Church of North America. Within that international organization, most belonged to the Native American Church of Navajoland. There were two other Navajo organizations, the Native American Church of the Four Corners and the Northern Navajoland Native American Church Association. Some Navajos probably belonged to more than one of these (Stewart 1972–1980). The Native American Church of Navajoland has its center in the southern part of Navajoland but has members in the north, while the other two organizations focus on the north, thus manifesting organizationally a difference in outlook that goes back to the early days of Navajo Peyotism (Aberle 1967:190–193). The Church as an organization does not concern itself with the training or ordination of Roadmen ("Peyote priests"—those who conduct ceremonies), with questions of proper ritual, or with theological issues. Roadmen are trained by other Roadmen and begin to run meetings when they feel ready to do so. Conflicts over proper ritual are sometimes taken to officers of the Church, whose usual response is that all members are united in worshiping the same God and using Peyote and that variations of ritual depend on the training and inspiration of particular Roadmen. There is no formal creed. The Church is an organization for opposition: for defending its members against repeated efforts to make the sale, use, possession, transportation, or mailing of Peyote illegal.

In the Navajo country, the four state branches were brought under a single Navajo coordinator in 1964. By 1966 the arrangement had been formalized, and there was a Native American Church of Navajoland with its own officers (Aberle 1949–1980, 1967:124; Anonymous 1966:1,4).

Ideology and Ritual

The ideology and ritual of the Native American Church in the Navajo country does not differ from that of the majority of Peyotists elsewhere (see La Barre 1964; Slotkin 1956). Peyotists believe in an all-powerful, transcendent God, who, they say, is the same supreme being worshiped by all people everywhere. Peyote is a symbol of the Church, a means of communication with God, a power in its own right, and a cure of unique potency for spiritual and physical disease. Peyotists use the generic Navajo term for medicine, *'azee'*, to refer to Peyote. To a Navajo, "medicine" refers not only to herbal or Western medicine but also to the entire complex of ritual that is brought to bear to use supernatural power for the benefit of the sick (Haile 1950–1951,1:22–23). When Navajos call Peyote "medicine," they refer to its inseparable physical and spiritual potency. Peyote—its ritual and itself—is a gift of God for Indians. Although God is transcendent, the world is infused with spirit, and the Indian is a natural man, embedded in, not opposed to, this inspirited world of nature. Whites have separated themselves from nature. Man is a mixture of good and evil. He is weak and prone to err, but capable of individual spiritual improvement.

Through prayer, and in particular through the communication with God achieved in a Peyote meeting, and through the power of Peyote, man may be cured of physical and psychic ill health, come to abstain from alcohol, recover from ill fortune and find good fortune, overcome witchcraft directed at him, come to understand his place in the world and his responsibilites to his family, see his path through life, and comprehend the world in which he lives. Although many experienced Peyotists would regard these as core beliefs, each would have his own additions and variations.

A Peyote meeting is held for a purpose, such as curing, blessing children about to go to boarding school or thanking God for their safe return, asking for help in economic stress or for success in livelihood, celebrating a holiday such as Thanksgiving, Christmas, Easter, or the Fourth of July, solemnizing a marriage (after a Roman Catholic, Protestant, traditional Navajo, or civil marriage service), or memorializing the dead. The meeting is held for a "patient" or "patients," who need not be ill, but for whose benefit it is conducted. It has a sponsor or sponsors, normally the patient and his or her spouse, but sometimes the parents of a child or the children of an aged person. Most of the participants are likely to be relatives of the patient, the sponsors, the Roadman, and his wife, but others may be present.

The ritual of Navajo Peyotism as practiced by most Roadmen follows normal Plains patterns (La Barre 1964:43–53; Stewart 1944:103–121). The ritual is minutely prescribed, except for three features. All the songs sung during the night except four are freely chosen by the singers. All the prayers are spontaneous rather than memorized. On the occasions when quiet talk occurs, its content is not prescribed. There are four officiants, the Roadman (Road Chief, Peyote Chief), Drummerman, Cedarman, and Fireman. The Roadman provides the following items of equipment: a cane or staff, jointed and ornamented with beads, with horsehair decoration at the top in red and white, two eagle feather fans, a single eagle feather, a bunch of sage, an eagle bone (or more rarely a reed) whistle, Bull Durham smoking tobacco and sometimes Indian tobacco (which may or may not be mixed with anise- or fennel-like seeds), cigarette papers, cornhusks for rolling cigarettes, and the drum (a cast iron, brass, or steel kettle, with a buckskin head, tied with a rope fastened on bosses made by pressing the buckskin over seven stones), drumsticks, and a Chief Peyote (a particularly fine specimen that he keeps and uses in all his meetings). He usually provides the Peyote. Other participants may have, but need not have, their own fans and drumsticks, sometimes made by Navajos and sometimes made by other Indians. The meeting is held in a hogan or a Plains-type canvas tepee, which some Navajos have procured for this purpose. If it is held in a hogan, the hogan is emptied of furniture, blankets are often hung on the walls, and mattresses, blankets, and cushions are laid down for people to sit on. Hogans and tepees are oriented with the door to the east. A crescent moon altar, a raised mound of damp sand, is prepared. An arc, drawn from tip to tip along the center of the crescent, symbolizes the Peyote road of life. The crescent is west of the center of the hogan, with the horns pointing toward the east. A fire of four sticks arranged in a particular fashion is kindled in the center of the hogan, and a firestick, used at intervals to light cigarettes, is placed east of the fire, oriented east-west (fig. 2).

A meeting falls into four segments: the opening, the midnight water ceremony, the morning water ceremony, and the Peyote breakfast. Ritual acts include smoking, praying, drumming, singing, and eating Peyote, all of which are conceived of as types of prayer; purification of people and equipment with cedar incense; whistle-blowing, to invoke supernatural power; blessing and drinking of holy water; and eating the Peyote breakfast. Discussion and instruction in the Peyote

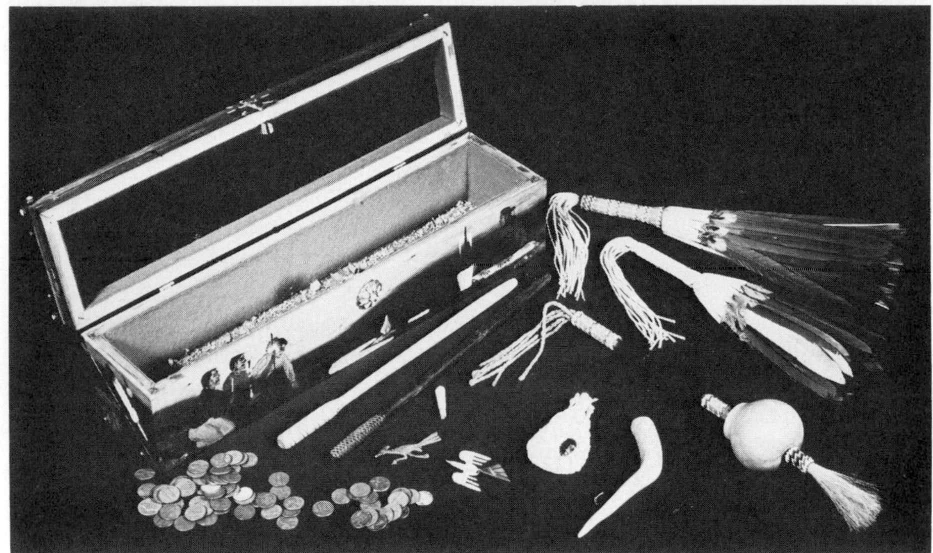

San Diego Mus. of Man, Calif: SDM 1969–6.

Fig. 1. Peyote kit. Wooden box with scenes relating to the Native American Church painted on all surfaces (except the bottom); glued to the center front is a small pink plastic and gilt crucifix and below that a silver and turquoise button. The box holds items used in the peyote ceremony including a piece of antler used to attach the drumhead, a bag for cedar, some drumsticks, a fan with beaded handle, a gourd rattle also decorated with beadwork and peyote jewelry—silver pins depicting a roadrunner and a Waterbird (anhinga). For a description of the box and its contents see Fintzelberg (1969). Length of box about 38 cm; made near Ft. Wingate, N. Mex., 1955.

way occur at some points in the service. Circulation of objects and of people is normally clockwise, but counter-clockwise movement sometimes occurs to avoid coming between someone who is praying, smoking, drumming, singing, or eating Peyote, and the altar, since this would disturb his communication with God through the Chief Peyote.

The participants, led by the Roadman, enter the hogan about eight o'clock in the evening and remain there, except for brief intervals for a few people at a time, until about 7:30 the next morning. A Peyote meeting is regarded by most people as an arduous experience. After purification of the equipment and the transmission of the single eagle feather to the Fireman, people roll cigarettes and light them from the firestick. The sponsor or the patient explains the purpose of the meeting; the Roadman says he will do his best to help; and all pray for the purpose of the meeting. The cigarette butts are collected by the Fireman and placed at the two ends of the altar. Sage is passed; it is a medicine. Peyote is passed and eaten. It may be whole and dried, powdered, steeped as a tea, soaked (ordinarily the product of preparing the tea), or more rarely, green. After purification, the equipment comes into use. The Roadman sings the opening song (a fixed song), and any other three he chooses, while the Drummerman drums for him. The Roadman holds the staff, a bundle of sage, a rattle, and an eagle feather fan while singing. Another eagle feather fan remains with him throughout the night. These items now move on to the next singer, while the drum follows behind, sometimes with the Drummerman, who may or may not do most of the drumming during the night. The prayers during the rest of the night are all made while the person praying smokes a cornhusk cigarette. Whether or not such cigarettes are initiated by the Roadman, they pass to him in the end, and the remainder of the cigarette is then buried in the coals behind the fire. The Fireman tends the fire continually, breaking off coals, rearranging sticks, and adding new sticks. Before midnight he shapes the coals, sometimes into the shape of a heart. The Roadman makes two prayers before midnight, one for the four officiants and one for all the fans and ritual equipment, followed by incense purification. The participants can then use their own fans for the first time, to fan themselves, to shield themselves from the firelight, and to shake in time with the music. The singing stops during incensing.

The Fireman prepares for the midnight water ceremony, reshaping the ashes, perhaps into a crescent, a full moon, or an eagle, fixing the fire, sweeping the floor, and burning the cigarette butts, an act that destroys people's sins and shortcomings and carries their prayers to God. The midnight water song, a fixed song, is sung; and after two more songs the Roadman blows his whistle four times, the Fireman brings in the midnight water, and the fourth song is sung. The Cedarman prays for the cedar and water, and then the Fireman lights a cornhusk cigarette and prays. After passing to the other officiants, with a seconding prayer and an expression of thanks to the participants from the Roadman, the remains of the cigarette are burned. The Roadman performs a ritual with the water, first blowing a whistle in it four times, making the shape of a cross, then moving his fan through it in the same shape, and then asperging the participants. The drum is given water to drink. Before the meeting, it was partly filled with water and with pieces of charcoal from the fire. There may then be teaching about Peyote by the Roadman. The holy water then goes round the room, and all drink. The Roadman goes out with his equipment and blows his whistle in the cardinal directions. Thereafter the patient uses a cornhusk cigarette to pray. No singing occurs at this time. This prayer, too, is seconded by the Roadman. The patient is purified with incense and is given specially prepared Peyote, normally four boluses chewed by the Roadman. He has thus rid himself of his sins. Singing and drumming continue until the morning water ceremony, and after gaining permission from the Roadman, some participants roll cornhusk cigarettes and offer prayers. Although these prayers, like those at the midnight water, morning water, and Peyote breakfast ceremonies, should be for the purpose of the meeting, it is also customary to seek God's blessing for oneself and help for one's own troubles, and to reach out to pray as well for others in the meeting, absent kin and friends, and indeed the welfare of the United States. There is some feeling that the primary focus should be on the purpose of the meeting, and an excessive amount of attention to the needs of others is

Denver Mus. of Nat. Hist.: Crane Coll. 4125 and 4653.

Fig. 2. Peyote-related watercolor paintings. left, *Peyote Way Ceremony*, depicting cross-sectional view of tepee, showing arrangement of participants and paraphernalia. The participants are probably (clockwise from left): Drummerman (with drum), Roadman (holding peyote staff, fan, and bundle of sage in left hand, and rattle in right), Cedarman (holding peyote fan and sitting just in front of the wooden box in which equipment is held), patient and 2 general participants, Fireman (holding single eagle feather), and Dawn Woman (with bucket of water placed immediately in front of her) (see Aberle 1967:129, diagram 1). Also shown are the crescent moon earth altar (against which a reed or eagle bone whistle is leaning) and ashes, central fire (shown here with logs in an unusual configuration), firestick (just to the right, or east, of the fire). A bucket of peyote tea and covered container of peyote are on Drummerman's right. right, *Peyote Altar*, includes a symbolic depiction of the Christian cross, behind Roadman (whose face painting may represent symbolically the hallucinatory effects of peyote). He is about to sprinkle cedar incense from a beaded bag. The incised line on the earth altar represents the peyote road of life, with the peyote button known as Chief Peyote at its midpoint; the ashes in front of the altar are shaped into a bird form. Painted by Beatien Yazz, a Navajo member of the Native American Church (see Brody 1971:162–165), in 1959 or before.

regarded as not entirely seemly. Prayer is usually accompanied by weeping, as people call to mind the miseries of the patient, themselves, or others, and ask God's help, like children asking help of their parents in crisis.

The morning water ceremony occurs at about four o'clock. Preparations are like those for the midnight water ceremony, but the water is brought this time by a woman, referred to as Dawn Woman or the water woman. She is ordinarily the Roadman's wife, one of the sponsors, or a relative of a sponsor. Sometimes she is a participant; sometimes she has been outside all night. It is an honor to perform the ceremony. She brings in the water just after the first song, the morning water song, which is a fixed song in a group of four songs. On completion of the set, the Cedarman prays or selects someone else to pray in his stead. The spirit of the meeting has changed. Where the patient's prayer, the midnight water prayer, and the participants' prayers dwelt on suffering, sin, and shortcomings, the Cedarman's prayer does not discuss the bad things, which are now past, but deals with hopes for the future and with the right way to live. Dawn Woman, who has a parrot feather, rolls a cigarette after a ritual over the water, expresses her appreciation, and prays over the water, which the patient is to drink for a good future and a long life. The Roadman seconds the prayer. Dawn Woman offers water to mother earth; the Roadman performs the ritual with the whistle and fan in the water, as at midnight, the drum and drumstick are given water, and then the people drink. Singing continues after the morning water ceremony, and preparation for the Peyote breakfast begins.

The Fireman brings in water, corn, fruit, and boneless meat, in that order—four goods given to the Indians by God before the White man came. This time the Drummerman prays over the Peyote breakfast with a cornhusk cigarette, giving thanks for the purpose of the meeting, which is regarded as having had its desirable effect. Singing may continue at this point or may stop. Whenever the Roadman wishes, the drum and staff return to him, and he sings three songs of his own choosing, followed by the closing song. The drum is untied, the ritual equipment put away, and the drum water is passed around for people to drink a little. Before the equipment is put away, and ahead of the drum and its water, it is passed around the hogan, every one touching it reverently. The drum water is poured on the west side of the altar, the charcoal in the drum is returned to the fire, all the equipment is purified with incense, and the Fireman takes it out. The patient receives the sage cushion from under the Chief Peyote. The Peyote breakfast is passed round in the order in which it came in. It must all be eaten. It is holy food. People may talk about the meeting and their experiences. The dishes are purified with incense and removed. Then the people go out, at about 7:00 or 7:30, whether it is past sunrise or not. Some might be given incense at this time, if they had a hard time during the meeting.

The meeting is over. People smile shyly, shake hands, and thank one another for their efforts—their prayer, singing, or simple participation. The ashes are disposed of, the altar removed, and the firestick saved for another meeting, unless it is too short, in which case it is burned. People may lounge about, talk, sleep, or leave the area if they have things to attend to. Around noon, a large meal (not to be confused with the Peyote breakfast, which provides only a mouthful of each dish for each person) is served. It is preceded by a prayer, and the person selected to pray is honored. Not only traditional Navajo foods but also delicacies like sweet rolls, soda pop, and salads make their appearance. Ordinarily after this, in the hogan, a blanket is placed before the Roadman, on which people may place their offerings. No one need make an offering, but all those in the hogan will shake hands first with the Roadman and then with everyone else in the room. Some Roadmen refuse any offering on some occasions; some will accept no offering at a meeting conducted for a relative. In English, it is called a freewill offering. The sponsors may have given the Roadman a gift privately; the Roadman may well give gifts to other officiants, and particularly to the Drummerman for his arduous efforts.

No account of the ritual, however meticulous, can convey its atmosphere and spirit. The smell of cedar smoke and juniper incense, the flickering flames seen through the feathers of a fan, the drumming and singing, which fill the room and suffuse one's body, the hope and anxiety of the opening, the grief and acute anxiety from midnight until shortly before the morning water ceremony, and the increased happiness and hope from then on—these things, the longing prayers, and the fellowship of 12 hours of common effort toward the purposes of the meeting are easily sensed but described with difficulty.

A fuller account of a Navajo Peyote meeting as described by a Roadman is provided by Aberle (1967:127–141), who also gives variations in Navajo ritual (Aberle 1967:157–173). A Roadman tends to follow the practices of his own teacher and to introduce small-changes if inspired to do so. Navajo Roadmen have been trained by Utes (themselves principally trained by Cheyennes), by Cheyennes, and by Otos. Roadmen from other tribes, including Kiowa and Yuchi, have had some impact. Many non-Navajo Roadmen visit the Navajo, some staying for extended periods. Some have married into the tribe. Many of them "doctor" patients, using various Plains curing techniques. Cheyenne influence is marked in the northern reservation, where there is a tendency to stress the significance of visionary experience, and Oto in the south, where the stress is on inner reflection and the moral message of Peyotism. These variations are less impressive than the similarities among Navajo ritual, Plains ritual, and the ritual as first described by Mooney (1892, 1896, 1897). They unite the Church members of this Southwestern tribe with those of many other tribes of the United States and Canada.

Syncretism

There is little indication that traditional Navajo religious belief and ritual have had any major influence on Navajo Peyotist belief and ritual, or that the reverse has occurred. Most Peyote rituals in other tribes focus on curing, as do most Navajo Peyote rituals and most traditional Navajo rituals. There seems no reason to attribute this focus in Navajo Peyotism to influence from traditional Navajo ritual. Some of the minor variants found in a small sector of the reservation appear to have been influenced by traditional Navajo ritual, and perhaps by divination ritual, but more detail is needed for definite conclusions. Although some traditional Navajo singers are also Roadmen, they claim to keep the two rituals entirely separate, and there is no evidence of any mingling. Peyote meetings are held to pray for the success of Navajo ceremonies and to give thanks for a positive outcome. Some Navajos have learned "moons" (rituals) from several different Roadmen, which may be a Navajo analogue for knowing several Navajo chants. And for Navajo Peyotists, God and the Holy People of Navajo religion are "all part of the same thing" (Aberle 1967:198–199). There is some tendency to classify Peyote meetings as "in the manner of Blessingway" if their primary aim is to seek good fortune and "in the manner of Evilway" if their primary aim is to overcome bad fortune, an analogy with traditional rituals. Most Navajo Peyotists also use Navajo ceremonies. Many belong to Christian churches as well.

The Appeal of the Peyote Religion to Navajos

Since the 1890s in many tribes traditionalists, Christian Indians, and the agents of White society have opposed the spread of Peyotism. In the early phases of the appearance of the religion in a new tribe, an adherent must face the disapproval of most of his social world (for some instances of Indian opposition, see La Barre 1964:112, 114–116, 119–121; for opposition by Whites, see Slotkin 1956:50–56, 123–133). Nowhere has opposition gone to greater lengths than among the Navajo. The appeal of Peyotism must be strong for people to take up the religion under these conditions. Although enemies of the Native American Church are likely to explain the appeal as a simple matter of addiction to a "drug" or getting "kicks" from taking Peyote, Peyote is not physiologically addictive (see Seevers 1954), nor do users recognize a subjective craving for it (Aberle 1967:10). Using Peyote is not regarded as pleasurable by most members, although the religious experiences are regarded as highly valuable.

Peyotism in the form in which it has existed since the 1880s or earlier in the United States is best seen as a religion of the oppressed, which is responsive to the needs of Indians living under reservation conditions of domination, expropriation, exploitation, and dole. It is polyvalent, appealing to those deprived of power, status, economic goods, and a viable economy and polity and subjected to discrimination as Indians with attendant loss of self-esteem (Lanternari 1963; Aberle 1967:322–329, 336–337). After the terrible experience of defeat and confinement at Fort Sumner between 1863 and 1868, Navajos, unlike the vast majority of American Indian tribes, lived in at least a portion of their old territory, were able repeatedly to expand their reservation, and until the 1930s had an apparently viable economy based on farming, livestock (principally sheep), crafts (silversmithing and weaving), and some employment, which enabled them to maintain themselves and many of their traditional ways of life. From 1869 until the 1930s there were almost no religious movements among them. Livestock reduction, first on a percentage basis and later on a permit-ceiling basis, entered their lives in 1933 and became more intensive in 1936. The results of livestock reduction and the concomitant Depression were an initial reduction in standard of living and a suddenly increased dependency on wage labor, which had been a minor part of the economy since the 1880s.

These changes did not destroy traditional culture, although they added many novel cultural features. Livestock reduction brought to Navajos an experience of the power of the dominant American society such as they had not had since the removal to Fort Sumner. There was serious economic privation, loss of status for well-to-do livestock owners, and a widespread feeling of despair and confusion. Furthermore, changes over a longer period had brought new problems of other sorts, such as excessive drinking by a portion of the population. Religious orientations are attitudes toward power and appear to be related to a group's experience of social power (Swanson 1960; Burridge 1969:3–14). Faced by new experiences of external power and by new problems, some Navajos perhaps found that traditional Navajo religion, immanent in its view about power and rooted in the Navajo country, provided insufficient answers to new questions. This may explain why minor religious movements occurred shortly after livestock reduction began, arising in the northern Navajo country, long a focus of opposition to the Bureau of Indian Affairs (Aberle 1967:73–74). During the livestock crisis and at the same time as these other religious experiments, Peyotism, known to Navajos north of the San Juan living in close contact with the Utes, spread south of the San Juan in about 1936 and in a period of four years gained many adherents in a number of communities (Aberle and Stewart 1957). Although there is no proof of a causal connection between livestock reduction and consequent relative deprivation, on the one hand, and this spread, on the other, it is plausible to regard the phenomena as linked. In several communities members of the Native American Church were found on average to have lost more livestock during reduction than had nonmembers (Aberle 1967:252–277). Only a few Peyotists make a direct connection between the livestock crisis and their joining the Church, but there were Peyote meetings during livestock reduction aimed at finding out what the Bureau of Indian Affairs was going to do, at stopping reduction through supernatural means, and at retaining special permits (for amounts of stock above the normal maximum for a given district), also by supernatural means. Since these permits are still in existence, Peyotists believe they succeeded in that respect.

It is plausible that, for Navajos faced with new problems, a new source of supernatural power promised new answers, and that they quickly began to use the new power for old purposes as well. Peyotism promised them success in their endangered livelihood, abstinence from alcohol, new purpose in life, and a way of dealing with old and chronic problems—illness, witchcraft, and the effects of ghosts. God's power was not confined to the Navajo country but operated everywhere. In its affirmation of Indian identity and dignity, Peyotism offered some surcease for the miseries of being derogated for being an Indian. The two features most commonly mentioned in the 1950s as "good things" about the Native American Church are the curative powers of Peyote and the value of the morality (especially abstinence from alcohol), and the next most commonly mentioned are improvement of livelihood or finding a clearer sense of purpose in life, or both.

In the 1950s in random samples drawn from two communities, Navajo Peyotists could not be distinguished from non-Peyotists in terms of indices of acculturation (Aberle 1967:244–251). Nevertheless, it was evident that there were then no Peyotists among the most highly acculturated Navajos to be found in the Navajo country: well-paid, technically trained employees of the BIA with a fluent command of English. By the late 1960s this was no longer true. For one thing, the level of income and of job quality of some Peyotists with moderate education had improved greatly, and for another a new generation of birthright Peyotists had appeared. College-educated Navajos with excellent jobs with the BIA and the Navajo Tribe could be found attending Peyote meetings. Whether the proportions of such individuals among the Peyotists are higher or lower than in the non-Peyotist population is not known.

It has been suggested that Peyotism affords a synthesis of contradictions for Indians caught in a dilemma between their need for mutual aid and orientation to the Indian community on the one hand, and, on the other hand, the pressures of the contemporary economy, which drive them toward individual economic success. The Peyote ritual accepts their individualistic strivings but orients them to the Indian collective (Aberle 1967:142–143). Peyotism also attempts to make Indians abandon individualistic hedonism, such as drinking, lack of attention to family needs, and adultery. Thus it directs the person toward effortful striving, toward Indian identity and mutual aid, and away from either narrowly egotistical achievement or narrowly egotistical hedonism; it attempts to lead the individual to balance his own needs and those of his group (see Jorgensen 1972:231–236ff.).

Opposition to Peyotism

Navajo reasons for opposing the Native American Church were the same that have been expressed in any other place. There was objection to Peyotism because it was not the traditional Navajo religion, because it was not orthodox Christianity, and because of the alleged, and undemonstrated, negative effects of Peyote, which was said to produce addiction, insanity, stillbirths, and birth defects and to be responsible for numerous deaths. Peyotists were said to indulge in sexual orgies and incest during Peyote meetings and to be lazy, neglect their work, and fail to educate their children. They were also alleged to neglect their kinship oblications. Roadmen were said to exploit their patients economically, so that they lost their livestock paying for ceremonies. Peyote was grouped with certain plants believed by Navajos to affect the mind, and non-Peyotists believed that Peyotists tried to administer Peyote to them without their knowing it. To Peyotist claims that Peyote stopped people from drinking, anti-Peyotists replied that Peyote caused a form of intoxication. In answer to Peyotists' claims of superior moral behavior, anti-Peyotists replied with accusations of misbehavior on the part of some Peyotists. In some Peyote meetings, diagnoses of witchcraft, perhaps including the naming of the alleged witch, were made, and anti-Peyotists regarded such accusations as dangerous and disturbing to the community (Aberle 1967:195–223). It is evident that Peyotism is neither traditional Navajo religion nor establishment Christianity; it is also evident that not all Peyotists are saints, and hence that misdeeds can be realistically attributed to some Church members; and the problems resulting from witchcraft accusations are real. There is no evidence to support the allegations about the negative effects of Peyote (Aberle 1967:399–405; Bergman 1971).

It is likely that many allegations about the effects of Peyote were drawn from White anti-Peyote propaganda, and especially from a work prepared under the aegis of the Bureau of Indian Affairs (U.S. Bureau of Indian Affairs 1925) and from various missionary comments, and probably specifically from *The Christian Indian* and *The Missionary Monthly* (see Aberle and Stewart 1957:65–69). There would undoubtedly have been opposition to the Native American Church in any case, but White antagonism contributed to the conflict.

From the 1930s to the 1970s the Native American Church in the Navajo country was involved in conflict with the tribal council, the BIA, other branches of the federal government, and the courts and legislatures of various states, all of which were resolved successfully. The struggles of individual Peyotists with their kinsmen and friends were intense from the 1930s to the 1950s, but relations between Peyotists and non-Peyotists became increasingly peaceful in later decades. The Peyote religion among the Navajo had its significant beginnings in the 1920s when Navajos living north of the San Juan in close contact with the Southern Ute, and especially the Ute Mountain Ute, began to participate in Peyote meetings. Ute contacts were facilitated in 1933 and thereafter by the employment of Navajos in Civilian Conservation Corps projects on the Ute Reservation. In 1936 or 1937, the Peyote religion was carried across the San Juan and spread rapidly on the reservation (for a detailed history see Aberle and Stewart 1957; Marriott and Rachlin 1971:39 believe that the Peyote religion may have reached the Navajo as early as 1901).

New Mexican, Santa Fe, N. Mex.

Fig. 3. Peyote meeting at Sawmill, Ariz., in June or July 1954. Singer at center holds staff (decorated with beadwork and tipped with horsehair) and peyote fan in his left hand, and a rattle (moving too fast to have been caught by the camera) in his right. The drum is being played by someone other than the Drummerman (who is the man in the dark shirt at right). The peyote fans in right foreground are being held by the Roadman. This meeting, which occurred in the midst of the peyote controversy, was attended by photographers for the Santa Fe *New Mexican* and the *Arizona Republic* (see Aberle 1967:figs. 1–4, 6–25). Photograph by Dave Weber, from collection of David Aberle.

The Tribal Council

From the beginning, opposition was marked, and two Roadmen were arrested in 1938 for possessing Peyote, at a time when there was no tribal statute on the subject (Aberle 1967:110). In 1940 the tribal council banned the sale, use, or possession of Peyote in the Navajo country (Navajo Tribal Council 1940; see also Navajo Indians 1962:96–97, 168 for this and other anti-Peyote legislation). The resolution of 1940 attacked Peyote on grounds that it was unconnected with, and contradictory to, Navajo religious practice and was damaging to, and foreign to, traditional Navajo life. Peyotists found it ironic that a resolution spearheaded by councilmen who were Navajo Christians and in some cases Christian missionaries should be so concerned about traditional religion, but the wording permitted Christians and traditionalists to join hands in opposition to Peyotism. The resolution received only one dissenting vote, that of Hola Tso, the sole Peyotist then on the council, who later became a vice-president of the Native American Church of North America (fig. 4) (Navajo Tribal Council 1940; Aberle 1949–1980).

The resolution of 1940 faced John Collier, the commissioner of Indian affairs, with a conflict of legal and moral principles. Legally, a tribe retains sovereign powers that permit it, in the absence of constraint from its own constitution or laws, to limit freedom of religion (see Stewart 1961:15–17 for a list of some of the relevant cases and Cohen 1942:122 for the general principle). Nevertheless, a tribe's laws must be approved by the secretary of the interior. Finally, in the 1940s, the Navajo police force was paid out of federal funds and supervised by BIA officials. Collier accepted the view of tribal sovereignty espoused by Cohen (1942) and supported by many court decisions, favored tribal self-government, valued freedom of religion, and had a high opinion of the Peyote religion. He reluctantly accepted the resolution, which was approved by Secretary of the Interior Harold L. Ickes in late 1940; public acceptance of the resolution by the secretary was announced on January 15, 1941 (Collier 1940, 1941). Later Collier asked that the police take a minimum of initiative in enforcing it, by acting only on complaints. Nevertheless, arrests began in 1941 and continued. Hence in

April 1944 he ruled that no federal employee—that is, no tribal police officer—could be used to enforce the resolution, since federal funds could not be used to violate the federal Constitution. That is, the tribal council could have its resolution but in theory could not enforce it. A situation in which a tribal government cannot enforce its own legislation epitomizes the legal contradictions of tribes as quasi-sovereign entities.

In an earlier epoch, BIA paternalism had been reflected in the effort to stamp out Peyotism (see Slotkin 1956:50–55, 123–133). Then it appeared in new guise in a refusal to enforce a tribe's anti-Peyote legislation. In fact arrests continued to occur, with somewhat haphazard outcomes: trial, fine, and jail; trial and probation; release without trial; or any of the above, and illegal confiscation of ritual equipment, usually returned on appeal.

The council felt that its authority was mocked, but the Peyotists who were being arrested felt that their freedom of worship was threatened. In 1945–1946, following a common practice of Peyotists in other states since the 1920s, they responded by filing papers of incorporation in Utah, Colorado, New Mexico, and Arizona, as had been done in other states. In this instance the move was stimulated by Frank Takes Gun, then vice-president of the Native American Church (Slotkin 1956:161–164; Stewart 1972–1980). Although Peyote was illegal in all these states except Utah, incorporations were not challenged, and copies of the articles of incorporation, which mention the use of Peyote as a sacrament, were used by Peyotists as "charters" to dispute their arrests and to justify their rights.

There had been three arrests in 1941 (Young 1961:277–278). At least eight are known between 1942 and 1951, but this figure is undoubtedly low since systematic law and order data are not available (Aberle 1967:114–115). Peyotists also suffered from anti-Peyotist vigilante raids in 1947. Non-Navajo antagonism to Peyotism became manifest, perhaps because the BIA was not attempting to extirpate it. Largely through the efforts of a medical missionary, Dr. Clarence G. Salsbury, then head of the Presbyterian mission at Ganado, articles hostile to Navajo Peyotism appeared in newspapers and magazines. Counter-statements appeared, one signed by several anthropologists and one by Collier, no longer commissioner of Indian affairs. Perhaps as a response to tribal council and wider public reactions, the BIA supported anthropological study of the Peyote religion in the Navajo country, beginning in 1949 (Aberle 1967:115–116, 227–243). In 1953 the tribal police were paid in part out of tribal funds, and the argument that they could not be used to enforce the resolution lost its effect. By 1958 the tribe paid most law-enforcement expenses, assuming formal responsibility for almost all enforcement activities in 1959 (Young 1961:281–282). Arrest rates showed no change when the tribe began to pay its own police. There were 96 arrests in 1952, 89 in 1953, 102 in 1954, 99 in 1955, 86 in 1956, 91 in 1957, 70 in 1959, and 38 in 1960, for a total of 768 (Young 1961:278). Although membership was growing, arrests remained nearly constant from 1952 through 1958, decreasing thereafter. Probably prior to 1953 fewer arrests eventuated in trials. In 1954 the arrest and sentencing of 13 Peyotists rounded up at a single meeting resulted in a request from Navajo Peyotists for a hearing before the tribal council, in hopes of a cancellation of the 1940 resolution. After listening to two expert witnesses, a few Navajo Peyotists, and one opponent of Peyotism, the council left the resolution in force (Navajo Tribal Council 1954). Unable to change the council's views, the Native American Church attempted to nullify the 1940 resolution through federal court action. Under the leadership of Frank Takes Gun, the newly elected president of the Native American Church of North America, there were two efforts in 1956, one in 1958, and one in 1960. The 1958 case was reviewed by the Tenth Circuit Court of Appeals, in Denver, in 1959. The 1960 case was initiated in the U.S. District Court for the District of Columbia, was reviewed by the District of Columbia Court of Appeals in 1962, and was rejected for appeal by the U.S. Supreme Court in 1963. Thus the Native American Church failed in all its attempts to nullify the Navajo tribal anti-Peyote ordinance of 1940 through federal court action.

New Mexican, Santa Fe, N.Mex.

Fig. 4. Hola Tso. Photograph by Dave Weber, summer 1954.

Meantime the council further strengthened its stand in 1956, when it legalized destruction of Peyote confiscated in the course of an arrest. Even so, for the first time some non-Peyotist councilmen spoke against the legislation (Navajo Tribal Council 1956). In addition, the number of Peyotist councilmen was growing, from one in 1940, to at least two in 1954, to about a dozen in 1959. Increased Native American Church membership began to have political impact.

In 1963 Native American Church members threw their support to Raymond Nakai, a candidate for the chairmanship of the tribal council, a non-Peyotist whose speeches stressed religious liberty for Navajos, and thus by implication for Peyotists. After his election there were no more arrests of Peyotists, although he took no further steps until the beginning of his second term. On October 9, 1967, the tribal council passed resolution CO–63–67 on basic Navajo human rights, which included freedom of religion, and on October 11, by a vote of 29 to 26, with 19 councilmen absent, it passed resolution CO–65–67, which continued the prohibition against the sale, use, and possession of Peyote in the Navajo country, with a crucial exemption: "it shall not be unlawful for any member of the Native American Church to transport peyote into Navajo country, or to buy, sell, possess, or use peyote in any form, in connection with the religious practices, sacraments or services of the Native American Church" (Navajo Tribal Council 1967). Officials of the Native American Church wholeheartedly supported the legislation, which prevented nonmembers from trafficking in Peyote or using it casually, while leaving members free to practice their religion. Passage of the resolution was made possible by the votes of not only Peyotist members of the council but also some non-Peyotists, who by then favored tolerance of the Native American Church. For the first time in 27 years Peyotists could practice their religion without fear of legal sanctions.

Social Adjustments

From the late 1930s until around 1956, most non-Peyotists who had heard of Peyote were antagonistic to the Peyote religion; yet it was from the ranks of anti-Peyotists that new converts came. The early spread of Peyotism caused severe conflict between neighbors, between friends, and between kinsmen residing in different extended families. Rarely was there conflict within an extended family. In some cases mutual aid between Peyotist and anti-Peyotist kinsmen ceased; some traditional ceremonialists refused Peyotist patients; and Peyotists sometimes rejected traditional ceremonies. Even so, there were chapter officers and councilmen who said privately that in spite of their opposition to Peyotism, it would be better to tolerate it than to perpetuate conflict (Aberle 1967:205). Events during this period have been interpreted to show that Peyotists tended to reduce the scope of their kinship obligations, but this conclusion seems unwarranted. As Peyotists grew to become a sizable minority or a majority in a community, breaches between kinsmen healed, often through the conversion of the non-Peyotists. Cooperation returned. Navajo ceremonialists were unlikely to reject Peyotist patients and in some cases joined the Native American Church. There were more and more tolerant nonmembers. These changes occurred before the legal reform of 1967. By 1973 the acute tension of earlier decades was past, although some conflict and mutual derogation could be found at the community level.

Legislation and Litigation

Navajo Peyotists were involved in legal problems in Colorado, Utah, New Mexico, and Arizona; in California, where many Navajos found employment; and in Texas, the source of Peyote for all U.S. Peyotists. One method of struggle was to lobby for changes in state laws against the sale, use, and possession of Peyote, so as to provide exemption for members of the Native American Church. Another was to work through the courts when Peyotists were arrested, or even to arrange test cases. Peyotists supported an exemption clause in New Mexico, which the state legislature passed in 1959, after the same clause had been defeated by veto in 1957. In Colorado, the state legislature provided a similar exemption in 1969. Utah, which had no law against Peyote from 1935 to 1971, provided an exemption for members of the Native American Church in 1971. In Arizona, a successful court case in 1960 did not prevent the subsequent arrest of Peyotists, but another court case in 1969 led to an Arizona Court of Appeals, Division One, decision in 1973 that members of the Native American Church were exempt from the state law's penalties. The U.S. Supreme Court in 1974 refused to review the decision. Arrests of Navajos in California in the early 1960s led to a court case in 1962, followed by a California Supreme Court decision in 1964 that treated the 1959 California law as an infringement of religious liberty when applied to members of the Native American Church; however, in 1974 Peyotists were still being arrested in California, although they were being released when defense attorneys called attention to the 1964 decision. When the Texas legislature, by an oversight, omitted an exemption for Peyotists from new legislation in 1967, a Navajo was involved in a test case, which he won in local court in Laredo in 1968. The Texas legislature restored the usual exemption in 1969. Federal drug legislation in 1970 threatened the use of Peyote by members of the Native American Church, but implementing regulations circulated in 1971 retained their exemption. Legislative actions, federal and state, from 1965 on, were responses to the growing popularity of psychotropic substances among U.S. non-Indians. Efforts by White users of psychotropics to use Peyotism as a precedent for their behavior alarmed members of the Native American Church, who refused to make common cause with them.

In their struggles, Navajos have been aided by anthropologists, psychiatrists, the American Civil Liberties Union, the Texas Civil Liberties Union, and the Dinebeiina Nahiilna Be Agaditahe, the legal services program of the Office of Economic Opportunity in the Navajo country; however, the brunt has fallen on Navajo members of the Native American Church, who have had to gather funds to pay for legal services and to transport themselves to court hearings and legislative sessions, to leave their work and their families for these occasions, and to travel many miles. Their accomplishments in these many confrontations are notable.

Navajos and the Native American Church of North America

Between the 1930s and the 1950s Navajo Peyotists grew from a handful to become the largest single tribal element in the Native American Church, while at the same time their problems became the most pressing faced by the Church. From the beginning they sought the counsel of experienced Oklahoma Peyotists, and Hola Tso began to attend national meetings of the Church in 1946. Frank Takes Gun who became involved in the Navajos' struggle 1945–1946, was a Crow from Montana. Navajos achieved representation among the officers of the Native American Church of North America beginning in 1956, when Hola Tso became president. Takes Gun, elected president in that year, moved to Albuquerque to be close to the Navajo struggle. His preoccupation with the Navajo scene was not welcome among all sectors of the national organization, and perhaps there was resentment at the time and money expended on Navajo problems. In 1957 he succeeded in passing a resolution to hold elections every six years instead of every two years, in violation of the bylaws of the Church. This disturbed many members and raised questions of the legality of his actions. Opposition centered in more easterly and northerly tribes (Native American Church of North America 1957; letter of March 1958, J. Sidney Slotkin to Hola Tso in Stewart 1972–1980). Annual meetings were held most often in the Southwest, which also disturbed members of easterly and northerly tribes. Finally, in August 1964 a split-off group held its own conventions and elections, calling itself the Native American Church of North America. (The Native American Church newsletter of December 1964 listed the officers of this group, who were from tribes in Nebraska and Iowa.) Takes Gun continued his organization, with two Navajos on his executive board in 1965, while Hola Tso continued as vice-president. At the end of Takes Gun's second six-year term, in 1968, there were double elections, and Navajos then appeared as officers in both groups. Throughout these years, the majority of Navajos supported Takes Gun, partly because of his assistance with their problems and partly because the Native American Church of Navajoland, developed under his leadership and chartered by him, had proved valuable as a unitary organization for the Navajo struggle. Nevertheless, by 1968 some senior Navajo Peyotists were quietly uneasy about the split and uncertain about their support for Takes Gun. In 1972 an election reunited the Native American Church under James Atcitty, a Navajo prominent in tribal and New Mexico state politics, even though Takes Gun, who no longer had a following, still maintained that he was president of the organization (Omer C. Stewart, personal communication 1973). Thus the growth in Navajo membership and the Navajo struggle were factors in splitting the Native American Church, while its reunion under a Navajo president reflects the shift in the center of gravity of the Native American Church of North America.

By 1973 victory in the tribal arena brought the Native American Church in the Navajo country to a new phase. Following its acceptance in tribal legislation it began to cooperate with Navajo law and order personnel, sometimes informing the police if nonmembers attempted to sell Peyote. In addition, factional developments occurred, as evidenced by the existence in 1973 of three Peyote organizations among the Navajo. After 1967 Peyotism no longer needed a monolithic front against oppression.

Since 1974 a number of publications relevant to the Peyote religion in the Navajo country have appeared. E.F. Anderson (1979) provides an account of a variant type of Peyote ceremony, V-Way ritual (see Aberle 1967). Hultkrantz (1975) comments on interpretations of Navajo Peyotism. Wagner (1974, 1975, 1975a, 1978) provides new research on Navajo Peyotism bearing on the importance of relative deprivation and acculturation as factors influencing membership, on the kinship ethic of Peyotists, on syncretism, and on numerous other topics. Beaver (1979) and Dolaghan and Scates (1978) discuss the rapid expansion of evangelical fundamentalist, often independent, often charismatic Christian congregations, many led by Navajos, which has drawn away some Navajos from the practice of traditional ritual and Peyote ceremonies.

Summary

From a handful of participants in the 1930s, the Peyote religion in the Navajo country grew to embrace at least a substantial minority, and perhaps a majority of the tribe by 1974. This growth was stimulated by the fact that Navajos faced new problems growing out of their relationship with the larger society, and initially those surrounding livestock reduction. Opposition to Peyotism was stronger, more organized, and more prolonged than in the case of any other tribe for which there is a detailed history, but the Peyotists' struggle of more than 30 years was successful. Their success is a tribute to their determination, courage, and organizational abilities. Yet when one considers other valiant struggles for Indian rights—water, tribal control of tribal destiny, and justice for Indians—the question arises why there is success in the Peyote arena and failure in so many others. Granting the vigor of Peyotists and their willingness to face arrest and jail, one might nevertheless suspect that the struggle over Peyotism threatened White values but not White interests, while in the other conflicts, interests of powerful White groups are engaged in opposition to Indians. The Native American Church has proved itself strong in the face of threats. Its beautiful ritual, its moral code, its effort to maintain community against corrosive atomization of Indian groups, its significance as a vehicle for Indian identity, and its ways of reacting to Indian deprivation are likely to make it appeal to Navajo people and give meaning to the lives of tens of thousands of Navajos for many years to come.

Language and Reality in Navajo World View

GARY WITHERSPOON

What people or peoples, including Western scientists, call their knowledge of reality consists of images of it that they themselves have fashioned, and what they see in reality is to a considerable degree a reflex of the devices by which they render it visible (Geertz 1971:20). If we are to penetrate another culture's world view, we must see their world through the same devices by which they render it visible.

Concepts, views, and meanings are embodied in symbols. The craving for symbols and the impulse to create and use them are integral to the life of man. The mind seeks to express its concepts, ideas, and sentiments and to see these embodied in objective symbols or symbolic acts. What the poet does in words and rhyme, groups of men do in symbolic acts and creations. Symbols capture and express, frame and focus, recall and retain, synthesize and condense cultural beliefs of enormous proportions into simple symbols that are polysemous and multivocal.

Each culture has two principal symbolic systems: linguistic and nonlinguistic. The ideas and views of a people are embodied in and communicated by both symbolic systems, but together they form a single meaningful system. Nevertheless, an analysis of a people's world view as seen through linguistic symbols and as seen through nonlinguistic symbols will not produce a single view of the same world. Each symbolic system provides a different device, a different angle, a different point of view. This difference is not so much contradictory as it is complementary. Linguistic and nonlinguistic symbolic systems, for the most part, support, enhance, and supplement each other.

Although this account of Navajo world view focuses mainly on the analysis of a set of linguistic symbols, the linguistic symbols and their meanings are analyzed in the context of both linguistic and nonlinguistic symbolism, and meanings derived from the analysis of ritual and other nonlinguistic symbolism are included to complement and supplement the view of the world contained in the linguistic symbolism.

It is also important to remember that culture is more than the sum of its parts, and that a world view is more than a combination of domains and categories. This view of culture is based on the view of man as a symbolizing, conceptualizing, meaning-seeking animal who cannot live in an incoherent, disordered, and meaningless world. The need to make sense out of experience, to give it form and order, is as basic to man as the more familiar biological needs (Geertz 1958:436). World views arise out of man's quest for unity underlying apparent diversity, for simplicity underlying apparent complexity; for order underlying apparent disorder, for regularity underlying apparent anomaly.

Navajo World View

If a world view is to make sense out of experience, and give it form, direction, and purpose, it cannot be fragmentary or incoherent. It must be more than the sum of its parts. It must be a unified whole that has a central hub and theme where everything comes together. Rather than an admixture of diversified themes, world views tend to develop central, unifying themes.

In Navajo world view this central theme is found in the phrase *są'áh naagháí bik'eh hózhǫ́* or in its shorter version as simply *hózhǫ́.** Kluckhohn (1968:686) identified *hózhǫ́* as the central idea in Navajo religious thinking. But it is not something that occurs only in ritual song and prayer; it is referred to frequently in everyday speech. A Navajo uses this concept to express his happiness, his health, the beauty of his land, and the harmony of his relations with others. It is used in reminding people to be careful and deliberate, and when he says good-bye to someone leaving, he will say *hózhǫ́ǫgo naninâa doo* 'may you walk or go about according to *hózhǫ́*'.

The longer phrase SNBH denotes that according to which *hózhǫ́* exists. SNBH has been translated numerous ways, all of which have been inadequate. The most common of these translations is the one popularized by Haile (1943a). It describes *są'áh naagháí* as 'long life' and *bik'eh hózhǫ́* as 'happiness'. Other translations include: 'in-old-age-walking-the-trail-of-beauty', 'according-to-old-age-may-it-be-perfect', and 'according-to-the-

*Throughout this paper various spellings of Navajo words, including those within quotations from other sources, have been changed to accord with the standard Navajo orthography used in the *Handbook*.

ideal may-restoration-be-achieved' (Reichard 1950:46–47).†

After attempting to outline many of the Navajo concepts concerning the nature of man and the world, Reichard (1950:45) concluded:

> Consideration of the nature of the universe, the world, and man, and the nature of time and space, creation, growth, motion, order, control, and the life cycle includes all these and other Navaho concepts expressed in terms quite impossible to translate into English. The synthesis of all the beliefs detailed above and of those concerning the attitudes and experiences of man is expressed by *są'áh naagháí* usually followed by *bik'eh hózhǫ́*.

Nearly every song and prayer in the elaborate Navajo ceremonial system uses SNBH in its benediction. In fact, the entire ceremonial system is primarily designed to produce or restore the conditions symbolized by this phrase.

Są'áh

The etymology of *są'áh* makes it a derivative of the past tense form of the verb stem 'to grow, to mature'. This verb stem is used widely to denote someone or something that is mature, ripe, experienced, or aged.‡ Haile concluded that *są'áh* refers to old age as a goal in life (Wyman 1970a:29). For the Navajo death from old age is considered to be both natural and highly desirable.

Life is considered to be a cycle that reaches its natural conclusion in death from old age and is renewed in each birth. Death before old age is considered to be unnatural and tragic, preventing the natural completion of the life cycle. Premature death results from evil intentions and evil deeds. Ceremonies have been provided by the Holy People to combat the suffering and misfortune caused by both disharmony and evil.

It has been mistakenly reported that the Navajos have a terrible fear of death. Actually they have a tremendous respect for life, and an avoidance of the dead, not a fear of death. An 85-year-old singer, Bidaga, noted that he was getting old and it was time for him to die. He said that when he was young he wanted to live but with old age should come death. Death is described as the departing from the body of the breath (wind) of life. He noted that it was "just up to that wind when he will get out of the body, and then die. But this wind himself he knows just what year and what month and what time the person will die" (Ladd 1957:417).

In a study of Navajo philosophy, Ladd (1957) concluded that death per se was not considered evil or feared but that the desirability of a long life in effect meant the undesirability of dying before old age. Death as an experience is not feared. It is inastute contact with the dead that is avoided in order to prevent unnatural illness and premature death.

The term *są'áh,* therefore, expresses the Navajo concern for and emphasis upon life, and their attitude toward death of old age as a goal of life.

Naagháí

Naagháí is one of about 356,200 distinct inflected forms of the verb 'to go'. This particular form is the singular form of the third person of the continuative-imperfective mode, which refers to continually going about and returning. The prefix *náá-* of this verb is but one example of the great emphasis upon repetitions, continuations, and revolutions found in the Navajo language.

The Navajo verb distinguishes six modes and four aspects. Two of these modes and two of these aspects are concerned with the repetition, restoration, or continuous reoccurrence of an event or set of conditions, some of which imply the completion of a cycle or a revolution. There are also two verbal prefixes that denote various types of repetitions, restorations, or reoccurrences. One of these is the prefix *hi-*, which renders the idea of succession. An example of the use of this prefix from the verb 'to go' is *'ahiikai* 'we went away one after another'. Reichard (1951:262) calls *hi-* the "repetitive of action or motion."

The other verbal prefix of interest here is *náá-* or *ná-*. Reichard (1951:220) says that *náá-* refers to the repetition of an act or condition, while *ná-* refers to a restoration of a condition or an act, or to the completion of a revolution or a cycle. Paul Platero (personal communication 1973), a Navajo linguist, believes that actually *náá-* and *ná-* are the same prefix, and that this prefix has either a long or a short vowel depending on its position in a given verb or the sounds it combines with in a given verb. This prefix can refer to either a repetition or a revolution. If used together, *náádá-,* they

†Among the other forms and translations given for these archaic expressions in the literature (here transcribed into the standard Navajo orthography) are the following: *shą́'ą́naaghéí* or *sa'ą́naagháí* 'one who goes about at the brink of old age' (i.e., 'one who avoids old age, who never becomes old') and *bik'ehózhǫ́ǫ́d* 'the pleasant one', (literally 'by reason of him there is pleasantness, there is good', i.e., 'one who brings blessings'), *tsą́'ą́hnaagháí* or *tsą́'ą́hnahagháí* 'that which goes about at the rim of old age' (i.e., 'that (or those) which are everlasting') and *bik'ehózhǫ́ǫ́d* or *bik'ehózhǫ́ǫ́* 'that in accordance with which there is beauty' (Sapir and Hoijer 1942:76, 457, 398–400); *są'ah naagháí* 'Long-life' and *bik'eh hózhóón* 'Happiness' (Haile 1978:64, 130–131; cf. Haile 1938:318); *są'á naagháii bik'eh hózhǫ́ǫ́* 'Long-life Happiness-one' (Luckert 1977:99); *Tsá'ąh Naagháí* (untranslated) and *Bik'eh Hózhóón* 'Harmony, Order, Peace' (Young and Morgan 1980:200); *są́'ą́hnaagháí* 'he who goes about at the rim of old age' (Sapir and Hoijer 1967:47); *sá'ą́naagháí* or *tsą́'ą́naagháí* 'one who lives at the rim of old age (?)' (Hoijer 1974:271). (Linguistic Editor.)

‡Cf. *są́* 'old age' and perfective mode forms from the verbal root *-zé* 'to grow' like *nininísą́* 'I reached full growth' and *ninísą́* 'I reached a certain height' (Young and Morgan 1980:647–648, 684). (Linguistic Editor.)

refer to either a repetition of a repetition or a repetition of a revolution.§

Restoration is a particularly important concept in understanding the nature and purpose of curing rites. Illness occurs when the normal harmony of one's world becomes disrupted, and curing rites are designed to restore harmony through which the health of the patient is also restored. These ceremonial restorations are indicated in the Navajo language by the prefix *ná-*.

Words, like thoughts, are considered to have creative power. In mythology things came into being or happened as people thought or talked about them. Repeating something four times will cause it to occur. A request made four times cannot be easily denied. At the end of each major portion of a ceremonial prayer, the phrase *hózhǫ́ náhásdlį́į́'* is repeated four times. This phrase can be glossed as 'harmony, beauty, and health have been restored'.

The world operates daily and yearly on the basis of a four-phased cycle. This is accomplished daily in the four-pointed path of the sun and yearly in the four seasons of the annual cycle of the earth. Since the sun and the earth, days and years, operate according to a four-phased cycle, ritual drama designed to harmonize the patient's life with these important aspects of the universe must be repeated four times.

Reichard (1950:13) observed that a basic Navajo belief is that "if something happened once, it may happen again." Further, if something happens once, it will likely happen again, and maybe even again and again. *Są'áh* refers to the completion of the life cycle through death of old age, and *naagháí* refers to the continuous reoccurrence of the completion of the life cycle.

Bik'eh

Bik'eh is the easiest of the four terms to translate. It means 'according to it' or 'by its decree'. The *bi-* 'it' in this case refers to what preceded it, which is *są'áh naagháí*. What follows *bik'eh* is, then, the product of or exists in conjunction with *są'áh naagháí*. The byproduct of *są'áh naagháí* is *hózhǫ́*.

§Young and Morgan (1980), published after this chapter was written, distinguish several similar prefixes: *ná-*, indicating (inherent) repetition (*náshkad* 'I sew it'); reversionary *ná-*, indicating returning back, reverting to, or resuming an earlier state (*nánísdzá* 'I went back'; *nábidiiłna'* 'I stood it back up'; *baa nání'ą́* 'I gave it back to him'; *ná'iilghaazh* 'I went back to sleep'); semeliterative *náá-* (in some forms *náánáá-*), indicating a single repetition (*nínááhóółtą́* 'it rained again'; *baa náání'ą́* 'I gave it to him a second time'); and iterative-mode *ná-*, indicating multiple repetition (*nánítsis* 'it (fire) repeatedly goes out'). The form *naaghá* 'he's walking about, he lives (somewhere)' is analyzed to contain a prefix *na-* 'around about' (Young and Morgan 1980:593–594). (Linguistic Editor.)

Hózhǫ́

The term *hózhǫ́* is most often translated as 'beauty', although all writers recognize that this term means much more than just 'beauty' or 'beautiful conditions'. Wyman (1970a:7) translates *hózhǫ́* as everything that the Navajo thinks of as being good—that is, good as opposed to evil, favorable to man as opposed to unfavorable. He feels it expresses concepts such as beauty, perfection, harmony, goodness, normality, success, well-being, blessedness, order, and ideal. Reichard (1950:45) defines this term as perfection so far as it is obtainable by man and feels that it represents the end toward which not only man but also supernaturals, time and motion, institutions, and behavior strive.

Noting that *hózhǫ́* occurs in the names of two important ceremonials (Blessingway and Beautyway) and is frequently repeated in almost all prayers and songs, Kluckhohn (1968) translates it in various contexts as beautiful, harmonious, good, blessed, pleasant, and satisfying. In fact, Kluckhohn (1968:686) believes "the difficulty with translation primarily reflects the poverty of English in terms that simultaneously have moral and esthetic meaning."

The translations of Wyman, Reichard, and Kluckhohn provide a good general notion of the meaning of *hózhǫ́*, but they are all inadequate because they deal with only one of the two morphological components of *hózhǫ́*. They take into account only the meanings of the stem *-zhǫ́*, and ignore the semantic significance of the prefix *ho-*.‖ *Ho-* is a verbal prefix used widely in the Navajo language, but it has not been carefully defined by students of Navajo. The closest English gloss of *ho-* might be 'environment', considered in its total sense. When one is referring to environmental conditions as a whole, the term *hoot'é* 'it is' is used. *ho-* contrasts in meaning with the prefix *ni-*, which refers not to a total environment but to a particular item, event, or aspect of an environment. Thus when one says *nizhóní*, he means 'he, she, or it (something specific) is nice, pretty, or good', whereas *hózhóní* means that everything in the environment is nice, beautiful, and good.

As a verbal prefix, *ho-* refers to: the general as opposed to the specific, the whole as opposed to the part, the abstract as opposed to the concrete, the indefinite as opposed to the definite, and the infinite as opposed to the finite.

‖The analysis of Young and Morgan (1980:450), published after this chapter was written, defines *ho-* (in some forms *ha-* or *hw(i)-*) as a pronominal prefix indicating that the direct object or the subject (depending on the position in the prefixal complex) is a space, an area, 'it' in an impersonal sense, or 'things' (referring to the general situation). The variant with high tone, *hó-*, represents the contraction of *ho-* and *ni-*, the prefix used to form neuter imperfective (adjectival) stems. (Linguistic Editor.)

hózhǫ́ refers to the positive or ideal environment. It is beauty, harmony, good, happiness, and everything that is positive, and it refers to an environment that is all-inclusive. Concepts of positive health or well-being (*shił hózhǫ́* 'I am happy', *shił yá'áhoot'ééh* 'I'm contented', *hózhdiníilts'ííd* 'I feel good') all use the environmental signifier *ho-*. Positive health for the Navajo involves a proper relationship to everything in one's environment, not just the correct functioning of one's physiology.

The goal of Navajo life in this world is to live to maturity in the condition described as *hózhǫ́,* and to die of old age, the end result of which incorporates one in the universal beauty, harmony, and happiness described as *są'áh naagháí bik'eh hózhǫ́.*

SNBH in Navajo Belief

In the explicit belief of the Navajo, *są'áh naagháí* and *bik'eh hózhǫ́* are personified as two beings who form an inseparable pair. This pair originated out of First Man's medicine bundle. When they arose, they were said to be without equal in their beauty and radiance, each having long hair extending to their thighs. At this time it was said that this pair would never be seen again, although their existence would be constantly manifested in the power of the earth to reproduce and sustain life (Wyman 1970a:112).

In the creation story found in Blessingway, First Man speaks to these two recently formed beings, assigning to them names and functions:

> 'Of all these various kinds of holy ones that have been made, you the first one will be their thought, you will be called Long Life [*Są'áh Naagháí*],' he was told. 'And you who are the second one, of all Holy People that are put to use first, you will be their speech, you will be called Happiness [*Bik'eh Hózhǫ́*]. That much so happened. 'You will be [found] among everything [especially ceremonial affairs] without exception, exactly all will be long life by means of you two, and exactly all will be happiness by means of you two' (Wyman 1970a:398).

This passage from Navajo mythology identifies SN with thought and BH with speech. Thought is the power source of all creation, transformation and regeneration. In Navajo mythology First Man and First Woman, accompanied by some other Holy People, went into the sweathouse and *thought* the world into existence. Songs sung by the Holy People during the time they were organizing this world clearly express the power of directed thought (plans): "I plan for it, when I plan for it, it drops nicely into position just as I wish, ni yo o. Earth's support I first lean into position. As I plan for long life–happiness it yields to my wish as it nicely drops into position, ni yo o" (Wyman 1970a:115).

There is additional evidence from everyday life that indicates the power of thought. Navajos emphasize that if one thinks of good things and good fortune, good things will happen. If one thinks of bad things, bad fortunes will be one's lot. Among the Navajo it is believed that planning for a "rainy day" would bring about "rainy days."

Navajos believe strongly in the power of thought. The world was created by it; things are transformed according to it; life is regenerated from it. People are cured and blessed, vegetation is improved and increased, and health and happiness are restored by the power of thought.

Inner and Outer Forms

Thought (SN) is not without its inseparable companion, speech (BH). According to the Navajo, speech is the outer form of thought, and thought is the inner form of speech. Before we can fully understand what it means in Navajo ideology to say that thought is the inner form of speech and speech is the outer form of thought, we must briefly consider the whole phenomenon of inner and outer forms.

Natural phenomena such as earth and sky, sun and moon, rain and water, lightning and thunder, have inner forms. They are referred to as *bii'gistíín* 'that (animate being) which lies within it'. These 'in-lying ones' are humanlike in character and appearance, and retain their individual identity and agency. People also have inner forms. These are referred to as *níłch'i bii' sizíinii,* usually translated as the 'in-standing wind soul'. The in-standing wind soul is thought to be in total control of one's body, including one's thoughts and actions. The "goodness" or "badness" of a person is attributed to the nature of his wind soul. There are said to be seven general classes of wind souls, and a few other exceptional ones (in the sense of being either extremely good or extremely bad).

Like the inner forms of natural phenomena, these wind souls have an existence that is independent of the body that they occupy. They are dispatched into one's body at birth and become its source of life and breath, thought, and action. At death they leave the body and "return to Dawn Woman to report on the life of the person thus controlled" (Haile 1943a:87). It is assumed by many Navajo philosophers that the wind soul may then be dispatched to another person.

When the fetus acquires human form, a 'small wind' is dispatched to it. This small wind is what causes the fetus to move, and its movements are evidence to the mother that the small wind has taken its place inside the growing fetus. The distinction between the 'small wind' soul and the wind soul acquired at birth is important for understanding the nature of thought and speech. Haile (1943a:80) states that the small wind soul manifests its activity in 'four speeches.' These are found both in pre-natal movements of the child in the womb, and in post-natal cries for nourishment, which approximate the call *shimá* 'my mother.' T'was also told that this small wind 'grows with a person,' but does 'not think far ahead.' This 'planning and calculating of things beneficial to the future of the individual' is done by the 'wind placed into a person at birth.' This tradition assigns a definite function to small winds, which seem to control the vegetative life of the human being, as 'they grow with a person.' This function is not replaced by the wind which, from birth on, does the planning 'for the future'.

The capacity to think "far ahead" and speak a language is acquired from the wind soul dispatched at birth, and it is this capacity that distinguishes humans from other animals, who have only calls and cries.

Whereas the small wind controls the digestive system of the body, and, therefore, its growth and maturation, the in-standing wind soul controls one's thought and movements. Navajos believe that thought is located in the brain, but they contend that the in-standing soul controls the functioning of the brain. Bodily movements, actions, or behavior are extensions or externalizations of thought. They are indeed external and observable evidence of the power of thought.

Speech is an externalization of thought. Being the outer form of thought, speech is an extension of thought. To the Navajo, speech represents marvelous evidence of the varied character and extensive capacity of thought. Moreover, speech is a reinforcement of the power of thought; it is an imposition on the world of external reality. This reinforcement reaches its peak after four repetitions.

Although this world was *thought* into existence, the consummation or realization of the thoughts of the Holy People did not occur until they were spoken in prayer or sung in song. Thought, the inner form, and speech, the outer form, represent the two basic components of ritual creation or restoration. Thought is associated with form, and speech, as a kind of action, is associated with the transformation of substance (air); thus, ritual creation and restoration constitute a union of form and substance, or an imposition of form onto substance.

In the songs of creation these two components of ritual action are preceded by another form or component. Wheelwright (1942:60) records the "Beginning of the World Song" as follows (my translation of the Navajo text):

first verse: The earth will be,
The mountains will be,
(and so on, mentioning other things to be).

second verse: The earth will be, from ancient times with me there is knowledge of it.
The mountains will be, from ancient times with me there is knowledge of it
(and so on).

third verse: The earth will be, from the very beginning I have thought it.
The mountains will be, from the very beginning I have thought it
(and so on).

fourth verse: The earth will be, from ancient times I speak it.
The mountains will be, from ancient times
I speak it
(and so on).

fifth verse: (The fifth verse is a repetition of the first verse, rendering the sense "and so it will be" or "and thus it will be done").

In these verses thought precedes speech, and knowledge precedes thought. Knowledge appears to be the inner form of thought, and thought is the outer form of knowledge. In this sense, thought is the crystallization or conceptualization of knowledge.

As knowledge precedes thought, language precedes speech. In two of the best accounts of the origin myth (Goddard 1934:9, 127; Haile 1943a), *saad łá'í* 'first language' is listed as one of the primordial elements of the universe. It is obvious to the Navajo that speech cannot occur unless a language already exists. As in all creations or transformations, form precedes substance, and language is associated with form and speech with substance.

It may seem perplexing to non-Navajos that thought, an inner form of speech, could be the outer form of knowledge and that speech, an outer form of thought, could be the outer form of language, but it is entirely consistent with the Navajo view of the world. Many inner forms also have inner forms of which they are outer forms.

Knowledge and Ritual

From the propositions that knowledge is the inner form of thought, language is the inner form of speech, and thought is the inner form of speech, it may be presumed that knowledge is also the inner form of language. The structural arrangement of these components is illustrated in table 1. This structural arrangement illustrates how all ritual creation or restoration begins with knowledge and culminates in speech. For the Navajo, then, knowledge is power, and the greatest power to transform or restore various conditions comes from the knowledge of various rituals acquired from the Holy People. As such, ritual knowledge is highly treasured and not easily obtained.

Ritual knowledge can be purchased but it cannot be produced, it can be learned but it cannot be discovered, it can be communicated but it cannot be destroyed.

Ritual knowledge is fixed and complete; it cannot be expanded. All there is to know about this world is already known because the world was organized according to this knowledge. Earth-surface people can expand their awareness or command of knowledge, but they cannot expand knowledge itself.

Creation is the external manifestation of knowledge. When asked what they were planning in the sweathouse, the Holy People said "we are planning to extend knowledge endlessly" (Goddard 1934:26, my translation). In Navajo mythology there are four underworlds (sometimes extended to 12 when phases within the principal underworlds are enumerated) that preceded this, the fifth world. The first of these underworlds is called *saad łá'í* (first language), the second is called *saad naakií* (second language), and so on (Wheelwright 1949:3). This description of the underworlds may sound strange until it is recognized that language is the means by which form is projected onto substance; thus, these underworlds are really being described as "first form," "second form," and so on.

Navajos do not postulate the possibility that language may distort reality or the perception of reality. Such a proposition goes directly contrary to the Navajo scheme of things. This world was transformed from knowledge, organized in thought, patterned in language, and realized in speech (symbolic action). The symbol was not created as a means of representing reality; on the contrary, reality was created or transformed as a manifestation of language. In the Navajo view of the world, language is not a mirror of reality; reality is a mirror of language.

The language of Navajo ritual is performative (Austin 1962), not descriptive. Ritual language does not describe how things are; it determines how they will be. Ritual language is not impotent; it is powerful. It commands, compels, organizes, transforms, and restores. It disperses evil, reverses disorder, neutralizes pain, overcomes fear, eliminates illness, relieves anxiety, and restores order, health, and well-being.

The primary purpose of Navajo ritual is to maintain or restore *hózhǫ́*—everything that is good, harmonious, orderly, happy, and beautiful. The opposite of *hózhǫ́* is *hóchǫ́'***—the evil, the disorderly, and the ugly.

Navajo ritual can be divided into three general kinds, depending on how they maintain, insure, or restore *hózhǫ́*. The first of these, the Blessingway rites *(hózhǫ́ǫ́jí)*, maintain and reinforce *hózhǫ́* by attracting and incorporating the good and power of benevolent Holy People. A second general type of ritual, the Holyway rites *(diyink'ehgo)*, deals with Holy People who are potentially malevolent. These rites emphasize transformation, that is, transforming powers that are potentially

**Also transcribed *hóchxǫ́ǫ́'* (Robert W. Young, communication to editors 1981).

Table 1. Diagrammatic representation of the relations of key Navajo philosophical concepts as inner and outer forms one of another

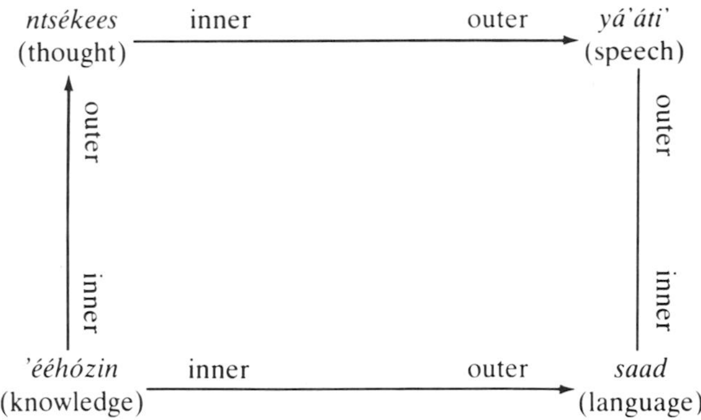

malevolent and dangerous into benevolent powers. This is done by ritual control and compulsion, creating in the patient an immunity to the potential evil of the Holy Person thus controlled. A third general class of ritual, the Evilway rites *(hóchǫ́'ójí)*, emphasize the exorcism of the evil powers of malevolent Holy People, thus eliminating *hóchǫ́'* and restoring *hózhǫ́*.

At the core of Navajo ritual is the relationship between the *Diyin Dine'é* 'Holy People' and the *nihookáá' dine'é* 'earth-surface people'. *Diyin* may be translated as 'immune' for the Holy People are people who are immune to danger, destruction, and death as a reflection of their inherent knowledge. Earth surface people may incorporate this power and immunity by knowing how to control and compel the Holy People who possess it. The symbolic action of ritual is the process by which the Holy People are controlled and compelled.

In most cases the Holy People of the fifth world are those who are the inner forms of various natural phenomena and forces, including animals. These in-lying ones are the controlling and animating powers of nature. Navajo ritual is not designed to control the elements directly; it is designed to control the Holy People who are the inner forms and controlling agents of those elements.

The goal of the earth-surface people is to live a long life of beauty, harmony, and happiness and die of old age; however, this must be done in a world of benevolent and malevolent forces. To reach the goal of old age successfully one must identify with and incorporate the good of benevolent powers and transform or exorcise the evil of malevolent powers.

The inner forms of various natural phenomena are beings of humanlike form and characteristics ("Navajo Views of Their Origin," fig. 1, this vol.). They can hear the speech of ritual and can see the movements and prestations involved in the symbolic action of ritual. These inner forms (in-lying ones) of natural phenomena also have inner forms (in-standing wind souls). Just as with the earth-surface people, it is the nature or class of the in-standing wind soul that determines whether the particular Holy Person is benevolent, malevolent, or a combination of these.

The world is an arena in which the inner forms of the Holy People and the inner forms of the earth-surface people interact. This is manifested in the movements and interactions of their outer forms. Since the movements of outer forms are representations of the thoughts and intents of inner forms, these actions or interactions are symbolic in nature. The world is, therefore, a stage of symbolic action, one of the most important aspects of which is found in language.

Songs of Blessingway illustrate the pattern of identifying with and incorporating the good of benevolent Holy People. Earth Woman is a Holy Person who is incapable of doing harm to anyone. She is only capable of blessing, aiding, and sustaining; and, as such, is the very essence of benevolence. The following excerpts from Blessingway songs illustrate how the patient identifies with and incorporates the benevolent power of Earth Woman:

> As I stand along the surface of the Earth
> she says child to me, she says grandchild to me. . .
>
> Now at Earth's soles, now dark cloud,
> now male rain, now dark water,
> rainbow, now pollen usually lies across.
>
> Now at my soles, now dark cloud,
> now male rain, now dark water,
> rainbow, now pollen usually lies across. . .
> (Wyman 1970a:123, 128).

This is followed by similar verses that make an identification with the tips of Earth's toes, the tips of her knees, the palms of her hands, her fingertips, the top of her body, the tips of her shoulders, her cheeks, eyes, lips and finally the top of her head. These verses, which constitute an identification of outer forms, are followed by an identification of inner forms:

> It is the very inner form of Earth that continues to move with me, that has risen with me, that is standing with me, that indeed remains stationary with me (Wyman 1970a:136).

The prayers of the Holyway chants are designed to transform evil and gain immunity from evil. This process is illustrated in excerpts from one of the Holyway chants, Male Shooting Way.

> At Rumbling Mountain,
> Holy Man with the eagle
> tail-feathered arrow glides out,
> This day I have come to be trustful
> This day I look to you. . .
>
> With your strong feet rise up to protect me.
> With your sturdy legs rise up to protect me.
> With your strong body rise up to protect me.
> With your healthy mind rise up to protect me.
> With your powerful sound rise up to protect me.
> Carrying the dark bow and the eagle
> tail-feathered arrow with which you transformed evil,
> By these means you will protect me. . .
>
> No weapon of evil sorcery can harm me as I go about.
> This day I shall recover.
> Safely may I go about.
> Your child I have become.
> Your grandchild I have become.
>
> I have recovered my energy, I say. . .
>
> Just as you are the one who is holy
> because of these things,
> So may I be holy because of them. . .
>
> This day the weapon of sorcery
> Has returned to normal. . .
> Just as you are the one who transforms evil,
> So may I transform evil.
> Just as you are the one dreaded by evil
> because of these things,
> So may I be dreaded by evil because of these things. . .
>
> We all survive
> My mind in safety repeatedly survives. . .
>
> [SNBH] I have become again. . .
>
> It has become beautiful again. . .
> (Reichard 1944:58–65).

The Evilway rites are designed to exorcise evil from the patient's body, mind, and presence. How ritual language is used in this process is shown in excerpts from an Evilway rite, Enemyway:

> From where threatens the weapon of the white man's ghost, its sorcery, its indispensable power, its parts naturally affected by evil, all of which bother me inside my body, which make me feverish, move deceitfully through me.
> From there they may be warned off (by winking), far away may they go.
> Along with its power of motion evil sorcery is moving far from me,
> Along with its power of motion its threatening sound is moving far from me,
> Far away with its evil power it has gone.
> It has gone back to its own dwelling place,
> It has become unknown water. . . .
> (Haile 1938:23–28; Reichard's 1944:31 translation).

In the translation above Reichard frequently includes "may," which gives a misleading sense of asking for permission. There is no "may" or requesting of permission in the Navajo versions. Phrases such as "so may I be dreaded by evil" should read "so I will be dreaded by evil."

There is another important source of *hóchxǫ́'* that must be brought under control and reversed or neutralized. It is found in witchcraft and has been part of the world from the beginning, having been part of the knowledge of First Man and First Woman. Witchcraft is associated with incest, and First Man and First Woman are both brother and sister and husband and wife. First Man is said to be the originator of "invisible witchcraft," and First Woman is the originator of "noisy medicine" and "gray witchcraft" (Haile 1943a:75).

The children of First Man and First Woman are called

'áńt'įįhjí SN and *'áńt'įįhjí* BH. *'Áńt'įį* is 'witchcraft', and these children, born of incest, are personifications of witchery SN 'thought' and witchery BH 'speech'. Whereas SN + BH produce, maintain, and restore *hózhǫ́*, witchery SN + witchery BH produce *hóchǫ́'*. One of the most common ways of producing *hóchǫ́'* is by reversing the order and sequence of the rites that produce *hózhǫ́*. Reichard (1950:275) notes that "the power of the word is as strong for evil as for good, an inverse wish being a curse." Haile (1943a:75) adds:

> The colored winds, too, which are assigned in proper sequence to the phenomena of the cardinal points, to wit: white wind soul to dawn, blue wind soul to horizontal blue, yellow wind soul to evening twilight, dark wind soul to darkness, are considered benevolent, if mentioned in this sequence in religious functions. But when a ceremonial, in its songs and prayers, disturbs this sequence, giving preference to darkness, malevolence and witchery may be suspected.

Whereas ritual language can be used to create order, it can also be used to create disorder. Ritual language was the means of transforming chaos into cosmos, but it can also be used to reduce cosmos to chaos. In the battle between the forces of disorder and evil and those of order and good, the "good" side has the advantage. This is based on the idea that through ritual knowledge and circumspect behavior one can acquire an immunity from evil, but there is no immunity from the ritual control and compulsion of good. There are no evil forces or deities that cannot be transformed or exorcised.

Evil and malevolence also have an advantage. They act secretly and deceptively. Before one can transform, exorcise, or reverse evil, one must know its nature and source. This is the function of the diviner or diagnostician. Often, however, serious misfortune or death is caused before the nature and source of the evil is discovered. If the source of the problem is witchcraft and the witch is discovered, the witch will die because his evil power can be reversed and returned. There is only one escape from this pronounced doom. He can confess and be treated by a Holyway rite by which he can gain an immunity from the evil forces that he himself has set in motion.

'Éého̧zin 'knowledge' is the awareness of a thing or being and its symbolic representation. To a great extent, the beginning of man's knowledge is found in learning the natures and names of things. Unlike Adam, First Man did not name things (creating symbols), he learned the names of things (interpreting reality through symbols).

Although First Man and First Woman were not the originators or inventors of symbol, they were the originators of form. The capacity to organize, arrange, and pattern symbols is found in the intellect. Symbols are the building blocks of mental images, and just as man cannot build a house without materials, so man cannot construct mental images of the universe without symbolic elements.

This is not to say that in the Navajo view man cannot or does not create symbols. After symbols have been organized in thought, and this organization or form has been imposed on substance, a new symbol is needed to symbolize the new world, and it is man who finds or creates a symbol to represent his own creations. This new or additional symbol becomes part of his symbolic resources for future thought and creation. The present world is the fifth world; it is organized out of symbols that originated and developed in four underworlds. Each of these successive worlds was organized out of the symbols of previous worlds, except the first underworld. The first underworld had substance but it possessed no inherent form. First Man and First Woman imposed form onto the substance of the first world. The capacity to originate and impose form is inherent to the intellect. Things do not think, symbols do not think; man thinks.

Having acquired the capacity to impose form and order onto the world, First Man and First Woman also acquired the capacity to return order to disorder, cosmos to chaos. Whereas SN 'thought' and BH 'speech' produce *hózhǫ́*, *'áńt'įįhjí* (witchery) SN 'thought' and BH 'speech' produce *hóchǫ́'*. *Hózhǫ́* may be conceived of as the imposition of form, order, harmony, beauty and, therefore, good upon the world. When *hóchǫ́'* occurs in one's world, it is as though things have returned to original chaos. The ritual takes the patient back to the beginning of things, or apparently it assumes he is already there because it is there that the ritual starts, and recreates the world according to *hózhǫ́*. The two states of being symbolized by the terms *hózhǫ́* and *hóchǫ́'* may be characterized as culture (ordered substance) and nature (unordered substance). Culture is the imposition by man of order and good on nature, resulting in beauty, harmony, happiness, and health. Disorder and evil constitute a return to the original ugliness and disorder of nature. Ritual reinforms nature with culture order, and that is why all rituals conclude with the phrase "*hózhǫ́* has been restored."

The first few sentences of the emergence myth are: "The one that is called 'water everywhere.' The one that is called 'black earth.' The one that is called 'first language.' " (Goddard 1934:9, 127). These phrases are significant in that they indicate that in the beginning was the word and the thing, the symbol and the object. The Holy People first became *aware* of things through their symbols and then later went into the sweathouse and organized these symbols through thought processes. Next the organized symbols were spoken in prayer and sung in song. Through these songs and prayers the inner forms of things to be were organized and controlled; that is, they were told where to go, how to position themselves, and what functions to fulfill.

Knowledge is the awareness of symbol, thought is the organization of symbol, speech is the externalization of symbol, and compulsion is the realization of symbol. Symbol is word, and word is the means by which substance is organized and transformed. Both substance and symbol are primordial, for in the beginning were the word and the element, the symbol and the symbolized.

A Taxonomic View of the Traditional Navajo Universe

OSWALD WERNER, ALLEN MANNING, AND KENNETH Y. BEGISHE

Navajo culture is very rich, as is the Navajo language. In order to translate the Bible into a given language Bible translators estimate that at least 25,000 words are needed. Navajo meets this requirement easily, and the Bible has been translated into this language. In addition there are thousands of recorded Navajo words that never appear in the Bible, and another few thousand words that have never been recorded before, including many that appear in print for the first time in this chapter. Considering that the bookshelf describing Navajo culture is at least 50 feet long (the bibliography by Correll, Watson, and Brugge 1969 on Navajo topics in print comes to 326 pages) this last may be surprising. The enormous complexity of human culture and cultural knowledge (Navajo and in general) is just beginning to be fully appreciated, even by anthropologists.

This chapter focuses on Navajo cultural knowledge, especially those aspects reflected in the Navajo language. At the simplest conceptual level these are the words of a language. However, here we are also talking about linkages of words, especially linkages by sentences. This includes classification: the way in which Navajos classify their universe. We describe only two kinds of classificatory systems: taxonomic classification and, much less frequently, part-to-whole classification.

The taxonomic classification of "objects" in the universe is a very fundamental part of all human languages. First, the principle of the poverty of language implies that human beings constantly make judgments involving classification, since any language in which every possible object was named differently would be very unwieldy. Since every blade of grass is unique, each and every one would need a separate name. Fortunately for the easy use of language we name only grass. Therefore, there exist considerably fewer words used to describe the universe than there are objects in the universe. In this chapter only the principal subdivisions of Navajo cultural knowledge are named; all or most specific terms are ignored. For example, in the classification of Navajo 'plants', the major subdivisions are given: 'woody plants', 'weeds', 'cacti', and 'lichen', but specific plants are not. Specifics are discussed only where the classification is very different from the classification in English, or if there are controversial items of classification on which Navajos disagree. In the above example the classification of 'yuccas' is controversial: some Navajos feel these are cacti because of their spines, others feel they belong to the weed category, because they are flexible (not woody).

This last is an example of the problem of variation. As the Navajo population increases and diversifies by religion, profession, income, and education, a greater heterogeneity of culture and language is introduced. On one analytical level this variation is all part of the "same" culture. On a lower level it may be equated with (among other largely unknown social factors) varying schools of thought in the Navajo population, or with exposure to similar experiences. The more we are able to say about the nature of the variation and disagreements among consultants who are native speakers of

Table 1. Navajo Creation

1.	→ 2.	→ 3.	→ 4.	→ 5.	→ 6.	→ 7.	→ 8.	→ 9.
Tó t'éí siyį́ 'Only water exists'	*Níłch'i diyinii 'ashdla'go tókáá'gi dah naháaztą́* 'Five sacred spirits are above the water'	*Nahasdzáán hazlį́į́'* 'The earth came into being'	*Nahasdzáán ni'iishchį́* 'The earth gave birth'	*Ni' bitł'áahdi* 'At the bottom of the world'	*'Ałnaashii 'adeezdéél* 'The separation of the sexes'	*Tó yíląąd* 'The flood'	*Hajíínáí* 'Emergence'	*Niilyáii nidaasya'* 'Placing of the creation'

NOTE: The arrows used in this diagram represent the lexical/semantic relation of succession, queuing, or grading. It can be represented by the frame "______ and then ______" (______ *'áádóó* ______).

Table 2. Classification of *niilyáii*

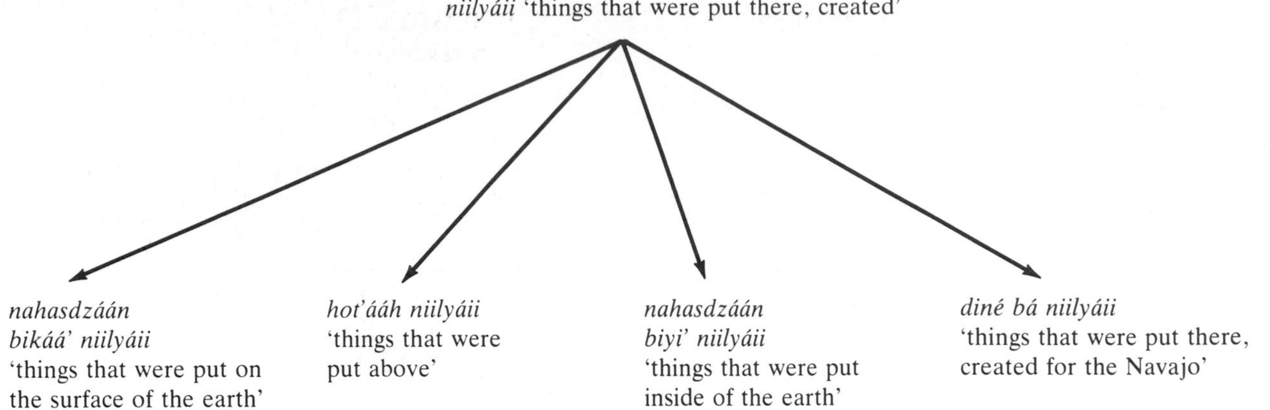

Navajo, the greater confidence the reader should have that we have captured the spirit of Navajo culture. Whenever only one version of a classification is given here it usually means that this presentation is based on very few consultants or on a homogeneous subgroup of Navajos.

The English translation labels that appear in single quotes after each italicized Navajo term represent the beginnings of a detailed accurate bilingual Navajo-English dictionary. These labels are rough and ready equivalents often selected because they are short enough to fit the limitations of space in the tree graphs rather than for their full and complete accuracy, and they are not standardized since the most appropriate label depends in part on its taxonomic context. The variations in English labels for the same Navajo term cast some additional light on Navajo usage. Ultimate accuracy cannot be reached until an *Encyclopedia Navajoana* is realized.

Taxonomies

A taxonomy is a system of interrelated sentences used for classifying objects. In the graphs in this chapter a taxonomic sentence is represented by two labeled nodes connected by an arrow. The node to which the arrow points is the subject of the sentence, while the arrow and the node from which it originates is the predicate. For example, in English, "A horse is an animal"; in Navajo, *Łį́į́' naaldlooshii 'át'é* 'A horse is a trotter':

A horse
o←——o
is an animal

łį́į́' 'horse'
o←————o
'át'é 'is', *naaldlooshii* 'trotter'

In the English case, "a horse" is the subject of the sentence and "is an animal" is the predicate; or, the two words or naming units* "horse" and "animal" are linked by the taxonomic relation (sentence) "________ is a (kind of) ________." In Navajo, *łį́į́'* 'horse' is the subject and *naaldlooshii 'át'é* 'trotter it is' is the predicate; or *łį́į́'* 'horse' and *naaldlooshii* 'trotter on four legs' are words or naming units which are linked by the taxonomic relation (sentence) in Navajo ______ ________ *'át'é.*

The taxonomic relation links two aspects of a pair of terms. On the one hand there are objects "in the real world," where the subject of a taxonomic sentence refers to a set of objects that is included in the class of objects mentioned in the predicate: in the previous example the class of all horses is included in the class of all animals. But this interpretation creates difficulties with objects that have no clear "real" referents. For such "abstract" terms the subordinate term can be considered to contain all the attributes of the superordinate term: in the same example the criterial attributes of the class 'horse' must include the criterial attributes of 'animal' (that is, every horse must have the characteristics that all other animals also have).

Human speakers at every point in their speech very rapidly perform complex taxonomic tasks, every sentence requiring several taxonomic decisions. A sentence includes a subject, a selection of what to talk about, usually something that speaker and hearer easily agree upon. This is the subordinate term; then by adding a predicate the speaker qualifies this term by means of attributes, that is, creates new information about the subordinate term.

*The term "naming unit" is used interchangeably with "words." The justification is that the units that relate taxonomically to other units are often larger than single words but are established conventional names for classes for things. The term "naming unit" is thus more flexible than the term "word" and allows for examples like *jack-in-the-pulpit* in English and *t'áá diné* 'the real Navajo or the Navajo proper' in the Navajo language (Mathiot 1962).

Table 3. Classification of *nahasdzáán bikáá' niilyáii*

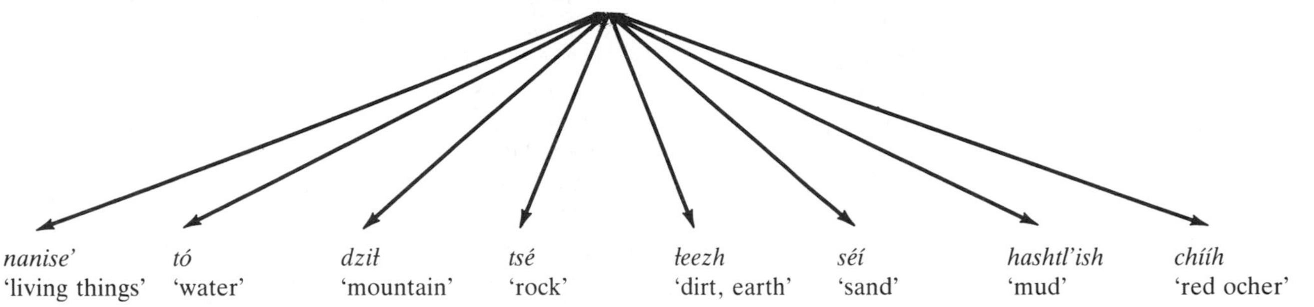

Table 4. Classification of *nanise'* I

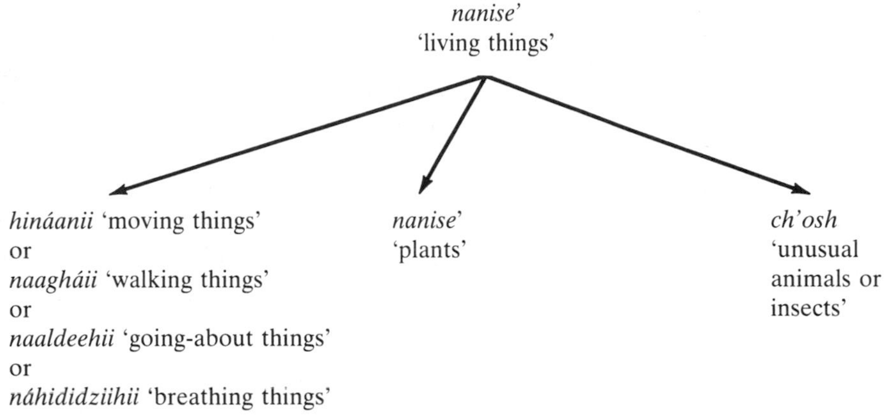

Systems of taxonomic relations are represented pictorially in so-called tree graphs. Since the arrows may on occasion converge (point from two different source nodes toward one destination node) the graphs are more correctly semi-lattices. Occasionally, for example in the case of body parts (anatomical terms), the graphs depict the part-to-whole relation rather than the taxonomic relation. To indicate the difference, for this relation double arrows instead of the single taxonomic ones are used. The double arrow therefore corresponds to the English sentence "_______ is part of ______" and the Navajo sentence ______ ______ *łahgo bił haz'ą́*.

One further convention is imposed on the taxonomies: the nodes and their labels are arranged according to an estimated frequency of occurrence and importance of the items in Navajo culture. These are only suggestive estimates, not well-refined conclusions. On each level of the taxonomies, the naming units of highest frequency or most importance appear first on the left. The more unusual or infrequent an item is, the farther to the right is its placement.

Elicitation of Taxonomies

The information presented here was obtained in a number of different ways. Frame elicitation, the method most often mentioned in the literature of ethnoscience, was used perhaps least. In this technique the investigator first elicits a question sentence; an English example might be "What kind of animals are there?" He then replaces the superordinate term "animal" by whatever his interests are. Thus he will obtain the frame "What kind of ______ are there?" If the anthropologist manages to convince his respondents to answer with a list, then each item on the list can be inserted into the frame until the lowest most specific terms are reached. These are simply those terms that when inserted into question frames precipitate no answers (or no further answers are possible).

We used various methods of textual analysis more consistently. Predominant among these was the elicitation of folk definitions and creation myths. Folk definitions are simply the answers to questions that ask about the meaning of a term. This method works especially well with abstract terms. Mythology was the most successful guide for working upward in the trees; almost all the very general Navajo terms were first encountered in creation myths.

Three further methods were sometimes useful. One was to ask knowledgeable Navajos to draw their own tree structures and then to discuss these with the anthropologist. For replication consultants were asked to sort into piles slips of paper with the terms written on them; this worked well for those who were literate. Illiterate consultants were sometimes able to provide useful data by sorting pictures. Most important for replication and for the discovery of disagreement was the technique of presenting Navajo consultants with the tree structure obtained from someone else (more often than not these were initially Kenneth Y. Begishe's taxonomic trees). As we became more sophisticated we tried to discuss first only items on which, and on the position of which, there was some agreement. We then would ask where other terms not in the diagram ought to be placed. This worked well because it checked the accuracy of earlier structures and brought in new information as well.

Sketch of the Navajo Creation

The sequence and content of the following nine major titles of the Navajo story of creation are not unique, being only one possibility out of several. The stories of the Underworld (Preworld) are associated with witchcraft because its origins are in incest: First Man and First Woman (and their siblings) are necessarily related. This association makes these stories supernaturally dangerous. Almost without exception systematic elicitation is difficult or nearly impossible. The following sequence is put together from bits and pieces.

The sequence of events leading up to the creation of the last, the present world, is as follows (table 1). In the beginning (1) 'Only water is in place' (*Tó t'éí siyį́*) and (2) 'Five sacred spirit winds are in place above the water' (*Nítch'i diyinii 'ashdla'go tókáa'gi dah naháaztą́*). Mysteriously through the Five Spirits (3) 'The Earth came into existence' *Nahasdzáán hazlį́į́'*. She (Earth is a woman) grows and matures until she unites sexually with the Sky, and (4) 'The Earth had a series of offspring' (*Nahasdzáán ni'iishchį́*). The results of this union are the Holy People (*Diyin Dine'é*). The story of the trials and tribulations of these beings who are between humans and the most Sacred Spirit Winds begins (5) 'At the Bottom of the Earth' (*Ni' bitł'áahdi*). As the population of this Underworld grows, animosities arise between the sexes. This is described in (6) 'Two groups of people (the sexes) separate' (*'Ałnaashii 'adeezdéél*). Their reunion leads to (7) 'The Flood' (*tó yíłą́ąd*). In the end the only way to escape the rising waters is by leaving the Underworld. This is the story of the (8) 'Emergence' (*Hajíínáí*). Then, after a series of complex events, 'Changing Woman' (*'Asdzą́ą́ Nádleehí*) is born and in turn bears the twins 'Monster Slayer' (*Naayéé' Neizghani*) and 'Born for Water' (*Tó Bájíshchíní*). The two rid the world of the horrible monsters that were the result of the self-gratification of the women during the separation of the sexes. This and the following creation of the universe in the present world of the Navajo is described in (9) 'the things that were established were put in place' (*niilyáii nidaasya'*). The taxonomic classification of the Navajo universe begins here with *niilyáii* 'the things that were established (created)'.

Story titles 1–2 and 5–8 probably have no further subtitles. Story 3 has two subtitles and a total of five more sub-subtitles. Story (4) has four subtitles but no further structures, while 9 has 12 subtitles.

Conceptually the Navajo creation story raises some interesting problems. The creation of water appears in the creation story yet the story of the universe begins with water. There are several parallel examples. Even more interesting is the fact that Navajo mythology (*diné baa hane'*), the collection of creation and other legends, were 'the things established (created) for the benefit of the Navajos' (*diné bá niilyáii*), yet at the same time these stories are the only source that explicitly details how this world came into being. Mythologies in general are full of similar examples of self-reference.

The Navajo Universe

The Navajo 'Creation' (*niilyáii*) consists of two parts: The 'Creation (proper)' (*niilyáii*) and 'Things created for the benefit of the Navajos' (*diné bá niilyáii*). The second term is difficult to re-elicit, perhaps because in

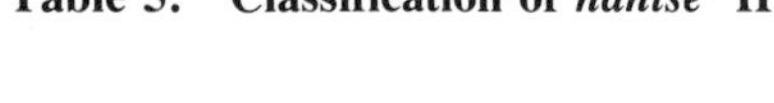
Table 5. Classification of *nanise'* II

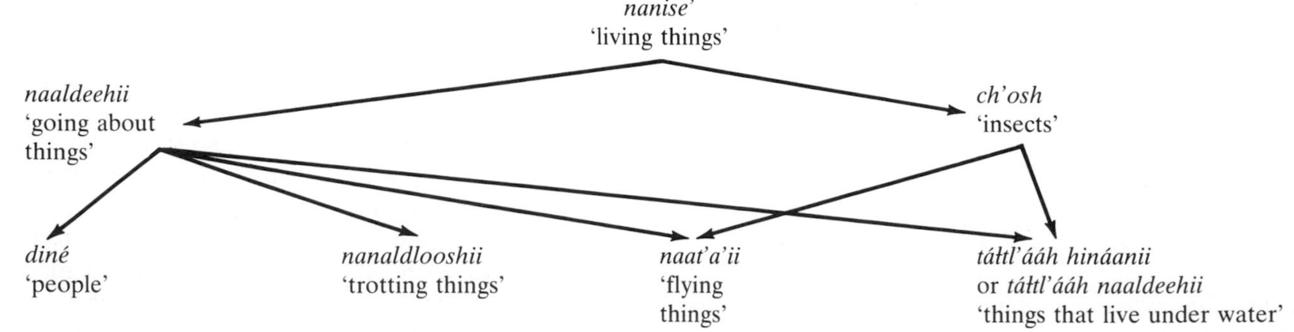

Table 6. Classification of *diné*

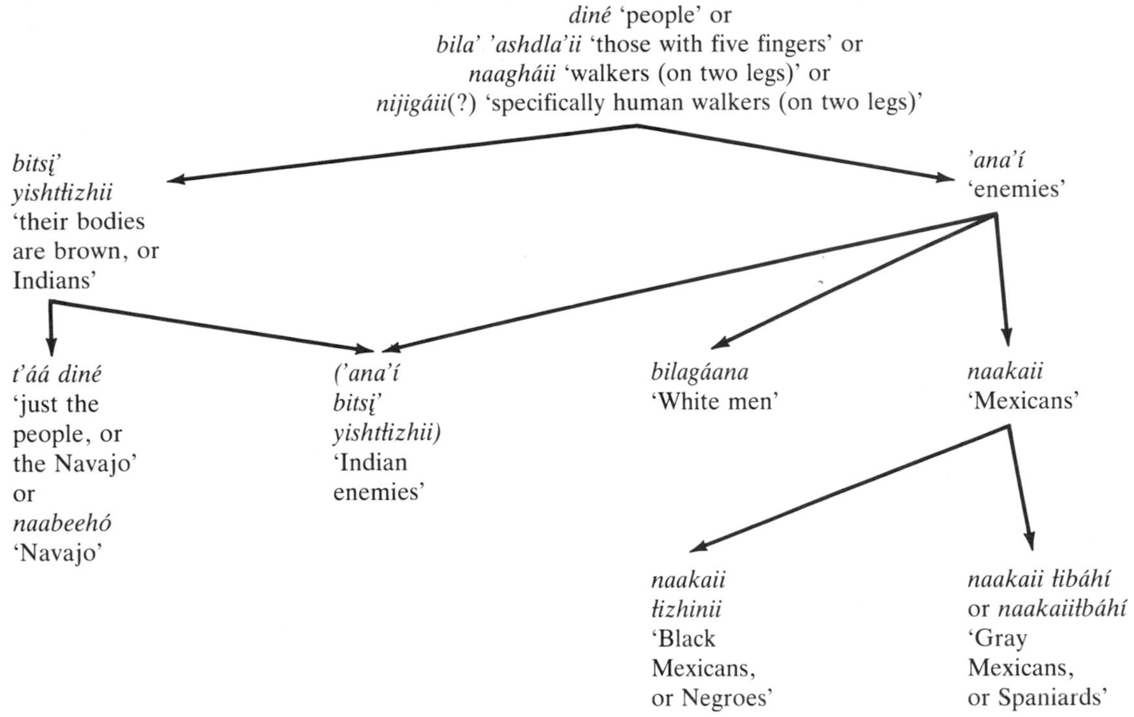

normal contexts all creation is considered for the benefit of the Navajo.

Only when speakers appear to be making the implicit contrast between themselves, the Navajo (*diné*), and their enemies (*'ana'í*) do they emphasize explicitly the Navajo items of the creation, such as their bodies, their conception of personhood or the good life, and incidentally the bad life. The term *diné be'ena'í bá niilyáii* 'The creation for the enemies of the Navajo' we assume is implicit and could probably be elicited only after a lengthy discussion, if at all; Gary Witherspoon (personal communication 1974) denies its grammaticality as well as its existence.

A second possible view of the creation is given in the fourfold division of table 2. 'Things that were set in place on the surface of the earth' (*nahasdzáán bikáá' niilyáii*) seem to be evoked most usually when Navajos speak of *niilyáii* 'the creation'. The most difficult term to (re)elicit is *bá niilyáii* 'the things created for their (the Navajo's) benefit', which is therefore placed last. This term may be part of the speech of sophisticated Navajos—most usually chanters (medicine men), who are intimately familiar with the creation story—but not that of Navajo laymen.

Except for *nanise'* 'living things' there seems to be very little disagreement on table 3 (although we did comparatively little work in this general domain).

In Navajo—as in languages in general—if two terms are used on different levels of generality (on different levels of the taxonomic tree), the more specific sense appears to be more focal, that is, it is usually given first. The focal sense of *nanise'* is usually given as 'plants'. Most consultants agreed that it may be used in both the specific 'plant' sense and the general 'living things' sense, while a few vigorously denied the appropriateness of the more general application. A group of young Navajo teachers argued that the more general sense of *nanise'* should be replaced by *hináanii,* which they interpreted as 'living things' (cf. *hiná* 'he is alive') and which we interpret as 'moving things' (cf. *naha'ná* 'he moves'). The term *nanise',* on the other hand, is related to the more general concept of growth seen in the verb stem *-sé* 'to grow progressively' (cf. *neesséét* 'I am growing'). In addition, unlike the teachers, traditional Navajo consultants never raised the above objection, nor did they object to the general use of *nanise'*.

The four synonyms for 'animate beings' (table 4) form an interesting set. *Hináanii* 'moving things' is perhaps the most generally or frequently accepted term in this context. Haile's (1943a) informants seem to have preferred *naaldeehii* 'things that go about'; this is also given by Young and Morgan (1980:581) as 'animal life, living thing'. Each of these synonyms is a metonym, in which one characteristic of animate beings is singled out for the naming process and becomes focally emphasized while all other attributes seem to become suppressed.

In table 5 we imply a separation of two of the four "synonyms" in table 4. More specifically we are placing *hináanii* 'moving things' and *naaldeehii* 'going-about things' on different hypothetical levels. In some con-

Table 7. Classification of *t'áá diné*

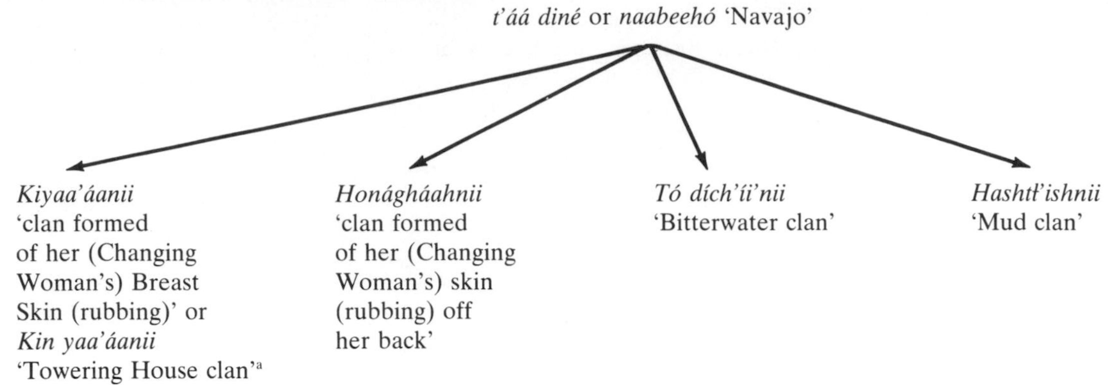

[a] The first appears to be a traditional interpretation (Franciscan Fathers 1910:428), while the second is a folk etymology by younger Navajos.

Table 8. Classification of *naaldlooshii* I

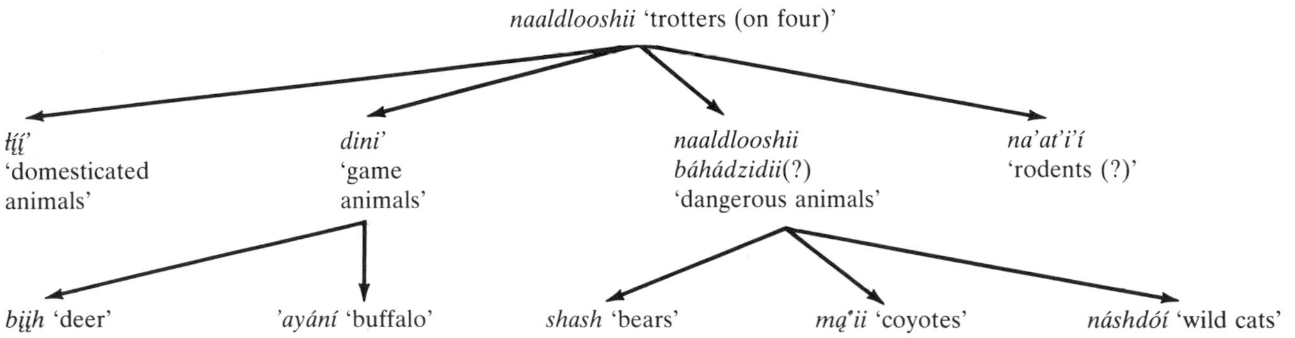

texts such a separation may be theoretically permissible. Some evidence may be marshalled by the following argument. It is controversial whether *ch'osh,* most generally perhaps 'unusual animals' or more specifically 'insects' are (kinds of) *naaldeehii.* Without doubt they are *hináanii* 'moving things', at least during the summer months. In *táłtł'ááh naaldeehii* 'things that go about under the water' the second term *naaldeehii* 'those that go about' implies literally walking about by means of legs. In Navajo, walking verbs are often used to imply living. It is through this extension of the sense of *naaldeehii* that Navajos are able to justify *łóó'* 'fish' to be (a kind of) *táłtł'ááh naaldeehii.* By a similar argument *ch'osh* may also be (a kind of) *naaldeehii,* though none of our consultants agreed to that. The same problem does not seem to arise with *hináanii.* This fact provides the context for questioning the synonymy of *hináanii* and *naaldeehii* and makes it difficult to establish the precise nature of the relationship between the two terms. It is equally unclear where *ch'osh* should be attached in addition to *nanise'* 'living things' and *hináanii* 'moving things' in its most general and most specific senses.

A partial explanation of the problem above may be found in a closer examination of registers of speaking. There are apparently (at least) two ways of talking about things in Navajo: naturally and supernaturally (ceremonially). Older people tend to switch back and forth between the two styles for selecting words. This often confuses younger Navajos. In the supernatural lexical domain *ch'osh* is (a kind of) *naaldeehii,* but in the natural order of things such an assignment is impossible. (The source of this information is Begishe.)

Bíla' 'ashdla'ii (table 6) is probably a ceremonial name for 'human beings'. *Naagháii* 'walkers (usually on two legs)' is sometimes used more generally but is usually reserved for human beings. *Nijigháii* should exist, emphasizing the human nature of the walkers, so marked by the prefix *ji-*, but we have never heard this term. *'Ana'í* 'enemies' were in the past (precontact) always Indians. Since the sixteenth century Mexicans and later Anglo-Americans were added. Since Navajos have participated in United States wars there is a whole group of names for enemies of the United States, like *bi'éé' daalchíí'ii* 'the Russians (Red Shirts)'. The situation is further complicated by the fact that Navajos do recognize other Athapaskan speakers and include them under *t'áá diné* 'the real people'. Several consultants included in this category the *Hak'az dine'é* 'the cold place people, or Eskimo'. There is still further complication due to the fact that the various Pueblo peoples are enemies, while at the same time many Navajo clans bear the names of Pueblo villages. It might be possible to clarify the situation by carefully controlling the con-

Table 9. Classification of *naaldlooshii* II

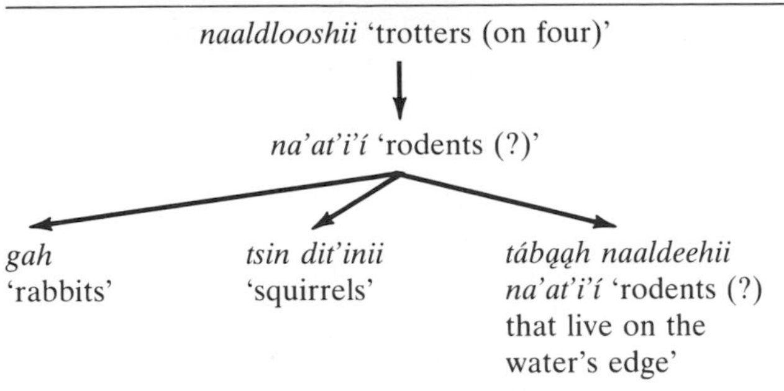

text of speaking. (For a different classification of human beings, see "Language and Reality in Navajo World View," this vol.)

One possible classification of Navajos is according to the four original clans (table 7). The set of four original clans given here is not the only one, for members of different clans claim a different set of original clans.

In other contexts *diné* 'the Navajo' are subdivided according to sex (*diné asdzání* 'Navajo woman' and *diné* 'Navajo man') rather than clan, and there are possibly also the designations for Navajos of various ages or life stages.

Another possibility, not checked with Navajo consultants, is a subdivision of *diné* according to religious affiliations, distinctions that are much discussed in Navajo.

The 'domesticated animals' (*łį́į́'*) are usually presumed to include 'trotters' (*naaldlooshii*) (tables 8–10). However, since domestication and the pet status are used in Navajo interchangeably, all domesticated birds and some wild birds that may be domesticated are also included. The 'game animals' (*dini'*) fall into two subcategories. *'Ayání* 'buffalo' is unique. The *bįįh* 'deer' category is controversial: some informants include all other game animals under the deer, while others would prefer to list them separately directly under *dini'*. This class includes elk, moose, deer proper, mountain goats, and possibly others.

The class *báhádzidii* 'dangerous things' is also controversial. Apparently all bears are dangerous, not only to life and limb but supernaturally through association with witchcraft. The foxes are considered by some to be *mą'ii* 'coyotes', while others see them as *na'at'i'í* 'scurriers (usually rodents)'. Only coyotes proper (*mą'ii*) are dangerous naturally and supernaturally. While *mą'iitsoh* 'wolves' are dangerous and perhaps also supernaturally dangerous, it is not clear whether wolf is (a kind of) *mą'ii* or independently attached to *naaldlooshii báhádzidii* (or simply *báhádzidii*) 'dangerous animals (trotters)'. Wildcats (*náshdóí*) and mountain lions (*náshdóítsoh*) are both dangerous, actually and supernaturally. The ordinary 'house cat' (*mósí* or *gidí*) falls into this class but is not considered dangerous in any sense.

Na'at'i'í 'rodents' are controversial for two reasons. First, the label 'rodent' is misleading. Although the class seems to include all or most of the rodents, perhaps a more appropriate name may be 'small animals'. The Navajo term *na'at'i'í* literally means something like 'scurriers'. Second, apparently not all *na'at'i'í* qualify as *naaldlooshii* 'trotters'. There is no question with the larger *na'at'i'í,* but most consultants were reluctant to have all the smaller ones subsumed under *naaldlooshii.* This may mean that *na'at'i'í* needs to be attached higher in the taxonomy with a later partial cross-classification with *naaldlooshii* (as in table 10).

The 'fliers' *naat'a'ii* (table 11) present interesting problems. First, the 'bats' (*jaa'abaní*) are difficult to classify. There is no doubt that they are fliers. It is questionable whether they attach directly to the fliers or are 'small birds' *tsídii,* or as several consultants suggested, they may, because of their unusual appearance, fall under the general *ch'osh* 'unusual animate beings' category. Second, there appears a generational or acculturational distinction. Younger Navajo tend to parallel English by assuming that *tsídii* is a generic term for all birds. For them all other birds fall under this term. Older monolingual Navajos include only 'small birds' in the *tsídii* classification with the large birds *'atsá* 'eagles' and *né'éshjaa'* 'owls' both directly attached to the 'fliers'. Also, both are dangerous, the owls especially because they are messengers of bad omens. In either case small birds of prey, for example *biizhii* 'nighthawk', are in the *tsídii* classification though all large hawks are *'atsá* 'eagles'. Crows and ravens (*gáagii*) are also in the unnamed class of large birds.

One irregularity of *tsídii* 'small birds' appears in several places in the Navajo taxonomies. It is subdivided into the 'domesticated birds' (*tsídii łį́į́'*), the 'birds dwelling near water's edge' (*tsídii tábąąh naaldeehi*) and a

Table 10. Overlapping classification of part of *naaldlooshii*

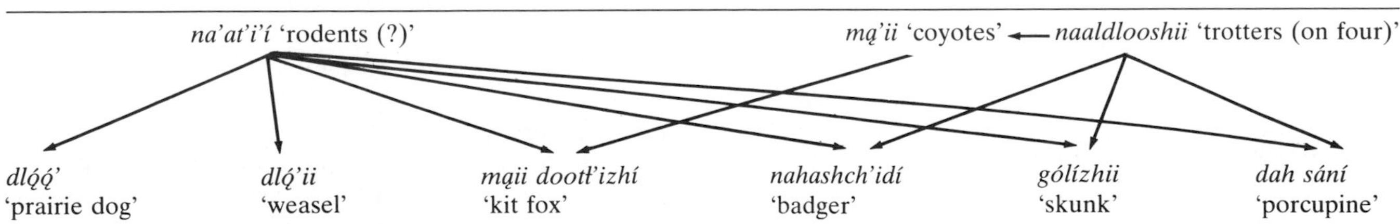

dummy node labeled *tsídii* proper.† The last includes several hundred (as far as we know) further unspecified and undifferentiated small birds.

The classification of the *táłtł'ááh hináanii* 'things that live under the water' is another one that cuts across the *naaldeehii* 'things that go about' and the *ch'osh* 'insects' category (table 12). Problems are presented by the classification of *tótł'iish* 'water snake', which can rightfully be considered a generalized *ch'osh* 'unusual animal'. The dummy node *táłtł'ááh hináanii* represents dozens of things that live under water, predominantly 'fish' (*łóó'*). Some consultants would want the fish under *ch'osh* 'unusual animals' also.

The classification of *ch'osh* (table 13) seems relatively straightforward (considering previously discussed cross-classification). Noteworthy is the inclusion of the *na'ashǫ́'ii* 'reptiles', or better, 'animals that drag themselves' or 'snakes' and 'lizards'. At the level of the dummy node *ch'osh* this term may imply some sort of bursting forth. In this case, insects, reptiles, and birds are all bursting forth from eggs. However, this generalization is based on one informant's responses and our rationalization is based on Reichard (1950).

The classification of the insects *ch'osh* as it appears on table 14 is the work of one consultant. Most consultants were unwilling or unable to subclassify this category.

All consultants agreed on the fourfold subclassification of plants (table 15). The only controversial genus was the four kinds of yucca plants *tsá'ászi'*. Some considered them cacti, others weeds (nonwoody plants). We have one extensive classification of plants by use, the most unusual feature of which is the division of dangerous plants into dangerous plants proper and antidotes to the various dangers they represent. This unique classification begins with an initial division into useful and useless plants (see Fowler and Leland 1967), but several plants that this consultant found useless had some uses according to another consultant. This may partly be explained by the fact that different species may be designated by the same name in different parts of the reservation.

William Morgan (personal communication 1973) assures us that *t'iis* 'cottonwood' and *ts'ah* 'sagebrush' may be used as generic terms for 'leafy tree' and 'bush' when the speaker does not know the specific leafy tree or bush in question. The term *tsin* 'woody plants' does not distinguish trees from bushes.

Hót'ááh niilyáii 'things that were set in place above' are not too well understood. We tried to subclassify this group further by creating subclasses I–III (table 16). This subclassification was done in part for reasons of space and the problem of presenting very shallow wide tree graphs. Consultants generally agreed that all three graphs are contained in the correct category *hót'ááh niilyáii* but were unwilling to sort them in the way we did.

Although the symmetry of table 17 is striking, the complexity is overwhelming. Here we have entered for the first time the domain of abstract Navajo terms (more precisely, Navajo terms that can no longer be defined by pointing at some object).

The double line represents the part-whole relation. On the left are the parts of Navajo religion. On the right side, all items of the bottom level are taxonomically related to 'Navajo life' *diné be'iina'* but may also be related to it through a parallel part/whole relation. This uncertainty is represented by the double line of which one is solid (the taxonomic relation) and the other is broken (the uncertain part-to-whole relation). At present there is no explanation for this unusual configuration of lexical/semantic relations.

Table 18 represents the Navajo perception of personhood. The entire graph shows personhood in the broader sense while the two part-to-whole relations on the left show it in the narrower use.

The only problem we are aware of is presented by the 'senses' *bee 'ákozhnízinii*. This term came originally from Begishe, but we have been exceptionally unsuccessful in re-eliciting it. If people understand it at all their responses are unpredictable. The explanation for this may be found in part on two levels above *bee 'ákozhnízinii*. There, all senses are represented under *diné yik'eh yigááłii* 'according to which Navajos live'. The sentience of human beings is also included under the senses (or what would correspond to a non-Navajo

†So-called dummy nodes are introduced for the following reasons. The situation of the *tsídii* 'small birds' classification may be resolved in two ways:

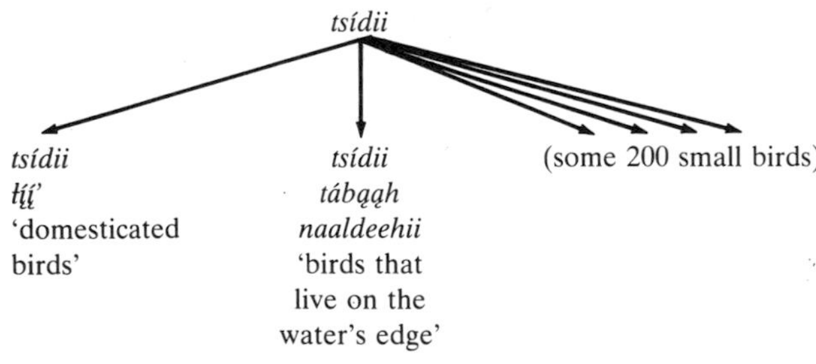

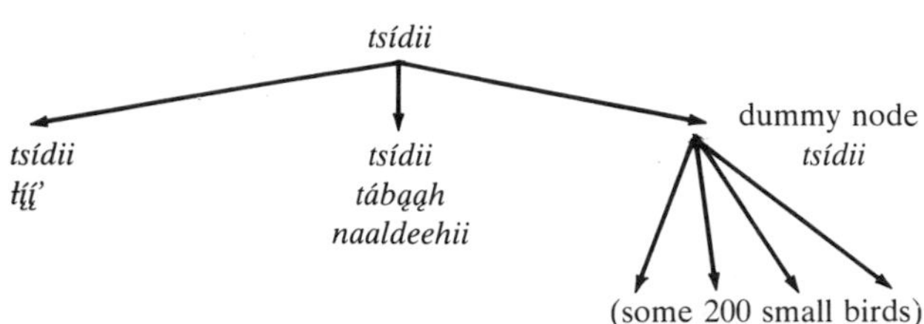

Although the bottom diagram is more elegant, there is no clear evidence for preferring it over the top one. The bottom diagram tries to preserve the unity of the *tsídii* in its ceremonial sense, perhaps best translated as 'brightly colored small birds'.

Table 11. Classification of *hináanii* I

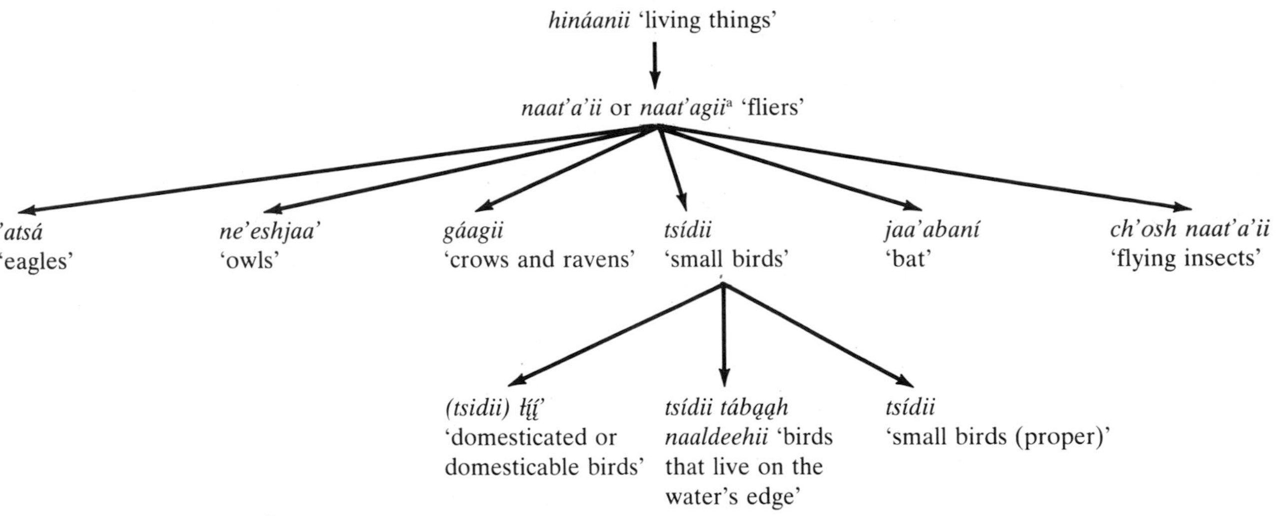

[a] Apparently a term from Navajo mythology.

Table 12. Classification of *hináanii* II

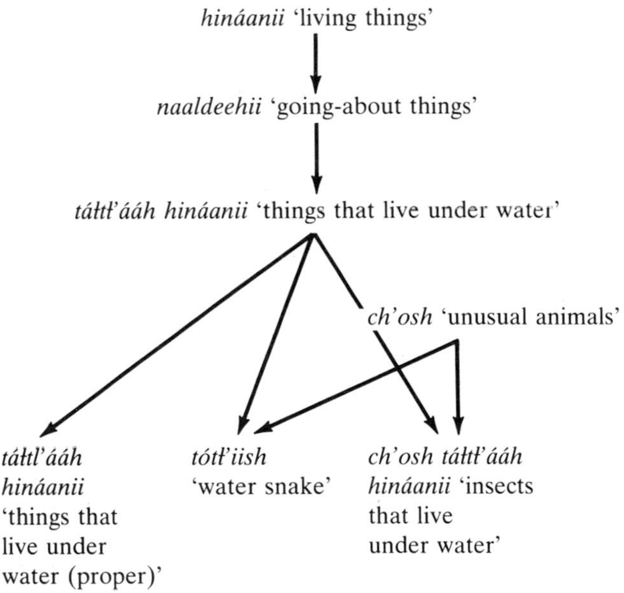

interpretation as the senses). However, the sense of taste appears nowhere, as far as we know. The terms *hanáá'* 'a person's eyes or sense of sight', *hajaa'* 'a person's ears or sense of hearing', *háchį́į́h* 'a person's nose or sense of smell', and *hanitsékees* 'a person's thought' may appear under *diné yik'eh yigááłii* 'according to which Navajos live' or under Begishe's term *bee 'ákozhnízinii* 'a person's perception or senses'.

In this context *honíłch'i* 'a person's spirit' (literally 'wind') is perhaps the central concept in the Navajo world view. The notion of harmony refers most generally to the harmony of the Spirit. As the outline of the creation story shows, the entire universe, underworld and this world, is ultimately the product of spiritual forces. A detailed explanation of this concept may require several monographs. The first one of these is by McNeley (1981).

The most unusual aspect of table 19 is that the part-to-whole classification of the parts of the human body is strictly ordered. Every one of a large number of consultants agreed with this order, which represents the presentation of the human body in prayers that are part of every Navajo ceremony (Begishe et al. 1981).

Although we spent an extraordinary amount of time during the summer of 1972 on the problem of the classification of Navajo religion and ceremonies we have very little confidence in the accuracy of tables 20–21. At times there appears to be a "modular" approach to classification, allowing many different combinations of freely movable subparts of ceremonies. Many parts at first included under Blessingway on the basis of Begishe's work were later excluded because these terms were not re-elicitable. This classification of Navajo religion and ceremonies should be considered as *one possible* arrangement, along with other classifications (Wyman and Kluckhohn 1938, 1940; Reichard 1950). There is probably no one correct arrangement.

The only controversy that was reasonably clear was the ambivalence of consultants with regard to the placement of 'Game Way' (*Dini'ee*) or 'Hunting Way' (*'Oozhék'eh*). With about equal frequency people confirmed or denied its place under *Hozhǫ́ǫ́jí* 'Blessingway', or directly under the more general heading *nahaghá* 'religion'.

There is some disagreement concerning the validity of the classification of ceremonies into small and large ones, with some consultants claiming that there are only ceremonies and on this level no reference should be made to duration.

Considering the very large number of Navajo ceremonies, tables 20–21 represent a bare skeleton of those

Table 13. Classification of *hináanii* III

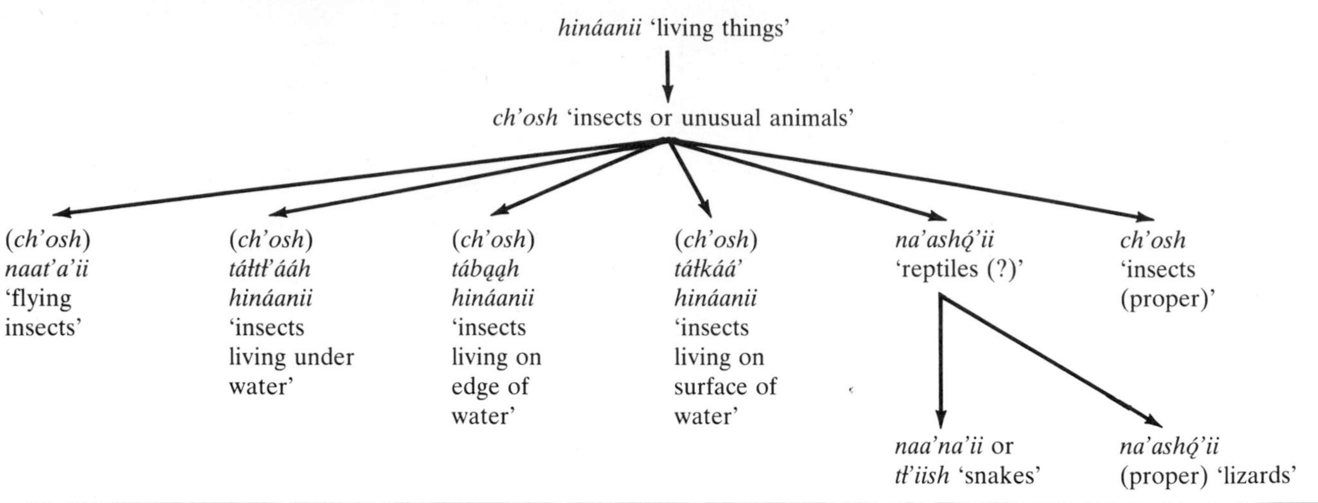

Table 14. Classification of *ch'osh*

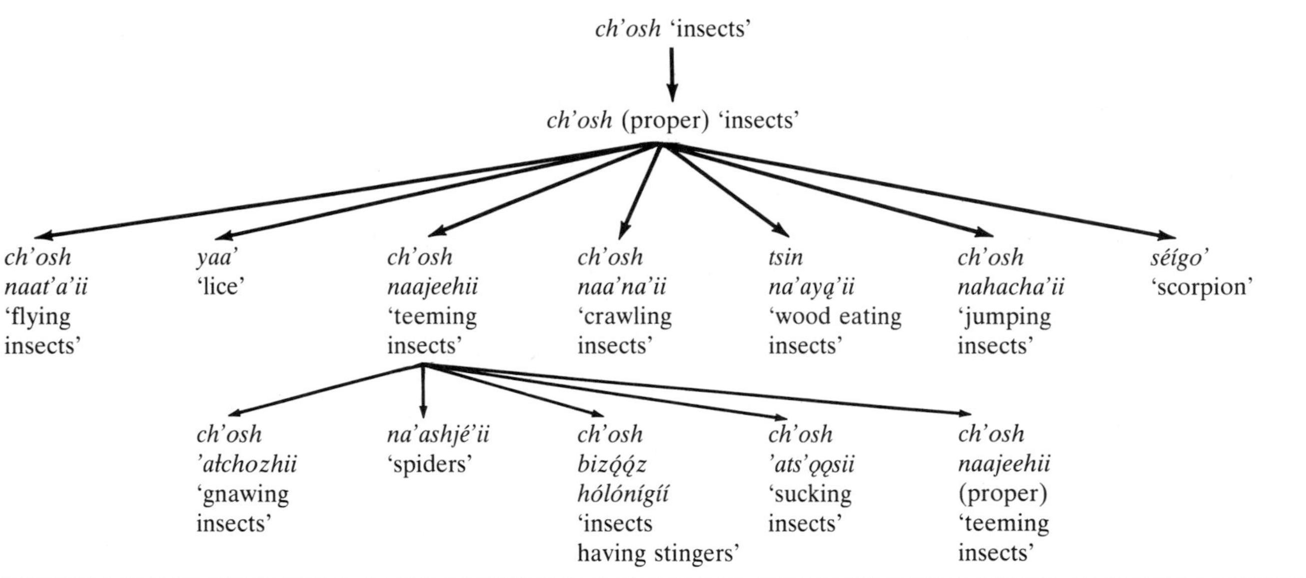

Table 15. Classification of *nanise'* III

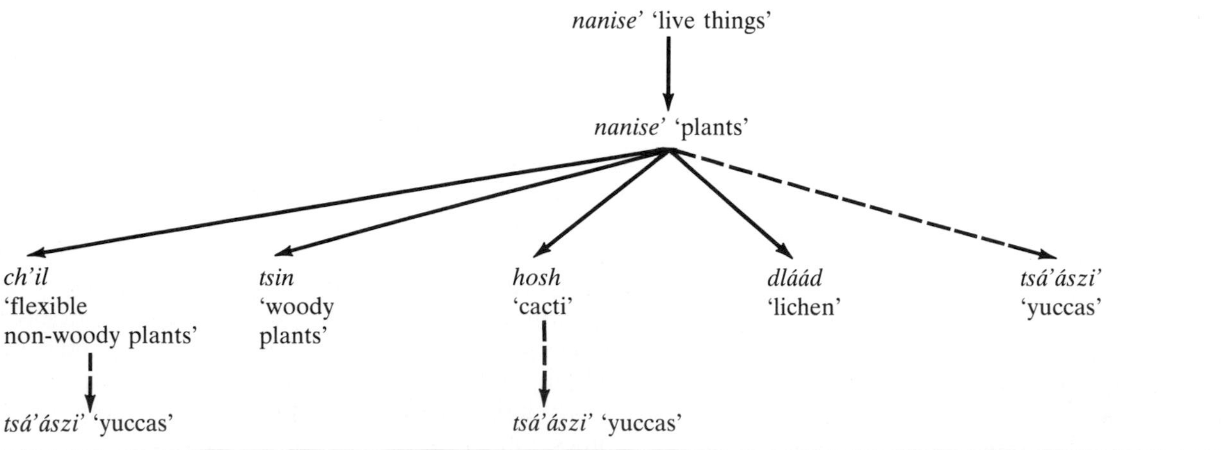

Table 16. Classification of *hót'ááh niilyáii*

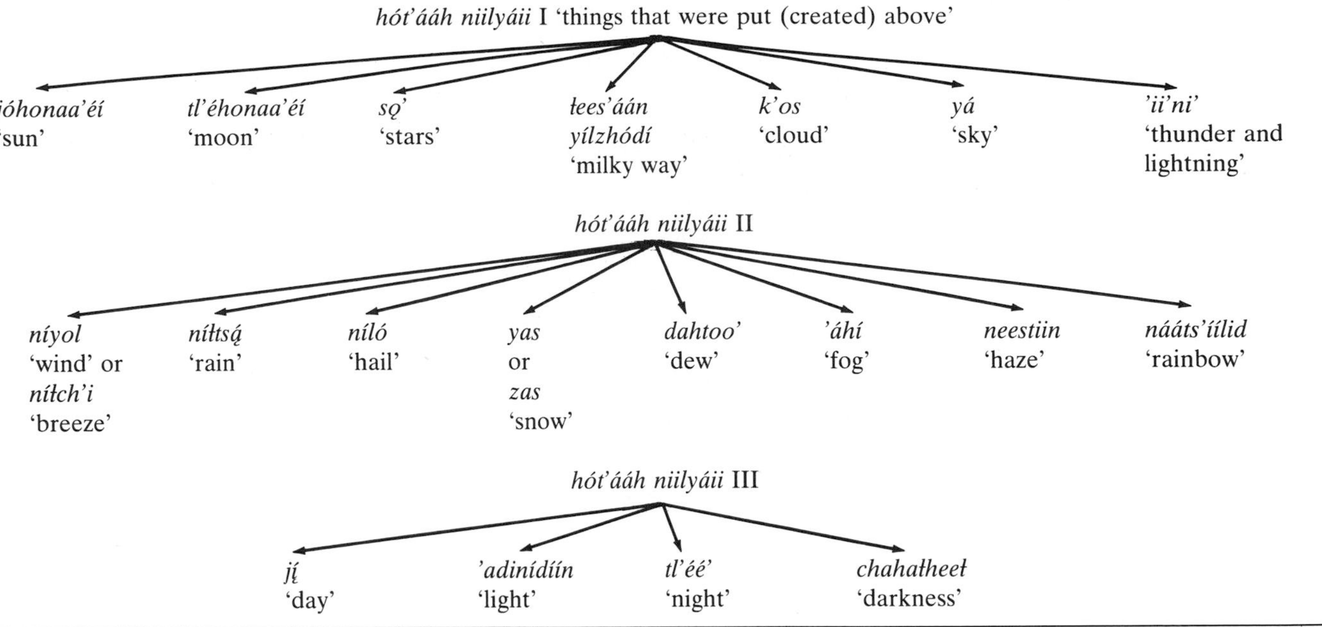

Table 17. Classification of *diné bá niilyáii* I

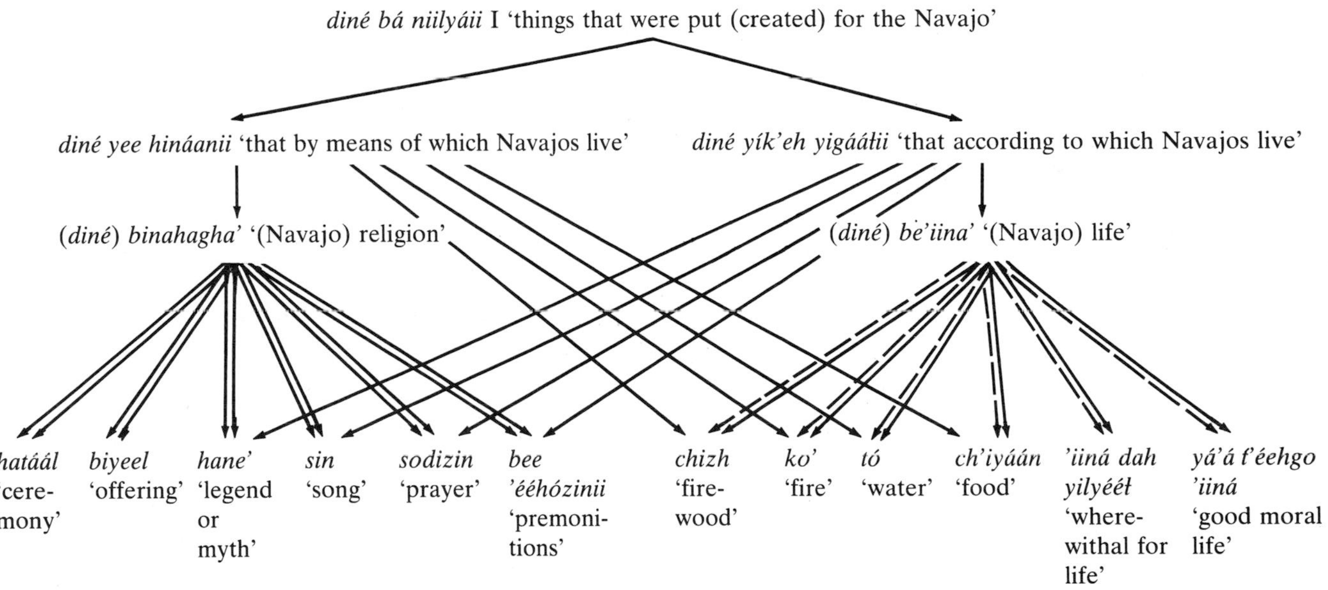

ceremonies or names of classes of ceremonies whose classification was reasonably consistent between consultants. All others varied so widely that we couldn't diagram even an approximate structure that could have represented the degree and amount of variation.

There is no disagreement that *'Anaa'jí* 'Enemyway' is different from all other ceremonies. 'Evilway' *Hóchxǫ́'ójí* and what consultants felt ought to be included in it varied widely. It has some part in almost every ceremony, though some are apparently inherently in this category. Almost all consultants agreed that there was a category *Diyink'ehgo* 'Holyway'; however, no one could agree on its composition. The *Na'at'oee Dziłk'ijí* 'Shooting Mountain Top Way' is possibly a unique combination of two previously independent ceremonies. Some consultants had never heard of the 'Corn Stalk Way' (*Kazee*). Dillon Platero (personal communication 1973) informed us that at present it is probably only known in the Cañoncito area.

Considering the importance of *níłch'i,* the 'Sacred Wind Spirit', in the Navajo world view the 'Navajo Windway' *Diné Biníłch'ijí* and the 'Chiricahua Windway' *Chíshí Biníłch'ijí* may be of special importance. Thus far, however, we have no evidence.

Table 18. Classification of *diné bá niilyáii* II

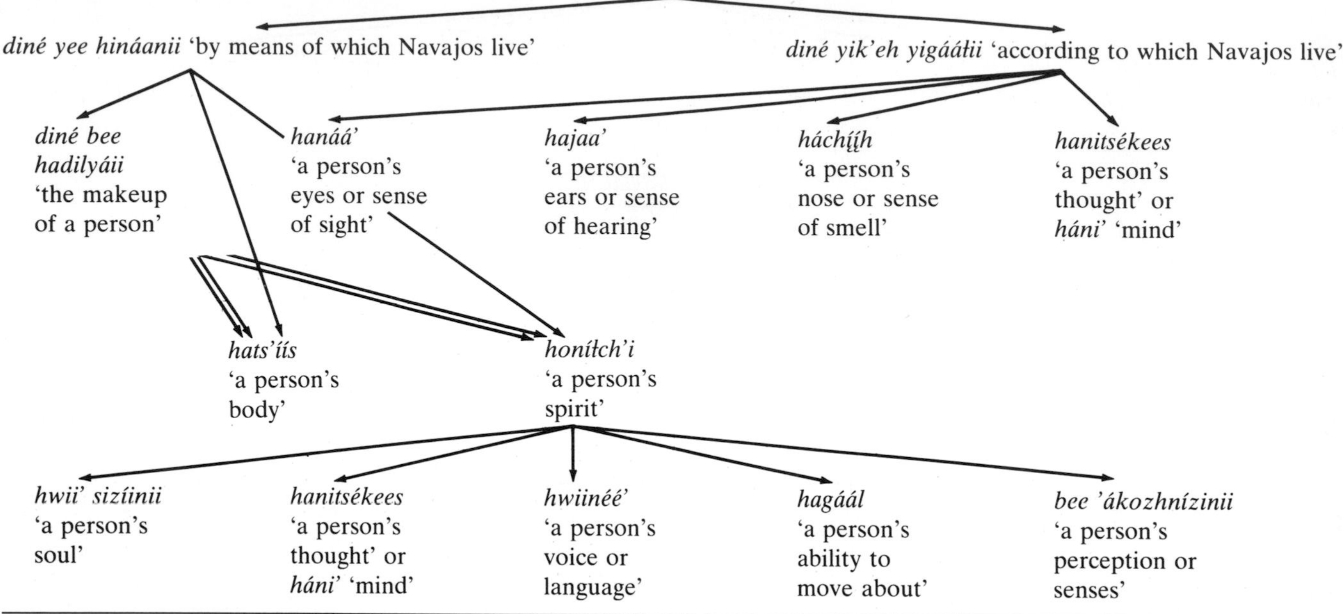

Table 19. Classification of *hats'íís*

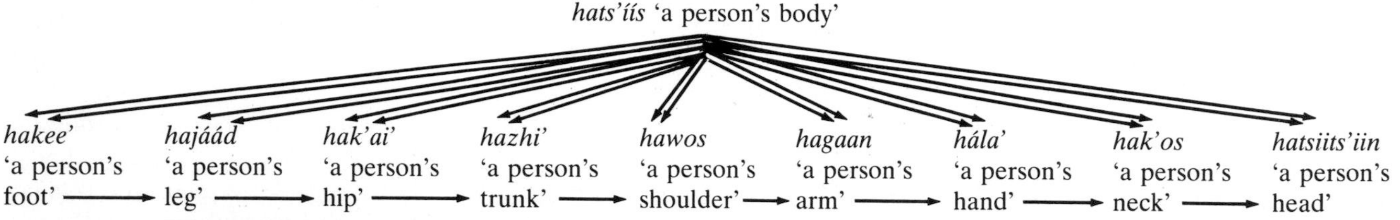

NOTE: The double arrows represent the lexical semantic relation of part to whole. The horizontal arrows represent the relation of succession, queuing, or grading.

Table 20. Classification of *hatáál*

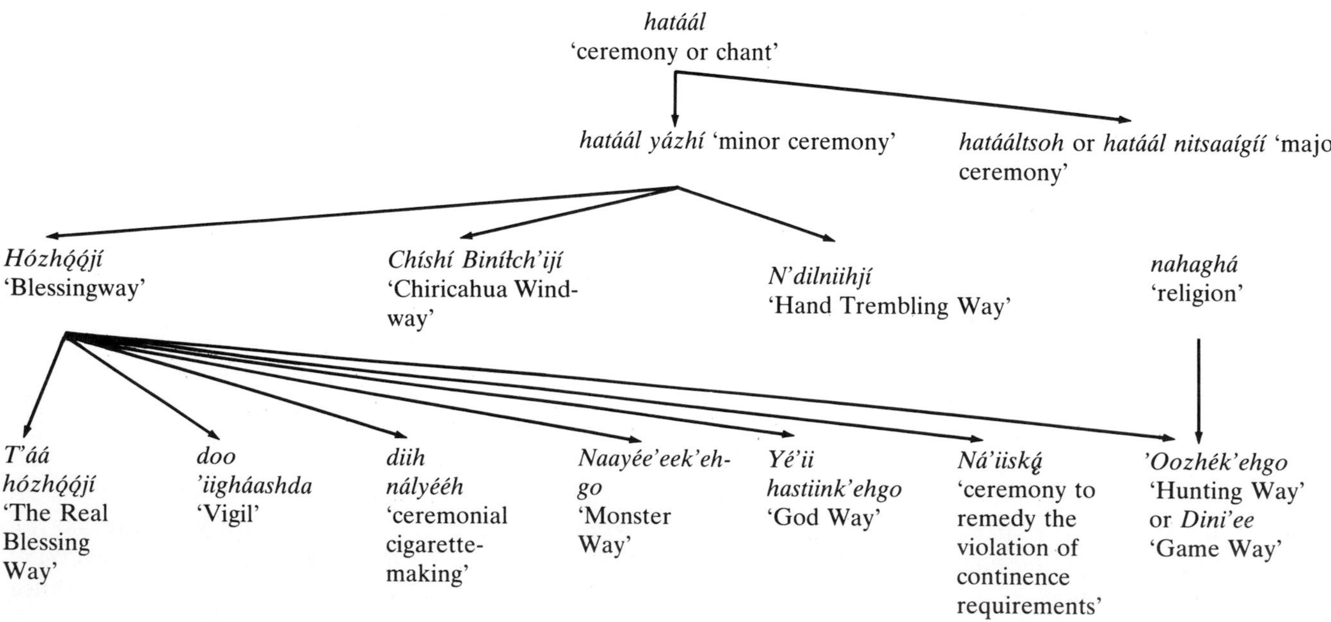

Table 21. Classification of *hatáál nitsaaígíí*

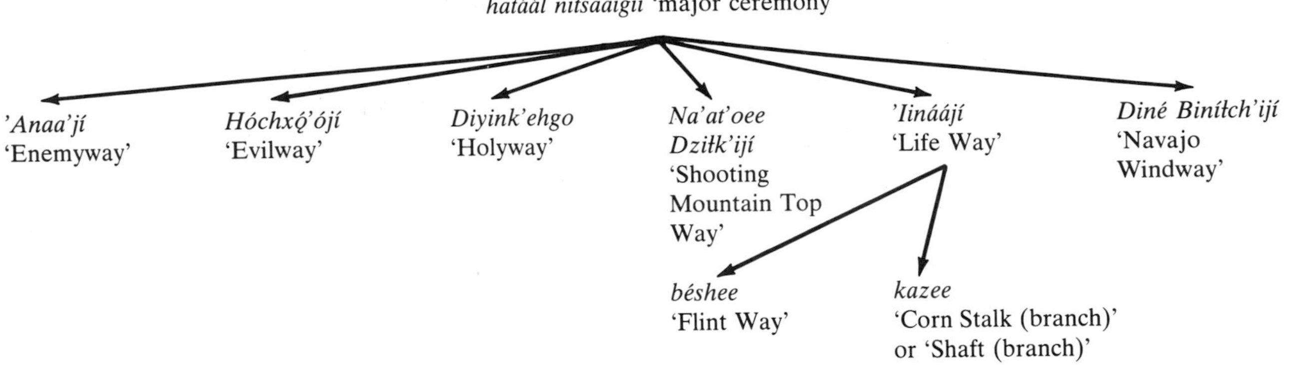

Sources

This chapter is a further development of Werner and Begishe (1970). The data were collected over many years, at first in the northwestern corner of the Navajo reservation (from Werner and Begishe's base at Tsegi Trading Post), later expanded with Manning to the north-central, Lukachukai area. The variations presented here are based on no more than three interviews with each of 28 people. Respondents were from the Tsegi area (8), Cow Springs (2), Shonto (2), Kayenta (6), Oljeto (4), Rough Rock (2), and Lukachukai (4). Of these, six were women, of whom three were from the Tsegi area.

Details on specialized Navajo knowledge are available for: classification in general (Franciscan Fathers 1910; Hoijer 1951; Kluckhohn 1948, 1960; Reichard 1948), anatomy (Begishe et al. 1981), astronomy (Haile 1947b), botany (Elmore 1944, 1952; Matthews 1886; Reichard 1948; Vestal 1952; Wyman and Harris 1941, 1951), color (Landar 1960), cosmology (Haile 1943a), entomology (Wyman and Bailey 1964), ethics and morals (Werner and Begishe 1968), daily activities (Topper 1972), food and eating (F.L. Bailey 1940; Berlin 1967; Landar 1964; Perchonock and Werner 1969), geography (Van Valkenburgh 1941; Young and Morgan 1947), kinship (Bellah 1952; D'Andrade 1970; Fenton 1974; Hoijer 1956; Landar 1962; Witherspoon 1970a), material culture (Kluckhohn, Hill, and Kluckhohn 1971), names (Young 1961a:539–561), medicine (Werner 1965; Begishe et al. 1981; Wyman and Bailey 1944), orientation (Casagrande 1964; Witherspoon 1971), religion (Wyman and Kluckhohn 1938, 1940; Reichard 1950), soul concept and Sacred Wind Spirit (Haile 1943a; McNeley 1981), values (Kluckhohn 1956), witchcraft (Kluckhohn 1944), zoology (Reichard 1948).

Navajo Arts and Crafts

RUTH ROESSEL

Weaving

Origin

Navajo stories and legends contain descriptions of Navajo weaving that go back to the earlier worlds than the one in which the Navajos now find themselves. In the lower worlds the ancestors of the Navajo are said to have used grass, yucca, and cedar bark in weaving. Navajo stories also discuss the use of mountain sheep hair, and there are the stories wherein Spider Woman taught the Navajo to use the material often described as being cotton.

The thrust of Navajo stories is to the effect that weaving was not a skill acquired by the Navajo after their entry into this world or into the Southwest but rather was a skill already known and practiced by the Navajo people. Certain authorities have suggested that this prior knowledge of weaving was very possible. While they are numerically fewer in number than the non-Navajo authorities who believe the Navajos learned weaving from the Pueblos after their entry into the Southwest, nevertheless even certain non-Navajo scholars suggest the possibility that Navajos learned weaving earlier. Reichard (1936:169), Roessel (1951:47–59), and James (1937:16) all discuss the probability that Navajos knew weaving before they entered the Southwest. The argument revolves around the fact that certain tribes on the Northwest Coast (near the Athapaskan homeland) did weaving that antedated the arrival of Europeans. Furthermore, these three authorities point out that among the Navajos, women do the weaving whereas with the Pueblo people it is the men that weave, yet among the Northwest Coast tribes it is also the women who weave (Jenness 1932:67, 155, 356; Curtis 1907–1930, 7:72, 9:43–44, 82).

In any event, the Navajo people believe they learned to weave from Spider Woman and that at the time they entered this world they had such knowledge and practiced the art of weaving blankets and also sashes or belts.

The majority of archeologists and ethnologists state that the Navajo learned to weave after their entry into the Southwest and they learned the craft from the Pueblos. In fact many of these authorities believe this learning took place immediately after the Pueblo Revolt in 1680 when many Pueblos moved to live directly with Navajos or moved adjacent to Navajo communities (Amsden 1934:129–130).

The earliest historical references to Navajo weaving date from the eighteenth century. The Rabal documents of 1706 through 1743 mention the weaving of cloth or textiles (Hill 1940:402, 411–413). Francisco Cuerbo y Valdes stated in 1706 that the Navajo "make their clothes of wool and cotton" (Hackett 1923–1937, 3:381–383). Teodoro de Croix in 1780 declared "the Navajos . . . weave their blankets and clothes of wool" (Thomas 1932:144). Fernando Chacón wrote in 1795: "They work their wool with more delicacy and taste than the Spaniards" (Bloom 1927:233). One of the earliest known examples of Navajo weaving that has survived was found by Sam Day, Jr., in 1903 (Morris 1925, 1948) in Massacre Cave in Canyon de Chelly ("Navajo Prehistory and History to 1850," fig. 6, this vol.); it dates from the infamous massacre by Spanish troops of Navajo women, children, and old people in the winter of 1804–1805 or 1805–1806.

During the period through The Long Walk, 1863–1868, all references to Navajo weaving relate to the weaving of blankets. Photographs of Navajos at Fort Sumner and also of other Indian tribes during approximately the same period show the use of many Navajo blankets. The designs include the traditional chief blanket design ("Navajo History, 1850–1923," fig. 2, this vol.), which evolved from a series of horizontal stripes to a series of stripes including diamonds and portions of diamonds. From 1788–1900, and especially 1800–1880, bayeta, which was a crimson red yarn unraveled from woven goods obtained from the Spaniards and Americans, was often seen and used. Amsden (1934:150) stated: "The bayeta period marked the high point, the 'Golden Age' of Navajo weaving . . . only an expert could wed native wool and bayeta fiber in a harmonious and happy union" (fig. 1).

Types of Weaving

There are three basic types of Navajo weaving—regular

Southwest Mus., Los Angeles: left, 1317; right, 457-G-2.

Fig. 1. Loom and blankets. left, Navajo weaver manipulating a batten (the wide flat stick used to separate warp elements so that weft can be inserted) at a vertical loom; wooden comb in her hand is used to tamp weft elements into position. The vertical loom, probably borrowed from the Pueblos, continues to be used with no changes of basic form. Two trees or poles are used as uprights. The warp is strung in a figure 8 around upper and lower warp beams; the upper is then tied to a tension beam, which is then tied to the upper horizontal support beam; the lower is tied directly to a support beam (not visible here). There are 2 sets of string heddles. Since the tapestry weave is used the weft often does not make a complete pass from selvage to selvage but is worked in sections forming the characteristic lazy lines that add flexibity to Navajo textiles. Looms are set up both inside and outdoors. Here the weaver sits on a sheepskin and works on a serrate-pattern rug using handspun wool. For further information on the loom and weaving technique see Bennett and Bighorse (1971), Gallagher (1981), and Pendleton (1974). Photograph by Warren Dickerson, before 1934. right, Poncho serape in what is known as the classic style. The wool yarns are white and indigo blue handspun by Navajos, and red unraveled from bayeta (baize) trade cloth. After about 1890 Navajos rarely produced tightly spun and densely woven fabrics such as this. About 183.0 by 139.7 cm, collected by Charles F. Lummis in 1889, probably woven about 1850.

weaving ("Navajo History, 1850–1923," figs. 7a, 12, 18, "Inter-Indian Exchange in the Southwest," fig. 9, this vol.), double weaving, and two-faced weaving.

• REGULAR WEAVES From information available in 1973 it would appear that out of 100 Navajo weavers, 90 knew the regular weave, while 9 knew the regular weave and double weave, and only 1 knew all three kinds of weaving. Amsden (1934:50) describes the regular or plain weave as the simplest of all in terms of loom arrangement and operation, requiring the minimum number of sheds, which is two. The single heddle controls one shed and the shed rod the other, to give the necessary interplay of warp and weft to bond the fabric. Included within the plain weave are some variations such as tufting, in which a certain part of the weft projects above the surface of the fabric, resulting in a pile of massive fiber rising above the plane of the rug.

• DOUBLE WEAVES OR TWILLED WEAVES Double weaves are usually the type utilized for saddle blankets (fig. 3); the thickness is almost double that of the regular or plain weave. The technique was common among the prehistoric Pueblos, and the Massacre Cave fragments show its use presumably by Navajos, although it did not become common among them until the 1880s (Kent 1961:26). While the plain weave uses but two sheds, the double weave employs four sheds that are controlled by three heddles on the shed rod. Through use of these devices the pattern of the weave is reversed from one side of the material to the other; it usually is of some geometric shape. Among the major types of double weaves are the diagonal twill and the diamond twill.

top, Amon Carter Mus., Ft. Worth, Tex.: Laura Gilpin Coll.; center, Heard Mus., Phoenix, Ariz.: NA-SW-Na-R-263; bottom, Denver Art Mus.: 1948.445 (RN-86).

Fig. 2. Two Gray Hills style rugs, probably the best known and among the best woven type. The characteristic pattern (complex central motif surrounded by framing borders) may be based on J.B. Moore's designs and is woven in natural-colored wool (the black sometimes intensified by aniline dye). top, Daisy Tauglechee spinning the particularly fine-spun yarn that yields the high weft count for which Two Gray Hills rugs, especially hers, are famous. After being cleaned and carded, the wool is spun and re-spun (as is the case here), sometimes several times, especially for the warp yarn, on a wooden spindle. The use of the right hand to roll, from knee to upper thigh, a spindle that rests on the ground and the left to hold wool is standard, producing a Z-spun yarn (Maxwell 1963:17–19). Photograph by Laura Gilpin, Toadlena, N. Mex., about Jan. 1955. center and bottom, Rugs woven by Tauglechee. The center rug, with a weft count of 106 to the inch, won a First Award at the Gallup Intertribal Indian Ceremonial in 1960; the bottom rug, woven in 1947–1948, has a weft count of 90 to the inch. bottom, 179 by 126 cm, center to same scale.

The interchange of these basic kinds provides many possible variations for the Navajo weaver familiar with the very versatile double weave. The key to the double weave is counting, and if one does not know how to do this it is impossible to make such a rug.

• TWO-FACED WEAVES In 1973 there were a few Navajo women who knew how to string a loom and weave a two-faced rug. Basically, a two-faced rug is one that has different and unrelated designs on the opposite sides. Although Matthews (1900:638–640) believed that the development of the two-faced weave took place some time during the 1890s, there are earlier examples, including a huge piece dated 1885 in the Museum of Northern Arizona, Flagstaff (Joe Ben Wheat, communication to editors, 1981). The weave has always been at best a collector's item or novelty.

Types of Dye

Navajo weaving is generally divided into three categories with reference to color: the natural colors, vegetable dyes, and aniline dyes ("Navajo Education," fig. 4, this vol.).

Natural colors include white, a native brownish black, a brown, and a gray that is produced by carding black and white wool together. Vegetable dyes range through a broad array of pastel hues. The colors and tints available from vegetable sources are all but unlimited. They include shades of yellow-brown, pink, lavender, and green. Collecting the plants, roots, or bark used for the dye adds a time-consuming element to the production of a vegetable-dyed rug.

The majority of rugs woven in 1973 were produced using aniline dyes purchased from the trading post or neighboring towns. These dyes are much harsher and brighter than are the older and more traditional vegetable dyes. Many tourists like and expect bright reds and blues and greens, and this, coupled with the fact that rugs using aniline dyes require far less time to prepare the dyed wool, accounts for the prevalence of aniline-dyed rugs.

Economics of Weaving

The Navajo Studies Department of Navajo Community College, Many Farms, Arizona, undertook an experiment to determine the total amount of time involved in marketing a rug from shearing the sheep to the sale of the finished rug. The following figures are for making a rug of approximately three feet by five feet.

Catching and shearing the sheep	1 hour
Cleaning and washing the fleece	2 hours
Drying the washed wool	8 hours
Carding the wool	16 hours
Spinning the wool	24 hours
Preparing the vegetable dye and dyeing the wool	60 hours
Making the loom; stringing the loom	16 hours
Weaving the rug	215 hours
Brushing, cleaning and completing the rug	2 hours
Selling the rug	1 hour
Total	345 hours

The rug in question, which was of above-average quality, was sold to a trader in 1973 for $105. The weaver therefore received 30¢ per hour for her skilled work on the rug.

Receiving only 30¢ an hour for work as difficult, demanding, and intricate as weaving a Navajo rug may seem unfair if not unjust. However, the value and significance of weaving to Navajo life in the late twentieth century cannot be overemphasized. Whether the amount the weaver receives is considered too high or too low is not the crucial concern; rather, the fact remains for many, many Navajo families that the money earned by women for weaving may be the only predictable source of income the family has! With the unemployment percentage for Navajo adults exceeding 60 percent (in 1973) and with many of the limited jobs being seasonal and uncertain, such as fighting forest fires, working on the railroads, and farm labor, the role of the women in weaving to provide a reliable source of food and clothing is of extreme importance to the existence of Navajo family life. The Navajo have always been matrilineal with women holding a position of prestige in Navajo culture, and weaving helps assure the continuation of this position for women.

In 1890 the cash value of Navajo weaving was estimated to be $30,000; in 1923, $750,000, with some 5,500 weavers; in 1931, $1,000,000. This represents for Navajo women a wage of about five cents an hour (Amsden 1934:182). The amount of money a weaver received in 1973 for her time was, of course, many times that, but taking into account the effect of inflation, it may very well be that the hourly income received by Navajo weavers in 1980 buys less than the five cents an hour received by Navajo weavers in the 1930s.

Heard Mus., Phoenix, Ariz.: NA-SW-Na-R-344.

Fig. 3. Saddle blanket in a diamond twill of vegetable-dyed black and brown and natural white handspun wool. Used under the saddle, such blankets are the one type still produced primarily for Navajo use. They are usually woven in twill rather than the plain weave used for larger blankets. Because they are narrow, the tapestry technique with its "lazy lines" is not used. About 116.8 by 101.6 cm, woven by Agnes Dodge, Crystal, N. Mex., 1961.

Navajo Community College's Navajo Studies Department in 1973 collected for the first time information from every trading post on and adjacent to the Navajo reservation with reference to the rugs and silver they purchased from the Navajos; this included the wholesale firm serving the reservation. A questionnaire was prepared and an interview held with a knowledgeable person at each facility. One of the questions asked dealt with the amount of money paid by these establishments to Navajo weavers for their rugs.

Whether Amsden's 1934 figures are comparable with the material collected by Navajo Community College is unknown, since Amsden did not define what he meant by "cash value" or explain whether he referred to wholesale prices or retail prices or something else. In the Navajo Community College study the data referred specifically to the amount of money paid by the trader to the weaver for the rug; what the trader sold the rug for is something else. In 1972 a total of $2,799,232 was spent by traders to purchase Navajo rugs. There would seem to be no doubt but the total amount received by Navajo weavers for their rugs has increased over the years. Furthermore, there is no doubt that the quantity of rugs has also increased as well as the total number of Navajo women weaving.

Navajo Community College undertook another study to estimate the total number of Navajo weavers at work in 1973. Using a sampling procedure, which included all chapters (communities) located on the Navajo Reservation, it was determined that a total of some 28,000 adult Navajo women knew how to weave. With weaving being taught in many of the schools—elementary, secondary, and college—there should be little possibility that Navajo weaving will become extinct, at least so long as the unemployment rate is high and average family income remains so low. Yet many of the younger Navajo weavers weave because of pride in Navajo culture and not solely for economic reasons.

The price of Navajo rugs is also escalating at a rapid rate. A rug that sold for about $500 in 1980 would probably have sold for less than $50 some 20 years earlier.

Regional Styles

Chinle, Wide Ruins, and Klagetoh, Arizona, produce some of the best examples of vegetable-dyed rugs. From the Wide Ruins and Klagetoh area come the finest examples of Navajo weaving to be found anywhere on the reservation. These rugs usually are without borders and are characterized by a softness highlighted by warm pastel colors. Chinle also produces vegetable-dyed rugs but usually not of such superior quality.

Two Gray Hills in New Mexico is the headquarters for the finest examples of Navajo weaving in natural color fiber (fig. 2). Some of the handspun yarn used in the finer examples of Two Gray Hills weaving is unequaled in fineness anywhere on the Navajo reservation, and the rugs produced from this yarn are the most expensive per square inch of any type of Navajo weaving. The rugs are white, black, and gray and also sometimes contain a native brown. The designs are elaborate, intricate, usually geometric, and usually contained within a border.

Teec Nos Pos has a characteristic style and design that often includes the fineness of weave associated with

PLATE XIX

left, Moore 1911:12; center, U. of N. Mex., Maxwell Mus. of Anthr., Albuquerque: 63.34.105; right, Mus. of Northern Ariz., Flagstaff: 2994/E7117.

Fig. 4. John B. Moore and the Crystal style. Traders such as Lorenzo Hubbell and Moore, worried about the poor quality weaving resulting from sale by the pound and other factors at the turn of the century, took an active role in encouraging quality work. Moore from his post at Crystal, N. Mex., sent wool east to be cleaned and carded mechanically. He discouraged the use of gaudy colors and designed rugs probably based on oriental rug patterns. left, A plate from Moore's 1911 catalog from which clients could select their choice shows "one of the most popular" patterns. center, A rug purchased in 1915 from Moore's Crystal Trading Post, obviously based on the catalog, is done in natural white and aniline dyed black, gray, red, and camel colored handspun wool. right, Rug of natural-dyed yarns. With the revival of natural dyes in the 1930s the Crystal style began to incorporate vegetal-dyed yarns in banded patterns. About 1955 wavy lines were added, achieved by alternating the color of the weft (Erickson and Cain 1976:34–41). Collected in 1965. center, 203.5 by 137.5 cm, right to same scale.

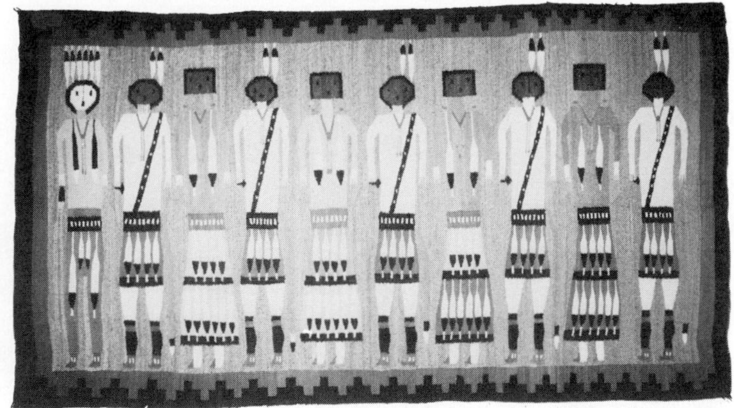

left, Heard Mus., Phoenix, Ariz.: NA–SW–Na–R–349; right, Smithsonian, Dept. of Anthr.: 325.883.
Fig. 5. Yei and yeibichai rugs depict gods (yeis) or masked dancers (yeibichais). The motifs are from sandpaintings, but only a portion of the total design is used. Like sandpainting rugs they have no ceremonial significance of their own. left, A two-faced rug, unusual in having patterns on both sides rather than stripes on one side. The reverse side, seen in the folded over corner, is a yei scene. It is woven entirely of vegetable dyed and natural colored handspun wool in contrast to most yei and yeibichai rugs, which utilize some commercially spun or aniline dyed wool. About 101.6 by 147.3 cm, woven by Sarah Williams, of Coal Mine Mesa, Ariz., the rug won several awards in 1962. right, Rugs with sandpainting designs are made for the tourist trade. Although there was much native disapproval when they were first woven (around 1900) the furor had died down somewhat by 1923 when Chee Dodge, Navajo leader and entrepreneur (Borgman 1948), presented this rug, 137.1 by 256.5 cm.

Two Gray Hills rugs with an added dimension of geometric designs, and with the use of bright aniline colors pleasantly combined with backgrounds in gray and white as well as black.

Crystal, New Mexico, produces rugs that are distinctive in often being composed of stripes or variation of stripes (fig. 4). They have a line of one color alternated with a line of another color, which gives a softness to the rug. Also, Crystal rugs frequently use vegetable dyes, which further the softness and pleasing quality of the rug.

Lukachukai, Arizona, is the center of an area where many of the present Yeibichai rugs are woven (fig. 5). These rugs usually consist of a number of the Yei figures standing in a row, usually surrounded by a rainbow guardian figure. The quality of weaving varies greatly. The demand for these rugs comes from the tourist who believes (erroneously) that he is purchasing something sacred.

Ganado, Arizona, is the center for what is known as Ganado red rugs. Here one finds geometric designs usually enclosed within a border. A deep red is one of the main colors and is usually combined with black, white, and gray. The weave is often very tight and the wool is spun beautifully but not with the fineness of the Two Gray Hills rugs.

Coal Mine Mesa in Arizona has enjoyed a strong revival of high quality weaving. There one finds a distinctive raised design in a double weave as well as some of the finest double weaves produced anywhere on the Navajo reservation. Coal Mine Mesa also produces large double weave rugs, some reaching as large as 6 by 12 feet.

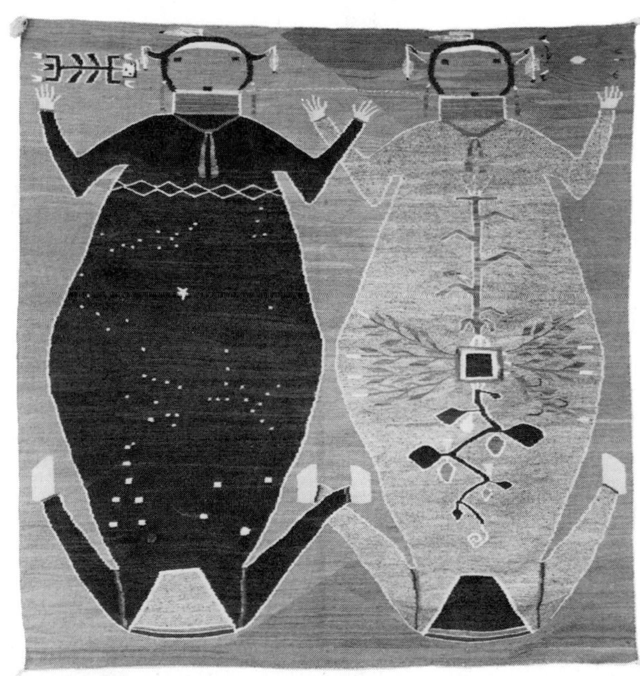

Wheelwright Mus., Santa Fe, N. Mex.: 44/517.
Fig. 6. Rug depicting Father Sky and Mother Earth. Although patterned after sandpaintings, such rugs have no ritual significance; however, there is still some objection to them among traditional Navajos. Hosteen Klah, himself a medicine man, began weaving sandpainting rugs in 1919 and taught his nieces, who wove this rug, his patterns (McGreevy 1981). About 166.0 by 160.0 cm, made 1920s–1930s.

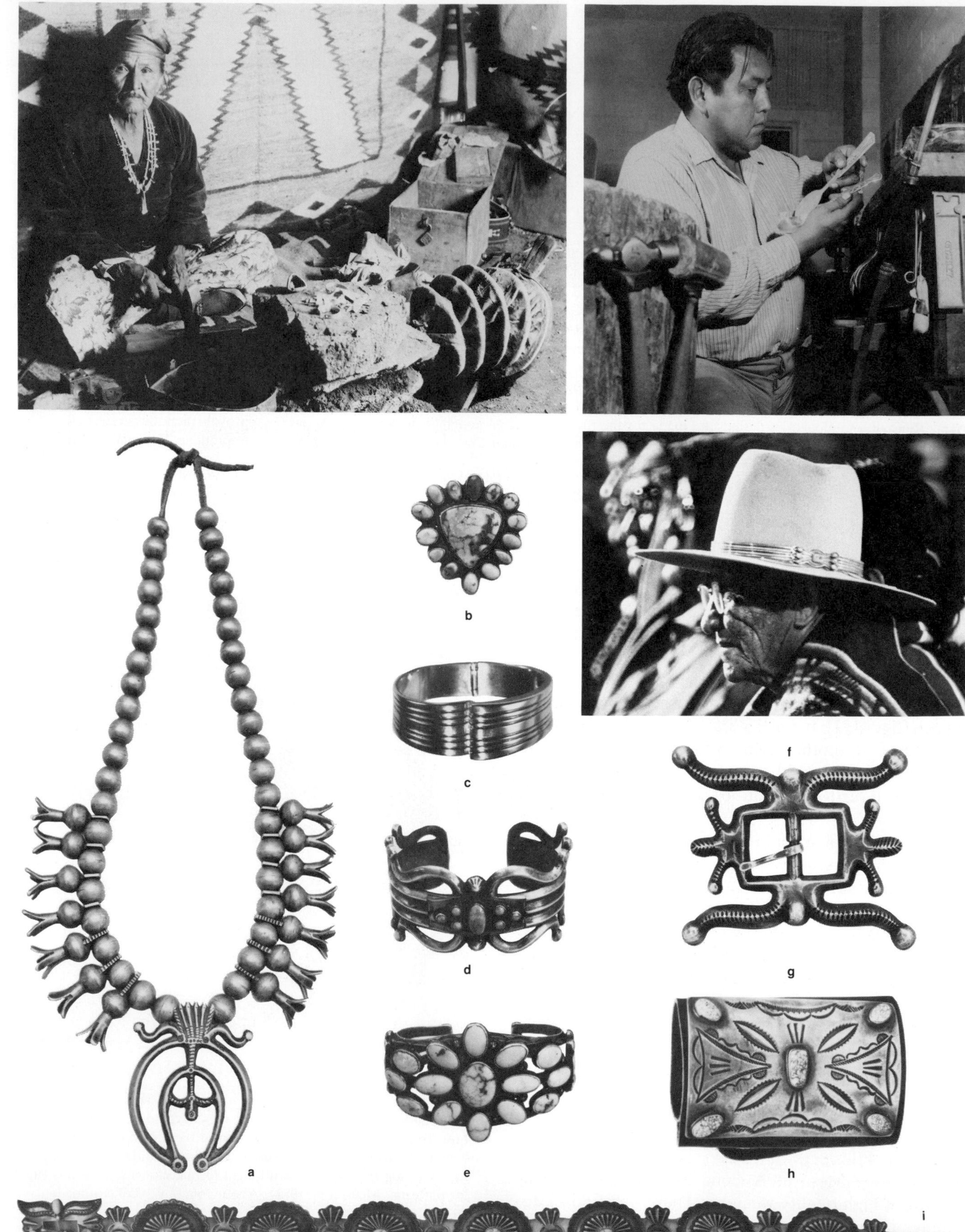

ROESSEL

top left, Smithsonian, NAA: 81-10468; top right, John Bonnell, Scottsdale, Ariz.; Wheelwright Mus., Santa Fe, N. Mex.: a, 47/153; b, 47/70; d, 47/168; e, 47/228; g, 47/279; h, 47/248; i, 47/571; c, Los Angeles Co. Mus. of Nat. Hist.: L2100.52-221; f, *The Gallup Independent*, N. Mex.

Fig. 7. Silverwork. top left, Tools of early smiths were limited including the goat skin bellows, crucible, anvil (here probably a piece of railroad tie), hammer, tongs, stamps, and punches. Photograph by G.H. Bate, location unkown, 1921 or before. By the 1930s commercial solder, saws, files, and blowtorches were being used. In the 1980s commercial jewelry-making machinery was employed. top right, Kenneth Begay in 1954–1955 at the White Hogan, Scottsdale, Ariz., where he was employed from 1946–1963. Begay did not limit himself to traditional forms, making also items such as the spoons he holds and the bracelet (c) made in 1952 that represents the innovative designing of some contemporary smiths. Traditional jewelry types still being made include a, Squash-blossom necklace with cast naja pendant. The beads, strung on a leather thong, are made by soldering 2 hemispheres together. This example is representative of the type made in the early 1900s; in the 1980s many have turquoise stones. b, Silver and turquoise cluster-set pin is similar to ring designs of the 1930s. Bracelets of cast silver with turquoise and silver buttons added (d), and of cluster-set turquoise on wrought and stamped band (e) represent 2 major techniques of silverwork, both post-1930. f, Silver hat band, in mid-1930s style, worn by a singer at the 1980 Gallup Intertribal Ceremonial. This typical part of Navajo costume developed around 1900. Photograph by Mark Lennihan. g, Bow guard developed from simple piece of leather worn by men on the arm to protect the wearer from snap of bow string. In the 1980s worn primarily for decoration, they were the one item not commercialized and still worn mostly by Indian men. The heavily stamped piece here with spider-web turquoise dates about 1950. h, Heavy cast belt buckle of the type made in the 1920s and later. i, Wrought belt, typical of the 1930s and later; the buckle is probably handwrought and the butterfly slides and the embossed centers of the conchas were produced by large dies; total length about 78.7 cm. Length of a, 37.7 cm, rest to same scale. Sources: Adair 1944; Bedinger 1973; Joe Ben Wheat, communication to editors 1981.

Silverwork

Origin

Authorities both Navajo and non-Navajo agree that silversmithing (fig. 7) is not an ancient craft among the Navajo. Adair (1944:3–11), Franciscan Fathers (1910:271–272), and Woodward (1971:16–25) state that the Navajo knew blacksmithing before they went to Fort Sumner but learned silversmithing after their return. The very first Navajo to learn the art of silverwork was *'Atsidí Sání* 'old smith', also known by his Spanish name Herrero 'smith' (Franciscan Fathers 1910:271).

The earliest Navajo silverwork contained no turquoise but rather was plain silver decorated with an awl (Matthews 1883). In this early period there was no stamping done nor any setting of stones. Adair (1944:20–25) declared that the first use of turquoise with silver occurred about 1880. The commercial aspects of the craft were recognized and exploited by the Fred Harvey Company in the early twentieth century (Adair 1944:25), and from that time on Navajo silversmithing has been an important economic activity.

The economic aspect of the craft and the great use of silver ornaments and objects by the Navajo themselves brought about a steady and spectacular development of the ability to work silver. Navajo silverwork and its place in Navajo culture must be distinguished from Navajo weaving. In the 1980s, with the exception of saddle blankets and often Navajo woven dresses, Navajo weaving is not used by the Navajo themselves; rather, it is sold for non-Navajo use. Silverwork is different because modern Navajos make extensive use of Navajo silver. While many hundreds of thousands of dollars of Navajo silver is sold to non-Navajos, it is equally true that many hundreds of thousands of dollars of Navajo silver is bought and used by Navajos. Although the best examples of old Navajo silver are to be found in museums and collections off the reservation, among contemporary Navajo silver, the best is to be found on the reservation being worn by Navajos. Adair (1944:202) estimated the total number of Navajo silversmiths in 1940 to be 600. Navajo Studies personnel from Navajo Community College conducted a survey in 1973 and estimated the number of Navajo silversmiths to exceed 1,300. In fact, the arts and crafts program itself at Navajo Community College produced over 150 qualified craftsmen in the period 1970–1973.

While silverwork is a relatively new craft among the Navajo it fits easily into the traditional Navajo concept of "hard goods."

Techniques and Design

In the early days of Navajo silversmithing the tools used were simple and few: a forge made of stones and adobe, bellows made from sheepskin, an anvil usually made of iron, and crucibles made of clay. Silver was obtained by melting Mexican pesos or American coins. During the early period of Navajo silversmithing items such as concha belts, buckles, bow guards or ketohs (Navajo *k'eet'oh*), bracelets, rings, earrings, bridles, necklaces, buttons and pins, and tobacco canteens were made ("Navajo History, 1850–1923," figs. 7, 12–13, this vol.).

The passage of time has not substantially increased the different kinds of silverwork produced by Navajo craftsmen, but rather the increase has been primarily in the types of design and style ("Navajo Social Organization," fig. 3, this vol.). A few especially gifted Navajo silversmiths, such as Kenneth Begay, have developed new forms, including the use of ironwood with silver. Also in response to demand a number of modern silversmiths make salad sets, jewelry boxes, flatware, and so forth. On the other hand, some of the old-time items such as silver bridles and bow guards are only infrequently made.

In the 1970s Navajo silversmiths used an array of tools and supplies that would have been not only unknown but also incomprehensible to the early-day silversmith. Modern torches using oxygen, diamond

Helga Teiwes Photography, Tucson, Ariz.

Fig. 8. Sally Black (center) finishing a large coiled basket after about 2 months' work. With her are her mother, Mary Black, who taught her basketry, and a sister. The yeibichai design—a motif derived from sandpaintings—is executed in willow bark (which she dyed herself) from a simple sketch. The size (diameter about 106.7 cm) and yeibichai design make it a unique basket; the 2 lower baskets are in the common Navajo style. The large basket is in the Heard Mus., Phoenix, catalog #NA–SW–Na–b–20. Photograph by Helga Teiwes, at the family's home on Douglas Mesa, north of Monument Valley, Utah, 1979.

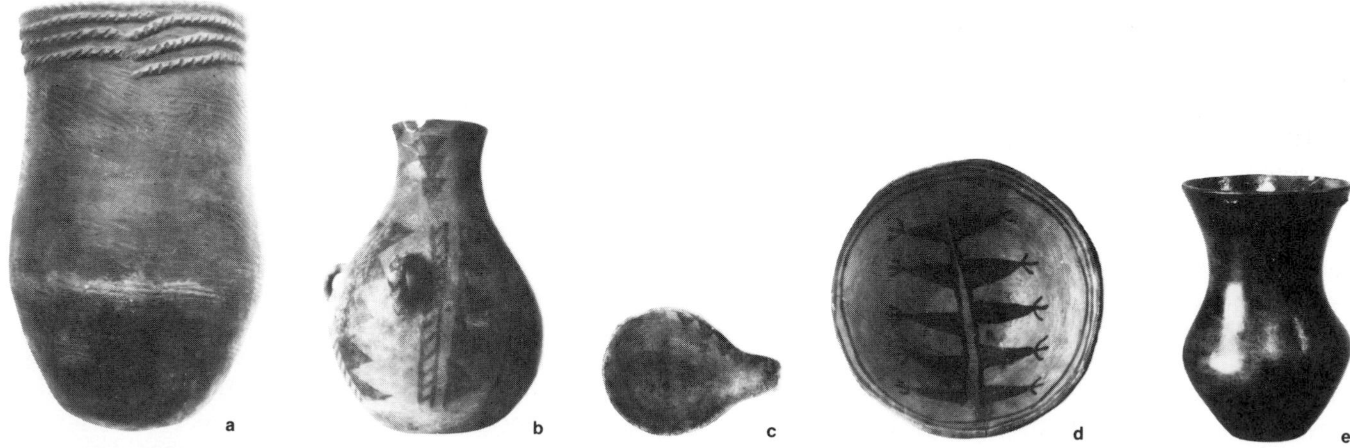

a, Smithsonian, Dept. of Anthr.: 292,723; U. of Calif., Lowie Mus., Berkeley: b, 2–8348; c, 2–8357; d, 2–8354; e, Milwaukee Public Mus., Wis.: 61964/22999.

Fig. 9. Pottery, although never a major craft, was made in several styles by women and berdaches (Hill 1937; Tschopik 1941). a, Cooking pot, the most common type, made in several sizes. Like all the vessels it is of sherd-tempered clay built up in coils, smoothed with a corncob or piece of gourd, and polished with a pebble. Here the rim is indented and there are 3 bands of fillet decoration. After firing, cooking pots are covered with pitch to make them waterproof. Painted pottery was formerly manufactured; color was rubbed on the vessel before firing and painted designs were added either before or after firing. b, Water bottle, shaped like a basketry water jar, with matte-black decoration on orange-buff ground. c, Ladle, shaped like a gourd dipper, with matte-black decoration on a pinkish-buff ground. d, Bowl with dark brown designs outlined in brownish black on a pinkish ground. Plain bowls were also made. Other pottery items included pipes and unfired figurines (see "Navajo Social Organization," fig. 6, this vol.). e, Modern adaptation of a traditional form. Height of a 33.5 cm, rest to same scale. a, collected by J.W. Fewkes, 1914. b–d, collected by George Pepper 1903. e, made by Alice Barlow about 1971.

saws, electric buffing and polishing equipment, pliers, and hack saws have become essential to Navajo craftsmen. Silver is bought from the trader or wholesalers in surrounding towns in sheet or wire form. Turquoise stones may also be purchased precut and polished. In fact most Navajo silversmiths do not cut and polish their own stones.

Turquoise is readily available although the cost has climbed tremendously since the 1940s. In 1940 good quality cut turquoise could be purchased for 10¢ to 25¢ a carat. In 1973 the same quality turquoise cost over $2.00 a carat. Furthermore, since the 1960s there have been many methods utilized to produce treated or artificial turquoise, with the result that there exist huge amounts of such turquoise, some of which finds its way into Navajo jewelry.

Silversmithing differs from weaving in that it usually is not a family-taught craft. Since 1969 the Navajo Community College has operated an extensive arts and crafts training program in which leading craftsmen from throughout the reservation teach students their skill. As a result, certain crafts that were all but extinct, such as basketmaking and pottery making, have staged a revival. In addition, the Rough Rock Demonstration School, Rough Rock, Arizona, has operated a similar program since 1966 and the Office of Economic Opportunity operated during the late 1960s a training program in silversmithing that was almost reservation wide.

Probably at no time in the past has there been such a demand for authentic Navajo silverwork. A leader in encouraging quality Navajo arts and crafts has been the Navajo tribe's own Arts and Crafts Guild with headquarters at Window Rock, Arizona, and branches at Cameron, Chinle, Kayenta, and Teec Nos Pos ("Navajo Education," fig. 4, this vol.). Some very skilled Navajo silversmiths earned over $15,000 a year from their trade in the early 1970s.

While the number of Navajos who make silverwork has increased over the years it is less certain that the total number of hours spent producing silverwork has increased proportionately. There were undoubtedly more Navajos in 1973 who could produce good silverwork, but many of them did not do so on anything like a full-time basis. Nevertheless, silversmithing more nearly approaches a full-time job than does weaving, which continues to be a woman's supplemental source of income and not a full-time endeavor.

The influence and tastes of the tourist upon Navajo silver are unmistakable. Many tourists want to buy souvenirs to take home ("Navajo Economic Development," fig. 13, this vol.), and cost is an overriding factor. Consequently certain dealers located in towns off the reservation have developed an assembly line for the production of "Navajo" silverwork. Here certain individuals perform specific steps in the manufacture of the item and pass the object to the next specialist who performs his particular step. As a result, the item was produced by a number of Indians or Navajos but not by a single craftsman. In spite of efforts to regulate mass-produced or production-line "Navajo" silver and the even more disturbing imitation Navajo silver, and imported "Navajo" rugs from Mexico and elsewhere, these attacks on handcrafted Navajo arts and crafts continue and are financially successful to the imitator. But there appears to be an ever-expanding number of people who want and are willing to pay the necessary high prices to purchase good quality Navajo silver.

In the arts and crafts study conducted by Navajo Studies personnel at Navajo Community College, it was discovered in 1972 that a total of $2,719,724 was spent by traders to purchase silverwork from Navajos. The figure does not include production firms in Albuquerque and elsewhere.

When one considers that in 1972 Navajo silver and weaving craftsmen received over $5.5 million, the economic importance of these crafts is obvious. Less obvious but probably more important is the relationship of arts and crafts to the Navajo belief in harmony and beauty. Navajo life and culture is intertwined with the belief in the significance of harmony and the necessity for beauty. Navajo crafts provide a means for this relationship to be expressed, revealed, and continued.

Basketry

The use of Navajo baskets is required in many Navajo ceremonies. In certain ceremonies baskets are used to hold sacred cornmeal or mush, in others baskets are used to bathe from, while in yet other ceremonies baskets are used as drums. Tradition demands the use of what is known as the "wedding basket," with two bands of mountain design usually in black and an interweaving band of dark russet ("Navajo Social Organization," fig. 4, this vol.). There is always an opening in the design so as to keep it from becoming a closed circle.

The Navajo basket is coiled counterclockwise, usually with a three-rod foundation (fig. 8). Split sumac is used for stitching, dyed black and russet as well as being used in its natural white state. The rim of the basket is usually twilled and must be completed in a single day. An awl is the only instrument used, but the sumac is split by the basketmaker using her teeth.

Navajos also make and use a wicker water jug, of sumac or willow waterproofed with melted piñon pitch. This type of Navajo basket was made more frequently in 1973 than even 20 years earlier, but nevertheless not nearly so frequently as the wedding baskets. Piñon gum is heated and, when liquid, poured into the inside of the water jug where it is rolled about by moving the jug back and forth. On the exterior a brush of grass of some sort is used to apply the pitch. The outside pitch is

Smithsonian, Dept. of Anthr.: left, 213, 274; center, 213,276; right, Smithsonian, NAA.

Fig. 10. Legwear. left, Knitted leggings made and worn primarily by men. The left and right are differentiated by the line of cable stitch worn on the outer side of each leg. Knitting was done on steel needles (either purchased from a trader or improvised from umbrella ribs) with dark blue (as here) or black wool yarn, or knitted with white wool and later dyed. Simple leather leggings (not shown) were wound around the leg from the ankle to below the knee, covering the knit pieces. The leather leggings were tied around the top with a woven garter and tucked into the moccasins at the bottom. center, Pair of red garters with green stripes at edges and center strip of raised red and white geometric design (Matthews 1884:389–391). They were woven on a belt loom. right, Woman weaving at belt loom with exterior frame (Shufeldt 1892), thought to be the precursor of the broader, vertical blanket loom (Amsden 1934:45). Belts were also woven on frameless looms. Amsden (1934:pl. 20) illustrates a similar loom with a partially woven belt, which differs in type and rigging from the Pueblo belt looms. Photograph by Ben Wittick or R.W. Shufeldt, 1880s, in northwestern N. Mex. left and center, collected by Walter Hough, 1901. Length of left 44.4 cm, center same scale.

colored with red clay to provide a soft reddish-brown hue.

Until the mid-1960s very few Navajos made the "Navajo wedding baskets." Primarily the baskets were made by Paiutes living with or near the Navajo, such as near Tuba City, or at Navajo Mountain. The traditional need to use Navajo wedding baskets has always been so great that there is a lively trade in used baskets with the trading posts. A Navajo who is going to have a "sing" (ceremony) will go to a trading post and purchase one or more baskets as required. Upon the completion of the "sing" the baskets usually are sold back to the trading post. The same basket may be sold and resold as many as 30 or 40 times a year.

The craft primarily is one wherein the finished product is used and sold almost exclusively by Navajos, in contrast to silversmithing and weaving where the majority of completed items are bought by non-Navajos. A well-made wedding basket, so named because it is used in the traditional Navajo wedding ceremony, sold for nearly $100 in 1980. Tourists do not appear to be very eager to pay that kind of money for a basket.

When the Rough Rock Demonstration School began in 1966, the all-Navajo school board hired a Navajo woman from the Inscription House area to teach basketmaking. Later the Navajo Community College hired one of the Rough Rock trainees to teach. The result is that while there were probably fewer than a dozen Navajo basketmakers prior to 1966 there were in 1973 over 100. Top quality new Navajo wedding baskets became available for the first time in many years.

Pottery

The Navajo have always made utilitarian-type pottery for their households (fig. 9). In certain ceremonies food must be prepared and cooked in a Navajo pot. A second continuing use for Navajo pottery is as a drum in the Enemyway ceremony (Squaw Dance), for which a pot is partly filled with water and covered with a leather head ("Navajo Music," fig. 4, this vol.). These two traditional uses for Navajo pottery combined with general resurgence of Navajo interest in all facets of Navajo

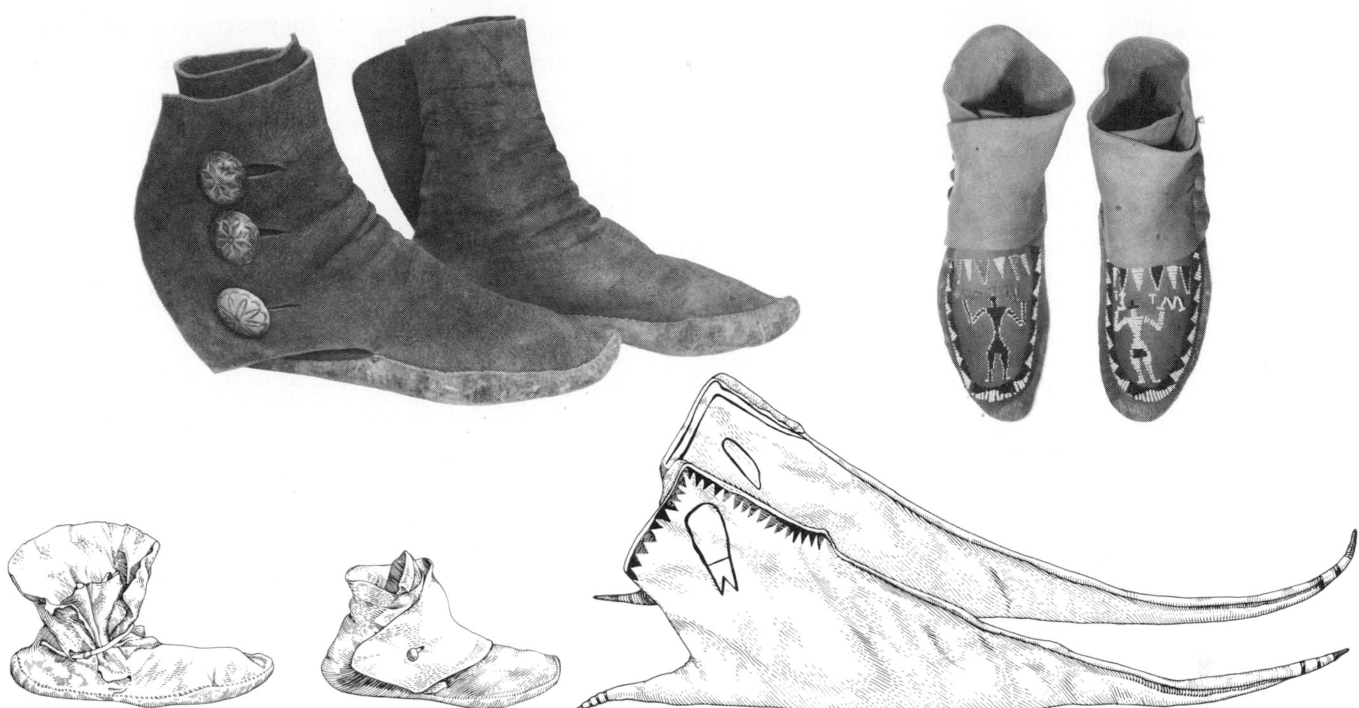

Smithsonian, Dept. of Anthr.: top right, 16,503; bottom left, 9550; bottom center, 9549; bottom right, 128,116. top left, Wheelwright Mus., Santa Fe, N. Mex.: 50/40.

Fig. 11. Footwear. Moccasins are usually made by men, who also tan the necessary hide (Shufeldt 1889). top left, The most common Navajo style consists of a one-piece wraparound upper of tanned leather dyed a reddish color that is fastened on the outer side of the foot with silver buttons. It has a rawhide sole that is molded around the foot and stitched using an awl and sinew thread. See Kluckhohn, Hill, and Kluckhohn (1971:282–290) for construction details. Variations include a style with a tongue that is either tied (bottom left) or buttoned (bottom center). Women, men, and children may wear these types, but women formerly wore Pueblo-style moccasins with attached leg wrappings. Early moccasins had bead and quill decorations (Franciscan Fathers 1910:309). top right, Pair decorated with white, black, and light blue seed beads. The pattern on the toes includes the initals W.F.M.A. of Agent W.F.M. Arny. They were probably made as a gift when Arny brought a Navajo delegation to Washington. bottom right, Another unusual pair, with long pointed toes and painted decoration, reported by the collector to be dance moccasins used in the Snake or Wind Dance (Stephen 1889). top left, Length about 25.5 cm, accessioned 1972. bottom left and center, Collected by Edward Palmer, 1869; top right, collected 1874; bottom right, length 75 cm (rest to same scale), collected 1887.

culture, including the crafts, has made Navajo pottery available in more adequate quantities than ever before.

Here again the Navajo Community College and the Rough Rock Demonstration School played an important role in teaching the craft to new learners. In 1954–1956 Ruth Roessel conducted a survey in the Chinle Agency seeking to identify the number of women who still knew pottery making and practiced it. Only two women were found, but by 1973 there were over 125 women in the same agency who could make pottery.

The Navajo formerly made decorated pottery, but their most frequently made pot, in the past as in the present, was an undecorated pot covered with piñon pitch with a pointed bottom or more often with a point partially flattened so the pot will stand by itself.

According to the Franciscan Fathers (1910:285–286), Navajo pottery once was "no wise inferior to that of the Pueblo." Navajo traditions tell that pottery making was learned from the Holy People, while most non-Navajo believe the Navajo learned pottery from the Pueblo people. Some archeologists maintain that Navajo pointed-bottom pottery has northern origins.

Pottery clay is found in many locations on the Navajo reservation. The primary temper used is ground-up potsherds. Long slender "ropes" of clay are rolled out and then coiled to make the pot. Piñon pitch is applied to both the inside and outside, in a manner similar to that used for basketry water jugs. The pottery is fired, usually with burning sheep or cow dung.

Another continuing traditional use of Navajo pottery is the making of elbow-shaped or cylindrical Navajo pipes, often inset with pieces of shell and turquoise. The pipes were still used in the 1980s to smoke sacred tobacco in certain ceremonies.

Other Arts and Crafts

Red or rust-colored moccasins (fig. 11) used by many Navajos in their ceremonies are made by a few Navajos who in 1980 primarily utilized commercial leather for the uppers as well as the soles. The production of traditional styles of clothing is a common craft, particularly the full velveteen skirts and blouses and the *biił* or two-piece woven wool dress.

Modern watercolors and other paintings are important. Beginning with the influence of the Santa Fe Indian School during the 1930s and 1940s numerous Navajos learned studio-style drawing and painting (for example, "Navajo Music," fig. 8, "Navajo Views of Their Origin," fig. 1, this vol.). In the 1980s a few Navajos gained their entire income from this kind of art, while most artists painted only part-time.

Navajo Music

DAVID P. McALLESTER AND DOUGLAS F. MITCHELL

The Navajo people distinguish categories of traditional music ranging from personal songs used for pleasure to deeply sacred chants that can be sung only in the appropriate ceremonial context. At a level that is essentially secular there are *diné biyiin* 'Navajo songs', a category that includes lullabies, children's songs, and social, comic, and topical songs. Strictly speaking, the term can include any songs used by Navajos, but its use usually implies "free style" nonceremonial singing.

At the other end of the spectrum are *hatáál sin* 'ceremonial songs' including all music from the great ceremonies, though there are many kind of songs within the ceremonies that also have more specific names applied to them. The traditional popular songs, *Nidáá' sin* or *Ndáá' sin* 'Squaw Dance songs' (literally 'War Dance songs'), are drawn from the Enemyway ceremonial and include *Yik'aash sin* 'Sway songs' ('high-pitched songs'), *Názhnoodahí sin* 'Circle Dance songs' ('people-dance-in-a-circle songs'), *'Ahidii'áhí sin* 'Two-step songs' ('linked-together songs'), and *'Iich'oshí sin* 'Round Dance songs', all of which can be readily distinguished from one another by their musical form.

Another style of traditional music, popular at occasions such as a Navajo fair, but not sung so widely as the Squaw Dance songs, is *'ak'áhí sin* 'corn-grinding songs'. Also from Enemyway but too sacred to be used as popular songs are categories such as the *'atsáłeeh* 'first songs', which initiate various ceremonial procedures, and the *chaashzhiní biyiin* 'Mud Dancers' songs', which accompany a special feature of some performances.

Songs from the ceremonials may be referred to generally by the name of the ceremony, such as *Na'at'oee sin* 'Shootingway songs', *Hózǫǫjí sin* 'Blessingway songs', and *'Anaa'jí biyiin* 'Enemyway songs'. Within these categories there are many specific terms such as *naaldlooshii biyiin* 'quadruped songs', *Tó Dine'é biyiin* 'Water People songs', *tsídii biyiin* 'bird songs', *naalyéhé biyiin* 'personal property songs', *ch'iyáán biyiin* 'food (gathering) songs', and *yiikááht'ááji̜' sin* 'dawn songs'. Specific function within the ceremony may give a name to a class of songs such as *Néigahí biyiin* 'Fire Dancer's songs' and *'Azhniidááh sin* 'Corral songs', both from Mountaintop Way.

Certain songs, such as *Késhjéé' sin* 'Moccasin Game songs' and *sodizin biyiin* 'prayer songs', are sacred and reserved for specific times and places even though the first group is not part of any ceremony and there are many kinds of prayer songs, some of which are personal with no ceremonial connections either (Gill 1980). There are other kinds of songs, such as weaving songs, that "have a story," the origins of which go back to mythical accounts: these too are sacred and reserved for specific occasions.

In addition to these traditional musics, an increasing number of outside musics are making themselves felt among the Navajo people. Churches and schools are powerful disseminators of Euro-American styles of music. Television sets and tape recorders are fairly common on the reservation and the battery-powered radio is widely used. At civic centers in Farmington, Window Rock, and Tuba City, teenagers fill the floor with the same kind of popular dance that can be seen anywhere else in the United States youth culture. The country and western or rock and roll or disco records or live music they dance to may come from Anglo or Navajo bands.

"Navajo hours" have been beamed to the reservation from stations in the neighboring large towns such as Gallup, Farmington, and Flagstaff since the 1940s. At first the music on these programs was traditional Navajo popular music (largely Squaw Dance songs), but since the 1950s, though the announcements and advertisements are still in Navajo, the music, by request, is largely Anglo popular music. A half-dozen record companies in 1981 supplied popular traditional music and Anglo popular music to a growing Indian audience. For several of these companies the major income was from Navajo sales. There were over 100 Navajo recordings commercially available in the 1980s.

Traditional Musics

Nonceremonial Songs

The *diné biyiin,* in the sense of songs that have no ceremonial purpose, often consist of only a few brief phrases, though some are cast in one or another of the Squaw Dance forms. Most are more or less casual and not sacred, but some are sacred even though nonceremonial.

• CASUAL SONGS The nonsacred songs may serve as

lullabies or entertainment for children and sometimes contain comic allusions to animals. The "Donkey Song" (Song 1) is a good example of the animal genre. This song is close to Circle Dance songs in melodic style. The triple meter and the formula (marked X in the transcription) that serves as beginning and ending and as an internal cadence are features of this type of Squaw Dance song. Certain rhythmic, melodic, and textual features set Navajo music apart from other American Indian styles of singing. So many of these features are present in this song that a brief list here will enable the reader to identify them in the other examples.

(1) Voice: robust and nasal with subtle ornamental grace-notes and quavers. Range is medium for women; men often sing in the same range, which gives a high tenor or a piercing falsetto effect.

(2) Melody: after an introductory formula on the tonic, or base note, the melody leaps up a fifth, octave or higher, then sweeps downward, often reaching thc tonic again at the end of every phrase.

(3) Formulas: There is an introductory formula that is often specific to a particular song style. It may be repeated as a cadence at the ends of many phrases and it usually concludes the song. The effect is to give song styles an unusual consistency and clear-cut identity.

(4) Scale: tone systems are heavily weighted and often limited to the tonic, the third, and the fifth (and the tonic again an octave higher). This emphasis on the triad is also a feature of Apache music and seems to occur in Northern Athapaskan music as well. It is not frequent in other American Indian music.

(5) Note Values: prevailingly limited to two, the eighth and the quarter note, throughout Navajo traditional music.

(6) Meter: usually duple with interest added by means of an occasional extra beat. A few styles use a triple meter.

(7) Text: usually brief meaningful texts surrounded by vocables (nonsense syllables) (Frisbie 1980:347–392). Older texts may be composed entirely of vocables. Ceremonial chants differ strongly from this in that they contain many lines of narrative poetry.

An old-time custom, rarely observed in the 1980s, was to sing a farewell serenade when friends were leaving. The "Women's Song" (Song 2) illustrates this form. More properly termed a farewell song, it conveys a message of regret and appreciation to those who must go. It is another song in the style of a Circle Dance song from the Enemyway ceremony. The triple meter, the Circle Dance formula, the heavy weight on the open triad, and the limitation on note values can all be observed, along with the combination of vocables with brief meaningful texts.

The *'iich'oshí sin* style of Squaw Dance song can be seen in Song 3, a song that has come to be associated specifically with silversmithing. Most of the features of Navajo musical style can be seen in it except that the tone system is an exception to the tonic-third-fifth-octave pattern. The formula here (the first seven notes) is specific to Sway songs and Skip Dance songs.

Another genre of occupational songs with their own characteristic style are the corn-grinding songs (Johnson 1964). Again, the distinguishing feature is the introductory and cadential formula with its many repeats (Song 4). The texts of corn-grinding songs tend to be jocular: the performance situation used to be a family corn-grinding bee in which the women did most of the work and the men urged them on with humorous singing. In the form of Blessingway ceremonial used for the girls' puberty ceremony *(kinaaldá),* there is a corn-grinding bee (fig. 1) in which these songs can be used in a ceremonial context (Frisbie 1967:36).

• SACRED SONGS There are several kinds of sacred songs that are not connected to any of the ceremonials. Examples are farm songs (Hill 1938:61–95) and hunting songs (Hill 1938:96–166). There are many other private rituals with songs and prayers. All of them are in the style of ceremonial chanting. Their performances are closed to outsiders and highly unlikely ever to appear on recordings.

Moccasin Game songs are supposed to be sung only in wintertime, like the songs of the major ceremonials. They are in the category of songs with a story, that is, songs with a mythical origin. For example, the Moccasin Game goes back to the creation times when the diurnal and nocturnal animals were gambling to determine whether it should always be day or night. Many of the songs mention different animals or the Moccasin Game itself in humorous contexts with the intention of distracting the players so they will guess wrong where the yucca-root ball is hidden (Song 5) (Reichard 1950, 1:287–288; Matthews 1889).

William R. Heick Photography, Mill Valley, Calif.

Fig. 1. Corn grinding in a hogan during a girl's puberty ceremony (*kinaaldá*); the women use stone manos and metates placed on goat or sheepskins (Frisbie 1967:26–66). Photograph by William R. Heick, Chinle, Ariz., June 1963.

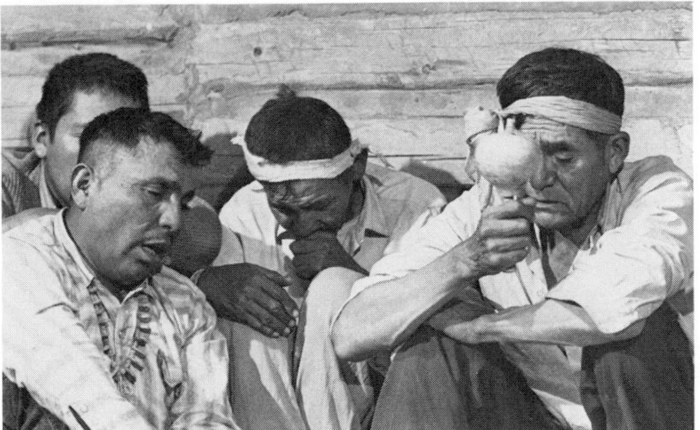

William R. Heick Photography, Mill Valley, Calif.

Fig. 2. Ceremonial singers at a Nightway, an elaborate 9-day Holyway ceremonial. Man at right, with gourd rattle, is lead ceremonial singer. See "Navajo Ceremonial System," this vol., for views of various ceremonies from this chantway, most of which are accompanied by music. Photograph by William R. Heick, Totso Trading Post (Lukachukai, Ariz.), Dec. 1963.

Smithsonian, Dept. of Anthr.: left, 74,730; right, 74,740; center, Brooklyn Mus.: Culin Coll. 3642.

Fig. 3. Rattles. Different ceremonies require different types of rattle. left, Pieces of the hoofs or dewclaws of a deer (as here), antelope, bighorn sheep, or other game animal are strung on buckskin thongs attached to a handle made of folded buckskin or buckskin-wrapped cane to make the rattle used in Flintway. right, Gourd containing turquoise, corn kernels, and other rattling pellets, and some pollen, with a wooden handle, is used in Nightway. center, Rawhide rattles, formerly of bison hide, but now of cow or horse hide, sewed and shaped when moist, attached to a wooden handle, and decorated with feathers, paint, and porcupine quills; used in a variety of chantways. For construction details see Kluckhohn, Hill, and Kluckhohn (1971:347–352). Length of center about 23.5 cm, collected by Stewart Culin at Chinle, Ariz., 1904. left and right collected by Washington Matthews, 1884.

Ceremonial Songs

The great chants or ceremonials of the Navajos may last from three to nine nights. During this time music, theater, poetry, and the graphic arts are brought together to prevent danger and restore harmony for a particular person, 'the one sung over', and for the Navajo people in general (see "Navajo Ceremonial System," this vol.). The texts of the chants constitute long epic sequences. The narrative deals with the creation story, and the thousands of lines of poetry contain the religion and philosophy of the people (McAllester 1980; Luckert 1979; Wyman 1957, 1970).

The music includes songs for blessing the ceremonial hogan, introducing prayers, performing specific ritual acts such as making offerings to the deities, making ritual fire, bathing, drying and blessing 'the one sung over', ritual dancing, and making drypaintings, to list a few examples. It is hardly too much to say that nearly every ceremonial act has its accompanying song (fig. 2). It is all these songs together that carry the story of the myth on which the ceremonial is based.

"When They Saw Each Other" (Song 6) from Blessingway (Mitchell 1978; Wyman 1970a) is a complete ceremonial song available on a record. It tells of when Changing Woman and the Sun saw each other in creation times, after which they became wife and husband as part of the continuing creation process. Though there are variations in chant form, there is a basic unity that Song 6 illustrates quite well. After an introductory formula, often in Sway song style or a reduction of it, there is a chorus of vocables or vocables plus a short refrain that may be picked up at the end of every line in the body of the song. Then come the meaningful verses, sometimes up to a dozen or more in number. They nearly always convey a sequence of meanings, enumerating parts of the body, a series of sacred mountains, or, as in this case, celestial bodies and regions. Often the verses alternate between male and female attributes so that the song has a two-part or a four-part structure. Usually the songs come in groups that also are sequential. The refrain, carried in the chorus and at the end of each verse, may be the only part that changes in such a series, creating a progression of ideas within a stable poetic frame.

Song 6 shows the tonic-third-fifth-octave tone system, the limitation to two note values, the characteristic vocables, the downward-moving melodic line, the use of melodic and textual formulas, and the same singing style noted in most of the other genres of traditional music. The only difference is the extended dimension of the form. The elements of balance, variation, extension, and alternation are carried further into the related groups of songs and indeed into the architecture of the entire ceremonial, which can be seen not only as a religious masterpiece but also as a work of art extending

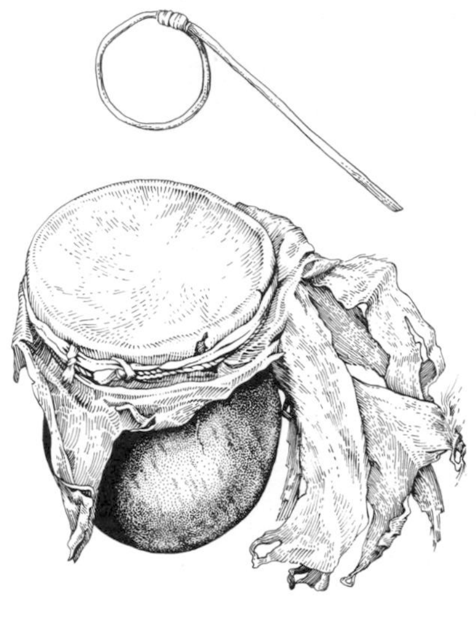

left, Mus. of N. Mex., Santa Fe: 3190/23P; right, Brooklyn Mus.: Culin Coll. 3640 and 3639.

Fig. 4. Squaw Dance (or War Dance) of the Enemyway. left, *Navajo N'da-a*, watercolor painted in 1938 by the Navajo artist Andy Tsihnahjinnie (Yazzie Bahe) (see Tanner 1973:312–319 for biography). Men either stand by the drummer (left foreground) where they sing with a swaying motion, or dance with the girls, one of whom (right foreground) carries a rattle stick that represents Enemy Slayer and much else in the Enemyway myth. (See Haile 1946:10–22). right, Drum used for Enemyway, made from a pottery cooking vessel. The head is buckskin (now sometimes goatskin) tightly stretched when wet, over a pot containing water. The drumstick is a slender twig with one end bent into a loop and secured with a leather thong. Baskets are inverted and used as drums in big ceremonies such as Shootingway and Mountainway; these are beaten with a drumstick of wrapped yucca leaves (Kluckhohn, Hill, and Kluckhohn 1971:353–359). See "Peyote Religion Among the Navajo," fig. 3, this vol., for iron or brass pots used as drums. Height of drum about 26 cm, collected by Stewart Culin, Chinle, Ariz., 1904.

over many days and sometimes involving hundreds of people (McAllester 1980a).

Reichard (1950, 1:286) believed the number of songs in Navajo ceremonial usage to be "incalculable," since any ceremonial practitioner knows hundreds of songs for any given ceremonial, other practitioners know further hundreds for various other branches or phases of the same chant, and all singers are constantly learning new ones.

Under the general category of *hatáál sin* come the several varieties of public songs in Enemyway, known as Squaw Dance songs (*Nidáá' sin*) (fig. 4). This repertory is so enormous as to be, in itself, "incalculable" as to numbers. New Squaw Dance songs are constantly being composed, reaching popularity, and then being forgotten. New styles, including borrowings from outside the traditional culture, come and go; certain old-time favorites remain in the canon for years. As in the other genres, each kind of Squaw Dance song is distinguished by stylistic features, most notably the formulaic phrases, that give it a unique definition.

Sway songs are sung by two groups of men from the two sponsoring parties whose joint efforts are required to perform Enemyway. They stand face to face and take turns singing, often swaying from side to side as they sing. There is a mercurial play of competition between the two sides involving slight changes of text for satiric effect and a thorough knowledge of what songs should follow each other. Sometimes a few women join in the singing. The songs are performed before there is any dancing on each night of the ceremony and again, after the dancing is over, until dawn. Many of the songs are old, and these often have only vocabalic texts (Song 7).

The introductory and cadential formula (the first five notes) characteristic of Sway songs is also used in other styles, such as Two-step songs, the "Silversmith's Song" (Song 3), in certain Gift songs, and others. Another way of putting it would be to say that Sway songs can be used for these other purposes. Another formula, which McAllester (1954:30) has termed the "Sway development," is labeled S in Song 6. This pattern of melody and vocables appears in many Sway songs and in no other Navajo or American Indian songs. Sometimes identified as a Riding song, this particular melody

Mus. of N. Mex., Santa Fe: 37683.

Fig. 5. Navajo Squaw Dance, location unknown, 1901. Spectators view the dance on horseback. Photograph by William H. Simpson.

can be used as a signal song to indicate that the dancing is over and that the all-night singing is to begin (McAllester 1954:57).

During that part of the three nights of the ceremony given over to dancing, two main styles of song are sung, Two-step and Round Dance (or Skip Dance) songs. The latter are somewhat more bouncy in style than the former and have been identified by some Navajos with Apache musical style. Elements of the formula in Skip Dance songs (the first four notes in Song 8) are used to connect phrases and to end the song as well. The formula in Two-step or Trotting songs is more flowing, and the dance to this music is correspondingly less bouncy, more of a steady stepping along. McAllester (1971:296–297) has advanced the idea that Two-step music is a "Navajoized" from of Skip Dance style since the formula is similar to the introductory and cadential formula of the older Sway songs.

Bonnie (1969) provides a comprehensive collection of the two kinds of dance songs. Song 7 serves as an example of a Two-step style, except for its "Sway development," and Song 8 illustrates the Skip Dance form and also the topical textual content of many of the dance songs in Enemyway. This is the most widely known song about World War II.

On the third day of the Enemyway ceremony a group of men performs the Circle Dance songs (Song 9) at about dusk. These are rather more sacred than the other dance songs, but some of them can be heard on commercial records (Sandoval and Winnie 1961:II-6-b; Navajo Chorus 1941a; Begay 1950). The identifying formula is the first three notes plus rest in Song 9, or like this but with the first two notes dotted. Circle Dance songs are often in triple meter (McAllester 1954:52).

The following three styles are widely known but are not used casually enough to be called popular. They are heard publicly in their ceremonial context, and they are used in displays at Navajo fairs. Of the three, Yeibichai songs are widely available on records, but only a few examples of Corral Dance songs and Gift songs have been published.

Yeibichai songs *(Ye'ii Bicheii biyiin)* (Song 10), performed by teams of masked dancers during the last two evenings of Nightway (fig. 6), are widely known as the most dramatic of Navajo songs. They have been described as being "piercingly powerful," having "hypnotic power," and "displaying almost acrobatic feats of bounding back and forth between octaves" (McAllester 1971a).

Well-known dance teams create these songs and perform them in the Nightway ceremony, at tribal fairs and on recordings. At least eight commercial recordings of this genre are available, and one of them (Bonnie 1968) is an entire album devoted to this one style. On this record the distinction is made between Night and Daylight Yeibichai songs. The former are said to have come from the the deities of Navajo Mountain and the latter from those of Mount Taylor. Bonnie (1968) states that the Daylight songs belong "to the children and the songs have the sounds of children talking and playing." Musically, the Daylight songs show a bouncy triple meter compared to the steady duple meter of the Night songs, and also a more complex melodic development based on partial variations of phrases. Criers may wake up the people and urge them to bring their children to hear the songs, since they were especially composed for children. The dancers often step higher and "act up" for the children.

In the case of Yeibichai songs not only is the introductory phrase specific to this song style, but also nearly all other aspects of these songs are unique. The vocables with the many *us* and *uwus* give the voices a sound unlike that of other Navajo (or other Indian) singing. The persistent, shifting syncopations, the shouts at the beginning and in the body of the song, the gourd rattles, and the held notes are additional special features. All these differences are intentional for it is the voices of the gods that are heard in Yeibichai songs and they should not sound like ordinary singing. There is also a strong prohibition against using ordinary speech while wearing the masks.

A very catchy melodic and rhythmic style can be heard in a series of songs from Shootingway. They are also performed in Red Antway and in Mountaintop Way as accompaniment for several dance forms that take place in a large enclosure made of evergreen boughs, hence the name Corral songs. Two of these songs appear on commercial records entitled "Feather Dance" after the particular Corral Dance with which they are associated (Song 11). During the dance a feather mysteriously rises on end in a basket and dances in time with four dancers. In the Shootingway myth, various animals came forward to offer their songs during the prototypical performance of the ceremony at the Sun's house in the sky. Many of these songs were in

top, Amon Carter Mus., Ft. Worth, Tex.: Laura Gilpin Coll.

Fig. 6. Yeibichai impersonators, led by Talking God, the first of the masked figures, at the ceremony of the First Dancers (see Matthews 1902:141–146), performed on the final night of a Nightway. The ceremonial singer and patient emerge from the ceremonial hogan to meet the approaching yeibichai impersonators, the patient carrying a basket containing sacred cornmeal. Following this ceremony, in which the masked dancers are approached individually and sprinkled with the cornmeal, begin the more spectacular public dances (Matthews 1902:146–155), which involve more yeibichai impersonators and may last all night. top, Photograph by Laura Gilpin, Oct. 15, 1952, at Pine Springs, Ariz. See Gilpin (1968:240) for description of this scene; patient and singer (in white headband) are at left facing Talking God. bottom, Watercolor painting of this same ceremony, by Navajo artist Robert Chee, 1967. Talking God is fully clothed under his deerskin robe and wears characteristic mask and headdress (see "Navajo Ceremonial System," fig. 4, this vol.). Behind him are 4 yeibichai impersonators, each representing a male divinity of a different character (see Matthews 1902:141 for descriptions of their dress). Above them is a representation in modified sandpainting style of the yeibichai that were painted on the hogan floor (compare with "Navajo Ceremonial System," fig. 15, this vol.). In private collection.

Corral Dance style, but they are sung in Shootingway without any dancing. It is the persistent dotted eighth- and sixteenth-note rhythmic figure and the pauses at the ends of phrases that especially set this style apart from others in the Navajo repertory.

Gift songs (Song 12) are used publicly in Enemyway but cannot be called popular music. The occasion is when gifts are exchanged between the two sponsoring camps. Small gifts are thrown out of the smoke hole of the hogan, first at the stick-receiver's camp and then at the home camp (McAllester 1954:11, 47–51). More valuable gifts are carried out and handed to the appropriate recipients. The texts of the songs may refer to gifts, but most of them are vocabalic.

There is a particular identifying formula for Gift songs (the first four notes in Song 12). In other respects the songs are like others in the Navajo tradition in their restricted note values, interrupted duple meter, range, and melodic line. Three of the four Gift songs by Joe Lee (1950) have the identifying formula, and half the published 10 Gift songs by McAllester (1954) have it or a variant of it. There is some indication that this song style came to the Navajos from the Utes (McAllester 1954:47). Sway songs can also be used for the music of this gift exchange.

There are several other genres of song from Enemyway and from other ceremonials that may be heard publicly but are not used in any way as popular or casual songs. The *'Atsáłeeh* 'First' songs of Enemyway are a good example. At several points in the ceremony these songs are performed to indicate the beginning of certain rituals. There was talk in the Navajo community that the early death of a singer while preparing recordings of them was because he was making these sacred songs public (Natay 1968). The Walking songs, the songs of the Mud Dancers (fig. 7), and the Closing songs are other examples from Enemyway.

There are sacred songs in the other ceremonials that may also be heard publicly, though usually only by a Navajo audience. The songs of the dancers in the Fire Dance in Mountaintop Way is another example (fig. 8).

New Musics

In the realm of new musics, there are hymns, introduced by the many sects of missionaries present on the reservation since the 1870s; the sacred songs of the Native American Church (Peyote songs), introduced particularly from the Utes in Colorado since the middle 1930s; the popular music from the Anglo culture, which has been taken over unaltered increasingly since World War II; and Indian show songs, adapted from the Plains. Since the late 1970s Navajo composers have been creating new forms mingling Navajo or pan-Indian musical and textual elements with Anglo popular music styles.

Christian Hymns

Though hymns are used by every mission congregation and are also heard on the reservation on religious broadcasts over the radio, they do not seem to be an active part of the daily musical life of the Navajo people.

top, Mus. of Northern Ariz., Flagstaff: MV 289; bottom, U. of Ariz., Ariz. State Mus., Tucson: 1094.

Fig. 7. Mud Dancers (also known as Black Dancers), so called because their bodies and breechclouts are daubed with mud and charcoal, performing in an Enemyway ceremonial, where they are an optional feature (Haile 1945:44–46) used to bring rain. Dancers pursue onlookers, smearing them with mud. The victims thereby become Mud Dancers themselves. top, Dancers, who have probably just emerged from the patient's hogan to the shelter, where the patient remains with ceremonial singer (visible in silhouette at right). Photographer and location unknown, 1933. bottom, Mud Dancers, with leader (clothed and carrying pottery drum). Photograph by Simeon Schwemberger, 1905 or before, Kayenta, Ariz.

There are hymnals printed in Navajo and there are records published by religious supply houses, but hymns do not carry over from church into many homes.

Navajo hymn singing has a striking, slow, portamento style and solemnity of manner. Part singing is rare; in this one feature traditional Navajo musical style could be said to carry over. Most congregations sing the texts in Navajo, and the melody is often altered to accommodate words with a different rhythm and a different number of syllables from the English ones. Part singing increased during the 1970s, especially in congregations that also contained Anglo participants. Since the late 1970s country gospel and gospel rock performed by Navajos have made their appearance in churches, other gatherings, and on records.

top, Amon Carter Mus., Ft. Worth, Tex.: Laura Gilpin Coll. 4340 [7]; bottom, James T. Bialac, Phoenix, Ariz.

Fig. 8. Fire Dance, also known as Corral Dance or Dark Circle of Branches because it is performed around a fire in a circle or "corral" of evergreen branches (see Wyman 1970:25). The term refers both to the general series of all-night dances, often including representative dances from various chantways that are performed on the final night of a Mountainway, as well as to the specific dance with which the series generally concludes. top, Fire or Corral dancers with Sun, Moon, and Wind wands performing at the Gallup Intertribal Ceremonial; the accompanying singers kneel behind them. This dance, which is a Shootingway specialty, is often performed on the last night of a Mountainway. The wands consist of triangularly segmented wooden frames to which feathers have been attached topped by blue Sun, white Moon, Black Wind, and Yellow Wind symbols, which are themselves surmounted by triangular cloud symbols and birds (see Wyman 1970:44, pls. 26–27). Photograph (detail) by Laura Gilpin, probably 1940s or 1950s. bottom, *Fire Dancer*, painting by Navajo artist Johnny Secatero, 1973 or earlier, representing the final dance of Mountainway, performed by dancers in white breechclouts and moccasins who throw firebrands consisting of bundles of shredded cedar bark. This visually spectacular dance is a popular subject for Navajo artists (see, for example, Tanner 1973:figs. 7.28, 7.32, 7.33). See Matthews (1887:431–444) for an account of other specific dances performed at a Fire Dance, including the dance in which great plumed arrows (*k'aatsoh yist'ání,* sg.) are "swallowed," and the "Re-whitening" dance of the *néigahí* 'one who repeatedly turns white'.

Peyote Songs

Though the Ute style of Peyote singing is widespread on the reservation, many other tribes have contributed to the Navajo repertory; and the tradition of individual composition, an important part of the ethos of the Native American Church, is also strong among the Navajos. In one recording session in 1950 the singers identified songs as Shoshoni, Cheyenne, Oto, and Navajo. The commercial recordings of Navajo Peyote singing show styles different in most respects from the traditional Navajo forms described above. The vocables are, for the most part, characteristic of Peyote songs and are not found elsewhere on the reservation. The drum and rattle accompaniment and the vocal style are all fully consistent with the well-established Peyote form (McAllester 1949:80–82). Peyote music does share with Navajo and other Athapaskan music the limitation to two note values, the prevailingly downward melodic direction, and the emphasis on a tone system based on the open triad. The first and last of these features have been considered significant enough to suggest Athapaskan influence in the makeup of the pantribal Peyote style (McAllester 1949:88; Nettl 1956:114).

Anglo Popular Music

All forms of Anglo popular music are heard at dances and on radio and television. The prevailing favorites are disco, rock and roll, and country and western music. There were six or seven Navajo groups in 1972 that performed country and western, including The Fenders, The Wingate Valley Boys, The Clansmen, and The Playboys. A favorite since the late 1970s has been the Navajo Sundowners, a very successful country and western group. Every mannerism of country and western, including the Nashville accent, is reproduced in this increasingly popular music. Writers such as Bobbie Price, Merle Haggard, Johnny Cash, Waylon Jennings, and Merle Travis are the favorites, but the Navajo bands also make up much of their own material. A lyric by The Fenders (1960) will illustrate:

Sugar Coated Babe

When the last of the liquor and the sun goes down
And they turn the lights on all over town
That's when you see me walking over the way (?)
I'm gonna go to eat my sugar coated babe.
I'm just like a kitten, a-playin' with with his shade (?)
When I'm a holdin' that pretty little babe,
She's the sweetest honey all the way around
She's sugar coated, all the way down!

Indian Show Songs

Though the Navajo tradition provides much of the material used for show purposes at tribal fairs and elsewhere, the Taos Hoop Dance has been adopted on the reservation as it has nearly everywhere in the American Indian world. The handsome Plains costumes and the intricate handling of the hoops are irresistible. The music is a generalized Plains song, simplified and with many repeats so that the music will last as long as the dancer needs to go through his maneuvers with the hoops (Song 13). The Plains features of this song are the use of transposition (the second A phrase is a repeat of the first a fourth lower) and the partial repeat that can be seen in the phrase pattern. The breakdown of the pattern after the fourth partial repeat suggests that the singer had the form in mind but was not quite comfortable with it. Both these features are characteristic of Plains songs (Herzog 1935:409) and are rare in Navajo music.

The Navajo elements are the Sway formula at the beginning and at the ends of the B phrases, the variation of the Gift song formula at the end of the song, the strict limitation to two note values, and the Navajo vocables.

The adaptation of Hoop Dance songs to a general Navajo style is what also happened to Anglo popular music on the reservation in the 1930s and 1940s and to Apache and Ute songs when they came in before that. This is also what occurred in certain of the other arts, such as weaving and silversmithing.

Other Modern Music

A wave of outside musical influences that seemed at first to have entered Navajo culture without significant changes have been Peyote singing; the war dances, gourd dances, and shawl dances of the pan-Indian powwow, increasingly important among the Navajos; and the popular forms of rock, country and western, and disco. However, there were in 1981 Peyote roadmen who were also active practitioners in traditional ceremonials such as Blessingway. Adaptation can also be seen in some of the Anglo popular music, though the native features are largely pan-Indian rather than specifically Navajo.

A cassette by Mr. Indian & Time includes "Grandmother," by Paul Beyale. It is in rock form but has a drumbeat and rattle introduction, a vocabalic chorus, a few lines of Navajo text, and lyrics in English urging a return to traditional values:

Go see grandmother, go see grandfather,
To listen to what they say, it's the only way home,
We've got to survive, our way of life,
We've got to revive our way to survive,
  O heya he, o heya he,
  O heya he, o heya he! (Beyale 1978: side 1, no. 2)

An urban Indian rock group, XIT ("Crossing of the Indian Tribes") in Albuquerque has published Indian protest songs as well as straight Anglo-style rock. Their

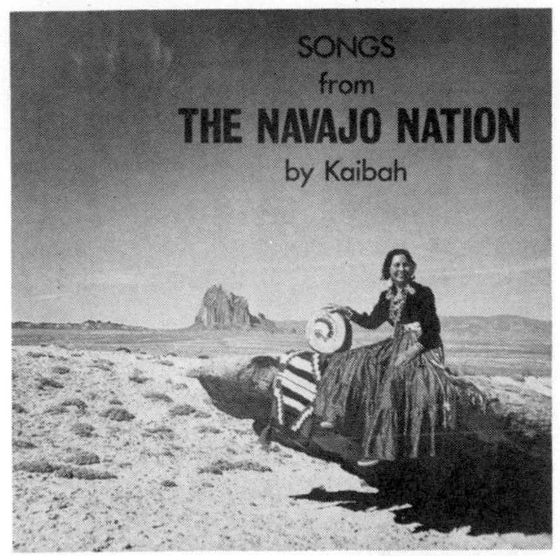

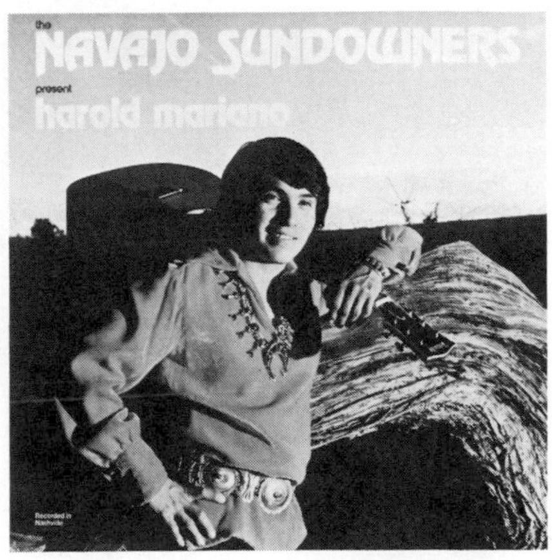

top left, Kay Bennett, Gallup, N. Mex.; top center, Canyon Records, Gallup, N. Mex; bottom left, Chinle Galileans, Chinle, Ariz; bottom right, The Fenders, Thoreau, N. Mex.

Fig. 9. Album covers from popular releases of Navajo music. Traditional music, top row, left and center: Kaibah 1972, Dine' Ba Aliil 1974. Country and gospel music, top right: Navajo Sundowners 1970; bottom row Chinle Galileans 1974, Rich Hubbell 1970, and The Fenders 1966. Cassette tapes, which can be played in motor vehicles, were replacing albums in the late 1970s and early 1980s.

release, "Plight of the Redman," contains "The Coming of the White Man" and "End," the latter having a Navajo introduction:

Aey, yah heh
'Ákódaaní,
Díí nihikéyah ho,
*'Ákónissin.**
The Indian has been out there on the ghetto of the
Reservation for a long time,
We have existed without adequate food, clothing,
Shelter, or medicine, to name but a few,
In their place we have been given malnutrition,
Poverty, disease, suicide, and bureaucratic promises
Of a better tomorrow . . . (Bee 1972:side 2, no. 4).

The same record contains a love song with Navajo and English texts:

Nihaa Shił Hózhǫ́
(I Am Happy About You)
Yinílyé hózhǫ́
Nihaa shił hózhǫ́ aah alah
T'áá 'áníidla,
Hóla
Yinílyé hózhǫ́
Aah *'ániid* aah *'at'ééd*
T'áá 'áníidla,
Hóla,†
I call you Sunflower,
You're the flower that happiness grows,
The beauty of your smile and the warmth in your
Eyes,
Brings sunshine into my soul.

Arliene Nofchissey, Navajo composer and actress, has written several songs in a genre that might be called Indian message music. "Proud Earth" is a good example: the music is a full orchestral score, produced in Nashville, Tennessee, but Indian effects are provided with echo chamber, drumbeats, and a few vocables. Part of the text, sung by Nofchissey and narrated by Chief Dan George, is:

*The Navajo words mean: 'That's what they say/ This is our country/ That's what I think'.

†The Navajo words are intended to mean: 'Your name is Happiness/ I am happy about you/ Both of us/ I don't know. /Your name is Happiness/ Young girl/ Both of us/ I don't know.' However, the Navajo used is unidiomatic and shows the influence of English. The Navajo second-person plural, 'you (people)', is used for the singular, and the order of the words in the lines 'Your name is Happiness' and 'young girl' follows the English rather than being the reverse of this, which would be correct for traditional Navajo.

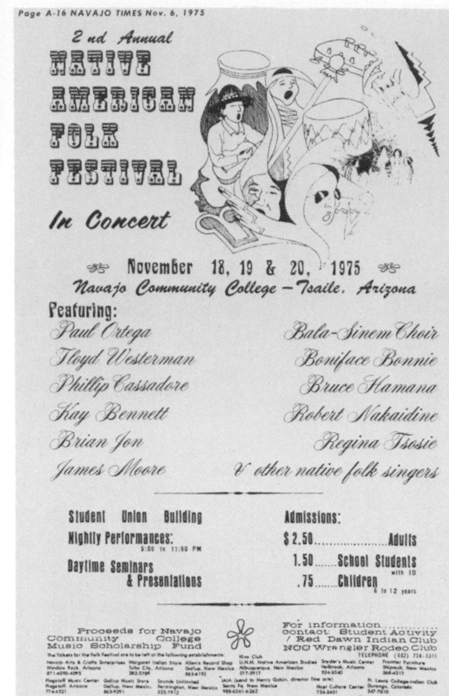

left, U.S. Dept. of Agriculture, Washington; right, *Navajo Times*, Nov. 6, 1975.

Fig. 10. Contemporary popular music. left, Teenagers congregating at juke box at a reservation trading post. Photograph by Jack Schneider, June 1971. right, Advertisement for the Second Annual Native American Folk Festival, which features non-Navajo entertainers such as Floyd Westerman (Sioux), A. Paul Ortega (Mescalero Apache), and Phillip Cassadore (San Carlos Apache) as well as Navajo singers such as Kay Bennett (Kaibah) and Boniface Bonnie. Proceeds from the concert were to go to a music scholarship fund at the Navajo Community College.

The beat of my heart is kept alive in my drum
And my plight echos in the canyons, the meadows, the plains,
And my laughter runs free with the deer,
And my tears fall with the rain,
But my soul knows no pain.

I am one with nature
Mother Earth is at my feet
And my God is up above me
And I'll sing the song, the song of my people . . .
(Nofchissey 1975:side 2 no. 1).

This style of music is much appreciated on the reservation. Nofchissey may be seen in the photos in *The Navajo Times* autographing her records or listed among the artists to be featured at an Indian folk festival at Window Rock or the Navajo Community College at Tsaile.

The coexistence of so many forms of music reflects the increasing enrichment of Navajo culture. The tribe offers scholarships to many young people for college studies, but also to those who wish to apprentice themselves to a ceremonial practitioner. Music is just one of the many areas in which a rich and persistent traditional culture continues side by side with, and exerts a strong influence on, the new ideas eagerly accepted from the outside.

Song 1. Donkey Song

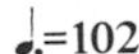

Kaibah, A-3001

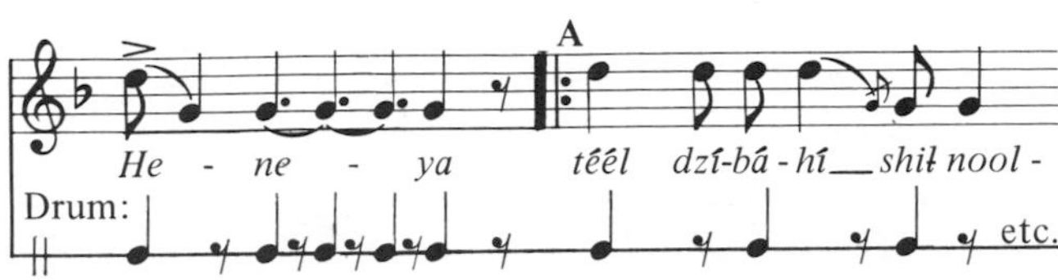

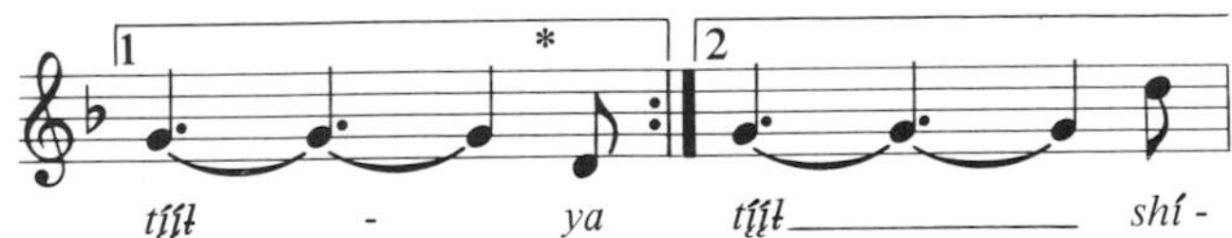

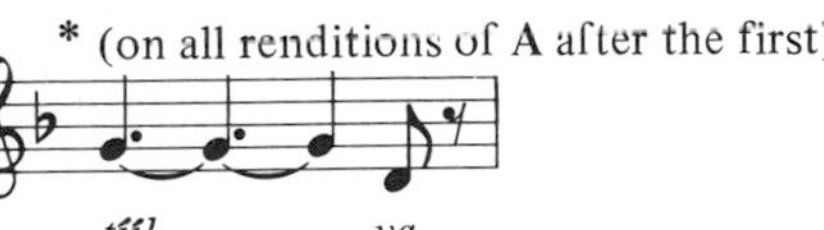

The entire pattern of the song is:

X A A A′ B C
A A A′ B C′ C′ D X
A A A′ B C C′ C′ D X
A A A′ B C C′ C′ D X

He-ne-ya,

Téél dzíbáhí shił nooltįįł ya
Breast light gray[1] with me trots along

Téél dzíbáhí shił nooltįįł
Breast light gray with me trots along

Shítágí (yi)sáłí nyiyi yiye, ehe lowo wowo,
My bangs

Aho[2] *wowo e, ne-ya!*

Téél dzíbáhí shił nooltįįł ya
Breast light gray with me trots along

Téél dzíbáhí shił nooltįįł
Breast light gray with me trots along

Shítágí (yi)sáłí nyiyi yiye, ehe lowo wowo,
My bangs

Aho, aho, haŋa, aho, aho, haŋahe

Yahe, yaho, ohe, ya'a hi, ne—ya!

[1] Gray breast means donkey.
[2] *Aho,* and *Yahe, yaho, ohe* imitate the donkey's bray.

Song 2. Farewell Song (Women's Song)

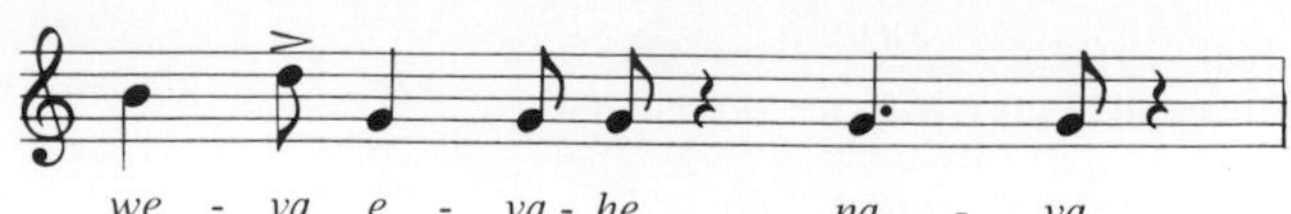
we - ya e - ya - he, na - ya

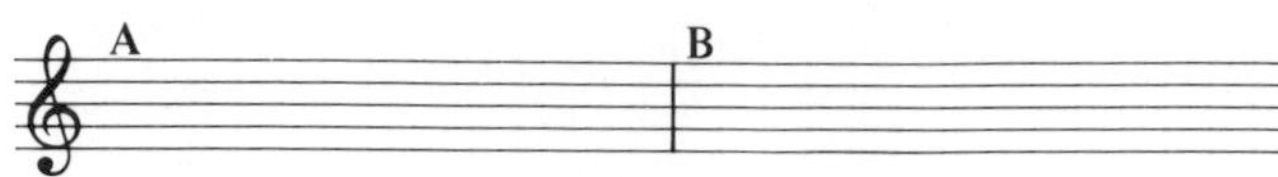
A
B

D
3. á-ko ni-de á-shi-di-ní-nę́ę bé-násh-niih - doo

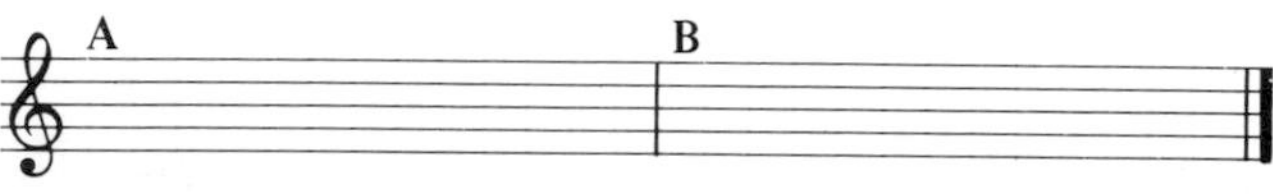
A
B

The entire pattern of the song is:

X	A	B	A	B
	C	B	A	B
	C	B	A	B
	D	D	A	B

The ♩ ♪ pattern of drumbeats is usually interrupted at the ends of phrases and occasionally elsewhere.

He - ne - ya - ,
Hene yahe yo'o o- o- o- ho- o'o o,
Ene yahe yo'o wo-wo weya eya he, na- ya,

Dooládo'shą' nikéyah nízaad at'é nihaa yíníyá
Ah, me! your land far away it is you came

Ene yahe yo'o wo-wo weya eya he, na-ya,

Dooládo'shą' naa ch'éná hóyéé' de doo nikííníyáago
Ah, me! you longing painful will be us you leaving

Ene yahe yo'o wo-wo weya eya he, na- ya,

Áko ndi áshidiniéę' bénáshniih doo
Even so what you said to me I remember will

Hene yahe yo'o o- o- o- ho- o o o,
Ene yahe yo'o wo-wo weya eya he, na- ya.

Song 3. Silversmith Song

A — Ambrose Roadhorse I:5

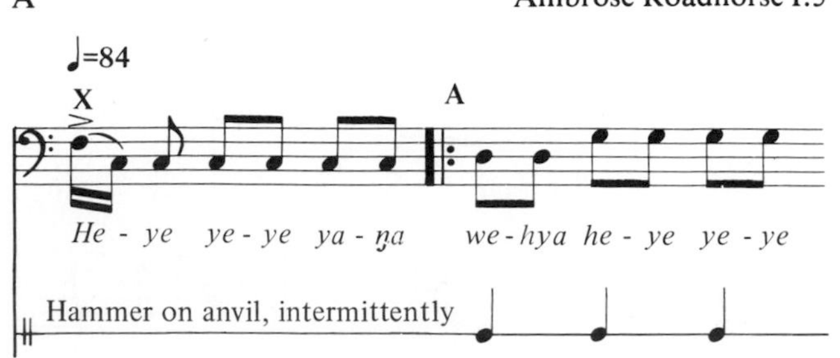
♩=84
X
A
He - ye ye - ye ya - ŋa we - hya he - ye ye - ye
Hammer on anvil, intermittently

B
a - ho a - ho a - ho we-ya he - hya
X
C
he - ye ye - ye - ya - ŋa Yo-shi-na yo-shi-na

B′
X
a - ho a - ho we-ya he - hya he - ye ye - ye ya - ŋa

Text: *Aho* from *ba'áhí*—an expression of feeling
Yoshina from *yoshi'ą́*—an expression of feeling

The entire pattern of the song is:

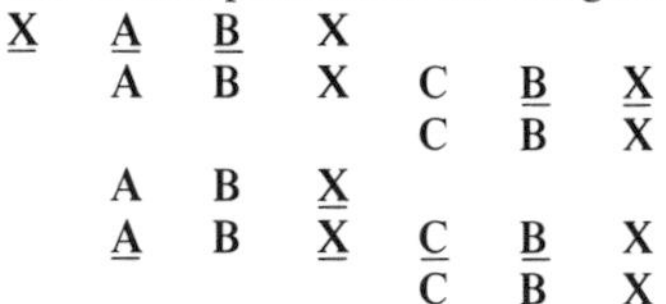

X	A	B	X		
	A	B	X	C	B	X
				C	B	X
	A	B	X		
	A	B	X	C	B	X
				C	B	X

Underlined phrases indicate where the hammer and anvil accompaniment was used.

Song 4. Corn Grinding Song

A♭ — Julia Deal II:5

♩=88
X
X′
Hę ŋa ghei a - ghei a ŋa - ŋa ghei a - ghei
Basket Drum:
etc.

A
B
a-we' m-ma o a-wé' m-ma o

Y
1
X
2
x
a-ghei ha-ghei hą ŋą ghei a - ghei hą a - ghei

B
C
a-we' m-ma o o a-wé' i cho wo - we' a - ghei

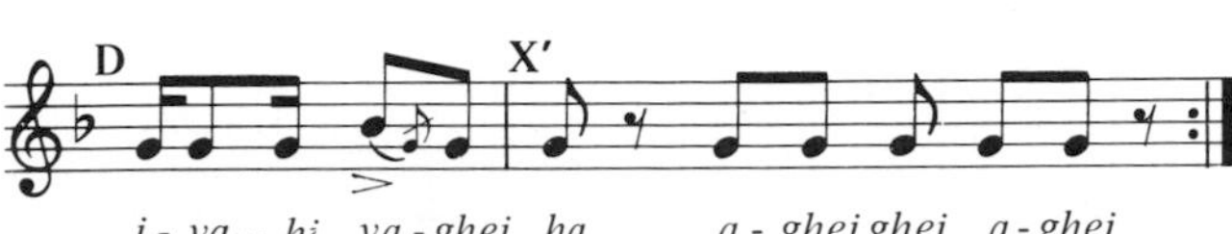
D
X'
i - ya - hi ya - ghei ha a - ghei ghei a - ghei

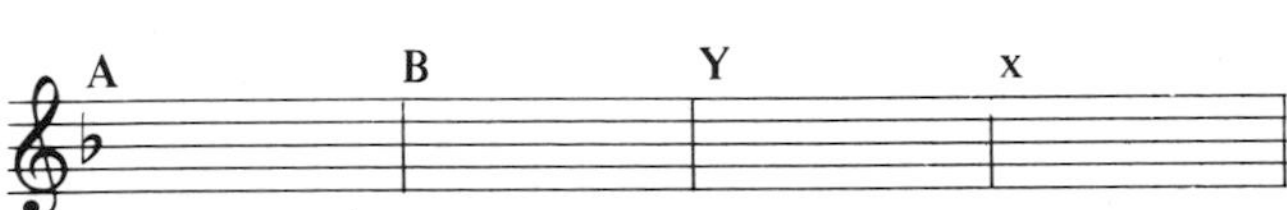
A
B
Y
x

B
C+
a-wé' i - cho - wo o - wo he-yo wo - wo - ho we a-we

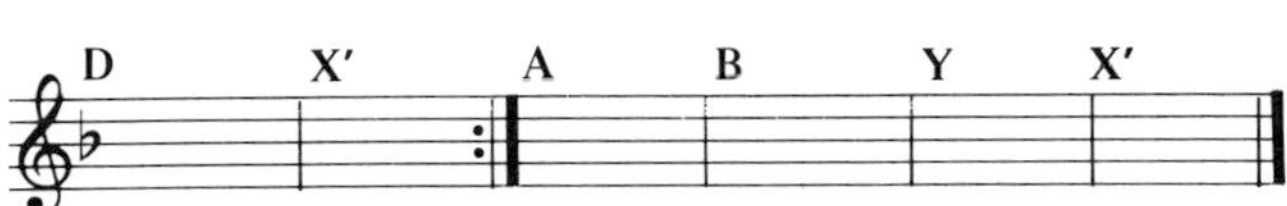
D
X'
A
B
Y
X'

The entire pattern of the song is:

X	X'	A	B	Y	X				
		A	B	Y	x	B	C	D	X'
		A	B	Y	x	B	C+	D	X'
		A	B	Y	X'				

The basket drum is struck with something fairly flexible like a doubled-up belt rather than with the yucca leaf drumstick of ceremonial usage.

Hę ŋa ghei aghei, a ŋaŋa ghei aghei,

Awéé'bimáo awéé'bimáo
Baby its mother! baby its mother!

Aghei haghei hą, ną ghei aghei

Awéé'bimáo awéé'bimáo
Baby its mother! baby its mother!

Aghei haghei ha, aghei,

Awéé'bimáo awéé'yicha wo we'aghei,
Baby its mother! baby crying

Iyahi yaghei ha aghei ghei aghei,

Awéé yicha wo owo heyo wo-wo-ho we awe
Baby crying.

Song 5. Shoe Game Song

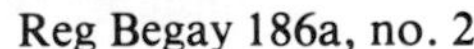
Reg Begay 186a, no. 2

A
♩=84
X
A
He-ye na - ŋa ya- ŋa di-ni-shíí-lí-shii yi- yí tó-i yó-ó' a - ŋa
B
di-ni-shíí - lí-shii yi - yi tó - i yó-ó' a-ŋa
C
di-ni-shíí-lí-shii yi -yí tó-i yó-ó' a - ŋa-ŋa e - ye-ye
D
Yí-ní - yáa - go dis-ní ts'ą́ą - go yí - ní - nii' go
yí - ní-yáa - go dis-ní ts'ą́ą - go doo-lá-dó'sh hó-yée'- da
C
di-ni-shíí - lí-shii yi-yí tó-i yó-ó' a-ŋa-ŋa -ye-ye

Heye neye yaŋa

Dinishíílíshii yiyí tói yóó'aŋa
Show it to us ball put in

Dinishíílíshii yiyí tói yóó'aŋa
Show it to us ball put in

Dinishíílıshii yiyí tói yóó'aŋaŋa eyeye,
Show it to us ball put in

Yíníyáago disínítsʼą́ągo
You having come you having heard it

yíníniiʼgo disínítsʼą́ągo
you having heard about it you having heard it

dooládóʼsh hóyéeʼda
Isn't it a pity?

Dinishíílíshii yiyí tói yóóʼaŋaŋa eyeye
Show it to us ball put in

The entire pattern of this song is:

X	A	B	C
		D	C
	A	B	C
		D	C
	A	B	C

Song 6. When They Saw Each Other

F

Song of Bead Chant Singer
side 5

♩=116

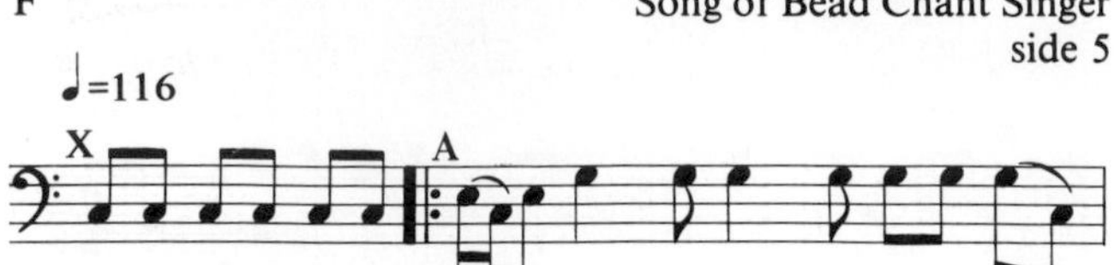

X
A
e-ye ne-ye ya-ŋa He-ya e - ya e - ya he-ye ye-ya,

B
he - ya e - ya e - ya he - ya e - ya na - ŋa

B′
he - ya e - ya e - ya he - ya e - ya - na

C
he - ya e - ya__ e - ya e - ya - ya

C′
*(A)
he - ya e - ya - e - ya e - na - ŋa

A
1. Ni - hos-dzáá - ne shi - nił - 'į́ - ni - ye,
2. K'ad Jo - ho - naa - 'éí - ye shi - nił - 'į́ - ni - ye,
3. Ya - dił - hi - łe shi - nił - 'į́ - ni - ye,
4. K'ad Tł'e-ho - naa - 'éí - ye shi - nił - 'į́ - ni - ye,
5. Ná - hoo - kǫ - she shi - nił - 'į́ - ni - ye,

B
ha - de - ge - ye ye - ye shi - nił - 'e - ye na - ŋa
ha - ya - 'e - ye ye - ye shi - nił - 'e - ye na - ŋa
ha - ya - 'e - ye ye - ye shi - nił - 'e - ye na - ŋa
ha - ya - 'e - ye ye - ye shi - nił - 'e - ye na - ŋa
ha' - na - ne - ye ye - ye shi - nił - 'e - ye na - ŋa

B′
ha - ya - 'e - ye ye - ye shi-nish - 'į́ - ye - ye,
ha - dai - ge - ye ye - ye shi-nish - 'į́ - ye - ye,
ha - dai - ge - ye ye - ye shi-nish - 'į́ - ye - ye,
ha - dai - ge - ye ye - ye shi-nish - 'į́ - ye - ye,
ha' - na - ne - ye ye - ye shi-nish - 'į́ - ye - ye,

C
shi - shi ye - le - shi - nił - 'į́ - ni - ye
shi - shi ye - le - shi - nił - 'į́ - ni - ye
shi - shi ye - le - shi - nił - 'į́ - ni - ye
shi - shi ye - le - shi - nił 'į́ - ni - ye
shi - shi ye - le - shi - nił - 'į́ - ni - ye

C
Shi - shi - ye - le__ shí - nish - 'į́ - ye - ne,

C′
e - ya e - ya e - ya e - na - ŋa

*A
He - ya e - ya e - ya e - ya - ye

The song ends with this after the fifth verse.

The entire pattern of the song is:

X	A	B	B′	C	C′		
	A	B	B′	C	C	C′	(five times)
	A	B	B′	C	C′	A.	

Eya neye yaŋa
Heya eya eya, heye yeya,
Heya eya eya, heya eyanaŋa,
Heya eya eya, heya eyana,
Heya eya eya, eyaya,
Heya eya eya, enaŋa,

Nihosdzááne shinił' į́ niye, hadeg eye yeye shinił' į́ ye naŋa
Earth it looks at me up it looks at me

Hayaa 'eye yeye shínísh'į́ yeye, shi shiyeel e shinił' į́ niye
Down I look at it I am happy it looks at me

Shi shiyeel e shínísh'į́ yene, eya eya eya e naŋa,
I am happy I look at it

Heya eya eya, heye yeya,
Heya eya eya, heya eyanaŋa,
Heya eya eya, heya eyana,
Heya eya eya, eyaya,
Heya eya eya, enaŋa,

K'ad Jóhonaa'éí ye shinił'į́ niye, hayaa'eye yeye shinił'į́ ye naŋa
Now Sun it looks at me down it looks at me

Hadeg 'eye yeye shínísh'į́ yeye, shi shiyeel e shinił'į́ niye
Up I look at it I am happy it looks at me

Shi shiyeel e shinish'į́ yene, eya eya eya e naŋa,
I am happy I look at it

Heya eya eya, heye yeya, (and the rest of the chorus as above)

Yadiłhił e shinił'į niye, hayaa'eye yeye shinił'į ye naŋa
Sky Dark it looks at me down it looks at me

Hadeg 'eye yeye shínish'į yeye, shi shiyeel e shinił'į niye
Up I look at it I am happy it looks at me

Shi shiyeel e shinish'į yene, eya eya eya e naŋa,
I am happy I look at it

Heya eya eya, heye yeya,
Heya, eya eya, heya eyananja (and the rest of the chorus as above)

K'ad Tłéhonaa'éí ye shinił'į niye, hayaa'eye yeye shinił'į ye naŋa,
Now Moon it looks at me down it looks at me

Hadeg 'eye yeye shínish'į yeye, shi shiyeel e shinił'į ye niye,
Up I look at it I am happy it looks at me

Shi shiyeel e shinish'į yene, eya eya eya e naŋa,
I am happy I look at it

Heya eya eya, heye yeya,
Heya eya eya, heya eyananja, (and the rest of the chorus as above)

Náhookǫs he shinił'į niye, ha'naa neye yeye shinił'į ye naŋa
North it looks at me across it looks at me

Ha'naa neye yeye shínish'į yeye, shi shiyeel e shinił'į niye,
Across I look at it I am happy it looks at me

Shi shiyeel e shinish'į yene, eya eya eya e naŋa,
I am happy I look at it

Heya eya eya, heya yeya,
Heya eya eya, heya eyananja,
Heya eya eya, heya eyana,
Heya eya eya, eyaya,
Heya eya eya, enaŋa,
Heya eya eya, eyaye

Song 7. Riding Song

Ab — Mesa Verde National Park Team 172b

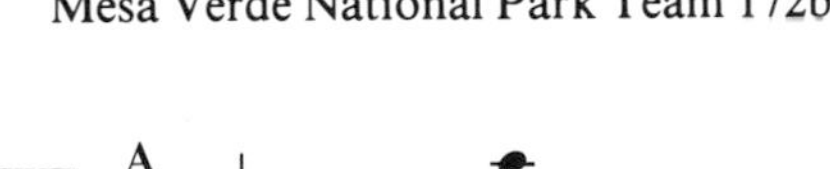

♪=78
X
A
E - ne - ya-ŋa Yo-'e ya-ŋa yo-'e yo
Drum:
etc.

B
wo - he yo - he yo - he ya - ŋa he - ye ye - ye ya - ŋa

A'
B
yo - 'e ya - he yo - 'e yo wo - he yo - he yo - he

S
ya - ŋa he - ye ye - ye ya - ŋa he - ya ha - ne hyo - e
S'
yo-'e hya-ŋe ŋa - ŋa he - ya ha-ne hyo-e yo-'e ha-ŋa

Text: all vocables

The entire pattern of the song is:

X	A	B	A'	B	S	S'
	A'	B	A'	B	S	S'
	A'	B	A'	B		

Song 8. Iwo Jima Flag Raising Song

G — Teddy Draper II:5

♩=116
X
A
He - ye ya- ŋa I - wo I - wo-ŋa I - wo I - wo-ŋa
etc.
Drum:

B
I - wo - ji - ma hol - yée - di ni-hi - si-láo

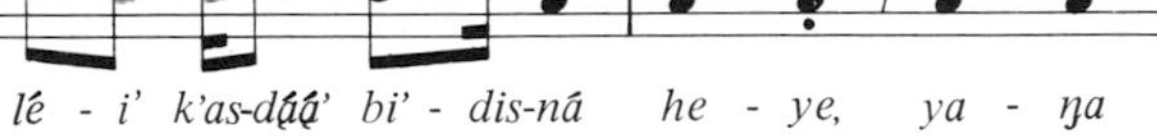
X
lé - i' k'as-dą́ą́' bi' - dis-ná he - ye, ya - ŋa

C
Sur - i - ba - chi - yí, Sur-i - ba - chi - yí

B
Sur - i - ba - chi bi-kááʼ - gi dah naat' - á'- í

X
lé - i'dah deis-tsooz hi - yi, ya - ŋa

C'
Sur - i - ba- chi - yí, Sur - i - ba - chi - yí, Sur-i -

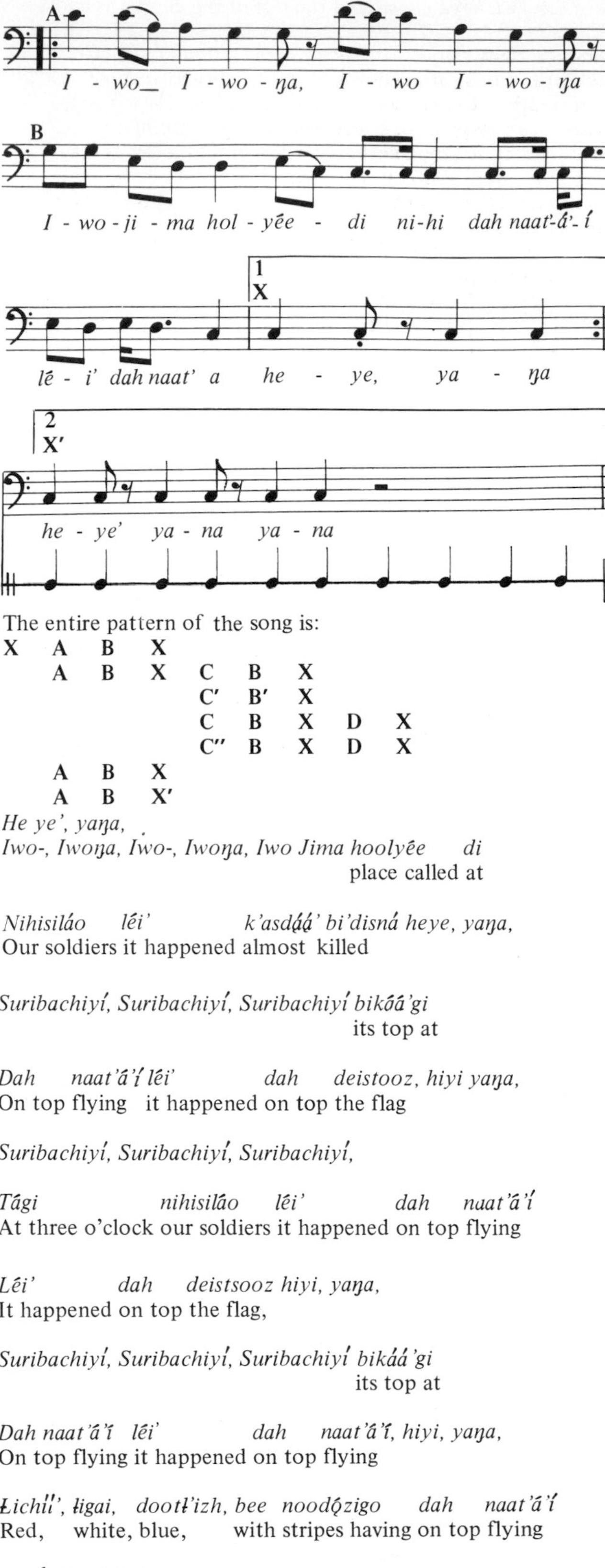

The entire pattern of the song is:

X A B X
A B X C B X
C' B' X
C B X D X
C'' B X D X
A B X
A B X'

He ye', yaŋa,
Iwo-, Iwoŋa, Iwo-, Iwoŋa, Iwo Jima hoolyêe di
place called at

Nihisiláo lêi' k'asdą́ą́' bi'disná heye, yaŋa,
Our soldiers it happened almost killed

Suribachiyí, Suribachiyí, Suribachiyí bikáá'gi
its top at

Dah naat'á'í lêi' dah deistooz, hiyi yaŋa,
On top flying it happened on top the flag

Suribachiyí, Suribachiyí, Suribachiyí,

Tágí nihisiláo lêi' dah naat'á'í
At three o'clock our soldiers it happened on top flying

Lêi' dah deistsooz hiyi, yaŋa,
It happened on top the flag,

Suribachiyí, Suribachiyí, Suribachiyí bikáá'gi
its top at

Dah naat'á'í lêi' dah naat'á'í, hiyi, yaŋa,
On top flying it happened on top flying

Łichíí', ɬigai, dootɬ'izh, bee noodǫzigo dah naat'á'í
Red, white, blue, with stripes having on top flying

heye, naŋa,

Iwo-, Iwoŋa, Iwo-, Iwoŋa, Iwo Jima hoolyêe di
place called at

Nihi dah naat'á'í lêi' dah naat'á'í heye, yaŋe, yaŋa,
Ours on top flying it happened on top flying

Free translation:

Heye', yaŋa,
Iwo-, Iwo-, Iwo-, Iwo-, at the place called Iwo Jima,
Our soldiers, it happened, were almost killed, heye, yaŋa,
Iwo-, Iwo , Iwo-, Iwo-, at the place called Iwo Jima,
Our soldiers, it happened, were almost killed, heye, yaŋa,
Suribachi, Suribachi, Suribachiyi, on top of it,
Up there, flying, it happened, up there was the flag, hiyi, yaŋa,
Suribachi, Suribachi, Suribachi,
At three o'clock, our soldiers, it happened, up there,
Flying, it happened, up there, the flag, hiyi, yaŋa,
Suribachi, Suribachi, Suribachi, on top of it,
Up there flying, it happened, up there, flying, hiyi, yaŋa,
Red, white, blue, striped, up there, flying, heye, yaŋa,
Suribachi, Suribachi , Suribachi, on top of it,
Up there flying, it happened, up there, flying, hiyi, yaŋa,
Red, white, blue, striped, up there, flying, heye, yaŋa,
Iwo-, Iwo, Iwo, Iwo-, at the place called Iwo Jima,
Ours, on top, flying, it happened, on top, flying, heye, yaŋa,
Iwo-, Iwo-, Iwo-, Iwo-, at the place called Iwo Jima,
Ours, on top, flying, it happened, on top, flying, heye, yaŋe, yaŋa.

Song 9. Circle Dance Song

A *8va* Navajo Chorus P-49-3a

Text: all vocables.

The entire pattern of the song is:

X A A B B C C
A B B

Song 10. Yeibichai Song

C♯*8va* Boniface Bonnie and group I:1

X
A
hi - ye hi - ye U-hu-wu hu hi - ye hi - ye hi - ye
wu! 3rd time.

hu-hu-wu hu hi - ye hi - ye hi - ye

The song ends here the fourth time through. Text: all vocables.

The entire pattern of the song: **introduction**:

A	B	B	C	C′	/C	C	**X**
A	B	B	C	C′	/C	C	**X**
A	B	B	C	C′	/C	C	**X**
A	B	B	C	C′	/C	C	**X**

Song 11. Feather Dance Song

G Navajo Chorus Group 100A

♩=126
A
Drum: hi-ya-na he-ya ho - we-na ho - we-na ho - we-na
etc.

B
he-ya - ha he-na ho - we-na ho - we-na ho - we-na

C
he-ya - ha he - na ho - we - na ho - ha we - na ya - ha

X
we - ne-ya he - ne ya - ha he ye ya
(last time) he nai ya
A
Są' - ah Naa-ghą́í haa-yá__ ya - ya-te__ ya - ya-te__ we-na

B
Bik'-eh Hó-zhǫ́ǫ́n haa-yá__ ya-ya-te__ ya-ya-te__ we-na

C
he - ya - ha he - na ho - we - na ho - ha we - na ya - ha

X
we - ne ya he - ne ya - ha he ye ya

The entire pattern of the song is
A B C X (eleven times);
the song ends at phrase **X**, with *he nai ya.*

Text:
vocables first time through, following text alternates with vocabalic text thereafter:

Są'ah Naagháí *haayá* *yayate yayate wena,*
Old age Returning it rose up

Bik'eh Hózhóón *haayá* *yayate yayate wena,*
Accordingly, Everywhere is blessed it rose up

Free translation:
Hiyana heya ho- wena, ho-wena, ho-wena,
Heyaha hena ho-wena, ho-wena, ho-wena,
Heyaha hena ho-wena, ho-hawena yaha weneya,
Hene yaha he ye ya.

Są'ah Naagháí shining over it, *yayate-, yayate-, wena*
Bik'eh Hózhóón shining over it, *yayate-, yayate-, wena*
Heyaha hena ho-wena, ho-hawena yaha weneya,
Hene yaha he ye ya.

Note: *Są'ah Naagháí* and *Bik'eh Hózhóón* are untranslatable terms centering around the concepts of an eternal return to life by means of which the cosmos is maintained in beauty and harmony. The most comprehensive discussion is by Witherspoon (1977:13-46).

Song 12. Gift Song

D *8va* Joe Lee and group ARP 159a #3

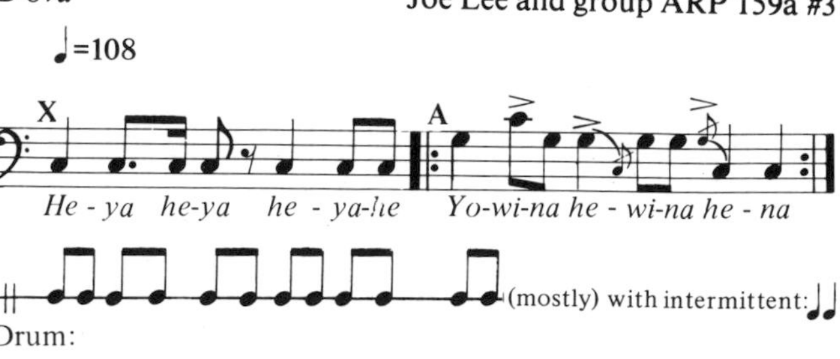
♩=108
X
A
He - ya he-ya he - ya-he Yo-wi-na he - wi-na he - na
(mostly) with intermittent:
Drum:

B
C
yo - wi - na he - na Yo - wi - na he - na

The entire pattern of the song is:

X	A	A	B	C	
	A	A	B	C	
	A	A	B	C′	X

Text is all vocables.

Song 13. Hoop Dance Song

A *8va* — Laughing Boy ARP 159b

There is also a jingling of bells as on a Plains dancer's costume.

The entire pattern of the song is:

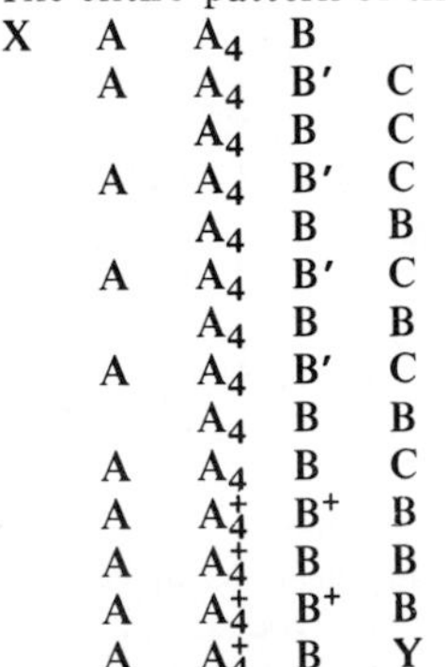

X	A	A_4	B	
	A	A_4	B′	C
		A_4	B	C
	A	A_4	B′	C
		A_4	B	B
	A	A_4	B′	C
		A_4	B	B
	A	A_4	B′	C
		A_4	B	B
	A	A_4	B	C
	A	A_4^+	B^+	B
	A	A_4^+	B	B
	A	A_4^+	B^+	B
	A	A_4^+	B	Y

Note: A^+ or B^+ means that this figure has been added to the end of the **A** or **B** phrases:

Development of Navajo Tribal Government

MARY SHEPARDSON

The short span of years since 1923 marks the rise, consolidation, and acceptance of the Navajo Tribal Council as an indispensable part of modern Navajo life. This emergence of a centralized government in a tribe previously lacking in any overall political organization has often been treated as the intrusion of an alien institution, a creature of federal policy, born out of a dizzying conflict of treaties, congressional acts, court decisions, and executive promulgations dealing with Indians. The setting for the emergence was one of struggle, among three states (Arizona, New Mexico, and Utah), among special interests of cattlemen, sheepmen, oil and mineral developers, and with local state pressure for authority and taxes. In descriptions of this welter of controversy and confrontation the Indians themselves tend to become lost, and yet it is the Navajos who in the end must present the demands, institutionalize the rules, accept or reject in daily life the policies of constituted authority. Essentially, then, this is the story of how Navajos became decision makers not alone for a family or a region but for a whole tribe, the largest tribe of Indians in the United States.

Nine Navajos led their government between 1923 and 1971 when the tenth chairman of the Navajo Tribal Council was inaugurated. Twelve men had served as vice-chairman. These leaders (fig. 1), their backgrounds, and the problems they faced form an important part of the political development story.

The Early Council

The establishment of a Navajo Tribal Council to replace the more or less sporadic use by the federal agent of scattered headmen came in response to the pressure of outsiders who wished to prospect for oil on the Navajo Reservation. By the 1920s the reservation had been divided into six jurisdictions, each with a non-Indian superintendent appointed by the Bureau of Indian Affairs. There was no overall agency or permanent Indian council. It had been the custom of a local superintendent to call meetings of adult males in his area at the request of a prospector seeking permission to search for minerals, principally because the Metalliferous Minerals Act recognized Indian ownership of subsurface resources found on treaty reservation land. This act applied to Navajos because the original reservation had been delimited by the peace treaty of 1868, which they had signed in order to be able to return to at least a part of old Navajo land from their exile at Fort Sumner. Eight extensions had been made to the original treaty reservation by executive order of various presidents between 1878 and 1917 when the policy was forbidden by Congress. Some of this additional land had been returned to the public domain.

The question of Indian rights to minerals found on executive order reservations was still moot in 1922, not to be legally decided until 1927.

The immediate precipitating event for the birth of the Navajo Tribal Council was the calling of a meeting of adult Navajo men in the San Juan Jurisdiction by Superintendent Evan Estep to discuss oil leasing. Seventy-five Navajos attended and voted to disapprove all such requests. However, a meeting held later in the year granted a lease for oil exploration in the Hogback area, probably because the Midwest Refining Company

U.S. Indian Service (Bureau of Ind. Affairs).
Fig. 1. First 5 chairmen of the Navajo Tribal Council, photographed outside the Navajo Tribal Council House at Window Rock, Ariz. They are, in order of tenure: Chee Dodge, center; Deshna Clah Cheschillige, holding hat; Tom Dodge, right of his father, Chee Dodge; Marcus Kanuho, far left; and Henry Taliman, far right. (Kanuho was not an elected chairman; he served as acting chairman following Tom Dodge's resignation in 1936.) Photograph by Milton Snow, Nov. 1938, from Mary Shepardson's collection.

had promised to employ Navajos at good wages on the site. The meeting also granted power of attorney to the superintendent to negotiate leases for the tribe. A day later, the company struck oil and a boom was on. Superintendent Estep wrote that "the Arabian Nights Tales are modest compared to this country."

In the following year, a business council was established in the Fort Defiance Jurisdiction where Chee Dodge, Dugal Chee Bekiss, and Charley Mitchell signed oil leases, which were later canceled. Dodge was already a recognized leader, the son of a Mexican man and a Navajo woman. Orphaned early, he was raised by an aunt and a non-Indian stepfather who gave him some education. He had experience as an interpreter, a headman, and a businessman. Above all, he possessed oratorical ability, a traditionally appreciated qualification for leadership. Superintendent Estep requested aid from someone with technical skill, feeling himself inadequate to handle the oil leasing. Herbert J. Hagerman, the former territorial governor of New Mexico, was appointed special commissioner to the Navajo Indians, empowered to exercise general authority over the six jurisdictions. Oil leases in future would be approved by a council representing all the Navajos, not those of one jurisdiction.

The first Navajo Council was established under a directive from the Bureau of Indian Affairs in Washington. It was composed of 12 delegates and 12 alternates, three each from the San Juan Jurisdiction, two each from the Western Jurisdiction, four each from the Southern Jurisdiction and one of each from Pueblo Bonito, Leupp, and the Moqui Jurisdictions. There was no fixed term for chairman or vice-chairman, and vacancies could be filled either by election or by appointment of the secretary of the interior.

The first meeting was held on July 7, 1923, at Toadlena, New Mexico. This council, assembled as it was under a restricted, promulgated set of administrative orders with no specific definition of authority, was intended to be no more than a consultative body (Young 1972:191). However, it proved to be the germ of self-government for the organized tribe. Dodge was elected chairman. One of the problems he faced was the opposition of the northern Navajos who objected to sharing oil royalties with Navajos outside their jurisdiction. Nevertheless, the meeting gave authority to Hagerman to sign all oil and mineral leases for the tribe on the treaty portion of the reservation. This wide authority was obtained by an enticing federal promise to secure more land for the tribe, which was feeling the pinch of overgrazing and drought. Opposition to Dodge was not expressed in open meeting, but Estep forwarded a petition to the BIA commissioner signed by the San Juan Navajos: "Whare by the old order of doing business of the Navijo indians has been taken from us & placed in the hands of Tche Dodge & a committee of six apointed by or through the Secritary of Interior" (Kelly 1968:67). Their fears were not ungrounded. Some kind of central authority had been envisioned by Dodge as early as 1918 when he wrote to Commissioner of Indian Affairs Cato Sells:

> I take a deep interest in all the Navajos; not only those of my immediate neighborhood. I would like to see them all make equal progress, but I am sure that it is only possible if we have one man at the head of the tribe, an active, strong, energetic and able man. . . . A uniform educational system, uniform treatment, uniform orders and regulations, and uniform progress would be the result. The whole tribe would advance as one unit (Kelly 1968:66).

The early tribal council has customarily been characterized as an acquiescent group, but Kelly (1968) makes a good case for rejecting this facile assumption by analyzing a number of decisions of the delegates that show that they were deliberating with care and taking strong policy positions. For example, they decided against dividing the oil money per capita. Instead they voted to divide the royalties by jurisdiction where delegates and superintendent could make agreements on how the money was to be spent. This by no means reflected the general climate of Indian affairs at the time. Congress had voted, without consultation with the Indians, to pay out of Navajo funds in the U.S. Treasury half the cost of a bridge across the Colorado River at some distance from the reservation. Once alerted to this scheme, the Navajo Tribal Council roundly condemned the unauthorized use of any of their money. Jacob C. Morgan, a council member, called upon the federal government to consult with the council whenever appropriation of tribal monies was contemplated. Clearly this "consultative" body was pressing for more decision-making authority.

Overgrazing, with consequent deterioration of the range, was another problem that had been recognized as early as 1910. In 1926 the council passed a resolution to limit the number of horses. This followed upon a federal threat that unless the number of useless horses was reduced it would be impossible to enlarge the reservation. Dodge recognized the necessity for cutting down the sheep herds but, his ear well to the ground, he advised postponement of a vote until the matter could be "talked over with the people."

Mineral rights on executive order reservations was another issue. Secretary of the Interior Albert B. Fall believed that these did not belong to the Indians. He testified in 1922 that such "reservations are merely public lands temporarily withdrawn by Executive order" (Kelly 1968:57). The Navajo Tribal Council disagreed, contending that the subsurface rights on such land belonged to the Indians. A contrary policy would, of course, substantially limit the royalties that could accrue to the tribe. The Cameron bill pending in Congress recognized the right of the Indians to 100 percent of the royalties on executive order reservations. A tax of 37.5% would go to the state in which oil was found, with the proviso that the tax money be spent in consultation with the Indians on projects for their benefit. Dodge and Deshna Clah Cheschillige attended the congressional hearings on the bill, which they supported. Dodge presented the Bureau of Indian Affairs with a plan for spending one million dollars of oil money for the purchase of land in New Mexico (Kelly 1968:120). The Cameron bill was signed into law as the Indian Oil Act of 1927, a law that still governs the use of oil revenue from Navajo land in Utah.

Reorganization of the Tribal Council

In 1928 regulations for the Navajo Tribal Council were amended to give Navajo women the right to vote, an ironic gesture since Navajo women had always taken part traditionally in meetings where public decisions were made. The terms of office for council delegates, chairman, and vice-chairman were fixed at four years. No legislative or substantive powers were conferred on the council, and the body could not meet without the presence of Hagerman, the special commissioner to the Navajo. Cheschillige, a farmer and stockman from Shiprock who had served for six years as interpreter to the superintendent of the San Juan Jurisdiction, was elected chairman, a post he held until 1932. Maxwell Yazzie, the vice-chairman, came from the western side of the reservation. He was educated at Sherman Institute in California.

Jacob C. Morgan, a member of the first Tribal Council, soon emerged as spokesman for the northern Navajos as well as a strong policy leader for the reservation as a whole. He had been educated at Hampton Institute and, like Dodge and Cheschillige, had served as interpreter. He was also a missionary for the Christian Reform Church. His political positions were frequently in opposition to those of the older leader, Dodge. For example, if Dodge called for the purchase of more land, Morgan would stress water development on the existing reservation.

The Police, the Courts, the Chapters

The Navajo Police Force and the Navajo Tribal Courts and the local Chapters had separate origin dates and paths of development. It was not until the 1950s that these organs of government were formally incorporated into the Tribal Council system. The first Navajo police force was established for the purpose of retrieving stolen cattle in 1870 under the old war leader, Manuelito. In a few months it was disbanded after its total success. In 1881 a second force was recruited, again under Manuelito, to deal with liquor problems. Since that time, there has been some form of police corps responsible to the Navajo agent, to a federal officer or chief of the Navajo Patrol, or to the Branch of Law and Order of the Bureau of Indian Affairs.

Navajo Courts of Indian Offenses were organized in 1891 after some prodding by the secretary of the interior, who had authorized the courts in 1883. Judges received three dollars a month until their salary was raised to eight dollars. Superintendent Albert Kneale (1950:343) describes a court session in Shiprock in the 1920s in which two judges and the entire police force participated with Kneale presiding.

The first local Chapter was established in 1927 by Agent John Hunter in the Leupp Jurisdiction as a grassroots organization to discuss land and grazing problems. This useful type of forum soon spread to other districts, until by 1933 there were nearly 100 Chapters in operation. When they became centers of resistance to stock reduction, the Bureau of Indian Affairs ceased to provide encouragement and operating funds. The number dropped to 60 in 1936 and to 30 in 1945 (Van Valkenburgh 1945:73). They revived with tribal aid in 1959 (fig. 2).

The New Deal Era, 1933–1945

The period from 1933 to 1945 should, if all had proceeded smoothly, have merited the title of "Rise of Navajo Self-Government." When a new era dawned for Navajos with the election of Franklin D. Roosevelt as president and the appointments of Harold L. Ickes as secretary of the interior and John Collier as commissioner of Indian affairs, the Navajo Tribal Council was already functioning. The new federal policy was a reversal of the aim of the Indian Allotment Act of 1887, which had been to make individualistic, property-owning farmers out of Indians. The Collier program called for respect for the diversity of Indian cultures, preservation and extension of the Indian land base, the right of self-determination for the tribes to be expressed in Indian governments and Indian courts, and the right of consultation in the shaping of federal policy. Deloria (1969:144) wrote that "Collier began to move the Bureau of Indian Affairs in a new direction. He figured that the movement to make white men out of Indians had not succeeded in four centuries and there was no reason to expect it to succeed in his lifetime." But of this same man and this same policy the Navajo Chapter at Houck stated:

> John Collier promised to help us more than any other white man but before he made these promises he forced us to agree to some hard things that we didn't like. . . . We Indians don't think it is right for Collier to tell us we should govern ourselves, and then tell us how to do it. Why does he want to fool us that way and make us believe we are running our country when he makes us do what he wants?

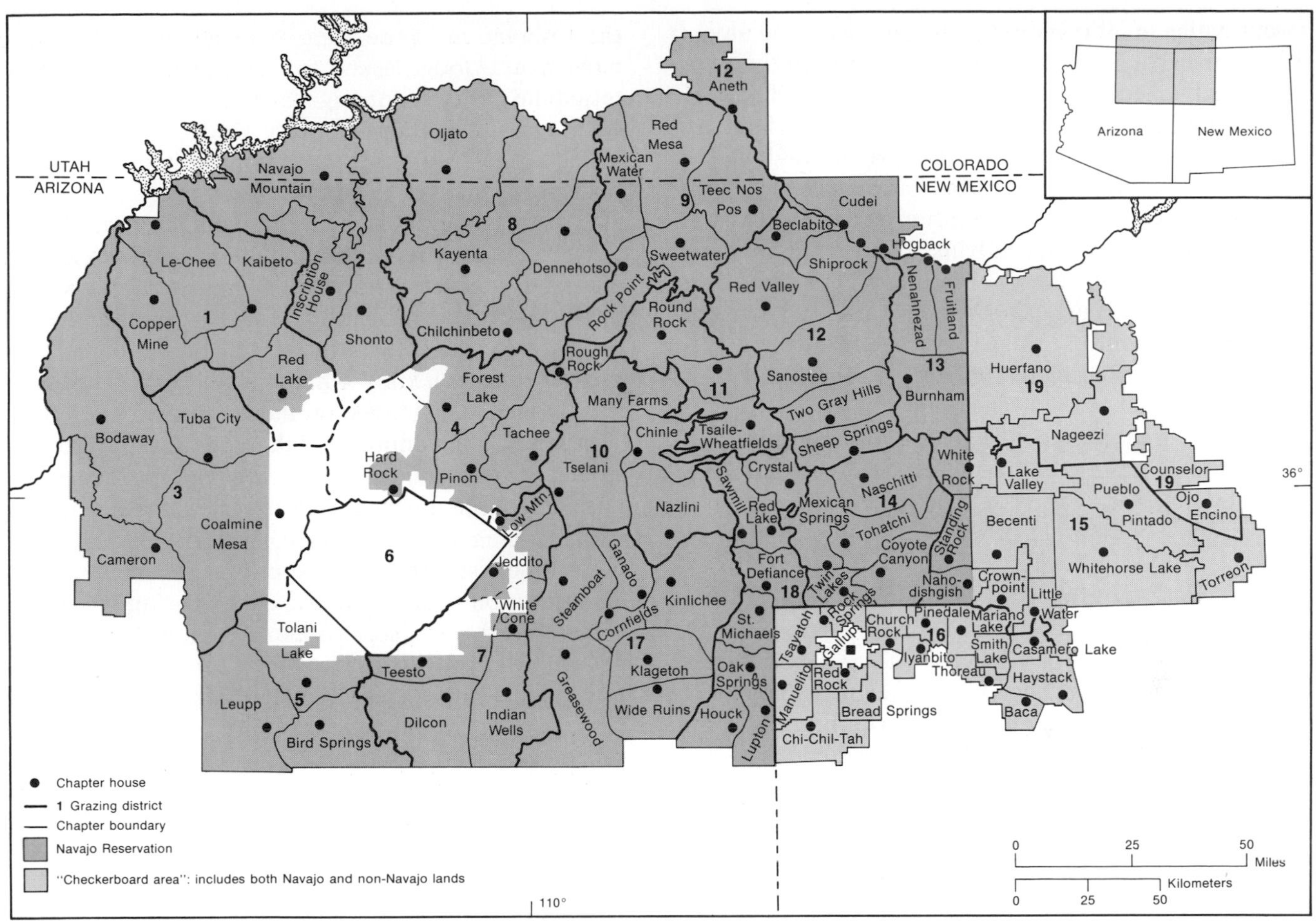

Fig. 2. Political subdivisions of Navajo territory in the 1980s. See "Navajo History, 1850–1923," fig. 16, this vol., for Cañoncito, Alamo, and Ramah reservations, which are also chapters.

(U.S. Congress. Senate. Committee on Indian Affairs 1937:18015).

What intervened between Collier's sincerely high aims, crystallized as they were in legal terms in the Indian Reorganization Act of 1934, and the creation of widespread Navajo support for his policies was stock reduction. Collier, the federal government, conservationists, and the builders of Hoover Dam were convinced that Navajo stock had to be reduced in order to preserve the range and to keep the dam from silting up through erosion. When the leadership of the fledgling Tribal Council tried to mediate between the federal government and the resistant stock owners, modern Navajo self-government nearly foundered.

Aberle (1966:52) suggests dividing stock reduction into three periods—voluntary stock reduction from 1933 to 1936, the systematic reduction program from 1937 to 1941, and from 1942 to 1945, continuing limitation in a war economy. Thomas Dodge, the only Navajo lawyer, a son of Chee Dodge, bore the brunt of the early period. He was elected chairman in 1932 and served until 1936, when he accepted employment with the Bureau of Indian Affairs. His vice-chairman was Marcus Kanuho from the Leupp Jurisdiction.

Among the benefits Collier was determined to institute was erosion control. In his first meeting with the Navajo Tribal Council in October, he proposed voluntary stock reduction. In compensation for cutting their flocks, Navajos would receive more land, soil conservation, water development, day schools, and jobs on the Emergency Conservation Works program. The Navajos took these promises as guarantees, but unfortunately for them and for Collier an Indian commissioner cannot control Congress. Collier began to move immediately when funds for the purchase of sheep and goats became available through the Federal Emergency Relief Administration. All the problems of this period were aggravated by the low prices and the collapse of the world market during the economic depression.

During the years 1933–1943 the Council passed a number of resolutions appearing to favor stock reduction, each resolution earning the delegates a reputation of treachery. It is more realistic to view their decisions as the delaying, temporizing, "horsetrading" tactics of men caught in an untenable situation than as the complacent affixing of a rubber stamp to federal proposals.

The first decision was for a 10 percent across-the-board cut, which allowed large holders to cull their flocks while small owners had to sacrifice good stock. The council then proposed to buy goats from the poor to be exchanged for sheep from the wealthy. The year of 1935 marked the end of voluntary stock reduction.

In the meantime, a resistance movement was building up under the leadership of Jacob Morgan, who organized the Navajo Rights Association as part of this campaign. Headmen in the outlying districts led sporadic moves of refusal to sell, to brand, to round up horses. In the midst of this upheaval, which the Navajos viewed not too unrealistically as the destruction of their livelihood, an all-tribal plebiscite rejected the Indian Reorganization Act of 1934. The act would have permitted Navajos to organize a council and Indian courts and to borrow money as a corporation without complete BIA control. However, it also contained a clause authorizing the secretary of the interior to limit livestock on Indian reservations.

The rejection of this act was a hard blow to Collier, who interpreted the move as showing a great lack of political sophistication. He reacted with an even stronger show of authoritarianism as a "benevolent dictator," firmly convinced that he had discharged his obligation to consult fully with the Indians. He assured them that he had the authority to enforce grazing regulations with or without their consent. He also threatened that the Navajo Boundary bill, designed to return to the reservation some of their previously withdrawn land that had been restored to the public domain, would not be acceptable to Congress if Navajos failed to cooperate. He himself would not undertake land improvements unless they reduced their stock (Aberle 1966:57). Through no fault of Collier's, the Boundary bill was never enacted into law.

In 1935 the six jurisdictions were consolidated into one agency with headquarters at Window Rock, Arizona. The move was opposed by the Council because Navajos preferred to deal face-to-face with a local superintendent. The new general superintendent was E. Reesman Fryer, who saw as his first responsibility the enforcement of erosion control.

The reactions of the Navajo leaders were expressed in Washington during the hearings on the Navajo Boundary bill and the hearings in the Senate committee on Indian affairs in 1936. Among the witnesses were Chee Dodge, Morgan, Cheschillige, Paul Jones, Robert Martin, Allen Neskahi, and Scott Preston—all men destined to be important in Navajo politics. Jones spoke in favor of an erosion-control demonstration area in Mexican Springs. Neskahi objected to the fact that Navajos had been promised 20 acres of land in the Fruitland Irrigation Project but in the end had received only 10 acres. Preston stated that stock reduction had never been approved by the tribe as a whole, only by a few delegates. Morgan presented a number of letters and petitions from the northern and eastern parts of the reservation, quite clear evidence of a resistance movement. Dodge asked for land extension and protested the policy of forcing Navajos off their allotments on the public domain. Because Dodge is so often pictured as the leading "cooperator" it is interesting to read his testimony: "You take sheep away from a Navajo, that's all he knows. He isn't going to farm or anything like that; you might give a few acres to the poor ones, but stock raising is in their heart. That's their work. If you keep on cutting down sheep after a while the Government will have to feed these people; give them rations; you know what that will cost" (U.S. Congress. Senate. Committee on Indian Affairs 1937:17905).

In 1936 Collier announced that the tribal government would be reorganized under regulations of the Department of the Interior as an aftermath to the rejection of the Indian Reorganization Act. The old executive committee was authorized to call an assembly to draft a constitution. The assembly, once constituted, was to declare itself a de facto tribal council. The committee decided to canvass the reservation for the names of the real leaders in the communities. Father Berard Haile, Chee Dodge, and Albert (Chic) Sandoval, among others, went throughout the reservation and collected 250 names of which the executive committee chose 70 to serve as delegates to the constitutional assembly on the assumption that these men had been informally "elected."

The first meeting of the constitutional assembly was held in 1937. Morgan demanded that the tribe be allowed to vote on the illegality of disbanding the old council. Nevertheless, the assembly voted, with only two dissents, to declare itself the de facto council. Morgan was offered the chairmanship but he stormed out of the meeting (fig. 3). Henry Taliman, an army veteran who had been educated off the reservation, was elected chairman with Roy Kinsel from Lukachukai as his vice-chairman.

The Council voted a constitution based on the type authorized by the Indian Reorganization Act, except that the approval of the secretary of the interior would be required on each council resolution. The constitution was not approved in Washington because there was a difference of opinion among Collier's advisers. Some objected that the constitution was based on an administrative action that could arbitrarily be changed; others believed that the concept of self-government had first to be built up among Navajos through education, and they were fearful that stock reduction had impaired the prestige of the Council. A third opinion held that under the doctrine of residual sovereignty, the tribe already possessed all the powers contained in the document. Collier decided to limit temporarily the powers of the Navajo tribe because the time was not ripe for holding a referendum on the constitution (Young 1972:203–205).

The new executive committee accepted the proposed

U.S. Indian Service (Bureau of Ind. Affairs).

Fig. 3. Members of the committee to draft a Navajo tribal constitution, appointed by Henry Taliman on the second day of the constitutional assembly (following Morgan's protest exit). Morgan, who never participated, was originally appointed chairman with 4 other tribal delegates (facing blackboard, left to right): Robert Curley of Leupp, Roy Haskon of Gray Mountain, Frank Mitchell of Chinle, and Jim Shirley of Ft. Defiance (chairman). standing, left, is Father Berard Haile, linguist and resident of the reservation since 1901, who had earlier helped canvass the reservation with Albert (Chic) Sandoval (at desk). Alfred Bowman (standing) and Sandoval served as interpreters. The constitution, which was begun in April 1937, was never adopted. An election was held in 1938, based on an election code and by-laws drafted by this group, and the new Tribal Council leaders took office without a constitution. Both proposed constitution and by-laws are reproduced in Young (1961:400–411). See also Parman (1968), Young (1978). Photograph by Milton Snow, spring 1938, from Mary Shepardson's collection.

U.S. Indian Service (Bureau of Ind. Affairs).

Fig. 4. Jacob Morgan, at his inauguration as chairman of the Navajo Tribal Council following his election in Sept. 1938. Seated just to his right is Howard Gorman, who was installed as vice chairman. Seated at far right is Henry Taliman, retiring chairman of the constitutional assembly (then the acting or de facto council), in which he and Morgan so emphatically clashed. Photograph by Milton Snow, Window Rock, Ariz., Nov. 8, 1938, from Mary Shepardson's collection.

federal grazing regulations, which were then immediately approved by Secretary Ickes. They called for an assessment of the carrying capacity of each land-management district into which the reservation had been divided and the assignment of permits to individuals on the basis of the relation between population and the size and condition of the range in the management district.

New Regulations

In 1938 rules for the Navajo Tribal Council were promulgated by the secretary of the interior. The regulations authorized a membership of 74 delegates to be elected for four years by popular vote and secret ballot. Nominations for chairman and vice-chairman were to be held in four election provinces. An executive committee was to be chosen from among the delegates to represent the land-management districts. Elections would be conducted by the general superintendent who would sit beside the chairman at all meetings of the Council. Once again the rules contained no statement of substantive legislative powers (Young 1972:207–208).

Jacob Morgan was elected chairman with Howard Gorman, a Presbyterian and interpreter from Ganado, as vice-chairman (fig. 4). The great tragedy of Morgan's life, according to Esanapa Martin, the widow of his close friend and colleague Bob Martin, was that he could not hold back the onrush of stock reduction. The new Council refused to choose an executive committee because the former executive committee had accepted the federal grazing regulations, so for nearly 10 years Navajo government functioned without continuing committee leadership.

A measure initiated by Morgan was to have far-reaching repercussions. That was the 1940 resolution banning the use of "the bean known as peyote." This hallucinogen was central to the ceremonies of the Native American Church, a religion that had spread to the reservation through the Towaoc Utes. The use of peyote was officially condemned by the Council as dangerous to health and productive of irrational and orgiastic behavior. Sanctions for possession and use were set as high as nine months' imprisonment and a fine of $100.

Chee Dodge was reelected in 1942 with Sam Ahkeah as vice-chairman. Ahkeah was from the Shiprock area, a farmer on irrigated land and an interpreter for the National Park Service at Mesa Verde. With General Superintendent Fryer at the helm, a vigorous policy of erosion control went forward. In 1943 the federal government instituted legal reprisals for trespass, that is, failure to reduce one's flocks, with widespread arrests, fines, and jail sentences.

The Council agreed to reduce surplus horses and to help in the issuance of grazing permits, but they requested special permits for small stock owners. According to Aberle (1966:68) the Council, "unable to stop reduction, in effect swapped surplus horses for special permits, mercy to transgressors, and delayed deadlines in enforcement." In 1945 the Council requested a return to the six-agency system and the suspension of stock reduction because "the people could not stand any more." Such resolutions, of course, were not approved by the secretary of the interior. Resistance increased, Superientendent Fryer was threatened with death, and a supervisor and his range rider from Teec Nos Pas were kidnapped and rescued only in time to save their lives. By the end of World War II Navajo livestock holdings were below the permitted level (Aberle 1966:75–76).

World War II and After

During World War II some 3,600 Navajos served in the armed forces. A number of men and women swelled the wartime labor pool, and their earnings pumped money into the dwindling reservation economy. But when the war and wartime industry ended, Navajos were in economic crisis.

In 1946 Ahkeah defeated Chee Dodge who was running for a third term as chairman. This is reputed to have been a cruel blow to the aging leader; nevertheless, he served as vice-chairman until his death in 1947. Zhealy Tso, a graduate of Sherman Institute, and a trading post owner in the Chinle valley, replaced Dodge.

Congress established an Indian Claims Commission and authorized suits against the federal government by Indian tribes for payment for lands that had been taken from them without compensation. The tribes were permitted to hire their own lawyers. Norman Littell, a former assistant attorney general in the Justice Department, was Ahkeah's choice. Littell signed a contract with the Navajo tribe as land claims attorney on a contingency basis, that is, a certain percentage of all monies recovered. A second contract bound him as general counsel to the tribe on a salary basis. He immediately adopted a strong policy of asserting Navajo rights against the federal government, the local states, and other Indians. A strident publicity campaign, aimed at strengthening his Navajo support, consisted of an unending attack against the "Collier cult" and the horrors of stock reduction. Ironically, Littell himself, while in the Justice Department, had signed the punitive orders to enforce the special grazing regulations (U.S. Congress. Senate. Committee on Interior and Insular Affairs 1948:453).

In 1947 the chairman of the Council took up residence in Window Rock as the capital (figs. 5–6), and an executive committee (called Advisory Committee) (fig. 7), was appointed to act with powers delegated by the Navajo Tribal Council. Questions as to the legality of methods being used to enforce the grazing regulations were plaguing the secretary of the interior, and he was impelled to send his assistant on land utilization, Lee Muck, to survey conditions. The result of the report was a "freeze order" to halt punitive measures against trespass and to direct the tribe to formulate its own grazing regulations and to enforce them.

Rehabilitation

Because of poor economic conditions following the war, a bill was proposed in Congress to appropriate nearly 90 million dollars over a 10-year period for the rehabilitation of the Navajo and Hopi Reservations. Sam Ahkeah, Zhealy Tso, Jacob Morgan, and Howard Gorman testified for the Navajos in 1948 and 1949, pointing out the need for roads, schools, health facilities, and water development. The Navajo-Hopi Rehabilitation Act was passed in 1950. Included in its provisions was a guarantee that the Indians be consulted at each stage of the planning, that they have the right to lease reservation land, and that tribal funds be made available for such purposes as the Council saw fit (with Interior Department approval, of course). Navajos would also have the right to adopt a constitution. This last clause "gave a statutory base for the adoption of a constitution that could not be arbitrarily cancelled or modified by the Secretary of the Interior" (Young 1972:212). However, the tribal attorney was seeking wider powers and on his advice the framing of a constitution was indefinitely delayed.

In 1950 election procedures were revised to include registration of voters, the popular election of judges, and the election of a chairman and vice-chairman as a team. Ahkeah was chosen for a second term with John C. Claw, a war veteran of Many Farms, as vice-chairman. Two years later Claw resigned to accept a position with the Presbyterian church. Adolph Maloney, also a veteran and a small businessman from Tuba City, replaced Claw.

Termination Policy

Another new era was ushered into Indian Affairs with a survey of Indian conditions by the Hoover Commission. House Concurrent Resolution 108, passed in 1953, calling for "termination" of special conditions for the Indians stated: "the sense of Congress" to be "that, at the earliest possible time, all the Indian tribes and the individual members thereof . . . should be freed from federal supervision and control and from all disabilities and limitations specially applicable to Indians" (Shepardson 1963:17). Navajos were frightened by the prospect of losing their land and of falling to the mercy of the states, but because their reservation was not slated for early termination, they did not experience the panic

Bureau of Ind. Affairs, Branch of Land Operations, Concho, Okla.

Fig. 5. Window Rock, Ariz., selected as the site of the capital of the Navajo Nation by John Collier, in the 1930s, with construction begun under federal work programs. The Council House, one of the earliest buildings, is the octagonal stone building at right center (1). Other buildings and named rock formations in use in 1981 (Russell P. Hartman, communication to editors 1981) are: (2) executive offices (including tribal officers', tribal legal department, and BIA area director's office), (3) Needle Rock, (4) tribal census office, (5) office of the legislative secretary, (6) old schoolhouse serving as the Public Health Service Building, (7) tribal motor pool, (8) Saddle Rock, (9) Old Club Building, used for offices, (10) recreational building and Window Rock Public Library, (11) St. Michael's housing area, (12) Tribal housing area, (13) office of the controller. Photographer unknown, 1963.

that seized so many tribes. Actually, the BIA's policy of "piecemeal withdrawal" worked to the advantage of the Navajos as more and more responsibilities and more and more areas of freedom were accorded to them.

The team of Paul Jones and Scott Preston won the elections of 1955. Jones, from Naschitti, had studied both on and off the reservation, served in the armed forces, and worked for a tea company in Chicago. Returning to the reservation, he became a BIA official and was interpreter and liaison officer between the BIA and the Tribal Council shortly before his election. Preston was a ceremonial leader from Tuba City who had learned English while acting in motion pictures in Hollywood.

The rapid development and maturing of the Navajo Tribal Council, begun during the chairmanship of Ahkeah, was accelerated under Jones. When at last it became apparent that the tribal delegates needed some local organization to help formulate demands and implement central policy, the council certified local chapters (figs. 9–10) as part of the formal political organization. A few were still functioning; some defunct chapters revived; new ones were organized. In 1974 more than 100 were operating as an integral part of tribal government (Williams 1970; Shepardson 1963).

Bonanza

In 1956 and 1957 the large Four Corners oil and gas fields were discovered, and millions of dollars poured into the tribal treasury, as much as 33 million in one year. This permitted a greatly expanded program of reservation development, the tribe again refusing to divide the funds per capita. Attorney Littell won some

©Thomas Y. Crowell Company: Farber and Dorris 1975:140; Smithsonian, NAA.

Fig. 6. Tribal Council Headquarters at Window Rock, Ariz., in front of the distinctive rock formation after which the capital is named. Photograph by Joseph C. Farber, early 1970s.

Navajo Tribal Mus., Window Rock, Ariz.

Fig. 7. Meeting of the Advisory Committee, tribal officers, and staff about 1957. They are, left to right: John Perry, Lee Tom, Dillon Platero, Ned Hatathli, Margery Allen (transcriber), Laurence Davis (assistant general counsel), Norman Littell (general counsel), Maurice McCabe (executive secretary of the tribe), Paul Jones (tribal chairman), Scott Preston (tribal vice-chairman), Carl Beyal (tribal interpreter), Howard Gorman, Manuel Begay (administrative assistant), and Richard Van Valkenburg (supervisor of land use survey). Photograph by James Bosch, Window Rock, Ariz., from Mary Shepardson's collection.

spectacular legal decisions for his employers: the exchange of land at Glen Canyon Dam site for land on McCracken Mesa; a suit to protect the rights of Navajos to graze livestock on the public domain in Utah (*Hatathley* v. *United States*), and a suit against a trader whose action in seizing a Navajo's sheep in payment of a bad debt had been supported in the Arizona courts. Littell took the case to the U.S. Supreme Court (*Williams* v. *Lee*) and secured a reaffirmation of John Marshall's 1832 decision, that a treaty tribe was a "domestic dependent nation" and as such, sovereign as opposed to the states, but not completely sovereign as opposed to the federal government.

The administrative branch of the tribal government was rapidly expanding. Tribal policy was to hire competent non-Indian specialists as department heads, with the understanding that they were to train Navajos to fill their positions eventually. The tribe accepted re-

left, Navajo Tribal Mus., Window Rock, Ariz.; right, Jerry Jacka Photography, Phoenix, Ariz.

Fig. 8. Navajo Tribal Council in session. left, Some of the 74 members of the Tribal Council in about 1957. Photograph by James Bosch, Window Rock, Ariz., from Mary Shepardson's collection. right, Council in session, 1979. This view from the back of the hall shows the interior architecture of the Council House, which was modeled after an 8-sided hogan. The murals are by Navajo artist Gerald Nailor. Photograph by Jerry Jacka.

Navajo Tribal Mus., Window Rock, Ariz.

Fig. 9. Chapter meeting at Shiprock, N. Mex., June 1957; Lee Tom speaking. Chapter meetings were initially held outdoors, often on the occasion of a Squaw Dance, Yeibichai Dance, or other public gathering. Several chapter houses were built in the 1930s, often resembling hogans; by 1980, most chapter districts had a chapter house. The tribal officials are seated on chairs, with women to their left, following the normal arrangement inside chapter houses (Williams 1970:43) and reflecting prescribed social divisions of space within a hogan. Photographer unidentified.

top, Mary Shepardson, Palo Alto, Calif.; bottom, *Navajo Times*, Window Rock, Ariz.

Fig. 10. Dedication of Navajo chapter houses. top, Dedication of Chilchinbito, Ariz., chapter house, probably involving the performance of a Blessingway by medicine man Tom Wilson (second from right). Photograph by John D. Wallace (later a delegate to the Navajo Council), May 12, 1962. bottom, Flag-raising at the opening of Cudei, Ariz., chapter house, performed by Navajo code-talkers (U.S. Marine Corps veterans who used Navajo for radio communication in World War II battles in the Pacific; see Johnston 1964). The community of Cudei was formerly represented by the Beclabito Chapter. Photograph by Paul Natonabah, May 3, 1980.

sponsibility for water development, irrigation, emergency grain distribution, emergency welfare, the distribution of surplus commodities, the building of chapter houses, a public works program, tribal scholarships, and tribal enterprises, among which were the Navajo Forest Products Industry, the Arts and Crafts Guild, and two motels.

Jones and Preston won their second terms in 1959 in an uncontested election after they were nominated in all four provinces. The disappointed aspirants regarded this procedure as illegal and even solicited the BIA to overturn the elections, without success. They did succeed as a result of their agitation in bringing about a revision of the election procedures in 1966 to authorize a single nominating convention for the reservation as a whole.

The executive branch of the Tribal Council was reorganized in 1959. The council assumed complete control of, and financial responsibility for, the legal system reorganized as the judicial branch. The court system was separated from the police force, with seven judges to be appointed by the Council for life.

Tribal policy forbidding the use of peyote in religious ceremonies, which had been a source of conflict in many of the districts since 1940, was exacerbated as membership in the Peyote religion increased. Constant police harassment finally forced Navajo Peyotists into political opposition to the council leadership. The Native American Church lost a suit against the Council when a U.S. District Court in New Mexico decided that the Navajo tribe retained authority over religious issues and therefore the secretary of the interior and the federal government had no right to overrule the peyote ban.

Raymond Nakai was elected chairman in 1963 with Nelson Damon as his running-mate. Nakai was born in Lukachukai and had been educated on the reservation. After serving in the navy during World War II he was employed at the Navajo Ordnance Depot near Flagstaff. His Navajo hour, broadcast on a Flagstaff radio station, brought the sound of his voice and his critical views of Navajo tribal leadership into hundreds of hogans on the reservation. Damon had served as delegate to the Council from Coyote Canyon on the eastern side, and before he ran for election he was employed as a supervisor by the Arizona State Highway Department.

Nakai's election program called for more concern for the individual Navajo, the termination of the tribal attorney's contract, better relations with the BIA, and a constitution to guarantee the Four Freedoms, particularly freedom of religion. Preelection efforts of the tribal lawyer and some powerful leaders to "muzzle" Nakai left him embittered. He refused to appoint any of the old leaders to the Advisory Committee. The opposition crystallized into a faction called the "old guard" with the result that tribal government was thrown into four years of unrelieved factionalism that brought all but routine business to a halt. Attempts by Nakai to dismiss the powerful executive secretary, Maurice McCabe, as a "Littell man" and to terminate the attorney's contract failed because neither faction could claim the majority of the Council's support. Mutual harassment was the order of the day (Shepardson 1971).

Nakai and Damon were returned to office in 1966. Nakai's support in the Council had increased. He had mellowed enough to appoint to the Advisory Committee some of the old guard such as Howard Gorman and Annie Wauneka, the daughter of Chee Dodge and winner of a U.S. presidential award for her work on the Health Committee. The problem of the tribal attorney came to a head when Littell obtained only a compromise decision from a federal district court on the Navajo-Hopi dispute case *(Healing* v. *Jones*). The court ordered exclusive occupancy rights for the Hopis to Land Management District 6 and the sharing of both surface and subsurface rights to the remainder of the executive order reservation of 1882. Navajos interpreted this ruling as a defeat. Accusing Littell of malfeasance in employing salaried tribal lawyers in the preparation of a contingency case, the Department of the Interior, after a series of court cases, was able to secure his dismissal.

A Navajo Bill of Rights, based on the U.S. Constitution, was passed in 1967. This was followed by a specific resolution permitting the use of peyote in the religious ceremonies of the Native American Church.

A significant event in Nakai's second term was the appropriation of federal funds through the Office of Economic Opportunity. Despite some routine friction between the Council and an independent agency, it was not until a legal aid association, Dinebeiina Nahiilna Be Agaditahe 'Lawyers Who Contribute to the Economic Revitalization of the People' (DNA), was set up with OEO funds that strong opposition arose within the Advisory Committee. DNA did not confine its activities to advising individual Navajos of their legal rights but also advised them how to oust a school board and how to control the behavior of the traders as well as alerting them to proposals in the Council to "give away" Navajo water rights. Congressional passage of the Indian Civil Rights Bill of 1968 weakened the often arbitrary exercise of the council's powers and strengthened the position of DNA. Nevertheless, the non-Indian director, Theodore Mitchell, was expelled from the reservation until DNA successfully brought suit in a federal district court on the grounds that Mitchell had not even been accused, much less found guilty, of any of the offenses previously established as grounds for expulsion from the Navajo Reservation.

Navajos were gradually taking over most of the directorships of administrative departments. Eventually Leo Haven replaced Mitchell as director of the OEO legal activities. Outside industry had been invited to enjoy free land and cheap labor on the reservation and the invitation had been accepted by Fairchild Semiconductor Electronics Corporation and General Dynamics Corporation. The most controversial decision of the Council was to permit the Peabody Coal Company to stripmine on Black Mesa and transport the coal to generators at Glen Canyon Dam. This action was attacked by conservationists both from within and from without the reservation on the basis that it would destroy the land for further use.

Leadership, Land, Culture

With termination policy by now fallen well into disrepute, a new emphasis was placed on the preservation of the Navajo cultural heritage, on bilingualism, and on local control of the schools. Rough Rock Demonstration School, directed in the early stages by Robert Roessel, Anita Pfeiffer, and Dillon Platero, pioneered. A few Navajo schools were contracted to local school boards by the Bureau of Indian Affairs. A community college under the direction of Robert Roessel, later under Ned Hatathli, was established and a beautiful campus at Tsaile was constructed.

A new wind began to blow out of Washington with the policy of appointing Navajos to important BIA positions. In 1968, Edward Plummer, Supervisor of Land

Bureau of Ind. Affairs, Washington.

Fig. 11. Peter MacDonald (at the podium) delivering his inaugural address following his first election as tribal chairman. The great seal of the Navajo Tribe is hung below the yei figure, partly visible, at left and on the podium. Photographer unidentified, Window Rock, Ariz., Jan. 5, 1971.

Investigation for the tribe, was appointed superintendent of the Crownpoint Agency. Two years later Anthony Lincoln, the son of the Chief Justice of the Navajo Tribal Courts, was appointed general superintendent of the Navajo Area Office. In 1970, Peter MacDonald and Wilson C. Skeet were elected chairman and vice-chairman of the council (fig. 11). MacDonald was born in Teec Nos Pas. He had an engineering degree from the University of Oklahoma and was employed by Hughes Aircraft Company in Los Angeles before his return to work for the Navajo tribe. In 1965 he was made director of the Office of Navajo Economic Opportunity. Skeet was educated on the reservation and at Nashville Business College in Tennessee. A veteran, he served as councilman from Two Wells before his election to higher office.

Navajo leadership since the 1920s has shown a progression with few breaks from older to younger, less-educated to better-educated men with more off-reservation experience. Navajo Indians, through the Tribal Council, have taken a long stride toward self-government (see Young 1978). Navajo leaders have become the most important decision makers as well as the executors of self-determined policies.

The Emerging Navajo Nation

PETER IVERSON

The Navajo Nation has been the official designation for the Navajo Tribe since 1969, when the Tribal Council's Advisory Committee called for the use of that term. The resolution represented in part a response to escalating demands by the outside world upon the Navajo people and their resources. Council members noted that the *Diné* "existed as a distinct political, cultural, and ethnic group" long before the Southwestern states had been established, that they had entered into treaties as "the sovereign Navajo Tribe" with the United States, that the Congress and the Supreme Court had "recognized the inherent right of the Navajo People to govern themselves." Yet, they observed, it had become "increasingly difficult for the Navajo People to retain their identity and independence." Thus it was "essential" to "remind" both Navajos and non-Navajos "that both the Navajo People and Navajo lands are, in fact, separate and distinct" (Navajo Indians 1969:7–8).

Navajo nationalism, therefore, must be viewed as an effort by the *Diné* to gain greater control over their social, economic, and political lives. The election of Peter MacDonald in 1970 as Council chairman mirrored this mood of emerging nationalism. Reelected both in 1974 and again in 1978 for an unprecedented third term, MacDonald sought a middle road between insensitive and immediate exploitation by outsiders of Navajo resources and total separation from the needs, demands, and influences of the Anglo Southwest and the United States. Self-determination may be a cliché, but by the end of the 1970s the Navajos had achieved substantial progress in that direction. For the Navajo Nation, it was a time of achievement, but pressing problems were not fully resolved (Iverson 1980:228).

From the time of his first inaugural address in January 1971, MacDonald gave notice that his administration would seek greater sovereignty and self-sufficiency. He said the Navajos must protect what was rightfully theirs, claim what was rightfully due them, replace with their labor and skills what they depended on from others, and bring into being what they desired but did not have (MacDonald 1971). MacDonald's first term witnessed important developments in law, education, health care, economy, and politics.

The chairman's selection of new legal counsel suggested the more aggressive tone of his administration. MacDonald had scored former chairman Raymond Nakai's attorney, Harold Mott, for not possessing a background in Indian law or in matters of concern to the Navajos. The new counsel was the Phoenix firm of Brown, Vlassis, and Bain. Partner George Vlassis and firm attorney Lawrence Ruzow later seceded to form their own partnership and continued to represent the Tribe. While not universally beloved, Vlassis and Ruzow in the view of most observers provided the Navajos with more experienced and sophisticated legal assistance. They played a central role in advising the chairman and in offering opinions on economic development and the Navajo Nation's relationship to the states, the Bureau of Indian Affairs, and the neighboring Hopis. In 1981 Vlassis and new associates represented the Tribe.

The legal assistance program, Dinebeiina Nahiilna Be Agaditahe, had been under fire during the Nakai years but initially enjoyed firm support from MacDonald. DNA lawyers continued their efforts to gain more equitable treatment of Navajo people by traders, bordertown merchants, and the states. They filed a class action suit against the Pinon trading post operators and won an out of court settlement, while helping local people to found an alternative, a cooperative store. Additional suits encouraged changes in pawn practices. In *McClanahan* v. *Arizona State Tax Commission*, DNA affirmed the right of Navajo employees not to pay state income taxes on wages earned within the Navajo Nation.

Two additional Navajo community schools, operated under the contract system with the BIA, were started during this era. At Ramah, residents established a high school, and at Borrego Pass a third community school was established, following the lead of Rough Rock and Rock Point. All four institutions served as models of local control and bilingual, bicultural instruction. They represented a larger pattern of greater parental involvement in the education of their children. More children enrolled in the public school system. In districts such as Window Rock and Chinle, Navajos gained a majority on school boards. This new majority attempted to hire principals more sympathetic to Navajo culture and to begin to fashion a curriculum more in keeping with their wishes. While its personnel wrestled with problems in the decision-making process, Navajo Community College moved to its permanent campus site at Tsaile,

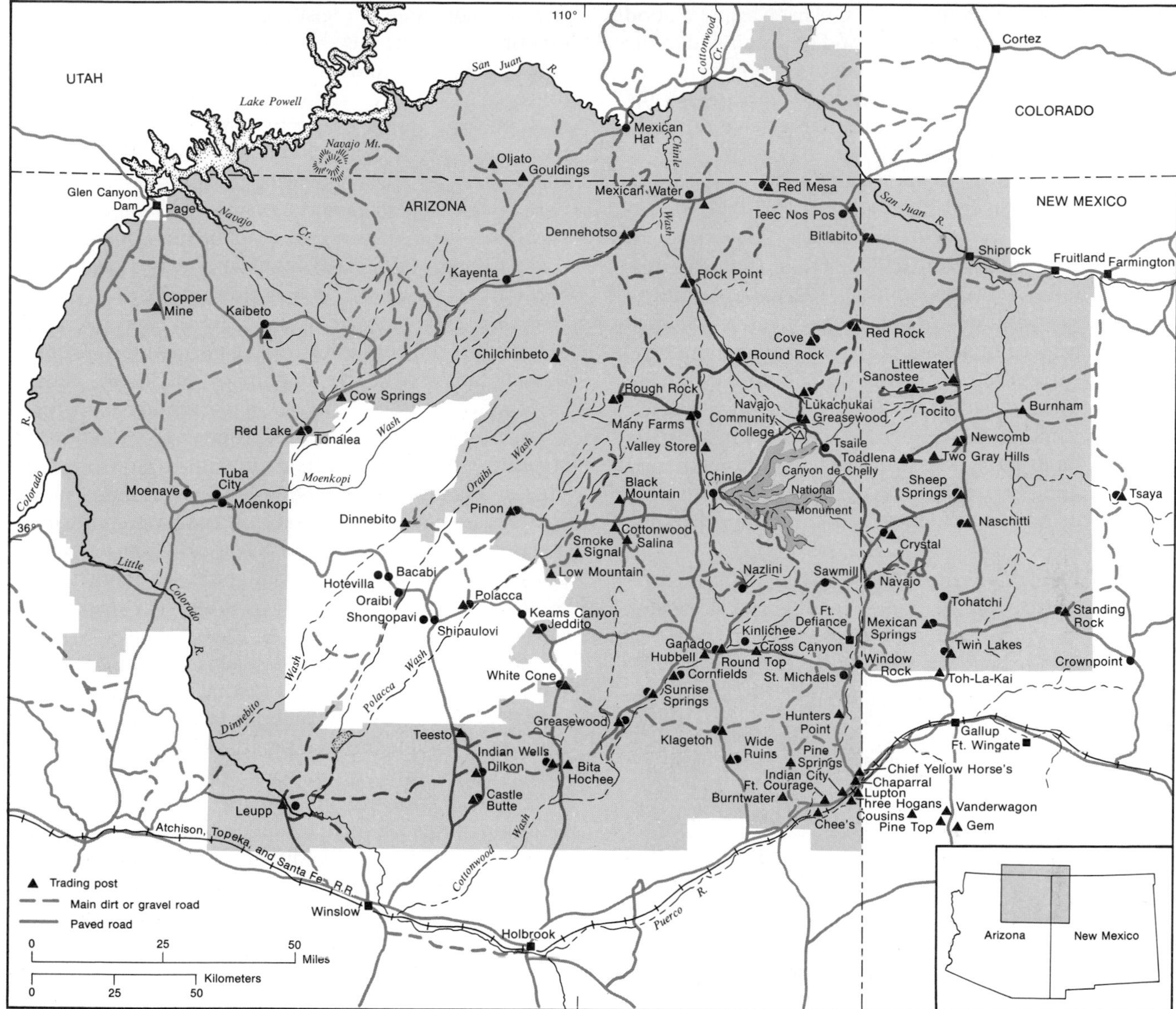

Fig. 1. The Navajo reservation in the 1970s.

Arizona, and offered courses in arts and sciences, vocational-technical areas, and basic English and mathematics. On June 17, 1971, the Tribal Council created the Navajo Division of Education to coordinate the movement for Navajo control of education. Its most significant program was the Navajo Teacher Education Program, initiated in cooperation with the University of New Mexico and the University of Arizona, to increase the numbers of Navajo teachers.

In the area of health care, Navajos also sought a more national approach. The Tribal Council in June 1972 established the Navajo Health Authority. This new agency was charged with several responsibilities, including the promotion of professional health careers and the retention of traditional ways of healing. Distinguished Navajo artist Carl Gorman headed a department of Native healing sciences to assist with the latter effort. Dr. Taylor McKenzie, one of only two Navajo physicians at this time, assisted in trying to develop the Health Authority and to boost Navajo influence within the workings of the Public Health Service.

Mineral development remained as a critical component within the Navajo economy. Political leaders such as MacDonald encouraged the evolution of a joint venture approach between the Navajo Nation and Exxon to develop Navajo uranium resources. Local chapters in the affected area, such as Sanostee, registered firm opposition to the idea. In general, Navajos took a far more critical view of mineral exploitation than they had in the 1960s. Local opposition to proposed coal gasification plants in the Burnham region forced Navajo government officials to reconsider their plans.

MacDonald also argued in a manner different from his predecessors in asserting that the Navajos would press for their full water rights. The Navajo Nation obviously would not make the kind of deal it had in the previous decade when it sacrificed its right to 34,000 acre-feet of Upper Basin Colorado River water for the life of the Page power plant in order to have the plant built near Page, Arizona.

The tribal enterprise approach to economic development, utilized so profitably in the case of the Navajo Forest Products Industry (fig. 2), was scrutinized for wider possible applicability. The Tribal Council's Advisory Committee created the Navajo Agricultural Products Industry on April 16, 1970, as a potential means of taking full advantage of the forthcoming Navajo Indian Irrigation Project. Other enterprises sought to reduce the flow of the Navajo dollar off the reservation. Tribal officials also tried to create more small businesses and more jobs within the Navajo Nation.

During the early 1970s Navajos became involved in an unprecedented way in local and state political affairs.

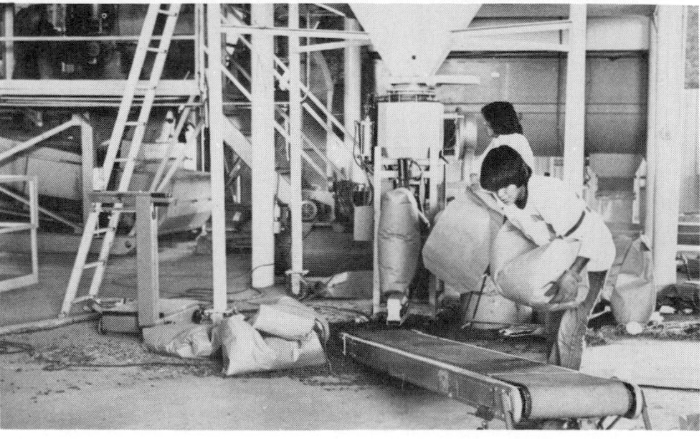

Navajo Times, Window Rock, Ariz.

Fig. 2. Navajo Agricultural Products Industry (NAPI). top, Members of the Navajo tribal Budget and Finance Committee and others being given a tour of NAPI, which (with the Navajo Forest Products Industry and the Navajo Tribal Utility Authority) is one of 3 major Tribal enterprises. bottom, Workers filling bags of feed pellets (made from compressed hay) at the pellet mill and fertilizer plant on the NAPI farm. Photographs by Paul Natonabah, at NAPI headquarters, near Farmingon, N. Mex., about 1979.

Initially motivated to register in many instances by local school board elections, Navajo voters rapidly began to vote at the county and state level. Anglo voters in southern Apache County, Arizona, frightened by the specter of a Navajo voting majority, unsuccessfully tried to carve out a separate Navajo county. Sen. Barry Goldwater decried the Navajo swing toward the Democratic party, which aided in the election of Democrat Raul Castro to the Arizona governorship. In general, such protests clearly indicated that the Navajos could be a force that mattered in regional politics (Iverson 1980:228–232).

In the 1974 election for tribal chairman, MacDonald handily defeated three opponents, including Nakai. Characterizing the election as "a referendum on Navajo dependence or Navajo self-sufficiency," MacDonald stated the theme of his second administration would be "the emerging Navajo Nation." The chairman said he and his associates would "continue the program we have begun to fully develop the Navajo Nation as an important economic, social, and political force in the Southwest and in the United States" (MacDonald 1975).

While there was important progress realized during the late 1970s, MacDonald's second term proved considerably more troubled than his first. To some extent this was inevitable: expectations had been raised among the people and yet serious questions persisted. MacDonald later argued that the success of his first term guaranteed efforts to undermine him in his next four years. In any event, difficulties soon appeared.

Economic development remained a continuing dilemma. Little expansion took place in the private sector, the Fairchild Semiconductor Electronics Corporation plant in Shiprock closed, and Navajo Agricultural Products Industry experienced a shaky beginning. Mineral development had to be depended upon, but protests against it escalated on several fronts. MacDonald advocated expansion of mineral exploitation, with more royalties to the Navajo Nation and better environmental protection. He became a leader in the Council for Energy Resources Tribes. Tribal Council actions displayed more steadfastness than in earlier times, including the rejection of one coal gasification plan and the renegotiation of a coal mining lease. But at the end of the1970s pressures continued upon the Navajos to use their resources in rapid fashion. Tribal leaders faced the recurring quandary of how best to employ those resources (Reno 1981).

The Navajo Nation attempted to gain greater dominion over the corporate development of their land's wealth. In addition to renegotiating leases, the Tribe also tried to control sulfur emissions by passing a Council resolution requiring any industry discharging sulfur or sulfur compounds to purchase a permit. The new regulation contained stiff penalties for noncompliance.

Power companies immediately and unsurprisingly took the matter to the courts. Also, the Tribal Council voted in 1978 to institute a possessory interest tax on companies leasing Navajo land and to tax large business concerns such as General Dynamics Corporation. The legitimacy of these new taxes also would be decided in the courts.

The Navajo-Hopi land dispute also confronted the Navajo tribal government. The issue dated back to the 1882 executive order establishing a reservation for the Hopis "and other Indians as the Secretary of the Interior may see fit to settle thereon." Eventually some of the reserve became assigned exclusively to the Hopis, while the remainder, about 1.8 million acres, became a "joint use" area. In the late 1970s, thousands of Navajos whose families had resided on the land for generations were threatened with immediate eviction. They often were the most traditional, least acculturated people among the Tribe, and given the demands for land elsewhere, they had nowhere to go. At the beginning of the 1980s, the final act of the tragedy was being played out, with relocation seemingly inevitable (fig. 3). As one study observed, Hopi property rights clashed with Navajo human rights, with compromise apparently impossible to achieve (Kammer 1980).

In education and health care, promising beginnings were followed by the challenge of maturation. Though gaining full accreditation, Navajo Community College faced problems of leadership and finances. The Navajo Division of Education continued to sponsor programs to train more Navajo teachers and school administrators and also administered Johnson-O'Malley Act funds but

Navajo Times, Window Rock, Ariz.

Fig. 3. Navajos moved off the Navajo-Hopi Joint Use Area, protesting near the U.S. Capitol against BIA programs for relocation and livestock impoundment on the occasion of a hearing by the Senate Committee on Indian Affairs. Photograph by Paul Natonabah, in Washington, May 18 or 19, 1981.

©Mark Lennihan/*The Gallup Independent*, N. Mex.

Fig. 4. Navajo Tribal Chairman Peter MacDonald at his desk in 1978. Photograph by Mark Lennihan, Window Rock, Ariz.

had no more control than before over the basic, dispersed pattern of curriculum provided by BIA, public, mission, and community schools. More Navajos were seeking health careers, with three completing medical school in the 1970s, but the tribal government did not exercise significantly greater control over the Public Health Service. The Division of Health Improvement Services within the Navajo Health Authority made beginnings in planning and organizing health care delivery. The American Indian Indian Medical School earned approval by the Council but attracted little financial support either from the Tribe or the federal government.

Navajo politics included several controversial incidents. The Navajo Nation had been moving to increase its jurisdiction over non-Navajos when the *Oliphant* v. *Suquamish Indian Tribe* (435 U.S. 191) decision of March 1978 authored by U.S. Supreme Court Justice William Rehnquist contended Indians did not have criminal jurisdiction over non-Indians. The Council then retreated in its efforts. The Navajo Housing Authority's director, Pat Chee Miller, pleaded guilty in March 1977 to conspiring to defraud the government in a kickback scheme involving millions of dollars. The scandal raised larger questions about the Navajo government's financial dealings and prompted several audits. MacDonald was one of the targets of a federal grand jury in Phoenix investigating alleged misuse of federal funds in the Navajo Nation. Though indicted on several counts, MacDonald had all charges dismissed after the jury could not reach a consensus. The chairman probably benefited from the episode, being perceived as harassed by outsiders such as Senator Barry Goldwater. Nonetheless, the indictment diverted his attention from policy issues facing the people.

Given the disappointments of his second term and the tradition of Navajos not to return a chairman to a third term, MacDonald took an unsual step in running for reelection. Challengers came forth in great numbers and the size of the field worked to MacDonald's advantage. His strongest potential opponent, DNA director Peterson Zah, decided not to run and no other candidate generated substantial support. MacDonald easily won reelection as chairman in November 1978 (fig. 4) and pledged that the Navajo Nation would guard its resources carefully and develop its human potential.

The Navajo Nation opened an office in Washington, D.C., on June 1, 1981. Once fully staffed, this office will be responsible for lobbying on behalf of the tribe, and of Native American causes in general, and will monitor relevant action in Congress. In addition, professional researchers, aided by a Navajo youth intern program, will gather information and assist in formulating policy. The Washington office, equipped with computer systems, is a necessary component of the tribe's efforts in nation building and economic development.

The tribal government in the 1970s had shown its willingness to address difficult political and economic questions. It is the primary agency through which solutions to those questions have to be worked out (Iverson 1981).

Navajo Economic Development

DAVID F. ABERLE

In the 1970s the Tribal Council and Tribal administration of the Navajo Nation was trying to cope with many economic and political problems that stem from the colonial situation of the Navajo people. The Navajos' resources are extracted and their labor exploited for the benefit of United States corporations, which largely prevent profitable manufacturing and commercial activities from passing into Navajo hands. Since the Navajo Nation is not an overseas colony but is in the heart of the United States, it may be called an internal colony. Like many non-Indian populations, it is a dependent satellite of the centers of economic and political power in the country, and like other satellite populations, Navajos can vote in state and federal elections (and, as Navajos, in tribal elections). But it resembles other Indian satellite groups more than it does non-Indian satellites, in the degree of control the federal government maintains over the lives of the Navajos. Final approval of Tribal Council actions is in the hands of the secretary of the interior, and the Department of Interior and Bureau of Indian Affairs also have initiatory powers over affairs on the Navajo reservation. Although the ultimate legal repository of power is, of course, the Congress, the Navajos, unlike other satellite groups such as the people of Appalachia, live under the shadow of immediate federal executive control of local government. Because of its relationship to the dominant society's economy and polity, the Navajo Nation's resources are being developed rapidly, while its overall economy stagnates (see Baran 1957; Frank 1967; and especially Jorgensen 1971 for perspectives on the problems of internal colonial, satellite economies). Nevertheless, there has been some economic development since World War II, and the Tribe hopes for more (see Navajo Nation 1972). Tremendous thought, ingenuity, and effort are directed toward economic progress and Navajo control of the Navajo economy (fig. 1).

Navajo Times, Window Rock, Ariz.

Fig. 1. Cartoon accompanying a *Navajo Times* editorial (Anonymous 1980) urging that budgetary priority be given to the Division of Resources. In 1980 the division, headed by Ray Lancer and Ron Izzo, included more than a dozen departments and commissions, such as Land Administration, Water Commission, Navajo Environmental Protection Commission, Fish and Wildlife, Forestry, Range Conservation, Forestry and Recreational Resources, as well as the *Navajo Times*, Film and Media, and the Navajo-Hopi Land Dispute Commission. Cartoon by Jack Jhasteen, 1980.

In what follows, Tribe and Tribal are used to refer not to the Navajo people but to the Tribal government, both the Council and its administrative organization.

The Economy from 1868 to 1933

The first reservation was created in 1868, when the Navajos were released from Fort Sumner. Navajo legal boundaries were repeatedly expanded thereafter, while population increased rapidly from perhaps 9,800 in 1870 to about 38,800 in 1930 (Aberle 1967:162). The territorial expansion, from 3.5 million acres in 1868 to about 16 million in the 1930s, represented more a slow confirmation of actual Navajo occupancy and increasing density than a movement into previously unoccupied land (see Correll 1972; Brugge 1972a; Stokes and Smiley 1964; Kemrer 1974). Eventually, movement of Anglo stockmen into the region halted further expansion of the legal boundaries of the reservation and led to a contraction in the east, where Navajos lived interspersed with non-Navajo ranchers.

Starting with about 15,000 sheep and goats issued to them after the Fort Sumner captivity, besides the residue kept by Navajos who escaped going to Fort Sumner, the Navajos built up their herds to peak at one and one-half million or more sheep and goats in 1885, 1892, and 1915. The range became overcrowded as early as the 1880s; per capita holdings peaked in 1890–1891 at about 100 sheep and goats. In spite of agents' repeated suggestions to increase irrigation and farming and to encourage Navajos to limit livestock numbers and improve livestock quality, the BIA, with limited funds, did little to implement these suggestions or to plan alternative means of livelihood. The BIA provided the Navajos with agricultural tools, some irrigated land, some development of wells and windmills (which permitted denser utilization of the range), some roads and schools, and some instruction in animal husbandry and agriculture.

Meanwhile, Navajo external economic relationships were being transformed. Between 1868 and 1933 the Navajos became increasingly dependent on manufactured goods, provided for them in quantity from 1868 to 1877 in accordance with the treaty of 1868, and therefore increasingly involved in producing goods for the U.S. market to get the manufactured products. They moved from weaving mainly to make their own clothing and bedding to weaving primarily for the market, began to sell wool on the market as early as 1871, and sold sizable amounts even before the railroad reached Gallup in 1882. Thereafter, sales of blankets and wool increased, until by 1890 more than two million pounds of wool were sold. The railroad also made possible large-scale sales of livestock. Traders linked Navajos to the external market and introduced them to more and more manufactures: food, dry goods, clothing, utensils, and tools. The traders began with barter and cash, then briefly used due bills, and moved on to traders' tokens (called "seco"), to credit secured by pawned jewelry, and finally to unsecured credit based on futures in wool, rugs, silver jewelry, sheep, and wages. Pawn was known as early as the 1880s, and unsecured credit by 1910, and probably much earlier, following the creation of border-town wholesale houses. With unsecured credit institutionalized, Navajos became debt peons to traders, a relationship that existed for many Navajos in the 1970s, while the traders themselves came increasingly under the control of large wholesalers. Thus the traders transformed the Navajos into customers for consumer goods and producers of carpet wool, livestock, and luxury crafts. The railroad provided the means for this traffic to expand. The increasing indebtedness of the Navajos suggests increasingly unfavorable terms of trade, but quantitative studies are lacking. Navajos were probably under pressure to build up their herds to cope with a shrinking standard of living. At any rate, their increase of population, environmental degradation, and productive and consumptive roles all have their parallels in other colonial situations (Adams 1963; Amsden 1971:171–187ff.; McNitt 1962; Underhill 1956:176–195; Van Valkenberg and McPhee 1938:37–48ff.).

The Economy from 1933 to 1975

Livestock Reduction

In 1933 the BIA's livestock reduction program initiated direct government intervention in the Navajo householding economy and terminated an economy based primarily on Navajo production of Navajo goods. By 1928 overgrazing, apparent from the 1880s, was regarded by the BIA as critical. Reduction began under Secretary of the Interior Harold L. Ickes and Commissioner of Indian Affairs John Collier. Both were conservation-minded. A supposedly voluntary percentage reduction occurred between 1933 and 1935. It damaged small holders, allowed large owners to cull their herds, and was ineffective. Purchased at low prices during the Depression to distribute to Americans on relief, the stock were sometimes burned on the spot when transportation arrangements broke down—something the Navajos have never forgotten. In 1936 systematic reduction began with the division of the reservation

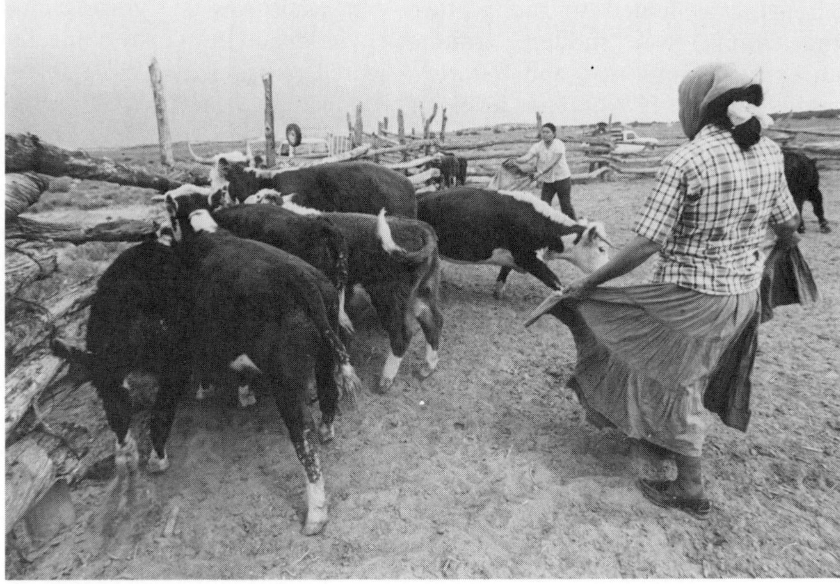

U.S. Dept. of Agriculture, Washington.

Fig. 2. Separating cattle in the corral, preparatory to loading them on trucks to take to auction. The women use skirts and blankets to haze the cattle, while the men more generally use ropes or lariats. Often this is done on horseback. Photographs by John Running, Sept. 20, 1975, near Dinnebito Wash (Hard Rocks area), Ariz.

U.S. Dept. of Agriculture, Washington.

Fig. 3. Cattle auction at Tuba City, Ariz. Photograph by John Running, Sept. 22, 1975.

into Grazing Districts (also called Land Management Units or LMUs; "Development of Navajo Tribal Government," fig. 2, this vol.), the livestock carrying capacity of which was then calculated. In 1937 livestock were tallied and listed by owner, and a maximum permit set for each district; if each person above the maximum sold down to that level and each person below the maximum was frozen at his current level, total livestock for each LMU would equal carrying capacity. Between 1933 and the 1950s, partly because of reduction and partly because of neglect of livestock during the war years, total Navajo holdings declined by some 50 to 65 percent of the prereduction herds. Government-instigated improvement in the quality of Navajo sheep compensated for some of the loss, so that, for example, when the number of livestock units had dropped by 45 percent, the total amount of meat and wool on the hoof had increased slightly. Nevertheless, because of Navajo population growth, per capita holdings dropped drastically—some 65 to 80 percent between 1933 and the early 1950s. The BIA attempted to use public works employment to compensate for the lost livestock, but as Navajos said, those who got the jobs were often not the ones who sold the sheep.

Livestock reduction was the most disturbing event in Navajo life since the Fort Sumner captivity. In the absence of BIA intervention, there would presumably have been an ecological crisis as Navajo population grew, herds increased, and no new acreage was added to the pasture, but as it was, the change was sudden, traumatic, induced by an external authority, and bitterly resented (Roessel and Johnson 1974). The level of production was externally regulated through the permit system. The household urgently required income from sources other than farming, herding, weaving, and silversmithing; seasonal or full-time employment and, later, welfare payments became vital to Navajo survival. Permits established not only who might raise how many livestock but also where, so that movement of a herd from, for example, one's parents' use-right area to one's spouse's area was difficult even within Grazing Districts and almost impossible between them (Aberle 1967:52–90).

Reduction made Navajo life hard from 1936 to 1941, but World War II afforded some relief, since many Navajos were drafted or employed in war industries. Instead of using reservation resources, they provided cash to those they left behind. Their return in 1945 and 1946 precipitated an economic crisis as incomes dropped and more people depended on local resources. An outcome of a Congressional investigation was the Navajo-Hopi Rehabilitation Act of 1950, which authorized more than $80 million during the years 1951–1960 for a variety of programs (Young 1961). In this way the BIA moved from its benignly neglectful caretaker role of the years 1868 to 1932, through the decisive intervention of livestock reduction in the 1930s, to a low-keyed development program in the 1950s.

The Underdevelopment of Livestock and Agriculture

In the 1940s the Tribal attorney called into question the legality of the punitive provisions of the grazing regulations, and they were suspended in 1948, although they continued for some years to inhibit the increase of herds that began slowly in the 1950s. In 1956 the Tribe enacted its own grazing regulations (Young 1961:157–159; Navajo Indians 1962, 1:xi–xii, 1969:T. 3, par. 301–520; Aberle 1967:257–259). By the 1970s, although the permit system continued to prescribe who could graze where, it was largely unenforced and had lost its effect in limiting numbers. In 1970 the Tribe's count showed livestock holdings as numerous as in some years just before reduction, and more meat and wool were produced because of the improvement of the stock. Per capita figures, of course, were far lower than those in the 1930s because of population growth—perhaps one-third of the 1930s figures for small stock (1970s figures from memoranda in author's possession; prereduction figures, Aberle 1967:69–72). Every piece of usable grazing land in the Navajo country has been claimed by some family (Bahe Billy, personal communication 1974).

The BIA, and later Tribal planners, tend to treat traditional farming and herding as relatively insignificant parts of the Navajo economy (Navajo Nation 1972, 1974:41 passim), partly because of the small dollar value of animals and animal and farm products sold plus animals and farm products eaten. Yet most families own some livestock, and no source of income that provides at least some cash and food to so many families can be trivial. Furthermore, the value of livestock consumed is underrated when its price on the hoof is used as a measure, rather than the price of a comparable quantity and quality of meat purchased retail. In addition, since Navajos consume the entire animal, their home-killed meat has higher health value than the muscle meat bought in the store. Finally, a herd is a constantly renewable source of food and income and hence a cushion against employment. No alternative investment of the dollar value of a herd is likely to produce so large a percentage yield, and in fact a family that sells all its stock is more likely to spend the cash for daily necessities than to reinvest the funds.

Prior to the 1960s neither farming nor herding was the focus of much BIA or Tribal development effort. Some irrigated land was developed, especially in the 1930s; from earliest days, watering facilities for stock were increased; and intensive efforts to

Natl. Geographic Soc., Washington/Western Ways, Tucson, Ariz.
Fig. 4. Navajo family collecting water, which was and remains a scarce and valued resource, preparatory to hauling it home by wagon for domestic use. Photograph by Charles Herbert, near Leupp, Ariz., Dec. 1955.

Southwest Mus., Los Angeles:4603.

Fig. 5. Navajo cornfield about 1900, with nearby hogan, lean-to shelter, and 4-posted shade or ramada. Most agricultural work was done by men, as among the Pueblos. Corn was planted in isolated clumps rather than in rows. For discussion of more modern techniques of Navajo farming, see Bingham and Bingham (1979). Photograph by P.G. Gates.

improve Navajo sheep occurred in the 1930s in conjunction with livestock reduction. Livestock increased after World War II, and the range, instead of improving under conservative practice, was further downgraded. It is not surprising that, without adequate alternative means of livelihood, many Navajos tenaciously cling to their livestock.

In the 1960s, with federal funds, active range improvement began in some areas, by chaining and reseeding tracts, providing plastic catchment basins for stock water, and fencing the tracts. Many, but not all, parts of the reservation can thus yield 2- to 40-fold more fodder and hence graze more livestock. Stockmen were given permission to raise additional stock on improved tracts as long as the range was properly maintained, an approach that gave a positive incentive to conservation. By contrast, the regulation of livestock in the 1930s and 1940s required extreme sacrifice and had no appeal for Navajos. The Tribal government has made its own contributions to the livestock industry. Beginning in the 1950s it purchased and operated a number of Tribal ranches. It built wells and, during climatic crises, hauled water and provided emergency fodder. In the early 1970s it began a program of buying wool and marketing livestock, hoping to expand its purchases and to begin to transport both wool and stock. The plan was to increase livestock owners' income by cutting out middleman profits and by holding wool as necessary to stabilize wool prices (MacDonald 1973:76–77, 89). It remains to be seen whether the Tribe can replace the trader in livestock and wool sales without providing new credit facilities, supportive efforts in cooperative buying, and extension services.

Under 1970s conditions, Tribal planners believe that only about 2,500 workers can be supported at an adequate income level in the traditional agrarian sector (livestock and farming) and that even with improvements the number cannot rise above 5,000 (Navajo Nation 1972:4, 5, 25, 26). Evidently the tribe will have to plan for a major restructuring of the work force to lessen agrarian dependency. Unable to survive on either jobs or livestock and farming alone, in the 1970s many Navajos used the extended family to draw sustenance from both sectors, keeping some men at home and deploying others in intermittent wage labor (Uchendu 1966; Aberle 1963, 1969:243–245). Younger people were shifting from sheep and goats to cattle, to reduce the need for daily herding and thereby improve their chances for steady work in border towns or administrative centers.

After 1945 subsistence farming declined, while commercial farming on irrigated land remained more or less stationary. Over the years the BIA had constructed six irrigation projects on which crops were produced for the market, but the allotments were too small for allottees to live on farm income alone. Hence, like families partly dependent on herding, they sought part-time employment in the job market, with a corresponding loss of efficiency in farming (Sasaki 1960). Subsistence farming declined because of the competition of the summer job market.

There is a potential for more irrigated farming for the Navajos. When the San Juan–Chama water diversion to central New Mexico was planned, the Navajos were promised 110,630 acres of irrigated land in return for their rights to San Juan water. Predictably, the government completed all other portions of the San Juan development before turning to the Navajo Indian Irrigation Project (NIIP) (fig. 6), and so the project was slow to start. In the late 1970s some acreage was under irrigation. Whether the Navajo Tribe will be able to secure the water supposedly assigned to them is uncertain because of various complications, including over-commitment of the water estimated to exist in the San Juan and Chama systems and overestimation of that water (Christiansen 1967; U.S. Department of the Interior. Bureau of Reclamation 1967; Navajo Agricultural Products Industry 1974; Reno 1975; Weatherford and Jacoby 1975).

In the 1970s planners hoped this project would provide the basis for a major, modern Navajo agrarian development. The planning agency, Navajo Agricultural Products Industry (NAPI), took over a farm training program near Farmington, New Mexico, in 1970 and then began to plan the development, but many features remained to be worked out. It was estimated that up to 2,400 farm workers might be required if all the acreage was irrigated, and up to another 2,000 in skilled and supervisory activities (Reno 1981:78). It is unlikely that the Tribe can go much beyond NIIP acreage in irrigated farming, since irrigation water will apparently not be available. The Tribe has made its water settlement with the state of New Mexico for 508,000 acre-feet, for NIIP. In Arizona, for complex reasons, it has limited itself to about 50,000 feet from the Colorado River mainstream, of which it allows 34,110 feet to be used for a power plant at Page, until either the plant is terminated or 50 years has elapsed, whichever is sooner, leaving a mere 15,900 feet to the Tribe for all other purposes. Its compensation for this sacrifice has been trivial, and water is crucial to Navajo agrarian development. But barring legal remedies, Navajo access to water from the Colorado Basin will remain limited, due to the actions and inactions of the Tribe and the BIA in the 1960s (MacMeekin 1971).

Given the number of people with some dependency on farming and herding and the plans for expansion of NAPI, the agrarian sector of the economy seems destined to remain critical for the Navajo people for decades to come. At a time when large agribusinesses are squeezing out less technically advanced producers

U.S. Dept. of Interior, Bureau of Reclamation, Farmington, N. Mex.

Fig. 6. Navajo Indian Irrigation Project (NIIP), a BIA project to irrigate over 110,000 acres of land on or adjacent to the Navajo Reservation in northwestern N. Mex., with construction arranged by the Bureau of Reclamation. left, Lee Barber, Navajo farm assistant at the N. Mex. State U. San Juan Branch Agriculture Experiment Station on the reservation, checking gated irrigation pipe in newly planted rye field. Photograph by T.R. Broderick, near Farmington, N. Mex., Sept. 1968. right, First-year crop of milo (a drought-resistant grain sorghum) in a field irrigated by side-roll sprinkler; pumping station with elevated water tank in background. Photograph by unidentified photographer, July 1976.

in the United States as a whole (Jorgensen 1971), the Navajo badly need the agrarian sector as insurance against their uncertain place in the labor market.

Tribal Enterprise

The most profitable resources in the Navajo country are not under Tribal management. They are oil, natural gas, coal, uranium, helium, and water. The extraction of energy resources and helium is in the hands of outside corporations, and so, in significant respects, is water. Other resources are pasture and farmland, utilized by Navajo families in a householding economy, and timber. Given the role granted to the energy corporations and that traditionally assumed by Navajo families, it is not surprising that the scale and scope of Tribal enterprise is small.

In the 1930s the Tribe began to operate the Arts and Crafts Guild, and in 1939 a Tribal sawmill (fig. 7), but there was no other Tribal enterprise until the federal funds under the Navajo-Hopi Rehabilitation Act, augmented by Tribal funds, provided a little money. Between 1951 and 1960 most enterprises developed with these funds were small-scale, labor-intensive, characterized by inelastic demand, and short-lived. The sawmill became the Navajo Forest Products Industry (NFPI) in 1958, later expanded the range of its products and moved to a planned community at Navajo, New Mexico (fig. 8), and in 1974 planned a particle-board plant. The Navajo Tribal Utilities Authority (NTUA), activated in 1959, has expanded ever since. The *Navajo Times,* an English-language newspaper, began publication in 1958. With the exception of these three enterprises, a housing project, and a small coal mine, all the developments of the 1950s are gone (based on Young 1961:178–197).

As for NTUA, by 1973 nearly 40 percent of households had electrical service, but only 20 percent had water and sewer service (Navajo Nation 1974:124). By comparison with 1958, the change was startling; by comparison with national averages, far more change was needed. There is room for expansion, since NTUA has rights to up to 12.5% of the power generated at the Four Corners Power Plant in Fruitland, New Mexico, and the Navajo Generating Station in Page, Arizona, at wholesale prices. The access to this power is somewhat roundabout. The coal that powers these plants is Navajo in origin. The Tribe receives royalties for the coal and then purchases power generated by the coal, while most of the power goes to Phoenix and southern California, the pollution remaining in Navajoland (see Gordon 1973).

Efforts in the 1970s to expand Tribal enterprises by using the model of NFPI, NTUA, and NAPI were not successful. Tribal authorities in the fields of heavy construction, housing, and aviation were created and collapsed. The Navajo Arts and Crafts Enterprises, which replaced the Guild, suffered misfortunes. The role of NAPI was not clarified. A health authority remained active. It was concerned with health statistics and planning, health training for young Navajos, and eventually the development of a medical school for American Indians. However, it was not an economic venture like the terminated ones. If there is a potential for further Tribal enterprises, as there should be, it had not yet been fulfilled.

Private Enterprise

Corporate Development of Energy Resources

As is characteristic for American Indians, while the agrarian sector of the economy remained underdeveloped and Tribal enterprise stayed small, the resources of special interest to corporate industry were being extracted at a rapid rate and with the most up-to-date technology. In the Navajo case, these were nonrenewable energy resources: coal, oil, gas, and uranium. Indeed, the desire of U.S. enterprises to extract these resources led to the creation of the Navajo Tribal Council. In 1921 the first oil lease in the Navajo country was signed shortly after oil was discovered, by an assembly of the adult men of the San Juan Jurisdiction. A year later a short-lived "Business Committee" of three men signed an oil lease of questionable legality on behalf of all Navajos. The oil companies and the Washington office of the BIA, however, wanted an easier avenue than "general councils" of a given region or of the whole Nation, and a more easily defensible legal entity than an appointed Business Committee (see Kelly 1968:47–75). To that end the BIA established the first Navajo Tribal Council in 1923. Essentially its charter provided for BIA control of the Council, which nevertheless sometimes managed to take independent positions. This small Council was replaced in 1938 by an elected Council of 74 members, which continues as the governing body of the Tribe (see Young 1968:60–87, 1972:185–192).

Oil revenues became increasingly important to the Tribe. From 1921 to 1937, inclusive, royalties averaged about $70,000 a year (Kelly 1968:102). Between 1938 and 1956, inclusive, income from lease bonuses, royalties, and rentals, for oil and natural gas, jumped to nearly one million dollars a year (Young 1961:269). An important oil strike in the Four Corners area in the 1950s caused income from oil and gas to jump again, between 1957 and 1968, to about $18 million a year, with wide annual variations (Aberle 1969:234). In the

Bureau of Ind. Affairs, Washington.

Fig. 7. Group touring the tribal sawmill near Fort Defiance, Ariz., on the occasion of its dedication on July 22, 1940. The mill continued to operate until 1963, made obsolete by a sawmill completed the year before at Navajo, N. Mex. Photograph by Milton Snow, Sawmill, Ariz.

left, Jerry Jacka Photography, Phoenix, Ariz.; right, U. of Ariz., Ariz. State Mus., Tucson: 38757.

Fig. 8. Navajo Forest Products Industry (NFPI). left, NFPI's sawmill operation, located about 15 miles northeast of Fort Defiance at Navajo, N. Mex. It markets ponderosa pine under the name Navajo Pine, as well as a variety of wood by-products. Photograph by Jerry Jacka, 1979. right, Housing at Navajo, N. Mex., a development primarily created for Navajo workers at NFPI (sawmill in background). Photograph by Helga Teiwes, March 1974.

late 1960s and early 1970s production of oil dropped, but this was offset to some degree by the rising price of crude oil. At least until 1960, income from helium, uranium, vanadium, and coal was small by comparison with these figures (Young 1961:268).

As the demand for energy increased, coal became more interesting to the mining industry. By the 1970s the Tribe was receiving significant amounts of income from coal royalties, although they did not match the oil income of the 1960s. Portions of the reservation were being made ugly by strip-mining (fig. 9), and fixed royalties, whether for oil or coal, became increasingly disadvantageous to the Navajo as world prices rose. In late 1972 the Tribe expanded and restaffed its Office of Minerals Development, which set forth new policies: monitoring of mining operations, Tribal assessment and evaluation of mineral resources, long-term planning of minerals policy, and improved royalty agreements. Few policies had been implemented by the late 1970s. There was a thrust toward partnership agreements with minerals-extracting corporations. In January 1974 a contract with Exxon attempted to realize some of these goals in connection with uranium exploration, mining, and milling. It provided for possible Tribal participation of up to 49 percent in each uranium venture, royalties based on the selling price of the uranium, development of water wells for the Tribe by Exxon, provision to the Tribe by Exxon of information about other minerals found in the course of uranium explorations, and maximum feasible Navajo employment (author's field interviews; Anonymous 1974). These apparently favorable arrangements concealed grave issues of economic inequities, forced relocation, and radiation pollution. As a royalty taker the Tribe would receive small gains

top left, Bureau of Ind. Affairs, SMC Cartographic Section, Concho, Okla.; bottom left, U. of Ariz., Ariz. State Mus., Tucson: 28896; right, Deborah Confer, Washington, D.C.

Fig. 9. Peabody Coal Company strip-mining at Black Mesa, in northeastern Ariz. top left, General view of strip-mining (a method of exploiting shallow subsurface coal deposits) on the Navajo Reservation. Photograph by unidentified BIA photographer, 1964. bottom left, Closer view of the strip-mining operation by Peabody Coal at Black Mesa, in 1970. Two separate strip-mining leases had been signed with Peabody Coal or its representatives by 1970: a 1964 lease gave the company access to 40,000 acres on the Navajo Reservation, and a 1966 lease added 25,000 acres in the Joint Use Area of the Hopi Reservation (Clemmer 1978:17). Photograph by Helga Teiwes, Sept. 1970. right, Poster distributed by the Committee to Save Black Mesa and the Black Mesa Defense Fund in 1971 or 1972, when Black Mesa was receiving much public attention (see Clemmer 1978:27–31; S. Gordon 1973). Poster features photograph by Marc Gaede of April 17, 1971 demonstration at Black Mesa.

left, Amon Carter Mus., Ft. Worth, Tex.: Laura Gilpin Coll.

Fig. 10. Uranium mining. right, Navajo miner in a uranium mine in the Lukachukai Mountains in N. Mex. Photograph by Laura Gilpin, Aug. 1963. left, Dr. Leon Gottlieb (center) interviewing a family living in a home made of uranium-irradiated materials, as part of a study for the Navajo Tribe. Many houses in the Red Valley and Lake Valley areas were found to have been built with radioactive materials (Anonymous 1980a). Photograph by P.B. Rosen, Jan.–Feb. 1980.

in exchange for its secure return, but to become a profit-taker the Tribe had to provide cash that it could not readily find for its partnership, although it was already supplying the venture's resources. Furthermore, unless the Tribe could inspect and evaluate the books, it might get little return from a venture, as a result of corporate bookkeeping policies. Experience does not indicate that Navajos will benefit greatly in terms of skilled employment or that the "multiplier effect" of resource development will have much impact on the reservation. Exploration and mining would necessitate the forced relocation of Navajos and the disruption of cooperative networks of kin. Most serious, Navajo acceptance of the lease was not based on informed consent, since the Tribal Council had inadequate information, especially about health hazards and problems of land restoration, and because the communities affected by the contract were not consulted. Little of what Exxon knew reached the Department of the Interior, and little of *that* reached the Council or local Navajos. Indeed the draft environmental impact statement was released more than two years after the Council accepted the agreement (see U.S. Department of the Interior. Bureau of Indian Affairs 1976). Aware of the dangers of radiation and fearful of forced relocation, some members of Sanostee and Two Gray Hills Chapters attempted unsuccessful legal action to prevent the secretary of the interior from signing the lease (*Manygoats* v. *Kleppe,* 558 F. 2d 556, 10th Circ. 1977), but he approved it in January 1977. As more and more evidence about increased Navajo morbidity and mortality resulting from uranium mining became available (fig. 10), Navajo complaints grew. Hidden problems had become manifest. The Tribe had signed another disadvantageous minerals contract, with an unusual potential for causing Navajo forced relocation, illness, and death.

Navajo coal is mostly used to generate electricity at the Mohave, Page, and Four Corners plants. Some was slurried to Page from the stripmine on Black Mesa before construction of a railroad to transport it, the only one on the reservation. There are plans for a number of coal gasification plants at the eastern edge of the reservation. These will require extensive planned community facilities to service them, although the scale and location of such facilities is not certain. Slurrying, coal gasification, and urban development all require Navajo water. Furthermore, Navajos gave up water for the sake of employment at the Page power plant—employment to which their access has been sadly limited (U.S. Department of the Interior 1972). By using Navajo water, the energy corporations are setting limits on the future of Navajo economic development.

Since 1954 or before, the Tribal budget has depended on energy revenues. Between 1954 and 1971 these revenues comprised from 50 to 94 percent of total Tribal income, varying over the years but dropping with time. They ranged from as much as 800 percent of the Tribal budget in 1954 to 42 percent in 1966. Income from minerals and total Tribal income vary widely, whereas Tribal budgets have climbed regularly, from $.03 million in 1951 to $20 million in 1971 (communication from the Tribal Chairman's Office, December 13, 1973, providing data on 1954 and for 5-year intervals, 1956–1971). Although the large energy resource income of the late 1950s and early 1960s provided surpluses that made unbalanced budgets possible for a while, the decline of this income in the late 1960s brought a need for balanced budgets.

In sum, the biggest business in the Navajo country is the extraction of energy resources, but all this extraction is in the hands of major U.S. corporations, operating under leases negotiated with the Navajo Tribe and approved by the secretary of the interior, who might or might not approve a partnership arrangement in the future. There is no present prospect of Navajo control of the extraction or processing of these nonrenewable resources. BIA policy and later Tribal policy (under BIA and corporate persuasion) has been to encourage this state of affairs. Tribal planners assert that Tribal resources are constantly depleted, while most of the income from the extraction and most of the immediate benefits of energy consumption accrue to people other than the Navajo, who own the resources (Navajo Nation 1974:136). If exploitation is defined as 'taking undue advantage of another', the Navajo Tribe has been and is being exploited. Although its royalties are larger than those of non-Indian owners of similar resources, it has suffered from the fact that the rate and timing of extraction, and in many ways the terms of payment, have been outside its control, while it has had to make many undesirable concessions to outside interests. The Tribal government's lack of expertise, lack of risk capital, and lack of encouragement all contributed to the situation. Within a capitalist framework, only the availability of venture capital could make possible Navajo extraction and processing of energy resources. Most such activities would require large federal loans or subsidies to provide the capital.

Although the federal government subsidized the railroads in the nineteenth century, through land grants and in other ways, and the war industries in the twentieth, through cost-plus contracts and other devices, it does not subsidize large, profitable business enterprises for tribal operations. Instead, by various actions, it has diverted Navajo Tribal income from potential development activities to service and welfare activities. That is, it has encouraged the Tribe to expend mineral income on the police force and many other items (Robert W. Young, personal communication 1974), some of which might legitimately be considered to be federal responsibilities. Alternatively, the Tribe might have been encouraged to tax corporations on the reservation, as well as draw royalties, rents, and bonuses from them. As examples, in the mid-1970s, it was expected that taxes on the operation of the Navajo Generating Station at Page would provide about $10.5 million a year to the state of Arizona, more than the Navajo Tribe would receive each year from a grand total of coal royalties, coal leases, and the wages of Navajos working in the energy industries (Robbins 1975). The state of New Mexico expects to collect $12.6 million a year in sales taxes alone from coal gasification plants on Navajo lands, or about two-thirds of annual Navajo petroleum revenues in the years 1957–1968 (Anonymous 1975:3). Such a figure illuminates the extent of exploitation of Navajos. In sum, Navajos have no control over their nonrenewable energy resources; profits from extracting and processing them flow elsewhere; and Tribal income from these resources goes to operate government and to supply welfare but not to develop the Navajo economy.

Other Private Industry

Except for extraction and conversion of energy resources, there has been little private industrial development in the Navajo reservation, which has few attractions except cheap wage labor and a favorable tax situation. In the 1960s federal policy provided new inducements for industry to locate in depressed areas, among them Indian reservations. These included preference in sales to federal procurement agencies and federal support for manpower training. For its part, the Tribe offered concessions in the form of low-cost land leases and construction of buildings for low-cost rent and use by new industry (Navajo Nation 1972a). Not surprisingly, the first industries attracted to the Navajo country were those manufacturing goods, mainly electronic, for the U.S. military effort. There was a high rate of turnover of such firms in the 1960s, and in 1972 and thereafter they were adversely affected by the diminishing U.S. participation in the war in Vietnam and by the recession of 1974. The largest of these firms, Fairchild Semiconductor Electronics Corporation, radically reduced its labor force in 1975, in response to the recession. Members of the American Indian Movement (AIM) reacted by occupying the plant for a week. Fairchild then closed the plant and removed the equipment, ostensibly because of the occupation, but inferrably because among its operations in the U.S. and abroad, this one could be closed with minimal cost to Fairchild, and, after the AIM occupation, with minimal damage to Fairchild's public relations. This episode supplies further evidence that these industries were exotic growths in the Navajo country, unrelated to the assets of the region and held by minimal stakes to Navajoland, especially since the buildings used by the firms were owned by the Tribe (Aberle 1968–1974). Nevertheless, the Tribe continued to hope it could attract "footloose" industry in the future (Navajo Nation 1974:56, 135, 140–142).

Amer. Mus. of Nat. Hist., New York: 60001, 60002.

Fig. 11. Street scenes in Gallup, N. Mex., showing 2 of the numerous trading posts. Signs painted on the wall of one of these offer to sell beadwork while picturing a Navajo making it, and to buy sheep (presumably from the Navajo). Photographs by an unidentified photographer during the Gallup Intertribal Ceremonial, held in Aug. 1954.

Retail Business

During the twentieth century the major and almost sole retail businesses on the reservation have been the trading posts. Initially the traders were a powerful force for changing Navajo material culture. After livestock reduction, the traders' hold on Navajos through debt peonage provided the leverage to force Navajos into off-reservation, part-time employment. Control of credit also made it possible for traders to decide whether a given family could afford a ceremony involving large expenditures. After World War II, the trader was no longer the principal source of consumer novelties. With better roads and more trucks, Navajos found these in expeditions to border towns. Nevertheless, traders retained their hold on their customers by providing credit to absorb future income, whether from livestock or from wage work (credit saturation), and by physical control of welfare, social security, and railroad retirement checks, sent through the mail to Navajos for whom the trader was also the postman. By various kinds of pressures, traders managed to make most Navajos turn over these checks in payment of debts or to expend the funds at the post if there were surpluses. The Federal Trade Commission investigated trading posts in 1972, providing publicity for abuses well known in the area: excessively high prices, a tendency for jewelry pawned by Navajos to be "lost" when the time came for redemption, credit saturation, and illegal control of Navajo checks. It criticized the BIA and the Tribe for failure to curtail these abuses—a failure that had gone on for a century in the case of the BIA and a shorter time for the Tribe, which has had the power to cancel leases for cause since 1954 (U.S. Federal Trade Commission 1973; Navajo Indians 1969:T. 5, par. 766). Yet it seems doubtful that regulation of trader conduct can be effective unless Navajos can find some other source of credit against futures in wool, crafts, livestock, or wages; traders had a virtual monopoly on consumer credit except for automobile financing.

Amon Carter Mus., Ft. Worth, Tex.: Laura Gilpin Coll.:4261[1].

Fig. 12. Trader (at left), examining wool in the warehouse of the Red Rock Trading Post (built in 1908), prior to purchasing it. In addition to the shorn wool (stacked at far right), complete pelts (stacked in background at right) and live sheep were normally purchased or taken as barter. Photograph by Laura Gilpin, July 2, 1951.

Smithsonian, Dept. of Anthr.: 404082, 404072, 404065.

Fig. 13. Silver souvenirs. Silver jewelry made specifically for the tourist trade as early as 1899; it was lighter in weight than that made for Navajo use. In the 1920s and 1930s smiths began producing different forms for sale as souvenirs—cigarette boxes, ashtrays, and the like. The nontraditional arrow, swastika, and thunderbird designs stamped on such objects increased their apparent Indianness and thus their salability (Bedinger 1973:115–118). Ashtray width 10.1 cm, rest to same scale.

Few Navajos own trading posts; fewer own large ones. Most trading is in Anglo hands. By the 1970s some large trading posts resembled supermarkets rather than the more familiar old-fashioned country stores. The trader's scope is somewhat circumscribed by the availability of border-town stores and by the greater amounts of cash in Navajo hands. In the 1960s a large discount house opened a branch at Window Rock, providing Navajos with a wider range of goods at lower prices than they could find in trading posts or in border towns and further circumscribing the scope of the trading posts. Most traders' licenses are due to expire in the decade 1980–1990, and the Tribe hopes that Navajos will then take over many of the posts. Because of competition from discount houses and border-town businesses, it seems likely, however, that if Navajos take over posts, they will have to operate smaller-scale establishments than those of the past. Meanwhile, cooperatives showed a modest growth in the early 1970s. Adams (1963) gives details on trading practices until the 1950s.

There is a shortage of other commercial establishments on the reservation. Indeed, there are five or six times as many people for each retail business on the Navajo reservation as in most counties adjacent to the reservation, in the mountain states, or in the United States as a whole (Gilbreath 1972:10, 1973:3–30). Lack of garages, shoemakers, and many other facilities make life unduly complicated for Navajos on the reservation. Although some expansion of service establishments seems likely, the projection is that a rise in on-reservation income will have its principal multiplier effect in border towns, rather than on the reservation, just as it has in the past (David C. Brunt, personal communication 1974). The headstart of the border-town merchants, their incentive to expand where they are, and the lack of Navajo capital alike point in this direction.

Sources of Income

Taxation

The Navajo Tribe has the power to tax and intends to tax industries and large-scale enterprises on the reservation. It is meeting resistance to its efforts in the courts (Levy 1980:17). In the past it has signed contracts that agreed to refrain from taxing, because of its eagerness to attract industry. To an increasing degree, the states in which the reservation lies have preempted potential areas of taxation (see Boyle 1973). The adjacent states benefit more from taxing corporations extracting and processing Navajo energy resources than the Navajos do from selling the resources (Levy 1980; Robbins 1980). Because it has thus far supported itself from nontax revenues, especially from minerals, without the benefit of tax revenues, using its income for government functions and welfare features, the Tribe has been handicapped by lack of funds for economic development.

Navajo Times, Window Rock, Ariz.

Fig. 14. Woman being instructed on how to fill out a pawn registration slip (which includes information such as census number) by a clerk at Little Bear's Market, a trading post in Gallup, N. Mex. Photograph by Paul Natonabah, 1978–1979.

Individual Income

In the 1970s most Navajos were poor and under- or unemployed, but there was income polarization, with a few well-off Navajos and many poor ones. U.S. census data analyzed by Boyle (1972) showed a 1969 median per capita income for Navajos of $831, compared with a U.S. median of $3,700, or 22 percent of the national average. Median Navajo family income was $3,484, as compared with a Black median of $6,000, a White median of $9,794, and a U.S. median of $9,400. Like other Indians, Navajos have incomes far lower than those of non-Indian ethnic minorities. Over the years between 1950 and 1972 while Navajo income rose, the dollar gap between Navajo and general U.S. income increased, and Navajo income stayed at about 22–24 percent of general U.S. income (Navajo Nation 1972:8). In 1969 of more than 21,000 Navajo consumption units (families and isolated individuals), there were about 1,900 with incomes ranging upward from $10,000 to more than $50,000. Yet there were nearly 5,600 units with incomes of less than $1,000. The top 25 percent of consumption units garnered 75 percent of all money income, whereas the bottom 25 percent received less than 3 percent.

Most Navajos who farm and herd are best thought of not as entrepreneurs in the livestock business but rather as agrarians involved in a householding economy. They use their agrarian products for a combination of sustenance and cash income, rather than estimating profit and loss, maximizing income, and reinvesting capital. They normally combine income from farming and herding with that from wage work and sometimes with welfare. Some may shift from this combination to full-time wage work, especially those who are young, educated, and fortunate in finding steady employment, but they tend to have stock cared for by their close relatives. Others may shift toward truly entrepreneurial cattle raising. Some, by reason of misfortune, become almost totally dependent on welfare. Probably there are more livestock-owning householders with wage and welfare income supplements than there are of other categories. Full-time employment, which is perhaps the next largest, is divided into those who spend part of each year on the reservation or live in border towns, and those who have left the reservation with no definite plans to return. These steady workers have incomes from low to high and occupations ranging from common labor to administration. Many of them are close kin of the householders, to whose income they contribute, and who care for the wage earners' livestock. In spite of this sharing, there is polarization, with the agrarian sector largely in the low-income category and the administrative sector in the high-income category.

In 1974, according to the BIA, of a Navajo labor force of 47,000, 45 percent were employed full time and 20 percent part time, yielding a participation rate of 65 percent, an unemployment rate of 35 percent, and an underemployed and unemployed rate of 55 percent. The unemployment rate does not take into account those who have "disappeared" from labor-force accounting because they have become discouraged, no longer seek employment, and retreat to the traditional sector (Navajo Nation 1974:37).

According to the Tribe's own figures, there were only about 14,000 Navajos employed full time in 1974, 66 percent of them in public services. Nine percent were in manufacturing and processing; commercial trades and services, construction, and agriculture and forestry (excluding the traditional sector) employed about 5 or

IT'S A GOOD TIME TO DEAL ON A
Ford
TRUCK
Gurley's takes livestock in trade. When you want to make a down payment, buy parts, pay for repairs or insurance, or make a car or truck loan payment, bring your livestock to Gurley Motor Co. A Gurley employee will go with you to a person who deals in livestock. This person will help set a fair market value on your stock agreeable to you and to Gurley Motor Co. Then you will be credited with that amount toward the purchase or payment you want to make.
Miles Above the Rest
GURLEY MOTOR COMPANY
New Mexico's Oldest Ford Dealership
GURLEY MOTOR CO.
GURLEY'S TRUCK CENTER
one block west and one block south of our car showroom.
701 W. COAL GALLUP, NEW MEXICO

Navajo Times, April 24, 1980:15.

Fig. 15. Advertisement, placed in the *Navajo Times* by a Gallup Ford dealership, offering to take livestock in trade or as down payment on a truck or car. The practice of barter in sheep and other livestock reflects a long tradition of trading post economics.

Navajo Times, Window Rock, Ariz.

Fig. 16. Tseyi' Shopping Center, in Chinle, Ariz., owned by Dineh Cooperative Incorporated (a local community development organization), and developed in cooperation with various agencies of the federal government and the Navajo Tribe (which contributed $900,000 toward the project). Intended to rival privately owned trading posts and retail stores, the development features a large supermarket (at left). Photograph by Paul Natonabah, shortly after its opening on March 14, 1981.

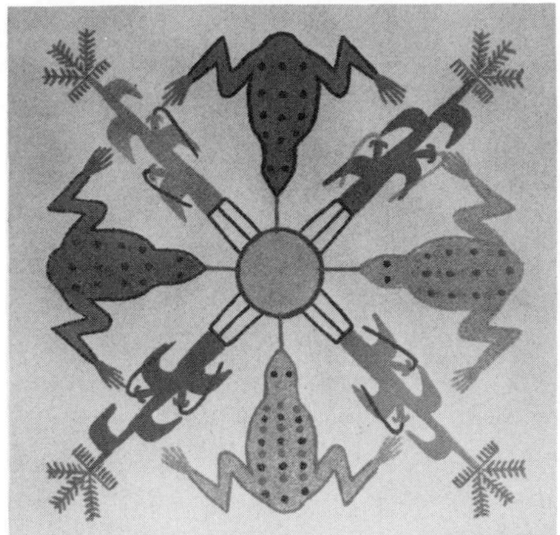

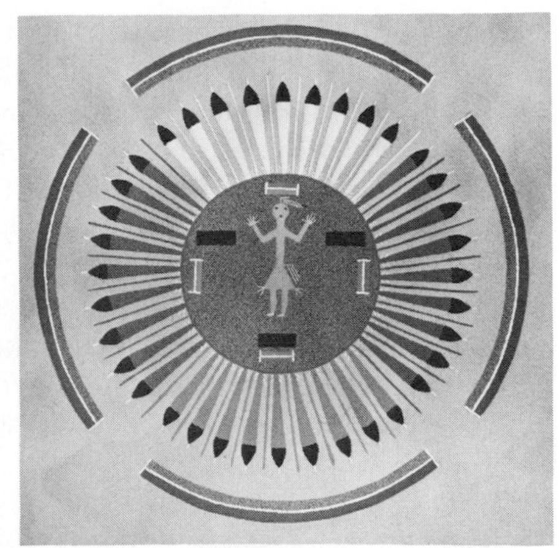

top, U. of Ariz., Ariz. State Mus., Tucson: left, E–8363, center, L–296, right, L–297.

Fig. 17. Commercial sandpainting, a nontraditional art form developed in the 1940s for sale to non-Navajos. In the 1980s over 500 men and women earned their living by the craft (Parezo 1980). top, Sandpaintings of subjects from Navajo mythology: left, *Frogs* by Lucy Curtis, 1969, 30.5 by 30.3 cm; center, *Big Wind* by Francis Miller, 1970, about 70.0 by 70.0 cm; right, *Sun and Eagle* by James Joe, 1970, about 45.7 by 45.7 cm. Nonreligious and non-Navajo subjects are also being produced as individual styles develop. bottom, Alfred Watchman producing paintings by gluing dry materials to particle board, masonite, or plywood. Cardboard stencils and a knife are usually used to make an outline and guide application of materials. Photograph by Richard Erdoes, Ft. Defiance, N. Mex., 1978.

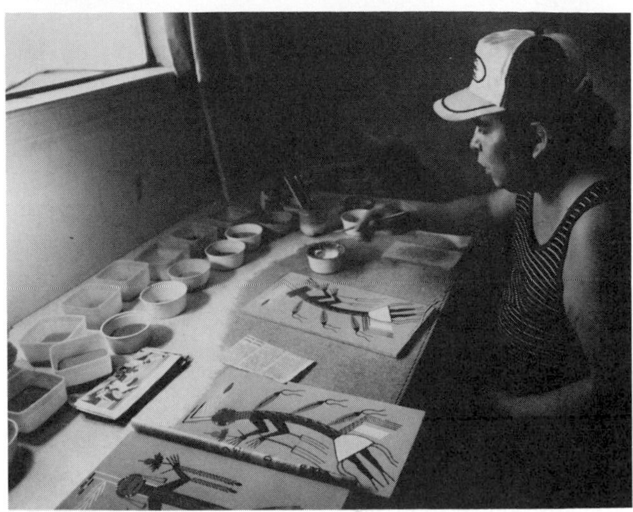

6 percent each; the remainder were distributed among the categories of mining, tourism, transportation, communications, and utilities (Navajo Nation 1974:35–65; see Carter 1970 and Reno 1970 for similar figures).

If "major" employers of full-time Navajo employees are considered, in 1974 the Navajo Tribe was the largest employer in the huge public service category, with the BIA next, followed by the Office of Navajo Economic Opportunity, the public schools, and the Public Health Service, in that order. Employees in agriculture and forestry worked for Tribal authorities, NAPI and NFPI. A sizable minority of employees in transportation, communication, and utilities was employed by NTUA and the Navajo Communications Company, further enlarging the role of the Tribe as employer. The largest single nongovernmental employer on the reservation was Fairchild Semiconductor Electronics, with a payroll of about 1,000, contributing greatly to the employment rate at Shiprock, where the plant was located (all from Navajo Nation 1974:44–45) (these figures are on a slightly different base from those cited in the prior paragraph). Employment in energy industries in 1974 amounted to about 9 percent of the total (Navajo Nation 1974:35–65), but the closure of Fairchild on the one hand, and the expansion of mining, use of a railroad to ship coal, and construction of power plants and perhaps coal gasification plants on the other hand promised an absolute and relative expansion in this sector of employment.

The largest average paychecks, $10,000 a year and up, went to employees in mining, pipeline work, public utilities, and private construction firms, while Fairchild's average was about $6,100, and several Navajo Tribal activities and retail businesses had averages of $4,300 and above (Navajo Nation 1974:35–65).

At the bottom, of course, are Navajos dependent on welfare, whose exact numbers are not known. A minimal estimate emerges from summing the average number a month who receive welfare from the state programs of Arizona, New Mexico, and Utah: 23,000 in 1972. At the same time the BIA provided assistance to nearly 30,000 (figures in author's possession), while the Tribe's emergency relief fund involved 6,330 cases or about 21,000 people (MacDonald 1973:79), and there were people employed on various Tribal public works programs. BIA and Tribal figures cannot be summed or added to state figures because of overlapping recipients.

The colonial character of the Navajo economy is evident (see Frank 1967; Jorgensen 1971). The traditional sector provides the people with insufficient support, while the industrial sector provides almost no employment; the major employer is government. Direct welfare and public works are required to support many people. Conditions would be worse if Navajos did not share income in cash and kind so widely. The major modern technological developments are capital-intensive and use Navajo energy resources for the benefit of large corporations and their customers far from Navajoland. Navajo resources have been developed; a rounded economy for the benefit of the Navajo people has not.

Welfare

The Depression of the 1930s and livestock reduction vastly increased Navajo indigence and led to a considerable dependence on welfare. As the Navajo Tribe's income grew in the 1950s, so did its contribution to a welfare economy. The term is intended to apply to many kinds of benefits other than money payments to indigents: work programs, medical benefits, housing benefits, scholarships, for example. It has two aspects: it supports on salaries and wages many people who deliver services and funds (including the wages for works projects) to a far more numerous clientele. Although the federal contribution to the Navajos' welfare economy was much larger than the Tribal, the Tribal purse contributed 15 percent of all federal and Tribal monies spent in Navajoland in 1967 and 1968, and the Tribe's energy revenues, making up perhaps 60 percent of its budget, supplied perhaps 9 percent of the total (see Harman, O'Donnell, and Henninger 1969:app. L(1):3). The Tribe's funds provide several million dollars for direct welfare in forms specifically tailored to reservation conditions and family crises. They also support perhaps 25 percent of all full-time employed Navajos on the reservation, excluding various Navajo Authorities like NAPI, NFPI, NTUA, and others. The Tribe's major contribution to the welfare economy is evident (Navajo Nation 1974:43–45).

The Tribe is in a bind. If it reduces its income from energy resources, the result will be a reduction in employment and in various welfare benefits, creating serious hardship and popular resentment against the Tribal Council. Therefore, since it cannot easily forego immediate opportunities to sell energy resources in favor of potentially better arrangements at a later date, its bargaining position with the great energy corporation is weak. Yet at prevailing rates of extraction its most easily available resources may be exhausted between A.D. 2000 and 2025, depending on the resource under consideration and future rates of consumption. Hence, if present trends continue, the Tribe is headed for a time when welfare needs will be larger and income from energy far smaller than at present. The Tribe badly needs to develop sectors of the economy that do not draw on these resources, but in the absence of taxation or federal subsidy, the Tribe's own funds for other developments are sharply limited.

Although some of the Tribe's welfare activities might better have been treated as federal responsibilities, it developed a variety of imaginatively conceived programs after the great oil discoveries of the 1950s: emergency transportation, baby layettes, prostheses, burial expenses, emergency relief, housing expenses for the needy, and other programs. Capital funds were set aside, their income to be used for college scholarships for Navajo students. The principal stood at $15 million by 1975. Several millions a year were used for public works programs for students home for the summer and for needy Navajos. These and many other programs provide significant community services.

Factors Contributing to Underdevelopment

The basic obstacle to development is the colonial status of the Tribe. The principal political agency that controls the relationships of the Tribe and of individual Navajos with the larger society is the Department of the Interior, and within Interior, the BIA. It can decide whether Tribal proposals to use funds will be accepted and can make an infinity of other decisions as well. It can also delay decisions, for instance, taking up to nine years to process a Navajo's application for a business site (Aberle 1968–1974; see Gilbreath 1973:41–45). The BIA itself is the weakest arm of Interior and has failed to guard Indian interests against powerful divisions in Interior such as Reclamation, Land Management, Parks, and others. The BIA also fails to protect the Navajos against powerful national and local business interests. The BIA's lack of power stems ultimately from Congressional decisions. Thus Interior has tight control over Tribal affairs, but within Interior the BIA cannot protect the Tribe's interest and often seems actively to oppose it. Congress also limits Navajo development by failing to provide adequate funds for large-scale Tribal endeavors, by its marked tendency to side with non-Indians whenever there is a conflict of interest between Indians and non-Indians, and in many other ways. Obstacles to development also inhere in relations with large-scale energy-extracting and energy-converting corporations, which are interested in their own profits and not in the development of a well-rounded Navajo economy or the economic well-being of the Navajo people. Border communities are concerned with their own development, not the Navajos', and with siphoning the income of individual Navajos into border-town commerce. All these external obstacles to Navajo economic development inhere in the status of the Navajo Nation as an internal colony, and all are shared with other Indian groups.

Internally, the Navajo economy suffers from an underdeveloped infrastructure, an undereducated labor force, lack of capital for Tribal economic enterprises, and lack of capital and credit for individual Navajo entrepreneurial efforts. In 1974 the reservation had about 40 percent of the linear mileage of surfaced roads per square mile found in the non-Indian Southwest and lacked any public transportation system. There was relatively little development of electrical, gas, water, and sewage systems by comparison with non-Indian regions. Average Navajo education in the late 1960s was 5 years, compared with a national average of 12 (Navajo Nation 1968). That implied an inadequately trained labor force and a shortage of all sorts of Navajo technicians, scientists, professionals, managers, and administrators. Without federal subvention, the Navajo Tribe cannot underwrite the kinds of large-scale energy projects that have been so profitable for U.S. corporations. Even without these, if the Tribe had had to use less of its revenues from the 1950s on for welfare, it might have been in a better position to support NAPI, to expand NFPI, and to plan partnership ventures with some energy-extracting and processing corporations. These are some of the obstacles to development that the Tribal government and individual Navajos faced in 1975, more than 100 years after the return from Fort Sumner.

Summary

After Fort Sumner, the Navajo economy was gradually shifted to specialized production for the American market, accompanied by debt peonage. Population growth, fixing of reservation boundaries, lack of agrarian development, and lack of economic alternatives, combined with livestock reduction and control, brought catastrophe after 1933. Few Navajos were or are willing to give up all dependency on livestock or to abandon their place in the Navajo country. To retain both, they are willing to supplement their agrarian income by seeking off-reservation employment, by accepting industrial development on or near the reservation for the sake of the employment it provides, and as a last resort, by falling back on welfare. Some local resistance to industrial development began in the late 1960s and early 1970s, because development displaced Navajos from pastures and farms. The Tribal Council has apparently committed itself to technological change and economic development. It hopes to develop NAPI, to turn NFPI more toward processing timber products, to get increasing control over its energy resources and over processing them, and to use income from these resources for other kinds of industrial development. Some of this might involve processing on-reservation products, such as agricultural produce and wool, and some might involve attracting "footloose" industry (Navajo Nation 1974:121–153). The success of these efforts is unpredictable, but it is a question whether the Tribe can bend the powerful energy-extracting corporations to its own purposes and achieve a more rounded pattern of development. Although in the 1970s most Navajos wanted to maintain a foothold on the reservation, if the population doubles by A.D. 2000, living in Navajoland will become impossible for more and more Navajos.

In the early 1970s local cooperatives were growing—both retail cooperatives and marketing cooperatives of weavers, smiths, and other producers. Since it appears that Tribally-centralized coordination of the economy may become stronger, it is possible that in the future there will be some conflict between local autonomy and Tribal planning. More serious is the conflict between immediate needs of the Navajo people and long-range development, which is apparent to Tribal planners (see Navajo Nation 1974:114–115).

Up to half the surface of the disputed portion of acreage of the executive-order area of 1882 was awarded to the Hopi, and several thousand Navajos were required to move from it (see U.S. Congress 1974). Additional land may be lost in the Moenkopi area. So, to the problems raised by shrinking mineral income will be added those of aiding 6,000 or more Navajos facing relocation and of paying the costs of legal battles to prevent some of the displacement, at a time when all utilizable land is already claimed by some family.

The prospects are for increased extraction of Navajo energy resources by outside agencies, along with local resistance to industrial development. A welfare state is likely to continue. Navajo nationalism and general opposition to manipulation by the dominant society will probably increase, but so, it seems, will conflict within communities, between Chapters and Council, between individuals and Council, between those who want to carry on a traditional life in comfort and those who want on-reservation wage work, and between the small but important sector of the population with fairly high and rising income and the large sector below the poverty level. Many Navajos will need part-time or full-time off-reservation employment, while within the Navajo country, under- and unemployment in the Navajo country are likely to persist. There have been significant changes in the Navajo economy since World War II. Nevertheless, in spite of Navajo effort and thought, the economy remains underdeveloped. Pre-industrial subsistence technology coexists with capital-intensive, complex technology for the extraction of resources, and Navajo poverty goes hand-in-hand with the enrichment of large-scale corporations.

Sources

This article is based both on interviews by Aberle (1968–1974) and on published materials and memoranda. Particularly important were the data acquired through cooperation of the Navajo Nation, and specifically of its Chairman, Peter MacDonald; the former head of the Office of Minerals Development, Robert Schryver, and his staff; the former head of the Office of Labor Relations, Thomas Brosé, and his staff; the then head of Tribal Operations, Cato Sells; the then head of the Office of Range and Livestock, Richard Lynch; the Administrator of Planning and Education for the Navajo Agricultural Products Industry, Bahe Billy; Navajo Community College Economist Philip Reno; and the former head of the Navajo Area Office of Information and Statistics, Melvin Wise.

There are no quantitative data on some important features of the Navajo economy and contradictory data on others. It was necessary to use data based on conflicting estimates for such basic variables as population (see U.S. Commission on Civil Rights 1973:A–62; memoranda in the author's possession from the Office of Information and Statistics of the Navajo Area Office of the Bureau of Indian Affairs; Boyle 1972).

The situation is described, for the most part, as it was in the early 1970s, except for sections on the Exxon lease and on taxation, which reflect the late 1970s. Since the mid-1970s, numerous relevant publications have appeared. Reno (1981) has presented a book-length analysis of the contemporary Navajo economy and its problems, with a brief historical section. Kelley (1980) has made a reconstruction of the pre-Fort Sumner political economy of the Navajo. Jorgensen (1978) has provided a historical analysis of American Indian underdevelopment. Lamphere (1979) has discussed the Navajo pastoral economy and (1976) the process of colonization of the Navajo. Historical treatment of the Collier years has supplied new information on the Navajo case (Parman 1976) and in general, including the Navajos (Philp 1977; Taylor 1980). Aberle (1978) has re-examined the livestock reduction of the Collier period. Kunitz (1977) has dealt with economic variation on the Navajo reservation. Robbins (1978) and Henderson (1979) give information on Navajo wage workers. Some of the problems of NAPI are dealt with by Keller (1979). There have been numerous papers on problems raised for American Indians in general and for Navajos in particular by mineral leases and patterns of mineral exploitation, including uranium contamination (Anonymous 1979; Barry 1979, 1979a, 1980; Barry and Wood 1978; Jorgensen et al. 1978; Levy 1980; Lipton 1980; Richardson 1980; Robbins 1979, 1981; Ruffing 1978, 1978a, 1979, 1980, 1980a). Wood (1979), Wood, Vannette, and Andrews (1979), Scudder (1979), and Kammer (1980) have discussed the effects of the Navajo-Hopi land dispute, including economic impacts. Most of the publications mentioned have brought out clearly the underdeveloped, colonial character of the Navajo economy and analyzed the serious obstacles to development that the Navajo Nation faces. Those who discuss the future favor Navajo control of Navajo resources, the goal sought by so many Navajos, but are well aware of the difficulties of achieving it.

Navajo Education

GLORIA J. EMERSON

The history of Navajo education is the history of the creation and imposition of westernized institutional forms, with varying and often conflicting goals and means. The Navajo were one people sharing a common language, culture, history, and land base, yet this did not seem to matter to the institutional forces. Thus, in 1981, there existed a patchwork of four basic institutions providing formal education for the Navajo—the Bureau of Indian Affairs (BIA) schools, the public schools, the community-controlled (contract) schools, and the mission schools (table 1). Except for the contract schools, these institutions have been educating Navajo children to become "biological Navajos" without knowing their tribal history, culture, language, or land. All but the mission schools are dependent upon the federal government for funding. Each funding agency dictates its own organizational goals and philosophy, which are reflected on the reservation as a microcosmic target of federal monies. Within the microcosm the empires coexist uneasily, often competing for the same pot of monies, for public support for their goals, and inevitably, for children to justify their budgets.

Because of the commitment the federal government made to educate Navajo people in the peace treaty of 1868, and because the Navajo Tribe is dependent upon the federal government for school funding, the government has been responsible for the westernization of Navajo education.

Historical Overview

After the United States government conquered the Navajo in 1868, and placed them as wards on the reservation, public interest in Indian affairs waned. This resulted in Indian agents' running reservation affairs for several decades without active supervision. The compulsory school attendance provision of the peace treaty of 1868 further alienated Navajo parents who tried to protect their children from meddlesome Indian agents bent on sending children off the reservation to far away schools. This continued until the 1930s. Throughout this time, education programs, resource development, jobs, and paved roads were all nonexistent.

In the 1930s, when John Collier became commissioner of Indian affairs, he was determined to eradicate the extremely impoverished conditions on Indian reservations, particularly among the Navajo, and so he generated a furor of zealous activity and national sympathy to vitalize decaying Indian programs. Collier supported community development processes; as a result he helped to create a network of community day schools on the Navajo reservation.

Much of what was started by Collier in the 1930s was delayed by the national priorities of World War II. Schools idled. Facilities deteriorated. School-age children were not being served because there were no facilities to accommodate them. Still, a few communities voluntarily kept their day schools open. Then the returning Navajo war veterans accelerated the Tribe's interest in education. Although only a fledgling interest, it was a change from the anger and resistance of the 1800s and the apathy of the early 1900s.

In the 1950s the prevailing national policy was similar to that before the 1930s. Public sentiment to see Indian people assimilated into the American mainstream and public interest in terminating Indian trust responsibilities recurred. This sentiment influenced BIA education. In the 1950s public schools on the reservation were established, while mission schools continued.

In the 1960s different policies were espoused in the administrations of Presidents John F. Kennedy and Lyndon B. Johnson. The Office of Economic Opportunity (OEO) endeavored to make war on poverty and outlined ways to create change, by involving local people in the formation and development of government agencies. Those policies and funds dramatically increased Navajo participation in programs that proliferated on the reservation, from Headstart (with 114 centers) to legal aid and similar community action pro-

Table 1. Enrollment in Navajo Schools, 1973

School System	*Enrollment*
Mission	1,000
Federal-BIA	24,248
Public	29,404
Community controlled	946
Tribal (Headstart and Homestart)	2,431
Special Education	414
Total	58,443

SOURCE: U.S. Department of the Interior 1973.

grams. The Collier ideas of the 1930s re-emerged in new forms.

The OEO program was a catalyst for curriculum development in the BIA. The public schools received additional funds from OEO for innovations such as parental involvement, pilot bilingual education classes, curriculum and materials development, and teacher training. These were funds over and above those due from the Johnson-O'Malley Act of 1934, Public Law 81–815, and Public Law 81–874, all three known as impact-aid legislation, which usually supported the public schools in areas heavily affected by the presence of the federal government.

During the 1960s and 1970s many Navajos had graduated from colleges or were working on degrees. Some planned to wrest control from non-Indian school officials and staff, not only on the reservation but wherever there was a heavy enrollment of Navajo students (table 2). In 1966 a community-controlled contract school, the Rough Rock Demonstration School, in Rough Rock, Arizona, emerged. It contracted with the BIA to open a school based upon the principles of community action, bilingual education, and Navajo cultural studies.

In the early 1970s more community-controlled contract schools were opened. The use of a bilingual curriculum expanded, and other instructional innovations were experimented with. Student dissatisfaction in the early 1970s forced an articulation of a "student rights code" in BIA school policies. The Navajo Tribe created a Navajo Division of Education in 1971 but tied its hands by not giving it sufficient powers to establish an authoritative Tribal governmental educational agency similar to a state education agency. In spite of some dramatic improvements in Navajo education since the 1940s, the educational institutions in 1981 were still dominated by the mercurial demands of the taxpayers, the politicians, policy-makers in Washington, D.C., and elsewhere, and the local bureaucrats running the schools.

Since the 1960s, the BIA has suffered a steady decline in student enrollment. From 1971 to 1976 the number of boarding students decreased at the rate of 1,000 students per year (Resta and Kelly 1980). The BIA is property owner of deteriorating facilities, many of which are empty, due to demographic changes following economic change as well as to the attitude of Navajo parents who believe their children should attend better-equipped White schools. The deterioration of the BIA facilities in the 1970s is related to the crash construction phase of the 1950s when the BIA economized by buying quantity rather than quality (Resta and Kelly 1980) at the urging of the Navajo Tribe in order to speed up the school construction (Young 1961). In addition, many of the buildings were poorly designed.

Table 2. Schools Serving Navajo Students, 1978–1979

Bureau of Indian Affairs Schools	*Contract Schools*
11 day schools	5 in Arizona
44 boarding schools	2 in New Mexico
Bordertown BIA Dormitories	*Off-Reservation BIA Schools*
4 in Arizona	Intermountain Indian School (Utah)
3 in New Mexico	Albuquerque Indian School (N. Mex.)
1 in Utah	Haskell Institute (Kan.)
1 in Colorado	
Reservation Public Schools	*Off-Reservation Public Schools*
22 in Arizona (14 districts)	29 in Arizona
20 in New Mexico (2 districts)	55 in New Mexico
1 in Utah (1 district)	7 in Utah
	11 in Colorado
Reservation Private Schools	*Reservation Mission Schools*
A School For Me (N. Mex.)	9 in Arizona
Navajo Academy (N. Mex.)	5 in New Mexico
Shiprock Alternative High School (N. Mex.)	*Off-Reservation Mission Schools*
Navajo Special Education Early Childhood Development Program (N. Mex.)	2 in Arizona
Coyote Canyon Special Education (N. Mex.)	3 in New Mexico
St. Michaels School (Ariz.)	
114 preschools, Office of Navajo Economic Opportunity (Ariz., N. Mex.)	
Reservation Colleges	*Near-Reservation Junior Colleges*
College of Ganado (Ariz.)	2 in Arizona
Navajo Community College, Tsaile, Ariz.	2 in New Mexico
Navajo Community College at Shiprock, N. Mex.	
Vocational Schools	
Navajo Skills Center (N. Mex.)	
Southwest Indian Polytechnic Institute (N. Mex.)	
Technical-Vocational Institute (N. Mex.)	
Holbrook Vocational Training Center (Ariz.)	
Cortez Mission School (Colo.)	

SOURCE: Resta and Kelly 1980.

Navajo educators have not developed quantitative instruments to measure "quality." Using general American criteria of education, the scholastic achievement scores of the Navajo student were far below national norms in the 1930s. In the 1970s the scores were still below national norms, with a few exceptions, notably Rock Point Community School (contract).

Because the Navajo Tribe has not authorized its own Division of Education (NDOE) to set up curriculum, teaching certification, or instructional standards, or otherwise established these, the BIA, public, mission, and contract schools all follow their own standards and have created a fragmented approach to Navajo education. The results are a costly duplication of efforts and uneven accountability, with most of the curriculum still dominated by the textbook approach designed by commercial publishers. On the other hand, the school institutions fear the day when the Tribe assumes responsibility for the systems because of the incredible maze of politics in the Tribal government that may impede constructive evolution.

Four Concurrent School Systems

BIA Education

BIA education during the 1950s was the foundation on which changes were made during the 1960s and 1970s, and it remains a significant part of the Navajo educational process. The BIA helped create the off-reservation public school program during the 1950s. It was the BIA that furnished information to Congress in support of Public Law 81–474 (Navajo-Hopi Rehabilitation Act of 1950), which encouraged the BIA to transfer responsibilities for the education of Navajo children to the public schools. The federal government pledged funds for public schools under Public Laws 81–815, 81–874, and 81–474, as well as the Johnson-O'Malley Act.

It was the paternalism of the BIA at the regional level that resulted in the establishment of the community-controlled contract school. In reaction to the paternalism, the Navajo people proposed an alternative to BIA education. During the hearings and discussions leading to Public Law 93–638 (Indian Self-Determination and Education Reform Act) and later Public Law 95–561 (amendments to education laws), administrators in the BIA saw many obstacles to the contract school.

• 1950–1980 In the 1940s the BIA hired George Sanchez to review the state of Bureau education. Sanchez recommended the construction of a new system of schools and a dramatic increase in funds to meet the needs of out-of-school students. He estimated that such changes would provide space for 75 percent of the 1946 school-age population. He recommended 10 elementary school districts on the reservation and a centralized high school, while the older students should continue their education outside the reservation. But in a survey of the water supply for the proposed school facilities, G.A. Boyce found that it was insufficient to build the recommended constellation of reservation schools. He recommended that students be placed in semipermanent dormitories in the towns bordering the Navajo reservation.

These two documents went into a report prepared by Secretary of the Interior Julius A. Krug, who had visited the reservation, that spelled out a state of emergency, identified a list of needs, and recommended assimilative-type resolutions. Public Law 81–474, the Navajo-Hopi Rehabilitation Act of 1950, grew out of Secretary Krug's report. This act outlined a comprehensive program to conserve and to develop Tribal natural resources and to generate employment and rehabilitative resources on and off the reservation. Nearly 25 million dollars was allocated for school construction. Since Navajo natural resources were seen as completely inadequate for development, the BIA decided to implement Krug's recommendations to assimilate the Navajo as rapidly as possible, and emphasized plans for off-reservation schooling. At the urging of the Bureau of the Budget, the BIA acted contrary to Sanchez's (1948) recommendations and used existing off-reservation facilities rather than constructing new buildings on the reservation.

Calif. Histl. Soc., Los Angeles: Title Insurance Coll.: top, 3251; bottom, 3218.
Fig. 1. Government boarding school at Tohatchi, N.Mex., around 1900. bottom, Children entering the school wear government issue clothing with older boys in long pants and jackets. Photographer(s) unidentified.

Public Law 81–474 provided for construction of school facilities on the Navajo reservation to accommodate all school children on a boarding or day basis, implementation of elementary and vocational education for 12–18 year olds (the Special Navajo Education program), development of high school opportunities on and off the reservation, and transfer of responsibility for the education of Navajo and Hopi children to public school systems as rapidly as possible.

The Tribe felt that the BIA was "too slow in constructing schools for children who were not in school" and urged the BIA to move more quickly (Young 1961).

Smithsonian, NAA: 54624, 54624A.

Fig. 2. Navajos at Carlisle Institute, Carlisle, Pa. top, Capt. R.H. Pratt (seated on porch) with a group of newly arrived students, probably among the group of 17 Navajos recruited (with missionary support) in 1882, which included 3 of Chief Manuelito's sons (one is seated second from left) and Tom Torlino (standing at left), the son of Torlino, an influential headman. Sons of both leaders died at Carlisle (Woerner 1941:30–36). bottom, Some of the same students in the more "civilized" haircuts and uniforms of Carlisle 6 months after their arrival. Photographs by J.N. Choate.

Both the Tribe and the BIA decided that school allocations should be reprogrammed to secure more for the money, a decision informally called the "two for one" formula (Resta and Kelly 1980).

The BIA then proposed the Navajo Education Emergency Program (NEEP), which called for (1) construction of trailer schools, (2) construction of public schools on the reservation, (3) expansion of boarding schools, (4) conversion of Shiprock High School to an elementary school, (5) creation of the Special Navajo Education program, and (6) establishment of border-town dormitories. On March 3, 1954, the Navajo Tribal Council unanimously passed a resolution endorsing NEEP (Young 1961:16–17) and granting Commissioner of Indian Affairs Glenn Emmons permission to implement the NEEP plans swiftly. Construction was begun and programs developed immediately. The Council later regretted its rash action of unanimously approving NEEP because the border-town dormitory concept became controversial (Roessel 1979:30).

Public Law 81–474 vitalized programs on the Navajo reservation. Unfortunately the vigor was colored by an assimilative thrust as the federal government was determined to relocate Navajos off the reservation "to become civilized." This perpetuated the educational philosophy of Capt. R.H. Pratt, founder of the Carlisle Institute in Pennsylvania in 1879, who advocated moving students into boarding schools far away from their homeland and keeping them from Indian ways of life (fig. 2) (Dale 1949:178).

• SPECIAL NAVAJO EDUCATION PROGRAM In 1946 only 6,000 out of 24,000 Navajo school-age children were in school; the need to enroll students was paramount (Coombs 1962). Since the Bureau of the Budget was against building new schools on the reservation Hildegard Thompson, director of education in the BIA, was forced to improvise. A Special Navajo Education Program, also called the Five Year Program, was designed and launched in 11 schools off the reservation. The goal was to reach as many of the 12-to-18 year old students as possible. Between 1951 and 1961, 4,347 students graduated from eight schools (Young 1961:46).

Under this program for the first time the BIA allowed the use of the Navajo language for instruction. Use of the Navajo language was decreased as the proficiency of the students in English increased.

The criticism of this program is that many students were channeled into it who should have gone into a full academic program and did not. Yet otherwise thousands of Navajos might never have gone to school at all. This program was one of the BIA's successful ones, even if the intention was to "assimilate" Navajos.

• SCHOOL OPERATIONS, 1950S From 1951 to 1961 the BIA operated six types of schools: boarding schools (table 3; fig. 3); day schools (43 were built in the 1930s; in the early 1950s there were 13; by the end of the 1950s, 11); trailer schools (there were 37 in 1954); reservation dormitories (there were 3 in 1959); border-town dormitories; and off-reservation schools, several of which had been built between 1880 and 1902 (Young 1961).

• BORDER-TOWN DORM PROGRAM Another NEEP program, the border-town dormitory project, became of concern to the Navajo people. The BIA negotiated a 20-year agreement with several towns that border the Navajo reservation. The BIA would pay the town public schools $1,000 per Navajo enrolled. The BIA would maintain boarding facilities for the students while they attended the public schools. In 1955, six towns were involved, serving 1,030 students. When four more were added, there were 2,441 students in 1971. In 1976 there were 1,346 students; in 1978, 1,359 students.

The controversy over border-town schools was that

Table 3. Enrollment in BIA Schools, 1939–1976

Year	Day School	*Enrollment Percent*	*Boarding School*	*Enrollment Percent*
1939	2,262	49%	2,401	51%
1955–1956	2,348	14	13,997	86
1965–1966	1,865	10	17,255	90
1969–1970	2,736	13	18,967	87
1970–1971	3,925	17	19,205	83
1971–1972	3,600	16	18,494	84
1972–1973	3,380	16	17,216	84
1973–1974	3,429	17	16,431	83
1974–1975	3,432	18	15,488	82
1975–1976	2,560	16	13,904	84

SOURCE: Roessel 1979.

the program was originally conceived for students 12 years old and older. However, the BIA maintained a practice of enrolling younger pupils in order to fill empty beds; from 1957 to 1964, from 33 to 45 percent of the students enrolled were under 12 years old. Paul Jones, Tribal chairman, condoned the practice since the expansion of the off-reservation facilities went faster than on-the-reservation construction, creating vacancies in the dormitories (H. Thompson 1975). This program significantly altered Navajo family structure by creating institutional surrogates for thousands of young children.

Another point of contention was that the BIA was building off the reservation instead of on the reservation. In 1959, two prominent Navajo educators, Dillon Platero and Allen Yazzie, who were also council members, questioned the BIA's construction plans (Roessel 1975:25).

In 1975 some of the agreements between the BIA and the town public schools lapsed. There was less interest in the partnership arrangement since there was no money available for school construction. Perhaps some of the problems inherent in this program were also reasons for the waning interest in this approach.

• TRAILER SCHOOLS The BIA installed 37 trailer schools around the reservation. These portable, modest schools played a vital function in the Navajo communities wherever they were located. The trailer school helped to localize education and to reinforce community interaction with the school (Roessel 1979:34). Ernest Magneson, assistant chief of special programs for the Navajo area, believed that the BIA might have done well to invest more in the trailer school approach (personal communication 1981).

• 1970S In the 1970s, the Navajo Area School Board Association (NASBA) was organized. Its main function was to train local school board members for their duties. It also reviewed and interpreted the complex and continuous changes in federal legislation that affect Navajo education, acting as a liaison between the BIA and the board members. Its mission is to prepare school boards to exercise their responsibilities under Public Law 93–638.

John Collier Jr., San Francisco, Calif.

Fig. 3. Navajo Mountain Community BIA School. top, Hogan-like structures. bottom, Children playing trading post, one of them holding what appears to be a Navajo-woven checkerboard. Photographs by John Collier Jr., about 1950.

Mission Schools

Although smaller in enrollment than BIA schools, mission schools have had a great influence by educating many who became Navajo leaders. The major schools are the Navajo Methodist Mission, established at Farmington, New Mexico, in 1912, and the Ganado Mission (Presbyterian), Arizona, established in 1906 and closed in the 1950s after the opening of the Ganado Public School. The Saint Michael's Mission School (Roman Catholic), Saint Michael's, Arizona, was opened in 1902, while the Rehoboth Mission School (Christian Reformed) opened in 1903. In 1960, there were about 20 mission schools, with a total enrollment of 1,300 students. In 1973, there were 21 mission schools with a total enrollment of 1,000 students (table 1) (Young 1961).

Reservation Public Schools

During the 1940s public schools were established for the children of non-Indian BIA employees on the reservation and were called "accommodation schools" (H. Thompson 1975).

The BIA, wishing to relinquish its education responsibilities to the states, requested the states to review the situation. Both New Mexico and Arizona conducted an exhaustive study of Navajo schools. In 1952–1953 New Mexico took over the Mexican Springs and Church Rock BIA schools while Arizona took over Sawmill.

top, Amon Carter Mus, Ft. Worth, Tex.: Laura Gilpin Coll. 3792: [7]; bottom left, Natl. Arch., Washington: Bureau of Ind. Affairs Coll.: 75–N–Nav. 237; bottom right, Heard Mus., Phoenix, Ariz.: NA–SW–Na–R–405.

Fig. 4. Crafts programs at the federal Indian school at Fort Wingate, N. Mex., a vocational school from 1926 until the mid-1950s. The school held annual arts and crafts exhibitions beginning in the 1930s and pioneered an arts and crafts guild that was a model for the later Navajo Arts and Crafts Guild (Parman 1976:210). top, Silversmithing class taught by Ambrose Roanhorse (standing at right), an influential Navajo silversmith. Photograph by Laura Gilpin, Sept. 1955. bottom left, Weaving room. In addition to weaving experiments, various programs in sheep raising and wool processing were conducted in cooperation with a nearby sheep breeding station (Shiskin 1944). Formal instruction in weaving at federal Indian schools dates from at least 1905 (Woerner 1941:51). Photograph by BIA photographer, 1940. bottom right, Rug woven at the school, about 1943. The DuPont chrome dyes (blue-gray, brown, purple, peach, green, and light green) used on the weft wool were an attempt to achieve the colors of vegetable dyes with a commercial product. Size about 84.0 by 134.6 cm.

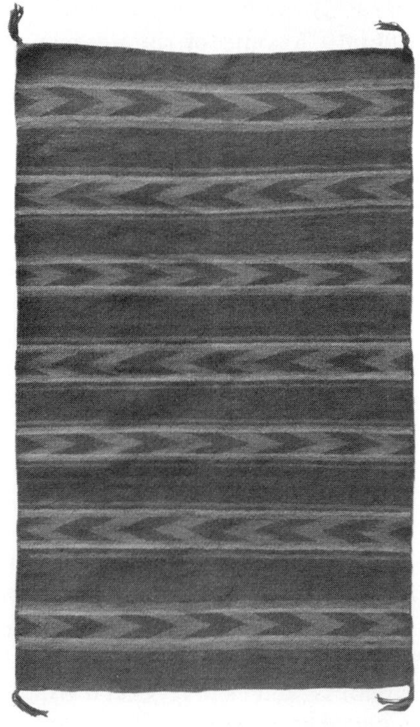

In 1953–1954 Arizona took over the Window Rock schools.

The reservation public school was sanctioned in 1934, with the passage of the Johnson-O'Malley Act (48 Stat. 996), which made it possible for the secretary of the interior to contract with individual states and others, to provide education, medical care, and other services for Indian people. However, it was not used until the 1950s on the Navajo reservation. Public Law 81–815 provided for public school construction. The first school built under this law was opened in January 1954 at Fort Defiance, Arizona. Public Law 81–874 allocated money for school operations. Combined, Public Laws 81–815 and 81–874, known as the School Assistance in Federally Affected Areas Acts, have accelerated the construction and operation of public schools since the 1950s.

The BIA implemented a policy that all students who lived within one and one-half miles of a paved road could not attend BIA schools, with some "social exceptions" for students who had behavioral or family problems. This policy coupled with the paving of highways throughout the reservation helped to increase enrollment in the public schools.

By the end of 1960 there were 21 public schools on the reservation with an enrollment of 7,470 students. In 1954 there had been only 2,830 students. Table 4 shows the dramatic increase in public schools by the 1970s. These students were transfering from the BIA schools to the public schools, resulting in an uneven distribution of money and facilities between the BIA and public schools.

In the early 1970s there was a public outcry over misuse of federal funds by public school officials, including funds from Title I of the Elementary and Secondary Education Act (Public Law 93–380) and Johnson-O'Malley. Monies earmarked for Indian students were being used for all students, which only helped to sharpen the inequities between the non-Indian student and the Indian student.

By the middle of the 1970s and later, the most pressing issue was the continuous struggle with the state public school officials over school finance inequities. The reservation public school officials said they were underfunded and that most public school monies went to the richer school districts off the reservation. The state school officials counter-claimed that the reservations did not have a state tax base and thus created a burden on the states. Reservation school officials countered that the industries on the reservation and the natural resources being extracted yielded revenues to the surrounding states far exceeding any taxes spent on schools.

The Window Rock Public School district compiled evidence and position statements that detail the issues. Central to the conflicts are questions of jurisdiction and responsibilities among the federal government, the state governments of Arizona, Utah, and New Mexico, and the Navajo Tribe (Roessel 1979:179–192).

Table 4. Enrollment by Type of School, 1939–1976

Year	*Total in School*	*BIA*	*Public*	*Other*	*Out of School*
1939–1940	5,120	4,663	98	359	6,010
1969–1970	51,860	23,164	25,002	3,694	5,757
1970–1971	55,081	23,679	26,973	4,429	4,776
1971–1972	55,846	22,146	29,404	4,296	4,061
1972–1973	54,134	20,446	29,378	4,310	4,223
1973–1974	54,210	20,128	29,427	4,655	3,965
1974–1975	52,804	18,913	29,288	4,603	7,532
1975–1976	55,099	18,057	32,369	4,673	4,832

SOURCE: Roessel 1979.

In the 1970s, there were several issues with respect to public schools. One was the lack of Navajo representation on the boards of schools with significant Navajo enrollment. The other was the lack of relevant and appropriate curriculum for the Navajo students. Concern over these and other issues prompted greater Navajo participation in these schools.

Community-Controlled Contract Schools

A community-controlled contract school is a school in which the educational services have been contracted for by an established and recognized school board made up of local community people. Provisions for such an arrangement are made possible under the guidelines of Public Law 93–638, enacted in 1975.

Public Law 93–638 was a tremendous boost to local Navajo education without the hindrance of bureaucratic governmental structures. In the 1960s, the OEO funds created a sweeping change on the Navajo reservation. In the 1970s, Public Law 93–638 has also dramatically speeded up the efforts of the Navajo people "to take control of their own destinies" in a variety of different types of programs. The community-controlled contract school has become sophisticated in the art of contracting, in negotiations, and in contract management.

In 1977–1978 there were five contract schools with an enrollment of over 1,300 students (see table 5). The pioneer Rough Rock Demonstration School was established at Rough Rock, Arizona, in 1966 (fig. 5). The emphasis of contract community-controlled schools was community relevancy, use of the Navajo language and culture, and community control. Rough Rock Demonstration School was followed by the Ramah Navajo High School, established in 1970 by the Ramah Navajo School Board. The high school was later expanded and moved to a new location and called the Pine Hill Schools of Pine Hill, New Mexico. The other community-controlled contract schools in 1981 were in the communities

Table 5. Enrollment in Contract Schools

Year	*Rough Rock*	*Rock Point*	*Ramah*	*Borrego Pass*	*Black Mesa*
1966–1967	260				
1972–1973	409	359	130	80	
1973–1974	461	355	142	105	
1974–1975	267	315	164	121	
1975–1976	338	316	395	104	
1976–1977	426	345	399	110	
1977–1978	471	327	410	123	40

SOURCE: Roessel 1979.

of Borrego Pass and Shiprock, New Mexico, and Bird Springs, Black Mesa, Kitsillie, and Rock Point, Arizona.

Of all the contract schools, the Rock Point model is the most structured and contains a self-evaluation procedure. It has a fully integrated Navajo language and an English-as-a-second language model that has been under extensive evaluation. The preliminary findings indicate that bilingual education has influenced a steady increase of student achievement at Rock Point.

The primary issues of the contract school have been over funds, of streamlining the inefficient Public Law 95–561 contracting process, in promulgating contract school goals in the face of BIA opposition, and of stabilizing internal managerial, curricular, and evaluation processes. In 1981 the community-controlled school model was of great interest to Navajo people, legislators, and other educators.

• CURRICULUM AND INSTRUCTION, 1946–1980 Until the 1970s curriculum and instruction on the reservation followed the pattern of Navajo education: haphazard, insensitive, and often the result of the powers of the time. In the late 1970s and early 1980s numerous curriculum development production projects and centers sprang up around the reservation to address the array of curricular concerns.

Curriculum and instruction in most of the school systems was largely textbook-oriented, selected by well-meaning teachers trained to review and select such commercial programs. Prior to coming to the reservation, many of the non-Indian teachers had limited exposure to Indian people or to cross-cultural, linguistic, and Indian history courses. Moreover, reservation public school systems adhering to state school standards purchased materials from the state textbook list, which is a selection of the commercial programs.

During the 1940s Robert Young and William Morgan, linguists, had done much to codify and to write Navajo language materials (fig. 6). But the Navajo language was banned from use in the reservation classrooms until the 1950s. During the late 1960s and 1970s with the renewed interest in bilingual education, Morgan and Young went back to work writing more materials, and they were joined by others.

Although the OEO War On Poverty influenced parts of the BIA education process, in the 1960s the BIA maintained the course it had established in the 1950s. The main influence of OEO on the BIA was that OEO provided supplementary monies that stimulated several

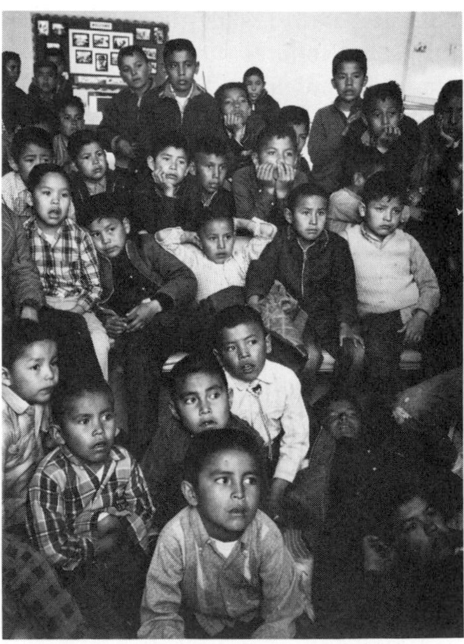

Robert Roessel, Jr., Chinle, Ariz.

Fig. 5. Rough Rock Demonstration School programs. left, Students resting at a hogan during an annual 3–4 day field trip to Canyon de Chelly. right, Boys in the boys' dormitory listening to a talk by a Navajo medicine man, part of a regular program to bring medicine men to the school to give lectures. The school also sponsored an apprenticeship program for medicine men (see "Navajo Health Services and Projects," fig. 6, this vol.). Photographs by Robert Roessel, Jr., 1970 (left), and Paul Conklin, 1976.

my mother cards the wool.
shimá 'aghaa' hanéiniłcha'.

my mother spins the wool.
shimá 'aghaa' hanéiniłdis.

my mother cards the wool.
she takes out the knots.
she makes soft rolls of the wool.
my sisters help my mother card the wool.
shimá ha'niłchaad.
'aghaa' yikáá' yits'ih.
'aghaa' yilzhóólígo dayiidis.
shádí dóó shideezhí shimá yił ha'niłchaad.

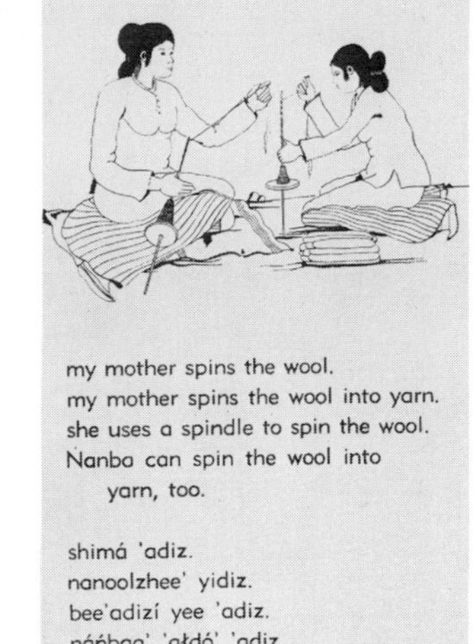

my mother spins the wool.
my mother spins the wool into yarn.
she uses a spindle to spin the wool.
Nanba can spin the wool into yarn, too.
shimá 'adiz.
nanoolzhee' yidiz.
bee'adizí yee 'adiz.
náńbaa' 'ałdó' 'adiz.

In the morning
when my father
leaves for meeting
he says to us,
"When I come here again
then I will know
if it is best
to have many sheep
or few sheep,
to use the land
or let it sleep."

'Ahbínígo
shizhé'é
' áłah ńda'adleehgóó
dah diigháahgo
'ánihiłnii łeh,
"Áádę́ę́' nínáánísdzáago
'áko 'índa shił bééhózin dooleeł
dibé t'óó 'ahayóígo daats'í,
dibé 'áłch'į́įdígo daats'í
yá'át'ééh dooleeł,
'áádóó kéyah daats'í
bik'i ndadiilnish
t'óó daats'í bíni' 'ałhosh doo."

top left, Enochs 1940:26–27; top right, Enochs 1940a: 22–23; bottom, Clark 1950:94–95.

Fig. 6. Text and illustrations from the first bilingual English-Navajo readers, which represented "the first publication in Navajo of anything save the Bible, religious tracts and scientific monographs" (Enochs 1940a:3). The readers employ a Navajo spelling system designed by John Peabody Harrington and Oliver LaFarge with the assistance of Robert W. Young and William Morgan (see Parman 1976:213) that with minor changes has been adopted as the standard Navajo orthography. top left, Facing pages from *Little Man's family*, a 1940 pre-primer, illustrated by Navajo artist Gerald Nailor with text adapted from material prepared by J.B. Enochs, a teacher at the Kayenta Sanatorium School. top right, Equivalent pages from the primer in the same series; pencilled glosses are by Clyde Kluckhohn. bottom, Facing pages from *Little Herder in Spring* (one of a second set of bilingual readers originally published in 1940) illustrated by Navajo artist Denetsosie and written by Ann Nolan Clark, previously a teacher at Tesuque Pueblo, who had pioneered the use of Indian-illustrated readers (see Bader 1976:160–166). Both series were commissioned and published by the U.S. Office of Indian Affairs under Commissioner John Collier and Director of Education Willard W. Beatty. Like other Indian readers of the period, they were composed in English and then translated. All pages slightly cropped.

important curricular and instructional innovations, beginning in 1966. In this period BIA and public schools began to develop a limited number of curriculum guidelines and materials, some of which were bilingual or bicultural in nature. Rough Rock Demonstration School established a curriculum center that began the design and publication of discrete products in Navajo and English. In the early 1970s, the University of New Mexico was funded to organize a Navajo Reading Study project. The research was augmented by a curriculum and materials production team who developed a number of Navajo language products.

In the late 1960s and through the mid-1970s the Dine Biolta Association sponsored many workshops to sensitize Navajo professionals to bilingual education. It also sponsored curriculum and materials development workshops. The DBA inventory of materials was an important beginning and is integral to the curriculum and instructional innovations of the 1970s.

In the 1970s several other curriculum production projects and centers responded to the paucity of linguistically and culturally relevant materials. The Rough Rock Demonstration School Curriculum Center continues to distribute classroom materials that were produced during the early 1970s. There is another curriculum production center sponsored by Title IV of the Indian Education Act (Public Law 92–318) and the Chinle Public School District, which produces materials for teaching English as a second language.

By 1981, there were three major curriculum centers: the Blanding, Utah, Curriculum Center (sponsored by the San Juan School District, a Utah public school dis-

JASON CHEE
Stock reduction—taking away the sheep, with a white man giving orders and a Navajo policeman standing near.

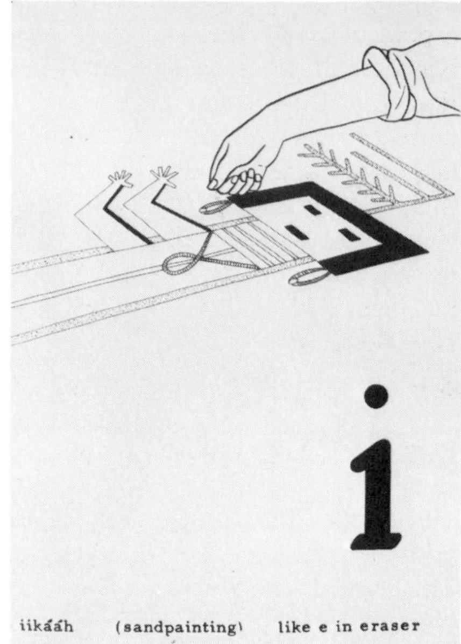
i
iikááh (sandpainting) like e in eraser

Navajo Community College Press: R. Roessel 1971: left, 34; right, 86.

Fig. 7. Illustrations from *Navajo Studies at Navajo Community College* (R. Roessel 1971), a publication specifically intended to present the Navajo Studies program at the college; the program was developed by the "all-Navajo" Board of Regents for the college (see R. Roessel 1971:ix–xi). left, Illustration by Jason Chee titled "Stock reduction—taking away the sheep, with a white man giving orders and a Navajo policeman standing near," a reference to the stock reduction program of the 1930s. right, One of a series of alphabet illustrations of Navajo consonants and vowels by either Raymond Johnson or Jason Chee accompanying an article on teaching the Navajo language by William Morgan, who had helped with the first standardized Navajo orthography. The source illustrated uses a common variant that omits word-initial glottal stop (').

trict) begun in 1970; the Navajo Community College Press, Tsaile, Arizona; and the Native American Materials Development Center, in Albuquerque, New Mexico. Each has contributed to addressing the curricular and materials vacuum.

The Blanding Center produces audio-visual materials intended primarily for the San Juan School District and distributes the materials to other schools only as a secondary function. The Navajo Community College Press produces materials intended for secondary and postsecondary use (fig. 7). Most of the materials are in English, on topics of Navajo history and culture. Another small materials production project is located at Rock Point Community School, Rock Point, Arizona. It produces materials for the fourth to eighth grade level and addresses current Navajo topics, publishing in English.

The Native American Materials Development Center, established in 1976, is sponsored by the Ramah Navajo School Board, Inc., and funded by the Office of Bilingual Education and the Office of Indian Education in the U.S. Department of Education. Since its inception, NAMDC has been the leading producer of curricula and materials. Its focus has been on the development of a language and culture-based core curriculum, kindergarten through eighth grade, in social studies, science, and language arts. The curriculum and materials are tested in a network of BIA, public, and contract schools; the Center has made an effort to avoid limiting its services to one type of institution. The test process is also crucial since it helps to assure linguistic, cultural, and curricular quality prior to publishing.

A concern expressed by bilingual educators is the need for more materials in the sciences and mathematics. Most products and curricula are in the language arts and social studies area, for kindergarten through third grade. Another concern is for high-quality materials that have been carefully tested. Training materials to implement the programs are also essential.

BIA Curriculum

In the 1940s Hildegard Thompson, a BIA education official, wrote curriculum guidelines entitled *Essential Goals in 1949*. Thompson's *Goals* contained the first formal educational goal statement made by the BIA. These goals, which the BIA used until 1966, were criticized for not recognizing Indian values, languages, and cultures. They were also faulted for their generalities, which led to local interpretation.

In 1966, the BIA published new goals for the elementary school level. Although this second curricular effort recognized Indian values, languages, and cultures, it did not contain a curricular philosophy.

The BIA contracted for curriculum development in four areas: English as a second language, social studies, language, and guidance and counseling. The important aspect of this effort was the intent to legitimize the Navajo culture as a social studies curriculum. In addition, the work in language was noted as having done more to sensitize teachers to the complexities of dual language development and bicognitive development than at any time in BIA history. Roessel (1979) reviewed the guidance and counseling outlines and found them excellent and insightful. The social studies project has been criticized because it is difficult to use, culturally inaccurate, and with inappropriate art work.

Role of the Tribal Government in Education

The role of the Navajo Tribe in education has been primarily through the Navajo Division of Education, which was created in 1971 following the vision of Dillon Platero, its first director. In the early 1970s NDOE undertook to learn what were the educational needs of the Navajo people. To accomplish this task, NDOE bypassed the existing institutions and went directly to each Navajo community. This was the first time that Navajo people were asked to voice their opinions about education in a formalized way.

With the results of the study, NDOE outlined educational goals in two policy position statements and recommended alternatives to the Navajo Tribal Council. NDOE recommended that it be sanctioned and authorized to assume functions similar to a state education agency. NDOE wanted to develop curricula and establish teaching and administrative standards. It requested power to unify the disunited school institutions and in essence, "to give education to the people." It was the desire of NDOE to legitimize Navajo language and culture within the schools and to assure that school districts were sensitive to the needs of the people (Navajo Tribe. Division of Education 1973, 1973a). Its other stated mission was to take over BIA education under contract. In 1981 NDOE had not received the sanctions it needed from the Navajo Tribal Council to assume these responsibilities.

Despite this drawback, NDOE has undertaken several important functions. For example, it is monitoring certain contracts, such as those provided under Johnson–O'Malley, to the public and contract schools, preparing reports about the schooling and boarding processes in the BIA and contract schools. A significant report in 1980 indicated the uneven quality of services provided by the BIA from one agency to another. Education administration was cited as being exemplary in Tuba City agency in 1980, and as being mediocre in the Shiprock agency (Navajo Tribe. Division of Education 1980).

Other findings substantiate the claim that curriculum in public schools is not Navajo-oriented and that the reason the school officials give is that there are not enough native language materials and curriculum and that teaching staff are not trained in bilingual methods.

Another important role of NDOE has been to administer the Navajo Tribal Scholarship Program, which has greatly increased the number of Navajo college graduates, thus creating an expanding corps of Navajo professionals. In 1953 the Navajo Tribe established a scholarship fund of $30,000. In 1958 it set up a $10 million trust fund from tribal revenues garnered from the Four Corners oil and gas leases. By 1977–1978 it had a budget of more than $4 million. The demand for scholarships has risen faster than allocations so that many students have had to be denied aid. For example, in 1977, 4,579 students applied, and 2,197 were funded. The average scholarship grant was $1,492 in 1977. The grant increase has not been significant in spite of national inflationary rises (Roessel 1979:39–43).

In 1973 NDOE created and sponsored the Navajo Teacher Education Development Program at the University of New Mexico and the University of Arizona. In 1973 there were 1,800 teachers, of which fewer than 200 were Navajos. By 1981 the University of New Mexico had graduated 153 teachers, most of whom were certified. Since 1973 NDOE has moved the Arizona teacher training program to Northern Arizona University, Flagstaff, and added a program at Arizona State University, Tempe. The University of New Mexico program is funded by the Office of Indian Education in the Department of Education. Most of the candidates recruited were formerly teacher aides so that most teachers speak Navajo and have classroom experience.

Since at least 1960 Navajos who wanted a college education had to leave the reservation and struggle through a college curriculum that often seemed meaningless to them. Many could not afford to leave their homes and jobs, in spite of the tribal scholarship programs. The type of technical assistance that the non-Indian colleges and universities were providing was fragmented and superficial.

For these and other reasons, two reservation colleges were created.* The Navajo Community College, Tsaile, Arizona, was conceived by the Navajo Tribal Council in 1968 (figs. 8–9). It opened in January 1969 and received accreditation in July 1976. Since that time the Tsaile campus has become a 15-million dollar facility, with a branch campus in Shiprock, and four regional centers, all of which are accredited.

The college consists of eight divisions that offer associate degrees. One of these is a degree in bilingual and bicultural education. Certificate programs in welding, auto mechanics, general clerical, data processing, and child development are available.

*The following was written by Nikki L. Lanza from telephone interviews in March 1982 with college officials.

Jerry Jacka Photography, Phoenix, Ariz.

Fig. 8. Two of the buildings on the Navajo Community College campus at Tsaile, Ariz.: left, a traditional hogan used for ceremonials and prayer; right, the Ned A. Hatathli Culture Center, which houses a museum, the Navajo Community College Press, a computer center, a research center, and various offices. In 1979–1980, the campus also included 10 dormitories, a gymnasium, student union building, library, a day care center, classrooms, the Dine Center for Human Development, and several facilities for an animal health care program. Photograph by Jerry Jacka, 1979.

The college has grown significantly since its inception. In spring 1969, 329 students were enrolled; by fall 1981, enrollment had risen to 2,009. In 1969 the faculty numbered 19; in fall 1981 there were 48 full-time professors on the staff. The college's first graduating class in June 1970 had 2 students; 119 students received diplomas in June 1981.

Tuition costs have necessarily risen from $200 a semester in 1969 to $1,200 in fall 1981. In 1982 the total operating budget was $5,129,333; of that sum, 71 percent was financed by the federal government through Public Law 96–374. Seed money from the Navajo tribe contributed 13 percent and tuition and fees made up the over 15 percent remaining. About 90% of the primarily Indian student body are recipients of student aid. The aid is in the form of: Pell (basic) grants, work-study programs, loans, tribal scholarships, and scholarships earmarked by corporations, organizations, and universities for specific certificate programs and academic specialties.

The Navajo Tribal Council offers scholarships and contributes to the financial operation of the college; but in addition, control of the college lies with the Navajo Tribe. The 10 members of the Navajo Board of Regents, each of whom is selected and sanctioned by the Navajo Tribal Council, represent various locations on the reservation.

The other reservation college is the College of Ganado that was founded in 1972 by the United Presbyterian Church in the U.S.A. Mission Board. Northern Arizona University, Flagstaff, certified the courses for the first year, making all credits fully transferable. The College of Ganado received accreditation in April 1979. It has since expanded to include an extension center in Oraibi, Arizona, which is located on the Hopi reservation.

The College of Ganado provides a two-year program with eight departments offering associate degrees. Certificate programs for teachers' aides and archeological technicians are also available. Unlike the Navajo Community College, which emphasizes Navajo culture, the College of Ganado has been geared toward a classic academic curriculum. However, Navajo is one of the

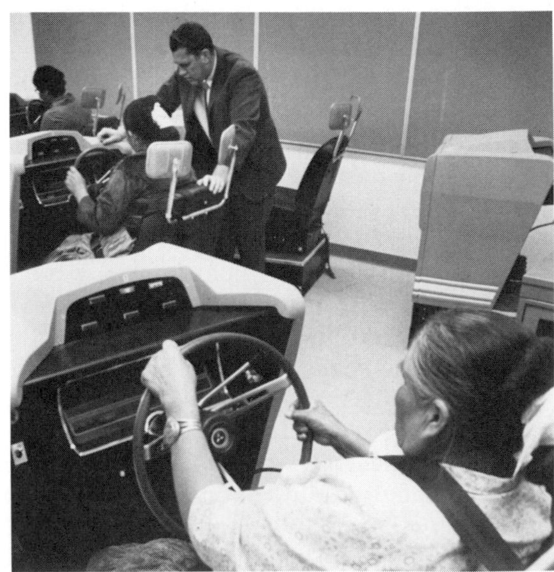

Robert Roessel, Jr., Chinle, Ariz.

Fig. 9. Classes at the Navajo Community College. left, Art class; right, adult education class in driver training. Photographs by Paul Conklin, 1975 (left) and 1976.

languages taught. About one-half of the graduates continue their education at four-year institutions. For most of the students, who come from many different tribes, English is a second language.

In fall 1981 there were 158 students (full and part-time) enrolled at the college. In the same school year there was a 24-member faculty, all non-Indian with the exception of one part-time Navajo instructor. The college had 15 students in its June 1981 graduating class.

The College of Ganado originally was solely funded by the United Presbyterian Church in the U.S.A. In 1978 the college became an independent, nonprofit institution sanctioned by the Hopi tribe and recognized by the Navajo tribe. The Hopi sanction allowed the college to receive federal funds under Public Law 95–471.

Tuition in fall 1981 was $35 per credit, or, $525 for a 15-hour semester. For the 1981 fiscal year the operating budget was 1.3 million dollars. Of that sum, 47 percent was financed from Public Law 95–471, federal grants, and contracts; 24 percent from auxiliary enterprises (food coop, employee housing); 10 percent from student financial aid (for housing); 8 percent for tuition and fees; and 7 percent were private gifts, primarily from the United Presbyterian Church. All the students receive some form of federal financial aid.

The College of Ganado, as with the Navajo Community College, is Indian controlled. The primary authority in the direction and control of the college rests with the Native American Board of Regents. The college president, and three of the 15 members of the Board of Regents are Hopis. The remaining regents—all of whom are Indian—represent, like the students, various tribes throughout the Southwest. Both colleges are important alternatives to the state public institutions of higher learning outside the reservation.

Navajo Health Services and Projects

ROBERT L. BERGMAN

The health of the Navajo people improved so rapidly in the first decades after World War II that relatively recent accounts of conditions became highly misleading, and a fairly hale and hearty people were sometimes surprised to hear themselves described as being among the world's least healthy by well-wishing outsiders whose sources were slightly out of date. In 1945, a Navajo infant had a 50 percent chance of living to enter school. In 1967 his chance was better than 98 percent. The infant death rate in 1967 was half the 1955 rate and the tuberculosis death rate declined 70 percent in those years. The prevalence and seriousness of infectious diseases in general were greatly reduced, and morbidity lessened in almost every category of illness (McCammon 1970.) This progress was accomplished by discoveries of improved methods of treatment, by greater availability of care for the Navajo people, and by increased understanding and cooperation between the Navajo community and those employed to provide its medical care.

Euro-American Medicine until the 1950s

The relationship between Navajo people and the first doctors who came to help them was marked by anxiety and mistrust. The elaborate and well-established methods of Navajo medicine men were preferred by most patients to the foreign and seemingly whimsical techniques of the White doctors whose persons, tools, and hospitals were contaminated by contact with the dead. The White doctors generally regarded Navajo medicine as dangerous superstitious nonsense. Until the 1950s, patients of the government-operated Fort Defiance Hospital were almost invariably refused permission to leave temporarily for treatment by a medicine man, and they were often refused care later if they should leave, against advice, to have a curing ceremony (McCammon 1970). In those days, many Navajos spoke of hospitals as death houses and considered their merit to be their availability to a patient obviously about to die. If death occurred in the hospital, then the family's home did not have to be abandoned because someone had died in it.

A government hospital in Fort Defiance opened in July 1912. It failed to do a very big business. The hospital record book shows 15 admissions the first month, followed by a steady decline for months afterwards. In the first two years of operation there were only 207 admissions, an average of nine per month. The first woman to enter the hospital for the delivery of a baby seems to have done so under duress. She was admitted in October 1912, delivered in January 1913, and discharged the following August. The only record of the discharge bears the notation, "Held until married." It was a year before another child was born in the hospital and in the first two years there were only five births there. Several of the earliest patients were assigned the diagnosis of "malingering." One of these presumed fakers died. In the first two years, one patient's record is marked "left would not stay" and two "ran away, returned by police" (Ft. Defiance Hospital 1910–1920).

Had the Navajos had more faith in the hospitals, a new difficulty would have been created: not enough space or staff. Though there have been physicians on the reservation since 1880, there were never many until after 1955. In 1948 there were only 16 doctors of all kinds on the reservation (McCammon 1970). In 1950, even though many Navajos still did not want non-Navajo treatment for tuberculosis, there were still more than 1,000 people with active tuberculosis who did want hospital treatment and who were being kept on a waiting list for hospital beds.

Until 1955, health care for the Navajo people was provided by medical missionaries and by the Bureau of Indian Affairs. Health was only one of many concerns of the BIA, and as part of the Department of the Interior, it paid more attention to land management than disease prevention and treatment. The branch of health had to compete with other BIA branches for funds and personnel, and agency superintendents had the authority, which they often exercised, to transfer health funds to other branches. Hospitals would occasionally run out of drugs and other essential supplies before the end of the fiscal year and then they had to wait until the next year to get some more. In 1928, the Meriam Report observed that the branch of health "has seemingly given too much consideration to the fact that the economic and social conditions of the Indians are low and it has assumed, therefore, that it is unnecessary to supply them with facilities comparable with those made available by states, municipalities, and private philanthropists for the poorest white citizens of progressive communities" (Meriam 1928).

Natl. Arch.: Bureau of Ind. Affairs Coll. 75–N–Nav–Med. Men–2

Fig. 1. Pause during the ceremonial blessing of the Crown Point Hospital, by Navajo medicine men, at its opening in 1940. Left to right, Navajo medicine men Hatalh Chee, Jeff King (leading the blessing and holding basket with medicine bundles), Mariano Bey, Frank Biyal, Paul Charley, Charley Bedazha Badani, Willie Charley, Be na ka asmille, Hosteen Lichee, and John Perry (Navajo Tribal Council delegate), Hoskie Largo (policemen), Sam Jim (judge), and Dr. W.W. Peter (U.S. Indian Service medical director for the Navajo Area). Identifications and orthography, possibly provided by Dr. Peter, from original print. Photographer unidentified.

Even though insufficient medical care of the European tradition was made available, native American methods were scorned and attacked. Missionaries, including medical missionaries, often attempted to break down Navajo health practices. As late as 1969, one Navajo woman was told by missionaries with headquarters on the reservation that she would go to hell because she had been the patient in a Blessingway ceremony. Even the usually insightful Meriam report, though it did praise cooperation between medicine men and White doctors, expressed the hope that traditional medical practice, which it referred to as "the old undesirable custom" was breaking down (Meriam 1928).

Not all the doctors and missionaries, of course, were in opposition to the survival of Navajo religion and medicine. Father Berard Haile of the Franciscan mission at Saint Michaels, Arizona, not only devoted much of his life to studying Navajo language and custom but also was one of the first to try to harmonize elements of Navajo and European culture. Ethnologists and their work were increasingly familiar to reservation doctors and led to the beginnings of appreciation of the richness and usefulness of Navajo medicine. The studies of Clyde Kluckhohn and the fiction of Oliver LaFarge have helped to introduce several generations of reservation doctors to Navajo ways. Leighton and Leighton (1941) were probably the first writers to describe in detail the beneficial effects of traditional curing ceremonies, and their paper on this subject has been endlessly duplicated for distribution among medical personnel newly arrived in the area.

In its last years, the Bureau of Indian Affairs Branch of Health became increasingly dependent on the United States Public Health Service. Many of the physicians working in the Branch of Health were Public Health Service Officers detailed for this work. This arrangement brought to the reservation a number of young physicians who were more receptive than their predecessors had been to the idea of understanding and working with Navajo ideas, and who were more sensitive because less inured to the inadequacy of the health facilities. Dissatisfaction was high among the doctors and resulted in rapid turnover. There was a series of 30 physicians at the Crownpoint Hospital between 1946 and 1955 (Adair and Deuschle 1970). Though the conditions that caused the personnel to leave and the frequent departures themselves were damaging to health care at the time, the increasing number of people with some familiarity with the sad situation helped to bring about its end.

Improvement of Medical Care After 1950

With the Navajo-Hopi Rehabilitation Act of 1950, appropriated money became available for contracts between the Branch of Health and private hospitals, and the backlog of untreated, active cases of tuberculosis began to be overcome as patients were admitted to hospitals and sanatoria all over the Southwest. It was as part of this program that Navajo patients were first transported by chartered light aircraft to and from remote areas— a practice that was to become increasingly important in health care on the reservation. The new appropriations also made possible the construction of a 75-bed hospital in Tuba City, Arizona (Young 1961).

An epidemic of hepatitis in Tuba City in 1952 occasioned bringing infectious disease experts from Cornell University medical school to the reservation for the first time and was the beginning of an important helpful association of that school with Navajo health programs. It was known that the incidence of tuberculosis was high, but accurate and precise knowledge of the problem did not exist. In the course of combating the hepatitis outbreak, it was learned that there was also a tuberculosis epidemic among children, and a number of cases of miliary tuberculosis were found. Miliary tuberculosis was usually fatal at that time, but a new drug, isoniazide, was just then being tested for the first time at Cornell's New York hospital. It had been determined that isoniazide was safe to use, but no large-scale clinical trial had yet been made. The Cornell group sought the approval of the Navajo Tribal Council for the use of the new medicine in Tuba City. The Council not only gave approval but also appropriated a $10,000 contribution toward the expenses of the program. The drug proved effective, and previously incurable cases were cured. Isoniazide later was in world-wide use (Adair and Deuschle 1970).

By 1953 great progress was being made in catching up on the backlog of untreated tuberculosis patients, but even though the lack of funds was no longer so great a problem, a new obstacle was encountered: many of the patients left the sanatoria before they were medically ready for discharge. The aid of the Tribal Council was again asked. Chairman Sam Ahkeah asked Annie D. Wauneka, the chairman of the health committee, to undertake the task, thus beginning her career as health educator and leader in the progress of Navajo health programs (fig. 2). She began by asking for as much information as possible on all aspects of tuberculosis and its treatment. She then began visiting the Navajo patients in the off-reservation hospitals. They expected her to help them in getting out and getting home, but instead she talked to them in Navajo about their illness and helped them to understand why it was best for them to stay. In 1953 Navajo patients suddenly left the Oshrin Sanatorium in Tucson, Arizona. Wauneka was consulted and learned that a tree on the hospital grounds had been struck by lightning. She suggested that a Blessingway ceremony be performed at the hospital and found a medicine man to perform it. He was flown to Tucson; he purified the hospital, and the patients returned. The success of this early incident of cooperation between the two medical systems led to a growing awareness of the need of each for the other. Knowing that the medicine men were crucial in the decisions of other Navajos, Wauneka traveled to the homes of many of them to show x-ray pictures and tell case histories in order to convince them that the non-Navajo doctors had something valuable to offer in the treatment of tuberculosis. Wauneka's recognition of their importance and her careful translation of medical concepts into Navajo convinced most of the medicine

top, Natl. Arch.: Bureau of Ind. Affairs Coll. 75–N–Nav–F–2; bottom, Navajo Tribal Mus., Window Rock, Ariz.

Fig. 2. Annie D. Wauneka, Tribal Council member and long-time Chairman of the Committee on Health and Welfare. top, Wauneka explains an exhibit relating to the diagnosis and treatment of tuberculosis, a disease that she was particularly active in combatting. bottom, Wauneka on a field visit to a Navajo family, probably with a Public Health Service nurse. Photographs by Gene Price, undated (bottom), and by unidentified photographer (possibly Milton Snow), probably late 1950s (top).

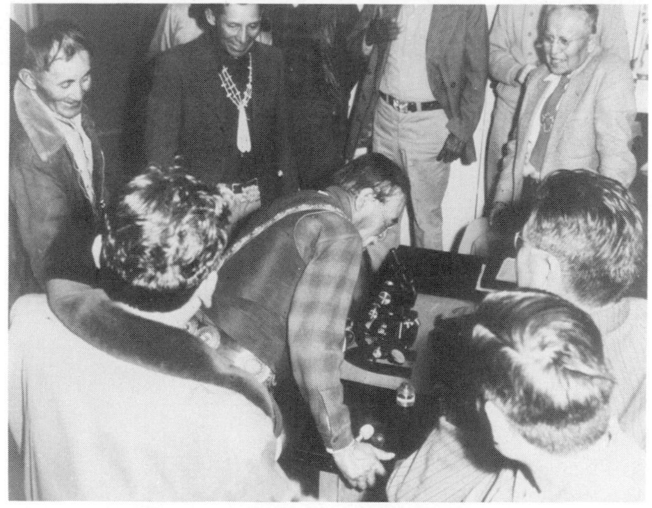

U.S. Ind. Service (Bureau of Ind. Affairs).

Fig. 3. One of several community meetings in the early 1950s to discuss tuberculosis, in which Navajo medicine men, medical doctors, and general members of the community participated (Adair and Deuschle 1970:33–34). Manuelito Begay, medicine man and delegate to the Tribal Council from Crown Point, examines tubercle bacilli under a microscope that was set up by doctors from the hospital at Ft. Defiance as part of a demonstration showing medical causes and methods of detecting tuberculosis. Photograph by Milton Snow at Crown Point Hospital March 1954, from the collection of John Adair.

Amon Carter Mus., Ft. Worth, Tex.: Laura Gilpin Coll. 4316 [1].

Fig. 4. Children lined up for throat cultures at the clinic at Many Farms, Ariz. The clinic was part of the Navajo-Cornell Field Health Research Project, organized by the Navajo Tribe, the U.S. Public Health Service, and Cornell University Medical College in 1955. From its inception, an attempt was made to staff the clinic with as many Navajos as possible. Photograph by Laura Gilpin, Sept. 1957.

men and thus greatly increased the acceptance of hospitals and drugs. In 1963 Wauneka was awarded the Presidential Medal of Freedom for this work (Wauneka 1970; McCammon 1970; Adair and Deuschle 1970).

As Navajo people learned more about non-Indian concepts of disease (fig. 3), and its treatment, they became increasingly dissatisfied with the inadequate facilities of the Bureau of Indian Affairs Branch of Health. For several years, outside observers as well as members of the Branch of Health had suggested a transfer of responsibility for Indian health care to the United States Public Health Service. In 1954 Dr. Ray Shaw of the United States Public Health Service conducted a study of the feasibility of such a transfer. He toured Navajo health facilities with Wauneka and reported his findings to the Tribal Council, who then passed a resolution requesting the transfer, which took place in 1955. The Division of Indian Health of the Public Health Service was created with Dr. Shaw as director, and expansion and improvement of Indian health facilities throughout the country were begun as rapidly as possible.

Cornell–Many Farms Project

On the Navajo Reservation, the Public Health Service made use of the already extensive local knowledge and experience of the Cornell University group. Under contract with the government, Cornell set up a research team to conduct a pilot project in the provision of health care to a representative Navajo community with the objective of learning what was most needed and how best to provide it (fig. 4). The contract originally covered the years 1955 to 1960 and was extended to 1962. The Cornell–Many Farms project was directed by Dr. Kurt W. Deuschle, a physician who had taken part in the earlier tuberculosis research and treatment, and by Dr. John Adair, an anthropologist with many years of fieldwork experience among the Navajo people. It provided information about Navajo epidemiology and health practices, methods of adapting medical record keeping to the structure of Navajo families and communities, ways of introducing technological change, and probably most important, it demonstrated the value of Navajo health-care workers (Adair and Deuschle 1970).

In 1955 there were few Navajo people trained in the non-Navajo medical tradition. The earliest were the registered nurses trained at the Sage Memorial Hospital in Ganado, Arizona, where the first class had graduated in 1933, but the classes were small and Navajo nurses remained rare (Salsbury 1969). Most health workers knew relatively little about Navajo ways, and almost none spoke the Navajo language. Since many patients could not speak English, interpretation was a constant problem. Translation was generally accomplished in a haphazard manner, with any handy Navajo who seemed to be able to speak both languages pressed into service by hurried physicians who often did not appreciate the difficulty or possible embarrassment of the task. Great misunderstanding often resulted as was the case with a patient in the early days of the Public Health Service Division of Indian Health whose doctor advised an operation on the thyroid, but who fled the hospital when told in Navajo that the doctor wanted to cut his throat (Bock 1971; Adair and Deuschle 1970).

The Cornell–Many Farms project recruited and trained a group of Navajo health visitors. These people learned the basic principles of non-Navajo medicine and how to interpret them in Navajo, to perform certain nursing procedures such as giving tuberculin skin tests, to take medical histories, to collect demographic and health information, and to recognize emergencies and administer first aid. During the seven years that the project provided care to the people of the Many Farms area, the health visitors were essential in performing direct services and in bringing two traditions together. However, at the end of the project, it proved more difficult to introduce health visitors into the government medical culture than it had been to introduce the government doctors into the Navajo culture. Civil service job series did not include anything like the health visitors, and many government supervisors were anxious about giving medical responsibilities to nonprofessionals (Adair and Deuschle 1970). After an initial hesitation lasting several years, many Navajo people were trained and put to work as medical paraprofessionals in a variety of Public Health Service programs. The dental technicians not only assisted the dentists but also performed a number of procedures independently. Mental health workers and social work associates provided counseling to individuals and families in the Navajo language. Community health representatives, employed by the tribal government under contract with the Public Health Service, acted as liaison agents between clinic and community much as the original health visitors had. In 1973, the first class of community health medics graduated from a Public Health Service school operated in Gallup and went to work throughout the reservation as physicians' assistants performing a wide variety of medical tasks.

In addition to the Cornell project, there was also a contract made in 1955 between the Public Health Service and the School of Public Health of the University of California at Berkeley for the development of a health education program suitable to the Navajo Nation (fig. 5). This project brought Dr. Jerrold E. Levy to the reservation where he remained as an employee of the Division of Indian Health. He not only increased the knowledge of the health practices of the Navajo people but also taught many physicians and administrators the importance of adapting the medical program to suit the needs of the culture of the patients.

Expansion of Services

At the same time that government medical systems changed to better fit the situation, there was considerable increase in facilities and staff. A 200-bed referral hospital providing specialized care opened in Gallup, New Mexico, in 1960. Many clinics were constructed, and in 1973, there were 566 available beds in six hospitals; one hospital was under construction and another was scheduled for construction within a year. There were five medical centers where routine care was available daily and emergency care at all times. Thirty-six other clinics were in operation on an intermittent basis. The number of government, missionary, and private doctors on the reservation had increased from the 16 of 1948 to more than 140. The overall staff of government medical programs had more than tripled since 1955 (Bock 1971). Utilization of government services also tripled in these years. Dental services that had been almost unavailable 20 years before were used by 42,000

Fig. 5. Navajo staff members of the University of California Navajo Health Education Project at a home demonstration of infant formula. top, Rosemary Goldtooth, a Navajo health education aide trainee, demonstrates formula preparation at the home of a Navajo woman. bottom, Dan Vicenti, a Navajo community health specialist trainee, photographs the proceedings for use in further home demonstration materials. Photographs by Jerrold E. Levy, July 1961.

Navajo people during fiscal year 1972. Care in almost all medical specialties was available on the reservation, and in cases where unavailable specialized care was needed it was usually possible to fly the patient to Albuquerque or some other city where it was provided at government expense. Away from the hospitals and clinics, public health nurses, health educators, sanitarians, and many other kinds of workers met with families and organizations to provide care and do preventative work. Public Health Service sanitarians and engineers insured the safety of community water systems and individual wells, and between 1961 and 1972 they constructed sanitary and water facilities in more than 5,000 Navajo homes (Bock 1971). Although in 1973 clinics were overcrowded and understaffed, hospital wards had too few nurses, and many patients received less than ideal care, still there did exist a widespread comprehensive health program where there had been essentially nothing a few decades before, and services were available free to Navajos that remained unavailable at any price to non-Indians in nearby towns.

In 1967 the Navajo Field Office of the Division of Indian Health was separated from the Albuquerque Area Office of which it had formerly been a part and became an area office in its own right, and Dr. George E. Bock became area director. This change was significant in that it meant that most decisions affecting Navajo health were thereafter made in Window Rock, Arizona, where there could be full participation by tribal leaders. The Tribal Council had included a health committee since 1937, and over the years—especially under the leadership of Annie Wauneka—its role in setting health policy had grown. In 1970 the Tribal Council set up a new group to act as directors of the Public Health Service Navajo operations. The membership consisted of five tribal councilmen, the chairman of the Human Resources Division of the Navajo Tribe, and eight community health representatives—one from each agency of the reservation. After its formation this group took part through its monthly meetings in planning, evaluating, and implementing the health program; for example, they reviewed and selected among the applications for all administrative positions.

Perpetuation of Traditional Navajo Medicine

While the new medical system grew and developed on the reservation, the old one continued to go about its work. Navajo patients, though they also went to hospitals and clinics, still sought the advice of hand tremblers and other diagnosticians and the care of ceremonialists. Major ceremonies appeared to be as numerous and effective as ever. The adaptation that evolved was usually to regard hospital treatment as useful in relieving a crisis of some dangerous symptom, and the ceremony as removing the underlying causative

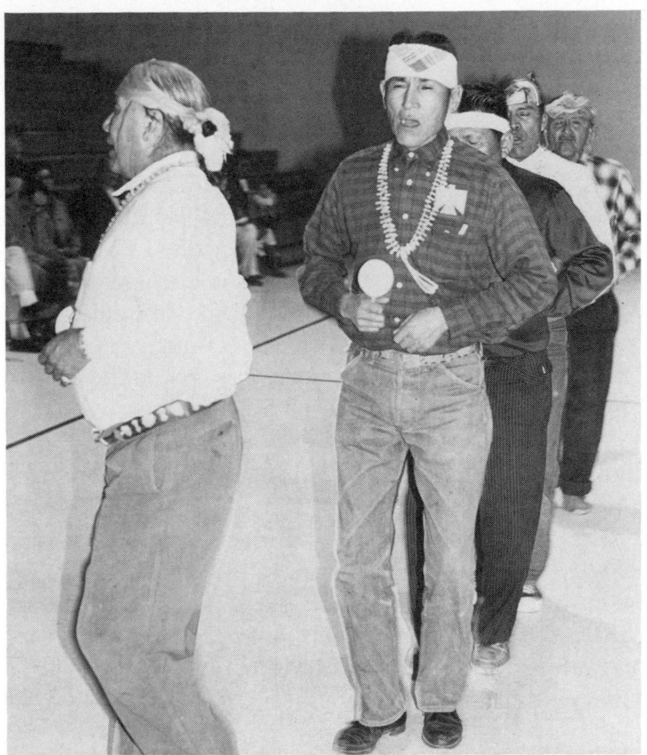

Robert Roessel, Jr., Chinle, Ariz.
Fig. 6. Navajo men practicing a Yeibichai dance in the gymnasium of the Rough Rock Demonstration School as part of a training program for Navajo medicine men and ceremonial singers (see "Navajo Music," fig. 6, this vol., for views of Yeibichai dancers during a Nightway). The first 2 dancers are Yazzie Begay (in profile) and Oshie Tsosie (holding gourd rattle), both members of the school board at the time. Photograph by Paul Conklin, 1968.

disharmony responsible for the trouble in the first place. The Public Health Service mental health program, new in 1966, was able to make connections with the traditional medical systems and referred many patients to medicine men with usually good results. Unfortunately, because it became economically difficult for young men to undertake the study of Navajo medicine, a shortage of medicine men appeared to be in the offing.

In 1966, when the Rough Rock Demonstration School, the first truly Navajo-controlled school, was founded, members of the Rough Rock Chapter suggested to the school board that a program to train new medicine men be started (fig. 6). The idea was taken up enthusiastically by the board and the details worked out over the course of the next year. It was decided to alter as little as possible the traditional method of teaching and learning sings. Each medicine man involved was to teach two apprentices of his own selection at his own home and at the homes where he performed ceremonies. Trios of medicine men and trainees were to be selected by the Rough Rock school board—mostly themselves medicine men—on the basis of the reputation of the medicine man, the apparent ability of the trainees, and the importance and threat of extinction to the ceremony that was proposed to be taught. The medicine men were to be paid a modest salary, and the trainees considerably less for their subsistence. The Public Health Service Mental Health Program had been consulting with the Rough Rock school on other matters, and its help was enlisted in finding money to operate the medicine man program. Ultimately a grant from the National Institute of Mental Health was secured and the medicine man school, called the Rough Rock Navajo Mental Health Project, began work in 1969 under the direction of John Dick. In addition to the usual teaching methods used, the trainees and their teacher ceremonialists met for a day biweekly with a Public Health Service psychiatrist to discuss the two systems—Navajo and European—of physical and psychological medicine. There were chances for the Navajo group to observe therapy at the Gallup hospital, to look at x-rays and microscope slides, to see demonstrations of hypnosis; and, on the other hand, the psychiatrist was taught about the Navajo view of health and illness. The first group of trainees completed the program, having each learned one or two ceremonies, in June 1972. A new group then started (Bergman 1973).

Navajo Physicians

While more of the old kind of Navajo doctor were being trained there was a need for a new kind. When Dr. Taylor McKenzie, the first Navajo to receive an M.D. degree, graduated from medical school in 1960, he expected, he later told a group of Navajo community health medics, to be "the first of a flood of Navajo physicians." The flood was slow in developing. Dr. McKenzie, a general surgeon, in 1973 directed the Shiprock Hospital. Dr. Joanna Dietz, a Navajo, was practicing psychiatry in Dallas, Texas. They were the only ones. There were by that time many Navajo nurses and technicians, but Navajo doctors did not appear to be on the way in any great numbers. For this reason the tribe took steps to start its own medical college. The idea originated in 1971 with Annie Wauneka and was endorsed by the Tribal Council and its chairman. The tribe set up its own health authority and secured a contract from the U.S. Department of Health, Education, and Welfare to develop a Center for Health Professions Education to foster the careers of prospective American Indian doctors and to plan a school of medicine. The Navajo Health Authority quickly drew community support and appeared to be well under way. Many medical educators came to Window Rock to consult; a conference for Indian medical and premedical students was conducted, but by 1981 it remained to be seen if the Navajo Reservation would ever become the site of the American Indian Medical School.

The Navajo Nation Today

MARSHALL TOME

To understand the Navajo people you must understand our Navajo country, which lies within the four sacred mountains. These mountains symbolize the Navajo hogan. When a new hogan is built (always facing east), or any other shelter, it must be blessed with corn pollen and white corn powder inside at all four cardinal directions. In the beginning of time, Talking God instructed the Navajo how to make hogans out of existing resources and to maintain a home in tranquillity. Navajos are religious people influenced by several deities that shape their behavior and destiny. In addition, the Holy People live among the Navajo. Thus, the religious philosopy has a major influence on Navajos who have been brought up with the religious trainings in the home.

Talking God is the foremost deity and the influential element of all Navajo religious teachings. In time of a need for prayer, Navajo people turn to Talking God, who helps with the Night Chant, who can answer questions that Earth Surface People cannot answer, who travels on rainbows, and who helps keep the Fifth World, which we now live in, as it should be.

Now I walk with Talking God.
It is with his feet I go;
It is with his legs I go;
It is with his body I go;
It is with his mind I go;
It is with his voice I go;
I go with twelve feathers of the white eagle.
With goodness and beauty in all things around me I go;
Thus being I, I go.

Some people may ask why the Navajo refuse to change or to accept the mainstream of American society and technological progress. Navajos want to maintain customary cultural ways when changes take place. But can we go on being Navajos when this place where we live, this place that is all of us and we are all of it, is changing so much and so fast? Can we keep our place in this terrible and wonderful Fifth World and not stop being Navajos? Perhaps only Talking God can answer this question. What will he tell us? His words are not easy to listen to, because he tells us only what is, and not what we like to hear.

Talking God says to us, "Look first at the environment around you. Look at Window Rock and Fort Defiance as the White people see them when they come here. How does this area appear to them?" As they drive along the highway from Gallup they see piles of wine and beer bottles scattered here and there. A few sheep wander across the sand and rocks followed by their herders. Several dozen wrecked automobiles rust quietly on the edge of an arroyo. There are some "Indian goods" stores selling jewelry, rugs, and baskets that few Navajos can afford to buy. The car stops at a restaurant-motel. The place is clean, and well run. The food is excellent but the Navajo waitress thinks that "Filet mignon well-done" means "Virginia Ham Steak without french fries." Usually no Navajos talk to these Whites as they sit eating and looking out through large glass windows that show what is left of rock formations that used to be beautiful enough to be put on picture post cards that were sold all over the world. Some of these rocks have now been used to make reservation roads. The Whites think that roads are now more important to us than just scenery. If the Navajos in the restaurant would talk to these White visitors they could tell them that scenery won't help children get to school in bad weather or make it possible for sick people to be taken quickly to a hospital. And scenery won't help you get to Gallup for what happens on Saturday night or for what follows on Sunday morning.

The tourists finish eating and go to their motel room that compares favorably to anything of its kind in price and comfort off the reservation. In Des Moines, Iowa, or Green Bay, Wisconsin, not as much red sand drifts underneath the door or the wind doesn't blow as hard against the windows all night, but it is still a nice place to stay. Maybe the Whites were here once before. Our sky looked a lot clearer in 1960. There was less dust in the air then, especially the gray- and brown-colored dust that comes from the west around Black Mesa and is made by the large machines that destroy the land to find coal that is burned to make electricity for Los Angeles. We are paid money to let this coal be taken from our ground. We use this money to pay tribal councilmen to work for us and to buy layettes for our women having babies and for thousands of other things that we want. But once the coal is gone and our money has been spent, we are left with worthless land and we need still more money. Before they leave the reservation to go back to the Rotary Club, their golf scores, and to worry about the weeds that grow in their yards, they stop at

top, Dr. and Mrs. Byron C. Butler, Phoenix, Ariz.; bottom, Roben Co., Sedona, Ariz.

Fig. 1. Tourism, which became economically important with the coming of the Santa Fe Railroad in the 1880s, continues as a major source of income and activity (see Anonymous 1979c). top, *Tourist Season*, watercolor painting by the Navajo artist Quincy Tahoma, 1947. With the possible exception of a peculiarly tied kerchief on the female tourist, details of clothing are meticulously rendered. (See Tanner 1973:319–329 for biography of the artist.) bottom, "Navajo Women sit in front of their log and mud Hogan . . .", color postcard purchased from a trading post in Arizona in 1980. Postcards of this type have been available since about 1900.

the Tribal Council headquarters and talk to some councilmen. These are Navajos who think much, work very hard, and truly want to help all other Navajos live as the free men that they would like to be. These Whites ask, "How do things get done around here?" The councilmen think carefully, look at the horizon for a while and then answer:

> Usually things don't get done around here. They just happen. The government like the Bureau of Indian Affairs, the Public Health Service, the Small Business Administration, the Navajo Tribal government, all Navajos elected to office and other Navajos who are appointed to jobs and work for the tribe all try to do their jobs. Anthropologists, economists, and others who tell us that they can solve problems swarm all over our Navajo Country. They go home and write long reports. Sometimes we read them. Sometimes we accomplish a lot and other times we get in each other's way and once in a while we try to work against each other because we are afraid that we might lose our jobs or make someone who has more influence than we do mad at us. Sometimes we think that the best thing to do is nothing because then no one can say that we made a mistake. We want to hold on to our jobs for as long as we can. There aren't many jobs here that pay money and we all need money if we are going to live. We are often like little children playing in our small sand piles. The sand piles of course are the reservation with its people and natural resources. Since it's all the same sand, the father should come along and make one big sand pile where we could all work together. But there is just one question here that we would like to ask you. Who is the father?

The White tourists cannot answer the councilmen. But perhaps they can understand better why many Navajos are concerned about their land.

Talking God now asks, "What are the Navajos really like?" Navajos are many things that cannot be said in a few words or even several thousand printed pages. Many Navajos follow as closely as they can the ways of their grandfathers. They herd sheep, goats, cows, and horses. They often wonder why it is getting harder and harder to find good grazing areas with enough water. They wonder much, but worry very little because something has always come along in the past to help. Why should it be any different today, tomorrow, or next year? They are living now and not yesterday or 10 years from now. With the coming of frost in the fall the

Richard Erdoes Photography, Sante Fe, N. Mex.

Fig. 2. Outside the Window Rock Motor Inn. Next door is a Navajo arts and crafts store. Photograph by Richard Erdoes, Window Rock, Ariz., 1977.

The Gallup Independent, N. Mex.
Fig. 3. Young Navajo shepherd with part of his flock in front of the Four Corners Power Plant at Fruitland, N. Mex. Foreground and background represent traditional and modern sources of livelihood. Photograph by Mark Lennihan, 1979.

masked dancers of the Night Chant appear with their blessings and our singers pray:

In beauty may fair corn of all kinds to the ends of the earth come with you.
In beauty may fair plants of all kinds, to the ends of the earth, come with you.
In beauty may fair goods of all kinds, to the ends of the earth come with you.
In beauty may fair jewels of all kinds to the ends of the earth come with you.
In beauty may you be.
In beauty may your roads home be on the trail of pollen.

From the time of the little eagles (January) through the time of the great cold winds (December), these Navajos believe that all will be beauty as the years pass.

Other Navajos know nothing of the old ways, laugh at those who do respect them, but want to learn nothing about living in the way that Whites believe that they must do. Some of these people really know nothing about living in any way, so they try to exist in strange places like taverns drinking too much of the whiskey and wine that is served there. Such people do not live well or long. There are other Navajos who know that life here on the reservation can never be as it was 50 years ago and who know that the tribe can survive here on this land for which we have all paid so much for so long, only if we all realize that we are in danger now of losing everything that we care for and can be as Navajos. The world of the Anglos, the Chicanos, and the Blacks has not stopped at the edge of the reservation. It is all around us now and grows stronger every day even as our ways seem to be forgotten. Some Navajos ignore their sacred heritage because they will work, act, and think only if they will benefit immediately by doing so. They must own their house, they must have a new car, and they must go to Washington often to fight with the government. They need to have and do these things to feel important. They do not seem to be interested in how much or how little their jobs help all the Navajos. Finally there are many Navajos who know only that some things on our lands are very wrong, but they have no idea as to how to work to improve the situation.

This is what Talking God tells us. Yes, we Navajos are like this. Now Talking God asks, "What must Navajos do to survive in this Fifth World?" Will they be like the Menominees of Wisconsin who because of individual interests allowed the federal government to terminate their reservation, so that their land could be sold to Whites in small pieces? Do you want your children to watch the land within our four sacred mountains become a place where wealthy Whites build houses to hide in when they cannot stand their cities that they have ruined?

If Navajos do not want this to happen they must start acting like Navajos and not confused sheep. We Navajos have always had to struggle to survive as individuals and as a people. We have made it this far because we have never fooled ourselves about the difficulties that we have faced. Now we must decide exactly how we will live as Navajos in this radically changing world. If we want to follow several different ways each must not be so different that any one style of life will be impossible for others to follow. We next must consider the very high cost of our decisions. We all will pay a great price in terms of peace of mind, financial security, and sheer hard work. Do we want to pay that much? Remember, we will have to follow this difficult road for a long time, and we who are here today will not benefit from these sacrifices, but our great grandchildren will. If we say "yes" and make this great effort to remain Navajos forever we will maintain our heritage and its bright promise. If we say "no" we will have no grandchildren. When other peoples at other times think of us, they will point to museum cases full of silver and turquoise jewelry, rugs, and baskets. As they look at photographs of us in large books written by anthropologists they will say that these were people who saw their own extinction coming but did not care.

What do you say now? How shall we Navajos answer Talking God?

And Where do the Whites fit in?

Land that once was occupied by Navajos is now owned by Whites. We freely acknowledge our mistakes and the fact that we are not now or will ever be perfect, but most of our major problems come from the Whites. Whites have convinced us that we must fight them in their own way if we are to survive to have a chance to live as we desire. We have lawyers on our payroll to fight for us and to protect our land and interests.

The Navajo people have learned and understand the art of politics, and the majority of eligible voters participate in local, state, and national elections. Furthermore, the Navajo people realize that they must protect their land and interests through the political process.

The Navajo people want to utilize coal, timber, and rare minerals for Navajo industries and to sell the excess but they will not sell their precious Navajo heritage. To destroy our land, and to prevent us from running our affairs in our own fashion is to deny our right to be Navajo. We will no longer stand idle and allow state and federal White politicians to have their own way and only their own way.

U. of Ariz., Ariz. State Mus., Tucson: 34,358, 34,638.

Fig. 4. 26th Annual Navajo Tribal Fair, at Window Rock, Ariz. top, Miss Navajo Contest, and bottom, contestants in a fry-bread making contest. In addition to such contests and arts and crafts exhibitions, the Navajo Fair features a rodeo and powwow. In 1980, attendance may have reached 60,000 people, with the tribe allocating $43,000 for awards and trophies to rodeo participants and $35,000 for powwow winners (Anonymous 1981:1, 1981a:1). Photographs by Helga Teiwes, Sept. 1972.

The Holy People have this message for Whites:

Hear us well!

There will be no more Kit Carson and the Long Walk.

There will be no more John Collier and his stock reduction.

There will be no more interference by senators who think they know everything but really know nothing, and thus prevent us from living in peace with our Hopi friends.

There will be no more brutality from corrupt police in Gallup, Farmington, Winslow, and Flagstaff.

Think carefully of what we say now, or tomorrow the fruits of your ignorance and hatred will be returned to you ten-fold!

There is a prayer that gives the Navajo person spiritual strength and inspiration. It is uttered at the close of traditional ceremonies and business affairs:

In beauty may we dwell.
In beauty may we walk.
In beauty may our male kindred dwell.
In beauty may our female kindred dwell.
In beauty may it rain on our young men.
In beauty may it rain on our young women.
In beauty may it rain on our chiefs.
In beauty may it rain on us.
In beauty may our corn grow.
In the trail of pollen may it rain.
In beauty all around us, may it rain.
In beauty may we walk.
The beauty is restored.
The beauty is restored.
The beauty is restored.
The beauty is restored.

Comparative Traditional Economics and Ecological Adaptations

JOSEPH G. JORGENSEN

Environment (biological and nonbiological) has been an extremely important general factor in the explanations and counter-explanations offered by ethnologists and archeologists to account for economic, kinship, and ritual organization among Pueblo cultures in the American Southwest. Beginning, perhaps, with Bryan (1929) and Steward (1937), anthropologists and geographers have sought to correlate variations in Pueblo environment with variations in Pueblo social and ritual organization (see Dozier 1970; Eggan 1950, 1966; Longacre 1970; and Ortiz 1972 for a sampling of this extensive literature). Pueblos have been central in these discussions; other Southwestern peoples have not had their social and religious organizations probed and explained in reference to environment on nearly so large a scale. Because of the unusually wide variation of cultures, languages, and, for want of a better term, microenvironments in the Southwest, there existed the need for all Southwestern tribes to be analyzed for cultural and environmental similarities and differences. In this fashion the explanations of Pueblo culture can be controlled through comparisons with non-Pueblo culture, and vice versa. Such comparisons are controlled here by working with 37 tribes or culture units representing all the language groups in the Southwest. (The term tribe is used here, even though some of these units do not correspond to the usual definitions of tribe.) The topic analyzed is restricted to economics and ecological adaptations: not ecology, kinship, or ritual. Whereas kinship and ritual are distinguished from economy for analytical purposes, "traditional economy" is deeply embedded in kinship and ritual organization. Examples for analysis are: whether or not land-owning and land-inheriting groups are organizations of kinsmen; whether or not producers of crops share their products, and if so with whom (kinsmen or others); whether or not ritual is a part of the sharing, reciprocity, redistribution, or gifting of economic resources; and the like. This is to say that whereas kinship and ritual, as such, are not the central topics of concern, they are critical to the following analysis nevertheless. Thus, in comparing traditional economics among Southwestern peoples it was necessary to define and measure information about (1) technology and material culture—tools and their uses, techniques of food extraction and production, and other products and techniques by which people articulated with their environments; (2) subsistence economy—the contributions of various types of foods to the local diet, the manner and places in which the foods were procured, the ways in which economic goods were transported, and the manner and duration of food storage; and (3) economic organization—the organization of extraction and production including the division of labor by sex, age, task groups, and specialization; the reciprocity, distribution, gifting, and sharing of access to resources; the ownership and the inheritance of property. It was also deemed important to compare Southwestern tribes for demographic information on the sizes of local community populations and the population densities in their approximate tribal territories. For information about how and what information was selected, collected, and analyzed see the explanation of methodology at the end of this chapter.

In order to analyze the ecological adaptations and to measure the relations between ecology and economy, ecological areas are defined as physical contexts, including physiography and climate, and the animals and plants that occupy those contexts. The measures of ecology are, of course, selected from an indefinitely large amount of information about biological and nonbiological environments and the relations that obtain within these environments. It is important to stress that within environments, no matter how environmental space is circumscribed (that is, as some definite or indefinite form), the phenomena and the relations among phenomena are infinite. For instance, indefinitely many surface phenomena can be intercorrelated, as can subsurface phenomena, and these two sets can, in turn, be intercorrelated.

"Ecological adaptations" has come to convey the meaning in some quarters of anthropology that human, other animal, and plant populations interact in physical space in such ways that the human population—usually unwittingly, but not necessarily so—has optimized its viability. It has, in brief, enhanced its survival probabilities by "adapting" to other aspects of a nonrational (human intentions, or reasons, or dispositions for causing them to act as they do are not required), self-regulating system. This chapter does not make such claims for ecological adaptation. Because all Southwestern tribes were practicing customs of one sort or another and occupying definable spaces at contact, it is a trivial truth to say that all were ecologically adapted. Ultimately an adaptation is anything that works. It is quite another thing to allege that "whatever is" (the nature of the tribes' economic organization), "had to be" (the tribe's economy is organized as it is because it had to be so organized). The lawlike explanation is a nonsequitur.

This chapter assesses the relations between environment and economy to learn whether scholars can postdict why economies of particular constellations of resource production and management features correlate with constellations of environmental features. It tests several hypotheses about environment-economy relations through nonmetric, multivariate techniques, or through a method of explicitly controlled and formally measured comparisons. This is not a review of the various ecological explanations that have been advanced to account for Pueblo society. The methodology employed in making these comparisons is described in the final section so as not to detract from the discussion in the text. Yet at a few points some relatively technical information must be introduced.

The sample used here of 37 Southwestern culture units (fig. 1) was drawn from a larger study of 172 culture units in Western North America (Jorgensen 1980). The culture units follow, organized by language family and subfamily membership. Elsewhere in this chapter they are referred to by means of partially overlapping classifications. For example, sometimes the Tewa are referred to separately, and sometimes the term Eastern Pueblos is used to include the Tewa (represented by Santa Clara, Nambe, San Juan, and San Ildefonso) and Taos. This use of the term Eastern Pueblos is different from that in "Pueblos: Introduction" (vol. 9). The term River Yuman is used as a cultural label to include both the River branch and the California-Delta branch of this linguistic classification.

All these groups are also treated elsewhere in *Handbook* volumes 9 and 10, except for the Tipai, who are described in volume 8, and the Lipan, in volume 13.

Yuman
- Upland Yuman—Havasupai, Walapai, Yavepe Yavapai (Verde Valley), Kewevkapaya Yavapai
- River Yuman—Mohave, Quechan, Maricopa
- Delta-California Yuman—Cocopa, eastern Tipai

Uto-Aztecan
- Pima, Papago; Hopi

Apachean (Athapaskan)—Western Apache: Northern Tonto, Southern Tonto, San Carlos, Cibecue, White Mountain; Chiricahua Apache: Warm Spring, Huachuca; Mescalero Apache; Lipan Apache; Jicarilla Apache; eastern Navajo, western Navajo

Zuni

Keresan—Acoma, Zia, Santa Ana, Santo Domingo, Cochiti

Tanoan (Kiowa-Tanoan)
- Tewa—San Juan, San Ildefonso, Santa Clara, Nambe
- Tiwa—Taos, Isleta
- Towa—Jemez

The 37 culture units in the sample are not the total universe of Southwest culture units. Because the ethnographic information was meager, it was necessary to eliminate some River Yumans, such as Halchidhoma and Kavelchadom; Tolkapaya Yavapai; some Tanoan Pueblos, such as Pecos and the doubtfully classified Piro; some Pima and Papago (especially the Salt River, Santa Cruz River, and San Pedro River Pimas, and the Río de la Concepción Papagos); and most of the Mexican groups. Nevertheless, the sample is extremely large relative to the total number of sixteenth-, seventeenth-, and eighteenth-century culture units in the Southwest.

An Overview of Southwest Environment and Culture

It will be helpful to know whether the measures employed to evaluate the relations among the environments of the 37 tribal territories in these comparisons reproduce a distribution of environments that is consonant with traditional expectations. That is, will the mountainous regions of central and southeastern Arizona occupied by Apaches be distinguished from the Colorado Plateau occupied by western Navajos and Western Pueblos, and the river plains occupied by the Yuman speakers? and so forth. Figure 2 is a two-dimensional mapping of the relations among the environments of the 37 tribes. The shorter the distance between any pair of tribal territories represented by points, the more similar the environments of the tribes.

The ordering of the environments is based on 134 separate variables for each tribal territory covering 334 different items of information about, among other things, the altitude range in each territory, the annual average precipitation, the range of average temperatures in January and July, the latitude and longitude ranges, and the numbers of species and the intensities of distributions of oaks, pines, cacti, mesquite, screw bean, mescal, yucca, sotol, berries, roots, grasses, ferns, lilies, mammals, fishes, and birds.

It is apparent that the Papago of the Sonoran Desert occupied an environmental niche most different from all other groups, and that the Tewa Pueblos (San Juan, San Ildefonso, Nambe, Santa Clara) and the Eastern Keresan Pueblos (Zia, Santa Ana, Santo Domingo,

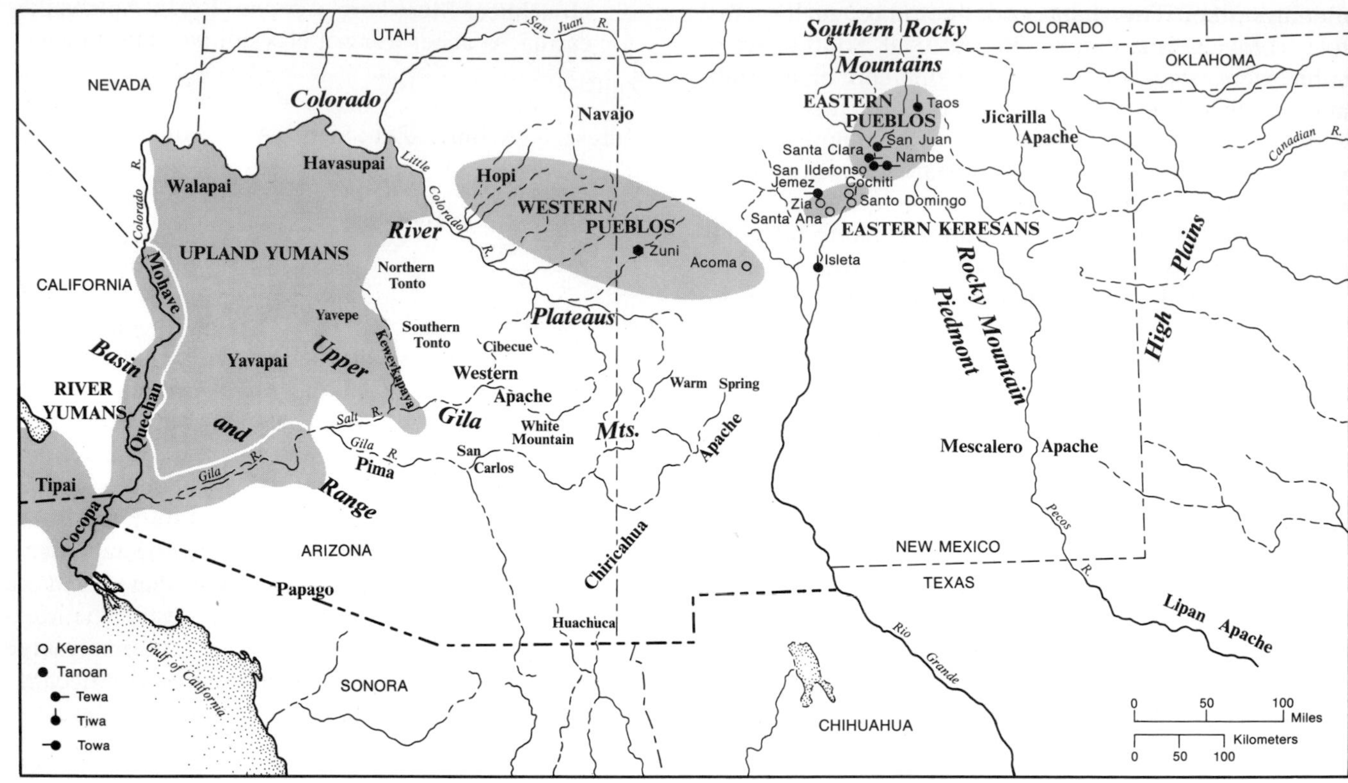

Fig. 1 Major physiographic regions of the Southwest (after U.S. Geological Survey 1970:61) and tribes evaluated in this chapter.

Cochiti) occupied the most similar micro-environmental niches. Indeed, the Pueblos in general, plus the Navajos and the Jicarilla Apache of the Colorado Plateau and the northern New Mexico Rocky Mountain and Rio Grande region shared a relatively similar environment overall. On the other hand, internally the Pueblo groups were much more similar to each other in their articulations with the environment and their economies generally than they were to their Athapaskan-speaking neighbors.

The western and eastern Navajos occupied territories that covered predominantly steppe and mountain life zones and that generally had meager precipitation (7 to 11 inches, although up to 26 inches in the mountain regions above 7,500 feet). Most of the precipitation came from summer storms, although winter storms helped account for the precipitation at higher elevations. The growing seasons varied from 170 days in the lowest elevations to 95 days in the mountain zones. Except for the relatively inaccessible Colorado River, and the somewhat more accessible San Juan River, most Navajos relied upon intermittent springs, seeps, streams, and small lakes for water. Furthermore, in this high (3,500–10,000 feet), arid (high evaporation rates), diverse area, high winds occurred periodically.

It is possible that for perhaps 700 years prior to A.D. 1000 the area in question received more precipitation than after A.D. 1000. Furthermore, the greatest amount of annual precipitation appears to have occurred during the winter periods (see R.G. Vivian 1970:75–78 for a review of the literature on this topic). After 1000 the pattern seems to emphasize a dwindling precipitation rate and a focus on summer accumulation. The recession of far-flung Pueblo occupations from the length and breadth of the entire area between about 1000 and 1300 is well documented (Longacre 1970). People who once farmed maize, beans, and squashes in scattered homesites located almost wherever it was practicable to farm—and to hunt deer, rabbits, antelope, sage hens, Rocky Mountain bighorn sheep, and to collect sundry wild plant products—evacuated the vast majority of territory. By the time the Athapaskan-speaking Navajos and Apaches entered and began to spread across the area, perhaps no earlier than the sixteenth century (Gunnerson and Gunnerson 1971:7–22), Puebloans were using it only for hunting, gathering, and religious and trade excursions. The question has not been answered about whether Navajos and other Athapaskans who took up farming initially learned the techniques from Pueblo Indians (Hester 1962:51; Opler 1971:32), or from Plains village farmers (Driver 1966), or both; that is to say, some Athapaskan speakers learned farming and pottery-making from Plains farmers whereas others learned it from Pueblo farmers (Gunnerson and Gunnerson 1971:7–22). The question is not trivial as it has become part of a larger question about the origin of matrilocal residence, matrilineal descent, and parent-in-law and children-in-law avoidances among Navajos and Western Apaches (Driver 1966; Kaut 1974; Dyen and Aberle 1974).

Sidestepping the question about the origin of matri-centered kinship organization (the Western Pueblos and the Eastern Keresan Pueblos are predominantly matricentered) and the origin of in-law avoidance customs among Navajos and most Apaches (no Pueblo group practiced these customs, whereas most Plains farmers did), it is not too daring to speculate that prior to about 1550 the Southern Athapaskans were, for the most part, scattered along the western Plains. They were predominantly hunters of bison, although some Athapaskan groups—the proto-Navajo in particular—might well have gained some sustenance from horticulture. The proto-Navajos moved into some unoccupied niches and contested for other niches with Pueblos, hunting large game (deer) as well as small (rabbits and prairie dogs), collecting plants, and, where there was sufficient water on alluvial plains, washes, or near springs, also farming. The diversity of the environment, no matter how meager the resources, tolerated a wide range of simple extractive pursuits, as well as farming. In preceding centuries Pueblo Indians had proved that farming could be done on river plains at 3,500 feet and on foothills and mesas at 7,500 feet.

The Pueblo groups occupied environments much like parts of the Navajo environment. The Hopi and Zuni lived on arid mesas, or steppe life zones. The Hopi did not have permanently flowing streams and, whereas the Zuni had a stream, it was not used for farming. Indeed, Hopi, Zuni, and Acoma (the Western Pueblos), lived in environments more similar to the western Navajos than to the Eastern Pueblos. Similar to the western Navajos, the Acoma, Zuni, and Hopi relied on rainfall, seeps, springs, and wash-offs for their farming.

The Eastern Pueblos, on the other hand (represented by Taos, Santa Clara, Nambe, San Juan, and San Ildefonso in figure 2), located their villages and farm sites on the banks of the Rio Grande and its tributaries. Not only did the Eastern Pueblo villages get greater precipitation from storms attracted by the mountains, as in the mountainous regions occupied by some Navajos, but also they had regular sources of water from the river system. Furthermore, Eastern Pueblo groups positioned their farmland at elevations lower than the river, thus availing themselves of a longer growing season than was enjoyed in the steppe areas, yet also placing themselves to draw water from the river by gravity flow.

As was pointed out by Eggan (1950) and others, Eastern Keresans and the Jemez Towa were situated on tributaries of the Rio Grande that were not nearly so conducive to farming as were the areas occupied by the Eastern Pueblos. The tributaries ran only intermittently, the rainfall was more sparse (about 10 inches) than in the adjacent Eastern Pueblo areas, and although they hunted and gathered, their hunting range was restricted by Navajos.

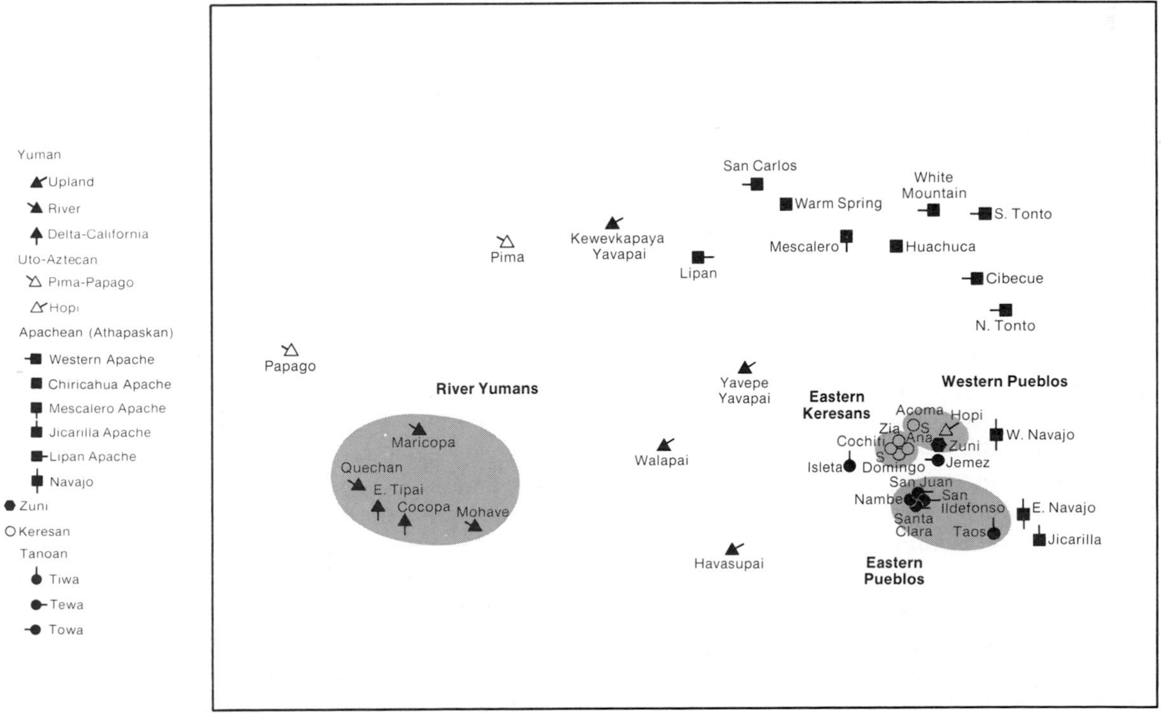

Fig. 2. Total environment in aboriginal Southwest. MINISSA smallest space analysis in 2 dimensions. Ranked G-coefficients based on 134 variables (334 attributes). K = .10 in 24 iterations.

Whereas the Eastern Pueblos did practically no dry farming, the Eastern Keresans did some dry farming and some irrigation farming, and the Western Pueblos relied almost wholly on rainfall and wash-offs.

South and west of the Pueblo-Navajo area the Western Apaches (Northern Tonto, Southern Tonto, Cibecue, White Mountain, San Carlos) occupied the desert, steppe, and mountainous areas of central and eastern Arizona. Both the desert areas and the steppe areas were at lower elevations (2,000 to 5,000 feet) than were the comparable areas farther north. Concomitantly, the growing seasons were somewhat longer (116 to 295 days) in the Western Apache territory. The annual precipitation was somewhat greater (10 to 30 inches) than in the north, and there was definitely a greater variety of edible plants, including cacti, mescal, and mesquite, in the more southerly area. The Salt and Gila rivers and their tributaries traversed Western Apache territory, and whereas some local groups farmed on the river bottoms, others farmed near seeps and springs at the higher elevations in the transitional biotic zones of the steppe (see Goodwin 1942; Griffin, Leone, and Basso 1971).

The Chiricahua (Huachuca, Warm Spring) and Mescalero Apache occupied environments that were more similar to those of their Western Apache congeners than to any other groups in the Southwest, and this is demonstrated in figure 2. Furthermore, except that the Mescalero, who were located east of the Rio Grande in what is now New Mexico, had access to bison on the southern Plains, the Chiricahua and Mescalero exploited contiguous territories that were very large—ranging throughout deserts, steppe, and mountains from the Pueblo villages in the north through the northern states of Mexico in the south (Castetter and Opler 1936). The Mescalero and Chiricahua were mountain dwellers who regularly exploited the mescal, mesquite, cacti, oak, piñon, grasses, large and small mammals, and other food resources throughout their ranges. Castetter and Opler (1936:3–63) analyze over 100 plants used by these people for food, drink, and narcotics, and they do not pretend to present a complete inventory of all plants used.

Unlike their Western Apache and Navajo counterparts, Mescalero and Chiricahua Apache did very little farming, although they did some. Castetter and Opler (1936:27) are of the opinion that these mobile hunters and gatherers did practically no farming in the aboriginal period, presumably extending back to the sixteenth century. They do not consider whether these Apaches began to rely less upon horticulture either with their acquisition of the horse and the greater range horses provided for hunting and gathering, or with their movement from the western plains to the less salubrious, for horticultural purposes, mountains, steppe, and deserts of southeastern Arizona and New Mexico during the competitive equestrian hunting period. It is known, for instance, that Cheyenne and, perhaps, Crow Indians gave up most or all of their horticultural pursuits during the equestrian hunting period. The Mescalero and Chiricahua could have done likewise.

Several mountain ranges and high basins, as well as steep canyons and low flatlands are distributed in the area. The low, desert areas had extremely meager water supplies, and the highest mountains had springs and heavy snow packs. To the east the Pecos River and Rio Grande cut through some of the valley floors and provided nearly constant water, but for the most part streams in the Chiricahua and Mescalero areas ran intermittently. The Apaches are said to have been masters of their huge territories, moving with the seasonal changes and pursuing the wild food harvests, plant and animal, as they occurred (Castetter and Opler 1936:10–15).

In figure 2 the crescent-shaped distribution of Apache environments and the ball-like distribution of Pueblo-Navajo environments are separated from the River Yuman environments (Maricopa, Quechan, eastern Tipai, Cocopa, Mohave) by a string of steppe-desert dwellers, the Upland Yumans (Havasupai, Walapai, Yavapai).

The Havasupai once occupied the territory as far east as Moenkopi near what is now Tuba City, Arizona. But according to Spier (1928) the Havasupai were displaced by Navajos and from the early nineteenth century occupied Supai canyon (3,200 feet) in the Grand Canyon from March through September. During these months they farmed, yet in October they split into small groups of families and returned to the Coconino Plateau, a semiarid limestone plateau 6,000 to 7,000 feet above sea level, staying there until the following spring. Whereas Supai was much warmer during the late fall and winter months, the Havasupai scaled the plateau in order to hunt bighorn sheep, and to collect yucca, grasses, mesquite, and mescal on the way up, and juniper berries, piñon, and seeds on top. The winter snow accumulation provided water and also made it easier to track rabbits, deer, and antelope on the plateau.

The Walapai, near neighbors of the Havasupai, did not have rich canyon farmland. Rather, they were strung out along the bases of several cliffs and mountains, occupying dry transitional steppe areas between desert and mountains. Cacti and mescal were available, as were some acorns, walnuts, and piñons at the highest elevations. Yet the Walapai territory was primarily washes and undissected plains, basins, or valleys. The rains were in the late summer and early winter and the precipitation was very sparse, averaging about six inches a year.

The Walapai convened winter camps of several families and hunted bighorn sheep, antelopes, and rats but split into even smaller hunting and gathering groups during spring through fall as they sought edible plants, small game, and water. Thus, they convened and dispersed in a pattern completely opposite to the Havasupai. According to Kroeber (1935) these mobile people claimed to have tried farming in only two locales in the territory they occupied in the nineteenth century.

The Yavepe (Northeastern Yavapai) occupied upper Verde Valley in central Arizona and were separated from the Walapai and Havasupai to the north by uninhabited land that was used periodically by the Northern Tonto Western Apache. The Yavepe hunted antelope in Lonesome Valley and deer, rabbits, and rats wherever available. Mescal was the most important single wild food in their diet, but they also relied on the giant saguaro cactus, sunflower seeds, and many more wild plants. The Yavepe farmed maize and tobacco at contact, but not beans and squashes, nor did they plant panic grasses and other wild grasses used by their River Yuman congeners.

The Kewevkapaya (Southeastern Yavapai) were located in the desert canyon country south and west of the Yavepe and bordered on the south and east by the San Carlos Apache. They farmed even less than their northeast counterparts in the period when they were adjacent to Western Apache. Whereas the Yavapai had access to waters of the Gila and Salt rivers and their environment was as similar to the Gila River Pima as it was to the San Carlos Apache, by the nineteenth century they primarily supported themselves by collecting mescal, mesquite, acorns, cacti, seeds, berries, roots, and bulbs, and by hunting deer and bighorn sheep. The growing season was long (290 days), and the precipitation was meager (3 to 10 inches per year), but the Salt and Gila provided water—even two floods a year in some locales.

It is interesting that the Kewevkapaya did not farm more, and that they did not rely more upon domesticates in their diet. Of course, the same can be said for the Western Apaches and the River Yumans.

The River Yumans are set off from all other groups. The Mohave, Quechan, eastern Tipai, and Cocopa occupied the floodplains of the Colorado River and the hot deserts above (rainfall about four inches a year, mean temperature about 70° F., growing season 300 days). A flood of the Colorado deposited silt on the river plain at least once each year, yet the plain remained moist all year through subsurface capillary action, and it supported mesophytic vegetation. The rocky, arid mesas above the plain supported only xerophytic plants (Castetter and Bell 1951).

Bottomlands supported mesquite and screw beans in considerable numbers, as well as many wild grasses (which they planted), roots, nuts, cacti, and yucca (Castetter and Bell 1951:187–188, 200–201, 204, 205). The desert environment did not provide either abundance or variety of animals. Small groups of deer, mountain sheep, and antelope browsed in the mountains at some distance and were not especially important. Rather, rats (*Dipodomys* spp.), rabbit (*Sylvilagus audubonii*), jackrabbit (*Lepus californicus*), migratory ducks, and freshwater fish were the most important of all. The Cocopa even fished for ocean fishes and shellfishes. Other small animals eaten occasionally included lizards (*Sceloporus clarkii, S. magister*), ground squirrels, beavers, and coyotes. The humpback sucker, the Colorado squawfish (*Ptychocheilus lucius,* a three-foot-long minnow), the bonytail (*Gila elegans*), and the mullet were the most important fishes.

The Maricopa were located on the Gila River, upriver from its confluence with the Colorado. The Gila had more fertile land than the Colorado and regularly flooded twice a year. Two floods on the Colorado were much less predictable but did occur from time to time. In general the Maricopa had access to practically all the types and quantities of subsistence resources that were available to their Colorado River congeners, but in addition they had land and water that made farming a more stable source of food products than was the same pursuit on the Colorado. Two floods, even when the farmer relies upon capillary action of subsurface water to irrigate the crops, allows for two plantings and two yields a year. Nevertheless, the Maricopa culled less of their diet from farm products than some of the Colorado River groups, and substantially less than their neighbors on the Gila, the Uto-Aztecan-speaking Pima. The Pima and Papago spoke the same language and shared many culture traits but occupied different environments. The Papago had considerably fewer water resources and therefore possessed a very different subsistence economy.

The Pima, situated on the fertile plains of the Gila with an annual growing season of 295 days, not only utilized the two floods a year for two plantings but also developed a canal system of irrigation with dams and ditches. Not even the Maricopa developed canals until very late (about 1850 according to Castetter and Bell 1942). Nevertheless, the Pima and their desert-dwelling relatives, the Papago—who had an "impoverished marginal version of the Gila Pima irrigation system" (Castetter and Bell 1951:239)—exploited the mescal, mesquite, screw bean, cacti, grasses, and small game in their areas. The major differences were that the Pima used wild food sources much less, and the Papago used wild food sources much more than any of the Yuman-speaking farmers.

It is apparent from these generalizations about tribal environments in the Southwest that four major types of environments prevail. Most Apacheans reside in territories that encompass mountains, steppe, and deserts. The Western Apache have access to more water than most other Apachean speakers, whereas Mescalero and Chiricahua had a wider range of wild foods available to them spread over a much wider and more diverse desert terrain than did their Western Apache neighbors.

The Pueblos and Navajo and Jicarilla reside on the high Colorado Plateau and Rocky Mountain zones of the northern Southwest. Only the Eastern Pueblos of these groups have regular, year-round sources of water, as well as abundant fish. The growing seasons were much shorter in the north than in the south, and the cacti, mescal, mesquite, screw bean, and several species of grasses distributed in the more southerly areas had much narrower distributions in the north. On the other hand deer, mountain sheep, and several species of small mammals, including rabbits, rats, and prairie dogs, were as abundant in the mountains and on the mesas of the north as in the south.

In the south and west of the Southwest, along the courses of the Gila, Salt, and Colorado rivers, Pima-Papago and Yuman speakers enjoyed year-round water, abundant fish, long growing seasons, and rich silt deposits from river floods. Yet their terrains did not provide large mammals, small mammals, or even wild plants in the amounts available in the eastern half of the Southwest. Nevertheless, mescal, mesquite, screw bean, panic grass, and scores of other species were available, if in sparser distributions. The desert-dwelling Papago did not, except for a very few local communities, enjoy continuous running water.

Between the river dwellers in the south and west, and the mountain-steppe-desert dwellers in the east, were the Upland Yumans situated throughout the mesas and deserts of what is now central Arizona. Only the Walapai occupied land not suitable for horticulture, yet only the Havasupai engaged in much farming.

To get an impression about overall culture similarities and differences for the 37 tribes in this sample, see figure 3, which is a two-dimensional mapping of the cultural distances among the tribes. As in the previous figure, the closer any pair of the constellation of points, the more similar the cultures. The measure for "total culture" is based on 292 variables covering information about technology, subsistence economy, economic organization, settlement pattern, community organization, kinship organization, political organization, sodalities, warfare, ceremonies, life cycle observances, shamanism, and magic. Figure 3 shows that the Yuman speakers form a chain from Quechan at the top to Kewevkapaya and Walapai at the bottom. The clear break between River Yuman and Upland Yuman environments, so noticeable in figure 2, does not occur. Indeed, language relations are a much better fit with overall similarity of Yuman cultures than are environmental areas. The riverine farmers and fishers are linked to the nonfarming or very minimally farming Walapai and Yavapai through the riverplain farming Havasupai. The Uto-Aztecan-speaking Pima and Papago with critically different environments—fertile river plain versus desert—are separated from all other Southwestern cultures, even though the Pima environment was more similar to the Kewevkapaya and the Maricopa than it was to Papago.

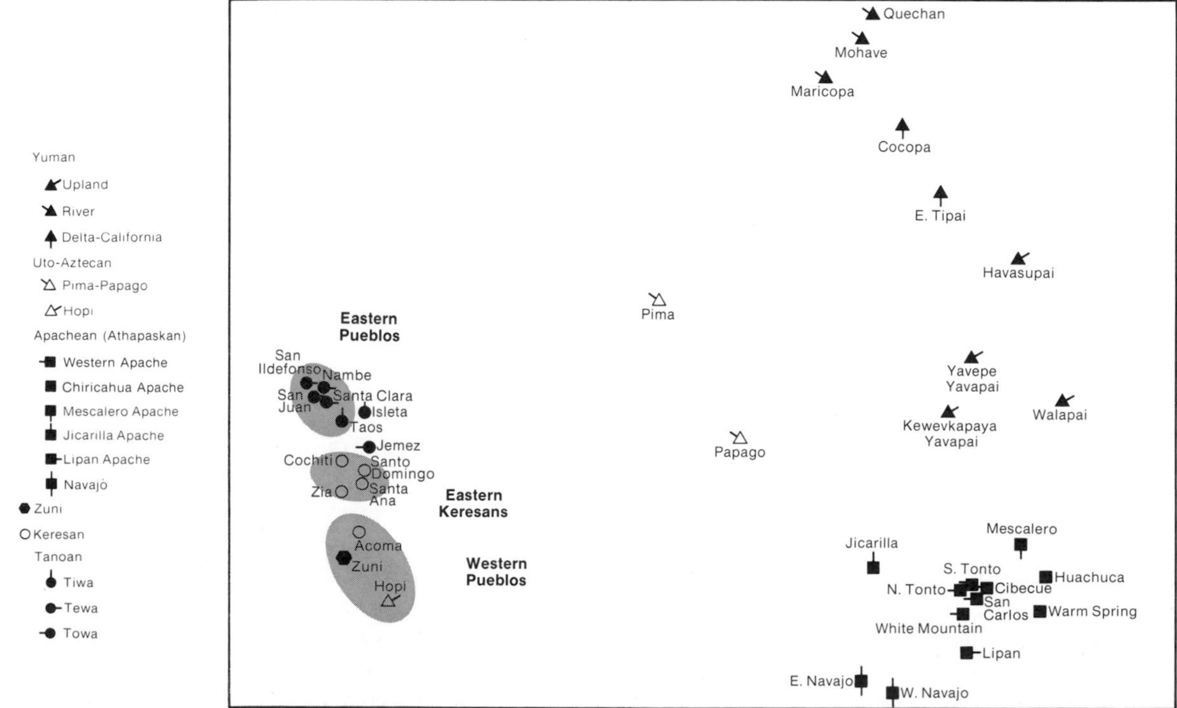

690 Fig. 3. Total culture in aboriginal Southwest. MINISSA smallest space analysis in 2 dimensions. Ranked G-coefficients based on 292 variables (1,577 attributes). K = .13 in 13 iterations.

The Athapaskan speakers form a third recognizable distribution. The Western Apache are in the center with the Mescalero, Chiricahua, and Lipan forming a semicircle on one side, while the Navajo and Jicarilla are pulled off toward the other side. The cultural affiliations of the Navajo and Jicarilla are much better accounted for by language affiliation than by environmental similarities, as figure 2 attests. The Athapaskan speakers who probably began moving into the Southwest during the early sixteenth century maintained considerable similarities even though they came to occupy a vast area.

The double column of Pueblo cultures, separated a considerable distance in the euclidian space from the other three distributions of cultures, reproduces a predictable order among the Tanoan-speaking Eastern Pueblos at the top through Hopi at the bottom. Indeed, while addressing ecological, kinship, sodality, and ritual information, Eggan (1950) suggested that all the Pueblos once shared a common "social structure." The Tanoan speakers moved east into a new environment and their structures were reshaped. Keresans, Eggan averred, lent support to this view by retaining some early Pueblo features but changing others toward forms similar to the Tanoans. They formed a "bridge" between Eastern and Western Pueblos. The Western Pueblos retained the basic structures and were used as the bases for comparison. Figure 3 demonstrates that the Tanoan speakers (San Ildefonso through Jemez) are linked to the Eastern Keresan speakers (Cochiti through Zia), who are linked to the Western Keresan-speaking Acoma, who are linked to the Zuni, who are linked to the Hopi.

It is doubtful that the differences in environments account for the differences in culture, but a look at figure 2 will attest that the Keresan speakers occupy environments more similar to the Western Pueblos than to the Eastern Pueblos, except for Jemez. Thus it is reasonable to ask whether environmental differences, or the organization for agricultural production with irrigation, made possible by bottomland of the Rio Grande and its tributaries, or both, accounts for the differences among Eastern Pueblos, Eastern Keresans, and Western Pueblos—keeping in mind that culture similarities for the Pueblos, as for other groups in the Southwest, fit more closely with language similarities than with environmental similarities, and furthermore increasing the scope of the question to account for other environments and economic organizations in the Southwest.

Technology, Subsistence, and Economic Organization

At contact some form of horticulture was practiced by all groups in this Southwestern sample, except perhaps for the Kewevkapaya, Mescalero, Chiricahua, and Lipan Apache, and albeit minimally for the Yavepe and the Walapai. Figures 4 and 5 are two representations of the relations among tribal technologies as they are

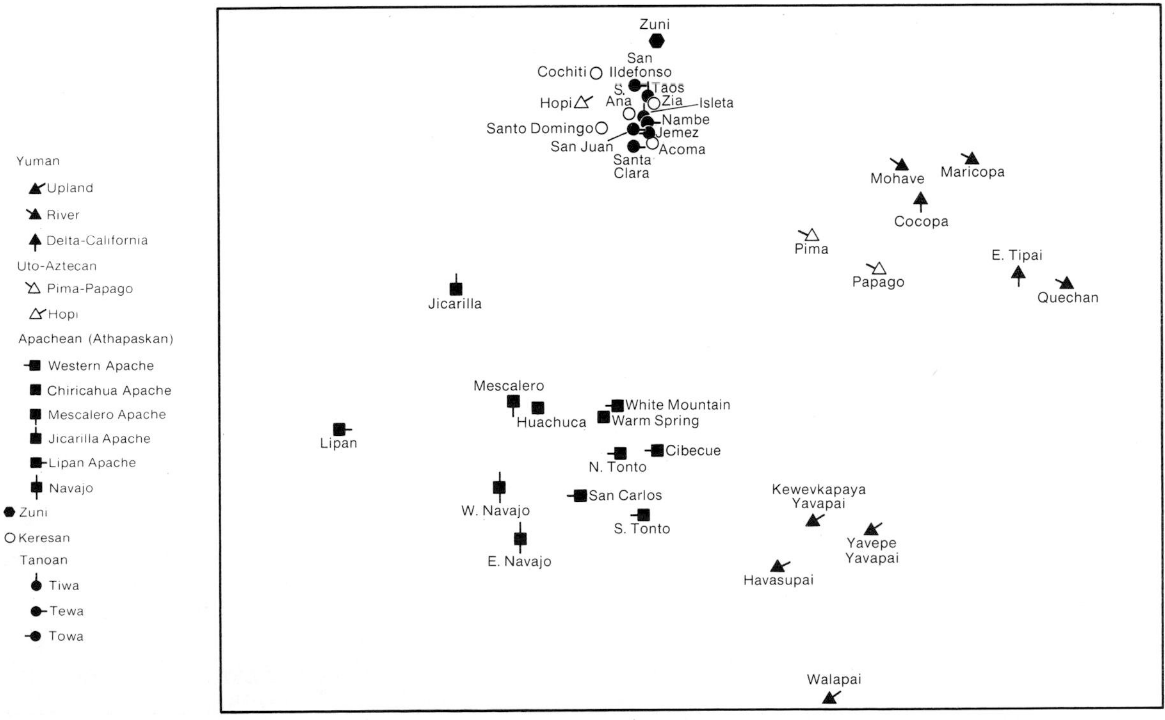

Fig. 4. Technology in aboriginal Southwest. MINISSA smallest space analysis in 2 dimensions. Ranked G-coefficients based on 46 variables (204 attributes). K = .15 in 12 iterations.

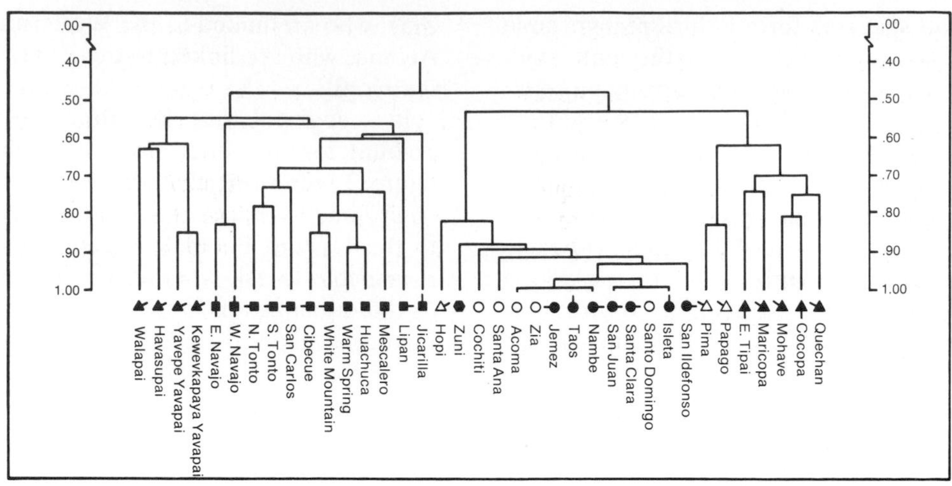

Fig. 5. Technology in aboriginal Southwest. Jorgensen's nonmetric tree in one dimension. G-coefficients based on 46 variables (204 attributes).

measured from 46 variables covering information on techniques and equipment for hunting, fishing, gathering wild plants, horticulture, food preparation and preservation, boats, housing, clothing, and weaving. Figure 4 represents the relations in two dimensions but does not preserve metric information. Figure 5 represents the relations in one dimension, but it preserves the information about the strength of the associations between pairs and among sets.

It is evident that the groups in the Southwest, when compared for technology, organize into: Pueblo, River Yuman and Pima-Papago, Upland Yuman (Pai), and Athapaskan clusters. The overall resemblance among the Pueblos is obvious from both figures, even though the Eastern Pueblos practice farming with an irrigation system of canals, dams, and ditches and gravity flow; Eastern Keresans use dams, ditches, and terraces; and Western Pueblos use dams and terraces. The various forms of water impoundment and diversion—from the Western Pueblo forms of controlled wash-offs and heavy rains to the Eastern Pueblo uses of main canals and a tributary system—are used in a context of marked similarity of technological items and techniques. This is quite remarkable considering that the Rio Grande and mountainous areas inhabited by most of the Tanoan speakers had relatively abundant fish resources (annually 50–100 pounds of fish per average square mile of territory), more grass species, a greater amount of browse, more abundant large game, and, for the more southerly Tanoans, even more species of mesquite, mescal, and cacti than the Keresans and Western Pueblos. Nevertheless, farming tools and techniques (aside from differences in irrigation), food storage, gathering poles and tongs, digging sticks, fence enclosures for hunting, pitfalls, clothing, and the like, are remarkably similar for these groups.

Most similar to the Pueblos are the Pima, Papago, and River Yuman farmers, referred to collectively as the Pima-Yuman group. Although the environments of the Pueblo and Pima-Yuman sets are very different, the similarities among their gathering, farming, and hunting technologies help set them off from the Upland Yuman and Athapaskan groups. It is important to note that the River Yumans, including the Maricopa of the Gila River, used simple fish-procuring tools such as hand nets, weirless traps, and obstructions, and obtained large quantities of fish. The Pima had weirless traps, but procured very little fish. On the other hand, for centuries the Pima, probably the Papago (wherever the conditions permitted), or their precursors had extensive canal irrigation systems replete with dikes, dams, and tributary systems. Yet in aboriginal times the River Yumans, including the Gila-dwelling Maricopa, did not borrow irrigation practices from the Pima or Papago. The Pima and Papago had more formal and extensive food storage than the Yumans.

The Athapaskans shared many features of clothing, housing, hunting, and gathering; and their farming technology did not include irrigation, except for the Navajo and Jicarilla, who used natural floods and some dams to control runoff. Apparently some Western Apaches used some irrigation techniques, where practicable, in the nineteenth century (Griffin, Leone, and Basso 1971).

The Upland Yumans, probably erstwhile farmers, are positioned somewhat closer to the Athapaskan group than to the River Yumans. In that all but the Havasupai seem to have given up farming, or were forced to give it up, their technology reflects their gathering and hunting subsistence economies.

Compare the distribution of the Southwestern cultures for environment (fig. 2) and technology (fig. 4). Except for the Navajo, Jicarilla, and Pima, the fit between environment and technology is very close, much closer than between environment and any other subclassification of cultural phenomena. These distributions suggest that people in similar environments tend to have similar technologies. On the other hand, the Navajo and Apache in the Pueblo area did not adopt all the Pueblo farming technology or Eastern Pueblo fishing techniques. And in the Pima-Yuman group, Pimas did not adopt all River Yuman fishing techniques while River Yumans did not adopt Pima irrigation techniques. In example after example, regardless of the multidimensional measures of environment-culture relations, cultural similarity aligns more along the lines of linguistic relatedness than it does along the lines of environmental similarity.

In order to compare similarities and differences, subsistence economy was measured using 30 variables covering information about the relative importance of agriculture, fishing, hunting, and gathering in the diet; whether the resources were produced or procured locally or whether they were obtained extra-locally, and the amounts for each source; the nature or types of resources procured or produced, the manner in which they were transported and stored, and the duration of the storage.

Practically every farming group in the Southwest raised maize, beans, and squashes, although the Yavapai and Walapai, at least by the mid-eighteenth century farmed only maize (and perhaps squashes), and very little at that, while the River Yumans also planted sunflowers and several varieties of wild grasses. It cannot be inferred from the presence of farming that farm products were dominant in the diets of all farmers.

A comparison of technology with subsistence economy shows how different two distributions can be. Technology articulates people with their environments, and subsistence economy (as it is measured here) shows relative differences in the outcomes of those articulations. For instance, Castetter and Bell (1951) referred to the Papago as desert-dwelling Pima, a retrogression from the Gila River Pima subsistence economy, which was a simple function of different environments. There is no doubt about the similarity of Pima-Papago technology, but in different environments this rather similar technology yielded very different subsistence economies. Whereas the Pima obtained 60 to 70 percent of their subsistence from maize, beans, and squashes produced locally, the Papago probably obtained no more than 20 percent of their subsistence from farm products, and perhaps one-third of these products came from trade with River Yumans and Pimas, feasts given by Pimas, and ceremonial gifts from the Pima. The Papago obtained the bulk of their food from wild plants, and some of those resources, too, were obtained extra-locally through gathering on Pima territory and through gifting. The smallest amount of Pima subsistence came from game and fish, and the Papago from game alone. So the harsh desert environment with its diffuse and sparse resources did not provide much game; furthermore, considerable distances were covered by the Papago to collect plants. Yet on the river floodplains the Pima obtained a predictable, abundant, localized food supply—enough to allow for gifting and exchanging for meat and so forth.

Figures 6 and 7 display distributions of the Pima and River Yumans, whose cluster is far removed from the Papago. The Pima and River Yumans obtained their dominant or co-dominant sources of food from agriculture, although the probable percentages of contribution varied from a low of perhaps 25 to 30 percent for the Maricopa on the rich Gila River to 60 to 70 percent for the Pima on the same river. The Colorado River Yumans probably obtained 30 to 50 percent of their sustenance from agriculture. All these people used multiple storage techniques (jars, ollas, room storage, platform storage, even caves, and every household had a separate, semisubterranean storage structure) but tended not to store crops for seed or for food more than one year. The River Yumans obtained as much of their diets from fish as they did from mescal, mesquite, and other wild plants, while the Pima did not fish so intensively or so well. None of these groups traded for agricultural products, although the Pima, and to a much lesser extent the River Yumans, traded agricultural products for animal products. There is no good environmental reason for the variation in the use of farm products among these people (see Castetter and Bell 1951:248–251). The River Yumans could have developed canal irrigation, but they did not. Furthermore, they could have planted more agricultural land, but they did not. Even the Maricopa on the Gila River did not begin to develop canal irrigation until after 1850. The paucity of water in Papago environments accounts for Papago difference from Pima and River Yuman subsistence.

Among the Pueblos, all of whom obtained more than 50 percent of their total sustenance from agricultural products, there is a looser grouping than for technology. The grouping reflects the roles played by hunting among the Keresans and Taos, pulling them somewhat toward the Athapaskans, and a modest amount of fishing among the Tewa, putting them at the top of the distribution. All the Pueblos stored their food and seed crops in rooms, and some also used walled-in overhangs. They tended to store foods, especially seed crops, for more than one year as a hedge against a poor yield. All the Pueblos collected wild plants in their areas as an important source of food (probably no more than 20%). The Zuni obtained some wild plants extra-locally, and all the Pueblos, except the Keresans, traded agricultural products for game. The Keresans seem to have had too little of the former and enough of the latter.

It is relevant to mention that not one of the groups whose major or codominant sources of food were agricultural products traded for agricultural products, yet

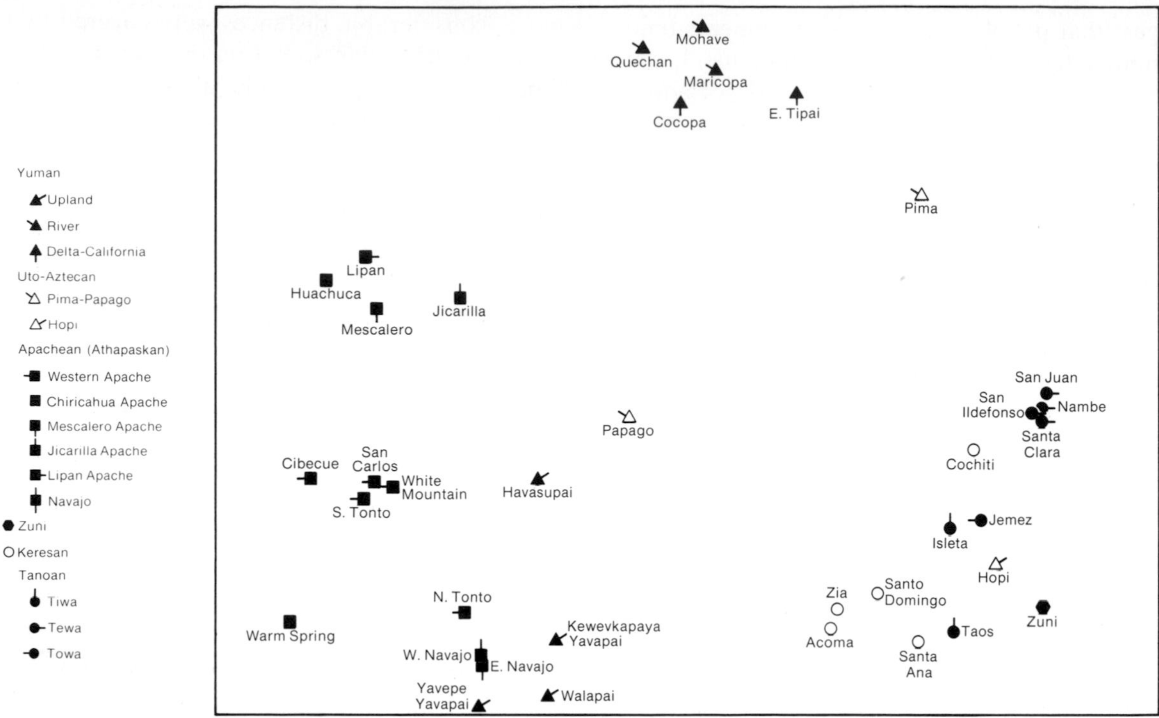

Fig. 6. Subsistence economy in aboriginal Southwest. MINISSA smallest space analysis in 2 dimensions. Ranked G-coefficients based on 30 variables (182 attributes). K = .16 in 11 iterations.

the Mohave, Quechan, Pima, Hopi, Zuni, and Tanoans traded for game. Virtually all other groups in the sample (Upland Yumans, Athapaskans, and Papagos) acquired food products through trade, raid, gifts, or some combination of these. Thus, of all the farming groups whose productive resource areas were relatively localized to river plains, river bottoms, washes, and fertile areas on mesas, those whose territories were bordered or crossed by the Athapaskans were (1) most dependent on agriculture, whether or not they practiced canal irrigation, and (2) most circumscribed in the amount of area available to them to pursue the more diffusely distributed wild plants and game. The Mohave, who were not bordered by Athapaskans, traded crops to the innocuous Walapai, and also gifted them regularly, perhaps partly out of good will because the relationship was markedly assymetrical, with the Mohave giving and the Walapai receiving. The Papago stood in somewhat the same relationship to the Quechan.

Some generalizations should be offered at this point, but they should be regarded as concluding hypotheses that require confirmation from further information provided below, as well as comparative ethnohistoric tests that have not been conducted. When the Athapaskans moved into the Southwest, filling much space left unoccupied by the contractions of Pueblo, Mogollon, and Hohokam farming settlements, they also began to crowd Pueblos, Pimas, Papagos, and Upland Yumans out of hunting territories and potential farming territories. Whereas Athapaskans began trading products of the hunt for products of the farm with the Pueblos, and even attending ceremonies at which they were feasted, they intermittently raided the crops of these farmers and they also raided and battled the Pima, Papago, and Yavapai. It is doubtful, but remotely possible, that these new relationships caused Pueblos and Pimas to become more dependent on crops than they had been, say, prior to the sixteenth century. The development of forms of irrigation since about A.D. 1000 argues against such a view. On the other hand, it is quite possible that the reduction of the territory available to the Yavapai, coupled with Apache threats, helped push the Yavapai groups to give up most of their farming and to accommodate to the Western Apache (for which the evidence is very strong), and it undoubtedly helped restrict Papago territory and divide the Pima population. Partly because they desired products from the hunt and partly to deflect some raids, the Pueblo farmers might well have continued to host Athapaskans.

The Athapaskans certainly helped to cause many changes in aboriginal Southwest economies, but Ute raiders and traders (Jorgensen 1965; Schroeder 1965) and River Yuman warriors and traders also helped to shape the seventeenth- and eighteenth-century configurations.

The Navajo farmed more extensively than the Yavapai or Walapai, at least during the eighteenth and nine-

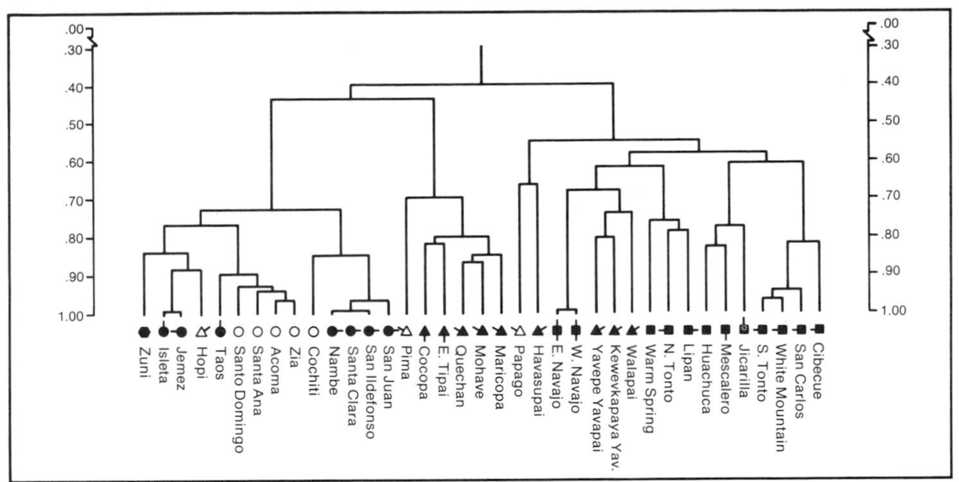

Fig. 7. Subsistence economy in aboriginal Southwest. Jorgensen's nonmetric tree in one dimension. G-coefficients based on 30 variables (182 attributes).

teenth centuries, and the Yavapai and Walapai were more dependent on wild plant foods, particularly mescal and saguaro cactus, than were the Navajo. They were probably equally dependent on large and small game. The Yavapai traded with Navajo and Apaches. The Kewevkapaya intermarried with Northern Tonto (Western Apache), organized into matricentered clans and band organizations, and came to be known as Yavapai Apaches (Schroeder 1974). Furthermore, Yavapai often joined Western Apache raids on Pima and Maricopa villages and conducted their own raids on Walapai and Havasupai. Like the Athapaskans, however, they did not raid the Quechan and Mohave, who were formidable opponents. It seems as though the Western Apaches, the Navajos, and the Quechan and Mohave used the Upland Yuman groups as buffers between them. The Colorado River Yumans used the Yavapai and the Walapai as trade connections to the Pueblos, and even the Mohave did not stop the Yavapai from attacking their friends the Walapai. The Yavapai groups maintained internal friendships.

The Warm Spring Chiricahua and the Northern Tonto component of the Western Apache are outliers between the Navajo–Upland Yuman group and the Western Apache group (figs. 6–7). They relied less on farming and more on gathering than the Navajos or the Western Apaches. On environmental evidence alone one would expect the Warm Spring Chiricahua to be placed closer to Huachuca.

The Western Apache cluster represents a subsistence economy in which wild plants contributed the most to the diet, followed by large and small game, and finally agriculture. The Western Apaches did not get much more than 25 percent of their sustenance from agricultural products, whether they raised their own crops or plundered them from Yavapai, Pima, Papago, or Maricopa. Nevertheless, the exceptional storability and nutritional qualities of agricultural products enhanced their value, and these facts were not lost on Western Apaches as either farmers or raiders (see Griffin, Leone, and Basso 1971).

The cluster of most easterly Apacheans represents people in several micro-environments, but what they shared was a modest amount of fishing (only the Warm Spring among the other Athapaskans fished). The Jicarilla farmed more than the other members of the set, and the Lipan and Huachuca were most dependent on gathering. The other similarities are that all four groups covered enormous territories in quest of game, plants, and plunder.

Some generalizations from subsistence economic comparisons are that those who produced the most food did not raid or trade for agricultural products. Those who produced little or no food raided, traded, or received agricultural products as gifts. The Yavapai were raided for food but also joined the Western Apaches and did some raiding to get food. The Athapaskans dominated hunting in the Southwest, but only the Navajo among all Athapaskans depended more on hunting than gathering, and for them, hunting was secondary to farming. The Athapaskan response to diffusely distributed resources was to use large territories while restricting the movements of non-Athapaskans.

Figures 8 and 9 represent the relations among the 37 culture units in this Southwest sample as measured by information on 67 variables pertaining to economic organization. The variables cover questions about the organization of labor by sex, age, specialization, and task groups for subsistence pursuits, housing, the production of tools, and so forth. They also cover the organization of reciprocity and distribution of goods, including sharing of access to resources, gift exchange,

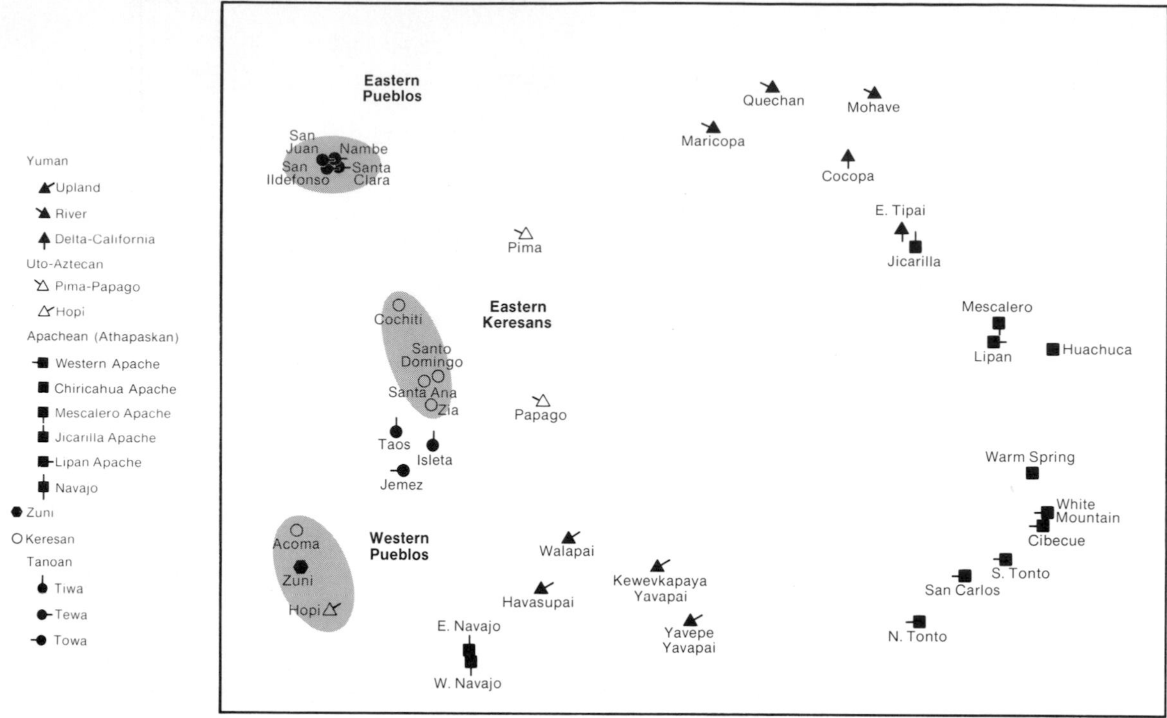

Fig. 8. Economic organization in aboriginal Southwest. MINISSA smallest space analysis in 2 dimensions. Ranked G-coefficients based on 67 variables (409 attributes). K = .13 in 12 iterations.

barter and trade. Two further sets of variables deal with the ownership and inheritance of property including strategic resources for production. In these distributions the differences among the Western Pueblos (Hopi, Zuni, Acoma), most of the Eastern Pueblos (San Juan, Nambe, Santa Clara, San Ildefonso), and the Eastern Keresans (plus the Tanoan Pueblos of Jemez, Isleta, and Taos) are apparent, yet they still form one large group. The Upland Yuman group is separated a considerable distance from the River Yumans, as are the Pima and Papago. Except for the Navajo, the Athapaskans form an uninterrupted semicircle distribution in figure 8 from the easternmost Apaches at the top to the westernmost at the bottom.

Among the Pueblos, it was the nuclear or perhaps bilateral stem family that either owned or had usufruct rights to garden plots and house sites among all the Eastern Keresans and all the Tanoan speakers, except for the Jemez and Isleta, in the sample. The Isleta sites were owned by individual men, whereas among the Jemez ownership was vested in the matriclan. Among all the Western Pueblos garden plots and houses were owned by matriclans.

In terms of the supervision of these resources, the dike, dam, and canal systems of the Eastern Pueblos required some communal effort, although farming itself was a family affair. The Eastern Pueblos, apparently prior to Spanish contact, developed political and religious sodalities composed of men (not necessarily related) of special status and real power capable of causing the villagers to maintain the central canals and dams, contribute labor toward producing crops for the leaders of the village sodality, participate in communal rituals, and so forth. Indeed, these leaders can be viewed as the supervisors of each village's communal property—corporeal such as land and houses, and incorporeal such as the major ceremonials. Thus, family "ownership" of farm and house sites is better defined as usufruct rights because the political-religious leaders of the villages could confiscate houses and land from village members who did not perform their communal duties.

Among the Eastern Pueblos, none of the villages or bilateral families within villages claimed ownership to fishing sites on the rivers; and of all Pueblos, Eastern and Western, only the ambilocal bilateral families among the Tewa villages (San Juan, Nambe, San Ildefonso, Santa Clara) claimed ownership of key gathering sites and key hunting sites. Thus, the key strategic resources for all Pueblos, as is inferred from the contribution of food to the diet, are farming sites, which are located in environments with relatively scarce and diffuse resources in the west, and more abundant and localized resources in the east. All Pueblos recognized ownership of farm plots, but ownership of other food resource sites was very rare. Furthermore, access to game for Pueblos was somewhat restricted by Athapaskan and Ute hunters.

The farming work—clearing, planting, weeding, harvesting—among all Pueblos was done predominantly by kin-related men working in task groups on family

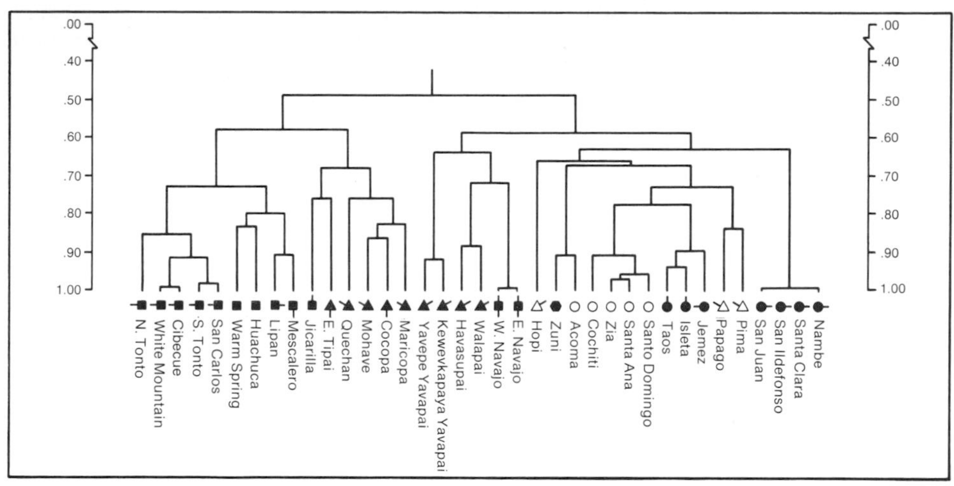

Fig. 9. Economic organization in aboriginal Southwest. Jorgensen's nonmetric tree in one dimension. G-coefficients based on 67 variables (409 attributes).

or extended family gardens.* In the west the men were matrikinsmen, and in the east they were bilateral kinsmen. Except for the communal tasks in the east of constructing and maintaining the major dams and canals, work on lateral ditches and dikes, whether to control flow from the canals in the east or from runoffs in the west, was done by the family farmers.

Except for the Tewa villages and Santo Domingo (Keresans), who organized themselves into small hunting task groups of men and women, kin and nonkin, the Pueblos generally organized themselves into small groups of male kinsmen to hunt and dress skins. The women did the gathering of wild plants in all the villages, but they did not organize task groups to do so. Nevertheless, a few women would gather in the same area at the same time to keep mutual company.

Women did the cooking and made the pottery in all the Pueblos. They also did the bulk of the weaving everywhere but among the Hopi and at Santa Ana, where men predominated, and among the Tewa villages, where both sexes did weaving. Houses were made jointly by men and women. The men shaped the stones and built the walls and roofs, and the women plastered the walls. Whereas weaving and potting were individual pursuits, houses were built by task groups of matrikinsmen in the west and bilateral kinsmen in the east.

There were no intravillage markets, although the Pueblos engaged in some intervillage trade and were incorporated into trade networks through the Upland and River Yumans to shells from California, and through Athapaskans and Utes to meat and hides from the mountains and plains. The vast majority of all exchanges of food and goods within villages and between villages was reciprocal and equal, and it was conducted by individuals rather than by special agents of some sort. Among kin and friends—within or between villages—the exchanges were recognized as gifts, although gift reciprocation could occur at a later date. Among strangers, between Utes and Taos, for instance, there was bargaining. At Hopi and Zuni practically all reciprocity of goods and food was attended by ceremonial etiquette, but among all other Pueblos some reciprocity was ceremonial and some was not.

Redistribution† of food and goods within a village was primarily conducted by individual families in various ceremonials and life cycle–attendant rituals. The amount collected in any family redistributed to kin and others in a year was modest and conformed to local etiquette, while the amount collected and redistributed by any single kinship-based sodality in the west or sodality in the east was somewhat greater. There was no explicit extra-local redistribution, although kin and friends from other Pueblo villages were feasted, and non-Pueblos too were often hosted at ceremonies.

Among the Tewa villages the political-religious leaders had storehouses, filled with produce derived from communal labor. The products were used to feed themselves and to be redistributed among needy people from time to time. Overall, however, reciprocity was the dominant mode of exchange within and among villages, and redistribution was tied to ceremonialism. Whole villages did not redistribute to other villages, even

* As used here, "task groups" are defined as units of co-workers who regularly (daily, seasonally, or annually) coalesce to accomplish jointly some task. Each member need not provide the same resources, or skills, or labor to accomplish the task. Membership is rather stable over a period of a few years.

† "Redistribution" is defined as the centralized collection of food or chattels by kinship groups, or sodalities, or villages, or some authority, followed by the distribution of these chattels or food to people other than those who produced and collected it, but perhaps including those who collected it.

among the Eastern Pueblos where there was centralization of political control over the key economic resources.

In this assessment it is not intended to make light of the real differences in the organization of production between Eastern and Western Pueblos. The centralized authorities in the east demanded communal labor and ritual behavior and ultimately controlled the garden and house sites. In the west clans controlled garden and house sites. Whether canal irrigation demanded the development of centralized control in the hands of people who represented whole villages rather than kinship groups is an unsolved problem, but to help answer the question a comparison of the Eastern Pueblo economic organization with the Pima and Papago economic organization is needed.

Among the Pima, and for the Papago who had access to regular sources of water for canal irrigation purposes, fishing, gathering, and hunting sites were not owned, but farming land was owned by each village. A village was a group of bilateral kinsmen who predominantly resided patrilocally and who inherited garden plots, which became inalienable, from fathers to sons. Nevertheless, this inalienable land was considered to be owned ultimately by all Pima or all Papago, past and present. A village, then, was a patrideme (patrilocal bilateral kinship unit), composed of several related families under the direction of a headman whose only coercive force was public opinion. The land that was farmed and inherited through the generations by specific patrilocal bilateral families was, as among the Eastern Pueblos, owned only in usufruct. Yet a village headman among the Pima had no coercive authority to reassign lands and to command communal services, whereas Eastern Pueblo sodality leaders exercised such powers.

The differences between the organization of production for the canal irrigation Pueblos and the Pima-Papago are dramatic. For the latter a village headman, himself the leader of the village kinship group, helped organize his kinsmen to clear fields, build dams, and dig major canals. There were no community fields, and the work on the major canals as well as the minor ditches was done communally. When new land was to be opened, perhaps three such villages would join together under their headmen and construct the canal network and clear the land. The work was reciprocal and each participant chose his own land when the work was completed. The multiple-village reciprocity was stimulated by threats of attacks from Apaches, so that several villages chose to locate their fields close to one another. It is also possible that villages joined together because of the desirability of enlisting many hands to build the major canal systems and subsequently to keep them clean and operable. After the main canal was dug for each set of villages located on the canal, the men of the villages kept their sections of the main canal cleaned and there was no one with overarching authority to see to it that the canals were maintained.

In marked contrast to the Eastern Pueblos, the Pima-Papago developed and maintained extensive canal irrigation systems with nothing more than kinship group labor, nominally directed by headmen who, from time to time (during the seventeenth and eighteenth centuries and the nineteenth century prior to the reservation period) brought their villages together in labor-reciprocating farming efforts. It took more than individual or family effort to irrigate, but the Pima-Papago coordinated their efforts without centralized political and religious authority, and without community fields and storehouses for the benefit of the authorities. Needy families among Pima and Papago were given food, and they reciprocated in kind when possible. Sometimes the men of the village worked in their kinsman-headman's field as a form of generosity and appreciation. The headman, in fact, was being reciprocated with labor for his managerial contributions. The labor was not compulsory.

Intervillage reciprocity of food was ceremonial. Each year a harvest ceremony was held by one Pima village for perhaps three or four other villages. The villagers of the host village fed the visitors and gifted them with corn. In subsequent years the visiting villages served as hosts. Furthermore, as the giant saguaro cacti ripened each year, the Pima-Papago villages took turns sequentially in the same year in holding rainmaking ceremonies. The ceremonies were attended with the consumption of an alcoholic beverage made from the cactus.

The reciprocal and convivial organization of labor under nominal authority, and the reciprocal distribution of food products—whether or not the distributions were attended by ceremonialism—stands in marked contrast to the organization of production of the Eastern Pueblos, even though farming was ultimately a family enterprise for all farmers in the Southwest. The Pima-Papago division of labor by sex, task groups, and specialization was about the same as for the Pueblos. Task groups of male kinsmen did the bulk of the farming and hunting. Men worked the hides individually, yet they joined into reciprocating task groups to do the heavy work on the houses. Women did the collecting of wild plants, and the weeding and harvesting of crops. Women also made the pottery and basketry whereas men made the tools that men used. There was no pronounced craft specialization.

It is interesting to encounter among the Colorado River Yumans and the Maricopa some differences from other Southwest farmers in the division of labor by sex. It is likely that the organization of Yuman production is not derived from the same base as the rest of the Southwest but was shaped from a California base (Jorgenson 1980). The Yuman speakers form a separate cluster in this nonmetric analysis. It seems that River Yuman women contributed more labor to the farming enterprise than did their female counterparts everywhere except among the Western Apache. The River Yumans could have gained all their sustenance from farming their well-watered and fertile river plains, and although farming contributed more to the food supply than any other food source for most groups, River Yumans varied from 30 to 50 percent agricultural dependency. Except for some Mohave, who carried water to their fields in large basketry ollas, the River Yumans relied on flood irrigation for which they exercised some controls with dams, dikes, and ditches (but not canals).

Critical differences from the other Southwestern farmers, beyond the amount of River Yuman dependence on agriculture, were: the totally individual nature of farm-site ownership by the male who cleared the site (or sites as one man often used several sites), and the individual family nature of farming. There were no task groups of kinsmen to reciprocate labor, and the larger kinship groups, such as the multi-local patriclans, did not retain ultimate ownership of land. If disputes occurred between men about property boundaries following a flood that obliterated markers, the disputants, more or less in this order, settled their problem by: talking, enlisting friends to help in a shoving fight, or finally by means of a controlled stick fight. The winner set the boundary markers. Often these disputes were between men of the same patriclan, as River Yuman settlements tended to be dispersed homesteads of patrikinsmen. Indeed, a segment of a clan might fraction from a settlement and resettle several miles distant from their closest kinsmen in order to open new fields. Each patriclan came to be located in many dispersed locales.

Along with garden sites, key gathering sites too were owned by individual men, even though women did the gathering. Gathering sites for mescal, screw bean, and mesquite were localized on the river plains. Fishing was extremely important for the River Yumans, and good fishing sites were used repeatedly; nevertheless, sites were not owned, and fishing was an individual affair for all but the Mohaves who organized into task groups of patrikin to fish. None of the River Yumans had fishing specialists. Hunting areas, like fishing sites, were free and available to all.

Of all the important localized resources, then, only garden and gathering sites were owned. And for these resource areas, owners did not grant access to other people who wished to use them. On the other hand, food was reciprocated locally and extra-locally, so people in need as well as people who were not in need received food. Furthermore, mourning ceremonies, hosted by the near kinsmen and friends of a recent decedent, were times to collect, redistribute, and even destroy property on behalf of the departed member. These ceremonies were used to invite kinsmen and friends from near and distant settlements, and the hosts for one ceremony were soon the visitors at several others.

Ceremonialism, in general, was not developed nearly so much among the River Yumans as it was among the Pima, and it was focused more on war exploits and honoring deceased individuals (one at a time as well as groups of specific people) than on propitiating gods, crops, or the natural elements and their relations to gods and crops. The differences in River Yuman ritual organization from the organization of Pima ritual, say, is not explainable by environmental or ecological variables.

All River Yumans were warriors. The Maricopa, Cocopa, Halchidhoma, Cocomaricopa, Kavelchadom and several others were primarily defensive warriors, whereas the Mohave and Quechan were offensive warriors, raiders, and traders. Warfare goals were neither to acquire crops nor to destroy crops. Yumans had plenty of food. The explicit motive for warfare was personal gain. Furthermore, the greatest warriors were also the most ambitious farmers and traders (Mohave and Quechan).

It is possible, and should be treated as a concluding hypothesis, that the Mohave and Quechan displaced several Yuman-speaking groups (such as the Kavelchadom) from their positions on the Colorado River and usurped their territories. The Mohave and Quechan were friendly—allowing each other to farm—but through harassment of their downriver and Gila River congeners, caused them to farm less. It is possible that the Pima and Papago, suffering attacks from the Apaches, and the Maricopa and Kavelchadom, suffering attacks from the Quechan and Mohaves, served as buffers between Apache expansion westward and Mohave-Quechan raiding eastward. In contrast the Mohave and Quechan had good relations with Papago, Walapai, Yavapai, and Havasupai and did not raid them. They used them as middlemen in some trade with Pueblos and crossed Upland Yuman territory in order to conduct other trade. It is significant that the closest Apache neighbors of the Yavapai were friendly, and they did not move west beyond the Upland Yumans for raiding. Yet out of fear the Yavapai and Walapai farmed almost not at all, although farming potentialities in much of the Yavapai territory were good. It is possible that the Yavapai, in particular, became the preeminent gatherers in the Southwest because they were allowed to occupy that subsistence niche and only that niche. It is suggested, then, that the organization of economic production for the River Yumans was focused on warfare whose causes might have been economic at one time, but whose effect might have become its own cause. It is clear that no overriding ecological factors stopped River Yumans from fishing more, farming more, using canal irrigation, storing more crops, or organizing themselves into centrally controlled governments. Indeed, the Quechan recognized themselves as a tribe with war leaders of definite rank. They joined together to wage war, to conduct mesquite ceremonies, and to help their tribal mates should they come under attack. But there was no communal labor and no authority to exact it.

The Apaches form a crescent-shaped distribution in figure 8, and as can be seen in figure 9, the internal relations among the Western Apaches are closer than those among the more easterly Apaches. The great differences between Western and Eastern Apaches were the role that horticulture played in their respective subsistence economies and the nature of ownership of key productive resources.

Goodwin's (1942) epic work on the Western Apache has been supplemented, often from Goodwin's notes, by the works of Basso (1970, 1971) and Kaut (1974). The Western Apache were organized into multilocal matrilineal clans whose local segments owned farmland, sometimes as clans and sometimes as individual members of clans. But farming was only one Western Apache subsistence pursuit, and the local clan segments or even individuals also owned some key gathering sites for mescal and mesquite. The farmland, in particular, was guarded against trespass, although members of other clans could join the owners and be given access to farming and choice collecting sites. There is no doubt that farming and farm-site ownership were critical to the Apache clan organization, for as populations grew or droughts occurred there seems to have been leapfrogging of clan segments in search of land. The movement for land in the eighteenth and nineteenth centuries, coupled with raiding for crops and goods, established adversary relations with the Pima and more friendly relations with the Yavapai.

The Western Apache farmers and raiders were organized much differently from the sedentary Pueblos, Pima, and River Yumans. Whereas the Yumans left their home areas for brief periods to raid and trade, Western Apaches ranged seasonally through several biotic zones, moving less often in summers (near their farm sites and water) than in winters.

Although farmland ownership seems to have been critical to the multilocal distribution of matrilineal clans, key gathering and some hunting sites, too, were claimed by local clan segments. Male affines hunted in small units of two to five, while young boys formed teams to hunt rabbits and other small game. Women matrikin formed small groups to go collecting, but they retained individual ownership of their goods. Men, women, and children formed work groups for farming, as among the River Yumans, yet men did the heaviest work as among other Southwest groups.

Hunting and gathering areas were made freely available to anyone who wished to use them, although protracted use by nonowners generally required permission from the owners. The more communitarian ethic toward hunting and gathering areas contrasted sharply with the private clan ethic toward farm-site ownership, and it is certainly a possibility that the availability of access to hunting and gathering sites made it easier for clans to fission and establish new farm sites, hunting and gathering across the lands of other clans while looking for new areas for themselves.

The local clan segments often let people from other clans join them and use farmland, if it was available. These local groups formed bands along with adjacent local groups. Band chiefs were influential, nominal leaders, but bands and even combinations of bands, such as the San Carlos, were egalitarian units that formed to conduct raiding for food, booty, and perhaps territorial expansion. Contributions of food to Western Apache diets from raiding were important during the winters. Clan segments could join and leave bands at their own instigation. So the Western Apache had all the flexibility and aggressiveness of hunting and raiding bands, yet the food supplies and definite territories of farmers. They could protect as well as attack, provide as well as steal. This was a considerable advantage over the Pueblo, Pima, Papago, and Upland Yuman groups, but no advantage over the Quechan and Mohave who engaged in trade and conducted devastating raids—but not for food—yet had more than enough to eat. It is very possible that attempts by Western Apache clan segments to establish farms and summer residences on the Gila River west of what is now Phoenix would have been short-lived and that the beleaguered Pima and Maricopa served as useful buffers between Apaches and Colorado River Yumans.

The eastern Apacheans, except for the Jicarilla, did not farm in the eighteenth and nineteenth centuries (prereservation), and their economic organizations show differences from their western congeners that seem to stem from the presence or absence of agriculture.

The various eastern Apacheans were organized into matrilocal and bilateral bands under the nominal authority of a good speaker. Yet families from several local residence groups representing more than one band might coalesce under one man to conduct a raid. Raiding was an important part of Apachean subsistence economy as it was in the west. Furthermore, eastern Apachean hunting and gathering was conducted in nearly the same fashion as in the west: individuals or small groups of male affines or boys hunted, while females related through the matriside kept one another company while gathering. Each woman kept whatever she gathered for her own family.

A difference was that men not only shared the game among the hunters but also gave away as much as one-half of their catch of deer and antelope beyond their own families. A difference with the Pueblo, Pima, and River Yumans is that women, rather than men, dressed the skins. This labor custom dominates in the Great Basin and on the Plains.

It should be emphasized that a communitarian ethic attended the reciprocity of food not only within the local groups but also between groups. Life-crisis events were attended by distributions of food to guests from local and extra-local groups. Although Chiricahua local residence groups recognized ownership to key gathering and hunting sites, they provided access to anyone who desired to use the resources.

The fluidity of movement of the matrilocal, bilateral, extended-family camps of the eastern Apaches as they temporarily joined raiding and hunting parties, and the regular movements of larger residence groups in order to obtain wild plants, rendered them considerably less sedentary than Western Apache farmers, at least during summer months. Although the local residence groups among eastern Apacheans had as many as 300 people, most of the organization of work was on the family level, and reciprocity, ritual distributions, and free access to resource areas moved goods among families.

The Jicarilla Apache farmed as well as gathered, hunted, and raided. Their farming sites were owned by the matrilocal, bilateral extended families. In all other respects their economy was organized very similarly to the other eastern Apacheans, except that men usually carried the wild plants collected by the women. The role played by farming in Jicarilla economic organization has located the Jicarilla more closely to the Kamia, who are River Yumans, than to the Western Apaches. Jicarilla agriculture, which employed dikes and ditches, fishing, and dual organization of Holiness rites combined to pull Jicarilla toward Eastern Pueblos and River Yumans, while maintaining their outlier position in relation to other Athapaskans.

The Navajo were the most aberrant of all Athapaskans. They were similar to the Western Apache and Jicarilla in that they farmed, hunted, gathered, and raided. And as among the Western Apache, local clan units owned farmland. Indeed, the relation between the multilocal distributions of Navajo clans and the availability of farmland appears to parallel the relations among those phenomena for the Western Apache.

As can be seen in figures 8 and 9, the Navajo are placed between the Upland Yuman and Western Pueblo clusters, emphasizing the Navajo's greater dependence on farming and organization for farming than other Athapaskans, as well as greater organization for hunting and gathering than the Pueblos. Although raiding parties were formed and the booty that they garnered was important, Navajos spent more time each year near their farm sites than did Western Apaches. When sheep, too, were added as an overlay to farming, clan units became still more sedentary, even though the population continued to expand and fill more geographic niches.

The organization of production among the Navajo was more similar to Pueblo organization than for the other Athapaskans. For instance, men worked the hides and built the houses, and they also formed small task groups to clear land and divert flood water for farming. The farming was not so codominant as among the Apaches. On the other hand, Navajo women herded the sheep in postcontact times.

The local clan elements (Aberle 1961) reciprocated food internally and redistributed food while serving as hosts to several ceremonies. Much of the reciprocity and redistribution was laden with ceremonial etiquette, although access to local resources was granted without ceremonial fanfare. Extra-local units were not granted access to key farming sites, so that redistribution through ceremonial giving was the manner in which local clan units had access to the resources of other units from time to time. For barter and trade, Navajos bargained with nonkin whether in their own local community or elsewhere.

Thus, on the one hand the Navajo were in many ways organized more similarly to the Western Pueblos than to the Western Apache. On the other hand, they exploited a wider range of resources than the Pueblos, whose movements they restricted, and they also engaged in extensive hunting and raiding.

These analyses of intertribal relations for technology, subsistence economy, and organization of extraction and production have demonstrated that time and time again the people who spoke most similar languages tended to be most similar in culture. It has also been shown that environment is fairly closely related to technological and economic organizations, but that the fit is loose at best: River Yumans could have employed canal irrigation, but did not, and so forth. Furthermore, canal irrigation was organized much differently among Pueblos and Pima-Papagos.

Relations Among Environment, Subsistence, Organization of Production, and Demography

In the note on methodology at the end of the chapter there is a discussion of some technical information about the differences between tests for the relations among tribes (Q-mode) and tests for the relations among variables (R-mode). In order to manage the enormous data set, the information has been reduced to 13 ordinal variables pertaining to the environment, and 70 ordinal variables pertaining to subsistence economy, economic organization, and demography. The 83 variables are analyzed in figure 10 (61 variables) and figure 11 (22 variables). It was necessary to separate the analyses because each variable in figure 10 has three

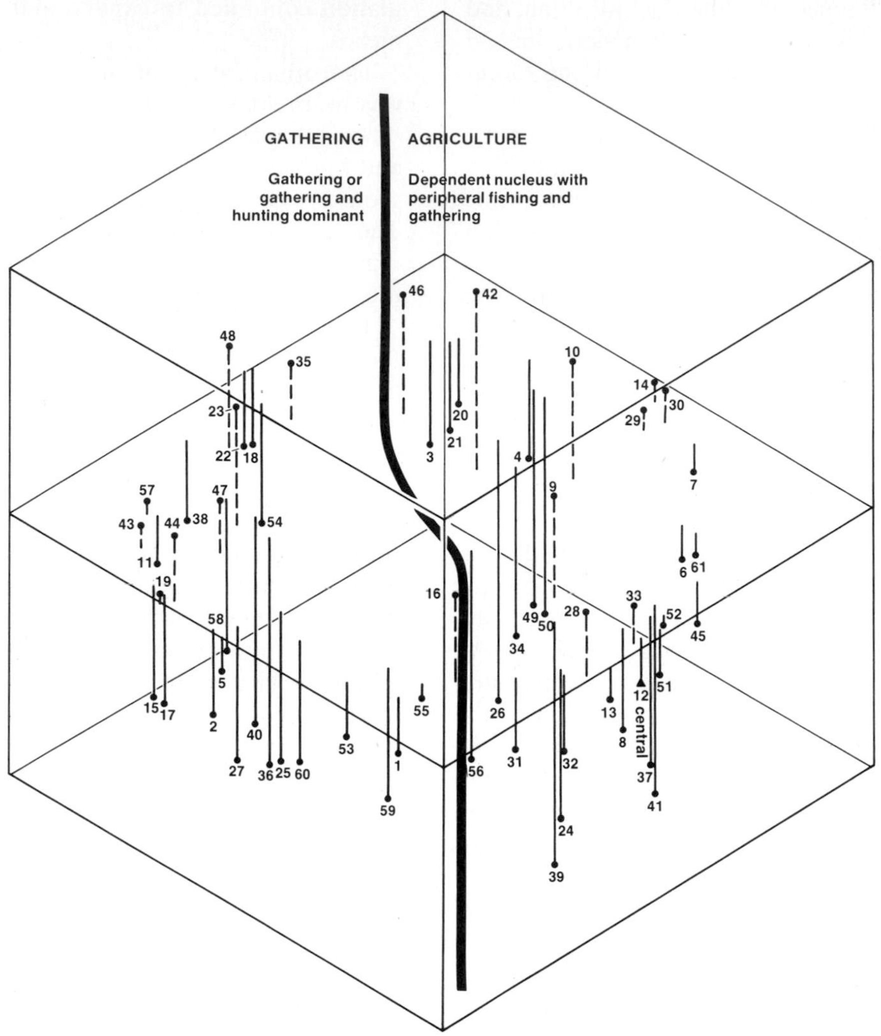

or more ordered categories while each variable in figure 11 has only two ordered categories. Both figures depict the relations among the variables in three dimensions. In general, relations among variables are more complex than relations among tribes, so higher dimensionality (three dimensions rather than two) is needed to show the complexity of the distances among variables. In figure 10 Goodman and Kruskal's (1954) Gamma has been employed in order to determine whether the order of pairs of ranks in one variable changes in the same direction, changes in the opposite direction, or shows no relation to the order of pairs of ranks in the other variable. Points, or variables, at opposite sides and opposite heights in the cube are negatively related (when one changes, the other changes in the opposite direction).

The complex relations between economy and environment in the aboriginal Southwest are most obvious in figure 10. But they are evident in figure 11 too. Indeed, the relations in figure 11 form a microcosm of the relations in figure 10. Practically all aborginal groups farmed, or once farmed; all gathered; all hunted; and some fished. How, then, to account for the various adaptations? Figure 10 forms a rather continuous circle in multidimensional space with variables pertaining to dominant hunters and gatherers on one side and variables pertaining to agriculture dependence on the other (this is true for fig. 11 also). On the righthand side of the circle the greatest concentration of points occurs, and this part of the distribution is broken into small arcs and semicircles that separate clusters of variables whose ordered ranks are most nearly similar. It is not surprising that these points focus on agricultural variables. Indeed, the tightest distribution occurs around variable 12, which measures the probable contribution to diets from agricultural foodstuffs that are produced locally—not bartered for, borrowed, stolen, or received as gifts. The order of ranks for this variable, and for the others in the cluster, tends to change in the same direction, yet variables, such as numbers 37 and 41, so closely related to variables 13, 8, 33, 52, and 51 in two dimensions, are also closely related to variables 24 and 39, as is demonstrated in the third dimension. Understanding the meaning of distances in three dimensions

Fig. 10. Environment, demography, subsistence economy and the organization of production in aboriginal Southwest. MINISSA smallest space analysis in 3 dimensions obtained from Gammas. K = .17 in 12 iterations. Based on the following 61 ordinal variables: 1, tribal altitude in 1,000-feet intervals; 2, tribal area annual average precipitation; 3, tribal area average temperature in January; 4, tribal area average temperature in July; 5, total number of the 19 types of land mammals available in tribal area; 6, quantity of fish available in tribal territory (average annual production in pounds per average square mile); 7, relative amount of fish used as food by tribe; 8, agriculture production; 9, agricultural products—nonfood; 10, agricultural products grown—food; 11, agricultural products grown—beverages, leaves, etc., procured locally; 12, probable contribution to diet of agricultural foodstuffs acquired locally; 13, animal husbandry—precontact; 14, probable contribution to diet of fish, shellfish, and large aquatic mammals procured locally; 15, local hunting—all types of game; 16, predominant types of animals for which groups hunt; 17, probable contribution to diet of hunting of large game, small mammals, and fowl procured locally, and leaves, etc., procured locally; 18, local gathering—contributions from all types of nuts, seeds, berries, roots, etc.; 19, predominant foods gathered; 20, external sources for roots, seeds, berries, fruits, tubers, leaves, etc.; 21, probable contribution to diet of gathered items procured extralocally; 22, probable contribution to diet of gathered items procured locally; 23, major storage place for food: most frequent or preferred; 24, maximum length of time stored food kept; 25, specialized pottery manufacture; 26, production task groups in gathering; 27, specialization in hunting; 28, production task groups in hunting; 29, production task groups in fishing and other aquatic animal procurement; 30, specialization in fishing and other aquatic animal procurement; 31, specialization in agriculture; 32, production task groups in agriculture; 33, sharing of access of local food resources as a form of distribution within the society (intracommunity); 34, ceremonialism or etiquette in intracommunity reciprocity of food and chattels; 35, ceremonialism or etiquette in intracommunity redistribution of food and chattels; 36, ceremonialism or etiquette in intracommunity use of privately owned food resources and chattels; 37, reciprocity distribution of food and chattels between (or among) societies; 38, sharing of access to local food resources as a form of distribution between (or among) societies; 39, ceremonialism or etiquette in intercommunity reciprocity of food and chattels; 40, ceremonialism or etiquette in intercommunity use of privately owned food resources and chattels; 41, barter or trade within communities for food and chattels; 42, gift exchange within communities for food and chattels; 43, barter or trade between (or among) communities for food and chattels; 44, agents of barter or trade between communities; 45, gift exchange between (or among) communities for food and chattels; 46, ownership of key gathering sites; 47, ownership of key hunting sites; 48, ownership of farming sites, including cultivated trees, but not tobacco plots; 49, ownership of men's chattels (movable property such as blankets, bows, knives); 50, ownership of women's chattels (such as blankets, clothes, tools); 51, density of community organization; 52, population density within territory controlled by community; 53, total number of 5 types of pines available in tribal territory; 54, total number of 13 types of cactus, mescal, mesquite, and yucca available in tribal territory; 55, total number of 12 types of grasses available in tribal territory; 56, total number of 11 types of roots, lilies, nuts, and berries available in tribal territory; 57, total number of herbs, roots, and tubers available; 58, total number of nuts and leaves available; 59, small land mammals available; 60, large land mammals available; 61, total number of 4 types of freshwater fishes in tribal territory.

aids the interpretation. Refer to the list of variables to coordinate numbers with variable definitions.

In the aboriginal Southwest, the more (as measured by ordered ranks) that people relied on local agricultural products, the larger was the size of the local community, the greater was the population density, the more probable was the local bartering for food and chattels between nonkin and the gifting between kin, and the more probable and the more varied were forms of extra-local (intercommunity or intertribal) reciprocity of goods and chattels. Somewhat less central to the cluster (variable 45), gift exchanges of food and chattels between people of different communities increased with population density, dependency on local agriculture, extra-local reciprocity, and the like.

Following these interrelations in the other direction, the more the agricultural dependence, the more likely that productive resource areas, such as garden sites, were owned by kin groups or political units, and access to these sites was not shared with nonowners; and that dogs and turkeys were raised.

Somewhat removed is a circle of points with interesting relations to the core variables. The top of the circle (variable 28) shows that male task groups tended to form to conduct the hunting and the farming (variable 32); that the maximum time that food was stored tended to increase, that people with special authority or knowledge were more apt to organize the agricultural pursuits, and that intercommunity reciprocity of food or chattels was probably attended by ceremonial etiquette. A special point in interpretation is that the ranked order for length of food storage period varies systematically with the local barter, extra-local reciprocity, and ceremonialism in extra-local reciprocity variables.

The larger cluster of variables on the righthand side represents high dependency on local agriculture, of course, and it is significant that access to garden sites is not shared with nonowners, that local barter occurs with nonkin, and that extra-local reciprocity, extra-local gift exchange, and ceremonialism in extra-local reciprocity organize intra- and intercommunity distributions of food and chattels. It can be inferred from these tests and from the previous analyses that the most dense populations produced the greatest amount of food, yet they maintained themselves in threatening social environments by formally gifting, hosting, and reciprocating with their neighbors. Perhaps it was better to give in a ceremonial fashion, than to lose one's productive resources to Athapaskans and Utes. The notable thing about this distribution is that no environmental variables are central or peripheral to it. That is to say, no environmental variables measured here increase their order in the same fashion as the demographic, subsistence economy, and economic organization variables. This result supports the expectation that farming dependency in the Southwest varies more because of cultural reasons than because of environmental reasons. Some people (for example, Hopi, Zuni, Acoma, some Eastern Keresans) were agriculture-dependent on meager environmental resources; some were much less agricultural-dependent than they could have been on their rich resources (for example, Mohave, Quechan); and so forth.

The agriculture-dependent cluster forms a still larger semicircle with variables 6, 61, 7, 29, 30, and 14. It is instructive to note that the quantity of fish available in pounds per average square mile of tribal territory (variable 6), and the number of species of freshwater fishes available (variable 61), are closer to the agriculture cluster than are the variables associated with the use and procurement of fish. In short, the environmental variables that are most closely related to the agriculture cluster show that year-round running water sources are distantly related to farming dependency, yet the fish in these waters (not for Hopi, Zuni, etc.) are exploited little in relation to availability. Those who use the most fish also farm, and of those, only the Mohave had fishing task groups and only the Cochiti had fishing specialists. It does not follow that those who had the most fish available also used the most fish.

Everyone in the Southwest collected wild plants, and even where wild-plant foods were the dominant subsistence resource they were not so dominant as agriculture among the Pueblos and the Pima; therefore, it is not surprising that gathering-dependency does not form so neat a distribution as the agriculture-dependency semicircle. Indeed, variables related to gathering occur in several Euclidean microspaces as measured in figures 10 and 11. Of interest is that the two variables relating to gathering that are most closely related to farming dependency are organization of extraction variables. The circle of variables 26, 42, 4, 49, 50, and 34 form to the left of the agriculture-dependent distribution. Between the two are the variables, distantly related, measuring the types of nonfood agricultural crops grown (variable 9) and the types of agricultural crops grown (variable 10). The distribution of variables 9 and 10 demonstrates that neither is critical to agriculture-dependency, so that the societies that experiment with the greatest variety of food and nonfood crops are not the most agricultural-dependent (specifically the River Yumans). Yet there is a positive, distant, and complex set of relationships between these variables and the organization of agricultural production and gathering extraction.

Variable 42 measures the nature of the ownership of gathering sites. If key gathering sites are owned privately or by kinship groups, the gathering is probably done by task groups of women (variable 26). Where there are gathering task groups, there is ceremonialism in local reciprocity, male chattels tend to be owned individually and the same holds for female chattels (variables 49 and 50). Finally, temperatures increase in the summer months as measured by ranked order much as ceremonialism in local reciprocity, gathering task groups, and chattel ownership increases. Much more distantly there is a gift exchange of food and chattels within the local community (variable 46 is most closely related to ownership of gathering sites).

A last arc in the righthand side of the cube completes the "agriculture-dependent with peripheral fishing and gathering" variables. Variables 3, 21, and 20 show that as the ranks of mean January temperatures increase so do the types of wild food plants procured extra-locally and the ranked contribution of these plants to the diet.

It is not trivial to learn from these tests that if people are dependent on agriculture, they also collect wild plants, and that the organization of extraction for wild plants is somewhat similar to its organization of agricultural production counterpart, to wit: key gathering sites are owned, and they are worked by task groups; food and chattels are reciprocated with ceremonial etiquette locally, and gifts are exchanged extra-locally. The stress seems to be on the recognition of property rights, attended by formal etiquette to distribute products from these properties.

In the entire righthand section of the cube, the few environmental variables that occur—temperature variables, fish and water course variables, and the outlier variable 56, measuring the types of roots, berries, lilies, and nuts available—are not central, and the temperature variables are more closely related to the organization of gathering extraction than to anything else.

At the lefthand side of the cube (fig. 10) is a loose rectangle of points (variables 55, 1, 59, and 53) with a more distant relative (variable 16). Attention is focused on these points because they are primarily environmental and because they are not closely related to variables of subsistence economics or economic organization. They show that as altitude, as measured by ranked intervals, increases, so does the number of species of grasses available, the number of species of small land mammals available, the number of species of pines available and, more distantly, the number of species of mammals and birds hunted. In the other direction these variables vary most closely and positively in ordinal ranks with the number of large, nonherd, land mammals (for example, deer and mountain sheep) available (variable 60), the presence of specialists to organize or administer hunts (variable 27), the number of species of land mammals of all kinds (large and small, herd and nonherd) available (variable 5), and the amount of annual precipitation (variable 2). Except for the hunting specialists and the number of types of mammals and birds hunted—and the two are not closely related—there are scant relations between the availability of animals, the fodder and browse available for the animals, and the subsistence adaptations made by aboriginal Southwest inhabitants. There is one surprising result: pottery specialization (people with special skills or power, rather than people who support themselves solely from their craft) is more closely related to hunting

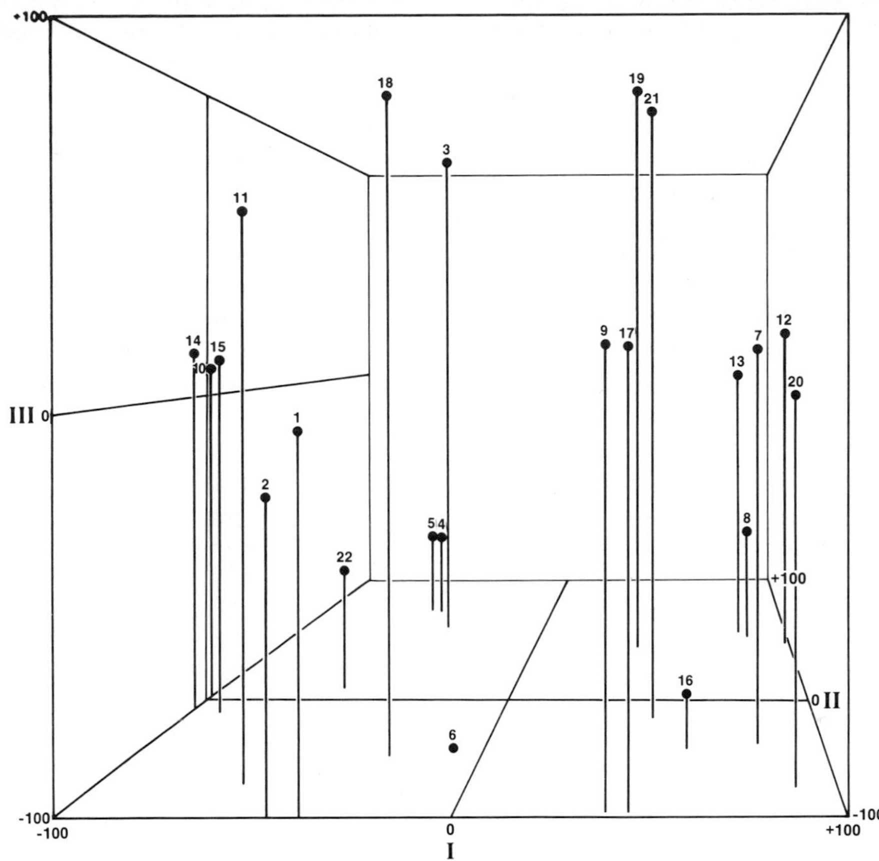

Fig. 11. Environment, subsistence economy, and the organization of production in aboriginal Southwest. MINISSA smallest space analysis in 3 dimensions obtained from combined Taus. K = .15 in 11 iterations. Based on the following 22 ordinal variables (2 ranks per variable): 1, external sources for agricultural products—food; 2, probable contribution to diet of agricultural foodstuffs acquired extralocally; 3, external sources for agricultural products—nonfood or beverage; 4, focal "fishing"—all types of aquatic animal procurement; 5, predominant aquatic animals for which groups fish, or hunt, or collect; 6, probable contribution to diet of fish, shellfish, and large aquatic animals procured extralocally; 7, external sources for game, small mammals, fowl; 8, probable contribution to diet of large game, small mammals, and fowl procured extralocally; 9, dominant land transportation of food or other goods; 10, dominant water transport of food or other goods; 11, specialized weaving of nets, baskets, or mats; 12, specialized weaving of cotton, wool, or hair garments; 13, production task groups for weaving cotton, wool, or hair garments; 14, specialization of boat building: all types of watercraft; 15, production task groups in boat building; 16, specialization in gathering; 17, reciprocity distribution of food and chattels within society; 18, redistribution of chattels and food within a society; 19, ceremonialism or etiquette in intercommunity redistribution of food and chattels; 20, ownership of common property following divorce; 21, total number of 11 types of oaks available in tribal territory; 22, large land mammals available (large herds including bison).

specialization and the availability of land mammals than to the agriculture-dependent cluster. This is probably because eastern Apacheans specialized in pottery, while Pimas, Papagos, and River Yumans did not. It is doubtful that pottery specialization is stimulated by the availability of mammals or even hunting specialists, because the Western Pueblos and Kewevkapayas had pottery specialists and relatively meager game, whereas all Southwesterners except the River Yumans had hunting specialists.

Continuing in a counterclockwise fashion, one can ferret out the intricate relations among variables pertaining to hunting and gathering and, wherever possible, the environmental variables related to them. The lefthand half of the cube is weakly linked to the righthand side through the mammal and mammal environment variables, and whereas the righthand side showed the agriculture-dependent, fishing, and gathering production relations, the lefthand side shows the organization of production and extraction when gathering is dominant or gathering and hunting are co-dominant. Except for perhaps one Upland Yuman and three Apachean groups, all 37 units in the sample gained some of their livelihood from local agriculture.

The close relations in two dimensions of variables 19, 44, 15, 17, 11, 43, and 57 show that as hunting contributes more to the diet, more types of wild plants are gathered, and the more likely that trade will be conducted and that special agents, or political unit leaders, will conduct trade between communities. Because only the Western Apache, the Navajo, and the Hopi used special agents (as well as anyone else who wished to trade), it is obvious that use of special traders was inversely related to agricultural dependence. Although the relations are demonstrated in figure 11 rather than figure 10, it is also true that the number of types of agricultural foods acquired extra-locally (variable 1) and the ranked contribution of these foods to the diet (variable 2) are part of the complementary cluster in figure 11, while the extra-local sources for mammals and birds (variable 7) and the contribution to the diet of mammals and birds acquired extra-locally (variable 8) are part of the agriculture-dependent cluster in figure 11. Farmers received animal products through trade, while hunter-gatherer-farmers received agricultural products through trade, gifts, ceremonial feasts, and raids.

Although they play peripheral roles to the organization of production variables, the number of types of available herbs, roots, and tubers (variable 57) and the number of types of nuts and leaves available (variable 58) are linked to the hunting and gathering adaptations. Furthermore, the types of cactus, mescal, mesquite, and yucca available (variable 54) are also linked to hunting and gathering, but more specifically to the amount that wild plants contribute to the total diet. Analyses show that it was mescal, mesquite, screw bean, and the cacti that the Apachean, River and Upland Yuman, and Papago groups gathered in great quantities. It is important to know as well that other wild plants were rather more abundant where hunting and gathering outstripped or equaled agriculture in prominence, even if grasses, pines, oaks (variable 21, fig. 11), mammals, and birds were not more abundant.

One variable (38) on the edge of the distribution, and two variables (36, 40) that are centered among the wild plant variables (58, 54) and the large, nonherd mammal variable (60) show that access was provided to private (say, kinship unit–owned) hunting and gathering sites to both local residents and extra-local residents following some etiquette. Variable 47 shows that key hunting sites tended to be owned more as a function of the ownership of farm sites (variable 48), the number of types of storage structures used (variable 23), and, perhaps, the presence of barter and trade (variable 44), than as a function of the presence or absence of game. So whereas the agriculture-dependent people did not provide access to their key resources, hunters and gatherers did. On the other hand, extra-local reciprocity and gift exchange moved goods among dominant farmers, while that was much less true for the hunters and gatherers. However, the communitarian ethic applied to gathering resources generally required that people ask to use resources that they did not own, yet the farming sites owned by these same people were generally not available for use by nonowners, as the farming variable 48 demonstrates. So there was a marked difference between extractive-resource areas (hunting, gathering, fishing) and productive-resource areas (garden sites), and the people who were most dependent on garden sites had worked out several ways to make their farm and gathering products available short of providing access to their resource areas.

It is of interest to examine one last question. Figure 11 shows that whereas local redistribution of goods and chattels (variable 18) was most closely related to the variously co-dominant gathering-hunting-farming-fishing distributions of variables, ceremonial redistribution (variable 19) was most closely related to the agriculture-dependent distribution. They were closely related to each other only in the third dimension (height). It seems to follow that the dominant farmers were less communitarian and more formal in their property relations overall than those who relied less on farming. Farming sites and farming products were always controlled more carefully by their owners than nonfarm, or extractive, goods.

Some Brief Conclusions

These systematic comparisons of aboriginal environments and economies in the aboriginal Southwest in both Q-mode (the relations among tribes) and R-mode (the relations among variables) have yielded many nontrivial empirical generalizations, not the least of which is that although environment-culture relations are generally positive in the Q-mode, that is, as environments vary cultures tend to vary in the same direction, practically everywhere features of culture tend to override features of environment. For example, many people who once farmed or who could have farmed (Kewevkapaya, Mescalero Apache) did not. People who could have produced more from farming (Western Apache) did not. People who could have irrigated (River Yumans) did not.

In looking at the interplay of environment with the organization of production, it was found that, contrary to the hydraulic hypothesis, there was no clear relation between canal irrigation and centralized political-economic control. Localized kinship groups among the Pima joined together to accomplish on ad hoc bases tasks that were annual and obligatory among Eastern Pueblos.

Task groups were more characteristic of the agriculture-dependent people than those who were not; nevertheless, for all but some River Yumans and Western Apaches where agriculture labor tended to be co-dominated by the sexes, men did the bulk of the farming. Men also hunted and dressed skins, obviously an old complex in the Southwest. Only among some Apacheans (not the Navajo), who were recent interlopers in the Southwest, did women dress the skins. Among all groups in the Southwest the women did the bulk of the gathering, but where gathering contributed much to subsistence, the men often helped the women carry the wild plants back to camp.

The organization of distribution analysis made it clear that all societies practiced reciprocity. Even the modest ceremonial distributions among River Yumans were reciprocal. Redistribution, except in the form of gifting of food, chattels and feasts that attended life crises and other ritual events among the Pueblos and Pima, were rare. These redistributions were sponsored by families, larger kinship groups, or kiva societies and shifted among several of these units depending on the year and the context.

These analyses have suggested that the behavior of the Athapaskans, Mohave, and Quechan seem to have exerted greater influence in shaping the nature of Southwest subsistence economies and economic organizations in the seventeenth and eighteenth centuries than did environment. Whereas it is trivially true that all units in the sample were "adapted," it is not trivial to learn that Yavapais were afraid to farm because of threats from some Western Apache raiders, that Pimas and Papagos were regularly attacked in the winters and had crops stolen by Apacheans and many were dislocated, and that Mohaves and Quechans attacked other River Yumans, but not for chattels or food, or, since the early nineteenth century, for land.

It seems that the predatory expansion of Athapaskans for farmland, hunting and gathering areas, and bounty, at least in late aboriginal times, was contained only by Upland Yuman buffers and the threat of River Yuman warfare. Pueblos and Pimas helped maintain themselves, after having their hunting and gathering territories restricted, by gifting and bartering crops and other moveable properties for products of the hunt with their sometimes adversaries.

The gathering base, which was women's work, and the farming base, which was men's work, were embedded in cultures (fig. 3) that demonstrated overall similarities associated more closely to language (a measure of historical inheritance and interaction) than to environments (fig. 2).

The importance of trade and raiding among River Yumans clearly influenced the shape of aboriginal adaptations in the Southwest, but it would be unnecessary sophistry to seek an explanation for River Yuman trade and noneconomic warfare, individual ownership of key resources, and failure to develop canal irrigation in terms of negative feedback mechanisms that, unknown to the participants, adapt the cultural system to the biological and abiological systems and the like, even though it is suggested above that at one time Mohave and Quechan might have garnered new farmland by dislocating some of their River Yuman congeners.

Although Kroeber (1939) did not test for relations between environment and culture, he showed again and again the "powerful dominance of history and culture over geography" (Driver 1962:8). Kroeber (1939:1) argued that while "cultures are rooted in nature . . . . they are no more produced by nature than a plant is produced or caused by the soil in which it is rooted."

It can be inferred from this analysis that canal irrigation was not possible where there was no source of predictable, running water; that hunting was not dominant where mammals and birds were sparse; and so forth. In the aboriginal context the environment provided some broad ranges within which people worked. Indeed, it is very probable that prehistoric farmers (Anasazi, Mogollon, and Hohokam) contracted their distributions following sustained drought, or some other deleterious and protracted environmental forces. Some groups survived and others probably did not, but even the canal irrigation people (Pima, Papago, Eastern Pueblos) "adapted" in different fashions.

Note on Ecological Adaptation

One point of logic that is most relevant, but that has been obscured by some advocates of "system ecology" in accounting for ecological adaptations, is that at any point in time any culture unit is "adapted" to its environment. Unless relations among phenomena are specified and measured through systematic comparisons and controls for a sample of culture units, there is no way to evaluate a generalization about the fit between natural environment and cultural environment, or natural environment and social structure, or cultural systems and biological systems, or whatever else one purports to explain. In talking about adaptation anthropologists have acted as if any and all ecological systems are composed of sets of populations that operate in definable natural environments. These natural environments, given the types of populations that operate within them, are alleged to have minimum to maximum carrying potential in reference to the several populations in their embrace. The natural environments, and all the relations among biological populations, are said to stand in specifiable relations with the human populations. Thus, it is alleged that farmers are dependent not only upon their seeds, the techniques they use to manage their crops, their storage techniques, their knowledge of precipitation patterns and soils and the like, but also upon things that the farmers need not or do not understand. For instance, it is alleged that in order for the human population to *survive* (a key term), it must *adapt* (a key term because it is a relational statement) to the other biological populations, and that these populations must adapt in their many interrelations in the environment. There is an interesting paradox here: on the one hand human populations (culture units) must maximize their survival potential by creating and optimizing customs to adjust to threats of all types. Thus, the human population is conceptualized as a rational, economic man. On the other hand, the maximizing model of economic man is eschewed and the system is explicated as a nonrational, self-regulating mechanism making lawful adaptations. If the populations get out of balance—for instance, if the population of farmers outstrips its food supply because of a drought, and that drought likewise affects the wild plant and animal populations—survival is threatened. The human population, it is alleged, adapts to the environment without even knowing it. Adaptation, then, is interpreted as is adaptation in evolutionary biology: it is a nonrational or nonintentional process of adjustments. That is to say, the human population is part of a larger system of multivariate relations wherein an impulse generated or felt in one part influences the other parts, and the various populations must adapt to these impulses or be selected out. Human populations, it is contended, adapt themselves to the ranges of behavior of the other populations and the natural environment through customs that control and regulate their own population. Thus, human populations create and borrow techniques for subsistence and, often in unwitting responses to impulses from elsewhere in their system, create customs that serve as controls and regulatory mechanisms so that the human population can survive. The notion of controls and regulatory mechanisms allows the analyst to understand systems as organization of phenomena separate from the intentions, reasons, motives, and dispositions of the human agents in the system. Indeed, the system is alleged to be self-regulating (a nonrational model), and its behavior obeys lawful processes. In a fashion reminiscent of the British functionalists of the 1930s and 1940s, Ford (1972:1–17) has claimed that certain ritual customs of Eastern Pueblos are not at all what Eastern Pueblos think they are. He says that they are regulatory feedback mechanisms for assisting the survival of the population by storing and redistributing food to people in need. The customs, then, are unwittingly integrated into a system that "assists" survival of the population when the needs of some people outstrip their ability to satisfy those needs. Moreover, the nature of the system is such that the needs of some people will become dire at regular intervals, and the regulatory mechanisms will "assist" survival at these periods. It is not clear that anything of theoretical or empirical import turns on this view of environment (biological and nonbiological) and culture relations, because the key relational terms, that is, the explanatory statements or argument clinchers, such as "assist" and "survival" are not defined and measured, the ranges for the variables in the system are not specified and measured, the meaning of the key term "effective" variable is not clear because it is not demonstrated why some variables are "effective" and others are not, and the like. Furthermore, no differential equation models have been deployed to simulate a dynamic system, showing how survival is achieved through adaptations.

Note on Methodology

In conducting this comparative analysis it was of critical importance to follow formal procedures in order to demonstrate that relations were real and determinate. The goal was to compare the relations among tribes (Q-mode in matrix analysis language) and among variables (R-mode in matrix analysis language) to demonstrate that one tribe, say, was more closely related to another on the basis of the measurements of the shared cultural inventories of all tribes in the sample. "Real" in statistical language means that whenever tribes A and B practice the same customs 1, 2, and 3, they will be more similar than if they do not practice those customs. It is not enough to know whether a pair of tribes are very similar, or very different; it must also be known how similar a pair of tribes is in relation to all other tribes. In order to assess the meaning of any relationship between a pair of tribes, that relationship must be controlled by comparing each member of the pair with all other tribes in the sample. The relations among every pair of tribes in the sample must be measured to determine the closest relations among tribes. In figure 2, for instance, the 37 tribes form 666 pairs of relations, and all these pairs had to be analyzed in order to reduce the 666 relations to a two-dimensional mapping.

Thus, formal comparisons are controlled, whether in the analyses of tribes or variables. The methodology for comparisons and controls will require brief explication and can best be understood as part of the overall research design (see Jorgensen 1974 for a more extended discussion of comparative method).

The Variables

In order to measure relations among tribes and among variables it was necessary to formulate hypotheses about relations among environments and cultures, and to define and operationalize variables so that these hypotheses could be formally (statistically) and empirically evaluated. As part of the larger study Jorgenson (1980) defined 134 variables to measure environment, and 292 variables to measure culture. It was necessary to consult ethnographic, biological, historical, and other sources to rate each culture unit and culture-unit territory for the information pertinent to each variable.

The variable code is 180 pages long and cannot be reproduced here. It is available in Jorgensen (1980). The titles, but not the definition of each rank, for the

83 ordinal variables used for tests in the R-mode are listed with figures 10 and 11.

The Measures of Relationship

In order to determine the similarity or dissimilarity of a pair of tribes on several variables it is necessary to compare the tribes and measure the comparison. For measures in the Q-mode Driver and Kroeber's (1932) G was chosen, a measure of association closely related to Pearson's (Pearson and Heron 1913) r, which is exceptional in that it eliminates the d cell in a conventional four-cell table. Driver and Kroeber's

$$G = \frac{a}{\sqrt{a + b}\sqrt{a + c}}.$$

A four-cell table is, conventionally,

		Tribe 1 +	Tribe 1 −
Tribe 2	+	a	b
	−	c	d

where a = attributes of variables that are the same for tribes 1 and 2, b = the attributes of variables that are present in tribe 2 but absent in tribe 1, c = the attributes of variables that are present in tribe 1 but absent in tribe 2, and d = the attributes of variables in the total sample of variables for all tribes that are absent in both tribes 1 and 2. By excluding the d cell, the relations between pairs of tribes are not inflated by common absences.

For example, to measure a pair of tribes for their relationship on subsistence economy variables, of which there are 30 in this sample, each society would be rated for each variable. Each variable is composed of mutually exclusive attributes, that is to say, each society must be rated on one, but only one attribute for each variable. The variable "local agricultural products in the diet" has five ranked (ordinal) attributes: 0 percent, 1–10 percent, 11–25 percent, 26–50 percent, and 51–100 percent. Each culture unit must be rated for one of these ordinal attributes. By rating each culture unit for all 30 variables (encompassing 182 attributes, or 6 attributes per variable) the relationship can be measured for each pair of tribes on the subsistence economy information in question.

If the Mohave were the same as the Pima on 13 variables, but different from the Pima on 17 variables, the four-cell table would look like this:

		Mohave +	Mohave −	
Pima	+	13	17	30
	−	17	135	152
		30	152	182

$$G = \frac{13}{\sqrt{13 + 17}\sqrt{13 + 17}}$$

$$G = \frac{13}{30}$$

$$G = .43$$

In brief the table shows that whenever the same attribute is shared, an entire variable is accounted for in the a cell. Because variables are mutually exclusive and inclusive, whenever the Pima practices a custom that the Mohave do not practice (cell b), the Mohave practice a custom that the Pima do not practice (cell c). As a consequence, b = c. The d cell represents all 152 attributes of the 182 that neither culture unit practices. Because the number of attributes that neither member of a pair shares is potentially unlimited, and because b = c, Driver and Kroeber's G can be interpreted as the percentage of agreement between each pair of tribes. That is, a G of .43 for subsistence economy means that a pair of tribes are similar on 13 variables and different on 17, or 43 percent in agreement. G varies between .00 and 1.00.

The measures employed in the R-mode analysis were developed by Goodman and Kruskal (1954) as "regression free" measures of relationship between ordinal and between nominal variables. The 83 variables used in the R-mode tests are ordinal, that is, the attribute categories are ranked to mean that 1 is less than 2, 2 is less than 3, and so forth. On the other hand, ordinal ranks do not assume that the distance between each pair of ranks is equal. Thus, Goodman and Kruskal's Gamma measures whether the order of ranks in one variable predicts the order of ranks in the other, and vice versa. Gamma = $\frac{Ns - Nr}{Ns + Nr}$ where Ns = the number of pairs of cases having the same order on both variables, and Nr = the number of pairs of cases having reverse orders on both variables.

Gamma, which varies between −1.00 and +1.00, shows that there is no relation between ordered ranks at zero, that the ranks change in the same order at +1.00, and that they change in the reverse order at −1.00. Thus, in measuring the relation between the "contribution to diet from gathering" and the "species of herbs, roots, and tubers available" the ordered categories are being measured.

Species of herbs, roots, and tubers available	Contribution to diet from gathering		
	Tertiary	Secondary	Dominant
1–2	13	6	4
3–4	1	6	3
5–6	0	3	1

Gamma = .57

The Gamma is calculated using the 37 tribes as cases. In the Q-mode the variables are cases. Whereas the majority of tribes that depended least on wild plants had the fewest herbs, roots, and tubers in their territories, the relation between increased order of use and increased order of plants available is only modest.

For 22 of the 83 ordinal variables it was necessary to employ Goodman and Kruskal's (1954) Tau for nominal variables. That is because Gamma behaves erratically in four-cell tables, as well as in 2×N tables. So the 22 variables that have only two ordered categories each were ferreted out and measured separately from the other 61. For a four-cell table

$$\text{Tau} = \frac{\sum_{1}^{r}\sum_{1}^{c}\frac{n^2ij}{ni} - \frac{\sum_{1}^{c}n^2i}{n}}{n - \frac{\sum_{1}^{c}n^2i}{n}}$$

For example, to measure the relationship between "agricultural food acquired extra-locally" and "extra-local agricultural products in the diet" the two variables are placed in a table.

Extra-local agricultural products in diet	Agricultural food acquired extra-locally	
	None	Maize, beans, squashes
0%	18	1
1–10%	0	14

Tau = .88

There was no information on this question for four tribes, so those cases are excluded. The Tau shows that knowledge of either the column or the row variable allows a reduction in errors in predicting the distribution of the categories of the other variable by 88 percent. In the multivariate analysis in figure 11, signs (+ and −) were assigned to the Tau values so that negative predictions would separate variables and positive predictions would bring them together.

The Unidimensional and Multidimensional, Nonmetric, Multivariate Analyses

In analyzing the relations among culture units (Q-mode) two multivariate techniques have been used. Both are nonmetric techniques for finding the shortest distances in Euclidean spaces, but based on different algorithms. The unidimensional method referred to as Jorgensen's nonmetric trees (Jorgensen 1969) preserves some metric information in that bridges between the closest pairs show the Driver and Kroeber's G level at which the pair is joined (the largest G level is the shortest distance between the two points). For groups larger than two members, the bridges show the centroid (geometric center of gravity, or the shortest distance among all points in the group) for all G's among all culture units in the group.

The second method, called MINISSA by its authors (Roskam and Lingoes 1970; Lingoes and Roskam 1971), as used here is a multidimensional scaling program that converts coefficients of similarity (Driver and Kroeber's G, Goodman and Kruskal's Gamma and Tau) for a square matrix (Q- or R-mode) to distances from a specified Euclidean distance function and maps the distances into a set of ranks using special tie-breaking procedures. The relations among variables or tribes, as measured by ranks, are solved in as many dimensions up to 10 as are necessary. For complete analyses also see Guttman (1968) and Lingoes (1965, 1968, 1971).

The Guttman-Lingoes Coefficient of Alienation K is used to measure the amount of variation explained for solutions in two dimensions or greater. As a rule of thumb, K = .15 is employed as a reasonable fit. That is, about 85 percent of the variance among all of the points in the matrix is explained when K = .15. In general, the higher the dimensionality the lower the K. On the other hand, the lower the dimensionality, the simpler the interpretation of complex phenomena.

In the Q-mode the mapping of ranked variables required only two dimensions for extremely good fits. But in the R-mode three dimensions were required. The dimensions can be interpreted by looking at the front-to-back and side-to-side relations among points in two dimensions, and adding the up-to-down dimension in three dimensional solutions.

Inter-Indian Exchange in the Southwest

RICHARD I. FORD

General discussions of Southwestern exchange are numerous, but detailed studies have been rare. Bandelier (1890–1892, 1) and Parsons (1939) both recognized the vast array of goods that circulated throughout the Southwest by a variety of means, and Beaglehole (1937), Spier (1928, 1933), Hill (1948), and Ford (1972a) have all focused on traditional exchange conducted by a particular tribe or linguistic group. Most studies have failed to quantify the amount of each good exchanged, to mention the frequency of intercommunity contacts for purposes of trade, or to identify why economic interaction occurred.

Intercommunity exchange is a complex of social and economic processes. It may involve the physical transfer of raw materials and finished goods or it may entail social and ceremonial services that are rewarded by immediate payment, continuous hospitality and obligations, or deferred expressions of gratitude. A variety of social mechanisms may be employed to consummate exchange. The participants may travel over great distance or only to a neighboring camp, the routes may be well-marked or expedient, and communication may range from fluency between friends to a few words or signs barely intelligible to total strangers. The exchange of goods and services in the Southwest encompassed great variation from prehistoric times until the early twentieth century, and despite changes in transportation and economics, it continued to be a vital part of Indian interaction in the 1980s.

Traditional Southwestern exchange was conditioned by differentiated biological productivity, scarce natural resources, and contrasting social and ceremonial organizations. Within a framework of environmental heterogeneity, exchange was an equalizer and at times a means to survival.

The physical environment for every Southwest society was typified by unpredictability and great variation. A good piñon nut harvest by the Navajo or Havasupai might not be followed by another for five years, while a bumper crop of corn might precede several years of drought or destruction. Under these conditions a basis of exchange—the good will of trade partners and friends—was a requisite for survival. Moreover, these social contacts were reinforced on a regular basis, leading to dependence upon another's crafts. Certainly this was the case with Jemez supplying Zia with surplus food in exchange for its domestic pottery (Stevenson 1894:11).

Since not all products could be stored for prolonged periods of time, some exchange was for the purpose of "banking." Commodities that were nonperishable, universally convertible, and always desired were used for this purpose. Shell beads, turquoise, silver jewelry, buckskins, and blankets fell into this category. When one had a surplus of some good, it was traded for these; when other wants were great, they were reconverted into food and necessities.

Finally, dependency upon other tribes for ritual paraphernalia was universal in the Southwest, and at the same time it helped to maintain contacts for obtaining other essential items. The Tewa ceremonially used Ute red ocher, Comanche and Taos buffalo hides, and feathers and shells from the Keresans; Cochiti required Comanche buffalo chin beards; Zia needed Jicarilla coiled baskets in naming ceremonies; Navajo ceremonial objects came from the Southern Ute, Hopi, and Zuni. The need for foreign goods was so pervasive that the individual costumes worn in every Indian dance had items obtained from outside the tribal territory. Only through trade could these ritual symbols be obtained. As they were consumed, trade was reinforced.

Prehistoric Exchange

Archeologists have unearthed the antiquity of trade in the Southwest. Obsidian from west of the Rio Grande has been identified in the Paleo-Indian Clovis area, and long-distance trade for saltwater shells is known in Archaic times ("Prehistory: Hohokam," figs. 6–7, "Prehistory: Southern Periphery," figs. 10–11, vol. 9). With the advent of sedentary horticultural villages and later the adoption of ceramics, evidence from sites for nonlocal material goods increased. Cotton textiles were traded from southern Arizona to the Colorado plateau for several hundred years before cotton was grown by the Anasazi. Pottery was exchanged throughout the Southwest (cf. Shepard 1965 and Warren 1969), and by A.D. 1000 turquoise, copper, and macaws were added to the continuing exchange of stone, marine shell, and ceramics.

The mechanisms of this prehistoric exchange are under investigation. Schroeder (1965a) regards the earlier patterns of exchange as a result of informal contacts and Ruby (1968) has applied a similar model based on egalitarian groups using trade partners to explain the long-recognized trade between southern California and the Southwest. This model is not universally applicable if Di Peso (1974) is correct in supposing that the Southwest was linked by *pochteca*-type traders to centers in Mexico. The northernmost of these centers was Casas Grandes where Di Peso revealed storage areas for many exotic items and pens for raising macaws and turkeys. The stockpiles found in this ruin suggest a regulated trade with monopolistic control by resident middlemen. Similar interpretations have been offered for the Hohokam (Schroeder 1966) and for Chaco Canyon, which is reputed to have possessed an actual resident *pochteca* colony (T.R. Frisbie 1971).The extent of these possible Mesoamerican contacts has been detailed by Schroeder (1981). The presence of nonlocal exports in limited quantity elsewhere supports the idea that several mechanisms operated simultaneously.

Early Historic Observations

Explorers to the Southwest were impressed by the amount of trade they witnessed and the distances walked by Indian traders. On the eastern periphery contrasting adaptations brought Plains nomads with buffalo hides and dried meat to Taos, Pecos, and the Piro Pueblos where they obtained corn, cloth, and turquoise, and where they sometimes wintered (Kenner 1969). Below Yuma, Arizona, Spaniards interviewed well-traveled Indians who were familiar with the Zuni. They saw Hopi cotton textiles worn by lower Colorado River Yuman farmers and the ubiquitous buffalo-skin robes available throughout the area. Sonoran Indians knew that parrot feathers were traded to the Pueblos for turquoise (Hammond and Rey 1940:140–151).

It appears that some Indian traders traveled the breadth of the Southwest from Pecos to the Colorado River and often down into Mexico. Certainly the late prehistoric trade routes in west Mexico, across southern California, and to Pecos and the Plains that enabled the distribution of marine shells, parrot and macaw feathers, buffalo robes and meat, and turquoise in the Southwest were observed by the Spaniards before depopulation and international conflict disrupted these contacts.

Goods

A plethora of raw materials and handicrafts was exchanged between villages. Wild and cultivated plant products, animal body parts, birds, shells, minerals, and an array of finished goods were produced in one village and were desired by another community because they were not locally available or because they confirmed social bonds.

Native plants required for ceremonies, cures, charms, crafts, and food were supplied by villages with access to them. Picuris, for example, provided Taos, San Juan, and San Felipe with ceremonial plants. San Juan and Santa Clara obtained osha (*Ligusticum porteri*), an indispensable medicine and charm, from the Jicarilla Apache. Isleta, Cochiti, and San Juan received another powerful plant, cachana (*Liatris* sp.), from Jemez. Comanches supplied Santa Clara with redbean charms (*Sophora secundiflora*), and all the Tewa Pueblos with walnuts. Plant fibers constituted trade items in the Colorado and Gila river drainages. Cotton was traded by the Pima and Hopi to the Papago and Navajo, respectively. The Pima also sent devil's-claw pods to the Quechan while the Papago supplied their neighbors with agave fibers. Furthermore, native plant foods were commonly exchanged. All the Western Apache and Upland Yumans people supplied dried mescal (*Agave* spp.) sheets to the Mohave, Papago, Maricopa, Hopi villages, Zuni, and Navajo. Saguaro cactus syrup, fruit, and seeds were primarily traded by the Papago to the Pima and Maricopa, and by the Yavapai to the Western Apache. Acorns reached the Mohave from the Ipai-Tipai, the Quechan from the Tipai, and the Cocopa from the Paipai. Mesquite pods went from the Pima to the Maricopa. Piñon nuts were supplied to Hopi by Upland Yumans and Navajos, and Western Apache brought sunflower seeds to Zuni. Finally, the wood from depleted Hopi mesas was supplemented by firewood brought by Santo Domingo Pueblo, Navajo, and Paiute traders.

Domesticated plant trade included prehistoric cultigens and Spanish-introduced wheat and fruits. Wheat bread was a common product of the irrigated fields in the Eastern Pueblos for the Comanche, Kiowa, Ute, and Jicarilla Apache and from the Pima for the Papago. Hopi-grown peaches were exchanged with the Navajo and other fruits raised by Eastern Pueblos went to nomadic groups to the east. The Tewa Pueblos provided the Jicarilla Apache and northern Tiwa with chile peppers. Corn was the most popular pre-Hispanic trade food. All the Pueblos had a regular commerce for maize with their nomadic neighbors and with one another when crops failed. Farther west the Havasupai, Sonoran Desert people, and Colorado River Yumans traded corn to Walapai, Yavapai, Western Apache, and Paipai. The Papago got tepary beans from the Pima. Gourds also were traded. The Mohave gave gourds to the Quechan who then exchanged gourd seeds to the Ipai-Tipai and rattles to the Cahuilla. The eastern Navajos received gourd rattles from Zuni and Laguna while Picuris and Taos were dependent upon San Juan and Santa Clara traders.

Unfortunately, most ethnographies do not specify the species of tobacco that were traded or the part of the plant involved. In the Eastern Pueblos the Tewas and Keresans grew *Nicotiana rustica* and traded its leaves widely. Taos and Picuris collected wild *N. attenuata* and exchanged its capsules and leaves to the Rio Grande Pueblos. Elsewhere the Hopi received tobacco from the Havasupai, the Pima produced surplus tobacco for the Maricopa and Halchidhoma, and an unknown species came to the Quechan from the Tipai and to the Cocopa from the Paipai and Ipai-Tipai.

Hide trade was extensive in the Southwest ("Taos Pueblo," fig. 3, vol. 9). Buffalo robes originating with the Comanche and some Eastern Pueblo hunters reached every group including the Colorado River tribes and northern Mexico. Buckskin was produced by the northern Tiwa, Tewa, Navajo, Apaches, Utes, and Upland Yuman people for the southern Pueblos, Zuni, Hopi, Papago, and Colorado River tribes. Mountain lion skins came to the Navajo from Tonto Apache and Yavapai. Rabbitskin blankets were made by the Yavapai, Hopi, Paiute, and Jemez; mountain sheep skins were prepared by the Walapai and Havasupai; beaver skins were processed by the Havasupai; and elk skins came from the Utes.

Jerked buffalo meat, tallow, and pemmican were brought by Plains tribes and Eastern Pueblos to western groups and deer meat followed the same trade networks as buckskin.

The exchange of live birds and feathers awaits fuller documentation. Macaws and parrot feathers reached the northern Rio Grande Pueblos from Opata, Zuni, and Santo Domingo traders. Most groups exchanged eagle feathers with friends in other tribes, although this exchange was quite intensive in the Colorado River area. Western Apache supplied turkey-feather caps to the Navajo and Yavapai and turkey feathers to Zuni. San Juan provided the Jicarilla with songbird feathers, and the Papago supplied the Maricopa with doves.

Saltwater shells came into the Southwest from coastal California groups, the Cocopa, Seri, and Papago. They were traded to all groups although Zuni and Santo Domingo traders were most influential in their dispersal as well as in the production of shell beads and ceremonial objects (T.R. Frisbie 1974).

Minerals for food, ceremonial use, and crafts were common exchange items. Salt was in great demand and was supplied from four major sources. Isleta obtained it from the Estancia basin in eastern New Mexico, Laguna and Zuni from their own salt lakes (fig. 1), and the Papago from the Gulf of California. From these groups most other tribes obtained this seasoning. Pigments and stone for rituals came from a number of sources. The Utes, Havasupai, Papago, and Quechan were major sources of red ocher. Nambe Pueblo provided other Tewas with mica for kachina dancers. The Quechan supplied a black paint to the Pima, and the Mohave were a source of yellow paint for the Havasupai and Walapai. Laguna made travertine rod fetishes for other villages. Certainly for craft production turquoise and clay were important in Southwest commerce. Turquoise from the Cerrillos mines in New Mexico was quarried primarily by Santo Domingo and Cochiti men. It was worked in most Pueblos into beads, pendants, and fetishes and traded as a finished product as well. Acoma traded a white kaolin pottery slip and San Felipe a black mineral pottery paint to Zuni and other pottery-producing Pueblos. Of the remaining minerals, jet from the Navajo was used in jewelry.

Finished goods were identifiable to individual villages and in some cases to a particular artisan. Pottery, basketry, textiles (fig. 2), leather goods, and utensils all circulated among groups. Taos, Picuris, and the Jicarilla Apache specialized in micaceous cooking pots, the other Pueblos made a variety of distinctly decorated vessel forms, and Papago, Maricopa, and Mohave produced trade wares for tribes in the western area. Basketry was almost universally produced and traded because different people made different functional types. The Jicarilla, Navajo, and Utes coiled baskets, San Juan produced a wicker form, the Yavapai made dippers and parching trays, Jemez made yucca wheat-washing baskets, the Western Apache made burden baskets and pitch-covered canteens, the Pima made trays, and the Papago wove storage jars. The weaving industry was dominated by Hopi textile blankets, mantas, sashes, leggings, and other ceremonial items. By the end of the nineteenth century Navajo blankets also were highly prized. Belts were woven in many Eastern Pueblos for trade. Leather clothing and bags were commonly made by the Upland Yumans, Utes, Comanche, and Apache. Various wooden and bone items were made for inter-

Southwest Mus., Los Angeles: 20,926.

Fig. 1. Zuni Indians bagging salt, an item traded to many groups, at Zuni Salt Lake, an important sacred area. Photograph by Donald Cadzow about 1921.

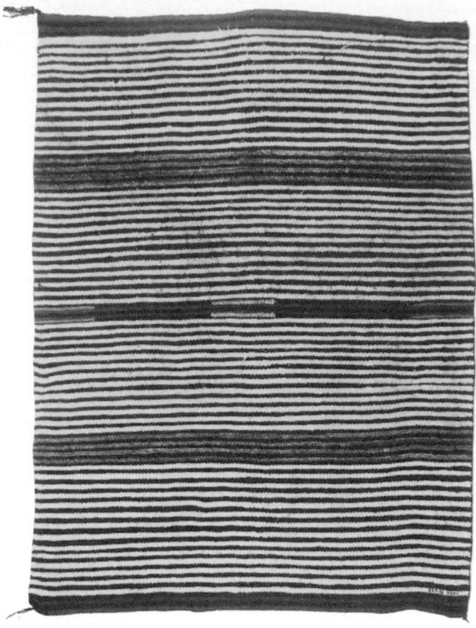

left, Smithsonian, NAA: 34011-B; right, Smithsonian, Dept. of Anthr.: 22,976.

Fig. 2. Striped blankets, a common type throughout the Southwest (Kent 1976:90). left, Chiricahua Apache camp, with trade blanket, probably Navajo, on brush shelter. Photograph by A.T. Willcox or A.F. Randall, probably 1880s. right, Blanket, probably Navajo, with modified woman's pattern has blue and dark brown stripes at the ends and center (which also has red blocks); the body is alternating dark brown and white stripes with 2 bands of a gray and dark brown. Size 116.0 cm by 162.5 cm, collected from the Hopi at Tusayan, Ariz., in 1876.

community exchange. Cochiti drums were found in all the Pueblos. Osage-orange bows from the Comanche were familiar to the Eastern Pueblos. Bows and arrows were given in trade by the White Mountain Apache and Yavapai.

The complexity of intercommunity exchange is exemplified by the Hopi villages (table 1). Numerous goods and linguistic groups were involved in these interactions, and the Hopi depended upon this vast network of contacts.

References that discuss trade goods are, for Taos, Curtis (1907–1930, 17), Ford (1972a), Parsons (1936); for Picuris, Ford (1972); for Sandia, U.S. Census Office. 11th Census (1893); for Isleta, Bloom (1936), Curtis (1907–1930, 12), Ford (1972a), Parsons (1932); for Tewa, Ford (1972a); for Jemez, Ford (1972a), Parsons (1925); for Cochiti, Curtis (1907–1930, 17), Eickemeyer and Eickemeyer (1895), Goldfrank (1927), Lange (1959); for Santo Domingo, Densmore (1938), Ford (1972a), White (1935); for San Felipe, Densmore (1938), White (1935); for Santa Ana, White (1942); for Zia, Stevenson (1894), White (1962); for Laguna, Ford (1972a), Hill (1948); for Acoma, Beaglehole (1937), Parsons (1939). Among the Apache, sources are, for the Jicarilla, Ford (1972a), Gifford (1940), Opler (1971a); for the Mescalero, Basehart (1974); for the Chiricahua, Gifford (1940), Opler (1941); for the Western Apache, Goodwin (1942); for the Tonto, Gifford (1940), Goodwin (1942); for the San Carlos, Gifford (1940). References that discuss Navajo exchange are, Gifford (1936), Hill (1948), Kluckhohn and Leighton (1946), Kluckhohn and Wyman (1940), Kroeber (1925), Spier (1928), Tschopik (1941). Zuni trade is treated by Bandelier (1890–1892), Bunzel (1932b), Curtis (1907–1930, 17), Cushing (1896, 1920). Items exchanged by the Yumans are given for Havasupai, Cushing (1882), Ewing (1960), Spier (1928); Walapai, Curtis (1907–1930, 2), Kroeber (1925), Spier (1928); Yavapai, Gifford (1936), Goodwin (1942); Mohave, Kroeber (1925), Spier (1933); Halchidhoma, Spier (1933), Forbes (1965); Quechan, Curtis (1907–1930, 2), Forbes (1965), Forde (1931), Gifford (1936); Cocopa, Castetter and Bell (1951), Gifford (1933); Maricopa, Spier (1933). Trade goods among the Pima are discussed by Russell (1908); among the Papago, by Castetter and Bell (1942), Gifford (1936), Underhill (1939, 1946).

Services

Just as each community was not self-sufficient in raw materials and craft production, it often lacked the proper complement of ceremonial specialists and eligible marriage partners. Here, again, intercommunity cooperation was indispensable.

Marriage between communities was sometimes essential as well as beneficial. Small Pueblos, like Picuris, which frequently married San Juan and Jicarilla mates, and Sandia, which sought Isleta partners, had to maintain themselves and to avoid incest violations by means of exogamy. In the Eastern Keresan and Western Pueblos incoming female partners were the genesis of new

Table 1. Hopi Exchange With Other Tribes

Hopi Products	*Items Traded to Hopis (Tribe Received From)*
maize	silver (Eastern Pueblos, Navajo, Zuni)
foodstuffs, peaches	turquoise (Zuni, Keresans, Jemez, Sandia)
rabbitskin robes	shell beads (Zuni, Acoma, Eastern Keresans, Jemez)
skin pouches	salt (Zuni)
spoons	buckskin (Zuni, Havasupai, Walapai, Northern and Southern Tonto)
pottery (First Mesa)	buffalo skins (Zuni, Eastern Pueblos)
coiled baskets (Second Mesa)	mountain lion quivers (Navajo, Paiute, Northern Tonto)
wicker baskets (Third Mesa)	firewood (Navajo, Paiute)
salt	vigas, sheep, mutton, blankets, antelope skins, water (Navajo)
cooking pots	horses (Navajo, Paiute, Havasupai)
bottles	bows, arrows (Havasupai, Paiute)
yucca sieves	mescal (Havasupai, White Mountain Apache, Walapai)
shell beads	piñon nuts (Havasupai, Walapai)
buckskin	baskets, leather clothing, horn ladles, sea shells, abalone, red ocher, copper stones, tobacco, grass, willows, cottonwood roots, yellow pigment, mountain sheep skins (Havasupai)
mantas, kilts, belts	green bows, arrows, moccasins (White Mountain Apache)
leggings, yarn	cotton (Pima, Zuni)
blankets	macaw feathers (Pima, Havasupai)
buffalo hides	deer meat (Paiute, Jemez)
turquoise	piñon gum (Paiute)
silver	maize (Isleta, Santo Domingo, San Felipe)
livestock	tools (Eastern Pueblos)
red ocher	feather caps (Southern Tonto)
iron tools	
tinklers	
ceremonial items	

SOURCES: Beaglehole 1937; Colton 1938; Curtis 1926; Hill 1948; Parsons 1939; Stephen 1936.

clans or a means to augment underpopulated clans. Sometimes marriage partners from outside introduced new songs, dances, and societies. The Ant society was brought to Santo Domingo by a Zuni, and eventually it was petitioned to cure in other Eastern Keresan villages (White 1935:68).

Mutual assistance by ritualists was commonplace in the conduct of ceremonies and the initiation of new members. The caciques at Jemez and Cochiti aided each other, and the winter cacique at Tesuque initiated his counterpart at Nambe. Tewa Koshares frequently performed together, while the Quiranas at Cochiti had ties with Tesuque, Nambe, and San Ildefonso (Ford 1972a:37; Lange 1959:350). Ceremonial participation between Hopi-Tewa and First Mesa Hopi villages provides an example of village interdependence through ceremonial service (Dozier 1954:364).

Individuals or troupes of dancers frequently performed in other communities. Zuni dancers came to First Mesa in the past (Parsons 1936), and most large-scale dances in the Rio Grande Pueblos have a component of nonresident performers. In return for their participation they received not only the benefit of the ceremony but also food and ritual items.

Specialists aided individuals in neighboring communities. Navajo and Hopi-Tewa exchanged cures. San Juan Bear medicine men cured Picuris and Taos patients; the Taos employed Ute doctors as well. Chiricahua treated other Apache. Furthermore, San Juan and Tesuque midwives were called upon by other Tewa villagers. Each practitioner was remunerated with food or goods by the patient's family according to its ability to pay.

Another intercommunity service was the teaching of new songs and dances. To accomplish this, one requested permission to learn the song or dance. The village owning it was not obligated to agree, as when Zunis were rebuked by First Mesa Hopis in their attempt to purchase the Snake-Antelope ceremony (Stephen 1936:679). If they did agree, a price was established and instruction began. Possibly by this method Taos obtained the Southern Ute Dog Dance, San Ildefonso learned the Jicarilla Basket Dance, Nambe obtained the Ute Serpent Dance, the Jicarilla Apache derived the Holiness rite from Taos, and the Navajo started the Ute Circle Dance. These dances were recognized as distinct from older, more sacred dances among the Pueblos and their performance was an occasion when fancy trade goods could be worn. Certainly this practice pertained when the Tewa presented the Comanche Dance ("San Ildefonso Pueblo," fig. 13, vol. 9) and Cochiti performed a Navajo Dance ("Cochiti Pueblo," fig. 14, vol. 9).

Exchange Mechanisms

The means for exchanging goods and services varied along a dimension of social distance. One series of rules and conventions applied to fellow villagers, while another affected relations with nonrelatives in neighboring communities. Long-distance trade required several alternative mechanisms to guarantee peace of trade under less than ideal circumstances.

Within a village or encampment four general methods of exchange were recognized: mutual assistance, gambling and gaming, ceremonial redistribution, and trading parties. Sharing was continuous, gambling was spontaneous or seasonal, while the other two occurred less frequently. Yet each gave everyone access to food raised in the village and materials imported from afar.

Milwaukee Public Mus., Wis.: 44433.

Fig. 3. Isleta woman offering bread and melons at a shrine dedicated to St. Stephen. Later the food will be shared among the dancers. Photograph by Sumner W. Matteson, 1899–1905.

Intracommunity lending, borrowing, and sharing was constant. Children ate with grandparents or unrelated neighbors. Tools were borrowed or ceremonial costumes lent upon request. The fundamental characteristic of these reciprocal interactions was that repayment was equalized only in the long run.

Gambling and games of skill were informal and voluntary mechanisms by means of which possessions circulated throughout a community and often allowed booty or newly acquired trade goods to pass to new owners. Opler (1941:398) noted this mechanism worked for the Chiricahua of all ages and both sexes, but the same applies to all Southwestern groups. Horse racing and cañute and other hand games (cf. Culin 1907) permitted informal redistribution of goods and food.

Ceremonial redistributions were familiar to all Southwestern tribes. At times of life crisis rites, relatives contributed payment for feasts and for specialists performing the ceremony. Among the Tewa the initiation of a new society member required the contribution of cornmeal, feathers, and other items from near kinsmen. But their generosity was not without recompense because once the initiate became an active participant in ceremonial affairs, payment in food for his services was shared with them. At the Mohave mourning ceremony food and presents were given to visitors. Similar fetes attended namings and weddings elsewhere. Ceremonies organized for the benefit of the community, such as calendrical rites, included contributions of food and other items to be consumed by participants, families, and friends (figs. 3–4; "San Ildefonso Pueblo," fig. 3, "Acoma Pueblo," fig. 16, vol. 9). These periodic rituals were often essential in providing food to those in need (Ford 1972a).

The intravillage mechanism of the trading party was probably more extensive than the literature suggests. Only the Hopi-Tewa, Hopi, and Zuni have been described as employing variants of this neighborly general exchange. Although individuals did trade privately, it was more common for Hopi to engage in a quasi-market (*ná·mi hɨ̂·yaya* 'they sell to one another') (fig. 5). Conducted principally by women, it consisted of goods displayed outside the house in the plaza. Stephen (1936:245–246) saw trays of dried peaches, salt, beans, cornmeal, mescal, and mealing stones offered in return for specific items. He was struck by the lack of bargaining. Dozier (1954:365) noted that a friendly, noncompetitive atmosphere prevailed among the Hopi-Tewa also. Here a household initiated the party but anyone could join. Women were most active, while men were expected to pay with meat. The Zuni variety was called auctioneering by Stevenson (1904:379).On these occasions, which sometimes lasted three days, goods were brought into the plaza and the auctioneer who conducted it announced what the owner desired, usually food. Visitors from other villages were always welcome participants.

Mus. of N. Mex., Santa Fe: Parkhurst Coll.

Fig. 4. San Ildefonso women's dance, with participants wearing stocking masks and carrying bread later distributed within the community. Photograph by T. Harmon Parkhurst, about 1935.

Sometimes one had a relative in another community to provide shelter and protection and to whom one could turn for assistance, but intercommunity exchange with nonrelatives generally had an accompanying expectation of immediate return. Visitors brought gifts; yet no gift was freely received. By accepting it, exchange transactions were assured. Bartering was minimal between "friends," but a return was always made before a guest departed. These visitations frequently occurred during dances or fiestas (fig. 7). At Hopi as elsewhere a guest might remain beyond the time of the dance for the purpose of trading. The host was obligated to go from door to door announcing the guest's intention. Beaglehole (1935:82) reported that women primarily did this.

The next degree removed from this guest-host relation was best observed in the Eastern Pueblos where the close proximity of neighboring villages permitted itinerant traders, usually with very specific items such as specialty foods, plant medicines, or jewelry, to visit several Pueblos on the same day and to trade their products at a seemingly fixed rate.

Milwaukee Public Mus., Wis.: 44744.

Fig. 5. Hopi women gathered at a quasi-market in Oraibi. Photograph by Sumner W. Matteson, 1901.

Smithsonian, NAA: Judd Coll.

Fig. 6. A Hopi wagon store selling goods to visitors to the Snake ceremony. Photograph by Neil M. Judd at Hotevilla, Aug. 1920.

Other forms of intercommunity exchange were more formal, scheduled, and involved many more participants. Saint's day fiestas brought traders from many tribes together. With the peace of the market assured by the host Pueblo, the solemnity of the dances contrasted with the joyous market atmosphere beyond the plaza punctuated by earnest haggling. While trading was in progress, other visitors danced or assisted in the conduct of the ceremonial. They were given food and sometimes ceremonial ornaments in return for their service.

In the arid Sonoran Desert and along the Colorado River intervillage entertainment was rewarded with food and gifts. Papago villages had a method for "investing" against the dire effects of harvest losses. A ceremony lasting two or three days was arranged after the harvest by sending a messenger with a bundle of sticks to the host village, with each stick representing a "singing" family. These were distributed to the local households. When the singers arrived, they sang and danced for rain, fertility, and general good fortune, and were hosted by local families (Underhill 1939:106). This mechanism of ceremonially singing for food extended to other tribes along the Gila and Colorado rivers. Periodically Cocopas danced in Quechan villages at harvest time and returned with maize and various foods (Gifford 1933:262). The Pimas, Papagos, and Maricopas sang in one another's villages in times of need. A Pima family gave its guest 50 to 100 pounds of wheat following the two- or three-day performance (Castetter and Bell 1942:43). These ceremonial services had two ecologically significant results. First, the visitors, who may have had a poor year, would materially benefit from their more fortunate neighbors. Second, these ceremonics created trading friendships. Some remained gift-exchanging partners for several generations, and other friendships became permanent through marriage. In subsequent years the guest village became the host, reciprocating hospitality and friendship, and receiving the benefits of the ritual.

Long-distance trade linked tribes who were not immediate neighbors. Since the farther from home one traveled, the more perilous the journey, women rarely went on these trips, ceremonialists were often forbidden to go, and many men preferred to send their goods with others. Attacks and accidents could waylay even the most experienced trader, despite superb knowledge about the trails, water supplies, and pasturage.

Major trails connecting villages were well-known (fig. 8) and sometimes marked by shrines, petroglyphs, and debris (potsherds). Many trails originating in antiquity became the routes followed by early explorers and settlers, and have become highways. The marine-shell trails are among the better documented. One originated near Los Angeles and crossed the desert to Needles and then followed the Gila before branching to major vil-

Mus. of N. Mex., Santa Fe.

Fig. 7. Navajos encamped at Laguna Pueblo, perhaps to attend the Fiesta of San José on Sept. 19 (see Goggin 1964:21–22). Photograph by T. Harmon Parkhurst, about 1935.

lages and Pueblos (Farmer 1935). A second trail began near Guasave and came up the west coast of Mexico before crossing the Sierras and heading north to the Pueblos (Di Peso 1974). Brand (1938) and Colton (1941) have shown how these trails formed a network of interaction in the Southwest. Indeed, an impressive network of trails linked the Plains, Great Basin, Sonora, and California with all areas of the Southwest. Although individual traders did go considerable distances along them, mostly the trails were maintained by a trade-chain linking one group to the next. To illustrate, Hopi blankets reached the Quechan through exchange from the Havasupai, Walapai, and Mohave. Sea shells, on the other hand, reached Hopi through the Chumash, Mohave, Walapai, and Havasupai. Coming from the east, Comanche buffalo robes passed from Eastern Pueblo traders to Zuni, Hopi, Navajo, and then along the old shell trade networks to the Colorado River Yuman tribes and into Mexico.

The time needed to reach another group created logistic problems even with Spanish-introduced horses and burros. Zuni was four days away from Hopi, Acoma six days away, and Jemez a week. Cocopas required 10 days to reach the Pacific, while Rio Grande traders allowed several weeks to locate a Comanche band. In each case food was carried for the traders to eat on the way, to be supplemented along the trail. For the return trip, food had to be purchased or conserved.

The visitor placed himself into the custody of a stranger. This was done by making an initial gift. Since each gift was actually a request to trade, to accept the gift obligated the recipient to feed and protect his guest. The two might trade or the host might inform others about his guest's desires. Upon the visitor's leaving, the host would give a present. If he wanted to obligate his visitor in the future, he might give something of greater value than the initial gift. Conversely, he could guarantee the termination of the association by giving something of lesser value. This type of visitation was common throughout the Southwest, and the process of making a formal friend is well illustrated by the Hopi. Although the Hopi preferred traders to come to them, some men did gather woven textiles, baskets, buckskins, or ocher from their fellow villagers and go in winter to other Pueblos to trade. Arriving after six days of travel at Acoma to the public announcement of the war chief, the Hopi displayed his goods in the plaza for all to see. During this episode he made a "friend" by symbolically becoming one when he and his sponsor "put their arms around one another and mutually inhaled each other's breath" (Beaglehole 1937:84).

Sometimes these new friendships became enduring

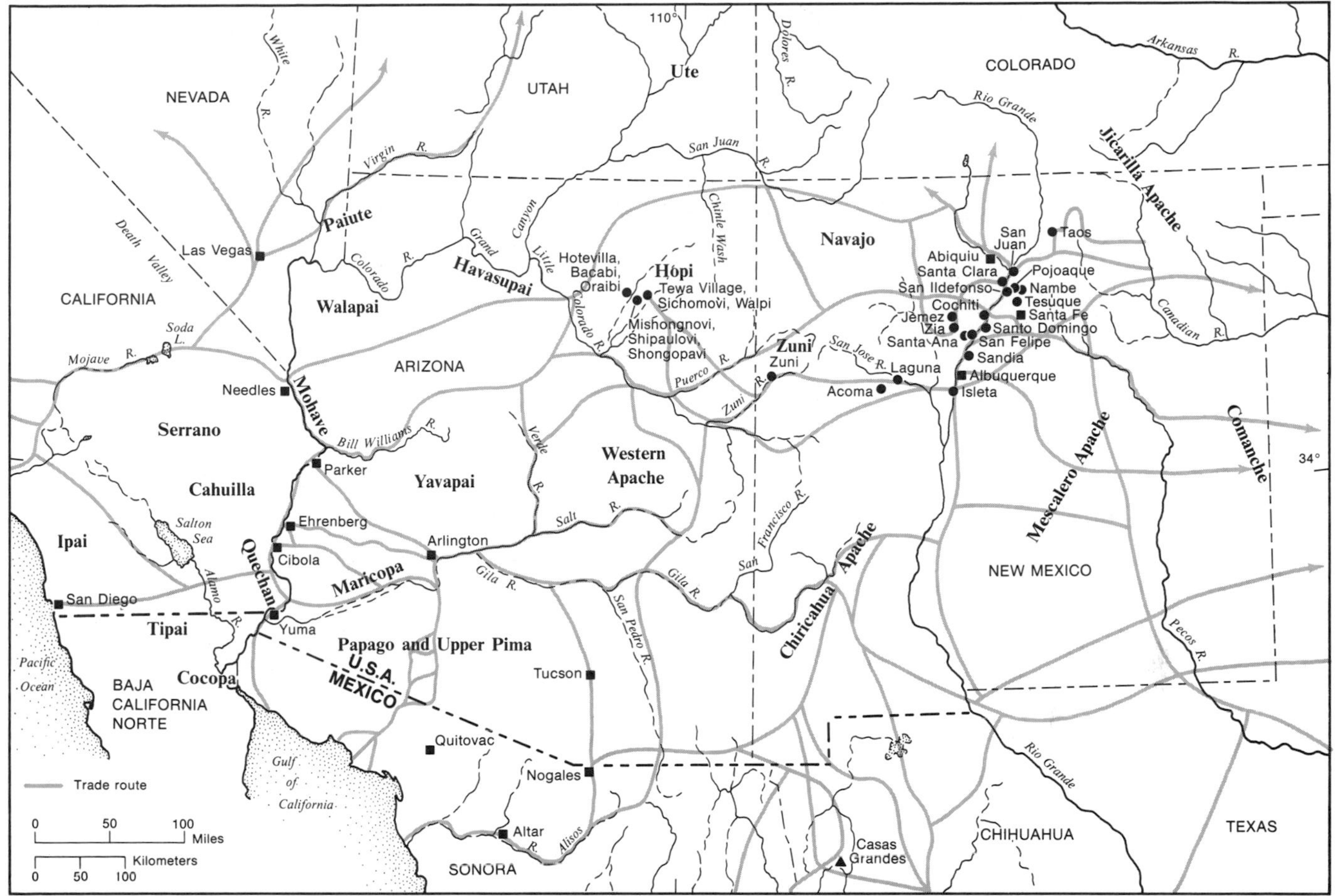

Fig. 8. Traditional trade routes in the Southwest.

and actually developed into recognizable trade partnerships. Quechan-Papago, Papago-Pima, and Maricopa-Pima sings often led to these individual arrangements. Navajo-Zuni family "friendships" have lasted two or three generations. In a spirit of quasi-kinship San Juan and Jicarilla partners rarely bargained and often "like brothers" let repayment lapse from one year to the next.

Strangers could also be enemies and a community kept a close watch for inauspicious signs to determine the intent of visitors. The Havasupai living in the lower recesses of the Grand Canyon watched for the smoke signals of friends and kinsmen as a sign of friendly relations (Spier 1928:246). The Hopi, who had periodic difficulties with Apache raiders yet welcomed traders, watched the sky in the south as Apaches approached. If a small raincloud hung over them, they were seen as coming in peace, but if no cloud was present, this was interpreted as a bad omen and they were forbidden to enter the village until peaceful intentions were proved (Beaglehole 1937:85). Within the community each member was protected by charms against potential harm brought by the stranger. This anxiety, a fear of involvement, was always present despite a proven need for maintaining trade relations.

Trade fairs were still another institution that brought distant traders together. Trade caravans from Mexico came under the auspices of Spanish officials, to obtain native products—hides, jerked meat, salt, horses, and slaves. Taos, Abiquiu, and Pima fairs were prominent places for inter-Indian contact and trade as well. However, unlike intertribal trade, rates were set by the Spaniards, to the disadvantage of the Indians, of course. These were also raucous affairs accentuated by drunkenness, brawls, and thievery (Thomas 1940).

Since many dangers haunted the trails, various supernatural precautions guided traders. Virtually every tribe had a ceremony to protect travelers before departing and a purification rite upon returning to protect the community from any bad spirits that might have accompanied the trader. Prayer feathers were carried by the Hopi for a safe trip. Each Tewa and Apache traveler carried a number of medicinal plant charms to ward off evil.

Trade Languages

Three modes of communication facilitated exchange between traders: the native language of one participant, a common third language, and sign language.

Some community members engaged in distant trading ventures more frequently than did others and they learned basic words and phrases in the language of the people they visited. In each Eastern Pueblo, for example, someone knew Comanche and could negotiate for others in a trading party. A few people at Jemez and Zia knew Navajo, while many Hopi-Tewas, Hopis, and Zunis were almost fluent in Navajo. Farther west, many Pimas and Maricopas spoke each other's language. Of course, many languages within a language family are mutually intelligible to some extent and this permitted easy communication among Keresan, Yuman, Tewa, or Tiwa traders.

The most common languages used by Indians who did not know each other's language were Spanish and Navajo. Navajo was used by the Hopi-Tewa and Zuni to communicate with each other (Parsons 1936:xxvii). Spanish, known to some degree by people in the Rio Grande Pueblos and even by the Jicarilla, Mescalero, and some Comanche, was the lingua franca of New Mexico.

Hand signs common to the southern Plains were tried when a mutually intelligible language was lacking. Sign language was needed between Tewa and Ute traders, Navajos and Paiutes, and Navajo and Tolkapaya Yavapai. However, rarely did an individual know more than a few signs and many people, particularly women, knew none.

The stimulus to exchange resulted in extensive bilingualism, which aided information processing, thus establishing trust and reducing possible chicanery.

Rates of Exchange

No commodity actually became money but several were so universally desired that exchange rates were phrased in terms of these items (see table 2). Long and short strings of shell beads (hishi) were convertible into any good at any time. The Navajo and Pueblos in particular desired these and used them more often than did people to the west. T.R. Frisbie (1974) has argued that a standard 30-inch length was a form of money. By the end of the nineteenth century Navajo blankets (fig. 9) were highly esteemed throughout the Southwest, and most published data on equivalencies state them in terms of blankets (cf. Spier 1928).

Beaglehole (1937), Goodwin (1942), Hill (1948), and Spier (1928) have published long lists of rates of exchange. The lists, which demonstrate a remarkable homogeneity and near universal knowledge of the rates, suggest that bargaining was quite restricted, although not absent. Generally, a large Havasupai buckskin, a

Table 2. Equivalent Values of Selected Paired Goods

Items	*Tribes*	*Source*
1 buckskin :: 1 blanket	Yavapai—Navajo	Gifford 1936
2 buckskins :: 1 large blanket	Yavapai—Navajo	Gifford 1936
1 buckskin :: 1 blanket	Hopi—Navajo	Beaglehole 1937
2 buckskins :: 1 large blanket	Ute—Navajo	Hill 1948
1 small buckskin :: 1 saddle blanket	Havasupai—Hopi	Beaglehole 1937
3 buckskins :: 1 big blanket	Walapai—Havasupai	Spier 1928
1 buckskin :: 1 blanket	Havasupai—Navajo	James 1903
1 large buckskin :: 1 big blanket	Western Apache—Zuni	Goodwin 1942
1 buckskin :: 1 blanket	Western Apache—Navajo	Goodwin 1942
1 buckskin :: 1 manta	Eastern Pueblos—Hopi	Beaglehole 1937
2 large buckskins :: 1 saddle blanket	Paiute—Havasupai	Spier 1928
1 sack wheat :: 1 pony	Santa Clara—Comanche	Parsons 1939
1 burden basket corn :: 1 horse	Havasupai—Hopi	Iliff 1954
1 burden basket corn :: 1 horse	Havasupai—Navajo	Spier 1928
1 blanket :: 1 poor horse	Maricopa—Papago	Spier 1933:112
2 blankets :: 1 good horse	Maricopa—Papago	Spier 1933:112
1 "chief's" blanket :: 1 horse	Navajo—Ute	Hill 1948
1 buffalo skin :: 1 horse	Hopi—Havasupai, Paiute	Beaglehole 1937
1 buffalo robe :: 1 "chief's" blanket	Ute—Navajo	Hill 1948
1 large buckskin :: 1 pony	Havasupai—Navajo	James 1903
1 large buckskin :: 1 horse	Havasupai—Hopi	Iliff 1954
2 buckskins :: 1 horse	Southern Tonto—Navajo	Gifford 1940
1 shell necklace :: 1 wedding blanket	Havasupai—Hopi	Beaglehole 1937
1 long string shell beads :: 2 mantas	Eastern Pueblos—Hopi	Beaglehole 1937
1 string turquoise :: 1 large blanket	Pueblos—Navajo	Hill 1948
Few strands beads :: 1 horse	Cochiti—Navajo	Eickemeyer 1895
1 strand of beads :: 1 buckskin	Zuni—Western Apache	Goodwin 1942

Smithsonian, Dept. of Anthr.: 220,194.

Fig. 9. Finely woven serape collected from a Ute chief in 1873. Navajo blankets were widely traded and used by Indians of other tribes. This one has a dark blue and black striped background with red, white, green, and yellow decorative elements. Size 195 cm by 140 cm, collected by Matilda C. Stevenson.

good-sized blanket, a buffalo skin or robe, a horse (fig. 10), and a large burden basket of shelled corn were interchangeable. A single gun could also be traded for any one of these items. These rates also recognized changes in the value of items resulting from processing. For example, undressed hides had half the value of a finished white buckskin. Thus two large buckskins brought by the Paiute would buy a Navajo saddle blanket from the Havasupai; the same skins refinished by the Havasupai would bring two blankets from the Navajo or Hopi.

Between some groups other commodities had recognized, standard values. Yavapai saguaro fruit cakes were exchanged at an almost set rate for Western Apache buckskins, blankets, and handicrafts (Goodwin 1942:91). The Papago made measuring baskets whose spiral design formed three parallel levels within the basket (fig. 11). Cornmeal, beans, and other items were given according to the amount as measured by these levels. Women's carrying nets served the same purpose, being equal to two measuring baskets (Underhill 1939:101).

Theft

Raiding and plundering are forms of negative reciprocity by which goods and services are obtained without giving a return. For some Mescalero and Chiricahua Apaches raiding was a primary source of even basic commodities. In fact, the Chiricahua reinforced this by asserting "you are ashamed to borrow . . . for that shows you are not a real man and have not been on the raid and obtained things for yourself" (Opler 1941:399).

Smithsonian, NAA: 43,091-A.

Fig. 10. Navajos selling ponies and blankets to Apaches. Photograph by A. Miller at Ft. Apache, Ariz., about 1890s.

Smithsonian, Dept. of Anthr.: 174,529.

Fig. 11. Papago coiled basketry bowls. The horizontal lines created by the black patterns could serve to measure contents when goods were exchanged. bottom, Fret pattern with braided rim; top, whirlwind pattern with coiled rim. bottom, Width 39.5 cm, top, same scale. Both collected by WJ McGee at San Xavier, Ariz., 1894–1895.

But this attitude was the exception in the Southwest. Warfare was expensive; men were killed and retaliation was fearsome. Moreover, the results were often unpredictable since one's efforts might be thwarted or seeming success vanished when desired items were lacking. In addition, constant raiding could jeopardize future trading, so some precautions were present that actually reduced the possibility for theft.

Ritual was a major force in stymying promiscuous raiding. The Hopi warrior returning from hostilities was secluded in a kiva for 20 days (Beaglehole and Beaglehole 1935:23–24), and Tewa combatants and their booty also underwent purification (Ford 1972a).

Interestingly, the threat of unexpected attacks from enemies encouraged exchange. The Rio Grande Pueblos found it advantageous to trade with marauding Comanches and Navajos, even when they were ill-provisioned, in an effort to avoid crop thefts and wanton destruction (Ford 1972a:34).

Stolen livestock and slaves were traded to the Pueblos. Comanches brought horses to the Eastern Pueblos and Apaches disposed of burdensome Mexican cattle, sheep, and goats with the Navajo and at Zuni. Indian children and slaves taken in intertribal skirmishes were sold to individuals in various villages or to Spanish dealers at trade fairs; however, these commodities were not significant in most intervillage transactions.

Conclusion

Inter-Indian exchange was a complex of interactions among kinsmen, neighbors, formal friends, and distant strangers. The social and ceremonial fabric encouraged outside contacts, thus assuring that all had equal information about rates of exchange and access to goods. All groups provided some special resource or craft or functioned as middlemen for some commodities. However, a network of alternative sources for every good prohibited monopolistic and exclusionary practices. Contacts were most frequent in the fall and winter between the harvest and new field preparation. The ecology of the Southwest necessitated a variety of means to maintain a maximum number of trade contacts expressed through social relations.

Mechanisms facilitating exchange were perpetuated to overcome disparities in food production between families or within a subregion. Ceremonial distributions were a reward for ritual service. These accompanied intravillage rituals as well as intervillage singing and dancing. Throughout the area food was the appropriate reward for service to man and gods.

Exchange as a social aspect of foreign relations made friends of potential enemies. Each gift made a foreigner a quasi-kinsman. Kinsmen did not bargain and could defer payment; strangers bartered and paid immediately. A kinsman or trade partner was protected and provisioned; a stranger was feared as a potential enemy. Through the creation of social dependency, desired goods became easier to obtain and unrecognized ecological differences were corrected with a minimum necessity for theft, except for Apaches in conflict with Mexicans.

Traditional Southwestern exchange was a splendid example of multiple means for moving goods within an open communication network to insure the adequate provisioning of politically independent, egalitarian communities.

Comparative Social Organization

FRED EGGAN

The American Southwest is the most complex cultural region north of Mexico, and its native Indian populations exhibit a bewildering variety of social structures. The Pueblo Indians range from matrilineal organizations in the west to bilateral and patrilineal institutions in the east, with a central region in which various combinations of east and west are found. The Navajo and Apache populations who surround the Pueblo regions show a variety of matrilineal and matrilocal groupings, and within the Navajo and Western Apache there are variations that are not yet fully understood. The Yuman populations along the lower Colorado River were patrilineal and patrilocal, with clan segments scattered along the river in favorable localities. In between, the Pima and Papago had bilateral social institutions with patrilocal residence, as did the Yuman-speaking Walapai, Yavapai, and Havasupai. The Pimans also had a set of patrilineal clans grouped into a pair of patrilineal moieties.

The Pueblo Indians, along with their neighbors, have been in contact and interaction for a long period and have been the subject of intensive investigations by anthropologists and historians since the late nineteenth century. These two volumes on the Southwest provide a summary of what has been learned with regard to culture and social organization, tribe by tribe, and this information will be referred to rather than repeated.

The Pueblos

The Pueblo Indians form a distinctive cultural unit in the Southwest, so far as externals are concerned, but exhibit important differences in their social and ceremonial organizations. The basic cultural division is between the Western Pueblos of the Colorado Plateau and the Eastern Pueblos of the Rio Grande and its tributaries, but the line of cleavage is not a sharp one. Parsons (1924) pointed out that there is a gradual shift in many aspects of Pueblo organization and belief as one moves from the Hopi in the west to Taos in the east, and Eggan (1950) presented some hypotheses to account for the apparent changes involved, including the role of the Keresan Pueblos as a "bridge" between west and east. Fox (1967) challenged this interpretation on the basis of his research at Cochiti and argued that the Keresans in the center of the Pueblo crescent should be considered a third basic division, so far as social organization is concerned: "The present system is *not* a bilateral imitation of Anglo, Spanish, or Tewa models; it is an intelligible system in its own right, based on a form of double descent and dual affiliation, and an organization of extended families. I have conjectured that this system in its outlines has characterized Cochiti since the move to the Rio Grande about 700 years ago" (Fox 1967:187).

Ortiz (1969), a Tewa from San Juan Pueblo, demonstrates that the Summer and Winter moieties are not exogamous and do not control marriage in any major way. Dozier (1970), a Tewa from Santa Clara Pueblo, both confirmed Ortiz's views of the Tewa dual divisions and analyzed the Keresan social system in general confirmation of Eggan's (1950) position with regard to Keresan kinship and the changes that had taken place. Ortiz's (1969) work required Fox to rethink his extreme position; he concludes that "there *need not have been* an exogamous patrimoiety system even if our reconstruction of the terminology and its history is correct" (Fox 1972:85).

The studies of Titiev (1944) and Eggan (1950) at Old Oraibi in the 1930s provided an account of Hopi social organization that emphasized the household and lineage as basic units. These works are particularly concerned with the "splitting" of Old Oraibi in 1906 and the founding of Hotevilla, with the later settlement of Bacabi and New Oraibi and the development of Moenkopi as a colony of Old Oraibi.

The Hopi belong to the Uto-Aztecan family of languages and are generally recognized as a member of the Numic branch. Some linguists conjecture that the homeland of northern Uto-Aztecan was in the western Mohave desert and the adjacent Sierra Nevada foothills, from which region the proto-Hopi apparently migrated eastward into the Grand Canyon region and Black Mesa, where they developed agriculture and shifted from a hunting and gathering subsistence characteristic of the Desert culture to a more sedentary life. In this process they apparently gave up their Great Basin bilateral organization and their marriage practices in favor of matrilineal and matrilocal institutions and monogamous marriage (Eggan 1980).

Hopi social structure is based upon matrilineal exogamous clans, matrilocal households, and a Crow or matrilineal lineage type of kinship system. By studying Shongopavi on Second Mesa and generalizing from earlier accounts of Hopi social structure in terms of "mother," colony, and guard villages on each mesa, it can be shown that the clans and the phratry system are interrelated in important ways, as are the households and lineages ("Hopi Social Organization," vol. 9).

Hopi social organization is "characterized by a pattern of maneuverable management groups. A theoretical order of social prestige is rooted in the origin myths, which established highest status for the earliest arrivals, with descending positions of importance for later-arriving groups. Living in a semidesert with an unpredictable and narrow growing season and crops subject to destruction from violent spring sandstorms, prolonged drought, or torrential summer rains, the tightly knit small units of social structure are highly significant" (vol. 9:549). The management processes assure continuity and provide a means for survival of the whole, both in the face of destructive natural events and in the pressures resulting from the modern world.

The Zuni Indians occupied six villages in the Zuni River valley at the time of the Spanish conquest in 1540 but consolidated their surviving villages into one after the Pueblo Revolt of 1680, when they were persuaded to come down from their refuge on Corn Mountain nearby. The Zuni speak a language with no close relatives.

Ladd ("Zuni Social and Political Organization," vol. 9), himself a Zuni, has clarified several of the controversial aspects of Zuni social organization, particularly those relating to kinship and clanship. Eggan's (1950) analysis of Zuni social organization interpreted Zuni kinship on the Hopi model and was critical of Kroeber's (1919) pioneer studies and his application of psychological principles to the analysis of the kinship system, especially his view that the Zuni "has the broad, vague outlines of his kinship system well in mind; but is not the least interested in following out basic principles into consistent detail" (Kroeber 1919:76–77).

Eggan's (1950:82) conclusion that "there is a marked structural resemblance to the Crow type in general and the Hopi system in particular" was supported by Murdock (1949:247) and criticized by Schneider and Roberts (1956:22), who came to the conclusion that the Zuni system "can best be described as 'modified Crow.'" Later, Roberts utilized seven Zuni informants in scaling kin and nonkin terms along a dimension of probable economic support, utilizing the 31 "kin expressions" used by Schneider and Roberts. His findings suggest not only that "kinsmen are much more highly valued in Zuni culture than non-kinsmen" (Roberts 1965:38), but also that the rank order of kin terms strongly favors relatives in the wife's or mother's clans as against the father's or other clanspeople (1965:table 1, 41), so far as willingness to provide support is concerned.

Ladd's authoritative account of Zuni social organization utilizes only 16 terms for blood kin in the mother's and father's clans, and for "children of the mother's clan" and "father's clan children." No terms are extended to the mother's father's clan. In addition there are a limited number of affinal terms, and some 10 kinship terms used to denote ceremonial relatives, in part used in smoking rituals, as well as special usages for particular kin.

Ladd makes no decision as to the type of kinship system the Zuni have, but he notes that the system is well understood by the users and that there are no wrong or inconsistent usages. Linguistic conventions are used for more distant clan and ceremonial relatives, depending on how close the speaker wishes to bring the person into the circle of kin. His clarification of the kinship system suggests that it is closer to the Hopi model than previously recognized and that the term "modified Crow" should be adequate.

The Zuni clan is matrilineal, totemically named, and exogamous; clans are lost through extinction but larger clans often divide into subclans. In the 1880s the clans were organized into phratries on a directional basis, probably as a result of the consolidation into one village after the Pueblo Revolt, but in 1981 such groupings have only a tenuous existence. Zuni clans once had roles similar to those of the Hopi but have lost many of their prerogatives since the early 1900s though they still control marriage. In 1981 marriage is an "agreement between two people," and the former exchanges between the families concerned are reduced or omitted.

One important factor is demographic. The Dogwood clan in 1977 had some 500 members and controlled many of the ceremonial positions that required that a clan member, or child of the clan, take responsibility. This clan also had three subclans, which may ultimately become clans in their own right, and occasional marriages between such subclans, though condemned, now occur. But more important may be the centralized socioceremonial system that was constructed on Corn Mountain during the Pueblo Revolt.

The Zuni socioreligious system is composed of four subsystems: the clans, the kiva groups making up the kachina society, the curing societies, and the priesthoods, which include the Rain Priests and the Bow Priests. "The Zuni clan system overlaps and interlocks with the kinship and religious systems to enforce, regulate, and to a degree, control the socioreligious behavior patterns" (vol. 9:485). The curing societies are similar in organization and activities to those of the Keresans to the east and there is evidence that they were borrowed from Keresan sources. The Rain Priests represent the six directions, and together they are the highest ceremonial officials in Zuni. They also formerly selected the secular officials, the governor, lieutenant governor, and councilors, who make up the tribal council, though these have been separately nominated and elected since the 1930s.

The Rain Priests, headed by the Priest of the North, very likely derive from a consolidation of the traditional villages during and after the Pueblo Revolt. The Bow Priests of the different villages were also united at that time, under the leadership of the elder-brother and younger-brother Bow Priests, representing the Twin War Gods. Membership requires the taking of a scalp from the enemy, and in 1981 there were only two Bow Priests remaining.

The decision to consolidate into a single village and the rapid increase in population in the mid-twentieth century have resulted in relatively few individuals carrying the ritual and ceremonial burdens for the rest of the population and have reduced the role of clan groups rather considerably from their traditional responsibilities. And on the economic side the upsurge in demand for silver jewelry greatly increased production by families who shifted almost entirely to a cash economy. In addition there were many new jobs on the reservation in terms of federally aided projects of various kinds that provided new opportunities for educated students.

The Keresan-speaking Pueblos are the least known of the Pueblo populations and have been the most controversial so far as interpretations of their social organization are concerned. The forms of speech of the seven Keresan Pueblos "are so closely related that it is commonly assumed that they are dialects of a single language" (vol. 9:173). Acoma and Laguna are very close and are opposed to the Rio Grande dialects, within which Zia and Santa Ana form another pair and San Felipe, Santo Domingo, and Cochiti a third group. The dialect distribution corresponds generally with the spatial order and the time-depth is said not to exceed 500 years.

Keresan is a language isolate, so far as it is known. The archeological record for Acoma and Laguna, the westernmost of the Keresan Pueblos, has been clarified in connection with the claims cases. Acoma has been occupied since the thirteenth century, at least, but has become more of a "ceremonial home" in the twentieth century as the farming villages, Acomita and McCartys, became permanent year-round residences except for ceremonies.

Laguna was established in 1697 by refugees from the Pueblos of Cochiti, Cieneguilla, Santo Domingo, and Jemez who had fled to Acoma after the reconquest of Diego de Vargas and, with dissident Acomas, had then moved northeast to the San Jose River, where they were visited by Gov. Pedro Rodríguez Cubero and given a patron saint in 1699. Laguna's population was 330 in 1707 and almost equaled that of Acoma by 1782. The dialectal differences between Acoma and Laguna are slight, and it is evident that prehistorically the two groups had a common culture. Oral tradition holds that their ancestors came from Mesa Verde, and the two groups shared a common origin myth, though there are some differences in the migration accounts.

Acoma had suffered greatly in 1599 when they were defeated by the Spaniards and sentenced to mutilation and "personal service" in retaliation for killing a detachment of Spaniards the year before. As a result the Acomas became a closed community and are highly conservative to the present day. It is probable that the dissidents who helped found Laguna were more progressive, and there were disputes over land use and other matters that continue in the 1980s. After the 1850s an influx of Anglos, who married into Laguna and took control of the school system and the governorship while introducing Protestantism, led to the conservatives migrating to Isleta on the Rio Grande, taking their religious societies and masked dances with them.

The social organization of Acoma outlined by Garcia-Mason ("Acoma Pueblo," vol. 9) presents the first authoritative account by a member of the Pueblo and helps greatly to clarify the hypotheses and reconstructions presented by Eggan (1950), which were largely based on White's (1932) monograph. Garcia-Mason reported 19 clans at Acoma in 1979. They were matrilineal, exogamous, and totemically named and corresponded closely with White's clan census, with additional subdivisions of some clans through in-marriage. There was no phratry grouping or moiety division for exogamic purposes, but Garcia-Mason reported a previously unknown item: "There are two main kivas that could be considered comparable to the Eastern Pueblos' moieties, with two kiva groups in one moiety and three kivas in the other. There is one other kiva that remains independent" (vol. 9:463). Since children join the kiva of their father, this suggests a patrilineal emphasis, and it is probable that the two divisions are responsible for major kachina rituals. The grouping of kivas may also be a later development since it is unique in the Keresan Pueblos.

The Acoma clans have limited economic, political, and ritual functions in comparison with Zuni and Hopi, but Garcia-Mason confirms the important position of the Antelope clan, whose members select the cacique and have authority over government and land allocations. The cacique selects the members of the tribal council for indefinite terms and appoints the governor and his staff on an annual basis. He likewise has authority over the medicine men and kiva chiefs and is closely associated with the kachina society. In the origin myth there is a more extensive allocation of duties on a clan basis, but there has been a shift from clan to village control in certain instances.

Little is known about the medicine societies that are central to most Keresan Pueblos. For Acoma, in the origin myth, Iatiku asked the chiefs to select a man to be the first medicine man, and they selected the oldest man in the Oak clan. After he was instructed as to how to set up the Fire Society altar and cure the sick he was told to select the leaders of the other groups of medicine men who were to assist him, but in 1979 there were no associations with particular clans.

The household in Acoma is generally matrilocal, though in the farming villages nuclear families were becoming the norm. In 1974 there were 866 family groups in a population of some 3,127, an average of less than four per family (vol. 9:465). Marriage ceremonies were conducted through the Roman Catholic Church; there were few Indian-custom marriages and little divorce.

Spier (1925) in his pioneer classification of North American kinship systems was not clear as to where the Acoma system belonged since there were several alternative terms for cross-cousins, so he provided a separate classification for the Pueblo. Eggan's (1950) hypothesis was that Acoma originally had a Crow type of kinship system, as at Laguna, but that acculturative changes, particularly with regard to the father's lineage, were in the direction of a "bilateral" system, in which the father's sister was classed with the mother and the cross-cousins were siblings. The kinship systems of both Acoma and Laguna make extensive use of self-reciprocal terminology, and Laguna has adjusted the grandparent-grandchild reciprocals to the lineage pattern. It seemed probable that Acoma had done the same.

Mickey (1956), who collected kin terminologies from a man and a woman in Acoma, emphasized the importance of the speaker's sex as well as the need to distinguish terms of reference and address. Her female informant corroborated several of Eggan's reconstructed terms for a woman's matrilineage, but her male informant presented a bilateral arrangement for his matrilineal relatives, suggesting a probable shift to a bilateral system.

In the 1950s Wick Miller, a linguist, was able to work intensively with an Acoma woman off the reservation and to record the terms phonemically. His results (Miller 1959) agree on almost every point with Parsons (1932a) and he disagrees with Mickey with regard to the shift to bilaterality. He finds only two major differences between Acoma and Laguna kinship. "One is the difference in cross-cousin terms; the Laguna consistently use grandparent terms for this class of relatives," whereas Acoma has a variety of alternatives. "The other is the use of *s'ak'ú·yá* for 'my father's clansmen' at Acoma, but 'my father's sister' at Laguna" (Miller 1959:183).

Data on Acoma kinship (vol. 9:463–465) demonstrate that the system is of the Crow type and in general conforms to the Laguna system, but there are still some differences. There are parallels between the mother's matrilineage and the father's matrilineage, in particular, in the use of *ňá·ya* 'mother' for the 'father's sister' as well. Cross-cousins use the grandparent-grandchild reciprocals, which are also utilized in alternate generations, so that there is a generational grid superimposed on the lineage patterns. What apparently has happened is that the father's clan and one's own clan have come to be treated similarly, so far as the kinship patterns are concerned. The use of *ňá·ya* for 'father's sister' is correlated with the extension of the Laguna term for 'father's sister' to the 'female members of my father's clan', a pattern that is characteristic of the Hopi and to a lesser extent the Zuni. The confusion with regard to cross-cousins in the earlier literature may have resulted from the difficulties of translating grandparent-grandchild reciprocals into English, since the children of a 'mother' should normally be 'brother' and 'sister,' rather than 'grandparent' or 'grandchild'.

The Laguna clans are matrilineal, named, and exogamous and they parallel Acoma in many respects. Seven original clans are believed to have come from Mesa Verde, and later clans were added by migrants from other Pueblos. Clans controlled farmlands, and control of ceremonial activities was often in the hands of individual clans, or the "children" of such clans. Each clan had a head and possessed a fetish that passed through the matrilineal line of the leading family who had to "feed" and otherwise care for it.

The kachina society was village-wide and had strong conceptual and other associations with Zuni, from whom a number of kachinas were borrowed. Of six small kivas, one was used by the Fire Society, and two big kivas were used for alternating dance groups, as in the Rio Grande Pueblos. These are reported to have been to the east and west of the plaza, but there is no information as to how membership was arranged, though the Acoma arrangement, with a set of kiva groups in each moiety, is a possibility.

The most important groups were the medicine societies—Flint, Fire, Shahaye, and Shikami—along with the associated clown groups, Quirana and Koshare, plus possibly the war society and the Scalp Takers, and the Mountain Lion (hunt) society (vol. 9:444). The leaders of these societies traditionally came from certain clans, but they gained their members by a variety of techniques—curing, trapping, and dedication—so that they were not dependent on clan survival. The village chief formerly came from the Water clan but was installed by the leader of the Flint-Koshare and the leader of the Shikami-Quirana. The chief never went to war but acted as father to the kachinas and offered prayers for fertility and general welfare. The outside chief, or war chief, was selected from the Scalp Takers' Society and was responsible for security and guarding the boundaries of the Pueblo.

The kinship system is presented in Parsons (1932a) in considerable detail and Eggan's (1950) analysis stands, except that the mother's father's matrilineal lineage should be omitted, since no evidence has come to light as to its presence in either Acoma or Laguna. Parsons analyzed the Laguna system in terms of Kroeber's (1909) psychological principles of generation, sex, age, etc., but found many inconsistencies, most of which are clarified by organizing the terminology on a lineage rather than a generation basis. Self-reciprocal patterns are here well developed, and there is a strong tendency to link alternating generations by means of the terminology, and Laguna carries alternation to an extreme. Little information on the changes in social organization taking place in the farming villages is available.

The Eastern Keresan Pueblos have a common set of social institutions, but there are a number of variants that are of interest. Of these Pueblos only Cochiti has been relatively open to study, and Lange's (1959) monograph is outstanding in its coverage, since he was able to reside in the community in the postwar period, as was Fox (1967). Linguistically Zia and Santa Ana are intermediate between Acoma-Laguna and the Rio Grande communities of San Felipe, Santo Domingo, and Cochiti.

All the Eastern Keresans have matrilineal exogamous clans and a dual ceremonial organization associated with two kivas, usually Turquoise and Squash, with generally patrilineal affiliation through initiation, and with wives changing affiliation if necessary to join their husbands' kivas. Zia shows some modifications in that clan exogamy is preferential rather than prescriptive, and the kivas, there Turquoise and Wren, have their membership in terms of residence in the north plaza and southern half of the town, respectively (vol. 9:411). Residence is bilocal rather than matrilocal, depending on who owns the house, and sons and daughters, married or unmarried, may continue to reside therein. Resources are shared within the household and it is a tightly knit group. The clans do not act as corporate bodies, nor do they own property, rituals, masks, or medicine bundles. The medicine societies are central in Zia, having responsibility for the fertility of crops and people, the bringing of rain, and the control of illness, as well as the protection of the village from enemies outside and witches within.

Santa Ana shares a generally similar social organization but the Squash and Turquoise ceremonial groups, each with its own kiva, are composed of sets of matrilineal clans, an apparently unique situation among the Keresans (vol. 9:401). The Turquoise and Squash kiva groups are reported to be in charge of the medicine societies and certain dances but do not act as social units otherwise (White 1942:142–144).

The kachina organization is composed of five groups, each of which is controlled by a medicine society, and membership appears to be voluntary. Both sexes can join, and women are reported to participate in the masked kachina dances, which is also unique for the whole Pueblo region.

For the Rio Grande Keresans, there is only reasonably full information from Cochiti. Santo Domingo, the largest and most conservative of the Rio Grande Keresans, has not allowed any study of their Pueblo since they expelled Adolph Bandelier in the 1880s, and San Felipe, though traditionally an offshoot of Cochiti, has generally followed the lead of Santo Domingo. The Cochiti clans are matrilineal and, ideally, exogamous, and the oldest woman is considered to be the head, but there are few clan functions or ceremonial affiliations. The dual kiva organization, there Turquoise and Pumpkin, is based on patrilineal affiliation, with transfer possible after marriage and for other reasons. The moieties or kiva groups are not considered kin associations: "The two kiva groups assume prominence in many ceremonials, the 'sides' complementing each other's activities, as they alternate as dance teams" (vol. 9:372).

Medicine societies have a central role in Cochiti political and ceremonial organization, the head of the Flint Society becoming the cacique and being considered the foremost medicine man. In turn the headmen of the three medicine societies select the principal officers of the Pueblo from the two kivas so that a balance is maintained between the two groups. Two societies, the Koshare and the Quirana, are responsible for "managing" the numerous ceremonies throughout the year, and the two alternate annually at Cochiti.

In social structure the simple family prevails in the late twentieth century, though Cochiti households have been traditionally matrilocal. Lange (1959:388–389) has collected kinship terms reported in the literature and has generally supported Eggan's guess "that Cochiti once had a kinship structure based on the matrilineal lineage and household, but that it has been the most acculturated [of the Keresans] toward Tewa and/or Spanish patterns."

It is this conclusion that Fox (1967) has denied, offering his own hypotheses based upon Claude Lévi-Strauss's analysis of the shift from "elementary structures" to "complex structures" and suggesting that the Cochiti were in a process of changing from a system of "restricted exchange" toward becoming a Crow system with modifications. Fox postulates that the Western Keresans "never went the whole way towards a Crow system. . . . This reinterpretation of the terminology and its possible history makes very much more sense than the theory of degeneration from a Crow to a bilateral system" (Fox 1967:178).

Eggan's (1950) formulation was in part based on the assumption that the bulk of Laguna's population were refugees from the Rio Grande villages, an assumption only partly true. But Fox's assumption of patrilineal exogamous moieties among the proto-Keresans has become untenable in the light of Ortiz's (1969) account of Tewa moieties, as Fox (1972) has recognized. Lange, whose data Fox praises as indispensable, has expressed no opinion on the controversy. As Fox (1967:183) indicates, "What is needed is a thorough review of Aztec-Tanoan and Keresan linguistic and social systems, in conjunction with archaeological findings and an examination of the results in the light of the theories of Lévi-Strauss, Murdock and Service." The data available so far are not convincing one way or the other.

The Tanoan-speaking Pueblos reside in the upper and middle Rio Grande region and are divided linguistically into three subgroups: Tiwa in the north and south, Tewa in the center, and Towa in west and (formerly) east. With Kiowa, they make up a separate language family, Kiowa-Tanoan. One group predominantly of Tanos (Southern Tewa speakers) was active in the Pueblo Revolt of 1680 and, after the Reconquest, moved westward and ultimately ended up at First Mesa in the Hopi country, where they were given land and a village site in exchange for aid against the Utes and Spaniards. In 1981 they were still there as the Hopi-Tewa inhabiting a village formerly called Hano, but now known generally as Tewa Village.

The Tiwa Pueblos very possibly had their major development in the Rio Grande region. In the north, Taos and Picuris have a kinship system that is bilateral and no clans are present. At Taos there are two house blocks, one on either side of the Taos Creek, but it is apparently the three kivas on each side who provide a dual ceremonial grouping and express the moiety principle. The nuclear family resides together, but it is the bilaterally extended family that is of most importance to the individual for socialization and security. Beyond the extended kinship group there is a strong sense of community in the obligation to carry out various duties with regard to irrigation projects, plastering the church, repairing the house blocks, and participating in the dances and ceremonies. These community-wide obligations are mandated by the religious hierarchy and enforced by the threat of loss of privileges or actual expulsion from the community.

The six kiva groups, with their constituent societies, are central to Taos life, and boys are initiated into the kivas of their parents' choice, but only a select few go through the initiation rituals that culminate in the annual tribal pilgrimage to Blue Lake (vol. 9:262). The uninitiated "boys" cannot take part in the esoteric rituals nor can they hold important positions in the Pueblo government.

Picuris, a few miles away, also is divided into two ceremonial groups, Northside People and Southside People, but affiliation was based on patrilineal descent, with women changing to their husband's group at marriage, if different from their own. These two groups participated in an annual relay race on San Lorenzo's Day and in long-distance races as part of the Summer rain ceremonials. The Northside People used Cloud kiva, while the Southside People were associated with the Sky kiva.

Within the major ceremonial groups there were smaller ceremonial associations, the Spring People who conducted the first three summer rain ceremonials in June, the Summer People who conducted similar ceremonies in August, and the Fall People, who had a third series in September. All three groups utilized the Round House, on the north side of the Pueblo. There was a fourth group, the Winter People, who were concerned with weather control and the fertility of game animals and held their ceremonies in Ice kiva.

The Tewa Pueblos occupy a large block of territory to the south of Taos, beginning with San Juan at the mouth of the Chama River and continuing with Santa Clara, San Ildefonso, and Tesuque along the Rio Grande and Pojoaque and Nambe on tributaries to the east. The languages spoken are mutually intelligible, and there is communication and considerable intermarriage among them. Ortiz (1969) has contributed greatly to the knowledge of Tewa culture and world view. Dozier provides new material on the social structure of the Tewa Pueblos.

Dozier notes that there are differences in detail in the social and ceremonial organizations of the five major Tewa communities, but the general outlines appear similar in each village. As with the Rio Grande Pueblos the village is the autonomous political unit, and there is no overall political organization to unite them. There is voluntary cooperation among members of the same esoteric associations across the five villages, and a limited number of marriages are outside the village.

The dual divisions or moieties are the most important organizations from a governmental and religious point of view. The members of each Pueblo are divided approximately equally between the Winter and Summer people. Children generally join the moiety of their father, but membership must be confirmed by initiation. Adults can change their moiety for a variety of reasons.

The moieties are mirror images of one another and are run by the moiety association, a small group composed of a head or chief priest, right and left arm assistants, and a body composed of the members of the association. Men and women may join through dedication after recovery from illness, or as a child. Ceremonial trapping is a further technique for maintaining an adequate number of members. Each moiety has responsibility for a number of governmental and ceremonial tasks during half the year, with transference ceremonies at or near the equinoxes, and all members of the village are required to conform to the dictates of the moiety in control with eviction from the Pueblo or loss of property for nonconformity.

In all the Tewa villages the secular officers are appointed annually and the moiety priests alternate in the selection of the officers. The moiety associations are assisted by a number of other associations or societies whose membership cross-cuts the moieties and thus serve to integrate the village.

The moieties utilize patrilineal descent in recruitment but tend to be endogamous in several cases rather than exogamous. They are not territorially localized nor are they kinship units, and the mechanism for changing affiliations makes it possible to keep them in demographic balance.

The kachina organization is concerned with ancestral spirits who are impersonated by masked performers, and who bring rain and general well-being to the community. Each moiety has its own kachina organization, and all males automatically become members, with an initiation after puberty to formalize membership. The ceremonial activities center in the kiva, and masked dances are performed at the equinoxes and on other occasions, under the supervision of the Kachina Father, who is appointed by the moiety association and serves for life. The clown associations, Koshare and Quirana, appear with the dancers and bring the kachinas from underneath the mythical "lake of emergence" in the north.

Village associations, such as the medicine societies, clown associations, a hunt association, and men's and women's war associations, cross-cut the moiety organization. Parents select the association that they want the child to join, and adults may be "called" to a particular association by persistent thoughts or dreams. Only the medicine men have specific rituals for curing and exorcism, using a variety of shamanistic practices and cooperating to rid and cleanse the village of witches. In addition each village association holds separate monthly retreats and conducts one or more ceremonies for the benefit of the villagers. The clowns prescribe conformance to Pueblo mores by ridiculing individuals who have been reported for deviant behavior and inflicting various indignities on their persons.

The household group is responsible for domestic affairs and is composed of extended families headed by a grandparental couple with some or all of their sons and daughters plus spouses and children. There is no discernible "lineage" arrangement or standard number of members. The members of the household share foodstuffs and work cooperatively at necessary tasks. The actual households diagrammed range from 10–15 members, and when there are major projects such as house building or agricultural activities the household members work together and eat together. Ceremonial occasions bring all the nuclear families of the household together, and formerly the winter was a special time for gathering to hear Tewa folktales.

The household is an exogamic unit and its members refer to one another as *matuin*, 'relatives'. Marriage with first cousins is also prohibited, regardless of household affiliation, and Dozier believes that all first cousins were included in the term *matuin*, at an earlier time when the household embraced a wider circle of kin.

A newly married couple may make their own decision as to where to reside, depending on housing and agricultural land available. While land is owned in theory by the village, which has the right to confiscate land and houses, the distribution usually operates within the household without interference from the authorities.

The kinship system of the Tewa is bilateral, essentially along the model of the Eskimo type. They are familiar with the ritual godparent system of their Spanish neighbors but have not adopted it to any important degree, and the Tewa have been resistant to adopting Spanish terms to any great extent.

The Tewa kinship system operates primarily within the context of the household, though terms for father, mother, parent's younger brother, and parent's younger sister—with their reciprocals—are extended to include the whole community. The arrangement of the terms is bilateral, with alternate terms for most relatives, except those in ego's generation, where the same terms are used for parallel and cross-cousins on both sides, derived from terms for parent's younger brother and parent's younger sister and not from siblings. There is an emphasis on age or generation, a frequent lack of sex distinctions, and an extensive use of senior and junior reciprocals, the latter indicated by a linguistic suffix. The pattern is logical but confusing to outsiders, though Harrington (1912) long ago provided a chart of the generalized system.

Kinship behavior has its locus in the household unit and the grandparents provide a warm and familiar gathering place for the younger members, who may be living elsewhere but come to share food and companionship. While males are nominally dominant the older women share in authority and discipline, and elders are respected regardless of sex. Children are normally disciplined by their parents though a grandfather or uncle may handle serious cases. Occasionally an offense may be handled by the moiety priest who may prescribe a whipping to be performed by the war captain.

There is a close bond between siblings that is extended to all cousins, if they are members of the same household, and all cousins are included in exogamic rules, though those not members are not bound by the loyalties and ties that characterize the interaction of household members. Uncles and aunts behave toward their nephews and nieces very much in the pattern of parents and children—with respect and obedience being accorded to relative age. When there are continuing difficulties the household is usually restructured.

In his comparative discussion of Keresan and Tanoan social organization Dozier (1960) notes that while the Keresan Pueblos are organized along a lineage pattern where the matrilineal clan is an important unit of organization, among the Tanoans, with the exception of Jemez, there are no clans. He considers the "clan names" in the literature to be ceremonial terms thought to be inherited from one's father or mother and useful in visiting Pueblos that have a clan system.

Within the Keresan Pueblos he finds a diminishing importance of the matrilineal clan from west to east, with the corporate functions found in the west being taken over by the medicine societies in the east, resulting in a highly centralized political and ceremonial community. He does not find a comparable shift in the Tanoan communities where governmental and ceremonial functions appear to have always been the responsibility of associations rather than clans. In the origin legends the Summer and Winter people migrated down opposite sides of the Rio Grande before uniting at *ṗosiˀówînge* 'village at the hot springs', northwest of modern San Juan.

The kachina organization, on the other hand, is strong among the Keresan Pueblos, but relatively weak among the Tewa, and absent among the Northern Tiwa, suggesting that the Tewa have borrowed this institution from the Keresans. In turn the dual ceremonial divisions associated with kivas and dancing may well have been adapted from the Summer and Winter divisions of the Tewa since they are strong among the Eastern Keresans and gradually fade out in the Western Keresans.

Dozier makes a strong case for the irrigation hypothesis following Wittfogel and Goldfrank's article on the influence of irrigation on Pueblo society, which suggested that we look at "certain forms of civil and magic leadership, for institutionalized discipline, and a specific social and ceremonial organization" (1943:20). Dozier (1958:9) notes that "the construction of dams and ditches and their maintenance, plus the complicated problems of the allocation of water rights demand a social organization which can mobilize a fairly large adult force and satisfy the irrigational needs of the society." The argument, though appealing, is not proved.

Dozier (1960) concluded that both Keresan and Tewa kinship systems have been remarkably resistant to change. Here he notes that the "Keresan system appears to be adjusting to a bilateral system, rearranging terminology and behavior to equalize the relationship between maternal and paternal relatives" (1960:434). He feels that the causes are more complex than simple diffusion, and he illustrates how the Wittfogel and Goldfrank hypothesis might operate to decrease the importance of clan and lineage among the Keresans in favor of an emphasis on centralized societal controls representing the whole community. The Spanish policy of forced acculturation is an alternate or supporting explanation for the "development of tighter village controls with attendant loss of clan importance" (1960:435). Since the Tanoans were probably earlier in the Rio Grande region they may well have been more adapted to the ecological and environmental resources.

Dozier's (1958:35) conclusions are relevant:

> Tewa social structure illustrates a society operating on the community level with organizations adapted to communal enterprises. Perhaps the most important factor of the Tewa pueblos is that kinship plays no role on the community level, but is functionally restricted to the household. Organizations which control the political and religious destinies of the Tewa communities are the moiety associations who divide the governmental and ceremonial functions of the village semi-annually. These associations and the moieties they represent exhibit some characteristics of bilateral organizations, but labels for similar structures extant in the literature seem inappropriate for Tewa moiety structures.

The Towa-speaking Jemez Indians, with the descendants of the few survivors from Pecos, occupy a Pueblo on the Jemez River, along with Zia and Santa Ana, and represent an exception to many of the statements as to Tanoan social organization. The Jemez Indians have matrilineal, exogamous clans with ceremonial functions; and membership in specific clans is required for certain ceremonial-political offices. Jemez families, however, have a patrilineal emphasis, with members of a nuclear family taking the surname of the male head of the household. There are two kiva moieties, Turquoise and Squash, which are basically patrilineal but tend to be endogamous. These two groups compete in races during work on the irrigation ditches, and they put on ceremonial dances as well as those performed on the saint's day and other holidays.

In addition, there are two societies, Eagle and Arrow, that are concerned with defense and war, with which affiliation is patrilineal, though two brothers may divide in membership. In addition there are over 20 religious societies, with affiliation determined on various nonhereditary bases, that form the basic social and political units of Jemez society. As Joe Sando, a native of Jemez notes, "there is no room for anything new" (vol. 9:426). It would be highly useful to have some data on kinship so that it might be possible to see what has happened to the Tanoan patterns. But the above brief statements, authoritative as they are, are of considerable value.

Ellis's (1964) reconstruction of the basic Jemez pattern of social organization is useful, though Sando is critical of some details. Ellis believes that the social structure of Jemez is basically Tanoan despite Keresan influences. This social system had two moieties, each controlled by a society (Eagle or Arrow) and using a single kiva; a bilateral kinship system; and only one society to begin with, which expanded into a number of societies, some borrowed from the Keresans. The

Keresan-derived additions are the second kiva, patrilineal inheritance of kiva membership, the clan system, and some additional societies, such as the Quirana. The clan system is considered to be the result of intermarriage with Keresan Pueblos. Fox finds it difficult to fit Jemez into his theoretical formulation and notes that his "assumption that Jemez is just another Keresan Pueblo speaking a different language is incorrect" (Fox 1967:203).

The Southern Tiwa Pueblos are Isleta and Sandia, and there is little detailed information available for either. At Isleta, both patrilineal and matrilineal relationships are officially recognized (vol. 9:356). A child is born into a bilaterally extended family, and there are marriage restrictions beyond fourth or fifth cousins. Children are inducted into one of five directionally oriented Corn groups that are not clans but ceremonial groups, with aspects of medicine societies and ritual functions that have some similarities to Taos kiva groups. Children are "given" by their parents to a chosen group, often that of one of the parents. In addition, there is a moiety division, the Red Eyes, or Summer, and the Black Eyes, or Winter, to which children are allocated on an alternate basis, the first child going into his father's moiety, the second into the mother's. Each moiety has charge of ceremonial activities during its own season with transfer at the March and October periods. Each moiety is also responsible for one major dance each year. Parsons (1939, 1:129, 349, 1962:7) has pointed out that these moiety performances are in reality the old kachina dances from which masks were omitted under Spanish pressures. The kachina dances were re-introduced by the conservatives from Laguna in the 1870s, and the Laguna Kachina Father is in charge of the moiety dances (Harvey 1963). There are also two medicine societies with curing functions, one of which, the Laguna Fathers, was introduced at the same time.

Sandia is a little-known pueblo whose ancestral population spent several decades at Payupki in the Hopi country in the 1700s before being resettled at Sandia. In general Sandia is closest to Isleta, but with more Keresan influence. There are two groups, Turquoise and Pumpkin, to which children are assigned alternately at birth, a kiva organization, Corn groups in which recruitment is matrilineal, and curing groups. The Turquoise and Pumpkin moieties have permanent leaders and are responsible for Eagle and Buffalo Dances, but there are few other details available (vol. 9:347).

In general the linguistic groupings provide the best basis for analyzing and interpreting Pueblo social organization, and it is clear that Eggan's (1950) attempt to provide a single broad framework for Pueblo development was too simple. Fox's (1967) emphasis on a central role for the Keresan Pueblos is acceptable, though the linguistic evidence does not support an ancient basic pattern but rather developments taking place in the 1300s and 1400s as the Keresans broke up into dialect groups and influenced, and were influenced by, their neighbors to the west and east.

For the Hopi-Tewa Dozier's (1954) monograph provides excellent material. "The Hopi-Tewa social system is almost identical to the matrilineal, matrilocal, extended-family, exogamous clan system of the Hopi," and the kinship system, though using different terms, is clearly a Crow type, "very similar in meaning to that of the Hopi" (vol. 9:596). The Hopi-Tewa went to First Mesa in 1700 and are still there. Dozier, as a visitor from Santa Clara Pueblo, one of the sources for the original migration, had unusual facilities for investigation, and his account is convincing as to the processes by which the Eastern Tewa social system was transformed.

The new developments in understanding of Pueblo social organization, as well as other aspects of life, are coming about through the interest of native scholars in their own history and culture. With their knowledge of the native languages and training in the analysis of scholarly problems, their contributions to the solutions of such problems are already making an important difference.

The Southern Athapaskans

There are seven Southern Athapaskan–speaking tribes, all but the Kiowa-Apache and Lipan associated with the Southwest. The ancestors of these Apachean groups split off from the northern Athapaskans about 1300 and moved southward, gradually occupying the region surrounding the Pueblos. Hoijer (1971) has stated that Navajo, Western Apache, Chiricahua, Mescalero, Jicarilla, and Lipan "are closely related dialects of a single language," with Kiowa-Apache a second Apachean language, and lexicostatistics suggests a time-depth of less than half a millennium for the linguistic differentiation, a figure that accords with the archeological data.

Apache

The Apachean groups moved into areas earlier abandoned by the Anasazi and Mogollon and gradually modified their ancestral hunting and gathering subsistence patterns through interaction with the Pueblos and later the Spaniards. The Navajo borrowed agriculture from the Eastern Pueblos, and later sheep herding from the Spaniards, as they settled down in the Chama Valley; the Western Apache, traditionally derived from three archaic Navajo clans, continued agriculture in the region south and west of the Mogollon Rim; the Chiricahua and Mescalero Apaches, in the region south of the Pueblos, continued their hunting and gathering with the addition of limited amounts of agriculture, while the Jicarilla and Lipan did the same on the margins of the Plains west and north of the Tewa and Tiwa. After the acquisition of horses in the seventeenth century all the Apachean groups participated in raiding and trading activities and were engaged in periodic warfare with Utes and Comanches, as well as with the Spaniards and Mexicans.

Opler's (1937) account of the Chiricahua was the first modern, comprehensive account of the social structure of an Apache tribe and the kinship system was particularly interesting. The Chiricahua kinship system was bilateral and organized in generational terms. All terms, except those of parent and child, were self-reciprocal. The father's siblings are classified together, regardless of sex, as are the mother's siblings, and these terms are extended to nephews and nieces. The four grandparental terms are similarly extended to their respective siblings and used self-reciprocally for grandchildren. In ego's generation two terms are used self-reciprocally: one which means sibling, parallel cousin, or cross-cousin of the same sex as the speaker, the other a sibling, parallel cousin, or cross-cousin of the opposite sex from the speaker. There are no regular terms to indicate age distinctions in ego's generation (Opler 1937:186–188).

Opler (1936) published a classification of the kinship systems of the Southern Athapaskan–speaking peoples in terms of two types, Chiricahua and Jicarilla. The Chiricahua type included the Chiricahua, Mescalero, and Western Apache; and the Jicarilla type was comprised of the Jicarilla, Navajo, Lipan, and Kiowa-Apache. These two types utilized mostly the same terms but in different kinship patterns. The Jicarilla type used no self-reciprocal terminology, with one exception. There are two grandparent terms, with a separate grandchild term. The mother and her sister are classed together, as are the father and his brother, and there are separate terms for mother's brother and father's sister. In ego's generation there are terms for older brother, older sister, and younger sibling, with parallel cousins equated with siblings and separate terms used for cross-cousins. Correlatively nephews and nieces are either son and daughter or addressed by special cross-sex terms.

These two types are clearly differentiated with the grouping being based on contrasting principles. There is no accepted name as yet for the Chiricahua system, with its emphasis on self-reciprocal terminology, but verbal reciprocity is widespread in the Great Basin, among the Yumans, and in most of the Pueblo kinship systems. The Jicarilla system is more familiar as the widespread Dakota-Iroquois type. The other members of each type clearly belong with their assigned systems but in some characteristics they resemble the usages in the other type. Very often there are alternate usages that lean one way or the other. There are likewise differences in behavior patterns, particularly with avoidance and joking relationships, that characterize the two types, and these are sometimes found in the opposite groups.

An arrangement of the kinship charts from Chiricahua to Mescalero to Western Apache and from Navajo to Jicarilla to Lipan to Kiowa-Apache offers a series of transitions from the Chiricahua type to the Jicarilla type, and Opler (1936:632–633) suggests that this may be "a clue to the actual developmental process." This would make the Chiricahua the older form of Southern Athapaskan kinship, a conclusion reinforced by the cultural and geographical positions of the Chiricahua and Mescalero and their lack of common elements with the Jicarilla. In addition Jicarilla, Lipan, and Kiowa-Apache share a phonetic shift from *t* to *k*, as well as cultural parallels not found in the Chiricahua type groups.

With linguistic and cultural evidence for such a dichotomy making a strong case for the existence of the two kinship types, with the further suggestion that the Jicarilla kinship type developed mainly after the initial dialect division, one important problem in Apachean social systems seemed well on the way to solution; however, this hope proved illusory as more was learned about the Athapaskans, both Northern and Southern, and as research into Navajo social life progressed.

Kroeber, impressed by Opler's demonstration, thought it worthwhile to look at the Northern and Pacific Athapaskans to see whether it was possible to provide a tentative reconstruction of "primitive" Athapaskan kinship that would clarify the Southern Athapaskan situation. He concluded that better linguistic data were essential to reconstruct "the original Athapaskan kinship system" but suggested (Kroeber 1937:605–606) that certain salient features emerge as probable: four grandparent terms, more than two children terms, four sibling terms, two cross-cousin terms, and an unstable pattern of aunt-uncle terms, including the equation of step-parents with father's brother and mother's sister.

These data support Opler's conclusions at some points but not others, and Kroeber suggests that the Chiricahua–Mescalero–Western Apache kinship systems have been influenced by Uto-Aztecan and Yuman contacts, the Jicarilla series by Plains influences, and the Navajo by Pueblo, as well as Plains via the Jicarilla. He also guesses that Navajo "may prove to preserve a greater number of features of original Southern Athapaskan than any one Apache group" (Kroeber 1937:607) and concludes that "Opler's excellent typological classification cannot in the main be read historically."

Kroeber encouraged Hoijer to carry out a more detailed linguistic reconstruction of the proto-Athapaskan kinship system, based on a comparative study of the kin terms in the daughter languages, using both cognate terms and kinship categories. Hoijer (1956a) concluded that the proto-Athapaskan kinship system had: two grandparent terms, six terms for parents and parent's siblings, four sibling terms denoting sex and age, no cousin terms, with the probability that cousins were classed with siblings, two terms for children, and a single grandchild term.

On the basis of these findings, Hoijer suggested the possibility of two subdivisions among the Southern Athapaskans: (1) Jicarilla, Lipan, and Kiowa Apache forming an eastern group with greater similarity to proto-Athapaskan and (2) Navajo, Western Apache, Chiricahua, and Mescalero forming a western group and possibily representing an earlier migration, since Navajo and Western Apache had lost practically all the proto-Athapaskan features.

In the meantime Murdock (1949:323–352) had developed a technique for the historical reconstruction of the social organization of particular societies based on descent and cross-cousin terminology, which provided a series of social organizational types. Two members of his 250-society sample, Chiricahua and Kiowa Apache, and probably Navajo as well, were considered to derive from a Hawaiian type having bilateral descent and Hawaiian kinship terminology (the equation of siblings and cousins) in a generational pattern, and with matrilocal residence providing a matri-Hawaiian subtype.

Bellah (1952) finds that a more intensive structural-function analysis is required to interpret the Apache kinship systems and that Opler is in error in considering that chance plays a major role. He also believes that Chiricahua, far from being the oldest system among the Southern Athapaskans, is probably one of the more divergent systems, and that clan systems are a late development rather than part of the original pattern.

C.B. White (1957: table 6) has provided a comparison of these various theories with regard to Southern Athapaskan kinship systems. He notes that while Kroeber and Hoijer depend upon linguistics and comparative-historical methods, Opler, Bellah, and Murdock depend more on the underlying social structures, and that the disagreements in terms of a developmental sequence depend in part upon these different emphases. His own conclusion (1957:448) is that "future reconstructions of kinship systems for any linguistic stock or substock might profit by utilizing a combination of social data with a linguistic and comparative-historical analysis rather than emphasizing one approach to the exclusion of others."

In 1957 Dyen and Aberle began a collaboration that resulted in a major contribution on Proto-Athapaskan kinship. Building on Hoijer's (1956a) study, which utilized the comparative method and Edward Sapir's division of the Athapaskan languages into 14 subgroups, Dyen and Aberle (1974) enlarged Hoijer's 73 cognate sets of kinship terms and provided reconstructed Proto-Athapaskan forms with their probable meanings. Dyen rejected Hoijer's subgrouping in favor of one based on comparative lexicostatistics, which provided six Athapaskan languages, each with a number of dialects: Tanaina, Ingalik, Ahtna, Canadian, Pacific, and Apachean; he also rejected his comparison of the kinship categories represented in the daughter languages as unnecessary. Even so, Hoijer (in Dyen and Aberle 1974:xii) states that the method "has resulted in reconstructions far more convincing than have been achieved heretofore."

Aberle has been primarily responsible for the additional data on kinship and for much of the broader analysis. As he notes (Dyen and Aberle 1974:1): "Reconstructions have differed chiefly in that some have concluded that Proto-Athapaskan or the early forms of its various branches had Iroquois cousin terms and others that they had Hawaiian cousin terms, and that some have favored matrilineal, matrilocal prototypes and others have preferred different prototypes. Since it is commonly believed that various kinship terminological patterns are associated with various forms of descent, residence, and marriage rules, the reconstruction of proto-kinship terminology appears to have implications for the reconstruction of non-terminological attributes."

After presenting the details of the terminological pattern of early Apachean, and interpretations based on statistics and on experience and intuition, as well as on the internal differentiation of the subgroups and the ethnological record, Dyen and Aberle (1974:chap. 8) provide a reconsideration of Apachean kinship and its differentiation. The early Apachean system is bifurcate in the first ascending and descending generations, with Iroquois cousin terms and evidence of the equation of cross cousins with in-laws and spouses. The terminal state for Apachean dialect groups shows Navajo and San Carlos (Western Apache) retaining bifurcate terminology and Iroquois cousin terms, but losing the equation of in-laws and cross-cousins, while the easterly dialects retain bifurcation, for the most part, but supplement or replace Iroquois cousin terms with Hawaiian cousin terms, all losing the equation of in-laws with cross-cousins.

The interpretation of early Apachean is that it was unilineal or double unilineal, non-neolocal, and characterized by the sororate, sororal polygyny, the levirate, sister exchange, and normative bilateral cross-cousin marriage, and the universality of matrilocal residence suggests that the early pattern was matrilocal. The modern situation is that the westerly tribes are matrilineal and matrilocal, with sororal polygyny and the sororate and levirate, but with no formal sister exchange or normative cross-cousin marriage, though there are suggestions of recent cross-cousin marriage among the Navajo and the San Carlos have statistical classificatory cross-cousin marriage. The eastern tribes are bilateral and matrilocal, and generally have sororal polygyny and the sororate and levirate, but no formal sister exchange and a rigorous prohibition of cousin marriage.

The reasons for these variant shifts are analyzed in terms of population dynamics and adaptive responses during the seventeenth and eighteenth centuries. In the west the Navajo and San Carlos Apache patterns of kinship seem to have developed in connection with the management and transmission of farm sites and expanding populations, with the Navajo acquisition of sheep adding mobility and the need for a wider network of kinship ties. In the east the situation is not clear, but the contractions and reorganizations required for groups on the edge of the Plains suggest that the development of bilateral systems, with Hawaiian kinship terms and a prohibition of cousin marriage, would be adaptive for the mobile hunting and raiding activities that dominated the later Plains life.

Navajo

The Navajo who returned from captivity in 1868 to occupy a new reservation made up of part of their earlier homeland numbered around 12,000–15,000, and they have since increased to become the largest tribe in the Southwest. The modern study of their social organization was inaugurated by Reichard (1928).

Witherspoon (1975a) provides a native rationale for the matrilineal clan system and the most general categories of kinship, as well as the basic kinds of solidarity that hold Navajo society together.

These categories and relationships are demonstrated in an analysis of the residence group and its possessions, particularly the sheep herd and any agricultural lands, and the changes that occur at death or divorce. The role of the sheep herd as a symbol of social integration and its relation to status and leadership are emphasized, and the changes in shifting to a cattle herd are noted. And in the realm of philosophy Navajos are able to blend the concept of individual need with that of community need.

Aberle (1980) has found this account of use in his evaluation of the conflicting views of Navajo exogamic rules and marital preferences by means of frequency data on marital choices, utilizing his own research in the Piñon area as a base and comparing the results of other studies. He is concerned with five types of marriage: marriage into own clan and clan group; marriage into father's clan and clan group; marriage of persons whose fathers are in the same clan or clan group; marriage into mother's father's clan and clan group; and marriage into father's father's clan and clan group. He presents evidence that both Navajo specialists and Navajos disagree about exogamic rules and preferred marriages. Establishing the clan groups themselves is a difficult task, and some clans were found to be more distantly related than others. Utilizing the data available, Aberle tested two rank orders as alternative models of Navajo prohibitions and preferences and found both to be useful under given conditions. A sample of expert Navajo opinion was provided that showed some variations but indicated considerable consensus that while marriage into the father's clan was not permitted, marriage into the father's clan group was permissible, as it was into the grandparent's clans and clan groups.

The rank order models utilize Witherspoon's cultural analysis and also build on Shepardson and Hammond's (1970) study, among others. Aberle also compares Navajo and Western Apache data, using Goodwin's (1942) monograph, and Kaut's (1957) reworking of Goodwin's data. Kaut has also prepared a further analysis of the Western Apache clan system (1974) in which the changes through time can be related to changing ecological and demographic factors. Three of the four phratry groups are considered by Goodwin to be related "archaic clans," which are believed to be of Navajo origin, a view which Kaut (1957) supports. Here marriage to close relatives is not acceptable, but marriage into the father's clan and related clans is preferred and is much higher than the Navajo rates.

The Navajo and Western Apache kinship systems are similar and Aberle finds that their conceptions of marriage are likewise similar, with Western Apache cognates for Navajo categories. Part of the variation with regard to the father's clan may lie in a differential emphasis on father's kin as affines or kinsmen, but the demographic situation may also be an important factor, particularly with the Western Apache who have fewer potential spouses available in many areas.

Another factor Aberle mentions is the intensive contact with Puebloan populations after the Pueblo Revolt of 1680, which may well have reinforced Navajo matriliny and introduced a prohibition of marriage into the father's clan. This prohibition reduces the number of potential partners considerably and thus "forces the network of alliances to broaden" (Aberle 1980).

The possibility that the Western Apache are "early" Navajos who retained the pristine clan system to a greater degree than the modern Navajos offers a historical insight into their respective developments that goes beyond parallels brought about by common agriculture and Pueblo influences.

The problems of lexical reconstruction with regard to the Athapaskans, Northern and Southern, are now a matter less of the data base than of the subclassification of language families and stocks. Whereas the Athapaskans were formerly organized into 14 language families, Dyen and Aberle (1974) reduced the number to some six or seven. Krauss (Dyen and Aberle 1974), working with the Northern Athapaskans in Alaska, considers Athapaskan as a "dialect complex" or chain, rather than a set of languages with definite boundaries, a finding that would make lexical reconstruction both difficult and different.

Here the Southern Athapaskans may be of considerable assistance. Since the initial group or groups apparently broke up into subgroups at about the same time, and since there is an outline of their contacts and separations, it may be possible to estimate what happened in the north at an earlier period, both with regard to dialect and language formation and with regard to social institutions. This would require a much more intensive analysis of each of the Apachean groups and a comparison of each with the others, a procedure that might result in a single developmental account.

The Pima-Papago and Their Neighbors

The Pima and Papago speak closely related dialects of Piman, a member of the Uto-Aztecan language family with linguistic relatives in southern California, the Great Basin, and among the Hopi, and extending well into Northwest Mexico. They are divided from the Takic-speaking Uto-Aztecans of southern California by a block of Yuman-speaking tribes who occupy the Lower Colorado River region and adjoining deserts, and much of Baja California. The Yumans are assumed to belong to the larger Hokan stock, and may be intrusive into the once solid Uto-Aztecan distribution.

The Pima and Papago and their linguistic relatives to the south, sometimes classed together as the Southern or Sonoran branch of Uto-Aztecan, share a basic social organization that has been modified by interaction with Yuman-speaking tribes and by later Hispanic and North American acculturation. "Pima and Papago Social Organization," this volume, is based in part on Underhill's (1939) comprehensive account, and Shimkin (1941) provides a glimpse of the earlier social organization with his reconstruction of Uto-Aztecan kinship.

Shimkin's reconstruction indicates a bilateral social structure with four grandparental terms used reciprocally for grandchildren, and with a separation of lineal and collateral relatives in the parental generation, with age as well as sex differentiation. In ego's generation a Hawaiian pattern of extending sibling terms to all cousins was used. Affinal terms were limited and were supplemented by teknonymy. Shimkin (1941) sums up the Uto-Aztecan system as highly consistent, with careful discrimination of the line of descent, and emphasis on seniority and self-reciprocity, and he would make them a separate type within Spier's (1925) classification of North American kinship systems (Eggan 1980:176).

The Pimans are divided into "patrilineal" moieties whose totems are Buzzard and Coyote, and the five patrilineal clan "names" are grouped—two in the Coyote moiety and three in the Buzzard. There is no present evidence that these moiety divisions were ever exogamous and the modern kindreds are bilateral, with rules forbidding the marriage of relatives on either side. The kinship system, likewise, gives equal weight to the paternal and maternal lines and is not influenced by the moiety division. The only trace of moiety functions is in connection with ceremonies, and some aspects of joking are often across moiety lines.

The clan name influences the kinship term used for father and hence everyone knows his or her clan name, and there is some evidence for an earlier localization of clans as well as a few ceremonial functions. The clan-moiety practices suggest the patterns found among Uto-Aztecan speakers in southern California, where the moieties are similarly named and are generally exogamous, and where Strong (1929) found a patrilineal lineage system with lineage territories and chiefs.

The Pima-Papago kinship system is thoroughly bilateral, extending up to great-great-grandparents and reciprocally down to great-great-grandchildren, with age and sex distinctions among parental siblings, and older and younger sibling terms extended to parallel and cross cousins. However, the moiety totems are described by a cross-cousin term, as are villages related to one's own. Polygyny was possible, and the junior sororate and levirate were in operation and reflected in kinship, but marriage was generally outside of known relatives.

In Underhill's (1939:40–41) summary of the kinship system, "the whole ancestral line thus seems to be viewed in segments of nine generations with the great great grandparents as the connecting link. This terminology shows the Papago as making use of a kinship system apparently worked out by a group with bilateral descent and strong emphasis on the levirate and sororate. It is the system used, in one form or another, throughout the desert area," including the Great Basin and the Plateau.

Three modes of Piman adaptation are distinguished: a sedentary One Village adaptation along streams with permanent running water, a Two Village adaptation where people moved between field villages and winter mountain wells, and a No Village completely migratory adaptation in the dryest regions. While these participate in a generally common sociocultural series of patterns the emphases are necessarily different. The Pima and Papago may be the direct descendants of the Hohokam peoples who disappeared in the fourteenth century or a little later, a hypothesis that, if further demonstrated, would be of great interest (see "Prehistory: Hohokam" and "Prehistory: O'otam," vol. 9), since the Anasazi Hopi are clearly related to northern Uto-Aztecan, and the Mogollon are very likely represented in the Zuni and Keresan populations.

In particular, the nonexogamous patrilineal moieties of the Pimans may well have been involved in the irrigated agriculture practiced by the Pimas, whether continuing Hohokam practices or moving into the region soon after from farther west, and the parallels with the Tanoan-speaking populations in the Rio Grande may be relevant to the disputes over the effects of irrigation on social and political organization.

Spicer (1969:777–791) provides a summary of what is known of Uto-Aztecan speakers and their cultures in Northwest Mexico. None of these Uto-Aztecan groups had peacetime tribal organizations, and they generally lived in autonomous rancherias before Spanish control resulted in consolidations into larger local groups and pueblos.

Spicer (1969:788) notes that bilateral forms of kinship organization characterized all the Uto-Aztecans. Kinship terminology was bifurcate collateral with Hawaiian cousin terminology, and the largest kinship units were generally extended families. Only among the Upper Pima, where there was a strong tendency "toward the development of patrilineal extended families and who possessed a unique patrilineal system of descent names," was there any major variation.

Religious acculturation under the Jesuits was strong and resulted not only in an effective "reduction" program and consolidation of local groups with civil officials but also in the introduction of ceremonial organizations, Roman Catholic marriage practices, and ritual kinship. Spanish contacts not only reinforced native rituals but also led to native reactions and to strong resistance, particularly among the Yaqui and others who developed a strong war organization, elaborated the war cults, and increased the authority of war leaders.

Romney (1967:209) provides data on the kinship patterns of nine of the Uto-Aztecan groups. He states that

> these systems are characterized by certain features: (1) Hawaiian cousin terminology, within which there is a distinction between elder and younger relatives; (2) a distinction between direct and collateral relatives in plus-one and minus-one generations; (3) four grandparental terms that distinguish each of the grandparents and merge grandparent siblings with the respective grandparents; (4) frequent use of self-reciprocal terms for grandparent, grandchild, and collateral relatives in plus-one and minus-one generations; (5) a recurring pattern in which ascending kinsmen are distinguished on the basis of sex of relative, whereas kinsmen in descending generations are distinuished by sex of speaker.

The charts Romney presents indicate that the geographically central west Mexican groups have more characteristic features than do the peripheral groups. Thus the northern groups distinguish relative age to a greater extent, and the Pima, Papago, and Ópata have developed nonreciprocal terms for grandchildren and first descending collaterals, a specialization that Romney (1967:211) thinks may be the result of contact with Yuman groups. The extreme southern groups, on the other hand, have much simplified bilateral systems, probably representing recent acculturation.

In his conclusions, Romney (1967:228) asks for more study on the functional interpretation of individual systems and suggests that historical reconstructions would be most useful for the major linguistic groups, for which he supplies some of the data in the form of lists of kinship terms.

Underhill (1939:235–273) provides an extensive summary of the distribution of "the elements from which the Papago built their social system," which is both detailed and perceptive, and she presents her tentative conclusions in a chart (1939:234) which compares the Papago traits with the Basin and California Uto-Aztecans, the Western Pueblos, the Eastern Pueblos, Mexico, and the River and Upland Yumans.

Underhill (1939:270–273) finds the greatest number of resemblances with the Uto-Aztecans of Mexico, and the second greatest number with those of the Great Basin and Plateau. The Uto-Aztecans of southern California are third in order, and the River Yumans fourth, with the Western Pueblos next and the Eastern Pueblos and Upland Yumans last. It would be useful to bring Underhill's account up to date and to test her hypotheses as to the nature of the relationships between different groups by a more intensive analysis. She has done this to a considerable extent (1948, 1954) with ceremonial patterns and intercultural relations in the Greater Southwest, but the data on kinship and social organization now available would make this a useful activity, as well.

The Yumans

The Yuman-speaking populations, centering on the Lower Colorado River and extending into California on the west and Arizona on the east, form a series of distinctive groups. The River tribes were organized into strong tribal groups who waged war against their neighbors and fellow Yumans alike, forcing some of their linguistic relatives to resettle along the Gila River or elsewhere. The riverine tribes were agricultural, planting their crops in the annual overflow areas along the Colorado and living in rancheria settlements at convenient places, but their environment also provided mesquite beans and other wild plant foods, along with fish and small game, which made up much of the food supply. In more marginal areas away from the river gathering and hunting were more important. Tipai-Ipai (vol. 8) and other Yuman-speaking groups of Baja California (Owen 1969) aboriginally lacked organized social and political unity and, except for the Kamia (eastern Tipai) in the Imperial Valley who practiced a little agriculture, lived on gathering of wild plants supplemented by hunting and fishing.

The Paipai, Kiliwa, and their neighbors, described by Owen (1969:877), seem to have the simplest social organization extant. They have remnants of named patrilocal bands, with bilateral descent and inheritance, though names are inherited patrilineally. The kinship systems vary somewhat, but all are basically Yuman. Marriage is monogamous and exogamy is extended to all known bilateral relatives.

The Tipai-Ipai to the north have, in addition to autonomous, seminomadic bands, some 30 or more patrilineal, named clans. The bands were not named and an individual identified himself by his clan and its places of settlement. Clans were localized, except for the Kamia, so that the clan name implied band and territory as well. There was no standard tribal name, and the terms Tipai and Ipai have been applied by anthropologists in the relative absence of self-designations. One of the western groups, the Cocopa, earlier moved to the Colorado delta region, where it developed a more complex social organization, related to that of the Quechan and other river peoples.

The River Yumans were made up of the Mohave, Quechan, Maricopa, and Cocopa, the Maricopa on the adjoining Gila River being composed of several tribes originally on the Colorado River but driven off by the Mohave and Quechan in aboriginal wars. The Mohave and Quechan in particular had a strong tribal unity and a sense of nationality that was unique for the Southwest. In alliance they dominated the river region and periodically made war against the Maricopa, who were allied with the Pima. The tribal chiefs had little authority and had to validate a status that was acquired by dreaming, with successful leadership.

The River tribes were organized into a series of patrilineal, exogamous clans that were named and had an association with totemic beings. Residence after marriage was generally patrilocal, and an extended family made up the core of the small rancheria settlements. In earlier times there were large semisubterranean earth lodges used for long-term habitation and simpler shelters for temporary residence during the agricultural season.

Marriage was without ceremony and was monogamous, for the most part. Clan exogamy brought in women from outside clans, and these women were identified in terms of their clan names, rather than by personal names. This may be the source of the Pima-Papago identification of the father's clan by utilizing the clan name as part of the kinship term for father.

The Upland Yumans to the northeast are the Walapai and Havasupai tribes south of the Colorado River and the Yavapai in central and western Arizona. The Walapai ranged over a wide area, hunting and gathering food; the Havasupai, originally part of the Walapai with the same language and culture, farmed in a well-watered canyon tributary to the Grand Canyon for part of the year and spent the winters hunting and gathering on the Coconino Plateau adjoining their farming territory. The Yavapai to the south and west relied mainly on hunting and gathering and were enemies of the Walapai and Havasupai. In later periods there were three subtribes of Yavapai, one of which, the Kewevkapaya, apparently had matrilineal clans, a possible result of close contact and intermarriage with the Western Apache (see also "Yavapai," this vol.).

All the Upland Yumans were organized into bands that ranged over large territories. They farmed in favorable locations but except for the Havasupai, who borrowed their agricultural practices from the Hopi, they were mainly hunters and gatherers. The Walapai were divided into some seven large territorial groupings, within which small related family groups owned tracts that were patrilineally inherited. The Havasupai lived on a small area in Cataract Canyon where each family possessed a plot of irrigated land that the males of the family owned jointly and that in-marrying wives helped cultivate. In the late fall and winter they moved to the plateau where small groups gathered piñon nuts and hunted, returning to the Canyon in early spring. The Yavapai subtribes and bands were generally more nomadic than either the Walapai or Havasupai, though a few planted crops along the Colorado River during the summer.

Steward (1937) suggests a historical development of the social organizations of the Southwest, with the patrilineal clans of the Colorado River tribes being derived from patrilineal bands, and he finds a gradation from the bands of the Diegueño type (i.e. the Tipai-Ipai except those in Imperial Valley) through the Kamia to the true clans of the River Yumans, which he thinks came about through the concentrations of population brought about by agriculture. This may be correct in broad outline but does not take into account the probable role of the California Uto-Aztecans with their development of localized lineages, who very likely influenced the bilateral bands of the Baja California Yumans in a patrilineal direction as can be noted among the Kamia, who have lineage names that are found among the other Ipai and Tipai.

According to Halpern (1942:440) there is "some evidence that the former local groupings of the Yuma [i.e., Quechan] were in effect patrilineal lineages with patrilocal residence. The males and unmarried females of the group were all related in the male line and members of the same clan. The married females of the group were the wives of the male members, therefore not related by blood to the others and not belonging to the clan of the others. The affinal kinship terminology is congruent with this type of organization." He notes that this outline of the local group makes sense of the peculiar naming practices of the Quechan, where an unmarried female has a personal name referring to some characteristic of the eponym or "namesake" of the clan but after marriage is addressed by her clan name. In small groups the clan name would normally distinguish one in-marrying female from the others.

The Yuman-speaking peoples all have kinship systems that share certain distinctive traits, and Spier (1925) recognized the Yuman systems as a separate type in his pioneer classification of North American kinship systems. According to Spier (1925:75–76) "the distinguishing feature here is the unusual development of age distinctions," which he illustrates in some detail. There are four grandparental terms and conversely four grandchild terms. There are four sibling terms, parallel cousins are called siblings, and cross-cousins either have special terms or are 'siblings'. In a number of cases the relative age of the connecting relatives is more important than the actual age.

In addition to the Cocopa, Quechan, Mohave, Havasupai, Kamia, and Ipai and Tipai, Spier found similar terminology among the California Uto-Aztecans, several Great Basin tribes, and the Papago and Northern Tepehuan.

M. F. Halpern's (1941) study of Yuman kinship systems provided a tripartite division of types of kinship systems based on a regional division. She finds that there has always been a stress on age differences in all generations, based primarily on the relative ages of connecting relatives.

The Western Yumans, including the Tipai-Ipai, Kamia, and the Cocopa (whose kinship system is basically western despite their delta location), show relationships in their kinship terminology both to the River Yumans and to their southern California Uto-Aztecan neighbors to the north. As one moves eastward among the Western Yumans there is a gradual shift from kinship terms and usages that are typical of these Uto-Aztecans toward those of the River Yumans. The Kamia, in particular, are very close to the River Yumans despite their linguistic connections with the Tipai-Ipai. The Cocopa, likewise, show Western Yuman patterns despite their later residence on the river.

The Western division is established primarily on the use of sibling terms for parallel cousins and a common pattern of terms for cross-cousins. The Eastern Yumans utilize a different pattern of terms for cross-cousins and have a unique set of terms for affinal relatives. The River Yumans share in the terminology of both the Western and Eastern Yumans and have a number of special developments of their own. But it is not yet clear that the River tribes represent either the most ancient or the basic pattern, though a detailed comparative linguistic study of cognates might enable a tentative decision to be made.

With regard to the local groups there are also differences. In the Western Yuman regions, the lineage or clan was the important local group, with territories of its own, and a chief, who was responsible for important ceremonies. The Cocopa and Kamia have similar groups but there are no clan officials or ceremonial activities, and territories are vague.

The River tribes had denser populations but the changes in flooding patterns led to considerable movement along the river and a general lack of correlation of local groups and clan organization. It is probably these conditions that led to some of the variant kinship usages, and to Halpern's (1942:425) conclusion that "the conceptual classification of kin among the Yuma [i.e. Quechan] is less complex than the terminological classification, taken at face value, would indicate," which he illustrates with the example that an individual recognizes three kinds of cousins, to whom he refers by five terms.

The Eastern Yumans had a variety of social institutions, all of which differed from the others. The Walapai local unit was the small village or camp made up of a number of families who were settled in areas with water for some agriculture. The families, when extended, were generally patrilocal. There were seven larger subdivisions occupying a territory and with a headman who was often a war leader and required to be a fluent speaker. Such a position often was inherited by a son or younger brother. The feeling of belonging to a particular territory was strong, and formerly five or six families might live around a spring and keep others away. Such land was inherited from parents and was kept undivided by the children. Marriage was forbidden with parallel cousins, who were called by sibling terms, but cross-cousins could and did marry.

The Havasupai, as a small group closely related to the Walapai, recognized only the immediate family as an important group, and there were no other definite social units up to the tribal level. Land is inherited in the male line and title is in the hands of the men, but the family jointly worked the land. Marriage was usually monogamous and blood relatives were not supposed to marry, but little attention was paid to distant ties.

The Yavapai had several subtribes and a more complex social organization. The important group was the local camp or small band unit, named after some geographical feature, whose territory was exploited for food. In some of these groups the band was matrilocal and children were considered members of the mother's group. In addition, the Kewevkapaya may have had exogamic, nontotemic, matrilineal clans, the members of which considered themselves to be "relatives." These were named after geographical features that referred to one-time homelands, but contemporary localization of clans no longer existed. Residence was neither matrilocal nor patrilocal, and hence there was no localization of clan members. Marriage, however, was forbidden with either the mother's or father's clan, and between cousins of any degree.

Bee (1963) has carried out field research among the Quechan Indians, with special reference to changes in Quechan social organization that have taken place since the mid-nineteenth century, comparing the situation in the 1880s with that of 1961, and considering settlement patterns, residence patterns, kinship terminology, clans, kinship behavior, descent and inheritance, and marriage. Bee finds (1963:207) an increasing tendency toward bilateral organization under the influence of American culture, a corresponding decline of the former unilineal organization, and particularly profound effects of contact on residence patterns and inheritance. With the breakdown of the large rancherias, the building of dams on the Colorado River, and the allotment of reservation lands, the preferred pattern of residence with the husband's family has broken down as the reservation shifted to a wage-based economy. About half the residence choices in 1961 were neo-local, and matrilocal residence had become more popular than patrilocal.

Kinship terminology is still complicated to unravel but Bee (1963:214) ultimately ascertained "that no basic terminological change had occurred over the past twenty years." However, he also notes that the entire terminology is disappearing, along with the Quechan language, as English takes over as the major language. Thus the highly complicated Quechan cousin terminology is simplified to English *cousin*, and the emphasis on age and sex is being overridden.

The clan is still an object of interest but when asked to describe its functions the general response of informants was, "It's just a name." It was still possible in 1961 to record the clan names, and there is evidence that a few clans were also local groups in the past. Halpern (1942:440) states that "there is some evidence that the former local groupings of the Yuma were in effect patrilineal lineages with patrilocal residence."

Bee had hypothesized that "the highly specialized kinship terminology of the Yuma [i.e., Quechan] might reflect a highly specialized system of standardized behavior patterns among kinsmen," but he soon found that the structuring of behavior in kinship was based on general criteria, such as age and sex, rather than on the specific relationships of kinsmen to one another. However, the general changes are very interesting.

Bee (1963:225–226) concludes that "the kinship terminology lays stress on the distinctions among kinsmen rather than on their similarity," and that Yuman patterns of social life always had a considerable degree of flexibility. The patrilineal clan groups and the residence patterns apparently could not maintain themselves in the face of seasonal movements in connection with agriculture and flooding, and the shift to allotments and wage work. Bee (1963:226) concludes that the effects of American culture on Quechan social organization in the twentieth century have reinforced, rather than drastically altered, a trend that was apparent in the late nineteenth century.

Summary and Conclusions

The complexities of social organization that have been summarized above do not fit neatly into even the enlarged Southwest. To provide an adequate base for historical reconstruction and comparison would involve a consideration of much of western North America, including portions of southern California, the Great Basin and adjoining Plateau regions, northwest Mexico, and the western Plains.

With regard to the Pueblos, while they share a common culture type, it seems clear that the Hopi and Zuni in the west, the Keresan-speaking villages in the center, and the Tanoans in the east represent three distinctive configurations of social structure, despite the overlapping on their borders due to mutual borrowings of social institutions and parallel adjustments to ecological conditions. Specific structural or institutional organizations run across linguistic boundaries: matrilineal lineages and clans are central to the Hopi and Zuni, and occur among the Keresans in diminishing importance from west to east, and among the Jemez, who live adjacent to Keresans. Moiety organizations of various types are strong among the Tewa and occur in various forms among the Tanoans generally and in the ceremonial dance organizations of the Keresans and the Jemez. The medicine societies, which are central to the Keresans, have spread both east and west—to the Zunis and to most of the Tanoan-speaking Pueblos. In addition, the kachina societies, thought to have been introduced from the south in the fourteenth century, are found in every group, except the northern Tiwa pueblos of Taos and Picuris.

Some progress has been made in relating these divisions to archeological data, and Ford, Schroeder, and Peckham (1972) illustrate the agreements and differences with regard to Puebloan prehistory that exist among archeologists. Most differences relate to the earlier time periods, and there is essential agreement on the developments after A.D. 1300 in each region.

Linguistic relationships have the greatest potential for historical reconstruction, and research on Pueblo languages promises important results. Hopi belongs to the widespread Uto-Aztecan language family, which extends from the Great Basin and southern California well into Mexico, with a time-depth estimated to be about 5,000 years. Zuni has no close relatives. Keresan, with no known relatives, apparently remained a single language until about 500 years ago. Tanoan, with its three divisions, is closely related to Kiowa, in the adjacent Plains area.

On the basis of Uto-Aztecan linguistic and kinship studies Eggan (1980) has considered Shoshoni kinship structures in connection with a delineation of Great Basin backgrounds for Western Pueblo social and cultural development, utilizing Steward's (1938) work. Beginning around 3,000 years ago, the northern Uto-Aztecan groups began to expand from their homelands, with the proto-Hopi moving eastward and the California Uto-Aztecans south and west, followed by the Numic populations—Northern Paiute, Shoshoni, and Southern Paiute, who expanded into the Great Basin about the twelfth century. The early Hopi reached the Grand Canyon by A.D. 900 and the Black Mesa region and the Hopi Buttes by about the same time; they had left these areas by A.D. 1150 to join linguistic or cultural relatives on the present Hopi mesas.

While the Hopi retain many traits characteristic of the Desert culture, and about half the kinship terms as reconstructed by Shimkin (1941), Hopi social organization was almost wholly transformed in comparison with the Numic groups. With the development of agriculture and small permanent settlements in favorable localities, the bilateral social system shifted to a matrilineal lineage pattern, giving up patterns of seniority and self-reciprocity in favor of a Crow type of kinship system, and changing from the varied marriage patterns based on brother-sister exchange to monogamy and clan exogamy.

From a broader standpoint Shaul has been concerned with the interrelations of the Western Pueblos—in terms of sociolinguistics as well as historical reconstruction. Shaul (1981) suggests that there was early contact and diffusion among the Keresan, Zuni, and Hopi speech communities that ended by A.D. 1300, when language apparently became a marker for ethnicity as the language populations coalesced. Shaul (1980) examines the position of Hopi within the Uto-Aztecan language family, finding that it is basically a northern language, but with strong southern connections. Shaul (1981a) provides lexical materials that suggest a participation in the Mogollon cultural sphere to the south, in contrast to the ethnohistoric data that places them in the Chaco and Mesa Verde regions.

Plog (1978) attempts to account for the variations in social organization in terms of ecological and archeological data. He utilizes Ford's (1972) ecological discussion to demonstrate that the Pueblo environments are subject to greater variation than is commonly assumed, particularly with regard to precipitation, hydrology, temperature, soils, and wind; and he contrasts the dry farming techniques of the Hopi with the irrigation systems in the eastern regions, noting that the former "provide the only basis for dealing with the immense environmental variation of the area" (Plog 1978:359). The irrigation hypothesis, as proposed by Wittfogel and Goldfrank (1943) and supported by Dozier (1970), is important but is clearly only one factor among many in bringing about a "more complex and centralized society." After considering the irrigation hypothesis with regard to the Pueblo of Picuris Ford (1977:150) concluded that the assumptions underlying the hypothesis "are not supported by the Picuris study." The political and ceremonial controls of secular and ritual activities in the Eastern Pueblos go far beyond the requirements for cleaning ditches and involve a system whose authority covers all aspects of social life.

Plog (1978:362–365) proposes to account for the differences in social structure between east and west in terms of irrigation, land use, cropping practices, and demography, and he suggests that there are "important links between variability in environment, variability in subsistence and variability in social organization." These are important considerations, but his belief that the early Western Pueblos were utilizing irrigation on a large scale about A.D. 1100 (Plog 1978:366) goes well beyond the available evidence. The origins of the present diversity, he believes, "reflect a common evolutionary process—experimentation with subsistence strategies, experimentation with organizational patterns, and the survival of a few relatively more successful combinations" (Plog 1978:370). The relations between variations and their spatial positions suggest that additional factors are involved, since the changes from west to east in the Pueblo crescent are regular, rather than random.

In contrast to the Pueblos, the Southern Athapaskans are recent intruders into the Southwest, speaking languages that are related to the Northern Athapaskans of Canada and Alaska and bringing a hunting and gathering culture and a social organization quite different from that of the Pueblo populations. Apparently coming as a single ancestral group, the Navajo, Western Apache, Chiricahua, Mescalero, Jicarilla, and Lipan still speak closely related dialects of Apachean, but as C.B. White's (1957) comparison of the various theories of development indicates, there is no agreement on their order. And Dyen and Aberle's (1974) attempt to solve the problem does not answer all the questions. Dyen and Aberle's solution parallels that of Kroeber (1937) who made a tentative reconstruction of the "original Athapaskan kinship system" and concluded that better linguistic data were essential. Hoijer (1956a) has provided the linguistic data for some 73 cognate sets of kinship terms, with their reconstructed meanings, and Dyen has provided exemplary rules for selection among competing cognate sets. Dyen, however, rejected Hoijer's comparison of the kinship categories in the daughter languages as "unnecessary," so that the comparison of a reconstructed proto-Athapaskan set of terms with the Apachean kinship systems may skip several important steps.

In the 1970s there has been great interest and debate on the social organization of Northern Athapaskan groups, summarized by Krech (1980). Here some 27 "tribes" are scattered in five physiographic-ecological zones. The Pacific drainages and Cordilleran regions are occupied by peoples with matrilineal and matrilocal organizations, which De Laguna (1975) suggests may have a proto-Athapaskan basis; but Arctic drainage lowland groups are generally bilateral with regard to kinship, and there are suggestions that bilaterality is adaptive to the ecological conditions in this area, with large composite bands and a dependence on caribou requiring flexible groupings. Since matrilocality was widespread in all areas in the early historic period the shift in the Arctic drainage to bilocal residence is considered to be relatively recent, but remains to be demonstrated.

The origins of the Southern Athapaskan groups have not been clearly shown as yet, but D.R. Wilcox (1981) provides an exhaustive analysis of the data and concludes that after a long sojourn in the Black Hills, the Apacheans entered the Southwest via the Plains soon after the Spaniards arrived. This conclusion is strengthened by C.F. Schaafsma's (1981) report on excavations of early Navajo sites in the Piedra Lumbre Valley near Abiquiu, New Mexico, dated between A.D. 1640 and 1710. These are almost certainly the "Apaches de Nabaju" of the Benavides *Memorials* who were reported living in the Chama River Valley, a day's journey from Santa Clara Pueblo, in 1629. With the collapse of the proposed dating for the Dinetah phase, the assumed earliest Navajo archeological period, the Chama Valley is the earliest well-documented Navajo occupation in the Southwest and confirms the Plains region as the probable place of entry of Apachean peoples.

If the Southern Athapaskans migrated via the Plains it is highly probable that they broke off from groups living on the southern margins of the Arctic drainage lowlands and might not have been organized in matrilineal and matrilocal groups, but rather in bilateral ones. Aberle (in Dyen and Aberle 1974) has recognized this possibility, but without a reconstruction for intermediate language groups he had little basis for such a choice.

Dyen and Aberle (1974) reconstruct the early Apachean kinship system as bifurcate in the first ascending and descending generations, with Iroquois cousin terms and evidence for the equation of cross-cousins with spouses and in-laws. The terminal state for Apachean dialect groups shows Navajo and San Carlos Apache retaining all but the equation of cross-cousins and in-laws, while the eastern groups retain bifurcation but supplement or replace Iroquois cousin terms with Hawaiian ones, as well as losing the cross-cousin equations. They further interpret early Apachean as matrilineal and matrilocal, and characterized by the sororate and levirate, sororal polygyny, sister exchange, and bilateral cross-cousin marriage.

They thus conclude that the Navajo and Western Apache, whom many ethnologists consider to have changed the most with regard to social organization and general culture, have retained the early patterns of kinship and descent to a greater extent than the eastern groups. Before such a conclusion is accepted the reverse hypothesis should be seriously considered: that the Navajo and Western Apache developed their clan system and kinship patterns after reaching the Southwest. The alternative is to believe that all the Apachean groups, except the Navajo and Western Apache, have lost their matrilineal clan systems in the Southwestern environment.

Neither hypothesis is of much assistance in understanding the Chiricahua Apache kinship system. Opler (1937) considered Chiricahua the older form of Southern Athapaskan kinship. Kroeber (1937) dissented, believing that Chiricahua–Mescalero–Western Apache kinship systems had been influenced by Uto-Aztecan and Yuman contacts and that Navajo might prove to be closer to original Southern Athapaskan. C.B. White (1957:442), who thinks that Western Apache and Navajo mark the final stage of differentiation, quotes Goodwin (1942:162–163) who states, "if a historical reconstruction of Western Apache stimulus toward formation of clans is made, strong social tendencies already present, adoption of agriculture, and contact with people already having clans must be equally stressed." It is obvious that the nature of early Apachean social organization and the order of development of the modern systems will require additional thought and effort, and perhaps a new view of the nature of Athapaskan linguistic units in the directions being advocated by Krauss (discussed in Dyen and Aberle 1974).

Turning to the Pima and Papago and their neighbors, there is little that can be added to what has been said above. Much of the region to the west and south of the Puebloan and Apachean populations has been characterized as a rancheria culture area, based on the characteristic settlement patterns, but within this broad region it is useful to differentiate the Uto-Aztecans from the Yumans.

As Underhill (1939:235–273) notes, the elements from which the Papago built their social system were shared over a large area. The Piman patrilineal moieties, "with their animal names and distinguishing paints and colors and their occasional ceremonial functions most resemble those of the southern California Shoshoneans [Takic Uto-Aztecans]" (1939:238). In these Takic-speaking tribes the moieties, Coyote and Wildcat, are patrilineal and exogamous and have important ceremonial functions, but moieties are absent in the intervening Yumans and have a different organization and function among the Eastern Pueblos. Patrilineal clans have a broader distribution with lineages and clans important among the Takic speakers, as well as among the River Yumans and some of the Western Yumans. Here the Piman clan names seem related to the Takic ones, though the associated fetish bundles, sacred house, and ceremonial leadership have apparently been transferred from the lineage or clan to the village.

The family structure of the Pimans and their linguistic relatives, as well as the kinship system, is bilateral rather than patrilineal, and the restrictions on marriage are in terms of blood kin rather than lineage or clan exogamy. This suggests that the Pima may have borrowed clan names and other items rather than formerly having a fully developed lineage system with moiety exogamy, most of which they later lost. It is possible that close comparison using linguistic cognates might solve this problem.

With regard to the kinship systems Shimkin's (1941) reconstruction of Uto-Aztecan kinship terminology makes it possible to compare the changes which have gone on in the daughter languages. Shimkin found that roughly half the reconstructed terminology was retained in the daughter languages, but it would now be possible to take the comparison further, utilizing the additional data that has become available in Romney's (1967) contributions, and the kinship cognates provided by Wick Miller and others.

Underhill (1939:245–250) provides a rather detailed analysis of Papago kinship terminology with regard to selected features: the equating of cross- and parallel cousins with siblings, the use of four grandparental terms, age and sex distinctions with regard to parental siblings, and age distinctions among siblings. She concludes that underneath the varied overlappings with surrounding groups, the Piman system shares a basic similarity with that of the Northern Uto-Aztecans, particularly with the Great Basin groups, rather than with the Yumans, with whom Spier (1925) classified them.

The Yuman-speaking population divides the Northern Uto-Aztecan speakers from the Southern Uto-Aztecan–speaking Pima-Papago and their Sonoran relatives, and their relations with each are important in understanding the role they play with regard to the development of social institutions in the lower Colorado River valley. It is probable that the Takic or Southern California Uto-Aztecan expansion took place in the first millennium B.C. The proposed Hokan affiliations of the Yumans suggest that the groups in extreme southern California and extending well into Baja California may be located in part of the old Yuman homeland, since they have apparently more divergent languages and a simpler social system. Cochimi is apparently extinct, but Kiliwa may be the most aberrant language, and Kiliwa and Paipai, with remnants of patrilocal bands, may represent an earlier form of social structure. The Tipai-Ipai have both band groups and patrilineal named clans that were localized and that may well be related to contacts with the Takic-speaking Uto-Aztecans to the north. Both the Kamia and the Cocopa appear to have moved from this region to the Imperial Valley and the Colorado delta region, respectively.

The River Yumans have probably been in place for a considerable period ("Prehistory: Hakataya," vol. 9). Not enough work has been done in the lower Colorado River valley to indicate when the River Yumans' distinctive adjustments, including floodwater agriculture and patrilineal clans that were named and exogamous, took place, but it is clear that the kinship system was not reoriented in a patrilineal direction to any great degree.

The warfare patterns of the River Yumans, and their relative fear of alien women, restricted the degree of intermarriage with neighboring non-Yuman groups, and the periodic shifting of local groups in connection with the biannual floods may have restricted the development of more complex patrilineal institutions, such as moieties. Rather there were tribal alliances for purposes of warfare, which had some of the aspects of a game.

With Halpern's (1942) analysis of kinship terms and Bee's (1963) study of changes in Quechan social organization, it may be possible to analyze the kinship systems of the variant Yuman groups more adequately, both in terms of the ancestral system and the relations of the variants to ecological and contact situations. At present the Yuman systems have a general relationship to the kinship systems of their neighbors but do not seem to be adjusted in any direct way to the patrilineal and patrilocal groupings that characterize the River Yumans as a whole. Underhill (1939:273) characterizes the Yumans as a "half assimilated group, highly resistant to some of the traits considered." Perhaps the attitudes engendered by war extended to other aspects of social and cultural life, as well. Or it may be that Bee's (1963:225–226) observation that the Quechan stress the distinctions among kinsmen, rather than their similarities, is an important key to the proliferation of Yuman kin terms.

Southwestern Ceremonialism

LOUISE LAMPHERE

For the native peoples of North America, unlike the European settlers who populated the continent and who confined Native American populations to reservations, the land and the natural environment itself had and continues to have important religious significance. In the Greater American Southwest (as in other parts of North America), native religion is rooted in a sense of place, and concepts of the supernatural are closely tied to the natural world. Plants, animals, and natural phenomena (sun, wind, lightning, rain) are not only important for the economic survival of Indian communities but also are intimately related to Indian concepts of supernatural power and to the ways in which ritual preserves the Indian way of life. Indian identity itself is closely tied to the local environment and, where Native American groups have been removed from their traditional habitat, not only have their economies been drastically changed or destroyed, but also their own identities, their collective sense of being, and their religious practices have been critically altered.

Ceremonialism is a broad term that covers a variety of religious practices or rituals; in the Southwest, these have centered on the maintenance of the natural and cultivated animal and plant life that sustains the Indian community, and the restoration of the individual's health and the continuation of a long life for the individual and the community. Rituals, then, focus on cultivation and hunting (sources of community sustenance) and on curing and warfare (related to the continued longevity of the individual and the community). Any ceremony or ritual is a set of actions recognized by members of a group to be sacred; these are usually performed by a specialist (a shaman or a priest) in order to communicate with the supernatural world and to influence worldly events (for example, to provide for a good harvest, to assure the abundance of wild game, to cure a sick individual, or to protect warriors in a raid). Finally, ritual contexts usually include the use of singing or chanting (often by the ritual specialist but also by a chorus) and dancing (usually by men impersonating various supernaturals). Both music and dance are crucial in communicating with the supernatural and in actually bringing the presence of supernatural forces into the human community.

The comparison of Southwestern ceremonialism will be developed by examining four aspects of religion in each of the cultural groupings discussed: concepts of supernatural power; images of the cosmos and social world; the organization of ceremonies and ritual that, in turn, reflect the cosmologies already outlined and communicate with the supernatural to accomplish a particular goal; and the symbolism of particular sacred objects and actions used in ritual.

Much of the data on which the analysis is based was gathered in the early part of the twentieth century, culminating in field studies made in the 1930s. The richness of Southwestern ceremonialism as portrayed in these early materials has been altered by the impact of Western culture; many practices have died out and many ceremonies have been altered or discontinued. Many Indians in the Southwest have adopted Christianity or become members of the Native American Church. On the other hand, traditional ceremonies among many groups, particularly among Pueblo cultures, are thriving. This essay emphasizes continuity and stresses the similarities and differences in ceremonial practices among Southwestern cultures as they existed at a time when their traditional economies and social structures were relatively undisrupted by Anglo-American society.

Yumans: the Shaman, the Dream, and the Mountain

In discussing shamanism throughout the New World, Furst (1973–1974:40) outlines the characteristics of a shamanic world view where the universe is depicted as multi-layered or stratified, with an underworld below and an upperworld above. The layers of the universe are interconnected by a central axis (*axis mundi*). Man and animals and all the phenomena of the environment are qualitatively equivalent, as suggested in the "primordial capability of man and animal to assume each other's outer form." Thus, in mythic first times, "there is no difference in the outer shape of animals and people, each sharing the form of the other, but this condition finally gave way through transformation to the present division of form and function" (Furst 1973–1974:48). In a shamanic belief system, cultural and physical survival depends on a multidimensional equilibrium of various natural and supernatural forces of which the shaman is guardian and for whose maintenance he marshals all his gifts (Furst 1973–1974:45).

In some groups, this focuses on the problem of hunting, while in others it centers on the techniques of healing, either counteracting soul loss or removing a foreign spirit or hostile object of supernatural origin (Furst 1973–1974:54–55).

Many of these general characteristics of North American shamanic religion were apparent in the practices of the Yuman peoples of the Colorado River, both the agricultural peoples of the Lower Colorado (Mohave, Maricopa, Quechan, and Cocopa) and the predominantly hunter-gatherer groups of the Upland area (Havasupai, Walapai, and Yavapai). The River Yumans, whose patrilineal descent patterns, inherited chiefdomship, and close settled pattern along the river banks set them apart from the Upland groups, also have differing religious patterns. Their origin myths involve two quarreling brothers, one of whom creates humans and is the source of shamanic power. The other dies, and it is his cremation at a sacred mountain center that becomes the prototype for the mourning ceremony among the River Yumans (Quechan *karˀúk*), a communal ritual that features songs, speeches, a mock battle, and the burning of images representing the dead ("Mohave," fig. 10, this vol.) (Forde 1931:262–264; Kroeber 1925a:750). The Mohave, Quechan, and those groups now amalgamated under the name Maricopa also have long song cycles (see Kroeber 1925a:776–770 for Mohave examples) that tell of ancestral wanderings or conflict with other groups and that are sung by those who have dreamed the power to do so.

In the remainder of their religious practices, the River Yumans share with the Upland groups an emphasis on curing ("Yavapai," fig. 10, this vol.). The shaman who has the power to cure acquires it through a dream experience. Only among the Kewevkapaya Yavapai (Gifford 1932:233) is power acquired through a trance, not a dream. The connection between dreaming and power can be seen in the Maricopa word *kʷṣtma·ṣ* 'one who has power', literally 'the one who dreams'. The Maricopa word for dream and spirit are the same: *ṣma·k* (Spier 1933:237–238, phonemicized). The dream is usually one in which the shaman travels to a sacred mountain place; there he encounters either a spirit of the mountain, a bird, or an animal who teaches him songs, gives him the opportunity to cure a sick person, or in some other way gives him the power to cure. In some instances, the spirit comes to the shaman and carries him to the "mountain home" (Gifford 1933:312–313). Among the Walapai (Kroeber 1935:188) a man may actually go to a mountain, build a fire in a cave, and spend four nights, during which time he dreams and acquires power from a spirit. In the Quechan, Mohave, and Kewevkapaya cultures, the spirits derive their power from the creator god or goddess. The power that a shaman acquires may be either positive or negative; it could be used to restore health or harm or bewitch a person. Among the Quechan, Mohave, and Cocopa, shamans believed to be harmful have been killed (Forde 1931; Gifford 1933:312; Kroeber 1925a:778).

Yuman groups do not have a well-developed cosmology or a model of the universe that associated animals, birds, and supernatural beings with direction and color symbolism; however, origin myths contain the theme of emergence from a flooded world to a mountain refuge (Kroeber 1935:245; Forde 1931:176; Spier 1933:35). Among the Quechan and Cocopa in particular, the cosmos has four layers, with the Quechan soul at death traveling through these four planes to a final afterworld that is an ameliorated version of the world of the living (Forde 1931:179; Gifford 1933:306). Some of the song cycles of the River Yuman groups (Mohave, Maricopa, and Quechan) recount the travels of supernaturals or spirits in animal forms as they travel from mountain, river, or other locale overcoming crises and creating human life and culture. The places they visit may be thought of as constituting a cosmology, though not a rigidly patterned one, where supernatural events are associated with important features of the local environment. Among the Upland Yumans, where song cycles are absent, spirits seem associated with particular places and the symbolism of sacred mountains associated with the four directions is often used (Kroeber 1935:188). Power-giving spirits may derive from a mountain, a bird, or an animal, but spirits are not related to one another in an ordered or hierarchical manner. Furthermore, the source of power and its use are not always systematically connected; for example, songs from the eagle or the buzzard may be used to cure a variety of symptoms.

Curing rituals themselves are usually directed toward the removal of a foreign object or spirit from the patient's body. The Quechan shamans (Forde 1931:191) also treat patients for sickness due to soul loss, but this seems less prevalent than illness due to the intrusion of an animal or mountain spirit or an object sent by that spirit (its "arrow"). Accounts of cures indicate a variety of methods used by the shaman, but all involve his possession by a spirit helper and his consequent ability to extract and remove the troublesome source of illness.

Among the Havasupai, during the cure the spirit helper enters the shaman, becomes lodged in his chest and, when he sings, it is really the spirit that sings. The shaman sucks the patient and, in the process of applying his mouth to the patient's body, his spirit enters the patient and is able to draw out the trouble (Spier 1928:279). Among the Maricopa tribes, the shaman sings two or four songs over the patient and smokes to gain strength himself; he may also blow smoke over the patient's body (Spier 1933:384). The shaman may attempt to relieve the patient by brushing him with his hand, blowing spittle over him, and sucking his body (Spier 1933:283). The brushing motion is toward the patient's feet in order to avoid driving the sickness toward the heart.

The Walapai shaman (in a cure described in Kroeber 1935:188–189) sends his own spirit to the mountain asking for help in curing the patient. The shaman prays to the mountains in the four directions, and the mountain spirit enters him through the mouth. Through a process of sucking, singing, and shuffle dancing, the shaman sends the mountain spirit into the patient's body and extracts blood, stone, and wood (the object in which the spirit causing the sickness resides) and thus sends the evil spirit back to the mountain.

The Havasupai, as well as the Quechan (Forde 1931:197), have weather shamans (fig. 1), who obtain their power by dreaming of clouds, thunder, and lightning (Spier 1928:281–282). The Havasupai also held masked dances (discontinued around 1900), a practice possibly borrowed from the nearby Hopi, which, like the Hopi masked dances, brought rain and good fortune (Spier 1928:266–267). Several Yuman groups have shamans who are specialists in curing rattlesnake bites (Forde 1931:196; Gifford 1936:310; Spier 1928:283).

Calif. Histl. Soc., Los Angeles: Title Insurance Coll., 3790.

Fig. 1. Rock Jones, seated in center, an important Havasupai shaman. In 1918 he was known as a weather shaman who had inherited his rain-making powers from his maternal uncle (Spier 1928:277–278). Later he also became a curing shaman (Smithson and Euler 1964:5, 11). Photograph by Charles C. Pierce, about 1900.

Smithsonian, Dept. of Anthr.: 277,924.

Fig. 2. Mohave clay pipe used by a doctor. The dark coloration is due to rubbing with green mistletoe. Length 13.5 cm, collected by J.P. Harrington in 1911.

Underhill (1948) discusses Yuman ceremonialism in terms of the broader pattern of "the vision," which, in her view, provides the underlying stratum in Greater Southwestern ceremonialism. The essence of this vision complex is the "vision recipient" (usually a male) armed with a fetish representing his power and possibly a song or formula that this power has given to him. The power may be any natural phenomenon, but it acts as a universal, impersonal force. The power provides the shaman with a permanent miraculous ability in return for prayer and offerings directed toward the power (Underhill 1948:11–12).

The dream or vision should be viewed within the context of the shamanic world view, which consists of a layered universe, where there is an intimate connection and ultimate transformability of human beings and certain aspects of the natural environment; these aspects are charged with supernatural power and the shaman is the guardian of the equilibrium of supernatural forces. The symbolism of curing is consistent with this world view. The acquisition of power includes the theme of a "journey," an expedition through the medium of a dream to the natural/supernatural world beyond human society. The process of curing entails the reverse, the transportation of the supernatural spirit from the external world into the shaman's body, where it can be used to see the source of the disease or enter into the patient's body and combat the cause. Disease-causing agents are extracted from the patient through sucking, spraying the body with spittle, or brushing the body. The symbolism of penetration and removal is dominant.

Color, number, and direction symbolism are only weakly developed. There is some use of the number four in association with the idea of boundaries, as with the Maricopa four sacred mountains, the use of four songs to cure a patient (Maricopa), the Walapai division of the night into four dream periods, and the seclusion of the Walapai shaman during his quest for power for four days (Kroeber 1935:186). Red and white are the only symbolic colors; red is used by the Havasupai weather shaman to attract a mountain (earth) spirit, and white attracts the natural phenomena associated with the sky (white clouds, rain, lightning, and thunder).

The song and the use of the gourd rattle (fig. 3) provide the means of attracting the supernaturals that

Mus. of N. Mex., Santa Fe: School of Amer. Research Coll., 10871/12.

Fig. 3. Walapai gourd rattle with wooden handle. Length about 20.3 cm, collected by A.L. Kroeber in 1929.

actually possess the shaman, rather than being represented through masked figures, drypaintings, prayersticks, or other ritual paraphernalia used in other Southwestern cultures.

Underhill (1948) has emphasized the contrast between the individual orientation found in the hunting-gathering Yuman cultures (where the focus is on curing) with the more communally oriented rituals of the Pueblos, and the Pima-Papago, and even the mourning ceremonies of the River Yuman peoples. Within the vision-oriented, individualistic rituals of the Yumans, it is important to emphasize three themes: power is acquired through a dream "journey" where a shaman travels outside the social world to meet the supernatural; curing is begun through a first stage of penetration and possession during which the supernatural comes into the social world, directly entering the shaman's body and the patient's body; and curing is finally achieved through the removal (by sucking, brushing, or cutting) of the malevolent agents from the patient.

Apaches: Reciprocity and Long Life

Apache curing and ceremonialism illustrate the ways in which these themes are transformed in another cultural context to reflect a different relationship among the human world, the supernatural, and the natural environment. Apache and Navajo ceremonialism, like Yuman religion, focuses mainly on curing, though preparation for warfare was a secondary theme in all the Apache groups (Hill 1936; Opler 1941; Basso 1971). Navajo curing is quite different from the general Apache pattern, making it appropriate to deal separately with Navajo concepts of power, their cosmology, ritual, and symbolism.

For the Apache groups, particularly the Mescalero (Opler 1969), the Chiricahua (Opler 1941), and the Jicarilla (Opler 1946), the theme of the vision is important. Power (*diγį*) is obtained through a dream or visionary experience where the individual travels outside the social world. Accounts of the acquisition of power by shamans among the Chiricahua (Opler 1941:269–272) and Mescalero (Opler 1969:40–46) show that power reaches man through animals, plants, and supernatural phenomena that take human form to instruct an Apache man or woman in the appropriate ceremonies. During a vision experience, the potential curer is guided on a journey to a "holy home," often a cave in the mountains (Opler 1969:24), where supernatural powers reside (Bear's Home, Summer's Home, Medicine's Home, the Home of the Puberty Ceremony, etc.). Appropriate songs are taught the shaman, and he is given the necessary ritual objects that are used during a curing rite to attract supernatural beings (Opler 1969:133). "Assurances were given that supernatural power would appear and lend help when it was summoned and when it heard its songs and prayers" (Opler 1969:24).

Power, therefore, refers to a set of abstract and invisible forces that derive from certain kinds of animals, plants, and natural phenomena. Any of the various "powers" may be acquired by man, either by dreaming about the particular class of objects or by purchasing the requisite chants, prayers, and paraphernalia that activate that class (Basso 1966:150). Among the Jicarilla and Western Apache, some ceremonies, particularly the girls' puberty rite and the Bear ceremony (a Jicarilla rite) are learned from other practitioners, while other ceremonies are acquired through dreams. In other words, the Apache seem to have a traditional system, part way between the vision-oriented Yuman system and the Navajo system, where all ceremonies (except for divination) are learned through a period of apprenticeship.

Basso (1969) lists 28 sources of power among the Western Apache, ranging from natural phenomena (water, fire, thunder, lightning, wind) to flying bipeds (eagles, bats), cold-blooded creatures (snakes, lizards), and quadrupeds (elk, deer, mountain lion, bear, and horse). Basso makes it clear that it is not the animal, bird, or natural object that is "holy" or sacred, but the power itself. As in the Yuman case, sources of power are located outside the social world, either in the mountains (the habitat of the elk, deer, bear, and mountain lion) or the sky (lightning, rain, wind, the eagle, and bat).

Like the Yuman quest, Apache power acquisition has the quality of a dream-journey, but the curing rituals of the Apache include a different relationship with the supernatural. While Yuman curing seems to involve direct possession (that is, the spirit enters the shaman's body), Apache curing entails an indirect system of reciprocity. As Aberle (1967a) has elaborated this theme for the Navajo, the patient presents the shaman or medicine man with ritual prestations (*biyeel* 'his fee'); during the ceremony, through the use of the proper songs and ritual actions the shaman attracts the spirit to come and use his power to cure the sick person. An "unbroken chain of reciprocity" binds the supernatural spirit, the shaman, and the patient. "Indeed, the chain is a circle; in the course of the ceremony the patient becomes one of the Holy Ones, a figure possessing temporary mana, not through trance or seizure, but through ritual contact and identification" (Aberle 1967a:27).*

The notion of a layered universe is implicit in the Apache belief in an underworld (Opler 1941:477–478), a mirror image of the Apache world, but where sickness and death are absent and where the environment is fertile, full of green grass and flowing streams. The world above ground is more structured than the Yuman cosmos, but there is no clear model of the universe that lays out the relationship of geographical entities like mountains and rivers, in terms of color and directional symbolism with associated birds, animals, and supernatural creatures. Among the Jicarilla, there is some indication of the bounding of territory by mountains and by four rivers (two male and two female; Opler 1971a), and the human body is used as a model for structuring the natural environment, as indicated in the texts collected by Goddard (Opler 1971a:313).

The number four is important and all Apache groups associate colors with each of the four directions, beginning with the east and proceeding in a sunwise or clockwise motion (the sacred direction). East is associated with black, the south with blue, the west with yellow, and the north with white. However, these associations are not nearly so prominent as similar ones are in Navajo and Pueblo ritual.

As part of the relationship of reciprocity among the Apache shaman, supernatural power, and the patient, during a curing ceremony the shaman's efforts are to attract the supernatural to the ceremony itself, through the correct prestations, prayers, and songs. There is less of a sense that the shaman himself becomes possessed during the ceremony. Instead, the ritual objects (for example, plants used as medicine, the fetishes constructed of animal parts or bird feathers) become imbued with the power of the supernatural. White shell and turquoise are sacred substances, and pollen (either tule pollen or corn pollen among the more agricultural Jicarilla and Western Apache) is used especially to impart sacred power to the participants in the ceremony.

The emphasis on removing evil influences from the patient's body, a central aspect of Yuman curing, is also part of the Apache ceremony. The shaman can often find the sickness by making the patient transparent through holding an eagle feather over his body. Techniques for extracting the sickness among the Jicarilla, for example, include pulling, sucking and blowing, brushing, and frightening by gesticulating.

In addition to the themes of the attraction of supernatural power through prestation and the removal of evil influence, a third is apparent: the identification of the patient with the supernatural, with the result that the patient's body becomes "holy" or *diyį*, full of supernatural power. This theme is especially emphasized in the girls' puberty rite, a ceremony that is important in all Apache groups and that is learned rather than acquired through a dream or vision experience (figs. 4–5). In the Western Apache version, the girl is given ritual paraphernalia, including a sacred cane, a buckskin dress, and a white abalone shell to carry and wear throughout the ceremony. These symbolize longevity and protection and identify her with with White Shell Woman, the female supernatural for whom the first puberty rite was performed. At one crucial point in the ceremony, the girl's identification with White Shell Woman becomes most apparent: while the medicine man sings, she kneels, raising her hands to the sun and, swaying back and forth, she assumes the posture in which White Shell Woman is generally believed to have experienced her first menstruation (Basso 1970:65).

The symbolism of long life is prominent throughout the ritual and is associated first with the pubescent girl and then with the entire community. The girl is given a ritual massage in order to assure a strong body in her adult life and, by running around the sacred cane, she progresses through the four phases of life and assures longevity. Toward the end of the ceremony and in the four days afterward, her identification with White Shell Woman means that she can bring good fortune to others and possesses the power to cure and make rain (Basso 1970:68; "The Apachean Culture Pattern and Its Origins," this vol.).

In the Mescalero and Chiricahua versions, supernatural presence is apparent not only through the identification of the girl with White Shell Woman, but also in the appearance of the *gą́hę́* spirits, impersonated by masked dancers (figs. 6–7; "Chiricahua Apache," fig. 11, this vol.). In preparation for the dancing, each dancer's body is painted and, when he dons the mask, he becomes sacred (*diyį*). The identification of the supernatural and the dancer (and, hence, the presence of the spirits at the ceremony) is clearly recognized in the songs sung at the ceremonial grounds during their dance performance.

In sum, the characteristics of the shamanic world view and ritual practice are seen in an altered form in Apache religion. The theme of the layered universe is apparent, slightly elaborated with a greater use of the number four, color, and directional symbolism. The acquisition

*Opler (1968, 1969a) has presented evidence for the Apache groups that there is a distinction between a ceremonial *yeel* presented to the medicine man (which is actually intended for the supernaturals) and a secular payment for the medicine man's services; however, this perspective does not alter Aberle's analysis that reciprocity unites supernatural, medicine, and patient in a circle of relationship.

bottom left, Natl. Geographic Soc., Washington; top right, Mus. of N. Mex., Santa Fe; bottom right, U. of Ariz., Ariz. State Mus., Tucson: 24746.

Fig. 4. Apache girl's puberty ceremony (Sunrise Dance). The masked dancers, called Crown Dancers (Western Apache *gaan*), were frequently asked to participate to ward off potential evil. They usually performed at night and have become a standard source of entertainment at this ceremony (Opler 1941:87). top left, Tapping the sacred yellow pollen from cattail reed blossoms. The pollen is mixed with a little water and sprinkled on the pubescent girl (bottom left). top left, photograph by Tad Nichols at Whiteriver, Ariz., July 1941; bottom left, photograph by Bill Hess, Whiteriver, Ariz., Sept. 1976. top right, Western Apache ceremony at Ft. Huachuca, Ariz. The girl is being massaged by her sponsor. Members of a Black cavalry or infantry unit look on, while one uniformed soldier is participating as a drummer. Photographed about 1920s. bottom right, Crown Dancers. Photograph by Helga Teiwes, Beaver Creek, San Carlos Reservation, Ariz., 1969.

Smithsonian, Dept. of Anthr.: 270,076.

Fig. 5. Apache painting on tanned deerskin, depicting the girl's puberty ceremony. Figures are outlined in black and colored blue, yellow, pink, and orange. Length at center 47 cm, collected before 1910, probably at Ft. Sill, Okla.

of supernatural power through a dream journey, found in Yuman curing, is also a prominent idea. However, connection with the source of power is much more indirect and abstract; the curing shaman still experiences the dream, but the practitioner of the puberty ceremony (and other Apache rituals), through the correct prestations, learns the ceremony from a specialist. During the cure and the puberty rite, the supernaturals are attracted to the situation through songs and the prescribed use of ritual paraphernalia. This is most dramatically seen when the *gą̂hę́* spirits arrive during the puberty ceremony, while in the curing rites, the ritual objects themselves symbolize the presence of powerful forces. The use of color, directional, and number symbolism, alluding to the cosmos, structures ritual actions and reinforces the connection between the ceremonial setting and the supernatural world.

Much of the action during a curing ceremony is directed toward removing evil objects or supernatural power from the patient's body. In addition, a second, more abstract process occurs, more in keeping with the nature of Apache prestation and reciprocity. Rather than being possessed with supernatural power, sent into the patient's body by the shaman, the Apache becomes identified with the supernatural. Likewise the pubescent girl, through appropriate dress and activity, becomes equated with White Shell Woman. The result of this combination of attracting the supernatural, removing intrusive influences, and identifying the patient with the sacred is to assure longevity, either in terms of a cured state for the patient or, in a puberty ceremony, long life for the young girl and blessings for the entire community.

Navajos: Reciprocity, Long Life, and a Structured Cosmos

Ritual reciprocity (or prestation), and the concomitant themes of removal and sanctification (or identification) become elaborated in the context of Navajo ceremonialism, where the cosmology and structure of rituals are more formalized and where the symbolism of song, ritual objects, and actions becomes more apparent.

Among the Navajo, power is not acquired through dreaming or the vision experience. The Navajo "singer" or medicine man is not a shaman but a priest. He learns the appropriate songs, medicines, and ritual actions necessary for curing a patient through apprenticeship

left, Ariz. Histl. Soc. Lib., Tucson: Hanna Coll.; right, Smithsonian, Dept. of Anthr. 372,990.

Fig. 6. Apache Crown Dancers. Traditional costume includes high moccasins (with upturned toes), skirts or kilts fringed and decorated with tinklers held up by a broad belt, bodies painted with specific designs, streamers with eagle feathers attached above the elbow, and elaborate hoods fitted closely over the head and tied around the neck (Opler 1941:109–110). The dancers carry pointed wooden sticks in each hand. The Crown Dancers represent mountain-dwelling spirits and their performance was used not only to keep evil spirits away but also to cure illness (Opler 1941:87). left, After painting themselves and preparing for the ceremony, the Crown Dancers move in single file down the mountain side. Costumed dancers include a clown on the far left. Photograph of Western Apache by Forman G. Hanna, Dec. 1925. right, Crown Dancer mask of wooden slats painted white, black, red, blue, and green atop a black cloth hood. The wooden wands are also painted. Height of headdress 61.0 cm, collected at White Mountain, Ariz. before 1935.

to a singer who already knows the rite he wishes to learn. Rather than a vision experience, the source of the ritual is a myth that relates how the ancestors of the Navajo acquired the ritual procedures from the supernaturals (Spencer 1957). The myth typically tells of a hero who experiences a series of misfortunes. He is aided by various supernaturals and in the process learns the ceremony that is instrumental in curing his illness or restoring conditions to their normal state. On his return, the hero teaches the ceremony to the people. There are important similarities between Apache dream-visions and Navajo myths including the visit to sacred "homes" of the supernatural and the kinds of help given. The main difference is that the Apache protagonist is a living shaman while the Navajo protagonist is a mythical figure; the Navajo hero is placed in a predicament of superhuman proportions while the Apache shaman is only seeking power. Thus, for the Navajo, the circle of reciprocity that links humans and the supernatural takes on an additional step. Prestations are given by the mythical hero to the supernatural in exchange for power. The singer offers prestations to his teacher in return for learning the ritual and, in a parallel fashion, the patient offers ritual prestations to the singer. In turn, the singer offers prestations to the supernaturals during the ceremony, attracting them to the ritual for the benefit of the patient. Then, finally, at some phase of the ceremony, the patient becomes "holy" or *diyin* (powerful) (Aberle 1967a:27).

Like the Apache, the Navajo believe that sickness is contracted by improper contact with objects that are dangerous (*báhádzid*). The list given by Wyman and Kluckhohn (1938:13, 14) is similar to Basso's (1970:37–38) list of Apache sources of illness. Wyman and Kluckhohn discuss contact in terms of "infection," but the animal (or its supernatural power) sends its weapon or arrow into the patient (Haile 1938a:648). Kaplan and Johnson (1964:208) suggest that illness is the result of possession by the "breath" or "instanding one" of the dangerous animal, witch, ghost, or natural phenomenon.

As among the Apache groups, Navajo power can be used for positive effects (restoring health) or negative ones (causing sickness through witchcraft). This is seen in two pairs of Navajo concepts, the contrast between *diyin* (becoming sacred or sanctified) and *'áńt'į́į́h*, referring to witchcraft by other human beings or the action of etiological factors such as snakes, bears, and lightning. A parallel contrast is between *hózhǫ́* and *hóchxǫ́ǫ́'*. *Hózhǫ́* is a state of "pleasant conditions," of beauty or

Denver Art Mus., Col.:Pac-2.

Fig. 7. Chiricahua Apache Crown Dancers (*gą́hę́*). Men with drums and curved drumsticks accompany the dancers. Original painting in tempera on paper by Allan Houser, Chiricahua artist, in 1953.

harmony (see Wyman and Kluckhohn 1938; Wyman 1970a:7). The prefix *ho-* indicates that it is the environment, the locale (not just an individual) that is nice, beautiful, and good. *Hóchxǫ́ǫ́'* indicates the opposite, a state of "unpleasant conditions" or "the ugly, unhappy and disharmonious environment." The purposes of a chant or sing are to counteract the "action against" the patient (*'áńt'į́įh*) and remove "ugly conditions" (*hóchxǫ́ǫ́'*), and to produce immunity by making the patient *diyin* and thus create "pleasant conditions" (*hózhǫ́*) (see "Language and Reality in Navajo World View," this vol.).

Navajo cosmology contains many of the same elements as are found among the Apache, but these are utilized in a more systematic and structured manner. The Navajo think of their cosmos as a circle where the "sky horizon edge" (*yák'ashbąąh*) meets the "earth horizon edge" (*ník'ashbąąh*). The circular horizon is divided into "light phenomena." Each has an "inner form" (*bii'gistíín*) that is male or female, and each is associated with one of the four directions and one of four colors. As one Navajo informant depicted the circle (Haile 1943a), Dawn Man (associated with whiteness) lies on the horizon from east to south; Horizontal Blue Man lies from south to west; Evening Twilight Woman (associated with yellow) lies from west to north; and Darkness Woman (associated with black) lies from north to east. The Navajo world is also bounded by four sacred mountains, each associated with a direction and a color. Four precious stones, four types of corn, and four birds are also associated with the mountains (Reichard 1945:215). The Navajo color-direction scheme has equations different from the Apache one. East is associated with white, south with blue, west with yellow and north with black. There is a definite pairing of north and black with *hóchxǫ́ǫ́'* or evil things, and of white and east with the sacred or *diyin*.

The Navajo origin myth tells of the emergence of the ancestors of the Navajo from a series of four worlds into a fifth and also includes details of the origin of Navajo clans (Yazzie 1971).† Like Apache origin stories (Opler 1969:150), the Navajo myth tells of the impregnation of Changing Woman (White Shell Woman in Apache versions) by the Sun and the birth of her twins

†Some sources imply that there were only four worlds; the confusion seems to be based on whether the flood in the fourth world led to an emergence into a fifth world or whether the waters simply receded with the people still occupying the fourth world. Other sources differ; see "Navajo Views of Their Origin," this vol.

U. of New Mexico, Santa Fe.

Fig. 8. Born for Water or *Tó Bájíshchíní* (far right), one of the slayer twins, on an 18th-century pictograph in Pine River Canyon (Los Pinos) Navajo Reservoir district, N. Mex. He is drawn in red and resembles his masked dancer impersonator (the inverted triangle on the mask is characteristic) and his representations in modern sandpaintings (Schaafsma 1966:11–12). The two gods (*yé'ii*) at the left of the panel, under the rainbow, are red, green, and white. Photographer unknown, about 1960.

U. of Ariz., Ariz. State Mus., Tucson: top, 28643; bottom, 28646.

Fig. 9. Sweat house, used for purification before many Navajo rituals. top, Sweat house being prepared; bark pieces hold colored sand used in making the small sand painting running down the side of the house. bottom, Navajo man emerging from the sweat bath. Plumed wands are on either side of the entrance. Photographs by Simeon Schwemberger, St. Michael's, Ariz., before Dec. 1905.

(fig. 8), who slay various monsters that had been endangering the people. The theme of an emergence and the notion of a layered cosmos is much more elaborated than in the Yuman cultures. The myth is more detailed: each world is associated with a particular color and, within each incident, the four colors and the four directions are utilized in patterning the events that explain the origin of important aspects of the natural environment (animal and bird species, the four sacred mountains and other important places) and of Navajo cultural items. Myths that tell the origin of each curing ceremony and the exploits of a hero—one of the *diyin dine'é* or Holy People—are filled with incidents that show how social relations between the Holy People parallel those among the Navajo themselves (Spencer 1957). There are two parallel worlds, the supernatural one, populated by the *diyin dine'é* and the social world of the *diné* or people. The pantheon of Holy People is not hierarchically structured, and there is no division of Holy People into various categories with certain prerogatives, privileges, or powers—quite different from Pueblo cosmologies. Likewise, the Navajo social world is relatively undivided, and even distinctions by age and sex, especially in the division of labor, are minimal.

Navajo ritual itself is centered on the restoration of "pleasant conditions" for the individual. Navajo chants are two, five, or nine nights in length (a "night" being counted from one sunset to the next). They are composed of component ceremonies, strung together in a specified order. Many chants include a bath, a sandpainting ritual, a sweat (fig. 9) and emetic ceremony, and an all-night sing the last night. Each component ceremony is composed of ritual acts that are directed against the etiological factor (for example, bears, snakes, lightning) causing the illness (see "Navajo Ceremonial System" and "Navajo Music," this vol.).

The Navajo model of the cosmos outlined above is expressed in the setting of the ceremony itself. The chant takes place in a Navajo hogan, which is circular like the horizon. Movement during a ritual is always clockwise or "in the direction of the sun." Men sit on the south side of the hogan; women sit on the north side. The singer sits on the southwest side and the patient, when resting, sits on the northwest side. The east (where the door is located) is associated with *diyin*; prayersticks and other offerings are deposited toward the east and the chant fetishes are arranged to face in this direction. The north is associated with *hóchxǫ́ǫ́'* and objects that have been pressed against the patient in order to remove *hóchxǫ́ǫ́'* are deposited toward the north. Each chant uses color and directional symbolism, though not always the same associations as in the cosmological model. The fourfold color-direction scheme is a condensed code for ordering and interpreting the myriad of ritual actions, using symbolic objects, that are performed during the chant. For instance, the cutting of prayersticks, the making of a sandpainting, and the text of a song-set all repeat this pattern, which, in turn, mirrors Navajo cosmology (Lamphere 1969:289).

The three themes outlined for Apache curing occur again and again throughout a Navajo ceremony: prestation through the presentation of a *yeel,* identification of the patient with the *diyin* by "applying to" or "taking in," and removal of *hóchxǫ́ǫ́'*. They are repeated in each subceremony, in each prayer, and in each song-set; however, one of these themes may be dominant or emphasized in a particular subceremony. For example, during the prayerstick ceremony, prestations are important; during the sweat and emetic ceremony, the removal of *hóchxǫ́ǫ́'* is crucial; and during a sandpainting ceremony, the identification of the patient with the *diyin* is the focus of the effort (fig. 10).

The total impact of the Navajo sing is that it brings a patient to a new state where he or she has become holy and where pleasant conditions have returned. This is often indicated at the end of a prayer or song; for example, "with pleasant conditions before me I go about" (Reichard 1944:92, line 383, retranslated), "These I have become again" (line 392), "pleasant conditions have returned" (line 396). Thus, Navajo curing is centered around the attainment of long life and the restoration of an ideal environment, often described by anthropologists in terms of universal harmony, happiness, and beauty.

Clearly, there are striking similarities between Apache and Navajo ceremonialism. Both place emphasis on the central theme of longevity, and both center on the individual, changing his or her state through prestation, removal of evil objects, and identification with supernatural power. However, there are also some important contrasts. In Navajo ritual, power is more abstract, attained through apprenticeship rather than through a vision experience. The cosmos is more structured, a bounded universe where the present world is the top of four layered worlds through which the Navajo emerged. Navajo ritual seems to replicate the cosmos more clearly, and color, sex, and directional symbolism is more fully utilized. Navajo ritual includes more agricultural symbolism as well. For example, corn pollen, as well as pollen from wild plants, is an important symbol of pleasant conditions. It is the symbol par excellence of sanctification. The sun is a more important

Natl. Geographic Soc., Washington.

Fig. 10. A Navajo priest with rattle treating an ill child. The patient is seated in the center of a Chiricahua Windway sandpainting. Photograph by John B. Breed, before 1939.

symbol than among the Apache, and the contrast between Father Sun and Mother Earth in Navajo world view reflects both agricultural influence and the importance of a male-female duality. Supernaturals representing corn (Corn Pollen Boy, Corn Beetle Girl) are important in myth and ceremony, and four domesticated plants—maize, beans, squash, and tobacco—are symbolized in many sandpaintings. During the Navajo girl's puberty rite, the central activity is grinding corn and preparing batter for a huge corn cake (*'ałkąąd*) to be baked in the ground during the last night of singing. The cake represents Mother Earth and, baked as a special offering to the Sun, brings special health and longevity to the girl (Frisbie 1967:12, 362).

Nevertheless, some of the themes prominent in Yuman and Apache ceremonialism are also important among the Navajo. Though encapsulated in a mythical contect, the theme of "the journey" to find supernatural power is still present. The myth hero travels outside the social world and gains power through contact with supernatural power located above or beyond the human arena. Mountains, mountain animals, and birds, as well as natural phenomena, are the sources of power, though they are depicted as *diyin dine'é* and contrasted to humans or *diné.* Power can be used for positive or for harmful purposes. The positive implementation of power for curing involves a reversal of the "journey to power" theme. The supernaturals are attracted—by proper prestations, songs, and prayers—to the human world to counteract those evil forces (*hóchxǫ́ǫ́'*) acting against the individual.

Pueblos: the Agricultural Cycle, the Masked Dancer, and Fertility

The Pueblo cultures of northern Arizona and New

Mexico are perhaps the best known of the agricultural groups in the Southwest. Although speaking languages of diverse affiliation (Kiowa-Tanoan, Keresan, Zuni, and Uto-Aztecan), they share a common agricultural economy, a commitment to adobe-village living, and a communally oriented religion focused on the agricultural cycle.

Pueblo ceremonialism is part of a larger group of maize ceremonies practiced throughout the Southwest, which celebrate the life cycle of Indian corn (planting, maturity, and harvest) (fig. 11). These maize ceremonies are an elaborate version of the vision situation, except that the vision itself is relegated to mythology. The officiant is a ceremonialist who has learned, not one song, but a complex ritual. According to tradition, this was dictated by the supernaturals to the first priest, who passed it on. Supernatural power in Pueblo religion has the same ambivalence—that is, the potentiality for harmfulness or for helpfulness—that is found in other Southwestern groups. However, as Underhill (1948:15–16) points out, the powers have become "differentiated and personalized, attaining almost the status of gods."

Among the Pueblos the idea of two parallel worlds, one supernatural and the other social, is taken even further than among the Navajo. The supernatural world becomes divided into classes or groups in the same way in which the social world is divided. Furthermore, there is a clear transformability of the social world into the supernatural one. In contrast to Yuman, Apache, and Navajo beliefs (where death releases the soul or "breath" to become a malevolent, sickness-producing ghost), among the Pueblo groups death transforms humans into ancestors who become supernaturals themselves. This is illustrated in table 1, which compares Tewa and Zuni cosmology.

The Hopi world view retains this same aspect of "conversion" or transformability, though without the more elaborate classes of humans and supernaturals found among the Tewa and Zuni. The Hopi cosmos is divided into an upper and a lower world, circumscribed by the sun's circuit (Titiev 1944:171–178). At death, the Hopi go to the lower world of the dead and return as kachinas. All kachinas are believed to take cloud form—to be Cloud People—and their substance (navala) is liquid that is manifested as rainfall. Navala means "spirit substance of their fathers" (see "Hopi World View," vol. 9).

The Tewa, Zuni, and Hopi cosmologies also have a horizontal, as well as a vertical, dimension, based on either the number four or six. For the Tewa, the four directions orient the horizontal plane and at the outermost edge are the four sacred mountains. Nearer the village are four sacred flat-topped hills, one in each

Mus. of N. Mex., Santa Fe: Dorothy Dunn Kramer Coll., 3314-23P.

Fig. 11. *Blessing the Seed Ceremony* as depicted in a watercolor by Gilbert Atencio (Uah-Peen) of San Ildefonso Pueblo in 1955. The Tewa summer chief blesses cultigens from each household in late Feb. or early March. This blessing will make the cultigens grow healthy and bountiful, when they are planted a month or so later. In San Juan a traditional shinny game followed the blessing of the seeds (Alfonso Ortiz, personal communication 1981).

Table 1. Examples of Pueblo Cosmologies

	Tewa		*Zuni*	
Supernatural	Moist People	*Dry Food Who Never Did Become* (souls of the Made People and all deities recognized by Tewa, some of whom appear as kachinas) *ṫowaʔê·* (6 pairs of sibling deities who were the Tewa before emergence)	Raw People (*kʔapin ʔa·hoʔʔi*)	*Sun, Moon, Earth Mother* *Rain Priests (ʔuwanam ʔa·šiwani)* (deceased human Rain Priests) *Beast Priests (wema· ʔa·šiwani)* (deceased human Beast Priests) *Bow Priests* (*ʔa·piʔła ʔa·šiwani*) (deceased human Bow Priests)
	Dry Food People	*Dry Food Who Are No Longer* (dead Dry Food People)		*Kachinas (kokko·kʷe) and ancestors in general* (*ʔa·laššina·we*)
Human	Dry Food People	*Made People* (*pa·ṫowa*) (members of moieties, medicine men, clowns, and members of Hunt, War, and Women's societies) *ṫowaʔê·* (human counterparts of supernatural *towaʔê·* *Dry Food People* (ordinary Tewa who serve in no official capacity)	Cooked People (*ʔakna ʔa·hoʔʔi*) or Daylight People (*tekʔohannan ʔa·hoʔʔi*)	*Beast Priests* (priests of medicine societies) *Bow Priests* *Ordinary Zunis* (*tewukoʔliya*)

Note: Members of each category of humans at death become members of the corresponding category in the tripartate hierarchy of supernaturals. The Zuni concepts of Raw and Cooked do not correspond exactly to the Tewa notions of Dry Food People and Raw or Moist People. The highest level of the Tewa hierarchy consists of supernaturals who never become "Dry Food People." Thus Zuni kachinas are Raw People, and Zunis are Cooked People in life but become Raw after death, while Tewa Dry Food People do not move into the equivalent category in the afterlife. Adapted from Ortiz 1969 and "Zuni Religion and World View," vol. 9.

direction, while nearer still are four sacred shrines of the directions. Finally, there are four dance plazas within the village and a sacred center of the village, "the Earth mother earth navel middle place" (see Ortiz 1969:18–21). The Zuni cosmology is based on the number six (the four cardinal directions, the zenith, and nadir) but shows the same characteristics as the Tewa one: vertical layers that correspond to horizontal distances, the use of directional symbolism associated with colors, the importance of the middle, and the internal differentiation of a human and a sacred world, each a replica of the other. The Hopi also have a system of correspondences of direction and color based on the number six. In contrast to the Zuni and Tewa models, the concept of "middle" is not centered on the village itself but in Sipapu, the place of emergence in the bottom of the Grand Canyon, west of the Hopi villages. Sipapu is represented symbolically in each kiva floor (vol. 9:568, 579). Thus, there are many middles, one in each kiva, that are replicated in various shrines in and around the village.

Thus, Pueblo cosmologies vary in form but, in comparison to the Navajo model of the universe, they are more structured. Ortiz (1972a) has summarized their characteristics as including: the setting of careful limits or boundaries of the world; a well-elaborated conception of the middle or center of the cosmos; a dominant spatial orientation characterized as centripetal or "inward"; the importance of the *axis mundi,* or central pole, as a vertical bridge between the various layers of the Pueblo cosmos; and the use of dualism, for example, between Father Sun and Mother Earth, between "raw" and "cooked," and between moiety divisions in Tewa and Keresan villages.

All these features of Pueblo cosmology are reminiscent of the shamanistic world view described earlier, except that priests of powerful societies rather than shamans are the real guardians. Hunting and curing continue to be important concerns of Pueblo ceremonialism, but the agricultural cycle becomes the central focus of most ritual activity (fig. 12). Shamanic practice appears, for example, in the spectacular magical feats performed by members of the Zuni medicine societies (Tedlock 1976). In other words, Pueblo religion seems to be based on an essentially shamanistic world view adapted to the needs of an agricultural people.

N. Mex. Dept. of Development, Santa Fe: 12,105.
Fig. 12. The Basket Dance at San Juan Pueblo, an agricultural rite. Photograph by Wyatt Davis, 1942.

Pueblo ceremonialism is coordinated in terms of a calendrical cycle where the solstices and equinoxes are the orienting points. There is an implicit dualism between the summer agricultural part of the cycle and the winter portion, when warfare and hunting are stressed (Ortiz 1969:106). Different portions of the year are emphasized by different Pueblo groups. For the Tewa, the most intense ritual period is between the autumnal and vernal equinox, while for the Hopi it is between the winter and summer solstices (Ortiz 1969:105).

Ritual involves two phases. One important set of activities revolves around the retreats and prayer sessions of the ritual specialists, which take place in the kivas. For example, the annual cycle of "works" are performed by the Made People in Tewa villages, led particularly by the Summer or Winter chief. At Zuni, the rain priests go into seclusion during the summer to establish direct contact with the *ʔuwanammi* or *ʔuwanam ʔa·šiwani* (supernatural rain priests). A second set of activities focuses on the coming of the supernaturals, the kachinas, who appear at specified times of the year and for specific rituals (fig. 13) ("Zuni Religion and World View," vol. 9).

The three themes apparent in Navajo and Apache ritual—prestation, removal, and sanctification—assume a different character in Pueblo ceremonialism, as indicated by a closer examination of priestly retreats and public dances. Pueblo relationship with the supernatural is also one of reciprocity, with the added dimension that the living take their places in the supernatural world at death. As Bunzel (1932:618) characterizes the Zuni relationship with the gods, "Zunis do not humble themselves before the supernatural; they bargain with it." Central to Pueblo ceremonialism is the offering of correct prestations: appropriate prayers, songs, and ritual objects to attract the supernaturals to the village. The most important prestation or offering is the prayerstick. As the Zuni data show, the symbolism of prayerstick offerings is quite different from that of Navajo prestations. The main offerings made by the Zuni to the "raw" people are those of food and clothing. Food is offered by Zuni women at every evening meal by throwing cooked food into the fire; other "food" offerings consist of tobacco, cornmeal tossed into the air, or large portions of food offered by men who take quantities to the river (Bunzel 1932:620). "Clothing" consists of *telikina·we* or prayersticks, small smoothed sticks to which feathers are attached. Sticks are offered by each family at the winter solstice and as part of every ceremony and are usually made to a particular supernatural (Bunzel 1932a:500).

B. Tedlock (1971) argues that the offering of prayersticks is really an act of sacrifice. The markings on the prayerstick symbolize a person—with eyes, mouth, and feathered clothing—who is called a "sacred younger sister or relative" and who stands for the maker (B. Tedlock 1971:10). The supernaturals, in accepting the prayerstick (representing both the person and clothing for the supernaturals), take the "life," "breath," "thoughts" of the prayerstick. They also hear prayers for long life, food, clothing, and good fortune. "The sacrifice is the vehicle of communication or the mediator between these people (the profane) and their gods (the sacred). The message is the paradox: a life for a life. My life (in surrogate form) for the necessities of my life" (B. Tedlock 1971:16). The gods receive the self-sacrifice and prayer that went into the making and presentation of the prayersticks, and the Zuni receive the good will of the supernaturals.

The theme of removal is much less important among the Pueblo groups, being associated mainly with curing ritual rather than with agricultural, hunting, or war ceremonies. Curing is in the hands of societies rather than the prerogative of individual medicine men. Among the Hopi, each kiva society cures diseases connected with improper contact with its paraphernalia, while Zuni and Keresan groups have distinct and important curing societies. Much curing revolves around the counteracting of witchcraft, for example, White's (1932:118–122) description of recapturing the "heart" of a patient stolen by a witch at Acoma. During the ceremony, medicine men suck intrusive objects from those present and evil is brushed away with eagle plumes dipped in ashes—both practices reminiscent of Yuman curing. The im-

left, John E. Wilson, Tulsa, Okla: Mora #178; right, Smithsonian, Dept. of Anthr.: 128.739 and 128.744.

Fig. 13. Musical instruments of the kachinas. left, White-faced Alo Manas of Walpi playing rasps for the Heheya Dance. They scrape an animal shoulderblade across the notched stick to produce the rhythmic sounds. Photograph by Jo Mora, 1904–1906. right, Hopi hand-held gourd rattles. These decorated examples are painted with pottery clay, but plain gourd rattles were also used. top right, Black design on green ground, with wooden handle and cloth wrist strap; bottom right, Buffalo rattle, black crosses on white ground with pieces of white wool attached, and wooden handle with string wrist strap. Feathers are also used as rattle decorations. Length of top right 24 cm, both collected by Matilda C. Stevenson at Mishongnovi in 1885.

portant differences are that the ceremony is communal, with most members of the village participating as patients, and that agricultural symbolism is central. The heart, rather than the soul, is the human aspect that has been taken away. It is represented by a bundle of rags containing corn kernels and is recaptured through a symbolic fight involving medicine men who represent bears and mountain lions. The heart bundle is then untied, and each member of the audience receives a kernel to eat. In the final phases of the ritual, each participant is given medicine to drink, and medicine is blown over them to drive away malevolent influences.

In contrast to the minor theme of removal, actions signaling the arrival of the supernaturals include some of the most public and dramatic aspects of Pueblo ceremonialism. The gods or kachinas are represented through masked impersonation and dancing by members of the kachina societies, one of the most important ceremonial associations among Pueblo groups. The kachina organizations are tribal-wide in all the Western Pueblos, joined by all children at Hopi, Acoma, and Laguna, but restricted to males at Zuni. The kachina society is less important among the Keresan and Tewa Pueblos and is of a completely "underground character," with dancing performed inside the kivas rather than in public plazas. At Taos, Picuris, and Isleta, masked dancing is absent from ritual. Masked impersonation plays a role in Apache and Navajo ceremonialism, but among Pueblo groups, it is part of a religion tied to the agricultural cycle, to a more elaborate cosmology, and to a configuration of symbols where fertility, as well as longevity, are important themes.

Kachinas appear in a large number and variety of Pueblo public ceremonies, but perhaps the most dramatic are those rituals that celebrate the annual coming of the supernaturals to the village (for example, the Zuni Shalako ceremony and the Tewa water-pouring ceremony) or their return to their sacred home (the Hopi Niman ceremony). The Zuni Shalako takes place at the end of the ritual year, in late November or early December before the winter solstice ceremonies. On the final day of the ceremony, five masked supernaturals arrive from the west, cross the river into the village, and plant prayersticks at six excavations representing the six kivas. They retreat to one of the new houses that has been repaired or built for the ceremony and will be blessed by the presence of the gods. Late in the afternoon, the Shalakos (six impressive birdlike figures) arrive in a procession, and each is escorted to a house that is blessed by planting prayersticks and seeds inside the threshold. During the evening, in each of the six houses a dialogue is started between the house owner and the Shalako. This songlike litany recounts the story of the creation and the migration of the Zuni people to "The Middle Place." Food is served to the Shalako, offered to the ancestors at the river, and fed to other guests. After midnight, the two Shalako impersonators take turns donning the Shalako mask and dancing while other masked supernaturals (including the Koyemshi or clowns) appear and dance also. In the morning, after a ritual washing, receiving gifts of food, and participating in a final closing ceremony, the six Shalakos and other masked supernaturals depart to their home (Kachina Village) in the west (Bunzel 1932:702–777). See "Zuni Religion and World View," volume 9, for illustrations of these ceremonies.

The coming of the supernaturals to Hopi is less dramatic and occurs in late November with the appearance of the Soyal kachina, who arrives in the village in old garments, dancing with the movements of an aged man to symbolize the belief that the kachinas are "locked up" at rest in their underworld homes during the period between the winter and summer solstice. At the last public appearance of the kachinas each year (the Niman or Home ceremony), when the dancing ends in the village plaza, the kachinas are blessed with smoke and medicine-water and are given prayer-feathers and sacred cornmeal. The Kachina clan chief makes a long speech of farewell, thanking them for past favors and praying for continued help from the supernaturals. Then the dancers are led to a special hollow shrine; the cover is lifted and each impersonator drops some of his prayerstick offerings into the shrine. The closing of the lid symbolizes the close of the kachina dances and their departure until the winter solstice, when the cycle begins again (Titiev 1944:110, 128). See "Hopi Ceremonial Organization," volume 9, for views of these ceremonies.

In the Tewa villages, supernaturals appear at the water-pouring ceremony given by either the Winter People or Summer People to mark the transition from childhood to the status of a Dry Food Person for Tewa boys and girls (Ortiz 1969:38–40). Their presence is preceded by a litany called "shouting the emergence path" where either the moiety chief or two sacred clowns trace the journey of the gods from distant lakes to the kiva. The kachinas arrive, are received by the sacred clowns, and their messages are interpreted by the moiety chief. The kachinas bless the people by "catching goodness from six directions" and passing it on to the people, who reach out and take it in. The people eat the sacred melons brought by the kachinas, and the two moiety chiefs also offer a thanksgiving prayer. The final response of the villagers emphasizes the "life of abundance" that will result from the coming of the supernaturals (Laski 1959:34–59).

These ritual pageants express the theme of the "journey" in a completely different context. In Yuman religion, the shaman journeys outside the social world to find power, and the process of curing involves the journey of supernatural power to the shaman and the patient's body. This same process became more and more stylized in Apache and Navajo curing, the journey for power even taking place in a myth in the Navajo case. Supernatural presence is realized through identification rather than possession. For the Pueblos, the supernaturals come in impressive visual form, and their arrival in the village may even dramatize the group's origin and migration to the present village. The presence of the kachina is an important occasion for feeding the supernaturals or offering other prestation in return for their blessings and good will.

In the public dances, as well as during the secret retreats that precede them, ritual actions and objects symbolize two important themes: longevity and fertility. Long life, also the goal of Navajo and Apache ritual, is found most strikingly in the Zuni concept of the "road." At birth, "the Sun Father sets the proper span for each Zuni's life and gives long roads to some and short roads to others" (Tedlock 1975:259). Zunis often end their prayers asking that their roads be completed and fulfilled, that is, that they lead long and abundant lives.

The theme of fertility is seen in the broadest sense in the desire for a life of abundance. But, more concretely, there is a concern with rain, which will bring good crops. The prevalence of water symbolism is striking in Pueblo religion, if only in contrast to the Yuman, Apache, and Navajo, where water symbolism is much less important.

Examples are numerous. The Pueblo cosmos is often bordered by oceans or lakes. In the Tewa water-pouring ceremony, the kachinas emerge from these lakes before coming to the village. Zuni prayersticks are made from red willow because willow roots are connected to a common root stock, just as Zuni springs are connected to an underground water system (B. Tedlock 1971:4; Bunzel 1932:710). The willows thus symbolize the bringing of long life and rain to humans. Sacred water is placed on Tewa altars contained in a bowl with jagged edges, indicating a cloud-shaped design. During the Cochiti Green Corn or Tablita Dance (vol. 9:373, 376) dancers use gestures that invoke the rain-bringing kachinas, lightning, clouds, fog, and growing crops (Kurath 1959:545). For the Hopi, the navala, the life-giving spiritual essence is essentially liquid, manifested as rainfall. Finally, at death, initiated Hopi and Zuni themselves become kachinas or "cloud people," who bring rain to the living.

Pima-Papago: the Shaman, the Communal Feast, and the Pilgrimage

The Piman peoples, like the Pueblos, had a set of communal rituals celebrating the life cycle of corn and focused on fertility and rainmaking; while these ceremonials have fallen into disuse, shamanism and curing have been preserved, becoming the center of traditional religion. The villages along the Gila River constituted the Pima (called 'the River People' in Pima-Papago) but, by the time Russell (1908) visited them in 1902,

Fig. 14. Santa Clara Corn (tablita) dancers. Photograph by Richard Erdoes, summer 1975.

there were only fragments of an old ceremonial cycle in evidence. Russell was able to collect versions of the origin myth, examples of oratory, and material on shamanism; but it is Underhill's (1946) fieldwork in the 1930s with the Papago (called 'the Desert People') to the south that must be consulted for a fuller picture of what the communal rituals in these loosely organized villages must have been like. Bahr et al.'s (1974) subtle and extensive analysis of a Papago shaman's theory of illness gives a clearer picture of Papago curing, which remained viable on the Arizona reservations in the 1960s.

Supernatural power was acquired in several ways by Piman men and a few women; some individuals became powerful shamans (*má:kai*), while others remained laymen who could use their songs for curing. In the nineteenth century, shamans performed magic feats in relation to warfare, hunting, and rainmaking, while in the twentieth century they have become private diagnosticians and healers. Russell (1908:257–258) gives several examples of the hereditary passing of power from father to son, but the most frequent method of gaining power was visionary. Like the Yumans, power was acquired through a dream vision while the recipient was asleep, rather than in a waking state as among some of the Plains cultures. In some dreams, the supernatural visitor, in animal form, takes the recipient on a journey to the mountains or to the sea (Underhill 1939:169); but often the dream is more "stationary," with the spirit instructing the dreamer. As one shaman expresses it, the animal "appears" (in visions) and "confronts" the person, teaching him songs and other knowledge (Bahr et al. 1974:308).

For the Papago, these dreams often came as a result of contact with powerful supernatural forces through slaying an enemy, killing an eagle, or taking a salt pilgrimage. (Among the Pima, only warfare was elaborated as a source of power.) All three activities took the individual outside the social world, placing him in contact with the supernatural and necessitating a purification ritual on return home (Underhill 1946:192–252). Afterward, an individual might be visited by an animal spirit who becomes his tutelary and source of power (see Underhill 1946:268). Songs acquired through these visions are often taught to other Papago men, who sing them during curing rituals (Bahr et al. 1974:242).

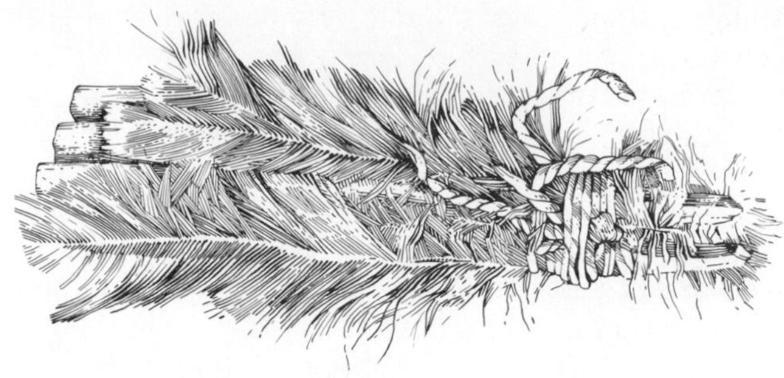

Smithsonian, Dept. of Anthr.: 218,057.

Fig. 15. Pima medicine sticks (*ʔo·mina*), an important part of a shaman's equipment. Always bundled together, with string (as here) or cloth. This set of 4 is sharpened at one end and painted green. Originally each stick had feathers attached. The sticks would be distributed at feasts to ensure health with some being buried later, to keep fields moist (Lumholtz 1912:107). Length 16.0 cm, collected by Frank Russell in 1901–1902.

The Piman universe is not highly structured. The origin myth tells of the creation of the earth by Earthmaker, a subsequent flood from which the supernaturals escape, and the final prominence after emergence of *ʔIʔitoi* 'Elder Brother' who creates the Pimans and their neighbors, teaching them various arts and ceremonies (Underhill 1946:8–12; Russell 1908:206–230). In subsequent episodes, *ʔIʔitoi* is killed and revived many times, an example of the "dying god" theme also found in Yuman mythology. In fact, the origin myth combines elements prevalent in Yuman and California mythology with other themes (such as the flood and the emergence) that are found in Pueblo and Navajo origin stories (Underhill 1946:12–13). The number four is prominent in both myth and ritual and there is some use of color symbolism, but Piman cosmology is relatively "unshaped" in clear contrast to the elaborate Navajo and Pueblo use of number, color, and direction to orient ritual and replicate the universe in a ceremonial context.

Piman rituals of diagnosis and curing, on the surface, seem similar to Yuman practices, but the theory of illness recalls Navajo and Apache curing. Piman 'staying sickness' (*ká·cim múmkidag*), much like Navajo and Apache sickness, is caused by dangerous objects or parts of dangerous objects. These include animals (coyote, deer, bear, rabbit, dog), birds (hawk, eagle), some insects and rodents, and some natural phenomena (cloud, lightning). All have both "strength" and "way," which sicken people. When a patient misbehaves toward one of these dangerous objects, he is said to have trespassed on the "way" of that object. As a result, the "strength" of that class of objects will create symptoms of illness within the patient's body (Bahr et al. 1974:21). As in the Apache system, it is not a particular animal, bird, or object that causes sickness but an impersonal, abstract "power," or strength, of that kind of object.

In practice, various "strengths" from different objects may enter the patient's body and only at a later date cause the person to become ill. The task of the shaman is initially that of diagnosis: to "see" the various strengths and disambiguate them, since they may have penetrated the body in various ways and become layered within it. Two kinds of diagnosis are possible, a shorter ritual performed during the day (*kúlañmada*) and a longer ritual (*dóajida*) performed during an entire night. Both involve diagnosis by "blowing"; the shaman's own breath is augmented by blowing tobacco smoke over the patient's body and, in some cases, by fanning the body with an eagle feather or by using a divining crystal. All these actions "illuminate" the strengths within the patient's body and may lead to a cure if the "strength" does not show up again (Bahr et al. 1974:189). The songs the shaman sings make his tutelary spirits happy and draw them from their mountain haunts, so that they communicate the nature of the illness to the shaman (Bahr et al. 1974:182). After disambiguating the strengths, sucking is done in order to manipulate the strengths and extract them from the patient's body. See "Pima and Papago Medicine and Philosophy," this volume.

The Piman curing ceremony is performed by laymen rather than a shaman; it does not involve sucking, but blowing and singing are important ritual acts. In contrast to the shaman's diagnosis, the songs sung by the curer (which have been learned) persuade the spirit to stop causing the illness. Blowing, rather than illuminating the strengths, also persuades spirits and introduces "breath" into the patient's body to cure the illness. Fetishes are also pressed onto the body to introduce the curative strength of the fetish (Bahr et al. 1974:220–221). In other words, during a *dóajida,* the shaman brings a spirit (usually the tutelary from whom he learned the song) into the curing setting and pulls the strengths out of the body once they are "illuminated" and separated from each other. The symbolism is one of penetration and removal. The curing ritual, in contrast, is "prayerful." When the curer sings the songs the spirit likes to hear, the spirit responds automatically and brings its skill to bear on the illness, causing the strengths within the patient's body to cease or diminish (Bahr et al. 1974:230). The curer is concerned with asking for help on the patient's behalf rather than grappling with the sickness directly (Bahr et al. 1974:232). This ritual exhibits indirect and reciprocal relationships comparable to those between Navajo singers and the supernatural rather than the directness of shamanism of the Yuman type. In the Papago case, as well as the Navajo, power to cure has become more abstract; the songs are learned (though, for the Papago, they ultimately come from a vision experience) and the spirits are petitioned with the proper song. A sort of bargain or reciprocal relationship is struck.

In contrast to this individualized curing system, many of the Papago villages, even as late as the 1930s, held one or more of the communal ceremonies centered around the themes of fertility and rainmaking. Each traditional Papago village had a Rain House (*wáʔaki*) or ceremonial shelter lived in by the Keeper of the Smoke, the most prominent village leader, and his family (Underhill 1946:233). This ceremonial house was large enough to hold all the older men of the village and was used for the brewing of liquor for the summer rainmaking ceremony. Each village had a fetish bundle wrapped in eagle down and kept in a basket in the hills away from the village. The village officials included a crier, war leader, hunt leader, and game leader. This set of hereditary offices was extremely flexible compared to the hierarchy and range of secret societies found among the Pueblos. Songs and speeches, which were an important part of each ceremony, were performed by ordinary men of the village ("Pima and Papago Social Organization," fig. 1, this vol.) rather than by initiates into secret societies or a hierarchy of priests.

Prominent among the rituals of the old ceremonial cycle in the Papago villages were the rainmaking ceremony, ceremonies to promote the growth of corn, and the *wí·gida* 'Prayerstick Festival' ("History of the Papago," fig. 3, "Kachinas and Masking," fig. 5, this vol.). The rainmaking ceremony, performed in July of each year, involved the fermenting and drinking of a liquor made from the fruit of the giant cactus. "The idea is that the saturation of the body with liquor typified and produces the saturation of the earth with rain" (Underhill 1946:41). Songs and speeches made during the two-day fermentation process and the final drinking ceremony establish the purpose of the ceremony as a petition for rain and allude to the association between drinking, white clouds, and rain. At the high point of the ceremony, the cactus liquor is offered to each of four men representing the four directions with the exhortation: "Drink, friends! Get beautifully drunk! Hither bring the wind and the cloud" (Underhill 1946:59).

In the period following the rainmaking ceremony, when the corn was planted and growing, some Papago villages held ceremonies to "sing up the corn." These may have involved replenishing a shrine or, more usually, included the singing of "scraping stick" songs, which describe the growing of corn and the coming of rain. The Prayerstick Festival was held every four years at the village of Achi, Arizona, and a similar ceremony was held at Quitovaca, Sonora, every August. This elaborately planned ceremony, "to keep the world in order," took 10 days of preparation in which men from each of the five participating villages composed songs and prepared prayersticks made from turkey down (symbolizing rain and renewal). The central event was a day-long pageant in which masked dancers from each village paraded around the ceremonial plaza, each group carrying an effigy (usually a cloud or mountain) while singing the specially composed songs that referred to the image. Other important participants were corn dancers, corn sprinklers who blessed cornmeal on participants and spectators by throwing cornmeal, masked dancers representing the Sun and Moon, and ceremonial clowns (or *náwijhu*) who had the power to cure and grant special favors. At the end of the ceremony, the prayersticks were distributed to villagers (at least to the older men) and were kept in storerooms or houses for good luck.

Without the complex ceremonial organization of the Pueblos, these Papago ceremonies utilized much of the same symbolism. Masked dancers were present at the Prayerstick Festival but, except for the clowns and the Sun and Moon figures, they did not represent particular supernaturals. There were village leaders and officials for particular ceremonies, but there was no hierarchical arrangement of these offices, which, in turn, replicated a supernatural hierarchy. However, the use of prayersticks, the importance of cloud and water symbolism ("History of the Papago," fig. 5, this vol.), the use of corn sprinkling as a blessing, and the association of feathers and water all recall symbols utilized in Pueblo ritual. Underhill (1946) refers to these ceremonies as communal food ceremonies, stressing their celebratory aspect more than the presence of supernatural forces. The Hopi Niman ceremony, the Zuni Shalako, and the Tewa water-pouring ceremony focus on the pilgrimage of the supernaturals into the human world. Papago religion stresses this theme, as well as its opposite: the pilgrimage of humans outward toward a supernatural source. The quest for power took men out of the Papago village (to kill an enemy, slay an eagle, or find salt) to confront power away from home. In addition, these journeys, especially the Papago salt pilgrimage, seem to fuse individual encounters with power (important in the shamanic side of Papago religion) and the community need for rain and good crops.‡ The salt pilgrimage incorporated the symbolism of individual power dreams with the symbolism of agricultural plenty as represented by planting prayersticks along the pilgrimage route, throwing cornmeal on the waves of the ocean, and casting prayersticks into the sea. On the one hand, the men who went on the salt pilgrimage had to undergo hardships and individual tests of strengths, such as running along the beach, advancing into the ocean (viewed by the Papago as the edge of the world and fraught with power and death); on the other hand, the speeches and songs sung on the journey mix the imagery of clouds, water, feathers, smoke, and rain. Again, the aspects of a shamanic world view combine

‡Salt pilgrimages are described for Zuni, Hopi, Cochiti, and Laguna, but they were not so elaborate as those of the Papago.

Kachinas and Masking

JAMES SEAVEY GRIFFITH

One of the most striking and dramatic aspects of Southwestern Indian religion, at least in the eyes of outside observers, is the use of masks. Much of the surviving ceremonialism features masking in one form or another. A large number of the major ethnographic documents refer at least in passing to the use of masks. A dramatic exchange in the professional literature was brought about by a difference of opinion between Parsons (1930), who felt masking to be a Spanish introduction, and Beals (1932), White (1934), and others, who felt it to be aboriginal in origin. Later investigations have borne out the latter viewpoint but have left open the strong possibility that much of the masking now visible in the Greater Southwest has a pre- or postcontact origin in Mexico.

There are two main masking traditions in the area. The first and oldest is of pre-Hispanic date. It is obvious that Pueblo, Apache, Navajo, and Papago masking are all related. It also appears that the Pueblo area has seen this tradition for the longest time and was the staging area from which mask use spread to the other groups. There is another group of ceremonies that is equally obviously of European origin. These ceremonies and the masked participants that they feature have analogues in Mexican and Western European folk practices. They include impersonations such as the Sandaro of Santo Domingo as well as the masked clowns that appear in Matachine ceremonies.

In addition to these two categories of masking, there is also a body of characters and ceremonies that appears to be the result of Spanish reinterpretations of aboriginal kachinalike personages. The prime examples of these are the *fariseos* of the Yaqui and Mayo of Northwest Mexico. (The *fariseos* of other groups such as the Lower Pima and the Opata may well be simple Spanish introductions.)

Precontact Masking

It is indisputable that some form of masking existed in the Greater Southwest in pre-Hispanic times. Kiva paintings (Smith 1952; Dutton 1963), petroglyphs (Dockstader 1954:34–38), and pottery from the Mimbres area (Cosgrove and Cosgrove 1932:229, 230) all unite in providing evidence in support of this conclusion. (Much of this evidence was not available at the time of Parsons's strongest statements on behalf of a Spanish origin for Southwest masking. In later publications she modified her opinions in order to comply with new evidence as it appeared.) Most of this evidence comes from periods later than A.D. 1000.

It should also be stated that no actual masks have been found. This is not surprising, considering the perishable nature of the materials from which contemporary masks are made as well as the fact that among the present-day Hopi, for example, masks are neither buried with their owners nor are they left behind at abandoned sites. Instead they are used until they are worn out and then discarded in unrecognizable condition (Dockstader 1954:33). Papago masks are left out in the desert to disintegrate (Steen 1937). On the other hand, Yaqui *čapayeka* masks are buried with members of the society, as are Zuni, Laguna, and Jemez kachina masks (Parsons 1939, 1:342). At any rate, all present evidence for prehistoric mask use comes from representations of masked beings.

Of the available evidence, petroglyphs are at once the most prolific and the hardest to date ("Prehistory: Eastern Anasazi," fig. 14, vol. 9). Several sites containing recognizable kachina masks have been found, both in the Hopi area and in West Texas. Another source is pottery. Mimbres sherds with obviously masked personages date from about 950 to perhaps 1350. Finally, polychromed kiva murals show masked figures. Two sets of murals, from Awatovi, Arizona ("Hopi Prehistory and History to 1850," figs. 6–7, vol. 9) (Smith 1952), and Pottery Mound, New Mexico, are particularly rich in representations of apparently masked figures. Dockstader (1954:44–53) has dealt extensively with the possible correspondences between Awatovi figures and contemporary Hopi kachinas; these can only be described as imprecise but tantalizing.

What is the origin of the masked deities of the Southwest? It is most likely that they were introduced into the area from elsewhere. There are string similarities between various aspects of the ceremonial material culture of the Pueblo area and that of Casas Grandes, Chihuahua. Similar fetishes, human figurines, and painted representations of ceremonially attired individuals that are found in both areas (Sayles 1936:56, 57; DiPeso 1974, 2:546–580) point to a probable strong

Smithsonian, NAA: 41,317.

Fig. 1. Zuni kachinas, probably as they appear in the Navajo Dance ("Zuni Religion and World View," fig. 7, vol. 9). Top row, fourth from left, is a yeibichai, wearing shirt and trousers, mask with eagle wing feathers tipped with ribbon streamers, and a spruce collar, and holding a young deer in his hand. The central figure in the bottom row is probably a *heheʔa* kachina, whose mask shows tears from eyes and a crooked mouth, and who wears a rabbitskin around his neck and a dark breechclout. The figures on the far right (both rows) are Koyemshi clowns. (Identifications from Bunzel 1932:1077–1078, 1082–1083, pls. 54, 57; Dennis Tedlock, communication to editors 1982.) Pencil and crayon drawing by an unidentified Zuni artist, 24.2 by 30.1 cm; probably collected by Frank Hamilton Cushing, 1879–1884.

connection. In the light of known Central Mexican influence in the Casas Grandes area, it is likely that the Casas Grandes people influenced the Southwesterners, rather than the other way around. DiPeso (1969) postulates programs of heavy trade, accompanied by deliberate religious proselytization.

The thinking of many contemporary scholars appears to involve several clusters of material and ceremonial traits coming into the Southwest from Mexico at different times (Ferdon 1955; Brown 1967, 1971; Di Peso 1969). The probable distribution point for cultural influences heading north was Casas Grandes, Chihuahua. More archeological work will be necessary before anything resembling the full story can be ascertained.

Anderson (1955:417) says that the kachina performances are probably not very old, although they definitely predate the Spanish conquest. It is a fact that rasps, the musical instruments most heavily associated with the kachinas, first appear in the area at around A.D. 1200, which is also close to the date for the first appearance of masked beings on pottery (Brown 1971:375). There is petroglyphic evidence that masks were introduced into the Mimbres area from the south after A.D. 900 (Schaafsma 1972). This earlier date might reflect a sequence of diffusion, with the Mimbres area receiving the ceremonies first. Anderson (1960:377) feels that Zuni is probably the most important surviving local source for most of the kachina ideas. Thus, there

top, U. of Ariz., Ariz. State Mus., Tucson: 858; bottom, Amer. Mus. of Nat. Hist., New York: (left to right) 50.1/4796, 50.1/4666, 50.1/4815, 50.1/4575.

Fig. 5. Papago *wí·gida* ceremony. top, Procession at Achi (Santa Rosa), Ariz., with masked singers in the foreground and the *nánawijhu* clowns (pl.; *náwijhu* sg.) behind them. At least two "floats" are visible to the right, possibly depicting a bird and Baboquivari Mountain. There were about 75 dancers, many with their arms and legs painted with white clay. Photograph probably by Rosamond Norman, Dec. 1921 (Norman 1960:98–101). bottom left, Clown mask, with canvas hood painted with black designs on the front symbolizing clouds, a large feather headdress attached to the top, horsehair braids tied with red cloth, and a canvas-backed red flannel flap, hanging from the crown down the back. A belt with tinklers was worn around the clown's waist, and around the ankles rattles made from cocoons of the giant silkmoth—both reminiscent of Yaqui and Mayo clown costuming. Comical items carried by the clowns include a wooden machete (tucked into the belt), a bow of crooked mesquite, and arrows of saguaro ribs. bottom right, Gourd masks, worn by singers, divided into 3 zones—the top is painted with red ocher, the central band is bluish-black (a mixture of mesquite and iron oxide), and the lower portion is white (chalk). The white dots in the upper band symbolize corn kernels, and the zigzags, clouds. In the white area, clouds and lightning are represented. The upper body of the singers is nude and the lower covered with a shawl or scarf; they also wear cocoon ankle rattles (Lumholtz 1912:92–98). Length of bottom left, about 100 cm, bottom right 18 cm, rest to same scale; all collected by Carl Lumholtz at Santa Rosa, 1909–1910.

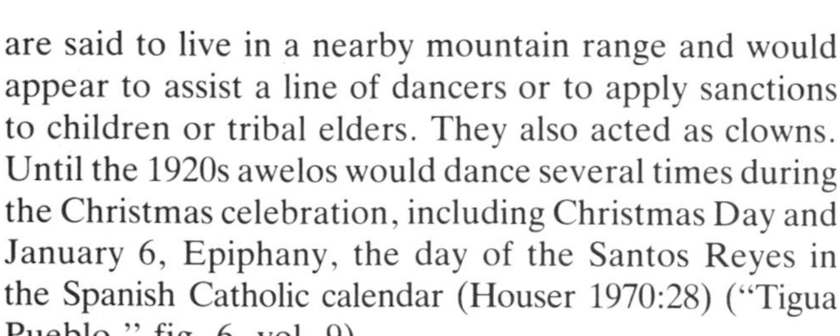

are said to live in a nearby mountain range and would appear to assist a line of dancers or to apply sanctions to children or tribal elders. They also acted as clowns. Until the 1920s awelos would dance several times during the Christmas celebration, including Christmas Day and January 6, Epiphany, the day of the Santos Reyes in the Spanish Catholic calendar (Houser 1970:28) ("Tigua Pueblo," fig. 6, vol. 9).

Papago, Navajo, Apache

The Papagos of southern Arizona and northern Sonora used masks on at least two occasions. One of these, the so-called Northern *wí·gida*, used to be held every four years near the village of Santa Rosa, in Arizona (Hayden 1937). This ceremony, which took place in the autumn, featured singers with perforated gourd face masks, clowns (*náwijhu*) with sack masks covering the entire head, and other performers (fig. 5). The main event of the ceremony was a procession including the masked figures as well as other people carrying "floats" or portable displays of a symbolic nature. Many of the features of the ceremony were strongly reminiscent of, and quite possibly derived from, various aspects of Pueblo ceremonialism. Another ceremony, also called the *wí·gida*, was held every August in Quitobac, Sonora. It also featured masked clowns. A final ceremony involving masked clowns and a small boy wearing a snouted case mask was held occasionally at Big Fields, to the east of the other two places (Underhill 1946:135–161; Jones 1971). All these events point to a strong tradition of masked processions and clowns that was probably of northern origin.

Navajos and Apaches also have masked ceremonies whose ultimate origins probably lie with Pueblo kachinas. It is fairly well established among anthropologists that Navajo masking, which includes the appearance of a group of gods during one night of the Night Chant ceremony ("Navajo Music," fig. 6, this vol.), was learned from Pueblo Indians in the period following the 1680 Pueblo Revolt (Underhill 1948:40). The Apache crown dancers (Western Apache *gaan, gáán,* "Southwestern Ceremonialism," fig. 6, this vol.) with their concealed faces and tablita headdresses are probably also of Pueblo origin.

U. of Ariz., Ariz. State Mus., Tucson: 15814.
Fig. 6. Manso Matachine dancers from San José, Ciudad Juárez, Chihuahua. The young girls in white dresses are the Malinches. Behind them stand the fiddler in street clothes and hat, and the masked clown with a bushy beard and mustache, which was typical of this type of clown mask before the mid-1960s. Since then, a wider range of mask variation has been observed. Photographed around 1900.

Spanish-Derived Masking in New Mexico

When the Spaniards arrived in the Southwest, they brought with them a form of Christian worship that permitted the use of popular ceremonialism and drama. Dance and drama had been important parts of worship in both Spain and Mexico prior to the conquest, and their importance continued with the Christianization of Mexico. In fact, both were recognized as valuable educational techniques in the business of conversion (McAndrew 1965:216–219). Therefore, the explorers and early colonists of New Mexico were well aware of masking both as a part of their own ceremonial lives and as a device for dramatizing various stories of the Christian tradition. Consequently, one can still find traditions of European-derived masking among both the aboriginal and Spanish populations of that area.

The occasions for masking are usually saints' day celebrations. The most common masked personage who appears is the clown, often a solo figure, who accompanies the Matachine dance groups of both Indian and Spanish-American fiestas (figs. 6–7). This clown is usually dressed in old clothes and often wears a bearded mask. He can carry a whip or some weapon. A rag doll is often attached to his costume or carried in his hand. His function is usually that described for the grandfathers of Isleta Pueblo. He makes the long hours of dancing easier for his presence, while also easing the burden of the spectator. He interacts with dancer and spectator alike, often speaking in a falsetto voice. These clowns have various names including *diablo* 'devil' and *viejo de la danza* 'old man of the dance'. They are, in fact, found all over Mexico in association with Matachine dances (Kurath 1949; Griffith 1969). There is, apparently, no feeling that these clowns become anything other than men during the masking process.

There are other Spanish-derived masks used by Pueblo groups in New Mexico, as well. The Pecos Bull

Mus. of N. Mex., Santa Fe.
Fig. 7. San Ildefonso Matachine dancers, Dec. 25, 1950. The Matachines have formed a barrier with their 3-pointed wands; the Monarca and then the Malinche will step over the sticks. The Abuelo or clown and his small masked apprentice are in the foreground. Photograph by John L. Champe.

("Pecos Pueblo," fig. 6, vol. 9) (Brown 1962), the bull impersonators that accompany many Indian Matachine groups (Robb 1961:96), and the Santo Domingo Sandaro dancers are among these. The Sandaro ceremony is put on annually in late January or early February by alternating kivas. Like other ceremonies in the Pueblo, it is preceded by a four-day retreat for the participants. These include Santiago and San Geronimo with hobby horses, a bull impersonator, and a double file of unmasked "Spanish soldiers." These dance in the morning, after which all are fed. Then the bull is fought in turn by pairs of soldiers, San Geronimo, and finally by Santiago, who kills him. The ceremony ended, the Sandaro return "to Mexico." Santiago and San Geronimo visit horse corrals in order to convey some of their power to the horse herds on their way out of town (White 1935:149–155). While the use of masks is confined to the bull impersonator (the Sandaro have blackened faces and long beards), this is an excellent example of a European-derived ceremony as performed by Pueblo Indians.

Northwest Mexico

The picture in Northwest Mexico is somewhat different from that presented in the American Southwest. There were connections between Zuni and the Opata country in late prehistoric times (Hammond and Rey 1940:67–72). Although the first historic reference to mask use in the Yaqui-Mayo area is comparatively late (Beals 1932a:217) and may possibly refer to an imported Spanish custom, there are bits of evidence that point to an earlier occurrence of masking, though possibly not to a continuum. Small pottery faces called miniature masks have been found in prehistoric sites in Sinaloa (Ekholm 1946:85–87; I.T. Kelly 1945:141). Such masks have occurred in much of Mesoamerica over a long period of time (De Borhegyi 1955). The fact that they are not currently used in Sonora and Sinaloa may be due to the withdrawal and later destruction of Mesoamerican culture in that area in late prehistoric and early historic times. Another suggestion lies in the fact that contemporary Yaqui and Mayo pascola masks are decorated with a variation of the paint cloisonné method, which was used prehistorically in the area (Ekholm 1946:91–96). This and other evidence, when considered as a whole, points to the existence of pre-Hispanic masking in the area, probably derived from the north.

The historic record is also different from that in New Mexico. Religious conversion was undertaken in the seventeenth century by members of the Society of Jesus, whose policies toward native ceremonialism were different from those of the Franciscans, who were entrusted with the Indians of New Mexico. A good deal of native ritual was permitted to survive in syncretic and reinterpreted form, thus presenting a picture far different from that in New Mexico, where compartmentalization is the rule (Dozier 1961:175).

The most important and widespread of the syncretic ceremonies of Northwest Mexico is the Lenten and Easter cycle, which is found in some form among the Yaqui, Mayo, Lower Pima, Papago, Opata, Tarahumara, Cora, and Huichol. The Yaqui ceremony, which has been the most thoroughly discussed in print, will be presented here as a basis for comparative discussion.

During Lent, beginning with the first Friday, each Yaqui village in Sonora and Arizona is the scene of a late afternoon or evening Friday procession. These processions, called *konti*s or 'surroundings' (Spicer 1954:139), are made up of members of various village religious sodalities and follow the stations of the cross through the village. The *konti*s are accompanied by one or more masked beings called *čapayekam*, or 'slender-nosed ones' (Spicer 1954:91). Each *čapayeka* wears a case mask, usually painted white, with horns, ears, and a long nose attached (fig. 8). It is further painted with eyes, mouth, and geometric designs in red and black. The *čapayeka* carries a wooden sword and dagger. A blanket or overcoat, a belt of deer-hoof rattles, trousers, sandals, and leg rattles complete the costume. Around his neck he wears a wooden rosary, the cross of which is held between the teeth while he is masked.

The *čapayeka* is a sinister (and left-handed) yet comic character. His role in the drama is to find, capture, and crucify Christ. He is defeated only in the final charge on the church. This takes place on Holy Saturday morning and is followed by an all-night fiesta. The *čapayekam* have an important role in village organization as well, for they, along with unmasked members of the same general ceremonial group, assume total control of religious and temporal affairs for the duration of Lent. Like the kachinas, they are present for a fixed season including the spring, and like them they exert a certain amount of social control during their stay. They are alien creatures, organized as soldiers, who behave in a structured manner, often in direct opposition to the way things usually are or should be. They never speak and at their funniest are always threatening. A good deal of ceremonial restraint and precaution is involved with assumption of the role of *čapayeka*. A man becomes a *čapayeka* as the result of a lifelong commitment made by himself or his parents, usually on the occasion of a cure.

The *čapayekam* grow in numbers and confidence during Lent, appearing at each *konti*. During Holy Week, they take a leading role in the drama, capturing and crucifying Christ, charging the church, being defeated (by being pelted with flowers), and removing their masks. After this, the ceremonial focus shifts to other groups, and the prevailing mood changes to one of light and joy. The *čapayekam* and other members of their

Edward H. Spicer, Tucson, Ariz.

Fig. 8. Yaqui *čapayekam*. left, Playing and communicating by pantomime with each other by rapping their painted wooden sticks together as they wait for a Friday Lenten procession to begin. The costume includes a belt hung with deer or pig hoof rattles that are used in their sign language and an elaborate mask, each unique (Spicer 1980:110–113). Behind the *čapayekam* stand unmasked *fariseos*. right, A typical pose while listening for the name of the Virgin Mary in a church service; if it is heard the *čapayeka* will shiver and pretend to wipe himself clean. Photographs by David J. Jones, Jr., at the plaza of the Church of San Ignacio, Old Pascua Village, Tucson, Ariz., March 1937.

group do not appear for another year, although they remain in charge of fiesta arrangements until Easter Sunday (Crumrine 1977:87–97).

The Yaquis are not the only group to give this sort of drama, although the Yaqui ceremony is more intense and in many ways the least Europeanized of its kind. Mayos in northern Sinaloa and southern Sonora have essentially the same cycle, with the masked characters being called *fariseos* or *judíos* (Pharisees or Jews) (fig. 9) (Crumrine 1977). Tarahumaras and Lower Pimas employ *fariseos* during Holy Week, but they are unmasked (Bennett and Zingg 1935:312–317). Cora *fariseos* are masked (fig. 10), but only on the culminating days of the ceremony (Hinton 1972). In the mountain valleys of eastern Sonora, the drama is produced by mestizo descendants of Ópatas (fig. 11), Lower Pimas, and Upper Pimas, with occasionally a greater emphasis on spoken dramatic lines during Holy Week. In Toníchi, Sonora, for example, Pontius Pilate, Saint Veronica, and the Virgin Mary all have spoken lines. The *fariseos* are still masked clowns, who still suffer public penance on Holy Saturday, after their unmasking. In the Sonora and Moctezuma valleys most ceremonies have been attenuated and expelled from the mission towns of their origin, presumably at the request of the priest and other "decent" townsfolk. This is usually due to the fact that masking for many *fariseos* is an excuse for license and drunkenness. The farthest north the ceremony has traveled is Cowlik, Arizona, on the Papago Reservation, where immigrants from Sonora produced a Holy Week ceremony complete with masked *fariseos* (fig. 12) but lacking in the Christian narrative elements (except for the burning of Judas). This practice apparently originated in the early twentieth century and continued through the 1930s.

Another masked figure appearing in Sonora and Sinaloa is the pascola of the Yaqui and Mayo (fig. 13). This dancer, whose name is a hispanicization of the Cahitan name (Mayo *pahkóˀola* 'old man of the fiesta'), appears at all Yaqui and Mayo fiestas. He opens and closes the fiesta and, by his clowning and dancing, provides a public focus of attention for the ceremony. The pascola is possibly not strictly a masked performer, as his black wooden face mask is worn over the face only at certain times during his public appearance. At other times it is worn on the back or side of the head, or over the shoulder (Griffith and Molina 1980).

Yaqui and Mayo pascolas are involved with a "religion of the woods" (Beals 1945:190) and derive much of their power from a non-Christian supernatural world. They wear distinctive costumes, which include black wooden face masks that feature long white beards and brows and often have an open mouth, with tongue and teeth visible. They can represent human or goat faces. They almost always have painted or inlaid crosses on the forehead (Griffith 1967, 1972).

Although the pascola and his dances have diffused to other peoples in Northwest Mexico, the Yaqui and Mayo are the only ones who employ special masks and costumes and the only group whose pascolas are in-

bottom, Taylor Mus., Colorado Springs Fine Arts Center, Colo.: left 7117, center 7126; right, Smithsonian, Dept. of Anthr.: 420,819.

Fig. 9. Mayo *fariseos*. top left, Clowning on Palm Sunday, April 7, 1968, in Charay, Sinaloa. Throughout the area, religious clowning frequently has a sexual theme. The mock phallus here is the wooden machete carried by one of the *fariseos*. Masks of the 3 main types found in Sinaloa are visible: all hide, hide with wooden features appended, and masks with wooden faces inserted into the hide case. Other traditional costume details include shawl and blanket, cane rattle belt, locally made sandals, and cocoon leg rattles. top right, At Capomos, Sinaloa, on Good Friday, April 12, 1968. *Fariseos* are carrying the Holy Cross of the village down from the hill where it normally lives, after having "shot" it with a skyrocket tied to the barrel of a B.B. gun. Later it will be placed on a bier and mourned. The cross is on the litter in the center of the picture, being held in place by a rawhide whip around its "throat." The masked individual in the left foreground is the military leader of the *fariseos*. The unmasked man in the rear is the sponsor of the *fariseos* for this year. Photographs by James S. Griffith. bottom left and center, Hide helmet-type masks typically worn by *judíos* or *fariseos*. bottom left, mask made of brown goatskin with the several dehaired areas decorated with red, blue, and green ink. In the Mochicahui area of Sinaloa there are mask-making specialists and a distinctive style is produced with a goatskin case but carved wooden face (Griffith 1967a). bottom center, Human female face (human male, devils, and pigs are also carved) painted pink with facial features also painted on and a headdress of colored tissue and crepe paper. bottom right, Portion of ankle rattles worn by clowns made of the cocoon of the giant silk moth (*Rothschildia jorulla*) with inserted pebbles, tied in pairs along a hemp cord. bottom left, Height about 35.6 cm, rest to same scale. Masks collected by James S. Griffith in 1967, left made by Manuel Savala, San Miguel Zapotitlan, Sinaloa; center, collected by Donald Cordy in Júpare, Sonora, in 1963.

Arizona State Mus., Tucson: Hinton Coll.

Fig. 10. Cora *judíos* on Good Friday, April 15, 1960, in Jesús María, Nayarit. These characters, analogous to Sonoran *fariseos*, are also called soldiers of the 'centurion'. The 3 masks in the picture are of papier-mâché, a craft introduced to the village by a Mexican government program in the 1940s. Other masks in the same village may be of hide or of wood, or they may be commercially produced rubber "monster masks." The stripes on the body (which, like the masks, are of different colors on the different days of Holy Week) present an interesting similarity with body stripes on Pueblo clowns, Tarahumara *fariseos*, and some Mayo *fariseos*. Note also the typical Cora woven bags and the tortoise-shell rattles at each man's waist. Photograph by Thomas B. Hinton.

volved in a separate religious cult. Among other groups such as the Tarahumara and Papago, the pascola simply serves as a clown and dancer whose appearance enlivens certain fiestas. Yaqui and Mayo pascolas can also appear at non-Indian fiestas and even at secular celebrations.

Masks in Representational Art

Although there is some evidence for the prehistoric manufacture of kachina figurines (Dockstader 1954:99), the earliest known historic kachina doll was collected at Hopi in 1852 by Ten Broeck (Dockstader 1954:101). These earliest dolls were flat wooden slabs with little carved detail. While later Hopi kachina figures have been more elaborately carved, possibly in part as a response to the heavy demand from Anglo collectors and scientists (Dockstader 1954:104), the slab figures are still produced. They are the more common type of doll in the eastern Pueblos (Harvey 1963), although a few fully carved figurines are currently being made in these villages for sale to Anglos.

The Hopi kachina doll (*tíhi*) is traditionally carved of cottonwood root, coated with a layer of kaolin, and painted (Colton 1959; Wright 1977). In addition to the slab-shaped doll, there are two other styles, showing more elaborate carving. The older "kachina doll" is usually depicted in a static position, with the arms simply raised out from the body and the legs separated by a notch. The more modern "kachina statuette" depicts the kachina in a more dynamic pose, often engaged in some typical activity. All three styles of carving place the heaviest artistic emphasis upon the details of the head and face. The Zuni doll is similar in appearance to the second of these three Hopi styles, except that it is usually given more slender proportions and has movable arms and feet. Zuni dolls are usually dressed in miniature costumes, while the costume details of the Hopi doll are painted on.

Pueblo kachina figurines have several functions within the cultures that produce them. At Hopi, they are given to children by kachinas on different occasions. Hung in the house, they serve as didactic devices to assist the child in learning the appearance and characteristics of the different kachinas. At most Pueblos, they are also fertility symbols. "The baby kachina is given so that there won't be an end to this world" (Harvey 1963a:5). In New Mexico, dolls are also given during the course of curing ceremonies. New Mexican Pueblo Indians regard their dolls as being more sacred than the Western Pueblos do, and consequently the carvings are little seen by outsiders. At most villages, however, the doll is a vital part of the kachina religion.

The success of the kachina doll as a commercial craft item has inspired members of other tribes to produce figurines for the Anglo market. Navajo Yeibichai dancers and Apache crown dancers have both been carved for the arts and crafts market. One mestizo in Sinaloa has started carving cottonwood statuettes of Mayo *fariseos* and pascolas. These commercial productions must not be considered part of the inward-facing aspects of any of the cultures concerned.

Kachinas appear in other media as well. Hopi pottery and baskets often are embellished with kachina faces of figures. Modern watercolors by artists of many tribes and villages of the Southwest give details of the appearance of various ceremonies, including those featuring masked figures (Tanner 1973; Brown 1962).

For illustrations see "Zuni Religion and World View," fig. 1, "Hopi Ceremonial Organization," figs. 9, 11, "Pueblo Fine Arts," fig. 5, volume 9.

left, U. of Ariz., Ariz. State Mus.: E-2872.

Fig. 11. Opata-descended *fariseos*. left, Wooden as well as cloth *fariseo* masks are made. This example is unfinished (they are usually painted), but eyebrows and beard of hair have been added. The masks are given to children after use. Height 22.3 cm, collected by Thomas B. Hinton in Tepupa, Sonora, 1955. right, Participants in Molinote, near Baviacora, Sonora, on Good Friday, March 31, 1972. They all wore skirts over their trousers, and most had sack masks with tied ears and painted features. A stick was also a regular part of their equipment. Several masks have a reference to a *chivo* 'goat' written on them, as does the central one in this picture (*Yo soy chivo* 'I am a goat'). They appeared only on this one afternoon, clowning outside a small rural chapel while the people adored the Holy Cross. Photograph by James S. Griffith.

San Xavier del Bac Mission, Oblasser Lib., Tucson, Ariz.

Fig. 12. Papago *fariseos* at Cowlik, Papago Reservation, Ariz., wearing horned masks and carrying long poles that they use to touch and frighten people (Underhill 1934:515). They are readying an image of Judas, preparatory to parading with it. Judas's shirt is apparently made of a Calumet flour sack. Photographed on a Holy Saturday, late 1920s or 1930s.

Conclusions

It will be seen from this brief survey that there are two main streams of masking tradition in the Southwest. The first and oldest one is that in which alien spirits, either benevolent or hostile, visit this world during certain specified, recurring periods of time and appear at their host villages, usually in groups. Kachinas belong to this tradition, as do the *čapayekam* and *fariseos* of Northwest Mexico, albeit in slightly altered form. In the case of this tradition, the identity of the visitor is assumed with the mask, and the performance with its attendant regalia is a very sacred and dangerous matter. There are many accounts of evil things that happen if the masks are not respected or if the ritual is incorrectly carried out.

In the second tradition, the masked beings are usually solo performers. In most cases they are of obvious European derivation, although the pascola is undoubtedly a syncretic figure. The masked figures are not so powerful, nor are there the ritual restrictions on them and their equipment that appear in the older tradition. *čapayeka* masks are dangerous and are, with few exceptions, burned after the ceremony. It is improper

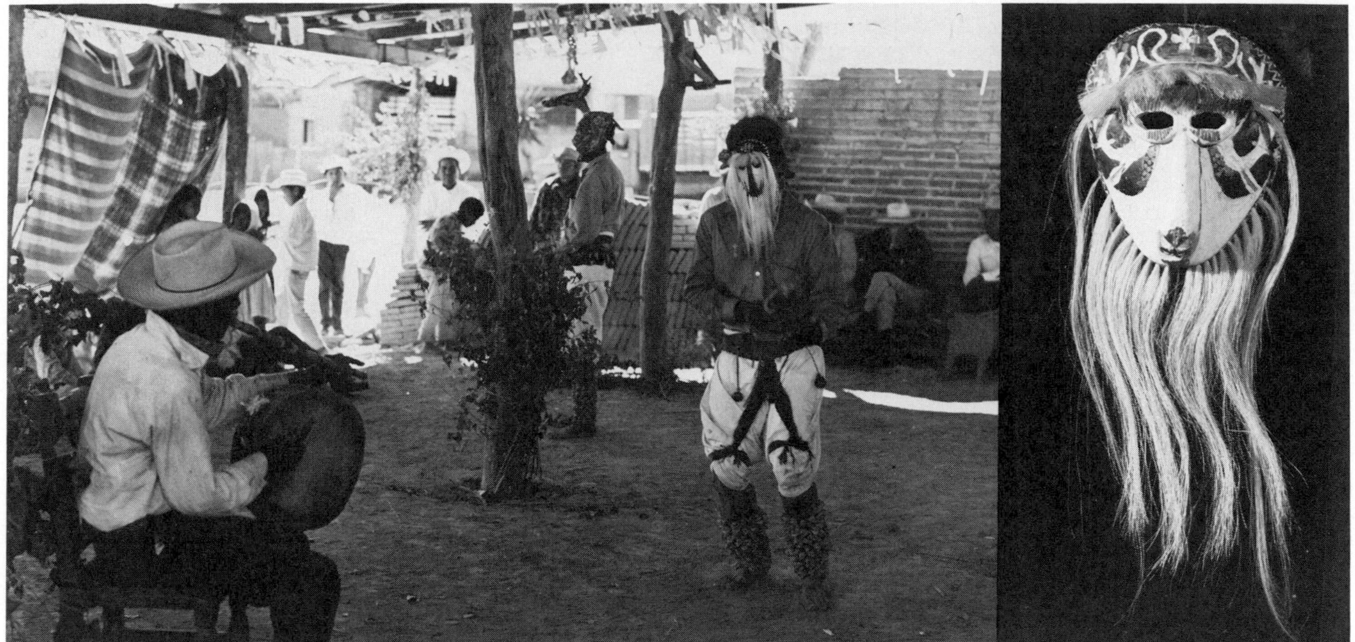

right, Taylor Mus., Colorado Springs Fine Arts Center, Colo.: 3941.

Fig. 13. Pascola. left, Mayo dancer at New Year's Day fiesta, Jan. 1, 1970, in La Playa, Sinaloa. His face covered by a wooden goatlike mask, the pascola dances to the music of the whistle and drum played by the man in the foreground. When music is supplied by the fiddle and harp orchestra, seen resting in the background, the pascola wears the mask over his shoulder or on the back of his head (Griffith 1972:185–198). In the center background a deer dancer is resting, with his headdress in position. The setting is a ramada in front of the village chapel. Photograph by James S. Griffith. right, Yaqui mask, probably representing a goat, painted black and white, with white horsehair eyebrows and beard and rhinestones inset under each eye. Height, about 18 cm, collected in Sonora, before 1950.

even to photograph them. Pascola masks are sacred in that they are used for religious purposes, but there is little harm in selling old masks and none at all in making new ones for sale to tourists.

It is perhaps too simple to equate these two traditions with aboriginal and European-introduced masking on a one-to-one basis. Solo masked clowns appear to antedate the Spanish conquest. One wonders whether Lower Pima and Opata *fariseos* have the aboriginal roots that Yaqui *čapayekam* do. Isletan grandfathers are not kachinas, but they are not certainly a Spanish introduction. This historical framework does serve, however, as a convenient organizational device for an examination of the incredibly rich masking traditions of this area. The organization itself is relatively unimportant. What matters is that many if not all the inhabitants of this region have at one time or another found their lives enriched by the "many faces of God in the Southwest" (Alfonso Ortiz, personal communication 1972).

Contributors

This list gives the academic affiliations of authors at the time this volume went to press. Parenthetical tribal names identify Indian authors. The dates following the entries indicate when each manuscript was (1) first received in the General Editor's office; (2) accepted by the editors; (3) sent to the author (or, if deceased, a substitute) for final approval after revisions and editorial work.

ABERLE, DAVID F., Department of Anthropology and Sociology, University of British Columbia, Vancouver. Navajo Economic Development: 9/23/74; 6/22/76; 6/23/81. Peyote Religion Among the Navajo: 4/16/73; 10/14/75; 5/22/81.

BAHR, DONALD M., Department of Anthropology, Arizona State University, Tempe. Pima and Papago Medicine and Philosophy: 7/17/72; 11/6/81; 12/22/81. Pima and Papago Social Organization: 3/22/73; 11/6/81; 12/22/81.

BASSO, KEITH H., Department of Anthropology, University of Arizona, Tucson. Western Apache: 10/10/72; 2/2/73; 3/12/82.

BEE, ROBERT L., Department of Anthropology, University of Connecticut, Storrs. Quechan: 5/8/72; 3/31/81; 10/2/81.

BEGISHE, KENNETH YAZZIE (Navajo), Department of Elementary Education, University of New Mexico, Albuquerque. A Taxonomic View of the Traditional Navajo Universe: 7/20/73; 4/15/81; 6/26/81.

BERGMAN, ROBERT L., Department of Psychiatry, University of New Mexico Medical School, Albuquerque. Navajo Health Services and Projects: 6/11/73; 4/7/81; 5/18/81.

BOWEN, THOMAS, Department of Anthropology, California State University, Fresno. Seri: 8/17/72; 6/20/74; 12/18/81.

BRUGGE, DAVID M., Interpretation and Visitor Services, National Park Service, Santa Fe, New Mexico. Navajo Prehistory and History to 1850: 4/23/72; 1/19/74; 5/15/81.

CAMPBELL, T.N., Department of Anthropology (emeritus), University of Texas, Austin. Coahuiltecans and Their Neighbors: 7/7/81; 11/5/81; 12/15/81.

CRUMRINE, N. ROSS, Department of Anthropology, University of Victoria, Victoria, British Columbia. Mayo: 5/29/72; 1/19/74; 12/22/81.

DUNNIGAN, TIMOTHY, Department of Anthropology, University of Minnesota, Minneapolis. Lower Pima: 7/13/72; 9/8/75; 12/22/81.

EGGAN, FRED, Department of Anthropology (emeritus), University of Chicago, Chicago. Comparative Social Organization: 7/6/81; 8/14/81; 10/13/81.

EMERSON, GLORIA J. (Navajo), Shiprock, New Mexico. Navajo Education: 6/4/81; 7/20/81; 7/7/81.

EZELL, PAUL H., Department of Anthropology (emeritus), San Diego State University, San Diego, California. History of the Pima: 8/14/72; 12/16/81; 12/22/81.

FONTANA, BERNARD L., University of Arizona Library, Tucson. History of the Papago: 8/21/73; 11/6/81; 12/22/81. Pima and Papago: Introduction: 8/21/73; 11/6/81; 12/22/81.

FORD, RICHARD I., Museum of Anthropology, University of Michigan, Ann Arbor. Inter-Indian Exchange in the Southwest: 8/6/73; 7/20/81; 7/20/81.

GILL, SAM D., Religious Studies Department, University of Colorado, Boulder. Navajo Views of Their Origin: 6/8/81; 7/20/81; 7/16/81.

GRIFFEN, WILLIAM B., Department of Anthropology, Northern Arizona University, Flagstaff. Southern Periphery: East: 4/28/72; 12/8/81; 12/16/81.

GRIFFITH, JAMES SEAVEY, Southwest Folklore Center, University of Arizona, Tucson. Kachinas and Masking: 6/26/72; 1/17/74; 7/14/81.

HACKENBERG, ROBERT A., Institute of Behavioral Science, University of Colorado, Boulder. Pima and Papago Ecological Adaptations: 12/27/73; 11/6/81; 12/22/81.

HARWELL, HENRY O., Center for Public Affairs, Arizona State University, Tempe. Maricopa: 7/20/81; 12/16/81; 10/2/81.

HINTON, THOMAS (deceased), Department of Anthropology, University of Arizona, Tucson. Southern Periphery: West: 6/1/74; 9/18/75; 3/23/82.

IVERSON, PETER, Department of History, University of Wyoming, Laramie. The Emerging Navajo Nation: 6/1/81; 7/20/81; 6/29/81.

JORGENSEN, JOSEPH G., Program in Comparative Culture, University of California, Irvine. Comparative Traditional Economics and Ecological Adaptations: 5/22/74; 1/19/76; 7/8/81.

KELLY, MARSHA C.S., Novato, California. Maricopa: 7/21/75; 12/16/81; 10/2/81.

KENDALL, MARTHA B., Department of Anthropology, Indiana University, Bloomington. Yuman Languages: 8/6/81; 9/22/81; 10/29/81.

KHERA, SIGRID, Department of Anthropology, University of Alaska, Fairbanks. Yavapai: 6/4/80; 11/5/81; 10/16/81.

LAMPHERE, LOUISE, Department of Anthropology, Brown University, Providence, Rhode Island. Southwestern Ceremonialism: 9/30/74; 7/20/81; 2/2/82.

MCALLESTER, DAVID P., Music Department, Wesleyan University, Middletown, Connecticut. Navajo Music: 5/18/72; 1/19/74; 7/9/81.

MCGUIRE, THOMAS R., Department of Social Science, Carnegie-Mellon University, Pittsburgh, Pennsylvania. Walapai: 5/27/75; 9/23/81; 10/7/81.

MANNING, ALLEN, Syracuse, New York. A Taxonomic View of the Traditional Navajo Universe: 7/20/73; 4/15/81; 6/26/81.

MARIELLA, PATRICIA S., Phoenix, Arizona. Yavapai: 6/4/80; 11/5/81; 10/16/81.

MATHIOT, MADELEINE, Department of Linguistics, State University of New York, Buffalo. Papago Semantics: 8/31/72; 6/25/76; 12/22/81.

MERRILL, WILLIAM L., Department of Anthropology, Smithsonian Institution. Tarahumara Social Organization, Political Organization, and Religion: 10/5/81; 12/9/81; 12/23/81.

MILLER, WICK R., Department of Anthropology, University of Utah, Salt Lake City. Uto-Aztecan Languages: 10/26/81; 12/10/81; 12/22/81.

MITCHELL, DOUGLAS F. (Navajo) (deceased), Window Rock, Arizona. Visiting Artist in American Indian Music and Dance, Music Department, Wesleyan University, Middletown, Connecticut. Navajo Music: 5/18/72; 1/19/74; 7/9/81.

NEWCOMB, WILLIAM W., JR., Department of Anthropology, University of Texas, Austin. Karankawa: 10/30/72; 11/4/81; 12/17/81.

OPLER, MORRIS E., Department of Anthropology (emeritus), University of Oklahoma, Norman. The Apachean Culture Pattern and Its Origins: 8/27/74; 5/7/75; 3/10/82. Chiricahua Apache: 5/14/74; 5/7/75; 3/12/82. Mescalero Apache: 12/29/81; 1/4/82; 3/17/82.

PABLO, SALLY GIFF (Pima), Laveen, Arizona. Contemporary Pima: 1/10/74; 11/6/81; 12/17/81.

PENNINGTON, CAMPBELL W., Department of Geography, Texas A & M University, College Station. Northern Tepehuan: 10/6/75; 9/28/81; 10/16/81. Tarahumara: 6/6/72; 7/28/75; 12/23/81.

ROESSEL, ROBERT, Chinle, Arizona. Navajo History, 1850–1923: 12/10/73; 4/15/81; 7/13/81.

ROESSEL, RUTH (Navajo), Chinle, Arizona. Navajo Arts and Crafts: 8/6/73; 4/15/81; 7/13/81.

SCHWARTZ, DOUGLAS W., School of American Research, Santa Fe, New Mexico. Havasupai: 10/24/73; 1/25/79; 10/9/81.

SHEPARDSON, MARY, Department of Anthropology (emeritus), San Francisco State University, San Francisco, California. Development of Navajo Tribal Government: 1/18/74; 5/15/74; 7/1/81.

SPICER, EDWARD H., Department of Anthropology (emeritus), University of Arizona, Tucson. Yaqui: 9/28/72; 1/18/74; 12/10/81.

STEWART, KENNETH M., Department of Anthropology (emeritus), Arizona State University, Tempe. Mohave: 5/22/72; 10/1/81; 10/30/81. Yumans: Introduction: 5/22/72; 12/17/81; 12/21/81.

TILLER, VERONICA E. (Jicarilla), Department of History, University of Utah, Salt Lake City. Jicarilla Apache: 2/12/79; 11/5/81; 3/15/82.

TOME, MARSHALL (Navajo), Navajo Tribal Office, Window Rock, Arizona. The Navajo Nation Today: 9/16/74; 1/21/82; 6/26/81.

WERNER, OSWALD, Department of Anthropology, Northwestern University, Evanston, Illinois. A Taxonomic View of the Traditional Navajo Universe: 7/20/73; 4/15/81; 6/26/81.

WILLIAMS, ANITA ALVAREZ DE, Mexicali, Baja California, Mexico. Cocopa: 11/24/75; 12/12/77; 10/13/81.

WITHERSPOON, GARY, Ignacio, Colorado. Language and Reality in Navajo World View: 3/27/75; 8/13/74; 7/1/81. Navajo Social Organization: 5/15/72; 1/19/74; 7/6/81.

WYMAN, LELAND C., Sønderborg, Denmark. Navajo Ceremonial System: 3/9/72; 1/18/74; 7/9/81.

YOUNG, ROBERT W., Department of Linguistics, University of New Mexico, Albuquerque. Apachean Languages: 9/15/81; 12/16/81; 12/22/81.

Bibliography

This list includes all references cited in the volume, arranged in alphabetical order according to the names of the authors as they appear in the citations in the text. Multiple works by the same author are arranged chronologically; second and subsequent titles by the same author in the same year are differentiated by letters added to the dates. Where more than one author with the same surname is cited, one has been arbitrarily selected for text citation by surname alone throughout the volume, while the others are always cited with added initials; the combination of surname with date in text citations should avoid confusion. Where a publication date is different from the series date (as in some annual reports and the like), the former is used. Dates, authors, and titles that do not appear on the original works are enclosed by brackets. For manuscripts, dates refer to time of composition. For publications reprinted or first published many years after original composition, a bracketed date after the title refers to the time of composition or the date of original publication.

ARCIA = Commissioner of Indian Affairs
1849- Annual Reports to the Secretary of the Interior. Washington: U.S. Government Printing Office. (Reprinted: AMS Press, New York, 1976-1977).

Abel, Annie H., ed.
1915 The Official Correspondence of James S. Calhoun While Indian Agent at Santa Fe and Superintendent of Indian Affairs in New Mexico. Washington: U.S. Government Printing Office.

Aberle, David F.
1942 Mythology of the Navaho Game Stick-dice. *Journal of American Folklore* 55(217):144-154.

_____
[1949-1980] [Interviews, Journals, and Notes from Intermittent Fieldwork Among the Navajo Indians of Arizona, New Mexico, and Utah.] (Manuscripts in Aberle's possession.)

_____
1961 Matrilineal Descent in Cross-cultural Perspective. Pp. 655-727 in Matrilineal Kinship. David M. Schneider and Kathleen Gough, eds. Berkeley and Los Angeles: University of California Press.

_____
1961a Navaho. Pp. 96–201 in Matrilineal Kinship. David M. Schneider and Kathleen Gough, eds. Berkeley and Los Angeles: University of California Press.

_____
1963 Some Sources of Flexibility in Navaho Social Organization. *Southwestern Journal of Anthropology* 19(1):1-8.

_____
1966 The Peyote Religion Among the Navaho. *Viking Fund Publications in Anthropology* 42. New York.

_____
1967 The Peyote Religion Among the Navaho. 2d printing. Chicago: Aldine.

_____
1967a The Navaho Singer's "Fee:" Payment or Prestation? Pp. 15-32 in Studies in Southwestern Ethnolinguistics: Meaning and History in the Languages of the American Southwest. Dell H. Hymes and William E. Bittle, eds. The Hague, Paris: Mouton.

_____
[1968-1974] [Interviews, Journals, and Notes on Economic Development from Intermittent Fieldwork Among the Navajo Indians.] (Manuscripts in Aberle's possession.)

_____
1969 A Plan for Navajo Economic Development. Pp. 223-276 in Vol. 1 of Toward Economic Development for Native American Communities, a Compendium of Papers Submitted to the Subcommittee on Economy in Government of the Joint Economic Committee. *91st Congress, 1st sess. Joint Committee Print.* Washington: U.S. Government Printing Office.

_____
1978 The Lessons of Navajo Livestock Reduction. Pp. 62-66 in Proceedings of the First International Rangeland Congress, Denver, August 14-18. Donald N. Hyder, ed. Denver: Society for Range Management.

_____
1980 Navajo Exogamic Rules and Preferred Marriages. Pp. 105-143 in The Versatility of Kinship: Essays Presented to Harry W. Basehart. Linda S. Cordell and Stephen Beckerman, eds. New York: Academic Press.

Aberle, David F., and Omer C. Stewart
1957 Navaho and Ute Peyotism: A Chronological and Distributional Study. *University of Colorado Studies, Series in Anthropology* 6. Boulder.

Acosta, Roberto
1949 Apuntes históricos sonorenses: La conquista temporal y espiritual del Yaqui y del Mayo. Mexico City: Imprenta Aldina-Rosell y Sordo Noviega.

Adair, John
1944 The Navajo and Pueblo Silversmiths. Norman: University of Oklahoma Press.

Adair, John, and Kurt Deuschle
1970 The People's Health: Medicine and Anthropology in a Navajo Community. New York: Appleton-Century-Crofts.

Adams, William Y.
1963 Shonto: A Study of the Role of the Trader in a Modern Navaho Community. *Bureau of American Ethnology Bulletin* 188. Washington.

Adams, William Y., and Gordon V. Krutz
1971 Wage Labor and the San Carlos Apache. Pp. 115-133 in Apachean Culture History and Ethnology. Keith H. Basso and Morris E. Opler, eds. *Anthropological Papers of the University of Arizona* 21. Tucson.

Aguirre Beltrán, Gonzalo
1953 Formas de gobierno indígena. Mexico City: Imprenta Universitaria.

_____
1967 Regiones de refugio: El desarrollo de la comunidad y el proceso dominical en mestizo América. *Instituto Indigenista Interamericano, Ediciones Especiales* 46. Mexico City.

Aikens, C. Melvin
1966 Fremont-Promontory-Plains Relationships, Including a Report of Excavations at the Injun Creek and Bear River Number 1 Sites, Northern Utah. *University of Utah Anthropological Paper* 82. Salt Lake City.

_____
1967 Plains Relationships of the Fremont Culture: A Hypothesis. *American Antiquity* 32(2):198-209.

_____
1972 Fremont Culture: Restatement of Some Problems. *American Antiquity* 37(1):61-66.

Alamán, Lucas
1825 [Memoria sobre los indios pimo y maricopa.] (Manuscript in Archivo Militar, Mexico City.)

Alcocer, José Antonio
1958 Bosquejo de la historia del Colegio de Neustra Señora de Guadalupe y sus misiones, año de 1788. Rafael Cervantes, ed. Mexico City: Editorial Porrúa.

Alegre, Francisco Javier
1956-1960 Historia de la provincia de la Compañia de Jesús de Nueva España [1780]. Ernest J. Burrus and Felix Zubillaga, eds. (*Biblioteca Instituti Historici S.J.* Vols. 9, 13, 16, 17) Rome: Institutum Historicum S.J.

Alessio Robles, Vito
1938 Coahuila y Texas en la época colonial. Mexico City: Editorial Cultura.

Almada, Francisco R.
1952 Diccionario de historia, geografía y biografías sonorenses. Chihuahua, Mexico: Sandoval.

——— 1955 Resumen de historia del estado de Chihuahua. Mexico City: Libros Mexicanos.

——— 1968 Diccionario de historia, geografía y biografía chihuahuensis. 2d ed. Ciudad Juárez, Mexico: Impresora de Juárez, S.A.

Alpher, Barry
1970 [Maricopa Fieldnotes.] (Manuscript in Alpher's possession.)

Altschuler, Constance Wynn
1977 Poston and the Pimas: The "Father of Arizona" as Indian Superintendent. *Journal of Arizona History* 18(1):23-42.

Alvarado, Anita L.
1970 Cultural Determinants of Population Stability in the Havasupai Indians. *American Journal of Physical Anthropology* 33(1):9-14.

Alvarez, Albert
1969 The Expressions of Papago. English Version by Kenneth Hale. Cambridge: Massachusetts Institute of Technology, Department of Linguistics.

Alvarez, Albert, and Kenneth L. Hale
1970 Toward a Manual of Papago Grammar: Some Phonological Terms. *International Journal of American Linguistics* 36(2):83-97.

Amsden, Charles A.
1934 Navaho Weaving: Its Technic and History. Santa Ana, Calif.: Fine Arts Press in Cooperation with Southwest Museum. (Reprinted: University of New Mexico Press, Albuquerque, 1949.)

——— 1971 Navaho Weaving: Its Technic and History. Glorieta, N.M.: Rio Grande Press.

Anderson, Edward F.
1979 Peyote, the Divine Cactus. Tucson: University of Arizona Press.

Anderson, Frank G.
1955 The Pueblo Kachina Cult: A Historical Reconstruction. *Southwestern Journal of Anthropology* 11(4):404-419.

——— 1956 Early Documentary Material on the Pueblo Kachina Cult. *Anthropological Quarterly* 29(2):31-44.

——— 1960 Intertribal Relations in the Pueblo Kachina Cult. Pp. 377-383 in Men and Cultures: Selected Papers of the 5th International Congress of Anthropological and Ethnological Sciences. Philadelphia, 1956.

Anderson, J.O., Frances Berdan, and James Lockhart, trans.
1976 Beyond the Codices: The Nahua View of Colonial Mexico. Berkeley and Los Angeles: University of California Press.

Andrews, J. Richard
1975 Introduction to Classical Nahuatl. Austin and London: University of Texas Press.

Anonymous
1596 Carta anua. (Transcript in Bolton Collection, Bancroft Library, University of California, Berkeley.)

——— 1777-1825 Patentes y comunicaciones que se refieren a la Tarahumara. (Manuscript in Convento de Guadalupe, Guadalupe, Zacatecas, Mexico.)

——— 1778 Descripción topográfica de las misiones de propaganda fide de Nuestra Señora de Guadalupe de Zacatecas de la Sierra Madre. (Manuscript in Convento de Guadalupe, Guadalupe, Zacatecas, Mexico.)

——— 1824 Nabijos. *Missouri Intelligencer* 3(cols. 2-4), April 3, 1824.

——— 1853-1857 Descripción topográfica de las misiones de propaganda fide de Nuestra Señora de Guadalupe de Zacatecas de la Sierra Madre. Pp. 92-131 in Vol. 4, ser. 4 of *Documentos para la Historia de Méjico*. 21 vols. in 19. Mexico City: Impr. de J.R. Navarro.

——— 1894 [Report No. 22512 from San Carlos Agency.] (In Letters Received, Commissioner's Office, Record Group 75, National Archives, Washington.)

——— 1900 Smithsonian Party Returns. *Arizona Sentinel*, December 12:3. Yuma, Ariz.

——— 1900a [Census of Verde Valley Indians.] (Unpublished manuscript in Sharlot Hall Museum, Prescott, Ariz.)

——— [1913-1922] [Allotment Register.] (Manuscript in Bureau of Indian Affairs Office, Sacaton, Ariz.)

——— 1948 Franchise for Southwestern Indians. *Masterkey* 22(5):170.

——— 1950 El IV Congreso Indígena Tarahumara. *Boletín Indigenista* 10:164-175. Mexico City.

——— 1964 Salt River Pima-Maricopa and Fort McDowell Mohave-Apache Communities Joint Tribal Position Paper on Proposed Orme Dam. (Unpublished manuscript in Tribal Office, Fort McDowell, Ariz.)

——— 1966 Native American Church Denies Use of Peyote as Tribal Political Issue. *Navajo Times* 7(26):1, 4. Window Rock, Ariz.

——— 1974 Exxon Uranium Venture Looms as Major Move. *Navajo Times* 15(4):A-1, A-5. Window Rock, Ariz.

——— 1975 Coal Project Tax Issue. *Wassaja* 3(2):3. San Francisco.

——— 1979 An Interview with Peter MacDonald. *American Indian Journal* 5(6):11-18.

——— 1979a Hubbell's Trading Post Vividly Portrays Southwest. Pp. 22-23 in Navajoland U.S.A., 1979 Tourist Guide. *Navajo Times* 4 (Special issue, May 1979). Window Rock, Ariz.

——— 1979b Boards to Bucks. *Indian Arizona News* 2(7). Phoenix.

——— 1979c Navajoland, U.S.A.: Tourist Guide 1979. *Navajo Times* 4 (Special issue, May 1979). Window Rock, Ariz.

——— 1980 Resource Division Must Be Top Priority. *Navajo Times* 22(19):6. Window Rock, Ariz.

——— 1980a Tribe Investigates Radioactive Homes. *Navajo Times* 22(19):1. Window Rock, Ariz.

——— 1981 Navajo Fair a Success. *Navajo Times* 22(37):1. Window Rock, Ariz.

——— 1981a Record Breaking Crowd Expected at Navajo Fair. *Navajo Times* 22(36):1. Window Rock, Ariz.

Anza, Juan Bautista de
1770 [Letter of May 1, to Governor Juan de Pineda, Tubac.] (Manuscript, carpeta 253/931, Provincias Internas, Sinaloa y Sonora, Archivo Franciscano, Biblioteca Nacional, Mexico City.)

——— 1776 Informe del Teniente Coronel Don Juan Bap.ta de Anza, México, November 20, 1776. (Manuscript, tomo 23, Provincias Internas, Archivo General de la Nación. Mexico City.)

Arizona. State Employment Service
1970 Manpower Services to Arizona Indians: Annual Report 1969. Phoenix: Arizona State Employment Service, Unemployment Insurance Division.

Arlegui, José, comp.
1851 Crónica de la provincia de N.S.P.S. Francisco de Zacatecas compuesto por el M.R.P. José Arlegui.... Mexico City: Reimpresa por Cumplodo.

Armagost, James L.
1980 Comanche Language. Suppl. to A Comanche-English, English-Comanche Dictionary and Grammar, by Lyla Wistrand-Robinson. (Unpublished manuscript in Armagost's possession.)

Arriaga, Julian D.
1775 [Letter to the Viceroy, 6 Sept.] (Manuscript, tomo 36, Correspondencia de los Virreyes, Archivo General de la Nación, Mexico City.)

Ascher, Robert
1962 Ethnography for Archeology: A Case from the Seri Indians. *Ethnology* 1(3):360-369.

Ascher, Robert, and Francis J. Clune Jr.
1960 Waterfall Cave, Southern Chihuahua, Mexico. *American Antiquity* 26(2):270-274.

Aschmann, Homer
1959 The Central Desert of Baja California: Demography and Ecology. *Ibero-Americana* 42. Berkeley, Calif.

Atwater, Elizabeth V.
1974 The Jicarilla Apaches, 1601-1849. Pp. 187-252 in Apache Indians, VIII. (*American Indian Ethnohistory: Indians of the Southwest*) New York: Garland.

Austin, John L.
1962 How to Do Things With Words. Cambridge, Mass.: Harvard University Press; Oxford, England: Clarendon Press.

Bader, Barbara
1976 American Picturebooks from Noah's Ark to the Beast Within. New York: Macmillan.

Bahr, Donald M.
1975 Pima and Papago Ritual Oratory: A Study of Three Texts. San Francisco: Indian Historian Press.

Bahr, Donald M., and J. Richard Haefer
1978 Song in Piman Curing. *Ethnomusicology* 22(1):89-122.

Bahr, Donald M., Joseph Giff, and Manuel Havier
1979 Piman Songs on Hunting. *Ethnomusicology* 23(2):245-296.

Bahr, Donald M., Juan Gregorio, David I. Lopez, and Albert Alvarez
1974 Piman Shamanism and Staying Sickness (*ká:cim múmkidag*). Tucson: University of Arizona Press.

Bahre, Conrad J.
1967 The Reduction of Seri Indian Range and Residence in the State of Sonora, Mexico (1536-Present). (Unpublished M.A. Thesis in Geography, University of Arizona, Tucson.)

———
1980 Historic Seri Residence, Range, and Socio-political Structure. *The Kiva* 45(3):197-209.

Bailey, Flora L.
1940 Navaho Foods and Cooking Methods. *American Anthropologist* 42(2):271-290.

Bailey, G.
1858 Report of November 4 by Special Agent G. Bailey in Regard to the Indians of Arizona. Pp. 202-208 in Report of the Commissioner of Indian Affairs for the Year 1858. Washington: Wm. A. Harris.

Bailey, Lynn R.
1964 The Long Walk: A History of the Navajo Wars, 1846-68. Los Angeles: Westernlore Press.

———
1966 Indian Slave Trade in the Southwest: A Study of Slave-taking and the Traffic of Indian Captives. Los Angeles: Westernlore Press.

———
1970 Bosque Redondo: An American Concentration Camp. Pasadena, Calif.: Socio-Technical Books.

Balbás, Manuel
1927 Recuerdos del yaqui: Principales episodios durante la campaña de 1899 á 1901. Mexico City: Sociedad de Edición y Librería Franco Americana.

Balke, Bruno, and Clyde Snow
1965 Anthropological and Physiological Observations on Tarahumara Endurance Runners. *American Journal of Physical Anthropology* 23(3):293-301.

Bancroft, Hubert H.
1874-1876 The Native Races of the Pacific States of North America. 5 vols. New York: D. Appleton.

———
1886-1889 The History of the North Mexican States and Texas. 2 vols. San Francisco: The History Company.

———
1889 The History of Arizona and New Mexico, 1530-1888. San Francisco: The History Company. (Reprinted: Horn and Wallace, Albuquerque, 1962.)

Bandelier, Adolph F.A.
1890 The Delight Makers. New York: Dodd, Mead. (Reprinted: Harcourt Brace Jovanovich, New York, 1971.)

———
1890-1892 Final Report of Investigations Among the Indians of the Southwestern United States, Carried on Mainly in the Years from 1880-1885. 2 vols. *Papers of the Archaeological Institute of America, American Series* 3 and 4. Cambridge, Mass.

Bannister, Bryant
1964 Tree-ring Dating of the Archeological Sites in the Chaco Canyon Region, New Mexico. *Southwestern Monuments Association, Technical Series* 6(2). Globe, Ariz.

Bannon, John F.
1955 The Mission Frontier in Sonora, 1620-1687. James A. Reynolds, ed. *United States Catholic Historical Society, Monograph Series* 26. New York.

Baran, Paul A.
1957 The Political Economy of Growth. New York: Monthly Review Press.

Barbastro, Francisco Antonio
1792 Sermones en la lengua ópata. (Manuscript in the Pinart Collection, Bancroft Library, University of California, Berkeley.)

———
1793 [Letter of December 1, to Revillagigedo.] (Manuscript, tomo 33, Provincias Internas, Archivo General de la Nación, Mexico City.)

Barnes, William C.
1960 Arizona Place Names. Rev. and enl. by Byrd H. Granger. Tucson: University of Arizona Press.

Barnett, Franklin
1968 Viola Jimulla: The Indian Chieftess, a Biography. Yuma, Ariz.: Southwest Printers.

Barnett, H.G.
1953 Innovation: The Basis of Cultural Change. New York: McGraw-Hill.

Barrett, S.M., ed.
1906 Geronimo's Story of His Life. New York: Duffield. (Reprinted as: Geronimo, His Own Story, Frederick W. Turner, III, ed., Dutton, New York, 1970.)

Barry, Tom
1979 Navajo Legal Services and Friends of the Earth Sue Six Federal Agencies Over Alleged Careless Uranium Mining Policies. *American Indian Journal* 5(2):3-7.

———
1979a The Navajo and Hopi's History of Inequitable Mining Leases. *American Indian Journal* 5(3):16-20.

———
1980 An Energy Dichotomy for the 80's. *American Indian Journal* 6(2):18-20.

Barry, Tom, and Beth Wood
1978 Uranium on the Checkerboard: Crisis at Crownpoint. *American Indian Journal* 4(6):10-13.

Bartlett, John R.
1854 Personal Narrative of Explorations and Incidents in Texas, New Mexico, California, Sonora, and Chihuahua Connected with the United States and Mexican Boundary Commission, During the Years 1850, '51, '52, '53. 2 vols. New York: D. Appleton.

Basauri, Carlos
1929 Monografía de los tarahumaras. Mexico City: Talleres Gráficos de la Nación.

____
1940 La Población indígena de México, etnografía. 3 vols. Mexico City: Secretaría de Educación Pública.

Bascom, Burton W.
1965 Proto-Tepiman (Tepehuan-Piman). (Unpublished Ph.D. Dissertation in Linguistics, University of Washington, Seattle.)

Basehart, Harry W.
1971 Mescalero Apache Band Organization and Leadership. Pp. 35-49 in Apachean Culture History and Ethnology. Keith H. Basso and Morris E. Opler, eds. *Anthropological Papers of the University of Arizona* 21. Tucson.

____
1974 Mescalero Apache Subsistence Patterns and Socio-political Organization. Pp. 9-153 in Apache Indians, XII. New York: Garland.

Basehart, Harry W., and Tom T. Sasaki
1964 Changing Political Organization in the Jicarilla Apache Reservation Community. *Human Organization* 23(4):283-289.

Basso, Keith H.
1966 The Gift of Changing Woman. *Anthropological Papers 76, Bureau of American Ethnology Bulletin* 196. Washington.

____
1969 Western Apache Witchcraft. *Anthropological Papers of the University of Arizona* 15. Tucson.

____
1970 The Cibecue Apache. New York: Holt, Rinehart and Winston.

_______, ed.
1971 Western Apache Raiding and Warfare: From the Notes of Grenville Goodwin. Tucson: University of Arizona Press.

Battey, Thomas C.
1968 The Life and Adventures of a Quaker Among the Indians [1875]. Norman: University of Oklahoma Press.

Beaglehole, Ernest
1937 Notes on Hopi Economic Life. *Yale University Publications in Anthropology* 15. New Haven, Conn.

Beaglehole, Ernest, and Pearl Beaglehole
1935 Hopi of Second Mesa. *Memoirs of the American Anthropological Association* 44. Menasha, Wis.

Beals, Ralph L.
1932 Masks in the Southwest. *American Anthropologist* 34(1):166-169.

____
1932a The Comparative Ethnology of Northern Mexico Before 1750. *Ibero-Americana* 2. Berkeley, Calif.

____
1933 The Acaxee: A Mountain Tribe of Durango and Sinaloa. *Ibero-Americana* 6. Berkeley, Calif.

____
1943 The Aboriginal Culture of the Cáhita Indians. *Ibero-Americana* 19. Berkeley, Calif.

____
1945 The Contemporary Culture of the Cáhita Indians. *Bureau of American Ethnology Bulletin* 142. Washington.

Beaver, R. Pierce, ed.
1979 The Native American Christian Community: A Directory of Indian, Aleut, and Eskimo Churches. Monrovia, Calif.: Missions Advanced Research and Communication Center.

Beck, Warren A., and Ynez D. Haase
1969 Historical Atlas of New Mexico. Norman: University of Oklahoma Press.

Bedinger, Margery
1973 Indian Silver: Navajo and Pueblo Jewelers. Albuquerque: University of New Mexico Press.

Bee, Robert L.
[1961] [Ethnographic Notes from Two Months' Fieldwork Among the Quechan.] (Manuscripts in Bee's possession.)

____
1963 Changes in Yuma Social Organization. *Ethnology* 2(2):207-227.

____
[1966] [Ethnographic Notes from Seven Months' Fieldwork Among the Quechan.] (Manuscripts in Bee's possession.)

____
1967 Sociocultural Change and Persistence in the Yuma Indian Reservation Community. (Unpublished Ph.D. Dissertation in Anthropology, University of Kansas, Lawrence.)

____
[1969] [Ethnographic Notes from One Month's Fieldwork Among the Quechan.] (Manuscripts in Bee's possession.)

____
1969a Tribal Leadership in the War on Poverty: A Case Study. *Social Science Quarterly* 50(3):676-686.

____
1970 "Self-Help" at Fort Yuma: A Critique. *Human Organization* 29(3):155-161.

____
1981 Crosscurrents Along the Colorado: The Impact of Government Policy on the Quechan Indians. Tucson: University of Arizona Press.

Bee, Tom
1972 End, in Plight of the Redman, by XIT. [Sound recording] Rare Earth R536L. 1 disc. 33⅓ rpm. 12 in.

Begay, Gishin
1949 Emergence Myth 1. Pp. 3–85 in Emergence Myth According to the Hanelthynayhe or Upward-reaching Rite. Recorded by Father Berard Haile; rewritten by Mary C. Wheelwright. (*Navajo Religion Series* 3) Santa Fe: Museum of Navajo Ceremonial Art.

Begay, Harrison
1967 The Sacred Mountains of the Navajo; in Four Paintings. Text by Leland C. Wyman. Flagstaff: Museum of Northern Arizona.

Begay, Reg
[1948] Shoes Game Song (Navajo). Recorded and edited by Raymond A. Boley. [Sound recording] Canyon ARP 186a.1 disc. 78 rpm. 10 in. (Reissued as Traditional Navajo Songs, LP No. 6064 in 1969; also available on 8-track tape, No. 8-6064 and as cassette, No. 6064c.)

____
[1950] Three Round Dances, More Round Dances. Recorded and edited by Raymond A. Boley. [Sound recording] Canyon ARP 197a and 197b. 2 discs. 78 rpm. 10 in.

Begishe, K.Y., M.A. Austin, O. Werner, J. Werner, et al.
1981 The Anatomical Atlas of the Navajo. Albuquerque: Native American Materials Development Center.

Bell, A.W.
1869 On the Native Races of New Mexico. *Journal of the Ethnological Society of London* n.s. 1:222-274.

Bell, Fillman, Keith M. Anderson, and Yvonne G. Stewart
1980 The Quitobaquito Cemetery and Its History. Tucson: National Park Service, Western Archaeological Center.

Bellah, Robert N.
1952 Apache Kinship Systems. Cambridge, Mass.: Harvard University Press.

Benavides, Alonso de
1630 Memorial que Fray Ivan de Santander de la Orden de San Francisco, comisario general de Indias, presente a la magestad católica del rey don Felipe quarto nuestra señor. Madrid: La Imprenta Real.

——— 1916 The Memorial of Fray Alonso de Benavides, 1630. Mrs. Edward E. Ayer, trans. Frederick W. Hodge and Charles F. Lummis, ann. Chicago: Privately printed. (Reprinted: Horn and Wallace, University of New Mexico Press, Albuquerque, 1965.)

——— 1945 Fray Alonso de Benavides' Revised Memorial of 1634. Frederick W. Hodge, George P. Hammond, and Agapito Rey, eds. Albuquerque: University of New Mexico Press.

——— 1954 Memorial of 1630. Peter P. Forrestal, trans. Washington: Academy of American Franciscan History.

Bender, Averam B.
1952 March of Empire: Frontier Defense in the Southwest, 1848-1860. Lawrence: University of Kansas Press.

——— 1974 A Study of Mescalero Apache Indians, 1846-1880. Pp. 61-279 in Apache Indians, XI. (*American Indian Ethnohistory: Indians of the Southwest*) New York: Garland.

——— 1974a A Study of Western Apache Indians, 1846-1886. Pp. 9-15 in Apache Indians, V. (*American Indian Ethnohistory: Indians of the Southwest*) New York: Garland.

——— 1974b A Study of Jicarilla Apache Indians, 1846-1887. Pp. 9-194 in Apache Indians, IX. (*American Indian Ethnohistory: Indians of the Southwest*) New York: Garland.

Bennett, Harry
1889-1894 [Mescalero Apache Vocabulary.] (Manuscript No. 80 in National Anthropological Archives, Smithsonian Institution, Washington.)

Bennett, Kay, *see* Kaibah

Bennett, Noël, and Tiana Bighorse
1971 Working with the Wool: How to Weave a Navajo Rug. Flagstaff, Ariz.: Northland Press.

Bennett, Wendell C., and Robert M. Zingg
1935 The Tarahumara: An Indian Tribe of Northern Mexico. Chicago: University of Chicago Press. (Reprinted: Rio Grande Press, Glorieta, N.M., 1976.)

Bergman, Robert L.
1971 Navajo Peyote Use: Its Apparent Safety. *American Journal of Psychiatry* 128(6):695-699.

——— 1973 A School for Medicine Men. *American Journal of Psychiatry* 130(6):663-666.

Berlandier, Jean L.
1969 The Indians of Texas in 1830. John C. Ewers, ed. Washington: Smithsonian Institution Press.

Berlant, Anthony, and Mary Hunt Kahlenberg
1977 Walk in Beauty: The Navajo and Their Blankets. Boston: Little, Brown for the New York Graphic Society.

Berlin, Brent
1967 Categories of Eating in Tzeltal and Navaho. *International Journal of American Linguistics* 33(1):1-6.

Betzinez, Jason
1959 I Fought with Geronimo. With the assistance of William S. Nye. Harrisburg, Pa.: Stackpole Company.

Beyale, Eugene
1978 Medicine Dream, by Mr. Indian and Time. Diné Records. [Cassette tape].

Bigelow, John
1958 On the Bloody Trail of Geronimo. Arthur Woodward, ed. Los Angeles: Westernlore Press.

Biggs, Bruce
1957 Testing Intelligibility Among Yuman Languages. *International Journal of American Linguistics* 23(2):57-62.

Bigler, Henry W.
1962 Chronicle of the West: The Conquest of California, Discovery of Gold, and Mormon Settlement, as Reflected in Henry William Bigler's Diaries. Erwin G. Gudde, ed. Berkeley: University of California Press.

Bingham, Sam, and Janet Bingham
1979 Navajo Farming. Chinle, Ariz.: Rock Point Community School.

Bittle, William E.
1961 [Letter of November 10 to Morris E. Opler.] (In possession of Morris E. Opler.)

——— 1963 Kiowa-Apache. Pp. 76-101 in Studies in the Athapaskan Languages, by Harry Hoijer and Others. *University of California Publications in Linguistics* 29. Berkeley.

——— 1971 A Brief History of the Kiowa Apache. *University of Oklahoma Papers in Anthropology* 12(1):1-34. Norman.

Blaine, Peter, Sr.
1981 Papagos and Politics. As Told to Michael S. Adams. Tucson: Arizona Historical Society.

Blair, W. Frank
1950 The Biotic Provinces of Texas. *Texas Journal of Science* 2(1):93-117. San Marcos.

Blanco, Jacobo
1873 Informe sobre la exploración del Río Colorado. (*Memoria—1873, Documento* 35) Mexico City: Secretaría de Fomento.

Bloom, Lansing B.
1927 Early Weaving in New Mexico. *New Mexico Historical Review* 2(3):228-238.

——— 1928 Barreiro's Ojeada sobre Nuevo-Mexico. *New Mexico Historical Review* 3(1):73-96, (4):145-178.

———, ed.
1936 Bourke on the Southwest, X. *New Mexico Historical Review* 11(3):217-282.

Bloom, Lansing B., and Lynn B. Mitchell
1938 The Chapter Elections in 1672. *New Mexico Historical Review* 13(1):85-119.

Blount, Bertha
1919 The Apache in the Southwest, 1846-1886. *Southwestern Historical Quarterly* 23(1):20-38. Austin.

Boas, Franz
1911 Introduction. Pp. 5-85 in Pt. 1 of Handbook of American Indian Languages. 2 Pts. *Bureau of American Ethnology Bulletin* 40. Washington.

——— 1917 El Dialecto méxicano de Pochutla, Oaxaca. *International Journal of American Linguistics* 1(1):9-44.

Boas, Franz, and Ella Deloria
1941 Dakota Grammar. *Memoirs of the National Academy of Sciences* 23(2). Washington.

Bock, George E.
1971 Report of the Director, Navajo Area, Indian Health Service to the Tribal Council, Window Rock, Ariz. Mimeo.

Bohorquez, Juan María de
1792 [Informe del Comisionado...] (Manuscript, carpeta 137/815, Provincias Internas, Archivo Franciscano, Biblioteca Nacional, Mexico City.)

Bollaert, William
1956 William Bollaert's Texas. W. Eugene Hollon and Ruth Lapham Butler, eds. Norman: University of Oklahoma Press.

Bolton, Herbert E.
1906 The Founding of Mission Rosario: A Chapter in the History

of the Gulf Coast. *Quarterly of the Texas State Historical Association* 10(2):113-139. Austin.

____
1911 The Jumano Indians in Texas, 1650-1771. *Quarterly of the Texas State Historical Association* 15(1):66-84. Austin.

____
1913 Guide to Materials for the History of the United States in the Principal Archives of Mexico. *Carnegie Institution of Washington Publication* 163. Washington.

____
1915 The Location of La Salle's Colony on the Gulf of Mexico. *Mississippi Valley Historical Review* 2(2):165-182.

____
1916 Spanish Exploration in the Southwest, 1542-1706. New York: Charles Scribner's Sons.

_______, ed. and trans.
1919 Father Escobar's Relation of the Oñate Expedition to California. *Catholic Historical Review* 5(1):19-41.

_______, ed.
1919a Kino's Historical Memoir of Pimería Alta. 2 vols. Cleveland: Arthur H. Clark. (Reprinted: University of California Press, Berkeley, 1948.)

_______, ed.
1930 Anza's California Expeditions. 5 vols. Berkeley: University of California Press.

____
1930a Spanish Exploration in the Southwest, 1542-1706. New York: Charles Scribner and Sons.

____
1950 Pageant in the Wilderness: The Story of the Escalante Expedition to the Interior Basin, 1776; Including the Diary of Father Escalante. *Utah Historical Quarterly* 18(1-4). Salt Lake City.

____
1960 Rim of Christendom: A Biography of Eusebio Francisco Kino, Pacific Coast Pioneer. New York: Russell and Russell.

____
1970 Texas in the Middle Eighteenth Century: Studies in Spanish Colonial History and Administration [1915]. Austin: University of Texas Press.

Bonillas, Antonio
1774 [Informe sobre la provincia de Sonora.] (Manuscript, ff. 10-33, tomo 88, Provincias Internas, Archivo General de la Nación, Mexico City.)

Bonnie, Boniface
1968 Night and Daylight Yeibichai. Sung by Boniface Bonnie and Singers from Klagetoh, Ariz. Recorded and edited by Tony Isaacs. [Sound recording] Indian House IH 1502. 1 disc. 33⅓ rpm. 12 in.

____
1969 Navajo Skip Dance and Two-step Songs. Recorded and edited by Tony Isaacs. [Sound recording] Indian House IH 1503. 1 disc. 33⅓ rpm. 12 in.

Booth, Curtis G.
1979 Postpositions as Verbs in Kawaiisu. *International Journal of American Linguistics* 45(3):245-250.

Borgman, Francis
1948 Henry Chee Dodge, the Last Chief of the Navaho Indians. *New Mexico Historical Review* 23(2):81-93.

Bourke, John G.
1884 The Snake Dance of the Moquis of Arizona....with an Account of the Tablet Dance of the Pueblo of Santo Domingo, New Mexico, etc. New York: Charles Scribner's Sons. (Reprinted: Rio Grande Press, Glorieta, N.M., 1962.)

____
1886 An Apache Campaign in the Sierra Madre: An Account of the Expedition in Pursuit of the Hostile Chiricahua Apaches in the Spring of 1883. New York: Scribner. (2d ed. in 1958.)

____
1889 Notes on the Cosmogony and Theogony of the Mojave Indians of the Rio Colorado, Arizona. *Journal of American Folk-Lore* 2(4):169-189.

____
1890 Notes Upon the Gentile Organization of the Apaches of Arizona. *Journal of American Folk-Lore* 3(9):111-126.

____
1891 On the Border with Crook. New York: Charles Scribner's Sons. (Reprinted: University of Nebraska Press, Lincoln, 1971.)

____
1892 The Medicine-men of the Apache. Pp. 443-603 in *9th Annual Report of the Bureau of American Ethnology for the Years 1887-1888.* Washington.

Bowden, Charles
1977 Killing the Hidden Waters. Austin: University of Texas Press.

Bowen, Thomas
1973 Seri Basketry: A Comparative View. *The Kiva* 38(3-4):141-172.

____
1976 Estado actual de la arqueología en la costa central. Pp. 347-363 in Sonora: Antropología del desierto. Beatrice Braniff and Richard S. Felger, eds. *Instituto Nacional de Antropología e Historia, Colección Científica* 27. Mexico City.

____
1976a Seri Prehistory: The Archaeology of the Central Coast of Sonora, Mexico. *Anthropological Papers of the University of Arizona* 27. Tucson.

Bowen, Thomas, and Edward Moser
1968 Seri Pottery. *The Kiva* 33(3):89-132.

____
1970 Seri Headpieces and Hats. *The Kiva* 35(4):168-177.

____
1970a Material and Functional Aspects of Seri Instrumental Music. *The Kiva* 35(4):178-200.

Boyer, Ruth McDonald
1962 Social Structure and Socialization Among the Apaches of the Mescalero Reservation. (Unpublished Ph.D. Dissertation in Anthropology, University of California, Berkeley.)

Boyle, Gerald J.
1972 Income Status of the Navajos, 1969. [Preliminary analysis.] Albuquerque: University of New Mexico, Department of Economics. Mimeo.

____
1973 Revenue Alternatives for the Navajo Nation: A Report to the Regents and President of Navajo Community College. (Working Papers in Economics) Albuquerque: University of New Mexico, Department of Economics. Mimeo.

Boyle, Henry G.
1931 Trials of the Mormon Batallion Told in Diary of Company "C" Soldier. *Arizona Republic,* April 16:1,10. Phoenix.

Brambila, David
1953 Gramática rarámuri. Mexico City: Editorial Buena Prensa.

____
[1980] Diccionario rarámuri-castellano (tarahumara). Mexico City: Editorial Buena Prensa.

Brand, Donald D.
1938 Aboriginal Trade Routes for Sea Shells in the Southwest. *Yearbook of the Association of Pacific Geographers* 4:3-10. Cheney, Wash.

Brandes, Ray
1960 Frontier Military Posts of Arizona. Globe, Ariz.: Dale Stuart King.

Brant, Charles S.
1949 The Cultural Position of the Kiowa-Apache. *Southwestern Journal of Anthropology* 5(1):56-61.

____
1951 The Kiowa Apache Indians: A Study in Ethnology and Acculturation. (Unpublished Ph.D. Dissertation in Anthropology, Cornell University, Ithaca, N.Y.)

Bautista Pino, 1812; the Ojeada of Lic. Antonio Barreiro, 1832; and the Additions by Don José Agustin de Escudero, 1849. Albuquerque: The Quivira Society.

Carson, William G.B., ed.
1964 William Carr Lane, Diary. *New Mexico Historical Review* 39(3):181-234, (4):274-332.

Carter, James R.
1970 Navajo Employer Demand Survey—1969. *Arizona State Employment Service, Research and Information Series* MNP-2-70. Phoenix.

Casad, Eugene
[1981] Cora. In Studies in Uto-Aztecan Grammar. Ronald W. Langacker, ed. Arlington: Summer Institute of Linguistics and the University of Texas. In press.

Casagrande, Joseph B.
1954 Comanche Linguistic Acculturation, II. *International Journal of American Linguistics* 20(3):217-237.

———
1964 On "Round Objects:" A Navaho Covert Category. Pp. 49-54 in Vol. 2 of *Actes du VIe Congrès International des Sciences Anthropologiques et Ethnologiques.* Paris, 1960.

Casañas, Francisco
1927 Descriptions of the Tejas or Asinai Indians, 1691-1722. Mattie A. Hatcher, trans. *Southwestern Historical Quarterly* 30(3):206-218, (4):283-304.

Castañeda, Carlos E.
1936-1958 Our Catholic Heritage in Texas, 1591-1936. Paul J. Folk, ed. 7 vols. Austin: Von Boeckmann-Jones.

Castetter, Edward F., and Willis H. Bell
1942 Pima and Papago Indian Agriculture. Albuquerque: University of New Mexico Press. (Reprinted: AMS Press, New York, 1980.)

———
1951 Yuman Indian Agriculture: Primitive Subsistence on the Lower Colorado and Gila Rivers. Albuquerque: University of New Mexico Press.

Castetter, Edward F., and Morris E. Opler
1936 The Ethnobiology of the Chiricahua and Mescalero Apache. A: The Use of Plants for Foods, Beverages and Narcotics. (Ethnobiological Studies in the American Southwest 3) *Biological Series 4(5), University of New Mexico Bulletin* 297. Albuquerque.

Castetter, Edward F., and Ruth M. Underhill
1935 The Ethnobiology of the Papago Indians. *Biological Series 4(3), University of New Mexico Bulletin* 275. Albuquerque.

Cavazos Garza, Israel
1964 Cedulario autobiográfico de pobladores de Nuevo León. Monterrey, Mexico: Universidad de Nuevo León, Centro de Estudios Humanísticos.

———
1966 El Municipio de Santa Catarina en la historia. *Humánitas: Anuario del Centro de Estudios Humanísticos, Universidad de Nuevo Léon* 7:301-311. Monterrey, Mexico.

———
1966a Catálogo y sínteses de los protocolas del Archivo Municipal de Monterrey, 1599-1700. *Publicaciones del Instituto Tecnológico y de Estudios Superiores de Monterrey, Serie Historia* 4. Monterrey, Mexico.

Century Geophysical Corporation
1970 Interim Planning Report No. 7004 on Analysis of Existing Conditions, Fort Apache Indian Reservation. Mimeo.

Cerda Silva, Roberto de la
1943 Los Tepehuanes. *Revista Mexicana de Sociología* 5(4):541-567. Mexico.

Cerny, Charlene
1975 Navajo Pictorial Weaving. Santa Fe: Published by the Museum of New Mexico Foundation for the Museum of New Mexico.

Chacón, Fernando
1801 Extracto de las Novedades occuridas en la Provincia del Nuevo Mexico desde 1° de Abril hasta 12 de Junio de 1801 (Unpublished manuscript SANM II No. 1548, State Records Center and Archives, Santa Fe.)

Chafe, Wallace L.
1962 Estimates Regarding the Present Speakers of North American Indian Languages. *International Journal of American Linguistics* 28(3):162-171.

Chamberlain, Samuel E.
1956 My Confession: The Recollections of a Rogue. New York: Harper Brothers.

Chamberlain, Sue A.
1975 The Fort McDowell Indian Reservation: Water Rights and Indian Removal, 1910-1930. *Journal of the West* 14(4):27-34.

Champe, John L.
1949 White Cat Village. *American Antiquity* 14(4):285-292.

Champion, J.R.
1955 Acculturation Among the Tarahumara of Northwest Mexico Since 1890. *Transactions of the New York Academy of Sciences,* ser. 2, Vol. 17:560-566. New York.

Chenowith, JoEllen
[1976] Maricopa Pottery, as Told by Phyllis Johnson, Maricopa Pottery Maker. Phoenix and Sacaton: Heard Museum, and Gila River Arts and Crafts Center.

Ch'iao, Chien
1971 Continuation of Tradition in Navajo Society. *Academia Sinica, Institute of Ethnology Monograph Series* B(3). Taipei.

Childs, Thomas
1954 Sketch of the "Sand Indians" (as written by Henry F. Dobyns). *The Kiva* 19(2-4):27-39.

Chinle Galileans
1974 Navajo Country Gospel. [Sound recording] Benson Sound Studio LPS 9039. 1 disc. 33⅓ rpm. stereo. 12 in.

Chittenden, Newton H.
1901 Among the Cocopahs. *Land of Sunshine* 14(3):196-204. Los Angeles.

Christiansen, J.Y.
1967 History of the Navajo Indian Irrigation Project: Prepared for Presentation at the Annual Land Operations Conference Held at Farmington, New Mexico, March 7. Mimeo.

Chung, Sandra
1976 Compound Tense Markers in Tolkapaya. Pp. 119-128 in Proceedings of the First Yuman Languages Workshop Held at the University of California, San Diego, June 16-21, 1975. James E. Redden, ed. *Southern Illinois University Museum Studies, Research Record* 7. Carbondale.

Clark, Ann Nolan
1950 Little Herder in Spring, in Summer: Na'niłkaadí yázhí dąągo, shį́įgo. Hoke Denetsosie, illus. Phoenix: Phoenix Indian School.

Clauser, Charles E.
1947 The Relationship Between a Coastal Algonkin and a Karankawa Cranial Series. *Proceedings of the Indiana Academy of Science* 57:18-23. Indianapolis.

Clemmer, Richard O.
1978 Black Mesa and the Hopi. Pp. 17-34 in Native Americans and Energy Development. Joseph G. Jorgensen et al., eds. Cambridge, Mass.: Anthropology Resource Center.

Clum, Woodworth
1936 Apache Agent: The Story of John P. Clum. Boston, New York: Houghton Mifflin.

Clune, Dorris
1960 Textiles and Matting from Waterfall Cave, Chihuahua. *American Antiquity* 26(2):274-277.

Cockrum, E. Lendell
1960 The Recent Mammals of Arizona: Their Taxonomy and Distribution. Tucson: University of Arizona Press.

Coffeen, William R.
1972 The Effects of the Central Arizona Project on the Fort McDowell Indian Community. *Ethnohistory* 19(4):345-377.

Cohen, Felix S., ed.
1942 Handbook of Federal Indian Law. Washington: U.S. Government Printing Office.

Collard, Howard, and Elisabeth Scott Collard
1962 Vocabulario mayo. (*Vocabularios Indígenas* 6) Mexico City: Instituto Lingüístico de Verano.

Collier, John
1940 [Memorandum for Secretary Ickes, December 6, 1940 on Navajo Tribal Council Resolution Against Peyote; with Approval by Oscar Chapman, Acting Secretary of Interior, of December 18.] (Manuscript in Office Files of Commissioner John Collier, 1933-1945, in National Archives, Washington.)

——— 1941 [Memorandum to Indian Office Personnel, January 15, Announcing Approval of Navajo Tribal Council Resolution Against Peyote.] (Manuscript in Office Files of Commissioner John Collier, 1933-1945, National Archives, Washington.)

——— 1962 On the Gleaming Way: Navajos, Eastern Pueblos, Zunis, Hopis, Apaches and Their Land; and Their Meanings to the World. Chicago: Sage Books.

Colton, Harold S.
1939 Prehistoric Culture Units and Their Relationships in Northern Arizona. *Museum of Northern Arizona Bulletin* 17. Flagstaff.

——— 1941 Prehistoric Trade in the Southwest. *Scientific Monthly* 52(April):308-319.

——— 1945 The Patayan Problem in the Colorado River Valley. *Southwestern Journal of Anthropology* 1(1):114-121.

——— 1959 Hopi Kachina Dolls with a Key to Their Identification. Rev. ed. Albuquerque: University of New Mexico Press.

Colyer, Vincent
1872 Report on the Apache Indians of Arizona and New Mexico. Pp. 41-68 in Report of the Commissioner of Indian Affairs for the Year 1871. Washington: U.S. Government Printing Office.

Comaduran, Antonio
1843 [Letter to Elias Gonzalea, 5 May.] (Manuscript No. 28 in Pinart Collection of Documents for the History of Sonora, Bancroft Library, University of California, Berkeley.)

——— 1843a [Despatch to Jose Maria Elias, 31 March.] (Manuscript No. 49 in Pinart Collection of Documents for the History of Sonora, Bancroft Library, University of California, Berkeley.)

Conner, Daniel E.
1956 Joseph Reddeford Walker and the Arizona Adventure. Donald J. Berthrong and Odessa Davenport, eds. Norman: University of Oklahoma Press.

Cook, Charles H.
1893 Among the Pimas; or, The Mission to the Pima and Maricopa Indians. Albany: Printed for the Ladies' Union Mission School Association.

Cook, Minnie A.
1976 Apostle to the Pima Indians: The Story of Charles H. Cook, the First Missionary to the Pimas. Tiburon, Calif.: Omega Books.

Cooke, Philip St. George
1848 Report of Lieut. Col. P. St. George Cooke of His March from Santa Fe, New Mexico, to San Diego, Upper California. Pp. 549-563 in *U.S. Congress. House. 30th Cong., 1st sess., House Executive Doc.* No. 41 (Serial No. 517). Washington.

——— 1952 The Conquest of New Mexico and California: An Historical and Personal Narrative [1878]. Oakland, Calif.: Biobooks.

Cooke, Ronald U., and Richard W. Reeves
1976 Arroyos and Environmental Change in the American South-West. Oxford, England: Clarendon Press.

Cooley, Maurice E.
1962 Late Pleistocene and Recent Erosion and Alluviation in Parts of the Colorado River System, Arizona and Utah. *U.S. Geological Survey Professional Paper* 450-B:48-50. Washington.

Coolidge, Dane, and Mary Roberts Coolidge
1939 The Last of the Seris. New York: E.P. Dutton. (Reprinted: Rio Grande Press, Glorieta, N.M., 1971.)

Coombs, L. Madison
1962 Doorway Toward The Light: The Story of the Special Navajo Education Program. Washington: U.S. Department of the Interior, Bureau of Indian Affairs, Branch of Education.

Corbalan, Pedro
1778 Instrucciones del Gouor de Sonora...Para la asignacion, y repartimto de tierras en los Pueblos de Yndios.... (Manuscript, carpeta 91/769, Provincias Internas, Archivo Franciscano, Biblioteca Nacional, Mexico City.)

Corbusier, William H.
1886 Apache-Yumas and Apache-Mojaves. *American Antiquarian and Oriental Journal* 8(5):276-284, (6):325-339.

——— 1921 [A Revised Yavapai or Apache Mojave Vocabulary.] (Manuscript No. 2249-b in National Anthropological Archives, Smithsonian Institution, Washington.)

——— 1921a [Additions to the Yavapai Vocabulary Made in 1873.] (Manuscript No. 2249-c in National Anthropological Archives, Smithsonian Institution, Washington.)

——— 1923-1925 [Walapai Vocabulary.] (Manuscript No. 2259 in National Anthropological Archives, Smithsonian Institution, Washington.)

——— 1925-1926 [Yuman, Cuchan, Homkwachin Vocabulary; Legend.] (Manuscript No. 2933 in National Anthropological Archives, Smithsonian Institution, Washington.)

Corbusier, William T.
1969 Verde to San Carlos: Recollections of a Famous Army Surgeon and His Observant Family on the Western Frontier, 1869-1886. Tucson: Dale Stuart King.

Cornell, John R.
[1971] [Tape Recordings of Onabes Pimas.] (Stored as part of the Doris Duke American Indian Oral History Project, Arizona State Museum, Tucson.)

Cornell, Lois A.
1929 The Jicarilla Apaches: Their History, Customs, and Present Status. (Unpublished M.A. Thesis in Anthropology, University of Colorado, Boulder.)

Correll, J. Lee
1972 Report Showing Traditional Navajo Use and Occupancy of Lands in the 1882 Executive Order re Reservation. [Window Rock]: The Navajo Tribe, Research Section. Mimeo.

——— 1979 Brief History of the Navajo Tribal Council. Pp. 42, 43-44 in Navajoland USA, 1979 Tourist Guide. *Navajo Times* 4 (Special issue, May 1979). Window Rock, Ariz.

Correll, J. Lee, and Alfred Dehiya
1972 Anatomy of the Navajo Indian Reservation: How It Grew. Window Rock, Ariz.: The Navajo Nation.

Correll, J. Lee, Editha L. Watson, and David M. Brugge
1969 Navajo Bibliography with Subject Index. Rev. ed. 2 vols.

(*Research Report* 2) Window Rock, Ariz.: The Navajo Tribe, Parks and Recreation Research Section.

———
1973 Navajo Bibliography with Subject Index. (*Research Report* 2, *Suppl.* 1) Window Rock, Ariz.: The Navajo Tribe, Parks and Recreation Research Section.

Cosgrove, H.S., and C.B. Cosgrove
1932 The Swarts Ruin: A Typical Mimbres Site in Southwestern New Mexico; Report of the Mimbres Valley Expedition Seasons of 1924-1927. *Papers of the Peabody Museum of American Archaeology and Ethnology, Harvard University* 15(1). Cambridge, Mass.

Coues, Elliott
1895 The Expeditions of Zebulon Montgomery Pike, to the Headwaters of the Mississippi River, Through Louisiana Territory, and in New Spain, During the Years 1805-6-7. 3 vols. New York: Francis P. Harper.

———, ed.
1900 On the Trail of a Spanish Pioneer: The Diary and Itinerary of Francisco Garcés (Missionary Priest) in His Travels Through Sonora, Arizona, and California, 1775-1776. 2 vols. New York: Francis P. Harper.

Coult, Allan D.
1961 Conflict and Stability in a Hualapai Community. (Unpublished Ph.D. Dissertation in Anthropology, University of California, Berkeley.)

Couro, Ted, and Christiana Hutcheson
1973 Dictionary of Mesa Grande Diegueño: 'Iipay Aa-English; English-'Iipay Aa. Banning, Calif.: Malki Museum Press.

Couro, Ted, and Margaret Langdon
1975 Let's Talk ʔIipay Aa: An Introduction to the Mesa Grande Diegueño Language. Banning. Calif.: Malki Museum Press and Ballena Press.

Couts, Cave Johnson
1961 Hepah, California! The Journal of Cave Johnson Couts from Monterrey, Nuevo León, Mexico, to Los Angeles, California, During the Years 1848-1849. Henry F. Dobyns, ed. Tucson: Arizona Pioneers' Historical Society.

Covey, Cyclone, trans.
1961 Cabeza de Vaca's Adventures in the Unknown Interior of America. New York: Collier Books.

Cowles, Lucy, ed.
1969 Perspectives in the Education of Disadvantaged Children. Scranton, Pa.: International Textbook Company.

Cox, Isaac J., ed.
1905 The Journeys of René Robert Cavelier, Sieur de La Salle, as Related by His Faithful Lieutenant, Henry de Tonty... 2 vols. New York: A.S. Barnes.

Cozzens, Samuel W.
1876 The Marvelous Country, or Three Years in Arizona and New Mexico: Containing an Authentic History of This Wonderful Country and Its Ancient Civilization...Together with a Full and Complete History of the Apache Tribe of Indians... Boston: Lee and Shepard.

Crapo, Richley H.
1970 The Origins of Directional Adverbs in Uto-Aztecan Languages. *International Journal of American Linguistics* 36(3):181-189.

Crawford, James M.
1966 The Cocopah Language. (Unpublished Ph.D. Dissertation in Linguistics, University of California, Berkeley.)

———
1976 The Cocopa Auxiliary Verb ya·, *be located, happen.* Pp. 18-28 in Proceedings of the First Yuman Languages Workshop Held at the University of California, San Diego, June 16-21, 1975. *Southern Illinois University Museum Studies, Research Record* 7. Carbondale.

———
1978 More on Cocopa Baby Talk. *International Journal of American Linguistics* 44(1):17-23.

Crawford, Judith G.
1976 Seven Mohave Texts. Pp. 31-42 in Yuman Texts. Margaret Langdon, ed. *International Journal of American Linguistics, Native American Text Series* 1(3).

———
1976a The Reduction of *idu: be* in Mohave. Pp. 45-54 in Proceedings of the First Yuman Languages Workshop Held at the University of California, San Diego, June 16-21, 1975. *Southern Illinois University Museum Studies, Research Record* 7. Carbondale.

———
1976b Seri and Yuman. Pp. 305-324 in Hokan Studies: Papers from the First Conference on Hokan Languages, San Diego, April 23-25, 1970. Margaret Langdon and Shirley Silver, eds. (*Janua Linguarum, Series Practica* 181) The Hague, Paris: Mouton.

Crawford, J.W.
1894 [Letter No. 50886 of December 22, to Commissioner's Office re Palomas Area Yavapai.] (Manuscript in Letters Received, Commissioner's Office, Record Group 75, National Archives, Washington.)

Crespo, Francisco Antonio
1774 [Letter to Hugo O'conor, 25 November.] (Manuscript, carpeta 51/79, Provincias Internas, Archivo Franciscano, Biblioteca Nacional, Mexico City.)

Crittenden, H.W., and Roy Maddison
1958 Apache Enterprise. *New Mexico Magazine* 36(5):16-17.

Crocchiola, Stanley F.
1967 The Jicarilla Apaches of New Mexico, 1540-1967. Pampa, Tex.: Pampa Print Shop.

Crook, Donald
1974-1976 [Linguistic Fieldnotes with the Serrano.] (Manuscripts in Crook's possession.)

Crook, George
1946 General George Crook: His Autobiography. Martin F. Schmitt, ed. Norman: University of Oklahoma Press.

———
1971 Crook's Resumé of Operations Against Apache Indians, 1882-1886. Barry C. Johnson, ed. London: The Johnson-Taunton Military Press.

Crook, Rena, Leanne Hinton, and Nancy Stenson
1977 The Havasupai Writing System. Pp. 1-16 in Proceedings of the 1976 Hokan-Yuman Workshop. James E. Redden, ed. *Southern Illinois University Museum Studies, Research Record* 11. Carbondale.

Crosby, Alfred W., Jr.
1972 The Columbian Exchange: Biological and Cultural Consequences of 1492. (*Contributions in American Studies* 2) Westport, Conn.: Greenwood Publishing Company.

———
1976 Virgin Soil Epidemics as a Factor in the Aboriginal Depopulation in America. *William and Mary College Quarterly,* 3d ser., Vol. 33(2):289-299. Williamsburg, Va.

Crow, Lester D., Walter I. Murray, and Hugh H. Smythe
1966 Educating the Culturally Disadvantaged Child: Principles and Programs. New York: David McKay.

Crowe, Rosalie, and Sidney B. Brinckerhoff, eds.
1976 Early Yuma: A Graphic History of Life on the American Nile. Flagstaff, Ariz.: Yuma County Historical Society and Northland Press.

Crumrine, Lynne S.
1969 Ceremonial Exchange as a Mechanism in Tribal Integration Among the Mayos of Northwest Mexico. *Anthropological Papers of the University of Arizona* 14. Tucson.

Crumrine, N. Ross
1961-1972 [Fieldwork on the Mayo.] (Unpublished manuscript in Crumrine's possession.)

———
1964 The House Cross of the Mayo Indians of Sonora, Mexico: A Symbol of Ethnic Identity. *Anthropological Papers of the University of Arizona* 8. Tucson.

———
1968 The Easter Ceremonial in the Socio-cultural Identity of Mayos, Sonora, Mexico. (Unpublished Ph.D. Dissertation in Anthropology, University of Arizona, Tucson.)

———
1969 Čapakoba, the Mayo Easter Ceremonial Impersonator: Explanations of Ritual Clowning. *Journal for the Scientific Study of Religion* 8(1):1-22.

———
1970 Ritual Drama and Culture Change. *Comparative Studies in Society and History* 12(4):361-371.

———
1974 El Ceremonial de Pascua y la identidad de los mayos de Sonora, México. Mexico City: Instituto Nacional Indígenista.

———
1975 A New Mayo Indian Religious Movement in Northwest Mexico. *Journal of Latin American Lore* 1(2):127-145.

———
1976 Mediating Roles in Ritual and Symbolism: Northwest Mexico and the Pacific Northwest. *Anthropologica* 18(2):131-152.

———
1977 The Mayo Indians of Sonora: A People Who Refuse to Die. Tucson: University of Arizona Press.

———
1977a El Ceremonial Pascual mayo de Banari, un drama ritual sagrado. *Folklore Americano* 24:111-139.

———
1978 A Transformational Analysis of Mayo Ceremonialism and Myth. *Journal of Latin American Lore* 4(2):231-242.

———
1979 Mayo Indian Myth and Ceremonialism, Northwest Mexico: The Dual Ceremonial Cycle. Pp. 89-111 in Ritual Symbolism and Ceremonialism in the Americas: Studies in Symbolic Anthropology. *University of Northern Colorado, Museum of Anthropology, Occasional Publications in Anthropology, Ethnology Series* 33(1). Greeley.

———
1981 The Ritual of the Culture Enclave Process: The Dramatization of Oppositions. Pp. 109-131 in The Persistent Peoples. George P. Castille and Gilbert Kushmer, eds. Tucson: University of Arizona Press.

———
1981a The Mayo of Southern Sonora: Socioeconomic Assimilation and Ritual—Symbolic Syncretism—Split Acculturation. Pp. 22-35 in Themes of Indigenous Acculturation in Northwest Mexico. Thomas B. Hinton and Phil C. Weigand, eds. *Anthropological Papers of the University of Arizona* 38. Tucson.

———
[1982] Transformational Processes and Models—with Special Reference to Mayo Myth and Ritual. In The Logic of Culture. Ino Rossi, ed. Brooklyn, N.Y.: J.F. Bergin. In press.

Crumrine, N. Ross, and Lynne S. Crumrine
1967 Ancient and Modern Mayo Fishing Practices. *The Kiva* 33(1):25-33.

———
1969 Where Mayos Meet Mestizos: A Model for the Social Structure of Culture Contact. *Human Organization* 28(1):50-57.

Crumrine, N. Ross, and M. Louise Crumrine
1977 Ritual Symbolism in Folk and Ritual Drama: The Mayo Indian San Cayetano Velación, Sonora, Mexico. *Journal of American Folklore* 90(355):8-28.

Crumrine, N. Ross, and B. June Macklin
1974 Sacred Ritual vs. the Unconscious: The Efficacy of Symbols and Structure in North Mexican Folk Saints Cults and General Ceremonialism. Pp. 179-197 in The Unconscious in Culture: The Structuralism of Claude Lévi-Strauss. Ino Rossi, ed. New York: E.P. Dutton.

Cruse, Thomas
1941 Apache Days and After. Eugene Cunningham, ed. Caldwell, Ida.: Caxton Printers.

Culin, Stewart
1907 Games of the North American Indians. Pp. 1-846 in *24th Annual Report of the Bureau of American Ethnology for the Years 1902-1903.* Washington. (Reprinted: Dover Press, New York, 1975.)

Curtin, L.S.M.
1949 By the Prophet of the Earth. Santa Fe: San Vicente Foundation.

Curtis, D.
1871 [Letter to General Act. Assistant Adjutant Department of Arizona, Dated November 5, Headquarters Camp McDowell, re Yavapai Ready to Settle on Reservation at Camp Reno.] (Manuscript in Record Group 393, National Archives, Washington.)

Curtis, Edward S.
1907-1930 The North American Indian: Being a Series of Volumes Picturing and Describing the Indians of the United States, and Alaska. Frederick W. Hodge, ed. 20 vols. Norwood, Mass.: Plimpton Press. (Reprinted: Johnson Reprint, New York, 1970.)

Curtis, Natalie
1919 The Winning of an Indian Reservation: How Theodore Roosevelt and Frank Mead Restored the Mojave-Apaches to Their Own. *The Outlook* (June 25):327-330.

Cushing, Frank H.
1882 The Nation of the Willows. *Atlantic Monthly* 50:362-374, 541-559. (Reprinted: Northland Press, Flagstaff, Ariz., 1965.)

———
1896 Outlines of Zuni Creation Myths. Pp. 321-447 in *13th Annual Report of the Bureau of American Ethnology for the Years 1891-1892.* Washington.

———
1920 Zuñi Breadstuff. *Museum of the American Indian, Heye Foundation. Indian Notes and Monographs* 8. New York. (Reprinted in 1974.)

Cutler, Hugh
1960 Cultivated Plant Remains from Waterfall Cave, Chihuahua. *American Antiquity* 26(2):277-279.

Cutter, Donald C.
1974 An Inquiry into Indian Land Rights in the Jicarilla Apache Area in the American Southwest Under Spain, Mexico, and the United States, with Particular Reference to the Jicarilla Apache Area of Northeastern New Mexico. Pp. 245-280 in Apache Indians, VI. (*American Indian Ethnohistory: Indians of the Southwest*) New York: Garland.

Dabdoub, Claudio
1964 Historia de El valle del Yaqui. Mexico City: Librería de Manuel Porrúa.

Dajevskis, Peteris
1974 Tribal Management Procedures: Study of the Hualapai Reservation. Tucson: University of Arizona, Bureau of Ethnic Research.

Dakin, Karen
1979 Phonological Changes in Nahuatl: The Tense/Aspect/Number Systems. *International Journal of American Linguistics* 45(1):48-71.

———
1981 The Characteristics of a Nahuatl *Lingua Franca.* Pp. 54-67 in Nahuatl Studies, in Memory of Fernando Horcasitas. Frances Karttunen, ed. (*Texas Linguistic Forum* 18) Austin: University of Texas, Department of Linguistics.

Dale, Edward E.
1949 The Indians of the Southwest: A Century of Development Under the United States. Norman: University of Oklahoma Press.

D'Andrade, R.G.
1970 Structure and Syntax in the Semantic Analysis of Kinship Terminology. Pp. 87-143 in Cognition: A Multiple View; Symposium on Cognitive Studies and Artificial Intelligence Research, University of Chicago, 1969. Paul L. Garvin, ed. New York: Spartan Books.

Davenport, Harbert, ed.
1924 The Expedition of Pánfilo de Narváez, by Gonzalo Fernández Oviedo y Valdez. Chapters IV and V. *Southwestern Historical Quarterly* 27(4):276-304. Austin.

Davis, Britton
1963 The Truth About Geronimo [1929]. M.M. Quaife, ed. New Haven, Conn.: Yale University Press.

Davis, Edward H.
1920 The Papago Ceremony of Vikita. *Museum of the American Indian, Heye Foundation. Indian Notes and Monographs* 3(4):158-178. New York.

Davis, Edward H., and E. Yale Dawson
1945 The Savage Seris of Sonora. *Scientific Monthly* (March):193-203.

Davis, Irvine
1966 Numic Consonantal Correspondences. *International Journal of American Linguistics* 32(2):124-140.

Davis, W.W.
1869 The Spanish Conquest of New Mexico. Doylestown, Pa.: no publisher.

Dayley, Jon
[1971] [Linguistic Fieldwork with the Panamint of Death Valley and Lone Pine, California.] (Notes in the Archives of the Survey of California Indian Languages, Linguistics Department, University of California, Berkeley.)

Deal, Julia
[1949] Music of the Sioux and Navajo. Recorded and edited by Willard Rhodes. [Sound recording] Folkway Records FE 4401. 1 disc. 33⅓ rpm. 12 in.

Debo, Angie
1976 Geronimo: The Man, His Time, His Place. Norman: University of Oklahoma Press.

DeBorhegyi, Stephan F.
1955 Pottery Mask Tradition in Mesoamerica. *Southwestern Journal of Anthropology* 11(3):205-213.

Decorme, Gerard
1941 La Obra de los Jesuítas mexicanos durante la época colonial, 1572-1767. 2 vols. Mexico City: Antigua Librería Robredo de J. Porrúa e Hijos.

Deimel, Claus
1980 Tarahumara: Indianer im Norden Mexikos. Frankfurt, Germany: Syndikat-Verlag.

______
1980a Les Indiens Tarahumaras: Au présent et au passé. Béatrice Dexmier and Jacques Dexmier, trans. Lyon, France: Fédérop.

De Laguna, Frederica
1975 Matrilineal Kin Groups in Northwestern North America. Pp. 17-145 in Vol. 1 of Proceedings: Northern Athapaskan Conference, 1971. A. McFadyen Clark, ed. 2 vols. *Canada. National Museum of Man, Mercury Series, Ethnology Service Paper* 27. Ottawa.

Del Hoyo, Eugenio *see* Hoyo, Eugenio del

Deloria, Vine, Jr.
1969 Custer Died for Your Sins: An Indian Manifesto. London: Collier-Macmillan.

Deniker, J.
1907 The Races of Man. New York: Charles Scribners' Sons.

Densmore, Frances
1929 Papago Music. *Bureau of American Ethnology Bulletin* 90. Washington.

______
1932 Yuman and Yaqui Music. *Bureau of American Ethnology Bulletin* 110. Washington.

______
1938 Music of Santo Domingo Pueblo, New Mexico. *Southwest Museum Paper* 12. Los Angeles, Calif.

Derby, George H.
1852 Reconnoissance of the Gulf of California and the Colorado River. *U.S. Congress. Senate. 32d Congress, 1st sess., Senate Executive Doc. No.* 81. (Serial No. 620) Washington: U.S. Government Printing Office.

De Solís, Gaspar José
1931 Diary of a Visit of Inspection of the Texas Missions Made by Fray Gaspar José de Solís in the Year 1767-1768. Margaret K. Kress, trans. *Southwestern Historical Quarterly* 35(1):28-76. Austin.

Detrick, Charles H.
1894 [Comanche Vocabulary and Phrases.] (Manuscript No. 788 in National Anthropological Archives, Smithsonian Institution, Washington.)

Devereux, George
1937 Mohave Soul Concepts. *American Anthropologist* 39(3):417-422.

______
1950 Education and Discipline in Mohave Society. *Primitive Man* 23(4):85-102.

______
1951 Mohave Chieftainship in Action: A Narrative of the First Contacts of the Mohave Indians with the United States. *Plateau* 23(3):33-43.

______
1951a Cultural and Characterological Traits of the Mohave. *Psychoanalytic Quarterly* 20:398-422.

______
1956 Mohave Dreams of Omen and Power. *Tomorrow* 4(3):17-24.

______
1957 Dream Learning and Individual Ritual Differences in Mohave Shamanism. *American Anthropologist* 59(6):1036-1045.

______
1961 Mohave Ethnopsychiatry and Suicide: The Psychiatric Knowledge and the Psychic Disturbances of an Indian Tribe. *Bureau of American Ethnology Bulletin* 175. Washington. (Reprinted in 1969.)

Devin, Thomas C.
1868 [Letter to Major Therburne, Dated Headquarters in Prescott in the Field, January 3.] (Manuscript in Record Group 393, National Archives, Washington.)

DeWald, Terry
1979 The Papago Indians and Their Basketry. Tucson: Terry DeWald.

Diné Ba' Aliil of Navajoland
1976 Produced and recorded by Raymond A. Boley. [Sound Recording] Canyon Records 6117. 1 disc. 33⅓ rpm. stereo. 12 in.

Di Peso, Charles C.
1953 The Sobaipuri Indians of the Upper San Pedro River Valley, Southeastern Arizona. *Amerind Foundation Publication* 6. Dragoon, Ariz.

______
1956 The Upper Pima of San Cayetano del Tumacacori: An Archaeohistorical Reconstruction of the Ootam of Pimeria Alta. *Amerind Foundation Publication* 7. Dragoon, Ariz.

______
[1969] Casas Grandes and the Gran Chichimeca. Santa Fe: Museum of New Mexico Press.

______
1974 Casas Grandes: A Fallen Trading Center of the Gran Chichimeca. 3 vols. *Amerind Foundation Series* 9. Dragoon, Ariz.

Di Peso, Charles C., and Daniel S. Matson, eds. and trans.
1965 The Seri Indians in 1692 as Described by Adamo Gilg, S.J. *Arizona and the West* 7(1):33-56.

Dittert, Alfred E., Jr., Jim J. Hester, and Frank W. Eddy
1961 An Archaeological Survey of the Navajo Reservoir District, Northwestern New Mexico. *Monographs of the School of American Research and the Museum of New Mexico* 23. Santa Fe.

Dobyns, Henry F.
1951 Papagos in the Cotton Fields, 1950. Tucson: Privately printed.

———
1963 An Outline of Andean Epidemic History to 1720. *Bulletin of the History of Medicine* 37(6):493-515.

———
1966 Estimating Aboriginal American Population; 1. An Appraisal of Techniques with a New Hemispheric Estimate. *Current Anthropology* 7(4):395-416.

———
1971 The Apache People. Phoenix: Indian Tribal Series.

———
1972 The Papago People. Phoenix: Indian Tribal Series.

———
1973 The Mescalero Apache People. Phoenix: Indian Tribal Series.

———
1974 Hualapai Indians, I: Prehistoric Indian Occupation Within the Eastern Area of the Yuman Complex: A Study in Applied Archaeology, 3 vols. *(American Indian Ethnohistory: Indians of the Southwest)* New York: Garland.

———
1974a The Kohatk: Oasis and ak-chin Horticulturalists. *Ethnohistory* 21(4):317-327.

———
1976 Spanish Colonial Tucson: A Demographic History. Tucson: University of Arizona Press.

———
1977 The Decline of Mescalero Apache Indian Population from 1873 to 1913. *University of Oklahoma Papers in Anthropology* 18(2):61-69. Norman.

———
1981 From Fire to Flood: Historic Human Destruction of Sonoran Desert Riverine Oases. *Ballena Press Anthropological Paper* 20. Socorro, N.M.

Dobyns, Henry F., and Robert C. Euler
1960 A Brief History of the Northeastern Pai. *Plateau* 32(3):49-57.

———
1967 The Ghost Dance of 1889 Among the Pai Indians of Northwestern Arizona. *Prescott College Studies in Anthropology* 1. Prescott, Ariz.

———
1970 Wauba Yuma's People: The Comparative Sociopolitical Structure of the Pai Indians of Arizona. *Prescott College Studies in Anthropology* 3. Prescott, Ariz.

———
1976 The Walapai People. Phoenix: Indian Tribal Series.

Dobyns, Henry F., Paul H. Ezell, and Greta S. Ezell
1963 Death of a Society: The Halchidhoma. *Ethnohistory* 10(2):105-161.

Dobyns, Henry F., Paul H. Ezell, Alden W. Jones and Greta Ezell
1957 Thematic Changes in Yman Warfare, Pp. 46-71 in Cultural Stability and Cultural Change. Verne Ray, ed. *(Proceedings of the 1957 Annual Spring Meeting of the American Ethnological Society)* Seattle: University of Washington Press.

———, 1960
What were Nixoras? *Southwestern Journal of Anthropology* 16(2):230-258.

Dobyns, Henry F., Richard W. Stoffle, and Kristine Jones
1975 Native American Urbanization and Socio-economic Integration in the Southwestern United States. *Ethnohistory* 22(2):155-179.

Dockstader, Frederick J.
1954 The Kachina and the White Man. *Cranbrook Institute of Science Bulletin* 35. Bloomfield Hills, Mich.

———
1961 A Figurine Cache from Kino Bay, Sonora. Pp. 182-191 in Essays in Pre-Columbian Art and Archaeology. Samuel K. Lothrop, ed. Cambridge, Mass.: Harvard University Press.

Documentos para la Historia de Méjico
1853-1857 Documentos para la Historia de Méjico. F. Garcia Figueros, ed. 21 vols. in 4 series. Mexico City: Impr. de J.R. Navarro.

Dolaghan, Thomas, and David Scates
1978 The Navajos Are Coming to Jesus. South Pasadena, Calif.: William Carey Library.

Dolan, Darrow, comp. and ed.
1972 The Plomo Papers. *Ethnohistory* 19(4):305-322.

Dolan, Thomas A.
1929 Report of Council Proceedings with the Jicarilla Apache Indians. *New Mexico Historical Review* 4(1):59-72.

Dolores, Juan
1910-1951 [Field Notebooks, Books VII and VIII.] (Manuscript No. 134 in Alfred L. Kroeber Collection, Department and Museum of Anthropology, University of California, Berkeley.)

Downs, James F.
1964 Animal Husbandry in Navajo Society and Culture. *University of California Publications in Anthropology* 1. Berkeley.

Dozier, Edward P.
1954 The Hopi-Tewa of Arizona. *University of California Publications in American Archaeology and Ethnology* 44(3):259-376. Berkeley.

———
1958 Social Structure of the Rio Grande Tewa Pueblos. (Paper prepared for a Seminar on Non-unilineal Kinship, held at the Center for Advanced Study in the Behavioral Sciences, Palo Alto, Calif.)

———
1960 A Comparison of Eastern Keresan and Tewa Kinship Systems. Pp. 430-436 in Men and Cultures: Selected Papers of the Fifth International Congress of Anthropological and Ethnological Sciences. Philadelphia, 1956.

———
1961 Rio Grande Pueblos. Pp. 94-186 in Perspectives in American Indian Culture Change. Edward H. Spicer, ed. Chicago: University of Chicago Press.

———
1970 The Pueblo Indians of North America. New York: Holt, Rinehart and Winston.

Draper, Teddy
[1960] Song Commemorating Flag Raising on Iwo Jima. Recorded and edited by Willard Rhodes. [Sound recording] Library of Congress AFS L41. 1 disc. 33⅓ rpm. 12 in.

Driver, Harold E.
1962 The Contribution of A.L. Kroeber to Culture Area Theory and Practice. *Indiana University Publications in Anthropology and Linguistics, Memoir* 18. Bloomington.

———
1966 Geographical-historical vs. Psycho-functional Explanations of Kin Avoidances. *Current Anthropology* 7(2):131-182.

Driver, Harold E., and Wilhelmine Driver
1963 Ethnography and Acculturation of the Chichimeca-Jonaz of Northeast Mexico. *Indiana University Research Center in Anthropology, Folklore, and Linguistics, Publication* 26. Bloomington.

Driver, Harold E., and Alfred L. Kroeber
1932 Quantitative Expression of Cultural Relationships. *University of California Publications in American Archaeology and Ethnology* 31(4):211-256. Berkeley.

Driver, Harold E., and William C. Massey
1957 Comparative Studies of North American Indians. *Transac-*

tions of the American Philosophical Society n.s. 47(2). Philadelphia.

Drucker, Philip
1941 Culture Element Distributions, XVII: Yuman-Piman. *University of California Anthropological Records* 6(3). Berkeley.

Dumke, Glenn S., ed.
1945 Mexican Gold Trail: The Journal of a Forty-niner [Evans], by George W.B. Evans. San Marino, Calif.: The Huntington Library.

Dunbier, Roger
1968 The Sonoran Desert: Its Geography, Economy, and People. Tucson: University of Arizona Press.

Dunn, Dorothy
1968 American Indian Painting of the Southwest and Plains Areas. Albuquerque: University of New Mexico Press.

Dunn, William E.
1911 Apache Relations in Texas, 1718-1750. *Quarterly of the Texas State Historical Association* 14(3):198-274. Austin.

Dunne, Peter M.
1944 Pioneer Jesuits in Northern Mexico. Berkeley: University of California Press.

——— 1948 Early Jesuit Missions in Tarahumara. Berkeley: University of California Press.

Dunnigan, Timothy
[1966] [Pima Texts and Tapes Collected at Maycoba, Sonora.] (Texts and tapes in Dunnigan's possession.)

——— 1970 Subsistence and Reciprocity Patterns Among the Mountain Pimas of Sonora, Mexico. (Unpublished Ph.D. Dissertation in Anthropology, University of Arizona, Tucson.)

——— 1981 Ritual as Interethnic Competition: Indito Versus Blanco in Mountain Pima Easter Ceremonies. Pp. 132-150 in Persistent Peoples: Cultural Enclaves in Perspective. George Pierre Castile and Gilbert Kushner, eds. Tucson: University of Arizona Press.

——— 1981a Adaptive Strategies of Peasant Indians in a Biethnic Mexican Community: A Study of Mountain Pima Acculturation. Pp. 36-49 in Themes of Indigenous Acculturation in Northwest Mexico. *Anthropological Papers of the University of Arizona* 38. Tucson.

Dustin, C. Burton
1960 Peyotism and New Mexico. Farmington, N.M.: no publisher.

Dutton, Bertha P.
1963 Sun Father's Way: The Kiva Murals of Kuaua, a Pueblo Ruin, Coronado State Monument, New Mexico. Albuquerque: University of New Mexico Press.

Dyen, Isidore, and David F. Aberle
1974 Lexical Reconstruction: The Case of the Proto-Athapaskan Kinship System. London and New York: Cambridge University Press.

Dyk, Walter, ed.
1967 Son of Old Man Hat: A Navajo Autobiography [1938]. Lincoln: University of Nebraska Press.

Dyk, Walter, and Ruth Dyk, eds.
1980 Left Handed: A Navajo Autobiography. New York: Columbia University Press.

Earle, Edwin, and Edward A. Kennard
1971 Hopi Kachinas. 2d rev. ed. New York: Museum of the American Indian, Heye Foundation.

Eaton, John H.
[1854] [Navajo Vocabulary, with Notes by George Gibbs.] (Manuscript No. 145 in National Anthropological Archives, Smithsonian Institution, Washington.)

Eckhart, George B.
1960 A Guide to the History of the Missions of Sonora, 1614-1826. *Arizona and the West* 2(2):165-183.

Eddy, Frank W.
1966 Prehistory in the Navajo Reservoir District: Northwestern New Mexico. 2 Pts. *Museum of New Mexico Papers in Anthropology* 15. Santa Fe.

Eggan, Fred
1950 Social Organization of the Western Pueblos. Chicago: University of Chicago Press. (Reprinted in 1970.)

——— 1966 The American Indian: Perspectives for the Study of Social Change. Chicago: Aldine.

——— 1980 Shoshone Kinship Structures and Their Significance for Anthropological Theory. *Journal of the Stewart Anthropological Society* 11(2):165-193. Urbana, Ill.

Eguilaz, Isabel *see* Eguilaz de Prado, Isabel

Eguilaz de Prado, Isabel
1965 Los Indios del nordeste de México en el siglo XVIII. *Seminario de Antropología Americana, Publicaciones* 7. Seville, Spain.

——— 1966 Los Indios del nordeste de México en el siglo XVIII: Areas de población y areas culturales. Pp. 177-194 in Vol 2 of *Proceedings of the 36th International Congress of Americanists.* Seville, Spain, 1964.

Eickemeyer, Carl, and Lilian W. Eickemeyer
1895 Among the Pueblo Indians. New York: The Merriam Company.

Ekholm, Gordon F.
1939 Results of an Archaeological Survey of Sonora and Northern Sinaloa. *Revista Mexicana de Estudios Antropológicos* 3:7-10. Mexico.

——— 1946 Excavations at Guasave, Sinaloa, Mexico. *Anthropological Papers of the American Museum of Natural History* 38(2). New York.

Elias, Simon
1826 [Letter of August 11 to the Secretary of State and the War Office and Navy.] (Manuscript in Archivos del Estado, Hermosillo, Mexico.)

Ellis, Florence Hawley
1964 A Reconstruction of the Basic Jemez Pattern of Social Organization, with Comparisons to Other Tanoan Social Structures. *University of New Mexico Publications in Anthropology* 11. Albuquerque.

——— 1968 What Utaztecan Ethnology Suggests of Utaztecan Prehistory. Pp. 53-105 in Utaztekan Prehistory. Earl H. Swanson, Jr., ed. *Idaho State University Museum Occasional Paper* 22. Pocatello.

——— 1974 An Anthropological Study of the Navajo Indians. *(American Indian Ethnohistory: Indians of the Southwest)* New York: Garland.

Elmore, Francis H.
1944 Ethnobotany of the Navajo. *Monographs of the School of American Research* 8. Santa Fe.

——— 1952 [Review of] The Ethnobotany of the Kayenta Navaho, by Leland C. Wyman and Stuart K. Harris. *American Antiquity* 17(3):276.

Emory, William H.
1848 Notes of a Military Reconnoissance, from Fort Leavenworth, in Missouri, to San Diego, in California, Including Parts of Arkansas, Del Norte, and Gila Rivers. Made in 1846-1847. *U.S. Congress. Senate. 31st Cong., 1st sess., Senate Executive Doc.* No. 7 (Serial No. 505). Washington.

———
1951 Lieutenant Emory Reports. Ross Calvin, ed. Albuquerque: University of New Mexico Press.

Enochs, J.B.
1940 Little Man's Family: Diné yázhí ba'ałchini. Pre-primer. Phoenix: Phoenix Indian School.

———
1940a Little Man's Family: Diné yázhí ba'ałchini. Primer. Gerald Nailer, illus. Phoenix: Phoenix Indian School.

Erasmus, Charles J.
1961 Man Takes Control: Cultural Development and American Aid. Minneapolis: University of Minnesota Press.

———
1967 Culture Change in Northwest Mexico. Pp. 1-131 in Contemporary Change in Traditional Societies. Vol. 3: Mexican and Peruvian Communities. Julian H. Steward, ed. Urbana: University of Illinois Press.

Erickson, Jon T., and H. Thomas Cain
1976 Navajo Textiles from the Read Mullan Collection. Phoenix, Ariz.: The Heard Museum.

Escalante H., Roberto
[1960] [Census of the Maycoba Pimas.] (Manuscript in Escalante's possession.)

———
1962 El Pima Bajo. *Anales del Instituto Nacional de Antropología e Historia* 14(43):349-352. Mexico City.

———
1964 Material lingüístico del oriente de Sonora: Tonichi y Pónica. *Anales del Instituto Nacional de Antropología e Historia* 16(45):149-177. Mexico City.

Escovar y Llamas, Christóval de
1745 [Acknowledgement to the King of the Real Cédula Dated November 3, 1744.] (Manuscript, folio 128r, tomo 67, Reales Cédulas, Archivo General de la Nación, Mexico City).

Escudero, D. José Agustin de
1849 Noticias estadísticas de Sonora y Sinaloa compiladas y amplificadas para la comisión de estadística militar. Mexico City: Tipografía de R. Rafael.

Espinosa, Isidro Félix de
1964 Crónica de los Colegios de Propaganda fide de la Nueva España. Washington: Academy of American Franciscan History.

Espinosa, J. Manuel, ed. and trans.
1940 First Expedition of Vargas into New Mexico, 1692. Albuquerque: University of New Mexico Press.

———
1942 Crusaders of the Rio Grande: The Story of Don Diego de Vargas and the Reconquest and Refounding of New Mexico. Chicago: Institute of Jesuit History.

Euler, Robert C.
1958 Walapai Culture History. (Unpublished Ph.D. Dissertation in Anthropology, University of New Mexico, Albuquerque.)

Everett, Michael W.
1970 Pathology in White Mountain Apache Culture. *Western Canadian Journal of Anthropology* 2(1):180-203.

———
1971 Drinking, Talking, and Fighting: An Apache Dilemma. (Unpublished manuscript at University of Kentucky, Lexington.)

———
1971a White Mountain Apache Medical Decision-making. Pp. 135-150 in Apachean Culture History and Ethnology. Keith H. Basso and Morris E. Opler, eds. *Anthropological Papers of the University of Arizona* 21. Tucson.

———
1972 'Drinking' and 'Trouble.' (Unpublished manuscript at University of Kentucky, Lexington.)

Ewing, Henry P.
1960 The Pai Tribes. Robert C. Euler and Henry F. Dobyns, eds. *Ethnohistory* 7(1):61-80.

———
1961 The Origin of the Pai Tribes. Henry F. Dobyns and Robert C. Euler, eds. *The Kiva* 26(3):8-23.

Ezell, Greta S., and Paul H. Ezell
1970 Background to Battle: Circumstances Relating to Death on the Gila, 1857. Pp. 168-187 in Troopers West: Military and Indian Affairs on the American Frontier. Ray Brandes, ed. San Diego, Calif.: Frontier Heritage Press.

Ezell, Paul H.
1951-1954 [Fieldnotes on the Pima.] (Unpublished manuscripts in Ezell's possession.)

———
1955 Indians Under the Law: Mexico 1821-1847. *America Indígena* 15(3):199-214.

———
1957 The Conditions of Hispanic-Piman Contacts on the Gila River. *America Indígena* 17(2):163-191.

———
1961 The Hispanic Acculturation of the Gila River Pima. *Memoirs of the American Anthropological Association* 90. Menasha, Wis.

———
1963 The Maricopas: An Identification from Documentary Sources. *Anthropological Papers of the University of Arizona* 6. Tucson.

———
1963a Is There a Hohokam-Pima Culture Continuum? *American Antiquity* 29(1):61-66.

———
1968 The CocoMaricopa Mail. Pp. 28-34 in Brand Book 1. Ray Brandes, ed. San Diego, Calif.: Corral of the Westerners.

Fabila, Alfonso
1940 Las Tribus yaquis de Sonora, su cultura y anhelada autodeterminación. Mexico City: Departamento de Asuntos Indígenas.

———
1957 Los Pápagos de Sonora. *Acción Indigenista: Boletín Mensual del Instituto Nacional Indigenista* 47:3-4. Mexico City.

———
1958 La Tribu yaqui de Sonora. (Unpublished manuscript in Instituto Nacional Indigenista, Mexico City).

Farber, Joseph C., and Michael Dorris
1975 Native Americans: 500 Years After. Photographs by J.C. Farber; text by Michael Dorris. New York: Crowell.

Farish, Thomas E.
1915-1918 History of Arizona. 8 vols. Phoenix: The Filmer Brothers Electrotype Company.

Farmer, Malcolm F.
1935 The Mojave Trade Route. *Masterkey* 9(5):154-157.

———
1942 Navajo Archaeology of Upper Blanco and Largo Canyons, Northern New Mexico. *American Antiquity* 8(1):65-79.

Fathauer, George H.
1951 The Mohave "Ghost Doctor." *American Anthropologist* 53(4):605–607.

———
1951a Religion in Mohave Social Structure. *Ohio Journal of Science* 51(5):273-276.

———
1954 The Structure and Causation of Mohave Warfare. *Southwestern Journal of Anthropology* 10(1):97-118.

Faubert, J.B. Edmundo
[1975] Los Indios pimas de Sonora y Chihuahua. (Manuscript, copy in the Arizona State Museum Library, Tucson.)

Faulk, Odie B.
1970 Arizona: A Short History. Norman: University of Oklahoma Press.

Fay, George E.
1955 A Preliminary Report of an Archaeological Survey in South-

ern Sonora, Mexico: 1953. *Transactions of the Kansas Academy of Science* 58(4):566-587. Topeka.

Felger, Richard S.
1966 Ecology of the Gulf Coast and Islands of Sonora, Mexico. (Unpublished Ph.D. Dissertation in Biology, University of Arizona, Tucson.)

——— 1976 The Gulf of California: An Ethno-ecological Perspective. *Natural Resources Journal* 16:451-464.

Felger, Richard S., and Mary B. Moser
1970 Seri Use of Agave (Century Plant). *The Kiva* 35(4):159-167.

——— 1971 Seri Use of Mesquite *Prosopis glandulosa* var *torreyana*. *The Kiva* 37(1):53-60.

——— 1973 Eelgrass (Zostera marina L.) in the Gulf of California: Discovery of Its Nutritional Value by the Seri Indians. *Science* 181(4097):355-356.

——— 1974 Seri Indian Pharmacopoeia. *Economic Botany* 28(4):414-436.

——— 1974a Columnar Cacti in Seri Indian Culture. *The Kiva* 39(3-4):257-275.

Felger, Richard S., Kim Clifton, and Philip J. Regal
1976 Winter Dormancy in Sea Turtles: Independent Discovery and Exploitation in the Gulf of California by Two Local Cultures. *Science* 191(4224):283-285.

Félix Váldes, Luís C.
1966-1967 El Informe anual, investigación. Hermosillo, Sonora: Escuela de Agricultura y Ganadería.

The Fenders
[1960] Introducing the Fenders. [Sound recording] Indian Arts R-3004. 1 disc. 33⅓ rpm. 12 in.

——— 1966 Second Time 'Round. Vol. 2. [Sound recording] Western Records 2.0.1.6. 1 disc. 33⅓ rpm. stereo. 12 in.

Fenton, Joann C.
1974 A Cultural Analysis of Navajo Family and Clan. (Unpublished Ph.D. Dissertation in Anthropology, Northwestern University, Evanston, Ill.)

Ferdon, Edwin N., Jr.
1955 A Trial Survey of Mexican-Southwestern Architectural Parallels. *Monographs of the School of American Research* 21. Santa Fe.

Ferg, Alan
1981 Amos Gustina: Apache Fiddle Maker. *American Indian Art Magazine* 6(3):28-35.

Fernald, Mary L.
1973 A Study of Maricopa Pottery. (Unpublished M.A. Thesis in Anthropology, Arizona State University, Tempe.)

Fernández del Castillo, Francisco
1926 Luz de tierra incognita. *Publicaciones del Archivo General de la Nación* 10. Mexico City.

Ferran, Manuel A.
1964 Mescalero Apache Reservation: A Case Study in Area Development. (Unpublished M.A. Thesis in Anthropology, University of New Mexico, Albuquerque.)

Feudge, John
1866 [Letter Dated November 21, from Special Indian Agent John Feudge at the Colorado River Reservation to D.N. Cooley, U.S. Commissioner of Indian Affairs, Washington.] (Manuscript in Letters Received, Commissioner's Office, Record Group 75, National Archives, Washington.)

Fewkes, J. Walter
1912 Casa Grande, Arizona. Pp. 25-179 in *28th Annual Report of the Bureau of American Ethnology for the Years 1906-1907*. Washington.

——— 1923 Clay Figurines Made by Navaho Children. *American Anthropologist* 25(4):559-563.

Figueroa, Gerónimo de
1853-1857 Puntos de Anua de estos diez años que he asistido en este partido de San Pablo. Pp. 217-221 in Vol. 3 of *Documentos para la Historia de Méjico*. 4th ser. Mexico City: J.R. Navarro.

Figueroa, José
1825 [Letter of September 6 from Arizpe, to Secretario de Estado y del Despacho de la Guerra y Marina, México.] (Manuscript No. 72 in Archivo Histórico Militar, Secretaria de la Defensa Nacional, Mexico City.)

Figueroa Torres, J. Jesús
1963 Fr. Juan Larios: Defensor de los indios y fundador de Coahuila, 1673-1676. Mexico City: Editorial Jus.

Fintzelberg, Nicholas M.
1969 Peyote Paraphernalia. (*Ethnic Technology Notes* 4) San Diego, Calif.: San Diego Museum of Man.

Fish, Paul R., and Suzanne K. Fish
1977 Verde Valley Archaeology: Review and Prospective. *Museum of Northern Arizona Research Paper* 8. Flagstaff.

Fishler, Stanley A.
1953 In the Beginning: A Navaho Creation Myth. *University of Utah Anthropological Paper* 13. Salt Lake City.

Fitzpatrick, W.S., Joan Fitzpatrick, and T.N. Campbell
1964 A Rockport Black-on-Gray Vessel from the Vicinity of Corpus Christi, Texas. *Bulletin of the Texas Archaeological Society* 35:193-204. Austin.

Font, Pedro
1951 The Colorado Yumans in 1775. Pp. 201-203 in The California Indians: A Source Book. Robert F. Heizer and Mary A. Whipple, eds. Berkeley and Los Angeles: University of California Press.

Fontana, Bernard L.
1958 A Detailed History of the Pima Indians of Arizona, with Special Emphasis on Their Location and the History of Their Water Supply—Between the Years 1846 and 1883. (Unpublished manuscript in the Arizona State Museum Library, Tucson.)

——— 1963 The Hopi-Navajo Colony on the Lower Colorado River: A Problem in Ethnohistorical Interpretation. *Ethnohistory* 10(2):163-182.

——— 1964 An Archaeological Survey of the Cabeza Prieta Game Range. (Unpublished manuscript in the Arizona State Museum Library, Tucson.)

——— 1968-1974 Man in Arid Lands: The Piman Indians of the Sonoran Desert. Pp. 489-528 in Vol. 2 of Desert Biology. 2 vols. George W. Brown, ed. New York: Academic Press.

——— 1971 The Seri Indians in Perspective. Introduction to The Seri Indians, by WJ McGee. Glorieta, N.M.: Rio Grande Press.

——— 1974 The Papago Tribe of Arizona. Pp. 152-226 in Papago Indians, III. *(American Indian Ethnohistory: Indians of the Southwest)* New York: Garland.

——— 1975 Meanwhile Back at the Rancheria... *Indian Historian* 8(4):13-18.

——— 1976 The Papago Indians. Pts. 1-3. Sells, Ariz.: Indian Oasis Schools.

——— 1976a Desertification of Papagueria: Cattle and the Papago. Pp. 59-69 in Desertification: Process, Problems, Perspectives. Patricia Paylore and Richard A. Haney, Jr., eds. Tucson: University of Arizona, Office of Arid Land Studies.

——— 1976b The Faces and Forces of Pimería Alta. Pp. 45-54 in Voices from the Southwest. Donald C. Dickinson, David Laird, and Margaret F. Maxwell, comps. Flagstaff, Ariz.: Northland Press.

———
1979 Tarahumara, Where the Night Is the Day of the Moon. Photographs by John P. Schaefer. Flagstaff, Ariz.: Northland Press.

———
1979a Tarahumara Pottery. *American Indian Art Magazine* 4(2):40-43.

———
1979b The Material World of the Tarahumara. Flagstaff, Ariz.: Northland Press.

———
1981 Pilgrimage to Magdalena. *The American West* 18(5):40-45, 60. Salt Lake City.

———
1981a Of Earth and Little Rain: The Papago Indians. Flagstaff, Ariz.: Northland Press.

Fontana, Bernard L., Edmond J.B. Faubert, and Barney T. Burns
1977 The Other Southwest: Indian Arts and Crafts of Northwestern Mexico. Phoenix: Heard Museum.

Fontana, Bernard L., William J. Robinson, Charles W. Cormack, and Ernest E. Leavitt
1962 Papago Indian Pottery. (*Monographs of the American Ethnological Society* 37) Seattle: University of Washington Press.

Forbes, Jack D.
1957 The Janos, Jocomes, Mansos and Sumas Indians. *New Mexico Historical Review* 32(4):319-334.

———
1959 The Appearance of the Mounted Indian in Northern Mexico and the Southwest to 1680. *Southwestern Journal of Anthropology* 15(2):189-212.

———
1959a Unknown Athapaskans: The Identification of the Jano, Jocome, Jumano, Manso, Suma, and Other Indian Tribes of the Southwest. *Ethnohistory* 6(2):97-159.

———
1960 Apache, Navaho, and Spaniard. Norman: University of Oklahoma Press.

———
1965 Warriors of the Colorado: The Yumas of the Quechan Nation and Their Neighbors. Norman: University of Oklahoma Press.

———
1966 The Early Western Apache, 1300-1700. *Journal of the West* 5(3):366-354.

Ford, Richard I.
1972 An Ecological Perspective on the Eastern Pueblos. Pp. 1-17 in New Perspectives on the Pueblos. Alfonso Ortiz, ed. Albuquerque: University of New Mexico Press.

———
1972a Barter, Gift, or Violence: An Analysis of Tewa Intertribal Exchange. Pp. 21-45 in Social Exchange and Interaction. Edwin N. Wilmsen, ed. *University of Michigan Museum of Anthropology, Anthropological Paper* 46. Ann Arbor.

———
1977 The Technology of Irrigation in a New Mexico Pueblo. Pp. 139-154 in Material Culture: Styles, Organization, and Dynamics of Technology. Heather Lechtman and Robert S. Merrill, eds. (*1975 Proceedings of the American Ethnological Society*) St. Paul: West Publishing Company.

Ford, Richard I., Albert H. Schroeder, and Stewart L. Peckham
1972 Three Perspectives on Puebloan Prehistory. Pp. 19-39 in New Perspectives on the Pueblos. Alfonso Ortiz, ed. Albuquerque: University of New Mexico Press.

Forde, C. Daryll
1931 Ethnography of the Yuma Indians. *University of California Publications in American Archaeology and Ethnology* 28(4):83-278. Berkeley.

Foreman, Grant, ed.
1941 A Pathfinder in the Southwest: The Itinerary of Lieutenant A.W. Whipple During His Exploration for a Railway Route from Fort Smith to Los Angeles in the Years 1853 and 1854. Norman: University of Oklahoma Press.

Fort Defiance Hospital
[1910-1920] [Original Logbook.] (Manuscript in Navajo Tribal Museum, Window Rock, Ariz.)

Foster, George M.
1962 Traditional Cultures and the Impact of Technological Change. New York: Harper.

Foster, Kenneth E.
1964 Navajo Sandpaintings. (*Navajoland Publications Series* 3) Window Rock, Ariz.: Navajo Tribal Museum.

Fowler, Catherine S.
1972 Some Ecological Clues to Proto-Numic Homelands. Pp. 105-121 in Great Basin Cultural Ecology: A Symposium. Don D. Fowler, ed. *Desert Research Institute Publications in the Social Sciences* 8. Reno.

———
1980 Some Lexical Clues to Uto-Aztecan Prehistory. (Paper given at the Uto-Aztecan Historial Symposium, at the Linguistic Institute, University of New Mexico, Albuquerque.)

Fowler, Catherine S., and Joy Leland
1967 Some Northern Paiute Native Categories. *Ethnology* 6(4):381-404.

Fowler, Jacob
1898 The Journal of Jacob Fowler, Narrating an Adventure from Arkansas Through the Indian Territory, Oklahoma, Kansas, Colorado, and New Mexico, to the Sources of Rio Grande del Norte, 1821-22. Elliott Coues, ed. New York: F.P. Harper.

Fox, Robin
1967 The Keresan Bridge: A Problem in Pueblo Ethnology. (*London School of Economics, Monographs on Social Anthropology* 35) London: Athlone Press.

———
1972 Some Unsolved Problems of Pueblo Social Organization. Pp. 71-85 in New Perspectives on the Pueblos. Alfonso Ortiz, ed. Albuquerque: University of New Mexico Press.

Franciscan Fathers
1910 An Ethnologic Dictionary of the Navaho Language. St. Michaels, Ariz.: The Franciscan Fathers.

———
1912 A Vocabulary of the Navaho Language. Vol 1: English-Navaho. St. Michaels, Ariz.: The Franciscan Fathers.

Frank, André Gunder
1967 Capitalism and Underdevelopment in Latin America: Historical Studies of Chile and Brazil. New York: Monthly Review Press.

Frank, Larry
1978 Silver Jewelry of the Southwest, 1868-1930. New York: Little, Brown for the New York Graphic Society.

Frazer, Robert W.
1965 Forts of the West: Military Forts and Presidios, and Posts Commonly Called Forts, West of the Mississippi River, to 1898. Norman: University of Oklahoma Press.

Freeze, Ray, and David E. Iannucci
1979 Internal Classification of the Numic Languages of Uto-Aztecan. *Amerindia* 4:77-92.

Freire-Marecco, Barbara
1910-1912 [Yavapai Vocabulary Cards.] (Manuscript No. 2624b in National Anthropological Archives, Smithsonian Institution, Washington.)

French, Benjamin F.
1846-1875 Historical Collections of Louisiana. 7 vols. New York: Wiley and Putnam.

French, David
1942 Comparative Notes on Chiricahua Apache Mythology. Pp. 103-111 in Myths and Tales of the Chiricahua Apache Indians, by Morris E. Opler. *Memoirs of the American Folklore Society* 37. Menasha, Wis. (Reprinted: Kraus Reprint, New York, 1969.)

Fried, Jacob
1953 The Relation of Ideal Norms to Actual Behavior in Tarahumara Society. *Southwestern Journal of Anthropology* 9(3):286-295.

——— 1969 The Tarahumara. Pp. 846-870 in Pt. 2 of *Ethnology*. Evon Z. Vogt, vol. ed. Handbook of Middle American Indians. Vol. 8. Robert Wauchope, gen. ed. Austin: University of Texas Press.

——— 1977 Two Orders of Authority and Power in Tarahumara Society. Pp. 263-269 in The Anthropology of Power: Ethnographic Studies from Asia, Oceania, and the New World. Raymond D. Fogelson and Richard N. Adams, eds. New York: Academic Press.

Frink, Maurice
1968 Fort Defiance and the Navajos. Boulder, Colo.: Pruett Press.

Frisbie, Charlotte Johnson
1967 Kinaaldá: A Study of the Navaho Girls' Puberty Ceremony. Middletown, Conn.: Wesleyan University Press.

——— 1977 Navajo *Jish* or Medicine Bundles and Museums. *Council for Museum Anthropology Newsletter* 1(4):6-23.

——— 1977a Jish—and the Question of Pawn. *Masterkey* 51(4):127-139.

——— 1978 Burial as a Disposition Mechanism for Navajo Jish or Medicine Bundles. *American Indian Quarterly* 4(4):347-392.

——— 1980 Southwestern Indian Ritual Drama. Albuquerque: University of New Mexico Press.

Frisbie, Theodore R.
1971 An Archaeo-ethnological Interpretation of Maize Deity Symbols in the Greater Southwest. (Unpublished Ph.D. Dissertation in Anthropology, Southern Illinois University, Carbondale.)

——— 1974 *Hishi* as Money in the Puebloan Southwest. Pp. 120-142 in Collected Papers in Honor of Florence Hawley Ellis. Theodore R. Frisbie, ed. *Papers of the Archaeological Society of New Mexico* 2. Albuquerque.

Frisch, Jack A., and Noel W. Schutz, Jr.
1967 Componential Analysis and Semantic Reconstruction: The Proto Central Yuman Kinship System. *Ethnology* 6(3):272-293.

Frost, Joe L., and Glenn R. Hawkes, eds.
1966 The Disadvantaged Child: Issues and Innovations. Boston: Houghton Mifflin.

Furst, Peter T.
1973-1974 The Roots and Continuities of Shamanism. *Arts Canada* 184/185/186/187:33-60.

Gallagher, Marsha
1981 The Weaver and the Wool: The Process of Navajo Weaving. *Plateau* 52(4):22-27.

Gallegos Lamero, Hernán
1927 The Gallegos Relation of the Rodriguez Expedition to New Mexico. George P. Hammond and Agapito Rey, eds. *Historical Society of New Mexico Publications in History* 4. Santa Fe.

Galloway, Tod, trans.
1905 Private Letters of a Government Official (John Greiner) in the Southwest. *Journal of American History* 3 (July):541-554.

Gálvez, Joseph de
1769 Instruccion dada en el Real de los Alamos el 23 de Junio de 1769...para la asignacion y repartimiento de Tierras en los Pueblos tanto de Yndios como de Españoles de las Prouas. de Sinaloa y Sonora. (Manuscript, carpeta 72/750, caja 33, Provincias Internas, Archivo Franciscano, Biblioteca Nacional, Mexico City).

Gámiz, Everardo
1948 Monografía de la nación tepehuana que habita en la región sur del estado de Durango. Mexico City: Ediciones Gámiz.

Garcés, Francisco T.H.
1770 Diario que se ha formado por el viaje hecho al río Gila...San Xavier del Bac. (Manuscript, tomo 396, Historia, Archivo General de la Nación, Mexico City.)

García, Alexo
1798 [Decreto.] (Manuscript, carpeta 77/750, Provincias Internas, Archivo Franciscano, Biblioteca Nacional, Mexico City.)

García, Bartholomé
1760 Manual para administrar los santos sacramentos de penitencia, eucharistia, extrema-uncion, y matrimonio...Mexico City: no publisher.

García Manzanedo, Héctor
1963 Notas sobre la medicina tradicional en una zona de la Sierra Tarahumara. *América Indígena* 23:61-70.

Gardiner, Arthur D., trans.
1957 Letter of Father Middendorf, S.J. Dated from Tucson 3 March 1757. *The Kiva* 22(4):1-10.

Gatewood, Charles B.
[1929] Lieutenant Charles B. Gatewood, 6th U.S. Cavalry, and the Surrender of Geronimo. Major C.B. Gatewood, comp., Edward S. Godfrey, ed. Baltimore: no publisher.

Gatewood, J.S.
1950 Use of Water by Bottom-land Vegetation in Lower Safford Valley. *U.S. Geological Survey, Water Supply Paper* 1103. Washington.

Gatschet, Albert S.
1877-1892 Der Yuma Sprachstamm nach den neuesten handschriftlichen Quellen. *Zeitschrift für Ethnologie* 9:341-350, 365-418; 15:123-147; 18:97-122; 24:1-18.

——— [1879-1885] [Isleta Words and Phrases.] (Manuscript No. 613 in National Anthropological Archives, Smithsonian Institution, Washington.)

——— [1880] [Dictionary of the Isleta Language, New Mexico.] (Manuscript No. 2506 in National Anthropological Archives, Smithsonian Institution, Washington.)

——— 1883 [Pinal Apache; Vocabulary and Texts with Interlinear Translation.] (Manuscript No. 1567 in National Anthropological Archives, Smithsonian Institution, Washington.)

——— 1883a [Apache Mohave (Yavapai) Words and Sentences.] (Manuscript No. 1144 in National Anthropological Archives, Smithsonian Institution, Washington.)

——— 1884 [Tonkawe Language, Collected at Fort Griffin, Shackleford County.] (Manuscript No. 1008 in National Anthropological Archives, Smithsonian Institution, Washington.)

——— 1884a [Lipan, a Dialect of the Apache-Tinné Family; Collected at Fort Griffin, Texas.] (Manuscript No. 81-a-b, National Anthropological Archives, Smithsonian Institution, Washington.)

——— 1884b [Apache Dialects and Navaho from Various Informants.] (Manuscript No. 186 in National Anthropological Archives, Smithsonian Institution, Washington.)

——— 1884c [Comanche Vocabularies and Notes from Various Informants.] (Manuscript No. 748 in National Anthropological Archives, Smithsonian Institution, Washington.)

——— 1884d [Apache-Tinné Language; Dialect of the Ná-isha Band. Collected at Kiowa, Apache, and Comanche Agency, Anadarko, Indian Territory.] (Manuscript No. 62 in National Anthropological Archives, Smithsonian Institution, Washington.)

———
1884e [Kiowa (Kayowe) Vocabulary and Notes on the Language.] (Manuscript No. 520 in National Anthropological Archives, Smithsonian Institution, Washington.)

———
1890 [Collection of Words, Names, Phrases and Sentences from the Kora Dialects of New Mexico.] (Manuscript No. 499 in National Anthropological Archives, Smithsonian Institution, Washington.)

———
1891 The Karankawa Indians: The Coast People of Texas. *Papers of the Peabody Museum of American Archaeology and Ethnology, Harvard University* 1(2). Cambridge, Mass.

———
1899 [Language of the Sandia Pueblo or Nafin ab, in the Central Parts of New Mexico; Tewa Linguistic Family, from Mariano Carpintero, Governor of Sandia.] (Manuscript No. 614 in National Anthropological Archives, Smithsonian Institution, Washington.)

Gearing, Fred
1962 Priests and Warriors: Social Structures for Cherokee Politics in the 18th Century. *Memoirs of the American Anthropological Association* 93. Menasha, Wis.

Geertz, Clifford J.
1958 Ethos, World-view and the Analysis of Sacred Symbols. *Antioch Review* 17(Winter):421-437.

———
1971 In Search of North Africa. *New York Review* (April 22):20-24.

Gentry, Howard S.
1963 The Warihio Indians of Sonora-Chihuahua: An Ethnographic Survey. *Anthropological Papers 65, Bureau of American Ethnology Bulletin* 186. Washington.

Geronimo
1887 Correspondence [of the War Department] with General Miles Relative to the Surrender of Geronimo, March 2, 1887. *U.S. Congress. Senate. 49th Cong., 2d sess., Senate Executive Document No.* 117. (Serial No. 2449) Washington.

Getty, Harry T.
1963 The San Carlos Indian Cattle Industry. *Anthropological Papers of the University of Arizona* 7. Tucson.

———
1964 Changes in Land Use Among the Western Apaches. Pp. 27-33 in Indian and Spanish American Adjustments to Arid and Semiarid Environments, a Symposium, April 28, 1964. Clark S. Knowlton, ed. *Committee on Desert and Arid Zone Research, Contribution* 7. Lubbock, Tex.

Gibbs, George
[1856] [Mohave Vocabulary; Copied form Lt. Sylvester Mowry.] (Manuscript No. 1135a in National Anthropological Archives, Smithsonian Institution, Washington.)

———
1868 [Isleta Vocabulary Recorded from Ambrosia Veita and Alejandro Padia, of Isleta.] (Manuscript No. 1019 in National Anthropological Archives, Smithsonian Institution, Washington.)

Giddings, Ruth Warner
1959 Yaqui Myths and Legends. *Anthropological Papers of the University of Arizona* 2. Tucson.

Giff, J.
1980 Pima Blue Swallow Songs of Gratitude. *Arizona State University Anthropological Research Paper* 20:127-139. Tempe.

Gifford, Edward W.
1931 The Kamia of the Imperial Valley. *Bureau of American Ethnology Bulletin* 97. Washington.

———
1932 The Southeastern Yavapai. *University of California Publications in American Archaeology and Ethnology* 29(3):177-252. Berkeley.

———
1933 The Cocopa. *University of California Publications in American Archaeology and Ethnology* 31(5):257-334. Berkeley.

———
1936 Northeastern and Western Yavapai. *University of California Publications in American Archaeology and Ethnology* 34(4):247-354. Berkeley.

———
1940 Culture Element Distributions, XII: Apache-Pueblo. *University of California Anthropological Records* 4(1):1-207. Berkeley.

Gifford, Edward W., and Robert Lowie
1928 Notes on the Akwa'ala Indians of Lower California. *University of California Publications in American Archaeology and Ethnology* 23(6):339-352. Berkeley.

Gila River Indian Community
1977 Population and Housing Census. Mimeo.

———
1981 Annual Report to the Bureau of Indian Affairs, Division of Industrial Development for 1980. Mimeo.

Gilbreath, Kent
1972 Business Development on the Navajo Reservation. *New Mexico Business Review* 25(March):3-10.

———
1973 Red Capitalism: An Analysis of the Navajo Economy. Norman: University of Oklahoma Press.

Gill, Mario
1957 La Conquista del Valle del Fuerte. Mexico City: ITM, S.A.

Gill, Sam D.
1974 A Theory of Navajo Prayer Acts: A Study of Ritual Symbolism. (Unpublished Ph.D. Dissertation in Anthropology, University of Chicago, Chicago.)

———
1977 Prayer as Person: The Performative Force in Navajo Prayer Acts. *History of Religions* 17(2):143-157.

———
1979 Songs of Life: An Introduction to Navajo Religious Culture. Leiden, The Netherlands: E.J. Brill.

———
1980 Sacred Words: A Study of Navajo Religion and Prayer. (*Contributions in Intercultural and Comparative Studies* 4) Westport, Conn.: Greenwood Press.

Gilpin, Laura
1968 The Enduring Navaho. Austin: University of Texas Press.

Givón, Talmy, ed.
1979 Ute Dictionary. Preliminary ed. Ignacio, Colo.: Ute Press, The Southern Ute Tribe.

Gladwin, Harold S., Emil W. Haury, E.B. Sayles, and N. Gladwin
1937 Excavations at Snaketown, I: Material Culture. *Gila Pueblo, Medallion Paper* 25. Globe, Ariz. (Reprinted: Arizona State Museum, Tucson, 1965.)

Gladwin, Winifred, and Harold S. Gladwin
1930 The Western Range of the Red-on-Buff Culture. *Gila Pueblo, Medallion Paper* 5. Globe, Ariz.

———
1935 The Eastern Range of the Red-on-Buff Culture. *Gila Pueblo, Medallion Paper* 16. Globe, Ariz.

Goddard, Ives
1979 The Languages of South Texas and the Lower Rio Grande. Pp. 355-389 in The Languages of Native America: An Historical and Comparative Assessment. Lyle Campbell and Marianne Mithun, eds. Austin: University of Texas Press.

Goddard, Pliny E.
[1906] [Lipan Texts.] (Manuscript in Archives of the Languages of the World, Indiana University, Bloomington.)

———
1909 Gotal: A Mescalero Apache Ceremony. Pp. 385-394 in Putnam Anniversary Volume: Anthropological Essays Presented to Frederic Ward Putnam in Honor of His Seventieth Birth-

day, April 16, 1909, by His Friends and Associates. Franz Boas, ed. New York: G.E. Stechert.

———
1911 Jicarilla Apache Texts. *Anthropological Papers of the American Museum of Natural History* 8. New York.

———
1919 San Carlos Apache Texts. *Anthropological Papers of the American Museum of Natural History* 24(3):141-367. New York.

———
1920 Myths and Tales from the White Mountain Apache. *Anthropological Papers of the American Museum of Natural History* 24(2). New York.

———
1920a White Mountain Apache Texts. *Anthropological Papers of the American Museum of Natural History* 24(4):369-527. New York.

———
1934 Navajo Texts. *Anthropological Papers of the American Museum of Natural History* 34(1):1-179. New York.

Goggin, John M.
1964 Calendar of Eastern Pueblo Ceremonies. Pp. 21-31 in Indian and Spanish Selected Writings, by John M. Goggin. Coral Gables, Fla.: University of Miami Press. (Reprinted from *New Mexico Anthropologist* Vols. 2 and 3, 1937-1939.)

Goldfrank, Esther S.
1927 The Social and Ceremonial Organization of Cochiti. *Memoirs of the American Anthropological Association* 33. Menasha, Wis.

Gómez Canedo, Lino
1968 Primeras exploraciones y poblamiento de Texas (1686-1694). *Publicaciones del Instituto Tecnológico y de Estudios Superiores de Monterrey, Serie Historia* 6. Monterrey, Mexico.

Gómez González, Filiberto
1948 Rarámuri, mi diario tarahumara. Mexico City: Talleres Tipográficos de Excelsior.

González, José Eleutereo
1885 Collección de noticias y documentos para la historia del estado de Nuevo León...Monterrey, Mexico: Tip. de A. Mier.

———
1887 Lecciones orales de historia de Nuevo-León. Monterrey, Mexico: no publisher.

Goodman, Leo A., and William H. Kruskal
1954 Measures of Association for Cross Classification. *Journal of the American Statistical Association* 49(December):732-764.

Goodwin, Grenville
1933 Clans of the Western Apache. *New Mexico Historical Review* 8(3):176-182.

———
1935 The Social Divisions and Economic Life of the Western Apache. *American Anthropologist* 37(1):55-64.

———
1938 White Mountain Apache Religion. *American Anthropologist* 40(1):24-37.

———
1938a The Southern Athapascans. *The Kiva* 4(2):5-10.

———
1939 Myths and Tales of the White Mountain Apache. *Memoirs of the American Folklore Society* 33. New York.

———
1942 The Social Organization of the Western Apache. Chicago: University of Chicago Press. (2d ed., University of Arizona Press, Tucson, 1969.)

———
1945 A Comparison of Navaho and White Mountain Apache Ceremonial Forms and Categories. Clyde Kluckhohn and Leland C. Wyman, eds. *Southwestern Journal of Anthropology* 1(4):498-506.

Goodwin, Grenville, and Charles Kaut
1954 A Native Religious Movement Among the White Mountain and Cibecue Apache. *Southwestern Journal of Anthropology* 10(4):385-404.

Gorbet, Larry P
1976 A Grammar of Diegueño Nominals. New York: Garland.

Gordon, Burton L., et al.
1974 Environment, Settlement, and Land Use in the Jicarilla Apache Claim Area. Pp. 7-244 in Apache Indians, VI. (*American Indian Ethnohistory: Indians of the Southwest*) New York: Garland.

Gordon, Lynn M.
1980 Relative Clauses in Maricopa. Pp. 15-24 in Proceedings of the 1979 Hokan Languages Workshop Held at the University of California, Los Angeles, June 26-28, 1979. James E. Redden, ed. *Southern Illinois University Occasional Papers in Linguistics* 7. Carbondale.

———
1981 Maricopa Morphology and Syntax. (Unpublished Ph.D. Dissertation in Linguistics, University of California, Los Angeles.)

Gordon, Suzanne
1973 Black Mesa: The Angel of Death. Photographs by Alan Copeland. New York: John Day.

Goss, James A.
1965 Ute Linguistics and Anasazi Abandonment of the Four Corners Area. Pp. 73-81 in Contributions of the Wetherill Mesa Archaeological Project. Douglas Osborne, comp. *Memoirs of the Society for American Archaeology* 19. Salt Lake City.

Goulding, William R.
1849 Diary. (Manuscript in Yale University Library, New Haven, Conn.)

Gouy, Cécile
[1976] Un Cas de resistance indienne: Les Yaquis du Mexique. (Unpublished Ph.D. Dissertation, Université de Paris, Paris.)

Gracy, Davis B., II
1964 Jean Lafitte and the Karankawa Indians. *East Texas Historical Journal* 2(1):40-44.

Grant, Campbell
1978 Canyon de Chelly: Its People and Rock Art. Tucson: University of Arizona Press.

Greenberg, Joseph H.
1980 The External Relationships of the Uto-Aztecan Languages. (Paper given at the Uto-Aztecan Historical Symposium, at the Linguistic Institute, University of New Mexico, Albuquerque.)

———
[1981] Language in the Americas. Palo Alto, Calif.: Stanford University Press. In press.

Greenfeld, Philip J.
1972 The Phonological Hierarchy of the White Mountain Dialect of Western Apache. (Unpublished Ph.D. Dissertation in Linguistics, University of Arizona, Tucson.)

———
1978 Some Special Phonological Characteristics of the White Mountain Dialect of Apachean. *Anthropological Linguistics* 20(4):150-157.

Gregg, Andrew K.
1968 Drums of Yesterday: The Forts of New Mexico. Santa Fe: The Press of the Territorian.

Gregg, Josiah
1844 Commerce of the Prairies: Or, the Journal of a Santa Fé Trader, During Eight Expeditions Across the Great Western Prairies, and a Residence of Nearly Nine Years in Northern Mexico. 2 vols. New York: Henry G. Langley. (Reprinted: University of Oklahoma Press, Norman, 1954.)

Griffen, William B.
1959 Notes on Seri Indian Culture, Sonora, Mexico. (*School of Inter-American Studies, Latin American Monograph Series 10*) Gainesville: University of Florida Press.

———
1961 Seventeenth Century Seri. *The Kiva* 27(2):12-21.

———
1969 Culture Change and Shifting Populations in Central Northern Mexico. *Anthropological Papers of the University of Arizona* 13. Tucson.

———
1979 Indian Assimilation in the Franciscan Area of Nueva Vizcaya. *Anthropological Papers of the University of Arizona* 33. Tucson.

Griffin, P. Bion, Mark P. Leone, and Keith H. Basso
1971 Western Apache Ecology: From Horticulture to Agriculture. Pp. 69-76 in Apachean Culture History and Ethnology. Keith H. Basso and Morris E. Opler, eds. *Anthropological Papers of the University of Arizona* 21. Tucson.

Griffith, James S.
1967 Legacy of Conquest: The Arts of Northwest Mexico. Colorado Springs: Taylor Museum of Colorado Springs Fine Arts Center.

———
1967a Mochicahui Judio Masks: A Type of Mayo Fariseo Mask from Northern Sinaloa, Mexico. *The Kiva* 32(4):143-149.

———
1969 Mestizo Matachines Dancers in Los Mochis, Sinaloa, December 11, 1968. *The Kiva* 35(2):103-104.

———
1972 Cáhitan Pascola Masks. *The Kiva* 37(4):185-198.

Griffith, James S., and Felipe S. Molina
1980 Old Men of the Fiesta: An Introduction to Pascola Arts. Phoenix: Heard Museum.

Grimes, Joseph E.
1964 Huichol Syntax. The Hague: Mouton.

Grossmann, F.E.
1871 [Report of May 23 to George L. Andrews.] Pp. 10-15 in *U.S. Congress. House. 41st Cong., 3d sess. House Executive Doc. No.* 139 (Serial No. 1460). Washington.

———
1873 The Pima Indians of Arizona. Pp. 407-419 in *Annual Report of the Smithsonian Institution for 1871*. Washington.

Guadalajara, Tomás de
1683 Compendio del arte de la lengua de los Tarahumares. Puebla de los Ángeles: Por Diego Fernández de León.

Guardián de San Bernardo, R.P.
1849 Esposición a la Dirección de Colonización e Industria, Ures, 13 Sept. (Manuscript in Sección de Archivo Histórico, Biblioteca y Museo de Sonora, Hermosillo, Mexico.)

Guenther, Arthur
1958 Apache Mountain Wonderland. *Arizona Highways* 34(5):32-33.

Gunnerson, Dolores A.
1956 The Southern Athabascans: Their Arrival in the Southwest. *El Palacio* 63(11-12): 346-365.

———
1974 The Jicarilla Apaches: A Study in Survival. De Kalb: Northern Illinois University Press.

Gunnerson, James H.
1956 Plains-Promontory Relationships. *American Antiquity* 22(1):69-72.

———
1960 An Introduction to Plains Apache Archeology: The Dismal River Aspect. Pp. 131-260 in *Anthropological Papers 58, Bureau of American Ethnology Bulletin* 173. Washington.

———
1968 Plains Apache Archaeology: A Review. *Plains Anthropologist* 13(41):167-189.

———
1969 Apache Archaeology in Northeastern New Mexico. *American Antiquity* 34(1):23-39.

Gunnerson, James H., and Dolores A. Gunnerson
1971 Apachean Culture: A Study in Unity and Diversity. Pp. 7-27 in Apachean Culture History and Ethnology. Keith H. Basso and Morris E. Opler, eds. *Anthropological Papers of the University of Arizona* 21. Tucson.

Gursky, Karl-Heinz
1964 The Linguistic Position of the Quinigua Indians. *International Journal of American Linguistics* 30(4):325-327.

Guttman, Louis
1968 A General Nonmetric Technique for Finding the Smallest Coordinate Space for a Configuration of Points. *Psychometrika* 33(4):469-506.

Habig, Marion A.
1968 The Alamo Chain of Missions: A History of San Antonio's Five Old Missions. Chicago: Franciscan Herald Press.

Hackenberg, Robert A.
[1955] On Piman Warfare. (Unpublished manuscript in Hackenberg's possession.)

———
1961 Indian Administration and Social Change. (Unpublished Ph.D. Dissertation in Anthropology, Cornell University, Ithaca, N.Y.)

———
1962 Economic Alternatives in Arid Lands: A Case Study of the Pima and Papago Indians. *Ethnology* 1(2):186-196.

———
1967 Parameters of an Ethnic Group: A Method for Studying the Total Tribe. *American Anthropologist* 69(5):478-492.

———
1968 Cultural Microevolution in a Southwest Reservation Indian Community. (Paper read at the Annual Meeting of the American Anthropological Association, Seattle.)

———
1972 Restricted Interdependence: The Adaptive Pattern of Papago Indian Society. *Human Organization* 31(2):113-125.

———
1974 Ecosystemic Channeling: Cultural Ecology from the Viewpoint of Aerial Photography. Pp. 28-39 in Aerial Photography in Anthropological Field Research. Evon Z. Vogt, ed. Cambridge, Mass.: Harvard University Press.

———
1974a Aboriginal Land Use and Occupancy. Pp. 23-308 in Papago Indians, I. *(American Indian Ethnohistory: Indians of the Southwest)* New York: Garland.

Hackenberg, Robert A., and Bernard L. Fontana
1974 Aboriginal Land Use and Occupancy of the Pima-Maricopa Indians. 2 vols. *(American Indian Ethnohistory: Indians of the Southwest)* New York: Garland.

Hackenberg, Robert A., and C. Roderick Wilson
1972 Reluctant Emigrants: The Role of Migration in Papago Indian Adaptation. *Human Organization* 31(2):171-186.

Hackett, Charles W., ed.
1923-1937 Historical Documents Relating to New Mexico, Nueva Vizcaya and Approaches Thereto, to 1773. Adolph F.A. Bandelier and Fanny R. Bandelier, colls. 3 vols. *Carnegie Institution of Washington Publication* 330(2). Washington.

———, ed.
1931-1941 Pichardo's Treatise on the Limits of Louisiana and Texas...3 vols. Austin: University of Texas Press.

———, ed.
1942 Revolt of the Pueblo Indians of New Mexico and Otermín's Attempted Reconquest, 1680-1682. Charmion Shelby, trans. 2 vols. Albuquerque: University of New Mexico Press.

Haefer, J. Richard
1977 Papago Music and Dance. *Navajo Community College Occasional Papers, Music and Dance Series* 3(4). Tsaile, Ariz.

———
1980 O'odham Celkona: The Papago Skipping Dance. Pp. 239-273 in Southwestern Indian Ritual Drama. Charlotte J. Frisbie, ed. Albuquerque: University of New Mexico Press.

Haile, Berard
1938 Origin Legend of the Navaho Enemy Way: Text and Trans-

lation. *Yale University Publications in Anthropology* 17. New Haven, Conn.

———
1938a Navaho Chantways and Ceremonials. *American Anthropologist* 40(4):639-652.

———
1943 Origin Legend of the Navaho Flintway. (*University of Chicago Publications in Anthropology, Linguistic Series*) Chicago: University of Chicago Press.

———
1943a Soul Concepts of the Navaho. *Annali Lateranensi* 7:59-94. Rome.

———
1945 The Navaho War Dance: A Brief Narrative of Its Meaning and Practice. St. Michaels, Ariz.: St. Michaels Press.

———
1946 The Navaho Fire Dance, or Corral Dance: A Brief Account of Its Practice and Meaning. St. Michaels, Ariz.: St. Michaels Press.

———
1947 Prayerstick Cutting in a Five Night Navaho Ceremonial of the Male Branch of Shootingway. Chicago: University of Chicago Press.

———
1947a Head and Face Masks in Navaho Ceremonialism. St. Michaels, Ariz.: St. Michaels Press.

———
1947b Starlore Among the Navajo. Santa Fe: Museum of Navajo Ceremonial Art.

———
1949 Navaho or Navajo? *The Americas* 6:85-90.

———
1950 Legend of the Ghostway Ritual and Sucking Way. St. Michaels, Ariz.: St. Michaels Press.

———
1950-1951 A Stem Vocabulary of the Navaho Language. Navaho-English; English-Navaho. 2 vols. St.Michaels, Ariz.: St. Michaels Press.

———, comp.
1978 Love-magic and Butterfly People: The Slim Curly Version of the *Ayiłee* and Mothway Myths. (*American Tribal Religion Series* 2) Flagstaff: Museum of Northern Arizona Press.

———
1979 Waterway: A Navajo Ceremonial Myth Told by Black Mustache Circle. (*American Tribal Religion Series* 5) Flagstaff: Museum of Northern Arizona Press.

———
1981 The Upward Moving and Emergence Way. (*American Tribal Religion Series* 7) Lincoln and London: University of Nebraska Press.

———
1981a Women Versus Men: A Conflict of Navajo Emergence. (*American Tribal Religion Series* 6) Lincoln and London: University of Nebraska Press.

Haines, Francis
1966 Horses for Western Indians. *The American West* 3(2):4-15, 92. Salt Lake City.

Hakluyt, Richard
1969 The Principal Navigations, Voyages, Traffiques & Discoveries of the English Nation...[1589] 12 vols. New York: A.M. Kelley.

Hale, Kenneth L.
1958 Internal Diversity in Uto-Aztecan, I. *International Journal of American Linguistics* 24(2):101-107.

———
1959 Internal Diversity in Uto-Aztecan, II. *International Journal of American Linguistics* 25(2):114-121.

———
1959a A Papago Grammar. (Unpublished Ph.D. Dissertation in Linguistics, Indiana University, Bloomington.)

———
1965 Some Preliminary Observations on Papago Morphophonemics. *International Journal of American Linguistics* 31(4):295-305.

———
1969 Papago /čɨm/. *International Journal of American Linguistics* 35(2):203-212.

Hale, Kenneth L., and Albert Alvarez
1972 A New Perspective on American Indian Linguistics. Pp. 87-133 in New Perspectives on the Pueblos. Alfonso Ortiz, ed. Albuquerque: University of New Mexico.

Hall, Edward T., Jr.
1944 Recent Clues to Athabascan Prehistory in the Southwest. *American Anthropologist* 46(1):98-105.

———
1944a Early Stockaded Settlements in the Governador New Mexico: A Marginal Anasazi Development from Basket Maker III to Pueblo I Times. *Columbia Studies in Archaeology and Ethnology* 2(1):1-96. New York.

Hall, Ruth K.
1961 Last of the Apache Traders. *New Mexico Magazine* 39(2):14-17, 39.

Hall, Sharlot M.
1907 The Story of a Pima Record Rod. *Out West* 26(5):413-424. Los Angeles.

Hallenback, Cleve
1940 Alvar Núñez Cabeza de Vaca: The Journey and Route of the First European to Cross the Continent of North America, 1534-1536. Glendale, Calif.: Arthur H. Clark.

Halpern, Abraham M.
1942 Yuma Kinship Terms. *American Anthropologist* 44(3):425-441.

———
1946-1947 Yuma I-IV. *International Journal of American Linguistics* 12(1):25-33, (3):147-151, (4):204-212; 13(1):28-30, (2):92-107, (3):147-166.

Halpern, Mary Fujii
1941 The Kinship Systems of the Yuman-speaking Peoples. (Unpublished M.A. Thesis in Anthropology, University of Chicago, Chicago.)

Hamilton, John M.
1948 A History of the Presbyterian Church Among the Pima and Papago Indians of Arizona. (Unpublished M.A. Thesis in Anthropology, University of Arizona, Tucson.)

Hammack, Laurens C.
1969 A Preliminary Report of the Excavations at Las Colinas. *The Kiva* 35(1):11-28.

Hammond, George P., and Agapito Rey, eds. and trans.
1928 Obregón's History of the Sixteenth Century Explorations in Western America, Entitled: Chronicle, Commentary, or Relation of the Ancient and Modern Discoveries in New Spain and New Mexico, 1584. Los Angeles: Wetzel.

———, eds.
1929 Expedition into New Mexico by Antonio de Espejo. *Quivira Society Publication* 1. Los Angeles.

———, eds.
1940 Narratives of the Coronado Expedition, 1540-1542. Albuquerque: University of New Mexico Press.

———, eds. and trans.
1953 Don Juan de Oñate, Colonizer of New Mexico, 1595-1628. 2 vols. Albuquerque: University of New Mexico Press.

———
1966 The Rediscovery of New Mexico, 1580-1594: The Explorations of Chamuscado, Espejo, Castaño de Sosa, Morlete, and Leyva de Bonilla and Humaña. Albuquerque: University of New Mexico Press.

Hardy, Heather
1979 Tolkapaya Syntax: Aspect, Modality and Adverbial and Modal Constructions in a Yavapai Dialect. (Unpublished Ph.D. Dis-

sertation in Linguistics, University of California, Los Angeles.)

Hardy, Heather, and Lynn Gordon
1979 Types of Adverbial and Modal Construction in Tolkapaya. *International Journal of American Linguistics* 46(3): 183-196.

Hardy, Robert W.H.
1829 Travels in the Interior of Mexico in 1825, 1826, 1827 and 1828. London: H. Colburn and R. Bentley.

Haring, Clarence H.
1947 The Spanish Empire in America. London: Oxford University Press.

Harman, O'Donnell and Henninger Associates
1969 Program Design Study for the Navajo Tribe. [Denver]: no publisher.

Harrington, Carobeth T.
1920 [Isleta Language; Texts and Analytical Vocabulary.] (Manuscript No. 2299 in National Anthropological Archives, Smithsonian Institution, Washington.)

Harrington, Gwyneth
[1930] The Cattle Industry of the Southern Papago Districts. (Unpublished manuscript in Harrington's possession.)

Harrington, John P.
1908 A Yuma Account of Origins. *Journal of American Folk-Lore* 21(82):324-348.

———
1909 [Jemez Vocabulary.] (Manuscript in John P. Harrington Papers, National Anthropological Archives, Smithsonian Institution, Washington.)

———
1912 Tewa Relationship Terms. *American Anthropologist* 14(3):472-498.

———
1913 [Zuni Vocabulary from George Piro.] (Manuscript in John P. Harrington Papers, National Anthropological Archives, Smithsonian Institution, Washington.)

———
1913a [Linguistic Fieldnotes Based on Work with a Speaker of Oraibi Hopi.] (Manuscript in John P. Harrington Papers, National Anthropological Archives, Smithsonian Institution, Washington.)

———
1913b [Hopi Vocabulary.] (Manuscript in John P. Harrington Papers, National Anthropological Archives, Smithsonian Institution, Washington.)

———
1914-1930 [Gabrielino Fieldnotes.] Manuscript in John P. Harrington Papers, National Anthropological Archives, Smithsonian Institution, Washington.)

———
1916 The Ethnogeography of the Tewa Indians. Pp. 29-36 in *29th Annual Report of the Bureau of American Ethnology for the Years 1907-1908*. Washington.

———
1917 [Kitanemuk Fieldnotes.] (Manuscript in John P. Harrington Papers, National Anthropological Archives, Smithsonian Institution, Washington.)

———
[1918] [Taos Vocabulary.] (Manuscript in John P. Harrington Papers, National Anthropological Archives, Smithsonian Institution, Washington.)

———
[1918a] [Taos Geographical Terms and Names of Tribes.] (Manuscript in John P. Harrington Papers, National Anthropological Archives, Smithsonian Institution, Washington.)

———
[1920] [Tewa Vocabulary.] (Manuscript in John P. Harrington Papers, National Anthropological Archives, Smithsonian Institution, Washington.)

———
1925-1926 [(Hopi) Linguistic Notes and Texts.] (Manuscript in John P. Harrington Papers, National Anthropological Archives, Smithsonian Institution, Washington.)

———
1928 Vocabulary of the Kiowa Language. *Bureau of American Ethnology Bulletin* 84. Washington.

———
[1934-1939] [Notes: Mostly Biographical and Names of Persons.] (Manuscript in "Notes and Drafts for Proposed Publication on Geronimo and Apache," John P. Harrington Papers, National Anthropological Archives, Smithsonian Institution, Washington.)

———
[1936] [Place Names, and Tribe Names Questionnaire.] (Manuscript in "Apache and Kiowa Vocabularies," John P. Harrington Papers, National Anthropological Archives, Smithsonian Institution, Washington.)

———
[1936-1941] [Informants, Addresses, etc. in Navajo Fieldnotes.] (Manuscript in John P. Harrington Papers, National Anthropological Archives, Smithsonian Institution, Washington.)

———
[1937] [Notes and Drafts for Proposed Publications on Geronimo and Apache.] (Manuscript in "Apache and Kiowa Apache," John P. Harrington Papers, National Anthropological Archives, Smithsonian Institution, Washington.)

———
[1939] [Notes for the Article "Etymology of the Word Apache."] (Manuscript in "Apache and Kiowa Apache," John P. Harrington Papers, National Anthropological Archives, Smithsonian Institution, Washington.)

———
[1939-1945] [Apache and Kiowa Apache.] (Manuscript in John P. Harrington Papers, National Anthropological Archives, Smithsonian Institution, Washington.)

———
1940 Southern Peripheral Athapaskawan Origins, Divisions, and Migrations. Pp. 503-532 in Essays in Historical Anthropology of North America. *Smithsonian Miscellaneous Collections* 100. Washington.

———
[1940a] [Notes on the Name Navaho.] (Manuscript in John P. Harrington Papers, National Anthropological Archives, Smithsonian Institution, Washington.)

———
[1940b] [Notes on the Spelling of the Name Navaho.] (Manuscript in John P. Harrington Papers, National Anthropological Archives, Smithsonian Institution, Washington.)

———
[1943] [Kiowa Vocabulary: Tribal Names.] (Manuscript in John P. Harrington Papers, National Anthropological Archives, Smithsonian Institution, Washington.)

———
1944 [Kiowa-Apache Vocabulary from Harry Soontay.] (Manuscript in John P. Harrington Papers, National Anthropological Archives, Smithsonian Institution, Washington.)

———
1944a [Keresan Vocabulary and Notes.] (Manuscript in John P. Harrington Papers, National Anthropological Archives, Smithsonian Institution, Washington.)

———
1944b [Cochiti Vocabulary and Ethnological Notes from John Dixon.] (Manuscript in John P. Harrington Papers, National Anthropological Archives, Smithsonian Institution, Washington.)

———
1945 [White Mountain Apache Vocabulary from Philip Cosen.] (Manuscript in John P. Harrington Papers, National Anthropological Archives, Smithsonian Institution, Washington.)

———
[1945a] [The Name Navaho.] (Manuscript in John P. Harrington Papers, National Anthropological Archives, Smithsonian Institution, Washington.)

Harrison, Mike, and John Williams
1977 How Everything Began and How We Learned to Live Right. Pp. 40-46 in The Yavapai of Fort McDowell: An Outline of

Their History and Culture. Sigrid Khera, ed. Fort McDowell, Ariz.: Fort McDowell Mohave-Apache Indian Community.

Hartman, C.W.
1897 The Indians of North-western Mexico. Pp. 115-135 in *Proceedings of the 10th International Congress of Americanists*. Stockholm, 1894.

Harvey, Byron, III
1963 Masks at a Maskless Pueblo: The Laguna Colony Kachina Organization at Isleta. *Ethnology* 2(4):478-489.

———
1963a New Mexican Kachina Dolls. *Masterkey* 37(1):4-8.

Harvey, H.R.
1972 The Relaciones geográficas, 1579-1586: Native Languages. Pp. 279-323 in Pt. 1 of *Guide to Ethnohistorical Sources*. Howard F. Cline, vol. ed. Handbook of Middle American Indians. Vol. 12. Robert Wauchope, gen. ed. Austin: University of Texas Press.

Harwell, Henry O.
1971-1978 [Fieldnotes on the Maricopa.] (Unpublished manuscript in Harwell's possession.)

———
1979 Maricopa Origins: An Ethnohistorical Approach to a Riverine Yuman Community. (Unpublished Ph.D. Dissertation in Anthropology, Indiana University, Bloomington.)

Hastings, James R., ed.
1964 Climatological Data for Sonora and Northern Sinaloa. Preliminary ed. (*Technical Reports on the Meteorology and Climatology of Arid Regions* 15) Tucson: University of Arizona, Institute of Atmospheric Physics.

Hastings, James R., and Robert R. Humphrey, eds.
1969 Climatological Data and Statistics for Sonora and Northern Sinaloa. (*Technical Reports on the Meteorology and Climatology of Arid Regions* 19) Tucson: University of Arizona, Institute of Atmospheric Physics.

Hastings, James R., and Raymond M. Turner
1965 The Changing Mile: An Ecological Study of Vegetation Change with Time in the Lower Mile of an Arid and Semiarid Region. Tucson: University of Arizona Press.

Haury, Emil W.
1945 Excavation of Los Muertos and Neighboring Ruins in the Salt River Valley, Southern Arizona. Based on the Work of the Hemenway Southwestern Archaeological Expedition of 1887-1888. *Papers of the Peabody Museum of American Archaeology and Ethnology, Harvard University* 24(1). Cambridge, Mass.

———
1950 The Stratigraphy and Archaeology of Ventana Cave, Arizona. Kirk Bryan, Edwin H. Colbert, Norman E. Gabel, Clara Lee Tanner, and T.E. Buehrer, collaborators. Tucson: University of Arizona Press; Albuquerque: University of New Mexico Press.

———
1976 The Hohokam: Desert Farmers and Craftsmen; Excavations at Snaketown, 1964-1965. Tucson: University of Arizona Press.

Hayden, Carl, comp.
1965 A History of the Pima Indians and the San Carlos Irrigation Project, 1924. *U.S. Congress. Senate. 89th Congress, 1st sess., Senate Doc. No.* 11. Washington.

Hayden, Julian D.
1935 Pima Creation Myth, as Told by Juan Smith, Snaketown, Arizona. (Manuscript in University of Arizona Library, Tucson.)

———
1937 The Vikita Ceremony of the Papago. Pp. 263-277 in Western Monuments Monthly Report, Supplement for April. Coolidge, Ariz.: U.S. Department of the Interior, National Park Service.

———
1942 Seri Indians on Tiburon Island. *Arizona Highways* 18(1):22-29, 40-41.

———
1956 Notes on the Archaeology of the Central Coast of Sonora, Mexico. *The Kiva* 21(3-4):19-22.

———
1967 A Summary Prehistory and History of the Sierra Pinacate, Sonora. *American Antiquity* 32(3):335-344.

———
1970 Of Hohokam Origins and Other Matters. *American Antiquity* 35(1):87-93.

Hayes, Benjamin I.
1849-1850 Diary of a Journey Overland from Socorro to Warner's Ranch. (Manuscript in the Bancroft Library, Berkeley, Calif.)

Heath, Jeffery
1977-1978 Uto-Aztecan Morphophonemics. *International Journal of American Linguistics* 43(1):27-36; 44(3):211-222.

Hedrick, Basil C., and Carroll L. Riley, trans.
1974 The Journey of the Vaca Party: The Account of the Narváez Expedition, 1528-1536 as Related by Gonzalo de Oviedo y Valdés. *Southern Illinois University Museum Studies* 2. Carbondale.

Heider, Karl G.
1956 Fort McDowell Yavapai Acculturation: A Preliminary Study. (Unpublished B.A. Honors Thesis in Anthropology, Harvard College, Cambridge, Mass.)

Heintzelman, Samuel P.
1857 [Report of August 2, 1853 to Major E. D. Townsend.] Pp. 34-58 in Indian Affairs on the Pacific: Message from the President of the United States Transmitting Report with Regard to Indian Affairs. *U.S. Congress. House. 34th Cong., 3d sess. House Executive Doc.* No. 76 (Serial No. 906) Washington: U.S. Government Printing Office.

Helm, June
1965 Bilaterality in the Socio-territorial Organization of the Arctic Drainage Dene. *Ethnology* 4(4):361-385.

Henderson, Eric
1979 Skilled and Unskilled Blue Collar Navajo Workers: Occupational Diversity in an American Indian Tribe. *Social Science Journal* 16(2):63-80.

Henshaw, Henry W.
1883 [Panamint Vocabulary.] (Manuscript No. 786 in National Anthropological Archives, Smithsonian Institution, Washington.)

———
1910 Yuma. Pp. 1010-1012 in Vol. 2 of Handbook of American Indians North of Mexico. Frederick W. Hodge, ed. 2 vols. *Bureau of American Ethnology Bulletin* 30. Washington.

Hernández, Fortunato
1902 Las Razas indígenas de Sonora y la guerra del yaqui. Mexico City: Talleres de la Casa Editorial "J. de Elizalde."

Herold, Joyce
1979 Havasupai Basketry: Theme and Variation. *American Indian Art Magazine* 4(4):42-53.

Hertzberg, Hazel W.
1971 The Search for an American Indian Identity: Modern Pan-Indian Movements. Syracuse: Syracuse University Press.

Hervas, Lorenzo
1800-1805 Catálogo de las lenguas de las naciones conocidas...6 vols. Madrid: Ranz.

Herzog, George
1935 Plains Ghost Dance and Great Basin Music. *American Anthropologist* 37(3):403-419.

———
1936 Note on Pima Moieties. *American Anthropologist* 38(3):520-521.

Hester, James J.
1962 Early Navajo Migrations and Acculturation in the Southwest. (*Museum of New Mexico Papers in Anthropology 6, Navajo Project Studies* 5) Santa Fe: Museum of New Mexico Press.

Hester, James J., and Joel L. Shiner
1963 Studies at Navajo Period Sites in the Navajo Reservoir District. (*Museum of New Mexico Papers in Anthropology 9, Navajo Project Studies* 8) Santa Fe: Museum of New Mexico Press.

Heuett, Mary L.
1974 Boulder Springs: A Cerbat-Hualapai Rock Shelter in Northwestern Arizona. (Unpublished M.A. Thesis in Anthropology, Northern Arizona University, Flagstaff.)

Hewett, Edgar L.
1906 Origin of the Name Navaho. *American Anthropologist* 8(1):193.

Hewitt, J.N.B.
1897 [Papago Material Obtained from Jose Lewis Brennan.] 3 vols. (Manuscript No. 1744 in National Anthropological Archives, Smithsonian Institution, Washington.)

———
1898 Comparative Lexicology. In The Seri Indians, by WJ McGee. Pp. 299-344 in Pt. 1 of *17th Annual Report of the Bureau of American Ethnology for the Years 1895-1896*. 2 Pts. Washington.

Hewitt, J.N.B., and C.V. Hartman
[1893] [Tarahumare Vocabulary.] (Manuscript No. 2866 in National Anthropological Archives, Smithsonian Institution, Washington.)

Hibben, Frank
1934 [Interview with Juan Dedios.] (Mimeo, at Jicarilla Apache Tribe, Dulce, N.M.)

Hill, Faith
1963 Some Comparisons Between the San Carlos and White Mountain Dialects of Western Apache. Pp. 149-154 in Studies in the Athapaskan Languages, by Harry Hoijer. *University of California Publications in Linguistics* 29. Berkeley.

Hill, Jane H.
1966 A Grammar of the Cupeño Language. (Unpublished Ph.D. Dissertation in Linguistics, University of California, Los Angeles.)

Hill, Jane H., and Rosinda Nolasquez
1973 Mulu'wetam: The First People; Cupeño Oral History and Language. Banning, Calif.: Malki Museum Press.

Hill, Kenneth C.
1967 A Grammar of the Serrano Language. (Unpublished Ph.D. Dissertation in Linguistics, University of California, Los Angeles.)

Hill, W.W.
1936 Navaho Warfare. *Yale University Publications in Anthropology* 5. New Haven, Conn.

———
1937 Navajo Pottery Manufacture. *Anthropological Series 2(3), University of New Mexico Bulletin* 317:7-23. Albuquerque.

———
1938 The Agricultural and Hunting Methods of the Navaho Indians. *Yale University Publications in Anthropology* 18. New Haven, Conn.

———
1940 Some Navaho Culture Changes During Two Centuries. Pp. 395-415 in Essays in Historical Anthropology of North America Published in Honor of John R. Swanton in Celebration of His Fortieth Year with the Smithsonian Institution. *Smithsonian Miscellaneous Collections* 100. Washington.

———
1943 Navaho Humor. *General Series in Anthropology* 9:1-28. Menasha, Wis.

———
1948 Navaho Trading and Trading Ritual: A Study of Cultural Dynamics. *Southwestern Journal of Anthropology* 4(4):371-396.

Hills, Jim
1977 The Finishers. *American Indian Art Magazine* 2(2):32-38, 95.

Hills, Richard James
1973 An Ecological Interpretation of Prehistoric Seri Settlement Patterns in Sonora, Mexico. (Unpublished M.A. Thesis in Geography, Arizona State University, Tempe.)

Hilton, K. Simon
1959 Tarahumara y español. (*Serie de Vocabularios Indígenas Mariano Silva y Aceves* 1) Mexico City: Instituto Lingüístico de Verano en cooperación con la Dirección General de Asuntos Indígenas de la Secretaría de Educación Pública.

Hine, Robert V.
1963 Edward Kern and American Expansion. New Haven and London: Yale University Press.

Hinton, Leanne
1977 Havasupai Songs: A Linguistic Perspective. (Unpublished Ph.D. Dissertation in Linguistics, University of California, San Diego.)

———
1980 When Sounds Go Wild: Phonological Change and Syntactic Re-analysis in Havasupai. *Language* 56(2):320-344.

Hinton, Leanne, and Margaret Langdon
1976 Object-subject Pronomial Prefixes in La Huerta Dieguenо. Pp. 113-128 in Hokan Studies. Margaret Langdon and Shirley Silver, eds. The Hague: Mouton.

Hinton, Thomas B.
1955 A Seri Girls' Puberty Ceremony at Desemboque, Sonora. *The Kiva* 20(4):8-11.

———
1959 A Survey of Indian Assimilation in Eastern Sonora. *Anthropological Papers of the University of Arizona* 4. Tucson.

———
1969 Remnant Tribes of Sonora: Opata, Pima, Papago, and Seri. Pp. 879-888 in Pt. 2 of *Ethnology*. Evon Z. Vogt, vol. ed. Handbook of Middle American Indians. Vol. 8. Robert Wauchope, gen. ed. Austin: University of Texas Press.

———
1972 Cora Masking. (Tape, on File at Arizona State Museum Library, Tucson.)

Hirst, Stephen
1976 Life in a Narrow Place. Photographs by Terry Eiler and Lyntha Eiler. New York: David McKay.

Hockett, Charles F.
1958 A Course in Modern Linguistics. New York: Macmillan.

Hodge, Frederick W.
1895 The Early Navajo and Apache. *American Anthropologist* 8(3):223-240.

———
1907 The Narrative of Álvar Núñez Cabeza de Vaca. Pp. 1-126 in Spanish Explorers in the Southern United States, 1528-1543 Frederick W. Hodge, ed. New York: Charles Scribner's Sons.

———, ed.
1907a Apache. Pp. 63-67 in Vol. 1 of Handbook of American Indians North of Mexico. 2 vols. *Bureau of American Ethnology Bulletin* 30. Washington.

———, ed.
1907-1910 Handbook of American Indians North of Mexico. 2 vols. *Bureau of American Ethnology Bulletin* 30. Washington.

———
1910 Querecho. Pp. 338-339 in Vol. 2 of Handbook of American Indians North of Mexico. Frederick W. Hodge, ed. 2 vols. *Bureau of American Ethnology Bulletin* 30. Washington.

———
1911 The Jumano Indians. *Proceedings of the American Antiquarian Society for 1909-1910,* Vol. 20:249-268. Worcester, Mass.

———
1949 The Name "Navaho." *Masterkey* 23(3):78.

Hoijer, Harry
1938 The Southern Athapaskan Languages. *American Anthropologist* 40(1):75-87.

———
1938a Chiricahua and Mescalero Apache Texts (with Ethnological Notes by Morris Edward Opler). Chicago: University of Chicago Press.

———
1939 [Letter of May 29, 1931 to John P. Harrington.] (In John P. Harrington Papers, National Anthropological Archives, Smithsonian Institution, Washington.)

———
1943 Pitch Accent in the Apachean Languages. *Language* 19(1):38-41.

———
1945 Navaho Phonology. *University of New Mexico Publications in Anthropology* 1. Albuquerque.

———
1945-1949 The Apachean Verb. 3 Parts. *International Journal of American Linguistics* 11(4):193-203; 12(1):1-13, (2):51-59; 15(1):12-22.

———, ed.
1946 Linguistic Structures of Native America. *Viking Fund Publications in Anthropology* 6. New York.

———
1949 An Analytical Dictionary of the Tonkawa Language. *University of California Publications in Linguistics* 5(1). Berkeley.

———
1951 Cultural Implications of Some Navaho Linguistic Categories. *Language* 27(2):111-120.

———
1956 Athapaskan Kinship Systems. *American Anthropologist* 58(2):309-333.

———
1956a The Chronology of the Athapaskan Languages. *International Journal of American Linguistics* 22(4):219-232.

———
1960 Athapaskan Languages of the Pacific Coast. Pp. 960-976 in Culture and History: Essays in Honor of Paul Radin. Stanley Diamond ed. New York: Columbia University Press.

———
1963 The Athapaskan Languages. Pp. 1-29 in Studies in the Athapaskan Languages, by Harry Hoijer and Others. *University of California Publications in Linguistics* 29. Berkeley.

———
1971 The Position of the Apachean Languages in the Athapaskan Stock. Pp. 3-6 in Apachean Culture, History and Ethnology. Keith H. Basso and Morris E. Opler, eds. *Anthropological Papers of the University of Arizona* 21. Tucson.

———
1974 A Navajo Lexicon. *University of California Publications in Linguistics* 78. Berkeley.

———
1975 The History and Creation of the Lipan, as Told by Augustin Zuazua. *Linguistics* 161:5-37.

Hoijer, Harry, and Edward Sapir
1967 The Phonology and Morphology of the Navaho Language. *University of California Publications in Linguistics* 50. Berkeley.

Holden, W.C., C.C. Seltzer, R.A. Studhalter, C.J. Wagner, and W.G. McMillan
1936 Studies of the Yaqui Indians of Sonora, Mexico. *Texas Technological College Bulletin* 12(1). Lubbock.

Holm, Wayne S.
1972 Some Aspects of Navajo Orthography. (Unpublished Ph.D. Dissertation in Linguistics, University of New Mexico, Albuquerque.)

Holzkamper, Frank M.
1956 Artifacts from Estero Tastiota, Sonora, Mexico. *The Kiva* 21(3-4):12-19.

Hoover, J.W.
1929 The Indian Country of Southern Arizona. *Geographical Review* 19(1):38-60.

———
1935 Generic Descent of the Papago Villages. *American Anthropologist* 37(2):257-264.

Houser, Nicholas P.
1970 The Tigua Settlement of Ysleta del Sur. *The Kiva* 36(2):23-39.

Howard, Oliver O.
1872 [Report of June, 1872 from Washington, D.C. to the Secretary of the Interior.] Pp. 148-159 in Report of the Commissioner of Indian Affairs for the Year 1872. Washington: U.S. Government Printing Office.

———
1907 My Life and Experiences Among Our Hostile Indians: A Record of Personal Observations, Adventures, and Campaigns Among the Indians of the Great West with Some Account of Their Life, Habits, Traits, Religion, Ceremonies, Dress, Savage Instincts, and Customs in Peace and War. Hartford, Conn.: A.D. Worthington.

Hoyo, Eugenio del
1960 Vocablos de la lengua quinigua de los indios borrados del nordeste de México. *Humanitas: Annuario del Centro de Estudios Humanísticos, Universidad de Nuevo León* 1:489-515. Monterrey, Mexico.

———
1963 Indice del ramo de causas criminales del Archivo Municipal de Monterrey (1621-1834). *Publicaciones del Instituto Tecnológico y de Estudios Superiores de Monterrey, Serie Historia* 2. Monterrey, Mexico.

———
1972 Historia del Nuevo Reino de León (1577-1723). 2 vols. *Publicaciones del Instituto Tecnológico y de Estudios Superiores de Monterrey, Serie Historia* 13. Monterrey, Mexico.

Hrdlička, Aleš
1904 Notes on the Indians of Sonora, Mexico. *American Anthropologist* 6(1):51-89.

———
1908 Physiological and Medical Observations Among the Indians of Southwestern United States and Northern Mexico. *Bureau of American Ethnology Bulletin* 34. Washington.

Hubbell, Rich
[1970] This Is the Country Indian. [Sound recording] Dineh 1001. 1 disc. 33⅓ rpm. stereo. 12 in.

Hultkrantz, Åke
1975 Conditions for the Spread of the Peyote Cult in North America. Pp. 70-83 in New Religions Symposium Held at Åbo on Sept. 1-3, 1974. Haralds Biezais, ed. (*Scripta Instituti Donneriani Åboensis* 7) Stockholm: Almquist and Wiksell International.

Humphrey, Robert R.
1958 The Desert Grassland: A History of Vegetational Change and an Analysis of Causes. Tucson: University of Arizona Press.

Huscher, Betty H., and Harold A. Huscher
1942 Athapaskan Migration via the Intermontane Region. *American Antiquity* 8(1):80-88.

———
1943 The Hogan Builders of Colorado. Gunnison: Colorado Archaeological Society. (Reprinted from *Southwestern Lore* 9(2) 1943.)

Huson, Hobart
1953 Refugio: A Comprehensive History of Refugio County from Aboriginal Times... Vol. 1. Woodsboro, Tex.: Rooke Foundation.

Hyde, Villiana
1971 An Introduction to the Luiseño Language. Ronald W. Langacker et al., eds. Banning, Calif.: Malki Museum Press.

Hymes, Dell H.
1957 A Note on Athapaskan Glottochronology. *International Journal of American Linguistics* 23(4):291-297.

———
1960 Lexicostatistics So Far. *Current Anthropology* 1(1):3-44.

Hymes, Dell H., and Harold E. Driver
1958 Concerning the Proto-Athapaskan Kinship System. *American Anthropologist* 60(1):152-155.

Iannucci, David E.
1972 Numic Historical Phonology. (Unpublished Ph.D. Dissertation in Linguistics, Cornell University, Ithaca, N.Y.)

Iliff, Flora G.
1954 People of the Blue Water: My Adventures Among the Walapai and Havasupai Indians [1901]. New York: Harper and Brothers.

Irigoyen Rascón, Fructuoso
1974 Cerocahui: Una comunidad en la Tarahumara. Mexico City: Universidad Nacional Autónoma de México, Facultad de Medicina.

Iverson, Peter
1976 The Navajos: A Critical Bibliography. (*The Newberry Library Center for the History of the American Indian Bibliographic Series*) Bloomington: Indiana University Press.

———
1980 Peter MacDonald. Pp. 222-241 in American Indian Leaders: Studies in Diversity. R. David Edmunds, ed. Lincoln: University of Nebraska Press.

———
1981 The Navajo Nation. Westport, Conn.: Greenwood Press.

Ives, Joseph C. *see* U.S. Army. Corps of Topographical Engineers

Ives, Ronald L., ed. and trans.
1939 Sedelmayr's Relacion of 1746. *Anthropological Papers 9, Bureau of American Ethnology Bulletin* 123:99-117. Washington.

———
1964 The Pinacate Region, Sonora, Mexico. *Occasional Papers of the California Academy of Sciences* 47. San Francisco.

Jacobs, Roderick A.
1975 Syntactic Change: A Cupan (Uto-Aztecan) Case Study. *University of California Publications in Linguistics* 79. Berkeley.

James, G. Wharton
1903 Palomas Apaches and Their Baskets. *Sunset Magazine* 11:146-153.

———
1903a The Indians of the Painted Desert Region: Hopis, Navahos, Wallapais, Havasupais. Boston: Little, Brown.

———
1937 Indian Blankets and Their Makers. New York: Tudor.

James, Thomas
1953 Three Years Among the Indians and Mexicans. Milo M. Quaife, ed. Chicago: Lakeside Press.

Jefferis, Cl[arence] R.
1915 [Letter from Clarence R. Jefferis, Superintendent, Mescalero Agency, Mescalero, New Mexico, to Commissioner of Indian Affairs, Washington, D.C., Dated March 25.] (Manuscript in Letters Received, Commissioner's Office, Record Group 75, National Archives, Washington.)

Jenness, Diamond
1932 The Indians of Canada. *Anthropological Series 15, National Museum of Canada Bulletin* 65. Ottawa. (Reprinted in 1934.)

Jett, Stephen C.
1964 Pueblo Indian Migrations: An Evaluation of the Possible Physical and Cultural Determinants. *American Antiquity* 29(3):281-300.

Jett, Stephen C., and Virginia E. Spencer
1981 Navajo Architecture: Forms, History, Distributions. Tucson: University of Arizona Press.

Jiménez Moreno, Wigberto
1944 Tribus e idiomas del Norte de México. Pp. 121-133 in El Norte de México y el sur de Estados Unidos. Mexico City: Tercera Reunión de Mesa Redonda sobre Problemas Antropológicos de México y Centro América, Sociedad Mexicana de Antropología.

———
1958 Estudios de historia colonial. (*Serie Historia* 1) Mexico City: Instituto Nacional de Antropología e Historia.

Joël, Judith
1964 Classification of the Yuman Languages. Pp. 99-105 in Studies in Californian Linguistics. William Bright, ed. *University of California Publications in Linguistics* 34. Berkeley.

———
1966 Paipai Phonology and Morphology. (Unpublished Ph.D. Dissertation in Linguistics, University of California at Los Angeles.)

John, Elizabeth A.H.
1975 Storms Brewed in Other Men's Worlds: The Confrontation of Indians, Spanish, and French in the Southwest, 1540-1795. College Station: Texas A and M University Press.

Johnson, Barbara
1959 Seri Indian Basketry. *The Kiva* 25(1):10-13.

Johnson, Broderick, ed.
1977 Navajos and World War II, by Keats Begay et al. Tsaile, Ariz.: Navajo Community College Press.

———, ed.
1977a Stories of Traditional Navajo Life and Culture, by 22 Navajo Men and Women. Tsaile, Ariz.: Navajo Community College Press.

Johnson, Charlotte I.
1964 Navaho Corn Grinding Songs. *Ethnomusicology* 8(2):101-120.

Johnson, Frederick
1940 The Linguistic Map of Mexico and Central America. Pp. 88-114 in The Maya and Their Neighbors. C.L. Hays, ed. New York and London: D. Appleton-Century.

Johnson, Jean B.
1950 The Opata: An Inland Tribe of Sonora. *University of New Mexico Publications in Anthropology* 6. Albuquerque.

———
1962 El Idioma yaqui. Mexico City: Instituto Nacional de Antropología e Historia.

Johnston, Abraham R.
1848 Journal of Captain A.R. Johnston, First Dragoons. Pp. 567-614 in *U.S. Congress. House. 30th Cong., 1st sess., House Executive Doc. No.* 41 (Serial No. 517). Washington.

Johnston, Bernice
1968 Seri Ironwood Carving. *The Kiva* 33(3):155-168.

———
1970 The Seri Indians of Sonora, Mexico. Tucson: Arizona State Museum.

Johnston, Philip
1964 Indian Jargon Won Our Battles. *Masterkey* 38(4):130-137.

Jones, Delmos J.
1962 Human Ecology of the Papago Indians. (Unpublished M.A. Thesis in Anthropology, University of Arizona, Tucson.)

Jones, Richard D.
1971 The Wi'igita of Achi and Quitobac. *The Kiva* 36(4):1-29.

Jones, Roger
1870 [Letter of July 21, 1869 to R.B. Marcy, Inspector General's Office, San Francisco.] Pp. 214-225 in Annual Report of the Commissioner of Indian Affairs for the Year 1869. Washington: U.S. Government Printing Office.

Jorgensen, Joseph G.
1965 The Ethnohistory and Acculturation of the Northern Ute. (Unpublished Ph.D. Dissertation in Anthropology, Indiana University, Bloomington.)

———
1969 Salish Language and Culture: A Statistical Analysis of Internal Relationships, History, and Evolution. (*Language Science Monographs* 3) Bloomington: Indiana University.

———
1971 Indians and the Metropolis. Pp. 66-113 in The American Indian in Urban Society. Jack O. Waddell and O. Michael Watson, eds. Boston: Little, Brown.

———
1972 The Sun Dance Religion: Power for the Powerless. Chicago: University of Chicago Press.

———
1974 On Continuous Area and Worldwide Studies in Formal Comparative Ethnology. Pp. 195-203 in On Comparative Methods and Explanations in Anthropology. Joseph G. Jorgensen, ed. New Haven, Conn.: Human Relations Area Files Press.

———
1978 A Century of Political Economic Effects on American Indian Society, 1880-1980. *Journal of Ethnic Studies* 6(3):1-82.

———
1980 Western Indians. San Francisco: W.H. Freeman.

Jorgensen, Joseph G., et al.
1978 Native Americans and Energy Development. Cambridge, Mass.: Anthropology Resource Center.

Joseph, Alice, Rosamund B. Spicer, and Jane Chesky
1949 The Desert People: A Study of the Papago Indians. Chicago: University of Chicago Press.

Joutel, Henri
1713 Journal historique du dernier voyage que M. de La Sale fit dans le golfe de Mexique pour trouver l'embouchure le cours de la rivière Missicipi . . . Paris: no publisher.

Kaczkurkin, Mini Valenzuela
1977 Yoeme: Lore of the Arizona Yaqui People. *Sun Tracks: An American Indian Literary Magazine*. Tucson.

Kaemlein, Wilma R.
1954-1955 Yuma Dolls and Yuma Flutes in the Arizona State Museum. *The Kiva* 20(2-3):1-10.

———
1967 An Inventory of Southwestern American Indian Specimens in European Museums. Tucson: Arizona State Museum.

Kahlenberg, Mary H., and Anthony Berlant
1972 The Navajo Blanket. Los Angeles: Praeger Publishers for Los Angeles County Museum of Art.

Kaibah [Kay Bennett]
[1960] Songs of the Diné. [Sound recording] Indian Arts of America A-3001. 1 disc. 33⅓ rpm. 12 in.

———
1972 Songs from the Navajo Nation. Album 3. [Sound recording] KB 4172. 1 disc. 33⅓ rpm. stereo. 12 in.

Kammer, Jerry
1980 The Second Long Walk: The Navajo-Hopi Land Dispute. Albuquerque: University of New Mexico Press.

Kaplan, Bert, and Dale Johnson
1964 The Social Meaning of Navaho Psychopathology and Psychotherapy. Pp. 203-229 in Magic, Faith and Healing: Studies in Primitive Psychiatry Today. Ari Kiev, ed. New York: Free Press.

Kappler, Charles J., comp.
1904 Indian Affairs: Laws and Treaties. 5 vols. Washington: U.S. Government Printing Office. (Reprinted: AMS Press, New York, 1971.)

Kari, James M.
1976 Navajo Verb Prefix Phonology. New York and London: Garland.

Kate, Herman F.C. ten, Jr.
1884 Sur la synonymie ethnique et la toponymie chez les Indiens de l'Amérique du Nord. Amsterdam: J. Müller.

———
1885 Reizen en Onderzockingen in Noord-Amerika. (Travels and Researches in North America) Leiden, The Netherlands: E.J. Brill.

Kaut, Charles R.
1956 Western Apache Clan and Phratry Organization. *American Anthropologist* 58(1):140-146.

———
1957 The Western Apache Clan System: Its Origin and Development. *University of New Mexico Publications in Anthropology* 9. Albuquerque.

———
1974 The Clan System as an Epiphenomenal Element of Western Apache Social Organization. *Ethnology* 13(1):45-70.

Keleher, William A.
1942 Maxwell Land Grant: A New Mexico Item. Santa Fe: Rydal Press. (Reprinted: Argosy-Antiquarian, New York, 1964.)

———
1952 Turmoil in New Mexico, 1846-1868. Santa Fe: Rydal Press.

Keller, Robert H., Jr.
1979 The Navajo Agricultural Industry: Subsistence Farming to Corporate Agribusiness. *American Indian Journal* 5(7):2-6.

Kelley, J. Charles
1952-1953 The Historic Indian Pueblos of La Junta de los Rios. 2 Pts. *New Mexico Historical Review* 27(4):257-295; 28(1):21-51.

———
1955 Juan Sabeata and Diffusion in Aboriginal Texas. *American Anthropologist* 57(5):981-995.

Kelley, Klara B.
1980 Navajo Political Economy Before Fort Sumner. Pp. 307-332 in The Versatility of Kinship: Essays Presented to Harry W. Basehart. Linda S. Cordell and Stephen Beckerman, eds. New York: Academic Press.

Kelly, Isabel Truesdell
1945 Excavations at Culiacán, Sinaloa. *Ibero-Americana* 25. Berkeley, Calif.

Kelly, Lawrence C.
1968 The Navajo Indians and Federal Indian Policy, 1900-1935. Tucson: University of Arizona Press.

———
1970 Navajo Roundup: Selected Correspondence of Kit Carson's Expedition Against the Navajo, 1863-1865. Boulder, Colo.: Pruett Press.

Kelly, Marsha C.
1972 The Society That Did Not Die. *Ethnohistory* 19(3):261-265.

Kelly, William H.
1942 Cocopa Gentes. *American Anthropologist* 44(4):675-691.

———
1949 Cocopa Attitudes and Practices with Respect to Death and Mourning. *Southwestern Journal of Anthropology* 5(2):151-164.

———
1949a The Place of Scalps in Cocopa Warfare. *El Palacio* 56(3):85-91.

———
1953 Indians of the Southwest: A Survey of Indian Tribes and Indian Administration in Arizona. *University of Arizona, Bureau of Ethnic Research Report* 1. Tucson.

———
1977 Cocopa Ethnography. *Anthropological Papers of the University of Arizona* 29. Tucson.

Kemrer, Meade F.
1974 The Dynamics of Western Navajo Settlement, A.D. 1750-1900: An Archaeological and Dendrochronological Analysis. (Unpublished Ph.D. Dissertation in Anthropology, University of Arizona, Tucson.)

Kendall, Martha B.
1968 [Fieldnotes Collected in Clarkdale, Arizona from Harold Sine and Ruth Beecher.] (Manuscript in Kendall's possession.)

———
1975 A Preliminary Survey of Upland Yumans. *Anthropological Linguistics* 17(3):89-102.

———
1976 Selected Problems in Yavapai Syntax: The Verde Valley Dialect. New York: Garland.

———
1977 The Upland Yuman Numerical System. Pp. 17-28 in Proceedings of the 1976 Hokan-Yuman Languages Workshop

Held at the University of California, San Diego, June 21-23, 1976. *Southern Illinois University Museum Studies, Research Record* 11. Carbondale.

———— 1980 From Myth to History: The Word for Old Woman in Northeastern Yavapai. *International Journal of American Linguistics* 46(3):224-227.

Kendall, Martha B., and Alan V. Shaterian
1975 Yavpe Alphabet Book. [Prescott, Ariz.]: The Yavapai Tribe.

Kennedy, John G.
1963 Tesguino Complex: The Role of Beer in Tarahumara Culture. *American Anthropologist* 65(3):620-640.

———— 1966 Tarahumara Joking Relationships: Some Theoretical Implications. Pp. 179-186 in Vol. 3 of *Proceedings of the 36th International Congress of Americanists*. Seville, Spain, 1964.

———— 1969 La Carrera de bola tarahumara y su significación. *América Indígena* 29(1):17-42.

———— 1970 Inápuchi: Una comunidad tarahumara gentil. Mexico City: Instituto Indigenista Interamericano.

———— 1970a Bonds of Laughter Among the Tarahumara Indians: Toward a Rethinking of Joking Relationship Theory. Pp. 36-68 in The Social Anthropology of Latin America: Essays in Honor of Ralph Leon Beals. Walter Goldschmidt and Harry Hoijer, eds. Los Angeles: University of California, Latin American Center.

———— 1978 Tarahumara of the Sierra Madre: Beer, Ecology, and Social Organization. Arlington Heights, Ill.: AMH Publishing Corporation.

Kennedy, John G., and Raúl A. López
1981 Semana Santa in the Sierra Tarahumara: A Comparative Study in Three Communities. *University of California, Occasional Papers of the Museum of Cultural History* 4. Los Angeles.

Kenner, Charles L.
1969 A History of New Mexican-Plains Indian Relations. Norman: University of Oklahoma Press.

Kent, Kate Peck
1961 The Story of Navaho Weaving. Phoenix: Heard Museum.

———— 1981 From Blanket to Rug: The Evolution of Navajo Weaving after 1880. *Plateau* 52(4):10-21.

Kerr, Carol
1959 Education on the Jicarilla Apache Reservation. (Unpublished M.A. Thesis in Anthropology, Staten Island College, Staten Island, N.Y.)

Kessell, John L.
1970 Mission of Sorrows: Jesuit Guevavi and the Pimas, 1691-1767. Tucson: University of Arizona Press.

———— 1975 Friars, Bureaucrats, and the Seris of Sonora. *New Mexico Historical Review* 50(1):73-95.

———— 1976 Friars, Soldiers and Reformers: Hispanic Arizona and the Sonora Mission Frontier, 1767-1856. Tucson: University of Arizona Press.

Khera, Sigrid
1974-1980 [Ethnographic and Ethnohistorical Fieldnotes Among the Fort McDowell Yavapai Community.] (Unpublished manuscript in Khera's possession.)

———— 1977 The Yavapai: Who They Are and from Where They Come. Pp. 1-16 in The Yavapai of Fort McDowell: An Outline of Their History and Culture. Sigrid Khera, ed. Fort McDowell, Ariz.: Fort McDowell Mohave-Apache Indian Community.

Kidder, Alfred V.
1924 An Introduction to the Study of Southwestern Archaeology with a Preliminary Account of the Excavations at Pecos. New Haven, Conn.: Yale University Press.

Kilcrease, A.T.
1939 Ninety Five Years of History of the Papago Indians. Pp. 297-310 *(Southwestern Monuments Monthly Report for April)* Coolidge, Ariz.: U.S. National Park Service.

King, Dale S.
1976 Indian Silverwork of the Southwest. Tucson: University of Arizona Press.

Kino, Eusebio F.
1698 [Letter to Polici.] (Manuscript in Ramo de Historia, Archivo General de la Nación, Mexico City.)

———— 1948 Kino's Historical Memoir of Pimeria Alta: A Contemporary Account of the Beginnings of California, Sonora, and Arizona, by Father Eusebio Francisco Kino, S.J., Pioneer Missionary Explorer, Cartographer, and Ranchman, 1683-1711, Published for the First Time from the Original Manuscript in the Archives of Mexico. Herbert E. Bolton, ed. and trans. 2 vols. in 1. Berkeley: University of California Press.

———— 1971 Kino's Biography of Francisco Xavier Saeta, S.J. Charles W. Polzer, trans., Ernest J. Burrus, ed. (*Sources and Studies for the History of the Americas* 9) Rome: Jesuit Historical Institute; St. Louis, Mo.: St. Louis University

Kirchhoff, Paul
1944 Los Recolectores-cazadores del norte de México. Pp. 133-144 in El Norte de México y el sur de Estados Unidos: Tercera reunión de mesa redonda sobre problemas antropológicos de México y Centro América: 25 de agosto a 2 de septiembre de 1943. Mexico City: Sociedad Mexicana de Antropología.

Kissell, Mary L.
1916 Basketry of the Papago and Pima. *Anthropological Papers of the American Museum of Natural History* 17(4):117-264. New York. (Reprinted: Rio Grande Press, Glorieta, N.M., 1972.)

Klah, Hasteen
1942 Navajo Creation Myth: The Story of the Emergence. Recorded by Mary C. Wheelwright. (*Navajo Religion Series* 1) Santa Fe: Museum of Navajo Ceremonial Art.

Klar, Kathryn, Margaret Langdon, and Shirley Silver
1980 American Indian and Indo-European Studies: Papers in Honor of Madison Beeler. The Hague, Paris: Mouton.

Klein, Sheldon
1959 Comparative Mono-Kawaiisu. *International Journal of American Linguistics* 25(4):233-238.

Kluckhohn, Clyde
1942 Myths and Rituals: A General Theory. *Harvard Theological Review* 35(1):45-79.

———— 1944 Navaho Witchcraft. *Papers of the Peabody Museum of American Archaeology and Ethnology, Harvard University* 22(2). Cambridge, Mass. (Reprinted: Beacon Press, Boston, 1967.)

———— 1948 The Navaho. Garden City, N.Y.: Natural History Press.

———— 1956 Some Navaho Value Terms in Behavioral Context. *Language* 32(1):140-145.

———— 1960 Navaho Categories. Pp. 65-98 in Culture and History: Essays in Honor of Paul Radin. Stanley Diamond, ed. New York: Columbia University Press.

———— 1968 The Philosophy of the Navaho Indians. Pp. 674-699 in Vol. 2 of Readings in Anthropology. Morton H. Fried, ed. 2d. ed. 2 vols. New York: Thomas Y. Crowell.

Kluckhohn, Clyde, and Dorothea C. Leighton
1946 The Navaho. Cambridge, Mass.: Harvard University Press.

———— 1947 *See* Leighton and Kluckhohn 1947.

———
1962 The Navaho. Rev. ed. Garden City, N.Y.: Natural History Library.

Kluckhohn, Clyde, and Katherine Spencer
1940 A Bibliography of the Navaho Indians. New York: J.J. Augustin.

Kluckhohn, Clyde and Leland C. Wyman
1940 An Introduction to Navaho Chant Practice: With an Account of the Behavior Observed in Four Chants. *Memoirs of the American Anthropological Association* 53. Menasha, Wis.

Kluckhohn, Clyde, W.W. Hill, and Lucy W. Kluckhohn
1971 Navaho Material Culture. Cambridge, Mass.: Belknap Press of Harvard University Press.

Kneale, Albert H.
1950 Indian Agent. Caldwell, Ida.: The Caxton Printers.

Kniffen, Fred B.
1931 The Primitive Cultural Landscape of the Colorado Delta. *University of California Publications in Geography* 5(2):43-66. Berkeley.

Knight,
1858 Indian Affairs. *Daily Alta California*, June 28. San Francisco.

Krauss, Michael E.
1964 [Review of] Studies in the Athapaskan Languages, by Harry Hoijer et al. *International Journal of American Linguistics* 30(4):409-415.

———
1964a Proto-Athapaskan-Eyak and the Problem of Na-Dene. Pt. 1. *International Journal of American Linguistics* 30(2):118-131.

———
1973 Na-Dene. Pp. 903-978 in *Linguistics in North America*. Current Trends in Linguistics. Thomas A. Sebeok, ed. Vol. 10. The Hague, Paris: Mouton. (Reprinted: Plenum Press, New York, 1976.)

———
1979 Na-Dene and Eskimo. Pp. 803-901 in The Languages of Native North America: An Historical and Comparative Assessment. Lyle Campbell and Marianne Mithun, eds. Austin: University of Texas Press.

———
1980 On the History and Use of Comparative Athapaskan Linguistics. Fairbanks: University of Alaska, Native Language Center.

Krech, Shepard, III
1980 Northern Athapaskan Ethnology in the 1970's. *Annual Review of Anthropology* 9:83-100. Palo Alto, Calif.

Krieger, Alex D.
1955 Un nuevo estudio de la ruta seguida por Cabeza de Vaca, a través de Norte América. (Unpublished Ph.D. Dissertation, Universidad Nacional Autónoma de México, Mexico City.)

———
1961 The Travels of Alvar Núñez Cabeza de Vaca in Texas and Mexico, 1534-1536. Pp. 459-474 in Homenaje a Pablo Martínez del Río en el XXV aniversario de la primera edición des Los Orígines americanos. Mexico City: Instituto Nacional de Antropología e Historia.

Kroeber, Alfred L.
1907 Shoshonean Dialects of California. *University of California Publications in American Archaeology and Ethnology* 4(3):65-165. Berkeley.

———
1909 Classificatory Systems of Relationship. *Journal of the Royal Anthropological Institute of Great Britain and Ireland* 39:77-84. London.

———
1909a Notes on Shoshonean Dialects of Southern California. *University of California Publications in American Archaeology and Ethnology* 8(5):235-269. Berkeley.

———
1915 Serian, Tequistlatecan, and Hokan. *University of California Publications in American Archaeology and Ethnology* 11(4):279-290. Berkeley.

———
1916 Thoughts on Zuñi Religion. Pp. 269-277 in Holmes Anniversary Volume: Anthropological Essays Presented to William Henry Holmes in Honor of His Seventieth Birthday. Washington: J.W. Bryan Press.

———
1919 Zuni Kin and Clan. *Anthropological Papers of the American Museum of Natural History* 18(2):39-204. New York.

———
1925 Handbook of the Indians of California. *Bureau of American Ethnology Bulletin* 78. Washington. (Reprinted in 1953.)

———
1925a The Mohave. Pp. 726-780 in Handbook of the Indians of California. *Bureau of American Ethnology Bulletin* 78. Washington.

———
1931 The Seri. *Southwest Museum Paper* 6. Los Angeles.

———
1934 Uto-Aztecan Languages of Mexico. *Ibero-Americana* 8. Berkeley, Calif.

———, ed.
1935 Walapai Ethnography, by Fred Kniffen, Gordon MacGregor, Robert McKennan, Scudder Mekeel, and Maurice Mook. *Memoirs of the American Anthropological Association* 42. Menasha, Wis.

———
1937 Athabascan Kin Term Systems. *American Anthropologist* 39(4):602-608.

———
1939 Cultural and Natural Areas of Native North America. *University of California Publications in American Archaeology and Ethnology* 38. Berkeley.

———
1943 Classification of the Yuman Languages. *University of California Publications in Linguistics* 1(3):21-40. Berkeley.

———
1948 Seven Mohave Myths. *University of California Anthropological Records* 11(1):1-70. Berkeley.

———
1972 More Mohave Myths. *University of California Anthropological Records* 27:1-160. Berkeley.

———
1974 Report on Aboriginal Territory and Occupancy of the Mohave Tribe. (*American Indian Ethnohistory: Indians of the Southwest*) New York: Garland.

Kroeber, Alfred L., and George W. Grace
1960 The Sparkman Grammar of Luiseño. *University of California Publications in Linguistics* 16. Berkeley.

Kroeber, Alfred L., and Michael J. Harner
1955 Mohave Pottery. *University of California Anthropological Records* 16(1):1-30. Berkeley.

Kroeber, Clifton B.
1980 Lower Colorado River Peoples: Hostilities and Hunger, 1850-1857. *Journal of California and Great Basin Anthropology* 2(2):187-190.

Kunitz, Stephen J.
1977 Economic Variation on the Navajo Reservation. *Human Organization* 36(2):186-193.

Kunstadter, Peter
1961 Culture Change, Social Structure, and Health Behavior: A Quantitative Study of Clinic Use Among the Apaches of the Mescalero Reservation. (Unpublished Ph.D. Dissertation in Anthropology, University of Michigan, Ann Arbor.)

Kurath, Gertrude Prokosch
1949 Mexican Moriscas: A Problem in Dance Acculturation. *Journal of American Folklore* 62(244):87-106.

———
1959 Cochiti Choreographies and Songs. Pp. 539-556 in Cochiti: A New Mexico Pueblo, Past and Present, by Charles H. Lange. Austin: University of Texas Press.

———
1967 La Danza de los matachines entre los indios y los mestizos. *Revista Méxicana de Estudios Antropológicos* 21:261-285. Mexico City.

Kurath, William
1945 A Brief Introduction to Papago, a Native Language of Arizona. *Social Science Bulletin 13, University of Arizona Bulletin* 16(2). Tucson.

Kuykendall, J.H.
1903 Reminiscences of Early Texans: A Collection from the Austin Papers. *Quarterly of the Texas State Historical Association* 6(3):236-253, (4):311-330. Austin.

La Barre, Weston
1964 The Peyote Cult. New enlarged ed. Hamden, Conn.: Shoestring Press.

Ladd, John
1957 The Structure of a Moral Code: A Philosophical Analysis of Ethical Discourse Applied to the Ethics of the Navaho Indians. Cambridge, Mass.: Harvard University Press.

Lafora, Nicolás de
1939 Relación del viaje que hizo a los presidios internos situados en la frontera de la América septentrional, perteneciente al rey de España. Vito Alessio Robles, ed. Mexico City: P. Robredo.

———
1958 The Frontiers of New Spain: Nicolás de Lafora's Description, 1766-1768. Lawrence Kinnaird, ed. and trans. Berkeley, Calif.: The Quivira Society.

Lamb, Sydney M.
1958 Linguistic Prehistory in the Great Basin. *International Journal of American Linguistics* 24(2):95-100.

———
[1958a] Monachi-English, English-Monachi Dictionary. (Manuscript in the Archives of the Survey of California Indian Languages, Linguistics Department, University of California, Berkeley.)

———
1958b Northfork Mono Grammar. (Unpublished Ph.D. Dissertation in Linguistics, University of California, Berkeley.)

———
1964 The Classification of the Uto-Aztecan Languages: A Historical Survey. Pp. 106-125 in Studies in Californian Linguistics. William Bright, ed. *University of California Publications in Linguistics* 34. Berkeley.

Lamphere, Louise
1969 Symbolic Elements in Navajo Ritual. *Southwestern Journal of Anthropology* 25(3):279-305.

———
1976 The Internal Colonization of the Navajo People. *Southwest Economy and Society* 1(1):6-13.

———
1977 To Run After Them: Cultural and Social Bases of Cooperation in a Navajo Community. Tucson: University of Arizona Press.

———
1979 Traditional Pastoral Economy. Pp. 78-90 in Economic Development in American Indian Reservations. Roxanne Dunbar Ortiz, ed. (*Native American Studies Development Series* 1) Albuquerque: University of New Mexico.

Landar, Herbert J.
1960 Navajo Color Categories. *Language* 36(3):368-382.

———
1962 Fluctuation of Forms in Navaho Kinship Terminology. *American Anthropologist* 64(5):925-1000.

———
1964 Seven Navaho Verbs of Eating. *International Journal of American Linguistics* 30(1):94-98.

———
1968 The Karankawa Invasion of Texas. *International Journal of American Linguistics* 34(4):242-258.

Langacker, Ronald W.
1976 Non-distinct Arguments in Uto-Aztecan. *University of California Publications in Linguistics* 82. Berkeley.

———
1977 An Overview of Uto-Aztecan Grammar. Studies in Uto-Aztecan Grammar. Vol. 1. Ronald W. Langacker, ed. (*Publication* 56) Arlington: Summer Institute of Linguistics and the University of Texas.

———
1977a The Syntax of Postpositions in Uto-Aztecan. *International Journal of American Linguistics* 43(1):11-26.

Langdon, Margaret
1970 A Grammar of Diegueño: The Mesa Grande Dialect. *University of California Publications in Linguistics* 66. Berkeley.

———
1974 Comparative Hokan-Coahuiltecan Studies: A Survey and Appraisal. (*Janua Linguarum, Series Critica* 4) The Hague: Mouton.

———
1975 Boundaries and Lenition in Yuman Languages. *International Journal of American Linguistics* 41(3):218-233.

———
1976 Syntactic Diversity in Diegueño Dialects. Pp. 1-9 in Proceedings of the First Yuman Languages Workshop Held at the University of California, San Diego, June 16-21, 1975. James E. Redden, ed. *Southern Illinois University Museum Studies, Research Record* 7. Carbondale.

———
1976a The Proto-Yuman Vowel System. Pp. 129-148 in Hokan Studies. Margaret Langdon and Shirley Silver, eds. The Hague, Paris: Mouton.

———
1976b Introduction. Pp. 1-3 in Yuman Texts. Margaret Langdon, ed. *International Journal of American Linguistics, Native American Text Series* 1(3).

———
1977 Yuma (Kwtsaan) After 40 Years. Pp. 43-51 in Proceedings of the 1976 Hokan-Yuman Languages Workshop Held at the University of California, San Diego, June 21-23, 1976. James E. Redden, ed. *Southern Illinois University Museum Studies, Research Record* 11. Carbondale.

Langdon, Margaret, and Pamela Munro
1980 Yuman Numerals. Pp. 121-136 in American Indian and Indo-European Studies: Papers in Honor of Madison S. Beeler. M. Klar, M. Langdon, and S. Silver, eds. The Hague, Paris: Mouton.

Langdon, Margaret, and Shirley Silver, eds.
1976 Hokan Studies: Papers from the First Conference on Hokan Languages Held in San Diego, California, April 23-25, 1970. (*Janua Linguarum, Series Practica* 181) The Hague, Paris: Mouton.

Lange, Charles H.
1959 Cochití: A New Mexico Pueblo, Past and Present. Austin: University of Texas Press. (Reprinted: Southern Illinois University Press, Carbondale, 1968.)

Lanternari, Vittorio
1963 The Religions of the Oppressed: A Study of Modern Messianic Cults. Lisa Sergio trans. New York: Alfred A. Knopf.

Las Casas, Gonzalo de
1936 Noticias de los Chichimecas y justicia de la guerra que se les ha hecho por los españoles. Pp. 123-215 in Quellen zur Kulturgeschichte des präkolumbischen Amerika. H. Trimborn, ed. and trans. Stuttgart, Germany: Strecker und Schröder.

Laski, Vera
1959 Seeking Life. *Memoirs of the American Folklore Society* 50. Philadelphia.

Lastra, Yolanda
1975 Panorama de los estudios de lenguas yutoaztecas. Pp. 157-229 in Las lenguas de México, I. Evangelina Arana de Swadesh et al., eds. Mexico City: Instituto Nacional de Antropología e Historia.

———
[1981] Las Areas dialectales del náhuatl. (Unpublished manuscript in Lastra's possession.)

Laughing Boy
[1953] Hoop Dance Song. Recorded and edited by Raymond Boley. [Sound recording] Canyon ARP 159b. 1 disc. 78 rpm. 10 in. (Reissued as LP 6055 in 1967; also available on 8-track tape, No. 8-6055 and as cassette No. 6055c.)

Law, Howard W.
1961 A Reconstructed Proto-culture Derived from Some Yuman Vocabularies. *Anthropological Linguistics* 3(4):45-57.

Lee, Joe, and Group
[1950] Gift Dance Song. Recorded and edited by Raymond Boley. [Sound recording] Canyon ARP 159a. 1 disc. 78 rpm. 10 in.

Leighton, Alexander H., and Dorothea C. Leighton
1941 Elements of Psychotherapy in Navaho Religion. *Psychiatry* 4:515-523.

Leighton, Dorothea C., and Clyde Kluckhohn
1947 Children of the People: The Navaho Individual and His Development. Cambridge, Mass.: Harvard University Press.

León, Alonso de, ed.
1909 Historia de Nuevo León, con noticias sobre Coahuila, Tejas, Nuevo México. G. García, ed. (*Documentos inéditos o muy raros para la Historia de México* 25) Mexico City: Librería de la Vda. de C. Bouret.

León, Alonzo de, Juan Bautista Chapa, and Fernando Sánchez de Zamora
1961 Historia de Nuevo León, con noticias sobre Coahuila, Tamaulipas, Texas y Nuevo México. Monterrey, Mexico: Universidad de Nuevo León, Centro de Estudios Humanísticos.

[León Pacheco, Ignacio]
[1975] Consejo supremo tarahumara. Guachochi, Chihuahua, Mexico. Mimeo.

Leopold, Luna B.
1951 Rainfall Frequency: An Aspect of Climatic Variation. *Transactions of the American Geophysical Union* 32:347-357. Washington.

Levy, Jerrold E.
1963 Navajo Health Concepts and Behavior. Window Rock, Ariz.: U.S. Public Health Service.

———
1980 Who Benefits from Energy Resource Development: The Special Case of Navajo Indians. *Social Science Journal* 17(1):1-19.

Lewis, Alexander, Sr.
1977 Gila River Indian Community, Population and Housing Census. Sacaton, Ariz.: Gila River Indian Community. (Manuscript, copy in Henry O. Harwell's possession.)

Liebe-Harkort, M.L.
1980 Recent Developments in Apachean Language Maintenance. *International Journal of American Linguistics* 46(2):85-91.

Liljeblad, Sven S.
[1939-1981] [Linguistic Fieldwork Among the Bannock and Northern Paiute of Idaho, Oregon, Nevada, and California.] (Fieldnotes in Liljeblad's possession.)

———
1950 Bannock I: Phonemes. *International Journal of American Linguistics* 16(3):126-131.

Lindenfeld, Jacqueline
1973 Yaqui Syntax. *University of California Publications in Linguistics* 76. Berkeley.

Lindig, Wolfgang H.
1964 Tree Burial Among the Seri Indians. *Ethnology* 3(3):284-286.

Linford, Laurence D.
1979 Archaeological Investigations in West-central Arizona: The Cyprus-Bagdad Project. With revisions by David A. Phillip, Jr. and R.G. Erven. (*Archaeological Series* 136) Tucson: University of Arizona, Arizona State Museum, Cultural Resources Management Series.

Lingoes, James C.
1965 An IBM-7090 Program for Guttman-Lingoes Smallest Space Analysis—I. *Behavioral Science* 10(2):183-184.

———
1968 The Multivariate Analysis of Qualitative Data. *Multivariate Behavioral Research* 3(January):61-94.

———
1971 Some Boundary Conditions for a Monotone Analysis of Symmetric Matrices. *Psychometrika* 36(2):195-203.

Lingoes, James C., and Edward Roskam
1971 A Mathematical and Empirical Study of Two Multidimensional Scaling Algorithms. *Michigan Mathematical Psychology Program (MMPP)* 1:1-169. Lansing.

Link, Martin A., ed.
1968 Navajo: A Century of Progress, 1868-1968. Window Rock, Ariz.: The Navajo Tribe.

Lionnet, Andrés
1968 Los Intensivos en tarahumara. *Anales del Instituto Nacional de Antropología e Historia* 19:135-146. Mexico City.

———
1972 Los Elementos de la lengua tarahumara. *Universidad Nacional Autónoma de México, Instituto de Investigaciones Históricas, Sección de Antropología, Serie Antropológica* 13. Mexico City.

———
1977 Los Elementos de la lengua cahita (yaqui-mayo). *Universidad Nacional Autónoma de México, Instituto de Investigaciones Antropológicas, Serie Antropológica* 29. Mexico City.

———
1978 El Idioma tubar y los tubares, según documentos inéditos de C.S. Lumholtz y C.V. Hartman. Mexico City: Universidad Iberoamericana.

Lipton, Charles J.
1980 The Pros and Cons of Petroleum Agreements. *American Indian Journal* 6(2):2-10.

Lister, Florence C., and Robert H. Lister
1966 Chihuahua: Storehouse of Storms. Albuquerque: University of New Mexico Press.

Littell, Norman M.
1967 Navajo Indians. Proposed Findings of Fact in Behalf of the Navajo Tribe of Overall Navajo Claims (Docket No. 229). Window Rock, Ariz.: The Navajo Tribe.

Lizasoain, Ignacio
1763 Noticia de la visita general de P. Ignacio Lizasoain visitador general de las misiones de esta provincia de Nueva España, que comenzio dia quatro de abril de 1761 años y se concluyo a fines de henero en 1763 con algunas notas y adiciones q. pueden servir para el conocimiento (Manuscript No. 47 in Stevens Collection, University of Texas Latin American Collection, Austin.)

Lloyd, John W.
1911 Aw-aw-tam Indian Nights: Being Myths and Legends of the Pimas of Arizona.... Westfield, N.J.: The Lloyd Group.

Lombardo, Natal
1702 Arte de la lengua Teguima llamada vulgarmente Ópata. Mexico City.

Longacre, William A., ed.
1970 Reconstructing Historic Pueblo Societies. Albuquerque: University of New Mexico Press.

López Batista, Ramón
1980 Qui'yá Irétaca Nahuisárami: Relatos de los tarahumaras. Mexico City: Instituto Nacional Indigenista.

López Batista, Ramón, Ignacio León Pacheco, Albino Mares Trías, and Luis Castro Jiménez
1981 Rarámuri Ri'écuara: Deportes y juegos de los tarahumaras. Chihuahua, Mexico: Don Burgess.

López-Velarde López, Benita
1964 Expansión geográfica franciscana en el hoy norte central y oriental de México. (*Cultura Misional* 12) Mexico City: Universidad Pontificia Urbaniana de Propaganda Fide.

Lowe, Charles H., ed.
1964 The Vertebrates of Arizona: Annotated Check Lists of the Vertebrates of the State: The Species and Where They Live. Tucson: University of Arizona Press.

Lowell, Edith S.
1970 A Comparison of Mexican and Seri Indian Versions of the Legend of Lola Casanova. *The Kiva* 35(4):144-158.

Lowie, Robert H.
1953 Alleged Kiowa-Crow Affinities. *Southwestern Journal of Anthropology* 9(4):357-368.

Luckert, Karl W.
1975 The Navajo Hunter Tradition; with Field Assistance and Translations by John Cook, Victor Beck and Irvy Goossen, and with Additional Translation by Father Berard Haile. Tucson: University of Arizona Press.

———
1977 Navajo Mountain and Rainbow Bridge Religion. (*American Tribal Religion Series* 1) Flagstaff: Museum of Northern Arizona Press.

———
1978 A Navajo Bringing-Home Ceremony: The Claus Chee Sonny Version of Deerway *Ajiłee*. (*American Tribal Religion Series* 3) Flagstaff: Museum of Northern Arizona Press.

———
1979 Coyoteway: A Navajo Holyway Healing Ceremonial. Tucson and Flagstaff: University of Arizona Press and Museum of Northern Arizona Press.

———
1979a An Approach to Navajo Mythology. Pp. 117-131 in Native Religious Traditions. Earle H. Waugh and K. Dad Prithipaul, eds. Waterloo, Ont.: Wilfrid Laurier University Press.

Ludlam, A.B.
1880 [Report of September 5, from Pima Agency, Arizona to the Commissioner of Indian Affairs.] Pp. 3-4 in Report of the Commissioner of Indian Affairs for the Year 1880. Washington: U.S. Government Printing Office.

Lumholtz, Carl S.
1894 Tarahumari Life and Customs. *Scribner's Magazine* 16(3):296-311.

———
1902 Unknown Mexico: A Record of Five Years' Exploration Among the Tribes of the Western Sierra Madre, in the Tierra Caliente of Tepic and Jalisco, and Among the Tarascos of Michoachan. 2 vols. New York: Charles Scribner's Sons.

———
1912 New Trails in Mexico: An Account of One Year's Exploration in North-western Sonora, Mexico, and South-western Arizona, 1909-1910. New York: Charles Scribner's Sons. (Reprinted: Rio Grande Press, Glorieta, N.M., 1971.)

Maas, P. Otto
1915 Viajes de misioneros franciscanos á la conquista del Nuevo México. Seville, Spain: Impr. de San Antonio.

McAllester, David P.
1949 Peyote Music. *Viking Fund Publications in Anthropology* 13. New York.

———
1954 Enemy Way Music: A Study of Social and Esthetic Values as Seen in Navajo Music. *Papers of the Peabody Museum of American Archaeology and Ethnology, Harvard University* 41(3). Cambridge, Mass.

———
1971 [Review of] Navajo Skip Dance and Two-step Songs. Recordings and Commentary by Tony Isaacs. (Indian House IH 1503, 1969.) *Ethnomusicology* 15(2):296-297.

———
1971a [Review of] Night and Daylight Yeibichei. *Ethnomusicology* 15(2):167-170.

———
1980 Shootingway: An Epic Drama of the Navajos. Pp. 199-238 in Southwestern Indian Ritual Drama. Charlotte J. Frisbie, ed. Albuquerque: University of New Mexico Press.

———
1980a The First Snake Song. Pp. 1-27 in Theory and Practice: Essays Presented to Gene Weltfish. Stanley Diamond, ed. (*Studies in Anthropology* 7) The Hague: Mouton.

McAllister, J. Gilbert
1949 Kiowa-Apache Tales. Pp. 1-141 in The Sky Is My Tipi. Mody C. Boatright, ed. *Publications of the Texas Folklore Society* 22. Dallas.

———
1955 Kiowa-Apache Social Organization. Pp. 97-169 in Social Anthropology of North American Tribes. Fred Eggan, ed. 2d ed. Chicago: University of Chicago Press.

McAllister, Martin E.
1980 Hohokam Social Organization: A Reconstruction. *The Arizona Archaeologist* 14. Phoenix.

McAndrew, John
1965 The Open-air Churches of Sixteenth-Century Mexico: Atrios, Posas, Open Chapels, and Other Studies. Cambridge, Mass.: Harvard University Press.

McCammon, Charles
1970 [Notes of an Interview with Charles McCammon, Director, Indian Health Service, Phoenix Area.] (Notes in Robert L. Bergman's possession.)

McCarty, Teresa
1977 Yavapai Weapons and Games. Pp. 52-62 in The Yavapai of Fort McDowell: An Outline of Their History and Culture. Sigrid Khera, ed. Fort McDowell, Ariz.: Fort McDowell Mohave-Apache Indian Community.

McCord, Thomas T., Jr.
1946 An Economic History of the Mescalero Apache. (Unpublished M.A. Thesis in Anthropology, University of New Mexico, Albuquerque.)

MacDonald, Peter
1971 Text of MacDonald's Inaugural Address. *Navajo Times*, January 7:2. Window Rock, Ariz.

———
1973 Annual Report to the Navajo Tribal Council for Period Covering January Through December, 1972; Winter Session—February, 1973. Mimeo.

———
1975 Second Inaugural Address, January 7. (Copy in Peter Iverson's possession.)

Mace, William E., and Pamela Munro
[1981] A New Tübatulabal Dictionary. (Manuscript in Wick R. Miller's possession.)

McGee, WJ
1898 The Seri Indians. Pp. 1-344 in Pt. 1 of *17th Annual Report of the Bureau of American Ethnology for the Years 1895-1896*. 2 Pts. Washington (Reprinted as: The Seri Indians of Bahia Kino and Sonora, Mexico. Rio Grande Press, Glorieta, N.M., 1971.)

———
1900 [Cocopa (Yuman) Vocabulary.] (Manuscript No. 1546a in National Anthropological Archives, Smithsonian Institution, Washington.)

McGinnies, William G., Bram J. Goldman, and Patricia Paylore, eds.
1971 Food, Fiber and the Arid Lands. Tucson: University of Arizona Press.

McGraw, Kate
1975 Mescalero—Big Stop on the Powwow Trail. *New Mexico Magazine* 53(5):30-32.

McGreevy, Susan
1981 Navajo Sandpainting Textiles at the Wheelwright Museum. *American Indian Art Magazine* 7(1):54-61.

McIntosh, John B.
1949 Huichol Texts and Dictionary. In Huichol and Aztec Texts and Dictionaries, by John B. McIntosh et al. (Microfilm Collection of *Manuscripts on Middle American Cultural Anthropology* 27) Chicago: University of Chicago Library.

McKee, Barbara, Edwin McKee, and Joyce Herold
1975 Havasupai Baskets and Their Makers: 1930-1940. Flagstaff, Ariz.: Northland Press.

McKenzie, A.S.
1889 Yaqui of Mexico. *American Anthropologist* 2(4):299-300.

McMahon, Ambrosio, and María Aiton de McMahon
1959 Cora y español. (*Serie de Vocabularios Indígenas* 2) Mexico City: Instituto Lingüístico de Verano.

McMahon, M.
1860 [Report to Charles E. Mix, Acting Commissioner of Indian Affairs, Dated Dec. 18, 1860, at Fort Yuma, California.] (Manuscript in Letters Received, Commissioner's Office, Record Group 75, National Archives, Washington.)

MacMeekin, Daniel H.
1971 The Navajo Tribe's Water Rights in the Colorado River Basin. [Window Rock, Ariz.: Dinebeiina Nahiilna Be Agaditahe, DNA—A Legal Services Program.] Mimeo.

McNeill, William H.
1976 Plagues and Peoples. Garden City, N.Y.: Anchor Press/Doubleday.

McNeley, James K.
1981 Holy Wind in Navajo Philosophy. Tucson: University of Arizona Press.

McNitt, Frank
1962 The Indian Traders. Norman: University of Oklahoma Press.

———
1972 Navajo Wars: Military Campaigns, Slave Raids, and Reprisals. Albuquerque: University of New Mexico Press.

———
1973 The Long March: 1863-1867. Pp. 145-169 in The Changing Ways of Southwestern Indians: A Historic Perspective. Albert H. Schroeder, ed. (El Corral de Santa Fe Westerners Brand Book 1973) Glorieta, N.M.: Rio Grande Press.

Mails, Thomas
1974 The People Called Apache. Englewood Cliffs, N.J.: Prentice Hall.

Malkin, Borys
1962 Seri Ethnozoology. *Occasional Papers of the Idaho State College Museum* 7. Pocatello.

Mange, Juan Mateo *see* Manje, Juan Mateo

Manje, Juan Mateo
1954 Unknown Arizona and Sonora, 1693-1721, from the Francisco Fernández del Castillo Version of Luz de Tierra Incógnita. Harry J. Karns et al., trans. Tucson: Arizona Silhouettes.

Manners, Robert A.
1957 Tribe and Tribal Boundaries: The Walapai. *Ethnohistory* 4(1):1-26.

———
1974 Hualapai Indians, II: An Ethnological Report on the Hualapai (Walapai) Indians of Arizona. *(American Indian Ethnohistory: Indians of the Southwest)* New York: Garland.

Manrique Castañeda, Leonardo
1959 Sobre la clasificación del otomi-pamé. Pp. 551-559 in Vol. 2 of *Proceedings of the 33d International Congress of Americanists*. San José, Costa Rica, 1958.

———
1967 Jiliapan Pame. Pp. 331-348 in *Linguistics*. Norman A. McQuown, vol. ed. Handbook of Middle American Indians. Vol. 5. Robert Wauchope, gen. ed. Austin: University of Texas Press.

———
1969 The Otomi. Pp. 682-722 in *Ethnology*. Evon Z. Vogt, vol. ed. Handbook of Middle American Indians. Vol. 8. Robert Wauchope, gen. ed. Austin: University of Texas Press.

Manuel, Henry F., Juliann Ramon, and Bernard L. Fontana
1978 Dressing for the Window: Papago Indians and Economic Development. Pp. 511-577 in American Indian Economic Development. Sam Stanley, ed. The Hague, Paris: Mouton.

Manuel-Dupont, Sonia
1980 [Maricopa Material.] Albuquerque: American Indian Language Development Institute. (Manuscript, copy in Henry O. Harwell's possession.)

Mares Trías, Albino
1975 Jena Ra'icha Ralámuli Alué 'Ya Muchígame Chiquime Níliga: Aquí relata la gente de antes lo que pasaba en su tiempo. Mexico City: Instituto Lingüístico de Verano.

Margry, Pierre, ed.
1876-1886 Découvertes et établissements des Français dans l'ouest et dans le sud de l'Amérique septentrionale, 1614-1754. Paris: D. Jouaust.

Maria of Portugal [Queen of Spain]
1759 [Letter to the Viceroy.] (Manuscript folio 34r, tomo 107, Reales Cédulas, Archivo General de la Nación, Mexico City.)

Mariella, Patricia S.
1975-1980 [Ethnographic and Ethnohistorical Fieldnotes on the Fort McDowell Yavapai Community.] (Unpublished manuscript in Mariella's possession.)

———
1977 Yavapai Farming. Pp. 28-35 in The Yavapai of Fort McDowell: An Outline of Their History and Culture. Sigrid Khera, ed. Fort McDowell, Ariz.: Fort McDowell Mohave-Apache Indian Community.

Marino Flores, Amselmo
1967 Indian Population and Its Identification. Pp. 12-25 in *Social Anthropology*. Manning Nash, vol. ed. Handbook of Middle American Indians. Vol. 6. Robert Wauchope, gen. ed. Austin: University of Texas Press.

Mark, Albyn K.
1961 Description of and Variables Relating to Ecological Change in the History of the Papago Indian Population. (Unpublished M.A. Thesis in Anthropology, University of Arizona, Tucson.)

Marriott, Alice L., and Carol K. Rachlin
1971 Peyote. New York: Thomas Y. Crowell.

Martin, John F.
1966 Continuity and Change in Havasupai Social and Economic Organization. (Unpublished Ph.D. Dissertation in Anthropology, University of Chicago, Chicago.)

———
1968 A Reconsideration of Havasupai Land Tenure. *Ethnology* 7(4):450-460.

———
1973 On the Estimation of the Sizes of Local Groups in a Hunting-gathering Environment. *American Anthropologist* 75(5):1448-1468.

Martín Bernal, Cristóbal
1858 Diario... In Relación del estado de la Pimería que remite el padre visitador Horacio Polici, 1697. *Documentos para la Historia de Méjico, 3d ser., Vol.* 1:799-809. Mexico City.

Martinez del Río, Pablo
1954 La Comarca lagunera a fines del siglo XVI y principios del XVII según las fuentes escritas. *Publicaciones del Instituto de Historia, Primera Serie* 30. Mexico City.

Mason, J. Alden
1917 Tepecano: A Piman Language of Western Mexico. *Annals of the New York Academy of Sciences* 25:309-416. New York.

———
1936 The Classification of the Sonoran Languages. Pp. 183-198 in Essays in Anthropology Presented to A.L. Kroeber in Celebration of His Sixtieth Birthday, June 11, 1936. Robert H. Lowie, ed. Berkeley: University of California Press.

———
1940 The Native Languages of Middle America. Pp. 52-87 in The Maya and Their Neighbors. Clarence L. Hay et al., eds. New York: D. Appleton-Century.

———
1948 The Tepehuán and Other Aborigines of the Mexican Sierra Madre Occidental. *América Indígena* 7(4):289-300.

———
1950 The Language of the Papago of Arizona. *University of Pennsylvania Museum Monograph* 3. Philadelphia.

———
1952 Notes and Observations on the Tepehuán. *América Indígena* 12(1):33-53.

Mason, J. Alden, and David M. Brugge
1958 Notes on the Pima Bajo. Pp. 227-297 in Vol. 1 of Miscellanea Paul Rivet, Octogenario Dicata: 31st International Congress of Americanists. 2 vols. Mexico City: Universidad Nacional Autónoma de México.

Mason, Otis T.
1896 Influence of Environment Upon Human Industries or Arts. Pp. 639-665 in *Annual Report of the Smithsonian Institution for 1895*. Washington.

Masse, W. Bruce
1980 Excavations at Gu Achi: A Reappraisal of Hohokam Settlement and Subsistence in the Arizona Papagueria. *U.S. National Park Service, Western Archeological Center Publications in Anthropology* 12. Tucson.

Massey, William C.
1966 Archaeology and Ethnohistory of Lower California. Pp. 38-58 in *Archaeological Frontiers and External Connections*. Gordon F. Ekholm and Gordon R. Willey, vol. eds. Handbook of Middle American Indians. Vol. 4. Robert Wauchope, gen. ed. Austin: University of Texas Press.

Mathiot, Madeleine
1962 Noun Classes and Folk Taxonomy in Papago. *American Anthropologist* 64(2):340-350.

———
1967 The Cognitive Significance of the Category of Nominal Number in Papago. Pp. 197-237 in Studies in Southwestern Ethnolinguistics: Meaning and History in the Languages of the American Southwest. Dell H. Hymes with William E. Bittle, eds. The Hague, Paris: Mouton.

———
1968 An Approach to the Cognitive Study of Language. *Indiana University Research Center in Anthropology, Folklore and Linguistics, Publication* 45. Bloomington.

———
1973 A Dictionary of Papago Usage. 2 vols. *Indiana University Language Science Monograph* 8(1-2). Bloomington.

Matson, Dan S., and Albert H. Schroeder
1957 Cordero's Description of the Apache, 1796. *New Mexico Historical Review* 32(4):335-356.

Matson, Richard G.
1971 Adaptation and Environment in the Cerbat Mountains, Arizona. (Unpublished Ph.D. Dissertation in Anthropology, University of California, Davis.)

Matthews, Washington
1883 Navajo Silversmiths. Pp. 167-178 in *2d Annual Report of the Bureau of American Ethnology for the Years 1880-1881*. Washington. (Reprinted: Filter Press, Palmer Lake, Colo., 1968.)

———
1883a A Part of the Navajo's Mythology. *American Antiquarian* 5(3):207-224.

———
1884 Navajo Weavers. Pp. 371-391 in *3d Annual Report of the Bureau of American Ethnology for the Years 1881-1882*. Washington.

———
1886 Navajo Names for Plants. *American Naturalist* 20(9):767-777.

———
1887 The Mountain Chant: A Navajo Ceremony. Pp. 379-467 in *5th Annual Report of the Bureau of American Ethnology for the Years 1883-1884*. Washington.

———
1889 Navajo Gambling Songs. *American Anthropologist* 2(1):1-19.

———
1893 Some Sacred Objects of the Navajo Rites. *Archives of the International Folklife Association* 1:227-247.

———
1894 The Basket Drum. *American Anthropologist* 7(2):202-208.

———, coll. and trans.
1897 Navaho Legends. *Memoirs of the American Folk-Lore Society* 5. Menasha, Wis. (Reprinted: Kraus Reprint, New York, 1969.)

———
1900 A Two-faced Navaho Blanket. *American Anthropologist* 2(4):638-642.

———
1902 The Night Chant: A Navaho Ceremony. *Memoirs of the American Museum of Natural History* 6. New York.

Maxwell, Gilbert S.
1963 Navajo Rugs—Past, Present and Future. Palm Desert, Calif.: Best-West Publications.

Mayhall, Mildred P.
1939 The Indians of Texas: The Atákapa, the Karankawa, the Tonkawa. (Unpublished Ph.D. Dissertation in Anthropology, University of Texas, Austin.)

Mecham, J. Lloyd
1927 Francisco de Ibarra and Nueva Vizcaya. Durham, N.C.: Duke University Press.

Meighan, Clement W.
1971 Archaeology of Sinaloa. Pp. 754-767 in *Archaeology of Northern Mesoamerica*. Gordon F. Ekholm and Ignacio Bernal, vol. eds. Handbook of Middle American Indians. Vol. 11. Robert Wauchope gen. ed. Austin: University of Texas Press.

Meigs, Peveril, III
1939 The Kiliwa Indians of Lower California. *Ibero-Americana* 15:1-114. Berkeley, Calif.

Mera, Harry P.
1947 Navaho Textile Arts. Santa Fe: Laboratory of Anthropology. (Reprinted: Peregrine Smith, Santa Barbara, Calif., 1975.)

———
1960 Indian Silverwork of the Southwest, Illustrated. 2d ed. Globe, Ariz.: Dale Stuart King.

Meriam, Lewis
1928 The Problem of Indian Administration. Baltimore: Johns Hopkins Press.

Meritt, E[dgar] B.
1915 [Letter from E[dgar] B. Meritt, Assistant Commissioner [of Indian Affairs, Washington, D.C.], to Clarence R. Jefferis, Supt., Mescalero School [and Agency, Mescalero, N.M.], Dated February 25.] (Manuscript in Record Group 1, National Archives, Washington.)

———
1920 [Letter from E[dgar] B. Meritt, Assistant Commissioner [of Indian Affairs, Washington, D.C.], to Ernest Stecker, Superintendent, Mescalero School [and Agency, Mescalero, N.M.], Dated September 20.] (Manuscript in Letters Sent, Commissioner's Office, Record Group 75, National Archives, Washington.)

Merrill, William L.
[1977-1981] [Ethnographic Notes, from Approximately 27 Months' Fieldwork Among the Rarámuri of Basihuare Pueblo, Chihuahua, Mexico.] (Manuscripts in Merrill's possession.)

———
1978 Thinking and Drinking: A Rarámuri Interpretation. Pp. 101-117 in The Nature and Status of Ethnobotany. Richard I.

Ford, ed. *University of Michigan, Museum of Anthropology Anthropological Paper* 67. Ann Arbor.

———
1981 The Concept of Soul Among the Rarámuri of Chihuahua, Mexico: A Study in World View. (Unpublished Ph.D. Dissertation in Anthropology, University of Michigan, Ann Arbor.)

Mesa Verde National Park Team
[1950] Riding in the Thunder. Recorded and edited by Raymond Boley. [Sound recording] Canyon ARP 172b. 1 disc. 78 rpm. 10 in.

Metzler, William H.
1960 [Livestock on the Papago Reservation.] (Unpublished report to the Papago Tribal Council; copy in Bernard L. Fontana's possession.)

Mexican Boundary Survey
1898 Report of the Boundary Commission Upon the Survey and Re-making of the Boundary Between the United States and Mexico West of the Rio Grande, 1891-96. 2 Pts. Washington: U.S. Government Printing Office.

México. Dirección General de Estadística
1963 VIII Censo general de población, 8 de junio de 1960. Localidades de República por entidades federativas y municipios. Mexico City: no publisher.

Mickey, Barbara Harris
1956 Acoma Kinship Terms. *Southwestern Journal of Anthropology* 12(3):249-256.

Mierau, Eric
1963 Concerning Yavapai-Apache Bilingualism. *International Journal of American Linguistics* 29(1):1-3.

Miguel, Patrick
[1950] The Quechan Tribe. (Unpublished manuscript in Miguel's possession.)

Miles, Nelson A.
1896 Personal Recollections and Observations of General Nelson A. Miles, Embracing a Brief View of the Civil War, or From New England to the Golden Gate and the Story of His Indian Campaigns with Comments on the Exploration, Development and Progress of Our Great Western Empire. Chicago and New York: The Werner Company.

Miller, Wick R.
1959 Some Notes on Acoma Kinship Terminology. *Southwestern Journal of Anthropology* 15(2):179-184.

———
1964 The Shoshonean Languages of Uto-Aztecan. Pp. 145-148 in Studies in Californian Linguistics. William Bright, ed. *University of California Publications in Linguistics* 34. Berkeley.

———
1965 Acoma Grammar and Texts. *University of California Publications in Linguistics* 40. Berkeley.

———
1966 Anthropological Linguistics in the Great Basin. Pp. 75-112 in The Current Status of Anthropological Research in the Great Basin, 1964. Warren L. d'Azevedo et al., eds. *Desert Research Institute, Technical Report Series S-H, Social Sciences and Humanities Publication* 1. Reno.

———
1967 Uto-Aztecan Cognate Sets. *University of California Publications in Linguistics* 48. Berkeley.

———
1968 [Linguistic Fieldwork with the Panamint of Beatty, Nevada.] (Unpublished manuscript in Miller's possession.)

———, comp.
1972 Newe Natekwinappeh: Shoshoni Stories and Dictionary. *University of Utah Anthropological Publication* 94. Salt Lake City.

———
1977 [Preliminary Notes on the Guarijío Language.] (Manuscript in Miller's possession.)

———
1978 [Vocabulario preliminar guarijío.] (Manuscript in Miller's possession.)

———
1980 The Classification of the Uto-Aztecan Languages Based on Lexical Evidence. (Paper given at the Uto-Aztecan Historical Symposium, at the Linguistic Institute, University of New Mexico, Albuquerque; to appear in *International Journal of American Linguistics* 49(3), 1983.)

———
1980a [Linguistic Fieldwork with Papago.] (Unpublished manuscript in Miller's possession.)

———
1980b Preaspirated Consonants in Central Numic. Pp. 151-157 in American Indian and Indo-European Studies: Papers in Honor of Madison S. Beeler. Kathryn Klar et al., eds. The Hague, Paris: Mouton.

———
1981 [A Note on Extinct Languages of Northwest Mexico of Supposed Uto-Aztecan Affiliation.] (Unpublished manuscript in Miller's possession.)

Mindeleff, Cosmos
1898 Navaho Houses. Pp. 469-517 in Pt. 2 of *17th Annual Report of the Bureau of American Ethnology for the Years 1895-1896*. 2 Pts. Washington.

Mindeleff, Victor
1891 A Study of Pueblo Architecture: Tusayan and Cibola. Pp. 3-228 in *8th Annual Report of the Bureau of American Ethnology for the Years 1886-1887*. Washington.

Miranda, Joan de
1871 Relación hecha por Joan de Miranda, clérigo, al doctor Orozco, Presidente de la Audiencia de Guadalajara; sobre la tierra y población que hay desde las minas de San Martín a las de Santa Barbara, que esto último entonces estaba poblada—año de 1575. (*Collección de Documentos Inéditos Relativos al Discubrimiento, Conquista y Organización de las Antiguas Posesiones Españolas de América y Oceania Sacados de los Archivos del Reino* 16) Madrid: Imprenta del Hospicio.

Mitchell, Emerson Barney Blackhorse, and T.D. Allen
1967 Miracle Hill: The Story of a Navaho Boy. Norman: University of Oklahoma Press.

Mitchell, Frank
1978 Navajo Blessingway Singer: The Autobiography of Frank Mitchell, 1881-1967. Charlotte J. Frisbie and David P. McAllester, eds. Tucson: University of Arizona Press.

Mixco, Mauricio J.
1972 Kiliwa Grammar. (Unpublished Ph.D. Dissertation in Linguistics, University of California, Berkeley.)

———
1976 Oblique and Non-oblique Surface Case in Kiliwa Syntax. Pp. 29-34 in Proceedings of the First Yuman Languages Workshop Held at the University of California, San Diego, June 16-21, 1975. James E. Redden, ed. *Southern Illinois University Museum Studies, Research Record* 7. Carbondale.

Möllhausen, Balduin
1858 Diary of a Journey from the Mississippi to the Coasts of the Pacific with a United States Government Expedition. Mrs. Percy Sinnett, trans. 2 vols. London: Longman, Brown, Longmans, and Roberts.

Moisés, Rosalio, Jane H. Kelley, and William C. Holden
1971 The Tall Candle: The Personal Chronicle of a Yaqui Indian. Lincoln: University of Nebraska Press.

Molina, Alonso de
1977 Vocabulario en lengua castellana y mexicana y mexicana y castellana 1555-1571. Miguel León Portilla, ed. Mexico City: Editorial Porrúa.

Montezuma, Carlos
1901-1922 [Correspondence.] (Manuscripts in Carlos Montezuma Collection, Heyden Collection at Arizona State University, Tempe.)

Monthan, Doris Born
1978 R.C. Gorman: The Lithographs. Flagstaff, Ariz.: Northland Press.

Mooney, James
1892 Eating the Mescal. *Augusta Chronicle,* January 24:11. Augusta, Ga.

——— [1892a] [Mooney Notebooks, Vol. 4: Kiowa Dictionary.] (Manuscript No. 2531 in National Anthropological Archives, Smithsonian Institution, Washington.)

——— [1895] [Notebook Containing Tewa Vocabulary and Miscellaneous Notes on the Hopi; Vocabulary of Hopi Foods.] (Manuscript No. 30 in National Anthropological Archives, Smithsonian Institution, Washington.)

——— 1896 The Mescal Plant and Ceremony. *Therapeutic Gazette,* 3d ser., Vol. 12:7-11.

——— 1896a The Ghost-Dance Religion and the Sioux Outbreak of 1890. Pp. 641-1136 in *14th Annual Report of the Bureau of American Ethnology for the Years 1892-1893.* Washington.

——— 1897 The Kiowa Peyote Rite. *Der Urquell* n.s. 1:329-333.

——— 1897a [Jicarilla Apache Tribal Names.] (Manuscript No. 454 in National Anthropological Archives, Smithsonian Institution, Washington.)

——— 1897b [Tribal Names and Divisions of the Jicarilla, Lipan, and Mescalero Apaches.] (Manuscript No. 3785 in National Anthropological Archives, Smithsonian Institution, Washington.)

——— 1898 Calendar History of the Kiowa Indians. Pp. 129-445 in Pt. 1 of *17th Annual Report of the Bureau of American Ethnology for the Years 1895-1896.* 2 Pts. Washington.

——— 1898a The Jicarilla Genesis. *American Anthropologist* 11(7):197-209.

——— 1928 The Aboriginal Population of America North of Mexico. *Smithsonian Miscellaneous Collections* 80(7). Washington.

Moorhead, Max L.
1968 The Apache Frontier: Jacobo Ugarte and Spanish-Indian Relations in Northern New Spain, 1769-1791. Norman: University of Oklahoma Press.

Morfí, Juan Agustín de
1932 Excerpts from the Memorias for the History of the Province of Texas... Frederick C. Chabot, trans. San Antonio: Naylor Printing Company.

——— 1935 History of Texas, 1673-1779. Carlos Eduardo Castañeda, trans. 2 vols. *Quivira Society Publication* 6. Albuquerque.

——— 1958 Viaje de indios y diario del Nuevo México. Pp. 331-431 in Viajes y viajeros: Viajes por Norteamérica. Vito Alessio Robles, ed. Madrid: Aguilar.

Morgan, Fred C.
1922 [Letter from Fred C. Morgan, Superintendent, (Mescalero Agency), Mescalero, New Mexico, to Commissioner of Indian Affairs, Washington, D.C., Dated December 16.] (Manuscript in Letters Received, Commissioner's Office, Record Group 75, National Archives, Washington.)

Morgan, Lewis H.
1871 Systems of Consanguinity and Affinity of the Human Family. *Smithsonian Contributions to Knowledge* 17. Washington.

Morris, Clyde P.
1971 A Brief Economic History of the Camp and Middle Verde Reservations. *Plateau* 44(2):43-51.

——— 1972 Yavapai-Apache Family Organization in a Reservation Context. *Plateau* 44(3):105-110.

Morris, Earl H.
1925 Exploring in the Canyon of Death. *National Geographic Magazine* 48:263-300.

——— 1948 Tomb of the Weaver. *Natural History* 57(2):66-71, 91.

Morrow, Mable
1975 Indian Rawhide: An American Folk Art. Norman: University of Oklahoma Press.

Moser, Edward
1961 Number in Seri Verbs. (Unpublished M.A. Thesis in Linguistics, University of Pennsylvania, Philadelphia.)

——— 1963 Seri Bands. *The Kiva* 28(3):14-27.

——— 1973 Seri Basketry. *The Kiva* 38(3-4):105-140.

——— 1976 Guia bibliográfica de las fuentes para el estudio de la etnografía seri. Pp. 365-375 in Sonora: Antropología del desierto. B. Braniff C. and R.S. Felger, ed. *Instituto Nacional de Antropología e Historia, Colección Científica* 27. Mexico City.

Moser, Edward, and Mary B. Moser, comps.
1961 Seri-castellano, castellano-seri. (*Serie de Vocabularios Indígenas* 5). Mexico City: Instituto Lingüístico de Verano en cooperación con la Dirección General de Asuntos Indígenas de la Secretaria de Educación Pública.

——— 1965 Consonant Vowel Balance in Seri (Hokan) Syllables. *Linguistics* 16(September):50-67.

——— 1976 Seri Noun Pluralization Classes. Pp. 285-296 in Hokan Studies: Papers from the First Conference on Hokan Languages, Held in San Diego, California, April 23-25, 1970. Margaret Langdon and Shirley Silver, eds. (*Janua Linguarum, Series Practica* 181) The Hague, Paris: Mouton.

Moser, Edward, and Richard S. White, Jr.
1968 Seri Clay Figurines. *The Kiva* 33(3):133-154.

Moser, Mary Beck
1964 Seri Blue. *The Kiva* 30(2):27-32.

——— 1970 Seri Elevated Burials. *The Kiva* 35(4):211-216.

——— 1970a Seri: From Conception Through Infancy. *The Kiva* 35(4):201-210.

——— 1978 Switch-reference in Seri. *International Journal of American Linguistics* 44(2):113-120.

Mota y Escobar, Alonso de la
1940 Descripción geográfica de los reinos de Nueva Galicia, Nueva Vizcaya y Nuevo León. Joaquín Ramíroz Cabañas, ed. 2d ed. Mexico City: Robredo.

Mowry, Sylvester
1858 [Letter to J.W. Denver, Commissioner of Indian Affairs, Dated Washington, D.C., November 10, 1857.] Pp. 296-305 in Annual Report of the Commissioner of Indian Affairs for the Year 1857. Washington: William A. Harris.

——— 1860 [Report of November 21, 1859 to Alfred B. Greenwood, Commissioner of Indian Affairs.] Pp. 353-362 in Annual Report of the Commissioner of Indian Affairs for 1859. Washington: George W. Bowman.

Munro, Pamela
1972 The Proto-Yuman p-v-w Question: The Problem Re-examined with Evidence from Mojave. (Unpublished manuscript in Munro's possession.)

——— 1976 Mojave Modals. Pp. 55-62 in Proceedings of the First Yuman Languages Workshop Held at the University of California, San Diego, June 16-21, 1975. James E. Redden, ed. *Southern Illinois University Museum Studies, Research Record* 7. Carbondale.

———
1976a Two Stories by Nellie Brown (Mojave). Pp. 43-50 in Yuman Texts. Margaret Langdon, ed. *International Journal of American Linguistics, Native American Text Series* 1(3).

———
1976b On the Form of Negative Sentences in Kawaiisu. Pp. 308-319 in *Proceedings of the Second Annual Meeting of the Berkeley Linguistic Society*. Berkeley, Calif.

———
1977 The Yuman *n- Prefix. Pp. 52-59 in Proceedings of the 1976 Hokan-Yuman Languages Workshop Held at the University of California, San Diego, June 21-23, 1976. James E. Redden, ed. *Southern Illinois University Museum Studies, Research Record* 11. Carbondale.

———
1980 Types of Agreement in Mojave. Pp. 1-14 in Proceedings of the 1979 Hokan Languages Workshop Held at the University of California, Los Angeles, June 26-28, 1979. James E. Redden, ed. *Southern Illinois University Occasional Papers on Linguistics* 7. Carbondale.

Munsell, Marvin R.
1967 Land and Labor at Salt River: Household Organization in a Changing Economy. (Unpublished Ph.D. Dissertation in Anthropology, University of Oregon, Eugene.)

Murdock, George P.
1949 Social Structure. New York: Macmillan.

Murphy, Lawrence, R.
1972 Philmont: A History of New Mexico's Cimarron Country. Albuquerque: University of New Mexico Press.

———
1972a Frontier Crusader: William F.M. Arny. Tucson: University of Arizona Press.

Murray, William B.
1981 A Tarahumara Body-painting Ritual. *Ornament* 5:18-21, 56.

Nabhan, Gary P.
1979 The Ecology of Floodwater Farming in Arid Southwestern North America. *Agro-Ecosystems* 5:245-255. Amsterdam, The Netherlands.

———
1979a Tepary Beans: The Effects of Domestication on Adaptations to Arid Land Environments. *Arid Lands Newsletter* 10:11-16. Tucson.

Natay, Ed Lee
[1968] Memories of Navajoland. Recorded and edited by Raymond Boley. [Sound recording] Canyon ARP 6057. 1 disc. 33⅓ rpm. 12 in.

Native American Church of North America
1957 [Minutes of the Annual Convention of the Native American Church of North America, June 6-10.] Mimeo.

Navajo Agricultural Products Industry
1974 Revised Comprehensive Plan for the Development of Farming and Related Activity, Block 1, Navajo Indian Irrigation Project. Farmington, N.M.: Navajo Agricultural Products Industry. Mimeo.

Navajo Chorus
1941 Circle Dance Song, in Indian Music of the Southwest. Recorded and edited by Laura Bolton. [Sound recording] Victor P-49-3a. 1 disc. 78 rpm. 10 in.

———
1941a Squaw Dance, in Indian Music of the Southwest. Recorded and edited by Laura Bolton. [Sound recording] Victor P-49-3. 1 disc. 78 rpm. 10 in.

Navajo Indians
1962 Navajo Tribal Code. 2 vols. Orford, N.H.: Equity Publishing Corporation.

———
1969 Navajo Tribal Code. 2d ed. 3 vols. Orford, N.H.: Equity Publishing Corporation.

Navajo Nation
1968 Navajo Manpower Survey: Data for 1967. [Window Rock, Ariz.]: Navajo Tribe, Indian Health Service, Bureau of Indian Affairs, and Arizona State Employment Service, Office of Navajo Economic Opportunity. Mimeo.

———
1972 The Navajo 10-Year Plan. [Window Rock, Ariz.]: The Navajo Tribe.

———
[1972a] New Business and Industrial Opportunity in Navajoland. (Mimeographed circular issued by the Tribal Council.)

———
1974 Overall Economic Development Program for the Navajo Nation: Prepared by the Office of Program Development of the Navajo Tribe. Window Rock, Ariz.: The Navajo Nation. Mimeo.

The Navajo Sundowners
[1970] The Navajo Sundowners Present Harold Mariano. [Sound recording] Nav-006. 1 disc. 33⅓ rpm. stereo. 12 in.

Navajo Tribal Council
1940 Resolution CJ-1-40. Pp. 107-108 in Navajo Tribal Council Resolutions; Proceedings of the Meeting of June 3-6, 1940. Window Rock, Ariz. Mimeo.

———
1954 [Proceedings of the Meeting of June 1-10. Window Rock, Ariz.] Mimeo.

———
1956 [Proceedings of the Meeting of May 7-25, 1956. Window Rock, Ariz.] Mimeo.

———
1967 Resolutions CO-63-67 and CO-65-67: A Declaration of Basic Navajo Human Rights and Revocation of Resolution Inconsistent Therewith, 9 October, 1967. Window Rock, Ariz. Mimeo.

Navajo Tribe. Division on Education
1973 Eleven Programs for Strengthening Navajo Education. Richard F. Tonigan, planning consultant. Window Rock, Ariz.: The Navajo Tribe.

———
1980 Report of Monitoring Visits to Bureau of Indian Affairs Contract Schools and Reservation Public Schools. Window Rock, Ariz.: The Navajo Tribe.

Navajo Women
[1960] Farewell Song, in Folk Music of the United States, Navaho. Recorded and edited by Willard Rhodes. [Sound recording] Library of Congress AFS L41. 1 disc. 33⅓ rpm. 12 in.

Navarro García, Luis
1964 Don José de Gálvez y la Commandancia General de las provincias internas del norte de Nueva España. Seville, Spain: Consejo Superior de Investigaciones Científicas.

———
1966 La Sublevación yaqui de 1740. Seville, Spain: Consejo Superior de Investigaciones Científicas.

———
1967 Sonora y Sinaloa en el siglo XVIII. Seville, Spain: Escuela de Estudios Hispano-Americanos de Sevilla.

Neighbours, Kenneth F.
1958 The Assassination of Robert S. Neighbors. *West Texas Historical Association Year Book* 34:38-49.

———
1960 Indian Exodus Out of Texas in 1859. *West Texas Historical Association Year Book* 36:80-97.

Nelson, Al B.
1936 Campaigning in the Big Bend of the Rio Grande in 1787. *Southwestern Historical Quarterly* 39(3):200-227. Austin.

———
1940 Juan de Ugalde and Picax-Ande Ins-Tinsle, 1787-1788. *Southwestern Historical Quarterly* 43(4):438-464. Austin.

Nelson, Jean Ware
1974 Anthropological Material on the Jicarilla Apaches. Pp. 171-185 in Apache Indians, VIII. *(American Indian Ethnohistory: Indians of the Southwest)* New York: Garland.

Nentvig, Juan
1863 Rudo Ensayo, tentativa de una descripción geográphica de la provincia de Sonora [1762]. San Augustin de la Florida. [Albany: Munsell].

——— 1894 Rudo Ensayo. (Translated from edition by J.B. Smith) Eusebio Guiteras, trans. *Records of the American Catholic Historical Society of Philadelphia* 5:109-264.

——— 1951 Rudo Ensayo: A Description of Sonora and Arizona in 1764. Tucson: Arizona Silhouettes.

——— 1980 Rudo Ensayo: A Description of Sonora and Arizona in 1764. Albert Francisco Pradeau and Robert R. Rasmussen, eds. and trans. Tucson: University of Arizona Press.

Nettl, Bruno
1956 Music in Primitive Culture. Cambridge, Mass.: Harvard University Press.

Neumann, Joseph
1682 [Letter of February 20.] (Manuscript in Bolton Collection, Bancroft Library, University of California, Berkeley.)

——— [1725] Historia seditionum quas adversus Societatis Jesú missionarios eorumque auxiliatoris moverunt nationes indicae ac potissimum Tarahumara in America Septentrionali regnoque Novae Cantabriae, jam toto ad fiden catholicam propemodum redacto. Prefacio 15 April 1724. (Manuscript in Bolton Collection, Bancroft Library, University of California, Berkeley.)

——— 1969 Révoltes des Indiens Tarahumars (1629-1724). Luis Gonzalez, ed. and trans. Paris: Institut des Hautes Études de l'Amérique Latine de l'Université de Paris.

Newcomb, Franc Johnson
1964 Hosteen Klah: Navaho Medicine Man and Sand Painter. Norman: University of Oklahoma Press.

Newcomb, Franc Johnson, and Gladys A. Reichard
1937 Sandpaintings of the Navajo Shooting Chant. Text by Gladys Reichard. New York: J.J. Augustin.

Newcomb, William W., Jr.
1956 A Reappraisal of the "Cultural Sink" of Texas. *Southwestern Journal of Anthropology* 12(2):145-153.

——— 1961 The Indians of Texas, from Prehistoric to Modern Times. Austin: University of Texas Press.

Newman, Stanley
1958 Zuni Dictionary. *Indiana University Research Center in Anthropology, Folklore, and Linguistics, Publication* 6. Bloomington.

——— 1967 Classical Nahuatl. Pp. 179-199 in *Linguistics*. Norman A. McQuown, vol. ed. Handbook of Middle American Indians. Vol. 5. Robert Wauchope, gen. ed. Austin: University of Texas Press.

Nichols, Michael J.P.
1971 Linguistic Reconstruction of Proto Western Numic and Its Ethnographic Implications. Pp. 135-145 in Great Basin Anthropological Conference 1970: Selected Papers. C. Melvin Aikens, ed. *University of Oregon Anthropological Paper* 1. Eugene.

——— 1973 Northern Paiute Historical Grammar. (Unpublished Ph.D. Dissertation in Linguistics, University of California, Berkeley.)

Nicklason, Fred
[1972] Report on the Jicarilla Apache Accounting Claim, Docket 22-K for the Years 1887-1907 and 1907-1940. 2 vols. (Mimeo., copy in possession of the Jicarilla Apache Tribe, Dulce, N.M.)

——— 1980 The American Indians' "White Problem:" The Case of the Jicarilla Apache. *Prologue* 12(1):41-55.

Nofchissey, Arliene
1975 Proud Earth, on Stan Bronson. Elppa Rednet Production. [Sound recording] Salt City Records, SC-60. 1 disc. 33⅓ rpm. 12 in.

Nolasco Armas, Margarita
1964 Los Pápagos, habitantes de desierto. *Anales del Instituto Nacional de Antropología e Historia* 17:375-448. Mexico City.

——— 1967 Los Seris, desierto y mar. *Anales del Instituto Nacional de Antropología e Historia* 18:125-194. Mexico City.

——— 1969 Los Pimas bajos de la Sierra Madre occidental (yécoras y nébomes altos). *Anales del Instituto Nacional de Antropología e Historia, Época 7,* 1(49):185-244. Mexico City.

Norman, Rosamond
1960 A Look at the Papago "Vikita." *Masterkey* 34(3):98-101.

North, Arthur W.
1910 Camp and Camino in Lower California: A Record of the Adventures of the Author While Exploring Peninsular California, Mexico. New York: Baker and Taylor.

Northern Cheyenne Language and Culture Center
1976 English-Cheyenne Student Dictionary. Lame Deer, Mont.: Northern Cheyenne Language Research Department.

Norwood, Susan
1976 Kwtsaan *lyvii* as an Enclitic. Pp. 78-87 in Proceedings of the First Yuman Languages Workshop Held at the University of California, San Diego, June 16-21, 1975. James E. Redden, ed. *Southern Illinois University Museum Studies, Research Record* 7. Carbondale.

Núñez Cabeza de Vaca, Alvar
1542 La Relación que dio Alvar Núñez Cabeza de Vaca... Zamora, Mexico: Impr. por Augustin de paz y Juan Picardo.

——— 1904 The Journey of Alvar Núñez Cabeza de Vaca, and His Companions from Florida to the Pacific, 1528-1536. Fanny Bandelier and A. F. Bandelier, eds. and trans. New York: Allerton. (Reprinted: Rio Grande Press, Glorieta, N.M. 1964.)

——— 1907 The Narrative of Núñez Cabeza de Vaca. Pp. 1-126 in Spanish Explorers in the Southern United States, 1528-1543. New York: Charles Scribner's Sons.

——— 1961 Cabeza de Vaca's Adventures in the Unknown Interior of America. Cyclone Covey, trans. New York: Collier Books.

Oakes, Maud
1943 Where the Two Came to Their Father: A Navajo War Ceremonial. Given by Jeff King; Text and paintings recorded by Maud Oakes; commentary by Joseph Campbell. (*Bollingen Series* 1) New York: Pantheon Books.

Oberste, William
1942 History of Refugio Mission. Refugio, Tex.: Refugio Timely Remarks.

O'Bryan, Aileen
1956 The Dîné: Origin Myths of the Navaho Indians. *Bureau of American Ethnology Bulletin* 163. Washington.

Ocampo, Manuel
1950 Historia de la Misión de la Tarahumara, 1900-1950. Mexico City: Editorial Buena Prensa.

——— 1966 Historia de la Misión de la Tarahumara (1900-1965). 2d ed. Mexico City: Editorial Jus.

Ocaranza, Fernando
1937-1939 Crónicas y relaciones del occidente de México. 2 vols. Mexico City: Antigua Librería Robredo de J. Porrúa e Hijos.

——— 1942 Parva crónica de la Sierra Madre y las Pimerias. Mexico City: Instituto Panamericano de Geografía e Historia.

Ogle, Ralph H.
1970 Federal Control of the Western Apaches, 1848-1886 [1940]. Albuquerque: University of New Mexico Press.

Ohannessian, Sirarpi
1969 Conference on Navajo Orthography. (Report of Conference, May 2-3, 1969, Albuquerque, N.M.) Washington: Center for Applied Linguistics for the Bureau of Indian Affairs.

Opler, Morris E., coll.
[1931-1934] [Chiricahua Autobiography, Collected in 1931-1932 and 1933-1934.] (Manuscript in Opler's possession.)

____
1931-1935 [Fieldnotes on the Mescalero.] (Unpublished manuscripts in Opler's possession.)

____
1935 The Concept of Supernatural Power Among the Chiricahua and Mescalero Apaches. *American Anthropologist* 37(1):65-70.

____
1936 The Kinship Systems of the Southern Athapaskan-speaking Tribes. *American Anthropologist* 38(4):620-633.

____
1936a An Interpretation of Ambivalence of Two American Indian Tribes. *Journal of Social Psychology* 7:82-116.

____
1936b A Summary of Jicarilla Apache Culture. *American Anthropologist* 38(2):202-223.

____
1937 An Outline of Chiricahua Apache Social Organization. Pp. 171-239 in Social Anthropology of North American Tribes. Fred Eggan, ed. Chicago: University of Chicago Press. (Reprinted in 1955.)

____
1938 A Chiricahua Apache's Account of the Geronimo Campaign of 1886. *New Mexico Historical Review* 13(4):360-386.

____
1938a Myths and Tales of the Jicarilla Apache Indians. *Memoirs of the American Folklore Society* 31. New York.

____
1938b Dirty Boy: A Jicarilla Tale of Raid and War. *Memoirs of the American Anthropological Association* 52. Menasha, Wis.

____
1940 Myths and Legends of the Lipan Apache Indians. *Memoirs of the American Folklore Society* 36. New York.

____
1941 An Apache Life-way: The Economic, Social, and Religious Institutions of the Chiricahua Indians. Chicago: University of Chicago Press. (Reprinted: Cooper Square Publishers, New York, 1965.)

____
1942 Myths and Tales of the Chiricahua Apache Indians. *Memoirs of the American Folklore Society* 37. Menasha, Wis.

____
1942a Adolescence Rite of the Jicarilla. *El Palacio* 49(2):25-38.

____
1943 The Character and Derivation of the Jicarilla Holiness Rite. *Anthropological Series 4(3), University of New Mexico Bulletin* 390. Albuquerque.

____
1944 The Jicarilla Apache Ceremonial Relay Race. *American Anthropologist* 46(1):75-97.

____
1945 The Lipan Apache Death Complex and Its Extensions. *Southwestern Journal of Anthropology* 1(1):122-141.

____
1946 Childhood and Youth in Jicarilla Apache Society. (*Publications of the Frederick Webb Hodge Anniversary Publication Fund* 5) Los Angeles: The Southwest Museum.

____
1946a Chiricahua Apache Material Relating to Sorcery. *Primitive Man* 19(3-4):81-92.

____
1946b Mountain Spirits of the Chiricahua Apache. *Masterkey* 20(4):125-131.

____
1946c Reaction to Death Among the Mescalero Apache. *Southwestern Journal of Anthropology* 2(4):454-467.

____
1946d The Slaying of the Monsters, a Mescalero Apache Myth. *El Palacio* 53(8):215-225, (9):242-258.

____
1947 Notes on Chiricahua Apache Culture, I: Supernatural Power and the Shaman. *Primitive Man* 20(1-2):1-14.

____
1960 Myth and Practice in Jicarilla Apache Eschatology. *Journal of American Folklore* 73(288):133-153.

____
1968 Remuneration to Supernaturals and Man in Apachean Ceremonialism. *Ethnology* 7(4):356-393.

_______, ed.
1969 Apache Odyssey: A Journey Between Two Worlds. New York: Holt, Rinehart and Winston.

____
1969a Western Apache and Kiowa Apache Materials Relating to Ceremonial Payment. *Ethnology* 8(1):122-124.

____
1971 Pots, Apache, and the Dismal River Aspect. Pp. 29-33 in Apachean Culture History and Ethnology. Keith H. Basso and Morris E. Opler, eds. *Anthropological Papers of the University of Arizona* 21. Tucson.

____
1971a Jicarilla Apache Territory, Economy, and Society in 1850. *Southwestern Journal of Anthropology* 27(4):309-329.

____
1972 Cause and Effect in Apachean Agriculture, Division of Labor, Residence Patterns, and Girls' Puberty Rites. *American Anthropologist* 74(5):1133-1146.

____
1974 Lipan Ethnology. (Manuscript in Opler's possession.)

____
1975 Applied Anthropology and the Apache. *University of Oklahoma Papers in Anthropology* 16(2):1-77. Norman.

Opler, Morris E., and William E. Bittle
1961 The Death Practices and Eschatology of the Kiowa Apache. *Southwestern Journal of Anthropology* 17(4):383-394.

Opler, Morris E., and Harry Hoijer
1940 The Raid and War-path Language of the Chiricahua Apache. *American Anthropologist* 42(4):617-634.

Opler, Morris E., and Catherine H. Opler
1950 Mescalero Apache History in the Southwest. *New Mexico Historical Review* 25(1):1-36.

Orozco y Berra, Manuel
1864 Geografía de las lenguas de México y carta etnográfica de México. Mexico City: J.M. Andrade y F. Escalante.

Ortega, José de
1732 Vocabulario en lengua castellana y cora. Mexico City: no publisher.

Ortiz, Alfonso
1969 The Tewa World: Space, Time, Being, and Becoming in a Pueblo Society. Chicago: University of Chicago Press.

_______, ed.
1972 New Perspectives on the Pueblos. Albuquerque: University of New Mexico Press.

____
1972a Ritual Drama and the Pueblo World View. Pp. 135-161 in New Perspectives on the Pueblos. Alfonso Ortiz, ed. Albuquerque: University of New Mexico Press.

Oviedo y Valdés, Gonzalo Fernández de
1851-1855 Historia general y natural de las Indias.. 4 vols. Madrid: Impr. de la Real Academía de la Historia.

Owen, Roger C.
1956 Some Clay Figurines and Seri Dolls from Coastal Sonora, Mexico. *The Kiva* 21(3-4):1-11.

____
1959 Marobavi: A Study of an Assimilated Group in Northern Sonora. *Anthropological Papers of the University of Arizona* 3. Tucson.

———
1965 The Patrilocal Band: A Linguistically and Culturally Hybrid Social Unit. *American Anthropologist* 67(3):675-690.

———
1969 Contemporary Ethnography of Baja California, Mexico. Pp. 871-878 in *Ethnology*. Evon Z. Vogt, vol. ed. Handbook of Middle American Indians. Vol. 8. Robert Wauchope, gen. ed. Austin: University of Texas Press.

Padfield, Harland, and William E. Martin
1965 Farmers, Workers and Machines: Technological and Social Change in Farm Industries of Arizona. Tucson: University of Arizona Press.

Pailes, Richard A.
1972 An Archaeological Reconnaissance of Southern Sonora and Reconsideration of the Rio Sonora Culture. (Unpublished Ph.D. Dissertation in Archaeology, Southern Illinois University, Carbondale.)

Palerm, Ángel
1979 Sobre la formación del sistema colonial: Apuntes para una discusión. Pp. 93-127 in Ensayos sobre el desarollo de México y América Latina (1500-1975). Mexico City: Fondo de Cultura Económica.

Palou, Francisco
1926 Historical Memoirs of New California. Herbert E. Bolton, ed. Berkeley: University of California Press.

Parezo, Nancy J.
1980 Navajo Sand Paintings on Boards: From Religious Act to Commercial Art. *Discovery* (School of American Research):31-50. Santa Fe.

———
1981 From Religious Act to Commercial Art. (Unpublished Ph.D. Dissertation in Anthropology, University of Arizona, Tucson.)

Parker, Samuel A.M.
1942 Journal of an Exploring Tour Beyond the Rocky Mountains, Under the Direction of the A.B.C.F.M. in the Years 1835, '36, and '37...3d ed. Ithaca, N.Y.: Mack, Andrus, and Woodruff.

Parman, Donald L.
1976 The Navajos and the New Deal. New Haven, Conn.: Yale University Press.

Parmee, Edward A.
1968 Formal Education and Culture Change: A Modern Apache Indian Community and Government Education Programs. Tucson: University of Arizona Press.

Parsons, Elsie Clews
1924 Tewa Kin, Clan, and Moiety. *American Anthropologist* 26(3):333-339.

———
1925 The Pueblo of Jemez. (*Papers of the Phillips Academy Southwestern Expedition* 3) New Haven, Conn.: Published for the Phillips Academy by Yale University Press.

———
1928 Notes on the Pima, 1926. *American Anthropologist* 30(3):445-464.

———
1930 Spanish Elements in the Kachina Cult of the Pueblos. Pp. 582-603 in *Proceedings of the 23d International Congress of Americanists*. New York, 1928.

———
1932 Isleta, New Mexico. Pp. 193-466 in *47th Annual Report of the Bureau of American Ethnology for the Years 1929-1930*. Washington.

———
1932a The Kinship Nomenclature of the Pueblo Indians. *American Anthropologist* 34(3):377-389.

———
1936 Taos Pueblo. *General Series in Anthropology* 2. Menasha, Wis. (Reprinted: Johnson Reprint, New York, 1971.)

———
1939 Pueblo Indian Religion. 2 vols. Chicago: University of Chicago Press.

———
1962 Introduction. Pp. 1-12 in Isleta Paintings. Esther S. Goldfrank, ed. *Bureau of American Ethnology Bulletin* 181. Washington.

Parsons, Elsie Clews, and Ralph L. Beals
1934 The Sacred Clowns of the Pueblo and Mayo-Yaqui Indians. *American Anthropologist* 36(4):491-514.

Paso y Troncoso, Francisco del, comp.
1950- Relaciones del siglo XVIII relativos a Chihuahua. Vol. 8: Guaguachic. (*Biblioteca de Historiadores Mexicanos*) Mexico City: Vargas Rea.

Passin, Herbert
1942 Sorcery as a Phase of Tarahumara Economic Relations. *Man* 42:11-15.

———
1943 The Place of Kinship in Tarahumara Social Organization. *Acta Americana* 34:360-383, 471-495.

———
1944 A Note on the Present Indigenous Population of Chihuahua. *American Anthropologist* 46(1):145-147.

Pattie, James O.
1833 The Personal Narrative of James O. Pattie of Kentucky. Timothy Flint, ed. Cincinnati: E.H. Flint. (Reprinted: R.R. Donnelly, Chicago, 1930; University Microfilms, Ann Arbor, 1966.)

Pearson, Jim B.
1961 The Maxwell Land Grant. Norman: University of Oklahoma Press.

Pearson, Karl, and David Heron
1913 On Theories of Association. *Biometrika* 9:159-315.

Peirce, H. Wesley
1964 Seri Blue: An Explanation. *The Kiva* 30(2):33-39.

Pendleton, Mary
1974 Navajo and Hopi Weaving Techniques. New York: Macmillan.

Pennington, Campbell W.
1963 The Tarahumar of Mexico: Their Environment and Material Culture. Salt Lake City: University of Utah Press.

———
1969 The Tepehuan of Chihuahua: Their Material Culture. Salt Lake City: University of Utah Press.

———
1970 La Carrera de bola entre los tarahumaras de México: Un problema de difusión. *América Indígena* 30(1):15-40.

———
1979-1980 The Pima Bajo of Central Sonora, Mexico. 2 vols. Salt Lake City: University of Utah Press.

———, ed.
1981 Arte y vocabulario de la lengua dohema, heve o eudeve: Manuscript of an Anonymous Eighteenth Century Author. Mexico City: Universidad Nacional Autónoma de México, Instituto de Investigaciones Filológico.

Pepper, George H.
1908 Ah-jih-lee-hah-neh, a Navaho Legend. *Journal of American Folk-Lore* 21(81-82):178-183.

Perchonock, Norma, and Oswald Werner
1969 Navaho Systems of Classification: Some Implications for Ethnoscience. *Ethnology* 8(3):229-242.

Pérez de Luxán, Diego
1929 Expedition into New Mexico Made by Antonio de Espejo, 1582-1583, as Revealed in the Journal of Diego Pérez de Luxán, a Member of the Party. George P. Hammond and Agapito Rey, eds. Los Angeles: The Quivira Society.

Pérez de Ribas, Andrés
1645 Historia de los trivmphos de nvuestra Santa Fee entre gentes las más barbaras y fieras del Nuevo Orbe. Madrid: A. de Paredes.

———
1944 My Life Among the Savage Nations of New Spain. Tomas Antonio Robertson, trans. Los Angeles: Ward Ritchie Press.

———
1944a Historia de los triunfos de nuestra Santa Fé entre gentes las más bárbaras y fieras del Nuevo Orbe... 3 vols. Mexico City: Editorial "Layac."

Perry, Edgar, comp.
1972 Western Apache Dictionary. Fort Apache, Ariz.: White Mountain Apache People.

Pfefferkorn, Ignaz
1949 Sonora: A Description of the Province. Theodore E. Treutlein, ed. and trans. (*Coronado Cuarto Centennial Publications* 12) Albuquerque: University of New Mexico Press.

Phillips, Allan R., Joe Marshall, and Gale Monson
1964 The Birds of Arizona. Tucson: University of Arizona Press.

Philp, Kenneth R.
1977 John Collier's Crusade for Indian Reform, 1920-1954. Tucson: University of Arizona Press.

Pichardo, José Antonio
1931-1946 Pichardo's Treatise on the Limits of Louisiana and Texas. Charles W. Hackett and Charmion C. Shelby, trans. and eds. 4 vols. Austin: University of Texas Press.

Pilles, Peter
1979 Yavapai Archeology. (Paper read at Southern Arizona Protohistoric Conference, Arizona State University, Tempe.)

Pimentel, Francisco
1862-1865 Cuadro descriptivo y comparativo de las lenguas indígenas de México. 2 vols. Mexico City: Impr. de Andrade y Escalante.

———
1874-1875 Cuadro descriptivo y comparativo de las lenguas indígenas de México...3 vols. Mexico City: Tip. de I. Epstein.

Pinart, Adolph
1879 [Seri Vocabulary.] (Manuscript No. 1449 in National Anthropological Archives, Smithsonian Institution, Washington.)

Plancarte, Francisco M.
1954 El Problema indígena tarahumara. *Memorias del Instituto Nacional Indigenista* 5. Mexico City.

Platero, Paul R., ed.
1974 Foreword to Vol. 1. Diné Bizaad Náníl'įįh/ *Navajo Language Review* 1(1):1.

Plog, Fred
1978 The Keresan Bridge: An Ecological and Archeological Account. Pp. 349-372 in Social Archeology: Beyond Subsistence and Dating. Charles L. Redman et al., eds. New York: Academic Press.

Pollard, William G.
1965 Structure and Stress: Social Change Among the Fort Sill Apache and Their Ancestors. (Unpublished M.A. Thesis in Anthropology, University of Oklahoma, Norman.)

Polzer, Charles W.
1976 Historiografía de la costa. Pp. 377-378 in Sonora: Antropología del desierto. B. Braniff C. and R.S. Felger, eds. *Instituto Nacional de Antropología e Historia, Colección Científica* 27. Mexico City.

Porras Muñoz, Guillermo
1966 Iglesia y estado en Nueva Vizcaya (1562-1821). Pamplona, Spain: no publisher.

Portillo, Estebán L.
1886 Apuntes para la historia antigua de Coahuila y Texas. Amado Prado, ed. Saltillo, Mexico: Tipografía "El Golfo de México" de S. Fernandez.

Poston, Charles D.
1864 [Letter of April 1, 1863, to William P. Dole, Commissioner of Indian Affairs.] Pp. 503-510 in *U.S. Congress. House. 38th Cong., 1st sess. House Executive Doc. No.* 1 (Serial No. 1182). Washington.

Powell, James
1964 Nothing Is as Lonely as the Gran Desierto. *Desert Magazine* 27 (12):19-21, 34.

———
1966 In the Gran Desierto. *Explorers Journal* 44(1):66-70.

Powell, John Wesley
1873-1874 [Ute Vocabulary; Komas and Wonroen Informants, Spanish Fork Cañon, Utah, and Washington, D.C.] (Manuscript No. 828b in National Anthropological Archives, Smithsonian Institution, Washington.)

———
1874 Report of the Explorations in 1873 of the Colorado of the West and Its Tributaries. Washington: U.S. Government Printing Office.

———
1891 Indian Linguistic Families of America North of Mexico. Pp. 7-142 in *7th Annual Report of the Bureau of American Ethnology for the Years 1885-1886.* Washington. (Reprinted: University of Nebraska Press, Lincoln, 1966.)

Powell, Philip W.
1945 The Chichimecas: Scourge of the Silver Frontier in Sixteenth-century Mexico. *Hispanic American Historical Review* 25 (August): 315-338.

———
1952 Soldiers, Indians and Silver: The Northward Advance of New Spain, 1550-1600. Berkeley: University of California Press.

Powskey, Malinda, Lucille J. Watahomigie, and Akira Y. Yamamoto
1980 Language Use: Explorations in Language and Meaning. Pp. 60-67 in Proceedings of the 1979 Hokan Languages Workshop Held at the University of California, Los Angeles, June 26-28, 1979. James E. Redden, ed. *Southern Illinois University Occasional Papers in Linguistics* 7. Carbondale.

Press, Margaret L.
1975 A Grammar of Chemehuevi. (Unpublished Ph.D Dissertation in Linguistics, University of California, Los Angeles.)

Preuss, Konrad-Theodor
1932 Grammatik der Cora-Sprache. *International Journal of American Linguistics* 7(1-2):1-84.

Prieto, Alejandro
1873 Historia, geografía, y estadística del estado de Tamaulipas...Mexico City: Tip. Escalerillas.

Quinn, Charles R., and Elena Quinn, eds.
1965 Edward H. Davis and the Indians of the Southwest United States and Northwest Mexico: A Harvest of Photographs, Sketches and Unpublished Manuscripts of the Indefatigable Collector of Artifacts of These Border Indians. Downey, Calif.: Elena Quinn.

Ramusio, Giovanni B.
1554-1603 ...Delle Navigationi et Viaggi. 3 vols. Venice: Stamperia de Giunti.

Ratkay, Juan María
1683 [An Account of the Tarahumara Missions and a Description of the Tribe of the Tarahumaras and of Their Country.] (Manuscript in Bolton Collection, Bancroft Library, University of California, Berkeley.)

Reagan, Albert B.
1931 Notes on the Indians of the Fort Apache Region. *Anthropological Papers of the American Museum of Natural History* 31(5). New York.

Redden, James E.
1966 Walapai. I: Phonology; II: Morphology. *International Journal of American Linguistics* 32(1):1-16, (2):141-163.

———, ed.
1976 Proceedings of the First Yuman Languages Workshop Held at the University of California, San Diego, June 16-21, 1975. *Southern Illinois University Museum Studies, Research Record* 7. Carbondale.

———, ed.
1977 Proceedings of the 1976 Hokan-Yuman Languages Workshop Held at the University of California, San Diego, June 21-23, 1976. *Southern Illinois University Museum Studies, Research Record* 11. Carbondale.

———, ed.
1978 Proceedings of the 1977 Hokan-Yuman Languages Workshop Held at the University of Utah, Salt Lake City, June 21-23, 1977. *Southern Illinois University Occasional Papers in Linguistics* 2. Carbondale.

———, ed.
1979 Proceedings of the 1978 Hokan Languages Workshop Held at the University of California, San Diego, June 27-29, 1978. *Southern Illinois University Occasional Papers in Linguistics* 5. Carbondale.

———, ed.
1980 Proceedings of the 1979 Hokan Languages Workshop Held at the University of California, Los Angeles, June 26-28, 1979. *Southern Illinois University Occasional Papers in Linguistics* 7. Carbondale.

Redondo, L.M.
1957 Translation of a Letter to John C. Fremont, Government of Arizona, from L.M. Redondo, Prefect of Altar, State of Sonora, [August 26, 1879]. (Film 169, Reel 21 in Letters Received by the Office of Indian Affairs, 1824-1881, National Archives, Washington.)

Reed, Erik K.
1954 Transition to History in the Pueblo Southwest. *American Anthropologist* 56(4):592-597.

Reeve, Frank D.
1938 The Federal Indian Policy in New Mexico, 1858-1880, IV. *New Mexico Historical Review* 13(3):261-313.

———
1956 Early Navaho Geography. *New Mexico Historical Review* 31(4):290-309.

———
1957 Seventeenth Century Navaho-Spanish Relations. *New Mexico Historical Review* 32(1):36-52.

———
1958 Navaho-Spanish Wars, 1680-1720. *New Mexico Historical Review* 33(3):204-231.

———
1959 The Navaho-Spanish Peace: 1720's-1770's. *New Mexico Historical Review* 34(1):9-40.

———
1960 Navaho-Spanish Diplomacy. *New Mexico Historical Review* 35(3):200-235.

Reichard, Gladys A.
1928 Social Life of the Navajo Indians. *Columbia University Contributions to Anthropology* 7. New York.

———
1936 Navajo Shepherd and Weaver. New York: J.J. Augustin.

———
1939 Navajo Medicine Man: Sandpaintings and Legends of Miguelito. New York: J.J. Augustin.

———
1944 Prayer: The Compulsive Word. (*Monographs of the American Ethnological Society* 7) New York: J.J. Augustin.

———
1945 Distinctive Features of Navaho Religion. *Southwestern Journal of Anthropology* 1(2):199-220.

———
1945a Linguistic Diversity Among the Navaho Indians. *International Journal of American Linguistics* 11(3):156-168.

———
1948 Navajo Classification of Natural Objects. *Plateau* 21(1):7-12.

———
1948a Significance of Aspiration in Navaho. *International Journal of American Linguistics* 14(1):15-19.

———
1950 Navaho Religion: A Study of Symbolism. 2 vols. (*Bollingen Series* 18) New York: Pantheon Books.

———
1951 Navaho Grammar. (*American Ethnological Society Publication* 21) New York: J.J. Augustin.

Reiter, Paul
1938 The Jemez Pueblo of Unshagi, New Mexico, with Notes on the Earlier Excavations at "Amoxiumqua" and Giusewa. 2 Pts. *Monographs of the School of American Research* 5-6. Santa Fe.

Relación de Cerocahui
1777 (Original Manuscript in the Biblioteca Nacional de Madrid. Copy in Department of Geography, University of California, Berkeley.)

Relación de Cusihuiriachic
1777 (Original Manuscript in the Biblioteca Nacional de Madrid. Copy in Department of Geography, University of California, Berkeley.)

Relación de Guaguachic
1777 (Original Manuscript in the Biblioteca Nacional de Madrid. Copy in Department of Geography, University of California, Berkeley.)

Relación de Guazápares
1777 (Original Manuscript in the Biblioteca Nacional de Madrid. Copy in Department of Geography, University of California, Berkeley.)

Relación de Tónachic
1777 (Original Manuscript in the Biblioteca Nacional de Madrid. Copy in Department of Geography, University of California, Berkeley.)

Reno, Philip
1970 Manpower Planning for Navajo Employment: Training for Jobs in a Surplus-labor Area. *New Mexico Business Review* 23 (November-December):8-16.

———
1975 The Navajos: High, Dry and Penniless. *The Nation* 220(12):359-363.

———
1981 Mother Earth, Father Sky, and Economic Development: Navajo Resources and Their Use. Albuquerque: University of New Mexico Press.

Resta, Paul, and Donald E. Kelly
1980 Navajo Educational Facilities Planning Study. Window Rock, Ariz.: Bureau of Indian Affairs.

Richardson, Douglas
1980 What Happens After the Lease Is Signed? *American Indian Journal* 6(2):11-17.

Riley, Carroll L.
1954 A Survey of Navajo Archaeology. *University of Colorado Studies, Series in Anthropology* 4:45-60. Boulder.

Rinaldini, Benito
1743 Arte de la lengua tépeguana, con vocabulario, confessionario y catechismo, en que se explican los mysterios de nuestra santa fè catholica, mandamientos de la Ley de Dios, y de nuestra Santa Madre Iglesia. Mexico City: Viuda de J. de Hogal.

Roadhorse, Ambrose
[1960] Folk Music of the United States, Navaho. Recorded and edited by Willard Rhodes. [Sound recording] Library of Congress AFS L41. 1 disc. 33⅓ rpm. 12 in.

Robb, J.D.
1961 The Matachines Dance—A Ritual Folk Dance. *Western Folklore* 20(1):87-101.

Robbins, Lynn A.
[1975] The Impact of Power Developments on the Navajo Nation. (Unpublished manuscript in Robbins' possession.)

———
1978 Navajo Labor and the Establishment of a Voluntary Workers Organization. *Journal of Ethnic Studies* 6(3):97-112.

———
1979 Navajo Energy Politics. *Social Science Journal* 16:93-119.

———
1980 Native American Experiences with Energy Developments. Pp. 21-32 in The Boomtown: Problems and Promises in the Energy Vortex. Joseph Davenport, III and Judith Ann Davenport, eds. Laramie: University of Wyoming, Department of Social Work, Wyoming Human Services Project.

———
[1981] Energy Developments and the Navajo Nation—II. In Native Americans and Energy Development—II. Joseph Jorgensen et al., eds. Cambridge, Mass.: Anthropology Resource Center. In Press.

Roberts, John M.
1951 Three Navaho Households: A Comparative Study in Small Group Culture. (Reports of the Ramah Project 3) *Papers of the Peabody Museum of American Archaeology and Ethnology, Harvard University* 40(3). Cambridge, Mass.

———
1965 Kinship and Friends in Zuni Culture: A Terminological Note. *El Palacio* 72(2):38-43.

Robertson, Thomas A.
1964 A Southwestern Utopia: An American Colony in Mexico. Los Angeles: Ward Ritchie Press.

Robinson, Alambert E.
1954 Basket Weavers of Arizona. Albuquerque: University of New Mexico Press.

Robinson, Jacob S.
1932 A Journal of the Santa Fe Expedition Under Col. Doniphan [1848]. Carl I. Cannon, ed. Princeton, N.J.: Princeton University Press.

Robles Ortiz, Manuel, and Francisco Manzo Taylor
1972 Clovis Fluted Points from Sonora, Mexico. *The Kiva* 37(4):199-206.

Rodee, Marian E.
1981 Old Navajo Rugs: Their Development from 1900-1940. Albuquerque: University of New Mexico Press.

Roessel, Robert A.
1951 Sheep in Navajo Culture. (Unpublished M.A. Thesis in Anthropology, Washington University, St. Louis.)

———
1979 Navajo Education. Rough Rock, Ariz.: Navajo Curriculum Center.

———
1980 Pictorial History of the Navajo from 1860 to 1910. Rough Rock, Ariz.: Rough Rock Demonstration School, Navajo Curriculum Project.

Roessel, Ruth, ed.
1971 Navajo Studies of Navajo Community College. Raymond Johnson and Jason Chee, illus. Many Farms, Ariz.: Navajo Community College.

———, ed.
1973 Navajo Stories of the Long Walk Period. Tsaile, Ariz.: Navajo Community College Press.

Roessel, Ruth, and Broderick Johnson, eds.
1974 Navajo Livestock Reduction: A National Disgrace. Tsaile, Ariz.: Navajo Community College Press.

Rogers, Malcolm J.
1945 An Outline of Yuman Prehistory. *Southwestern Journal of Anthropology* 1(2):167-198.

Romney, A. Kimball
1957 The Genetic Model and Uto-Aztecan Time Perspective. *Davidson Journal of Anthropology* 3:35-41. Seattle.

———
1967 Kinship and Family. Pp. 207-237 in *Social Anthropology*. Manning Nash, vol. ed. Handbook of Middle American Indians. Vol. 6. Robert Wauchope, gen. ed. Austin: University of Texas Press.

Roosevelt, Theodore
1909 Executive Order [No. 862], Dated March 2, re Mescalero Apache Indian Reservation Boundaries. Pp. 638-641 in Vol. 3 of Indian Affairs: Laws and Treaties, by Charles J. Kappler. Washington: U.S. Government Printing Office.

Roskam, Edward, and James C. Lingoes
1970 Minissa-I: A Fortran IV (G) Program for the Smallest Space Analysis of Square Symmetric Matrices. *Behavioral Science* 15(2):204-205.

Ruby, Jay W.
1968 Culture Contact Between Aboriginal Southern California and the Southwest. (Unpublished Ph.D. Dissertation in Anthropology, University of California, Los Angeles.)

Rudisill, Richard. comp.
1973 Photographers of the New Mexico Territory, 1854-1912. Santa Fe: Museum of New Mexico.

Ruecking, Frederick H., Jr.
1953 The Economic System of the Coahuiltecan Indians of Southern Texas and Northeastern Mexico. *Texas Journal of Science* 5(4):480-497. San Marcos.

———
1954 Ceremonies of the Coahuiltecan Indians of Southern Texas and Northeastern Mexico. *Texas Journal of Science* 6(5):330-339. San Marcos.

———
1954a Bands and Band-clusters of the Coahuiltecan Indians. *University of Texas, Department of Anthropology, Student Papers in Anthropology* 1(2):1-24. Austin.

———
1955 The Social Organization of the Coahuiltecan Indians of Southern Texas and Northeastern Mexico. *Texas Journal of Science* 7(4):357-388. San Marcos.

———
1955a The Coahuiltecan Indians of Southern Texas and Northeastern Mexico. (Unpublished M.A. Thesis in Anthropology, University of Texas, Austin.)

Ruffing, Lorraine Turner
1978 Navajo Mineral Development. *American Indian Journal* 4(9):2-16.

———
1978a Navajo Mineral Development. *The Indian Historian* 11(2):28-41.

———
1979 A Mineral Development Policy for the Navajo Nation. Window Rock, Ariz.: no publisher.

———
1980 Fighting the Substandard Lease. *American Indian Journal* 6(6):2-8.

———
1980a Agenda for Action. *American Indian Journal* 6(7):14-23.

Ruggles, Levi
1870 Report of June 23, 1869 from Pima Villages, Arizona Territory to George W. Dent, Superintendent of Indian Affairs, La Paz, Arizona Territory. Pp. 206-212 in Report of the Commissioner of Indian Affairs for the Year 1869. Washington: U.S. Government Printing Office.

Rusling, James F.
1874 Across America; or, The Great West and the Pacific Coast. New York: Sheldon.

Russell, Frank
1898 [Jicarilla Apache Vocabulary from Juan and Reuben Quintana.] (Manuscript No. 1302a in National Anthropological Archives, Smithsonian Institution, Washington.)

———
1898a Myths of the Jicarilla Apaches. *Journal of American Folk-Lore* 11(43):253-271.

———
1902-1903 [Pima Lexical Data.] (Manuscript No. 2507 in National Anthropological Archives, Smithsonian Institution, Washington.)

———
1908 The Pima Indians. Pp. 3-389 in *26th Annual Report of the Bureau of American Ethnology for the Years 1904-1905.* Washington.

———
1975 The Pima Indians. Re-edition with Introduction, Citation Sources, and Bibliography by Bernard L. Fontana. Tucson: University of Arizona Press.

Ryerson, Scott H.
1976 Seri Ironwood Carving: An Economic View. Pp. 119-136 in Ethnic and Tourist Arts: Cultural Expressions from the Fourth World. N.H.H. Grayburn, ed. Berkeley: University of California Press.

Sage, Rufus B.
1956 His Letters and Papers, 1836-1847, with an Annotated Reprint of His Scenes in the Rocky Mountains and in Oregon, California, New Mexico, Texas, and the Grand Prairies. LeRoy R. Hafen and Ann W. Hafen, eds. 2 vols. Glendale, Calif.: Arthur H. Clark.

Sahagún, Bernardino de
1978 The War of Conquest: How It Was Waged Here in Mexico: The Aztec's Own Story. Arthur J.O. Anderson and Charles E. Dibble, trans. Salt Lake City: University of Utah Press.

St. John, Silas
1859 [Letter Datelined Pimo Villages, New Mexico, September 16, 1859, to A.B. Greenwood, Commissioner of Indian Affairs, Washington.] (Manuscript in Letters Received—Pima Agency, 1859-1861, Record Group 75, National Archives, Washington.)

Saldívar, Gabriel
1943 Los Indios de Tamaulipas. *Instituto Panamericana de Geografía e Historia, Publicación* 70. Mexico City.

———
1945 Historia compendiada de Tamaulipas. Mexico City: Academia Nacional de Historia y Geografía.

Salsbury, Clarence G.
1969 The Salsbury Story: A Medical Missionary's Lifetime of Public Service. Tucson: University of Arizona Press.

Sanchez, George I.
1948 "The People:" A Study of the Navajos. Washington: U.S. Department of the Interior, Indian Service.

Sandner, Donald
[1979] Navaho Symbols of Healing: Essays, Aphorisms, Autobiographical Writings. New York: Harcourt, Brace, Jovanovich.

Sandoval, Albert G., and Ray Winnie
1961 Squaw Dance Songs. Recorded by David P. McAllester. Donald N. Brown, ed. [Sound recording.] Taylor Museum, KCMA—1205. 1 disc. 33⅓ rpm. 12 in.

Santamaría, Francisco J.
1974 Diccionario de méjicanismos. 2d ed. Mexico City: Editorial Porrúa.

Santa María, Vicente
1929-1930 Relación histórica de la colonia del Nuevo Santander y costa del Seno mexicano. 2 vols. Mexico City: Talleres Gráfica de la Nación.

Sapir, Edward
1913-1914 Southern Paiute and Nahuatl: A Study in Uto-Aztekan. 2 Pts. *Journal de la Société des Américanistes de Paris* n.s. 10:379-425; 11:443-488.

———
1920 The Hokan and Coahuiltecan Languages. *International Journal of American Linguistics* 1(4):280-290.

———
1925 The Hokan Affinity of Subtiaba in Nicaragua. *American Anthropologist* 27(4):491-527.

———
1930-1931 The Southern Paiute Language. *Proceedings of the American Academy of Arts and Sciences* 65(1):1-296, (2):297-535, (3):536-730. Washington.

———
1931 The Concept of Phonetic Law as Tested in Primitive Languages by Leonard Bloomfield. Pp. 297-306 in Methods in Social Science: A Case Book. Stuart A. Rice, ed. Chicago: University of Chicago Press. (Reprinted: Pp. 73-82 in Selected Writings of Edward Sapir, David G. Mandelbaum, ed., University of California, Berkeley, 1949.)

———
1936 Internal Linguistic Evidence Suggestive of the Northern Origin of the Navaho. *American Anthropologist* 38(2):224-235.

Sapir, Edward, and Harry Hoijer
1942 Navaho Texts. Iowa City: Linguistic Society of America.

———
1967 The Phonology and Morphology of the Navaho Language. *University of California Publications in Linguistics* 50. Berkeley.

Saravia, Atanasio G.
1956 Apuntes para la historia de la Nueva Vizcaya. 3 vols. Mexico City: Librería de Manuel Porrúa.

Sasaki, Tom T.
1960 Fruitland, New Mexico: A Navaho Community in Transition. Ithaca, N.Y.: Cornell University Press.

Sasaki, Tom T., and Harry W. Basehart
1961-1962 Sources of Income Among Many Farms–Rough Rock Navajo and Jicarilla Apache: Some Comparisons and Comments. *Human Organization* 20(4):187-190.

Sauer, Carl
1932 The Road to Cíbola. *Ibero-Americana* 3. Berkeley, Calif.

———
1934 The Distribution of Aboriginal Tribes and Languages in Northwestern Mexico. *Ibero-Americana* 5. Berkeley, Calif.

———
1935 Aboriginal Population of Northwestern Mexico. *Ibero-Americana* 10. Berkeley, Calif.

———
1971 Sixteenth Century North America: The Land and the People as Seen by Europeans. Berkeley: University of California Press.

Saxton, Dean F.
1956 [Report to the Summer Institute of Linguistics on the Pima Bajo of Sonora, Mexico.] (Unpublished manuscript in Saxton's possession.)

Saxton, Dean F., and Lucille Saxton, comps.
1969 Dictionary: Papago and Pima to English, English to Papago and Pima; O'odham-Mil-gahn, Mil-gahn-O'odham. Tucson: University of Arizona Press.

———
1973 O'othham hoho'ok a'agitha: Legends and Lore of the Papago and Pima Indians. Tucson: University of Arizona Press.

Sayles, Edwin B.
1936 An Archaeological Survey of Chihuahua, Mexico. *Gila Pueblo, Medallion Paper* 22. Globe Ariz.

———
1962 The Hohokam Culture as Related to Other Southwestern Cultures. Tucson: Arizona State Museum.

Sayles, Gladys, and Ted Sayles
1948 The Pottery of Ida Redbird. *Arizona Highways* (January):28-31.

Schaafsma, Curtis F.
1979 The Cerrito Site (AR-4): A Piedra Lumbre Phase Settlement at Abiquiu Reservoir. Santa Fe: School of American Research.

———
1981 Early Apacheans in the Southwest: A Review. Pp. 291-320 in The Protohistoric Period in the North American Southwest, A.D. 1450-1700. D.R. Wilcox and W.B. Masse, eds. *Arizona State University Anthropological Research Paper* 24. Tempe.

Schaafsma, Polly
1963 Rock Art in the Navajo Reservoir District. *Museum of New Mexico Papers in Anthropology* 7. Santa Fe.

——— 1966 Early Navaho Rock Paintings and Carvings. Santa Fe: Museum of Navajo Ceremonial Art.

——— 1972 Rock Art in New Mexico. Santa Fe: State Planning Office.

——— 1980 Indian Rock Art of the Southwest. Santa Fe: School of American Research; Albuquerque: University of New Mexico Press.

Schaedel, Richard P.
1949 The Karankawa of the Texas Gulf Coast. *Southwestern Journal of Anthropology* 5(2):117-137.

Schaffer, Dan
1978 Overall Economic Development Plan for Fort McDowell Community. (Unpublished manuscript in Schaffer's possession.)

Schermerhorn, John F.
1814 Report Respecting the Indians, Inhabiting the Western Parts of the United States. *Collections of the Massachusetts Historical Society,* ser. 2, Vol. 2:1-45. Boston.

Schneider, David M., and John M. Roberts
1956 Zuñi Kin Terms. *University of Nebraska, Laboratory of Anthropology Notebook* 3. Lincoln. (Reprinted: Human Relations Area Files Press, New Haven, Conn., 1965.)

Scholes, France V.
1937 Troublous Times in New Mexico, 1659-1670. *New Mexico Historical Review* 12(2):134-174, (4):380-452.

——— 1940 Documentary Evidence Relating to the Jumano Indians. Pp. 271-289 in *Contributions to American Anthropology and History 6(34), Carnegie Institution of Washington Publication* 523. Washington.

——— 1944 Juan Martinez de Montoya, Settler and Conquistador of New Mexico. *New Mexico Historical Review* 19(4):337-342.

Scholes, France V., and H.P. Mera
1940 Some Aspects of the Jumano Problem. *Contributions to American Anthropology and History 6(34), Carnegie Institution of Washington Publication* 523. Washington.

Schoolcraft, Henry R.
1851-1857 Historical and Statistical Information Respecting the History, Condition, and Prospects of the Indian Tribes of the United States. 6 vols. Philadelphia: Lippincott, Grambo.

Schroeder, Albert H.
1952 Documentary Evidence Pertaining to the Early Historic Period of Southern Arizona. *New Mexico Historical Review* 27(2):137-167.

——— 1952a A Brief History of the Yavapai of the Middle Verde Valley. *Plateau* 24(3):111-118.

——— 1952b The Significance of Willow Beach. *Plateau* 25(2):27-29.

——— 1953 A Brief History of the Havasupai. *Plateau* 25(3):45-52.

——— 1954 Comment on Reed's "Transition to History in the Pueblo Southwest." *American Anthropologist* 56(4):597-599.

——— 1955-1956 Fray Marcos de Niza, Coronado and the Yavapai. *New Mexico Historical Review* 30(4):265-296; 31(1):24-37.

——— 1957 The Hakataya Cultural Tradition. *American Antiquity* 23(2):176-178.

——— 1960 The Hohokam, Sinagua, and Hakataya. (*Archives of Archeology* 5) Madison: Society for American Archaeology and University of Wisconsin Press.

——— 1961 An Archaeological Survey of the Painted Rocks Reservoir, Western Arizona. *The Kiva* 27(1):1-28.

——— 1963 Navajo and Apache Relationships West of the Rio Grande. *El Palacio* 70(3):5-23.

——— 1965 A Brief History of the Southern Utes. *Southwestern Lore* 30(4):53-78.

——— 1965a Unregulated Diffusion from Mexico into the Southwest Prior to A.D. 700. *American Antiquity* 30(3):297-309.

——— 1966 Pattern Diffusion from Mexico into the Southwest After A.D. 600. *American Antiquity* 31(5):683-704.

———, ed.
1973 Changing Ways of Southwestern Indians: A Historic Perspective. *El Corral de Santa Fe; Westerners Brand Book 1973.* Glorieta, N.M.: Rio Grande Press.

——— 1974 A Study of Yavapai History. *(American Indian Ethnohistory: Indians of the Southwest)* New York: Garland.

——— 1974a A Study of the Apache Indians. Pts. 1-3. Pp. 27-583 in Apache Indians, I. *(American Indian Ethnohistory: Indians of the Southwest)* New York: Garland.

——— 1974b A Study of the Apache Indians. Pts. 4-5. Pp. 9-645 in Apache Indians, IV. *(American Indian Ethnohistory: Indians of the Southwest)* New York: Garland.

——— 1974c The Jicarilla Apaches. Pp. 311-469 in Apache Indians, I. *(American Indian Ethnohistory: Indians of the Southwest)* New York: Garland.

——— 1975 The Hohokam, Sinagua and the Hakataya. (*I.V.C. Museum Society Occasional Paper* 3) El Centro, Calif.: I.V.C. Museum Society.

——— 1981 How Far Can a Pochteca Leap Without Leaving Footprints? Pp. 43-64 in Collected Papers in Honor of Erik Kellerman Reed. Albert H. Schroeder, ed. *Papers of the Archaeological Society of New Mexico* 6. Albuquerque.

Schulman, Edmund
1938 Nineteen Centuries of Rainfall History in the Southwest. *American Meteorological Society Bulletin* 19:211-215.

——— 1956 Dendroclimatic Changes in Semiarid America. Tucson: University of Arizona Press.

Schumm, S.A., and R.F. Hadley
1957 Arroyos and the Semiarid Cycle of Erosion. *American Journal of Science* 255(3):161-174.

Schwartz, Douglas W.
1955 Havasupai Prehistory: Thirteen Centuries of Cultural Development. (Unpublished Ph.D. Dissertation in Anthropology, Yale University, New Haven, Conn.)

——— 1956 The Havasupai 600 A.D.—1955 A.D.: A Short Culture History. *Plateau* 28(4):77-85.

——— 1956a Demographic Changes in the Early Periods of Cohonina Prehistory. Pp. 26-31 in Prehistoric Settlement Patterns in the New World. G.R. Willey, ed. *Viking Fund Publications in Anthropology* 23. New York.

——— 1959 Culture Area and Time Depth: The Four Worlds of the Havasupai. *American Anthropologist* 61(6):1060-1070.

Schwatka, Frederick
1893 In the Land of Cave and Cliff Dwellers. New York: Cassell Publishing Company.

Scott, Richard B.
1959 Acculturation Among Mescalero Apache High School Stu-

dents. (Unpublished M.A. Thesis, University of New Mexico, Albuquerque.)

Scudder, Thayer
1979 Expected Impacts of Compulsory Relocation of Navajos with Special Emphasis on Relocation from the Former Joint Use Area Required by Public Law 93-531. Binghamton, N.Y.: Institute for Development Anthropology.

Secoy, Frank R.
1953 Changing Military Patterns on the Great Plains (17th Century Through Early 19th Century). *Monographs of the American Ethnological Society* 21. Locust Valley, N.Y.: J. J. Augustin.

Sedelmayr, P. Jacobo
1744 [Letter to Juan Antonio Balthasar.] (Manuscript, carpeta 37/65 in Provincias Internas, Californias, Archivo Franciscano, Biblioteca Nacional, Mexico City.)

———
1856 Relación. *Documentos para la Historia de Méjico*. 3d ser. Vol. 4(2):843-859. Mexico City: Biblioteca Nacional.

———
1939 Sedelmayr's Relacion of 1746. Ronald L. Ives, trans. and ed. *Anthropological Papers 9, Bureau of American Ethnology Bulletin* 123. Washington.

Seevers, Maurice H.
1954 Drug Addictions. Pp. 236-252 in Pharmacology in Medicine: A Collaborative Textbook. Victor A. Drill, ed. New York: McGraw-Hill.

Seiler, Hansjakob
1970 Cahuilla Texts with an Introduction. *Indiana University Language Science Monograph* 6. Bloomington.

———
1977 Cahuilla Grammar. Banning, Calif.: Malki Museum Press.

Seiler, Hansjakob, and Kojiro Hioki
1979 Cahuilla Dictionary. Banning, Calif.: Malki Museum Press.

Sellers, William D., and Richard H. Hill
1974 Arizona Climate, 1931-1972. 2d rev. ed. Tucson: University of Arizona Press.

Service, Elman R.
1969 The Northern Tepehuan. Pp. 822-829 in *Ethnology*. Evon Z. Vogt, vol. ed. Handbook of Middle American Indians. Vol. 8. Robert Wauchope, gen. ed. Austin: University of Texas Press.

Shaterian, Alan V.
1976 Yavapai [Sonorant] Segments: P. 87-95 in Hokan Studies: Papers from the First Conference on Hokan Languages Held in San Diego, California, April 23-25, 1970. (*Janua Linguarum, Series Practica* 181) The Hague, Paris: Mouton.

Shaul, David
1980 Toward a Linguistic Prehistory of Hopi. (Unpublished manuscript in Department of Linguistics, University of California, Berkeley.)

———
1981 A Preliminary Analysis of the Pueblo Culture Area as a Linguistic Area. (Unpublished manuscript in Department of Linguistics, University of California, Berkeley.)

———
[1981a] The Location of the Proto-Keresan Speech Community. (Unpublished manuscript in Department of Linguistics, University of California, Berkeley.)

Shaw, Anna Moore
1968 Pima Indian Legends. Tucson: University of Arizona Press.

———
1974 A Pima Past. Tucson: University of Arizona Press.

Shea, John G.
1852 Discovery and Exploration of the Mississippi Valley with the Original Narratives of Marquette, Allouez, Membré, Hennepin, and Anastase Douay. Clinton Hall, N.Y.: Redfield.

Sheldon, Charles
1979 The Wilderness of Desert Bighorns and Seri Indians: The Southwestern Journals of Charles Sheldon. D.E. Brown, P.M. Webb, and N.B. Carmony, eds. Phoenix: Arizona Desert Bighorn Sheep Society.

Shepard, Anna O.
1965 Rio Grande Glaze-paint Pottery: A Test of Petrographic Analysis. Pp. 62-87 in Ceramics and Man. Frederick R. Matson, ed. *Viking Fund Publications in Anthropology* 41. New York.

Shepardson, Mary
1963 Navajo Ways in Government: A Study in Political Process. *Memoirs of the American Anthropological Association* 96. Menasha, Wis.

———
1971 Navajo Factionalism and the Outside World. Pp. 83-89 in Apachean Culture History and Ethnology. Keith H. Basso and Morris E. Opler, eds. *Anthropological Papers of the University of Arizona* 21. Tucson.

Shepardson, Mary, and Blodwen Hammond
1966 Navajo Inheritance Patterns: Random or Regular? *Ethnology* 5(1):87-96.

———
1970 The Navajo Mountain Community: Social Organization and Kinship Terminology. Berkeley: University of California Press.

Sherer, Lorraine M.
1965 The Clan System of the Fort Mojave Indians: A Contemporary Survey. *Southern California Quarterly* 47(1):1-72. Los Angeles.

———
1966 Great Chieftains of the Mojave Indians. *Southern California Quarterly* 48(1):1-35. Los Angeles.

———
1967 The Name Mojave, Mohave: A History of Its Origin and Meaning. *Southern California Quarterly* 49(1):1-36. Los Angeles.

Sheridan, Thomas E.
1979 Cross or Arrow? The Breakdown in Spanish-Seri Relations, 1729-1750. *Arizona and the West* 21(4):317-334.

Sheridan, Thomas E., and Thomas H. Naylor, eds.
1979 Rarámuri: A Tarahumara Colonial Chronicle, 1607-1791. Flagstaff, Ariz.: Northland Press.

Shimkin, D.B.
1941 The Uto-Aztecan System of Kinship Terminology. *American Anthropologist* 43(2):223-245.

Shiskin, J.K.
1944 Experimental Weaving with the Navaho. *El Palacio* 51(10):199-200.

Shreve, Forrest
1934 Rainfall, Runoff, and Soil Moisture Under Desert Conditions. *Annals of the Association of American Geographers* 24(3):131-156. Washington.

———
1951 Vegetation of the Sonoran Desert. *Carnegie Institution of Washington Publication* 591. Washington.

Shreve, Forrest, and Ira L. Wiggins
1964 Vegetation and Flora of the Sonoran Desert. 2 vols. Stanford, Calif.: Stanford University Press.

Shufeldt, R.W.
1889 The Navajo Tanner. Pp. 59-66 in *Proceedings of the United States National Museum for 1888*. Vol. 11. Washington.

———
1892 The Navajo Belt-weaver. Pp. 391-394 in *Proceedings of the United States National Museum for 1891*. Vol. 14. Washington.

Sibley, John
1806 Message from the President of the United States Communicating Discoveries Made in Exploring the Missouri, Red River and Washita, by Captains Lewis and Clark, Doctor Sibley and Mr. Dunbar.... Feb. 19, 1806. Printed by order of the Senate. Washington: A. and G. Way.

———
1832 Historical Sketches of the Several Indian Tribes in Louisiana, South of the Arkansas River, and Between the Mississippi and River Grande. *American State Papers, Class II, Indian Affairs* 1:721-731.

Siméon, Rémi
1963 Dictionnaire de la langue nahuatl ou mexicaine [1855]. Graz, Austria: Akademische Druck und Verlagsanstalt.

Simmons, Hilah L.
1965 The Geology of the Cabeza Prieta Game Range. Mimeo.

Simmons, Norman M.
1967 Refuge in a Wilderness. *Explorers Journal* 45(2):127-133.

Simpson, James H.
1850 Journal of a Military Reconnaissance from Santa Fe, New Mexico, to the Navajo Country...in 1849, by James Simpson, A.M., First Lieutenant Corps of Topographical Engineers. Pp. 56-139 in *U.S. Congress. Senate. 31st Cong., 1st sess. Senate Executive Doc. No.* 64. (Serial No. 562) Washington: U.S. Government Printing Office.

———
1964 Navaho Expedition: Journal of a Military Reconnaissance from Santa Fe, New Mexico, to the Navaho Country Made in 1849. Frank McNitt, ed. Norman: University of Oklahoma Press.

Simpson, Lesley Byrd
1950 The Encomienda in New Spain: The Beginning of Spanish Mexico. Berkeley: University of California Press.

Sitgreaves, Lorenzo
1853 Report of an Expedition Down the Zuni and Colorado Rivers. Washington: U.S. Government Printing Office.

Sladen, J.A.
[1880] Making Peace with Cochise, Chief of Chiricaua [*sic*] Indians, 1872. (Manuscript of 82 pages, undated but compiled from pencilled notes made in the 1880's, in the Frank Phillips Collection, Bizzell Memorial Library, University of Oklahoma, Norman.)

Slater, Carole E.
1976 Not, in Yuman, I Say. Pp. 71-77 in Proceedings of the First Yuman Languages Workshop Held at the University of California, San Diego, June 16-21, 1975. James E. Redden, ed. *Southern Illinois University Museum Studies, Research Record* 7. Carbondale.

Slotkin, James S.
1956 The Peyote Religion: A Study in Indian-White Relations. Glencoe, Ill.: Free Press.

Smart, Charles
1868 Notes on the "Tonto" Apaches. Pp. 417-419 in *Annual Report of the Smithsonian Institution for 1867.* Washington.

Smith, Anne M.
1966 New Mexico Indians: Economic, Educational and Social Problems. *Museum of New Mexico Research Record* 1. Santa Fe.

Smith, Buckingham T., trans.
1851 The Narrative of Alvar Núñez Cabeza de Vaca. Washington: no publisher.

———, ed. and trans.
1861 A Grammatical Sketch of the Heve Languages. (*Shea's Library of American Linguistics* 3) New York: Cramoisy Press.

———, ed.
1862 Arte de la lengua névome, que se dice pima, propia de Sonora; con la doctrina cristiana y confesionario añadidos. (*Shea's Library of American Linguistics* 5) New York: Cramoisy Press. (Reprinted: AMS Press, New York, 1970.)

Smith, Charline G.
1973 Selé, a Major Vegetal Component of the Aboriginal Hualapai Diet. *Plateau* 45(3):102-110.

Smith, Watson
1952 Kiva Mural Decorations at Awatovi and Kawaika-a with a Survey of Other Wall Paintings in the Pueblo Southwest. *Papers of the Peabody Museum of American Archaeology and Ethnology, Harvard University* 37. Cambridge, Mass.

Smith, William N.
1951 Why Bring Seri Indians from Tiburón Island to Visit the United States? *Masterkey* 25(5):167-169.

———
1959 Observations Regarding Seri Indian Basketry. *The Kiva* 25(1):14-17.

———
1970 Introduction and Observations. Pp. 3-14 in The Seri Indians: A Primitive People of Tiburón Island in the Gulf of California, by Ted De Grazia with William N. Smith. Flagstaff, Ariz.: Northland Press.

———
1974 The Seri Indians and Sea Turtles. *Journal of Arizona History* 15(2):139-158.

Smithson, Carma Lee
1959 The Havasupai Woman. *University of Utah Anthropological Paper* 38. Salt Lake City.

Smithson, Carma Lee, and Robert C. Euler
1964 Havasupai Religion and Mythology. *University of Utah Anthropological Paper* 68. Salt Lake City.

Snyder, Richard G., Albert A. Dahlberg, Clyde C. Snow, and Thelma Dahlberg
1969 Trait Analysis of the Dentition of the Tarahumara Indians and Mestizos of the Sierra Madre Occidental, Mexico. *American Journal of Physical Anthropology* 31(1):65-76.

Song of Bead Chant Singer
1952 When They Saw Each Other. Recorded and edited by David P. McAllester, text recorded by Harry Hoijer. Navajo Creation Chants, Peabody Museum, Harvard University, Cambridge, Mass.

Sonnichsen, C.L.
1958 The Mescalero Apaches. Norman: University of Oklahoma Press.

Soustelle, Jacques
1937 La Famille Otomi-Pame du Mexique central. *Université de Paris. Institut d'Ethnologie, Travaux et Mémoires* 26. Paris.

Southworth, Clay H.
1919 The History of Irrigation Along the Gila River. Pp. 103-223 in Vol. 2, Appendix A of Indians of the United States: Hearings Before the Committee on Indian Affairs. *U.S. Congress. House. 66th Cong., 1st sess.* 2 vols. Washington: U.S. Government Printing Office.

———
1949 The River People. [Film narration.] Washington: U.S. Department of the Interior, Indian Service.

Spencer, Katherine
1947 Reflection of Social Life in the Navaho Origin Myth. *University of New Mexico Publications in Anthropology* 3. Albuquerque.

———
1957 Mythology and Values: An Analysis of Navaho Chantway Myths. *Memoirs of the American Folklore Society* 48. Philadelphia.

Spencer, Robert F., and Jesse Jennings
1965 The Native Americans: Prehistory and Ethnology of the North American Indians. New York: Harper and Row.

Spicer, Edward H.
1940 Pascua: A Yaqui Village in Arizona. Chicago: University of Chicago Press.

———
1947 Yaqui Villages Past and Present. *The Kiva* 13(1):1-12.

———
1954 Potam: A Yaqui Village in Sonora. *Memoirs of the American Anthropological Association* 77. Menasha, Wis.

———
1961 Perspectives in American Indian Culture Change. Chicago: University of Chicago Press.

———
1962 Cycles of Conquest: The Impact of Spain, Mexico, and the United States on the Indians of the Southwest, 1533-1960. Tucson: University of Arizona Press.

———
1964 Apuntes sobre el tipo de religión de los yuto-aztecas centrales. Pp. 27-38 in Vol. 2 of *Proceedings of the 35th International Congress of Americanists*. Mexico City, 1962.

———
1968 Developmental Change and Cultural Integration. Pp. 172-200 in Perspectives in Developmental Change. Art Gallaher, Jr., ed. Lexington: University of Kentucky Press.

———
1969 Northwest Mexico: Introduction. Pp. 777-791 in *Ethnology*. Evon Z. Vogt, vol. ed. Handbook of Middle American Indians. Vol. 8. Robert Wauchope, gen. ed. Austin: University of Texas Press.

———
1980 The Yaquis: A Cultural History. Tucson: University of Arizona Press.

Spicer, Edward H., and R.B. Spicer
1936-1970 [Fieldnotes on the Yaqui in 1936-1937, 1942, 1947, and 1970.] (Unpublished manuscripts in Edward H. Spicer's possession.)

Spier, Leslie
1923 Southern Diegueño Customs. *University of California Publications in American Archaeology and Ethnology* 20(16):297-358. Berkeley.

———
1925 The Distribution of Kinship Systems in North America. *University of Washington Publications in Anthropology* 1(2). Seattle.

———
1928 Havasupai Ethnography. *Anthropological Papers of the American Museum of Natural History* 29(3):81-392. New York.

———
1933 Yuman Tribes of the Gila River. Chicago: University of Chicago Press. (Reprinted: Cooper Square Press, New York, 1970.)

———
1936 Cultural Relations of the Gila River and Lower Colorado Tribes. *Yale University Publications in Anthropology* 3. New Haven, Conn.

———
1946 Comparative Vocabularies and Parallel Texts in Two Yuman Languages. *University of New Mexico Publications in Anthropology* 2. Albuquerque.

———
1953 Some Observations on Mohave Clans. *Southwestern Journal of Anthropology* 9(3):324-342.

———
1955 Mohave Culture Items. *Museum of Northern Arizona Bulletin* 28. Flagstaff.

Spolsky, Bernard
1970-1971 Navajo Language Maintenance. *University of New Mexico Navajo Reading Study, Progress Reports* 5, 13, 14. Albuquerque.

Stanford Research Institute
1958 Needs and Resources of the Jicarilla Apache Indian Tribe. 5 vols. Menlo Park, Calif.: Stanford Research Institute.

Steck, Francis B.
1932 Forerunners of Captain de Leon's Expedition of Texas, 1670-1715. *Southwestern Historical Quarterly* 36(1):1-28. Austin.

Stecker, Ernest
1920 [Letter from Ernest Stecker, Superintendent, Mescalero Indian Agency, Mescalero, N.M., to Commissioner of Indian Affairs, Washington, D.C., Dated October 4.] (Manuscript in Letters Received, Commissioner's Office, Record Group 75, National Archives, Washington.)

Steele, Susan
1973 Futurity, Intention, and Possibility: A Semantic Reconstruction in Uto-Aztecan. *Papers in Linguistics* 6:1-37.

———
1975 Past and Irrealis: Just What Does It All Mean? *International Journal of American Linguistics* 41(3):200-217.

———
1979 Uto-Aztecan: An Assessment for Historical and Comparative Linguistics. Pp. 444-544 in The Languages of North America. Lyle Campbell and Marianne Mithun, eds. Austin: University of Texas Press.

Steen, Charlie R.
1937 More About the Vikita Ceremony. Pp. 278-283 in *U.S. National Park Service. Southwest Monuments Monthly Report, Supplement for April.* Coolidge, Ariz.

Steen, Charlie R., and Volney H. Jones
1935 Ceremonial Cigarettes. Pp. 287-292 in *U.S. National Park Service. Southwestern Monuments Monthly Report for October.* Coolidge, Ariz.

Steffel, Matthäus
1809-1811 Tarahumarisches Wörterbuch, nebst einigen Nachrichten von den Sitten und Gebräuchen der Tarahumaren, in Neu-Biscaya, in der Audiencia Guadalaxara im Vice-Königreich Alt-Mexico, oder Neu Spanien. Pp. 293-374 in Vol. 1 of Nachrichten von verschiedenen Ländern des Spanischen Amerika. Christoph Gottlieb von Murr, ed. 2 vols. Halle, Germany: J.C. Hendel.

Stephen, Alexander M.
1889 The Navajo Shoemaker. Pp. 131-136 in *Proceedings of the United States National Museum for 1888*. Vol. 11. Washington.

———
1930 Navajo Origin Legend. *Journal of American Folk-Lore* 43(167):88-104.

———
1936 Hopi Journal of Alexander M. Stephen. Elsie C. Parsons, ed. 2 vols. *Columbia University Contributions to Anthropology* 23. New York.

Stevenson, James
1891 Ceremonial of Hasjelti Dailjis and Mythical Sand Painting of the Navajo Indians. Pp. 229-285 in *8th Annual Report of the Bureau of American Ethnology for the Years 1886-1887.* Washington.

Stevenson, Matilda Coxe
1894 The Sia. Pp. 3-157 in *11th Annual Report of the Bureau of American Ethnology for the Years 1889-1890.* Washington.

———
[1894a] [Sia Vocabulary of 930 Terms Prepared But Not Used in the 11th Annual Report of the Bureau of American Ethnology for the Years 1889-1890.] (Manuscript in National Anthropological Archives, Smithsonian Institution, Washington.)

———
1904 The Zuni Indians: Their Mythology, Esoteric Fraternities, and Ceremonies. Pp. 3-634 in *23d Annual Report of the Bureau of American Ethnology for the Years 1901-1902.* Washington.

Steward, Julian H.
1936 Pueblo Material Culture in Western Utah. *Anthropological Series 1(3), University of New Mexico Bulletin* 287. Albuquerque.

———
1937 Ecological Aspects of Southwestern Society. *Anthropos* 32:87-104.

———
1937a Ancient Caves of the Great Salt Lake Region. *Bureau of American Ethnology Bulletin* 116. Washington.

———
1938 Basin-Plateau Aboriginal Sociopolitical Groups. *Bureau of American Ethnology Bulletin* 120. Washington.

———
1940 Native Cultures of the Intermontane (Great Basin) Area. Pp. 445-502 in Essays in Historical Anthropology of North

America. *Smithsonian Miscellaneous Collections* 100. Washington.

———
1955 Theory of Culture Change: The Methodology of Multilinear Evolution. Urbana: University of Illinois Press.

Stewart, Irene
1980 A Voice in Her Tribe: A Navajo Woman's Own Story. Doris O. Dowdy, ed. *Ballena Press Anthropological Paper* 17. Socorro, N.M.

Stewart, Kenneth M.
[1946] [Mohave Fieldnotes.] (Manuscript in Stewart's possession.)

———
1947 Mohave Warfare. *Southwestern Journal of Anthropology* 3(3):257-278.

———
1947a An Account of the Mohave Mourning Ceremony. *American Anthropologist* 49(1):146-148.

———
1947b Mohave Hunting. *Masterkey* 21(3):80-84.

———
1957 Mohave Fishing. *Masterkey* 31(6):198-203.

———
1965 Mohave Indian Gathering of Wild Plants. *The Kiva* 31(1):46-53.

———
1966 The Mohave Indians and the Fur Trappers. *Plateau* 39(2):73-79.

———
1966a The Mohave Indians in Hispanic Times. *The Kiva* 32(1):25-36.

———
1966b Mojave Indian Agriculture. *Masterkey* 40(1):4-15.

———
1968 Culinary Practices of the Mohave Indians. *El Palacio* 75(1):26-37.

———
1968a A Brief History of the Chemehuevi Indians. *The Kiva* 34(1):9-27.

———
1969 A Brief History of the Mohave Indians Since 1850. *The Kiva* 34(4):219-236.

———
1969a The Aboriginal Territory of the Mohave Indians. *Ethnohistory* 16(3):257-276.

———
1969b Scalps and Scalpers in Mohave Indian Culture. *El Palacio* 76(2):25-30.

———
1970 Mojave Indian Shamanism. *Masterkey* 44(1):15-24.

———
[1970-1971] [Mohave Fieldnotes.] (Manuscript in Stewart's possession.)

———
1973 Witchcraft Among the Mohave Indians. *Ethnology* 12(3):315-324.

———
1974 Mortuary Practices of the Mohave Indians. *El Palacio* 79(4):2-12.

———
1974a Mojave Shamanistic Specialists. *Masterkey* 48(1):4-13.

———
1977 Mojave Indian Ghosts and the Land of the Dead. *Masterkey* 51(1):14-21.

Stewart, Omer C.
1944 Washo-Northern Paiute Peyotism: A Study in Acculturation. *University of California Publications in American Archaeology and Ethnology* 40(3):63-142: Berkeley.

———
1961 The Native American Church and the Law with Description of Peyote Religious Services. *Denver Westerners Monthly Roundup* 17(1):5-48.

———
[1972-1980] [Letters and Phone Calls to David F. Aberle.] (Letters in Aberle's possession.)

Stokes, M.A., and T.L. Smiley
1964 Tree-ring Dates from the Navajo Land Claim, II: The Western Sector. *Tree-ring Bulletin* 26(1-4):13-27.

Stoltzfus, Ron
1979 [Guarijío Phonology.] (Unpublished manuscript in Stoltzfus' possession.)

———
1979a [Guarijío Morphophonemics.] (Unpublished manuscript in Stoltzfus' possession.)

Stone, Connie L.
1981 Economy and Warfare Along the Lower Colorado River. Pp. 183-197 in The Protohistoric Period in the North American Southwest, AD 1450-1700. David R. Wilcox and W. Bruce Masse, eds. *Arizona State University Anthropological Research Paper* 24. Tempe.

Stottler, V.E.
1897 Pressure as a Civilizer of Wild Indians. *The Outlook* 56 (January 12):397-400.

Stout, J.H.
1872 Report to Gen. O.O. Howard of a Council Held by the Chiefs and Head-men of the Pima and Maricopa Indians at the U.S. Indian Agency, Gila Bend Reservation, Arizona, on the 11th of May 1872. Pp. 166-168 in Annual Report of the Commissioner of Indian Affairs for the Year 1872. Washington: U.S. Government Printing Office.

———
1878 Report of August 15, from the Pima Agency, Arizona to the Commissioner of Indian Affairs. Pp. 2-6 in Report of the Commissioner of Indian Affairs for the Year 1878. Washington: U.S. Government Printing Office.

Stratton, R.B.
1857 Captivity of the Oatman Girls: Being an Interesting Narrative of Life Among the Apache and Mohave Indians. New York: Carlton and Porter.

Strong, William D.
1929 Aboriginal Society in Southern California. *University of California Publications in American Archaeology and Ethnology* 26:1-358. Berkeley.

Sullivan, Thelma D.
1976 Compendio de la gramática náhuatl. (*Instituto de Investigaciones Históricas, Serie de Cultura Náhuatl, Monografías* 18) Mexico City: Universidad Nacional Autónoma de México.

Sundheim, Beth M.
1976 Internal and External Heads in Kwtsaan Relative Clauses. Pp. 88-92 in Proceedings of the First Yuman Languages Workshop Held at the University of California, San Diego, June 16-21, 1975. James E. Redden, ed. *Southern Illinois University Museum Studies, Research Record* 7. Carbondale.

Sunn, Nick, and Henry O. Harwell
1976 An Account of Maricopa Origins. Pp. 26-30 in Yuman Texts. Margaret Langdon, ed. *International Journal of American Linguistics, Native American Text Series* 1(3).

Swadesh, Morris
1955 Towards Greater Accuracy in Lexico-statistic Dating. *International Journal of American Linguistics* 21(2):121-137.

———
1959 Indian Linguistic Groups of Mexico: Published in Commemoration of the 58th Annual Meeting of the American Anthropological Association, Held in Mexico City in December 1959. Mexico City: Escuela Nacional de Antropología e Historia, Instituto Nacional de Antropología e Historia.

———
1963 Nuevo ensayo de glotocronología yutonahua. *Anales del Instituto Nacional de Antropología e Historia* 15:263-302. Mexico City.

———
1967 Lexicostatistic Classification. Pp. 79-115 in *Linguistics*. Norman A. McQuown, vol. ed. Handbook of Middle American Indians. Vol. 5. Robert Wauchope, gen. ed. Austin: University of Texas Press.

Swadesh, Morris, and Madalena Sancho
1966 Los Mil elementos del mexicano clásico. (*Instituto de Investigaciones Históricas, Serie de Cultura Náhuatl, Monografías* 9) Mexico City: Universidad Nacional Autónoma de México.

Swanson, Guy E.
1960 The Birth of the Gods: The Origin of Primitive Beliefs. Ann Arbor: University of Michigan Press.

Swanton, John R.
1915 Linguistic Position of the Tribes of Southern Texas and Northeastern Mexico. *American Anthropologist* 17(1):17-40.

———
1924 Southern Contacts of the Indians North of the Gulf of Mexico. Pp. 53-60 in *Proceedings of the 20th International Congress of Americanists.* Rio de Janeiro, 1922.

———
1940 Linguistic Material from the Tribes of Southern Texas and Northeastern Mexico. *Bureau of American Ethnology Bulletin* 127. Washington.

———
1946 The Indians of the Southeastern United States. *Bureau of American Ethnology Bulletin* 137. Washington.

———
1952 The Indian Tribes of North America. *Bureau of American Ethnology Bulletin* 145. Washington. (Reprinted in 1969.)

Taft, William Howard
1912 Executive Order No. 1481, Dated February 17, re Mescalero Apache Indian Reservation Boundaries. P. 685 in Indian Affairs: Laws and Treaties, by Charles J. Kappler. Washington: U.S. Government Printing Office.

Tamarón y Romeral, Pedro
1937 Demostración del vastísimo obispado de la Nueva Vizcaya—1765: Durango, Sinaloa, Sonora, Arizona, Nuevo México, Chihuahua y porciones de Texas, Coahuila y Zacatecas. Vito Alessio Robles, ed. (*Biblioteca Histórica Mexicana de Obras Inéditas* 7) Mexico City: Antigua Librería Robredo, de I. Porrúa e Hijos.

Tanner, Clara Lee
1946 Gathering Piñon Pitch for Apache Baskets. *Arizona Highways* 22(3):12-13.

———
1957 Southwest Indian Painting: A Changing Art. Tucson: University of Arizona Press. (Rev. ed. in 1973.)

———
1965 Papago Burden Baskets in the Arizona State Museum. *The Kiva* 30(3):57-76.

Taylor, Benjamin J., and Dennis J. O'Connor
1969 Indian Manpower Resources in the Southwest: A Pilot Study. Tempe: Arizona State University, Bureau of Business and Economic Research.

Taylor, Edith S., and William W. Wallace
1947 Mohave Tattooing and Face-painting. *Masterkey* 21(6):183-195.

Taylor, Graham D.
1980 The New Deal and American Indian Tribalism: The Administration of the Indian Reorganization Act, 1934-45. Lincoln: University of Nebraska Press.

Taylor, Morris F.
1969 Campaigns Against the Jicarilla Apache, 1854. *New Mexico Historical Review* 44(4):269-291.

———
1970 Campaigns Against the Jicarilla Apache, 1855. *New Mexico Historical Review* 45(2):119-136.

Tedlock, Barbara
1971 Prayer Stick Sacrifice at Zuni. (Manuscript in Department of Anthropology, Wesleyan University, Middletown, Conn.)

Tedlock, Dennis
1975 An American Indian View of Death. Pp. 248-271 in Teachings from the American Earth: Indian Religion and Philosophy. Dennis Tedlock and Barbara Tedlock, eds. New York: Liveright.

———
1976 In Search of the Miraculous Zuni. Pp. 273-283 in The Realm of the Extra-human: Ideas and Actions. Agehananda Bharati, ed. The Hague: Mouton.

Tellechea, Miguel
1826 Compendio gramatical para la inteligencia del idioma tarahumar: Oraciones, doctrina cristiana, pláticas, y otras cosas necesarias para la recta administración de los santos sacramentos en el mismo idioma. Mexico City: Impr. de la Federación en Palacio.

Tello, Antonio
1858-1866 Fragmentos de una historia de la Nueva Galicia, escrita hácia 1650, por el padre fray Antonio Tello de la orden de San Francisco. Joaquín García Icazbalceta, ed. *Colección de Documentos para la Historia de México* 2:343-438. Mexico City.

———
1891 Libro segundo de la crónica miscelánea, en que se trata de la conquista espiritual y temporal de la santa provincia de Xalisco en el Nuevo Reino de la Galicia y Nueva Vizcaya, y descubrimiento del Nuevo México. Guadalajara: Impr. de "La República literaria" de C.L. de Guevara.

Ten Kate, Herman F.C., Jr. *see* Kate, Herman F.C. ten, Jr.

Thomas, Alfred B., ed. and trans.
1932 Forgotten Frontiers: A Study of the Spanish Indian Policy of Don Juan Bautista de Anza, Governor of New Mexico, 1777-1787; from the Original Documents in the Archives of Spain, Mexico and New Mexico. Norman: University of Oklahoma Press. (Reprinted in 1969.)

———
1935 After Coronado: Spanish Exploration Northeast of New Mexico, 1696-1727; Documents from the Archives of Spain, Mexico and New Mexico. Norman: University of Oklahoma Press.

———
1940 The Plains Indians and New Mexico, 1751-1778: A Collection of Documents Illustrative of the History of the Eastern Frontier of New Mexico. Albuquerque: University of New Mexico Press.

———
1941 Teodoro de Croix and the Northern Frontier of New Spain, 1776-1783. (From the Original Document in the Archives of the Indies, Seville). Norman: University of Oklahoma Press.

———
[1958] The Jicarilla Apache Indians: An Outline, 1598-1848: Their History, Relationships and Customs. (Mimeo., copy in possession of Jicarilla Apache Tribe, Dulce, N.M.)

———
1959 The Chiricahua Apache, 1695-1876: A Report of the Mescalero-Chiricahua Land Claims Project, Contract Research No. 290-154. Albuquerque: University of New Mexico. Mimeo.

———
1974 The Mescalero Apache, 1653-1874. Pp. 9-60 in Apache Indians XI. *(American Indian Ethnohistory: Indians of the Southwest)* New York: Garland.

Thomas, Cyrus, and John R. Swanton
1911 Indian Languages of Mexico and Central America and Their Geographical Distribution. *Bureau of American Ethnology Bulletin* 44. Washington.

Thomas, George H.
[1868] [Vocabulary of Yuma Words.] (Manuscript No. 1107 in National Anthropological Archives, Smithsonian Institution, Washington.)

Thomas, Robert K.
1953 Papago Land Use West of the Papago Indian Reservation South of the Gila River and the Problem of Sand Papago Identity. (Dittoed, copy in the Arizona State Museum Library, Tucson.)

Thompson, Gerald E.
1976 The Army and the Navajo: The Bosque Redondo Reservation Experiment, 1863-68. Tucson: University of Arizona Press.

Thompson, Hildegard
1975 The Navajos' Long Walk for Education. Tsaile Lake, Ariz.: Navajo Community College Press.

Thompson, J.
1857 [Instructions to Leach.] (Manuscript M. 95-1 in Record Group 75, National Archives, Washington.)

Thord-Gray, I.
1955 Tarahumara-English, English-Tarahumara Dictionary and an Introduction to Tarahumara Grammar. Coral Gables, Fla.: University of Miami Press.

Thornthwaite, C. Warren, C.F. Stewart Sharpe, and Earl F. Dosch
1942 Climate and Accelerated Erosion in the Arid and Semi-arid Southwest, with Special Reference to the Polacca Wash Drainage Basin, Arizona. (*U.S. Department of Agriculture Technical Bulletin* 808) Washington: U.S. Government Printing Office.

Thrapp, Dan L.
1964 Al Sieber: Chief of Scouts. Norman: University of Oklahoma Press.

———
1967 The Conquest of Apacheria. Norman: University of Oklahoma Press.

———
1972 General Crook and the Sierra Madre Adventure. Norman: University of Oklahoma Press.

———
1974 Victorio and the Mimbres Apaches. Norman: University of Oklahoma Press.

Thwaites, Reuben G., ed.
1904-1907 Early Western Travels, 1748-1846: A Series of Annotated Reprints of Some of the Best and Rarest Contemporary Volumes of Travel, Description of the Aborigines and Social and Economic Conditions in the Middle and Far West, During the Period of Early American Settlement. 38 vols. Cleveland: Arthur H. Clark.

Tiller, Veronica V.
1976 A History of the Jicarilla Apache Tribe. (Unpublished Ph.D. Dissertation in History, University of New Mexico, Albuquerque.)

———
1982 The Jicarilla Apache Tribe: A History, 1846-1970. Lincoln: University of Nebraska Press.

Titiev, Mischa
1944 Old Oraibi: A Study of the Hopi Indians of Third Mesa. *Papers of the Peabody Museum of American Archaeology and Ethnology, Harvard University* 22(1). Cambridge, Mass.

Topper, Martin D.
1972 The Daily Life of a Traditional Navajo Household: An Ethnographic Study in Human Daily Activities. (Unpublished Ph.D. Dissertation in Anthropology, Northwestern University, Evanston, Ill.)

Torquemada, Juan de
1943-1944 Monarquía indiana. 3 vols. 3d ed. Mexico City: Chávez Hayhoe.

Tozzer, Alfred M.
1909 Notes on Religious Ceremonies of the Navaho. Pp. 299-343 in Putnam Anniversary Volume. New York and Cedar Rapids: G.E. Stechert.

Trager, George L., and Edith C. Trager
1959 Kiowa and Tanoan. *American Anthropologist* 61(6):1078-1082.

Tremblay, Marc-Adélard, John Collier, Jr., and Tom Sasaki
1954 Navaho Housing in Transition. *América Indígena* 14(3):187-219.

Trimble, Stephen, ed.
1981 Tension and Harmony. *Plateau* 52(4).

Trippel, E.J.
1889 The Yuma Indians. *Overland Monthly* ser. 2, Vol. 13(78):561-584; 14(79):1-11.

Troike, Rudolph C.
1976 The Linguistic Classification of Cochimi. Pp. 159-164 in Hokan Studies: Papers from the First Conference on Hokan Languages Held in San Diego, Calif., April 23-25, 1970. (*Janua Linguarum, Series Practica* 181) The Hague, Paris: Mouton.

Troncoso, Francisco P.
1905 Las Guerras con las tribus yaqui y mayo del estado de Sonora...Mexico City: Tipografía del Departamento de Estado Mayor.

Troncoso, Vicente
1788 Report to Don Fernando de la Concha, Santa Fe, April 12. (Manuscript, copy in files of Navajo Tribal Research Section, Window Rock, Ariz.)

Tschopik, Harry, Jr.
1938 Taboo as a Possible Factor Involved in the Obsolescence of Navaho Pottery and Basketry. *American Anthropologist* 40(2):257-262.

———
1940 Navaho Basketry: A Study of Culture Change. *American Anthropologist* 42(3):444-462.

———
1941 Navaho Pottery Making: An Inquiry into the Affinities of Navaho Painted Pottery. *Papers of the Peabody Museum of American Archaeology and Ethnology, Harvard University* 17(1). Cambridge, Mass.

Turnage, William V., and T.D. Mallery
1941 An Analysis of Rainfall in the Sonoran Desert and Adjacent Territory. *Carnegie Institution of Washington Publication* 529. Washington.

Turner, Paul R.
1967 Seri and Chontal (Tequistlateco). *International Journal of American Linguistics* 33(3):235-239.

———
1976 Pluralization of Nouns in Seri and Chontal. Pp. 297-303 in Hokan Studies: Papers from the First Conference on Hokan Languages, Held in San Diego, California, April 23-25, 1970. Margaret Langdon and Shirley Silver, eds. (*Janua Linguarum, Series Practica* 181) The Hague, Paris: Mouton.

Tweed, William C.
1973 The Seri Indian Frontier of New Spain: 1617-1762. (Unpublished M.A. Thesis in History, Texas Christian University, Fort Worth.)

———
1975 The Seri Indians of Sonora, Mexico: 1760-1790. (Unpublished Ph.D. Dissertation in History, Texas Christian University, Fort Worth.)

Twitchell, Ralph, comp.
1914 The Spanish Archives of New Mexico. 2 vols. Cedar Rapids, Iowa: The Torch Press.

Tyler, Daniel
1881 A Concise History of the Mormon Battalion in the Mexican War. Salt Lake City: no publisher.

Tyler, S. Lyman, and H. Darrel Taylor
1958 The Report of Fray Alonso de Posada in Relation to Quivira and Teguayo. *New Mexico Historical Review* 33(4):285-314.

Tyroler, H.A., and Ralph Patrick
1972 Epidemiologic Studies of Papago Indian Mortality. *Human Organization* 31(2):163-170.

Uchendu, Victor C.
1966 Navajo Harvest Hands (a Study of Agricultural Labor Migration Among Navajo Indians): A Report Submitted to the Bureau of Indian Affairs. Window Rock, Ariz. Mimeo.

Underhill, Lonnie E., and Daniel F. Littlefield, eds.
1976 Hamlin Garland's Observations on the American Indians, 1895-1905. Tucson: University of Arizona Press.

Underhill, Ruth M.
[1930] Acculturation at the Papago Indian Village of Santa Rosa. (Unpublished manuscript in Robert A. Hackenberg's possession.)

———
1934 Note on Easter Devils at Kawori'k on the Papago Reservation. *American Anthropologist* 36(4):515-516.

———
1936 The Autobiography of a Papago Woman. *Memoirs of the American Anthropological Association* 46. Menasha, Wis.

———
1938 A Papago Calendar Record. *Anthropological Series 2(5), University of New Mexico Bulletin* 322. Albuquerque.

———
1938a Singing for Power: The Song Magic of the Papago Indians of Southern Arizona. Berkeley: University of California Press. (Reprinted: Ballantine Books, New York, 1973.)

———
1939 Social Organization of the Papago Indians. *Columbia University Contributions to Anthropology* 30. New York.

———
1940 The Papago Indians of Arizona and Their Relatives the Pima. (*Indian Life and Customs Pamphlet* 3) Lawrence, Kans.: U.S. Bureau of Indian Affairs, Branch of Education.

———
1946 Papago Indian Religion. *Columbia University Contributions to Anthropology* 33. New York.

———
1948 Ceremonial Patterns in the Greater Southwest. (*Monographs of the American Ethnological Society* 13) New York: J.J. Augustin.

———
1951 People of the Crimson Evening. Lawrence, Kans.: U.S. Bureau of Indian Affairs, Branch of Education.

———
1953 Here Come the Navaho! Washington: U.S. Bureau of Indian Affairs, Branch of Education.

———
1954 Intercultural Relations in the Greater Southwest. *American Anthropologist* 56(4):645-656.

———
1956 The Navajos. Norman: University of Oklahoma Press. (Rev. ed. in 1967.)

———
1979 Papago Woman. New York: Holt, Rinehart, and Winston.

Underhill, Ruth M., Donald M. Bahr, B. Lopez, J. Pancho, and D. Lopez
1979 Rainhouse and Ocean: Speeches for the Papago Year. (*American Tribal Religions* 4) Flagstaff: Museum of Northern Arizona.

U.S. Army. Corps of Topographical Engineers
1861 Report Upon the Colorado River of the West Explored in 1857 and 1858 by Lieutenant Joseph C. Ives. *U.S. Congress. Senate. 36th Cong., 1st sess. Senate Executive Doc. No.* 90. (Serial No. 1058) Washington: U.S. Government Printing Office.

U.S. Bureau of Indian Affairs
1925 Peyote. An Abridged Compilation from the Files of the Bureau of Indian Affairs. Prepared by Dr. Robert E.L. Newburne... 3d rev. ed., Lawrence, Kans.: Haskell Institute.

U.S. Bureau of Reclamation
1976 [Draft Environmental Impact Statement, Orme Dam and Reservoir.] Mimeo.

U.S. Census Office. 11th Census
1893 Moqui Indians of Arizona and Pueblo Indians of New Mexico. Extra Census Bulletin. Eleventh Census of the United States. Washington: U.S. Government Printing Office.

U.S. Commission on Civil Rights
1973 Demographic and Socio-economic Characteristics of the Navajo. (Staff report by the Office of General Counsel). Mimeo.

U.S. Commissioner of Indian Affairs
1881 [Letter to Agent Tiffany 5/30/1881 re San Carlos Coal Strip.] (Manuscript in Letters Received, Commissioner's Office BIA Special Case: San Carlos Coal Strip; Record Group 75, National Archives, Washington.)

———
1900 [Letter of October 3, Received from San Carlos Agency re Yavapai Indians.] (Manuscript in Letters Received, Commissioner's Office, Record Group 75, National Archives, Washington.)

U.S. Congress
1974 H.R. 10337, an Act to Provide for Final Settlement of the Conflicting Rights and Interests of the Hopi and Navajo Tribes to and in Lands Lying within the Joint Use Area of the Reservation Established by Executive Order of December 16, 1882, and Lands Lying within the Reservation Created by Act of June 14, 1934, and for Other Purposes. Approved Dec. 22, 1974. Washington: U.S. Government Printing Office.

U.S. Congress. House of Representatives. Indian Affairs Committee
1911 Memorial and Papers from Mohave-Apache Indians of McDowell Reservation, Arizona, in Relation to Their Removal from McDowell Reservation to Salt River Reservation, Arizona. Washington: U.S. Government Printing Office.

U.S. Congress. Senate
1861 [Letter of September 9, 1860 from Col. Thomas T. Fauntleroy to General Scott.] Pp. 64-65 in *36th Cong., 2d. sess., Senate Executive Doc. No.* 1. (Serial No. 1112) Washington.

———
1867 Letters Relating to Indian Affairs in the Department of New Mexico During the Years 1862 and 1863. Pp. 98-362 in Appendix to Report on Condition of the Indian Tribes of the Joint Special Committee. *39th Cong., 2d sess., Report No.* 156. (Serial No. 1279) Washington: U.S. Government Printing Office.

———
1890 Letter from the Secretary of War, Transmitting in Response to Senate Resolution of March 11, 1890, Correspondence [Between Lieut. Gen. P.H. Sheridan and Brig. Gen. George Crook] Regarding the Apache Indians. *51st Cong., 1st sess. Senate Executive Doc. No* 88. (Serial No. 2686) Washington: U.S. Government Printing Office.

———
1936 Walapai Papers: Historical Reports, Documents, and Extracts from Publications Relating to the Walapai Indians of Arizona. *74th Congress, 2d sess. Senate Document No.* 273. Washington: U.S. Government Printing Office.

U.S. Congress. Senate. Committee on Indian Affairs
1931 Partial Report [by Mr. Lynn J. Frazier, Chairman]. Survey of Conditions of the Indians in the United States—Indian Tribal and Trust Funds, Mescalero Apache Reservation, N. Mex. *72nd Congress, 1st sess. Senate Report No.* 25. Washington: U.S. Government Printing Office.

———
1937 Survey of Conditions of the Indians in the United States, Pt. 34: Navajo Boundary and Pueblos in New Mexico. *75th Congress, 2d sess: Hearings on S. Res. 79,* a Resolution Directing the Committee on Indian Affairs of the United States Senate to Make a General Survey of the Condition of the Indians of the United States. Washington: U.S. Government Printing Office.

U.S. Congress. Senate. Committee on Interior and Insular Affairs
1948 Rehabilitation of Navajo and Hopi Indians. *80th Congress, 2d. sess: Hearings on S. 2363,* a Bill to Promote the Rehabilitation of the Navajo and Hopi Tribes of Indians and the Better Utilization of the Resources of the Navajo and Hopi Indian Reservations, and for Other Purposes. Washington: U.S. Government Printing Office.

U.S. Congress. Senate. Committee on the Judiciary. Subcommittee on Constitutional Rights
1965 Constitutional Rights of the American Indian. *89th Cong., 1st session. Hearings* June 22, 23, 24, and 29, 1965. Washington: U.S. Government Printing Office.

U.S. Department of Commerce. Economic Development Administration
1971 Federal and State Indian Reservations: An EDA Handbook. Washington: U.S. Government Printing Office.

U.S. Department of the Interior
1972 Special Investigation Report by the Office for Equal Opportunity, Western Region, Denver, on Navajo Project, Page, Ariz., January 10-12, 1972. Mimeo.

——— 1973 Statistics Concerning Indian Education. Lawrence, Kans.: Haskell Press.

U.S. Department of the Interior. Bureau of Indian Affairs
1976 Uranium Exploration, Mining and Milling Proposal, Navajo Indian Reservation, New Mexico: Draft Environmental Impact Statement. Billings, Mont.: Planning Support Group. Mimeo.

U.S. Department of the Interior. Bureau of Reclamation
1967 Information Summary of Navajo Indian Irrigation Project (revised March, 1967). Farmington, N.M.: Navajo Indian Irrigation Project. Mimeo.

U.S. Federal Trade Commission
1973 The Trading Post System on the Navajo Reservation. (Staff report) Washington: U.S. Government Printing Office.

U.S. Geological Survey
1970 National Atlas of the United States. Arch C. Gerlach, ed. Washington: U.S. Government Printing Office.

U.S. National Park Service
1963 Soldier and Brave: Indian and Military Affairs in the Trans-Mississippi West, Including a Guide to Historic Sites and Landmarks. (*National Survey of Historic Sites and Buildings* 12) New York: Harper and Row.

U.S. Treaties, etc. 1865-1869
1968 Treaty Between the United States of America and the Navajo Tribe Indians [June 1, 1868], with a Record of the Discussions That Lead to Its Signing. Las Vegas, Nev.: KC Publications.

Uriarte Castañeda, María Teresa
1974 Las Costumbres y los ritos funerarios de los indígenas de la Baja California. (Unpublished Ph.D. Dissertation in History, Universidad Nacional Autónoma de México, Mexico City.)

Urrea, Bernardo de
1773 [Letter to Bucareli.] (Manuscript in Vol. 82, Provincias Internas, Archivo General de la Nación, Mexico City.)

Utley, Robert M.
1967 Frontiersmen in Blue: The United States and the Indian, 1848-1865. New York: Macmillan.

Valenzuela, Dolores G., comp.
1981 The Emerging Pascua Yaqui Tribe. Tucson: The Pascua Tribe.

Van Roekel, Gertrude B.
1971 Jicarilla Apaches. San Antonio, Tex.: Naylor.

Van Valkenburgh, Richard F.
1941 Dinebikeyah. Window Rock, Ariz. Mimeo.

——— 1945 The Government of the Navajos. *Arizona Quarterly* 1(4):63-73.

——— 1946 Last Powwow of the Navajo. *Desert Magazine* 10(1):4-7. El Centro, Calif.

——— 1946a We Found the Hidden Shrine of Old Makai. *Desert Magazine* 9(11):20-22. El Centro, Calif.

——— 1974 A Short History of the Navajo People. Pp. 201-267 in Navajo Indians, III. *(American Indian Ethnohistory: Indians of the Southwest)* New York: Garland.

Van Valkenburgh, Richard, and John C. McPhee
1938 A Short History of the Navajo People. Window Rock, Ariz.: U.S. Department of the Interior, Navajo Service. Mimeo.

Velasco, José Francisco
1850 Noticias estadísticas del estado de Sonora, acompañadas de ligeras reflecsiones, deducidas de algunos documentos y conocimientos prácticos. Mexico City: Imprenta de Ignacio Cumplido.

Velasco, Juan B. de
1890 Arte de la lengua Cáhita por un padre de la Compañía de Jesús...Eustaquio Buelna, ed. Mexico City: Imprenta del Gobierno Federal.

Venegas, Miguel
1759 A Natural and Civil History of California. 2 vols. London: J. Rivington and J. Fletcher.

Vergára, Gabriel de
1965 El Cuadernillo de la lengua de los indios pajalates (1732) por Fray Gabriel de Vergára y el Confesario de indios en lengua coahuilteca. Eugenio del Hoyo, ed. *Publicaciones del Instituto Tecnológico y de Estudios Superiores de Monterrey, Serie Historia* 3. Monterrey, Mexico.

Vestal, Paul A.
1952 Ethnobotany of the Ramah Navaho. *Papers of the Peabody Museum of American Archaeology and Ethnology, Harvard University* 40(4). Cambridge, Mass.

Villa, Eduardo W.
1951 Historia del estado de Sonora. 2d ed. Hermosillo, Mexico: Editorial Sonora.

Villagra, Francisco Antonio de
1777 Relación de Navogame. (Manuscript in the Biblioteca Nacional de Madrid; Copy at Department of Geography, University of California, Berkeley.)

Villagrá, Gaspar Pérez de
1900 Historia de la Nueva México. 2 vols. Mexico City: Museo Nacional.

Villaseñor y Sanchez, José Antonio de
1748 Theatro americano, descripcion general de los reynas y provincias de la Nueva España, y sus jurisdicciones etc. Vol. 2. Mexico City: Impressora del Real.

Villiers du Terrage, M. de, and Paul Rivet
1919 Les Indiens du Texas et les expéditions françaises de 1720 et 1721 à la baie Saint-Bernard. *Journal de la Société des Américanistes de Paris* n.s. 11:403-442.

——— 1929 Deux vocabulaires inédits recueillis au Texas vers 1688. *Journal de la Société des Américanistes de Paris* n.s. 21(2):307-311.

Vivian, Patricia Bryan
1961 Kachina—the Study of Pueblo Animism and Anthropomorphism within the Ceremonial Wall Paintings of Pottery Mound, and the Jeddito. (Unpublished M.A. Thesis in Fine Arts, State College of Iowa, Ames.)

Vivian, R. Gwinn
1960 The Navajo Archaeology of the Chacra Mesa, New Mexico. (Unpublished M.A. Thesis in Anthropology, University of New Mexico, Albuquerque.)

——— 1965 An Archeological Survey of the Lower Gila River, Arizona. *The Kiva* 30(4):95-146.

——— 1970 An Inquiry into Prehistoric Social Organization in Chaco Canyon, New Mexico. Pp. 59-83 in Reconstructing Prehistoric Pueblo Societies. William A. Longacre, ed. Albuquerque: University of New Mexico Press.

Voegelin, Charles F.
1935 Tübatulabal Grammar. *University of California Publications in American Archaeology and Ethnology* 34(2):55-190. Berkeley.

——— 1935a Tübatulabal Texts. *University of California Publications in American Archaeology and Ethnology* 34(3):191-246. Berkeley.

———
1958 Working Dictionary of Tübatulabal. *International Journal of American Linguistics* 24(3):221-228.

Voegelin, Charles F., and Florence M. Voegelin
1957 Hopi Domains: A Lexical Approach to the Problem of Selection. *Indiana University Publications in Anthropology and Linguistics, Memoir* 14. Bloomington.

———
1965 Languages of the World: Native America Pt. 1. *Anthropological Linguistics* 7(7). Bloomington.

———
1966 Index to Languages of the World: *Anthropological Linguistics* 8(6); 8(7).

———, comps.
1966a Map of North American Indian Languages. (*American Ethnological Society Publication* 20, rev.) [n.p.]: American Ethnological Society.

Voegelin, Charles F., Florence M. Voegelin, and Kenneth Hale
1962 Typological and Comparative Grammar of Uto-Aztecan: I (Phonology). *Indiana University Publications in Anthropology and Linguistics, Memoir* 17. Bloomington.

Voegelin, Erminie W.
1933 Kiowa-Crow Mythological Affiliations. *American Anthropologist* 35(3):470-474.

Vogt, Evon Z.
1961 Navaho. Pp. 278-336 in Perspectives in American Indian Culture Change. Edward H. Spicer, ed. Chicago: University of Chicago Press.

Voth, H.R.
1905 Traditions of the Hopi. *Anthropological Series 8, Field Museum of Natural History Publication* 96. Chicago.

Waddell, Jack O.
1969 Papago Indians at Work. *Anthropological Papers of the University of Arizona* 12. Tucson.

———
1973 The Place of the Cactus Wine Ritual in the Papago Indian Ecosystem. Pp. 213-228 in The Realm of the Extra-human Ideas and Actions. Agehananda Bharati, ed. (*9th International Congress of Anthropological and Ethnological Sciences, Chicago*) The Hague and Paris: Mouton.

Wagner, Roland M.
1974 Western Navajo Peyotism: A Case Analysis. (Unpublished Ph.D. Dissertation in Anthropology, University of Oregon, Eugene.)

———
1975 Pattern and Process in Ritual Syncretism: The Case of Peyotism Among the Navajo. *Journal of Anthropological Research* 31(2):162-181.

———
1975a Some Pragmatic Aspects of Navaho Peyotism. *Plains Anthropologist* 20(69):197-205.

———
1978 Peyotism, Traditional Religion, and Modern Medicine: Changing Healing Traditions in the Border Area. Pp. 139-145 in Modern Medicine and Medical Anthropology in the United States-Mexico Border Population: Proceedings of a Workshop Held in El Paso, Texas, Jan. 20-21, 1977. Boris Velimirovic, ed. Washington: Pan American Health Organization.

Walcott, George A., Jr., ed.
1943 A Doctor Comes to California: The Diary of John S. Griffin, Assistant Surgeon with Kearny's Dragoons, 1846-47. *California Historical Society Quarterly* 21(3):193-224; 22(1):41-66. San Francisco.

Wallace, William J.
1947 The Dream in Mohave Life. *Journal of American Folklore* 60(237):252-258.

———
1947a The Girls' Puberty Rite of the Mohave. *Proceedings of the Indiana Academy of Science* 57:37-40. Indianapolis.

———
1948 Infancy and Childhood Among the Mohave Indians. *Primitive Man* 21(1-2):19-38.

———
1953 Tobacco and Its Use Among the Mohave Indians. *Masterkey* 27(6):193-202.

———
1955 Mohave Fishing Equipment and Methods. *Anthropological Quarterly* 28(2):87-94.

Walter, Paul A.F.
1933 The First Civil Governor of New Mexico Under the Stars and Stripes. *New Mexico Historical Review* 8(2):98-129.

Wares, Alan C.
1968 A Comparative Study of Yuman Consonantism. (*Janua Linguarum, Series Practica* 57) The Hague, Paris: Mouton.

Warren, A. Helene
1969 Tonque. *El Palacio* 76(2):36-42.

Watahomigie, Lucille J., Malinda Powskey, and Akira Y. Yamamoto
1979 The Structure of Nominal Modifiers. Pp. 11-18 in Proceedings of the 1978 Hokan Languages Workshop Held at the University of California, San Diego, June 27-29, 1978. James E. Redden, ed. *Southern Illinois University Occasional Papers in Linguistics* 5. Carbondale.

Wauneka, Annie D.
1970 [Notes of an Interview with Annie D. Wauneka, Chairman, Health Committee, Navajo Tribal Council.] (Notes in Robert L. Bergman's possession.)

Wayland, Virginia
1962 Apache Playing Cards. *Expedition* 4(3):34-39.

———
1972 The Indian Looks at the White Man: Playing-card Portraits of the Old West. *Expedition* 14(3):15-24.

Weatherford, Gary D., and Gordon C. Jacoby
1975 Impact of Energy Development on the Law of the Colorado River. *Natural Resources Journal* 15:171-213.

Weaver, Donald E., Jr.
1977 Investigations Concerning the Hohokam Classic Period in the Lower Salt River Valley, Arizona. *Arizona Archaeologist* 9. Phoenix.

Weaver, Thomas
1971 Political Organization and Business Management in the Gila River Indian Community. Tucson: University of Arizona, Bureau of Ethnic Research.

———
1973-1976 Social and Economic Change in the Context of Pima-Maricopa History. Pp. 579-592 in Vol. 2 of *Proceedings of the 40th International Congress of Americanists*. Rome-Genoa, 1972.

Webb, George
1959 A Pima Remembers. Tucson: University of Arizona Press.

Webb, Nancy
1977 Yuman Language Interrelationships: The Lexical Evidence. Pp. 60-68 in Proceedings of the 1976 Hokan-Yuman Languages Workshop Held at the University of California, San Diego, June 21-23, 1976. James E. Redden, ed. *Southern Illinois University Museum Studies, Research Record* 11. Carbondale.

Webb, William, and Robert A. Weinstein
1973 Dwellers at the Source: Southwestern Indian Photographs from the A.C. Vroman Collection in the Natural History Museum of Los Angeles County. New York: Grossman.

Weddle, Robert S.
1968 San Juan Bautista: Gateway to Spanish Texas. Austin: University of Texas Press.

———
1973 Wilderness Manhunt: The Spanish Search for La Salle. Austin: University of Texas Press.

Wedel, Waldo R.
1940 Culture Sequence in the Central Great Plains Pp. 291-352 in Essays in Historical Anthropology of North America. *Smithsonian Miscellaneous Collections* 100. Washington.

——— 1947 Culture Chronology in the Central Great Plains. *American Antiquity* 12(3):148-156.

——— 1947a Prehistory and Environment in the Central Great Plains. *Transactions of the Kansas Academy of Science* 50(1):1-18. Topeka.

——— 1950 Notes on Plains-southwestern Contacts in the Light of Archeology. Pp. 99-116 in For the Dean: Essays in Anthropology in Honor of Byron Cummings on His Eighty-Ninth Birthday, September 20, 1950. Erik K. Reed and Dale S. King, eds. Tucson: Hohokam Museums Association; Santa Fe: Southwestern Monuments Association.

——— 1953 Prehistory and the Missouri Valley Development Program: Summary Report on the Missouri River Basin Archeological Survey in 1948. Pp. 1-59 in River Basin Surveys Papers. *Bureau of American Ethnology Bulletin* 154(1). Washington.

——— 1953a Prehistory and the Missouri Valley Development Program: Summary Report on the Missouri River Basin Archeological Survey in 1949. Pp. 61-101 in River Basin Surveys Papers: Inter-Agency Archeological Salvage Program. *Bureau of American Ethnology Bulletin* 154(2). Washington.

——— 1953b Some Aspects of Human Ecology in the Central Plains. *American Anthropologist* 55(4):449-514.

——— 1959 An Introduction to Kansas Archaeology. *Bureau of American Ethnology Bulletin* 174. Washington.

——— 1961 Plains Archaeology, 1935-60. *American Antiquity* 27(1):24-32.

——— 1961a Prehistoric Man on the Great Plains. Norman: University of Oklahoma Press.

——— 1964 The Great Plains. Pp. 193-220 in Prehistoric Man in the New World. Jesse D. Jennings and Edward Norbeck, eds. Chicago: University of Chicago Press.

Welsh, Herbert
1887 The Apache Prisoners in Fort Marion, St. Augustine, Florida. Philadelphia: Office of the Indian Rights Association.

Werner, Oswald
1965 Semantics of Navajo Medical Terms: I. *International Journal of American Linguistics* 31(1):1-17.

Werner, Oswald, and K.Y. Begishe
1968 Styles of Learning: The Evidence from Navajo Thought. (Unpublished manuscript in its authors' possession.)

——— 1970 The Taxonomic Aspects of the Navajo Universe. Paper Prepared for the *39th International Congress of Americanists*. Lima, Peru, 1970.

West, Elizabeth Howard
1905 De Léon's Expedition of 1689. Elizabeth H. West, trans. *Quarterly of the Texas State Historical Association* 8(3):199-224. Austin.

West, Robert C.
1949 The Mining Community in Northern New Spain: The Parral Mining District. *Ibero-Americana* 30. Berkeley, Calif.

——— 1964 Surface Configuration and Associated Geology of Middle America. Pp. 33-83 in *Natural Environment and Early Cultures*. Robert C. West, vol. ed. Handbook of Middle American Indians. Vol. 1. Robert Wauchope, gen. ed. Austin: University of Texas Press.

Wetzler, Lewis
1949 History of the Pima Indians. (Unpublished Ph.D. Dissertation in History, University of California, Berkeley.)

Wheat, Joe Ben
1981 Early Navajo Weaving. *Plateau* 52(4):2-9.

Wheelwright, Mary C.
1942 Navajo Creation Myth: The Story of the Emergence. By Hasteen Klah. (*Navajo Religion Series* 1) Santa Fe: Museum of Navajo Ceremonial Art.

——— 1946 Hail Chant and Water Chant. (*Navajo Religion Series* 2) Santa Fe: Museum of Navajo Ceremonial Art.

——— 1949 Emergence Myth: According to Hanelthnayhe or Upward-Reaching Rite. Recorded by Father Berard Haile. (*Navajo Religion Series* 3) Sante Fe: Museum of Navajo Ceremonial Art.

——— 1956 The Myth and Prayers of the Great Star Chant and the Myth of the Coyote Chant. David McAllester, ed. (*Navajo Religion Series* 4) Santa Fe: Museum of Navajo Ceremonial Art.

Whipple, Amiel W.
1941 A Pathfinder in the Southwest. Grant Foreman, ed. Norman: University of Oklahoma Press.

Whipple, Amiel W., Thomas Ewbank, and William W. Turner
1855 Report Upon the Indian Tribes. Pt. 3 of U.S. War Department Reports of Explorations and Surveys to Ascertain the Most Practical and Economical Route for a Railroad from the Mississippi River to the Pacific Ocean. *U.S. Congress. Senate. 33d Cong., 2d sess., Senate Executive Doc. No.* 78 (Serial No. 752). Washington.

White, Charles B.
1957 A Comparison of Theories on Southern Athapaskan Kinship Systems. *American Anthropologist* 59(3):434-448.

White, Chris
1974 Lower Colorado River Area: Aboriginal Warfare and Alliance Dynamics. Pp. 113-135 in 'ANTAP: California Indian Political and Economic Organization. Lowell J. Bean and Thomas F. King, eds. *Ballena Press Anthropological Paper* 2. Ramona, Calif.

White, John B.
1873-1875 [Names of Indian Tribes as Spoken by the Tontoes.] (Manuscript No. 178b-2 in National Anthropological Archives, Smithsonian Institution, Washington.)

——— 1873-1875a [Names of Different Indian Tribes in Arizona and the Names by Which They Are Called by the Apaches.] (Manuscript 178a-2 in National Anthropological Archives, Smithsonian Institution, Washington.)

White, Leslie A.
1932 The Acoma Indians. Pp. 17-192 in *47th Annual Report of the Bureau of American Ethnology for the Years 1929-1930*. Washington. (Reprinted: Rio Grande Press, Glorieta, N.M., 1973.)

——— 1934 Masks in the Southwest. *American Anthropologist* 36(4):626-628.

——— 1935 The Pueblo of Santo Domingo, New Mexico. *Memoirs of the American Anthropological Association* 43. Menasha, Wis.

——— 1942 The Pueblo of Santa Ana, New Mexico. *Memoirs of the American Anthropological Association* 60. Menasha, Wis.

——— 1962 The Pueblo of Sia, New Mexico. *Bureau of American Ethnology Bulletin* 184. Washington.

Whited, S.
1894 Pima Agency. Pp. 137-146 in Report on Indians Taxed and Indians Not Taxed in the United States (Except Alaska) at the Eleventh Census, 1890. Washington: U.S. Government Printing Office.

Whittemore, Isaac T.
1893 Among the Pimas. Albany: The Ladies' Union Mission School Association.

Whorf, Benjamin L.
1935 The Comparative Linguistics of Uto-Aztecan. *American Anthropologist* 37(4):600-608.

——— 1935a The Hopi Language. (Microfilm Collection of *Manuscripts on Middle American Cultural Anthropology* 48) Chicago: University of Chicago Library.

——— 1935b [Review of] Uto-Aztecan Languages of Mexico, by A.L. Kroeber. *American Anthropologist* 37(2):343-345.

——— 1936 [Notes on Hopi Grammar and Pronunciation; Mishongnovi Forms.] Pp. 1198-1326 in Vol. 2 of Hopi Journal, by Alexander M. Stephen. Elsie C. Parsons, ed. 2 vols. New York: Columbia University Press.

——— 1936a Appendix to The Classification of the Sonoran Languages, by J. Alden Mason. Pp. 197-198 in Essays in Anthropology Presented to A.L. Kroeber in Celebration of His Sixtieth Birthday, June 11, 1936. Robert H. Lowie, ed. Berkeley: University of California Press.

——— 1946 The Hopi Language, Toreva Dialect. Pp. 158-183 in Linguistic Structures of Native America, by Harry Hoijer et al. *Viking Fund Publications in Anthropology* 6. New York.

Whorf, Benjamin L., and George L. Trager
1937 The Relationship of Uto-Aztecan and Tanoan. *American Anthropologist* 39(4):609-624.

Wilcox, David R.
1981 The Entry of Athapaskans into the American Southwest: The Problem Today. Pp. 213-256 in The Protohistoric Period in the North American Southwest, AD 1450-1700. D.R. Wilcox and W.B. Masse, eds. *Arizona State University Anthropological Research Paper* 24. Tempe.

Willett, Thomas L.
1978 The Southeastern Tepehuan Verb. *Anthropological Linguistics* 20(6):272-294.

Williams, Anita Alvarez de
1974 The Cocopah People. Phoenix: Indian Tribal Series.

——— 1975 Travelers Among the Cucapá. Los Angeles: Dawson's Book Shop.

——— 1975a Primeros pobladores de la Baja California; Introducción a la antropología de la península. Mexicali, Baja California: Talleres Gráficos del Gobierno del Estado.

Williams, Aubrey W.
1970 Navajo Political Process. *Smithsonian Contributions to Anthropology* 9. Washington.

Williams, J.W.
1962 New Conclusions on the Route of Mendoza, 1683-1684. *West Texas Historical Association Year Book* 30:111-134.

Williams, John, and Sigrid Khera
[1975] Ethnohistory of the Yavapai. (Manuscript in Khera's possession.)

Wilson, Edward F.
1889 [Jicarilla Vocabulary from List Furnished by Grover Cleveland, an Apache Pupil from Ramona School.] (Manuscript No. 4748 in National Anthropological Archives, Smithsonian Institution, Washington.)

Wilson, Eldred D.
1962 A Resume of the Geology of Arizona. (*Arizona Bureau of Mines Bulletin* 171) Tucson: University of Arizona Press.

Wilson, H. Clyde
1964 Jicarilla Apache Political and Economic Structures. *University of California Publications in American Archaeology and Ethnology* 48(4) Berkeley.

Winsor, Justin, ed.
1884-1886 Narrative and Critical History of America. 8 vols. Boston and New York: Houghton, Mifflin.

Winter, Joseph C.
1973 Cultural Modifications of the Gila Pima: A.D.1697-A.D.1846. *Ethnohistory* 20(1):67-77.

Winter, Werner
1957 Yuman Languages, I: First Impressions. *International Journal of American Linguistics* 23(1):18-23.

——— 1963 Stories and Songs of the Walapai. *Plateau* 35(4):114-122.

——— 1967 The Identity of the Paipai (Akwa'ala). Pp. 372-378 in Studies in Southwestern Ethnolinguistics. Dell Hymes with William Bittle, eds. The Hague, Paris: Mouton.

Wissler, Clark
1917 The American Indian: An Introduction to the Anthropology of the New World. New York: D.C. Murtrie.

Wistrand-Robinson, Lyla
1980 A Comanche-English, English-Comanche Dictionary and Grammar. (Unpublished manuscript in Wistrand-Robinson's possession.)

Witherspoon, Gary
1970 A Cultural and Social Analysis of Navajo Kinship and Social Organization. (Unpublished Ph.D. Dissertation in Anthropology, University of Chicago, Chicago.)

——— 1970a A New Look at Navajo Social Organization. *American Anthropologist* 72(1):55-65.

——— 1971 Navajo Categories of Objects at Rest. *American Anthropologist* 73(1):110-127.

——— 1974 The Central Concepts of Navaho World View. *Linguistics* 119:41-59.

——— 1975 The Central Concepts of Navajo World View, II. *Linguistics* 161:69-88.

——— 1975a Navaho Kinship and Marriage. Chicago: University of Chicago Press.

——— 1977 Language and Art in the Navajo Universe. Ann Arbor: University of Michigan Press.

Wittfogel, Karl A.
1957 Oriental Despotism: A Comparative Study of Total Power. New Haven, Conn.: Yale University Press.

Wittfogel, Karl A., and Esther S. Goldfrank
1943 Some Aspects of Pueblo Mythology and Society. *Journal of American Folklore* 56(219):17-30.

Woerner, Davida
1941 Education Among the Navajo: An Historical Study. (Unpublished Ph.D. Dissertation in Philosophy, Columbia University, New York City.)

Wood, John J.
1979 A Sociocultural Assessment of the Livestock Reduction Program in the Navajo-Hopi Joint Use Area: A Summary. Flagstaff: Northern Arizona University, Department of Anthropology.

Wood, John J., Walter M. Vannette, and Michael J. Andrews
1979 A Sociocultural Assessment of the Livestock Reduction Program in the Navajo-Hopi Joint Use Area. Flagstaff: Northern Arizona University, Department of Anthropology.

Woodbury, George
1937 Notes on Some Skeletal Remains of Texas. *Anthropological Papers of the University of Texas* 1(5):7-16. Austin.

Woodbury, George, and Edna Woodbury
1935 Prehistoric Skeletal Remains from the Texas Coast. *Gila Pueblo, Medallion Paper* 18. Globe, Ariz.

Woods, Clyde M.
1980 Native American Cultural Resources. San Diego: Wirth Associates. (Manuscript, copy in Henry O. Harwell's possession.)

Woodward, Arthur
1971 Navajo Silver: A Brief History of Silver-smithing. Flagstaff, Ariz.: Northland Press. (Originally published as *Museum of Northern Arizona Bulletin* 14, 1938.)

Woodward, John A.
1966 Recent Seri Culture Changes. *Masterkey* 40(1):24-32.

Worcester, Donald E.
1941 The Beginnings of the Apache Menace of the Southwest. *New Mexico Historical Review* 16(1):1-14.

____
1944 The Spread of Spanish Horses in the Southwest. *New Mexico Historical Review* 19(3):225-232.

____
1947 Early History of the Navaho Indians. (Unpublished Ph.D. Dissertation in History, University of California, Berkeley.)

_______, ed. and trans.
1949 Advice on Governing New Mexico, 1794. *New Mexico Historical Review* 24(3):236-254.

____
1951 The Navaho During the Spanish Regime in New Mexico. *New Mexico Historical Review* 26(2):101-118.

Wright, Barton
1977 Hopi Kachinas: The Complete Guide to Collecting Kachina Dolls. Flagstaff, Ariz.: Northland Press.

Wright, Harold B.
1929 Long Ago Told: Legends of the Papago Indians. New York: D. Appleton.

Wyllys, Rufus K., ed.
1931 Padre Luís Velard's Relación of Pimería Alta, 1716. *New Mexico Historical Review* 6(2):111-157.

Wyman, Leland C.
1936 Navaho Diagnosticians. *American Anthropologist* 38(2):236-246.

____
1950 The Religion of the Navaho Indians. Pp. 341-361 in Forgotten Religions. Vergilius Ferm, ed. New York: Philosophical Library.

____
1951 Notes on Obsolete Navaho Ceremonies. *Plateau* 23(3):44-48.

____
1952 The Sandpaintings of the Kayenta Navaho: An Analysis of the Louisa Wade Wetherill Collection. *University of New Mexico Publications in Anthropology* 7. Albuquerque.

____
1957 Beautyway: A Navajo Ceremonial. Told by Singer Man; Father Berard Haile, trans. (*Bollingen Series* 53). New York: Pantheon Books.

____
1959 Navaho Indian Painting: Symbolism, Artistry, and Psychology. Boston: Boston University Press.

____
1960 Navaho Sandpainting: The Huckel Collection. Colorado Springs: The Taylor Museum of Colorado Springs Fine Arts Center.

____
1962 The Windways of the Navaho. Colorado Springs: The Taylor Museum of Colorado Springs Fine Arts Center.

____
1965 The Red Antway of the Navaho. (*Navajo Religion Series* 5) Santa Fe: Museum of Navajo Ceremonial Art.

____
1966 Snakeskins and Hoops. *Plateau* 39(1):4-25.

____
1970 Sandpaintings of the Navaho Shootingway and The Walcott Collection. *Smithsonian Contributions to Anthropology* 13. Washington.

____
1970a Blessingway. With Three Versions of the Myth Recorded and Translated from the Navaho by Father Berard Haile. Tucson: University of Arizona Press.

____
1972 A Navajo Medicine Bundle for Shootingway. *Plateau* 44(4):131–149.

____
1975 The Mountainway of the Navajo. Tucson: University of Arizona Press.

Wyman, Leland C., and Flora L. Bailey
1943 Navaho Upward-Reaching Way: Objective Behavior, Rationale and Sanction. *Anthropological Series 4(2), University of New Mexico Bulletin* 389. Albuquerque.

____
1944 Two Examples of Navaho Physiotherapy. *American Anthropologist* 46(3):329-337.

____
1945 Idea and Action Patterns in Navaho Flintway. *Southwestern Journal of Anthropology* 1(3):356-377.

____
1964 Navaho Indian Ethnoentomology. *University of New Mexico Publications in Anthropology* 12. Albuquerque.

Wyman, Leland C., and Stuart K. Harris
1941 Navajo Indian Medical Ethnobotany. *University of New Mexico Bulletin, Anthropological Series* 3(5). Albuquerque.

____
1951 The Ethnobotany of the Kayenta Navajo: An Analysis of the John and Louisa Wetherill Ethnobotanical Collection. *University of New Mexico Publications in Biology* 5:1-66. Albuquerque.

Wyman, Leland C., and Clyde Kluckhohn
1938 Navaho Classification of Their Song Ceremonials. *Memoirs of the American Anthropological Association* 50. Menasha, Wis.

____
1940 An Introduction to Navaho Chant Practice: An Account of the Behaviors Observed in Four Chants. *Memoirs of the American Anthropological Association* 53. Menasha, Wis.

Wyman, Leland C., W.W. Hill, and Iva Osanai
1942 Navajo Eschatology. *Anthropological Series 4(1), University of New Mexico Bulletin* 377. Albuquerque.

Xavier, Gwyneth Harrington
1946 Seri Face Painting. *The Kiva* 11(2):15-20.

Yazzie, Alfred et al.
[1970] Navajo Squaw Dance Songs. [Sound recording] Canyon Records 6067. 1 disc. 33⅓ rpm. 12 in; also available as 8-track tape. 1 reel. Canyon Records 8-6067.

Yazzie, Ethelou, ed.
1971 Navajo History. Vol. 1. Written under the direction of the Navajo Curriculum Center, Rough Rock Demonstration School. Many Farms, Ariz.: Navajo Community College Press.

Young, Robert W
1940 [Linguistic Fieldnotes from One Month's Fieldwork with Edward Onespot at Sarcee, Alberta.] (Manuscript in Young's possession.)

_______, comp.
1961 The Navajo Yearbook, 1951-1961: A Decade of Progress, Rep. 8. Window Rock, Ariz.: Navajo Agency.

____
1961a Navajo Personal Names. Pp. 539-561 in The Navajo Yearbook, 1951-1961: A Decade of Progress. Rep. 8. Window Rock, Ariz.: Navajo Agency.

____
1968 The Role of the Navajo in the Southwestern Drama. Gallup, N.M.: Gallup Independent.

____
1972 The Rise of the Navajo Tribe. Pp. 167-237 in Plural Society in the Southwest. Edward H. Spicer and Raymond H. Thompson, eds. New York: Interbook.

———
1977 Written Navajo: A Brief History. Pp. 459-470 in Advances in the Creation and Revision of Writing Systems. J. Fishman, ed. The Hague and Paris: Mouton.

———
1978 A Political History of the Navajo Tribe. Tsaile, Ariz.: Navajo Community College Press.

Young, Robert W., and William Morgan
1947 Navajo Place Names in Gallup, New Mexico. *El Palacio* 54(12):283-285.

———, eds.
1954 Navajo Historical Selections. Phoenix: Bureau of Indian Affairs.

———
1980 The Navajo Language: A Grammar and Colloquial Dictionary. Albuquerque: University of New Mexico Press.

Young, Stella, and Nonabah Bryan
1940 Navajo Native Dyes: Their Preparation and Use. (*Indian Handcrafts* 2) Washington: Bureau of Indian Affairs.

Zapata, Juan Hortíz
1678 Relación de las misiones que la Compañía tiene en el Reyno y provincias de la Nueva Vizcaya en la Nueva España, echa el año de 1678 con ocasión de la visita general dellas que por orden del Padre Provincial Tomás Altamirano hizo el Padre Visitador Juan Hortíz Zapata de la misma Compañia. (Transcript in Bolton Collection, Bancroft Library, University of California, Berkeley.)

Zapata, Juan O.
1853-1857 Relación de las misiones que la Companía de Jesús tiene en el reino y provincia de la Nueva Vizcaya, 1678. In Vol. 3 of Documentos para la Historia de Méjico, 4th ser. F. García Figueroa, ed. Mexico City: J.R. Navarro.

Zárate Salmerón, Gerónimo de
1899-1900 Relating All the Things That Have Been Seen and Known in New Mexico as Well by Sea as by Land from the Year 1538 till that of 1626. Charles F. Lummis, trans. *Land of Sunshine* 11(6):336-341; 12(1):39-48, (2):104-113, (3):180-187. Los Angeles.

———
1966 Relaciones: An Account of Things Seen and Learned by Father Jerónimo de Zárate Salmerón from the Year 1538 to the Year 1626. Alicia R. Milich, trans. Albuquerque: Horn and Wallace.

Zigmond, Maurice L.
1975 A Kawaiisu Dictionary. (Manuscript in Wick R. Miller's possession.)

Zingg, Robert M.
1940 Report on Archaeology of Southern Chihuahua. *Contributions of the University of Denver 3, Center of Latin American Studies Publication* 1. Denver.

———
1942 The Genuine and Spurious Values in Tarahumara Culture. *American Anthropologist* 44(1):78-92.

Index

Italic numbers indicate material in a figure caption; roman numbers, material in the text.

All variant names of groups are indexed, with the occurrences under synonymy *discussing the equivalences. Variants of group names that differ from those cited only in their capitalization, hyphenation, or accentuation have generally been omitted; variants that differ only in the presence or absence of one (noninitial) letter or compound element have been collapsed into a single entry with that letter or element in parentheses.*

The entry Indian words *indexes, by language, all words appearing in the standard orthographies and some others.*

H

K

L